PRAISE FOR THE

ACADEMY OF NUTRITION AND DIETETICS
Complete Food and Nutrition Guide

"Nutrition is a confusing and ever-changing science. This book is a terrific guide, as Roberta Duyff boils down some of the most complicated issues into clear, concise, and easy-to-digest nuggets. From weight loss to healthy eating to physical activity, this book gives readers a bottom line that's solid, practical, realistic, and evidence-based. It's a trustworthy reference—and it has definitely secured a permanent spot on my bookshelf."
—Joy Bauer, MS, RDN, health and nutritition expert for NBC's *TODAY* show, best-selling author of *From Junk Food to Joy Food,* founder of Nourish Snacks

"Jam-packed with practical eating and food safety tips."
—USA Today

"Of the five books closest to my keyboard, this guide is one of the most frequently used. A dynamite resource!"
—Antonia Allegra, CCP, executive director, Symposium for Professional Food Writers; food, wine, and travel author

"Bottom line, this is the best consumer nutrition book out. It's user-friendly, and it's complete. From a tidbit to a chapter, if it matters in nutrition, Roberta Duyff has included it. This book is worth its weight in gold."
—Keith Ayoob, EdD, RD, Associate Professor of Pediatrics, Albert Einstein College of Medicine

"If you question what to eat, please don't surf the Internet. You'll end up confused and overwhelmed by too much information. Instead, trust this well-indexed resource for valid answers to any and all of your food and nutrition questions from brain health to gut health, infancy to aging, sports nutrition to mindful eating—apples to zucchini!"
—Nancy Clark, MS, RD, CSSD, author, *Nancy Clark's Sports Nutrition Guidebook*

"Sorting out the constantly changing world of nutrition information, diets, and weight loss fads can be tricky, but this book provides all the facts in an easy-to-read format."
—Connie Diekman, MEd, RD, Director of University Nutrition, Washington University

"Brimming with tips from baby food to eating for healthy aging."
—*Shape* magazine

"[The book] may be the ultimate healthy-eating primer. How often can it be said of a book that it may extend your life?"
—*Fitness* magazine

"Duyff really covers nutrition and healthy eating from all angles . . . without overusing the 'd' word [don't]."
—Tufts University Health & Nutrition Letter

"Brings healthy eating and the family table together."
—Art Smith, chef, author, *Back to the Table: Reunion of Food and Family*

"Tackles most of the nutritional issues that concern Americans today . . . up-to-date and helpful."
—Seattle Times

"In short, it's a winner!"
—Washington Post

"Excellent and thorough . . . includes solid, science-based content on many nutrition topics, up-to-date eating guidance and ways to evaluate current nutrition research."
—Johanna Dwyer, DSc, RD, professor, School of Nutrition and Medicine, Tufts University, Director of Frances Stern Nutrition Center

"Solid all-around guide to nutrition that's fun just to pick up and peruse . . . clear, straight-forward language . . . sure to become dog-eared over time."
—Environmental Nutrition

"[An] easy-to-follow, masterful guide covering virtually everything you need to know about eating for optimal health. If you have only one food and nutrition book in your library, make sure that it's this one."
—Sharon Palmer, RDN, editor, *Environmental Nutrition,* author, *Plant-Powered for Life*

"Roberta Duyff has once again done an excellent job of combing through the voluminous nutrition-related scientific research to update this indispensable resource . . . tried and true, belongs on everyone's book shelf."
—Kathleen M. Zelman, MPH, RDN, Director of Nutrition, WebMD

"[It's] no doubt my go-to resource for food and nutrition information I can trust for years to come. Written in straightforward, easy-to-understand language, this evidence-based reference is a must-have for both consumers and professionals."
—Regina Ragone, MS, RDN, Food Director, *Family Circle*

"[An] invaluable resource for navigating through the complex world of food and health . . . important guidance for evaluating current nutrition research, critical given today's scientific and media environment."
—Sylvia Rowe, Chair, Health and Medicine Division (Institute of Medicine) Food Forum, Adjunct Professor, University of Massachusetts Amherst and Tufts Friedman School of Nutrition Science and Policy

ABOUT THE ACADEMY OF NUTRITION AND DIETETICS

The Academy of Nutrition and Dietetics is the world's largest organization of food and nutrition professionals, with more than 75,000 members committed to improving health and advancing the profession of dietetics through research, education, and advocacy.

FOR MORE INFORMATION . . .

Visit the Academy's Web site at www.eatright.org, where you'll find nutrition news, tips, and information. Click on "Find an Expert" to locate a registered dietitian nutritionist (RDN) in your area.

For information about permission to reproduce selections from this book, write to trade.permissions@hmhco.com or to Permissions, Houghton Mifflin Harcourt Publishing Company, 3 Park Avenue, 19th Floor, New York, New York 10016.

www.hmhco.com

THIS BOOK PRESENTS THE RESEARCH AND IDEAS OF ITS AUTHOR. IT IS NOT INTENDED TO BE A SUBSTITUTE FOR CONSULTATION WITH A PROFESSIONAL HEALTHCARE PRACTITIONER. CONSULT WITH YOUR HEALTHCARE PRACTITIONER BEFORE STARTING ANY DIET OR SUPPLEMENT REGIMEN. THE PUBLISHER, AUTHOR, AND THE ACADEMY DISCLAIM RESPONSIBILITY FOR ANY ADVERSE EFFECTS RESULTING DIRECTLY OR INDIRECTLY FROM INFORMATION CONTAINED IN THIS BOOK.

Mention of product names in this book does not constitute endorsement by the author or the Academy of Nutrition and Dietetics.

Unless otherwise noted, the nutrient and calorie data in this book were derived from the U.S. Department of Agriculture, Agricultural Research Service, 2016. USDA Food Composition Databases, USDA National Nutrient Database for Standard Reference, Release 28, ndb.nal.usda.gov/ndb

Library of Congress Cataloging-in-Publication Data is available

ISBN 978-0-544-52058-5 (pbk)

ISBN 978-0-544-52059-2 (ebk)

Designed by Empire Design Studio

Printed in the United States of America

DOW 10 9 8 7 6 5 4 3

4500690980

eat right. Academy of Nutrition and Dietetics

ACADEMY OF NUTRITION AND DIETETICS

Complete Food and Nutrition Guide

5th Edition

Roberta Larson Duyff, MS, RDN, FAND, CFCS

HOUGHTON MIFFLIN HARCOURT
BOSTON NEW YORK 2017

Contents

Foreword ix

Acknowledgments x

Introduction xii

PART I Wellness: Eat Smart, Get Active, Live Well 1

Chapter 1 Making Your Food and Lifestyle Choices Count 3

Wellness: Your Overall Health ... 3
Your Food Choices: The Inside Story ... 5
Smart Eating, Active Living: Recipe for Health ... 8
Reaching SMART Goals, One Step at a Time! ... 18

Chapter 2 Plan Smart to Eat Smart 21

Eating Well: More than Nutrients! ... 21
A Plan for Healthy Eating: From MyPlate to Your Plate ... 25
DASH to Health ... 51
The Mediterranean Route to Healthy Eating ... 52
The Healthy Vegetarian Way ... 53

Chapter 3 Make Quick, Easy Meals and Snacks 60

Breakfast Matters ... 60
Eating Well at Work ... 66
Brunch, Lunch, Dinner ... 68
Snacks Count! ... 75
More Meal and Snack Challenges ... 78

Chapter 4 Think Your Drinks 81

Water: First for Thirst ... 81
Juice, Juice Drink, or Fruit Drink? ... 88
Dairy and Nondairy Beverages ... 90
Coffee and Tea: Caffeinated or Not? ... 93
Soda, Energy Drinks, and Enhanced Beverages ... 100
Alcoholic Beverages: In Moderation ... 102

PART II Food and Nutrition: Choices in the Marketplace 109

Chapter 5 Producing Your Food 111

Food for Today and Tomorrow ... 111
Today's Agriculture ... 113
Food Processing ... 127

Chapter 6 Shop with Nutrition Savvy 141

Today's Supermarkets: What's in Store? ... 142
Food Labels: Decode the Package ... 143
Your Food Dollar: More Nutrition, Less Waste ... 154
The Store: Shopping for Health, Flavor, and Convenience ... 159
Shopping Green: Opportunity, Responsibility ... 187
Food Safety and Quality: From Store to Home ... 188

Chapter 7 Keep Your Food Safe 191

Kitchen: Clean, Safe Zone ... 192
Food Storage: Safekeeping ... 197
Safe Food from the Start ... 208
Foodborne Illness: More Common Than You Think ... 218

Chapter 8 Cook for Flavor and Health 230

Home Cooking Matters ... 230
Culinary Basics: Plan, Prepare, Serve ... 231
Kitchen: "Well" Equipped, "Well" Stocked ... 233
Recipes: Culinary Roadmaps ... 234
Flavor on the Menu ... 238
The Waste-Less Kitchen ... 243
Culinary Know-How: Flavor Plus Health ... 246

Chapter 9 Eat Smart Away from Home 275

Eating Out for Health and Pleasure ... 276
Eating Out: Safe from "Bad Bugs," Free from Food Waste ... 285
Fast, Casual Food ... 287
Eating Ethnic, Eating Global ... 297
Traveler Alert: Eating "on the Road" ... 309

Chapter 10 Use Supplements Wisely 315

Dietary Supplements: More than Vitamin Pills ... 316
Supplements: Safe, Effective? ... 328
If You Take a Supplement ... 335

PART III Nutrients: What's Inside Your Food 343

Chapter 11 Carbs: Sugars, Starches, and Fiber 345

Carbs: Simple and Complex ... 345
Sugars and Starches: For Energy and Health ... 347
Fiber and Health ... 350
Carbohydrates: How Much? What Kind? ... 355
Carbohydrates in Foods and Drinks ... 358
Sugar Alternatives ... 368

Chapter 12 Protein Power 373

Protein Basics ... 373
Protein: Today's Health Issues ... 375
Protein: How Much? What Kind? ... 377
Protein in Foods and Drinks ... 378

Chapter 13 Fat Facts 385

Fats: Not Created Equal ... 385
Fats and Health ... 389
Fats: How Much? Too Much? What Kind? ... 394
Fats in Food ... 398
Cholesterol: Like Fat, Not Fat ... 404
Fat Replacers ... 406

Chapter 14 Vitamins and Minerals 408

Regulating Your Body's Work ... 408
Vitamins: From A to K ... 409
Minerals—Major and Trace ... 425

Chapter 15 Water, "Phytos," and Probiotics 443

Water: A Fluid Asset ... 443
Phytonutrients: Different from Nutrients ... 448
Prebiotics and Probiotics: A Bioactive Duo ... 453

PART IV Food: For Every Age and Every Stage 457

Chapter 16 Give Your Baby a Healthy Start 459

Breastfeeding: Ideal for Babies ... 460
Infant Formula: A Healthy Option ... 471
Solid Foods: Solid Advice ... 476

Chapter 17 Help Kids Grow Up Healthy 489

Raising Healthy Eaters ... 489
Learning about Food ... 493
Feeding Concerns ... 498
Toddlers and Preschoolers: Food and Active Play ... 508
School-Age Kids: Eat Smart, Move More ... 516
Feeding the Teen Machine ... 524

Chapter 18 Manage Women's Unique Nutrition Concerns 533

The Childbearing Years ... 533
You're Expecting! ... 541
Breastfeeding—Your Choice ... 555
Women: Midlife and Beyond ... 557

Chapter 19 Tackle Men's Nutrition Issues 564

Guys: Your 20s, 30s—Any Age ... 564
Men: Middle Years and Beyond ... 569

Chapter 20 Eat Healthy Beyond Midlife 574

Healthy Eating and Active Living Matter ... 575
When Lifestyles Change ... 587
Physical Changes: Challenges and Smart Strategies ... 592

Chapter 21 Eat Smart for Sports 599

Nutrients for Active Living 599
A High-Performance Diet 611
Making Weight 614
The Game Plan 616
Ergogenic Aids: No Training Substitute 619

PART V Smart Eating: Preventing and Managing Health Issues 623

Chapter 22 Reach and Maintain Your Healthy Weight 625

What's a Healthy Weight? 625
Weight and Health 628
Calories: A Matter of Balance 633
Weight Management: Strategies That Work! 637
Popular Diets: Truths and Half Truths 648

Chapter 23 Cope with Food Allergies and Other Food Sensitivities 653

Food Allergies: A Growing Concern 654
Lactose Intolerance: A Matter of Degree 667
Gluten Free: When It's a Must 670
Sensitive to Additives? Maybe, Maybe Not 678

Chapter 24 Manage Cardiovascular Disease, Diabetes, and Cancer 680

Your Healthy Heart 680
Blood Pressure: Under Control? 693
Diabetes: A Growing Concern 698
Cancer Connection 713

Chapter 25 Manage Other Diet-Related Health Issues 722

Anemia: "Tired Blood" 722
Arthritis: Getting Relief 726
Digestive Health: GI Upsets and Conditions 727
Eating Disorders: More Than a Nutrition Issue 732
Oral Health: Your Healthy Smile 735
Osteoporosis and Bone Health 738

PART VI Resources for Healthy Eating 745

Chapter 26 Keep "Well" Informed 747

Healthy Eating: Ten Reasons for Expert Advice 747
Truth or Half-Truth: Read between the Headlines 748
Case against Health Fraud 755
Nutrition Advice to Trust 758

Resources You Can Use 763

Appendix 769

Physical Activity Guidelines for Americans. 769
Estimated Calorie Needs per Day by Age, Gender, and Physical Activity Level 770
How Many Calories? Figuring Your Energy Needs. 771
Eating Patterns, 2015-2020 Dietary Guidelines for Americans 771
Healthy US-Style Eating Pattern 772
Healthy Mediterranean-Style Eating Pattern 774
Healthy Vegetarian Eating Pattern 775
DASH Eating Plan at Various Calorie Levels 776
BMI: What Does It Mean?. 777
CDC Growth Chart. 777
Sample Menus for a 2,000-Calorie Food Pattern 778
Alcoholic Drink-Equivalents of Select Beverages 780
Dietary Reference Intakes. 780
% Daily Values: What Are They Based On? 786

Index 787

Foreword

For the past 100 years, the Academy of Nutrition and Dietetics has been dedicated to fostering lifelong health through food and nutrition. In 1917, a visionary group of women pioneered our profession as they applied their knowledge and service to the biggest food and nutrition challenge of the day—nourishing the population in the face of severe food shortages in the U.S. and Europe during World War I.

Today, the Academy is the world's largest organization of food and nutrition professionals and represents more than 100,000 registered dietitian nutritionists (RDNs) and nutrition and dietetics technicians, registered (NDTRs) working in hospitals, food service, academia, business, wellness, agriculture, and private practice. As the Academy embarks on our second century, we're about to chart a new vision, with a focus on solving the food and nutrition challenges of the 21st century.

This year, 2017, not only marks our organization's 100th anniversary, but also celebrates this book's fifth edition and over 20 years that this guide has supported our mission of improving the nation's health through research, education, and advocacy. As an award-winning bestseller, we are proud that the *Complete Food and Nutrition Guide* continues to be an accurate and up-to-date food and nutrition resource for so many individuals and families.

With this edition, author Roberta Duyff again presents a wealth of science-based and practical advice in an entertaining and easy-to-read style, and Academy members have also contributed their knowledge and expertise. Once again, this book serves as an indispensable nutrition and healthy eating guide for the public, as well as an important reference for registered dietitian nutritionists and other health care professionals. As the Academy continues to expand its reach in its second century, I am confident the fifth edition will have an important place on many bookshelves, as well as on tablets, computers, and other electronic devices.

Like previous editions, this resource remains the most comprehensive, authoritative, and current reference available on healthy eating. This book is all about choice, allowing the reader to personalize his or her own path to healthier eating—a theme that fits closely with the Academy's goals to support better decision making around food and to create a world where people and communities flourish because of the transformational power of food and nutrition.

As the Academy has grown and evolved over the years, so has this book. This edition includes expanded and updated guidance on the role food and eating habits can play in promoting a heathy lifestyle, enjoying the pleasures of food, and preventing and managing today's leading health concerns, such as obesity, heart disease, diabetes, cancer, food allergies, and foodborne illnesses. There is more on healthy eating for every age and stage of life, and there is important information on nutrition for both men and women.

This book will arm you with information to make the best healthy eating choices for you and your family—and perhaps to inspire those around you. If we all take just a little information from this book and share it with those close to us, we'll soon be helping our communities thrive in unprecedented ways.

I welcome you to now dive into the fifth edition of the Academy's *Complete Food and Nutrition Guide.* Happy reading and healthy eating to you and yours!

Lucille Beseler, MS, RDN, LDN, CDE, FAND
President, 2016–2017
Academy of Nutrition and Dietetics

Acknowledgments

For this and every earlier edition of the *Academy of Nutrition and Dietetics Complete Food and Nutrition Guide*, I am indebted to and thankful for the many professional experts and colleagues—in the fields of nutrition and dietetics, health, culinary arts, food sciences, and agriculture and in communications, education, public policy, and research—who have shared their insights, knowledge, and experience for all five editions of this book.

I am especially grateful to the Academy of Nutrition and Dietetics, for the honor and opportunity to write this comprehensive food and nutrition resource on behalf of the Academy's more than 75,000 members—and especially to *Betsy Hornick*, editor and registered dietitian nutritionist, who, since this book's very first edition and all subsequent editions over these twenty-plus years, has shared her food and nutrition expertise, insights, and editorial guidance, always with a commitment to excellence and sound science.

For these five editions, Academy of Nutrition and Dietetics staff has provided editorial and marketing opportunity and support. For this edition, *Jennifer Herendeen*, Senior Director, Publications, Resources, and Products and *Ryan Baechler*, Director, Publications, Resources, and Products, who lead the highly respected publishing efforts of the Academy; *Sharon Denny, Wendy Marcason, Jill Kohn,* and *Eleese Cunningham* in the Academy Knowledge Center, for their expertise in answering today's nutrition questions with evidence-based answers; *Georgia Gofis*, Director of Marketing, for her enthusiastic and ongoing promotional efforts; the many other *Academy staff* who have supported this edition; and the earlier *Academy editors* who continually made each of the previous editions better.

Bringing their professional expertise as registered dietitian nutritionists from many specialized areas of food, nutrition, and dietetics, the following Academy members provided careful review of this fifth edition, helping to ensure its accuracy, clarity, and relevance with the most current scientific evidence:

Susan E. Adams, Torey Armul, Jennifer Autodore, Keith Thomas Ayoob, Carol Bradley, Sheila Campbell, Andrea Canada, Vanessa Carr, Angela Chalé, Kristine Clark, Nancy Clark, Neva Cochran, Jaime Schwartz Cohen, Sherry Coleman Collins, Diana Cullum-Dugan, Connie Diekman, Suzanne Dixon, Cheryl L. Dolven, Allison Dostal, Lynn Dugan, Dana Elia, Nancy Patin Falini, Susan Finn, Molly Gee, Heather A. Goesch, Patricia Grace-Farfaglia, Cheryl Harris, Alice Henneman, A. Christine Hummell, Barbara J. Ivens, Amy Jones, Wendy Reinhardt Kapsak, Kim Kirchherr, Sally Kuzemchak, Shelley Maniscalco, Caroline Margolis, Liz Marr, Leah McGrath, Beth Ogata, Christine M. Palumbo, Amber Pankonin, Catharine Powers, Jean Ragalie-Carr, Elizabeth Rahavi, Paula Ritter-Gooder, Bonnie Roill, Sarah Romotsky, Christine Rosenbloom, Tami A. Ross, Liz Sanders, Abby Sauer, Jodie Shield, Janelle Smith, Marianne Smith Edge, Toby Smithson, Kris Sollid, Cathie Squatrito, Theresa Stretch, Chris Vogliano, Jill Weisenberger, Sheila C. Weiss, and *Adam Woodyard*.

Many more registered dietitians also have shared their expertise over the years as reviewers in previous editions, where they are recognized by name. Many thanks to them, as well.

Fact checking and updates of nutrient and calorie information, as well as the extensive list of additional resources are attributed to the thorough work of *Morgan Cooper* during her dietetic internship.

Registered dietitian nutritionists and other food, nutrition, and health professionals in government agencies, the food industry, and educational institutions throughout the country have served as ongoing resources and insightful experts. Thanks also goes to the organizations who granted permission for the use of their supporting illustrations and graphics.

The HMH team of editors and designers have provided exceptional editing, a fresh and contemporary design, and expert management—and have been a joy to work with: *Cindy Kitchel,* Editorial Director; *Melissa Fisch*, Editorial Assistant; *Marina Padakis Lowry*, Managing Editor; *Tai Blanche*, Art Director, and *Kevin Watt,* Lead Production Coordinator; as well as *Mary Goodbody*, Content Editor; *Kristi Hart*, Copy Editor; and *Gary Tooth*, Designer. Thank you!

A special thanks is given to *Linda Ingroia*, former Executive Editor, who championed and acquired this fifth new edition for Houghton Mifflin Harcourt, and to *Natalie Chapman*, former Publisher, who began the editing process.

As the Academy celebrates its 100-year anniversary, it's important to recognize the publishing history of this highly successful book and the publishing teams who brought their expertise to previous editions: Chronimed Publishing for the first edition and John Wiley & Sons for the second through fourth editions.

Through these five editions, many colleagues, friends, and family members have provided their consumer and professional perspectives and support. Among them, *Anne Piatek* and *Nancy Schwartz*—colleagues and registered dietitians—who first encouraged my authorship. And my mentors and academic advisors, *Edith Syrjala Eash, Dr. Diva Sanjur*, and *Dr. Hazel Spitze*, who encouraged my early career as a registered dietitian and as a food and nutrition educator and professional.

Special thanks to my husband, *Phil*, who has read every word in all five editions to help ensure clarity of the content and its positive voice, who has been "nourished" by the message, and who provided the loving support needed to continually update this resource.

And most important . . . thank you to all who've called this book their "bible" of healthy eating through its many editions, who've shared their insights for subsequent editions, and who've helped make this book a bestseller from the start. Now fully updated, I hope this resource will continue to be your "go-to" source for sound, healthy eating information and advice . . . at every age and stage of your life!

To your health!
Roberta Larson Duyff, MS, RDN, FAND, CFCS
Author/Food, Nutrition, and Culinary Consultant
Duyff Associates, St. Louis, MO

About the Author

. . . an award-winning author, national speaker, media spokesperson, and food and nutrition consultant, Roberta Larson Duyff, MS, RDN, FAND, CFCS, promotes "the power of positive nutrition" to those of all ages with practical, science-based, great-tasting ways to eat and stay active for health.

As a food and nutrition educator, Roberta's writing for school audiences spans more than thirty years, authoring works such as *Food, Nutrition and Wellness* (for schools), several children's healthy eating books, and *Team Nutrition* and other educational resources. In popular media, her work and quotes have appeared nationally and regionally.

Focused on the "great tastes of good health," Roberta was the guiding force behind and contributor to the Academy's *Cooking Healthy Across America* cookbook. She has contributed to its *Food and Nutrition* magazine and is former Chair of the Academy's Food & Culinary Professionals Dietetic Practice Group. She serves in national and international leadership positions in the James Beard Foundation, Les Dames d'Escoffier, the Society for Nutrition Education and Behavior Foundation, and is an active member of the International Association of Culinary Professionals. She has held national positions within the American Association of Family and Consumer Sciences. Roberta has authored other titles for the Academy, including *365 Days of Healthy Eating*.

Among her professional awards, Roberta has been recognized by the Academy of Nutrition and Dietetics as an Academy Fellow and with its prestigious Medallion Award for professional excellence, its first Annual President's Lecture, and Missouri's Lifetime Achievement Award in nutrition and dietetics.

Both professionally and personally, Roberta embraces the cultural and global connections of food, nutrition, and good health.

Introduction

Making healthy food choices isn't always easy. Whether you want to provide healthy meals and snacks for your busy life . . . or stay fit to feel great, look good, and reduce your chances of a health issue . . . or simply sort through the latest nutrition news to find sound advice . . . this book is for you.

Now in its fifth edition, the *Academy of Nutrition and Dietetics Complete Food and Nutrition Guide* reflects the latest food and nutrition research; the 2015–2020 Dietary Guidelines for Americans; and many of today's food, culinary, and lifestyle trends. But it's much more!

Since its first edition, this resource has provided positive advice that's backed by sound, current science. It continues to be filled with practical (and often great-tasting) "can-do" ways to eat healthier and be more physically active, one step at a time.

What's new in this edition? It's all about food first—and your overall food and beverage choices over time, not a single food, meal, or snack.

As a complete resource on healthy eating, it covers:

- *A healthy eating plan*—flexible for your health needs, lifestyle, and food preferences . . . and how to judge food and drinks by their full powerhouse of nutrients. As a complete resource on healthy eating, it covers:
- *Today's food marketplace from farm to table*—food farming and processing, food shopping and labeling updates, food safety, nourishing and appealing meals and snacks prepared at home, and healthy, flavorful meals enjoyed away.
- *Healthy eating advice for every age and stage of life*—from feeding an infant, child, or teen, to the unique food and nutrition needs of women and of men (a new chapter), and the special challenges of aging.
- *Advice for common food-related health issues*—promoting gut health, a healthy weight, and immunity; preventing, slowing, and dealing with heart disease, cancer, diabetes, among others; managing a food allergy, celiac disease, or lactose intolerance; and addressing many other health issues.

You don't need to read this book from cover to cover. Instead use "Your Healthy Eating Check-ins" to assess your everyday food decisions and to find chapters and features that may relate to your own needs.

Look for countless topics—in-depth features and brief snippets—that capture your interest: perhaps eating meatless meals sometimes or always; limiting food waste; exploring uncommon fruits, vegetables, and whole grains; shopping online or at a farmers' market; doing recipe makeovers; making simple shifts to healthier eating; helping a child grow or prepare food; eating for sports performance; taking supplements wisely; knowing more about pre- and probiotics; judging food experiences in child or adult day care; overcoming mindless eating; using today's mobile or digital health options; finding trustworthy eating advice; supporting healthy eating for others; and so much more.

Questions posed by consumers like you have helped shape the *Academy of Nutrition and Dietetics Complete Food and Nutrition Guide*, from its successful first edition, and now to this fully updated one. Answers to their food and nutrition questions may answer many of yours as well.

This comprehensive resource can help you take easy, practical, and flavorful steps toward your everyday healthy eating decisions and good health.

From my table to yours, read, enjoy, be active, and eat healthy . . . for life!

Roberta Larson Duyff, MS, RDN, FAND, CFCS
Author/Food, Nutrition, and Culinary Consultant
Duyff Associates, St. Louis, MO

PART I

Wellness: Eat Smart, Get Active, Live Well

1

Make Your Food and Lifestyle Choices Count

In this chapter, find out about . . .

Wellness essentials

Nutrition basics: nutrients, calories, and more

Dietary Guidelines for Americans

Physical Activity Guidelines

Setting wellness goals and strategies

Your life is filled with choices! Every day you make thousands of choices, many related to food. Some seem trivial. Others are important. A few may even set the course of your life. But as insignificant as a single choice may seem, when made over and over, it can have a major impact on your health—and your life!

This book is about choices—those you, your family, and your friends make every day—about food, nutrition, physical activity, and health. Within its pages, you'll find food and nutrition information, as well as reliable and sound, positive advice, based on current scientific evidence. You'll find useful, practical tips, flexible guidelines, and simple tools to make healthy food and drink choices in almost any situation and at every stage of life—and to enjoy the pleasures and flavors of food and eating together, too. After all, taste is the number one reason most people choose one food over another. Eating for health is one of the wisest decisions you'll ever make!

Wellness: Your Overall Health

Let's start the journey with a question: What does wellness, or being healthy, mean to you? Perhaps it's just being free of disease or health problems? Or having plenty of energy for everyday work and living? Or having a trim or muscular body? Or being able to finish a 10K run or fitness walk?

Actually, wellness is even broader and more personal. It refers to your own optimal health and overall level of fitness. Wellness is *your* good health—at its very best!

WHAT IS "HEALTHY"?

Wellness, or being healthy, results from physical health, plus emotional and mental well-being. In fact, all three are interconnected. And smart eating and active living are fundamental to each one.

The benefits of being healthy throughout life are enormous. When you're fit, you have:

- Energy to do what's important to you and to be more productive
- Stamina and a positive outlook to handle the mental challenges and emotional ups and downs of everyday life and to deal with stress
- Reduced risk for many health problems, including serious, often life-changing diseases such as heart disease, cancer, type 2 diabetes, and osteoporosis
- The opportunity to look and feel your personal best
- The physical strength and endurance to protect yourself in case of an emergency

Your Healthy Eating Check-in

Healthier Eating: Are You Ready?

Where do you fit on this healthy eating readiness test?

- *"My food choices are okay as they are."* Okay, that's your decision. But read on to find out why you might consider making a few steps in the future to eat for better health (and perhaps to be more active, too).
- *"I'll change my eating habits sometime, but I can't make myself do it now."* Good initial thought. Consider the pros and cons as you decide. Consult these pages for sensible, realistic ways to eat smarter (and get active)—but now rather than later. The sooner you start, the greater the benefits.
- *"I'm ready to eat smarter, starting now."* Good—you can do it! Check the tips throughout the book for small steps to healthy eating that work for you. As you achieve them, try a few more. Be active, too.
- *"I'm already a 'healthy eater.'"* Great, keep it up! Flip through this book for more practical ways to eat smart. In fact, get adventuresome with your eating. And take time for active living.
- *"Healthy eating and active living are second nature to me."* Excellent! Share the practical advice provided here and your own success with someone else. The health benefits are your rewards. If you stray from time to time, identify why, address the reason or reasons, and get back on board. If you're ready for healthier eating, *"Reaching SMART Goals, One Step at a Time!" in this chapter, page 18, can show you "how."* The pages in between give a brief overview of the "whys" and "hows" covered in this book.

- A better chance for a higher quality of life, and perhaps a longer one, too!

Good nutrition helps ensure a healthy pregnancy and successful breastfeeding. Well-nourished, physically active children and teens grow, develop, and learn better. Healthful eating and active living help people at every age and stage of life feel their best and work productively. They may even slow aging—a benefit most people yearn for.

The sooner healthy eating and regular physical activity become your priorities, the better your overall health and quality of life will be!

YOUR PERSONAL HEALTH EQUATION

For your own best health, you don't need special or costly foods, fancy exercise equipment, or a health club membership. You don't need to give up your favorite foods or set up a tedious system of eating rules and calorie counting. Health habits don't need to take more time either. And you don't need to hit a specific weight on the bathroom scale or even become a serious athlete.

You do need sensible ways to eat smart and be active, with approaches that are right for you. You're in control. You can do that, one simple step at a time.

What and how much you eat and how much you move profoundly impact your health and body weight. Arguably, healthy eating and active living are among your best personal investments.

Smart Eating Fuels Fitness

You've heard the term "nutrition" all your life. In a nutshell, nutrition is how food nourishes your body. Being well nourished depends on getting enough of the nutrients and calories your body needs—but not too many calories.

Today's understanding of nutrition is based on years of scientific study. As recorded by the ancient Greeks, interest in food and health has a long history. Hippocrates, the "Father of Medicine" born about twenty-five hundred years ago, is quoted as saying, "If every individual could have the right amount of nourishment and exercise, not too little and not too much, we should have found the safest way to health."

Not until the nineteenth century, however, did the mysteries of nutrition begin to unravel. Although scientists have answered many nutrition questions, new ones arise as knowledge evolves. Research continues as scientists explore emerging food and nutrition questions about the many roles they play in promoting health and protecting against disease. New knowledge is evolutionary, not revolutionary!

Today it's known that healthy eating and active living can lower your risks for being overweight and having high blood pressure, high blood cholesterol, obesity, high blood glucose, and low bone density. All are risk factors for serious diseases such as heart disease, certain cancers, type 2 diabetes, stroke, and osteoporosis, which are among the main causes of disability and death in the United States.

Today's nutrition guidance is supported by scientific evidence. So unlike the ancients, you have a well-founded basis for making wise food choices for health and your own well-being.

Active Living Matters, Too

Wellness requires more than healthy eating. Regular physical activity is also part of the equation that promotes health, a sense of well-being,

? Have you ever wondered?

. . . why sleep is important to your health? Getting enough quality sleep—promoted by healthy eating habits and regular physical activity—is one more factor in the health equation.

The National Heart, Lung, and Blood Institute (NHLBI) cites these among the connections between sleep and physical health:

- Sleep helps keep a healthy balance of the hormones that make you feel hungry (ghrelin) and full (leptin). With inadequate sleep, ghrelin goes up and leptin goes down, so you may feel hungrier when you're sleep deprived. That may impact how much you eat and may indirectly impact body weight.
- Sleep affects how your body reacts to insulin, the hormone that controls your blood glucose level. With a sleep deficiency, a normal blood glucose level may be higher, increasing the risk for diabetes.
- Sleep promotes immunity. Ongoing sleep deficit changes the way your immune system responds. For example, it reduces the ability to fight common infections.
- Sleep supports healthy growth and development. With deep sleep, the body triggers the release of the hormone that promotes normal growth in children and teens and that helps build and repair body cells and tissues for those of any age. Sleep also affects puberty and fertility.
- Sleep is involved in the healing and repair of heart and blood vessels. An ongoing sleep deficit is linked to an increased risk of some chronic diseases such as heart disease, high blood pressure, stroke, diabetes, and kidney disease.

Besides helping to promote and protect your physical health, good sleep impacts your mental health, your physical safety and productivity, and the quality of your life. Adults are advised to get seven to eight hours of sleep a day; teens, nine to ten hours; and children, ten hours or more, depending on their age.

Click Here! Links to Know . . .

- 2015–2020 Dietary Guidelines for Americans
  health.gov/dietaryguidelines/2015
- 2008 Physical Activity Guidelines for Americans
  www.health.gov/paguidelines
- MyPlate (visual cue for healthy eating)
  www.ChooseMyPlate.gov
- Dietary Reference Intakes (DRI) Calculator
  fnic.nal.usda.gov/fnic/interactiveDRI

and a healthy body weight. Yet most Americans don't move enough. How about you?

Regular physical activity doesn't need to be a sport or gym-based exercise routine. Enough moderate physical activity just needs to be a regular part of your daily routine. These include everyday activities of living such as doing yard work, using the stairs, and walking the dog or walking with a friend.

More to the Wellness Equation

There's still more to the equation for wellness. Your genetic makeup, your age and gender, your surroundings and lifestyle, and the influences of culture strongly affect your health, as do the many ongoing choices you make throughout life.

Here are some clear-cut ways you can add value to your equation for wellness: Get enough quality sleep, avoid smoking, manage stress, drink alcoholic beverages only in moderation (if you drink and are of legal age), wear your seat belt, practice good hygiene, get regular medical checkups, and obtain adequate healthcare—to name a few.

FOOD CHOICES: ALL ABOUT YOU

You've likely heard the phrase, "You are what you eat." That's one way to say that the nutrition in your food choices has great bearing on your health and development. That said, there's no one "right" way to eat. There are many different paths to healthy eating.

It is also true that food choices reflect what's important to you: your culture, traditions, and perhaps religion, your surroundings, your food budget, the people around you, your view of yourself, the foods available to you and those foods you like, your emotions, and likely your knowledge about food and nutrition.

Besides its nutrition benefits, food can be a source of pleasure, adventure, and great taste, offering occasions to share with others. It's no surprise that people entertain and celebrate with food, or look forward to a special dish. Good nutrition can go hand in hand with pleasurable meals and snacks.

Your Food Choices: The Inside Story

While you enjoy the sensual qualities of food—the mouthwatering appearance, aroma, texture, and flavor—your body relies on the life-sustaining functions that the nutrients in food perform. Other food substances, including phytonutrients (or plant substances), appear to offer health benefits, too, beyond basic nourishment. *See "Phytonutrients: Different from Nutrients," in chapter 15, page 448, to learn about the roles of phytonutrients in health.*

NUTRIENTS: CLASSIFIED INFORMATION

Your body can't make most of the substances it needs to function normally, repair itself, produce energy, or grow. You need the varied and adequate nutrient supply that food delivers for nourishment—and for life itself.

To access these nutrients, what you eat and what you drink are digested, or broken down, before they are absorbed into your bloodstream and carried to every cell in your body. Most of your body's work takes place in your cells.

Food's nutrients are essential. More than forty nutrients in food, classified into six groups, have specific and unique functions. Their functions are linked as they work together as part of your body's many metabolic processes.

Carbohydrates. As your body's main source of energy, or calories, carbohydrates are both starches (complex carbohydrates) and sugars.

Fiber, another form of complex carbohydrate, aids digestion, promotes health (including gut health), and helps protect against several chronic and serious diseases. Despite its important role in health, fiber isn't a nutrient; it isn't digested and then absorbed into the body. *See chapter 11, page 345, to learn about carbohydrates.*

Fats. Fats from food not only supply energy, they also support many metabolic functions, such as nutrient transport and growth. Fat is also part of many body cells.

Fats are made of varying combinations of different types of fatty acids, with different effects on overall heath. Some fats are high in saturated fatty acids, making them solid at room temperature (butter, stick margarine, lard); others contain more poly- and monounsaturated fatty acids, making them soft, even at colder temperatures (tub margarine), or liquid (oils).

Some fatty acids are essential, or required for your health, but your body can't make them. *See chapter 13, page 385, to learn about fats.*

Proteins. Proteins are sequenced combinations of amino acids, which build, repair, and maintain body tissues. Your body makes nonessential amino acids; others, from food, are considered "essential" because your body can't make them.

Proteins also provide energy, especially when carbohydrates and fats are in short supply. If they're broken down and used for energy, amino acids can't be used to maintain body tissue, however. *See chapter 12, page 373, to learn about proteins.*

Vitamins. Vitamins work like spark plugs, triggering chemical reactions in body cells. Each vitamin regulates different body processes. Because their roles are so specific, one vitamin cannot replace another. *See chapter 14, page 408, to learn about vitamins.*

Minerals. Somewhat like the actions of vitamins, minerals also spark body processes. Each mineral also has a unique metabolic role. Some, such as calcium, are also part of your body's structure. *See chapter 14, page 408, to learn about minerals.*

Water. Water makes up 45 to 75 percent of body weight—and it's also a nutrient. It regulates body processes, helps regulate your body temperature, carries nutrients and other body chemicals to your cells, and carries waste products away. *See "Water: A Fluid Asset," in chapter 15, page 443, to learn about water as a nutrient—and why there's such a range of water weight in body composition.*

Nutrients: How Much?

Everyone needs the full range of the same nutrients—just in different amounts. For healthy people, age, gender, and body size make a difference. Children and teenagers, for example, need more of some nutrients for growth. Pregnancy and breastfeeding increase the need for some nutrients and for calories. Because their bodies are typically larger, men often need more of most nutrients than women do.

The Dietary Reference Intakes (DRIs) established by the Food and Nutrition Board of the Institute of Medicine, National Academy of Sciences, made daily nutrient recommendations for healthy people in the United

DRIs: Five Types of Recommendations

- *Recommended Dietary Allowances (RDAs):* Recommended nutrient levels that meet the needs of almost all healthy individuals in specific age and gender groups. Consider these recommendations as your goal for getting enough nutrients.
- *Adequate Intakes (AIs):* Similar in meaning to RDAs. They're used as guidelines for some nutrients that don't have enough scientific evidence to set firm RDAs.
- *Tolerable Upper Intake Levels (ULs):* Not recommended amounts. In fact, there's no scientific consensus for recommending nutrient levels higher than the RDAs for most healthy people. Instead, ULs represent the maximum nutrient intake that probably won't pose health risks for most healthy people in a specific age and gender group. As someone's intake increases above the UL, the potential risk for adverse health effects does, too.
- *Estimated Average Requirements (EARs):* Used to assess groups of people, not individuals. They're the average daily nutrient intake amount estimated to meet the requirement of half the healthy people in a life stage and gender group.
- *Acceptable Macronutrient Distribution Ranges (AMDRs):* Recommended ranges of intake for three macronutrients—carbohydrates, fats, and proteins—as energy sources. These ranges not only reflect amounts considered to be enough to provide essential nutrients, they are also the amounts linked to reduced risk for chronic diseases. An intake that goes outside these ranges carries a possible increased risk of some chronic disease and/or insufficient intakes of essential nutrients.

See the appendix, page 780, for details on recommended DRI amounts.

States and Canada based on age and gender. This advice is reviewed and updated regularly by groups of scientific experts to reflect the most current research evidence.

Smart Eating = Nutrient Balance

How do you use the DRIs? If you're healthy and follow the eating plans *discussed in chapter 2, page 23,* you likely get the right amounts of the all the nutrients you need. Those eating plans, from the 2015–2020 Dietary Guidelines for Americans *(discussed in this chapter, page 6)* take the DRIs into account.

If you choose to calculate your nutrient intake, some websites and apps can help you. But remember, the recommendations—RDAs and AIs—apply to your average nutrient intake over several days, not just one day and certainly not one meal. A registered dietitian nutritionist can assist you; *see "Nutrition Advice to Trust" in chapter 26, page 758, to find expert help.*

FOOD: MORE THAN NUTRIENTS

Food contains many more substances than nutrients. Science recognizes the health benefits of other components in food, such as phytonutrients (including fiber), plant stanols and sterols, and pre- and probiotics, to name a few.

Often described as "functional," these substances do more than nourish you. They appear to promote health and protect against health risks related to many major health problems, including heart disease, some cancers, type 2 diabetes, and macular degeneration, among others.

At least for now, no DRIs exist for functional components in food, except for fiber. Scientists don't yet fully understand their roles in health. However, within this book, you'll get a glimpse of emerging knowledge about some of them. You're bound to hear more as new studies unfold.

Note: Animal-based foods also contain cholesterol, which is a fat-like substance but not a nutrient. No DRIs exist for cholesterol.

CALORIE BASICS

Back in science class, you probably learned the technical definition: one calorie is the amount of energy needed to raise the temperature of 1 gram of water by 1 degree Celsius. In the world of nutrition and health, the term "calorie" refers to the energy in food and the energy the body uses to keep you alive and moving—and to help kids grow.

Calories: What Sources?

In food, calories are the energy locked inside the three macronutrients: carbohydrates, fats, and proteins. How much energy they provide differs. Carbohydrates (starches and sugars) in food are your body's main energy source, providing 4 calories per gram. Proteins also provide 4 calories per gram. Fats deliver 9 calories per gram, or twice the energy per gram that carbohydrates and proteins do. Although not a nutrient, alcohol provides 7 calories per gram, too.

These macronutrients are released from food during digestion, absorbed into the bloodstream, and at some point can be converted to blood glucose, often referred to as blood sugar. In your body, the energy in blood glucose is released into trillions of body cells. There it's used to power all your body's work—from your heartbeat, to push-ups, to the smile that spreads across your face.

As an aside, protein is an energy source only if you don't get enough calories from carbohydrates and fats. And when excess calories are consumed, they're stored as body fat.

Recognizing physical differences among people, as well as their personal preferences, a range of calories from each macronutrient is advised: for adults, 45 to 65 percent of calories from carbohydrates, 20 to 35 percent from fats, and 10 to 35 percent from proteins. In the DRIs, these are referred to as AMDRs; *see "DRIs: Five Types of Recommendations," in this chapter, page 6.* To lose, gain, or maintain your weight, you need to be mindful of your total calories—in and out.

Know that foods with solid fats (high in saturated fats and *trans* fats) and added sugars won't promote weight gain any more than other calorie sources do—*if* your calorie intake balances with the calories your body needs, or uses.

Be aware: The fewer calories you consume overall, the greater percentage of calories you need from proteins (within the AMDR range) to meet your protein need. To put that range in actual numbers, you need to know your daily calorie target.

Calories: Your Target?

Everyone has a personal calorie limit, yet most people are unaware of how many calories they need, how many calories they take in, or how to make adjustments to help manage their weight. Given the same height, age, and gender, calorie needs vary from person to person, and even for the same person, day to day.

Your energy (calorie) needs depend on how many calories you need to take in to match your body's energy expenditure. That's called calorie (or energy) balance. Your target depends on:

- The amount and intensity of your physical activity in your everyday living and in sports. The more physically active you are, the more calories you need to fuel your body, *as discussed in "Calories: A Matter of Balance" in chapter 22, page 635.*
- Your age and stage of life, your basal metabolic rate, your body size and composition, and your physical health, *as discussed in "Weight: What's Healthy?" in chapter 22, page 628.*
- Your weight goals: whether you want to lose, gain, or maintain your current body weight, *as discussed in "Personally Speaking: Your Healthy Weight" in chapter 22, page 627.* To manage your body weight, all calories matter, not just those from so-called "empty calorie," or nutrient-poor, foods.

Physical Activity: How Many Calories Will Your Body Burn?

Calories Burned per Hour, by Body Weight

Activity	120 lbs.	170 lbs.
Aerobic dance	335	500
Archery	190	270
Basketball	330	460
Bicycling (<10 mph)	220	310
Bowling	165	230
Calisthenics	190	270
Driving a car	110	155
Eating	80	115
Food preparation	120	175
Gardening	220	310
Golf (walking)	245	345
Hiking	325	460
Horseback riding	220	310
Housework	135	190
Jogging	380	540
Mowing lawn	245	345

Calories Burned per Hour, by Body Weight

Activity	120 lbs.	170 lbs.
Racquetball	380	540
Reading	70	100
Rowing, stationary	380	540
Running, 10 mph	870	1,235
Sitting (watching TV)	55	75
Sitting (writing, typing)	100	140
Skating, roller	380	540
Skiing, cross-country	435	615
Skiing, downhill	325	460
Sleeping	50	70
Soccer	380	540
Swimming, leisure	380	540
Tennis	380	540
Walking, brisk	205	295
Weight training	165	230

Calculated from: Ainsworth, BE. *The Compendium of Physical Activities Tracking Guide.* Prevention Research Center, Norman J. Arnold School of Public Health, University of South Carolina, 2002.

Are you on track with your calorie target? Monitor your body weight and any changes in weight over time, and then adjust the calories in your food and drink choices as you update your calorie target.

To estimate your calorie needs, see "How Many Calories? Figuring Your Energy Needs," in the appendix, page 771, and "Estimated Calorie Needs per Day by Age, Gender, and Physical Activity Level," also in the appendix, page 770. Or use the online Body Weight Planner—www.supertracker.usda.gov/bwp/index.html—which is one of the interactive tools available in the SuperTracker. The SuperTracker can generate an eating and a physical activity plan for you, too.

Smart Eating, Active Living: Recipe for Health

Healthy eating and active living are among the most powerful tools for preventing and delaying disease. There's no secret here, just solid, science-backed advice. Some advice never really changes—and may even sound like a lot like your mom: eat more vegetables and fruits, watch your portions, and get up and move. Whether it's healthy eating or physical activity, these concepts matter: variety, balance, and moderation.

Two sets of science-based guidelines have been established to help you put variety, balance, and moderation into action: the Dietary Guidelines for Americans and the Physical Activity Guidelines for Americans. Both support a "total approach" to your overall choices, over several days.

EAT SMART: DIETARY GUIDELINES FOR AMERICANS

The Dietary Guidelines for Americans is the nation's go-to source for advice about making informed food choices, consuming the right amount of nutrients and calories for you, and reinforcing advice for physical activity. The goals? To promote overall health and a healthy weight and to prevent or reduce the chance of getting many chronic diseases. These guidelines aren't meant to treat disease.

Most people in the United States, regardless of their current health status, could benefit from shifting their food and drink choices to better support healthy eating patterns.

Facts About the Guidelines

Issued jointly by the US Department of Health and Human Services (USHHS) and the US Department of Agriculture (USDA), the 2015–2020 Dietary Guidelines for Americans report was developed by a scientific advisory committee, and it presents science-based guidance for Americans ages two and older, including people who are at higher risk for chronic disease. The goal is to make recommendations about the components of a healthy, nutritionally adequate diet to help promote health and prevent chronic disease for current and future generations.

The recommendations reflect current scientific evidence. Experts have conducted a rigorous, systematic review of scientific evidence in a transparent process that's open to public review to establish this advice.

While relatively consistent since first established in 1980, the Dietary Guidelines for Americans report has been reviewed and updated every five years as scientific evidence about nutrition and health has evolved and grown. Nutrition is, after all, a dynamic science that continues to expand knowledge over time.

This advice doesn't apply to infants and toddlers. Their nutritional needs and eating patterns vary and depend on their developmental stage. What's more, their needs differ significantly from those of older children, teens, and adults. Dietary guidelines specific to infants and toddlers (birth to age two), with additional guidance for pregnant women, are underway and are projected for release with the 2020 Dietary Guidelines for Americans. Stay tuned!

The Dietary Guidelines' recommendations are used to establish policies related to food and nutrition and are applied in many places where you can access food. They provide the scientific basis that underlies many nutrition initiatives such as designing science-based nutrition programs for children and mothers; regulating the USDA's School Breakfast and School Lunch Programs; providing food assistance for needy people and older adults; teaching children and teens about nutrition; including nutrition information on food labeling; developing healthier foods and drinks by food companies; and communicating with consumers about sound nutrition and active living.

2015–2020 Dietary Guidelines for Americans: Five Key Messages

1. Follow a healthy eating pattern across your life span. All food and beverage choices matter. Choose a healthy eating pattern at an appropriate calorie level for you to help achieve and maintain your healthy body weight, to get an adequate amount of nutrients, and to reduce your risks of chronic disease.
2. Focus on variety, nutrient density, and amount in your food choices. To meet your nutrient needs within your calorie limits, choose a variety of nutrient-dense foods among and within all five food groups in recommended amounts.
3. Limit the calories you take in from added sugars and saturated fats, and reduce your sodium intake. Consume an eating pattern low in added sugars, saturated fats, and sodium. Cut back on foods and beverages higher in these components to amounts that fit within healthy eating patterns.
4. Shift to healthier food and beverage choices. Choose nutrient-dense foods and beverages among and within all food groups in place of less healthy choices. Consider your own cultural and personal preferences to make these shifts easier to do and maintain.
5. Support healthy eating patterns for you, your family, friends, and others. Everyone has a role in helping to create and support healthy eating from your home, to school, to work—and to your community and elsewhere.

Source: 2015–2020 Dietary Guidelines for Americans, USHHS and USDA.

Healthy Eating Patterns: Focus on Your Total Diet

How can you apply this guidance to your food decisions? How can you choose meals and snacks to stay within your daily calorie limit, to deliver the nutrients you need, and to keep you healthy? How can you use this advice to plan healthy meals and snacks for your family?

The Dietary Guidelines recognizes that eating patterns as a whole (your total diet), not just single foods, single drinks, and single nutrients, promote overall good health. For their effect on health, they—and their components—work synergistically, or together, for bigger results.

Your whole diet refers to the total nutrient package. It doesn't mean cutting out a nourishing food because it contains added sugars or sodium. Sometimes a little added sugars can make calcium-rich yogurt more appealing or a little salt adds flavor to vegetables or a hearty whole-grain dish. The big picture is what counts.

With this in mind, these guidelines advise healthy eating patterns, *discussed in chapter 2, page 21*, that support a healthy body weight and can help prevent and reduce the risk of chronic disease throughout periods of growth, development, and aging, as well as during pregnancy. These healthy eating patterns are built around three principles in the Dietary Guidelines that support its key recommendations of:

1. An eating pattern represents everything you eat and drink. In a healthy eating pattern, all foods and drinks are parts of a puzzle that fit together to meet your nutritional needs—if you don't exceed your limits for saturated fats, added sugars, sodium, and total calories. That includes all forms of foods: fresh, canned, dried, and frozen.
2. Nutritional needs should come mostly from nutrient-dense foods—not supplements. In some cases, fortified foods and dietary supplements may help provide one or more nutrients that otherwise may be consumed in less-than-recommended amounts.

? Have you ever wondered?

. . . what the term "nutrient dense" means? It describes nourishing foods and drinks with the right balance of calories and nutrients. These foods pack in plenty of important nutrients and are naturally lean or low in solid fats, with little or no added solid fats, sugars, refined starches, or sodium. And they have positive health benefits with relatively few calories. All vegetables, fruits, whole-grain foods, eggs, beans and peas (legumes), unsalted nuts and seeds, fat-free and low-fat milk and milk products, and lean meats, poultry, and fish fit this definition—if prepared with little or no saturated fats, sodium, and added sugars. Nutrient-dense foods are the foundation of a healthy eating pattern.

The terms "nutrient dense" and "nutrient rich" are often used interchangeably. For food labeling, the term "rich" has a regulated definition, however, meaning that the amount in one serving (as given on the label) has 20 percent or more of the Daily Value for the nutrient.

. . . what makes the 2015–2020 Dietary Guidelines different from the 2010 Guidelines? Scientific understanding evolves, and so every five years the guidelines are re-issued to reflect the most current scientific evidence.

The most recent Dietary Guidelines report expands on weight management, addressing the prevention of a broader range of diet-related chronic diseases, including type 2 diabetes, heart disease, and some cancers. And instead of focusing on specific, individual dietary components, such as foods, food groups, and nutrients, the 2015–2020 Dietary Guidelines takes a wider view, emphasizing overall eating patterns and the combinations of all the foods and drinks that people consume every day.

3. Healthy eating patterns are flexible. You have more than one way to achieve a healthy eating pattern. In fact, any eating pattern can be tailored to your sociocultural and personal food and drink preferences.

A healthy eating pattern for you matches your target calorie level. That calorie level considers the calories you consume from foods and drinks and how many calories your body uses for its daily functions and for physical activity.

Shifting your food choices—both within and among food groups—from less healthy to more nutrient-dense choices may offer health benefits. Some shifts you may need to make are probably minor, achieved with simple substitutions; others may take more effort. Regardless, even small shifts in your food and drink choices—over a week, a day, or even a meal—can make a big difference. They all add up!

Shift Your Choices: Eat More of These!

Today much more is known about the health-promoting nutrients found in vegetables, fruits, whole grains, fat-free and low-fat dairy foods, and lean protein foods, including fish, lean meats and poultry, eggs, beans and peas (legumes), soy products, unsalted nuts and seeds, and oils.

Together, these foods provide essential nutrients, including those that many people don't consume enough of. Yet, across nearly every age and gender group, Americans come up short on certain foods or food groups.

(For more about all of these food groups, see chapter 2, page 22.)

Vegetables and fruits. Despite the health benefits of vegetables and fruits, most people don't consume enough of them—and variety is lacking, too.

Whether they're fresh, frozen, canned, or dried, vegetables and fruits are major sources of often underconsumed nutrients, including folate, magnesium, potassium, fiber, and vitamins A, C, and K. If prepared without adding fats or sugars, vegetables and fruits are relatively low in calories.

Research has shown that eating enough vegetables and fruits is associated with a reduced risk of many chronic diseases, including cardiovascular disease, and may protect against some types of cancers.

Recommendations: Eat more vegetables and fruits in place of foods high in calories, saturated fats, or sodium, such as some meats, poultry, cheeses, and snack foods. Shift the proportions in mixed dishes to include more veggies and less of the ingredients often overconsumed. Include a variety of colorful vegetables, especially dark-green, red, and orange vegetables, and beans and peas (legumes). For canned and frozen vegetables, choose those lower in sodium.

Many children and young adults consume more than half of their fruits as juice. Instead, for the fiber benefits, choose mostly whole fruits rather than juice. Enjoy fruits as snacks, in salads, as side dishes, and as desserts in place of foods with added sugars, such as cakes, pies, cookies, doughnuts, ice cream, and candies. For juice, choose 100 percent juice. Also, choose fruit canned in juice rather than syrup to limit added sugars.

Grains. While most people eat enough grain products, very few consume enough whole grains. Why do the Dietary Guidelines emphasize whole grains? They're important sources of iron, magnesium, selenium, B vitamins, and fiber. Eating enough whole grains may help reduce the risk of heart disease and may be linked to a lower body weight. Although evidence is limited, eating whole grains also may be associated with a reduced risk of type 2 diabetes.

Refined grains differ from whole grains because two parts of the grain—the bran and the germ—are removed when grains undergo processing. That also removes dietary fiber, iron, and other nutrients. Although most refined grains are enriched with B vitamins and iron and are fortified with folic acid, all the nutrients and fiber found in whole grains aren't fully restored in refined-grain products.

2015–2020 Dietary Guidelines for Americans: Key Recommendations

Consume a healthy eating pattern that accounts for all foods and beverages within an appropriate calorie level.

A healthy eating pattern includes:

- A variety of vegetables from all of the subgroups—dark green, red and orange, beans and peas (legumes), starchy, and other
- Fruits, especially whole fruits
- Grains, at least half of which are whole grains
- Fat-free or low-fat dairy, including milk, yogurt, cheese, and/or fortified soy beverages
- A variety of protein foods, including seafood, lean meats and poultry, eggs, beans and peas (legumes), and nuts, seeds, and soy products
- Oils

A healthy eating pattern limits*:

- Saturated fats and *trans* fats, added sugars, and sodium*
  - Consume less than 10 percent of calories per day from added sugars
  - Consume less than 10 percent of calories per day from saturated fats
  - Consume less than 2,300 milligrams (mg) per day of sodium

If alcohol is consumed, it should be in moderation: up to one drink per day for women and up to two drinks per day for men—and only by adults of legal drinking age.

In tandem with the dietary recommendations above, Americans of all ages—children, adolescents, adults, and older adults—should meet the Physical Activity Guidelines for Americans to help promote health and reduce the risk of chronic disease. Americans should aim to achieve and maintain a healthy body weight. The relationship between diet and physical activity contributes to calorie balance and managing body weight. As such the Dietary Guidelines includes a Key Recommendation to meet the advice of the Physical Activity Guidelines for Americans.

*These components are of particular public health concern in the United States and should be limited. Specified limits can help individuals achieve healthy eating patterns within calorie limits.

Source: 2015–2020 Dietary Guidelines for Americans, USHHS and USDA.

Recommendations: Shift your choices so at least half the grains you eat are whole, replacing some refined grains with whole grains. The fiber in whole-grain products varies, so choose those with more fiber (at least 3 grams or more per label serving) for more health benefits. Making at least half your grains whole can be tricky.

If at least half of your grains are whole, what about the other half? Make them enriched refined-grain foods or whole grain, too. Enriched grains are fortified with folic acid, whereas whole grains may not be. Limit refined grains and products made with them, especially those high in saturated and *trans* fats, added sugars, and/or sodium, such as cookies, cakes, and some snack foods.

Fat-free and low-fat dairy foods. These foods deliver many important nutrients, including some that people often lack in their food choices: calcium, vitamin D (if vitamin D–fortified), and potassium. Fat-free and low-fat (1%) dairy products provide the same nutrients but less fat (and thus, fewer calories) than higher-fat options Beyond that, consuming dairy foods appears to be linked to better bone health, especially in children and teens.

Despite the benefits of milk, milk products, and fortified soymilk, most people ages four and older, and even some two- and three-year-olds, don't consume enough. Females consume less than males, and intake tends to decline with age, with low levels among adults of all ages.

Being similar to milk for nutrition and culinary uses, soymilk that's fortified with calcium and vitamins A and D is grouped with dairy foods. Other beverages sold as "milks," such as almond, coconut, hemp, and rice, may provide calcium but aren't similar to dairy milk and are not dairy alternatives.

Recommendations: Replace whole and full-fat products with low-fat and fat-free versions of milk, yogurt, and cheese as a way to consume less saturated fats. Switch the proportion, from less cheese to more low-fat and fat-free milk and yogurt, which have more potassium and vitamins A and D and less sodium and saturated fats than cheese does. Try yogurt as a snack or using yogurt as an ingredient in prepared dishes such as salad dressings or spreads.

If you are lactose intolerant, try low-lactose and lactose-free dairy products. If you don't choose to or can't consume dairy products, choose foods that provide the variety of nutrients that dairy foods provide (including protein, calcium, potassium, magnesium, vitamin D, and vitamin A), such as soymilk fortified with calcium and vitamins A and D.

Protein foods. Whether from fish, meats such as beef and pork, poultry, eggs, beans and peas (legumes), soy products, nuts, or seeds, these foods provide more than protein. They're all good sources of B vitamins, vitamin E, iron, zinc, and magnesium. However, their nutrients differ. While meat provides the most zinc, poultry provides the most niacin. Meat, poultry, and fish provide heme iron, which is more bioavailable than the non-heme iron in eggs, beans and peas (legumes), and nuts. Fish, nuts, and seeds deliver more unsaturated fats than meat does, while meat provides more saturated fats. And oily fish provides the most omega-3s. Eggs provide the most choline; nuts and seeds provide the most vitamin E. Like beans and peas (legumes), soy foods are a source of copper, manganese, and iron.

Most people consume enough protein foods overall, but shifting to more legumes, fish, and other lean protein foods to meet your protein food recommendation is eating-right advice.

Recommendations: Switch from fattier meats and poultry, which are higher in saturated fats, to lean protein foods; some, such as fish and nuts, are good sources of oils, too. Eating a variety of protein foods delivers a host of benefits.

More variety means eating more seafood in place of some meat and poultry, too. Among seafood's unique benefits are its omega-3 fatty acids. How much fish should you eat? Eight ounces or more a week (less for young children). *For guidelines on eating fish during pregnancy and breastfeeding, see "Who's at High Risk? Select Safer Food Alternatives" in chapter 7, page 222, and "Foodborne Illness and Pregnancy" in chapter 18, page 553.*

Because they are high in calories, eat nuts and seeds (unsalted) in small portions in place of other protein foods. Limit processed meats and processed poultry, which are sources of sodium and saturated fats; they can be included in your eating plan as long as you keep your overall intake of sodium, saturated fats, added sugars, and total calories within your limits. For meatless and vegetarian options, choose enough plant-based protein foods.

Oils. Why have advice about oils? Although not a food group, they contribute essential fatty acids and vitamin E. Oils that are high in unsaturated fats are heart healthier than solid fats, which are more saturated.

Tropical oils (coconut, palm, and palm kernel) are solid at room temperature and are not grouped with the healthy oils because they have high amounts of saturated fatty acids; they're considered solid fats. Most Americans consume more solid fats—and less oils—than advised.

Because oils are a concentrated source of calories, consume them as part of your total fat intake (recommended as range of 20 to 35 percent of total calories) without exceeding your calorie limits.

Recommendations: To consume the recommended amount of oils, whenever possible switch from solid fats to oils in food preparation rather than adding more oils to your foods. Small amounts are enough if your limit is 2,000 calories daily.

Switch from foods high in saturated fats (butter, stick margarine, shortening, lard, coconut oil) to vegetable oils when you cook. Among the common options are vegetable oils such as canola, corn, olive, soybean, peanut, and sunflower oils. Eat more of the foods such as avocados, nuts, olives, and some fish, that naturally contain oils, in place of some meat and poultry. Choose foods made with oils, such as salad dressings and spreads, instead of solid fats.

For more about all of these categories of foods, the amounts advised for you, and how to fit them into your daily meals and snacks, see chapters 2, page 12, and 3, page 60.

Under-consumed nutrients of concern. Potassium, calcium, vitamin D, and fiber come up short in the eating patterns of most Americans. For young children, pregnant women and those able to become pregnant, a low intake of iron also is a public health concern. *See chapter 14, page 408, to learn about these vitamins and minerals and chapter 11, page 350, to learn about fiber. See the appendix [DRI Tables], page 781, for the nutrient amounts recommended for you.*

Recommendation: Eat more vegetables, fruits, whole grains, and dairy foods to consume more of these nutrients.

Shift Your Choices: Eat Less of These!

Many people (children and teens included) consume too much sodium, solid fats (major sources of saturated fats and *trans* fats), and added sugars. Often they "hide" unexpectedly in foods and drinks. Overconsuming alcoholic drinks is a concern, too.

Consuming too much saturated fats, added sugars, and sodium, as well as alcoholic drinks, increases the risks of certain chronic diseases. It also makes it harder to meet nutrient recommendations and control calories. What should you cut back on?

Added sugars. Added sugars such as table sugar, honey, syrups, and other sugary sweeteners supply only calories without other nutritional value.

Then why are they added? To sweeten foods and drinks, to add flavor, to help preserve foods, and to provide other qualities, such as improved texture, that add appeal. Sugars that are naturally present in food and drinks, such as fructose in fruit and lactose in milk, are not added sugars.

When it comes to health concerns, it's hard to separate one factor in an eating pattern from another. However, eating patterns with less added sugars are associated with reduced risk of obesity, type 2 diabetes, and some cancers in adults—and perhaps reduced risk of cardiovascular disease.

What about tooth decay? Both added sugars and naturally occurring sugars may contribute to decay in children and adults, as do starches, another form of carbohydrate.

That said, a little sweetness can have a positive role in healthy eating by making nutrient-dense foods taste better. That's okay as long as calories from added sugars do not exceed 10 percent per day, total carbohydrate intake remains within the recommended daily amount, and total calorie intake remains within healthy limits. For example, fat-free yogurts and whole-grain breakfast cereals with a small amount of added sugar may encourage people to consume them and get the vitamin D, calcium, and/or fiber they provide. Tart fruits such as cranberries may be more palatable with a little added sweetener.

On average, people in the United States consume almost 270 calories daily, or more than 13 percent of their day's calories, from added sugars; the percentage is especially high among children, teens, and young adults. Cutting back on foods and drinks with added sugars can lower calories without compromising nutrition adequacy.

A Healthy Weight, a Healthy Life

The incidence of being overweight and obesity is much higher in the United States today than just a few decades ago. The risks are significant. At every age, a healthy weight is fundamental to a long, healthy, and productive life. For children and adults, even a few excess pounds may be riskier than you think. Research shows that being overweight or obese increases the risk for high blood pressure, unhealthy blood lipids (fats) levels, and prediabetes. But obesity also is linked to type 2 diabetes, heart disease, certain cancers, and even premature death. *Chapter 22, page 625,* addresses reasons for the rise in overweight and obesity, including scientific evidence that links food choices to weight.

Calorie balance is key to a healthy weight. Calorie balance is achieved when the calories consumed from foods and drinks equal the calories used for physical activity and metabolic processes. On the flip side, calorie imbalance, or consuming more calories than the body uses, has resulted in the growing national and global epidemic of overweight and obesity, and not just among adults. Incidences of being overweight among children and teens have risen dramatically in recent decades.

No matter what your age, pay attention to your weight. Set your goal on achieving or keeping a weight that's healthy for you. Your calorie needs will likely decrease gradually during adulthood. Strive to keep your healthy weight over the years; children and teens who keep their healthy weight as they grow have less chance of becoming overweight or obese as adults.

Reaching and keeping a healthy weight isn't always easy. Lifestyle, your food environment, and social pressure are among the many barriers that enable overeating and inactivity.

To achieve and maintain a healthy weight, improve your eating habits and be physically active. That means controlling the calories you consume from all your food and beverage choices and cutting back on your intake if you need to lose weight. Also, fit more physical activity into your day and spend less time in sedentary activities such as TV watching and computer time.

What's your measure of health? *See "Weight Management: Strategies that Work" in chapter 22, page 639.* For specific advice, *see "Growth and Weight" in chapter 17, page 503, "Healthy Weight Matters" in chapter 18, page 542.*

Almost fifty percent of added sugars in the typical US diet comes from drinks! That includes soft drinks, fruit drinks, and other sweetened beverages. Snacks and sweets, which include grain-based desserts such as cakes, pies, cookies, brownies, doughnuts, sweet rolls, and pastries are other sources, as are dairy desserts such as ice cream, other frozen desserts, and puddings; candies; sugars; jams; syrups; and sweet toppings.

Recommendations: Reduce calories from added sugars to less than 10 percent of your day's calories. That means less than 50 grams of added sugars for a 2,000-calorie daily eating plan. Consuming more than that makes it hard to follow a healthy eating pattern and stay within your calorie limit. (To make it easier to meet this guideline, the Nutrition Facts on food labels are being updated to include added sugars.)

Since so many drinks supply added sugars, make these switches. Replace sugar-sweetened drinks with water or with unsweetened options, reduce portions of sugar-sweetened beverages and drink them less often, and select beverages low in added sugars. Another strategy is to replace sugar-sweetened beverages with fat-free or low-fat milk or 100 percent fruit or vegetable juice within recommended amounts.

More strategies: limit or eat smaller portion sizes of grain-based and dairy desserts, as well as sweet snacks. Choose unsweetened or no-sugar-added versions of canned fruit, fruit sauces such as applesauce, and yogurt.

Consider replacing added sugars with high-intensity sweeteners, *discussed in "Sugar Alternatives" in chapter 11, page 368,* That may reduce calorie intake in the short term, but their role in managing weight for the long term is unclear.

See chapter 11, page 345, for more about carbohydrates.

Saturated and *trans* fats. Fat is another nutrient that's essential for health—and for children's growth. Besides supplying energy, fat contains essential fatty acids and carries fat-soluble vitamins (A, D, E, and K) and carotenoids (a category of phytonutrients) into your bloodstream. Fat has other roles in health as well. The AMDR for total fat intake for adults is 20 to 35 percent of total calories. This range allows for an eating plan that's flexible and with enough essential nutrients. *See "Dietary Fat: A Range of Advice" in chapter 13, page 396, for the ranges for other age groups.*

Scientific evidence shows that the type of fat consumed affects the risk of heart disease more than the amount of total fat. Too much solid fat (saturated fats and *trans* fats) is linked to a higher risk for unhealthy levels of blood cholesterol and to heart disease. Most people consume more saturated fats than the limit of 10 percent of total calories that's advised. As an aside, replacing total fat or saturated fats with carbohydrates isn't linked to a lower risk of cardiovascular disease.

Remember Your Drinks!

Beverages often get forgotten when people think about all their food choices during the day. Yet they're important and contribute more than you may think. Besides the obvious—the water they provide—beverages deliver varied amounts of nutrients and calories. Plain water doesn't contain calories, and some drinks such as soft drinks provide calories but little else. Others such as milk and 100 percent fruit and vegetable juices provide important amounts of nutrients—some which are often underconsumed—in addition to calories.

Why consider them in your whole day's eating pattern? Beverages account for nearly 20 percent of total calorie intake, with sweetened drinks accounting for 35 percent of those beverage calories, or about 7 percent of the total calories consumed, on average, each day. *See chapter 4, page 81, for more about how drinks can contribute to your good nutrition and overall eating pattern—without overdoing the calories.*

Have you ever wondered?

. . . why dietary cholesterol doesn't appear as a key recommendation in the 2015–2020 Dietary Guidelines? Not enough evidence exists to set a quantitative limit for dietary cholesterol, as part of the guidelines. On average, Americans consume 267 milligrams of cholesterol daily, less than the recommended limit of 300 milligrams daily that was set in the 2010 Dietary Guidelines, which means it's no longer considered a component of food that is overconsumed. Moreover, dietary cholesterol doesn't seem to play a key role in blood cholesterol levels.

This change doesn't suggest that dietary cholesterol in your overall eating pattern is no longer an important consideration. The Institute of Medicine advises eating as little dietary cholesterol as possible within an overall healthy eating pattern. Research indicates that eating patterns that include a lower intake of dietary cholesterol are associated with reduced risk of cardiovascular disease. In general, fatty meats and high-fat dairy products are high in cholesterol and saturated fats.

Your body uses cholesterol for its own physiological and structural functions, but you don't need it from food because your body makes more than enough for these purposes.

See *"Cholesterol: Like Fat, Not Fat" in* chapter 12, page 404, for more about dietary cholesterol.

Most saturated fats in the US diet come from mixed dishes with cheese, meat, or both, such as burgers, sandwiches, and tacos; pizza; grain-based dishes; and meat, poultry, and seafood dishes. *Trans* fats, found in partially hydrogenated fats, are in some processed foods such as desserts, frozen pizza, and coffee creamer; *trans* fats that occur naturally in dairy foods and meat are in small amounts and not a concern.

Recommendations: Limit saturated fats to less than 10 percent of your total calories per day by replacing them with foods containing unsaturated fats, especially polyunsaturated fats. Keep your total fat intake from food within the AMDR for your age to reduce your risk for cardiovascular disease. You need some saturated fats from food for various body functions, but your body makes more than enough to meet those needs. If you're aged two years or older, you don't have a dietary need for saturated fats.

Keep *trans* fats from processed foods as low as possible. Read the Nutrition Facts label on packaged foods to find out how much *trans* fats it contains.

Although some saturated fats are naturally part of foods, others are added. Make a switch: replace foods higher in saturated fats with those that contain unsaturated fats, for example oils instead of butter and stick margarine, or fish instead of higher-fat meats. Limit solid fats in your cooking and food choices, too. For example, trim fat from meat, remove skin from poultry, and choose fat-free and low-fat foods such as milk and milk products. Eat smaller portions of foods that contain solid fats, such as regular cheese, sausage, bacon, pizza, and grain-based desserts.

For your sources of fat, choose foods such as oily fish, nuts, and vegetable oils, which contain mostly heart-healthy oils (high in polyunsaturated and monounsaturated fatty acids).

See "Fats: Not Created Equal" in chapter 12, page 385, for more about saturated and trans fats.

Sodium. Sodium is an essential nutrient, and besides adding flavor, it has many important uses as a food ingredient. Unless you sweat a lot, you probably get plenty of sodium. So why the advice to eat less?

Most Americans consume 50 percent more sodium than they need—on average 3,440 milligrams a day—with men consuming slightly more and women slightly less. Most is consumed as salt (sodium chloride).

Generally speaking, evidence shows a relationship between higher sodium intake and higher blood pressure and heart disease. Conversely, when sodium intake goes down, so may blood pressure. Keeping blood pressure in a normal range decreases the risk for heart disease, congestive heart failure, and kidney disease. Moderate evidence also suggests an association between increased sodium intake and increased risk of cardiovascular disease in adults, but higher blood pressure is shown more consistently to be an indicator of cardiovascular disease risk.

Recommendations: Limit sodium intake to less than 2,300 milligrams daily (for adults and teens ages fourteen and older). Younger children should limit their sodium intake to the upper limit for their age and gender; *as given in "Dietary Reference Intakes" in the appendix, page 780.*

Those with hypertension or prehypertension can perhaps see a greater blood pressure reduction by limiting sodium to 1,500 milligrams daily.

Most of the sodium consumed in the United States comes from food that is commercially processed or prepared—not from the salt shaker at the table. Shift to more fresh, frozen (no sauce or seasoning), or no-salt-added canned vegetables, and to fresh lean meats, poultry, and fish, rather than processed options that are high in sodium.

Eat more foods prepared at home, where you control the amount of sodium. When you cook at home, use little or no salt or salt-containing seasonings. Flavor with herbs and spices instead. When you eat out, order lower-sodium items if you can, or ask that salt be left out.

Sodium is found in a wide range of foods, so the more foods consumed, the greater potential for high sodium intake. Cutting back on food portions to cut calories also may help to reduce sodium.

See "Sodium" in chapter 14, page 431, for more about sodium. See "DASH to Health" in chapter 2, page 51, which targets sodium at 2,300 milligrams or less daily.

Alcohol. Alcoholic beverages aren't part of any of the healthy eating patterns *discussed in chapter 2*, and there's no recommendation to start drinking them for any reason. However, if consumed, that should only be done in moderation—up to one drink a day for women and two for men—and only by adults of legal drinking age. Consuming more than the recommendation poses health risks and can lead to excess calorie intake. The Dietary Guidelines also address the risks related to excessive (high-risk) and binge drinking, *as discussed in "Alcoholic Beverages: In Moderation" in chapter 4, page 102.*

The alcohol and calories in different drinks vary. For the purposes of the Dietary Guidelines, a drink is a portion that's contains 14 grams (0.6 fluid ounces) of pure alcohol. That equates to 12 ounces of regular beer (5 percent alcohol), 5 ounces of wine (12 percent alcohol), or 1.5 fluid ounces of 80-proof (40 percent alcohol) distilled spirits.

Recommendations: When should you avoid drinking alcoholic beverages? Of course, this includes whenever you put yourself and others at risk. Don't drink at all if you can't control the amount; if you're taking certain prescription or over-the-counter medications that can interact with alcohol; if you have certain medical conditions (such as liver disease, hypertriglyceridemia, or pancreatitis); if you are recovering from alcoholism; or if you are driving, planning to drive, operating machinery, or taking part in other activities that require your attention, skill, and coordination.

Women who are pregnant or may be pregnant should not drink because drinking during pregnancy, especially in the first few months, may result in behavioral and nervous system problems for a developing baby. No safe amount during pregnancy has been established. Women who are breastfeeding should talk with their doctor or health care provider about consuming alcoholic drinks.

See "Alcoholic Beverages: In Moderation" in chapter 4, page 102, for more advice about alcoholic beverages; see "Pregnancy and Alcoholic Beverages Don't Mix!" and "Nonfoods: Effect on Breast Milk" in chapter 18, pages 551 and 559.

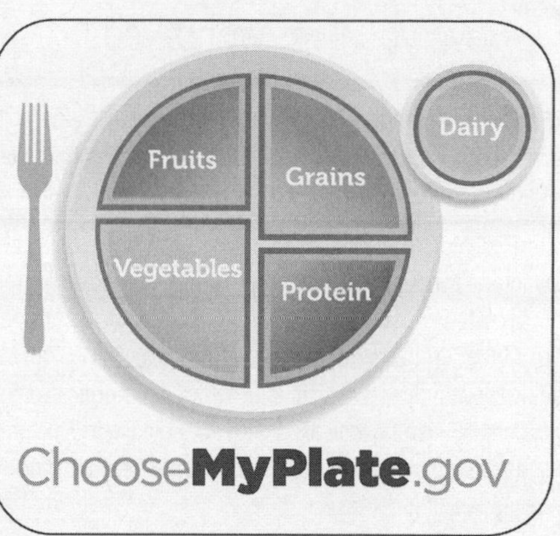

MyPlate is a reminder to find your healthy eating style and build it throughout your lifetime. Everything you eat and drink matters. The right mix can help you be healthier now and in the future. This means:

- All foods and beverage choices matter. Focus on variety, amount, and nutrition.
- Choose foods and beverages with less saturated fats, sodium, and added sugars.
- Start with small changes to build healthier eating styles.
- Support healthy eating for everyone.

Eating healthy is a journey shaped by many factors, including your stage of life, situations, preferences, access to food, culture, traditions, and the personal decisions made over time. All your food and beverage choices count. MyPlate offers ideas and tips to help you create a healthier eating style that meets your individual needs and improves your health.

Throughout this book, you'll find many more easy steps like these. *See chapters 2, page 21, and 3, page 60, to learn how to set your table using the advice from the ChooseMyPlate website.*

Source: USDA's Center for Nutrition Policy and Promotion, www.ChooseMyPlate.gov.

MOVE MORE! PHYSICAL ACTIVITY GUIDELINES

When it comes to behavior that poses health risks, some say: "Sitting is the new smoking." Why is regular physical activity so important to wellness?

Evidence shows that regular moderate physical activity reduces the risks for many health problems; some activity is better than none. Most

Have you ever wondered?

. . . if caffeine fits into a healthy eating plan? Caffeine isn't a nutrient but is a substance in some foods and drinks that works as a stimulant in the body.

The Dietary Guidelines advises that if you don't consume caffeine already in one form or another, you're not encouraged to start. Moderate coffee consumption (three to five 8-ounce cups per day, or up to 400 milligrams per day of caffeine) can be incorporated into healthy eating patterns. In healthy adults, moderate coffee consumption isn't associated with an increased risk of major chronic diseases such as cancer or premature death, especially from cardiovascular disease.

Alcohol and caffeine are generally not deemed to be a safe mix by the US Food and Drug Administration (FDA). Consuming them at the same time may lead to drinking more alcoholic drinks and becoming more intoxicated than people realize. Also caffeine doesn't change the levels of alcohol in the blood and so doesn't reduce risks related to drinking alcoholic beverages.

Women who are, may be, or are trying to become pregnant, and those who are breastfeeding should talk with their doctor or health care provider about their caffeine consumption.

See "Coffee and Tea: Caffeinated or Not?," in chapter 4, page 93, for more about caffeine and coffee.

Food Safety Principles and Guidance

Keeping food safe, an important part of healthy eating, is addressed in the Dietary Guidelines. Foodborne illness strikes an estimated one in six (forty-eight million) Americans each year, according to statistics from the Centers for Disease Control and Prevention (CDC), causing mild to severe and even life-threatening symptoms and leading to 128,000 hospitalizations and 3,000 deaths every year.

A substantial number of outbreaks likely come from unsafe food practices at home. Keeping food safe is up to you, not just farmers, food manufacturers, retailers, and restaurant workers. Many cases of foodborne illness could be avoided if consumers handled food carefully.

Four basic food-safety principles work together to reduce the risk of foodborne illness:

- Clean
- Separate
- Cook
- Chill

Clean your hands, food-contact surfaces, and vegetables and fruits. Separate raw, cooked, and ready-to-eat foods while shopping for, storing, and preparing them. Cook foods to safe internal temperatures. Chill (refrigerate) perishable foods promptly.

See chapter 7, page 191, for more about keeping food safe.

health benefits come from at least 150 minutes (2 hours and 30 minutes) a week of moderately intense physical activity. If you move longer or with more vigor, you get even more benefits. Endurance (aerobic) and muscle-strengthening (resistance) activities are beneficial, too.

Being physically active is important at every age, including for those with physical disabilities. Just choose activities that work for you. *The bottom line:* For almost everyone, the benefits of appropriate physical activity far outweigh possible injury or other health risks from being active. Unless you have a health concern, you probably can start moving more now.

The Physical Activity Guidelines for Americans (PAG), issued by the US Department of Health and Human Services (USHHS), provides science-based guidance on physical activity and health for Americans ages six and older. Although established in 2008, it still applies today; however, it was being reviewed for an update at the time of this writing.

Following the Physical Guidelines for Americans can help you improve your health through appropriate physical activity in your daily lifestyle, in sports, or in both. You can have fun at the same time, too! This advice complements the Dietary Guidelines' advice.

Talk to your doctor first if you have an ongoing health problem, including heart disease, high blood pressure, diabetes, osteoporosis, arthritis, or obesity. Also consult him or her if you're at high risk for heart disease, if you have a disability, or if you're pregnant. Determine together the amount and type of activities that are right for your abilities or condition.

See the appendix, page 769, for the Physical Activity Guidelines' key recommendations for each age group.

Get Active, Stay Active, Be More Active

How do you fit enough physical activity into your life? Whether you spread it out during the day or do it all at once, you get benefits:

- If you have been inactive, start gradually and build up slowly to longer, more intense activities. For your physical activity of choice, do a little more, a little longer, each time. Then do it more often. Move enough to keep fit without overdoing. You might keep track with a journal or app.

Ten Reasons to Get Up and Move

Whether you're involved in sports or live an active lifestyle, physical activity pays big dividends. The more you do, the greater the health benefits. Physical activity is the right move for fitness for almost everyone. Consider these reasons why:

1. *Trimmer body.* If you're physically active, you'll have an easier time maintaining a healthy weight or, if you're overweight, losing weight and keeping it off. *See chapter 22, page 627, for more about physical activity and weight management.*
2. *Less risk for health problems.* An active lifestyle—or a sports regimen—can help protect you from many ongoing health problems.

   Studies show that regular physical activity helps lower risk factors. For example, physical activity helps to lower total and LDL ("bad") cholesterol and triglyceride levels while boosting the HDL ("good") cholesterol level. It helps control blood pressure and improve blood glucose levels. Your risks for heart disease, high blood pressure, type 2 diabetes, and certain cancers go down when you fit physical activity into your daily life.

   Active living also may reduce or eliminate the need for medication to lower blood lipids, lower blood pressure, or manage diabetes.
3. *Stronger bones.* Regular, weight-bearing activities—such as walking, running, weight lifting, and cross-country skiing—help make your bones stronger. Even in adulthood, weight-bearing exercise helps maintain bone strength and reduces your chance of fractures and osteoporosis.
4. *Stronger muscles.* Strength-training activities, such as lifting weights, at least two times a week keep your body strong for sports and everyday living. When you're strong, it's easier to move, carry, and lift things. When you exercise your muscles, you also give your heart a workout. It's a muscle, too. A strong heart pumps blood and nutrients more easily through your sixty thousand miles of blood vessels.
5. *More endurance.* You won't tire as easily when you're physically active.
6. *Better mental outlook.* Active people describe feelings of psychological well-being and self-esteem when they make active living a habit. It's a great way to reinforce an empowered attitude and a positive outlook.
7. *Stress relief and better sleep.* Research shows that physical activity helps your body relax and release emotional tension. That promotes longer, better-quality sleep, and you may fall asleep faster.
8. *Better coordination and flexibility.* Your body moves with greater ease and range of motion when you stay physically active.
9. *Injury protection.* When you're in shape, you more easily can catch yourself if you slip or trip, and can move away from impending danger more quickly.
10. *Feel better and perhaps feel younger longer.* Research suggests that physical activity slows some effects of aging. Active people have more strength and mobility and fewer limitations.

One more reason: physical activities can be fun.

- Choose activities with moderate or vigorous intensity. *See "Moderate Activity: What Is It?" in this chapter, page 18.* You might gradually replace some moderate activity with vigorous activity for similar health benefits in half the time.
- Do it your way. Choose activities that fit your lifestyle. For kids, make them fun and appropriate for their physical ability.
- Vary your activities. Different activities use different muscles. For example, gardening works your arm muscles, power walking or bicycling uses your heart and leg muscles, and sit-ups help your abdominal muscles. For overall fitness, choose activities that build cardiovascular endurance (walking, running, distance biking), muscle strength (heavy gardening, working with resistance bands), bone strength (walking, tennis), and flexibility (stretching, yoga, dancing).
- Get a partner. Being active with family and friends can make it easy and fun!

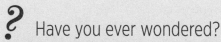

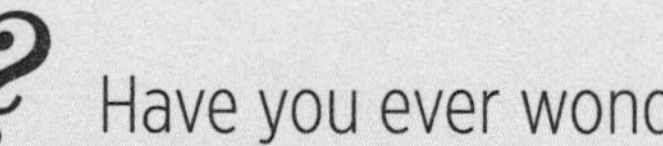

. . . if your own exercise level is of moderate intensity? Take the "talk-sing" test to find out.

- If you can talk comfortably as you move, that's moderate activity.
- If you can sing, that's light-intensity activity; step up your pace.
- If you're too breathless to talk, the activity may be vigorous. If your goal is moderate activity, you might need to slow down, but remember that vigorous activity has added benefits.

See "Your Physical Activity: How Intense?" in chapter 21, page 600, for another way to target your workout intensity. Also see "Moderate Activity: What Is It?" in this chapter, page 18.

Exercise Your Options

For more about the benefits of physical activity—and ways to be more physically active—check here:

- *For most healthy people, including those managing their body weight, see Quick Tips to Move More" in chapter 21, page 640.*
- *For children, see "Active Play: Toddlers and Preschoolers" and "Get Up and Move!" in chapter 17, pages 518 and 524.*
- *For teens, see "Move It: Sports and More!'" in chapter 17, page 531.*
- *For older adults, see "Physical Activity: How Much" in chapter 20, page 585.*
- *For travelers, see "On the Road? Keep Moving" in chapter 21, page 601.*
- *For athletes, see chapter 21, page 599.*

- Start with ten-minute chunks three times a day, three days a week. Perhaps walk; then gradually walk longer, more often, and at a faster pace. Try walking when you talk on the phone. Keep your head up for safety's sake and pay attention to where you walk!
- Limit screen time—especially important for kids. That's the amount of time spent watching TV, using a cell phone or other device, playing online games, and using social and online media. When you do watch TV, try to move around and "multitask" as you watch or listen; perhaps do some sit-ups, step in place, or do other exercises.

Reaching SMART Goals, One Step at a Time!

Are you ready to eat healthier or get more physically active? You will have more success setting and reaching those goals if your goals align with

Moderate Activity: What Is It?

If some activities use more energy than others, you may wonder what moderate physical activity really means. It equates to the energy you need to walk two miles in thirty minutes.

Moderate physical activity uses about 3½ to 7 calories a minute, 150 calories a day, or about 1,000 calories a week. For that amount of energy expenditure, you might spend more time on less vigorous activities such as brisk walking, or spend less time on more vigorous activities, such as running.* Most people don't need to see a doctor before they start a moderate-level physical activity.

Common Activities	Duration (in minutes)
Washing and waxing a car	45–60
Washing windows or floors	45–60
Gardening	30–45
Wheeling self in wheelchair	30–40
Pushing a stroller 1½ miles	30
Raking leaves	30
Shoveling snow	15
Stair walking	15

Less Vigorous, More Time* ↕ *More Vigorous, Less Time*

Sporting Activities	Duration (in minutes)
Playing volleyball	45–60
Playing touch football	45
Walking 2 miles	30
Shooting baskets (basketball)	30
Dancing fast (social)	30
Performing water aerobics	30
Swimming laps	20
Playing basketball	15–20
Walking 1 mile	15
Jumping rope	15
Running 1½ miles	15
Running 1 mile	10

*Some activities can be performed at various intensities. The suggested durations correspond to the expected intensity of effort.

Adapted from source: Your Guide to Lowering Blood Pressure, NHLBI, www.nhlbi.nih.gov/files/docs/public/heart/hbp_low.pdf.

Go Online

Track Your Food Choices, Make Your Eating Smart Plan!

Want a snapshot view of what you eat and how much you move in a day, several days, or even over weeks? There's an easy, personalized way to plan, track, and assess your overall eating pattern and physical activity level.

Whether from a cell phone or a home computer, use the SuperTracker at www.ChooseMyPlate.gov to compare your food choices to the Dietary Guidelines for Americans, to find out about foods in the marketplace, and to see steps you can take to improve your eating and physical activity decisions. Online and interactive, the SuperTracker can be your coach, journal, and source of social media support.

what matters to you—your values and knowledge about your health and lifestyle. Simply trying to follow rules doesn't usually work in the long run.

Life doesn't need to get in the way of your wise, wellness intentions. The sooner you invest in your health, the greater the benefits! Even if it takes effort, it's worth it. To reach your goals, take one easy step at a time. Here's how to get started:

Step one: Audit your food choices and lifestyle. Start by keeping track of what you eat or drink for several days, along with how much, when, and why. For example, do you snack when you feel stressed or bored?

Keep a food journal—on paper, online, or with an app. Track how active you are, too, with a physical activity log—many people find that wearable devices work well. This will help you pinpoint eating and lifestyle behaviors you wish to change.

These resources can help you: (1) "Food and Physical Activity Logs" in chapter 22, page 647, (2) the SuperTracker, noted in "Go Online," above, and (3) the personal assessments in "Your Healthy Eating Check-in" features throughout this book.

Step two: Set personal goals. Know what you want to achieve for better health—perhaps a healthier weight or a lower blood cholesterol level. Make your goals SMART: specific, measurable, achievable, relevant, and time-framed.

- *Specific (and strategic) goals*, such as "I will eat more vegetables" or "I will switch to more whole grains," have a greater chance of being accomplished than general goals such as "I will eat better."
- *Measurable goals* state how you'll determine your success, such as "I will count to three: three cups of colorful vegetables in my meals and snacks each day."
- *Achievable goals* are realistic, or do-able, for you, given your skills, resources, time, and commitment. For example, if you like to cook, your goal could be "I will try one unfamiliar vegetable each week." Remember: often there are many different ways to achieve a similar outcome.
- *Relevant (results-oriented) goals* match the result you expect—and match what truly matters to you. For example, if you want to lose weight, "I will switch from a big bag of chips or cookies, to sliced, raw veggies in my snack pack or lunch to cut calories" is a match. Goals that are relevant to you are more motivating.
- *Time-framed goals* have a clearly defined time frame or target date, such as for next week or in three months or by six months. Having a clear target date often helps.

The common New Year's resolution "to simply eat healthier" isn't a smart goal. Instead a SMART goal would be "to eat healthier by drinking a cup of milk instead of soda with lunch every day. That would provide another cup of calcium-rich dairy foods in my daily eating plan."

Step three: Make a plan for change. Divide bigger goals, such as "I will eat more vegetables" or "I will eat more whole-grain foods," into smaller, more specific goals with practical steps that are achievable. For example:

- *Smaller, specific goal:* Eat more vegetables.

  Practical steps: I will add a salad or vegetable dish to my supper every day. I'll pack baby carrots, cherry tomatoes, or mini bell peppers in my bag lunch. I'll layer my sandwich with sliced tomatoes, spinach leaves, or roasted peppers.
- *Smaller, specific goal:* Make at least half of all grain food choices whole grains.
- *Practical steps:* Make sandwiches and French toast with whole-grain bread. Switch to brown rice. Eat oatmeal for breakfast. Snack on plain popcorn. Add whole barley to vegetable soup.

Step four: Be patient. Change gradually. Long-term change takes time, commitment, and encouragement. Most health goals take a lifelong commitment. Stick to your plan. Remember that small steps toward a goal add up over time.

Step five: Monitor your progress. Keep track of the healthy choices you make, not just what you need to improve. If you get off track, pick up where you left off, and start again.

Realistically speaking, change doesn't mean giving up foods you like. Smaller portions, different ways of cooking, or being more physically active give you "wiggle room" to occasionally enjoy nearly any foods. Even when you're concerned with weight loss, you can eat small amounts of high-calorie foods now and then.

Step six: Seek help from a qualified health professional, as needed. A registered dietitian nutritionist can help you on your fitness journey; *see "Nutrition Advice to Trust" in chapter 26, page 758, for tips on finding a reliable nutrition expert.*

Step seven: Reward yourself for doing something right. Change takes effort that deserves recognition. "Pat yourself on the back" with a bike ride to a unique place, a walk with a friend, a new fitness app, new sneakers, or a bouquet of flowers. That said, feeling good is the best reward!

Step eight: Reevaluate your plan every month or two. See how the changes you made—the simple steps you took—fit with your goals. Leveraging your personal commitment can make a difference. Now plan a few more simple steps if you need to—even tackle a new goal.

Throughout this book, you'll find many easy ways to make your "plates" more appealing—and at the same time, more nourishing. You'll not only learn the whys of healthy eating and being physically active, you'll also learn how to be successful at managing your weight—and how to keep your family healthy. In addition, you'll gain insights and get tips about buying, preparing, serving, and eating foods you like in the right portion size—and about trying new foods—to promote good health.

And remember . . . it's your total diet, or all you eat and drink over several days, that counts. It all adds up!

2

Plan Smart to Eat Smart

In this chapter, find out about . . .

Your personal healthy eating pattern

The DASH Eating Plan: a "win-win" for nutrition and blood pressure

The Mediterranean approach to healthy eating

Eating the vegetarian way

Food, glorious, food! It's the wide array of foods, not their individual nutrients, that entice most people to eat. Aromas, flavors, textures, and the mouthwatering appearance of all kinds of foods stimulate your appetite, satisfy your taste buds, and give you the contented feeling that goes with a wonderful meal or a tasty snack.

The foods you eat deliver much more, of course. The food and drink choices you make every day provide nutrition. And along with physical activity, those food choices affect your health and how you feel today, tomorrow, and far into the future.

You may be ready to harness the power of healthy eating—to plan smart to eat smart—but aren't sure how to go about it. Help is here! Adopting a healthy eating style can easily be summed up as follows:

- Focus on variety, amount, and nutrition. All food and beverage choices matter.
- Choose foods and beverages to limit calories from saturated fats and added sugars and limit sodium. Shift to healthier choices.
- Start with small changes to build a healthier eating style.
- Support healthy eating for everyone.

Now put this advice into an action plan!

Eating Well: More than Nutrients

When you're looking for a sensible guide for healthful eating—one that's meant for you—rest assured that there is one that takes your food preferences into account. There are plans with enough flexibility to allow you to enjoy foods that match your lifestyle, your food preferences, and your personal nutrition and health needs, as well as your food budget.

What is an eating pattern? Simply said, it represents all the foods and drinks you consume over time. It's another way to say "your total diet"—and "diet" in this context doesn't necessarily refer to the act of cutting calories for weight loss.

Since there's no single eating plan that's right for everyone, this chapter offers several healthy eating patterns you might follow. Each reflects science-based advice from the Dietary Guidelines for Americans and can be used to guide your daily food and drink choices.

Smart eating plans are designed to help you get enough of all nutrients without overdoing some. Most people in the United States underconsume vegetables, fruits, whole grains,

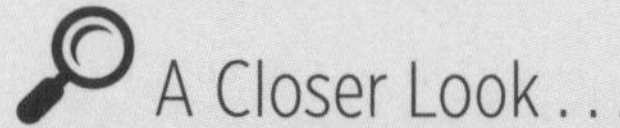

Ten Steps to Healthier Eating

Eating smart isn't just for today. For good health and a healthy weight, make wise food choices for a lifetime. Try this to make a healthy eating pattern that works for you:

Step 1. *Pick an eating pattern.* All of the patterns *described in this chapter* are great "templates" to follow. They match advice from the Dietary Guidelines for Americans. Each one classifies foods into groups with similar nutrient content:

- Healthy US-Style*
- DASH (Dietary Approaches to Stop Hypertension)**
- Healthy Mediterranean-Style*
- Healthy Vegetarian*

Step 2. *Figure your calorie target.* With your age, gender, height, weight, and physical activity level in mind, estimate your daily calorie needs; *"Estimated Calorie Needs per Day by Age, Gender, and Physical Activity Level" in the appendix, page 770,* can help you. As you get older or your activity level changes, adjust for your new calorie target.

Step 3. *Know how much you need from all five food groups.* The daily recommendations are based on your calorie needs. There are twelve food-group plans—from 1,000 to 3,200 calories. Getting the advised amount from each food group provides your body with enough essential nutrients and enough calories for your energy needs.

Step 4. *Get to know the food groups:* the amounts recommended, foods included, nutrients and benefits provided, and tips for making wise choices. Recommended amounts are given in cups and ounces for a whole day rather than in servings for a single meal or snack. Food group discussions in this chapter can help you convert daily recommendations to serving sizes and amounts.

Step 5. *Make the plan yours.* The beauty of these eating plans is their adaptability. And they still work if you need to eat gluten free or allergen free *(see chapter 23, page 653)*; to lose, gain, or maintain your weight *(see chapter 22, page 625)*; to follow a religious or cultural food tradition; or simply want to fit in the foods you like best.

Look inside the food groups. Make your food and drink choices mostly nutrient-dense with limits on saturated fats, added sugars, and sodium.

Step 6. *Take small steps.* Start by swapping one food for another so you eat healthier one step at a time. Modify your food choices and your physical activity level gradually. This may be easier than overhauling your whole eating plan and lifestyle at one time.

Perhaps start with a change in one meal or snack, just one food group, or one active-living strategy. Move on gradually toward a healthier you.

Step 7. *Stay within your day's calorie limit.* Eat and drink the right amounts from the different food groups to maintain a healthy weight. Balance the calories you eat with the amount your body uses. Move more if you want more calories to "spend." While sticking to your calorie budget, learn how to fit in foods you enjoy, even when they deliver "extra" calories.

Step 8. *Track your progress.* Self-monitoring can be a useful tool, especially when you're starting a new approach to meals and snacks.

You might use an app to track your food and drinks for the day. Or use the SuperTracker online at www.supertracker.usda.gov to keep track in an interactive way. The Food Tracker tool helps you track the foods you eat and compare them to your nutrition targets. This online tool also provides tips and support to help you make healthier choices and plan ahead.

Step 9. *Make your healthy eating plan your lifetime plan.* And know that your overall eating plan for several days is what really counts, not a single day.

Step 10. *Support healthier eating for everyone.* That includes your family and friends, and those in your community and workplace whose lives you touch. Do your part to support the chance to make healthy food choices available and affordable for all.

*One of three USDA Food Patterns

**Similar to the Healthy US-Style Eating Pattern

Refer to "Eating Patterns 2015–2020 Dietary Guidelines for Americans" and "DASH Eating Plan at Various Calorie Levels" in the appendix, pages 771 and 776.

and dairy foods. That has resulted in low intakes of calcium, vitamin D, potassium, and fiber—a public health concern with links to health risks. Food choices have also led to other concerns. For example, saturated fats, added sugars, and sodium, when overconsumed, are linked to health risks, too.

SMART EATING PLANS: THE BASICS

The best eating plan for good health and optimal nutrition is flexible, allowing for a variety of foods, beverages, and combinations. It considers your food preferences and lifestyle, your nutrient and calorie needs, and your health (including medical) goals.

Daily Recommendations in a Healthy Food Pattern

Food Group (Food group foods are assumed to be lean or low-fat and/or prepared without added fats, sugars, refined starches, or salt.)	**Daily Amounts***		
	1,600 Calories	**2,000 Calories**	**2,400 Calories**
Grains	5 ounce-equivalents	6 ounce-equivalents	8 ounce-equivalents
Vegetables	2 cups	2½ cups	3 cups
Fruits	1½ cups	2 cups	2 cups
Dairy	3 cups	3 cups	3 cups
Protein foods	5 ounce-equivalents	5½ ounce-equivalents	6½ ounce-equivalents
Oils	22 grams	27 grams	31 grams
Calorie limit for other uses** (% of calories)	130 calories (8%)	270 calories (14%)	350 calories (15%)
Added sugars	<10% of total calories	<10% of total calories	<10% of total calories
Saturated fats	<10% of total calories	<10% of total calories	<10% of total calories
Sodium (for 14 years or older)	<2,300 mg	<2,300 mg	<2,300 mg
Alcoholic drinks	Limit to 1 drink daily for women; 2 for men.		

**For the amounts that are right for more calorie levels, see "USDA Food Patterns," in the appendix, page 772, or go to www.ChooseMyPlate.gov. Food-group amounts are discussed in this chapter.*
** If all food group choices are in nutrient-dense forms, a small number of calories remain within the overall calorie limit of the pattern.
Source: 2015–2020 Dietary Guidelines for Americans, USDA/USHHS.

For any healthy eating plan, a few common basics matter: plenty of vegetables and fruits; an emphasis on whole grains (as opposed to mostly refined grains); moderate amounts and a variety of protein foods, including fish, lean meats, poultry, eggs, beans, nuts, and seeds; enough fat-free and low-fat dairy foods; limits on added sugars and solid fats (saturated and *trans* fats). The fats are mostly replaced with the appropriate amount of healthy oils. The USDA Food Patterns discussed in this chapter, exemplify healthy eating, showing how to fit recommendations for these foods at twelve different calorie levels, ranging from 1,000 to 3,200 calories daily.

- MyPlate, the building blocks of healthy eating and a daily checklist
  www.ChooseMyPlate.gov
- Food-A-Pedia, nutrition information for 8,000 foods
  www.supertracker.usda.gov/foodapedia.aspx

Beyond that, the best eating plans for health share these general guidelines:

- Vary your choices. Eating an appropriate mix of foods from the food groups and subgroups—within an appropriate calorie level—is important to promote health. No one food or food group supplies all the nutrients, fiber, and other components needed for energy, health, and, for kids, growth. Classifying foods and beverages into food groups based on nutrient content is the basis of food guides that can help you eat enough variety.

  Foods within each food group promote health in comparable ways. Even then, the nutrient content of the group's foods differs somewhat, which explains why variety among and within the food groups is advised. Variety also makes mealtime more flavorful, interesting, and pleasurable!

? Have you ever wondered?

. . . how food guides apply to ethnic and regional cuisines? The guidelines *discussed in this chapter* can apply to many of the cuisines you enjoy—perhaps Asian, Mediterranean, Latin American, Middle Eastern, and more. That said, more than 100 countries have their own food guides and healthy eating guidelines to match their foods, food-related health concerns, eating patterns, food availability, culinary culture, and eating habits. To learn about food-based dietary guidelines, see this link from the Food and Agriculture Organization (FAO) of the United Nations: www.fao.org/nutrition/education/food-dietary-guidelines/home/en/

Visual Guide to Portion Size

What do 3 ounces of cooked meat, poultry, or fish look like? How about ½ cup of vegetables, 1 cup of cooked pasta, 1½ ounces of cheese, or 1 teaspoon of spread on toast?

Visual cues are always "hand-y" equivalents!	**Use them to guesstimate these food amounts.**
Average-size fist =1 cup	cut-up vegetables sliced or whole fruit (equivalent to 1 medium apple, orange, or pear) cooked beans dry and cooked cereal cooked pasta, rice, other grains
Palm (no fingers) =3 ounces	cooked meat cooked poultry cooked fish
Small cupped handful =1 ounce	nuts, seeds
Large cupped handful =2 ounces	dried fruit, such as raisins pretzels, other dry snacks shredded cheese
Thumb (tip to base) =1 ounce	cheese cube meat, poultry, fish
Thumb tip (to first joint) =1 tablespoon	peanut butter
Fingertip (tip to first joint) =1 teaspoon	butter, margarine, spreads, mayonnaise, salad dressing vegetable oil sugar

- Make choices from all food groups nutrient-dense. These foods and drinks count. Nutrient-dense foods and beverages deliver vitamins, minerals, and phytonutrients (including fiber) with positive health benefits and relatively few calories. They're mostly lean or low in solid fats (saturated and *trans* fats) and have minimal or no added sugars or sodium.

  What foods meet this definition? Vegetables, fruits, whole grains, fish, eggs, beans and peas, unsalted nuts and seeds, low-fat and fat-free milk and milk products, and lean meats, poultry, and fish—if prepared with little or no saturated fats, sodium, or added sugars. *See "Where Do Extra Calories Come From?" in this chapter, page 25.*

- Think in proportions. You may benefit by eating more from some food groups than others. For example, consider having vegetables and fruit take up more room on your plate than protein foods. Check the advice for each of the five food groups.

- Balance calories (energy). Balance the calories you consume from everything you eat and drink with the calories your body uses for physical energy and all your body's metabolic processes.

  Healthy eating patterns, *as discussed in this chapter*, provide food group amounts for different calorie levels. The amounts recommended are associated with positive health outcomes. To estimate how many calories you need, *see "Calories, Your Target?" in chapter 1, page 7.* Then check daily food group advice for your calorie limit; check amounts for oils—and for added sugars and saturated fats, too. Be physically active to burn calories over the course of the day.

- Right-size your portions. Amounts matter, and knowing about how much of any given food to eat helps you balance your calories to manage your weight and avoid overeating. Some common foods may have more calories than you realize.

  Learn to estimate your food and drink portions (in cups and ounces). Portion out your foods before eating to avoid overeating. *See "Visual Guide to Portion Size," above, and "Portions: Be Size Wise!" in chapter 3, page 78.* That said, you don't need a tape measure or kitchen scale to determine the size of each piece of fruit or vegetable!

Where Do Extra Calories Come From?

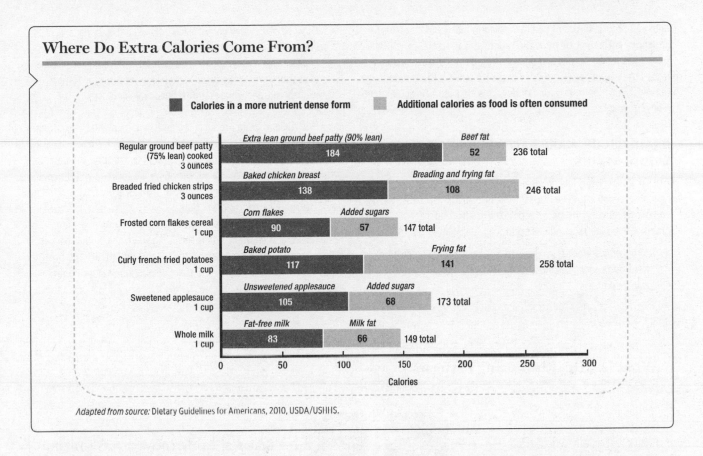

■ Calories in a more nutrient dense form ■ Additional calories as food is often consumed

Food as often consumed	Calories in a more nutrient dense form		Additional calories as food is often consumed		Total
Regular ground beef patty (75% lean) cooked 3 ounces	*Extra lean ground beef patty (90% lean)*	184	*Beef fat*	52	236 total
Breaded fried chicken strips 3 ounces	*Baked chicken breast*	138	*Breading and frying fat*	108	246 total
Frosted corn flakes cereal 1 cup	*Corn flakes*	90	*Added sugars*	57	147 total
Curly french fried potatoes 1 cup	*Baked potato*	117	*Frying fat*	141	258 total
Sweetened applesauce 1 cup	*Unsweetened applesauce*	105	*Added sugars*	68	173 total
Whole milk 1 cup	*Fat-free milk*	83	*Milk fat*	66	149 total

Calories (axis: 0, 50, 100, 150, 200, 250, 300)

Adapted from source: Dietary Guidelines for Americans, 2010, USDA/USHHS.

> ## MyPlate: Build a Healthy Meal
>
> MyPlate is your reminder to eat foods from the five food groups. To learn how to choose a variety of foods and drinks for a single day—in the right amounts for your calorie needs—visit the website www.ChooseMyPlate.gov
>
> 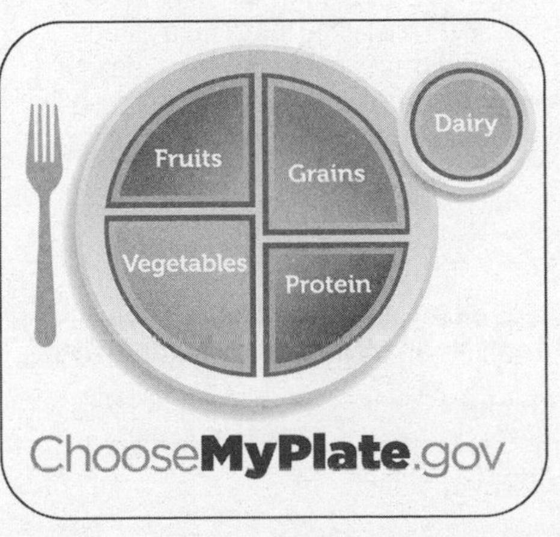
>

- Enjoy your food, but eat less. Slow down when eating. When you pay attention to your food, hunger, and fullness cues before, during, and after meals, you are more likely to eat the right amount rather than overeat.

No matter which eating pattern you choose, improve gradually. Take small steps to healthier eating. Small steps add up to big benefits. Remember to be physically active, too, a step at a time. It's the flip side of the calorie equation!

Remember: It's your total diet—what you eat and drink for the whole day and over time—that either benefits or deters health. No single food, or meal for that matter, is either good or bad.

Throughout this book, you'll find ways to follow a healthy eating pattern at every age and every stage of life.

A Plan for Healthy Eating: From MyPlate to Your Plate

Local foods, ethnic foods, your favorite foods, restaurant foods, snack foods, foods you grow yourself, supermarket foods—all kinds of foods can fit into a day's worth of healthy meals and snacks. With MyPlate as a visual reminder, healthy eating patterns are meant to help you put the basics of healthy eating in place and make nourishing choices. Think of them as the practical way to make the Dietary Guidelines for Americans and other nutrition standards work. Regardless of the eating pattern, choose foods from every food group to get the most nutrition from your calories. This also can help you to manage your weight.

GRAIN GROUP: MAKE HALF YOUR GRAINS WHOLE GRAINS

A grain product is any food made from wheat, rice, oats, cornmeal, barley, or another cereal grain. Bread, pasta, oatmeal, breakfast cereals, tortillas, and grits are among the many foods in the grain group made with whole grains, refined grains, or perhaps both:

- *Whole grains:* Made from the whole-grain kernel, with the bran, germ, and endosperm intact. *See "What Is a Whole Grain?" in this chapter, page 27.*
- *Enriched and refined grains*: Made from refined flour that's been milled for a finer texture or a longer shelf life. The bran and germ are removed, taking dietary fiber, iron, and many B vitamins with them. White refined flour, degermed cornmeal, most white bread, and white rice are refined grain products.

Most refined grain products are enriched, meaning that nutrients (thiamin, riboflavin, niacin, and iron) lost in processing are added back—but the fiber isn't. Most refined grain products and some whole grains are also fortified with folic acid, and some are fortified with fiber. The ingredient list on the package of a grain product is the best way to find out if it is enriched, fortified, or both.

Most Americans eat enough total grains. However, most are refined rather than whole grains, including white rice, traditional pasta, many breads, and more. Many items such as doughnuts and pastries are made with refined grains and are also high in saturated fats and added sugars.

What Is a Healthy Eating Pattern?

Fruits, especially whole fruits

Grains, at least half of which are whole grains

A variety of vegetables—dark green, red and orange, legumes (beans and peas), starchy, and other vegetables

A variety of protein foods, including seafood, lean meats and poultry, eggs, legumes (beans and peas), soy products, and nuts and seeds

Fat-free or low-fat dairy, including milk, yogurt, cheese, and/or fortified soy beverages

Oils, including those from plants (such as canola, corn, olive, peanut, safflower, soybean, and sunflower) and in foods (such as nuts, seeds, seafood, olives, and avocados)

Saturated & *trans* fats—limit saturated fats to less than 10% of daily calories and keep *trans* fat intake as low as possible

Added sugars—limit to less than 10% of daily calories

Sodium— limit to less than 2,300 mg a day (for adults and children 14 years and older)

Alcohol—limit to no more than 1 drink per day for women and no more than 2 per day for men

Source: 2015–2020 Dietary Guidelines for Americans, USDA/USHHS.

What Is a Whole Grain?

A whole grain is the intact, or entire, edible part of any grain, such as wheat, corn, oats, and rice, among others. In the life cycle of plants, the whole grain is the seed from which a new plant grows, and nutrients in the seed supply nourishment for the plant before the roots form. The whole grain, or seed, consists of three parts:

- *The bran,* which makes up the outer layers of the grain. It supplies antioxidants, B vitamins, trace minerals, and dietary fiber.
- *The endosperm,* which is the inner part of the grain. It contains most of the proteins and carbohydrates and only small amounts of vitamins and minerals. White flour is ground from the endosperm.
- *The germ,* which is small but very important because it sprouts, generating a new plant. It contains B vitamins, vitamin E, trace minerals, antioxidants, and essential fats.

While whole grains have more fiber than their refined forms, some grains have more fiber than others. *See "Grains, Grains, and More Grains" in this chapter, page 31, for examples of whole grains.*

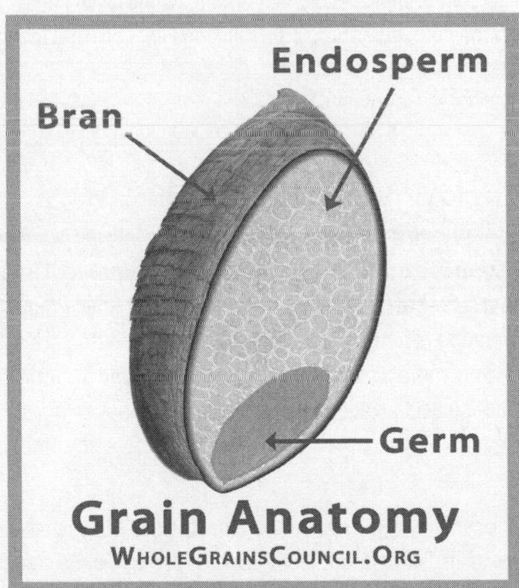

The bran and germ of a whole grain supply most of its fiber. When milled to produce white flour, only the endosperm remains. Most of the fibrous bran and the germ are removed—along with important nutrients and phytonutrients, including fiber. Since they contain nutrients, fiber, and other phytonutrients found naturally in grains, whole-grain foods are usually a healthy choice!

Source: Whole Grains Council.

Many grain products contain gluten, a type of protein. *See "Gluten Free: When It's a Must" in chapter 23, page 670, if you need to avoid gluten due to celiac disease or non-celiac gluten sensitivity.*

Why Eat Grains, Especially Whole Grains?

Grain products, especially whole grains, offer a bundle of nutrients and phytonutrients.

Key nutrients: Grain products deliver starches (complex carbohydrates), several B vitamins (thiamin, riboflavin, niacin, and folate), and iron. Whole-grain foods also supply magnesium, selenium, and, in varying

? Have you ever wondered?

. . . if cornmeal is a whole grain? Yes—but only if it's made with the whole corn kernel. Cornmeal that's labeled degerminated or degermed has been refined and is not whole grain.

. . . if couscous is a grain? Although it is made from grains, it's actually a form of pasta. Traditional couscous (made from ground millet) has long been the pasta of northern Africa. In the United States, it's made from ground semolina wheat—a good source of B vitamins—and is often used in salads, mixed with fruit, and added to other grain dishes. Look for whole-wheat couscous.

. . . what ancient grains are—and are they healthier? All whole grains trace their history to ancient times. Although not officially defined, those often referred to as "ancient" have been mostly unchanged over the past few centuries. In the wheat family, they include einkorn, emmer/farro, freekah, kamut, and spelt. Amaranth, millet, quinoa, sorghum, and teff are also considered ancient grains, and sometimes buckwheat, black barley, black and red rice, blue corn, and wild rice are, too—although some are really pseudo-grains.

Nutritionally speaking, these grains provide more nutrition than refined grains. Many grow well with less irrigation, pesticides, and fertilizers, notes the Whole Grains Council. Every whole grain offers somewhat different nutritional benefits, so choose a variety.

. . . what graham flour is? It's whole-wheat flour that's a little coarser than regular whole-wheat flour and is used to make graham crackers and rustic breads. Substitute graham flour for some of the regular whole wheat flour in bread baking if you prefer. Besides having a hearty texture, it may create higher volume in baked bread.

amounts, dietary fiber. The Dietary Guidelines for Americans 2015 Scientific Report notes that whole and enriched grains provide 42 percent and 20 percent of iron consumed today, respectively (more than protein foods do). *See chapter 11, page 345, and chapter 14, page 408, to learn about these nutrients and their health benefits.*

Important health benefits: Grain products are a key source of carbohydrates, your body's main energy source. Their B vitamins help cells produce energy. Their folic acid from fortified grains, consumed before and during pregnancy, helps protect against birth defects.

Switching to more whole grains with their higher fiber content as part of healthy eating may help reduce the risk of some chronic diseases, including heart disease, and may help you manage your weight as well. Limited evidence suggests this switch might lower the risk for type 2 diabetes, too.

Grain Products: How Much?

Hit your carb goal with mostly whole-grain, nutrient-rich foods! Just how much do you need? Specific advice for you depends on your calorie need. If you need 2,000 calories a day, the recommended daily amount adds up to 3 ounces of whole-grain products and three ounces of enriched refined-grain products. *See "Eating Patterns: 2015–2020 Dietary Guidelines for Americans" in the appendix, page 771, for the amounts that match your calorie level.*

Make at least half of your daily grain choices whole grains for their fiber and other benefits. And replace many refined-grain foods, especially those with more added sugars and saturated fats, with nutrient-rich whole-grain foods.

One ounce-equivalent of grain equals: In general, one ounce of grain equals 1 slice of bread, 1 cup of ready-to-eat cereal, or ½ cup of cooked rice, pasta, or cereal. *See "Grain Products: How Much Is One Ounce? How Much Is a Common Portion?" in this chapter, page 29.*

Grain Group: Ten Quick Tips

Choose grain products that deliver more nutrition for fewer calories. Not only do whole grains provide unique nutrition benefits, but most refined grains are enriched with B vitamins and, by law, fortified with folic acid. Folic acid fortification is voluntary in whole-grain products. To make wise choices from the grain group, try this:

1. Go easy on grain-based foods that are high in saturated fats and added sugars, such as regular tortilla chips, croissants, pastries, doughnuts, hushpuppies, and fried rice.

   For refined-grain products, opt for a bagel instead of a croissant or sweet roll, a soft tortilla instead of a crispy one, or an English muffin instead of a doughnut. Enriched and fortified pasta, white rice, bread sticks, Italian bread, hamburger buns, and pita bread are other options. *See the chart on the next page for portion sizes.*

2. Replace refined-grain products with whole grains when you can, rather than add more. For example, eat brown rice instead of white rice, or whole wheat bread instead of white bread. *See "Grains, Grains, and More Grains," in this chapter, page 31, for whole-grain options.*

3. Check the food label and ingredient list for the words "whole" or "whole grain" before the grain's ingredient name. Choose foods that name a whole-grain ingredient.

   Know that many grain products combine whole-grain and refined-grain ingredients. These don't count as a full whole-grain portion. Check the ingredient list; look for those with whole grain or whole wheat among the first ingredients, and use the whole-grain label with the grams of whole grain as another clue to find whole grains. *See "Three Ways to Make at Least Half of Total Grains Whole Grains," in this chapter, page 30, and "Is It Really Whole Grain? Tricky to Know" in chapter 6, page 184.*

4. Check the Nutrition Facts on food labels to find whole-grain foods that are good or excellent sources of fiber. A good source has 10 to 19 percent Daily Value per serving; an excellent source has 20 percent or more. Many, but not all, whole grains qualify. (Note: With the new regulations for Nutrition Facts on food labels, the

? Have you ever wondered?

. . . if sprouted grains are healthier than unsprouted grains? Sprouted corn, oats, and wheat—and sprouted grain flour—have been trending recently. Research notes that sprouted grains have slightly more vitamin C and carotenoids, and a somewhat better amino acid profile, but the differences appear small. Sprouted grains may provide benefits for those with some grain allergies.

While a positive effect from higher enzyme activity such as phytase has been claimed, the biological effect may not be significant. Another enzyme called amylase may be higher in sprouted grains. It could aid the digestion of starch into sugars. Stay tuned as more is learned.

Before adding sprouted grains to your meals, however, be aware that eating raw sprouts has been linked to foodborne illness. The Food and Drug Administration (FDA) advises some people to avoid them: children, older adults, pregnant women, and those with weakened immune systems.

Grain Products: How Much Is One Ounce? How Much Is a Common Portion?

WG = whole grains *RG = refined grain*

Grain Product	Available Grain Form(s)	Amount that Counts as 1 Ounce-Equivalent of Grains	Common Portions and Ounce-Equivalents
Bagels	WG: whole wheat RG: plain, egg	1 mini bagel	1 large bagel = 4 ounce-equivalents
Biscuits	RG: baking powder/buttermilk	1 small (2″ diameter)	1 large (3″ diameter) = 2 ounce-equivalents
Breads	WG: 100% whole wheat RG: white, wheat, French, sourdough	1 regular slice 1 small slice, French 4 snack-size slices rye bread	2 regular slices = 2 ounce-equivalents
Bulgur	WG: cracked wheat	½ cup, cooked	
Cornbread	RG or WG. Depends on type of corn-based flour	1 small piece (2½″ × 1¼″ × 1¼″)	1 medium piece (2½″ × 2½″ × 1¼″) = 2 ounce-equivalents
Crackers	WG: 100% whole wheat, rye RG: saltines, snack crackers	5 whole-wheat crackers 2 rye crisp breads 7 square or round crackers	
English muffins	WG: whole wheat RG: plain, raisin	½ muffin	1 muffin = 2 ounce-equivalents
Muffins	WG: whole wheat RG: bran, corn, plain	1 small (2½″ diameter)	1 large (3½″ diameter) = 3 ounce-equivalents
Oatmeal	WG only	½ cup, cooked 1 packet instant 1 ounce (⅓ cup), dry (regular or quick)	
Pancakes	WG: whole wheat, buckwheat RG: buttermilk, plain	1 pancake (4½″ diameter) 2 small pancakes (3″ diameter)	3 pancakes (4½″ diameter) = 3 ounce-equivalents
Popcorn	WG only	3 cups, popped	1 mini microwave bag or 100-calorie bag, popped = 2 ounce-equivalents
Ready-to-eat breakfast cereal	WG: toasted oat, whole-wheat flakes RG: corn flakes, puffed rice	1 cup, flakes or rounds 1¼ cup, puffed	
Rice	WG: brown, wild RG: enriched, white, polished	½ cup, cooked 1 ounce, dry	1 cup, cooked = 2 ounce-equivalents
Pasta: spaghetti, macaroni, noodles	WG: whole wheat RG: enriched, durum	½ cup, cooked 1 ounce, dry	1 cup, cooked = 2 ounce-equivalents
Tortillas	WG: whole wheat, whole-grain corn RG: flour, corn	1 small flour tortilla (6″ diameter) 1 corn tortilla (6″ diameter)	1 large tortilla (12″ diameter) = 4 ounce-equivalents

Adapted from source: www.ChooseMyPlate.gov/grains

Three Ways to Make at Least Half of Total Grains Whole Grains*

1. 3 ounces of 100% whole grains and 3 ounces of refined-grain products

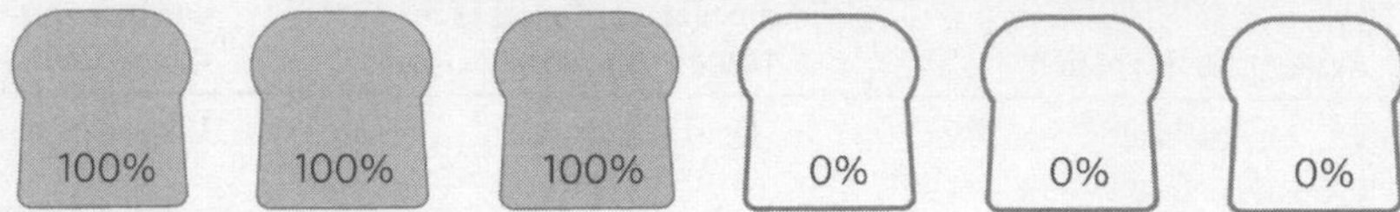

2. 2 ounces of 100% whole grains, 2 ounces of partly whole-grain products,** and 2 ounces of refined-grain products

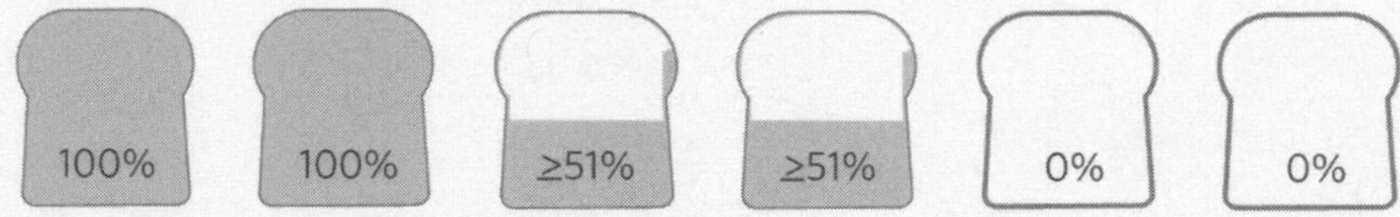

3. 6 ounces of partly whole-grain products

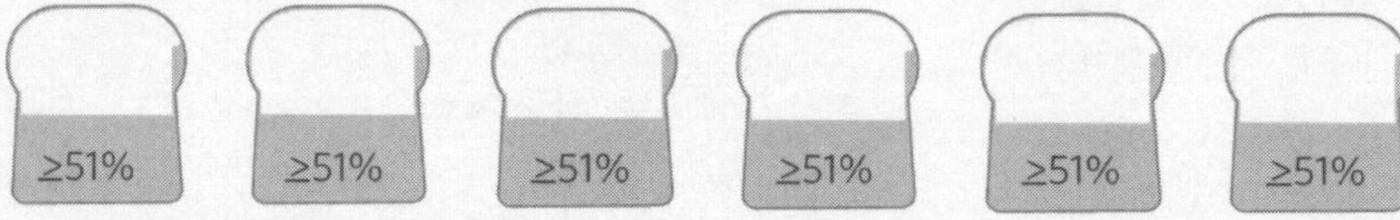

*Each 1-ounce slice of bread represents 1 ounce-equivalent to grains: One 1-ounce slice bread; 1 ounce uncooked pasta or rice; ½ cup cooked rice, pasta, or cereal; 1 tortilla (6″ diameter); 1 pancake (5″ diameter); 1 ounce ready-to-eat cereal (about 1 cup cereal flakes). This chart is for a person whose recommendation is 6 ounces of total grains with at least 3 ounces from whole grains per day.

**Partly whole-grain products depicted are those that contribute substantially to whole-grain intake. For example, products that contain at least 51% of total weight as whole grains or those that provide at least 8 grams of whole grains per ounce-equivalent.

Source: Dietary Guidelines for Americans, USDA/USHHS, 2010.

amount of fiber required to label a food as a good or excellent source of fiber will increase slightly since the Daily Value for fiber will be higher; *see "Nutrition: Fact Check!" in chapter 6, page 148 to learn how to read the nutrition label.*

5. Choose whole-grain versions of breakfast cereals, bread, crackers, rice, and pasta. Choose whole-grain or oat bread for sandwiches and toast, oat breakfast cereal, brown rice with stir-fries, whole barley in soup, or bulgur in salads and casseroles.
6. When you choose food made with refined grains, combine them with high-fiber ingredients as in pasta primavera, which is a classic pasta dish made with vegetables.
7. Change up familiar meals by adding or substituting different whole grains; their nutrient benefits differ somewhat. Try quinoa, buckwheat, millet, or whole-wheat couscous in casseroles and grain-based salads, such as pasta salad, rice pilaf salad, tabbouleh (made with bulgur), or polenta (made with cornmeal). *See "How to . . . Cook Whole Grains" in chapter 8, page 253, to learn how to prepare many of these whole grains.*
8. Experiment with other refined- or whole-grain products to add variety to meals: perhaps risotto (made with arborio rice); Asian dishes made with rice noodles or soba (buckwheat) noodles; or naan, injera, or pumpernickel bread.
9. For snacks, choose whole grains such as air-popped popcorn, baked tortilla chips, and rye and whole-grain crackers. (When corn is dried and may be popped, it's considered a whole grain; otherwise, it's classified as a vegetable.) When eating refined grains, choose lower-fat and lower-calorie options such as graham crackers, matzos, pretzels, rice cakes, saltines, baked pita chips, and bread sticks.
10. For dessert, consider angel food cake topped with fruit, graham crackers, and low-fat granola with a dollop of frozen yogurt. These are lower in calories than frosted cake, brownies, and pie, which are high in solid fats and/or added sugars.

See "Grains: Make Half Whole" in chapter 8, page 252, for more tips for including healthy grain foods in meals and snacks.

Grains, Grains, and More Grains

Looking for creative ways to eat more grains? Most of today's "new" grains are really as old as the hills. Although less familiar in the United States, some are staples that nourish millions of people around the world.

Both whole and enriched, refined grains deliver health benefits. Seeds such as amaranth and wild rice are high in protein and often are used as grain substitutes. Of the grains listed here, their nutrient contents vary somewhat, making variety a health benefit.

Some of these grains are gluten-free (GF); others are (or may be) whole-grain (WG). For the record, popcorn, whole oats and oatmeal, whole rye, and whole wheat are the most common whole grains in the United States.

Several are not true grains but instead are pseudo-grains, or false grains: amaranth, buckwheat, quinoa, and wild rice. While these four have different botanical origins, they are similar to cereal grains in their composition and use.

- *Amaranth (AM-ah-ranth)*, a seed rather than a true grain, is a protein-rich food. Use the seeds as a cereal grain. (GF)
- *Arborio (ar-BOH-ree-oh) rice*, a plump medium- or long-grain rice, absorbs a lot of liquid. The result is a creamy-textured rice. Use it to make Italian risotto, a rice-based dish. It's usually cooked in broth. (GF)
- *Barley* is an ancient, hardy grain. Pearl barley with the bran removed is the polished and most common form; it's generally enriched with the vitamins and minerals lost during processing. It makes a hearty addition to stews, soups, salads, and casseroles. Whole-grain barley, which is hulled, is sold, too. Barley typically is served in soups. Look for barley grits, flakes, and flour, which is hull-less, but still uses the whole-grain kernel. (WG if whole barley, not pearl barley).
- *Basmati (bahz-MAH-tee) rice*, a long-grained aromatic rice, has a distinctive nutlike, fruity flavor. It may be polished or brown (whole-grain) rice. It's often used in Asian and Middle Eastern recipes and in salads because it's light and fluffy. (GF)
- *Black rice*, also called purple rice, forbidden rice, or longevity rice, is glutinous and has a mild, nutty flavor. Its purple-black color, which is dark-purplish when cooked, comes from its high anthocyanin content, especially in the bran. It's used in some Asian foods, including cooked cereal, sticky rice, black rice cakes, and desserts. (GF, WG)
- *Brown rice* is whole-grain rice with only the inedible outer husk removed. Unlike refined white rice, brown rice contains the bran, germ, and endosperm of the grain. Any variety of rice—long-, medium-, or short-grain—can be brown rice. (GF, WG)
- *Buckwheat*, a whole grain, often is prepared like rice. The crushed, hulled kernels, called buckwheat groats, most commonly are used in dishes of Russian origin, such as kasha. (GF, WG)
- *Bulgur*, whole-wheat kernels that have been parboiled, dried, and crushed, has a variety of textures, from coarse to fine. It provides a soft but chewy texture in many grain-based dishes such as pilaf and tabbouleh. Add it to bread dough, too. It's similar to cracked wheat. (WG)
- *Einkorn (AHYN-korn)*, a very ancient wheat variety that is drought tolerant, is now produced so that it's more satisfactory for baking and cooking than it once was. It retains its antioxidants better than other varietals. (likely WG)
- *Farro (FAHR-oh), (emmer wheat)*, a wheat variety that dates back twenty thousand years! Used in bread, pasta, and risotto-type dishes, it's dense and chewy, rich and nutty. As a flour, the hull is removed, but it can still contain the whole-grain kernel. (WG if whole farro)
- *Freekeh (FREE-kah)* is made from roasted green wheat in an ancient Middle Eastern process. The soft and yellow grains are harvested and then sun-dried and roasted before being threshed into small pieces that look like green bulgur. (WG)
- *Glutinous rice*, either black or white, is very sticky because it's high in starch, making it chopstick friendly. Either short- or medium-grain, this type of rice is typically served in Japanese and Chinese restaurants. (GF)
- *Hominy (HAH-mih-nee)* is the dried whole-kernel corn with the hull removed. It's usually soaked in liquid to soften before it's cooked in soups, stews, and casseroles. Note: Although corn is eaten as a vegetable, it's really a whole grain. (GF, WG)
- *Jasmine (JAZ-mihn) rice*, an aromatic rice, is used in many Asian dishes. It's equally nice as a subtle "sweet" side dish, perhaps with pork or fruit-glazed poultry. A polished rice, it's often sold in specialty stores. (GF)
- *Job's tears*, a gluten-free grain, comes from a tropical plant. It can be cooked and used in dishes such as rice or barley. (GF)
- *Kamut (kah-MOOT)*, a high-protein wheat, has a nutty flavor. Its contribution of other nutrients is higher than traditional wheat, too. (may be WG)

(continued)

Grains, Grains, and More Grains *(continued)*

- *Kaniwa (kah-nyee-wah)*, native to Bolivia and Peru, is a tiny grain that is high in protein and, similar to quinoa, has a more complete amino acid balance than most grains. Unlike quinoa, it doesn't have bitter saponins that must be rinsed off before cooking. (GF, often is WG)
- *Millet*, a group of small, related whole grains that are staples in Europe, Asia, and northern Africa, but less common in the United States. Mild in flavor, millet cooks fast. Use it for pilafs, casseroles, cooked cereal, and, when ground, for bread. (GF, WG)
- *Quinoa (KEEN-wah)*, a whole grain native to South America, cooks much like rice but faster. Nutritionally it stands out because it's higher in protein (with all essential amino acids) than other grains and is a good source of iron and magnesium. The grain is small, bead-shaped, ivory in color, and bland in flavor. Use quinoa in place of rice in soups, salads, and casseroles. (GF, often is WG)
- *Sorghum (SOR-guhm)* (also called *ormilo*), a gluten-free whole grain, can be eaten as a cooked cereal or used as a flour for baked foods. (GF, WG)
- *Spelt*, another ancient grain, is nutty and mellow in flavor. Among its benefits, it's easily digested and higher in protein than other grains. Substitute spelt flour for wheat flour in baking. (may be WG)
- *Teff (TEHF)* is a gluten-free grass that cooks like millet and quinoa. (GF, likely WG)
- *Texmati rice* (sometimes called popcorn rice), from Texas, is a cross between American long-grain rice and basmati rice. Less fragrant than basmati rice, it's an all-purpose aromatic rice. (GF)
- *Triticale (trih-tih-KAY-lee)* is a modern whole grain developed as a hybrid of rye and wheat. The result is a nutty-flavored grain with more protein and less gluten than wheat alone. Cooked as a whole berry (not as flour), it's used in hearty grain-based salads, casseroles, and other grain dishes. Look for flaked and cracked varieties to add to bread dough. (often is WG)
- *Waxy rice*, or sweet rice or sticky rice (opaque white or deep, dark purple in color), is moist and very sticky when cooked. The purple variety has a subtle fruity flavor. (GF)
- *Wehani (weh-HAH-nee) rice*, a basmati rice, is sold with the bran intact. When cooked, it looks like wild rice. (GF)
- *Wheat berries* are whole grains that haven't been processed. They're often cooked and used in grain-based dishes. Cracked wheat isn't bulgur but instead is whole-berry wheat that has been crushed into coarse, medium, or fine particles. Also look for rye berries in specialty stores. (WG)
- *Wild rice* isn't a grain but instead is the seed of a grass that grows in water. With its nutlike flavor, it's often used in place of grains or perhaps mixed with them. As a seed, it's higher in protein yet somewhat lower in carbohydrates than brown rice, and it's a good fiber source. (GF)

See "Gluten: Know Its Sources" in chapter 23, page 673, for more about gluten-free grains.

VEGETABLE GROUP: VARY YOUR VEGGIES

Raw or cooked; fresh, frozen, canned, or dried/dehydrated; whole, cut up, mashed, or juiced—no matter how you like them, a wildly colorful and bountiful array of foods fits within this food group. In fact, vegetables belong in five subgroups, based on their nutrient content: dark-green leafy vegetables, red and deep-orange vegetables, starchy vegetables, beans and peas, and other vegetables. The more variety and color you eat, the better! *See "Vegetables: Have You Tried These?" in this chapter, page 36, and "Paint Your Plate with Color" in chapter 15, page 452.*

Even if fresh, raw veggies aren't available, you have other healthy options. In fact, both frozen and canned vegetables are picked and processed at their peak, and their nutritional content is comparable to cooked fresh vegetables. *See "How to . . . Keep Nutrients In" in chapter 8, page 248, for ways to cook vegetables and retain nutrients.*

Why Eat Vegetables?

More than a colorful garnish on your plate or a crisp texture in a sandwich, vegetables are loaded with nutrition, vital for your body's health and maintenance. Eating a variety as part of a healthy eating pattern overall may help reduce the risk for some chronic diseases.

Key nutrients: Vegetables are important sources of many nutrients, including potassium, magnesium, iron, beta carotene (which forms vitamin A), vitamins C and K, folate, other vitamins, dietary fiber, and phytonutrients. Unless you add sauces and other seasonings, most are naturally lower in fat and calories. None has cholesterol. *See chapter 11, page 345, chapter 14, page 408, and chapter 15, page 443, to learn about these nutrients, phytonutrients, and their health benefits.*

The nutrient content of vegetables' subgroups differs somewhat, which explains the importance of variety:

- *Dark-green leafy vegetables:* beta carotene (forms vitamin A) as well as vitamin C, folate, calcium, magnesium, and potassium

- *Red and deep-orange vegetables:* beta carotene (which forms vitamin A). Some others have more vitamin C; many are rich in folate.
- *Starchy vegetables:* in addition to their complex carbohydrates, vitamin B_6, zinc, and potassium
- *Beans and peas (legumes):* protein as well as thiamin, folate, iron, magnesium, phosphorus, zinc, potassium, and fiber
- *Other vegetables:* It varies!

"Different Vegetables and Fruits, Different Nutrients," in this chapter, page 38, provides examples of vegetables that supply various nutrients.

Important health benefits: The vitamin C found in vegetables not only helps to heal wounds and keep teeth and gums healthy, but also aids iron absorption. The vitamin A keeps eyes and skin healthy and helps to protect against infections. The vitamin E works as an antioxidant. The folate helps form red blood cells and may help reduce the risk of some birth defects. The potassium, as part of overall healthy eating, may help maintain healthy blood pressure and may also reduce the risk of developing kidney stones and help to decrease bone loss. And finally, the fiber may help maintain digestive health and possibly fill you up with fewer calories.

Vegetables in an overall healthy diet are linked to reduced risk of many chronic diseases, including stroke and heart disease. Some vegetables may be protective against certain cancers.

Another potential benefit: Eating foods such as vegetables that, cup by cup, are lower in calories than some other higher-calorie foods and may help you cut calories.

See "Eating Patterns: 2015–2020 Dietary Guidelines for Americans," in the appendix, page 771, for the amount that matches your calorie level.

Beans and Peas: Uniquely Healthy!

In the food world, pulses refer to dry beans such as kidney beans, pinto beans, black beans, lima beans, black-eyed peas, garbanzo beans (chickpeas), split peas; lentils; and others, which are harvested dry. Green (English) peas and green beans are not pulses.

Beans and peas (aka mature legumes) are unique because they belong in two food groups. Plus, they're a nutrient powerhouse. Here's why:

- *Protein foods group:* Like meat, poultry, and fish, beans and peas are good sources of protein and deliver iron and zinc, yet they're low-fat or fat-free. With their plant protein, they are great options for all vegetarians and especially important for vegans.
- *Vegetable group:* Like other vegetables, beans and peas are great sources of fiber and other nutrients, such as folate and potassium. Plan to eat at least 1½ cups of legumes a week.

When ground, some legumes such as lentils, chickpeas, and dry peas are used as gluten-free flour.

Count them in either food group—but not in both food groups at the same time. If you usually eat meat, poultry, and fish, you might prefer to count beans and peas as vegetables. If you're a vegetarian or eat "meatless" regularly, you may count them as protein foods instead. Determine how much counts toward the recommendations from each food group as you continue to read this chapter. If you need to count carbs for managing diabetes, remember that ½ cup counts as 15 grams of carbohydrates.

Vegetables: How Much, What Kind?

Have you heard, "Make half your plate vegetables and fruit"? Do you get enough? The amount of vegetables advised for you depends on your calorie level.

For 2,000 calories a day, the recommendation adds up to 2½ cups of vegetables daily. Most people come up short. To get the nutrient variety and health benefits that different vegetables provide, spread them out this way over the week:

- Dark-green vegetables: 1½ cups per week
- Red and orange vegetables: 5½ cups per week
- Beans and peas (legumes): 1½ cups per week
- Starchy vegetables: 5 cups per week
- Other vegetables: 4 cups per week

One cup of vegetables equals: For most vegetables, 1 cup is either 1 cup of raw or cooked vegetables or vegetable juice, or 2 cups of raw, leafy greens. To extend the list, here are some more vegetables that count as 1 cup:

DARK-GREEN VEGETABLES:

- 2 cups raw, leafy greens (spinach, romaine lettuce, watercress, dark-green leafy lettuce, endive, escarole, other leafy greens)
- 1 cup cooked greens (collards, mustard greens, kale, spinach)
- 3 spears (5 inches long) broccoli or 1 cup chopped broccoli or 1 cup broccoli florets

RED AND ORANGE VEGETABLES:

- 1 cup sliced or mashed carrots, pumpkin, sweet potatoes, winter squash (acorn, butternut, hubbard), tomatoes, red bell peppers, cooked or raw
- 1 large (2¼-inch-diameter or more) sweet potato, baked
- 1 large (3-inch-diameter) tomato

- 1 large (3-inch-diameter) red bell pepper
- 1 cup (12) baby carrots
- 1 cup tomato or mixed-vegetable juice

BEANS AND PEAS:

- 1 cup whole or mashed cooked dry beans or peas (black, garbanzo, kidney, pinto, or soybeans, or black-eyed peas or split peas)

STARCHY VEGETABLES:

- 1 cup corn, green peas, or diced or mashed potatoes
- 1 large ear (8 to 9 inches long) corn, yellow or white
- 1 medium (2½- to 3-inch-diameter) potato, baked or boiled

OTHER VEGETABLES:

- 1 cup chopped, mashed, or sliced other vegetables (cauliflower, celery, cucumbers, green or wax beans, green bell peppers, mushrooms, onion, summer squash, zucchini), cooked or raw
- 1 cup cooked bean sprouts
- 2 large stalks (11- to 12-inch-long) celery
- 2 cups raw iceberg or head lettuce, shredded or chopped
- 1 large (3-inch-diameter) green bell pepper

Vegetable Group: Ten Quick Tips

Eat more veggies! Vary the types and colors—their nutrient and phytonutrient contents differ. Ease up on French fries, fried onion rings, and salads with heavy dressings.

1. Enjoy your vegetable favorites and eat more of them! Fresh veggies are especially delicious in peak season—and they cost less, too.
2. Broaden your vegetable repertoire, perhaps with seasonal vegetables. Besides green beans, broccoli, and corn, try okra, snow peas, or Brussels sprouts. Roast parsnips and beets with carrots and potatoes; *see, "How to . . . Roast Vegetables" in chapter 8, page 249.* Shred fresh spinach, broccoli stalks, and fennel for slaw.

   Need more ideas? Besides the vegetables *noted in this chapter and in chapter 8*, a walk through the produce department and grocery aisles may spark your creativity! *See "Vegetables: Have You Tried These?" in this chapter, page 36.*
3. Make a vegetable dish the focus of your meal. Start with familiar dishes—vegetable lasagna, bean enchiladas, vegetable stir-fry—and then get more creative with vegetarian (meatless) main dishes.
4. Try different greens such as Bibb lettuce or watercress and include dark, leafy ones such as beet greens, chard, chicory, collard greens, fennel greens, kale, romaine lettuce, and spinach in salads. Beet greens, collard greens, and kale are great in stews and soups, too.
5. Enjoy more beans and peas in soup (split peas or lentils), salads (kidney or garbanzo beans), and side dishes (baked beans or pinto beans). Or eat them in a main dish. They have a split personality—count them in either the vegetable group or the

? Have you ever wondered?

. . . where salsa fits in the food groups? That depends on the ingredients. An all-vegetable salsa, perhaps made with beans, counts in the vegetable group. If the salsa has mango or another fruit as well as veggies, your portion counts toward a little from both the fruit and the vegetable groups.

. . . what cruciferous vegetables are? Members of the cabbage family, they get their name from their four-petal flowers, which look like a crucifer, or cross. They include a diverse variety: arugula, bok choy, broccoli, Brussels sprouts, cabbage, cauliflower, collards, kale, kohlrabi, mustard greens, radishes, rutabagas, chard, turnips, turnip greens, and watercress. In addition to nutrients, cruciferous vegetables contain phytonutrients with unique health-promoting benefits. This vegetable family has something else in common: a strong cooking aroma.

Proper food handling enhances their flavor without intensifying the aroma. First, eat them soon after buying, whether raw or cooked. Second, cook them quickly, just until tender-crisp. Third, eat leftovers within a day.

. . . if potatoes can substitute for bread since they're both high in starches? Although both provide complex carbohydrates, starchy vegetables such as potatoes have different nutrients and phytonutrients than foods in the grain group such as bread. Potatoes, for example, supply vitamin C and potassium; grain group foods supply some B vitamins and iron. Breadfruit, cassava, corn, green peas, hominy, rutabaga, taro, and yautia are some other starchy vegetables in the vegetable group.

. . . if corn is a good vegetable choice? As part of the variety of vegetables on your plate, corn deserves more credit than it often gets. Besides being a rich source of fiber, it also delivers lutein and zeaxanthin, two carotenoids with antioxidant power, as well as some B vitamins, iron, selenium, and some incomplete protein. Cooking and heating corn makes the antioxidants more available to your body.

protein foods group; the same bowl of beans can't count for both.

6. Snack on raw veggies. Keep cleaned broccoli and cauliflower florets, red and green pepper strips or minis, cucumber sticks, celery sticks, sliced kohlrabi, or baby carrots in the fridge, ready for a quick nibble. They taste great with a low-fat dressing or dip!
7. Add color, flavor, and appeal. Top pizza and toss pastas with chopped or sliced vegetables such as zucchini, carrots, broccoli, and bell peppers. Top sandwiches with a layer of spinach and slices of tomato, zucchini, or cucumber, or try portobello mushrooms as a topper. Top baked potatoes with vegetable salsa or stir-fried veggies.
8. Drink your veggies. Make smoothies with kale, shredded carrots, pureed pumpkin, or any vegetables you like. Or enjoy 100 percent vegetable juice, perhaps just tomato juice or a mix, with other vegetables such as carrots and kale, or try a mix of vegetables and fruit juices.
9. Eating out? Order vegetables as a starter or side dish. Or order a main-dish salad or vegetarian dish. Ask for slaw or a garden salad rather than fries with fast food.
10. Blend pureed cooked vegetables, such as pumpkin, carrots, potatoes, or beans, and use the puree as a thickener in stews, soups, and gravies.

See "Fruits and Vegetables: Fit More In" in chapter 8, page 246, for more tips for including colorful vegetables in meals and snacks.

FRUIT GROUP: FOCUS ON WHOLE FRUITS

What's in the fruit bowl? All of America's favorites: apples, bananas, and oranges, as well as berries, grapes, melons, peaches, and some you may eat less often, such as kiwifruit, mangoes, and nectarines. For more variety, you can fill your fruit bowl with less common fruits, too, such as lychees, loquats, and pomegranates! *See "Fruit: What's New to You?" in this chapter, page 39.*

Any fruit or 100 percent fruit juice counts in the fruit group, whether it's fresh, canned, frozen, or dried. Fruit may be eaten whole, cut up, or pureed.

Why Eat Fruit?

Fruit tastes good! More than that, fruit provides nutrients and phytonutrients that are essential for maintaining overall good health and reducing the risk of some chronic diseases.

Key nutrients: As in vegetables, the nutrient content differs from fruit to fruit—a reason for varying your choices. Overall, fruit supplies carotenoids, including those that form vitamin A, as well as vitamin C, folate, potassium, fiber, and many other phytonutrients. *See "Different Vegetables and Fruits, Different Nutrients," in this chapter, page 38, for some sources of each.*

Fruit's sweet flavor comes from its natural sugar, or fructose. Sometimes sugars are added to canned and frozen fruit and fruit juice to enhance their flavor or to help maintain their quality; choose unsweetened fruit whenever you can. Most fruits are low in fat, sodium, and calories, and all are cholesterol free. Two fruits, avocados and olives, contain monounsaturated fat. Avocados also supply beta carotene (which forms vitamin A).

Most juices have little or no fiber, so choose whole or cut-up fruit more often than juice.

See chapter 11, page 345, chapter 14, page 408, and chapter 15, page 443, to learn about these nutrients, phytonutrients, and their health benefits.

Important health benefits: Fruit's vitamin C promotes growth and repair of all body tissues, helps heal cuts and wounds, and keeps teeth and gums healthy. Its fiber aids digestion, and its folate helps the body form red blood cells and, for many women, helps reduce the risk of birth defects.

As part of your overall healthy eating strategy, fruit is linked to some potential health benefits, such as reduced risk for heart disease, and for some fruits, protection from some cancers. As a good potassium source, fruit may help maintain healthy blood pressure, and perhaps help reduce the risk of developing kidney stones or possibly help reduce bone loss with age. Fruit's dietary fiber may help reduce the risk of heart disease, high blood cholesterol levels, constipation, and diverticulosis, when fruit is part of an overall healthy eating pattern.

As a sweet food, unadorned fruit is lower in calories per cup than a serving of many sugary desserts. For that reason, fruit may help you control the calories in your meals and snacks. And fruit's fiber and water may help you feel full with fewer calories.

Fruit: How Much?

Sweeten your day with fruit! The specific amount recommended depends on your calorie needs, which in turn, depends on your age, gender, and level of physical activity. For 2,000 calories a day, you need about 2 cups of fruit a day. *See "Eating Patterns, 2015–2020 Dietary Guidelines for Americans" in the appendix, page 771, for the amount that matches your calorie level.*

Make most of your fruit choices whole fruit rather than juice. Fruit drinks, even if they provide 100 percent Daily Value for vitamin C, are considered sugar-sweetened beverages—not juice—and don't belong in the fruit group. *See "Juice, Juice Drink, or Fruit Drink" in chapter 4, page 88, for why 100 percent fruit juices are advised over fruit drinks.*

One cup of fruit equals: As a rule of thumb, 1 cup of fruit is 1 cup of cut-up fruit, grapes, or berries, 1 cup of 100 percent fruit juice, or ½ cup of dried fruit. To limit added sugars, choose fruit canned in 100 percent juice instead of heavy syrup. What counts as 1 cup of whole fruit takes more estimating and reflects typical portion sizes. To extend the list, these also count as one cup of fruit:

- 1 cup cut-up fresh, frozen, or canned fruit (apples, bananas, berries, grapes, grapefruit or orange sections, melons, peaches, pears, pineapples, plums, other)

Vegetables: Have You Tried These?

Looking for new ways to enjoy vegetables? Identify vegetables you've never tried. Buy and try one or two the next time you shop or eat out. Look for recipes online, in magazines, or a vegetable cookbook.

- *Arugula (ah-ROO-gu-lah)* is a green, leafy vegetable with a distinctive peppery flavor. Use it raw in mixed garden salads or cook and toss it with pasta or risotto.
- *Beet greens* are the edible and hearty greens from fresh bunches of the beetroot. Similar in flavor, these nutrient-rich greens can be used like kale, turnip greens, or collard greens.
- *Bok choy (bahk CHOY)* (also called *pak choi*) is a Chinese cabbage. It doesn't form a head but instead has several white, bunched stems with thick, green leaves. Eat it raw or cooked, and in stir-fry dishes.
- *Breadfruit* looks like a green, bumpy melon (brown when ripe) on the outside and is creamy-white inside. Like other starchy vegetables, it's peeled before it's baked, boiled, fried, grilled, or cooked in stews and soups. Its flavor is slightly sweet, yet mild. Some Caribbean dishes include breadfruit.
- *Broccoli raab* (also called *rapini*), with 6- to 9-inch stalks and small broccolilike buds, is strong and bitter. Use it raw in salads, cooked as a side dish, or in mixed dishes.
- *Cactus pads* (also called *nopales [noh-PAH-lays]*), which are cactus leaves, are used in Mexican and Southwest dishes. Their thorns are removed before cooking. They're usually sliced and then simmered or cooked in a microwave oven. You can buy canned nopales.
- *Cassava (kah-SAH-vah)* (also called *manioc [MA-nee-ahk]* and *yucca* [YOO-kah] root), a starchy root vegetable, has a thick, brown peel, and inside it's white or yellow like a potato. Cook and use it as you would potatoes.
- *Celeriac (seh-LER-ee-ak)*, a member of the celery family, is enjoyed for its root, not its stalks. It has a fibrous, brown, bumpy peel and a sweet, celery flavor inside. Once peeled, enjoy it raw, perhaps in salads, or cooked—boiled, steamed, or fried. Use it in soups or stews, perhaps in place of celery.
- *Chard*, a white-rooted beet, is grown for its leaves and its creamy-white or red stalks and dark-green leaves. With its mild yet distinctive flavor, use it like spinach.
- *Chayote (cheye-OH-tay)* is a pale-green, pear-shaped vegetable with a mild flavor. Baked, boiled, braised, or stuffed, it complements the flavors of other ingredients in mixed dishes. Use it like squash.
- *Chicory* (also called *curly endive*) has a frizzy leaf in a loose head of greens. In small amounts, its bitter flavor adds interest to salads.
- *Daikon (DEYE-kuhn)* is a Japanese radish that looks like a smooth, white parsnip. It has a stronger, more bitter flavor than a red radish. Often it's used in sushi (fish rolled with rice in seaweed) and in vegetable carvings.
- *Dasheen (dah-SHEEN)* is a large, round root vegetable with a coarse, brown peel, similar to taro. Usually prepared boiled or baked, it is starchy, somewhat like a potato.
- *Escarole (EHS-kah-role)* is a somewhat bitter salad green. Sometimes its green leaves have a reddish tinge. Unlike iceberg lettuce, it forms a loose head.
- *Fennel* looks like a squat, flattened bunch of celery with feathery leaves. Its flavor is like sweet, delicate anise. The bulb and stalks are often braised, steamed, sautéed, or used in soups, and they also can be served raw. Use the feathery leaves in salads, as an herb, or as a garnish.
- *Jerusalem artichoke*, native to North America, has nothing in common with a globe artichoke. Like a potato, it's a tuber and grows underground. But it's knobby and irregularly shaped, with a sweet flavor and a light-brown or purplish-red peel. It's often cooked in its skin; a little lemon juice in the cooking water keeps peeled Jerusalem artichokes from browning. Use it in dishes that call for potatoes, or eat it raw.
- *Jicama (HEE-kah-mah)*, a root vegetable, is crisp and slightly sweet. Peel, slice, and eat it raw, perhaps in salads. Or cook it in stews and stir-fries.
- *Kale*, a leafy vegetable in the cabbage family, doesn't form a head. It has a curly, purple-tinged, green leaf. Use it in salads, or prepare it like cooked spinach.
- *Kelp* is brown seaweed, often used in Japanese cooking and wrapped around sushi.
- *Kohlrabi (KOLE-rah-bee)*, a member of the cabbage family, looks and tastes like a turnip. It's light green in color. Use it in recipes that call for turnips; slice and use it in stir-fry dishes; or peel and eat it raw or in salads.
- *Leek* is an onion. It looks like a bigger, sturdier, flat-leaved version of a green onion. Clean it to remove soil between the leaves and layers of onion. Slice the bulb; steam it in soups, or bake it in casseroles. Use the leaves in salads.

Vegetables: Have You Tried These? *(continued)*

- *Lotus root*, the water lily root, has the texture of a potato and a flavor similar to fresh coconut. Peel and slice it, then stir-fry, steam, or braise it in mixed Chinese dishes.
- *Mushrooms* of all kinds include chanterelle, enoki, morel, oyster, porcini, portobello, shiitake, straw mushrooms, and wood ears. Each has a unique flavor and qualities. Some are sold dried.
- *Parsnip*, a root vegetable, is a starchy vegetable that becomes sweet when harvested after the first frost. Choose small or medium-size roots that are not limp or shriveled. Bake, broil, roast, sauté, or steam them, and perhaps mash them as you would other root vegetables.
- *Plantain (PLAN-tihn)* belongs to the banana family, but it's longer and thicker, starchier, and less sweet. It's never eaten raw but can be cooked at any stage of ripeness—green, yellow, or black; it's sweetest when black. Eat it as a vegetable, cooked in or out of the peel. Bake, fry, or boil plantains, perhaps in a stew.
- *Radicchio (rah-DEE-chee-oh)* is a small, purplish head of leaves with white ribs. It's somewhat bitter. Use it in salads, pasta, and stir-fries.
- *Rhubarb (ROO-bahrb)*, eaten as a fruit, is a celerylike vegetable with an intense tart flavor. Choose crisp, brightly colored stalks; use them right away. (The leaves contain oxalic acid and should be removed; leaves are not edible.)
- *Rutabaga (ROO-tuh-bay-guh)* is a root vegetable with a turnip-like flavor and appearance. Use them in place of turnips in stews, soups, and casseroles.
- *Salsify (SAL-sih-fee)* is a white root vegetable that tastes like delicate oysters. Eat it as a cooked side dish or perhaps in soups.
- *Seaphire (SEE-fyre)* is a halophyte, or salt water crop. With an asparagus-grass look, seaphire is crisp, crunchy, and salty. Since it's high in sodium, enjoy small amounts as a flavoring in salads, stir-fries, and vegetable dishes. Three ounces have 1,350 milligrams of sodium.
- *Seaweed*, used most often in Asian dishes and some Irish, Welsh, and Scottish dishes, has many varietals. Kelp may be the most common in the United States. Many Japanese dishes use nori *(NOH-ree)*. See also "*Kelp*" above.
- *Taro (TAIR-oh)* is a rough, brown or purplish tuber. Some, not all, resemble yams. Peel taro and boil, bake, or fry it much like potatoes. Hawaiian poi is made from taro. Its edible leaves, called *callaloo* in the Caribbean, are cooked in a soup.
- *Tomatillo (tohm-ah-TEE-oh)*, a member of the tomato family, has a paperlike husk. Under the husk, it looks like a small green tomato. Often prepared like a green tomato, its flavor is citruslike. Use it in Southwest and Mexican dishes, including salsa and salads.
- *Winter squash*—acorn, bitter melon, buttermilk, crookneck, delicata, golden nugget, hubbard, kabocha, minipumpkin, spaghetti (as a pasta alternative), sunburst, and turban—is used in cooked dishes.

- 1 cup applesauce
- 1 small (2½-inch-diameter) apple
- ½ large (3¼-inch-diameter) apple
- 1 large (8- to 9-inch-long) banana
- 32 seedless grapes
- 1 medium (4-inch-diameter) grapefruit
- 1 large (3-inch-diameter) orange
- 1 large (2¾-inch-diameter) peach
- 2 halves canned peaches
- 1 medium pear (2½ pears per pound)
- 3 medium or 2 large plums
- About 8 large strawberries
- 1 small (1-inch-thick) wedge watermelon or 1 cup diced (balls) watermelon
- ½ cup dried fruit (raisins, dried plums, dried apricots)
- 1 cup 100 percent fruit juice (orange, apple, grapefruit, other)

Fruit Group: Ten Quick Tips

Eat more fruits! Mix up the variety, including seasonal fruits, for more nutrition and more enjoyment. Choose whole or cut-up fruits more often than 100 percent fruit juices.

1. Keep frozen, canned, and dried fruits on hand, especially when fresh fruits aren't in season. Choose canned fruits that are packed in juice for less added sugars and fewer calories.
2. Add variety, color, flavor, and nutrition to your meals with less familiar fruits, such as prickly pear, papaya, mango, star fruit, figs, or guava. Try new-to-you varieties of apples, pears, plums, or melons. *See "Fruit: What's New to You?" in this chapter, page 39.*
3. Keep rinsed, fresh fruits and dried fruits handy on the counter or in the fridge. Cut up and refrigerate melon or pineapple so

Different Vegetables and Fruits, Different Nutrients

SOURCES OF VITAMIN A

- Bright-orange vegetables such as carrots, sweet potatoes, and pumpkin
- Tomatoes, tomato products, and red bell peppers
- Leafy greens such as spinach, collards, turnip greens, kale, beet and mustard greens, green-leaf lettuce, and romaine lettuce
- Orange fruits such as mangoes, cantaloupe, apricots, and red or pink grapefruit

SOURCES OF VITAMIN C

- Citrus fruits and juices, kiwifruit, strawberries, guava, papaya, and cantaloupe
- Broccoli, peppers, tomatoes, cabbage (especially Chinese cabbage), Brussels sprouts, and potatoes
- Leafy greens such as romaine lettuce, turnip greens, and spinach

SOURCES OF FOLATE

- Cooked dry beans and peas (legumes)
- Orange and orange juice
- Deep-green leaves such as spinach and mustard greens

SOURCES OF POTASSIUM

- Baked white or sweet potatoes, cooked greens (such as spinach), winter (orange) squash
- Bananas, plantains, many dried fruits, oranges and orange juice, cantaloupe, and honeydew melons
- Cooked dry beans (legumes)
- Soybeans (green and mature)
- Tomato products (sauce, pasta, puree)
- Beet greens

it's ready to eat. Sliced bananas, apples, and pears will turn brown, so cut them just before you're ready to eat them. (Hint: tossing these cut fruits with citrus juice, such as lemon juice, delays browning.) Pack dried apricots, apple slices, cranberries, raisins, and prunes (dried plums) to go or keep in your desk or bag.

4. Enjoy fresh fruits in season when they are at peak flavor and cost less. (They don't need to be perfectly shaped to be nourishing!)
5. Choose 100 percent fruit juice when choosing juice. Mix it with sparkling water for a refreshing fizzy drink.
6. Enjoy a fruit smoothie from a smoothie bar or make one at home. Whirl cut-up fruit (canned, fresh, frozen), juice, and yogurt, frozen yogurt, or milk.
7. Add fruit to leafy-green salads or slaw: mandarin orange segments, grape halves, berries, raisins, dried cranberries, chopped apples, or pomegranate seeds.
8. Top breakfast cereal, pancakes, pudding, or frozen yogurt with cut-up or pureed fruit instead of sugar syrup or other sweet toppings.
9. Blend dried fruits with stuffing and rice dishes. Mix them in muffin batter and bread dough.
10. Choose whole fruit or 100 percent frozen fruit juice bars for your snack or dessert.

See "Fruits and Vegetables: Fit More In" in chapter 8, page 246, for more tips for including fruits in meals and snacks.

DAIRY GROUP: MOVE TO LOW FAT AND FAT FREE

Dairy foods, including milk, yogurt, and cheese, are calcium- and protein-rich. Fluid milk and many foods made from milk that retain their calcium content fit here. Low-fat and fat-free dairy foods—milk and yogurt—are the most nutrient-dense.

A few dairy foods—butter, cream, cream cheese, and sour cream—don't count as foods from the dairy group since they contribute fat and few other nutrients. They're made from the cream that naturally separates from unhomogenized milk.

What about soymilk (soy beverages)? They too contain protein, and if fortified with calcium and vitamins A and D, they're considered part of the dairy group. From a nutrition standpoint and for their use in meals, they're similar to milk, although their whole nutrient package isn't the same as in dairy foods. Other nondairy drinks do not fit the nutrient criteria for this food group. *See "The Healthy Vegetarian Way" in this chapter, page 53, for more about the vegan dairy group.*

Why Consume Dairy Foods?

Over a lifetime, an adequate amount from the dairy group reduces the risk of low bone mass and osteoporosis. That said, dairy delivers more nutrition than just calcium and vitamin D and does more than promote bone health. Milk's nutrients are good for your whole body.

Key nutrients: Dairy foods are the body's best sources of calcium, vitamin D, and riboflavin. Without these foods, getting enough calcium and vitamin D isn't as easy. Most milk and yogurt are fortified with vitamin D.

Fruit: What's New to You?

In addition to reaching for fruit you know already, try something new! Many tropical and subtropical fruits aren't well known in much of the United States. Look for less common fruits in the produce department or as canned foods. Visit Asian and Hispanic food markets.

Try different varietals of common fruits, too, such as red bananas, manzano bananas, apple bananas, and plantains. Different varietals of apples, oranges, plums, and pears also offer unique flavors, textures, and even cooking qualities.

- *Açai (ah-SAH-ee)* is a dark-purple, grape-sized fruit that grows on the açai palm. The inedible nut is surrounded by a small amount of pulp with a delicate berry flavor. Because it's highly perishable, it's generally sold as juice, frozen pulp, or powder. Use it in fruit drinks and smoothies.
- *African horned melon* (also called *kiwano [kih-WAH-no]*) is spiked (yellow "horns"), oblong, and golden-orange. Its juicy green fruit tastes like cucumber, banana, and lime. Mild in flavor, it's like a juicy, seed-filled cucumber. Scoop the pulp, and enjoy it in salads, drinks, and sauces.
- *Asian pear* looks like a yellow apple and has a similar firm, crunchy texture. It's sweet, juicy, and eaten whole or cut for mixed salads.
- *Atemoya (a-teh-MOY-ah)* is a cross between a cherimoya *(see below)* and a sweetsop *(see below)*. With a green skin, it looks petallike. Its cream-colored, custardlike pulp is studded with large black seeds and has a mango-vanilla flavor.
- *Blood orange* is a tart yet sweet orange with flesh that's either bright red or white with red streaks. Enjoy as juice or like other whole citrus fruit.
- *Cherimoya (chair-ih-MOY-ah)* (also called custard apple) has a custardlike consistency and flavor. It looks like a little green pineapple without leaves. The inside has little black seeds and tastes like a mix of strawberry, banana, pineapple, and mango. To eat it, cut it in half, remove the seeds, and scoop out the fruit.
- *Cape gooseberries* are juicy and bittersweet beneath their Chinese lantern skin. Serve them with meat, savory dishes, and desserts.
- *Date*, sold both fresh and dried, is very sweet and has a shiny, thin skin. Enjoy dates as a snack or in mixed-greens dishes, sweet-savory sauces, and salads.
- *Dragon fruit*, in the cactus family, is yellow to shocking pink, shaped like a hand grenade, and has spines on the outside. The fruit inside is juicy and grainy, with edible seeds that taste like kiwifruit or grapes. To eat it, peel and scoop out the fruit.
- *Feijoa (fay-YOH-ah* or *fay-JOH-ah)* looks like a kiwifruit without fuzz. Inside, its cream-colored flesh is sweet, fragrant, and pearly white. To eat it, remove the skin, which may be bitter, cut it in half, and scoop out the fruit. Use it in place of apples or bananas.
- *Goji (GOH-jee) berry* (also called *wolfberry*) is a bright red berry shaped like a plump almond. Enjoy them raw, dry in trail mix, or as juice, or perhaps in mixed juices or smoothies.
- *Guava (GWAH-vah)* (also called *guayaba [gway-AH-bah]*) is a sweet, fragrant fruit that's about the size of a lemon. Its peel varies from yellow to purple; the fruit inside may be yellow, pink, or red. Eat guavas as whole fruit or in sauces, salads, juices, frozen desserts, and jams.
- *Jackfruit*, a relative of breadfruit and fig, is a tropical fruit, and considered the world's largest fruit. When ripe, the skin is yellow-brown; the flesh is yellow, slightly sweet, and juicy. Prepare in cooked dishes such as curry or sweet and sour dishes, or cut up raw in salads or desserts.
- *Kumquat (KUHM-kwaht)*, a citrus fruit that looks like a small, olive-shaped orange. Kumquats are eaten with their thin peel on—either uncooked or cooked with meat, poultry, or fish. Slice them for a garnish or salads.
- *Longan (LONG-uhn)* is a small, round, cherry-sized fruit with a thick, inedible brown shell. The white, juicy fruit around the large black seed is sweet and fragrant. Enjoy as a snack or in fruit salads.
- *Loquat (LOH-kwaht)*, a small, pear-shaped fruit, is light orange inside and out. Somewhat tart, the pit must be removed. Eat loquats whole, in salads, or in cooked poultry dishes.
- *Lychee (LEE-chee)* (also called *litchi*) is 1 to 2 inches in diameter with a pink to red shell. Inside, the fruit is white and sweet with a consistency similar to a grape. Its seed isn't edible. Eat lychees as a snack or dessert just as they are.
- *Mango*, sweet-tart and juicy, ranges in size and shape. It can weigh anywhere from six ounces to five pounds and be round or elongated. Its inedible peel is orange when ripe, with orange fruit inside and a large seed. To easily eat a mango, either peel back the skin and eat it with a spoon, or remove both the peel and seed and cut it into pieces. Use mangoes in fruit salads, smoothies, and desserts, and prepare them with cooked meat, poultry, rice, or grains.
- *Mangosteen (MAN-goh-steen)* has an inedible leathery, brown skin. Inside, the soft, white, juicy fruit is segmented. Buy it canned; it's rarely available fresh.

(continued)

Fruit: What's New to You? *(continued)*

- *Papaya (pah-PEYE-ah)* (also called *pawpaw*) weighs from one to twenty pounds and has elongated, oval shape. Its inedible peel is yellow or orange, with orange fruit inside and many black seeds. Tart and sweet, it's delicious as is or in salads.
- *Passion fruit* (also called *granadilla [gra-nah-DEE-yah]*) is a small, round fruit with a leathery peel, which may seem shriveled. It has a sweetly tart, perfumed flavor, and its color varies from light yellow to reddish-purple. Eat it whole or add it to salads, sauces, desserts, or drinks.
- *Pepino (peh-PEE-noh)*, ranging in size from a plum to a papaya, is a fragrant melon with a smooth, golden skin that's streaked with purple. Inside, the yellow flesh is juicy sweet. Peel it and eat it whole, or use it in salads or as a garnish.
- *Persimmon (puhr-SIHM-uhn)* looks somewhat like an orange-red tomato with a pointy end. If it's ripe, it's sweet. If not, it's mouth-puckering, bitter, and sour. Eat it whole, or use it in desserts and baked foods.
- *Plumcot* is a cross between a plum and an apricot. It has an intensely sweet, fruity flavor. Enjoy this whole fruit as a snack, or in desserts or salads.
- *Pomegranate (PAH-meh-gran-uht)* is unlike any other fruit. It has a red, leathery peel. Inside, membranes hold clusters of small, edible seeds encased in juicy red fruit. The flavor is tart and sweet. Use pomegranate seeds in salads and many cooked dishes.
- *Pomelo (POM-eh-loh)*, a huge citrus fruit, can be as big as a watermelon but is more commonly the size of a cantaloupe. In many ways, it looks and tastes like a grapefruit, but the sections are not as juicy. Use like other citrus sections in salads.
- *Prickly pear* (also called *cactus pear*), which is yellow-green to deep yellow, is the fruit of a cactus plant. It has a sweet, mild flavor. Peel and seed it before eating. It may have small hairs or needles in the peel that can be uncomfortable if they get into your skin. Eat it whole or in salads, sauces, and other dishes.
- *Rambutan (ram-BOOT-uhn)*, with its dark, bristlelike rind, is a small fruit. Peel the rind to reveal translucent, grapelike flesh that surrounds a seed and tastes like a lychee (see above). Combine peeled rambutan in tropical fruit salad or as a snack.
- *Sapodilla (sah-poh-DEE-yah)* is a small, egg-shaped fruit with a rough, brown peel. Only the creamy pulp is edible—when the fruit is ripe. Its mild flavor is like vanilla custard.
- *Star fruit* (also called *carambola [kar-am-BOH-lah]*) gets its name from its unique shape, which forms stars when sliced. The flavor varies from sweet to tart. Eat it sliced, in salads, or as a garnish.
- *Sweetsop, or sugar apple*, is a round fruit that has segments that separate when ripe, exposing the interior flesh. The flesh is fragrant and sweet, creamy white to light yellow, with a custardlike flavor. Enjoy the flesh whole or as snacks.
- *Tamarillo (tam-uh-RIH-yoh)*, with its tough, thin peel, is a small, egg-shaped fruit. Being tart, it's often sweetened. Use it in baked or cooked foods.
- *Ugli (UHG-lee) fruit* is a cross between a tangerine and a grapefruit. It's sectioned on the inside but looks like a small grapefruit on the outside. Use like other citrus sections in salads.
- *Zapote (zah-POH-tay)* (also called *white sapote*) is a sweet, yellowish fruit about the size of an orange. Peel and enjoy, or puree for smoothies and mixed juice.

Dairy foods also are good sources of protein, magnesium, phosphorus, potassium, and vitamin B_{12}, a vitamin available only from animal sources of food. Without dairy foods, you may not get enough potassium. Many dairy foods, especially fluid milk, are fortified with vitamin A. For vegetarians (except vegans), dairy foods are an important protein source.

Low-fat and fat-free milk provide little or no fat, including saturated fat. If you occasionally choose full-fat dairy foods, know that fats contribute calories.

Cheese? The nutrient and calorie content of cheese varies. In general, cheese has more total and saturated fat, cholesterol, and sodium than milk does. That said, fat-free and reduced-fat cheeses are available; some have less sodium. Lower-fat cheeses usually have less cholesterol. Regardless of the fat content, the amounts of other nutrients—calcium, protein, phosphorus, and vitamin D—are comparable.

Dairy foods may contain two types of sugars: naturally occurring lactose and added sugars. Any added sugars (and extra calories) in dairy foods come from flavorings added to yogurt and milk, drinkable yogurt, dairy desserts such as ice cream, and other dairy foods.

Check the Nutrition Facts label on nondairy calcium sources. Calcium-fortified soymilk is an alternative to dairy milk and fits in this group. Coconut milk, rice milk, and almond milk do not; *see "Dairy and Nondairy Beverages" in chapter 4, page 90, for more about these and other nondairy beverages.*

Important health benefits: Eating patterns that include milk are generally higher in nutrition quality.

From childhood through adulthood, calcium in dairy foods helps build and maintain bones and teeth and reduce the risk of osteoporosis later in life. During childhood and adolescence, it is especially important for building bone mass.

Milk's full nutrient package is vital for health for many more reasons. For example, vitamin D helps maintain proper levels of calcium and phosphorus, thereby helping to build and maintain bones. The calcium and potassium in milk as well as yogurt help maintain healthy blood pressure. These foods also provide cell-building protein.

Consuming milk and milk products is linked to other health benefits, including reducing the risk of cardiovascular disease and type 2 diabetes.

Have you ever wondered?

. . . if frozen yogurt has the same nutrients as regular yogurt? Similar to low-fat ice cream, the nutrient content of frozen yogurt varies. No federal standards exist for frozen yogurt. To find the nutrient and calorie content, you need to read the food label; or if you order from a quick-service frozen yogurt bar, ask for the nutritionals. Regular yogurt—plain or fruit-flavored—typically supplies more calcium than frozen yogurt.

Some frozen yogurts contain active live cultures with possible probiotic health benefits; *see "Prebiotics and Probiotics: A Bioactive Duo" in chapter 15, page 453.* However, freezing temperatures slow the action of any live cultures, so the probiotic benefit may be limited.

. . . if Greek yogurt is a better yogurt choice than regular yogurt? Nutritionally speaking, yogurt is a great dairy option, whether it's Greek or not. You need to weigh the benefits of each.

Because Greek yogurt has been strained to remove liquid whey and some lactose and sodium, it has a thicker texture and tangier flavor than regular yogurt.

Although Greek yogurt provides twice the protein, it has less bone-building calcium than the same amount of regular yogurt—unless fortified with more calcium. Any yogurt containing live cultures has probiotic benefits as well. That said, check the Nutrition Facts label to see if the yogurt is fortified with whey protein and other nutrients.

Greek yogurt has a consistency like sour cream, with far less fat and far more nutrients. That quality makes it a great base for dips, salad dressings, and smoothies—and perfect as a dollop on creamy soup, a baked potato, or chili. Stick to low-fat and fat-free Greek yogurt to limit saturated fat, and to plain yogurt to limit added sugars.

Be aware that Greek yogurt costs more than regular yogurt. It takes more fluid milk to make than the same volume of Greek yogurt.

Choose low-fat and fat-free dairy foods to help you cut calories when they replace whole milk.

Dairy Foods: How Much?

How do your dairy food choices stack up? The specific amount advised depends in part on your age. For moderately active people ages eight and up, the recommended amount is equivalent to 3 cups of dairy foods daily. The advice for younger children who need fewer calories is 2 to 2½ cups daily. Many people, teens and adult women especially, don't consume enough. *See "Milk: A Great Calcium and Vitamin D Source" in chapter 4, page 93, to compare calories and nutrients in different milk options. See "Eating Patterns, 2015–2020 Dietary Guidelines for Americans" in the appendix, page 771, for the amount for your calorie level.*

One cup of dairy foods equals: One cup (8 ounces) of milk or yogurt, 1½ ounces of natural, hard cheese (cheddar, mozzarella, Swiss, Parmesan), or 2 ounces of processed (American) cheese. Choose low-fat or fat-free options most often.

These choices are also equivalent to 1 cup from the dairy group:

- 1 cup buttermilk
- ½ cup evaporated milk
- ⅓ cup shredded cheese
- ½ cup ricotta cheese
- 2 cups cottage cheese
- 1 cup pudding made with milk
- 1 cup frozen yogurt
- 1½ cups ice cream

If you choose sweetened milk, yogurt, drinkable yogurt, or desserts, count them toward your day's limit of calories from saturated fats and added sugars. Lactose-free and lower-lactose products are available. *See "The Healthy Vegetarian Way," in this chapter, page 53, for calcium-rich foods that are alternatives to dairy foods.*

Dairy Group: Ten Quick Tips

Consume more low-fat or fat-free milk and milk products such as milk, yogurt, cheese, and/or milk alternatives such as calcium-fortified soy beverages. And replace higher-fat milk and milk products with lower-fat versions. You'll cut calories but not calcium or other essential nutrients!

1. Make milk (preferably low-fat or fat-free) or calcium-fortified soymilk your beverage of choice for meals. That includes deli or fast-food meals. Try flavored milk (chocolate, strawberry, other flavors) if you prefer.
2. Start your day with dairy: low-fat or fat-free yogurt or a yogurt-fruit smoothie with breakfast, or low-fat or fat-free milk on cereal or oatmeal. (Drink your cereal milk.)

3. Make hot cereals, such as oatmeal, and creamy soups with milk rather than water.
4. Lighten up your coffee or tea with milk, not a powdered nondairy creamer. Instead of black coffee or plain tea, drink cappuccino, latte, or chai made with milk.
5. Drink thick, creamy buttermilk or kefir, or use it in smoothies. Even with its buttery name, buttermilk is usually made from low-fat or fat-free milk. Or make your own fruity drinks by blending milk or yogurt with fruit and ice in a blender.
6. Use plain, low-fat, or fat-free yogurt, Greek yogurt, or cottage cheese (pureed in a blender) in place of sour cream.
7. Enjoy sliced cheese on a sandwich, shredded cheese on soups, casseroles, stews, vegetables, or salads, or cheese cubes for a snack. Try low-fat cheese, or use a smaller amount of sharp cheese for less saturated fats and fewer calories.
8. Use evaporated fat-free milk instead of cream on cereals, whipped as a topping, and in recipes calling for cream. Evaporated fat-free milk has a creamy texture when whipped.
9. Top fruit with yogurt for dessert. Or make pudding with milk.
10. If you're lactose intolerant, you don't need to give up dairy. Instead, drink smaller amounts at a time; drink milk with a meal or snack; and eat yogurt, which often is tolerated better. Or try lactose-free milk or calcium- and vitamin D–fortified soymilk. *See "Lactose Intolerance: A Matter of Degree" in chapter 23, page 666, for more strategies for handling lactose intolerance.*

If you don't consume dairy foods, find other ways to get the calcium and vitamin D your body needs, perhaps from fortified soymilk and soy yogurt. Other calcium-fortified foods and drinks, such as juice, cereal, breads, rice milk, or almond milk, are options but don't provide other nutrients found in dairy milk; check the Nutrition Facts labels. As a result, they don't belong in the dairy group.

Also, nondairy foods that contain calcium, but not as much as dairy foods, include canned salmon or sardines with edible bones, some leafy greens (collard and turnip greens, kale, bok choy), some beans (legumes), tempeh, lime-treated corn tortillas, almonds, and tofu processed with calcium sulfates. The amount of calcium that can be absorbed from these foods varies. *See "Calcium" in chapter 14, page 425, for the calcium content of some of these foods.*

See "Dairy and More: Boost Calcium and Vitamin D" in chapter 8, page 263, for more tips for including low-fat and fat-free dairy foods in meals and snacks.

PROTEIN FOODS GROUP: VARY YOUR PROTEIN ROUTINE

Beef, veal, pork, chicken, turkey, finfish, shellfish, game, eggs, beans and peas, lentils, soybean products (tofu, tempeh, soyburgers, others), nuts, seeds, and nut butter belong in this food group. Beans, lentils, and peas actually lead a double life, *as discussed in "Beans and Peas: Uniquely Healthy," in this chapter, page 33.* They count toward the protein foods group or the vegetable group, but not both at the same time.

Why Eat Protein Foods?

Not only are meat, poultry, fish, beans and peas, lentils, eggs, nuts, and seeds protein-rich, but they also deliver a unique combination of essential vitamins and minerals. Some are high in saturated (solid) fats and cholesterol, and some fish, as well as nuts and seeds, contain healthy oils.

Meat includes all forms of beef, pork, lamb, veal, goat, and nonbird game such as venison, bison, and elk. Poultry includes all forms of chicken, turkey, duck, goose, guinea hen, and game birds, such as quail and pheasant.

Key nutrients: Animal-based foods—meat, poultry, fish, and eggs—deliver high-quality protein with all essential amino acids, as do soybeans. Protein in beans, seeds, and nuts is nearly as high quality, but low in one or more essential amino acids, *as discussed in "Completing the Protein Equation" in chapter 12, page 381.*

Protein supplies varying amounts of iron, zinc, magnesium, selenium, B vitamins (thiamin, niacin, vitamins B_6, and B_{12}), and vitamin E. Heme iron in meat, poultry, and fish is better absorbed than nonheme iron from eggs or plant sources of food. *(See "A Closer Look . . . Iron" in chapter 14, page 438, for more about heme and nonheme iron.)* Vitamin B_{12} is available only from meat, poultry, fish, and eggs. Eggs are also a good choline source. Beans and peas are good sources of fiber and complex carbohydrates (starches).

Nuts and seeds provide phosphorus, zinc, and magnesium, as well as vitamin E and selenium (two antioxidant nutrients). Their phytonutrients may have other health benefits. Small portions are a healthy choice. (Peanuts are actually legumes, not tree nuts; their phytonutrient benefits differ from that of nuts.)

The fat and cholesterol in protein foods vary. (Note: The total fat is both saturated and unsaturated, but the proportions and amounts differ.)

- Lean meat (including extra-lean or at least 90 percent–lean ground beef) and skinless poultry (not fried) have less total and saturated fats.
- Meat and poultry that are higher in total fat include: fattier cuts of beef, pork, and lamb (*see "Meat Counter" in chapter 6, page 164*); regular (75 to 85 percent–lean) ground beef; regular sausages, hot dogs, and bacon; some luncheon meats such as regular bologna and salami; skin-on poultry and some poultry such as duck and goose.
- Organ meats such as liver and giblets are high in cholesterol.
- Fish has less total fat than most meat. Most is heart-healthier mono- and polyunsaturated fats. Some fish are excellent sources of essential fatty acids. Oily fish, such as salmon, mackerel, swordfish, and herring, have more omega-3 fatty acids (EPA and DHA).

In a Nutshell: Tree Nuts and Seeds

Tree nuts contain protein, fiber, and a combination of vitamins, minerals, and antioxidants. They have cholesterol-lowering properties and are rich in heart-healthy monounsaturated and polyunsaturated fats. Their fiber, protein, and fat provide satiety to meals and snacks. The caveat: be aware of portion size. While healthy, nuts contribute a significant amount of calories, ranging from 160 to 200 calories per ounce. Seeds provide 120 to 150 calories per ounce (about 3 tablespoons).

It's easy to lump nuts and seeds into one category. What makes each special is its unique package of nutrients, taste, texture, origin, and culinary uses. Here are a few insights beyond their protein, fiber, and unsaturated fats.

TREE NUTS

- *Almonds:* Excellent source of vitamin E and magnesium, also provide calcium and folate. Versatile ingredient, can be used whole, sliced, blanched to remove skins, and as flour, paste, or butter. Almonds are enjoyed in savory and sweet dishes globally. (About 23 nuts per 1-ounce serving.)
- *Brazil nuts:* Largest nut commonly eaten. Grows wild on trees in Amazon rain forests. In addition to polyunsaturated and monounsaturated fats, one nut contains more than 100 percent Daily Value for the antioxidant selenium. Rich, creamy texture lends well to snacking, raw or roasted, and confections. (About 6 nuts per 1-ounce serving; however, the amount of selenium is 6 Brazil nuts exceeds its Tolerable Upper Intake Level, or UL.)
- *Cashews:* Excellent source of copper and magnesium. Soft consistency with delicate, sweet flavor. Native to South America but introduced by colonists to Africa and India. Commonly eaten as a snack, raw or roasted, but often used in Asian recipes and to make a rich, creamy nut butter or vegan cheese. (About 18 nuts per 1-ounce serving)
- *Macadamias:* Native to subtropical rain forests of Australia, this nut is high in fat, but 17 of the 22 grams are monounsaturated. Excellent source of manganese. Unique rich, buttery taste and smooth texture lend to eating as a snack, raw or roasted. Often baked into cookies and coated with chocolate. (About 10 to 12 nuts per 1-ounce serving)
- *Hazelnuts:* Also known as *filberts,* this nut is rich in monounsaturated fats and an excellent source of vitamin E, copper, and manganese. Available in-shell, whole, diced, sliced, and as meal for gluten-free baking. Pair well with savory, citrus, and sweet flavors, particularly chocolate, and commonly used in confections. (About 21 nuts per 1-ounce serving)
- *Pecans:* Rich in antioxidants and heart-healthy monounsaturated fats. Sweet, mellow flavor and meaty texture lend well to a variety of dishes, including salads, as a coating for fish, and in sweets such as pralines and pecan pie. (About 19 halves per 1-ounce serving)
- *Pine nuts:* Also called *pignoli,* this soft nut found inside the cone of several varieties of pine trees. Good source of vitamin E and phosphorus. Standard ingredient in Italian cuisine and best known as an ingredient in pesto. Light, delicate flavor also lends well to pastas, salads, sautés, breads, and other baked goods. (About 167 nuts per 1-ounce serving)
- *Pistachios:* Contain antioxidants, including lutein and zeaxanthin. Eating them from the shell helps you eat them more slowly. Bright green color makes for great addition to salads and grain dishes and as a coating for meats. Native to the Middle East, they are used in favorites like baklava, halvah, and ma'amoul, a shortbread pastry. (About 49 nuts per 1-ounce serving)
- *Walnuts:* Integral part of Mediterranean diet, contributing to health benefits of this style of eating. Rich in antioxidants and certain minerals, and an excellent source of alpha-linolenic acid (ALA), the plant-based form of omega-3 fatty acid. Their grooves hold onto flavors well and are delicious when seasoned sweet or hot. Oil can be used in dressings and sautés. (About 14 halves per 1-ounce serving)

Source: Food & Nutrition *Magazine, Academy of Nutrition and Dietetics.*

SEEDS

Here are a few insights beyond their significant amounts of protein, fiber, and unsaturated fats:

- *Chia seeds:* A member of the mint family, an excellent source of alpha-linolenic acid (ALA), vitamin E, and certain minerals. In a healthy diet, may promote satiety, or a feeling of fullness, may help slow the absorption of sugar, and may help remove cholesterol from the body; limited evidence, however.

  Ground or whole chia seeds may be sprinkled on cereal, rice, yogurt, or vegetables. Being very absorbent, they develop a gelatinous texture when soaked in water, which is easy to mix into cooked cereal or other dishes. Chia sprouts are also edible; add them to salads, sandwiches, and other dishes.
- *Flaxseeds:* Rich in lignans and alpha-linolenic acid (ALA). Need to be purchased as milled seeds or ground before using to get the benefits (whole flaxseeds pass through the body undigested). Have a nutty flavor. May be sprinkled over hot dishes, cooked with cereal or stir-fries, or ground and mixed with flour for baked goods. Whole flaxseeds can be sprouted for use in salads and sandwiches.

(continued)

In a Nutshell: Tree Nuts and Seeds *(continued)*

- *Hemp seeds:* Also a good source of omega-3s, as well as phytosterols and certain minerals. For the record, hemp seeds do not deliver psychoactive side effects as do other members of their plant species, *Cannabis sativa*. Use shelled hemp seeds as a crunchy topping on salads, cereal, frozen yogurt, yogurt, or creamy soups. Or combine with herb or spice rubs before cooking meat, poultry, or fish, or add to mixtures for meat loaf, to ground meat, to poultry patties.
- *Poppy seeds:* Good source of certain minerals. Tiny, dried, bluish-gray seeds from the poppy plant. Used in baked goods to provide a crunchy texture and nutty flavor. Can be purchased whole or ground for use as a filling, paste, or thickener.
- *Pumpkin seeds (pepitas [peh-PEE-tahs]):* Good source of B vitamins, iron, potassium, some other minerals, and lignans. Used as an ingredient in Mexican dishes such as mole. Delicate flavor, especially when roasted. Also enjoyed as a snack or in snack mixes, and can be added to mixed dishes, cereals, yogurt, and salads. As an experience of autumn, can also be roasted in their hulls at home, once removed from raw, whole pumpkins.
- *Sesame seeds (benne [BEHN-ee] seeds):* Rich in B vitamins, certain minerals such as magnesium, calcium, iron, and zinc, and in linoleic and oleic fatty acids. Tiny, flat seeds that may be ivory, brown, black, or red. Nutty sweet flavor, which complements the flavors in baked goods, often used as a topping on sesame rolls. Used as a seasoning as early as five thousand years ago. Used in snack bars, Asian dishes such as sushi, dim sum, and bowl meals. Came to Southern American cooking from Africa.
- *Sunflower seeds:* High in vitamin E, B vitamins, iron, and phytonutrients. Roasted or dried, unsalted (for less sodium) or salted, they are eaten as a snack, in trail mix, or added to cooked dishes such as stir-fries and rice dishes, salads, or baked goods.

Note: Technically, amaranth, quinoa, and wild rice are seeds, but they are eaten as grains, *as discussed in "Grains, Grains, and More Grains" in this chapter, page 31.* Nuts and seeds contribute more nutrients than *those noted above.*

Shellfish tend to be low in saturated fat but higher in cholesterol than finfish.

- While egg yolks contain cholesterol, egg whites are cholesterol free.
- Beans and peas are cholesterol free and virtually fat-free. Although nuts and seeds are higher in fat than many other protein foods, their fats are mostly oils and so mostly unsaturated. They are cholesterol free. *See "In a Nutshell: Tree Nuts and Seeds," in this chapter, page 43.*

Important health benefits: Protein provided by this food group not only builds body cells, enzymes, and hormones, it is also an energy source.

The vitamin and mineral package delivers more health benefits. For example, B vitamins help with energy production, formation of blood cells and body tissues, and nervous system function. Iron helps carry oxygen in your blood. Magnesium aids in bone building and energy release in your muscles. Zinc not only helps your immune system function, it's part of other body processes, too.

Lean protein foods are heart-healthier choices. In contrast, a diet high in solid fats may raise LDL ("bad") cholesterol levels in the blood, which increases the risk for heart disease. Eating eight ounces of fish, including those higher in omega-3 fatty acids, may help reduce LDL cholesterol and the risk of heart disease if they replace foods high in saturated fats. Replacing fatty meats with leaner meats is one way to cut back on calories, too.

See chapter 12, page 373, for more about the nutrients and health benefits of protein foods.

Protein Foods: How Much?

The recommended daily amount of protein foods for most adults is equivalent to 5 to 6½ ounces daily. This is based on what is advised for adults who get less than thirty minutes of moderate physical activity every day. This relatively small amount of protein foods is often a surprise to those who typically eat much more.

How much you need depends on the calories recommended for your age, gender, height, weight, and level of physical activity. *See "Eating Patterns, 2015–2020 Dietary Guidelines for Americans" in the appendix, page 771, for what matches your calorie level.*

Most Americans eat enough from the protein foods group. That said, you may need to make your choices leaner and more varied. That includes 8 ounces of fish weekly unless you're a vegetarian.

One ounce of protein foods equals: One ounce is generally 1 ounce of meat, poultry, or fish; ¼ cup of cooked beans or peas; 1 egg; 1 tablespoon of peanut butter; or ½ ounce of nuts or seeds. Here are some specifics:

- 1 ounce cooked lean beef, lean pork, or ham
- 1 ounce cooked chicken or turkey, without skin
- 1 sandwich slice (4½ × 2½ × ⅛ inches) turkey
- 1 ounce cooked finfish or shellfish
- 1 egg
- ½ ounce nuts (12 almonds, 24 pistachios, 7 walnut halves)

How Do You Count Protein Foods?

A Common Portion of . . .	Is Equivalent to . . .
1 steak, small eye or round, or filet	3½ to 4 ounces
1 small lean hamburger	2 to 3 ounces
1 small chicken breast half	3 ounces
½ Cornish game hen	4 ounces
1 small can tuna, drained	3 to 4 ounces
1 salmon steak	4 to 6 ounces
1 small trout	3 ounces
1 egg	1 ounce
3 egg yolks	1 ounce
3 egg whites	2 ounces
1 ounce nuts or seeds*	2 ounces
2 tablespoons peanut butter	2 ounces
1 cup split pea, lentil, or bean soup	2 ounces
1 soyburger or bean burger	2 ounces

*For example, 1 ounce is 23 almonds, 14 walnut halves, or 21 whole hazelnuts.

Adapted from www.ChooseMyPlate.gov/protein-foods

- ½ ounce seeds (pumpkin, sunflower, or squash seeds, hulled, roasted)
- 1 tablespoon peanut butter or almond butter
- ¼ cup cooked dry beans (such as black, kidney, pinto, or white beans)
- ¼ cup cooked dry peas (such as chickpeas, cowpeas, lentils, split peas)
- ¼ cup baked beans or refried beans
- ¼ cup (about 2 ounces) tofu
- 1 ounce tempeh, cooked
- ¼ cup roasted soybeans
- 1 (4-ounce, 2¼-inch) falafel patty
- 2 tablespoons hummus

Note: Beans and peas can count in either the vegetable group or protein group, but not in both at the same time.

Protein Foods Group: Ten Quick Tips

Vary your protein food routine. Choose different kinds of lean protein foods from both plant and animal sources, not just meat and poultry: fish, beans and peas, eggs, soy foods, nuts, and seeds.

1. Eat a variety of fish in place of some meat and poultry twice a week. Include oily fish, such as salmon, herring, mackerel, trout, anchovies, sardines, and Pacific oysters, which are rich in omega-3 fatty acids. *See "Food Safety Precautions" in chapter 18, page 552, for guidelines on eating fish during pregnancy and breastfeeding.*
2. Choose lean meat and poultry. To be considered lean, it must be at least 92 percent lean. Remove skin from poultry. Trim visible fat from meat and poultry.
3. Enjoy the flavors of meat and poultry—in small portions. Filling about a quarter of your plate with them is enough. You probably need only the equivalent of about 5 to 7 ounces total from the protein foods group daily. Occasionally, it's okay to eat larger portions, but a 12- to 16-ounce steak for dinner is way more than enough—in fact, enough for two days!
4. Broil, grill, roast, or use other low-fat cooking methods to cook meat, poultry, and fish. Frying and using some sauces deliver calories to these foods.
5. Several times a week, build menus around beans and peas, or soy foods, as a main dish, or make them part of a meal. They are naturally low in saturated fat and high in fiber. Try vegetarian chili or lasagna, vegetable tofu stir-fry, or bean soup. Or mix canned beans into a vegetable salad.
6. Enjoy eggs for lunch or dinner, not just breakfast. They're an excellent and economical protein source. If you are advised to control cholesterol, make egg dishes with egg whites or egg substitutes with no cholesterol and little or no fat.
7. Include nuts among your protein food choices. A small handful is enough for flavor and nutrition. Because they're a concentrated source of calories, eat small portions.

   Vary your choices—almonds, hazelnuts, pistachios, walnuts, sunflower seeds, pumpkin seeds, and more—since their nutrients and phytonutrients differ. Snack on unsalted nuts and seeds to keep sodium low. Use nuts in desserts or as a topping for frozen yogurt or fruit. Eat them in salads, in pesto sauce, sprinkled on vegetables, or in main dishes such as stir-fries to replace meat or poultry.
8. Experiment with plant-based protein foods: perhaps tofu, tempeh, and veggie/bean burgers (soyburgers). If you need to count carbs for managing diabetes, check the carbohydrate content of veggie/bean burgers, too.
9. Make a healthy sandwich with lean beef or turkey, canned tuna or salmon, or peanut butter. Many deli meats, such as regular bologna, salami, and other deli meats, are high in fat and sodium. Choose mostly lean turkey, roast beef, and ham, or low-fat luncheon meats for sandwiches.
10. Limit processed meats such as ham, sausage, and hot dogs, which are typically high in sodium. Be aware that consuming

? Have you ever wondered?

. . . how venison, buffalo (bison), and ostrich stack up as choices from the protein foods group? Their nutrient content is similar to that of other meat and poultry: good sources of protein and iron. Their fat content varies. Many types of game (venison, bison, caribou, elk, moose, rabbit, squirrel) and wild birds (goose, duck, pheasant, quail) are quite lean.

Ostrich tastes like red meat, even though it's poultry. It's very lean—fewer than 3 grams of fat in 3 ounces, less than in the same amount of beef round or chicken with skin.

. . . what offal is? It's just another way of saying organ meats or variety meats, commonly used in many ethnic cuisines and often considered delicacies: sweetbreads, pâté, chopped liver, Scottish haggis, Mexican menudo, Southern chitlins. These are mostly good sources of protein, iron, and other nutrients found in meat. Some, such as liver, are high in cholesterol. *See "Protein Foods: From Snout to Tail" in chapter 8, page 258, for more about offal.*

. . . if processed meats and processed poultry fit in the protein group? Most do fit in the protein group; however, they are generally high in saturated fat and sodium. That includes products preserved by smoking, curing, salting, and/or the addition of preservatives, such as meat or poultry sausages (bologna, frankfurters, luncheon meats and loaves, viennas, chorizos, kielbasa, pepperoni, salami, and summer sausages), as well as smoked or cured ham or pork shoulder, corned beef, pastrami, pig's feet, beef jerky, and smoked turkey products. You're advised to limit them; *see "Curing: Preserving Meat and Fish" in chapter 5, page 131.*

too much nitrates (which convert to nitrites) and nitrites from curing—used to manage bacteria growth—may increase cancer risk; *see "Curing: Preserving Meat and Fish" in chapter 5, page 131.*

Brining fresh chicken, turkey, and pork for flavor and tenderness in a salt solution makes them higher in sodium.

See "Meat, Poultry, Fish: Keep Lean" in chapter 8, page 254, for more tips for including lean protein foods in meals and snacks.

OILS: GO FOR HEALTHY FATS

Oils are fats that are liquid at room temperature. They come from various plant-based foods and from fish, and while they are not a food group, they provide essential nutrients.

Common oils include canola, corn, cottonseed, olive, safflower, soybean, and sunflower. Some others, such as walnut and sesame oils, make great flavorings. Several other foods are high in healthy oils, too: avocados, nuts, olives, and oily fish such as salmon and tuna.

Mayonnaise, certain salad dressings, and soft (tub or squeeze) margarine are mainly oils without *trans* fats. Check the Nutrition Facts labels to ensure that you are buying soft margarines with 0 grams of *trans* fat.

Note: Some fats are not part of this category because they are high in saturated fats. These include the tropical oils: coconut, palm, and palm kernel. Fats that are solid at room temperature such as butter, lard (pork fat), tallow and suet (beef and sheep fat), and the fat in cheese and other dairy foods are highly saturated, too. Partially hydrogenated oils, which are high in *trans* fats, are not considered healthy oils.

See chapter 13, page 385, to learn about the different types of fats, including trans *fats and tropical oils and their sources.*

Why Consume Oils?

Oils are a type of fat, which is an essential nutrient. For their health benefits, most fats in your food choices should be monounsaturated (MUFAs) and polyunsaturated (PUFAs), which are supplied mostly by foods' healthy oils. Some PUFAs are "essential." Saturated or not, all fats deliver 9 calories per gram.

Key nutrients: Oils are high in heart-healthier monounsaturated or polyunsaturated fats, and low in saturated fats, which are linked to heart disease. Oily fish supply omega-3s and omega-6s, which are types of unsaturated fatty acids. Oils also are the major source of vitamin E for most Americans.

Important health benefits: What makes MUFAs and PUFAs healthy? They don't raise LDL ("bad") cholesterol levels in blood, as saturated fats do. Essential fatty acids (from some nuts and seeds) are important for a healthy nervous system and skin—particularly important for kids' skin. Oils, your body's main source of vitamin E, are important antioxidants. And the omega-3 and omega-6 fatty acids in oily fish may help promote heart health.

Most of your fat intake should be MUFAs and PUFAs. Some PUFAs are essential for health since your body can't make them. Like all fats, oils deliver calories, so use them to replace saturated fats, not in addition to them.

Oils: How Much?

You need some healthy oils, including the essential fatty acids they contain. Like most Americans, you probably consume enough from nuts, fish, cooking oil, and salad dressing in the foods you normally eat.

The recommendation depends on your age, gender, and physical activity level. If you need 2,000 calories a day, the recommended daily amount is 27 grams, or about 6 teaspoons, of oils. (One teaspoon of oil weighs about 4.5 grams.) *See "Eating Patterns, 2015–2020 Dietary Guidelines for Americans" in the appendix, page 771, for the amount that matches your calorie level.* If you come up short, substitute oils for solid fats. Replace, don't add!

How Do You Count Oils?

	Portion	Amount of Oil	Calories from Oil	Total Calories
Oils				
Vegetable oil (such as canola, corn, cottonseed, olive, peanut, safflower, soybean, and sunflower)	1 tablespoon	3 teaspoons	120	120
Foods Rich in Oils				
Margarine, soft (*trans* fat–free)	1 tablespoon	2½ teaspoons	100	100
Mayonnaise	1 tablespoon	2½ teaspoons	100	100
Mayonnaise-type salad dressing	1 tablespoon	1 teaspoon	45	55
Italian dressing	2 tablespoons	2 teaspoons	75	85
Thousand Island dressing	2 tablespoons	2½ teaspoons	100	120
Olives, ripe, canned*	4 large	½ teaspoon	15	20
Avocado*	½ medium	3 teaspoons	130	160
Peanut butter*	2 tablespoons	4 teaspoons	140	190
Peanuts, dry roasted*	1 ounce	3 teaspoons	120	165
Mixed nuts, dry roasted*	1 ounce	3 teaspoons	130	170
Cashews, dry roasted*	1 ounce	3 teaspoons	115	165
Almonds, dry roasted*	1 ounce	3 teaspoons	130	170
Hazelnuts*	1 ounce	4 teaspoons	160	185
Sunflower seeds*	1 ounce	3 teaspoons	120	165

*Although they provide oils, avocados and olives belong in the fruit group; and nuts, including peanuts, and seeds belong in the protein foods group. Their oils contribute toward the recommended amount of oil for the day.

Source: www.ChooseMyPlate.gov/oils

Like solid fats, oils contain calories, about 40 calories per teaspoon or about 120 calories per tablespoon. Limit the amount to help balance your calorie intake with the calories your body uses.

One teaspoon of oils equals: One teaspoon of vegetable oils (canola, corn, cottonseed, olive, peanut, safflower, soybean, and sunflower) is easy to measure. *See "How Do You Count Oils?" above to learn how other sources stack up.*

Oils: Five Quick Tips

Make the switch. When you can, use foods with healthy oils instead of those with solid fats in food prep and as spreads.

1. Use mostly oil-based spreads and soft tub margarine with 0 *trans* fat in place of stick margarine, cream cheese, or butter. As a spread, use olive oil, pesto, or nut butter. If you use butter, use just a small amount. *Note:* Some stick margarine has 0 trans fat, but contains tropical oils, which are higher in saturated fat.
2. Use small amounts of oil in cooking, and dress salads with oil-based salad dressing. To control calories, limit yourself to 1 to 2 tablespoons of oil in a portion of food.
3. Check the ingredient list and the Nutrition Facts labels to find foods with unsaturated fats and with less saturated fats.
4. Prepare foods with vegetable oils (canola, corn, olive, safflower, or sunflower), rather than butter, stick margarine, shortening, or lard.
5. Include foods with healthy oils in your meals and snacks, such as olives, avocados, or nuts. Enjoy them in mixed dishes such as salads to replace some foods higher in saturated fats. For example, use less shredded cheese on a pizza and add sliced olives.

See "Lean Tips for Fats and Oils" in chapter 8, page 261, for more tips for including healthy oils in meals and snacks.

EXTRAS: CHOOSE WISELY AND WITHIN YOUR CALORIE BUDGET!

Small amounts of solid fats and added sugars in foods such as sweetened breakfast cereals, an oatmeal cookie, or a small bacon slice on a BLT (bacon, lettuce, tomato) sandwich add flavor. But they deliver calories, too! Consuming too much solid fats and added sugars is linked to some chronic health risks.

Empty calories? That term refers to foods high in saturated fats and/or added sugars but with few nutrients. A small amount of these foods or drinks is okay. However, many Americans consume too much.

Extras: Set Limits

If you follow the food pattern for your calorie level—and make most of your choices nutrient-dense—you'll likely have leeway for small amounts of foods with solid fats and/or added sugars within your calorie goal. Physically active? You'll have even more leeway.

That said, calories from these extras need to fit within your total estimated calorie needs, not in addition. Assume that your calorie budget is 2,000 per day. Of these calories, you need to spend at least 1,740 on nutrient-rich foods for their nutrient essentials—doable with wise food-group choices. That leaves 260 more calories yet to spend—if you keep saturated fats and added sugars each under their 10 percent of total calories limit for the day. To spend these extra calories, you can:

- Eat even more nutrient-rich foods from any food group.
- Or eat some higher-calorie versions of food-group foods, perhaps with somewhat more saturated fats or added sugars. A few examples of foods: whole milk, cheese, higher-fat meats, biscuits, sweetened cereal, sweetened baked foods, or honey-sweetened yogurt.
- Or flavor your healthy meal choices with some added fats or sweeteners, perhaps with sauces, salad dressings, sugar, syrup, or butter—or more healthy oils.
- Or enjoy a small portion of candy, soft drinks, wine, beer, or other calorie-dense foods or beverages.
- Or make trade-offs. *See "Trade-Offs: Save Calories, Spend Elsewhere," as noted on this page.*

Whatever option you choose, go easy. Your calorie allowance from fats, added sugars, and alcoholic drinks isn't very big. Typically, people have just 100 to 300 extra calories per day to spend, especially if they aren't very active. The good news is that the more you get your body moving, the more extra calories you have to spend.

See "Eating Patterns, 2015–2020 Dietary Guidelines for Americans" in the appendix, page 771, to estimate your calorie limit.

Trade-Offs: Save Calories, Spend Elsewhere

Are some of your favorite foods higher in calories—perhaps from added sugars or saturated fats? Rather than give them up, find ways to fit small amounts in occasionally. You can save at one meal or snack and then spend elsewhere. For example:

- Skip the butter and sour cream on a baked potato to save for a small dish of ice cream.
- Make pizza with reduced-fat, rather than regular, mozzarella to save for a cookie later.
- Top French toast with sliced fresh peaches rather than syrup, to save for sugar in your hot tea.

Information from the Nutrition Facts labels makes trade-offs easier. *See "Nutrition: Fact Check!" in chapter 6, page 148, to learn about reading food labels.*

Remember: Your goal is positive. Instead of eliminating some foods, moderate the calories from your day's meal and snack choices over the course of the day or several days—and then balance the calories you consume with those your body uses.

Fewer Calories per Bite!

"More food, fewer calories" may sound great if you love to eat! In fact, fiber-rich, watery foods deliver more volume to your plate for fewer calories. Ounce per ounce, foods with more fat and with less fiber and water are more calorie-dense.

To compare, 1 cup (about 4 ounces) of sliced raw carrots has 50 calories, and so does just ⅓ ounce of chips. Carrots give you more nutrients and fiber, take longer to eat, and can leave you feeling more satisfied with more food and far fewer calories. Even a small snack bag of chips weighs at least 1 ounce and provides about 150 calories!

Other foods high in volume but low in calorie density include broth-based soups, fruits and vegetables, low-fat and fat-free milk and yogurt, and beans. *See "Food: A Water Source" in chapter 15, page 446, for the percentage of water in common foods.*

Less Saturated Fats and Added Sugars: Ten Quick Tips

Saturated fats and added sugars can make a food or beverage more appealing. However, they also can add a lot of calories. In some foods, like most candies and sodas, all the calories are empty calories. To manage calories, either eat empty-calorie foods less often, or make portions smaller.

Typical vs. Nutrient-Dense Foods and Beverages

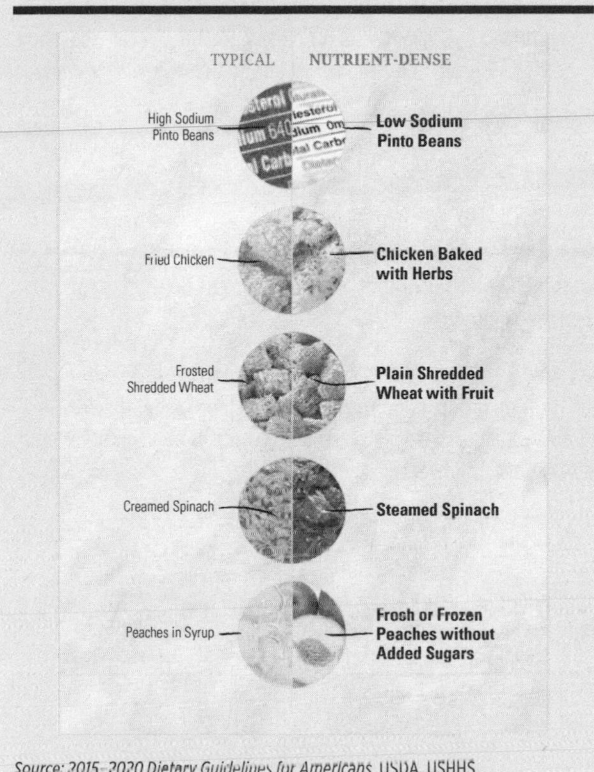

Source: 2015–2020 Dietary Guidelines for Americans, USDA, USHHS.

For less added sugars: Sweetened beverages (not milk or 100 percent fruit juice) provide 47 percent of the added sugars consumed by most Americans, and snacks and sweets deliver about another 31 percent according to the "What We Eat in America Food Category" analyses for the 2015 Dietary Guidelines Advisory Committee.

These are some ways you can limit added sugars in your food and beverage choices:

1. Remember, beverages count! Drink few regular sodas, sports drinks, energy drinks, and fruit drinks.
2. Eat cake, cookies, ice cream, other desserts, and candies less often. Or just consume small portions.
3. Choose fruit for dessert more often.
4. Drink water, fat-free plain milk, 100 percent juice, or unsweetened tea or coffee rather than sugar-sweetened drinks.
5. Use the ingredient list on food labels to find foods with little or no added sugars—don't rely on the amount of total sugars. Total sugars on the Nutrition Facts label represents sugars that are both naturally present and added. When the new Nutrition Facts appear on package labels, added sugars will be identified separately; *see "Nutrition Facts: Comparing the Old and New" in chapter 6, page 147, to learn about the Nutrition Facts labeling update.*

Have you ever wondered?

. . . where potato chips and corn chips fit in the food groups? Potato chips fit in the vegetable group; corn chips, in the grain group. Yet they supply more fat and more calories (less nutrient density) than most other foods in those groups. Eat them with discretion within your calorie budget; try baked varieties, which have fewer calories and less fat.

. . . where fortified foods fit in the food groups? Fortified foods fit in the same food group as their unfortified counterparts. With their added nutrients, they simply provide a nutritional bonus. For example, a cup of calcium- and vitamin D–fortified orange juice can't replace a cup of milk because milk has other nutrients that juice doesn't have. Like any juice, calcium-fortified orange juice counts in the fruit group, with a calcium bonus. Fortified foods can provide a benefit by either increasing the amount of certain nutrients or providing them in forms that the body can better absorb and use.

Can you overdo? It's possible, but eating fortified foods in the typical American diet rarely leads to overconsuming calcium, iron, folate, or vitamin D. But supplement use can, especially with high-dose supplements. Get advice from a registered dietitian nutritionist or pharmacist.

. . . where dietary supplements fit in? All healthy people need to get their nutrients from food first. Food group advice doesn't change if you take a multivitamin/mineral supplement. Supplements are merely what their name implies; they're intended to supplement nutrients from the foods you eat, only if needed, not to replace nutrient-rich foods. *See chapter 10, page 315, for more about supplements.*

. . . what the term "superfood" means? No regulations define a superfood. And no individual food is a "magic bullet" for health—although high amounts of certain nutrients or phytonutrients in some foods may offer health benefits. Over time a "super diet" will likely bring increased health benefits. Caution: Some foods marketed as superfoods are high in added sugars, solid fats, or sodium; nutrients or phytonutrients in others may have limited bioavailability to the body.

For less saturated fats: Burgers, sandwiches, and pizza provide about 25 percent of the saturated fats consumed by most Americans according to the "What We Eat in America Food Category" analyses for the 2015 Dietary Guidelines Advisory Committee. Snacks and sweets deliver about another 18 percent of saturated fats. Protein foods, dairy foods, and other mixed dishes also provide significant amounts.

These are some ways you can limit the saturated fats in your food and beverage choices:

1. Ease up on the major sources of solid fats: cakes, cookies, and other desserts (often made with butter, stick margarine, or shortening); pizza; cheese; processed and fatty meats (sausage, hotdogs, bacon, ribs); and ice cream. Switch to lower-fat versions

Mixed Foods: What Food Group?

Pizza, fajitas, lasagna, and cioppino (fish stew)—many foods don't fit neatly into a single food group. Prepared with ingredients from several food groups, mixed foods count toward your daily total from two or more groups, especially grains, vegetables, and protein foods. Fruit and dairy (except for cheese) are seldom part of mixed dishes.

Mixed dishes often contain substantial amounts of saturated fats, added sugars, and sodium. On the flip side, they can also contribute important amounts of nutrients that often come up short, depending on their ingredients.

Use your best guesstimates, as well as common sense, to determine the food group amounts these mixed-food dishes deliver. How might you change these popular dishes to add more vegetables and fruits, or perhaps lower the calories?

Food and Portion	Grain Group (oz. Equivalents)	Vegetable Group (cups)	Fruit Group (cups)	Dairy Group (cups)	Protein Foods Group (oz. Equivalents)	Calories (Estimated)
Apple pie (1 slice)	2	0	¼	0	0	280
Bean and cheese burrito (1)	2½	0	0	1	2	445
Beef stir-fry (1 cup)	0	½	0	0	1½	185
Cheese pizza—thin crust (1 slice from medium pizza)	1	⅛	0	½	0	215
Lasagna (1 piece, 3½ inches by 4 inches)	2	½	0	1	1	445
Tuna noodle casserole (1 cup)	1½	0	0	½	2	260

Adapted from source: www.ChooseMyPlate.gov

Here are five tips for creating healthier mixed-food choices:

1. Try whole-wheat pizza crust, burritos on a whole-wheat tortilla, or brown rice risotto. Add plenty of vegetables! Most mixed dishes are made with refined grains, and by trying whole grain alternatives, you are doing yourself a favor.
2. Fit fruit into mixed dishes. Try chopped apples or grapes in chicken salad, dried fruit in turkey dressing, or pineapple as a pizza topping.
3. Use reduced-fat or low-fat cheese in mixed dishes such as cheese enchiladas, lasagna, and macaroni and cheese. This will cut saturated fats. Or, if you prefer the fuller flavor of other cheeses, use less; a little strong-flavored cheese provides good flavor.
4. Seize the opportunity! Boost veggies in all kinds of mixed dishes. Double the amount in soups and stews. Layer more vegetables in sandwiches and wraps. *See "Fruits and Veggies: Fit More In" in chapter 8, page 246, for more ideas for food preparation.*
5. Instead of fruit pies, enjoy whole fruit, or perhaps have cut-up fruit with a dollop of Greek yogurt or frozen yogurt on top.

such as low-fat cheese, lower-fat sausages and hot dogs, and lower-fat ice cream.

2. Choose lean meat and poultry, and low-fat or fat-free dairy foods. If you choose foods with higher fat content such as regular ground beef (75 to 80 percent lean) or chicken with skin, the fat counts against your maximum limit for calories for other uses, which include from solid fats or added sugars.
3. Cook with oils, rather than butter, beef fat, chicken fat, lard, stick margarine, and shortening. Remember that consuming only a small amount of healthy oils is important; you need fat to help your body absorb the fat-soluble vitamins (A, D, E, and K) in food.
4. Choose baked, broiled, steamed, or stir-fried foods more often than fried foods.
5. Check the Nutrition Facts labels to ensure that you choose foods with little or no saturated fat and no *trans* fat. Use ingredient lists to limit foods with partially hydrogenated oils, which contain *trans* fats.

Less Sodium: Five Quick Tips

Mixed dishes provide about 44 percent of the sodium consumed by most Americans, according to the "What We Eat in America Food Category" analyses for the 2015 Dietary Guidelines Advisory Committee. It comes from a variety of other foods, too, in varying amounts: snacks, protein foods, grain-based foods, dairy, condiments, gravy, and salad dressings.

These are some ways you can limit the sodium in your food and beverage choices:

1. Prepare food from scratch at home. This enables you to control the amount of sodium you add as you prepare a meal or snack.
2. Choose fresh, frozen (no sauce or seasoning), or no-salt-added canned vegetables as well as fresh meat, poultry, and fish rather than processed meat and poultry.
3. Limit sauces, mixes, and "instant" products, including flavored rice, instant noodles, and ready-made pasta. Check the sodium content in sauces and dressings used in mixed dishes. Pick those with less sodium, cut back on the amount you use, or do both.
4. Season with spices and herbs instead of salt.
5. Check the Nutrition Facts labels to compare foods. Look for those with less sodium. Buy low-sodium, reduced sodium, or no-salt-added versions of products when available.

DASH to Health

Another healthy eating plan that may be right for you is called DASH, which stands for Dietary Approaches to Stop Hypertension. It was developed to help people prevent or manage high blood pressure. It's consistent with the Dietary Guidelines for Americans and is much like the Healthy US-Style Eating Pattern *just discussed*. DASH is a guide to healthy eating for everyone—even those not at risk for hypertension.

Like the USDA Food Patterns, the DASH plan provides enough nutrients for overall health, with recommended amounts from each food group and with no special foods or recipes. The DASH plan:

- Emphasizes fruit, vegetables, low-fat or fat-free milk and milk products, whole grains, fish, poultry, beans and peas (legumes), seeds, nuts, and vegetable oils.
- Limits foods that are high in saturated fat, such as fatty meats, full-fat dairy products, and tropical oils, such as coconut, palm kernel, and palm, as well as sugar-sweetened beverages and sweets.
- Provides less sodium (salt), saturated and *trans* fats, cholesterol, and added sugars, and more potassium, calcium, magnesium, and fiber than the average American diet. *See "DASH for Better Blood Pressure" in chapter 24, page 697.*

HEALTH BENEFITS OF THE DASH PLAN

As a way to lower blood pressure, the DASH eating plan can be a taste-appealing and arguably more beneficial switch from simply heeding the advice to cut out salt. And it may be an alternative to medication. The maximum sodium level in the DASH plan is 2,300 milligrams a day. However, following the DASH plan with even less sodium (no more than 1,500 milligrams of sodium per day) may be more effective.

The DASH plan also may reduce risk factors for heart disease, stroke, kidney stones, and type 2 diabetes. The lower sodium level matches the recommendation to reduce sodium to 1,500 milligrams daily for those with pre-hypertension and hypertension.

DASH DIET: HOW IT WORKS

Like other diets, the DASH plan has several calorie levels with daily food-group amounts for different calorie needs. *See "DASH Eating Plan at Various Calorie Levels" in the appendix, page 776.*

What's more, it's easy to adapt the DASH plan for vegetarians, for those eating gluten free or allergen free, and for anyone trying to lose weight. It's flexible enough to allow you to match to your own food preferences and lifestyle.

- DASH Eating Plan
  www.nhlbi.nih.gov/health/health-topics/topics/dash
  or www.dashdiet.org

? Have you ever wondered?

. . . what a plant-based diet is? It's a way of eating that focuses on vegetables, fruit, grains (especially whole grains), beans and peas, lentils, nuts, and seeds, rather than on meat, poultry, fish, eggs, and dairy foods. It's not necessarily meatless or vegan.

DASH PLAN: FIVE QUICK TIPS

1. Check the Nutrition Facts labels to compare sodium in packaged foods. Many processed and convenience foods are high in sodium, which can be challenging. *See "A Word About Ingredients" in chapter 6, page 150, and "Sodium" in chapter 14, page 431, for ways to spot ingredients with sodium.*
2. Take time to be a home cook. As you do with added fats, you have more control over the amount of sodium, as well as fruits and vegetables in your meals and snacks when you prepare food at home.
3. If cutting back on salt seems bland at first, use herbs, spices, or other flavor-enhancing techniques; *see "Herbs—and Spices, Too!" in chapter 8, page 266.*
4. Be aware that restaurant foods are typically higher in sodium than the food you cook yourself. Order simply-prepared plain foods, or choose a restaurant that can cook to order; *see "Order It Your Way" in chapter 9, page 278.*
5. Get creative with vegetables and fruit. The DASH plan advises more of both!

For optimal health benefits, physical activity, weight management, and limited alcohol consumption should part of the DASH approach.

The Mediterranean Route to Healthy Eating

Take your plate to the Mediterranean! As defined in the 2015–2020 Dietary Guidelines for Americans, the Mediterranean-style eating pattern, based on traditional cuisines of the regions bordering the Mediterranean Sea, offers another way to eat for good health. It provides enough of most nutrients, with the possible exception of calcium since the pattern is relatively low in dairy foods.

There's no single cuisine for this part of the world, but instead it offers a diverse, colorful, and flavorful eating pattern that includes the dishes of Greece, southern Italy, Spain, southern France, Tunisia, Lebanon, Egypt, and Morocco. Being more plant-based than some of the world's other cuisines, the ingredients and preparation styles have similar characteristics. For instance:

- Emphasizes grain products (often whole grains), fresh fruits and vegetables, beans and peas, and nuts.
- Focuses more on fish and perhaps poultry, less on red meat and dairy. Dairy is traditionally cheese and yogurt.
- Shifts to more monounsaturated fat (mostly from olive oil) and omega-3s (from some fish). In general, the total fat intake of the Mediterranean diet isn't lower than that of the typical American diet.
- Uses herbs and spices in place of salty flavorings.
- Includes fewer sugary sweets.
- Some people may choose to drink wine in moderation; this is optional.

HEALTH BENEFITS OF "MED-STYLE" EATING

Traditional Mediterranean eating is often described as heart healthy. Studies show reduced risk factors for and incidences of cardiovascular disease in addition to a lower death rate. Some research indicates links to lower risk of certain cancers, type 2 diabetes, and Parkinson's disease, as well as the possibility of protection from Alzheimer's disease. Overall, the Mediterranean eating pattern may promote healthy aging.

The overall Mediterranean lifestyle is relaxed with a good deal of time devoted to enjoying meals with family and friends, which suggests that health benefits may be linked to more than food. Traditionally, the people studied in the region were physically active, and their weight and genetics might have been factors in their health. Some studies indicate that those who stopped eating traditional Mediterranean diets experienced cardiovascular health problems, although the reasons for this are not yet clear.

MEDITERRANEAN EATING PATTERN: HOW IT WORKS

The Mediterranean style of eating focuses on a broad variety of plant-based foods—creatively planned with beans and peas, vegetables, fruit, whole grains, and nuts. It's not meatless, however. Poultry and fish in moderate amounts—and smaller amounts of lean red meat—are key protein sources in meals, along with yogurt and cheese. Healthy oils are the main source of dietary fat.

See "Healthy Mediterranean-Style Eating Pattern." in the appendix, page 774, for the various calorie levels.

MEDITERRANEAN EATING: TEN QUICK TIPS

1. Add more beans, peas, and lentils—whole or mashed—to your meals and snacks. Chickpeas are great in salads. Beans of all kinds work in pasta and other grain-based mixed dishes. Hummus-style dips can be made from any type of legume.

2. Prepare meals with whole grains when you can. Consume less-common types such as bulgur, farro, brown rice, and whole wheat couscous.
3. Enjoy roasted vegetables (eggplant, bell peppers, summer squash, mushrooms, and more) as starters, side dishes, salads, and flatbread toppings. Add extra vegetables to mixed pasta, rice, and other grain dishes. Top pizza after it's baked with fresh greens, as they do in southern Italy.
4. Fit a variety of fish—finfish and shellfish—in your meals. Grill, bake, or broil it, or prepare it in mixed dishes such as hearty stews, rice, or pasta dishes.
5. Make chicken and other types of poultry a protein option. Roast or grill it, or add it to mixed dishes. And make lean red meat—beef, pork, lamb—an option, too, but limit the size of the portions.
6. Enjoy yogurt in appetizer dips, cold soups, and more. Cheese makes a pleasing starter, or serve it at the end of the meal with fruit. What's more, it's a protein-rich ingredient in many mixed dishes. Remember that a little of this high-in-saturated-fats food goes a long way.
7. Use olive oil and other healthy oils such as canola as your main source of fat when preparing food—not just in salad dressings.
8. Enhance flavor with Mediterranean seasoning combinations, such as cinnamon, coriander, cumin, and oregano—or blends such as za'atar and dukkah (*see "Salt-Free Herb Blends" in chapter 8, page 274*)—instead of salt.
9. Snack on nuts and dried fruit (apricots, dates, dried plums, others). Add them to salads and mixed dishes.
10. Make fruit your main dessert choice. This means you will consume less added sugars as you benefit from the nutrients fruit provides, including vitamin C, potassium, fiber, and phytonutrients. If you want a bit more sweetness, sprinkle the fruit with a little honey and fragrant spices such as cardamom or cinnamon. Or sprinkle sesame seeds on top.

Take time to enjoy your meal—slow down and be mindful. Savoring food and enjoying the social time with family and friends is part of the Mediterranean mealtime tradition.

The Healthy Vegetarian Way

Meatless sometimes or all the time? Any eating style—vegetarian (including vegan) or nonvegetarian—can be healthy. The health benefits depend on the foods chosen and the amounts eaten over time. Planned well, a vegetarian eating style offers another USDA Food Pattern that follows the eating advice of the Dietary Guidelines for Americans.

Vegetarian and semi-vegetarian eating has of late become more mainstream for many reasons. Potential health benefits that either prevent or treat disease or enhance quality of life are cited. For other people, vegetarian eating reflects an ethical approach to addressing world hunger. Others express concerns about the use of environmental resources or animal welfare. Yet, all food production, even for plant-based foods, impacts the environment.

For some, religious, spiritual, or ethical reasons define a strict vegetarian lifestyle. Several religions advocate vegetarian eating—for example, Hinduism and the Seventh-Day Adventist Church.

Other people simply prefer the flavors and food mixtures of vegetarian dishes—always or sometimes. Some may recognize that a plant-based diet, such as a vegetarian diet, may cost somewhat less than one that includes red meat and poultry.

Whatever the reasons, eating for overall good health remains a common goal. And, well-planned, a vegetarian eating plan can provide the right nourishment for people at all stages of life, from infancy through the older years, for pregnant and breastfeeding women, and for athletes.

VEGETARIAN OR VEGAN?

Being a vegetarian may be a way of eating. For some, it's a lifestyle.

Broadly defined, a vegetarian diet means avoiding foods from animal sources. Instead, plant-based foods—grain products, beans and peas, lentils, vegetables, fruits, nuts, and seeds—form the basis of the diet. As a matter of choice, many vegetarians eat dairy products and perhaps eggs. Vegetarians are defined several ways:

- Lacto-ovo-vegetarians eat dairy products and eggs but no meat, poultry, or fish. The prefix "lacto" refers to milk; "ovo" refers to eggs. Most vegetarians in the United States fit here.
- *Lacto-vegetarians* avoid meat, poultry, fish, and eggs (and egg derivatives such as albumin or egg whites) but do eat dairy foods.
- *Ovo-vegetarians* avoid meat, poultry, fish, and dairy foods, but do eat eggs (and egg derivatives such as albumin or egg whites).
- *Strict vegetarians, or vegans*, eat no animal products: no meat, poultry, fish, eggs, milk, cheese, or other dairy products. Vegans typically also avoid foods made with animal products as ingredients, too: for example, refried beans made with lard; fries cooked in beef tallow; baked goods made with butter, eggs, or albumin (from eggs); margarine made with whey or casein (from milk); foods flavored with meat extracts; and foods, such as most marshmallows, made with gelatin (from animal bones and hooves). Some avoid honey, too.

- Vegetarian Resource Group
  www.vrg.org

- *Raw vegan* diets rely strictly on fresh and mostly uncooked foods, based on fruit, nuts, seeds, and vegetables.

Two eating patterns are nearly vegetarian:

- *Flexitarian, or semi-vegetarian*, diets usually follow a vegetarian eating plan with limited amounts of meat, poultry, and fish, perhaps as a condiment or side dish, or perhaps one or twice weekly.
- *Pesco-vegetarian* diets usually follow a vegetarian eating plan and includes fish occasionally.

Other people simply may enjoy the flavors of main dishes made with beans and peas, vegetables, and perhaps whole grains—regularly or as an occasional switch from everyday fare—and want their health benefits.

HEALTH BENEFITS OF A VEGETARIAN EATING PATTERN

Vegetarian diets also may have advantages in preventing some chronic health conditions. This style of eating is associated in some studies with lower blood pressure, lower body weight and rates of obesity, lower LDL ("bad") cholesterol levels, and improved blood glucose control for those with type 2 diabetes. A typical vegetarian diet with foods that contribute soy and phytonutrients is also associated with lower cancer risk.

Why these potential benefits? Perhaps it's the features of a vegetarian diet: the bounty of plant-based foods and little or no saturated fat. On average, vegetarians consume fewer calories; a smaller portion of calories from fat, especially saturated fat; less cholesterol; and more fiber, potassium, folate, vitamin C, and phytonutrients.

Beyond these attributes, vegetarians, including vegans, usually have a lower body mass index, an indicator of a healthy body weight. Lifestyle factors likely play a role, too; many vegetarians are physically active, avoid smoking, and drink alcoholic beverages in moderation.

Worth noting! A vegetarian eating approach isn't always healthier. Simply limiting meat, dairy, or eggs, doesn't guarantee adequate nutrition. Like any way of eating, even a vegetarian diet can be high in calories as well as in total fat, saturated fats, added sugars, and sodium. Poorly planned meals and snacks, with a heavy reliance on high-calorie foods such as many quick-serve options, may come up short in fruits, vegetables, whole grains, and calcium-rich foods—without enough of the nutrients and fiber they provide.

Alert: Some people "go vegetarian" to disguise an undiagnosed eating disorder; *see "Eating Disorders: More than a Nutrition Issue" in chapter 25, page 732.* That said, following a vegetarian diet does not increase the risk of eating disorders.

VEGETARIANS: NUTRIENTS TO FOCUS ON

Vegetarian eating plans can provide enough of all nutrient essentials. Nutrient adequacy is just a matter of making wise food choices and following food-group advice for your calorie level. And to dispel a common myth, this approach to eating won't leave you feeling hungry. Adequate amounts of both protein and fiber may leave nearly anyone feeling full.

Do you consume dairy products and perhaps eggs? If so, nutrition issues don't differ much from those of nonvegetarians. However, for vegans especially, including growing children and teens, getting enough calories to maintain a healthy weight may be challenging. Also, getting enough of some nutrients may need attention. These may include protein, iron, zinc, calcium, vitamin D, and vitamin B_{12}, among others.

Protein: Questions about protein often arise when vegetarian diets are discussed. The truth of the matter is that, except for some vegans, adequate protein generally isn't a concern, and even among vegans (strict vegetarians), it does not need to be.

Almost every food of plant origin except fruit contains protein—at least a small amount, with limited amounts of some essential amino acids. Beans, seeds, nuts, nut butters, and soy products (edamame, tofu, tempeh, textured vegetable protein, soyburgers) are good sources of protein. Whole grains provide some protein, but it's not high quality. For lacto-ovo-vegetarians, eggs and dairy foods contain complete protein.

Foods with complete proteins have an adequate supply of all essential amino acids. If you eat a variety of foods with incomplete vegetable proteins, and enough calories during the day (not necessarily at the same meal), your body will get all the essential amino acids it needs. You don't need to combine them (as in rice and beans or in peanut butter on bread) at every meal. *See "Completing the Protein Equation" in chapter 12, page 381.*

Because the protein in beans and peas and whole grains isn't digested as easily as the protein in meat, eggs, and dairy foods, vegans may be well advised to consume more protein.

Pregnant and breastfeeding women are advised to follow the protein recommendation for their life stage and then consume an additional 25 grams daily, which is advised for nonvegetarian women as well.

See "Protein for Vegans" in chapter 12, page 379, for tips for getting enough high-quality protein.

Essential fatty acids: Fats are made of fatty acids. Because the body cannot produce them, two fatty acids are considered essential: One is alpha-linolenic acid (ALA), an omega-3 fatty acid found in foods such as ground flaxseeds, chia seeds, hempseeds, walnuts, soy nuts, canola oil, soybean oil, and some other plant sources. The other is linoleic acid (LA), an omega-6 fatty acid from some plant oils, nuts, and seeds.

- Include plant-based ingredients such as canola oil, soy oil, walnuts, chia seeds, ground flaxseed, and soybeans in your meals and snacks. Walnuts are the only tree nut with significantly high ALA fatty acids.
- If you eat eggs, look for those with omega-3 fatty acids.
- If you eat fish, oily fish are good sources of omega-3s.
- Talk to a registered dietitian nutritionist about the appropriate use of supplements to ensure adequate intake of these essential fatty acids. Supplements with DHA and EPA fatty acids from microalgae are available for vegans.

See chapter 13, page 385, for more about these fatty acids.

Iron: Getting enough iron may be an issue for vegetarian children, teens, women of childbearing age, and pregnant women. Although many plant-based foods contain iron, it's nonheme iron, a form that isn't as well absorbed as the heme iron found in meat and other foods of animal origins (except eggs). (Iron carries oxygen in the blood.) For that reason, the recommendations are higher for vegetarians, including vegans.

Be aware that phytates, as well as polyphenolic compounds, in plant-based foods are significant inhibitors of iron absorption. *See "Phytonutrients: Different from Nutrients" in chapter 15, page 448, for more about phytonutrients.*

An eating pattern with enough calories can provide enough iron, so here are a few tips:

- Consume foods with nonheme iron: beans and peas; iron-fortified and whole-grain cereals and breads; some dark-green leafy vegetables (such as spinach and beet greens); seeds; prune juice; some dried fruits (dried apricots, prunes, raisins); and blackstrap molasses; and for ovo-vegetarians, eggs.
- Improve the absorption of foods with nonheme iron by pairing them with a vitamin C–rich food such as citrus fruits, 100 percent juice, broccoli, or bell peppers. Try beans and mango salsa, black-eyed peas and collards, broccoli and tofu, or oatmeal topped with strawberries. *See "A Closer Look . . . Iron" in chapter 14, page 438, for more ways to enhance iron absorption from plant-based foods.*
- If you're a flexitarian or pesco-vegetarian, eat a little poultry and fish to help with nonheme iron absorption.
- If you cook foods in iron pots or skillets, some iron from the pots or skillets may pass into food—a good thing! That's especially true when the ingredients being cooked are high in acid, such as tomatoes, and when you simmer foods, such as soups and stews, for awhile.

Zinc: A mineral essential for many body processes, growth, and immunity, zinc may come up short in a vegetarian diet. For lacto-ovo-vegetarians, dairy foods and eggs provide zinc. Many plant-based foods also contain zinc, but its bioavailability is less than that from animal-based foods. For this reason, the recommendation for zinc for vegetarians, especially vegans, may be as much as 50 percent higher than it is for nonvegetarians.

- Eat whole-grain foods, many types of beans and peas (white beans, kidney beans, chickpeas), zinc-fortified breakfast cereals, seeds, and nuts. Grains lose zinc when processed to make refined

Glossary for Vegetarians

A vegetarian diet may include these unfamiliar foods and ingredients.

- *Casein:* A milk protein sometimes used in otherwise nondairy products such as soymilk, soy cheese, and nondairy creamer
- *Legumes:* The vegetable family that includes beans, lentils, peas, and peanuts, all of which are excellent sources of vegetable protein
- *Nutritional yeast:* A supplement often grown on molasses or the pulp of sugar beets. Nutritional yeast is a rich source of vitamin B_{12} and protein.
- *Rennet:* An enzyme from the stomach of slaughtered calves used to coagulate cheese and found in many dairy cheeses
- *Seitan (also called wheat gluten):* A vegetarian meat replacement made of protein (gluten) that has been extracted from flour
- *Soybeans:* A legume that is an excellent, inexpensive source of protein and iron, used to make a number of vegetarian and vegan substitutions for meat, dairy, and eggs
- *Soy cheese:* A cheeselike product made from soybeans. Soy cheeses come in most of the same varieties as dairy cheeses, such as parmesan, mozzarella, and cheddar. However, some soy cheeses are not vegan because they contain the animal protein casein.
- *Soymilk:* A milklike product made from soybeans, with the same amount of protein and less fat than cow's milk. However, some soymilks are not vegan because they contain the animal protein casein.
- *Tempeh:* A replacement for meat made from fermented soybeans
- *Textured vegetable protein (TVP):* A product derived from soy flour, commonly used in vegetarian restaurants as a substitute for ground beef
- *Tofu:* A replacement for meat, eggs, and cheese made from curdled soymilk and pressed into blocks. Tofu can be eaten fresh or cooked in many different ways and is an excellent source of protein. Types and uses of tofu:
    - *Extra-firm tofu:* frying, roasting, grilling; can be marinated
    - *Firm tofu:* stir-frying, boiling, or as filling
    - *Soft tofu:* pureeing
    - *Silken tofu:* pureeing, simmering, egg substitution, used in vegan desserts and smoothies

Source: Vegetarian Nutrition, a dietetic practice group of the Academy of Nutrition and Dietetics.

flour. Be aware that phytates in plant-based foods can inhibit zinc absorption; however, phytates are broken down when yeast fermentation makes bread dough rise.

- Be cautious of zinc supplements. In large doses, they can have harmful side effects. If your doctor or registered dietitian nutritionist recommends a supplement, stick with a vitamin-mineral combination with 100 percent or less Daily Value for zinc.

Calcium: Except for vegans, dairy foods are excellent sources of calcium for vegetarians. Calcium is essential for building and maintaining bone and much more; *see "Calcium" in chapter 14, page 425*. Vegans can get enough calcium from calcium-fortified foods and some plant-based foods, but it may take more planning; a calcium supplement may be advised for them.

- Try tofu and tempeh processed with calcium, calcium-fortified soy or rice beverages, broccoli, almonds, soybeans, some greens (kale, collards, mustard greens, turnip greens), okra, rutabaga, bok choy, figs, or tortillas (made with slaked lime-processed corn).
- Look for calcium-fortified products: perhaps juice, bread, cereal bars, and cereal. Note that the grain products may not be vegan. Studies show that the body's ability to use the calcium carbonate–fortified soymilk is comparable to calcium in cow's milk.
- Be aware: beet greens, rhubarb, spinach, chard, and a grain called amaranth supply calcium. However, these foods contain oxalates that bind calcium, blocking its absorption. Some grain products also contain small amounts of calcium, but they also may contain phytates that block calcium absorption.
- As a vegan, if you can't consume enough calcium from food, talk to your doctor or a registered dietitian nutritionist about a calcium supplement with vitamin D if you need more.

Vitamin D: Lacto-vegetarians can get enough vitamin D from milk fortified with it. Some yogurt also is vitamin D fortified. Vegans, however, need another source of vitamin D to absorb calcium effectively.

- If you're a vegan, check the Nutrition Facts labels. Some breakfast cereals; some soy, rice, almond, and hemp beverages; some cereal bars; and some calcium-fortified juices are fortified with vitamin D.
- If in doubt, talk to your doctor or a registered dietitian nutritionist about taking a vitamin D supplement at the level that's right for you. Choose one that contains 100 percent Daily Value.

Talk to a registered dietitian nutritionist about different forms of vitamin D. Vitamin D_2 is vegan and made with yeast. Vitamin D_3 may be developed with a substance from sheep's wool or, more recently, from lichen. *See "Vitamin D" in chapter 14, page 413, for more about the different forms of vitamin D.*

Vitamin B_{12}: For vegetarians who consume dairy products or eggs, getting enough vitamin B_{12} isn't a concern. This vitamin is widely available in foods of animal origin. Plant-based foods supply vitamin B_{12} only when soil with vitamin B_{12}–producing microorganisms clings to fruits and vegetables. In the United States, fruits and vegetables are scrubbed clean before they're eaten, which washes away the vitamin.

Vegans of all ages need a reliable source of vitamin B_{12}. Foods fortified with vitamin B_{12} or a vitamin B_{12} supplement are good choices, and since vitamin B_{12} isn't absorbed as well with age, older adult vegetarians who consume dairy foods or eggs benefit by taking a supplement as well.

- Look for vitamin B_{12}–fortified products: ready-to-eat breakfast cereal, soy or rice beverages, or soyburger patties.
- Be aware that seaweed, algae, spirulina, and fermented plant foods such as tempeh and miso are not dependable sources of vitamin B_{12}, even if the package says so. Their vitamin B_{12} is either inactive or not in a form that the human body can use. Vitamin B_{12} in beer and other fermented foods isn't reliable, either.
- If your healthcare professional advises a supplement, find one with 100 percent Daily Value for vitamin B_{12}. Check the Supplement Facts. Cyanocobalamin is the most bioavailable, or easily absorbed, form of vitamin B_{12}. Vitamin B_{12} in fortified foods and supplements is produced synthetically from bacteria, not from animal sources.
- Consider nutritional yeast if it's grown in a medium that's enriched with vitamin B_{12}. Check the label. Don't count on yeast typically used to make baked goods (such as bread) because it typically doesn't supply vitamin B_{12}.

See chapter 14, page 408, for more about all of these nutrients.

VEGETARIAN PATTERN: HOW IT WORKS

Once you know how, being a smart vegetarian takes no more effort than any other healthy eating approach for getting enough nourishment, no matter what your age.

The general advice, *addressed earlier in this chapter*, applies to vegetarian eating, too. It's also been adapted for vegans who eat only plant-based foods and for lacto-ovo-vegetarians.

See "Healthy Vegetarian Eating Pattern," in the appendix, page 775, for the various calorie levels.

Grains the Vegetarian Way: Three Quick Tips

1. Make grain dishes, especially whole grains, a mainstay in your menus. Try tabbouleh, barley soup, brown rice risotto or pilaf, wild rice or buckwheat dishes, or polenta.
2. Prepare mixed dishes with cooked grain products. Stuff vegetables (eggplant, bell peppers, cabbage, zucchini, winter squash) with rice, oats, and barley, among others. Blend cooked grains with shredded vegetables and perhaps tofu for vegetable patties or croquettes. Toss cooked grains, perhaps quinoa or whole-wheat pasta, with stir-fried vegetables; quinoa is a high-protein, grainlike seed with substantial benefits for vegetarian eating.

Going Meatless: Making the Switch

How to make the switch to a meatless diet, sometimes or all the time? Start with small steps so you can gradually find foods you enjoy.

- Find a vegetarian pattern (lacto-, ovo-, vegan, other) that works for you.
- Take stock of the foods you like already. Keep whole-grain, vegetable, and fruit dishes on your menus—perhaps add more vegetables and beans to them.
- Adapt your recipes. Replace meat with beans, tempeh, or tofu in pizzas, sandwiches, tacos, chilies, soups, stews, and casseroles. *See "Recipe Makeovers: Healthy Vegetarian" in chapter 8, page 237.*
- Give meat alternatives, such as soy patties and soy hot dogs, a try when you're learning to prepare more plant-based foods. Go beyond hummus!
- Order a vegetarian meal when you eat out. Ask about vegetarian options if the menu doesn't clearly indicate them. Many ethnic restaurants may inspire you with new dishes to try.
- Get a vegetarian cookbook or search online for vegetarian recipes and meal ideas; check the nutrition information if available. Especially check Asian, Indian, and Middle Eastern cuisines. *See "A Global Kitchen: Meatless on the Menu" in chapter 9, page 288.*
- If you decide to go vegan, look for dairy substitutes: calcium- and vitamin D–fortified soy beverages and soy yogurts. Switch to soy cheese.
- When making meal and snack choices, consider your overall nutrition for the whole day—not just for a single food or dish. Even on a meatless diet, you can consume too many calories and too much solid fat, added sugars, and sodium!

3. Choose fortified breakfast cereals. Check the Nutrition Facts labels to compare nutrients added through fortification, including iron, vitamin B_{12}, calcium, and zinc.

Vegetables the Vegetarian Way: Three Quick Tips

1. Vary your veggies! Especially if you're vegan, choose vegetables with more calcium: dark-green leafy vegetables (such as kale and mustard, collard, and turnip greens), bok choy, and broccoli. Dark-green leafy vegetables also supply iron.
2. Choose vegetables that are high in vitamin C. For example, the vitamin C in broccoli, tomatoes, and green and red bell peppers helps your body absorb iron from eggs and plant-based sources of food.
3. Plan meals with different vegetables, not just garden salads, baked potatoes, and French fries, for the nutrient and phytonutrient benefits of variety.

Fruit the Vegetarian Way: Two Quick Tips

1. Enjoy a variety of fruits, including those rich in vitamin C, such as citrus fruits, melons, and berries. Among the other benefits, vitamin C–rich fruit is an important partner for nonheme iron.
2. Look for calcium- and vitamin D–fortified juice, especially if you're a vegan.

Have you ever wondered?

. . . if "vegetarian" on a food label means low-fat, too? No. Foods labeled as vegetarian on packages or restaurant menus may contain high-fat ingredients. Foods that can be high in fat include textured soy patties, soy hot dogs, soy cheese, refried beans, and snack bars. Even tofu may have more fat than you'd think: 4 ounces (about ½ cup) have about 95 calories and 6 grams of fat, but mostly from polyunsaturated fats. Compare that to about 145 calories and 4 grams of fat in 3 ounces of cooked lean beef round steak. Check the Nutrition Facts label to compare calories and nutrients in a single serving.

. . . if a macrobiotic diet is nourishing? First a description: a macrobiotic diet is predominantly vegetarian (or meatless), emphasizing fewer processed foods. Food choices are mostly grains (40 to 60 percent), vegetables (25 to 30 percent), and legumes (5 to 10 percent), with other foods eaten to a lesser extent, including miso soup, sea vegetables (seaweed), seeds, nuts, and fruits, among other foods,. Some who follow a macrobiotic diet consume limited amounts of fish.

Like any eating approach, the answer to its nutritional quality lies in the foods chosen, how much, and how the overall food choices stack up to healthy eating guidelines and nutrient needs.

For the record, the Zen macrobiotic diet, followed several decades ago, typically for spiritual reasons, is quite different and highly restrictive.

Dairy and Dairy Alternatives the Vegetarian Way: Six Quick Tips

1. Choose low-fat and fat-free dairy foods if you're lacto-ovo-vegetarian.
2. Especially if you're vegan, choose soy beverages that are fortified with calcium and vitamins A and D. They can provide calcium in amounts similar to milk, and they're usually low in fat and cholesterol free.
3. Check for added sugars in soy beverages. Many plain varieties use modest amounts of brown rice syrup. Flavored varieties, such as vanilla and chocolate, use significantly more sweetener. Calcium-fortified orange juice, rice milk, and other nondairy "milks" don't count in the dairy group.
4. Check the Nutrition Facts labels to compare products. Milk supplies about 300 milligrams of calcium per 8-ounce serving; choose soy beverages with at least this much. If soy-based products aren't calcium fortified, they do not count as a dairy group option.

For more tips for vegetarians, see . . .

- *"Meatless on the Menu," chapter 3, page 73*
- *"Stocking the Vegetarian Kitchen," chapter 6, page 187*
- *"Recipe Makeovers: Healthy Vegetarian" chapter 8, page 237*
- *"A Global Kitchen: Meatless on the Menu" chapter 9, page 288*
- *"For Vegetarian Babies . . . ," chapter 16, page 477*
- *"Feeding Vegetarian Kids," chapter 17, page 520*
- *"The Vegetarian Mom," chapter 18, page 546*
- *"Vegetarian Fare for Sixty-Plus Adults," chapter 20, page 580*
- *"The Vegetarian Athlete," chapter 21, page 614*

? Have you ever wondered?

. . . if a Paleo diet is a healthy option? Also called the stone age, caveman, warrior, or hunter-gatherer diet, the Paleo diet advises eating as our ancestors did ten thousand years ago. The premise is that this ancient approach matches human genetic makeup—and that today's diet-related health problems result from the changes in food production brought about by civilization.

Strictly defined, a Paleo diet recommends foods that can be hunted, fished, or gathered (meat, poultry, fish, eggs, vegetables such as roots, and fruits such as berries). No grains, no dairy, no beans or peas (legumes), no added sugars, no salt. Fasting occasionally is sometimes advised, too.

The premise of the Paleo diet evades a reality: human genetics have evolved over the past ten thousand years along with the transition to and evolution of agriculture. For example, as animals were domesticated for milking, many humans evolved, too, to develop the ability to digest milk. Genes related to digesting starch have also changed, likely in response to agriculture.

Another point to consider: Science cannot confirm how—and how well—the stone-age diet nourished our ancestors nor how perfectly they adapted their diet to their environmental conditions. Of necessity, the diet of prehistoric people had to be flexible. And what about more recent changes in eating patterns from 200 to 300 years ago?

This Paleo approach provides some good direction that aligns with the Dietary Guidelines for Americans: more fruits and vegetables; cutting out added sugars and excess sodium; and choosing whole, less-processed food.

However, a typical Paleo plan exceeds advice for the daily amounts of fat and protein and falls short on carbohydrate recommendations, a key energy source for both body and brain. The consequence of excluding nutrient-rich whole grains, legumes, and dairy means that it likely comes up short on important vitamins and minerals, among them calcium and vitamin D. Nutrient supplementation is advised.

The Paleo diet may be hard to sustain. Strict conformity isn't realistic because, among the reasons, plant-based foods today aren't grown and gathered in the wild. The lack of food variety, the need for planning and for nutrient supplementation, and the cost also can make it hard to follow. Many scientists point out that the validity of the Paleo premise isn't certain.

5. Look for calcium-fortified soy yogurt and soy cheese.
6. Avoid overloading menus with high-fat cheeses to replace meat in mixed dishes. Consider lower-fat cheese, readily available in most grocery stores.

Protein Foods the Vegetarian Way: Four Quick Tips

1. Feature beans and peas on your menu: bean burritos, chili with beans, pasta primavera with beans. Besides protein, they're also good sources of iron and zinc, similar to meat, poultry, and fish. They're also excellent sources of fiber, potassium, folate, and more. *See "How to . . . Cook Dried Beans" in chapter 8, page 252, for ways to cook them.*
2. Be creative with soy-protein foods such as tofu, tempeh, textured vegetable protein, and garden burgers. Try them in stir-fry dishes, casseroles, pasta dishes including lasagna, burger patties, and soups. Use them in place of meat; be mindful of their sodium content. *See "A Closer Look . . . Soy Protein and More" in chapter 12, page 383.*
3. If you eat eggs, plan meals around quiche, omelets, frittatas, scrambled eggs, French toast, egg salad, and egg foo yung. If your doctor advises you to limit eggs to manage your blood cholesterol level, make egg-based dishes with egg whites or egg replacers in place of some whole eggs.
4. Include nuts, nut butters (almond, cashew), peanut butter, seeds, and seed spreads (tahini, or sesame seed, spread) in your meals and snacks. They, too, supply protein and a variety of phytonutrients. Since they're fairly high in fat, go easy even though most fat from nuts is unsaturated. Choose unsalted nuts and nut butters without added salt, added sugars, or partially hydrogenated vegetable oil.

Oils the Vegetarian Way: Two Quick Tips

1. For nonvegetarians, choose oils over solid fats; for example, use oil or soft margarine instead of stick margarine. Oils from nuts, seeds, avocados, and olives are great options—in small amounts.
2. For vegans, consume plant-based foods: flaxseed, soybean, and canola oils, as well as walnuts, soy nuts, and ground flaxseed—with alpha-linolenic (ALA) fatty acids that convert to DHA and EPA fatty acids. *See "A Closer Look . . . Omega-3s and -6s" in chapter 13, page 392.*

Solid Fats and Added Sugars the Vegetarian Way: One Quick Tip

A vegetarian eating plan doesn't automatically mean low in saturated and *trans* fats, added sugars, sodium, or calories. Follow the same advice for nonvegetarians *described earlier in this chapter.*

3

Make Quick, Easy Meals and Snacks

In this chapter, find out about . . .

Fast, easy, healthy mealtimes

Eating at work

Better snacking

Eating mindfully (not mindlessly)

Right-sizing your portions

Do you prefer a hearty breakfast or a light morning bite? A big meal at lunchtime or in the evening? Three meals a day or several mini-meals? Snacks or no snacks?

No approach is healthier than another—if you make food choices that fit the healthy eating pattern that matches your calorie limits, *as described in chapter 2.* You don't need foods from all five food groups at every meal. And what you eat for one meal, one snack, or one day won't make or break your health either. What you eat consistently on most days—over the long term—is what counts!

As you plan breakfast, lunch, dinner, and snacks—or a series of mini-meals, consider the big picture and how they promote health in a way that's right for you—and your family and friends.

Breakfast Matters

"No time," "nothing to eat," "woke up too late," and "on a diet." People give many reasons for breakfast skipping or skimping.

Despite its benefits, breakfast may be the most neglected and skipped meal of the day. Some blame their body clock for a lack of hunger when they wake up. Some may not be hungry if they ate late the night before. "Not hungry" could result from stress; stress hormones can affect hunger cues. With today's hectic lifestyles, others come up short on time and energy first thing in the morning—or they'd rather spend a few more minutes in bed. Some falsely believe that breakfast skipping is effective for weight control.

Despite the reasons for breakfast skipping or skimping, most people acknowledge that eating breakfast is the healthy way to start the day, notes research from the International Food Information Council Foundation, even though fewer people today make breakfast a daily habit. Other surveys suggest that breakfast is on the upswing, perhaps a result of morning menu options becoming more creative.

Research into breakfast is complicated because there's no one definition or one type of breakfast food. You might say it's the first meal of the day, or food eaten before your daily routine kicks in, or what you eat within two to three hours of waking up, or anything eaten between 5:00 and

Your Healthy Eating Check-In

How Do You Solve Daily Food Dilemmas?

Take this simple quiz to see how your meal and snack planning measures up to healthy eating practices.

	Never 1 point	Sometimes 2 points	Usually 3 points	Always 4 points
1. I try to eat breakfast—even when I'm rushed.	☐	☐	☐	☐
2. I try to include nutrient-rich foods from at least three food groups in my morning meal.	☐	☐	☐	☐
3. For lunch, I put aside my work or other tasks and take time for a nourishing meal—and a mental or physical break.	☐	☐	☐	☐
4. I plan supper ahead so I can prepare and serve a healthy meal, even at the end of a very hectic day.	☐	☐	☐	☐
5. I pay attention to food and drink portions for myself and others so they're not oversized.	☐	☐	☐	☐
6. I keep my refrigerator, freezer, and pantry stocked with a variety of nutrient-rich foods for last-minute meals.	☐	☐	☐	☐
7. I try to make my meal and snack choices match the food-group advice that's right for me.	☐	☐	☐	☐
8. I prepare meatless meals—with good protein foods—for myself and my family.	☐	☐	☐	☐
9. I modify everyday favorites, such as breakfast cereal, pasta dishes, and pizza, to add more fruits, vegetables, or beans, and different whole grains.	☐	☐	☐	☐
10. I try to plan at least two meals with fish during the week.	☐	☐	☐	☐
11. I pre-portion my snacks rather than eat from a big package or bowl.	☐	☐	☐	☐
12. I like the adventure of trying unfamiliar foods from different regions, cultures, and countries.	☐	☐	☐	☐
13. I consider nutrition when I choose snacks and snack drinks, being careful about how many added sugars and calories they contain.	☐	☐	☐	☐
14. I snack when I'm hungry, not because it's the social thing to do.	☐	☐	☐	☐
15. I am mindful of food when I eat, rather than multitasking and giving attention elsewhere (perhaps a smart phone or TV).	☐	☐	☐	☐

Now, how did you fare? Add up your points.

46 to 60: Excellent! You seem to have mastered the art of planning and managing healthy meals and snacks.

31 to 45: Good. You have many skills for planning and managing healthy meals and snacks. Take a few more smart steps.

16 to 30: Okay. You're in the healthy eating zone sometimes. Use this quick check-in to see where you might take action—one step at a time—to plan and eat smarter. Every step you take is for your own good health.

15: You've got lots of opportunity for healthier eating. Choose one thing to do from this check-in for starters. And begin to take small steps toward solving your own meal and snack dilemmas.

Click Here! Links to Know . . .

- Ten Tips Nutrition Education Series (tips on menu planning)
  www.ChooseMyPlate.gov/tipsresources/tentips.html
- What's Cooking, USDA Mixing Bowl (recipes to build your cookbook)
  www.whatscooking.fns.usda.gov
- *Food & Nutrition Magazine* (ideas and recipes for healthy meals and snacks)
  www.foodandnutrition.org

9:00 a.m., or perhaps before 10:00 a.m. Or maybe you define it by the menu: cereal, milk, and sliced banana; eggs, toast, grapefruit half, and coffee; a protein bar and juice; steamed rice, miso soup, and vegetables. It can be all these, and more.

WHY BREAKFAST?

Do you eat, skip, or skimp on breakfast? That decision likely affects the rest of your morning, and perhaps your day. According to research, a regular morning meal is positive nutrition, linked to better overall health, including better diet quality, a healthier body weight, lower risk for some chronic disease, and some cognitive benefits.

Although not proven, research suggests that breakfast eaters tend to have better concentration and problem-solving ability, better attitudes toward work or school, and higher productivity in the late morning, as well as a better ability to handle tasks that require memory. Athletes have more endurance if they eat breakfast.

Is breakfast the most important meal of the day, as often heard? It's hard to say that one meal is any more important than another, but spreading nutrients out throughout the day is generally advised. That said, starting the day with a healthy meal can get you off to a good start.

Breakfast: An Energizing Start

Breakfast is your body's early morning refueling stop after eight to twelve hours without a meal or a snack. Your body needs to refuel for the sustained mental work—in school, at work, or for volunteer work or home projects—you do throughout the day. Your muscles also need an energy source to refuel for the day's activity.

Eating a variety of breakfast foods with a mix of carbohydrates, proteins, and fats provides a sustained release of energy that delays hunger symptoms for several hours.

Breakfast: The Nutrient Connection

Think of breakfast as a marker for healthy eating and a healthy lifestyle—not just as a source of food energy. Among other benefits, breakfast provides a jumpstart for fitting in enough fruits, vegetables, whole grains, and calcium-rich dairy foods to your day.

Those who regularly eat a morning meal usually consume more vitamins, minerals, and fiber for the day, which includes more of the nutrients that often come up short, such as calcium, potassium, fiber, folate, iron, or vitamin B_{12}. Those who skip breakfast may not make up the nutrients they miss in the morning. Tip: If you skip a meal, try to make up what you missed in other meals or with snacks.

These are some nutrients that common breakfast foods deliver:

- In addition to the carbohydrates, B vitamins, and iron you get from whole-grain and other fiber-rich cereals, eating whole grain breads, muffins, and waffles will boost your fiber intake. Fortified ready-to-eat cereals and bread also deliver folate. Make your carb food choices nutrient dense.
- Milk, yogurt, or fortified soymilk enjoyed with cereal, or on the side, adds calcium and vitamin D. To get the most out of your bowl of cereal, drink your cereal milk!
- Whole fruits or 100 percent fruit juices provide vitamin C and more. They're also good sources of potassium and some phytonutrients.
- Protein foods—eggs, peanut butter, nuts, leftover chicken, tofu, or other protein foods—help satisfy your appetite and perhaps improve the quality of your diet. Protein helps your brain release a hormone that signals fullness, and spreading protein over meals throughout the day is important for muscle health. Dairy foods deliver protein, too. Try to fit 20 to 25 grams of protein into your breakfast meals.

Breakfast and Learning

Breakfast helps prepare children and teens to learn, especially those at risk for poor nutrition. Although inconclusive, many studies indicate that kids who regularly eat a morning meal tend to perform better in school. The reasons? Limited data suggest links to better memory, better grades and test scores (especially math), better school attendance, and a better mood. Breakfast eaters often behave better in school, too, and have better muscle coordination.

Unlike many adults, children probably can't condition themselves to overcome the effects of skipping breakfast. The impact of short-term hunger may be particularly problematic for young children because basic skills—reading, writing, and arithmetic—often are taught first thing in the morning. And consider the long-term effect of transient hunger on learning. When children can't reach their learning potential day after day, they potentially fall farther and farther behind.

Classroom attendance? Stomachaches or hunger pangs caused by breakfast skipping or skimping may result in leaving class to see the school nurse. Breakfast skippers also tend to be tardy or absent from school more often. Many schools provide breakfast. If your child doesn't eat breakfast at home, encourage him or her to eat school breakfast if it's available. *See "Eating Right at School" in chapter 17, page 505.*

Breakfast: For a Healthy Weight

Eating a morning meal is linked to a healthier body weight—and to weight loss and maintenance—although the reasons or the cause and effect are unclear. It simply may be that eating, like being physically active, is a common behavior among those who maintain a healthier weight.

Breakfast foods that are particularly satisfying may factor in. For example, regularly choosing cereal, including high-fiber cereal topped with nuts or seeds, and milk, has been linked to healthy weight, perhaps because it's satiating. Protein in a breakfast meal can help you feel full, too.

Or, maybe it's the timing. Compared to breakfast skippers, people who eat breakfast may not be overly hungry for a midmorning snack or lunch. The likelihood of impulsive snacking or eating more for lunch may be less for those who eat breakfast.

Eating breakfasts that are very high in calories is associated with a higher body mass index (BMI).

Breakfast: More Good-for-You Benefits

Starting the day with a healthy meal may offer benefits for heart health, digestion, and bone health. This could be linked to foods typically consumed in the morning such as whole-grain breads and cereals, dairy foods, whole fruits, and 100 percent fruit juice—and the fiber, and pre- and probiotics they supply. *See "Prebiotics and Probiotics: A Bioactive Duo" in chapter 15, page 453.*

Emerging evidence suggests that breakfast eating also may positively affect blood glucose regulation, insulin levels, and fat metabolism as well as may reduce the risk of metabolic syndrome. Much more research is needed to explore if it does—and if so, why.

Finally, another benefit for some might be social: getting together with friends to eat breakfast, especially true for older adults and empty nesters.

WHAT'S A GOOD BREAKFAST?

There's no consensus among experts on what foods make the best meal, on their amounts, or on timing. The best breakfast depends on what and how much you eat the rest of day, what foods you enjoy in the morning, and your morning schedule.

The following criteria can help identify a high-quality breakfast:

- Foods from at least three food groups, *as discussed in chapter 2, page 21.* Including protein-rich food and whole grains, which are rich in fiber, appears to make a morning meal more satisfying. That also means you'll be getting the variety of nutrients your body needs. Try to fit in vegetables as well as whole fruits. Vegetables are often underconsumed, and this is a good way to get more. Remember a fat-free or low-fat dairy food or drink, too.
- A meal with between 15 and 25 percent of your day's total calorie recommendation—from a mix of carbohydrates (from fiber-rich whole grains, fruits, low-fat and fat-free dairy foods), lean protein foods, and healthy fats. (Enriched, fortified grain products with limited added sugars may be another carbohydrate source.) The amount from each food group depends on how much and what you eat at other meals and snacks.

Total Daily Calories	Calorie Range for Breakfast (15–25% of Total)
1,600	240–400
2,000	300–500
2,400	360–600

Breakfast: Six Ways to a Protein Boost

1. Eat a grab-and-go bran muffin and banana. Partner it with ½ cup cottage cheese, too, for 14 more grams of protein and 1 large hard-cooked egg for 6 more grams of protein.
2. Swap the spread on toast. Spread 2 tablespoons peanut butter on toast instead of butter or margarine to add 8 grams of protein, or replace them with 4 tablespoons hummus for 5 grams of protein.
3. Switch yogurt. Eat 6 ounces of Greek yogurt for 18 grams of protein. The same amount of regular yogurt has 9 grams of protein. (Unless fortified with calcium, Greek yogurt likely has less calcium than regular yogurt; check the Nutrition Facts label to find out.)
4. Make oatmeal with milk. Prepare 1 cup oatmeal with 1 cup milk instead of water for 8 grams of protein. Top with 2 tablespoons walnuts for 2 more grams of protein.
5. Add ham or Canadian bacon to a breakfast sandwich. Two ounces add 9 grams of protein. One ounce of Cheddar cheese adds 6 grams of protein.
6. Give smoothies a protein boost beyond the protein from its milk or yogurt. Add a 1-ounce scoop of whey protein for 16 more grams of protein; or ½ ounce (about 1 tablespoon) of chia seeds for about 2 more grams of protein.

Two Minutes: Breakfast, Lunch, Mini-Meal

Each easy menu here is packed with nutrients from three or more food groups. Good for a quick breakfast, light lunch, or a mini-meal!

- Ready-to-eat cereal topped with low-fat yogurt or milk, sliced banana, and sunflower seeds (or layer it in reverse with yogurt and bananas on the bottom, topped with cereal and sunflower seeds); coffee or tea
- Bran muffin or granola and Greek yogurt topped with berries; coffee or tea
- Hummus on whole-wheat toast or soft tortilla; yogurt drink or kefir
- Hard-cooked egg (cooked the night before); whole-wheat English muffin; peach or pear; chocolate milk
- Leftover cheese or lean-meat pizza slice; 100 percent juice
- Instant oatmeal made with milk or soymilk, topped with dried cranberries and grated cheese or nuts
- Breakfast smoothie (buttermilk or kefir, whole fruit, dry oats, chopped nuts)
- Whole-grain toaster waffle "sandwich" with sliced fruit, nuts, and ricotta or cottage cheese; tea or coffee
- Almond or peanut butter on whole-grain toasted bagel, topped with apple slices; low-fat milk
- Whole-grain bagel with fruit chutney spread; baby carrots; fat-free milk or soymilk
- Lean ham, Canadian bacon, or deli meat topped with low-fat cheese on a toasted English whole-wheat muffin; tangerine; water
- Banana dipped in low-fat yogurt and rolled in granola or nuts; coffee or tea
- Heated leftover rice with chopped apples, nuts, and cinnamon; 100 percent prune juice
- Breakfast wrap, made with cut-up fresh or canned fruit and Greek yogurt rolled in a whole-wheat tortilla; water, coffee, or tea
- Leftover quiche (reheated or not); vegetable juice
- Heated leftover quinoa or couscous mixed with beans, peppers, and cilantro; soymilk

- Limits breakfast foods high in sodium, added sugars, and saturated fats. This includes bacon, biscuits and gravy, and pastries.
- Portions appropriate to your calorie limits, based on the food pattern that's right for you, as *discussed in chapter 2*.
- A variety of foods from day to day that match your own preferences, lifestyle, and cultural traditions, with foods that are both available and affordable.

BEATING BREAKFAST BARRIERS

For you or your kids, every excuse or apparent breakfast barrier has a solution. If you have children, you're their best role model. Children who see their parent(s) eat breakfast are more likely to eat breakfast, too. To overcome breakfast barriers, try these strategies.

Barrier: Not hungry when you wake up

Solution: Since it may take some time to get used to eating breakfast if you've been a breakfast skipper, start with a light bite, perhaps 100 percent juice and whole-wheat toast. Later, perhaps midmorning, when you feel hungry, add some variety such as a hard-cooked egg, low-fat or fat-free yogurt, or a fruit-yogurt smoothie.

Barrier: No time, too busy

Solutions: Get the food (perhaps hard-cooked eggs, fruit-yogurt parfaits), bowls, spoons, and cups ready the night before as you clean up from supper. *See "Two Minutes: Breakfast, Lunch, Mini-Meal" above.*

Keep quick-to-fix foods on hand, such as ready-to-eat breakfast cereal, instant oatmeal, bagels, whole-grain toaster waffles, whole-grain bread, yogurt, fresh fruit, canned fruit in juice, dried fruit, 100 percent fruit

Have you ever wondered?

. . . if eating presweetened ready-to-eat breakfast cereal is okay for kids? These cereals may be options for getting kids to eat breakfast in the morning. Limit the portions to curtail the added sugars they contain. For younger children, ¾ to 1 cup cereal is likely enough. As another option, if your child prefers a sweeter taste, offer unsweetened cereal topped with fruit or fruit-flavored yogurt.

Research shows that children who eat ready-to-eat cereal as part of the School Breakfast Program have a healthier body weight. And children who eat breakfast are more likely to meet their nutrient needs.

A Day's Family Menu*: Three Calorie Levels

This chart shows how the same menu can be adjusted for family members with different calorie needs. When planning menus, remember that nutrient amounts vary among product—and what counts is how food choices average over several days.

The 2,000-calorie menu here has been adapted from a menu on www.ChooseMyPlate.gov/. *For a week's worth of sample menus that meet food-group guidelines and are planned for 2,000 calories, see "Sample Menus for a 2,000-Calorie Food Pattern" in the appendix, page 778.* These menus on the website show the full week's nutritional analysis.

	1,600 Calories*	**2,000 Calories***	**2,400 Calories***
BREAKFAST			
Ready-to-eat oat cereal topped with	¾ cup	1 cup	1 cup
Fat-free milk	½ cup	½ cup	1 cup
Banana	½ small	1 small	1 small
Almonds	¼ ounce (6 almonds)	½ ounce (11 almonds)	½ ounce (11 almonds)
Whole-wheat toast with	1 regular slice	1 regular slice	2 regular slices
Tub margarine	1 teaspoon	1 teaspoon	2 teaspoons
100% orange juice	½ cup	½ cup	¾ cup
LUNCH			
Tuna salad sandwich with			
Rye bread	2 regular slices	2 regular slices	2 regular slices
Tuna, canned, drained	2 ounces	2 ounces	3 ounces
Celery, chopped	1 tablespoon	1 tablespoon	2 tablespoons
Lettuce, shredded	½ cup	½ cup	½ cup
Tomato	1 medium slice	2 medium slices	2 medium slices
Mayonnaise	1 tablespoon	1 tablespoon	1½ tablespoons**
Peach	½ medium	1 medium	1 medium
Baby carrots, raw	6	8	8
Milk, fat-free	1 cup	1½ cups	1½ cups
SNACK			
Dried apricots	¼ cup	¼ cup	¼ cup
Flavored low-fat yogurt (chocolate)	6 ounces	1 cup	1 cup
DINNER			
Roasted chicken breast, skinless, boneless	2½ ounces	3 ounces	3½ ounces
Sweet potato, roasted	1 small	1 medium	1 large
Succotash (lima beans and corn) with	½ cup	½ cup	¾ cup
Tub margarine	1 teaspoon	1 teaspoon	1 teaspoon
Whole-wheat roll with	1 medium (2½ inches across)	1 medium (2½ inches across)	2 medium (2½ inches across)
Cheese spread	½ ounce	½ ounce	½ ounce
Chocolate low-fat pudding	½ cup	¾ cup	¾ cup
Water, coffee, tea (unsweetened)	1 cup	1 cup	1 cup

*Planned using the SuperTracker from www.ChooseMyPlate.gov

**½ tablespoon = 1½ teaspoons

Hidden Components in Eating Patterns

Many of the foods and beverages we eat contain sodium, saturated fats, and added sugars. Making careful choices, as in this example, keeps amounts of these components within their limits while meeting nutrient needs to achieve a healthy eating pattern.

Contributes:
● Sodium* ▒ Saturated Fats ▲ Added Sugars
Breakfast
Bagel with Peanut Butter & Banana ●▒▲
Whole Wheat Bagel ● ½ regular bagel (4 oz)
Creamy Peanut Butter ●▒▲ 2 tablespoons
Banana 1 medium
Coffee with Milk & Sugar ▒▲
Whole Milk ▒ ¼ cup
Sugar ▲ 2 teaspoons
Fat-free Strawberry Yogurt ●▲ 8 ounces
726 Calories
Lunch
Tuna Salad Sandwich with Lettuce & Mayo ●▒▲
100% Whole Wheat Bread ●▲ 2 slices
Canned Tuna ● 2 ounces
Mayonnaise ●▒ 2 teaspoons
Chopped Celery 2 tablespoons
Lettuce 1 medium leaf
Carrots 4 Baby Carrots
Raisins ¼ Cup
Low-fat Milk (1%) ●▒ 1 Cup
507 Calories
Dinner
Spaghetti & Meatballs ●▒▲
Spaghetti 1 cup, cooked
Spaghetti Sauce ●▲ ¼ cup
Diced Tomatoes (canned, no salt added) ¼ cup
Meatballs ●▒ 3 medium meatballs
Parmesan Cheese ●▒ 1 tablespoon
Apple, Raw ½ medium
Water, Tap 1 cup
Garden Salad ●▒▲
Mixed Greens 1 cup
Cucumber 3 slices
Avocado ▒ ¼ cup, cubed
Garbanzo Beans (canned, low sodium) ● ¼ cup
Cheddar Cheese (reduced fat) ▒ 3 tablespoons, shredded
Ranch Salad Dressing ●▒▲ 1 tablespoon
761 Calories
Total
Sodium: 2,253 mg
less than or equal to 2,300 mg
Calories From Saturated Fats: 153 (8% of Total Calories)
less than or equal to 10% of calories
Calories From Added Sugars: 164 (8% of Total Calories)
less than or equal to 10% of calories
1,995 Calories

* Foods very low in sodium not marked

Source: 2015–2020 Dietary Guidelines for Americans, USDA/USHHS

and vegetable juices, low-fat or fat-free milk, cheese, cottage cheese, nuts, peanut butter, and nut butter.

Also, set your alarm clock a few minutes earlier.

Barrier: Too much effort

Solution: Plan a light, easy breakfast that is grab-and-go to kick-start the day. This could be a carton of yogurt and a small bran muffin; a whole-wheat bagel spread with peanut butter, nut butter, or hummus; a high-fiber cereal bar and grapes; or whole-grain crackers, cheese, and dried cranberries.

Barrier: Want to eat less to lose weight

Solution: A morning meal with a lean-protein food and a whole-grain food may aid in weight management if it helps you feel full longer so you're less likely to be hungry and snack too much midmorning. Scientific evidence isn't clear whether eating breakfast or skipping it makes a difference in body weight.

One key to weight loss is making healthy choices with fewer calories over the whole day rather than skipping breakfast. And of course, limit higher-calorie breakfasts, such as those with bacon or breakfast sausage, hash browns, and biscuits with gravy, because their high fat contents can add up to more calories than you need!

Barrier: Don't like breakfast foods

Solution: That's okay.

If traditional breakfast foods seem boring, get creative. Mix it up with a new yogurt flavor, a new type of whole-grain cereal or toast, or a fruit you've not tried before on your cereal. Add chopped kale or shredded carrots to your morning smoothie. *See "Quick School-Day Breakfasts" in chapter 17, page 500, for more ideas.*

Breakfast can be any food you like: chicken-noodle soup; whole-grain toast topped with an egg and avocado and tomato slices; a lean-beef or turkey sandwich and milk; a quesadilla or burrito with scrambled eggs or beans, cheese shreds, and spicy salsa; scrambled tofu with veggies, cheese, and meatless sausage; a breakfast-bowl meal; or last night's leftovers.

See "BREAK-Fast Options" and "Breakfast on the Road" in chapter 9, pages 291 and 311, for advice about eating breakfast away from home.

Eating Well at Work

Because the world of work—and often volunteering—demands high productivity, eat for success. Your workday meals are regular eating events that can deliver good nutrition—and maybe even help increase your work output.

HEALTHY EATING = WORKPLACE PRODUCTIVITY

To make your day more productive:

- Kick-start your workday with breakfast. You'll replenish your supply of energy. A morning meal is linked to better health and may

Great Cereal Bowls

OVERNIGHT OATMEAL (MUESLI)

For a breakfast that's ready even before you awaken (or for a lunch, dinner, or snack):

1. Combine (in a 1:1 ratio) ½ cup raw oats and ½ cup low-fat or fat-free milk or yogurt in an 8-ounce container (perhaps a jar) that can be covered and tightly sealed.
2. If you like, add 2 teaspoons chia seeds, 1 teaspoon of cinnamon, a 1-ounce scoop of whey protein, and/or 2 teaspoons honey.
3. Cover and shake to combine.
4. Remove the lid and add ¼ cup berries or other cut-up fruit in any form (fresh, drained canned, frozen—but not packed in syrup).
5. Cover and refrigerate overnight so the oats absorb the liquid. Even a few hours is fine.
6. If you like, add nuts in the morning for a crunchy texture.

JAZZED-UP CEREAL

Whether it's overnight oatmeal or any cooked cereal (instant or not) such as oatmeal, cream of wheat, grits, quinoa, or brown rice, think creatively to vary your bowl meal:

- Instead of the usual low-fat or fat-free milk, use 100 percent juice, soymilk, or another nondairy alternative as the liquid. Or try quark (a type of cheese) or cottage cheese.
- Blend in grated cheese (perhaps low-fat), chopped fruit (apple, peach, banana, kiwifruit), dried fruit (chopped apricots, papaya, dates, raisins), wheat germ, or nuts. Or add flaxseeds, chia seeds, pumpkin seeds, or hemp seeds for fiber, some protein, and ALA fatty acids.
- Fortify the cereal by adding dry milk for more calcium and protein.
- Liven it up with spices—ground cinnamon, nutmeg, allspice, or cloves—or fresh mint; *see "Herbs—and Spices, Too!" in chapter 8, page 266,* *to learn about herbs and spices.*
- Make it a sweet-savory bowl by adding cooked vegetables such as sweet potatoes, butternut squash, kale, and carrots. These can be leftovers.

Have you ever wondered?

. . . why eating lunch may make you feel sleepy in the afternoon? Your overall sleep habits, age, and body cycle—or wine or beer with your meal—may be the cause, rather than lunch. New research also suggests that a mid-afternoon slump may be normal and induced by hormones. For some people, meals that are mostly carb foods increase serotonin, which contributes to drowsiness. Mixed meals with protein foods may help you avoid the slump, as might limiting foods with added sugars, such as sugary sodas.

To stay alert all day, get enough sleep at night. If you feel sleepy in the afternoon, a ten- to twenty-minute nap (if your workplace or situation allows) might be enough to revive you.

have cognitive benefits. A varied breakfast with a high-fiber food and a protein food will help stave off midmorning hunger. *See "Breakfast Matters" in this chapter, page 60.*

- Coffee break? Enjoy a cup of coffee or tea if that helps wake you up in the morning. Switch to decaf or water if caffeine bothers you. Or take a milk or water break instead; perhaps bring your beverage of choice from home in a clean, insulated water bottle. Milk as a regular break beverage may help reduce your risk of osteoporosis later in life.
- Take time for lunch—even when you're time pressured. Eating lunch may help you avoid an afternoon dip in energy levels, especially if your lunch provides a mix of foods, such as protein foods and whole grains that have staying power.
- Order "healthy options" in your worksite cafeteria, if available. For example, it may offer fresh fruit, offer a discount for a meal with vegetables, or sell healthier items in vending machines. Check if your company has access to a farmers' market or a wellness program with a healthy weight challenge.
- Lunch hour with coworkers? Order sparkling water with a lemon twist when you need to feel alert at work. An alcoholic drink may make you drowsy and deliver extra calories. Blood-alcohol levels from two drinks may stay with you for the better part of the afternoon—a risk, too, if you drive or use potentially dangerous equipment on your job.
- Snack breaks? Pre-portion your own single-serving snack packs at home to control amounts—¼ cup dried fruit or unsalted tree nuts

Your Workday: Time to Move, Too!

Many of today's jobs are sedentary. However, evidence shows that moderate to vigorous activity not only impacts overall health and body weight but also helps improve job performance and relieve workday stress.

- Take short stress breaks; stretch your legs. A brisk ten-minute walk may be enough. Stretch your muscles, and hold for thirty seconds. Relieve shoulder and neck tension by tilting your head from side to side and front to back. Use stretching or exercise bands or weights. Or switch tasks for a while. Avoid the urge to nibble for stress relief or as a break.
- If you have a desk job, get a standing desk as a way to change positions. Sit on a large yoga ball as you work to engage your core muscles.
- Schedule walking meetings, indoors or out, and in pairs or groups. Besides the benefit of physical activity, they may help to boost productivity, creativity, and team building. Set a start and end place and a walking course.
- Get your coworkers moving with you. Walk or take a fitness class during the lunch hour. Use the workplace fitness center if it's an employee benefit. Team up in an after-work volleyball, softball, or bowling league.
- Make time to move. If you work at home, you miss the routine walk from the parking lot, bus, or train. Use your unique opportunities for an action break: walk the dog, dig in the garden, or swim in the neighborhood pool.

or peanuts. If your snacks are perishable, keep them in the workplace fridge or a cold, insulated container; *see "Snacks Count!" in this chapter, page 75.*

- What about office parties? When it's your turn to bring doughnuts, bring fruit instead, hummus with unsalted pita chips, or a trail mix with nuts and dried fruit. When cake or cookies are offered, enjoy just a small piece to limit added sugars and saturated fats.

DESKTOP DINING: A GOOD IDEA?

Perhaps—if you're really in a time crunch. And it may be convenient. But if this is your regular mode of operation, give it extra thought. Here's why:

- First, food safety: Your desktop (likely your keyboard and phone, too) is among the most germy things you touch—even more than a toilet seat, according a university study! If you do eat at your desk, use a sanitizer to clean its surface, and wash your hands before eating.
- Eating solo at your desk or in your work cubicle doesn't give you a chance to connect with colleagues, staff, or your boss. Often, positive interaction over food is a chance to problem solve, provide feedback, and encourage collaboration. If you need to, schedule time with a colleague for a working lunch.
- Sometimes deciding to eat deskside results in forgetting to eat! Evidence shows that skipping meals doesn't promote productivity or health in the long run.
- Think your pack-and-carry meal is healthier? That depends on what you choose—and what's available if you prefer to buy a quick take-out meal. Think variety and nutrient-rich foods (food groups), along with food safety, when you pack a meal—and think beyond oh-so-common homemade sandwiches. *See "Packing Meals and Snacks Safely" in chapter 7, page 217, to learn how to avoid foodborne illness from carried meals.*
- Eating should be enjoyable. Take fifteen to twenty minutes to give yourself a mental break and to eat and enjoy your food—even if you're alone. Put aside your computer screen or cell phone to eat mindfully. If you're distracted from eating, you may eat more (too many calories) than your body needs.
- Choose desk-drawer snacks wisely. *See "Snacks: Easy, Convenient, Nourishing" in this chapter, page 77, for ideas.*

HEALTHY EATING: YOUR HOME OFFICE

Work from a home office? If you're used to a company cafeteria or a nearby deli, you may need to redesign your workday meal approach when you start working from home.

- Keep to a routine. Instead of rolling out of bed and into your home office, start with breakfast and perhaps a morning walk. Try to set a regular lunchtime.
- Stock your kitchen for nourishing, quick-to-prepare workday meals and snacks: chef's salads, leftovers, or made-ahead chili or hearty soups with whole-grain crackers and milk.
- Occasionally change your lunch venue. Make a lunch date with other home-based workers. The social context and networking may be as valuable as a nourishing meal.
- Take advantage of working at home for dinner food prep. As a work break, start after-work meals. Perhaps simmer a pot of bean soup, or put a turkey breast, roast, or dinner casserole in the oven.

Brunch, Lunch, Dinner

A morning meal is a great start to the day, but how do your other meals balance it out? Make sure they provide a variety of nutrient-rich foods to help complete your daily food plan.

GUIDELINES FOR MEALTIME

Turning healthy eating guidelines into healthy everyday meals, or even several mini-meals, starts with planning. There are key priorities: food variety—vegetables, fruits, whole and enriched grains, low-fat or fat-free milk and other dairy foods, and lean protein foods. Remember healthy oils, and restrict added sugars and saturated fats. *See chapter 2, page 21, for more about healthy eating guidelines.*

Consider these tips as you plan your meals:

- Make half your meal fruits and vegetables. Fit in red, orange, and dark-green vegetables, such as tomatoes, sweet potatoes, and broccoli as main and side dishes. Choose mostly whole fruits, rather than juice.
- Make half your grains whole grains. Try brown rice, farro, quinoa, and whole-grain pasta and bread; *see "Grains, Grains, and More Grains" in chapter 2, page 31, for more ways to vary your options.* For the rest, choose enriched grain foods without much added sugars or solid fats.
- Include a variety of lean protein foods—with about 25 grams of protein per person in a meal. Vary your protein choices. Occasionally consider eggs, perhaps in quiche or a frittata, or simply scrambled or hard cooked. Twice a week, make fish the protein food on your plate. Plan for beans such as garbanzo or black beans, and soy-based foods such as tofu or tempeh as protein options, too. Add nuts or seeds. For more protein, you can also choose grains with more protein such as quinoa. *See chapter 12, page 373, for more about protein and the protein content of typical foods.*
- Make beverages part of your meal planning—and make them count for good nutrition. Low-fat or fat-free milk and water are great choices,—or perhaps unsweetened tea or coffee. If you've missed out on fruit during the day, consider 100 percent juice. If you choose an alcoholic drink, plan for moderation. Limit or skip sugary drinks such as soda as they deliver a lot of added sugars. *See chapter 4, page 81, to compare drink options, including non-dairy alternatives.*
- Size your portions right. Eat the amount for the day to match your energy (calorie) need. *See "A Day's Family Menu: Three Calorie Levels" in this chapter, page 65.*
- Dessert? Make whole fruit a frequent option, perhaps served with a scoop of frozen yogurt. If you like cakes, cookies, and other sweet desserts, serve them but only occasionally, and keep portions small.

MEALS: QUICK, EASY, HEALTHY

Like many people, you probably don't spend much time preparing a family meal—at least on most weekdays—even if you're a foodie. According to current market research, most people devote less than fifteen minutes to daily dinner prep. Many don't decide on a menu until the end of the workday.

When time and energy are in short supply, don't give up on healthy eating. Just take shortcuts. A simple meal can be as healthy and delicious as one that takes more time. Make it easy!

Planning Matters

With busy schedules, planning makes a difference. Here's how:

- Have a week's worth of meals in mind. Include meals made from leftovers. For example, grilled-chicken Caesar salad could be made with sliced, leftover grilled chicken breasts.
- Plan ahead for speed-scratch meal prep. Buy foods ready for assembly and cooking such as precut stir-fry vegetables, shredded cabbage, prewashed bagged salad greens, kale, or spinach, already-cut melon, skinless chicken strips, prepared sauces and grated cheese. Thin-sliced, lean deli meats are great in quick stir-fry recipes.
- Stock up on quick-to-fix foods: pasta, rice, frozen and canned vegetables and fruits, bread, lean deli meats, eggs, prewashed greens, sliced fruits or vegetables, salsa, canned beans, milk, yogurt, and cheese, among others. Check the Nutrition Facts labels to make the healthiest choices; *see "Nutrition: Fact Check!" in chapter 6, page 148, for tips on reading food labels.* With a wide variety of great choices on hand, you won't need to worry about what's for dinner. *See "Shopping List: Stocking a Healthy Kitchen," in chapter 6, page 143.*
- Many of these and other prepared foods need nothing more than to be cooked, heated, or assembled on your plate. For example, it's easy to toss together a simple salad to go with a heat-and-eat pot roast or a rotisserie chicken and microwaved potatoes. Or pick up a prepared salad at the supermarket to use as a new side dish to complement last night's leftover main dish. Finally, be aware that many prepared foods are high in sodium, so be sure to check the Nutrition Facts labels to make the healthiest choices. *See "Keep Takeout Safe" in chapter 9, page 288, for tips on take-out food.* For prepared foods in your meals, such as soup, bread, and frozen meals, choose those with less sodium, added sugars, and saturated fats.
- Have a backup meal in mind for when you get home too late to prepare a meal, or when your original plan doesn't pan out. Improvise with ingredients you have on hand. Think omelets, chef's salads, pasta tossed with halved cherry tomatoes and shredded cheese, or grilled cheese sandwiches and an apple. *See "Quick Meals with Foods on Hand" in this chapter, page 72.*
- Organize your pantry and refrigerator so healthy options are visible and within easy reach for you and those in your family who cook.
- Keep your counters free of clutter and food so you have room to prepare meals without stress.
- Stay flexible. Switch your meal plans around if you need to accommodate unexpected family activities. You can always eat a breakfast menu for a light supper if time is short.

Global Table: Varied, Healthy, Enjoyable

Planning menus? Add great nutrition with a multicultural array of foods. Think about Mediterranean tabbouleh (bulgur salad) or a cucumber-yogurt dip; Brazilian black bean soup; a Korean bibimbap bowl of cooked rice, vegetables, and an egg; Indian vegetable curries; Spanish paella (a rice dish with meat, seafood, chicken, vegetables, and sometimes beans); Thai pad thai (a stir-fried dish with rice noodles, bean sprouts, eggs, peanuts, and shrimp, chicken, or tofu); or Ethiopian injera (bread) with meat, beans or peas, and vegetable dishes served on top. To continue to be adventuresome:

- Try unfamiliar foods at ethnic or regional restaurants or at local ethnic festivals. *See "Eating Ethnic, Eating Global" in chapter 9, page 297, for more tips about ethnic foods.*
- Be a foodie when you travel, rather than settle for familiar fast-food fare. Explore what the locals eat.
- Buy an ethnic cookbook or magazine; go online for recipes, a food prep video or blog; or check out the food shows on TV.
- Learn "hands on" from an ethnic cooking class, culinary trip, or local tour. Ask a friend who prepares his or her family's ethnic dishes to invite you to dinner or, even better, teach you a dish or two.
- Shop the ethnic food section of your supermarket, or go to an ethnic food store. If you try an ethnic market, ask other customers or store staff for food preparation advice.

Food Group/Item*	**Cuisine**	**Serving/Preparation Ideas**
GRAIN GROUP		
Whole-wheat couscous (tiny, round pasta)	Moroccan	Serve hot with tomato sauce and Parmesan cheese, or serve cold as a salad with raisins, mandarin oranges, and spices.
Kasha (buckwheat kernels)	Eastern European	Serve as a hot side dish with chicken or beef. Mix with pasta shapes.
Pozole (soup made with fermented corn kernels)	Mexican	Serve warm with diced onions, shredded cabbage, and a lime wedge.
Wonton wrappers (thin wheat dough used to wrap spring rolls)	Chinese, Vietnamese	Wrap with thin strips of cooked lean barbecued pork or chicken, shredded cabbage, and shredded carrots inside the wrappers, and then steam the spring rolls.
VEGETABLE GROUP		
Jicama	Mexican	Slice into thin strips, and dip into salsa or reduced-fat or fat-free ranch dressing. Use to replace water chestnuts in stir-fry dishes.
Collard greens	African American / Southern	Sauté with chopped, smoked turkey, vinegar, and seasonings.
Tomatillos	Mexican	Dice and mix with jalapeño peppers for salsa. Dice and combine with onions for an omelet.
Shiitake mushrooms	Japanese	Add raw to salads and sandwiches, or toss in stir-fry dishes.
FRUIT GROUP		
Lychee	Chinese	Serve on top of frozen yogurt.
Papaya	Mexican, Central American	Blend with pineapple for tropical juices, dice and add to salsas, or simmer in a chutney recipe.
Plantain	Puerto Rican, Central American	Cube and add to stews and soups.
Mango	Caribbean	Slice for fruit salads, or simmer in a chutney recipe.

Global Table: Varied, Healthy, Enjoyable *(continued)*

Food Group/Item*	Cuisine	Serving/Preparation Ideas
PROTEIN FOODS GROUP		
Squid	Mediterranean, Asian	Slice into rings and broil; serve with marinara sauce. Or cook in stir-fry dishes.
Veal, lamb	Mediterranean	Marinate in Italian vinaigrette and then grill.
Hummus (mashed chickpeas)	Middle Eastern	Serve as a dip for raw vegetables or pita triangles.
Chorizo (sausage)	Mexican	Slice into bite-size pieces; add to omelets or stews.
Tempeh	Japanese, Chinese	Slice for stir-fry dishes, or dice for salads or soups.
Black beans	Latin American	Use in place of red beans in chili or soup, mash for homemade refried beans, or mix with rice.
DAIRY GROUP		
Plain Greek yogurt	Middle Eastern	Top falafel sandwiches (chickpea- and vegetable-stuffed pita), or blend with mint to use as a dip or dressing for cucumbers.
Goat milk	Middle Eastern, African (some areas)	Serve plain for drinking, or mix with juice to make a thick drink. Use in place of cow's milk for baking.
Quark (curd cheese)	Central/Eastern Europe	Use as a spread or as an ingredient in mixed dishes and desserts.
Ricotta cheese	Italian	Use in lasagna or as a filling for jumbo pasta shells. Shred and melt over enchiladas and quesadillas.
Queso blanco (white cheese)**	Mexican	Shred and melt over enchiladas and quesadillas.

*These foods may be used in the dishes of many global cuisines.

**To reduce the risk of foodborne illness, look for queso blanco made from pasteurized milk.

See "Culinary Basics: Plan, Prepare, Serve" in chapter 8, page 231, for more about menu planning. See "Sample Menus for a 2000 Calorie Food Pattern" in the appendix, page 778.

Everyday Challenges, Everyday Meal Solutions

If you're a three-meal-a-day family, you have more than 1,000 meals a year to consider—with about 700 of them being lunch or supper! Some of those meals are likely to be eaten away from your home, some at school for kids, and some, perhaps, packed and carried. Still, many are apt to be prepared or eaten in your home.

For solutions to the challenges of preparing and serving healthy, everyday meals, consider these strategies:

Challenge: Tired, don't feel like cooking, no time for meal prep

Solutions: Preparing and serving a great meal doesn't need to take much time or energy. To put a meal on the table after a busy work or volunteer day, you can:

- Prep ingredients ahead. For example, wash and trim broccoli florets. Skewer kabobs with vegetable and meat pieces the night before as you clean up from dinner. Cook lean ground meat ahead for soft tacos. Assemble packets of fish and sliced vegetables in foil, ready to bake and serve.
- Give your slow cooker a workout. Start your meal in the morning, and it will be ready by suppertime. Tip: Pre-prep the ingredients the night before and refrigerate overnight so they're ready in the morning.

Quick Meals with Foods on Hand

Prepare these quick meals with the basics, or check your pantry and fridge for other ingredients to add variety and "jazz up" your meal. These ideas may get your creativity flowing:

- **Chef's salad:** Toss a chef salad with fresh greens, raw veggies, lean deli meats, and vinaigrette. Serve with whole-grain bread, fresh or canned fruit in juice, and low-fat or fat-free milk.

  Jazz it up: Toss in jarred artichoke hearts, Kalamata olives, reduced-fat feta cheese, garbanzo or other beans, sliced avocado, dried cranberries or cherries, sliced almonds, chopped hazelnuts, or hemp or sunflower seeds—and use homemade balsamic vinaigrette.

- **Veggie omelet:** Cook a vegetable omelet (or frittata) with leftover vegetables or no-salt-added canned vegetables, and shredded cheese. Serve with a whole-wheat bagel or toast and whole fruit. (It's not just for breakfast!)

  Jazz it up: Add sundried tomatoes, sliced mushrooms, shredded carrots, shredded kale, chopped green onions or bell peppers, or fresh herbs.

- **Chicken stir-fry:** Stir-fry sliced chicken breast with frozen, canned, or fresh vegetables (perhaps sliced mushrooms, bell peppers, carrots, radishes, summer squash, green beans, and asparagus). Serve over cooked brown rice, whole-wheat couscous, quinoa, or another cooked whole grain. Serve with frozen yogurt with fruit, and unsweetened tea.

  Jazz it up: Mix in chopped cashews or unsalted peanuts, pumpkin seeds (pepitas), or hemp seeds. Add more vegetables, such as sliced leeks, zucchini, or bell peppers, or cut-up butternut squash. Or serve over sautéed kale, spinach, or spaghetti squash.

- **"Homemade" pizza:** Load up a frozen pizza with more veggies, in any form—fresh, frozen, or canned. Serve with fruit and low-fat or fat-free milk. Or keep prepared pizza crust (perhaps whole grain) on hand to create your own.

  Jazz it up: Top with sundried tomatoes, sautéed spinach or kale (arranged under the cheese if built from scratch), shredded zucchini, or fresh herbs. You might even break an egg into the middle and bake the pizza until the egg is done.

- **Panini:** Make this grilled sandwich with bread (preferably whole grain), lean beef or ham, sliced chicken or turkey, cheese, and sliced tomatoes. Serve with water flavored with a lemon slice.

  Jazz *it up:* Switch the bread to ciabatta or a baguette. Spread the bread with pesto or sun-dried tomato paste, and layer on roasted portobello mushrooms, eggplant, bell peppers, or basil leaves.

For more time savings, prepackage your own slow-cooker freezer meals. Pack all the recipe ingredients in a zippered freezer bag or a covered freezer container. For efficiency, package several weeks' worth at a time, label, and freeze. For an easy meal, thaw in refrigerator overnight, then in the morning, pop them in the slow cooker and flip the switch to "cook." When it's time to eat, prepare appropriate sides such as a salad, cooked brown or white rice, or mashed potatoes. Search online for recipe ideas and cooking settings and times.

- For convenience, use frozen ingredients, such as vegetables or precooked meatballs, or microwaveable packaged fresh vegetables, such as spinach or green beans in any menu planning.
- Use quick cooking methods. Stir-frying, broiling, and microwaving are faster than baking or roasting. Slice meat and poultry thinly for faster cooking.
- Use kitchen equipment that cuts prep time. For example, rinse and dry vegetables in a salad spinner. Chop onions in a food processor. Puree soup with an immersion blender. Snip herbs with kitchen shears. Grate garlic and ginger faster with a kitchen grater or zester. Thaw foods faster in a microwave oven. *See "Tools of the Culinary Trade" in chapter 8, page 233, for more about kitchen tools.*
- Multi-batch. For example, cook double or triple batches of crumbled ground beef; freeze the extra for tacos or spaghetti later. Or simmer enough pasta for two days. Serve it hot one night with meat sauce, and then chilled in a salad with tuna or shrimp, chopped veggies, and low-fat salad dressing the next.
- Prepare meals that pack variety in just one dish. Try chicken fajitas with cooked veggies in a soft taco. Stuff tuna or vegetable salad into a pita. Prepare a smoked salmon and spinach quiche. Make a chef's salad—no cooking needed. Prepare risotto with seafood, chard or kale, and shredded cheese, or a stir-fry with noodles, tofu, and vegetables.
- Cook on weekends, and save food-prep time on weekdays. (It's a great time to package freezer slow-cooker meals.) Freeze leftovers in individual-meal containers for quick thawing midweek.
- Involve everyone in the family in meal prep, from start to finish, from planning to serving to clean up. Preparing a meal can be everyone's responsibility. *See "'I Can Help': Kitchen Tasks for Kids of Every Age" in chapter 17, page 498, for age-appropriate kitchen tasks for kids.*

Family Meals Matter

Can you get your family together at mealtime at least a few times a week? Research shows that shared meals promote healthier eating—more fruits, vegetables, and fiber; less fried food; and often fewer calories. And they do far more than put healthy food on the table.

In the haste to get meals prepared, you may forget that mealtimes are good times to talk, listen, and build family relationships. Plus, they're opportunities for parents and other adult caregivers to be good role models for healthy eating. Try to make it routine:

- Set a regular family mealtime. Pick a time together.
- Enjoy more table time and less cooking time. Make quick, simple meals (even a sandwich, fruit, and milk) to allow for more table time together.
- Turn off the TV. Set cell phones, tablets, and other hand-held digital devices aside. Focus mealtimes on family talk.
- Keep table talk positive. Everyone gets to talk and listen. Sitting around a table, not side by side at a counter, helps.
- Keep table time realistic—not so long that the pleasure goes away.

See "Shared Meals Matter" in chapter 17, page 491, for more about the benefits of eating together at the family table.

Challenge: In a rut; bored by the same menus

Solutions: You don't need to prepare the same menus over and over (except for family favorites). To switch up your menus for variety, you can:

- Reinvent your favorite dishes. *See the jazzed-up versions of popular dishes in "Quick Meals with Foods on Hand" on the previous page.*
- Go meatless sometimes, using ideas in this chapter.
- Eat breakfast for lunch or dinner (and vice versa). Many of the two-minute breakfast ideas in this chapter make nourishing, light, and quick midday or supper meals, too.
- Serve an old favorite in a new way. For example, for a pasta dinner, use spaghetti squash instead of linguini or spaghetti. Arrange grilled chicken over a bed of sautéed greens. Or make a classic tuna casserole with salmon instead, and add some chopped veggies!

Challenge: Different family schedules

Solutions: You don't need to be a short-order cook to provide healthy meals for family members with different schedules. On your own timetable, you can:

- Make "assemble-your-own" meals to allow for personal preferences and time schedules. Have the ingredients ready for foods such as deli sandwiches or wraps, mini-pizzas on English muffins, or tacos. Everyone makes his or her own.
- Prepare one-pot meals such as hearty chilies, stews, and similar dishes made in a slow cooker or not. These can be kept warm or simply reheated.
- Package your own frozen dinners in small freezer- and microwave-friendly containers, ready to pop in the microwave oven. When you multi-batch, you can make enough for a family meal and then divide the rest into single meals and freeze for later.

MEATLESS ON THE MENU

Pasta salad with tofu and vegetables. Polenta topped with homemade tomato sauce and freshly grated Parmesan cheese. Bean burritos. Portobello mushroom sandwiches layered with cheese, stir-fried onions, and bell peppers. Split-pea soup with rye bread. Whether you go meatless all the time or sometimes, vegetarian dishes can add food variety and flavor to healthy eating.

- Like any meal, vary the foods in your meatless meals with foods from all groups. Look for vegetarian recipes that use whole grains,

Your Healthy Eating Check-in

Does Your Supper Pass These Tests?

Color-Crunch Test: Try to choose fruits and vegetables with a variety of colors. Vary the textures, too!

Whole Test: Serve a whole-grain version of the bread, rolls, rice, or pasta in your meal to help you make at least half of your grains whole.

½-¼-¼ Test: Fill half your plate with vegetables and fruits, one quarter with grain foods (mostly whole grain), and one quarter with lean protein foods. (This general guideline isn't as easy to follow with mixed dishes, but try.) And did you add dairy as a beverage or other side?

Use MyPlate as a visual cue to healthy eating. *See "MyPlate: Build a Healthy Meal" in chapter 2, page 25, and www .ChooseMyPlate.gov.*

Vegetarian Menu*: How a Day's Choices Stack Up

To make food preparation fast and easy, choose dishes that everyone—vegetarians and nonvegetarians—around your table will enjoy. This sample vegetarian menu was planned for a 2,000-calorie-a-day eating plan, using the Healthy Vegetarian Eating Pattern, *described in chapter 2, page 53, and shown in the appendix, page 775.*

BREAKFAST

½ cup uncooked oats, made with ½ cup low-fat milk (or calcium- and vitamin D–fortified soymilk)

½ ounce slivered, unsalted almonds

2 tablespoons dried cranberries

½ cup carrot juice

12-ounce latte, made with low-fat milk (or calcium- and vitamin D–fortified soymilk)

LUNCH

1½ cups bean soup (mixed beans)

1 whole-wheat tortilla with ¼ cup mango salsa

2 slices jicama

2 slices red bell pepper

1 low-fat granola bar with oats, fruit, and nuts

10 ounces -fat-free milk (or calcium- and vitamin D–fortified soymilk)

SNACKS

8 pita chips

¼ cup hummus

½ cup seedless grapes

12 ounces sparkling water with lime slice

DINNER

1 cup tofu sir-fry with carrots, broccoli, and/or dark-green leafy vegetables, a soy-based sauce, and ½ ounce unsalted cashews

¾ cup cooked brown rice

½ cup fresh fruit salad (grapefruit and orange sections with mint)

1 medium scoop frozen vanilla low-fat yogurt or frozen soy yogurt topped with ½ cup sliced strawberries

2 small oatmeal cookies with raisins

12 ounces unsweetened iced tea

DAILY AMOUNTS

	Healthy Vegetarian Eating Pattern	This Menu
Calories	**2,000**	**1,998**
FOOD GROUP		
Grains	6½ ounce-equivalents (more than half as whole grain)	6½ ounce-equivalents (more than half as whole grain)
Vegetables	2½ cups	2¾ cups
Fruits	2 cup-equivalents	2 cup-equivalents
Dairy	3 cup-equivalents	3 cup-equivalents
Protein foods	3½ ounce-equivalents	4½ ounce-equivalents
Oils	6 teaspoons	6 teaspoons

*Planned using the SuperTracker from www.ChooseMyPlate.gov.

beans, and vegetables in unfamiliar ways—perhaps a lentil stew, a vegetable-quinoa tagine (North African stew), chickpea succotash with tomatoes and yellow squash, or tofu or tempeh stir-fried with bok choy and shiitake mushrooms.

- Create your menu so protein foods such as beans and lentils, tofu or tempeh, soyburgers, Greek yogurt, or eggs (if you eat them) take center stage. Go easy on cheeses since they're high in saturated fats; nuts and nut butters are high in heart-healthy oils. *See "Stocking the Vegetarian Kitchen" in chapter 6, page 187, for shopping tips.*
- Especially if menus are vegan (no dairy or eggs), fit fortified soymilk, tofu, and soy yogurt into your meals, as well as plant-based sources of calcium, such as bok choy, broccoli, and kale, and calcium-fortified foods, such as some juices. Be aware that some vegetables that deliver calcium, such as spinach and rhubarb, are also high in oxalates, which decrease calcium absorption.
- Experiment with vegetarian food products made with soy protein or beans created as meat alternatives. Try veggie burgers in place of beef or turkey patties. For outdoor grilling,

cook soy hot dogs, marinated tofu or tempeh, and veggie kabobs. These foods are usually lower in saturated fats than their animal-based counterparts and are cholesterol free. Check the Nutrition Facts label, however, as some are high in saturated fats and sodium.

- Use veggie crumbles to transform meat dishes into vegetarian ones. The crumbles, typically made with soy, work well in dishes such as lasagna, fajitas, meatloaf, and chili. When you use them, you'll boost the amount of vegetables in your meal and cut saturated fats at the same time. *See "Recipe Makeovers: Healthy Vegetarian" in chapter 8, page 237.*
- Look for vegetarian dishes within Asian, Indo-Pakistani, Middle Eastern, African, and Latin American cuisines. Perhaps find a recipe for kuku, an Iranian egg dish, or for chakalaka, a spicy South African vegetable dish. *For ideas, see "Global Table: Varied, Healthy, Enjoyable!" in this chapter, page 70, or "Eating Ethnic, Eating Global" in chapter 9, page 297.*

See "The Healthy Vegetarian Way" in chapter 2, page 53.

MINI-MEALS: ANOTHER MEALTIME APPROACH

Many Americans—young adults especially—have moved from three "square meals" a day to several mini meals, a shift that matches on-the-go lifestyles for some and small appetites for others. That's okay—as long as healthy eating goals for the day are met and as long as you don't overeat and so go beyond your calorie limits.

Eating patterns, *described in chapter 2, page 21,* are guidelines for how much to eat over an entire day or averaged over several days. Eating five or six mini-meals a day can be as healthy as eating three.

Little meals—several small portions eaten throughout the day—are nothing new. They've been part of many traditional cuisines for years:

- Small traditional Spanish dishes, such as garlic shrimp, cod croquettes, or potato tortilla, are served as tapas or pinchos.
- In Greece, Turkey, and parts of the Middle East, these small plates are called mezze and might include stuffed grape leaves or chickpea patties.
- A little meal, or spuntino, in Italy might be a mini pizza, grilled bread with tomatoes and cheese, or small skewers of meat and vegetables.
- Dim sum, meaning "to touch the heart" in Chinese, is a savory snack of spring rolls, pot stickers, and steamed dumplings, to name a few.

Chosen wisely and mindfully, mini-meals can contribute enough nutrient-rich foods from all the food groups. The challenge is eating enough variety of foods without overeating. Eating mini-meals mindlessly can lead to excesses: excess calories, excess solid fats, excess added sugars, and excess sodium.

So pay attention and follow advice from the USDA Food Patterns or the DASH Eating Plan, *discussed in chapter 2, page 21,* for the right amounts and food variety; an app to track your food choices and count calories may help. *See "Two Minutes: Breakfast, Lunch, Mini-Meal" earlier in this chapter, page 64, for menu ideas.*

Snacks Count!

What does the word "snack" imply to you: a type of food, an eating event, or eating frequently? There's no single definition, but generally snacks are foods and drinks consumed in addition to (and perhaps in between) meals. With many different definitions, researching the links between snacking and health gets complicated!

Are you hungry? Need a nutrient boost or a meal replacement? Crave something salty or sweet? Feel bored or upset? Enjoy the social interaction that goes with a snack? So . . . is snacking a positive or a negative? That depends on what you snack on, how much, and when.

SMART SNACKING: BENEFITS

When mindfully chosen to satisfy hunger, snacks can supply foods and nutrients that often come up short during the day. Snacks offer a way to eat more vegetables, fruits, whole-grain foods, and low-fat and fat-free dairy foods—all good things!

In fact, snacks can add positively to your nutritional bottom line—if you keep your calories under control and if your choices contribute toward your food-group goals. For example, munching on a handful of baby carrots can help you meet your day's vitamin A needs, and a planned snack may help prevent overeating later.

- For active children and teens, snacks can supplement meals. Because children's stomachs are smaller, they may need to eat more often to get the calories (food energy) they need—and to provide foods missing from their meals. Physically active, growing teens may need the added calories that snacks supply. No evidence shows that frequent eating is linked to overweight in very young children. *See "Snacking for Good Nutrition" in chapter 17, page 493, for more about snacking for kids and teens.*
- For adults, a snack can provide an energy boost and satisfy midday hunger.
- For older adults with small appetites or limited energy, several small meals may be easier to handle. Besides, there's social value in enjoying a snack with others. *See "Meals and Snacks: Make Calories Count!" in chapter 20, page 575, for more about snacking for older adults.*
- For athletes of every age, snacks help fuel the increased energy demands of their sports and help them to refuel afterwards. In fact, a light snack about two hours before exercise may improve performance. A low-fat snack with carbohydrates and some protein is a good choice—perhaps low-fat yogurt with fruit; crackers

A Closer Look . . .

Snacking: Myth or Truth?

Snacking: a smart habit—or not? Actually, there's no need to feel guilty about snacking. In fact, here's the truth behind common snacking myths.

Myth: Snacks are fattening!

Truth: There's no direct link between snacking and body weight. The issue is related to total calories in and out. Snacking may be advantageous for weight control. Eaten during the stretch between meals, snacks help take the edge off hunger, helping you avoid overeating at meals.

For smart snacking, choose foods carefully to fit within your day's calorie target; be sensible with mega-size and empty-calorie snacks and drinks. To dispel another snacking misconception: Frequent snacks won't boost metabolic rate enough for weight loss.

Myth: Snacking causes cavities.

Truth: Frequent snacking can promote cavities but not cause them. The longer teeth come into contact with food, particularly any food with carbohydrates (not just sugars), the more time the bacteria in plaque have to produce acids that damage tooth enamel. Foods with carbohydrates include grain products, fruits, vegetables, and milk, as well as regular sodas and candy.

To control a plaque attack, consume the whole snack at one time rather than nibble constantly. Choose snacks that aren't sticky. Brush and/or floss afterward to remove food that sticks to and between teeth, or rinse your mouth with water. Some cheeses have qualities that may protect against cavity formation. *See "Oral Health: Your Healthy Smile" in chapter 25, page 735, for more about oral health.*

Myth: Snack foods aren't good for you.

Truth: To the contrary, snacks can be any food! How healthy they are depends on what foods you choose. Snacks such as baby carrots or a tangerine can help fill the food-group gaps in your day's meal plan. Ease up on snacks that are high in solid fats, added sugars, and calories, such as cupcakes, cookies, candy, and regular soft drinks. Go easy on snacks high in sodium, too, such as chips and salted peanuts and nuts.

Myth: Snacking isn't a good habit for kids to learn.

Truth: With their high-energy needs and small stomachs, most children need snacks. And so do teens. *See "Snacking for Good Nutrition" and "Healthy, No-Cook Snacks for Kids" in chapter 17, pages 493 and 498, for more on snacks and kids.* Three daily meals often aren't enough to provide all the nutrients and calories (food energy) they need. The advice for parents: Help children learn good snacking habits that satisfy hunger without overeating.

Myth: Snacks spoil your appetite.

Truth: It's all about timing! Eaten two to three hours before meals, a small snack, such as a banana or half a turkey sandwich, won't ruin your appetite. Snacks may quell hunger pangs so you are less likely to overeat at the next meal.

Myth: Healthy snacking means giving up fun foods.

Truth: Any food can be a snack—even a small amount of chips, sweets, or soda. Keep the portion small:

1 ounce, or 22, potato chips (150 calories)

8 to 12 ounces regular soda (100 to 150 calories)

3 pieces hard candy or 15 jelly beans (about 60 calories)

Count these in your calorie and added sugars budgets for the day. These are the extra calories you may have after you meet your food-group goals—if it matches your calorie limit.

If you eat a small, higher-calorie snack, balance it with fewer calories at mealtime. Remember, the more physically active you are, the bigger your calorie budget. Again, use the USDA Food Patterns, *described in chapter 2, page 21,* as your guide.

and low-fat cheese; or a granola bar. Include fluid for hydration. Because timing is individual, adjust to what works best for you if you're active in sports. *See chapter 21, page 559, for more about eating right for athletes.*

POOR SNACKING: CONSEQUENCES

Benefits aside, snacking often gets a bad rap, for good reasons:

- Too often, people snack on energy-dense, low-nutrient foods and drinks and then skimp on nutrient-rich foods and drinks at meals.
- Oversnacking can lead to excess calories.
- Poor choices can result in too many added sugars and saturated fats and too much sodium. Compared with moderate snackers, research suggests that people who frequently

Snacks: Easy, Convenient, Nourishing

Snacks to . . .	Nutrient-Rich Options
Keep on hand at home	Whole fruits, washed and cut-up raw veggies, low-fat or fat-free yogurt and milk, cottage cheese, low-fat cheese, string cheese, lean deli meats, hummus or salsa, frozen juice bars, frozen yogurt, whole-grain crackers, pita bread, dried fruits, nuts, nut butter, yogurt drinks
Keep at work for late or busy workdays	Mini-cans of water-packed tuna, instant oatmeal or couscous, dried fruits or single-serve fruit cups, whole-wheat crackers, snack-size cereal boxes, boxes of raisins, soy nuts, plain microwavable popcorn, whole-grain granola or cereal bars. For cereal bars, check the Nutrition Facts label for calories per serving; choose those with whole grains, nuts, and dried fruits.
Pack to take along	Soy nuts, sunflower seeds, air-popped popcorn (sprinkled with dried herbs or chile powder), whole fruits, dried fruits, oatmeal-raisin cookies, dried fruit-nut mixes, whole-wheat crackers and low-fat cheese, or canned or boxed 100 percent juice
Choose from a vending machine—if available	Small bag of peanuts, almonds, trail mix; dried fruit (raisins, cranberries, apricots); whole-grain granola or cereal bars; 100 percent fruit or vegetable juice; whole-wheat crackers with peanut butter or cheese; microwaveable soup or oatmeal; and, if available, whole fruit, and low-fat or fat-free milk (flavored or unflavored)
Limit sugary drinks	Water or sparkling water (perhaps with a slice of fruit or a berry), low-fat or fat-free milk, fortified soymilk, yogurt drinks, juice spritzers (juice and mineral water), fruit smoothies (fruit or juice blended with milk or yogurt), hot chocolate. Be aware: fruit-flavored waters may be high in added sugars; check the Nutrition Facts label.
Include two food groups	• Fruit smoothie (fruit or 100 percent juice with low-fat or fat-free milk, fortified soymilk, or yogurt) • Apple or pear slices topped with sliced cheese • Dried berry and nut mix • Whole-wheat tortilla stuffed with roasted veggies, or with lettuce, tomato, cucumber, and low-fat dressing • Raw veggies with hummus or Greek yogurt dip • Grapes and yogurt drink • Microwaved sweet potato topped with Swiss cheese shreds

consume a lot of sugary drinks or sweets tend to take in less calcium.

- Snacking too close to mealtime may ruin an appetite for nutrient-rich meals.

MINDFUL SNACKING

Did you know that watching television tends to increase snacking and that people eat or drink more when the snack package or beverage cup is bigger? Snack mindfully, not mindlessly. Overeating is easy if you nibble mindlessly as you watch TV or spend time online. Consider these tips:

- Keep a variety of tasty, nutrient-rich, ready-to-eat snacks on hand for whenever you need a light bite to take the edge off hunger. If you do, you won't be limited by what's available from vending machines, fast-food restaurants, convenience stores, or your own randomly stocked kitchen.
- Portion out the snack. Put it on a plate or in a dish instead of eating directly from the package. That way you know how much you've eaten.
- Make snack calories count. Choose foods to fill food-group gaps in your day: perhaps fruits, vegetables, whole grains, and low-fat or fat-free dairy foods.
- Go easy on energy-dense, nutrient-poor snacks (candy, juice drinks, regular soft drinks, others) with high levels of fat, especially solid fats, added sugars, and/or sodium. Choose them only occasionally, and keep portions small.
- Snack when you're hungry—not because you're bored, frustrated, or stressed. Feed an emotional urge to munch by walking the dog, checking your e-mail, or calling or texting someone instead.
- Keep snack portions sensible. Choose a single-serve container, or put a small helping in a bowl. Skip mega- or super-size drinks and snacks.
- Use food labels to choose. If a snack package says two servings and you eat the whole amount, you double the calories, solid fats,

? Have you ever wondered?

. . . what slow food is? It's a term used to refer to the slow-food movement, which encourages people to take their time to enjoy food and food traditions. Consider how time at the table may add pleasure, great flavors, and social time to your life. Eating slower also may help you eat less as you pay attention to satiety cues. That's also called mindful eating! *See "Eating: Mindless or Mindful?" below, for more about mindful eating.*

and sodium in a single serving! *See "Food Labels: Decode the Package" in chapter 6, page 144, for more on reading labels.*

- Snack well before mealtime. A light bite two to three hours ahead probably won't interfere with your appetite—and may divert a temptation to snack heavily right before dinner. To stave off hunger longer, pick snacks with protein and fiber, such as peanut butter on celery, or cheese and whole-wheat crackers.

More Meal and Snack Challenges

Do you have "a lot on your plate"? Figuratively speaking, that is. A lack of time and energy for food prep, along with limited culinary know-how, are among the many challenges to making healthy meal and snack decisions. So is the ever-present availability of foods and drinks that can lead to mindless eating and the often-oversized portions.

EATING: MINDLESS OR MINDFUL?

Ever eaten a plate of food without registering the flavors or aromas in your mind? Tempted to graze on salty or sugary snacks without thinking?

Being mindful is being in control: eating when you're hungry, focusing on your food choices, and being aware of feeling full. In that way, you can eat with enjoyment and stop with satisfaction.

Mindful Solutions to Everyday Eating

Foodie or not, being "fully present" when you're eating has benefits! You'll likely eat less, perhaps eat healthier, and probably enjoy it more. To be more mindful, try these strategies:

- Take your "temperature." On a scale of one to ten, are you physically hungry before you reach for a snack or second helping? Paying attention to hunger and fullness cues makes it easier to regulate how much you eat.
- Take stock of your "food radius." Do you eat just because food is there or because the clock says it's mealtime? If your environment sets you up for mindless eating, change it. For example, fill the candy dish on your desk with paper clips instead of hard candy, or move it across the room. Keep tempting foods out of sight, and keep fruit and the healthiest snacks on the kitchen counter or within easy reach. Move your kitchen chair to look out the window, not at the fridge.
- Make your kitchen "friendly" for preparing veggies, fruits, and other nutrient-rich foods. Otherwise, you may find it easier to reach for convenient, nutrient-poor foods that take less effort. Keeping pre-cut veggies handy in your fridge increases the chance of eating more vegetables than simply keeping them whole in your refrigerator's crisper.

  This means keeping knives sharp and in a convenient knife block, having cutting boards within easy reach, and having enough lidded containers to hold the food once it's chopped or sliced.
- Get out of a mindless food rut or routine. The same breakfast or lunch every day can be monotonous with limited food variety.
- Take time to enjoy the "art" of cooking, instead of rushing through meal prep. Be mindful of the colors and textures. Breathe in the aromas. Savor the experience—the flavors of food from start to finish! Slow down and enjoy.
- Focus on what you're eating, rather than trying to do computer work or watch a movie at the same time. Studies suggest that TV watching prompts mindless eating.
- Take two or three bites of a food indulgence (perhaps candy, cookies, or chips). Enjoy. Put the rest away for later, and then distract yourself with something as simple as a phone call or word puzzle. You will likely feel just as satisfied by your small indulgence as if you'd eaten the whole thing.
- Keep a bottle or glass of water within arm's reach to avoid the urge for a sugary drink.

See "Eat More Mindfully" in chapter 22, page 644, for tips on mindful eating to manage weight.

PORTIONS: BE SIZE WISE!

Large portions may seem to call out: "Eat until you feel stuffed, not just until you're satisfied." Whether in restaurants or at home, more food served on larger plates and in larger bowls—and drinks in larger bottles and cups—have changed perceptions of portion sizes over the years.

Not surprising, large portions are linked to excess calorie intake and weight gain. Research shows that smaller portions are linked to weight loss. It also shows that diet-related health risks may go up with oversized portions that overdeliver total fat, including saturated fats, sodium, and added sugars.

Portion Shift: How They've Changed

During the last two or three decades, many Americans have gotten used to—and come to expect—larger and larger portions. Restaurants often serve portions that are big enough for two. Foods and drinks are often packaged in large amounts to sell more. People may not even know what a healthy portion is.

Here is a look at how portion sizes have grown over the years.

CALORIES IN PORTIONS

Food	Mid-1980s	20 or More Years Later
Bagel	140 calories (3-inch-diameter)	350 calories (6-inch-diameter)
Fast-food cheeseburger	333 calories	590 calories
Spaghetti and meatballs	500 calories (1 cup spaghetti with sauce and 3 small meatballs)	1,025 calories (2 cups pasta with sauce and 3 large meatballs)
Bottle of soda	85 calories (6½ ounces)	250 calories (20 ounces)
Fast-food French fries	210 calories (2.4 ounces)	610 (6.9 ounces)
Coffee	45 calories (8 ounces with whole milk and sugar)	350 calories (16 ounces mocha coffee with steamed whole milk and mocha syrup)
Blueberry muffin	210 calories (1½ ounces)	500 calories (4 ounces)
Pepperoni pizza	500 calories (2 slices)	850 calories (2 large slices)
Chicken Caesar salad	390 calories (1½ cups)	790 calories (3½ cups)
Popcorn, movie theater	270 calories (5 cups)	630 calories (11 cups)
Cheesecake	260 calories (3 ounces)	640 calories (7 ounces)
Chocolate chip cookie	55 (1½-inch-diameter)	275 calories (3½-inch-diameter)
Chicken stir-fry, restaurant	435 calories (2 cups)	865 calories (4½ cups)

Source: Department of Health and Human Services, National Institutes of Health, www.nhlbi.nih.gov. 2010. Tip. *Take the Portion Distortion quiz on this website to see how long it would take to burn these extra calories with physical activity!*

Excessive portions also lead to food waste—and a waste of all the resources that go into putting too much food on the table. Being portion savvy isn't just healthier. It also saves food dollars and the environment!

Portion Savvy

How big is your bowl of pasta? Your favorite bakery-fresh blueberry muffin or bagel? Your fast-food drink? Perhaps bigger than you think!

To find out, get out your measuring cups and a kitchen scale. For different foods or drinks, serve your normal portion on a plate or in a bowl or glass. Then measure or weigh them. Your amount may be bigger or smaller than you think! To right-size your portions try these strategies:

- Know visual clues for portions. Use a hand comparison for a quick estimate: Your fist is about 1 cup; your palm, about ½ cup, or 3 to 5 ounces; and your thumb, about 1 tablespoon. *See "Visual Guide to Portion Size" in chapter 2, page 24.*
- Use smaller serving utensils, dishes, bowls, mugs, and cups. A meal served on a lunch plate rather than a dinner plate looks like more. Buy smaller dishware and glasses if that helps.
- Serve beverages in a tall, narrow glass if you want less to seem like more. Consumer behavior research shows that the brain estimates more in a tall, narrow glass than a short, wide one—even when they hold the same volume.
- Let veggies, fruits, and grain products (mostly whole grain) fill most of your plate, leaving less plate space for meat, chicken, or fish.

- Eat from a plate, not a package, so you know how much you eat. Put the opened package out of sight to resist temptation.
- Repackage big packages of snack foods into several smaller containers—enough for one snack. Or buy portion-controlled singles if that helps.
- Portion out foods before you eat. Count out just two to four cookies, depending on the size, as your snack budget for TV watching.
- For yourself or serving others, start with small helpings. Put the rest out of sight. Then eat slowly, paying attention to hunger and fullness cues. Go for seconds only if you're still truly hungry.
- Check the Nutrition Facts labels to gauge serving sizes. *See "Nutrition: Fact Check" in chapter 6, page 148, which explains serving sizes on food labels.*

See "Control Your Restaurant Portions" in chapter 9, page 279, and "Get Portion Savvy" in chapter 22, page 644, for more ways to avoid oversizing your portions.

The good news: These days some foods are packaged in smaller portions, and some restaurants also offer small plate portions. These same strategies apply to mindful eating!

4

Think Your Drinks

In this chapter, find out about . . .

Water, a healthy thirst quencher

Milk's benefits, non-dairy options

Juice vs. fruit drinks

Coffee, tea—and a morning "buzz"

"Sometimes" drinks: sodas, energy drinks, enhanced beverages

Wine, beer, and spirits: drinking responsibly

What's to drink? Whether it's just plain water or something else, beverages are as much a part of your day's meals and snacks as your food choices are. They not only quench your thirst, but also replace the water in body fluids naturally lost throughout the day. Enjoyed with a meal, a beverage helps you soften and swallow solid foods. Consumed alone, beverages can add flavor and pleasure to a meal—and your lifestyle.

The drinks you choose matter—a lot! Do you know how many calories you drink each day? Your beverage calories may add up to more than you think. On average, drinks provide about 400 calories daily for people ages two years and over—and for some, much more. Many drinks, such as milk, 100 percent fruit juice, and soy beverages, supply nutrients. Others such as sodas, energy drinks, sports drinks, and many sugar-sweetened fruit drinks are among major sources of extra calories and added sugars. And what about coffee and tea, beer and wine, and today's overwhelming array of enhanced beverages?

When water just won't do, enjoy the beverage of your choice, but just cut back on those without much nutritional benefit. Make your drinks count—think your drinks!

Water: First for Thirst

Just plain water: It's the most available fluid around—and often your best choice. Plain water has no calories, and it's low in sodium. Watching your caffeine intake? Unlike many coffees, teas, and some soft drinks, water has no caffeine either. Whether tap or bottled—with very few and unusual exceptions—water in the United States is safe and stringently regulated.

To learn about water as a nutrient, see "Water: A Fluid Asset" in chapter 15, page 443.

TAP WATER: CONVENIENT, INEXPENSIVE

Just turn on your faucet! Most drinking water in the United States comes right from the tap. Most of us take this for granted, yet in many parts of the world, drinkable tap water is a luxury. Here, tap water is a thrifty option, whether you drink it at home or ask for water when you eat out. There's plenty to know about your drinking water.

Did you ever stop to think?

. . . that 8 ounces of milk provide a quarter to almost a third of your day's calcium recommendation? Great for bones! A 12-ounce diet soda provides "zero" calcium.

. . . that bottled drinks can deliver more calories than you realize? If a single bottled drink contains two or more "label servings," it provides at least twice the calories if you drink it all at one time. The serving sizes on new Nutrition Facts labels, being introduced gradually, more realistically reflect how much people really drink at one time. *See "Nutrition Facts: Comparing the Old and the New" in chapter 6, page 147, for more about updates on food labeling.*

. . . that a large, regular soda (32 ounces) has about 400 calories? Do the math! Drinking one soda that size three times a week adds up to 1,200 calories per week. Over time, that could add up to several pounds of weight if these "empty" calories put you over your daily calorie needs. Consider swapping out regular soda with low-calorie soda, low-fat or fat-free milk, or water—or for at least a smaller size drink. Small steps make a difference!

. . . that slowly sipping a regular soft drink, sweetened iced tea, or even juice bathes your teeth in cavity-promoting sugars? The effect continues for twenty or more minutes after your last sip. *See "Oral Health: Your Healthy Smile" in chapter 25, page 738, for more about oral hygiene.*

Your Healthy Eating Check-In

Compare What You Drink

Use this online feature to compare the calories, nutrients, added sugars, and fats in your favorite drinks.

- Food-A-Pedia in the SuperTracker, Food and Nutrition Service, US Department of Agriculture
  www.supertracker.usda.gov/foodapedia.aspx

Treated: For Safety's Sake

If you live in an urban area, your tap water probably comes from a surface water source such as a river, lake, or reservoir fed by a watershed or land area. In a rural area, you likely drink groundwater that's pumped from an aquifer or from your own private well.

No matter what the original source, water isn't naturally pure. Impurities dissolve in or are absorbed by water as it flows through rivers and streams, filters through soil and rocks, and collects in lakes and reservoirs. From any source, water must be treated and filtered to ensure its quality and safety. That may include adding chlorine to kill germs and perhaps fluoride to prevent cavities.

To make tap water safe to drink, the Environmental Protection Agency (EPA) has established standards for contaminants. Levels are set low enough to protect most people, including children. Treatment protects you from microbes such as bacteria and viruses, inorganic contaminants such as chemicals, and minerals such as lead and arsenic, among others. To find out about a public water supply, ask for the annual report, or Consumer Confidence Report, from your community water supplier. It indicates the water source, the presence or level of contaminants, and what you can do to protect your drinking water.

If you rely on a private well or spring, have it tested annually by a certified water-testing laboratory for coliform bacteria, nitrates, and perhaps other contaminants such as radon, pesticides, or industrial wastes. Do it more often if your sample exceeds the standard. People who draw their water from a private water source are responsible for its safety. *For tips on how to protect a private water supply, visit the EPA's website, www.epa.gov/safewater.*

Water may be disinfected chemically or by a physical process such as ultraviolet light. Chlorination is a tried-and-true method for effectively treating water to protect against most immediate microbial reactions, such as diarrhea and vomiting, and against outbreaks of cholera, hepatitis, dysentery, and other microbial diseases.

There's been some question about a by-product called trihalomethane (THM), created when chlorine breaks down the organic matter in water. The very low amount of THM created in the process of making water safe to drink isn't enough to create a cancer risk, as some people fear. Protecting the populace from waterborne disease outbreaks far outweighs the insignificant effect of THM. And yet, if you or someone in your family is undergoing kidney dialysis, talk to your doctor about your water supply.

To find out the THM level, check your municipal water quality report; home testing is unreliable. The THM standard from the EPA is an annual average of 80 parts per billion (ppb). Home water filters can reduce these compounds in drinking water.

Water quality is assessed continually for safety. For example, low levels of arsenic in drinking water (from natural and commercial sources), consumed over a long period of time, have been considered a potential health risk. For many years, the federal standard for arsenic in public drinking water was 50 parts per billion ppb. In recent years, the EPA set a stricter, more health-protective standard: a maximum level of 10 ppb. (If you have a private well, have your water checked; if the arsenic level is at or above 10 ppb, consider another source of water, or consider an arsenic-removal treatment system.) Boiling the water won't remove arsenic. *For more information, visit the EPA's website, www.epa.gov/dwreginfo/drinking-water-regulatory-information.* Tap water is regulated by the EPA; commercial bottled water, by the FDA.

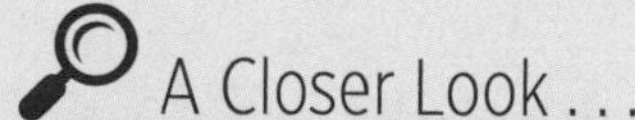

A Closer Look . . .

Water: The Fluoride Connection

For children and adults, a low level of the mineral fluoride helps harden developing tooth enamel and so protects teeth from decay each day and throughout life. It's also important for bone health. The Centers for Disease Control and Prevention (CDC) report that water fluoridation reduces tooth decay by about 25 percent over someone's lifetime.

FLUORIDATION AND TAP WATER

Many municipal water systems contain a natural supply of fluoride. In areas where fluoride levels are low, communities may decide to have their water system fluoridated to promote dental health. The current recommended fluoride level, set in 1962, is 0.7 to 1.2 milligrams of fluoride per liter of water. However, in 2011, the US Department of Health and Human Services proposed that the level be set at 0.7 milligrams of fluoride per liter of water to limit the possibility of fluorosis, *described on this page*.

Claims that fluoridation poisons the water source are unfounded. The trace amount of fluoride in fluoridated water will not cause harm.

If your water system has naturally occurring fluoride at 4.0 milligrams of fluoride per liter of water or above, the EPA requires systems to take action to reduce it. The EPA advises that some people who drink water containing fluoride in excess of 4.0 milligrams of fluoride per liter over many years could get bone disease, including pain and tenderness of the bones.

If you're not sure about fluoride in your tap water, check with your local water department or public health department. If you have your own well, have it tested for fluoride. If your community drinking water or home well is higher than recommended by the CDC, provide a different water source for your child to avoid fluorosis.

BOTTLED WATER: A SOURCE OF FLUORIDE?

People who drink mostly commercial bottled water may not consume enough decay-preventative fluoride. The fluoride content in commercial bottled water varies and may be naturally present depending on the source. Purified, distilled, or de-ionized bottled waters do not have fluoride unless it's added.

It's hard to know how much fluoride is in bottled water since the US Food and Drug Administration (FDA) only requires fluoride labeling on bottled water if it's added in processing. The limit set by the FDA is 0.7 to 2.4 milligrams per liter.

FLUORIDE: OTHER SOURCES

If needed, the US public has other fluoride sources, including toothpaste, mouthwash, prescription fluoride supplements, and fluoride applied by dental professionals.

In areas where water isn't fluoridated, dentists and pediatricians may prescribe fluoride supplements for children. "Topical" fluoride—applied directly to teeth with fluoride toothpaste, oral rinses, gels, foams, and treatments from a dental office—also helps strengthen tooth enamel.

Do you need fluoride in drinking water if you brush with tooth paste? Yes, because it protects your teeth differently. Both slow the action of decay-causing bacteria, and both combine with tooth surfaces for stronger teeth. Fluoride in water helps to keep a low level of fluoride in the mouth, offering protection; the higher concentration of fluoride in toothpaste lasts only an hour or two after brushing.

FLUOROSIS

Consuming too much fluoride can cause fluorosis, a splotchy discoloration of teeth, even though teeth are healthy in other ways. That most likely happens with excessive supplemental doses.

To reduce the chance for developing fluorosis and/or pitting, on permanent teeth, before they erupt from the gums, children shouldn't swallow fluoride toothpaste or rinses.

The Tolerable Upper Intake Level for fluoride is 2.2 milligrams daily for children ages four through eight; from age nine through adulthood, it's 10 milligrams of fluoride daily. The EPA advises that children under nine should not drink water that has more than 2.0 milligrams of fluoride per liter of water.

For more about fluoride and healthy teeth, see "Oral Health: Your Healthy Smile" in chapter 25, page 738, and "Caring for Baby Teeth" in chapter 16, page 480. See also "Fluoride" in chapter 14, page 436.

Water: Hard or Soft?

Surprisingly, water itself may not be the only nutrient in drinking water. Unless distilled, or demineralized, drinking water may contain minerals in varying amounts, such as fluoride, calcium, sodium, iron, and magnesium. The water source and how the water is processed determine the actual composition of the drinking water.

Water from underground wells, springs, and aquifers may contain high mineral concentrations. As water from rain and snow seeps through rocks, gravel, and sand, it picks up minerals along the way. This explains how some underground water becomes naturally fluoridated.

Water may be "hard" or "soft" depending on its mineral content. Hard water contains more calcium and magnesium, which dissolves into rainwater from the soil. Soft water has more sodium. With one exception (iron), there's essentially no flavor difference from the mineral content between hard and soft water. A small amount of iron gives a metallic taste to hard water—but it's not enough to make water a significant source of dietary iron.

Where water is naturally hard, some consumers choose to use a water softener, which often replaces calcium and magnesium in water with sodium. The reason? Softening water can make soap work more efficiently, extend the life of a water heater, and avoid mineral residue buildup in pipes.

If your water supply is softened, the amount of softening, or salt added, depends on how hard your water is. The average softened municipal water may contain less than 15 milligrams of sodium per cup. Most well water doesn't need to be fully softened. When it does, the amount of sodium per cup of water is about 39 milligrams or less; the level depends on how much is required to soften it. For most people, the amount of sodium in softened water isn't significant.

Water: Concerns about Lead and Nitrates

Since the spread of infectious disease from drinking water is under control in the United States, attention has shifted to other public health concerns.

Lead. Although lead exposure from breathing or swallowing lead paint chips and dust is riskier, too much lead from food and beverages, over time, has harmful effects, too. It can build up in the body, potentially damaging the brain, nervous system, kidneys, reproductive system, and red blood cells. It can also lead to high blood pressure. Infants, children under six, and unborn babies are more vulnerable to lead poisoning, which can lead to delays in physical and mental development.

Where does lead in tap water come from in a home? The answer is that often it's from plumbing inside the building or from service lines. Many older houses and multifamily dwellings were constructed with water pipes, fittings, or fixtures made of lead; corrosion causes lead to leach into water. The amount of lead in water also depends on other factors such as how long water stays in the pipes, the water temperature and acidity, and the wear-and-tear within the pipes. What's more, over time, dissolved oxygen in the water running through the pipes combines with the actual metal in the pipe to coat it with a metal oxide that essentially protects the water.

There's always the chance that the community water system may be a contributor. In older communities, lead service lines may connect a house with the municipal water system. According to 1996 amendments

Drinking Water: For Those with Health Risks

Some people are vulnerable to microbial contaminants such as Cryptosporidium (or "crypto"), which isn't destroyed by chlorination. More often found in surface water than ground water, "crypto" may cause nausea, diarrhea, or stomach cramps when healthy people ingest it. For people who are vulnerable, the symptoms may be severe and perhaps life-threatening. This includes people HIV/AIDS or other immune system disorders such as lupus or Crohn's disease, those who've had organ transplants, those undergoing anti-cancer therapies, older adults, and children.

EPA standards put controls on disinfecting procedures for microbial contaminants, including "crypto," for surface water. However, at-risk people should still talk to their doctor and take careful precautions.

Boiling tap water and pasteurizing bottled water destroys "crypto." Filters with an "absolute 1-micron" rating are relatively effective; *see "Have you ever wondered . . . if you need a water filter?" in this chapter, page 88.* Bottled waters—processed by distillation or reverse osmosis, or commercially filtered with an "NSF International Standard 53" filter before bottling—are safe. Not all bottled waters are handled in this way.

Water for Emergencies

Disaster can hit anyone, anywhere. To ensure a safe water supply, disaster experts advise these precautions:

- Store a week's supply of bottled water for everyone in your family: about one gallon per person per day.
- Store containers of water in a cool, dry place away from direct sunlight.
- Label bottles of tap water with the date. Replace them every six months for freshness. Use bottled water within two years if there is no expiration date.

to the US Safe Drinking Water Act (with more amendments effective in 2014), all pipes, fittings, and fixtures introduced into commerce must be lead-free. Uncontrolled contaminants in the local water supply also can be a cause of lead getting into the water that enters your home.

If you suspect high lead levels, get your tap water and pipes tested. Even copper pipes might use lead solder in the joints; brass faucets and fittings may contain lead, too. Your local public health department or water utility company may have a free testing kit or may refer you to a government-certified laboratory that tests for water safety.

If a lead problem is severe, you might install a water-filtering device or use bottled water for drinking and cooking. If less severe, here's how you can reduce your exposure:

- Avoid drinking water that has been in your home's plumbing for more than six hours. Before you use the water to drink, cook, or brush your teeth, run it until you feel the temperature change.
- Run cold water for sixty seconds or more to clear the pipes and faucet each time before use. This helps flush out water with the heaviest lead concentration.
- For cooking, drinking, and preparing baby formula, use either cold water from your tap or bottled water. Hot water dissolves lead from pipes more quickly than cold water does. Boiling water doesn't remove lead!
- If you use a faucet filter, get one that is NSF International Certified to remove lead. *See "Have you ever wondered . . . if you need a water filter?" in this chapter, page 88.*

Precaution: The American Academy of Pediatrics and the CDC advise lead screening for infants and toddlers at ages one and two. If you have a young child between six months and three years old, talk to your doctor about possible sources of lead in your home or childcare setting. When lead in children's blood tests goes above 10 micrograms per deciliter, lead sources in the child's environment should be identified and corrected.

? Have you ever wondered?

. . . where to get your water tested? Whether you want to check for lead, trihalomethanes, or other contaminants, or have a private well tested, skip the home testing kits. They're unreliable. Instead, contact the EPA or your local public health department.

. . . how to get the taste of chlorine out of tap water? Fill a pitcher, and let it sit uncovered on the counter or in the refrigerator overnight. The chlorine will evaporate. Chlorine in small, safe amounts is used to keep water supplies safe.

Note: EPA regulations for lead and copper in the water supply are under current review.

Nitrates. If your water supplier alerts you to nitrate or nitrite levels above EPA standards and if you have a child under six months old, talk to your doctor. Ingesting that water could cause "blue baby syndrome," which is potentially life-threatening without immediate medical attention. Symptoms are bluish skin tone and shortness of breath.

Find a different and safe water source for baby formula. Nitrates are inorganic and can't be destroyed as bacteria can be. As with lead, boiling water concentrates nitrates and so increases risk.

BOTTLED WATER?

In recent years, consumption of bottled water has soared. Except for soft drinks, people living in the United States drink more bottled water than any other bottled beverage! Since most tap water and bottled water is safe, why choose bottled water?

According to consumer research, some people prefer the taste. Bottled water usually doesn't contain chlorine, which can give water a slight flavor. It's convenient—portable for the office, a picnic, a drive, or a workout—and often easy to buy. You may buy bottled water instead of other bottled drinks for what it doesn't contain: calories, added sugars, caffeine, or alcohol.

Regulated: For Safety's Sake

Bottled water sold state to state is regulated by the FDA to assure its quality, safety, and accurate labeling.

Labels, such as "spring water" or "mineral water," are defined legally. If bottled water comes from a municipal water supply, the label must say so, unless it's been purified. By regulation, bottled water can't contain sweeteners or additives—besides flavors, extracts, or essences from food or spices (less than 1 percent by weight). It must be calorie- and sugar-free.

Instead of using chlorine, commercial bottled water usually is disinfected in other ways: filtration, reverse osmosis, ultraviolet (UV) light, or ozone, a highly reactive form of oxygen. Depending on the method, bottled water may or may not be 100 percent pathogen free. If you have suppressed immunity, talk to your healthcare provider to find sterile bottled water.

Ever see "NSF Certified" or "IBWA Bottler Member" on bottled water labels? NSF stands for National Sanitation Foundation (NSF International) and IBWA for International Bottled Water Association. These initials indicate that a voluntary inspection, with standards set by the NSF, was conducted with the water source and the finished product and was checked against FDA regulations. Perfectly safe water may not be labeled since inspections are voluntary. If you see "FDA Approved" or "EPA Certified," beware; neither agency conducts these inspections.

On bottled waters marketed for infants, look for the term "sterile." That means the water meets the FDA's standards for commercial sterilization,

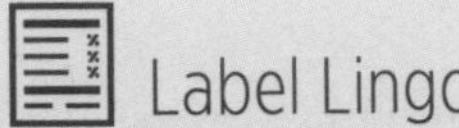

Label Lingo

Bottled Waters: What's in a Name?

Today's supermarket shelves offer bottled waters—some flavored, others plain. But what do the terms on the labels mean? According to the FDA:

- *Artesian water* is a certain type of well water collected without mechanical pumping. The well must tap a confined aquifer that has water standing much higher than the rock, gravel, or sand. An aquifer is an underground layer of rock or sand with water.
- *Distilled water,* which is one type of purified water, has been evaporated to steam, then condensed again to remove minerals.
- *Drinking water* is bottled water from an approved source. It must meet state and federal standards and go through minimal filtration and disinfection. It has no added ingredients, except perhaps some antimicrobial agents. Fluoride may be added.
- *Mineral water* contains minerals at a standard level, no less than 250 parts per million (ppm) of total dissolved solids, or minerals. These minerals must be naturally present, not added. If the level is less than 500 ppm, it will be labeled "low mineral content"; if higher than 1,500 ppm, "high mineral content."
- *Purified water* has been processed to remove minerals and other solids. The process may be distillation, deionization, reverse osmosis, or another suitable process. *Tip:* "Purified" on the label doesn't mean that purified water is any more "pure" or better for you than tap water.
- *Sparkling water* is water with a "fizz." Either carbon dioxide is added, or water is naturally carbonated. If carbon dioxide is added, the water can't have any more than its naturally carbonated level. It can be labeled as "natural sparkling water" only if there's no added carbonation. Sparkling water can't have added ingredients.
- *Spring water* comes from an underground source and naturally flows to the surface. It must be collected either at the spring above ground or through a bored hole that taps an underground source of the spring. If it's collected by an external (not natural) force, it must have the same composition and physical qualities (perhaps carbonated) as the naturally flowing spring water.
- *Well water* is collected from an underground aquifer, too, but with a mechanical pump that taps the source through a bored hole, instead of flowing naturally to the surface.

so it's safe from bacteria. If it doesn't meet those standards, the label must state that the product isn't sterile and should be used to prepare infant formula only as directed by a doctor or according to infant formula preparation instructions.

Flavored and Nutrient-Added Water Beverages

Some bottled waters are enhanced, sometimes with flavorings (perhaps a natural fruit essence), other times with added nutrients such as vitamins, electrolytes including sodium and potassium, and amino acids. Some also contain sugar or low-calorie sweeteners as well as artificial flavors. Read labels to find out what's in the beverages you choose to drink.

For these waters, such as for spring water with berry flavor, the labels provide Nutrition Facts and an ingredient list, and the water itself must meet the requirements for bottled water. Being clear doesn't mean that a beverage is simply water!

Buying Bottled Water

Calorie-free, yet thirst-quenching, bottled water is a good choice, especially when safe tap water isn't available or convenient. Weigh the pros and cons:

- Consider the cost. Bottled water may cost 240 to over 10,000 times more per gallon than tap water—and may not offer more health benefits.
- Compare for nutrition benefits. From a nutritional standpoint, there's no significant difference between tap and bottled water except that bottled may not have much, if any, fluoride. In fact, some bottled water is tap water, reprocessed to change its taste and composition.

  Look for fluoridated bottled water if your child or infant consumes only bottled water. Be aware that the fluoride content of bottled water varies; talk to your baby's healthcare provider about a low-fluoride bottled water to use for mixing infant formula.
- Choose for safety's sake. Both tap and bottled waters are usually safe options in the United States. In some situations, bottled water is a better choice.

  Those at high risk might benefit from commercial bottled waters; *see "Drinking Water: For Those with Health Risks" earlier in this chapter, page 84.*

  When the lead or nitrate content of water is a concern, bottled water is a good option, particularly for pregnant women or families with children. Bottled water doesn't contain lead. In homes with lead pipes or lead solder, bottled water is a good option for cooking foods that require relatively long cooking times, such as soups, stews, and braised dishes; any lead in tap water may become more concentrated during extended cooking times.

- Look for water in BPA-free plastic bottles. They may be labeled as BPA-free, perhaps with recycle codes "3" or "7." They're meant for recycling, not reuse. Some studies suggest low but potential risks for consuming food from plastic containers, such as plastic water bottles made with bisphenol A (BPA). *See "Have you ever wondered . . . about the safety of BPA in food containers?" in chapter 5, page 132.*
- Taste the difference? Because the taste of tap water differs throughout the country, some people prefer commercial bottled water. Bottled and filtered waters usually don't contain chlorine, which may slightly alter the flavor of soups, stews, coffee, tea, and similar preparations. If the appeal of flavored waters helps you drink more water, take advantage of them, but only if they don't contain added sugars.
- Think about the environment. Even when single-use plastic bottles are recycled, there's an environmental cost: from making the bottle to transporting it with water, and then to handling waste. Thinner-plastic bottles as well as aluminum cans and paper containers are more eco-friendly. Better yet: drink tap water!

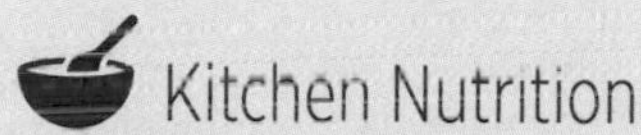

Kitchen Nutrition

Give Water a Flavor Spark!

Make your own flavored drinks using tap or bottled water. You'll save money and calories:

- Add citrus slices, berries, watermelon cubes, cucumber slices, or fresh mint.
- Go 50-50 with sparkling water or 100 percent juice.
- Freeze juice in the ice cube tray, and then use the cubes for chilled water.

YOUR RESPONSIBILITY: CLEAN WATER!

In many developed nations, including the United States, access to safe drinking water is taken for granted. Yet access to clean, safe water is an ongoing public health issue—and a basic human right—throughout the world.

Household Safety

Although regulations in the United States are in place to keep tap water safe under normal conditions, you need to keep water safety in mind—even without local disasters.

- Sanitize the ice bin in your freezer. Clean the icemaker and water dispenser regularly if you have them. Follow the guidelines that come with the appliance.
- Wash durable, reusable (BPA-free or perhaps stainless steel) water bottles well with soapy water after using them; only refill bottles meant for reuse. Sipping from a bottle without cleaning it for several days increases the risk of bacterial contamination.
- Avoid leaving a disposable water bottle in the car or sports bag to drink from over several days. That also increases the risk of bacterial contamination.
- Don't share the same bottle of water with someone else.

Your Environmental Responsibility

A staggering statistic: the World Health Organization says one in nine people around the world lacks access to safe drinking water! That said, everyone shares responsibility for keeping water safe and plentiful no matter where you are in your environment. Here are a few ideas:

- Protect your local drinking water by handling household chemicals safely. Learn how to dispose of toxic trash such as household cleaners and batteries with lead or mercury. Your town may have a collection site. Take used motor oil to a recycling center; don't discard it in your trash or storm sewer. Don't put any chemicals in places that seep into groundwater, such as septic systems, drainage wells, or dry wells.
- Limit use of single-use plastic water bottles to limit your carbon footprint! Use reusable water bottles; look for drinking fountains and water-bottle refilling stations, which are becoming increasingly common, especially in urban parks and open spaces, airports, university campuses, hiking trails, and similar places.

Local Disasters: Safe Drinking Water

In the United States, infectious diseases spread by untreated water are almost nonexistent, except during natural disasters such as floods, earthquakes, or accidental contamination of wells or municipal water. Because these incidents can devastate a community's drinking water supply, it's a good idea to know what to do in a water emergency. *See "Water for Emergencies" in this chapter, page 84.*

When the safety of your water supply is in doubt, don't drink it! Instead, take steps to make it safe:

- Report your concern to your water company or local public health department, or both. They may test the source of your water or, if the problem is specific to your house, refer you to a qualified private laboratory. If you have a private water source such as a well, check it for safety, *as described earlier in this chapter.*

Have you ever wondered?

. . . if you need a water filter? Probably not, unless you prefer the taste and smell of filtered water or, although uncommon, if your water supply needs filtration or boiling for safety. If you buy one, read the manufacturer's information to see what it filters out.

A water filter that meets the National Sanitation Foundation (NSF) International Standard of 53 for cyst removal or cyst reduction is the most effective (cyst refers to common waterborne microbiological material, such as *Giardia*). The filter uses reverse osmosis, which is a purification technology that passes water through a semi-permeable membrane to block larger particles.

A filter that meets NSF standards has an "absolute 1 micron" rating given on the label, meaning that the pore size is 1 micron or less in diameter, with or without NSF testing. Filters rated as "nominal 1 micron" aren't reliable for removing bacteria, such as *Cryptosporidium*. Replace the filter cartridges regularly and properly, according to the manufacturer's instructions. A filter may not eliminate smaller bacteria.

. . . how seltzer and club soda compare to sparkling bottled water? Soda water (or club soda), tonic water, seltzer, and other water with added carbonation are regulated by the FDA as soft drinks. Seltzer contains no added ingredients. However, club soda contains additives such as table salt, sodium bicarbonate, or potassium bicarbonate, adding a slightly salty flavor. Tonic water is sweetened (usually with corn syrup) and gets a slightly bitter taste from quinine. Water that is not naturally carbonated cannot contain any other ingredient and still be called "water."

. . . if oxygen-enhanced drinks offer unique benefits, such as a boost in athletic performance? No. It's just marketing hype. First, consider "oxygen-enhanced" water. Under pressure, only a tiny amount (about the amount in one breath) of oxygen can be forced into water. It quickly bubbles out as soon as you open the bottle.

Even if some "extra oxygen" in water made it into your mouth, your digestive tract is equipped to absorb nutrients, not oxygen. Your lungs process oxygen from the heme (iron) portion of blood.

- Purify contaminated drinking water by boiling it for at least one minute, then it can either be stored in a sterile container used immediately for drinking or cooking. At high altitudes, water boils at lower temperatures and also takes longer to reach the boil.
- Use iodine or chlorine tablets to disinfect your water supply; strictly follow the package directions. These products are available in camping stores. Campers, hikers, and others who rely on water supplied by wilderness lakes and streams might use water filtration and purification devices.
- Contact EPA's Safe Drinking Water Hotline or website for your state certification officer for referral to a certified water testing lab, or your local health department. *See "Resources You Can Use" in the appendix, page 763 for contact information.*

In some countries, contaminated water is an ongoing public health problem, spreading diarrhea and even life-threatening diseases such as cholera and hepatitis. For globe-trotters, water is a common source of travelers' diarrhea; *see "Safe to Drink?" in chapter 9, page 314, for more about water while traveling.* For added safety in less-developed areas, travel with a supply of iodine or chlorine tablets.

Juice, Juice Drink, or Fruit Drink?

When you're thirsty, a refreshing, fruity beverage often hits the spot. And a savory vegetable juice can complement a meal. Which one will you reach for: 100 percent juice, a juice drink, a fruit drink, or fruit-flavored water? Because their composition differs, some are far more nourishing than others.

- *Fruit or vegetable juices:* Only 100 percent juice can be labeled as "juice." It's nothing but the juice squeezed from flavorful fruits or vegetables. Labeled as 100 percent juice, it, by definition, contains no added sugars.
- *Juice drinks:* If juice is diluted (less than 100 percent juice), the product label must use a different name: "juice drink," "juice beverage," or "juice cocktail"; these terms can be used interchangeably.

  It must declare the percentage that is juice, such as "contains ___% juice" or "___ % juice." It must also say the name of the fruit or vegetable. A juice drink may be called "diluted ___ juice,"—for example, "diluted apple juice."

  If flavored with a minor amount of juice, it doesn't need a percent-juice statement; then it can say "flavor, "flavored," or "flavoring," but cannot use "juice" on its label except in the ingredient list and cannot give any other impression that it contains juice.

  Some beverages such as cranberry juice drink may be similar in nutrients and calories to 100 percent juice, but they have added sugars to make their tart flavors palatable.
- *Fruit drinks:* A "fruit drink" is simply flavored water (with no juice), perhaps fortified with vitamin C or other nutrients,

phytonutrients, or herbs. Some fruit drinks contain some concentrated juice as a flavoring. Many are sweetened with added sugars.

JUICE: A POUR OF GOOD NUTRITION

All these beverages are mostly water. For juice and juice drinks, the nutrition content—vitamins A and C, other nutrients, fiber, phytonutrients, and calories—depends on the fruits and vegetables they're made from. Any added ingredients and any pulp that may be left in also make these beverages more or less nutritious. Nutritionally speaking, a fruit drink cannot substitute for 100 percent juice!

Fruit Juices and Juice Drinks

Drinking 100 percent fruit juice packs in good nutrition: for example vitamins A and C as well as magnesium, folate, phosphorus, and potassium. They naturally contain other nutrients, including some that don't appear on the Nutrition Facts label.

Juices aren't all the same. Besides vitamin C, orange juice is high in potassium and folate. Blueberry juice—less common than some juices but gaining in popularity—is a good source of phytonutrients with antioxidant qualities.

Does 100 percent fruit juice have more vitamin C than a juice drink? Not necessarily. Some 100 percent fruit juices contain less than 100 percent of the Daily Value (DV) for vitamin C, while some juice drinks are fortified to supply at least 100 percent in a single label serving. You need to check the Nutrition Facts label, *as discussed in "Nutrition: Fact Check!" in chapter 6, page 148.*

¾ Cup	Percent Daily Value* of Vitamin C
Orange juice	100
Apple juice (fortified with vitamin C)	80
Apple juice (unfortified)	2
Grape juice (unfortified)	0

* Based on updated Daily Values for new Nutrition Facts Labeling; *see "% Daily Values: What Are They Based On?" in the appendix, page 786.*

Sweet flavor comes from sugar, either natural or added. Fruit juice gets its sweetness from fructose, a sugar that occurs naturally in fruit. Juice drinks may be sweetened either with juice concentrate or added sugars such as high-fructose corn syrup, as noted in the ingredient list. Some tart juices, such as cranberry, are blended with other juices (apple, grape, pear) to balance the tartness. Some blends contain green tea. Many juices, juice blends, and juice drinks are fortified with calcium, vitamin D, omega-3s (perhaps DHA), or others, identified on the label.

Vegetable Juices

Vegetable juice is another way to fit veggies into your day's meals and snacks. Bottled vegetable juice may be 100 percent juice (perhaps tomato, beet,

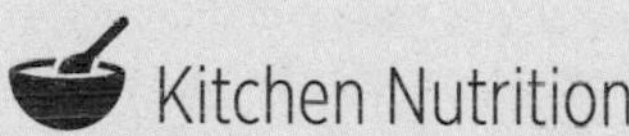

Juice, Dairy, and More: Super Sippers

CHILLED THIRST QUENCHERS

- Combine grapefruit juice or cranberry-mango cocktail concentrate with chilled club soda. Serve with a sprig of fresh mint.
- Make a fruit smoothie. In a blender, puree berries, sliced kiwifruit, chopped mango, or pineapple chunks with 100 percent juice and yogurt. Perhaps add fresh mint. For convenience, try canned and frozen fruit for smoothies.
- Create shakes. In a blender, puree melon chunks or peach slices with buttermilk, crushed ice, and a touch of ginger or cinnamon until smooth.
- Use silken tofu as a great nondairy alternative in a creamy shake. Add a little juice and frozen fruit; puree until smooth.
- For a hint of fruit flavor without adding calories, float citrus slices or berries (or add a splash of 100 percent juice) in ice water.
- Blend fruit and vegetable juices. Whirl fresh kale leaves, sliced cucumber, green grapes, and sliced kiwifruit or Granny Smith apple slices with a little water.

HOT BELLY WARMERS

- Simmer cranberry-apple juice with cinnamon, cloves, allspice, and orange peel for about 20 minutes. Strain. Stir in fat-free dry milk powder and vanilla extract. Heat through.
- Add anise seeds, ground cinnamon, and ground cloves to ground coffee. Prepare hot coffee using the spiced ground coffee. Lighten with warm milk.
- Scoop praline or chocolate frozen yogurt into a mug. Pour hot cocoa or coffee over the top. Stir with a cinnamon stick.

carrot, or cucumber) or a juice blend with several veggies such as beets, carrots, celery, parsley, lettuce, spinach, sweet potatoes, tomatoes, watercress, and more.

How does the nutrient content stack up? Vegetable juice provides the range of nutrient and phytonutrient benefits provided by the vegetables it's made from. It usually has fewer calories than fruit juice but often more sodium; look for low-sodium options. Vegetable juice may be less filling than whole vegetables and will have less fiber. Like fruit juice and juice drinks, it may be fortified with other nutrients.

Think Your Drink: Juice and Juice Drinks

Drinking 100 percent juice can conveniently squeeze more fruit and vegetables into your day's eating plan—a good thing since many people come up short on daily recommendations. Keep this in mind for your juice choices:

- Choose 100 percent juices. They deliver important vitamins, minerals, and phytonutrients, just less fiber, from whole fruit. (Most fiber is lost when whole fruits or vegetables are made into juice.) Polyphenols from grapes and some carotenoids in orange and tomatoes may be more available to the body when crushed to make juice.
- As with any food or drink, be prudent with amounts as juices deliver calories, too. Most research studies show that drinking moderate amounts of 100 percent juice isn't linked to overweight or obesity in children or adults.
- Be aware: Bottled fruit punch, "ades," and fruit drinks look like juice but may contain little or no fruit and provide calories but few nutrients. Check the Nutrition Facts label.

The American Academy of Pediatrics advises a limit on fruit juice for infants and children; *see "Have you ever wondered . . . when your baby can have fruit juice?" in chapter 16, page 480, and "Have you ever wondered . . . are fruit juices and fruit drinks good choices for kids?" in chapter 17, page 517.*

JUICING FRUITS AND VEGETABLES

Juices provide most of the vitamins, minerals, and phytonutrients found in whole fruits and vegetables. That's a good thing.

If you wonder whether juicing makes fruits and vegetables more healthy or their nutrients more available, the answer is somewhat complex.

Despite marketing promises, juicing using a juice extractor either in your own kitchen or at a juice bar does not make nutrients in fruits and vegetables any more bioavailable. In fact, juicing results in some nutrient loss. On the other hand, the juice itself is pure (no added sugar or other added sweeteners) and often described as refreshing and delicious.

Juice typically has less fiber than whole fruit. The juice extractor separates the juice from the pulp in short order. The pulp, which includes the edible peel, contains nutrients and phytonutrients, and so if you only drink the juice, you miss out on the fiber and other nutritional benefits from the pulp.

? Have you ever wondered?

. . . if a juice cleanse can help you lose weight or get rid of toxins? In spite of "cure-all" claims for juice cleanses, simply changing the form of food by juicing won't deliver added benefits. A juicing diet for weight loss, without other nourishing foods, can leave you short on essential nutrients. No studies support the idea of detoxing your body with a juice cleanse either; your body's liver is well equipped to do that. Enjoy juice as a way to get the benefits of fruits and vegetables—but don't expect miracles!

. . . what maple water is? First, what it's not: it's not water with added sugars, and it's not maple syrup. Instead, it's the watery sap from the maple tree that has not yet been concentrated and processed into thick maple syrup. The sweetness is from the sap, not from added sugars. The nutrient content is limited.

Juicing Wisely

If you decide to juice at home, return some pulp to the juice. Or use the pulp to fortify other foods: cake or muffin batter, mixed dishes, cooked rice, or soups. Because fiber helps you feel full, it may help curb your appetite so that you eat fewer calories.

Another option is to use a blender or food processor to make fruit or vegetable juice. This keeps the pulp in, and you won't have to buy a costly juicer.

Tip: When you make vegetable juice—perhaps from cucumber and kale—in a blender or food processor, add a splash of 100 percent fruit juice for sweetness. You also might want to thin the juice with a little water if it's too thick.

Dairy and Nondairy Beverages

Want milk with light taste that's low calorie? Try fat-free milk. Need milk for your toddler? Provide whole milk until two years of age. Prefer milk that's creamy yet not too rich? Enjoy low-fat milk. Have lactose intolerance? Consider lactose-free milk. Need a vegan or milk allergen-free option? Choose fortified soy beverage, as a nondairy alternative.

These options—and more—are nourishing and refreshing alone or when used as ingredients in other drinks, perhaps lattes, cappuccinos, chai, hot cocoa, or smoothies.

WHOLE TO FAT-FREE DAIRY MILKS

Like all beverages, milk supplies water. It's about 89 percent water by weight and, as one of the best sources of calcium, also offers significant amounts of nine more nutrients. Here's some of what just 1 cup (8 ounces) supplies:

Nutrients in Milk (8 Ounces)	% Daily Value*
Calcium (300 mg)	23
Vitamin D (3 mcg, or 120 IU)	15
Vitamin A (135 RAE, or 465 IU)	15
Protein (8 g)	16
Potassium (380 mg)	8
Riboflavin (0.4 mg)	31
Vitamin B_{12} (1.3 mcg)	54
Phosphorus (245 mg)	20

* Based on updated Daily Values for new Nutrition Facts Labeling; *see "% Daily Values: What Are They Based On?" in the appendix, page 786.*

Depending on which milk you choose, the fat and calorie contents will vary, yet other nutrient amounts remain about the same. No sugars are added to plain milk.

The choices include whole, 2 percent reduced-fat, 1 percent low-fat, and fat-free milk. Whole milk comes closest to the milk from a cow before processing removes different amounts of fat.

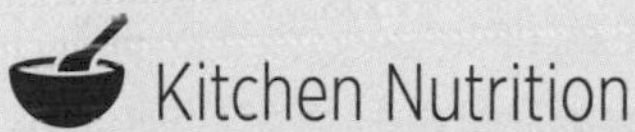

Kitchen Nutrition

Milk Plus: Add a Healthy Flavor

You say you're not a milk drinker? Whisk one or two ingredients, such as those below, with 1 cup of milk—cold or hot, fat-free or whole, cultured or lactose-free—and give it a refreshing new flavor. You might find you actually are a milk drinker! (And you'll get the benefits of 300 milligrams of calcium, and more.)

- ½ cup of fresh or frozen pureed berries: strawberries, raspberries, blackberries, or blueberries
- 2 tablespoons of fruit juice concentrate, or 1 pureed peach and ½ teaspoon of flavor extract
- ¼ teaspoon of almond, anise, hazelnut, maple, or vanilla extract. Or, perhaps cinnamon or peppermint. Use 2 drops of oil in place of ¼ teaspoon of extract.
- ½ cup of cranberry juice cocktail and a small scoop of low-fat vanilla ice cream or frozen yogurt
- 1 tablespoon of creamy peanut butter and 2 tablespoons of chocolate syrup

The FDA has set minimum nutrition standards for milk. By law, it's fortified with vitamin D, which helps the body absorb calcium; vitamin A is often added to reduced, low-fat, and fat-free milk.

For safety, most milk is pasteurized to destroy harmful bacteria and extend its shelf life. It's then homogenized so the milk fat doesn't separate from the fluid, keeping milk smooth. *See "Label Lingo: What Other Label Claims Mean" in chapter 6, page 155, for definitions of pasteurization and homogenization and "Have you ever wondered . . . if raw milk is healthier than pasteurized milk?" in chapter 7, page 201, for health risks related to raw (unpasteurized) milk.*

Flavored, Cultured, and Lactose-Free

Flavored milks. Whether whole, low-fat, or fat-free, flavored milk provides another way to get milk's nutrients. Flavored or not, the amounts of the milk's key nutrients are about the same. For chocolate milk, the added cocoa or chocolate and sweetener bumps up the calorie count by about 30 calories for an 8-ounce serving. Over the past few years, calories and added sugars in flavored milk have been lowered significantly to comply with the Healthy Hunger-Free Kids Act of 2010 for milk served in schools and other USDA Child Nutrition Programs.

Offering them flavored (often chocolate) milk encourages kids to get the recommended three cups daily of dairy—and benefit from the nutrients that often come up short for many people: calcium, potassium, magnesium, and vitamin D. And yet questions may arise from parents about giving children flavored and sweetened milk:

- What about added sugars? Today, an 8-ounce carton of chocolate milk has about 6 grams of added sugars. To compare, regular soda contains 25 to 30 grams of added sugars with few, if any, nutrients besides water and carbohydrates. Fruit drinks typically provide more added sugars than flavored milk does, too. Research shows that kids who drink flavored milk are more likely to eat a higher quality diet than kids who don't drink milk, regardless of the added sugars. The likelihood of being at a healthy weight is the same whether kids drink flavored or unflavored milk.
- Do the sugar and caffeine in chocolate milk cause hyperactivity? No scientific evidence suggests that sugar or caffeine is linked to hyperactivity, mood swings, or academic performance. The amount of caffeine in the chocolate or cocoa is very small. Some soft drinks provide much more caffeine. *See "Caffeine: What Sources, How Much?" in this chapter, page 98.*

Cultured milks. Among other dairy options are buttermilk, drinkable yogurt (perhaps yogurt shots), and kefir (keh-FEER), which is a yogurt-like drink made from cow's, goat's, or sheep's milk. These drinks are fermented, made by adding "friendly" bacteria such as lactobacilli to milk. They, too, deliver calcium and perhaps vitamin D. Check the ingredient list and Nutrition Facts label to compare the calories and other nutrients.

Most drinkable yogurt, yogurt drinks, and kefir have "active and live cultures" with desirable probiotic benefits; check the label. While buttermilk is fermented, too, it may not provide probiotic benefits. *See "Prebiotics and Probiotics: A Bioactive Duo" in chapter 15, page 453.*

Lactose-free milks. Meant for those with lactose intolerance, this is simply milk—whole, low-fat, or fat-free—without the lactose but with all of milk's essential nutrients. By adding lactase during milk processing, the lactose is predigested to simple sugars, making the taste slightly sweeter. Look for lower-lactose milk, too.

See "Dairy Foods: Buying Tips" in chapter 6, page 169, for more about these and other dairy options.

Think Your Drink: Dairy Drinks

Keep these guidelines in mind as you make dairy drink choices:

- Drink fat-free (skim) or low-fat (1 percent) milk. If you drink 2 percent or whole milk now, gradually switch to lower-fat options.
- Try some dairy-good new ideas to make milk more of a treat. *See "Milk Plus: Add a Healthy Flavor" on the previous page.*
- If you're lactose intolerant, try lactose-free milk. *See "Lactose Intolerance: A Matter of Degree" in chapter 23, page 666, for ways to manage lactose intolerance.*
- Try something new to you, perhaps drinkable yogurt or kefir! Both are sold in a variety of flavors.
- Raw, unpasteurized milk? Be aware that the potential danger from foodborne illness outweighs any claims for health benefits.

NONDAIRY DRINKS: SOY, ALMOND, AND MORE

Vegan, allergic to milk, or another reason for a nondairy choice? Try calcium-fortified soymilk as an alternative. While nutritionally not the same as dairy milk, the protein, as well as the added calcium and vitamin D when fortified, make it a good alternative.

Other plant-based beverage choices, such as almond, coconut, hemp, oat, quinoa, and rice milk, offer variety and flavor, but they don't provide comparable nourishment to dairy milk. There's no standard of identity, so the nutrient and calorie contents vary, even in the same type of drink.

Plant-based drinks often contain significant amounts of added sugars and perhaps sodium. They may be flavored or plain, sweetened or not, light or regular, fortified or not, or organic. Flavored options often contain significant amounts of added sugars and perhaps sodium.

Soymilk. For high-quality protein (if you're not allergic to soy), this is a good choice. Among nondairy options, only calcium- and vitamin D–fortified soy beverages come close to low-fat cow's milk in some nutrients, letting it count as a nutrient-rich alternative to dairy milk. *See "Have you ever wondered . . . how cow's milk and soymilk compare?" right.*

Almond milk. Smoother and less chalky than soymilk, this usually has fewer calories and carbohydrates than other nondairy options. It has more vitamin E, since it's made from ground almonds, but there's only 1 gram of protein per 8 ounces of almond milk. The presence and amount of other nutrients depend on fortification. Almond milk is low in saturated fat, and free of gluten, lactose, and soy; it is not for those with nut allergies.

Coconut milk. Made by soaking shredded coconut "meat," the fat (highly saturated) content of coconut milk is higher than other nondairy milk, and there is essentially no protein. To keep coconut milk from separating, thickening agents and emulsifiers are typically added. *See "Have you ever wondered . . . if coconut milk is high in fat?" in chapter 13, page 400, for more about coconut milk; for coconut water, see page 94 in this chapter.*

Hemp milk. Made with ground, soaked hemp seeds and water, hemp milk delivers a significant amount of omega-6 and omega-3 fatty acids

? Have you ever wondered?

. . . how cow's milk and soymilk compare? The nutrient content of soymilk isn't the same as cow's milk. Unless it's fortified, soymilk, made by pressing ground, cooked soybeans, is significantly lower in calcium. As a substitute for cow's milk, choose soymilk that's calcium fortified. Soy drinks range from 80 to 500 milligrams of calcium per cup; check the Nutrition Facts label.

The calcium absorbed by the body from fortified foods varies. For example, the calcium from 1 cup of milk and 1 cup of soymilk fortified with calcium carbonate is about the same. However, to get the same amount from soymilk with tricalcium phosphate, you'd need to drink 1⅓ cups because this form of calcium isn't absorbed as well in the body.

Compared with cow's milk, soymilk is lower in protein and riboflavin, and has little vitamin A or D naturally; some soy beverages are fortified with vitamins A and D and riboflavin. Soy protein may have cardiovascular benefits. The fat content is similar to 2 percent cow's milk. Also look for low-fat versions; however, they may have less protein. If you've been advised to limit cholesterol, soymilk is cholesterol free.

Isoflavones (phytoestrogens) in soy may offer unique benefits; *see "Phytonutrients: Different from Nutrients" in chapter 15, page 448.* Since soy is a weak estrogen, women at high risk for hormone-related sensitivities should consult their doctor about soymilk.

. . . how goat's milk stacks up against cow's milk? Either one is a nutritious option. Goat's milk has slightly more calcium, potassium, and vitamin A; cow's milk, slightly more B vitamins. Cow's milk is the only dairy milk that is routinely fortified with vitamin D; check the Nutrition Facts label on goat's milk. Goat's milk typically costs more. *See chapter 23, page 671, "Have you ever wondered . . . if goat's milk is a good substitute for cow's milk for someone with lactose intolerance or a milk allergy?"*

Milk: A Great Calcium and Vitamin D Source

Dairy and Non Dairy Beverages		Protein	Calcium	Vitamin D		Total Fat	Saturated Fat	Calories
(8 ounces)		(g)	(mg)	(mcg)	(IU)	(g)	(g)	
Buttermilk	1% low-fat	8	285	0	2	2	1.5	100
	2% reduced-fat	10	350	0	2	5	3	135
Milk, unflavored	Fat-free	8	300	3	115	<0.5	<0.5	85
	1% low-fat	8	305	3	115	2	1.5	100
	2% reduced-fat	8	295	3	120	5	3.0	120
	whole	8	275	3	125	8	4.5	150
Milk, chocolate	Fat-free†	9	290	3	120	1	<0.5	140
	1% low-fat†	8	290	3	115	2	1.5	180
	2% reduced-fat	7	275	3	120	5	3	190
	whole	8	280	3	130	8	5	210
Kefir, unflavored	Low-fat	8	195	2	95	2	1.5	95
Almond milk, sweetened, fortified*		1	380	3	120	3	0	60
Rice milk, unsweetened, fortified*		<1	285	2	100	2	0	115
Soymilk (all flavors) fortified*	Low-fat	4	200	2	100	2	0	105

Figures are rounded.

*Nutrient amounts vary based on fortification.

†With concerns about added sugars, many dairy producers have significantly reduced the amount of added sugars in flavored milk.

Source: U.S. Department of Agriculture, National Nutrition Database for Standard Reference Release 28, and Food-A-Pedia, Accessed 2016

and protein. Like other nondairy options made from grains or seeds, it has more carbohydrates than cow's milk. Although nutty in flavor, it's an option for those with nut allergies.

Oat milk. Low in protein and higher in carbohydrates, oat milk provides fiber and iron.

Rice milk. Also low in protein and fat, but higher in carbohydrates, rice milk (often made from brown rice) is an option for those with nut or soy allergies—but not the best option for those with diabetes. It's sweeter than cow's milk.

Think Your Drink: Nondairy Beverages

Consider these tips as you make your nondairy beverage choices:

- For the nutrients they provide, enjoy nondairy drinks in addition to cow's milk or a fortified soymilk, not as a substitute.
- Use the ingredient list and Nutrition Facts label to compare beverages. Choose fortified nondairy milk alternatives with added calcium, vitamin D, and vitamin B_{12}. Look for unsweetened and reduced-sugar options. Limit those with significant amounts of sodium.
- Use the label to compare other nondairy milks, including those made from flaxseed, hazelnuts, and other grains.
- Shake nondairy drinks before you drink them. Some solids, including nutrients, settle to the bottom.

See "Nondairy alternatives" in chapter 6 page 172, for more about buying nondairy alternatives.

Coffee and Tea: Caffeinated or Not?

Does coffee or tea in the morning go with your "wakeup" routine? Caffeine, a mild stimulant, has been part of the human diet for centuries. As far back as five thousand years ago, records suggest that the Chinese were brewing tea. About twenty-five hundred years ago, highly valued coffee beans were used in Africa as currency. In the Americas, first the Mayans and then the Aztecs enjoyed chocolate drinks. Today, caffeine-containing foods and beverages are consumed throughout the world.

A naturally occurring substance in some plants, caffeine is found in leaves, seeds, and fruits of more than sixty plants, among them coffee and cocoa beans, tea leaves, and kola nuts. They're consumed as coffee, chocolate, tea, soft drinks, and energy drinks. If added to a food or drink, caffeine must be listed as an ingredient on the food label. If naturally occurring, it does not need to appear on the label. Caffeine also is found in more than a thousand over-the-counter and prescription drugs.

Coffee remains the chief source of caffeine in the United States. This includes drinks made with coffee, such as lattes, mochas, and cappuccinos. The amount of caffeine varies depending on the type of coffee, the amount, and the brewing method.

Soft drinks, teas, and many energy drinks are common sources of caffeine for children and teens. Among soft drinks, cola isn't the only beverage with caffeine; some citrus-flavored beverages contain caffeine. While claims have been made for using caffeine as a flavor enhancer, this attribute has been scientifically disputed.

? Have you ever wondered?

. . . if sports drinks are good fluid replacers? The optimal drink for many athletes is water. Sports drinks are meant to replace fluids, supply calories for energy, and replace sodium and potassium lost through perspiration. Most athletes don't need a sports drink unless they've exercised for an hour or more. Even then, the body mainly needs fluids. If you're more likely to drink a sports drink than water during physical activity, then do. Just be aware that these drinks contain added sugars, so they also supply calories. If sports drinks are your regular beverage choice, their calories can add up: often 50 to 100 calories per 8 ounces. *See "Fluids for Sports: What's Best?" in chapter 21, page 603, for more about sports drinks.*

. . . if coconut water is a good fluid replacement? Sure. It's both refreshing and thirst quenching. Coconut water (not coconut milk), which is the clear liquid inside young, green coconuts, is naturally rich in potassium (670 milligrams per 11 ounces), with less sodium and fewer calories than a sports drink. For shorter workouts, coconut water (like water) is a good choice. If unflavored, it's low in sugar and provides (about 50 calories per 8 ounces), so it might be a better choice than a soft drink. But it won't make you lose weight or detoxify and won't be the perfect drink for endurance sports. Unlike commercial sports drinks, coconut water won't replace all the electrolytes lost through sweat.

CAFFEINE AND HEALTH

Among healthy people, moderate amounts of caffeine are safe and don't pose a danger to health. As a mild stimulant to the central nervous system, caffeine helps people stay mentally alert, overcome fatigue, and sustain their attention. And it may help enhance mental and physical effort.

What's considered moderate? Up to 400 milligrams of caffeine per day or about three to five eight-ounce cups of home-brewed coffee is a moderate daily amount. The FDA, as well as Health Canada and the European Food Safety Authority, advise that this amount isn't associated with adverse health effects for healthy adults.

Potential Health Benefits

Over the years, many studies have explored the connection between caffeine and health. A growing body of evidence suggests some potential health benefits of moderate caffeine intake—beyond being more alert in the short term. Among possible benefits linked to consuming moderate amounts of caffeine are lower risks for cardiovascular disease and type 2 diabetes, and perhaps helping to prevent cognitive decline associated with aging.

Most research on caffeine has been done with coffee. A growing body of research indicates that some potential long-term benefits of coffee drinking also may be linked to antioxidants, such as flavonoids, minerals, or other components, in coffee. Among the unanswered questions is what substances in coffee may confer long-term health benefits? More research is needed before recommendations can be made. In fact, the Dietary Guidelines for Americans advises: if you don't now consume caffeinated drinks, you don't need to start.

See "Have you ever wondered . . . if caffeine can boost your physical performance?" in chapter 21, page 604, for more about caffeine and physical performance.

Caffeine: Clarifying Confusion

Scientific evidence does not link moderate caffeine intake to higher risks for some cancers, fibrocystic breast disease (benign fibrous lumps), cardiovascular disease, elevated blood cholesterol levels, ulcers, inflammatory bowel disease, infertility, birth defects, or osteoporosis. Both the American Cancer Society and the American Medical Association (AMA) confirm the safety of moderate caffeine consumption.

The following information should help to dispel some misconceptions about caffeine consumption and certain health issues:

Blood pressure. Caffeine may cause a temporary rise in blood pressure that lasts only a few hours, adding up to less than that from climbing stairs. It doesn't cause chronic hypertension or a lasting increase in blood pressure. If you have high blood pressure talk to your doctor about caffeine intake.

Bone health. While caffeine can slightly increase the calcium lost through urine and feces and slightly decrease calcium absorption, adding a little milk to your coffee easily offsets this. (Or get calcium from other sources.) Moderate amounts of caffeine don't appear to increase osteoporosis or the risk of fractures.

Hydration. Dump the myth relating caffeine and hydration. Caffeinated drinks can help people meet the recommended amounts of daily water, as acknowledged by the Institute of Medicine. Although caffeine is a weak diuretic, it doesn't cause dehydration. In fact, the body develops a tolerance to caffeine after three to five days of regular use, allowing the body to keep its fluid balance.

Caffeinated drinks won't cause electrolyte imbalance, either. If you have diarrhea, avoiding caffeine might be advised, however.

Heart rate, heart disease, and anxiety. In varying degrees, excessive caffeine intake may cause "coffee jitters," anxiety, or insomnia. Caffeine also may increase the heart rate temporarily. The effects don't last long; caffeine doesn't accumulate in the body.

Most research concludes that moderate caffeine intake isn't associated with higher risk of cardiovascular disease or changes in blood cholesterol levels.

Caffeine "addiction." Can you get addicted to morning coffee or a caffeine drink? Not with a true addiction, although you might think or say so. Feeling dependent on coffee when you wake up is habitual, not a physical dependence to caffeine, as associated with addiction to some drugs.

Caffeine doesn't have addictive qualities as some drugs may. The term "addictive" is loosely used. If you consume caffeinated drinks regularly and then suddenly stop, you may have short-term symptoms—drowsiness, headache, perhaps less concentration—that disappear in a day or two.

Hyperactivity and attention deficit disorder. According to the National Institutes of Health, caffeine affects children and adults in the same way. No studies show that caffeine is linked to hyperactive behavior or attention deficit disorder.

"Sobering" effect. Many think coffee helps someone "sober up" after drinking too much alcohol, but caffeine won't counteract its effects and does not change blood alcohol levels. Drinking coffee or any other caffeinated drink will not reduce the harmful risks related to drinking alcoholic beverages. Neither will a cold shower or a long walk. Only time can make someone sober.

Sensitive to Caffeine?

Caffeine sensitivity varies. It depends on the amount and frequency of caffeine intake, body weight, physical condition, and overall anxiety level, among other factors. For that reason, "excessive" caffeine intake is subjective.

After ingesting caffeine, it takes thirty to forty-five minutes for it to reach the bloodstream. The effect lasts for three to four hours before it's excreted through urine. For smokers, it's slightly faster. Some people eliminate caffeine more slowly.

Some people feel caffeine's effects—perhaps "coffee jitters," anxiety, or insomnia—at very low levels; others are unaffected and can consume more. Moreover, a regular coffee drinker may not notice the effects as quickly as someone who drinks an occasional cup. And tolerance to caffeine develops over time.

Caffeine: What's Moderation?

For most healthy people, moderate amounts of caffeine pose no problems The Dietary Guidelines for Americans defines a "moderate level" for healthy adults—up to 400 milligrams a day, or about three to five 8-ounce cups of home-brewed coffee.

Those who may be more sensitive to caffeine, such as pregnant women and those with a history of heart attack or high blood pressure, should talk with their physician about their caffeine consumption.

For kids: No evidence shows that caffeine in levels normally found in food and beverages are harmful or that kids are any more sensitive to caffeine than adults—although too much is not advised, discussed in *"Have you ever wondered . . . how much caffeine is your child getting?" on the next page.* Current data show caffeine consumption among children and teens, although moderate, is from soft drinks and tea as well as coffee drinks and energy drinks; *see "Energy Drinks" in this chapter, page 604.*

Here is some advice to consider when choosing caffeinated drinks:

- If you're pregnant or nursing: Up to 200 milligrams of caffeine is advised by the American College of Obstetricians & Gynecologists and the March of Dimes as well as the FDA and the European Food Safety Authority. That's the average amount of caffeine in 12 ounces of caffeinated coffee (depending on preparation method and roasting degree of coffee beans).

  Moderation doesn't appear to cause adverse effects, such as miscarriage, preterm delivery, birth defects, or low-birth weight babies. And it doesn't affect fertility. Most physicians agree on its safety, but sensitivity to caffeine may increase during pregnancy.

  In breast milk, caffeine can pass to the baby; the amount in usual amounts of coffee or tea isn't enough to affect the infant. Still, the American Academy of Pediatrics advises you to limit caffeine during breastfeeding, but you don't need to avoid it altogether.

- If you have a medical issue: Ask your physician about caffeine intake, especially if you have gastritis, ulcers, or high blood pressure, or if you take beta-blockers. Caffeine doesn't cause gastric reflux disease (GERD). Not enough evidence exists to advise everyone with GERD to avoid caffeinated drinks, but limits may be advised for some.

- At any age: Pay attention to how caffeine affects you, especially if coffee, tea, soft drinks, or energy drinks replace more nutritious foods or drinks.

Think Your Drink: Caffeine in Moderation

If you drink caffeinated beverages, these are some ways to moderate your caffeine intake:

- If you need to cut back, do it gradually—to get your body accustomed to consuming less. A gradual cutback helps avoid any temporary headaches or drowsiness.

? Have you ever wondered?

. . . if powdered caffeine can be a good pick-me-up? No! In fact, the FDA warns against powdered pure caffeine because it is a powerful stimulant, which may lead to an unintended overdose. It's especially harmful for those with pre-existing heart conditions. A single teaspoon is about equal to twenty-five cups of coffee. Caffeine toxicity can include a dangerously erratic or rapid heartbeat, seizures, disorientation, diarrhea, vomiting, and even death. Although the suggested dose is between 1⁄32 and 1⁄16 teaspoon, measuring that amount with home measuring equipment is nearly impossible! (*Note:* powdered caffeine isn't the same as instant coffee.)

. . . how much caffeine your child is getting? Depending mostly on drink choices, your child may consume more caffeine than you realize. While small amounts may make people of all ages feel more energetic without causing harm, too much caffeine may affect your child's or teen's sleep pattern, and being tired may affect learning and more. If your child or teen has trouble sleeping and seems jittery or anxious, do a caffeine check: limit soft drinks, tea, and coffee, and keep energy drinks, gums, and candy with caffeine out of reach. (Encourage good sleep habits, too.)

Canada has established daily limits for caffeine for children: ages four to six years (about the amount in one twelve-ounce can of cola), 45 milligrams; ages seven to nine years, 62 milligrams, and ages ten to twelve, 85 milligrams. Most kids consume much less (15 to 22 milligrams daily), as noted by a report from the International Food Information Council (IFIC) Foundation.

. . . why caffeine isn't listed on a Nutrition Facts label? Since caffeine isn't a nutrient, it isn't listed on the Nutrition Facts label. However, if it's added to a food, it must appear on the ingredient list. Because coffee, tea, and cacao for chocolate contain caffeine naturally, caffeine won't be listed. Many companies, including those who make energy drinks, voluntarily list the caffeine content on their food or drink packages.

. . . how much caffeine a cup of chicory coffee contains? Chicory is an herb that's caffeine-free. The chicory root is roasted and then ground before it is brewed or steeped. Roasting gives it a flavor that's similar to coffee. To make chicory coffee, you might replace some of the coffee grounds with chicory. The result: less caffeine. Because chicory root costs less than coffee, you save money, too.

. . . what coffee flour is? A by-product of processing coffee beans, coffee flour is starting to "trend" as a high-fiber, gluten-free carbohydrate ingredient that can be used in cooking and baking. It's actually from the fruit of the coffee tree, or the cherry, which surrounds the coffee bean. It has a minimal amount of caffeine and essentially no coffee flavor. (It is not powdered caffeine.) And it may be one more way of processing by-products with a new culinary mission.

The leftover, dried coffee cherry can also be used to make cascara, a traditional coffee drink popular in Ethiopia and Yemen.

- Mix equal amounts of regular and decaffeinated coffee for "half caf."
- Drink decaffeinated varieties of tea or coffee, or caffeine-free herbal tea. Some bottled coffee drinks also are decaffeinated; check the label.
- Brew tea for a shorter time. Research shows that a one-minute brew may contain just half the caffeine that a three-minute brew contains.
- Keep a cup of water handy to sip. If you drink coffee mindlessly, you may be getting more caffeine than you realize.
- Read soft drink labels; look for soft drinks labeled "caffeine-free." Color doesn't indicate the presence of caffeine; both clear and caramel-colored soft drinks may have caffeine. Caffeine is listed in the ingredient list if it was added to make the product. Caffeine that's present naturally is generally not listed on the label.
- Go easy on energy drinks, *discussed later in this chapter, page 100*, and read the label. The caffeine content per label serving in energy drinks varies; a beverage container may contain more than one label serving—or may reflect the amount commonly consumed of the drink.
- Read medication labels carefully, or check with your pharmacist. One dose of an over-the-counter pain-relief capsule can contain as much caffeine as one or two cups of coffee, which is amplified if you're consuming caffeinated foods or beverages.
- For those with insomnia, avoid coffee or other caffeine sources six to eight hours before bedtime. *See "Drink Smart—and Get Your Zzzzs!" on the next page.*

See "Caffeine: What Sources, How Much?" in this chapter, page 98. Also see "Coffee: Morning Brew," "Tea Time," and "Soda, Energy Drinks, and Enhanced Beverages" in this chapter, pages 97 and 100.

COFFEE: MORNING BREW

Coffee, brewed from ground, roasted beans (actually seeds) comes from a tropical evergreen shrub called *Coffea*. Two species are the most common, arabica and the stronger robusta. The degree and conditions of roasting affect the coffee's flavor and body, or texture. Stronger roasting intensifies the flavor and aroma and darkens the color. A darker roast has a somewhat sweeter flavor; longer roasting caramelizes starches in the beans.

Coffee's Health Connections

A cup of black coffee is calorie free. Adding milk, cream, sugar, or other flavorings changes its nutrient content. Coffee is also a source of phytonutrients (polyphenols) and caffeine. These bioactive substances may have health benefits, *as discussed elsewhere in this chapter.* The mild, short-term diuretic effect from caffeine doesn't outweigh its fluid benefits.

Despite the chance of disturbed sleep patterns, coffee's caffeine may have some health benefits, *as noted earlier in this chapter.* How much caffeine per cup? That depends on the grind, brewing method, and type of coffee bean. *See "Caffeine: What Sources, How Much?" on the next page.* Experts say that steeping, as done with a French press, releases more caffeine from dark-roasted coffee beans, while espresso methods and percolating release more caffeine from light-roasted coffee beans.

Coffee also contains antioxidant compounds and diterpenes (in the coffee beans' oil), which may protect against some health issues.

Think Your Drink: Coffee

Consider these tips if you choose caffeinated coffee or coffee drinks:

- Enjoy the flavor of coffee black (no sugar, to limit added sugars) or with milk. Just 2 tablespoons of low-fat milk add 35 grams of calcium and only 12 calories.
- For a specialty coffee drink, choose one made with steamed milk only (no flavored syrup). A latte is typically espresso, steamed milk, and milk foam. Café au lait is coffee with warm, steamed milk and no foam. A cappuccino is like a latte but with additional steamed milk. And a macchiato is espresso with a milk foam topping.
- Chic coffee drinks? Go easy on added shots of caramel, chocolate, and other flavored syrups. Ditto for cream and sugars. Total fats, saturated fats, and calories add up! Remember that double espresso shots mean double the caffeine, too; order your drink made decaf if you prefer.
- Limit the size of coffee drinks. The larger the cup, the more calories and, if more sugary syrup is added in a larger cup, the more added sugars. A 16-ounce coffee drink can add up to 250 to 300 calories to your daily intake (for many, this is more than 10 percent of the day's calorie needs)! Many coffee drinks are often even bigger!
- Customize your coffee drink to make it healthier. Request fat-free milk (no or less whipped cream) or soymilk, and perhaps sugar-free syrup and a dusting of cocoa powder or cinnamon.

Drink Smart—and Get Your Zzzzs!

Do you wake up with a sleep deficit? Do you regularly have trouble sleeping? Adequate rest, along with good nutrition and regular physical activity, are part of any fitness formula. For the "rest" of your life:

- If you're caffeine sensitive, avoid caffeinated drinks six to eight hours before sleep time. To drink at meals and with snacks later in the day, opt for milk, juice, water, or decaffeinated drinks instead.
- Don't expect a glass of wine or other alcoholic beverage to help you sleep well. A drink might help you to feel drowsy at first, but even if you sip a drink two or three hours before bedtime, your sleep might be light and disrupted instead of the deep, most restful sleep pattern. Since alcohol stays in your system for a while, you'll sleep better if you avoid an alcoholic beverage several hours before bedtime.
- Will a glass of warm milk help you sleep? Perhaps. The reason is more likely the psychological impact of milk as a comfort food, not its relatively small tryptophan content.

An added note: Promote rest through regular physical activity. Being active actually helps your body relax and sleep soundly. Just refrain from exercise too close to bedtime. Exercise speeds up your metabolism for a while, perhaps keeping you "pumped up" and unable to sleep right away. *See "Have you ever wondered . . . why sleep is important to health?" in chapter 1, page 5, for more about sleep.*

For the record, a 12-ounce latte, made with fat-free milk (no added syrups or whipped cream), has about 400 milligrams of calcium and 110 calories. For cappuccino, you don't need whole milk to get a foam; low-fat or fat-free milk and soymilk will do the trick.

- Instead of syrup or sugar, flavor with a pinch of cardamom or cinnamon as you brew coffee, or blend a splash of vanilla or almond extract with brewed coffee.
- Check the Nutrition Facts label of bottled coffee drinks. They may not have as much calcium as you think—but perhaps a lot more calories!

TEA TIME

Next to water, tea is the most common beverage choice around the world—more popular today with growing numbers of tea shops and tea rooms, and myriad ways to enjoy traditional tea and its herbal options.

Caffeine: What Sources, How Much?

The amount of caffeine in foods or beverages depends on several factors: type of product, method of preparation, and portion size, and for teas and coffees, the plant variety. Caffeine occurs naturally in some products, such as coffee and chocolate, and is added as a flavoring in some others, such as soft drinks.

	Caffeine (mg)	
Beverage	**Typical**	**Range***
Coffee (8-ounces)		
Brewed, drip method	95	75–165
Instant	75	60–85
Decaffeinated	3	2–4
Espresso (1 ounce)	40	30–50
Tea† (8 ounces)		
Black	47	14–70
Green	25	24–45
White	15	15
Instant	30	11–47
Iced	2	59–50
Soft drinks (12 ounces)		
Cola	40	30–60
Citrus	40	37–47
Energy drinks (8 ounces)	80	27–164
Cocoa beverage (8 ounces)	6	3–32
Chocolate milk beverage (8 ounces)	5	2–7
Solid milk chocolate (1 ounce)	6	1–15
Solid dark chocolate (1 ounce)	20	5–35
Solid unsweetened chocolate (1 ounce)	26	26
Chocolate-flavored syrup (1 ounce)	4	4

*Due to brewing method, plant variety, formulation, etc.

†Herbal teas that are infusions with no tea leaves have no caffeine.

Simply Tea

Whether it's black, green, oolong, or white, tea comes from the same plant families, called *Camellia sinensis*. Differences in color and flavor depend on how it is processed:

- For black tea, the most popular type in the United States, tea leaves are exposed to air. Natural fermentation and oxidation colors them a deep red-brown and imparts a unique, rich flavor. Many flavored specialty teas start with black tea. For pu-erh tea, a type of black tea, the leaves are aged and pressed into cakes. *Note:* orange pekoe isn't made with orange flavor; instead "pekoe" or "orange pekoe" refers to the grade and size of tea leaves.
- For green tea, typically served in Chinese and Japanese restaurants, the tea leaves are not processed as much as those used for black tea. Instead, they're heated or steamed quickly to keep their green color and delicate flavor.
- Oolong tea is "in between," between black and green tea. It is semi-fermented, but not as much as black tea is.
- White tea, which is not as common in the United States as elsewhere, comes from uncured and unfermented tea leaves and buds from the *Camellia sinensis* plant. White tea is the most minimally-processed variety of all teas.

Tea-rific health benefits. Can tea drinking help keep you healthy? Indeed. Besides keeping you hydrated, it's calorie free if unsweetened. And its components may deliver more health benefits.

Tea ranks high as a source of polyphenols (including flavonoids); these antioxidants may help protect body cells from damage done by free radicals. Due to the fermentation and oxidation processes, the concentration of polyphenols is lower in black and oolong teas; they're still an antioxidant powerhouse. Decaffeinated teas have less flavonoids. *See "Rounding Up Free Radicals" in chapter 14, page 423, for more about antioxidants.*

Tea or tea's flavonoids may reduce the risk of gastric, esophageal, and skin cancers and offer protection from heart disease and stroke. Some evidence suggests these benefits are most likely to occur if you drink four to six cups a day. Other studies are investigating whether tea plays a role in relaxation or mental performance, and in lowering cholesterol, preventing diabetes, burning fat, or holding off dementia. Tea also may offer antimicrobial qualities.

Besides smaller amounts of caffeine, tea contains the amino acid L-theanine, which may have some calming effects. Research indicates that L-theanine and caffeine may have other cognitive benefits including heightening mental alertness. Stay tuned.

Tea, with its moderate amount of fluoride, may promote dental health. Fluoride, which helps strengthen tooth enamel, is a natural compound in black, green, and oolong tea leaves. Tea leaves may also be steeped in fluoridated water. Additionally, tea may help reduce plaque formation and hinder cavity-forming bacteria.

Herbal Teas

Take a sip of apple-cinnamon tea, mint tea, hibiscus tea, chamomile tea, or ginger tea. Like what you taste? Interest in herbal teas has grown as an alternative to caffeinated beverages and for those seeking other health benefits. For others, exploring herbal teas is simply for the flavor adventure.

? Have you ever wondered?

. . . what's rooibos tea (red bush tea)? Pronounced ROY-boss, rooibos is a fermented herbal brew, not a tea. First popularized in South Africa, this red brew that comes in nutty, flowery, and fruity flavors is purported to have antioxidant benefits. Research doesn't back up the advertised health claims, however. As with other herbals, be cautious, *as discussed in "Herbal Teas" on the previous page.* Its use as a drink appears safe for most healthy people; however, not enough is known about its components or its use or dosage as a medicine,

. . . what's yerba mate? Originating in South America, this is an infusion made by steeping yerba mate leaves in hot water and then drinking it through a special straw to strain it. High in caffeine and other compounds, it's a stimulant. Evidence for its purported health benefits is lacking. *Caution:* While likely safe in limited amounts for short periods of time for most healthy people, large amounts over time may be harmful, especially for those with certain health conditions. Health professionals advise that yerba mate can have mild to severe interactions with many medications, including alcoholic beverages. Talk to your doctor.

. . . how matcha compares to green tea? Actually, matcha is green tea that's milled into a fine powder, giving the tea itself a smooth texture and sweet taste. Traditionally enjoyed in Japanese tea ceremonies, it's getting attention today as a concentrated source of antioxidants, specifically catechin, since the whole tea leaf is consumed. Some call it "supercharged green tea." To date, there's not much research on the health benefits of matcha, except for what's known about its caffeine.

Being concentrated, its flavor is strong and grassy. Matcha also is used as a flavoring and coloring ingredient in foods such as soba noodles, green tea ice cream, and energy bars. Its deep-green color comes from its high chlorophyll content. Matcha powder is sold in Japanese tea shops and some specialty stores; you may use it to flavor and color smoothies, baked goods, and other foods.

. . . what kombucha is? In general, this is a fermented beverage made of steeped tea (any type), sugar, and yeast for fermentation. It may have fruit juice or other flavors added during production, too. Its alcoholic content varies, but if kombucha has at least 0.5 percent alcohol by volume, it's regulated as an alcoholic beverage.

Herbal teas can fit into two categories:

- Tea leaves with added herbs and perhaps fruit juice, honey, sweeteners, or flavor extracts when consumed: These have small amounts of caffeine unless the label indicates "decaf." The ingredient list will include "tea."
- Infusions made with herbs, flowers, roots, spices, seeds, or various other parts of many plants: The more correct term for them is "tisane," which means tea-like substance. They aren't tea.

Unique health benefits—or not? Despite claims that certain herbal teas may ease stress, promote sleep, aid weight loss, or fend off the common cold, little is known about the unique health benefits of herbal teas. Some research suggests that polyphenols in some may bind iron before it can be absorbed.

Most major branded herbal teas are considered safe to drink. Still, consume only common varieties sold by major manufacturers.

Some herbal teas interfere with over-the-counter or prescription medications. Talk to your doctor or pharmacist before drinking them if you're on medication.

Because of their potential harmful effects, be careful about using comfrey, lobelia, woodruff, tonka beans, melilot, sassafras root, and some others to make infusions; they may be harmful in large amounts. For example, comfrey may cause liver damage. Woodruff, an anticoagulant, may cause bleeding. Lobelia may cause breathing problems. Even chamomile may cause an allergic reaction. The FDA has also issued warnings about dieter's teas with plant-derived laxatives such as aloe, buckthorn, and senna.

See "Herbals and Other Botanicals" in chapter 10, page 320.

Think Your Drink: Tea

Keep these guidelines in mind if you choose tea or tea drinks:

- Enjoy tea, preferably unsweetened; steep it for at least three minutes to bring out the flavor, color, and health benefits.
- Add flavor and nutrition to your next cup of tea. *See "Kitchen Nutrition: Enjoy Tea for Flavor and Health!" on the next page.*
- Be aware: Many bottled or canned iced-tea drinks have as many added sugars and calories as regular sodas; read the label. Even instant tea may have added sugars and flavorings. For sweetness, you might look for those with low-calorie sweeteners.
- For herbal teas, be cautious—as noted above!
- Green tea extract as a dietary supplement? It may have health risks, *as noted in chapter 10, page 317.* Brewed tea may have health-promoting compounds that extracts don't.

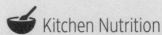

Kitchen Nutrition

Enjoy Tea for Flavor and Health!

Hot or cold, flavored or not, blended with milk or a nondairy alternative, tea can be a healthy drink choice:

- Watching calories? Enjoy cold or hot, unsweetened tea, steeped with a slice or citrus or ginger, or a sprig of fresh basil, lemon verbena, mint, or thyme.
- Add citrus or other fruit juice. Tea's flavonoids partly inhibit the absorption of nonheme iron (iron from legumes, grain products, and eggs). A squeeze of vitamin C–rich lemon, orange, or lime in tea can counteract some of the action.
- For more calcium and vitamin D, enjoy "milk tea": hot or cold tea blended with milk. Some believe that adding milk to tea lowers tea's antioxidant power. However, no scientific evidence proves that milk binds to and inactivates polyphenols.
- Take milk tea up a notch, and enjoy it as chai (rhymes with pie) or spiced milk tea! A favorite in India, chai blends black tea, milk, spices such as cardamom, cinnamon, ginger, cloves, and pepper, and a little sugar or honey to bring out the flavor of the spices. Serve it iced or as a milkshake. Be aware: Some chai mixes are very high in added sugars.

Soda, Energy Drinks, and Enhanced Beverages

When you want a switch from water, 100 percent juice, or milk, enjoy other beverages. But go easy!

SOFT DRINKS: OKAY?

Flavored, carbonated drinks have been around for about two hundred years. The term "soft drink" originally was coined to distinguish these beverages from "hard" liquor. A hundred years ago, consumers asked for "pop," named for the sound made by popping open the bottle cap. Today, a "soft drink"—or "soda" in some parts of the United States—is a beverage made with carbonated water and usually with flavoring ingredients.

What's in soft drinks? Whether regular or diet varieties, soft drinks contain water—about 90 percent by weight for regular soft drinks and about 99 percent for diet soft drinks. Carbon dioxide, added just before sealing the bottle or can, provides the fizz. Regular soft drinks are sweetened with sugar (perhaps high-fructose corn syrup); diet drinks, with aspartame, sucralose, or other low-calorie sweeteners; *see "Sugar Alternatives" in chapter 11, page 368, for more about low-calorie sweeteners.* Artificial and natural flavors may add more flavor. Acids such as citric acid and phosphoric acid give tartness and act as preservatives. Coloring may be added, while other ingredients may give consistency.

Enjoyed only sometimes, no one disputes that soft drinks are tasty, refreshing, and hydrating. But if your consumption goes up, nutritional concerns do, too. Sugar-sweetened beverages account for about 39 percent of added sugars in the US diet; 25 percent of total calories come from soft drinks, as noted in the Dietary Guidelines for Americans! Cutting back on regular soft drinks can reduce added sugars and calories, and depending on your calorie intake, perhaps help lead to initial weight loss.

Think Your Drink: Soft Drinks

Keep these guidelines in mind if you choose soft drinks:

- Limit regular soft drinks. Regular soft drinks deliver water, carbohydrates in the form of added sugars, and calories but little else nutritionally. A 12-ounce can of regular cola supplies water and about 150 calories (from almost 10 teaspoons of added sugars). A 20-ounce bottle has 250 calories!

  Be aware: Advice for healthy eating says that no more than 10 percent of your day's calories should come from added sugars. On a 2,000-calorie daily eating pattern, that would be no more than 200 calories from added sugars per day from all drink and food sources.
- Go for small cans, bottles, cups, or glasses. Resist the temptation to super-size. If a soda machine only sells 20-ounce bottles, save half for later; most bottles have screw tops. Some sodas are now sold in 8-ounce cans or bottles with just 100 calories.
- Make soft drinks a sometimes beverage, not a replacement for nutrient-rich drinks such as low-fat and fat-free milk, fortified soymilk, or 100 percent juice.
- For essentially zero calories, choose a diet soft drink. It's a source of water, and may contain caffeine, but nothing else. It might be a drink option for weight loss or control, or for diabetes management—but not a weight-loss tactic if you splurge elsewhere.
- Drink milk or water with a meal; break the habit of soft drinks as a regular accompaniment. Enjoy a soft drink as a now-and-then snack instead.
- If you're caffeine sensitive, look for caffeine-free options.
- Soft drinks fortified with antioxidants? *See "Enhanced Beverages" in this chapter, page 101.*

ENERGY DRINKS

Can energy drinks or energy shots make you alert or enhance physical and mental performances, especially on less sleep? The answer is perhaps for the short-term. But, cautions the FDA, they can't replace a good night's sleep. Reaction time and judgment still can be impaired by a lack of sleep.

Caffeine, often at very high levels, is the common stimulant in many energy drinks. There can be as many as 500 milligrams of caffeine in a 24-ounce can! Unlike colas, caffeine levels in energy drinks aren't regulated. Excessive amounts of caffeine or caffeinelike ingredients may lead to anxiety, insomnia, increased blood pressure, and rapid heartbeat. *See "Caffeine and Health" in this chapter, page 94.*

Many energy drinks, considered dietary supplements, contain other ingredients such as taurine (an amino acid), inositol, guarana (a potent caffeine-containing seed), ginseng, B vitamins, and carnitine that are added for their purported roles in physical or mental performance. Scientific evidence, however, is inadequate to support these claims. Energy drinks may also be high in added sugars. As an aside, food can provide some of these ingredients: taurine from animal sources and inositol from beans, brown rice, and corn.

What about energy drinks for athletes? Their caffeine may feel like an energy boost at first, but performance may suffer with excessive caffeine intake. Energy drinks are different from sports drinks.

See "Fluids for Sports: What's Best?" in chapter 21, page 603, for more about drinks for athletes.

Caution: Energy Drinks

Energy drinks aren't advised for people with certain health conditions, such as heart disease or high blood pressure. Limit their use during pregnancy and nursing, too. If you are considering drinking one of these products, consult your healthcare provider to make sure you don't have a medical condition that could worsen with regular consumption of energy drinks.

The American Academy of Pediatrics (AAP) advises against energy drinks for children and teens due to excessive amounts of caffeine, posing concerns about potential health risks of stimulants for young people; *see "Energy Drinks" in chapter 21, page 604.* In 2013, the American Medical Association adopted a policy that supports a ban on marketing high-stimulant/caffeine drinks to adolescents under the age of eighteen.

Caffeinated alcoholic drinks. Using energy drinks as mixers in alcoholic drinks is not advised. The stimulating effect of caffeine may mask the headache, weakness, and dry mouth that comes with consuming too much alcohol. Decreased motor coordination and slower reaction time is still a potential danger. Caffeine won't change blood alcohol levels, either, or reduce the potential risks related to alcoholic drinks.

The FDA warns against packaged alcoholic beverages that contain caffeine and other stimulants as additives. It does not consider them "generally recognized as safe." If you combine caffeinated drinks with alcohol, you may not be able to tell how intoxicated you are.

Think Your Drink: Energy Drinks

If you want the caffeine from an energy drink, go easy! Keep these guidelines in mind if you choose energy drinks:

- Check the serving size and the calorie and caffeine content per serving on the Nutrition Facts label. Choose those with less caffeine and added sugars. Many energy drinks contain as much as 25 to 50 grams of added sugars per serving; if you consume 2,000 calories daily, that's half or all the added sugars advised for a day. These added sugars are also a potential problem for those with diabetes or who have prediabetes.
- If the container has two to three servings, as shown on the Nutrition Facts label, drink one serving or less. A two- to three-serving can or bottle provides two to three times the caffeine and calories. As new food labeling regulations go into effect, Nutrition Facts will be shown in commonly consumed amounts. *See "A Closer Look . . . Nutrition Facts Update 2016" in chapter 6, page 146, for more about updates on food labeling.*
- If you're drinking wine, beer, or another alcoholic drink, skip the energy drink—and vice versa.
- If you're often tired or run-down, instead boost your energy with more sleep, less stress, regular physical activity, and healthy eating. If that doesn't work, talk with your doctor.

ENHANCED BEVERAGES

Improve your memory? Lift your mood? Build your immunity? Boost your energy? Aid weight loss? The popularity of enhanced beverages has grown in leaps and bounds! However, they often displace nutrient-rich beverages and water. And evidence may not support the marketing claims.

They include enhanced waters and juices, probiotic and protein drinks, and others, all formulated or fortified to provide health benefits beyond general nutrition. However, currently there's no regulatory definition for them. If they qualify as "enhanced," they might offer carry nutrient content claims or other claims on the label. For example, juice, juice blends, and juice drinks that are fortified with calcium, vitamin D, or omega-3s might carry these claims. Depending on their ingredients (herbs, phytonutrients, nutrients, tea, probiotics, and others), some are regulated as dietary supplements. *See chapter 10, page 315, for more about supplements.*

For many herbal drinks, such as acai berry drinks and noni juice (morinda), the scientific evidence for their marketing claims is limited and inconclusive. Many over promise on what they can deliver. Some are high in added sugars. The amount of the herbal ingredient is neither standardized nor usually stated on the Nutrition Facts label. The safety of consuming optimal amounts is not known. Talk to your healthcare professional about using them.

Vitamin-enhanced waters? Not necessary if you follow guidelines for healthy eating—and certainly not if you take a multivitamin supplement.

Enhanced drinks do provide hydration, but often as a pricey option!

Have you ever wondered?

. . . if diet soda can promote weight gain? Early research is exploring a possible physical response to artificially sweetened sodas and whether they lead to physiological confusion that might prompt overeating. So far, this hypothesis has not been proven, and data is too limited to know. Advice for now: many organizations, including the American Diabetes Association and the Academy of Nutrition and Dietetics, support the use of low- and no-calorie sweeteners to help maintain a healthy weight—as long as you also manage calories overall.

. . . if flavored or nutrient-added water drinks are good choices? They may be a thirst-quenching option, but check the Nutrition Facts and ingredient list, required on the label, to see what they contain. Some are simply bottled water with flavoring. Others may contain added nutrients such as vitamins, electrolytes such as sodium and potassium, and amino acids. A water beverage must meet the FDA's bottled-water regulations if the word "water" is highlighted on the label. This is the case, for example, with berry-flavored spring water.

Think Your Drink: Enhanced Beverages

Keep these guidelines in mind if you choose enhanced beverages:

- Go for naturally nutrient-rich beverages. Fortifying sugary drinks with vitamins or antioxidants doesn't make them healthy. Because they don't provide the full array of nutrients and the phytonutrients that are supplied by fruits and vegetables, their potential benefits may be limited.
- Check the labels for added sweeteners and calories. Go easy on those with added sugars.
- Enjoy these drinks if they fit within your limit, but know that they may not provide the added health benefits that you hope for. If you already eat smart, exercise regularly, manage stress, and get enough rest, they probably won't offer significant benefits. No enhanced or functional beverage can counter the effects of dysfunctional eating or living.

Alcoholic Beverages: In Moderation

No one's sure who first invented beer, wine, or spirits, but historians do know that societies have consumed them throughout recorded history.

Today, moderate amounts still may add pleasure to eating. For some, a single drink may be relaxing—perhaps in the company of others. The key to potential benefits is sensibility: moderation and understanding alcohol equivalency.

- *Moderation:* If you drink alcoholic beverages, moderation is essential. This means up to one drink per day for adult women and two drinks per day for adult men of legal drinking age.

  What is excessive? High-risk drinking for women is considered as four or more drinks per day, or eight or more per week. For men, five or more drinks per day, or fifteen or more per week is considered excessive. Even with low-risk drinking, problems can arise for those who drink too fast or have other health issues, as noted by the National Institute on Alcohol Abuse and Alcoholism (NIAAA) and the NIH. Binge drinking, as defined by NIAAA, is consuming four or more drinks for women and five or more for men within two hours.
- *Equivalency of one drink:* Twelve fluid ounces of regular beer (5 percent alcohol; about 150 calories), or 5 ounces of fluid wine (12 percent alcohol; about 120 calories), or 1.5 fluid ounces of 80-proof distilled spirits (40 percent alcohol; 100 calories). Each one of these drinks—one beer, one wine, or one drink made with distilled spirits—contains the same amount of alcohol—approximately 14 grams (or 0.6 fluid ounces) of pure ethanol. (Distilled spirits include bourbon, brandy, gin, rum, vodka, whisky, and liqueurs.)

Label Lingo

Alcoholic Beverages

You'll find the warning statement below on the label of beverages containing alcohol. On wine and beer labels, you may also find information on sulfite content. Sulfites are added to most wines to protect flavor and color. *See "Sulfite Sensitivity: Mild to Severe" in chapter 23, page 678.* (*Tip:* If you're sulfite sensitive, distilled spirits and sake, a type of rice wine, don't contain sulfites.)

GOVERNMENT WARNING:

(1) ACCORDING TO THE SURGEON GENERAL, WOMEN SHOULD NOT DRINK ALCOHOLIC BEVERAGES DURING PREGNANCY BECAUSE OF THE RISK OF BIRTH DEFECTS. (2) CONSUMPTION OF ALCOHOLIC BEVERAGES IMPAIRS YOUR ABILITY TO DRIVE A CAR OR OPERATE MACHINERY, AND MAY CAUSE HEALTH PROBLEMS.

CONTAINS SULFITES

Currently, the presence of major food allergens doesn't need to be disclosed on alcoholic beverage labels. There is an interim rule, in effect since 2006, for optional allergen-labeling statements.

Because packaged beer, wine, and mixed drinks vary in their alcohol content, it's important to be aware of their alcoholic-drink equivalents; *See "Alcoholic Drink-Equivalents of Select Beverages" in the appendix, page 780.*

Note: A 750-milliliter bottle of wine contains about five 5-ounce glasses of wine.

ALCOHOLIC DRINKS: RISKS AND BENEFITS

For most adults, one or two alcohol-containing drinks a day present little risk for problems related to drinking. What are the risks? Are there benefits?

Unlike nutrients, most alcohol isn't broken down through digestion. Its "pathway" to body cells moves much faster, including directly through the stomach lining and wall of the small intestine into the bloodstream. With no food in the stomach to slow it down, absorption is even faster (within about twenty minutes). From the bloodstream, it goes to every cell of the body, to some degree depressing cell activity.

Have you ever wondered?

. . . if a little "nip" of brandy will help fight a cold? To the contrary, if you have a cold or a chronic health problem that lowers your immunity, you're wise to abstain. Alcohol can impair the body's ability to fight infectious bacteria and may interfere with medication.

. . . if an alcoholic drink will warm you up in cold weather? No. Alcohol tends to increase the body's heat loss, making people more susceptible to the cold. If you're ice fishing, cross-country skiing, or watching outdoor winter sports, an alcoholic drink won't keep you warm and may make you more vulnerable to the effects of cold.

. . . if a few cold beers on a hot day are as good as water to replace fluids? Beer is 95 percent water and so provides refreshment on a hot day. Still, it's a good idea to limit alcoholic drinks and to drink water as well as a beer on a hot, sweaty day.

What about water in mixed drinks? They don't supply as much water per volume. For example, 80-proof vodka is only 60 percent water.

For the record, alcohol acts as a mild diuretic, which increases urine output. By itself, that's likely not enough to cause dehydration.

. . . if a nightcap will help you sleep? It may put you to sleep but not help you stay asleep—with the deep, restful sleep you need. A drink with dinner probably won't affect your sleep habits. *See "Drink Smart—Get Your Zzzzs! in this chapter, page 97.*

Although some people drink to be the "life of the party," alcohol actually is a depressant, not a stimulant. Any initial "lift" is short-lived. By dulling various brain centers, alcohol may reduce concentration, coordination, and response time; cause drowsiness; and interfere with normal sleep patterns. It can also result in slurred speech and blurred vision. Because of the short-term diuretic effect, some people may feel thirsty after drinking a lot—perhaps the morning after.

Blood alcohol level depends on the amount of alcohol consumed over a period of time as well as body composition, body size, metabolism, and medications. A healthy liver detoxifies the alcohol at a rate of about one-half ounce per hour. The higher the blood alcohol concentration level, the longer it takes. Two regular-size drinks consumed during a sixty-minute "happy hour" take about two to three hours to break down.

A single alcoholic drink affects women more than men, due in part to differences in body size and metabolism. Alcohol is carried in body fluids. Women's bodies have a smaller volume of water than men's, so the same amount of alcohol is more concentrated in the bloodstream and potentially has a greater effect. The enzyme that helps metabolize alcohol is also less active in women. As a result, women are at greater risk for problems related to alcoholism.

The risks. The hazards of heavy drinking are well known and include an increased risk for several health problems, including high blood pressure, cirrhosis of the liver, and several forms of cancer as well as motor vehicle accidents, other injuries, violence, and death. During pregnancy, drinking increases the chances for birth defects and brain damage. For women, moderate drinking may slightly increase the risk for breast cancer.

Over time, excessive drinking is linked to increased body weight. For those with diabetes, alcohol intake must be managed; excessive amounts increase diabetes risks.

Heavy drinkers may have social and psychological problems: for example, altered judgment and a potential dependency. With both heavy drinking and episodes of binge drinking, mental function is impaired. Excessive drinking can lead to brain and heart damage, cirrhosis of the liver, and an inflamed pancreas. For children and teens, alcohol consumption increases the risks of drowning, car accidents, and traumatic injury. Accidents are the number-one cause of death in this age group.

The NIAAA notes that alcohol factors into 60 percent of fatal burn injuries, drownings, and homicides; 50 percent of severe trauma injuries and sexual assaults; and 40 percent of fatal car crashes, falls, and suicides. *See "Caution: Drinking Is Riskier for Some" in this chapter, page 104.*

Potential benefits. Moderate drinking may be linked to some health benefits: lower risk for heart disease and all-cause mortality, mostly for middle-aged and older adults. Healthy eating and active living are essential to the equation, too. The benefits appear to come from moderation when consuming wine, beer, or distilled spirits.

An alcoholic drink before a meal may stimulate the appetite and make a meal more appealing. This can be especially beneficial for older adults and people with some chronic illnesses. Some evidence suggests that moderate drinking, along with a healthy eating pattern and regular physical activity, may help keep mental function intact as we age. Talk to your doctor if you have a health problem linked to appetite loss. That said, the potential benefits aren't reason enough to start drinking or to drink more frequently.

See "A Closer Look . . . Wine: A Toast to Heart Health?" in chapter 24, page 695, to learn about alcoholic drinks and heart health.

Calories in alcoholic drinks. Alcohol is a fermentation product of carbohydrates: both sugars and starches. In beverages or food, alcohol supplies calories: 7 calories for every gram, compared with 4 calories per gram of carbohydrate and protein, and 9 calories per gram of fat.

A 1½-ounce jigger or "shot" of vodka, brandy, or other 80-proof spirits, for example, may be, on average, 40 percent alcohol, or have up to 0.6 ounce of alcohol. That equals about 14 grams and contributes about 100 calories. Beer, wine, or liqueurs have more calories from carbohydrates; distilled spirits have no carbohydrates.

The alcohol content of a single drink depends on the type of alcoholic beverage, the proof, if it's a distilled spirit, and the serving size. As the alcohol content goes up, so do the calories. The calorie content also is determined by the amount of alcohol and, for mixed drinks, other ingredients: soft drinks, cream, and syrups. "Special" alcoholic drinks advertised on restaurant table tents often contain more alcohol because they tend to be generous in size. *See the "Alcohol Calorie Calculator" in this chapter, page 106, and "Alcoholic Drink-Equivalents of Selected Beverages," in the appendix, page 780.*

Does drinking lead to weight gain? Not as likely for moderate drinkers. In fact, a few scientific studies suggest that the body uses calories from alcohol differently than calories from other sources. Over time, heavier drinking—beyond two drinks a day—may lead to weight gain.

For some people who drink to excess, a "beer belly" is aptly named. Calories from alcoholic beverages can add up. For example, a six-pack of beer, consumed on a hot summer day, supplies 900 calories. A 5-ounce glass of dry wine before dinner supplies about 120 calories, or 840 calories if consumed every day of the week. Mixers add even more calories. For example, the soft drink in a rum-and-cola, coconut cream in a piña colada, and sugar in a daiquiri or hot buttered rum are all high in calories.

Alcohol: Not a nutrient. Because alcohol may interfere with nutrient absorption, heavy drinkers may not benefit from all the vitamins and minerals they consume elsewhere. Unless juice or milk beverages are mixers, alcoholic drinks supply few if any nutrients.

Moderate drinking isn't associated with poor nutrition, and so a glass of beer or wine with dinner is okay. Malnutrition is a significant concern for very heavy drinkers.

CAUTION: DRINKING IS RISKIER FOR SOME

Some people are wise to avoid alcohol entirely. Besides the risks mentioned earlier, those who should avoid drinking include:

- *Teens and children.* Young people—under age twenty-one—should not drink. That includes fortified fruit-flavored wines and hard (alcoholic) ciders. Since the risk of alcohol dependence goes up when drinking starts at an early age, kids who drink can set themselves up for the same health-related risks that adults have. Alcohol and inexperienced teenage driving is a very risky combination. Besides, buying alcoholic beverages is illegal in the United States for anyone under twenty-one.
- *Those who can't restrict drinking to moderate levels.* As part of a lifelong commitment, recovering alcoholics and problem drinkers should abstain from any alcoholic drink. Because of the genetic link to alcoholism, people with alcoholism in their family are wise to limit their intake of alcoholic beverages, too—or avoid them.
- *Those whose work requires attention, skill, or coordination.* Alcohol affects productivity, which can affect your work output and your personal safety. Even with moderate drinking—a glass of wine or a beer—alcohol stays in your blood for about one hour, and two glasses, for two hours or more.
- *Those who plan to drive or handle potentially dangerous equipment.* Even low levels of blood alcohol from a single drink can make you more accident-prone. If you plan to drink, designate another driver from the start who won't be drinking!
- *Women who are pregnant, trying to get pregnant, or are unsure.* In the United States, drinking during pregnancy is the leading known cause of birth defects. Fetal alcohol syndrome is characterized by mental retardation and behavioral and psychosocial problems. While there's not enough proof that an occasional drink is harmful during pregnancy, even moderate drinking may have behavioral and mental consequences. No safe level has been established for a woman at any time during pregnancy, including the first few weeks. Too often, women drink before they even know they're pregnant, potentially compromising their baby for life. *See "Pregnancy and Alcoholic Beverages Don't Mix" in chapter 18, page 549, for more about fetal alcohol syndrome.*

  Heavy drinking may not be wise for the prospective dad, either. According to research, excessive alcohol may decrease sperm count and potency and thus affect fertility. *See "Fertility: A Man's Health Counts" in chapter 19, page 567.*
- *Women who are breastfeeding.* The level of alcohol in breast milk will mirror that of blood alcohol content from alcoholic drinks. Even low to moderate drinking may adversely affect a baby's feeding and behavior—and may reduce the amount of breast milk. Although the data is limited, alcoholic drinks consumed while nursing may be linked to a baby's sleep patterns, psychomotor patterns, or growth. It's best to wait at least four hours after drinking alcohol before breastfeeding. Alcohol should not be consumed until consistent latching on and breastfeeding patterns are established. *See "Breastfeeding Cautions" in chapter 16, page 466, to learrn more about the effects of alcohol.*

? Have you ever wondered?

. . . what the term "80 proof" means on a bottle of liquor? The term "proof" indicates the amount of alcohol. The proof is twice the percentage of alcohol content. If a label on a bottle of liquor states "80 Proof," this means that the liquor contains 40 percent alcohol. The proof will vary with the type of liquor.

. . . how organic wine and beer are labeled? USDA organic labeling standards, addressed in *"Organic labeling" in* chapter 6, page 153, apply to alcoholic beverages, too.

. . . what cooking wine is? It is typically an inferior wine that lacks distinctive flavor and is usually high in sodium. Regular wine may be better for cooking.

. . . how to know the alcohol and calorie content of wine, beer, or distilled spirits? Check the label. Since not all beverages are required to list the alcohol content, check the bottler's website. As new restaurant menu labeling regulations are enacted, the FDA expects a separate calorie disclosure for alcoholic beverages, including beers by brand name or style. For example, caloric amounts for the beer must be specific to its style and to the serving sizes offered.

. . . what ABV and IBU for beers mean? On beer labels and on beer menus, you might see these two measurements.

ABV means Alcohol by Volume, usually given as a percentage, shows how much alcohol is contained in a given volume. The range might be 2 to 12 percent ABV; most American beer is 4 to 6 percent.

IBU is different and stands for International Bitterness Units. That measures the bitter flavor that comes from hops, given on a scale of 0 to 100. A very hoppy beer, such as some IPAs, can be 80 IBU. Malt also affects the flavor, so a stout with sweet malt may have a high IBU, but not taste too bitter.

. . . what hard cider is? Recently becoming popular, hard cider isn't beer, although it's often marketed in a similar way. Instead, hard cider is wine, fermented with yeast (not brewed), and usually made with ripe apple or pear juice.

It has no less than 0.5 percent and not more than 7 percent alcohol by volume. It's often chosen as a gluten-free alternative to beer. Although hard cider and beer may be similar in calorie content, hard cider generally has more sugar from natural sources and somewhat more calories.

- *Those with certain medical conditions,* such as liver disease, pancreatitis, or high triglyceride levels. If you have a medical condition, talk with your doctor.
- *Those on medication, even over-the-counter kinds.* Alcohol may interact with certain medicines, making them either less effective or more potent. The medication itself may raise blood alcohol levels or increase its adverse effects on the brain. The result: a single drink combined with medication may result in feeling drowsy, dizzy, or light-headed and may impair judgment, coordination, and skill.

  Labels on over-the-counter medications and herbal remedies may carry warnings about taking them with alcoholic drinks. Talk with your doctor or pharmacist about your prescribed and over-the-counter medications. *See "Food and Medicine: Some Don't Mix" in chapter 25, page 741.*
- *Those who suffer from allergies.* Sulfites in wine may trigger histamine production and allergy symptoms.

Even otherwise healthy people should exercise caution:

- *Those who drink caffeine and alcohol mixed in the same beverage* or drink them separately but at the same time may drink more alcohol and become more intoxicated than they realize, which increases the risk of alcohol-related adverse events.
- *With the legalization of cannabis in some states,* there's concern about the harmful effects of combining recreational drinking and smoking marijuana.

DRINK RESPONSIBLY!

If you choose to drink alcoholic beverages, always do so responsibly:

- Start with a nonalcoholic beverage. Satisfy your thirst first. Then drink an alcoholic beverage slowly.
- Don't drink on an empty stomach. Eating a little food helps slow the absorption of alcohol.
- Decide ahead to limit consumption: no more than one drink per day if you're a woman or two per day if you're a man. If you choose to drink more, pace yourself. On average, the body can detoxify only one standard-size drink (0.6 fluid ounces, or 14 grams of alcohol) per hour. The rest circulates until it's finally broken down.
- Slow your pace. Put your drink down. Socialize. Limit yourself to no more than one standard-size drink per hour.
- Alternate. If you have one alcoholic drink, make the next one nonalcoholic. Besides consuming less alcohol, your body has a chance to process the alcohol you've already imbibed.
- Measure liquor for mixed drinks with a measured jigger so you know how much to pour from the bottle.

Your Healthy Eating Check-In

Alcohol Calorie Calculator

Calories from alcohol add up, potentially contributing to unwanted weight gain. And they provide few nutrients. If you need to lose weight, your drinking habits may be a good place to start. Use the calculator below to figure how many calories you consume each week from alcoholic beverages.

Although their calorie content differs, each of these standard-size drinks supply approximately the same amount of alcohol—about 14 grams of pure ethanol. (*Note:* Alcoholic drinks are not 100 percent alcohol; that's why the volume that provides 14 grams of ethanol differs.) To estimate the calorie content, pay attention to the size of your servings. Adjust your calculation to the serving size on the chart.

For the interactive online version of this calculator, visit rethinkingdrinking.niaaa.nih.gov/Tools/Calculators/calorie-calculator.aspx. The website also provides other alcohol-related calculators such as cocktail content and drink size. *Also see "Alcoholic Drink-Equivalents of Select Beverages" in the appendix, page 780.*

Beverages	Serving Size (fluid ounces)	Calories (Average)	Average Number of Drinks per Week	Total Calories
Beer				
Regular	12	153	____	____
Light	12	103	____	____
Distilled spirits*				
80-proof† gin, rum, vodka, whiskey, tequila	1.5	97	____	____
Brandy, cognac	1.5	98	____	____
Liqueurs	1.5	165	____	____
Wine				
Red	5	125	____	____
White	5	121	____	____
Sweet	3.5	165	____	____
Sherry	2	75	____	____
Port	2	90	____	____
Champagne	4	84	____	____
Vermouth, sweet	3	140	____	____
Vermouth, dry	3	105	____	____
Cocktails				
Martini (traditional)	2.25	124	____	____
Martini (extra dry)	2.25	139	____	____
Cosmopolitan	2.75	146	____	____
Mojito	6	143	____	____
Margarita	4	168	____	____
Piña colada	9	490	____	____
Manhattan	3.5	164	____	____
Daiquiri	3.5	112	____	____
Whiskey sour	3.5	160	____	____
			Calories per week	____

*An added mixer, such as a soft drink, adds more calories.

†(*See "Have you ever wondered . . . what the term "80 Proof" means on a bottle of liquor?" on the previous page*).

Source: Adapted from *Rethinking Your Drinking: Alcohol and Your Health*, National Institute on Alcohol Abuse and Alcoholism.

Label Lingo

Beer and Wine: What's in a Name?

Today beer and wine can be found on supermarket shelves. But just what do the descriptions mean, and how much alcohol do they contain?

An average, regular American beer is 4 to 6 percent (alcohol by volume), and IPA (India pale ale) beers are typically 5.5 to 7.5 percent ABV. And some craft beers are higher. In the United States and Europe, pale beer (usually a lager) may be called light beer. The alcohol content is about the same as in regular beer, but the calories are somewhat less. An alcoholic beverage with more than 24 percent ABV is defined (and taxed) as a distilled spirit; some are closer to 40 percent alcohol or more.

- *Near beer:* Malt beverage with an alcohol content less than 0.5 percent by volume. It also can be labeled a "malt beverage" or a "cereal beverage." When the label says "contains less than 0.5 percent alcohol by volume," it can also be labeled as "non-alcoholic."
- *Low-alcohol or reduced-alcohol beer:* Malt beverage with less than 2.5 percent alcohol by volume.
- *Alcohol-free malt beverage:* Malt beverage that contains no alcohol.
- *Flavored malt beverage:* Malt beverage (beer, lager, ale, porter, stout) flavored after fermentation, perhaps with juice, fruit, or juice concentrate—for example berry-, lemon-, or orange-flavored beer.
- *Aperitif wine:* Wine with an alcohol content of 15 to 24 percent by volume, made from grape wine (from ripe grapes) and added brandy, or alcohol flavored with herbs or other natural aromatic flavorings. Vermouth is a type of aperitif wine.
- *Fortified wine:* Wine that has brandy or distilled spirits added to it.
- *Table wine:* Grape wine that is not in excess of 14 percent alcohol by volume. Light wine, red wine, and sweet table wine are all types of table wines.
- *Fruit wine:* Wine from ripe fruit, but not grapes or citrus. It cannot exceed 14 percent alcohol by volume.
- *Dessert wine:* Grape wine with an alcoholic content of 14 to 24 percent alcohol by volume and so more than table wine. A fruit dessert wine must meet these same regulations.
- *Low-alcohol wine:* Wine or any fermented fruit beverage with less than 7 percent alcohol by volume. Low-alcohol wine isn't necessarily lower in calories; it may have more sugars than other wine.
- *Wine cooler:* Diluted wine product (diluted with fruit juice, water, and/or added sugars) with less than 7 percent alcohol by volume. Check the Nutrition Facts label for calorie content. Wine coolers may have more alcohol and calories than you think since a serving is usually sizeable: often 12 ounces, rather than a 5-ounce glass of table wine.

Sources: Electronic Code of Regulations, PART 4—LABELING AND ADVERTISING OF WINE, and PART 7—LABELING AND ADVERTISING OF MALT BEVERAGES, Accessed November 30, 2016.

Need more strategies to boost your fluid intake? Check here for "how-tos":

- Buy dairy and nondairy drinks to match your needs; *see "Dairy Foods: Buying Tips" in chapter 6, page 169.*
- Drink sensibly when you eat out; *see "Drinks: Smart Choices, Sensibly Sized" in chapter 9, page 296.*
- Know about water as a nutrient, which is a vital part of your eating plan; *see "Water: A Fluid Asset" in chapter 15, page 443.*
- Get enough fluids when you're physically active; *see "Fluids for Peak Performance" in chapter 21, page 602.*
- Know how to fit milk in if you're lactose intolerant; *see "Managing Lactose Intolerance" in chapter 23, page 671.*

- Make an alcoholic drink last longer; you'll less likely order another. Learn to sip, not gulp; use a straw for mixed drinks. Dilute drinks with water, ice, club soda, or juice to increase the volume. Frozen drinks often take longer to sip.
- If you feel thirsty, drink bottled water or a soft drink instead. Remember: alcohol has a diuretic effect and may contribute to dehydration, especially if you're already sweating a lot.
- Prefer a wine cooler or spritzer? Mix your own using less wine and more sparkling water or fruit juice.
- Lighten up! Order low-alcohol beer, light wine, or a light distilled spirit instead. Each has somewhat less alcohol. Or try nonalcoholic beer or an alcohol-free malt beverage.
- At the table, have a glass of water by your plate. You'll probably drink less alcohol.

Click Here!
Links to Know . . .

If you drink, take a look at your drinking habits and how they may affect your health.

- National Institute of Alcohol Abuse and Alcoholism
  rethinkingdrinking.niaaa.nih.gov/

- Skip the last round before the bar closes. As a host, don't feel a need to refresh your guests' drinks as the evening progresses.
- Order a "virgin" cocktail: nonalcoholic mixers without the liquor. Mix in juice or carbonated water.
- Bring bottled water or soft drinks to a picnic or sports event so you have a nonalcoholic option.
- Account for the calories from these drinks within the limit of your healthy eating plan to avoid exceeding your limits. Remember that calories from these drinks vary. Consider the calories in mixers as well as the alcohol.
- Know your triggers. If you tend to drink in certain situations or with certain people, try to avoid them. If drinking at home is an issue, keep only a little alcohol or a few alcoholic beverages on hand—or none at all.
- Know your "no"—and when and how to politely decline a drink offer.

PART II

Food and Nutrition: Choices in the Marketplace

5

Producing Your Food

In this chapter, find out about . . .

Sustainable farming for a growing population

Today's agriculture and your food options

Roles of processed foods in healthy eating

Awareness of nearly every aspect of food is at an all-time high! The reasons? A greater demand for authentic flavors, healthy ingredients, safe food, convenience, affordability, and environmental conscientiousness. Familiar?

- Maybe you're interested in how food gets from the farm to your plate: where your food comes from and how it's produced, processed, and packaged.
- Perhaps you want to explore more health- or flavor-focused foods, or some foods produced by local farmers, or foods you've never tried before.
- Maybe you want to take steps to protect the natural resources needed to nourish you and your family, your community, and the world now and for years to come.

All this and more is part of being a savvy and responsible food consumer.

Food for Today and Tomorrow

As many people have become more food aware, the whole food system—from farm to table—has gained attention. Many in the food system are concerned about producing enough food to nourish a growing global population now and in the future, while conserving natural resources and minimally impacting the environment.

From food production, processing, and retail stores and farmers' markets, to restaurant and kitchen tables, the trending buzzword is "sustainability." Everyone has a role to play—including you as a consumer.

FEEDING A GROWING WORLD

You've likely heard this projection: To feed the growing global population, in the next 40 years, the world will need to produce as much food as it did in the past 8,000 years! The issues go further—to producing enough of the *right foods* for as many people as possible, protecting against food- and water-related health issues, and managing environmental resources. A tall order.

Sustainability is essential to meet the growing demand for food and the capacity to maintain resources, without compromising future generations' ability to do the same. The term "sustainable" is often misunderstood, however. In the context of food it doesn't mean "local" or "organic." Instead "sustainable" refers to a food system that can maintain itself in healthy and responsible ways. And it's about connections with the economy, the environment, and society as a whole—all important to ensure adequate food for future generations.

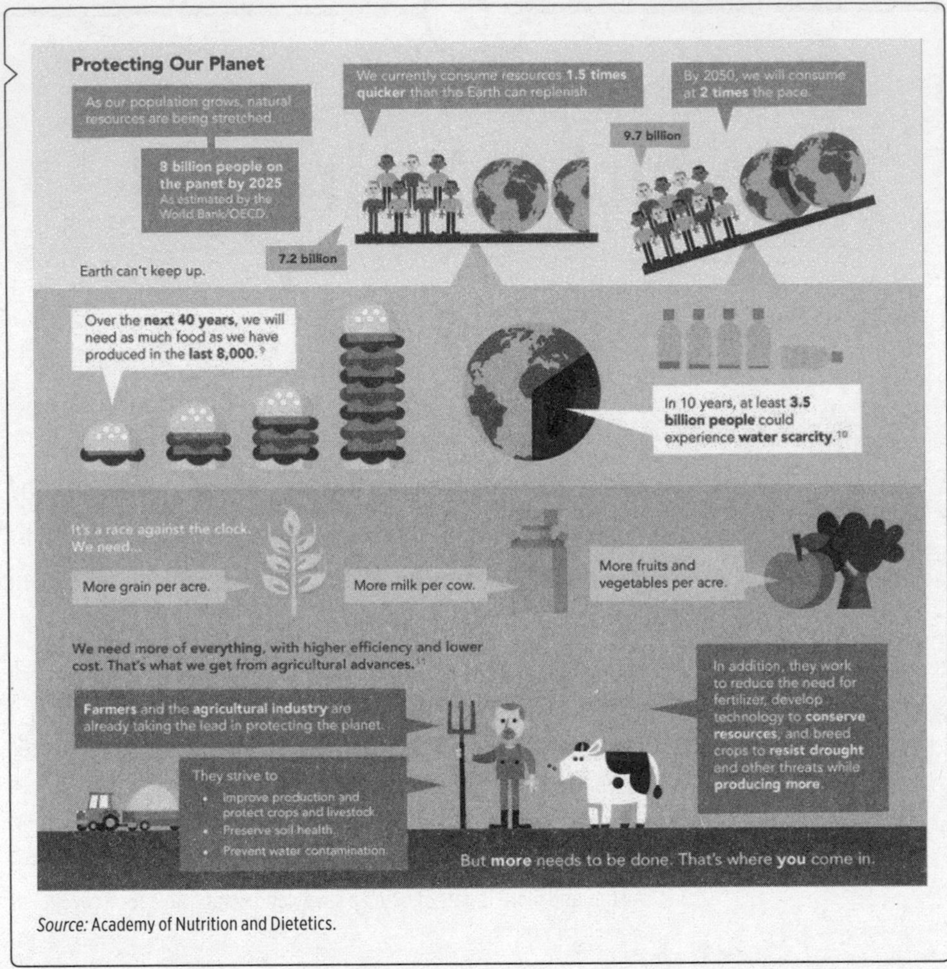

Source: Academy of Nutrition and Dietetics.

Sustainability in farming and ranching is important since they have so much potential impact on the environment. Sustainable agricultural production relies on (1) fertile soil with reduced soil erosion, (2) plenty of fresh water that's not impaired with polluters, and (3) available energy that limits greenhouse gas emissions. Issues, such as water scarcity for irrigation, a loss of soil productivity, air and water pollution related to farming practices, potential loss of biodiversity, and pesticide and herbicide resistance, are high priority. The whole system—from farm to plate—must be mindful of:

- Managing waste
- Conserving, protecting, and regenerating natural resources such as soil, water, and fossil fuels as well as landscapes
- Protecting the environment from practices that may harm public health
- Preserving the diversity of plants, animals, and soil nutrients
- Using ecologically sound practices when it comes to farming and food production and distribution
- Maintaining and working to improve the economic health and vitality of communities
- Distributing raw ingredients to food companies, processing and packaging them, and then getting the food to wholesalers, retail outlets, restaurants, and ultimately to your table

Tools of science and agricultural technology equip farmers and ranchers to manage natural resources. Food producers in the United States—helped by the US Department of Agriculture (USDA)—have reduced soil erosion by more than 40 percent in the past three decades. They've also encouraged wetland restoration and the production of renewable energy such as from wind and biofuels. Drip irrigation is controlling the amounts of water dispersed so that less is wasted. And with satellite guidance, farmers can plant and use pesticides and fertilizers more precisely. They also can match seeds and production practices to the soil type and climate. Yet, there is still so much to do.

The result can be better yields for lower cost and better, perhaps less, fertilizer and pesticide use. For you, these farming techniques can translate to lower food prices, more available food, and a healthier environment that we all live and work in.

Sustainable practices also help protect the business of agriculture. By caring for the land and for animal welfare, farms and ranches can be profitable and productive for future generations.

Access to enough food isn't the only global health issue. Did you know that 663 million people, or one in ten, in the world lack access to safe water, as reported in 2015 by the World Health Organization and UNICEF? In that same year, the World Economic Forum reported that the water crisis is the top global risk that can impact society (as a measure of devastation).

LIMITING FOOD WASTE

Did you know . . . that wasted food results in about 1,250 wasted calories per person each day in the United States? That 15 to 20 percent of fresh produce is wasted, or never eaten, according to the Produce for Better Health Foundation? That an estimated 25 to 40 percent of food grown, processed, and transported in the United States is never eaten? That's estimated to be seventy billion pounds of foods annually, reports the Food Waste Reduction Alliance (FWRA). Despite the abundance of food, many in the United States and around the world are hungry.

Reducing food waste—defined as post-harvest food that's available to eat but is not eaten for many reasons—is a priority for many reasons. First, it is a strategy for reducing hunger. Second, wasted food impacts the environment by wasting natural and other resources: water, fertilizer and pesticide, and fuel used to transport food. Moreover, rotting food produces methane, or harmful greenhouse gases, that in turn may be affecting our climate. And third, food that ends up in landfills wastes your own grocery and eating-out dollars.

The US Environmental Protection Agency (EPA) and the USDA have set an ambitious goal: to reduce food loss, including food waste, by 50 percent by 2030. To help achieve that goal, partners in the food industry—companies, retailers, restaurants—are working together as part of the FWRA.

To help make the food system more sustainable, see "Eradicate Food Waste!" above. Also see "Your Healthy Eating Check-In: How Sustainable Are Your Food Decisions?" in this chapter, page 115, for more ways.

Eradicate Food Waste!

For some ways you can limit wasted food and other natural resources in your kitchen, you can:

- Shop to make the most of your food dollar and limit wasted food; *see "Shopping Green: Opportunity, Responsibility" in chapter 6, page 187.*
- Prepare food in a waste-free kitchen; *see "The Waste-Less Kitchen" in chapter 8, page 243.*
- Eat out and limit wasted food; *see "Waste Not, Restaurant Savvy" in chapter 9, page 286.*
- Grow a vegetable garden with your kids; *see "Grow a Family Garden" in chapter 17, page 494.*

Today's Agriculture

Do you think much about where your food comes from? Large and small, conventional and organic, rural and urban: US farms and ranches produce a safe, affordable, and abundant supply of nourishing food for consumers like you. Whether by conventional or organic farming practices or both, this food supply not only feeds Americans, but also people in many other parts of the world.

Farming may conjure up images of vast corn and wheat fields, the crops slowly swaying in a gentle wind, or lush green pastures of grazing dairy cows. However, farming is much more. Think row crops of vegetables and vast fruit orchards and vineyards. Visualize hog and poultry farms and ranches with beef cattle and other livestock. Remember freshwater or saltwater fish farming, too.

Farming in the United States is mostly a family business; 97 percent are family farms. While these farms come in all sizes, the average is 434 acres, according to 2012 US census data, with small farms averaging 231 acres to make up 88 percent of American family farms. Very large family farms, with an average of 2,086 acres, make up only 4.6 percent of family farms. To clarify a misconception, only about 3 percent of US farms are organized as cooperative or nonfamily corporations run by hired managers.

In recent years, growing food has expanded to more and more urban farms. Small farmers and residents are transforming vacant lots, rooftops, and backyard gardens in cities and suburbs into places where fruits and vegetables flourish. School gardens and restaurant (chefs') gardens also are taking their place in small-scale farming. Many farmers—conventional and organic—produce both crops and livestock. That provides two income streams to reduce financial risk, support the family business, and protect the farm for future generations. Growing animal feed is also an efficient farming practice.

All types of farming and all sizes of farms are important for feeding the growing world population. Read on to learn a bit more about farming, and visit the US Farmers & Ranchers Alliance website—www.fooddialogues.com—to learn about daily life on the land and how farmers and ranchers cultivate their crops and care for livestock.

Have you ever wondered?

. . . what food insecurity is? It's not having reliable access to enough affordable nutritious food. It isn't just a problem for the future. In the United States today, one in six people, or forty-nine million, are food insecure, notes Feeding America. About sixteen million of them are children, who lack consistent access to enough nutritious food often due to poverty.

That may be surprising in a nation of plenty, with an obesity epidemic, and so much wasted food. Those who are food insecure might overeat when food is available to compensate for times when they're hungry. Those with food insecurity are often at the highest risk for long-term health conditions such as type 2 diabetes, high blood pressure, and obesity. When money is tight, many must make choices: to buy food or pay for medication or health care.

. . . how a food system may impact the carbon footprint? A carbon footprint is a measure of the total amount of carbon dioxide (CO_2) and other greenhouse gases released into the air. Some foods come with a greater carbon footprint than others, depending on how they're grown, produced, transported, prepared, and disposed of.

Some farming practices may reduce emissions and keep more carbon in the soil. For example, no-till and conservation tillage, which are practices that aim to disturb the soil as little as possible, prevent carbon dioxide from being released into the atmosphere. Improved weed control lets farmers keep residues from harvests on the ground so carbon is trapped in the soil. And farming practices that limit the use of mechanized farm equipment (less tilling, less pesticide application) mean less carbon emission from fuel.

Food waste also contributes to the carbon footprint. Waste from food processed by food companies and food used in restaurants can be used for animal feed and compost. To see how your food decisions may impact your carbon footprint, visit www3.epa.gov/carbon-footprint-calculator.

. . . what gleaning is? Gleaning is collecting excess fresh foods from farms, gardens, farmers' markets, grocers, restaurants, state/county fairs, or any other sources in order to provide it to those in need. To avoid wasting nourishing food, become part of a gleaning initiative in your community and donate to area food banks, pantries, and soup kitchens.

Click Here! Links to Know . . .

- Know Your Farmer, Know Your Food
  www.usda.gov/knowyourfarmer
- Food and Agriculture Organization of the United Nations
  www.fao.org/themes/en
- Feeding America
  healthyfoodbankhub.feedingamerica.org
- Organic Trade Association
  www.ota.com/organic-101
- Food Dialogues, US Farmers & Ranchers Alliance
  www.fooddialogues.com
- American Community Gardening Association
  communitygarden.org

CONVENTIONAL FARMING

If you've visited a modern farm, you've likely learned that conventional farming has become far more complex and precise than the agricultural practices of past generations. Today, modern technology and mechanization have advanced agricultural productivity, efficiency, and resource conservation, making farming more sustainable and offering a more abundant and affordable food supply in the United States. In fact, 70 to 90 percent of the increased food production throughout the world in recent years can be attributed to modern techniques for conventional agriculture rather than turning more land into farms. According to 2014 data from the American Farm Bureau Federation, American farmers use less than half as much land on a per-person basis to produce meat, poultry, and dairy than about 45 years ago. Now one farmer supplies food for more than 155 people worldwide, compared with only 25.8 people in 1960.

From farm to farm, region to region, and country to country, farming and ranching practices vary. Each operation must determine the best practices for its size, its natural resources (such as soil quality, water supply, and climate), and the type of crops or livestock. The people who run it must also consider how much farm labor is needed, what resources are required to efficiently produce and protect crops or livestock, how much financial investment is needed, and much more.

"Eating local" supports regional and local food production: a good thing. Different conditions—different soil, different climate, and different amounts of available water, among others—are one reason why producing all food locally isn't realistic or even efficient.

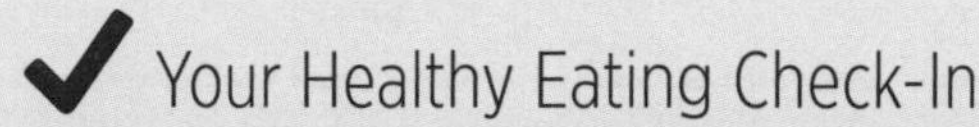

How Sustainable Are Your Food Decisions?

Caring for the environment is everyone's responsibility! From the list below, check off ways in which you can protect some natural resources that bring food to your table. Some of these actions might not work for you. That's okay; taking even a few small steps can help. And at the end of this list, you can write in a strategy or two that works for you.

COULD YOU . . .	Yes	No
1. Buy and eat just the amount of food that you need to reduce overconsumption?	☐	☐
2. Minimize wasted food in preparation and storage, and at your table?	☐	☐
3. Compost vegetable and fruit scraps?	☐	☐
4. Buy foods with recyclable packaging when possible? (*Note:* Minimal amounts of packaging protect food and keep it safe to eat.)	☐	☐
5. Recycle food packages if recycling is available in your area? Most packaging today is recyclable.	☐	☐
6. Conserve water and keep it free from contamination? Carry water in a clean, reusable water bottle rather than relying on buying bottled water.	☐	☐
7. Grow fruits or vegetables in your backyard or a container garden—perhaps share some with a friend or food bank if you have a big yield?	☐	☐
8. Volunteer at an urban or community garden, greenhouse, school garden, or food pantry?	☐	☐
9. Use Earth-friendly cleaning products in your kitchen? (Most household cleaning products are water-soluble, formulated for safe disposal, and don't contain ingredients in amounts harmful to the environment. Still, read the label.)	☐	☐
10. Walk or bike once a week, perhaps to a grocery store or a farmers' market?	☐	☐
11. Talk to farmers at a farmers' market, farm stands, food co-ops, local farms, or pick-your-own farms to learn about the food they produce and how they manage natural resources and care for their environment?* Take children so they learn, too.	☐	☐
12. Participate in a CSA (Community Supported Agriculture) program? *See "Have you ever wondered . . . how Community Supported Agriculture (CSA) works?" in chapter 6, page 163.*	☐	☐
13. Learn about and support public policies that both conserve natural resources and protect the environment: for example land use, local drinking water, energy use, and local issues of air pollution?	☐	☐
14. Figure out how you can conserve resources—water, energy, and more—at home, at work, and in your community?	☐	☐
15. Add your own "green" strategy (strategies) to this list?	☐	☐

*Or learn from the US Farmers & Ranchers Alliance (www.fooddialogues.com/)

Be mindful as you plan, buy, store, prepare, and enjoy food, and also repurpose, donate, and recycle. That can help you save money and reduce the amount of food you throw away.

America's Edible Heritage

Throughout history, the foods of one culture and region have traveled to others, infusing cuisines with vibrant food variety and new flavors. Along the way, those foods also became new sources of nutrients and food energy.

NEW FOOD PRODUCTION

The quest for the flavor provided by exotic Eastern spices launched the Age of Discovery and the exploration of the so-called New World. Among the discoveries for Europeans and other parts of the world was a vast array of foods, which at that time grew only in the Americas. In fact, about 50 percent of foods eaten globally today originated in the Americas, where for generations they had nourished native peoples.

American cuisine has strong roots in its native foods: chiles, corn, legumes, peanuts, peppers, pineapples, potatoes, pumpkins, squash, tomatoes, turkey, and wild rice, among many others. The Americas contributed tomatoes to Italy, potatoes to Ireland, peanuts (or groundnuts) to West Africa, and hot chiles to Thailand.

Likewise, foods unknown to Native Americans five hundred years ago came from all parts of the so-called Old World. With rich agricultural land in the Americas, these foods grew and thrived on fertile land with excellent growing conditions. For example, Europeans introduced Asian rice, bananas, barley, beef cattle and dairy cows, chickens, citrus fruits, lettuce, oats, okra, peaches, pears, pigs, watermelon, and wheat to the Americas, all of which became part of American cuisine.

NEW CUISINES

Each immigrant wave has contributed its culinary traditions to their new home. Regional specialties developed as cultural cooking styles were adapted for available foods. Early American settlers substituted native ingredients such as cornmeal and squash in traditional English dishes. Black-eyed peas (prepared with rice from the Old World), cooked collard greens, gumbo, and hoppin' john from the South were created by African American cooks, often from memories of foods with African origins.

Consider other regional favorites: bean burritos with cheese, cactus salad, and tamales with chicken from the Southwest; berry cobblers and smoked salmon from the Pacific Northwest; and clam chowder and crab cakes from the Atlantic coast. Many foods once eaten as regional specialties in the United States are now nationally popular.

In time, many foods inspired by immigrants have become "typically American"—for example, pizza, tacos, and chop suey. "Food immigration" continues as more recent waves of immigrants—mostly Asians, Eastern Europeans, Latin Americans, and Middle Easterners—influence American cuisine today.

Conventional farmers are allowed to use synthetic fertilizers and crop protection for crops as well as antibiotics and hormones (with strict FDA regulation) for farm animals. For this reason, foods from conventional farming typically cost less than organic foods. Like organic farmers, many who produce food conventionally also use renewable resources and employ sound techniques for soil and water conservation.

One commonly used technique for both conventional and organic farming is crop rotation, used to preserve the quality of the soil. Typically, one crop is planted in the spring and another in the fall or winter. That helps manage the fertility of the soil, limits the spread of pests and diseases during the growing season, reduces the effects of bad weather, and extends and the farm's productivity.

Some farmers have adopted other new technologies to use water, fossil fuels, and other natural resources more efficiently. Some examples include high-efficiency sprinklers and solar-powered wells.

Protecting Crops, Protecting You

The array of safe, wholesome food in your supermarket throughout the year doesn't happen by chance. To limit crop loss, successful growers must carefully manage croplands and orchards to control about eighty thousand plant diseases, thirty thousand weed species, more than ten thousand insect species, and a thousand species of nematodes. If you've ever struggled with insects, mildew, rodents, or weeds in your own garden, just multiply the problem!

The use of crop protection varies with the time of year, the soil conditions, the climate, and the presence of pests. Most farmers use several methods of crop protection. There's no way the ordinary consumer can tell the difference. If present, any residues in fruits and vegetables are at very low levels. Any that remain decrease significantly with harvesting, transport, exposure to light, washing, preparation, and cooking. It's safe to say that they're unlikely to pose any health risk.

Pesticides. Pesticides are one approach to crop protection. They must be applied safely and judiciously to control pests and protect human health and the environment. Herbicides control weeds. Fungicides control mold, mildew, and fungi that cause plant disease and inhibit molds that may be harmful to consumers. Insecticides control insects that damage crops or carry plant disease. Rodenticides control rodents in

? Have you ever wondered?

. . . what the term "precision farming" means? It's a method of field management that recognizes that no field and no sections of fields are exactly alike—and so they require different inputs for maximum efficiency. Farmers monitor and respond to the variations in their fields, such as differences in soil composition, slope of the land, and organic matter, texture, and pH levels. Many factors affect the fields, including cover crops, drainage, temperature, humidity, farming practices, previous crops, and weeds.

Modern technology such as satellite imagery, electromagnetic soil mapping, GPS-guided tractors, and drones as well as analysis of soil samples and crop yields provide data that enable farmers to manage large fields section by section. As a result, they can limit and properly apply fertilizers and crop protection, reduce agricultural waste, increase harvest, and be good stewards of the environment.

. . . if buying local food is a better choice? First consider what the term may or may not mean. The term "local" refers to the proximity of purchase. In practice, it often refers to foods that are produced, processed, distributed, and consumed in a small, defined area. Unregulated and undefined, it could mean one mile or one thousand miles away from the point of purchase.

Buying local foods often supports the local economy. Moreover, buying them may give you chances to connect with the farmer and learn how the food is grown and handled.

That said, restricting your food choices to local ones has some limitations. The variety of fresh fruits and vegetables may be limited at certain times of year, depending on the climate and geography. Growing some foods locally may not be economically or resource efficient.

A few cautions: Some retailers label foods with their place of origin or their distance, which may range from ten to five thousand miles away or more. If you want to know what "local" means for a specific product, ask the food retailer or the farm stand or restaurant owner. You may be surprised by the differences. *Tip:* If raw produce isn't in season locally, it probably isn't locally produced. As an aside, "local" doesn't mean "organic."

See "Fresh from the Farmers' Market?" and "Have you ever wondered . . . how Community Supported Agriculture (CSA) works?" in chapter 6, pages 159 and 163, for ways to support local growers.

the field. Disinfectants act against bacteria and other disease-carrying microorganisms.

Without prudent use of pesticides, many farmers couldn't control crop damage, crop yields would be much lower, and the variety of foods available to you likely would be limited and more costly. Still, pests damage a significant amount of crops each year. Even organic farming relies on acceptable, natural pesticides.

When people think of pesticides, synthetic chemicals often come to mind. However, naturally occurring substances in the environment, such as copper, nicotine, and sulfur, and some bacteria also are used to control pests. Many plants protect themselves by producing their own pesticides in low levels.

IPM—Partnering Agricultural Practices. IPM stands for integrated pest management—an approach that combines biological control, pesticides, farming practices, and biotechnology to reduce crop damage. As farmers work in partnership with nature, they use crop protection selectively, with the goal to use fewer pesticides. IPM uses several strategies:

- What does sex have to do with pest control? Interestingly, sex scents, called pheromones, can disrupt the mating patterns of pests and therefore reduce their numbers, allowing farmers to use fewer pesticides. It too is a part of a biological system of pest control.
- Farmers may use pest predators (when "good" bugs eat "bad" bugs) to help control pest diseases.
- Crop rotation—for example, switching from soybeans to corn—helps limit pest buildup in the field because insects lose their natural food source. Mulch, distance between plants, tillage practices, and field sanitation are some other ways by which farmers can control pests. Today's technology, including the use of computers and satellites, lets farmers apply pesticides, fertilizers, and irrigation water only in the amount and locations needed.
- Growers may choose plant varieties that are more pest resistant. Traditional plant breeding and today's biotechnology can help crops develop their own natural resistance.

Who Safeguards Pesticide Use? Responsibility for safe pesticide use in agriculture is three-way: growers, pesticide manufacturers, and government regulators.

- Safety starts with growers. Most use pesticides safely and prudently, and here are three reasons why:

Nature's Pest Control

Plants have built-in mechanisms for pest control: fungi, insects, and animal predators. Unlike animals, plants can't flee when they sense danger. Instead, they produce natural, toxic compounds to protect themselves.

Many of the foods you eat every day contain natural toxins—for example, cyanide in lima beans, nitrates in broccoli, oxalates in rhubarb, and solanine in green potatoes. In fact, the FDA estimates that Americans ingest many times more (by weight) natural pesticides than synthetic ones—with no apparent health risk.

There are risks even in nature. At high levels, some natural toxins might cause illness or may be carcinogenic. However, in amounts normally eaten in a varied diet, none has been shown to pose a cancer risk. Through advances in biotechnology, scientists can identify genes in food that produce natural toxins and then remove them or suppress their action.

Did You Know . . . ?

Around 10,000 plant species have been used for human food since the origin of agriculture.

- Today, only 150 plant species make up the diets of the majority of the world's population.
- Twelve plant species provide more than 70 percent of the world's food.
- Four plant species—maize, potatoes, rice, and wheat—make up over 50 percent of the food supply.
- Only thirty crops provide 90 percent of the world's calorie intake.

Source: Food and Agricultural Organization of the United Nations "Facts and Figures: about plant genetic resources," 2014.

- The first reason is cost. Crop protection is costly, so farmers use it judiciously to remain profitable.
- Second, successful growers plan for the future. Using too much pesticide with one year's crop may cause crop damage in the future since some residues may remain in the soil.
- Third, farmers and ranchers are more aware of and concerned about their environmental impact. Their long-range livelihood depends on it. Most farmers are trained in the responsible, legal use of agricultural products, which means some must be applied only by those certified or licensed to do so.

- Manufacturers also have some responsibility for the effects of the pesticides they develop. If research indicates that its use does not meet standards for toxicity, crop residues, or environmental impact, the Environmental Protection Agency (EPA) can stop or change its use.
- Several government agencies regulate and monitor the safety of pesticides in food. Because they can pose health risks, regulations are essential. The levels of pesticide residues legally allowed in food are set at amounts that are far below what is considered safe for the most sensitive part of the population, including infants and children.
  - The *EPA* regulates pesticide manufacture, labeling, and use—and sets maximum levels, or tolerances, for residues. The potential for harm is in the amount, not whether the pesticide is present.

    Before a pesticide can be used on crops, it is thoroughly tested for safety for the environment and human health. If approved, the EPA may limit its use—by the amount and frequency used or for application to specific crops—and require that these limits be listed on the pesticide label. Growers who misuse pesticides, even mistakenly, risk having their crop seized or destroyed. The grower may be charged with a civil or criminal lawsuit.
  - The *FDA* monitors residues in most foods (not meat, poultry, and eggs)—both raw and processed—and enforces tolerance levels set by the EPA. If residues exceed these levels, food can be seized or destroyed, and a lawsuit may be filed. Residues remaining on the skins or peels of produce are minimal and must be within safe levels set by the EPA and the FDA. Washing produce at home removes any residues that remain on raw foods.
  - Like the FDA, the *USDA's Food Safety and Inspection Service (FSIS)* monitors residues and enforces tolerance levels for meat, poultry, and eggs.
  - *Several states,* including California, that grow many fruits and vegetables have their own regulations, too.

Tolerances, or maximum levels, for pesticide residues are set in parts per million, parts per billion, and parts per trillion. For example, 1 part per million (ppm) would be 1 gram of residue in 1 million grams of food. To make that amount understandable, that compares to 1 cherry in about 20,000 one-pound cans of cherries or one drop of water in an Olympic-size swimming pool.

Tolerances for pesticide residues have legal limits. In most foods, levels are well below that. Tolerances are a hundred to a thousand times lower than the amount that might pose a health risk, so there's a very wide margin of safety.

Have you ever wondered?

. . . what hydroponically grown foods are? They're foods from plants raised in water, not soil; "hydro" means water. The hydroponic solution—which varies by crop and environmental conditions—supplies roots with nutrients found in soil and fertilizer. With hydroponic farming, high-quality food can be produced almost anywhere: a desert, outer space, and areas with poor soil. Food can also be grown in indoor vertical farms, perhaps sharing space with kitchens and office buildings.

Nutritionally, hydroponically grown foods are comparable to those grown in soil; undamaged by weather, they may look better. They also require fewer pesticides since growing conditions can be controlled more easily.

Also being experimented with in modern agriculture are (1) aeroponics, or growing plants by spraying the roots with nutrient solution, and (2) aquaponics, which is part hydroponic, relying on the symbiotic relationship between plants and fish.

. . . why some fresh fruit and vegetables are exposed to ethylene gas? Some, such as bananas, peaches, pears, and tomatoes, produce ethylene gas naturally as they ripen, and the gas causes the changes in texture, softening, and color that come with ripening. Some types of produce can be harvested before they're fully ripe and still be firm. This prolongs shelf life. Later, these same fruits and vegetables are exposed to ethylene gas to induce ripening. This allows them to be available even when they aren't in season.

. . . how Bt crops are used for crop protection? *Bacillus thuringiensis* (Bt), a common soil bacterium, produces proteins that kill certain insects. Bt corn, cotton, and soy have been developed through biotechnology as a way for crops to protect themselves from certain insects that eat and destroy them. That in turn can significantly reduce the need for insecticides.

While Bt is harmful to targeted insects, it isn't harmful to beneficial insects or to humans, other mammals, birds, or fish. Bt binds to specific receptors in the gut of certain insects, and the insects stops eating. Humans, birds, fish, and mammals do not have these receptors.

Over time, some insects may become tolerant to certain Bt proteins, which explains why farmers who grow a Bt crop also must practice Insect Resistance Management, which lets some susceptible insects survive. Farmers can either plant a strip or block of the same crop without the Bt trait or use a seed blend with some non-Bt seeds. These practices help growers enhance the sustainability of their agricultural systems. Bt itself isn't new. Organic and traditional farmers have used it for their crops for more than forty years.

. . . about aquaculture and its role in food production? Expanding globally, aquaculture is the breeding, rearing, and harvesting of finfish, shellfish, and plants in both freshwater and saltwater, including artificial earthen ponds, rivers, lakes, and oceans as well as high-tech recirculating water systems. As with agriculture, it's done in both natural and man-made environments. As a way to supplement the wild fish harvest, aquaculture helps provide enough finfish and shellfish to meet the dietary recommendation to consume eight ounces a week on a 2,000-calorie-per-day eating plan.

US aquaculture production is overseen by several federal agencies including the USDA, EPA, FDA, the US Fish and Wildlife Service, and the US National Oceanic and Atmospheric Administration. Many states have additional regulations. With this oversight, farm-raised fish in the United States must be raised with strict environmental and safety standards. Antibiotics and hormones to promote growth rates aren't allowed. Imported farm-raised fish is not always produced with such stringent regulations.

To help consumers stay informed, the USDA requires labels for fish sold in large retail stores; the label must include country of origin and state whether it is wild caught or farm-raised. Restaurants, small fish markets, and butcher shops are not required to provide this labeling.

. . . why farm-raised salmon have color additives? The pink or reddish color of wild salmon comes from what they eat: astaxanthin (a natural antioxidant related to beta-carotene in carrots) found in krill, plankton, and other small organisms.

To make farm-raised salmon meet consumer demand for appealing fish, carotenes (astaxanthin and the similar canthaxanthin) sometimes are added to the feed for farm-raised salmon. They are regulated as a color additive by the FDA. While some feeds have natural pigments, most have manmade additives; research is underway to improve the production of naturally occurring sources. The flesh of the salmon isn't dyed. By law, farm-raised salmon must be labeled as "color added" to indicate the addition of carotenes to their feed.

FDA testing has shown that foods rarely exceed limits; many samples are below the tolerance level or show no residues at all. To pass through US Customs, imported foods must meet the same stringent standards set for foods grown domestically.

Despite strict regulation, there are ongoing concerns about the potential effects of pesticides on wildlife and in water, soil, and air if leaching, runoff, or spray drift happens. Studies on the impact of pesticide use is ongoing, as is further regulation and use of safer pesticides, less dependence on them, alternative cropping systems, and the correct use of spraying equipment. For example, current research is investigating the effect of certain insecticides on honey bee populations, as well as ways to control the invasive varroa mite, which is a pest of honey bees.

Limiting Exposure to Residues. You can increase your safety net and protection from any residues—and get the nutritional benefits of fruits and vegetables—by the way you handle them and how you grow them in your garden.

- Wash raw fruits (including melons) and vegetables under running water. Doing so not only can reduce any remaining residues on the surface and in the crevices, but also removes foodborne microbes. Rinse well. Washing fruits and vegetables with soap, detergent, or a commercial produce wash is not recommended.
- Remove and discard (or compost) the outer leaves of cabbage, lettuce, and other leafy vegetables.
- If you eat the fiber-rich skin or peel on foods such as apples, carrots, pears, and squash, use a vegetable brush to clean them. Although you could peel some fruits and vegetables, recognize what you'd be giving up—the nutrients and fiber that the peel contains. Instead, wash them well.
- Clean organic produce, too. Being organic doesn't mean produce with no pesticides; instead, there may be nonorganic pesticides found naturally in nature.
- Eat a variety of foods. Not only do you get the nutritional benefits, but you also minimize pesticide risks. Variety limits exposure to any one type of crop protection.
- If you're a home gardener, minimize your use of pesticides, organic or not; follow directions for their safe use, storage, and disposal. Contact your county Cooperative Extension Service if you need guidance. *See "Resources You Can Use" on page 763, to help locate your local Cooperative Extension Service.*

The Surgeon General and many health organizations, including the National Institutes of Health, the American Medical Association, the American Cancer Society, and the American Academy of Pediatrics, recognize that the health benefits of eating more fruits and vegetables far outweigh any possible pesticide-related risks. Prudent use helps ensure a wide variety of fruits and vegetables, which supply vitamins, minerals, fiber, and other phytonutrients for human health.

Today's Leaner Meat

Through traditional breeding, feeding, and farm management, hogs and beef cattle are leaner than in past decades. One reason for leaner hogs is genetics. Some of the eight major hog breeds in the United States carry genes that produce leaner, meatier hogs. With selective breeding, hog farmers have changed the fat and muscle composition of hogs, gradually producing leaner animals. In fact, today's pork is 16 percent leaner and 27 percent lower in saturated fats compared with twenty years ago.

As with humans, hogs' food and "lifestyle" affect their body composition. With a scientifically balanced diet matched to age, current weight, and nutrient needs, they're fed without excess.

The next step in producing lean meat is with the meat packers or processors. They usually trim the fat surrounding meat cuts to ⅛ to 1/16 inch, rather than ½ to ¼ inch as in past decades. With beef, many cuts have no outside fat at all.

Even though many meats are produced and processed to have less fat than before, they can still be tender, moist, and flavorful. Look for lean ground beef and low-fat pork sausages: just 5 fat grams and 6 fat grams, respectively, per 3-ounce serving. That's about 50 percent less than for regular meat.

Finally, it's up to you to keep lean meat lean and flavorful by using low-fat cooking methods, avoiding high-fat sauces, and cooking it to a safe internal temperature without overcooking. *See "Meat, Poultry, Fish: Keep Lean" in chapter 8, page 254, and "Meat Counter" in chapter 6, page 164, for more about leaner cuts and buying lean meat.*

ORGANIC FARMING

With growing consumer demand, organic farming has expanded—not only with more organic vegetables, fruits, and grains, but also with meat, poultry, eggs, dairy foods, and oils. More organic production has also put more organic packaged foods in retail stores, including frozen and canned foods, baby foods, and even wine and beer.

Organic Production: What It Means

What are organic foods? To clarify misnomers, the marketing term "local" doesn't mean "organic," and "organic" doesn't mean more nutritious or safer, either.

"Organic" is a method of farming. It refers to producing food with little or no nonorganic fertilizers or pesticides and with no antibiotics or hormones. Crops cannot be genetically engineered. The term "organic"

? Have you ever wondered?

. . . why antibiotics are used and how they're regulated in animal agriculture? Like people when they get sick, animals need to be treated for illness, whether raised in a pasture or feedlot. Antibiotics have been used in animal agriculture for many years to prevent or cure diseases in animals—sometimes administered to just one animal, sometimes to the herd or the flock if many animals are infected at the same time.

The FDA and FSIS work together to provide safe food by regulating the proper use of antibiotics in animal agriculture. That includes the type of antibiotic, the dose and its duration, and how long before slaughter the animal or animals must be withdrawn from the market or, for dairy cows, ensuring how long milk that is free from antibiotic residues before milk can be sold. USDA regulations require that antibiotic use must stop for at least sixty days before slaughter.

The FDA regulates and monitors the use of animal antibiotics to ensure that any residues in meat and poultry are minimal and at very safe levels. When animals, raised to be "antibiotic free," get sick and need an antibiotic, they are separated, treated, and later sold as meat from conventionally raised meats—but then only after the withdrawal time for the antibiotic has elapsed.

For milk, a dairy cow can't return to the milking herd until tests show that her milk is free of antibiotics. In addition, every tank load of milk is strictly tested for antibiotics; if it tests positive for any antibiotic, the entire tank of milk is discarded without getting to the store. As a result, milk sold in stores—conventional or organic—does not contain antibiotics.

Because of concerns about overusing antibiotics, the FDA in 2015 (fully enacted in January 2017) issued new guidance for the use of antibiotics in animals that produce food. It requires that these drugs must be used only under veterinary supervision and only when necessary to treat, prevent, and control disease—and not for growth promotion. That requires veterinary oversight of antibiotics for prophylactic, or disease-preventing, use.

If the FSIS finds enough substantiated proof that animals were raised without antibiotics, meat and poultry may be labeled "no antibiotics added" or "raised without antibiotics."

. . . if antibiotics used in agriculture affect human health? Questions have been posed about the possibility of "antibiotic resistance" in humans if animal antibiotics are used in cattle production. Definitive research is needed to determine if there is any effect from the use of animal antibiotics on human health. There is very limited overlap in antibiotics given to both humans and animals. For example, penicillin, important to human health, is not used with cattle.

. . . about hormones used in beef production, and if they affect humans? The FDA and FSIS work together to ensure the safe, proper use of hormones in cattle. To clarify a misconception, exposure to high levels of hormones from beef has never been implicated in early puberty in young girls.

In very small amounts, certain hormones are used with FDA approval to improve feed efficiency or weight gain of most beef cattle. Ready for market faster, beef animals have more lean muscle and less fat—a desirable quality. Growth hormones are used with only a small percentage of dairy cows to increase milk production.

The amount of growth-promoting hormones used must fit within the same range as is naturally present in untreated animals. Producers must show that hormone levels in animals after treatment remain below a level that's too low to affect humans who consume the meat.

To put this in perspective, all meat, treated or not, contains hormones in very low levels; plant-based foods have them, too. A three-ounce serving of treated beef has 1.85 nanograms of estrogen, compared to 1.3 nanograms in the same amount of untreated beef. One serving of many plant-based foods contains several hundred nanograms of estrogen naturally. The natural estrogenic activity from many other common foods, including beans and eggs, is many times higher. The human body also produces thousands of nanograms of estrogen daily. One nanogram is very tiny: one billionth of a gram.

Beef may be labeled "no hormones administered" if the producer provides enough evidence to the FSIS showing that hormones weren't used to raise the animals. That gives you an option when you shop. Meat from untreated animals may cost somewhat more. The use of hormones reduces the cost of raising beef cattle.

Pork and poultry are hormone free. Federal regulations prohibit using added hormones in raising hogs or poultry, so the "no hormones added" claim can't be used on their labels unless it is followed by a statement that says "Federal regulations prohibit the use of hormones."

. . . what qualifies beef as being organic? Requirements for being "certified organic beef" extend beyond "no hormones administered." Beef labeled as "certified organic" must be from cattle that meet production requirements for livestock established by the USDA's National Organic Program (NOP). Feed must be certified as organic; livestock may be grain- or grass-finished as long as the feed is 100 percent organic. Certain vitamins and minerals may be given. Cattle cannot have been treated with antibiotics or be given anything that promotes growth such as hormones. If they were treated with antibiotics, they cannot be sold as organic. And like most cattle, they must have access to pasture unless temporarily confined for specific reasons. *See "Organic Farming" on the previous page.*

. . . how grain-finished and grass-finished beef differ? With either type of beef, cattle graze on pasture. However, for grass-finished beef, cattle spend their whole lives on pasture, which can be challenging in some climates. Grain-finished cattle eat a carefully balanced diet of grasses, grains, and other forages in the feedlot for the last four to six months before slaughter.

is legally defined by a set of standards set by the USDA, referring to a way of managing food production.

Pesticides in organic farming. Organic farmers may use methods such as insect traps, careful crop selection (disease-resistant varieties), predator insects, or beneficial microorganisms to help control pests that damage crops. Certain insects, for example, are natural predators of others that cause crop damage; *see "Nature's Pest Control" in this chapter, page 118*. Farmers also may use nonorganic chemicals found naturally in the environment, such as copper, nicotine, pyrethrins, or sulfur for crop protection.

When these methods don't work, organic farmers can use other substances (biological, botanical, or nonorganic) from a list approved by the USDA's National Organic Program (NOP). Their use follows the same toxicology principles as with conventional farming.

Fertilizers in organic farming. Manure, compost, and other organic wastes are used to fertilize organic crops as are some nonorganic natural fertilizers. As with conventional farming, soil can be managed with crop rotation, tillage, and cover crops.

Organic fertilizers are effective for agricultural production. That said, plants don't distinguish them from synthetic fertilizers. Both types of fertilizer nurture growing plants.

Organically raised livestock and poultry. From the last third of gestation (or for poultry, the second day of life), organically raised animals are fed only 100 percent organic feed, and they must have outdoor access. Although vitamin and mineral supplements are allowed, hormones for growth and antibiotics to treat or prevent infection and disease are not. Any animal treated with medication no longer meets organic criteria or standards. Organic criteria for animals raised for milk and eggs are equally stringent.

Organic Certification

The USDA's certified organic label identifies foods that meet federal organic farming standards. The NOP ensures that the production, processing, and certification of organic foods meet set standards. Organic farming must abide by these standards for three years before receiving certification and then must continue to follow them.

Under the Organic Foods Production Act, federal regulations require consistent and uniform standards. Organic farming or processing operations that take in more than $5,000 gross per year must be certified to use the label. Even smaller, uncertified organic operations must abide by the standards and may label their foods. In organic food production, food irradiation (to destroy foodborne bacteria), sewage sludge, and genetic engineering can't be used.

Certification allows organic labeling with consistent terminology: "100 percent organic," "organic," and "made with organic ingredients." The USDA organic seal may appear on any foods that contain at least 70 percent organic ingredients. A product with less than 70 percent organic ingredients can list only specific organically produced ingredients in the ingredient list. *See "Organic Labeling" in chapter 6, page 153.*

Farmers may follow organic practices even if they don't choose to be certified. Those who farm conventionally often use many agricultural practices that are associated with organic farming. Some farmers choose to practice both organic and conventional agricultural methods. Organic or not, caring for natural resources helps ensure successful agriculture now and into the future.

Going Organic

The availability of organic foods of all kinds has grown markedly in the last decade—with options in traditional supermarkets, not just specialty stores and farmers' markets. How do organic and nonorganic foods compare?

Comparing nutrition, safety, flavor, and cost. Organic foods must meet the same safety and quality standards as those of conventional foods.

Based on current scientific understanding, both approaches—organic and conventional farming—supply nutritionally comparable foods, although this is an issue of ongoing debate. For both farming practices, climate and soil conditions, genetic differences in plants, maturity at harvest, and the way food is handled affect the nutrient content of raw foods—and may account for minimal differences.

Studies show no significant flavor differences between growing methods; however, the food varietal, its growing conditions, maturity at harvest, and how it is handled and perhaps packaged may make differences in flavor.

Organically produced foods typically cost more. That's usually due to higher production costs (more labor, more intense management) and smaller scale (smaller farms or yields). However, in season, the price of organic produce is often comparable to out-of-season produce grown conventionally.

Quality? Some organic produce such as cucumbers may be more perishable since they aren't treated with a wax coating. Other specimens may be oddly shaped, smaller in size, or uneven in color. This is okay and doesn't impact their nutritional value. In fact, misshapen produce is trending!

Environmental considerations. Farming practices meant to care for the environment, such as reducing pollution and often conserving water and soil quality, and to ensure animal welfare drive some organic purchases. Some people buy organic foods to limit pesticide exposure. Organic or not, regulations don't allow residues that exceed government safety thresholds. The residue limit set by the EPA for all produce is many, many times lower than the lowest amount that may be harmful.

Both organic and conventional farming practices have a place in feeding a growing global population—and may coexist on the same farm. Today, both large and small farming operations produce food organically.

Shopping for organic foods. Whether you choose to buy organic or conventionally grown foods, shop wisely:

- Be a label reader. Being organic or containing organic ingredients doesn't mean more nutritious. Organic foods may still be high in added sugars, sodium, saturated fats, or calories—and low in fiber.
- Choose a variety of foods from a variety of sources. This reduces exposure to a single pesticide, organic or not, and produces a greater nutrient mix.
- At farmers' markets, talk to farmers. Locally grown doesn't mean organic. Some local farmers may use organic farming methods even though they aren't certified.
- Compare prices. You may elect conventional over organic if there is a big price gap, especially for produce you wouldn't consume with the skin or the peel on. This outside layer is where very small traces of pesticide residues may reside.
- Wash and scrub raw produce well under running water to remove dirt, bacteria, and any traces of pesticides. Organic residues are still residues.

Traditional and Modern Biotechnology

Food and agriculture are at the center of some of the world's biggest challenges in the years ahead. The population is growing dramatically, but the resources of the planet are not. Farmers are being challenged to produce more nutrient-rich food, more sustainably, on less land with less water. These are just some of the reasons why a form of agricultural science known as biotechnology is being applied to food production.

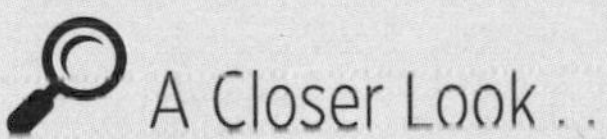

Understanding Biotechnology

The term "biotechnology" refers to the biological processes, organisms, or systems that improve yield and the quality of food. The earliest farmers used selective breeding to improve their crops and farm animals. At least two thousand years ago the technique of grafting trees transferred genes from one species to another. Today the term biotechnology has additional meaning: over the years, advances in science and an understanding of genetics have generated more sophisticated and faster ways to improve agricultural production.

Agricultural biotechnology includes a range of simple to sophisticated methods, developed over the course of time. These techniques can (1) improve the quality of plants or animals, (2) modify or make new plant varieties, (3) develop microorganisms for specific agricultural uses, (4) use the thousands of edible plant species yet unexplored, and (5) use resources—and, water, pesticides, fertilizers—for food production more efficiently and safely.

Selective and cross-breeding. Over the years, farmers planted seeds from their best crops or used controlled cross-pollination to develop hybrids. Likewise they've bred better livestock such as today's leaner hogs from their best animals.

These traditional biotechnology techniques have intentionally changed the genetic makeup of plants and animals for millennia. The goal: to obtain desirable traits and eliminate undesirable ones. Even organic vegetables, fruits, and grains sold commercially have been developed by traditional breeding over time by these techniques. *See "Methods of Plant Breeding" on the next page.*

- Selective breeding likely began ten thousand years ago when farmers saved the best of their crop as seed for the next crop. In fact, nearly every fruit, vegetable, and grain eaten today began this way.
- By selecting and raising plants and animals with desirable traits and then selecting and raising them again and again, new, more desirable plant varieties or breeds are established. For example, thousands of years ago, the tiny teosinte plant, a wild grass, was gradually altered by selective breeding to become today's corn. Five thousand years ago in today's Peru, potatoes were grown with selective breeding with the end results on today's plates.
- By cross-breeding plants, pollen from one variety of a plant species pollinates another to create new hybrids; animals are cross-bred too to improve their traits.

Starting in the 1700s, cross-breeding within plant species was used to develop crops—such as barley, corn, oats, potatoes, rice, soybeans, and wheat—with traits for higher yield, better taste, and pest resistance. By the late 1800s techniques developed that allowed a genetic exchange between different plant species that don't cross

(continued)

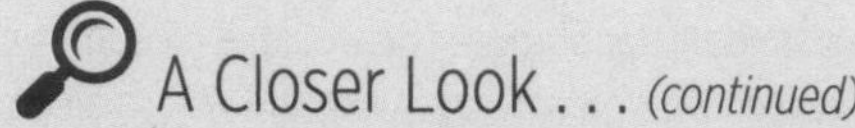

A Closer Look . . . *(continued)*

naturally. That gave us products such as pluots, tangelos, and some varieties of apples, rice, and wheat.

While used to improve agricultural products today, selective breeding takes time. Often it's unpredictable. For cross-breeding, each time one plant pollinates another, or one animal inseminates another, thousands and thousands of genes cross; that transfer is random since it's unknown which genes are affected. Along the way, less desirable traits—and the genes that cause them—may pass along with desirable ones. Several generations of breeding, perhaps ten to thirty years, may go by before desirable traits are established and less desirable qualities are finally bred away.

Mutagenesis. Starting in the 1930s other methods—chemical and radiation—were developed to change plant genetics and produce traits of many foods enjoyed today, such as some apples. bananas, mint, pears, and yams. As with selective and cross-breeding, these techniques randomly transfer hundreds perhaps thousands of genes, taking more than five years to develop.

Genetic engineering. A genetic engineering technique using GMOs, or genetically modified organisms, is a form of modern biotechnology. This is a process of changing the way a plant expresses genes, and is an extension of traditional plant breeding. Unlike selective or cross-breeding, genetic engineering transfers just one to three specific genes for a specific trait at a time.

As scientists learned more about DNA (deoxyribonucleic acid), genes, and the genetic code of living things, they applied this knowledge to transferring genes for valuable traits from one plant into the genetic code, or DNA, of another. To understand how this new science of farming works, think about writing a book on a computer. With a click of your mouse, you can copy a single quote from one document to another without merging the two, or you can highlight or delete a single phrase.

Likewise, agricultural scientists can pinpoint specific genes that carry traits they want, such as disease resistance, better nutrient quality, or flavor. Then they can transfer a single gene from one plant or from an unrelated species, such as a bacterium, to another. Or they can extract a certain gene, leaving only desirable traits behind.

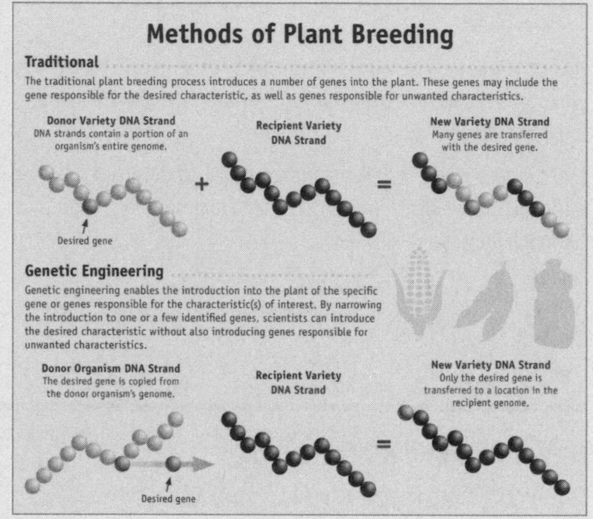

Source: gmoanswers.com/ask/what-gmo.

Three US crops (corn, cotton, and soybeans) are grown mostly from genetically engineered seed. They have been developed for two key traits, insect resistance and herbicide resistance. Corn (sweet and field) also has been developed to be drought tolerant. Three other field crops (alfalfa, canola, and sugar beets) are also approved as genetically engineered; these crops are also grown from seeds developed by other agricultural techniques. Many foods contain ingredients made from these six foods. To clarify a common misconception, there is no genetically engineered wheat on the market.

Currently the only fruits and vegetables sold in the United States that may be produced from seeds with genetic modification are papaya, sweet corn, and summer squash. Apples that won't brown when cut and non-browning potatoes have been approved and are coming to the market.

With advances in the understanding of plant science and genetics, the science of farming helps improve the nutritional quality and expand the varieties of food, improve food safety, reduce environmental impacts, limit pesticide use, and reduce crop loss and food waste from disease and pests. This in turn makes the global food system more sustainable.

Why Biotechnology?

Today's biotechnology—from traditional breeding to genetic engineering—are used not only to enhance the quality, safety, abundance, and wholesomeness of the food supply, but also to protect the environment, manage waste, provide alternative fuels, and develop products for medical treatment, among other applications.

Different methods are used to change different crop traits. Cross-breeding and hybridization have been used to create traits such as increased crop size and seedless varieties of melons. Genetic engineering has been used to develop commercial crops with other traits: insect resistance, drought resistance, increased/enhanced nutritional content, disease resistance for the plant, and herbicide tolerance.

More Food, Better Harvest. Within the next forty or so years, the world will need about 70 percent more food than is needed today to feed the world's rapidly growing population, which is expected to be about 9.7 billion by 2050. (In 2016, the world's population was about 7.4 billion.)

Using food biotechnology (all types) and good farming practices, higher-yielding crops can feed more people on less farmland and thus contribute to a more sustainable food supply with increased yields while reducing production costs and effort for farmers. All advances must be balanced against their carbon footprint.

Weather-resistant crops can turn regions with poor climate (extreme temperatures and drought) or poor soil conditions into productive agricultural land, able to withstand severe conditions, and can help lengthen the growing season and expand the size of the growing region. In developing countries, these advancements are critical when crop loss can result in devastating health and economic conditions.

Environmental protection. Crops produced using all forms of biotechnology can thrive with less environmental impact, including reducing the amount of pesticides. With enhanced farming techniques, greater crop yields may reduce the need to clear forests for farmland, thus protecting the environment. Better weed control with herbicide-tolerant crops allows farmers to use herbicides only when needed and to fight weeds with a no-till system or other forms of conservation tillage. That leads to less erosion of valuable topsoil because soil isn't turned over as much; therefore, there is less runoff and fewer greenhouse gas emissions.

Some crops, developed through genetic engineering, can resist plant viruses and other diseases. An example is papaya, which can resist the potentially devastating papaya ringspot virus. Other crops require less insecticide use or more environmentally friendly herbicides. Crops with traits that repel pests require fewer pesticides, which results in fewer residues that can pass into water supplies. With "environmentally friendly" animal feed, less unwanted phosphorus passes into manure and then into the water supply. Crops genetically engineered to be insect resistant can be protected from specific insects throughout the growing season and therefore lower pesticide use and production costs.

Drought-resistant crops can protect yield during times when water is scarce. Others can be developed to be more resistant to flooding. As a related use, biotechnology may provide cost-effective options for renewable, nonpolluting fuel—for example, fuel made from corn (ethanol). These fuel sources may reduce dependence on nonrenewable energy sources such as petroleum.

New food varieties, better flavors. By understanding the plant genome, traditional cross-breeding has developed food varieties and foods with better flavor, other agronomic qualities, and a better nutrient profile. By transferring desirable genetic traits through cross-breeding, fruits and vegetables have been developed with different ripening qualities that can be shipped without spoilage or damage—bananas, pineapples, and strawberries, for example, that resist mold. This can provide better-tasting produce that stays fresh longer, such as sweeter peppers, or potatoes with fewer dark spots.

Cross-breeding also has created baby kiwi, baby pineapples, blood oranges, doughnut peaches, mini avocados, red sweet corn, and seedless melons as well as broccoflower (broccoli crossed with cauliflower), broccolini (broccoli crossed with Chinese broccoli), and kalettes (Brussels sprouts crossed with kale). And did you know that ugli fruit is a hybrid of grapefruit, orange, and tangerine?

Foods with more nutrition benefits. For example, highly pigmented carrots (purple, red, and yellow) were originally developed by the USDA with traditional breeding to contain more beta carotene, the red-orange pigment that gives carrots their color, as well as other new pigments including red lycopene, purple anthocyanins, and yellow xanthophylls, which may help guard against heart disease, help the eyes, and act as antioxidants, too. In the future, fruits and vegetables such as sweet potatoes developed with higher levels of antioxidants (vitamins C and E, beta carotene) may help reduce heart disease and cancer risk.

Already, some vegetable oils have an improved fatty-acid profile—less saturated fats and more monounsaturated fats—to promote heart health. Food biotechnology also has enhanced soybeans, canola, and other oil seeds so they have more oleic acid, an unsaturated fatty acid that is beneficial to health. Heart-healthier high-oleic soybean oil has been developed so fewer *trans* fats are formed with high heat. No genetically modified foods from livestock or poultry are on the market at this time.

Biotechnology, Food Safety, and the Environment

As with any new technology, public health and environmental impact are top concerns. Except for a specific trait, most foods enhanced through today's biotechnology don't differ in composition, nutritional quality, or safety from those developed with traditional agricultural techniques. Foods developed with any form of food biotechnology are subject to the same stringent standards of safety as all foods sold in the United States. Unlike seeds and crops developed by selective or cross breeding methods or by mutagenesis, those produced with genetic engineering undergo extensive safety scrutiny by regulatory agencies.

The environmental impact of and potential concerns about disrupting the ecosystem with genetically modified crops must be addressed and researched, too. Seed manufacturers are required to conduct thorough research and demonstrate proof of testing for every crop brought to market—for example, showing proper nutrient levels, status of allergens or natural toxins, how the improved crop functions as food or animal feed, scientific procedures for product development, environmental effects, and the history of safe use. The development, testing, and review and approval process typically take more than a decade before genetically engineered foods can reach the marketplace.

The USDA assesses the safety of crops growing in the field and the crop's potential impact on the environment and agriculture. Before a crop can move from the greenhouse to field testing, the USDA must give approval to the developer. At the same time, the FDA or the EPA reviews the documentation on the safety and potential for allergic reactions to the crop.

Growing Possibilities

Modern food biotechnology may make foods such as these available in the future:

- Tomatoes with more lycopene, an antioxidant that may protect against some cancers
- Low-fat potato chips or French fries made from higher-starch potatoes that absorb less fat
- Vegetables and fruits with higher levels of antioxidants (vitamins C and E, and beta carotene) that may help reduce risks for some chronic diseases such as cancer and heart disease
- Rice with higher-quality protein (more amino acids) produced with genes from pea plants; golden rice with more beta carotene
- Vegetable oils—canola, corn, soybean, and others—with more stearate (a form of stearic acid, which is a saturated fat that doesn't appear to affect blood cholesterol levels) for use in margarine and spreads
- Garlic with more allicin, a phytonutrient that may help lower cholesterol levels
- Peanuts with less of the naturally occurring protein that causes allergic reactions
- Strawberries with more ellagic acid, a cancer-fighting phytonutrient
- Drought-resistant rice for growing in regions with extreme heat and drought
- Fruits that can deliver vaccines in regions without adequate refrigeration to store vaccines
- Folate-rich grains

- The FDA's key role is assuring the safety of the product and its nutritional value as a crop, as a food for humans, or as animal feed. It must show that known or suspected allergens were not increased inadvertently.
- The EPA regulates the safety of pest-control properties of crops, including their impact on the environment and food supply. For example, if a crop is genetically engineered to carry a gene for a Bt toxin, the EPA requires the developer to verify that the toxin is safe for the environment and to conduct a food-safety analysis to ensure that the foreign protein is not allergenic. *See "Have you ever wondered . . . how Bt crops are used for crop protection?" earlier in this chapter, page 119.*

Current evaluation procedures used by manufacturers and regulators to ensure safety for consumers are endorsed internationally by the Food and Agriculture Organization (FAO) of the United Nations and the World Health Organization (WHO). In the United States, the National Academy of Sciences, the American Medical Association, the Society of Toxicology, and the Academy of Nutrition and Dietetics, among others, recognize the safety of foods produced by genetic engineering. To clarify, there is no scientific evidence attributing any health conditions—including allergic reactions, autism, cancer, and gluten issues—or death to foods that have been genetically engineered.

With new technology comes change, controversy, and more research questions to explore and answer. The use of food biotechnology must be weighed against all outcomes for overall health and the environment.

Labeling: When You Want to Know

Foods developed through biotechnology—selective and cross breeding and genetic engineering—are subject to the same FDA labeling regulations and carry the same food labels, including allergen labeling, as any other foods. Food labels must provide information for consumers in these cases:

- *If a food contains a known allergen.* Allergic reactions come from proteins; genes direct protein production. If a gene were taken from a food known to cause allergic reactions (such as peanuts), then transferred to another (such as corn), the new food would be required to be labeled as potentially containing that allergen.

  To date, no foods introduced into the food supply are known to contain proteins from known allergenic foods. (Through biotechnology, research is underway to remove known allergens from foods, such as to develop allergen-free or allergen-reduced peanuts.)

- *If the nutritional content changes.* Foods that are enhanced through any form of modern biotechnology (including selective or cross breeding or genetic modification) to change their nutritional content must be labeled. For example, the labels on rice with protein or oranges with additional vitamin C must indicate the modifications.

- *If the food composition changes substantially.* Perhaps it would be labeled with a new varietal name or maybe, like broccoflower, be given a new identity.

If you want to eat GMO-free, you have some options:

- *Choose foods with organic labeling.* The use of GMOs is prohibited in the production of organic-labeled products. Many non-GMO foods are not organic. *See "Organic Labeling," in chapter 6, page 153.*
- *Look for "non-GMO" labeling.* Until new federal regulations are fully in place, foods may be labeled voluntarily, as produced with or without the use of ingredients that are enhanced or produced through GMO technology. Labeling must be truthful and not misleading

That said, be aware of misleading or confusing labeling. Currently foods can claim to be "non-GMO" even though that food was never developed or approved with genetic engineering. So seeing a product, such as orange juice or vanilla extract, marketed as "non-GMO" does not mean that there's an option that is genetically engineered. A new law signed in 2016—with compliance sometime in 2019 for big companies and 2020 for smaller companies—requires food companies to disclose GMOs.

Food Processing

Several questions come to mind these days, such as what exactly is food processing? Do processed foods contribute more or less nutrition? When did we start processing food?

Throughout much of recorded history, people have "processed" foods to make them edible and safe, and to preserve foods for times of scarcity. About eight thousand years ago, foods were smoked and dried in Europe and elsewhere. Cheese-making developed forty-five hundred years ago in the Middle East to preserve milk. About twenty-five hundred years ago, both Egyptians and Europeans preserved foods with salt. In the 1800s, canning gave perishable foods a longer shelf life, followed by freezing in the early twentieth century, making a variety of fruits and vegetables available year-round. And in the nineteenth century, pasteurization made milk safe by using heat to kill disease-causing bacteria.

Food preservation has played an important role in advancing civilization, too. Because of processing, food can be preserved so people can spend less time growing food and more time in other endeavors such as science, literature and the arts, exploration, and manufacturing.

FOOD PROCESSING: DEFINED

The term "processed food" often gets mischaracterized as food that's highly processed, less nourishing, and unhealthy. The term is generally perceived as a catch-all for foods to avoid.

Yet, many ways you prepare and cook foods in your own kitchen are similar to the practices employed by food companies. Your food processor can grind flaxseed or oatmeal into flour, or puree whole fruit into a sauce. Your pressure cooker can be used to can and preserve garden vegetables to enjoy next winter. You might dry fresh herbs you've grown to season hearty soups and stews, or pickle an overabundant crop of garden cucumbers or okra. And you've likely shaken heavy cream in a jar until it turned to butter back when you were in school. These are all examples of "processing."

In truth, processing methods differ from each other in many ways, and there is no regulated definition for processing. You may not think of prewashed bagged kale, yogurt, or brown rice as processed, but they

Fruits and Vegetables: Processed or Not?

The flavor of produce in season is hard to beat when it's freshly picked, handled properly, and eaten right away. However, the moment you pick fruits or vegetables, or even catch a fish or milk a cow, food starts to degrade in texture, taste, nutrient content, and perhaps color. That's why most food companies process food as fast as possible, while the nutrient content and the overall quality are at their peak.

Immediate processing, such as freezing, canning, and drying, helps lock the best qualities into foods. Tomatoes may be canned just yards away from the fields. The same is true for commercially frozen foods. In canneries on board some fishing vessels, fish is processed as soon as it's hauled in.

Research shows that canned and frozen ingredients are nutritionally comparable to their cooked fresh counterparts when handled properly. If processed foods are handled properly—from the manufacturer, to store, to home—there's little nutrient loss.

Whether fruits and vegetables are purchased raw or processed, it's up to you to minimize nutrient loss from store to table. The nutritional quality of fresh fruits and vegetables depends on their care after harvest, all along the food distribution and food preparation chain. If they are handled or cooked improperly or stored too long, they may not be quite as nutritious as their canned or frozen counterparts. *See "How to . . . Keep Nutrients In" in chapter 8, page 248.*

Have you ever wondered?

. . . why boxed fluid milk can be sold on the grocery shelf, not in the dairy case? Aseptic packaging allows fluid milk to be stored at room temperature from six months to a year without preservatives. Sterilization is the key to preventing spoilage. To sterilize it, food is first heated quickly (three to fifteen seconds) to ultrahigh temperatures to kill bacteria. It is then packaged in a sterilized container, such as the aseptic boxes you find on the market shelves, within sterile surroundings. Flash heating minimizes loss of nutrients, texture, color, and flavor—and extends shelf life. Once opened, milk processed and packaged like this needs refrigeration.

Besides milk, look for many other grocery items sold in aseptic packaging—for example, juice and juice drinks, liquid eggs, nondairy creamers, soups, soy beverages, syrup, tofu, tomatoes, and wine.

. . . why some fruits and vegetables have a wax coating—and if it's safe to eat? The thin, waxy coating on foods such as apples and cucumbers is applied after picking to replace the natural wax that gets washed off with dirt and soil after harvest. Wax helps retain moisture, protect food from bruising, inhibit mold growth, prevent other physical damage and disease, and enhance appearance.

The amount of wax used is tiny—just a drop or two. The coating must meet FDA food-additive regulations for safety. By long-standing federal law, waxed produce must be labeled. While there is no need to peel waxed produce, wash it with fresh running water, not soap. And use a brush to remove any dirt, bacteria, and residues.

. . . why the US food supply is considered among the safest in the world? Although not risk free, government regulations for food production help to safeguard and minimize potential health risks. For example, a system called HACCP, or Hazard Analysis and Critical Control Points, used in food processing and food service—from food production and packaging to distribution—helps detect, reduce, eliminate, and track potential foodborne pathogens. For some foods, such as meat and juice, HACCP is mandatory; for others, its use is voluntary. The process allows for recalls if a food safety problem occurs. Restaurants and other food-service institutions rely on HACCP.

are. Processed foods, in part, are any food that is not still in its raw agricultural state.

Food processing includes the many deliberate practices that transform raw plant and animal commodities such as grains, produce, meat, poultry, fish, and dairy into food products you can consume. It's as basic as milling wheat into flour so grains are edible, and freezing or canning vegetables to make them available all year long. It's as complex and valuable as developing appealing gluten-free baked foods for those who need them or fortifying bread with folic acid for public health reasons.

Food processing generally refers to what takes place in a food manufacturing plant: washing, cleaning, concentrating, cutting, chopping, emulsifying, enriching, fermenting, heating, milling, pasteurizing, blanching, cooking, canning, freezing, drying, dehydrating, mixing, packaging, refining, and so on to alter the food from its natural state. In reality, most foods are processed in some way.

Processing also may include adding ingredients, such as preservatives, flavors, nutrients, and other food additives or substances accepted for specific food functions, such as tenderness, thickening, or leavening (as in bread). Processing also may reduce, increase, or leave unaffected the nutritional qualities of the unprocessed food—making some more nourishing and others less so.

REASONS FOR FOOD PROCESSING

Food processing, much of which requires a keen understanding of food science and the chemistry of food, is part of food's journey from farm to plate and serves a number of purposes.

Food safety and preservation. From farm to plate, keeping food safe and preserving its quality and nutrition are top priorities. Canning, drying, freezing, and pickling are some methods that preserve food and destroy bacteria that cause foodborne illness. These processes help keep food safe and extend its shelf life, providing more food variety year-round.

Practices such as pasteurizing milk and juice and fermenting dairy products into yogurt and cheese extend shelf life and ensure food safety, as does the prudent use of certain additives. Today, other regulated food-processing methods, such as irradiation and antimicrobial washes and sprays done by food companies, also help in removing substances that may be harmful.

The packaging of processed foods also helps keep foods safe and extend their shelf life. That helps to protect a food's quality and nutritional value longer and also potentially reduce wasted food. The package label is also an important source of information on a food's proper storage and use.

See chapter 7, page 230, for more about food safety and foodborne illness.

Flavor, acceptability, and food variety. No matter how nourishing it may be, a food without appeal likely won't be eaten. Some processing methods preserve the appealing aromas, colors, textures, and flavors of raw foods. Other methods modify these sensory qualities, adding appeal and more food variety from which to choose.

Nutrition and health benefits. Food processing can improve the nutrition and health benefits of foods and, with some methods, perhaps lower the chance for some nutrient deficiencies.

Most foods are processed in some way before they're consumed. Processing transforms raw products, such as wheat grains, into edible foods and ingredients. Some processing methods such as freezing and canning help to retain the nutritional value of foods. Others—enrichment and fortification—*discussed in this chapter, page 134*, raise or restore a food's nutritional value.

Food processing contributes to good nutrition in other ways, too. For example, it makes a wide variety of nourishing and appealing foods available; it formulates food and drink options to solve nutrition challenges such as allergen-, lactose- or gluten-free foods; and it changes nutritious foods to a form such as baby carrots and flavored yogurt that increases their appeal. And while refining grain removes some key nutrients, it also removes phytic acid in the bran, improving the body's absorption of iron from food.

Without enriched and fortified foods, many people wouldn't meet their recommendations for calcium, iron, potassium, folate, vitamin B_{12} (for vegans), vitamin D, and fiber, all nutrients that come up short for many people, as noted in the Dietary Guidelines for Americans. *Caution*: Some processed foods may contribute more of what most people need to limit, including calories, saturated fats, added sugars, and sodium.

Bottom line: The nutrients a food contains, not whether it's processed or not, should be a major factor when it comes to making food choices. The package label is your "go-to" source of information about the nutritional value of the food inside.

Convenience and shelf life. Many consumers lack the time, skills, energy, and/or interest to prepare food from scratch. Convenience foods make it easy to serve a meal with little or no food prep: (1) pre-cleaned and processed produce (fruit slices, guacamole, and salad and stir-fry kits), (2) ready-to-eat foods (breakfast cereals, cheese, crackers, deli meats, simmering sauces, and yogurt), and (3) frozen and canned vegetables, frozen pizza, and microwavable meals. With convenience, you can get meals on the table with very little effort.

Sustainability and cost. Food processing also can help reduce food waste—a perspective that needs to be balanced against the use of resources and the carbon footprint for processing and packaging. Processes that preserve and prevent spoilage, inhibit rancidity, protect vitamins, and keep foods' color and flavor appeal help keep food out of your trash can.

Processing can turn cosmetically imperfect foods into mixed convenience foods such as canned soups, frozen entrees, sauces, slaw mixes, and stews. And the by-products of processing can be used for other purposes: fish bones and blood for fertilizer, oat hulls for producing electricity, and vegetable oils for biodiesel fuel.

PROCESSING: A CONTINUUM OF CHOICES

Many people think of foods as either processed or not. Yet food processing varies from a little to a lot. The amount of processing can be simply canning or freezing fruits or vegetables to preserve nutrients and extend freshness, or can be formulating a food product, perhaps for a health benefit or other quality.

Minimally processed foods keep most of their original physical, chemical, sensory, and nutritional qualities. They aren't fundamentally altered. Most are as nourishing as their unprocessed counterparts.

Not all processed foods are healthy options, however (true of home-cooked foods, too). Some more highly processed foods are best enjoyed only occasionally since they're often high in saturated or *trans* fats, added sugars, and sodium, and the processing method may minimize their nutritional value.

- Minimally processed foods don't require much preparation, perhaps just washing and simple "pre-prep" for convenience: for example, washed and packed fruits and vegetables, bagged salads, and roasted and ground nuts. Raw, uncooked meat, pasteurized milk, and dry beans aren't changed much from their unprocessed form and keep most of their nutritional properties.
- Foods are processed at their peak to keep and enhance the nutritional quality and freshness, such as with canned beans, tomatoes, and tuna; frozen fruits and vegetables; and jarred baby foods.
- Ingredients are added to some foods for safety, flavor, and perhaps visual appeal. That includes colors, flavors, oils, spices, sweeteners, and preservatives in packaged foods such as cake mixes, instant potato mixes, jarred tomato sauces, salad dressings, sauces, and spice mixes.
- Ready-to-eat foods need minimal or no preparation by consumers. Some examples include breakfast cereal, crackers, granola bars, ice cream, luncheon meats, and yogurt.
- Some processed foods are packaged for convenience, safety, and time-saving, such as frozen meals, pizza, and prepared deli foods.

Instead of choosing food based on whether it's processed or not, consider its ingredients and nutrient content: what's lost or added, and how it contributes to the nutrients you need. For the most nutrition and fewer added sugars, sodium, and perhaps saturated fats, less processed is often best. Although foods may sometimes be marketed as "clean foods," there is no accepted definition of this trending phrase; only that there may be a shorter list of ingredients.

That said, by lowering fats or carbohydrates, a food's qualities may change. For example, cookies might be made to have less fat but may need more sugar to ensure an acceptable texture and flavor. Some changes may alter a food's flavor and mouth feel. Formulating foods

Grains of Truth

Your ancestors consumed much more fiber than you do! Before advanced milling technology, gristmills were used to grind corn, wheat, and other grains into meal or flour. Using the water power of a river, grain was milled between two coarse stones. Then it was sifted to remove the inedible chaff, or husk, leaving all the edible parts of the grain: the bran and germ that contain fiber and many essential nutrients. Whole grains were the foods of the masses. In some parts of the world, that continues to be true. In fact, some people still pound their grain by hand to make flour.

As technology improved, the bran and germ were separated and removed, leaving refined white flour. With this new process came new status. White bread, with its softer texture and high-class appeal, became more desirable than coarser, darker bread. But white bread was more expensive and available only to those who could afford it—as far back as Roman times. For the same reasons, white rice became more desirable than brown rice. Simply put, refined was in!

With the switch to refined grains, people became shortchanged on some nutrients and fiber. In the 1940s, recognizing the health consequences, manufacturers began enriching many grain foods with some of the nutrients lost during processing—thiamin, riboflavin, niacin, and iron. In some foods, fiber was added back, too. Since the late 1990s, enriched grain foods also have been fortified with folic acid.

Only in recent years have health experts recognized that fiber offers more than bulk to food. It's loaded with many health benefits; *see "Fiber and Health" in chapter 11, page 350*. Today, whole-grain foods, along with other fiber-rich foods—vegetables, fruits, and beans—are in again. And today's experts recommend that whole grains make up at least half of your daily grain intake.

with less sodium may make them less flavorful unless other flavor-intense ingredients such as herbs or spices are added.

PRESERVING FOOD FOR NUTRITION, FOOD SAFETY, AND APPEAL

Foodborne illness often involves raw foods—vegetables, fruits, and animal products—contaminated by bacteria and toxins. Heat processes such as canning, cooking, and pasteurization destroy pathogens. Many other processing methods either slow or stop their growth, keeping a nourishing and safe supply of food year-round.

The method used, such as canning, curing, drying, freeze-drying, freezing, or irradiation, depends on the type of food, the length of storage desired, and its ultimate use. Advances in food science have developed other methods to preserve food as well to help maximize quality, shelf life, and nutrition.

Canning: It's Cooking

Canning began about 200 years ago as a way to preserve food safely. It's simply cooking food in a can or jar after it's sealed. Whether it's commercial or home canning, the process (high temperature and a sterile container) destroys organisms that would cause spoilage—with no need for preservatives. Any salt as an ingredient is added for flavor, not preserving. Lacking oxygen during storage, the food's quality and nutrient content remain relatively stable as long as the container and its seal or lid remain intact.

Unopened canned or jarred foods have a long shelf life. Washing, peeling, and other steps done before canning remove nearly all pesticide residues. Foods sold in cans have another safety advantage: tamper resistance. Any opening is clearly evident. Rust spots on the outer surface or dents don't affect the contents of the can as long as it isn't bulging or leaking.

While some nutrients are lost during any heating process, canned foods are nutritionally comparable to their cooked fresh and frozen counterparts—and can even deliver somewhat more nutrition than fresh and frozen foods that aren't stored and prepared properly. A few examples: Heat from canning makes lycopene in tomatoes and lutein in corn more bioavailable (available to the body); heat also increases the bioavailability of folate, thiamin, niacin, and vitamin B_6. The amount of beta carotene (provitamin A) in canned pumpkin is three times higher than in cooked fresh pumpkin because canning concentrates the pumpkin. Canning softens edible bones in canned salmon, making it a source of calcium. Calcium chloride may be used in canned tomatoes to keep them from becoming mushy.

Caution: Salt or added sugars may be used to enhance the flavor of many canned foods. As alternatives, look for fruits packed in natural juices, and choose vegetables, soups, stews, and other mixed savory foods with reduced salt or no salt added. Fish such as tuna may be packed in oil such as olive oil; drain if you prefer.

Beyond that, canned foods of all kinds are convenient, portable, and quick to prepare. To retain their nutrients, heat them or eat them at room temperature since they're already cooked during canning.

Freezing: Ice Cold

Whether peas or green beans, a pizza or waffles, lasagna, or a whole dinner, freezing preserves perishable foods by storing them well below the temperature at which harmful microorganisms thrive. The freezing process depends somewhat on the foods to be frozen. Vegetables, for example, are blanched before freezing to destroy enzymes that cause deterioration over time.

Freezing temperatures also help retain much of the original texture, color, and flavor, as well as the nutrition of foods, over several weeks or months. This is longer than storage for fresh foods, but not as long as for canned and dried foods.

As consumed, frozen foods are comparable in nutrition to cooked fresh and canned foods—if properly stored. *See "The Cold Truth: Food Storage" in chapter 7, page 202, for freezer storage times.* Frozen foods also offer convenience for busy consumers. Check the Nutrition Facts and the ingredient list to find those with less added sugars, saturated fats, and sodium.

Drying and Freeze-Drying: Removing Moisture

Drying is among the oldest methods of preserving foods. By removing moisture from fruits, vegetables, beans, and nuts—even meat, poultry, and fish—bacteria no longer have access to water, needed for them to grow. To keep dried protein-rich foods such as meat or fish safe, a preservative generally is used.

Freeze-dried foods are frozen first, and then any ice crystals or vapor are removed with a vacuum. The food is then packaged and sealed immediately before it can absorb moisture. When used in food prep, these foods quickly reabsorb moisture. Freeze-drying retains foods' color, texture, and flavor better than other methods of dehydration. In dry, covered conditions, even at room or cool temperatures, dried foods in well-sealed containers remain safe and retain their quality.

Fermentation: Old Process, New Interest

Fermentation is an age-old process. It uses microorganisms such as friendly bacteria and yeast to make chemical changes in carbohydrates that alter the appearance and flavor of foods, extend their shelf life, and often add health benefits, particularly for gut health. In fact, gut health is behind the renewed interest in fermentation.

Many common foods are produced when starches and sugars they contain ferment: buttermilk, cheese, and yogurt are produced by fermenting milk; sauerkraut by fermenting cabbage; kimchi by fermenting various vegetables such as cabbage and radishes; vinegars by fermenting various foods, such as apples for apple cider vinegar or rice for rice vinegar. Olives are fermented, too, to make them palatable. Beer and wine are fermented, and bread rises due to the fermentation of yeast. Because their friendly bacteria may promote digestive health, many other raw vegetables, such as cabbage, green beans, okra, and turnips are being fermented, too. Fermented foods taste tart because the process produces acid.

Note: Pickling isn't the same as fermenting. Instead pickling is preserving in a brine (salt or salty water) or an acid such as vinegar. That said, the fermentation of some foods such as sauerkraut and traditional dill pickles begins with a brine.

Curing: Preserving Meat and Fish

Sausage, bacon, and many deli meats are cured, which is another way to process meat and fish for preservation. Foods that are salt cured are dried and then packed in a salt preparation, which draws out the moisture through osmosis. Sugar is sometimes used in the curing process as well. Smoke-cured foods can be cured at temperatures of 70°F to 90°F for a longer time or more quickly at 100°F to 190°F. Nitrites and nitrates that convert to nitrites are often used to cure meat and inhibit *Clostridium botulinum*, the bacteria that causes botulism.

Caution: Eating large amounts of meat and fish that have been processed by curing, fermentation, salting, and smoking to enhance flavor or improve preservation is associated with a higher risk of colorectal cancer: (1) Added nitrates/nitrites are one factor that may increase the cancer risk. (2) The smoke curing and high heat associated with some processing methods that lead to formation of polycyclic aromatic hydrocarbons (PAHs), a group of organic substances considered carcinogenic, increase the risk of cancer, too. (PAHs also can be found in charred foods as well as in cigarette smoke and exhaust fumes.) (3) High amounts of salt may promote the development of stomach cancer.

In 2015, the World Health Organization advised limiting processed meat. It reported that eating 50 grams of processed meat—equivalent to about four strips of bacon or one hot dog daily—increased the average lifetime risk of colorectal cancer. An occasional hot dog or bacon strip is okay. By limiting processed meats such as bacon, ham, hot dogs, sausage, and some deli meats, you reduce potential cancer risks as well as the high levels of sodium they typically provide.

Irradiation: Cold Pasteurization

Irradiation improves the safety and extends the shelf life of foods by reducing and eliminating microorganisms and insects. It can also delay sprouting (potatoes) and ripening (fruit) to increase their shelf life.

The irradiation process passes food through a field of radiant energy, much like sunlight passes through a window or like microwaves pass through food in cooking. It leaves no residue. These changes are the same as those caused by pasteurization, roasting, steaming, and other cooking.

Irradiation uses no heat yet destroys disease-causing bacteria and other organisms. Meat and poultry can be irradiated to ensure that pathogens that are especially harmful to children, the elderly, and people with weak immune systems are destroyed. That includes *Escherichia coli* (*E. coli*) 0157:H7, *Salmonella*, and *Campylobacter*.

? Have you ever wondered?

. . . if convenience foods usually cost more than cooking from scratch? That may be the intuitive response. But factoring in the value of time spent in food prep, along with the dollar cost of the ingredients, convenience foods may cost less.

You can determine this for yourself. Use the online Food Value Analysis tool (www.foodvalueanalysis.org) to compare the cost, nutrition, storage time, prep time, and food safety of foods you can make at home, compared to its store-bought, processed/prepared counterpart.

. . . what sous vide is and how it's used? Sous vide (soo VEED) is a way to cook food at low temperatures in a vacuum pack, which helps ensure even cooking and retain flavor and moisture, and also can extend the storage time. As a processing method, it may help food retain its sensory qualities longer—but it needs to be carefully controlled since bacteria multiply at these lower temperatures.

. . . about the safety of BPA in food containers? First, a definition: Bisphenol A (BPA) is a compound used in some reusable plastic food and beverage containers and can liners (as a barrier between the metal and the food inside). Some cans and plastic containers are BPA free. In 2012 the FDA banned the use of BPA in baby bottles.

Having been researched and deemed safe for decades, it's being reviewed again for health issues, such as some cancers and certain hormonal changes. Evidence shows no clear risk to human health, nor does it appear to build up in the human body. Any amount that migrates from plastic containers or cans to food is extremely low, many times lower than the safe exposure levels set by the FDA and international regulatory agencies.

While the risk is likely minimal, you can limit exposure to BPAs:

- Buy BPA-free plastic or glass baby bottles *as discussed in "Bottles and Nipples: Baby Feeding Supplies" in chapter 16, page 472*, storage containers, and plastic plates.
- Hand wash plastic containers with BPA, and avoid exposing them to the high heat in microwave ovens and dishwashers as well as filling them with hot ingredients.
- Use stainless steel, glass, or porcelain bowls for hot foods or liquids instead.

Like canning, drying, freezing, and pasteurization, irradiation results in minimal nutrient loss, often too insignificant to measure. Irradiation can't replace good food-handling practices—or improve the quality of food. As a consumer, you still need to store, prepare, and cook food using clean, safe methods to avoid foodborne illness.

Besides food safety, irradiation offers potential advantages. Agricultural losses (waste) caused by insects, parasites, or spoilage can be cut dramatically. Like other processing methods, irradiation is regulated and approved by the FDA.

By law, whole foods that have been irradiated must be labeled on the package. Look for the international Radura symbol (shown here) and the phrase "Treated by Irradiation" or "Treated with Radiation." Irradiated ingredients in prepared, deli, or restaurant foods usually aren't labeled.

To control foodborne illness, irradiation—studied for safety by the FDA for forty years—was approved twenty years ago by the FDA for fresh and frozen meats, including beef, pork, lamb, and poultry as well as finfish and shellfish. The process protects these foods from contamination—for example, by *E. coli* O157:H7 and *Salmonella*—but doesn't compromise their nutritional quality, taste, texture, or appearance. Irradiation also is used for some vegetables and fruits, beans, wheat flour, cereals, and spices. Research continues to evaluate irradiation as part of the overall system of ensuring food safety. To debunk a myth, irradiation doesn't make food radioactive.

ADDITIVES: THEIR PLACE ON THE PLATE

Does it ever occur to you that most peanut butters don't separate into oil and nut solids? That prepared baking mixes rise in the oven? That ice cream is smooth and creamy? Or that milk is fortified with vitamin D for your bone health? Most likely you take many desirable qualities of food for granted. And while you may not attribute the qualities you expect to them, food additives are used for purposes such as these.

Adding substances to food for preservation, flavor, or appearance is centuries old. Before refrigeration, salt preserved meat, poultry, and fish; vegetables were pickled in vinegar; and sugar was added to cut fruit to prevent spoilage. Ancient Egyptians used food colorings. Romans used sulfites to help preserve wine. The spice trade through Asia, the Middle East, and Europe flourished because people demanded the flavors that spices imparted to food.

Food additives, with their long unfamiliar names, may be confusing, even worrisome. Understanding what they do and how carefully they are regulated may allay many of your concerns.

Salt: Preserving Food for Centuries

Throughout recorded history, salt has played an important economic and political role—and has always been part of the world's food supply. It was only in the past 200 years that salt has not been heavily used for preserving meat, fish, vegetables, and even fruits. Especially in Mediterranean regions, cooks relied on herbs and spices to mask the strong, salty flavors caused by preservation. Cheese, too, was salted. Nations that controlled the salt trade also controlled distribution and preservation of food, especially in times of shortage.

Ancient Greeks valued salt so highly that they used it for currency. Salt was traded for slaves, hence the phrase "He's not worth his salt." Originally, Roman soldiers were given a handful of salt every day. Later they received money to buy their own salt, which was referred to as *salarium argentum*, meaning "salt money." The word "salary" comes from this Latin term. "Salad" also derives from the Latin word "*sal*," meaning salt.

Because of its value, salt has been used symbolically. To the ancient Romans, giving salt to a newborn meant giving wisdom. In Europe, a pinch of salt tossed three times over the left shoulder helped fend off evil. Even today, we reflect our doubts: "Take it with a grain of salt."

Until the late 1700s, common salty flavors came from food preservation. In the nineteenth century, tastes began to change, and people preferred less-salty foods. Concurrently, other food preservation methods took its place, namely canning, freezing, and refrigeration.

By the twentieth century, salt and other sodium-containing ingredients performed a variety of other functions in food processing. In the United States, salt was deemed "generally recognized as safe" as an additive recognized by the FDA, with no regulatory limits on its use, although of late, this regulation has come under scrutiny and may be amended. Over the last century, sodium intake also rose significantly, primarily because consumers cooked with fewer raw ingredients and more processed foods and ate out more frequently, often eating foods seasoned with sodium-containing ingredients, and so they consumed more sodium overall.

In ancient times, salt's ability to preserve food helped provide a varied supply of nutrients to the population. As science advanced, we learned that the blood pressure of some people might be sensitive to salt, or to the sodium it contains. Now we recognize that the blood pressure link to nutrition may be more complex, with potassium, magnesium, and calcium also playing a role; *see "Blood Pressure: Under Control?" in chapter 24, page 693.*

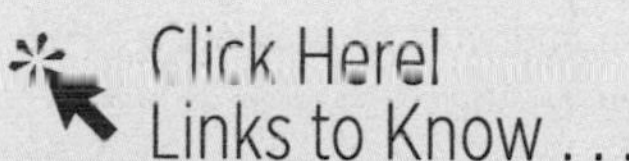

- Food Facts, Institute of Food Technologists
  www.ift.org/Knowledge-Center/Learn-About-Food-Science/Food-Facts.aspx
- Overview of Food Ingredients, Additives & Colors, US Food and Drug Administration
  www.fda.gov/Food/IngredientsPackagingLabeling/FoodAdditivesIngredients/ucm094211.htm

Additives Defined

What is a food additive? It's any substance added—directly or indirectly—to food for an intended purpose. Additives help foods retain original qualities that might otherwise alter through temperature changes, storage, oxidation, and contact with microbes. Benefits can include increased nutritional value, freshness and safety, convenience, affordability, color, and flavor appeal.

All additives must be listed by name in the ingredient lists on food labels. Ingredient names may seem long and unfamiliar, but all foods—including fresh strawberries, kale, sweet potatoes, and other fruits and vegetables—are made of complex chemical compounds, with chemical names, that provide their characteristic qualities.

You may wonder why a single food such as flour shows a string of ingredients on the label, perhaps extending over several lines. Federal labeling regulations are the reason. For example, flour must list all the nutrients used for enrichment and required for fortification.

Additives are subject to FDA review and safety regulations and some international organizations to ensure safety and accurate labeling. Today, more than three thousand substances are listed in the FDA's database named "Everything Added to Food in the United States (EAFUS)" (www.accessdata.fda.gov/scripts/fcn/fcnNavigation.cfm?rpt=eafusListing). Many are common household ingredients such as baking soda, salt, spices, sugar, vanilla, yeast, and colors.

Additives: For Good Nutrition

Vitamins, minerals, or fiber are added to almost every category of processed foods to maintain or improve their nutrition and health-promoting qualities. As recently as one hundred years ago, nutritional-deficiency

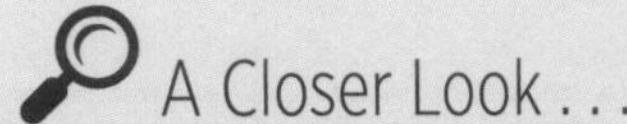

Functional Foods with Benefits beyond the Basics

Although there is no legal definition, the term "functional foods" describes foods and beverages that have health benefits beyond (and in addition to) basic nutrition due to their bioactive compounds. These foods or beverages may enhance your health and protect you from certain diseases. *See "Functional Nutrition: What's in a Name" in chapter 15, page 453.*

Rapid advances in science provide a growing body of credible evidence for functional nutrition. Agricultural and food-science technology can produce foods that offer more health benefits. In addition, changes in food regulations that began in the mid-1990s allow labels to provide health-related statements and claims that address some functional benefits of foods; *see chapter 6, page 141.*

FOODS WITH FUNCTIONAL BENEFITS

Technically, all foods, in one way or another, have functional health benefits. That includes traditional foods such as fruits, vegetables, whole grains, and yogurt as well as foods enhanced, enriched, or fortified with nutrients, phytonutrients, or other health-promoting substances.

The functional benefits of any food probably come from several, perhaps many, of its food components. For example, the heart-healthy benefits of oats not only come from its soluble fiber (beta glucan) but also from its antioxidants, amino acids, and natural plant sterols. Cancer protection from beans and peas may come from their fiber as well as isoflavones, saponins, and protease inhibitors.

Tried and true, or innovative and new, functional foods can be considered in several categories:

- *Conventional foods.* Most foods from all five food groups contain bioactive food components with benefits beyond basic nutrition.

  Many vegetables, fruits, and grain products naturally contain phytonutrients, or plant substances, such as carotenoids, flavonoids, indoles, or isoflavones, which may reduce the risk for certain diseases, including heart disease, macular degeneration, and prostate cancer. Fructooligosaccharides in shallots, as well as some other vegetables and fruits, may improve the balance of good intestinal bacteria. Phytonutrients that give health benefits are also the food components that deliver flavor and color.

  Probiotics such as *Lactobacillus* in some yogurts and other dairy foods may improve the balance of good intestinal bacteria. Dairy foods and some meat such as beef and lamb have another fatty acid, conjugated linoleic acid (CLA), which may help lower cancer risk. Oily fish such as salmon have omega-3 fatty acids, which may help lower the risk for heart disease, improve mental performance, and reduce joint pain.

- *Modified foods*, such as cereals and some juices, are enriched, fortified, or enhanced to deliver functional benefits. As examples: calcium-fortified orange juice (for bone health); folate-fortified breads (for proper fetal development); enhanced foods such as vegetable juice with added lutein; yogurt with DHA omega-3s; pasta with added fiber; and tea with ginkgo biloba. Through traditional selective plant breeding, some foods also are modified to provide additional functional benefits, such as tomatoes with more lycopene and rice that is high in beta carotene:

- *Foods created for functional and other health benefits*, such as shakes and snack bars with soy protein, omega-3s, and flaxseeds; spreads with plant stanol or sterol esters that help lower blood cholesterol; foods with resistant starch; and energy bars.

- *Medical foods* for (1) *specific health problems* such as a phenylalanine-free formula for an infant with PKU, as advised by a doctor, and (2) *foods for special dietary uses* such as infant

diseases such as goiter, pellagra, rickets, and scurvy were relatively common. Adding nutrients to foods has almost eliminated most of these nutritional-deficiency diseases. Eating vitamin C-rich fruit is why scurvy has been eliminated.

Today, nutrients are added to promote health, reduce risks of chronic disease, and contribute to a food's nutrient density or optimal nutrition.

- *Enrichment* is replacing or returning some nutrients that are lost. For example, when grains are milled to make white flour or white rice, they are enriched with B vitamins (thiamin, riboflavin, and niacin) and iron.

- *Fortification* increases the nutritional value of foods by adding nutrients not present before processing. Fortification is used to

foods, weight-loss foods, and gluten-free, allergen-free, and lactose-free foods.

FITTING IN FUNCTIONAL FOODS

Credible research shows that, along with overall healthy eating and regular physical activity, functional foods may help promote wellness, but they can't make up for poor eating habits or an unhealthy lifestyle. Although their bioactive components and their physiological action are full of unknowns, enjoy them for their potential benefits:

- Eat a variety of foods—conventional and perhaps modified—with functional benefits. Enjoy them as part of your health strategy, not in place of appropriate medical care or medications prescribed by your doctor.
- Be aware. Occasionally eating foods with potential functional benefits won't provide enough benefits to possibly make a difference. For plant sterols and stanols, for example, a daily amount is advised as a strategy for lowering cholesterol. For most foods, however, a recommended amount hasn't been determined.
- Enjoy food first, rather than supplements. Food has many more functional components that likely work best together, as nature provided.
- Choose wisely. Foods modified for functional benefits aren't always the best choices, especially if they have a lot of calories, added sugars, saturated or *trans* fats, and/or sodium.
- Look for label claims to find foods that match your needs. But turn to the ingredient list to judge the product. *See "A Word About Ingredients" in chapter 6, page 150.*
- Be savvy about foods promoted with functional benefits. Junk science abounds! Nutrition research that's either misinterpreted or oversimplified often makes headlines—and may not tell the whole story about a functional food. *See "How to . . . Find a Qualified Nutrition Expert" in chapter 26, page 759, to find a health expert to help you sort through the claims.*

add nutrients often lacking in a typical eating pattern or to address a public health problem. Although not required by law in most cases, the FDA advises appropriate fortification for these reasons:

- Correct a dietary insufficiency
- Restore nutrient levels to those prior to storage, handling, and processing
- Provide a balance of vitamins, minerals, and protein in proportion to the total caloric content of the food
- Prevent nutrient inferiority in a food that replaces a traditional food in the diet.

For example, some soymilk and juices are fortified with calcium and vitamin D for bone building. Refined-grain products as well as some whole-grain products are fortified with folic acid to reduce the risk of birth defects. Salt is iodized to avoid goiter. Some margarines and cooking oils are fortified with omega-3 fatty acids for heart health. Many breakfast cereals, some pasta, and other foods are fortified with a fiber boost. And for vegans, some fortified breakfast cereals may offer a reliable source of vitamin B_{12}.

Caution: Fortification is sometimes used as a marketing tool to make less-nourishing foods and beverages seem healthier than they are. To learn about the food, read the Nutrition Facts and ingredient list on the package label.

What's added to enrich or fortify a food? Check the food label. Any added nutrient must show up in two places: (1) the ingredient list and (2) the Nutrition Facts panel, stating the total amount or contribution (percent Daily Value) of that nutrient in a single serving. *See "Nutrition: Fact Check!" in chapter 6, page 148.*

Additives: For Preserving and Safety

Air, bacteria, fungi, mold, and yeast promote food spoilage. Some additives, called preservatives, slow spoilage and help maintain foods' appeal and wholesome qualities. Some preservatives work as antioxidants, protecting foods from chemical changes caused by contact with oxygen. Others are antimicrobials that inhibit the growth of bacteria, mold, and yeast. Some foods contain both. Antioxidants prevent rancidity or discoloration.

- *Calcium propionate*, produced naturally in Swiss cheese, is a preservative that keeps bread and other baked foods from getting moldy too quickly.
- *Citric acid*, a natural component of citrus fruits, works as an antioxidant, helping foods keep their color. Coating sliced apples with lemon juice does the same thing, keeping them from turning brown. Ascorbic acid (vitamin C) does this, too.
- *Sodium nitrite*, used as a preservative in processed meats such as ham, hot dogs, and deli meats, keeps meat safe from the very harmful botulism bacteria. It also adds to the flavor and pink color. *See "Foodborne Illness: More Common Than You Think" in chapter 7, page 281, for more on botulism and other food safety issues.*

While this preservative offers food-safety benefits, the American Institute of Cancer Research advises limiting processed meats,

Have you ever wondered?

. . . how natural and artificial additives differ? So-called natural ingredients come from natural sources such as soybeans or corn to make lecithin for product consistency or beets to make food coloring. Others are man-made and can be produced with greater purity, consistent quality, and perhaps more economically. For example, vitamin C made in a lab or from fruit is chemically the same. Whatever their source, food additives must follow the same federal standards for safety.

. . . if food additives are safe for everyone? Except for a very few people with sensitivities who may react, the answer is yes. In fact, a primary use of additives is protecting food quality and food safety to protect against foodborne illness.

Consuming a food additive rarely causes adverse reactions. When it does, the response is commonly a sensitivity—not a true allergy. And the food itself, not the additive, is more often the cause. If you have a food reaction and think it may be additive related, talk to your doctor or a board-certified allergist to assess any reaction instead of self diagnosing. *See "Sensitive to Additives? Maybe, Maybe Not" in chapter 23, page 678.*

If you have a history of food-related allergies, you may be advised to limit or avoid foods with ingredients, including some additives, that you're sensitive to. Read the ingredient lists on labels; *see "A Word about Ingredients" in chapter 6, page 150.* For someone sensitive to a specific type of additive, any reaction should be similar whether the additive is natural or synthetic since the chemical makeup is similar.

. . . how people with food sensitivities can avoid certain ingredients including additives? Consistent and careful label-reading skills are important. With an array of foods available, consumers have choices about foods with additives. For those who need to manage celiac disease, food allergies, and other food sensitivities, some additives may need to be avoided; *see chapter 23, page 653.*

due to their possible links to some forms of cancer, but doesn't give a specific amount. Nitrites and nitrates may not be the only factor for potential increased cancer risk, and so it's advisable to limit processed meats.

- *Sulfites* help prevent color and flavor changes in dried fruits and vegetables. They're used to inhibit bacterial growth in wine and fermented foods. Some baked foods, snack foods, and condiments also may contain sulfites. Most people have no adverse reactions to sulfites. But packaged and processed foods containing sulfites are labeled for the small percentage who are sulfite sensitive. *See "Sulfite Sensitivity: Mild to Severe" in chapter 23, page 678.*
- *Tocopherols (vitamin E), BHA (butylated hydroxyanisole), and BHT (butylated hydroxytoluene)* help delay or prevent vegetable oils and salad dressings from rancidity. Working as antioxidants, they help protect naturally present nutrients in foods: essential fatty acids (linoleic and alpha-linolenic acids) and fat-soluble vitamins (A, D, E, and K). Studies verify the safety of BHA and BHT; the FDA has deemed them GRAS ("generally recognized as safe") substances.

Additives: For Functional Qualities

From helping bread rise to keeping chocolate suspended in chocolate milk and seasoning blends from clumping, some food additives provide food qualities or appeal that consumers want and expect.

- *Anticaking agents* prevent lumping and keep seasonings, baking powder, confectioners' sugar, table salt, and other powdered or granular products flowing freely. Because they keep foods from absorbing moisture, they won't clump. Calcium silicate and silicon dioxide are two examples of anticaking agents.
- *Emulsifiers* distribute particles evenly. As mixers, they keep ingredients and flavorings blended by holding fat on one end and water on the other end of their chemical structure. For example, they keep oil, vinegar, and seasonings in salad dressings from separating. In peanut butter, emulsifiers keep peanuts and oil from separating. Even in baked foods, they help keep dough uniform. Bread, breakfast cereals, chocolate, chocolate milk, cocoa, frozen desserts, margarine, mayonnaise, and pudding and pie filling mixes also may contain emulsifiers.

  Some emulsifiers come from food itself: for example, lecithin (from soybeans, milk, and egg yolks), alginates (salts from algae), and mono- and diglycerides (from vegetables and beef tallow).
- *Humectants* such as glycerine or sorbitol help foods stay moist and soft. Foods with humectants include shredded coconut and marshmallows.
- *Leavening agents* help food rise. They create a light texture in bread, muffins, waffles, and other baked goods. Baking soda (sodium bicarbonate) and baking powder (sodium bicarbonate and acid salts) as well as yeast produce carbon dioxide that makes

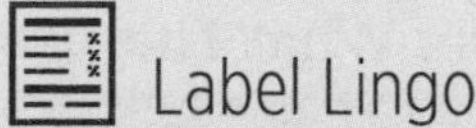

Label Lingo

Deciphering Additives in Food

By reading ingredient lists on food labels, you can identify specific additives in any food. Note the "contains" statement for food-allergen labeling.

Emulsifier to keep ingredients blended

Flavoring to add sweetness

INGREDIENTS: CRUST: WHEAT FLOUR WITH MALTED BARLEY FLOUR, WATER, PARTIALLY HYDROGENATED VEGETABLE OIL (SOYBEAN AND/OR COTTONSEED OIL) WITH SOY LECITHIN, ARTIFICIAL FLAVOR AND ARTIFICIAL COLOR (BETA CAROTENE), SOYBEAN OIL, YEAST, HIGH FRUCTOSE CORN SYRUP, SALT, CALCIUM PROPIONATE ADDED TO RETARD SPOILAGE OF CRUST, L-CYSTEINE MONOHYDROCHLORIDE; **SAUCE:** TOMATO PUREE (WATER, TOMATO PASTE), WATER GREEN PEPPERS, SALT, LACTOSE AND FLAVORING, SPICES, FOOD STARCH - MODIFIED, SUGAR, CORN OIL, XANTHAN GUM, GARLIC POWDER, **TOPPING:** LOW MOISTURE PART SKIM MOZZARELLA CHEESE (PASTEURIZED MILK, CHEESE CULTURES, SALT, ENZYMES). **CONTAINS WHEAT, MILK, SOY.**

Preservative to retard spoilage

Thickener to give a uniform texture

dough rise. Without these ingredients, textures would be compact and heavy.

- *Maturing and bleaching agents* improve baking qualities of foods made with wheat flour and improve the appearance of certain cheeses. When the yellow pigment of wheat flour is bleached, dough becomes more elastic and results in better baking results. White curd in some cheeses, such as blue cheese and gorgonzola, comes from adding a bleaching agent to milk.
- *pH control agents* are used to adjust the acidity or alkalinity in foods; this influences a food's texture, taste, and safety. Adding acids (acidulants) such as lactic acid or citric acid gives a tart taste to beverages and frozen desserts; they also inhibit bacterial growth in low-acid processed foods such as canned beets and help prevent discoloration and rancidity. Alkalizers neutralize acids in foods such as chocolate so the flavor is milder. Baked goods, chocolate, gelatin desserts, processed cheese, salad dressings, sauces, soft drinks, and vegetable oils may contain pH control agents.
- *Thickeners and stabilizers, binders and texturizers* give food a smooth, thick, uniform texture and improve mouth feel. In ice cream, they keep the texture smooth without forming ice crystals. In chocolate milk, they allow chocolate particles to stay in suspension. In salad dressings, they help keep oil and other liquid ingredients from separating and herbs and spices evenly distributed. Proteins and carbohydrates—such as alginates and carrageenan from seaweed, gelatin from animal bones, and pectin from fruit—commonly are used as thickeners and stabilizers. Foods such as chilis, soups, stews, and sausage may have whey protein concentrate as a binder. Baked goods, beverages, cream cheese, frozen desserts, jam, pie filling, pudding, salad dressings, sauces, and soups are among foods that often have these additives.

Additives: For Flavor and Appeal

Some additives add color, provide or enhance flavor, or sweeten food.

- *Colorings* won't affect the nutrients, safety, or taste of food, but they make a nutritional contribution by making nourishing food look more appealing. Cheese and margarine often get their yellow coloring from annatto, which comes from the tropical annatto tree. Mint ice cream wouldn't be green without a color additive. Many baked foods, gelatin mixes, jam, pie and pudding fillings, specialty pasta, and yogurt are among the many other foods with added coloring.

  There are numerous reasons why color is added to foods. It may offset color that's lost from exposure to light, air, temperature extremes, moisture, and storage; it may also correct natural color variations, enhance natural colors, and give color to colorless or fun foods for appeal.

  Both naturally and synthetically produced colors are used in foods. Nine certified colors are approved in the United States. They offer intense, uniform color at a low cost, without undesirable flavor. More and more natural pigments from vegetables, minerals, and animal sources are being used as colorings, which can be costly; they're exempt from certification yet must meet safety and purity regulations. For example, look for foods with annatto extract, beet juice, beta carotene, carrot oil, grape skin extract, paprika, or saffron.

  One food coloring—FD&C Yellow #5, or tartrazine—is known to cause allergic reactions (hives) in rare cases. Though controversial, data is insufficient to link additives with hyperactivity in children. No evidence shows that it provokes asthma attacks. By law, it must be identified in the ingredient list for those who may be sensitive to it. *See "Color Additives: Rare Reactions" in chapter 23, page 678.*
- *Flavorings*, which may be natural or artificial, make up about seventeen hundred approved additives in the United States for use in food. They include caffeine, essential oils and their extracts, fruit juices, herbs, spices, and other seasonings. Baked goods, gelatin pudding, milk, salad dressing mix, sauces, soft drinks, and yogurt are some foods with flavorings.

  Natural flavors come from food itself after minimal processing. They're often taken from one food and added to another. To make artificial flavorings, food scientists study the chemical makeup of natural flavors and create a flavor that is similar but perhaps not an exact match.
- *Flavor enhancers* don't add flavor. Instead, they heighten the natural flavors already present. A well-known flavor enhancer

is monosodium glutamate (MSG). MSG comes from a common amino acid, a protein called glutamic acid which comes mostly from vegetable protein. *See "MSG—Another Flavor Enhancer" in chapter 8, page 240.* Some other examples: citric acid, herbs, salt, spices, and vanilla. Canned vegetables, frozen meals, processed meats, sauce mixes, soups, and yogurt are among the foods with flavor enhancers.

- *Sweeteners* are also flavorings but are grouped separately from colorings and flavor enhancers. They're used in baked foods, canned and frozen fruit, frozen desserts, fruit juice drinks, fruit yogurt, gelatin mixes, jam, pudding mixes, pie filling mixes, and soft drinks, among others.

  Some, such as sucrose (table sugar), fructose, dextrose, and mannitol, are nutritive, meaning they add calories and produce energy in your body. Besides their sweet flavor, these sugars add mouth feel and work as browning agents in food. And they may be used as preservatives. These added sugars can also add significant amounts of calories to food, which can contribute to increased risk for weight gain and obesity. Read the Nutrition Facts and limit the amount.

  Nonnutritive sweeteners such as aspartame, saccharin, and sucralose, often used in sugar-free products, don't contribute calories; these foods aren't necessarily calorie free. People with PKU (phenylketonuria) need to avoid aspartame. *See "Aspartame: PKU Warning" in chapter 23, page 679.*

See chapter 11, page 345, for more about sugars and sugar alternatives.

Ingredients with Sodium: What They Do

Ingredient	Function
Baking powder	Leavening agent
Baking soda (sodium bicarbonate)	Leavening agent
Brine (salt and water)	Preservative
Disodium phosphate	Emulsifier, stabilizer
Monosodium glutamate (MSG)	Flavor enhancer
NaCl (salt or sodium chloride)	Flavor enhancer, preservative
Sodium benzoate	Preservative
Sodium caseinate	Thickener, binder
Sodium citrate	Acid controller, stabilizer
Sodium erythorbate	Antioxidant
Sodium nitrate/nitrite	Preservative
Sodium propionate	Preservative, mold inhibitor
Sodium sulfite	Preservative for dried fruits
Soy sauce	Flavor enhancer
Teriyaki sauce	Flavor enhancer

? Have you ever wondered?

. . . how nanotechnology might affect food in the future? Nanotechnology relates to extremely small particles of matter. In size, one nanometer equals about one millionth of a pinhead or one blade of grass on a football field. As a science, it's not new, but more potential uses are under study.

Applied to agriculture, food processing, and food packaging, nanotechnology is cutting edge. It also has potential uses in medicine and in helping the environment.

Eventually nanotechnology may provide more benefits, including helping to make agricultural production more efficient, making functional foods more effective, making flavors more prominent, and even using food packaging to decrease any foodborne pathogens or contaminants. More research is needed before nanotechnology will be approved in food application to ensure its long-term safety. Stay tuned!

Additives: Testing and Approval

New food additives must pass rigid safety tests before federal approval for use. During the past eighty or so years, the use of food additives has allowed a more varied and plentiful food supply in the United States and many other parts of the world. Beginning in 1938, US government regulations have helped guide and ensure their safety in food. Today, food additives are regulated more tightly than ever—with safety as the primary goal.

In 1958, the federal government passed the Food Additives Amendment, which gave the US Food and Drug Administration (FDA) responsibility for approving additives use in food. The FDA sets safety standards, determining whether a substance is safe for its intended use. If found to be safe, the FDA decides what types of foods the additive may be used in, in what amounts, and how it must be indicated on a food label. Federal food laws distinguish among additives: prior-approved additives, those "generally recognized as safe" (GRAS), regulated additives, and color additives.

Prior-approved substances. Before the 1958 Food Additives Amendment, some additives—such as nitrites used to preserve deli meats—had been approved by the FDA or the USDA. If used as originally approved, these substances didn't need to go through the approval process again; the government already had judged them safe in amounts commonly used, and with a safety net.

Prior-approved substances are monitored continually. Current scientific evidence of their link to health is reviewed, recognizing that the status of prior-approved substances can be changed.

Generally recognized as safe (GRAS) list. In 1959, the FDA established a list of about seven hundred additives that were exempted from the regulation process. These additives had an extensive history or existing scientific evidence of safe use in food. Additives on the GRAS list include salt, sugar, spices, vitamins, caffeine, and monosodium glutamate.

From time to time, GRAS ingredients are reevaluated by the FDA and perhaps removed from the list or reclassified. An example occurred in 2013 when the FDA preliminarily determined that partially hydrogenated oils, a major source of *trans* fats in processed foods, were no longer considered GRAS ingredients for any use in human food. Currently, initiatives are underway to help modernize the process for determining GRAS status for food ingredients in a clear, transparent, and scientific manner.

Regulated additives. Any additive not considered as GRAS or prior-approved must be evaluated and approved by the FDA before it can be marketed and used in foods.

For a new food or color additive, a petition must be filed by the manufacturer or other sponsor for FDA approval, with evidence that the substance is safe for its intended use.

In its evaluation of the additive's safety and approval, the FDA considers its composition and properties, the amount typically consumed, the immediate and long-term effects of consuming it, and other safety factors. If approved, the FDA establishes regulations that may include the types of foods in which the additive may be used, for what purposes, the maximum amount, and how it must be described on the label. The level approved is much lower than the amount that may have any expected adverse effect.

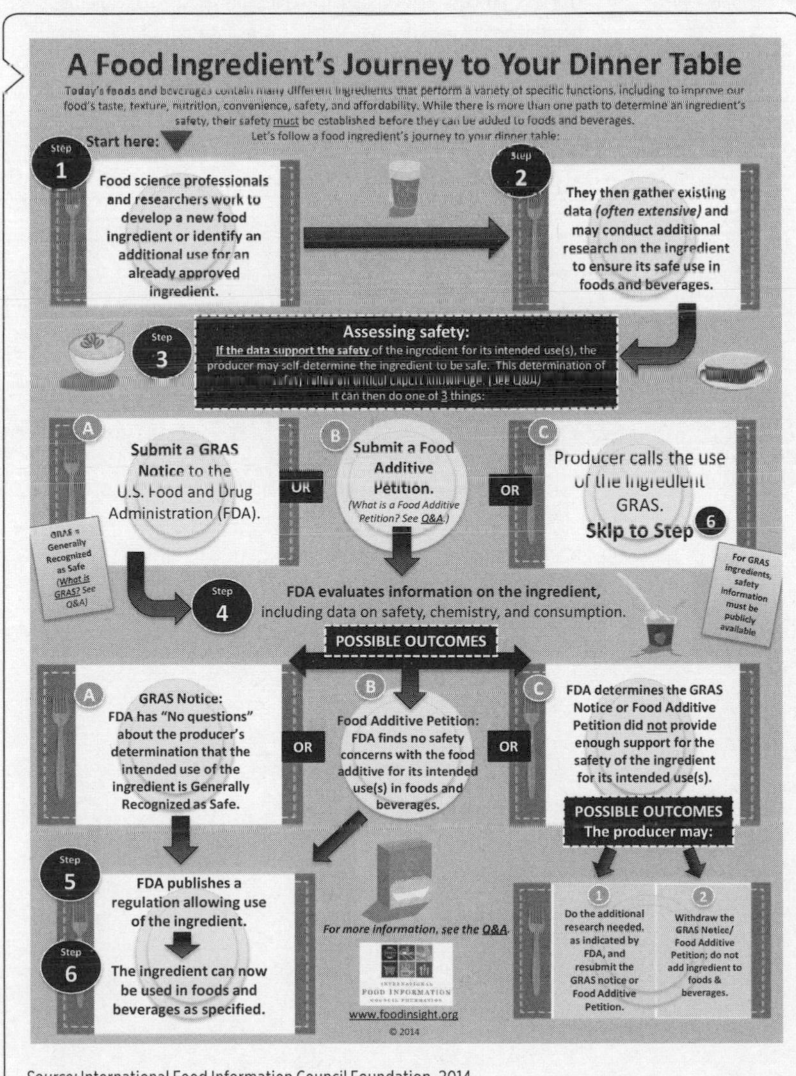

Source: International Food Information Council Foundation, 2014.

When a new food additive is proposed for use in meat or poultry products, another approval also is required—this time from the USDA's Food Safety and Inspection Service (FSIS)—with standards that consider the unique characteristics of meat and poultry. For example, the FSIS doesn't allow sorbic acid, an approved additive, in meat salads because it could mask spoilage.

Color additives. The FDA requires that dyes used in foods, drugs, cosmetics, and medical devices be evaluated, with tests similar to those for regulated food additives.

Additives: Safety Check

Approval of food additives, including those on the GRAS and prior-sanctioned lists, doesn't guarantee that they'll be used in food forever, nor does it imply absolute safety. However, based on the best available science, FDA approval reflects reasonable certainty of no harm to consumers when the additive is used as intended.

The FDA continues to review all categories of food additives and judges them by the latest scientific standards and current consumption of that additive. Based on new evidence, approval is either continued, withdrawn, or requires more research to determine its safety.

As another safety check, the Food Additives Amendment also has a section called the Delaney Clause, which states that no additive known to cause cancer in animals or humans can be put in food in any amount. One artificial sweetener, called cyclamate, was removed from the GRAS list in the

1970s for that reason. Tests showed that large amounts were linked to cancer in test animals. The safety of cyclamate is being reevaluated; it is approved for use in some other countries.

To monitor and investigate complaints of adverse reactions to additives, the FDA also maintains the Adverse Reaction Monitoring System (ARMS), which records updated safety data. Incidences of allergic reactions to food and color additives and to dietary supplements, reported by individuals or their doctors, are recorded. These reports help determine whether further investigation is warranted—and if action is needed to maintain public health. *See "Sensitive to Additives? Maybe, Maybe Not" in chapter 23, page 678.* Good Manufacturing Practices (GMP) regulations also limit additive use, saying that only the minimal amount needed for the desired result can be used.

PROCESSED FOODS: MAKING WISE CHOICES

How can you decide which processed foods to buy and which to skip or limit?

- Choose foods based on the calories and nutrients they provide rather than the level of processing. Some ready-to-eat foods provide significant amounts of nutrients, without excessive calories. Others are high in added sugars, saturated fat, or sodium and are nutritionally poor.
- Read labels, including ingredient lists, to make healthy choices when it comes to processed foods and drinks to prepare at home. *See "Food Labels: Decode the Package" in chapter 6, page 144.* That said, a food with just a short list of ingredients doesn't necessarily mean healthier. Some nourishing foods are nicely flavored with a longer list of herbs and spices.
- Consider trade-offs. If you have time to prepare and assemble a whole, nourishing meal from scratch, great. But if you would need to give up a walk or bike ride, nourishing ready-to-eat food may be a smart option.
- Before eschewing additives, remember that some protect you from harmful bacteria. Others make nourishing food more appealing.
- Use less-processed foods, such as a tossed salad, to complement healthy processed choices, such as frozen lasagna. Chosen carefully and eaten in moderation, processed foods can make your meals and snacks convenient, safe, flavorful, and nourishing.

6

Shop with Nutrition Savvy

In this chapter, find out about . . .

Making food labels work for you

Max-ing your food dollar

Food shopping with a healthy mindset

Being an eco-friendly shopper

Keeping food safe from store to kitchen

With thousands of items available in today's supermarkets, it's no wonder you have so many decisions to make! These days, you have more food facts and healthy eating information at your fingertips than ever before.

Think about food labels, brochures, and food TV. There also are in-store supermarket dietitians, pharmacists, and consumer-affairs professionals ready to help, and then there are the food blogs and websites available on handheld devices.

Where do you shop? A few decades ago traditional supermarkets handled most retail food business. Today, you have far more options (and many more food choices): specialty stores, natural- and health-food stores, restaurants, convenience stores—even gas stations, department stores, and drugstores. Online shopping (e-commerce) and mail-order businesses sell food to eat at home. More and more farmers' markets with local, fresh produce are cropping up in urban centers. And you can buy directly from farmers through farm stands and CSAs (Community Supported Agriculture).

MORE FOOD CHOICES, MORE FOOD DECISIONS

Every year US consumers have more variety and more new foods from which to choose. About twenty thousand new foods and drinks are introduced yearly, according to the USDA Economic Research Service, yet only a small percentage survive. And the average store stocks more than 42,000 items, according to the Food Marketing Institute.

Why not keep the status quo instead of introducing new foods every year? Changes in consumer demand and flavor preferences are the main reasons. For consumers, taste tops the list, notes 2016 consumer surveys from the International Food Information Council Foundation (IFIC), followed by price, healthfulness, convenience, and for many, sustainability (a term with no universal definition).

More food choices mean more to learn, more decisions to make, and more ways to eat for health. Today, you have options like these:

- *More local and regional foods.* If you're committed to local food, call yourself a locavore! Local food is generally grown or produced close to where it's purchased, perhaps in the same state or closer; "local" isn't a defined and regulated term—and it's not necessarily from a small or organic farm.

  Because it's closer in proximity, seasonal produce may be picked at the peak of ripeness. It may not be available all year long, so eating local means eating with the season. Supporting local and regional farmers' markets and agriculture offers a chance to explore foods from your region and perhaps reduce your carbon footprint.

- *More organic foods and more foods marketed as "GMO-free," "pesticide-free," or "hormone-free." See "Today's Agriculture" in chapter 5, page 113.*
- *More food marketed as environmentally friendly.* Increasingly, environmental responsibility from farm to store is part of the business bottom line. You're likely to see more marketing that deems the food "clean" or "sustainable" these days—although there's no regulated definition for either term.
- *More varieties of vegetables and fruits.* Produce departments, as well as the grocery and frozen-food aisles—stock a greater variety year-round, including exotics, tropicals, and different varietals. For example, a potato isn't just a potato anymore; it may be a Yukon Gold, a purple, or a fingerling. Depending on the season, a peach may be a Babcock, a doughnut, or a Honey Baby, and a watermelon may be an icebox Sugar Baby, a seedless Crimson, or a picnic Jubilee. *See "Vegetables: Have You Tried These" and "Fruit: What's New to You?" in chapter 2, pages 36 and 39.*
- *More grain varieties (including whole, ancient, and sprouted grains, nuts, and seeds.* For example, bread choices have shifted to more coarse-textured and dense whole-grain breads made with ancient grains. Breakfast cereals are made with amaranth, barley, kamut, and more, not just corn, oats, or wheat; pasta may be made with farro, quinoa, or spelt. And chia seeds, flaxseeds, and hemp seeds are finding their way into many food products. *See "Grains, Grains, and More Grains" in chapter 2, page 31.*
- *More fish options*: Fresh and frozen, wild-caught and farm-raised fish have found their way to supermarkets and specialty stores.

Today's Supermarkets: What's in Store?

No matter where you shop for food or what matters most to you, qualities of excellence matter:

- A store or market with clean display cases, grocery shelves, and floors
- Produce, meat, poultry, fish, and dairy foods with qualities of freshness
- Refrigerated cases that are cold, and freezer compartments that contain solidly frozen foods
- Salad bars, bulk bins, and other self-serve areas that are clean and properly covered
- Workers handling raw, deli, and other unpackaged foods who wear disposable gloves and change them after handling nonfood items and again after handling raw food

- *More simple, fresh, and raw foods.* Supermarkets from coast to coast are expanding the variety of fresh, raw vegetables and fruits they carry. They also offer more "just-baked" breads, "freshly caught" fish, and even "made-to-order" sushi. Farmers' markets and specialty stores present similar and even more choices.
- *More convenience, too.* You can buy restaurant-style take-out to eat at home, steamed-to-order shellfish, and made-to-order wraps. Fresh bagged salad and stir-fry mixes, as well as meal kits and marinated ready-to-cook roasts and chicken breasts, are among items that just need assembly or simple cooking or heating. The freezer section is full of frozen skillet meals, bean burritos, and vegetarian lasagna and preprepared items.
- *More nutrition- and health-focused products.* Traditional foods have been modified as consumers become increasingly health aware. That includes new and leaner cuts of meat; dairy and other foods with probiotics for gut health; foods made with chia seeds, or soy or whey protein for a protein boost; and myriad gluten-free products for those with celiac disease.
- *More flavor and taste adventure—and more ethnic and specialty foods.* Growing food experiences and sophistication have brought more gourmet, artisan, and ethnic foods to mainstream stores. Just consider the many flavored vinegars and oils as well as condiments such as wasabi mustard and Sriracha catsup on today's store shelves.

MORE SERVICES, TOO!

Today's supermarkets are more than a place to buy food. For example, many stores offer:

- *Culinary and nutrition education* through cooking classes; food demos and tastings; store or market tours conducted by registered dietitian nutritionists; websites and online magazines offering a wealth of food and nutrition information, healthy recipes, and meal ideas: some created by qualified nutrition experts and others, for mostly marketing.
- *More convenience*, provided by online ordering and home delivery, and store apps to locate what you need faster. Online or not, your supermarket may also offer meal kit delivery services with preportioned ingredients and step-by-step instructions, delivered to your home.
- *Neighborhood health services* such as blood pressure readings, vaccinations, in-store health seminars, discounts for local fitness clubs, personalized wellness plans, recipes for special health issues, and nutrition information and counseling.
- *Social space for gathering* with friends and community meeting space.
- *In-store cafes* for a quick meal, whether you're food shopping or not.
- *Support for community* food banks, local agriculture products, and "green" initiatives.

Food Labels: Decode the Package

Wrapped around almost every packaged food in the supermarket, you'll find a wealth of information. Regulated by the US Food and Drug Administration (FDA), packaged foods identify the common name of the product, name and address of the food manufacturer, net contents (by weight, measure, or count), ingredients, Nutrition Facts, and any common allergens it contains.

To make informed choices about nutrition and health, look for this label information, too:

- *Nutrient content claims* such as "no salt added" or "high-fiber" help you to easily find foods that meet specific nutrition goals. *See "Label Lingo" boxes in this chapter, as well as in other chapters for specific nutrient content claims.*
- *Nutrition Facts* give specifics about the calories and key nutrients in a single label serving/amount of the food. The Nutrition Labeling and Education Act (NLEA) of 1990 authorized the FDA to require nutrition labeling. Since 1994, this information has been required on virtually all food labels.

✔ Your Healthy Eating Check-In

What's Your Shopping Savvy?

Like most consumers, flavor likely tops your list when you buy foods. And healthiness, price, convenience, and safety are important to shoppers, too. If that sounds like you, do you . . .

	Yes	No
1. Use the nutrition and ingredient information on food labels to make sound shopping decisions?	☐	☐
2. Look for nutrition information displayed near fresh foods: produce, meat, poultry, and fish?	☐	☐
3. Know what the dates on packaged foods mean and don't mean so you get the best quality, yet avoid wasting food?	☐	☐
4. Check packaging and cans to be sure they're clean and not damaged?	☐	☐
5. Know what to look for when picking peak-quality, fresh produce; raw meat, poultry, and fish; and refrigerated and frozen foods?	☐	☐
6. Try new-to-you ingredients from time to time to experience new flavors?	☐	☐
7. Take perishable foods home within thirty minutes of shopping and immediately refrigerate or freeze them?	☐	☐
8. Pack refrigerated and freezer foods in separate, insulated shopping bags to keep them cool until you get home?	☐	☐
9. Ask to have fresh meat, poultry, and fish bagged separately so their juices don't drip on other foods?	☐	☐
10. Take advantage of cents-off coupons and in-store specials found online or in print flyers?	☐	☐
11. Monitor prices as items are scanned at checkout?	☐	☐
12. Skip the urge to buy a food or drink just because you sampled it or see it in a big store display?	☐	☐
13. Buy only foods in the amount you'll use to avoid wasting food and expense?	☐	☐
14. Use unit-price codes on shelves to compare the cost of similar products?	☐	☐
15. Keep a shopping list to save shopping time and avoid impulse buys?	☐	☐
16. Keep shopping trips to a minimum—if so, you tend to buy no more than once or twice a week?	☐	☐
Total	___	___

The more times you checked "yes," the more savvy a shopper you are. Read on to learn more about these and other ways to shop smart and boost your score.

Now, after more than two decades, the format and nutrition information of this consumer resource are undergoing a transition—from the original, approved in 1993, to a new format, required by July 28, 2018 for larger food manufacturers. Companies with less than $10 million in annual sales have more time to comply. *See "Nutrition Facts: Comparing the Old and New" and "Nutrition Facts Update 2016" in this chapter, page 146.*

- *Ingredient lists* give an overview of the makeup of the contents, with the ingredients listed in order by weight from most to least.
- *Health claims* describe the potential health benefits of a food, nutrient, or food substance to perhaps reduce the risk of a chronic disease or condition.
- *Structure/function claims* describe the way a nutrient or food substance maintains or supports a normal body function. For example, it may say "helps maintain bone health" or "supports a healthy immune system."
- *Allergen labeling* identifies common allergens.

Beyond that, the label may provide voluntary information, including safety guidelines, preparation and storage tips, organic labeling, gluten-free labeling, and freshness dates, among other things. Some products also show nutrition information on the front of the package, provided voluntarily by the manufacturer for marketing, but this is not FDA regulated or required. When described on websites, products are subject to these same FDA labeling regulations.

Nutrition Facts: Comparing the Old and New

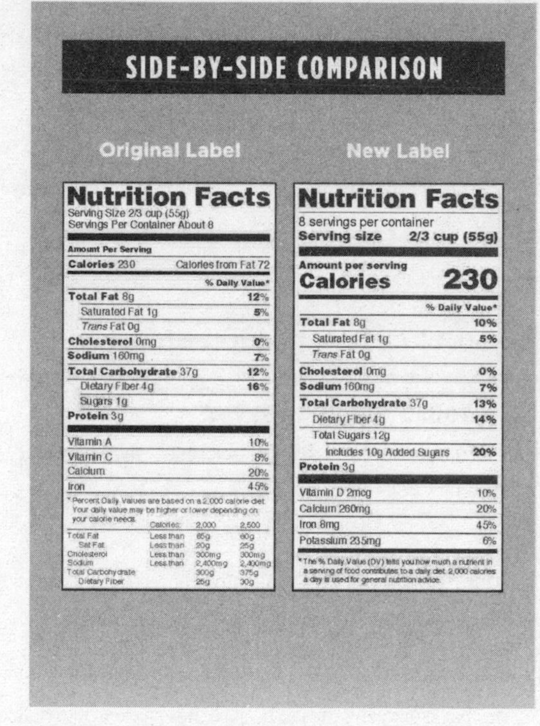

Source: US Food and Drug Administration.

NUTRIENT CONTENT CLAIMS: AT A GLANCE

Imagine rolling your cart through the supermarket. Your eyes dart from one food product to another. Some canned peaches say "no added sugar." Certain breakfast cereals are "high in fiber"; others are "fortified." On packages of deli meats you see the term "lean." The words "high in calcium" on a milk carton or "excellent source of calcium and vitamin D" on a juice carton catch your eye. And a box of cookies says "fewer calories." What does all this label language mean?

Known as nutrient content claims, these terms describe the amount of nutrients, fiber, or calories in food. They often appear on the front of the package for quick comparisons. Some claims can say "contains [*x amount*] of [*nutrient*]."

A nutrient content claim can help you spot the item you prefer, while the Nutrition Facts give more specifics about the nutrient content. For example, suppose you're comparing the fat in hot dogs. A term such as "lean" offers a general idea. For the amount of total fat—and saturated and possibly *trans* fats—in one label serving, you need to check the Nutrition Facts.

Nutrient content claims mean the same thing for all foods, no matter what food or which manufacturer makes the product. That's because these claims are defined strictly by regulation. Like Nutrition Facts, nutrient content claims are defined for a single label serving. However, the amount, or serving size, is set by FDA regulations—and may not necessarily be what you eat as one helping.

With the new Nutrition Facts labeling, some foods may no longer meet the criteria for a nutrition content claim; others may now comply. Food companies may also change the ingredients somewhat, too, to keep a nutrient content claim. For example, the FDA has begun a process of redefining what the term "healthy" means on food labels, to better reflect current knowledge on nutrients' contributions to health.

While the language of nutrient content claims is regulated, their use is optional by food companies. Many foods that meet the criteria for these claims don't carry these terms on the label. If you see a product with a nutrient content claim, use the % Daily Value (DV) in the Nutrition Facts to compare it to a similar food that doesn't carry a claim. *See "Label Lingo: What Nutrient Content Claims Mean" in this chapter, page 145, as well as in other chapters for definitions of nutrient content claims.*

NUTRITION: FACT CHECK!

Claims such as "low-fat, "no added sugar," or "calcium rich" may not mean the food is the healthiest option. You've got to check the Nutrition Facts, as well as the ingredient list, for specifics, and then decide what works best for your own nutrition needs.

- Use the Nutrition Facts to pick nutrient-rich foods and to compare calories and nutrients in similar foods.
- Use the ingredient list, *discussed in "A Word About Ingredients" in this chapter, page 150*, to identify allergens and other ingredients of interest—type of oil or other fat, added sugars, whole grains, ingredients with sodium, and others.

Nutrition Facts appear on almost every packaged food. That includes packages of ground or chopped meat and poultry, such as hamburger or ground turkey. Most raw cuts of meat and poultry also have nutrition information on the label or on a store display.

Today, many fresh vegetables and fruits may be labeled voluntarily with nutrition information, too, either on the package or on a poster or pamphlet displayed nearby. If you don't find this information, ask the store manager to start providing it, or find this information online.

Nutrition Facts: Why Use Them

Nutrition Facts specifically state the amount of required nutrients and number of calories in one label serving of a food, as well as some that are listed voluntarily. Nutrient content claims on the product label such as "low in fat" or "more fiber" are quick-to-read descriptions and won't provide specific amounts. Check the Nutrition Facts for more specific information to help you make informed decisions, such as:

Label Lingo

What Nutrient Content Claims* Mean

Label term . . .	Means . . .
LOW	An amount specifically defined for each term, such as "low-calorie," "low-fat," or "low-cholesterol." Other terms: "few," "contains a small amount of," "low source of," "low in," "little," "a little."
REDUCED	Contains at least 25 percent fewer calories and 25 percent less fat, saturated fat, cholesterol, sugars, or sodium than a regular food. Look for information about the food it's being compared to. Other terms: "reduced in," "% reduced," "fewer," "lower," "lower in," "less."
HIGH	Contains 20 percent or more of the Daily Value** for a nutrient—for example, "high in vitamin C" or "high-calcium." Other terms: "excellent source of," "rich in."
GOOD SOURCE	Contains 10 to 19 percent of the Daily Value** for a nutrient—for example, "good source of fiber." Other terms: "contains," "provides."
MORE	Contains 10 percent or more of the Daily Value** for a nutrient—for example, "more fiber" or "more iron." You won't find it on meat or poultry products. Other terms: "enriched," "fortified," "added," "extra," "plus." *See "Additives for Good Nutrition" in chapter 5, page 133, for definitions of enrichment and fortification.*
LIGHT	Contains one-third fewer calories or 50 percent less fat than the traditional version. A "low-calorie" or "low-fat" food with 50 percent less sodium might also be called "light." Other term: "lite." When "light" describes a product characteristic, such as "light brown sugar," it isn't a nutrient content claim.
HEALTHY	Low in fat and saturated fat, and contains 60 milligrams or less cholesterol per serving, 480 milligrams or less sodium per serving, and at least 10 percent of the Daily Value per serving of vitamin A, vitamin C, calcium, iron, protein, or fiber. Vegetables, fruits, and enriched cereal products can be labeled "healthy" without having 10 percent of the Daily Value or more of these nutrients per serving, but they must meet low-fat, low-saturated-fat, cholesterol, and sodium criteria. A meal or main-dish product must have 600 milligrams of sodium or less. (*Note:* The FDA is reevaluating this definition of "healthy" in light of evolving scientific evidence and changes in Nutrition Facts labeling.)

On meat, poultry, or fish, look for:

LEAN	Contains less than 10 grams of total fat, 4.5 grams or less saturated fat, and less than 95 milligrams cholesterol per 3-ounce (and per 100 grams) cooked serving.
EXTRA LEAN	Contains less than 5 grams of total fat, less than 2 grams saturated fat, and less than 95 milligrams cholesterol per 3-ounce (and per 100 grams) cooked serving.

* FDA regulatory definition

**When compared with a label serving size of the traditional food.

Front-of-Package Nutrition Labeling

Many consumers want quick ways to identify and choose healthier foods. These often come in the form of seals, icons, or symbols that call out nutrition information and may appear on the front of a package (FOP) or next to FDA-regulated nutrient content or health claims.

The challenge: With many different symbols and systems, FOP labeling isn't consistent. Some FOP labeling programs simply bring information from the Nutrition Facts panel to the front of the package. Others have their own nutrient criteria (or scoring algorithms) to identify food products as better choices, or more nutrient rich; the way they score differs, and it's often proprietary. Without consistency, some FOP systems may overrate products' healthy qualities or may be more lenient with their own definitions. Just remember: They're used for marketing.

In recent years, the Grocery Manufacturers Association and the Food Marketing Institute established a voluntary FOP labeling initiative called "Facts Up Front." It's meant to help consumers easily find key facts about a single serving: the number of calories and the amounts of the nutrients that are best to limit: saturated fat, sodium, and sugar content per serving. It may also show one or two of the nutrients that many people need more of: If the product contains 10 percent or more of the Daily Value per serving of the nutrient and meets the FDA requirements for a "good source." The facts displayed come from the Nutrition Facts label, *see www.FactsUpFront.org*.

Although currently there's no standardized, science-based criteria for FOP nutrition labeling, FDA regulations may come in the future. Until then, use FOP labeling as only one tool for quick information. However, just because a product provides FOP facts doesn't mean the food is more nutritious. Turn to the Nutrition Facts label, which is regulated by law, to make informed judgments about the calories and nutrients in food products.

- To compare calories and nutrients in similar foods
- To find foods with nutrients you may underconsume, such as calcium, as well as fiber
- To find foods with fewer of the nutrients you may need to limit, such as saturated fat, *trans* fat, and sodium
- To help you make food tradeoffs. (If you plan to eat a higher-calorie snack, the label can help you trade off and find other foods with fewer calories.)
- To choose foods that match a special health need, perhaps to cut calories to manage weight, to limit sodium (salt) to manage blood pressure, or to count carbohydrates to manage diabetes

This may surprise you: Fat-free products aren't always low in calories, and sugar-free products aren't always low in calories or low in fat! That's why you need to read and understand the Nutrition Facts.

Nutrition Facts: How to Use Them

As Nutrition Facts transition to the new format, you'll gradually find products displaying the new Nutrition Facts alongside products with the original Nutrition Facts. Original or new, here's how to make the Nutrition Facts work for you:

Step One: Start with label servings—the serving size and number of servings per container.

Serving sizes—set by government regulations—are expressed in familiar kitchen measures (e.g., teaspoon, tablespoon, cup). A label serving may be different from the portion size you actually eat; studies show that most people underestimate portion sizes.

By law, the serving size on the label must be based on amounts of food and drink that people customarily consume, not on what people *should* be eating—and not necessarily what *you* may consider to be one helping. For the new Nutrition Facts format (*"Nutrition Facts Update 2016" in this chapter, page 146*), serving sizes will more realistically reflect what people eat and drink these days.

Nutrition Facts apply to the amount of food or beverage in one label serving, not necessarily to the amount in the whole container. A 14-ounce can of ready-to-eat soup or 1½ ounces of chips may look like a single serving to you, but the Nutrition Facts may show a different serving size.

If you eat the amount for two servings, you eat twice the calories and nutrient amounts, too. Check the number of servings in a container and the size of each serving so you won't be misled. If you compare two or more similar foods, check to be sure the serving size is the same.

Step Two: Check the calories in a label serving.

Calories count, so pay attention. To help manage your weight, know the calories per serving and in the portion size you eat. If a label says that three cookies and 100 calories equal a serving, and you eat six cookies, you've doubled the calories and eaten two servings.

Step Three: Note the nutrients.

Unless their amounts are insignificant, some nutrients must appear in the Nutrition Facts. Required nutrients are those that are typically over- or underconsumed and so are linked to major health issues. *You'll read more about these nutrients later in this book.*

Those required on the original Nutrition Facts label are total fat, saturated fat, *trans* fat, cholesterol, total carbohydrates, sugars, protein, vitamins A and C, calcium, and iron. In addition to these required nutrients, others may be listed: some are voluntary; others are mandatory when a nutrient content claim is made. For example, if the label says "fortified with vitamin E" or "high in folate," then vitamin E or folate must appear in the Nutrition Facts.

Step Four: Use the % Daily Values (DVs) to get the most nutrition for your calories.

Generally speaking, % DVs show how the amount in one label serving of a food contributes to the total 2,000-calorie-a-day diet for some nutrients. If it shows 15% DV for iron, one serving has about 15 percent of the iron many people need for the day, which means the whole day, not a single meal or a snack.

Use % DVs to help you: (1) limit some nutrients such as sodium to the maximum advised for the day, and (2) get enough of others such as calcium to meet your daily nutrient recommendation. For example, for bone health, look for foods such as fat-free or low-fat milk or yogurt that have 20% DV or more for calcium. To limit sodium, find foods with 5% DV or less for sodium. For heart health, choose foods with less saturated and *trans* fats.

A few points of clarification:

- Daily Values used for labeling are averages for healthy adults, not necessarily optimal nutrient amounts advised for you. You may need more or less than the % DV for some nutrients. Be aware that the Daily Values for many nutrients—including calcium, vitamin D, sodium, and fiber—were revised for the new Nutrition Facts label; *see "% Daily Values: What Are They Based On?" in the appendix, page 786, for a complete list of Daily Value (original and new).*
- Daily Values aren't the same as the Dietary Reference Intakes (DRIs), *described "Nutrients: How Much?" in chapter 1, page 6. Also see "Dietary Reference Intakes" in the appendix, page 780, for details about the DRIs.*
- No Daily Values were established for *trans* fats or sugars for the original Nutrition Facts; sugars in the original Nutrition Facts reflect both natural and added sugars. The new Nutrition Facts provide % DVs for added sugars, listed separately.
- The % DV for total fat is not the same as the dietary advice: "Eat 20 to 35 percent of total calories from fat." The latter applies to the DRIs for everything you eat and drink for the day, not to a single food, beverage, meal, or snack. The % DV for total fat shows whether the food itself is high or low in fat.

Use the "5–20 guide" as a quick guide to label reading. For any nutrient:

- Five percent or less is low: For nutrients you need to limit, look for foods with a 5% DV or less.
- Twenty percent or more is high: For nutrients you need more of, look for foods with a 20% DV or more.

Note: The "5–20 guide" doesn't define a food as good or bad. Instead, it helps interpret how much of certain nutrients the food contains.

Step Five: Check the footnote.

The footnote on the original Nutrition Facts label shows Daily Values for some nutrients for two calorie levels—2,000 and 2,500 a day. They're maximum amounts for total fat, saturated fat, cholesterol, and sodium—and target amounts for total carbohydrate and fiber. This footnote is general advice and may not be right for you. The new Nutrition Facts has a different footnote.

Step Six: Check the calories-per-gram conversion.

In the original Nutrition Facts, this is the math that shows the number of calories in 1 gram each of fat, carbohydrate, and protein. *Note:* Fat supplies more than double the calories per gram (9 calories) than carbohydrate and protein do (4 calories per gram each).

See "A Closer Look . . . Nutrition Facts Update 2016," in this chapter, page 146, for a summary of the new Nutrition Facts.

A WORD ABOUT INGREDIENTS

Imagine that you reach for a can of vegetable soup. The ingredient list is like a recipe and differs from the Nutrition Facts. This list tells you what ingredients are in the soup.

Next time you reach for any mixed food, check what ingredients are listed first, second, and third on the label. By regulation, any food with more than one ingredient must carry an ingredient list on the label. All ingredients are listed in descending order by weight, from most to least. Canned vegetable soup that lists tomatoes first contains more tomatoes by weight than anything else.

Sometimes the ingredient list gives the source as well. For example, "tomato puree" may be followed by "(water and tomato paste)," and "Vegetable Oil" would be followed by "(contains one or more of the following: Corn Oil, Soybean Oil, or Safflower Oil)."

Looking for foods with less sodium, saturated fats, and added sugars, and without *trans* fats? The ingredient list can help you.

What else may appear on the ingredient list? Nutrients added for enrichment or fortification, or additives used to retain the appeal (color, texture, shape), add flavor, prevent spoilage, or provide a function such as yeast to make dough rise. *See "Additives: Their Place on the Plate" in chapter 5, page 132.*

The ingredient list is a useful tool for people with special food needs, such as:

- Those with cultural preferences or religious needs including, for example, those who avoid pork or other meats, or shellfish
- Vegetarians, including vegans, who avoid foods made with ingredients from animal sources
- Those with a food allergy (perhaps to peanuts or eggs), a food intolerance (perhaps to lactose, sulfites, or other ingredients), or celiac disease or non-celiac gluten sensitivity (to avoid gluten-containing ingredients)

A Closer Look . . .

Nutrition Facts Update 2016

Ready for the "new look"? The Nutrition Facts is getting a "face-lift" to make it easier for you to use the latest scientific evidence and healthy eating recommendations for your food and drink decisions.

Most Nutrition Facts updates fit into three categories:

1. *Updated nutrition information* to reflect current scientific evidence and nutrition advice, to reduce the risk of chronic diseases such as cardiovascular disease, obesity, high blood pressure and stroke, and to encourage an adequate intake of essential nutrients.

- *Nutrients of public health concern:* The mandatory list of vitamins and minerals is changing to those that aren't adequately consumed—and are linked to chronic disease risk: calcium, vitamin D, potassium, and iron. Metric amounts as well as DVs are required for mandatory vitamins and minerals. Vitamins A and C are no longer required.
- *No "calories from fat":* Since scientific evidence indicates that the type of fat is more important to public health than total fat, this will no longer appear.
- *Added sugars:* The mandatory listing of added sugars with a % DV will provide consumers with more information about added sugars in foods and drinks.
- *Daily Values:* DVs have been revised for some nutrients, including calcium, sodium, dietary fiber, and vitamin D. In addition, amounts of vitamins A, D, and E will be shown in metric measures instead of international units (IU)—milligrams or micrograms—as well as in the %DV. *See "% Daily Values: What Are They Based On" in the appendix, page 786, for the new DVs.*

2. *Updated serving size requirements and labeling for certain packages:*

- *Serving sizes:* The serving sizes, or Reference Amount Customarily Consumed (RACCs), are changing to more realistically reflect what people really eat and drink. And they may differ from servings shown on www.ChooseMyPlate.gov/. For example, the reference amount for yogurt is decreasing from 8 to 6 ounces. The amount for ice cream has been ½ cup and is increasing to ⅔ cup. Soda has been 8 ounces, now increasing to 12 ounces. On average, people eat more today than they did when Nutrition Fact labeling began more than 20 years ago.
- *Servings in a package*: Some food products previously labeled as more than one serving will instead be labeled as a single serving, for example a 20-ounce can of soda or a 15-ounce can of soup. That's because people typically drink or eat them in one sitting.
- *Dual columns*: Some foods that are packaged as larger than a single serving must be labeled in two ways: amounts "per serving" and "per package"/"per unit." They're foods or drinks such as a pint of ice cream or a 24-ounce soda that could be consumed either all at once or as several smaller servings. That shows how many calories and nutrients you get if you consume the whole package or container at one time.

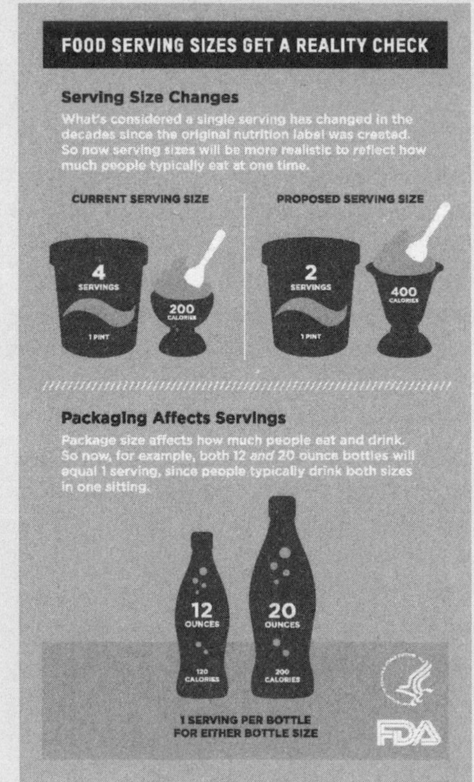

For those sensitive to artificial food color, the colors are named individually, not just listed as "coloring." If an ingredient list isn't clear to you, write or call the food manufacturer.

See chapter 23, page 653, for more about food sensitivities, including food allergies and lactose intolerance, and celiac disease; also see "Food-Allergen Labeling," and "Gluten-Free Labeling," page 151, in this chapter.

3. *Refreshed design to feature information that reflects links to key public health issues such as obesity.*

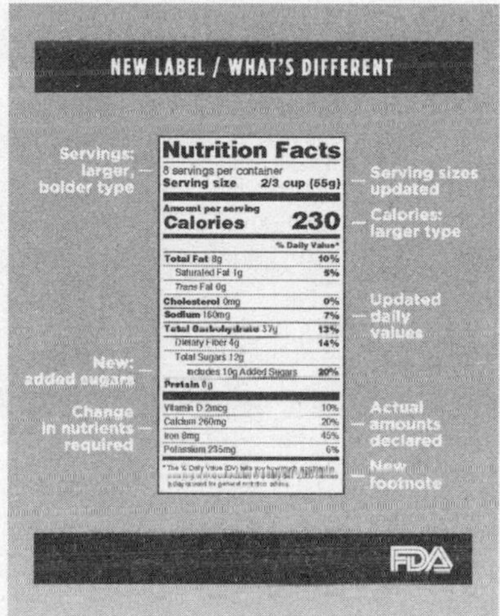

You also will see these changes:

- *Bolder and larger type:* "Calories," "servings per container," and the "Serving size" declaration will be more prominent and easier to see.
- *New footnote:* To make the % Daily Values easier to understand, it will read: "The % Daily Value tells you how much a nutrient in a serving of food contributes to a daily diet. 2,000 calories a day is used for general nutrition advice." The original footnote will be gone.
- *New information for carbs:* "Includes Added Sugars" will show right below "Total Sugars," And "Total Sugars" is a part of "Total Carbohydrates."

Approved Health Claims

To date, health claims have been approved by the FDA for use on food labels for the following categories:

- Calcium, Vitamin D, and Osteoporosis
- Dietary Lipids (Fat) and Cancer
- Dietary Saturated Fat and Cholesterol and Risk of Coronary Heart Disease
- Dietary Non-cariogenic Carbohydrate Sweeteners and Dental Caries
- Fiber-containing Grain Products, Fruits, and Vegetables and Cancer
- Folic Acid and Neural Tube Defects
- Fruits and Vegetables and Cancer
- Fruits, Vegetables, and Grain Products that Contain Fiber, Particularly Soluble Fiber, and Risk of Coronary Heart Disease
- Sodium and Hypertension
- Soluble Fiber from Certain Foods and Risk of Coronary Heart Disease
- Soy Protein and Risk of Coronary Heart Disease
- Stanols/Sterols and Risk of Coronary Heart Disease

Source: U.S. Food and Drug Administration, 2016.

This list does not include approved qualified health claims. *To learn the details of these approved health claims, visit www.fda.gov/Food/IngredientsPackagingLabeling/LabelingNutrition/ucm2006876.htm*

To use health claims:

- Remember, your food choices are just one factor that can reduce your risk for certain health problems. Genetics, physical activity, and smoking are among other factors that affect your health and risks for disease.
- Make shopping decisions using information from the whole label, not just the health claim. Check the Nutrition Facts to see if the product is right for you.

HEALTH "INFO": CLAIMS AND MORE

The "real estate" on a product label may carry useful health information that goes beyond its nutrient and ingredient content.

Health Claims

How might a food promote your health? Check the health claims. They link food or food components—in part of an overall healthy eating plan—with a lowered risk for some chronic diseases. Strictly regulated by the FDA, health claims are supported by scientific evidence. Foods that do meet the criteria may not carry a health claim.

With so much emerging science on nutrition and health, you might find approved qualified health claims on packages, too. They also indicate a relationship between a food component and health or reduced disease risk; however, qualifying language must appear with it. The reason? Supportive scientific evidence isn't conclusive.

Structure/Function Claims

Structure/function claims such as "helps promote urinary tract health" describe how a nutrient or food substance may affect your health. These claims *cannot* suggest any link to lowered risk for disease.

Unlike health claims, structure/function claims don't need prior FDA approval or review before putting them on the package label, but they are subject to FDA enforcement. They must be truthful and not misleading.

? Have you ever wondered?

. . . why you don't see % Daily Values for protein? Adjustments for protein's digestibility make calculating a % DV difficult. If the food is touted with a nutrient content claim—perhaps "high in protein"—then % DV for protein must be shown on the Nutrition Facts. All foods meant for infants, toddlers, and young children must show % DV for protein on the Nutrition Facts. Getting enough protein isn't a health concern for most older children, teens, and adults, except for some older adults, so it usually isn't listed with a % DV.

. . . why a food with "no sugar added" shows grams of total sugars on the Nutrition Facts? Vegetables, fruits, milk, grains, and beans and peas have naturally occurring sugars. "Sugars" in the original Nutrition Facts represent the total grams of added plus naturally occurring sugars. The new Nutrition Facts show a % DV for added sugars, as well as grams of total sugars. To identify added sugars, such as corn syrup, invert sugar, and corn sweeteners, in a food product, check the ingredient list. *See "Check the Ingredients" in chapter 11, page 367.*

. . . if either of these foods has added sugars: raw apple slices or honey? While both are sweet, the answer is neither one. The apple slices contain only natural sugars, so they have 0 grams of added sugars.

Honey is more complicated. Straight from the jar, the sugar in honey is naturally present, so the new Nutrition Facts will show it as 0 grams of added sugars, too. However, if honey was added to sweeten a packaged food, then the Nutrition Facts will show honey as added sugars.

. . . if a product labeled "0 grams *trans* fats per serving" is really *trans*-fat free? A product with less than ½ gram *trans* fat per label serving can be labeled as "0 *trans* fats."

Labels—and You

What's the best way to shop for good nutrition? Use food labels—nutrient content claims, health claims, ingredient lists, and Nutrition Facts—to choose nutrient-rich foods that fit your healthy eating plan, your nutrient and health needs, and your calorie target!

With the Nutrition Facts, always start with the serving size and the servings in the container, considering the portions you usually eat, too. Then consider other factors—are you:

- Concerned about weight? Compare the calories.
- Managing blood glucose (blood sugar)? Pay special attention to carbohydrates, including added sugars in the ingredient list and in new Nutrition Facts, and the fiber content.
- At risk for heart disease or high blood pressure? Check the saturated fat, *trans* fat, and sodium content. Key in on fats (for heart health) and sodium (for blood pressure).
- Concerned about loss of bone density? Look at the % DV for calcium and vitamin D.

Consider these two examples:

Example 1: Spaghetti sauce. To decrease sodium:

1. Look for a product with the nutrient content claim of "reduced sodium" or "low sodium."
2. Check the Nutrition Facts for the exact sodium content in one label serving. Compare it to other spaghetti sauces before you buy.
3. Check the ingredient list to find the sodium-containing ingredients.

Example 2: Granola bar. To limit calories:

1. Check how many calories are in one label serving.
2. Check how many servings the package contains and what the serving size is.
3. Calculate the calories in the amount of the granola bar you'll eat.

Dietary Guidance Statements

Dietary guidance statements describe the health benefits of broad categories of foods. For example, "Diets rich in fruits and vegetables may reduce the risk of some types of cancer and other chronic diseases."

Food-Allergen Labeling

Allergen labeling is required on foods or food groups containing a major food allergen or a protein from these allergens: milk, eggs, fish (e.g., bass, cod, flounder), crustacean shellfish (e.g., crab, lobster, shrimp), peanuts, tree nuts, (e.g., almonds, pecans, walnuts), wheat, and soybeans. These allergens account for over 90 percent of all food allergies and represent the foods most likely to result in severe or life-threatening reactions. Allergen labeling may appear in the ingredient list or in a statement at the end of that list. Wherever it appears, allergens must be identified by common names. For example, the label may say: "Contains milk, egg, peanuts." The label also might provide a disclaimer, such as "Made in a facility that also processes peanuts."

Food Safety and Handling Tips

For your good health, some food labels offer guidance on food safety and handling. To reduce the risk of foodborne illness, raw and partially cooked meat and poultry products must be labeled with guidelines for safe handling. Each of the simple graphics—a refrigerator, hand washing, fry pan, and meat thermometer—represents a safe-handling tip.

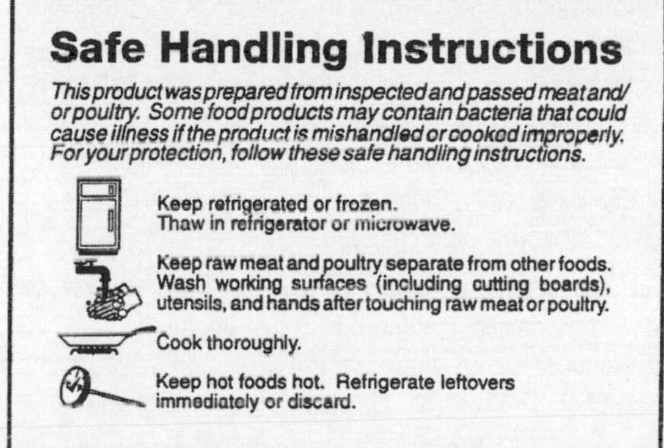

Safe Handling Instructions

This product was prepared from inspected and passed meat and/or poultry. Some food products may contain bacteria that could cause illness if the product is mishandled or cooked improperly. For your protection, follow these safe handling instructions.

Keep refrigerated or frozen. Thaw in refrigerator or microwave.

Keep raw meat and poultry separate from other foods. Wash working surfaces (including cutting boards), utensils, and hands after touching raw meat or poultry.

Cook thoroughly.

Keep hot foods hot. Refrigerate leftovers immediately or discard.

Cartons of shell eggs also have safe-handling instructions (*see below*) to help control *Salmonella* contamination. Eggs that have been treated to destroy *Salmonella*—by in-shell pasteurization, for example—are not required to carry safe-handling instructions.

> **SAFE HANDLING INSTRUCTIONS:**
> To prevent illness from bacteria: keep eggs refrigerated, cook eggs until yolks are firm, and cook foods containing eggs thoroughly.

See chapter 7, page 191, for in-depth information on food safety and handling.

Gluten-Free Labeling

"Gluten-free," "no gluten," "without gluten," "free of gluten." Foods with less than 20 parts per million (ppm) of gluten can be labeled voluntarily as gluten-free, even if naturally gluten-free, such as fresh vegetables and fruits and spring water. That applies to all foods regulated by the FDA including imported foods as well as dietary supplements. Meat, poultry, unshelled eggs, which are regulated by the USDA, distilled spirits, many wines, and malted beverages aren't covered by this regulation.

Why not zero ppm? Amounts below 20 ppm can't be detected reliably. Experts in celiac disease indicate that 20 ppm can be tolerated by those with celiac disease. Any grain, including oats—other than the gluten-containing grains of wheat, rye, barley, or their crossbred hybrids like triticale—can be labeled gluten-free if any unavoidable gluten from cross-contact situations is less than 20 ppm.

Several organizations have developed symbols that identify certified gluten-free foods, such as these:

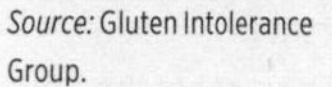

Source: Gluten Intolerance Group.

Source: National Foundation for Celiac Awareness.

Source: Celiac Support Association.

The use of a gluten-free logo isn't required. If used, it must be consistent with FDA labeling regulations and can't interfere with required labeling. A symbol can't substitute for the terms "gluten-free," "no gluten," "free of gluten," or "without gluten."

Since gluten-free labeling is voluntary, a food may be gluten-free even if it doesn't say so. Some products may include a statement such as "Produced in a facility that also produces wheat." If you have celiac disease, contact the brands or food manufacturers for information on their testing and safety protocols.

Health Warnings

Some foods are required to carry health warnings:

- Foods and beverages made with aspartame (a nonnutritive sweetener) carry a warning for those with phenylketonuria (PKU). Aspartame contains the amino acid phenylalanine, which people with PKU can't metabolize; *see "Aspartame" in chapter 11, page 369; "Have you ever wondered . . . if nonnutritive sweeteners are safe to consume during pregnancy?" in chapter 17, page 554; and "Aspartame: PKU Warning," in chapter 23, page 679.*
- The term "Contains Sulfites" appears on beer and wine labels, dried fruit, and some salad seasonings for those who are sulfite sensitive; *see "Sulfite Sensitivity: Mild to Severe" in chapter 23, page 678.*
- Alcohol-containing beverages carry warnings for pregnant women; *see "Pregnancy and Alcoholic Beverages: Don't Mix!" in chapter 18, page 549.*
- Unpasteurized juice and juice products, including cider, must carry a food-safety warning if sold across state lines. For example:

> **WARNING:** This product has not been pasteurized and therefore may contain harmful bacteria that can cause serious illness in children, the elderly, and persons with weakened immune systems.

MORE FOR FOOD LABEL READERS

A few more moments with food labels can teach you even more about the food inside the package.

Type of food. The product name tells what's in the container. Besides specifically naming the food, it tells the form. This could be a description such as smooth or chunky, sliced or whole, or miniature—often important to know when following a recipe.

Net contents. Food labels tell the total amount in the container, either in volume, count, or net weight. Net weight refers to the food amount inside the container, including any liquid.

For juice products, total percent juice content. Fruit and vegetable juices that are only juice may be labeled "100 percent juice." Juice drinks, which contain other ingredients, can't carry this statement.

A "100 percent juice" may—or may not—supply 100 percent of the Daily Value for vitamin C. That said, juices offer more nutrients and phytonutrients than just vitamin C. Many juices are fortified with additional nutrients, too.

Juice "drinks," "beverages," or "cocktails" (containing some juice, but not 100 percent juice) may be fortified to provide 100 percent of the Daily Value for some nutrients. Typically, these beverages have added sugars but probably not the full array and amounts of nutrients and phytonutrients in 100 percent juice. *See "Juice, Juice Drink, or Fruit Drink?" in chapter 4, page 88.*

Name and full address of the manufacturer, packager, or distributor. Need to contact a food company with your consumer questions and concerns? Look for a consumer service phone number or website address. If the food manufacturer, packager, or distributor is not in the United States, the label must state the country and mailing code.

Country of origin. As of 2009, many food commodities were required to carry a country-of-origin label (COOL). This included wild and farm-raised fish and shellfish; fresh and frozen vegetables and fruits; peanuts, pecans, and macadamia nuts; and ginseng. For some items such as produce or seafood, this information might appear on a display tag, too. In 2016, cuts of beef and pork as well as ground beef and pork were removed from the list of commodities that were subject to the COOL regulation.

COOL *only* tells you where the food is from—not more, not less. It's not a food-safety program. Specialty stores such as fish markets are exempt, although they may provide the information voluntarily.

Organic labeling. The Organic Foods Production Act and the National Organic Program, part of the USDA's Agricultural Marketing Service, ensure that the production, processing, and certification of organic foods are standardized. The term "organic" has legal label definitions. Knowing what they mean will help you make informed decisions.

Products that are certified organic are produced without genetic engineering. Natural fertilizers and pesticides are allowed in organic farming, but synthetic substances are prohibited. They may bear the "USDA Organic" seal. *See "Organic Farming" in chapter 5, page 122.* Food labels may indicate one of three classifications for "organic":

- *"100 percent organic"*: The product must contain only organically produced ingredients (except for water and salt).

A Closer Look . . .

Deciphering Package Dates, Reducing Food Waste

You can't see inside the package, so how do you know if it's fresh or safe to eat? Billions of dollars of food are wasted annually because people don't understand product dating. Learn what these dates mean so you don't waste food!

Product dating isn't standardized. Except for infant formula, product dating usually isn't mandatory, either. For formula, the date applies to when the formula is at peak nutritional quality, not the safety of the formula.

Dates often indicate peak flavor and freshness, not when the food is unsafe to eat. Many nonperishable foods remain safe to eat long after the package date. Contact the food manufacturer if you questions. And check FoodKeeper App from the US Department of Health and Human Services: www.foodsafety.gov/keep/foodkeeperapp/. *See "Cupboard, Pantry, Fridge, and Freezer Storage" in chapter 7, page 197, for more about storage times.*

Food manufacturers determine both the way dates are expressed and what they mean. The date could be meant for the store or for you. Product dates are written in several different ways, too, such as "12-15" or "1215" or "Dec. 15," all meaning December 15.

- *"Sell by" or pull date:* This is the last day the store should sell a food so it remains fresh for home storage. This allows you a reasonable time to enjoy it at peak quality after purchase. It is not an "eat or toss by" date.
- *"Use by" date:* This is the last date advised for use while the product is at peak quality, as determined by the manufacturer. These are *not* food-safety dates.
- *"Best if used by" date:* This is the last date advised for use for optimal flavor and quality. For example, the label may say, "Best if used by 1-31-18." It's *not* a purchase-by or food-safety date.
- *"Closed or coded" dates:* These are packing numbers for use by the manufacturer. You might see a pack date, which is when the item was produced or packaged.

Remember, these dates are for quality and optimum freshness—not for food safety. Depending on the food and whether it has been stored properly, it's likely safe beyond this date and until it reaches your table.

- *"Organic"*: The product must contain at least 95 percent organically produced ingredients (except for water and salt). The other 5 percent are ingredients that aren't available in organic form or that appear on an approved list.
- *"Made with organic ingredients"*: Processed foods may bear this label if they contain at least 70 percent organic ingredients—for example, "soup made with organic peas, potatoes, and carrots." The regulation also identifies production methods that can't be used.

If it's labeled organic, the product's name and the address of the certifying organization must appear—with one exception. Small farmers (less than $5,000 in organic sales annually), including those who may sell in small farmers' markets, don't need certification. Still, their label claims must be truthful and in compliance with organic labeling laws—but talk to the farmer to learn more.

Organic labeling regulations don't change food labeling regulations, administered by the FDA and the USDA's Food Safety and Inspection Service. Being labeled as organic doesn't mean a food is more healthy or more nutritious. Terms such as "all-natural," "free-range," or "hormone-free" don't mean organic.

Labeling for foods produced with or without genetic engineering. Currently the FDA has provided guidance for the voluntary labeling by manufacturers to inform consumers who want to know if a food was produced using genetic engineering. This labeling must be truthful and not misleading. Although the terminology used is not yet regulated, the FDA has made recommendations for a food product (or its ingredients):

- If not developed using bioengineering, genetic engineering, or modern biotechnology, the FDA advises claims such as "not bioengineered," "not genetically engineered," and "not genetically modified through the use of modern biotechnology."
- If developed using bioengineering, genetic engineering, or modern biotechnology, the FDA advises claims such as "genetically engineered," "This product contains cornmeal from corn that was produced using modern biotechnology," or "Some of our growers plant soybean seeds that were developed through modern biotechnology to be drought tolerant."

In 2016, regulations were passed that will require food companies to disclose GMO (genetically modified organism) ingredients as a text label, a symbol, or an electronic code readable by smart phones. Rules for this labeling are expected to be written in two years (2018), with a compliance date later. With this regulation, federal regulations pre-empt state laws. *See "Labeling: When You Want to Know" in chapter 5, page 126, for more about non-GMO labeling.*

Grading and inspection symbols on some products. These symbols indicate that foods have met certain standards set by the government:

- *Inspection stamps* on fresh and packaged meats and poultry mean the food is wholesome and was slaughtered, packed, or processed under sanitary conditions.

Have you ever wondered?

. . . what the code on the lid or the bottom of canned foods means? A series of letters or numbers identifies the plant location, exact date of processing, and perhaps even the work shift or time. This lets manufacturers rotate the stock and locate it in case of a recall. These codes aren't meant as "use by" dates. Codes differ from one food company to another. If you can't read the code but wish to, contact the company, using the toll-free number, website address, or address on the label.

. . . what "natural" on a label means? Defining a food product as "natural" is difficult because the food has probably been processed and is no longer only a product of the earth. That said, the FDA has not developed a definition over the years for using the term "natural" or its derivatives, and it hasn't objected to the use of the term if the food does not contain added color, artificial flavors, or synthetic substances. However, due to consumer requests and changes in food ingredients and production, the FDA is exploring the use of the term "natural" in food labeling. Stay tuned. For meat and poultry, the term is defined by the US Food Safety and Inspection Service (FSFS) to mean no artificial ingredients or added color and is only minimally processed. "Minimally processed" means that processing can't fundamentally change the product and the label must state the meaning of the term "natural."

Label Confusion?

Food packages may carry other attention-grabbing, marketing terms implying a ""halo" of health. But what do these terms really mean? There are no consistent definitions—and some may lead to shopper confusion. These are among the terms with no current federal government–regulated definitions for food labeling, but which may turn up on packaging:

- doctor-recommended
- eco-friendly
- energy
- green
- naturally raised, naturally grown
- high-quality
- local
- no additives
- sustainable
- wholesome

Label Lingo

What Other Label Claims Mean

Besides nutrition and health claims, some labels carry other label terms.

Label Term . . .	Means . . .
FRESH	Food in its raw state. The term can't be used on food that has been frozen or heated, or on food that contains preservatives.
FROZEN FRESH OR FRESH FROZEN	Food that is quickly frozen while very fresh shortly after harvest
QUICKLY FROZEN	Food that is frozen using a system that freezes the center of the food fast but with virtually no deterioration
HOMOGENIZED	Milk that has been processed to break up and separate the milk fat, which makes its texture smooth and uniform
NATURAL	No regulatory definition by FDA, which has not objected to the use of the term if the food contains no artificial ingredient or added color or synthetic substances. The label must explain the use of the term "natural" (e.g., "no added colorings or artificial ingredients"). For meat and poultry, the term is defined by FSIS to mean no artificial ingredients or added color, and only minimal processing.
PASTEURIZED	Food such as raw milk, raw eggs, and fresh juice that has been heated to a temperature high enough to destroy bacteria and inactivate most enzymes that cause spoilage
ULTRA- PASTEURIZED	Food such as cream that has been heated to a temperature higher than for pasteurization, which extends the time it can be stored in the refrigerator or on the shelf
UHT (ULTRA-HIGH TEMPERATURE)	Food that has been heated to a temperature even higher than for ultra-pasteurization and packaged in a sterile container; this allows it to be stored unopened without refrigeration for up to three months. Once opened, it must be refrigerated.

- *Food grades*—for example, on some types of meat, poultry, eggs, dairy foods, and produce—suggest standards of appearance, texture, uniformity, and perhaps taste. With the exception of marbling fat in meat, food grading does not suggest nutrient value. *Grading for meat, poultry, and eggs is discussed in "Meat: Buying Tips" and "Eggs: Buying Tips" in this chapter, pages 164 and 172.*

Preparation instructions. Some products suggest oven or microwave times and temperatures, or perhaps other preparation or serving tips. Some offer recipes.

Kosher symbols. The term "kosher" means "proper" or "fit" in Hebrew. Kosher symbols indicate that the food has met the standards of a Jewish food inspector, done in addition to a government safety inspection. The kosher code, which may appear on foods throughout the store, doesn't imply any nutritional qualities.

Often the word "Pareve" is written next to these symbols, meaning the food has neither meat nor dairy ingredients. During March and April, a large "P" next to the symbols means it's kosher for Passover.

Star-K

OU

OK

KOF-K

Halal and Zabiah Halal symbols. Products prepared by federally inspected meatpacking plants and handled according to Islamic dietary law and under Islamic authority may bear Halal and Zabiah Halal references.

Universal Product Code (UPC). Black bars of different widths, which identify the manufacturer and the food, on package labels are used by stores and manufacturers for inventory control, marketing information, and price scanning.

Your Food Dollar: More Nutrition, Less Waste

Good news: You don't need to give up good nutrition for a reasonable grocery bill! But how do you save money, as well as time and hassle, when you shop for food? And how do you get the most nutrition for your food dollar—and limit waste? Being an educated consumer who has smart shopping habits and knows what's needed is the main way. It's also important to be aware of marketing ploys that tempt you to buy beyond your shopping list. Know thyself!

PLAN AHEAD

Planning menus ahead lets you buy just what you need, avoid wasted food, lower your food costs, and prevent the time and stress of unneeded shopping trips and the last minute dilemma: "what's for dinner?" To plan well, keep the following in mind:

- Know your food budget; know what you typically spend. Adjust your menus, as needed, to get the most nutrition for your food dollar.
- Keep a running grocery list, written and posted in your kitchen, or use an app with a built-in database on your smart phone or tablet. Track routine purchases, and note ingredients for recipes you plan to prepare. Some apps convert recipes into shopping lists.

  Organize your list by category to match the store layout—for example, produce department, dairy case, meat counter, deli, bakery, frozen foods, and grocery aisles. Before you shop and as you plan, check your food inventory—pantry, fridge, freezer—to use what you have on hand.

  Whatever method you use, a shopping list jogs your memory, saves money at the store, saves shopping time, and simplifies any online shopping or shopping by those who assist you. It also may keep you from buying what you don't need. Stick to your list.
- Stock up on staples, or the foods you use often, so you can prepare healthy meals without a trip to the store. That includes vegetables and fruits in all forms: fresh, frozen, canned, dried, and 100 percent juice. When available in your own kitchen, you're more likely to eat enough vegetables and fruits. Every cook has his or her own unique list of staples.
- Buy and prepare the right amount. If food goes uneaten, you've wasted food and money.

USE COUPONS, STORE SPECIALS, AND APPS

Use these tools to stretch your food budget:

- Download or clip coupons, but only for items you really need. Some apps aggregate coupons from many store flyers; some can alert you to their expiration date.

  Be alert: Items with coupons aren't always the best buy. Another brand or a similar food might be cheaper and perhaps more nourishing, even without a coupon.
- Check supermarket specials in store circulars, newspaper inserts, or online. Plan menus around them; some apps can help. If the store runs out of an item on special, ask for a rain check. Be aware of "limit" signs ("limit three per customer") and messages such as "two for $5.00" (not "$2.50 each"), which are marketing ploys to get you to buy more. Research shows they work!
- Choose apps that make shopping trips easier. Besides being a handy place to keep shopping lists, the best apps also scan bar codes, deliver coupons, and let you share family shopping tasks.
- Sign up for a loyalty program—if it offers benefits that match your needs. Besides savings, you may get advance e-mail/online notices of in-store specials, cash-back offers, reward cards, coupons, recipes, nutrition and health tips, and reminders of products you buy frequently.
- Take advantage of seasonal produce. In season, the price for fresh vegetables and fruits may be lower, and the produce may be more flavorful with more varietals. Depending on where you live, you might shop at a farm or local farmers' market. What's seasonal depends on the growing season and conditions where you live.

CONSIDER YOUR TIMING

Timing your shopping trip right can help in many ways:

- Try to shop less often for major stock-ups if that works for you. Likely you'll spend less on impulse items—and save time and fuel cost. More trips for major shopping can add up to more money spent and potentially to more food waste if you buy more than used and needed. A quick after-work stop for a fresh item for a meal is different.
- Eat before you shop. Even a small snack can prevent you from being hungry when you shop. This helps you avoid impulse buys from store sampling, buying too much, and being tempted to buy a candy bar at checkout.
- Shop during off-hours if you can: early morning, late evening, or midweek. You'll shop faster, perhaps with less stress.
- If you can, walk or bike to the store for small purchases when you have time. If you need to hand carry food home, you may skip the urge to buy extras—and you'll get exercise, too!

SHOP WITH INTENT

Being a mindful shopper is as important as being a mindful eater. These are ways to "mind" your food expenses and the quality of your food choices:

- Shop with a basket or smaller cart, which may encourage you to buy less or only what you need.
- Use food labels to find foods that match your needs and compare their nutrition, *as discussed in "Food Labels: Decode the Package" in this chapter, page 144.*
- Decide what quality and form of food you need. For example, if you're making a casserole, chunk light tuna may be fine. But more expensive solid white tuna has more eye appeal in a tuna-vegetable salad.

Shopping List: Stocking a Healthy Kitchen

In Your Kitchen Cabinet . . .

Baking ingredients (baking soda, baking powder, cocoa powder)
Barley (whole)
Beans (canned, dry)
Beans, refried (canned, fat-free, reduced fat, vegetarian)
Bread and rolls (whole wheat or mixed grain)
Broth (beef, chicken, vegetable; canned, reduced sodium, reduced fat)
Bulgur
Cereal (whole-grain, fortified)
Condiments (ketchup, mustard)
Cornstarch
Couscous (perhaps whole wheat)
Flour (whole wheat, unbleached white whole wheat)
Fruit (canned in own juice or light syrup, dried)
100 percent fruit spread
Gingersnaps or vanilla wafers
Herbs and spices (dry)
Juice (100 percent), fruit and vegetable, (boxed)
Milk, evaporated fat-free (skim)
Milk powder (nonfat dry)
Nuts
Pasta (spaghetti, macaroni, others, perhaps whole grain or fiber rich)
Pasta sauce
Peanut butter, other nut butters (almond, cashew)
Rice (brown, white)
Salad dressing (perhaps reduced fat)
Salsa or picante sauce
Sugar (granulated, brown, powdered/confectioners')
Tuna or salmon (canned and packed in spring water, vacuum packed)
Vegetable oil cooking spray
Vegetable or other oil (canola, olive, peanut, soybean, others)
Vegetable soup (canned, perhaps reduced sodium)
Vegetables (canned, perhaps reduced sodium)
Vinegar (apple cider, balsamic, rice, others)

In a Cool, Dry Place . . .

Garlic
Onions
Potatoes, sweet potatoes
Shallots

In Your Refrigerator* . . .

Apples
Celery
Cheese (regular, reduced fat)
Cheese, Parmesan
Deli meats, lean, perhaps reduced or low sodium (sliced turkey or chicken breast)
Eggs (or egg substitute)
Garlic
Green onions (scallions)
Greens (kale, lettuce, spinach, others)
Juice (100 percent), fruit and vegetable
Lemons
Milk (fat-free, low-fat, perhaps whole)
Mushrooms
Oranges
Tortillas (perhaps whole wheat, corn)
Vegetables (carrots, green beans, others)
Yogurt (perhaps Greek)

In Your Freezer* . . .

Frozen cut fruits and berries (assorted)
Frozen fish fillets
Frozen green bell peppers (chopped)
Frozen onions (chopped)
Frozen vegetables without sauce (assorted)
Frozen whole-wheat waffles or bagels
Frozen yogurt or fruit sorbet
Fruit juice (100 percent) concentrate
Lean ground beef
Pork loin
Skinless chicken breasts or thighs

*Buy fresh produce, meat, poultry, and fish as you need them.

- Buy the economy size or a family pack only if it's cheaper, and if you have enough storage space.
- While warehouse stores may charge less, you may not save if you must buy large amounts, especially if food spoils and must be discarded. For foods that freeze, take time to repackage them into smaller amounts in freezer bags and then freeze for later use.
- Check unit prices on supermarket shelves. They make cost comparisons easier, especially for similar foods in different-size containers. Prices are given as cost per unit rather than price per package or container. The unit might be an ounce, a pint, a pound, or some other measurement. The largest container isn't always the cheapest.

- Compare the prices of private-label brands, store brands, and generic brands. Store brands and generic products may cost less since they don't have the same promotional costs. The quality is likely similar.
- Stock up on canned and other nonperishable foods when they're on sale. At home, rotate your food supply so that the "first in" is the "first out."
- Buy perishable foods in amounts that will be consumed during their peak quality. An extra bunch of broccoli that spoils in the refrigerator is no savings.
- Consider buying from bulk bins if your store has them. Without the expense of packaging or branding, bulk foods often cost less, and they're usually the same foods you find on supermarket shelves. For best advantage, buy just the amount you need. Foods such as dried fruit, pasta, rice, other grains, snack mixes, and spices are among those sold in bulk.

  While buying unpackaged bulk foods has advantages, packaging has different benefits, such as offering convenience and providing product information about nutrition, storage and use and about the food manufacturer. By protecting a product's cleanliness and safety and perhaps extending its shelf life, packaging can contribute to less wasted food.
- Consider the cost of convenience. Prepared, presliced, and precooked foods usually cost more. For example, ready-to-grill beef kabobs cost more than buying beef to make your own. However, depending on your schedule, labor-saving and step-saving, these ingredients may be worth the price.

  Convenient, innovative packaging such as squirt bottles and ready-to-serve pouches often add to the cost; decide if the benefits are worth the added packaging cost.
- If available, and if you qualify, take advantage of senior citizen discount days.
- Remain flexible. If you see a better bargain or a new food (perhaps a vegetable or fruit), adjust your menu.
- Plan menus that combine more costly ingredients with more affordable ingredients, such as fruits, vegetables, whole grains, and low-fat or fat-free dairy foods as the main feature. Use small amounts of lean meats.

"Small-Household" Shopping

If you're a household of one or two, how can you maximize your food dollar? Besides general cost-saving tips, you might save in other ways:

- Buy frozen, free-flow vegetables and fruits in bags. As long as they aren't thawed, you can pour out as much as you need and then reseal and return the bag to the freezer.
- Look for single-serving foods: juice, yogurt, frozen meals, soup, and pudding, among others. These give you a greater variety of food on hand. "Singles" may help with portion control, too.
- Economy-size packages? Share with a friend.
- Decide if the bigger package with the lower unit price is really a saving. If you can't use it all, it's not.
- Shop from bulk bins for small amounts.
- At home repackage meat, poultry, and fish into single portions in freezer wrap or plastic freezer bags. Freeze for later.
- Ask the butcher or the produce manager to repackage a smaller amount of fresh meat, poultry, or produce.
- Buy produce that keeps longer in the refrigerator: broccoli, Brussels sprouts, cabbage, carrots, parsnips, potatoes, sweet potatoes, turnips, apples, grapefruit, melons, oranges, pears, and tangerines.
- Shop for convenience. Often, mixed salad greens (perhaps from the salad bar) or raw vegetables already cut and mixed for stir-fry dishes or salads cost less than individual foods bought in quantity.
- Buy small loaves of bread, or wrap and freeze what you won't use right away.

- Be aware of marketing tactics. End-of-the-aisle displays, called endcaps, and store sampling are meant as attention grabbers. When you stop and look, you are more likely to buy. In the aisles, the best bargains may be at the top or bottom of the shelf, not at eye level.
- Be savvy about the marketing approach, referred to as "green washing" or "green sheen." The term "green" is undefined and unregulated. This type of marketing may suggest that foods are more environmentally friendly than they really are. Marketing phrases that imply the product is better for the Earth don't necessarily mean better for you.

  To buy with sustainability in mind, learn about the food, such as how and where it's grown and produced—and consider your own food preparation and eating: are you wasting food?
- Pay attention at checkout. Put down the magazine or your cell phone. See that prices scan as advertised or as indicated on the shelf label, especially for sale items. Common checkout errors are: sale items not programmed into the computer; charging for the weight of packaging; and in some states, taxing nontaxable items. Check your receipts.

Click Here!
Links to Know . . .

- Food Value Analysis, comparing the cost of homemade to prepared food
  www.foodvalueanalysis.org

Shopping for Food Online

Here's a projection to chew on: Online grocery shopping will add up to $100 billion sales by 2019, four times a much as in 2014, according to Packaged Facts!

With improved ordering and better delivery services, the convenience of online shopping is trending among those who have less time or less ability to shop in traditional supermarkets. Many online grocers are designed for time-pressed families; you might multitask with food shopping while waiting for an appointment. Online shopping may also be a good solution for older adults or those with physical limitations. *Bonus:* You may avoid impulse buying (although the ease of shopping may add food expense).

If you decide to be an online food shopper, these tips may save you time, energy, and money:

- Find the right online service for your needs. A few questions to ask: Do you want nonperishables only, fresh produce only, or both? Does the service offer the brands you like? Is there a membership or delivery fee that costs more than any savings? Is the delivery the same day or next day? Where will it be delivered; will you be home? Is there a minimum order? Does it offer easy online coupons or other promotions? Does it keep an order history? Does your local grocer offer a delivery service, perhaps without a membership fee?
- Keep a list of staples you want to keep on hand. Some online services have an interactive list you can use and modify for your needs.
- Use your label savvy. Since you can't see or touch food items, you need to be especially attentive to the label information and unit prices as you compare and choose.
- Click around the website for recipes and to learn more about the food, its ingredients (perhaps allergens), its preparation and storage, and perhaps its producer. If you count on package labeling for information such as high fiber, gluten free, or low saturated fat, look for that too.
- For specials, check the sales expiration date before confirming your order to make sure an item is charged to you within the sale period.
- Scroll through your options. Often a grocery search lists more costly items before generic or store brands.
- Be cautious with auto-reorder to avoid food waste. Before clicking "yes" to items you've bought before, check your kitchen inventory and consider whether you'll use the item.
- For perishables, find a service that provides the freshness and quality you want, at affordable prices. Check that the delivery matches your schedule. You might decide to order only produce that doesn't bruise easily such as apples, corn, and pineapple and save other items for trips to the store.
- Assess the benefits. Calculate your time and money savings and decide if this was the best option for you. If products are mishandled, contact customer service.
- Look for more, such as information about new or better-for-you foods, shopping and food safety tips, and perhaps online "talk time" with a supermarket dietitian.

More and more brick-and-mortar supermarkets offer online shopping. As this option grows, look for more online stores that sell specialty foods or foods from small producers.

? Have you ever wondered?

. . . if it's healthier to just shop the outside perimeter of the store? If you've heard advice to shop mostly the perimeter, that's old school. Today's stores have many different layouts. For example, some have themed areas in center store, while others display their fresh produce there. Some stores have in-store cafes that occupy part of the perimeter.

Even if your supermarket displays fresh vegetables and fruits, fresh meat and poultry, fresh fish, dairy, and bakery around the perimeter, you'll miss a lot of good flavor and good nutrition if you avoid the middle. Mid-store grocery aisles display items such as barley, brown rice, oatmeal, quinoa, nuts, dried fruit, olive and canola oils, and healthy convenience foods such as canned vegetables and fruits, low-sodium broth, and 100% vegetable juice. And freezer aisles provide many nourishing frozen items including vegetables and fruits. Wherever you shop, get to know the store layout to make the best use of your time and supermarket savvy.

. . . what a "food desert" is? It refers to geographic areas (often urban) without access to affordable fruits, vegetables, whole grains, low-fat or fat-free milk, and other foods that make up the full range of a healthy diet. The result? The ability to make nourishing food choices is limited. Since higher-caloric, lower-nutrient foods might be the options instead, food deserts may play a role in the obesity epidemic and some chronic health problems.

Do you think you live in a food desert? There's no precise definition, but this government website offers insight: www.ers.usda gov/data/fooddesert. Even if you do, you can take steps to eat healthy—maybe even start or participate in an urban garden.

The Store: Shopping for Health, Flavor, and Convenience

Filling your shopping cart? Let's tour the supermarket, department by department, focusing on shopping tips for high-quality, nutritious, and safe foods—that match your needs.

Certainly the "shopping trip" on the next few pages won't cover all the foods sold today; and new products, including more variety and more better-for-you products, constantly come on the market. However, some shopping savvy for each food category can help you make healthy and perhaps more economical shopping decisions. *See chapter 5, page 511, for more about food—from farm to market.*

PRODUCE DEPARTMENT

Supermarkets carry about 300 types of vegetables and fruits. They're most nutritious and best tasting at peak quality.

Raw Veggies and Fruits: Buying Tips

1. Check the produce department. Besides being clean, organized, and appealing, raw vegetables and fruits should be held at a proper temperature. Most are chilled; a fine mist helps keep greens crisp; being soggy promotes growth of mold or rot.

Fresh from the Farmers' Market?

With thousands of farmers' markets in operation in the United States and more opening every year, you get a chance to talk directly to growers and producers and perhaps find products you can't find elsewhere: different varietals of vegetables and fruits; artisan cheeses; fresh or potted herbs; cut flowers; homemade sauces; oven-fresh baked goods; organically certified foods; meat, poultry, or eggs from nearby producers; or fresh fish. And it's a great shopping option for getting more vegetables and fruits in your food plan!

Be aware that the produce sold may—or may not—be fresh from the field. Some markets feature only nearby growers. Others sell brokered products from the same commercial markets that supermarkets buy from. And some sell both. Ask the market manager.

For food safety and great shopping:

- Bring a clean carry bag, basket, or several, perhaps insulated. Use separate bags for raw and cooked foods. Also keep uncooked meat, poultry, and fish separate from other foods, including dairy foods, to avoid cross contamination. Some markets don't allow plastic bags.
- Pay attention to the food-safety practices of the vendor: cleanliness, gloves or clean utensils for handling food, covered garbage cans, clean bags.
- Go early for the best selection; check the market website ahead of time if there is one. Walk through the market first to see what's available and then make your choices.
- Shop with flexibility. Markets change with the season and the local growers and vendors who come to market.
- Take time to talk to the growers and learn from them. Many small farmers are eager to talk about their growing methods and how they care for their animals. They may even invite you for a farm visit!
- Pack your purchases so they don't get crushed; take perishables home right away.

Freshness: How to . . . Judge Produce

Here are guidelines for choosing the freshest produce for optimal flavor and quality.

FOR FRUITS . . .

APPLES	Firm with smooth, clean skin and good color. Avoid fruit with bruises or decay spots.
APRICOTS	Plump with as much golden-orange color as possible. Blemishes, unless they break the skin, will not affect flavor. Avoid fruit that is pale yellow, greenish-yellow, very firm, shriveled, or bruised.
ASIAN PEARS	Fragrant, unbruised fruit with little or no brown spots. They are hard when ripe, unlike traditional pears.
AVOCADOS	Green to purplish-black skin with a smooth to bumpy texture, and yellow-green, soft flesh. When ripe, it yields to gentle pressure. Most are sold unripe.
BANANAS	Plump with uniform shape at the desired ripeness level. Avoid fruit with blemished or bruised skins.
BLUEBERRIES	Plump and firm with a light-grayish bloom, which is the thin coating on the surface. Check the carton to avoid signs of mold.
CANTALOUPES	Slightly oval shape, 5 inches or more in diameter, with yellow or golden (not green) background color and heavy for size. Signs of sweetness include pronounced netted (netlike markings) rind and a few tiny cracks near the stem end. Smell the melon; it should be noticeably fragrant. At home, check for ripeness before you eat it; the stem area will be slightly soft when ripe.
CHERRIES	Plump, firm sweet or sour cherries with stems attached. Sweet cherries with reddish-brown skin have the best flavor. Avoid fruit that is overly soft or shriveled or has dark stems.
DATES	Plump and soft with smooth, shiny skin. Avoid fruit that is shriveled or has sugar crystals or mold on the skin.
GRAPEFRUITS	Firm, thin-skinned, smooth, and heavy for its size, and flat at both ends. Avoid fruit with a pointed end or thick, deeply pored skin.
GRAPES	Plump, firm grapes that are firmly attached to pliable green stems. Avoid fruit that is soft or wrinkled and that has bleached-looking areas at the stem end.
HONEYDEW MELONS	Waxy white rind barely tinged with green and weighs at least five pounds. Fully ripe fruit has a cream-colored rind; the blossom end should give to gentle pressure.
KIWIFRUIT	Evenly firm fruit with a rough, fuzzy brown skin. For ripeness, slightly soft with gentle handling.
LEMONS	Firm, thin, bright-colored, and smooth skin. Generally, rough-textured lemons have thicker skins and less juice than fine-skinned varieties.
LIMES	Firm, thin, bright-colored, and smooth skin.
MANGOES	Usually quite firm when sold and must be ripened further at home before eating. Avoid fruit with shriveled or bruised skin. When ripe, it will give to gentle pressure.
NECTARINES	Orange-yellow (not green) background color between areas of red. Ripe nectarines feel slightly soft with gentle handling, but not as soft as ripe peaches.
ORANGES	Firm, thin-skinned, and bright-colored. Avoid fruit with any hint of softness or whitish mold at the ends.
PAPAYAS	Soft like a peach and has more yellow than green in the skin. Most must be ripened further at home in a loosely closed paper bag at room temperature. Avoid bruised or shriveled fruit showing any signs of mold or deterioration.
PEACHES	Creamy or yellow background color. Ripe peaches feel slightly soft with gentle handling. Avoid green, extra-hard, or bruised fruit.
PEARS	Firm. Pears gradually ripen after picking. When the stem end yield to gentle pressure, it's ready to eat.
PINEAPPLES	Plump with dark-green leaves, heavy for size, and a sweet smell. Avoid fruit with soft or dark spots, areas of decay, or fermented odor, or with dry leaves.
PLANTAINS	Firm when green, yields to gentle pressure when yellow, and slightly soft and black when ripe. Avoid fruit that is moldy or cracked.

Freshness: How to . . . Judge Produce *(continued)*

PLUMS	Plump, smooth skins. Ripe plums are slightly soft at the tip end and feel somewhat soft with gentle handling. Avoid fruit soft spots, bruises, or shriveled skin.
POMEGRANATE	Plump, round, and heavy for its size. Avoid fruit that is shriveled.
RASPBERRIES AND BLACKBERRIES	Firm, plump, and well shaped. If soft or discolored, they are overripe. Avoid containers that look stained from overripe berries or have signs of mold.
STRAWBERRIES	Firm, shiny, and bright red colored, with fresh, green, and intact cap. Avoid leaky, mushy, or shriveled berries. Check the carton to avoid signs of mold.
WATERMELONS	Heavy for its size, well shaped, and with rind and flesh colors characteristic of the variety. Ripe melons are fragrant and slightly soft at the blossom end. A melon that sloshes when shaken may be overripe. Stem should be dry and brown, not green. When thumped, you should hear a low-pitched sound, indicating a full, juicy interior.
FOR VEGETABLES . . .	
ARTICHOKES	Tight, compact heads that feel heavy for their size. Surface brown spots don't affect quality.
ASPARAGUS	Firm, brittle spears that are bright green almost their entire length, with tightly closed tips.
BEANS (GREEN OR WAX)	Slender, crisp, bright-colored, and blemish free. Avoid mature beans with large seeds and swollen pods.
BEETS	Small to medium size, firm, and smooth-skinned, with fresh-looking, deep-green leaves.
BELL PEPPERS	Bright-colored, glossy, firm, and well shaped. Avoid peppers with soft spots or gashes.
BOK CHOY	Heads with bright-white stalks and glossy dark leaves. Avoid heads with slippery brown spots on the leaves.
BROCCOLI	Compact clusters of tightly closed, dark-green florets. Avoid heads with yellow florets or thick, woody stems.
BRUSSELS SPROUTS	Firm, compact, fresh-looking, bright-green, and heavy for their size.
CABBAGE	Firm heads that feel heavy for their size and outer leaves that have good color and are blemish free.
CARROTS	Firm, clean, and well shaped with bright, orange-gold color. Carrots with their tops still attached are likely to be freshest.
CAULIFLOWER	Firm, compact, creamy-white heads with florets pressed tightly together, and crisp, bright-green leaves. A yellow tinge and spreading florets indicate over-maturity. Avoid heads with brown spots.
CELERY	Crisp, rigid, green stalks with fresh-looking leaves. Avoid celery with limp stalks.
CELERY ROOT (CELERIAC)	Small and firm, with few knobs and rootlets. Avoid those with soft spots.
CORN	Fresh-looking ears with green husks, moist stems, and silk ends free of decay or worm injury. When pierced with a thumbnail, kernels should squirt some juice. Tough husks indicate over-maturity.
CUCUMBERS	Firm, dark-green, and slender but well shaped. Soft or yellow cukes are over-mature.
DAIKON (ASIAN RADISH)	Firm and not wrinkled.
EDAMAME (IMMATURE SOYBEANS IN THE POD)	Tender, bright-green pods with no yellowing.
EGGPLANTS	Firm, heavy for their size, with taut, glossy, deeply colored skin and bright-green stems.
FENNEL	Fragrant, celerylike stalks with a bulbous base and feathery leaves.

(continued)

Freshness: How to . . . Judge Produce *(continued)*

GREENS	Fresh, tender, blemish-free leaves. Avoid bunches with thick, coarse-veined leaves.
JICAMA	Firm, well-formed tubers free of blemishes. Size does not affect flavor, but larger roots do tend to have a coarse texture.
KALE	Dark-green, with small to medium leaves. Avoid kale with brown or yellow leaves.
KOHLRABI	Young, tender bulbs with fresh green leaves. Avoid bulbs with scars and blemishes. The smaller the bulb, the more delicate the flavor and texture.
LEAF LETTUCE	Crisp leaves. Avoid dark edges.
LEEKS AND GREEN ONIONS	Clean, white bottoms and crisp, fresh-looking bright-green tops.
MUSHROOMS	Blemish-free mushrooms without slimy spots or signs of decay.
OKRA	Small to medium pods that are deep green and free of blemishes. Pods should snap or puncture easily with slight pressure.
ONIONS	Firm and dry with brittle outer skin. Avoid onions with sprouting green shoots or dark spots.
PARSNIPS	Small to medium, firm, smooth, and well shaped. Avoid large roots because they may have a woody core.
PEAS	Small, plump, bright-green pods that are firm, crisp, and well filled.
POTATOES	Firm, smooth, with no wrinkles, sprouts, cracks, bruises, decay, or bitter-green areas (caused by exposure to light).
RUTABAGAS	Small to medium, firm, smooth, and heavy for their size.
SNOW PEAS	Shiny, flat with small peas barely visible through the thin pod.
SPINACH	Fresh, crisp, green, with no signs of insect damage.
SUGAR SNAP PEAS	Bright green, firm, and free of blemishes.
SUMMER (YELLOW) SQUASH	Firm, smooth, glossy, tender skin, small to medium size, heavy for their size. Avoid any with cuts and bruises.
SWEET POTATOES AND YAMS	Firm, well shaped, with bright, uniformly colored skin.
TOMATOES	Firm but not hard, smooth, well formed, and bright-shiny skin.
TURNIPS	Firm, smooth, small to medium size, and heavy for their size.
WINTER SQUASH	Hard, thick-shelled.
ZUCCHINI	Shiny, firm with slightly prickly skin. Avoid any with cuts and bruises.

2. For fruits, consider ripeness. Some fruits—for example, bananas, apples, mangoes, and pears—continue to ripen after picking and get sweeter as their starches convert to sugar. Avocados only ripen after picking. Apricots, blueberries, cantaloupe, honeydew, nectarines, and peaches don't get sweeter, but their juiciness, texture, and color ripen after picking.

   If you plan to eat them today, buy ripe fruit! *Tip:* To hasten ripening, put fruit in a loosely closed paper bag at room temperature. Putting an apple or a banana in the bag, too, speeds the process because they give off ethylene gas, which is a ripening agent. Check to make sure they're not left in the bag too long to get overripe. Many other fruits—soft berries, cherries, citrus, grapes, pineapples, and watermelon—won't ripen further after picking.
3. Buy only the amount you need since they're perishable. Produce at peak quality contains the most nutrients.
4. Look for signs of quality—not beauty. Bruised or wilted produce suggests improper handling or produce that's past its peak. Some nutrients may be lost as a result. *See "Freshness: How to . . . Judge Produce" in this chapter, page 160.*

Click Here! Links to Know . . .

- Local Food Directories: National Farmers Market Directory www.ams.usda.gov/local-food-directories/farmersmarkets
- Produce for Better Health Foundation (selection, storage, and nutrition of fruits and vegetables) www.fruitsandveggiesmorematters.org/vegetable-nutrition-database www.fruitsandveggiesmorematters.org/fruit-nutrition-database
- Produce for Better Health Foundation, What's in Season? www.fruitsandveggiesmorematters.org/what-fruits-and-vegetables-are-in-season

5. Handle produce gently. (Don't squeeze to check for ripeness.) Damage and bruising hasten spoilage. Place produce in the shopping cart where it won't get bruised. At checkout, pack it on top or in separate bags.

6. Choose a colorful variety of vegetables and fruits. Rather than just the old standbys, buy a new vegetable or fruit each week or two; try some that are locally grown. *See "Vegetables: Have You Tried These?" and "Fruit: What's New to You?" in chapter 2, pages 36 and 39.*

Explore different varieties of a familiar food. For example, try different apples such as Cortland, Granny Smith, Newtown Pippin, and Rome Beauty. Or choose one of each variety of plums such as Laroda, Queen Ann, Santa Rosa, and Wickson.

7. For flavor, buy small fruit. They often are sweeter than larger versions of the same fruit. Look for tender mini-vegetables, too: for example baby artichokes, bok choy, Brussel sprouts, and potatoes. (While there are mini carrots, the "baby carrots" commonly sold in the supermarket are baby-cut carrots, or cut from slim, tender carrots.)

8. Look for nutrition information. Packaged produce may carry Nutrition Facts, but if not available, check for a nearby poster or pamphlet. Ask the store manager to provide this information otherwise. Check for preparation and handling tips for unfamiliar produce.

Have you ever wondered?

. . . if misshapen, or "ugly," vegetables or fruits are less nourishing? Picking the best produce isn't a beauty contest. In fact, rescuing "ugly fruit" has become a consumer movement!

Misshapen apples, tomatoes, and other produce with normal bumps and blemishes are as delicious and nutritious as those that are perfectly shaped. Yet, being flawed, too big or too small, they often go to a landfill. If you see "cosmetically challenged" produce, buy it as a way to cut food waste and likely save money, too. If you plan to cut, shred, or cook them, looks don't matter anyway.

. . . what heirloom vegetables, fruits, and grains are? Heirlooms are grown from open-pollinated (without human intervention) seed varieties, typically grown for at least fifty years. They're often considered "Old World breeds" with distinct flavors and traits common before more recent growing and breeding practices. The unique genetics of many heirloom varietals often make them naturally resistant to certain pests and diseases. As a result, they are great gene banks for agriculture. They are sometimes considered to be especially flavorful, and farmers' markets and specialty stores often sell them.

If you're a gardener, try growing less-common and heirloom varietals of vegetables and fruits. Examples include pinkish-red Brandywine tomatoes (Amish), purple-striped Cherokee Trail of Tears pole beans (Native American), and sweet, lime-green Jenny Lind melons.

Heritage grains, often fiber rich with unique baking or cooking qualities, are finding their way back into breads as well as grain based dishes. Consider amaranth, emmer, and millet.

As an aside, it's not just plant-based foods that are being reintroduced. Heritage breeds of livestock and poultry are being conserved to help retain biodiversity in animal agriculture. You may even find heirloom ingredients in popcorn, rice, tea, and other packaged foods.

. . . how Community Supported Agriculture (CSA) works? CSAs provide a way to buy local, seasonal vegetables and fruits directly from farmers—often at a more affordable price. Farmers sell a set number of shares, or memberships, to customers. The shares usually provide a container or containers of vegetables or other seasonal farm products on a weekly or biweekly schedule during the growing season, depending on growing conditions. CSAs provide a market for local farmers, and both raw products and a farm connection for consumers. To find one near you, visit www.localharvest.org.

9. For convenience, choose ready-to-eat/use vegetables and fruits: prewashed bags of salad greens, sliced stir-fry veggies, precut fruits, and packaged baby carrots and celery sticks. Choose packaged, sliced fruits, such as melon and pineapple, without added sugars. For precut fruits, make sure they're refrigerated or displayed on chipped ice.
10. For cost saving, buy unpackaged produce. You can buy just what you need and pick items at their peak of quality.
11. Look for fresh herbs in the produce department. Choose fresh herbs that look fresh, not wilted. They're sometimes found growing in a pot! Sun-dried tomatoes are sometimes displayed with the herbs. *See "Storing Herbs and Spices" in chapter 8, page 269.*
12. Another option: Dried fruits. Often sold in the produce department, dried fruits are relatively nonperishable. They supply the same nutrients as fresh fruits. If you're sensitive to sulfites, check the label; sulfites are used to prevent browning in many dried fruits.

MEAT COUNTER

Shopping for health at the meat counter starts by recognizing quality and freshness, and then making most meat choices lean. For example:

- For freshness, check the color. Choose beef that is bright cherry red, unless it has been cured or cooked. Beef that's vacuum-packaged might have a darker purplish-red color, which will get brighter when exposed to oxygen. Both young veal and pork are reddish-pink and firm. Older veal is darker pink. Lamb can be light to darker pink, depending on the animal feed eaten.
- Check the date on meat. Only buy fresh and processed meats that still will be fresh when you're ready to eat them. Or plan to freeze meat immediately for later use.
- Check the Safe Handling Instructions label. A sample label is shown in this chapter, page 152. *See "Safe Food from the Start" in chapter 7, page 208, for more about handling meat safely.*

If you need help, ask the butcher, who may also trim, bone, or slice meat to your specifications.

Meat: Buying Tips

Through advanced breeding and feeding practices, today's livestock is leaner than ever. Newer meat cuts and closer trimming of beef, veal, pork, and lamb also make more lean cuts available. *See "Today's Leaner Meat" in chapter 5, page 120.* For good health: make most choices lean.

1. Know meat's lean cuts. Look for "round" or "loin" in the name when shopping for beef, and "loin" or "leg" when buying pork or lamb.
   - *Beef:* eye of round, top round steak, top round roast, sirloin steak, top loin steak, tenderloin steak, flank steak, and chuck arm pot roast
   - *Veal:* cutlet, blade or arm steak, rib roast, and rib or loin chop
   - *Pork:* tenderloin, New York pork chop (top loin chop), Porterhouse pork chop (loin chop), bone-in chop (rib chop center), sirloin roast, rib-eye pork chop (rib chop), and shoulder blade steak
   - *Lamb:* loin chop, rib or rack, arm chop, and shoulder blade

   Unsure of the cut? Check the meat label. It identifies the kind and cut, along with the net weight, unit price, and cost per package. Or ask the butcher. *See "Meat, Poultry, Fish: Keep Lean" in chapter 8, page 254, for more about preparing leaner cuts of meat.*

2. Choose leaner grades. "Select" grades of beef are the leanest meaning they have the least marbled fat (or thin streaks of fat between the muscle), followed by "choice" grades with more marbling, and then finally "prime" grades, which have the most marbling. Veal and lamb use the same grading system; however, the term "good" is used instead of "select." Grading, determined by the USDA, is based on fat content, appearance, texture, and the age of the animal. Pork is not graded.

More costly prime grades of beef—more often found on restaurant menus than sold in supermarkets—have webs of finely marbled fat, which helps make the meat juicy and flavorful. With

Meat Buying Guide

How much raw meat should you buy? For about 3 ounces of cooked, lean meat per person, you'll need approximately 4 ounces of raw meat per person. For some meats, you'll need to take the amount of bone and fat into account.

Type of Meat	Servings per Pound*
Boneless or ground meat	4
Meat with a minimum amount of bone (steaks, roasts, chops, etc.)	2 to 3
Meat with a large amount of bone (shoulder cuts, short ribs, neck, etc.)	1 to 2

*Three ounces of cooked, trimmed meat equal one serving.

the right method of cooking, such as stewing and braising, and of carving, leaner "select" and "choice" meats can be tender, juicy, and flavorful, too. Nutritionally speaking, nutrients in meat—protein, thiamin, niacin, iron, and zinc, among others—are the same, regardless of grade.

3. Buy well-trimmed meat: one-eighth-inch fat trim or less. "Trim" refers to the fat layer surrounding a steak, roast, or other cut of meat. *Note:* Marbled fat cannot be trimmed away. Only cooking removes some, but not all, marbled fat when it melts out of the meat.

4. Check the "numbers" for ground meat—look for packages that have the highest ratio of lean meat to fat stated as a percentage. Ground beef labeled as 95 percent lean also may include the nutrition description "Lean" because it meets the definition of a lean product. *Note:* "Percent lean" refers to the weight of the lean meat in relation to the weight of the fat. For example, 80 percent lean ground beef has 20 percent fat, while 95 percent lean ground beef has 5 percent fat.

5. Look for nutrition information for fresh meat as well as poultry. Nutrition Facts are required for single-ingredient raw meat and poultry on packages or point-of-purchase signs. This labeling can help you compare different meat and poultry cuts and ground products. The Nutrition Facts are based on a label serving of 4 ounces (not the whole package) of raw meat or poultry as packaged—and not as cooked or eaten. Nutrition Facts don't account for what happens in your food prep, such as removing poultry skin or draining away fat drippings.

6. Use Nutrition Facts to find lean packaged meats: deli meats, hot dogs, luncheon meats, and sausages that are leaner and have less sodium. For ready-to-slice luncheon meats from the deli counter, ask for nutrition information if you're unsure of its leanness. Some lean products will be identified with a nutrient content claim such as "low-fat," "% fat-free," or "lean."

What about jerky? It's lean meat (often beef or bison) that's trimmed to remove fat, cut into thin strips, and then dried, usually with salt and at a low temperature. This removes moisture and prevents spoilage from bacterial growth. While jerky makes a flavorful protein snack to pack and carry, it also contains a significant amount of sodium. Some recipes also use sugar. You may also find jerky made from fish such as salmon, as well as turkey. Kept dry, jerky needs no refrigeration.

7. Buy enough meat without overdoing portion sizes. For moderate-size portions (3 ounces cooked), figure 4 ounces of uncooked, boneless meat per person. *The "Meat Buying Guide" on page 164 will help you determine how much meat to buy.*

8. For bacon, compare the nutrition slice to slice. There are many choices when it comes to bacon: traditional, Canadian, turkey, and center cut (tends to be meaty) bacon. Canadian bacon is lean, much like ham. In contrast, traditional bacon is mainly fat and not a lean protein food; nearly 70 percent of its calories come from fat, and about half of that is saturated. No matter what kind, bacon delivers a lot of sodium, too; check the label.

9. If you eat organ meats, called variety meats, buy them only occasionally: brain, chitterlings (pig intestines), heart, kidney, liver, sweetbreads (thymus gland), tongue, and tripe (stomach lining of cattle). Organ meats are good sources of many nutrients; liver especially is high in iron. Most are higher in cholesterol than lean meat. Some such as chitterlings, sweetbreads, and tongue have more fat.

10. For convenience, look for meat that's already seasoned, prepared, and ready to cook, such as meat and vegetable kabobs or marinated pork loin. Be aware: Precooked, packaged heat-and-eat meats in the refrigerated case may be higher in sodium. Check the Nutrition Facts.

POULTRY COUNTER

Besides being economical, chicken and turkey offer high-quality protein, and they're generally lean. For cost savings, it's usually best to buy a whole bird and carve it yourself.

Recognize the qualities of fresh poultry. Look for meaty birds with skin that's creamy-white to yellow and that are free of bruises, tiny feathers, and torn or dry skin. Check for product dating on food labels.

Reading Meat Labels

1. The kind of meat—Listed on every label
2. The primal (wholesale) cut—Tells where the meat came from on the animal
3. The retail cut—Tells which part of the primal cut the meat came from

Have you ever wondered?

. . . what is meant by "grass-fed" beef? The FDA standard is that animals have been fed fresh grass throughout life, but that doesn't mean free-roaming or pasture-raised livestock.

Certification from the American Grassfed Association is stricter, meaning that meat comes from livestock grazed in pastures their whole lives. It generally grades as "Select" meat. Conventional beef cattle graze most of their lives in the pasture, too, but they're "finished" on a balanced, grain-based diet in a feed lot. Grass-fed meat isn't necessarily organic. Be aware that in some parts of the country, winter conditions keep cattle from grazing on pasture year 'round.

. . . what milk-fed veal is? It's a USDA classification, for veal meat, a creamy white to pale pink meat, from calves produced by the dairy industry. They are fed a nutrient-rich milk formula or milk replacer typically made from whey and whey protein. Both are by-products of cheese making. Most farmers also feed some grain and forages. (Forage is grass, hay, and other bulky feed for cattle and horses.) Veal calves are raised to about 475 to 500 pounds (about five months) before slaughter.

. . . if free-range chicken has less fat? It's a common misperception that free-range chickens—those that "roam the barnyard and forage for food"—are always leaner than chickens raised in coops. Whether raised in a coop or a barnyard, their exercise level often is about the same. Genetic stock, age, and growth rate have more influence on fat levels. Older, larger chickens and those that grow faster tend to have more fat—no matter how they're raised.

According to the USDA's Food Safety and Inspection Service, which regulates poultry labeling, the terms "free-range" and "free-roaming" may be used on poultry labels if the producers can demonstrate that the poultry has been allowed access to the outside for a significant portion of their lives. Free-range chickens usually cost more; blind taste tests haven't shown significant differences in flavor perception.

While free-range chickens are raised outdoors or have daily outdoor access, in reality, most stay indoors. Because free-range chickens may be exposed to outdoor pollutants, food-safety questions have been raised. Cage-free chickens aren't caged but may not have outdoor access. Mortality rates of these chickens are higher since they tend to peck at and injure each other.

. . . about the difference between a hen turkey and a tom turkey? It's just gender. A "hen" is female and a "tom" is male. It suggests size, not tenderness.

Poultry: Buying Tips

1. Choose mostly lean varieties of poultry—turkey and chicken. Pheasant and quail, especially without the skin, are lean, too. Domesticated duck and goose are higher in fat. A 3½-ounce cooked portion of roasted, skinless chicken (light and dark meat) has about 7 fat grams. Compare that with 11 fat grams in the same portion of roasted, skinless duck.
2. Shop for skinless poultry—chicken and turkey. Compared to skin-on poultry, the grams of total fat and saturated fat are cut in half. Or buy skin-on poultry if it costs less, and remove the skin before or after cooking it.
3. For less total fat and saturated fat, choose light meat turkey or chicken breast. Compare: 3 ounces of roasted, skinless, dark-meat (thigh) chicken have about 170 calories, 9 grams of total fat, and 3 grams of saturated fat; the same amount of roasted, skinless, light-meat (breast) chicken has about 140 calories, 3 grams of total fat, and 1 gram of saturated fat. Dark meat, however, has a somewhat richer flavor, which you may prefer.
4. When you buy whole turkey or chicken, know that self-basting varieties are higher in fat and sodium. "Basted" or

Poultry Buying Guide

How much poultry? Here's how many servings come from 1 pound of uncooked chicken, duck, goose, game hens, or turkey.

Poultry	Servings per Pound*
Chicken, whole (broiler-fryer or roaster)	2
Boneless chicken breast	4
Duck, whole	1
Goose, whole	1½ to 2
Rock Cornish game hen, whole	1
Turkey, whole, bone in	2
Boneless turkey roast	3
Ground turkey	4

*Amounts are based on three ounces of cooked poultry without bone per serving.

"self-basting," they're moist and flavorful because they're injected or marinated with a solution of butter or another fat, broth, stock or water plus spices, flavor enhancers, and perhaps other ingredients.

Instead, baste it yourself with broth, juice, or juices from the poultry. *Hint:* Roasting any whole bird with the breast side up makes it more moist.

5. If ground meat is on your shopping list, try lean ground turkey breast. Ground turkey or chicken can be as lean as 99 percent fat-free. The fat content is higher if ground with dark meat and skin—sometimes even higher than for ground lean sirloin.
6. Read the Nutrition Facts before you buy turkey dogs, turkey ham, or turkey bologna. They may—or may not—be low in fat. Compare the sodium content with that of traditional processed meats; processing typically adds sodium. For fresh cuts of meats and poultry, look for the Nutrition Facts, which may be posted on the package or in the retail case.
7. Check the Nutrition Facts for sodium content. Uncooked poultry may be plumped, or injected with a saltwater solution, to keep in moisture, flavor, and tenderness.
8. Buy enough poultry for moderate portions. *The "Poultry Buying Guide" in this chapter on page 166 will help you determine how much to buy for a cooked 3-ounce portion per person.*
9. For food safety, don't buy fresh, pre-stuffed poultry.

FISH COUNTER

Fifty to a hundred varieties of fish are commonly on the market today. Barramundi, bass, catfish, cod, flounder, sardines, haddock, herring, mahi mahi, monkfish, salmon, snapper, tilapia, tuna, and trout are among the many types of finfish. Shellfish are both crustaceans (crab, crayfish, lobster, and shrimp) and mollusks (abalone, clam, conch, mussel, octopus, oyster, scallop, snail, and squid).

Much of this fish is wild, coming from oceans and freshwater lakes, ponds, and rivers. As the demand for fish grows, aquaculture, or fish farming, has become an important source for fish, especially for barramundi (Asian sea bass), bass, catfish, salmon, shrimp, tilapia, and trout, as well as clams, mussels, oysters, and scallops. *See "Have you ever wondered . . . about aquaculture and its role in food production?" in chapter 5, page 119.*

How do you know what fish to buy?

- Know what form you need: finfish—fillets, steaks, whole fish, or dressed (head, tail, and fins removed), or shellfish—whole live or just "meat."
- Choose what's best for the recipe. Lean fish is great for baking, microwaving, and poaching. Fish with more fat tends to be better for grilling and roasting because it doesn't dry out as quickly and holds its shape better. For example, the firmer, fattier, steak-like texture of salmon and tuna are better for kabobs or grilled fish steaks. Mild-flavored fish, such as barramundi, cod, flounder, haddock, snapper, sole, and tilapia, tends to be the lowest in fat and so has a more flake-like texture.
- Substitute one fish for another. When the store doesn't have the fish you want or if it costs more than you anticipate, switch the type of fish. Sometimes lesser-known or underused species such as mackerel and whiting cost less. For example, when a recipe calls for flounder, almost any mild finfish (perhaps haddock, halibut, or perch) can take its place.

Fish: Buying Tips for Freshness

Learn to choose high-quality, safe, and fresh fish that also matches your personal needs and preferences.

1. Check the fish counter. Always buy fresh or frozen fish from a reputable source. Fresh fish should be displayed for food safety: properly iced, well refrigerated, and in clean display cases. To reduce the chance of spoilage, fish should be displayed "belly down" so that melting ice drains away beneath it.

   Check for general fish-counter cleanliness: clean look and smell; free of insects; employees wearing disposable gloves (changed after handling nonfood and again after handling raw fish); and knowledgeable workers who can answer your questions about the freshness and qualities of the fish. Ask when and how often fresh and flash-frozen fish come in. Be flexible; buy the freshest fish if you don't need a specific type.
2. *Fresh fish.* Give fish a sniff test. For all fish—finfish and shellfish—a strong "fishy" odor is a sign that the fish is no longer fresh. Fresh, raw shrimp will have a mild odor. Look for these qualities:
   - *Finfish.* At peak quality, whole finfish have a fresh, ocean-breeze scent, not a fishy or ammonialike smell. They're naturally firm to the touch, with stiff fins and scales that cling tightly to the skin. The skin is shiny and "metallic," not dull. The gills are pink or bright red and free from mucus or slime. If undamaged, their eyes are clear, bright, and protruding. Walleyes are among the few fish with naturally cloudy eyes. Fish fillets or steaks also have a mild scent, firm and moist flesh, a translucent appearance, and no browning around the edges. If the fish is wrapped, packaging should be tight and undamaged.
   - *Crustacean shellfish.* These are sold live. In fact, unless frozen, canned, or cooked, crabs, crayfish, and lobsters should be alive when you buy them. They'll move slightly if they're alive, and live lobsters curl their tails a bit when handled. For food safety, buy from a reputable source.
   - *Mollusks.* If their shells are still on, clams, mussels, and oysters must be sold alive, too. For the sake of safety, the shells

shouldn't be damaged. When the mollusks are alive, their shells are slightly open but close tightly when tapped. As another test, hold the shell between your thumb and forefinger and press so that one part of the shell slides across the other. If the shells move, the mollusk is not alive. Ask to see the tag on the bag of mollusks; it's best if the shellfish were purchased within five days of harvest. They should be displayed nestled in ice that can drain away from them so that they never stand in water.

Freshly shucked mollusks (shells removed) have a mild, fresh scent. A somewhat clear liquid, not too milky or cloudy, should cover shucked "meat."

Scallops are removed from their shells at sea. They vary in size and color, from creamy white to light orange, tan, or somewhat pinkish. When fresh, they're not dry or dark around the edges.

Squid (calamari) sold fresh should be small and whole with clear eyes and an ocean-fresh aroma.

3. *Frozen fish.* Frozen fish should be solidly frozen, mild in odor, and free of ice crystals and freezer burn. Freezer burn is indicated by drying and discoloration. The package shouldn't be damaged or water stained, and it should be stored below the frost line in the store's display freezer. These qualities apply to frozen fish as well as to frozen prepared items such as crab cakes and breaded shrimp.

   Note: "Previously frozen" (thawed for sale) fish—harvested and frozen in remote locations—may be superior in quality to fresh fish that's been transported for several days.

   Check the product dating on the label of frozen fish. Choose packaged fish that doesn't show signs of thawing and refreezing. Check the "sell by" date, if it has one. *See "A Closer Look . . . Deciphering Package Dates, Reducing Food Waste" in this chapter, page 153.*

4. *Cooked fish.* Look for cooked crabs, crayfish, lobsters, and shrimp that are moist with a mild odor and a characteristic color. When cooked, the shells of cooked shrimp should be pink to reddish. For other crustaceans, the shells should be bright red. Some stores cook them for you.

   For food safety, don't buy cooked fish that's displayed alongside raw fish. Bacteria from raw fish can contaminate cooked fish, creating a potential for foodborne illness.

5. *Smoked fish.* Look for fish such as smoked salmon or smoked trout that is bright, glossy, and free of mold. Since it may not be cooked before serving, smoked fish should be wrapped and kept away from raw fish to avoid cross-contamination. Smoked fish often has more sodium.

? Have you ever wondered?

. . . how the fat and cholesterol in surimi compares with crabmeat? Surimi is imitation crabmeat, made from pollock or another mild-flavored fish. The fish is processed by rolling out "sheets" of fish and adding color so it looks like crab legs. The nutrient content reflects the fish it's made from. Surimi is comparable in fat content but lower in cholesterol than crabmeat.

. . . what eco-labeling on seafood means? You might see a blue label from the Marine Stewardship Council (www.msc.org), indicating that the wild-caught seafood comes from fisheries that meet strict standards for sustainability, consistent with the United Nations' best practice guidelines.

Fish: More Buying Tips

Besides being a good protein source, most fish such as cod, grouper, and haddock is low in fat, especially saturated fat. Oily fish such as salmon offers potential health benefits from omega-3 fatty acids. *See "Common Foods: How Much Omega-3s and Total Fat?" in chapter 13, page 401.*

1. Buy a variety of fish to get their range of nutrients. Check the Nutrition Facts on packaged products or, for fresh fish, displayed nearby.

2. Recognize the fat content of various fish. In general, most fish has less fat than many other protein-rich foods, including meat and poultry with skin. And most fat in fish is polyunsaturated.

   Oily fish that is firm and darker in color, such as king mackerel, salmon, and tuna, tends to have more fat and omega-3 fatty acids; omega-3s may offer heart-healthy benefits. Try to eat fish, including oily fish, at least twice a week.

3. Be aware of differences when you substitute one fish for another. If you need to watch cholesterol, lobsters, shrimp, and squid, for example, have more than clams, crabs, mussels, and scallops. Three ounces of boiled shrimp supply about 165 milligrams of cholesterol; the same amount of scallops has about 55 milligrams.

4. Go easy on breaded items such as shrimp and fish sticks. The breading often contains more calories and fat.

5. Buy only the amount of fish you need. Because of waste, you need more when preparing whole or dressed fish. A dressed fish has the head, tail, and fins removed. Fish steaks, fillets, and shellfish have less waste but usually cost more per pound. Without the waste, the price may equal out. *The "Fish Buying Guide" in this chapter on page 169 will help you estimate how much to buy for a cooked 3-ounce portion per person.*

Fish Buying Guide

How much fish? Here's approximately how much you will need to buy for a single portion of cooked fish per person.

Type of Fish	Approximate Amount of Raw Fish Needed per Adult Serving*
Whole fish	¾ pound
Dressed or pan-dressed fish	½ pound
Fish fillets	¼ to ⅓ pound
Fish steaks with bone	½ pound
Fish steaks without bone	⅓ pound
Live clams and oysters	6 to 8
Shucked clams and oysters	⅓ to ½ pint
Live lobsters or crabs	1 to 1½ pounds
Cooked lobster or crabmeat	¼ to ⅓ pound
Scallops	¼ to ⅓ pound
Shrimp, headless and unpeeled	⅓ to ½ pound
Shrimp, peeled and deveined	¼ to ⅓ pound

*The smaller amounts in the ranges shown provide a cooked portion that is approximately 3 ounces when prepared by most common cooking methods.

Source: New York Seafood Council, 2010.

REFRIGERATED CASE

Although you'll find tortillas, refrigerator rolls, and biscuits among the many products in the refrigerated case, dairy foods, eggs, and juice are prominent.

Dairy Foods: Buying Tips

Milk. Which milk for you? Because milk solids make up at least 8.25 percent for each type of milk, their protein, vitamin, and mineral content is about the same. Eight ounces is an excellent source of calcium, vitamin D, riboflavin, vitamin B_{12}, and phosphorus, and a good source of protein, vitamin A, niacin, and potassium. (Milk solids are the part of milk that's neither milk fat nor water; percentages of milk fat are percent by weight, not by calories.)

1. Consider milk's calorie and fat content, using the Nutrition Facts. Choose mostly fat-free and low-fat milks. Almost all milk in the U.S. is fortified voluntarily with vitamin D. *See "Milk: A Great Calcium and Vitamin D Source" in chapter 4, page 93, to see how different milks compare.*
   - *Whole milk* has no less than 3.25 percent milk fat
   - *2% reduced-fat milk* has 2 percent milk fat; is vitamin A–fortified
   - *1% low-fat milk (or light milk)* has 1 percent milk fat; is vitamin A—and D–fortified
   - *Fat-free (or nonfat or skim milk)* has less than 0.5 percent milk fat; is vitamin A–fortified
2. Look for *flavored milk* (added chocolate, cocoa, or fruit flavoring, and sweetener) with added vitamin D. You can find whole, 2 percent reduced-fat, 1 percent low-fat, or fat-free options.
3. Lactose-sensitive? Buy *lactose-reduced or lactose-free milk* (whole, low-fat, or fat-free). To be "lactose-reduced," lactose must be reduced by 70 percent. Lactose-free milk is 100 percent lactose-reduced. The lactase enzyme, added to milk, "predigests" lactose (naturally occurring sugar in milk), so you can enjoy milk without discomfort. Because lactose converts to simple sugars (glucose and galactose), this milk tastes slightly sweeter. *See "Lactose Intolerance: A Matter of Degree" in chapter 23, page 666, for more about lactose intolerance and malabsorption.*
4. Use Nutrition Facts to compare various *nutrient-enhanced milks* and those with added health benefits.
   - *Protein-fortified milk* has added nonfat milk solids and perhaps thickeners. Enhancing fat-free or low-fat milk with milk solids adds a fuller flavor, a creamier consistency, and more protein and calcium.
   - *Skim deluxe or skim supreme milk* is fat-free but has the mouth feel (from some added fiber) of 2 percent reduced-fat milk.
   - *Milk with functional benefits* may be enhanced with omega-3 fatty acids or with plant stanols or sterols to help reduce heart disease risk, or with probiotics for gut health. Other enhanced milks might have added DHA, a form of omega 3s, which may promote vision and the health of the nervous system.
5. Enjoy *acidophilus milk* and *kefir* (a yogurt drink). They're made by adding "friendly" bacteria cultures to dairy products—often to fat-free or low-fat milk. The bacteria culture produces their unique flavor, aroma, and acidity, as well as gives it a thick texture. Salt may be added for flavor. Live, active "friendly" bacteria work as probiotics in fermented dairy foods and may help improve digestion and promote healthy bacteria in the gastrointestinal tract. The probiotic benefits are specific to the bacterial strain. *See "Prebiotics and Probiotics: A Bioactive Duo" in chapter 15, page 453, for more about probiotics.*
6. Enjoy tangy, cultured *buttermilk* as another great source of calcium. It, too, is made with the action of "friendly" bacteria cultures but doesn't have probiotic benefits from live cultures. Despite its name, butter isn't added to cultured buttermilk. Sweet cream buttermilk is the by-product of churning cream into butter, but it's not available in stores.

? Have you ever wondered?

. . . why cottage cheese has less calcium than other cheese? During processing, the whey is drained away, along with 50 to 75 percent of the calcium. Check food labels for cottage cheese processed with extra calcium. Good news: Cottage cheese still provides plenty of protein and riboflavin, without much fat.

. . . what labneh (labna) is? It's yogurt cheese, sold in some Middle Eastern and Central Asian stores and some specialty food stores. Can't find it in the store? You can make this nutrient-rich spread by straining yogurt or Greek-style yogurt to the consistency of cream cheese. *See "Kitchen Nutrition: Greek Yogurt Blends—or Add-ins?" in chapter 13, page 402.*

. . . how skyr compares to regular yogurt? Skyr is an Icelandic-style yogurt, typically made from fat-free milk. It is thick and creamy like Greek yogurt with a milder, tangy flavor. Unlike regular yogurt, it's strained to remove whey, so skyr is more concentrated, higher in protein, and a bit lower in calcium than regular yogurt. (Greek yogurt is also strained.) Strained yogurt also has less lactose than regular yogurt. Look for "live and active cultures" on the label for probiotic benefits.

. . . where buttermilk got its name? The term "buttermilk" sounds like a misnomer. Its name refers to the way buttermilk was first made—from the whey, or liquid, left after butter was churned from cream. Today, most buttermilk is made from fat-free or low-fat milk.

7. *Organic milk?* It must comply with organic standards, *as explained in "Organic Labeling" in this chapter, page 153, and in "Organic Farming" in chapter 5, page 122.*
8. Try *eggnog* during the winter holidays. It's a blend of milk, pasteurized eggs, sugar, cream, and flavor ingredients. Or you might prefer eggnog-flavored milk, made with reduced-fat or fat-free milk. Vegans might enjoy soy eggnog.
9. Try *goat's milk* for its strong, tangy-sour flavor—great for smoothies, too.

See "Dairy and Nondairy Beverages" in chapter 4, page 90, for more about dairy drinks.

Yogurt. Flavored or plain . . . whole, low-fat, or nonfat . . . split yogurt cups with mix-ins . . . Greek-style and Icelandic-style, too, which are thicker . . . yogurt is a high-calcium, high-protein dairy food. Made with "friendly" bacteria, it has a tangy taste and thick consistency.

Nutritionally speaking, 8 ounces of yogurt supply about 300 milligrams of calcium, as does 8 ounces of milk. Yogurt's calorie and fat content reflect the milk it's made from. Yogurt may be sweetened with fruit, fruit preserves, honey, or other sugars, or flavored with extracts such as vanilla or coffee. It may contain pectin, found naturally in fruit, or gelatin to make it thicker and creamier; oats or chia seeds for more fiber; or beets or butternut squash for a savory flavor.

1. For fewer calories and/or added sugars, reach for plain fat-free or low-fat yogurt, or perhaps yogurt flavored with a low-calorie sweetener such as aspartame. With plain yogurt, including Greek yogurt, you can add your own flavoring: fruit for sweetness, or even pureed or shredded vegetables for a savory flavor.
2. Look for vitamin D–fortified yogurt, especially if you don't drink milk.
3. For potential health benefits, look for the "Live and Active Cultures" seal from the National Yogurt Association. "Made with active cultures" doesn't mean the cultures are alive; heat from processing may destroy bacteria. The ingredient list shows the probiotic, or live, cultures: often *Lactobacillus acidophilus, L. casei, L. reuteri*, and *Bifidobacterium bifidum (Bifidus). See "Prebiotics and Probiotics: A Bioactive Duo" in chapter 15, page 453, for more about probiotics.*
4. For the thick creaminess (without the high calories and fat) of sour cream, try Greek-style yogurt, plain or flavored. It's made by straining whey from whole, low-fat, or fat-free yogurt, which concentrates the nutrients. Greek yogurt is especially high in protein.
5. Check the carton size—and Nutrition Facts. The smaller (4- or 6-ounce) carton of yogurt isn't a complete calcium swap for 8 ounces of milk.
6. Enjoy flavored yogurt-juice beverages, drinkable yogurt, yogurt shots, or kefir—other sources of calcium and perhaps vitamin D. Ingesting thick, frothy kefir is like drinking yogurt; like flavored yogurt beverages, some are high in added sugars, which will show on new Nutrition Facts labels.
7. Try other yogurts: They may be enhanced nutritionally in other ways—for example, with DHA or with inulin, a prebiotic. Read the label's structure/function claim, the Nutrition Facts, and the ingredient list to learn more. Organic yogurt? Like milk, it must comply with organic standards, *as explained in "Organic Labeling" in this chapter, page 153.*
8. Vary the flavors—great for those who dislike the tangy flavor of plain yogurt. Today's yogurt choices offer more flavor options, with some blended with yogurt and others as mix-ins: fruit, granola, nuts, oats or other grains, peanut butter, vegetables, and even chocolate. Read the Nutrition Facts; check the ingredient list.

Cheese. It's milk in concentrated form—more compact and portable, with a longer shelf life—and with milk's naturally occurring nutrients. Many cheeses have considerably more fat (including saturated fat) per serving than a serving of milk. Some cheeses are vitamin D–fortified.

Cheese of any kind and made from any kind of milk can be considered a minimally processed food. In the United States, most cheeses are made from cow's milk, but it's increasingly easy to find cheeses made from goat's or sheep's milk. Many cheeses are made by coagulating the casein, a milk protein, and then separating the solids and pressing them into their final form.

What accounts for differences in style, texture, and flavor? The type of milk, its origin, its butterfat content, the bacteria or mold used, its processing, its aging time, and any herbs, spices, and perhaps wood smoke for flavoring.

1. Consider the use, flavor, texture, and food-preparation qualities of the cheese when you buy it.
   - *Soft, semisoft, semihard, or hard cheeses.* Their differences reflect their moisture content and aging time. With less moisture, harder cheeses have a longer shelf life. Without preservatives, soft cheeses such as feta and ricotta spoil quickly. Semisoft cheeses such as Muenster and Monterey Jack melt well. Semihard cheeses such as Cheddar and Gouda are great for sandwiches. Very hard cheeses such as Parmesan and Romano are most often grated before using.
   - *Processed cheeses.* These blends of traditional cheeses are shredded, mixed, and heated with emulsifying salts, and perhaps milk, preservatives, and food coloring. They melt well. Some, such as American cheese, are sold presliced.
   - *Veined cheeses.* Either soft or hard, these cheeses, such as blue and Roquefort, get their strong, distinctive flavor from blue or green veins of "friendly" mold in the interior.
   - *Soft-ripened cheeses.* These are firm to start with, but as they age, the centers soften, the flavor gets more intense, and a white edible mold grows on the outside. Three examples: Brie, Camembert, and Mascarpone.
2. Check the Nutrition Facts to compare the calories, fat, sodium, and other nutrients in various cheeses. For example, the fat content of double- and triple-cream soft cheeses is much higher than in hard cheeses.
3. For less fat, including saturated fat, and perhaps fewer calories, look for lower-fat cheeses such as low-fat ricotta, part-skim mozzarella, string cheese, or reduced-fat Cheddar. Made with reduced-fat or fat-free milk, they usually have less fat and fewer calories than other cheeses. Cheese with less fat usually has less cholesterol, too, but check the label if you need to limit cholesterol.
   - *Low-fat cheese* has 3 grams or less fat per serving; that's 1 ounce for most cheeses and 4 ounces for cottage cheese.
   - *Reduced-fat cheese* has 25 percent less fat than the same full-fat cheese.
   - *Fat-free cheese* has less than 0.5 gram of fat per serving.
4. Look for reduced-sodium cheeses to lower sodium intake. Traditional cheeses have sodium, which is a key ingredient in cheese making. *Note:* Reduced-sodium cheese has a shorter shelf life.
5. To savor the flavor but control the fat, use grated, shredded, and sharp-flavored cheeses. When grated, you may use less than sliced or chunk cheese. Grate your own, or buy grated or shredded cheese, which likely costs more per ounce.

   Sharp flavor develops with aging. With sharp cheeses such as sharp Cheddar, Provolone, or Parmesan, you can get more flavor with less cheese.
6. Buy cheese in well-sealed packaging. Check the "use by" or "sell by" dates. Avoid any shredded, crumbled, or sliced cheese with mold; same goes for soft cheeses such as ricotta cheese, cottage cheese, and cream cheese.Make sure there are no cracks on hard or semihard cheese. Mold is used to make some cheeses such as Brie and Camembert; this mold rind is safe to eat—unless you have a mold allergy.

Cream, sour cream, and dairy and non-dairy spreads. Go easy on how much you use of these products. Many are high in calories and fat and contain little calcium, even though they're in the dairy case. The Nutrition Facts are your go-to source to compare calories and saturated and *trans* fats in a label serving.

1. *Cream or sour cream*? Try lower-fat and fat-free products. Other options: half-and-half or fat-free half-and-half instead of coffee cream or heavy cream; and/or fat-free sour cream. An exception: If you need (or want) whipped cream, you'll need heavy or whipping cream to make it.
2. Compare: Both regular *butter* and *stick margarine* contain about 35 calories and 4 grams of total fat per teaspoon. Either way, they're mostly fat. Butter contains cholesterol and more saturated fats than margarine. Made from vegetable oil and used mostly for baking, stick (hard) margarine is cholesterol free and has more poly- and monounsaturated fats than butter; it may be high in *trans* fats. If the ingredient list says "partially hydrogenated vegetable oil," it has *trans* fats.
3. For *spreads,* buy soft tub, liquid, or spray margarines. More common than stick margarine, they have less saturated fat than butter, and all national brands have 0 grams of *trans* fat per serving. The first ingredient is probably liquid vegetable oil or water with no partially hydrogenated vegetable oil.

   Whipped butters or margarines have less fat and fewer calories per tablespoon because air adds volume. They can't be substituted for regular butter or margarine in recipes that require baking or frying; they're fine for melting on veggies or spreading on bread.

   Because reduced-fat butter and margarine have more moisture, they're not suitable in some recipes. As an alternative, look for cholesterol-lowering spreads with plant stanol and sterol esters. *See "Functional Nutrition: Plant Stanols and Sterols" in chapter 13, page 405.* If you like a buttery flavor, try blends of butter and olive or canola oil. They likely have less saturated fat and cholesterol. Read the Nutrition Facts.
4. Enjoy small amounts of *cream cheese*, but don't confuse its nutrient content with other cheeses. Cream cheese is mainly milk fat, with very little milk solids. For a creamy texture with less fat, look for reduced-fat or fat-free cream cheese. Or buy regular cream cheese, and spread a little less on your morning bagel.

Cream: Fat and Calories?

Cream	% Milk Fat Content	Total Fat Grams per Tablespoon	Saturated Fat Grams per Tablespoon	Calories per Tablespoon
Half-and-half	10.5 to 18	2	1	20
Light or coffee cream	18 to 29	3	2	30
Light whipping cream	30 to 36	5	3	44
Heavy cream	36 or more	6	3	52
Cream, whipped in aerosol cans	0.5	1.0	0.5	8

Whipped cream cheese is often easier to spread, so you may be able to use less.

Nondairy alternatives. For vegans and those with milk allergies, look for nondairy alternatives in the dairy case. Their flavor differs from cow's milk products; some are flavored; unsweetened soymilk has a beany flavor. Plant-based beverages may be packaged in aseptic boxes and sold in the grocery aisle, not just the refrigerated case.

Many are made with soy: soymilk, soy yogurt, soy cheese, soy sour cream, soy eggnog, and soy smoothies. Although likely lower in total and saturated fats, and cholesterol free like all plant-based foods, soy foods don't have the same sensory or cooking characteristics as milk products. However, they are good sources of plant-based protein and phytoestrogens—and refreshing drink options. Choose soy drinks that are fortified with calcium and vitamin D. Their nutrient content varies, so read the Nutrition Facts.

If you choose other nondairy alternatives—for example, almond milk, flax milk, hemp milk, rice milk, and others—check the Nutrition Facts on the carton. They don't provide all the nutrients in cow's milk or fortified soymilk. *See "Nondairy Drinks: Soy, Almond, and More" in chapter 4, page 92, for more about nondairy beverage options.*

See "A Closer Look . . . Soy: Protein and More" in chapter 12, page 383, for more about the nutrition and health benefits of soy protein and soy products.

Eggs: Buying Tips

For an economical, convenient, and easy-to-prepare source of high-quality protein, try eggs. One egg supplies 6 grams of protein (about 10 percent of the protein you need in a day), along with good amounts of vitamins A, D, and B_{12}, choline, as well as phytonutrients (lutein and zeaxanthin).

Although eggs are high in cholesterol, 185 milligrams per large egg, they have 5 grams of total fat—no more than an ounce of cheese. Of that, only 1.5 grams are saturated fat. The American Heart Association notes that saturated fat affects blood cholesterol levels more than cholesterol in food. One large egg has about 1.5 grams of saturated fat, less than one-quarter of the amount in a tablespoon of butter.

Shell color—brown or white—doesn't affect the nutritional quality of eggs; the color varies with the breed of hen. Yolk color depends on the feed eaten and doesn't affect the quality, flavor, nutritive value, or cooking characteristics.

Eggs are sold in sizes ranging from jumbo to small. What-size to buy? The bigger the egg, the more it has of everything: nutrients, cholesterol, calories. *As a shopping and food preparation tip:* Four jumbo eggs equal five large eggs or six small eggs. Most recipes are written for large eggs, but most supermarket eggs will do. It's not easy to find small eggs in supermarkets.

Eggs are graded AA, A, and B. Grading refers to the interior and exterior quality of the eggs when they're packed. Most eggs sold in supermarkets are Grade A; they're almost the same as Grade AA eggs, which are considered slightly higher in quality.

1. To determine the freshness of shell eggs, check the date on the carton. If eggs come from a USDA-inspected plant, the carton will display a number (called a Julian date) for the packing date. A Julian date will be between 001 (January 1) and 365 (December 31).

   You can refrigerate fresh shell eggs in their carton for four to five weeks beyond the Julian date without losing quality. The carton also may carry an expiration date; after that it can't be sold.

   The yolks of fresher eggs hold their shape when they're cracked open. As eggs age, the white thins and the yolk flattens. However, the nutrition and functional qualities don't change.
2. Open egg cartons before you buy. Avoid cartons with cracked eggs. They may be contaminated with *Salmonella.*
3. Buy eggs that are refrigerated, not kept at room temperature. Even though eggs are stored in their own natural package, unrefrigerated eggs spoil quickly.
4. If advised by your doctor to limit egg yolks, try cholesterol-free or reduced-cholesterol egg substitutes. The yolk, which contains the cholesterol, is left out. Other ingredients, such as nonfat milk, tofu, and vegetable oils, take its place; for coloring, substitutes may contain beta carotene. You also can buy eggs and use just the whites to replace some or all whole eggs.

Look for egg substitutes, including soy-based egg replacers for vegans, made with potato starch and lecithin, in the store's freezer or refrigerated sections.

See "Eggs: If Advised to Limit Cholesterol" in chapter 8, page 255.

5. Want convenience? Consider frozen and refrigerated whole-egg products. They're pasteurized, or heat treated, to kill potential *Salmonella* bacteria inside. The heat processing slightly lowers heat-sensitive nutrients, but not much. Use them immediately after opening the container. Refrigerated, peeled, and ready-to-eat hard-cooked eggs are available in some stores.
6. For safety's sake, buy pasteurized (not pastured) whole shell eggs if you have a recipe for raw eggs, perhaps for homemade salad dressings or mayonnaise, or for preparing eggs softly cooked or sunny-side up. Pasteurization is a process that eliminates the risk of *Salmonella* in eggs.

Juice and Juice Drinks: Buying Tips

Juice options are more than orange and apple juice! And you can find juices with "lots of pulp" and "no pulp"; 100 percent juice that's fortified with calcium, vitamin D, DHA, omega-3s, and more; juice blends; and juice drinks. *See "Juice, Juice Drinks, or Fruit Drink?" in chapter 4, page 88, for a comparison of these products.*

1. Read the label before you choose. Remember that juice drinks have added sugars; 100 percent juice does not.
2. Know that most packaged juices and juice drinks are pasteurized or processed to destroy harmful bacteria and naturally occurring enzymes that hasten spoilage. More and more cold pasteurized juices are showing up on the market; this processing method uses very high pressure to preserve juices for safety. Cold-pressed and unpasteurized juices have a very short shelf life and an increased risk for foodborne illness.

   If sold in interstate commerce, fresh juice and juice products that have not been pasteurized or appropriately treated must show a warning on the package label, *as shown in "Health Warnings" in this chapter, page 152.*

   Juices made locally, such as apple cider from a nearby orchard, aren't required to provide this warning unless there is a state ruling. Juice bars and restaurants that sell freshly squeezed juice in glasses to drink right away don't need to provide this warning, either.

Tofu, Tempeh, and More Plant-Based Options: Buying Tips

The refrigerated section of the store sells far more than dairy foods, juices, and eggs. Try these:

Tofu. High in plant-based protein, tofu is a cheeselike curd made from curdled soybean milk and pressed into soft cakes. Its calcium content is highest when calcium fortified, often with calcium sulfate.

Have you ever wondered?

. . . if fertile eggs, organic eggs, free-range, or cage-free eggs contain more nutrients? They don't, but they're an option if you prefer them. Fertile eggs, which can become chicks, won't keep as long. Organic eggs are produced by hens fed on organic rations. "Free-range" or "cage-free" eggs come from chickens raised outdoors or that have daily outdoor access. These eggs usually cost more.

. . . if modified-fat eggs or lower-cholesterol eggs are worth the extra cost? That depends on your food budget, your other food choices, and your health needs. Hens raised on feed with flaxseed, fish oil, or Maine algae can produce eggs with more omega-3 fatty acids; flaxseed is a great source of omega-3 fatty acids, which may offer health benefits. Eggs with more omega-3s also have more vitamin E. *See "A Closer Look . . . Omega-3s and -6s" in chapter 13, page 392.*

You might also find specialty eggs that are high in lutein or vegetarian eggs, from hens raised on feed containing no animal by-products.

. . . if soybeans or tofu are good fiber sources? Half a cup of soybeans has more than 5 grams of fiber. But when soybeans are processed to make tofu, fibrous substances are strained out. What's left is high in soy protein. One-half cup of tofu has less than 1 gram of fiber.

1. Buy the form you need:
   - *Soft or silken tofu* for dressings, smoothies, soups, dips, and sauces
   - *Medium-soft tofu* for puddings, cheesecakes, pie fillings, and salads
   - *Firm or extra-firm tofu* for grilling, marinating, slicing, and stir-frying and using in casseroles, soups, and sandwiches
2. Choose between tofu that's unpackaged and sold in water, or tofu sold in aseptic packaging. Unpackaged tofu should be refrigerated in water, which is changed daily, and used within a week. Tofu in aseptic packaging doesn't need refrigeration until after it's opened. Try flavored tofu such as smoked, teriyaki, Mexican, and Italian tofu. For more variety, check an Asian food specialty store.

Tempeh. Another plant-based protein option with less calcium than tofu, tempeh is a rich, fermented soybean cake made from a mixture of soybeans, millet, rice, or other grain. Grilled or marinated, it adds a smoky or nutty flavor to soups, casseroles, chilis, or spaghetti sauce.

Nondairy spreads. Look for refrigerated spreads with more nutrients and less fat or spreads made with healthy oils found in foods such as tapenade and hummus. Try protein-rich hummus, made with chickpeas, or hummus-like spreads made with edamame (soybeans) or other beans (legumes). They may be flavored with sun-dried tomatoes, roasted red pepper, spinach and artichoke, jalapenos, and more!

Other spreads, such as pesto, have more fat in the form of healthy oils, usually olive oil. Guacamole, sometimes enjoyed as a spread, is made from avocados, a source of healthy oils, too.

FREEZER CASE

Bagels and bread dough; waffles and tortillas; cookies and pastries; fruits and fruit juice; vegetables, plain and mixed; pizza, burritos, and quiche; vegetables and fruits, full dinners and quick snacks; meat, poultry, and fish; ice cream and frozen yogurt—the freezer case is well stocked with nearly any convenience food you can think of.

Frozen foods offer convenience, time saving, consistent prices, year-round availability, longer storage, and less chance for food waste. Commercial quick freezing preserves freshness, flavor, color, and nutritional quality.

Frozen at their peak, minimally processed frozen foods are nutritionally comparable to cooked fresh products—if handled properly. Pre-portioned or partly or fully cooked items can be prepared and served with little time or effort.

1. Buy only clean, firm packages. Discoloring, frost, or ice may mean improper storage.
2. For the best nutrition, choose frozen products that are minimally processed. Read the Nutrition Facts and ingredient lists to compare. More-highly processed items can be high in sodium and added sugars, and perhaps limited in other nutrients.

Frozen Vegetables and Fruits: Buying Tips

Stock up on these frozen products for quick, easy food prep! Frozen vegetables and fruits have been harvested at their peak of quality and ripeness, then flash frozen to minimize nutrient loss and extend storage time—and they're available year-round.

1. Shop for the rainbow in the freezer case, as well as in the fresh produce department. Look beyond fries and corn for frozen veggies and beans and peas: perhaps frozen sweet potato fries, artichoke hearts, bell peppers, butter beans, and edamame. When shopping for fruit consider frozen blueberries, mangoes, and peaches.
2. To control fat and perhaps calories, choose frozen plain vegetables. Some sauces mixed with frozen vegetables add fat, sodium, and calories; check the Nutrition Facts.
3. When fresh fruits aren't in season, consider frozen fruits. Be aware of any added sugars. Frozen fruits may lose their shape when thawed, so consider serving them while still somewhat frozen.
4. If you only want to use a small amount at a time, buy frozen vegetables and fruits in a flow pack so they don't stick together. This allows you to pour out what you need and immediately reseal it and return the rest to the freezer.
5. Want more convenience? Buy frozen sliced stir-fry veggies and mixed veggies or fruits.
6. Frozen juice? Consider 100 percent juice concentrate. It often costs less than juice in cartons, takes less space to store, and stores longer than refrigerated juice.
7. For a nutrient-rich snack, buy frozen fruit bars. Read the ingredient list to know if they're made with 100 percent juice or with flavored water and sweeteners.

Frozen Meals, Entrées, and Mixed Dishes: Buying Tips

Need a quick-to-fix meal or entrée in the freezer? You can make your own, or have a prepared meal ready to heat and eat. Consider nutrition along with flavor, convenience, and cost.

1. Use the Nutrition Facts and ingredient list to compare frozen prepared meals, bowl meals, soups, stews, and entrées. When comparing one frozen dinner with another, check the label serving size. For example, some may be 7-ounce dinners; others, 11 ounces.
2. For mixed dishes (burritos, enchiladas, lasagna, and pizza), frozen dinners, and others, look for products with more fruits, vegetables, and whole grains; and with less fat, including saturated fats and *trans* fats, cholesterol, and sodium.
3. Go easy on breaded frozen fish, poultry, or vegetables. They supply more calories and fat. Check the package directions for oven cooking or heating, rather than deep-fat frying.
4. Be adventuresome. Try frozen entrées and sides, perhaps from a specialty food store, that may be new to you. Consider chicken paella, an Indian curry dish, or shrimp pad thai. Although they'll cost more than homemade, they offer a way to try new culinary experiences!

Frozen Desserts: Buying Tips

Frozen ice cream, sherbet, sorbet, and yogurt—plenty of refreshing flavors! To compare, Nutrition Facts tell the calorie, nutrient, and ingredient story. Check the serving size: if your portion is bigger than the label serving, you'll consume more calories, fat, and added sugars.

Frozen yogurt (hard-frozen or soft). For the same amount, most frozen yogurt has fewer calories and less saturated fat than ice cream does. The amount depends on its main ingredient (whole, 1 percent low-fat, or fat-free milk). Although made with lactic acid cultures, frozen yogurt may or may not contain active, live cultures; if present, freezing slows their action. Look for the "Live and Active Cultures" seal from the National Yogurt Association.

Shopping for Soy

Fresh, canned, dried, or frozen, soybeans are found in many areas of the grocery store. The following are among the many soy-based products you'll find:

- *Dairy case:* soymilk, soy cheese, soy eggnog, soy smoothies, soy sour cream, soy yogurt, soy beverage juice blends, and dairy milk and dairy yogurt with added soy protein. (Although cholesterol free, soy products differ in some culinary characteristics and nutrition content from milk products.)
- *Egg case:* egg replacers
- *Freezer case:* edamame, soy bacon, soy-based burgers, soy crumbles, soy entrées, soy ice cream, and soy sausage and patties
- *Grocery aisle:* canned black and yellow soybeans, dried soybeans, miso, seasoning mixes with soy (for burgers, chilis, and tacos), soy baking mixes (for pancakes, muffins, brownies), soy cereal (granola, soy flakes, soy grits, soy mixed with other cereals), soy flour, soy jerky, soy pasta (sold in many shapes), soy pudding, soynut butter (like peanut butter), and textured soy protein (TSP) and soy beverage powders (to add to drinks and other foods)
- *Meat counter:* gardenburgers or soyburgers, soy hot dogs (*Note:* If you choose a veggie burger for the soy benefits, be aware that not all are made with soy protein. If you want the benefits of isoflavones, choose burgers made with soy protein isolate. Veggie burgers made with soy protein concentrate may contain little isoflavones, depending on the processing method.)
- *Produce department:* edamame (in the pod or shelled), soy sprouts, tempeh, tofu
- *Snack aisle:* soy protein bars, soynut trail mix, and soynuts

Ice cream and other frozen desserts. The creamy texture and rich flavor of premium ice cream come with more saturated fat and more calories than frozen yogurt. Remember that mix-ins such as cookies, brownies, candies, and cake add to the calorie, added sugars, and fat contents. And ingredients such as green tea, mango, and pumpkin provide more flavor experiences.

For great flavor and less "indulgence":

1. Try slow- or double-churned ice cream for fewer calories. Because the churning makes the fat particles and ice crystals smaller, it still has a creamy texture with less fat.
2. Choose ice cream labeled as having less fat. In a half-cup serving:
   - *Reduced-fat (2 percent) ice cream* has at least 25 percent less fat than regular ice cream.
   - *Low-fat (1 percent) ice cream* has 3 grams or less of fat.
   - *Light ice cream* has at least 50 percent less fat or 33 percent fewer calories.
   - *Fat-free ice cream* has less than 0.5 fat grams.
3. Special needs? Although the flavor and mouth feel may differ, look for ice cream with sugar substitutes (labeled "no sugar added" or "low sugar") or with added calcium or other nutrients. Today, you can also find gluten-free, lactose-free, and for vegans, soy or nondairy options.
4. Consider some of these other frozen dessert products, which may offer slight advantages over ice cream. Compare labels to see the differences.
   - *Frozen custard.* It's about the same as ice cream. The only difference is that more egg yolks are used in custard. It's also called semifreddo.
   - *Gelato.* Often served semifrozen, it has less milk fat than ice cream. It also contains egg yolks, sweeteners, and flavoring.
   - *Sherbet.* It's made with sweetened fruit juice and water, 1 to 2 percent milk fat, 2 to 5 percent milk solids, and stabilizers, such as egg white and gelatin. It has less fat but more sugar than ice cream.
   - *Sorbet.* Frozen fruit juice that is whipped, it can be counted in the fruit group. It's dairy free and may be slightly sweetened—a good option for vegans and those with milk allergies or lactose intolerance.
   - *Whipped topping.* Frozen whipped toppings are convenient to keep in the freezer. Many have the same calories and ingredients as real whipped cream, but check the label. Toppings made with coconut or palm oils are high in saturated fats. If you enjoy the taste of whipped cream, buy it—then use just a dollop, not a heaping spoonful. Or look for light or low-calorie versions of frozen whipped toppings.

GROCERY AISLES

The inside aisles of the supermarket are stocked with foods that range from low nutrition to nutrient-rich, as well as herbs and spices. Use your label-reading skills to choose mostly items that are less processed.

Canned, Jarred, and Dried Vegetables and Fruits: Buying Tips

For a nonperishable supply of vegetables and fruits, buy canned, jarred, and dried varieties. They're convenient for boosting vegetables and fruits in mixed dishes, such as in soups, stews, other cooked dishes, and for fruits, in smoothies or as sides or snacks. They're often more economical, and they're always available, especially when fresh options aren't in season.

Canned and jarred fruits. Canned fruits are more than just applesauce, apricots, mandarin oranges, peaches, pears, and pineapple. For more fruit variety, consider blueberries, mangoes, papaya, and other less-common fruits, as well as items such as raspberry-flavored peaches and cinnamon-flavored pears.

1. For less or no added sugars, look for label descriptions such as "packed in its own juices," "packed in fruit juice," "unsweetened," or "in light syrup." Fruits packed in juice have fewer calories than fruits packed in syrup or "in heavy syrup."
2. Check the ingredient list to identify added sugars, too.

Juice, juice cocktail, or juice drinks. Which should you buy? *See "Juice, Juice Drink, or Fruit Drink?" in chapter 4, page 88.*

Canned and jarred vegetables. Besides the basics (corn, green beans, peas, and tomatoes, for example), check grocery shelves for more variety: beets, collards, hominy, pumpkin, and zucchini, among others, to use in mixed dishes. Sauerkraut, which is fermented cabbage, makes a flavorful side dish. For more flavor, look for canned vegetables that are seasoned with other ingredients, such as tomatoes with chilies or herbs, and corn with chopped bell peppers.

1. To limit sodium, read the Nutrition Facts and look for package claims such as "no salt added" and "reduced sodium." The sodium in canned vegetables is a flavoring, not a preservative. Heat from the canning process does the preserving.
2. Check the ingredient list to identify sodium-containing ingredients, too.
3. Stock up on special items—perhaps canned or jarred artichokes, olives, and roasted peppers—to add flavor to everyday dishes.

Dried fruits. Think apples, berries, dates, dried plums (prunes), peaches, pears, raisins, and more. Drying takes out water, leaving the concentrated flavors of the fruit and its nutrients in place. When buying dried fruits:

1. Check the label for added sugars; for example, dried banana chips are often sugar or honey coated.
2. If you're sulfite sensitive, look for sulfite-free or unsulfured options. To protect dried fruits from browning, sulfites may be added. *See "Sulfite Sensitivity: Mild to Severe" in chapter 23, page 678.*

Fruit snacks, "made with real fruit." Snacks that claim to contain real fruit may have very little whole fruit, or the fruit may instead be in the form of juice concentrate used as a flavoring. Read the ingredient list and see where it falls in the order of most-to-least ingredients. Added sugars and fruit flavoring may be key ingredients, with just a little real fruit.

Canned or Pouched Meat, Poultry, and Fish: Buying Tips

Protein foods (not just legumes and nuts) appear on grocery shelves, too: another way to put convenience in your food inventory.

Canned or pouched meat, chicken, or turkey. Buy these protein foods to keep on hand for convenience and emergencies. Check the Nutrition Facts. Some are water packed; some are sodium reduced.

Canned or pouched fish. Tuna is a best-seller, but clams, mackerel, salmon, sardines, and shrimp are sold in the grocery aisle, too.

1. Decide among fish packed in water or oil, typically canola, vegetable, or olive oil.
   - *Oil-packed.* Even when drained, the fish has more fat (oil) than water-packed varieties, but it's mostly unsaturated. Some heart-healthy omega-3 fatty acids transfer to the oil, which gets discarded when drained.
   - *Water-packed.* For a milder flavor and drier texture, choose fish packed in spring water. Also look for "flavored" fish in shelf-stable pouches, often infused with lemon, herbs, or other flavorings.
2. To limit sodium, read the label. Look for fish with reduced sodium content.
3. Compare the form and cost. "Chunk" tuna has many cut pieces and generally costs less; "solid" tuna is an intact portion that fits in the can. Buy the form to fit your use.
4. For a calcium boost, buy canned fish (salmon and sardines), which typically has some edible bones. Three ounces of salmon eaten with the bones has about 200 milligrams of calcium, comparable to 6 ounces of milk. (Not all canned salmon has edible bones; check the ingredient list.) Canning softens bones, making them edible. Canned tuna and crabmeat don't have edible bones.
5. Although tuna outsells other canned fish, enjoy a change in flavor with canned salmon or sardines. Salmon is higher in omega-3 fatty acids. Use it in salads, stir-fries, and soups, and as a pizza topping.

Soups, Stews, and Other Convenience Foods: Buying Tips

Shelf-stable soups, stews, and other packaged foods are convenient, but many are high in sodium. Many food manufacturers are gradually cutting back on sodium.

1. Look for products labeled "less sodium" or "no salted added," especially if you eat them regularly. Use the Nutrition Facts and ingredient lists to compare.
2. On soups, stews, and chilis (canned, jarred, or boxed), check the fat content, too. Clear soups and stews are usually lower in calories and fats than creamy varieties or stews with gravy. Many creamy soups, such as cream of celery and cream of mushroom, are sold in low-fat and fat-free versions.
3. Ready-to-eat, condensed, or dehydrated? Buy the type that fits your needs; compare nutrition first. With ready-to-eat soups, stews, or entrées, such as chow mein or pasta with meat, the Nutrition Facts represent what's served; open the container, heat, and

serve. For condensed and dehydrated soups, what you add—water, broth, or milk—contributes nutrients and perhaps calories.

4. To trim fat and calories, buy defatted broth. You also can put canned broth or stews in the refrigerator prior to use; the fat will congeal so you can easily skim it off after opening.
5. Know that many instant noodle (Asian-style) mixes, dehydrated soups, and entrée mixes (macaroni and cheese) are typically high in sodium. If you buy them, use half the seasoning packet to cut sodium; for more flavor and nutrition, mix in chopped vegetables or herbs. For fewer calories, plan to use less butter or margarine than the directions call for; for less saturated fat, use oil instead.

Shopping Tips: Three Easy Ways for Less Sodium (Salt)

- Compare sodium in processed and prepared foods such as soups, breads, and frozen meals. Read food labels for sodium content in milligrams and % DV for sodium per serving. Choose foods with lower numbers.
- Choose food-group foods with less sodium: fresh meats, poultry, and fish, beans and peas, unsalted nuts, eggs, milk, and yogurt. Plain rice, pasta, and oatmeal don't have much sodium, either. Their sodium content goes up if high-sodium ingredients are added during processing or food prep.
- Let your eyes scan the nutrient content claims on the front of the label. From canned fish, soups, vegetables, and vegetable juice to crackers, popcorn, and snack foods, look for products labeled "unsalted," "no salt added," "reduced sodium," "sodium free," or "low in sodium."

Pasta, Rice, and Other Grains: Buying Tips

From traditional and ancient grains to gluten-free and fiber-rich grains, a greater "field of grains" has sprouted on supermarket shelves.

Pasta. Buying pasta is about more than considering its shape these days. Besides being made with traditional durum wheat or whole wheat for Italian-style pasta, different pastas also are made with flours of buckwheat, kamut, quinoa, rice, spelt, and others, as well as a flour-legume blend. They may provide more protein or fiber, and some are gluten free.

Today the refrigerated part of the store sells a wide variety of fresh pastas, too. The flavor, nutrition, and texture of fresh pasta is comparable to that of dry pasta. However it's perishable and needs to be kept in your fridge. It also cooks faster than dry pasta.

Pasta Buying Guide

How much dry pasta should you buy? Figure the amount based on its cooked volume. For example:

Dry Pasta	Uncooked Amount to Buy	Cooked Amount Needed
Egg noodles	8 ounces (2 cups)	4 cups
Macaroni, shells, bow ties, penne, other small to medium shapes	8 ounces (2 cups)	4 cups
Spaghetti, fettuccine, other long shapes	8 ounces (1½-inch-diameter bunch)	4 cups

1. Use food labels to compare. The fiber and nutrients in pasta and noodles depend on the grains they're made from. Check both the Nutrition Facts and the ingredient list; pay attention to serving size. When the first ingredient is semolina or durum flour, it's made mostly from refined white flour. Also notice the cooking instructions, which will be important when you cook and may differ from one pasta to another.
2. Choose the pasta shape to match its use:
   - For thick sauces, use thicker pastas: fettuccine, lasagna, and tagliatelle.
   - Chunky sauces are best with sturdy pasta shapes: farfalle (bow ties), fusilli (twists), macaroni, rigatoni, and ziti.
   - With smooth, thin sauces, use thinner strands of pasta: cappellini (angel hair), spaghetti, and vermicelli.
3. For more fiber, look for whole-grain pastas: fettucine, lasagna, macaroni, and spaghetti. Like traditional pasta, whole-wheat pasta is high in starches (complex carbohydrates). However, the fiber content is almost three times higher; half a cup of whole-wheat pasta has about 3 grams of fiber, compared with about 1 gram of fiber in traditional pasta. Another option: Some are made with a blend of whole-wheat flour and white flour if you prefer a more familiar texture.
4. For more variety, savor the appeal of vegetable and herbed pastas. The addition of beets, carrots, spinach, tomatoes, and other vegetables imparts color and flavor to pasta dough before it's shaped; herbs add a delicate flavor.

   What about the nutrients? Spinach pasta and tomato pasta don't count toward your vegetable intake. Nutrient amounts in the vegetable purees used to make commercially flavored pasta are too small to matter. It's the vegetables or tomato sauce tossed with the pasta that provide extra nutrients.

5. Experiment with Asian-style noodles, which are made with many ingredients besides wheat flour. Look for noodles made with buckwheat flour, potato flour, rice flour, and soybean starch.
   - *Japanese soba noodles* are made with buckwheat and wheat flour.
   - *Japanese wheat noodles* are called udon (thick noodles) and somen (thin noodles).
   - *Rice noodles, mung bean noodles, wonton wrappers* (sheets of wheat dough), and *rice paper* (a thin dough used somewhat like a tortilla) offer more variety.
   - *Ramen noodles,* which are Japanese instant-style deep-fried noodles, are often packaged with dehydrated vegetables and broth mix; the mix is typically high in sodium and saturated fats. They were previously cooked, then dehydrated.
6. Egg noodles? While pasta is made from flour and water, noodles also may contain eggs, egg yolks, or egg whites. Non-egg pasta contains no cholesterol and very little fat. Egg noodles may have small amounts of cholesterol and a little more fat but still are low in fat and cholesterol. If you have an egg allergy, skip egg noodles.
7. More options in the pasta aisle: soy pasta for soy-protein health benefits; wheat-free or gluten-free pasta; and pasta with added fiber and perhaps protein for more health benefits. Bean-based pasta is also a good source of fiber, and it's high in protein as well as gluten free. *See "Gluten Free: When It's a Must" in chapter 23, page 670, for more about wheat-free and gluten-free products.*
8. Couscous? It's pasta, too! Look for whole-grain options for more fiber. Israeli couscous, or pearl couscous, is toasted and has bigger granules, or pearls, than regular couscous. Toast regular couscous before cooking for a nuttier flavor and chewier texture.

Rice. Try different varieties. Brown rice contains the most nutrients, followed by polished white rice, then instant white rice with the least amount.

Rice Buying Guide

How much rice should you buy? That depends on the type of rice, so check the package label to figure the amount based on its cooked volume. For example:

Rice	Uncooked Amount to Buy	Cooked Amount Needed
Brown rice	8 ounces (1¼ cups)	4⅓ cups
Polished, long-grain white rice	8 ounces (1¼ cups)	3¾ cups
Converted white rice	7 ounces (1 cup)	3½ cups
Instant white or brown rice	8 ounces (2 cups)	4 cups

? Have you ever wondered?

. . . what makes some whole-wheat flour white? White whole-wheat flour comes from a type of wheat that's naturally lighter in color and milder in flavor than red wheat—with its darker color and slightly bitter taste—used to make traditional whole-wheat flour. For consumers who prefer products made with refined white flour, white whole-wheat products are appealing. Nutritionally speaking, they're comparable to traditional whole-wheat flour.

. . . which to buy: wheat germ or wheat bran? They're two different parts of the grain, so their benefits differ. The germ is the nutrient-rich inner part, and the bran is the outer coating. From a nutritional standpoint, 1 ounce (⅓ cup) of wheat bran has a lot more fiber, about 13 grams, compared to 4.4 grams of fiber in 1 ounce (¼ cup) of wheat germ. Wheat germ has more protein and more of some vitamins and minerals.

1. Use the labels to compare their nutrients. Being a whole grain, brown rice—with 1.5 grams of fiber per half cup cooked—has about three times the fiber of white rice. When you read the label, look to see if it's for uncooked and cooked rice; it may also show the nutritional content for prepared rice including added butter or salt.
2. Long, medium, or short grain? Whether brown or white, long-grain rice is lighter, fluffier, and separates when cooked. Medium-grain rice is more moist and tender and clings together more than long-grain rice. And short-grain rice is soft and clingy when cooked. Choose the type with the qualities that match your need.
3. Change the flavor and texture of a dish with specialty rice. Jasmine rice and white or brown basmati rice have a fragrant flavor and aroma, especially nice with Thai and Indian food. Arborio rice and sweet brown rice, both short-grain varieties, give Italian risotto its creamy texture. Chinese black rice is medium-grain rice that takes on a deep-purple color when cooked, as does purple Thai rice with a somewhat sweeter flavor. Himalayan red rice is a long-grain rice with a reddish bran layer and a complex nutty flavor.
4. What about rice mixes, such as boxed pilaf? Enjoy the convenience; however, to watch sodium, consider using just half the dry seasoning mix.

Other grains. Add variety, and even more whole-grain options.

1. Sometimes referred to as a pseudo-grain, wild rice is actually a long-grain marsh grass. From a nutritional standpoint, it has a little more protein, riboflavin, and zinc and a little less carbohydrate than brown rice. The fiber content is about 1.5 grams per half cup cooked. To experience its nutty flavor, serve wild rice in salads, side dishes, soups, stir-fries, and stuffing. Or mix it fifty-fifty with regular or brown rice.

2. Browse the grocery shelves for other grain products or products made with barley, bulgur, couscous, farro, kasha, and quinoa, to name a few. Many are whole grain; some such as quinoa are high in protein. *See "Grains, Grains, and More Grains" in chapter 2, page 31, for descriptions and "How to . . . Cook Whole Grains" in chapter 8, page 253, for tips on cooking with various grains.*

3. And the grain options are even greater still. For example, cornmeal, ground as coarse, medium, or fine from blue, white, or yellow corn, is used in baking as well as for thickening. Grinding removes most of the husk and germ. Polenta, a coarsely ground cornmeal, may be packaged as an instant or quick-cooking product on grocery shelves; it may also be sold in a tube-shaped package, fully cooked.

Breakfast Cereals: Buying Tips

From product to product, brand to brand, the nutritional value of breakfast cereals varies. Why? They're made with differing amounts of different parts of the grain—bran, germ, and endosperm. Many are made from corn, oats, rice, or wheat, but the cereal aisles are full of cereals made with ancient and other grains.

More choices: Most breakfast cereals are ready-to-eat; some are ready-to-cook. Many are fortified with vitamins, minerals, and fiber. Some contain dried fruit; others have nuts or seeds, such as flaxseed or chia seeds, for somewhat more protein. Some are gluten free. Sweetened cereals, often with honey, are high in added sugars; some have more sodium or fat than you would think. Lots of choices!

Nutrition Facts on cereal boxes are often given for both cereal only and for cereal with added milk. Adding milk or topping it with yogurt makes cereal a great vehicle for delivering calcium, protein, and other nutrients that milk provides. For all the benefits of your morning cereal, drink the cereal milk. During processing, fortified vitamins and minerals are often sprayed onto cereals and may dissolve in milk.

1. *Unsweetened or sweetened cereals?* Use the same criteria used for any food to compare their calories and nutrients. Note that portion sizes on the Nutrition Facts may differ and range from one-half cup to two cups, cooked or not, with milk and without.

   For less added sugars, buy unsweetened cereals, and then sweeten them with fruit (not table sugar). For oral health, sweetened cereals are no more cavity promoting than unsweetened cereals; both contain starches and sugars that can linger on tooth surfaces. *See "Oral Health: Your Healthy Smile" in chapter 25, page 738.*

2. *"Multigrain," "whole-grain," "bran" cereals.* Do they have more fiber? Check the Nutrition Facts and ingredient list. *See "Is It Really Whole Grain? Tricky to Know" in this chapter, page 184.*

   Cereals that are good sources of fiber supply at least 2.5 grams of fiber per serving; whole-grain cereals typically have more. (*Note:* With updates in the Nutrition Facts label, the Daily Value for fiber will go up, so a cereal would need to provide somewhat more per serving to be considered a good fiber source.) The ingredient list reveals the whole grains and bran in the cereal's "recipe." Although high in fiber, bran lacks the vitamins and minerals supplied by the germ portion of grain.

3. *Fortified cereals.* Check the Nutrients Facts. Most supply about 25 percent of the Daily Value for vitamins and minerals. Some have much more—100 percent—making these cereals comparable to a dietary supplement. Since other foods you eat have these nutrients, too, 100 percent of the Daily Value may be more than you need from cereal. Like any food, decide if you need a highly fortified cereal in your day's eating plan.

4. *Cooked cereals.* Cream of rice, grits, rolled oats (for oatmeal), and toasted wheat—consider cooked cereals that are whole grain.

   Think they take too long to prepare? The packaging may give microwave instructions for quick prep. Many—cream of wheat, grits, oatmeal—also are sold in "instant" varieties. Their nutritional content is comparable to traditional cereals; however, instant cereals may have more sodium. Check the Nutrition Facts.

5. *"Natural" cereals or granola.* These may have more fat, sugars, or sodium than you'd think; many are high in saturated fats from coconut and palm oils. To make granola, the grains are often toasted with oil and honey to give a crisp texture and a sweet glaze. Instead, try muesli (meaning "mixture"), generally made of raw or toasted grains, nuts, dried fruit, bran, wheat germ, and perhaps milk solids—and typically having less fat and added sugars. Muesli is usually eaten with milk, yogurt, or fruit juice. *See "Have you ever wondered . . . what 'natural' on a label means?" in this chapter on page 154.*

Beans, Peas, Lentils, Nuts, and Peanut and Nut Butters: Buying Tips

Dry beans, peas, and lentils. With the demand for nutrient-rich, high-fiber recipes, as well as more interest in ethnic cuisines, stores are stocking different kinds of dry beans, peas, and lentils, not just the expected black-eyed peas, cannellini beans, cranberry beans, garbanzos (chickpeas), Great northern beans, limas, navy and black beans, pinto beans, and soybeans, as well as split peas and lentils. In addition to packaged dry and frozen beans, you may find fresh dry beans in the produce department.

Nutritionally, most beans and peas are about the same, even though their appearance, texture, and flavor differ somewhat. They're economical protein sources that can be used to extend or replace meat in many mixed dishes.

1. For freshness, look for these qualities in dry, uncooked (not canned) beans: no pinhole marks or discoloration, dry and firm beans, not shriveled, and bags that aren't torn.

2. Stock up on canned beans (black, kidney, red, and more) for a quick way to fit fiber-rich beans into your meals—faster than soaking and cooking uncooked dry beans for hours before they can

? Have you ever wondered?

. . . why canned beans are often called dry beans? Beans such as cannellini, kidney, and pinto used for canning aren't picked until they're fully mature in their dry pods. Canning is cooking dry beans in the can; dry beans are also sold in dry form.

. . . what dal (dhal, dhall) is? It's a Hindi term in India that refers to most pulses (beans, peas, or lentils) that have been split and often hulled. The term is popularly used to mean all beans, peas, or lentils. A spicy or mild Indian dish made with lentils or other pulses also may be called dal.

be cooked. For less salt and sodium, buy reduced-sodium beans. Or buy regular canned beans, and then drain and rinse them under cold running water to reduce sodium significantly.

3. For less fat, buy vegetarian or fat-free baked beans and refried beans. Some are sodium reduced. Some refried beans are made with lard, which contains saturated fat and cholesterol.
4. If you can't find the type of bean you want, substitute. For example, adzuki, black, and pinto beans can substitute for kidney beans, giving a dish a slightly different look. Cannellini, lima beans, and navy beans are the same color, just a different size.
5. Experiment with heirloom varieties that cost a bit more, such as anasazi, appaloosa, black turtle, flageolet, lupini, and scarlet runner. (Lupini beans need to be soaked longer than other beans before cooking to remove their bitterness.)
6. Give lentils a try. Lentils are legumes, too, and look like dry peas, but they are flat, not round. Sold whole or split in half, they too are great sources of protein, fiber, and more. If you're pressed for time, they don't need soaking and cook faster than dry beans and peas. You can also buy them canned. Green lentils keep their shape best when cooked, followed by brown, lentils and whole (not split) lentils of any kind.

Peanut butter and nut butters. All are good protein sources, but added ingredients make a difference. Salt or small amounts of sugar may be added for flavor; unsalted and sugar-free varieties are available. Many tree nuts also are ground to make nut butters, which offers a way to benefit from their protein and their healthy oils. Peanut butter is simply roasted peanuts ground into a paste. The style—smooth, chunky, or crunchy—doesn't affect the nutrient content.

The oil in "natural" peanut butter and nut butter may separate from the "butter" without added stabilizers. Avoid the urge to make peanut butter lower in fat by pouring that fat away because it will become too stiff to spread. Instead mix it well, or turn the jar upside down to let the oil run through. Check the Nutrition Facts and ingredient lists on peanut butter, nut butter, and soynut butter to see whether it has added sugars or sodium, and if so how much.

Reduced-fat peanut butter often has the same number of calories (about 200 calories per two tablespoons) as traditional varieties because some fat is replaced by sugars (perhaps molasses or corn syrup). Starchy fillers are added, too, to enhance the flavor and texture.

Tree nuts, peanuts, and seeds. Great for snacks and great in salads, baked foods, and mixed dishes, they're all good sources of plant-based proteins. Their nutrient and phytonutrient benefits differ somewhat, so mix up your choices; their fats are mostly mono- and polyunsaturated. Peanuts are really legumes, but often are eaten like nuts. See *"In a Nutshell: Tree Nuts and Seeds" in chapter 2, page 43.*

1. Besides popular tree nuts (almonds, cashews, pecans, walnuts), use hazelnuts, macadamias, pine nuts, and pistachios, among others.
2. For unshelled tree nuts, choose those with no signs of insect or moisture damage. They should be heavy for size and not rattle when shaken, which is a sign of being dried out and aging. The shells shouldn't be broken or cracked. For shelled nuts a rancid smell and rubbery, shriveled nuts signal aging.
3. Be aware that tree nuts and peanuts often are sold both salted and unsalted. Some are sugar-coated; others are spiced. Unsalted nuts typically are found in the baking aisle; salted, spiced, and sugared nuts, with the snack foods. To limit sodium and added sugars, limit salted and sugar-coated nuts as snacks.
4. Raw, dry-roasted, or oil-roasted nuts or peanuts? Buy what you prefer. An ounce of dry- or oil-roasted tree nuts has about the same amount of fat and calories—almost 14 fat grams per ounce. Nuts and peanuts don't absorb much oil when they're roasted. The fat comes from the nuts and peanuts themselves. Either way, they're a good protein source and provide fiber and varying amounts of different phytonutrients. *Tip:* You can roast or toast nuts at home without using oil.
5. Add seeds to your shopping cart, too: chia, flax, hemp, pumpkin, sesame, and sunflower. Like nuts, they're a great source of fiber, protein, healthy fats, and various vitamins, minerals, and phytonutrients.

Beverages: Buying Tips

Think about the meal and snack drinks purchased in supermarkets, vending machines, and convenience stores. *These tips reinforce a much more complete discussion of beverages in chapter 4, page 81.*

1. Buy flavored waters, but remember that waters sold in plastic bottles aren't the "greenest" beverage choice. Lemon, mango, peach, and other fruit-flavored waters are refreshing. For the "fizz," some are made of sparkling water and juice. Others are flavored with sweeteners but contain little juice. Unlike plain water, they may not be calorie free. *See "Bottled Water?" in chapter 4, page 85.*

2. For a no-calorie beverage, buy club soda, mineral water, and plain seltzer. Don't confuse these beverages with quinine or tonic water, which have 125 calories per 12 ounces.
3. For to-go meals, camping, and emergencies, stock up on boxed, or UHT, milk. Because boxed milk is ultra-pasteurized, or heated to an ultra-high temperature (UHT) to kill bacteria, chilled and sealed in a sterile aseptic container, it can be stored unopened at room temperature for about three months without spoiling or losing nutrients. Once opened, UHT milk is as perishable as milk sold in the refrigerated dairy case.
4. For more convenience, keep nonfat dry milk or evaporated canned milk on hand. They're both shelf-stable or able to keep their quality and stay safe on your shelf for a long time. When reconstituted, nonfat dry milk powder has the same amount of nutrients as fat-free fluid milk. It may cost less than fat-free fluid milk, too.

   Evaporated milk has about 60 percent of the water removed, so its nutrients are more concentrated than in regular fluid milk. It's also fortified with vitamins A and D. If reconstituted, the nutrients are equivalent to the same-size serving. Evaporated milk may be whole or fat-free (skim). Sweetened condensed milk—whole or fat-free—is concentrated, too, but because sugars are added, it's higher in calories. *Tip:* Once evaporated and condensed milks are opened and dry milk is reconstituted, all should be refrigerated.
5. Alternatives to cow's milk? For vegans and those allergic to milk, look for some plant-based products (almond milk, flax milk, rice milk, soymilk, and others), packaged in shelf-stable, aseptic boxes and sold in the grocery aisle. *See "Dairy and Nondairy Beverages" in chapter 4, page 90, to compare them with cow's milk.* Fortified soy milk is considered a nondairy alternative to cows's milk; the others are not.
6. Nondairy creamers, either dry or liquid, may be high in solid fats (saturated fat or *trans* fat). Although nondairy creamers are made with vegetable oil, the fats—if coconut or palm oil—are highly saturated. To lighten your coffee or tea, nonfat dry milk or evaporated fat-free (skim) milk are both good substitutes from the grocery aisle—or use fluid milk or fat-free half-and-half instead.
7. Sensitive to caffeine? Then look for decaffeinated coffee and tea, and caffeine-free soft drinks. Also, seltzer, sparkling water, and most fruit-flavored soft drinks have no caffeine. *See "Coffee and Tea: Caffeinated or Not?" in chapter 4, page 93.* Blended coffee drinks, often bottled, are often loaded with added sugars—and calories!
8. For soft drinks, consider the calorie differences as you shop. A regular soda has 150 to 200 calories per 12-ounce can—with carbohydrates (from added sugars) and water as the only significant nutrients. Buy sensibly sized cans or bottles, perhaps 8-ounce cans to control your portions.

   Diet sodas and other beverages with nonnutritive sweeteners are calorie-free options. If you're sensitive to their nonnutritive sweetener, avoid these products. *See "Soft Drinks: Okay?" in chapter 4, page 100.*
9. Buy single-serving containers of juice and boxed milk for carried meals or snacks, rather than rely on vending machine drinks.
10. To control your intake of alcohol, look for low-alcohol versions of beer and wine. For a single serving, buy 12-ounce cans or small bottles of beer instead of a bigger size. You may find wine in a pop-top can for picnics, too. For calories, check the label. *See "Alcoholic Beverages: In Moderation" in chapter 4, page 102.*

Crackers and Snack Foods: Buying Tips

Crackers and dry snacks may promise "more fiber," "less fat," "0 gram *trans* fat," "less sodium," "gluten-free," "whole grains," and "fewer calories." To sort through the options, check the serving sizes and servings per package, and compare the Nutrition Facts and the ingredient lists.

1. To control calories, buy small snack packs (chips, crackers, dry snacks, and candy). With them, it's not as easy to overindulge. Just limit yourself to one pack!
2. Consider trail mix; to lower the cost, buy the ingredients to make your own. The most nutrient-rich mixes combine dry fruit, nuts, and seeds, but no candy. Some have mini-pretzels.
3. Many chips, crackers, and cookies are made with oil, but what kind? Those made with partially hydrogenated vegetable oils have more *trans* fats. Those with coconut or palm oil have more saturated fats. For healthier fats, look for those made with olive, corn, peanut, and soy oils, or with high-oleic canola or sunflower oil, or low-linolenic soybean oil.
4. What about chips made with other vegetables: beets, blue potatoes, broccoli, kale, parsnips, plantain, sweet potatoes, taro, or yucca? Just because they are made from colorful vegetables doesn't mean they're nutrient rich. In fact, they may have more sodium and calories than you might think. Use the Nutrition Facts label to judge for yourself.
5. Crackers? For less fat, try bread sticks, graham crackers, matzos, melba toast, rice crackers, rusk, saltines, and zwieback. For more fiber, look for those made with whole grains and perhaps seeds; remember that multi-grain doesn't mean whole grain. Some are gluten free. Check the information on the label.
6. For a crunchy snack with fewer calories, buy pretzels or plain popcorn. They're lower in fat than most snack chips or buttered popcorn. Microwave popcorn often has high-fat flavorings.
7. Less sodium? Look for chips and crackers with less salt, and for unsalted popcorn. One way that manufacturers have cut sodium is

by sprinkling salt on the surface instead of adding salt to the dough; this process gives a salty taste with less sodium.

8. Buying cookies or candy? "Sugar-free" and "low-fat" don't mean "low-calorie." Animal crackers, fig bars, gingersnaps, and vanilla wafers are usually lower in calories, fat, and added sugars; today's supermarkets have many more options.
9. Breakfast bars, energy bars, granola bars, protein bars, and more: sound healthy? They're not all the same. Looking for fiber or protein? That varies from bar to bar. And many are higher in added sugars and saturated fats than you might think. Use the Nutrition Facts to compare. Look for those with more fiber and protein, and less added sugars and saturated fat. If it's low in carbs, it's likely low in fiber, too.

Oils and Dressings: Buying Tips

Oils. Although they are used in place of some stick margarine and butter, healthy oils have about the same number of calories (about 120 calories per tablespoon). Canola, flaxseed, and olive oils are higher in monounsaturated fatty acids; corn, safflower, and sunflower oils are higher in polyunsaturated fatty acids. All plant-based oils are cholesterol free. *See "Solid Fats and Oils: How Do They Compare?" in chapter 13, page 386.*

"Light" oil refers to the color or mild flavor, not the fat content. Although you may see coconut oil and palm oil sold alongside other plant-based oils, they are high in saturated fats and not your healthiest choices.

1. Choose the right oil for its use. Refined oils are more stable and suitable for high-heat cooking such as frying, stir-frying, and searing because they have a high smoke point. Avocado, canola, corn, peanut, refined safflower oils have a high smoke point. Canola, high-oleic safflower, and sunflower oils are good for baking. Unrefined oils such as many cold-press oils and others with low smoke points such as flaxseed oil, unrefined sesame oil, and extra-virgin olive oil are good for low- and no-heat uses, such as salad dressings or marinades.

   Try avocado or grapeseed oils instead. Grapeseed oil is neutral in flavor and great for sautéing and roasting on medium heat, while avocado oil can be used for high-heat cooking such as frying, searing, and stir-frying.
2. Look for nonstick cooking oil (avocado, canola, grapeseed, olive, others) sprays. With these sprays, you can use less oil in a fry pan or casserole dish, or on a baking pan.
3. Experiment with aromatic oils: for example, hazelnut, pecan, sesame, or walnut oils. These are finishing or dipping oils, not cooking oils, made by pressing nuts or seeds to extract the mostly unsaturated fats. Flavored oils, perhaps olive or other oils infused with herbs, chiles, citrus, or truffles, also add distinctive flavors. Just a splash on salads, grains, soups, and vegetables—even fruits—will do.

Salad dressing, mayonnaise, vinegar. These pantry staples can build flavor in nourishing foods.

1. For fewer calories, choose "light," "reduced-fat," or "low-calorie" varieties of salad dressings, or buy regular dressings to lightly dress your salads. Fat-free dressings typically have 5 to 20 calories per tablespoon, compared with 75 calories and 6 to 8 fat grams per tablespoon of regular salad dressing. Vinegar and water usually are the first two ingredients in fat-free dressing.

   Look for mayonnaise with fewer calories, or those made with canola or olive oil.

? Have you ever wondered?

. . . if snack foods labeled "0 grams *trans* fat per serving" are a better choice if made with palm oil? Palm oil and palm kernel oil are highly saturated. They're often used in place of partially hydrogenated oils to lower or eliminate *trans* fats. But the switch doesn't make snacks healthier for your heart.

. . . if a beverage made with corn syrup or high-fructose sweetener has more calories? Used in the same amount, these sweeteners are equal in calories to table sugar, or sucrose. They are slightly sweeter than sucrose, however, so a little less might be used, perhaps resulting in somewhat fewer calories. Either way, it's added sugar, which you're advised to limit.

? Have you ever wondered?

. . . if virgin olive oil has fewer calories than pure olive oil? No matter what the type, olive oil is high in monounsaturated fatty acids, and the calories are the same. Terms that may confuse consumers, such as "virgin" and "extra-virgin" olive oil, refer to the acid content—not the nutrient content. Extra-virgin olive oil has less acid and a fruitier flavor than "pure" or "virgin" olive oil. Because it has more aroma and flavor, you can use less.

What about light olive oil? The term "light" refers to the color and fragrance, not to the calories and fat content, or if it has an olive-oil flavor. Light olive oil has a neutral flavor and a higher smoke point.

. . . about the differences between refined and unrefined oils? Unrefined oils are processed simply by pressing and bottling them, which helps retain their color and full-bodied flavor. Refining has the advantage of making oils more stable at high temperatures (higher smoke point), but it neutralizes the flavor and color.

2. Soy mayonnaise, typically made with tofu, is another option. For vegans and those with an egg allergy, read the ingredient list to find out if it's made with eggs.

3. Buy dry blends to mix into your own salad dressing. This way, you can control the amount and type of oil and vinegar you add. Often you can use less oil and more vinegar, water, or other flavorful liquid than the package directions specify.

4. Stock your kitchen with a variety of vinegars to pair with oils in salad-making and more: apple cider vinegar, balsamic vinegar, herb vinegars, fruit-flavored vinegars, and red wine vinegar. Aged vinegar has a deeper flavor. The strong flavor of sweet balsamic vinegar complements salad greens. Vinegars are fat-free and considered sodium free since they have less than 5 milligrams of sodium per tablespoon.

Condiments, Sauces, and Jams: Buying Tips

1. Buy ketchup, mustard, and pickle relish as tasty spreads, with just 2 fat grams or less per tablespoon. Check the label for sodium content. Unless prepared with less salt or sodium, most of these condiments provide 150 to 200 milligrams of sodium per tablespoon. For more flavor with fewer calories, buy prepared horseradish. Look for chutney—a condiment with fruits or vegetables, spices, sugar, and vinegar—that's low in sodium and fat.

   Kimchi, a spicy fermented vegetable-soybean condiment from the Korean culinary tradition, is more often sold in the refrigerated section of the store. It's often high in sodium.

2. Olives, pickles, sauerkraut, and other vegetables packed in brine: they too are high in sodium. When you buy them, plan to serve or eat small amounts.

3. Try salsas: chunky or pureed. They're low in calories and bursting with flavor, but check the sodium. Experiment with the different levels of spiciness—usually labeled as mild, medium, or hot—to see which you like best. Salsas have less fat than cheese dip or spreads.

4. Shopping for prepared pasta sauce? Alfredo, clam, marinara, meat, and primavera: the clue to its nutrient content is its name. (Creamy sauces such as Alfredo and clam usually have more fat). Read the Nutrition Facts. *See "What's That Sauce?" in chapter 9, page 280, for descriptions of these and other sauces.*

5. For any sauce—chutney, peanut, pesto, sambal, Sriracha, and more—check the Nutrient Facts and ingredient list for sodium and added sugars—and choose judiciously to make healthy dishes flavorful and appealing.

6. To cut back on sodium, look for reduced-sodium chile sauce, soy sauce, teriyaki sauce, and marinades. Their traditional counterparts may be quite high in sodium. Tamari is a wheat-free variety of soy sauce; shoyu is not.

7. Fruit jams and jellies—nutritionally, they're much the same. Both have relatively small amounts of nutrients. *Hint:* Fruit jams and jellies supply extra calories from added sugars. Fruit spreads—sweetened with juice—can have the same number of calories as jam or jelly, or they may have less sugar. And they provide some nutrients. Check the Nutrition Facts.

Baking Aisle: Buying Tips

Every purpose has a flour. Every flour has a purpose.

Flour. Recognize the different types and qualities of wheat flour. Ideal for bread making, "hard" wheat flour is higher in protein, including gluten (a protein), giving dough the qualities needed as the dough rises. "Soft" wheat flour has less protein and less elasticity and so is better for pastries and cakes.

1. Choose whole-wheat flour for more fiber and other nutrients. Because its bran layer and germ are still intact, the grain has more fiber and B vitamins, iron, selenium, potassium, and magnesium. Know that bread made with whole-wheat fiber is heavier. *See "What Is a Whole Grain?" in chapter 2, page 27, for an illustrated description.*

2. Make refined flour, with its snowy-white appearance, a pantry staple, perhaps to use in combination with other flour.

   Because the refining process removes the fiber- and nutrient-rich bran and germ, the resulting flour (from only the endosperm) is missing almost all of the fiber and many of the vitamins and minerals. When enriched, four nutrients that were lost in processing—thiamin, riboflavin, niacin, and iron—are added back. Fiber is not. The amounts of these four nutrients compare to those of whole-grain flour. Enriched flour also is fortified with folic acid, whole-wheat flour may or may not be folic-acid fortified. Some refined flour is also fortified with calcium and vitamins A or D.

   Refined flour may be bleached or unbleached. Bleaching simply whitens the somewhat yellowish unbleached flour. From a nutritional standpoint, bleached and unbleached flours are almost the same. Forms of refined flour:

   - *All-purpose flour,* often used for baking, thickening, or breading, is a mixture of high-gluten hard wheat and low-gluten soft wheat.
   - *Bread flour* is mainly high-gluten hard wheat, suitable for yeast bread.
   - *Cake, or pastry, flour* made from low-gluten soft wheat has a finer texture that makes pastry and cakes more tender.

Is It Really Whole Grain? Tricky to Know

Whole grains have all three parts of the grain kernel: bran, endosperm, and germ. Refining takes away the bran and the germ, leaving only the endosperm.

MISUNDERSTOOD LABEL TERMS

- "Made with whole grains" may mean it just has a small amount of whole grains. "Wheat flour" or "100 percent wheat" doesn't mean that it's whole grain; it could be refined wheat.
- "Wheat bread" or "100 percent wheat" doesn't mean it's whole grain, just that it's only made with wheat. "Wheat bread" may contain both white refined and whole-wheat flours; proportions vary.
- "Seven-grain" or "multigrain" is no assurance that bread is whole grain. Those two terms simply mean that the bread is made with flour from more than one grain, refined or whole. "Stone ground" and "cracked wheat" don't mean whole wheat, either.
- Fiber on the Nutrition Facts? Whole-grain breads may or may not be high in fiber. Even products that are "good sources" of whole grains may not be high in fiber.

MISUNDERSTOOD APPEARANCE

- Being brown doesn't make bread whole wheat. Being white may not mean that bread is made with just refined white flour. Whole-grain breads usually are browner than breads made with refined white flour.
- A rich brown color may come from coloring, often listed on the label as caramel coloring. Some whole-wheat bread is made from a white wheat grain variety with a lighter color and milder flavor.

LABELS: THE "WHOLE" STORY

- Does the package claim link whole grains to a reduced risk for heart disease or some cancers? If so, the food must contain at least 51 percent whole grains by weight (it doesn't mean 100 percent whole grain), and it must meet specific levels for fat, cholesterol, and sodium. An FDA labeling guideline: a "whole-grain food" must contain the bran, endosperm, and germ in natural proportions.
- Is it labeled "whole wheat"? If so, the bread must contain 100 percent whole-wheat flour, noted on the ingredient list. The flour listed first is in the greatest amount.
- Is the first grain on the ingredient list whole grain? Even if a refined grain is listed first, the sum of several whole-grain products listed next may add up to more by weight than the refined grain.

Source: The Whole Grains Council.

To help you, the package may have a voluntary Whole Grain Stamp sponsored by The Whole Grains Council, indicating whether one label serving of the food contains a dietarily significant amount of whole grains: at least 8 grams of whole grains. To get the amount of fiber provided by the advice "make at least half your grains whole," you'd need to eat at least 48 grams of whole grains daily. Some food companies have their own whole-grain symbol, too.

- *Gluten flour* is made from hard wheat with most of the starch removed. Higher in protein (gluten) than all-purpose flour, it gives more strength and rising power to dough. It's often blended with lower-gluten flours for making bread and may be called bread flour.
- *Self-rising flour* is all-purpose flour with baking powder and salt added for making quick breads, generally not for yeast breads.

3. Look for nonwheat flour in the supermarket and specialty stores. These flours may or may not be whole grain, so check the label. Some are gluten free.

- *Buckwheat flour* has a grassy and hearty flavor. Whole buckwheat flour has a strong flavor and more nutrients than white buckwheat flour.
- *Corn flour*, made from the whole corn kernel, is finely ground cornmeal; masa harina is a specialty corn flour used to make tortillas. Yellow corn flour—and yellow cornmeal—has more vitamin A than white corn flour.
- *Oat flour* has a nutty flavor and denser texture than all-purpose flour and, in dough that needs to rise, it must be mixed with other flour.

   - *Rye flour* is a heavy, dark whole-grain flour with less gluten than all-purpose or whole-wheat flour.
   - *Triticale flour* is a blend of wheat and rye flours. It has less gluten than all-purpose flour and makes a dense bread. To lighten the texture of baked goods, go fifty-fifty with triticale and bread flour.
4. Try other types of flour, such as almond, amaranth, banana, black bean, buckwheat, coconut, flaxseed, millet, peanut, potato, rice (white and brown), sorghum, and soy flours, which are especially useful for people who have a wheat allergy or are sensitive to gluten. Be aware that their cooking and baking qualities and flavors differ from wheat flour. If you don't need to eliminate wheat or gluten, you might experiment by replacing some wheat flour with these specialty products.
5. Look for other types of flours in ethnic specialty stores, such as cassava (manioc), chickpea (garbanzo), dal, fufu, kamut, and teff. Today, most supermarkets carry specialty flours.

See "Shopping for Gluten-Free Foods and More" in chapter 23, page 674, for tips on finding wheat- or gluten-free flour.

Sugar. Know the differences between various types of sugar. Most cooking and baking is done with granulated, refined sugar. Superfine sugars, which are more finely granulated, may be used in meringues or in recipes that call for granulated sugar. Powdered or confectioners' sugar is granulated sugar that's been crushed into a fine powder. *See chapter 11, page 345, for information on honey, brown sugar, and raw sugar as well as sugar alternatives, and to learn about nonnutritive sweeteners.*

Baking mixes. Bread, cake, muffin, and waffle mixes—and more: just add ingredients (as stated on the package), and bake.

1. Buy them for convenience, and control the type of ingredients (eggs, fat, liquid) you add. For example, for less saturated fats, use soft margarine or oil instead of butter. An egg substitute or egg whites might substitute for a whole egg. The liquid might be fat-free milk, soymilk, or even 100 percent juice. And you might add dry fruit and nuts.
2. Look for gluten-free or wheat-free mixes if needed. They might be made from other grains or plant sources, such as fava bean flour, garbanzo bean flour, potato starch, rice flour, sorghum flour, and tapioca four.
3. Check the label; some manufacturers provide tips for ingredient substitutions and variations. Whole-grain mixes have more fiber.

Dry Seasonings: Buying Tips

Herbs and spices enhance the flavor of food without adding sodium. Dry or fresh, add them to your list.

1. Buy herbs and spices in the amounts you need. Dry herbs can be stored for up to a year and still retain their peak flavors. Fresh herbs last in the refrigerator for only a short time. *Tip:* Many ethnic food stores and supermarkets sell herbs and spices in bulk at lower prices.
2. Know that seasoned salts are high in sodium. This includes garlic salt and onion salt. As an alternative, look for garlic powder and onion powder. *To compare different types of salt, see "Salty Terms" in this chapter, page 186, to compare different types of salt.*
3. Look for salt- or sodium-free herb and spice blends and dry rubs. Bouquet garni, fines herbs, herbs de Provence, and Italian herb blends take the guessing out of seasoning blends.
4. Buy seasonings, both common types and some that may be new to you, for unique culinary pairings, such as cumin in chili, epazote or chipotle chili powder in Mexican dishes, fennel on roasts or in stew, and turmeric in curries. Or look for unique blends, such as za'atar or dukkah for Middle Eastern dishes, or Chinese five-spice for Chinese dishes.
5. Try liquid smoke, smoked black pepper, or smoked paprika. They add the smoky flavor of curing without salt.

See "Quick Guide: Herbs and Spices" in chapter 8, page 272, for a comprehensive list of seasonings.

BREADS AND BAKERY PRODUCTS

Baked products are found in several places: the grocery aisle, the deli, and the in-store bakery, where you can buy baked goods, fresh from the oven. Products baked in the store may not have nutrition labeling to help you compare. (Packaged dough is sold with frozen and refrigerated foods and carries nutrition information on the package label.)

1. Use food labels—the ingredient list and Nutrition Facts—to compare in-store bakery products to packaged bakery products.
   - Limit those with more saturated fat and added sugars: croissants, doughnuts, sweet rolls, and many cookies, cakes, and muffins. Half of a croissant has about 5 fat grams compared with 1 fat gram in half of an Italian roll. A doughnut has about 10 fat grams. And a premade toaster pastry may deliver 15 to 20 grams of sugar with 200 calories; double that if you eat two toaster pastries!
   - Choose mostly bread and other bakery products with less saturated fat and added sugars such as most bagels, corn tortillas, English muffins, French bread, Italian bread, Kaiser rolls, pita bread, pumpernickel bread, and rye bread, which have 2 grams of fat or less per label serving. Be aware: some are oversized.
   - For white bread and rolls, look for "enriched" with B vitamins and iron. Most products made with refined grains, including bread, are fortified with folic acid but not necessarily fiber or other vitamins and minerals. And most store-bought rye and pumpernickel breads are made with mainly refined white flour.

Salty Terms

When a recipe calls for salt, which one will you buy?

- *Finishing salt:* Gourmet salts, such as black salt, fleur de sel, and Himalayan pink salt, bring out flavor with a crunchy texture. A small amount is used at the end of cooking.
- *Iodized salt:* Table salt with iodine added. It's a good choice in most recipes. By using iodized salt, people get enough iodine—even when they go easy on salt. An important nutrient, iodine helps prevent goiter, a thyroid gland condition. Specialty salts may not be iodized.
- *Kosher salt:* Coarse-grain salt that adds a crunchy texture to some dishes and drinks, such as margaritas. Kosher salt is used to prepare meat in accordance with Jewish dietary laws, referred to as "koshering." *Tip:* One-quarter teaspoon of kosher salt has somewhat less sodium than one-quarter teaspoon of table salt simply because kosher salt has a coarser grain and so less fits in the spoon. For the same saltiness in a cooked dish, you need the same amount by weight—which provides the same amount of sodium, kosher or not.
- *Lite salt:* Salt that is fifty-fifty: half sodium chloride (table salt) and half potassium chloride. It has less sodium than table salt, but it's not sodium free.
- *Pickling salt:* Fine-grained salt used to make brines for sauerkraut or pickles. Unlike table salt, it has no iodine or anticaking additives. Additives would make the brine cloudy or would settle to the bottom.
- *Popcorn salt:* Very finely granulated salt that sticks well to popcorn, fries, and chips.
- *Rock salt:* Large, chunky crystals of salt used in a crank-style ice-cream maker or as a "bed" for serving foods such as clams or oysters. Not commonly used in recipes, rock salt contains some harmless impurities.
- *Salt substitute:* Made by substituting some or all of the sodium with potassium, magnesium, or another mineral. It may be recommended by a doctor for people on a sodium-restricted diet.
- *Sea salt:* Either fine-grained or larger crystals produced by evaporation of seawater—for example, Black Sea, Celtic, French (fleur de sel), or Hawaiian sea salt. It has trace amounts of other minerals that may offer a somewhat different flavor. Still, it's sodium chloride. Even though sea salt is often promoted as a healthy alternative to table salt, the sodium content is comparable; the small amount of other minerals offers no known health advantages. As with other salts, use sea salt judiciously. If the grain is coarse, it may have less sodium per teaspoon, but not by weight. It may or may not be iodized. *Tip:* When canning, trace minerals in sea salt may discolor food.
- *Seasoned salt:* Salt with herbs and other flavorings added, such as celery salt, garlic salt, onion salt, or other seasoned salts. Seasoned salt has less sodium than table salt but more than herbs alone. *Tip:* For less sodium in cooking, use just herbs—for example, celery seed, garlic powder, or onion flakes. Check the ingredient list for salt.
- *Table salt:* Fine, granulated salt commonly used in cooking and in salt shakers. Table salt generally is iodized. An anticaking additive—calcium silicate—helps table salt flow freely and not get lumpy.

2. Make an effort to buy more whole-grain and whole-wheat bakery products. For more fiber, check the Nutrition Facts and ingredient list to find those made with mainly whole-wheat flour. Whole grains should be among the first ingredients. *See "Is It Really Whole Grain? Tricky to Know" in this chapter, page 184.*

   On the Nutrition Facts, you'll see that a 1-ounce slice of whole-wheat bread has about 1.6 fiber grams compared to 0.5 to 1 gram of fiber in the same-size slice of enriched white bread. Bakery products that supply 2.5 or more grams of fiber per serving are a good fiber source.
3. Be portion savvy. A small muffin or sweet roll, or a small bagel or bun, is likely to be big enough.
4. Check the label's product date for freshness. Packaged bakery products, with preservatives added, may have a longer shelf life than those from the in-store bakery. *See "Additives: Their Place on the Plate" in chapter 5, page 132.*

DELI, PREPARED, AND TAKE-OUT FOODS

Consumers increasingly shop at supermarkets for the most convenient and fastest home-served meals of all: foods that are ready to eat and might come from salad bars or deli counters, such as rotisserie chicken, steamed shrimp, sushi, and deli sandwiches, as well as a variety of heat-only main dishes, appetizers, and side dishes and cold salads.

If you're pressed for time, buy your main dish—or a whole meal—already prepared. Then just heat and serve as a healthy eating solution on a hectic day. For food safety, eat the food the same day you buy it. Guidelines for buying supermarket take-out foods are similar for buying and handling foods from a carry-out restaurant. *See "Keep Takeout Safe" in chapter 9, page 286.*

Stocking the Vegetarian Kitchen

Supermarkets carry all the foods needed for a healthy, vegetarian diet—even vegetarian versions of popular convenience foods as well as specialty foods.

As for any kitchen, stock up on vegetables and fruits; grain products; condiments, seasonings, and other flavorings; and perhaps dairy and eggs. For the vegetarian kitchen, also stock up on meat and dairy alternatives; *see "Shopping for Soy" in this chapter, page 175.* Buy foods that provide high-quality protein, iron, calcium, vitamin B_{12}, and other nutrients that may come up short; *see "The Healthy Vegetarian Way" in chapter 2, page 53.*

Ingredient lists help you identify products with animal-derived ingredients. The Vegan Awareness Foundation has a registered trademark Certified Vegan label for products that don't contain animal products and that have not been tested on animals.

BEANS AND PLANT-BASED PROTEIN FOODS

(Choose mostly with less saturated and *trans* fats and less sodium)

- Canned, frozen, fresh, and dry beans, peas, and lentils such as black beans, garbanzos, pinto beans, soybeans, and split peas
- Vegetarian refried beans
- Dry bean mixes such as falafel, hummus (mashed chickpeas), and refried beans
- Tofu and tempeh
- Miso
- Natto (fermented Japanese soy food)
- Soy-protein patties, soy bacon, soy sausages
- Lentil or veggie burgers
- Soy flour, soy grits
- Soy nuts
- Textured soy protein
- Peanut butter
- Nut butters and seed spreads, such as almond butter and tahini (sesame seed spread)
- Nuts, such as almonds, cashews, hazelnuts, pecans, and walnuts
- Seeds such as pumpkin, sesame, and sunflower
- Eggs or egg substitute*

*For vegans, egg replacer powder made from tapioca starch and leavenings (not a meat alternative)

GRAIN PRODUCTS

Read the Nutrition Facts and ingredient lists if you're vegan; some breads have ingredients derived from eggs, or they've been brushed with eggs to make them shine.

DAIRY AND DAIRY ALTERNATIVES

(Choose mostly low-fat and fat-free.)

- Vitamin D–fortified milk, reduced-fat or fat-free
- Calcium- and vitamin D–fortified soymilk
- Cheese (dairy or soy based)
- Yogurt (dairy or soy based)
- Dry milk powder
- Ice cream, frozen yogurt, or nondairy ice cream

COMBINATION FOODS

(Choose those with less sodium.)

- Canned and frozen vegetarian soups
- Frozen vegetarian entrées, such as bean burritos or vegetable pot stickers
- Canned vegetarian dishes, such as meatless chili
- Vegetable pizza

If you don't eat meatless all the time, *see "Shopping List: Stocking a Healthy Kitchen" in this chapter, page 143,* *for a list of foods to help you stock your kitchen for good nutrition.*

Shopping Green: Opportunity, Responsibility

Ready to reduce waste, your carbon footprint, and your environmental impact with your shopping behavior? Then you're on the upward trend of "greener" shopping.

Being "green" or sustainable in the marketplace is defined by several attributes, including energy efficiency; reduced, recyclable, and biodegradable packaging; limited food waste; and fewer "food miles," or the distance food travels from production to purchase. According to the US Department of Agriculture in 2015, food waste costs each consumer $370 per year! Consider if you buy a watermelon for $5.00, but half goes bad before you use it. You've just wasted $2.50. *See chapter 7, page 191, for safe and proper food storage.*

As the consumer, you're the last stop on the purchasing chain. So you can be a "green" shopper, too. For starters, you can:

- Plan ahead. Limit your shopping trips or shop for groceries when you do other errands. You'll use less gasoline to go to and from the store. Walk or bike there if you can.
- Buy only as much as you need without waste. Discarding food wastes more than money. It also wastes the human energy, packaging, fuel energy, and other resources used to produce, distribute, and sell it!
- Buy products with less packaging. Or buy in bulk, and package them yourself. Be aware that single-serve products generally have more packaging per serving. A larger container may serve the same purpose and cost less. Do you need individual boxes of juice if you drink the same amount from a larger carton, in your own kitchen?
- Choose products in recyclable, recycled, or biodegradable packaging. Be aware that the "chasing arrows" symbol may mean (1) the package is made of recycled materials or (2) the package itself can be recycled. If just one claim is true, the manufacturer must say so. Even if a package carries the symbol, your community may not accept it for recycling. Check first. The number inside the symbol indicates how it can be recycled.

- Get and use reusable shopping bags. Don't forget to bring the bags with you when you shop!
- Recycle paper and plastic grocery bags, perhaps in the store's recycling program—or reuse them at home in your trash container. Either way, it helps lessen the impact of 100 billion petroleum-based plastic bags, which often end up as litter and landfill, used annually in the United States.
- Handle food you buy with care. You've bought it, so care for it. Food that's tossed is money and other resources wasted and in landfills.

See "Limiting Food Waste" in chapter 5, page 113, for more about limiting food waste and using resources wisely.

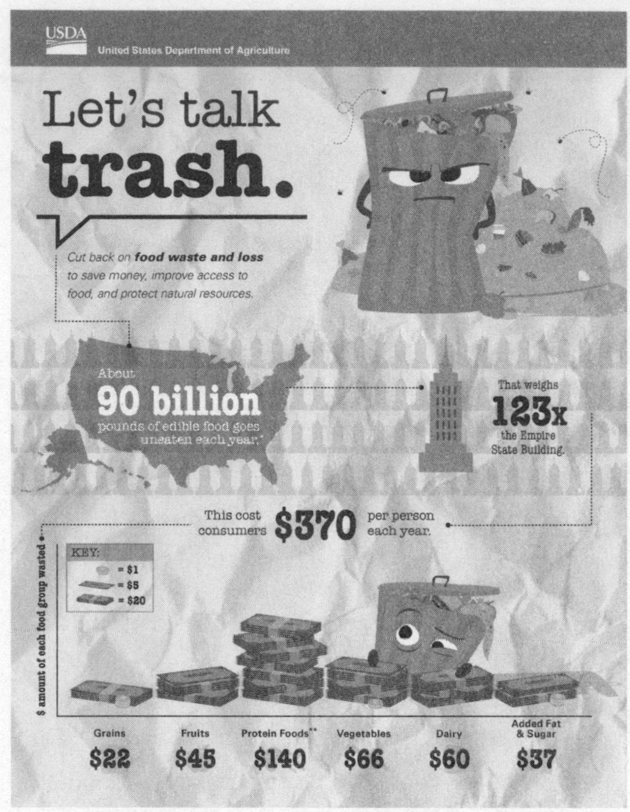

Food Safety and Quality: From Store to Home

While the safety of the food supply is monitored and regulated all along the food chain, it's your responsibility to select foods carefully at the store and to employ safe food-handling practices at home.

FOOD SAFETY: AT THE STORE

Here's how you can keep food safe as you shop:

- Only buy food from reputable food businesses that follow government regulations for food safety. *Note:* Imported foods are subject to the same safety regulations as those produced domestically.
- If you bring reusable grocery bags to pack your groceries, make sure they're clean—not doing double duty as a book bag or travel bag.
- Make a clean start. If provided, use the hand sanitizer at the store's entrance. Wipe the handle of the shopping cart with sanitizer, too.
- Be careful when sampling food as you shop—clean your hands first! If you plan to sample, bring moist towelettes or carry a bottle of hand sanitizer to use before you taste.
- Check food packages. They should have no holes, tears, or open corners. Frozen foods should be solid, and refrigerated foods should feel cold. Frozen foods shouldn't show signs of thawing; if so, report the product to the store manager.
- Check safety seals and buttons. Safety seals may appear on milk, yogurt, and cottage cheese. Jars of foods often are vacuum-sealed

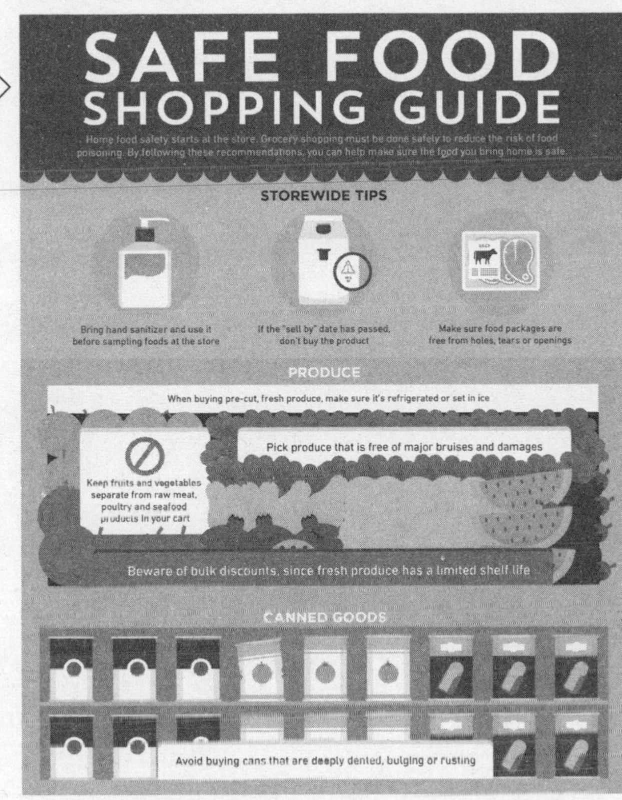
SAFE FOOD
SHOPPING GUIDE
Home food safety starts at the store. Grocery shopping must be done safely to reduce the risk of food poisoning. By following these recommendations, you can help make sure the food you bring home is safe.
STOREWIDE TIPS
Bring hand sanitizer and use it before sampling foods at the store
If the "sell by" date has passed, don't buy the product
Make sure food packages are free from holes, tears or openings
PRODUCE
When buying pre-cut, fresh produce, make sure it's refrigerated or set in ice
Pick produce that is free of major bruises and damages
Keep fruits and vegetables separate from raw meat, poultry and seafood products in your cart
Beware of bulk discounts, since fresh produce has a limited shelf life
CANNED GOODS
Avoid buying cans that are deeply dented, bulging or rusting

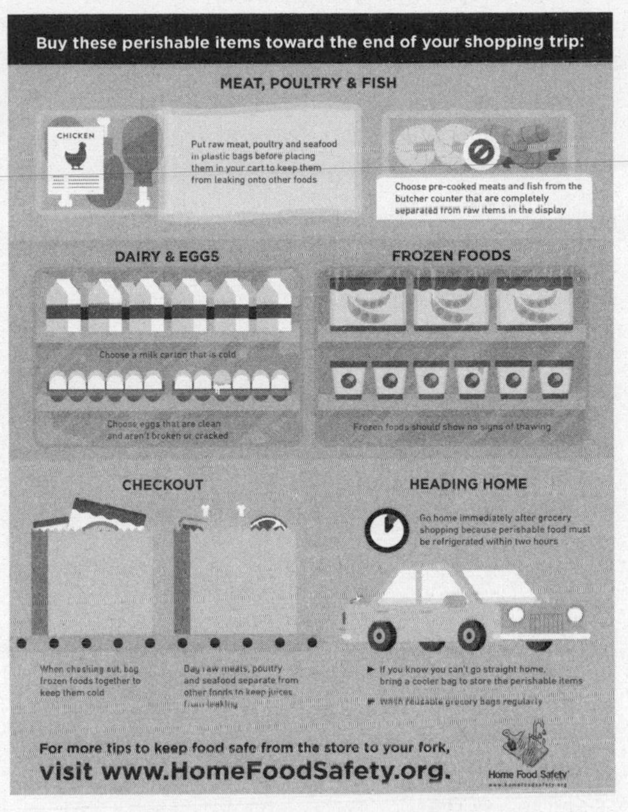
Buy these perishable items toward the end of your shopping trip:
MEAT, POULTRY & FISH
CHICKEN
Put raw meat, poultry and seafood in plastic bags before placing them in your cart to keep them from leaking onto other foods
Choose pre-cooked meats and fish from the butcher counter that are completely separated from raw items in the display
DAIRY & EGGS
Choose a milk carton that is cold
Choose eggs that are clean and aren't broken or cracked
FROZEN FOODS
Frozen foods should show no signs of thawing
CHECKOUT
When checking out, bag frozen foods together to keep them cold
HEADING HOME
Go home immediately after grocery shopping because perishable food must be refrigerated within two hours
If you know you can't go straight home, bring a cooler bag to store the perishable items
For more tips to keep food safe from the store to your fork,
visit www.HomeFoodSafety.org.
Home Food Safety

for safety. Check their safety buttons or seals with your finger. If the indented safety button on the cap is indented (down), the vacuum is still active; if it's raised (popped up), don't buy or use the food. Report a defective cap to the store manager.

- Reject cans that are swollen, damaged, rusted, or dented. These are warning signs for bacteria that cause botulism. Report these to the store manager, too. *See "Bacteria: Hard Hitters" in chapter 7, page 220.*
- If you suspect food tampering, report it to the store manager. Once you're home, contact your county public health department, your local police, or, for meat and poultry, the USDA's Meat and Poultry Hotline (800-535-4555); for other foods, contact the US Food and Drug Administration (888-SAFEFOOD).
- When possible, put raw meat, poultry, and fish in separate plastic bags before placing them in your cart. Occasionally, their packaging may leak and drip onto unprotected foods.
- Pay attention to food's perishability. Purchase only those items that will be at peak quality when you're ready to eat them. *See "A Closer Look . . . Deciphering Package Dates, Reducing Food Waste" earlier in this chapter, page 153, to understand what the dates on packages do and don't mean.*
- If your shopping excursion is apt to take awhile, select perishable foods such as frozen foods, meat, poultry, and fish last before checkout.
- At checkout, pack cold foods together, preferably in paper bags, which keep foods cold longer than plastic bags do.

Add More Variety

Need more strategies to enjoy the food varieties from today's marketplace? Check here for how-tos:

- Include a variety of less common vegetables, fruits, and grains in your eating plan; *see "Grains, Grains, and More Grains," "Vegetables: Have You Tried These?," and "Fruit; What's New to You?" in chapter 2, pages 31, 36, and 39.*
- Make over your everyday recipes with new foods, seasonings, and cooking techniques; *see "Recipe Revamp" and "Flavor on the Menu" in chapter 8, pages 235 and 238.*
- Be adventurous with food when you eat out to get familiar with new ways to eat for health; *see "Eating Ethnic, Eating Global" in chapter 9, page 297.*

FOOD SAFETY: ON THE WAY HOME

Here's how you can keep food safe on its way from the store to your kitchen:

- During warm weather, transport your groceries inside the air-conditioned vehicle, not in the hot trunk. Take groceries home and store them immediately.
- If you must run a few quick errands after food shopping that could take longer than thirty minutes, bring a cooler with chill packs for perishable foods. This is especially important in warm weather since the temperature of refrigerated foods can go up eight to ten degrees Fahrenheit on a trip home from the store. *See chapter 7, page 191, for guidelines on keeping food safe at home.*

7

Keep Your Food Safe

In this chapter, find out about . . .

Food safety basics: clean, separate, cook, and chill

Safe food handling and storage

Preparing food safe to the plate

Foodborne illness: if food makes you sick

Is the food you serve your family safe? Outbreaks of foodborne illness associated with restaurant and store-bought foods get plenty of media attention despite the reality—that more foodborne illnesses are caused by mishandling food in our own kitchens. These cases usually aren't diagnosed or reported, and neither are many foodborne illnesses with less severe, nuisance symptoms.

Sometimes called food poisoning, foodborne illness is caused by eating contaminated food. Its symptoms often are mistaken for other health problems because they vary from chills, diarrhea, dizziness, fatigue, headaches, a mild fever, an upset stomach, and vomiting to dehydration, severe cramps, and vision problems. Even death can result.

Those who are especially vulnerable include the very young, pregnant women and their unborn babies, the elderly, and those with a weakened immune system caused by a medical condition or treatment. *See "Foodborne Illness: More Common Than You Think" in this chapter, page 281, for more about causes and symptoms.*

To reduce the risks of foodborne illness, following good food safety practices—from farm to fork—is essential. Proper food handling helps maintain the nutrients that promote health and keep harmful bacteria at bay. You may already know the four basic food safety rules for serving, handling, and storage:

1. *Clean:* Always wash your food, hands, countertops and cooking tools.
2. *Separate:* Don't cross-contaminate! Keep raw foods to themselves. Germs can spread from one food to another.
3. *Cook:* Cook foods to a proper temperature. Foods need to get hot and stay hot. Heat kills germs.
4. *Chill:* Refrigerate food right away.

Do you always practice these food safety rules at home? Many people don't, even though they know better. All along the food chain—from farms and food companies to supermarkets and restaurants—food safety regulations must be followed to minimize the risks for foodborne illness. Once food leaves the store or farmers' market, however, that responsibility is yours.

Click Here!
Links to Know . . .

- Home Food Safety, Academy of Nutrition and Dietetics
  www.homefoodsafety.org
- Fight Bac, Partnership for Food Safety Education
  www.fightbac.org
- Gateway to Federal Food Safety Information
  www.foodsafety.gov
- Food Safety, Centers for Disease Control and Prevention
  cdc.gov/foodsafety
- Be Food Safe, USDA Food Safety and Inspection Service
  www.befoodsafe.gov

Kitchen: Clean, Safe Zone

Thoroughly washing all kitchen surfaces, appliances, utensils, and equipment—along with proper hand washing—is essential for keeping your food safe and significantly reducing the spread of the common cold and flu.

EVERYDAY HABITS FOR KITCHEN CLEANLINESS

A clean, sanitized kitchen and eating space offer a first-line defense against the spread of foodborne illness. Cleaning is removing dirt. Sanitizing is reducing microorganisms to safe levels.

Sanitizing your kitchen and other food-prep places eliminates breeding grounds for harmful bacteria, viruses, parasites, and mold. Besides obvious places, such as the faucet, refrigerator door, dishcloths, sponges, and towels, remember to sanitize your keyboard and cell phone if you eat while you work!

Clean Hands

Bacteria live and multiply on warm, moist hands. Hands can spread germs from surface to surface, food to food, and person to person. Proper hand washing can prevent nearly half of all cases of foodborne illness.

Proper hand washing. Wash your hands before and after handling food and while multitasking. Run your hands under clean, running warm or cold water. Turn off the tap. Apply soap and lather up for at least twenty seconds. Wash the front and back of your hands, between your fingers, and under your fingernails. Rinse well under clean, running water. Dry your hands completely with a clean towel, or air dry them.

Tip: Have young helpers sing "The Alphabet Song" or "Happy Birthday" twice while washing their hands. That takes about twenty seconds.

Hand sanitizer? Use when soap and water are not available. Just be aware that hand sanitizers may not eliminate all germs, including norovirus. Apply hand sanitizer in the amount noted on the label to the palm of one hand. Rub your hands and fingers together over all surfaces until dry. A rinse-free hand sanitizer with at least 60 percent alcohol is better than no hand washing when washing with soap isn't possible. Hand sanitizers are not as effective when hands are visibly dirty or greasy. The FDA is taking a closer look at ingredients in hand sanitizers to ensure the safety and effectiveness of their frequent use to reduce bacteria on the skin.

Plastic gloves? If you use them, perhaps when handling food at a community event, wash and dry your hands properly before putting on clean, dry disposable gloves. Change to new, clean gloves between food-preparation tasks and if they tear.

Plastic gloves aren't enough for food safety. Although a barrier for foodborne contamination, even clean disposable gloves, used properly, can't substitute for regular, thorough hand washing and drying. The moist, warm conditions inside gloves are perfect breeding grounds for bacteria.

Other reminders: If you have an open cut or sore, wear latex gloves to handle food. Open food bags with a clean knife or scissors. Remember to direct your coughs and sneezes away from food. Cover your mouth and nose with tissue. Then wash your hands! No tissue? Cough or sneeze into your upper sleeve or elbow, not your hands.

Clean Countertops and Tabletops

Do grocery bags go from your car trunk or floor to your kitchen countertop? Even though you can't see bacteria, your countertops aren't clean.

Clear away anything that doesn't belong there such as cookbooks (unless you're using them), mail, newspapers, purses, cell phones, and keys. Keep these and similar items off countertops and away from food and utensils. Kitchen counters shouldn't become permanent landing pads.

Clean your countertops often, especially before food preparation. Use hot, soapy water and clean cloth towels or paper towels (not a sponge, which can harbor bacteria). Sanitize with a solution: 1 tablespoon of unscented liquid chlorine bleach to 1 gallon of water. Using any more bleach offers no advantage. In fact, sanitizing solutions that are too strong can be toxic and corrosive.

Clean Equipment

Utensils. Wash dishes and cookware carefully in the dishwasher or in hot (at least 140°F), soapy water. Rinse well. Be aware that 140°F is very hot and higher than most consumers use in their homes.

Dishcloths and towels. Change them often. When they're damp, they're perfect breeding grounds for bacteria; dry them between each use. Wash them in the hot cycle of your washing machine, and dry on high heat. Or consider paper towels. Use different dishcloths for different purposes, such as hand washing and dish drying.

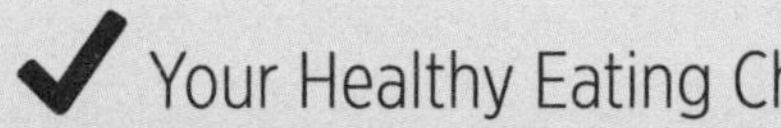

What's Your Kitchen Safety Savvy?

Are you careful enough in your kitchen to avoid foodborne illness? Answer these questions, and then total your points to see how you're doing on kitchen safety.

DO YOU . . . ?	Never 1 point	Sometimes 2 points	Usually 3 points	Always 4 points
CLEAN				
1. Wash your hands for twenty seconds or more with warm soapy water before and after handling food? Dry them with a clean cloth?	☐	☐	☐	☐
2. Clean up surfaces with paper towels or with or cloth towels that you wash often?	☐	☐	☐	☐
3. Clean up splatters in your microwave oven immediately with hot, soapy water?	☐	☐	☐	☐
4. Wash cutting boards, utensils, and work surfaces with hot soapy water after each food item, before starting the next?	☐	☐	☐	☐
5. Store raw meat, poultry, and fish on the bottom of your refrigerator in containers that won't leak?	☐	☐	☐	☐
6. Wash raw produce under cool running tap water, including those with inedible skins?	☐	☐	☐	☐
7. Clean the outdoor grill and picnic cooler after every use?	☐	☐	☐	☐
8. Clean the top of the lids on canned foods before opening?	☐	☐	☐	☐
9. Avoid the urge to use the stirring spoon for a quick taste?	☐	☐	☐	☐
SEPARATE				
10. Use a clean plate and fork for cooked food from the grill?	☐	☐	☐	☐
11. Use one cutting board for fresh produce and a separate one for raw meat, poultry, or fish?	☐	☐	☐	☐
12. Avoid using marinades from raw foods on cooked foods without boiling them first?	☐	☐	☐	☐
COOK				
13. Cover food, stir, and rotate for even microwave cooking?	☐	☐	☐	☐
14. Follow cooking instructions when microwaving packaged foods?	☐	☐	☐	☐
15. Cook hamburger patties until they're 160°F inside?	☐	☐	☐	☐
16. Use a food thermometer to judge when meat and poultry are cooked to a safe internal temperature, and cook eggs until the yolk and white are firm?	☐	☐	☐	☐
17. Use leftovers within three to four days? Heat leftovers to 165°F?	☐	☐	☐	☐
18. Bring gravies, sauces, and soups to a boil when reheating?	☐	☐	☐	☐

(continued)

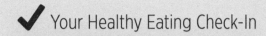

✔ Your Healthy Eating Check-In *(continued)*

DO YOU . . . ?	Never 1 point	Sometimes 2 points	Usually 3 points	Always 4 points
CHILL				
19. Thaw foods in the refrigerator, not on the countertop?	☐	☐	☐	☐
20. Marinate meat, poultry, and fish in the refrigerator?	☐	☐	☐	☐
21. Refrigerate leftovers and perishables from the buffet within two hours of cooking? Or within one hour if the outside temperature is over 90°F?	☐	☐	☐	☐
22. Use refrigerator and freezer thermometers to check their temperatures?	☐	☐	☐	☐
23. Rotate foods in your freezer and cupboards, putting the oldest foods in front?	☐	☐	☐	☐
24. Remove stuffing from chicken and turkey before refrigerating leftovers?	☐	☐	☐	☐
25. Clean your refrigerator each week, discarding foods that are too old?	☐	☐	☐	☐
Subtotals	____	____	____	____

Add up your total points: ________

When it comes to food safety, you need a perfect score: 100 points! Anything less, and you're putting yourself—and anyone who eats with you—at risk for a foodborne illness. It's safe to assume that the higher your score, the lower the risk. If you scored 3 or less for any item, exert a conscious effort to change to "always." Keep reading for more food safety advice.

Sponges. Clean sponges daily. Toss them in the dishwasher with a drying cycle, or microwave a damp sponge for one minute. That kills about 99 percent of bacteria, yeasts, and molds. Replace sponges frequently, even if you clean them daily. If a sponge starts to smell, toss it out immediately. Store them in a dry location, wring them out completely after each use, and wash off any loose food or debris.

Sink. Use a cleaner to sanitize the sides, bottom, faucet, and handles of your sink. Although you may think that soapy water will keep it clean, grease and other residues can build up. Plug the drain; fill the sink with about a gallon of warm water; swish in a tablespoon of bleach; dip a clean sponge in the water; and wipe off the faucet, handles, and sides before draining and rinsing. Clean the dish drainer, too.

Appliances. Clean spills right away, including liquids from opened hot dog and deli meat packages. Wash surfaces thoroughly with hot, soapy water or a chlorine bleach–water solution; rinse. Clean the outsides of appliances with a soft cloth and a mild dishwashing detergent or an appliance cleaner. Pay attention to buttons and handles where cross-contamination to hands can happen.

When cleaning the refrigerator and freezer, remember the shelves, sides, doors, knobs, handles, and food compartments such as the meat and vegetable drawers. While cleaning and defrosting your refrigerator-freezer, pack perishables in coolers with ice. Scrub mold (usually black) on rubber casings of refrigerators with a bleach-water solution. At least once a week, throw out refrigerated foods that should no longer be eaten.

The inside and turntable of a microwave oven easily become splattered with food, allowing bacteria to grow. By washing both the inside and outside, including handles and buttons, foodborne illness may be prevented.

Remember to clean small appliances such as the food processor, coffee maker, blender, and more. Clean them well after each use.

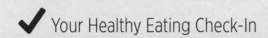

✔ Your Healthy Eating Check-In

Do You Wash Your Hands Enough?

	Yes	No
BEFORE YOU:		
Handle or prepare food	☐	☐
Eat meals	☐	☐
Feed children	☐	☐
AFTER YOU:		
Prepare food	☐	☐
Touch raw food, especially meats and poultry	☐	☐
Switch food preparation tasks	☐	☐
Touch eggs and egg-rich foods	☐	☐
Use the bathroom	☐	☐
Change a diaper	☐	☐
Clean an appliance	☐	☐
Handle garbage or dirty dishes	☐	☐
Smoke a cigarette	☐	☐
Pet animals and scoop animal feces	☐	☐
Use the computer, cell phone, or other handheld device	☐	☐
Touch face, hair, body, or other people	☐	☐
Touch a cut or a sore, cough, or sneeze	☐	☐
Clean or touch dirty laundry	☐	☐

Adapted from: homefoodsafety.org, Academy of Nutrition and Dietetics.

PREVENTING CROSS-CONTAMINATION

The term may be unfamiliar, but cross-contamination can easily happen in your kitchen. It occurs when bacteria from one food spread to another, often from a cutting board, knife, plate, spoon, or your hands. For example, drippings from raw meat, poultry, and fish left on a cutting board can transfer bacteria to the fruits or vegetables that are sliced next on the same cutting board.

Cutting boards. Always use a clean cutting board—separate boards for fresh produce and for raw meat, poultry, and fish, especially if you prefer wooden cutting boards. Mark them or get colored cutting boards to avoid confusion.

Choose cutting boards that clean easily: smooth, made of hard maple, acrylic, plastic, or marble, and free of cracks and crevices. Avoid boards made of soft, porous materials. Discard cutting boards that are heavily worn or have deep, hard-to-clean grooves and knife scars.

Rinsing or wiping isn't enough! After each use, wash cutting boards in hot, soapy water, rinse, and dry well, perhaps in the dishwasher. That's especially important after using a cutting board to cut raw meat, poultry, or fish.

Sanitize cutting boards with a chlorine bleach–water solution after each use: Mix 1 tablespoon of liquid, unscented bleach with 1 gallon of water. Let the boards air dry. Brush to get into the grooves and other hard-to-reach places.

Utensils. Unless it's cleaned well in between uses, avoid using the same knife to slice meat and chop vegetables. Although it's hard to resist, remind everyone who ventures into the kitchen to never taste with the stirring spoon! If children reach for a finger-licking taste, be sure they wash their hands first. Another reason to resist tasting: If food (perhaps meat sauce) isn't cooked through yet, it still may harbor harmful bacteria!

Sponges and dishcloths. Cleaning up spills from ground beef or poultry with a sponge or dishcloth can increase your chances of spreading harmful foodborne pathogens. Instead, use a paper towel or disinfectant wipe to clean up meat and poultry juices. Germs and bacteria can spread from the sponge or dishcloth to your countertops, so use a paper towel or disinfectant wipes to clean countertops instead.

Common Food Safety Mistakes?

- Thawing foods on the countertop
- Cooling leftovers on the countertop before putting them in the fridge
- Tasting food to see if it's still good
- Washing meat or poultry
- Forgetting to wash your hands
- Forgetting to replace sponges and dishcloths
- Eating raw cookie dough or cake batter
- Undercooking high-risk foods such as meat, poultry, fish, and eggs
- Putting cooked or ready-to-eat foods back on a plate that held raw meat (a common grilling blunder)
- Marinating at room temperature
- Delaying refrigerating a "doggie bag"
- Stirring and tasting with the same spoon
- Using the same knife (without cleaning) to trim raw meat and chop vegetables

? Have you ever wondered?

. . . if lemon juice and salt can clean and sanitize a cutting board? No; you first need to wash it with hot water and soap and then sanitize with a diluted chlorine-bleach solution: 1 tablespoon bleach per 1 gallon of water. You can sanitize a nonporous board but not a porous board such as wood.

. . . if antibacterial cutting boards really minimize cross-contamination? Depending on the antibacterial rating, these cutting boards may reduce some common organisms, but research on their effectiveness is limited. These boards are treated with silver ions, which deliver some antimicrobial properties. Even if you use them, follow food safety basics!

. . . if antimicrobial soap is a better choice? Not necessarily. For long-term home use, wash with regular soap instead unless your doctor advises otherwise. Over time microbes may resist antibacterial soaps—so you may not get all the protection you expect.

. . . if the "five-second rule" is a good food safety rule? The idea that food that hits the floor is safe to eat—if you pick it up right away—is an urban myth. Instead of taking a chance, toss it or wash well.

SAFE FROM KITCHEN INJURIES

Protecting against foodborne illness isn't the only safety concern in the kitchen. With sharp utensils, hot ovens, messy spills, and more, kitchens are risky places for injury.

Avoid Slips, Falls, and Bumps

- Wipe up floor spills immediately so no one slips.
- Invest in a stable stool to reach a high cabinet.
- Keep cabinets, drawers, and doors closed so you don't bump into them. Put safety catches on drawers so they won't fall out when they're opened too far.

Avoid Burns

- Keep pot holders handy—and use them. Be careful if they get wet; water conducts heat.
- Turn handles on pots and pans inward and away from the stove's edge, where they may be bumped into or where children can grab them.
- Avoid overfilling pots and pans. Too much hot soup, stew, or pasta can burn you if it spills or boils over.
- Be careful with the hot-water tap, especially if you have small children.
- Allow enough time for the pressure to release if you use a pressure cooker.
- Avoid dropping water into hot oil. Splatters may burn you. *Remember:* Water and oil don't mix!
- Douse grease fires at the base of the flames with baking soda—not water! Or put a lid on it to control flames.
- Keep electrical cords away from stove burners.
- Keep a fire extinguisher in your kitchen. Check it regularly to make sure it works.

Avoid Cuts and Other Injuries

- Handle knives safely. Store them carefully, perhaps in a knife holder. Never leave them loose and perhaps unseen in the kitchen drawer. Use sharp knives; dull knives are harder to use and promote injury. Always cut on a cutting board with the sharp edge pointing away from you.
- Watch out for broken glass. If glass breaks in the sink, empty the water so you find all the pieces.
- Watch your fingers near your garbage disposal! Teach children to use it safely.
- Use safety latches on cabinets with alcoholic beverages, household chemicals, matches, plastic bags, and sharp utensils (knives, toothpicks) so children can't reach them.

Alert: What to Do If Someone's Choking

Perform the Heimlich Maneuver. If a victim can't talk, can't breathe, is turning blue in the face, or is clutching at his or her throat, get behind the person and wrap your arms around his or her waist. Make a fist with your thumb outside the fist and against the victim's upper abdomen, below the ribs and above the navel. Grasp your fist with your other hand and press into the victim's upper abdomen with a quick upward thrust. Repeat until the object is expelled. (Don't slap the victim's back—this can make matters worse.)

When you choke and no one is there to help, use the same technique as described above on yourself. You also can lean over a fixed horizontal object (chair, table edge, railing), pressing your upper abdomen against the edge until the object is expelled.

See "Safety from Choking: Infants, Toddlers, and Preschoolers" in chapter 16, page 486, for choking prevention and first aid for infants.

Source: Courtesy of The Heimlich Institute, Cincinnati, Ohio.

FOOD STORAGE SAVVY: YOUR GUIDE TO WHAT GOES WHERE

First comes shopping, then comes putting food away – but where? You may be surprised to learn the best places to store your groceries! Here's a helpful guide from the Academy of Nutrition and Dietetics.

Wrap and label meat, fish and poultry that you plan to freeze.
FREEZER
Dairy and eggs should be stored in the coldest part of the fridge, usually near the back and away from the door.
FRIDGE
Put meat in the meat drawer or on the lowest shelf of the refrigerator.
Use the crisper or produce drawers for veggies!
MAYO
RICE
PANTRY
Canned goods last 2+ years but can be damaged by temperatures above 100°F.
Mayo and peanut butter can be stored in the pantry; move mayo to the fridge when it's been opened.
Keep potatoes in a cool, dark part of the pantry and remove any that start to go bad. Onions like the same conditions, but don't put them together. Potatoes and onions should be separated!
Fruits with pits, like peaches and plums, should be placed in a closed paper bag until ripe – then refrigerated. Keep tomatoes in the pantry only if they'll be eaten within 1-2 days – otherwise, they go in the fridge.

Source: Academy of Nutrition and Dietetics.

Food Storage: Safekeeping

Did you know . . . billions of pounds of good food are wasted each year in the United States because home cooks aren't sure about their quality or safety? The USDA estimates thirty-six pounds of food waste per month per person!

To keep food safe and avoid food waste, store food right: *right* container, *right* place, *right* temperature, and *right* length of time. *See "A Closer Look . . . Deciphering Package Dates, Reducing Waste" in chapter 6, page 152, to learn how dates can help determine the freshness of packaged foods.*

CUPBOARD, PANTRY, FRIDGE, AND FREEZER STORAGE

The first task after a shopping trip is to store food properly. Foods stay safe and keep their quality, nutrients, and flavor longer when properly stored. Besides, you stretch your food dollar when you don't need to discard spoiled food.

Your Cupboards and Pantry

How long do nonrefrigerated foods keep peak quality and safety? That depends on how carefully they're stored. For safe, dry storage, follow these guidelines:

- Keep shelf-stable food in cupboards and a pantry that are clean, dry, dark, and cool and preferably away from heat-producing appliances. The best temperature range is 50°F to 70°F. High storage temperatures (more than 100°F) lower the quality of canned foods.
- Store, prepare, and eat foods away from kitchen chemicals and household and kitchen trash.
- Store dry pet food away from the kitchen and your food. Leftover canned pet food should be refrigerated. For your own food safety, feed pets outside the kitchen.

Canned and jarred foods. Stored properly, most *unopened* canned and jarred foods stay edible and keep their nutritional quality well beyond two years. Although the food is still safe to eat for longer, its color and texture may change after a while even when unopened. Stored at high temperatures (over 100°F), the quality is lowered. *Note:* Heed package labels if they say "Refrigerate after opening."

- Organize your cupboards or pantry with older cans and jars up front so you can use them first. The good news: they have a long shelf life.
- Be alert for food spoilage. Never use food from cans that are cracked, bulging, or leaking or that spurt liquid when opened. Food may be contaminated with deadly botulism organisms. Toss—never taste!

Dry and other shelf-stable foods. Store opened packages of dry food, such as breakfast cereal, pasta, and rice, in dry, airtight containers to keep out insects, rodents, and moisture. This also keeps food from absorbing odors.

With nonperishable foods such as canned foods, honey, spices, and packaged cereals and crackers, safety isn't an issue. However, these foods may taste less flavorful after a long storage time.

- Most dried fruits and vegetables can be stored for four to twelve months. For peak quality, keep dried fruits in the fridge in a well-sealed container.
- Use nuts and seeds right way. Or refrigerate them for up to one year for best quality. Nuts and seeds are high in unsaturated fats. This makes them fragile and means they can develop rancid, "off" flavors that may be unpleasant but are not unhealthy.
- Like the flavor of freshly baked bread? Store bread at room temperature. Bakery bread with fewer preservatives generally won't stay fresh as long. Keeping any bread in the fridge causes it to turn stale faster. If you can't use it right away, freeze it. What if bread has black or green fuzzy spots (mold)? Since the mold may have spread, toss the whole loaf.

Your Refrigerator

Do science experiments ever grow in your refrigerator? Is yesterday's meat loaf hiding behind tomorrow's juice carton? Has that special cheese become as dry as old leather? With the pace of today's life, these things happen even in the best kitchens. Refrigeration helps foods retain their quality and safety longer because it slows the growth of bacteria.

Chilling for keeps. Twenty-three percent of consumer refrigerators aren't cold enough!

- Keep your refrigerator cold—no higher than 40°F. Even at this temperature, bacteria that spoil food can grow, although slowly.
- Keep a refrigerator thermometer on the middle, inside shelf to monitor the temperature. Buy one at your supermarket.
- Cool leftovers and cooked food meant for later use in the refrigerator or freezer, not on the countertop. Never keep perishable foods or leftovers at room temperature for longer than two hours.
- Avoid overloading your refrigerator. Cold air needs room to circulate.
- Remind your family to make refrigerator raids quickly so the door doesn't stay open too long.

Packing food for refrigeration. Besides keeping food safe from foodborne bacteria, careful packing keeps food from drying out and absorbing off flavors.

- Unless the package is torn, leave food in its store wrapping. The less food is handled, the better. Follow safe handling instructions on food packaging.

The Danger Zone

Effects of temperature (°F) on growth of bacteria in food. The most dangerous temperature zone is between 40°F and 140°F.

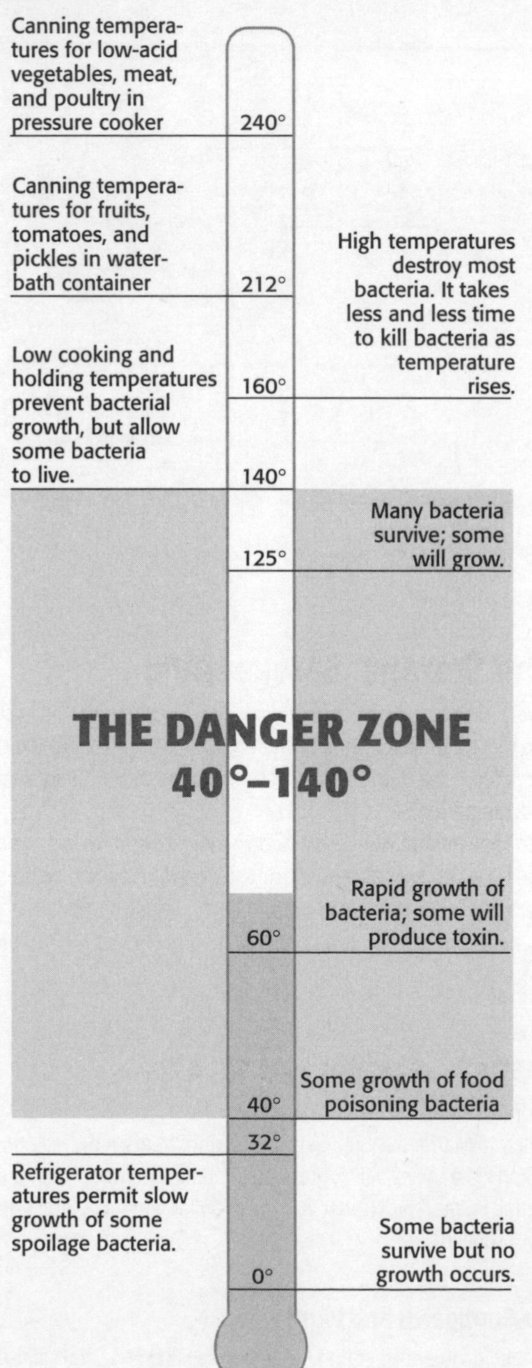
Canning temperatures for low-acid vegetables, meat, and poultry in pressure cooker
240°
Canning temperatures for fruits, tomatoes, and pickles in water-bath container
212°
High temperatures destroy most bacteria. It takes less and less time to kill bacteria as temperature rises.
Low cooking and holding temperatures prevent bacterial growth, but allow some bacteria to live.
160°
140°
Many bacteria survive; some will grow.
125°
THE DANGER ZONE
40°–140°
Rapid growth of bacteria; some will produce toxin.
60°
Some growth of food poisoning bacteria
40°
32°
Refrigerator temperatures permit slow growth of some spoilage bacteria.
Some bacteria survive but no growth occurs.
0°

Have you ever wondered?

. . . how to check refrigerator or freezer temperatures? Put a refrigerator thermometer in a glass of water in the middle of the refrigerator. Check in five to eight hours. If it's not 38°F to 40°F, adjust the temperature control; check again in another five to eight hours. Put the freezer thermometer between frozen-food packages. Check in five to eight hours. If it's not 0°F to 2°F, adjust the temperature control; check again in five to eight hours.

Keep appliance thermometers in your fridge and freezer all the time. During a power outage, the food is safe if the refrigerator is still 40°F and the freezer is 0°F or below.

. . . if opened ketchup and syrup can keep safely in the cabinet? Better to keep them in the refrigerator. The high acid content of ketchup keeps most bacteria in check, but refrigeration preserves the quality. Maple syrup actually has a short shelf life—in the fridge for up to one year; toss if mold appears. Chocolate syrup keeps its flavor quality better in the fridge; keep it for up to six months.

. . . if using a vacuum sealer is good for storing food longer? Yes, but only if done with food safety in mind. Freezing is as effective. A vacuum sealer shrink-wraps food, removing air (oxygen), and so preserves some qualities longer and potentially extends the storage time. Vacuum sealing nonperishable dry foods such as dried nuts or crackers may be useful because their moisture content is so low that an airtight container works well.

Vacuum sealing doesn't ensure food safety and doesn't provide the same long, shelf-stable benefits of home canning. If perishable, keep vacuum-sealed perishable foods refrigerated or frozen (not at room temperature). Clean them beforehand, then handle them like other perishable foods to keep them safe. Be aware that removing oxygen may eliminate the growth of spoilage bacteria, but not bacteria that thrive in low-oxygen environments, such as *Clostridium botulinum*, which give no visible indicators. *See "Bacteria: Hard Hitters" in this chapter, page 202, for more about harmful bacteria.*

. . . if some food-storage containers are safer than others? For plastic, know the code. Inside the tiny triangle on the bottom, there's a number from 1 to 7. The safest choices for food storage are 1, 2, 4, and 5. Number 3 is polyvinyl chloride (PVC), 6 is polystyrene, and 7 can be various plastics. Glass is always a safe bet!

. . . what to do if you suspect that food is contaminated? Don't even taste or smell it. Instead, securely wrap it and discard it where humans and animals can't get at it. If you've just purchased the food, consider taking it back to the store for a replacement or a refund.

- Wrap or store foods in covered containers or sealable bags.
- If you rewrap, seal storage containers well to prevent moisture loss and absorption of off odors. Remove as much air as possible from storage bags.

Managing the fridge. Eat perishable foods at peak quality.

- Store more perishable foods, such as milk and eggs, on the shelves and in the drawers of the fridge, not in the refrigerator door. The door temperature fluctuates more than the inside temperature does.
- Once weekly, clean out the refrigerator. Discard perishable foods, rather than risk foodborne illness, after they are past their prime.
- When in doubt about a food's safety, toss it out! Never trust its odor or appearance. Food may look, taste, and smell okay, even when no longer safe to eat. Sniffing moldy food may cause respiratory trouble.
- Discard moldy food in a bag or a wrapper so mold spores don't spread. Clean the food's container, the refrigerator, the cupboard, or the pantry to remove mold spores. Mold spreads fast in fruits and vegetables.
- Be aware of recommended food storage times. *See "The Cold Truth: Food Storage" in this chapter, page 202.*

Refrigerating meat, poultry, and fish. Before refrigerating these foods, they need to be packed carefully.

- Keep packages of raw meat, poultry, and fish in separate plastic bags, in a bowl or pan, and on the lowest refrigerator shelf so juices won't drip onto other foods. The lowest shelf usually is coldest.
- Another option: Store them in the refrigerator's meat keeper. It's extra cold, so these foods stay fresher longer. Keep raw and cooked meat, poultry, and fish separate.
- Use fresh meat, poultry, and fish, within a few days, *as noted in "The Cold Truth: Food Storage" in this chapter, page 202.*
- Refrigerate salami and other cured meats. Curing is a time-honored way to preserve meat, yet although cured meat is less likely to carry bacteria than fresh meat, cured meats aren't 100 percent bacteria free.
- For the very short time you keep them (within two days), refrigerate live mollusks in a container with a damp cloth on top so they don't dry out and die. Be sure other foods don't drip on them.

Don't store them in an airtight container or in water. They're saltwater fish that need air to stay alive. Scrub with a stiff brush just prior to shucking or cooking.

- Discard meat, poultry, and fish with an off odor, a sticky or slimy surface, and perhaps a color change.

See "Food Safety and Handling Tips" in chapter 6, page 151, to learn about fresh meat and poultry labeling.

Refrigerating eggs. Proper storage keeps the qualities of eggs fresh longer.

- Refrigerate eggs. At room temperature, eggs can age as much in a day as they would in a week if kept in the fridge! Aging isn't strongly related to safety—if the shell isn't cracked. However, eggs lose moisture and carbon dioxide as they age. The white thins and spreads; the yolk flattens and its yolk membrane weakens. That affects its cooking qualities.
- Refrigerate fresh shell eggs in their carton, not in the egg tray or door shelf, so they stay fresher longer.
- Use eggs *within* three weeks of purchase if there is no Julian date on the carton. If there is a Julian date, they keep their quality four or five weeks *beyond* the date. A Julian date is a number system, sometimes used on egg cartons to indicate the day the eggs are packed. Starting with January 1 as 001 and ending with December 31 as 365, they represent the consecutive days of the year. *See "Eggs: Buying Tips" in chapter 6, page 172.*

Refrigerating fruits and vegetables. Fresh fruits and vegetables are perishable, and differ in the way they're stored.

- Keep raw, whole fruits and vegetables in the proper place, at the right temperature:
  - *Refrigerate* certain fruits and vegetables: for example apples, apricots, berries, cantaloupe, figs, kiwifruit, and plums; and broccoli, Brussels sprouts, cabbage, cauliflower, cucumbers, lettuce, and mushrooms. Refrigerate herbs right away to keep them safe and at peak quality. (Exception: To keep the leaves from turning brown, trim the stems and keep basil at room temperature in a cup of water, as you do with a bouquet of flowers.) *See "Storing Herbs and Spices" in chapter 8, page 269.*
  - *Ripen* avocados, bananas, nectarines, and peaches on the countertop. Once they're ready to eat, put them in the fridge. *Tip:* Even if banana peels turn brown when refrigerated, they're okay to eat.
  - *Do not refrigerate* garlic, onions, potatoes, sweet potatoes, or winter squash. They are cold sensitive. Instead, keep them in a cool, dark, dry cabinet for up to a month or more. Separate them so their flavors and smells don't migrate.
- Unless you dry produce thoroughly with clean paper towels, wait to wash them until just before using. Washing before storing can promote bacterial growth and speed spoilage if the produce is stored while still wet.
- If you do wash produce, store it in clean bags or containers, not in the store's bag, which isn't clean.
- Keep produce in crisper bins in the refrigerator to retain moisture. Don't crowd the crisper but rather leave space for air to circulate. Keep fruits in a separate crisper from vegetables if you can; fruits give off ethylene gas that can shorten storage life.
- Refrigerate cut or peeled produce, or cooked fruits or vegetables, including those purchased precut or peeled. Discard any that have been left at room temperature for more than two hours.
- Discard cooked vegetables after three to four days.
- Keep dried fruits in the fridge, too, for up to six months for maximum freshness.

Refrigerating grain products. While most grain products keep well at room temperature, some are best refrigerated.

- Refrigerate or freeze whole-grain foods such as brown rice unless you plan to use them right away. They tend to turn rancid faster than refined-grain products.
- Extend the shelf-life of flour of all kinds, too, by keeping it in the refrigerator or freezer.
- Check the label on tortillas. It may recommend refrigerating after opening to avoid mold.

Refrigerating fresh dairy products. Safety is one reason for proper storage; retaining flavor and quality is another.

- Refrigerate promptly, preferably in the back of the fridge, where it's colder. Cover well so they don't pick up off odors. Pasteurization doesn't mean it's safe to leave milk unrefrigerated for an extended time, especially if the carton has been opened.
- Once milk is poured, never return it to its original container. Pouring it back increases the chance of contaminating the milk with outside organisms that cause spoilage and foodborne illness.

Refrigerating leftovers. Properly stored, most leftovers keep for three to four days.

- Refrigerate promptly—even if leftovers are still warm—to remove them from the danger zone. Today's refrigerators are powerful enough to cool food quickly. Store large amounts, such as soup or stew, in small, shallow containers to cool faster.
- Transfer opened canned food to a clean, covered container before refrigerating. You can refrigerate opened canned foods in the can if covered, but off flavors may develop.
- Carefully date leftovers on the container.
- Keep leftovers where you can see them. Remember: many bacteria that cause foodborne illness don't affect the look, smell, or

? Have you ever wondered?

. . . if prepackaged ground beef that's red on the outside but grayish-brown on the inside is safe to eat? These color differences don't mean that the meat is spoiled or old. Myoglobin, a protein in meat, is responsible for most of the red color. When oxygen from the air reacts with the myoglobin in freshly cut meat, it turns a bright red. You may see that on the surface of ground beef you buy at the store. The interior may be grayish-brown because no oxygen penetrates below the surface. Once exposed to air, meat will turn the familiar bright red.

. . . if blood spots on eggs are okay? Yes, they are harmless. Blood spots happen naturally while eggs are forming. You can remove them.

. . . about the safety of wild mushrooms? Stick with exotic mushrooms from the store if you're a mushroom lover. Telling the difference between edible and poisonous (some deadly) mushrooms takes expertise. Unless you know that the mushrooms were gathered by a trusted mushroom expert, avoid them.

. . . if mold on cheese is dangerous? That depends. Few molds on hard cheese produce toxins, or poisons. To be safe, discard at least one inch of cheese on all sides where mold is visible. Keep the knife out of the mold. Cover cheese with fresh, clean wrapping.

Discard soft cheeses such as Brie, Camembert, cream cheese, and cottage cheese with mold; however, the white fuzzy surface (rind) on Brie and Camembert is natural and the result of mold used to ripen these cheeses. For other mold-ripened cheeses such as blue, Gorgonzola, Roquefort, and Stilton, check the mold's color and pattern. If different from the usual blue or green veins and if you see furry spots or white, pink, blue, green, gray, or black flecks, cut off the cheese around and below the mold and discard. For all crumbled, shredded, and sliced cheeses, discard if moldy.

. . . if raw milk is healthier than pasteurized milk? No; even if it's certified, raw milk—from cows, goats, or sheep—can harbor *E. coli*, *Listeria*, *Salmonella*, and other harmful bacteria! Raw milk and unpasteurized cheese can be especially dangerous to those at risk, *as noted in "Who's at High Risk? Select Safer Food Alternatives" in this chapter, page 222.* In contrast, pasteurization, or heating milk quickly to a high temperature, kills harmful bacteria. *See "Bacteria: Hard Hitters" in this chapter, page 220, for more about harmful bacteria.*

To refute myths, raw milk won't prevent certain health problems. Pasteurization doesn't destroy nutrients or cause lactose intolerance or allergic reactions. For those who are lactose sensitive or have a milk allergy, the reaction to raw milk is the same as for pasteurized milk. Buying raw milk isn't really a strategy for sustainability—and being "organic," "certified," "grass fed," or local doesn't guarantee the safety of raw milk.

. . . if you can freeze milk? Yes, it's okay—and may be a good option if you can't use it all by its package date. Since milk expands when frozen, make sure there's still enough room in the carton or jug. Thaw it in the fridge or in cold water. Be aware that the flavor and texture may change, so you might prefer to use it in smoothies or an ingredient, rather than enjoy it as a beverage.

taste of food. Discard after four days, *or as noted in the "Refrigerator Calculator" in this chapter, page 204.* If you can't remember when you refrigerated them, toss! Once deli meat is opened, it's a leftover—even if its sell-by date is a week or more away.

Your Freezer

Freezing extends the safety and quality of many foods. Stored constantly at 0°F or below, it will stay safe, but the quality may suffer if stored too long.

Freezing preserves food by slowing the movement of molecules so microbes become dormant, and microorganisms won't grow. Freezing also slows the action of enzymes naturally present in fruits, vegetables, and animal-based foods. At higher temperatures, enzymes can lead to the deterioration of food. Enzyme activity doesn't harm frozen meat, poultry, and fish, and the acids in fruit neutralize them. However, for most vegetables, blanching and quickly chilling them prevents enzymatic deterioration.

Freezing for keeps. For freezer storage, the colder, the better.

- For long-term storage and top food quality, maintain a freezer temperature of 0°F or below. A free-standing freezer can stay that cold, while the freezer compartment of most refrigerators usually can't. Plan to use foods stored the freezer compartment more quickly, and avoid opening the door too often.
- To check the temperature, install a freezer thermometer, available at kitchen stores or supermarkets. That's especially important if you experience power-out or mechanical problems. *See "Have you ever wondered . . . how to check refrigerator or freezer temperatures?" in this chapter, page 199.*
- Freeze food as fast as possible to keep its quality and keep large ice crystals from forming. Large ice crystals melt as the food thaws and cause food such as meat to lose its juiciness. Ideally, a food that's two inches thick should freeze completely in about two hours.

The Cold Truth: Food Storage

How long can refrigerated and frozen foods keep safely and remain at top quality? Freezer and refrigerator times vary.

These short but safe time limits for home-refrigerated foods will keep them from spoiling or becoming dangerous to eat. The guidelines for freezer storage are for quality only. Frozen foods remain safe indefinitely, notes www.foodsafety.gov

As long as the food is properly packaged, these are basic guidelines for storing food for freshness and quality.

Food*	Refrigerator (40°F or below)	Freezer (0°F or below)
EGGS		
Raw eggs, in shell	3 to 5 weeks	Don't freeze. Instead beat egg yolks and whites together, then freeze.
Hard-cooked eggs	1 week	Don't freeze
Liquid pasteurized eggs or egg substitutes		
Opened	3 days	Doesn't freeze well
Unopened	7 days	Doesn't freeze well
Commercial mayonnaise (refrigerate after opening)	2 months	Don't freeze
DAIRY PRODUCTS		
Milk	1 week	3 months
Cottage cheese		
Opened	1 week	Doesn't freeze well
Unopened	2 weeks	Doesn't freeze well
Yogurt	1 to 2 weeks	1 to 2 months
Cheese, hard (such as Cheddar, Swiss)		Doesn't freeze well
Opened	3 to 4 weeks	3 to 4 weeks
Unopened	6 months	6 months
Cheese, soft (such as Camembert, Brie)	1 to 2 weeks	6 months
Cream cheese	2 weeks	Doesn't freeze well
Butter	1 to 2 months	6 to 9 months
HOT DOGS†		
Opened package	1 week	1 to 2 months
Unopened package	2 weeks	1 to 2 months
DELI MEATS		
Opened package or deli-sliced	3 to 5 days	1 to 2 months
Unopened	2 weeks	1 to 2 months

Food*	Refrigerator (40°F or below)	Freezer (0°F or below)
FRESH BEEF, VEAL, PORK, LAMB		
Steaks	3 to 5 days	4 to 12 months
Chops	3 to 5 days	4 to 12 months
Roasts	3 to 5 days	4 to 12 months
FRESH POULTRY		
Chicken or turkey, whole	1 to 2 days	1 year
Pieces	1 to 2 days	9 months
Giblets	1 to 2 days	3 to 4 months
FRESH FISH		
Lean fish (cod, flounder, etc.)	1 to 2 days	6 to 10 months
Fatty fish (salmon, etc.)	1 to 2 days	2 to 3 months
Smoked fish	14 days or date on vacuum package	2 months in vacuum package
Shrimp, crayfish	1 to 3 days	6 to 18 months
Cooked shellfish	3 to 4 days	1 to 3 months
HAM AND CORNED BEEF		
Canned ham, unopened (labeled "Keep refrigerated")	6 to 9 months	Doesn't freeze well
Ham, fresh, cooked	1 week	1 to 2 months
Corned beef, in pouch with pickling juices	5 to 7 days	1 month, drained, wrapped
HAMBURGER AND OTHER GROUND MEATS	1 to 2 days	3 to 4 months

The Cold Truth: Food Storage *(continued)*

Food*	Refrigerator (40°F or below)	Freezer (0°F or below)
BACON AND SAUSAGE		
Bacon	1 week	1 month
Sausage, raw (beef, pork, chicken, turkey)	1 to 2 days	1 to 2 months
Precooked, smoked breakfast links, patties	1 week	1 to 2 months
Hard sausage (pepperoni, jerky sticks)	2 to 3 weeks	1 to 2 months
VARIETY MEATS		
Tongue, brain, kidneys, liver, heart, chitterlings	1 to 2 days	3 to 4 months
DELI AND SELF-SERVE FOODS		
Salads: egg, ham, chicken, tuna, macaroni	3 to 4 days	Does not freeze well
Entrées, cold or hot	3 to 4 days	2 to 3 months
FROZEN DINNERS AND CASSEROLES		3 months; keep frozen until ready to serve

Food*	Refrigerator (40°F or below)	Freezer (0°F or below)
SOUPS AND STEWS		
Vegetables or meat added	3 to 4 days	2 to 3 months
LEFTOVERS		
Cooked meat, poultry, fish, or egg dishes	3 to 4 days	2 to 3 months
Cooked vegetable, rice, potato, and other dishes without meat, poultry, fish, or egg	3 to 4 days	1 to 2 months
Pizza	3 to 4 days	1 to 2 months
FRESH PRODUCE	For storing individual fruits and vegetables, refer to the Produce for Better Health Foundation's www.fruitsandveggiesmorematters.org.	

*Use the FoodKeeper app, noted below, to find storage times for other egg products, other types of ham and fish, and many other foods.

†Some may have package dates that are inconsistent with these guidelines.

Source: Adapted from the FoodKeeper App, www.foodsafety.gov/keep/foodkeeperapp/index.html. Accessed December 15, 2016. Use this app to find storage times for many other foods as well.

- Use the "quick-freeze" shelf if your home freezer has one.
- Spread food out in a single layer on several shelves if possible to speed up freezing. Stack them after they're frozen solid. Never stack packages before they're frozen.

Managing your freezer. Keeping the fresh qualities of frozen food takes good management.

- Before freezing, label each package with the food's name, the date, and the amount. Freeze food in serving sizes appropriate for your meals or cooking needs.
- Organize your freezer. Rotate foods, keeping the oldest foods in front so they're used first. Stack similar foods together for an easier find.
- Remember that some foods don't freeze well: bananas, celery, custard, cream (unless whipped), eggs in the shell, fresh tomatoes, gelatin salads, lettuce, mayonnaise, raw potatoes, sour cream, unblanched vegetables, and foods made with these ingredients. When frozen, cultured foods such as yogurt lose their smooth texture. Freezing affects quality, not safety.
- Be aware of recommended storage times. *See "The Cold Truth: Food Storage," above, for freezer storage times.*

Packing foods for the freezer. Proper packaging helps maintain food quality and prevents freezer burn. These leathery dry spots happen when air contacts the surface of food. Although still safe to eat, food quality is lost.

- Store foods purchased frozen in their original packaging. This includes meat and poultry. Commercial packaging is usually airtight. For long storage, overwrap these packages in something else as well. The original packaging may be permeable to air, and the quality may diminish over time. The extra layer of wrapping will help protect the food.

Refrigerator Calculator

Do Your Leftovers Make a Safe Meal?

Perishable Food	Keeps Refrigerated Up To
MEAT	
Cooked beef, bison, lamb, pork, and poultry	3 to 4 days
Cooked ground beef and ground turkey	3 to 4 days
Deli meats	3 to 5 days
FISH	
Raw (e.g., sushi, sashimi)	Must consume on day of purchase
Cooked fish	3 to 4 days
SOUPS AND CHILIS	
Chili with or without meat	3 to 4 days
Soup and stew	3 to 4 days

Perishable Food	Keeps Refrigerated Up To
OTHER ENTRÉES	
Casserole	3 to 4 days
Pasta and rice	7 days
Pizza	3 to 4 days
SIDE DISHES	
Fresh salad	1 to 2 days
Pasta and potato salad	3 to 5 days
Potato (any style)	3 to 5 days
Cooked vegetables	3 to 4 days
Hard-cooked egg	7 days
Deviled egg	3 to 4 days
DESSERT	
Cream pie and fruit pie	3 to 4 days
Pastries, cake, and cheesecake	7 days

Source: Adapted from www.homefoodsafety.org. Academy of Nutrition and Dietetics.

- Freeze unopened vacuum packages without opening them. If a package has been torn or opened while food is in the freezer, overwrap or rewrap it.
- Are you freezing home-prepared foods? Use freezer containers, moisture-proof paper, zippered plastic bags meant for freezing, or other freezer wraps. Traditional plastic wrap isn't suitable. Use freezer tape to help keep the package airtight and free of freezer burn. Remove as much air as you can to avoid freezer burn.

Freezing vegetables. For best quality, freeze fresh vegetables at their peak. Blanch fresh vegetables to lengthen their freezer life and stop enzymatic actions that cause loss of flavor, texture, and color. Blanching also cleanses the surface, brightens the color, helps slow vitamin loss, and softens vegetables so they're easier to pack.

- To blanch vegetables: Put them in a wire basket, and then immerse the basket in boiling water for one to three minutes. Plunge them into cold (60°F or below) water to stop the cooking. Freeze in airtight plastic bags after draining well. Blanching times vary; visit the National Center for Home Food Preservation at nchfp.uga.edu/how/freeze.html for blanching times for freezing specific vegetables. You can also blanch vegetables by steaming or microwaving; the latter may not inactivate some enzymes, however.
- Take care when packaging the vegetables for freezing. They can turn a dull color if they dry out from improper packaging or storing them for too long.

Freezing eggs and dairy foods. With some "know how," these foods can keep their quality when frozen.

- Extra eggs? They can't be frozen in their shells. Freezing makes the yolk thick and syrupy, and it won't flow like an unfrozen yolk or blend very well with the egg white or other ingredients. Instead, beat whole eggs just until blended and then pour them into freezer-safe containers. Seal tightly and freeze for up to a year. Label with the date and number of eggs in the container. Thaw in the fridge.
- Fresh milk? Freeze it while it's fresh, and thaw in the refrigerator. Although still safe and nutritious, the flavor and the texture will change. Still, it's great for smoothies and cooking.
- Cheese? Hard and semi-hard cheese will be crumbly when frozen, but the flavor will be fine. Freeze in small pieces.

? Have you ever wondered?

. . . if freezer burn is harmful? The grayish-white, dried-out patches on improperly wrapped frozen food won't make you sick, but it will make food tough and tasteless. It happens when air comes in contact with the surface of food.

To prevent freezer burn, wrap food that hasn't been previously frozen in proper freezer wrap (aluminum foil, heavy freezer paper, or plastic freezer bags), push air out, and then seal with freezer tape. Well-sealed freezer containers work, too; before putting on the lid, cover food with plastic wrap to avoid freezer burn from air inside the container. If portions of food have freezer burn, cut it away before cooking. If heavily freezer burned, discard because the quality of the food is poor.

. . . if freezing destroys bacteria and parasites? Freezing food to 0°F inactivates microbes—bacteria, yeasts, and molds. Once thawed, these microbes can again become active, multiplying under the right conditions to levels that can lead to foodborne illness. Since they then grow at about the same rate as microorganisms on fresh food do, handle thawed items as you would any perishable food.

Trichina and other parasites can be destroyed by subzero freezing temperatures. However, home freezing may not be reliable. Thorough cooking destroys parasites.

. . . if you can refreeze food without cooking it after it's thawed in the refrigerator? Yes, it's safe, but some quality may be lost since it will lose moisture during thawing.

After cooking raw foods that were previously frozen, it is safe to freeze the cooked foods. If previously cooked foods are thawed in the refrigerator, you may refreeze the unused portion. If you purchase previously frozen meat, poultry, or fish, you can refreeze it if has been handled properly.

- Ice cream and frozen yogurt? Once opened, cover the surface lightly with plastic wrap. That helps keep crystals from forming, although the milk solids and gelatin in commercial ice cream help prevent this.

Thawing safely. Thawing is primarily used for frozen meats, poultry, and fish. Most vegetables can be cooked without thawing.

Thaw food safely in three ways: in the refrigerator or, for a faster thaw, either submerged in cold water or in the microwave oven. Never thaw food on the countertop, outdoor porch, or in a cool place such as your garage or basement. Bacteria thrive when left for more than two hours in the temperature "danger zone," between 40°F–140°F; *see "The Danger Zone" in this chapter, page 198.*

- *In the refrigerator:* Put food that's thawing into a plastic bag or on a plate to collect any juices. Plan ahead to defrost frozen meat and poultry in the refrigerator. Here's how long it takes to thaw in the fridge:
  - Ground beef, 1-inch-thick package—twenty-four hours
  - Large roast—four to seven hours per pound (A six-pound roast takes at last twenty-four hours to thaw in the fridge.)
  - Small roast—three to five hours per pound
  - Steak, 1 inch thick—twelve to fourteen hours
  - Turkey—one day for every five pounds of weight
- *In cold water:* To thaw frozen meat, poultry, or fish, place it in a leakproof package or plastic bag so bacteria and water can't get into it. Submerge the bag in cold water, changing the water every thirty minutes. Cold water keeps the surface chilled while thawing occurs. After thawing, cook immediately.
- *In the microwave oven:* Remove the store wrapping first. Put the meat, poultry, or fish in a microwave-safe container, and cover. Defrost on low or use the defrost settings on your microwave oven. The time for thawing depends on the amount of food you need to thaw. Once thawed, cook the food right away. Some parts of the food may become warm and begin to cook during microwave thawing.

POWER'S OUT: HANDLING STORED FOOD SAFELY

Suppose a storm, an accident, or some other natural or man-made event shuts off power to your home—and to your refrigerator and freezer. If you take precautions, maybe you won't need to toss food out.

Before Emergencies Happen

Wherever you live, keep a three-day emergency supply of food and water for you, your family, and your pets. *See "Disaster Planning: Emergency Supply Checklist" in this chapter, page 207.*

- Stock up on nonperishable foods: ready-to-eat canned meat, fruits, juices, milk, soups, and vegetables. Keep high-energy foods on hand, such as nuts, peanut butter, and trail mix. Food in cans is preferable to food in glass jars, since cans won't break. Choose single-serving portions, too; you may have no way to keep leftovers cold.
- Keep a manual can opener on your emergency shelf. An inability to open canned food adds to any disaster! Keep an appliance thermometer in the refrigerator and freezer to check the temperature in case of a power outage.
- Plan for one gallon of water per person per day. Buy commercially bottled, well-sealed water, or store your own water in sanitized,

Foods from the Fridge: After the Power Is Back On

If the power has been out for more than 4 hours (and the fridge has remained closed), follow these guidelines for what is safe to keep and what should be tossed. See www.foodsafety.gov/keep/charts/refridg_food.html for a complete list of foods.

What to Keep	What to Toss*
Hard cheese, including grated Parmesan, processed cheese	Milk, poultry, fish
Butter, margarine	Soft cheese, shredded cheese
Opened fruit juice and canned fruit	Milk, cream, yogurt, other dairy foods
Jelly, relishes, catsup, mustard, taco sauce	Opened baby formula
Worcestershire, soy, barbecue, and Hoisin sauces	Eggs and egg products
Opened vinegar-based dressings	Dough, cooked pasta or rice
Breads, muffins, tortillas, waffles	Cooked or cut fruit and vegetables
Fresh, uncut fruits	
Uncut, unwashed raw vegetables	

*Discard perishable foods that have been above 40°F for over 2 hours.

food-grade containers (not milk cartons or jugs). *See "Local Disasters: Safe Drinking Water" in chapter 4, page 87, for how to make contaminated water safe to drink.*

- Rotate emergency food and water supplies every year or so. This way, they're fresh when you need them.
- Store food and water in a way to prevent it from being contaminated in case of flooding.

If a Possible Emergency Is Projected

Alerts for hurricanes, tornadoes, ice storms, and other weather events often broadcast a "heads up" several days ahead. If so, you may have enough time to plan.

- Freeze containers of water and ice packs to help keep food cold.
- Freeze refrigerated items such as leftovers, milk, and fresh meat and poultry that you don't need right away.
- Pack foods closely in the freezer to help them stay colder longer.
- If you think your power may be out for an extended time, buy dry or block ice to keep your fridge or freezer cold.
- In case of flooding, keep foods on higher shelves to avoid flood water.

- Gateway to Federal Food Safety Information, Refrigerated Food and Frozen Food and Power Outages: When to Save and When to Throw Out
  www.foodsafety.gov/keep/charts/refridg_food.html
  www.foodsafety.gov/keep/charts/frozen_food.html

When the Power Goes Out

Keep refrigerator and freezer doors closed! Unopened, most refrigerators will keep food safely cold for about four hours, depending on the warmth of your kitchen. If the power is out longer, dry ice or block ice can help to keep the refrigerator and freezer cold—but not as cold is if the power was on.

Frozen foods can hold for about two days (forty-eight hours) in a full, freestanding freezer if it stays closed. Half full, an unopened freezer remains cold for about one day (twenty-four hours). Freezers are well insulated; each frozen food package is an ice block, protecting the foods around it.

Once the Power's Back On

Appearance, taste, or odor isn't a guide to food safety. Never taste! Always discard any items in the freezer or refrigerator that have come in contact with raw meat or poultry juices. And follow these guidelines:

Refrigerated foods. If the power's been out for the refrigerator for no longer than four hours, food should be safe. Discard perishable foods such as meat, poultry, fish, eggs, soft cheese, and leftovers that (1) have been kept above 40°F for more than two hours or (2) if the power has been out for four hours or more.

In that time, bacteria can multiply enough to cause illness. Dispose of foods safely, where animals can't eat them.

Fresh whole fruits and vegetables, hard and processed cheeses, butter, stick margarine, and condiments often keep for several days at room temperature. Although still safe, soft margarine (in tubs) loses its shape, texture, and flavor at room temperature and may get rancid.

- Is My Food Safe?—Find out proper internal cooking temperatures, learn how long to keep leftovers, and test your kitchen safety knowledge (from the Academy of Nutrition and Dietetics)
- FoodKeeper—Advice for how and how long to store hundreds of food items at home (from the USDA, Cornell University, and the Food Marketing Institute)

Disaster Planning: Emergency Supply Checklist

Stocking up on emergency supplies—and rotating (using and replacing) them regularly—can contribute safety and comfort during and after a disaster. Store enough supplies for at least seventy-two hours. If you're in a flood area, store foods and eating utensils where they'd likely be away from contaminated water.

Food and Water*

- Drinks: instant coffee, tea bags, hot chocolate
- Fruits and vegetables: canned fruits, vegetables, juice; dried fruits, raisins; other dried foods
- Grain products: whole wheat crackers, instant oatmeal, pasta, pretzels, ready-to-eat cereals, instant rice
- Milk or soymilk: evaporated, powdered, or ultra-pasteurized milk; boxed soymilk
- Mixed foods: canned soups, chili, spaghetti
- Pet food, if appropriate
- Protein foods: canned beans, canned meats (beef, ham, chicken, tuna), peanut butter
- Ready-to-eat infant formula, infant foods, food for elderly people and those with special needs, if appropriate
- Snacks: granola bars, nuts, trail mix
- Staples: sugar, salt, pepper, mayonnaise, ketchup, mustard
- Water: One gallon per person per day (for pets, too)

Avoid salty foods since they'll make you thirsty, a problem when water is in short supply.

Cooking

- Appliance (refrigerator) thermometer
- Barbecue grill, camp stove, pots/pans (*Warning:* Barbecue grills and camp stoves should not be used inside your home.)
- Can opener (manual)
- Fuel for cooking (charcoal, propane, etc.)
- Heavy-duty aluminum foil
- Matches in a waterproof container
- Plastic knives, forks, spoons
- Paper plates, cups
- Paper towels

The National Disaster Education Coalition provides more food- and water-related advice at www.disastereducation.org

Sanitation

- Bar soap, shampoo, liquid detergent
- Feminine and infant supplies
- Hand sanitizer, wet wipes
- Household bleach
- Large plastic trash bags for trash, waste, water protection
- Large trash cans
- Newspaper (to wrap garbage and waste)
- Toothpaste, toothbrushes
- Toilet paper

Safety and Comfort

- Candles and matches in a waterproof container
- Change of clothing, sweatshirts
- Garden hose for siphoning and firefighting
- Heavy gloves for clearing debris
- Sturdy shoes, socks

Other Supplies

- Alternative power for your mobile device
- Ax, shovel, broom
- Blankets or sleeping bags
- Coil of ½-inch rope
- Copies of personal identification, medication prescriptions, credit cards
- Crescent wrench for turning off gas
- Essential medications, spare glasses
- Extra keys for car and house
- Fire extinguisher: A-B-C type
- First-aid kit and book
- Multi-tool pocket knife
- Plastic tape
- Portable battery-powered radio or television, flashlight, spare fresh batteries
- Screwdriver, pliers, hammer
- Suntan lotion, hats
- Tent

*In case distribution is disrupted after an emergency, store a two-week supply if you have special food or medical needs.

Frozen foods. Check the freezer temperature using an appliance thermometer. If the temperature reads 40°F or below, the food is safe and may be refrozen. Quality may be lost with refreezing, but the food is still safe to eat. However, use it as soon as possible. Another option: cook it before refreezing it.

If previously cooked foods thaw in the refrigerator, refreeze them if they haven't been left outside the refrigerator longer than two hours (one hour in temperatures above 90°F). Use these foods within two to four months.

For more advice about handling and perhaps discarding food and kitchen equipment after disasters (fires, floods, hurricanes) and power outages, contact experts: US FDA Food Safety Hotline (1-888-SAFE-FOOD), USDA Meat and Poultry Hotline (1-800-535-4555), or your local American Red Cross, Cooperative Extension Service, Civil Defense, or emergency management office.

Safe Food from the Start

Handle food properly from prep to serving—for freshness, nutrition, quality, and safety. Food is a delicate commodity. You can't fix it once those qualities are lost.

HOW TO PREP UNCOOKED FOOD SAFELY

Whether you're prepping food prior to cooking or planning to enjoy the flavors of fresh fruits and vegetables, food safety must be top-of-mind.

Preparing Fruits and Vegetables Safely

Whether grown conventionally or organically—or gathered from the supermarket, farmers' market, or garden—wash produce thoroughly with clean, running water before eating, cutting, or cooking it. Start by washing your hands properly.

- Firm produce, such as melons and cucumbers, should be scrubbed with a clean produce brush. A diluted vinegar wash is no more effective than plain water, and soap and commercial produce washes aren't recommended either. To debunk a myth: Misting produce at the grocery store doesn't wash it!
- Even if you plan to cut or peel avocados, bananas, grapefruit, lemons, melons, oranges, and squash, wash them well first. Cutting through unwashed peels can carry bacteria and dirt from the surface to the interior. Remove outer leaves.
- Dry wash produce with clean cloths or paper towels when you aren't sure you will eat it right away. Moisture left on fruits and vegetables may attract bacteria and promote its growth.
- Remove spots caused by bruising or damage. They may harbor bacteria or mold. "Rust" spots on lettuce aren't harmful; they occur as cells in the leaf break down naturally after harvest. On the other hand, discard or compost produce that looks rotten.
- Check the package label on precut, packaged produce such as bagged lettuce. If it says "prewashed, ready to eat," the FDA notes that it's safe to use without more washing so long as it's kept refrigerated and used by the "use by" date. In fact, you actually run the risk of cross-contamination by washing produce again. If you do choose to wash a product marked "pre-washed" and "ready-to-eat," be sure that it does not come in contact with unclean surfaces or utensils.
- For leafy greens, remove damaged leaves or stems. For iceberg lettuce, remove the core. Wash loose leaves by running them under cold running water or by immersing them in cold water in a clean bowl or salad spinner. Rinse for 30 seconds or more and then drain. Repeat twice. Pat lettuce dry with a clean towel or use a salad spinner to remove excess moisture.

Preparing Canned and Jarred Foods Safely

Cleanliness is a key to keeping foods in cans and jars safe.

- Check cans and jar lids before opening. Safety buttons on jar lids should be depressed. Unopened cans shouldn't bulge or leak. Use the oldest cans and jars first.

? Have you ever wondered?

. . . how to handle sprouts for food safety? Sprouts such as mung bean and alfalfa tend to harbor *E. coli*, *Listeria*, and *Salmonella*; moist conditions that sprouts need to grow are perfect for breeding bacteria, too. The Centers for Disease Control and Prevention (CDC) advises you to cook sprouts thoroughly (alfalfa, clover, mung bean, radish, and other sprouts) before eating them to destroy bacteria. High-risk individuals should avoid sprouts entirely! The FDA also recommends cooking sprouts. Even carefully washed sprouts can harbor bacteria. Especially if you're at high risk, ask for sandwiches and salads in restaurants to be made without raw sprouts.

For healthy people, sprouts can be a source of important nutrients. Only buy sprouts that have been refrigerated properly and do not have a musty smell or slimy appearance. Refrigerate sprouts to slow bacterial growth; wash them under cold, running water; and buy them fresh with the buds on (no musty smell or slimy appearance). To cook them, add them to soups, stews, or stir-fries at the end of cooking, or oven roast them until crisp and lightly browned.

. . . is a raw-food diet safe? Certainly raw fruits and vegetables are safe and nourishing—if they're properly cleaned. If eaten at their peak, they can provide more heat-labile nutrients than their cooked counterparts.

Eating raw or uncooked meat, poultry, fish, or eggs is a different story. These foods provide perfect conditions for harboring and growing bacteria. A raw-food diet is especially risky for infants, young children, and those with impaired immune functions.

- Wash lids before opening them so particles don't fall into food (this includes soft drink and soup cans). Vacuum-packed canned foods may hiss softly when opened. That's probably the normal release of air pressure. But a loud hiss or spurting may indicate food spoilage.
- Wash can openers after each use.

Preparing Meat, Poultry, and Fish Safely

Keeping raw meat, poultry, and fish safe is not only about cleanliness, but also about avoiding cross contamination.

- Never rinse raw meat, poultry, or fish. You can't rinse away all bacteria. *Salmonella* and *Campylobacter jejuni* can only be killed by cooking to an internal temperature of 165°F. Besides being unnecessary, rinsing increases the chance of cross-contamination by splashing from the sink to other foods, utensils, and surfaces.
- Keep juices from raw meat, poultry, or fish away from contact with other foods—cooked and raw. Use separate or thoroughly cleaned cutting boards, plates, trays, and utensils.
- Deveining shrimp is only needed for cosmetic purposes. Cooking destroys any bacteria in the intestinal vein so it's safe to eat. However, in large shrimp, the vein may contain a lot of grit.
- Marinate meat, poultry, and fish in the refrigerator in covered glass or plastic containers. Even with acidic ingredients (citrus juice, wine, and vinegar), bacteria can grow fast at room temperature. Why glass or plastic? Acidic ingredients react with metals, which can migrate into food.
- To use the marinade as a dip or sauce, make a double batch and reserve half for serving time. Discard the half that's used to marinate the food.
- Brush sauces onto cooked burgers when they're nearly cooked. Sauces made with dark-colored sauces (barbecue, soy, teriyaki, or Worcestershire sauces), when mixed into the meat, make it hard to judge visual doneness of ground meat or poultry. That said, check with a food thermometer.

Preparing Herbed Oils Safely

If you infuse oil with herbs or garlic, use it right away; don't store it. Botulism has been linked to some home-prepared herb and garlic oils. Commercially prepared herb and garlic oils contain additives that prevent bacterial growth. For added precaution, always refrigerate commercial herb- and garlic-oil products.

HOW TO COOK FOOD SAFELY

Is it done yet? That's a question on any cook's mind to make sure the food is flavorful and visually appealing. Another should be: Is it cooked right so it's safe to the plate?

- Cook and hold cooked foods at temperatures higher than 140°F. High temperatures (160°F to 212°F) kill most bacteria. Slightly lower temperatures (between 140°F and 159°F) prevent their growth, but bacteria may survive. You may need to set your oven temperature higher than 140°F to keep food hot enough if you're holding it before serving.
- Use a food thermometer to know if you've cooked foods to safe minimum internal temperatures. Use an oven thermometer to check your oven temperature and a timer to cook accurately.

Is Raw Seafood Safe to Eat?

Many people like sushi and sashimi as well as seviche (seviche is a popular Mexican and Caribbean appetizer, also spelled ceviche). This means eating raw finfish or shellfish that has been marinated in a lime juice–based mixture (or similar). However, the lime juice in seviche doesn't guarantee safety! (*Note:* some recipes for seviche use cooked or canned fish.)

Shellfish, especially mollusks (clams, mussels, oysters, scallops), may carry *Vibrio vulnificus* bacteria, which multiply even during refrigeration. *See "Bacteria: Hard Hitters" in this chapter, page 220, for risks related to* Vibrio.

High-risk individuals—those with cancer, diabetes, hemochromatosis, HIV, impaired immune systems, inflammatory bowel disease, kidney disease, liver and gastrointestinal disorders, steroid dependency, or stomach problems—should avoid eating any raw or partly cooked fish. Pregnant women and their unborn children, infants, young children, older adults, and those with alcohol problems also are considered at high risk.

With careful control, the following foods can be safe for those who are not at high risk. Precautions to reduce the risks include:

- If you prepare raw fish at home, start with high-quality, sushi-grade fish—very, very fresh—and use it the day of purchase. Buy from a licensed, reputable dealer.
- For mollusks (clams, mussels, oysters), ask to see the certified shipper's tag. If you harvest your own, make sure the waters of origin are certified for safety.
- Follow rules for safe food handling. Still, eating raw fish at home isn't advised. You're wiser to cook fish to an internal temperature of 145°F to destroy parasites, according to government food-safety guidelines.
- If fish is sushi grade or high quality, sushi, sashimi, seviche, and oyster bars are generally safe for those not at risk. Reputable restaurants have highly trained chefs who know how to buy fish for safety and sanitation standards—and to handle fish safely.

Cook to Safe Internal Temperatures

Three numbers to remember for safe cooking: 145°F for whole meat, 160°F for ground meats, and 165°F for all poultry! These are safe internal temperatures; use a food thermometer to check (instant-read thermometers are easy to use and generally reliable). For reasons of personal preference, you may cook meat to a higher temperature.

Remember, you can't tell whether meat is safely cooked just by looking at it. Any uncured red meats, including pork, might be pink, even when the meat has reached a safe internal temperature.

For safety and quality, let meat rest for at least three minutes before carving or consuming. During the resting time, its temperature remains constant or continues to rise, which destroys harmful germs.

Food Item	Internal, Cooked Temperature
GROUND MEAT, POULTRY, AND MEAT MIXTURES	
Beef, pork, veal, and lamb	160°F
Hamburgers (patties, meatballs, etc.)	160°F
Chicken and turkey	165°F
FRESH BEEF, PORK, VEAL, LAMB	
Roasts, steaks, and chops	
Medium rare	145°F*
Medium†	160°F
Well done†	170°F
HAM	
Fresh ham (raw)	145°F*
Precooked ham (to reheat)	140°F
POULTRY	
Chicken and turkey, whole	165°F
Poultry breasts, roasts, thighs, legs, and wings	165°F
Duck and goose	165°F
Stuffing (cooked alone or in bird)	165°F

Food Item	Internal, Cooked Temperature
EGGS AND EGG DISHES	
Eggs	Cook until yolk and white are firm.
Egg dishes	160°F
SEAFOOD	
Finfish	145°F or cook until flesh is opaque (milky white) and flakes (separates) with a fork.
Shellfish	
Shrimp, lobster, and crabs	Cook until flesh is opaque and pearly white.
Clams and mussels, and oysters in their shells	Cook until shells open during cooking. Discard those that don't open.
Shucked clams and oysters†	Cook until opaque or milky white and firm.
Scallops	Cook until flesh is milky white, or opaque and firm.
Leftovers and Casseroles	165°F

*For food safety, the USDA advises cooking to an internal temperature of 145°F even if pink in the center, then allowing it to rest for at least three minutes (called standing time) before carving or consuming it.

†Not shown in source.

Source: www.foodsafety.gov. Accessed November 30, 2016.

See "Cook to Safe Internal Temperatures" and "How to Choose and Use a Food Thermometer" in this chapter, above and on page 212, respectively. This website can help as well: www.isitdoneyet.gov

- If you baste or brush sauces on food as it cooks, switch to a clean brush and fresh sauce once the food is cooked so you won't transfer bacteria from raw to cooked foods. Discard the marinade from raw meat, poultry, or fish, or boil it for a least one minute before using it on cooked food.
- Cook food thoroughly, and don't interrupt cooking. Food that's partly cooked and held, and then cooked more, may not get hot enough inside for food safety. These conditions may encourage bacterial growth.

- Know how to use a slow cooker safely. Even though food is cooked at a lower temperature, usually between 170°F and 280°F, food prepared in a slow cooker is safe; lengthy periods of time in moist heat are lethal to bacteria. Set the cooker on high until the food begins to bubble, and then turn to simmer or low. Cover and check the internal temperature, which should be at least 160°F (165°F for chicken) when done. Always choose a recipe with a liquid. Use small, thawed pieces of meat or poultry. Fill the cooker from half to two-thirds full. Once cooked, food inside will be safe—if the slow cooker is on.

  If the power goes out and you're not home to know for how long, toss the food! An added safety tip: A slow cooker is not for reheating.

Cooking Meat and Poultry Safely

Cooking meat and poultry to safe internal temperatures is essential to helping ensure safe eating.

- If you stuff poultry, do so just before roasting and stuff loosely. Once roasted, both the internal temperature of the bird and the center of the stuffing must reach 165°F before they're safe to remove from the oven. Another option is to cook the stuffing separately. Even so, still check the temperature of the center of the stuffing for doneness. Never cook stuffed poultry in a microwave oven. Refrigerate leftover poultry and stuffing separately.
- Use a food thermometer to check the internal temperature of meat and poultry for doneness—even if you brine. When properly cooked, their juices shouldn't be pink and poultry joints should move easily. That said, visual cues alone are inaccurate!
- Cook ground meat and ground poultry thoroughly—until the internal temperature reaches 160°F for meat and 165°F for poultry. Thorough cooking is especially important with ground meat and poultry; bacteria on the outside can easily get mixed with the interior meat during grinding and mixing. According to USDA research, one in four burgers browns on the outside before it reaches a safe internal temperature.
- Instead of going for rare beef, pork, veal, or lamb, cook roasts and steaks until medium rare (to an internal temperature of 145°F) for safety.
- Before carving any beef, pork, veal, or lamb roast, let it rest for about 15 minutes after removing it from the oven; steaks take less. The internal temperature will rise, and the roast will continue to cook a bit for a short time. The purpose of resting is more than this: to allow the juices to be reabsorbed so they aren't lost during carving. The meat will firm up, making carving easier and make the meat more tender and juicy.
- Avoid very low oven temperatures (below 325°F) for roasting meat and poultry, or for long or overnight cooking for meat. Low oven temperatures for roasting encourage bacterial growth before the meat is cooked.
- When in doubt, cook a ham. If the label says the ham is "cooked," it's safe without cooking or heating. If not, don't take chances; cook it. Label terms such as "smoked," "aged," or "dried" are no guarantee of safety without cooking. The smoked flavor may come from added flavoring, and not from curing.

Cooking Fish Safely

As with other protein foods, cook fish to keep them safe. Here's how:

- Follow the ten-minute rule for finfish, which includes whole fish, steaks, and fillets. For every inch of thickness, cook for ten minutes. If the fish is cooking in a sauce or a foil wrap, cook for five minutes longer. If one end is thinner than another, fold it underneath so the thickness is uniform. This rule applies to baking, broiling, grilling, poaching, and steaming. Cooking times for frying and microwaving are generally shorter. If fish is cooked from a frozen state, double the cooking time.
- Cook scallops, shrimp, and lobster properly. Scallops and shrimp take three to five minutes, depending on size, and regardless of the cooking method. Scallops turn milky-white and firm; shrimp turn pink. Boiling lobsters takes five to six minutes per pound after the water returns to a boil; when fully cooked, the lobster shells turn bright red.
- Be sure that mollusks are still alive before cooking them. If the shells don't close tightly when tapped or if they're open, toss them! Cook them in a pot that's big enough to cook them all thoroughly—even shells at the top or the middle. For live clams, mussels, and oysters, keep the water boiling for three to five minutes after the shells open, or steam them for four to nine minutes. Cook until they open. Discard any that don't open during cooking.

  If the mollusks are shucked:

  - Bake for about ten minutes at 450°F.
  - Boil for at least three minutes or until the edges curl.
  - Broil for at least three minutes.
  - Fry for at least ten minutes at 375°F.

Cooking Eggs Safely

If handled improperly, eggs and egg-rich foods are a perfect medium for *Salmonella* growth.

- Avoid washing eggs. You'll remove the coating applied during processing that protects them from bacteria while stored.
- Toss cracked or dirty eggs.
- Separate egg whites and yolks with an egg separator or a funnel. Passing the egg from shelf half to shell half can contaminate the egg with pathogens from the outside of the shell.
- Cook eggs until done—slowly over gentle heat until the yolks and whites are firm. *See "When Are Cooked Eggs Safe?" in this chapter, page 213.* For people with a compromised immune system, even

How to Choose and Use a Food Thermometer

The only way to know if meat, poultry, casseroles, and egg dishes are done is to use a food thermometer! Doing so takes away guesswork and, besides reducing risk for foodborne illness, it helps to prevent overcooking.

Buy the food thermometer for your intended use. Use as directed in the manufacturer's instructions. (*Note:* A food thermometer is different from a candy thermometer.)

Test the food thermometer to confirm an accurate reading. If improperly calibrated, it could be off by as much as 30 degrees. Calibrate, if possible, according to the manufacturer's directions.

Place the food thermometer properly (*as shown in "Where to Place an Oven-Safe Food Thermometer" on the next page.*) in the thickest part of the food, not touching bone, fat, or gristle. Start checking toward the end of the cooking time and before you think the food should be done. (For roasts, the temperature may rise from 5 to 10 degrees, depending on the size; it must reach a safe internal temperature before carving.) Check irregularly shaped meat and poultry, egg dishes, and ground meat and poultry in several places.

Give the thermometer reading enough time to respond. Allow enough rest (standing time), *as discussed on the previous page,* before carving and consuming. Know the safe internal temperature for the food (*as given in "Cook to Safe Internal Temperatures" in this chapter, page 210*).

After each use, wash the thermometer stem well in hot, soapy water. Most thermometers should not be immersed.

Safety tip: Remove the food from the heat source to a clean plate or spatula if you're cooking on a grill or in a frying pan before inserting a food thermometer sideways in the food.

TYPES OF FOOD THERMOMETERS

- *Dial oven-safe (bimetal):* Should be inserted 2 to 2½ inches deep into the thickest part of the food and can remain there throughout cooking. Reads in 1 to 2 minutes. Can be used in roasts, casseroles, and soups. Not appropriate for thin foods. Easy to read; placement is important. Some can be calibrated. *Note:* Heat conduction of the metal stem can cause a false high reading.
- *Digital instant-read (thermistor):* Not designed to stay in the food while cooking; reads in 10 seconds when the stem is inserted into the food about ½ inch deep. Can measure a temperature in thin and thick foods; works well in shallow-tray frozen dinners as well as thin foods such as meat patties, pork chops, and chicken breasts. Check at the end of cooking time. Some can be calibrated.
- *Dial instant-read (bimetal):* Not designed to stay in the food while cooking; reads in 15 to 20 seconds when the stem is inserted into the food about 2 to 2½ inches deep in the thickest part. Can be used in roasts, casseroles, and soups. Appropriate for thin foods if inserted sideways into the center of the food. Check at the end of the cooking time. Some can be calibrated.
- *Pop-up:* Often found already inserted into poultry when purchased; pops up when the food reaches the final temperature for safety and doneness. Always verify doneness with a conventional food thermometer.
- *Thermometer-fork combination:* Not designed to stay in the food while cooking; reads in 2 to 10 seconds. Insert at least ¼ inch deep into the thickest part of the food, with the sensor in the fork tine fully inserted. Can be used in most foods. Convenient for grilling. Check at the end of the cooking time. Cannot be calibrated.
- *Disposable temperature indicators:* Use once and toss. Reads in 5 to 10 seconds. Temperature-sensitive material changes color when the desired temperature is reached. Meant only for specific temperature ranges; for example, for burgers or chicken. Insert about ½ inch deep, according to the manufacturer's directions. Use only for the foods intended. Useful for grilling at picnics and tailgate parties. They're Inexpensive; find them in the meat case of your supermarket. Use as directed by the manufacturer.
- *Other types of food thermometers*: An oven probe with cord, or a thermocouple. Use them according to the manufacturer's directions. Microwave-safe food thermometers are designed for microwave ovens only.

lightly cooked egg dishes such as soft custards and French toast can be risky and should be avoided.

- Use slightly cooked eggs when making soft meringues and mousse to destroy any *Salmonella,* or use pasteurized egg whites. To prepare the eggs, put the whites in a double boiler or a heavy pan. Add two tablespoons of sugar for each egg white. Cook over low heat, beating with a mixer on low speed as you cook, until the whites reach 160°F. Increase the speed to high, and beat until soft peaks appear. Proceed with the recipe as directed.

Avoid foods made with raw eggs—such as Caesar salad dressing, eggnog, hollandaise sauce, and homemade mayonnaise—unless they're made with an unopened carton of pasteurized eggs. Once pasteurized eggs are open, treat them like other eggs because at this point they can be contaminated by bacteria.

Where to Place an Oven-Safe Food Thermometer

Poultry (Whole Bird)

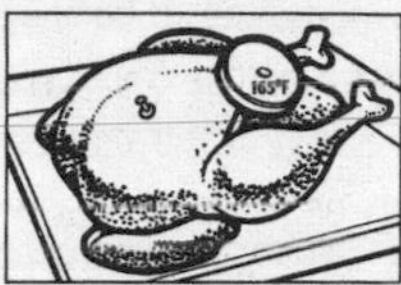

Insert into the thickest part of the thigh, avoiding the bone. For a whole turkey, insert into the innermost part of the thigh and wing and into the thickest area, avoiding the bone. Each area should reach 165°F. It's okay to cook turkey to a higher internal temperature. If stuffed, the stuffing temperature must also reach 165°F.

Ground Meat and Poultry

Insert into the thickest area of the meat loaf or patty. For thin patties, insert sideways, reaching the very center with the stem of the thermometer.

Beef, Pork, Lamb, Veal, Ham (Roasts, Steaks, or Chops), and Poultry Pieces

Insert into the center of the thickest part, away from bone, fat, and gristle.

Casseroles and Egg Dishes

Insert into the center or the thickest part.

See "Look to Safe Internal Temperatures" in this chapter, page 210, to know what temperature your food should reach for safety. *Remember:* Allow at least three minutes of resting, or standing time, before carving or consuming for safety and quality.

When Are Cooked Eggs Safe?

When eggs are properly cooked, *Salmonella* bacteria are destroyed. Look for these doneness signs.

Cooking Method	Signs of Doneness
Scrambled, omelets, frittata	No visible liquid egg remains
Poached, fried over easy, sunny-side up	White completely set; yolk starting to thicken but not hard (*Hint:* For sunny-side up eggs, cover with lid during cooking to ensure adequate cooking.)
Soft-cooked	White completely set; yolk starting to thicken but not hard (Bring to a boil; turn off heat. Let eggs stand in water for four to five minutes.)
Hard-cooked	White and yolk are completely set (Bring to a boil; turn off heat. Let eggs stand in water for fifteen minutes.)
Stirred custard, including ice cream, and eggnog	Mixture coats the spoon; temperature reaches 160°F
Baked custard, including quiche	Knife placed off center comes out clean (*Note:* Cheese in a properly cooked quiche will leave particles on the knife, too.)

- How about if you—or your kids—eat homemade cookie dough or batter? Especially if it contains raw eggs, don't! Some other ingredients have the potential for creating risk, too. When you make ice cream, make an egg-based version from a cooked stirred custard.
- As another option, use cooked yolks in recipes that call for raw eggs. Cook the yolks in a double boiler or a heavy skillet with liquid from the recipe, using two tablespoons of liquid for each yolk. Beat the yolks while they cook until they coat a spoon or until bubbles form around the edges, and the temperature reaches 160°F.
- Pasteurized egg products? They're great options for use in any cooked products, especially for people who are at risk for foodborne illness. Buy only pasteurized liquid and pasteurized shell egg products with a USDA inspection mark. *Tip:* Read the label carefully when you buy pasteurized egg products to make sure you get "pasteurized" eggs, and not eggs from "pastured" chickens.
- Cook casseroles and other dishes with eggs to 160°F. Check with a food thermometer.
- Keep cooked eggs and egg-rich foods, including pumpkin and custard pies, at 40°F to 140°F for no longer than two hours, including serving time. Otherwise, refrigerate them. Use leftovers made with eggs within two to three days.
- Use hard-cooked eggs, including Easter eggs, within a week of cooking. Store them in the refrigerator. Like other high-protein foods, they shouldn't sit out at temperatures of 40°F or above for longer than two hours. If they do, toss them!

Have you ever wondered?

. . . how to check and calibrate a food thermometer? Check for accuracy in one of two ways: (1) Fill a large glass with finely crushed ice, pour tap water on top, and stir. Dip the thermometer stem two inches into the glass without touching the bottom. In 30 seconds, it should read 32°F. (2) Bring a deep pot of water to a rolling boil. Dip the thermometer stem two inches into the water without touching the bottom. Within 30 seconds, it should read 212°F.

Calibrate according to the manufacturer's directions, usually by using pliers to turn the nut under the dial. Some digital thermometers can't be calibrated.

. . . why you need to worry about bacteria once food is cooked? Actually, bacteria growth can increase after cooking. As food cools enough to eat and enters the "danger zone," its temperature allows bacteria, which may be present from handling or cross contamination, to thrive if kept too long at these temperatures.

. . . if plenty of hot sauce kills harmful bacteria in fish such as raw oysters? No; neither does the beer or vodka (for oyster shooters) "downed" with them. Only prolonged exposure to a high enough cooking temperature kills bacteria. Love raw oysters? Don't rely on your senses as a safety gauge—even experienced oyster eaters can't tell.

. . . if cooked ground beef can be safe and still be pink inside? Yes, that's why the internal temperature, not the color, should be your test for doneness and food safety. The pink color may result from a reaction between the oven heat and the myoglobin in meat. It can also occur when vegetables with their naturally contained nitrites cook along with meat. Use a food thermometer to be sure harmful bacteria are destroyed when cooking ground beef. Cook to an internal temperature of 160°F.

. . . if dishwasher cooking is safe? Using the dishwasher to cook some foods has gotten some recent media attention. Among the concerns: Is the water temperature high enough to kill pathogens and cook the food? Is there a risk of cross-contamination if dirty dishes are in the dishwasher, too? If the food isn't sealed tightly in an airtight container, will soap and water get into the food? Other issues: It's neither efficient nor appealing!

. . . if it's okay to cook meat just to rare or medium rare? For ground meat, no, since grinding can bring potentially harmful bacteria from the meat's surface into the ground meat. For steaks, roasts, or chops, cooking just to medium-rare is fine.

. . . if adding acid to a food will destroy bacteria? No. It's true that bacteria like a neutral environment—not too acid, not too basic. But adding lemon juice, vinegar, or wine, as when making seviche, won't necessarily destroy the bacteria.

- Handle hard-cooked eggs destined for the Easter basket or egg hunt carefully while decorating; cracked eggs invite bacteria. Hide them so they stay clean and do not come in contact with pets, dirt, and other bacterial sources. Toss cracked or dirty eggs or those that aren't found within two hours.

Microwaving Food Safely

For microwave cooking, the higher the oven wattage, the faster the cooking time. Fast cooking helps retain nutrients—and no added fat is needed.

Microwave-safe containers and wrappings. Use only microwave-safe containers and wraps in a microwave oven. Any utensil—glass, ceramic containers, and all plastics—if labeled for microwave use is okay.

- Check glass bowls, dishes, or cups before using if you're unsure. Place the empty container in the microwave oven alongside a separate cup of water. Microwave it on high for one minute. If the empty container stays cool, it's microwave safe; if slightly warm, use it for reheating; and if it gets hot, it's not microwave safe.
- Unless labeled microwave safe, don't microwave food in its packaging. Containers from store-bought microwave meals are for one-time use only; toss them.
- Use straw or wood baskets for quick bread warm-ups; line the basket first with napkins to absorb moisture. White, unprinted paper plates, towels, napkins, and bags as well as waxed paper, parchment paper and heavy microwave-safe plastic wrap are okay, too.
- Don't microwave foods in tubs that have held margarine, butter, cottage cheese, or yogurt. Stay away from other plastic tubs as well as polystyrene boxes and trays. Plastic bags, brown paper bags, and printed paper plates, towels, and napkins aren't safe either. Chemicals from these products may migrate to food.
- Remember other containers that aren't microwave safe, too: aluminum foil, metal pans, Chinese take-out containers with metal handles, metal package "twist ties," and dishes with metallic paint or trim. Any container or packaging that has warped or melted with heat isn't safe either.

For the High-Altitude Cook

At high altitudes, you need to cook food longer to kill bacteria. Thin air—less oxygen and lower atmospheric pressure—affects the time and temperature for nearly everything that's cooked. At higher altitudes, water evaporates faster and boils at a lower temperature, so it's less effective for killing bacteria. Above 3,000 feet, you need special cooking methods for meat and poultry. In breads and cakes, leavening gases expand more.

Most cooking and canning temperatures are based on food preparation at sea level, yet about one-third of the US population lives at high altitudes. If you're a high-altitude cook, adjust the time, temperature, and moisture accordingly. The Food and Safety Inspection Service website, *noted in "Resources You Can Use" in the appendix, page 763,* can lead you to more advice about high-altitude cooking and food safety.

? Have you ever wondered?

. . . if liquid smoke is safe to eat? Bottled liquid smoke is sold alongside herbs and sauces in many supermarkets. It gives a smoky flavor without grilling. The flavoring is created by burning wood and then trapping the smoke; most potential carcinogens are removed. About 60 percent of processed meats sold in supermarkets are "smoked" with liquid smoke.

. . . if acrylamide is a health risk? In your own kitchen and in food processing, acrylamide forms naturally in foods such as browned breads, chips, coffee, fries, and toasted cereals. It happens when sugars react with certain amino acids when some foods are cooked at high temperatures—perhaps baked, fried, or toasted. The darker the browning, the more acrylamide that forms. Likely around since cooking began, acrylamide has been detected only recently at very low levels in foods. To clarify, acrylamides don't form, or form only at low levels, in grilling meat, poultry, and fish.

There's not enough research to conclude that acrylamide, in the small amounts consumed, is a human health risk. Yet the FDA is one of many institutions involved in long-term research. The best advice based on what's known now: There's no reason to change your food or cooking habits. Eat a variety of healthy foods, eat plenty of fruits and vegetables, and go easy on fatty and fried foods.

. . . what to do with the food if the cooking oil smells bad or darkens, or starts to smoke when heated? Toss it out. Overheating and overuse lowers the smoking point of oils and breaks down the fat. When heavily overcooked oils form unhealthy compounds, the oil is likely past the point of being palatable.

Microwaving safely. General cooking guidelines apply, as do these precautions to ensure that food is thoroughly and adequately cooked for food safety.

- To defrost, remove food from the packaging (foam trays, plastic wraps, others) first; thaw using the defrost button on the microwave oven. Cook food right away since food that's been heated can cause any bacteria in it to start multiplying.
- Cut food for microwaving into same-size pieces. This helps ensure even cooking.
- Whether preparing prepackaged, frozen microwaveable meals or following a microwave recipe, read and follow cooking instructions carefully.
- Cover food well during cooking to keep it moist and provide safe, even cooking. Use waxed paper, microwave-safe plastic wrap, or a lid that fits. For safety, allow a little space for some steam to escape.
- Flip, rotate, and stir food for even cooking. Halfway through cooking, turn the dish, stir or reposition the food on the plate or bowl, turn large foods over, or reposition the dish on the turntable. Check for cold spots.
- Be aware of differences in the power, or wattage, of microwave ovens. Cooking times may differ. In fact, check the wattage of your oven periodically; read the manual to learn how.
- Allow "standing" time. Food keeps cooking—and the internal temperature can go up—after the microwave oven turns off, spreading heat more evenly. Use a food thermometer to check, even if you're just reheating. Check in several places but not near the bone. Without standing time, food may not be cooked to a safe temperature.
- Don't use your microwave oven for canning. Pressure that builds up in the jar may cause it to explode.

For more on microwave oven safety, see "Play It Safe: Warming Baby's Bottle and Food" in chapter 17, page 471, and "Microwave Oven Safety for Kids" in chapter 18, page 495.

Grilling Food Safely

Before you put a burger, a steak, chicken—or even vegetables—on the grill, take precautions.

- Clean the grill between each use with hot, soapy water. Removing charred food debris from the grill reduces exposure to bacteria.
- Adjust the grill so foods cook evenly—inside and out. When meat or poultry are too close to the heat source, the outside surfaces cook

quickly and may appear done, but the inside may not be cooked well enough.

- If you're grilling at a picnic site, do all the cooking there—from start to finish. Partly cooked meats transported to the picnic may still carry bacteria.
- Grill on both sides. Turn meat, poultry, and fish over at least once for even cooking. If fish is less than ½ inch thick, you don't need to turn it.
- Use a food thermometer to check for doneness; pack one in your picnic basket.
- Cook meat to medium doneness, rather than well done. If you fully precook meat first, you can then quickly grill for flavor. Grill poultry and fish until the internal temperature reaches its target but the surface isn't blackened.
- Grill meat, poultry, and fish until cooked through but not charred. High-heat cooking such as grilling can cause two potentially carcinogenic compounds to form: polycyclic aromatic hydrocarbons (PAHs), mostly from fat drippings that form when meat is cooked over open flames and produces smoke, and heterocyclic amines (HCAs), mostly from charring, as in a well-done steak. These compounds form naturally during cooking and grilling.

  While research on the health effects isn't conclusive, the quality of the meat is better if you avoid the "black stuff." That said, the potential risk is in the amount; there's not enough in properly cooked meat to make a difference. To reduce charring, especially if you grill a lot, be certain the food reaches a safe internal temperature.
- Marinate to help keep meat, poultry, and fish from drying out. Emerging research indicates that marinating, especially with certain spices and herbs such as turmeric and rosemary, may reduce HCAs.
- Control hot coals to avoid flare-ups that cause smoke and charring. Trim visible fat. Cook in the center of the grill—coals on the side—so fat and juices won't drip on them. Drain away high-fat marinades.
- For charcoal flare-ups have a spray bottle filled with water ready. On a gas grill never use water to control flames; instead turn down the gas.
- Scrape off charred areas before eating the meat, poultry, or fish.
- Cooking in a smoker? It's a slow way to cook outdoors, it is good for less tender meat cuts, as well as poultry and fish steaks, and it gives a smoky flavor. For safety's sake, make sure the smoker stays at 250°F to 300°F—and that meat is cooked to a safe internal temperature.
- Again, remember to transfer grilled or smoked foods to a clean plate—not the unwashed plate used to bring raw foods to the grill or the smoker. Use a clean utensil, not your fingers!

Reheating Leftovers Safely

Heat leftovers to 165°F—and steaming hot. That includes precooked foods such as stuffed chicken breasts and preroasted chickens from takeout; eat them the same day you purchase them. Reheat sauces and gravies to a rolling boil for at least one minute.

- Use a food thermometer to make sure reheated food reaches 165°F before you eat it—even takeout food from the store or order from a restaurant as well as doggie-bag food.
- Toss (don't reheat) pizza that sits out longer than two hours.
- If you reheat in the microwave oven, be sure to rotate food midway through for even heating, and allow for standing time.

Caution—Decorative Dishes

For years, lead has been an ingredient in the glaze, or coating, on ceramic bowls, dishes, and pitchers. With proper firing or heating in a kiln, glazes with lead are safe. However, when dishes are fired incorrectly or when copper is added to the glaze, hazardous amounts of lead can leach from dishes into food. Lead can collect in bones and some soft tissues. Among other problems, lead poisoning can cause learning disabilities, organ damage, and even death. Infants, children, and pregnant women are particularly sensitive to lead's toxic effects. *See "Water: Concerns About Lead and Nitrates" in chapter 4, page 84.*

To be sure your dishes are safe enough for food:

- Inspect the surface of ceramic dishes. The surface that contacts food should be smooth and shiny, not rough or painted on top of the glaze.
- Check both sides of dishes, bowls, and pitchers. If it says "Not for Food Use" or "For Decorative Purposes Only," don't use it for food!
- Don't store food in ceramic dishes or leaded crystal. Lead can leach out when acidic foods and beverages such as coffee, fruit juice, or wine come in contact with glaze or leaded crystal over time.
- Beware of ceramic ware made by untrained potters or obtained from foreign travel as well as older dishes imported before government monitoring. Most of today's hobbyists know the problems of lead glazes.
- If you're concerned about a possible lead hazard, have the item tested professionally. Check with the US Consumer Product Safety Commission (CPSC) at www.cpsc.gov. Results from home lead-test kits are unreliable.

HOW TO SERVE FOOD SAFELY

Keeping food safe extends beyond the kitchen. How food is served is yet another step in protecting against foodborne illness and in retaining foods' quality and flavor.

- Use clean dishes and utensils for serving; use nothing that touched raw meat, poultry, or fish unless it was cleaned in hot, soapy water first.
- Avoid keeping perishable foods on a serving table or at room temperature for more than two hours (one hour at 90°F or above). This includes cooked meat, poultry, fish, eggs, and dishes made with them.
- For buffet-type service, keep cold foods cold and hot foods hot. Serve cold foods on ice, at a temperature of 40°F or below. Use heated servers such as a chafing dish to keep hot foods hot. After two hours, discard even these foods.
- When replenishing serving dishes, don't mix fresh food with food that's been sitting out. *See* "Clostridium perfringens" *in this chapter, page 220, for more about contamination on buffets.*

HOW TO TRANSPORT FOOD SAFELY

Whether it's a picnic, a bag lunch, or take-out food, simple steps can ensure that unwanted bacteria won't have a place at your table.

Packing Picnic Foods Safely

Summer picnics and autumn tailgate parties are times of increased risk for food poisoning. Before you pack the picnic basket, know ways to keep food fit to eat in your fresh-air kitchen. The basics: Keep hot food hot and cold food cold, and keep the food clean. That includes proper hand washing!

- Use clean and dry insulated coolers, chilled with ice or chemical cold packs. As a rule of thumb, pack your cooler with 75 percent food and 25 percent ice or frozen cold packs. Freeze cold packs at least twenty-four hours ahead so they stay cold as long as possible. Chill the cooler ahead, too, with ice or cold packs. Secure the lid and keep it closed—no peeking!
- Store nonperishable foods in a clean basket, with the heaviest foods on the bottom.
- Seal all foods tightly in bags, jars, or plastic containers. This keeps out moisture and bugs.
- Chill or freeze foods before packing them. Your cooler can't cool foods adequately if packed at room temperature. Pack perishables between ice or cold packs; they'll stay cold longer.
- Pack uncooked meat, poultry, or fish carefully—in well-sealed containers—for grilling at the picnic spot. Put them in the bottom of the cooler so any juices won't leak onto other foods. Bring a food thermometer in your picnic basket. Remember: Avoid cross-contamination by packing enough clean plates and utensils for serving the food when cooked.
- Keep your cooler in a cool place (under a tree or a picnic table), not in the hot trunk of your car or the sun. Melted ice signals that food isn't safe anymore. Toss the leftovers, and throw out the used bags and wrappers.
- Keep ice for drinks in a sealed bag. Loose ice for chilling food and drinks isn't safe for using in drinks. If possible, keep drinks in a separate cooler since it may be opened frequently.
- Serve only the amount of food you'll eat right away. Return any perishable foods to the cooler immediately after serving.
- For picnics nearby when you'll eat right away, consider a hot dish—covered and wrapped well. Wrap the dish in several layers of newspaper and then place in an insulated container. Baked beans are a great choice.
- Bring premoistened towelettes to wash up after handling meat, poultry, or fish—or any food, for that matter. Or bring soap and a bottle of water to wash your hands and cooking surfaces. Another option: Bring a hand sanitizer, usually formulated with alcohol that kills bacteria on your hands.
- Be prepared to clean the grill at the picnic site before grilling. Pack a brush, soap, and perhaps water. Make sure you have a safe water source for rinsing the grill after washing.
- After the picnic, toss perishable leftovers. Or repack them in a cold cooler if they have been out for less than two hours (one hour at 90°F or above) and are clean (no flies, dirt, or improper handling).

? Have you ever wondered?

. . . if you need to worry about mayonnaise in picnic foods and brown-bag lunches? Mayonnaise is a perishable spread, so it must stay chilled. Homemade mayonnaise, made with uncooked eggs, is potentially more hazardous than its commercial counterpart and isn't considered appropriate for people at high risk. Commercial mayonnaise and salad dressings, made with pasteurized ingredients, contain salt and more acid, which slow bacteria growth. In unrefrigerated mayonnaise-based salads such as chicken, tuna, or egg salad, it's usually not the mayonnaise that poses the risk but the chicken, tuna, or eggs. That said, keep any opened jars of mayonnaise in the fridge.

Packing Meals and Snacks Safely

Whether you pack it at home or buy ready-to-eat take-out foods, any perishable foods left at room temperature for two hours or more are at risk for foodborne illness. That's especially true when food is stuffed in a school locker with a dirty gym bag, carried in a handbag, or left on a warm windowsill at work! For safety's sake:

- Use a clean insulated bag or a lunch box, not your gym bag, brief case, tote, or purse filled with potentially contaminated items, including cell phone, keys, a wallet, or lipstick.
- Tuck a small refreezable ice pack in the clean bag or lunch box to keep food cold. Or freeze a juice box or small plastic container of water to keep the lunch box and the food cold. Pack a moist towelette or hand sanitizer, too, if there's no chance for hand washing with soap and water.
- For cold beverages, refrigerate an insulated vacuum bottle ahead of time, and then fill it with milk or juice. Or keep milk or juice in the fridge at work.
- Rinse raw produce, including peel-and-eat fruit, before packing it.
- For hot soups, stews, and chilis, heat an insulated container, and then fill it with boiling water. Let it sit for several minutes before pouring out the water. Fill it with very hot food, and keep the container closed until you eat the food.
- If you assemble your meal the night before, refrigerate perishables. Pack nonperishable foods, too: unopened canned soup or stew to heat up in the microwave oven at work, raisins or dried apple slices, crackers and peanut butter, boxed juice or milk, and beef jerky, to name a few.
- Keep transported perishable food in an insulated container in a clean, cool place, away from sunlit windowsills, radiators, or warm vehicles. If a refrigerator is available, use it.
- Discard any perishable foods that you don't eat. Remind your school kids to do the same, too!
- If you keep food in the office fridge, label and date it. Discard anything perishable, usually after three to four days. Check to make sure the refrigerator is regularly cleaned and is cold enough (40°F or below). You may need to initiate the cleaning!
- If you're in charge of cleaning the office kitchen, skip the corporate sponge. Use paper towels and hot, soapy water instead. Wipe up splatters in the microwave oven right away.
- If possible, keep a food thermometer handy at work to check the temperature when you reheat your lunch.
- Launder your lunch bag regularly, or wash your lunch box with soapy water after every use.

HOW TO SHIP FOOD SAFELY

Do you buy food online or by mail-order, get home-delivered groceries, or ship perishable-food gifts? These tips can help ensure its safety:

- *When you place an order,* ask how and when perishable foods will be sent. Ask that food be packed with dry ice or cold packs; order for one-day delivery. Reputable mail-order companies take food safety seriously, but it's always wise to ask. If the food is a gift, let the recipient know it's coming so it won't sit on the doorstep.

Need more strategies for food safety? Check here for "how-tos":

- Purify unsafe water: *see "Local Disasters: Safe Drinking Water" in chapter 4, page 87.*
- Know about food safety in food production: *see "Preserving Food for Nutrition, Food Safety, and Appeal" in chapter 5, page 130.*
- Shop with food safety in mind: *see "Food Safety and Quality: from Store to Home" in chapter 6, page 188.*
- Learn to eat out safely: *see "Safe to the Restaurant Plate" in chapter 9, page 285.*
- Take food safety precautions when you travel: *see "Food Safety in Faraway Places" in chapter 9, page 312.*
- Keep food safe for infants and young children: *see "Play It Safe: Warming Baby's Food" in chapter 16, page 482, and "Food Safety" in chapter 17, page 490.*
- Teach microwave-oven safety to kids: *see "Microwave Oven Safety for Kids" in chapter 17, page 495.*
- Follow food safety advice when pregnant: *see "Foodborne Illness and Pregnancy" in chapter 18, page 551.*

- *If you're packing a perishable food gift,* freeze the food solid or refrigerate it until cold before packing it. Pack food in an insulated cooler or a heavy corrugated box with cold packs or dry ice. Talk to your shipper or the post office about proper forms, packing materials, and warning labels for shipping packages with dry ice. Mark the package as "Perishable—Keep Refrigerated." Use one-day delivery. Let the recipient know it's coming.
- *If you receive a food gift,* open it immediately. Some mail-order foods, such as dry-cured ham and hard salami, don't require refrigeration. Perishable meats (including most hams), poultry, fish, and other perishable foods should be packed in dry ice and arrive frozen. If cold enough, freeze or refrigerate the food. If it does not arrive cold, toss it out and then contact the mail-order company for a replacement or a refund.

Foodborne Illness: More Common Than You Think

An upset stomach, diarrhea, a fever—do you have the flu? Your illness actually may be foodborne illness. Even if you believe you're not vulnerable, remember that anyone can fall victim!

Have you ever wondered?

. . . who keeps track of outbreaks of foodborne illness? Several government agencies are responsible for food safety surveillance. One is FoodNet, a collaboration between the CDC, the FDA, the USDA's Food Safety and Inspection Service, and several state health departments, which give an annual report of food safety in the United States. That said, local and state public health agencies are often the first to detect an outbreak and start to investigate it.

. . . why there seem to be more outbreaks of foodborne illness these days? One reason is better surveillance and detection. Beyond that, the FDA reports that new disease-causing organisms have emerged, some of which are spreading globally as food production and distribution methods change. Some are hard to detect. An increased demand for less-processed foods and the globalized food system can sometimes make it harder to identify the food source of an outbreak.

. . . what is being done to improve protection from foodborne illness? Among recent government initiatives, the FDA Food Safety Modernization Act of 2010 (FSMA) aims to ensure the US food supply is safe by shifting the focus of federal regulators from responding to contamination to preventing it. The law gives the FDA new authority to regulate the way foods are grown, harvested, and processed. This includes mandatory recall authority. The law enables the FDA to better protect public health by strengthening the food safety system in the United States.

. . . why the spectrum of foodborne illness changes? Over the years, food safety practices such as pasteurization, safe canning, and water treatment have resolved many foodborne diseases in the United States such as typhoid fever, tuberculosis, and cholera. Today, new foodborne risks have emerged. Why?

- The food supply has changed. Today, we are dealing with a bigger global food supply; new food production and processing methods (for example, precut, bagged produce and sous vide packaging, *explained in chapter 5, page 132*); and more demand for year-round and fresh produce and for minimally processed and ethnic foods.
- The number of people at higher risk for foodborne illness is greater.
- Microorganisms themselves change and evolve over time.
- According to consumer studies, many people lack food safety knowledge or don't take responsibility for proper food handling at home.

In the future, environmental changes may affect food safety risks related to food production, storage, and distribution if the temperature changes.

Just how common is foodborne illness? The actual incidence is unknown. A 2011 CDC report estimates that one in six (forty-eight million) Americans get sick, 128,000 are hospitalized, and three thousand Americans die each year from foodborne illness. Reducing foodborne illness by just 10 percent would keep five million people in the United States from getting sick. In fact, the simple act of proper hand washing alone could wipe out a significant amount of foodborne illness in this country.

Although the actual incidence is unknown, foodborne illness may be linked to a small percentage of some long-term health problems, including arthritis, acute kidney failure, and Guillain-Barré syndrome.

Foodborne illness is a huge economic burden, linked to medical expenses, lost productivity, and even death. The CDC identifies fifteen pathogens as responsible for more than 95 percent of illnesses and deaths from foodborne illness in the United States. It advises that preventing a single fatal case of *E. coli* O157:H7 infection could save about $7 million!

People react differently to foodborne bacteria and contaminated food. One person may show no symptoms, while another may get very ill. The reaction depends on the type of bacteria or toxin, how much of the food was contaminated, how much food was eaten, and the person's own susceptibility. Foodborne illness is riskier for some than others. *See "Who's at High Risk? Select Safer Food Alternatives" in this chapter page 220.*

Bacteria are the root of many cases of foodborne illness, usually due to improper food handling. Viruses, parasites, toxic molds, heavy metals (such as lead and mercury), and environmental pollutants and household chemicals, such as cleaning supplies stored near food and food preparation areas, also can contaminate food.

BACTERIA: BAD BUGS

Most bacteria won't harm you. In fact, some are essential in the fermentation process used to make yogurt, some cheeses, vinegar, and some other foods. Friendly bacteria, including those in probiotics, also are essential for gut health; *see "The 'Pre' and 'Pro' of Gut Health" in chapter 15, page 453, and "How to Keep 'Gut Healthy'" in chapter 25, page 727.* Harmful bacteria, however, are among the main causes of foodborne illness in the United States. Being everywhere, they can't be avoided completely.

In most healthy adults, the body can handle small amounts of harmful bacteria with no health threat. Risks for foodborne illness rise when bacteria multiply to very large numbers in mishandled food. That said, even small amounts of harmful bacteria put young children, pregnant women, older adults, and people whose immune systems don't function normally at greater risk.

Bacteria Basics

Life begins at 40! Between 40°F and 140°F, a single bacterium can multiply to become trillions in just twenty-four hours. Why the exponential leap? Under the right conditions, bacteria double in number about every twenty minutes. The more plentiful the bacteria are to start with, the greater the risk for getting sick.

Even with so many, you can't see bacteria without a microscope. Unlike microorganisms that cause food spoilage, you can't taste or smell most bacteria. Yet they live everywhere—in many foods, on your skin, under your fingernails, on all manner of surfaces, and on pets and other live animals.

To survive and multiply, bacteria need time and the right conditions: food, moisture, and warmth. Many need oxygen, too. With their rich nutrient supply and moist quality, many foods offer the perfect medium for bacterial growth. Bacteria thrive on protein; that's why raw meat, poultry, fish, eggs, and milk are linked to foodborne illness. Ideal temperatures for bacterial growth are between 40°F and 140°F. Above 160°F, heat destroys bacteria. Refrigerating foods below 40°F slows their growth. Freezing stops but doesn't kill bacteria. *See "The Danger Zone" in this chapter, page 198.*

Foods of animal origin—raw meat, poultry, fish, eggs, unpasteurized raw milk—are the most common food sources of bacteria. Although it's less common but equally important, harmful bacteria also can be transferred to fresh produce, perhaps through contaminated water or soil residue.

Bacteria: Hard Hitters

Although as many as a hundred types of bacteria cause foodborne illness, those responsible for most cases are *Campylobacter jejuni, Clostridium perfringens, Escherichia coli (E. coli)* O157:H7, *Listeria monocytogenes, Salmonella, Staphylococcus aureus,* and *Vibrio vulnificus.* (The other pathogens most responsible for foodborne illnesses are a virus called norovirus and a parasite called *Toxoplasma gondii.*) Other commonly known bacterial sources of foodborne illness include *Bacillus cereus*; *Clostridium botulinum; Shigella*; and *Yersinia enterocolitica.* *See "Quick Reference: Foodborne Illness–Causing Organisms in the United States" in this chapter, page 227.* Get to know these hard hitters:

- *Bacillus cereus* produces toxins that can cause diarrhea and perhaps vomiting. Contaminated fish, meat and poultry, milk, and vegetables as well as some mixed foods (casseroles, cooked rice, puddings, and salads, and sauces) are sources.
- *Campylobacter jejuni* is estimated to be the major bacterial cause of diarrhea in the United States. Like *Salmonella, Campylobacter* grow in raw and undercooked meat and poultry, unpasteurized milk, and contaminated water. Safe food handling and water treatment systems destroy it.
- *Clostridium botulinum* contamination is rare. Yet, untreated, botulism is often fatal. The toxin affects the nervous system, requiring immediate medical attention.

  Botulism-causing bacteria can come from improperly home-canned or commercially canned foods. Usually, these are low-acid canned foods such as meats and vegetables that were not processed or stored properly. Foods improperly canned at home, such as cheese sauce, garlic, and honey, pose a higher risk.

  Look for warning signs: swollen or leaking cans or lids, cracked jars, loose lids, and clear liquids turned milky. Never eat—or even taste—foods from cans or jars that spurt or fizz when they're opened! *Other cautions:* Always use approved methods for home canning. Heat home-canned meats and vegetables thoroughly, about fifteen to twenty minutes, before serving. Serve or refrigerate baked potatoes and grilled vegetables right away. Cooked root vegetables held at room temperature, instead of refrigerated, can be problems, too. That's especially true when they're wrapped in foil; *C. botulinum* spores thrive without air.
- *Clostridium perfringens* is present everywhere, growing where there's little or no oxygen. Sometimes called the buffet germ, it grows fastest in large portions of food, such as casseroles, stews, and gravies, held at low or room temperatures in the danger zone.

  Chafing dishes that aren't hot enough and large portions that don't cool quickly in the refrigerator are breeding grounds. Rather than put out large portions of food for an extended time, replace buffet foods often. Refrigerate leftovers in shallow containers as soon as you can. When the food is divided into smaller containers, it cools down more quickly in the refrigerator.
- *Escherichia coli (E. coli)*, a common bacterium, is found in the lower intestinal tract and is mostly harmless. In fact, harmless strains in normal intestinal flora not only aid vitamin K production; they also help to keep harmful bacteria from establishing there. Some strains of *E. coli*, however, are associated with foodborne illness. Travelers' diarrhea, often caused by contaminated drinking water, as well as diarrhea among infants are examples.

  One strain—*E. coli* O157:H7—has received attention because its effects can be so severe. This strain, associated with eating raw or undercooked ground beef or drinking unpasteurized milk or unpasteurized cider, has been known to cause life-threatening health problems such as hemorrhagic colitis with severe abdominal cramps, bloody diarrhea, nausea, vomiting, and perhaps hemolytic uremic syndrome (HUS), which may cause kidney failure, brain damage, strokes, seizures, and death, especially in young children and the elderly. Each year, there are about twenty to forty thousand cases!

To combat harmful *E. coli* strains, cook and reheat meat thoroughly. Be especially careful of ground meat, for example, hamburgers; bacteria on the surface can get mixed into the center of the meat, which takes longer to cook. Keep cutting surfaces clean. Avoid cross-contamination. Raw milk, cheese from raw milk, unpasteurized juice, and contaminated water also may be sources and should not be consumed.

- *Listeria monocytogenes* can cause a less common, potentially fatal foodborne illness, called listeriosis. Pregnant women, infants, older adults, and those with weakened immune systems are most susceptible. In fact, pregnant women are twenty times more likely than other healthy adults to get this infection, which can lead to premature delivery or stillbirth.

  Listeria are part of your surroundings, including places where food is processed. It grows even when foods are properly refrigerated, below 40°F. Because it's common in unpasteurized milk and in cheese made from it, avoid eating any raw, unpasteurized milk products. *Listeria* may be found in soft-ripened cheeses, such as Brie, Camembert, feta, ricotta, and traditional Mexican-style cheese.

  Raw and under-cooked meat, poultry, and fish also may contain *Listeria*. As with any packaged food product, follow the label's "keep refrigerated" advice and all reheating instructions. Follow safe storage guidelines; *see "The Cold Truth: Food Storage" in this chapter, page 202.* This is also why pregnant women are advised to avoid hot dogs, luncheon meats, and deli meats unless properly reheated to steaming hot (or 165°F).

  To avoid *Listeria*, high-risk individuals are advised by the FDA to avoid certain foods. *See "Who's at High Risk: Select Safer Food Alternatives" in this chapter, page 222.*

- *Salmonella*, the leading cause of estimated hospitalizations and deaths from foodborne illness, is found mostly in raw or undercooked meat, poultry, fish, eggs, and unpasteurized (raw) milk, cheese, and juice. It is also found in contaminated raw fruits and vegetables, such as melon and alfalfa sprouts. Control is simple enough: proper cooking kills *Salmonella*. Combat this bacterium by cooking raw foods thoroughly, especially meat, poultry, and eggs; by keeping foods clean; and by consuming only pasteurized milk.

- *Shigella*, one source of bacterial diarrhea, is transmitted through improper handling of food or water. It originates in the feces of infected humans and can pass easily through improper hand washing. Proper cooking eliminates it. Salads such as chicken salad, potatoes, or tuna are more likely sources because they're typically handled more during food preparation.

- *Staphylococcus aureus* (staph) spreads from someone handling food. It's carried on the skin, nose, and throat, in skin infections, and on food preparation surfaces and equipment; and from these places, it spreads to food. Toxins, or poisons, produced by staph aren't killed by ordinary cooking, which is why personal hygiene and cleanliness in the kitchen are so important!

- *Vibrio* bacteria, which thrive in warmer waters, infect shellfish, especially raw or undercooked mollusks such as oysters. Pollution isn't a cause. These bacteria multiply even during refrigeration. Thoroughly cooking contaminated finfish and shellfish destroys them. For most healthy people, *Vibrio* are destroyed in the intestinal tract or by the immune system. However, for high-risk

? Have you ever wondered?

. . . how food irradiation affects food safety? Food irradiation breaks down the DNA molecules in harmful organisms such as *Salmonella*, *E. coli*, and other foodborne bacteria. In that way it can dramatically reduce or eliminate disease-causing bacteria and other harmful bacteria and so reduce or prevent outbreaks of foodborne illness. Regardless, handle food properly to keep it safe. *See "Irradiation: Cold Pasteurization" in chapter 5, page 131.*

. . . if you can catch bird flu from eating chicken, turkey, or eggs? Bird flu isn't transmitted through properly cooked poultry or eggs. The strains of bird flu (avian influenza) that have been identified haven't affected humans and aren't considered a public health risk. The USDA and other government agencies are working to protect poultry and eggs as well as to prevent infected poultry and eggs from reaching consumers. If you travel to places affected by bird flu, check with the CDC for current travelers' advice.

The USDA advises proper food handling and cooking to protect against avian influenza and other viruses and bacteria such as *Salmonella*. Cooking eggs properly and cooking poultry to safe internal temperatures of 165°F destroys any foodborne virus.

. . . if you can get H1N1 from eating pork? No. H1N1 is a respiratory disease spread by coughing and sneezing, not a foodborne illness. According to the CDC, H1N1 isn't transmitted by food. For protection, wash your hands properly; avoid touching your eyes, nose, and mouth.

. . . what to do about a food recall? First, don't panic; most recalls are precautionary for possible contamination, not for outbreaks of foodborne illness. Nevertheless, don't eat the food; wash your hands if you've opened the package. The recall notice explains what to do, perhaps returning the food or disposing of it properly.

Recall announcements come from the FDA and USDA, which monitor the safety of food products and issue recall announcements. Get recall updates or report a food problem at www.recalls.gov/index.html, or download an app for your smart phone. *See "A Closer Look . . . Deciphering Package Dates, Reducing Food Waste" in chapter 6, page 152, for more about product codes on packages.*

Who's at High Risk? Select Safer Food Alternatives

Foodborne illness can affect anyone who eats food contaminated by bacteria, viruses, parasites, toxins, or other substances. But certain groups of people are more susceptible. They are more likely to get sick from contaminated food and, if they do get sick, the effects are much more serious. Some of these groups of people include: cancer patients, pregnant women, children under the age of five, older adults, and people with weakened immune systems (autoimmune diseases and HIV/AIDS, among other chronic illnesses.

By following basic rules of food safety, *addressed in this chapter*, you can help prevent foodborne illness for yourself and others. For those at high risk, follow general advice for food safety and avoid riskier foods.

Type of Food	Recommended Foods for Lower Risk	High Risk Foods
Meat and poultry	• Meat or poultry cooked to a safe minimum internal temperature	• Raw or undercooked meat or poultry
Fish	• Cook fresh fish to 145°F. • Heat previously cooked fish to 165°F. • Canned fish and shellfish	• Any raw or undercooked fish or shellfish, or food containing raw or undercooked fish (e.g., sashimi, sushi, or seviche) • Refrigerated smoked fish • Partially cooked shellfish, such as shrimp and crab
Milk	• Pasteurized milk	• Unpasteurized (raw) milk
Eggs	• Use pasteurized eggs or egg products when preparing recipes that call for raw or undercooked eggs.	• Foods that contain raw or undercooked eggs, such as: homemade Caesar salad dressing homemade eggnog homemade mayonnaise homemade raw cookie dough
Sprouts	• Cooked sprouts	• Raw sprouts (alfalfa, bean, or any other sprout)
Vegetables	• Washed fresh vegetables, including salads • Cooked vegetables	• Unwashed fresh vegetables, including lettuce/salads
Cheese	• Hard cheeses • Soft cheeses that are clearly labeled "made from pasteurized milk" • Processed cheeses • Cream cheese • Mozzarella	• Soft cheeses made from unpasteurized (raw) milk, such as: blue-veined Brie Camembert feta Mexican-style (asadero, panela, queso blanco, and queso fresco)
Hot dogs and deli and luncheon meats	• Reheat hot dogs, deli meats, and luncheon meats to steaming hot or 165°F	• Hot dogs, deli meats, and luncheon meats that have not been reheated
Pâtés	• Canned or shelf-stable pâtés or meat spreads	• Unpasteurized and/or refrigerated pâtés or meat spreads

Source: www.foodsafety.gov/risk. Accessed November 30, 2016.

Information on food safety is constantly emerging. Recommendations and precautions for people at high risk are updated as scientists learn more about preventing foodborne illness. If you are among those at high risk, be aware of and follow the most current information on food safety. For the latest information and precautions, talk to your doctor. Check the government's food safety website (www.foodsafety.gov), or call the government information numbers *listed in "Resources You Can Use," page 763.*

Flu or Foodborne Illness?

How do flu symptoms, caused by a virus that infects the respiratory tract, compare to foodborne illness?

Symptom	The "Flu"	Foodborne Illness
Body aches and pains	Common: headache and muscle aches	Common: headache, backache, and stomach cramps
Fatigue	Common (often extreme)	Common (often extreme)
Fever	Common	Common
Gastrointestinal: nausea, diarrhea	Rarely prominent	Common (often extreme)
Respiratory: chest discomfort, cough	Common (often extreme, can become severe)	Rare
Respiratory: nasal, congestion, sore throat, runny or stuffy nose	Common	Rare
Prevent or lessen risk	*Annual vaccination*	*Proper food handling*

Adapted from: www.homefoodsafety.org.

individuals, *Vibrio* infection can be very serious, even fatal within two days of developing it. Symptoms include sudden chills, fever, nausea, vomiting, and stomach pain.

- *Yersinia enterocolitica* most often is found in contaminated raw or undercooked pork products (including chitterlings, or pork intestines). The most common symptoms for young children are fever, abdominal pain, and diarrhea, often bloody. For older children and adults, symptoms include fever and abdominal pain that feels like appendicitis. Unpasteurized milk or untreated water also may transmit this bacterium. In most cases, the body can handle a yersiniosis infection without antibiotics.

  As prevention, avoid eating raw or undercooked pork and unpasteurized dairy foods, wash hands well, avoid cross-contamination, and dispose of animal feces in a sanitary way. If you're making chitterlings, have someone else care for your children until your hands are well washed. *See "Cook to Safe Internal Temperatures" in this chapter, page 210, for cooking pork.*

Have you ever wondered?

. . . if your food is safe from foot-and-mouth disease and mad cow disease? These are different diseases.

Although *foot-and-mouth disease (FMD)* is highly contagious among livestock and is economically disastrous, it poses no known risk to humans; FMD hasn't been found in US livestock for about seventy-five years. Because travelers who visit agricultural areas can bring it back, the government prohibits the importing of agricultural products by people entering the United States who have been on a farm abroad or in contact with livestock abroad, and inspects their baggage.

Before returning to the United States from FMD-infected areas, the USDA advises that you avoid agricultural areas for five days before returning; clean and disinfect footwear with detergent and bleach; and wash or dry-clean clothing. After returning, avoid contact with livestock or wildlife for five days.

As other safety measures, the USDA regularly monitors US cattle herds and has banned animals and animal products from infected areas. *Note:* FMD is different from hand, foot, and mouth disease (HFMD), common among infants and children.

Mad cow disease, or bovine spongiform encephalopathy (BSE), affects the nervous system in cattle; it may be linked to a brain-wasting illness in humans known as Creutzfeldt-Jakob disease. BSE is a prion disease in cattle. Prions are infectious agents linked to neurodegenerative disease, which may be passed from cattle to humans.

To protect the US food supply, government regulations include import bans to make sure no live cattle or products from these animals are imported from areas where BSE is known to exist or is at risk, a ban on most mammalian protein in cattle feed, and a USDA surveillance program. A feed ban is in place to reduce the risk of BSE. Since 2004, the FDA and, similarly, USDA regulations have excluded potentially risky cattle products from human food, dietary supplements, and cosmetics. In 2009, an enhanced feed ban harmonized the United States' and Canada's feed control measures. No research indicates that BSE is transmitted to cow's milk.

If you travel to Europe, where BSE is known to exist, your risk for getting this disease is very small, according to the National Institutes of Health. If you're concerned, however, avoid beef or beef products, including brain, or eat only solid pieces of meat rather than ground-beef products such as burgers or sausage when you travel there.

PARASITES AND VIRUSES

Parasites and viruses—other tiny microorganisms—also can contaminate food. Parasites survive by drawing on nutrients in a living host. Viruses such as hepatitis A and norovirus, or Norwalk virus, act like parasites. Through the food chain, parasites and viruses can infect humans.

- *Amebiasis (Entamoeba histolytica),* a parasite, comes from polluted water and vegetables grown in soil polluted with human feces. It's a problem mostly for travelers in less developed areas. Symptoms include intestinal cramps and diarrhea.
- *Cryptosporidium*, a parasite traditionally linked to travelers' diarrhea, or cryptosporidiosis, in developing nations, has become a more common illness in the United States. It enters the environment through feces of warm-blooded animals, including humans. Contaminated water or ice is the usual source. Municipal water filtration controls this parasite; chlorine doesn't destroy it.
- *Cyclospora cayetanensis,* a parasite, can cause intestinal illness, perhaps with appetite loss, nausea, abdominal cramps, vomiting, fatigue, muscle pain, and low-grade fever. It comes from consuming food or water contaminated with feces. Reduce the risk with proper hand washing and by washing, peeling, and cooking raw fruits and vegetables properly.
- *Giardia lamblia* is a parasite that causes an intestinal illness called giardiasis, which is most often contracted by swallowing contaminated water. It also can be contracted by eating contaminated food or through person-to-person contact. In recent years, giardiasis has become one of the most common causes of waterborne disease among humans in the United States.

  Gastrointestinal symptoms are more likely to strike campers and hikers, travelers, diaper-age children who go to day-care centers, and others who drink untreated water from contaminated sources. Symptoms typically appear one to two weeks after infection and may last several weeks. Boiling destroys *Giardia* in water; chlorine may not if the chlorine concentration isn't high enough. Good hand-washing habits are essential.

  What if there's a giardiasis outbreak in your child's day-care center? If it continues despite control efforts, children with or without symptoms might be screened and perhaps treated. If your child has symptoms (diarrhea, abdominal cramps, nausea), contact your doctor. The American Academy of Pediatrics doesn't advise treatment for children diagnosed with giardiasis who don't have diarrhea unless poor appetite, weight loss, or fatigue are observed.
- *Hepatitis A* is a virus that comes from food contaminated by feces. Conditions caused by hepatitis, such as jaundice and liver problems, can be severe. Sometimes hepatitis A comes through the food chain from shellfish harvested from contaminated waters—perhaps where raw sewage is dumped. More commonly, an infected person who handles food without proper hand washing can transmit the disease, most often in a food-service operation. Cooking may not kill the virus. As a precaution, always choose a restaurant known for cleanliness. Eat only well-cooked shellfish. The CDC advises getting a hepatitis A vaccine for prevention; that is especially important for food-service workers, who may be more susceptible than others.

  Note: Hepatitis C, which is getting media attention, is not a foodborne illness. The CDC notes that it is not spread through food or water or by sharing eating utensils, breastfeeding, hugging, kissing, holding hands, coughing, or sneezing.
- *Norovirus*, or Norwalk virus, is very common, resulting in about 60 percent of estimated foodborne illnesses but a much smaller proportion of severe illnesses. It causes acute gastrointestinal

What If You Suspect Foodborne Illness?

Call or see a medical professional if you observe the symptoms *noted in "When Should You Call a Doctor?" in this chapter, page 226.* For a health emergency, call 911. Physicians and laboratories must contact the health department to report a diagnosis of foodborne illness.

If the suspected food came from a public place or a large gathering—restaurant, street vendor, employee cafeteria, company picnic, or grocery store, among others—report the incident to your city, county, or state health department as soon as possible. You also can report it to the Centers for Disease Control and Prevention (CDC), 1-800-CDC-INFO (1-800-232-4636), or www.foodsafety.gov

If you report the incident, try to preserve the suspected food. Ask authorities how to package and store the food until they can collect it. If possible, keep the original packaging; it identifies where the product was produced. Label it with a warning so no one consumes it.

If you suspect food contamination from a household chemical:

- Check the label for an antidote or a remedy. Likely you'll find an 800 or other toll-free number for first-aid advice, too. Follow the advice.
- Call the national hotline of the American Association of Poison Control Centers: 1-800-222-1222. This number will automatically link you to the closest poison control center to you. Another option: Contact your local health department, or use a local poison-control-center number. As a precaution, post their phone numbers in a convenient spot, or load them on your phone so you'll have them handy if needed.

illness usually lasting two days. This virus is passed primarily from one infected person to another, often on the hands of kitchen workers who handle salads, sandwiches, and bakery products such as cream pies.

Reduce the risk with proper hand washing. If you are sick with symptoms of *norovirus*, including vomiting and diarrhea, avoid preparing food or caring for others—and continue doing so for at least two to three days after you recover.

- *Taenia saginata* (beef tapeworm) and *Taenia solium* (pork tapeworm) are parasitic worms. Consuming undercooked beef or pork when traveling to places with poor sanitation increases the risk. The symptoms include abdominal pain, weight loss, digestive disturbances, and possible intestinal obstruction.
- *Toxoplasma gondii* is the parasite that causes toxoplasmosis. It can be contracted by eating undercooked, contaminated meat and poultry, unwashed fruits and vegetables, and contaminated water as well as by using utensils or cutting boards that have had contact with contaminated raw meat. It is also directly transferred to humans from cat feces.

Most healthy people who contract the parasite show no symptoms. If they do feel ill, the symptoms may resemble the flu. However, for some (including pregnant women), toxoplasmosis can cause serious problems. For those at higher risk, the symptoms may be severe, causing damage to the brain, eyes, or other organs.

To combat *Toxoplasma*, cook meat, especially pork, lamb, and poultry to proper doneness temperatures; after handling raw meat, wash hands, utensils, and surfaces thoroughly with soap and water; and wash raw fruits and vegetables before eating. When possible, keep your cat indoors. If you do handle cats, wash your hands well with soap and water.

Pregnant women are at special risk because they can pass the parasite to their unborn baby. For pregnant women, avoid handling a cat's litter box; have someone else clean it daily. People with severely weakened immune systems are also at risk, such as those

? Have you ever wondered?

. . . if fish you catch are safe to eat? About 20 percent of the fish eaten in the United States are caught for personal use. They're safe to eat if caught in safe waters—and if properly handled and cooked, and not eaten raw. However, seafood toxins, which occur naturally in some waters, and fish contaminated by chemicals in the water, pose health risks. Check for advisories from your local and state health department or state fishery agency for a current safety status.

. . . if you need to be concerned about red tide? No, unless you harvest your own shellfish. Red tide happens when marine algae are in a time of excessive growth, which is when they produce shellfish toxins that may cause illness. These areas are monitored carefully to protect the shellfish supply. Heed red tide warnings from local authorities if you harvest your own shellfish.

. . . if you should only eat oysters during months with an R in their name? That advice goes back more than four hundred years when the risk of *Vibrio* was high during warm-weather months and when the quality of oysters wasn't as good. Today, commercial oyster operations monitor oysters for safety and quality all year long, including during warm-weather harvesting. This allows for safe, quality oysters any time of year.

. . . if mercury in fish is risky? Mercury is naturally present in all living things as well as in soil, air, and water. Pollution also releases mercury into the air, which falls into water or onto land, where it then washes into lakes, rivers, and oceans. Bacteria in water change mercury to methylmercury, which is toxic. Over time, methylmercury can build up in large, predatory, long-lived fish.

The Dietary Guidelines for Americans advises that the health benefits to most healthy adults from consuming at least eight ounces a week (in a 2,000-calorie-per-day eating plan) of a variety of cooked fish outweigh the risks linked to exposure from methylmercury. Consumers also should follow local seafood advisories and limit ingestion of large, predatory, long-lived fish.

Because methylmercury is a potential risk to the developing nervous system of the fetus or the child, the FDA and EPA provide advice about eating fish for women who are pregnant or who might become pregnant, nursing mothers, and young children: avoid eating king mackerel, shark, swordfish, marlin, orange roughy, tuna (bigeye), and tilefish (Gulf of Mexico). The 2017 advisory also lists fish that are "best choices" to eat two to three times per week and "good choice" to limit to once per week; see www.fda.gov/Food/FoodborneIllnessContaminants/Metals/ucm393070.htm.

To get the health benefits of fish and limit methylmercury exposure, pregnant and nursing women are advised: eat up to twelve ounces (two to three servings) a week of a variety of fish lower in mercury (for example, canned light tuna, catfish, pollock, salmon, shrimp); that can include up to six ounces of albacore (white) tuna.

Check local fishing advisories about the fish you catch. No advice? You can eat up to six ounces of locally caught fish if that's the only fish you eat in a given week. This advice also applies to young children, but serve smaller portions. *Note:* Fish in fish sticks and fast-food sandwiches are usually made with fish that is low in mercury.

When Should You Call Your Doctor?

Should you just "tough it out" until the discomfort goes away in a day or so? Some foodborne illnesses result in long-term health conditions, even death. Know the symptoms, and take the right action!

Imagine that you or a family member have an upset stomach, diarrhea, vomiting, fatigue, abdominal discomfort, or a fever. Symptoms can appear from thirty minutes to three weeks after eating contaminated food. Most often, symptoms appear within four to forty-eight hours after eating and usually pass within twenty-four to forty-eight hours. Rest and plenty of fluids are the best ways to treat most cases. Some foodborne illnesses can affect your health for weeks, months, or even years. Talk to your doctor or other healthcare provider if you think that food has made you sick. In some circumstances, you need a doctor's care:

- Diarrhea is bloody. This may be a symptom of *E. coli* O157:H7.
- Diarrhea or vomiting is excessive. This may lead to dehydration if fluids aren't replaced.
- These three symptoms all appear: stiff neck, severe headache, and fever. The victim may have *Listeria*, which can be life-threatening.
- You suspect illness from *Clostridium botulinum* or *Vibrio vulnificus*, which can be fatal.
- The victim is at high risk—perhaps a young child, an elderly person, or someone whose immune system is compromised due to illness.
- Signs of dehydration appear; *see "Dehydration: Body Signals" in chapter 15, page 444.*
- Symptoms persist for longer than three days.

who have HIV/AIDS, who are undergoing certain types of chemotherapy, and who have recently received an organ transplant.

- *Trichinella spiralis*, a parasitic worm that causes trichinosis, is contracted by consuming undercooked pork or game that has been infested with its larvae. With careful food-industry control and advancements in food processing, trichinosis is much less common today than it was a generation or two ago. However, still cook pork, game, and other meat to the recommended and safe internal temperature to destroy any live *Trichinella* larvae.

MOLDS

Molds, or fungi, that live on plant and animal matter, are another food safety issue. Why? Under the right conditions, some produce harmful mycotoxins.

Unlike bacteria, you can see some molds, such as the furry growth on food that's been forgotten in your fridge. But you can't always see the thin threads of mold branching and growing deep inside food, the mycotoxins that molds produce, or the bacteria that grow with mold. That's why simply cutting off surface mold may not remove the problem. Mold on certain cheeses may be handled differently, *as noted in "Have you ever wondered . . . if mold on cheese is dangerous?" in this chapter, page 201.*

Like bacteria, most molds like warm temperatures, but they also grow in the refrigerator. Because they tolerate sugar and salt, jams and cured, salty meats can get moldy, too. Discard foods with obvious signs of mold. A sanitary refrigerator and clean dishcloths, sponges, and other cleaning utensils are essential for mold control.

Quick Reference: Foodborne Illness–Causing Organisms in the United States

The chart below includes foodborne disease-causing organisms that frequently cause illness in the United States. As the chart shows, the threats are numerous and varied, with symptoms ranging from relatively mild discomfort to very serious, life-threatening illness. While the very young, the elderly, and persons with weakened immune systems are at greatest risk of serious consequences from most foodborne illnesses, some of the organisms shown below pose grave threats to all persons.

Organism	Common Name of Illness	Onset Time After Ingesting	Signs & Symptoms	Duration	Food Sources
Bacillus cereus	*B. cereus* food poisoning	10–16 hours	Abdominal cramps, watery diarrhea, nausea	24–48 hours	Meats, stews, gravies, vanilla sauce
Campylobacter jejuni	Campylobacteriosis	2–5 days	Diarrhea, cramps, fever, and vomiting; diarrhea may be bloody	2–10 days	Raw and undercooked poultry, unpasteurized milk, contaminated water
Clostridium botulinum	Botulism	12–72 hours	Vomiting, diarrhea, blurred vision, double vision, difficulty in swallowing, muscle weakness. Can result in respiratory failure and death	Variable	Improperly canned foods, especially home-canned vegetables, fermented fish, baked potatoes in aluminum foil
Clostridium perfringens	Perfringens food poisoning	8–16 hours	Intense abdominal cramps, watery diarrhea	Usually 24 hours	Meats, poultry, gravy, died or precooked foods, time and/or temperature-abused foods
Cryptosporidum	Intestinal cryptosporidiosis	2–10 days	Diarrhea (usually watery), stomach cramps, upset stomach, slight fever	May be remitting and relapsing over weeks to months	Uncooked food or food contaminated by an ill food handler after cooking, contaminated drinking water
Cyclospora cayetanensis	Cyclosporiasis	1–14 days, usually at least 1 week	Diarrhea (usually watery), loss of appetite, substantial loss of weight, stomach cramps, nausea, vomiting, fatigue	May be remitting and relapsing over weeks to months	Various types of fresh produce (imported berries, lettuce, basil)
E. coli (*Escherichia coli*)-producing toxin	*E. coli* infection (common cause of "travelers' diarrhea")	1–3 days	Watery diarrhea, abdominal cramps, some vomiting	3–7 days or more	Water or food contaminated with human feces
E coli O157:H7	Hemorrhagic colitis or *E. coli* O157:H7 infection	1–8 days	Severe (often bloody) diarrhea, abdominal pain and vomiting. Usually, little or no fever is present. More common in children 4 years or younger. Can lead to kidney failure.	5–10 days	Undercooked beef (especially hamburger), unpasteurized milk and juice, raw fruits and vegetables (e.g., sprouts), and contaminated water

(continued)

Quick Reference: Foodborne Illness–Causing Organisms *(continued)*

Organism	Common Name of Illness	Onset Time After Ingesting	Signs & Symptoms	Duration	Food Sources
Hepatitis A	Hepatitis	28 days average (15–50 days)	Diarrhea, dark urine, jaundice, and flu-like symptoms, i.e., fever, headache, nausea, and abdominal pain	Variable, 2 weeks–3 months	Raw produce, contaminated drinking water, uncooked foods and cooked foods that are not reheated after contact with an infected food handler, shellfish from contaminated waters
Listeria monocytognes	Listeriosis	9–48 hours for gastrointestinal symptoms, 2–6 weeks for invasive disease	Fever, muscle aches, and nausea or diarrhea. Pregnant women may have mild flu-like illness and infection can lead to premature delivery or stillbirth. The elderly or immunocompromised patients may develop bacteremia or meningitis	Variable	Unpasteurized milk, soft cheese made with unpasteurized milk, ready-to-eat deli meats
Noroviruses	Variously called viral gastroenteritis, winter diarrhea, acute non-bacterial gastroenteritis, food poisoning, and food infection	12–48 hours	Nausea, vomiting, abdominal cramping, diarrhea, fever, headache. Diarrhea is more prevalent in adults, vomiting is more common in children	12–60 hours	Raw produce, contaminated drinking water, uncooked foods and cooked foods that are not reheated after contact with an infected food handler; shellfish from contaminated waters
Salmonella	Salmonellosis	6–48 hours	Diarrhea, fever, abdominal cramps, vomiting	4–7 days	Eggs, poultry, meat, unpasteurized milk or juice, cheese, contaminated raw fruits and vegetables
Shigella	Shigellosis or bacillary dysentery	4–7 days	Abdominal cramps, fever, and diarrhea. Stools may contain blood and mucus	24–48 hours	Raw produce, contaminated drinking water, uncooked foods and cooked foods that are not reheated after contact with an infected food handler
Staphylococcus aureus	Staphylococcal food poisoning	1–6 hours	Sudden onset of severe nausea and vomiting. Abdominal cramps. Diarrhea and fever may be present	24–48 hours	Unrefrigerated or improperly refrigerated meats, potato and egg salads, cream pastries

Quick Reference: Foodborne Illness–Causing Organisms *(continued)*

Organism	Common Name of Illness	Onset Time After Ingesting	Signs & Symptoms	Duration	Food Sources
Vibrio parahaemo-lyticus	*V. parahaemolyticus* infection	4–96 hours	Watery (occasionally bloody) diarrhea, abdominal cramps, nausea, vomiting, fever	2–5 days	Undercooked or raw sea-food, such as shellfish
Vibrio vulnificus	*V. vulnificus* infection	1–7 days	Vomiting, diarrhea, abdomi-nal pain, bloodborne infection. Fever, bleeding within the skin, ulcers requiring surgical removal. Can be fatal to persons with liver disease or weakened immune systems	2–8 days	Undercooked or raw sea-food, such as shellfish (especially oysters)

Source: US Food and Drug Administration.

8

Cook for Flavor and Health

In this chapter, find out about . . .

Culinary basics: terms, tips, tools

Recipe revamps for ease, flavor, and health

Healthy how-tos for home "chefs"

Eco-friendly kitchens

Herbs, spices, rubs, and more

Kitchen nutrition—cooking for health and flavor—isn't new. More than 150 years ago, *The Book of Household Management* described the kitchen as "the great laboratory of the household . . . much of the 'weal and woe' as regards bodily health, depends on the nature of the preparations concocted within its walls."

Throughout the decades, food preparation methods, recipes, and food itself have changed dramatically. Many of today's home cooks didn't grow up learning to cook from their parents. They have less time to prepare food, and they use more convenience foods and time-saving appliances than previous generations did. Despite the changes, the kitchen remains the place where foods can be transformed into the nourishing, flavorful dishes that you enjoy.

Home Cooking Matters

Delicious, home-cooked meals often bring compliments, satisfaction, and much more. As a strategy for good nutrition and shared family meals, cooking skills matter.

Healthy for you. With home-prepared meals, you have control over the nutrition and safety of the food served at your table: the ingredients, their nutrient quality and calorie content; the ways food is stored and prepared; the flavors, freshness, and visual appeal; and the portion sizes. For these reasons, home-cooked meals can be deliciously healthy, allow for more variety with fewer calories, and be served in sensible portion sizes.

Home cooking also makes it easier to meet the challenges of special food needs, perhaps to manage diabetes, high blood pressure, a food allergy, celiac disease, or other health conditions. Some evidence indicates that home cooking, where you control the calories in a meal or snack, can be a good strategy for weight loss or maintenance.

Economical. Home-cooked meals, especially made with raw or minimally processed ingredients, can cost significantly less than most meals eaten out or purchased fully prepared.

Time-saving. Preparing a home-cooked meal can be faster than going to and from a restaurant, ordering, and waiting for food. If you're pressed for time, planning ahead, cooking enough for two meals at a time, and using some partly prepared foods such as salad kits can help you save time; *see "Meals: Quick, Easy, Healthy" in chapter 3, page 69.* Once learned, home cooking doesn't need to take much time, energy, or effort.

Bonding and teaching experience. Sharing cooking experiences can teach others, including children, about food, health, and how to cook; *see "Cooking Together" in chapter 17, page 495.*

Click Here!
Links to Know . . .

- Academy of Nutrition and Dietetics
  www.eatright.org/resources/food/planning-and-prep/cooking-tips-and-trends
- National Heart, Lung, and Blood Institute (delicious heart healthy recipes)
  healthyeating.nhlbi.nih.gov
- *Food & Nutrition Magazine* (ideas and recipes for healthy meals and snacks)
  www.foodandnutrition.org
- What's Cooking? USDA Mixing Bowl (recipes to build your cookbook)
  WhatsCooking.fns.usda.gov
- Food Value Analysis (compare the cost, nutrition, storage and prep times, and food safety of homemade foods to processed foods)
  www.foodvalueanalysis.org

Cooking traditional or regional foods is a way to experience, share, and celebrate cultural diversity as well as your family's own roots.

Perhaps most important of all, cooking together can help instill healthy eating habits and offer positive opportunities to build relationships and bring people together. For health and much more, home cooking matters a lot! *See "Family Meals Matter" in chapter 3, page 73, and "Family Mealtime: A Priority" in chapter 17, page 491, for benefits of shared meals, enjoyed together.*

Culinary Basics: Plan, Prepare, Serve

Whether you cook from scratch or prefer speed-scratch (which relies on convenience foods and raw ingredients), basic kitchen skills are your key to successful, flavorful meals. The better your kitchen literacy, the better the end result. But relax . . . food you prepare doesn't need to look perfect to be delicious and nutritious.

If you're just learning to cook, take a class. Look for free classes and cooking demos in your community: stores, places of worship, food banks, schools, or farmers' markets. Invest in a step-by-step illustrated cookbook or find similar online instruction. Cook alongside a "foodie" friend.

Practice; each time you try, a recipe or cooking technique gets easier. Tight on time? Cook when you can, even just one or two dishes to serve with store-bought prepared food. Set a goal to cook once or twice a week, and then work up gradually to cook more often. *See "20 Skills for 'Kitchen Literacy'" on the next page.*

PLAN AHEAD

A healthy, home-prepared meal or snack starts with nourishing ingredients on hand and some pre-planned ideas for how to use them. Along with better nutrition, planning ahead can translate to time, effort, and money saved. You're wise to consider:

- *Your food budget, time, and energy. To maximize your food dollar, see "Your Food Dollar: More Nutrition Less Waste" in chapter 6, page 155.*
- *Foods you have on hand* (pantry, refrigerator, and freezer). Check before you shop, and make a shopping list. Plan a "fridge clean out meal" each week to limit food waste. *See "Shopping List: Stocking a Healthy Kitchen" in chapter 6, page 156.*
- *Seasonality.* Seasonal produce is abundant and economical, with more varietals to pick from. It's also at peak flavor.
- *Nutrition and health needs.* Plan for sensibly sized portions. Consider the ingredients and cooking methods, and how a meal or snack fits into other meals and snacks during the day. *See chapters 2, page 21, and 3, page 60, for planning a day's meals and snacks.*
- *Food preferences, lifestyles, and ages,* as well as cultural and religious needs and restrictions of those you're cooking for.
- *Meal appeal.* Think about the colors, textures, flavors, and shapes of food on the plate and in the meal. *See "Variety for Flavor Appeal" in this chapter, page 241.*
- *Kitchen skills.* Simple speed-scratch dishes can be as nourishing and delicious as those prepared with lengthy recipes. Speed-scratch cooking is shortcut cooking, preparing or simply assembling a dish with partly prepared, convenience ingredients. If you cook this way, choose mostly minimally processed ingredients for better nutrition and less added sugars and sodium. For example, make a quick main-dish salad with pre-washed salad greens tossed with precooked roasted chicken and salad dressing.
- *Kitchen equipment.* Mixing bowls and spoons, pots and pans, measuring cups and spoons, ladle, spatula, and cutting boards are among the basics. You don't need every kitchen gadget to make a healthy meal, but you do need some good tools for success! *See "Tools of the Culinary Trade" in this chapter, page 233.*

PREPARE CAREFULLY

Preparation saves time and helps ensure a flavorful and successful meal. Consider these tips as you prepare your next family meal:

- Read through the recipe before you start! Make sure you have all the ingredients and kitchen equipment you need. Missing something? Substitute wisely.
- For recipes, look up terms you don't know. *See "Food-Prep Skills to Know," page 235, and "Cooking Methods to Know," page 236, in this chapter.*
- Get the ingredients ready: perhaps wash, chop, or slice them and measure them into small bowls or containers. The French call this *mise en place*, translated as "everything in its place."

20 Skills for "Kitchen Literacy"

Knowing kitchen basics makes food preparation easier, faster, and perhaps even healthier. Do you . . .

1. Choose recipes that match your family's needs?
2. Always make proper hand washing your first food prep step?
3. Measure dry and liquid ingredients accurately?
4. Follow recipe terms for cutting, combining, and cooking, such as dice, mince, fold, whip, reduce, and sauté?
5. Use knives correctly—and safely?
6. Use and clean kitchen equipment properly?
7. Know how to perform basic food preparation skills, such as cook pasta, marinate meat, or make a hard-cooked egg?
8. Use dry-heat and moist-heat cooking techniques to cook meat, poultry, and fish?
9. Prepare fruits and vegetables to retain their nutrients and fiber?
10. Make an effort to fit more vegetables and fruits into mixed dishes, such as casseroles and pizza?
11. Prepare different whole grains, such as brown rice, quinoa, and whole barley?
12. Modify recipes and substitute ingredients for better nutrition such as sweetening food with fruit or fruit juice instead of added sugars, thickening food with beans or starchy vegetables, or substituting oils for ingredients with solid fats?
13. Incorporate dairy ingredients, including low-fat or fat-free products, or fortified soymilk in your meals for a calcium boost?
14. Use herbs and spices for flavoring as well as to limit salt and other high-sodium ingredients?
15. Cook foods to their proper and safe temperatures, relying on a food thermometer?
16. Know how to perform basic skills for making baked foods, such as how to knead dough, sift dry ingredients, and whip egg whites?
17. Limit waste in your kitchen, including wasted food and wasted water—and recycle or reuse when you can?
18. Consider the age, health, preferences and cultural needs of others as your plan meals and snacks, and serve appropriate portions?
19. Plan appealing meals with a variety of flavors and ingredients from several food groups—and perhaps add a simple, edible garnish to the plate?
20. Plan menus to match your budget and to use seasonal ingredients?

- Pick the right knife—for example, a paring knife for peeling and trimming vegetables and fruits, a serrated knife with a jagged edge for cutting bread, and a chef's or French knife for slicing and dicing all kinds of foods.
- Keep knives sharp and use a clean cutting board. When cutting, be safe: hold food so your fingertips are under your knuckles, and cut away from yourself.
- Measure carefully. Although a pinch here or there may work in some recipes, exact measuring is critical in others such as those for baked breads and cakes.
- Use liquid measuring cups for liquids. Put the glass or plastic cup on a flat surface and pour liquid to the line. Check at eye level; the correct measure is the bottom of the curve.
- Use graduated dry-volume measuring cups for dry ingredients. Fill to the top of the cup and level off with the back of a knife. For brown sugar and solid fats, you'll need to press or pack it firmly.
- Follow recipe instructions, cooking times, and temperatures. Know the signs of doneness for cooked meat, poultry, fish, and eggs; *see "How to Cook Food Safely" in chapter 7, page 209.*

SERVE WITH APPEAL

A nourishing meal that looks and smells appealing is more likely to be eaten and enjoyed. Consider these tips:

- Serve sensible portions on the plates: enough but not too much. Let those who are still hungry go back for more. For good nutrition, think in these proportions: half the plate with fruits and veggies, a quarter of the plate with whole-grain or enriched-grain foods, and another quarter of the plate with a lean protein food. Serve fat-free or low-fat milk or water. Every meal doesn't need to look this way, and mixed dishes are hard to gauge. As noted before, it's the whole day (or several days) that counts. Another option: serve family style, or in serving bowls and platters, for self-service.

- Serve food so it looks appealing. Consider the aroma and temperature (hot food hot, cold food cold), too. A simple fruit, vegetable, or herb garnish adds appeal yet few calories. *See "Beyond Parsley . . . Quick, Easy Garnishes" in this chapter, page 243.*
- Keep mealtime the event—no distractions. So that all enjoy the food and table talk, turn off the television and ban hand-held devices. Remove table clutter; set the table nicely.

Kitchen: "Well" Equipped, "Well" Stocked

A healthy plate of food starts with a well equipped kitchen and a pantry and fridge stocked with nourishing food.

TOOLS OF THE CULINARY TRADE

To cook for deliciousness and health and with the ease of a chef, equip your kitchen. Besides major appliances, counter or table space, and a sink, gather some basic equipment. Buy only what you think you'll really use. You can always add to your kitchen equipment as you become more proficient at cooking.

Bakeware. For general oven baking and cooking: nonstick baking sheet, pizza pan, roasting pan and rack, 9-by-13-inch baking pan, and 3-quart rectangular and 8-inch-square glass baking dishes.

Basting brushes. For lightly coating meat, poultry, fish, and baked goods with marinades and sauces. Label them for savory and sweet dishes. You don't want to brush a sweet syrup on a cake with the brush you used for a garlicky marinade, regardless of its cleanliness.

Bowls. For mixing all kinds of nourishing foods. A three-bowl nesting set saves space.

Colander. For draining pasta and washed fruits and vegetables. Choose one that fits in your sink.

Cutting boards. One for cutting fruits, veggies, breads, and cooked foods, and one for cutting raw protein foods (meat, poultry, and fish).

Egg separator. For easily separating yolks from whites when required in a recipe. Compared to the technique of transferring the yolk back and forth between the two shell halves, an egg separator reduces the chance of transferring bacteria from the outside of the shell to the uncooked egg.

Fat-separating pitcher. For pouring out the liquid from gravies and sauces and leaving the fat behind. The position of the spout lets you pour from the bottom; the fat rises to the top.

Food processor or blender. For pureeing sauces and soups to a thick, creamy consistency; for chopping, grating, or pureeing vegetables for soups, sauces, salads, and side dishes; and for pureeing fruits, yogurt, and milk for thick, lower-calorie, and nourishing smoothies and shakes.

Food (instant-read) thermometer. For helping to ensure that meat, poultry, and other foods are cooked to a safe internal temperature and to your preference. *See "How to Choose and Use a Food Thermometer" in chapter 7, page 212.*

Grater. For shredding cheese as well as vegetables such as carrots and summer squash, or for grating citrus rinds for flavorful zests. When cheese is grated, a small portion still can deliver plenty of flavor. A zester grater gives a finer grate, often preferred for citrus and ginger.

Grill pan or indoor grill. For high-heat cooking, a grill pan, an indoor grill that either fits over the burners on your stovetop or is a freestanding appliance. Either way, you can easily discard the excess fat, which drips through the grates into a drip pan.

Hand mixer. For mashing cooked potatoes, sweet potatoes, and winter squash; whipping egg whites; and making quick batters.

Hot-air popcorn popper. For making a quick, low-fat, low-calorie snack. This popper requires no oil. (You can also use a heavy-bottom saucepan with a lid.)

Immersion blender. For easily preparing fruit smoothies and pureed fruit and vegetable soups. This blender is handheld.

Juicer. Either electric or manual, for extracting juice from fruits and perhaps vegetables.

Kitchen scale. For measuring in ounces to help determine portion sizes and for recipes that call for ingredients to be weighed. If you have a hard time determining the amount of your meat, poultry, fish, or cheese servings, a kitchen scale is helpful.

Kitchen shears. For trimming visible fat from meat and poultry and for snipping herbs. These also are useful with stubborn packaging.

Knives. For cutting fruits, vegetables, and more. Good-quality knives that feel good in your hand are important. You need just three: a paring knife, a serrated knife, and an 8-inch-long chef's knife.

Measuring cups and spoons. For controlling ingredient amounts. Get both dry and liquid measuring cups, and a full set of measuring spoons.

Microwave oven. For faster cooking, without the need for added fat. Fast cooking time also helps food retain vitamins and minerals. Why so speedy? Microwaves, which cause food molecules to vibrate and create friction, travel fast; the friction heats and cooks food.

Microwave-safe strainer. For cooking vegetables in a microwave oven and collecting juices in a container underneath.

Mini food processor. For chopping or mincing small amounts of nuts, seeds, and grains, as well as dried herbs and spices. A coffee grinder that is not also used for coffee is another option.

Miscellaneous tools. For basic food prep: can opener, garlic press, ladle, meat mallet, rubber scraper, heat-resistant nonstick spatulas, wire whisk, tongs, vegetable peeler, wooden spoons.

Nonstick pots and pans. For stovetop cooking. Nonstick cookware (small and large pots, pans, and skillets with lids) lets you cook with little or no added fat. Although today's nonstick finishes last a long time, care for them properly. Use nonmetal utensils to prevent scratching; avoid abrasive cleaners that strip away coatings. Many are dishwasher safe.

Pizza, or baking, stone. For baking or heating bread or for cooking pizza or flatbread. Because it has a high heat retention and absorbs moisture, it gives a crisper, browner crust.

Pressure cooker. For saving time and cooking quickly without much water, helping to retain vitamins. It's great for cooking dry beans, which have less salt than canned beans. Today's pressure cookers are easy and safe to use.

Pump spray bottle. For using instead of buying a vegetable or olive oil spray. A refillable oil pump can be filled with the type of oil you like. By spraying olive oil on bread, you may use less.

Refrigerator thermometer. For helping to keep your fridge cold enough for food safety.

Ribbed fry pan. For letting meat or poultry cook above the fat drippings so less fat gets absorbed.

Rice cooker. For cooking rice and other grains easily. With this countertop appliance, just add rice (white, brown, wild—or various whole grains), the right amount of the liquid of your choice (perhaps juice or broth), and perhaps herbs, and turn it on. It turns off automatically when the rice or other grain is cooked. Note: Experiment with the time setting since wild rice, brown rice, and some other grains take longer to cook than white rice does.

Roasting pan with a grate. For collecting fat drippings on the bottom so roasted and broiled meat or poultry can't absorb them.

Salad spinner. For easily removing excess water from fresh salad greens using centrifugal force. It has a removable strainer.

Slotted spoon. For lifting food out of the pan, leaving any fat drippings behind.

Slow cooker. For cooking food with low, steady, moist heat. This countertop appliance can be used to tenderize tougher cuts of meat. Perfect for a nourishing, convenience soup or casserole-type dish that's thrown together in the morning and enjoyed for dinner.

Steamer. For steaming, rather than frying, food. There are several kinds of steamers: an electric steamer for vegetables, rice, fish, or chicken; a stackable bamboo steamer set that fits in a wok or a stockpot; and a small aluminum vegetable steamer that fits in a saucepan.

Storage containers with lids. For keeping leftovers and ingredients you haven't used yet. It's one more tool to help you avoid wasting food!

Wok. For fast cooking without much oil because of a wok's sloped sides. Unless it has a nonstick surface, "season" a new stainless-steel wok to keep food from sticking. Here's how: First coat the cooking surface with vegetable oil, then heat in a 350°F oven for about an hour. Oil will work its way into the porous surface.

NOURISHING KITCHEN "STAPLES"

Every household has its own staples, or foods consumed routinely, that make up an important part of everyday meals and snacks.

The "secret" to healthy meals and snacks is keeping an inventory of nutrient-dense staples on hand. Many of these foods are sold with reduced amounts of added sugars, saturated fats, or sodium. Decide which form to buy to fit your overall meal and snack goals. Buy fresh ingredients only as you need them so they don't go to waste!

See chapter 6, page 141, to be a savvy food shopper.

Recipes: Culinary Roadmaps

Recipes differ in style and detail. Some are very specific, explaining or illustrating each food-prep step. Others assume basic culinary knowledge and skills. Many suggest substitutions or offer side notes with food-prep hints, ingredient factoids, or menu tips. Most aren't "cast in stone." Many can be adapted as needed if you have some culinary know-how and an inventory of ingredients on hand.

RECIPES: JUDGE FOR YOURSELF!

Cookbooks, websites, blogs, phone and tablet apps, magazines, newspapers, package labels, social networks, and more: all these sources provide you with millions of recipes to choose from. Some are kitchen tested; some aren't. Some don't provide adequate direction. Some have online reviews or comments; most don't.

How do you pick recipes that are worth your time, food budget, and effort? And how do you choose those that taste good, that match your schedule, cooking skills, and family preferences, and that fit your health goals?

If there's a photo, that's a place to start. Photos may grab your attention, especially if they feature the nourishing qualities you're looking for, such as colorful vegetables and fruits and hearty whole grains. But you need to read the recipe carefully—headnotes, ingredients, and directions—from start to finish, before you judge:

- *Ingredients.* Are all the ingredients included in the directions, and vice versa? Are they listed in the order of use, as is the convention? Do the amounts make sense? Do you have the ingredients or need to substitute or shop? Do you prefer a recipe with fewer or more common ingredients?
- *Directions.* Are the directions clear and complete? Do you have the time to prepare the recipe? The skills? Do you need a simpler

Food-Prep Skills to Know

CUTTING

CHOP	to cut foods into smaller pieces of no particular size or shape
CUBE	to cut foods into square pieces, usually ½ inch per side
DICE	to cut foods into small, cubed pieces.
GRATE	to rub foods against a serrated surface to create fine shreds
JULIENNE	to cut foods into thin, matchstick-size strips
MINCE	to cut foods into very small pieces
SLICE	to cut foods either lengthwise or crosswise into slices
ZEST	to cut thin, narrow strips of the thick outer part of the citrus rind with a grater or peeler

COMBINING

BEAT	to mix briskly until the mixture is smooth using a spoon, whisk, or mixer
BLEND	to mix and so distribute the ingredients
CREAM	to soften a fat, such as butter, with a spoon or mixer, perhaps with another ingredient, until smooth
FOLD IN	to blend ingredients gently, such as beaten egg whites or whipped cream, so the volume remains and air bubbles don't break
KNEAD	to repeatedly fold, press, and turn dough by hand to mix ingredients and develop gluten in dough
MIX	to combine ingredients until they're evenly distributed
STIR	to mix ingredients with a circular or figure-eight motion until they're evenly distributed or combined
WHIP	to beat rapidly to incorporate air and increase volume
WHISK	to combine or fluff by whipping with a light, rapid movement

OTHER

BASTE	to brush or spoon juices, a marinade, or liquid fat (such as melted butter) over food as it cooks to help retain surface moisture
DEGLAZE	to add liquid to a pan after food has been sauteed or roasted to soften and dissolve bits of food on the pan
DREDGE	to coat in flour and then shake off the excess
MARINATE	to tenderize and add flavor by letting food, such as meat or chicken, remain in a flavorful liquid, such as Italian dressing, for a period of time
PUREE	to finely mash to a smooth, thick consistency
SEASON	to add herbs, spices, salt, or pepper for flavor

recipe? Can you complete some steps ahead? Look for illustrated step-by-step recipes or online video demos that show technique if it's a new recipe or uses a technique that's new to you.

- *Equipment.* Do you have the equipment to prepare the recipe? If not, can you adjust the cooking technique?
- *Yield.* What's the portion size, and what does it deliver to your day's eating plan? How many people does it serve? Are the portions sensible?
- *Nutrition analysis (if provided).* It gives you an idea of the nutrients and calories in a serving of the recipe, but it may not be precise. Unlike food labels, nutrition information and serving sizes for recipes aren't standardized, and your own measurements and ingredients may vary somewhat. Recipes may list some, but not all, the nutrients you find on a label.

When comparing nutrition information in similar recipes, be alert: serving sizes vary from one recipe to another, and your homemade dish may differ in portion size and ingredients from a label-size serving of its counterpart sold as a convenience food.

Choose recipes to create a varied meal—to balance with other meals and snacks for the whole day. Consider variety of colors, flavors, textures, tastes—and nutrition. If the recipe you choose is higher in calories, saturated fats, added sugars, or sodium, consider substitutions or plan your menu with other foods that have less of what needs to be limited.

Most important, choose recipes that appeal to you and your family. No matter how nutritious a recipe sounds, a great recipe should be something you enjoy—or a food you're willing to experience. And a poor recipe, or one that doesn't appeal, can result in food waste.

RECIPE REVAMP

Chefs and test-kitchen experts change recipes all the time. In fact, there's nothing sacred about most recipes (except perhaps Mom's or other family recipes).

Recipes get altered when new ingredients come on the market, when cooking equipment changes, when consumers want recipe shortcuts, when ingredients are in or out of season or become more or less costly, when consumers shift food preferences, when yields must change to feed more or fewer, and when nutrition and health issues arise.

Recipe Makeovers: Healthier, Easier

In your own "test kitchen," you can modify many recipes to make them healthier or cut calories, often without much flavor change. Or you may need to adjust them for a health condition such as a food allergy, celiac disease (gluten free), or high blood pressure (less sodium).

Recipes can be adapted in several ways: change or substitute ingredients, modify the steps, cut or increase portion sizes, or do all three. Even one or two small recipe changes may net significant nutrition differences.

Whatever your approach, keep flavor, texture, and appeal in mind. Depending on the goal, a single indulgent dish may not need a makeover—if you don't eat it often, if the rest of your day's choices are nourishing or have fewer calories, or if you eat just a small amount.

Because ingredients in recipes serve specific functions, some recipes don't lend themselves well to appealing makeovers. *See "Fats, Sugars, Salt: What These Ingredients Do" in this chapter, page 246.* Reducing or taking out an ingredient may cause the recipe to fail—or at least lose its appeal.

If you decide to make over a recipe, know your goals; then you might:

1. *Change the ingredients.* Review the recipe and the ingredient list before you identify the ingredient changes you want to make—perhaps less saturated fats or added sugars, more fiber or calcium, or more vegetables. Other goals you may have: to have leftovers, boost the flavor, take advantage of a supermarket sale, or match a family preference.

Cooking Methods to Know

BAKE	to cook surrounded by hot air, usually in an oven
BLANCH	to partly cook vegetables in water, then cool quickly in cold water
BOIL	to cook in liquid brought to a rapid boil
BRAISE	to brown or sear (usually meat or vegetables) and then simmer over low heat in a small amount of liquid—water, broth, or even fruit juice—in a covered pot for long, slow cooking, either on the stovetop or in the oven
BROIL	to cook with direct heat, usually beneath a heating element in the oven
BROWN	to cook briefly over high heat, so the surface turns brown without cooking the interior
DEEP-FRY	to cook by submerging in hot oil
GRILL OR BARBECUE	to cook with direct heat directly over hot coals or another heat source
PANBROIL	to cook uncovered in a preheated, nonstick skillet without added fat or water
PANFRY	to fry in a small amount of fat (not enough to cover the food)
POACH	to cook gently in liquid, at about 160° to 180°F. The surface of the liquid starts to shimmer.
REDUCE	to boil a stock, wine, or sauce until evaporation reduces the volume, the consistency thickens, and the flavor intensifies
ROAST	to cook uncovered with dry heat in the oven
SAUTÉ	to cook quickly in a small amount of fat so the food browns evenly
SEAR	to cook, or caramelize, the surface (usually meat, poultry, or fish) as part of grilling, baking, braising, roasting, etc., at a high temperature
SIMMER	to cook gently in liquid, at about 185° to 200°F, often called a "gentle boil." Tiny bubbles will begin to break the surface.
STEAM	to cook with steam heat over (not in) boiling water in a covered pot, or wrapped in foil packets or leaves (such as lettuce or banana leaves), over boiling water or on a grill
STEW	to simmer slowly, barely covered by a liquid, such as water, juice, wine, broth, or stock, in a tightly covered pot over low heat
STIR-FRY	to cook small pieces of meat, poultry, fish, and/or vegetables in a very small amount of oil, perhaps with added broth, over high heat, stirring as you cook

- *Consider the ingredient's functions.* Use suitable substitutions, knowing why it's in the recipe. Sometimes the switch is easy, such as changing the flavor. For example, in meat, poultry, fish, and vegetable dishes, salt enhances taste; herbs make flavorful substitutes.

  Experiment, perhaps by changing just one ingredient at a time so you know what works. That's especially important when the ingredient serves a functional purpose, such as eggs or sugar in baked foods. When the recipe makeover works, jot it down—in your cookbook or your file.
- *Reduce or eliminate.* In some recipes, you may cut back on sugar by a third with good results. With sautéed foods, try less cooking oil. Optional ingredients are easy to take out; removing others may alter the appearance or the flavor. If you cut back on salt, season with more herbs, spices, or other flavorings.
- *Shift proportions.* For example, serve a bowl of fruit with a dollop of ice cream instead of a bowl of ice cream topped with a spoonful of fruit.
- *Add or increase.* Fortifying casseroles with wheat bran or dry milk powder may go unnoticed. Adding shredded carrots or mashed cauliflower to mashed potatoes, beans to salads, or dried cranberries to muesli gives extra flavor and color along with more nutrients and phytonutrients.
- *Substitute.* For example, use Greek yogurt in place of sour cream in dips and some creamy sauces, reduced-sodium canned tomatoes in place of out-of-season fresh tomatoes, or ground lean turkey in place of regular ground beef. Switch to brown rice in recipes, or to canola or olive oil for less saturated fats.

2. *Modify food preparation.* Changes in cooking techniques and preparation may require little or no extra time—just know-how.

   Some changes are simple: scrub potatoes rather than peel away the fiber-rich skins, oven-bake rather than fry them, or brown them in a nonstick pan coated with vegetable oil spray instead of butter or oil. Instead of one-quarter cup of cheese sauce on a baked potato, use two tablespoons; top with steamed, chopped vegetables and/or herbs for flavor.

   Other changes in cooking techniques may require more skill: sautéing in a small amount of fat instead of deep-frying, thickening with pureed beans instead of flour, or making a reduction sauce instead of gravy. If you make changes, it's okay to write in your own notes if it's your cookbook. That way you'll remember next time. Keep a file of successful recipes.
3. *Reduce portion sizes.* For recipes high in calories, saturated fats, or added sugars, serve less. Trick the eye so less looks like more by serving smaller portions on smaller plates. Later in this chapter, you'll find many tips to help make over recipes for health, flavor, and personal preferences.

Recipe Makeovers: Healthy Vegetarian

Looking for vegetarian recipes? Many recipes can be transformed to make them meatless—even to avoid eggs and dairy products for vegan dishes.

Instead of meat, poultry, or fish . . .

- *Casseroles, stews, soups, lasagna, and chili.* Substitute cooked or canned dried beans and lentils for meat: perhaps kidney beans in chili or stew; red lentils in spaghetti sauce or stuffed cabbage rolls; or vegetarian refried beans in burritos, tacos, or enchiladas. Or add veggie crumbles (soy protein), often sold in granular form.
- *Grilled kebobs.* Cube and skewer firm tofu and tempeh with vegetables. Tofu has a chewier texture if frozen for up to three months.
- *Pasta sauces, pizza, soups, stews, other mixed dishes.* Prepare as directed—but skip the meat. Add more chopped vegetables and beans. If you eat dairy products, top with cheese for more protein and calcium.
- *Pizza, hot sandwiches, sloppy joes, and other dishes that typically call for meat.* Use soy or other legume alternatives: patties (gardenburgers or beanburgers), falafel (chickpea patties), soy bacon, soy hot dogs, or soy sausage links.
- *Stir-fry dishes.* Use firm tofu, tempeh, soyburgers or soy sausage, cooked beans, nuts, or sesame seeds in place of meat, poultry, or fish. *Hint:* For more flavor, marinate tofu before adding it to other ingredients.

Instead of Eggs . . .

Eggs offer functional qualities to recipes—for example, thickening, binding ingredients together, clarifying stock, coating breaded foods, and leavening. Leavening lightens the texture and increases the volume of baked goods. Without eggs, the qualities of foods often change. So experiment.

- Try one of these ingredients in place of one egg. Know that the results may differ from the original recipe. For example, when you make muffins, quick breads, pancakes, and scrambled eggs, try replacing one egg with one of these options:
  - Half of a mashed banana
  - Two tablespoons of cornstarch or arrowroot
  - One-quarter cup of applesauce or pumpkin puree
  - One-quarter cup of cooked oatmeal or mashed cooked beans
  - Egg replacer powder or vegetarian egg replacement (often sold in specialty stores)
  - One-quarter cup of cooked oatmeal, mashed potatoes, mashed beans, or tofu (in vegetarian burgers or loaves)
- Scramble tofu with herbs for breakfast.

Instead of Dairy Foods . . .

- *Baked foods.* Use one cup of soy beverage or another milk alternative plus one tablespoon of vinegar to replace one cup of buttermilk.
- *Cheese dishes.* Use crumbled tofu to replace ricotta cheese in lasagna. Soft tofu or soy cheese is great in dips or sauces; blend it with other ingredients.
- *Frozen desserts.* Enjoy fruit sorbet in place of sherbet and ice cream.
- *Spreads.* Use soy margarine instead of butter and margarine. Some margarine has ingredients derived from milk, such as whey or casein. Cookies, pastries, and other baked goods made with margarine may have a different texture than those made with butter. Remember that lard is another fat of animal origin and that stick margarine may contain undesirable *trans* fatty acids; use mostly soft or liquid margarine. Hummus is another option. *See "Stocking the Vegetarian Kitchen" in chapter 6, page 187, for more options.*
- *Thick, creamy fruit shakes.* Blend fruit with soft tofu, soy beverage or other milk alternatives, soy yogurt, or nondairy ice cream—or make all-fruit smoothies!

Instead of Gelatin . . . Use kosher gelatin, made from a sea vegetable, if you're vegetarian or vegan. Find it in a specialty food shop.

Edible Flowers: Please Don't Eat the Daffodils

Edible flowers add a distinctive flavor (sweet lilac, spicy nasturtium, minty bee balm) and a unique splash of color on the plate. But you can't eat just any flower!

Some are poisonous, and even edible flowers may be contaminated by chemicals if they weren't grown for eating. Don't eat flowers from a florist or a greenhouse—or flowers you pick along the road, not even as a garnish. Flowers that are not edible include buttercup, delphinium, lily of the valley, foxglove, goldenseal, periwinkle, oleander, sweet pea—and daffodils, to name a few.

Only eat flowers if you're absolutely sure of their safety! *Tip:* If you have hay fever, allergies, or asthma, be cautious about eating flowers. Buy edible flowers in the produce section of a grocery store. They should be labeled as "edible flowers."

Grow edible flowers in your kitchen garden: bee balm, borage, calendula (pot marigold), chrysanthemum, day lilies, dianthus, scented geraniums, marigolds, nasturtiums (enjoy leaves and blossoms), pansies, roses, squash blossoms, sunflowers, tulips, and violets. Enjoy blossoms from any herb plant: try basil, chive, lavender, oregano, sage, savory, and thyme blossoms.

After harvesting, wash edible flowers well, and gently pat them dry. To keep for a few days, refrigerate them. Keep the stems in water, or put short-stemmed blossoms in a plastic bag or between damp paper towels. For most flowers, enjoy the petals.

Flavor on the Menu

Imagine . . . the aroma of homemade, whole-wheat bread baking in your oven . . . the sweet, juicy taste of a ripe peach—just picked . . . the cool sensation of ice-cold milk . . . the crispy crunch of a raw carrot . . . the creamy texture of chocolate ice cream . . . or the fiery spiciness of a hot chile pepper.

Foods that appeal to your senses are probably those you enjoy most. Sensory stimulation evokes food memories. The more senses a food or meal affects, the more vivid the flavor memory, positive or not. For most Americans, enjoyment is an important part of eating; it may even be the reason. Like good nutrition, food appeal needs to be a kitchen priority. When it comes to nutrition, think flavor . . . and when it comes to flavor, think nutrition!

FLAVOR AND HEALTH

Food that delivers great flavor can help you eat healthier. Why—and how? And just what is flavor?

What Is Flavor?

Flavor comes from a combination of sensory experiences: taste plus smell, as well as touch (temperature and mouth feel). Arguably, sound, perhaps the crunch of an apple, and sight contribute to flavor, too.

Taste. Average adults have about ten thousand taste buds, which respond to five different taste sensations: sweet, sour, salty, bitter, and umami (the savory flavor of a protein called glutamate). Some flavor experts suggest "fat" may be a sixth sense; *see "Your 'Fat Tooth'" in chapter 13, page 389.*

You experience all these tastes throughout your mouth, not only on your tongue. Some parts of the tongue may be especially sensitive to certain tastes. Even the lining of your mouth, the back of your throat, your tonsils (if you still have them), and your epiglottis (the flap of tissue that covers your larynx, preventing food and liquids from entering the airway) have some taste buds, with more in childhood. The way your taste receptors are configured, which is determined by your genes, influences how you detect these tastes.

To some degree, all five tastes can be perceived at birth. Not surprisingly, infants are born with an ability to perceive flavors. In fact, the first experiences with flavors happen before birth. The flavors of amniotic fluid change along with a mother's food choices. Early exposure to flavors, starting in the prenatal years, enhances a child's acceptance and enjoyment of them. That includes foods of a family's culture, as well as vegetables.

Smell. Aromas that waft through the room get picked up by more than 400 different olfactory (smell) receptors (with millions of nerve cells) in the back of your nasal passages. With so many receptors, the body is capable of detecting millions of aromas. A single aroma—perhaps from a ripe peach or sizzling bacon—is really a combination of many odor molecules connecting on many receptors.

When an odor molecule connects with these receptors, sensory neurons send signals to your body's olfactory bulb. These signals get relayed to other parts of the brain. There they become integrated with taste information and register as flavor.

Aromas of certain foods may evoke certain emotions and memories for you. That's because smell information is sent to parts of the brain linked to memory and learning. Because they are so complex and numerous, aromas aren't classified the way tastes are.

Touch. Mouth feel also affects perceptions of food and its flavor—and what you may describe as its "taste." Cold sorbet and steamy hot soup, the "irritation" from eating a spicy jalapeño pepper, or the "numbing" from a persimmon are "touch points" of flavor. So are the crunchy textures of crisp apples and crackers, the stickiness of peanut butter, the chewiness of a granola bar, the greasiness of fried food, and the smoothness of yogurt and mashed potatoes.

The Flavor Experience

With one sensation diminished, perhaps when you have a head cold, a flavor experience may be entirely different. As an experiment, hold your nose so you can't smell, then bite into an onion. The flavor may be somewhat sweet, like an apple. Now open your nose; consider the difference! Think

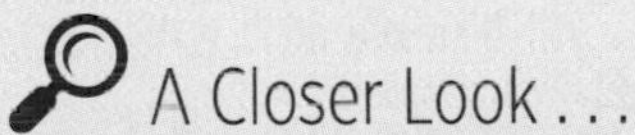

New Flavors: From Ethnic to Fusion

Global communications, travel, and food imports make the world of food highly connected. Just a few decades ago, bagels, pita bread, pastas of every shape, and tortillas were trendy; salsa and hummus were new flavor experiences, as were Cajun dishes and California rolls (sushi). Today, ethnic and regional foods such as these are supermarket mainstream.

Moroccan or Lebanese, Peruvian or Brazilian, Korean or Thai, Indian or Ethiopian: today, many want to try these and go beyond ethnic basics such as Italian, Chinese, and Mexican. Regional ethnic foods—Tuscan, Liguria Roman, Calabrian, and Lazio (Italian); Sichuan, Peking, and Cantonese (Chinese); and Yucatán, Oaxacan, and Michoacán (Mexican)—have also captured consumer interest, at least among foodies.

GROWING DEMAND FOR ETHNIC AND REGIONAL FOODS

What sparks interest in and availability of ethnic and regional foods? Perhaps a sense of curiosity and adventure, and a desire to try nutritious, flavorful alternatives. Celebrity chefs entertain by preparing ethnic foods and by taking us to global markets and kitchens. Travel, cooking classes, websites, blogs, print media, cookbooks, and restaurants introduce unique ingredients, seasonings, and dishes.

Supermarkets are stocked with ethnic and regionally inspired foods, partly to meet the demand from diverse populations and partly to match flavor trends. That offers you more food variety and more ways to fit beans and peas, fish, fruits, vegetables, whole grains, and other nutrient-rich foods into your meals and snacks.

See "The Global Kitchen: Meatless on the Menu" in chapter 9, page 288, and "Global Table: Varied, Healthy, Enjoyable" in chapter 3, page 70.

A FLAVOR FUSION

The blending of cuisines, sometimes called fusion cuisine, is a culinary phenomenon. It combines the ingredients or cooking techniques of two or more cultures not geographically close together. The result is new cuisines such as Thai-French, Southwest-Asian, Cuban-French, and unique dishes such as Moroccan couscous topped with Chinese stir-fried vegetables. Even fast-food menus reflect fusion, such as Mexican pizza, chili in a pita pocket, or a Thai wrap in a tortilla.

The fusion of ingredients and flavors isn't new. It has happened for centuries as people gradually adapted their cuisines to the available food supply, sometimes by choice and often by necessity.

Today, fusion cooking brings an explosion of new dishes to the table. In many cases, new fused dishes uniquely combine grain products, fruits, and vegetables. Simply adding seasonings from an ethnic or a regional cuisine also creates fusion; perhaps a touch of curry powder from India in pumpkin soup, or basil and garlic, borrowed from Italian cooking, in beef stew. *See "Ethnic Flavor Profiles" in this chapter, page 269, for seasoning combinations.*

Are You a Supertaster?

Why do you like the foods you like? The reasons are partly genes, gender, and age. Even in the same family, people experience tastes differently. The intensity of taste depends partly on how many fungiform papillae (tiny, smooth red bumps with clusters of taste receptor cells, or taste buds) a person has on his or her tongue.

Supertasters have a lot of papillae, experience the flavors of foods more intensely, and tend to strongly like or dislike certain foods. Supertasters perceive bitter flavors—perhaps in pungent vegetables, tea, coffee, and grapefruit juice—and sweet flavors more intensely, too. Those with few papillae tend to be indifferent to one flavor over another, and those in the middle are likely to enjoy all kinds of foods if prepared well.

Children have more papillae than adults, perhaps one of many reasons why a child may be a picky eater. Taste sensitivity seems to decline with age, which is explained in part by the decrease in the number of papillae.

Have you ever burned your tongue on steamy hot soup, or the roof of your mouth on the hot cheese topping a pizza? Hot foods may damage papillae. Fortunately, your body repairs its papillae fairly quickly.

Are you a supertaster? Find out. First punch a hole (with a hole punch) in a small piece of wax paper. Put the hole on the tip of your tongue; wipe it with blue food coloring. With a mirror, magnifying glass, and flashlight, count the papillae. Nontasters have fewer than fifteen, but supertasters have dozens of them! (More women than men are supertasters.)

about how food tastes when your nose is stuffed up—not much flavor and not much pleasure, either. About 80 percent of a food's flavor is aroma.

Why does the same food taste too spicy or bitter for some, and not for others? Why might you like asparagus, but your best friend doesn't? People sense foods differently. Saliva (affected by diet, genes, and health), the number and configuration of taste receptors on taste buds, the number of olfactory receptors, medications, some illnesses, smoking, and aging contribute to the difference. *See "Are You a Supertaster" above.*

One reason why some older people say that foods just don't taste the way they remember is that taste and smell diminish with age; *see "Flavor Loss? Aging with 'Taste'" in chapter 20, page 592.* Likewise, children may be more sensitive to some tastes than their parents, so they eat in a different "flavor world."

Chewing makes a difference, too. Eating slowly and taking time to chew stimulates saliva flow, enhancing flavor as foods' components dissolve and blend. Textures change as you chew, too. Another benefit: by taking time to savor the flavor, you may eat more slowly—and avoid overeating, too.

MSG—Another Flavor Enhancer

You probably know about monosodium glutamate, or more simply, MSG. Common in some ethnic cooking, MSG enhances flavor. It blends well with salty and sour flavors, and brings out flavors of many foods including prepared foods, such as "heat 'n' eat" meals, sauces, and canned soups.

MSG has nutrition-related benefits that often go unrecognized. Since a little goes a long way, MSG provides a bigger "bang" for the "shake." With only a third as much sodium as a comparable amount of table salt, its use may help control sodium intake. Using MSG instead of salt can lower the sodium in a recipe by 20 to 40 percent while still enhancing flavor. In food preparation, one-half teaspoon of MSG is enough to season one pound of meat, or four to six servings of vegetables.

Besides accenting natural flavors, MSG adds a unique taste of its own. Called "umami," it's described as "meaty" or "brothlike." Studies show "umami" elicits a fifth taste sensation, distinctive in cheese, meat, and tomatoes.

As its name implies, MSG contains sodium and glutamate, or glutamic acid. Glutamic acid is an amino acid found naturally in your body and in high-protein foods. Meat, fish, dairy foods, and some vegetables, such as tomatoes and mushrooms, get their umami taste from glutamate.

Adding MSG to foods such as soups and stews may perk up the flavor, making eating more enjoyable for older adults. With age, the sense of smell may weaken, and fewer taste buds may change a food's flavor appeal. That decline often causes older adults to lose interest in eating, putting them at nutritional risk. *See "Flavor Loss? Aging with 'Taste'" in chapter 20, page 592, for more about flavor perception and older adults.*

The US Food and Drug Administration considers MSG "generally recognized as safe" (GRAS) for consumption. *See "Additives: Testing and Approval" in chapter 5, page 138, for more about the GRAS list and "Have you ever wondered . . . if you can be sensitive to MSG?" in chapter 23, page 679.*

Flavor and Nutrition

Besides your flavor experience, there's a lot wrapped up in why certain foods appeal (or don't) to you, including social, emotional, and health reasons. In any case, the foods you enjoy are likely the ones you eat most. The more often you eat them, the more they'll affect your overall nutrition and health.

Flavor matters. If food tastes good, people likely will eat it. If you like a healthy food once, you'll likely eat it again. If it doesn't taste good to you, even the healthiest food may be left on your plate—wasted and nourishing no one.

? Have you ever wondered?

. . . what makes chile peppers taste "hot"? Capsaicin in chile peppers stimulates pain receptors in your mouth. The irritation, or "heating" effect, depends on the amount of capsaicin, measured in Scoville heat units (SHU)—anywhere from 1 to 300,000 SHU (mild to very hot). A sweet bell (pimento) pepper is rated at 0 to 5; an Anaheim pepper at 500 to 1,000; an ancho or poblano pepper at 1,000 to 1,500; a jalapeño or chipotle pepper at 2,500 to 5,000; a Serrano pepper at 5,000 to 15,000; and a habañero (Scotch bonnet) pepper at 80,000 to 300,000!

. . . how to reduce the "fire" caused by eating hot chile peppers? Try dairy foods. Caesin, the main protein in milk, washes away the capsaicin that makes your mouth and throat "burn." Hot chile peppers do "fire up" the flavors of Thai dishes, Mexican salsas, and Cajun foods, among others. To tone down the heat, remove the seeds and inner membranes of hot chiles. To avoid a burning sensation on sensitive skin as you handle hot chiles, use latex or rubber gloves. Never touch or rub your eyes—or any other sensitive areas—when you're handling chiles.

Since people eat for flavor, there's good reason to consider how nutrition and health are linked to food's taste, aroma, and texture. That's why agriculture has developed some fruits and vegetables that are more flavorful, why food companies look for ways to enhance flavor as they also lower salt in processed foods, and why flavor-enhancing techniques are used to make foods more flavorful for older adults. Equally important is knowing how to make and keep food flavorful for you, as you cook at home.

VARIETY FOR FLAVOR APPEAL

Like a well-decorated room or a beautifully landscaped garden, an appealing meal follows basic principles of design. Different foods add a variety of colors, tastes, textures, shapes, and temperatures to meals or snacks. In fact, the more variety, the more satisfying the eating experience. At the same time, food variety supplies different nutrients and phytonutrients. When planning menus, think variety:

Vary the color. Contrast the visual differences: meat loaf, mashed potatoes with gravy, corn, and applesauce . . . as opposed to meat loaf, baked sweet potato with chopped chives, asparagus, and spinach salad with orange slices. Which one has more interest? The meal with an artist's palette of color! Phytonutrients that give fruits and vegetables their colorful appeal and health benefits also contribute different flavors.

Vary the flavors. Different ingredients and seasonings in a dish or meal add layers of flavor. Instead of serving sweet orange-glazed chicken, candied sweet potatoes, and fruit compote, complement chicken with wild rice pilaf and a crisp spinach salad with herbed balsamic dressing. Include sweet, sour, salty, bitter, and umami tastes in a meal. Other sensations, such as the "burn" of chiles and smoky aromas, add to the flavor, too.

Vary the texture. Crunchy foods contrast with soft foods—for example, chopped nuts in brown rice, or raw veggies with herbed yogurt dip. Varied textures (soft, smooth, creamy, crunchy, crispy) add appeal as much as variety of color.

Vary the shape and size. Round meatballs, round peas, round new potatoes, and round grapes may look somewhat boring if plated together. Add variety to the plate with baby carrots or pea pods instead of peas, pasta spirals instead of potatoes, or sliced peaches instead of grapes.

Vary the temperature. Hot and cool in the same meal maximize the flavor perception of a meal. For example, a cold summer supper or a picnic from the cooler can be refreshing. However, a warm whole-wheat roll offers a nice contrast to a cool chef's salad. And frozen yogurt makes a nice ending to a hot dinner.

FOOD PREP: THE FLAVOR CONNECTION

What makes foods taste so good? As a home cook, the way you handle, store, prepare, and serve food matters for its best flavor, appeal, and ultimately its ability to nourish.

Flavor: Handle with Care

Proper food handling and storage can build and preserve food's natural flavors without relying on much fat, salt, or added sugars, and also keep nutrient loss to a minimum.

- Start with high-quality ingredients, at their peak of quality. For example, fresh produce often tastes best in season. Stored properly and used at their peak, nuts and seeds avoid developing rancid flavors. Airtight wrapping and proper storage times keep frozen produce, meat, poultry, and fish from developing freezer burn. *See "Freshness: How to . . . Judge Produce" in chapter 6, page 160.*
- Store foods properly. Poor storage destroys flavor and quality. Poor packaging can result in one food absorbing flavors from others. *See "Food Storage: Safekeeping," chapter 7, page 197, for ways to store food to retain flavor and freshness.*
- Prepare foods in ways that retain and enhance their flavor, color, and texture, as well as nutrients. Cooking cannot improve foods that have passed their peak quality. Overcooking destroys flavor and nutrients. *See "How to . . . Keep Nutrients In" in this chapter, page 248 for ways to retain nutrients in food prep.*
- Serve hot foods hot—and cold foods cold. Enticing flavors in hot foods come partly from aromas released with heat. Cold foods, properly chilled, give a refreshing mouth feel. Some foods such as cheese release their full flavor at room temperature. Whatever the temperatures, food safety for perishable foods must be top of mind.

Give It a Little Salsa

Salsa is the Spanish word for "sauce." By combining a variety of cold ingredients—chopped vegetables, fruits, herbs, and even hot sauce—you can prepare a salsa to enjoy as a dip or sauce.

- *Black bean salsa:* Combine canned, drained and rinsed black beans with chopped tomato, chopped onion, chopped cilantro, and a little jalapeño and red wine vinegar. Chill.
- *Pineapple or mango salsa:* Combine chopped, fresh, or canned pineapple or mango with chopped bell pepper, cilantro, fresh lime juice, and a touch of sugar and minced garlic. Chill.
- *Tomato salsa*: Combine chopped plum tomatoes, onions, canned green chiles, cilantro, tomatillos, and lime juice. Add red pepper flakes or hot sauce for more zip. Chill. *Tip:* Plum tomatoes, especially when they're in season, often have more flavor than salad tomatoes.

Flavor: Use Good Culinary Techniques

Good culinary techniques not only retain foods' natural appeal, but may enhance nutrition and build flavor at the same time.

- Poach fish, poultry, or meat by gently cooking it in flavorful hot broth, just below boiling, rather than cooking in oil; poach fruit in juice rather than cooking in sugary syrup.
- Roast or grill vegetables in a very hot (450°F) oven or grill for a sweet, smoky flavor. Brush or spray lightly with oil so they don't dry out. Sprinkle with herbs.
- Reduce, by simmering meat, poultry, and fish stocks to concentrate their flavors and evaporate some or most of the water. Then use reduction sauces as a flavorful glaze or gravy.
- Intensify flavor with high-heat cooking techniques. Pan-searing, grilling, and broiling meat, poultry, and fish brown the surface and seal in juices and so add flavor.
- Caramelize sliced onions, garlic, root vegetables, and other vegetables to bring out and deepen their natural sugar flavor. Just cook them slowly over low heat in a small amount of oil. Use them to make a rich, dark sauce for meat or poultry. Caramelize sliced apples and some other fruits, too.
- Infuse oils and vinegars with herbs or garlic for more flavor.
- Marinate, or soak, food in tangy, sweet, or savory sauces to infuse flavor and moisture from the outside in. For protein foods such as meat and poultry, marinades typically contain an acidic ingredient such as fruit juice to tenderize the meat.
- Switch the liquid. Cooking grains that absorb fluid, such as rice, buckwheat, and barley, in low-fat, fat-free, and perhaps reduced-sodium chicken or beef broth makes them more flavorful than cooking in water. Risotto, an Italian rice specialty, typically is prepared by cooking arborio or white medium-grain rice in broth, along with herbs and other ingredients.
- Substitute or add ingredients with big, bold flavors, but perhaps in small amounts. Try feta or blue cheese, pomegranate seeds, chipotle peppers (with a smoky taste), cilantro, or bitter broccoli rabe. Switch to more whole grains, with their fuller flavors, such as brown rice or quinoa, or experiment with amaranth and wild rice. *See "How to . . . Cook Whole Grains" in this chapter, page 253.*
- Balance tastes within a dish or meal—for example, a fruit sauce for fish, made with mango (sweet), tarragon (bitter), vinegar (sour), broth (umami), and a touch of salt. A touch of acid from citrus juice or other fruit or a sprinkle of salt can brighten the flavor.
- Layer flavors with a variety of contrasting ingredients—as easy as a mixture of many greens, citrus fruits, nuts, and balsamic dressing in a salad.
- Season creatively with herbs and spices: perhaps a sweet spice such as cinnamon with meat, or a savory herb such as rosemary with fruits or desserts. Try less common spices such as smoked paprika, Chinese five spice, or sichuan pepper. *See "Quick Guide: Herbs and Spices" in this chapter, page 272.*

More Flavor, More Texture: Nuts, Seeds, Nut Butters

A small handful of nuts and seeds not only adds flavor, but they're also good sources of protein and healthy oils. Go easy since their calories can add up. The nutrients and phytonutrients in different nuts and seeds vary. Toasting adds flavor to some, such as almonds, pecans, and seeds. Enjoy a variety. You have choices: buy them whole, slivered, sliced, ground, salted, or unsalted. For example, try:

- Almonds, pecans, or sunflower seeds in salads, waffles, and sweet potatoes
- Cashews in stir-fries
- Macadamia nuts or walnuts in quick breads
- Nut butters and tahini (sesame paste) as a light spread
- Pine nuts or pistachios in pasta sauces and casseroles
- Sesame seeds on green veggies, soups, and stews
- Any nuts on cereal or yogurt, or in trail mix

See "In a Nutshell: Tree Nut and Seeds" in chapter 2, page 43.

How to . . . Give Food an Easy Flavor Lift!

- Enhance sauces, soups, and salads with a splash of flavored, balsamic, or rice vinegar, or a touch of fish sauce, Sriracha sauce, or soy sauce.
- Add a splash of tangy citrus juice or grated citrus peel: lemon, lime, or orange. Acidic ingredients help lift and balance flavor.
- Pep it up with peppers! Use red, green, and yellow peppers of all varieties—sweet, hot, and dried. Or add a dash of hot pepper sauce or chile oil.
- Intensify flavor by simply adding dried ingredients: apricots, cranberries, figs, plums (prunes), mushrooms, sun-dried tomatoes, or red pepper flakes. Try plump sun-dried tomatoes and dried mushrooms in broth or cooking wine, and dried cranberries or dried plums (prunes) in apple juice.
- Serve food with good-quality condiments on the side or on top, instead of butter or margarine: try bean purees, chutney, flavored mustard, horseradish, tapenade (anchovy-olive spread), wasabi, and salsas of all kinds.
- Blend herbs, spices, sun-dried tomatoes, and shredded cheese into bread dough before baking it.
- Sharpen the flavor with cheese. Add a little Asiago, blue cheese, sharp Cheddar, feta, Parmesan, or Romano to vegetables, rice, or pasta.
- Add a little nut oil: almond, hazelnut, or walnut. A little drizzle as a finishing oil will do! (Finishing oils have a lot of flavor, but may not be good for high-heat cooking because they break down with high heat. They're often drizzled on food after its cooked, or use in salad dressings or for dipping.)
- Fire up the flavor with kimchi, a pungent condiment of fermented vegetables, such as cabbage or turnips. Go easy, since it's high in sodium.

- Cook with aromatics, or fresh vegetables that give a deep, rounded flavor and aroma when heated or crushed: carrots, celery, chile peppers, garlic, ginger, leeks, onions, parsnips, peppers, scallions (green onions), and shallots. They'll bring flavor to soups, stews, sauces, and more, along with health benefits, too. A mixture of diced carrots, onions and celery, and herbs, called "mirepoix" in culinary terms, is often used to enhance the flavors of soups, stews, and meat dishes.
- Experiment with unique ingredients, including local or ethnic foods and seasonings.

Beyond Parsley: Quick, Easy Garnishes

Garnishes do more than add eye appeal with color and texture contrasts. Meant to be eaten, too, they also deliver flavor and some nutritional value. Garnishing doesn't require special culinary skills.

- Use a garnish to bring attention to an ingredient in the dish, perhaps a sprig of basil on an Italian dish with pesto.
- Garnish food with edibles that complement the ingredients in the dish, perhaps a slice of lemon or lime on many fish dishes.
- Arrange garnishes artistically—around, under, or on top of the food.
- Go beyond parsley, the most common garnish, which serves as a freshener, too. "Paint your plate" simply, with other edibles:
  - *On salads:* apple (tossed with lemon juice to prevent browning); red, green, and yellow bell pepper strips; blueberries or raspberries; rinsed capers; grated cheese; fennel slices; shredded jicama; marigold petals; red onion slices; orange sections; toasted, chopped pecans or walnuts; pomegranate seeds; sesame seeds; snow peas; or watercress. *See "Edible Flowers: Please Don't Eat the Daffodils" in this chapter, page 238.*
  - *On soups:* an avocado slice dipped in lemon juice; shredded green, yellow, and red bell peppers; shredded carrot; grated cheese; minced chives; croutons; edible flowers; sprigs of fresh herbs; minced fresh herbs; a lemon slice; orange peel strips; pesto sauce; plain air-popped popcorn; snow peas; or a dollop of plain yogurt.
  - *On cooked vegetables:* toasted, sliced almonds; grated Parmesan cheese; chopped lean ham; fresh herbs; stir-fried mushroom slices; chopped olives or pimiento; stir-fried onion slices; toasted pine nuts.
  - *In beverages:* apple, kiwifruit, or sliced starfruit; fresh berries; a cinnamon stick; scented geranium leaves; lemon, lime, or orange slices; or a mint sprig.
  - *Beside or atop meat, poultry, or fish:* crab apple slices; chutney or salsa; a small bunch of grapes; lemon or lime wedges; a grilled peach or pear half; fresh herb sprigs.

The Waste-Less Kitchen

Go green in your kitchen by conserving fuel, water, and other resources, and minimizing food waste. The home kitchen is one place where you're in control. There's no secret to using resources wisely and limiting waste, but it does require intentional effort. *See "How Sustainable Are Your Food Decisions?" in chapter 5, page 115.*

CONTROLLING FOOD WASTE

Food is too precious to waste, *as addressed in "Food for Today and Tomorrow" in chapter 5, page 111.* Yet at least 25 percent of edible food in the United States is never eaten. Food spoilage, oversupply, and shopping habits, food preparation, and eating all contribute to waste.

Most Americans think they do better than average at controlling food waste, and yet a family of four typically tosses about $1,600 of food per year. Limiting household food waste is one way you can conserve this nourishing resource:

- Resist the urge to buy food you don't need or really want. Buy only the amount and types of food you or your family will eat. Be especially careful about overbuying fresh produce. *See "Your Food Dollar: More Nutrition, Less Waste" in chapter 6, page 154.*
- Use all edible parts of produce: fronds, leaves, peels, roots, seeds, stalks, and stems. You may need to get creative with your food prep. Of any type of food, fruits and vegetables have the highest rate of waste. Compost what you can't eat. *See "Waste Not: Use It All" on the next page.*
- "Shop" your refrigerator and freezer regularly. Use perishable foods and food leftovers before they need to be discarded. "Shop" your pantry, too, to use and enjoy the shelf-stable products you've overlooked.
- Freeze or use leftovers right away if you prepared too much food. Again, you might give them a new identity, perhaps in soups or stews.
- Have a "use it" meal. A leftover meal also may make a good "brown-bag" lunch.
- Give any extra food to a neighbor or friend before it goes bad. Traveling? Give it away while it's still fresh.
- Serve smaller, sensible portions to keep uneaten food from being scraped from the plate to the garbage can or sink disposal. Sensible portions, *see "Portions: Be Size Wise!" in chapter 3, page 78*, also limit the chance of overconsuming calories. Or avoid plate waste by switching to family style service; everyone takes just the amount they want to eat.
- Donate unopened canned and packaged foods, instead of throwing them away, perhaps to a food pantry or someone in need.

For more about limiting food waste, see "Shopping Green: Opportunity, Responsibility" in chapter 6, page 187, and "Waste Not, Restaurant Savvy" in chapter 9, page 286.

CONSERVING WATER, ENERGY, AND MORE

There's more to conserving resources—and saving money—in the kitchen than limiting food waste.

Water Savers

Do this to conserve water:

- Choose the proper-size pots and pans for what you're cooking. Equipment that's too big may use more cooking water.
- Cook in a microwave oven or a pressure cooker to conserve water—and time.
- Avoid overcooking foods such as soups and stews and braised dishes that need to boil or simmer so you don't waste water through evaporation. Use a timer. Cook with the lid on to limit evaporation and loss of volatile (lost in vapor with evaporation) nutrients.
- Keep cold water in the fridge rather than running the faucet until the water is cold.
- Washing dishes? Turn the faucet on and off as you rinse rather than allowing the water to run continually.
- Run your dishwasher only when full. Scrape soiled dishes. Don't rinse them if your dishwasher is efficient enough or if you wash them right away.
- Repair your faucet if it leaks. One drop a second can add up to 700 gallons of water a year!

Energy Savers

Do this to conserve electricity and perhaps gas for appliances:

- Preheat your oven shortly before you use it. Older ovens may need 20 minutes to preheat to 350°F, while new, more efficient ovens need only 10 to 15 minutes.
- Use equipment that speeds up cooking, such as a microwave or convection oven, a pressure cooker, or ovens that also use radiant or halogen heat. Use small appliances when you can: a toaster oven rather than the standard oven.
- Trim the flame. Use a burner that matches the size of the cooking pot. Turn it off when cooking is done.
- Cook the whole meal in the oven at the same time: for example, meat loaf, baked potatoes, and roasted vegetables.
- Arrange baking pans in the oven so air circulates. Baked goods, such as breads, cakes, and cookies, will bake more evenly, and other foods will cook faster and more efficiently.
- Use the old-fashioned approach: mix by hand when you can. (You burn your own calories, too!)
- Turn off lights when you leave the kitchen.
- Turn off your coffee pot when you're done. Better yet, unplug your coffeemaker and other appliances that suck energy from the grid even when not in use.

Waste Not: Use It All

DAIRY

- Grate small bits of cheese, including Parmesan and other hard cheeses, to top salads, soups, and vegetables or to blend into scrambled eggs or macaroni and cheese.

VEGETABLES AND FRUITS

- Leave the edible peels on potatoes, carrots, cucumbers, apples, and more. Scrub them well. Peels add texture and flavor and plenty of nutrients, phytonutrients (pectin, quercetin, others), and fiber. If you remove them, use the peels to make stock.
- Sauté chopped broccoli and cauliflower stalks along with the florets. Or shred or shave them for slaw, stir-fries, soups, and stews. Chopped beets, chard, or kale stems and leaves, and asparagus bottoms can be used this way, too.
- Clean beet, radish, and turnip tops. Chop and add them to pasta sauces, soups, and casseroles. Sauté and add them to omelets. Or blanch and puree for a pesto or for extra flavor in hummus or salsa.
- Use fennel fronds, carrot tops, or celery leaves as quick garnishes. Use them to make a pesto—even puree them in a smoothie. Wilted kale and spinach make good pestos, too.
- Save the stems from herbs and mushrooms for soups and stews. It's okay to freeze them for later.
- Freeze small amounts of fresh berries, cranberries, a banana (skin on), or a half apple before they go bad. Use them in smoothies.
- Use arugula, escarole, romaine, and other sturdy greens in stews, soups, and slow cooker dishes.
- Use overripe bananas for banana bread. Or store them in the freezer until you're ready to make the bread or add to a smoothie.
- Roast seeds from squash. Enjoy them as a snack or salad garnish.
- Use citrus rinds to flavor simmering rice or beverages.
- Save "tired" vegetables in the freezer to make later into a savory stock. Or use them in a frittata, stir-fry, or stew.
- Remember, in mixed dish, shape, size, and color don't matter, especially if fresh fruit and vegetables are chopped or cooked. "Ugly" produce is fine. It's texture, flavor, and aroma that matter.

GRAIN PRODUCTS

- Turn stale (not moldy) bread into bread crumbs in your blender or food processor; freeze them for later use as a thickener for soups and stews, as a topping (with a little cheese or oil) for casseroles, or for breading.
- Add leftover cooked pasta, rice, or other grains to cooked soups and stews. Turn leftover rice into fried rice; go easy on the oil. Cooked grains can be frozen for later.
- Use slightly stale or dry bread to make croutons, French toast, bread pudding, or egg casseroles (strata). It's also great for Mediterranean Spanish panzanella (bread salad).

MEAT AND POULTRY

- Turn leftover bits of meat, chicken, or turkey into pasta salads. Add them to soups and stews.
- Freeze the uncooked giblets (neck, heart, liver) from a whole chicken or turkey. Simmer them to make soup later.
- Use the carcass (bones) from rotisserie or home-roasted poultry, or meat bones to make broth. Simmer it with mirepoix (a mixture of diced aromatic vegetables: carrots, onions, celery, and herbs).
- Cook snout-to-tail, *as discussed in this chapter, page 258.*

- Buy Energy Star–certified appliances when you need new major appliances. This voluntary certification from the US Environmental Protection Agency (EPA) was initiated to help businesses and individuals save money and protect the climate through superior energy efficiency.
- Use the energy-saving cycle if available on your dishwasher. It will use less hot water and save energy, too. Also be aware: appliances draw less energy for clocks and lights in their "off" mode.
- Keep the oven and refrigerator doors shut. Each peek inside uses more power to regain its set temperature. For the refrigerator, decide what you want before you open the door; keep foods you need often within easy reach. When using the oven, use a timer. *Tip:* An open oven isn't efficient or safe for heating your kitchen!
- Save energy with a slow cooker. Eight hours in a slow cooker uses less energy than one hour of oven cooking.
- For energy efficiency, defrost your freezer regularly if it isn't self-defrosting.
- Keep appliances clean and in good condition: tighten gaskets around the oven and refrigerator doors; clean refrigerator coils regularly. For efficiency, a gas stove should burn with a blue, not a yellowish, flame in the pilot light—if it has one. Most gas stoves no longer do.
- Use the self-cleaning oven feature judiciously, only when it needs cleaning. For a head start, start it while the oven is still hot.

More Resource Savers

Do this to recycle, reuse, or conserve other resources in your kitchen:

- Buy only the basic kitchen tools you need—not unneeded specialty gadgets.
- Limit disposable packaging. Buy products with less packaging or in recyclable packaging, such as aluminum cans, steel cans, glass containers, recyclable plastic, and paperboard cartons. On plastic containers, look for the recycling symbol with a number in the center. *See "Shopping Green: Opportunity, Responsibility" in chapter 6, page 187, for the symbol.*
- Keep a recycling bin. Dispose of recyclables according to municipal regulations and services.
- Reuse glass and some plastic food packages for storage. Clean them well with hot, soapy water if used to store food.
- Skip disposable tableware. Use stainless steel flatware, ceramic or glass plates and cups, and cloth napkins. Rely on reusable plastic plates and bowls only when you take the meal outside.
- Compost food scraps and other kitchen waste outside or in an indoor compost pail—for example, corn husks, potato peels, apple cores, and melon rinds. Composting recycles nutrients that will nourish your garden later. Once in landfills, food breaks down to produce methane, a potent green-house gas, which may contribute to climate change.

Culinary Know-How: Flavor Plus Health

Making meals and snacks healthier, without compromising flavor doesn't require extra time, effort, or cost—just kitchen know-how.

Have you ever wondered?

. . . if cooking makes fruits or vegetables more nutritious? Interestingly, sometimes yes. Cooking won't add nutrients to a food (unless ingredients are added), but it can make food safer from foodborne bacteria and perhaps more edible and appealing. For example, you probably prefer eating a potato that's cooked, not raw.

Sometimes cooking enhances nourishment. For example, lycopene, a phytonutrient in tomatoes, is absorbed in the body better from cooked or processed tomatoes; lycopene may offer some protection from some cancers. Carotenoids (which form vitamin A) are more available for absorption when cooked, as is lutein, a phytonutrient in corn. Heat has also been shown to increase the bioavailability of thiamin, niacin, folate, and vitamin B_6.

These next few pages offer many ways to make your food preparation flavorful, while including more fruits, vegetables, beans, whole grains, and calcium-rich, low-fat and fat-free dairy foods in everyday meals and snacks. You'll learn how to keep lean protein foods lean, to retain foods' precious nutrients and fiber, and to trim away calories, solid fats (saturated and *trans* fats), added sugars, and sodium.

FRUITS AND VEGETABLES: FIT MORE IN

As a child, you probably enjoyed fruits and vegetables for their vibrant colors, their crunch, and perhaps their different flavors. You probably also

Fats, Sugars, Salt: What These Ingredients Do

Fats, sugars, and salt are basic ingredients. While the Dietary Guidelines for Americans advises limits, each (in controlled amounts) also plays important culinary functions.

- Cut the fats, not the flavor! Fats carry, blend, and stabilize flavors. With less fats, flavors may be more volatile and fade quickly. In baked foods, fats tenderize, add moisture, and hold air in place so the crumb (texture of the soft inner part) stays light and holds its shape. In sauces, fats keep foods from curdling and emulsify with water and other liquids. Fats in recipes conduct heat—for example, when sautéing and stir-frying. Fats lubricate foods so they don't stick to the pan, and they help seal in moisture when foods are basted. Fats make meat more moist and tender.

  Beyond that, fats also carry some nutrients (vitamins A, D, E, and K) from foods into your body, so a little oil in salad dressing partners well with nutrients in greens. In cooking, substitute healthy oils for solid, or more saturated, fats. *See "Why Foods Contain Fat" in chapter 13, page 395.*

- "Just a spoonful of sugar," notes Mary Poppins! Besides adding a sweet taste, sugar adds to the aroma, texture, color, and bulk of many foods. Sugar is the "food" for yeast that helps bread rise. In baked foods, it contributes to the light-brown color and to crisp textures. In canned jams and jellies, sugar helps inhibit the growth of molds and yeasts. *See "Sugars as Added Ingredients" in chapter 11, page 364.*
- Salt: often just a pinch will do! Salt brings out the flavor in foods, but that's not its only culinary function. Among its roles, salt increases and stabilizes the volume of whipped cream and egg whites, controls the speed of fermentation in cheese and in yeast for bread dough, and helps give yeast bread a finer texture. For centuries, salt has been an important preservative. *See "Salt and Sodium: More than Flavor" in chapter 14, page 434.*

✔ Your Healthy Eating Check-In

Does Your Food Prep Make Meals Healthier?

Do you cook with good nutrition, as well as flavor, in mind? You may have checked your culinary literacy earlier in this chapter, but how about your kitchen nutrition skills?

DO YOU . . .	Never 1 point	Sometimes 2 points	Usually 3 points	Always 4 points
LEAN MEAT, POULTRY, AND FISH				
Trim visible fat from meat and poultry?	☐	☐	☐	☐
Remove the skin from poultry before eating it?	☐	☐	☐	☐
Drain fat off meat after it's cooked?	☐	☐	☐	☐
Use lower-fat cooking methods: broil, grill, roast, stir-fry, steam, microwave, or braise?	☐	☐	☐	☐
HEALTHY FRUITS, VEGETABLES, AND BEANS				
Keep edible peels on fruits and vegetables—just wash, not peel them?	☐	☐	☐	☐
Sweeten foods with fruit, fruit juice, or fruit purees?	☐	☐	☐	☐
Cook vegetables with the lid on the pot—in just a small amount of liquid, or steam them in the microwave?	☐	☐	☐	☐
Try to include different colors of fruits and vegetables?	☐	☐	☐	☐
Use cooking water from vegetables for soups, stews, or sauces?	☐	☐	☐	☐
Cook vegetables only until they're just tender-crisp?	☐	☐	☐	☐
Plan meals with many different and colorful fruits and vegetables?	☐	☐	☐	☐
Add beans (legumes) to salads, soups, or other foods?	☐	☐	☐	☐
WHOLE GRAINS				
Cook with more whole grains, such as whole barley or whole-wheat pasta, or bake with whole-wheat flour?	☐	☐	☐	☐
Replace some refined-grain ingredients with whole grains, such as brown rice in place of white rice?	☐	☐	☐	☐
CALCIUM-RICH DAIRY				
Sprinkle cheese on salads, soups, or vegetables for more flavor and calcium?	☐	☐	☐	☐
Boost calcium in creamy soups, cooked cereals, and casseroles with nonfat dry milk, plain yogurt, buttermilk, or calcium-fortified soy products?	☐	☐	☐	☐
HEALTHY OILS				
Cook mostly with healthy oils such as canola, olive, and vegetable?	☐	☐	☐	☐
FOR FLAVOR AND MEAL APPEAL	☐	☐	☐	☐
Use herbs, spices, or lemon juice and ease up on salt to flavor food?	☐	☐	☐	☐
Taste before deciding to add salt to foods?	☐	☐	☐	☐
Use garnishes to make food look more appealing?	☐	☐	☐	☐
Subtotals	___	___	___	___

Add up your total points: ______

61 to 80 points: You're "kitchen nutrition–savvy."

41 to 60 points: Improving your food preparation skills would make a nutritious difference! Read on.

21 to 40 points: You're starting to get the hang of it. Now turn those "sometimes" answers into "usually" and "always." Read the rest of the chapter for "food prep" tips.

20 points: Read the chapter. There's lots to learn!

learned that fruits and vegetables were good for you. Today, health experts better understand why. Although their nutrient and fiber content varies, fruits and vegetables provide relatively few calories for the many nutrients, fiber, and phytonutrients they deliver; *see "Fruit Group: Focus on Whole Fruits" in chapter 2, page 35.* Today's culinary experts have created many delicious ways to fit them into your daily eating patterns.

Fruits and Veggies: Made Deliciously Easy

- Blend grated, shredded, or chopped vegetables such as carrots, collards, spinach, and zucchini, as well as beans and peas, into lasagna, casseroles, meat loaf, pasta sauce, risotto, soups and stews, and mashed potatoes.
- "Sandwich" in fruits and vegetables in sandwiches, wraps and pita pockets; sliced fruit (apple, avocado, pineapple); sliced raw vegetables (bell pepper, cucumber, tomato); greens (arugula, spinach, watercress); and roasted vegetables (bell peppers, eggplant, portobello mushrooms).
- Liven up frittatas and omelets with colorful veggies: bell peppers, broccoli, carrots, kale, mushrooms, onions, squash, spinach, or

How to . . . Keep Nutrients In

Proper food preparation techniques keep nutrient loss to a minimum and food quality at its peak. Some minerals and water-soluble vitamins dissolve in cooking water and are lost when the cooking water is discarded. High temperatures and long cooking times can destroy heat-sensitive nutrients such as B vitamins, including folate, and vitamin C.

FRUITS AND VEGETABLES

- Clean thick-skinned vegetables and fruits well with a soft brush and water. Avoid soaking because some vitamins dissolve in water.
- Leave edible skins on vegetables and fruits—for example, on carrots, potatoes, or pears. Trim as little as possible. Most vitamins and minerals are found in the outer leaves, the skin, and the area just below the skin—not in the center. A medium baked potato with the skin on has about twice the fiber of a "naked" potato: 5 fiber grams compared to 2.5 fiber grams. Peels also are natural barriers that help protect against nutrient loss.
- Eat vegetables and fruits raw; clean properly first.
- Cook vegetables such as asparagus, green beans, broccoli, and snow peas, quickly—just until tender-crisp. Some nutrients, such as B vitamins and vitamin C, are destroyed easily by heat. The color and texture can become less appealing, too. The flavor of some vegetables, such as Brussels sprouts and turnips, can get stronger when the food is overcooked.
- Cook fruits or vegetables in a small amount of water—better yet, steam them in a vegetable steamer. Steaming retains most nutrients because vegetables usually won't come into contact with the cooking liquids.
- Microwave! Because microwaving is so fast, heat-sensitive nutrients aren't subjected to heat for long. Also, microwaving doesn't require added fat, so you limit calories. There's a flavor advantage, too: unless overcooked, vegetables retain the color and tender-crisp qualities that make them appealing.
- Cut vegetables that need long cooking times into larger pieces. With fewer surfaces exposed, fewer vitamins are lost.
- Cook vegetables and fruits in a covered pot. Steam doesn't escape, and the cooking time is shorter.
- Reheat canned vegetables on the stovetop or in the microwave oven. Because canning is a form of cooking, canned vegetables don't need to be cooked again.
- Save liquid from cooking vegetables for soups, stews, and sauces; perhaps freeze it for later. That's one way to "recycle" water-soluble vitamins and minerals that would be tossed with cooking water.
- For beets and red cabbage, add a little lemon juice or vinegar to the cooking water. This helps retain their bright-red color.
- Don't add baking soda to the vegetable cooking water. Although the alkali in baking soda keeps vegetables looking greener, it also destroys vitamin C and makes veggies mushy because it causes cellulose to break down. *Tip:* Adding acid (lemon juice) to green vegetables while cooking turns them olive green; add juice or sauce after cooking.

GRAINS

- Skip the urge to rinse grains, such as rice, before cooking. That may wash nutrients, down the drain, especially B vitamins added to enriched and fortified grain products.

  An exception: for quinoa, rinsing removes its natural coating called saponin, which can make it taste bitter or soapy. Check the package label. Often boxed quinoa is pre-rinsed, but not always.

MILK

- Keep milk refrigerated in opaque containers. Leaving it in a clear, glass pitcher on the table allows some riboflavin to be destroyed.

tomatoes. Chop, sauté, and then add them to the eggs as they cook. This is also a way to use leftover veggies.

- Toss a rainbow in your salad bowl. Brighten it, for example, with sliced red beets, black beans, chopped orange bell peppers, deep-green spinach, and sweet peas. Change the "leaves": arugula, endive, massaged kale, red leaf lettuce, romaine lettuce, shredded red cabbage, and watercress. Add fruits such as berries, figs, kiwi-fruit, mandarin oranges, and chunks of melon.
- Order pizza loaded with vegetables, or make it yourself. Top it with artichoke hearts, asparagus, red and green bell pepper strips, broccoli florets, shredded carrots, sliced mushrooms, chopped spinach, sliced tomatoes, thinly-sliced zucchini, or other firm vegetables. For more flavor, roast them first. *See "How to . . . Roast Vegetables" on this page.*
- Let vegetables and fruits take center stage in a meal, with smaller portions of meat, poultry, and fish. Kebobs threaded with fruits or vegetables (mangoes, peaches, pineapple, carrots, eggplant, mushrooms, peppers, potatoes, squash, sweet potatoes) are one way to do it. Brush with a little oil so they don't dry out when grilled.
- Stir-fry to cook quickly. All kinds of sliced vegetables—green beans, sugar snap peas, summer squash—make an easy side dish.
- Try a new-to-you fruit or vegetable in a favorite recipe—perhaps seasonal produce. Go online to learn how to prepare it, perhaps broccoli rabe (a vegetable related to broccoli with smaller heads, also called rapini) in stir-fries, fennel in salad, or parsnips or turnips (a starchy vegetable) in stews. *See "Vegetables: Have You Tried These?" and "Fruit: What's New to You?" in chapter 2, pages 36 and 39, for ideas.*
- Make dips, sandwich spreads, and toppings with vegetables and fruits:
  - Baba ghanouj, made with eggplant
  - Caponata, made with eggplant and tomato
  - Guacamole, made with avocado
  - Hummus, made with mashed chickpeas or any type of cooked dried beans (black, white kidney, others), or a spin-off with beets or shredded carrots
  - Salsa, made with tomato, bell pepper, onion, and cilantro. Some salsas include fruit such as pineapple, mango, papaya, or peaches as an ingredient. *See "Give It a Little Salsa" in this chapter, page 242.*
- Mix dried fruits or fruit chutney into stuffing, rice dishes, salads, main-dish salads, casseroles, and dough for cookies and bread. Go beyond raisins and dried cranberries: try dried apples, apricots, bananas, dates, mangoes, papayas, pears, pineapples, and plums (prunes). One-quarter cup of raisins adds 2 grams of fiber; three dried plums have almost as much.

How to . . . Roast Vegetables

Roasting caramelizes the natural sugars in vegetables and browns and crisps the surface, enhancing the flavors and helping them keep their vibrant colors.

- Cut vegetables such as beets,* Brussels sprouts, carrots, cauliflower, eggplant, mushrooms, onions, parsnips, peppers, potatoes, sweet potatoes, squash, turnips, and zucchini into uniform 1½- to 2-inch pieces to increase the cut surfaces. For others such as asparagus and green beans, simply trim them. For corn on the cob, remove the husks.
- Toss the vegetables with a little oil, perhaps canola or olive. Figure about 1 tablespoon per 3 cups or 1 pound of vegetables.† Porous vegetables such as eggplant and mushrooms need more oil than root vegetables and tubers such as carrots and potatoes.
- Arrange the vegetables in a single layer, without crowding them, on a nonstick baking sheet.
- Roast them at 400° F to 450°F for 35 to 45 minutes, tossing once or twice.*

*Since beets bleed when cut, turning other vegetables pink or red, toss them in oil and roast them separately.

†Add herbs and garlic for more flavor: garlic and sturdy herbs such as rosemary and thyme while roasting, and delicate herbs such as basil, dill, or parsley after roasting.

- Puree apples, berries, cherries, peaches, pears, and other fruits for a thick, sweet sauce to spoon over grilled or broiled poultry or fish, pancakes, French toast, or waffles.
- Bake with fruits and vegetables. Use pureed fruit such as apple-sauce, bananas, peaches, or dried plums (prunes) in place of

Have you ever wondered?

. . . how to massage kale—and why? Kale is deliciously enjoyed in many ways: baked as chips, sautéed or stir-fried, and mixed in hearty stews. Massaged for a few short moments, this fibrous, bitter, leafy green loses any toughness and adds color, sweetness, and nourishment to raw garden salads.

To massage kale, remove the ribs, and rub the leaves for several minutes. As you do so, the fiber (cellulose) breaks down, and the leaves darken, soften, and shrink. Even the flavor becomes less bitter.

Bean Bag

Beans of all kinds are sold as dried, canned, frozen, and fresh. Each has a distinctive appearance and flavor, varying cooking times, and somewhat different uses. Combining a variety of beans makes a more interesting dish.

On average, 1 pound of dried uncooked beans yields about 2¼ cups of dry uncooked beans, or 5 to 6 cups of cooked beans.

The yield for lentils is less. For 2¼ cups of dry lentils, figure about 3½ to 4 cups cooked.

One can (15½ ounces) of drained, canned beans or lentils equals about 1⅔ cups cooked. Draining and rinsing canned beans reduces the sodium content by about 40 percent.

Note: Soak beans—but not lentils or split peas—before simmering to help tenderize them; *see "Beans, Peas, and Lentils: Prep with Ease" and "How to . . . Cook Dried Beans" in this chapter, pages 251 and 252.*

Beans and Peas	Size and Color	Flavor	Simmering Time (Hours)*	Common Uses†
Adzuki or azuki bean	Small, red, shiny	Slightly sweet	½ to 1	Salads, soups, poultry stuffing, casseroles, Asian dishes
Black bean	Small, black, shiny, kidney-shaped	Slightly sweet	1½ to 2	Soups, stews, Brazilian feijoada, Cuban rice and beans
Black-eyed pea or cowpea	Small, cream-colored ovals with black spots	Vegetablelike, full-flavored	1 to 1½	Southern dishes with ham or rice, bean cakes, curries, *Hoppin' John* (Southern rice and peas dish)
Cannellini or white kidney bean	Elongated, slender, creamy white	Mild	2	Salads, soups, stews, casseroles, Italian side dishes, *pasta e fagioli* (Italian dish, meaning rice and beans)
Chickpea or garbanzo bean	Golden, hard, pea-shaped	Nutty	2¼ to 4	Soups, stews, casseroles, cooked with cous-cous, hummus, *caldo gallego* (Spanish, typically with cabbage, collard and turnip greens potatoes; white beans, and perhaps pork, chorizo, ham, or bacon)
Fava or broad bean	Large, broad, oval, light brown	Nutty	1½ to 2	Stews, side dishes, *ful medames* (Middle Eastern dish of cooked fava beans with oil, cumin, and perhaps other vegetable, herb and spice ingredients)
Flageolet or green haricot bean	Small to medium, pale green	Nutty	1½ to 2	Mixed-bean salads, side dishes, French bean dishes
Great northern bean	Large, white	Mild	1 to 1½	Soups, casseroles, mixed-bean dishes
Lentils‡	Yellow, green, orange, or brown	Earthy	¾	Soups, English pease pudding, Indian *dhal*, curry dishes
Lima bean	Large or small, creamy white or pale green, kidney-shaped	Like chestnuts	1½	Salads, soups, casseroles, Southern succotash
Mung bean	Small, olive green	Earthy	1	Soups, casseroles, purees, Asian and Indian dishes, "sprouted" for salads

(continued)

Bean Bag *(continued)*

Beans and Peas	Size and Color	Flavor	Simmering Time (Hours)*	Common Uses†
Navy bean	Small, oval, white	Mild	1 to 1½	Boston baked beans
Pigeon pea	Small, round, slightly flat, beige with brown flecks	Mild	¾ to 1	Caribbean peas and rice
Pinto bean	Oval, orange-pink with rust- colored flecks	Earthy, full-flavored	1 to 1½	Stews, Mexican rice and beans, refried beans
Red kidney bean	Dark red-brown, kidney-shaped	Full-flavored, "meaty"	1½ to 2	Mixed-bean salads, stews, Cajun bean dishes, chili con carne
Soybean	Small, yellow or black	Full-flavored	3½ to 4	Soups, side dishes, used to make tofu (bean curd), "sprouted" for salads

*Simmering time for uncooked dry beans.

†Traditional and ethnic dishes, italicized throughout the chart, commonly use the type of bean indicated.

‡Lentils don't require soaking, only shorter cooking times.

about half the fat in recipes for homemade breads, muffins, pancakes, and other baked goods. Add fresh berries and cranberries to your favorite muffin recipe. For flavor, texture, and nutrients, blend in shredded zucchini, carrots, or dried fruits. Experiment. These substitutions may alter the texture or volume of the end result.

- Flip the dessert. For example, serve sliced fruit and berries with a shortbread garnish on top, rather than shortbread with a spoonful of fruit.
- Fill your fridge with "nature's fast food." Clean and cut fresh vegetables and fruits to make them ready to eat. Consider baby carrots, edamame, and sliced kohlrabi. Keep canned and frozen vegetables and fruits on hand for convenience.
- Make a habit of tucking an apple, kiwifruit, peach, plum, or tangerine, or a small serving of cherries, dates, grapes, dried fruits, or other fruits into your briefcase, tote, or lunch bag, as a great to-go snack.
- Make smoothies as a snack or dessert: 100 percent juice with almost any fruit, or use juicing greens (beet tops, chard, and kale).

BEANS, PEAS, AND LENTILS: PREP WITH EASE

Beans, peas, and lentils are packed with fiber, which many people tend to underconsume. A half-cup serving of cooked beans and peas supplies 4 to 10 grams of fiber. (Healthy adults are advised to consume 21 to 38 grams of fiber a day, depending on age and gender.) They also are packed with protein, folate, iron, potassium, other nutrients, and phytonutrients, yet little sodium or fat and no cholesterol. Adding them to meals and snacks several times each week is well worth it.

Starting with dried beans, peas, and lentils means a lengthy cooking time. For beans, it also means soaking before they can be cooked. This is not hard, but it does take time. As an alternative, canned, frozen, or fresh forms take little effort.

When boiled and served plain, beans don't have much flavor. When combined with other ingredients, they're versatile, taking on savory, sweet, and robust flavors.

Boosting the Bean Factor

- Make minestrone soup with drained, canned kidney or garbanzo beans and vegetables, or by replacing meat with beans. Add beef or chicken broth or canned tomatoes for umami flavor. Split pea, navy bean, or lentil soup is a light lunch; top with shredded carrot or apple.
- Fill tacos, burritos, or enchiladas with drained, cooked or canned pinto beans, or refried beans, instead of meat. Accent the flavor with grated cheese and salsa, tomatoes, onions, cilantro or parsley, and/or chopped lettuce or cabbage.
- Add cooked, canned or frozen legumes or lentils to green salads, casseroles, and pasta dishes.

- Puree all kinds of cooked beans to use as a low-fat, high-fiber base or thickener in sauces and soups, and as a flavorful sandwich spread, a base for hummus, or a baked potato topping.
- As an easy side dish, baked potato topping, or pasta sauce, simply heat frozen or canned beans with a tasty sauce of tomatoes, molasses, or jalapeño peppers. Or mix up a three-, four-, or five-bean salad with several cans of drained, rinsed beans, chopped bell peppers and onion, and a savory vinaigrette.
- Substitute beans or lentils for some or all the meat in mixed dishes: kidney beans in chili, lentils in meat loaf, pinto beans in enchiladas, black beans in chunky soups, mashed kidney or pinto beans in meatballs, soybeans in casseroles, and white beans in stews. *See "Recipe Makeovers: Healthy Vegetarian" in this chapter, page 237.*
- Create a high-fiber pasta sauce that's low in fat. Puree cooked or drained, canned beans with beef or chicken stock. White cannellini beans make a creamy white sauce, but any variety of beans will do. Add fresh herbs: basil, chives, garlic, marjoram, and oregano, among others. Fresh tomatoes or tomato sauce add flavor and color.
- Roast chickpeas and lentils (red, brown, green), and season, for a crunchy snack, perhaps to add to trail mix.
- Experiment with using chickpea or other legume flour in pancakes, waffles, and baking, or in other ways you might use flour. (Flour from beans is gluten free and so it won't behave like wheat flour.)

How to . . . Cook Dried Beans

If you're short on time, go for canned, frozen, or fresh beans. If not, use dried beans, prepared the traditional way by soaking them first. (Or cook in a slow cooker.) *Tip:* Uncooked dry legumes need soaking; lentils or split peas don't.

To soak beans, do this:

- *Leisurely method.* Reduce cooking time by up to half by soaking beans for at least four hours or overnight in a pot filled with room-temperature water. Choose a pot that's big enough; beans expand!
- *Quick method.* Time short? Bring water to a boil, and let the beans soak in hot water for one to four hours, depending on the variety of beans.

To reduce the intestinal gas often experienced when you eat beans, rinse the beans after soaking them, discard the soaking water and any debris, and cook them in fresh water. Not to worry—beans, not the soaking water, retain most of the nutrients.

To cook beans, cover them with fresh water. You need about six cups of fresh water for each pound of dried beans. Add seasonings to the cooking water. Salt toughens beans by taking out the moisture; and acid foods, such as tomatoes or vinegar, slow their softening. Wait until the end of the cooking time to add these ingredients.

Cover the pot partially. To keep the beans from foaming, add a little cooking oil (one-quarter teaspoon) to the water. Simmer until cooked; rapid boiling causes beans to break down. *See the "Bean Bag" chart in this chapter, page 250, for simmering times.* Add cooked beans or peas to your favorite dish.

GRAINS: MAKE HALF WHOLE

Does your plate lack fiber? You're not alone. With refined-grain ingredients in many breads, pasta, and other grain products and too few fruits and vegetables consumed, many people come up short.

Make at least half your grains whole! Substituting whole-grain foods for refined-grain foods not only boosts the fiber in meals and snacks, but provides other important nutrients and phytonutrients, too. Many whole-grain foods have fewer calories than refined-grain foods made with sugary or higher-fat ingredients. Moreover, whole grains add different textures and hearty flavors, making meals more interesting.

Advice for the home cook: Don't give up ingredients or foods with refined grains, just use them judiciously in foods that limit added sugars. By law, refined grains are fortified with folic acid, important for pregnant women and those who may become pregnant to reduce the chance of birth defects.

Healthy Makeovers with Whole Grains

- Stack sandwiches on whole-grain breads, English muffins, and pita pockets. Or roll them up in a whole-wheat tortilla or wrap. *See "Is It Really Whole Grain? Tricky to Know" in chapter 6, page 184.*
- Make pasta dishes and salads with whole-grain and other high-fiber pasta—lasagna noodles, macaroni, spaghetti, and pasta cuts. For better texture, some are blends made with refined wheat. (Try whole-grain couscous, too; remember that it is a type of pasta.)
- Swap brown or wild rice (2 grams and 1.5 grams of fiber, respectively, per one-half cup cooked) for some or all white rice (<0.5 fiber grams per one-half cup cooked).
- Swap in other whole grains, too, in all kinds of savory mixed dishes, such as pilaf, rice salads and risotto. Use brown rice, bulgur, farro, buckwheat (kasha), quinoa, sorghum, or whole-grain couscous. Go 100 percent whole or fifty-fifty. Substitute whole grains for refined ones, rather than just adding more whole-grain foods.
- Make soups, stews, and stuffing healthier and heartier by adding your choice of whole grain. Some good options: barley, brown rice, or bulgur wheat. For soups and stews, use uncooked grains that cook as the pot simmers.

How to . . . Cook Whole Grains

Wonder how to cook whole grains? You can use the same simple steps outlined here for all the listed whole grains. *See "Grains, Grains, and More Grains" in chapter 2, page 31, for descriptions of these and other grains.* Use cooked grains in salads and soups; as side dishes flavored with sauces or seasonings.

1. Bring the cooking water (or other liquid such as vegetable stock, or both) to a boil; stir in the grain. (*Tip:* toast them first in a dry skillet for nuttier flavor.)
2. Cover, reduce heat, and simmer for the time indicated below. Don't stir.
3. Let stand, covered, if indicated below.

1 Cup Uncooked Grain	Cooking Water (Cups)	Cooking Time (Minutes)	Standing Time (Minutes)	Yield (Cups)	Common Uses
Amaranth*	2	20–25	—	3½	Side dish, cereal
Barley, whole	3	20	5	3½	Side dish, cereal, soup
Buckwheat (kasha)	2	20	10	4	Side dish (buckwheat groats flour also used in baked foods)
Bulgur	2	**	15–20	3	Side dish, salad (tabbouleh), stew
Farro, whole	2¾	25–30	—	3	Side dish, salad, soup
Hominy (corn) (soak overnight first)	4	30	5	3½	Side dish, stew, soup, cereal
Millet, hulled	2½	30	15	4	Side dish, bread
Quinoa (rinsed if desired)	2	15	—	3	Side dish, salad, stuffing, soup, stew
Rice, brown	2½	25–45	5	3–4	Wherever rice is used
Rice, wild*	3	45–55	—	3½	Side dish, salad, stuffing, soup
Rye berries (soak overnight first)	4	45–60	—	3	Side dish, bread
Sorghum	4	25–40	—	3	Salad, side dish
Spelt berries (soak overnight first)	4	45–60	—	3	Wherever rice is used
Triticale (wheat and rye) (soak overnight first)	2½	40	—	4	Side dish, soup, cereal, bread
Wheat berries (soak overnight first)	4	45–60	—	3	Side dish, bread

*Amaranth and wild rice are seeds, not grains.

**Bulgur doesn't need to be cooked. Put it in a bowl, pour boiling water over it, and let stand until the water is absorbed.

- In some doughs and batters, substitute whole-wheat flour or oat flour for up to half of the refined white flour. If more is used, the texture will be too dense and the flavor possibly less acceptable. Try white whole-grain flour or whole-wheat pastry flour. Whirl dry oatmeal in a blender to make oat flour, or use oatmeal to replace up to a third of the white flour in a recipe.
- When substituting a whole-grain flour (graham, stone-ground, whole-wheat) for some traditional white flour, you may have to adjust the recipe to get an acceptable result. The composition of flours differs. For example, whole-wheat flour absorbs more liquid.
- Add uncooked oatmeal (or wheat or oat bran) to mixed dishes such as meat loaf, casseroles, stuffing, salmon patties, crab cakes, and

? Have you ever wondered?

. . . how to cook with flaxseed? To get the benefits of flaxseed, you need to grind it in a blender, food processor, or coffee grinder (or buy it ground). Add it to dough or batter, or use it as a topping on puddings, cereal, and other foods. Flaxseed is high in fiber and is a source of omega-3 fatty acids, yet has little saturated fat.

. . . if you should soak ham, bacon, or salt pork to get rid of some salt? No. Very little salt is removed. More important, for food safety, washing meat is not advised.

burgers. Figure about one-half cup per pound of ground meat, ground poultry, or fish. (One tablespoon of bran adds a little more than 1 gram of fiber.)

- Build homemade pizza on a whole-wheat pizza crust or flatbread, available in most supermarkets.
- Make polenta, grits, and cornbread with whole cornmeal.
- Toast whole-wheat bread, wheat germ, or bran if you need crumbs.
- Use several different grains, perhaps in a pilaf or risotto, to build layers of flavor. Blending less-familiar grains with brown rice or corn may make them more approachable.

MEAT, POULTRY, FISH: KEEP LEAN

Enjoyed as a key source of protein, iron, zinc, and several B vitamins, meat, poultry, and fish have an important place at the table. These foods deliver two nutrients that come up short for some: iron and B_{12}. Meat also delivers saturated fats that you need to limit. As a home cook, choose mostly lean cuts of meat, poultry, and fish and then use low-fat cooking techniques to keep them tender and flavorful—and lean.

Cooking Tips to Limit Sat Fats

- Trim off visible, solid fat on meat and poultry before cooking to help limit saturated fats. Even on lean meat, you'll find some fat.

What Are the Lean* Cuts of Beef, Pork, Lamb, and Poultry?

BEEF CUTS†

Eye round roast and steak
Sirloin tip side steak
Top round roast and steak
Bottom round roast and steak
Top sirloin steak
Brisket, flat half
93% lean ground beef
Round tip roast and steak
Shank cross cuts
Sirloin tip center roast and steak
Chuck shoulder steak
Bottom round (Western Griller) steak
Top loin (strip) steak
Shoulder petite tender and medallions
Flank steak
Shoulder center (ranch) steak
Tri-tip roast and steak
Tenderloin roast and steak

VEAL CUTS†

Cutlet
Foreshank
Loin chop
Shoulder blade chop

LAMB CUTS†

Foreshank
Leg, shank half
Leg, sirloin
Loin
Shoulder arm

PORK CUTS†

Tenderloin
New York pork chop (top loin chop)
Boneless top loin roast
Bone-in center loin chop
Bone-in rib chop
Bone-in sirloin roast

CHICKEN CUTS†

Skinless chicken breast
Skinless chicken leg
Skinless chicken thigh

TURKEY CUTS†

Skinless turkey, dark meat
Skinless turkey, light meat

*"Lean" is defined by the FDA as less than 10 grams of total fat, 4.5 grams or less of saturated fat, and less than 95 milligrams of cholesterol per 3-ounce cooked serving (per 100 grams).

†Three-ounce cooked servings, visible fat removed.

Advised to limit cholesterol? Trimming fat from the edges removes some, but not all, of the cholesterol. Cholesterol is in both the lean tissue and the fat in meat, poultry, and fish.

- Go "skinless" on poultry. Under the skin there's a layer of fat. Remove the skin before or after cooking to cut the fat content about in half before you eat it! With whole birds, most fat is near the cavity opening. *Tip:* Cooking poultry with the skin on helps keep it tender and moist. The same is true for meat; trim remaining fat after cooking.
- Brown meat, poultry, and fish in a nonstick skillet with little or no added fat, except for vegetable oil spray, or use only a little oil. Browning also adds flavor.
- Drain off fat from ground-meat crumbles as they're cooked. To reduce the fat further:
    - Transfer cooked ground-meat crumbles to a large plate lined with three layers of white paper towels. Blot the top of the meat, and let it sit one minute.
    - Or, place the meat in a strainer or a colander. Pour about 1 quart of hot tap water over the meat. Drain for about 5 minutes. You may rinse away 2 to 5 grams of fat per 3-ounce cooked serving.
    - Blot cooked ground meat burgers, meatballs, and meat loaf with several layers of clean paper towels, too.

? Have you ever wondered?

. . . how lamb rates as a lean source of protein? As a flavorful, nourishing meat option, lamb is popular in many parts of the world—and enjoyed in kebobs, roasts, gyros, and much more. It's the tender meat of sheep less than one year old. Spring lamb is usually younger, three to five months old. Most lamb raised in the United States is finished ("fattened") on grain, which makes the meat more tender and milder in flavor.

Lamb is good source of many important nutrients besides protein, including iron, selenium, zinc, niacin, and vitamin B_{12}. Like many other red meats, lamb is relatively high in saturated fats. However, it's also a source of unsaturated fats, including more omega-3s if grass fed.

If lamb fits into your menus, know that the leanest cuts come from the leg, loin, and shank. On average, many qualify as "lean." The same cut from domestic and imported lamb may vary. The loin is a good choice for dry-heat cooking. The shoulder is tougher and has more fat, making it a better choice for moist-heat cooking. For fattier cuts, you can trim away visible fat.

As when buying ground beef, check the label when buying ground lamb for the "percent lean." And drain fat away when you cook ground lamb.

- Use low-fat cooking methods. Match the method to the meat cut for a tender, flavorful end result. Cook to a safe internal temperature, *see "Cook to Safe Internal Temperatures" in chapter 7, page 210*; avoid overcooking to keep it tender.
- Grill, broil, or roast meat and poultry on a rack so fat drips through and drippings aren't reabsorbed. Drain away any fat that appears during cooking.
- Marinate meat, poultry, and fish in marinades with a little oil and an acidic ingredient to tenderize it: lemon, lime, or orange juice; tomato juice; reduced-fat salad dressings; salsas; soy sauce; vinegar; wine; plain low-fat yogurt; or buttermilk. Add fresh herbs to the marinade for more flavor. Use it as a basting sauce, too, which may be enough fat to keep the surface moist.
- To keep poultry or fish moist, steam it wrapped in heavy aluminum foil with fruits, herbs, onions and other vegetables, and other flavorings. Secure the "package" and then put it in the oven or on the grill. For the oven, you can wrap and cook meat, poultry, or fish in parchment paper (chefs call this en papillote, or paper package) or leaf packets (such as banana leaves). *Tip:* Take care when you open these packages because the escaping steam is very hot.
- Oven-fry chicken or fish, instead of deep-frying it. Dip it first in beaten egg whites. Bake on a nonstick baking pan coated with vegetable oil spray.
- When using dry-heat cooking methods, use a rub on raw meat, poultry, or fish; for a spicy taste, rub a mixture of chile powder, cinnamon, coriander, cumin, and red and black peppers on a pork roast. Or coat meat, poultry, or fish with salsas or chutneys. *See "How to . . . Make Rub Combos" in this chapter, page 271.*
- In recipes that call for ground beef, such as meat loaf, burgers, and meat sauce for pasta, swap in lean (at least 90 percent lean).
- When recipes call for bacon or sausage, use lean ham, Canadian bacon, smoked turkey, or turkey bacon for the smoky flavor. Although leaner, these foods have significant amounts of sodium, so go easy. Go easy on processed meats for another reason: higher intakes increase some cancer risks.
- Bake fish with a splash of white wine, tomatoes, and fresh herbs, or poach fish in a flavorful broth rather than frying or panfrying it.

See "How to Cook Food Safely" in chapter 7, page 209, *for safety tips related to cooking meat and other protein foods, including cooking to safe internal temperatures and limiting the formation of heterocyclic amines (HCAs) and polycyclic aromatic hydrocarbons (PAHs) in cooked meats.*

EGGS: IF ADVISED TO LIMIT CHOLESTEROL

A great meat alternative, eggs supply protein, iron, choline, selenium, biotin, and lutein. Many people underconsume choline, a B vitamin, and iron.

Meat, Poultry, and Fish: Lean Cuts, Low-Fat Cooking Methods

	Dry Heat					Moist Heat			
	Roast	Broil	Grill	Panbroil	Stir-fry	Braise	Stew	Steam	Poach
BEEF									
Eye round*		X				X	X		
Top round*	X	X	X	X	X				
Round tip*	X	X	X	X	X	X	X		
Bottom round*	X					X	X		
Sirloin	X	X	X	X	X				
Top loin	X	X	X	X	X				
Tenderloin	X	X	X	X	X				
Flank*		X	X		X				
95% lean ground beef	X	X	X	X	X				
VEAL									
Cutlets	X	X	X	X					
Loin chop	X	X	X	X					
Foreshank						X	X		
Shoulder (blade chop)		X	X	X					
PORK									
Tenderloin	X	X	X	X	X				
Boneless top loin roast	X	X	X						
Porterhouse pork chop (loin chop)		X	X	X					
Loin strips					X				
Boneless sirloin chop		X	X	X					
Boneless rib roast	X		X			X	X		
Ribeye pork chop (rib chop)		X	X	X					
Boneless ham	X	X	X	X	X				
LAMB									
Foreshank						X	X		
Leg, shank half	X								
Leg, sirloin	X	X	X						
Loin	X	X	X						
Shoulder arm		X	X						
POULTRY[†]									
Whole chicken	X		X			X	X		
Whole turkey	X		X			X			
Cornish game hen	X		X			X	X		

Meat, Poultry, and Fish: Lean Cuts, Low-Fat Cooking Methods *(continued)*

	Dry Heat					Moist Heat			
	Roast	Broil	Grill	Panbroil	Stir-fry	Braise	Stew	Steam	Poach
Breast	X	X	X	X	X				X
Drumstick	X	X	X						
FISH									
Cod	X	X	X	X	X		X	X	X
Flounder	X	X	X	X				X	X
Halibut	X	X	X	X	X		X	X	X
Orange roughy		X	X	X	X			X	X
Shrimp		X	X	X	X		X	X	X

*May be cooked by dry-heat methods if they are tenderized first by marinating or pounding.

†White meat has less fat than dark meat. Skin should be removed before eating.

Until recently, health experts advised healthy Americans to eat whole eggs and egg yolks in moderation to control dietary cholesterol (to less than 300 milligrams daily). The 2015–2020 Dietary Guidelines for Americans notes that there isn't scientific evidence to put a quantitative limit on dietary cholesterol; but still be prudent, advises the Institute of Medicine.

Egg yolks, not whites, contain cholesterol and a small amount of saturated fat. (A yolk from one large egg has about 185 milligrams of cholesterol and 1.5 grams of saturated fat.) If your doctor advises you to limit cholesterol in food, here's how to fit eggs into your meals and snacks:

- Use two egg whites in place of one whole egg in baked goods, pancakes, pudding, and other recipes that call for whole eggs. Or for two whole eggs, use two egg whites and one whole egg. That way you'll get the color and the flavor of the yolk. This idea works well for scrambled eggs, quiche, and omelets. (Recipes that require egg yolks, such as custards or cream puffs, are best made with whole eggs.)
- Use a cholesterol-free liquid egg product in place of whole eggs. Read the package label; usually one-quarter cup equals one egg.

Have you ever wondered?

. . . how the fat content of deep-fried turkey compares to roasted turkey? If the cooking oil stays high enough—350°F for the entire frying process—it makes little difference. A 3½-ounce portion of deep-fried turkey with the skin on has about 12 grams of fat, compared with 10 grams in a 3½-ounce portion of roasted turkey (white and dark meat) with the skin on. However, if the cooking oil remains at 340°F or less, more oil will seep into the turkey meat, adding to the fat content. For the record, without the skin, the same amount of roasted turkey (white and dark meat) has 5 fat grams.

SOUPS, STEWS, SALADS, SIDES, SPREADS, AND MORE: REDUCE FAT OR SWITCH

All of these dishes can be prepared and cooked to trim saturated and *trans* fats and calories without losing flavor. Use cooking methods that require little or no added fat; try to boil, braise, broil, grill, poach, roast, steam, stew, stir-fry, or microwave foods, rather than fry them, most of the time. *See "Cooking Methods to Know," "How to . . . Cook with Dry Heat," and "How to . . . Cook with Moist Heat" in this chapter, pages 236, 259, and 260.*

Stretch higher-fat ingredients. For example, grate cheese so less looks like more; you can also get more flavor with less cheese if you use sharp (not mild) cheese such as sharp cheddar. Spread one, not two, tablespoons of peanut butter on toast.

Lean Tips for Soups, Stews, and Sauces

- Thicken soups and stews with pureed beans (legumes), low-fat refried beans, potatoes, potato flakes, or other starchy vegetables, whole-grain bread crumbs, and nonfat dry milk. That increases the nutrient and phytonutrient content, too, without adding fat.

Protein Foods: From Snout to Tail

As people are valuing and using all edible parts of an animal for food, variety meats, called "offal" by the British, are finding their way into today's menus. Often economical, these meats are protein rich and flavorful, but often tough. They may require slow cooking, chopping, or grinding. And some call for careful preparation to minimize food safety risks.

BLOOD	From blood pancakes to soups, sausages to puddings, the culinary use of blood differs among cultures. Blood sausage is high in protein, total fats, saturated fats, and cholesterol.
BRAIN	Despite the potential risk of Variant Cruetzfeldt-Jakob disease, brain appears in dishes worldwide, including breaded and fried as fritters. Brain is a good source of protein and iron and very high in cholesterol.
FEET (HOCK)	Sinewy, flavorful, and gelatinous, hocks require long, slow cooking. They are high in protein and total fats and low in iron.
HEART	Grilled on skewers or simmered with other organ meats, onions, and more, heart is a good source of protein and iron, but extremely high in cholesterol.
INTESTINES	For food safety, intestines must be thoroughly cleaned and then cooked well. As the first prep step, simmering for hours helps tenderize them. They're a good source of protein and high in total fats, saturated fats and cholesterol.
LIVER	Strong in flavor, liver can be sautéed or simmered, but it toughens when overcooked. Liver from younger animals is more tender and mild. High in protein and iron, liver is also very high in vitamin A and cholesterol.
PANCREAS AND THYMUS (SWEETBREADS)	Typically poached, braised, or sautéed, sweetbreads are most tender and flavorful when from veal and young lamb. A good source of iron, sweetbreads are high in protein, total fats, saturated fats and cholesterol.
STOMACH LINING (TRIPE)	Intact tripe requires long, moist cooking, but it can be stir-fried in small slices. Tripe is a good source of protein and is high in total fats and saturated fats.
TAIL	Bony yet flavorful, tail is tough and requires long, slow braising. Gelatinous oxtail is used as a stock base for soups.
TESTICLES	Typically scalded, skinned, and soaked before cooking, testicles can be sautéed, braised, or poached.
TONGUE	Tongue's toughness requires slow moist-heat cooking. Tongue is a good source of protein and iron and is high in saturated fats (less so for veal tongue).

Source: Food & Nutrition Magazine, R. Duyff. Academy of Nutrition and Dietetics, January, 2013, www.foodandnutrition.org/January-February-2013/.

- Puree part of the soup; add it back as a thickener.
- Use tempeh, tofu, or beans and peas as a low-fat, high-protein ingredient in soups, stews, pasta dishes, and other mixed foods. *See "Tofu, Tempeh, and More Plant-Based Options: Buying Tips" in chapter 6, page 173, for more about tempeh and tofu.*
- Enhance flavors of soups, stews, and sauces with fat-free ingredients: garlic, ginger, lemon juice, onions, tomatoes, herbs, and spices, among others, instead of bacon.
- Cut back on oil in homemade marinades. Or marinate with reduced-fat or fat-free salad dressing (may be high in sodium, however).
- If the recipe calls for a rich sauce, go easy. The goal is to add flavor, not overwhelm the food.
- Use pureed vegetables or reduction sauces rather than cream-based sauces. For a creamy texture, add milk, yogurt, or Greek yogurt as you puree vegetables. Reheat gently.
- For a "creamy" sauce, use fat-free, plain yogurt or cottage cheese as a base. Blend in fresh herbs for a sauce with chicken or fish, and horseradish to serve with lean beef, and heat gently. Thin with a little milk if needed.
- Skim fat, or degrease, from pan juices, soups, and stews that rises to the top.

Lean Tips for Salads

- Dress lightly. Salad dressing should lightly coat the ingredients and blend and enhance their flavors—not overwhelm them! Start with a little; you can always add more.
- Adjust the proportions in homemade vinaigrettes. Make it with three parts vinegar to one part oil (three-quarter cup vinegar to one-quarter cup oil) instead of the other way around, if you'd like. Too acidic? Substitute broth or fruit or vegetable (tomato) juice for some oil.

How to . . . Cook with Dry Heat*

BROILING

1. Preheat the broiler for ten minutes.
2. Place the meat, poultry, or fish on the rack in the broiler pan.
3. Season with herbs or spices as desired. Position thinner pieces (¾ to 1 inch) so that the surface of the meat is 2 to 3 inches from the heat; thicker pieces, 3 to 6 inches from the heat.
4. Broil to the desired doneness, turning once.† After cooking, season with salt if desired.

GRILLING

1. For gas grilling, set the heat to medium. For charcoal grilling, coals should be ash-covered and medium temperature (allow about thirty minutes for them to reach this temperature). To test the heat intensity of the charcoal grill, spread the coals in a single layer. Carefully hold the palm of your hand above the coals at cooking height. If you can keep it there for about four seconds, the heat is medium hot.
2. Before cooking, season the meat, poultry, or fish with herbs or spices as desired. Trim fat, if needed, to avoid flare-ups. Remove meat from marinade and pat dry with a paper towel for even browning and to avoid steaming.

   For smaller pieces of meat, poultry, or fish (chops, steaks, burgers, breasts, fillets, or kebobs), place them on the cooking grid directly over the coals. For roasts, thick steaks or chops, whole chicken or turkey, place the meat on the grill with the coals or heat source on each side. Turn occasionally for even cooking and browning. Baste with sugary sauces glazes at the end of grilling to avoid charring.
3. Grill the food to the desired doneness, turning it occasionally with a spatula or tongs.† Don't press, flatten, or pierce the meat; otherwise juices will be lost. After cooking, season with salt if desired.

PANBROILING

1. Heat a heavy nonstick skillet over medium heat for meats ¾ inch thick or thicker, or medium-high heat for meats ½ inch or thinner until hot, about five minutes.
2. Season the meat, poultry, or fish with herbs or spices as desired. Place in the preheated skillet. Do not crowd. Do not add oil or water. Do not cover.
3. Cook to the desired doneness, turning once.† For thicker pieces, turn occasionally. Remove excess drippings as they accumulate. After cooking, season with salt if desired.

ROASTING

1. Heat the oven to the recommended temperature (varies based on the cut of meat).
2. Place the roast (straight from the refrigerator) fat side up, on a rack in a shallow roasting pan. Season as desired. Insert an oven-proof food thermometer into the meat so the tip is centered in the thickest part of the roast but not resting in fat or touching bone (or use an instant-read thermometer later). Do not add water; do not cover.
3. For beef, pork, veal, and lamb, roast to 5° to 10°F below the desired doneness.† Transfer it to a carving board, and tent loosely with aluminum foil. Let the meat stand for fifteen to twenty minutes. (The temperature will continue to rise by 5° to 10°F to reach the desired doneness.) For whole poultry, cook until the desired temperature is reached.†

STIR-FRYING

1. Partially freeze the meat, poultry, or fish (about thirty minutes) for easier slicing. Cut into thin, uniform strips or pieces. Marinate to add flavor and tenderize while preparing the other ingredients, if desired.
2. Heat a small amount of oil in a wok or large heavy nonstick skillet over medium-high heat until hot.
3. Stir-fry in half-pound batches (do not overcrowd), continuously turning with a scooping motion, until cooked to desired doneness. Add additional oil for each batch, if necessary. (Cook meat and vegetables separately, and then combine everything and heat it through.)

*These cooking methods apply to fruits and vegetables, too.

†*See "Cook to Safe Internal Temperatures" in chapter 7, page 210.*

How to . . . Cook with Moist Heat

BRAISING

1. Slowly brown meat or poultry on all sides in small amounts of oil in a heavy pan. Pour off the drippings. Season as desired.
2. Add small amounts (½ cup to 2 cups) of liquid such as broth, juice, water, beer, or wine.
3. Cover tightly and simmer gently over low heat on the stovetop or in a preheated 325°F oven until meat or poultry is fork-tender. (The cooking liquid may be reduced or thickened for a sauce after removing the fat, as desired.)

POACHING

1. Season the meat, poultry, or fish as desired. For roasts, tie with heavy string at 2-inch intervals, if needed. Brown on all sides in a nonstick pan. Pour off excess drippings.
2. Cover the meat, poultry, or fish with liquid such as defatted broth, juice, water, beer, or wine. Season with additional ingredients, if desired.
3. Bring to a boil. Reduce the heat, cover, and simmer until fork-tender.

STEAMING

1. For fish, put it on a steamer pan or perforated tray. Vegetables, such as onions, leeks, celery, and bok choy, can be added.
2. Set the steamer in a pan above simmering liquid.
3. Cover the pan and continue simmering over low heat until the fish flakes.

STEWING

1. Lightly coat meat, poultry, or fish with seasoned flour if desired. Slowly brown on all sides in small amounts of oil, if necessary, in a heavy pan. Pour off the drippings. Season as desired.
2. Add liquid such as defatted broth, water, juice, beer, or wine to the pan. You will need enough liquid to cover the food. Some dishes, such as stew, require more liquid than others, such as chili. Bring to a boil and then reduce the heat.
3. Cover tightly and simmer gently over low heat on the stovetop or in a preheated 325°F oven until the meat, poultry, or fish is fork-tender. (Cooking soups in the oven is not practical.) Thicken or reduce defatted liquid as desired.

MICROWAVING*

1. Place fish in a microwave-safe dish. If cooking more than one piece, arrange the fish in spoke fashion for even cooking.
2. Add a small amount of liquid or seasoned vegetables, if desired. (Some vegetables may take longer to cook; choose vegetables with similar cooking times, or cook the vegetables separately.)
3. Cover with microwave-safe plastic wrap, and vent or lift one corner.
4. Following manufacturer's directions, microwave on high until the fish flakes and any added vegetables are tender.

* Microwaving affects the water molecules, thus helping to steam these foods.

That said, vinaigrette is a way to enjoy healthy oils. Experiment with different types of flavored oils and vinegars, or make your own herbed vinegars. *See "How to . . . Make Herbed Vinegars" in this chapter, page 270.*

- On taco salads, use lots of salsa with tomatoes, chiles, onions, herbs, and lime juice. Use a light touch with sour cream by going fifty-fifty: 50 percent sour cream, 50 percent plain low-fat yogurt (or perhaps Greek yogurt); use reduced-fat or fat-free sour cream; or enjoy a taco salad without it.
- Instead of making creamy slaw with regular mayonnaise, moisten shredded cabbage, broccoli, carrots, and other shredded vegetables with low-fat or fat-free yogurt or mayonnaise, flavored with herbs and other seasonings. Or use a vinaigrette.
- Main-dish salads? Limit ingredients that are high in fat or calories, such as bacon, cheese, creamy dressings, fried meats or poultry, and fried onions.

Lean Tips for Vegetables

- Sauté vegetables such as onions and mushrooms in just a little oil. Or cook them in a little defatted broth, juice, wine, or water in a covered, nonstick pan.
- Steam, stir-fry (in a nonstick wok or skillet), simmer, or microwave vegetables. If you really enjoy the crispiness of French fries and fried onion rings, oven-bake instead of frying them.
- Use lean ham instead of bacon for flavor when cooking beans and peas, collard and turnip greens, and other vegetables. Or just

How to . . . Degrease Pan Juices, Soups, and Gravies

Remember your science lessons? Fat rises to the top because it's lighter than water. The same thing happens in cooking. Fat in pan juices, soups, gravies, and canned broth collects on the surface, making it easy to skim off. Every tablespoon of fat you discard removes about 120 calories and 13 fat grams from the dish you're preparing.

- Remove fat from meat and poultry juices with a wide-mouthed spoon or a fat-separating pitcher.
- Refrigerate soups and stews before they're served. Do the same with homemade and canned broth, soups, and chilis and leftover refrigerated gravy. Fat, which hardens when chilled, is easy to remove with a spoon.
- When time is short, add a few ice cubes to the broth or gravy. Fat will rise and congeal around the ice, but the ice may dilute the broth slightly and cool it down.

reduce the amount of bacon if you want the flavor that bacon gives.

- Puree or mash potatoes, sweet potatoes, cauliflower, and other vegetables with milk, yogurt, buttermilk, reduced-sodium broth, or liquid from cooking potatoes. If you use butter or margarine, go easy; instead consider adding a splash of finishing oil such as pumpkin seed oil after they're cooked instead to add a spark. Boost the flavor and nutrients by blending in shredded carrots or zucchini or a little olive oil.
- For flavor on vegetables, toss with a small amount of butter (or finishing oil such as sesame oil or truffle oil), but just before serving. Cooking dilutes the flavor. You also need less butter if you add it just before serving.
- Roast or grill vegetables and fruits (bell pepper chunks, sliced eggplant, pineapple slices, sliced zucchini) as a low-fat way to bring out the flavor. They're great as kebobs! *See "How to . . . Roast Vegetables" in this chapter, page 249.*
- Sprinkle some grated Parmesan or Romano cheese on vegetables for flavor; go easy to limit fat and calories.

Lean Tips for Grain-Based Mixed Dishes

- Skip the oil or use just a little when cooking pasta or vegetable sauces. For more flavor, add herbs but use plenty of water. Just drain—don't rinse—cooked pasta; toss it with sauce immediately so the pasta doesn't stick together.
- Use a lower-fat sauce such as tomato- or other vegetable-based sauces. For more flavor, add herbs or spices such as basil or garlic; *see "Herbs—and Spices, Too!" in this chapter, page 266.*
- Cook grains including rice with herbs and defatted broth or with some fruit or vegetable juice in place of some water.

Lean Tips for Spreads

- Serve breads, rolls, muffins, bagels, and biscuits with low-fat spreads: fruit butter, chutney, mustard, nonfat mayonnaise, pureed beans such as hummus, reduced-fat or nonfat cream cheese, or reduced-fat soft margarine spread.
- Make a savory or sweet spread with Greek yogurt or yogurt cheese, or with silken tofu puree, instead of higher-calorie, higher-fat cream cheese.

Lean Tips for Fats and Oils

- In place of butter only, use half butter and half oil for less saturated fats.
- Coat pans with a thin layer of oil and then wipe them with a paper towel. Two tablespoons of oil add 240 calories and 28 fat grams; a thin coating of vegetable oil spray provides just 10 calories and 1 fat gram. Using nonstick pans makes it easier to use less fat.
- Skip or limit breading, which adds fat and calories because it enables food to soak up more fat during frying or panfrying.
- Drain panfried foods on a paper towel to absorb extra fat. Go easy on oil in the fry pan; cook in a nonstick pan.
- When adding ingredients to packaged mixes (such as macaroni and cheese, scalloped potatoes, or brownies), try soft margarine or oil instead of stick margarine or butter to limit *trans* and saturated fats. Or use half the fat called for in casserole and rice mixes.
- Match the cooking oil to the recipe. Avocado, canola, corn, peanut, refined olive, safflower, and soybean oils have high smoke points (the temperature at which oil starts to break down). These oils can be used for high-heat cooking such as stir-frying and frying. When oil smokes or burns, it loses some nutritional value and can impart an unpleasant, bitter flavor to food. If this happens, discard it.

  The unique flavor of extra-virgin olive oil may not be appropriate for some foods. A mild-flavored oil such as canola oil is versatile. Hazelnut, walnut, and some other specialty oils have low smoke points. They are nice for salad dressings and as finishing oils to add a splash of flavor at the end of cooking.
- When you do fry food, use good techniques. Keep the oil at the proper temperature (375°F for frying). A lower temperature

Smart Swaps for Less Total Fats and Saturated Fats

When cooking calls for . . .	Use . . .
Bacon	Canadian bacon, lean ham; or smoked deli turkey
Baking chocolate, 1 ounce unsweetened	3 tablespoons (unsweetened) cocoa powder and 1 tablespoon oil
Butter, lard, stick margarine	Soft, tub margarine; squeeze margarine; oil (canola, olive, vegetable, other)
Cream	Evaporated fat-free (skim) milk, fat-free half-and-half
Cream soups	Defatted broths; broth-based soups; fat-free milk-based soups; evaporated fat-free milk
Egg yolk (one)	One egg white
Egg, whole (one)	Two egg whites; ¼ cup liquid egg substitute; one egg white plus 2 teaspoons oil
Egg, whole (one); as thickener	1 tablespoon flour
Ground beef	95-percent lean ground beef; lean ground turkey or chicken; crumbled tempeh; beans (legumes)
Ice cream	Low-fat or fat-free ice cream; frozen low-fat or fat-free yogurt; frozen fruit-juice products such as sorbet
Mayonnaise	Low-fat, reduced-fat, or fat-free mayonnaise or whipped salad dressing; plain low-fat yogurt combined with pureed low-fat cottage cheese
Milk, whole	Fat-free (skim), 1 percent, or 2 percent milk as a beverage or in recipes
Ramen noodles	Rice or pasta (spaghetti, other)
Salad dressings	Low-fat or fat-free dressing; homemade dressing made with less saturated oil (canola, olive, peanut, soy, others), water, and vinegar or lemon juice
Sausage	Lean ground turkey, or 95-percent fat-free sausage
Sour cream	Greek yogurt; plain low-fat yogurt; ½ cup cottage cheese blended with 1½ teaspoon lemon juice; light or fat-free sour cream; ¾ cup Greek yogurt combined with ¼ cup sour cream
Whipped cream	Chilled, whipped evaporated fat-free (skim) milk; nondairy whipped topping

increases cooking time, and the food absorbs more oil. Too hot, and the food may not be fully cooked inside. Avoid overcrowding the pan, too, because that lowers the oil's temperature, which makes it take longer to cook and so absorb more oil.

BAKED DESSERTS: LESS FAT, STILL FLAVORFUL

Fat plays both functional and flavor roles in many baked foods. Reducing fat or switching to oil may affect the texture, making cakes, quick breads, and cookies less moist and tender. *See "Fats, Sugars, Salt: What These Ingredients Do" in this chapter, page 246.*

As a home baker, you may be able to reduce fat by as much as 30 percent—if a recipe hasn't already been adjusted to reduce it. Experiment, but know it's a matter of trial and error. Saturated fats are considered a nutrient of concern because they are overconsumed and need to be reduced, *as discussed in chapter 13, page 385.*

For ways to reduce sugar in baked goods and make them healthier, see "Sugar Shakers" in this chapter, page 265.

Lean Tips for Baked Goods

- Take out some fat—but not all. Some recipes work well with less fat; others don't. For example, with less fat, baked goods may not brown well and their texture may be dry. Shortbread, butter cookies, butter cakes, and many pound cakes need fat for the flavor and texture you expect.

  In baked breads, cakes, muffins, and brownies, try substituting an equal amount of applesauce, mashed bananas or dried plums (prunes), pureed other fruits, mashed garbanzos, pumpkin or squash puree, or cottage cheese for at least half the oil, margarine, or butter in recipes. Make sure they are well pureed or mashed. For bar and drop cookies, this substitution often works well; drop cookies with less butter won't spread as much.

Try buttermilk or fat-free or low-fat yogurt in place of sour cream and perhaps some butter. Try margarine in biscuits, muffins, and other breads; soft margarine spreads usually aren't good substitutes in baked goods.

- Instead of flaky pastry shells (high in fat), make graham cracker or gingersnap crumb crusts. Try using one-third to half of the margarine or butter called for in the recipe. If the crumbs seem dry, add just a little liquid such as water or juice to moisten, or a little honey to help hold it together.
- Prepare single-crust pies. Either make the pie open-faced, or arrange the fruit in the pie pan first and then put the crust on top. Or instead of a top crust, cover the top with uncooked oatmeal mixed with a little oil or other fat as well as a few finely chopped nuts.
- Enjoy a nutty flavor? Since nuts deliver heart-healthy oils and other nutrients, as well as texture and flavor, enjoy them in baked goods. To make fewer nuts seem like more, chop or toast them—toasting brings out the flavor.
- For more flavor—yet no more fat—mix in chopped dried fruits such as apples, apricots, cranberries, plums (prunes), or raisins.
- Coat baking pans very lightly with nonstick vegetable oil spray rather than butter, margarine, or oil. Perhaps spray a little on top of the dough for a gently browned crust.
- To cut down on saturated fats, experiment with cooking oil instead of butter, lard, or stick margarine. Be aware: the texture of baked goods will differ, being coarser, more mealy, and perhaps more oily. This substitution isn't suggested for quick breads, pie crusts or other pastry dough, or sweet baked goods that are higher in fat to start. When you do substitute, the recipe probably needs less oil than the amount of solid fat called for.
- Instead of whipped-cream toppings, whip chilled, evaporated fat-free milk—with a touch of sugar—for a creamy topping. Serve it right away since it's less stable and may get runny. Evaporated fat-free milk can be substituted for heavy cream in some recipes.
- Replace some (not all) whole eggs with whites if you need to reduce cholesterol in food. Baked goods can be rubbery when made only with whites.
- Packaged mixes? Use fat-free milk in brownies or instant pudding.
- What about fat substitutes? *See "Fat Replacers" in chapter 13, page 406*? Go online to learn how to use them successfully.

In place of solid fat . . .	Try liquid oil . . .
1 tablespoon	¾ tablespoon
⅓ cup	4 tablespoons (¼ cup)
½ cup	6 tablespoons
¾ cup	9 tablespoons
1 cup	12 tablespoons (¾ cup)

DAIRY AND MORE: BOOST CALCIUM AND VITAMIN D

Like many Americans, the calcium and vitamin D in your diet probably need a boost! People of all ages need these nutrients for healthy bones and teeth, and for other bodily functions. Yet they often come up short. *See "A Closer Look . . . Calcium, Vitamin D, and Bone Health" in chapter 14, page 427, for recommendations for calcium and vitamin D.*

Calcium and Vitamin D: More from Dairy

- Fortify casseroles, mashed potatoes, thick soups, and vegetable purees with nonfat dry milk, evaporated fat-free milk, buttermilk, or plain regular or Greek yogurt. A little dry milk added to meat loaf won't be noticed! One quarter cup of dry milk powder adds 375 milligrams of calcium to a recipe.
- Use milk instead of water when preparing creamy canned or packaged soups, or instant mashed potatoes, rice, oatmeal, or stuffing.
- Sprinkle shredded cheese on salads, baked potatoes, soups, stews, and vegetables. One ounce (one-quarter cup) of Cheddar cheese has 200 milligrams of calcium. Reduced-fat or fat-free cheese doesn't blend or melt as well as whole-milk cheese, but it has the same nutrients as regular cheese. For best results, shred lower-fat cheeses finely, or use them in a mixture with whole-milk cheese. Blend them with other ingredients rather than just sprinkle them on top.
- Make oatmeal, hot cereal, and hot cocoa with milk or with calcium- and vitamin D–fortified soymilk instead of water. One-half cup of milk adds 150 milligrams of calcium. Fortify them even more with nonfat dry milk powder for more of a calcium boost.
- Instead of black coffee in the morning, try caffe latte (made with steamed milk, perhaps fat-free). One-half cup (4 ounces) of milk added to coffee adds 150 milligrams of calcium. Or drink chai (spiced tea with milk).
- Use plain regular or Greek yogurt, or pureed cottage or ricotta cheese for some or all of the mayonnaise or sour cream in

How Much Cheese?

1 cup shredded cheese = 4 ounces*

1 cup grated cheese (Parmesan, Romano) = 3 ounces

*Eight ounces of milk is equivalent to ½ cup (2 ounces) of shredded processed cheese or about ⅓ cup (1½ ounces) of natural cheese such as Cheddar or mozzarella.

Try This: Give It a Shake!

How much salt do you typically add to food? Take the "shaker test" to find out. Cover a plate or a bowl with foil or plastic wrap. Now pretend your dinner is on the plate—or that the bowl is filled with popcorn. Salt your "food" just as you would if the bowl or plate was full of food. Measure how much salt you added. If you shook as much as one-quarter teaspoon of salt, you added almost 600 milligrams of sodium to your meal or popcorn. That's about 25 percent of the advised limit for sodium for a day.

salad dressings, sandwich spreads, and dips. Add herbs for flavor.

- Boost calcium, not fat, by using yogurt cheese or Greek yogurt. Made by draining the whey from the solids, yogurt cheese may substitute for cream cheese or sour cream. *See "Greek Yogurt Add-Ins" in chapter 13, page 402, for tips with yogurt cheese.*
- For a different flavor, try goat cheese. It has a strong and unique flavor. A half-ounce portion of semisoft goat cheese has about 42 milligrams of calcium. Serve it on crackers, in salads, or as a vegetable garnish. A half ounce of hard goat cheese has about 130 milligrams of calcium. *Hint:* You might find herb-flavored goat cheese in your supermarket.

Calcium from Other Foods

- Add vegetables with more calcium to many dishes: salads, soups, and stews, for example. One serving of broccoli, collard greens, kale, mustard greens, okra, and turnip greens all provide calcium, although not as much as a serving of milk.
- For casseroles, main-dish salads, pasta dishes, other mixed dishes, salmon cakes, and sandwich spreads use salmon with bones as an occasional change from tuna. Fish with edible bones—salmon, sardines, perch—all supply calcium.
- Make casseroles, chilis, dips, salads, smoothies, stir-fries, and other dishes with tofu (soybean curd), preferably made with calcium sulfate. One-quarter cup of tofu with calcium sulfate has about 130 milligrams of calcium. The same amount of tofu without calcium sulfate has 65 milligrams of calcium.
- Blend a delicious fruit smoothie with calcium-fortified beverages: almond milk, orange juice, and/or soy milk. *See "Dairy and Nondairy Beverages" in chapter 5, page 90, for more about other calcium- and vitamin D–fortified beverages.*

SALTY FOODS: SHAKE THE SODIUM

Cooking with salt may seem so natural that it goes unnoticed. However, with potential links to high blood pressure and excessive sodium intake by many, sodium is considered a nutrient to reduce, *as discussed in chapter 14, page 431.*

For the average American, only a small percentage of sodium comes from food prep and salt added at the table. A salt preference and the habit of cooking with salt are learned. You can relearn a healthier way.

You don't need to eliminate sodium from your cooking. In fact, you probably can't—and shouldn't. Sodium occurs naturally in many foods, such as artichoke, beets, and celery. Seaweed has a lot. Just a pinch of salt may help bring out other tastes (bitter, sweet, umami) and so enhance the flavor of many nourishing foods. Learn to choose and prepare foods with just a little salt. Cut back gradually, especially if you're a salt lover. After a while, your preference for saltiness probably will change. You might be surprised when some foods seem too salty!

Except for recipes with yeast, you can cut back on salt, in most traditional recipes, by as much as 50 percent—or just use a pinch in other food prep. Baked goods made with yeast need salt to control yeast fermentation, or the rising of dough. *See "Fats, Sugars, Salt: What These Ingredients Do" earlier in this chapter, page 246, for salt's other functions.*

Salt Shakers

- Taste before you reach for the salt shaker. Food may taste great just as it is.
- Remove the salt shaker from the kitchen counter and the table. A single ⅛-teaspoon "salt shake" adds about 300 milligrams of sodium to your dish.
- Instead of adding salt or high-sodium seasonings to sauces, spark up the flavor with herbs and spices, garlic, onions, vinegars, or citrus juice. *See "How to . . . Give Food an Easy Flavor Lift" in this chapter, page 243.*
- Make a little salt go further for flavor. Salt lightly just before serving. When it's on the surface of food, the salty taste seems more intense. Get a bigger flavor burst (and use less salt) with a large-granule, coarse salt, such as kosher or coarse sea salt.

- Instead of salt, add a touch of flavor to dishes by adding ingredients that contain salt already plus a little fat, such as cheese, ham, olives, salted nuts, or salty fish (anchovies)
- Limit added salt if a dish or meal has other salty ingredients such as mustard, kimchi, brined relishes (pickles, capers), and soy sauce. If foods have ingredients with salt or sodium already, you likely don't need to add more during cooking or when serving.

? Have you ever wondered?

. . . if draining and rinsing canned beans reduces the sodium content? If you drain and rinse canned beans under cool running water, you can reduce their sodium content by about 41 percent. If you drain only, sodium is reduced by about 36 percent. You also rinse away some nutrients, such as some B vitamins, that leach from the beans into the canning liquid. Most recipes made with canned beans do not include the canning liquid.

. . . if salting cooking water speeds up the cooking? That's mostly urban legend. It's true that the boiling point of water may rise very slightly with added salt but not enough for a noticeable difference. Salt added to cooking water will, however, make food a bit saltier.

As an aside, adding salt to oil when frying or stir-frying doesn't prevent splattering. It actually does the opposite. It increases the chance of splatters because salt draws moisture from the surface of food. It also lowers the oil's smoke point.

. . . how you can spot chicken or turkey that isn't injected (marinated) with saltwater solution? Sometimes uncooked poultry is injected with a saltwater solution to keep it moist, tender, flavorful, and plump, and it will say so on the label. Usually fresh poultry has less sodium, but read the Nutrition Facts label, or talk to your butcher, to find out.

Brining, advocated at times by chefs and home cooks, is done for similar reasons. If poultry has already been injected with a saltwater solution, don't brine it, too.

. . . how brining chicken, turkey, or pork affects the sodium content? Significantly! Brine is a solution of a liquid and salt, and perhaps a sweetener, spices, or herbs. It helps bring moisture into the muscle but adds a significant amount of sodium, too—a problem for those who need to reduce their intake. The amount depends on the type of meat or poultry, the length of brining time, the salt concentration of the brine, and how much surface is covered.

- Reduce or skip salt in cooking water, even if a recipe or package label says to add it. Instead, season pasta, rice, vegetables, and cereals with spices or herbs after they're cooked. Salt toughens many vegetables, including beans, as they're cooked, drawing water out of the plant cells.
- Use prepared or processed ingredients with less sodium—perhaps low-sodium broth, light soy sauce, salt-free seasoning mixes, and no-salt-added canned vegetables. Read the Nutrition Facts label.
- Salt substitutes? They may give food an off flavor. If they contain potassium, they may create health risks for those taking medications for high blood pressure or for those with kidney conditions. Check with your doctor before turning to salt substitutes.
- Savory foods enhanced with monosodium glutamate have less salt because MSG has significantly less sodium than salt. It also contains glutamic acid, an amino acid that gives umami, or yumminess, to food. *See "MSG—Another Flavor Enhancer" in this chapter, page 240, for more details.*

SWEET FOODS: CUT ADDED SUGARS, NOT FLAVOR

A preference for sweetness is innate, with sweet foods adding to the flavor and pleasure of eating. Some foods contain sugars naturally: fruits (fructose) and dairy products (lactose). Yet most sugars in a typical American diet are added during food processing, food preparation, and at the table.

On average, added sugars account for almost 270 total calories, or more than 13 percent of calories per day in the US population, as noted in the Dietary Guidelines for Americans. That contributes to overweight and other health risks. For that reason, added sugars are considered a nutrient of concern to be reduced, *as discussed in chapter 11, page 346.*

As a home cook, you can reduce sugars by using ingredients with fewer added sugars, by serving smaller portions of foods with added sugars, and by using your culinary skills to reduce added sugars without compromising flavor.

Sugar Shakers

Be mindful, but before reducing or eliminating sugar in a recipe, consider its function and whether the change will give the baking or cooking result you want. *See "Fats, Sugars, Salt: What These Ingredients Do" in this chapter, page 246.*

- In breads, cakes, cookies, and other baked goods, try using less sugar. Often you can reduce sugar by a fourth to a third yet hardly notice the difference. Be aware: many recipes already have done this, so take time to experiment. *See "Baking with Sugar" on the next page, for guidelines on how much to use.*

- Instead of sugary frosting, top cakes with pureed fruit, sliced fresh fruits, or a dusting of powdered sugar, cocoa powder, or powdered "sweet" spices such as cinnamon and nutmeg. A half cup of strawberries and half of a peach (skin on) each add 2 grams of fiber, too! Or top a cake or slice of toast with a 100-percent fruit spread.
- Enhance sweetness, especially in warm foods, with extracts and so-called "sweet" spices. Almond, lemon, orange, peppermint, vanilla, and other sweet extracts get their concentrated flavors from aromatic substances. Fragrant spices, such as allspice, cardamom, cinnamon, cloves, coriander, ginger, mace, and nutmeg, enhance the sweet, natural flavors in other ingredients. By themselves, spices aren't sweet. *See "Kitchen Nutrition: Sweet Seasonings" in chapter 11, page 265 for more tips.*
- Puree fruit with a blender or a food processor (perhaps add applesauce, even pureed baby-food fruit) for a flavorful "syrup," or coulis, on pancakes, waffles, French toast, fruit salads, and ice cream or frozen yogurt; serve warm or cold. It also makes a tasty glaze for meat, fish, and poultry. Too thick? Add a little fruit juice. More flavor? Add "sweet" spices or a few drops of flavored liqueur or extract.
- Instead of eating fruit-flavored yogurt, add flavor to plain yogurt with chopped fresh, canned, frozen, or dried fruits, or whole berries, or fruit puree.
- Deconstruct and shift the proportion in fruit desserts for less sugar. Instead of fruit pie, bake an apple, peach, or pear in fruit juice and any "sweet" spice. Top with small cookies or crumbled graham crackers or gingersnaps. The warm temperature enhances their sweet flavors!
- Sweeten lemonade and other drinks with fresh fruits such as berries or citrus slices instead of sugar.
- Make frozen strawberry popsicles with a blend of low-fat strawberry milk and strawberry slices. Freeze them in a frozen pop mold or an ice-cube tray with a wooden pop stick.

Baking with Sugar

To ensure good results when reducing sugar in baked foods, follow these guidelines:

In these baked foods . . .	For each cup of flour use . . .
Cakes and cakelike cookies	½ cup sugar (cookies made with juice, milk, water)
Muffins and quick breads	1 tablespoon sugar
Yeast breads	1 teaspoon sugar

? Have you ever wondered?

. . . if sweetening with honey is a way to reduce calories? It's true that most honey is slightly sweeter than sugar, so you might use less honey for the same level of sweetness. However, one teaspoon of honey has 21 calories, compared to 16 calories in one teaspoon of table sugar. From a calorie standpoint, there's no net calorie advantage. Honey produced from different flowers delivers subtle and pleasing flavors.

. . . how much alcohol burns off or evaporates during cooking? That depends on the cooking time, temperature, and amount of distilled spirits, wine, or beer used. When added to uncooked foods, the alcohol content doesn't change. However, when added to boiling liquid at the end of cooking, about 85 percent of the alcohol may be retained, compared to only about 5 percent if the dish was braised for two and one-half hours. A flamed (flambé) dish may retain about 75 percent of its alcohol content.

- Consider using sugar alternatives such as aspartame, stevia, or other choices in some foods. They're almost calorie free—and can be a useful option for those managing diabetes. However, sugar alternatives don't function in food like sugars do, so their use has limits. *See "How to . . . Cook with Nonnutritive Sweeteners" on the next page.* Try replacing one-third of the sugar with a sugar alternative.
- Making a gelatin salad or a dessert? Rather than using flavored gelatin, dissolve unflavored gelatin in fruit juice and then sweeten with a sugar alternative.

HERBS—AND SPICES, TOO!

Herbs and spices have a long culinary tradition. If you're a history buff, you know that spices have been traded throughout the Mediterranean and the Middle East for more than two thousand years. In the first century, Apicius, who was a Roman epicure, described herb combinations to enhance flavor. Spices were a motive for Christopher Columbus's forays across the ocean.

Today, innovative uses of herbs and spices offer new flavor opportunities as chefs and home cooks reduce fats, sugars, and sodium in food preparation. Just a spoonful or pinch of herbs or spices can help transform a dish! Interest in ethnic flavors and food adventures brings a new fusion of flavor to the table with a greater use and more combinations of spices and herbs. Many people confuse the terms "herb" and "spice."

How to . . . Cook with Nonnutritive Sweeteners

With their sugarlike flavor, the nonnutritive sweeteners listed below can replace sugars and so reduce calories in many recipes. For example, sweetening an apple cobbler with saccharin rather than brown sugar might save 67 calories per serving (if a recipe to serve four calls for one-half cup of brown sugar). Use according to the directions on the package or the manufacturer's website.

If you use nonnutritive sweeteners, remember that their unique cooking qualities such as browning, crystallization, and inhibiting bacterial growth differ from those of sugar. You likely need to adjust your recipe or food preparation technique. The manufacturer's website may give sugar equivalents. Low-calorie sweeteners may have ingredients added for bulk, so substitution equivalents vary among products.

For baking, you might buy a blend—part sugar, part nonnutritive sweetener. Blends have fewer calories and carbohydrates than sugar, but they aren't calorie or carbohydrate free.

Heat stable or not? Use any nonnutritive sweetener in recipes that do not require heat, such as cold beverages, salads, chilled soups, frozen desserts, or fruit sauces. Consider these examples:

- Saccharin-, acesulfame K-, and sucralose-based sweeteners are heat stable and retain their sweetness when heated. Even then, you may get better results if you substitute only some of the sugar with a nonnutritive sweetener. (*Note:* acesulfame K is acesulfame potassium.)
- Aspartame isn't heat stable. Prolonged and high heat breaks it down so that it loses sweetness. Add aspartame-based sweeteners near the end of the cooking or baking. If heated, aspartame is still safe to consume.

Recipes prepared with nonnutritive sweeteners may not turn out the same as recipes made with sugar, especially baked products such as cookies, cakes, muffins, and quick breads. Sugar does more than add flavor. With a nonnutritive sweetener, expect:

- Lower volume and different texture. Sugar adds bulk, but nonnutritive sweeteners may not unless they have a bulking agent to help bring up the volume. Another option: go fifty-fifty by substituting saccharin- or acesulfame K–based sweeteners for half the sugar, according to the package directions. The volume still won't be as high as with 100 percent sugar. Crispy cookies may not have the same texture.
- Lighter color. Sugar caramelizes and has a browning effect. Nonnutritive sweeteners don't.
- Different baking time.
- Somewhat different flavor—an issue if you're sensitive to the sweetener's aftertaste.
- Shorter keeping time. Sugar holds moisture. With nonnutritive sweeteners, baked foods may dry out faster.
- Intensely sweet. Experiment. Add just a little sweetener until you get the sweetness you want. Adding too much can ruin the flavor.

See "Sugar Alternatives" in chapter 11, page 368, for more about nonnutritive sweeteners, including brand names and cooking tips.

- Herbs, which grow in temperate climates, are the fragrant leaves of plants.
- Spices, which grow in tropical areas, come from the bark, buds, fruit, roots, seeds, or stems of plants and trees. Usually they're dried. Garlic and gingerroot are two common exceptions.

The same plant may supply both spices and herbs. For example, the seeds of coriander often are used in curry powder, while the leaves of the same plant are called cilantro, a favorite seasoning in Mexican dishes.

See "Phytonutrients: Different from Nutrients" in chapter 15, page 448, to learn about the potential health and phytonutrient benefits of some herbs and spices.

Growing Herbs

Even if you don't have a green thumb, herbs are easy to grow and ready to use with a snip.

- Grow most herbs in a sunny spot—indoors or out—that gets at least four to six hours of full sun daily. Some tolerate shade, such as mint, oregano, and parsley. Herbs thrive in well-drained soil (not overwatered) with good air circulation.
- Experiment with less common herb varieties: lemon basil, borage, burnet, chervil, culinary lavender, lemongrass, lovage, orange mint, pineapple sage, and savory, among others.
- Grow scented geraniums: lemon, peppermint, and rose, to name a few. Their aromatic leaves and flowers offer a nice garnish and flavor to salads, sauces, vinegars, and baked foods.
- Harvest herbs at their peak of flavor—just before they bloom—by removing no more than one-quarter of the plant from the top at one time. Prune the flower so the herbs flourish and don't become bitter. Remember: That said, the flowers on many herb plants are flavorful, too.

Substitutions for Alcoholic Ingredients

Baby back ribs, chicken, or fish tenderized in a beer marinade . . . a touch of distilled spirits to enhance the flavor of cooking juices . . . light biscuits or bread made with beer . . . chicken braised in wine. Wine, beer, and distilled spirits can add to the flavor, tenderness, and texture of your culinary creations. Cooking wine and cooking sherry have added sodium, so it's better to use regular wine or sherry.

If you choose to skip the wine, beer, or distilled spirits called for in a recipe, it's easy to make a quick, flavorful substitution. To equal the amount of liquid from the alcoholic ingredient, you may need to add water, broth, or apple or white grape juice. (*Note:* Extracts may have small amounts of alcohol.) Adjust the recipe if you eliminate alcoholic ingredients because the flavor may be affected by ingredient substitutions.

In a recipe that calls for . . .	**Use this instead . . .**
2 tablespoons almond-flavored liqueur, such as amaretto	¼ to ½ teaspoon almond extract
¼ cup or more beer	*For soups, stews, and other cooked dishes:* Equal amount of nonalcoholic beer, apple cider, or broth
2 tablespoons bourbon	1 to 2 teaspoons vanilla extract
¼ cup or more brandy, port wine, rum, or sweet sherry	Equal amount of apple juice or apple juice plus 1 teaspoon vanilla extract
2 tablespoons chocolate/coffee-flavored liqueur	½ to 1 teaspoon chocolate extract plus ½ to 1 teaspoon instant coffee in 2 tablespoons water
2 tablespoons coffee liqueur, such as Kahlúa	2 tablespoons double-strength espresso *or* 2 tablespoons instant coffee, made with 4 to 6 times the usual amount in a cup of coffee
2 tablespoons orange-flavored liqueur, such as Grand Marnier	2 tablespoons orange juice concentrate *or* 2 tablespoons orange juice plus a little orange rind
2 tablespoons rum or brandy	½ to 1 teaspoon vanilla, rum, or brandy extract *or* 2 tablespoons orange or pineapple juice
2 tablespoons dry sherry or bourbon	2 tablespoons orange or pineapple juice *or* 1 to 2 teaspoons vanilla extract
1 tablespoon dry vermouth	1 tablespoon apple cider
¼ cup or more red wine	Equal amount of: *In any dish:* red grape juice, cranberry juice, or nonalcoholic wine (plus 1 tablespoon vinegar to balance its sweetness) *In salad dressings:* lemon juice *In marinades:* vinegar *In savory dishes:* tomato juice, fruit-flavored vinegar, or beef, chicken, or vegetable broth
¼ cup or more white wine	Equal amount of: *In any dish:* apple juice, white grape juice, or nonalcoholic wine (plus 1 tablespoon vinegar to balance its sweetness) *In salad dressings:* lemon juice *In marinades:* vinegar *In savory dishes:* chicken, vegetable, or clam broth (Use ⅞ cup broth plus 2 tablespoons lemon juice or vinegar.)

Have you ever wondered?

. . . what a flavor extract really is? Extracts are concentrated flavorings from foods and plants dissolved in alcohol. Some are made by distilling fruits, seeds, or leaves; almond, anise, peppermint, and vanilla extracts are made this way. Because they are so concentrated, use just a few drops.

Meat, poultry, and vegetable extracts (such as Kitchen Bouquet) are made by concentrating stock, or cooking juices; use them in marinades and sauces. Infused culinary or flavoring, oils such as orange oil or peppermint oil are even more concentrated than extracts. Handy if you cook or bake, use even less than you would with extracts.

. . . why some people think cilantro tastes like soap? It's all about genes. It seems that a small percentage of people have an olfactory receptor that picks up the smell of aldehydes, fragments of fat molecules found both in cilantro and in soap and lotions. By substituting parsley for cilantro, that soapy flavor is avoided. If you plan to use cilantro in a dish, ask guests beforehand and prepare a portion with parsley.

. . . what garam masala is? It's a blend of dry-roasted ground spices that give distinctive flavors to the dishes of India. The word "garam" means "hot" or "warm"—and that's the flavor experience they provide. It may contain up to twelve different spices, such as cardamom, chiles, cinnamon, cloves, cumin, mace, nutmeg, and pepper. Buy it—or make it yourself.

Ethnic Flavor Profiles

Would you combine a tomato with basil, cinnamon, or chile powder? The subtle blend of just two ingredients often defines the distinctive flavor of an ethnic cuisine—in these examples, Italian, or Middle Eastern, or Mexican. Ingredient blends—or at least some of these ingredients—are common in dishes of various ethnic cuisines.

China	Ginger, rice wine, and soy sauce
France	Marjoram, rosemary, sage, thyme, and tomato
Greece	Lemon, olive oil, and oregano
Hungary	Onion and paprika
India	Cumin, curry, garlic, and ginger
Italy	Basil, garlic, olive oil, and tomato
Mexico	Chile and tomato
Middle East	Lemon and parsley
Morocco	Coriander, cinnamon, cumin, fruit, and ginger
West Africa	Chile, peanut, and tomato

Storing Herbs and Spices

Herbs and spices won't keep indefinitely. To lock in the aromatic flavors, store them carefully.

- *Dried herbs and spices.* Store them in tightly covered containers—in a cool, dry, dark place (not in the refrigerator). Avoid placing your spice rack near a window, by the dishwasher, or above the stove. Heat, bright light, and air destroy their flavor and color. Moisture can promote mold. Keep them in airtight containers, close tightly after each use.

  Label dried herbs and spices with the purchase date, try to use them within a year or less. After a while, even properly stored seasonings lose their full "bouquet," or strength.

  Stored properly, the shelf life of quality dried spices and herbs is approximately four years for whole spices, two to three years for ground spices, and one to three years for leafy herbs, depending on the herb. Figure one to two years for seasoning blend.

  To check the freshness, rub seasonings between your fingers or shake the closed container and then smell the aroma. If there isn't much, get a new supply. When the color fades, the aroma has likely faded, too. To avoid waste, buy just enough dry herbs and spices for a few months for the most freshness and flavor. *Tip:* Avoid introducing moisture into stored herbs and spices. Use a dry measuring spoon if you dip into the container, and don't sprinkle them from the container into a steaming pot.

- *Fresh herbs.* To keep them longer, treat herbs like a bouquet of flowers! Snip the stem ends, and stand them in water. Cover them with a plastic bag and then store in the fridge. Change the water every couple of days. *Note:* Basil is best in a vase of water at room temperature; otherwise, the leaves turn brown.

  Before using fresh herbs, gently wash them under cold, running water. Spin them in a salad spinner to dry them, or pat them dry with paper towels.

  To preserve home-grown herbs for cold-weather months, either freeze or dry them, or add fresh herbs to vinegars. Be aware that some herbs are better dried—for example, bay leaves, marjoram, oregano, and summer savory.

  - *To freeze herbs:* Wash them and dry them well. Seal the herbs intact in plastic freezer bags; chop chives and lemongrass before freezing. Push the air from the bag before sealing. Label and date. Use them within twelve months.

Other options: snip them and then freeze them in water or oil in ice cube trays. Adding an "herb ice cube" to soups and stews is easy! Basil, chives, dill, fennel, parsley, rosemary, and tarragon are among the herbs that freeze well. Or grind them in a paste (or a pesto), mixing ⅓ cup oil with 2 cups chopped herbs. These are some herbs to try: basil, chervil, dill, fennel, marjoram, mint, parsley, rosemary, sage, savory, and tarragon.

- *To dry herbs in the oven:* Wash them, blot them dry or spin in a salad spinner, and remove the leaves from the stems. Place the herbs on baking sheets in a single layer. Heat them in the oven at 100°F for several hours keeping the door slightly open. Remove the leaves before they brown. Cool, crumble, and store them in tightly covered containers.

How to . . . Make Herbed Vinegars

Although today's supermarket shelves are stocked with herbed vinegars, why not make your own? They may cost less—and they're satisfying to make, especially if your herbs are home grown. Herbed vinegars also make great gifts from your kitchen!

- First, sterilize the bottle: immerse it in water, simmer for ten minutes, and then let it cool. Wash the cap or obtain a clean cork.
- Insert a combination of fresh herbs (stems and leaves) and spices into the bottle. Three or four herb sprigs per pint are usually enough.
- Fill the bottle with vinegar. You can use any vinegar as a base: cider, red wine, or white vinegar. Herbs and spices may go better with some vinegars than others. For example, try tarragon and garlic cloves in red or white wine vinegar, and delicate herbs in distilled white vinegar.

  Is wine or rice wine vinegar okay to use? Be aware that a protein they contain may promote bacteria growth if the herbed vinegar isn't stored properly.
- Put on the cap, or insert the cork. Store the bottle in a cool, dark place. Allow the flavor to develop for two to three weeks.

Try these flavorful combinations: fresh sage or thyme in red wine vinegar; garlic cloves, fresh rosemary or sage, and lemon peel in white wine vinegar; and fresh mint and orange peel in cider vinegar. For fun, make herbed vinegar with edible flowers—for example, nasturtiums with garlic cloves, whole cloves, peppercorns, and cider vinegar.

- *To dry herbs in the microwave oven:* Wash them, then place them between paper towels. Dry them on the lowest power setting for two to three minutes.

- *Spices.* Since whole spices last longer than ground, you may decide to grind your own. Freezing spices isn't advised because condensation can form in the container. Some whole spices such as allspice, cardamom seeds, and nutmeg stay fresh longer because they are protected by their outer shell. Sesame and poppy seeds have a shorter shelf life than other spices, just one to two years.
- *Jarred herbs and spices.* Keep herb purees, sold for convenience in jars or tubes, in the refrigerator. Once opened, refrigerate jarred minced garlic and ginger.

Building Flavor with Herbs and Spices

Add a pinch of this and a pinch of that. Dry or fresh—which herbs and spices should you use?

Nothing beats the delicate flavor of fresh herbs or the intense flavors of spices. Fresh herbs aren't always available, and unless you have your own herb garden, they can be expensive. Whether you use fresh or dried seasonings, use them correctly to ensure their peak flavor:

- Mince fresh herbs (chop very fine). Kitchen shears are great for mincing and snipping. With more cut surfaces, more flavor and aroma are released.
- If fresh herbs have woody stems, strip off the leaves before using them. Discard damaged leaves. If the stems are soft and pliable, use them, too. Stems often carry a lot of flavor and aroma.
- To release more flavor and aroma, crumble dried, leaf herbs—basil, oregano, savory, and tarragon, among others—between your fingers. Or use a mortar and pestle or coffee grinder.
- When substituting dried herbs for fresh, and vice versa, figure about one tablespoon of fresh herb equals one teaspoon of crumbled dried herb and about one-quarter teaspoon powdered dried herbs. Dried herbs are stronger than fresh; powdered herbs are stronger than crumbled herbs.
- Use seasonings with care—especially if you're not familiar with their flavor. They should enhance, not disguise, the aroma and taste of food. Start with one-quarter teaspoon of dried herbs or spices for one pound of meat or one pint of sauce or soup. The pungency and how it affects flavor depends on the seasoning; for example, use just one-eighth teaspoon of cayenne and garlic powder. You can always add more, but you can't take them away! (As an aside, the heat of red chiles intensifies with cooking, so go easy.)
- Avoid overwhelming a dish with seasonings. A few simple herbs and spices bring out the flavors of foods without confusing your taste buds.

- Add dried herbs and spices to liquid ingredients. They need moisture to bring out their flavors.
- In dishes that require a long cooking time, such as soups, stews, and braised dishes, add fresh herbs toward the end of cooking. That way their flavor won't cook out. Dried herbs and spices are best added at the start of cooking to release and blend their flavors.
- For chilled foods such as salads and dips, add herbs and spices several hours ahead so the flavors can blend. Again, basil is an exception; add just before serving.
- If doubling a recipe, you may not need to double the herbs or spices. Use just 50 percent more. If you triple the recipe, start by doubling the seasonings.
- Toast dried spices, such as coriander, cumin, fennel seeds, and mustard seeds, in a dry nonstick skillet for two to five minutes or until the spices are fragrant and lightly browned to bring out their aromatic oils. Stir constantly to prevent burning, and remove from heat right away.
- Use seasoning blends—a blend of herbs and maybe spices, too.
    - *Bouquet garni* is a bundle of fresh and/or dried herbs, often bay leaf, parsley, and thyme, that's added to soups, stews, and braised meat or poultry. Usually they're tied up in cheesecloth or placed in a metal teaball to easily remove and discard later.
    - *Curry powder* is a pulverized mixture of as many as twenty different spices, herbs, and seeds. The spice turmeric is the ingredient that makes curried dishes yellow. For a recipe to make your own curry blend, *see "Salt-Free Herb Blends" in this chapter, page 274.*
    - *Dukkah* is an Egyptian spice blend, often combining hazelnuts or chickpeas with coriander, cumin, pepper, and sesame seeds. It's often sprinkled on vegetables and meats or blended in dips (with olive oil).
    - *Fines herbes* usually refers to a mixture of chopped herbs often used in French cooking, such as basil, chervil, chives, lavender, parsley, savory, tarragon, and thyme.
    - *Za'atar* is a pungent, lemony blend of dried marjoram, toasted sesame seeds, ground sumac, and dried thyme that is used as an ingredient in Middle Eastern dishes or blended with olive oil to use as a dipping oil. Ground sumac, a spice that grows as a deep-red berry, can be purchased in Middle Eastern markets. (It should not be confused with poison sumac, which grows wild in parts of the United States.)

See "Ethnic Flavor Profiles" in this chapter, page 269, for seasonings that define ethnic cuisines.

How to . . . Make Rub Combos

Experiment with your own favorite blend of herbs and spices for all sorts of great rubs. You don't need a recipe; just combine flavors that taste good to you.

Use rubs on tender cuts of meat, poultry, and fish. To apply a rub, gently press the mixture onto the surface of the meat prior to cooking. Flavors usually become more pronounced the longer the seasoning is on the meat.

- *Citrus rub.* Combine grated lemon, lime, and/or orange peel with minced garlic and cracked pepper.
- *Herb rub.* Combine fresh or dried basil, marjoram, and thyme.
- *Italian rub.* Combine fresh or dried basil, oregano, and rosemary with minced garlic and minced Italian parsley.
- *Pepper-garlic rub.* Combine garlic powder, cracked black pepper, and cayenne pepper.

? Have you ever wondered?

. . . if homemade herbed oils and garlic oils, or flavored vinegars, can pose a food safety risk? If not used right away, these homemade infused oils can result in foodborne illness, caused by *Clostridium botulinum* bacteria! (*See "Bacteria: Hard Hitters" in chapter 7, page 220.*) Make homemade oils infused with garlic and herbs or with vegetables just before any meal or snack. Avoiding leaving them out at room temperature. Refrigerate and use leftovers within three days or discard.

What about herb-, fruit-, and vegetable-flavored vinegars? They're generally safe if made in sterilized containers—and kept in a cool, dark place for up to three months or refrigerated for six to eight months. Being high in acid, vinegar keeps them safe from *Clostridium botulinum* growth. Be cautious with wine and rice vinegars, however, since the protein they contain is a medium for bacterial growth if not stored properly.

For any flavored vinegar, if you see signs of mold or fermentation (bubbling, cloudiness, sliminess), toss without tasting or using it. If you choose to display flavored vinegars in a kitchen window, enjoy them only as decoration, not as food-prep ingredients.

Using Herbs and Spices in Mixed Dishes

Herbs and spices not only enhance the flavors and appeal of nourishing foods, their phytonutrients may contribute health benefits as well; *see "Phytonutrients: Different from Nutrients" in chapter 15, page 448*. These are some ways you might enjoy their flavors in your food preparation.

Quick Guide: Herbs and Spices

Not sure what herbs and spices to use? Use this quick reference to enhance the flavor of foods in every part of your meal. This is just a partial list—add your flavor creativity to the list, too.

In these foods . . .	Try these herbs and spices . . .
BREAD	
Sweet breads, rolls	Allspice, cinnamon, cloves, ginger, lavender, nutmeg
Other breads, rolls	Any herb, spice, or seed
EGGS	Basil, black pepper, chervil, chives, cilantro, garlic, marjoram, oregano, paprika, tarragon, thyme
FISH	
Finfish	Basil, bay leaf, chile powder, dill, fennel, ginger, oregano, paprika, sage, tarragon, thyme
Shellfish	Basil, black pepper, curry powder, dill, garlic, ginger, tarragon
FRUIT	Cinnamon, cloves, ginger, lavender, mint, nutmeg, rosemary
MEAT	
Beef	Bay leaf, basil, black pepper, celery seeds, curry powder, fennel (in sausage dishes), marjoram, onion, oregano, savory, thyme
Ham	Cloves, ginger, mustard seeds, tarragon
Lamb	Garlic, marjoram, mint, oregano, rosemary
Liver	Garlic, onion, thyme
Pork	Cayenne pepper, chile powder, cinnamon, cloves, fennel (in sausage dishes), sage, thyme
Veal	Basil, curry powder, lemongrass, oregano, rosemary, sage, thyme
POULTRY	
Chicken, turkey	Curry powder, ginger, marjoram, paprika, sage, tarragon
Stuffing	Basil, marjoram, onion, parsley, sage, savory
PASTA, RICE	
Pasta (including couscous)	Basil, chives, marjoram, oregano, saffron
Rice (brown and wild)	Ginger, onion, parsley
Rice (white)	Cinnamon, cumin, fennel, onion, parsley, saffron, turmeric
SALADS	
Chicken, turkey	Chives, celery seeds, oregano, tarragon
Egg	Marjoram, onion, paprika, parsley, tarragon
Fish (finfish, shellfish)	Chives, curry powder, ginger, marjoram, oregano, tarragon
Fruit	Cinnamon, ginger, lavender, mint
Greens	Basil, black pepper, chervil, chives, cilantro, garlic, marjoram, mint, onion, parsley, tarragon, thyme
Beans (legumes)	Basil, onion, oregano, parsley, tarragon
Vegetables	Basil, onion, oregano, parsley, tarragon

Quick Guide: Herbs and Spices *(continued)*

In these foods . . .	Try these herbs and spices . . .
SAUCES	
Cheese	Chervil, chile powder, chives, paprika, parsley, smoked paprika
Cream (or milk based)	Basil, curry powder, marjoram, tarragon, thyme
Tomato	Basil, bay leaf, cayenne pepper, cilantro, fennel seed, oregano, paprika, parsley, sage, thyme
SOUPS AND STEWS	
Beef, ham, lamb, pork, sausage (chorizo, wurst, others), veal	Basil, clove, coriander (cilantro), oregano, rosemary, savory, smoked paprika, thyme
Chicken, turkey	Bay leaf, lemongrass, mace, marjoram, paprika, parsley, sage, savory, thyme
Clear broth	Basil, lemongrass, paprika, parsley
Cream (or milk based)	Chervil, chives, rosemary, sage, tarragon, white pepper
Fish (finfish, shellfish)	Bay leaf, celery seeds, chives, curry powder, ginger, saffron, tarragon, thyme
Bean (legume)	Bay leaf, celery seeds, saffron, tarragon, thyme
Mushroom	Basil, bay leaf, garlic, marjoram, onion, oregano, parsley, tarragon, thyme
Potato	Chives, curry powder, dill
Vegetable	Allspice, basil, bay leaf, black pepper, cloves, garlic, marjoram, sage
VEGETABLES	
Asparagus	Chervil, savory
Baked beans	Allspice, chile powder, cinnamon, cloves, mace, parsley, red pepper
Broccoli	Oregano
Brussels sprouts	Caraway seeds, celery seeds, dill, marjoram, mint, sage, savory, tarragon
Cabbage	Caraway seeds, celery seeds, dill, marjoram, mint, sage, savory, tarragon
Carrots	Basil, bay leaf, ginger, marjoram, mint, oregano, parsley, thyme
Cauliflower	Marjoram, nutmeg, parsley
Corn	Chile powder, chives, smoked paprika
Green beans	Basil, cloves, marjoram, parsley, sage, savory
Lima beans	Marjoram, sage, savory
Mushrooms	Marjoram, oregano, parsley, tarragon, thyme
Onions	Basil, oregano, sage, thyme
Peas	Basil, chervil, marjoram, mint, oregano, parsley, sage, tarragon, thyme
Potatoes	Basil, caraway seeds, chives, dill, garlic, parsley
Spinach	Marjoram, ginger, nutmeg, parsley, savory
Sweet potatoes	Allspice, cinnamon, cloves, ginger, nutmeg, savory, thyme
Tomatoes	Basil, bay leaf, cilantro, cloves, marjoram, nutmeg, oregano, sage
Winter squash	Allspice, cinnamon, cloves, ginger, nutmeg, savory, thyme
SWEET DESSERTS	Allspice, cinnamon, cloves, ginger, lavender, mace, mint, nutmeg

Looking for more food-prep tips for healthy eating? Check here for "how-tos":

- Find more creative food-prep ideas: *see "Kitchen Nutrition" in many chapters.*
- Add nutrition to speed-scratch meals: *see "Planning Matters" in chapter 3, page 69.*
- Cook healthy and "small" for one or two: *see "When Lifestyles Change" in chapter 20, page 587.*
- Cook with kids: *see "Cooking Together" in chapter 17, page 495.*

- For baked chicken, fill the cavity with herbs and citrus peel—perhaps rosemary and lemon peel—and then roast it in the oven. Instead of lemon peel, try lemongrass or lemon-scented geranium.
- Cook strong-flavored vegetables, such as cabbage, with savory (the herb) to cut down on the strong aroma of cabbage while enhancing the flavor.
- Use herb and spice rubs on meat and poultry. *See "How to . . . Make Rub Combos" in this chapter, page 271.* For a simple rub, just combine garlic and lemon pepper, or try smoked paprika.
- Use herbed yogurt as a flavorful dip or vegetable topping. Perhaps blend dill, chives, garlic, and parsley into plain low-fat or Greek yogurt.
- Make no-fat marinades with an acid ingredient—vinegar or fruit juice—and herbs or spices. For example, combine orange juice and nutmeg. Splash herbed vinegar on salads and soups.
- Flavor mineral water, iced tea, lemonade, and spritzers with the leaves of scented geraniums, sprigs of fresh herbs, or edible flowers. Allow enough time for the flavor infusion. *See "Edible Flowers: Please Don't Eat the Daffodils" in this chapter, page 238.*
- "Reverse" the flavors. Use a "sweet" spice with meat or poultry, and a savory herb in dessert. Try cinnamon in tomato sauce, rosemary or thyme in pound cake, and chiles in brownies.

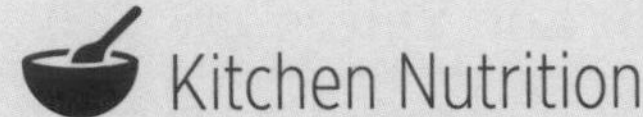

Salt-Free Herb Blends

Enhance the flavor of food with salt-free herb-and-spice blends. Herbal seasonings don't taste like salt but do add flavor to food! To make one-half cup of these blends, combine the ingredients in a jar. Cover tightly and shake. Keep in a cool, dark, dry place. Rub or sprinkle it on food for flavor. (*Tip:* They make great gifts!)

Chinese five-spice—for chicken, fish, or pork.

Blend ¼ cup of ground ginger, 2 tablespoons of ground cinnamon, 1 tablespoon each of ground all-spice and anise seeds, and 2 teaspoons of ground cloves.

Curry blend—for chicken and for lentil, rice, and vegetable dishes.

Blend 2 tablespoons each of turmeric and ground coriander, 1 tablespoon of ground cumin, 2 teaspoons each of black pepper, ground cardamom, and ground ginger, and 1 teaspoon each of cinnamon, powdered cloves, and ground nutmeg.

Easy dip blend—for mixing with cottage cheese, yogurt cheese (*see "Kitchen Nutrition: Greek Yogurt Add-Ins" in chapter 13, page 402*), or low-fat sour cream; also nice on chicken and fish.

Blend ¼ cup of dried dill weed and 1 tablespoon each of dried chervil, dried chives, garlic powder, and dried lemon peel.

Greek blend—for fish (finfish and shellfish), herbed bread, and poultry.

Blend 3 tablespoons each of garlic powder and dried lemon peel, 2 tablespoons of dried oregano, and 1 teaspoon of black pepper.

Italian blend—for chicken, focaccia, herbed bread, pasta dishes, pizza, and tomato-based soups

Blend 2 tablespoons each of dried basil and dried marjoram, 1 tablespoon each of garlic powder and dried oregano, and 2 teaspoons each of crushed red pepper, crushed dried rosemary, and thyme.

Mexican chile blend—for beef, chicken, chili with beans, enchiladas, fajitas, pork, and tacos.

Blend ¼ cup of chile powder, 1 tablespoon each of ground cumin and onion powder, 1 teaspoon each of garlic powder, dried oregano, and ground red pepper, and ½ teaspoon of cinnamon.

Mixed-herb blend—for fish, salads, pasta salads, vegetable soup, or steamed vegetables.

Blend ¼ cup of dried parsley flakes, 2 tablespoons of dried tarragon, and 1 tablespoon each of dried celery flakes, dill weed, and oregano.

9

Eat Smart Away from Home

In this chapter, find out about . . .

Eating right when eating out

Fast meals: healthy choices

Ethnic menus: more healthy options

Food and travel

Food safety when eating out

A quick meal at a fast-food chain, a food truck, the company cafeteria, or a casual dinner at a family restaurant doesn't mean you have to abandon your healthy intentions. Nor does trying a new flavor experience at an ethnic restaurant or enjoying an elegant evening of fine dining in a relaxing atmosphere.

Hungry or not, food bombards your senses nearly everywhere you go. In addition to sit-down, buffet-style, quick-service, and fast-casual restaurants, supermarket cafés let you "take out" to "eat in"—at home or in the store. Convenience stores, bookstores, drugstores, recreational centers, institutions (schools, hospitals, businesses, others), sports and cultural events, and vending machines make it convenient to eat away from home. No planning, no shopping, no cooking, no cleanup!

Busy lifestyles often compete with time in the kitchen. If you work during the day, you likely won't be home for lunch. With evening activities, grabbing a quick dinner out may make sense. Eating out may be the antidote for a long work day or a chance to socialize. A lack of cooking skills drives others to eat out.

Chew on this. The US Census Bureau reported in recent years that slightly more was spent in restaurants than on groceries. And the National Restaurant Association projected that total restaurant sales (food and drinks) for 2016 was nearly $785 billion, sold at over one million restaurant locations in the United States, compared to about $43 billion spent in current dollars in 1970.

These data show that eating out truly is an essential part of today's American lifestyle. The more often you eat away from home or get take-out food, the greater the impact may be on your overall nutrition, health, and well-being (and perhaps your food budget). If you eat out just occasionally, a little splurge is likely okay.

The US Department of Agriculture (USDA) reports that meals eaten out, on average, deliver more calories than home-cooked meals do. Depending on your choices, they often deliver more saturated fats and less calcium, fiber, and iron than recommended, and not enough vegetables and fruits. Yet, 2016 data from the National Restaurant Association say that eating out is trending healthier and that seven in ten adults are trying to eat out healthier than two years before.

The good news: The restaurant scene is changing—with more to come! Many chefs and restaurants are meeting expectations and demand for fresh flavor, healthier menu options with higher-quality foods, and more variety of vegetables, fruits, and whole grains on their menus. That results in menus with more interesting and different flavor profiles and eating experiences.

Eating Out for Health and Pleasure

Besides providing nourishment, eating out is part of everyday life—and a chance to socialize, celebrate, and experience flavors that typically aren't prepared at home. More and more, it's also a chance to connect you to how food is produced and prepared.

What's cooking? You've got choices—plenty of them! The explosion of eating-out establishments offers every type of food imaginable: traditional family menus and gourmet dining; regional, ethnic, and fusion cuisine; vegetarian choices; sushi, tapas, and other small plates; quick foods of all kinds; breakfast bagels and smoothies to go; and specialty coffees and teas, to name a few.

With forethought, culinary knowledge, and menu savvy, you can make great-tasting, enjoyable, even adventuresome choices when eating away from home—while keeping your nutrition in check.

ENJOY YOUR MEAL!

Eating out can be one of life's pleasures. It offers easy access to unique and varied flavors. More than ever, chefs use culinary techniques to enhance foods' natural flavors while retaining their nourishing qualities. This phenomenon isn't reserved for table-service or upscale restaurants. Many fast-food, deli, casual-dining, and family restaurants have expanded their menus, with a greater variety of vegetables, fruits, whole grains, seasonings, and flavors.

When you eat out, keep these tips in mind:

- Seize the chance to experience unfamiliar ingredients, perhaps new vegetable or whole-grain dishes, an ethnic dish, or new ways to prepare popular dishes. Order something you usually don't eat at home. Cautious about a new food or dish? Try an appetizer portion.
- Double the experience. Turn a cooking class into a dining-out experience to sharpen your culinary skills and eat out at the same time.
- Savor each bite. Be mindful of the layers of flavors at a leisurely pace. Eat to feel satisfied—perhaps even be inspired by unique foods and flavors—not until you feel too full. *See "Eating: Mindless or Mindful?" in chapter 3, page 78.*

Trending Today: Eating Out

- Chefs and registered dietitian nutritionists are partnering and often adopting "California fresh" concepts (seasonal, local foods, simply prepared). Some dietitians are trained chefs.
- Display or open-kitchen cooking let you see food being prepared.
- Chefs and farmers are collaborating—"farm-to-fork"—with more local and regional foods on restaurant menus. Called "hyper-local food sourcing," some chefs grow restaurant gardens, even on their rooftops. You might even enjoy seasonal meals on a farm.
- Restaurants kitchens and guest areas continue to become more environmentally friendly, often marketing to socially conscious customers. For example, from root to frond, chefs are creating new ways to use all nutritious, edible parts of plants and so waste less. Consider how they may use beets: roasted roots, sautéed greens, and pickled stems.
- Vegetables are being celebrated at center plate, as protein foods traditionally have been. One example is a "cauliflower steak," which is the center of a cauliflower head, cut down the center and then cut into ¾-inch-thick slices. It's then seasoned and roasted or grilled. Other examples: Vegetarian lasagna, flatbreads, and sandwiches with layers of grilled vegetables put a rainbow on the plate. Microgreens, mini vegetables, root vegetables (parsnips, rutabaga), fresh fava beans, kale, purple potatoes, and sunchokes are among those vegetables appearing on more vegetable-centric menus.
- Many mainstream and upscale restaurants are featuring meatless (even vegan), gluten-free, and allergen-free options; zucchini "spaghetti" and cauliflower "rice" are trendy examples.
- Meal kits provide portion-controlled, chef-quality meals for home delivery, often purchased from your supermarket.
- "Pop up" and mobile truck restaurants move restaurants to their customers, often with innovative menus that go beyond traditional "street food."
- Fast-food and chain restaurants offer menus with vegetable and fruit sides, kids' entrée salads, and fewer foods. In fact, menus in many of these places are getting a "face-lift" for all customers with fresher, healthier, and higher-quality foods and menu items.
- Chef-to-school partnerships offer flavorful, kid-friendly ways to put nutrition on the lunch tray.
- Restaurants contribute significant amounts of nourishing foods to food banks and soup kitchens as part of their social-responsibility commitment, including volunteering their chefs at community events.
- Passionate chefs lead initiatives in food policy and sustainability issues. And restaurants around the nation are taking initiatives to use energy and water more efficiently and divert food waste.

Service-focused restaurants are eager to accommodate special needs if they can. Check here for advice:

- Eating out with children—*see "Eating Out" in chapter 17, page 507.*
- Helping children and teens make the most of school breakfast and lunch options—*see "Eating Right at School" in chapter 17, page 505.*
- Managing food allergies, celiac disease, non-celiac gluten intolerance, and other food sensitivities when eating out—*see "Eating Allergen Free Away from Home" and "Eating Gluten Free Away from Home" in chapter 23, pages 664 and 676.*

- Order the tasting menu—with small portions of many different dishes served in several courses—as a way to experience new foods.
- If you eat with others, enjoy the social time. Make it a relaxing time with family and friends. *See "Eating Out" in chapter 17, page 507.*
- Enjoy dining out for celebrations. Unless you have a dietary restriction, it's okay to enjoy occasional splurges without going overboard.
- If the service and food are good and if your special food needs are met, tip well and let others know. Your good word about flavorful and healthy food items may also encourage restaurants to keep them on the menu.

No matter where you eat out or what you'd like to order, plan ahead, consider the menu, ask questions, order wisely, and enjoy.

CHOOSE THE RIGHT RESTAURANT

To enjoy a meal, pick a restaurant with the type of food (cuisine), the ambiance, the menu prices, and the convenience you want. Prepare before leaving home to help you stick to your nutrition goals and address any food concerns.

- Get familiar with restaurant and menu options. Use restaurant websites, blogs, Facebook pages, or a restaurant app. With some online apps, you can preorder as well as make a reservation, choose a table, and find out the waiting time. Check nutrition information if available. *See "Nutrition Labeling on the Menu: Your Right to Know" in this chapter, page 285.*
- Read online restaurant reviews from other patrons and restaurant critics.

Food Allergy Alert

Studies indicate that half the fatal episodes from food allergens occur outside the home. The restaurant industry is taking many steps to train their staff to keep foods safe. You must also do your part. Be savvy about menu terms, and ask questions about the ingredients and food preparation. *See chapter 23, page 653, for managing food allergies and other food sensitivities.*

- Call ahead to see if food can be prepared to order. This gives you more control if you have a special need, such as eating vegan, gluten free, or allergen free. If you're time pressed, order ahead: online or by phone or app for some restaurants.

Be aware: Restaurants that let you order on a digital, touch-screen tablet or online—and before you arrive at the restaurant—may not allow customized orders.

KNOW MENU LANGUAGE

"Primavera," "aioli," "al dente": What do they mean? Knowing menu terms and culinary basics makes ordering easier—especially important if you need to control calories, sodium, saturated fats, and other nutrients, or need to manage a food allergy, a food intolerance, or conditions such as celiac disease or diabetes. Menu literacy also makes eating out more fun. For example, here's how these three terms are defined:

- *Primavera*, translated from Italian, means "spring style." It refers to dishes prepared with raw or lightly cooked fresh vegetables.
- *Aioli* is a garlic-flavored mayonnaise, popular in southern France, made with olive oil. Often it's served with meat, fish, and vegetables.
- *Al dente* describes how pasta and vegetables are cooked: only until firm when bitten, not soft or overdone. Literally translated, it means "to the tooth." Vegetables cooked al dente retain more nutrients.

Throughout this chapter, you'll find many other menu terms explained. Ask your server about unfamiliar menu terms and ingredient names. Especially in some ethnic restaurants, the name of a dish, its ingredients, or its preparation method may be unfamiliar.

BALANCE EATING OUT WITH EATING IN

When you choose a restaurant and order from a menu, consider all your food choices for that day or several days: food variety, balance, and moderation. Order dishes with vegetables, fruits, and whole grains—not

- Healthy Dining Finder, partnered with the National Restaurant Association (healthy choices at a variety of restaurants)
  www.healthydiningfinder.com
- DietFacts.com (nutrition information for many chain-restaurant menus)
  www.dietfacts.com/fastfood.asp
- SafeFARE, dining out with allergies, Food Allergy Research & Education, Inc.
  safefare.org/for-diners
- Dining Out, Celiac Disease Foundation
  celiac.org/live-gluten-free/lifestyle/social-eating/dining-out

just protein foods. Think your drinks, too; *see chapter 4, page 81.* This way, you can fit in the variety of nourishing foods and drinks without overdoing the calories. These are some important considerations:

- Plan a light dinner out at a restaurant if you ate a big lunch. Look for "small plate" menus.
- To curb a big appetite, start with a salad, cup of soup, or small appetizer—easy on dressings and dips. A bite-size appetizer, or "amuse-bouche," may be just enough to whet your appetite. A bigger appetizer, perhaps with a small salad, may be enough for a meal without an entrée.
- Conversely, skip the starter, or appetizer, if you plan to order an entrée and need to lighten your meal. Many appetizers have as many calories as the entree!
- If you plan a three-course meal, skip the bread, or take just one whole-grain roll or bread stick. Then you'll have room for the pasta, pilaf, rice, or other grain dish.
- Order menu items to fill in your nutrition gaps, perhaps an extra side of vegetables or milk as a beverage choice.
- Save up for a more indulgent restaurant dinner. Eat small meals earlier in the day, but don't skip breakfast or lunch. Meal skipping may backfire—you might overindulge when you eat out if you're overly hungry.
- If an enticing dish is a "calorie splurge," take half home to eat later, or split it with someone else. That cuts the calories in half, at least for that meal.
- Remember: If you eat out regularly, every meal out is *not* a special occasion with permission to splurge.

ORDER IT YOUR WAY

When others cook for you, it's not easy to know what's in a dish—or how much saturated fats, added sugars, or salt it may have. Knowing menu terms and asking questions help you make healthy choices.

Since today's restaurant patrons often are food savvy, servers expect questions and are generally willing to find out answers they don't know. Restaurants are service oriented. Most servers are eager to please and will ask the kitchen to customize your order if they can. They want you back.

- Be assertive—and realistic—with special requests. Your server may have recommendations to match a special need. If your request is unclear to the server, it's generally okay to ask for the chef or manager.
- Ask about ingredients, if you can make substitutions, or how the food is prepared or served—especially if the menu description is unclear or the item is unfamiliar. Be prepared to order your second choice.
- Be specific about a special menu request. For example, ask to have it "broiled without butter," "bring dry toast," or "serve dressing on the side." Or if you have an allergy, perhaps to nuts, be sure that "no nuts" is clearly understood with kitchen follow-through. *See "Chef Card: Food Allergy Alert" in chapter 23, page 667, for a chef's card, which you can use to describe your special food need such as gluten free.*
- If you don't plan to eat a side dish or sauce, ask to have it left off your plate. Perhaps skip the tartar sauce served with fish or the chips served with a sandwich.
- Nothing on the menu that's right for you? Ask if you can order "off the menu." For fewer calories and less saturated fats, you might request broiled chicken breast or fish seasoned with herbs and lemon juice, or fresh fruit for dessert, or low-fat or fat-free milk.
- If you choose a higher-calorie entrée, balance it by ordering a lower-calorie side dish and dessert. For example, balance fettuccine Alfredo, which is high in calories and saturated fats, with fresh fruit to end the meal.
- If the food isn't prepared as ordered, politely ask to have it prepared correctly. Or request something else.
- If you have special food needs, request a special meal ahead of time for organized meal functions.

Menu Clues

Looking for foods with fewer calories or sodium? Check the menu. For some foods, limiting calories also limits saturated fats. Although they offer no guarantees, descriptive terms often provide clues.

Clues to Fewer Calories

Baked	Lightly sautéed
Braised	Poached
Broiled	Roasted
Cooked in its own juices or in lemon juice or wine	Steamed
Grilled	Stir-fried

Clues to More Calories

Aioli (garlic mayonnaise)	Hollandaise
Au gratin or in cheese sauce	Lightly fried
Batter fried	Marinated (in oil)
Béarnaise	Panfried
Breaded	Pastry
Beurre blanc	Prime
Buttered	Rich
Creamy	Sautéed
Crispy	Scalloped (escalloped)
Deep-fried	Smothered
Double crust	With cream sauce
En croûte	With gravy
Flash-fried	With mayonnaise
French-fried	

Clues to More Sodium

Barbecued	Smoked
Charcuterie	Teriyaki
Cured	With cocktail sauce
In broth	With Creole sauce
Marinated	With soy sauce
Pickled	

CONTROL YOUR RESTAURANT PORTIONS

You control portions—and calories—by what you order and how you handle what comes on your plate. Sensible portions mean less wasted food. They're also a way to manage your eating-out budget.

Before eating out:

- Look for restaurants with early-bird specials. They may offer smaller portions at a lower price. Or eat out at midday for a lunch-size portion.
- Plan ahead if you want a multicourse tasting menu. Even enjoying many small portions can add up to a lot of food—and calories!

Before ordering:

- Think: "how hungry am I?" If restaurant portions seem too big (or a dish seems like a splurge), remember that you have choices.
- Look around at what other customers have ordered to get a sense of the portions being served.
- Ask about portion sizes. Large portions may not mean better value—and the calories add up. A 6- or 12-ounce filet mignon? A 5- to-6-ounce meat portion probably is enough, especially if you eat other protein foods during the day. Many restaurants offer appetizer portions, half portions, and full portions. Or try tapas, "little plates," mezzes, or dim sum. Order one or two dishes at a time. You can order more if you're still hungry. Instead of the full entrée and other courses, order two appetizers, an appetizer and a salad, or a small-plate or lunch-size portion.

When ordering:

- Order before your meal companions do, if possible. Then you won't be influenced by their orders.
- Split a menu item such as an entrée or a dessert with a dining partner. You might make that decision before you even see the menu. Ask for two plates. Half the order means half the calories.
- Order à la carte. À la carte means that each item is separately ordered and priced. Then you may not be tempted by more food than you need.
- Order dessert—but in trendy bite-size, mini portions for fewer calories.

When you're satisfied:

- Turn some of today's dinner into tomorrow's lunch. Ask for a to-go container. Even before your food is served, ask your server to put half in a take-away container. *Tip:* Store perishable foods in the refrigerator within two hours, or within one hour if the outdoor temperature is more than 90°F.
- Leave some food on the plate. Ask the server to remove your plate (perhaps pack it to go when you're done), even if a little food is left. Why pay twice, with your pocketbook and your waistline?

What's That Sauce?

What's in the sauce? Tomato- and other vegetable-based sauces are typically lower in calories and fat than cream-based sauces. And they count as another vegetable in your day's food choices.

- *Alfredo:* Creamy Italian sauce, typically prepared with butter, heavy cream, and Parmesan cheese
- *Arrabbiata*:* Spicy Italian sauce made from garlic, tomatoes, and red chili peppers cooked in olive oil
- Béarnaise*:* Thick French sauce made with white wine, tarragon, vinegar, shallots, egg yolks, and butter
- *Béchamel:* Basic white sauce made with flour, milk, and butter
- *Bolognese:* Italian meat sauce made with ground beef and sometimes pork and ham, sautéed in a small amount of butter and/or olive oil with tomatoes, other vegetables, herbs, and sometimes wine. Also referred to as ragù bolognese sauce.
- *Bourguignonne*:* French sauce made with red wine, carrots, onions, flour, and a little bacon
- *Beurre blanc:* Thick, smooth French sauce whisked with wine, vinegar, shallot reduction, and cold butter
- *Carbonara:* Italian sauce made with cream, eggs, Parmesan cheese, and bits of bacon
- *Chermoula*:* North African sauce often made with herbs, oil, lemon juice, pickled lemons, garlic, cumin, and salt, and may include onions, fresh cilantro, ground chili peppers, black pepper, or saffron
- *Chimichurri*:* Uncooked sauce popular in parts of South America and often used for grilled meat, often made of finely chopped parsley, minced garlic, vegetable oil, oregano, and white vinegar
- *Coulis*:* Thick puree or sauce, such as tomato or squash coulis
- *Demi-glace*:* Reduction sauce that gets its intense flavor by slowly cooking beef stock and perhaps Madeira or sherry to a thick glaze
- *Hollandaise:* Thick sauce with white wine, vinegar, or water, egg yolks, melted butter, and lemon juice
- *Marinara*:* Italian sauce made with tomatoes and basil and perhaps other seasonings such as onions, garlic, and oregano
- *Mornay:* Béchamel sauce with Parmesan or Swiss cheese, and sometimes egg yolks or cream added for creaminess
- *Pesto:* Uncooked sauce made of fresh basil, garlic, pine nuts, Parmesan or Pecorino cheese, and olive oil. It's a favorite with Italian pasta. Pistou is similar but without pine nuts.
- *Reduction sauce:* Sauce of usually broth or pan juices boiled down to concentrate the flavor and thicken the consistency. Unlike many other sauces, flour or other starches aren't used as thickeners.
- *Romesco:* Classic sauce from Catalonia, Spain, made with ground almonds, garlic, onions, red bell peppers, tomatoes, and olive oil
- *Sriracha**: A Thai hot sauce made from a paste of chili peppers, vinegar, garlic, sugar, and salt
- *Sweet-and-sour*:* Sugar and vinegar added to a variety of sauces; typically added to Chinese and German dishes
- *Velouté:* Light, stock-based white sauce. Stock is the broth left from cooking meat, poultry, fish, or vegetables. It's thickened with flour and butter; sometimes egg yolks and cream are added.

*These sauces tend to be lower in calories and fat. But the ingredients vary, and so do the calories and fat content.

SIZE UP FOOD BARS AND BUFFETS

So goes the idiom: are your eyes bigger than your stomach? If this applies to you, pass on all-you-can-eat specials, buffets, and unlimited salad and food bars. When they are offered, these tips may help limit overindulgence:

- Pace yourself. Check out the buffet or salad bar from end to end before filling your plate.
- Use a small salad plate, not a dinner plate, because it holds less.
- If buffet-style eating is your choice, fill up on salad (easy on the dressing) and vegetables first to appease your appetite. Take only two trips to the buffet: one for veggies, fruits, and salads; one for anything else.
- Sit facing away from the buffet and as far away as you can.

Salad Bars

A salad bar can serve up a healthy meal all by itself—or provide a starter or side dish. The rainbow of vegetables and fruits is not only a calorie bargain, it's also often loaded with vitamins A and C, folate, fiber, and an array of phytonutrients, with antioxidant potential.

That said, a salad-bar plate can top out at more than 1,000 calories, depending on your choices and portions! Where do excessive calories come from? Not from lettuce, tomatoes, cucumbers, and other fresh vegetables. Depending on the amount, regular salad dressings, along with higher-fat toppings such as bacon bits, cheese, croutons, and fried onions, can heap calories onto a bed of raw vegetables, and so can mayonnaise-based mixed salads.

Build a Healthy Salad

Whether it's in a restaurant or in your supermarket, a salad bar with bowls and bowls of vegetables, fruits, and lean protein foods is an option for building your own healthy salad. To build a great salad, choose ingredients wisely, and take sensible amounts.

Food	Amount	Calories*
GREENS		
Bean sprouts	¼ cup	8
Lettuce	1 cup	8
Spinach	1 cup	7
OTHER VEGGIES		
Artichoke hearts	¼ cup	20
Beets	¼ cup	20
Bell peppers	2 tbsp.	5
Broccoli	¼ cup	8
Carrots, shredded	¼ cup	10
Cauliflower	¼ cup	6
Cucumbers	¼ cup	4
Green peas	2 tbsp.	15
Mushrooms	¼ cup	4
Onions	1 tbsp.	4
Radishes	2 tbsp.	2
Tomatoes	¼ cup	8
FRUITS		
Avocados	¼ cup	60
Canned peaches, in juices	¼ cup	25
Fresh melons	¼ cup	15
Fresh strawberries	¼ cup	10
Mandarin oranges, segments in juice	¼ cup	20
Olives, ripe	2 tbsp.	20
Raisins	2 tbsp.	60
BEANS, NUTS, AND SEEDS		
Almonds, sliced	1 tbsp.	55
Chickpeas (garbanzo beans)	¼ cup	65
Kidney beans	¼ cup	55
Sunflower seeds	1 tbsp.	45
Tofu (raw, firm)	¼ cup (about 3 oz.)	90

Food	Amount	Calories*
MEAT, POULTRY, FISH, AND EGGS		
Eggs, chopped	2 tbsp.	25
Lean ham, chopped	1 oz.	40
Popcorn shrimp	1 oz.	30
Surimi	1 oz.	30
Tuna in spring water	1 oz.	35
Turkey in strips	1 oz.	40
CHEESE		
Cheddar cheese, grated	2 tbsp.	55
Cottage cheese, creamed	¼ cup	60
Cottage cheese, 1% low-fat	¼ cup	40
Feta cheese	2 tbsp.	50
Mozzarella cheese, grated (part skim)	2 tbsp.	45
Parmesan cheese	2 tbsp.	45
OTHER TOPPINGS		
Bacon bits	1 tbsp.	25
Chow mein noodles	1 tbsp.	15
Croutons, seasoned	2 tbsp.	25
MIXED SALADS		
Potato (with mayonnaise)	¼ cup	90
Three-bean (in vinaigrette)	¼ cup	60
Tuna (with mayonnaise)	¼ cup	95
DRESSINGS		
Blue cheese, regular	2 tbsp.	145
French, regular	2 tbsp.	145
Honey mustard	2 tbsp.	140
Italian, fat-free	2 tbsp.	15
Italian, regular	2 tbsp.	85
Lemon juice	2 tbsp.	6
Oil and vinegar	2 tbsp.	145**
Ranch	2 tbsp.	130
Thousand Island, regular	2 tbsp.	120
Vinegar	2 tbsp.	6

*Nutrient values have been rounded.

** Calorie amount varies, based on ratio of oil and vinegar.

Sources: US Department of Agriculture, National Nutrient Database for Standard Reference, Release 28, 2016.

Salt Alert!

Unlike supermarket foods, you usually don't know the sodium content of items on restaurant menus. Yet, if you eat out a lot, the sodium from foods you eat out can quickly add up to more than you need. To eat less salt from foods you order out:

- Taste before you use the salt shaker. Ask for a lemon wedge, or bring your own herb blend to enhance the food's flavor.
- Recognize menu terms that may indicate a high sodium content: "au jus," "cured," "in broth," "pickled," "smoked," or "soy sauce."
- Skip salty snacks often served as bar food. Besides their sodium, they'll likely make you more thirsty so you are apt to drink more.
- Ask the server to have your vegetables and other food prepared without added salt. Perhaps they could just be steamed.
- Ask for sauces and salad dressings on the side since they're often high in sodium. For a salad, use a twist of lemon, plain oil, and a splash of vinegar, or a light drizzle of dressing.
- Keep your order simple. Order broiled or grilled meat—without salty seasonings—rather than entrées cooked in sauces. Condiments such as ketchup and mustard also add a lot of sodium.
- Look for sodium amounts in nutrition information for restaurant chains. And know that many restaurants are cutting back quietly and gradually on salt in their menu items.

To control salad bar calories:

- Start with a base of dark-green leafy vegetables such as arugula, romaine, and spinach, and perhaps shredded red cabbage. They supply more nutrients and phytonutrients than iceberg lettuce does.
- Spoon on plenty of brightly colored vegetables (beets, bell peppers, broccoli, or carrots, to name a few), fruits, and beans (such as kidney and garbanzo). They too are loaded with nutrients and phytonutrients, yet they're limited in calories.
- Pump it up with lean protein foods: beans and peas, lean meat, turkey, salmon, tuna, crabmeat or surimi, shrimp, and eggs. Cottage cheese, other cheese, and yogurt on the salad bar add calcium as well as protein. Just a ¼ cup of beans also provides 3 grams of fiber as well as protein for just 50 calories.
- Go easy on shredded cheese; ¼ cup can add about 100 calories and some saturated fats too. With strong-flavored cheese, such as feta or Parmesan, you can use less and still get plenty of flavor.

? Have you ever wondered?

. . . if dipping oils are a better choice than butter on bread? To decide, think about the amount you dip or spread on bread and its calorie and fat content.

Although usually made with olive oil, a healthy oil with unsaturated fats, the calories in dipping oils can add up. One slice of bread may soak up 3 to 4 teaspoons of oil, which adds up to 126 to 171 calories. For comparison's sake, 3 to 4 teaspoons of butter has about the same number of calories, with many of those calories from saturated fats. However, you likely won't spread that much on a single slice of bread.

As another option, ask for a vegetable-based spread, such as squash puree or hummus. Besides providing fewer calories, it's another way to fit vegetables in. Hummus, prepared with some olive oil, provides some healthy oils.

. . . what the ingredients "lardo" or "lardons" on some menus are? Compare them to bacon. More likely found on some upscale menus, these ingredients are strips of cured (and sometimes smoked) pork fatback seasoned with garlic, herbs, and spices. Used as a flavor ingredient, perhaps in some Italian- and French-inspired dishes, lardo and lardons are high in saturated fats. As an aside, "bacon jam" on some of today's menus, typically made with bacon, onions, and a sweetener such as brown sugar, is also high in saturated fats and has added sugars.

. . . where to go for nutrition information on restaurant menus? A restaurant's own website is the most accurate source—if nutrition information is available. Because menus, ingredients and ingredient sources change frequently, larger restaurant chains, which are required to provide nutrition information, must update continually. For some restaurants, the website may also provide information needed if you have a food allergy or must eat gluten free. *See "Nutrition Labeling on the Menu: Your Right to Know" in this chapter, page 285.*

- Dress lightly! A 2-tablespoon ladle of blue cheese, French, Italian, or Thousand Island dressing adds about 85 to 145 calories to an otherwise low-calorie salad. Doubling or tripling that amount loads on calories and overpowers the delicate flavor of salad ingredients. Another option: Drizzle the salad with a little flavored vinegar or lemon juice, and a splash of oil, which helps your body absorb some of the vitamins in your veggies.
- Go easy on higher-fat toppings such as bacon bits, croutons, crunchy noodles, and fried onions.

Calorie Alert!

Most people underestimate the calories in their restaurant meals. Once menu labeling laws are enacted, by May 2017, it will be easier to estimate calories from foods served in many restaurants. Even without menu labeling, there are a few ways you can limit calories as you order food.

- Order a smaller portion for fewer calories. Large steaks and burgers, and big helpings of pasta and other cooked grain foods can really add up!
- If you're apt to indulge on complimentary tortilla chips or bread when you're seated or to nibble mindlessly on chips, nuts, and pretzels with a beverage order, instead take a small amount on a plate or napkin and ask to have the rest removed from the table.
- Not sure what to order? As a rule of thumb:
    - *Starters:* Fresh fruit, broth-based soup, pureed vegetable soups (not finished with butter or cream), marinated vegetables, or raw vegetables (crudités) with hummus or salsa dip, ceviche or seafood cocktail
    - *Salads:* Dressing on the side
    - *Entrées:* Lean meat, poultry, or fish that is broiled, grilled, or roasted, with any sauces served on the side. If breaded and fried, or cooked in butter or margarine, it has more calories.
    - *Meatless entrees:* Dishes that go easy on cheese or cheese sauces. Make beans your protein choice.
    - *Vegetables:* Steamed vegetables, plain or with a lemon wedge, or grilled, roasted, or dry-sautéed vegetables
    - *Grain-based sides:* Brown rice, farro, wild rice, other whole grains
    - *Breads:* Hard rolls or whole-wheat buns, French or Italian bread, or bread sticks
    - *Desserts:* Angel food cake with fruit, cappuccino, chocolate-covered fruit, frozen yogurt, Italian ice or sorbet, or seasonal fresh fruit
    - *Non-alcoholic drinks:* Mineral water, tap water, or club soda with a twist of lemon, lime, or other fruit
- Order a leaner cut of meat (for example, filet mignon; flank, flat iron, round, sirloin tip, or tenderloin steak). On fattier cuts, ask if visible fat can be trimmed before cooking. You'll limit calories and saturated fats.
- Ask what's in the sauce or dressing. That's your clue to the calories and nutrient content. If possible, ask for higher-calorie sauce on the side so you can control the amount. For salad dressing, a drizzle will do, but don't give it up. Most salad dressings are made with healthy oils, which you need in your day's food plan. Just as important, salad ingredients such as kale, romaine, and spinach as well as carrots, tomatoes, and other plant-based foods, have fat-soluble vitamins that need fat to be well absorbed.
- Swap in a baked potato, vegetables, or a salad in place of fries or chips. Many vegetables are great sources of fiber, phytonutrients, vitamins A and C, folate, and potassium.
- Substitute vegetables or salsa for cheese and cheese sauces. Top your baked potato with salsa instead of sour cream.
- If you can't resist rich desserts, don't even peek at the dessert tray or menu. If you're tempted, share.
- Limit wine, beer, and other alcoholic drinks, including flights (several smaller portions of wine, beer, sake, or other distilled spirits). Order by the glass, not the bottle or pitcher, to make it easier to limit yourself to one drink or two. Have a designated driver. *See "Alcoholic Beverages: In Moderation" in chapter 4, page 102, for more about alcoholic drinks.*
- Skip drinks—alcoholic or not—containing a lot of high-sugar mixers.

- For crunch, sprinkle on some sunflower seeds and chopped nuts for protein and some heart-healthy fats. One tablespoon of nuts or seeds is about 50 calories, so go easy; their calories can add up quickly.
- To limit sodium, go easy on bacon bits, pickles, and other pickled foods and relishes.
- Go easy on creamy mixed salads (ambrosia, macaroni salad, pasta salad, and potato salad), creamy soups, and crackers, even desserts—all with more calories—that often line up on a salad bar.

EAT OUT VEGETARIAN-STYLE

Whether you're vegetarian or simply enjoy meatless meals, many of today's restaurant menus—casual and upscale—cater to you with flavor and menu creativity. Even a number of fast-food restaurants serve meatless main-dish salads as well as vegetarian versions of deli sandwiches, pita pockets, pizzas, and tacos.

- If the menu has no meatless entrées, order a salad with vegetable soup and perhaps bread, or several vegetable appetizers. A side of fruit—with or without cheese or yogurt—can serve as a satisfying entrée.

Healthier Menu Options: More Often, Less Often

The choices on the left have fewer calories than their counterparts on the right.

Enjoy more often . . .	**Enjoy less often . . .**
Clear soups, consommé, or gazpacho	Bisques, cream soups, or soups topped with cheese
Vegetable plate with salsa; grilled, roasted, or steamed vegetables	Pâté, quiche, or stuffed appetizers
Garden, spinach, or tossed salad with dressing on the side; or crisp and crunchy vegetables	Salads with large amounts of dressing, bacon, cheese, and croutons; and mayonnaise-laden salads such as macaroni, potato, and tuna
Broiled or grilled meat, poultry, or fish	Batter-dipped or breaded or meat, poultry, or fish; or extra gravy
Baked, broiled, poached, roasted, or steamed; Cajun, or blackened entrées	Au gratin, breaded, creamed, en casserole, en croûte, escalloped, fried, Kiev, or sautéed entrées
4- to 8-ounce steak	More than 8-ounce steak
Filet mignon or flat iron steak	Rib-eye steak or ribs
Au jus, marinara, Provençal, or fruit sauces	Gravy or Alfredo, béarnaise, béchamel, beurre blanc, carbonara, hollandaise, pesto, or velouté sauces
Baked or roasted potatoes (plain or with a small amount of butter, margarine, or sour cream) or redskin potatoes	Buttered noodles, croquettes, deep-fried or home-fried potatoes, fried onion rings, fries, mashed potatoes with gravy, or twice-baked potatoes
Sandwiches on whole-wheat, pita, or rye bread with hummus or vegetable spreads	Sandwiches on white bread, croissants, or biscuits and with butter or mayonnaise
Brown rice, farro, quinoa, or whole-grain pilaf	White rice
Plain whole-wheat or multigrain rolls or bread sticks	Garlic bread, rolls or bread with cheese spreads or flavored butters
Fruit or fruit sorbet	Cheesecake, crème brûlée, French pastries, ice cream, and pie

- Ask to omit meat, poultry, or fish from stir-fries or other mixed dishes; add more vegetables, beans, or tofu in its place. Ask for meatless sauces. It's easier to substitute at restaurants that make food to order.

Have you ever wondered?

. . . how to make healthier choices from the kids' menu? Many restaurants now feature more vegetables and fruits, and other healthy options, on menus for kids—with kid's meals of 600 calories or less, and limits on saturated fats, added sugars, and sodium. Look for more vegetable and fruit sides on the kids' menu as well as more whole-grain foods, entrée salads, ethnic inspired foods (tacos, even sushi), fish, and oven-baked fries and chicken fingers.

To go with the common grilled-cheese sandwiches, chicken nuggets, hot dogs, and burgers, you can also encourage an order of steamed broccoli, fruit, carrot sticks, and low-fat or fat-free milk. Or offer something from the adult menu, perhaps to share. *See "Eating Out" in chapter 17, page 507.*

- Choose a restaurant with a salad bar where you have choices. Start with greens and other vegetables, including ones with more vitamin C, to help your body absorb iron from plant sources of food. Then toss with chickpeas (garbanzo beans), kidney beans, and sunflower seeds. If you're lacto-ovo-vegetarian, spoon on cottage cheese, shredded cheese, and/or chopped hard-cooked eggs. If you're vegan, find out if the dressing has ingredients derived from milk or eggs; if so, dress with vinegar and oil.
- Enjoy many of the vegetarian options and specialties served in ethnic restaurants such as African, Indo-Pakistani, and Middle Eastern. *See "A Global Kitchen: Meatless on the Menu" in this chapter, page 288.* (For vegans: Note that ghee, used in many dishes from India, is melted, clarified butter.)
- Look for restaurants that participate in the Meatless Monday campaign (www.meatlessMonday.com).
- For chain restaurants, go online or contact the company to ask what ingredients they use, especially if you're vegan and frequently dine there.
- For organized meal functions, request a vegetarian meal ahead of time.

? Have you ever wondered?

. . . how to feel comfortable when you dine alone? Any discomfort shouldn't make you skip a meal. In reality, you're likely the only one who notices that you're a solo diner. If you feel conspicuous, ask for a table off to the side. Take an avid interest in your surroundings. Talk with the server; study the menu and the decor. While you wait, be productive: read, make notes on your to-do list, do a little office work, or simply reflect on your day.

Once your meal is served, put down your book, turn off your handheld device, or put work away. Eat slowly and savor the flavors. When you're traveling and truly need to wind down and be alone, choose a hotel with room service.

. . . what spa cuisine is? Although the term isn't regulated, spa cuisine often refers to health-positioned food preparation, perhaps in resorts or health club cafés. A menu that offers spa cuisine may have foods with fewer calories, more vegetables, fruits, and fiber-rich grains, or perhaps smaller portions. Typically, preparation techniques are very basic and use, for example, a minimal amount of oil, no frying, and more steaming. Like any cuisine, ask about the menu; order with savvy.

Eating Out: Safe from "Bad Bugs," Free from Food Waste

A great meal is more than delicious food, good service, and pleasing surroundings. It's also a meal free from food-safety risks—with the responsible use of resources in its preparation.

SAFE TO THE RESTAURANT PLATE

Almost nothing can ruin a trip or a pleasant meal more than foodborne illness. Although restaurants in the United States, Canada, and many other developed nations must operate under strict public-health regulations, any restaurant can have an occasional cleanliness lapse. In some parts of the world, these regulations may not exist. Most of the time, wherever you are, hotel staff, perhaps the concierge, can recommend places to eat out with high public-health standards.

Following these tips helps ensure that food eaten away from home won't come back to bite you:

- Check for cleanliness. Although you probably can't see into the kitchen, just looking at the public areas tells a lot about a restaurant. Look for these indicators:
    - Tables that are wiped clean with clean cloths; chairs and tables free of crumbs and dried food

Nutrition Labeling on the Menu: Your Right to Know

How many calories does a burger, a pasta salad, delivery pizza, a smoothie drink, or box of movie theater popcorn provide? How many calories do your restaurant meals contribute? Most people underestimate, as in one study, by as many as 500 calories! And from chain to chain, the calories and nutrient amounts in the same item vary.

With the new menu labeling laws, requiring compliance by May 2017, many restaurants and vending machines must display calorie and nutrient amounts. Since Americans eat and drink about one-third of their calories away from home, having this information available matters. It can help you make more informed choices when you eat out. This transparency also may help chain restaurants edge their way to healthier menus, too.

With the new law, if a restaurant (or other place selling restaurant-type food, such as a supermarket or ballpark) is part of a chain with twenty or more locations doing business under the same name and offering substantially the same menu items, calories must be disclosed. The information must be clear and conspicuous on menus and menu boards, including drive-through menus, next to the name or price of the item. Menu exceptions: daily specials, temporary seasonal items, and condiments for general use on the counter or table. Restaurants with fewer than twenty locations also can provide this same information voluntarily. Likewise, those who own or operate twenty or more vending machines need a sign or an electronic or digital display with nutrition information, unless the calories are visible on the food package before purchase.

Want more nutrition information? Just ask. The regulations state that restaurants also need to have additional information on their menu items available, including total fat, calories from fat, saturated fats, *trans* fats, cholesterol, sodium, total carbohydrates, sugars, fiber, and protein. Use this information to:

- Compare menu items before ordering.
- Choose smaller portions, or an appetizer instead of a larger entrée.
- Manage larger portions by splitting an entrée with someone else, or taking some home.
- Choose healthy menu options.
- Watch out for calories in drinks.

- Well-groomed servers and cooks (if you can see into the kitchen)
- Clean silverware, tablecloths, glasses, and dishes
- Adequate screening over windows and doors to keep out insects
- No flies or roaches, which can spread disease
- Clean restrooms with soap, hot water, and paper towels or air dryers (wash your hands before sitting down to eat)
- A clean exterior with no uncovered garbage

- Be cautious about raw meat and fish; they may carry bacteria and parasites. The following menu items are served raw: steak tartare (raw ground beef and raw eggs), carpaccio (thin-sliced raw beef), and sashimi (raw fish). Sushi, often made with raw fish, is popular among many restaurant goers. *See "Is Raw Seafood Safe to Eat?" in chapter 7, page 209, for guidance on sashimi.*
- Ask the server if menu items such as Caesar salad dressing, Hollandaise, mousse, and tiramisu are made with raw or lightly cooked, unpasteurized eggs. If so, skip them. (Foods made with pasteurized eggs are okay.)
- Ask that raw sprouts be left off wraps, sandwiches, salads, and Asian spring rolls. Even raw sprouts that have been properly washed can carry harmful bacteria, warns the US Food and Drug Administration.

Eat Safely from Food Bars

- Use the hand sanitizer if available. Some restaurants ask you to hand sanitize if you use serving spoons and tongs for self-service.
- Select food from food bars, buffets, and displays only if the food is properly covered with a sneeze guard or a hood. This includes appetizer and dessert displays.
- Check the temperature. A hot buffet should be piping hot. A cold salad bar should be well chilled or placed on ice.
- Use a clean plate when returning to the food bar.

If you have a food allergy, celiac disease, non-celiac gluten sensitivity, or another food sensitivity, *see chapter 23, page 653, for food safety advice related to these health conditions.*

Keep Takeout Safe

Whether from restaurants, delis, or supermarkets, many "to-go" meals are perishable. Keep hot takeout foods hot and cold takeout foods cold. *See "How to Transport Food Safely" in chapter 7, page 217.*

If takeout food is hot already . . .

- Eat it right away: within two hours or within one hour if the air temperature is 90°F or more. Longer than that, toss it out.
- If it won't be eaten for more than two hours, refrigerate it in shallow, covered containers. Reheat it to a temperature of 165°F, or until it's hot and steaming. Check the temperature with a food thermometer. For reheating in a microwave oven, let the food stand for a few minutes after removing it from the oven; cooking continues as heat is conducted throughout the food during this "standing time." *See "How to Choose and Use a Food Thermometer" in chapter 7, page 212.*
- Keep hot takeout food in your oven or slow cooker at a temperature of 140°F or above—but for not much longer than two hours so it does not lose its appeal. Cover with foil to keep it moist.

For cold takeout food . . .

- If you don't eat it right away, refrigerate or store it in a chilled, insulated cooler until meal- or snack time.
- For takeout food that requires heating or cooking, follow food safety precautions.

WASTE NOT, RESTAURANT SAVVY

Reducing food waste and managing all resources is a priority among many of today's restaurateurs. Among the many tactics chefs embrace to make their operations sustainable, cost efficient, and socially responsible are these: re-inventing unserved leftovers, perhaps in soup, to avoid food waste; using more seasonal foods; donating excess food to local hunger-relief organizations; recycling paper products and cooking oil; and even composting.

You can help limit waste and promote sustainability by taking these actions:

- Support restaurants with a sustainable, environmentally focused mission. You may find their "green" initiatives on their website.
- If a restaurant runs out of an item, it is likely managing resources wisely to avoid wasting food.
- Order only what you plan to eat, share, or take home. For a social meal when you have more time, order something small, and then order again if you're still hungry. Uneaten food contributes huge amounts of restaurant waste.
- Patronize and value restaurants that serve sensibly sized portions. Avoid the lure of promotions for extra-large servings, which may add to restaurant waste as well as more to your own waistline.
- Portions too big? As noted before, take some home to enjoy later. For example, roasted vegetables you take home can top a poached egg in the morning, and uneaten cooked chicken or meat can turn tomorrow's lunchtime garden salad into a hearty chef salad.
- Only take condiment or sauce packets available with fast food if you really use them. Same goes for paper napkins and other disposables. If these items are packed with your take-out meal but they aren't used, save them for a picnic lunch or meal on a road trip.
- When eating in restaurants where you bus your own tray, sort trash as posted for recycling.

Fast, Casual Food

Quick-service food has been part of American food culture for many more years than most people realize. If your great (or great-great) grandparents traveled by train in the early 1900s, they likely devoured quick meals from the dining car. When the automobile took over, the dining-car concept was reinvented as fast-food restaurants dotted the roadside.

Eating in the car? That isn't new either. The popular drive-in restaurant of the 1950s evolved into today's drive-through window. The so-called fast-food chain, or quick-service restaurant, is a phenomenon that was launched for a post–World War II, speed-oriented, mobile society, at a time when eating out also became more than an occasional treat. At the start, fast food was limited to mainly fried chicken, hamburgers, French fries, ice cream, shakes, and soft drinks. In recent years, the fast-food counter has changed dramatically.

Today's fast-food and fast-casual menus offer these traditional foods, but also many "fast" and healthy menu choices such as grilled chicken or fish sandwiches; paninis, stuffed pitas, and wraps; main-dish salads and bowl meals; low-fat and fat-free milk and fruit smoothies; meatless entrées; "artisan" pizza; sushi; and much more. Some let you customize your order. Many offer nontraditional breakfast menus; others, late-night food.

There's more. Food trucks sell "street food," bringing food variety into different neighborhoods. Their menus often feature innovative foods and global flavors. Bakery cafes sell drinks, baked goods, and sandwiches all day, not just for breakfast. Food courts in shopping malls may let you travel a world of flavors to buy Chinese stir-fry bowls, Japanese domburi, Mediterranean dishes, Mexican bean burritos, Middle Eastern stuffed pitas with cucumber-yogurt dressing, or Vietnamese banh mi sandwiches.

Even the convenience store where you gas up your car sells food—truly the "dining car" of the highway. These days, some offer fresh, healthier options, such as fresh whole fruits; containers of ready-to-eat, cutup vegetables; nuts; and yogurt. Some offer sandwiches and other typical fast foods. That said, healthier convenience-store food is starting to trend toward the future. Bottom line: You have choices—and lots of them—whether it's mealtime or time for "grazing."

Eating and Driving: A Safety Issue

When time is short, many people assume that the fastest food comes from the drive-up window. Not so. Many times waiting in a drive-through line takes longer than making something to eat at home. Beyond that, eating or sipping while driving not only can be messy, it's also dangerous when one hand is on the wheel and the other hand is holding a burger or a steaming hot beverage.

If you do eat in the car, pull over in a parking lot or city park or by the curb. Enjoy those few minutes of eating without thinking about driving, too. Better yet, relax with your food in a mall or on a park bench. Then take a brisk walk.

FAST, CASUAL MEALS AND SNACKS: THREE QUALITIES THAT COUNT

For both convenience and speed, you have many opportunities for quick, healthy, and flavorful meals or snacks. Just be mindful and choose carefully. And be aware that changing how the food is prepared in many restaurant chains may not be easy—or even possible. This is because very often the food comes into the kitchen partially prepared.

One: Enjoy a Variety of Foods and Flavors

When you're rushed, buying the same quick meal—perhaps a burger, fried chicken, pizza, or a sandwich—is easy and often convenient. Yet these meals are high in calories, saturated fats, and sodium—and typically short on vegetables, fruits, whole grains, and dairy foods.

If you choose these meals and snacks, consider how they fit into your whole scheme of healthy eating for the day, *as discussed in chapter 2, page 287.* Whether you order bowls, salads, wraps, or ethnic-inspired foods, or even traditional fast food, consider these tips:

- Make vegetables, fruits, or both part of your meal or snack—in a bowl meal or an omelet, on a pizza or sandwich, in a salad or wrap, or as a side dish or some other menu item.

  Unless fried or prepared with a high-fat sauce, vegetables are low in calories. And the sweetness of whole fruits comes from naturally occurring (and not added) sugars. Besides their vitamins A and C, both vegetables and fruits deliver nutrients that some people often underconsume: potassium, folate, and fiber.
- Order whole grains for a fiber boost when you can, perhaps for sandwich bread, a burger bun, pita, wrap, pizza crust, or a bowl meal with noodles, rice, or other grains.
- Fit in dairy foods. As your beverage choice, order low-fat or fat-free milk or fortified soymilk—flavored or not—to boost your calcium and vitamin D intake. Balance your meal with yogurt, a yogurt parfait, or a smoothie. Or add a cheese slice or sprinkle of grated cheese.
- Boost the protein and iron with lean meat, poultry, or fish—broiled, grilled, roasted, or stir-fried—in sensible amounts in bowl meals, pizza, salads, sandwiches, and more. Eggs are another good protein source. Or enjoy plant-based alternatives, such as beans, lentils, or tofu. Nuts, seeds, and nut butters are good options, too, and they deliver healthy oils, but go easy to keep calories under control.

See chapters 2, page 21, and 3, page 60, for more about planning healthy meals and snacks to meet your nutrient and calorie needs for a day.

A Global Kitchen: Meatless on the Menu

Delicious and nutritious—vegetarian dishes are typical fare in many parts of the world. As you glance through the menu of an ethnic restaurant or flip the pages of ethnic cookbooks, you may find dishes such as these. They're typically made without meat, poultry, or fish. Internationally, rice and beans—a high-protein food combination—is popular nearly everywhere, but uniquely prepared and seasoned depending on the cuisine.

Caribbean

BLACK-EYED PEA PATTIES	Black-eyed peas mashed with eggs and seasonings and then quickly pan-fried in a small amount of oil
CALLALOO	One-pot meal (stew) made with dark-green leafy vegetables, a variety of other vegetables, seasonings, and often chili peppers
GUNGA	Pigeon peas and rice
MOROS Y CRISTIANOS	Cuban black beans and rice with seasonings

China

EGG FOO YUNG	Frittata-like dish made by combining slightly whipped eggs with sliced vegetables and then frying in a skillet until browned; also may be prepared with meat or poultry
HOT AND SOUR SOUP	Hot (spicy) soup with tofu
SOYBEAN CAKES	Stir-fried tofu with steamed rice
VEGETABLE POT STICKERS	Steamed vegetable dumplings
VEGETABLE-TOFU STIR-FRY	Variety of thinly sliced vegetables and cubed bean curd, stir-fried with soy sauce and perhaps vegetable broth

East Africa

INJERA AND LENTIL STEW	Flat bread served with cooked lentils; this is an Ethiopian dish
KUNDE (BEAN AND GROUNDNUT STEW)	Stew made of black-eyed peas, onions, peanuts (groundnuts), and tomatoes; a similar stew is made in West Africa, often without peanuts

France

RATATOUILLE	Soup or stew made of eggplant, green bell peppers, onions, tomatoes, and other vegetables; enjoy with crusty French bread
VEGETABLE QUICHE	Pie with a custard of egg and cheese mixed with chopped vegetables such as asparagus, leeks, mushrooms, and spinach

Greece

SPANAKOPITA (SPINACH PIE)	Phyllo-dough turnover filled with a mixture of spinach, feta cheese, and eggs. It's high in fat, so split the order.
TZATZIKI (CUCUMBER-YOGURT SALAD)	Plain yogurt mixed with shredded cucumber, garlic, and perhaps black olives; served with crusty bread
VEGETABLE-STUFFED EGGPLANT	Eggplant hollowed out and filled with chopped vegetables, cooked grains, and sometimes nuts

India

IDLI	Steamed cakes made of a batter of rice and fermented lentils
VEGETABLE CURRY DISHES	Combination of chopped vegetables and lentils flavored with a garam masala mix and perhaps served with basmati rice

Indonesia

GADO-GADO	Cooked vegetable salad with a peanut sauce; often seasoned with chiles

A Global Kitchen: Meatless on the Menu *(continued)*

Italy	
ANTIPASTI	An array of roasted or marinated vegetables, and perhaps bread and cheese
EGGPLANT PARMESAN	Sliced eggplant prepared by dipping it into a mixture of eggs and milk, coating it with bread crumbs and Parmesan cheese, and then sautéeing it; served with tomato sauce. Because the breading absorbs fat, go easy on your portion.
PASTA PRIMAVERA	Cooked pasta tossed with lightly cooked vegetables, with or without Parmesan cheese
PASTA E FAGIOLI	Pasta and white bean "stew" seasoned with herbs; usually prepared without meat
VEGETABLE RISOTTO	Arborio rice cooked in vegetable broth and combined with cooked vegetables and perhaps cooked beans or nuts. Made with grated cheese and often finished with butter, it's high in saturated fats. You might order it without butter and cheese.
Mexico	
BEAN BURRITO	Vegetarian refried beans wrapped in a soft tortilla, with or without cheese topping
CHILES RELLEÑOS	Poblano peppers stuffed with cheese, dipped in an egg batter, and baked or fried; if fried, they're high in fat, so share.
HUEVOS RANCHEROS (MEXICAN EGGS)	Scrambled eggs prepared with onions and served with tomato salsa, vegetarian refried beans, and tortillas
VEGETABLE FAJITAS	Stir-fried vegetables and perhaps tofu rolled in a soft tortilla; often served with guacamole
Middle East	
FALAFEL SANDWICH	Ground chickpea patties (fried) tucked in pita bread with chopped tomato and lettuce shreds and topped with tahini (sesame seed spread). Frying and tahini make this higher in fat.
FUL	Brown bean casserole made with eggs, lemons, parsley, and tomatoes
MUJADDARA	Lentils and rice seasoned with cumin, lemon, and onions
TABBOULEH	Salad made with bulgur, parsley, mint or chives, lemon juice, tomatoes, and perhaps cooked white beans
Morocco	
ROASTED VEGETABLES WITH COUSCOUS	Roasted veggies and couscous (perhaps whole grain) often with dried fruit and nuts mixed in
Native American Southwest	
MARICOPA BEAN STEW	Stew made of beans, corn, and cholla buds
South America	
OCHOS RIOS	Kidney beans and rice flavored with shredded coconut
Spain	
TORTILLA À LA ESPAÑOLA (SPANISH OMELET)	Egg omelet made with onions, potatoes, and other vegetables
VEGETABLE PAELLA	Saffron-flavored rice dish with tomatoes and other vegetables
Switzerland	
CHEESE FONDUE	Cheese melted with wine and served with chunks of crusty bread
RACLETTE	Cheese "scraped" from a melted piece of hard cheese, then spread on a boiled potato or dark bread

Two: Order Sensible Portions

Portion size is often a challenge when eating out—especially in many fast-food places. To right-size your fast-food or fast-casual order, consider these tips:

- Think before ordering. Order takers may try to increase the sale with marketing questions such as "Would you like fries with that?" or "Do you want the value size?" Just say "No, thank you."
- Before you order, decide if the "value meal" is a good deal. If you don't need the extra food, there's no extra value; smaller may cost less. Sharing may be the better deal.
- Choose the right-size portion for you. For most people, the small or regular sizes are healthy choices, so you don't need "deluxe," "super," and "mega" portions. Whether it's a sandwich, fries, a shake, or another option, bigger portions can mean more calories and likely more saturated fats, added sugars, and sodium.
- Order the kids' meal for a smaller portion, which also is likely to have fewer calories and less sodium and saturated fats. Good news: In many restaurants, kids' meals are being prepared in healthier ways: more whole-grain foods, oven-baked chicken fingers and fries, and more vegetable and fruit sides.
- Go smaller with side items and snacks. A large order of fries and a large soft drink can add up to a hefty 650 or more calories! Even small orders can vary greatly from chain to chain. For example, a small order of fries can differ by more than 100 calories.
- Split your order. Halve the calories, and double the pleasure. Share fries or a sandwich with a friend.

See "Control Your Restaurant Portions" in this chapter, page 279.

Three: Limit Saturated Fats, Added Sugars, Sodium

All three—saturated fats and added sugars (and their calories), and sodium—can add up quickly in fast-food and fast-casual meals. For example, a typical meal—a large cheeseburger with fries and a regular soda—can range from 1,150 to 1,750 calories (on average, adults need 2,000 calories daily), and well over half the sodium limit for a day. Yet,

Your Healthy Eating Check-In

How Do Your Fast-Food Meals Stack Up?

If you're a patron of traditional fast-food places, how did your last meal or snack rate? What did you order? Rate your choices. Which of these strategies do you use to make your fast-food meals healthy?

DO YOU . . .	Yes	No
1. Order the regular size: burgers, fries, drinks, shakes, and smoothies?	☐	☐
2. Make burgers a single: a single meat patty, no bacon (or just a little, if you want the flavor)?	☐	☐
3. Build it with whole grains: whole-wheat and other whole-grain bread, buns, pita, pizza crust, or tortillas—and brown rice in bowl meals and wraps?	☐	☐
4. Switch it up, with more menu variety: fast-food bowl meals, main-dish salads, stir-fries, stuffed pitas, and more if they're offered?	☐	☐
5. Layer on veggies: bell peppers, cucumbers, lettuce, shredded carrots, tomatoes, and more for burgers, sandwiches, and wraps or in a bowl meal?	☐	☐
6. Lighten the mayonnaise, sauce, or spread: Ask for hummus, another mashed-vegetable spread, or nut butter instead?	☐	☐
7. Go for grilled: grilled (not breaded or fried) chicken sandwich (same for a fish sandwich)?	☐	☐
8. Swap: a baked potato, fruit, or a side salad instead of fries or fried onion rings?	☐	☐
9. Substitute: water, 100 percent juice, or low-fat or fat-free milk instead of regular soda or sugar-sweetened tea?	☐	☐
10. Order a sweet and healthy ending: fruit or low-fat frozen yogurt rather than a fruit pie or a sundae?	☐	☐

The more times you said "yes," the better—especially if you're a fast-food regular! Each of these tips adds good nutrition to your fast meals and snacks.

you can enjoy the food and limit these nutrients that are so easily over-consumed.

Limit calories and saturated fats in ways like these:

- Ease up on condiments, special sauces, and dressings. One packet of mayonnaise (about 1 tablespoon) adds about 60 calories and 5 fat grams. The same-size packet of tartar sauce has about 70 calories and 8 fat grams. Instead, ask for ketchup, mustard, salsa, Sriracha sauce, or low-fat condiments and spreads—and add flavor with mushrooms, onions, peppers, and other savory vegetables.
- For fried foods, pay attention to the oil used for frying. The good news: Most fast-food chains use 100 percent vegetable oil that is also *trans* fat free. This oil may be identified on the menu. Compared to lard, which is high in saturated fats, vegetable oil is high in polyunsaturated fats, which are healthier for you.
- Choose fried foods only sometimes. Rely mostly on broiled, grilled, oven-baked, roasted, or steamed menu items instead.
- Enjoy full-fat cheese—but in small portions—since they can add to the flavor and satisfaction of the meal.
- When you need a dressing or spread, go light and choose those made with healthy oils such as canola oil, olive oil, nut and seed oils, and nut spreads. All these contain unsaturated fats.
- On sandwiches and burgers, watch the amounts of meat and cheese because both deliver saturated fats. Instead of bigger portions, add interest with vegetable toppings.

Limit calories and added sugars in ways like these:

- Limit sugary desserts, and pastries. All these can provide more calories than you may think. Substitute whole fruits.
- Order milk or water as your drink choice instead of soda. Water may be free.

Limit sodium in ways like these:

- Taste any food before salting it.
- Go easy on condiments that tend to be high in sodium such as ketchup, mustard, olives, pickles, relish, tartar sauce, and other sauces. Add flavor with savory vegetables such as onions, peppers, and tomatoes instead.
- Since bacon, ham, sausage, and deli meats are high in sodium, limit them, too.
- Limit salty snack foods and sides, such as salted fries.

BREAK-FAST OPTIONS

Today's fast-food and fast-casual restaurants provide more breakfast options than ever. Traditional items—often high in calories, saturated fats, added sugars, and sodium—have often been re-invented with a healthier spin. Innovative menus offer more ways to fit fruits, dairy foods, lean protein foods, whole grains, and even vegetables into your morning meal. And some restaurants offer all-day breakfast menus—for lunch and dinner.

Quick or not, what makes a great breakfast? That's up to you, but consider these options when you order:

- Sensible portions with reasonable calories, perhaps 400 to 500 calories for most people
- Lean protein food, which helps you feel full longer
- Fiber-rich choices such as whole-grain foods, vegetables, and some fruits
- A good source of calcium such as yogurt or milk
- Fruit, as a source of vitamin C
- Limited foods with added sugars, such as donuts, pastries, and sugary coffee or tea drinks

See "Breakfast Matters" in chapter 3, page 60, for more benefits from having a healthy breakfast.

Breakfast Sandwiches and Eggs

Many people buy breakfast on the run: a quick breakfast sandwich from a drive-up window, or perhaps a meal of eggs and hash browns or another side from the fast-food counter. When these quick breakfasts become a regular eating pattern, it's time to take stock of their nutritional impact.

For example, a typical bacon, egg, and cheese biscuit sandwich can provide about 440 calories, 24 fat grams (many as saturated fats), and 1,250 milligrams of sodium. Try these options instead:

- Order a breakfast egg sandwich (perhaps just egg whites) with avocados, vegetables (onion, spinach, tomato), and a small amount of flavorful cheese such as feta. Perhaps flavor with a little salsa. Build it on "skinny" bread—and maybe add a "slim slice" of meat. Egg whites are a good option if you want meat or cheese on the breakfast sandwich as well. (However, if you order just the whites, you get the protein but miss the choline from the egg yolk.)
- Skip bacon or sausage on your breakfast sandwich. Or substitute a "slim slice" of Canadian bacon or ham for less saturated fats. All these choices still have a lot of sodium, however. Substitute grilled chicken tenders if available on the breakfast menu.
- Order your sandwich on a bagel, an English muffin, panini, flatbread, or even a hamburger bun—whole grain if available—instead of on a biscuit or croissant. A typical fast-food breakfast biscuit can have about 18 fat grams and a croissant about 10 fat grams, compared to 1 fat gram in an English muffin.
- Try a breakfast burrito, pita pocket, or wrap stuffed with scrambled eggs, perhaps beans, and salsa occasionally—easy on the cheese. Be aware: A typical breakfast (bean-and-cheese) burrito has about 375 calories and 12 fat grams, yet 1,170 milligrams of sodium, nearly half the sodium limit for the whole day!

- Ease up on egg entrées if your doctor has advised you to watch cholesterol. A two-egg breakfast has about 370 milligrams of cholesterol (about 185 milligrams of cholesterol per one large egg). Omelets are often made with three eggs. Since cholesterol is only in the yolk, ask for either egg whites only, for one whole egg and one white, or for an egg substitute.
- If you get an omelet to order, load it with lots of vegetables—again, easy on the cheese. If you want a three-egg omelet, ask for at least one to be an egg white only.
- Keep it simple with no added ingredients. Just order a plain scrambled egg; flavor it with a little hot sauce or salsa. Or get a hard-cooked shell egg to go, which you can peel when you're ready.
- Enjoy your eggs in a breakfast quiche, perhaps prepared with asparagus, broccoli, mushrooms, or sun-dried tomatoes. Since quiche is typically made with cream and cheese, one slice is likely enough, especially if it's complimented with a garnish of fruits or vegetables.

Breakfast Sides

Many breakfast meals—eggs, pancakes, and waffles—come with breakfast sides. Keep these in mind as you add more to your order:

- Hash browns or breakfast fries? Being cooked in so much oil, they're high in calories and likely in sodium, too. Ask for fruit on the side instead—or even a salad or raw or roasted vegetables if available.
- Biscuits and gravy? To cut calories and saturated fats, skip the gravy. Use a low-calorie nut butter or spread on the biscuit instead.
- If you want a side order of meat, choose lean ham instead of bacon or sausage for less saturated fats. Ham, like bacon and sausage, is high in sodium, so keep the portion small.
- Order a side of whole fruits: bananas, berries, melon, and peaches, among others. Breakfast is a good time to fit fruit in. It's great on its own or as a topping for popular breakfast foods: cereal, French toast, pancakes, and yogurt.
- If you prefer juice, order 100 percent fruit juice, and not fruit drink. An 8-ounce carton of orange juice provides more than 100 percent of the vitamin C needed in a day.

More Hot Breakfast Entrées

A hot breakfast is the perfect morning meal anytime, especially on a cold autumn or winter morning. These are other menu items to consider:

- Order hot oatmeal—made with milk instead of water—or other cooked grains if available such as farro or quinoa. Top it with dried or fresh fruits, a handful of nuts or seeds, and raisins. These grains are all fiber-rich whole grains.
- If pancakes or waffles are on the menu, skip the butter or margarine. Use a light touch with syrup, or top with sliced fruit or berries instead—or maybe almonds, walnuts, or other nuts, or sunflower seeds.
- For French toast, try to order it made with whole-grain bread. Easy on the syrup! Sweeten with fruit instead.
- For more variety, look for less traditional fare, such as breakfast bowl meals (beyond cold cereal and oatmeal) and breakfast pizza. Consider a savory breakfast bowl of cooked grains, steamed vegetables, and a savory sauce, topped with a cooked egg!

Cold Breakfasts: Quick and Healthy

When it's a quick continental breakfast (bakery item, juice, and coffee) or ready-to-eat cold cereal with milk, make these options healthier yet:

- Order the fastest breakfast of all: ready-to-eat cereal or muesli with low-fat or fat-free milk. Cereal delivers starches (complex carbohydrates), B vitamins, iron, and almost no fat. Whole-grain or bran cereal provides fiber, too.
- Eat it with an 8-ounce carton of milk for about 300 milligrams of calcium, or about 25 to 30 percent of the calcium you need daily (plus vitamin D). Pour some on your cereal, perhaps some in your coffee or tea, and drink the rest!
- Ask for nuts, seeds, or sliced fruit to sprinkle on top.
- Look for other breakfast choices: yogurt, including Greek yogurt, or a fruit-yogurt parfait. An 8-ounce carton of low-fat fruit yogurt supplies about 315 milligrams of calcium and 225 calories. Greek yogurt has more protein than the same volume of regular yogurt. Enjoy it with a small bagel and piece of fruit or 100 percent fruit juice.
- Drink a nourishing breakfast in a fruit-yogurt smoothie. Complement it with hearty whole-grain bread.

Bakery Items

When you order a morning bakery item, again consider the nutrients and calories in your options:

- Make your bakery order whole grain: bagel, English muffin, toast, or plain, soft-baked pretzel. Cinnamon buns, croissants, doughnuts, fruit pies, muffins, scones, and sweet rolls can deliver a lot of calories, added sugars, and often saturated fats.
- Order the small size, or share. Today's oversized muffins and bagels can be double or triple the calories. For example, a small 1½-ounce blueberry muffin has about 210 calories; today, many muffins weigh in at 5 ounces! A plain 3-inch-diameter bakery bagel has about 140 calories, while a 6-inch-diameter bagel provides about 350 calories. If it's big, eat half and save the rest for later.
- Ask for a spread—soft margarine, jam, or jelly—on the side; then spread it lightly yourself. Better yet, order a nut butter or hummus so you're spreading on some protein.

See "Breakfast on the Road" in this chapter, page 311, for more tips.

BOWL MEALS: NOODLES, RICE, AND MORE

From breakfast to dinner, bowl meals have become popular on fast-food and fast-casual menus. They're generally nutritious, usually combining protein foods, whole grains, and vegetables into a single dish and getting their unique flavors from flavorful sauces.

At some restaurants, you can customize your order, creating a bowl meal to suit your preferences. The combinations are endless, often with ethnic twists:

- Start by choosing the base. Make it about a third of your bowl meal. It may be noodles; try a whole-wheat or buckwheat noodle, or rice noodles for a Thai bowl. Whole grains such as cooked brown rice, farro, spelt, wheat berries, whole barley, or wild rice—even cooked oats are great—or try cooked amaranth or quinoa if available. Cooked starchy vegetables (roasted or mashed) such as parsnips, sweet potatoes, and squash make a good base, too.
- Add veggies for another third of the bowl meal. Choose leafy greens such as arugula, chard, kale, or spinach and a colorful combo of other chopped or shredded, roasted, or stir-fried vegetables—and perhaps some fresh herbs such as chives, cilantro, lemon grass, or Thai basil for flavor.
- Choose your protein foods. Make it meatless, if you prefer, with beans, lentils, nuts and seeds, seitan, tempeh, or tofu. Or add lean cooked meat, poultry, or fish such as salmon or shrimp. Even top it with a fried, hard-cooked, or poached egg.
- If you like, add some cheese of your choice.
- Sauce it up—lightly. Try guacamole, hummus or other bean dip, salsa, tahini, sambal, sriracha, or chimichurri. Or dress it lightly with salad dressing. Be aware that some dressings such as peanut sauce can deliver a lot of calories.

BURGERS, BBQS, HOT DOGS, CHICKEN, AND FISH: GOING LEAN

Hamburgers may be America's all-time favorite fast food, but fast-food chicken and fish have gained a significant market share in part because of "health-washing": consumers perceive them as lower in calories and fat. Chicken and fish do have a lean advantage, if they're broiled or grilled. However, battering, breading, and frying bump up the calorie and fat content significantly. A fried chicken or fried fish sandwich may supply more calories and fat than a burger!

Burgers and Other Hot Meat Sandwiches

When you order a burger or other hot sandwich, consider the size, as well as the nutrients and calories, in your options:

- Order the regular, junior, or single-size burger or other sandwich; 3 to 4 ounces of meat is enough for a single meal. The larger the burger, the higher the calories, saturated fats, and sodium. A regular hamburger, for example, can supply about 275 calories, while a large burger may have 510 calories. Double patties are higher still.
- Top all kinds of hot sandwiches—burgers, chicken, or fish—and garden burgers (soy or bean) with tomato slices and other vegetables such as avocados, mushrooms, roasted bell peppers, sautéed onions, or spinach. While avocados add fat, it's the healthier, unsaturated kind. If you're short on calcium, add cheese—but go easy.
- For a fiber boost, ask for a whole-wheat bun or bread if available.
- Skip the bacon—or bacon jam. While it adds flavor, bacon also boosts calories, saturated fats, and sodium.
- Cut calories and sodium by ordering sandwiches with condiments, sauces, or spreads on the side. Then you control the amount. As a rule of thumb, calories go up with the number of extras. Instead of mayonnaise-based spreads and tartar sauce, use ketchup or salsa.
- On a brat or hot dog, go easy on the sauerkraut. Sausages of all kinds are high in saturated fats—and like sauerkraut, they're high in sodium!

Chicken: Broiled, Fried, Grilled, and Roasted

Ordering chicken? Keep it lean; here's how:

- Order a broiled or grilled chicken sandwich most often. Skip creamy special sauces to reduce the calories. Try salsa instead.
- Remove the skin from rotisserie chicken before you eat it. Poultry skin is high in fat.
- Order "regular" fried chicken rather than "extra crispy," which soaks up more oil during cooking. Batter or breading may have a high-sodium seasoning, too; lower the calories and sodium by removing the crust. Chicken nuggets or tenders are usually fried and may contain skin and meat (white and dark); order roasted nuggets or tenders if available.
- For fried chicken, get a single-piece, rather than a two- or three-piece, order.

Fish: Baked, Broiled, Fried, and Grilled

When you follow advice to fit fish twice into your weekly meal plan, keep it lean. Here's how:

- Choose baked, broiled, or grilled fish fillets, shrimp, and other seafood if you have a choice. Most fish sold in fast-food restaurants is battered and fried, even on a fish taco.
- Change it up. Vary the types of fish you order; salmon, for example, is a great source of omega-3s!
- Go easy on the tartar sauce. Ask for tomato-based cocktail sauce instead. Better yet, just use a squeeze of lemon, which has no added sodium.

DELI SANDWICHES, POCKETS, AND WRAPS: HEALTHY INSIDE AND OUT

Delis, sandwich shops, and sub shops: you often can order a sandwich as you like it. And—although sandwiches take center stage at these outlets—most have a broader menu from which to choose as well: perhaps yogurt, fruit, salads, soups, bagels and muffins, milk, flavored waters, coffee, and tea. Consider these tips to customize your sandwich for good nutrition:

- *Bread:* Choose a whole-grain bread, roll, or pita pocket for more fiber. Get a sandwich "wrap" in a soft tortilla. Or try a thin-sliced bagel (small), flatbread, or herbed focaccia. Skip the croissant, as its buttery flavor is partnered with more fat.
- *Spread:* Choose a spread that adds flavor and fewer calories, such as mustard, light mayonnaise, hummus, or another vegetable puree. Ask the server to go easy on higher-fat spreads, including cream cheese, or opt for a spread made with mashed avocado for heart-healthy fats.
- *Filling:* Consider all the great nutrition you can pack inside your sandwich:
  - Want meat? Go lean. Fill a sandwich with lean roast beef, ham, chicken breast, or turkey; these meats contribute protein, iron, and other nutrients. Some delis use meats that are 90 percent or more lean. On a club sandwich, replace bacon with Canadian bacon or lean ham. Go easy on bologna, liverwurst, salami, and other deli meats that are high in saturated fats and sodium. Two to 3 ounces of lean meat or poultry are likely enough.
  - Unless premixed, request chicken, egg, seafood, tuna, or another mixed salad to be made with less mayonnaise or with a reduced-fat alternative.
  - Add a slice of cheese, perhaps low-fat, to boost the calcium content. One slice may be enough since cheese is also high in saturated fats.
  - Layer on vegetables—carrot shreds, cucumbers, grilled veggies, jalapeños, onions, roasted bell peppers, spinach, or tomatoes. They're low in fat and calories, and supply vitamins A and C, fiber, and other nutrients.
  - Make it vegetarian. A roasted large portobello mushroom makes a hearty filler, with sliced avocado and a variety of other veggies.
  - Enjoy wrap fillings that typically are low in fat, such as brown or white rice blended with seafood, grilled vegetables, grilled chicken tenders, or shredded chicken.
- *Sides:* Ask for carrot or green bell pepper sticks, fruit salad, or vegetable salad rather than creamy slaw. For less sodium, enjoy a cucumber spear instead of a pickle.

For large sandwiches, subs, and wraps, buy one to share. Or keep half in the fridge for the next day. And order a Reuben sandwich only very occasionally since it's filled with high-fat, high-sodium ingredients.

PIZZA AND FLATBREAD: MADE TO ORDER

Those of every age eat pizza—or flatbread as it's called in some restaurants. Made with foods from three or more food groups, pizza is more nutritious than it often gets credit for. Crust supplies carbohydrates and B vitamins (and fiber if whole grain). Cheese is a good source of calcium and protein—although it often delivers saturated fats, too. Tomato sauce and vegetables top it with vitamins A and C, potassium, and phytonutrients. Add meat, poultry, or fish and you're adding protein, iron, and some vitamins, too.

Smart Toppings and More

The nutrition challenge comes mostly with portion control. It's easy to consume too many slices, especially from a pizza that's oversized for your needs or when a slice or two left on the pizza pan seems irresistible.

The nutrition opportunity comes when ordering a pizza, or a flatbread, your way, with healthy toppings, the right crust, and in the right size. Be a smart pizza architect:

- *Crust:* Consider the crust:
  - Build pizza or flatbread on a whole-wheat crust for more fiber if available.
  - Order a thin-crust pizza rather than a thick-crust pizza if you choose to trim the calories and carbs. Flatbread is usually built on a thinner crust. Although thin crusts generally aren't sturdy enough to hold a lot of toppings, they are a calorie saver.
  - Think before ordering a stuffed-crust pizza. With cheese and perhaps other stuffing, the calories and saturated fats can be considerably higher than with a thinner-crust pizza. For example, one slice (one-eighth of a pizza) of a 14-inch stuffed-crust cheese pizza may have 14 fat grams and 320 calories or more, compared to about 10 fat grams and 285 calories in one same-size slice of a regular cheese pizza.
- *Sauce:* While tomato sauce is most common, some restaurants are getting more creative, using barbecue sauce, pesto, or even peanut sauce for a Thai-style pizza or flatbread. Be aware that "white" pizza, made with an Alfredo sauce, can be high in calories.
- *Toppings:* Go beyond sausage and pepperoni to make your pizza healthier and more interesting.
  - Choose more vegetables and even fruits, which add up to better nutrition and often fewer calories. Flatbread may come topped with fresh greens such as arugula, dried figs, and other unique toppings.

Pizza and Flatbread Toppings: More Often, Less Often

Enjoy More Often			Enjoy Less Often
Artichoke hearts	Chicken, grilled	Onions	Anchovies*
Asparagus spears	Crabmeat	Pancetta	Bacon
Beans (legumes)	Eggplant	Pineapple chunks	Extra cheese
Bell peppers	Green onions	Shrimp	Olives*
Broccoli florets	Jalapeño and other peppers	Spinach	Pepperoni
Calamari	Lean ground meat	Sun-dried tomatoes	Prosciutto
Canadian bacon	Lean ham	Tomato slices	Sausage
Carrot shreds	Lean turkey	Tuna or salmon	
Cheese, part skim or reduced fat	Mushrooms	Zucchini	

*Enjoy in judicious amounts. They provide heart-healthy oils, but go easy since they deliver calories, too.

- Limit higher-fat toppings, which often add sodium, too. Many combination or deluxe pizzas have several high-fat toppings. Stick with one, not several. Limit double cheese since it's high in saturated fats. Flatbread is often cheese-less.
- Choose a lean protein topping, such as beans, Canadian bacon, grilled chicken, or shrimp.
- More flavor? Sprinkle on herbs or hot pepper flakes for no calories but lots of flavor.
- Order strong-flavored cheese if available, such as sharp Cheddar; you can use less of a more flavorful cheese and get great flavor with fewer calories. Fresh mozzarella on a traditional margherita pizza (fresh sliced tomatoes, basil, tomato sauce, and mozzarella) can be lighter and lower in sodium than typical mozzarella cheese.
- Enjoy wood-fired oven-baked pizza, or pizza with a regional twist for more flavor: perhaps Cajun style, Hawaiian with pineapple and lean ham on top, or Southwest style.
- Go halfsies. Order half the pizza your way if someone else prefers toppings with more calories on the other half. In that way, you both get what you want.

See "Pizza and Flatbread Toppings: More Often, Less Often" above.

Pizza-Size Wise

The bigger the pizza, the bigger the temptation!

- Order a reasonably sized pizza. Limit yourself to two or perhaps three slices—or just one slice if you're really watching calories. Calories from any pizza, even a veggie pizza, add up! A typical slice—one-eighth of a 14-inch thin-crust sausage and cheese pizza—may supply a hefty amount of fat and sodium. A thick crust can add another 30 or so calories per slice.
- If a bigger size is really the better deal, wrap the extra slices before you start eating. Store them in the fridge at home for later, or freeze slices in packs of one or two for easy reheating.
- Prefer a Chicago-style deep-dish pizza? Load it with vegetables, but take just one slice! As delicious as it may be, the rich, thick crust is layered with extra cheese, making it more like a high-calorie, baked casserole.
- Order a salad to complement your pizza. Salad not only adds nutrients and fiber, but it also helps you fill up. You may be less likely to eat that second or third slice.

SALADS, SIDES, AND DESSERTS: THINK HEALTHY

Your meal entrée likely provided protein foods and grain foods. Use salads, side dishes, and desserts to round out your meal and perhaps include more nutrient-rich vegetables, fruits, and dairy foods.

Salads

Whether it's a fast-food meal or fast-casual dining, complete your meal with a salad to fit in vegetables or fruits—or load up a main-dish salad. Consider these tips:

- Order a garden salad with dressing on the side. Lightly dress it with an oil-and-vinegar dressing, as a source of healthy oils. *See "Size Up Food Bars and Buffets" in this chapter, page 280.*
- Go easy on prepared salads made with mayonnaise or creamy salad dressing, such as creamy coleslaw, macaroni salad, or potato

salad. They often have more calories than salads with a vinaigrette dressing, such as coleslaw or three-bean salad.

- Order raw veggies or fruit chunks, or whole fruits when you can.
- Enjoy entrée salads (easy on the dressing) from most fast-food chains and fast-casual restaurants. Consider ingredients such as grilled or charbroiled chicken, shrimp, red beans and garbanzo beans, dried fruits such as apple slices and cranberries, sliced avocado, fennel, nuts such as pine nuts and pecans, and seeds—and sauces such as salsa verde, vinaigrette, and more. And be aware: The calories in a main-dish salad cut across a wide range from modest to 1,000 calories or more, depending on the ingredients you choose.

Potatoes and Other Cooked Vegetables

For nourishing hot sides, consider these tips:

- Order a baked potato, mashed potatoes, oven-roasted potatoes, or a baked sweet potato rather than fries as a side dish, or even as part of an entrée—if you have the option. Served plain, a baked potato supplies complex carbohydrates including fiber, vitamin C and other vitamins, and some minerals—but almost no sodium or saturated fats.
- For a baked potato, go easy on higher-fat toppings—bacon, butter, and sour cream. For more nutrients and usually fewer calories, top with sautéed or steamed vegetables, cottage cheese, plain Greek yogurt, or salsa. Chili as a topping? The calories and sodium content depend on the ingredients; check the nutrition information in the restaurant if it's a larger chain. When accompanied by a salad and milk, chili on a baked potato can make a nutritious entree.
- For mashed potatoes, ask for gravy on the side to control how much you add. Gravy is high in calories, mostly from fat. Find out how mashed potatoes are prepared, perhaps with butter and salt; check the nutrition information if it's posted.
- Ask for a small, not large, order of fries (even sweet potato fries) to limit calories and fat, especially if you already have a higher-fat meal. French fries provide some vitamin C. Sweet potato fries supply beta carotene (preformed vitamin A).
- For fewer calories, order baked beans, corn on the cob, green beans, broccoli, or a side salad instead of French fries, hush puppies, fried okra, or fried onion rings. For corn, ease up on butter and salt.

Desserts

Think about your choices with sweet snacks and desserts, too. Keep these tips in mind:

- Go easy on fried fruit fritters or turnovers. Eat them only if they fit within your daily calorie and fat budget. They usually have added sugars and solid fats.
- Check to see if fresh whole or cutup fruit is available; skip the fruit pie.
- For a cold dessert, enjoy a single scoop of frozen yogurt, ice cream, or sherbet. You may find low-fat and nonfat versions on the menu. Even though frozen yogurt is usually low-fat or fat-free, the flavoring often makes it high in added sugars—and may provide more calories than you think. Either way, the small or kids' portion offers a taste without indulging.
- If you order frozen yogurt for purported probiotic benefits, be aware: Probiotic bacteria don't always survive the freezing process, so you may not get the benefits you hope for. *See "Prebiotics and Probiotics: A Bioactive Duo" in chapter 15, page 453, for more about probiotics.*
- For fewer calories, go easy on candy pieces or mix-ins, fudge sauce, or syrup toppings. A little of these toppings goes a long way. Instead, ask for cutup fresh or dried fruits, granola, or nuts.

DRINKS: SMART CHOICES SENSIBLY SIZED

Ideal as a meal accompaniment, water is calorie free. Unless it's bottled, water is usually offered free of cost. For flavor, add a lemon wedge. If you choose to buy other drinks, make them count for good nutrition. Here's how:

- Round out your meal with milk. For a flavor switch, try chocolate or other flavored milk; ask if it can be low-fat or fat-free. An 8-ounce carton of milk supplies about 300 milligrams of calcium as well as protein, riboflavin, vitamin D, and other nutrients. If you choose low-fat or fat-free milk, you limit saturated fats, too.
- Consider 100 percent juice if you've come up short on whole fruits during the day. An 8-ounce carton of 100 percent orange juice supplies 75 milligrams of vitamin C, which more than meets your daily need.
- If you choose regular soft drinks, keep the amounts reasonable. In small amounts, they provide fluid, food energy (calories), and enjoyment. However, added sugars in large-size drinks provide a lot of calories: 150 for every 12 ounces of regular soft drink, and 400 calories for a 32-ounce cup. Diet drinks supply essentially no calories—and no nutrients (except water).
- For coffee drinks, consider these options:
    - Order a cappuccino, latte, or coffee or hot tea (chai) with low-fat or fat-free milk—and get the calcium and vitamin D benefits. Milk, rather than cream, is a good calcium booster. Creamers are typically high in solid fats.
    - Opt for sugar-free syrup and unsweetened tea. Sweetened iced tea and many flavored coffee and tea drinks can be high in calories and have added sugars. Add a slice of lemon instead.

- If you don't want to substitute lower-calorie ingredients, order a small, not a large, drink.

See chapter 4, page 81, for more about choosing these drinks as well as energy drinks and fruit drinks.

SMOOTHIES AND SHAKES

Consider a smoothie or shake as part of a meal such as breakfast or as a snack, not simply as a beverage or thirst quencher. With their varied ingredients, they can provide a way to fit in a variety of nutrient-rich foods. They can also provide a hefty amount of calories, depending on the portion size and what they contain. When you order, consider these tips:

- *Smoothie:* Ask about the ingredients before ordering a smoothie. Choose a blend of 100 percent juice, whole fruits (bananas, berries, dates, figs, mangoes, melon, peaches, pineapple, others), and perhaps Greek yogurt, low-fat or fat-free milk, or soymilk, and sources of healthy fats such as chia or flax. Or try grated carrots and chopped kale if available. Skip fruit syrup, which adds sugar but not all the nutrients that whole fruits or 100 percent juice contain. Consider size. A smoothie that's 20 ounces or more may supply more than you need, especially calories.

  Herbal mix-ins? Bee pollen, ginseng, and other herbal mix-ins may cost extra in smoothies yet not offer the benefits you think. *See "Herbals and Other Botanicals" in chapter 10, page 320, to learn about herbals.* Raw wheatgrass? It's a concentrated source of nutrients, but it doesn't offer miracle health benefits. Caution is advised, especially for those with weakened immunity, since wheatgrass can be contaminated with bacteria or mold from the soil or water it's grown in.

- *Shake:* If you can fit the calories into your eating plan, order a small milk shake. In any flavor, it's a good calcium source—if it's made with milk. Be aware: A 10-ounce strawberry shake contains about 320 calories; let it serve double duty, as both beverage and dessert. Super-size shakes, with their 18 ounces, may supply a hefty 575 calories. Another option: Ask to have your shake made with low-fat or fat-free milk or fat-free ice cream if possible.

Eating Ethnic, Eating Global

As a nation of mostly immigrants, the United States always has been home to ethnic cuisines. Interest in foreign-themed restaurants grew in the 1960s with pizza parlors and Japanese tabletop cooking. Mexican and more Asian flavors became common in the restaurant repertoire a decade or so later.

Most popular today? Italian, Mexican, and Chinese (Cantonese) cuisines are so mainstream that they're no longer considered ethnic—unless they feature an authentic regional cuisine. French and fine Italian have been upscale restaurant cuisines for years.

Today, ethnic restaurants offer far more culinary diversity and sophistication. Japanese (sushi), Thai, Vietnamese, Indo-Pakistani, and Middle Eastern restaurants have found popularity. Korean, Peruvian and other Latin American, and some African cuisines are among those getting attention among chefs. Urban areas offer even more ethnic flavors from every corner of the globe, including authentic ethnic, ethnic fusion, and regional ethnic cuisines.

For fun, find restaurant websites in your locale. Now count. How many different ethnic cuisines could you enjoy? To expand the variety in your food choices—and discover new ways to eat for good nutrition—try a new cuisine the next time you eat out!

ITALIAN: MORE THAN PIZZA AND PASTA!

Italian foods are simple, flavorful, and nourishing. Traditional Italian cuisines rely on small meat and fish portions. Grated cheese, especially hard cheese such as Parmesan, flavors many dishes. Pasta, polenta, risotto, and crusty breads deliver complex carbohydrates (starches). Pasta dishes, salads, and soups are among the many ways that vegetables fit in. Herbs deliver flavor: basil, garlic, oregano, parsley, and more.

Particularly with the foods of southern and central Italy, olive oil is the main cooking fat. In many northern Italian dishes, butter is used. High in heart-healthier monounsaturated fatty acids, olive oil has nutritional benefits. Regardless, go easy; any oil is still fat, with the same number of calories per ounce as margarine and butter. *See "The Mediterranean Route to Healthy Eating" in chapter 2, page 52.*

When you eat in an Italian restaurant, consider these tips:

- Know menu lingo. For example, "fritto" (fried) or "crema" (creamed) dishes are higher in fat. "Fresco" means fresh. "Primavera" means "spring style" (lots of veggies); in cooking, it refers to dishes prepared with raw or lightly cooked fresh vegetables. For fewer calories, order primavera dishes, without a creamy sauce made with butter or cream.

- Enjoy crusty Italian bread, focaccia, and bread sticks—a slice or two, but not the whole basket! Bruschetta, a crusty slice of toasted bread with tomatoes and olive oil, is another option. For less fat, go easy on butter or olive oil for dipping, or enjoy the flavor of fresh bread as it is, without a spread. A dipping sauce? Perhaps just balsamic vinegar with little or no olive oil. Some restaurants offer a pureed vegetable spread.

  Garlic bread usually is lathered in high-fat spreads, Parmesan cheese, and garlic before it arrives at your table. Plain bread is a lower-calorie, lower-fat choice.

- Enjoy—and go easy on antipasto. "Antipasto" means "before the pasta." It usually refers to a variety of hot or cold appetizers. In the Italian tradition, they include cheese, olives, marinated

? Have you ever wondered?

. . . what makes pesto sauce high in calories? It's not the basil. In a traditional pesto sauce, it's the olive oil, grated cheese, and pine nuts. Used judiciously, pesto is a flavorful way to enjoy and get the benefits of heart-healthy oils.

. . . how to keep these terms straight—cannoli, cannelloni, and cannellini? Cannoli are deep-fried pastry shells filled with ricotta cheese or whipped cream and perhaps chocolate bits, nuts, and candied fruit. Cannelloni are pasta tubes filled with meat and cheese and topped with sauce. Cannellini are white kidney beans. The memory trick is up to you.

vegetables and fish, and smoked meats (charcuterie). While nutritious, some may be high in calories, fat, and/or sodium—even the olives. Nibbling appetizers, followed by a heavy meal, can add more calories than you expect.

- Order a fresh garden salad, or *insalata*, to round out your meal, with salad dressing, perhaps herbed or balsamic vinegar and olive oil, served on the side. Salads in Italian restaurants often are tossed with a variety of raw vegetables and mixed greens, including arugula, bell peppers, onions, radicchio, and tomatoes. As an entrée, salad with bread makes a nourishing, light meal.

  Caesar salad, typically made with salty anchovies and grated cheese, can be dressed with a creamy dressing or with a healthier option (vinegar and oil). If the dressing is made with raw eggs, restaurants usually use pasteurized eggs for food safety to avoid *Salmonella*. It's worth asking your server.
- Look for traditional bean dishes, soups, and vegetable dishes. White beans, called fagioli, are featured in soups and in pasta and risotto dishes. Minestrone is a hearty, tomato-based soup with beans, pasta, and vegetables. Florentine dishes, usually egg or fish, are prepared with spinach.
- Enjoy pasta—but in a sensibly sized portion. One-half to one cup may be enough, especially if it's a side dish. Order different types of pasta dishes—in shapes, sizes, even flavors (like squid ink)—that you may not find on supermarket shelves. For more fiber, order whole-wheat pasta if available. Fat, and perhaps higher calories, come from the sauces and other ingredients tossed with pasta.
- Pick pasta sauce wisely because that's how calories often add up. Ask for extra vegetables. Look for marinara or other tomato-based sauces that usually have more vegetables and fewer calories and less fat, too, than creamy white sauces such as Alfredo and carbonara do. *See "What's That Sauce?" in this chapter, page 280, for descriptions of these and other sauces.*
- For another pasta option, order ravioli, square "pillows" of pasta filled with cheese, fish, meat, or pureed or minced vegetables. Usually they're served with a sauce. Ask about preparation before you order; as appetizers, ravioli may be fried; go easy.
- Ask how the following dishes are prepared before ordering to manage calories, fat, and sodium.
  - *Polenta*, similar to a cornmeal mush, typically is served (on top or on the side) with sauce, vegetables, and meat; some ingredients may have more fat than others.
  - *Gnocchi*, usually made from potatoes or flour, means dumplings. Sometimes cheese, chopped vegetables or vegetable purees (such as squash or sweet potato), eggs, or whole wheat are mixed into the dough. After they're cooked in boiling water, they may be baked or fried and then served with a flavorful sauce.
  - *Risotto*, typically made from arborio rice, usually is cooked in broth and perhaps butter, often with additional ingredients such as cheese, fish, meat, or vegetables. Be aware that the broth may be salty.
- To watch calories and fat in main-course dishes, choose grilled chicken or fish, perhaps with herbs and lemon. Go easy on veal scaloppini, and chicken or veal parmigiana, which are panfried or sautéed. Parmigiana (Parmesan cheese) entrées such as chicken or eggplant are breaded, so they absorb more fat.

  As an alternative and a lower-fat option, order chicken or veal cacciatore, marsala, or piccata. Cacciatore is a tomato-based sauce; marsala is broth-based and cooked with wine; and piccata is a pan sauce made from pan drippings, lemon juice, and chopped parsley.
- Instead of salt, spark up the flavor with the red pepper flakes in the shaker on the table.
- Dessert? Order Italian ice or sorbet (sorbetto), or fresh berries. Or split desserts with more calories, such as cannoli, gelato (Italian ice cream with a dense texture), panna cotta, or tiramisu.

From the Italian Menu

ENJOY MORE OFTEN:

- Tomato and broth-based soups (minestrone and Italian wedding soup)
- Roasted bell peppers and other vegetables
- Garden salad

- Vinegar-and-oil dressing
- Bread sticks
- Pasta e fagioli
- Pasta with red sauce, such as marinara
- Cacciatore, marsala, and piccata dishes
- Grilled chicken, fish, and shellfish
- Cappuccino (with low-fat or fat-free milk)
- Italian ice and fresh fruit

ENJOY LESS OFTEN:

- Antipasto plates
- Fried croutons
- Buttered garlic bread
- Creamy Italian dressing
- Pasta with butter or white sauce such as Alfredo or carbonara
- Deep-fried calamari
- Double-cheese pizza
- Italian sausage, prosciutto (Italian ham), and pancetta (Italian bacon)
- Parmigiana and scaloppine dishes
- Cannoli and tiramisu

Italian Fare: How It Fits in the Food Groups

Grains

- Bread sticks
- Gnocchi (dumpling)
- Italian bread
- Polenta (cornmeal mush)
- Risotto (rice specialty)
- Spaghetti, linguini, other pasta

Vegetables

- Artichokes
- Beans (fava, garbanzo, white kidney)*
- Bell peppers
- Eggplants
- Grape leaves
- Greens
- Mushrooms
- Tomatoes, tomato sauces
- Spinach

Fruits

- Dates
- Figs
- Grapefruit
- Grapes
- Olives
- Oranges
- Pomegranates
- Dried fruits

Dairy

- Cheese: mozzarella, Parmesan, pecorino, ricotta, others
- Gelato
- Milk
- Yogurt

Protein Foods

- Beef
- Chicken
- Fish (anchovies, tuna, others)
- Beans (fava, garbanzo, white kidney)*
- Nuts (almonds, pine nuts)
- Pork: Italian sausage, pancetta (Italian bacon), prosciutto (Italian ham)
- Shellfish (calamari, clams, shrimp)
- Veal

Oils

- Olive oil
- Oils in nuts, olives, anchovies, tuna, other oily fish

*Beans (legumes) fit into either food group: vegetables or protein foods.

GREEK FOOD: MORE MEDITERRANEAN!

For many, experience with Greek restaurants comes from fast-food courts in malls. Gyros (sandwich), Greek salad, moussaka, rice pilaf, souvlaki, and baklava are best known. As with other cuisines, full-service restaurants offer far more variety.

The qualities enjoyed in other Mediterranean cuisines define Greek cuisine, too. *See "The Mediterranean Route to Healthy Eating" in chapter 2, page 52.* When you eat in a Greek restaurant, consider these tips:

- Enjoy small amounts of baba ghanouj, which is a dip with eggplant and olive oil, and of hummus made with mashed chickpeas (garbanzo beans) and sesame seed paste. Olive oil and the oil in sesame seeds are good sources of unsaturated, healthy oils; however, their calories can add up. For example, one-quarter cup of hummus can add up to 100 calories and 6 grams of mostly unsaturated fats.
- Make a meal of reasonable amounts of a few small plates, or meze, such as beans, cheese, eggplant, fish and shellfish, nuts, olives, whole-grain breads, and other Greek staples.
- Enjoy, but go easy with flavored olive oil for dipping, often served with a basket of pita bread. Although high in monounsaturated fats, low in saturated fats, and cholesterol free, olive oil contains just as many calories as butter or margarine does. Bread can soak up a lot of oil.
- Order Greek salad with dressing on the side. Go easy on higher-fat, higher-sodium ingredients: anchovies, feta cheese, and olives.
- For a creamy dressing on salads or a sauce on pita sandwiches, enjoy tzatziki. It's made with yogurt, cucumbers, and garlic. Sometimes tzatziki is listed on the menu as a salad. Try it as an appetizer dip with pita bread, too, but watch the amount.
- Ordering saganaki as an appetizer? Saganaki is thick kasseri cheese that's fried and sometimes flamed in brandy. For fewer calories and less fat, share.
- For nutritious fast food, order pita bread stuffed with Greek salad, lean meat, tabbouleh, or other ingredients. Tabbouleh is bulgur wheat mixed with chopped tomatoes, lemon juice, mint, olive oil, and parsley. For more fiber, ask for whole-wheat pita.

  For a gyro in a pita, make it just an occasional choice. Gyro meat is typically made from minced lamb, although other types of meat can be used. If the meat doesn't have enough fat, strips of fat are added. The meat is molded so it can be roasted vertically on a rotisserie and then thinly sliced. It's often tucked into pita bread with grilled bell peppers, onions, and tzatziki sauce. Gyro meat tends to be high in calories, sodium, and saturated fats.
- As a main dish, look for broiled and grilled meat, poultry, and fish: perhaps shish kebob, which is meat and vegetables that are skewered and then broiled; souvlaki, which is lamb marinated in lemon juice, olive oil, and herbs, then skewered and grilled; or plaki, fish broiled with tomato sauce and garlic.
- Try dolmades, or stuffed vegetables. Grape leaves are commonly stuffed with ground meat and rice. Other vegetables, such as bell peppers, cabbage leaves, eggplant, and squash, are stuffed with mixtures of ground meat, rice, dried fruit, and pine nuts. Because they're steamed or baked, fat usually isn't added with cooking.
- To boost fiber, order mixed dishes and soups made with beans and peas such as fava beans.
- Enjoy pastitsio, which is a Greek casserole made with pasta, ground beef or lamb, grated cheese, and seasonings; or order moussaka, made with ground lamb or beef, eggplant, and perhaps other vegetables. Both are made with a creamy béchamel sauce, which adds more calories; *see "What's That Sauce?" in this chapter, page 280*. Enjoy a small serving.
- Go easy on rich Greek desserts such as baklava. Made with phyllo and plenty of butter, honey or sugar, and nuts, this sweet, compact pastry is very high in calories, fat, and sugar. It may taste wonderful to you, but a small serving can be enough to satisfy a sweet tooth!

From the Greek Menu

ENJOY MORE OFTEN

- Tabbouleh
- Dolmades
- Tzatziki
- Greek salad
- Fresh fruit
- Pita bread
- Pita sandwiches
- Baba ghanouj and hummus (Middle Eastern but on some Greek menus)
- Broiled, grilled, simmered, and stewed dishes

ENJOY LESS OFTEN

- Deep-fried calamari
- Falafel (Middle Eastern dish on some Greek menus, made of spiced ground chickpeas)
- Gyro (shawarma in Middle Eastern cuisine)
- Moussaka and other creamy casseroles
- Panfried dishes
- Savory pastries such as spanakopita (spinach pie) and tyropita (filled with cheese)
- Baklava and phyllo pastry dishes

MEXICAN FOOD: TACOS, TAMALES, AND MORE

From fast-food to fast-casual to full-service restaurants, Mexican food and its Tex-Mex offspring are among America's favorite ethnic foods. Mexican flavors appear in pizzas, entrée salads, soups, wraps, and stir-fries. Yet, regional Mexican restaurants with authentic dishes, and a more varied menu, are popping up in some urban areas.

The staples of Mexican fare—beans, corn, rice, and tortillas—are great sources of complex carbohydrates, and black or pinto beans (cooked, mashed, or refried) supply protein and fiber as well. Moderate portions of meat and poultry contribute adequate amounts of protein. The combination of beans and rice, or beans and tortillas, supply high-quality protein. Tomatoes, and chiles of all kinds, give distinctive flavors and nourishment to all sorts of dishes, soups, and sauces.

Depending on the choices, Mexican or Tex-Mex cuisine can be high in fat and sodium. In most restaurants, vegetable oil (not lard) is used in cooking (except perhaps in refried beans)—but ask. Saturated fats in Mexican dishes may be lower than in the past but not the calories or the total fat.

As with foods of every culture, enjoy variety; however, go easy. Portions are often large in Mexican restaurants. When you order in a typical Mexican restaurant, consider these tips:

- For chips and salsa (or pico de gallo), enjoy one basket or less with your meal partners. Then have it taken away if you can't resist. Or skip the tortilla chip basket altogether.
- Order a low-fat soup as an appetizer in a cup (not a bowl, unless it's your entrée): gazpacho (chilled tomato soup), black bean soup, posole, or tortilla soup. Or make the bowl the main part of your entrée. Sliced jicama with salsa makes a great vegetable starter.
- Go easy on nachos and cheese, or chile con queso, especially if it's just your appetizer. To cut half the calories and the solid fats from cheese, ask for half a ladle of cheese sauce, or half as much cheese shreds.
- Ask for soft tacos instead of crispy tacos or tostadas, which are deep-fried. Corn tortillas have slightly fewer calories and less fat than flour tortillas—plus corn is whole grain.
- Taco salad? Enjoy, but go easy on the big, crisp tortilla shell it's served in—or the taco chips on top—to trim calories and fat. Instead enjoy warmed, soft tortillas on the side. Dress the salad with salsa.
- Check the menu for salads with nopales, or cactus pads; chayote and jicama, which are starchy vegetables; and tomatillos, a type of green tomatoes.
- Choose mostly baked, grilled, roasted, or stir-fried entrées such as enchiladas or fajitas with vegetables and a soft tortilla.
- Go easy on fried dishes such as chiles relleños, chimichangas, or flautas; ask for less cheese and sour cream. Quesadillas can also be high in fat since they have so much cheese.
- Order guacamole and sour cream on the side to control the amount. For more vitamins A and C and potassium, use a heavy hand with tomato-based salsa instead. Made with tomatoes, onions, chiles, and herbs, it's virtually fat-free, yet bursting with flavor. So are the cilantro, hot sauce, and peppers!
- Although burritos, enchiladas, tacos, and tamales are among the most popular items (especially in Tex-Mex restaurants), Mexican and Southwestern restaurants offer a far broader menu, especially in authentic restaurants. Look for chicken with mole sauce, grilled fish in soft tacos, or tamales. Or try Veracruz-style fish dishes, which are cooked in an herbed tomato sauce, or chile verde, which is pork simmered with vegetables and green chiles.
- A margarita? "On the rocks" has fewer calories than "frozen." Skip the salt or sugar around the rim of the glass to reduce sodium, or added sugars and calories, respectively. Order the smaller size, or order sparkling water with a lime slice or strawberry instead.

Mexican Menu Language

Learn to speak Mexican menu talk. Look for descriptions that offer clues to the calorie content.

Menu clues—perhaps fewer calories and saturated fats:

- Asada (grilled)
- Mole sauce (chile-chocolate sauce)
- Served with salsa verde (green chile sauce)
- Simmered
- Tomato sauce, picante
- Topped with lettuce and tomato
- Veracruz-style (tomato sauce)
- With chiles
- Wrapped in a soft tortilla

Menu clues—perhaps more calories and saturated fats:

- Con queso (with cheese)
- Layered with refried beans (if made with lard or bacon)
- Mixed with chorizo (Mexican sausage)
- Served in a crisp tortilla basket
- Smothered in cheese sauce
- Topped with guacamole and sour cream

From the Mexican Menu

ENJOY MORE OFTEN:

- Black bean soup, gazpacho, and menudo (spicy soup made with tripe and hominy)
- Jicama with fresh lime juice
- Salsa, pico de gallo
- Taco salad (without sour cream; perhaps a few tortilla chips or strips instead of the taco shell)
- Soft tacos, perhaps grilled fish tacos with lime
- Burritos, enchiladas, fajitas, and tamales
- Arroz con pollo (chicken with rice)
- Grilled or roasted meat (carnes asadas), poultry, and fish
- Red beans and rice or Spanish rice
- Black beans, frijoles à la charra, and refried beans (no lard)
- Steamed vegetables
- Fruit for dessert such as guava, mango, and papaya
- Flan (custard) and pudding

ENJOY LESS OFTEN:

- Guacamole or queso (cheese) dip with taco chips
- Sour cream (crema) and extra cheese
- Crispy, fried tortillas (chips or taco shells)
- Chicharrones (fried pork rinds)
- Chalupas, chiles relleños, chimichangas, flautas, and tostadas
- Carnitas (simmered pork or beef, then fried in pork fat)
- Chorizo (pork sausage)
- Honey-sweetened pastry (churros and sopaipillas)
- Fried ice cream

Mexican Fare: How It Fits in the Food Groups

Grains

Posole (soup made with corn kernels)
Rice
Sopa (thick rice soup)
Taco shells
Tortillas, corn and flour

Vegetables

Beans and peas (black, garbanzo, kidney, and red beans; pigeon peas)*
Chayote
Corn
Jicama
Nopales
Peppers
Refried beans*
Salsa
Tomatillos
Tomatoes

Fruits

Avocados
Mangoes
Papayas
Plantains (cooking bananas)
Zapotes (sweet yellow fruit)

Dairy

Café con leche (coffee with steamed milk)
Flan (custard)
Jack cheese
Leche (milk)
Queso blanco (cheese)

Protein Foods

Beans and peas (black, garbanzo, kidney, and red beans; pigeon peas)*
Beef
Chicken
Chorizo (pork sausage)
Eggs
Fish
Refried or mashed beans*
Shrimp

Oils

Corn oil
Vegetable oil

*Beans (legumes) fit into either food group: vegetables or protein foods.

CHINESE FARE: SIMMERED, STEAMED, AND STIR-FRIED

Chinese cuisine, complex and highly developed, contributes significantly to world cuisine. With its focus on vegetables, rice, and noodles, Asian-style cooking has earned its place as a nutritious option when prepared without high-fat cooking methods.

Chinese cuisine represents many cooking styles, ingredients, and flavorings from China's many regions:

- Cantonese cuisine of southeastern China features roasted and grilled meat, steamed dishes, stir-fried dishes, and mild flavors. This cuisine is the most common in the United States, largely influenced by Cantonese immigrants in the mid-1800s.
- Szechuan and Hunan foods tend to be hot and spicy, and perhaps higher in fat.
- Peking cuisine, from northeastern China, is noted for skillful, subtle uses of seasonings.
- Shanghai-style has more fish.
- The term "Mandarin" on menus usually refers to aristocratic cuisine, featuring the finest aspects of all regional cuisines.

Chinese meals emphasize rice or noodles, and vegetables, contributing complex carbohydrates. Vegetables are good sources of fiber, beta carotene (which forms vitamin A), vitamin C, and phytonutrients. Meat, poultry, and fish are served in small portions, often sliced, and cooked with vegetables. Tofu, or soybean curd, is a common, high-protein, low-fat, cholesterol-free ingredient. Many Chinese dishes are roasted, simmered, steamed, or stir-fried in a wok.

Chinese cuisines can be high in fat and sodium. Deep-fat frying is a common cooking technique. Sometimes foods are stir-fried in large amounts of oil. For those who are sodium sensitive, flavoring sauces such as soy sauce, black bean sauce, Hoisin sauce, and oyster sauce can be high in sodium. Monosodium glutamate (MSG), used in many Chinese dishes, contributes sodium, too, but about one-third the amount in table salt. *See "MSG—Another Flavor Enhancer" in chapter 8, page 240.* Plum sauce and sweet-and-sour sauces are high in added sugars.

Calcium-rich foods are limited on Chinese menus since milk, cheese, and yogurt aren't part of the traditional cuisines. Most calcium comes from fish with edible bones and from vegetables such as bok choy, broccoli, and greens, although the amount of calcium per half-cup portion is much lower than in eight ounces of milk. Whether you eat in or carry out from a Chinese restaurant, consider these tips:

- Enjoy flavorful soup as a starter or a main dish. Many are made with clear broth and small amounts of meat and vegetables. Made by cooking eggs in the broth, egg drop soup and hot-and-sour soup are good choices; however, hot-and-sour soup is high in sodium.
- Go easy on fried appetizers. Crab rangoon, fried wontons, and many egg rolls are deep-fried. As an option, order steamed appetizers instead: dumplings, egg rolls, spring rolls, or wontons.
- Enjoy the vegetable variety in Chinese dishes—ask for more, even if you need to pay a little more. Besides familiar bean sprouts, bell peppers, broccoli, cabbage, carrots, chile peppers, green onions, and mushrooms, Chinese dishes feature bamboo shoots, bok choy, lily pods, napa cabbage, snow peas, and other vegetables. Flip to the vegetarian section of the menu for dishes featuring beans (legumes) and tofu. As an aside, being vegetarian doesn't make these Chinese dishes lower in calories. Many meatless dishes are deep-fried.
- For less fat, look for braised, roasted, simmered, steamed, and stir-fried dishes. Ask that stir-fried dishes be cooked in just a small amount of oil. Some Chinese restaurants offer steamed dishes with your choice of protein food (chicken, shrimp, tofu) mixed with vegetables and with sauce on the side. Ask for steamed vegetables without any added oil.
- Order plain rice and noodles rather than fried versions. If available, order brown rice or whole-grain noodles for more fiber. Plain rice and noodles usually are lower in sodium than fried options, which are flavored with soy sauce. Crispy skin on poultry dishes such as Peking duck is high in fat.
- Be aware that the meat, poultry, or fish in sweet-and-sour dishes is typically breaded and deep-fat fried. Instead, ask for grilled or roasted meat with sweet-and-sour sauce to cut down on fat.
- For less sodium, ask for a light touch with MSG and high-sodium sauces such as bean and oyster sauces. You might ask for light or reduced-sodium soy sauce to add yourself. Or instead, choose dishes with hoisin sauce that have somewhat less sodium, or dishes with hot-mustard, sweet-and-sour, plum, or duck sauces, which have even less sodium. Ask for these sauces on the side instead so you control the amount.
- For a small bite, enjoy dim sum. Translated as "little heart," these small portions include steamed dumplings and steamed spring rolls. Go easy on fried dim sum. An array of dim sum is often sold on a cart or tray by a server, who passes your table with one dish after another. Result: It's easy to over order and overeat!
- Enjoy your fortune cookie—and the fortune inside! A single cookie has just 15 calories and 0 grams of fat. Typically, Chinese meals don't give much attention to sweet desserts. Usually, you can have almond cookies, fresh fruit, or ice cream.

- Control the urge to overeat. In Chinese restaurants, portions are often quite ample. For a sit-down meal, order the amount you need, not necessarily the meal "special" with several courses. Order fewer dishes than those you dine with if food is served family style. Ask for half a portion if you can. Plan to share a dish; perhaps order two or three dishes to serve four people. Or take leftovers home. Skip popular Chinese buffets, or go easy.
- Use chopsticks, especially if that helps you eat slower so you enjoy your meal more and perhaps eat less.

From the Chinese Menu

ENJOY MORE OFTEN:

- Egg drop, hot-and-sour, and wonton soups
- Steamed spring rolls
- Chicken, scallops, or shrimp with vegetables
- Whole steamed fish
- Steamed and simmered dishes
- Stir-fried dishes (with a small amount of oil)
- Steamed rice (preferably brown rice)
- Steamed dumplings and other dim sum
- Soft noodles
- Tofu
- Fortune cookies

ENJOY LESS OFTEN:

- Fried wontons
- Fried egg rolls or spring rolls
- Peking duck
- Fried fish with lobster sauce
- Fried rice
- Fried dim sum
- Fried noodles
- Fried "crispy" dishes, such as sweet-and sour dishes with breaded, deep-fried ingredients

THAI AND VIETNAMESE CUISINE: MORE ASIAN!

For restaurant patrons who enjoy an Asian kitchen, "spicy hot" defines many Thai dishes. Although similar to Thai dishes, Vietnamese dishes are not known for spiciness. Both cuisines are noted for plenty of vegetables, fruits, rice, and noodles and for stir-frying. The unique flavors come from contrasting seasonings, unique herbs and spices, and fresh ingredients.

Rice is a staple that's simply cooked or enjoyed as an ingredient in rice noodles, rice flour, and rice-paper wrappers. Another common grain-based ingredient is wheat-flour noodles.

Vegetables and fruits add flavor, nutrients, and interest to Thai salads, soups, and mixed dishes. Look for dishes made with bamboo shoots, banana blossoms, bananas, bitter melons, green mangoes, green papaya, pummelos, or straw mushrooms as well as bean sprouts, cucumbers, eggplant, green peppers, or snow peas. For Asian cuisine, Thai restaurants are unique because salads may be cooked.

In mixed dishes, portions of protein foods—meat, poultry, and fish—are typically reasonable. Look for all kinds of seafood, including mussels, shrimp, and scallops as well as beef, pork, chicken, and duck. Meatless dishes may feature egg or tofu, too, or combinations with noodles or rice, and vegetables.

The unique flavors in Thai cooking? Menu descriptions may identify a unique variety of herbs native to Thailand that add flavor but no sodium: for example, coriander (cilantro), galangal, ginger, kaffir lime leaves (citrus leaf), lemongrass, mint, and Thai basil. Look for spices in curry dishes. Peanuts and cashews, common to Thai cooking, may add texture and flavor as well as protein. The distinctive flavors of Thai curries come from a blend of nam pla (Thai fish sauce) combined with chiles, garlic, and seasonings such as coriander (cilantro), cumin, and turmeric in Indian-type curries, or gingerroot, lemon grass, and shrimp paste.

Small, green or red bird's eye chiles (prik kii noo suan) are viciously hot and distinctively Thai, although they aren't the only chiles used in Thai cooking. Check the menu for clues to the "heat." If you can't take the heat, ask for "toned-down Thai." Many dishes can be prepared to suit your taste.

Consider the nutritional bounty in these cuisines—especially because it can deliver fewer calories, less fat and sodium, and great flavor! Most dishes are cooked to order in a Thai or Vietnamese restaurant, so you have more control over the ingredients. When you order, consider these tips:

- If you enjoy Thai food often, go easy on soups, curries, desserts, and other dishes made with a Thai staple: coconut milk or cream. The fat in regular coconut milk is highly saturated and high in calories. (Vietnamese cuisine uses more broth and fewer coconut-based sauces.)
- Satay (grilled chicken or meat skewers)? It's usually marinated in curried coconut milk and served with a dipping sauce of peanuts and coconut milk. To control calories and fat, cut back on the peanut dipping sauce.
- Know that some starters are fried, such as egg rolls and crab rangoon. Choose steamed spring rolls with fresh ingredients, and perhaps cooked crab or shrimp, in rice-paper wrappers.

Popular Chinese Fare: How It Fits in the Food Groups

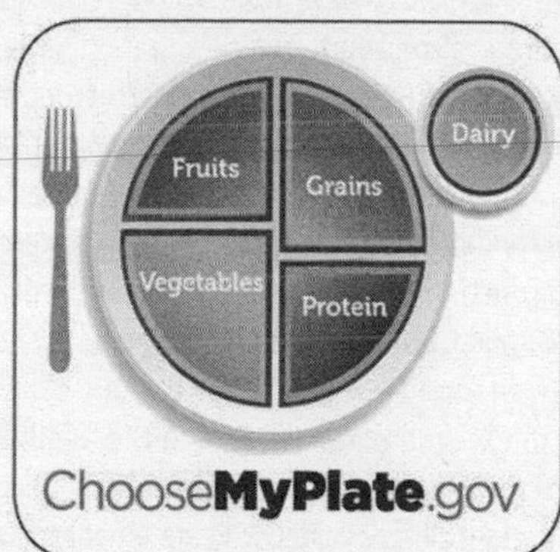

Grains
- Dumplings (pot stickers, others)
- Fortune cookies
- Noodles
- Rice
- Rice congee (rice soup)
- Rice noodles, rice sticks
- Wonton or egg roll wrappers

Vegetables
- Asparagus
- Baby corn
- Bamboo shoots
- Bean sprouts
- Bell peppers
- Bok choy
- Broccoli
- Carrots
- Chives
- Long beans
- Mushrooms (straw, wood ear, others)
- Napa cabbage
- Pea pods
- Water chestnuts

Fruits
- Guavas
- Kumquats
- Lychees
- Oranges, mandarin oranges
- Pineapples
- Persimmons
- Pummelos (large citrus fruit)

Dairy
- Milk
- Soy beverage (calcium fortified)
- Soy cheese (calcium fortified)

Protein Foods
- Beef
- Cashews
- Chicken
- Eggs
- Fish
- Mung beans
- Pork
- Shellfish (crab, lobster, octopus, scallops, shrimp)
- Tofu

Oils
- Healthy oils from cashews, oily fish
- Peanut oil
- Sesame oil
- Vegetable (soybean) oil

- Look for braised, grilled, sautéed, steamed, and stir-fried dishes on the menu. Limit deep-fried foods and heavy sauces made with coconut milk.
- Ask about the oil the kitchen uses. If lard or coconut oil, ask for sautéed and stir-fried dishes cooked in vegetable oil instead for less saturated fats. Curry dishes and some soups are typically made with coconut milk.
- Enjoy plain rice—long-grained jasmine rice with its perfumelike flavor; or sticky, plump rice—or try chopped, cooked vegetables, meat, poultry, or fish and fresh herbs, wrapped in moistened rice paper. Another option: translucent rice noodles, cooked and tossed in salads and stir-fries.
- Ask for just a light touch with nam pla, a high-sodium sauce, and with soy sauce. Or see if the kitchen can use light (low-sodium) soy sauce instead.
- Enjoy the popular pad Thai (with noodles, eggs, green onions, peanuts, sprouts, and perhaps chicken or tofu). Because pad Thai can be high in fat and sodium, depending on preparation and portion size, ask for a smaller portion, less soy sauce, less cooking oil, and more vegetables.
- Build a banh mi sandwich, a Vietnamese specialty made with a French baguette and traditional ingredients such as cucumber, pickled carrots and daikon, cilantro, tofu, and lean meat; go easy on pork sausages or belly. It may also be offered for breakfast, made with scrambled or fried eggs, and perhaps onions and soy sauce.
- To ease up on sodium, limit dishes made with salty condiments such as dried shrimp, fish paste, and salty eggs. Be aware that many Asian sauces are often seasoned with MSG, which contains

sodium, too; *see "MSG: Another Flavor Enhancer" in chapter 8, page 240.*

- In all kinds of dishes, ask for more vegetables.

If you pick a Vietnamese restaurant, the cuisine will be similar to Thai and based on rice, noodles, similar vegetables, meat, and fish. Order with the same mind-set. Vietnamese cuisine also is flavored with fish sauce but contains more fresh coriander root and leaf (cilantro), and less garlic and chile pepper.

From the Thai and Vietnamese Menu

ENJOY MORE OFTEN:

- Broth-based soups such as Thai tom yum koong, made with shrimp, coriander, ginger, lemongrass, and other herbs and spices; or pho, an aromatic Vietnamese broth-based noodle soup
- Spring rolls in moistened rice paper (also called summer rolls)
- Banh mi sandwich
- Stir-fried noodle dishes such as pad Thai (fat and calorie content varies depending on the preparation method)
- Sautéed or stir-fried vegetables with meat, poultry, fish, or tofu
- Broiled or steamed dishes
- Steamed rice, sweet sticky rice, brown rice
- Tropical fruits such as lychees, and fruit juices
- Grilled or charbroiled meat, poultry, or fish
- Fruit ice

ENJOY LESS OFTEN:

- Soups made with coconut milk such as tom ka gai
- Fried spring rolls
- Peanut–coconut milk sauce
- Fried shrimp toast
- Dishes (including curries) made with coconut milk
- Deep-fried eggplant or tofu
- Dishes with deep-fried duck, fish, or meat
- Fatty short ribs
- Fried rice and fried noodles
- Fried bananas
- Desserts made with coconut milk such as coconut pudding or custard

JAPANESE CUISINE: SUSHI AND MORE

Interest in Japanese-style restaurants started with the Japanese (teppanyaki) steakhouse. There, Americans experienced the flair of tabletop, stir-fry cooking, seated around the grill. In either full-service or fast-food restaurants, today's Japanese menus offer more variety—and plenty of sushi!

With its use of rice, noodles, tofu, vegetables, fish, and small meat portions as staples, and its limited use of oils, Japanese cooking is noted for being low in fat. Glazes and sauces typically are made with broth, rice vinegar, sake (rice wine), and soy sauce. While some foods are fried, more common cooking methods are low in fat, such as braising, broiling, grilling, simmering, and steaming. Some sauces and dishes have a touch of sugar added.

Rice, noodles, and vegetables contribute complex carbohydrates, and vegetables supply fiber, beta carotene, and vitamin C. Meat, poultry, fish, tofu, and other soy foods are high-protein ingredients usually served in moderate-size portions. Calcium-rich foods are limited. For those trying to reduce sodium, high-sodium flavorings are a nutrition concern.

To the Japanese cook, artistry and balance rank as high as nourishment in a traditional meal. Edible garnishes of ginger or vegetables, seaweed carefully wrapped around raw fish and rice, and an artful arrangement of foods on a plate are among the aesthetic touches that make Japanese food beautiful and harmonious. Enjoyment of food has always been an important dietary guideline in the Japanese diet!

When you eat in a Japanese restaurant, consider these tips:

- Know that tempura is a popular battered, fried dish. Agemono and katsu dishes also are breaded in panko (Japanese bread crumbs) and fried. To control calories and fat, go easy on fried dishes, but don't avoid them altogether or you'll miss some outstanding taste treats! Just eat small portions, and balance these foods with other, lower-calorie and lower-fat choices.
- Look for menu terms that suggest less fat, such as nimono (simmered), mushimono (steamed), yaki (broiled), and yaki-mono (grilled). Two examples for meat, poultry, or fish: yakitori, which is skewered and then broiled or grilled; and teriyaki, which is marinated in soy sauce and mirin (rice wine) and then grilled.
- Looking for another low-fat choice? Try sashimi (raw fish) or sushi (vinegared, sweetened rice prepared with seaweed, raw fish, and/or vegetables). For less sodium, go easy on the soy sauce for dipping. *See "Is Raw Seafood Safe to Eat?" in chapter 7, page 209, for choosing a sushi restaurant and for advice to those who need to avoid raw fish.*
- As another bowl meal, try domburi, or rice covered with meat, poultry, or vegetables, and perhaps egg and soy sauce.
- For less sodium, go easy on sauces such as soy sauce, miso sauce, or teriyaki sauce, as well as broth and pickled vegetables. A single tablespoon of regular soy sauce can add up to about 1,000 milligrams of sodium! The trendy ponzu sauce, often used as a dipping sauce, is made with soy sauce, rice vinegar or lemon juice, mirin or sake, kombu (seaweed), and dried fish flakes.

  Many dishes, such as soups, noodle dishes, and stir-fried dishes, also are flavored with soy sauce; ask for low-sodium soy sauce. Or instead, ask for dishes prepared without soy sauce—for example, shabu shabu, steamed seafood, or foods that aren't marinated; you can dip them in a low-sodium soy sauce if you choose.

  A little shredded or mashed green wasabi adds flavor but no sodium. Beware: The very strong, hot-horseradish taste of a little wasabi goes a long way for flavor.

- For more vegetables, order salad (aemono or sunomono) as a side dish, perhaps made with greens, seaweed, or tofu. Try edamame (fresh, steamed soybeans, often in the pod). For less sodium, ask for a lemon slice to squeeze on top, rather than miso dressing. Miso, a common flavoring in Japanese cooking, is derived from fermented soybean paste and is high in sodium.
- Enjoy Japanese noodles—rice noodles and bean thread noodles, soba (buckwheat noodles), and udon (wheat noodles). Soba noodles are higher in fiber than udon noodles. Noodles often are served with cooked dishes such as sukiyaki or in soups.
- Order fresh fruit for dessert. Japanese menus typically don't offer rich pastries.
- Take time to enjoy the aesthetics of a Japanese meal. Learn to use chopsticks. They may slow your eating, and that can be a good part of the dining experience!

From the Japanese Menu

ENJOY MORE OFTEN:

- Edamame
- Clear soups such as miso and suimono
- Sashimi and sushi
- Dumplings such as gyoza and shumai
- Salad
- Stir-fried dishes such as sukiyaki
- Simmered dishes such as shabu shabu
- Grilled dishes such as yakitori
- Stir-fried tempeh and tofu
- Steamed rice (brown rice for more fiber)
- Noodles and broth
- Steamed vegetables, including bok choy, mushrooms, seaweed, and yams
- Green tea

ENJOY LESS OFTEN:

- Deep-fried dishes such as tempura
- Breaded and fried dishes such as katsu and tonkatsu
- Fried rice
- Fried tofu (bean curd)

Passport to Flavor: More Ethnic Cuisines

When you eat out, try these cuisines for variety and adventure! Order menu items with fewer calories if you eat out often. If you prefer a higher-calorie food, share or have smaller portions.

Enjoy More Often	Enjoy Less Often
Caribbean	
Beans and rice dishes	Fried chicken and fish
Chicken and rice	Fried plantains
Grilled meat and chicken (jerk chicken or goat)	Fritters (conch fritters)
Vegetable stews (callaloo, tubers)	
Tropical fruit	
German	
Potato salad with a sweet-sour dressing	Breaded and fried meat and poultry (schnitzel)
Cooked cabbage	Creamy soups
Dumplings	Noodle and cheese dishes
Roast pork (lean) with gravy on the side	Sausages
	Thick, creamy gravy

(continued)

Passport to Flavor: More Ethnic Cuisines *(continued)*

Enjoy More Often	Enjoy Less Often
Cuban	
Black beans (frijoles negros)	Breaded, fried rolls with creamed ham (croquetas)
Black beans and rice (Moros y Cristianos)	Caramel-flavored custard (flan and dulce de leche)
Ground lean beef, vegetables, and spices (picadillo)	Chorizo (sausage)
Rice with chicken (arroz con pollo)	Fried dough ball (buñuelo)
Shredded beef simmered in tomato sauce (ropa vieja)	Fried empanadas
	Pasteles (flaky turnovers filled with cheese, meat, or sweets)
	Roast pork from the whole pig (lechón asado)
	Sweet fried plantains (tostones)
French	
Broth-based fish soup (bouillabaisse)	Cheese
Demi-glace, Bordelaise, and other wine sauces	Cream soups
Poached fruit	Soups with gratinée (cheese)
Provençal dishes (with tomatoes)	Creamy sauces
Roasted or braised meat, poultry, and fish	Croissants
Salad greens with vinaigrette	French fries (pommes frites) and au gratin potatoes
Steamed or sautéed vegetables	Liver pâté
Vegetable casserole (ratatouille)	Rich desserts (mousse and Napoleon)
Indo-Pakistani	
Baked roti (bread, such as naan) and chapati	Dishes, such as curry dishes, made with coconut milk, coconut oil, or cream
Chicken or beef tikka (roasted with mild spices)	Fried bread (pakora, paratha, poori)
Dishes prepared with yogurt	Fried dishes (samosa, shami)
Fragrant steamed rice	Ghee (clarified butter)
Lassi (mango-yogurt smoothie)	Korma (meat dish with rich cream sauce)
Lentil dishes and curries with vegetable or lentil sauce	Sauced rice dishes
Papadum (lentil wafers)	
Rice pilaf with peas	
Roasted chicken or fish dishes with vegetable sauces	
Grilled kabobs	
Tandoori chicken or fish (baked by direct heat in a brick oven)	

Passport to Flavor: More Ethnic Cuisines *(continued)*

Enjoy More Often	Enjoy Less Often
Korean	
Bibimbap (rice topped with sautéed vegetables, meat, or chicken, perhaps an egg and pepper-soy sauce or fermented soybean paste)	Barbecued dishes (bulgogi) if sauce is high in sugar ingredients
Buckwheat noodle dishes (myon)	Dumplings
Parboiled vegetables (sukchae)	Kimchi (salted, fermented vegetables)
Stir-fried rice noodles with stir-fried vegetables (chopchae) if made with little oil	Scallion pancakes
Middle Eastern	
Bean and bulgur salad	Baba ghanouj
Cold yogurt soup	Fried chickpea cakes (falafel)
Couscous	Fried meat-bulgur patties (kibbeh)
Dukkah, a condiment of nuts (usually hazelnuts), herbs, and spices	Rich pastries, often with honey (baklava)
Fatoosh (bread salad)	Shawarma
Lamb and vegetable stew	
Rice and lentil/bean dishes	
Tzatziki and hummus	
Russian	
Boiled or baked dumplings (pelmeni)	Blini
Broiled meat skewers (shaslyk)	Dishes made with sour-cream gravy (stroganoff)
Kasha	Fried dumplings
Meat-stuffed cabbage	Salads with mayonnaise or sour cream
Whole-grain breads	Soups made with cream or sour cream (borscht)

To be more adventuresome with new ingredients, new flavors, new cuisines, and new ways to fit in nutrient-rich foods, look for the ethnic restaurants that also are getting a good deal of attention: Ethiopian, Malaysian, North African (Moroccan), Peruvian, and Spanish. Or try regional American food, perhaps Cajun, California-style, Low Country, New England, or Southwest cuisine—or Native American dishes.

Traveler Alert: Eating on the Road

Does eating as you travel challenge your waistline and good nutrition sense? In addition to good nutrition, be aware of food and water safety, and take steps to avoid dehydration when you travel.

FARE AT 35,000 FEET

Airline food service? That depends on the carrier, where you sit on the plane (first class or not), and the length and time of your flight. As airlines cut back to control costs, food service on most domestic flights has become just a beverage and a pack of crackers, cookies, pretzels, or peanuts—or no food at all. On some airlines, you can opt to buy a sandwich or snack in-flight. In the end, don't count on an airline meal except for long (usually international) flights.

For food and beverages to eat and drink in flight or at the airport; use the guidelines *addressed earlier in this chapter.* In recent years, food at many airport terminals has become comparable to restaurant food elsewhere, even some local fare and local brews. You may even find an aeroponic garden in an airport restaurant!

What about food carried with you? Follow Transportation Security Administration (TSA) rules: www.tsa.gov/travel/security-screening/prohibited-items. The TSA allows frozen liquid items through the checkpoint if frozen solid at screening. If partially melted, slushy, or having any liquid at the bottom of the container, they must meet the 3-1-1 liquids rule.

Food in Flight

For in-flight meals and snacks, consider this:

- If you or someone you're traveling with has a peanut allergy, advise the airline ahead. In that case, a different dry snack may be served to all passengers in-flight.
- Want a special meal? That may be possible on major carriers on a long international flight—if you or your travel agent make a request through the airline at least twenty-four hours before your flight.
- If you take food on board, make portable, safe choices. If you travel with small children, it's a good idea to bring simple snacks; if brought from home, make sure they pass TSA regulations. Dried fruit such as an apple, apricots, or a banana, raw vegetables, packaged crackers and sliced cheese, bagels, muffins, pretzels, and protein bars travel well.

  For safety's sake, don't keep a sandwich with meat or another perishable food purchased at the airport for too long at cabin temperature—no more than two hours. That includes transit time from your kitchen if the food comes from home.
- If you buy airport food to take on board or eat as you wait, or if you buy a meal or snack on board, try to order sensibly—*as noted above*—even if choices are limited.

Drinks in Flight

For in-flight beverages, consider this:

- Especially on a long trip, drink plenty of liquids before, during, and after flying—eight ounces every hour of your flight—even if you aren't thirsty. With the low humidity and recirculating air in the pressurized cabin, airline travel can be dehydrating because you lose body fluids through evaporation on your skin. Dehydration causes fatigue. Good beverage choices: water, club soda, and 100 percent fruit juice. Pack an empty water bottle in your carry-on bag to fill, or buy bottled water, after passing through security.
- When the beverage cart rolls by, consider calories as well as overall nutrition. Instead of regular soda, ask for water, 100 percent fruit juice, tomato juice, or low-fat milk (if available). That said, it's okay to say "no" to the beverage cart. You don't need to take a snack or soda just because it's offered.
- Want to relax or sleep on the flight? If you're sensitive to caffeine, avoid caffeinated beverages: coffee, tea, and colas. For some people, too much caffeine can promote sleeplessness, anxiety, and overstimulation, especially for those anxious about flying.
- If you drink alcoholic beverages, go easy—even if you're in a class of service where drinks are usually free. Stop after one or two drinks. On a long flight, wine or cocktails may not help you sleep or relax. Instead, larger amounts may have the opposite effect, making you more restless.

Overcoming Jet Lag

Best advice: Organize ahead so you're well rested and relaxed before traveling. Avoid skipping meals as you rush to pack. On your trip, stick to healthy eating.

Being dehydrated promotes jet lag. To minimize the effects, drink a glass of water or 100 percent juice before your flight and then again each hour in-flight. Alcoholic beverages also can promote dehydration and may increase jet lag. Go easy if you drink them. During long flights, get up, stretch, and walk around the cabin. Try to sleep rather than spending all your flight time on the entertainment program.

On the ground, keep drinking fluids. After a long flight, drink extra fluids for several days. Immediately adjust your meals and sleep to the new time if you've traveled over several time zones. If your body clock skips from late afternoon to early morning and you lose the night (as you often do with overseas flights), take a short nap when you arrive, and then continue with a normal day—lunch, dinner, and an early evening. If you leave in the morning and arrive at night, have dinner and go to bed—even if your body clock says it's midday.

No evidence shows that anti–jet lag formulas or diets are effective. You may have heard anti–jet lag claims about a dietary supplement called melatonin. This claim may be partially true; the amount of melatonin that may promote sleep is far less than the amount in over-the-counter products. *See chapter 10, page 331, for more information on melatonin and other supplements.*

TRAVEL FARE—ON THE GROUND

For business travelers and leisure travelers alike, calories from eating out can add up, especially when food is a main event of the trip. Overdoing is all too easy when you eat most meals out and if portions are big, desserts are rich, and the menus are tantalizing. If you aren't watchful, excess calories can add up to extra body fat!

The advice: Be a wise restaurant patron, *as addressed earlier in this chapter.* Take advantage of the mini-fridge and microwave oven if available.

? Have you ever wondered?

. . . how to enjoy the floating feast on a cruise ship without overeating—or feeling guilty? Food is a wonderful part of the cruise experience, but because it's available 24/7, it's easy to eat and drink more than you realize.

- Take advantage of the built-in variety on cruise ship menus. Many of today's cruise ships offer lighter or "spa" fare. Children's areas may be peanut-free or nut-free zones.
- If you can't resist the urge to order another course, ask for a small tasting portion. Having prepaid meals isn't a reason to over order.
- If you stay up to enjoy late-night food, balance it by going easy at other meals.
- Don't feel forced to buy a beverage package or to order a beverage when you sit down to an evening show or sit around the pool.
- If you have a special food need, advise the booking agent when you make your reservation. Confirm your request again on embarkation and with your server.
- If a cooking class or ship's galley tour is offered, join in!
- Use the ship's outer deck as a running or walking track, or take advantage of the ship's fitness center, pool, or workout classes so you can enjoy and indulge a little more.

Some of these cautionary tips also apply to vacationing at all-inclusive resorts.

Problem with seasickness? Skipping food entirely isn't the answer. Instead, ask the guest services desk for motion-sickness medication; eat something light, perhaps crackers, to keep something in your stomach.

To help control infectious disease, always use hand sanitizers available to passengers near dining areas and throughout the ship. If you do get sick, tell a crew member right away.

Whether you're a leisure or business traveler, make time to move: explore museums, historic spots, parks, and shops on foot. Use fitness centers and athletic facilities at the hotel or a local park. Get up early enough for a walk or a workout. Too often, people complain that travel upsets their workout routine. *See "On the Road? Keep Moving" in chapter 21, page 601, for tips on fitting physical activity into your travel schedule.*

Business Travelers: Alert

For tips for business travel, consider this:

- On an expense account? Avoid the urge to overeat just because you don't pay the bill personally. Promising to cut down when you get home may not be enough to keep trim, especially if you travel frequently.
- When work continues through the cocktail hour or a meal, be mindful of your food and drinks and your body's hunger and satiety signals as well as your business issues. A second round of drinks or another basket of chips can appear without much notice.

  Drinking is often part of the social side of business travel or is viewed by travelers as a way to relax. The calories in a cocktail or two, and perhaps wine with dinner, add up fast. Depending on the size, a single drink can supply 10 percent or more of your day's calorie needs! A drink or two also may increase your appetite and lessen your personal discipline at the table. Be careful, too, that cocktails and salty snacks don't replace a nourishing meal.

Breakfast on the Road

A 2-egg omelet, 3 strips of bacon, ½ cup of hash browns, 1 slice of toast with 2 teaspoons of butter or margarine, ¾ cup of fruit juice, and coffee: This hearty restaurant breakfast can total up to 685 calories and 40 fat grams. Consider the calories if you travel a lot and this kind of breakfast is your daily fare!

Continental breakfast (bread, juice, and coffee)? Add a protein food, such as a hard-cooked egg or yogurt, for more staying power. For breads with less fat, ask for a bagel, an English muffin, or toast (perhaps whole-wheat or rye), and ask for jam, butter, or margarine on the side. Skip croissants, doughnuts, sweet rolls, and other pastries to cut down on calories, saturated fats, and added sugars.

For a quick, yet nutritious start (typical at moderately priced hotel chains), choose a nourishing breakfast with fewer calories:

- Fresh fruit, small bagel with peanut butter, perhaps a hard-cooked egg, and low-fat or fat-free milk
- Ready-to-eat dry cereal (preferably low in added sugars), grits or oatmeal (made with low-fat or fat-free milk), fresh or dried fruit, a handful of nuts, and coffee or tea
- Low-fat yogurt, whole-wheat English muffin with spread served on the side, fruit juice or fresh fruit, and coffee or tea

Traveling Abroad? Eating for Safety's Sake

In some parts of the world food safety, particularly in places that are less developed, is a greater public health issues issue than in the United States. In those places, be cautious.

Skip these foods . . .	**Eat these foods instead . . .**
Salads, fruit with the peel on, and raw vegetables	Fruit peeled by you and cooked vegetables (in uncertain areas)
Raw, rare, or partly cooked meat, poultry, and fish	Well-cooked meat, poultry, and fish
Softly scrambled or sunny-side-up eggs	Well-cooked scrambled or hard-cooked eggs
Unpasteurized milk	Canned or ultrapasteurized (UHT) boxed milk, and pasteurized milk from a large commercial dairy (ask to be sure)
Juice or juice drink with added "local" water	Canned or boxed juice or juice drink from a commercial processor (ask to be sure)
Cheese made from unpasteurized milk	Cheese made from pasteurized milk
Food and drinks sold by street vendors	Only commercially bottled drinks and commercially packaged foods from vendors
Local water and ice made with local water	Commercially bottled water and drinks without ice

If you have more time, or if you choose a sit-down restaurant:

- Whole-wheat pancakes or waffles topped with fruit and hot cocoa or a latte made with milk
- One poached or scrambled egg, whole-wheat toast with jam, half a grapefruit, and fat-free milk
- Vegetable omelet. Consider a side of Canadian bacon, whole-wheat toast, 100 percent fruit juice, and a latte.

Allow time for breakfast. An early morning meal is, after all, a smart way to start an effective work or vacation day. A light breakfast service may be part of the room rate. Or for room service, order the night before.

See "Break-FAST Options" in this chapter, page 291, for more breakfast advice.

Road Trips, Carried Food

If your job, vacation, or weekend outings take you on a road, train, or bus trip, brown-bag it or fill a cooler. This way, you don't need to rely on the limited options in vending machines, convenience stores, or snack bars.

- Pack nonperishables, such as:
  - Single-portion beverages: bottled water, boxed low-fat or fat-free milk, canned or boxed 100 percent fruit juice, and canned tomato juice
  - Crackers, dried fruit, nuts, peanut butter, plain popcorn, pretzels, raisins, single-serving cans of tuna or fruit, small boxes of ready-to-eat cereal, and snack bars
  - Packages of instant oatmeal and perhaps dry milk powder to make a quick, easy, hot breakfast in your hotel room
- Stock an insulated cooler with perishables: cheese, deli sandwiches, salad, and yogurt, among others. Keep fresh fruit and raw vegetables in the cooler, too, to keep them crisp. *See "How to Transport Food Safely" in chapter 7, page 217, for more tips.*
- Fill sealable plastic bags with vegetable finger foods: raw vegetables (bell pepper rings, broccoli and cauliflower florets, carrot and jicama sticks, snow peas, and zucchini slices). Take seasonal fruit. Besides taking the edge off hunger, fruit can be a thirst quencher.
- Bring a refillable water bottle. It costs less to refill than to buy bottled water, and it's a healthy drink choice.
- When you're hungry, stop to eat if you're driving. Get out of the car, stretch, and take a short walk. You'll enjoy your meal more—and feel more relaxed as you continue driving.
- To help prevent constipation—a frequent complaint on long-distance road trips—stop every hour or two for a brisk walk and drink of water.

FOOD SAFETY IN FARAWAY PLACES

From cozy cafés, open-air markets, and food stalls to rice paddies, tropical fruit plantations, and fishermen hauling in their nets, new foods and flavors, as well as local farming and food markets, offer unique cultural experiences for adventurous travelers. Americans' growing enjoyment of ethnic foods comes in part from their travel experiences, including agritourism and culinary travel.

Today, more business and pleasure travelers (adults and youths) venture to places where sanitation standards are less strict than in the United States. In some environments, bacteria, parasites, and viruses can transfer to food from poor sanitation or agricultural practices.

To help control the spread of disease, immigration forms required to enter the United States ask if the traveler has visited a farm. Most food items, including meat and fresh produce, are not allowed into the United States (most duty free is allowable). Travelers and their baggage also go through an agricultural inspection.

An Ounce of Pre-Travel Precaution

No matter what you call it—Montezuma's Revenge, Delhi belly, turista, or something else—travelers' diarrhea most often is caused by contaminated food and/or water. Typically, it lasts no more than three to four days, and is rarely serious or life-threatening. However, it's enough to upset or even ruin an otherwise wonderful vacation—and certainly puts a business trip into a tailspin.

With this in mind, prepare before you travel abroad. Research your destination. Consider these tips:

- Talk with your doctor at home; take recommended precautionary medication with you, including prescription and over-the-counter diarrhea medication.
- If you will travel to developing or rural areas, ask your doctor and county health department about immunizations and preventive medication suggested for your destination. The Centers for Disease Control and Prevention (CDC) (wwwnc.cdc.gov/travel) provides food, water, and immunization alerts and advice for travelers throughout the world. The CDC provides additional advice for those on mission or disaster-relief trips. Another resource to help you prepare for international travel: www.cdcfoundation.org/businesspulse.

  Even if you will stay with friends and relatives abroad, take pre-travel preventive care. In some places, hotels with International standards may have more public health protection than a home-stay can offer.

  For an infant, child, or someone at high risk (*see "Who's at High Risk? Select Safer Alternatives" in chapter 7, page 222*) who travels, immunizations generally are a must, as is taking the pre-travel advice just discussed for avoiding foodborne and other infectious illness.

Precautions on Your Trip

Like other types of foodborne illness, travelers' diarrhea is caused most commonly by bacteria—probably 80 percent of all cases. Improperly handled and contaminated food and drink also can cause *E. coli* infections, hepatitis A, giardiasis, shigellosis, typhoid, and other contagious diseases.

The first bout won't provide immunity from the next. You can reduce your risk by being cautious and careful with everything you eat and drink.

Food safety precautions apply wherever you eat away from home. In less developed places of the world, you need to take added precautions: "Boil it, cook it, peel it, or forget it." *See "Safe to the Restaurant Plate" in this chapter on page 285, and chapter 7, page 285, for more about food safety.*

- Check travel guides and talk to staff in the better hotels, or talk to your tour guide, to find restaurants with high sanitation standards. Restaurants in better hotels usually have high standards. Be especially wary of food and drinks from street vendors.
- When you aren't sure what you may encounter, carry packable, nonperishable foods. Single-serve packaged foods, such as energy bars, are great for travelers.
- As at home, always wash your hands with warm, soapy water, and dry them before eating. *Remember:* Your hands can transfer diarrhea-causing bacteria to your mouth. Carry an antibacterial hand wash and maybe a small bar of soap and commercially bottled water. The CDC advises using an alcohol-based hand sanitizer containing at least 60 percent alcohol or an antibacterial hand wipe.
- Like anywhere, avoid buffets if food is just rewarmed after sitting for a while, or if it's been kept at room temperature for longer than one to two hours. Avoid raw foods such as meat, fish, and eggs.
- *Be aware:* Fresh dairy products in developing countries may not be pasteurized. They also may be diluted with untreated water. Avoid them. When in doubt, avoid foods prepared with tap or well water.
- If you travel with a baby, breast milk guarantees food safety. If your infant takes formula, prepare it from commercial powder and boiled or commercially bottled water. Wash pacifiers, teething rings, and toys that fall to the floor, too. *See "Infant Formula: A Healthy Option" in chapter 16, page 471, for more about infant formula.*
- Be cautious about eating different types of fish and shellfish when you travel. The CDC advises that foodborne illness from marine toxins is under-recognized as a hazard for travelers, especially seafood from the tropical and subtropical waters of the Caribbean Sea and the Pacific and Indian Oceans. Warmer sea water, coral reef damage, and the spread of toxic algal blooms are among the factors that are increasing the incidence. The CDC notes the following traveler recommendations:
  - Carnivorous reef fish, including amberjack, barracuda, grouper, moray eel, sea bass, and sturgeon, are most likely to cause ciguatera poisoning. Omnivorous and herbivorous fish such as parrot fish, red snapper, and surgeonfish also can be a risk.

    Avoid or limit ingestion of these reef fish, particularly if they weigh more than six pounds, and avoid parts of the fish where the toxin may be concentrated (such as head, intestines, liver, and roe). Never eat barracuda, moray eel,

Click Here!
Apps to Know . . .

- Can I Eat This? and TravWell (apps from the CDC) wwwnc.cdc.gov/travel/page/apps-about

To use apps, make sure your mobile device has access while you are traveling.

or puffer fish. Ciguatera toxins do not affect the texture, taste, or smell of fish, and they aren't destroyed by cooking, smoking, freezing, canning, salting, or pickling, or by gastric juices during digestion.

  - Be cautious to avoid scombroid poisoning, a foodborne illness which occurs after eating fish that has been improperly refrigerated or preserved, causing it to contain high levels of histamine. From both temperate and tropical waters worldwide, the fish to avoid include amberjack, anchovy, blue fish, herring, mackerel, mahi-mahi (dolphin fish), marlin, sardines, and tuna. Cooking, smoking, canning, or freezing will not destroy histamine in contaminated fish. The key to prevention is proper refrigeration or freezing.
  - Be aware that foodborne illness may also come from bivalve mollusks (such as clams, cockles, mussels, oysters, and scallops) that contain potent toxins, contaminated by harmful algal blooms ("red tides" or "brown tides"). Avoid this seafood from areas during or shortly after algal blooms. If you travel to developing countries, avoid eating all shellfish because they carry a high risk of viral and bacterial infections; marine shellfish toxins cannot be destroyed by cooking or freezing.

- Curb the adventure if you're a foodie. Exotic foods—even if cooked—such as unusual wild game, monkey, and bushmeat are best avoided. The same is true for unknown roadside and street vendors.

For other issues related to seafood safety if fishing is part of your travel, visit the website: wwwnc.cdc.gov/travel. If you have health conditions that require special dietary needs such as diabetes, celiac disease, or a food allergy, plan with your doctor and prepare well in advance of your travel.

Safe to Drink?

You're always smart to play it safe. In developed countries, tap water generally is fine. Still, be cautious. Better hotels in less-developed areas may filter and chlorinate their tap water for safety. Especially in less-developed areas, follow these precautions:

- Before you use water from the faucet, find out if the hotel has a water-purification system. When you're not sure, don't drink or brush your teeth with tap water. Instead, use factory-sealed bottled or canned water, making sure the seal or cap is intact when you get it; keep some in your carry bag.
- Be aware that in some places, bottled water may not be superior to tap water. Knowing how to disinfect water may be important, especially for long-term travel. Visit the CDC's Traveler's Health website to learn how: wwwnc.cdc.gov/travel/page/yellowbook-home, also downloadable on a mobile device.

Soft drinks, canned or bottled juices, beer, and wine are safe to drink. Coffee, tea, and other hot beverages usually are safe, too. The long heating times destroy most and perhaps all bacteria, viruses, and parasites that might be present in the water. You also can boil or chemically treat the water you drink.

In addition, the CDC advises drying wet cans or bottles before opening them and then wiping clean any surfaces where your mouth contacts the can or the bottle. *See "Your Responsibility: Clean Water!" in chapter 7, page 87, for guidelines on treating water.*

In less-developed areas, avoid beverages made with water or that contain ice cubes unless you know that factory-sealed bottled water was used. Avoid bottled water without an intact seal or cap; it may have been refilled with local tap water. Be cautious of locally bottled water; the standards may not be high for bottling. Even crystal-clear water in wilderness areas anywhere, including the United States and Canada, should be treated before drinking it.

If You Do Get Sick

- In most cases of travelers' diarrhea, dehydration is the biggest concern. If it strikes you, increase your fluid intake—with plenty of safe water, canned juice, and hot soup. Canned or bottled soft drinks (preferably without caffeine) are okay, too.
- If the problem persists (for more than three or four days) or if your symptoms are severe, seek qualified medical care. Your hotel or tour guide should be able to suggest a doctor.
- If symptoms persist after you return home, see your doctor.

See "Digestive Health: GI Upsets and Conditions" in chapter 25, page 727, for more about dealing with diarrhea.

10

Use Supplements Wisely

In this chapter, find out about . . .

Nutrient, herbal, and probiotic supplements

Safe and unsafe use of dietary supplements

Making wise supplement buys

Would a supplement replace a nourishing dinner—or provide an easy approach to better health? For all those who enjoy the pleasure of eating, there's good news. The answer is unequivocally "no"!

Only food can provide the unique mixtures of vitamins, minerals, phytonutrients, and other substances needed for health—qualities that can't be duplicated with dietary supplements. Fortunately for most Americans, there's plenty of quality, quantity, and variety in the food marketplace, and so for most people, supplements aren't needed for good health. In fact, taking them may result in some unintended risks.

Despite this fact, the nutritional supplement business is big and growing. The US Food and Drug Administration (FDA) recognized that the industry has grown dramatically in 20 years with an estimated 200 million Americans now taking supplements.

Although dietary supplements are big business, manufacturing standards for their quality, potency, and effectiveness have lagged behind their phenomenal market growth. Product information is often misleading, despite limited government regulations. While scientific claims may be used in marketing, well-designed scientific studies for supplements are often limited. Pharmaceuticals (drugs), meant to cure or prevent disease, are well regulated, but government regulations for supplements are less stringent.

Why do so many consumers take dietary supplements? The reasons are varied—often medically valid, often not. In appropriate dosages, some supplements offer health benefits under some circumstances. Some people use supplements with good intention and with advice from qualified health professionals. Perhaps they fill dietary gaps, prevent nutrient deficiencies, or offer protection from health problems such as depression, postmenopausal symptoms, aging skin, cancer, or arthritis. Some supplements may be effective for other benefits such as promoting more restful sleep, better athletic performance, or improved gut health. Too often, however, supplement use is encouraged with scientifically unfounded marketing promises or by a friend, a family member, or health "gurus" not adequately trained to deliver supplement and health advice. Supplements may be recommended to you without regard to possible risks—and your own health needs and conditions.

Being sold in the marketplace doesn't make a supplement safe or effective. Many supplements are full of unknowns: unknown benefits; unknown interactions with food, medicines, and other supplements; undetermined standards; and unknown levels of safety and effectiveness, making dosages on package labels confusing.

Scientific evidence for the use of supplements is being gathered, but many answers about their safety and effectiveness remain unclear. Regardless, no supplements provide a quick, easy road to health. Good nutrition depends on overall healthy eating and active living. Good health requires much more than a supplement or two, or more.

What about regulation? Under the Dietary Supplement Health and Education Act (DSHEA) of 1994, the FDA monitors the marketplace and can issue public warnings, take legal action, and work with a company to recall a product in question. Because the supplement industry continues to grow, in late 2015 the FDA established the Office of Dietary Supplement Programs (ODSP) to focus more on safety problems and support supplement regulation.

What, then, is the appropriate, safe, and effective use of dietary supplements? How are they regulated? And just what is a dietary supplement anyway? Read on and find out.

Dietary Supplements: More than Vitamin Pills

Dietary supplements are neither food nor drugs. Instead, they're products taken orally that contain a "dietary ingredient" meant to supplement, not substitute for, healthy foods. According to the Dietary Supplement Health and Education Act, "dietary supplements" refers to a broad range of products: vitamins, minerals, herbs or other botanicals, amino acids, as well as substances such as enzymes, hormones, concentrates, extracts, metabolites, and probiotics. Supplements may seem like drugs, some with druglike effects. But unlike drugs, dietary supplements aren't intended to treat, diagnose, reduce, prevent, or cure disease, and they aren't regulated in the same way.

Thousands of dietary supplements are marketed in the United States, with new products launched each year. They're sold in many forms—for example, tablets, capsules, softgels, gelcaps, liquids, powders, and energy bars. Supplements can be easier to spot than you think. One way to tell is to look for the Supplement Facts label, which is required by the FDA on the packaging of a dietary supplement, *see "Shop with Supplement Savvy" in this chapter, page 337.*

NUTRIENT SUPPLEMENTS

Should you take a vitamin and mineral supplement? Maybe, maybe not. A fundamental premise of good nutrition is that nutrients should come mostly from foods. Food provides not only nutrients often contained in supplements, but also fiber and other naturally occurring substances that promote health. No sufficient evidence supports taking, or not taking, a multivitamin/mineral supplement as the best way to prevent chronic disease for healthy people. A supplement is not meant to replace a healthy diet.

In some cases, notes the 2015–2020 Dietary Guidelines for Americans, dietary supplements may be useful in providing one or more nutrients that otherwise may be consumed in less-than-recommended amounts.

Nutrient supplements can be used safely if the total intake from your food and drink choices plus supplements does not exceed the Tolerable Upper Intake Level (UL) in the Recommended Dietary Allowances (RDAs); *see "Dietary Reference Intakes" in the appendix, page 780, for the ULs of vitamins and minerals.* Taking high doses should be discussed with a registered dietitian nutritionist or doctor.

That said, taking certain nutrient supplements—for some people, under some circumstances—may be beneficial for overall health and managing some health conditions. Conversely, some supplements may be harmful to other subgroups of people. So, is a supplement right for you?

Vitamin/Mineral Supplements: For Whom?

With some exceptions, supplements usually aren't necessary—*if* you're healthy and *if* you're able and willing to eat a balanced, varied diet. You probably can get the vitamins and minerals you need from smart food choices. According to national studies, most Americans have enough nourishing foods available to do that. So the advice: Food first! Then under some circumstances vitamin/mineral supplements may be advised.

Many vitamins and minerals are sold as single supplements—for example, vitamins C and E, beta carotene, calcium, and iron—sometimes in doses larger than you need. Others are sold as combinations in multivitamin/mineral supplements.

Your doctor or registered dietitian nutritionist may recommend a dietary supplement if you are:

- *A woman with heavy menstrual bleeding.* You may need an iron supplement to replace iron from blood loss. *See "A Closer Look . . . Calcium and Iron Supplements," in this chapter, page 320.*
- *A pregnant or breastfeeding woman.* You need more of some nutrients, especially folate and iron—and perhaps calcium (with vitamin D) if you don't consume enough calcium-rich foods. Ask about a prenatal vitamin/mineral supplement. *See "Prenatal Nutrition: Preparing for Pregnancy" in chapter 18, page 539.*
- *A woman able to become pregnant.* Consume 400 micrograms of folic acid (the synthetic form of folate) daily from fortified foods, vitamin supplements, or a combination of the two—in addition to folate found naturally in some fruits, vegetables, and beans and peas. In case you become pregnant, the extra folic acid reduces the risk of spinal-cord defects in a developing fetus. Synthetic folic acid is better absorbed than food folate. Foods fortified with folic acid include enriched grains such as flour, breads, cereals, pasta, and rice. If you take a supplement, choose one with a dosage of no more than 1,000 micrograms of folic acid daily.
- *Someone on a restrictive diet.* You likely won't consume enough food to meet all your nutrient needs. Your doctor or registered dietitian nutritionist may recommend a multivitamin/mineral

Supplements—Fact or Myth?

Misconceptions about dietary supplements are rampant. What do you think about using them?

Fact?	or	Myth?	
_____		_____	**1.** Nutrient supplements can make up for my poor food choices.
_____		_____	**2.** Taking supplements can prevent, treat, or cure disease.
_____		_____	**3.** Nutrient supplements boost my energy.
_____		_____	**4.** If it's herbal, it's not harmful.
_____		_____	**5.** "Stress" vitamins help me cope better with a lot of emotional stress.
_____		_____	**6.** A nutrient supplement can help me build muscle or get more from my physical performance.
_____		_____	**7.** A vitamin pill could protect my body from the harmful effects of smoking or alcohol.
_____		_____	**8.** Supplements make up for foods grown in depleted soil.
_____		_____	**9.** Taking the right supplement can help with weight loss.
_____		_____	**10.** If I can buy it, it's safe.

All ten statements are myths. Here are the facts!

1. No supplement can fix an ongoing pattern of poor food choices. Supplements may supply some vitamins and minerals, but not all the substances in food, for optimal health. Only a varied, balanced eating pattern provides enough nutrient variety, phytonutrients, and other substances for health. If you eat smart, you probably don't need a daily supplement.
2. No scientific evidence in humans proves that vitamin and mineral supplements prevent, treat, or cure cancer or other chronic illnesses. Extra vitamin C won't prevent colds but may reduce symptoms or shorten the duration if taken before symptoms start. Some antioxidant nutrients may be protective; research is preliminary. *See "Vitamins as Antioxidants" in chapter 14, page 423.*
3. Boosting your nutrient intake won't cause your cells to produce extra energy or more brain power. Only three nutrients—carbohydrates, fats, and proteins—supply energy (calories). Vitamins don't. Although B vitamins do help body cells produce energy from energy nutrients, they aren't energy sources.
4. Many powerful drugs and toxic chemicals, as well as herbal supplements, are plant based. As with some medications, taking herbal supplements may lead to side effects, some possibly harmful, depending on the herbal supplement, the dosage, and any interaction with medications.
5. Emotional stress doesn't increase nutrient needs. Claims promoting dietary supplements to "de-stress" your life are misleading, too. The best dietary advice for the physical demands of stress is to follow a healthy eating pattern, *as discussed in chapter 2.* More "de-stressing" advice: stay active, get enough rest, and take time to relax.
6. Athletes and other physically active people need about the same amount of nutrients as others do—just more calories for the increased demands of exercise. The extra amount of food that active people eat supplies the small amount of extra vitamins needed for energy production. Although protein needs are somewhat higher for some athletes, especially for those in strength-training sports, food can easily provide the extra. On another note, physical activity, not extra amino acids (protein), builds muscle. *See "Ergogenic Aids: No Training Substitute" in chapter 21, page 619.*
7. Dietary supplements won't protect you from the harmful effects of smoking or alcohol abuse. Smoking increases the need for vitamin C; beta carotene supplements may increase lung cancer risk among some smokers. Drinking excessive amounts of alcoholic beverages can interfere with the body's use of most nutrients.
8. If soil can grow crops, the food produced is nutritious. When soil lacks minerals, plants don't grow properly and may not produce their potential yield. The growing locale does affect a food's iodine and selenium contents.
9. Weight-loss supplements touted to trap fat, block carbs, or boost metabolism typically are no more effective than placebos. Except for some that may temporarily help curb your appetite, no over-the-counter supplement effectively causes someone to shed pounds. Some touted for weight loss, such as ephedra and high-dose green tea extracts, can have adverse, potentially harmful side effects. *See "Weight Management Strategies That Work!" and "Weight Loss Supplements" in chapter 22, page 649, for healthy ways to manage your weight.*
10. Unlike medications, supplements don't undergo the same scrutiny, so they may not be as safe as you hope. Marketing claims are related to effectiveness, not safety. Claims on product labels and marketing materials are regulated by the FDA. Most reliable companies don't make unsupported or illegal label claims.

supplement. *Caution:* Unless under a doctor's supervision, very-low-calorie eating plans aren't advised. *See "Popular Diets: Truths and Half Truths" in chapter 22, page 648.*

- *Someone with limited milk intake and sunlight exposure.* If you have lactose intolerance, a milk allergy, or simply don't consume enough dairy foods, you may be advised to take a calcium supplement with vitamin D for bone health—perhaps a vitamin D supplement, too. This could be the case, too, if you aren't able to get outside in the sunshine on a regular basis. *See "A Closer Look . . . Calcium, Vitamin D, and Bone Health" in chapter 14, page 427.*
- *A vegetarian.* You may be advised to take a supplement with calcium, iron, zinc, and vitamins B_{12} and D—if your regular eating pattern doesn't supply much, if any, meat, dairy, and other animal products or if you don't consume enough from fortified foods. *See "Vegetarians: Nutrients to Focus On" in chapter 2, page 54.*
- *Someone with a health condition that affects the body's nutrient use.* Your doctor may prescribe a supplement if a health problem affects your appetite, eating, or how nutrients are absorbed, used, or excreted. For example, this may apply for those with digestive or liver problems. Surgery or injuries may increase the need for some nutrients, as do some medications, such as antacids, antibiotics, diuretics, and laxatives that may interfere with the bioavailability of some nutrients. If a food allergy, gluten intolerance, or other health problem restricts what you eat, a supplement may be advised.
- *An older adult.* For bone health, you may be advised to take a calcium and vitamin D supplement. Evidence indicates the effectiveness in reducing fractures and falls (which can cause fractures) in older adults in institutionalized care. However, the benefits aren't clear for other adults over age fifty.

  Taking more vitamin B_{12} in its crystalline form from a supplement or fortified food may be recommended, too. Why? Ten to 30 percent of adults over age fifty have atrophic gastritis, which causes damage to stomach cells and so reduces vitamin B_{12} absorption. *See "B Vitamins: 6, 12, and Folate" in chapter 20, page 581.*
- *Some babies after age six months, children, and teens.* They may need a fluoride supplement—and perhaps iron or vitamin D. *See "Supplement Advice: For Breastfed Babies" in chapter 16, page 469.*
- *Someone unable—or unwilling—to regularly consume a healthy diet.* You may need a dietary supplement to fill in nutrient gaps, as directed by a doctor or registered dietitian nutritionist. For example, postmenopausal women who don't consume enough calcium from food may be advised to take a calcium (with vitamin D) supplement.

Except for rare medical conditions, few people need more than 100 percent of their RDAs of any nutrient (except perhaps for protein). Large mineral or vitamin doses are prescribed only for certain medically diagnosed health problems. Even then, their use should be monitored carefully by a doctor.

If you have any questions about your own nutrient needs—or think you need a supplement—talk to a registered dietitian nutritionist or your doctor first. *See "Nutrition Advice to Trust" in chapter 26, page 758.*

More Isn't Always Better!

A little is good, but a lot may *not* be healthier. As with other nutrients, moderation is the smart guideline for vitamins and minerals: enough, but not too much.

Supplements carry labeling, showing the amounts of vitamins and minerals in a single dose. If you already eat a healthy diet, a low-dose supplement is likely enough. Taking a multivitamin/mineral supplement, with about 100 percent of the Daily Values (DVs) as a safety net, is generally considered safe. "High potency" (significantly higher than the DVs) supplements may be sold as single-nutrient supplements or in vitamin-mineral combinations. Because high-potency supplements can be harmful, consult your doctor before taking them.

Risks. Consuming nutrients in amounts that exceed the Tolerable Upper Intake Level (UL) (*see "Dietary Reference Intakes" in the appendix, page 780*) from some supplements can have undesirable side effects: some serious and harmful, such as kidney stones, liver or nerve damage, birth defects, or even death. The UL is the maximum amount considered safe for most healthy people.

Because fat-soluble vitamins (A, D, E, K) are stored in the body, taking high levels of them for a prolonged time can be toxic. For example,

Antioxidant Nutrients: Enough, or Too Much?

Antioxidant supplements are taken by many—even though there's no conclusive evidence that taking daily amounts of antioxidant nutrients beyond their Recommended Dietary Allowance (RDA) offers health benefits or protection from cancer or heart disease—whether from food or supplements. That said, research investigating the potential health benefits of antioxidants is ongoing, looking at links to aging, chronic diseases, asthma, allergies, and much more. Listen for science-based updates.

Antioxidants occur naturally in food, but supplements only provide a small number of them. When antioxidants are extracted from food to make supplements, some beneficial qualities may be lost. Excessive amounts from supplements could be harmful.

If you choose to take them for their potential benefits, talk to your doctor first. Then avoid exceeding the Tolerable Upper Intake Level (UL) set for safety. Use the Supplement Facts on product labels to know how much one dose-serving contains. *See "Antioxidants in Supplements" in chapter 14, page 425.*

Have you ever wondered?

. . . if ridges or marks on your fingernails suggest a vitamin deficiency? No, but it's a common misconception. Instead, they're often caused by a slight injury to the nail, not a nutrient deficiency.

. . . if a biotin supplement can strengthen your hair? If your hair is fine and easily damaged, this sounds like a great solution, but no evidence shows that a biotin supplement makes a difference. While biotin, a B vitamin, is important for hair health, most people get enough from their everyday food choices. If you're healthy, good hair care is the best way to keep hair strong!

. . . why a nutrient supplement label may list the percentage of vitamin A from beta carotene? The supplement may contain beta carotene but not vitamin A itself. However, the body converts beta carotene to vitamin A.

. . . if zinc lozenges can help people with a cold feel better and recover faster? Different studies show different results, so the answer isn't clear. But a caution: Some people have temporarily lost their sense of smell after using nasal sprays and gels with zinc. Talk to your doctor before using them.

. . . if taking a vitamin C supplement will cure or at least protect against the common cold? When taken regularly before getting a cold, a vitamin C supplement might shorten the length of a cold slightly and make its symptoms somewhat milder. For most people, scientific evidence doesn't justify taking large doses of vitamin C regularly to boost immunity and lower the chance of getting a cold. And taking a supplement after getting a cold doesn't appear to be helpful. Research suggests that any benefits from a vitamin C supplement may be the placebo effect.

Vitamin C in supplements is usually ascorbic acid. But you might find sodium ascorbate, calcium ascorbate, other mineral ascorbates, and ascorbic acid with bio-flavonoids. Research hasn't shown that one is better than another.

. . . about the difference between vitamins D_2 and D_3 in supplements? Either form increases vitamin D in the blood. However, D_3 (cholecalciferol) has been shown to be more effective in raising the circulating form of vitamin D in blood and keeping the level up longer. Today, many supplements provide D_3 instead of D_2.

. . . if you need more potassium when you're taking a diuretic medication? That depends on the diuretic prescribed, but it's generally not needed. Talk to your doctor or a registered dietitian nutritionist. Many foods are great sources, including many fruits and vegetables, and milk.

. . . if vitamin nasal sprays or patches are effective? No research evidence says so, even though they're promoted for faster, more efficient absorption. In fact, they may not be absorbed at all. Here's the reality check: Fat-soluble vitamins need fat from food to aid absorption. Vitamin C in your intestine aids iron absorption—a problem if vitamin C comes from a spray. Vitamin B_{12} binds with an intrinsic factor made in the stomach during digestion. That cannot happen with a spray or a patch.

. . . if supplements with "phytonutrients" are a good choice? Named for *phyto*, Greek for "plant," these botanical substances are extracted from vegetables and other plant foods. Plants have thousands of phytonutrients. Science hasn't yet revealed which one, if any, or what amount in a supplement might offer any health benefits. And there's not enough scientific evidence to know if supplement manufacturers have picked the right active substance from plant sources for any benefit.

Better advice: Get "phytos" from food. Any health-promoting benefit might come from the interaction of many phytonutrients provided naturally in food. *See "Phytos: Different from Nutrients" in chapter 15, page 448.*

. . . if taking a dietary supplement can protect against biological threats? No, although some supplement promoters may make this claim. According to the Centers for Disease Control and Prevention (CDC) and the Food and Drug Administration (FDA), no current and credible scientific evidence suggests that supplements on the market today offer protection from or treatment for biological contaminants such as anthrax, SARS, or bird (avian) flu.

excess amounts of vitamin D in the blood from a supplement overdose can cause kidney damage, and high blood levels of calcium can cause confusion, disorientation, and problems with heart rhythm. Too much vitamin A, taken over time, can cause bone and liver damage, headaches, diarrhea, and birth defects.

Supplements with water-soluble vitamins or minerals can be risky, too, if taken in excess over time. For example, taking extra vitamin B_6 may help relieve premenstrual cramps, although no convincing evidence supports large vitamin B_6 doses for relief of these symptoms. Many women have viewed large vitamin B_6 doses as harmless, since the supplement is water soluble. Instead, it may cause irreversible nerve damage in very large doses (500 to 5,000 milligrams of vitamin B_6 per day. The UL for vitamin B_6 is 100 milligrams per day).

Other examples: Very high vitamin C doses can cause diarrhea and nausea. Excessive folic acid can hide symptoms of pernicious anemia, so the disease gets worse without being detected.

Click Here!
Links to Know . . .

- Dietary Supplement Label Database
  dsld.nlm.nih.gov
- Office of Dietary Supplements
  ods.od.nih.gov/
- US Pharmacopeia
  www.usp.org/dietary-supplements/overview
- National Center for Complementary and Integrative Health
  nccih.nih.gov
- National Agriculture Library
  fnic.nal.usda.gov/dietary-supplements

Children are especially vulnerable to overdoses of vitamins and minerals. In fact, excessive iron—perhaps mistakenly taken from iron supplements intended for adults—can be fatal to children.

Many factors affect how your body handles a nutrient megadose from a dietary supplement—and whether it's toxic for you. Body size, dosage (amount and frequency), and how long it's taken matter. On the other hand, overdosing on vitamins or minerals delivered naturally in food choices is highly unlikely. The vitamin and mineral content of food is much more balanced than in dietary supplements. In amounts of food normally consumed, even with extra helpings, you won't consume toxic levels of nutrients. If you are taking dietary supplements, nutrient amounts can add up if you consume a lot of highly fortified cereal, drinks, and other foods; some are classified as supplements because they have as many vitamins and minerals as a multivitamin supplement.

See chapter 14, page 408, for more about vitamins and minerals, which may be sold in supplement form.

Nutrient-nutrient interactions. High doses of some nutrients may result in deficiencies of others. For example, high calcium intake may inhibit the absorption of iron and other trace nutrients. High doses of vitamin E can interfere with the action of vitamin K and make anticoagulant drugs such as warfarin more powerful.

Even low levels of dietary supplements may contribute to health problems for some. For example, those at risk for hemochromatosis need to be careful of taking iron in supplements. Folic acid can mask a vitamin B_{12} deficiency, which may cause neurological damage. Zinc supplements in excess of the UL can decrease levels of HDL ("good") cholesterol, impair immunity, and reduce copper status.

HERBALS AND OTHER BOTANICALS

Herbs and other botanicals have been used as traditional medicines for thousands of years. They are still common in many cultures and countries, and interest and use for health purposes is growing today in the United States. Despite consumer attention to alternative treatments, little research backs up their safety or effectiveness. For the most part, their purported benefits are shared mostly in individual reports, not well-controlled scientific studies.

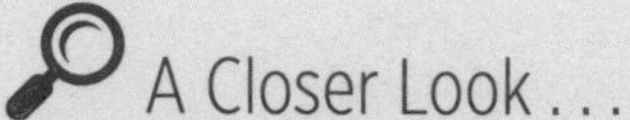

A Closer Look . . .

Calcium and Iron Supplements

ABOUT CALCIUM SUPPLEMENTS . . .

People of every age need an adequate amount of calcium; food is the best source. Some are more likely to be advised to get extra calcium: postmenopausal women, women with amenorrhea, individuals with lactose intolerance or milk allergy, and vegetarians, as noted by the National Institutes of Health (NIH). If you're advised to take a calcium supplement:

- Choose the dosage and form of calcium that's right for you. Products differ. Check the Nutrition Facts label to know whether the dosage provides what you need. The calcium amount in a multivitamin/mineral supplement is generally less than in a calcium supplement.
- Calcium supplements are generally compounds, such as calcium carbonate (often found in antacids) and calcium citrate. Calcium carbonate, often less expensive, is best absorbed when taken with food; calcium citrate can be taken any time. Because of lower levels of stomach acids after age fifty, calcium citrate is absorbed more easily. Chewable and liquid calcium supplements dissolve before entering the stomach, aiding absorption, too. You might also find calcium gluconate, calcium lactate, or calcium phosphate.
- Choose a calcium supplement or a multivitamin/mineral with vitamin D, essential for calcium absorption.
- Avoid calcium supplements with dolomite, unrefined oyster shell, or bonemeal, packaged without a USP symbol, *discussed in "Independent Quality Standards" in this chapter, page 333.* They might contain small amounts of hazardous contaminants: lead, arsenic, mercury, or cadmium. Dolomite is a mineral compound found in marble and limestone.
- Coral calcium? No evidence shows that it's better. People with shellfish allergies may react since it's from coral reefs. It also may contain lead, which can be dangerous.
- Take calcium supplements as intended—as a supplement, not as your only important calcium source. Although calcium

supplements may boost calcium intake, they don't provide other nutrients your bones and body need: vitamin D, boron, magnesium, and phosphorus. Milk provides vitamin D, a nutrient that helps deposit calcium in your bones.

- If you take two or three low-dose tablets daily, space them throughout the day for better absorption. Calcium is absorbed best in doses of 500 milligrams or less.
- Take most calcium supplements with food. Stomach acid produced when eating helps absorb calcium. Calcium citrate, an exception, absorbs well with or without food. Milk's lactose and vitamin D enhance calcium absorption.
- Take calcium and iron supplements at different times of the day for better absorption.
- Follow the dosage advised by your doctor. The amount not to exceed, or the UL, for calcium is 2,500 milligrams daily from food and supplements.
- If you take medications or other supplements, ask your doctor or registered dietitian nutritionist about interactions. For example, calcium and tetracycline bind; neither is adequately absorbed as a result. Calcium also inhibits magnesium, phosphorus, and zinc absorption.
- If you don't drink milk and want an alternative to calcium pills, consider calcium- and vitamin D–fortified juice or soymilk. One cup of either one can contain about 300 milligrams of calcium, the same amount as in a cup of milk; fortified juice also provides vitamin C, folate, and other nutrients.

Are calcium supplements for everyone? Getting enough from food is best, with supplements advised only when that isn't feasible. For people with kidney damage or urinary tract stones, calcium supplements pose risks. If you have a history of kidney stones, take them only under your doctor's care. A topic of current scientific debate, warranting further study, is whether calcium intake from supplements is linked to an increased risk of cardiovascular disease.

Are antacids as effective as an extra calcium source? That depends. Look for an antacid without aluminum hydroxides. Aluminum in antacids increases calcium loss in urine.

See "Osteoporosis and Bone Health" in chapter 25, page 738.

ABOUT IRON SUPPLEMENTS . . .

Physicians may advise iron supplements for premenopausal and pregnant women and for some children and teens. If you are advised to take an iron supplement:

- Pick one with a better-absorbed form of iron (ferrous sulfate, rather than ferric sulfate).
- Check the dosage. Fifteen to 30 milligrams per day is likely adequate. Only take higher amounts if prescribed by your doctor. Because iron absorption goes down as the dosage goes up, your doctor may recommend two or three smaller doses during the day.
- Take an iron supplement on an empty stomach—between meals or before bedtime—to enhance absorption. Absorption may go down by as much as 50 percent when taken with food. But if nausea and constipation are problems, take iron supplements with food.
- Take it with water or juice—not milk, coffee, or tea, which can inhibit absorption. Drinking vitamin C–rich juice with an iron supplement isn't necessary. Unlike nonheme iron in plant-based foods, the iron in supplements is in an absorbable form.
- Drink plenty of water. Choose foods with fiber to help avoid constipation, a common side effect from taking an iron supplement.
- Store the iron supplements where children can't reach them. Adult iron supplements can be extremely toxic to children!

Adult men and postmenopausal women: be cautious! For you, iron deficiency is uncommon. Taking an iron supplement or a multivitamin/mineral supplement with iron could result in iron overload and lead to hemochromatosis.

Fresh or dried, liquid or solid extracts, tablets, capsules, powders, and tea bags: botanicals are sold in many forms. Consider ginger: fresh gingerroot, dried ginger in tea bags, and liquid ginger extract. Some, such as phytoestrogens from soy, are isolated substances sold as dietary supplements.

Benefits or Risks?

Although Dietary Reference Intakes (DRIs), with recommended intakes, exist for vitamins and minerals, no recommendation for safe dosages exists for herbals, other botanicals, and other nonnutrient supplements. The Office of Dietary Supplements provides advice on many botanicals.

Herbal and other botanical supplements may seem safe. After all, they come from natural, fresh herbs or other parts of plants: flowers, leaves, roots, and seeds. In reality, there's nothing inherently harmless about botanical supplements just because they're labeled "natural." Many have ingredients with strong biological effects. While safe for some people in some circumstances, they may not be safe for everyone. In combination, perhaps with medications, or as substitutes for prescribed medications, they may be harmful. Their safety depends on many things, including their chemical makeup, how they work in the body, how they're prepared, and the dosage taken.

The effects of herbal and botanical supplements can range from mild to potent. The mild action of chamomile and peppermint, for example, often enjoyed in tea, may be gently relaxing and aid digestion. In contrast, kava has an immediate, powerful action and is potentially dangerous. The form—whether it's in a cup of tea, a few teaspoons of tincture, or even less as an herbal extract—makes a difference, too. While peppermint tea is generally safe, concentrated peppermint can be toxic if taken incorrectly.

Herbals and other botanical supplements should be taken with caution. Much needs to be learned about the safety and effectiveness of botanicals, as noted in research initiatives from the National Center for Complementary and Integrative Health (NCCIH). Enough scientific evidence has been collected on only a handful of botanical supplements to support their limited use.

Many herbals and other botanicals have known medicinal qualities; like many of today's drugs, they come from plants. Many claims have only limited scientific evidence. Dosages aren't always standardized and vary among different brands of the same product. Some treatments may offer promise in certain circumstances.

For those with allergies or asthma, some herbal supplements can induce symptoms. For example, chamomile, some herbal teas, and echinacea may cause an unpleasant, allergic reaction for people with a ragweed pollen allergy. Ingredient labels may not adequately identify allergenic ingredients.

Until more is known, alternative approaches to healthcare shouldn't replace treatment that's known to be safe and effective. If you do choose to try alternative or complementary care, talk to your doctor first. Some alternative approaches may interfere with the effectiveness of your doctor's prescribed treatment.

Herbals: Health Warnings!

The FDA has warned against the use of botanical supplements with these active ingredients, due to their serious, *even deadly,* side effects:

- *Aristolochic acid.* A substance in some traditional Chinese herbal products, aristolochic acid causes kidney damage and is a potent carcinogen. It's known, or suspected to be, in many products, including those with guan mu tong, ma dou ling, birthwort, Indian ginger, wild ginger, colic root, and snakeroot.
- *Chaparral.* This Native American medicine can cause rapid, potentially irreversible liver damage.
- *Comfrey.* Supplements with comfrey (common, prickly, or Russian) pose serious health risks, notably for liver damage and as a possible carcinogen.
- *Ephedrine, ma huang* (ephedra sinica), *epitonin.* Being medicinal herbs, supplements with these ephedrine alkaloids have been touted as energy enhancers. Ephedrine also has been a component of weight-loss teas and aids. It's a stimulant closely related to methamphetamine, and is especially dangerous when combined with other stimulants. Hazards range from nervousness, dizziness, rapid heartbeat, and changes in blood pressure to muscle injury, seizures, nerve damage, heart attack, hepatitis, psychosis, stroke, and even death. People with health problems, such as high blood pressure, heart disease, or diabetes, are at special risk. Bitter orange peel, sometimes used to replace ephedra in weight loss products, contains synephrine, which may be no safer than ephedra; avoid it, too. Because dietary supplements with ephedra are so risky, an FDA regulation prohibits their sale; some medications, however, contain a form of it.
- *Germander.* Its use may lead to liver disease and possibly to death.
- *Kava.* An herbal ingredient promoted for relaxation and relief of sleeplessness and menopausal symptoms, kava is linked to liver-related injuries. It's especially risky for those with liver problems or disease, or persons who are taking drugs that can affect the liver.
- *Magnolia-stephania preparation.* Its use may lead to kidney disease and permanent kidney failure.
- *Willow bark.* Marketed as an aspirin-free product, willow bark contains an ingredient that converts to the active ingredient found in aspirin. Potential health hazards include Reye's syndrome, a potentially fatal disease that's linked to aspirin intake in children with chicken pox or flu symptoms. Adults can have an allergic reaction.
- *Wormwood.* Its use may cause neurological symptoms such as numbness in the legs and arms, loss of intellect, delirium, and paralysis.
- *Yohimbe.* Marketed for sexual arousal and derived from tree bark, yohimbe has several active ingredients, including yohimbine, with potentially dangerous side effects: kidney failure, seizures, nervous system disorders, paralysis, fatigue, stomach problems, and death. Because it is a MAO (monoamine oxidase) inhibitor, yohimbine is especially harmful when taken at the same time as tyramine-containing foods such as cheese, liver, or red wine, and with over-the-counter medications containing phenylpropanolamine (some nasal decongestants and diet aids).

Other ingredients, often found in herbal supplements, have potential health hazards. For example, germanium (a nonessential mineral) may result in kidney damage, possibly death. Colloidal silver—a nonessential mineral with no known physical benefits when consumed—may cause

? Have you ever wondered?

. . . if any herbal supplement can replace or enhance medication for depression? If your doctor has prescribed medication for depression, follow the directions; don't mix or change antidepressants. Mixing may result in harmful interactions—for example, St. John's wort interacts with antidepressants such as Prozac and amoxapine. The combination may be additive. An herbal treatment may not yield the intended outcome. If you choose to try an herbal, talk to your doctor first.

. . . if acai can help with weight loss or antiaging? The acai (pronounced ah-sigh-EE) berry comes from the acai palm, indigenous to Central and South America. While acai, in juices, powders, tablets, and capsules delivers antioxidants, no evidence indicates unique qualities that promote weight loss, burn body fat, boost metabolism, cleanse the body of toxins, or slow aging. Other fruits, including other berries, and vegetables also deliver antioxidants at much less expense. And many acai drinks are high in calories and added sugars.

. . . if supplements promoted as "memory enhancers" or "cognitive enhancers" will improve mental abilities? Some so-called "smart drugs," or nootropics, are marketed as dietary supplements. Others aren't, even if they contain vitamins or other dietary supplement ingredients. Regardless, not enough reliable evidence shows if they're either safe or effective.

permanent grayish or bluish discoloration of the skin, nails, gums, and conjunctiva (clear membrane covering the white of the eye).

PROBIOTIC SUPPLEMENTS

Due to interest in gut health and immunity, sales of probiotic supplements have skyrocketed in recent years. In fact, consumer interest and marketing have moved faster than the research on their effectiveness and safety. Sold as dietary supplements, probiotics must comply with FDA regulations.

Some early evidence suggests that probiotics may help prevent diarrhea caused by infections and antibiotics. They may help improve symptoms of irritable bowel syndrome. A growing body of evidence suggests that the benefits of probiotics may extend to heart health, blood sugar control, and more. For most conditions, strong evidence for specific uses of probiotics is lacking.

While food is the best source, supplements with live cultures such as *Lactobacillus* and *Bifodobacteria* and the yeast *Saccharomyces boulardii*, may deliver benefits. Be aware that probiotic supplements have different types of probiotic bacteria, with different effects for different people. Moreover, their benefits haven't been demonstrated conclusively.

For healthy people, any side effects, such as intestinal gas, are usually minor. However, those with weakened immunity, those who have had recent surgery, or those who are critically ill may develop infections or some other serious complications.

If you choose to take a probiotic supplement:

- Talk to your doctor to determine if it is right for you—and to discuss the benefits you hope for—especially if you have a medical condition. That's very important if you are pregnant or breastfeeding or are considering a probiotic supplement for a child. Probiotics may complement, not replace, health care advised by your doctor.
- Taking antibiotics? Talk to your doctor about their use and timing to get the most from each.
- Know that the "friendly" bacteria in probiotics are of many types: different genera, species, and strains. One probiotic product is not the same as another even if they contain the same species. Some experts suggest choosing a probiotic with several strains, not just one.
- Be label savvy. To provide benefits, they must be alive when consumed. Check the expiration date and CFUs (colony forming units). A CFU is a unit used to estimate the number of live bacteria in a given dose. That said, the National Center for Complementary and Integrative Health reports that some products have been found to have fewer live microorganisms than expected, and some contain bacterial strains other than those listed on the label.
- Check the package label for dosage and storage instructions.
- Remember that probiotics feed on prebiotics, or the fermentable fibers in many plant-based foods, which is another reason to fit vegetables, fruits, and whole grains into your meals and snacks. In addition, you might look for a probiotic supplement containing a prebiotic such as inulin.

Probiotics can be sold as supplements without FDA approval. Marketing claims about their function in the body are also allowed without FDA approval. No claims for preventing or treating any health problem have FDA approval; this would require stringent evidence on safety and effectiveness from clinical trials.

See "Prebiotics and Probiotics: A Bioactive Duo" in chapter 15, page 453, to learn more about probiotics and foods with prebiotic and probiotic benefits.

OTHER SUPPLEMENTS

As supplement categories, nutrient and herbal supplements—and now probiotic supplements—come to mind. But stores and Internet sites sell others. *Many are addressed in "Other Supplements (Selected): Effectiveness, Cautions" in this chapter, page 329.*

HERBALS AND OTHER BOTANICALS (SELECTED): EFFECTIVENESS, CAUTIONS

- The FDA warns against the use of several botanicals due to serious, even deadly, side effects, *as discussed in this chapter, "Herbals: Health Warnings!" page 322.*
- Tell all your doctors about any complementary health approaches you use. Give them a full picture of what you do to manage your health. This will help ensure coordinated and safe care.
- For more about these and other botanicals, see "Herbs at a Glance" on the National Center for Complementary and Integrative Health website: nccih.nih.gov/health/herbsataglance.htm. For each botanical, it lists common names, what the science says, potential adverse effects and cautions, and resources for more information.

Herbal or Other Botanical Supplement*	Effectiveness	Side Effects and Cautions (Selected)**
Acai	• No definitive scientific evidence to support use for weight loss or other health purpose • May have antioxidant properties and anti-cancer and anti-inflammatory activity	• Little reliable information about the safety of acai as a supplement; widely consumed as an edible fruit or juice • Should not be consumed by those allergic to acai or to plants in the palm family • Might affect MRI test results
Aloe vera	• Applied topically as a gel, may help heal burns and abrasions • Has not been shown to prevent burns from radiation therapy • Not enough scientific evidence for other uses	• Topical use: not associated with significant side effects • Oral use: may be carcinogenic • Oral use: possible abdominal cramps and diarrhea (laxative effect can decrease the absorption of many drugs) • Oral use: for people with diabetes who use glucose-lowering medication, may lower blood glucose levels
Bitter orange	• No definitive scientific evidence to support use for weight loss or other health purposes	• May cause chest pain, anxiety, faster heart rate, and higher blood pressure • Contains the chemical synephrine, which is similar to the main chemical in ephedra (banned by the FDA because it raises blood pressure and is linked to heart attacks and strokes) • Often used in place of ephedra, unclear whether bitter orange has similar effects; little evidence that bitter orange is safer than ephedra
Black cohosh	• May help relieve menopausal symptoms, but results are mixed • No definitive scientific evidence to support use to relieve hot flashes and night sweats in post-menopausal women or those approaching menopause • Not enough reliable data to determine whether effective for rheumatism or other uses	• Safety of long-term use uncertain; in general, no serious side effects with use for menopausal symptoms • Possible effects on liver; discontinue use and consult a doctor if you have a liver disorder or develop symptoms of liver trouble, such as abdominal pain, dark urine, or jaundice • May cause side effects such as stomach discomfort, headache, or rash • Unclear if safe for women who have had hormone-sensitive conditions such as breast cancer or for pregnant women or nursing mothers • Should not be confused with blue cohosh, which has different properties, treatment uses, and side effects

HERBALS AND OTHER BOTANICALS (SELECTED): EFFECTIVENESS, CAUTIONS *(continued)*

Herbal or Other Botanical Supplement*	Effectiveness	Side Effects and Cautions (Selected)**
Cinnamon	• Does not appear to affect factors related to diabetes and heart disease • High-quality clinical evidence (for any medical condition) is generally lacking	• Safe for most people, up to 6 grams daily for 6 weeks or less • Possible allergic reactions • Should not be used to replace or delay care for symptoms of concern, particularly for those with diabetes
Echinacea	• May help prevent or treat upper respiratory tract infections such as the common cold, but results are mixed	• Oral use: usually does not cause side effects; some have allergic reactions, including rashes, increased asthma, and anaphylaxis • Potential allergic reactions, especially for those with asthma, allergies to plants in the daisy family (which includes chrysanthemums, marigolds, and ragweed), and those with a genetic tendency toward allergic reactions
Evening Primrose Oil	• *Note: See Gamma-linolenic acid (GLA) in "Other Supplements (Selected): Effectiveness, Cautions" in this chapter, page 329.*	
Fenugreek	• May help lower blood glucose levels for those with diabetes • Not enough scientific evidence to support use for other health purposes	• Oral use: possible intestinal gas, bloating, and diarrhea • Topical use: may cause skin irritation • Use caution when taking during pregnancy
Garlic	• May slightly lower blood cholesterol levels, but evidence is mixed • May slightly lower blood pressure, particularly for those with high blood pressure • May slow development of atherosclerosis (hardening of arteries) • No evidence that long-term use prevents stomach cancer; no clinical trials for other cancers	• Appears to be safe for most adults • May cause undesirable body and breath odors, heartburn, upset stomach, and allergic reactions • Can thin the blood (reduce the ability of blood to clot); may be a problem during or after surgery or dental work • Interferes with the effectiveness of some medications including saquinavir, a drug used to treat HIV infection
Ginger	• May relieve pregnancy-related nausea and vomiting safely with short-term use • Mixed results for treating nausea caused by motion, chemotherapy, or surgery • Unclear if effective in treating rheumatoid arthritis, osteoarthritis, or joint and muscle pain	• Few side effects in small doses • Most-often reported side effects (mostly associated with powdered ginger): gas, bloating, heartburn, and nausea
Ginkgo biloba	• Appears ineffective in lowering the overall incidence of dementia and Alzheimer's disease in the elderly	• Side effects may include headache, nausea, gastrointestinal upset, diarrhea, dizziness, or allergic skin reactions; more severe allergic reactions occasionally reported

(continued)

HERBALS AND OTHER BOTANICALS (SELECTED): EFFECTIVENESS, CAUTIONS *(continued)*

Herbal or Other Botanical Supplement*	Effectiveness	Side Effects and Cautions (Selected)**
	• Appears ineffective in slowing cognitive decline, lowering blood pressure, or reducing the incidence of hypertension • Conflicting evidence on the efficacy for tinnitus (ringing in ears) • May offer improvement of symptoms of intermittent claudication (pain caused by too-little blood flow, usually during exercise)	• May increase bleeding risk, so caution advised for those on anticoagulant drugs, those with bleeding disorders, or prior to surgery or dental procedures • Consuming fresh (raw) ginkgo seeds can cause serious adverse reactions, seizures, and death; roasted seeds can also be dangerous • Products from standardized ginkgo leaf extracts appear safe when used orally and appropriately • May be carcinogenic
Ginseng, Asian	• May affect blood glucose level and blood pressure • May have beneficial effects on immune function	• Appears safe for most people at recommended doses for short-term use; prolonged use might cause side effects • Most-common side effects: headaches, sleep and gastrointestinal problems • Can cause allergic reactions • Extra caution needed by those with diabetes, especially if using medicines to lower blood glucose or taking other herbs, such as bitter melon and fenugreek, also thought to lower blood pressure
Goldenseal	• Little scientific evidence to support its use for any health problem	• Considered safe for adults at recommended doses for short-term use • Rare side effects may include nausea and vomiting • Little information about the safety of high doses or the long-term use of goldenseal • May cause changes in the way the body processes drugs; could potentially alter the effects of many drugs • Should be avoided by women who are pregnant or breastfeeding since berberine (compound in goldenseal) can cause or worsen jaundice in newborns and could lead to a life-threatening problem (kernicterus) • Should not be given to infants or young children
Green coffee extract	• Possible modest effect on body weight	• Few safety concerns reported but not rigorously studied; contains caffeine • Reported adverse effects include headache and urinary tract infections
Green tea and green tea extract	• Possible modest effect on body weight	• No safety concerns reported when used as a beverage; contains caffeine; some safety concerns reported for green tea extract • Reported adverse effects (for green tea extract) include constipation, abdominal discomfort, nausea, increased blood pressure, liver damage

HERBALS AND OTHER BOTANICALS (SELECTED): EFFECTIVENESS, CAUTIONS *(continued)*

Herbal or Other Botanical Supplement*	Effectiveness	Side Effects and Cautions (Selected)**
Hawthorn	• Leaf and flower: may be safe and effective for milder forms of heart failure; conflict ing results • Insufficient evidence to determine whether hawthorn works for other heart problems	• Considered safe for most adults for short-term use • Rare side effects can include upset stomach, headache, and dizziness • Evidence suggests interactions with a number of different drugs, including certain heart medications
Hoodia	• No reliable scientific evidence to support its use; no published studies of use in people	• Unknown safety; potential risks, side effects, and interactions with medicines and other supplements not studied • Quality of hoodia products varies widely; news reports suggest that some products sold as hoodia do not contain hoodia • Safety concerns reported: increases heart rate and blood pressure • Reported adverse effects include headache, dizziness, nausea, and vomiting
Milk thistle	• Mixed results and no evidence linking milk thistle to protection from liver disease	• Appears to be well tolerated in recommended doses; gastrointestinal side effects occasionally reported • Can produce allergic reactions, more commonly among those allergic to plants in the same family (for example, chrysanthemum, daisy, marigold, and ragweed) • May lower blood sugar levels; caution for those with diabetes or hypoglycemia, or taking drugs or supplements that affect blood glucose levels
Red clover	• Likely no significant beneficial effects on menopausal symptoms • Not enough scientific evidence for effectiveness with other health conditions	• Appears safe for most adults for short-term use • No serious adverse effects reported • Because of estrogenlike compounds, possibility that long-term use would increase the risk of women developing cancer of the lining of the uterus • Unclear if safe for women who are pregnant or breastfeeding, or who have breast cancer or other hormone-sensitive cancers
Saw palmetto	• Not enough scientific evidence to support the use of saw palmetto for reducing the size of an enlarged prostate or for any other associated conditions such as urinary conditions • Does not appear to affect readings of prostate-specific antigen (PSA) levels	• Appears to be well tolerated by most adults • May cause mild side effects, including stomach discomfort

(continued)

HERBALS AND OTHER BOTANICALS (SELECTED): EFFECTIVENESS, CAUTIONS *(continued)*

Herbal or Other Botanical Supplement*	Effectiveness	Side Effects and Cautions (Selected)**
St. John's wort	• Mixed results on alleviating depression, perhaps no more effective than a placebo	• Not a proven therapy for depression • Interacts with many medications in ways that can interfere with their intended effects, such as antidepressants, birth control pills, cyclosporine (prevents the body from rejecting transplanted organs), digoxin (heart medication), indinavir and possibly other drugs (to control HIV infection), irinotecan and possibly other drugs (to treat cancer), seizure-control drugs, and warfarin and related anticoagulants • May cause increased sensitivity to sunlight • Side effects can include anxiety, dry mouth, dizziness, gastrointestinal symptoms, fatigue, headache, or sexual dysfunction • Taken with certain antidepressants, may lead to increased serotonin-related side effects, which may be potentially serious

*FDA health warnings for other herbals are addressed in "Herbals: Health Warnings!" in this chapter, page 329.

** See "Warning: Supplement-Drug Interactions!" in this chapter, page 335, for other side effects and cautions.

Sources: "Dietary Supplements for Weight Loss," National Institutes of Health, ods.od.nih.gov/factsheets/WeightLoss-HealthProfessional, and "Dietary Supplements Fact Sheets," ods.od.nih.gov/factsheets/list-all. Accessed September 1, 2016.

- Enzymes and hormones—for example, coenzyme Q10, dehydroepiandrosterone (DHEA), melatonin
- Ergogenic aids—for example, chromium picolinate, creatine
- Others—for example, bee pollen, carnitine, conjugated linoleic acid, fish oil, flaxseed, glucosamine, lecithin, royal jelly, shark cartilage

Caution: The FDA warns against using any products that are being marketed for bodybuilding and that claim to contain steroids or steroidlike substances. These products are potentially harmful and could lead to serious liver injury, stroke, kidney failure, or other serious conditions.

Supplements: Safe, Effective?

If you buy a supplement, do you get what you think you paid for? It may be hard to tell from the label. Just because a supplement is on the market doesn't mean it's safe or effective.

QUALITY, EFFECTIVENESS: WHO'S IN CONTROL?

Responsibility for the safety of supplements rests with the manufacturers and distributors before these products hit the market. The FDA has limited authority over supplements. Although it can remove supplements from the market if they are unsafe or if the claims are misleading, the FDA isn't required to review dietary supplements for safety and effectiveness before they appear on store shelves.

FDA Regulated, Not FDA Approved

Dietary supplements are regulated differently than food and drugs. Enacted in 1994, the FDA's Dietary Supplement Health and Education Act requires that supplements are (1) safe, unadulterated, and properly labeled; (2) produced with good manufacturing practices; and (3) promoted with truthful label information. However, dietary supplements aren't "FDA approved" for safety and effectiveness.

In 2007, the FDA issued Current Good Manufacturing Practice (CGMP) regulations for supplements, requiring manufacturers to guarantee the identity, purity, strength, and composition of their dietary supplements. The aim: to prevent contamination, wrong ingredients,

OTHER SUPPLEMENTS (SELECTED): EFFECTIVENESS, CAUTIONS

- Tell all your doctors about any complementary health approaches you use. Give them a full picture of what you do to manage your health. This will help ensure coordinated and safe care.
- For much more updated information—and more warnings—about many of these and other dietary supplements, visit the Office of Dietary Supplements website: ods.od.nih.gov/factsheets/list-all.

Other Supplement	Effectiveness	Side Effects and Cautions (Selected)
Carnitine	• No consistent evidence for improving exercise or physical performance in healthy subjects—at doses of 2 to 6 grams per day for up to 28 days • Does not appear to increase the body's use of oxygen or improve metabolic status when exercising, nor necessarily increase the amount of carnitine in muscle • No conclusive evidence for use in male infertility therapy *Note:* Not needed because the liver and kidneys produce sufficient amounts from the amino acids lysine and methionine to meet daily needs (meat, poultry, fish, milk provide plenty)	• Side effects at approximately 3 grams per day can include nausea, vomiting, abdominal cramps, diarrhea, and a "fishy" body odor; rarer side effects include muscle weakness in uremic patients and seizures in those with seizure disorders • May be metabolized to form a substance that might increase cardiovascular disease risk, especially among those who consume meat • Interacts with certain antibiotics used in the long-term prevention of urinary-tract infections
Chitosan	• Minimal effect on body weight • Small, mostly poor-quality studies	• Few safety concerns reported; could cause allergic reactions • Reported adverse effects include flatulence, bloating, constipation, indigestion, nausea, and heartburn
Chromium	• Minimal effect on body weight and body fat, according to studies of varying quality	• No safety concerns reported at recommended doses of 25 to 45 micrograms per day for adults • Reported adverse effects include headache, watery stools, constipation, weakness, vertigo, nausea, vomiting, hives • With limited data on chromium absorption in humans, unclear which forms are best to take; chromium chloride in particular appears to have poor bioavailability. • Interactions with many medications, including insulin, especially when taken regularly
Coenzyme Q10 (ubiquinone)	• May benefit some patients with cardiovascular disorders • Inconclusive research on other conditions	• Generally well tolerated or mild side effects • May make warfarin, an anticoagulant (blood thinner), less effective • Most common side effects include insomnia, increased liver enzymes, rashes, nausea, upper-abdominal pain, dizziness, sensitivity to light, irritability, headaches, heartburn, and fatigue • Should not be used by women who are pregnant or breastfeeding

(continued)

OTHER SUPPLEMENTS (SELECTED): EFFECTIVENESS, CAUTIONS *(continued)*

Other Supplement	Effectiveness	Side Effects and Cautions (Selected)
Colloidal silver	• No quality scientific evidence to support the safe or effective use for any disease or condition *Note:* Silver is not a nutritionally essential mineral or a useful dietary supplement.	• Can cause serious side effects, the most common being argyria, a bluish-gray discoloration of the skin, which is usually permanent • Can cause poor absorption of some drugs, such as certain antibiotics and thyroxine to treat thyroid deficiency • Oral use: no legally marketed prescription or over-the-counter drugs containing colloidal silver • Topical silver (used on the skin): some appropriate medical uses, such as in bandages and dressings to treat burns, skin wounds, or skin infections and in medicines to prevent conjunctivitis (an eye condition) in newborns
Conjugated linoleic acid (CLA)	• Minimal effect on body weight and body fat	• Few safety concerns reported • Reported adverse effects include abdominal discomfort and pain, constipation, diarrhea, loose stools, dyspepsia (possibly), adverse effects on blood lipid profiles
Fish oil, contains omega-3s (DHA, EPA)	• No convincing evidence of protection against heart disease • Some evidence of modest relief from symptoms of rheumatoid arthritis	• May interact with drugs that affect blood clotting and reduce the risk of bleeding • Uncertain whether safe for those with fish or shellfish allergies • Usually no negative side effects; if any, typically of minor gastrointestinal symptoms, such as belching, indigestion, or diarrhea • Conflicting evidence about omega-3 fatty acids and an increased risk of prostate cancer *Note:* Fish liver oils (not the same as fish oils) contain vitamins A and D as well as omega-3 fatty acids; these vitamins can be toxic in high doses.
Flaxseed, flaxseed oil	• Contains soluble fiber, like that found in oat bran and may have a laxative effect • Mixed results on benefits for decreasing hot flashes • May benefit people with heart disease alpha-linolenic acid, but evidence is insufficient reliable to support this use • May reduce the risk of certain cancers, but insufficient research	• Appears to be well tolerated with few reported side effects • Should be taken with plenty of water; otherwise, could worsen constipation or, in rare cases, even cause intestinal blockage • Can cause diarrhea • Flaxseed: its fiber may lower the body's ability to absorb medications taken by mouth; should not be taken at the same time as any conventional oral medications or other dietary supplements

OTHER SUPPLEMENTS (SELECTED): EFFECTIVENESS, CAUTIONS *(continued)*

Other Supplement	Effectiveness	Side Effects and Cautions (Selected)
Gamma-linolenic oil (evening primrose oil, black currant oil, borage seed oil)	• Not enough evidence to support its use for any health condition • Does not appear to affect menopausal or PMS symptoms • Taken orally, not helpful for relieving symptoms of eczema	• Well tolerated by most people for short-term use • Mild side effects include gastrointestinal upset and headache • Safety of long-term use not established • May increase bleeding in people who are taking the anticoagulant (blood thinning) medication warfarin
Glucosamine and Chondroitin	• Limited research for osteoarthritis of joints other than the knee and hip • Unclear if glucosamine lessens osteoarthritis knee pain or if either supplement lessens osteoarthritis pain in other joints • Research suggests that chondroitin isn't helpful for osteoarthritis knee or hip pain	• May interact with the anticoagulant (blood-thinning) drug warfarin (Coumadin) • No other serious side effects shown • Glucosamine: may affect blood glucose level, especially for those with diabetes, insulin resistance, or impaired glucose tolerance • For those with joint pain: some diseases such as rheumatoid arthritis may need immediate treatment. • Caution: if pregnant or breastfeeding, discuss with your healthcare provider before taking any medication or supplement, including glucosamine or chondroitin. • Uncommon side effects can include drowsiness, headache, dizziness, or nausea. No reported significant side effects of melatonin in children
Guar gum	• No effect on body weight	• Few safety concerns reported with currently available formulations • Reported adverse effects include abdominal pain, flatulence, diarrhea, nausea, cramps
Melatonin	• May help some people with certain sleep disorders, including jet lag, sleep problems related to shift work, and delayed sleep-phase disorder (one in which people go to bed but can't fall asleep until hours later), and insomnia • Insufficient research to support use for other health conditions	• Appears safe for short-term use; less is known about long-term safety • Limited research indicates possible worsening of mood in people with dementia • Has not been shown to relieve ADHD symptoms • Uncommon side effects can include drowsiness, headache, dizziness, or nausea. No reported significant side effects of melatonin in children
Noni (morinda)	• May have antioxidant, immune-stimulating, and tumor-fighting properties, but not well studied	• Should be avoided by those with kidney problems on potassium-restricted diets because noni is high in potassium • Few side effects reported, but safety not adequately studied • Reports of liver damage, so should be avoided by those with liver disease

(continued)

OTHER SUPPLEMENTS (SELECTED): EFFECTIVENESS, CAUTIONS *(continued)*

Other Supplement	Effectiveness	Side Effects and Cautions (Selected)
S-adenosyl methionine (SAM-e)	• No conclusive evidence about benefits for treating depression, osteoarthritis, or a liver condition that can occur during pregnancy *Note:* Produced in the body from methionine, an amino acid found in foods	• May interact with medication • Limited data on the long-term safety and safer use during pregnancy are too limited to draw any conclusion
Soy protein and isoflavones	• From daily intake of soy protein, may slightly lower levels of LDL ("bad") cholesterol • From soy isoflavone supplements, may reduce hot flashes in women after menopause, although results are inconsistent • Not enough scientific evidence to determine whether soy supplements are effective for any other health uses	• Considered safe for most people when used as a food or when taken for short periods as a dietary supplement • May cause minor stomach and bowel problems such as nausea, bloating, and constipation • In rare cases, allergic reactions such as breathing problems and rash • Safety of long-term use of not established • No evidence for an effect of dietary soy on risk for endometrial hyperplasia, a thickening of the uterus lining that can lead to cancer • Possible role in breast-cancer risk uncertain; until more is known about soy's effect on estrogen levels, women who have or who are at increased risk of developing breast cancer or other hormone-sensitive conditions (such as ovarian or uterine cancer) should be particularly careful about using soy and should discuss it with their doctors.
Shark cartilage	• Mixed results in the human studies of cartilage as a cancer treatment; not FDA approved as a cancer treatment	• Side effects of cartilage treatment are usually mild or moderate • Most-common side effects include gastrointestinal discomfort, vomiting, constipation, lower-than-normal blood pressure, higher-than-normal blood sugar, general weakness, higher-than-normal calcium in blood
Spirulina/blue-green algae	• Insufficient evidence to determine effectiveness for use with any health condition *Note:* no better than meat or milk as a protein source	• Possibly safe for most people if free of contaminants • Likely unsafe, especially for children, if contaminated with substances such as microcystins, toxic metals, and harmful bacteria; can cause liver damage, stomach pain, nausea, vomiting, weakness, thirst, rapid heartbeat, shock, and death (Safe products should be tested and found free of mycrocystins and other contamination.)

Sources: "Dietary Supplements for Weight Loss," National Institutes of Health, ods.od.nih.gov/factsheets/WeightLoss-HealthProfessional, and "Dietary Supplements Fact Sheets," ods.od.nih.gov/factsheets/list-all. Accessed September 1, 2016.

too much or too little of dietary ingredients, and improper packaging and labeling.

The responsibility for proof lies with the manufacturer, not the FDA. The FDA doesn't currently require testing—for safety, effectiveness, or interactions—before a supplement is produced or launched into the marketplace. If, however, an ingredient is new (marketed after October 1994), manufacturers must provide the FDA with evidence that the supplement is "reasonably expected to be safe" at the labeled dosage. The manufacturer is expected to ensure that the supplement's package label information (Supplement Facts and ingredient list) is accurate, its ingredients are safe, and the declared contents match what's in the container.

Supplements sold in the United States before October 15, 1994, are presumed safe, based on their history of human use. By law, manufacturers are required to notify the FDA if they receive any serious adverse reaction that's reported from taking a dietary supplement, but these reactions usually are under-reported.

While many supplements are labeled accurately and completely, some aren't; what's stated on the label may not be what's in the container. The potency or purity may be misrepresented or inconsistent. Herbs may be misidentified, indicating the wrong part of the herb or type of herb. Potentially dangerous allergens may not be identified. *Bottom line:* It's up to you to be a discriminating consumer.

The FDA can take action by issuing a warning or requiring that the product be removed from the market if the supplement is either unsafe or mislabeled. The FDA's Office of Dietary Supplement Programs, established in late 2015, is elevating the regulation of dietary supplements within the FDA, making it a higher priority.

Independent Quality Standards

For a growing list of dietary supplements, US Pharmacopeia (USP), an independent, not-for-profit organization, sets quality standards for strength, quality, purity, and consistency of supplements. If manufacturers voluntarily comply, they can display the USP Verified Mark on product labels, packaging, and promotional materials—and if the products and ingredients meet standards after testing. The mark signals that the supplement:

- contains the ingredients listed on the label, in the declared potency (or strength) and amounts;
- doesn't contain harmful levels of specified contaminants, such as lead, mercury, pesticides, bacteria, molds, toxins, and others;
- will break down and release into the body within a specified amount of time so the consumer gets its full benefit; and
- is made according to the FDA's Current Good Manufacturing Practice. That said, this is industry-reported compliance. Supplements are not FDA-tested before they're sold.

Several other independent organizations—e.g., NSF International, and ConsumerLab.com—also have certification programs, designed to assess whether a supplement really contains what the manufacturer declares on the label. A fee-based service to industry, each certifying organization sets its own assessment criteria; some are more in-depth than others. Some audit manufacturing practices; some do ongoing surveillance.

While certification programs are a step in the right direction, it's hard to discern precisely what a specific certification mark on a supplement label means and how each mark's criteria differs. Although a certifying mark helps you know if you're getting what you paid for, it does not verify a supplement's overall safety or effectiveness.

What if there is no certifying mark? It could mean several things: the supplement didn't meet certification criteria, the assessment is in progress, or perhaps the supplement hasn't been submitted for review.

What about advertising supplements? The Federal Trade Commission (FTC) regulates supplement advertising, including media infomercials and Internet promotions. Like the FDA, its resources for monitoring are limited.

MARKETPLACE CONFUSION

Many supplement manufacturers provide reliable product information. By law, supplement labels must bear a Supplement Facts panel. If the label carries one or more claims, the claims are supposed to be truthful and not misleading.

For well-intentioned consumers eager to take responsibility for their health, the sea of science and fiction is often confusing and misleading, and ultimately may be costly and harmful. Misleading marketing tactics for supplements may include:

- *Borrowed research.* Study results that may or may not apply to the product: perhaps supplements with different potencies or formulations, or derived from different parts of the plant.
- *Distorted data.* Information that's "spun" to match the product claim. Again, the formulation or dosage may differ from the supplement used in the original study. Less reputable manufacturers may present their "proof" in a format that looks like a reliable research study, such as charts, tables, or cited references.
- *Claims that research is underway.* In other words, no specific data are available.
- *Unreliable studies.* Poorly designed research that hasn't been published in peer-reviewed publications.
- *Testimonials.* Statements, not based in sound science, from "satisfied" customers or celebrities.

SCIENCE BEHIND SUPPLEMENT USE: MORE NEEDED

Sound scientific evidence supports the benefits of some dietary supplements for managing certain health conditions. However, high-quality research is needed to understand the effectiveness and active ingredients of many other supplements. Good research provides data from randomized, placebo-controlled, double-blind studies—not just one study, but several that duplicate the results. Manufacturers of supplements are not required to conduct research on their products. *See "A Closer Look . . . Scientific Studies: Research Terms Worth Understanding" in chapter 26, page 751, for defined research terms.*

To further complicate what's known and unknown, many supplements—for example, botanicals—have two or more active ingredients. Yet, all the bioactive substances haven't been identified, nor do we know what they do. Potencies differ when the same herbal supplement derives from different parts of a plant or different varieties. Growing conditions may affect the potency of bioactive substances.

Even if sound research exists for the safety and effectiveness of one active ingredient, it may not exist for all ingredients, and usually not for the combination. Typically the potency of active ingredients in combination products is less than the amount used in single-ingredient studies. In addition, there's not enough scientific evidence to know how much of a supplement or its bioactive substitutes offers benefits, how much may be harmful, the health effects of dosages beyond the label dosage, or any interaction with food or medication.

Good news: When published, sound research on supplements is available from the NIH, including the Office of Dietary Supplements and the National Center for Complementary and Integrative Health. Until then, the best advice is to maintain a healthy skepticism.

See chapter 26, page 747, for more about judging nutrition information, scientific reports, and nutrition quackery.

For more on supplements, read about . . .

- *"Weight-Loss Supplements" in chapter 22, page 649:* general information
- *Caffeine in "Have you ever wondered . . . if powdered caffeine can be a good pick-me-up?" in chapter 4, page 96:* caffeine powder
- *"Supplement Watch: Fiber Pills, Powders, and More" in chapter 11, page 357:* fiber pills and powders
- *"Prebiotics and Probiotics" in chapter 15, page 453:* fructooligosaccharides, inulin, others
- *Menopausal symptoms in "Have you ever wondered . . . if herbal and other botanical supplements are safe, effective treatments for menopause symptoms or rebalancing hormones?" in chapter 18, page 561:* black cohosh, dong quai, red clover, soy foods and isoflavones, St. John's wort, or Mexican yam
- *Athletic performance in "Ergogenic Aids: No Training Substitute" in chapter 21, page 619:* amino acid supplements, androstenedoine ("andro"), carnitine, creatine, dehydroepiandrosterone (DHEA), ergogenic aids, spirulina, wheat germ and wheat germ oil, whey protein
- *"If You Are Lactose Intolerant: More Ways to Fit Dairy In" in chapter 23, page 670:* lactase
- *Chronic health issues in chapters 24, page 680, and 25, page 722:* fish oil supplements, garlic supplements, glucosamine, lecithin, mangosteen

Questions to Ask an Expert

With so many supplement products on the market, and so many unknowns about them, talk with a qualified nutrition expert to make a judgment.

- What is it for? What are the claims? Who's making them? Why? Are the claims valid?
- Where did the product information come from? Is the manufacturer a trusted, nonbiased source?
- Is the supplement generally safe? Can it cause harm in any dosage?
- Does the product come from a company that's known, or highly likely, to follow safe, appropriate manufacturing practices?
- What's known about the supplement's effectiveness for its proposed benefit?
- How do the active ingredients work in the body?
- What plant or plants and part of the plant or plants do the main active ingredients come from?
- How much of the active ingredients does the supplement have? What else does it contain?
- What are its intended potential benefits for anyone, for you?
- Are there any precautions or warnings to know about (for example, an amount or "upper limit" that should not be exceeded)?
- What scientific evidence supports this product formula or brand?
- Are there any possible safety risks or side effects from taking it?
- What's the proper dose?
- How, when, and for how long should you take it?

Warning: Supplement-Drug Interactions!

Are you dealing with cancer, diabetes, heart disease, immune problems, kidney problems, thyroid problems, ulcers, allergies, celiac disease, or other health problems? Talk with your doctor before using dietary supplements and about the potential for biological effects and harmful interactions with medications.

Are you taking prescription or over-the-counter medication? Supplements, when combined with medications or other treatments, may interfere with or boost their action, and even may be harmful or life-threatening. *See "Food and Medicine: Some Don't Mix" in chapter 25, page* 743. For example:

- Folic acid can interact with anticonvulsant medications and with methotrexate, used in cancer treatment.
- Vitamin E, garlic, and ginkgo biloba may thin blood—dangerous when taken with blood-thinning medication such as warfarin and aspirin.
- Ginkgo biloba can interact with some psychiatric drugs and some drugs that affect blood glucose levels.
- Garlic supplements may interact with drugs used in HIV therapy such as saquinavir, which is a protease inhibitor.
- The combination of foxglove (the source of digitalis, or digoxin) and cardiac medication is dangerous for those with heart disease.
- St. John's wort may reduce the effect of heart drugs, antidepressants, antiseizure drugs, anticancer drugs, birth control drugs, certain HIV drugs, and transplant anti-rejection drugs.
- Ginseng can lower blood glucose levels, perhaps interfering with diabetes medication. It can also increase caffeine's effects as a stimulant.
- Calcium can reduce absorption of osteoporosis medication (bisphosphonates) and some antibiotics. Antacids with aluminum and magnesium increase calcium loss in urine, and mineral oil and stimulant laxatives reduce absorption. Glucocorticoids such as prednisone can cause calcium depletion.
- Magnesium can interact with thiazide, loop diuretics (for example, Lasix), some cancer drugs, antibiotics, and antacids with magnesium. Over time, prescription drugs for acid reflux or peptic ulcers can cause low blood levels of magnesium.
- Vitamin K may reduce the ability of warfarin to keep blood from clotting.
- Antioxidant supplements, such as vitamins C and E, may lessen the effectiveness of some cancer chemotherapy treatments.
- Antioxidant supplements, including vitamin C supplements, during chemotherapy or radiation can alter the effectiveness of these treatments.
- Taking prescription medications with synthetic forms of vitamin A, along with a vitamin A supplement, can make vitamin A blood levels dangerously high.
- Taking some medications, such as beta-blockers, insulin, ibuprofen, aspirin, and more, with chromium may impact the effects of one or both.

This isn't a complete list. For more interactions between medications and supplements, visit the ODS website: ods.od.nih.gov/factsheets/list-all. *Some nutrient-nutrient interactions are noted in "Nutrient Supplements" in this chapter, page 316.*

Planning for any surgery? Avoid all supplements two to three weeks ahead, advises the American Society of Anesthesiologists. Herbal supplements may seem "innocent," but their use can cause complications such as bleeding, cardiac instability, low blood glucose level, blood pressure changes, and others. Among those linked to surgical complications are ephedra, garlic, ginkgo biloba, ginseng, kava, St. John's wort, and valerian.

If You Take a Supplement

So, you think a dietary supplement should be part of your strategy for wellness. Before making a decision, do some homework to determine what, if anything, may offer benefits to improve or enhance your health. Put their potential use in perspective: supplements aren't meant to treat, cure, or alleviate the effects of diseases. And they can't completely prevent diseases.

REMEMBER: FOOD BEFORE PILLS

Before you decide to take a dietary supplement, go with the tried-and-true. If you're healthy, do you really need it? Plenty of scientific evidence supports that physical activity, healthy eating, getting enough sleep, and a healthy lifestyle may be enough.

- Give up some notions. Supplements *cannot be*:
  - simple, immediate solutions to your health problems. Even beneficial supplements require safe, appropriate use before they can offer potential benefits.
  - replacements for healthy eating, conventional health care and perhaps prescription medications, or a doctor's visit. Never self-diagnose a health problem! Self-medicating with herbal,

If You Have an Adverse Reaction . . .

- Immediately inform or see your doctor if you think you have suffered a serious harmful effect or illness from a dietary supplement.
- Report any adverse reactions to the FDA's MedWatch hotline (1-800-FDA-1088), by fax (1-800-FDA-0178), or online (www.fda.gov/Food/DietarySupplements/ReportAdverseEvent/default.htm). Both you and your doctor should do this right away. Be prepared to identify the suspected product. You can also make a report to the product's manufacturer or distributor using contact information on the product label; they are required to forward the report about serious adverse effects to the FDA within fifteen days.
- For a general nonserious concern or complaint about any supplement, contact the Consumer Complaint Coordinator at your nearest FDA District Office. Find the phone number at www.fda.gov/Safety/ReportaProblem/ConsumerComplaintCoordinators/default.htm.

other botanical, or any supplement may delay known treatment that can help you.

- With a few exceptions, remember: supplements are meant for short-term use only.
- Consider your everyday food choices and the nutrients they provide. If you follow a healthy eating pattern, *as described in chapter 2, page 21,* you likely get all the nutrients you need already.

No supplement provides the full complement of vitamins, minerals, and other important nutrients in food. Supplements only have what's listed on the label. By relying on them, you miss out on all the nutrients, as well as fiber and phytonutrients, that food supplies.

GET SOUND ADVICE

Keeping up with the explosion of supplements and supplement claims can be overwhelming. Skip the lure of this myth: "Even if a supplement won't help me, at least it won't hurt me." High dosages, taken long enough or combined with other supplements, can be harmful.

Best practice: Before taking any supplement, talk to a registered dietitian nutritionist, pharmacist, or your doctor. That's especially important if you're under age eighteen, pregnant or breastfeeding, chronically ill, elderly, have a food allergy or intolerance, are taking prescription or over-the-counter medicines, or are planning to have surgery. *Use "Your Healthy Eating Check-In: If You Take Dietary Supplements" in this chapter, page 338, when you talk to your doctor.*

Good practice: If you're already taking a supplement, tell your doctor about it to make sure it's safe and appropriate for you and your health status. Some interfere with medications. Prepare to discuss:

- Supplement name, type, and daily or weekly dose. (Bring the container if you can because it will have Supplement Facts on the package.)
- How long you have taken it, how much, and how often; how long you plan to take it; and why you think you need it.
- How long you've had symptoms you're treating with supplements; if your symptoms have improved.
- Your typical day's food choices, including fortified foods such as some cereals and drinks. The combined intake from all supplements and fortified foods needs consideration.
- Other medications (over-the-counter and prescription), other supplements you take, and other alternative health practices. *See "Warning: Supplement Interactions!" in this chapter, page 335.*
- Any health issues or illnesses you have, such as:
  - pregnant or breastfeeding
  - allergies or intolerances
  - chronic health condition(s)
  - special diet (self- or medically prescribed)
- Known cautions or warnings about the supplement, including amount and upper limit.
- Whether you drink alcoholic beverages or smoke; if so, how often and how much.

Have you ever wondered?

. . . if supplements are safe if you have allergies or other sensitivities? If you're prone to allergic reactions, check with your doctor. The supplement should not contain anything that's restricted for you, such as wheat-, gluten-, or milk-containing ingredients. If you're sensitive to histamine, avoid niacin in your multivitamin; instead, choose one with niacinamide. Chitosan, promoted for weight loss (with limited effectiveness), comes from the hard outer shells of shellfish (crabs, lobster, shrimp)—a problem if you have shellfish allergies. *See chapter 23, page 653, for more about food sensitivities.*

Caution: Herbals Not for Kids!

Even though supplement companies aggressively target kids and parents, herbal and other botanical supplements may not be as safe or effective for your child or teen as you may think. Some are useless; others, potentially harmful. As noted in this chapter, little evidence exists on the safety and effectiveness of botanical supplements for adults. Their use among children and teens is virtually untested. In other words, the short- or long-term benefits and, more importantly, the risks are mostly unknown.

Warning: Despite the FDA ban against ephedra for everyone—including for those under age eighteen—medications with a form of ephedra may be available to teens. *See "Herbals: Health Warnings" in this chapter, page 322.*

Caution: For Chronic Health Conditions

Taking dietary supplements for potential health benefits can be risky for people diagnosed with cancer, AIDS, or other life-threatening health problems. They may put their hopes and healthcare dollars into supplements and other alternative treatments.

Supplements may offer a false sense of security—and cause a serious problem if well-proven approaches to health care or medical treatment are delayed. If you have a health problem, seek medical attention and proven treatment first.

More wise practices: Before taking a supplement, consider this too:

- If you're pregnant, planning for pregnancy, or breastfeeding, talk to your doctor about supplements. You're at greater risk for side effects.
- Unless your pediatrician prescribes them, avoid giving supplements, including herbals, to your child or teen. *See "Supplements for Kids?" in chapter 17, page 519.*
- Skip the urge to "prescribe" a supplement for someone else. Even if it works for you, it may not be safe or effective for someone else.
- Use noncommercial websites to search for information on published research studies about supplements. The Office of Dietary Supplements is an excellent science-based resource on specific dietary supplements: ods.od.nih.gov.
- Ask a registered dietitian nutritionist, pharmacist, or your doctor about the effectiveness of specific supplements—and research behind the claims—and how to distinguish between reliable and questionable information. Show the supplement container.
- Remember that combining supplements, using them with prescription or over-the-counter medications, and taking too much of some supplements is risky. They can have unwanted and harmful effects taken before, during, and after surgery.

SHOP WITH SUPPLEMENT SAVVY

Before you head down your store's supplement aisle, order online, or pick up a product at the fitness center, get supplement savvy. Buy and use dietary supplements with the same consumer wisdom you use when you buy a car or make any major investment.

- Choose a supplement for your unique needs, and as advised by your doctor. Consider your age, gender, and medical status. *Note:* If you're under stress, don't count on a stress vitamin pill to help. Stress doesn't increase nutrient needs.
- Stay skeptical of supplement marketing—and label or advertising claims. Besides being ineffective, the supplement may be costly and harmful. *See "Food and Nutrition 'Info': Judging the Message" in chapter 26, page 752, to help you evaluate their claims.* Don't be lured by extra ingredients: inositol, lecithin, PABA, herbs, and enzymes. They add to the cost but deliver no proven nutritional benefits. Also, just because there is no cautionary information on the product label doesn't mean it's safe. Warnings of potential adverse effects may not appear on product labels.
- Unless you know the source is reputable, avoid buying supplements online.
- For a vitamin-mineral combination, limit the potency to 100 percent of the DVs for your age for most nutrients; use the label's Supplement Facts to judge the product. A supplement with close to 100 percent DV for most nutrients is likely more than enough, especially if your diet is healthy.
- Look for products labeled with the voluntary USP Verified Mark or NSF Mark (certification), *as described in "Independent Quality Standards" in this chapter, page 333.* Although some reputable companies choose to pay for independent certification, others don't. Often, national brands from larger companies have stricter quality controls. Certification marks represent differing criteria; most importantly, they indicate whether a label matches the contents of the supplement, not its safety or effectiveness. The FDA has found contaminants in some products marketed as "natural."
- Be cautious about buying supplements online. They may or may not cost less. And their quality is uneven.
- Especially if you have a food allergy, celiac disease, or a non-celiac gluten sensitivity, check the ingredients list on the food label for any you need to avoid. In addition, you can contact the manufacturer to learn more about what the supplement contains.

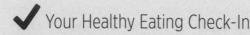

Your Healthy Eating Check-In

If You Take Dietary Supplements . . .

Use this checklist when you talk with your doctor about your nutritional status and whether taking a dietary supplement(s) is right for you.

TELL YOUR DOCTOR IF THESE STATEMENTS DESCRIBE YOU

1. I currently take a dietary supplement(s).
2. I eat fewer than two meals a day.
3. My diet is restricted (e.g., don't eat dairy or meat, and/or eat fewer than five servings of vegetables and fruits a day).
4. I eat alone most of the time.
5. Without wanting to, I have lost or gained more than ten pounds in the last six months.
6. I take three or more prescription or over-the-counter medicines a day.
7. I have three or more alcoholic drinks a day.

GENERAL QUESTIONS ABOUT DIETARY SUPPLEMENT USE

1. Is taking a dietary supplement important to my total diet?
2. Are there any precautions or warnings I should know about (e.g., is there an amount or "upper limit" that I should not go above)?
3. Are there any known side effects (e.g., loss of appetite, nausea, headaches, etc.)?
4. Are there any dietary supplements I should avoid while taking certain medicines (prescription or over-the-counter) or other supplements?
5. If I'm scheduled for elective surgery, when should I discontinue use of dietary supplements?

QUESTIONS TO ASK ABOUT SUPPLEMENTS YOU ARE CONSIDERING

1. What is this product for?
2. What are its intended benefits?
3. How, when, and for how long should I take it?

Companies that provide sound scientific information about their products are more likely to be reliable resources; still, be cautious. Supplements aren't standardized by regulation. So even if the label says "standardized" or "certified," the supplement may have more or less than the label says. In addition, manufacturing and storage methods may affect the contents.

Decipher the Label

A supplement label looks somewhat like a food label. Required by the Dietary Supplement Health and Education Act, the label must provide specific information that you can use to make informed decisions:

- *Statement of identity.* Look for the product name, perhaps "ginseng." The term "dietary supplement" or a descriptive phrase, such as "vitamin and mineral supplement," also must appear. If the product is a botanical, the plant part must be identified.
- *Net quantity of the ingredients.* This might be the number of capsules, perhaps "sixty capsules," in the package or container, or the weight.
- *Disclaimer with any structure/function claim. See "Check the Claims" in this chapter, page 340.*

? Have you ever wondered?

. . . if the same supplement can be sold by several names? Yes; that adds to consumer confusion. However, the ingredient list must list the common name.

Botanical supplements may have a common name and a botanical name—for example, St. John's wort, often promoted to treat mild to moderate depression, is also known as *Hypericum perforatum*. The common name also may refer to a category. Ginseng may refer to Panax ginseng or *Panax japonicus* (Asian ginsengs) or to *Panax quinquefolius L.* (American ginseng), each with different effects. Siberian ginseng (*E. senticosus*) isn't botanically related to either one!

. . . what "high potency" on a dietary supplement label means? According to government regulations, "high potency" means that a nutrient in a food or a dietary supplement provides 100 percent or more of the DV for that vitamin or mineral. The term also can refer to a product with several ingredients if two-thirds of its nutrients contribute more than 100 percent of the DVs. *See "Nutrition: Fact Check!" in chapter 6, page 144, for more about DVs.*

. . . if chelated mineral supplements are any better? Chelation binds minerals to other substances, supposedly making minerals easier for the body to absorb. While that may be true, many minerals found naturally in food aren't very bioavailable; that's considered when their Dietary Reference Intakes are established. In the overall picture, chelation isn't important—if you're meeting your day's mineral recommendation.

. . . if dietary supplements contain saturated and *trans* fats? Some may. Energy and nutrition bars are often classified as supplements. If they have 0.5 grams or more of *trans* or saturated fats, those fats must be in the Supplement Facts.

- *Supplement Facts.* This gives the serving size (dose), the amount, the % Daily Values (DVs) per serving if appropriate, and the active ingredient.
- *Directions for use.* This might indicate how often to take the supplement, perhaps "Take one capsule daily"; whether the supplement is best taken with or without food; safety tips; or storage guidelines. Suggested dosage is meaningless when little is known about the benefits and risks of many supplements.
- *Ingredients.* The list must be in descending order and by common name or proprietary blend. *See "Check Ingredients Labeling, Too" in this chapter, page 340.*
- *Name and address of the manufacturer, packager, or distributor.* Use this contact information to get more product information.

Supplement labels also may carry product claims: nutrient content, health, or structure/function claims. Although not required, the label may have a cautionary statement if adverse effects are linked to the product. In other words, it may or may not carry a warning.

For Herbals and Other Botanicals . . .

Helpful or harmful? Natural or not? Even though herbal and other botanicals are sold over the counter, use them with caution and discretion. Besides other advice you've learned in this chapter, remember this:

- Know that "natural" doesn't mean safe or milder. For example, peppermint leaf tea is thought safe; concentrated peppermint oil from leaves can be toxic. Having a "mark" on the container isn't necessarily an indicator of quality.
- Seek unbiased, science-based sources for information about herbals. Relying on product claims may not be a good idea. The poorly defined term "natural" doesn't mean safe or healthy. Ask a registered dietitian nutritionist or other qualified nutrition expert for help and advice.
- Find out about the risks and potential side effects. Then decide with your doctor if an herbal is safe and appropriate for you—or if other known health strategies would yield safe, effective results instead.
- Always consult a qualified health professional—preferably one properly trained in herbal medicine. The National Center for Complementary and Integrative Health advises that's especially important when taking herbs as part of medical care, including traditional Chinese medicine or Ayurvedic medicine. Be very cautious of those who call themselves an "herbalist," "herb doctor," "health counselor," or "master herbalist." These job titles aren't regulated.
- Talk to your doctor about herbal remedies if you take medication—either prescription or over-the-counter. The combination could

Need more strategies for appropriate supplement use? Check here for "how-tos":

- Find out about *safe* supplement use for children: *see "Supplements for Kids?" in chapter 17, page 519.*
- Get savvy about ergogenic supplements for athletic performance: *see "Ergogenic Aids: No Training Substitute" in chapter 21, page 619.*
- Sort through misleading information about supplements: *see "Food and Nutrition 'Info': Judging the Message" in chapter 26, page 752.*
- Talk to a qualified nutrition expert about safe and appropriate supplements for you and your family: *see "Food and Nutrition 'Info': Judging the Message" in chapter 26, page 752.*

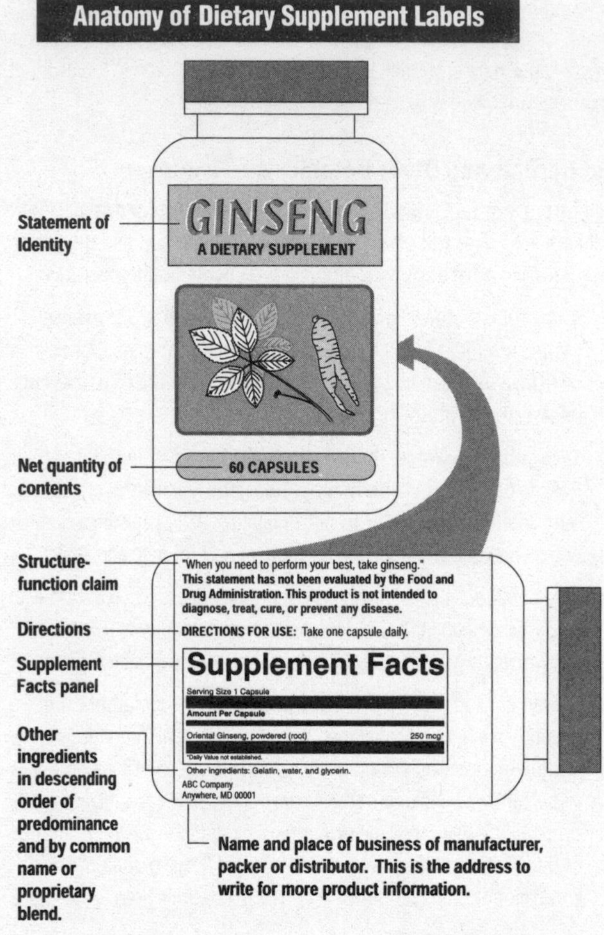
Anatomy of Dietary Supplement Labels
Statement of Identity
GINSENG
A DIETARY SUPPLEMENT
Net quantity of contents
60 CAPSULES
Structure-function claim
"When you need to perform your best, take ginseng."
This statement has not been evaluated by the Food and Drug Administration. This product is not intended to diagnose, treat, cure, or prevent any disease.
Directions
DIRECTIONS FOR USE: Take one capsule daily.
Supplement Facts panel
Supplement Facts
Serving Size 1 Capsule
Amount Per Capsule
Oriental Ginseng, powdered (root) 250 mcg*
*Daily Value not established.
Other ingredients in descending order of predominance and by common name or proprietary blend.
Other ingredients: Gelatin, water, and glycerin.
ABC Company
Anywhere, MD 00001
Name and place of business of manufacturer, packer or distributor. This is the address to write for more product information.

make your medication ineffective or create a harmful side effect. *See "Warning: Supplement-Drug Interactions!" in this chapter, page 335.*

- Take single-herb products, not herbal mixtures, unless recommended by a qualified practitioner with expertise in herbal therapies. If you have an adverse effect, you can identify the source more easily if you're taking single-herb products.

Check the Supplement Facts

How do you know about the nutrition in a dietary supplement? Check the Supplement Facts panel, which must appear on *all* supplements. Its format is similar to the familiar Nutrition Facts you see on food products. The FDA is making minor changes to the Supplement Facts label to make it consistent with the new Nutrition Facts label; *see "A Closer Look . . . Nutrition Facts Update 2016" in chapter 6, page 148.*

To use the Supplement Facts panel:

- Check the serving size, or an appropriate unit, such as a capsule, packet, or teaspoonful. That's what the facts are based on. Unlike Nutrition Facts for foods, serving size isn't standardized for supplements; neither is the potency, or nutrient amount, per serving. Manufacturers make that decision.
- Check the quantity and the % DVs for the required nutrients in the supplement, listed if the levels are significant. Other vitamins or minerals must be listed, too, if they are added or referred to with a nutrient content claim on the label.

Be aware: Daily Values aren't the same as the Recommended Dietary Allowances for nutrients for your age and gender; % DVs suggest how much is in a dose-serving of the supplement in the context of a total day's food intake. The % DVs may differ from what you need in a day. *See "% Daily Values: What Are They Based On?" in the appendix, page 786, for a list of Daily Values used for the original, as well as new, Supplement Facts labeling.*

On the Supplement Facts, a nutrient probably won't appear if it isn't present. For example, cod liver oil lists fat on the panel, but a calcium supplement won't because it doesn't contain fat. For a substance with no % DVs, the quantity per serving must be listed—for example, "15 mg omega-3 fatty acids."

Check the Claims

Confused about marketing claims for supplements? Not surprising! Some nutrient content claims and health claims are backed by scientific consensus, yet many (structure/function claims) aren't, at least not yet. One exception: "Calcium helps build strong bones." Loose supplement regulations, including many product claims that push "over the edge" of credibility, leave many consumers misguided, bewildered, or both.

Some product claims are clearly illegal—for example, "cures cancer," "treats arthritis," "prevents impotence." According to FDA regulation, no dietary supplement can legally state or imply that it can help diagnose, lessen, treat, cure, or prevent disease. A supplement cannot be labeled legally as "FDA Approved" either no matter what it does!

Here's what marketers can claim about supplements—and how the claims are regulated—on package labels. Since claims for food and for dietary supplements are similar, *see "Food Labels: Decode the Package" in chapter 6, page 143.*

Effective August 2014, dietary supplements (vitamins, minerals, herbs, amino acids) were covered by the FDA gluten-free labeling rule; *see "Gluten-Free Labeling" in chapter 6, page 151, and "Gluten: Know Its Sources" in chapter 23, page 673.*

Nutrient content claims. "High in calcium." "Excellent source of folate." "Iron-free." Like food labels, dietary supplement labels can carry nutrient content claims if they contain a specific level of a nutrient in a serving. The claims, regulated by the FDA, are similar to nutrient content claims for food. For example, any product with at least 20 percent of the Daily Value per serving can be labeled as "high" or "excellent source" of that nutrient.

What does a nutrient content claim tell you? It's just a clue for the relative amount. You need to read the Supplement Facts to know the specific nutrient content of one dose, or "serving."

Why would a supplement be labeled as "iron free"? It's for the age fifty-plus market, when women's iron needs drop. Most men's supplements are also iron free.

Health claims. "Calcium may reduce the risk of osteoporosis." "Folic acid may reduce the risk of some neural tube defects." Health claims must be based on scientific evidence of a strong link between nutrients or food substances and a health condition; it can only state that it reduces the risk. These FDA-regulated statements are based on scientific consensus—you can trust these claims.

Some qualified health claims have been approved for supplements but not for food products: for example, B vitamins (folic acid, vitamins B_6 and B_{12}) and reduced risk for cardiovascular disease.

Structure/function claims. Echinacea "boosts the immune system." Zinc "helps maintain good immunity." Garlic "helps maintain cardiovascular health." Lutein "helps maintain healthy eyes."

Structure/function claims may appear on dietary supplements, as on food labels. They describe what the ingredient is intended to do in the body or state that it is to promote health. But they can't mention a specific disease. Research to support these claims may be limited, with little or no scientific consensus.

By regulation, the manufacturer, not the FDA, must substantiate that structure/function statements are truthful and not misleading. Because the FDA does not approve them, supplement labels also must carry a disclaimer: "This statement has not been evaluated by the Food and Drug Administration. This product is not intended to diagnose, treat, cure, or prevent any disease."

Check Ingredients Labeling, Too

The label shows ingredients, with their common name or proprietary blend, in descending order by weight. If an ingredient isn't in the Supplement Facts, it must be in the ingredients statement—for example, rose hips as the vitamin C source. Besides active ingredients, other substances—fillers, colorings, flavors, sweeteners—must be listed.

For herbal and other botanical supplements, potency often differs when different parts of a plant are used. The label must identify what part of the plant it comes from—for example, ginseng may come from a root. The ingredient source may appear on an ingredients statement or near the statement of identity. If the dietary ingredient is the exclusive blend of a manufacturer, the total weight of the blend must be stated in addition to its components being listed in descending order by weight. Non-dietary ingredients such as fillers, artificial colors, sweeteners, flavors, or binders must be listed, too, in descending order by weight and by common name or proprietary blend.

As an online reference, the Dietary Supplement Label Database (DSLD) contains the full label contents from a sample of dietary supplement products marketed in the United States. It is a joint project of the NIH's Office of Dietary Supplements and National Library of Medicine (NLM); visit www.dsld.nlm.nih.gov.

STORE SUPPLEMENTS SAFELY

Like food and medications, supplements need to be stored properly for safety.

- Keep supplements in a safe place—away from where children may reach them! Adult iron supplements are the most common cause of poisoning deaths among children in the United States.
- Keep supplements in a cool, dry, and dark place—preferably away from the stove and not in the bathroom. Heat, moisture, and light affect their quality and effectiveness. Keep them in their original containers (label still on).
- Keep fish oil and any other fat-based supplements in the refrigerator to protect against rancidity. Some supplements with probiotics should be refrigerated, too; check the label.
- Check the expiration date. Supplements lose some potency as they get closer to their expiration date.

USE SUPPLEMENTS AS DIRECTED

If your doctor recommends a supplement—either a vitamin-mineral combination or a single nutrient such as calcium—follow his or her professional guidance. The same advice applies to any supplement.

- Take only the recommended dosage. Instead of double-dosing on nutrient supplements on days when you've missed a meal, make up for foods you missed with your food choices on the next day.
- Be cautious about doubling up. If you already take a multivitamin/mineral supplement, taking a single vitamin or mineral supplement, or a food fortified with that nutrient, on a regular basis as well may be too much. Read the label.
- Stick with the label dosage; heed warnings. The dosage is set by the manufacturer—not by FDA regulations. Increasing the dosage without medical supervision can be dangerous, even for an insignificant substance. *Be aware:* For the same supplement in the same dosage, people may react differently.
- Follow label directions. Some supplements are more effective taken with food; others, on an empty stomach. Ask your doctor or pharmacist for a list of foods and drinks to avoid consuming with the supplement. Usually water is the best drink.
- If you get a doctor's okay, use herbal products only as directed. Because herbal supplements can have druglike effects, too much taken at one time can be dangerous.
- If an herbal product—or a supplement—seems to cause any negative side effects, stop taking it and contact your doctor right away. Your doctor should contact the FDA's MedWatch hotline, which monitors adverse reactions to food and dietary supplements. *See "If You Have an Adverse Reaction . . ." in this chapter, page 336.*

- Keep a daily supplement journal for you and your doctor: what supplement(s), how often, how much, why, and any adverse reactions (appetite loss, headaches, nausea). Keep track of medication, too, both prescription and over-the-counter.
- Be alert for unexpected side effects; many supplements contain active ingredients with the potential for strong effects on the body. And know that harmful side effects more likely happen when people take a combination of many supplements or use supplements instead of prescribed medication.

PART III

Nutrients: What's Inside Your Food

11

Carbs: Sugars, Starches, and Fiber

In this chapter, find out about . . .

- Sugars, starches, and fiber differences
- Carbs: why, how much, and what sources
- Carb foods for good nutrition
- Low-calorie and calorie-free sweeteners

When you think of carbohydrates, what comes to mind? "Good carbs" and "bad carbs"? Eating "low carb" or not? Or maybe getting enough fiber? "Good carbs" and "bad carbs" are just popular jargon. To some people, the term "bad carbs" may casually mean added sugars, refined flour, or foods made with these ingredients that have few other nutrients. And in casual use, "good carbs" often refers to foods with more fiber and complex carbs that have other nutrients, too, such as whole grains, vegetables, fruits, and beans.

That said, all carbohydrate foods can have a place in healthy meals and snacks—with wise planning and some limits. Carbohydrates are essential as an energy source; in the form of fiber, carbohydrates protect your health in many important ways. So going "low carb" may not be a smart approach.

Many nourishing and flavorful foods—crunchy celery, summer-fresh corn on the cob, juicy peaches, sweet mangoes, hearty whole-grain breads, enriched white rice, savory baked beans, and yogurt—put carbohydrates, in one form or another, on your plate. If you choose them wisely, you may have room for some sweet treats from time to time, too.

Carbs: Simple and Complex

Sugars, starches, and fiber all belong to the nutrient category called carbohydrates. As a category of energy nutrients, sugars (simple carbohydrates) and starches (complex carbohydrates) are your body's main fuel sources. Fiber, another complex carb, has different and unique health benefits, but it's technically not a nutrient.

For the record, "carbs" is the nickname for a nutrient category. However, the words "carbohydrates" and "carbs" often are used loosely by many people to mean bread, pasta, rice, and other carbohydrate-containing foods.

All carbohydrates are made of the same three elements: carbon, hydrogen, and oxygen. The name comes from their chemical makeup: "carbo-" means carbon, and "-hydrate" means water, or H_2O. To make different types of carbohydrates, these elements are arranged into single sugar units. Then these units are often linked together. Sugars are made of one unit or a small number of units. That's why sugars are considered simple carbohydrates. Starches and fiber, on the other hand, are complex carbohydrates, made of chains of sugar units.

SUGARS: CARBOHYDRATES' SHORT FORM

When you hear the word "sugar," table sugar may come to mind. Yet that's just one form of sugar, or simple carbohydrate. Some sugars occur naturally in foods. Others are added. Regardless, both provide the same number of calories per gram. In scientific language, here's how they are named: "mono-" means one, "di-" means two, "oligo-" means few, "poly-" means many, and "-saccharide" means sugar.

- Monosaccharides are made of one sugar unit. Glucose, fructose, and galactose are monosaccharides. Glucose, used for energy in body cells, is the form of sugar that circulates in the blood. It is referred to as blood sugar or blood glucose. Fructose is the naturally occurring sugar in fruit, root vegetables, and honey. When fructose occurs naturally, it's always in food with other sugars, such as glucose. Galactose is structurally similar to glucose, but less sweet. It is found in milk as a part of lactose.
- Disaccharides are two sugar units linked together. When two monosaccharides join chemically, they become disaccharides:
    - lactose = glucose + galactose
    - maltose = glucose + glucose
    - sucrose = glucose + fructose

  Lactose is the naturally occurring sugar in milk. During digestion, lactose is broken down into glucose and galactose. Maltose is formed when starch breaks down; in turn maltose can become simpler yet. Sucrose is another name for table sugar. This same sugar is found naturally in many fruits, some vegetables, and some grains.
- Oligosaccharides have three to ten sugar units.

STARCHES: MADE OF MANY SUGARS

Starches and fiber have something in common. Called complex carbohydrates, they're long-branched (like a tree branch and twigs) or unbranched (straight) chains of up to hundreds, even thousands, of sugar units.

Starch comes from plant-based foods such as beans and peas, rice, pasta, potatoes, and other vegetables and grain products. Whole-grain foods as well as beans and peas, fruits, and other vegetables also deliver fiber.

Glycogen is the form of carbohydrate that's stored in your liver and muscles. During endurance sports, glycogen is an important energy source. *See "Energy to Burn: Fuel Your Workout" in chapter 21, page 604, for more about energy for sports.*

? Have you ever wondered?

. . . if honey, coconut sugar, or other so-called natural sweeteners are more nutritious than white, or table, sugar? That's a common misconception. While promoted as healthier options, sweeteners such as agave nectar, honey, grape juice concentrate, date sugar, maple sugar, and coconut sugar don't differ significantly from other sugars in calories and nutrients.

Honey, formed from nectar by bees, is composed of several sugars (fructose, glucose, sucrose, and others). Ounce for ounce, the nutrients in honey and table sugar are nearly the same. A teaspoon of honey has slightly more calories and carbohydrates because honey weighs slightly more. One teaspoon of table sugar has about 16 calories and 4.5 grams of carbohydrates; one teaspoon of honey, about 21 calories and 6 grams of carbohydrates. Both are broken down into glucose and fructose in your body. Honey is sweeter than table sugar, so you need slightly less honey to sweeten foods at the same level—you could say it equals out.

For anyone, including those with diabetes, these sugars affect blood sugar in similar ways. If you like the flavor, enjoy them but only in limited amounts, as with any added sugars.

. . . if molasses, a natural sugar, is more nutritious than other sweeteners? Molasses has measurable amounts of some nutrients. Because the flavor is strong, the amount generally consumed isn't usually enough to provide an appreciable nutrient contribution—and it does supply calories. One teaspoon of molasses has about 13 milligrams of calcium, 0.3 milligrams of iron, and 20 calories.

. . . how sweeteners compare for calories? Sugars of all kinds deliver about 15 to 20 calories and about 4 grams of sugar per teaspoon. Compare calories in 1 teaspoon of each of these sugars:

honey	21 calories
agave nectar/syrup	21 calories
corn syrup, light or dark	19 calories
turbinado sugar	18 calories
brown sugar (packed)	17 calories
maple syrup	17 calories
jelly	16 calories
table sugar	16 calories
coconut (palm) sugar	15 calories

Have you ever wondered?

. . . what refined sugar is? Refined sugar is described most simply as sugar separated either from the stalk of sugarcane or from the root of a sugar beet. The sugar-containing juice of the plant is extracted and then processed into dried sugar crystals, which are sold as granulated or white sugar, also called table sugar. Molasses is the thick syrup that's left (spun out) after sugar beet or sugarcane is processed for table sugar.

Brown sugar is merely sugar crystals flavored with molasses. Nutrition-wise, it too has about 17 calories and 4 grams of carbohydrate per teaspoon—about the same amounts as white sugar.

. . . what raw sugar is? Raw sugar is a coarse, granulated solid sugar left when clarified sugarcane juice evaporates during sugarcane processing. Light-tan turbinado sugar is raw sugar washed in a centrifuge to remove surface molasses. Nutritionally speaking, its caloric and carbohydrate contents are the same as in refined sugar.

. . . about evaporated cane juice? Although it has a natural-sounding name, it's simply sugar from the sugarcane plant, with a hint of molasses that gives it a light-golden color. Evaporation is part of sugar's crystallization process.

. . . if starch is made of sugars, why it doesn't taste sweet? Molecule size makes the difference. Starch molecules are bigger. Unlike sugars, starch molecules are too big to fit on the receptors of your taste buds, so they don't taste sweet. But keep a starchy cracker in your mouth for a while. Once digestive enzymes in saliva break down its starch into sugars, the cracker starts to taste sweet.

FIBER: COMPLEX, TOO

Fiber is often referred to as a single food component, but it's not that simple. Actually, fiber is a general term referring to different polysaccharides and lignin. Polysaccharides have more than ten sugar units.

Like starch, fiber is a complex carbohydrate, made of many linked sugar units. Unlike starch, fiber can't be digested, or broken down, into simple sugars for absorption into the bloodstream. Humans lack the right enzymes to digest fiber in the small intestine. Instead, it passes through to the large intestine undigested.

Various types of fiber have differing qualities, promoting health in different ways. One quality that describes different fibers is their solubility. Some dissolve in water; others don't. Known as "roughage," insoluble fibers give structure to plant-cell walls. Other qualities that may be more important for fibers' health benefits are their viscosity or fermentability; some fibers have both. Viscous, or gelatinous, fibers are soluble fibers that gel or thicken in water. Many fiber-rich foods have a mixture of fiber types.

DIGESTION: COMPLEX TO SIMPLE

Both sugars and starches break down to single sugars during digestion. From a calorie standpoint, the body doesn't distinguish their food source.

In a nutshell, going from a complex carbohydrate to a simple sugar happens when starches are digested. Before they can be absorbed from your digestive tract into your bloodstream, starches are broken down by human enzymes in several places (mouth, stomach, intestines) to the simplest sugars: glucose, galactose, and fructose. Then, in the bloodstream, single sugars move into body cells where they're converted to energy.

Monosaccharides such as the fructose in fruits can be absorbed as they are. That's not true for disaccharides: sucrose, lactose, and maltose. Digestive enzymes must break them down. That said, some people don't produce enough of a digestive enzyme called lactase; as a result, they may feel discomfort after eating lactose, or milk sugar. *See "Lactose Intolerance: A Matter of Degree" in chapter 23, page 666.*

Only fiber remains relatively intact through the body's small intestine. Digestive enzymes in the intestine can't break down fiber to sugar units, which is why fiber isn't a significant source of energy, or calories.

Different fibers work in different ways in the large intestine. Fibers can bind to water and add bulk to waste, or they can be fermented by friendly bacteria in the gut to form gases and short-chain fatty acids. Short-chain fatty acids, created through fermentation, are absorbed and provide a small amount of calories and other unique health benefits.

Sugars and Starches: For Energy and Health

Carbohydrates are one of six nutrient categories. They are your body's preferred and major energy source.

YOUR BODY'S POWER SOURCE

Carbohydrates power everything from jogging to breathing to thinking and even to digesting food. Actually, glucose is the main form of carbohydrate used for energy—and the only energy source your brain normally can use. Because glucose circulates in your bloodstream, it's often called blood glucose. It's carried to all body cells. Each cell has its own powerhouse, which uses blood glucose to fuel the cell, and so everything you do.

When carbohydrates are absorbed, blood glucose levels rise. Insulin helps glucose enter cells, where it's used for energy. But your body doesn't turn all blood glucose to energy at once. As blood glucose levels rise above normal, insulin (a pancreatic hormone) signals your liver, muscles, and some other cells to store the extra. Some gets stored in the muscles and liver as glycogen, a storage form of carbohydrate. Some glucose may be converted to body fat—if you consume more than your body uses, or burns.

When blood glucose levels drop below normal, another hormone, called glucagon, triggers the conversion of glycogen to glucose. That's how blood glucose levels stay within a normal range between meals. Once glucose is back in your bloodstream, it's again ready to fuel body cells.

Your body also obtains energy from fat and protein. However, carbohydrates should be your main energy source. When your body doesn't have enough carbohydrates for energy, fat becomes an energy source. If you limit calories and carbs and stored glucose is depleted, ketones form from a process of incomplete fat breakdown and build up in the bloodstream (complete fat breakdown requires glucose). Excess ketones in the blood, or ketosis, has been linked to health problems such as kidney damage and gout.

If your calorie intake is less than what your body needs and if your limited glycogen stores are spent, body proteins are broken down for energy. Getting enough carbs from food choices also can spare, or save, protein for what only protein can do: build and repair body cells and tissues. *See chapter 12, page 373, for more about protein.*

Whether from sugar or starch, a single gram of carbohydrate fuels your body with the same amount of energy, 4 calories per gram. By comparison, protein also supplies 4 calories per gram, and fat supplies 9 calories per gram. (Fiber fermentation in the gut is estimated to provide 2.5 calories per gram. However since not all fiber is fermentable, calculating fiber's energy value poses problems and can lead to calorie miscalculations.)

The bottom line: For your health's sake, make nutrient-rich carbohydrate foods your body's main energy source.

? Have you ever wondered?

. . . what resistant starch is? It's a complex carbohydrate that resists digestion in the small intestine. Instead, it passes into the large intestine, where it's fermented and may promote the growth of healthy bacteria. Resistant starch performs like fiber and so contributes fewer calories than other complex carbohydrates.

Naturally occurring resistant starch, which works like low-viscous fiber, is found in beans and peas; underripe and slightly green bananas; cold, cooked potatoes; and unprocessed whole grains. It also may be produced through food processing and added to food as a functional fiber.

. . . what inulin is? Inulin—not to be confused with insulin—is a soluble and fermentable fiber found naturally in many vegetables and fruits, including Jerusalem artichokes, asparagus, leeks, onions, bananas, and raisins. It's also added to many foods in the marketplace (such as some breads and pasta) to increase fiber, and sometimes as a fat replacement, without affecting the taste and texture.

Inulin isn't digested or absorbed in the stomach or small intestine. Instead, it passes into the large intestine, where it has health benefits as a fermentable prebiotic fiber. As a prebiotic, inulin is food for good bacteria such as *Bifidobacteria* and *Lactobacilli*, the same bacteria in yogurt with active cultures and fermented dairy foods. *See "Fermentation: for Gut Health" in this chapter, page 353, and see "Prebiotics and Probiotics: A Bioactive Duo" in chapter 15, page 453, for more about prebiotics and probiotics.* When replacing starch as a food ingredient, inulin doesn't affect blood glucose levels, offering possible benefits for those with diabetes. Too much inulin can result in gas (*see "Fiber and Health" in this chapter, page 350*) and diarrhea. Try to eat a variety of fiber sources, not just inulin.

. . . what fructooligosaccharides (FOS) are, and what they do? FOS, which are polymers, or chains, of fructose, are found naturally in some foods such as artichoke, asparagus, banana, chicory, garlic, and onion. Like inulin, FOS are only partially digested by humans and may help improve gastrointestinal health. Providing fewer calories than sugars or starches, they're often used as an alternative sweetener. They, too, work as a prebiotic. There's not enough evidence to suggest whether they're effective as supplements or as prebiotics for preventing traveler's diarrhea, constipation, high blood cholesterol levels, or other conditions, as sometimes claimed.

. . . what the difference is between lignin and lignan? The terms often get confused. Classified as an insoluble fiber, lignin actually isn't a carbohydrate but a complex molecule that's a woody part of the stems and seeds of vegetables and fruits and the bran in cereals. Its properties may help prevent cancers. Lignans are phytonutrients in whole grains and flaxseeds; research is examining their roles as phytoestrogens and anticancer agents. *See "Phytonutrients: Different from Nutrients" in chapter 15, page 448, to learn about phytonutrients.*

Carbs and Health: Myths or Truths?

Myth: Carbs cause an unhealthy blood-sugar spike.

Truth: It's true that insulin levels rise when carbohydrates are absorbed. That's normal and temporary. Insulin regulates energy storage, allowing your body to move blood glucose out of your bloodstream, perhaps to your cells for energy or to your muscles or liver for storage. Once that's accomplished, insulin and glucose levels drop to a normal level, and the after-meal blood glucose rise, or spike, is hardly noticed if you're healthy. The idea of unhealthy sugar spikes, or sugar highs, isn't scientifically founded for healthy people.

Myth: Eating carbs makes you fat.

Truth: Contrary to some popular beliefs, sugars won't cause your body to make or store fat unless you consume them to excess. Glucose is converted to body fat only if you consume more calories than your body needs. Eating too many calories from any source—carbohydrates, fats, proteins, or alcohol—contributes to weight gain when calorie intake exceeds calorie output. The same goes for any type of sugar (added or naturally occurring) or starch; all have calories and share equally in the potential for weight gain when calorie balance tips toward excess calorie intake.

When you eat a variety of foods with enough carbohydrates, excess calories from fats turn into body fat first before extra calories from carbohydrates do. Neither sugar itself nor a carbohydrate-rich diet causes an insulin reaction that will result in weight gain; again, it's only if carbs are consumed in excess. And consuming carbohydrate-rich foods doesn't cause insulin resistance. People who are overweight and sedentary may have symptoms of insulin resistance, a condition often diminished with moderate physical activity and weight loss.

Myth: Carbs cause diabetes.

Truth: Neither sugars nor other carbohydrates cause diabetes. Although the scientific community debunked this myth decades ago, this misconception persists.

With diabetes, the body can't handle blood glucose (blood sugar) normally, which affects the body's ability to produce energy from food. The causes are complex. Genetics and a sedentary lifestyle certainly play roles, but illness, being overweight or obese, prior gestational diabetes, or simply getting older may trigger type 2 diabetes. Being overweight seems to be a key factor in the growing epidemic of type 2 diabetes, and not just for adults, but among kids, too.

In the past, people with diabetes were warned to avoid or strictly limit sugar in their food choices. Today, experts recognize that both sugars and starches affect blood glucose levels. According to current advice from the American Diabetes Association, moderate amounts of sugar—in fact, all carbohydrates—can be part of a well-balanced diet for controlling diabetes if managed carefully.

To control blood glucose levels, people with type 2 diabetes need to manage all carbohydrates as well as proteins, fats, and alcoholic drinks, in their meals and snacks. Physical activity and perhaps medication also are part of managing diabetes.

A registered dietitian nutritionist or certified diabetes educator can help people with diabetes plan and monitor their diet. *See "Diabetes: A Growing Concern" in chapter 24, page 698, for more on diabetes as well as insulin resistance.*

Myth: Carbs trigger hypoglycemia.

Truth: This is highly unlikely. Yet many people explain away anxiety, headaches, and chronic fatigue as hypoglycemia caused by eating foods with sugar. Often self-diagnosed, hypoglycemic disorders are actually rare.

Hypoglycemia, or low blood glucose, is a condition, not a disease. Between meals, glucose levels naturally drop, but they remain fairly constant, between 60 and 110 milligrams per deciliter (mg/dL). A signal for hypoglycemia is when levels drop below about 40 mg/dL. When blood glucose falls below normal levels, there's not enough glucose immediately available for cells to produce energy. That can cause several symptoms, including sweating, rapid heartbeat, trembling, and hunger.

Among people with diabetes, hypoglycemia is caused by taking too much insulin, by exercising too much, or by not eating enough. In most other cases, low blood glucose is linked to other serious medical problems, such as liver disease or a pancreatic tumor.

Although uncommon, a disorder called reactive hypoglycemia may occur. As a rebound effect, the body secretes too much insulin after eating a large meal. The result is a drop in blood glucose well below normal, with symptoms such as shakiness, sweating, rapid heartbeat, and trembling—within about two to four hours after eating. These symptoms shouldn't be confused with being extremely hungry. Some people have similar symptoms without having low blood glucose.

If you think you're among the few with symptoms of reactive hypoglycemia, pay attention to how you feel two to four hours after eating. Talk to your doctor about testing your blood glucose level while you're experiencing symptoms. Be cautious of so-called health clinics that diagnose sugar-induced hypoglycemia and offer treatment with costly remedies.

(continued)

Carbs and Health: Myths or Truths? *(continued)*

Myth: Carbs cause hyperactivity, or a "sugar high."

Truth: Following an afternoon of sweet snacks, friends, and active play, kids may be wired up. But don't blame candy, cupcakes, or sweet drinks for a sugar high. Sugar has been wrongly accused as a cause of hyperactivity or attention deficit-hyperactive disorder (ADHD). Although scientific evidence doesn't support a link between sugar intake and hyperactivity, many parents and other caregivers seem reluctant to put this notion aside.

Causes of nervous, aggressive, and impulsive behavior and a short attention span aren't understood completely. But experts advise adults to take stock of a child's overall environment. The excitement of a party or a special event, such as trick-or-treating or visiting Santa—not the sweet snacks that go with the fun—may account for unruly behavior. To the contrary, some studies suggest that sugars (and carbohydrates, in general) may have a calming effect. A body chemical called serotonin produced in and released from the brain may be a factor.

Myth: Sugar is addictive.

Truth: A liking for sweetness is innate from birth. A sweet tooth may be a habitual or an emotional response, but not a physiological dependency. Although it may take getting used to, cutting back on sweets or sugary drinks won't cause a physical response.

Fiber and Health

Life doesn't depend on fiber, but your overall health may. Fiber promotes health, including optimal digestive and gut health and bowel regularity. A high-fiber eating pattern—with fiber-rich whole grains, vegetables, fruits, beans, peas, and lentils, and nuts—also may help reduce the risks for obesity, heart disease, type 2 diabetes, and other chronic diseases. Here's why.

Foods contain different types of fiber with different qualities that provide different health benefits. Fiber found naturally in most fiber-rich foods is a combination of types. Some fibers are fermentable, being degraded in the intestine by friendly bacteria and so yield gases and short-chain fatty acids. How fermentable they are depends on the type of fiber, the time it takes to pass through the digestive tract, and the bacteria in the gut.

Some fibers, such as cellulose, hemicellulose, and lignin, aid digestion. Although they don't dissolve, these fibers do hold on to water; they are sometimes referred to as insoluble. And they move waste through the intestinal tract without being broken down, earning fiber its title as "nature's broom." By adding bulk and softness to stools, fiber promotes regularity and helps prevent constipation. And by moving wastes through the colon, fiber increases the rate at which wastes are removed.

Other fibers, such as gums, mucilages, pectin, and some hemicelluloses, dissolve, becoming gummy or gelatinous (viscous). They are sometimes referred to as soluble. Gelatinous fibers help reduce dietary cholesterol and fat absorption, helping to lower blood cholesterol levels. They help control the amount of glucose in the bloodstream, a benefit to those with insulin sensitivity. Gelatinous fibers also may slow the time it takes to empty the stomach, giving a feeling of fullness. They're often used in low-fat and fat-free foods to add texture and consistency. Soft, liquid foods may have fiber, but usually it's not gelatinous.

If you've ever made jam or jelly, you're probably familiar with pectin. Pectin provides their thick, gel-like consistency. In your body, pectin binds to fatty substances and promotes their excretion as waste. This quality seems to help lower blood cholesterol levels. Gelatinous fibers also may help regulate the body's use of sugars.

HEALTHY WEIGHT AND FIBER

A fiber-rich diet may help you reach and keep your healthy weight. In fact, research shows that a fiber-rich diet is linked to lower body weight. The reasons are not clear. But these factors are being studied:

- Fiber-rich foods are often lower in calories than the same volume of high-fat foods and may displace other sources with more food energy (calories).
- Fiber itself isn't digested, so it provides few calories. Its few calories come from short-chain fatty acids, which are produced when fiber ferments in the large intestine.
- Many fiber-rich foods are more satiating than low-fiber foods, meaning they help you feel full on fewer calories, so you may be less likely to overeat. Because many fiber-rich foods take longer to chew, you may eat more slowly, giving your body time to register that you're full.

Fiber adds bulk to food, slowing the time it takes to pass through your gastrointestinal tract. A fiber-rich meal or snack may help fill you up and stay with you longer. Fiber that ferments in the intestine may affect satiety, too. Some types of fiber are more satiating than others, and some types added to food and drinks have little or no satiating effect.

To make a fiber-rich diet work for your waistline, avoid excess calorie intake, too, and stay physically active. *See chapter 22, page 624, to learn more about healthy weight.*

Glycemic Index and Glycemic Load

WHAT IS GLYCEMIC INDEX?

Glycemic index (GI) rates carbohydrate-containing foods for their effects on blood glucose levels after eating them: how high the glucose level rises and for how long. Depending on their characteristics, some foods enter the bloodstream faster; others, more slowly because they take longer to digest.

A food's GI is ranked against a glucose solution on a scale of 1 to 100: 55 or under is low; 56 to 69 is medium; and 70 or above is high. Foods with a higher glycemic index produce a greater increase in blood glucose levels (response) than low GI foods. Figuring the body's response sounds simpler than it really is.

Glycemic index is calculated for a specific amount of food, usually the amount that provides 50 grams of available carbohydrate. Fiber is not a factor. The glycemic index of a food depends on many factors, so even the same foods can differ:

- Differences in cooking and processing techniques, a plant's chemical composition (including its ripeness and variety), and how much fiber or sugar naturally occurs in a carbohydrate food can affect the GI.
- How long it takes to digest matters.
- The size of the portion factors in when figuring what counts as the standard 50 grams of available carbohydrate.

In general, nonstarchy vegetables, most fruits, beans and peas, and milk tend to have a low glycemic index. For example, ½ cup of kidney beans has a glycemic index of 52; a medium apple, 38. White bread (from refined flour), crackers, and cornflakes are high-GI foods. The glycemic index of a medium baked potato (no skin) is 85, considered high. Perhaps surprisingly, lower-calorie, nutrient-rich foods may have a higher GI than you think. Both ½ cup of carrots and 2 cups of watermelon have a high glycemic index, 92 and 72, respectively.

WHAT IS GLYCEMIC LOAD?

Glycemic load (GL) takes both the quality and the quantity of carbohydrates into account. The rise and the fall of blood glucose levels after eating depend on both.

The GL equals the food's GI multiplied by the amount of carbohydrates in grams divided by 100. For example, a small apple has a GI of 40×20 grams of carbohydrate, then divided by 100=a GL of 8. In contrast, a small baked potato with a GI of 60×30 grams of carbohydrate, then divided by 100=a GL of 18, or more than twice the metabolic impact. For GL, less than 10 is low, 11 to 20 is medium, and 21 or over is high.

GI: A USEFUL TOOL?

The glycemic index of a single food isn't reliable for helping most healthy consumers make food choices. Here's why:

- GI doesn't measure what happens with mixed foods, and so a high-GI food eaten with a low-GI food may give a moderate GI response. The presence or absence of fat or protein in the meal affects the total GI value of that meal. For example, spread butter on bread, and the GI goes way down.
- How much of a food you eat matters. If it's more or less than the amount used to calculate glycemic response, your own response may differ.
- Food preparation makes a difference. For example, overcooked pasta has a higher GI than pasta cooked al dente.
- The GI response to the same food can vary from one person to another, and from day to day for the same person.

By choosing foods based on GI or GL alone, you may miss out on some foods with considerable amounts of nutrients and phytonutrients. Think again about the example of carrots and watermelon. A lower GI value does not necessarily make the food healthier. A smarter approach is to heed the calories, nutrient density, and fiber content. If you choose to use the GI or GL, avoid using it as your only way to judge a food. Choose lower-GI foods more often, and make overall balanced nutrition your goal. And don't disregard sound nutritional advice.

Can glycemic index (GI) and glycemic load (GL) help you choose foods to manage your weight, blood glucose level, or other health condition?

Regarding weight management, eating foods with a lower GI and/or GL isn't associated with body weight, and using GI or GL as tools to select foods doesn't lead to more weight loss or better weight maintenance, according to research evidence. And currently, no evidence shows that eliminating foods with a higher glycemic index, such as baked potatoes or cornflakes, promotes weight loss or helps with appetite control.

If you have diabetes, glycemic index may be a tool to help you make food choices to manage your blood glucose level. However, it cannot replace the need to monitor the total grams of carbohydrate you consume and your blood glucose level. That said, glycemic index is being used in research related to type 2 diabetes, heart disease, and obesity. *See "If You Have Diabetes" in chapter 24, page 702, to learn about GI and diabetes management.* Sometimes endurance athletes use high-GI foods to resynthesize muscle glycogen.

Defining Fiber

If you read about fiber, you'll likely find a cluster of terms: dietary fiber, functional fiber, added fiber, total fiber, and a few more. What's the difference? What we understand about fiber is in flux—with more to learn about measuring food's fiber content and its many physiological effects. This includes fiber's ability to bind cholesterol, how it speeds intestinal transit time to protect against cancer and constipation, and how its fermentation benefits gut health. These issues affect how we talk about fiber.

The Dietary Reference Intakes (DRIs) use "total fiber," defined as dietary fiber plus functional fiber. In this book, dietary fiber is the indigestible carbohydrates and lignin that are naturally present in plant-based foods. Nutrition Facts for food labeling in the United States use dietary fiber, too.

Also with health benefits, functional fibers consist of isolated, nondigestible carbohydrates that are either extracted from natural sources or are manufactured plant or animal products and added to foods, beverages, and supplements.

The term "added fiber" refers to fiber added to food during processing. For example, inulin and FOS (fructooligosaccharides or fructan) work as prebiotics; methylcellulose is a bulking agent.

As more is learned, the definitions of fiber will be clarified. For example, the definition of dietary fiber differs around the world. Nutrition truly is an evolving science.

Functional Nutrition

A Quick Look at Dietary Fiber

Fiber/Component	Potential Benefit	Some Food Sources
Beta glucan*	May reduce the risk of coronary heart disease (CHD)	Oat bran, oatmeal, oat flour, barley, rye
Insoluble fiber	Supports maintenance of the digestive system; may reduce the risk of some types of cancer	Wheat bran, corn, bran, fruit skins
Soluble fiber*	May reduce the risk of CHD and some types of cancer	Psyllium seed husk, peas, beans, apples, citrus fruit
Whole grains*	May reduce the risk of CHD and some types of cancer; supports maintenance of healthy blood glucose levels	Cereal grains, whole-wheat bread, oatmeal, brown rice

*The US Food and Drug Administration has approved a health claim for this food component.

Source: International Food Information Council Foundation, 2011.

TYPE 2 DIABETES AND FIBER

For people with type 2 diabetes, a fiber-rich diet (especially gelatinous fiber from foods such as oats and beans) may help to control the rise of blood glucose levels after eating. The reason it may help lower blood glucose levels isn't fully understood. Perhaps it's because some types of fiber make the stomach contents more gelatinous (more sticky and gummy) and so prolong its emptying. Because carbohydrates break down more slowly, sugars are released and absorbed more slowly, too. That in turn may slow the rise of blood glucose levels.

A fiber-rich meal, which is "bulkier," less calorie dense, and takes longer to eat, is another plus for diabetes management. All these factors promote satiety and may help prevent overeating. For some with diabetes, fiber's role in blood glucose control may help reduce the need for insulin, or medication.

Some research suggests that increasing dietary fiber, particularly with low-GI foods, may reduce the risk of type 2 diabetes. However, more research is needed to understand the role of dietary fiber in preventing prediabetes.

If you have diabetes and want advice for consuming more fiber for blood glucose control, talk to a registered dietitian nutritionist or certified diabetes educator.

See "Diabetes: A Growing Concern" in chapter 24, page 698, to learn more.

DIGESTIVE HEALTH: FIBER LINK

Fiber is well recognized for sweeping waste through the digestive tract. It's also key to fermentation that promotes gut health. *See "A Closer Look . . . How to Keep 'Gut Healthy'" in chapter 25, page 727.*

An Intestinal "Broom"

As discussed earlier, some types of fiber hold on to water, helping to soften and add bulk to waste. For example, wheat bran has been shown to have a bulking effect since it resists digestion and fermentation. This action promotes gastrointestinal health, helping stools pass through the intestinal tract more quickly and with normal frequency and ease—and gives some fiber the reputation of being an "intestinal broom." As a result, fiber helps prevent constipation and the discomfort that goes with it. It

Have you ever wondered?

. . . if carbohydrates affect your mood? Maybe, but the evidence isn't conclusive. Studies have investigated the link between stress and serotonin, a body chemical synthesized as more tryptophan (a nonessential amino acid) enters the brain. Serotonin, a mood regulator, breaks down to help relieve stress. Although carbohydrates may help replenish the body's serotonin, no conclusive research suggests a calming effect. Does a bowl of ice cream or a mug of hot chocolate give you a feeling of comfort or calm? Perhaps it's really a link to pleasant memories.

. . . why fiber isn't classified simply as "soluble" and "insoluble" fiber as it was in the past? Being soluble or not doesn't tell the whole fiber story. Other properties of various fibers may be as important for different health benefits, among them their viscosity, their ability to ferment, and their physical and chemical structures.

. . . what FODMAPs are? FODMAP is an acronym that stands for "fermentable oligosaccharides, disaccharides, monosaccharides, and polyols." These various types of sugars and carbohydrates are found in many different foods, making a low-FODMAP diet challenging to follow. When FODMAPs can't be digested or absorbed, they pass to the large intestine, where they are fermented and may cause gastrointestinal discomfort. Polyols, or sugar alcohols, are found naturally in some vegetables and fruits and can be made by processing some sugars, *as discussed in "Sugar Alcohols in Foods" in this chapter, page 369.*

For some people, managing FODMAPs can be a way to manage some gastrointestinal discomfort such as irritable bowel syndrome (IBS). *See "A Closer Look . . . FODMAPs" in chapter 25, page 730.*

also may help solidify loose, watery stools. Other fibers, for example in vegetables, fruits, oats, and corn, increase the weight of stools.

When soft stools easily pass out of the body, there's no need for strained bowel movements. As a result, hemorrhoids—a painful swelling of the veins near the anus—are less likely to form. Softer, bulkier stools put less pressure on the colon walls, too, and so reduce the chance of hemorrhoids and the discomfort of constipation. This also may reduce cancer risk. *See "Digestive Health: GI Upsets and Conditions" in chapter 25, page 727.*

Fermentation for Gut Health

Potential benefits to gut health also come into play when health-promoting, intestinal bacteria cause fiber to ferment. Fibers, such as inulin, beta glucans, and pectins, are fermentable, helping to create an environment for colonies of healthy bacteria to thrive. That may help promote immunity, may help the body eliminate waste, and may help reduce discomfort from some food intolerances.

Short-chain fatty acids (SCFAs), produced from fermentable fiber, help the body absorb some key minerals, especially calcium, iron, and magnesium; provide some energy; and may help support immunity. The production of SCFAs during fermentation also may help suppress harmful bacteria that create inflammation and so may lower the chance of infections and colorectal cancer. SCFAs also may help to lower blood cholesterol and triglyceride levels, improve the HDL-LDL cholesterol ratio, and lower blood glucose response.

FIBER: FOR HEART HEALTH, TOO

Another potential benefit of fiber: Differing types of fiber (from foods or supplements) may help reduce the risk of cardiovascular disease in different ways: by improving blood cholesterol levels, by lowering blood pressure, and by reducing inflammation in the body.

Research suggests that 12 to 33 grams of fiber per day from food, or up to 42.5 grams of fiber per day from supplements with gelatinous fiber, such as psyllium and beta glucan, may provide these benefits. Studies indicate that whole grains also protect against heart disease and that bran is likely protective, as well.

Some fibers (mostly beta glucan) may help lower the level of total blood cholesterol, mainly by lowering LDL, or "bad," cholesterol. Research evidence indicates these factors:

- In the small intestine, soluble fiber acts like a sponge, binding cholesterol-rich bile acids so they can't be reabsorbed, but instead pass through the intestine as waste. Thus the body absorbs less dietary cholesterol, and the liver pulls more cholesterol from the blood to replace the lost bile acids. That may make blood cholesterol levels drop.
- Fermentation of some soluble fibers in the large intestine to form short-chain fatty acids also helps inhibit cholesterol synthesis in the liver. Other fibers may resist fermentation and may pass through the digestive tract mostly unchanged.
- Fiber may also protect against inflammation and high levels of C-reactive protein, which are both linked to increased risk of cardiovascular disease. *See "A Closer Look . . . Inflammation, Health, and Food" in chapter 24, page 699.*

There's enough sound research relating fiber and heart health for the US Food and Drug Administration (FDA) to allow some foods to carry health claims linking oats, psyllium, and whole grains to heart health. (*See "Health 'Info': Claims and More" in chapter 6, page 149.*) Those same high-fiber foods may be lower in fat, too, and may have other substances besides fiber that affect the way the body uses lipids (fats), such as omega-3 fatty acids. Yet another benefit is that fiber-rich foods may displace fattier foods in meals and snacks. Research also suggests a potential link between higher fiber intake and reduced blood pressure.

As more is learned about fiber and heart health, it's a good idea to consume fiber-rich foods of all kinds—and follow other advice for heart health. *See "If You Need to Improve Your Lipid Levels" in chapter 24, page 689.*

How to . . . Deal with Intestinal Gas

People complain and sometimes joke about beans and vegetables in the cabbage family, saying they cause gas. Yet, intestinal gas is a temporary and normal side effect of moving to a high-fiber diet. It lessens over time—often two to four weeks—as your body adjusts.

Intestinal gas forms in the colon when undigested carbohydrates are fermented by intestinal bacteria. Nutrient-rich, high-fiber foods such as beans, peas, and lentils often create the most discomfort, but vegetables, fruits, and whole grains can cause gas and bloating, too. Cruciferous vegetables, such as broccoli, Brussels sprouts, and cabbage, may produce gas with unpleasant odors. Nonetheless, this fermentation may have health benefits.

If your typical eating plan is low in fiber, and you decide to increase your fiber intake, minimize any discomfort that comes with bulking up by adding fiber slowly to your diet over several months. Drink enough water to help reduce the effects of intestinal gas and prevent impacted stools, and chew thoroughly (don't gulp your food!).

To help tame the chance of gas caused by beans try this:

- Soak uncooked, dry beans overnight in cool water. Discard the soaking water because it will contain some gas-producing carbohydrates. Cook the beans in fresh water. Allow enough time to cook dry beans thoroughly, which makes them easier to digest.
- De-gas canned beans by draining and rinsing them. This also reduces the sodium significantly.
- Take small helpings.

If you need more relief from intestinal gas, several nonprescription products may help:

- Products containing activated charcoal (a type of charcoal made for use in medicine) and taken at the end of a meal help trap body chemicals so they aren't absorbed. However, the charcoal can interfere with the absorption of medications and aren't recommended for children.
- Products such as Beano® with a food enzyme called alpha-galactosidase help convert gas-producing carbohydrates to more easily digestible sugars. They're sold as tablets or drops and are meant to be taken before a meal.
- Products with simethicone help relieve gas symptoms but don't prevent them. This substance works by breaking large pockets of gas in the intestines into smaller bubbles.

Other gas-reducing or gas-preventing products are sold, some with questionable claims. Check with your doctor before using any gas-reduction products.

Be aware that intestinal gas can have other causes. Some need medical attention, such as lactose intolerance and celiac disease, *discussed in "Lactose Intolerance: A Matter of Degree" and "Gluten Free: When It's a Must" in chapter 23, pages 666 and 670,* and health conditions such as constipation, diverticulitis, or inflammatory bowel disease, *discussed in "Digestive Health: GI Upsets and Conditions" in chapter 25, page 727.* Carbonated drinks, fiber supplements with psyllium, and sugar alcohols (polyols) such as sorbitol, mannitol, and xylitol, may also cause gas; *they're discussed in "Sugar Alcohols in Food" in this chapter, page 369.*

FIBER: CANCER PROTECTION

The link between a high-fiber diet and lowered risk for some cancers, such as colorectal cancer, and for colon polyps hasn't been clearly established, although they seem associated. Despite the inconsistency in studies, most scientific research shows there are benefits to consuming a fiber-rich diet. A high-fiber diet may help reduce colorectal cancer risk in several ways, among them:

- By speeding up the time it takes for waste to pass through the digestive tract. Slow movement of food waste through the digestive tract allows more time for potentially harmful substances to come in contact with intestinal walls.
- By forming a bulkier, heavier stool. Bulkier stools help dilute the concentration of potential carcinogens.
- By controlling the intestinal pH balance (the level of acidity or alkalinity). Insoluble fibers help keep the pH at a level that reduces the ability of intestinal microbes to produce carcinogens.

Fiber may play a protective role from other forms of cancer, too. However, research evidence is limited at this time. Is fiber the potential protector, or is it something else? It's difficult to know. Many fiber-rich foods supply plenty of nutrients, including antioxidants and phytonutrients. Any anticancer power of fiber-rich foods may come from the complex interaction or the additive benefits of their many components.

MORE FIBER BENEFITS

Ongoing research suggests that fiber plays other roles in health, too. Some types of fiber, such as inulin, may work as prebiotics. *See "Functional Nutrition: Prebiotics and Probiotics" in chapter 15, page 456.* Other types of fiber may affect the absorption of minerals such as calcium and, as a result, bone health.

Understanding fiber's benefits is complicated in other ways. Foods with dietary fiber (as opposed to functional fiber) also contain vitamins, minerals, and phytonutrients that may work together and with fiber to promote health. And food patterns that are high in dietary fiber are often lower in saturated and *trans* fats, added sugars, and sodium, too.

Carbohydrates: How Much? What Kind?

Many subscribe to the notion that "cutting carbs" is an easy path to healthy eating. Yet, smart advice is more complicated than that. It's really about choosing carb-containing foods more wisely. Carbohydrates are the best energy source for your brain and the rest of your body. And limiting added sugars and consuming more fiber are also part of carbohydrate advice.

CARBS FOR ENERGY: THE RIGHT AMOUNT FOR YOU

While the optimal amount of carbohydrates is unclear, the Institute of Medicine (IOM) offers recommendations in two ways: an Adequate Intake (AI) level for carbohydrates, and an Acceptable Macronutrient Distribution Range (AMDR) for carbs along with the other two energy nutrients.

Adequate Intake. The AI is based on the minimum level of sugars and starches needed to provide enough glucose (blood glucose) daily just for your brain to function normally. For people ages one year or over, that's a minimum of 130 grams of carbohydrate, which equals 520 calories, or 25 percent of the calories in a 2,000-calorie daily diet. (As an aside, the early stages of some weight loss regimens may recommend less.) The AI for pregnancy is 175 grams; for breastfeeding, 210 grams. Beyond the energy needed for brain function, you need carbohydrates to fuel the rest of your body.

An eating plan that simply meets the AI for carbohydrates likely won't provide enough of some other nutrients and fiber overall, and it may be high in fat or protein, depending on the total calories.

Acceptable Macronutrient Distribution Range. For that reason, the IOM also established an AMDR. For carbohydrates, that's a recommended range of 45 to 65 percent of total daily calories (or 225 to 325 grams of carbohydrates daily—providing 900 to 1,300 calories—in a 2,000-calorie-a-day eating plan). The range for young children is somewhat different; *see "Dietary Reference Intakes" in the appendix, page 780.*

The actual amount of carbs (in grams) recommended within the AMDR depends on your total calorie needs:

- If you're physically active, consume on the high end of the AMDR—about 65 percent of total daily calories from carbohydrates.
- If you're on a low-calorie eating plan, consume at the low end of the AMDR—about 45 percent of total daily calories from carbohydrates. Be aware, however, that at the lowest end of this range, it is difficult

High-Fructose Corn Syrup

Does high-fructose corn syrup (HFCS) contribute to obesity differently than other sugars? That's a question that's gotten plenty of media and research attention. And HFCS has been replaced in some products with other sweeteners due to consumer perceptions. However, a sugar is a sugar.

The amount, not the type, of sugars may lead to weight gain. Calorie for calorie, HFCS contributes no more than other sugars do. Like sucrose (table sugar), HFCS delivers 4 calories per gram. Also like sucrose, HCFS has about equal parts of fructose and glucose. When absorbed into the bloodstream, the metabolites of these sugars are indistinguishable. Flavor wise, HFCS is no sweeter than sucrose.

Despite the recent controversy, no convincing scientific evidence indicates that HFCS is processed by the body differently than sucrose, that it increases body fat in a unique way, or that it boosts appetite or causes sugar cravings. In fact, the American Medical Association (AMA) concluded that HFCS doesn't appear to contribute to obesity any more than other caloric sweeteners.

Why the attention then? Perhaps because HFCS is one of the most common sweeteners used in processed foods and beverages in the United States. And, because many people consume significant amounts of highly processed foods and drinks with added sugars, they might consume too much of it.

Why is it used? HFCS is commonly used because it blends well with other ingredients, and it costs less than sugar. It derives from cornstarch and has virtually the same composition and taste as sucrose. Crystalline fructose, which is pure fructose, can be manufactured from any source of glucose, and it looks and tastes much like sucrose, although slightly sweeter.

Some advice: As an added sugar, HFCS provides calories, and the more calories consumed from any source, the greater their influence on weight gain. To help trim your calorie intake, ease up on added sugars of all kinds, including HFCS. If you consume fruit drinks, regular soft drinks, sports drinks, and other sugary drinks, consider moderation and portion size. And go easy on all kinds of foods with added sugars, such as baked goods, candies, condiments, jams, salad dressings, sugary desserts, syrups, and yogurts as well as canned and packaged foods, and other sweetened foods.

The bottom line: Rather than trying to avoid HFCS altogether, limit your intake of all added sugars.

Your Healthy Eating Check-In

How Do Your Sweet Choices Stack Up?

Are your sweet choices packed with nutrients? Or do they provide mostly added sugars, calories, and few nutrients? Check the box that best describes what choices you make, then total the points for each column and see how you're doing with sugar management.

DO YOU . . . ?	Never 1 point	Sometimes 2 points	Usually 3 points	Always 4 points
1. Drink water, 100 percent juice, or milk rather than soft drinks as a meal or snack beverage?	☐	☐	☐	☐
2. Reach for fruit rather than candy or cookies as a snack?	☐	☐	☐	☐
3. Top your cereal with fruit rather than honey or sugar?	☐	☐	☐	☐
4. Sweeten French toast, pancakes, or waffles with fruit or fruit puree rather than syrup?	☐	☐	☐	☐
5. Top ice cream with fruit, not just chocolate or caramel syrup?	☐	☐	☐	☐
6. Check food labels to limit foods with added sugars?	☐	☐	☐	☐
7. Choose fruit rather than a sugary, high-calorie dessert?	☐	☐	☐	☐
8. Go for a small rather than a big slice of cake or pie?	☐	☐	☐	☐
9. Snack on two or three cookies with milk rather than the whole package?	☐	☐	☐	☐
10. Choose 8- or 12-ounce sodas rather than a 20-ounce (or larger) serving—and limit them regardless of size?	☐	☐	☐	☐
Subtotals	____	____	____	____

Add up your total points: ______

IF YOU SCORED . . .

30 points or above: Your sweet choices are mostly high in nutrients, too. In fact, it's okay to enjoy a bit of sugar now and then to add pleasure to eating.

20 to 29 points: If your overall diet is balanced and you're not overspending your calorie budget, your preference for sweets is probably okay.

10 to 19 points: Your sweet tooth may be crowding out nutritious foods. Check their content, and consider some sweet options such as fruit with few or no added sugars. You'll find great ideas for nutrient-rich options in this chapter.

to consume enough fiber. Usually proteins replace carbohydrates as an energy source for those on a low-calorie diet.

Tolerable Upper Intake Level (UL). There is no UL set for carbohydrates. Most people consume adequate amounts of total carbohydrates. However, depending on the food choices, too much can result in not only more added sugars, but also to more foods with refined grains that have added fats and little dietary fiber.

ADDED SUGARS: WHAT'S THE LIMIT?

Added sugars are defined as sugars, syrups, and other caloric sweeteners added to food and drinks for sweetness, preservation, and other qualities such as browning or texture. They may be added during food processing or preparation, or at the table. They don't include sugars that occur naturally in foods such as fruit or milk.

Supplement Watch: Fiber Pills, Powders, and More

Taking a fiber supplement or eating foods with added fiber may help fill the fiber gap. But they may not offer all the health benefits that fiber-rich foods provide—even if, depending on the type of fiber, they help soften stools and relieve constipation.

Most fiber in supplements and in fiber-fortified foods is called functional fiber, derived from plant or animal sources. Different functional fibers deliver different benefits. Psyllium, inulin, and oligofructose are fermentable, promoting the growth of healthy bacteria for gastrointestinal health. Psyllium also gives bulk to stools and may help lower cholesterol levels. An ingredient list on a food label may show many other functional fibers, including acacia fiber, guar gum, methylcellulose, pectin, resistant dextrins, and more.

If you do choose to take a fiber supplement for regularity, your body eventually may rely on it if your overall diet lacks fiber. Taking too much may cause intestinal issues, such as bloating, diarrhea, or gas. Ten grams of fiber per day from a supplement, spread out during the day, is likely enough.

Fiber supplements can bind with and inhibit the absorption of some minerals including calcium, iron, magnesium, and zinc as well as some medications such as aspirin and warfarin. If you take insulin to manage your blood glucose levels, you also may need to adjust your insulin dosage if you take a fiber supplement. Some fiber supplements offer only small amounts of fiber, so even if they have a laxative effect, it would take many fiber pills to meet the fiber recommendation.

Can fiber supplements help you lose weight and keep it off? No scientific evidence supports this claim. Research doesn't show a link between fiber supplements and reduced cancer risk, either.

While fiber supplements are generally safe, talk to your doctor or pharmacist before taking them, especially if you have intestinal problems. With some digestive disorders, a doctor may recommend taking a fiber supplement. If you take a fiber supplement, also drink plenty of fluids.

Fiber-rich foods—vegetables, fruits, beans, and whole grains—are better options. They supply vitamins, minerals, and phytonutrients along with other benefits associated with a high-fiber diet.

The 2015–2020 Dietary Guidelines for Americans recommends limits for added sugars: less than 10 percent of total calories from all you consume—meals, snacks, and drinks—during a single day. If you eat 2,000 calories daily, that's fewer than 200 calories (from fewer than 50 grams of added sugars). Currently, added sugars account for almost 270 calories—more than 13 percent of the total calories—per day, on average, in the US population.

Why does the Dietary Guidelines set limits? There are several reasons:

- Added sugars are used to sweeten foods and drinks. Doing so adds calories but no other nutrients.
- Limiting added sugars to no more than 10 percent of total calories provides some flexibility in your food choices. When added sugars exceed this recommendation, it's hard to keep within your calorie limit and still meet your nutrient needs.
- Sugar-sweetened drinks, snacks, and sweets that are high in calories from added sugars may contribute to excess calorie intake, with few or no other nutrients or dietary fiber. They may contribute to being overweight for children, teens, and adults.
- Meal and snack patterns that are lower in added sugars are associated with lower risks of type 2 diabetes, obesity, some types of cancer, and cardiovascular disease among adults.
- Fermentable carbohydrates—added sugars as well as starches and naturally occurring sugars—can promote tooth decay, especially with frequent snacking. Poor oral hygiene and sticky foods enhance sugars' ability to promote decay. *See "Oral Health: Your Healthy Smile" in chapter 25, page 735.*

With limits, there's some room for added sugars in a healthy eating plan. Added sugars can make nourishing foods more palatable. For example, a whole-wheat muffin, lightly sweetened with honey or dab of jam, is a way to get the benefits of whole grains. Tart cranberries are more palatable with some added sweetness. For some people, chocolate-flavored milk is a way to get the calcium and vitamin D benefits that dairy foods provide.

And if you're prudent about your food and drink choices and meet your day's food-group recommendations with your calorie limit, you may have a little "wiggle room" left for occasional extras, or sweet treats.

FIBER: WHAT'S ENOUGH?

If you're like most Americans, your day's meals and snacks come up seriously short on fiber, supplying only about half (about 15 grams) of the amount advised per day.

Fiber recommendations depend on age and gender. The IOM advises an AI for total fiber, established at a level to protect against coronary heart

? Have you ever wondered?

. . . what psyllium is? (When you pronounce it, the "p" is silent.) Psyllium—high in soluble fiber—is a seed husk used in some bulk-forming natural laxatives; it also has potential cholesterol-lowering qualities. Some supplements have it. Its source is plantago, a plant that grows in India and the Mediterranean. Although some people may be allergic to psyllium, in moderate amounts, it's safe for most people.

. . . if "whole grain" is "high fiber"? And if "high fiber" is "whole grain"? In either case, not always. First, some whole grains are higher in fiber than others, and both moisture and other ingredients in whole-grain foods also affect fiber content. Second, some foods, such as some bran cereals, are high in fiber even though they aren't whole grain. To be "whole grain," they must contain all parts of the grain (bran, endosperm, and germ).

The ingredient list and the Nutrition Facts on the food label are your best clues to foods higher in fiber. As another clue, check for a whole-grain labeling claim, *described in "Is It Really Whole Grain? Tricky to Know" in chapter 6, page 184.*

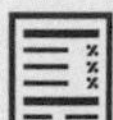

Label Lingo

Calories, Sugars, and Fiber

Although the FDA hasn't approved nutrient content claims for total carbohydrates, you may find claims related to calories, sugars, or fiber. Look for these terms on food products:

Label term . . .	Means . . .
CALORIE FREE	Contains less than 5 calories per serving
SUGAR-FREE	Contains less than 0.5 gram sugars per serving
REDUCED SUGAR OR LESS SUGAR	Contains at least 25 percent less* sugar or sugars per serving
NO ADDED SUGARS, WITHOUT ADDED SUGAR, NO SUGAR	Contains no sugars added during processing or packing, including ingredients that contain sugar, such as juice or dry fruit
HIGH FIBER	Contains 5 grams or more fiber per serving
GOOD SOURCE OF FIBER	Contains 2.5 to 4.9 grams per serving**
MORE OR ADDED FIBER	Contains at least 2.5 grams or more* fiber per serving**

*As compared with a standard serving size of the traditional food
** The updated Daily Values for use with new Nutrition Facts labeling may change these values.

disease and, as a secondary factor, to reduce the risk of type 2 diabetes. The AI for fiber is:

- Men up to age fifty years: 38 grams daily
- Women up to age fifty years: 25 grams daily. During pregnancy and breastfeeding, the recommendation is slightly higher.
- Men age fifty-one years or older: 30 grams daily
- Women age fifty-one years or older: 21 grams.

See "Dietary Reference Intakes" in the appendix, page 780, for fiber recommendations for children and teens.

Many minimally processed foods with naturally occurring fiber are the best fiber sources because they have other inherent nutrition benefits plus a mixture of fiber types.

Most healthy people can get enough fiber by eating more plant-based foods while also consuming fewer calories from foods that are high in added sugars and fat and low in fiber. *To meet your fiber goal, follow the healthy eating patterns addressed in chapter 2, page 21.*

Fiber: Too Much of a Good Thing?

No UL has been set for fiber since high intakes of dietary fiber have not been confirmed to cause adverse health effects in adults. Vegetarian diets may provide more than 50 grams of fiber per day.

Although uncommon, it's possible to overconsume fiber by eating a lot of bran or very-high-fiber cereals. It's more likely to occur by consuming too much from a fiber supplement, especially for those who also eat plenty of vegetables, fruits, and whole grains.

Consuming more than 50 to 60 grams of fiber a day may lower your body's ability to absorb vitamins and minerals, among them zinc, iron, magnesium, and calcium. An excessive amount of fiber may cause gas, diarrhea, and bloating. *See "Supplement Watch: Fiber Pills, Powders, and More" in this chapter, page 357.*

Carbohydrates in Foods and Drinks

We casually refer to a vast array of foods as "carbs" when we really mean carbohydrate-containing foods. The fact is that some are better choices than others. Most carbohydrates come from plant-based foods. Through photosynthesis, plants transform the sun's energy into carbohydrates as food for their own growth. As a result, carbohydrates—sugars and starches—are found naturally in vegetables and fruits, including beans and peas, grain products, nuts, and seeds. It may surprise you, but asparagus, broccoli, celery, and kale as well as berries, melons, and peaches, have carbohydrates, too. All these foods are good sources of other nutrients.

Carbohydrates in foods change as plants mature:

- As a fruit matures and ripens, its carbohydrates shift from starches to sugars, making it sweeter and more appealing. Serve fruits when they're ripe; you may need to allow ripening time after you buy them. *See "Freshness: How to . . . Judge Produce" in chapter 6, page 160, to learn about buying ripe and unripe fruit.*

How Much Total Carbohydrate and Fiber?

How do the total carbs in these nutrient-dense foods compare? What might 25 to 38 grams of fiber a day look like in a day's worth of meals and snacks for you? It isn't as easy as you might think to figure out. Using this list of nutrient-dense foods, consider how your fiber-rich choices can provide up to 7 to 10 grams of fiber for each of your meals. Pick fiber-rich snacks, too.

Remember that the total carbohydrates may include added sugars, depending on how these foods are processed and prepared. For packaged foods, check the label, or use Food-A-Pedia on the USDA's SuperTracker to see the added sugars in your food choices (www.supertracker.usda.gov/foodapedia.aspx).

Selected foods	Serving size	Calories	Total Carbohydrates (grams)	Dietary Fiber (grams)
LEGUMES AND LENTILS				
Kidney beans, canned	½ cup	108	19	5.5
Lentils, cooked	½ cup	115	20	7.8
Navy beans, cooked	½ cup	127	24	9.6
Peanut butter, smooth	2 tablespoons	191	7	1.6
Peanuts, roasted	1 ounce	166	6	2.9
Soybeans, cooked, mature	½ cup	148	7	5.2
Split peas, cooked	½ cup	116	21	8.1
VEGETABLES				
Artichoke, globe, hearts cooked	½ cup	45	10	4.8
Asparagus, cooked, chopped	½ cup	20	4	1.8
Broccoli, cooked, chopped	½ cup	27	6	2.6
Carrot, raw, strips	½ cup	25	6	1.7
Collard greens, cooked	½ cup	31	5	3.8
Green beans, cooked	½ cup	22	5	2
Green peas, cooked	½ cup	67	13	4.4
Lettuce, leaf, shredded	1 cup	5	1	0.5
Mixed vegetables, canned	½ cup	40	8	2.4
Okra, sliced, cooked	½ cup	18	4	2.0
Potato, baked, with skin	1 medium	161	37	2.9
Pumpkin, canned	½ cup	42	10	3.6
Spinach, raw	1 cup	7	1	0.7
Sweet potato, baked, with skin	1 medium	105	24	3.8
Tomato, red, ripe, chopped	½ cup	15	4	1.1
Tomato paste	¼ cup	54	12	2.7
Turnip, cubed, cooked	½ cup	17	4	1.6
Winter squash, acorn, cubed, mashed, baked	½ cup	57	15	4.5

(continued)

How Much Total Carbohydrate and Fiber? *(continued)*

Selected foods	Serving size	Calories	Total Carbohydrates (grams)	Dietary Fiber (grams)
FRUITS				
Apple with skin	1 small	77	21	3.6
Banana	1 medium	105	27	3.1
Blueberries	½ cup	42	11	1.8
Cantaloupe, cubed	½ cup	27	65	0.7
Dates, chopped	¼ cup	104	28	2.9
Figs, dried	¼ cup	93	24	3.7
Orange	1 medium	62	15	3.1
Peach	1 medium	58	14	2.2
Pear	1 medium	101	27	5.5
Pineapple, raw, chunks	½ cup	41	11	1.2
Plums, dried (prunes), no added sugars, stewed	¼ cup	66	17	1.9
Raspberries	½ cup	32	7	4.0
Strawberries, whole	½ cup	23	6	1.4
BREADS, PASTA, AND OTHER GRAINS				
Bran flakes ready-to-eat cereal	¾ cup	98	24	5.5
Bread, white	1 slice	64	12	0.6
Bread, whole-wheat	1 slice	81	14	1.9
Bulgur, cooked	½ cup	76	17	4.1
Crackers, whole-grain	1 ounce	121	20	2.9
English muffin, whole-wheat	½ muffin	67	13	2.2
Oat bran muffin	1 small	178	32	3.0
Oatmeal, cooked	½ cup	83	14	2.0
Pearled barley, cooked	½ cup	97	22	3.0
Quinoa, cooked	½ cup	111	20	2.6
Rice, brown, cooked	½ cup	109	23	1.8
Rice, white, cooked	½ cup	103	22	0.3
Rye wafer crackers, plain	2 wafers	73	18	5.0
Shredded wheat, ready-to-eat, spoon size	1 cup	172	40	6.1
Spaghetti, enriched, cooked	½ cup (not packed)	98	19	1.1
Spaghetti, whole-wheat, cooked	½ cup (not packed)	87	18	2.3
Waffle, whole-wheat, plain, low-fat, frozen	1 (4-inch)	90	17	1.5

How Much Total Carbohydrate and Fiber? *(continued)*

Selected foods	Serving size	Calories	Total Carbohydrates (grams)	Dietary Fiber (grams)
NUTS AND SEEDS				
Almonds	1 ounce	164	6	3.5
Chia seeds, dry	1 tablespoon	69	6	4.9
Flaxseeds, whole	1 tablespoon	55	3	2.8
Sesame seeds, dry	1 tablespoon	53	2	1.3
Sunflower seeds	1 tablespoon	94	4	1.0
Walnuts	1 ounce	185	4	1.9

Source: US Department of Agriculture, National Nutrient Database for Standard Reference, Release 28, 2016.

- By contrast, many vegetables—among them carrots, corn, and peas—are sweetest when young. As they mature, their sugars change to starches. What's the culinary lesson? If you're buying fresh produce, look for young vegetables and serve them at their peak. Don't store them too long.

NUTRIENT-RICH CARB FOODS

When it comes to carbohydrate-containing foods, you have choices. Many are nutrient-rich. Others qualify as empty-calorie foods. The best choices deliver a nutrient bundle without excess calories.

Enjoy more often:

- Many fruits and vegetables contribute folate, potassium, and fiber, as well as antioxidant vitamins such as beta carotene and vitamin C, which may help protect against some cancers. From a nutrition standpoint, they're a calorie bargain.
- Low-fat and fat-free dairy foods contain a naturally occurring sugar called lactose. Milk and some other dairy foods not only contain lactose, but also significant amounts of high-quality protein, calcium, vitamin D, and six more nutrients.
- Along with starches and fiber, whole grains contain vitamin E and selenium as well as iron, magnesium, zinc, and B vitamins. Some whole-grain foods supply lignan, which may block estrogen activity in cells and perhaps reduce the risk of some cancers. Whole grains also supply phytic acid, which may prevent free radicals from forming and perhaps reduce cancer risk by binding to minerals.
- Refined-grain foods that are enriched and fortified—especially those limited in added sugars and solid fats—also are bundled with important nutrients (B vitamins, iron, and folic acid).
- Dry beans and peas supply protein, B vitamins, and iron, along with starches and fiber.

Eat less often: Some carb-containing foods qualify as nutrient poor, being high in added sugars and solid fats and providing little else nutritionally, except calories. Sugary drinks such as soda and fruit-flavored drinks, candy, and grain-based desserts and pastries that are high in added sugars and/or solid fats are among those to limit.

Foods with Naturally Occurring Sugars

Whether naturally occurring or added, sugars make many foods more appealing. They contribute to the taste, aroma, texture, color, and body of the foods we all enjoy. For overall good health, enjoy sweet flavors from naturally occurring sugars in fruit and milk more often, and limit foods sweetened with added sugars. Consider these tips:

- Enjoy fruit—in salads, salsas, sauces, toppings, and more. For bitter or sour fruits, such as cranberries and limes, add a touch of sweetness to make these nutritious fruits or their juices more enjoyable.
- Snack mostly on fruit. Tuck an apple, a banana, grapes, a peach, a pear, or dried fruit into your carry bag. Keep a bowl of fresh fruit in your kitchen.

- Switch to whole or sliced fruit for dessert rather than cake, cookies, ice cream, or other sugary desserts.
- Drink milk. It derives some of its pleasing flavor from its own naturally occurring lactose. For a sweeter taste, choose flavored low-fat or fat-free milk. The benefits of its calcium and vitamin D outweigh the calories from added sugars in flavored milk. Many dairies are reducing added sugars in flavored milk; check the label to compare. *See "Lactose Intolerance: A Matter of Degree" in chapter 23, page 666, to learn how those with lactose intolerance may include milk in their meals and snacks.*
- Choose 100 percent fruit juice rather than fruit drinks, soda, or sweetened tea.

Starchy Foods: Healthy Options

Many starchy foods deliver more nutrients than complex carbohydrates. And many are fiber rich. Consider these nourishing ways to fit them in:

- Prepare or order starchy vegetables and beans in soups, salads, casseroles, and sides: for example, chickpeas, kidney beans, lima beans, peas, pumpkin, squash, and sweet potatoes.
- Switch to whole-grain products—whole-wheat bread and pasta, and oat muffins. Make at least half of your grain choices whole grain.
- Pair grain foods with other nutrient-rich foods. For example, serve whole-grain pasta or brown rice with vegetable stir-fry, whole-wheat pita stuffed with garden salad, or skin-on baked potato topped with chili beans.
- Choose starchy foods with fewer fats and added sugars—for example, bagels instead of doughnuts, whole-grain crackers instead of cookies, and baked potatoes instead of fries.
- Be sensible with portions. It's all too easy to serve three cups of pasta when half that may be enough.
- For refined-grain foods, choose those that are enriched with B vitamins and fortified with iron and folic acid.

? Have you ever wondered?

. . . if chocolate milk is okay for kids? While limiting added sugars is wise advice, check the full nutrition package when making choices. Flavored milk has all the nutrients of plain milk, including three nutrients that often come up short for kids: calcium, vitamin D, and potassium. So for children and teens who don't like plain milk, flavored milk is a way for them to get those nutrients, along with milk's protein, for growth, development, and health. When available, low-fat or fat-free flavored milks are best.

Research shows that kids who drink flavored or white (unflavored) milk have better nutrient intakes overall and similar body weights, compared to those who don't drink milk. Evidence also shows that kids who drink flavored milk don't consume more added sugars overall but do drink more milk. Sugars in flavored milk are no more cavity promoting than naturally occurring sugars and other carbohydrates.

Flavored milk contributes a very small amount (about 3 percent) of the added sugars that youth, aged two to eighteen years, usually consume. And most flavored milks sold in schools these days have less added sugars than in the past—perhaps 6 grams of added sugars per 8-ounce carton.

What about the sugars on the Nutrition Facts label? Eight ounces of both plain and flavored milks have 12 grams of naturally occurring lactose. Flavored milk provides an additional 6 to 12 grams of added sugars. To compare, an 8-ounce regular soft drink or fruit drink has about 24 grams of added sugars but no other nutrients besides water. Most of these drinks come in 12-ounce or larger containers and so have significantly more added sugars.

As new Nutrition Facts appear on labels, you'll see added sugars listed separately on flavored milk as well as on nondairy alternatives.

FIBER-RICH FOODS

Do you like to nibble on popcorn? This whole-grain snack is a fiber booster, with 3.5 grams of fiber and just 95 calories in 3 cups of plain popcorn.

Most vegetables, fruits, and whole grains provide about 1 to 3 grams of fiber per standard serving, but some are better fiber sources than others. For example, you might think that a heaping bowl of fresh salad greens is loaded with fiber. The fact is: greens are mostly water. Two cups of lettuce contain only about 1 gram of fiber. Toss greens with ¼ cup of kidney beans for at least 3 more grams of fiber. And top the salad with chopped bell peppers and sunflower seeds for another easy fiber boost.

The fiber content of whole grain foods varies greatly. Some are much better sources than others, so eating a variety is important. *See "For a Fiber Boost" in this chapter, page 364.* Minimally processed foods generally contain more fiber than highly processed foods. The fiber content drops when the fiber-rich part of a food, such as the bran, is removed during processing. The same happens when you remove the edible peel on fruit or a potato. However, some processed foods are fiber fortified; although their fiber amount may be higher, these foods still may lack other important nutrients.

Which Apple for Fiber?

Apple juice, applesauce, a whole apple—which has the most fiber? An apple of any variety with the peel on has more fiber than an apple without the peel. And as food changes form, its fiber content may change, too.

1 whole medium apple with peel	3.3 grams fiber
1 whole medium apple without peel	1.7 grams fiber
½ cup applesauce	1.5 grams fiber
¾ cup apple juice	0.2 gram fiber

Different Foods, Different Fiber

If foods such as bread or pasta made from refined flour are your main sources of carbs, chances are you'll fall short on fiber. You need to eat a variety of fiber-rich foods—vegetables (including beans and peas), fruits, whole-grain foods, and nuts and seeds—to get the different benefits from different types of fiber.

- Plant-based foods contain a mixed bag of fibers. The tough, chewy texture of some fiber-rich foods comes from insoluble fibers. When cooked, the soft, mushy texture of other fiber-rich foods comes from their soluble fibers.
- Vegetables and fruits have both pectin and cellulose. Vegetable skins have more cellulose, which is an insoluble fiber. Fruits usually have more pectin, which is generally soluble (but some pectins are insoluble).
- The fiber in oatmeal and beans is both soluble and insoluble. Beta glucan is the soluble fiber in oats and barley.
- Wheat bran has a higher concentration of fiber than most other brans, and its bran is mainly insoluble; oat bran contains mainly soluble fiber.

"Fiber Up" Your Food Choices

To boost your fiber intake, do so gradually over several weeks. If you don't give the friendly bacteria in your intestines time to adjust, you may end up with gas, diarrhea, cramps, and bloating.

When you eat more fiber, drink plenty of water and other fluids so fiber can do its job. Fiber acts like a large sponge in your gastrointestinal (GI) tract. It holds water as it keeps waste moving along. That's how it helps prevent constipation and related intestinal problems.

Note: Older adults (age sixty-five or older) and those who have had gastrointestinal (stomach, intestines, or rectum) surgery may feel the effects of added fiber more than others. They should use caution and check with their doctor before adding fiber to meals and snacks.

To put your fiber intake within recommendations—and boost other nutrients, too—fit more veggies, fruits, and whole grains into your meals and snacks. Keep fiber-rich foods on hand so they're easy to add during food prep or have as snacks. Consider these tips:

- Start with breakfast. Choose a fiber-rich breakfast cereal, perhaps bran; check food labels to find one with 5 or more grams of fiber per serving. Top cereal or yogurt with fruit, nuts, or wheat bran for a little more fiber. Or enjoy foods such as oatmeal, bran muffins, whole-wheat waffles or toast, or fiber-rich breakfast and cereal bars.
- Switch to whole grains. Make at least half of your grain choices fiber-rich whole grains (3 ounces of whole-grain foods or more) each day. Choose breads, buns, and bagels with whole-grain flour as the first ingredient on the label—for example, whole-wheat flour, oat flour, rye flour, whole ground cornmeal. Check the % Daily Value (DV) for dietary fiber per label serving. It's an excellent fiber source if it has 20 percent or more DV; a good source is 10 to 19 percent DV per serving. Eat breads made with bran, too, such as bran muffins. Try whole-wheat tortillas and pasta, too.
- Eat about 4½ cups total of vegetables and fruits a day if you eat 2,000 calories a day—and slightly more if you need more calories. Perhaps plan to have cooked vegetables and a salad for dinner, and whole fruit and carrot sticks for lunch. How about a veggie or fruit snack?

  Enjoy vegetables and fruits with the edible skin on. With the skin, a medium potato has 3.8 grams of fiber. Skinless, it has 2.3 grams. Also enjoy the flavor, crunch, and fiber benefits of edible seeds in berries, figs, and kiwifruit. Choose whole fruit more often than juice. Fiber comes mainly from the peel and pulp; usually both are removed when fruit is juiced. Juice usually has almost no fiber.
- Speaking of snacks, go fiber-rich with raw veggies, whole fruits (including dried fruits), whole-grain pretzels or crackers, plain popcorn, or a small handful of nuts. A high-fiber granola bar may provide 5 grams of fiber.
- Eat beans and peas (legumes) and lentils often—about 1½ cups a week on a 2,000-calorie-a-day eating plan. They're among the best fiber sources around—and add flavor and texture to salads, soups, casseroles, salsas, and more.
- Consider filling the fiber gap with some fiber-fortified foods. Be aware: highly processed foods with added fibers such as dextrin, polydextrose, and soluble corn fiber may not offer all the other nutrition benefits of less processed, fiber-rich foods.
- Fiber-ize your cooking style. Substitute higher-fiber ingredients in recipes, such as whole-wheat flour in baked goods. Fortify

? Have you ever wondered?

. . . if soybeans or tofu are good fiber sources? Half a cup of soybeans has more than 5 grams of fiber. That's great! But when soybeans are processed to make tofu, fibrous substances are strained out. What's left is high in soy protein, and one-half cup of tofu has less than 1 gram of fiber.

mixed dishes with high-fiber ingredients, perhaps crushed bran cereal, chia seeds, or oatmeal added to meat loaf or ground flaxseeds added to baked goods. Add veggies of all kinds to soups, stews, pizzas, and pasta sauces.

FOODS WITH ADDED SUGARS

Over the years people have baked with white and brown sugar and honey; prepared jellies, jams, and syrups with sugar; and flavored homemade baked beans with molasses or sorghum molasses. As a home cook, you likely prepare food with some types of sugar, too, especially if you bake.

Today, much of the sugar consumed is added during food processing—not just in home food preparation. For many foods and drinks—desserts, sweet baked goods, candy, other sweet snacks, and most soft drinks—sugars are basic ingredients. In many processed foods, added sugars may not be so obvious.

Sugars as Added Ingredients

Sugars contribute far more than sweetness. They work as multipurpose ingredients with functions that you may not even think about:

- In all kinds of food, including nutrient-rich foods, sugar adds flavor, aroma, texture, color, and body. Just a small amount can bring out the flavors and balance acids in other ingredients, such as in brines, rubs, salad dressings, and tomato-based sauces.
- In yeast breads, sugars are "food" for yeast, allowing dough to rise. Yeast doesn't consume all the sugar. What's not consumed adds flavor and contributes to the aroma and the delicate-brown crust (the "Maillard reaction").
- In cakes, sugars contribute to the bulk, tenderness, smooth crumb texture, and lightly browned surface. In cakes that have air whipped in, such as angel food cake and sponge cake, sugars help hold their form.
- In cookies, as sugars and shortening are creamed together, sugars help bring air into the dough. Sugars contribute to the light-brown

For a Fiber Boost . . .

Compare This . . .

Food	Calories	Fiber
½ cup refried beans, canned	107	4.4
1 cup orange juice	112	0.5
1 English muffin (refined wheat)	127	2.6
1 cup cooked cream of wheat	126	1.3
1 ounce potato chips	152	1.4
1 ounce pretzels (refined wheat)	109	1.0
½ cup mashed potatoes	87	1.6
½ cup unsweetened applesauce	51	1.3
1 ounce jelly beans	105	0.1
1 ounce cheese puffs snack	161	0.2
1 large (21 grams) fruit leather	78	0
½ cup cooked white rice	102	0.3

With This . . .

Food	Calories	Fiber
½ cup cooked red beans	123	7.7
1 cup orange sections	85	4.4
1 whole-wheat English muffin	134	4.4
1 cup cooked oatmeal	166	4.0
1 ounce (3 cups) air-popped, plain popcorn	93	3.6
1 ounce almonds	164	3.5
1 small baked potato, flesh and skin	134	3.2
1 small banana	90	2.6
¼ cup dried cranberries	123	2.1
6 baby carrots	24	1.8
½ cup sliced strawberries	27	1.6
½ cup cooked brown rice	124	1.6

Source: US Department of Agriculture, National Nutrient Database for Standard Reference, Release 28, 2016.

What Foods and Drinks Deliver the Most Added Sugars?

As noted in the 2015–2020 Dietary Guidelines for Americans, sugar-sweetened drinks, snacks, and sweets top the list for added sugars. In fact, beverages account for almost half (47 percent)! Together, these three categories provide more than 75 percent of all added sugars that Americans consume.

Here's how the food category sources of added sugars rank in terms of the percentage of the total amount consumed by the US population:

Beverages (not milk or 100% fruit juice)	47%
Sugar-sweetened beverages (soft drinks 25%, fruit drinks 11%, sport and energy drinks 3%)	
Coffee and tea 7%	
Alcoholic drinks 1%	
Snacks and sweets*	31%
Grains	8%
Mixed dishes	6%
Dairy	4%
Condiments, gravies, spreads, salad dressings	2%
Vegetables	1%
Fruits and fruit juice	1%

*Includes grain-based desserts such as brownies, cakes, cookies, doughnuts, pastries, pies, and sweet rolls; dairy desserts such as ice cream, other frozen desserts, and puddings; candies; jams; sugars; sweet toppings, and syrups

color, crisp texture, and cracked surface of sugar cookies and gingersnaps.

- In baked goods, sugars absorb water and inhibit the development of flour gluten, giving it the expected texture. A little sugar in a bread roll gives a dense texture; a lot of sugar gives a light cakelike texture.
- In canned jams, jellies, and preserves, sugars help inhibit the growth of molds and yeast by tying up the water that these microorganisms need to multiply, killing them and preventing spoilage. For this reason, sugars act as preservatives.
- When it comes to candy, sugar contributes to the texture. It is partially responsible for the smoothness of hard candy and the creaminess of fudge. As it cooks and caramelizes, turning from white to yellow to brown, sugar develops a unique, tasty flavor.

Sweetened with Less Added Sugars

While it is important to limit added sugars, attempting to strictly avoid them is challenging, unnecessary, and unrealistic. In fact, a little sweetener, perhaps a little honey, won't hurt you and can deliver flavor that makes a nutrient-rich food, such as plain yogurt, more appealing. Instead consider these tips:

- Limit regular soft drinks, sport drinks, energy drinks, and fruit drinks. A 12-ounce can of soda has about 10 teaspoons of sugar! Quench your thirst with water (with a citrus slice), unsweetened beverages, or 100 percent fruit juice instead.
- Use a light touch with the sugar spoon. Sweeten coffee or tea with just a bit of sugar, use low-calorie sweeteners, or add a hint of sweetness with a sprinkle of cinnamon. Use the same approach with cereal or French toast. Better yet, sweeten them with sliced or pureed fruit instead.

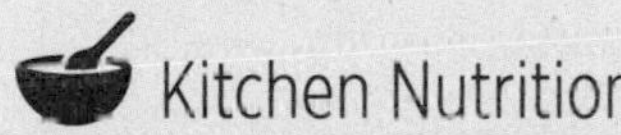

Sweet Seasonings

Bring out the flavors of foods with seasonings that offer the perception of sweetness: allspice, cardamom, cinnamon, ginger, mace, nutmeg, and citrus juices.

- Add ginger to a fruit glaze. Blend frozen raspberries with a pinch of ginger and a small amount of fruit juice concentrate or sweetener. Toss the glaze with fresh berries or sliced fruit.
- Add a "sweet" or fragrant spice, such as those noted above, of your choice to dry, ground coffee before brewing.
- Add zest and the sense of sweetness to oatmeal and other cooked breakfast cereals with allspice, mace, or nutmeg. In place of water, cook it in fruit juice (or milk for more calcium and phosphorus). Toss with dried fruits such as apricots or cranberries, or top with fresh fruit.
- For a hint of sweet flavor in rice, cook with cardamom, cinnamon, or ginger. You might substitute juice for part of the cooking liquid. Perhaps toss in raisins or other dried fruits, too.
- Add a touch of sweetness to cooked vegetables. For example, add cinnamon to mashed sweet potatoes, ginger to carrots, and a sprinkle of nutmeg to spinach.
- Squeeze citrus juice—lemon, lime, or orange—over fresh fruit to enhance the flavor. *Calorie-saving tip:* You save about 45 calories with a squeeze of juice rather than one tablespoon of sugar.
- Make your own syrup for pancakes or waffles. In a blender, puree apples, berries, or sliced peaches with a little fruit juice, honey, and a pinch of cinnamon.

? Have you ever wondered?

. . . if a "sugar-free" food is also "calorie free"? Not necessarily, so don't let the term confuse you. Although a sugar-free food doesn't have sugar, it likely has calories from other carbohydrates and perhaps fats and proteins. To find out about the calories and sugars, read the Nutrition Facts, *as discussed in "Nutrition: Fact Check!" in chapter 6, page 144.*

. . . what goes in when food manufacturers take carbs out? Traditional products may use higher-protein ingredients in place of some carbohydrates—for example, soy flour, soy protein, or wheat protein in place of wheat flour. Or, as in candy, ice cream, and other sweets, sugar alcohols may replace some sugars. High-fiber fillers also may replace whole grains in products promoted as high fiber; however, by replacing whole grains with fillers, a product won't have all the whole-grain nutrient and phytonutrient benefits.

. . . what "no sucrose" or "no refined sugar" means? Perhaps not what you think. Instead of sweetening with added sugars, such as high-fructose corn syrup, the food may be sweetened with ingredients such as agave syrup, date sugar, or juice concentrates. Check the Nutrition Facts; the calories from these sugars may be about the same.

. . . if "low carb" is "low calorie"? No again. If protein or fat replaces carbohydrates, the calories per label serving may be comparable. If you're out to manage your weight, you can't cut carbs and ignore the calories.

. . . what "net carbs," "low carb," or "net-impact carbs" mean—and don't mean? Although currently allowed, none of these terms are regulated by the FDA, at least not now. And they're not used as much today as in recent years. Their meaning is unclear, varying among food manufacturers and weight-loss plans.

"Net carbs" or "net-impact carbs" on a label may be total carbohydrates minus fiber, or minus fiber and sugar alcohols, meant to indicate how much carbohydrates in the product will cause an increase in blood glucose. The idea behind them is that because fiber isn't digested and absorbed and sugar alcohols aren't completely absorbed, their carbohydrates don't count. However, this issue is under scientific debate.

Until regulated, the FDA recommends that labels explain the term and its calculation. For diabetes management, talk to your registered dietitian nutritionist or certified diabetes educator about how foods labeled with these terms fit into your food plan.

- Go fifty-fifty to cut calories in half. Share a sugary dessert or snack with a friend; eat it slowly for the most enjoyment.
- Eat small, infrequent portions of sugary snacks. Choose a miniature instead of a large candy bar, a 6-ounce can of soda instead of a 20-ounce bottle, or a stick of chewing gum (sugarless for better oral care) instead of a sugary snack. Be mindful: portion out just fifteen or so jelly beans as a day's budget instead of having a small bowl of them on your desk or counter to eat mindlessly.
- Choose fruit for dessert; limit high-calorie desserts.
- Read food labels to compare breakfast cereals and other packaged foods. Choose mostly those with little or no added sugars on the ingredient list. Look for "no sugar added" on canned and frozen fruit as a nutrient content claim. Some foods, such as baked goods, beverages, candy, and yogurt may be sweetened with a sugar alternative (*discussed in "Sugar Alternatives" in this chapter, page 368*) with few or no calories.

Can you cut back on sugar in recipes? That depends. For some recipes, the results wouldn't be much different—except for taste. In others, the volume, texture, color, and aroma may not be the same. In jams, jellies, and preserves, mold grows quickly without added sugar, even if refrigerated. *See "Sugar Shakers" in chapter 8, page 265, for tips on preparing food with less added sugars. "Kitchen Nutrition: Sweet Seasonings" in this chapter, page 365, offers ways to add a sense of sweetness without adding sugar.*

CARBS ON FOOD LABELS

Hunting for the carbohydrate content of food? Check the food label. Clues come in three places: nutrient content claims, the Nutrition Facts, and the ingredient list.

Check the Claims

Nutrient content claims such as "sugar-free" or "no added sugar" appear on some food containers, such as breakfast cereal, canned fruit, and flavored yogurt. You may see a "high fiber" or "added fiber" claim on packages of bread, breakfast bars, or cereal. These claims are regulated by the FDA. You may see front-of-package labeling, too; *see "Front-of-Package Nutrition Labeling" in chapter 6, page 146.*

If they catch your attention, check the Nutrition Facts for specific amounts. *See "Label Lingo: Calories, Sugars, and Fiber" earlier in this chapter, page 358, to know their meaning.*

Check the Facts

Almost all food labels carry Nutrition Facts with the amount of calories and total carbohydrates, sugars (and added sugars on the new Nutrition

Facts label) and fiber in a single label serving. As defined by the FDA, the Nutrition Facts must state the following:

- *Total carbohydrates*, given in grams, include starches, all naturally occurring and added sugars, sugar alcohols, and fiber as well as organic acids and preservatives (which don't weigh much).
- *Dietary fiber* is listed separately and is also counted in the total carbohydrates because it includes naturally occurring and added fiber. Whole-grain foods usually have more fiber than those made from refined grains. The label won't say the amount of soluble and insoluble fiber.
- *Sugars* are listed differently on the original and the new Nutrition Facts label.

On the original Nutrition Facts label, *Sugars* represents all naturally occurring and added sugars. They are given in grams with no percent Daily Value (DV). Because added sugars aren't listed separately, you need to check the ingredient list to estimate a relative amount.

The new Nutrition Facts label refers to *Total sugars*, which is naturally occurring and added sugars, in grams. Under that, the grams and a % DV for just is shown separately. *See "Nutrition: Fact Check!" in chapter 6, page 144, for more about Nutrition Facts labels.*

- *Sugar alcohols, discussed later in this chapter, page 369*, might appear on a separate line in the Nutrition Facts.

Check the Ingredients

Added sugars. To identify added sugars in processed foods, check the ingredient list (naturally occurring sugars aren't listed). If a sugar appears

Chocolate and Sugars: A Flavorful Pair

Melting Away Chocolate Myths

A love for chocolate can be traced through the centuries. Known as a food of the gods, chocolate was highly prized in the Americas in pre-Columbian times. Native Americans from what is now Mexico served chocolate to European explorers as early as the 1500s.

By itself, chocolate has a bitter taste, but sugar, transported from plantations in the American and Caribbean colonies, made chocolate tasty to the European palate. By the mid-1600s, the popularity of chocolate, sweetened with sugar, had spread throughout Europe. In 1847, milk chocolate was created, and it quickly became popular around the world.

CHOCOLATE AND HEALTH

As an ingredient with a distinctive flavor, chocolate and its main ingredient, cocoa, can fit within a healthy eating plan. They may add a flavor spark that makes nutritious foods, such as milk, more appealing.

Chocolate, a plant-based ingredient, also contains a category of phytonutrients called flavanols that may offer some heart-health benefits according to recent research. Chocolate's stearic acid, a saturated fat with unique qualities, may have a neutral effect on blood cholesterol levels. Chocolate appears to have significant antioxidant potential; dark chocolate has more flavanols than milk chocolate does. Unfortunately, Dutch process chocolate doesn't have these benefits; the alkali used in processing removes flavonoids. *See "Phytonutrients: Different from Nutrients" in chapter 15, page 448, for more about flavanols and other phytonutrients.*

The chocolate challenge? Sugary, chocolate-flavored foods are typically high in calories, added sugars, and fats, and often low in other nutrients. If they crowd out more nutritious foods (if a chocolate bar replaces fruit in your lunch bag or if you can't control a chocolate urge), their calories may add up. Much of the chocolate consumed is in confectionery and baked products that are fat-laden, too. *The bottom line:* Enjoy, but go easy on chocolate!

Myth: Chocolate causes acne.

Truth: That misconception has captured the attention of teens for years. However, hormonal changes during adolescence, not chocolate, are the usual cause of acne.

Myth: Carob bars are more healthy than chocolate bars.

Truth: Actually, a carob bar has the same amount of calories and fat as a similar-size chocolate bar. Carob, a common substitute for chocolate, comes from the seeds of the carob tree, which are different from cocoa beans.

Myth: Chocolate has a lot of caffeine.

Truth: Chocolate supplies caffeine, but the amount is quite small. Eight ounces of chocolate milk have about 5 milligrams of caffeine, compared with 3 milligrams in 5 ounces of decaffeinated coffee. In contrast, 8 ounces of regular-brew coffee contains about 95 milligrams of caffeine.

Myth: Some people are "chocoholics."

Truth: Not true—although some people do have a stronger preference for chocolate than others, perhaps because of its taste, aroma, and texture. While popping chocolate candies may become a high-calorie habit with a pleasurable sensation, eating chocolate itself can't become truly addictive. Research is exploring any potential role of chocolate in the function of brain neurotransmitters that regulate serotonin and dopamine, often referred to as feel-good body substances.

as the first or second ingredient, or if several sugars are listed, the food likely has a lot of added sugars.

Even if you don't see the word "sugar" in the ingredient list, it may have added sugars. Terms ending in "ose" mean sugars. Dextrin and corn syrup are sugars, too, often made of several types of sugars. Among the many sugars that may appear, besides those ending in "ose," are:

Brown sugar

Cane sugar

Confectioners' sugar

Corn sweetener

Corn syrup

Crystallized cane sugar

Evaporated cane juice

Fruit juice concentrate

Honey

High-fructose corn syrup (HFCS)

Invert sugar

Malt syrup or malt sugar

Maple syrup,

Molasses

Nectars (apricot, peach, pear, etc.)

Pancake syrup

Raw sugar

Syrup

Turbinado sugar

Evaporated fruit juices and jams are mostly sugars, too.

Fiber. To spot fiber-rich grains, learn which ones are whole grain. Look for terms such as "bran," "whole grain," or "whole-wheat flour," too. *See "What Is a Whole Grain?" in chapter 2, page 27, and "Is It Really Whole Grain? Tricky to Know" in chapter 6, page 184.* The ingredient list also will list any added functional fibers, such as beta glucans, cellulose, fructooligosaccharides, guar gum, inulin, pectin, and polydextrose.

Sugar Alternatives

"Low in calories" and "sugar-free"! As a way to minimize added sugars and calories, these may be sweet messages, especially for those looking to manage their weight, control their blood glucose levels, or limit their exposure to tooth-decay-promoting sugary foods.

Two types of sugar alternatives can help achieve those goals: sugar replacers (a category of nutritive sweeteners) and nonnutritive (high-intensity) sweeteners. Stevia, extracted from the leaves of the stevia plant, is another option.

SUGAR ALCOHOLS (POLYOLS)

Sugar alcohols, or polyols, are a category of nutritive sweeteners. Usually, they replace sugar on an equal basis by weight, but most aren't quite as sweet. Like sugars, they provide energy, or calories, but not as much.

Why the term "sugar alcohol"? To clarify, the words "sugar" and "alcohol" in this context refer only to their chemical structure. They're neither sugar nor alcohol. Sugar alcohols don't contain ethanol, as alcoholic beverages do. They also may be referred to as sugar replacers or reduced-calorie sweeteners.

Sugar alcohols are carbohydrates naturally present in many foods you already enjoy, including berries, other fruits, and vegetables. Derived from sucrose, glucose, and starch, sugar alcohols also can be produced by adding hydrogen to their chemical makeup—for example, erythritol, isomalt, lacititol, maltitol, mannitol, sorbitol, xylitol, and hydrogenated starch hydrolysates.

Their sweetness varies from 25 percent to 100 percent as sweet as sugar. Sorbitol and mannitol, for example, may be half as sweet as table sugar (sucrose); however, xylitol is just as sweet. They're often combined with low-calorie, or intense, sweeteners such as aspartame or saccharin for a sweeter flavor. *See "Sugar Alternatives: Comparing Sweetness" in this chapter, page 371.* As sugar replacers, they are more likely used in packaged foods rather than home cooking.

Sweet Benefits

Sugar alcohols supply energy, but fewer calories per gram than sugar does: on average 2 calories per gram. (Sugars provide 4 calories per gram.) To compare, sorbitol has 2.6 calories per gram; mannitol, 1.6 calories per gram. Since they're lower in calories than sugars, sugar alcohols have potential advantages for people managing their weight or diabetes.

For those with diabetes, sugar alcohols offer another benefit. As an energy source, they're absorbed more slowly than sugars and incompletely, and require little or no insulin for metabolism. Their glycemic response is low. Still, for diabetes management, sugar alcohols aren't "free foods." Instead, 2 grams of sugar alcohols are generally counted for 1 gram of carbohydrate. If you're managing diabetes, have a registered dietitian nutritionist or certified diabetes educator help you fit foods with sugar alcohols into a healthy eating plan.

Another benefit: sugar alcohols don't promote cavities. Why? They aren't converted to acids by the oral bacteria that produce cavities. The FDA has approved a health claim for beverages, candies, gum, and snack foods with sugar alcohols, noting that their sugar alcohols don't promote tooth decay.

For some people, sorbitol and mannitol may produce abdominal gas, bloating, or other digestive discomfort or may have a laxative effect when consumed in excess. Excess is individual. For you, it's an issue of trial and error, often depending on whether it's consumed after a meal or instead on an empty stomach.

You might see this statement on a label: "Excess consumption may have a laxative effect. Eat foods with these sweeteners in moderation or perhaps with other foods if your tolerance is lower." This is required if a food product has more than 50 grams of sorbitol per serving; most foods have only a few grams. These products can cause digestive discomfort because they're not fully digested and absorbed. Fermentation in the large intestine can cause gas.

What about safety? The FDA regulates their use. The following sugar alcohols are on the GRAS ("generally recognized as safe") list or are approved as additives: D-tagatose, erythritol, hydrogenated starch hydrolysates (HSH), isomalt, isomaltulose, lactitol, maltitol, mannitol, sorbitol, trehalose, and xylitol. *See "Additives: Testing and Approval" in chapter 5, page 138, to learn about the GRAS list.*

Sugar Alcohols in Foods

Besides adding sweetness to some sugar-free foods, sugar alcohols add texture and bulk to a wide range of foods such as baked goods, candies, frozen desserts, fruit spreads, and ice cream. They also help food stay moist, prevent browning when heated, and add a cooling sensation. Baked goods made with sugar alcohols won't have a crisp brown surface unless the color comes from another ingredient. Sugar alcohols also are used in chewing gum, mouthwash, and toothpaste.

How can you spot foods with sugar alcohols?

- The ingredient list on a food label may give the specific name, perhaps sorbitol.
- They're listed on the Nutrition Facts label as part of the amount of total carbohydrates. If a nutrition content claim is made, such as "sugar-free," the sugar alcohol content must appear separately under total carbohydrates on the Nutrition Facts label. Look for grams of sugar alcohols or of the specific sugar replacer.
- The food label also may say that the food has fewer calories per gram than other similar foods with nutritive sweeteners, such as corn syrup, honey, or sucrose.

NONNUTRITIVE SWEETENERS: FLAVOR WITHOUT CALORIES

When it comes to sweetness, sugar is at the top of one's mind. Yet nonnutritive sweeteners, also called very-low-calorie or high-intensity sweeteners, deliver sweetness while providing virtually no calories. Being many times sweeter than the same amount of sugar, they're also aptly called intense sweeteners. Just a very small amount delivers a lot of sweetness. In comparison, nutritive sweeteners (sugars and sugar alcohols) supply calories.

Just about anyone can safely consume nonnutritive sweeteners. Alone or blended with other sweeteners, they sweeten beverages and foods such as pudding and yogurt without adding calories or promoting tooth decay.

Foods and drinks with nonnutritive sweeteners may substitute for higher-calorie foods and drinks as a way to cut calories. That may reduce calorie intake in the short term. However, evidence that this is effective as a long-term weight loss strategy is limited.

Sweet Options

When it comes to safety, perhaps no ingredients have been scrutinized by researchers as much as nonnutritive sweeteners. Before being used in foods or drinks—or as a tabletop sweetener—they're tested extensively to ensure they meet the guidelines and safety standards of the FDA. That includes assigning Acceptable Daily Intakes (ADIs) for nonnutritive sweeteners used as food additives. The ADI for each one, set at a very conservative level, is the amount that can be consumed daily over a lifetime without posing a risk. Available scientific evidence indicates that these sweeteners are considered safe as used by the general population, even among those people who consume high amounts.

Currently in the United States, six intense sweeteners have been approved: acesulfame K, aspartame, luo han guo extract, neotame, saccharin, and sucralose. But watch for news about others. Approval from the FDA has been sought for alitame and cyclamate. Both are approved in some other countries, including cyclamate in Canada. If you travel abroad, you may hear of neohesperidine or thaumatin, too.

Acesulfame Potassium. Approved for use in the United States in 1988, acesulfame potassium, or acesulfame K, was first marketed as a tabletop sweetener. More recently, it was approved for use in beverages and then for general use.

A white, odorless, crystalline sweetener, it provides no calories. Like saccharin, acesulfame K can't be broken down by the body, and it's eliminated in the urine unchanged. Because it is calorie free, it has a potential benefit for people with diabetes.

Acesulfame K is 200 times sweeter than table sugar, adding its sweet taste to alcoholic drinks, baked goods, candies, dairy products, desserts, noncarbonated drinks, sauces, and tabletop sweeteners such as Sweet 'n' Safe®, Sweet One®, Swiss Sweet®, and Sunette®. By itself in some foods, a high concentration of acesulfame K may leave a slight aftertaste, so it's often combined with other sweeteners, both traditional and intense.

Cooking tip: Because acesulfame K is heat stable, you can use it in cooked and baked foods. Like saccharin, it gives no bulk, or volume, as sugar does, so it may not work in some recipes.

Aspartame. Sweeter than table sugar by 160 to 200 times, aspartame was developed in 1965 and approved by the FDA in 1981. It was first marketed as NutraSweet® and sold as the tabletop sweeteners Equal®, NutraSweet®,

Have you ever wondered?

. . . what stevia is? It's a sweetener extracted from the leaves of the stevia plant. It's much sweeter than sugar yet virtually calorie free. Harvested from a bush, stevia has been used in South America as a sweetener for hundreds of years; it's also used for medicinal purposes.

In 2008, the FDA granted GRAS ("generally recognized as safe") status to Rebaudioside A, a highly purified compound in stevia. It's sold under brand names such as Pure Via® and Truvia®. This very refined stevia product can be used as a replacement for calorie-containing sweeteners—with a reminder that it's not a magic bullet for weight loss or blood glucose control and that it may cause nausea, bloating, or other mild side effects. In higher amounts it might have a bitter taste. GRAS status has not been given to whole-leaf stevia or its crude extracts, sold as supplements, due to concerns about potential unhealthy side effects of other active compounds in the whole leaf.

The best advice is to talk to your doctor before using it. Sometimes stevia is marketed as "natural," but remember that this term has no legal FDA definition. While stevia is safe as a tabletop sweetener and as an ingredient, no data show that it has benefits over other nonnutritive sweeteners.

. . . what tagatose is? It's a GRAS-approved, low-calorie sweetener derived from lactose, found in dairy foods. It's 75 to 92 percent as sweet as table sugar. Unlike lactose, it passes through the stomach and small intestine without being digested or absorbed. Instead, it's fermented in the large intestine, providing about 1.5 calories per gram; it also works there as a prebiotic. Sold as Nutralose®, it may be used as a food and beverage ingredient; check the ingredient list to find out. Because it doesn't promote tooth decay, as other sugars do, it can carry a health claim about dental health.

. . . what allulose is? Another GRAS-approved, low-calorie sweetener, allulose is sold as Dolcia Prima® and listed as an ingredient in processed foods. It delivers a sweet flavor and texture, similar to table sugar, to foods and beverages—with 90 percent fewer calories than table sugar. Allulose doesn't convert to glucose when absorbed as sugar does. Because it doesn't metabolize, allulose doesn't affect blood glucose or insulin production.

and NutraTaste®. Aspartame is in many other tabletop sweeteners as well, such as SweetMate®.

Aspartame isn't sugar. Instead, it's a combination of two amino acids—aspartic acid and the methyl ester of phenylalanine. While amino acids are the building blocks of protein, aspartic acid and phenylalanine are joined in a way that's perceived as sweet to your taste buds. These same two amino acids are also found naturally in common foods such as fat-free milk, fruit, meat, and vegetables. When digested, they're treated like any other amino acid in food. Like other proteins, aspartame has 4 calories per gram. Because so little is used, the calorie impact is negligible.

Because aspartame contains phenylalanine, people with the rare genetic disorder called phenylketonuria (PKU) need to be cautious about consuming foods and beverages that contain it. Food labels must list "aspartame" in the ingredient list as well as display this statement: "Phenylketonurics: Contains Phenylalanine." PKU doesn't allow the body to handle phenylalanine properly. PKU afflicts about one in fifteen thousand people in the United States, where all infants are screened for PKU at birth. *See "Aspartame: PKU Warning" in chapter 23, page 679.* If you don't have PKU, you can drink diet soda without this concern.

Contrary to rumors spread by unidentified online sources, aspartame has been intensely studied for its safety. No consistent scientific evidence shows links between aspartame and health problems, including attention deficit disorder and seizures among children. It is approved as safe by the FDA.

Because it's not heat stable, aspartame is used mostly in foods that don't require cooking or baking. Most aspartame consumed in the United States is in soft drinks. Other commercial uses are in frozen desserts,

Have you ever wondered?

. . . why nonnutritive sweeteners don't promote tooth decay? As sweeteners, they aren't broken down by bacteria in plaque. Since they don't feed bacteria, no acids form. Sugarless gum, flavored with a nonnutritive sweetener or sugar alcohol, may actually promote dental health. Not only does it not have carbohydrates, but it also increases saliva flow, which helps neutralize plaque acids.

. . . if foods with nonnutritive sweeteners increase your appetite and potentially promote weight gain? Although inconclusive, research evidence doesn't show that these sweeteners stimulate appetite. That said, they may aid weight management by adding flavor to food and beverages while limiting calories.

gelatins, puddings, yogurt, hot cocoa mix, powdered soft drinks, teas, breath mints, chewing gum, and tabletop sweeteners.

Cooking tip: When aspartame is heated for a long time, it may lose its sweetness. When you prepare food with a tabletop sweetener containing aspartame, add it toward the end of cooking. Or sprinkle it on a cooked or baked product after removing it from the heat.

Luo han guo. Also called monk-fruit extract or Swingle-fruit extract, this sweetener was recently approved as GRAS. It is 150 to 300 times sweeter than table sugar and may leave an aftertaste if consumed at high levels. Use it as a tabletop sweetener.

Neotame. Approved by the FDA in 2002, neotame is a noncaloric sweetener that's 7,000 to 13,000 times sweeter than table sugar; to date, it's rarely used in food. Although it contains aspartic acid and phenylalanine as aspartame does, the chemical structure differs. Because the amount used is so very small, the amount released into the body is negligible. Neotame doesn't need to carry a warning label for PKU.

Saccharin. Developed in 1879, saccharin has been used as a noncaloric sweetener for more than a hundred years. It's produced from a naturally occurring substance in grapes. Today, saccharin is used in soft drinks and tabletop sweeteners such as Sweet'N Low® and Sweet 10®. The benefits? It's calorie free, not cavity promoting, not metabolized by humans, and safe to consume.

Being 300 times sweeter than table sugar, saccharin adds a lot of flavor, even in small amounts, without adding calories. Just 20 milligrams of saccharin give the same sweetness as one teaspoon (4,000 milligrams or 4 grams) of table sugar. Because the body can't break it down, saccharin doesn't provide energy. Instead, it's eliminated in urine. What about its bitter aftertaste? It's usually blended with other sweeteners to make the flavor pleasing.

After decades of research, saccharin was removed from the government's list of potential carcinogens and, since the 1970s, has had interim approval. Scientific consensus in the US National Institute of Environmental Health Services' May 2000 "Report on Carcinogens, 9th Edition" deemed that cancer data on rats was not relevant to human physiology. In the past, a few studies hinted that saccharin—in very large amounts (equivalent to 750 cans of soft drinks or 10,000 saccharin tablets daily)—may cause cancer in laboratory rats. No human studies have ever confirmed the findings. As of 2000, a warning label hasn't been required for products that contain saccharin. As with any food or food substance, keep moderation in mind.

Cooking tip: Saccharin keeps its sweet flavor when heated, so it can be used in cooked and baked foods. Because it doesn't have the bulk that sugar has, it may not work in some recipes. *See "How to . . . Cook with Nonnutritive Sweeteners" in chapter 8, page 267.*

Sucralose. Of the nonnutritive sweeteners, sucralose is the only one that's made from sugar. It's actually 600 times sweeter than table sugar. Developed in 1976 and approved in 1998 for use in the United States, sucralose is marketed as Splenda®, among other brands.

Sugar Alternatives: Comparing Sweetness

Many ingredients have a sweet flavor. Some much more than others. Most sugar alcohols aren't as sweet as sucrose (table sugar). For sweeteners such as saccharin, a little bit goes a long way!

For the same amount by volume, here's how sugar alcohols and nonnutritive sweeteners compare to table sugar.

Sweetener*	Comparing the Sweetness to Sucrose (White or Table Sugar)†
SUGAR ALCOHOLS	
Hydrogenated starch hydrolysates	0.25–0.5
Lacititol	0.3–0.4
Isomalt	0.45–0.65
Trehalose	0.45
Isomaltulose	0.5
Sorbitol	0.5–0.7
Mannitol	0.5–0.7
Erythritol	0.6–0.8
Maltitol	0.9
D-Tagatose	0.75–0.92
Xylitol	1.0
SUCROSE (TABLE SUGAR)	1.0
NONNUTRITIVE SWEETENERS	
Aspartame	160–200
Luo han guo extract	150–300
Acesulfame K	200
Stevia	250
Saccharin	300
Sucralose	600
Neotame	7,000–13,000

†An amount below 1 means, less sweet, for example 0.5 means it is half as sweet as table sugar; above 1 means it is sweeter, for example, 160 means it is 160 times as sweet as table sugar.

*Sweeteners approved in the United States by the FDA.

Source: "Use of Nutritive and Nonnutritive Sweeteners," Position Paper, Academy of Nutrition and Dietetics, 2012

Need more carb-smart strategies for healthy eating? Check here for how-tos . . .

- Shop to make carb foods count for good nutrition: *chapter 6, page 141.*
- Sweeten food and boost the fiber as you cook for health: *chapter 8, page 230.*
- Cook with nonnutritive sweeteners: *see "How to . . . Cook with Nonnutritive Sweeteners" in chapter 8, page 267.*
- Enjoy sweet flavors in restaurant foods—and eat smart, too: *chapter 9, page 275.*
- Manage carbs if you're an athlete: *see "Carbs: Your Main Energy Source" in chapter 21, page 605.*
- Handle carbohydrates on an eating plan to manage diabetes: *see "If You Have Diabetes" in chapter 24, page 702.*

Unlike sugar, sucralose is not recognized as a carbohydrate by the body. As a result, it doesn't promote tooth decay and supplies no calories. Most sucralose (85 percent) can't be digested, absorbed, or metabolized for energy, so it doesn't affect blood glucose levels or insulin production, either. Instead, it passes through the body unchanged—a benefit for people with diabetes. As a nonnutritive powder, it's used in beverages, chewing gum, processed foods, and tabletop sweeteners.

Cooking tip: Sucralose offers the sweet sugar flavor without the calories, and performs like sugar in cooking and baking. However, it doesn't give bulk to baked goods. It's highly heat stable, even for a prolonged time, and it keeps its flavor in foods even when stored for a long time. Like sugar, it dissolves easily in water. Use sucralose as a sweetener in food preparation and beverages.

Nonnutritive Sweeteners: For Whom?

The 1970s brought a focus on slimness and the 1980s on fitness, and from the 1990s until today, diabetes and obesity have become bigger issues. The growing use of nonnutritive sweeteners paralleled these health interests and concerns. From a health perspective, almost anyone can consume foods and beverages flavored with nonnutritive sweeteners. It's a matter of personal choice.

Nonnutritive sweeteners can be part of a weight-management strategy. However, just consuming foods or drinks with these sweeteners won't result in weight loss or keep you from gaining weight. You must limit calories from other sources, too, and avoid replacing the calories saved with higher-calorie foods.

For people with diabetes, foods and drinks with nonnutritive sweeteners can satisfy a taste for sweetness without affecting insulin production or blood glucose levels. And they can help with weight control, which is important for managing diabetes.

Nonnutritive sweeteners are safe but not intended for infants and young children. Kids need ample calories for rapid growth and active play. Foods and beverages sweetened with low-calorie sweeteners are okay for kids occasionally if they eat enough from a variety of nutrient-rich foods.

12

Protein Power

In this chapter, find out about . . .

Amino acids: building blocks of proteins

Protein: why, how much, what kind

Lean protein foods: plant and animal sources

Protein for meatless eating

Protein is once again getting the attention it deserves. This is good news since protein (the nutrient) and its related health issues have often been overlooked until recently, primarily because of its ready availability in typical eating patterns in the United States and other developed countries. Most health professionals figured we were getting enough and didn't talk about it much.

Today, scientific evidence is revealing key roles for protein beyond the basics you may have learned in school. Protein has a role in promoting weight loss and managing weight, maintaining muscle mass and bone health as you age, helping reduce risks for diabetes and heart disease, and more. At the same time, the benefits of plant-based sources of protein are gaining more recognition.

The word "protein" may conjure up thoughts of steak, chicken, milk, soy, beans, or high-power protein smoothies. And like many people, you may think you get enough protein from foods like these. Yet, even if you are not protein deficient, it doesn't mean you're protein sufficient.

Protein Basics

We often think of protein as a single nutrient, but there are many proteins in both foods and body cells. Each are made of different amino acids. Although hundreds appear in nature, the body uses about twenty amino acids as raw materials to make at least ten thousand unique body proteins, each with a somewhat different structure. In food, it's the unique composition and arrangement of amino acids that also make protein in meat or cheese so different from protein in beans or tofu.

Like carbohydrates and fats, proteins and their constituent amino acids are composed of carbon, hydrogen, and oxygen. However, proteins also have nitrogen—one more element that makes them different from other energy nutrients.

BUILDING BLOCKS OF PROTEIN

Amino acids, the building blocks of protein, are classified into groups based on the body's ability to produce them. Nine of these twenty amino acids are considered essential, or indispensable. Because the body can't make them, food choices must supply them. Their names may sound unfamiliar: histidine, isoleucine, leucine, lysine, methionine, phenylalanine, threonine, tryptophan, and valine. (*Note:* While arginine isn't essential for adults because their bodies can make it, it is essential for young people.)

The other amino acids are nonessential, or dispensable, because the body can make sufficient amounts. They're made by breaking other amino acids or nitrogen-containing compounds apart and then reusing the components; a great example of nature's own recycling program! Alanine, asparagine, aspartic acid (aspartate), glutamic acid (glutamate), and serine are some nonessentials.

Several other nonessential amino acids have conditional status: arginine (for adults), cysteine, glutamine, glycine, proline, and tyrosine. Under normal bodily conditions, the body makes them as long as you consume enough essential amino acids and enough calories during the day from a variety of different foods. For example, to make tyrosine you need to consume enough phenylalanine.

Amino acids are described as protein's building blocks. Like notes in a music scale or letters of the alphabet, they are arranged in countless ways, and some combinations are used more often than others. The same musical notes create symphonies, jazz, and pop hits, and the same twenty-six letters of the alphabet form thousands of words in many languages, each word with its own meaning. It's the same for amino acids. In a single body cell, ten thousand different proteins may exist. Short- or long-chain, intricately folded, each body protein has a unique arrangement of amino acids.

Just as words must be spelled correctly to express their intended meaning, the chains of amino acids that make up the unique proteins in different foods and in the body must be arranged in a precise number, combination, and order. In body cells, the genetic code (genes)—called DNA, or deoxyribonucleic acid—carries spelling instructions for making each protein. If the amount of an essential amino acid is limited, the body's ability to make certain proteins for muscles and all body tissues is limited, too. Your body can't store these essential amino acids, so you need a fresh and regular supply.

PROTEINS: WHAT THEY DO

Protein obtained from food has several functions in the body, including making new proteins and enzymes for your body's internal use. In fact, nearly everything your body does requires protein. Protein is an energy nutrient, too.

Proteins for Growth, Repair, and Every Body Cell

Proteins are part of every cell in your body. Except for bile and urine, they're also part of all body fluids. Amino acids are the raw materials needed to make and repair the many types of body proteins. Different tissues—skin, muscles, bone, blood, and organs, for example—are unique because the amino acid patterns of their proteins differ.

You need a constant supply of proteins to make and repair your body cells. That's obvious during times of growth (infancy, childhood, adolescence) and, for women, during pregnancy and nursing. It's also needed to heal skin from a burn or replace blood after bleeding. Perhaps not so obvious is that your body needs proteins to replace cells as they wear out.

Body cells—including muscle cells—are in a constant state of turnover, always being made and broken down and remade. All body proteins need to be replaced every three to four months. In physiology terms, this is a constant balance between anabolism (growth) and catabolism (breakdown). The pool of amino acids used for cell growth and repair comes from proteins in food and from recycled body proteins.

To do this work, your food choices must supply the essentials: essential amino acids, in sufficient amounts, in the right balance—and when you need them. Digestion releases amino acids from foods' proteins for absorption. When the right amino acids aren't available, the body needs to break down its own protein stored in muscle to get what it needs for hormones, enzymes, and more. Consuming protein throughout the day helps ensure that you have a steady source of amino acids to pull from instead of breaking down muscle.

Kids need more protein for their body size than adults do, not just for their growth, but also for hormones, enzymes, and all body tissues. While growth hormones are the key drivers of protein synthesis for children, in adulthood an amino acid called leucine is the driver.

Proteins to Regulate Body Functions

Protein does more than build muscle and body tissue. Of the possible one hundred thousand different proteins in your body, many help regulate body processes. Here are some examples:

- As enzymes and hormones, proteins help speed up or expedite many chemical reactions in the body. For example, a nonessential amino acid, L-arginine, may play a role in heart health by helping to keep blood vessels open. Insulin and glycogen are hormones that help maintain normal levels of blood glucose. Some of the body's proteins help regulate fluid balance in and out of body cells.
- Proteins are part of your body's defense mechanism. Skin, which is made of protein, is your first line of defense against bacteria and injury. Blood-clotting proteins limit blood loss from injury, and antibodies in your immune system help fight disease-causing bacteria and viruses.
- Actin and myosin, two muscle proteins, help muscles contract to help your body move. Your heart muscle also relies on proteins so it can contract and beat normally. Another amino acid, tyrosine, is part of epinephrine and norepinephrine, two neurotransmitters (brain chemicals) that relay messages in the nervous system. And tryptophan is a material needed for serotonin, thought to contribute to feelings of well-being.
- Proteins work as transport carriers. For example, hemoglobin is a protein that helps transport the oxygen in blood to body cells. Lipoproteins carry lipids (fats) to body cells from the liver and intestines. Some vitamins need a protein carrier. Other body substances, including glucose, use proteins to help move across cell membranes.

? Have you ever wondered?

. . . how much of your body is protein? That, of course, depends on each individual. But if you figure an average 170-pound person, it's about 16 percent. About half of that is in skeletal muscle, and the rest is in every body cell and fluid except urine and bile.

. . . why diet soda offers a warning about the amino acid phenylalanine? Diet sodas don't contain protein, but they're typically sweetened with aspartame, a nonnutritive sweetener that releases phenylalanine when digested. People with the rare genetic disease phenylketonuria (PKU) can't metabolize this amino acid properly due to a lack or deficiency of an enzyme needed to process phenylalanine. This causes a harmful build-up of this amino acid. In infants and young children, unmanaged PKU can cause tissue damage and brain damage. High phenylalanine levels can also affect mental and central nervous system functioning in adults with high phenylalanine levels. . *See "Aspartame: PKU Warning" in chapter 23, page 679, for more about PKU.*

. . . if tryptophan in milk helps you sleep? Perhaps. Tryptophan is an amino acid used to make serotonin, a neurotransmitter (brain chemical) that helps control sleep patterns. However, it's more likely that the act of drinking milk has a calming effect because the amount of tryptophan in milk is too small to make a difference. Similarly, tryptophan in turkey is often credited with drowsiness; however, the amount is comparable to that in most other meats. Feeling sleepy after a Thanksgiving dinner likely comes from many other factors, not feasting on turkey. As an aside, if you consider taking tryptophan as a dietary supplement, talk to your doctor first, as it may have harmful side effects.

Protein in Food: Complete and Incomplete

The quality of protein depends on which essential amino acids the food contains as well as on their digestibility. Protein sources are often categorized as complete or incomplete:

- *Complete:* Animal-based protein foods—meat, poultry, fish, eggs, milk, and milk products such as cheese and yogurt—supply complete protein with all nine essential amino acids in the right amounts needed to make new body proteins. Soybeans and quinoa are unique in the plant world since they, too, are sources of high-quality, or complete, proteins. *See "A Closer Look . . . Soy: Protein and More" in this chapter, page 383, for more about soy protein.*
- *Incomplete:* Most other plant-based foods supply amino acids but are lacking in one or more of the essentials. Their proteins are considered of lower quality and are sometimes called incomplete. Beans and peas, lentils, nuts, and seeds are good sources of incomplete proteins. Grain products and most vegetables supply some incomplete proteins but even less of the amino acid "essentials." Even fruits provide small but insignificant amounts.

A variety of foods with incomplete protein, eaten during the day, can provide enough essential amino acids. What one food lacks in essential amino acids, another can provide. When consumed at the same or different meals during the day, their proteins complement each other and are considered complete. You just have to be aware to consume the right variety of plant-based foods to get enough essentials.

See "Completing the Protein Equation" in this chapter, page 380, to learn about complementary proteins.

Proteins for Energy

Along with carbohydrates and fats, proteins supply energy: 4 calories per gram of protein. To compare, carbohydrates also provide 4 calories per gram, and fats provide 9 calories per gram. Unlike fats, proteins can convert to glucose, the fuel used for brain function.

Protein isn't the body's preferred fuel source. When carbohydrates and fats provide enough food energy, proteins are spared so they can do the work that only proteins can do: build and repair body cells and perform other body functions just noted. Muscle loss can be an unintended consequence when fat and carbohydrate intake is too low so that amino acids from recycled body proteins are used for energy instead of making body proteins.

Protein: Today's Health Issues

Considering protein's importance to health, there's surprisingly little research linking protein intake to many health conditions. The exceptions are the allergic reactions to some proteins in foods such as eggs, fish, shellfish, milk, peanuts, soy, tree nuts, and wheat. *See "Food Allergies: Growing Concern" in chapter 23, page 698.* Increasingly, research questions are being raised to help address protein's links to public health concerns, including being overweight, diabetes, heart health, high blood pressure, obesity, osteoporosis, and sarcopenia.

Does the source of your protein—animal- or plant-based foods—make a difference to your health? Most people consume both, so it's hard to know until more controlled research is done. Other factors also confound the question. For example, those who follow a vegetarian eating pattern also tend to eat less solid fats and more whole grains and perhaps more vegetables and fruits.

HEALTHY WEIGHT AND PROTEIN

Whether you consume high-protein foods or not, you can lose weight or maintain a healthy weight. If calories are controlled, vegetarian diets and meat-containing diets are comparable when it comes to weight loss.

That said, does a higher-protein diet have unique benefits? It's likely that it may, so don't skimp on protein as a way to cut calories. Some research indicates a high-protein diet—25 percent or more calories from protein—may help with weight loss if calories are reduced and may help preserve lean body mass, which itself may increase energy expenditure. And a diet with more protein may be easier to follow.

As calorie intake goes down for weight loss, the percentage of calories you need from protein should go up, perhaps to the upper amount of the range recommended in the Acceptable Macronutrient Distribution Range, *discussed further in "AMDR: A Range of Protein Advice" in this chapter, page 378.*

Beyond that, protein may help keep hunger at bay by enhancing satiety, or feeling full, and by reducing the urge to snack between meals. In fact, eating more protein at breakfast can start the day with a sustained feeling of fullness for the morning. Protein helps steady blood glucose levels and so helps control the brain signals for hunger. In addition, protein is more thermogenic than other macronutrients, meaning your body actually burns slightly more calories during protein digestion.

A pound of weight loss is composed mostly of body fat and some body protein. Eating a bit more protein may help protect muscle and shift the loss to more body fat. As an aside, preserving muscle mass has another weight management benefit. Body composition is important. Ounce for ounce, muscle burns more calories than body fat does.

For a healthy weight, remember that protein contributes calories. Eating portions of protein-rich foods that exceed your daily calorie needs adds up—and potentially leads to weight gain. Extra calories also may come from the company these foods keep: for example, from the fat in a juicy steak, fried chicken, gravy, or full-fat cheese. Instead choosing low-fat, fat-free, and lean protein foods with fewer calories usually means eating fewer solid fats.

See "Have you ever wondered . . . if a high-protein/low-carb diet has any weight-loss advantage?" in chapter 22, page 648, for more about high-protein diets for weight management.

MUSCLE, SARCOPENIA, AND PROTEIN

Protein is well known for its role in maintaining healthy muscles. And the amino acid leucine is powerful for building muscle. Protein—for both strength and muscle recovery—is a priority for many athletes, *as discussed in "Protein and the Athlete: How Much?" in chapter 21, page 607.* That said, no matter how much protein you consume, physical activity (resistance training) increases the efficiency of protein use in muscle building and repair.

Sarcopenia. The term "sarcopenia" may be unfamiliar. However, if you're an older adult or if you're caring for an aging person, you've likely seen it. Coming from a Greek term meaning "poverty of the flesh," sarcopenia is the natural progressive loss of skeletal muscle and its function, quality, and strength.

Several factors contribute to muscle loss. With aging, the body doesn't convert amino acids to muscle tissue as efficiently as it once did. Inadequate protein intake and less physical activity, when muscles don't get enough of a workout, contribute further to muscle loss.

Muscle loss may start earlier than you think. For every decade of life after age thirty, lean muscle mass can decline by 3 to 8 percent. That's a concern because preserving muscle as you age helps retain your physical endurance and strength, which enables you to engage in the activities of everyday life. Down the line, that includes such common things as lifting objects, getting up from a chair, and reducing your risk of falling. In its advanced stages, sarcopenia is seen as the frailty of age, associated with higher risks of falls and disability.

Sarcopenia may be slowed or even partly reversed with sound nutrition and regular strength-building physical activity. This includes consuming enough protein, more than the current recommendation for protein, *discussed in "RDA: Minimum Advice for Protein" later in this chapter, page 378.* If you're an older adult, a moderate increase in the amount of high-quality protein, along with resistance exercise, may help you retain muscle mass and strength.

Spreading out high-quality protein foods during the day (not just eating protein foods for dinner) also improves protein synthesis and so helps to build and maintain muscle mass. For those who are physically active, evidence suggests that timing a higher-protein meal or a protein shake after a workout may promote muscle building.

Although most people in the United States consume more protein than the current minimum advice in the Recommended Dietary Allowances (RDAs), protein intake often declines in later years. That may be because older people eat less food overall—or perhaps eat fewer high-quality protein foods. As a result, they may not meet current protein recommendations; some older adults risk energy-protein malnutrition.

See "Protein: Pump It Up" in chapter 20, page 578, for more about sarcopenia.

BONE HEALTH AND PROTEIN

While calcium and vitamin D are well recognized for their roles in reducing the risks of osteoporosis, protein also plays a role in your bone health. That's not surprising, since about 50 percent of bone volume is protein. Like other body tissues, bone tissue also undergoes ongoing repair that needs protein.

Although research isn't consistent or conclusive, there appears to be a positive link between higher protein intake and greater bone mass and fewer fractures—if calcium intake is adequate, too. More research is needed to determine protein's role in maintaining bone density and lowering fracture risk among older adults.

OTHER HEALTH ISSUES AND PROTEIN

Diabetes. No consistent evidence shows that protein intake from any source is linked to an increased risk for developing type 2 diabetes. In fact, a higher-protein diet may help with glycemic (blood glucose) control, when combined with an eating pattern that also factors in amounts of calories, fats, and carbohydrates (including fiber).

The National Institute of Diabetes and Digestive and Kidney Diseases advises that people with disease-related kidney disease follow protein recommendations but avoid high-protein diets. The reason is that damaged kidneys need to work harder to remove protein waste products from the bloodstream. For those with greatly reduced kidney function, reducing protein intake may help delay the start of kidney failure; working with a registered dietitian nutritionist can help ensure adequate nutrition.

Cancer prevention. No consistent evidence links protein intake—from either plant-based or animal-based sources—to either higher or lower risk of most cancers. However, go easy on processed meats because high intakes of them may increase some cancer risks. Some studies suggest a link between colon cancer and eating large amounts of red meat, especially processed meats such as bacon, ham, and hot dogs, but research isn't conclusive. More studies are needed to show if the type of meat, how it's prepared, or how much is eaten is linked to cancer risk, and if other substances factor in. The best advice for now: use moderation and eat a variety of protein-rich foods.

Heart disease, high blood pressure, and protein. Again, no consistent evidence links protein intake—from either plant-based or animal-based sources—to heart disease or high blood pressure. Some research indicates that increased protein intake may reduce the risk of heart disease when protein foods replace those high in carbohydrates. Lean protein may play a role in lowering blood lipids. There's not yet enough research to offer advice, however.

? Have you ever wondered?

. . . why protein foods make meals more satisfying? Satisfaction may come in part from what you define as a meal. Perhaps the protein food—such as meat, fish, poultry, eggs, or a soyburger—served as "center plate" makes a meal satisfying to you.

Satisfaction from protein foods extends beyond meal preferences, however. Recent research indicates that protein can add satiety, or feelings of fullness, perhaps more than fat or carbohydrates. Protein takes longer to move through the digestive tract than carbohydrate does, which may reduce the desire to overeat or eat as often.

By helping to stave off hunger longer, protein foods may aid weight management—if your calorie intake remains within your energy budget. Eating enough protein, along with getting adequate physical activity, also may help you lose fat, not muscle, as you manage your weight.

The bottom line: Include lean protein foods in sensible amounts in all your meals. *See "Visual Guide to Portion Size" in chapter 2, page 24.*

Protein: How Much? What Kind?

How much protein do you need in a day? Actually, the optimal amount—and even the types—of protein needed for health isn't fully understood. Certainly the amount, the quality, and perhaps the timing matter. Age, gender, body size, and level of physical activity all make a difference, too.

PROTEIN: HOW MUCH IS ENOUGH?

Recommendations for protein intake come from the Institute of Medicine's Dietary Reference Intakes (DRIs), in two ways:

- The Acceptable Macronutrient Distribution Range (AMDR) provides "wiggle room," or a range, for the recommended amount of protein you need daily.
- The Recommended Dietary Allowance (RDA) for protein is a minimum, not an optimum, recommendation.

Recommendations for protein are the same for vegetarians and nonvegetarians.

See "Protein: How Much?" below for recommended amounts.

Protein: How Much?

Age	AMDR: Percentage of Total Calories	RDA: Minimum Daily Advice
Boys and girls, 1 to 3 years	5 to 20%	13 grams
Boys and girls, 4 to 8 years	10 to 30%	19 grams
Boys and girls, 9 to 13 years	10 to 30%	34 grams
Teen boys, 14 to 18 years	10 to 30%	52 grams
Teen girls, 14 to 18 years	10 to 30%	46 grams
Adult men, 19 years and older	10 to 35%	56 grams
Adult women, 19 years and older	10 to 35%	46 grams
Pregnant and breastfeeding women	10 to 35%	71 grams

Source: Dietary Reference Intakes, Institute of Medicine, 2005.

AMDR: A Range of Protein Advice

As a protein recommendation, the AMDR lets you take your food preferences, physical needs, and personal eating patterns into account. Because it is a range, you can increase your protein intake to a higher or optimum level for more potential health benefits.

For adults, the recommended range is 10 to 35 percent of total calories. For a 2,000-calorie daily eating that's 50 to 175 grams of protein, or 200 to 700 calories from protein, per day. If you need more than 2,000 calories daily, the recommended grams of protein go up—but still within the range. To help you put this protein advice in a food context: one ounce of lean meat or plant-based protein foods (beans, tofu, others) delivers about 7 grams of protein, and an eight-ounce cup of milk or soymilk provides about 8 grams of protein.

For weight loss, as your calorie intake goes down, the percentage of calories from protein should go up. That's also true for those who eat fewer calories as they get older—a key nutrition issue with aging.

Consuming only the minimum (lower number in the AMDR) helps prevent a protein deficiency. Most adults in the United States average between 15 and 16 percent of their calories from protein. That amount is near the lower end of the range and likely not enough for optimal health benefits or adequate muscle synthesis. Scientific evidence indicates that targeting the upper end of the AMDR for protein offers more health benefits.

Those with kidney disease (perhaps related to type 2 diabetes) may be advised to limit protein intake to less than 10 percent of calories. If you're advised to limit protein, work with a registered dietitian nutritionist or a certified diabetes educator to ensure you get adequate nutrition.

See chapter 2, page 21, for a healthy eating plan that helps you consume enough protein. See "Protein: Muscles and More" in chapter 21, page 607, to explore protein and protein supplements for competitive and weekend athletes.

RDA: Minimum Advice for Protein

Now, the minimum advice: The RDA for protein is the amount advised daily for protein balance, or to repair your body proteins as they wear out and break down. It's enough, based on body weight and age, for most healthy people to prevent a deficiency. The RDA is at the lower end of the AMDR.

For most healthy adults aged nineteen and older, the RDA is 0.8 grams of protein per kilogram of body weight (about 59 grams daily for a 160-pound adult). For infants, children, teens, and pregnant or nursing women, the RDA is higher than for most adults. In fact, protein needs per pound of body weight are the highest for infants: not surprising since most babies double their birth weight in the first 6 months! As a child's growth rate slows, protein needs per pound of body weight decrease, even while the total protein need goes up.

Pregnancy and breastfeeding increase protein needs. A mother's increased blood volume, breast and uterine tissues, and placenta, as well as the fetus, are reasons that new and expecting mothers require more protein.

Some experts believe that the current RDAs for protein may not be enough, especially for older adults, for optimum health benefits. Twice the protein recommendation in the RDA may optimize the benefits.

Protein needs may increase for healing after injury, burns, and surgery, or with some other health problems, including type 2 diabetes, significant muscle loss, and critical illness. If you have diabetes or kidney disease, the recommendation may differ; talk to your doctor or registered dietitian nutritionist.

PROTEIN: WHAT IF YOU GET TOO LITTLE?

When protein intake, especially high-quality protein, isn't enough, the body can't make or repair body cells adequately. Instead, proteins in body tissues, including muscle, break down, releasing their pool of amino acids for recycling. Without enough energy (calories from food), the body uses its fat stores and perhaps its muscle protein for energy. With severe calorie restriction—common among those with anorexia—muscle loss is the outcome. *See "Eating Disorders: More Than a Nutrition Issue" in chapter 25, page 732.*

Most adults in the United States and other developed countries get enough protein to avoid a deficiency. But where poverty or a limited food supply exists, protein deficiency is common. Growing children are at special risk. Kwashiorkor is a form of protein malnutrition; among its outcomes are loss of muscle, failure to grow, reduced immune response, increased risk for disease, and weakened respiratory and cardiovascular systems. Marasmus, a type of severe protein-energy malnutrition, is a serious lack of food energy, causing debilitating muscle loss and often death.

PROTEIN: CAN YOU GET TOO MUCH?

No upper limit, or Tolerable Upper Intake Level (UL), for protein has been set in the Dietary Reference Intakes. And going beyond the RDA can result in health benefits. However, no evidence shows an advantage for excessive amounts beyond the AMDR for supplying body proteins or for building skeletal muscles.

Your body doesn't store excess protein from food. Instead, your body breaks it down for conversion to body fat or to glycogen for energy storage. Its nitrogen-containing components, released in the process, are removed and excreted through the kidneys in urine. And if excess protein contributes to excess calories, it's one more factor that tips energy balance toward weight gain.

A high-protein diet and protein supplements can be risky for those with kidney disease. *See "Other Supplements (Selected): Effectiveness, Cautions" in chapter 10, page 329, to learn about protein supplements.*

Protein in Foods and Drinks

Meat, poultry, fish, eggs, milk, cheese, and yogurt: These animal-based food sources all deliver high-quality protein with all the essential amino acids in amounts that your body needs. In fact, three ounces of lean meat and poultry each provide about 25 grams of protein. And one cup of milk or yogurt provides about 8 grams of protein, as does one cup of soymilk.

RDAs for Protein: Figuring the Minimum

The RDA for protein is based on the minimum recommendation for your body weight. You can calculate the target amount for you. Here's the advice, given for both kilograms and pounds of body weight.

Age	Protein per Kilogram of Body Weight	Protein per Pound of Body Weight
0 to 6 months	1.52 grams	0.69 grams
6 to 12 months	1.20 grams	0.55 grams
1 to 3 years	1.05 grams	0.48 grams
4 to 13 years	0.95 grams	0.43 grams
14 to 18 years	0.85 grams	0.39 grams
19 years and older	0.80 grams	0.37 grams

Use this formula to determine your target:

body weight × minimum protein amount per kilogram or pound = RDA

For example, for a 120-pound, 16-year-old girl, the RDA would be 46.8 grams daily (120 × .39).

Source: Dietary Reference Intakes, Institute of Medicine, 2005.

? Have you ever wondered?

. . . how much protein a vegan meal might have? Of course, that varies, but here's the protein in a sample meal: A one-cup serving of rice and beans (half rice, half beans) supplies about 10 grams of protein. Add one cup of soymilk for about 8 grams of protein, a green vegetable side dish topped with nuts for 4 to 5 grams of protein, and one whole-wheat roll for about 4 more grams of protein. That adds up to at least 26 grams of protein in just one meal (without dessert). If you're a vegan, make sure your meals deliver lysine, the essential amino acid that is most likely limited.

. . . if you can get enough protein in a vegan diet if you're allergic to soy? You have many other plant-based options. Other legumes (garbanzos, lentils, pinto and black beans, split peas, peanuts), nuts, foods made from legumes and nuts (almond and peanut butter, chilis, falafel, hummus, soups, and more), and quinoa are great options.

. . . what tempeh is? Another soy food, tempeh is made from cooked, slightly fermented soybeans, spices or herbs, and sometimes grains, giving it a firm texture and a nutty flavor. Low in fat yet high in protein, it's a great meat substitute that's easy to slice or cube for chilis, soups, stir-fries, and other mixed dishes.

. . . what natto is? Popular in Japanese cooking, often as a condiment, perhaps with rice, natto is steamed, fermented, mashed soybeans, with a strong cheeselike flavor and glutinous texture. Nutritionally speaking, it is rich in isoflavones and fiber, is a good source of calcium, iron, and potassium, and provides protein.

A Closer Look . . .

Protein for Vegans

Carefully planned meals and snacks can provide enough total protein and essential amino acids for vegetarians. That's easy for lacto- and lacto-ovo-vegetarians, who eat eggs and/or dairy foods—but like others, they need to be mindful of spreading protein choices throughout the day. Vegans can get enough protein, too, if they consume a variety of plant-based foods with protein since the amino acid content of foods differs.

For vegans, lysine is the essential amino acid most likely to come up short. Because cereals are low in lysine, vegans may wisely consume more beans, peas, lentils, and soy products, which are good sources of lysine. Amaranth, pistachios, pumpkin seeds, quinoa, and seitan are all high in lysine, too. Another option for vegans: Consume more protein from all other sources of plant-based foods, too, to insure enough lysine.

Consuming a significant amount of legumes makes it easier to get adequate protein. Amino acids from soybeans, a complete protein source, have the same health effects as amino acids from dairy foods or poultry. However, proteins from some plant-based foods, such as legumes and some cereals, may not be digested as well, so protein recommendations for vegans may be slightly higher.

With careful planning, most vegetarians, including vegans, don't need a protein supplement. *See "The Healthy Vegetarian Way" in chapter 2, page 53.* If you're vegan, check with a registered dietitian nutritionist if you need guidance.

Boost the Benefits: Spread Protein Out

Many people distribute their protein intake throughout the day like this: a little protein for breakfast, perhaps cereal with milk; more for lunch, in chicken soup, tuna salad, or a peanut butter sandwich; most at dinnertime, in a generous portion of meat, poultry, or fish. (And maybe none at snack time.) That could be 12 grams, 20 grams, and 60 grams spread out over three meals: not the best way to maximize protein's potential in your body!

Redistributing those 90 or so grams of high-quality protein more evenly throughout your day's meals and snacks—starting early—may provide the most benefits for promoting weight loss or aiding weight maintenance, and preserving muscle mass and strength as you age.

Single meals with about 30 grams of high-quality protein each—three times daily—seems to stimulate protein synthesis more effectively than meals with less protein (20 grams per meal) among healthy adults.

For 25 to 30 grams of protein in your daily meals, with perhaps a little protein from a snack, consider these tips:

- Give your breakfast a protein boost. Replace some carbohydrate foods at breakfast with protein foods: a carton of yogurt, peanut butter on toast, or a handful of nuts with your cereal. Top your bagel with an egg; add whey protein to your smoothie.
- Consider this for about 26 grams of protein: cereal with milk may provide 10 grams of protein. A carton of Greek yogurt to go with it can add another 13 grams or so. Top it with ½ ounce of almonds for another 3 grams of protein.
- Enjoy a protein-rich drink with lunch. Choose low-fat or fat-free milk or fortified soy beverage instead of water, iced tea, or soda. Make salads with quinoa and soup with lentils.
- Snack smartly. Choose hummus, peanuts, a protein bar, or string cheese as a quick snack. Enjoy a latte or chai with milk.
- Make your meat or poultry portion reasonable at dinnertime: a three- to four-ounce portion provides about 25 grams of protein. That allows room for more protein foods at other meals and snacks, and perhaps in a dinner side dish.

See "Breakfast: Six Ways to a Protein Boost" in chapter 3, page 63.

Beans and peas, nuts, and seeds are good sources of protein, too, but lack sufficient amounts of one or more essential amino acids. Grains provide some protein, including some essential amino acids that beans and peas lack.

See "Your Healthy Eating Check-In: Do You Eat Enough Protein?" in this chapter, page 381, for the protein amounts in various foods. The Healthy Eating Patterns, *discussed in chapter 2,* page 21, can help you eat enough high-quality protein.

Label Lingo

Protein

While the Nutrition Facts label gives the specific amount of protein in one label serving of the food item, "protein lingo" in nutrient content claims may offer a quick description. Look for these terms on food labels as you walk the supermarket aisles.

Label term . . .	Means . . .
HIGH-PROTEIN	Contains 10 grams or more per serving
GOOD SOURCE	Contains 5 to 9.9 grams per serving
MORE, EXTRA, PLUS, OR ADDED	Contains at least 5 grams more* per serving
FORTIFIED OR ENRICHED	Contains at least 5 grams more* per serving

*As compared with a standard serving size of the regular food.

COMPLETING THE PROTEIN EQUATION

Beans plus grains: it's a combination enjoyed around the world. What one lacks, the other has. Together they deliver complete protein; together they're often referred to as foods with complementary proteins, providing all essential amino acids without adding animal protein.

Except for soybeans and quinoa, plant-based foods (beans and peas, grains, nuts, and seeds) are limited in one or more essential amino acids—often cysteine, lysine, methionine, and tryptophan:

- Beans are high in lysine but limited in cysteine and methionine.
- Nuts, seeds, and grains are high in methionine and cysteine but limited in lysine.
- Rice is high in methionine but limited in lysine.
- Corn is a good source of methionine but is limited in lysine and tryptophan.

Pair them for complete protein. Legumes plus grains can be enjoyed as a bean burrito, beans and rice, hummus (mashed chickpeas/garbanzo beans) with pita bread, lentil–brown rice soup, meatless bean chili and cornbread, or peanut butter on a bagel.

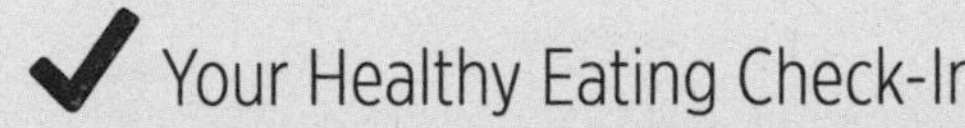

Do You Eat Enough Protein?

What might 25 to 30 grams of protein per meal look like? Many people get most of their protein at dinner, but it's better to spread it out.

Using this list of common foods, what protein-rich foods and drinks might you choose to add up to 25 to 30 grams of protein in each meal in your day? Start with breakfast, and then consider snacks with protein, too.

Ask yourself these questions: Do I get at least the minimum amount of protein recommended daily? How about the optimal amount? Did I spread my protein foods and drinks out over the day?

Selected Foods	Serving Size	Calories	Protein
SOURCES OF ANIMAL-BASED PROTEINS			
Chicken breast, skinless, meat only, grilled	3 ounces	128	26 grams
Lean beef, sirloin, broiled, 0-inch trim	3 ounces	160	26 grams
Pork, loin, roasted	3 ounces	147	23 grams
Ground beef, 90 percent lean, broiled	3 ounces	184	22 grams
Salmon, sockeye, baked	3 ounces	133	23 grams
Tuna, canned in water, drained	3 ounces	109	20 grams
Whey protein powder	1 ounce	103	17 grams
Cottage cheese, low-fat	½ cup	81	14 grams
Greek yogurt, nonfat, vanilla	5.3 ounces	117	13 grams
Yogurt, nonfat, vanilla	8 ounces	177	7 grams
Milk, low-fat	8 ounces	102	8 grams
Cheese, cheddar	1 ounce	115	6 grams
Egg	1 large	72	6 grams
SOURCES OF PLANT-BASED PROTEINS			
Tempeh	½ cup	160	17 grams
Soy nuts, dry roasted	¼ cup	104	10 grams
Soybeans (edamame), frozen, prepared	½ cup	94	9 grams
Tofu, regular, with calcium sulfate	½ cup	88	9 grams
Lentils, cooked	½ cup	113	9 grams
Kidney beans, canned, drained	½ cup	108	8 grams
Peanut butter, smooth, reduced fat	2 tablespoons	187	9 grams
Soymilk, all flavors	1 cup	80	7 grams
Hummus, commercial	⅓ cup	136	6 grams
Almonds	1 ounce, 23 nuts	170	6 grams
Sunflower seeds, roasted	1 ounce	165	5 grams
Pumpkin seeds, roasted	1 ounce	126	5 grams
Quinoa, cooked	½ cup	111	4 grams
Walnuts	1 ounce, 14 halves	185	4 grams
Miso	2 tablespoons	67	4 grams
Natto	2 tablespoons	46	4 grams
Cowpeas (black-eyed) peas, cooked	½ cup	80	3 grams
Bulgur, cooked	½ cup	75	3 grams
Pecans	1 ounce, 19 halves	196	3 grams
Rice, white, long-grain, cooked	½ cup	105	2 grams
Corn, yellow, cooked	½ cup	72	2 grams
Almond milk, unsweetened	1 cup	39	2 grams

Source: US Department of Agriculture, National Nutrient Database for Standard Reference, Release 28, 2016.

Use Food-A-Pedia in the USDA's SuperTracker to see the protein amounts in more of your food choices (www.supertracker.usda.gov/foodapedia.aspx).

Have you ever wondered?

. . . if you need a protein supplement, especially if you're physically active? If you're healthy, you probably get all the protein you need from your everyday meals and snacks. Protein-rich foods, especially those from animal sources, have plenty of amino acids. Vegans likely don't need protein supplements, either, if they eat a variety of plant-based foods and enough calories in their day's meals and snacks. "Meatless" doesn't mean low protein!

Protein supplements may be useful for some health conditions or for older adults who can't consume enough protein. However, talk to your doctor before taking protein supplements. *See "Other Supplements (Selected): Effectiveness, Cautions" in chapter 10, page 329, for more about protein supplements.*

. . . what casein is? What whey protein is? They're the two high-quality proteins in dairy foods. While casein is about 80 percent of milk's protein, whey protein makes up the rest. Whey—composed of fats, minerals, lactose, protein, other carbohydrates, and other substances—is the liquid left after milk is separated and curdled to make cheese. At one time considered a waste by-product, today whey protein is often used in beverages, drink mixes, protein bars, and yogurt. Whey protein contains all essential amino acids, including high concentrations of leucine, which may play an important role in glucose metabolism and insulin sensitivity. Whey protein also is very efficient in helping to stimulate the synthesis of muscle protein after a strenuous workout and may help increase satiety (feeling full) after a meal.

Casein is also an excellent source of all the essential amino acids, but it is digested and absorbed more slowly than whey. Both are beneficial in regulating protein balance.

. . . what makes pea protein unique? Unlike whey and soy proteins, it has no common allergens. Research is underway to understand its benefits, but like whey protein, it may have benefits for muscle synthesis and may promote satiety. Pea protein is high in arginine, which helps form creatine, important for providing energy to muscles.

Good news, especially if you're a vegetarian: For protein benefits, you don't need to combine foods with complementary proteins at each meal as once thought. But you can if you want to in dishes like those *mentioned in "Completing the Protein Equation" in this chapter*, page 380. That said, you do need to eat a variety of plant-based foods—beans and peas, grains, nuts, seeds, and vegetables and fruits—and enough calories throughout the day. The limited amino acid(s) in one food can come from foods in other meals or snacks.

Kitchen Nutrition

Easy Protein Boosters

- Sprinkle chopped nuts or seeds over breakfast cereal, fruit, ice cream, oatmeal, waffles, or yogurt.
- Use finely chopped nuts instead of, or in addition to, breadcrumbs as a breading.
- Spoon cottage cheese or Greek or soy yogurt over a baked potato, cereal, or fruit.
- Spread nut butter (almond, macadamia, or peanut) on apple or pear slices.
- Whisk an egg or egg whites into simmering chicken soup.
- Toss canned beans (drained, rinsed) or chopped tofu with a garden salad.
- Steam edamame as a finger-food meal starter. Or try soynuts as a dry snack.
- Blend whey protein or dry milk into smoothies, creamy soups or pasta sauces, or add it to cooked breakfast cereal (oatmeal), mashed potatoes, or milk-based desserts.
- Enjoy hummus as a raw veggie dip.
- Grate cheese as a topper for chilis, salads, or soups. Or mix it into casseroles, pasta, or rice dishes.
- Mix leftover chopped meat, poultry, or fish into vegetable soup or pasta sauce.
- Layer a slice of cheese on any sandwich.
- Add sliced hard-cooked eggs to salads.

Be wary of plant-based foods advertised as having all essential amino acids. Most plant-based foods do. But the amount of one or more amino acids may be quite limited and not adequate for protein synthesis or for building and repairing your body's proteins.

PROTEIN KEEPS GOOD COMPANY

It's not just the protein, but the nutrients packaged in foods and beverages along with it that make protein foods so nourishing.

- *Animal proteins:* Foods from animal sources have more solid fats than plant-based foods but in varying amounts. Fish has more unsaturated fats, including beneficial omega-3 fatty acids (DHA and EPA) in oily fish. Milk, yogurt, and cheese deliver calcium, among other important nutrients; their fat content varies. Heme iron and zinc are among the other important nutrients in meat, poultry, and fish.
- *Plant proteins:* Along with essential amino acids, beans and peas (legumes), nuts, and seeds provide fiber; certain vitamins and minerals, including nonheme iron; and more poly- and monounsaturated fats than animal sources of protein. Plant-based protein foods are low in solid fats and, for those advised to limit cholesterol, they're cholesterol free.

For good nutrition, consider the whole nutrient package. Choose protein-rich foods with less saturated fat. Those with less fat often have fewer calories, too. Consider these tips as you prepare protein foods:

- Eat a variety of protein foods, which include lean meat, poultry, fish, eggs, beans and peas, soy products, and unsalted nuts and seeds. A meatless (no animal-based foods) eating pattern can provide enough high-quality protein.
- Increase the amount and variety of fish consumed by choosing fish in place of some meat and poultry.
- Replace protein foods that are higher in saturated fats with choices that are lower in saturated fats and calories and/or are sources of oils.
- Prepare protein foods to keep them lean. Choose lean meat; trim off any visible fat.
- For chicken and turkey, remove the skin to reduce the fat.
- Bake, broil, or grill meat, poultry, and fish instead of frying them.

? Have you ever wondered?

. . . if chia seeds are a good protein source? Eaten tradtionally by Native Americans in the Southwest, chia seeds offer a good source of protein. One ounce contains nearly 5 grams of protein and about 140 calories. They're also an excellent source of omega-3 fatty acids and a good source of several minerals and vitamins, as well as fiber. While chia seeds are promoted for contributing to reduced risk of heart disease and weight loss, there's no evidence to support these claims. Enjoy them raw or ground as an ingredient in biscuits, bread, cake, or porridge.

A Closer Look . . .

Soy: Protein and More

Made into many food products, soybeans are versatile and nourishing. Compared with many other legumes, soybeans are a rich source of plant-based protein—unique because soybeans contain complete protein. That's why many soy products make good protein alternatives in meatless meals. Soybean oil is not a protein source.

Beyond that, soybeans are a good source of B vitamins and other nutrients. A source of essential fatty acids (including ALAs, which are omega 3-fatty acids that convert to DHA and EPA), soybeans contain fat that is mostly poly- and monounsaturated. Tofu (made with calcium sulfate), calcium-fortified soymilk, and calcium-fortified soy yogurt deliver calcium and often are vitamin D–fortified, too.

The health benefits of soy extend to its phytonutrients. Although research hasn't yet provided clear answers, soy's isoflavones are credited with helping to lower risks for some women's health issues, such as hot flashes and menopause symptoms; evidence for these benefits isn't consistent. Soybean's two main isoflavones—genistein and daidzein—have weak estrogenlike effects. *See "Phytonutrients: Different from Nutrients" in chapter 15, page 448.*

Some evidence suggests that soy foods may be heart healthy, especially if they replace higher-fat options. Possible reasons? They're low in solid fats but provide fiber and polyunsaturated fat. Soy protein itself may have a small effect on lowering total and LDL (bad) cholesterol levels. Vegetable protein including soy protein also may be linked to lower blood pressure; however, other components of plant-based foods, such as fiber, might factor in.

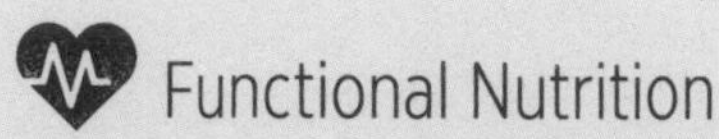

A Quick Look at Soy Protein

Class/Components	Potential Benefit	Some Food Sources
Soy protein*	May reduce risk of cardiovascular disease	Soybeans and soy-based foods such as cheese, milk, tofu, and yogurt

*The US Food and Drug Administration has approved a health claim for this food component.

Source: Adapted from the International Food Information Council Foundation, 2014.

See "Functional Nutrition: A Quick Look at Key Phytonutrients" in chapter 15, page 449, to learn the functional benefits of phytoestrogens: isoflavones and lignan.

- Eat smaller portions of meat, and eat fish more often (twice a week).
- Make beans and peas, including soybeans and soy-based foods, an important part of your meal plans. Substitute black or pinto beans or soy products for meat in chilis, pasta sauce, and tacos to make them high protein and meatless.
- Choose low-fat or fat-free milk, yogurt, and cheese. Limit full-fat cheese.

See "Meat Counter" in chapter 6, page 164, and "Meat, Poultry, Fish: Keep Lean" in chapter 8, page 254, for more ways to buy and prepare lean protein-rich foods.

Have you ever wondered?

. . . how the protein in almond milk, rice milk, and soymilk compares with cow's milk? The Nutrition Facts label shows the protein content per eight-ounce serving. Like cow's milk, soy beverages, such as soymilk, provide high-quality, complete protein. However, even though they're referred to as "milk," almond milk, coconut milk, and rice milk don't provide much protein, and their proteins lack some essential amino acids. While cow's milk and soymilk provide about 8 grams of protein per eight-ounce serving, almond milk and rice milk generally provide only about 1 gram or less of protein per eight ounces. Since these milks are poor protein sources, Nutrition Facts labels on almond and rice milk state: "Not to be used as an infant formula." All these milk alternatives may be calcium- and vitamin D–fortified.

. . . if a protein shake is a good meal replacement or snack? It certainly provides protein's nutrient and health benefits. However, research shows that protein shakes and other protein beverages may not curb hunger for as long as other sources of protein do. They move through the stomach faster than solid protein foods do and may get absorbed more quickly. A protein shake probably won't supply the other nutrients and fiber that a varied meal with protein-rich foods does. Enjoy a protein shake as a beverage choice or as snack.

. . . why soy products may carry a health claim on their food labels? A health claim indicating a link between soy protein and the lowering of total and LDL (bad) cholesterol levels was approved in the year 2000.The claim was based on the need for 25 grams of soy protein per day for the potential benefit. For a label to carry the claim, a food must contain at least 6.25 grams of soy protein per serving. Since that time, research indicates that the effect may be smaller, from a greater soy protein intake, than once thought. Still, soy products are heart healthy. *See "Health Claims" in chapter 6, page 149.*

13

Fat Facts

In this chapter, find out about . . .

"Good" fats and "bad" fats

Fats, food, and health

Clarifying cholesterol

Fat replacers in food

For nearly half a century, dietary fat and cholesterol have been in the limelight. The advice to limit fat because it was unhealthy was simple—and arguably shortsighted.

Today, scientific knowledge of dietary fats and their relationships to health is known to be far more complex, yet still full of unknowns. The balance of the types of fats appears to be far more important to health than trying to eat low-fat. In fact, you need certain fats—chosen wisely—to be healthy!

As scientists learn more, advice for dietary fats as well as dietary cholesterol has shifted. Today's guidance reflects the most current science and understanding of dietary fats, nutrition, and health.

So . . . how do different fats impact your health? Which fats are healthy? How much is enough? What fats should you limit—and how do you do that? To understand the role of fats in food, health, and chronic disease and to comprehend today's advice about dietary fats in healthy meals and snacks, first explore the basic facts about this often misunderstood nutrient.

Fats: Not Created Equal

Whether solid or liquid, fats are compounds that aren't soluble in water. All fats in food are blends of different fatty acids—some saturated, some not. Each fatty acid is composed of carbon, hydrogen, and oxygen. These same elements are found in carbohydrates and proteins, just arranged differently.

Fats in food are broken down during digestion, which releases fatty acids and glycerol in the body. In turn, the body uses those to form other lipids (fats). When fat is stored in your body, it's in the form of a triglyceride. Aside from their different structures, fatty acids have different physiological effects in the body. Some are essential for health, some not.

See "Fats 101: A Dictionary of Terms" in this chapter, page 387.

FATS: SATURATED AND UNSATURATED

The differences among fats and their fatty acids are all about their chemistry. In scientific terms, fatty acid molecules may be saturated or unsaturated, differing significantly in three main ways: the length of their hydrocarbon chains, their degree of saturation, and the shape of their molecules, all of which determine their characteristics and their functions in food and health.

"Saturation" refers to the number of hydrogen atoms linked to each carbon in the chain. So, here's a quick chemistry lesson.

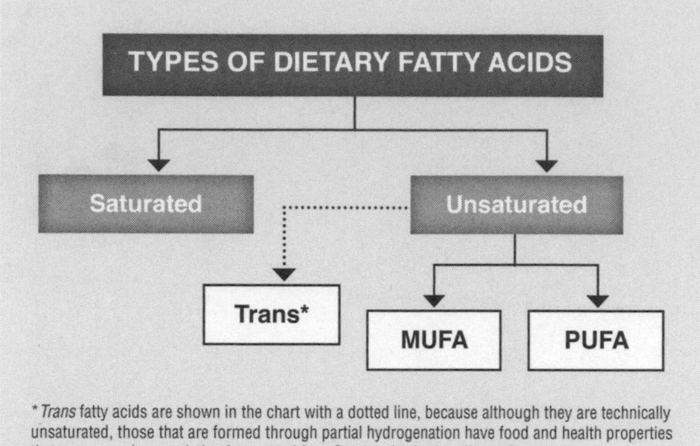

* *Trans* fatty acids are shown in the chart with a dotted line, because although they are technically unsaturated, those that are formed through partial hydrogenation have food and health properties that are more characteristic of saturated fats. See text for further discussion.

Source: Dietary Fats: Balancing Health and Flavor, IFIC Foundation, 2015.

Saturated. When carbon atoms have as many hydrogen atoms attached as possible on their molecular chain, the fatty acid is saturated—or completely filled with hydrogen. As a result, there are no double bonds on the chain.

Fats made mostly of *saturated fatty acids (SFAs)* usually are solid at room temperature and also more stable. This makes them less likely to spoil or turn rancid than fats with more unsaturated fatty acids.

Fats in animal-based foods are mostly saturated. For example, think about butter, lard, and the fat in cheese and meat. Tropical vegetable oils (coconut, palm kernel, and palm) and cocoa butter also are higher in saturated fatty acids than fats from other plant-based foods. Fully-hydrogenated vegetable oils are also highly saturated.

Unsaturated. When hydrogen atoms are missing and double bonds form between neighboring carbon atoms, the fatty acid is unsaturated, or not saturated with hydrogen.

- *Monounsaturated fatty acids (MUFAs)* are missing one hydrogen pair on their chemical chain, so there's just one double bond.

  Fats with mostly MUFAs are liquid at room temperature. Some vegetable oils, such as canola, olive, peanut, high-oleic safflower, and sunflower oils, have significant amounts of MUFAs. Avocados are high in MUFAs, too. Omega-7 fatty acid (palmitoleic acid) and omega-9 fatty acids are MUFAs. The body can make omega-9s if enough omega-3s and -6s are consumed. *Note:* palmitic acid is a different, and saturated, fatty acid.)

Solid Fats and Oils: How Do They Compare?

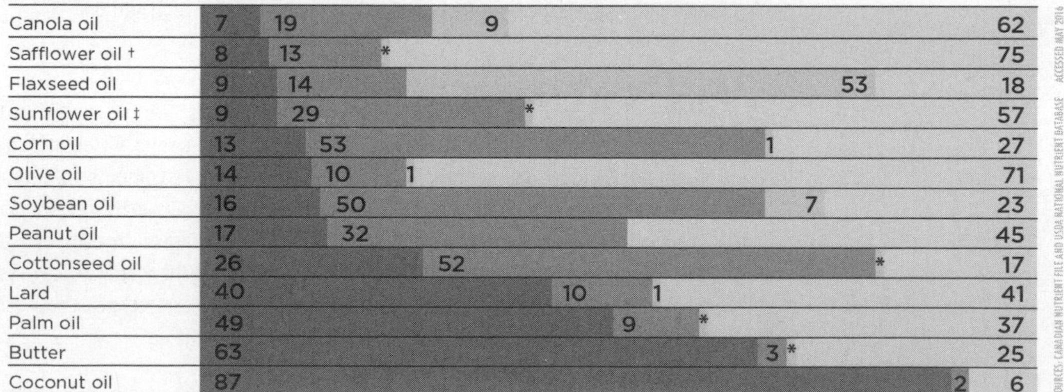

Each of these fats has minor amounts of other fatty acids, not shown on this chart. For that reason, the total for each line in this bar graph will come close to, but not equal, 100.

Source: CanolaInfo, Canola Council of Canada, 2016.

- *Polyunsaturated fatty acids (PUFAs)* are missing two or more hydrogen pairs, so two or more double bonds are formed. PUFAs themselves differ in another way: the location of their double bonds determines whether they are omega-3 or omega-6 fatty acids.

  Fats with mostly PUFAs usually are liquid at room temperature. Corn, cottonseed, flaxseed, soybean, and sunflower oils contain the highest amounts of PUFAs. Fatty acids in fish are mainly polyunsaturated, too.

The fat in nearly all foods is a mixture of fatty acids: saturated, monounsaturated, and polyunsaturated. Their proportions account for their varying health effects and culinary characteristics. For example, fish and meat both have saturated and unsaturated fatty acids. However, fish has a higher proportion of PUFAs, and meat, more SFAs. Yet, both generally have more MUFAs than SFAs.

TRANS FATS: SEMISOLID FATS

"*Trans*" fats are unsaturated fatty acids, too. Surprised? This may be so, but their chemical makeup is different from other unsaturated fats, making them more solid, and more like saturated fats.

Trans fatty acids (TFAs) come from two sources: first, most are created by processing (partially hydrogenating) vegetable oils, and second, some are found naturally in small amounts in foods from ruminant animals such as cows and sheep. In recent years, the main sources have been partially hydrogenated oils (PHOs) in processed foods. (Oils that aren't hydrogenated can contain very small amounts of TFAs from processing.)

The process of partial hydrogenation, which creates most *trans* fatty acids, changes the structure of unsaturated fatty acids in oils. Hydrogen is added to chains of unsaturated fatty acids, making them 5 to 60 percent saturated, depending on how much hydrogen is added. The resulting

? Have you ever wondered?

. . . if melting butter, stick margarine, or lard makes them less saturated? While unsaturated fats are liquid at room temperature, simply heating and melting doesn't change saturated fatty acids to unsaturated fatty acids. As soon as butter, margarine, or lard is cooled to room temperature, it's solid again.

. . . what high-oleic safflower and sunflower oils are? These oils, from high-oleic hybrid plants, are very high in oleic acid, a type of monounsaturated fatty acid, which is more shelf stable. They're used in baked goods, cereals, crackers, and nondairy creamers, and for frying as a substitute for saturated or *trans* fats.

. . . what an interesterified oil is? It's a fully hydrogenated oil that has been blended with liquid vegetable oil to make it more stable and firm, without creating *trans* fats. The intent is a healthier replacement for PHOs and a way to avoid *trans* fats in foods. What's unknown so far is their impact on health. The label may not say if the fully hydrogenated oil has been interesterified. Best advice for now: limit hydrogenated oils.

. . . what shortening is? It's another term that refers to fat. Solid at room temperature, shortening is vegetable oil (often partially hydrogenated coconut, cottonseed, palm, or soybean oil) sometimes combined with animal fat. Traditional shortening has been high in *trans* fats. Today *trans*-free shortenings are produced through blending, interesterifying, and emulsifying techniques. Check the food's package label.

Fats 101: A Dictionary of Terms

Suppose your doctor said, "You need to get your serum cholesterol level down. Your triglycerides are borderline high. And cut the fat, especially the saturated fats, in your diet. Try to eat more omega-3s."

Just what would all these terms mean to you?

Nutrition terms like these may seem endless and often confusing. Some apply to different fats in food; others to fatlike substances in the body; and some to both. Differences in the fatty acid makeup of food account for their differing effects on your health. Here's what they mean:

Cholesterol. Waxy, fatlike substance in foods of animal origin and in every body cell. It's essential for cell building.

- *Blood (serum) cholesterol:* Cholesterol that travels in the bloodstream. The body manufactures most of its blood cholesterol; some is also absorbed from foods you eat.
- *Dietary cholesterol:* Cholesterol in food, found only in foods of animal origin, and not from plant sources, even if they contain fat.
- *HDL ("good") blood cholesterol:* Cholesterol carried by high-density lipoproteins (HDLs) in the blood. HDLs carry cholesterol and other blood lipids away from body cells to the liver so they can be broken down and excreted. HDLs, with a higher ratio of protein to cholesterol, are made in the liver in response to physical activity and some foods. Foods don't have them.
- *LDL ("bad") blood cholesterol:* Cholesterol carried by low-density lipoproteins (LDLs) in the blood. LDLs circulate to body cells, carrying cholesterol and other lipids, where they may be used. LDL cholesterol may form deposits on artery and other blood vessel walls. LDLs, with a higher ratio of cholesterol to protein, are also manufactured in the liver. Foods don't have them.

(continued)

Fats 101: A Dictionary of Terms *(continued)*

Fats. Compounds made of glycerol and fatty acids.

- *Adipose tissue:* Body fat.
- *Dietary fat:* Fats in food. They are one of three macronutrient groups that supply energy; the other two are carbohydrates and proteins.
- *Lipids:* Refers to all fats, cholesterol, and other fatlike substances; lipids do not dissolve in water.
- *Lipoproteins:* Protein-coated packages that carry lipids, including cholesterol, in the bloodstream. Without the protein coating, lipids cannot travel through the bloodstream.
- *Oils:* Fats in liquid form. They are made of mostly unsaturated fats.
- *Solid fats:* Dietary fats that usually aren't liquid at room temperature. They contain more SFAs and/or *trans* fatty acids and less MUFAs and PUFAs than most oils do. Beef tallow (beef fat), butter, lard (pork fat), and stick margarine are some examples of solid fats.
- *Triglycerides:* The common form of fat found both in the body and in foods. Most body fat is stored in the form of triglycerides; they also circulate in the blood. Triglycerides, made of three fatty acids and glycerol, act like saturated fat: they trigger the liver to make more cholesterol so levels of total and LDL cholesterol may rise. (In some people, triglycerides may be high, but total and LDL cholesterol may not rise.)

Fatty acids: Basic units of fat molecules arranged as chains of carbon, hydrogen, and oxygen. Fats are mixtures of different fatty acids, categorized by their structure. Each has its own unique physiological effect in your body. The terms "fats" and "fatty acids" are often used interchangeably, but they are not technically the same. Fatty acids are the building blocks of fat.

- *Monounsaturated fatty acids (MUFAs):* Chemically speaking, fatty acids that are missing one hydrogen pair on their chemical chain. They have just one double bond. They trigger less total or LDL cholesterol production and more HDL cholesterol production in the body. Foods high in unsaturated fats are liquid at room temperature. Omega-7s and -9s are MUFAs.
- *Polyunsaturated fatty acids (PUFAs):* Fatty acids missing two or more hydrogen pairs on their chemical chains. They have two or more double bonds. They also promote lower total blood cholesterol as well as lower LDL and HDL cholesterol production. Two are essential—linoleic acid (an omega-6) and alpha-linolenic acid (an omega 3)—because the body cannot make them; the location of their double bonds is what makes them different. Fats with mostly PUFAs usually are liquid at room temperature,
    - *Omega-3 fatty acids:* A group of polyunsaturated fatty acids that include alpha-linolenic acid (ALA), eicosapentaenoic acid (EPA), and docosahexaenoic acid (DHA). They may help promote heart health by helping to lower total and LDL cholesterol when replacing saturated and *trans* fatty acids. *See "A Closer Look . . . Omega-3s and -6s" in this chapter, page 392, to learn more.*
    - *Omega-6 fatty acids:* A group of polyunsaturated fatty acids. Linoleic acid (LA) is a short-chain omega-6 fatty acid; arachidonic acid (AA) is one type of long-chain omega-6. They may promote heart health by helping to lower total and LDL cholesterol when replacing saturated and *trans* fatty acids. *See "A Closer Look . . . Omega-3s and -6s" in this chapter, page 392, to learn more.*
- *Saturated fatty acids (SFAs):* Fatty acids with all the hydrogen they can hold on their chemical chains. They have no double bonds. Except for stearic acid, saturated fats trigger the liver to make more total and LDL cholesterol than unsaturated fats do. Foods high in saturated fatty acids are solid at room temperature.
    - *Stearic acid*: A type of saturated fatty acid that appears to have a neutral effect on blood lipid levels, neither raising nor lowering total or LDL cholesterol levels. Effects on thrombosis, inflammation, and blood pressure are unclear. Stearic acid is found in animal products such as beef tallow (beef fat) and lard (pork fat). Dark chocolate and shea nut oil also contain stearic acid.
- Trans *fatty acids (TFAs):* Unsaturated fatty acids formed during the process of partial hydrogenation. Although they're also found naturally in some foods from ruminant animals, most TFAs in the diet come from partially hydrogenated oils (PHOs). They are structurally different from unsaturated fatty acids that occur naturally in plant-based foods and differ in their health effects. In the body, they act like saturated fats and may raise total and LDL cholesterol levels.

Hydrogenation: The process of adding hydrogen to chains of unsaturated fatty acids in vegetable oils.

- *Partially hydrogenated oils (PHOs):* Unsaturated fats that are processed and so have more TFAs, which are more saturated as well as more stable and solid at room temperature—for example, they're in many packaged foods (such as cookies and crackers) and some stick margarine. *See "Trans Fats: Semisolid Fats" in this chapter, page 387.*
- *Hydrogenated oils:* An unsaturated oil, often shown on a food label's ingredient list, that is fully saturated and has no *trans* fats.

semisolid fat is more saturated, with characteristics that are similar to saturated fats. That makes them more stable and firm at room temperature.

The extent of hydrogenation determines whether they become partially hydrogenated or fully hydrogenated. When partially hydrogenated, the fat is semisolid, forming *trans* fats. When fully hydrogenated, these fatty acids become saturated (solid), and there are no *trans* fats.

Why hydrogenate? This processing technique was created more than one hundred years ago. The reasons? It offered an affordable way to use vegetable oils, which cost less than animal fats. In addition, there was a shortage of butterfat at the time, and so with hydrogenation, margarine could be produced.

Over the years, hydrogenation has given desirable qualities to many processed foods. For example, being more stable, PHOs have extended the shelf life of foods such as crackers and cookies so they don't develop a rancid flavor and odor as quickly as they would otherwise. Partial hydrogenation of the oil in peanut butter gives it a creamy consistency; oil stays mixed in and doesn't rise to the top. With hydrogenation, stick margarine and shortening stay firm at room temperature.

Before the 1990s, no consensus science showed that the TFAs created by partial hydrogenation had their own health risks. Instead, using PHOs was believed to create heart-healthy alternatives because *trans* fats are less saturated. Stick margarine, for example, was recommended over butter. Now, after years of study, more is known, and this processing method isn't used as much and continues to decline for public health, and now for regulatory, reasons. *See "TFAs: The Ban" in this chapter, page 404.*

Why be concerned about *trans* fats? Your body treats TFAs much like most saturated fats, increasing risks related to cardiovascular disease. They contribute to the buildup of plaque inside the arteries, which increases risk for heart attack and may contribute to diabetes and metabolic syndrome, as well. As a result, TFAs have been removed from the GRAS (Generally Recognized as Safe) list by the US Food and Drug Administration. *See "Fats and Cardiovascular Disease" in this chapter, page 391; also see "Additives: Testing and Approval" in chapter 5, page 138, to learn more about the GRAS list.* It's unclear if *trans* fats that occur naturally have the same or different metabolic effects.

Fats and Health

With their full workload of body functions, you can't live without dietary fat. Besides, a fat-free diet is virtually impossible!

Despite years of negative publicity, fats (an essential nutrient category) have fundamental and essential health functions and positive benefits. In fact, emphasis on restricting total fat is outdated advice. Based on nutrition research, the 2015–2020 Dietary Guidelines for Americans has focused advice on the types of fat, not total fat.

Various types of fat in foods have different health effects. Some may offer health-protective benefits—a reason to consume enough unsaturated fats, from foods such as fish, nuts, and vegetable oils. On the other hand solid fats (saturated and *trans* fats) may increase health risks if overconsumed.

FATS: A POWER SOURCE

Like carbohydrates and protein, fats supply energy, or calories, to power your physical activity and the many body processes that keep you alive. (Remember: A calorie is a unit of energy.) As a concentrated energy source, fats supply 9 calories per gram. To compare, carbohydrates and protein both provide 4 calories per gram. Although your body uses fats for energy, it's not your body's preferred fuel source.

DIETARY FAT: ROLES IN HEALTH

Besides being an energy source, dietary fat has many essential—often overlooked roles—in health:

As part of body cells and more. Your brain is about 60 percent fat. In fact, fat is part of every body cell, including brain and nervous tissue. Fats also are part of the hormones that regulate many body functions, including smooth muscle contraction, immune function, blood clotting, and blood pressure.

For absorbing and transporting fat-soluble vitamins. Just as sugar dissolves in water, some vitamins dissolve in fat. That's how vitamins

Your "Fat Tooth"

Have a craving for rich chocolates or desserts? Your "fat tooth," not your "sweet tooth," may account for that urge. In this world of high-fat foods, a preference for them may be culturally conditioned. Research suggests this happens early, when infants and young children learn through experience that fat is associated with satiety, a satisfying feeling of fullness.

A smooth, creamy milkshake; a flaky, tender pastry; and a juicy steak: the appeal of high-fat foods may come from qualities that fat imparts. Or perhaps the appeal stems from on-again, off-again dieting. Some studies say that dieting may amplify a fat craving, or more likely, the craving for sweetened fat like that found in many rich desserts.

No matter what the reason for a "fat tooth," you can overcome, or manage, your preference for fatty foods:

- Fool your taste buds. Get a smooth, creamy consistency with low-fat and fat-free ingredients: low-fat yogurt in savory dips; thick, pureed fruit as a dessert sauce; and creamy buttermilk as a milkshake base.
- Indulge your "fat tooth." Share a rich dessert to cut your fat grams and calories in half.
- Gradually shift to lower-fat foods.

As an interesting side note, fat is being studied as a possible sixth sense (with sweet, sour, bitter, salty, and umami as the five others).

A, D, E, and K, as well as carotenoids (which form vitamin A), are carried in food and absorbed into and carried by your bloodstream. On a very low-fat diet, these vitamins may not be able to fully nourish your body or allow it to function normally. *See "Vitamins: From A to K" in chapter 14, page 409, to learn about their functions.*

For brain and visual development, growth, and more. For an infant's brain and eye development, for normal growth and development for infants and children, and for adults and children to maintain healthy skin, food must supply certain essential fatty acids: linoleic acid (LA), which is an omega-6, and alpha-linolenic acid (ALA), which is an omega-3. Because your body lacks the enzymes to make these fatty acids, they are considered essential in the human diet.

Breast milk supplies the essential fatty acids babies need. Many infant formulas are supplemented with these fatty acids in amounts similar to breast milk.

If your food choices are varied, getting enough of these fatty acids is easy. Both LA and ALA are widely available in food; for example, LA comes from vegetable oils and poultry fat, and ALA, from canola and soybean oils, nuts, and seeds.

See "A Closer Look . . . Omega-3s and -6s" in this chapter, page 392.

For heart health and more. Omega-3s and omega-6s may promote immunity, help reduce inflammation, help reduce the risk of cardiovascular disease, and contribute to the hormones that regulate blood clotting.

Some ALA converts to other omega-3s: eicosapentaenoic acid (EPA) and to docosahexaenoic acid (DHA), which have their own unique and potential health benefits. Advice for you: Because ALA from plant sources converts to DHA ineffectively, consume fish with omega-3s, too.

See "A Closer Look . . . Omega-3s and -6s" in this chapter, page 392.

For satiety. A little fat in food adds more than flavor. Fat helps satisfy hunger by helping you feel full and by providing the mouthfeel that makes food so appealing. As an aside, if lower-fat food doesn't taste as satisfying or if you don't feel full, you may eat until you do. *See "Your 'Fat Tooth'" in this chapter, page 389.*

Dietary Fat: Effects of Too Little

What happens if your fat intake is too low? For one, fat-soluble vitamins in food may be less available. Second, diets low in PUFAs may negatively impact cardiovascular health. And third, inadequate omega-3s and vitamin E may be linked to cell membrane damage, altered cell DNA, and a disruption in cell function.

FATS: LINKS TO HEALTH CONCERNS

If fat is a nutrient that's essential for health, why are some fats cited as a nutrient of concern?

While total fat has gotten attention as a health issue for many years, the quality, or fatty acid content, appears to be more important, according to current science. Although much needs to be learned, here's the thinking among many researchers about some links among the types (saturated vs. unsaturated fats), the amounts consumed, and some health risks.

At a Glance: How Dietary Fat May Affect Blood Lipids and Other Body Functions

Type of Fatty Acids	Physiological Effects
All	Component of cell membranes, brain and nervous tissue Absorption, transportation, storage of fat-soluble vitamins Production and proper functioning of hormones that regulate blood pressure, blood clotting, immune function, smooth muscle contraction
Saturated	May raise both LDL and HDL cholesterol
Trans	May raise total and LDL cholesterol and triglycerides
Unsaturated	When saturated and *trans* fatty acids are replaced with unsaturated fatty acids, may lower LDL and total cholesterol and improve the ratio of total to HDL cholesterol. When unsaturated fatty acids replace carbohydrates or saturated or *trans* fatty acids, may improve insulin sensitivity
Omega-9 MUFA	May help lower LDL and maintain HDL blood cholesterol levels MUFAs may improve insulin sensitivity
Omega-3 and -6 PUFAs	When saturated and *trans* fatty acids are replaced with omega-3 and -6 PUFAs, may lower total and LDL cholesterol Omega-3 PUFA DHA assists visual and cognitive development of young infants. Omega-6 PUFA may improve insulin sensitivity.

Source: Dietary Fats: Balancing Health and Flavor, IFIC Foundation, 2015.

? Have you ever wondered?

. . . if fish really is brain food? Today's science would say "yes" to that old wives' tale! DHA, the omega-3 fatty acid from oily fish, is found in the brain and throughout the body. *See "Dietary Fat: Roles in Health" in this chapter, page 389.*

. . . if coconut oil has special health benefits? Despite the "health halo" for coconut oil, no clinical evidence shows that coconut oil (from the coconut palm) is any more healthy than other sources of saturated fats.

Coconut oil is about 90 percent saturated fat—more than many animal sources of saturated fats (butter is about 63 percent saturated) and much more than liquid vegetable oils (canola oil is 7 percent, and olive oil is 15 percent).

It's true that the type of saturated fatty acids in coconut oil differ chemically from most other oils and solid fats, in part based on their chain length. While some saturated fatty acids in coconut oil are medium length (medium-chain triglycerides, or MCTs), potentially having less impact on heart disease, many of them are long chain, more likely to increase heart health risks. Coconut oil does tend to raise HDL cholesterol, but unlike PUFAs, it has been shown to raise LDL cholesterol, too.

There's no good evidence that supports claims that coconut oil helps with weight loss, thyroid function, Alzheimer's disease, HIV/AIDS, or irritable bowel syndrome, among other claims, either. Some products, such as milk alternatives and spreads, claim unfounded benefits from coconut oil.

If you enjoy the flavor of coconut oil, consider using it in place of butter or shortening, or pairing it with other cooking oils. Limit the amount, and avoid using it in place of other plant-based oils. *See "Have you ever wondered . . . if coconut milk is high in fat?" in this chapter, page 400.*

. . . if cocoa butter in chocolate increases blood cholesterol levels? Cocoa butter does contain saturated fats. The main fatty acid is stearic acid, which doesn't appear to raise blood cholesterol levels. And although product formulations vary, darker chocolate has less dairy fat and therefore somewhat less saturated fat. Eating just moderate amounts of chocolate may not affect cholesterol levels. Heart-healthy benefits may come from the flavonoids in chocolate; *see "Chocolate and Sugars: A Flavorful Pair," in chapter 11, page 367, to learn more about chocolate.* However, chocolate is often partnered with added sugars, and chocolate candy and desserts are typically high-calorie foods.

. . . if omega-7 fatty acids in macadamia nuts have special health benefits? Found in blue-green algae, too, these fatty acids have gotten recent media attention for some purported benefits, among them weight loss, increased satiety, reduced inflammation, improved insulin sensitivity, and lower levels of cholesterol. However, the limited body of research to support these claims isn't clear or conclusive, in part because there are two forms of this fatty acid and they contribute little to the American diet. Before you snack on macadamia nuts, remember that 10 to 12 nuts (1 ounce) also deliver a whopping 200 calories!

. . . if a vegetarian or vegan diet can provide enough omega-3s? ALA, which converts to EPA and/or DHA, is available in plant sources of food. However, without fatty fish, DHA may come up short since ALA doesn't appear to convert efficiently to DHA for most people. It's still unknown if those on a vegetarian eating plan have the ability to convert ALAs to omega-3s more efficiently than others do. EPA and DHA are available in supplements derived from algae.

Fats and Cardiovascular Disease

Dietary fat remains a key factor in the risk for cardiovascular disease. However, the links between dietary fat and cardiovascular disease are more complicated than once thought.

The type of fat and the balance of different fatty acids, not just the amounts, make a difference. Reducing solid fats (saturated and *trans* fats) and replacing them with unsaturated fats appears to be more effective for cardiovascular health than just reducing total fat intake.

As noted earlier, some unsaturated fatty acids, including omega-3s and -6s, may promote heart health and help decrease inflammation; others may have a neutral effect. *See "At a Glance: How Dietary Fat Affects Blood Lipids and Other Body Functions" on page 390.*

Evidence shows that solid fats—most saturated fatty acids and *trans* fatty acids—raise blood cholesterol levels. That, in turn, may increase the risk for fatty deposits on blood vessel walls and for heart attacks. For that reason, the advice has been to limit solid fats by replacing foods high in solid fats with foods that have more unsaturated fats.

Trans fatty acids (TFAs) in foods act like saturated fats, raising LDL cholesterol levels. TFAs from partially hydrogenated vegetable oils also may increase the risk of metabolic syndrome and diabetes.

Should you try to go totally "low-fat" or "fat-free" for heart health? No. Eating less total fat and more carbohydrates doesn't lower cardiovascular risk. Current evidence indicates that lowering your total fat intake too much may have unintended consequences if the balance swings toward a higher carbohydrate intake. That may cause triglycerides in blood to rise and HDL cholesterol levels to drop, which are potential negatives for heart health.

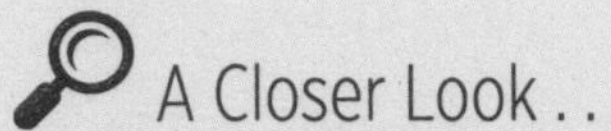

Omega-3s and -6s

No doubt about it: fish can be good for your health. Generally speaking, it has less saturated fat than meat and poultry. And oily fish is a great source of omega-3s, which are polyunsaturated fatty acids. For these reasons, eating fish regularly (at least twice a week) may help lower your blood cholesterol levels. Moreover, fish supplies several vitamins and minerals. And there are omega-6 benefits, too!

OMEGA-3S AND HEALTH

Depending on the source, food provides either "long chain" or "short chain" omega-3s. The difference in their chemical structure affects their function. Long-chain omega-3 fatty acids (EPA and DHA) are found mostly in fish, especially oily fish such as albacore tuna, Atlantic herring, lake trout, mackerel, salmon, and sardines. Canola oil, chia seeds, flaxseed oil, and soybean oil, as well as walnuts, supply short-chain omega-3s, in the form of alpha-linolenic acid (ALA), some of which converts to EPA and DHA. Some eggs contribute significant amounts of omega-3s if the chicken feed contained it. Fortification also adds EPA and/or DHA to many foods including breading for fish sticks, cooking oil, juice, snack foods, soymilk, and spreads.

Research suggests that EPA and DHA may have an effect on reducing the risk of heart disease, although it's not conclusive. They may help thin blood and prevent blood platelets from clotting and sticking to artery walls. That, in turn, may help reduce the risk for blocked blood vessels and heart attacks and strokes. These omega-3s may help prevent arteries from hardening, lower levels of triglycerides, and modestly reduce blood pressure levels. They may also help reduce inflammation.

For those with cardiovascular disease, getting more ALAs from plant-based foods may offer benefits, but evidence is limited. In fact, more research is needed to know whether the amount of omega-3s produced from ALAs is sufficient to protect against heart disease.

Even if science eventually confirms these health benefits, omega-3 fatty acids by themselves aren't a magic remedy for heart disease—and you can't simply add them to your meals and snacks to get the potential benefits. Combined with eating less saturated fats in an overall healthy diet, they may have a protective effect.

Omega-3s, especially DHA, appear to have another potential benefit. Consuming two servings of fish (about eight ounces total) per week during pregnancy and breastfeeding is linked to higher DHA levels in breast milk as well as better cognitive development and vision in infants. *See "Food Safety Precautions" in chapter 18, page 552, for guidance on making educated fish choices during pregnancy and breastfeeding.*

Researchers are exploring other links between omega-3 fatty acids and health: eye health, rheumatoid arthritis, immunity, cognition, and inflammation in the body that's linked to cardiovascular disease. Evidence is currently inadequate to support advice for these conditions. Look for future updates.

OMEGA-3 SUPPLEMENTS

Although fish oil supplements contain omega-3 fatty acids, they shouldn't be your first choice or be used in place of eating fish, but they may provide heart health benefits. Popping a fish oil capsule won't undo the effects of an unhealthy diet. Better yet, enjoy fish for its nutritional benefits, flavor, and variety in your meals.

For those with cardiovascular disease who don't consume enough omega-3s from food alone, the American Heart Association suggests talking to the doctor about fish oil supplements and safe dosages, especially for people with high levels of triglycerides; *see "Have you ever wondered . . . if fish-oil supplements can protect your heart?" in chapter 24, page 691.* Fish oil supplements are Generally Recognized as Safe (on the USDA's GRAS list) at up to 3 grams daily of EPA and DHA for healthy people. For vegetarians, EPA and DHA are available from algal sources. Other omega-3 (ALA) supplements—from flaxseed oil and chia seed oil—are widely available, too.

Food first, however! Foods with omega-3s provide other nutrients, phytonutrients, and perhaps other healthy fats, which work together for heart health.

OMEGA-6S AND HEALTH

What about omega-6s (polyunsaturated fatty acids in vegetable oils)? They, too, may help reduce cardiovascular disease risk. Most people consume more than enough omega-6s, which may be unhealthy.

Linoleic acid (LA), an omega-6 fatty acid, is converted to another fatty acid, arachidonic acid (AA), which may be linked to inflammation and other chronic health conditions. LA cannot be made by the body. It comes from foods such as meat, vegetable oils (such as corn, safflower, and soybean), and processed foods made with these vegetables oils.

Another type of omega-6 fatty acid—conjugated linoleic acids (CLA)—may offer functional benefits. CLA is naturally found in dairy foods and some meat (beef, lamb). Research is exploring a potential link between CLA and decreased risk for certain cancers as well as a role in improved

A Closer Look . . . *(continued)*

body composition. Little human research has yet been done. CLA is also available as supplements, made from vegetable oils.

Some experts question if the substantial imbalance—more than ten times as much omega-6s as omega-3s in food choices for many people—may interfere with the positive heart-health benefits of omega-3s by promoting inflammation. However, research on human health is needed to understand the effects of the ratio between omega-3s to omega-6s in the diet.

OMEGA-3s AND -6s: ADVICE

To enjoy both nutritional and omega-3 benefits from some fish, make fish a regular part of your eating style; eat oily fish twice or more weekly (eight ounces total per week). And try eating foods with omega-3s in place of foods with more saturated fats.

The National Institutes of Health reports general agreement: consuming more omega-3s and fewer omega-6s may promote health since the balance affects their function. That can happen by switching from oils high in omega-6s to those with more omega-3s such as canola and flaxseed oils.

See "More Advice: Omega-3s and -6s" in this chapter, page 392, for daily Adequate Intake (AI) amounts and, also in this chapter, "Common Foods: How Much Omega-3s and Total Fat?" on page 401, for amounts provided in food.

Fats and Body Weight

It's time to set the record straight: dietary fat doesn't automatically convert to body fat. Eating more calories than you use, not just calories from fats, is the issue in increased body fat and weight gain.

Weight control is a good reason to go easy on high-fat foods since many are high in calories, too. However, simply replacing fats with calories from carbohydrates and protein doesn't shift the calorie balance toward weight loss.

Fat intake needs to be part of the calorie balance equation along with other energy nutrients. Remember that 1 gram of fat provides 9 calories, more than twice the amount in 1 gram of carbohydrate or protein. Whether fats are saturated or unsaturated, their calorie contributions are the same.

Without attention to calorie intake, cutting back on fats isn't a weight-loss solution. If you consume more calories from any nutrient source than your body needs, the extra gets converted to fat and stored

Have you ever wondered?

. . . if olive oil has fewer calories and less fat than butter? Because liquid oils are concentrated, and solid fats may contain small amounts of other ingredients besides fat, oils generally contain slightly more fat and calories than equal amounts of solid fats. Per tablespoon, olive oil contains about 14 grams of fat and 120 calories as compared to butter, with about 12 grams of fat and 100 calories. The main difference is the types of fatty acids they contain. Olive oil has a higher proportion of monounsaturated fatty acids; butter has a higher proportion of saturated fatty acids.

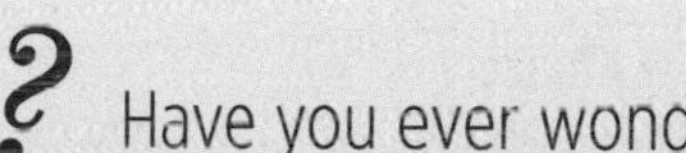

Have you ever wondered?

. . . why ground flaxseed often is recommended over whole flaxseed? Whole flaxseed passes through the gastrointestinal tract without being digested and absorbed so it won't provide potential omega-3 benefits. Flaxseed oil does, however, but it doesn't contain the beneficial fiber and lignan supplied by ground flaxseeds. To get all of flaxseed's benefits, buy ground flaxseed, or grind whole flaxseed in a coffee grinder. Add it to baked goods, sandwich spreads, smoothies, yogurt, or your morning cereal.

. . . if inhaling aromas of essential plant oils (aromatherapy) helps relieve pain, migraines, nausea, or other health conditions? Although lavender and some other essential oils may have a calming effect—perhaps caused by a brain response—there's not enough research to know how or if inhaling essential oils relieves medical discomfort.

Inhaling the fragrant vapors of diluted essential oils is safe but may cause drowsiness. Consuming these oils in undiluted states isn't advised and may cause serious kidney problems and seizures.

To clarify any confusion, essential oils are not the same as essential fatty acids. "Essential" oils refer instead to their concentrated essence.

as body fat. When you need an extra energy supply, your body can draw on this stored fat.

See "Obesity: The Risks" in chapter 22, page 630, to learn about the health risks of excess body fat.

Fats and Other Health Concerns

Different fatty acids affect your body differently. Among the areas of study are the potential benefits of some omega-3 fatty acids on health conditions, such as Alzheimer's disease, dementia, and depression. Essential fatty acids—EPA and DHA—may also play a role in reducing symptoms of rheumatoid arthritis. Evidence linking fat intake to increased cancer risk is still unclear. Stay tuned!

Fats: How Much? Too Much? What Kind?

FATS: THE RIGHT AMOUNT FOR YOU

Advice for fat intake from foods applies to your total diet, not to a single food or a single meal. So how many grams of fat is enough—and too much? That depends. (*Note:* The guidance here is for healthy people, not for those with chronic health issues since advice about dietary fat may differ.)

Dietary Fat: A Range of Advice

The Dietary Reference Intakes (DRIs) recommend an Acceptable Macronutrient Distribution Range (AMDR), not a single amount: 20 to 35 percent of calories from total fat for adults. That includes less than 10 percent of calories from saturated fats as advised by the Dietary Guidelines for Americans. The AMDR is linked to a reduced risk of chronic disease yet allows for overall food choices for the day with enough essential nutrients.

Age is factored into the recommendations. Infants and toddlers have energy needs that are higher than for any other age group based on body weight. For them, fats are an especially important source of calories—and some essential fatty acids. For children aged 1 to 3 years, the AMDR for fat is 30 to 40 percent of calories; for children aged 4 to 18, it's 25 to 35 percent of calories.

(The Adequate Intake [AI] levels for infants are: 31 grams daily for ages 0 to 6 months and 30 grams daily for those aged 6 to 12 months. There are no AIs for older age groups.)

What if you eat less than 20 percent of your daily calories from total fat? You might come up short on vitamin E, a fat-soluble vitamin with antioxidant powers that may protect against heart disease. Another possibility: missing out on essential fatty acids, which only food provides. Yet another potential concern is that lower fat intake may result in higher carbohydrate intake, which can lead to higher triglycerides and lower HDL ("good") cholesterol levels.

In real numbers, how does the AMDR equate to fat grams per day? The amount depends on your overall energy (calorie) needs, which in turn depend on your age, gender, body size, and physical activity level. *See "What's the Advice for Total Fat and Saturated Fat Intake?" in this chapter, page 398. See "Calories: Your Target?" in chapter 1, page 7, and "How Many Calories? Figuring Your Energy Needs," in the appendix, page 771.*

Bottom line: The focus of advice for dietary fat is not to reduce total fat, but to replace saturated and *trans* fats with unsaturated fats.

More Advice: Omega-3s and -6s

The quality of the fat—or balance of saturated and unsaturated fatty acids—may be as important to your health and reduced health risks as the total amount of fat you consume. For example, as part of total fat advice, the DRIs also advise a range of intake for omega-3 and omega-6 fatty acids.

For omega-3s, the AMDR for all ages (except infants under 12 months), including during pregnancy and breastfeeding, is 0.6 to 1.2 percent of total calories, or 1.3 to. 2.7 grams of omega-3s daily for those who consume 2,000 calories daily. For those aged nineteen and older, the AI for ALA, one type of omega-3, is 1.6 grams daily for men and 1.1 grams daily for women.

For omega-6s the AMDR for all ages (except infants under 12 months), inducing during pregnancy and breastfeeding, the AMDR is 5 to 10 percent of total calories. The AI for LA, one type of omega 6, is 17 grams for men and 12 grams daily for women, ages 19 to 50.

See the "Dietary Reference Intakes" in the appendix, page 780, for the AI for both the ALA and LA for children, and for pregnant and breastfeeding women. There are no Recommended Dietary Allowances for either omega 3s or 6s.

SOLID FATS AND *TRANS* FATS: YOUR LIMITS

You know you need fat for health, energy, and for kids, growth. And you know that all fats are made of saturated, monounsaturated, and polyunsaturated fatty acids. How you proportion those fats in your food choices impacts your health.

What's the Advice for Total Fat and Saturated Fat Intake?

If You Consume This Amount of Calories a Day . . .	Your AMDR for Daily Total Fat Intake Is* within 20 to 35 Percent of Calories . . .	You Should Limit Your Daily Saturated Fat Intake* to Less Than 10 Percent of Calories . . .
1,600	36 to 62 grams	18 grams or less
2,000	44 to 78 grams	22 grams or less
2,200	49 to 86 grams	24 grams or less
2,500	56 to 97 grams	28 grams or less
2,800	62 to 109 grams	31 grams or less

*Reflects the adult recommendations in the 2015–2020 Dietary Guidelines for Americans.

✓ Your Healthy Eating Check-In

How Does Your Fat Intake Stack Up?

What's the fat quotient of your eating style? To be fat savvy, limit solid fats as well as calories from total fat. Remember: Your overall intake of solid fats is what counts—not each individual choice. Small steps to healthier eating—like these "healthy dozen"—add up. The more "yes" boxes you check, the further along you are on the path.

DO YOU . . .	Yes	No
1. Buy lean meats and skinless poultry?	☐	☐
2. Choose mostly low-fat and fat-free milk and yogurt?	☐	☐
3. Limit cakes, cookies, and other desserts made with butter, margarine, or shortening, as well as full-fat cheese, full-fat ice cream, meats such as bacon and ribs, hot dogs, and sausages?	☐	☐
4. Cook with vegetable oils instead of butter, beef tallow (beef fat), chicken fat, lard (pork fat), stick margarine, and traditional shortening when possible?	☐	☐
5. Bake, steam, or broil foods more often than fry them?	☐	☐
6. Read ingredient lists to limit foods with partially hydrogenated oils?	☐	☐
7. Check the Nutrition Facts labels to choose foods with little or no saturated fats and no *trans* fats?	☐	☐
8. Choose soft tub margarines with zero *trans* fats as a sandwich spread?	☐	☐
9. If you use butter, use just a small amount?	☐	☐
10. Switch from butter, stick margarine, shortening, and lard to vegetable oil, such as canola, corn, olive, safflower, or sunflower oil?	☐	☐
11. Use small amounts of oils in food preparation to control calories?	☐	☐
12. Eat eight ounces or more of fish per week, including some oily fish?	☐	☐

An eating pattern that's high in saturated and *trans* fats is linked to higher blood cholesterol levels and increases the risks of cardiovascular disease and diabetes. *See "Heart Disease: The Blood Lipid Connection" in chapter 24, page 684, to learn more.*

Saturated Fats. Consume less than 10 percent of calories from saturated fatty acids, advises the Dietary Guidelines for Americans and the DRIs. Replace them with unsaturated fatty acids while also keeping total dietary fats within the age-appropriate AMDR. That said, saturated fats account for about 11 percent of calories per day, on average, for the US population, as noted in the Dietary Guidelines for Americans—more than what's advised.

American Heart Association guidelines for saturated fats are lower. For heart health, it advises aiming for an eating pattern with 5 to 6 percent of calories from saturated fatty acids. If you need about 2,000 calories daily, that's about 13 grams of saturated fats a day, providing no more than 120 calories.

***Trans* Fats.** Keep *trans* fatty acid consumption as low as possible, advises the Dietary Guidelines for Americans. Limit foods that contain synthetic sources of *trans* fats, such as partially hydrogenated oils.

You don't need *trans* fats for normal health. In fact, any *trans* fat intake increases cardiovascular risk. No recommendation or upper limit for *trans* fatty acids has been set in the DRIs.

At the same time, make your total eating plan healthy. Still, be prudent, especially if your blood cholesterol levels are high. Because small amounts of TFAs occur naturally in nutrient-rich foods such as beef and milk, you can't eliminate *trans* fats completely.

HEALTHY OILS: REPLACE SOLID FATS

Polyunsaturated fats contain essential fatty acids, necessary for health. That's why the three USDA Food Patterns (Healthy US-Style, Healthy Mediterranean-Style, and Healthy Vegetarian) have a category for oils; *see chapter 2, page 21, to learn more.* Besides their essential fatty acids, oils are the major source of vitamin E for most Americans.

Oils such as canola, corn, olive, safflower, soybean, and sunflower are heart healthier. For heart health, replace foods with solid fats with those having more saturated fats whenever possible. Neither monounsaturated nor polyunsaturated fats raise total or LDL ("bad") cholesterol levels in

Common Foods: How Much Total Fat and Saturated Fats?*

- To figure the approximate amount of unsaturated fats, simply do the math:

  grams of total fat – (grams of saturated fats + grams of *trans* fats) = grams of unsaturated fats

- Since the amount of *trans* fats varies from product to product, you will need to check the Nutrition Facts label. Due to new FDA regulations, many foods no longer contain *trans* fats.

Food Group	Total Fat (grams)	Saturated Fat (grams)	Calories
GRAINS GROUP			
Bagel (½ small, 3-inch diameter)	Trace	Trace	90
Biscuit, homemade (2½-inch diameter)	10	3	210
Blueberry muffin (2¾-inch diameter)	11	2	250
Bread (1 slice)			
White (from refined wheat) (1 oz.)	1	Trace	65
Whole wheat (1 oz.)	1	Trace	80
Croissant (1 medium)	12	7	230
Danish pastry, cinnamon (4¼-inch diameter)	15	3.5	260
Doughnut, yeast, glazed (3¾-in. diameter)	15	6	270
Fried rice (without meat), restaurant (½ cup)	2	0.3	120
Granola, homemade (⅓ cup)	10	1.5	200
Oatmeal, cooked (½ cup)	2	0.4	85
Pancake (4-inch diameter)	1	0.2	75
Rice, white, cooked (½ cup)	Trace	Trace	105
Roll, dinner (1 oz.)	4	2	85
VEGETABLE GROUP			
Potatoes			
Baked potato with skin, plain (5 oz.)	3	Trace	130
Chips (1 oz.)	10	1	150
French fries (10 fries)	5	1	205
Potato salad, homemade (½ cup)	10	2	180

Food Group	Total Fat (grams)	Saturated Fat (grams)	Calories
FRUIT GROUP			
Apple (2¾-inch diameter)	Trace	Trace	75
Avocado, sliced, ½ cup	11	1.5	115
Olives, ripe (5 large)	2.5	0.3	25
DAIRY GROUP			
Cheese (1 oz.)			
Natural Cheddar	9.5	5	115
Low-fat Cheddar	2	1	50
Mozzarella, part-skim milk	4	3.0	70
Processed American	9	4.5	100
Cottage cheese (½ cup)			
Creamed	5	2	110
1% low-fat	1	1	80
Ice cream, vanilla (½ cup)	7	4	135
Milk (1 cup)			
Whole	8	4.5	150
2% reduced-fat	5	3	120
1% low-fat	2	1.5	100
Fat-free	Trace	Trace	85
Yogurt, frozen (not chocolate) (½ cup)	3	2	110
Yogurt, plain, low-fat (1 cup)	4	2.5	155
PROTEIN FOODS GROUP			
Beef			
Lean cut (eye of round), roasted (3 oz.)			
Lean and fat, ⅛-inch trim	8	3	175
Lean only, ⅛-inch trim	4	1.5	145

Common Foods: How Much Total Fat and Saturated Fats?* *(continued)*

Food Group	Total Fat (grams)	Saturated Fat (grams)	Calories
Fattier cut (chuck blade), braised (3 oz.)			
Lean and fat, ⅛-inch trim	21	8.5	290
Lean only, 0-inch trim	11	4.5	215
Ground, patty, broiled (3 oz.)			
70% lean/30% fat	16	6	235
85% lean/15% fat	13	5	210
95% lean/5% fat	6	3	150
Frankfurter, beef (48 g)	14	5.5	155
Beef liver, braised (3 oz.)	4.5	2.5	160
Pork center loin, boneless, roasted (3 oz.)			
Lean and fat	13	4	215
Lean	8.5	3	185
Chicken, breast, roasted (½ breast)			
With skin	8	2	195
Without skin	3	1	140
Salmon, Atlantic, farmed, cooked (3 oz.)	10.5	2	175
Tuna, canned (3 oz.)			
In oil	7	1	160
In water	2.5	Trace	110
Shrimp, steamed or boiled (8 large)	0.5	Trace	52
Egg (1 large)			
Whole	4.5	1.5	72
Yolk	4.5	1.5	55
White	Trace	0	17
Dry beans, cooked (½ cup)	0.5	Trace	105
Peanut butter (2 tbsp.)	16	3	190
Sunflower seeds (1 oz.)	14	1.5	165
SOLID FATS AND OILS			
Butter (1 tbsp.)	11.5	7	100
Cream (1 tbsp.)			
Light (table)	3	2	30
Heavy (whipping) cream	5	3.5	50
Cream cheese (1 tbsp.)	5	3	50
Margarine, stick (1 tbsp.)	11.5	2	100
Salad dressing (1 tbsp.)			
Mayonnaise, regular	10	1.5	95
Mayonnaise, light	3	0.5	35
Italian, regular	3	0.5	35
Italian, reduced-fat	1	Trace	15
Sour cream, regular (1 tbsp.)	2.5	1.5	25
Vegetable oil, corn (1 tbsp.)	14	2	120
SWEET SNACKS AND DESSERTS			
Cake, chocolate, frosted (1⁄12 of cake)	28	8	537
Cheesecake, commercial (3 oz. piece)	20	18	260
Cookie, chocolate chip, made with butter (2¼-inch diameter)	4.5	2	78
Milk chocolate, bar (1.55 oz.)	13	8	235
Pie, apple (⅛ of 9-inch pie)	19.5	5	410

*Values are rounded.

Source: US Department of Agriculture, National Nutrient Database for Standard Reference, Release 28, 2016.

the blood. That said, oils do provide calories: 120 calories per tablespoon, about the same as solid fats. Limit how much you consume to stay within your calorie limit; *see "Oils: How Much?" in chapter 2, page 46.*

Fats in Food

Fats—both saturated and unsaturated—contribute in many ways to the foods you eat and enjoy. Rather than trying to give up the fat, spend your fat calories wisely. And make the switch to healthy oils when appropriate.

WHY FOODS CONTAIN FAT

Fat offers sensory qualities that make food taste good. As an ingredient, fat carries flavor. It also gives a smooth, creamy texture to foods such as ice cream and peanut butter. When a brownie seems to "melt in your mouth," that's just what's happening—the fat is melting! From meat to baked goods, fat makes many foods moist and tender, or brown and crispy. And oils work well in liquid foods such as salad dressings and for frying.

Can you cut the fat in a recipe? To a certain extent, yes. The recipe may work if you use less, but by doing so or trying to eliminate fat altogether, you may not get the result you expect. Here's why:

- *In all kinds of food.* Fat helps carry and absorb flavor and nutrients, helps with browning, provides texture (mouthfeel), gives a glossy look, and adds to satiety.
- *In baked goods.* Fat tenderizes, adds moisture, holds in air so baked foods are light, and affects shape—for example, in cookies. With too little fat, baked goods might be tough or dry, or may not rise properly. Solid fats often work well in baked goods for the texture and stability they provide, although oils are used, too.
- *In cooked meat, poultry, and fish.* Fat seals in moisture as foods are basted or brushed with liquid during cooking. Sometimes the surface dries out if it isn't basted.
- *In other cooked foods.* Fat helps conduct heat as food cooks—for example, when food is sautéed (cooked quickly in a small amount of fat) or fried.
- *For foods cooked in a pan.* Fat lubricates the pan so foods won't stick.
- *In sauces.* Fat keeps sauces from curdling and forms part of an emulsion. An emulsion is a mixture of two substances such as fat and water that stay together instead of separating, as they normally would.

FATS: VISIBLE OR NOT

Visible or not, almost all foods contain fat in varying amounts. Some foods are very high in fat; others have only trace amounts.

Fat in some foods is obvious—butter, margarine, and oil—but not in others. In meat and skin-on poultry, some fat is easy to see—and easy to trim off. Although not always visible, fat also is a "hidden" ingredient in cheese, chips, crackers, fries, many grain-based desserts and other baked goods, and pizza, as well as salad dressings and some sauces.

While many foods contain fat, the proportion and amount of saturated and unsaturated fatty acids varies significantly:

- *In most animal-based foods.* Fat in meat, poultry, egg yolks, cheese, and other dairy varies in amount and is generally more saturated than in plant-based foods.
- *In fish.* Fish has a higher proportion of unsaturated fats (both MUFAs and PUFAs) than most other animal-based foods do. Oily, cold-water fish have the most omega-3 fatty acids. These oils stay fluid and insulate fish in cold water.

Have you ever wondered?

. . . why using olive oil and canola oil in your food prep is healthy—if you substitute them for solid fats? Both oils are high in monounsaturated fatty acids and low in saturated fatty acids. You may be surprised to know that canola oil contains more omega-3s, more polyunsaturated fats, and even less saturated fats and somewhat less monounsaturated fats than olive oil.

Fats higher in monounsaturated fatty acids may help lower blood cholesterol levels when they replace fats higher in unsaturated fatty acids. However, simply adding olive or canola oil to an already high-fat diet is not the point. These oils are still 100 percent fat, with about 120 calories per tablespoon.

. . . what the source of canola oil is? Extracted from the seeds of the canola plant, canola oil is a healthy oil. Like broccoli, cauliflower, kale, and mustard seed, canola is part of the brassica family. Its name derives from Canada oil ("can" and "ola," referring to oil), where it was originally developed.

To clarify a misperception: Although the canola plant derives from the rapeseed plant, it differs in a significant way. Erucic acid from rapeseed has been virtually eliminated in developing the canola plant through traditional plant breeding in the 1970s; oil from canola seeds has essentially no erucic acid. (While erucic acid hasn't been shown to affect human health, it has been linked to cardiac abnormalities in experimental animals.)

The *Codex Alimentaris* has defined a maximum amount of erucic acid and glucosinolates that may be found in a seed before it can be called canola. The FDA declares that canola is GRAS approved, deeming

Have you ever wondered? *(continued)*

canola oil safe in food. *Codex Alimentarius* means "Food Code" in Latin; it provides internationally recognized standards, relating to foods, food production, and food safety.

Today's canola oil is produced with both genetically engineered seeds and organic sources that don't use biotechnology.

As an aside, the FDA has approved a Qualified Health Claim for canola oil, "Limited and not conclusive scientific evidence suggests that eating 1½ teaspoons (19 grams) of canola oil daily may reduce the risk of coronary heart disease due to the unsaturated fat content in canola oil. To achieve this possible benefit, canola oil is to replace a similar amount of saturated fat and not increase the total number of calories you eat in a day."

. . . what tropical oils are, and how they stack up for nutrition? Tropical oils come from the fruit (palm oil), seeds (palm kernel oil), or nuts (coconut oil) of the tropical plants they're named for. They are solid or semisolid at room temperature because they are highly saturated. More than 80 percent of the fat in palm kernel oil is saturated, compared to about 50 percent in palm oil. Palm oil also has quite a bit of polyunsaturated fat. For nutritional purposes, they are considered solid fats.

The saturated fatty acids in palm oil, suggests some research, may not raise cholesterol—but the Dietary Guidelines for Americans advises limiting them. Palm oil also has heart-healthy carotenoids, which impart a golden or reddish color. Coconut oil contains a fatty acid called lauric acid, also a saturated fat, with possible health benefits.

You may not think you consume coconut, palm, or palm kernel oils, but they're often used in processed foods, imparting qualities similar to partially hydrogenated oils. Until more is known about the links between these oils and health, limit foods made with tropical oils. Read the ingredient list on food labels to identify them in foods.

- *In plant-based foods*. Some plant-based foods are rich sources of unsaturated fatty acids: avocados, nuts, olives, peanuts, seeds, and soybeans. Most other vegetables and fruits don't supply much fat naturally—it's added during food preparation or processing, as with French fries, fried okra, or fried onion rings. (That's true for most grain products, too; consider the hidden fat in croissants, flaky pastries, and hush puppies.) Nuts are other examples: almonds and peanuts have a higher percentage of MUFAs, while walnuts have more PUFAs: omega-3s and omega-6s.
- *In salad dressings*. Salad dressings are high in unsaturated and low in saturated fatty acids. The types of unsaturated fats vary. For example, canola, olive, safflower, and sunflower oils are high in MUFAs. Corn oil has the most omega-6 fatty acids of the major cooking oils, while flaxseed oil has a significant amount of omega-3s. *See "Solid Fats and Oils: How Do They Compare?" in this chapter, page 386.*

See "Common Foods: How Much Total Fat and Saturated Fats?" in this chapter, page 396, for amounts in many foods.

GO LEAN, CHOOSE WISELY

Trying to count the amount of fat in your food choices gets tedious—and it's the solid fats that matter most for health anyway. When you shop or eat out, focus on the types of fat in your food, the portion sizes of foods that contain them, and the other important nutrients that these foods deliver—not just the amount of fat. Remember that most foods have a mix of fats, so the healthy approach is to think "replacement": choose foods with more unsaturated fats and less saturated fats.

Making a switch to less saturated fats or trimming fat to save calories doesn't need to be a big deal. Even small changes add up. Eating a smaller portion of a high-fat dessert, switching to lean meat and low-fat or fat-free dairy products, or eating broiled rather than fried foods can make a difference!

Foods with Solid Fats: Eat Less and Switch

With that in mind, substitute, rather than add, fat to your eating plan. Replace foods and ingredients high in solid fats with those higher in unsaturated fats. Here's how:

- Know where solid fats come from. Use the Nutrition Facts and the ingredient list on food labels to compare the saturated fats and *trans* fats. Look for *trans*-fat-free options; limit foods with partially hydrogenated oils.
- Switch from butter or stick margarine to soft tub or squeeze (liquid) margarine. Or use oil in recipes calling for melted butter or shortening.
- Choose lean meat (beef, veal, and/or pork) and skinless poultry. Loin and round cuts of meat have less total fat (and saturated fats). Trim visible fat from meat and poultry; remove skin from poultry. Lean meat isn't fat-free; it just has less fat.
- Lean meat contains cholesterol in both the fat and the lean muscle tissue. Trimming the fat and buying lean cuts help reduce the cholesterol if you're advised to do so.
- Enjoy fish at least twice a week, especially oily fish such as salmon, prepared in a low-fat way, to get potential omega-3 benefits.

- Limit doughnuts, sweet rolls, higher-fat muffins, croissants, cakes, and cookies often made with solid fats. Choose lower-fat products: bagels; breakfast cereal; pasta; pita, tortillas, and other lower-fat breads; and rice.
- Choose mostly low-fat or fat-free dairy foods. The amount of bone-building nutrients in whole, low-fat, and fat-free-milk products is about the same.
- If you use butter as a spread or to sauté, use just a small amount. Or use oil, or perhaps only part oil, instead.
- Watch "snack fats." Some popular snack foods are higher in fat, especially solid fats, than you may realize. Read the ingredient list and the Nutrition Facts on the label.

You can also trim fats, including solid fats, and calories from fat in these ways:

- Be aware of portion sizes. For higher-fat foods, the fat and calorie content rises when portions get bigger.
- De-fat your cooking style—without losing flavor. Bake, boil, broil, microwave, steam, or stir-fry foods, rather than fry them.
- Add flavor with herbs and spices instead of high-fat sauces. Rub seasoning mixtures on tender cuts of meat before cooking. Use low-fat or fat-free marinades to add flavor to lean cuts.
- Make beans the "main event" at meals. As a protein source, most bean dishes are lower in total fat and saturated fats, yet higher in fiber and starches than those made with meat or cheese.
- Eat more vegetables and fruits in place of some food with more fat. Besides being low in fat, they fill you up and help curb your appetite.
- Order "lean" when you order out. In a quick-service or table-service restaurant, look for menu clues that suggest less fat, such as "broiled" or "grilled." Ask questions about food prep. Go easy on foods that are breaded or fried, or prepared with rich sauces or gravy.

As you've read before, what you eat over several days—not just one day—impacts health.

Oils and Foods with Oils: Enjoy in Sensible Amounts

Get the health benefits of oils. Switch to oils instead of solid fats whenever you can.

Have you ever wondered?

. . . if nuts and seeds are heart healthy? Research evidence suggests "yes"! If they're part of an overall eating pattern that's nutritionally adequate and without excess calories, nuts and seeds positively impact risk factors for cardiovascular disease, especially blood lipid levels. Also a good source of protein, they're high in fat, but it's mostly unsaturated. An important reminder: enjoy them (preferably unsalted) in small portions, as their calories can add up quickly. Or enjoy them in place of some meat or poultry.

Like oils, different nuts have different amounts of fats: total fat, as well as different amounts of saturated, monounsaturated, and polyunsaturated fatty acids. Walnuts, for example are higher in PUFAs, while macadamia nuts are higher in MUFAs. Be aware that types of nuts vary in nutrient, fiber, and calorie content, too. *See "In a Nutshell: Tree Nuts and Seeds" in chapter 2, page 43, for more about nuts.*

The FDA has approved a Qualified Health Claim for nuts and heart disease: "Scientific evidence suggests but does not prove that eating 1.5 ounces per day of most nuts [such as walnuts] as part of a diet low in saturated fat and cholesterol may reduce the risk of heart disease."

. . . if coconut milk is high in fat? One cup of canned coconut milk (made by combining grated coconut meat and coconut water) contains 445 calories and 48 fat grams (of which 43 fat grams are saturated). In contrast, coconut water, or liquid, drained from a fresh coconut—without any grated coconut meat—has just 46 calories and less than 1 fat gram per cup. Just one-quarter cup of dried, sweetened coconut has 87 calories and 6 fat grams. Look for canned low-fat coconut milk. *See "Have you ever wondered . . . if coconut oil has special health benefits?" in this chapter, page 391.*

. . . if popcorn is always a low-fat snack? Not always. If you buy it ready-made, check the Nutrition Facts label for total fat, saturated fat, and *trans* fat content. Although the package may say "air-popped," oil may be added after popping as a flavoring. For microwave popcorn, check the label to see if oil is added—and how much and what kind. The bucket of popcorn you buy in malls or movie theaters usually is loaded with fat. Satisfy your appetite with the small-size order.

. . . if ghee is a good butter substitute? Common in the cuisine of India, ghee is clarified butter. It's been heated and then strained to remove milk solids so the fat is slightly concentrated—with more fat and calories per teaspoon. Why clarify butter? Without milk solids, it can be heated to a higher temperature without burning, which works well in Indian cooking. It's still high in saturated fat.

. . . how the fat in feta cheese compares with that in other cheeses? It's somewhat lower—but not much. One ounce of feta cheese has 6 grams of fat, which includes 4 grams of saturated fat. By comparison, 1 ounce of Cheddar cheese has about 9 total fat grams, including 5 grams of saturated fat. With their intense flavors, small amounts of strong cheeses such as blue, feta, and Parmesan go a long way in delivering taste.

Common Foods: How Much Omega-3s and Total Fat

Animal-Based Foods	Omega-3s (grams)*	Total Fat (grams)*
OILY FISH, ABOUT 3 OUNCES, COOKED		
Atlantic salmon, farmed	2.0	10
Anchovy, canned in oil, drained	1.8	8
Atlantic herring	1.8	10
Chinook salmon	1.7	11
Atlantic mackerel	1.1	15
Rainbow trout, farmed	0.8	6
LESS OILY FISH, ABOUT 3 OUNCES, COOKED		
Tuna, white, canned in oil, drained	1.0	7
Tuna, white, canned in water, drained	0.7	2
Flounder	0.3	2
Halibut, Atlantic and Pacific	0.2	1
Tuna, light, canned in water, drained	0.2	1
Catfish, farmed	0.1	6
Cod, Atlantic	0.1	1
Plant-Based Foods	**ALA (Converts to EPA and DHA) (grams)*†**	**Total Fat (grams)***
Ground flaxseed (2 tbsp.)	3.2	6
Walnuts (14 halves, or 1 oz.)	2.6	18
Canola oil (not high oleic) (1 tbsp.)	1.3	14
Soy nuts, dry roasted (¼ cup)	0.3	3.5
Chia seeds, hemp seeds, and some other nuts also provide ALA.		

*Figures have been rounded.

†About 2 to 10 percent of ALA is converted to omega-3s.

Source: US Department of Agriculture, National Nutrient Database for Standard Reference, Release 28, 2016.

See "A Closer Look . . . Omega-3s and -6s" in this chapter, page 392, to learn more about omega-3s.

Have you ever wondered?

. . . how to use a Nutrition Facts label to know how much unsaturated fats a food has? Do the math. Using the Nutrition Facts, subtract saturated and *trans* fats from the total fat to determine the amount of unsaturated fats that one serving of a food provides.

A label may also list omega-3s (one type of polyunsaturated fatty acid) elsewhere on the label, perhaps on the front of the package. Some food manufacturers list mono- and polyunsaturated fatty acids in the Nutrition Facts, but it's not required.

. . . what a label stating "98% fat-free" means? You might think this means that only 2% of the total calories come from fat. Actually, the percentage is referring to weight and not calories. So "98% fat-free" means that 2% of the weight of the total serving comes from fat. By law, when manufacturers state "% fat-free" on a label, the amount of total fat must be less than 3 grams of total fat per serving. This amount is quite low but may be more than you'd think when reading the "% fat-free" claim.

. . . what *trans*-free spreads are? They're usually margarine-type products, processed with little or no *trans* fatty acids. Most don't contain fat substitutes, but they may contain tropical oils. With the FDA ban coming into effect, *trans* fats in spreads have been mostly eliminated.

. . . if a food that's "low-fat" is "low calorie," too? Not necessarily. It's true that fat is a concentrated source of energy, or calories. However, cutting back on high-fat foods may not trim calories if too many carbohydrates or proteins take their place.

The calorie content of the regular and low-fat versions of a food may be similar because carbohydrate-containing ingredients often are added to help replace flavor that's lost when fat is removed. To find out, read the Nutrition Facts label. Even if the calories are less, go easy on your amount of low-fat or fat-free foods. Eating a whole box of fat-free cookies isn't a low-calorie experience!

. . . if a reduced-fat food is always low-fat? Not necessarily. It just may have less fat (at least 25 percent less) than its full-fat counterpart. Read the Nutrition Facts label to find out. *See "Label Lingo: Fats and Cholesterol" in this chapter, page 403, to learn what these terms mean.*

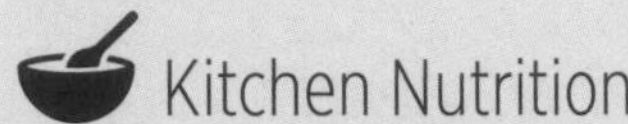

Greek Yogurt Add-Ins

Do you like Greek yogurt? If so, use it as a base for a thick spread, creamy dip, or baked potato topper. It's low in fat yet high in calcium. For the least amount of fat, use low-fat or fat-free yogurt. Flavor it in your own distinctive way. Blend with:

- Apricot preserves and chopped nuts
- Crumbled blue cheese and grated apple or pear
- Salmon and chopped green onion
- Horseradish and lemon zest
- Frozen chopped spinach (thawed and squeezed to remove liquid) and pesto
- Mashed berries and honey
- Fresh or dried herbs or spices
- Cinnamon, pumpkin spice, nuts, dark chocolate

- Fit avocados, nuts, oily fish, olives, peanuts, seeds, and soybeans into your daily meals and snacks. Oily fish are great sources of unsaturated fats, too. And mashing avocados and olives can make a flavorful spread; mix mashed olives with garlic and herbs to make a tapenade.
- Prepare food with vegetable oils—canola, corn, cottonseed, olive, safflower, soybean, sunflower—in place of butter, shortening, or stick margarine. Mayonnaise, some salad dressings, and soft (tub or squeeze) margarine with no *trans* fats are mainly oils, too. Use only small amounts to control calories.

FATS ON FOOD LABELS

The food label is the way you can compare the amount and types of fat in foods as you shop. Several parts of a food label provide that information: ingredient list, Nutrition Facts, and perhaps nutrient content claims, health claims, and front-of-pack labeling.

You may find fat-modified foods on supermarket shelves such as fat-free salad dressing, low-fat snacks, *trans*-free spreads, and eggs with omega-3s. But be aware: These fat-modified foods may have the same or more total calories as their traditional counterparts! Read each part of the label as you compare. To retain the flavor and texture that consumers look for, fat may be replaced by sugar, other refined carbohydrates, or sodium.

Check the Claims

Nutrient content claims, perhaps "low-fat," "fat-free," or "lean," may guide your food purchases. *See "Label Lingo: Fats and Cholesterol" in this chapter, page 403, to learn what these claims mean.*

Fats in Snacks: Shift Your Choices

Snacks	Total Fat (grams)	Saturated Fat (grams)	Calories
Apple (1 medium)	0	0	70
Apple pie (⅛ of 9-inch pie)	20	8	410
Banana (1)	Trace	0	105
Milk chocolate bar (1½ oz.)	13	8	235
Tangerine (1 medium)	Trace	Trace	45
Chocolate chip cookie (2¼-inch diameter)	4	2	80
Salsa (¼ cup)	Trace	0	20
Ranch dressing, regular (¼ cup)	26	4	255
Saltines (10 crackers, or 1 oz.)	4	Trace	130
Potato chips (1 oz.)	10	1	150
Frozen yogurt (½ cup)	3	2	110
Ice cream, vanilla (½ cup)	7	4	135
Angel food cake, commercially prepared (1⁄12 of cake)	0	0	130
Pound cake, butter, commercially prepared (⅙ of loaf cake, or 2 oz.)	8	3	215
Bagel, plain (3-inch diameter)	1	Trace	90
Bagel with jam (2 tbsp.)	1	0	220
Bagel with cream cheese (2 tbsp.)	11	6	190
Doughnut, yeast, glazed (1)	15	6	270

Source: US Department of Agriculture, National Nutrient Database for Standard Reference, Release 28, 2016.

Many food manufacturers have reformulated their food products to reduce or remove *trans* fats. However, a food claiming " 0 *trans* fat" may have more saturated fats that you expect. Sometimes ingredients with saturated fats replace *trans* fatty acids when foods are reformulated. Tropical oils, which are high in saturated fats, may replace some or all partially hydrogenated oils.

Why might a product with partially hydrogenated oil say "0 *trans* fats" on the label? Due to rounding, less than (<) 0.5 grams of *trans* fat is considered zero according to the FDA. That's why checking the Nutrition Facts and ingredient list may be more important than just reading nutrient content claims.

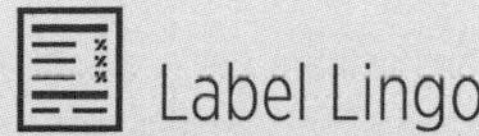

Label Lingo

Fats and Cholesterol

Check food labels for clues about fat and cholesterol. You may find these nutrient content claims.

Label term . . .	Means . . .
FOR FAT CONTENT . . .	
FAT-FREE	Contains less than 0.5 gram fat per serving
LOW-FAT	Contains 3 grams or less of fat per serving
REDUCED OR LESS FAT	Contains at least 25 percent less fat* per serving
LIGHT OR LITE	Contains ⅓ fewer calories or 50 percent less fat* per serving
____% FAT-FREE	Meets the criteria for "low-fat" or "fat-free" (as noted above) If stated as "100% fat-free"‡
LIGHT OR LITE MEAL	May be used to mean "low-fat," contains at least 50 percent less fat per serving*; or "low-calorie," contains at least ⅓ fewer calories per serving*
LOW-FAT MEAL	Contains 3 grams or less fat per 100 grams and 30 percent or less calories from fat per serving
FOR SATURATED FAT CONTENT . . .	
SATURATED FAT-FREE	Contains less than 0.5 gram saturated fat and less than 0.5 gram *trans* fatty acids per serving
LOW SATURATED FAT	Contains 1 gram or less saturated fat and no more than 15 percent of calories from saturated fat per serving
REDUCED OR LESS SATURATED FAT	Contains at least 25 percent less saturated fat* per serving

Label term . . .	Means . . .
FOR CHOLESTEROL CONTENT . . .	
CHOLESTEROL-FREE	Contains less than 2 milligrams cholesterol and 2 grams or less of saturated fat per serving
LOW CHOLESTEROL	Contains 20 milligrams or less cholesterol and 2 grams or less of saturated fat per serving
REDUCED OR LESS CHOLESTEROL	Contains at least 25 percent less cholesterol* and 2 grams or less of saturated fat per serving
FOR FAT, SATURATED FAT, AND CHOLESTEROL CONTENT . . .	
LEAN†	Contains less than 10 grams total fat, 4.5 grams saturated fat, and 95 milligrams cholesterol per 3-ounce serving and per 100 grams
EXTRA LEAN†	Contains less than 5 grams total fat, 2 grams saturated fat, and 95 milligrams cholesterol per 3-ounce serving and per 100 grams

*Compared with a standard serving size of regular food

†On packaged fish or game meat, cooked meat, or cooked poultry

‡ *See "Have you ever wondered . . . what a label stating '98% fat-free' means?" in this chapter, page 401*

Note: Although not a nutrient content claim per se, look for packages that say "0 g *trans* fat" or "no *trans* fat."

Need more strategies for managing fat in your meals and snacks? Check here for "how-tos":

- Shop for food with a fat-savvy mind-set; *see chapter 6, page 141.*
- Prepare meals and snacks with fewer solid fats and fat calories, without giving up flavor; *see chapter 8, page 230.*
- Be fat-savvy when eating out; *see chapter 9 page 275.*
- Manage dietary fat for heart disease, type 2 diabetes, and other health issues; *see chapter 24, page 680.*

Health claims related to a food's fat content may appear on food labels, too. *See "Health 'Info': Claims and More" in chapter 6, page 149.*

Check the Facts

The Nutrition Facts on food labels show how many grams of fat, including saturated and *trans* fats, that a single label serving contains. You'll also find the % Daily Value (DV). Remember this general rule of thumb: 5% DV or less is low for total fat and saturated fats, and 20% DV or more is high. *Trans* fats have no DV amount assigned.

Since the Nutrition Facts were first introduced, "Calories from Fat" have been listed, too. However, the new Nutrition Facts label, *discussed in "A Closer Look . . . Nutrition Facts Update 2016" in chapter 6, page 148*, no longer shows that. The reason is research shows that the type of fat is more important than the amount.

TFAs: The Ban

In 2015, the FDA declared that partially hydrogenated oils (PHOs), a primary source for *trans* fatty acids (TFAs),—are not Generally Recognized as Safe (GRAS) for use in food, based on extensive research; *see "Additives: Testing and Approval" in chapter 5, page 138, to learn more about the GRAS list.* It stated that removing them from processed foods could prevent thousands of heart attacks and deaths each year.

The FDA gave the food industry three years to reformulate their products to remove PHOs from food or to get permission to use them for some specific reasons. In recent years, even before the ruling, many food companies have been removing PHOs from processed foods to be free of *trans* fat.

You're still advised to be prudent. Check the Nutrition Facts label. A product that no longer contains *trans* fat may be high in saturated fats, not necessarily a healthy alternative. Check the ingredient list on food labels for partially hydrogenated oils because they are the main source of TFAs in food.

TFAs are found naturally in small amounts in ruminant animals (cows and sheep), and so products such as beef, lamb, milk, and butter have small amounts of TFAs; it is unclear if they have different physiological effects than most synthetic forms of TFAs. Edible oils have very small amounts, too, since TFAs are unavoidably produced during the manufacturing process.

See "Trans *Fats: Semisolid Fats" in this chapter, page 387, to learn more.*

Fats are identified in the Nutrition Facts this way:

- *Total fat* includes all saturated, unsaturated, and *trans* fats.
- *Saturated fat* is also shown separately.
- *Polyunsaturated and monounsaturated fats* may be shown at the discretion of the manufacturer. Omega-3s may be noted somewhere on the food package but not specifically in the Nutrition Facts.
- Trans *fat* shows the *trans* fatty acid content from partially hydrogenated oils. When *trans* fats are present at 0.5 or more grams per serving, the amount is required on the Nutrition Facts label, along with total and saturated fats. This is true for supplement labeling, too.

  Note: For nutrition labeling, the FDA excludes naturally occurring *trans* fats from its definition of *trans* fats.

See "Nutrition: Fact Check!" in chapter 6, page 144, to learn how to use the Nutrition Facts panel.

Check the Ingredients

To limit solid fats, use the ingredient list on the label. For example, look for vegetable oils. Rather than stick margarine, buy soft margarine that lists liquid vegetable oil as the first ingredient and contains no more than 2 grams of saturated fat per tablespoon, as advised by the American Heart Association. Or buy *trans* fat-free spreads, such as those that combine cottonseed, soy, and sunflower oils.

As an aside: Tub and squeeze margarines contain more water and may have air whipped in so they may be lower in fat and calories. Yet, by law, margarine must contain at least 80 percent fat. To compare, table spreads may have 0 to 80 percent fat.

If the ingredient list shows partially hydrogenated vegetable oil, it has *trans* fatty acids, too. Although TFAs in foods are being eliminated, stick margarine, vegetable shortening, many prepared foods such as fried foods, packaged baking mixes, some snack foods, and other processed foods may still have them.

Tropical oils such as coconut and palm, often used to replace partially hydrogenated oils, are highly saturated. They are often used to enhance texture. (*Note:* Some stick margarine is made with tropical oils instead of partially hydrogenated vegetable oils.)

Cholesterol: Like Fat, Not Fat

What about dietary cholesterol? Current evidence shows that unless you have diabetes, consuming moderate levels of cholesterol doesn't appear to affect health risks—even for heart disease—for most people.

With ongoing research, cardiovascular health and its links to cholesterol and fat intake are better understood today. Until recently, advice in the Dietary Guidelines for Americans has been to limit cholesterol to 300 milligrams or less daily to lower the risk of heart disease. Current evidence indicates that consuming too much solid fat—not too much cholesterol—is what increases heart disease risk for most people.

CHOLESTEROL BASICS

What is cholesterol? To clear up a misperception, cholesterol is a fat-like substance, not a fat. The biochemical makeup of cholesterol differs from dietary fat. Chemically speaking, cholesterol is a sterol instead and functions differently in the body from dietary fat.

Dietary vs. Blood Cholesterol

Cholesterol terms often cause confusion. Actually, "cholesterol" refers to two types: dietary cholesterol and blood cholesterol.

- Dietary cholesterol comes from foods and beverages of animal origin: meat, poultry, fish, eggs, and dairy foods. Animals produce cholesterol, but plants don't. Phytosterols (stanols and sterols) that occur naturally in plant cells are different from cholesterol, which is a natural sterol, in animal-based foods. *See "Functional Nutrition: Plant Stanols and Sterols" in this chapter, page 405.*

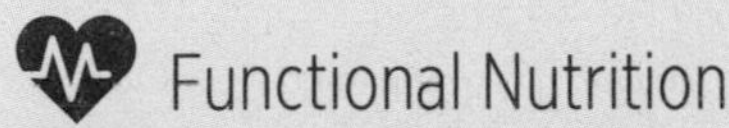

Functional Nutrition

Plant Stanols and Sterols

Phytosterols (plant stanols and sterols) are found naturally in fruits, vegetables, vegetable oils, whole grains, nuts, and seeds. Although similar in structure to cholesterol, they function differently. They reduce cholesterol absorption in the intestines, which includes cholesterol from bile that normally would be reabsorbed and reused. This, in turn, helps to reduce blood levels of total and LDL ("bad") cholesterol—but they don't affect HDLs or triglycerides.

Getting enough phytosterols from food isn't easy. The average person consumes less than 500 milligrams (0.5 grams) of phytosterols a day, not enough to lower blood cholesterol levels. For that reason, food manufacturers are fortifying some products with plant stanols and sterols, such as some cereals, chocolate, mayonnaise, milk, orange juice, snack bars, butterlike spreads, and yogurt beverages. Check the ingredient list on the label to find out if they contain stanols and sterols, and how much.

Studies show that stanols and sterols in significant amounts may lower LDL cholesterol levels by about 6 percent on average and, for some people, perhaps as much as 14 percent in four weeks. The National Cholesterol Education Program of the National Institutes of Health recommends consuming 2 grams total of plant stanols and/or sterols every day as part of an overall heart-healthy diet. For example, two to three tablespoons of margarine spread with plant stanols or sterols contain that much, as do two cups of orange juice fortified with plant sterols.

Two spreads—Promise Activ® and Benecol®—contain these unique dietary ingredients. Use them in food preparation, not only as a spread. Benecol regular spread (with plant stanol esters) can be used in cooking and baking without changing the flavor of food. Use it like any margarine, substituting it equally for the fat, oil, or shortening in a recipe. A spread with plant sterols (Promise Activ) isn't recommended for baking or frying; use it in foods that aren't cooked.

Foods fortified with plant stanols and sterols offer cholesterol-lowering benefits. Research shows that people with elevated cholesterol levels benefit most. Plant stanols and sterols aren't meant to replace statin drug therapy, but they may help lower blood cholesterol further as part of a healthy eating plan.

The FDA-approved health claim on phytosterols states: "Foods containing at least 0.65 gram per serving of vegetable oil plant sterol esters, eaten twice a day with meals for a daily total intake of at least 1.3 grams, as part of a diet low in saturated fat and cholesterol, may reduce the risk of heart disease." Read the label for a serving size that provides that amount.

Plant stanols and sterols in soft-gel form are available as supplements, but talk to your doctor before taking them.

One caution: High intake of phytosterols, more likely from supplements, may reduce the absorption of beta-carotene.

- Blood, or serum, cholesterol circulates in the bloodstream. Your body produces enough for your needs. Your liver makes most of it, but every body cell can make cholesterol, too.

How does your body use cholesterol? First, it's part of every cell in your body and some hormones, including sex hormones such as estrogen and testosterone. As part of a body chemical called bile, cholesterol helps your body digest and absorb fat. And with the help of sunlight, a form of cholesterol in your skin can change to vitamin D, a nutrient essential for bone building.

Blood cholesterol contains both lipids (fats) and lipoprotein. Two kinds of lipoproteins are HDLs and LDLs. HDLs, or "good" cholesterol, are high-density lipoproteins that carry cholesterol from the tissues to the liver for removal from the body. LDLs, or "bad" cholesterol, are low-density lipoproteins that carry cholesterol to arteries and tissues, and may lead to a buildup of cholesterol in the arteries.

Dietary cholesterol doesn't automatically become blood cholesterol. Solid fats (saturated fats and *trans* fats) in your food choices affect blood cholesterol levels more than dietary cholesterol alone does. *See "Heart Disease: The Blood Lipid Connection" in chapter 24, page 684, for more about risk factors for heart disease.*

DIETARY CHOLESTEROL: TODAY'S GUIDANCE

Since the human body can make enough, no Dietary Reference Intakes (DRIs) for cholesterol have been established. Unlike adults, infants and young children don't produce much cholesterol. Whether dietary cholesterol plays a role in early development hasn't been resolved; recommendations have not been made.

In the Dietary Guidelines for Americans no longer advises a specific daily limit for dietary cholesterol for most healthy people. Still, it advises keeping cholesterol to a minimum in a healthy eating pattern. For some health problems, such as diabetes, limiting cholesterol may be advised. Talk to your doctor.

By following the eating patterns from the Dietary Guidelines, *discussed in chapter 2, page 21,* cholesterol intake comes in at about 100 to 300 milligrams daily anyway. That's good since the Guidelines notes that a lower intake of dietary cholesterol is associated with a reduced risk for cardiovascular disease.

CHOLESTEROL IN FOOD

If your doctor advises limiting dietary cholesterol, which foods do you target? Only foods of animal origin contain cholesterol. Egg yolks and organ meats are especially high in cholesterol. In varying amounts, meat, poultry, fish, dairy products, and animal fats such as butter or lard all supply cholesterol, too.

Because cholesterol and saturated fatty acids often occur together in animal-based foods, they sometimes get confused. Sirloin steak, butter, and Cheddar cheese, for example, contain both; organ meats and shellfish such as shrimp and squid are high in cholesterol yet low in saturated fatty acids.

In foods of animal origin, both lean and fatty tissues contain cholesterol. The sauce or butter on fish can boost their cholesterol content, too.

Food	Cholesterol (milligrams)
Beef liver, braised (3 oz.)	337
Egg, cooked (1 large)	
Whole	185
Yolk	185
White	0
Shrimp, steamed or boiled (8 large)	93
Beef, ground, cooked (3-oz. patty)	
70% lean/30% fat	70
95% lean/5% fat	65
Pork, center loin, roasted (3 oz.)	
Lean	69
Lean and fat	69
Salmon, Atlantic, farmed, cooked (3 oz.)	54
Butter (1 tbsp.)	31
Milk (1 cup)	
2% reduced fat	20
Fat-free	5
Margarine, stick (1 tbsp.)	0

Plant-based foods have no cholesterol. Although they're high in fat, nuts, seeds, vegetable oils, and margarine are cholesterol free. Egg whites have no cholesterol either.

So why do some vegetable dishes and grain-based baked goods contain cholesterol? It's from the added ingredients: butter, cheese, egg yolks, lard, meat, milk, or poultry. Some other examples: refried beans made with lard, greens cooked with bacon, and muffins made with butter and egg yolks. The amount of cholesterol per serving varies with the recipe.

? Have you ever wondered?

. . . if cholesterol supplies calories? Often confused with fat, cholesterol isn't a source of energy, or calories. Unlike fats, carbohydrates, and proteins, cholesterol isn't broken down, so the body cannot derive any energy from it.

. . . if it's okay to eat eggs? Yes! Despite being a great source of protein and other nutrients, people have been advised for years to restrict eggs to limit dietary cholesterol. With more scientific evidence, it's now known that eating eggs doesn't increase the risk of heart disease significantly for healthy people, although people with diabetes may be at higher risk if they consume too much cholesterol. Besides their many other nutrient contributions, eggs provide more choline than many other foods, which is a nutrient that often comes up short.

CHOLESTEROL: IF ADVISED TO CUT BACK

Scrambled, hard-cooked, or in omelets, eggs are great nutrition for most people. Although dietary cholesterol in the amounts usually consumed are no longer considered a health concern for most people, those with some health conditions, such as diabetes, may be advised to limit cholesterol intake by following these tips:

- Go easy on egg yolks, including eggs in prepared foods such as bread, cakes, and pancakes. The yolk has all the cholesterol—about 185 milligrams from a large egg. *Tip:* Substitute two egg whites for one whole egg in baked goods, or use an egg substitute.
- Go easy on organ meats such as liver. Even though they're nutritious, they're high in cholesterol.
- Look for lean meat, poultry, fish, and low-fat and fat-free dairy foods. You'll trim away some cholesterol along with fat.
- Check the package labels to find low-cholesterol or cholesterol-free foods. If you spot a food "no cholesterol" or "cholesterol-free" claim, it cannot have any more than 2 grams of saturated fat. However, read Nutrition Facts to find out about the fat content; it could be high in total fat or *trans* fats. *See "Label Lingo: Fats and Cholesterol" in this chapter, page 403.*

Fat Replacers

Today's supermarkets sell options. Foods made with fat-reduction ingredients mimic their higher-fat counterparts, with much of the same tastes, textures, and appearance. Usually they're lower in saturated fats, perhaps cholesterol, and calories as well.

Fat gives food some unique characteristics. When it's removed from a "recipe," perhaps to make a low-fat cookie, some of the more appealing qualities of the food change, too. Many fat replacers or substitutes are meant to prevent these kinds of changes.

Ingredients used to replace fat fit into three categories: carbohydrate, fat, or protein replacers. Most contribute calories, although less than fat does. Because none acts exactly like fat, most reduced-fat and fat-free products contain a mixture of fat substitutes to get a desirable result.

From a food safety standpoint, scientific research and review by the FDA recognize fat replacers or substitutes as safe. New products must go through a thorough review.

FAT REPLACERS: WHAT TYPES?

Carbohydrate-Based Fat Replacers

These fat replacers combine with water to retain moisture and provide texture, appearance, and mouth feel similar to fat. They are made with plant polysaccharides and include carrageenan, cellulose, dextrins, gelatin, gellan gum, gels, guar gum, inulin, maltodextrins, oatrim, polydextrose, starches, xanthum gum, and modified dietary fibers. Fat-free salad dressings, for example, contain carbohydrate-based substitutes.

Calories in these replacers range from almost nothing to 4 calories per gram, compared to 9 calories per gram of fat. The difference is that some, such as modified starches and dextrins, are digested; others, such as cellulose and other fibers, aren't, which makes them essentially calorie free.

Most carbohydrate-based fat replacers can withstand some heat. However, they can't be used for frying.

Pureed dried plums (prunes) and unsweetened applesauce—both high in carbohydrates are used as fat substitutes in baked goods, too. They're an easy fat replacement that you can try yourself. Pureed plums and applesauce add bulk, flavor, and nutrition.

Protein-Based Fat Replacers

Made with protein from egg whites or whey from milk, protein-based fat replacers provide a creamy sensation and improve the appearance and texture when fat is removed. Low-fat cheese made with a protein-based substitute gives an appearance and texture that come close to full-fat cheese. Most protein-based replacers aren't used in foods prepared at high temperatures because when the protein coagulates, it no longer functions in ways similar to fat. Microparticulated protein, used in baked goods, dairy foods, margarine- and mayonnaise-type products, salad dressings, sauces, and soups, is made from whey protein or milk and egg protein.

Protein-based replacers contribute 1 to 4 calories per gram, compared with 9 calories per gram of fat. What accounts for the calorie range? These replacers may be blended with ingredients such as cellulose that can't be digested. Protein-based replacers provide small amounts of amino acids.

> **?** Have you ever wondered?
>
> **. . . if foods made with fat substitutes cause digestive discomfort?** In the amounts generally consumed, likely not. However, consuming large amounts of fat-based replacers, such as olestra, and some carbohydrate-based replacers may cause short-term digestive discomfort, which comes from the added bulk from these ingredients.

Fat-Based Fat Replacers

These fat replacers are barriers to fat absorption. They provide few or no calories because the body is unable to fully absorb their fatty acids. Because they're made from fats, their physical properties—taste, texture, and mouth feel—are the same as fat. They may be used in baked goods, cake mixes, frosting, dairy foods, and some prepackaged (such as frozen) fried foods.

Olestra is a calorie-free fat replacer made from vegetable oils and sugar. It contributes no calories because it passes through the body without being digested and absorbed. Olestra provides the characteristics of fat in cooking, especially for frying, and in snack foods. Because olestra isn't digested, some vitamins (A, D, E, and K) carried by fat in these foods aren't fully absorbed, either. For this reason, fat-soluble vitamins are added to products with olestra to make up for possible losses.

Salatrim, caprenin, emulsifiers and mono- and diglycerides are other fat-based replacers used in baked goods, confection-type products, and dairy products. Salatrim provides calories, but only 5 calories per gram (as compared to 9 calories per gram of fat) because it is only partially absorbed in the body.

FAT REPLACERS: FOR WHOM? WHAT FOODS?

Foods with fat replacers can be a safe and effective option for making meals and snacks appealing while, at the same time, reducing fat and calories in your food choices.

Check the ingredient list on reduced-fat, low-fat, or fat-free foods: for example, baked goods, butter, candy, cheese, gravy, ice cream, margarine, mayonnaise, processed meats, pudding, salad dressing, sour cream, and yogurt. A combination of fat replacers may be used for the best texture and taste in fat-reduced foods.

Fat replacers supply calories in varying amounts, so fat-modified foods may or may not be fewer calories than the original food. For the calories and fat per serving, check the Nutrition Facts label. And go easy. Less fat is no license to overeat!

14

Vitamins and Minerals

In this chapter, find out about . . .

Vitamins and minerals: why, how much, and what kind

Shortchanged: nutrients of concern

Antioxidants and their health benefits

Vitamins and minerals: your body needs them—more of some, less of others. How much do you need of each for optimal health? What are the best sources? How do these nutrients help keep you well?

Although headlines often seem confounding, there's plenty that's well known about the roles of vitamins and minerals for good health. True deficiencies are rare in developed countries, such as the United States, although not consuming enough over an extended time can result in adverse health effects, *as discussed in this chapter.* Consuming too much of many of them can be detrimental, too.

Today's nutrition breakthroughs focus on how nutrients and other food components promote health and how they may help protect you from heart disease, cancer, and osteoporosis, among other health concerns. In general, here's what's known today:

- More than forty nutrients, including vitamins and minerals, have been identified. Their functions, the amount you need at different stages of life, and their food sources are better understood than ever before. Today's vitamin and mineral research extends well beyond their well-known, important roles in health.
- The balance of vitamins and minerals—and the variety of foods that provide them—is better understood. A great deal is known about how the body absorbs and uses them most efficiently. And science is discovering what's enough, but not too much, for unique, individual needs.
- Science is exploring a new frontier: food components, including phytonutrients, that offer health benefits beyond basic nourishment, *as discussed in "Phytonutrients: Different from Nutrients" in chapter 15, page 448.*

Bottom line? A variety of foods, with plenty of vitamins, minerals, and phytonutrients, is part of your ticket to good health.

Regulating Your Body's Work

Vitamins and minerals are key to every process that takes place in your body. They don't work alone, but instead work in close partnership with other nutrients to make every process in your body happen normally. This includes helping carbohydrates, fats, and proteins produce energy, assisting with protein synthesis (creation of new proteins), building healthy bones, and helping you think about the words on this page. Vitamins and minerals work as part of your body's spark plugs that help make things happen.

Vitamins are complex substances that regulate body processes. Often, they act as cofactors, or partners with enzymes, to the proteins that trigger reactions in your body.

Minerals are part of many cells, including (but not only) the hard parts: bones, teeth, and nails. Minerals also are cofactors in enzymes, triggering many body reactions to happen.

Compared with carbohydrates, fats, and proteins, your body needs vitamins and minerals in only small amounts, so they're called micronutrients. Don't let these small amounts fool you, however. Vitamins and minerals don't supply energy directly, but they do regulate and enhance processes that produce energy—and do a whole lot more!

"Dietary Reference Intakes" in the appendix, page 780, provides specific recommendations—for vitamins and minerals for different ages and for both genders including infants, children, and teens. In this chapter, you also will learn about the vitamins and minerals that the Dietary Guidelines for Americans identify in this way:

- *Underconsumed:* Many Americans underconsume vitamins A, C, D, and E, choline, calcium, magnesium, and potassium. Iron is also underconsumed by adolescent girls and women ages nineteen through fifty. Intakes of calcium, potassium, and vitamin D are low enough to be considered a substantial health concern. For young children, women capable of becoming pregnant, and women who are pregnant, a low intake of iron also is of public health concern.
- *Overconsumed:* Sodium is a mineral of public health concern linked to high blood pressure; most people consume too much sodium.

Please note in this chapter: Unless another source is cited, the amounts of vitamins and minerals in food have been rounded and reflect amounts from the National Nutrient Database for Standard Reference (Release 28). *Nutrient interactions with some medications are addressed in "Doctor Prescribed: Diets and Medications" in chapter 25, page 743.*

Alphabet Soup: Nutrient Recommendations

- *Dietary Reference Intakes (DRIs):* Daily nutrient recommendations—expressed as RDAs, AIs, ULs—based on age and gender; set at levels to decrease the risk of chronic disease.
- *Recommended Dietary Allowances (RDAs):* Recommended daily intake levels of nutrients to meet the needs of nearly all (97 to 98 percent) healthy individuals in a specific age, life-stage, and gender group; used when there's scientific consensus for a firm nutrient recommendation.
- *Adequate Intakes (AIs):* Similar to RDAs and used for nutrients that lack sufficient scientific evidence to determine a firm RDA.
- *Tolerable Upper Intake Levels (ULs):* Not a recommendation; maximum intake (daily average) that most likely won't pose risks for health problems for almost all healthy people in that age and gender group based on current research findings. As the intake increases above the UL, the potential risk of adverse health effects increases.

The DRIs for age groups other than those noted in this chapter are provided in the appendix, page 780.

Daily Values (DVs) for nutrients aren't DRIs, although they are based on RDA values. For the new Nutrition Facts labels, the DVs have been updated, *as noted in "% Daily Values: What Are They Based On?" in the appendix, page 786.* DVs are used primarily for food labeling for a quick comparison to daily recommendations.

Source: Institute of Medicine, National Academy of Sciences.

How do your favorite foods stack up for vitamins and minerals? Other nutrients? Calories?

What more does science say about the vitamins and minerals discussed in this chapter? More in-depth information is just a click away.

- USDA National Nutrient Database for Standard Reference, US Department of Agriculture, Agricultural Research Service
  ndb.nal.usda.gov/ndb
- Vitamin and Mineral Fact Sheets, National Institutes of Health, Office of Dietary Supplements
  ods.od.nih.gov/factsheets/list-VitaminsMinerals
- Food-A-Pedia in the SuperTracker, US Department of Agriculture
  www.supertracker.usda.gov/foodapedia.aspx

Do your daily food choices provide enough vitamins and minerals? Use this interactive tool to track the foods you eat and compare your nutrient intake to your personal targets.

- Food Tracker in the SuperTracker, US Department of Agriculture
  www.supertracker.usda.gov/foodtracker.aspx

Vitamins: From A to K

Vitamins belong in two groups: fat soluble and water soluble. Their category explains how they are carried in food and transported in your body.

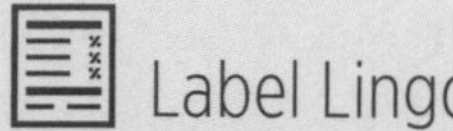

Label Lingo

Vitamins and Minerals

The lingo on the front of many food packages describes the amount of vitamins or minerals found in a single serving. For specific amounts of those nutrients, check the % Daily Value (%DV) on the Nutrition Facts label.

Label term . . .	Means . . .
HIGH, RICH IN, OR EXCELLENT SOURCE OF	20 percent or more of the Daily Value
GOOD SOURCE, CONTAINS, OR PROVIDES	10 to 19 percent of the Daily Value
MORE, ENRICHED, FORTIFIED, OR ADDED	10 percent or more of the Daily Value

Fat-soluble vitamins (A, D, E, and K). These vitamins dissolve in fat, which is how they're carried in food and into your bloodstream. Once absorbed, they attach to substances within your body made with lipids, or fat. These vitamins are one reason why you need moderate amounts of fat in your overall food choices.

Your body can store fat-soluble vitamins in body fat, so consuming excessive amounts of any fat-soluble vitamins for too long can be harmful. Vitamin A, for example, can build up to harmful levels. High intakes of vitamins E and K usually aren't linked to unhealthy symptoms since higher levels of either are the least toxic of excess vitamins.

It's About the Food!

Think food—to get enough (and not too much) of the vitamins and minerals discussed in this chapter. You'll find practical food tips and how-tos throughout the book to fit them in. Start here:

- Plan a day's food choices (vegetables and fruits, grain foods, dairy foods, and protein foods) that deliver enough vitamins and minerals and plenty of phytonutrients; *see chapters 2 and 3, pages 21 and 60.*
- Scout for nutrient-rich, phytonutrient-rich foods when you shop; *see chapter 6, page 141.*
- Lock vitamins in, boost calcium, and cut sodium when you store and prepare food; *see chapters 7 and 8, pages 191 and 230.*
- Use vitamin and mineral supplements wisely; *see chapter 10, page 315.*

Water-soluble vitamins (B-complex vitamins and vitamin C). These vitamins dissolve in water. For the most part, water-soluble vitamins aren't stored in your body—at least not in significant amounts. Instead, your body uses what it needs, then excretes the excess through urine. Since they aren't stored, you need a regular supply of water-soluble vitamins from your food choices.

For water-soluble vitamins, you need enough, but not too much. Even though you excrete excess amounts of water-soluble vitamins, moderation is advised. For example, taking large doses of vitamin C from a dietary supplement may create extra work for your kidneys, which might result in kidney stones, as well as cause diarrhea. Likewise, too much niacin, vitamin B_6, folate, or pantothenic acid also may have health risks.

FAT-SOLUBLE VITAMINS

Vitamin A (and Provitamin A Carotenoids)

Vitamin A from foods comes in two forms: (1) preformed, meaning completely made in animal-based foods, or (2) as carotenoids (provitamin A) such as beta-carotene that convert to vitamin A in the body. Beta-carotene is the form of vitamin A in plant-based foods. *See "Carotenoids: 'Color' Your Food Healthy" in this chapter, page 424.*

What it does:

- Promotes normal vision and helps your eyes see normally in the dark, helping them adjust to the lower level of light
- Promotes the growth and health of cells and tissues throughout your body. During pregnancy, it's important for reproduction and the developing baby.
- Protects you from infections by keeping your skin and the tissues in your mouth, stomach, and intestines, as well as your respiratory, genital, and urinary tracts healthy
- Helps your heart, lungs, kidneys, and other organs work properly
- Helps regulate your immune system
- Works as an antioxidant (in the form of carotenoids) and may help reduce the risk for some diseases of aging. Some carotenoids may have other health benefits.

How much you need: That depends on your age and reproductive status.

For males aged fourteen and older, the Recommended Dietary Allowance (RDA) is 900 micrograms Retinol Activity Equivalent (RAE) (equivalent to 3,000 International Units, or IUs) daily; for females of the same age, it's 700 micrograms RAE (2,333 IUs) daily. Children under age fourteen need less, depending on their age. During pregnancy, the RDA increases to 750 micrograms RAE (2,500 (IUs) daily for those under age eighteen and to 770 micrograms RAE (2566 IUs) daily for ages eighteen and older; during breastfeeding, it increases to 1,200 micrograms RAE (4,000 IUs) daily for those under age eighteen and to 1,300 micrograms (4,333 IUs) for ages eighteen and older.

See "Calculating Vitamin A in Foods" for more about RAEs.

On the Label

Without looking, do you know which vitamins and minerals appear on food labels? Four have been required on the original Nutrition Facts label: vitamins A and C, calcium, and iron. The new label, *discussed in "A Closer Look . . . Nutrition Facts Update 2016" in chapter 6 page 148,* requires these four instead: vitamin D, calcium, iron, and potassium.

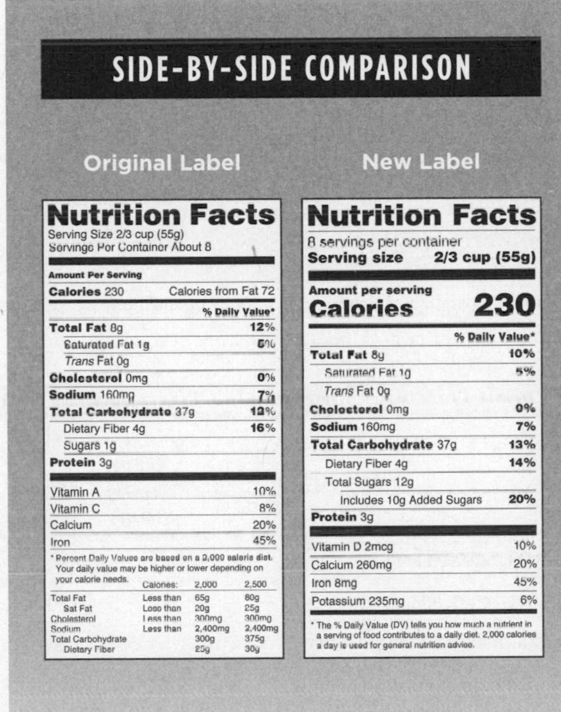

SIDE-BY-SIDE COMPARISON

Original Label

Nutrition Facts
Serving Size 2/3 cup (55g)
Servings Per Container About 8

Amount Per Serving	
Calories 230	Calories from Fat 72
	% Daily Value*
Total Fat 8g	**12%**
Saturated Fat 1g	**5%**
Trans Fat 0g	
Cholesterol 0mg	**0%**
Sodium 160mg	**7%**
Total Carbohydrate 37g	**13%**
Dietary Fiber 4g	**16%**
Sugars 1g	
Protein 3g	
Vitamin A	10%
Vitamin C	8%
Calcium	20%
Iron	45%

* Percent Daily Values are based on a 2,000 calorie diet. Your daily value may be higher or lower depending on your calorie needs.

	Calories:	2,000	2,500
Total Fat	Less than	65g	80g
Sat Fat	Less than	20g	25g
Cholesterol	Less than	300mg	300mg
Sodium	Less than	2,400mg	2,400mg
Total Carbohydrate		300g	375g
Dietary Fiber		25g	30g

New Label

Nutrition Facts
8 servings per container
Serving size 2/3 cup (55g)

Amount per serving	
Calories	**230**
	% Daily Value*
Total Fat 8g	**10%**
Saturated Fat 1g	**5%**
Trans Fat 0g	
Cholesterol 0mg	**0%**
Sodium 160mg	**7%**
Total Carbohydrate 37g	**13%**
Dietary Fiber 4g	**14%**
Total Sugars 12g	
Includes 10g Added Sugars	**20%**
Protein 3g	
Vitamin D 2mcg	10%
Calcium 260mg	20%
Iron 8mg	45%
Potassium 235mg	6%

* The % Daily Value (DV) tells you how much a nutrient in a serving of food contributes to a daily diet. 2,000 calories a day is used for general nutrition advice.

Consume enough of these nutrients to reduce your risk for some common health problems. Other nutrients may appear on the label, too, some voluntarily and others required if these nutrients are added.

Be aware: Daily Values (DVs) for nutrients, used with food labeling, may differ from the DRIs for you. *See "% Daily Values: What Are They Based On?" in the appendix, page 786.*

If you don't consume enough: Night blindness; other eye problems; dry, scaly skin; problems with reproduction; diminished immunity; and poor growth signal a significant deficiency. Deficiencies aren't common in the United States except perhaps for premature infants during their first year.

Xerophthalmia, an inability to see in low light, is a common symptom of vitamin A deficiency in young children and pregnant women, and it can lead to blindness if untreated.

If you consume excess amounts: Because it's stored in your body, high intakes of some forms of preformed vitamin A (usually from supplements or some medicines), if taken over time, can be quite harmful. They may cause headaches, dizziness, vomiting, coma, nerve damage, and even death—and birth defects if high intakes are taken during pregnancy. High doses of beta-carotene supplements aren't advised for smokers.

High beta-carotene (provitamin A) intake from vegetables and fruits may turn skin yellow once the body stores enough vitamin A, but that's

? Have you ever wondered?

. . . if you need more—or less—of some vitamins or minerals if you're on medications? Maybe. That depends on your health condition and the interactions between some medications and vitamins and/or minerals. *As addressed in "Doctor Prescribed: Diets and Medications" in chapter 25, page 743,* some medications affect the absorption of some nutrients, and some foods and nutrients affect the effectiveness of some medications. For example:

- Orlistat, a weight-loss drug, and the cholesterol-lowering drug cholestyramine can lower vitamin A absorption, lowering vitamin A blood levels in some people. They can also reduce the absorption of other fat-soluble vitamins (D, E, and K).
- Antacids with aluminum or magnesium increase calcium loss through urine.
- Glucocorticoids (such as prednisone) can cause calcium depletion and eventually osteoporosis when used for months at a time.
- Metformin, a drug used to treat type 2 diabetes, can interfere with the body's absorption or use of vitamin B_{12}.
- Calcium might interfere with iron absorption. Taking calcium and iron supplements at different times of the day might prevent this problem.
- Vitamin K can seriously interact with the blood thinner warfarin (Coumadin).

This is a very short list—and it's a reminder to check on interactions with nutrients and nutrient supplements if you take any medication. The Vitamin and Mineral Fact Sheets from the Office of Dietary Supplements, National Institutes of Health, provide more details about nutrient-medication interactions for each nutrient; visit the website ods.od.nih.gov/factsheets/list-VitaminsMinerals.

More importantly, consult your doctor, pharmacist, or registered dietitian nutritionist about any nutrient-drug interactions if you take medications—whether they're sold by prescription or over the counter.

Calculating Vitamin A in Foods

RAEs or IUs: Both are used to measure vitamin A. The RDAs for vitamin A are given in RAEs. The amount in food and supplements may be given in RAEs or IUs. The Daily Values (DVs) for vitamin A on the original Nutrition Facts and Supplement Facts labels are figured with IUs; the updated labeling bases DVs for vitamin A on RAEs.

The reasons for different measurements relates to different food sources of vitamin A, and so to bioavailability, or the amount available to your body, of different forms of vitamin A. Provitamin A carotenoids (plant based), which form vitamin A, differ from vitamin A as retinol (animal based). These differences are recognized in calculating the amount of vitamin A from a variety of foods.

Retinol Activity Equivalents (RAEs) measure vitamin A equivalency from all sources. They reflect the conversion of vitamin A from retinol units (animal-based sources) and from carotenoid units (plant-based sources) to one common unit. They take bioavailability into account.

Converting between micrograms of RAEs and IUs isn't easy, and cannot be done accurately if you don't know whether vitamin A comes from a plant- or animal-based source. Here's how it is calculated:

1 IU retinol (animal-based) = 0.3 mcg RAE

1 IU beta-carotene from food (plant-based) = 0.05 mcg RAE

1 IU beta-carotene from daily supplements (plant-based) = 0.15 mcg RAE

Know how many IUs or RAEs you need daily—and make plant-based foods an important source of vitamin A in your meals and snacks. This chart shows both RAEs and IUs for a few common foods.

VITAMIN A AND CAROTENOIDS: SOURCES

Food	RAE per Serving (mcg)	IU* per Serving
Beef liver, panfried (3 oz.)	6,582	22,175
Sweet potato, baked, in skin (1 whole)	1,403	28,058
Spinach, frozen, boiled (½ cup)	573	11,458
Carrots, raw (½ cup)	459	9,189
Ice cream, French vanilla, soft serve (1 cup)	278	1,014
Cheese, ricotta, part skim (1 cup)	263	945
Herring, Atlantic, pickled (3 oz.)	219	731
Milk, fat-free, with added vitamins A and D (1 cup)	149	500
Ready-to-eat cereal, fortified with 10 percent of the DV for vitamin A (¾ to 1 cup) (more heavily fortified cereals might provide more of the DV)†	127–149	500
Cantaloupe, raw (½ cup)	135	2,706
Bell peppers, red, raw (½ cup)	117	2,332
Mangoes, raw (1 whole)	112	2,240

Food	RAE per Serving (mcg)	IU* per Serving
Egg, hard cooked (1 large)	75	260
Black-eyed peas, boiled (1 cup)	66	1,305
Apricots, dried, sulfured (10 halves)	63	1,261
Broccoli, boiled (½ cup)	60	1,208
Salmon, sockeye, cooked (3 oz.)	59	176
Tomato juice, canned (¾ cup)	42	821
Yogurt, plain, low-fat (1 cup)	32	116
Tuna, light, canned in oil, drained solids (3 oz.)	20	65
Baked beans, canned, plain or vegetarian (1 cup)	13	274
Summer squash, all varieties, boiled (½ cup)	10	191
Chicken breast, meat and skin, roasted (½ breast)	5	18
Pistachio nuts, dry roasted (1 oz.)	4	73

*The % Daily Values (DVs)—used on the original food labels and many dietary supplements—are based on International Units (IUs) for vitamin A. *Note:* under FDA's new labeling regulations for foods and dietary supplements, vitamin A will be listed only in mcg of RAEs and not IUs; *see "Nutrition: Fact Check!" in chapter 6, page 148*. The amounts in IUs are approximate.

†Many fortified foods, including breakfast cereals, supply vitamin A, too. Read the Nutrition Facts label to see how much.

Source: Office of Dietary Supplements, National Institutes of Health, Department of Health and Human Services, ods.od.nih.gov/factsheets/VitaminA-HealthProfessional. Accessed December 1, 2016.

not considered harmful. Converting beta-carotene to vitamin A in your body decreases once it stores enough vitamin A.

For preformed vitamin A (from animal-based sources), the Tolerable Upper Intake Level (UL) for RAE daily is this: for males and females aged nine through thirteen, it's 1,700 micrograms daily; for those fourteen through eighteen, it's 2,800 micrograms daily; and for ages nineteen and older, it's 3,000 micrograms daily. The levels remain the same during pregnancy and breastfeeding. RAEs cannot be directly converted into IUs without knowing the source(s) of vitamin A. No ULs for provitamin A (beta-carotene) have been established. *See "Dietary Reference Intakes" in the appendix, page 780, for ULs for other age groups.*

Caution: Some prescription medications have synthetic forms (preformed vitamin A, provitamin A, or a combination); taking these with a vitamin A supplement can raise vitamin A in blood to a dangerously high level.

Where it's mostly found:

- Preformed vitamin A in animal sources of foods is in the form of retinol. Vitamin A comes from liver, other organ meats, some fish (salmon, for example), eggs, milk fortified with vitamin A, and other vitamin A–fortified foods such as breakfast cereal.
- Provitamin A comes from vegetables, fruits, and other foods of plant origin. Some carotenoids form vitamin A; the most common is beta-carotene. Carotenoids are found in red, yellow, orange, and many dark-green leafy vegetables. As a source of vitamin A, beta-carotene from plants is especially important to those who eat few, if any, animal-based foods. To get enough vitamin A from its conversion from beta-carotene, you need to eat plenty of colorful vegetables and fruits.

In dietary supplements, vitamin A is usually retinyl acetate or retinyl palmitate (both preformed vitamin A), or beta-carotene (provitamin A), or a combination. Note: under FDA's new labeling regulations for foods and dietary, vitamin A will be listed only in mcg and not IUs.

Vitamin D

What it does:

- Helps almost every part of the body, from muscle movement to carrying messages through the nervous system to every body part
- Promotes absorption of calcium and phosphorus; regulates how much calcium remains in the blood
- Helps deposit calcium and phosphorus in bones and teeth and helps keep them strong and so reduces fracture risk
- Helps regulate cell growth
- Plays a role in immunity

Compelling evidence shows that vitamin D is linked to bone health in preventing and treating osteoporosis. Although studies are exploring other links of vitamin D to health, including cancer, diabetes, and autoimmune conditions such as multiple sclerosis, among others, the evidence isn't sufficient to offer guidance. Some research suggests that vitamin D may protect against colon cancer and perhaps prostate and breast cancer; again, evidence isn't sufficient.

Vitamin D is unique because sunlight, or ultraviolet (UV), that touches skin, even on a cloudy day, lets the body make vitamin D. (Be aware, however, that tanning beds, as well as too much sunlight, also increase risks for skin cancer and early aging of skin.) That is why vitamin D is known also as the "sunshine vitamin." Your skin makes less vitamin D if you are dark skinned, if sunlight is filtered through windows, or if you are outside on cloudy days or in shade on sunny days.

To lower your risk for sunburn, wear protective clothing, and apply sunscreen to exposed skin if you're outside longer than a few minutes. The American Academy of Dermatology recommends broad-spectrum sunscreen with an SPF (sun protection factor) of at least 30. Broad-spectrum sunscreens protect against both ultraviolet A and ultraviolet B rays; choose a water-resistant product if you're in the water or sweat a lot.

How much you need: The RDAs are listed in micrograms (mcg) and show a conversion to IUs. In the form of cholecalciferol, 1 microgram = 40 IU.

For ages one through seventy, the RDA is 15 micrograms (600 IU), cholecalciferol daily; for those over seventy, it's 20 micrograms (800 IU), daily. The level remains the same during pregnancy and breastfeeding.

The RDA for vitamin D assumes little or no sunlight exposure. The recommendation also allows for a margin of safety that recognizes differences in season, latitude, and skin pigment as well as genetic differences, among other factors, and also considers risks for skin cancer with more sun exposure.

The Dietary Guidelines for Americans recognizes vitamin D as a nutrient that is low enough in the diets of many Americans to be a public health concern. *See "A Closer Look . . . Calcium, Vitamin D, and Bone Health" in this chapter, page 427.*

If you don't consume enough. A vitamin D deficiency could occur if you don't consume or absorb enough vitamin D from food or if your kidneys can't convert vitamin D to its active form. In your older years, you may have greater loss of bone mass (osteoporosis), and your risk of softening of the bones (osteomalacia) increases with insufficient vitamin D intake.

Another reason: Limited sun exposure also affects vitamin D status, so you must consume good food sources of vitamin D and perhaps take a vitamin D supplement. If you avoid the sun, cover up with clothing or sunscreen, or live in the northern half of the United States during the winter, your skin can't make vitamin D. During cold months in the northern half of the United States, the sun's energy isn't strong enough. For the recommendation, this region is designated as the area above a line drawn between Boston and the northern border of California.

Identifying a vitamin D deficiency can be confusing since lab tests don't have standardized cutoffs to define it. According to the National Academy of Sciences, blood levels of vitamin D that are equal to or above 20 nanograms per milliliter (ng/mL), or equal to or above 50 nanomoles per liter (nmol/L) are generally considered adequate for bone and overall health in healthy people. Other sources advise a higher level of vitamin D for optimal benefits; research to learn optimal levels is ongoing. (Be clear about the units of measure if you get a lab test since they can be confusing.)

Those more likely to be vitamin D deficient include the following:

- Breastfed infants, since human milk is a poor source
- Older adults since their skin doesn't make vitamin D when exposed to sunlight as efficiently as when they were young, and their kidneys are less able to convert vitamin D to its active form
- Those with dark skin since it doesn't produce vitamin D as efficiently from sunlight
- Obese people because body fat binds with vitamin D, and so it doesn't get into the bloodstream as efficiently
- Those with health issues, such as celiac disease or Crohn's disease, who don't handle fat properly, since vitamin D needs fat for absorption

Children with a significant vitamin D deficiency may develop rickets or defective bone growth. Fortifying milk with vitamin D had virtually wiped out rickets in the United States. However, rickets is reemerging as a concern, possibly related to regular consumption of juice or soft drinks in place of milk, despite vitamin D fortification of some juices and other foods.

Curing Vitamin Deficiencies

Nutrition history is full of fascinating stories of nutrient-deficiency diseases that confounded doctors of the past.

- *Beriberi*, a deficiency of thiamin, was noted in Asia as polished, or white, rice became more popular than unrefined, or brown, rice. The cure was discovered accidentally when chickens with symptoms of beriberi ate the part of rice that was discarded after polishing. It contained the vitamin-rich germ. Today, the process of enrichment adds thiamin and other B vitamins back to polished rice, which also is fortified with folic acid.
- *Night blindness*, often caused by a deficiency of vitamin A, was known in ancient Egypt. The recommended cure of the day: eating ox or rooster livers. Today, it's well known that liver contains more vitamin A than many other foods.
- *Rickets* was prevented in the nineteenth century by giving cod liver oil to children. But not until 1922, when vitamin D was discovered, did scientists know what substance in cod liver oil gave protection.
- *Scurvy*, the scourge that plagued seafarers several hundred years ago, was finally cured by stocking ships with lemons, oranges, and limes; hence, British sailors were called "limeys." Scurvy is caused by a deficiency of vitamin C, a nutrient that citrus fruits provide in abundance.

If you consume excess amounts: Because it's stored in your body, too much vitamin D can be toxic, possibly leading to confusion, problems with heart rhythm, and kidney stones or damage. Symptoms include poor appetite, weakness, constipation, nausea, and weight loss.

An overdose usually comes from dietary supplements, not food. For ages nine and older, the UL is 100 micrograms (4,000 IU), daily. ULs remain the same during pregnancy and breastfeeding. *Note, however:* Low serum levels of vitamin D may call for greater intakes of vitamin D or for supplements; there isn't much evidence for adverse effects from higher amounts. Stay tuned.

Because the body limits its own vitamin D production, excessive sun exposure won't result in vitamin D toxicity.

Where it's mostly found: Few foods are natural sources of vitamin D. Some oily fish supply vitamin D—another reason to enjoy salmon, tuna,

	Vitamin D*	
Food	**IU**	**mcg**
Mushrooms, brown, cremini, or Italian, exposed to UV light, whole (1 cup)	1110	28
Mushrooms, white, exposed to UV light, raw (1 cup diced)	976	24
Salmon (sockeye), cooked, dry heat (3 oz.)	570	14
Cod liver oil (1 tsp.)	450	11
Tuna fish, light, canned in oil, drained solids (3 oz.)	228	5.7
Halibut, cooked, dry heat (3 oz.)	196	5
Milk, fat-free (1 cup)	115	3
Soymilk, all flavors, unsweetened vitamin D-fortified (1 cup)**	119	3
Yogurt, fruit variety, nonfat, vitamin D-fortified (8 oz.)**	127	3
Orange juice, vitamin D-fortified (1 cup)**	100	2.5
Fortified ready-to-eat cereals (about 1 oz.)	35–100	1–2.5
Egg (1 large) (vitamin D in yolk)	41	1
Tuna fish, light, canned in water, drained solids (3 oz.)	40	1

*Note that conversions vary due to rounding.

**Check the label; amounts vary. Vitamin D is required on the new Nutrition Facts label and will be shown in micrograms; *see "A Closer Look . . . Nutrition Facts Update 2016" in chapter 6, page 148, to learn more.*

See "A Closer Look . . . Calcium, Vitamin D, and Bone Health" in this chapter, page 427.

? Have you ever wondered?

. . . why mushrooms exposed to UV light have more vitamin D? Many types of mushrooms are grown commercially in dark growing rooms. Like wild mushrooms, they respond to ultraviolet light (the type of light in sunlight) once exposed to it for just a few seconds. This begins their natural process of vitamin D production.

and mackerel. As a public health strategy, most milk is vitamin D fortified, with 100 IU, or 2.5 micrograms, of vitamin D in an eight-ounce serving, but many foods made with milk aren't fortified. Today's supermarkets carry vitamin D–fortified foods: breads, breakfast cereals, cereal bars, cheese, juices, soy drinks, and yogurt, as well as eggs from hens raised on vitamin D-fortified feed. Mushrooms are another source. Some mushrooms sold today have been exposed to sunlight (or another source of ultraviolet light), which boosts their vitamin D content.

Fortified foods and dietary supplements supply vitamin D in two different forms: D_2 (ergocalciferol) and D_3 (cholecalciferol). Both increase vitamin D in your bloodstream. Current research shows that vitamins D_2 and D_3 are equally good for bone health.

Vitamin E

See also "Vitamin E: One Main Mission" in this chapter, page 424.

What it does:

- Neutralizes free radicals, which may damage cells. *See "Rounding Up Free Radicals" in this chapter, page 423.*
- Allows cells to interact to carry out their functions
- Works as an antioxidant, preventing the oxidation of LDL ("bad") cholesterol, and perhaps lowering the risk for heart disease and stroke
- Contributes to immune function
- As an antioxidant, protects essential fatty acids and vitamin A. *See "Vitamins as Antioxidants" in this chapter, page 423.*

How much you need: For ages fourteen and older, including during pregnancy, the RDA is 15 milligrams of alpha-tocopherol (22.4 IU) daily. Children under age fourteen need less, depending on their age. During breastfeeding, the RDA increases to 19 milligrams (28.4 IU) daily.

If you don't consume enough: Most healthy Americans don't show clear signs of a deficiency of vitamin E. Coming up short on vitamin E over time may cause nerve and muscle damage and make your body less able to fight off infection. Premature, very low–birth weight infants and people with poor fat absorption, cystic fibrosis, or some other chronic health problems may be deficient in vitamin E. In these cases, the nervous system and immune response can be affected.

Calculating Vitamin E

Vitamin E is a group of substances called tocopherols with different potencies. Alpha-tocopherol is its most potent form. On the original Nutrition Facts labels, the amount has been given in IUs of alpha-tocopherol. The new Nutrition Facts label will give vitamin E in milligrams.

Here's how the adult RDA of 15 milligrams daily translates to IUs for natural and synthetic forms of vitamin E:

15 mg alpha-tocopherol = About 22 IU of d-alpha-tocopherol ("natural" vitamin E from some foods and supplements)

15 mg alpha-tocopherol = About 33 IU of dl-alpha-tocopherol (synthetic vitamin E from fortified foods and some supplements)

The "natural" form of vitamin E is more fully used than the synthetic form. That's why there's a difference in the conversion factor: 100 IU of natural vitamin E equals about 150 IU of vitamin E in its synthetic form.

Because vegetable oils are good sources of vitamin E, people who cut back on total fat may not get enough. Vitamin E–fortified cereal may be a good choice.

If you consume excess amounts: Eating plenty of vitamin E–rich foods doesn't appear problematic. Taking large doses of vitamin E as a supplement hasn't been shown conclusively to have benefits—but isn't recommended. Too much may increase the risk of bleeding, may impair vitamin K action, and may increase the effect of anticoagulant medication.

For ages fourteen through eighteen, the UL of alpha-tocopherol is 800 milligrams daily; for nineteen and older, it's 1,000 milligrams daily. The levels remain the same during pregnancy and breastfeeding. If you take a supplement, 1,000 milligrams equal about 1,500 IU of natural vitamin E or 1,100 IU of dl-alpha-tocopherol (synthetic) vitamin E.

Where it's mostly found: The best sources of vitamin E are vegetable oils, such as cottonseed, safflower, and sunflower oils. That includes margarine, salad dressings, spreads, and other foods made with these oils. Nuts, especially almonds and hazelnuts, seeds (such as sunflower seeds), wheat germ—all high in oil—are good sources, too, as are peanut butter and some fortified foods, such as breakfast cereals. Green leafy vegetables also supply small amounts.

Some oils and nuts are better sources of vitamin E than others. To boost vitamin E intake, make substitutions among oils and foods with oils, without increasing your calorie intake: for example, sunflower oil in place of soybean oil, and almonds or hazelnuts in place of cashews.

Note: Heating vegetable oils to high temperatures, as in frying, destroys vitamin E.

Food	Vitamin E (mg alpha-tocopherol)
Fortified ready-to-eat cereals (about 1 oz.)*	3–15
Almonds (1 oz. or 24 nuts)	7
Sunflower seeds (1 oz.)	7
Sunflower oil, linoleic (1 tbsp.)	6
Safflower oil, high oleic (1 tbsp.)	5
Hazelnuts (1 oz.)	4
Peanut butter, smooth (2 tbsp.)	3
Corn oil (1 tbsp.)	2
Spinach, cooked (½ cup)	2
Turnip greens, cooked (½ cup)	1

*Check the label; amounts vary.

Have you ever wondered?

. . . if hair analysis is a valid way to diagnose a vitamin or mineral deficiency? Good nutrition certainly promotes healthy hair. However, except to detect poisonous elements such as lead or arsenic, hair analysis isn't a valid way to check your nutritional status. Why? Hair grows slowly; the condition of hair strands differs along their length. Chemicals used to clean and treat hair affect its composition. Differences in age and gender also affect the quality of hair. Too often, those who promote hair analysis for nutrition reasons are also trying to promote dietary supplements. Buyer, beware!

. . . if vitamin E or other nutrients in skin moisturizers gets rid of wrinkles? Vitamins, amino acids, cocoa butter, or other nutrients in skin creams and cosmetics can't remove or prevent aging skin. The possible exception is Retin-A, sold by prescription, which may slow the process. However, there's no research on its long-term effects.

Protecting your skin from damage caused by ultraviolet light (sunshine and tanning booths) is the most important way you can slow the process of wrinkling. Moisturizing your skin daily with skin cream, preferably one containing a sun block of SPF 30 or higher, will help, too.

Healthy eating overall promotes healthy skin. Skin creams with vitamins don't necessarily affect blood levels for those vitamins and cannot replace the nutrients from food.

Vitamin K

What it does:

- Makes proteins that cause your blood to coagulate, or clot, when you bleed so that the bleeding stops
- Regulates calcium metabolism
- Plays a key role in cellular signaling and proliferation
- Helps your body make some other body proteins for your blood, bones, and kidneys

How much you need: For ages fourteen through eighteen, the Adequate Intake (AI) is 75 micrograms daily. For those aged nineteen and older, it increases to 120 micrograms daily for men and 90 micrograms daily for women. The levels remain the same during pregnancy and breastfeeding. To make sure infants have enough, newborns typically receive an injection of vitamin K.

If you don't get enough: Blood doesn't coagulate normally. A deficiency may reduce bone strength and increase the chance of osteoporosis. Except due to rare health problems, a deficiency of vitamin K is very unlikely. With some gastrointestinal conditions such as celiac disease, the body may not absorb as much vitamin K. Prolonged use of antibiotics could be a problem since they destroy some bacteria in the intestines that produce vitamin K.

If you consume excess amounts: No symptoms have been observed, but moderation is still the best approach. People taking blood-thinning drugs, or anticoagulants, need to eat foods with vitamin K in

Food	Vitamin K (mcg)
Spinach, cooked (½ cup)	445
Spinach, raw (1 cup)	145
Kale, raw (1 cup)	115
Broccoli, cooked, chopped (½ cup)	110
Broccoli, raw, chopped (½ cup)	45
Cabbage, raw, chopped (½ cup)	35
Green peas, frozen, cooked (½ cup)	20
Pumpkin, canned (½ cup)	20
Blueberries (½ cup)	15
Pine nuts (1 oz.)	15
Canola oil (1 tbsp.)	10
Raspberries (½ cup)	5
Hazelnuts (1 oz.)	4
Pistachios, dry roasted (1 oz.)	4

moderation. Too much can make blood clot faster. No ULs have been established.

Where it's mostly found: Like vitamin D, vitamin K can be produced on its own—this time from certain bacteria in your intestines.

The best food sources are green, leafy vegetables such as spinach and broccoli. However, a variety of foods provide smaller amounts, including some vegetables, some fruits, and some nuts.

WATER-SOLUBLE VITAMINS

Thiamin (Vitamin B_1)

What it does:

- Is essential for producing energy from carbohydrates in all cells of your body
- May contribute to maintaining mental function
- Helps regulate metabolism

How much you need: The RDA for thiamin is tied to your energy needs. For males aged fourteen and older, it's 1.2 milligrams daily. For females aged fourteen through eighteen, it's 1.0 milligram daily; for nineteen and older, it's 1.1 milligrams daily. During pregnancy and breastfeeding, the RDA increases to 1.4 milligrams daily.

If you don't consume enough: Because most people consume many grain products, a thiamin deficiency is rare in the United States today, with one exception: chronic alcoholics may not consume enough, or their body might not convert thiamin to a bioactive form. Symptoms include fatigue, weak muscles, and nerve damage. Before refined grains were enriched with thiamin, a deficiency was common, sometimes resulting in a disease called beriberi, which mainly affects the cardiovascular and nervous systems.

If you consume excess amounts: Since your body excretes any excess amount you may consume, no ULs have been established. Contrary to popular claims, extra amounts have no energy-boosting effect.

Where it's mostly found: Whole-grain and enriched grain products such as bread, rice, pasta, tortillas, and fortified cereals provide much of the thiamin you eat. Enrichment adds back nutrients, including many B vitamins, lost when grains are refined. Pork, liver, and other organ meats provide significant amounts, too.

Food	Thiamin (mcg)
Breakfast cereals, fortified with 100% DV for thiamin (1 cup)*	1.5
Pork, lean, broiled (3 oz.)	0.9
Trout, cooked, dry heat (3 oz.)	0.4
Beef liver, braised (3 oz.)	0.2
Black beans, boiled (½ cup)	0.2
Egg noodles, enriched, cooked (½ cup)	0.2
Enriched flour tortilla (1)	0.2
Rice, brown, cooked (½ cup)	0.2
Macaroni (elbow), whole wheat, cooked (½ cup)	0.1
Rice, white, long grain, enriched, cooked (½ cup)	0.1
Whole-grain bread (1 slice)	0.1

*Check the label; amounts vary.

? Have you ever wondered?

. . . what B complex vitamins are? They're a "vitamin family" with related roles in health: thiamin (vitamin B_1), riboflavin (vitamin B_2), niacin (vitamin B_3), pantothenic acid (vitamin B_5), pyridoxine (vitamin B_6), biotin (vitamin B_7), folate (vitamin B_9), and cobalamin (vitamin B_{12}). Besides their varied, unique functions in the body, most B vitamins help the body produce energy within its trillions of cells.

. . . how cooking affects the vitamin content of foods? Water-soluble vitamins are destroyed more easily during food preparation, processing, and storage than fat-soluble vitamins are. *See "How to . . . Keep Nutrients In" in chapter 8, page 248, for food handling tips to retain vitamins.*

Riboflavin (Vitamin B_2)

What it does:

- Helps produce energy in all cells of your body
- Helps convert the amino acid called tryptophan in your food to niacin
- Helps support cell growth
- Works as an antioxidant to protect against free radicals, which may inhibit damage to body cells
- Helps regulate metabolism

How much you need: As with thiamin, the RDA for riboflavin is tied to your energy needs. For males aged fourteen and older, it's 1.3 milligrams daily. For females aged fourteen through eighteen, it's 1.0 milligram daily; for nineteen and older, it's 1.1 milligrams daily. During pregnancy, the RDA increases to 1.4 milligrams daily, and during breastfeeding, to 1.6 milligrams daily.

If you don't consume enough: Except for people who are severely malnourished, a deficiency isn't likely. Deficiency symptoms include eye disorders (including cataracts); dry, flaky skin; and a sore, red tongue. Contrary to popular myth, riboflavin deficiency doesn't cause hair loss.

If you consume excess amounts: There are no reported problems from consuming excess amounts; no ULs have been established. Riboflavin is not known to interact with any medications.

Where it's mostly found: Milk and other dairy foods are major sources of riboflavin. Some organ meats—liver, kidney, and heart—are excellent sources. Enriched bread and other grain products, eggs, meat, nuts, and green, leafy vegetables supply smaller amounts. Because ultraviolet light, such as sunlight, destroys riboflavin, most milk is packed in opaque plastic or cardboard containers, not clear glass.

Food	Riboflavin (mg)
Beef liver, braised (3 oz.)	3.5
Milk, low-fat (1 cup)	0.5
Yogurt, fruit variety, fat-free (8 oz.)	0.4
Almonds, dry roasted (1 oz.)	0.3
Pork, loin, lean, roasted (3 oz.)	0.3
Egg (1 large)	0.2
Spinach, cooked (½ cup)	0.2
Bread, white, enriched (1 slice)	0.1
Bread, whole grain (1 slice)	0.1
Cheese, Cheddar or Swiss (1 oz.)	0.1
Quinoa, cooked (½ cup)	0.1

Niacin

What it does:

- Plays a key role in all aspects of metabolism, including cell growth and energy production
- Helps enzymes function normally in your body
- Helps your body use sugars and fatty acids

How much you need: Niacin recommendations are given in NE, or niacin equivalents. This is because it comes from two sources: niacin itself and from the amino acid called tryptophan, part of which converts to niacin.

As with thiamin and riboflavin, the recommendation is tied to your energy needs. For males aged fourteen and older, the RDA is 16 milligrams NE daily; for females, it's 14 milligrams NE daily. During pregnancy, the RDA increases to 18 milligrams NE daily, and during breastfeeding, it is 17 milligrams NE daily.

If you don't consume enough: For people who consume adequate amounts of protein-rich foods, a niacin deficiency isn't likely. Pellagra is caused by a significant niacin deficiency. Symptoms include diarrhea, mental disorientation, and skin problems.

If you consume excess amounts: Consuming excessive amounts, not likely from food, may cause flushed skin, rashes, or liver damage. For ages fourteen through eighteen, the UL is 30 milligrams NE daily; for nineteen and older, it's 35 milligrams NE daily. The levels remain the same during pregnancy and breastfeeding. Self-prescribing large doses of niacin to lower blood cholesterol may lead to adverse effects—and may not give cholesterol-lowering benefits. If your doctor prescribes niacin, take it in the recommended dosage.

Where it's mostly found: Foods high in protein are typically good sources of niacin: meat, poultry, fish, beans and peas, and peanut butter. Niacin is also added to many enriched and fortified grain products.

Food	Niacin (mg NE)
Turkey breast, roasted, meat only (3 oz.)	10.0
Beef, ground, 95 percent lean, broiled (3 oz.)	5.0
Peanut butter, smooth (2 tbsp.)	4.5
Tilapia, cooked, dry heat (3 oz.)	4.0
Brown rice, cooked (½ cup)	2.5
Enriched pita bread (one 4-inch diameter)	1.5
Enriched spaghetti, cooked (½ cup)	1.0
Lima beans, boiled (½ cup)	1.0
Pinto beans, canned, drained (½ cup)	0.4
Yogurt, fruit variety, fat-free (8 oz.)	0.2

Vitamin B_6 (Pyridoxine)

What it does:

- Helps your body make nonessential amino acids, or protein components, which are then used to make body cells
- Helps turn the amino acid called tryptophan into two important body substances: niacin and serotonin (a messenger in your brain)
- Helps produce other body chemicals, including insulin, hemoglobin, and antibodies that fight infection
- May contribute to maintaining healthy immune function
- Helps regulate metabolism

? Have you ever wondered?

. . . about the difference between the terms "enriched" and "fortified"? Both terms indicate that nutrients—usually vitamins or minerals—were added to make a food more nutritious.

- *Enriched* means adding nutrients that were lost during food processing. For example, B vitamins and iron lost when wheat is processed are added to refined white flour. Enrichment of refined grains is not mandatory; however, those that are labeled as enriched (e.g., enriched flour) must meet the standard of identity for enrichment set by the FDA.
- *Fortified* means deliberately adding one or more nutrients to food whether or not they were present originally. For example, milk is fortified with vitamin D, a nutrient that helps your body absorb milk's calcium and phosphorus. Fortification may be used to prevent or correct a demonstrated nutrient deficiency, perhaps for a population or specific population groups; to restore naturally occurring nutrients lost during processing, storage, or handling; or to add a nutrient to a food at the level found in a comparable traditional food.

  When cereal grains are labeled as enriched, they must be fortified with folic acid. Grain products are fortified with folic acid to reduce the incidence of certain birth defects.

. . . if microwave cooking destroys vitamins? Even if you cook foods properly, some water-soluble vitamins, such as B vitamins and vitamin C, can be destroyed. For several reasons, more vitamins are retained with microwave cooking than with most other methods: very short cooking time, covered cooking, and little or no cooking water contribute to this.

How much you need: For females aged fourteen through eighteen, the RDA for vitamin B_6 is 1.2 milligrams daily; for nineteen through fifty, it's 1.3 milligrams daily; for fifty-one and older, 1.5 milligrams daily. For males aged fourteen through fifty, the RDA is 1.3 milligrams daily; for fifty-one and older, it's 1.7 milligrams daily. During pregnancy, the RDA increases to 1.9 milligrams daily, and during breastfeeding, to 2.0 milligrams daily. For infants, breast milk and properly prepared infant formulas contain enough.

If you don't consume enough: A deficiency can cause confusion, mental convulsions, depression, a sore tongue, or greasy, flaky skin. A deficiency also may increase blood levels of homocysteine, an amino acid. Some evidence suggests that an elevated homocysteine level may increase the risk for heart disease and stroke.

If you consume excess amounts: Large doses, over time from supplements, can cause nerve damage and other symptoms. For ages fourteen through eighteen, the UL is 80 milligrams daily; for nineteen and older, it's 100 milligrams daily. The levels remain the same during pregnancy and breastfeeding. *See "Dietary Reference Intakes" in the appendix, page 780, for ULs for other age groups.*

Where it's mostly found: Vitamin B_6 is found in a wide variety of foods including fortified cereals, meat, poultry, fish, beans and peas, and some vegetables and fruits.

Food	Vitamin B_6 (mg)
Ready-to-eat cereal, 100% fortified (¾ cup)*	2.0
Garbanzo beans, canned, drained (½ cup)	0.9
Chicken breast, meat only, roasted (3 oz.)	0.5
Banana, raw (1 medium)	0.4
Potato, small, baked, with skin (5 oz.)	0.4
Pork, loin, lean only, cooked (3 oz.)	0.4
Trout, rainbow, cooked (3 oz.)	0.3
Squash, acorn, baked (½ cup)	0.2
Walnuts, English (1 oz.)	0.2
Peanut butter, smooth (2 tbsp.)	0.1

*Check the label; amounts vary.

Folate (Folic Acid or Folacin)

What it does:

- Plays an essential role in making new body cells by helping to produce DNA and RNA, the cell's master plan for cell reproduction. It also helps prevent changes to DNA that may lead to cancer.
- Works with vitamin B_{12} to form hemoglobin in red blood cells and prevent anemia
- May help protect against heart disease
- Helps lower the risk of delivering a baby with a brain or spinal-cord defect such as spina bifida
- Helps control plasma homocysteine levels, linked to increased cardiovascular disease risk

How much you need: Folate can come from foods with naturally occurring folate as well as from foods that are fortified with folic acid and from supplements. For ages fourteen and older, the RDA is 400 micrograms daily. During pregnancy, it increases to 600 micrograms daily, and during breastfeeding, to 500 micrograms daily.

If you don't consume enough: A deficiency affects normal cell division and protein synthesis, especially impairing growth. Anemia, caused by malformed blood cells that can't carry as much oxygen, may result from a deficiency. This type of anemia differs from the form caused by a lack of iron in the diet, *addressed in "Anemia: Tired Blood" in chapter 25, page 722.* Other symptoms include fatigue, heart palpitations, headache, and shortness of breath.

Pregnant teens and women who don't get enough folate, especially during the first trimester, have a greater risk of delivering a baby with neural tube defects such as spina bifida. A deficiency also increases the chance of delivering a premature or low-birth weight baby.

Those with a greater chance of not getting enough folate include females aged fourteen through thirty (especially before and during pregnancy), those who have disorders that lower nutrient absorption such as celiac disease and inflammatory bowel disease, and those with alcoholism.

If you consume excess amounts: Consuming too much makes it hard to diagnose a vitamin B_{12} deficiency and may interfere with some medications yet offer no known benefits.

For ages fourteen through eighteen, the UL is 800 micrograms daily of folic acid, the form of folate in fortified foods and supplements. For ages nineteen and older, the UL is 1,000 micrograms daily. The levels remain the same during pregnancy and breastfeeding. Adults over age fifty should talk to their doctor about their vitamin B_{12} status before taking a supplement containing folic acid; *see "The B Vitamins: 6, 12, and Folate" in chapter 20, page 581, to learn more.*

Where it's mostly found: Fruits (especially avocadoes and oranges), fruit juices, beans and peas, lentils, liver, nuts, peanuts, and many vegetables (especially dark-green leafy vegetables, asparagus, and Brussels sprouts) are among the good sources of naturally occurring folate.

Food	Folate (mcg)
Breakfast cereals, fortified with folic acid (¾ to 1 cup)*	100–400
Spinach, boiled (½ cup)	130
Navy beans, boiled (½ cup)	125
Wheat germ (¼ cup)	80
Orange juice, 100 percent (1 cup)	75
Rice, long grain, white (enriched, fortified), cooked (½ cup)	75
Romaine lettuce, shredded (1 cup)	65
Avocado, sliced (½ cup)	60
Bread, white (enriched, fortified) (1 slice)	35-45
Peanuts, dry roasted (1 oz.)	25
Bread, whole wheat (1 slice)	15
Rice, brown, cooked (½ cup)	10

*Check the label; amounts vary.

Enriched grain products (breads, crackers, flour, macaroni, noodles, and rice) must be fortified with folic acid. Some breakfast cereals are fortified at 400 micrograms per serving—100 percent of the RDA for many. Unenriched grain products, such as some imported pastas, may not be fortified; check the Nutrition Facts label.

Many whole-grain breads and other whole-grain products are not fortified with folic acid; again, check the Nutrition Facts. If you prefer mostly whole-grain foods, then choose some that are folic-acid fortified, as advised by the Dietary Guidelines for Americans.

Vitamin B_{12} (Cobalamin)

What it does:

- Works with folate to make red blood cells and also helps make DNA, the genetic material in cells
- Serves as a vital part of many body chemicals and so occurs in every body cell
- Helps use fatty acids and some amino acids
- May contribute to maintaining mental function
- Plays a critical role in cell division and growth

How much you need: For ages fourteen and older, the RDA is 2.4 micrograms daily. During pregnancy, it increases to 2.6 micrograms daily, and during breastfeeding, to 2.8 micrograms daily.

Those aged fifty and older may be advised to consume foods fortified with vitamin B_{12}, such as fortified cereals, or dietary supplements. On average, adults of this age consume enough vitamin B_{12}. However, some may not be able to absorb naturally occurring vitamin B_{12}; the crystalline form in fortified foods and supplements is well absorbed.

If you don't consume enough: A deficiency may result in megaloblastic anemia, fatigue, and nerve damage such as numb or tingling hands and feet, as well as problems with balance, depression, poor memory, a smooth tongue, or very sensitive skin. A deficiency of vitamin B_{12} can be masked—and even progress—if extra folic acid is taken to treat or prevent megaloblastic anemia.

For either genetic or medical reasons, some people develop a deficiency—pernicious anemia—because they can't absorb vitamin B_{12}. They're missing a body chemical called "intrinsic factor" that comes from their stomach lining. This problem can be medically treated with injections of vitamin B_{12}.

Vegans, who eat no animal products, and infants of vegan mothers are at risk for developing a vitamin B_{12} deficiency. This could cause severe anemia and irreversible nerve damage. Older adults also are at risk. Consuming foods fortified with vitamin B_{12} or dietary supplements can prevent a deficiency.

If you consume excess amounts: No symptoms are known, but there is no basis in science for taking extra vitamin B_{12} to boost energy. No ULs have been established.

Where it's mostly found: Vitamin B_{12} comes from animal products—meat, poultry, finfish, eggs, milk, and other dairy foods. Some fortified foods may contain it.

Food	Vitamin B_{12} (mcg)
Liver, beef, cooked (3 oz.)	58.0
Breakfast cereals, fortified with vitamin B_{12}* (¾ to 1 cup)	1.5–6.0
Salmon, sockeye, cooked (3 oz.)	3.8
Beef, ground, 95 percent lean, broiled (3 oz.)	2.1
Milk, fat-free (1 cup)	1.2
Yogurt, fruit variety, fat-free (8 oz.)	1.1
Egg (1 large)	0.4
Cheese, cheddar (1 oz.)	0.3
Chicken breast, meat only, roasted (3 oz.)	0.3

*Check the label; amounts vary.

Biotin

What it does:

- Helps your body produce energy in all cells of your body
- Helps metabolize (or use) proteins, fats, and carbohydrates from food
- Helps regulate hormone synthesis

How much you need: For ages fourteen to eighteen, the AI is 25 micrograms daily; for nineteen and older, including during pregnancy, it's 30 micrograms daily. During breastfeeding, the AI increases to 35 micrograms daily.

If you don't consume enough: That's rarely a problem for healthy people who eat a healthy diet because the body also produces biotin from intestinal bacteria. In rare cases of deficiency, these symptoms may appear: heart abnormalities, appetite loss, fatigue, depression, or dry skin.

If you consume excess amounts: There are no reported effects of consuming excess amounts. No ULs have been established.

Where it's mostly found: Biotin is found in small amounts in a wide variety of foods. Eggs, liver, tree nuts, peanuts, and some vegetables are among the best sources.

Food	Biotin (mcg)
Beef liver, cooked (3 oz.)	34
Egg (1 large)	10
Peanuts, dry roasted (1 oz.)	5
Salmon, pink, canned in water (3 oz.)	5
Sunflower seeds, roasted (1 oz.)	2
Sweet potato, cooked (½ cup)	2
Almonds, roasted (1 oz.)	1

Source: Journal of Food Composition and Analysis, December, 2004.

Pantothenic Acid

What it does:

- Helps produce energy in all cells of your body
- Helps metabolize (or use) proteins, fats, and carbohydrates from food
- Helps regulate hormone synthesis

How much you need: For ages fourteen and older, the AI is 5 milligrams daily. During pregnancy, it increases to 6 milligrams daily, and during breastfeeding, to 7 milligrams daily.

If you don't consume enough: That's rarely a problem for healthy people who eat a healthy diet. In rare cases of a deficiency, symptoms may include depression, fatigue, insomnia, irritability, stomach pains, vomiting, or upper-respiratory infections.

If you consume excess amounts: The only apparent effects are occasional diarrhea and water retention, no ULs have been established.

Food	Pantothenic Acid (mg)
Yogurt, plain, fat-free (8 oz.)	1.3
Sweet potato, mashed, cooked (½ cup)	1.0
Milk, fat-free (1 cup)	0.9
Turkey, meat only, roasted (3 oz.)	0.9
Avocado, (¼ cup puree)	0.8
Egg (1 large)	0.8
Corn, yellow, canned (½ cup)	0.6
Ham, lean, 11 percent (3 oz.)	0.4
Kidney beans, cooked (½ cup)	0.2
Whole-wheat macaroni, cooked (½ cup)	0.2

Where it's mostly found: Pantothenic acid is widely available in food. Meat, poultry, fish, whole-grain cereals, and beans and peas are among the better sources. Milk, vegetables, and fruits also contain varying amounts.

Choline

What it does: A vitamin-like substance, choline plays a role in many body processes.

- Promotes the transport of fats and helps make substances that form cell membranes
- Helps make acetylcholine, which is a neurotransmitter needed for many functions, including muscle control and memory storage
- Plays a role in liver function and reproductive health
- Works with folate during pregnancy for the development of a baby's brain and nervous system

How much you need: For males aged fourteen and older, the AI is 550 milligrams daily. For females aged fourteen to eighteen, it's 400 milligrams daily; for nineteen and older, it's 425 milligrams daily. During pregnancy, the AI increases to 450 milligrams daily and during breastfeeding, to 550 milligrams daily.

If you don't consume enough: Although there's little evidence of significant deficiencies in the United States, many people still come up short on choline. Inadequate intake may have health risks. A choline deficiency may be linked to an increased risk of heart disease because it results in increased homocysteine levels.

If you consume excess amounts: For ages fourteen to eighteen, the UL is 3.0 grams daily; for nineteen and older, it's 3.5 grams daily. The levels remain the same during pregnancy and breastfeeding.

Where it's mostly found: Choline is a natural food component found in a wide variety of foods. Consuming eggs and beans and peas in place of some meat and poultry may provide enough. Meat, eggs, soybeans, and peanuts are especially good sources. With the FDA approval of a nutrient-content claim for choline on food labels, more choline-fortified products have appeared in the marketplace.

Food	Choline (mg)
Beef liver, braised (3 oz.)	358
Egg (1 large)	147
Salmon, pink, canned (3 oz.)	96
Beef, ground, 95 percent lean, broiled (3 oz.)	73
Chicken breast, meat only, roasted (3 oz.)	73
Tofu, firm, made with calcium sulfate (½ cup)	35
Peanut butter, smooth (2 tbsp.)	20
Pistachios (1 oz.)	20

Vitamin C (Ascorbic Acid)

What it does:

- Helps produce collagen, a connective tissue that holds muscles, bones, and other tissues together
- Helps keep capillary walls and blood vessels firm, and so protects you from bruising
- Helps your body absorb iron and folate from plant sources of food
- Helps keep your gums healthy so they don't bleed
- Helps heal any cuts and wounds
- Protects you from infection by stimulating the formation of antibodies and so boosting immunity
- Works as an antioxidant to neutralize free radicals, which may inhibit damage to body cells

Vitamin C works in partnership with iron, helping the body to absorb iron from plant sources of food. *See "A: Closer Look . . . Iron" in this chapter, page 438.* In fact, an adequate daily supply of vitamin C in your food choices can increase the absorption of nonheme iron (mostly from plant sources) by as much as two to four times. For those who get most of their iron from plant sources of food, including vegetarians, vitamin C is of special importance.

How much you need: For males aged fourteen to eighteen, the RDA is 75 milligrams daily; for nineteen and older, it's 90 milligrams (about the amount in ¾ cup of orange juice) daily. For females aged fourteen to eighteen, it's 65 milligrams daily; for nineteen and older, it's 75 milligrams daily. During pregnancy, the RDA increases to 80 milligrams daily for those under age eighteen and to 85 milligrams for ages eighteen and older, and during breastfeeding, it increases to 115 milligrams daily for those under age eighteen and to 120 milligrams daily for ages eighteen and older. *See "Dietary Reference Intakes" in the appendix, page 780, for RDAs for other age groups.*

For people who smoke, the RDA for vitamin C is increased by 35 milligrams daily to help counteract the oxidative damage from nicotine. Being regularly exposed to secondhand smoke may increase vitamin C needs as well.

If you don't consume enough: Eventually, a severe deficiency of vitamin C leads to scurvy, a disease that causes loose teeth, excessive bleeding, and swollen gums. Wounds may not heal properly either. Because vitamin C–rich foods are widely available, scurvy is rare in the United States today.

If you consume excess amounts: Because vitamin C is water soluble, your body excretes the excess; high levels of vitamin C in urine can interfere with the results of tests for diabetes. Very large doses may cause kidney stones and/or diarrhea, and for those with iron overload (hemochromatosis), excessive vitamin C (which enhances iron absorption) can worsen iron overload and damage body tissues. But the effects of taking

? Have you ever wondered?

. . . if bleeding gums mean you're not getting enough vitamin C? It's not likely unless you have a severe deficiency. Most cases of bleeding gums come from inadequate oral hygiene, especially a lack of regular flossing. Brushing and flossing regularly help keep your gums healthy. *See "Oral Health: Your Healthy Smile" in chapter 25, page 735, for more about healthy gums.*

large amounts for a long time aren't known. For ages fourteen to eighteen, the UL is 1,800 milligrams daily; for nineteen and older, it's 2,000 milligrams daily. The levels remain the same during pregnancy and breastfeeding. *See "Dietary Reference Intakes" in the appendix, page 780, for ULs for other age groups.*

Where it's mostly found: Vitamin C mainly comes from plant sources of food. All citrus fruits, including grapefruits, oranges, and tangerines, are good sources. And many other fruits and vegetables listed below supply significant amounts, too.

Some fruit drinks, bottled waters, and other processed foods are fortified with vitamin C. Check the Nutrition Facts label. If you rely only on fortified foods as your vitamin C source, you may miss out on other nutrients and compounds in foods with naturally occurring vitamin C.

Food	Vitamin C (mg)
Tomato juice, canned (6 oz.)*	130
Bell pepper, red, chopped (½ cup)	95
Orange juice, 100 percent (6 oz.)	95
Papaya (1 small)	95
Bell pepper, green, chopped (½ cup)	60
Strawberries, sliced (½ cup)	50
Grapefruit, white (½ cup)	40
Broccoli, raw, spear (5-in.)	30
Cantaloupe, cubes (½ cup)	30
Mango, chopped (½ cup)	30
Cabbage, red, raw, chopped (½ cup)	25
Collard greens, frozen, boiled (½ cup)	20
Potato, baked, with skin, small (5 oz.)	15
Tomato, raw (1 medium)	15

*Check the label; amounts vary.

VITAMINS AS ANTIOXIDANTS

You've probably read the headlines "Antioxidants Promote Health" or "Antioxidants Prevent Aging." Many food manufacturers are fortifying foods with beta-carotene (which forms vitamin A in the body), vitamin C, and vitamin E, as well as selenium (a mineral) which also work as antioxidants.

Antioxidants are a handful of vitamins, minerals, and some phytonutrients (carotenoids and polyphenols) present in a variety of foods that significantly slow or prevent damage from oxygen and so prevent or repair damage to body cells. Some may also improve immune function and perhaps lower the risk for infection and cancer.

What makes them unique? What foods supply them naturally? How might they work in your body? And how might they promote health and reduce risk for chronic disease? Since antioxidant research is new, evidence for their roles in health is still emerging.

Rounding Up Free Radicals

Just how do antioxidant vitamins work? First let's learn more about oxygen, which is basic to life. To produce energy, every cell in your body needs a constant supply of oxygen.

How free radicals form. When body cells burn oxygen as they produce energy (oxidation), they form free radicals, or oxygen by-products. Chemically speaking, free radicals are unstable molecules with a missing electron. They can damage body cells and tissues as well as DNA, your body's master plan for reproducing cells. Inflammation, stress, and environmental factors such as cigarette smoke, pollution, and ultraviolet light also cause free radicals to form.

Actually, you're probably familiar with damage caused by oxidation: for example, the quick browning on a cut apple or pear and rancidity in oils are caused by oxidation. But, if you dip your apple or pear in orange or lemon juice, which has vitamin C, it stays white. And if vitamin E is added as a preservative to vegetable oil, it doesn't turn rancid as fast.

In your body, the process is similar. Free radicals cause oxidation, or cell damage, as they "steal" an electron from body cells to become stable. While having some level of free radicals in your body is natural and offers some health benefits, excessive levels, over time, may damage cells and contribute to the onset of health problems such as cancer, artery and heart disease, cataracts, age-related macular degeneration, type 2 diabetes, Alzheimer's disease, and some deterioration that goes with aging. Antioxidants in your body counteract the damaging action of free radicals.

How antioxidants work. Three antioxidant vitamins appear to neutralize free radicals: beta-carotene and other carotenoids, vitamin C, and vitamin E. Some enzymes that have trace minerals—selenium, copper, zinc, and manganese—and some phytonutrients act as antioxidants, too; *see "Phytonutrients: Different from Nutrients" in chapter 15, page 448.*

As scavengers, antioxidant vitamins mop up free radicals by donating an electron of their own. The result? Antioxidants may control free radicals or convert them to harmless waste that your body eliminates before they cause damage. Antioxidants may even help undo some damage done to body cells.

Each antioxidant has its own biological job description. Being water soluble, vitamin C removes free radicals from fluids inside and outside of body cells. Beta-carotene and vitamin E, because they're fat soluble, are present in your body's lipids and fat tissues. Antioxidants seem to complement each other, and because they work together, an excess or a deficiency of one may inhibit the benefits of others.

Scientific evidence can't promise that antioxidant nutrients provide a "safety shield" from chronic diseases. Their role and potential interactions in reducing the risks are among many unknowns. And we don't know the potentially adverse effects of ongoing, high intakes of these nutrients from supplements, either. Still, a varied diet—that follows a healthy eating plan, *discussed in chapter 2*—with plenty of antioxidant-containing vegetables, fruits, and whole grains is smart eating!

Carotenoids: "Color" Your Food Healthy

Imagine a beautiful autumn day. Leaves of red, orange, and yellow rustle in the branches overhead. The colors of the season belong to carotenoids, or plant pigments that generally are red, orange, and deep yellow.

? Have you ever wondered?

. . . if beta-carotene supplements offer protection for smokers? No research supports any benefit. More importantly, a large study of smokers indicated that beta-carotene supplements may be harmful to smokers. Smokers who used supplemental beta-carotene had a higher incidence of lung cancer than those who didn't. For nonsmokers, it's still unknown whether higher intakes of beta-carotene offer benefits.

. . . what happened to the ORAC score for antioxidants? The ORAC (oxygen radical absorbance capacity) database, indicating a food's antioxidant capacity, has been withdrawn from the US Department of Agriculture's website for several reasons.

Research on antioxidants is relatively new, with many unanswered questions about foods' antioxidant capacity and the effects on the human body. Whether data on antioxidant levels from lab studies apply to effects on humans is uncertain. Also, it's known that antioxidants do far more than absorb free radicals. In addition, ORAC values have been misused in food and supplement marketing and by consumers in making their food and supplement choices.

Until more is known, the better guideline is to eat a variety and plenty of antioxidant-rich plant-based foods, including vegetables, fruits, beans, nuts, seeds, and whole grains.

The array of colors in vegetables and fruits also comes from carotenoids. Clues to their presence are obvious in the vibrant palette of produce in your supermarket. It's no surprise that apricots, cantaloupes, carrots, mangoes, red and yellow bell peppers, and sweet potatoes contain carotene. Broccoli, kale, romaine lettuce, and spinach have carotene, too—even though they're dark green. The orange-yellow color gets hidden by the chlorophyll in the leaves.

While beta-carotene is the best-known carotenoid, the plant world has more than six hundred known carotenoids. Of those, only a few have been analyzed in vegetables and fruits: alpha-carotene, beta-carotene, beta-cryptoxanthin, gamma-carotene, lycopene, lutein, and zeaxanthin—even then, data are limited.

Of the more than six hundred identified carotenoids, only about 10 percent, including beta-carotene, perform as precursors, or substances from which vitamin A is formed. Carotenoids also have other health-promoting functions. Various carotenoids seem to offer protection from some diseases, such as cancer, and degenerative changes, such as macular degeneration, that accompany aging.

Color is a clue, not an assurance, that vegetables and fruits are good sources of beta-carotene. Despite their color, neither corn nor snow peas have much beta-carotene—but do supply other nutrients and phytonutrients.

Try to choose red, orange, deep-yellow, and some dark-green leafy vegetables every day. *See "Vitamin A and Carotenoids: Sources" in this chapter, page 412.* No Dietary Reference Intakes (no RDA, AI, or UL) specifically for carotenoids have been established yet except as precursors to vitamin A. Be cautious: consuming too much of them from dietary supplements may have an adverse effect. *See "Nutrient Supplements" in chapter 10, page 316.*

Vitamin C: An Antioxidant

Over the years, vitamin C, also known as ascorbic acid, developed celebrity status with claims that it can prevent or cure the common cold. Although those claims have been overblown, an adequate intake of vitamin C does play an important role in fighting infection; *see "A Closer Look . . . How to Build Your Immunity" in chapter 25, page 724.*

As an antioxidant, vitamin C may protect your body in much the same way that beta-carotene and vitamin E do. However, vitamin C attacks free radicals in body fluids, not in fat tissue. Preliminary research is exploring a link to reduced risk for cataracts and cancer; no evidence exists to advise consuming more than the RDA for vitamin C.

Because vitamin C isn't stored in the body, you're wise to consume a vitamin C–rich food daily. A habit of including it with breakfast probably provides enough.

Vitamin E: One Main Mission

For years, vitamin E has been surrounded by pseudoscientific myths. It's been misguidedly acclaimed as a cure for almost all that ails you: for example, improving sexual prowess, curing infertility, preventing aging, curing heart disease and cancer, and improving athletic performance, to name a few. Vitamin E benefits don't extend this far, but this vitamin does seem to play a broad role in promoting health.

The main role of vitamin E—a fat-soluble vitamin—appears to be as an antioxidant. It may help prevent the oxidation of LDL ("bad") cholesterol, which contributes to plaque buildup in the arteries, and so help reduce the risk for heart disease and stroke. The jury is still out on these claims, however. Vitamin E also may help protect against cell damage that can lead ultimately to health problems such as cancer. Vitamin E appears to work with other antioxidants such as vitamin C and selenium.

Found in vegetable oils, nuts, and seeds, vitamin E protects unsaturated fats from oxidation. Foods such as these, which are high in unsaturated fats, are often good sources of vitamin E.

A "Garden" of Antioxidants

Vegetables and fruits are undisputed as the best sources of antioxidant vitamins. Antioxidant vitamins in vegetables and fruits may work together to reduce chronic disease risks, giving one more reason to eat a variety of them. Whole-grain foods and nuts containing vitamin E provide them, too.

Many foods are fortified with antioxidant vitamins: C, E, and beta-carotene. While fortified foods may not supply enough antioxidants for possible protective benefits, they're often good sources. For carotenoids and vitamin C, vegetables and fruits still are the best sources, as they contain other phytonutrients that may help protect against some health problems such as some cancers and heart disease. *See "Phytonutrients: Different from Nutrients" in chapter 15, page 448.*

Antioxidants in Supplements

Even if a little is good, a lot may not be better. So far, no research proves that taking beta-carotene, vitamins C or E, or other antioxidant supplements reduces disease risk.

To date, scientists haven't pinpointed which antioxidants offer specific benefits, how much would be enough, or how long you'd need to take them. Not enough is known about side effects from taking supplemental antioxidants over long periods of time. Also unknown: Might the mix of antioxidants in food, not just one or two from supplements, offer positive and powerful antioxidant action?

Many other antioxidant issues also need research. First, not all free radicals are harmful. Some protect by attacking harmful bacteria or cancer cells in the body. Second, high doses from antioxidant supplements may be harmful, perhaps by working to promote, rather than neutralize, oxidation. Very high intakes of antioxidants may destroy or hinder protective free radicals.

Until more is known, enjoy a wide variety of vegetables, fruits, whole-grain foods, and nuts and seeds, with their naturally occurring antioxidants. And avoid high doses from supplements. *See "Antioxidant Nutrients: Enough, or Too Much?" in chapter 10, page 318.*

Minerals—Major and Trace

The term "minerals" may conjure up thoughts of rocks or gems, but to your body, minerals are another group of essential nutrients. They are needed to both regulate body processes and give your body structure.

Like vitamins, minerals help trigger, or regulate, a myriad of processes that continually take place in your body, so they are life essentials. For example, various minerals regulate fluid balance, muscle contractions, and nerve impulses. Even though they make up only about 4 percent of your weight, minerals help give your body structure—and not only to bones and teeth. Muscles, blood, and other body tissues all contain minerals, too.

Unlike vitamins, minerals are inorganic. They can't be destroyed by heat or other food-handling processes. In fact, if you've ever completely burned food, perhaps while cooking over a fire, the little bit of ash left over is its mineral content.

From a dietary perspective, minerals belong in two categories—major minerals (some are electrolytes) and trace minerals—grouped by how much you need. Regardless of amount, they're essential.

Major minerals. You need major minerals in greater amounts than trace minerals—more than 250 milligrams are advised daily for each one. Calcium, magnesium, and phosphorus fit in this category, along with three electrolytes—chloride, potassium, and sodium.

> **Electrolytes.** Sodium, along with some other major minerals (chloride and potassium), are collectively called electrolytes, so named because they transmit nerve, or electrical, impulses in your body. Compare them to electrically charged particles, or ions, in flashlight batteries. Their work is interrelated, regulating fluid balance in and out of body cells. *See "A Closer Look . . . Sodium and Potassium, A Salty Subject" in this chapter, page 433.*

Trace minerals, or trace elements. Your body needs just small amounts—fewer than 20 milligrams daily—for each: chromium, copper, fluoride, iodine, iron, manganese, molybdenum, selenium, and zinc. Recommended Dietary Allowances (RDAs) have been set for some: copper, iodine, iron, molybdenum, selenium, and zinc. Others are in the Dietary Reference Intakes (DRIs) as Adequate Intakes (AIs).

Nutrition experts have reviewed research on other trace elements: arsenic, boron, nickel, silicon, and vanadium. They don't appear to have a role in human health. However, ULs have been set for some: boron (20 milligrams daily), nickel (1.0 milligram daily), and vanadium (1.8 milligrams daily) for adult levels.

All minerals are absorbed in your intestines and then transported and stored in your body in different ways. Some pass directly into the bloodstream, where they're carried to cells; any excess passes out of the body through urine. Others attach to proteins and become part of your body structure. Because they're stored, excess amounts can be harmful if the levels consumed are too high for too long.

MAJOR MINERALS

Calcium

What it does:

- Builds bones (length and strength) and maintains healthy bones, becoming part of bone tissue
- Supports the structure and hardness of bones and teeth

? Have you ever wondered?

. . . why tortillas made with corn have calcium? Made in the traditional Mexican way, corn tortillas can supply significant amounts of calcium, especially to people who eat them as the main bread in their everyday diet. Corn itself doesn't have calcium, but to prepare corn for tortillas, it's first soaked in a solution that contains calcium hydroxide to remove the hard coating on corn kernels. This process was developed by pre-Columbian cultures many centuries before contact with Europeans. This form of calcium is bioavailable, meaning it's in a form that the body can absorb and use.

- Helps your muscles contract and your heart beat
- Carries messages in the nervous system throughout every part of the body
- Helps your blood clot if you're bleeding
- Helps blood vessels move blood throughout the body; helps release hormones and enzymes
- May help control blood pressure. *See "DASH to Health" in chapter 2, page 51, and "DASH for Better Blood Pressure" in chapter 24, page 697, to learn about high blood pressure and its calcium link.*
- Although research is limited, calcium or dairy foods may help reduce the risk of colorectal and breast cancer and may play a role in cardiovascular health.

How much you need: For males and females aged four through eight and nineteen through fifty, the RDA is 1,000 milligrams daily; for nine through eighteen, it's 1,300 milligrams. For females aged fifty-one and older and for males seventy-one and older, the RDA is 1,200 milligrams daily. During pregnancy and breastfeeding, the RDAs for each age group stay the same. Following RDA advice for vitamin D is essential, too, as these two nutrients work in partnership; *see "Vitamin D" in this chapter, page 413.*

Like vitamin D, calcium is a nutrient cited by the Dietary Guidelines for Americans as a public health concern. Many people—teens, women over age fifty, and men over age seventy—don't get enough calcium from their food choices. As a safeguard, many doctors recommend a calcium supplement, especially for menopausal and postmenopausal women, to help slow bone loss that comes with hormonal changes.

If you're advised to take calcium supplements, use them to fill the calcium gap—not to substitute for calcium-rich foods. *See "A Closer Look . . . Calcium and Iron Supplements" in chapter 10, page 320.*

Others who may not get enough calcium include vegans who eat no animal products, those with unmanaged lactose intolerance, and women of childbearing age who have amenorrhea (when menstrual periods stop well before the menopause years) because they eat too little or exercise too much.

If you don't consume enough: In the short term, your body gets the calcium it needs from your bones. But even a mild deficiency over a lifetime can affect bone density and bone loss, increasing the risk for osteoporosis, or brittle bone disease. For children, not getting enough calcium may interfere with growth and may increase the risk of pediatric fractures. A severe deficiency may keep children from reaching their potential adult height, and for anyone, it can lead to numbness, convulsions, and abnormal heart rhythms.

If you consume excess amounts: Unless the doses are very large (more than 2,500 milligrams daily), adverse effects for adults are unlikely. Very large doses of calcium over a prolonged time may cause kidney stones and poor kidney function and may affect the absorption of other minerals such as iron, magnesium, and zinc. Regular consumption of milk and milk products won't result in excessive amounts of calcium.

For ages one through eight and nineteen through fifty, the UL is 2,500 milligrams daily; for nine through eighteen, it's 3,000 milligrams daily; for fifty-one and older, 2,000 milligrams daily. The levels remain the same during pregnancy and breastfeeding. Chronic heartburn may result from consuming antacids with calcium in amounts beyond the recommended dosage.

Food	Calcium (mg)
Tofu, regular, raw (prepared with calcium sulfate*) (½ cup)	435
Chocolate milk, low-fat (1 cup)	320
Yogurt, plain, low-fat (6 oz.)	310
Milk, fat-free (1 cup)	300
Soymilk, added calcium* (8 oz.)	300
Orange juice, added calcium* (6 oz.)	265
Cheese, Swiss (1 oz.)	250
Salmon, chum, canned with edible bones (3 oz.)	210
Cheese, cheddar (1 oz.)	200
Frozen yogurt, fat-free (½ cup)	100
Turnip greens, chopped, boiled (½ cup)	100
Mustard greens, chopped, boiled (½ cup)	85
Tempeh, cooked (3 oz.)	80
Cottage cheese, low-fat (½ cup)	70
Orange (1 medium)	50
Corn tortilla, made from slaked lime–processed corn* (one 6-inch diameter)	45
Pinto beans, boiled (½ cup)	40

*Check the label; amounts vary.

Calcium, Vitamin D, and Bone Health

The human body contains more calcium than any other mineral. For an average 130-pound adult, about 1,200 grams (almost 3 pounds) of the body is calcium. The amount in your body, of course, depends on the size of your body's frame, the density of your bones, and, if you're older, how much bone mass you've lost through aging.

About 99 percent of your body's calcium is in your bones. The remaining 1 percent is in other body fluids and cells. Calcium is as important in your food choices as an adult as it was during your childhood and teen years. The reasons aren't that different.

Your bones are in a constant state of change. Because bones are living tissue, calcium gets deposited and withdrawn daily from your skeleton, much like money in a bank, in a process called remodeling. Older bone tissue is replaced with new bone tissue. To keep your bones strong and to reduce bone loss, you need to make regular calcium deposits to replace the losses—even build up a little nest egg of calcium for when your food choices come up short.

BONE HEALTH = GOOD NUTRITION + PHYSICAL ACTIVITY

The sum of many nutrients equals good bone health. Calcium works in partnership with other nutrients, including phosphorus and vitamin D. Vitamin D helps absorb, carry, and deposit calcium in bones and teeth. Phosphorus is also an important part of the structure of bone. Magnesium helps build and maintain bone health, as do protein and some other minerals.

If you don't consume enough calcium—or if your body doesn't adequately absorb it (perhaps because you're short on vitamin D)—your body may withdraw more calcium from your bones than you deposit. You need calcium, for example, for muscle contraction and for your heartbeat.

Gradually depleting bone structure leaves a void where calcium otherwise would be deposited and eventually makes bones more porous and fragile.

Regular, weight-bearing physical activities—such as walking, strength training, dancing, kickboxing, and tennis—are essential to bone health, too. They trigger nerve impulses that, in turn, activate other body chemicals to deposit calcium in bones. When you don't put weight on your bones because you're bedridden or very sedentary, the body signals that it doesn't need bone, which results in calcium excretion.

BONING UP: A LIFELONG PROCESS

During the childhood and teen years, bones grow long and wide. Forty percent or more of the body's bone mass is formed during adolescence. (*See "Nutrients: Special Attention" in chapter 17, page 525, to learn more.*)

By age twenty or so, that phase of bone building is complete. But building peak bone mass continues into your early thirties. Bones become stronger and denser as more calcium becomes part of the bone matrix.

After age thirty or so, bones slowly lose minerals that give them strength. That's a natural part of aging. Whatever calcium a woman has stored away in her skeleton will be the amount in her bones when she enters menopause. Even then, consuming enough calcium and vitamin D can help women retain their bone density and lower the risk for osteoporosis later.

For women during their childbearing years, the hormone estrogen appears to protect bones, keeping them strong. With the onset of menopause, bone loss speeds up as estrogen levels go down; the body doesn't absorb calcium as well. If women achieve peak bone mass as younger adults, their risk for osteoporosis is reduced later in life.

For older adults, ages fifty-one and over, calcium and vitamin D remain essential for building and maintaining healthy bones. Even if you start now, you can benefit from consuming more calcium and vitamin D.

BASIC STRATEGIES FOR BONE HEALTH

- Consume adequate amounts of calcium and vitamin D—at every age and stage of life.
- Eat a variety of foods to get enough of all nutrients—not only calcium and vitamin D, but also phosphorus, magnesium, and protein—needed for strong, healthy bones.
- Participate regularly in weight-bearing activities—at least three times weekly.
- Be careful about weight loss. Eating plans that severely restrict food often restrict calcium and vitamin D, too.
- Avoid smoking and excessive amounts of alcoholic beverages. Both interfere with bone health.

See "Osteoporosis and Bone Health" in chapter 25, page 738.

Where it's mostly found: Milk and other dairy foods such as yogurt and most cheeses are the best sources of calcium. These products and the foods made from them provide about 72 percent of the calcium that people consume in the United States. In addition, some dark-green leafy vegetables (bok choy, broccoli, and kale), fish with edible bones, corn tortillas, calcium-fortified soymilk, and tofu made with calcium sulfate also supply significant amounts. Juice, bottled water, and bread may be calcium fortified.

Green, leafy vegetables and grain products supply some calcium; however, calcium from plant-based foods is less bioavailable than calcium from dairy foods. Some vegetables such as spinach contain oxalates; grains may contain phytates. Both bind with some minerals, including calcium, iron, and magnesium, partially blocking their absorption. If you eat a variety of foods, you don't need to worry since that's figured into calcium recommendations.

See "A Closer Look . . . Calcium, Vitamin D, and Bone Health" in this chapter, page 427.

Have you ever wondered?

. . . if calcium supplements or calcium-fortified foods can substitute for dairy foods? For most people, fortified foods and supplements are meant to supplement, not replace, foods naturally rich in calcium.

Although they may fill the calcium gap, supplements and calcium-fortified foods (such as some juice, cereal, pasta, and rice) don't supply all the other health-promoting nutrients and food substances found in dairy foods. Besides calcium, foods from the dairy group are key sources of protein, vitamins A, B_2, (riboflavin), B_{12}, and D (if fortified along with the minerals magnesium, phosphorus, potassium, and zinc). Beyond that, dairy foods offer substances with potential functional benefits: conjugated linoleic acid (CLA), sphingolipid, and butyric acid, which may help protect you from some cancers and other health conditions. *See "Functional Nutrition: Omega-3s and -6s" in chapter 13, page 392, for more about CLA; and "Nondairy Drinks: Soy, Almond, and More" in chapter 4, page 92, for more about calcium-fortified soy beverages.*

You can overdo calcium if you regularly consume calcium-fortified juice and/or calcium-fortified breakfast cereal—and take a calcium supplement as "insurance." What's the downside? Too much calcium, most likely from fortified foods and supplements, may limit the absorption of iron and zinc, two minerals that often come up short for many Americans. *See "A Closer Look . . . Calcium and Iron Supplements" in chapter 10, page 320, for more about taking calcium supplements.*

. . . if eggs count as a calcium-rich dairy food? Although they're typically sold in the dairy case, eggs aren't a dairy food. Since you don't eat the shell (your body can't use that form of calcium), eggs supply very little calcium.

Click Here! Links to Know . . .

Use the interactive calcium calculator to determine whether you get enough calcium in your daily food choices.

- Calcium Calculator, International Osteoporosis Foundation www.iofbonehealth.org/calcium-calculator

Magnesium

What it does:

- Serves as an important part of more than three hundred body enzymes and body chemicals that regulate body functions, including producing energy, making body protein, and helping regulate blood glucose levels
- Helps maintain body cells in nerves and muscles; signals muscles to relax and contract
- Keeps heart rhythm steady and promotes normal blood pressure
- Serves as a component of bones
- May help maintain immune response

How much you need: For males aged fourteen to eighteen, the RDA is 410 milligrams daily; for nineteen through thirty, it's 400 milligrams daily; for thirty-one and older, 420 milligrams daily. For females aged fourteen to eighteen, the RDA is 360 milligrams daily; for nineteen through thirty, it's 310 milligrams daily; for thirty-one and older, 320 milligrams daily.

During pregnancy, the RDA increases to 400 milligrams daily for ages eighteen and younger, to 350 milligrams daily for ages nineteen through thirty, and to 360 milligrams daily for ages thirty-one through fifty. During breastfeeding, it then decreases to 360 milligrams daily for ages eighteen and younger, to 310 milligrams daily for ages nineteen through thirty, and to 320 milligrams daily for ages thirty-one through fifty.

If you don't consume enough: A deficiency is rare since the body can maintain a healthy magnesium level by reducing its loss through urine—except for those with diseases that affect magnesium absorption, such as chronic digestive problems, celiac disease, kidney disease, and alcoholism.

Many consume less magnesium than advised—a concern if they don't have enough stored to protect against conditions such as heart disease and immune disorders. It's not considered a true deficiency, however.

If you consume excess amounts: Consuming too much magnesium from food probably is not harmful—unless it can't be excreted properly due to kidney disease. For ages nine and older, the UL is 350 milligrams daily. This amount is less than the RDA because it represents only the amount of magnesium from supplements or drugs, not from food or drinks. The level stays the same during pregnancy and breastfeeding.

High intake from supplements and medications can cause abdominal distress: cramping, diarrhea, and nausea, and in extreme cases, may lead to irregular heartbeat and cardiac arrest.

Where it's mostly found: Magnesium is found in varying amounts in all kinds of foods. The best sources are beans and peas, nuts, and whole grains. Dark-green vegetables are good sources, too, because chlorophyll contains magnesium.

Food	Magnesium (mg)
Almonds, dry roasted (1 oz.)	80
Spinach, boiled (½ cup)	80
Peanut butter, smooth (2 tbsp.)	55
Lima beans, boiled (½ cup)	40
Pigeon peas, boiled (½ cup)	40
Potato with skin, baked (one 5-oz.)	40
Pecans, dry roasted (1 oz.)	35
Spaghetti, whole-wheat, cooked, not packed (½ cup)	30
Parsnips, sliced, boiled (½ cup)	25
Whole-wheat bread (1 slice)	25

Phosphorus

What it does:

- Helps generate energy in every cell of your body
- Acts as the main regulator of energy metabolism in your body's organs
- Is a major component of bones and teeth, second only to calcium
- Serves as part of DNA and RNA, which are your body's master plan for cell growth and repair

How much you need: For ages nine through eighteen, including during pregnancy and breastfeeding, the RDA is 1,250 milligrams daily; for nineteen and older, including during pregnancy and breastfeeding, it decreases to 700 milligrams daily. Scientific evidence shows that people need less than previously thought.

If you don't consume enough: A deficiency is quite rare, except for small, premature babies who consume only breast milk, or for people who take an antacid with aluminum hydroxide for a long time. In those rare cases, the symptoms include bone loss, weakness, loss of appetite, and pain.

If you consume excess amounts: An excess amount may lower the level of calcium in the blood—a problem if calcium intake is low. As a result, bone loss may increase. Besides that, consuming too much phosphorus doesn't appear to be a problem in the United States. For ages nine through seventy, the UL is 4,000 milligrams daily; for those over seventy, it's 3,000 milligrams daily. During breastfeeding, the level stays the same; during pregnancy, it's 3,500 milligrams daily.

Where it's mostly found: Almost all foods contain phosphorus. Protein-rich foods—meat, poultry, fish, eggs, and milk—contain the most. Beans, peas, and nuts are good sources as well. Even bread and other baked goods have some. You'll also find phosphorus in colas and other dark-colored soft drinks.

Food	Phosphorus (mg)
Perch, cooked (3 oz.)	255
Milk, fat-free (1 cup)	245
Beef, ground, 95 percent lean, broiled (3 oz.)	175
Kidney beans, canned, drained (½ cup)	160
Almonds, dry roasted (1 oz.)	135
Cheese, cheddar (1 oz.)	130
Tofu, regular, raw (½ cup)	120
Peanut butter, smooth (2 tbsp.)	105
Egg (1 large)	100
Cola (12 oz.)	35

MAJOR MINERALS: ELECTROLYTES

Read about electrolytes earlier in this chapter, page 425.

Chloride

What it does:

- Helps regulate fluid balance in and out of body cells
- As a component of stomach acid, helps with the digestion of food and the absorption of nutrients
- Helps transmit nerve impulses, or signals

How much you need: For ages nine through fifty, including during pregnancy and breastfeeding, the AI is 2,300 milligrams daily. For ages fifty-one through seventy, it decreases to 2,000 milligrams daily; for those over seventy, it decreases further to 1,800 milligrams daily.

If you don't get enough: Because salt, which consists of 40 percent sodium and 60 percent chloride, is such a common part of the diet, a deficiency of chloride isn't likely. If it occurs, however, symptoms are similar to sodium deficiency.

If you consume excess amounts: Excess amounts of chloride may be linked to high blood pressure, especially among those who have blood pressure that is sodium sensitive. For ages nine through thirteen, the UL is 3,400 milligrams daily; for fourteen and older, it's 3,600 milligrams daily. The levels stay the same during pregnancy and breastfeeding.

Where it's mostly found: Salt and salty foods are the main chloride sources: one-quarter teaspoon of salt has 750 milligrams of chloride.

Potassium

See "A Closer Look . . . Sodium and Potassium, A Salty Subject" in this chapter, page 433.

What it does:

- Helps regulate fluids and mineral balance in and out of body cells
- Helps maintain normal blood pressure by blunting sodium's effects on blood pressure
- Helps transmit nerve impulses, or signals
- Helps reduce the risk of kidney stones and bone loss
- Helps muscles contract
- May help protect against muscle loss and help preserve bone density with aging

How much you need: For ages nine through thirteen, the AI is 4,500 milligrams daily; for fourteen and older, including during pregnancy, it's 4,700 milligrams daily. During breastfeeding, the AI increases to 5,100 milligrams daily. Those with kidney disease who take some diuretics and those with heart disease who take medicines such as ACE inhibitors should check with their doctor for guidance on potassium intake. Current evidence suggests that African Americans and those with high blood pressure especially benefit from increasing their intake of potassium because they are at higher risk for high blood pressure; potassium helps blunt the effects of sodium for those whose blood pressure is sodium sensitive.

The Dietary Guidelines for Americans cites potassium as a nutrient of concern because many people don't consume enough. Eating a variety of foods, notably vegetables, fruits, and dairy foods, can help you reach the recommended level of potassium for optimal health without over-consuming calories (energy).

If you don't consume enough: While many people underconsume potassium, a true potassium deficiency is rare among healthy people. When vomiting, diarrhea, or laxative use goes on for too long, the body may lose excess amounts. Kidney problems also may cause severe loss. Deficiency symptoms include muscle cramps, weakness, appetite loss, nausea, and fatigue. A potassium supplement may be prescribed by a doctor for those on blood pressure medication.

If you consume excess amounts: Harmful effects from consuming too much from food are rare. Since excess potassium is excreted through urine, no ULs have been established for those with healthy kidney function.

If an excess can't be excreted, it can cause heart problems and possible sudden death. People with kidney (renal) problems, including some with high blood pressure, may not be able to get rid of excess potassium and may be advised to limit potassium-containing foods and avoid high-dose potassium supplements or using potassium chloride as a salt substitute. People with certain cardiac issues, such as arrhythmia, are advised to consume under 4,700 milligrams daily.

Where it's mostly found: Getting enough potassium is another reason to eat a variety of fruits and vegetables. Beans and peas, dairy foods, meat, poultry, fish, and nuts also deliver potassium. Less-processed foods tend to have more potassium.

Food	Potassium (mg)
Potato with skin, baked (1 small, 5 oz.)	740
Banana (1 medium)	420
Spinach, boiled (½ cup)	420
Milk, fat-free (1 cup)	380
Sweet potato, mashed, canned (½ cup)	380
Orange juice, 100 percent (6 oz.)	370
Dates, medjool (2)	335
Yogurt, fruit variety, fat-free (6 oz.)	330
Raisins, seedless, packed (¼ cup)	310
Kidney beans, canned (½ cup)	305
Haddock, cooked (3 oz.)	300
Tomato, raw (1 medium)	290
Turkey, light meat only, roasted, skinless (3 oz.)	210
Almonds, dry roasted (1 oz.)	200
Carrot, raw (1 medium)	195
Peach, canned in juice, solids and liquid (½ cup)	160
Bell pepper, red, raw, chopped (½ cup)	160
Broccoli, raw (1 spear, 5 inch)	100

? Have you ever wondered?

. . . about sulfate—since it's considered an electrolyte?
Inorganic sulfate is a nutrient with electrolyte properties. No RDA, AI, or UL have been set for sulfate. Food, water, and the metabolic breakdown of amino acids in the body provide enough. Dried fruit, fruit juice, wine, beer, soy flour, bread, and meat supply sulfate. The odor and off flavor that come from sulfate usually limit how much people consume. That said, when the water supply has a high level of sulfate, diarrhea may result.

Sodium

See "A Closer Look . . . Sodium and Potassium, A Salty Subject" in this chapter, page 433.

To keep your body running normally, you need sodium, but you likely consume more than enough! Most Americans do—and significantly more than the UL. Due to its link to high blood pressure, sodium is a nutrient of public health concern. For Nutrition Facts labeling, the Daily Value is based on the UL and not the AI, given below.

What it does:

- Helps regulate fluid balance in and out of body cells
- Helps muscles, including your heart, relax
- Helps transmit nerve impulses, or signals
- Helps regulate blood pressure

How much you need: Your sodium needs are relatively small, as long as you don't sweat substantially.

Rather than an RDA, an AI is given. For mostly healthy people aged nine through fifty, the AI is 1,500 milligrams daily and accounts for sweat losses. The level stays the same during pregnancy and breastfeeding. For ages fifty through seventy, the AI decreases to 1,300 milligrams daily; for those over seventy, it decreases further to 1,200 milligrams daily. It's somewhat less for children aged eight and under.

Food	Sodium (mg)
Ham, regular, sliced, 11 percent fat (3 oz.)	960
Beef bologna (3 oz.)*	850
Cheese spread, American (1 oz.)	455
Olives, green, bottled (5, or ½ oz.)	210
Cheddar cheese (1 oz.)	185
Sunflower kernels, dry roasted, salted (1 oz.)	185
Pickle relish, hot dog (1 tbsp.)	165
Whole-wheat bread (1 slice)	140
Milk, fat-free (1 cup)	105

*Amounts vary. Some products are reduced sodium or salt free. The Nutrition Facts label tells how much sodium comes from a single label serving of food. Food manufacturers are gradually reducing the sodium in many foods. *See "Nutrition: Fact Check!" in chapter 6, page 144, for more about food labeling.*

Did You Know . . . ?

- One teaspoon of table salt contains 2,325 milligrams of sodium, or about a day's worth, according to the Dietary Guidelines.
- By eating fewer calories, you may also reduce sodium in your meals and snacks, too.
- By eating more fruits and veggies, you boost your potassium intake, which helps blunt the effect of sodium on blood pressure. *See chapter 4, page 81, and 9, page 275.*
- You can cut back. To learn how:
  - Follow the DASH Eating Plan; *see "DASH for Health" in chapter 2, page 51.*
  - Shop for foods with less sodium; *see "Food Labels: Decode the Package" in chapter 6, page 143.*
  - Cut salt in your cooking, and give food a flavor burst with herbs and spices, not salt; *see "Salty Foods: Shake the Sodium" in chapter 8, page 264.*
  - Order restaurant foods with less sodium; *see "Order It Your Way" in chapter 9, page 278.*

Label Lingo

Salt and Sodium

Does the term "sodium" or "salt" appear on the front of the food label? If so, here's what the claims mean. For the specific sodium content in a standard serving, check the Nutrition Facts label.

Label term . . .	Means . . .
SALT-/SODIUM-FREE	Less than 5 milligrams of sodium per serving*
VERY LOW SODIUM	35 milligrams or less of sodium per serving*
LOW SODIUM	140 milligrams or less of sodium per serving*
REDUCED OR LESS SODIUM	At least 25 percent less sodium than the regular product
LIGHT IN SODIUM OR LIGHTLY SALTED	At least 50 percent less sodium than the regular product
LOW-SODIUM MEAT	140 milligrams or less of sodium per 100 grams* (3½ ounces)
NO-SALT-ADDED OR UNSALTED	No salt is added during processing, but these products may not be salt-/sodium-free unless stated

* The updated Daily Values for use with new Nutrition Facts labeling may change these amounts slightly.

The Dietary Guidelines for Americans advises reducing daily sodium intake to less than 2,300 milligrams daily. Adults with prehypertension and hypertension especially benefit, as it's a way to help lower blood pressure; by reducing intake to 1,500 milligrams daily, these individuals can experience greater blood pressure reduction. In fact, every incremental decrease in sodium intake likely makes a difference.

The American Heart Association also advises that reducing daily sodium intake to 1,500 milligrams is desirable to lower blood pressure further. At a target level of 1,500 milligrams, it's challenging to choose foods that provide enough other nutrients, including potassium; sodium is an ingredient in many processed and prepared foods. There's also scientific debate on the benefits of setting this lower target for most people.

If you don't consume enough: Unless you have prolonged diarrhea or vomiting, or have kidney problems, a sodium deficiency isn't likely. If it happens, symptoms might include nausea, dizziness, and muscle cramps.

If you consume excess amounts: The average sodium intake in the United States—currently 3,440 milligrams (equivalent to 1½ teaspoons of salt) daily—is too high. For all adult men, the average intake is 4,240 milligrams daily; for adult women, it's 2,980 milligrams daily. There's no known advantage to consuming that much. Those at risk for—or already have—high blood pressure are better off with less.

For healthy people, excess sodium is excreted, but some kidney diseases interfere with sodium excretion, causing fluid retention and

? Have you ever wondered?

. . . how you know if you're sodium sensitive? There's no easy way to know. But about 20 percent of people in the United States are estimated to be sodium sensitive; in other words, their blood pressure varies with sodium intake. Testing for salt sensitivity is highly controlled and takes several days; often it's done in a hospital setting. This test usually isn't done except in research settings. Because blood pressure rises with sodium intake, especially for those with salt sensitivity, and because many people don't know if they have hypertension or are salt sensitive, it's advised that everyone reduces sodium intake to recommended levels.

. . . if a high-salt diet is okay if you're not salt sensitive? Moderation is always a better rule of thumb for anything you eat, so it's wise to reduce sodium and to consume foods with potassium. Choose and prepare foods with little salt, and hedge your bets with the DASH approach to eating: dairy foods, plenty of fruits and vegetables, whole-grain foods, and low-fat foods. The body excretes more calcium through urine when salt intake is high, so that's another reason to cut back on salt.

. . . if celery has a lot of sodium? Many people think so. But a celery stalk has only 35 milligrams of naturally occurring sodium.

. . . if drinking water has much sodium? The amount of sodium in drinking water varies from place to place. Unless you're on a sodium-restricted diet, you don't need to be too concerned. To know the sodium content of your tap water, contact your local water department. A water softener may add sodium to your water—but the contribution is typically small. Talk to the manufacturer of the water softener to find out how much sodium it adds to your water supply.

. . . if salt substitutes are good options for cutting back on sodium? That depends. Salt substitutes (potassium chloride) aren't appropriate—and may not be healthy—for everyone.

Many salt substitutes contain potassium in place of all or some of the sodium. For some people, potassium consumed in excess can be harmful. For example, those with kidney problems may not be able to rid their bodies of excess levels of potassium. If you're under medical care, especially for a kidney problem, check with your doctor before using salt substitutes. Those taking digoxin for heart failure or ACE inhibitors for high blood pressure should also talk with their doctor before using these substitutes.

Rather than salt substitutes, try herb-spice blends as a flavorful alternative—or try lemon or lime juice to bring out flavor. Today's supermarkets carry a variety of salt-free seasoning blends. Read the ingredient list and the Nutrition Facts on the label. Some herb-spice blends are neither salt nor sodium free. As an alternative, make your own; *see "Kitchen Nutrition: Salt-Free Herb Blends" and "Flavor on the Menu" in chapter 8, pages 274 and 238.*

. . . if you need extra salt from the shaker, a salt tablet, or a sports drink when you sweat after strenuous physical activity? Probably not. Food eaten after exertion normally replenishes sodium lost in sweat. That said, sodium's Adequate Intake level doesn't apply to highly active people, such as those doing endurance sports.

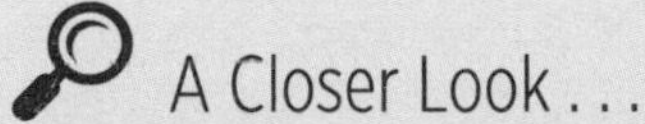

Sodium and Potassium, A Salty Subject

Salt . . . or sodium? Although we often refer to them interchangeably, salt and sodium are different. Table salt is the common name for "sodium chloride." It's 40 percent sodium and 60 percent chloride. And potassium? Like sodium and chloride, it's an essential mineral.

SODIUM AND POTASSIUM: WHY YOU NEED THEM!

The link between sodium and high blood pressure is well publicized, yet few people know the flip side of the sodium story, which explains why sodium is essential to health.

Sodium and potassium (electrolytes) occur naturally in food. Some of your body's most basic work depends on these minerals: maintaining fluid balance, controlling the movement of fluids in and out of your cells, and regulating your blood pressure. By transmitting nerve impulses, they help send messages from your brain to your muscles, causing them to relax or contract.

If you lick your upper lip after sweating a lot, you know that body fluids have salt. You can taste it! Sodium, chloride, and potassium dissolve in body fluids, where they become separate ions.

KEEPING THE BALANCE

Sprinkle salt on a sliced eggplant or potato and then watch liquid come to its surface. That happens because salt draws fluid out of plant cells. The same happens in your body, as sodium draws water from your cells into your bloodstream.

Electrolytes control and regulate fluid balance in and out of cells. Sodium and chloride mostly work outside body cells; potassium works mainly inside. They help to move nutrients into cells and to move waste out.

Your kidneys regulate your body's sodium and potassium levels. If you're healthy, your body doesn't retain, or store, excess sodium—even when you consume more than you need. Instead, your body gets rid of the extra through urine. If you eat foods high in sodium, you may urinate more. Your body also releases some sodium through perspiration. Because you lose fluids along with sodium, you may feel thirsty.

Is extra sodium in the body always removed? No, not when the kidneys don't work properly, perhaps due to kidney disease. This causes swelling, often in the face, legs, and feet. In medical terms, this swelling is called edema.

LINKS TO BLOOD PRESSURE

High blood pressure (hypertension) is a key risk factor for heart disease, stroke, kidney failure, and other conditions. In the United States, about one-third of adults have it; about one-third more are prehypertensive. Although many don't know it, more and more children are at risk.

Why is attention given to sodium? Think again about how sodium works. As a high-sodium diet draws water into the bloodstream, the volume of blood goes up. Over time, that can increase blood pressure, causing the heart to work harder.

Although a family history of high blood pressure, being overweight, excessive alcohol intake, advancing age, and smoking are linked to high blood pressure, there's also a direct, progressive link between excessive sodium intake and increased high blood pressure—perhaps in its early prehypertension stage. On average, the higher the sodium intake, the higher a person's blood pressure. Conversely, reducing sodium intake may help to lower blood pressure if it's higher than normal.

Normal blood pressure lowers the risks of heart and kidney diseases. Even a modest sodium decrease can make a difference! *See "Blood Pressure Levels: For Adults" in chapter 24, page 696, for blood pressure ranges that indicate prehypertension and hypertension.*

Three other minerals may help regulate blood pressure: potassium from fruits, vegetables, milk, and yogurt; calcium from dairy foods and some vegetables; and magnesium from beans and peas, green vegetables, milk, nuts, and whole grains. Although the scientific reasons aren't fully understood, potassium may offer some protection by blunting the effect of sodium on blood pressure.

The DASH (Dietary Approaches to Stop Hypertension) Eating Plan—low in fat, with low-fat and fat-free dairy foods and plenty of fruits and vegetables—may help lower blood pressure, even for those within a "normal" range. The DASH plan is high in calcium, magnesium, and potassium, with sodium upper limits of 2,300 milligrams daily. Especially for those with hypertension, reducing sodium to 1,500 milligrams daily with the DASH plan has been shown to have a better blood pressure–lowering effect. High blood pressure or not, the DASH plan is a healthy eating plan; *see "DASH to Health" in chapter 2, page 51.*

Research suggests that high sodium intake may be linked to other health concerns, including gastric cancer and cardiovascular

(continued)

A Closer Look . . . *(continued)*

disease, while inadequate potassium intake may increase risk for kidney stones and perhaps asthma and osteoporosis. A possible benefit of cutting back on salt: less calcium loss from bone, and as a result, reduced risk of osteoporosis and bone fractures.

ADVICE . . . EVEN FOR HEALTHY PEOPLE

Limit sodium and choose foods with potassium such as fruits and vegetables. Why this advice for healthy people? First, you probably won't know if your blood pressure is sodium sensitive. Second, blood pressure naturally rises with age, so limiting sodium can be considered "antiaging," or a good precaution. And third, consuming less sodium or little salt certainly isn't harmful if you're healthy. Even if you don't have high blood pressure now, cutting back may provide protection, just in case.

What about potassium? Research indicates that eating foods high in potassium may help lower blood pressure by reducing adverse effects of sodium on blood pressure.

Can your overall food choices be too low in sodium? Yes, but with the sodium naturally in foods and the current food supply, the likelihood is slim. The average person in the United States consumes more than 3,400 milligrams of sodium daily: about 50 percent more than the recommended 2,300 milligrams daily maximum for adults whose blood pressure isn't sodium sensitive, and more than double the 1,500 milligrams daily advised for some.

Your body conserves sodium when your intake is low and conserves potassium, too, but less effectively; make up for it by eating more potassium-rich foods. If a person vomits or has diarrhea for a prolonged period, or if he or she has a kidney problem, sodium levels might get too low.

Consult your doctor for the right sodium level for you, and a registered dietitian nutritionist to help you follow this advice. *See "Blood Pressure: Under Control?" in chapter 24, page 693.*

SALT AND SODIUM: MORE THAN FLAVOR

Salt and sodium: Are they in foods just for flavor? Or do they have other roles, too? Spotting foods with salt or sodium is easier if you know what they do.

A few grains of salt can enhance a food's natural flavors, even in sweet foods such as cakes and cookies and certainly in savory foods such as vegetables and soups. A pinch helps disguise metallic or chemical aftertastes, as in some soft drinks. Yet despite these roles, ingredients with sodium play an even broader role.

- Before refrigeration, people relied on salt to preserve food. Salt and sodium-containing ingredients draw water out of food and so inhibit the growth of bacteria, molds, and yeast, which need moisture to thrive. That helps prevent food spoilage and foodborne illness.

  Even today, many cured foods use salt or an ingredient made with sodium (such as sodium nitrate) as a preservative: Canadian bacon, corned beef, ham, prosciutto, and sausage, to name a few. Other foods may be brined in a water-and-salt solution. Cucumbers, okra, and peppers are among the veggies pickled in brine.
- In some foods, salt is added for a desired texture. For example, yeast breads with salt have a finer texture than their coarser-crumbed, salt-free, yeast-bread cousins. Salt also reduces the dryness of crackers and pretzels.
- Salt controls the speed of fermentation in foods such as bread dough, cheese, and sauerkraut. Fermentation changes the chemistry of food and, as a result, its appearance and flavor.
- When whipping egg whites, a pinch of salt increases and stabilizes the volume.
- In processed meats, including sausage, salt and sodium-containing ingredients help bind the meat.
- Some foods can't be produced without salt. Besides being essential for ripening cheese, salt is needed for the texture, flavor, quality, shelf-life, and safety of cheese. That said, the salt content of about 300 types of cheese in the US varies. For example, cheddar and mozzarella cheese have about half as much as the same-size portion of processed cheese. Read the Nutrition Facts label!

Since salt and sodium-containing ingredients do much more than enhance flavor, lowering sodium in processed foods is challenging. Yet many food companies are quietly cutting down, in fact—so gradually that you likely won't notice. As a consumer, periodically check the Nutrition Facts label to be up-to-date on the sodium content.

WHERE DOES SODIUM COME FROM?

Many people think their taste buds offer all the clues needed to detect sodium in food. Not true. Many foods that contain sodium don't taste salty.

A shake here, a shake there—only a small percentage of the sodium most people consume comes from salt added during cooking or at the table. However, it can add up, especially if you use the salt shaker before tasting.

Sodium occurs naturally in some foods—even if unprocessed. This isn't a concern since it provides only a very small amount of overall sodium intake.

Most sodium in the US diet comes from foods processed and prepared commercially (including chicken and beef mixed dishes, Mexican mixed dishes, pasta dishes, pizza, and yeast breads) and restaurant foods. Condiments such as mustard, soy sauce, and tartar sauce can add more sodium than you think.

Foods in every food group contain sodium. The differences—even in very similar foods—come from the way foods are prepared and processed. Because salt and sodium-containing ingredients serve many functions, it's not surprising that sodium amounts are often higher than you may realize. For example, two cookies or crackers may have from 25 to 270 milligrams of sodium. A frozen dinner might deliver 550 to 1,300 milligrams, and two slices of bacon, 500 to 800 milligrams. Even "reduced-sodium" foods may contain more than you think.

For clues to sodium in processed foods, check the label's ingredient list. "Na," "salt," "soda," or "sodium" indicates sodium. ("Na" is the scientific symbol for sodium.) Foods described as "basted," "brined," "broth," "corned," "cured," "marinated" "pickled," and "smoked" usually contain sodium; cured ham often has about 350 milligrams of sodium per ounce.

The Nutrition Facts help you know if a food has a lot of sodium, or a little. If one serving contains 5 percent or less of the Daily Value (DV) for sodium, that's low. If it contains 20 percent or more DV, that's a lot. *See "Food Labels: Decode the Package" in chapter 6, page 143 to learn about Nutrition Facts and ingredient lists.*

"SALTY"—AN ACQUIRED TASTE

Do you like the taste of salty snacks? Does food seem to taste better after a few shakes of the salt shaker?

A preference for strong, salty tastes is acquired, probably starting in infancy if a baby is exposed to salty tastes. It's the saltiness that people like, not the sodium. In fact, chloride in salt may have more to do with flavor than sodium does.

The body adjusts easily to less salt. When people gradually cut back, their desire for salty tastes usually declines, too. Over time, the less salt consumed, the less is desired.

For taste perception, even salt substitutes, suggested for some, don't give the same sensation as salt. They may taste somewhat bitter or sharp.

TAMING YOUR TASTE BUDS

Healthy foods don't need to taste bland just because they have less salt. And you don't need to give up your favorite high-sodium foods—just eat less of them. To slowly step down your sodium intake and your preference for saltiness:

- Cut back on high-sodium foods gradually. Because a preference for a salty taste is learned, it takes time to unlearn it, too—and to learn to appreciate new flavors.
- Taste before salting. Food may taste great just as it is! Keep the salt shaker in the cabinet, not on the kitchen counter or the table where it's too easy to use. Season with more herbs, spices, and citrus instead.
- Balance: If you enjoy some foods with more sodium, eat others with less. Use the Nutrition Facts label to compare sodium in processed foods. How much sodium consumed over several days is what counts.
- Cut back on portions to sensible amounts. Calorie intake is highly associated with sodium intake. In other words, too, the more calories you consume, the more sodium you consume.

swelling. Moderate evidence also suggests a link to higher sodium intake and increased risk of cardiovascular disease. For people with sodium sensitivity, including children, a high-sodium diet can increase blood pressure.

For ages nine through thirteen, the UL is 2,200 milligrams daily; for fourteen and older, it's 2,300 milligrams daily. The levels stay the same during pregnancy and breastfeeding. This advice is set for people who don't have high blood pressure; the UL may be too high for those who already have it.

Where it's mostly found: Foods that are processed and prepared commercially, including in restaurants, account for most of the sodium consumed. That includes salty snacks and prepared foods, canned and boxed soups and broth, and "instant" foods such as flavored rice and instant mixes and noodles (Ramen noodles).

Only a small percentage comes from sodium that occurs naturally in food and from salt or other flavorings added in home cooking and at the table. As a point of reference, one-quarter teaspoon of table salt contains about 500 milligrams of sodium.

TRACE MINERALS

Chromium

What it does:

- Works with insulin to help your body use blood glucose, or blood sugar
- May be involved in the metabolism of carbohydrates, fats, and proteins

How much you need: For males aged fourteen to fifty, the AI is 35 micrograms daily; for those over fifty, it decreases to 30 micrograms daily. For females, aged fourteen to eighteen, it's 24 micrograms daily; for nineteen through fifty, it's 25 micrograms daily; and for fifty-one and older, it decreases to 20 micrograms daily. During pregnancy, the AI increases to 29 micrograms daily for ages fourteen to eighteen and to 30 micrograms daily for ages nineteen through fifty. During breastfeeding, it increases to 44 micrograms daily for ages fourteen to eighteen and to 45 micrograms daily for ages nineteen through fifty.

If you don't consume enough: Because chromium works closely with insulin, a deficiency can look like diabetes. *See "Diabetes: A Growing Concern" in chapter 24, page 698.*

If you consume excess amounts: Consuming harmful amounts from dietary sources is highly unlikely. Few serious adverse effects have been linked to high intakes of chromium. No ULs have been established.

Where it's mostly found: Most foods have small amounts (fewer than 2 micrograms of chromium per serving). That said, meat, eggs, cheese, whole-grain products, beans and peas, and some fruits and vegetables are all reasonable sources.

Food	Chromium (mcg)
Red wine (5 oz.)	1–13
Broccoli, chopped, cooked (½ cup)	11
Grape juice (1 cup)	8
Garlic, dried (1 tsp.)	3
Potatoes, mashed (1 cup)	3
Beef cubes (3 oz.)	2
Turkey breast, meat only, roasted (3 oz.)	2
Apple, unpeeled (1 medium)	1
Green beans (½ cup)	1
Whole-wheat bread (1 slice)	1

Source: ods.od.nih.gov/factsheets/list-VitaminsMinerals/Chromium

Copper

What it does:

- Helps your body make hemoglobin, needed to carry oxygen in red blood cells
- Serves as a part of many body enzymes
- Helps your body develop connective tissue, myelin, and melanin
- Helps produce energy in all the cells of your body

How much you need: For ages fourteen to eighteen, the RDA is 890 micrograms daily; for nineteen and older, it's 900 micrograms daily. During pregnancy, it increases to 1,000 micrograms daily, and during breastfeeding, to 1,300 micrograms daily.

If you don't consume enough: A deficiency rarely occurs due to a lack of consuming enough copper, but rather due to genetic problems. Excess zinc from supplement sources can also hinder copper absorption.

If you consume excess amounts: For ages fourteen to eighteen, the UL is 8,000 micrograms daily; for nineteen and older, it's 10,000 micrograms daily. The levels remain the same during pregnancy and breastfeeding.

Where it's mostly found: Organ meats, especially liver; fish; nuts; and seeds are the best sources. Cooking in copper pots increases the copper in food.

Food	Copper (mcg)
Beef liver, braised (3 oz.)	9,710
Oysters, canned (3 oz.)	3,790
Oysters, cooked (3 oz.)	2,290
Sunflower seeds, dry roasted (1 oz.)	520
Mushrooms, white, cooked, drained (½ cup)	390
Almonds, dry roasted (1 oz.)	310
Peanuts, dry roasted (1 oz.)	120
Soybeans, cooked (½ cup)	110

Fluoride

See "Water: The Fluoride Connection" in chapter 5, page 83.

What it does:

- Helps harden tooth enamel and so helps protect teeth from decay
- May offer some protection from osteoporosis, or brittle bone disease, by helping to strengthen bones

How much you need: For males and females aged four through eight, the AI is 1 milligram daily; for nine through thirteen, it's 2 milligrams daily;

and for fourteen to eighteen, 3 milligrams daily. For males aged nineteen and older, the AI is 4 milligrams daily; for females, it's 3 milligrams daily. The levels remain the same for each age group during pregnancy and breastfeeding. A fluoride supplement may be prescribed by a dentist or doctor for some infants and children. *See "Supplement Advice: For Breastfed Babies" in chapter 16, page 469.*

If you don't consume enough: Tooth enamel may be weak, with greater risk for cavities.

If you consume excess amounts: With excessive fluoride, teeth become mottled, or marked with brown stains, although teeth are healthy in every other way. This condition is called fluorosis. Be aware that these stains may have other causes as well. For ages four through eight, the UL is 2.2 milligrams daily; for nine and older, it's 10 milligrams daily. The level stays the same during pregnancy and breastfeeding. Fluorosis among youth is becoming more common, and studies also are exploring other health risks related to excess fluoride.

Where it's mostly found: Fluoride is not widely available in food. Two significant food sources are tea, especially if it's made with fluoridated water, and fish with edible bones, such as canned salmon.

Many municipal water supplies are fluoridated; however, most bottled waters are not, nor is well water. The fluoride content in food varies and is affected by the environment in which the food originated. The current recommended level for fluoridation is a range of 0.7 to 1.2 milligrams per liter. Based on current scientific reviews, the US Department of Health and Human Services has proposed changing the recommended level for community water systems to 0.7 milligrams per liter.

See "A Closer Look . . . Water: The Fluoride Connection" in chapter 4, page 83.

Iodine

What it does:

- Serves as part of thyroid hormones such as thyroxin, which regulate the rate at which your body uses energy
- Plays an important role in fetal and infant development and proper health at all life stages. Iodine is important for fetal and infant brain development.

How much you need: For ages fourteen and older, the RDA is 150 micrograms daily. During pregnancy, it increases to 220 micrograms daily, and during breastfeeding, to 290 micrograms daily.

If you don't consume enough: With an iodine deficiency, the body can't make enough thyroxin, leading to hypothyroidism, often potentially accompanied by goiter. As a result, the rate at which the body burns energy slows down, and weight gain may become a problem. Goiter, an enlarged thyroid gland, is usually the first clinical sign of an iodine deficiency. With the use of iodized salt, goiter and other serious health problems rarely are caused by an iodine deficiency.

For those with marginal iodine status or with a thyroid condition, eating foods containing goitrogens, such as soy, broccoli, cabbage, cassava, cauliflower, and other cruciferous vegetables can be a concern. These substances interfere with the uptake of iodine in the thyroid and can worsen an iodine deficiency. For most people in the United States, this is not an issue.

If you consume excess amounts: Interestingly, high intakes of iodine—not at levels usually consumed in the United States—can cause some of the same symptoms as an iodine deficiency in some people. That's because excess iodine inhibits the production of the thyroid hormone. As a result, goiter can develop. Too much also can result in an irregular heartbeat and confusion.

For ages fourteen to eighteen, the UL is 900 micrograms daily; for nineteen and older, it's 1,100 micrograms daily. The levels remain the same during pregnancy and breastfeeding.

Where it's mostly found: Iodine is found naturally in saltwater fish. Sea vegetables such as seaweed (kelp, kombu, nori, wakame) are among the best sources, but the iodine content of different seaweed species varies widely. Food produced near coastal areas in soil that also contains iodine. The iodine content of food varies greatly, depending on how much iodine is in soil where foods grow, fertilizer use, and irrigation practices. For animal-based foods, it depends on the iodine in the feed and where animals graze.

Those who don't regularly eat foods that naturally contain iodine can get enough from iodized salt. Table salt, sea salt, and kosher salt may or may not be iodized; check the label. Other specialty salts (fleur de sel, Himalayan salt, pink salt, others) and salt substitutes probably aren't iodized.

Be aware that most salt intake in the United States comes from processed foods, which often isn't iodized, so don't count on salty snacks as a source. If iodized salt is used, it must say so in the label's ingredient list.

Food	Iodine (mcg)
Seaweed, whole or sheet (1 gram)	16–2,984
Cod, cooked (3 oz.)	99
Table salt, iodized (about ¼ tsp.)	71
Milk, reduced fat (1 cup)	56
Shrimp (3 oz.)	35
Egg (1 large)	24
Bread, white, enriched (1 slice)	23
Tuna, canned in oil, drained (3 oz.)	17
Corn, cream style, canned (½ cup)	14
Lima beans, mature, boiled (½ cup)	8

Source: ods.od.nih.gov/factsheets/list-VitaminsMinerals/Iodine-HealthProfessional/.

Iron

What it does:

- Serves as an essential part of hemoglobin, which carries oxygen in your blood from your lungs to every body cell, and so helps your body produce energy
- Is used to make myoglobin, a protein that provides oxygen to muscles, and to make some hormones and connective tissue
- Helps change beta-carotene to vitamin A, helps produce collagen (which holds body tissues together), and helps make body proteins (amino acids)
- Helps in brain development
- Supports a healthy immune system

How much you need: For males aged fourteen to eighteen, the RDA is 11 milligrams daily; for nineteen and older, it's 8 milligrams daily. For females aged nine through eighteen, the RDA is 15 milligrams daily; for nineteen through fifty, it's 18 milligrams daily; and for fifty-one and older, 8 milligrams daily.

During pregnancy at any age, the RDA increases to 27 milligrams daily. During breastfeeding, it's 10 milligrams daily for ages eighteen and younger, and it's 9 milligrams daily for ages nineteen and older; the lower RDA for iron (than for nonpregnant women) during breastfeeding assumes that menstruation hasn't resumed.

The Dietary Guidelines for Americans cites low intake of iron as a concern for young children, women capable of becoming pregnant, and women who are pregnant. Women who are pregnant are advised to take an iron supplement as recommended by an obstetrician or other physician.

With menopause, iron needs drop. That's the time to stop taking an iron supplement, especially for women at risk for hemochromatosis, a genetic disorder that results in high levels of stored iron in the body. Iron-rich foods can supply as much as most postmenopausal women need.

If you don't consume enough: When iron gets shortchanged or when iron stores in your body get too low, red blood cells can't carry as much oxygen, likely making you feel tired and maybe weak, inducing poor memory or the inability to concentrate, and lowering the ability to fight infection and to perform at peak efficiency. Iron deficiency increases the risk of low birth weight and premature births. For infants and children, it may delay psychological development and affect concentration.

Although there may be other causes, an iron deficiency can lead to anemia. All interfere with a person's physical ability to perform at full potential. *See "Anemia: 'Tired Blood'" in chapter 25, page 722, to learn more.*

Among menstruating women, iron deficiency is more common. Iron also is underconsumed by adolescent girls and women who are capable of becoming pregnant. Premature or low-birth weight babies may not get enough iron. Vegans are advised to consume more iron because the body doesn't absorb nonheme iron from plant-based foods as well as it does heme iron from animal-based foods.

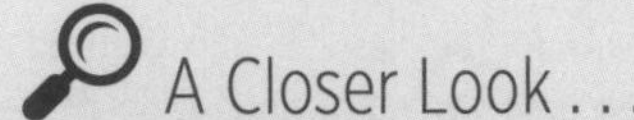

A Closer Look . . .

Iron

Iron, a mineral widely available in food, is needed in small amounts. Yet, iron deficiency is a common nutrition problem around the world and often leads to anemia. Symptoms of anemia include fatigue, weakness, and poor health, all interfering with a person's ability to perform to full potential.

IRON: ITS MAIN MISSION

Although iron has many biological functions, its main job is to carry oxygen in the hemoglobin of red blood cells. In fact, about two-thirds of your body's iron is in hemoglobin. Hemoglobin takes oxygen to your body cells where it's used to produce energy. Iron in red blood cells also helps take away carbon dioxide, a by-product of energy production.

Red blood cells have a life span of about four months. After that, some of their iron gets recycled. It's either stored or used immediately to make new red blood cells. This recycling action helps protect you from iron deficiency.

Your body is highly adaptive, absorbing more iron when its iron stores are low, and less when they're higher. Regardless, the RDAs are set to meet the needs of most people.

WHY THE CONCERN ABOUT IRON?

What happens when you don't consume enough iron—or when the iron stored in your body gets low? Red blood cells can't carry as much oxygen, likely making you feel tired, perhaps weak, and less able to perform at your peak efficiency. These are among the symptoms of anemia. However, anemia has several causes—not just iron deficiency. *See "Anemia: More Causes" in chapter 25, page 723.*

Iron needs are highest during periods of rapid growth: childhood, adolescence, child-bearing years for women, and pregnancy. Prior to menopause, women need enough iron to replace losses

If you consume excess amounts: Healthy adults have little risk of iron overload from iron in foods. However, consuming excessive amounts from supplements or medications can lead to abdominal pain, constipation,

from menstrual flow. Iron needs also go up to support increases of blood volume during pregnancy. Not surprisingly, iron-deficiency anemia is most common among people at these ages and stages of life when the dietary need for iron is highest. In fact, it's hard to get enough without taking an iron supplement.

IRON: HEME VS. NONHEME

The iron in the food you consume isn't absorbed into your bloodstream particularly efficiently. In fact, much never gets absorbed. Fortunately, the RDAs take this fact into account.

How much iron in your food gets absorbed depends on several factors: (1) Is the form—heme or nonheme iron? (2) How much iron do you consume overall? (3) Are there other nutrients in your meal or snack that enhance or hinder iron's absorption? and (4) How much iron does your body have stored already?

- *Heme iron:* Most iron from meat, poultry, and fish is heme iron. That term comes from the way it's carried in foods—as part of the hemoglobin and myoglobin in animal tissue.
- *Nonheme iron:* Foods of plant origin contain only nonheme iron. Egg yolks have mostly nonheme iron.

Heme iron is absorbed more readily than nonheme iron is. Depending on how much iron your body already has stored, 15 to 35 percent of heme iron from food gets absorbed. Only 2 to 20 percent of nonheme iron gets absorbed, even though foods with nonheme iron often contain more iron. In fact, the bioavailability of iron in a mixed US diet (animal- and plant-based foods) is about 18 percent; in a vegetarian diet, about 10 percent.

Conversely, some phytonutrients—oxalic acid in spinach and chocolate; phytic acid in some legumes and grains; polyphenols in coffee; and tannins in coffee and tea—seem to inhibit nonheme iron absorption. *Tip:* For better nonheme iron absorption, drink coffee or tea between meals, not with them. Consuming vitamin C or iron from meat, poultry, and fish at the same time helps overcome these "inhibitors."

IRON: POWER OF PARTNERSHIP

Pairing certain foods enhances the absorption of nonheme iron in eggs and in plant-based foods:

- Add a little meat, poultry, or fish, which contain heme iron, to foods containing nonheme iron. For example:

Absorption Enhancers	Nonheme Iron Sources
Barbecued beef	With refried beans and tortillas
Chicken	With brown rice
Ground lean beef	With a whole-grain roll
Ground lean turkey	With beans in chili
Lean ham	With scrambled eggs or an omelet
Pork	With bean soup
Sirloin strips	With spinach salad

- Eat vitamin C–rich foods with foods that have nonheme iron. For example:

Absorption Enhancers	Nonheme Iron Sources
Grapefruit	With bran cereal
Orange juice	With a peanut butter sandwich on whole-wheat bread
Papaya	With whole-wheat toast
Red bell pepper	With whole-grain pasta
Strawberries	With oatmeal

faintness, gastric upset, nausea, and vomiting, especially when taken without food.

Iron can build up to dangerous levels for people with a genetic problem called hemochromatosis, whereby the body absorbs and stores too much iron. That excess can cause an enlarged liver and bronze skin pigmentation, as well as cardiac, liver, pancreatic, and other organ damage. Ten times more common in men, symptoms of hemochromatosis usually begin to appear in adulthood, often in their thirties.

Taking adult iron supplements can be dangerous for children. Children should get immediate medical attention if they take an overdose of iron supplements. For ages one through thirteen, the UL is 40 milligrams daily; for fourteen and older, it's 45 milligrams daily. The levels remain the same during pregnancy and breastfeeding.

See "A Closer Look . . . Calcium and Iron Supplements" in chapter 10, page 320.

Where it's mostly found: Iron is widely available from foods of both animal (heme iron) and plant (nonheme) sources. The deep-red color of animal muscle comes from hemoglobin. The darker the color, the higher the heme iron content. For example, beef liver, which is redder than roast beef, has more iron; dark turkey meat has more heme iron than light meat. Many foods on today's supermarket shelves are enriched or fortified with iron: iron-enriched flour (also used in baked goods and pasta) and iron-fortified breakfast cereals.

Food	Iron (mg)
SOURCES OF MOSTLY HEME IRON	
Beef liver, braised (3 oz.)	5.4
Beef, ground, 95 percent lean, broiled (3 oz.)	2.4
Chicken, dark meat only, roasted (3 oz.)	1.1
Chicken, light meat only, roasted (3 oz.)	0.9
Pork, lean, roasted (3 oz.)	0.6
Salmon, canned with edible bones (3 oz.)	0.6
SOURCES OF NONHEME IRON	
Fortified breakfast cereal (1 cup)*	4.5–18
Spinach, boiled (½ cup)	3.2
Prune juice (1 cup)	3.0
Wheat bran (½ cup)	3.0
Lima beans, cooked (½ cup)	2.1
Red kidney beans, canned (½ cup)	2.0
Pretzels, hard, plain (1 oz.)	1.3
White rice, enriched, cooked (½ cup)	1.0
White bread, enriched (1 slice)	0.7
Apricots, dried (¼ cup)	0.9
Egg (1 large)	0.9
Raisins, seedless, packed (¼ cup)	0.8
Whole-wheat bread (1 slice)	0.8
Peanut butter, smooth (2 tbsp.)	0.6
Brown rice, cooked (½ cup)	0.5
Dried plums (prunes) (¼ cup)	0.4
Egg white (1 large)	<0.1

*Check the label; amounts vary.

? Have you ever wondered?

. . . if spinach will make you strong, as the famous cartoon character Popeye believed? It's true that spinach contains iron. But another food component in spinach, called oxalic acid, binds with iron, impairing its absorption, so spinach is not the best source. Only physical activity, not iron or any other nutrient, builds muscle strength.

. . . why cooking in an iron skillet may improve the iron content of food? Before aluminum and stainless steel cookware, great-great-grandma unknowingly supplemented her family's diet with iron from her iron pots and pans. Foods with acids such as tomato juice, citrus juice, and vinegar help dissolve small amounts of iron from cast-iron pots and pans into the cooking liquids—especially in foods that simmer for a while.

. . . if you need more iron if you seem tired all the time? Maybe—or maybe you need more sleep, less stress, or perhaps more physical activity to increase your stamina. Fatigue is a symptom of anemia, however. Check with your doctor for a blood test. *See "Anemia: 'Tired Blood'" in chapter 25, page 722, for more about anemia and blood testing.*

Manganese

What it does:

- Serves as a partner of many enzymes, including RNA and DNA
- Helps in bone formation
- Helps in the metabolism of energy from carbohydrates, fats, and proteins

How much you need: For males aged fourteen to eighteen, the AI is 2.2 milligrams daily; for females, it's 1.6 milligrams daily. For males aged nineteen and older, the AI is 2.3 milligrams daily; for females, it's 1.8 milligrams daily. During pregnancy, the AI increases to 2.0 milligrams daily, and during breastfeeding, to 2.6 milligrams daily.

If you don't consume enough: The chances of not getting enough are very low since manganese is so widely distributed in the food supply.

If you consume excess amounts: Consuming harmful levels from food is very rare, too. For ages fourteen to eighteen, the UL is 9 milligrams daily; for nineteen and older, it's 11 milligrams daily. The levels remain the same during pregnancy and breastfeeding.

Where it's mostly found: Whole-grain products are the best sources of manganese, along with some fruits and vegetables. Tea also is a good source.

Food	Manganese (mg)
Sweet potato, canned, mashed (½ cup)	1.3
Pecans, chopped (1 oz.)	1.1
Brown rice, cooked (½ cup)	1.0
Tea, instant powder (1 tsp.)	0.9
Pineapple, raw, chunks (½ cup)	0.8
Whole-wheat bread (1 slice)	0.7
Hummus (¼ cup)	0.5
Kale, boiled (½ cup)	0.3
Strawberries, halved (½ cup)	0.3

Molybdenum

What it does:

- Works with riboflavin to incorporate the iron stored in the body into hemoglobin for making red blood cells
- Is part of many body enzymes

How much you need: For ages fourteen to eighteen, the RDA is 43 micrograms daily; for nineteen and older, it's 45 micrograms daily. During pregnancy and breastfeeding, the RDA for both age groups increases to 50 micrograms daily.

If you don't consume enough: With a normal diet, there's no need to worry about a deficiency. However, a deficiency of the enzymes made with molybdenum affects the nervous system and, in extreme cases, causes death.

If you consume excess amounts: Too much may affect reproduction, but harmful levels are quite uncommon. For ages fourteen to eighteen, the UL is 1,700 micrograms daily; for nineteen and older, it's 2,000 micrograms daily. The levels remain the same during pregnancy and breastfeeding.

Where it's mostly found: Molybdenum is found mostly in beans and peas, breads, grain products, liver, and milk. The amount consumed in a typical eating pattern appears adequate. Little is known about the actual amounts in foods.

Selenium

What it does:

- Works as an antioxidant with vitamin E to protect cells from damage that may lead to heart disease and perhaps to cancer and other health problems
- Aids cell growth and thyroid function
- Boosts immune function

How much you need: For ages fourteen and older, the RDA is 55 micrograms daily. During pregnancy, it increases to 60 micrograms daily, and during breastfeeding, to 70 micrograms daily.

If you don't consume enough: A deficiency is rare in the United States. If it occurs, it can cause a type of heart disease or a type of arthritis that produces pain, swelling, and loss of motion in joints.

If you consume excess amounts: A normal diet with a variety of foods generally provides moderate levels of selenium. Getting too much over time can cause brittle hair and nails, diarrhea, irritability, nausea, and nervous system problems, among other problems. Very high levels from dietary supplements can cause more severe problems, including heart and kidney failure. For ages fourteen and older, the UL is 400 micrograms daily. The level stays the same during pregnancy and breastfeeding.

Where it's mostly found: The richest sources are fish, kidneys, liver, and other meats. Grain products and seeds contain selenium, but the amount depends on the selenium content of the soil where they're grown. Fruits and vegetables generally don't have much. Brazil nuts contain about 70 to 95 micrograms in just one nut; one's enough!

Food	Selenium (mcg)
Brazil nuts (1)	96
Tuna, yellowfin, cooked, dry heat (3 oz.)	92
Beef liver, panfried, (3 oz.)	30
Ham, roasted (3 oz.)	22
Chicken, white meat, roasted (3 oz.)	21
Spaghetti, enriched, cooked (½ cup, not packed)	16
Egg (1 large)	15
Whole-wheat bread (1 slice)	8
Brown rice, cooked (½ cup)	6
Cashew nuts, dry roasted (1 oz.)	3
White beans, canned (½ cup)	2

Zinc

What it does:

- Promotes cell reproduction and tissue growth and repair. Adequate zinc intake is essential for growth and for making DNA, the genetic material of all cells.
- Is associated with more than two hundred enzymes
- Helps wounds heal and helps the immune system work properly

- Promotes sensory responses (taste and smell)
- Helps your body use carbohydrates, fats, and proteins

How much you need: For males aged fourteen and older, the RDA is 11 milligrams daily. For females aged fourteen to eighteen, it's 9 milligrams daily; for nineteen and older, it's 8 milligrams daily. During pregnancy, the RDA increases to 12 milligrams daily for ages eighteen and younger, and to 11 milligrams daily for ages nineteen and older; during breastfeeding, it increases to 13 milligrams daily for those age eighteen and younger and 12 milligrams daily, respectively.

If you don't consume enough: A deficiency during childhood can impair growth, and during pregnancy, it can cause birth defects. Other symptoms include appetite loss, diarrhea, diminished ability to taste food, hair loss, impaired immune functions, and skin conditions, among other problems.

Those who may not get enough zinc include people who have had gastrointestinal surgery, women who breastfeed babies after six months of age (breast milk contains zinc), and vegetarians who don't eat meat (zinc from beans and grains isn't fully absorbed).

If you consume excess amounts: Some symptoms can include diarrhea, headaches, and nausea. Over time, excess amounts can lead to low copper levels, lower immunity, and low levels of HDL ("good") cholesterol. For ages fourteen to eighteen, the UL is 34 milligrams daily; for nineteen and older, it's 40 milligrams daily. The levels remain the same during pregnancy and breastfeeding.

Where it's mostly found: Good sources of zinc include foods of animal origin, including meat—especially liver, poultry, and fish. Eggs and milk supply smaller amounts. Beans and peas, fermented soybean paste (miso), nuts, and whole-grain products contain zinc but in a form that's less available to the body.

Food	Zinc (mg)
Beef, ground, 95 percent lean, cooked (3 oz.)	5.6
Wheat germ (¼ cup)	3.5
Crab, canned (3 oz.)	3.2
Wheat bran (½ cup)	2.1
Pork, loin, lean, roasted (3 oz.)	1.8
Sunflower seeds (1 oz.)	1.5
Milk, fat-free (1 cup)	1.0
Tofu, regular, raw (½ cup)	1.0
Almonds, dry roasted (1 oz.)	0.9
Chicken breast, meat only, roasted (3 oz.)	0.9
Kidney beans, canned (½ cup)	0.8
Peanut butter, smooth (2 tbsp.)	0.8
Egg (1 large)	0.6
Tuna, light, canned, packed in water, drained (3 oz.)	0.6
Whole-wheat bread (1 slice)	0.6

15

Water, "Phytos," and Probiotics

In this chapter, find out about . . .

Water, beyond thirst

Phytonutrients, a rainbow for health

Prebiotics and probiotics, for gut health and more

Food is a deliciously complex package of nourishment, but it can't be overlooked that water is an essential nutrient, too. What's more, other substances in food, including phytonutrients, probiotics, and prebiotics, promote health beyond—and in addition to—basic nutrition.

Water: A Fluid Asset

Unless your throat feels parched and sweat drips from your brow, you probably give little thought to water. Yet this clear, refreshing fluid is one of your body's most essential nutrients.

Water is vital. While you may survive for several weeks without food, you can't live longer than a few days without water. In fact, losing more than 10 percent of your body weight from dehydration, or water loss, causes extreme weakness and potential heat stroke. And a 20 percent loss is life-threatening. Water truly is the beverage of life!

Water is the most abundant substance in the human body as well as the most common substance on earth. On average, body weight is 50 to 65 percent water—or for many adults, or about eight to twelve gallons of water. That range may seem surprisingly large, but differences from person to person depend on body composition, age, and gender, among other factors.

So, compared with body fat, lean tissue holds much more water. The leaner you are, the higher the proportion of water in your body. Males, with more muscle, carry a higher percentage of water in their bodies than females do. Younger people usually have more than older adults. Water accounts for about 75 percent of a newborn's weight, while the amount dwindles in older adults to about 50 percent.

All body tissues contain water—some more than others. That blood contains water is certainly no surprise; your blood is about 83 percent water. Lean muscle tissue is about 70 to 75 percent water; body fat, about 10 to 40 percent, as reported by the National Academy of Sciences' Institute of Medicine. (IOM). As the amount of body fat increases, the percentage of water in body fat decreases. Even though bones seem hard, they, too, contain water, about 22 percent by weight.

AN ESSENTIAL NUTRIENT

What does water do in your body? Far more than satisfy your thirst! Thirst is like a warning light that's flashing on your car's dashboard. This physical sensation signals that your body needs more fluid to perform its many functions. To satisfy thirst, you drink fluids. That said, you needed water even before experiencing the signal of thirst.

Water itself is a simple substance, containing just one part oxygen and two parts hydrogen. It supplies no calories. Yet every body cell, tissue, and organ, and almost every life-sustaining body process, needs water to function. In fact, water is the nutrient your body needs in the greatest amount.

Whether inside or surrounding your cells, nearly every body function takes place in a watery medium. Water regulates body temperature, keeping it constant at about 98.6°F. Many body processes produce heat, including any physical activity. Through perspiration, heat escapes as water evaporates on your skin.

Think of water as a solvent in which other body substances dissolve. Water dissolves nutrients and transports them, along with oxygen, to your body cells and carries waste products away. It moistens body tissues such as those in your mouth, eyes, and nose. Water is the main part of every body fluid, including blood, gastric (stomach) juice, saliva, urine, and amniotic fluid (for a developing fetus). By softening stools, water helps prevent constipation. It helps lubricate joints and cushion organs and tissues.

To keep your body functioning normally and efficiently, your body needs an ongoing water supply. Feeling tired? Even mild dehydration can cause a drop in energy production. All the metabolic processes that produce energy in your cells need water.

During a strenuous workout, losing water weight is common, especially on hot, humid days. Losing just one or two pounds of your body's water weight can trigger thirst. With a little more fluid loss, the body loses strength and endurance; even mild dehydration can interfere with physical performance. With more water loss and prolonged exposure to high temperatures, a person may suffer from heat exhaustion or risk heat stroke.

Dehydration: Body Signals

The effects of dehydration, or loss of body water, can be significant and even lead to death. Watch for signals of water loss. All these steps won't happen in a single day.

Water Loss by Body Weight	Progressive Effects of Water Loss . . . That Can Lead to Dehydration (Partial List)
0 to 1%	Thirst
2 to 5%	Dry mouth, flushed skin, fatigue, headache, and impaired physical performance
6%	Increased body temperature, breathing rate, and pulse rate
8%	Dizziness, increased weakness, and labored breathing with exercise
10%	Muscle spasms, swollen tongue, delirium, and wakefulness
11%	Poor blood circulation and failing kidney function

See "Dehydration Alert" in chapter 21, page 602, for signs that you need to drink more when you work out or during sports activities.

WATER AS A NUTRIENT: YOUR SOURCES

Of all the nutrients in your diet, water is the most abundant. Drinking water and other beverages are the main sources of fluids. But you "eat" quite a bit of water in foods, too—perhaps more than you think. On average about 20 percent of someone's fluid intake comes from food. Juicy vegetables and fruits such as celery, lettuce, tomatoes, and watermelon contain more than 90 percent water. Even dry foods, such as bread supply some. *See "Food: A Water Source" in this chapter, page 446, for the amount in specific foods.*

Your body has one more water source. About 15 percent of your body's total water supply forms in your body cells when energy is produced from carbohydrates, fats, and proteins. Along with energy, water is an end product of metabolism.

FLUIDS: HOW MUCH IS ENOUGH?

The average adult loses about 2½ quarts or more (about 10 or more cups) of water daily through perspiration (even when sitting), urination, bowel movements, and even breathing. During hot, humid weather or strenuous physical activity, fluid loss may be much higher. Unlike some other nutrients, extra water isn't stored in the body. To avoid dehydration and to keep your body working normally, you need to replace lost fluids.

How much fluid do you need each day? The Dietary Reference Intakes (DRIs) set the Adequate Intake (AI) level at 3.7 liters (125 ounces, or about 15½ cups) of total water daily for males aged nineteen and older; for females nineteen and older, it's 2.7 liters (91 ounces, or about 11½ cups) daily. (A liter is about 1 quart or about 4 cups.) Children and teens need somewhat less. *See "Daily Reference Intakes" in the appendix, page 780, for DRIs for water.*

The AI is for generally healthy people living in temperate climates. The IOM notes that people can be properly hydrated at higher or lower levels of water intake, too. In fact, the AI is neither a specific requirement nor a recommended intake, but instead is based on the median total water intake, estimated from US dietary surveys.

These amounts may seem like a lot, but your "total water" can come from many sources—from drinking water, other beverages, and water in foods. If you're healthy and have access to drinking water and other beverages, you likely drink enough water. In fact, satisfying your thirst, along with a habit of drinking beverages with meals, is usually adequate. A little more than eight cups (about 1.9 liters) of fluids a day, along with food, is generally enough to replace the fluids you lose.

Thirst signals the need for fluids, but it isn't foolproof, especially for elderly people and children, and during illness, hot weather, or strenuous physical activity. Waiting until you feel thirsty to drink may be too

Your Healthy Eating Check-In

Are You Adequately Hydrated?

There's no perfect way to calculate your exact fluid needs for the day, but this simple equation provides a quick guesstimate if you're a healthy adult. Remember that the more you perspire, the more fluids you need. More important, let thirst (and urine color) be your guides.

1. For your fluid needs based on your body weight and activity level, use these formulas:

Activity Level	Body Weight	×	Fluids per Pound	=	Total Daily Fluids
Average:	______ pounds	×	0.5 fluid ounces	=	______ fluid ounces
More active:	______ pounds	×	0.66 fluid ounces	=	______ fluid ounces

For the total daily fluid amount in cups, use this formula:

Daily Fluids in Ounces	÷	Ounces per Cup	=	Daily Fluids In Cups
______ fluid ounces	÷	8 fluid ounces	=	______ cups

2. Now keep a beverage diary for a few days. Jot down what you drank and how much.

3. Did you drink enough?

(Remember that about 80 percent of the water you consume comes from beverages. The rest will come from your food choices.)

long. By then, two or more cups of body fluids may be gone—even when you're healthy. *See "Water" in chapter 20, page 594, for more on fluids for older adults.*

To see if you're drinking enough fluids, check your urine. A small volume of dark-colored urine indicates that you aren't consuming enough fluids. Besides feeling thirsty, this is your signal to drink more. If you're well hydrated, your urine will be pale yellow, like the color of lemonade.

If you participate in sports, weigh yourself before and after strenuous physical activity. For every pound of weight you lose, replace it with 2½ to 3 cups (20 to 24 ounces) of fluid (more than the water weight you lost).

Caution: If you always seem thirsty or urinate too much, talk to your doctor. This may signal diabetes or another serious health concern. Water retention, for reasons other than premenstrual syndrome, may suggest a kidney or liver problem.

Water: Too Much?

In healthy people, water intake and water loss balance out. When you don't consume enough, your body may trigger thirst. If you consume more than you need, your kidneys eliminate the excess, potentially about two cups of fluid an hour. You probably won't overdo on water.

While rare, water toxicity can happen if someone drinks too much water, especially a concern for some endurance athletes, who can drink too much water, or overhydrate. However, anyone can be a victim.

Have you ever wondered?

. . . why you feel thirsty after eating salty food? Salt is made of two minerals: sodium and chloride. When you eat a lot of salty foods, the salt is absorbed and circulates in your bloodstream, and the fluid around your body cells gets saltier. Your body responds by drawing water out of body cells. That sends a signal from your cells to your brain (your thirst center), alerting you to drink more water to restore the balance of sodium and body fluid.

Bars and cocktail lounges have figured this out. When you feel thirsty, you likely drink more. This explains why they often serve salty snacks with drinks.

. . . if you really need to drink eight cups of water a day to meet the recommendation? That's a common perception. Obviously, however, water is in every beverage as well as in soups, smoothies. Moreover, it's in nearly anything you eat. In fact, some vegetables and fruits are 90 percent water or more, *as shown in "Food: A Water Source" in this chapter, page 446.*

On average, about 80 percent of the water you consume comes from beverages. The rest—about 20 percent—comes from water in foods.

Food: A Water Source

It's not easy to calculate how much water you consume each day. While drinks supply most of your water needs, foods also provide a surprising amount.

Food	Serving Size	Amount of Water as Percentage of Food Weight	Amount of Water in Fluid Ounces per Serving
Lettuce, green leaf, shredded	1 cup	95%	1.2 ounces
Celery, raw	1 medium stalk	95%	1.5 ounces
Tomato, raw	½ cup	94%	3 ounces
Grapefruit, white	½ medium	91%	3.8 ounces
Watermelon, chunks	1 cup	91%	4.9 ounces
Milk, low-fat	1 cup	90%	7.7 ounces
Broccoli, raw, chopped	½ cup	89%	1.4 ounces
Carrot, raw, strips	½ cup	88%	1.9 ounces
Orange juice	½ cup	88%	3.8 ounces
Apple, with skin	1 medium	86%	5.5 ounces
Yogurt, fat-free, vanilla	8 ounces	79%	6.3 ounces
Tuna, canned in water, drained	3 ounces	78%	2.3 ounces
Potato, baked with skin	1 medium	75%	4.6 ounces
Rice, brown, cooked	½ cup	70%	2.5 ounces
Chicken, roasted, meat only	3 ounces	67%	2.0 ounces
Kidney beans, canned, drained	½ cup	67%	3.1 ounces
Spaghetti, cooked	½ cup	63%	1.4 ounces
Cheddar cheese	1 ounce	38%	0.4 ounce
Whole-wheat bread	1 slice	38%	0.4 ounce
Butter	1 tablespoon	16%	0.1 ounce
Raisins, packed	¼ cup	15%	0.2 ounce
Vegetable oil	1 tablespoon	0	0

Source: US Department of Agriculture, National Nutrient Database for Standard Reference, Release 28, 2016.

Kidneys can't excrete enough excess water through urine, diluting the mineral content of the blood. The result can be hyponatremia, an imbalance of water and electrolytes, when sodium levels in the blood are too low. With this imbalance, extra water swells body cells, including brain cells. The extra pressure affects vital functions, with potentially fatal outcomes.

This condition requires prompt medical attention, as serious symptoms can be life-threatening. *See "Fluids: Enough, Not Too Much" in chapter 21, page 601 to learn about the symptoms and how to avoid hyponatremia.* Since water toxicity is unlikely in most circumstances, a Tolerable Upper Intake Level (UL) for water wasn't set.

Your Water Needs

Your own water needs vary from day to day. The amount depends on your health, level of physical activity, the climate, and your exposure to heat, along with other factors. For example:

- *Heat or cold.* When you're exposed to extreme temperatures—very hot or very cold—your body uses more water to maintain its normal temperature. Very hot weather increases the risk of dehydration for older adults.

- *Heated or recirculated air.* When you're exposed to either one for a long time, water evaporates from your skin. Dry, recirculated air on planes promotes dehydration.
- *High altitudes.* Altitudes of about 8,200 feet, or about 2,500 meters, may increase urine output and raise your breathing rate; both result in more water loss.
- *Strenuous work or exercise.* Your body loses water through perspiration. How much depends on the type of exercise, the duration, the temperature—and how much you sweat. Drink before physical activity. During exercise, drink early and often—and afterwards, too. As a practical guide, check the color of your urine, as noted above. *See Thirst for Success!" in chapter 21, page 600, for more about water needs during physical activity.*
- *High-fiber diet.* Your body needs extra water to process more roughage and prevent the chance of constipation.
- *Pregnancy and breastfeeding.* Both increase the amount of fluid a woman's body needs. The AI for water advised for pregnancy is 3 liters daily, and for breastfeeding, 3.8 liters daily.

Water: Keeping Body Fluids in Balance

To maintain your body's fluid balance, replace the amount of water you lose each day. If you lose a little more, such as through perspiration, drink more to balance out.

YOUR BODY LOSES WATER DAILY THROUGH . . .	
Perspiration (loss through skin)	2 to 8 cups
Urine	2 to 4 cups
Breath (expired air)	1 to 1½ cups
Feces	⅔ cup

YOU REPLACE WATER IN YOUR BODY DAILY THROUGH . . .	
Water and other fluids	9 to 12½ cups* (depending on gender)
Solid foods	2⅓ to 3 cups (depending on gender)
Water from metabolism	1 to 1½ cups

*Based on estimated minimum losses and production of water in healthy sedentary adults. If you consume a little more than your body needs, your body will excrete any extra.

Source: Based on *Dietary Reference Intakes for Water, Potassium, Sodium, Chloride, and Sulfate*, The National Academies Press, 2005.

- *Fever, diarrhea, and vomiting.* These conditions cause increased water loss. Follow the advice of your doctor; drink plenty of water and other fluids to prevent dehydration. Depending on the illness, your doctor may advise an oral rehydration solution. Some health conditions, such as urinary tract stones and bladder infections, may increase the need for fluids. Others may cause fluid retention; your doctor may advise limiting fluid intake. For older adults, some health conditions make hydration a serious issue; *see "Water" in chapter 20, page 584 for more about fluids for older adults.*

Hydration: An Issue for All Seasons

From the bone-chilling days of winter to the hot, sultry days of summer, the body needs water to maintain its normal temperature. Your body perspires as a cooling mechanism. Cooling down is harder in hot, humid weather than in hot, dry weather because perspiration doesn't evaporate quickly from your skin. Instead, your skin feels sticky and hot.

Dehydration may seem like just a summer issue, but keeping your body well hydrated during winter is just as important. When the weather turns chilly, most people head indoors. There, heated air evaporates the moisture on your skin. Even in the cold outdoors, you may perspire and may not realize it—perhaps from the physical exertion of shoveling snow, skating or skiing, or from being bundled up with many layers of clothing.

SMART DRINKING: A HEALTHY HABIT

To keep your body well hydrated, consume enough water—and drink small amounts throughout the day, not mostly all at once. Follow your thirst; drink beverages with meals. Because milk, juice, and some other beverages are mostly water, they count toward your daily water intake. So does water from soups and solid foods, although you can't measure it. On average, moisture in food provides about 20 percent of total water intake, water and other fluids provide the rest.

To drink more water during the day, consider these tips:

- Take water breaks during the day instead of coffee breaks. If you're a mindless "sipper," keep a cup of water on your desk.
- When you buy a vending machine or convenience store drink, reach for bottled water.
- Complement meals and snacks with water, milk, or juice (instead of soda or other sweetened beverages). Occasionally, start your meals with soup. Limit the amount of juice, however, since its natural sugars can contribute more calories than you may realize.
- With a snack, drink 100% juice, milk, or sparkling water. Remember that sipping juice, milk, or sweetened drinks may increase the risk of tooth decay. You might dilute juice with water, or add a splash of juice to your water for a fruity beverage with less sugar.
- Keep a glass of water on your nightstand to drink when you awake during the night or first thing in the morning. After a night's sleep, you may be thirsty.

- Before, during, and after any physical activity, drink water, especially in hot weather. Consume one-half to two cups of water every fifteen to twenty minutes while you exercise. Don't wait until you feel thirsty. *See "Thirst for Success" in chapter 21, page 600, for more on drinking fluids during exercise.*
- Keep a bottle of water with you as you commute, while you work, and as you run errands. Periodically fill it up. Travel with water, too, even for day outings. Airline travel promotes dehydration. Use reusable water bottles when possible; always make sure they are clean! *See "Drinks in Flight" in chapter 9, page 310, for tips on staying hydrated.*
- Freeze water in freezer-safe reusable water bottles, available in retail stores. Take one with you for ice-cold water all day long.
- Add a lime or lemon wedge if it makes water more appealing so you drink more. Or try other flavors such as berries, fresh herbs, or apple, peach, or cucumber slices. Consider using a water bottle with an infuser basket for slices of your favorite vegetables or fruits.
- Keep the environment in mind. Instead of relying mostly on bottled water, carry water in a reusable, eco-friendly water bottle. Clean it after each use.
- Besides plain water, choose other drinks: fluids with few if any added sugars. Drinks such as fruit drinks, some sports drinks, and nondiet sodas deliver water—and calories you may not need. *Tip:* By drinking water instead of a 20-ounce sugar-sweetened drink, you save about 240 calories!
- Drink sparkling water at social gatherings. Limit alcoholic drinks. When eating out you'll save money and reduce calories.
- Consume caffeinated beverages such as coffee, tea, and some soft drinks in moderation along with enough water. They contribute to your day's total water intake, too, as noncaffeinated drinks do. While a high intake of caffeine may have a diuretic effect, fluid from these beverages should offset any small fluid loss. For that reason, they aren't dehydrating. Diuretic effect means water loss through increased urination.

  Also note: Any diuretic effect from alcoholic drinks appears to be short term, too. The effect may vary and may depend on how much water you drink before meals.

See chapter 4, page 81, for more about nutrition in drink options.

Phytonutrients: Different from Nutrients

Besides nutrients, plant-based foods (vegetables, fruits, beans and peas, whole grains, nuts, seeds, and teas, as well as herbs and spices) have another "crop" of naturally occurring compounds with potential health benefits. Collectively, they're called phytonutrients, also called phytochemicals, meaning plant chemicals. *Phyto* from Greek means "plant." Think "fight" for "phytos" since they appear to promote health by sparking

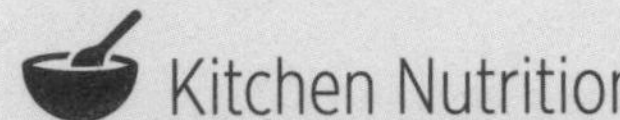

More from "Phytos" on the Menu

Research suggests that what you do in the kitchen can make a difference in food's phytonutrients benefits.

- Cooking, chopping, pureeing, and food processing may enhance the body's ability to use (the bioavailability of) some phytonutrients such as carotenoids (including lycopene). In addition, dietary fat may enhance the absorption of carotenoids; dietary fiber impedes it.
- Heat damages anthocyanins, which are flavonoids. On the flip side, the anthocyanin content may increase in many types of fresh fruit if stored for a few days.
- Flaxseed needs to be crushed or ground to get the benefits of its omega-3s.
- For the most benefit from tea's polyphenols, you need to brew each cup fresh (preferably in water that's not hard) and drink it soon. Three to five minutes of brewing for one tea bag brings out 80 percent of the catechins, which are flavonoids.
- You need to chop garlic about fifteen minutes before heating to allow allyl sulfides to fully develop.

? Have you ever wondered

. . . if the body stores phytonutrients like it does for fat-soluble vitamins A, D, E, and K? Carotenoids are fat soluble, too, and so can be stored. They can accumulate in the body to toxic levels when consumed to excess, more likely from high amounts in supplements than from food.

Flavonoids are water soluble. Like B vitamins and vitamin C, any excess is washed out of the body. Because they aren't stored, foods with flavonoids need to be eaten often to get their health benefits.

. . . if supplements are a good way to get phytonutrients like lutein and genestein? Not recommended. While the health benefits of phytonutrients from food appear positive, little is known about the long-term benefits or effects of large doses of phytonutrients from supplements. Beyond that, the relationship between health and food is complex, and so are the interactions among phytonutrients, nutrients, and fiber. Supplements with just one or a few phytonutrients are likely not to be as effective as those same phytonutrients from food.

Functional Nutrition

A Quick Look at Key Phytonutrients

A Handful of Phytonutrients	What They Appear to Do	Where They're Found (Some Food Sources)
CAROTENOIDS		
Beta-carotene	• Neutralizes free radicals that may damage cells • Bolsters cellular antioxidant defenses • Can be made into vitamin A in the body	• Yellow-orange vegetables such as carrots, pumpkins, sweet potatoes, winter squash; and fruits such as apricots, cantaloupes, papayas • Green vegetables such as broccoli, kale, and spinach
Lutein, zeaxanthin	• Supports maintenance of eye health	• Green vegetables such as asparagus, broccoli, Brussels sprouts, collard greens, kale, Romaine lettuce, spinach, Swiss chard • Corn, winter squash, citrus fruits, kiwifruit (Eggs have a small amount of zeaxanthin, too.) • Egg yolks
Lycopene	• Supports maintenance of prostate health	• Most red vegetables and fruits such as tomatoes, processed tomato products, guava, pink grapefruit, watermelon (*Note:* The red pigment in red peppers is from keto-carotenoids, not lycopene.)
FLAVONOIDS		
Anthocyanins: cyanidin, pelargonidin, delphinidin, malvidin	• Bolsters cellular antioxidant defenses • Supports maintenance of healthy brain function	• Berries, cherries, red grapes
Flavanols: catechins, epicatechins, epigallocatechin	• Supports maintenance of heart health	• Apples, chocolate, cocoa, grapes, tea (black, green, or oolong)
Flavanones: hesperetin, naringenin	• Neutralizes free radicals which may damage cells • Bolsters cellular antioxidant defenses	• Citrus fruits
Flavonols: quercetin: kaempferol isorhamnetin, myricetin	• Neutralizes free radicals that may damage cells • Bolsters cellular antioxidant defenses	• Apples, broccoli, onions, tea
Procyanidins, proanthocyanidins	• Supports maintenance of urinary tract health and heart health	• Apples, cinnamon, cocoa, cranberries, grapes, peanuts, strawberries, red wine, tea
ISOTHIOCYANATES		
Sulphoraphane	• May enhance detoxification of undesirable compounds • Bolsters cellular antioxidant defenses	• Broccoli, Brussels sprouts, cabbage, cauliflower, horseradish, kale
PHENOLIC ACIDS		
Caffeic acid, ferulic acid	• Bolsters cellular antioxidant defenses • Supports maintenance of eye and heart health	• Apples, citrus fruits, pears, some vegetables, coffee
PHYTOESTROGENS		
Isoflavones: daidzein, genestein	• For women, supports menopausal health • Supports maintenance of bone health, immune health, and healthy brain function	• Soybeans (edamame), soy-based foods such as tofu

(continued)

Functional Nutrition *(continued)*

A Handful of Phytonutrients	What They Appear to Do	Where They're Found (Some Food Sources)
Lignans	• Supports maintenance of heart health and immune health	• Broccoli, carrots, cauliflower, flaxseed (not flaxseed oil unless hull remains), lentils, nuts, rye, seeds, triticale
SULFIDES/THIOLS		
Allyl methyl trisulfide, diallyl sulfide	• Supports maintenance of heart, immune, and digestive health • May enhance detoxification of undesirable compounds	• Garlic, leeks, onions, scallions
Dithiolthiones	• Supports maintenance of immune health • May enhance detoxification of undesirable compounds	• Cruciferous vegetables such as bok choy, broccoli, Brussels sprouts, cauliflower, cabbage, garden cress, and similar green leaf vegetables.

Source: Adapted from International Food Information Council Foundation, 2011.

Other phytonutrients are addressed elsewhere: fiber and polyols (sugar alcohols) in *chapter 11, page 368*, plant stanols and sterols in *chapter 13, page 405*, and soy protein *in chapter 12, page 373*. Animal-based foods also contain some functional substances, e.g., some fatty acids, *see chapter 13, page 385.*

body processes that fight, or reduce the risk for, the development of some diseases.

Unlike nutrients, phytonutrients aren't essential for life. Yet, because of their potential to promote good health, they've captured attention from both the scientific community and the public. Today, many consumers are motivated to eat well as part of self-care. Adding foods with phytonutrients may provide health-enhancing benefits such as boost immunity, slow aging, and prevent or reduce the risks for chronic disease.

A common challenge is that public interest in phytonutrients is ahead of scientific evidence about them. Research on phytonutrients is a relatively young frontier in nutrition, as exciting today as vitamin discoveries were a hundred years ago—with much to learn about their composition in food and their roles in health. Here's some of what's known so far.

"PHYTOS": IN A CLASS OF THEIR OWN

Neither vitamins nor minerals, phytonutrients are substances that plants produce naturally to protect themselves against viruses, bacteria, and fungi, as well as insects, drought, and even the sun. Beyond that, they provide the color, aroma, texture, and flavor that give many foods so much sensual appeal.

An orange has more than 170 different phytonutrients! While all edible parts of vegetables and fruits contain phytonutrients, they're concentrated in the skin, or peel—a reason to eat edible peels.

Of the thousands of phytonutrients already identified, more than two thousand are plant pigments that put a rainbow of colors on your plate. Sometimes one color may mask another. And some are colorless—one more reason for variety! *See "A Closer Look . . . Paint Your Plate with Color!" in this chapter, page 452.*

Because growing conditions differ (soil, climate, altitude, temperature, plant maturity, and the presence of predators), the phytonutrient content in the same food may differ somewhat, depending on where it's from. Food processing and preparation also affect phytonutrient content.

Phytonutrient Categories

Like nutrients, phytonutrients are grouped according to their biochemical characteristics and similar protective functions in your body. Only a few hundred have been studied much.

Most phytonutrients in vegetables and fruits fit into several subgroups:

- *Carotenoids:* The yellow, orange, and red colors found in nature come from more than 600 carotenoids. These pigments are hidden by chlorophyll in some green plants. Beta-carotene, lutein, and lycopene are well-known leaders in the fight to reduce the damage from free radicals. Foods high in carotenoids may be effective in helping prevent certain cancers and may help reduce your risk of macular degeneration. *See "Carotenoids: 'Color' Your Food Healthy" in chapter 14, page 424.*

Spices and Herbs: More Ways to Boost "Phytos"

A pinch of this, a dash of that. From ethnic dishes to family favorites, herbs and spices help define the flavors and aromas we enjoy. They contribute taste without salt, added sugars, or fats. They add appeal to vegetables, fruits, whole grains, and other nutrient-rich foods, a positive strategy for weight management and healthy eating. Culinary herbs and spices, when used well, may encourage the enjoyment of nourishing foods that may otherwise be avoided and may help preserve the quality of food.

BENEFITS BEYOND FLAVOR

Like vegetables and fruits, herbs and spices are sources of phytonutrients, not surprising since they also come from plants. Many are phenolic phytonutrients with health-promoting potential: "potential" since research on antioxidants is still limited. For example, animal studies are researching the possibility that certain herbs and spices may promote immunity; reduce inflammation linked to heart disease; help to curb appetite; enhance satiety; boost metabolism; enhance insulin activity; and potentially protect against cancer.

These are among the common herbs and spices getting more research attention: black pepper, cinnamon, cloves, coriander, ginger, oregano, paprika (red pepper), rosemary, thyme, and turmeric.

Since dried herbs and spices have water removed, the antioxidants are concentrated. They also retain more of their phytonutrient potential. And a little bit can go a long way! Research indicates that some antioxidant-rich herbs and spices, when paired with certain foods, appear to enhance their beneficial qualities. For example, some herbs may help boost the antioxidant power of salad ingredients, protect vitamin E (alpha-tocopherol) in edible oils, or increase the bioavailability of beta carotene in vegetables; others may help reduce fat oxidation when grilling meat. That said, there is still much to be learned about the bioavailability of phytonutrients in herbs and spices and how they work.

HERBS AND SPICES IN MEAL PREP

Just as it's advisable to eat a variety of vegetables and fruits, it's a good idea to boost flavor with a variety of herbs and spices to get a variety of phytonutrients, too: cloves in coffee, ginger in tea, and oregano in nearly any Italian dish. Double the benefit by using paprika in chili in place of salt, sprinkling cinnamon on oatmeal in place of sugar, or using garlic in place of butter in mashed potatoes.

Herbs and spices can help improve the nutritional quality of your meals and snacks when they replace salt, added sugars, and unhealthy fats and when they add flavor appeal to all kinds of healthy foods such as vegetables.

See "Herbs—and Spices, Too!" in chapter 8, page 266, for more about herbs and spices and using them in food preparation.

- *Flavonoids:* As an abundant type of polyphenols, many flavonoids have been studied more than other phytonutrients. Many biological effects of flavonoids appear to be related to sending signals to cells rather than working as antioxidants.
- *Organosulfur compounds:* Phytonutrients that contain sulfur, called glucosinolates, come from cruciferous vegetables. Isothiocyanates are also released when these vegetables are chopped or chewed.

What's known about the phytonutrient composition of food is limited. The USDA National Nutrient Database for Standard Reference (Release 28) has limited databases for some phytonutrient categories: flavonoids, isoflavones, and proanthocyanidins: www.nal.usda.gov/fnic/phytonutrients. This site also offers a link to other databases, including some for carotenoids and flavonoids.

PHYTOS: ROLE IN HEALTH? HOW MUCH?

Phytonutrients are among the unique components of food that offer functional benefits. The term "functional foods" refers to foods or their components with health benefits beyond basic nutrition. *See "Functional Nutrition: A Quick Look at Key Phytonutrients" in this chapter, page 449.*

From any vegetable, fruit, herb, or spice, these substances appear to work together and with nutrients and fiber for your good health. How do their actions add up? An individual phytonutrient is unlikely to be the sole influence on heath and protection from disease. What we know today about phytonutrients is merely an "appetizer."

Phytonutrients: What They Do

These bioactive compounds may promote health in many different ways, for example by helping to slow the aging process or helping to reduce

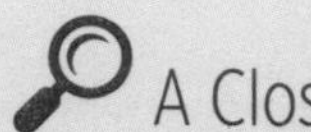

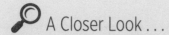

A Closer Look . . .

Paint Your Plate with Color

Toss blueberries in your yogurt. Garnish your salad with sliced beets. Tuck spinach leaves in your sandwich. Color offers much more than eye appeal to a wonderful meal! A rainbow of vegetables and fruits creates a palette of nutrients, *addressed in chapter 14, "Carotenoids: 'Color' Your Food Healthy," page 424*, and phytonutrients on your plate, each with a different bundle of potential benefits in a healthy diet. These benefits range from oxidizing free radicals that may damage healthy cells, to having anti-inflammatory qualities, to lowering LDL ("bad") cholesterol.

Color	Vegetables		Fruits		Potential Benefits
Green	artichokes asparagus broccoli Brussels sprouts green beans green cabbage green pepper	kale leafy greens okra snow peas spinach zucchini	avocado green apples green grapes honeydew	kiwifruit lime green pears	Their lutein and indoles may help promote healthy vision.
Orange and deep yellow	carrot sweet corn sweet potato	winter squash yellow beets yellow pepper	apricot cantaloupe grapefruit mango papaya	peach pineapple yellow apple yellow fig	Carotenoids, bioflavonoids, and the antioxidant vitamin C may promote heart, vision, and immune health, and reduce risk for some cancers. The deeper the yellow/orange color, the more carotenoids these foods have!
Purple and blue	eggplant purple cabbage	purple-fleshed potato	blackberries blueberries plums	purple figs raisins	Anthocyanins, which give a blue-purple color, and phenolics, may help with memory and urinary tract health and may help reduce cancer risks.
Red	beets red onions red peppers	red potatoes rhubarb tomatoes	blood oranges cherries cranberries pomegranate	red grapes red/pink grapefruit strawberries watermelon	Lycopene, a powerful carotenoid, and anthocyanins may help maintain heart, vision, and immune health, and may reduce cancer risks. When cooked or canned, lycopene is more available to your body.
White, tan, brown	cauliflower jicama kohlrabi mushrooms onions	parsnips turnip white corn white-fleshed potato	banana brown pear	dates white peaches	Of particular interest: allicin in garlic and onions, and selenium in mushrooms may promote heart health and may help reduce cancer risks.

See "Vegetable Group: Vary Your Veggies" and "Fruit Group: Focus on Whole Fruit" in chapter 2, pages 32 and 35, for more about vegetables and fruits.

the risk for many diseases. They may serve as antioxidants, enhance immunity, enhance communication among body cells, cause cancer cells to die, detoxify carcinogens, and repair damage to DNA that's caused by smoking and other toxins. Similar foods may have different health effects for two key reasons: their chemical structures differ and they're metabolized differently.

Researchers are investigating how certain phytonutrients protect against some cancers, heart disease, stroke, high blood pressure, cataracts, osteoporosis, urinary tract infections, and other chronic health conditions. Health claims or qualified health claims have been approved by the FDA for some. That said, the benefits and actions of phytonutrients are uncertain.

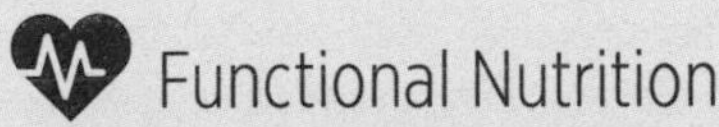

What's in a Name?

With the advent of functional foods, new terms have entered our vocabulary. Although not legally defined, here's what they generally mean and how they differ:

- *Functional foods:* Foods that provide health benefits beyond basic nutrition
- *Phytonutrients:* Substances in plant-based foods with physiologically active components that have functional food benefits; also called phytochemicals
- *Prebiotics:* Nondigestible food substances that stimulate the growth or activity of health-promoting, or "good," bacteria in the intestines (gut), providing health benefits to the body
- *Probiotics:* Live microorganisms (bacteria and some yeasts) that, when consumed in adequate amounts, may promote health by improving the balance of "good" bacteria in the intestines (gut)
- *Synbiotics:* Products with both prebiotics (usually an oligosaccharide) and probiotic microorganisms that work together to keep the growth and balance of "good" bacteria in the intestines (gut)
- *Zoonutrients:* A term sometimes used for substances, such as omega-3 fatty acids, with physiologically active components in animal-based foods; also called zoochemicals

Phytonutrients: How Much You Need

Since little is understood about their absorption or metabolism, no Dietary Reference Intakes exist for phytonutrients yet. Neither do we know how much of them people consume. We can surmise that those who eat more vegetables, fruits, and whole grains get more.

The bottom line: Already there's overwhelming evidence for the health benefits of plant-based foods as a key part of healthy eating: vegetables, fruits, beans and peas (including soy), nuts, seeds, and grains, especially whole grains. Research shows that you lower the odds for some cancers, heart disease, and other health problems by eating more vegetables, fruits, and whole grains. Check with a registered dietitian nutritionist for guidance on how much and what kind.

To reap the potential benefits of the thousands of phytonutrients, remember: food first! Enjoy a variety of plant-based foods rather than getting them isolated in supplements. The composition of "phytos" in food differs, as do phytonutrients' biological functions. Keep in mind that whether from food or supplements, phytonutrients aren't a magic bullet for health.

Prebiotics and Probiotics: A Bioactive Duo

Not so long ago, the word "probiotics" seemed to be a medical term. "Gut feelings" referred only to your intuition. And yogurt and kefir? You just knew they were good for you, but why?

Today, most people know about probiotics, especially if they focus attention on their gut health. Yet, with so many products—yogurt, drinks, granola bars, supplements, and more—marketed as probiotics, how do you know you're getting the benefits you're looking for?

THE "PRE" AND "PRO" OF GUT HEALTH

No matter their source, prebiotics and probiotics work in tandem. Their first syllable ("pre" and "pro") signals their functional difference. "Probiotic" literally means "for life"; "pre," meaning "before," indicates that prebiotics are prerequisites. Interestingly, the term "probiotics" was first used in 1965 to contrast them with antibiotics, which inhibit the growth of microbes. Probiotics help stimulate the growth, or repopulation, of microbes.

Probiotics are a group of live, active microorganisms (mostly bacteria, but other microbes such as yeast, too) with intended health benefits in the gastrointestinal (GI) tract. They help to ferment, decompose, and digest the food you eat. To provide these benefits, probiotics from food must be live, active bacterial cultures.

Interesting facts: It's estimated that human intestines are home to trillions of friendly microbes, mostly bacteria, including between five hundred to a thousand different bacterial strains. Amazingly, microorganisms in the human body outnumber human cells by ten to one!

Many of the probiotics in foods, and perhaps supplements, are the same or similar to the "good" bacteria found naturally in your body. In fact, you acquire gut microbes when you're born. Your food and drink choices, health, antibiotic use, and even stress level can affect the type and amount of microbes in your gut.

Among the more familiar probiotics are these: bacteria—*Bacillus coagulans*, *Bifidobacteria*, and *Lactobacillus*, and a yeast—*Saccharomyces boulardii*.

Prebiotics are components of nondigestible fibers, such as inulin, oligosaccharides, and polydextrose, found naturally in many plant-based foods. (One more reason to fit vegetables, fruits, and whole grains into your meals.) They are also added to some processed foods.

Prebiotics can be called "good" bacteria promoters. They pass through your digestive system without being digested. Instead, they promote the growth and activity of probiotic bacteria in your gut. Simply stated, prebiotics are food for probiotics.

Prebiotics are found naturally in many vegetables, fruits, and whole-grain foods. Asparagus, chicory root, garlic, Jerusalem artichokes (sunchokes), leeks, and onions are among the especially good sources. Many other foods are good sources, too, among them bananas, beans and peas, flaxseed, sweet potatoes, wheat bran, and whole wheat. Sugar alcohols may work as prebiotics, too.

Summing up, prebiotics stimulate or help activate bacteria growth; probiotics are the live cultures, or bacteria, themselves. Consumed together, prebiotics and probiotics work synergistically. Synbiotics are foods with a built-in team: both prebiotics and probiotics.

See "A Closer Look . . . How to Keep 'Gut Healthy'" in chapter 25, page 727.

PREBIOTICS, PROBIOTICS: WHAT THEY MAY DO

Overall, probiotics have a good safety profile. As functional components of foods and drinks, prebiotics and probiotics promote gut health, as just noted—and may improve your health and lower some health risks in other ways although evidence is limited.

For probiotics, different bacterial species and strains, even with the same genera (classifications), have different potential benefits; some may have no effect at all. To clarify terms: Scientists categorize bacteria by genus, species, and strains. As an example, for the probiotic bacterium identified as *Lactobacillus rhamnosus* GG, *Lactobacillus* is the genus, *rhamnosus* is the species, and GG is the strain. On a package label you might see the common genus and species.

Lactobacilli and *Bifidobacteria* in yogurt, kefir, and some other dairy foods with live, active cultures may improve gastrointestinal health and promote a healthy immune system. Yet a different genus or different species and strain within a genus may have different effects. For example, if one kind of *Lactobacillus* may help to protect against an illness, another may not. And one product with *Bifidobacteria* may not do the same thing as another.

Scientific understanding of their role is considered a work in progress. It's still largely unclear which probiotics are helpful and which ones aren't; how much would be needed to gain benefits; and who would likely benefit. That said, these are potential benefits.

GI functions. By maintaining the community of "good" bacteria in the gut, probiotics promote gastrointestinal (GI) health and may help maintain a barrier against unhealthy microorganisms or at least produce substances that inhibit their growth.

For example, they may help to reduce the severity and shorten the duration of diarrhea (perhaps including traveler's diarrhea) by helping the GI tract return to normal after a sickness or the use of an antibiotic. Probiotics may help colicky infants.

Evidence also indicates that some probiotics may help to reduce symptoms of lactose intolerance, to manage symptoms of irritable bowel syndrome, and to limit the growth of *Helicobacter pylori*, a bacteria in the GI tract that can cause stomach and intestinal ulcers. The benefits are not conclusive, and not all probiotics have the same effects.

See "Lactose Intolerance: A Matter of Degree" in chapter 23, page 666, and "Digestive Health: GI Upsets and Conditions" in chapter 25, page 727, for more about these conditions.

Immune function. Probiotic cultures appear to help support your immune system, too, by preventing the growth of harmful bacteria and aiding in their elimination. They also maintain a GI barrier as part of the body's defense systems. The National Institutes of Health cautions, however, that in people with underlying health problems such as weakened immune systems, using probiotics could result in serious infections.

Cardiovascular health. Probiotics lower the pH in the large intestine, which may help prevent cholesterol and bile acids from metabolizing.

Nutrient absorption. Certain prebiotics, along with dairy foods (some of which are rich in probiotics), also may enhance calcium and magnesium absorption.

Ongoing research on potential health benefits. Researchers are investigating the possible roles of different strains of probiotics in reducing the risks of some cancers and as well as high blood pressure, reducing blood cholesterol levels, and helping to prevent some allergy symptoms. Other areas of probiotic research: the role of gut microflora in obesity, obesity-related inflammation, insulin resistance, vaginal yeast infections, and brain and mental health. In the future, science may have answers to these many questions.

The FDA offers this caution: The rapid growth in the marketing and use of probiotics may have outpaced scientific research of their many proposed uses and benefits.

See "Functional Nutrition: A Prebiotics and Probiotics" in this chapter, page 456.

Pre- and Probiotics: How Much, How Often

There's no general recommendation or guideline for how much, how often, or what kind of prebiotics or probiotics anyone should consume, pending the need for strong evidence on which to base specific advice. That said, here are insights and cautions, based on what's understood today.

Eating a wide variety of high-fiber vegetables and fruits, along with other high-fiber foods every day provides the best possibility of getting enough prebiotics. Eating probiotic foods such as yogurt, kefir, and fermented vegetables with live cultures daily appears to be beneficial, as well. Researchers believe that potential health benefits are tied to many factors, including which strain of microbes (such as bacteria or yeast) is eaten. No generic equivalence exists between probiotic strains or products. Even with the same genus and species, one probiotic product may not provide the same benefits as another due to differences from the strain. A higher probiotic count or more probiotic strains isn't necessarily better either.

Much more research is needed to learn about the effectiveness, safety, different strains, and amount of probiotics needed for specific health benefits. Only a very few probiotics have been shown as effective in clinical trials. Even the microflora in your own gut make a difference in how your body's responds to various probiotics.

Just being labeled "probiotic" doesn't mean a product is effective for your specific health condition, and knowing the strain in a product can be hard to figure out, too. For example, someone taking antibiotics may not benefit from a bacteria-based probiotic. Why? Antibiotics will kill the bacteria. However, a yeast-based probiotic may be of benefit.

Consult a registered dietitian nutritionist to see if probiotics can help address your health needs, and if so, which type and at what level. While eating probiotic-rich foods is generally regarded as safe for everyone, those with compromised immune systems may be advised against taking supplemental probiotics. Be aware, too, that some prebiotics may aggravate some gastrointestinal conditions. *See "Probiotic Supplements" in chapter 10, page 323, for more information.*

PROBIOTICS: GOOD BUYS FOR GOOD BUGS

Some foods and drinks—and some supplements—deliver probiotics. Since what you eat and drink can deliver plenty of nutrients, too, they may be the best sources. Some also provide prebiotics.

Foods with Probiotics

These are ways to put probiotics in your shopping cart:

- Fermented dairy foods such as cheese, kefir, and yogurt are well-known sources of probiotics. The "friendly" (good) bacteria commonly used in the fermentation that produces these foods from milk are the bacterial strains in a healthy gut, too. For probiotic benefits, yogurt (including Greek yogurt and frozen yogurt) and kefir need to be labeled "live and active cultures." For those with milk allergies and for vegans, nondairy kefir and yogurt drinks (made from soymilk or coconut milk) with live, active cultures are available.

  For all these options, try to choose those with little or no added sugars; store brands are as good as major brands and typically cost less.
- Beyond dairy, other foods are fermented with live probiotic cultures. For example, try pickled vegetables such as kimchi (spicy-seasoned fermented vegetables) and unpasteurized sauerkraut, and some soybean products (miso, natto, and tempeh). *See "Fermentation: Old Process, New Interest" in chapter 5, page 131, for more about fermentation.*
- With probiotics as a buzzword for gut health, some shelf-stable foods—cereal, cookies, granola bars, and more—have probiotics added. They can be a more costly way to get probiotic benefits, and the potency isn't a sure thing. And some may not be the best choices for overall nutrition.

Labeling Probiotics

Because there are no universally established and/or enforced standards for content and label claims, no legal definition for "probiotic" exists. The World Gastroenterology Organization does, however, give minimum criteria for probiotic products: must be specified by genus and strain; alive; delivered in an adequate dose through the end of the product's shelf life; shown to be effective in controlled human studies; and safe for the intended use.

Because there are few guidelines regulating the labeling of probiotics, comparing and determining the best products can be difficult. For example, the ingredient label on yogurt indicates the genus and strain, but not the bacteria count. And even different species of the same bacteria aren't alike.

On the package label, you might see these common genus and species: *Lactobacillus rhamnosus*, *L. casei*, and *Bifidobacterium lactis*. Others—*L. bulgaricus* and *S. thermophiles*—are starter cultures in yogurt, which help break down lactose; stomach acid may break them down before they get to the intestine. Products with several strains may have more probiotic benefits.

No health claims for prebiotics or probiotics have been approved by the FDA for use in food labeling. However, a structure/function claim is allowed on a label, such as "promotes a healthy digestive system."

- Probiotics, National Center for Complementary and Integrative Health
  nccih.nih.gov/health/probiotics
- Medline Plus, US National Library of Medicine, National Institutes of Health: scientific evidence on the effectiveness (reported in the Natural Medicines Comprehensive Database) of *Bacillus coagulans, Bifidobacteria, Lactobacillus,* and *Saccharomyces boulardii.* The fact sheets also address their safety, possible interactions with food and medications, and the doses in supplements.
  medlineplus.gov/druginfo/herb_All.html

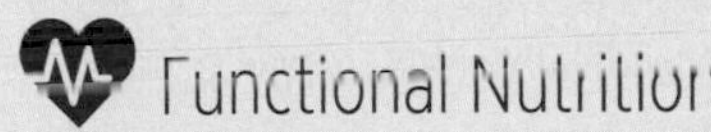

More to Learn!

Phytonutrients, prebiotics, and probiotics aren't the only food substances with functional benefits. Check here to learn more:

- *"Tea Time" in chapter 4, page 97*
- *"A Closer Look . . . Functional Foods with Benefits beyond Basics" in chapter 5, page 134*
- *"Sugar Alcohols (Polyols)" in chapter 11, page 368*
- *"Functional Nutrition: A Quick Look at Dietary Fiber" in chapter 11, page 353*
- *"Functional Nutrition: A Quick Look at Soy Protein" in chapter 12, page 384*
- *"Functional Nutrition: Plant Stanols and Sterols" in chapter 13, page 405*

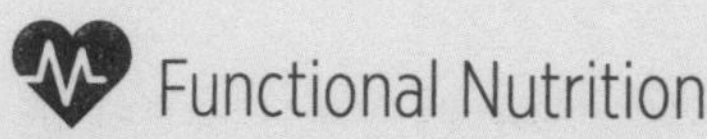

Prebiotics and Probiotics

	What They Appear to Do	Where They're Found (Some Food Sources)
Prebiotics		
Inulin, fructo-oligosaccharides (FOS), polydextrose	• Supports maintenance of digestive health; supports calcium absorption	• Bananas, some fortified foods and beverages, garlic, honey, leeks, onions, some fruits, whole grains
Probiotics		
Yeast, *Lactobacilli, Bifidobacteria*, and other specific strains of beneficial bacteria	• Supports maintenance of digestive and immune health; benefits are strain specific	• Certain yogurts and other cultured dairy and nondairy uses

Source: Adapted from International Food Information Council Foundation, 2011.

Have you ever wondered

. . . if kombucha tea is a good probiotic drink? This sharp-tasting, acidic tea is made by adding kombucha (a colony of bacteria and yeast) to sweetened black tea and letting it ferment. Kombucha tea is sometimes called kombucha mushroom tea because the result of the fermentation looks like a mushroom atop the tea.

While some people claim health benefits, others report adverse reactions from this fermented tea drink. Currently there's no evidence to support health claims. And depending on handling, the level of active cultures may be less than expected. With pasteurization, it loses its probiotic benefits and also reduces the risk of contamination.

Kombucha tea can be home brewed, made with a starter. The FDA cautions that home-brewed versions are at high risk of contamination from unsterile conditions. Most home brews are consumed raw and unpasteurized. Commercially prepared kombucha tea is the better choice for food safety.

. . . if probiotic supplements deliver the health benefits they claim? Maybe. In general, supplements don't require FDA approval before being marketed. While the label can offer a claim about a supplement's function in the body, it can't make a health claim, such as an ability to reduce disease risk, without FDA consent. Be aware that the label may indicate the probiotic count, but it may be the count when packaged, not as consumed. Having multiple probiotic strains doesn't necessarily mean it's effective for you.

Talk to your doctor before choosing a probiotic supplement or relying on one to address, rather than complement, management of a health concern. *See "Probiotic Supplements" in chapter 10, page 323.*

See "Structure/Function Claims" in chapter 6, page 150, to learn more about them.

For more information on the type (genus, species, and perhaps the strain) of probiotic in a food product, check the product label or manufacturer's website. While this information is provided voluntarily by manufacturers, either resource may provide information about the strain, the potential health benefits, proper storage, and recommended usage of the product, along with contact information.

Probiotic Foods and Drinks: Fitting Them In

If you choose to make probiotics part of your eating plan, consider these tips:

- Store most probiotic products in the refrigerator to keep their friendly bacteria alive. Enjoy them by the "best used by" date for the most benefit since the bacterial count goes down as products get older.
- Remember that different probiotic products contain different microbes—and that many factors influence these potential benefits. Consider products with several different strains.
- *Be aware:* Cooking and heating will destroy live, active cultures.
- Be cautious about choosing probiotic foods if you have a milk allergy since many probiotics are grown in a dairy medium. Because of this, even nondairy foods may have trace amounts of milk proteins.
- Try to fit in foods and drinks with probiotics every day since they aren't stored in your body. Instead, they pass through your GI tract.

PART IV

Food: For Every Age and Every Stage

16

Give Your Baby a Healthy Start

In this chapter, find out about . . .

Breastfeeding basics

Infant formula: a healthy option

Starting solid foods

"Should our baby be breastfed or bottle-fed?" "Can solid foods be given too soon?" "How do I know if my baby has eaten enough?" "Do I give my baby 100 percent juice from a cup or a bottle?" "Should solid foods be warmed?"

New and experienced parents ask so many questions! Wouldn't it be great for parents and other caregivers if newborns were delivered into their parents' arms with a "how-to" manual filled with feeding instructions? While it's amazing how fast infant feeding becomes routine, as soon as babies and parents master one feeding stage, they're all ready to move on and learn the next.

With infant feeding, keep two main goals in mind:

- Offer the right amount of food energy (calories) and nutrients at the right time to support your baby's optimal growth and development.
- Nourish the emotional bonds between you and your baby.

Consider this: A baby's birth weight doubles by about five months of age and triples by one year. And from birth, he or she grows about 30 percent in length (height) by five months of age and about 50 percent by twelve months. At birth, a baby's brain is about 25 percent of its adult size. It grows to 75 percent of its adult size by twelve months.

Good feeding practices are not only essential for proper growth. They set the stage for food and eating patterns and a healthy weight throughout life. From the very start, help your baby develop a positive relationship with food and eating. That includes learning and trusting his or her hunger and fullness signals.

Learning baby-feeding basics takes the guesswork out. Practical guidance from your pediatrician, pediatric nurse, registered dietitian nutritionist, and other parents is important. Your own patience, time—and creativity—build warm, memorable feeding experiences for your baby, your family, and you.

Your feeding relationship and how you shift from breast milk or formula to solid foods, too, and then to family foods can provide good, long-term health outcomes for you and your baby. Feeding practices during this first year will affect the quality of your baby's diet and your baby's weight status in childhood and beyond.

If you have concerns about how much your baby eats, how feeding is going, and how your baby is growing, talk with your pediatrician and ask for a referral to a registered dietitian nutritionist if needed. Public health programs such as the Women, Infants, and Children (WIC) Program and programs from the public health department offer good advice, too; *see "Credible Support for Healthy Eating" in chapter 26, page 763.*

Breastfeed or Formula-Feed?

If you're a new parent, either approach—breast- or formula-feeding—can provide adequate nourishment and the strong emotional bond that your growing baby needs. When possible, though, breast milk is best for baby during the first year. If you're not sure which approach to use, start with breastfeeding. If it isn't right for you, switch to formula-feeding. Starting with a bottle, then trying later to breastfeed is difficult. Either way—or both ways—you'll find guidance in this chapter.

Breastfeeding: Ideal for Babies

Nature provides ideal nourishment for babies: breast milk. Medical and nutrition experts recommend breastfeeding for at least the first twelve months of life. Breast milk alone can provide optimal nutrition and health protection for most babies' growth and development during the first six months of life. When solid foods are introduced, they complement breast milk as the ideal feeding pattern.

Deciding to breastfeed is personal. As parents, you need to consider your family's lifestyle, economic situation, and cultural beliefs. The mother's and the infant's physical ability are important considerations, too. (*Note:* If your infant was born prematurely, follow your pediatrician's advice. Breastfeeding is usually advised.)

ADVANTAGES OF BREASTFEEDING

Breastfeeding offers a host of physical, emotional, and practical benefits for both baby and mother. Most health benefits come when mother's milk is baby's exclusive source of nourishment. That usually continues when solids are introduced at about six months. The longer a baby breastfeeds, the greater the benefits. That said, babies benefit even when breastfeeding lasts for only a short time, perhaps during a six- to eight-week maternity leave.

Human Milk: Good for Baby

Mother's milk is uniquely designed to nourish an infant for several reasons.

Provides optimal nutrition and digests easily. Human milk has the right amount and balance of carbohydrates (lactose), protein (casein and whey), fat, water, and other nutrients for meeting an infant's growth, development, and energy needs. It's digested easily, and its nutrients are easily absorbed and used.

For most nutrients, what a mother eats has little if any effect on the nutrient content of breast milk. If her nutrient intake is low, her body's own stored nutrients may be used for breast milk, putting her at potential nutritional risk. That's especially true for calcium and folate. *See "Nutrients: Just a Little More" in chapter 18, page 555.*

Babies may react to something their mothers eat. However, they're rarely allergic or unable to handle their mother's milk.

Builds immunity and protects against common illnesses. Immunity and nourishment starts with colostrum, the clear or yellow fluid secreted by the breast for two to four days after delivery.

Colostrum helps protect a newborn's intestines from infection during the first few months. Think of colostrum as a newborn's first immunization! Not only rich in protein and vitamin A, colostrum has more antibodies than the mature milk that follows. Its color and thick consistency come from its protective factors. Colostrum also helps a baby pass his or her first stool.

Breast milk—unlike formula—has antibodies and other substances that help build the immune system and "friendly" (good) gut bacteria. They help protect a baby from illnesses such as diarrhea, ear infections, intestinal infections, and respiratory illnesses. In fact, human milk contains at least a hundred ingredients that infant formula doesn't have! Breastfed babies aren't sick as often and have fewer doctor's visits.

Changes with baby's changing needs. As a baby matures and grows, the composition and amount of breast milk that a mother produces naturally changes. From about the third to the tenth day after delivery, her body produces transition milk—a mix of colostrum and mature milk. Then mature milk, bluish in color and thinner in consistency, comes in. As a baby suckles more, a mother's breasts produce more milk.

Is bacteria-free (clean and safe). Breast milk is bacteria-free when it leaves the breast. Mothers who express milk for a later bottle-feeding need to use care to keep it safe. To express milk means to stimulate milk flow by hand or with a breast pump.

Promotes oral development. Breastfeeding requires more complex sucking than bottle-feeding. This helps strengthen and develop the baby's jaw and so helps teeth and speech patterns.

Reduces allergy risk. That's especially true of allergies to the proteins in infant formula and, later, to cow's milk.

May reduce the risk of some chronic diseases later in life. The evidence isn't well established, but breastfed babies may have a lower risk of asthma, celiac disease, sudden infant death syndrome (SIDS), and type 1 diabetes.

May promote healthy weight. Although research isn't conclusive, breastfed babies may be at less risk of overweight or obesity later, with potentially more benefits from each added month of nursing.

Possibly helps with mental development. That said, additional study is needed to know if there is a relationship.

Exposes the baby to flavors of the family culture. The flavor of breast milk is affected by what the mother eats. These early flavor experiences are likely the start of preferring family foods throughout life. Sensory experts have described this as nature's way of introducing babies to the foods and flavors of their family and culture.

Has added benefits. For unexpected disasters, breast milk is always available: no supplies needed. Your baby also gets protection from the risks of using contaminated water (for mixing formula), and protection against respiratory illness and diarrhea, which can be fatal if your family is displaced.

✔ Baby's Healthy Eating Check-In

How Do You Feed Your Baby?

There's a lot to know about feeding an infant and about ensuring a positive eating experience from day one. As you embark on this journey over the next year, consider how you will answer these questions.

	Yes	No
TO CAREFULLY BREASTFEED AND/OR FORMULA-FEED, DO YOU . . .		
1. Count the number of wet diapers (six or more every twenty-four hours) to make sure your breast- or formula-fed baby is getting enough to eat?	☐	☐
2. Offer breast milk if possible—or formula—to your baby up to twelve months of age (not cow's milk)?	☐	☐
3. If your baby is formula-fed, offer iron-fortified formula, unless your doctor advises otherwise?	☐	☐
4. Avoid putting your baby to bed with a bottle?	☐	☐
TO INTRODUCE SOLIDS—ONLY WHEN YOUR BABY'S READY—DO YOU . . .		
5. Wait to start solid foods until your doctor advises, perhaps at about six months?	☐	☐
6. Start with single foods, one new food at a time?	☐	☐
7. Offer infant cereal that's iron-fortified?	☐	☐
8. Try new foods several times rather than give up after two or three tries?	☐	☐
9. Offer smooth foods until your baby is ready for mashed or finely chopped foods?	☐	☐
TO STAY CLEAN AND CAREFUL, DO YOU . . .		
10. Always wash your hands before feeding your baby?	☐	☐
11. Clean all baby-feeding equipment with hot, soapy water, and then rinse well?	☐	☐
12. Check the temperature of food or bottles that are heated so they're evenly warmed, not hot?	☐	☐
13. Discard unused expressed breast milk or infant formula as well as uneaten food after feeding?	☐	☐
14. Monitor your baby's reaction to a new food in case of a physical reaction?	☐	☐
15. Always stay with your baby while he or she is eating?	☐	☐
TO ENCOURAGE GOOD EATING HABITS EARLY, DO YOU . . .		
16. Let your baby—not you—set the feeding pace, and do you know your baby's hunger and fullness cues?	☐	☐
17. Offer your baby enough healthy food, without worrying about restricting calories or fat?	☐	☐
18. Remain patient as your baby learns to feed himself or herself?	☐	☐
19. Bring your baby's high chair to the family table to encourage family mealtime?	☐	☐
20. Make infant feeding a special, unstressful time to nurture and enjoy your baby? These days don't last!	☐	☐

How did you do? Give yourself—and your baby—a big hug if you said "yes" to all twenty items; read on to learn more. If you said "no" to anything, *check this chapter for feeding advice*. Your baby's health depends on it!

Nursing: Good for Mom

Besides knowing that your baby is well fed, you, as a nursing mom, get many benefits from breastfeeding, too. The longer a woman breastfeeds, the greater the benefits to both baby and mother.

Nurtures a close bond between mother and baby. Skin-to-skin contact is often a gratifying, emotionally fulfilling extension of pregnancy and a chance to build self-esteem as a parent. In addition, breastfeeding may help to decrease the chance of postpartum depression.

? Have you ever wondered?

. . . if breast size affects breastfeeding success? No, nor does it affect the volume of milk production. When a woman isn't breastfeeding, glands that produce milk are very small, regardless of breast size. The amounts of fat and fibrous tissue a woman has, not the milk-producing glands, determine breast size. Surgery to reduce or enlarge breast size may affect milk production; a health-care professional who monitors a baby's growth can advise if he or she is getting enough milk.

. . . if premature babies can breastfeed successfully? Many premature babies can. But if your baby is born prematurely, get help from a lactation counselor, pediatric nurse, or your doctor. You may need to express milk at first; you'll still feed your milk to your baby, perhaps mixed with a nutrient supplement for preterm infants. For premature babies, breast milk offers benefits that help them grow and stay free from illness. There's another reason to start right away: you need to establish your milk supply if you plan to nurse.

. . . if the foods you eat during pregnancy or breastfeeding increase your baby's risk for food allergies? Plenty of research indicates that breastfeeding reduces the risk for food allergies, particularly if there's a family history of allergies. Food allergies are less common in breastfed babies than in formula-fed babies.

For pregnant and nursing mothers? The American Academy of Pediatrics (AAP) notes that avoiding known food allergens hasn't been shown to protect against developing food allergies. As a precaution, talk to your doctor or registered dietitian nutritionist if you have a food allergy, or a family history of food allergies, such as to peanuts. Avoiding certain foods during nursing possibly may prevent eczema; talk to your doctor. Exclusively breastfeeding doesn't appear to protect a child from allergic asthma that starts after early childhood (after age six years).

. . . what to do if your baby reacts to something you eat? Be watchful. If your baby seems to react poorly after you eat certain foods, including those with known allergens, you should stop eating them for a while. Any allergic reaction usually comes from a protein in a food that the mother consumes, not from breast milk. If your pediatrician identifies an allergy, eliminate that food or ingredient in your diet until your baby is weaned. *See "Food Allergies: A Growing Concern" in chapter 23, page 654.*

Click Here! Links to Know . . .

- American Academy of Pediatrics (AAP), for more about infant feeding
  www.healthychildren.org
- Bright Futures promoting optimal health for children
  www.brightfutures.org
- Centers for Disease Control and Prevention (CDC)
  www.cdc.gov/breastfeeding/resources/guide.htm
- Office on Women's Health, US Department of Health and Human Services, for more on breastfeeding
  www.womenshealth.gov/breastfeeding
- Nutrition.gov, National Agricultural Library, USDA, for more on infant feeding
  www.nutrition.gov/life-stages/infants
- Food and Nutrition Service, USDA, for more on infant feeding, including breastfeeding
  www.fns.usda.gov/wic/breastfeeding-promotion-and-support-wic

Helps reduce bleeding after delivery and regain a pre-pregnancy body figure. Because nursing stimulates the release of oxytocin, a hormone that helps the uterus to contract and shrink, a mother's abdomen trims down more quickly. This same hormone stimulates the release of breast milk, called the "let-down" reflex.

May promote weight loss. Milk production burns calories. Mother's body also uses the fat pad deposited on her hips and thighs during pregnancy as some of the fuel needed for milk production. Gradual weight loss during breastfeeding doesn't affect milk production.

Provides convenience. Always ready to feed, breast milk doesn't need measuring, mixing, or warming, so it's easy, especially in the wee hours of the night. With no bottles to prepare or wash and no infant formula to shop for, nursing moms have more time to relax with the baby, or to catch a nap as baby sleeps.

Costs less. Breastfeeding is economical, even accounting for the cost of the extra food for mom and her breastfeeding supplies, such as nursing bras and a breast pump. Your insurance company may provide a breast pump at no cost to you. An "eco-benefit": Less waste from packaging of formula containers and from formula production.

Since breastfed babies usually aren't sick as much, there's less cost for doctor visits and less lost income from missing work. Depending on the formula brand, breastfeeding can save $1,000 to $1,500 a year, according to the U.S. Department of Health and Human Services estimates!

May offer long-term health benefits. Women who have breastfed may have a lower risk of developing premenopausal breast cancer, ovarian cancer, type 2 diabetes, and high blood pressure; the evidence is limited, however. Breastfeeding also helps control blood glucose levels for women with gestational diabetes.

Do Babies Need Extra Water?

Newborns need little or no extra water. In fact, water before a feeding may interfere with a baby's interest in eating. Except for periods of hot weather when your baby perspires, breast milk or infant formula usually supplies enough fluid.

If water is needed, offer one to two ounces of plain water after a feeding; water shouldn't take the place of breast milk or formula. For safety's sake when your baby is less than four months of age, boil the water first, then chill before offering it, or offer sterilized bottled water. When babies begin eating solid foods, offer plain water.

Diarrhea and vomiting can lead to dehydration—and its complications—if fluids aren't replaced. Your baby then needs water in addition to breast milk or formula to replace fluids lost through diarrhea or vomiting. Rather than water or 100 percent juice (when your baby is ready), your doctor or pediatric nurse may recommend an oral electrolyte-maintenance solution, sold near baby foods in your grocery store. Besides fluid, the solution contains glucose (a form of sugar) and minerals (chloride, potassium, sodium) called electrolytes. Electrolytes help maintain fluid balance in your baby's body cells. These minerals are lost through body fluids.

Consult your doctor or pediatric nurse before feeding an oral electrolyte-maintenance solution to children under two years of age (and older children, too). Besides the risk of dehydration, diarrhea and vomiting signal possible illness that may require medical attention! If diarrhea, vomiting, or fever persist longer than twenty-four hours, consult your doctor or pediatric nurse. An electrolyte-maintenance solution won't stop diarrhea or vomiting, but it does prevent dehydration.

Has added benefits. With nursing, there's less odor involved. Diaper-changing odor is less offensive. If a breastfed infant spits up, there's very little smell, and it doesn't stain clothing. Feeding time gives a mother time to relax every few hours, often a welcome and needed change of pace from the added demands of being a new parent. That's true whether you breastfeed or formula-feed. Also important: Ovulation may be delayed, but that doesn't ensure birth control.

See "Breastfeeding—Your Choice" in chapter 18, page 555, to learn about staying well-nourished as you breastfeed.

BREASTFEEDING TECHNIQUES

While breastfeeding is nature's way of providing ideal nutrition for infants, the "art" of breastfeeding might not come as naturally. Like learning any new skill, success comes from knowledge, practice, and support of family, friends, and maybe coworkers and employers. If a mother chooses to continue breastfeeding after returning to work, support from coworkers and employers will be important.

Preparing Before Delivery

Preparing ahead helps new parents be more informed and confident with breastfeeding once the baby is born. The more you know, the more relaxed you'll be.

- Take a breastfeeding class. Read about it. Most hospitals and WIC clinics give assistance and instruction, often by registered dietitian nutritionists and dietitian technicians who are registered and trained and/or certified as International Board Certified Lactation Consultants.
- Discuss your decision to breastfeed with your doctor. Remind hospital staff when you arrive at the hospital. An increasing number of hospitals are certified through the Baby-Friendly Hospital Initiative, showing support and training for aiding breastfeeding moms.

Getting Started

To build confidence and help ensure an adequate milk supply, start nursing as soon after delivery as possible. The best time is within twenty to thirty minutes after your baby is born.

- Make the first feeding short, about ten minutes. "Rooming in" at the hospital may make your first days with nursing more successful. Having your baby in your hospital room lets you respond to his or her hunger cues right away.
- Relax and make yourself comfortable. Find a comfortable chair with good arm and back support. Or lie down with pillows strategically positioned to help you support your baby. If you are comfortable and well supported, it's easy to hold your baby, and you won't feel much tension in your neck, back, and shoulders.
- Plan to nurse on demand—that is, whenever your baby says it's time to eat and when your baby is wide awake and calm. Increased alertness or activity, rooting toward your breast, hand-to-mouth activity, lip smacking, and mouthing are all signs that your baby is hungry. *See "Know Your Baby's Cues: Hungry or Full?" in this chapter, page 464.*
- Continue feeding until your baby is satisfied. Avoid scheduling, restricting, or limiting the length of feeding time. Your baby knows how much to eat and how fast.
- Be prepared to nurse very frequently during the first months—about eight to twelve times every twenty-four hours. This is because a newborn's stomach is small and nutrient needs are exceptionally high during rapid growth and development. After about three months, babies feed less often and consume more at each feeding, and some start to sleep through the night.

Frequent nursing helps establish your milk supply and keeps your breasts from becoming hard and swollen. Full, heavy breasts signal that it's time to nurse. As milk "lets down," or moves from the inner breast to the nipple, you may get a tingling feeling.

Latching On

Some newborns instinctively suck when they're first put to their mother's breast. (They may have practiced sucking their thumb before birth.) Others nuzzle first, to get used to the warmth, security, and softness of their mother. Either way is normal.

- Remember to wash your hands before nursing.
- Help your baby by stroking his or her cheek nearest your breast. As your baby turns toward your nipple, guide your baby's mouth to take in as much of the areola (dark area of the nipple) as possible, not just the nipple. Newborns have a "rooting reflex" at the breast; they open their mouths naturally.
- Try to offer both breasts at each feeding. Let your baby nurse as long as he or she wants (about ten to twenty minutes on each breast). The last portion from each breast is "hind milk." This milk is higher in fat and helps the baby feel full and satisfied after feeding.
- Release your baby from the breast by gently putting your finger into the corner of his or her mouth. (This will ease the baby's grip and break the suction without discomfort. Wait until you feel the suction release before pulling away.

Latching on correctly helps your baby get enough milk and protects you from sore nipples. Ask your doctor or lactation counselor about breast compression as a way to create and maintain a natural flow of milk and to stimulate a natural letdown reflex.

After Breastfeeding

Is your baby done and feeling satisfied? Sometimes babies rest during a feeding, too, making it hard to know when one feeding stops and the next begins. Is your baby getting enough milk? Trust your baby to let you know when he or she has had enough to eat. When your baby feels full, he or she may close his or her mouth, turn away, or even fall asleep. *See "Know Your Baby's Cues: Hungry or Full?" on this page.*

When breastfeeding is done:

- Burp your baby when you change breasts and at the end of the feeding. This relieves any discomfort from air swallowed while nursing. Hold him or her upright, chin on your shoulder, or lay your baby "tummy-side down" across your lap. Gently rub or pat your baby's back. It's normal for a baby to spit up a bit of milk.
- Skip the urge to give your baby a pacifier or bottle nipple until after breastfeeding is fully established, at about three to four weeks, advises the AAP. Using a pacifier can interfere with your baby's ability to learn how to suck at the breast.
- Although a between-meal pacifier may help quiet your baby, crying is a sign that he or she is hungry, tired, or sick. A pacifier shouldn't be used to delay or replace a meal. It should be offered only if you are certain your baby isn't hungry. Excessive use of pacifiers when a baby is older and eating solids can interfere with normal development of oral motor skills, such as rotary chewing and up-and-down munching.
- Don't worry about the consistency of your baby's stools. It's normal for a breastfed baby to have loose, yellowish stools.

See "Nursing: Reassuring Signs of Success" in this chapter, page 467.

MOM: TAKING CARE OF YOU

Although you may think so, it's not all about the baby. Your health and well-being are essential to both of you while breastfeeding.

Know Your Baby's Cues: Hungry or Full?

These signs suggest that your baby is hungry:

- Your baby is more alert or active.
- Your baby may cry or make fussy sounds or make pre-cry facial expressions.
- Your baby may suck on his or her fists, with hand-to-mouth activity.
- Your baby may open his or her mouth to indicate more.
- If breastfeeding, your baby may root toward your breast.
- Your baby may smack his or her lips.

These signs suggest that your baby has had enough to eat:

- Your baby's sucking may slow or stop.
- Your baby may seal his or her lips together and turn away from the nipple.
- Your baby may fall asleep.
- Your baby may get interested in other things.
- Your baby may bite, spit out, or play with the nipple.
- Your baby may rest during a feeding.

See "Feeding Skills and Readiness Cues" in this chapter, page 483, for more on hunger and fullness cues.

Breastfeeding: Making a Good Connection

1. *Snuggle "tummy to tummy."* Cradle baby in your arms with his or her tummy against your tummy. Baby's head should rest in the bend of your elbow. Your forearm should support the baby's back, with your hand on his bottom.

2. *Place the nipple directly in front of your baby's mouth.* Make sure your baby is facing the nipple straight on and his or her head and body are in a straight line. If your baby's head is tilted back or he or she has to turn to reach your nipple, your baby is in the wrong position.

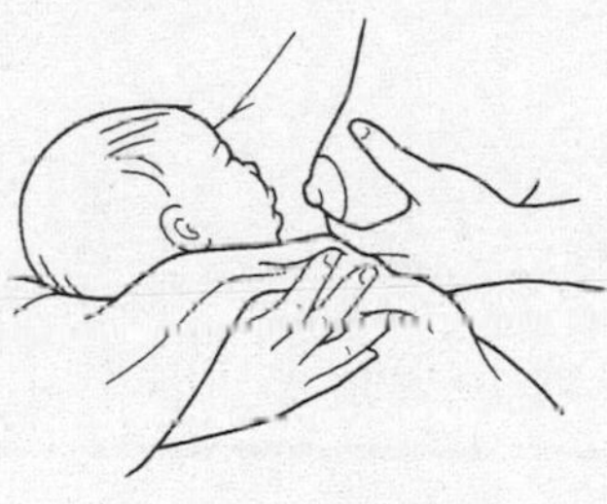

3. *Hold a good position.* Make sure your back is straight and you are not leaning over your baby. Keep your baby well supported. *See "Breastfeeding Positions" in this chapter, page 467.*

4. *Nurse as long as your baby wants.* Try to use both breasts at each feeding. To take your baby off the breast, release the suction by putting your little finger in the corner of his or her mouth. Wait until you feel the suction release before removing your baby.

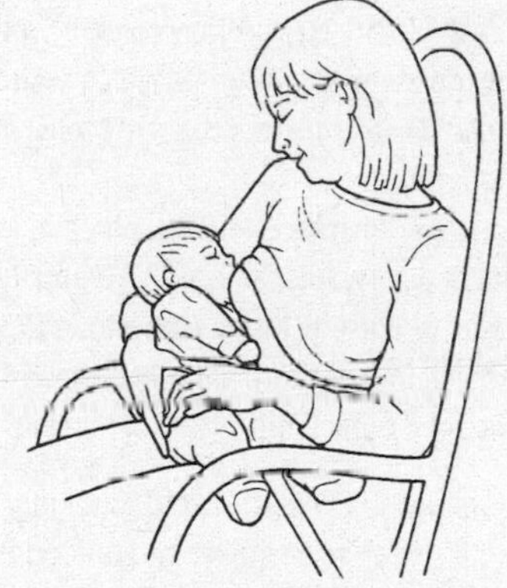

- Because babies nurse more vigorously when they start feeding, alternate the breast you offer first. Clip a safety pin to your bra as a reminder of where to start next time. Alternating ensures that both breasts are emptied regularly and helps prevent breast tenderness. Vary the nursing position, too, and allow your nipples to "air dry" after feedings to avoid breast tenderness and cracking.
- If your breasts are tender or reddened, or if you feel achy and feverish, contact your doctor. You may have a plugged duct or breast infection (mastitis). An antibiotic might be prescribed. Usually you can keep on nursing while an infection clears up.
- If your breasts feel tight and full, soften them with a warm shower, or express a small amount of milk. Fullness and discomfort are signs of engorgement and may happen when your milk supply first comes in or if you've gone too long between feedings. Feed your baby often. Wearing undergarments with proper support helps, too. When breasts become too full, your baby won't be able to latch on correctly, which can cause nipple soreness.
- Don't be surprised if your milk "lets down" and leaks a bit when you hear your baby cry, or even when you think about him or her. It's natural. You might choose to wear pads (without plastic liners) for protection.

- Take care of yourself. Pour some water or 100 percent juice before nursing for you to sip while doing so. Get enough rest, perhaps napping while your baby sleeps.

See "Breastfeeding—Your Choice" in chapter 18, page 555, for additional ways to care for yourself and precautions to take during breastfeeding for the health of your baby.

Breastfeeding Cautions

Smoking, drinking alcoholic beverages, using some herbal supplements, and taking medications may affect milk production and the let-down reflex. Some of these substances pass into the mother's milk, too, at the same levels as in her bloodstream. Foodborne bacteria and contaminants can pose health risks, too.

Alcoholic drinks. Alcohol concentrates in breast milk. If you breastfeed, be especially cautious about habitually drinking alcoholic beverages—if you drink at all. An occasional alcoholic drink doesn't mean you should give up nursing.

Contrary to popular belief, no scientific evidence suggests that an alcoholic drink promotes the "letdown" reflex. In fact, heavy drinking may inhibit your "letdown" reflex. So steer away from wine or beer for relaxation. Drinking alcoholic beverages also can decrease (not increase) milk production.

Alcohol that passes into breast milk may cause your baby to be less alert and may affect the taste of your milk, which your baby may not like, notes AAP. Repeated exposure to alcohol in breast milk may affect a baby's brain development.

An occasional single drink is okay—if consumed at least two hours before breastfeeding or afterwards, advises AAP, and if nursing is well established, consistent, and predictable. That allows time for the body to clear itself of alcohol before nursing. Another option: The mother also can offer a bottle of stored breast milk in lieu of nursing.

Smoking. When nursing, it's wise to avoid smoking, too. Nicotine passes into breast milk. If you're a smoker and quit during pregnancy, breastfeeding isn't the time to start again. Nicotine can reduce your milk supply and increase your baby's chance for colic, a sinus infection, or fussiness. Too close to a nursing session, smoking may inhibit your "letdown" reflex. Smoking is also linked to the increased rate of lung cancer.

When mothers smoke, babies are more likely to get sinus infections, colic, or become fussy. Even secondhand smoke is harmful, so dads and other caregivers should avoid smoking, too. Smoking around babies increases the possibility of getting burned and the risk for Sudden Infant Death Syndrome (SIDS).

Bottom line: Breastfeeding is still best, even in a smoking environment. If you choose to smoke, change your clothing before nursing, and don't smoke near your baby—not even in the same room. Try to avoid smoking for 2½ hours before nursing, and never smoke as you nurse.

Food Safety Issues. As during pregnancy, food safety precautions are advised during nursing. That includes prevention of foodborne illness and exposure to contaminants such as methyl mercury. *See "Food Safety Precautions" in chapter 18, page 552, which applies to breastfeeding, as well as pregnancy.*

Medications, supplements, and health issues. Consult your doctor about any prescription and over-the-counter medication you're taking. That includes any herbal supplements you take, too. Most medications pass into breast milk in concentrations that pose no harm to your infant. There are some exceptions, however. Take your own medications after nursing, not before—even if they're safe for babies.

In a few circumstances, breastfeeding isn't advised. Mothers who test positive for HIV can transmit the virus to their baby through breast milk. Women with untreated tuberculosis or who are undergoing chemotherapy should not breastfeed. And babies born with galactosemia, who can't tolerate breast milk, need a special diet free of lactose and galactose.

Recreational drugs are never advisable. During breastfeeding, they can pass to the baby in breast milk and cause serious, perhaps lasting, side effects.

Getting Help from Others

You and your baby are learning about breastfeeding together. It's okay to ask for help. Besides the delivery room nurse, certified lactation consultants in many hospitals teach breastfeeding techniques and answer parents' questions. Some may visit you at home later to

Have you ever wondered?

. . . if you can breastfeed when you're sick? Yes—usually it's safe to continue breastfeeding. It even offers added protection for your baby, who already has been exposed to any "bug" before you experienced any symptoms. In breast milk, you pass on some immunity through the antibodies your own body produces to fight the infection. (That doesn't happen with bottle-feeding.) If you're taking any medications to treat an illness, talk to your pediatrician to make sure they're compatible with breastfeeding. Severe illness may require weaning; again consult your doctor.

. . . if a baby can be sensitive to lactose in mother's milk? That's highly unlikely. A baby's body makes lactase, so he or she can digest lactose in breast milk. If a child does become lactose sensitive, that usually starts later. *See "Lactose Intolerance: A Matter of Degree" in chapter 23, page 666.*

Breastfeeding Positions

If you're a nursing mom, you may want to experiment with these positions as you feed your baby:

Cradle position. Sit up straight with your baby cradled in your arm. His or her head should be slightly elevated and resting in the crux of your elbow. You and your baby should be comfortably positioned "tummy to tummy," with baby's mouth level with your nipple. Be sure that your baby is facing straight toward you, without having his or her head, back, or neck turned.

Lying down. Lie on your side with the baby on his or her side, too. Place pillows under your head and behind your back for comfort. Position your baby "tummy to tummy" so his or her mouth is next to your nipple. Use a folded towel or a pillow to elevate your baby to the correct height. This position is especially comfortable for women who've had a cesarean delivery. You can feed your baby from both breasts on one side, or turn onto your other side to nurse from your second breast.

"Football" position. Hold your baby with the head facing your breast, and his or her body tucked under your arm at your side. Your forearm supports the baby's back, and his or her legs and feet should point toward your back. Rest the baby on a pillow near your elbow to give support and slightly raise his or her head.

Whatever the position, enjoy eye contact with your baby. This helps build the mother-baby bond and helps your baby feel secure.

help you perfect your skills. Some nursing support groups offer support for dads, too.

Within the first week or two, nursing mothers and their newborns should see their pediatrician or healthcare professional. That's a chance to check feeding techniques. If you're discharged from the hospital less than forty-eight hours after delivery, your first checkup should be within two to four days after birth.

You can also seek help and get support and reassurance from a registered dietitian nutritionist, a nurse midwife, or another healthcare professional with experience in lactation counseling. Women who have been successful at breastfeeding offer great support and practical advice to new mothers. *To find sound, reliable advice on infant feeding and breastfeeding, see "Nutrition Advice to Trust" in chapter 26, page 760, and "Resources You Can Use," page 765.*

NURSING: REASSURING SIGNS OF SUCCESS

Not knowing how much milk their infant consumes makes some parents feel uncomfortable about breastfeeding. As a new mom, you probably don't need to worry about producing enough milk. Your body is amazing. As your baby needs and demands more, your body will make more milk to satisfy the demands of nursing—even when you are gradually losing the weight gained during pregnancy. Mothers of twins and triplets can produce enough milk to nurse successfully. Look for these signs that nursing is going well:

- Following the third or fourth day after birth, your baby has six or more wet diapers soiled with light-colored urine every twenty-four hours. Most newborns wet fewer diapers in the first few days when they are only ingesting colostrum.
- Your baby nurses at least eight times every twenty-four hours, and maybe up to twelve times daily, in the first month. If your baby sleeps longer than a four-hour stretch, you may need to awaken him or her for a feeding. While nursing, you should feel sucking and hear the infant swallowing.
- Your baby's weight steadily increases. Be sure your baby is weighed and assessed at the doctor's office within a week or two after delivery to monitor weight gain, and after that during regular checkups. Doctors check measurements against reference growth curves. Infants who don't gain weight normally may have a feeding or medical problem.

Initially, babies may lose a little weight right after birth. That's normal. However, if your baby doesn't regain his or her birth weight by three weeks of age, your doctor or pediatric nurse will need to monitor him or her frequently. From birth to six months, babies typically gain four to eight ounces per week. Other signs of breastfeeding success: Your baby's urine will be pale yellow, not deep yellow or orange, and he or she will sleep well yet be alert when awake.

HELP FROM DAD

A father—and other family members—play a very important role in the success of breastfeeding. They can offer support, encouragement, and confidence to a new mother. Fathers can attend prenatal breastfeeding classes with an expectant mother, read a book on breastfeeding, arrange pillows, and bring a snack or beverage to mom when she's breastfeeding. A father also can burp the baby, change diapers, massage mom's neck and shoulders to encourage relaxation, and give baby a supplemental bottle.

By sharing household responsibilities, caring for other children, shopping, and doing other tasks, dad and others take some pressures and interruptions away from mom.

SUPPLEMENTAL BOTTLES

Milk production abides by the law of supply and demand. Nursing stimulates the flow of milk—and increases its production as baby demands more to meet his or her needs. Supplemental bottles usually aren't needed—unless your pediatrician advises them, perhaps if your baby loses weight and doesn't regain it.

Although nursing may temporarily limit your independence, offering a supplemental bottle too soon may discourage your baby from nursing. Until your milk supply is established, stay close for nursing.

Expressed breast milk or commercially prepared infant formula may be offered in a supplemental bottle. If you choose to offer a supplemental bottle, wait about four weeks after birth, or until breastfeeding is well established. Because the nipple on a bottle is different from the breast, it can confuse a baby who is just learning to breastfeed.

Once the milk supply is constant—and both you and your baby are comfortable with nursing—a supplemental bottle lets dad, siblings, and other caregivers share in feeding. *Note:* When nursing sessions are replaced regularly with supplemental bottles—without expressing milk—a mother's breasts will adapt by producing less milk.

See "Breast Milk: Safe Handling and Storage" in this chapter, page 470, for tips on storing breast milk, and "Infant Formula: A Healthy Option," also in this chapter, page 471, for more about infant formula and bottle-feeding.

BACK TO WORK: BREASTFEEDING OPTIONS

To continue breastfeeding beyond maternity leave, changing to a back-to-work schedule takes adjustment. Some moms express milk during their workday. In that way, their baby can have bottles of mother's milk when mom's away. Other moms breastfeed only when they can be with their baby; caregivers offer infant formula when mom can't. Some babies take both—bottles of expressed breast milk and of formula. Choose the option that works best for you and your baby. If you're a back-to-work nursing mom (or need to be away from home regularly), consider these guidelines for breastfeeding success.

Before Maternity Leave . . .

- Make a plan with your employer. Perhaps telecommute/work at home for a while, or plan your schedule for short workdays, flextime, or longer breaks. Other options to investigate: onsite child care, bringing your baby to work, or having your baby brought to you at work. Check your state law for breastfeeding at work: National Conference of State Legislatures, www.ncsl.org/research/health/breastfeeding-state-laws.aspx/. Benefit to your employer: Breastfed babies tend to be sick less often, so that means fewer missed workdays for a parent.
- Select a caregiver for your baby who supports breastfeeding.

When You Return to Work . . .

- Plan to nurse before you leave for work, soon after you return home, and during the evening to keep your milk supply strong. Routine helps.
- If your work schedule and the travel distance from work allow, schedule feeding visits during your work breaks. Let the caregiver know when you'll arrive so your baby won't be fed with a supplemental bottle too soon before your visits.
- Let the caregiver know when you'll pick up your baby after work. Together, schedule feedings so your baby won't eat too close to the end of your workday.

If You Decide to Express (Pump) Milk . . .

- Try to make a plan before your maternity leave. If necessary, arrange for a clean, private area to relax, free from interruptions. (You'll need fifteen to thirty minutes, usually twice a day.) Unoccupied offices or women's lounges may be options. You will need an outlet nearby if you use an electric breast pump. You'll also need access to a refrigerator or a small cooler with ice packs to store breast milk. *See "Breast Milk: Safe Handling and Storage" in this chapter, page 470, for tips.*

  By federal law, a nursing mother must have a reasonable break time and a clean place (not a bathroom) at work to express breast milk for one year after an infant's birth. Currently, some exemptions exist for those employed less than one year in certain professions. State laws may be stricter.
- Before you return to work, help your baby learn to take expressed breast milk or infant formula from a bottle. Wait at least four weeks after delivery so your own milk supply is well established. If you wait too long, your baby may be less willing to take a bottle. Experiment with different types of bottle nipples to find one your baby likes as well as different feeding techniques to find what works best. This may be the perfect chance to involve dad in feeding! *See "Bottles and Nipples: Baby Feeding Supplies" in*

this chapter, page 472, for more about the types available, and "Bottle-Feeding Techniques," also in this chapter, page 474, for the different options.

SUPPLEMENT ADVICE: FOR BREASTFED BABIES

Until solid foods are introduced—preferably at about six months—breast milk can be the complete source of nutrition for infants. Several nutrients warrant additional consideration. Ask your doctor.

Vitamin D. This vitamin helps your baby use calcium from breast milk (and infant formula) to help bones grow and develop. When skin is exposed to sunlight, the body can make vitamin D; however, because a baby's skin is delicate this isn't a good option; protect it from sunlight with sunscreen or clothing.

Unlike infant formula and fortified cow's milk, breast milk doesn't contain much vitamin D. That's why the AAP advises 400 IU of oral vitamin D drops a day, starting a few days after birth, even if the baby consumes supplemental formula. Check with your pediatrician for advice about a vitamin D supplement for your baby. For most children, a vitamin D supplement should continue throughout childhood.

Only use the dropper that comes with that vitamin D supplement so your baby gets the right amount. Too much vitamin D can have harmful side effects such as nausea, vomiting, appetite loss, frequent urination, constipation, muscle weakness, confusion, fatigue, and even kidney damage.

There's not enough evidence to know if an infant gets any benefit in breast milk if the mother takes a vitamin D supplement.

Iron. Iron is essential for a baby's brain development and growth. It's also important for the formation of hemoglobin, the part of red blood cells that carries oxygen throughout the body.

In the last trimester before birth, babies accumulate enough iron stores. They rely on their own stores for their first four to six months of life. Breast milk is quite low in iron. Then an iron-rich cereal and/or single-ingredient pureed meat can provide the additional iron babies need, in a form they can use.

Premature infants who breastfeed may need iron supplementation earlier as they had less time to build adequate iron reserves before birth. Low-birth weight babies may need an iron supplement, too. Talk to your pediatrician or registered dietitian nutritionist about what is best for your baby.

Fluoride. Your baby's teeth started to develop even before you could see them. Fluoride, a mineral often found in tap water, helps develop strong teeth and prevent cavities later.

Breast milk contains little fluoride—even if the mother's drinking water is fluoridated. If your breastfed infant takes supplemental formula made with fluoridated water—at least 0.3 ppm (parts per million) of fluoride—your baby may get enough fluoride. If your child is breastfed only or drinks formula made with well water, distilled water, unfluoridated bottled water, or city unfluoridated water, your doctor may advise a fluoride supplement starting at about six months. Breastfed infants who take supplemental ready-to-use formula also may need a fluoride supplement because these formulas usually are prepared with water low in fluoride.

At your baby's six-month checkup, ask your doctor if fluoride supplementation is needed. A fluoride supplement may be prescribed.

Vitamin K. Babies have very little vitamin K in their bodies at birth because only small amounts of the vitamin pass through the placenta. A vitamin K injection usually is given to newborns shortly after delivery to avoid the risk of bleeding due to a vitamin K deficiency, which can happen without warning. This is important because a newborn's blood doesn't have enough vitamin K to form a clot. Vitamin K prevents major blood loss and the risk of spontaneously bleeding into the intestines or brain, which can lead to brain damage and even death. The vitamin K injection is safe and is the only way for a baby to get vitamin K in these

? Have you ever wondered?

. . . if a human milk bank is an option if you can't breastfeed? Perhaps—but generally only for medical reasons and only for pasteurized human milk from screened donors. Talk to your doctor first. Human milk banks require a prescription. Currently supplies are limited, and the cost is high.

Unpasteurized shared human milk, perhaps from unscreened donors or informal milk sharing, especially milk purchased on the Internet, may have high bacterial levels, which can put your infant's health at risk. The Human Milk Banking Association of North America has established guidelines to assure the safety of human milk banks; this includes pasteurization and proper storage and shipping.

. . . how to successfully breastfeed twins? Wonder if you'll produce enough milk? Remember: Your milk supply operates on the principle of supply and demand. With more breastfeeding, your body produces more breast milk. In the early weeks, you may be able to feed both infants simultaneously—an efficient use of time.

Talk to your doctor about the need for supplemental bottles. If your babies are growing normally, they're probably not needed unless you need help from other caregivers. Seek help from a lactation counselor for any special guidance for successfully nursing "multiples," such as help with positioning for two infants.

early days. Breast milk has very little vitamin K, and it takes several weeks before a baby's gut bacteria can make it.

Other vitamins. Babies of strict vegetarian mothers may need a vitamin B_{12} supplement. *See "The Vegetarian Mom" in chapter 18, page 546, for more advice.* Always get advice from your baby's doctor or a registered dietitian nutritionist before giving any nutrient supplements to a baby.

Caution: For some infants, perhaps those who are premature, the doctor may advise providing fortified human milk so they get enough calories and a balance of nutrients. Follow preparation instructions carefully for proper nutrition and food safety—and to avoid toxic levels of vitamins A and D.

WEANING: WHEN? HOW?

When nursing moms encounter challenges, it's all too easy to wean too soon. In fact, you can continue to breastfeed when your baby starts teething. Experts encourage moms to breastfeed for at least twelve months. Babies benefit from breastfeeding for as long as it's mutually right for mother and baby. Some older babies naturally wean themselves.

Weaning is a slow, gradual process. As you wean your baby, introduce either infant formula or, depending on your infant's age, cow's milk. Start slowly. Replace breast milk with formula or cow's milk for just one feeding on one day. A few days later, change another feeding. If your baby is under twelve months of age, wean from breast milk to iron-fortified infant formula. If your baby is twelve months or older, whole cow's milk is appropriate.

Should you wean your baby to a bottle or a cup? That depends on his or her developmental readiness. For infants under six months of age, a bottle is probably the best choice. The AAP advises having infants start learning to drink from a cup at six months. Most infants will drink or suck small amounts of liquid from a cup when someone else holds it. Older babies and toddlers usually have the coordination to drink fluids from a cup or a straw. After twelve months, most healthcare professionals advise only water in a bottle, and by age fifteen months, to give up the bottle entirely.

Some babies develop feeding skills more slowly. Daily practice with a cup help helps develop drinking skills. Be consistent and patient as your baby learns.

No matter how long you choose to nurse, start complementary foods when your baby's ready, which is at about six months of age. Talk to your pediatrician about timing. When your baby eats other foods, too, you'll probably nurse less often: typically first thing in the morning, naptimes, and bedtime.

? Have you ever wondered?

. . . if self-weaning is a good approach for introducing solid food? Instead of being fed pureed foods from a spoon by someone else, with Baby-Led Weaning (BLW), the baby feeds him- or herself with hand-held foods—when he or she has the motor and oral skills to do so. Some parents like this since an infant can share family food and mealtimes. The baby still gets breast milk or formula on demand until he or she can self-wean. Research is underway to determine if this approach to infant feeding can encourage healthy eating patterns and a healthier body weight. It may not be an approach that works for all infants or families.

Breast Milk: Safe Handling and Storage

- Wash your hands before expressing milk.
- Before you use a breast pump, review the operation and cleaning instructions.
- Use clean plastic or glass collection bottles that are BPA-free. They can be stored in either the refrigerator or the freezer. *See "Bottles and Nipples: Baby Feeding Supplies" in this chapter, page 472, to learn more.*
- Store breast milk in two- to four-ounce portions to avoid wasting unused milk after a feeding. Because bacteria from the baby's mouth can contaminate milk in the bottle, always discard milk that's left in the bottle after feeding.
- Store breast milk in the refrigerator if you are going to use it within twenty-four hours. Otherwise, freeze it.
- If you work outside your home, or need to be away, consider stocking a breast milk supply in your freezer while you are on maternity leave:
    - In a freezer compartment inside the refrigerator, not the freezer door, store for up to two weeks.
    - In a refrigerator-freezer with a separate freezer door, store for three to four months.
    - In a separate freezer at temperatures below 0°F, store for six months or longer.
- Date the breast milk kept in the refrigerator or freezer. Then rotate the milk—first in, first out.
- Thaw breast milk in the refrigerator; under warm, running water; or in a pan of warm water, which has been heated on the stove. Do not thaw or heat it in a microwave oven. Before feeding thawed breast milk, gently shake the container to mix any layers that may have become separated. Once thawed, use breast milk within twenty-four hours; avoid refreezing it. *See "Play It Safe: Warming Baby's Bottle" on the next page.*

Play It Safe: Warming Baby's Bottle

Babies enjoy breast milk and infant formula either warm, room temperature, or cool. Unlike most adults, babies have no physical or emotional need for warmed liquids—or warmed foods.

- If you want to serve liquids at warm temperatures, play it safe so your baby won't get burned. Warm bottles of formula or breast milk in a pan of warm water that's removed from the stovetop, or under a stream of warm tap water. You can do the same with frozen breast milk, or defrost it overnight in the refrigerator.
- Be careful not to heat breast milk or formula to the boiling point. Boiling temperatures destroy some nutrients and, for breast milk, some protective properties.
- Avoid using the microwave oven to warm breast milk or formula because microwave heating produces destructive boiling temperatures quickly. And plastic bottle liners may explode if their contents become too hot.
- Shake the bottle during and after warming to evenly distribute the heat. And always test a few drops on the back of your hand, not your wrist; the back of your hand is more sensitive. The formula or milk should be tepid, or just slightly warm to the touch.

Healthy Weight Starts Early

Developing eating and physical activity habits that lead to a healthy weight starts as early as infancy.

- Respect your baby's appetite from the beginning; learn his or her hunger and fullness cues. *See "Know Your Baby's Cues: Hungry or Full?" in this chapter, page 464.* That helps your baby learn to eat the right amount, not over- or undereat.
- Know that your baby's brain needs a little time to signal a sense of fullness. Try to wait two to two and a half hours between bottle-feedings.
- Avoid overfeeding or forcing your baby to finish a bottle if he or she isn't hungry. The AAP advises talking to your doctor if your baby takes more than seven to eight ounces per feeding or more than thirty-six ounces a day.
- Not only can overfeeding make your baby feel uncomfortable, it also sets the stage for weight problems later. Even in the first few months, overfeeding is linked to childhood obesity; some babies drain a bottle fast because they suck so strongly. With breastfeeding, overfeeding is less likely.
- On the flip side, restricting food, or underfeeding, may keep your baby from getting nutrients and food energy (calories) needed to grow and develop, and may cause failure to thrive. Overly restrictive feeding also can keep your baby from learning the hunger and fullness cues that can lead to a healthy weight throughout life.
- When it's time for solids, offer nutrient-rich foods—at regular feeding times—even if your baby initially won't eat them.
- Too much juice can be an issue. Wait until your baby is at least six months old to offer juice, and start with only an ounce or two, perhaps diluted with water. The AAP suggests no more than four to six ounces per day for children aged one and younger—and only 100 percent fruit juice.
- Talk to your pediatrician about the right weight for his or her healthy growth and development. A healthy weight starts early—and helps prevent childhood obesity.

Infant Formula: A Healthy Option

For many reasons, breastfeeding may not be right for everyone. In rare cases, a woman may not be able to breastfeed for physical or health reasons. Some parents may feel uncomfortable with nursing. Other women may take medications that wouldn't be safe if passed through their breast milk to the baby. Still others have cultural or work-related reasons, or may need more time flexibility. Regardless, parents can feel assured that bottle-feeding is healthy, too.

Commercially prepared infant formulas are as similar to mother's milk as currently possible. Infant formulas have enough nutrients, in the right balance, and enough food energy (calories) for your baby until you introduce solid foods—at about six months. Whether generic or branded, infant formulas must meet the FDA's nutrient requirements. Unlike breast milk, however, formulas lack protective factors such as antibodies that promote immunity.

Formula-fed babies get vitamin D from fortified formula. The AAP advises 400 IU of oral vitamin D drops daily for a formula-fed infant who consumes less than a 1 liter (just under 1 quart, or 33.8 ounces) of infant formula per day. Talk to your pediatrician or registered dietitian nutritionist for the advised amount—and so your baby doesn't get too much. Too much vitamin D can have harmful side effects such as nausea, vomiting, appetite loss, frequent urination, constipation, muscle weakness, confusion, fatigue, and even kidney damage.

Most newborns will receive a vitamin K injection soon after birth, regardless of whether they will be formula- or breast-fed. For breastfed babies, *as noted in this chapter, page 469*, this is because babies have very little vitamin K in their bodies at birth since only small amounts of the vitamin pass through the placenta. Sufficient vitamin K is key in the ability to form blood clots and so prevents major blood loss and the risk of spontaneously bleeding into the intestines or brain, which can lead to brain damage and even death in some infants. It can take several weeks or months before the bacteria that produce vitamin K in the newborn's intestines are established and functional. Most infant formula is fortified with vitamin K in varying amounts. Once a baby eats solid foods, he or she will likely get enough vitamin K.

Even after babies take solids, continue feeding infant formula until your baby's first birthday. Similar to breastfeeding, cuddling a baby while he or she takes formula builds a close, nurturing relationship with all those who share the responsibility of feeding: dad, siblings, grandparents, and other caregivers.

FORMULA: WHAT TYPE?

Commercially prepared infant formulas are sold in three ways: powdered, liquid concentrate, and ready to feed. Powdered and liquid-concentrate formulas need to be diluted with boiled or sterile water. Sold in cans or bottles, ready-to-feed formulas can be fed to babies "as is," but they cost more. Regardless of type, commercially prepared infant formulas are usually cow's milk–based or soy-based. Formula that's based on modified cow's milk is appropriate for most babies.

A soy-based or specialty formula might be best for the small number of babies who are sensitive to protein in cow's milk. Vegetarian, including vegan, moms who don't choose to breastfeed may prefer a soy-based formula, too. As an aside, soy-based formulas do not seem to prevent allergies. For premature or low-birth weight babies, a soy-based formula probably won't be recommended. If you choose to feed your baby as a vegetarian (or vegan), ask your pediatrician about choosing the right formula.

Old-fashioned homemade formulas, made from canned evaporated milk and corn syrup, may have nourished your mother or grandmother, but they're nutritionally inferior to today's commercial formulas. And corn syrup and honey may contain spores of the *Clostridium botulinum* bacterium, which cause infant botulism. *Caution:* Homemade infant formulas aren't recommended and may be harmful. Recreating the nutrient balance babies need and get from commercial formulas is nearly impossible with a homemade formula.

Iron. Most infant formulas are iron fortified. Iron is a key mineral in the formation of hemoglobin, the part of red blood cells that carries oxygen to cells to make energy. Your baby also needs iron for brain development; an iron deficiency may cause irreversible developmental delays. Full-term babies are born with enough iron stores to last four to six months. An iron-fortified formula right from the start helps keep a baby's iron stores adequate.

Choose an iron-fortified formula, or ask your pediatrician, pediatric nurse, or a registered dietitian nutritionist to recommend one. If your baby starts on a formula without iron, switch to an iron-fortified formula by four months of age. To clear up a common misconception, iron added to infant formula won't cause constipation or other feeding problems. Continue an iron-fortified formula until twelve months, when your baby is already eating a variety of foods and starts drinking cow's milk.

Fluoride. This mineral helps your baby develop strong teeth and protects teeth from cavities. Use fluoridated water if available, but don't overdo it because too much fluoride during the first eight years of life can cause permanent stains in baby teeth as well as the developing permanent teeth, a condition called fluorosis. Talk to your baby's doctor about the water you use. When you mix powdered or liquid-concentrate formulas with water, you add fluoride, too—if your water supply is fluoridated. Ready-to-feed formulas aren't prepared with fluoridated water.

If you regularly offer ready-to-feed formula or if your water supply isn't fluoridated, talk to your pediatrician or pediatric dentist. After six months, a fluoride supplement may be advised.

Cow's Milk: When? What Type?

As a great source of calcium and other nutrients, cow's milk is ideal for toddlers, children, and adults, but not for infants younger than twelve months. Many formulas are made from cow's milk that is modified for infants.

Cow's milk itself isn't right for young infants for several reasons. Its high protein content is hard for a baby's immature system to digest and process. The potassium and sodium contents are higher than recommended for babies. Unlike formula, cow's milk is low in iron, vitamin E, and linoleic acid; the iron it does contain isn't absorbed well. And it doesn't provide enough vitamins C and E, copper, zinc, or essential fatty acids—nutrients needed for growth and development.

Goat's milk isn't suitable, either, for many of the same reasons. If you choose to offer goat's milk after age one, make sure it's vitamin D–fortified. To clear up a misconception, babies who are allergic to the protein in cow's milk are probably allergic to the protein in goat's milk, too. And about one in five babies who are allergic to cow's milk are also allergic to soymilk.

BOTTLES AND NIPPLES: BABY FEEDING SUPPLIES

Preparing for bottle feeding is more than having the right supplies. You also need to care for and clean them properly.

Baby bottles. Plastic or glass bottles, or disposable bottle bags? The choice is yours. Some parents keep a variety of baby bottle sizes and styles on hand for different purposes. For example, disposable bottle bags are handy when you're on the go and when washing facilities are limited. For convenience, bottles with disposable liners let you toss away the used liner when the feeding is done. Small bottles are perfect for holding two- or three-ounce feedings during the first weeks after delivery. Be cautious of bottles with cute shapes because they're often hard to clean.

Note: The FDA banned the use of BPA in baby bottles and sippy cups in 2012, so if you have some older bottles, consider replacing them.

Have you ever wondered?

. . . if your baby needs formula fortified with DHA and ARA? Added to almost all infant formulas in the United States, two fatty acids—docosahexaenoic acid (DHA) and arachidonic acid (ARA)—may provide developmental benefits (brain and vision), especially for premature infants. The formula label will indicate the presence of DHA and ARA. Evidence about the benefits of these formulas is still inconclusive, however. Ask your pediatrician before choosing these formulas for your infant.

Found naturally in breast milk, DHA and ARA are important components of cell membranes in the brain and retina. Infants also produce these fatty acids inside the body when adequate amounts of essential fatty acids—alpha-linolenic acid (ALA) and linoleic acid (LA)—are present in infant formula. *See "Fats and Health" in chapter 13, page 389, for more about fatty acids.*

. . . why carrageenan and mono- and diglycerides are added to some liquid formulas? They pose no health risks and are added to ensure that the formula doesn't separate during its shelf life.

. . . if formula fortified with probiotics helps build immunity? Perhaps. Probiotics are "friendly" bacteria that may help protect against unhealthy bacteria in the intestines that cause infections and inflammation. Breastfed babies already have friendly bacteria in their digestive system.

Probiotic-fortified formula may offer similar benefits while the baby consumes it. There's not enough conclusive evidence yet to confirm positive benefits. Formula with probiotics appears safe, but ask your pediatrician first. *See "Prebiotics and Probiotics: A Bioactive Duo" in chapter 15, page 453.*

. . . if there are dietary guidelines for infant feeding? Not yet, but they're coming in the next few years, projected for 2020. The federal government is developing a set of dietary guidelines for children from birth to twenty-four months, based on the best available science.

To reduce exposure, use glass baby bottles or plastic baby bottles and sippy cups labeled BPA-free. Avoid clear, plastic baby bottles or containers imprinted with "3" or "7" as the recycling number or the letters "PC" (which stands for polycarbonate, suggesting BPA); avoid heating or microwaving in these bottles or washing them in the dishwasher as heat releases BPA from plastic. *See "Have you ever wondered . . . about the safety of BPA in food containers?" in chapter 5, page 132.*

Baby bottle nipples. They come in many shapes and sizes. Choose nipples that match your baby's mouth size and developmental needs. A baby's comfort and ease of sucking are the criteria to use when choosing a nipple. There are four basic nipple types:

- Regular nipple with slow, medium, or fast flow (the number and size of the holes will determine the flow)
- Nipple for premature or very small babies
- Orthodontic nipple, which imitates the shape of a human nipple during breastfeeding
- Cleft-palate nipple for babies with a lip or palate problem that prevents them from sucking properly

Equipment care. Keep bottle-feeding equipment in good condition:

- Discard cracked or chipped glass bottles that could break and spill formula onto your baby. Toss scratched plastic bottles.
- Replace nipples regularly, as they can become "gummy" or cracked with age. Check them by pulling the tip before each use.
- Check the size of the opening on new nipples and then periodically as you use them. Formula should flow from the nipple in even drops—not a steady stream. If the milk flows too fast, your baby could choke; discard the nipple. If the milk flows too slowly for your baby, consider trying a nipple with more holes, designed for older babies.

Cleanliness. When it comes to preparing infant formula and washing bottles, cleanliness is essential. Your baby's immune system isn't fully developed, so he or she is very susceptible to foodborne illness from improperly cleaned feeding equipment.

- Sanitize bottles in boiling water for five minutes before their first use.
- Use hot, soapy water to wash your hands, work area, and measuring utensils before preparing the bottle.
- If possible, wash bottles right away when they're easier to clean. *See "How to Safely Clean Baby Bottles" in this chapter, page 475, to learn the daily cleaning routine for bottles and supplies.*
- *Remember:* The outer "shell" of bottles with disposable bottle bags and their nipples need regular washing to destroy bacteria.
- Opening a new can of formula? First, wash the can opener and the can's lid with soap and water; rinse well.

PREPARING INFANT FORMULA

For mixing infant formula, careful cleanliness, measurement, and refrigeration constitute the "recipe for success." When properly mixed, powdered, concentrated, and ready-to-feed infant formulas are identical in their nutritional composition. The primary differences are price and how much time you need to prepare formula.

Pay attention to the "use by" date on the label. If it's expired, don't use it.

Whatever formula chosen, follow these guidelines:

- Wash your hands first, and clean the preparation surface.
- Follow mixing instructions on the formula label carefully. Add the right amount of water.
  - Too much water dilutes the formula, so your baby may not get enough nutrients or food energy (calories). The AAP advises that babies don't need water in addition to formula.
  - Too little water concentrates the formula too much, making it harder for a baby to digest. It also supplies too much food energy at one feeding and not enough fluid to prevent dehydration.
- For powdered and concentrated formulas, mix with boiled or sterile water that's low in minerals. You have two options, unless your pediatrician advises otherwise:
  - Bring tap or bottled water to a rolling boil for one minute, and then cool it to room temperature for no more than thirty minutes. Boiling longer may concentrate the minerals too much. Cooling the water before mixing the formula lessens both clumping and the loss of heat-labile vitamins.
  - Use bottled water that's labeled "sterile." If the label on bottled water says it's meant for infants, the water must meet Environmental Protection Agency (EPA) standards for tap water, and it must say "sterile." *See "Bottled Water?" in chapter 4, page 85, for more information.*
- Shake ready-to-feed formula and concentrated formula before pouring it into a bottle since some solids may have settled to the bottom.
- If your baby does well with one type and brand of infant formula, stick with it unless advised otherwise. If you switch, check the label for preparation instructions. The "recipe" for mixing the new formula may differ from the brand you used before.
- Always use clean bottles and baby-bottle nipples. *See the "Bottles and Nipples: Baby Feeding Supplies" and "How to Safely Clean Baby Bottles" in this chapter, pages 472 and 475, for how to properly maintain and clean bottle-feeding equipment.*
- For convenience, prepare a supply of bottles—enough for the day ahead. Date and refrigerate the prepared infant formula as soon as you make it; use it within forty-eight hours. Once opened, ready-to-feed formula and liquid concentrates must be covered and refrigerated and used within forty-eight hours. Cover a powdered formula container that's been opened; use it within one month.
- Cool, room temperature, or slightly warm: any temperature for infant formula can be okay. Always test the formula to make sure it's not too hot; check by shaking a few drops on back of your hand. *Caution:* Avoid feeding cold formula to a newborn. Doing so may lower his or her body's core temperature. *See "Play It Safe: Warming Baby's Bottle" in this chapter, page 471, for safety tips and how to bring bottles to the proper temperature.*
- Prepare only as much formula as your baby needs. Discard formula left in the bottle within one hour after feeding. Bacteria and enzymes from your baby's saliva can contaminate leftover formula and cause spoilage. To avoid too much leftover, fill the bottle with less. Make or add more as your baby's appetite dictates.

How Much Formula?

Your baby's appetite is a good guide to the amount of infant formula he or she needs—and how often. That depends in part on the stage of development. In addition, some babies drink a little more or less depending on body weight and when solid food is introduced. On average, a baby should take in about two and a half ounces of formula a day for every pound of body weight, notes the AAP.

See "Know Your Baby's Cues: Hungry or Full?" in this chapter, page 464.

Use this chart only as a guide, knowing too that babies usually self-regulate the amount from day to day to get what they need.

Age	Bottle Feedings per Day	Amount of Formula per Day
Birth to 4 months	6 to 8	18 to 32 ounces
4 to 6 months	4 to 6	28 to 45 ounces
6 to 9 months	3 to 5	24 to 32 ounces
9 to 12 months	2 to 4	24 to 32 ounces

BOTTLE-FEEDING TECHNIQUES

Bottle-feeding can give the whole family warm, cozy moments with the baby. Nestled in the arms of a parent, sibling, grandparent, or other caregiver, babies feel safe and comfortable. Consider these tips for your bottle-feeding techniques:

- Find a comfortable place, perhaps a chair with an armrest. Hold your baby across your lap with his or her head slightly raised, resting on your elbow. That allows a baby to suck from the bottle and to swallow easily. Keep eye contact.
- Avoid propping your baby in bed or in an infant seat with a bottle, even if your baby can hold a bottle, to prevent choking. That's also uncomfortable for the baby and may lead to

How to Safely Clean Baby Bottles

You only need soap, hot water, and a baby bottle brush:

- Fill your sink with hot water, and add dishwashing liquid.
- Immerse bottles, nipples, caps, rings, preparation utensils, and other supplies in the water.
- Pour hot, soapy water into each bottle, and rotate a baby bottle brush inside until the bottle is clean. Thoroughly rinse under running water to remove all traces of soapy water. Place in the dish drainer to dry.
- Use a nipple brush to wash nipples and nipple holes. Squeeze the hot, soapy water through the nipple hole to flush out any trapped milk. Place in the dish drainer to dry.
- Scrub each utensil, then thoroughly rinse under running water to wash way all traces of soapy water. Place in the dish drainer to dry.

You can wash and dry in the dishwasher, too—but only dishwasher-safe items—using heated water and a hot drying cycle. Look for dishwasher baskets designed to hold bottle parts and keep them from falling to the dishwasher bottom.

Source: www.homefoodsafety.org

ear infections. And if he or she falls asleep with a bottle in the mouth, formula that bathes the teeth can promote baby-bottle tooth decay.

- Choose a feeding time when your baby is calm and wide awake. Remove the bottle promptly if your baby falls asleep while eating.

Need more parenting tips for feeding your baby?

Check here for "how-tos":

- Look ahead to toddler and preschool feeding; *see "Toddlers and Preschoolers: Food and Active Play" in chapter 17, page 508.*
- Eat smart during pregnancy and breastfeeding; *see "You're Expecting" and "Breastfeeding—Your Choice" in chapter 18, pages 541 and 555.*
- Know signs of food allergies or intolerances; *see "Symptoms? Something to Sneeze About" in chapter 23, page 655.*
- Find a nutrition expert experienced in infant feeding; *see "How to . . . Find a Qualified Nutrition Expert" in chapter 26, page 761.*

- Angle the bottle to help prevent your baby from swallowing too much air. The nipple should stay full of formula when your baby is eating.
- To ease discomfort from air bubbles swallowed during feeding, burp your baby in the middle and at the end of a feeding. Hold him or her upright, chin resting on your shoulder, or lay your baby tummy down across your lap. Then gently pat or rub your baby's back.
- Keep a clean burp-cloth handy. It's normal for babies to spit up some formula during burping.
- When your baby is done, take the nipple out of his or her mouth. Sucking on an empty bottle causes air bubbles in your baby's tummy.
- If your baby doesn't finish a bottle, don't refrigerate it for later. The remaining formula can be kept at room temperature for up to one hour; discard after that.

BABY'S BOTTLE-FEEDING ROUTINE

Newborns eat frequently in the first months after birth—every three to four hours. Since their stomachs are small, about two to four ounces of infant formula, may be enough for these early feedings. *See "How*

Physical Activity and Infants

Physical activity is important from the very beginning of life. Activity can encourage rolling over, crawling, and walking, as well as cognitive development, and can lead to a preference for active play. Conversely, inactivity may set the stage for childhood obesity.

Rather than confine your baby to a stroller or playpen too much, start a habit of safe, active living now. Be present, and give him or her chances to try different ways to move. During your baby's first year:

- Spend part of each day playing active baby games such as peekaboo and pat-a-cake.
- Find ways to help your baby safely and actively explore his or her surroundings. Floor play is great!
- Avoid restricting your baby's movements for prolonged periods of time.
- Choose activities that encourage your baby to move his or her large muscles (arms, legs, hands, and feet).
- Tell your child care provider about how much time you want them to provide in active play.
- Play when your baby is awake. Don't interrupt sleep to play.
- Avoid rough-and-tumble play. Gentle bouncing, rolling, and swaying are good from the start.

Parenting at Mealtime: Feeding Baby and Older "Sibs"

Are you an experienced parent with one or more other children? If so, feeding a newborn isn't new to you. Yet, every baby is different, so be prepared to learn new parenting skills. One may be a fussy eater; another, ready and eager to eat. One baby may be ready for solid foods a bit earlier than the other. Observe, respect, and enjoy their unique differences.

Do you wish that you had handled feeding differently with your first child? That's normal, too, especially after being a first-time parent. It's okay to change your feeding approach with your next child.

Perhaps the biggest change is trying to do several things at once: trying to feed a baby, older siblings, and others in your family—including you.

Enlist help from your preschooler or school-age child, without expecting too much. An older child can be your helper but shouldn't be responsible for your baby. Tasks as simple as wiping baby's sticky hands, getting a bib, or picking up a bottle that falls to the floor make your older child feel helpful and important. A younger child can listen to music or a story as you are nursing.

A new baby competes for your attention, which may lead to fussy eating from another child. Give your older child personal time at the table, too; include him or her in table talk. And try to keep mealtime calm and pleasant—despite all that's happening around the table.

Much Formula?" in this chapter, page 474, for guidelines during the first twelve months.

Formula-fed babies usually need twenty to thirty minutes to finish a bottle—but let your baby set the pace. If it takes less than fifteen minutes for your newborn to finish a bottle, use a nipple with smaller holes. If it takes longer and if the baby is sucking actively, make sure the holes aren't clogged. Or try a nipple with several more holes.

As with a breastfed baby, plan to formula-feed on demand—when a baby signals hunger: fussy sounds, hand-to-mouth activity, pre-cry facial grimaces, and waking and tossing around. Trying to impose a feeding routine may frustrate you both. A formula-fed baby may not eat as often as a breastfed one; formula digests more slowly.

Should formula be warm, cool, or at room temperature? That's up to you. Your baby will become accustomed to whatever temperature you usually provide. Just be careful that it isn't too warm so your baby doesn't get burned or too cold, which may lower a newborn's core body temperature. *See "Play It Safe: Warming Baby's Bottle" in this chapter, page 471, for safety tips.*

Let your baby decide how much to drink. Pay attention to his or her appetite; your baby doesn't need to finish a bottle. In fact, forcing him or her to finish focuses too much on eating—which may lead to overfeeding. To learn good eating habits, babies need to learn their own hunger and fullness cues. *See "Know Your Baby's Cues: Hungry or Full?" in this chapter, page 464, to know what signs to watch for.*

If your baby has six or more wet diapers a day, seems content between feedings, and his or her weight increases steadily, your baby is probably getting enough to eat. If those aren't the case, check with your doctor or pediatric nurse.

Transitioning to a cup? Start with a sippy cup, then move on to an open cup with two handles for ease. Between twelve and fifteen months, advises the AAP, phase out bottles. Only give your baby a cup when he or she needs to drink, not as something to hold or play with.

Solid Foods: Solid Advice

Just when you master breastfeeding or formula feeding routines, your baby indicates that he or she is ready to join the high-chair crowd! Starting solid foods is one more adventure in the journey of child feeding.

SOLID FOODS: WHEN READY, WILLING, AND ABLE

Although most babies are ready to start solid foods by about six months, don't rely solely on the calendar. Each baby is different. Age is just a general point of reference.

Well-meaning friends and family may tell you to start solid foods earlier, saying they'll help your baby sleep. However, babies sleep through the night only after their nervous system is more fully developed. It's important to wait. Babies must be physically and developmentally ready for solids.

Until about four months, babies are unable to effectively coordinate their tongue to push food to the back of their mouth for swallowing. Instead, they have a tongue-pushing reflex needed for breast- or bottle-feeding. Solid foods offered too soon also stress a baby's immature digestive system; most of it passes right through to the diaper.

According to the AAP, starting complementary solid foods before six months generally doesn't increase total calorie intake or contribute to growth rate. Instead, when solid foods replace breast milk or formula, it's more likely that some nutrients may be lacking. Solids don't have the protective factors in breast milk, so starting solids early may cut short the benefits of breastfeeding. The AAP also cautions that starting solid foods before a baby's body is ready may increase the risk of some chronic diseases later in life.

When is the right time to start? Usually, around six months or a little earlier if your infant is developmentally ready. Then, if your baby weighs at least thirteen pounds and has doubled his or her birth weight, it might be time. Let your baby be the judge. Remember to calculate his or her age from the time of gestation. At six months, a premature infant probably won't be at the same developmental level as a full-term baby.

It's important to complement breast milk or formula with solid foods after about six months. At this time, daily needs for many nutrients, such

For Vegetarian Babies

Breast milk is the best first food for babies. Commercial infant formulas, including soy formulas, are also healthy options for vegetarian babies. Since breast milk is so rich in nutrients, vegan mothers may choose to breastfeed for longer than one year.

At one year of age it's okay to start a full-fat commercial, fortified soy beverage (with calcium and vitamins D and B_{12}) or cow's milk. Before the age of two, babies need enough fat to develop a healthy nervous system—it's not the time to restrict fat in food.

Caution: Vegetarian milk, such as soymilk and rice beverages, are not healthy for babies. Wait until after two years of age to give these beverages, and then talk to your doctor, pediatric nurse, or registered dietitian nutritionist first. Rice and almond beverages in particular are often low in protein and other nutrients. They can't adequately substitute for breast milk or infant formula.

Give special attention to sources of vitamin D, vitamin B_{12}, zinc, and iron. Vegetarian or not, the AAP advises a vitamin D supplement for breastfed babies, starting within the first few days after birth, even if the baby consumes supplemental formula. Infant formula contains vitamin D; *see "Infant Formula: A Healthy Option" in this chapter, page 471, for more about vitamin D and formula-feeding.* For breastfed vegan babies, a vitamin B_{12} supplement may be recommended if the mother doesn't consume vitamin B_{12}–fortified foods. Your doctor may advise an iron supplement.

Time to introduce solid foods? Introduce them in the same way as for nonvegetarian babies. Instead of meat offer pureed or mashed, cooked egg, cottage cheese, soy or dairy yogurt, tofu, very pureed or strained beans and peas, and bean spreads. Later, start tofu cubes, dairy cheese or soy cheese, and soyburger pieces.

Most important: If you choose a vegetarian eating style for your baby, consult a registered dietitian nutritionist, your doctor, or a pediatric nurse for support and nutrition counseling.

as iron and zinc, increase, and some fairly substantially. Solid foods, along with breast milk or formula, will help to ensure that an infant is getting enough of a range of nutrients.

The following milestones suggest readiness for solid foods:

- Baby can sit with little support. Your baby can control his or her head and may be able to lift up his or her chest, shoulders, and head when lying tummy down. By now, your baby can turn away or keep his or her mouth shut to signal "enough."
- Baby has an appetite for more. If your baby is hungry after eight to ten breastfeedings or drinks more than thirty-two ounces of formula in a day, it may be time for solids.
- Baby shows interest in foods you're eating. As your baby watches, he or she leans forward and may even open his or her mouth in anticipation or perhaps grabs things to put in his or her mouth. Take a trial run with appropriate solid foods. If your baby doesn't seem interested, wait a few weeks and then try again. Avoid forcing him or her to eat solid foods.
- Baby can move foods from the front to the back of the mouth. As babies develop, the tongue becomes more coordinated and moves back and forth. This allows babies to swallow foods from a spoon. Eating solids helps with motor development, such as swallowing and speech.

SOLID FOODS: WHAT'S FIRST, WHAT'S NEXT?

Throughout the first year, breast milk or iron-fortified infant formula continues to be your baby's main nutrient and energy source. (Wait until after twelve months for cow's milk.) When your baby is ready, start solid foods to complement the nutrition from breast milk or formula.

No medical evidence indicates that introducing solids in a particular order has an advantage for a baby. What's important is providing your baby with an iron source and making sure that the consistency and texture are developmentally appropriate.

- Traditionally, iron-fortified, single-grain infant cereal (mixed with breast milk or formula) is introduced first.
- There is no evidence that a baby will develop a dislike for vegetables if fruits are given first. Strained single vegetables and fruits are developmentally appropriate at first.

  Early research indicates that the flavors of amniotic fluid from what the mother eats prenatally may affect how a baby accepts and enjoys food flavors during weaning. Think of it as a way to introduce the flavors of family foods.
- Pureed single-ingredient meats and poultry can be offered as first foods, especially for primarily breastfed infants. They are good sources of easily absorbed iron and zinc, which are needed by four to six months of age. They also provide high-quality protein. Check with your pediatrician.
- By ten to twelve months, your baby will likely be ready for chopped soft vegetables, fruits, and meats; unsweetened dry cereals; plain, soft bread; and pasta. Offer toast and teething biscuits when teething starts. Grinding food from the family table for older infants can help them make the transition from smooth, pureed foods.

Something New: Eating from a Spoon!

Learning to eat the first solid food—usually iron-fortified cereal—from a spoon is a big transition in infant feeding. It's a step toward independence. And it encourages chewing and swallowing skills.

Spoon feeding has challenges. It's messier. At first, more food may end up on the bib and face than in the mouth. Try these tips to make the transition pleasant:

? Have you ever wondered?

. . . if it's okay to offer solid foods in a bottle? No, not for most babies (unless recommended by your doctor or a registered dietitian nutritionist—for example, for a baby with reflux). One reason why: It may cause a delay in learning feeding skills. Other reasons: Cereal or other foods from a bottle also can cause choking and may encourage your baby to overeat (too many calories). With spoon-feeding, resting between bites gives your baby time to feel full and learn self-regulation. Cereal in a bottle also may be offered instead of breast milk or formula, so the baby misses out on the nutrients that breast milk or formula supply.

To clarify a misconception, offering cereal in a bottle won't help baby sleep or stop crying.

. . . how you can help relieve the discomfort of teething? Rub your baby's tender gums gently with your clean finger, perhaps with a little teething gel, along the gum line. A chilled teething ring—kept in the refrigerator, not the freezer—can help. Chewing on textured solid foods, such as teething biscuits, bagel pieces, breadsticks, or rice cakes may offer some comfort, but watch carefully that large chunks do not break off and cause your baby to choke. Offer these foods when your baby is sitting up; stay nearby. Chill baby foods, too; they may feel better on a baby's gums than warm foods. Another option is a mesh teething feeder, where the mesh portion can be filled with frozen (slightly thawed) fruits or vegetables. A screw on top and handle ensures that baby can easily handle the teething feeder.

Drooling more and swollen, tender gums signal teething. Be aware that a runny nose, diarrhea, fever, or rash probably are symptoms of illness, not teething.

. . . if you should comfort your baby with a bottle or food? No. Just cuddle, rock, or walk your baby instead. Comforting an infant with food may teach him or her to eat in response to emotions, not to hunger. A fussy baby may just need attention. Remember that it's normal for babies to cry, especially if they're hungry, wet, *or* tired. When a fussy baby is hungry, offering a bottle or nursing is appropriate.

. . . if your baby is growing at a healthy rate? Your pediatrician will assess his or her growth rate during regular visits. With support from the AAP, the Centers for Disease Control and Prevention (CDC) recommended using growth charts from the World Health Organization (WHO) to assess growth for infants and toddlers aged one to twenty-four months. After that, CDC growth charts are used. For both WHO and CDC charts, visit www.cdc.gov/growthcharts.

- Relax. This is a new eating adventure for baby *and* you! Pick a time when your baby is relaxed and not ravenously hungry. Smile and talk as you feed your baby. Your soothing voice will make new food experiences more pleasant. Talking helps with language development, too.
- Of course, wash your hands first. And keep baby food safe and clean.
- Seat your baby straight or propped upright, facing forward. This makes swallowing easier and helps prevent choking. Position yourself in front of your baby. Use the seat belt in a high chair. Have direct eye contact with your baby.
- Use a small spoon with a long handle, and just a little bit of food on the tip of the spoon. Wait until your baby opens his or her mouth before giving food.
- Start with a teaspoon or two of food. Then work up to one to two tablespoons (dry amount before mixing with formula or breast milk), two to three times a day. Gradually increase to three to four tablespoons of cereal.
- Let your baby set the pace for feeding. Don't try to go faster or slower.
- Introduce new foods at the start of the meal. Once his or her hunger is satisfied, your baby may be less willing to try something new. If he or she refuses a new food, that's okay; try again in a few days.

Infant Cereals: For Starters

As mentioned above, by tradition, single-grain cereal is typically introduced as the first solid food. Choose an iron-fortified infant cereal (often the most convenient iron source) to help your baby maintain his or her iron stores. Dry or premixed, cereals developed especially for babies are best; you can add breast milk, formula, or water to them. Infant cereals digest more easily than cereals for older children and adults.

- Although there's no strict order, you might start with rice cereal. It's the type of cereal least likely to cause allergic reactions. *To determine if a food may be causing a reaction, see "Food Sensitivities and Your Baby" in this chapter, on page 479.* Some infants are sensitive to wheat before one year of age. However, current advice is that unless a parent or sibling has a sensitivity, you don't need to avoid specific foods.
- For your baby's first cereal feedings, keep the cereal mixture thin. Start with just one part dry cereal to four parts of breast milk or formula. Once your baby develops eating skills—and a taste for cereal—mix in less liquid so the cereal is thicker.

  Caution: Don't mix in honey or corn syrup; they may contain small amounts of spores of the *Clostridium botulinum* bacterium, which can cause infant botulism, a severe foodborne illness. *See "Bacteria: Hard Hitters" in chapter 7, page 220.*

Food Sensitivities and Your Baby

Some babies are sensitive to certain foods. Their reaction—perhaps a rash, wheezing, diarrhea, or vomiting—is a tell-tale sign. Most babies outgrow these reactions once their digestive and immune systems mature. In the meantime, monitor your baby for food reactions:

- Keep track of the foods your baby eats. Serve single-grain infant cereals and plain vegetables, fruits, and meats instead of mixed varieties or "dinners" until you know what your baby can handle. If your baby has a reaction, stop that food.
- Offer one new food at a time. Wait three to five days before offering the next new food. That way, if your baby has a reaction, you'll more likely know what food may be the cause.
- After your baby has tolerated some less-allergenic solid foods, introduce eggs, dairy, peanuts, tree nuts, fish, and shellfish gradually—one at a time and ideally at home—advises the American Academy of Allergy, Asthma & Immunology.
- Be particularly watchful of foods that may contain common allergens: eggs, milk, peanuts, tree nuts, fish, shellfish, soy, and wheat. Use the ingredient list and allergen labeling on food labels to identify foods with these ingredients.
- If any food causes a significant or ongoing reaction such as moderate to severe eczema, stop giving it. Talk to your pediatrician, pediatric nurse, or registered dietitian nutritionist to establish an eating plan that's best for your baby.

As an aside, a baby's stool often changes color and consistency when new foods are eaten. These changes don't necessarily indicate a food sensitivity.

Whether a baby has a family history of food allergies or not, delaying or avoiding foods with common allergens, such as eggs, peanuts, fish, or wheat, doesn't appear to reduce the risk of developing food allergies.

New guidelines on peanuts: Released in early 2017 from the National Institutes of Allergy and Infectious Diseases of the National Institutes of Health, these guidelines indicate that exposing infants to peanuts early, as young as four to six months of age, may prevent or reduce the chance of developing a peanut allergy later. The timing and way to introduce peanuts depends on an infant's risk, such as whether he or she already has eczema, an egg allergy, or both, and should be with a doctor's approval and guidance. Peanuts should also be in a form that won't cause choking, such as thinned peanut butter, or perhaps mixed into pureed applesauce. In all cases, infants should start other solid foods before they are introduced to peanut-containing foods. *Important:* Follow the guidance of your pediatrician and perhaps an allergist to make sure your infant isn't already allergic to peanuts before offering them.

See "Food Allergies: A Growing Concern" in chapter 23, page 654, to learn more.

- If your baby refuses cereal at first, try again in a few days. Infant cereal tastes different from familiar breast milk or formula. The texture differs, too—not to mention the difference between a nipple and a spoon.
- Once your baby starts eating more cereal, be aware that he or she will take less breast milk or formula. Breast milk or iron-fortified formula still should be the mainstay during the first year.

Solids: From Strained to Family Foods

Once your baby accepts cereal, try strained solids. Meat, poultry, and beans and peas are good sources of vitamin B_6, iron, phosphorus, and zinc. Especially for breastfed babies, these nutrients are likely limited. Offer strained vegetables or fruits, too. It doesn't matter which is first: vegetables or fruits. Some pediatricians advise vegetables first.

Even if your baby refuses a food three or four times, don't give up! Babies often need twelve or even fifteen different tries before finally accepting a new food. Just be patient and persistent as your baby learns and grows. Try these tips to make the transition pleasant:

- One by one, add more variety of foods. This lays the groundwork for healthy eating throughout life. *See "Food Variety: Good for Baby" in this chapter, page 481.*
- Try single foods first: for example, beef, pork, chicken, turkey; eggs; beans or tofu (for vegetarian infants); vegetables—carrots, green beans; peas, squash, and sweet potatoes; and fruits—applesauce, bananas, peaches, pears, and prunes (dried plums).
- Start with smooth foods that are easily swallowed. Babies can eat mashed or finely chopped foods when their teeth start to appear and when they start to make chewing motions.
- Around six to nine months of age, most babies enjoy drinking from a cup—or at least trying to! Offer formula, breast milk, water, or pasteurized 100 percent fruit juices (not fruit drinks)

in a child-size unbreakable cup. *See "Have you ever wondered . . . when your baby can have fruit juice?" on this page, for guidelines.*

A cup without handles may be easier for a baby to hold. Covered, sippy cups with a spout are helpful at this stage. Babies are clumsy with a cup at first but usually catch on quickly.

- If you offer 100 percent juice, offer it from a cup, not a bottle. Give just a small amount: about two ounces. Sipping on juice too long from a bottle exposes a baby's teeth to natural sugars in fruit juice, and prolonged contact with sugars can promote tooth decay.
- As your baby gets more teeth and becomes interested in self-feeding—at nine to twelve months of age—introduce finger foods. Soft, ripe fruits without peels or seeds and cooked vegetables are good for tiny fingers. Avoid foods that a baby can choke on. *See "Safety from Choking: Babies, Toddlers, and Preschoolers" in this chapter, page 486.*
- Teething biscuits, bagel pieces, breadsticks, and rice cakes are good natural "teethers." Chewing on them eases a baby's sore gums while offering a healthy snack. *See "Feeding Myself" in this chapter, page 481, to learn how to help your baby master this skill. See "Have you ever wondered . . . how you can help relieve the discomfort of teething?" in this chapter, page 478.*

Caring for Baby Teeth

Good dental care begins at birth—even before baby teeth appear! Healthy teeth enable children to chew food more easily, learn to talk clearly, and smile with self-assurance.

Make cleaning your baby's teeth and gums part of the daily bathing routine. Starting a few days after birth, clean your baby's gums with a soft infant toothbrush and water, or use a clean, wet washcloth or gauze pad. Do this after every feeding. Skip toothpaste, which babies often swallow.

Schedule your baby's first visit to a pediatric dentist after the first tooth appears (at about six to twelve months).

Fluoride is a mineral that helps teeth develop and resist decay. In many places, various levels of fluoride are naturally present in local water supplies. If you live in an area that doesn't have fluoridated water or if you rely on well water, ask your pediatrician if he or she needs a fluoride supplement. Unless your baby's dentist advises otherwise, wait until after age two or three years to start with fluoridated toothpaste.

For more information on fluoride, see "Supplement Advice: For Breastfed Babies" and "Formula: What Type?" in this chapter, pages 469 and 482. For more about fluoridated water, see "A Closer Look . . . Water: The Fluoride Connection" in chapter 4, page 83.

To avoid tooth decay, do not put your infant, toddler, or young child to bed with a bottle of juice, formula, or milk. The liquid that bathes the teeth and gums from sucking on the bottle stays on the teeth and can cause tooth decay. This happens even if a baby's teeth haven't yet erupted through the gums. If your child won't nap or go to bed without a bottle, fill it with plain water instead.

For more about dental care, see "Oral Health: Your Healthy Smile" in chapter 25, page 735.

? Have you ever wondered?

. . . if it's okay to sweeten baby foods with honey or to dip a pacifier in honey? No. Before the baby's first birthday, avoid giving honey in any form. Although rare, honey can harbor spores of a toxic bacterium called *Clostridium botulinum*. For adults and older children, these spores are harmless, but for babies younger than twelve months, they can cause botulism, a severe foodborne illness that can be fatal. *Note:* Sucking on a sweetened pacifier also promotes cavities.

. . . when your baby can have fruit juice? Before six months of age, fruit juice offers no nutritional benefits, advises the AAP. After six months, pasteurized 100 percent fruit juice (not fruit drinks) is an option, as long as your baby doesn't drink too much of it. Four ounces of 100 percent juice a day are enough.

Offer 100 percent juice in a small cup at mealtime or snack time—not from a bottle, covered cup such as a sippy cup with a spout, or juice box, which promotes sipping juice throughout the day.

Juice shouldn't be given in a bedtime bottle or as a way to manage diarrhea. Other than the fact that fruit has more fiber, 100 percent fruit juice and fruit offer the same nutritional benefits for older babies.

. . . if your baby needs a vitamin supplement when he or she starts solid foods? Ask your pediatrician. A specially formulated infant supplement may be recommended if you're not sure if foods supply enough, if your family is vegetarian, or if your baby needs to restrict food for any reason.

. . . if almond milk, rice milk, or coconut milk are appropriate for infants? No. For infants, breast milk and formula provide the nutrition needed for growth, development, and health. Wait at least until the toddler years to offer whole cow's milk or, for vegans, fortified soymilk. Other drinks don't provide the nutrients in cow's milk or soymilk and may be high in added sugars. *See "Nondairy Drinks: Soy, Almond, and More" in chapter 4, page 92, for more about these options.*

- Babies need the opportunity to develop a taste for the natural flavor of foods without added sugars, salt, or other flavorings. Seasonings are not added to many varieties of commercially prepared baby foods. Read the product label to find out.
- Gradually expose your baby to foods containing herbs and spices, including flavors of your family's food culture. There's no need to keep food plain.
- As you choose foods for your baby, don't restrict fat during the first two years. Growing babies need the calories and essential fatty acids that fat provides for brain development.
- As your baby grows and develops a bigger appetite, offer more solid foods. *See "Feeding Skills and Readiness Cues" in this chapter, page 483, for a guide suggesting readiness at different ages.*

To refute a myth, feeding your baby cereal before bedtime doesn't lead to sleeping through the night.

FOOD VARIETY: GOOD FOR BABY

Variety certainly is the spice of life, and it's beneficial for your baby, too. Learning to enjoy a variety of nutrient-rich solid foods helps establish a lifetime of good eating habits.

- Offer a variety of foods with different flavors, colors, shapes, and textures to help ensure that your baby's nutrition needs are met. Variety makes mealtime more fun, too.
- Don't let your own food biases limit your baby's preferences. Your baby or toddler may like foods you don't like.
- Be aware that babies perceive sweet tastes first. Not surprising, since amniotic fluid and breast milk are sweet. Other taste perceptions develop during a baby's first year.
- Be patient. Like you, your baby may like some foods better than others. That's normal. Likes and dislikes also may change from week to week. It's okay if your baby doesn't like some foods at first; those first tries are only one to two tablespoons of food. Try again.
- Skip foods with added sugars or salt. Consuming them now may help establish a baby's preference for them later. Added sugars provide only added calories.
- If your baby has little or no interest in solids and continues to struggle with spoon feeding or more textured foods, talk to your pediatrician or registered dietitian nutritionist. Your baby may need professional help from someone who specializes in infant feeding issues.

Cereals, Breads, and Other Grain Foods

Offer iron-fortified cereal to babies and toddlers. To enhance iron absorption, serve iron-containing foods with vitamin C–rich foods, such as fruits and 100 percent fruit juice. Other grain products include dry cereals, crackers, teething biscuits, soft breads, and soft, cooked pasta or rice. *See "Infant Cereals: For Starters" in this chapter, page 478.*

Caution: Some high-fiber cereals, such as bran, are low in calories yet high in bulk. Avoid offering large amounts to infants; they fill a small stomach without providing many nutrients or calories. Infants and young children can get enough fiber from a variety of other foods such as vegetables and fruits.

Meats, Milk Products, and Other Protein Sources

These foods are valuable sources of protein, calcium, iron, zinc, and other minerals that your baby needs to develop bones and muscles, and for his or her blood supply and brain development.

Offer a variety of soft, pureed, or finely chopped meats such as lean beef or pork, or chicken or turkey without skin. Besides their protein and zinc, meat and poultry contain iron that is more bioavailable than iron from plant-based foods.

By age seven to eight months, well-cooked, pureed beans and peas (perhaps strained) or mashed tofu are options for vegetarian infants; since tofu is made of soy, be watchful for potential food allergies.

Feeding Myself

As babies master spoon feeding, they're gradually ready to feed themselves. Watch for signals that suggest your baby is ready. At eight to nine months, he or she may try to help you by taking a cup in his or her hand or putting his or her hand on yours.

- Start with finger foods. It's easy because eating by hand is utensil free.
- Give your baby a spoon to hold in one hand while you use another for feeding. This gives your baby practice grasping a utensil.
- Offer baby-friendly utensils: a small, rounded spoon with a straight, wide handle, and a dish with high, straight sides.
- Use the two-spoon approach. Give an empty one to your baby, and fill the other with baby food. Then switch so baby has a filled spoon for self-feeding.
- Be patient—and relaxed. Food will end up on the floor. Your baby will need lots of practice before being able to eat a whole meal without your help.
- Always stay with your baby when he or she is self-feeding. In that way, you'll be around if he or she starts to choke and be there to help make the meal a social one.

Tip: Start a lifelong habit of family mealtime. Bring your baby's high chair to the family table, even if you need to feed your baby first.

Offer only cooked eggs. Before age one, your doctor may advise only egg yolks in case your baby has a reaction to egg whites. The AAP advises that there is no evidence that introducing eggs after four to six month of age determines whether your baby will be allergic to them.

After twelve months, if a toddler no longer takes breast milk or infant formula, offer whole cow's milk, an important source of calories, calcium, vitamin D, proteins, essential fatty acids, and other nutrients. Growing bones need an adequate supply of calcium and vitamin D. Good calcium sources include milk, cheese, and calcium-fortified cottage cheese. Health experts advise that there is no need for children under two years of age to consume lower-fat versions of dairy foods such as low-fat or fat-free milk or low-fat yogurt.

Vegetables and Fruits

Vegetables and fruits are good sources of vitamin C, beta carotene, other nutrients, and phytonutrients. By offering these foods frequently at mealtime, children become familiar with vegetable and fruit flavors, which helps set the stage for accepting and enjoying them throughout life.

Introduce vegetables and fruits in any order. As already stated, no evidence indicates that introducing fruits before vegetables makes a baby prefer fruits. If you want to start with applesauce, bananas, and carrots, that's fine. Offer new flavors along with familiar vegetables and fruits as you go. Respect what your baby likes and may not like. No one vegetable or fruit is essential for health, so relax. Encourage a rainbow of colorful vegetables and fruits. The goal? Learning to like as many vegetables and fruits as possible.

See "Dietary Reference Intakes" in the appendix, page 780, for specific nutrient recommendations for healthy infants.

Have you ever wondered?

. . . what foods help your baby avoid constipation? Offer a combination of foods to keep stools soft enough to pass easily. Some foods produce softer stools: for example, apricots, peaches, pears, peas, and prunes (dried plums). Drinking enough fluid helps soften stools, too.

If your baby gets constipated, offer apple or pear juice twice a day, or prune juice for something stronger. Get advice from your pediatrician if this doesn't work.

. . . how to tell if your older baby is hungry or full? Older babies might signal hunger by opening and moving their mouth toward a spoon, by trying to swipe food toward their mouth, or by pointing, nodding, or grabbing a spoon. Fullness signals might be turning their head away from the spoon, spitting out or pushing familiar foods away, or being distracted. Learn your baby's hunger and fullness cues, as you help him or her learn to avoid overeating later in life.

. . . whether lead poisoning is an issue for your baby? You need to check! The AAP and the CDC advise lead screening at ages one and two. Talk to your doctor. *See "Water: Concerns about Lead and Nitrates"* in *chapter 4, page 84, for more about lead poisoning.*

. . . if organic baby food is worth the extra price? That's your choice. The AAP advises that organic baby foods are no more nutritious or safe than traditional options—and usually cost more. Organic or not, nutrient-rich foods from the start are the key to a lifetime of healthy eating.

PLAY IT SAFE: WARMING BABY'S FOOD

Babies enjoy baby foods either warm, cool, or room temperature, just as they do bottle-fed breast milk and infant formula. If you want to serve foods at warm temperatures, follow these guidelines:

- Read warming guidelines on baby food labels before heating them on the stovetop or in the microwave oven.
- Heat higher-fat foods such as meat and eggs on the stovetop, not in the microwave oven, for even, gentle heating.
- Warm jars of baby food in a pan of warm water that's removed from the stovetop. Heat baby foods until just lukewarm so your baby won't get burned. Test the temperature of the food before feeding it to your baby.
- Always use a clean spoon to feed your baby.

Be very cautious if you warm baby food in a microwave oven. Microwaving creates uneven heating, or "hot spots," that can burn a baby's mouth, throat, and skin. Food may feel cool on the outside while the inner contents reach scorching temperatures. And since food doesn't heat evenly, microwaving may not destroy bacteria that cause foodborne illness.

Follow these guidelines for proper heating in a microwave:

- Always use a microwave-safe dish to warm baby food.
- Heat only the amount you'll need. If you save the uneaten food, bacteria in leftovers can grow and may cause diarrhea, vomiting, and other symptoms of foodborne illness if used at a later feeding.
- So food isn't overheated, remember that less food heats faster than more food, and some microwave ovens heat faster than others. For example, for microwave heating, fifteen seconds on high (100 percent power) for four ounces of baby food are enough.
- After microwaving, stir the food to distribute the heat. Then let it "rest" for at least thirty seconds. As it rests, the food will continue to heat through.

See "Microwaving Food Safely" in chapter 7, page 214.

Feeding Skills and Readiness Cues

Babies differ in their size, appetite, and readiness for solid foods. This guide offers a general time frame for a baby's development and skills, and a guide to the signs of readiness for different solid foods. Some babies may be ready for certain foods a little sooner; others, somewhat later. Your pediatrician, pediatric nurse, or a registered dietitian nutritionist will make recommendations to meet your baby's individual needs.

Infant's Approximate Age	Mouth Patterns	Hand and Body Skills	Feeding Skills or Abilities	Hunger and Satiety (Fullness) Cues
BIRTH THROUGH 5 MONTHS	• Suck/swallow reflex • Tongue thrust reflex • Rooting reflex • Gag reflex	• Poor control of head, neck, and trunk • Needs head support • Brings hands to mouth around 3 months	• Swallows liquids but pushes most solid objects from the mouth • Coordinates suck-swallow-breathe while breast- or bottle-feeding • Moves tongue forward and back to suck	**HUNGER CUES:** • Wakes and tosses, is more alert or active • Sucks on fist • Cries or fusses, or make pre-cry expressions • Opens mouth while feeding to indicate wanting more • If breastfeeding, your baby may root toward your breast. **SATIETY CUES:** • Decreases or stops sucking • Spits out the nipple • Seals lips together • Turns head away • Falls asleep
4 MONTHS THROUGH 6 MONTHS	• Up-and-down munching movement • Transfers food from front to back of tongue to swallow • Draws in upper or lower lip as spoon is removed from mouth • Tongue thrust and rooting reflexes begin to disappear • Gag reflex diminishes • Recognizes spoon and holds mouth open as spoon approaches	• Sits with support • Good head control • Uses whole hand to grasp objects (palmer grasp)	• Takes in a spoonful of pureed or strained food and swallows without choking • Drinks small amounts from cup when held by another person, with spilling	**HUNGER CUES:** • Cries or fusses • Sucks on fist • If breastfeeding, your baby may root toward your breast. • Smiles, gazes at caregiver, or coos during feeding to indicate wanting more • Moves head toward spoon or tries to swipe food towards mouth **SATIETY CUES:** • Decreases or stops sucking • Spits out, bites, or plays with the nipple • Turns head away • May be distracted or pay attention to surroundings more

(continued)

Feeding Skills and Readiness Cues *(continued)*

Infant's Approximate Age	Mouth Patterns	Hand and Body Skills	Feeding Skills or Abilities	Hunger and Satiety (Fullness) Cues
5 MONTHS THROUGH 9 MONTHS	• Up-and-down munching movement • Begins to control the position of food in the mouth • Positions food between jaws for chewing	• Begins to sit alone unsupported • Follows food with eyes • Transfers food from one hand to the other • Tries to grasp foods such as toast, crackers, and teething biscuits with all fingers and pull them into the palm	• Begins to eat mashed foods • Eats from a spoon easily • Drinks from a cup with some spilling • Begins to feed self with hands	**HUNGER CUES:** • Reaches for spoon or food • Points to food **SATIETY CUES:** • Eating slows down • Clenches mouth shut • Pushes food away
8 MONTHS THROUGH 11 MONTHS	• Moves food from side to side in mouth • Begins to use jaw and tongue to mash food • Begins to curve lips around rim of cup • Begins to chew in rotary pattern (diagonal movement of the jaw as food is moved to the side or center of the mouth)	• Sits alone easily • Transfers objects from hand to mouth • Begins to use thumb and index finger to pick up objects (pincer grasp) • Plays with spoon at mealtimes but does not spoon feed yet	• Begins to eat ground or finely chopped foods and small pieces of soft foods • Begins to experiment with spoon but prefers to try feeding self with hands • Drinks from a cup with less spilling	**HUNGER CUES:** • Reaches for food • Points to food • Gets excited when food is presented **SATIETY CUES:** • Eating slows down • Pushes food away
10 MONTHS THROUGH 12 MONTHS	• Rotary chewing (diagonal movement of the jaw as food is moved to the side or center of the mouth)	• Feeds self easily with fingers • Begins to put spoon in mouth • Dips spoon in food rather than scooping • Reaches to spoon feed self • Begins to hold cup with two hands • Drinks from a straw • Good eye-hand-mouth coordination	• Begins to eat chopped foods and small pieces of soft, cooked table foods • Begins spoon-feeding self with help • Bites through a variety of textures	**HUNGER CUES:** • Expresses desire for specific food with words or sounds **SATIETY CUES:** • Shakes head to say "no more"

Adapted from: Infant Nutrition and Feeding: A Guide for Use in the WIC and CSF Programs, USDA, Food and Nutrition Service, March 2009.

Avoid Feeding Baby from the Jar

Feeding directly from the baby food jar or container introduces bacteria from your baby's mouth to the spoon and then into the food. If you save the uneaten food, bacteria in leftovers can grow and may cause diarrhea, vomiting, and other symptoms of foodborne illness if used at a later feeding.

- Instead, spoon small amounts of baby food into a feeding dish, and feed from there. Toss what's uneaten from the dish. If your baby needs a second helping, just take more from the jar with a clean spoon.
- As soon as you finish feeding your baby, replace the cap on opened containers of baby food that haven't come in contact with your baby's saliva. You may then safely refrigerate them: opened strained fruits for two to three days; strained meats and eggs, one day; and meat and vegetable combinations, one to two days.

Unopened containers of baby food have the same shelf life as other canned foods. Check the date on food the label or lid, and use the baby food while it's still at its peak quality. *See "More for Food Label Readers" in chapter 6, page 152, to learn how to interpret product dates.* Most jars of baby food have a safety button on top. If the button is depressed, the food should be safe. As the vacuum seal releases when you open the jar, you'll hear a "pop." Discard jars with chipped glass or rusty lids.

Travel and Day Care: Baby Foods To Go

- Pack unopened jars of commercial baby food. Even cereal comes in jars. Ready-to-feed formula in a prepackaged bottle is handy, especially since it doesn't require refrigeration. Or use powdered formula. Just pre-measure water and powder into separate containers, and then mix when it's needed.
- Keep perishable foods, such as bottles of prepared infant formula or breast milk, well chilled. Pack them in an insulated container with frozen cold packs or buried in ice in a plastic bag. When you arrive at your destination, refrigerate them.
- Bottles already cold from your refrigerator can stay safe for up to eight hours in sterile sealed bottles in an insulated bottle bag with cold packs—or for about four hours if they're stored in ice cubes in a plastic bag.
- Have everything handy: food, utensils, bib, and baby wipes or a clean, damp washcloth. If someone else is feeding your baby, provide feeding instructions, too, including the time and approximate amount.
- Keep food separate from soiled diapers. And don't put food and bottles in a diaper bag that's been exposed to soiled diapers.

BABY FOOD—MAKE IT YOURSELF?

Commercial baby foods are nutritious options for feeding baby. Today's commercial baby foods provide balance and variety with carefully controlled and consistent nutrient content. Yet, some parents get satisfaction from preparing baby food themselves.

If you choose to prepare homemade baby food, take care to keep it safe and to retain the nutrients from fresh foods:

- Wash your hands before preparing baby food.
- Always use clean cutting boards, utensils, and containers to cook, puree, and store homemade baby food.
- Wash, peel, and remove seeds or pits from fresh produce. Take special care to thoroughly wash and peel vegetables and fruits that are grown close to the ground such as melons and potatoes; they may contain spores for *Clostridium botulinum* or contain other harmful bacteria that can cause foodborne illness.
- Start with fresh or frozen vegetables and fruits. Cook them until tender by steaming or microwaving, then puree or mash them. There's no need to add salt, other seasonings, or sweeteners. A baby's taste preferences aren't the same as yours.
- Puree or mash fresh fruit or fruit canned in its own juice. Never add honey, sugar, or corn syrup. *See "Have you ever wondered . . . if it's okay to sweeten baby food with honey or dip a pacifier in honey?" in this chapter, page 480, for the dangers of honey.*
- Offer cooked eggs only, whether they're yolks only or whole eggs.
- Cook meats, poultry, and eggs until well done. Babies are especially susceptible to foodborne illnesses caused by eating undercooked meats, poultry, and eggs. Again, there's no need for added flavorings.
- Prepare foods with a texture appropriate for the baby's feeding stage. Puree foods in a food processor, blender, or baby-food grinder; mash them with a fork; or chop them well, so your baby won't choke.
- Cover, and refrigerate or freeze homemade baby food immediately after it's prepared. Homemade baby food keeps in a covered container for one to two days in the refrigerator. *See "The Cold Truth: Food Storage" in chapter 7, page 202, to check for freezer storage times.*
- For convenience, freeze prepared baby food for later using one of these methods. Make sure to label and date it.
    - Freeze it in small portions in a clean ice cube tray. Once frozen, put the cubes into clean, airtight, plastic bags for single-serve portions.

Food Labels: For Infants and Young Children

The 2015–2020 Dietary Guidelines for Americans doesn't apply to children under age two—and neither do the Nutrition Facts on labels for foods that are for adults, teens, and school-aged children.

Foods meant for infants, toddlers, and young children must carry Nutrition Facts that look much like the labels on your other foods. However, the information provided reflects the kinds and amounts of nutrients that children need—which differ somewhat from the needs of older children, teens, and adults. It's another tool to help parents compare and choose foods for infants and young children.

Nutrition Facts will show up in one of two ways until the revised label is shown on all foods:

- The original Nutrition Facts labels on these foods are categorized for infants and toddlers for under four years of age or for under two years of age.
- The new Nutrition Facts labels, which must be in use by late July, 2018, have new age categories that are more consistent with the nutrient recommendations for these ages: infants seven months through twelve months of age, when they are transitioning to solid foods; and children one year through 3 years of age.

Serving sizes are based on average amounts that infants and toddlers usually eat at one time. For example, for oatmeal, it's ¼ cup, which is about half an adult-size label serving.

Nutrition Facts for some nutrients such as fat, total carbohydrates, and dietary fiber are given in grams, but not the percent Daily Values (DVs), as labels do on your foods. This is because DVs for these ages haven't been established. Infants and toddlers under two years of age need fat as a concentrated energy source to fuel their rapid growth. Parents and other caregivers shouldn't try to limit an infant's or toddler's fat intake.

On the original Nutrition Facts label, look for protein, as well as vitamins and minerals. With the new Nutrition Facts label, the percent DV for protein will be shown for infants and children one through three years of age. Vitamin D will also be required on the new labels.

See "Nutrition: Fact Check!" in chapter 6, page 144, for details about the Nutrition Facts on foods for older children, teens, and adults.

Besides the Nutrition Facts, check the required use-by date on the food labels for infant formula and baby food, too. That date is for quality as well as for nutrient retention. *See "More for Food Label Readers" in chapter 6, page 152, to learn more about product dating.*

- Use the "plop and freeze" technique: Plop meal-size spoonfuls of pureed food onto a clean cookie sheet and freeze them just until firm. Then transfer the baby food to clean, airtight, plastic bags for continued freezing.

SAFETY FROM CHOKING: INFANTS, TODDLERS, AND PRESCHOOLERS

Having teeth doesn't mean children can handle all foods. Small, hard foods, slippery foods, and sticky foods can block the air passage, cutting off a child's supply of oxygen. Saying "no" to foods a child might choke on is one of his or her first safety lessons. Follow these guidelines to keep your child from choking:

- Have the child seated at the table or counter when eating. Anything can be a choking hazard if he or she is eating and crawling, walking, or running at the same time.
- Watch your infant or toddler while he or she is eating.
- Don't offer these foods to children younger than four years of age:
  - *Small, hard foods:* cherry tomatoes, dry flake cereal, nuts, popcorn, pretzels, raw carrots, raw celery, raw peas, seeds, snack chips, whole kernel corn, and whole olives. For toddlers and preschoolers, cut or break these foods into ½-inch pieces or smaller to bite and chew, but not to put whole into their mouths.
  - *Slippery foods:* large pieces of meat, poultry, and hot dogs; whole grapes; and hard candy, lollipops, and cough drops, which may be swallowed before they're adequately chewed. Chop grapes, meat, poultry, hot dogs, and other foods in small pieces.
- Be careful with sticky foods, too, such as peanut butter. Spread only a thin layer on bread. Avoid giving your baby peanut butter from a spoon or finger. Avoid giving chewing gum. If these foods get stuck in your baby's throat, he or she may have trouble breathing.
- Watch out for these foods that are a choking risk, too: caramels, fruit leather, jelly beans, marshmallows, soft candies with a firm texture such as gel or gummi candies, taffy, raw peeled apple and pear slices, cherries with pits, and dried fruits.
- Avoid propping your baby in bed or an infant seat with a bottle for feeding. Refrain from feeding your baby in the car, too.
- Offer nutrient-rich foods that your baby can handle for his or her developmental level. Finger foods for older babies and toddlers include pieces of banana, strips of cheese, graham crackers, or pieces of a bagel.
- Watch young children while they eat. That includes watching older brothers and sisters who may offer foods that younger children can't handle yet.

When an Infant Is Choking

Choking is when someone can't breathe because food or another object is blocking the throat or windpipe (airway). When a person doesn't get enough air, permanent brain damage can occur in as little as four minutes. Rapid first aid for choking can save a life.

This advice is for infants under one year of age.

SYMPTOMS

The danger signs of choking are bluish skin color, difficulty breathing (ribs and chest pull inward), loss of consciousness if the blockage isn't cleared, inability to cry or make much sound, weak and ineffective coughing, and soft or high-pitched sounds while inhaling.

FIRST AID

Do NOT perform these steps if the infant is coughing hard or has a strong cry. Strong coughs and cries can help push the object out of the airway.

If your child is not coughing forcefully or does not have a strong cry, follow these steps:

1. Lay the infant face down, along your forearm. Use your thigh or lap for support. Hold the infant's chest in your hand and hold the jaw with your fingers. Point the infant's head downward, lower than the body.
2. Give up to five quick, forceful blows between the infant's shoulder blades. Use the palm of your free hand.

If the object doesn't come out of the airway after five blows:

1. Turn the infant face-up. Use your thigh or lap for support. Support the head.
2. Place two fingers on the middle of the breastbone just below the nipples.
3. Give up to five quick thrusts down, compressing the chest one-third to one-half the depth of the chest.
4. Continue five back blows followed by five chest thrusts until the object is dislodged or the infant loses alertness (becomes unconscious).

If the child becomes unresponsive, stops breathing, or turns blue:

1. Shout for help.
2. Give infant CPR. Call 911 after one minute of CPR*.
3. If you can see the object blocking the airway, try to remove it with your finger. Try to remove an object only if you can see it.

DO NOT DO THIS

- Do NOT perform choking first aid if the infant is coughing forcefully, has a strong cry, or is breathing enough. However, be ready to act if the symptoms get worse.
- Do NOT try to grasp and pull out the object if the infant is alert (conscious).
- Do NOT do back blows and chest thrusts if the infant stops breathing for other reasons, such as asthma, infection, swelling, or a blow to the head. Do give infant CPR* in these cases.

WHEN TO CONTACT A MEDICAL PROFESSIONAL

If the infant is choking, tell someone to call 911 while you begin first aid. If you are alone, shout for help and begin first aid.

Always call your doctor after a child has been choking, even if you successfully remove the object from the airway and the infant seems fine.

*All parents and those who take care of children should learn infant and child CPR. See www.americanheart.org for classes near you.

Source: MedlinePlus, National Institutes of Health, www.nlm.nih.gov/medlineplus/ency/article/000048.htm. Accessed October 16, 2016.

- Insist that children sit to eat or drink. They should not drink beverages when they're lying down, walking, or running. As they develop eating skills, encourage them to take time to chew well.
- Look for warning labels on foods with a high choking risk.
- Be prepared to do first aid for choking quickly to dislodge solid foods that obstruct the air passage. *See "When an Infant Is Choking . . ." in this chapter, page 487.* The technique for infants and toddlers differs somewhat from that for older children, teens, and adults.

A FINAL WORD ON FOOD-SAFETY FOR INFANT FEEDING

Infants and young children are very vulnerable to foodborne illnesses. Their immune systems aren't developed enough to fend off foodborne infections. Safe food handling and preparation are essential, *as addressed earlier in this chapter.* When feeding an infant, avoid raw (unpasteurized) milk and any products made from unpasteurized milk; raw or partially cooked eggs and foods containing raw eggs; raw or undercooked meat and poultry; raw or undercooked fish and shellfish; unpasteurized juices (fruit and vegetable); raw sprouts; and honey and corn syrup. *See chapter 7, page 191, for more advice on food safety.*

17

Help Kids Grow Up Healthy

In this chapter, find out about . . .

Raising a healthy eater

Learning about food: cooking, gardening, shopping together

Feeding issues: growth and weight, school meals, eating vegetables, eating out

Healthy eating and physical activity: toddlers and preschoolers, school children, and teens

Food nourishes at every age and stage in a child's life: during infancy and throughout the toddler, preschool, school-age, and adolescent years. Careful food choices not only help to ensure the physical nourishment of a child's growing body and brain, but also to nourish his or her social, mental, and psychological development.

Whatever the age, kids need the same nutrients that adults do. Only the amounts differ. Like you, they need energy from food—in fact, more than you do relative to their body weight. They enjoy many of the same foods you like, but the form and combinations may differ.

Childhood and adolescence is a time to establish patterns of healthy eating and active living that lead to lifelong health and wellness. It's also a time for kids to learn eating skills for social times with family and friends. The implications of becoming healthy eaters can extend further, when they someday model these food behaviors for their own children.

As a parent, a grandparent, or an adult caregiver, you influence the well-being of your child in ways beyond role modeling. By taking good care of yourself (smart eating and active living), you not only have better health, but you're better able to care for your child and your family.

Raising Healthy Eaters

Just how do you raise healthy eaters? This chapter starts with some general perspectives and advice: who's responsible for what, strategies for feeding kids of all ages, the value of the family table, and what kids can learn from various food experiences. Next, it addresses some other issues, such as nutrition and learning, school meals, eating out with kids, kids and body weight—and vegetables. Finally, it covers specific nutrition issues for toddlers and preschoolers, school-age kids, and teens.

YOUR RESPONSIBILITIES—AND THEIRS

Simply stated: From tots to teens, parents, grandparents, and adult caregivers supply the three *w*'s of meals and snacks: *what* foods are offered, and *when* and *where* they're eaten. Kids fill in the other *w* and *h*: *whether* to eat the foods offered and *how* much.

Adults. Your responsibilities start with being a good role model for healthy eating, mealtime behavior, and active living. After all, parents and other caregivers are kids' first and most influential teachers. It's up to you to support your child's chances to make wise food choices and enjoy food:

- By recognizing and respecting his or her unique needs
- By choosing and preparing a variety of nourishing, appropriate foods (both familiar and new from which your child can choose)
- By setting a routine (time and place) for eating

Bottom line: Kids usually eat better when they feel in control of their food choices. Trust them. Let your child choose what and how much to eat from what you offer. Respect his or her food preferences and appetite. Help your child learn to eat slowly and pay attention to feeling full. By learning hunger and fullness cues, your child will learn to eat enough but not overeat. Give your child the freedom to politely refuse foods he or she doesn't want.

Children and teens. Their responsibilities are to learn the skills needed to make sound food choices from foods offered, to behave at meals, and to eat foods the family eats. Kids also are responsible for listening to their body cues so they eat the right amounts (eat when hungry, stop when full).

Physical activity—all responsible! Regular physical activity is also part of the health equation. As an adult, your role is to encourage your child to engage in regular physical activity as well as provide safe opportunities for regular active play or perhaps age-appropriate individual or team sports. Kids need to make active play—or, as they get older, perhaps a sport, too—part of their daily life. Age-specific ideas about physical activity *are provided later in this chapter.*

- Action for Healthy Kids
  www.actionforhealthykids.org
- Families, Food and Fitness; Cooperative Extension System
  articles.extension.org/families_food_fitness
- Kids Eat Right, Academy of Nutrition and Dietetics
  www.eatright.org/kids
- American Academy of Pediatrics
  www.healthychildren.org
- MyPlate (health and nutrition for preschoolers and kids), USDA
  www.choosemyplate.gov/health-and-nutrition-information
- Let's Move!
  www.letsmove.gov
- Team Nutrition, USDA
  www.fns.usda.gov/tn
- We Can! (children's activity and nutrition), National Heart, Lung, and Blood Institute, USHHS
  www.nhlbi.nih.gov/health/educational/wecan

SMART TACTICS FOR FEEDING HEALTHY KIDS

From tots to teens, basic advice for healthy eating applies to all ages. Offering healthy food choices, helping to ensure food safety, and establishing positive mealtime behavior—for everyone at the table, including you—are the smart ways to start. *Later in this chapter, you'll find more tactics specific to each age group.*

Food Safety

For both you and your child, remember that handling and eating food must always start with proper hand washing; *see "Hand-Washing Basics" in this chapter, page 496.* Food safety is a must whenever you or your child are around food; *see chapter 7, page 191, for complete details.*

Even if you can't eat together, be present when your child, especially a younger or school-age one, is preparing or eating food. Younger children particularly need supervision in case they start to choke. Someone who's choking may not be able to make sounds you can hear easily.

Food Choices for Kids and Families

Your role as a parent is to decide what foods to offer. As you make those choices, consider these tips:

- Offer nourishing meals and snacks regularly. Include a variety of nutrient-dense foods from all five food groups, *as discussed in chapters 2 and 3, pages 21 and 60. See "Snacking for Good Nutrition" in this chapter, page 493, for tips about snack time.*
- Involve your child—from preschooler to teen—in planning and preparing meals and snacks. It's his or her chance to practice making food decisions. Whatever their age, kids are more likely to eat foods that they help plan and prepare.
- Consider what your child eats overall. It's what he or she eats over several days that counts—not what is eaten for one meal or in one day. If your child occasionally skips some nourishing foods or doesn't eat a full meal, that's okay.
- Offer new foods often, including foods of cultures and cuisines other than your own. Trying new foods is like a new hobby; it expands your child's food knowledge, experience, and skills. Kids learn to like foods, including vegetables and fruits, that they're frequently exposed to—especially if they see their parents and siblings eating and enjoying them, too. Acknowledge that your child will like some, but not all, of those foods. That's okay.
- Bring into the house whatever foods and drinks you want your child to have. Remember, your responsibility as the adult is deciding what foods to offer. If you buy items such as sugary drinks,

candy, and cookies, store them out of sight to enjoy as "extras"; that helps avoid the chance for confrontation.

- Help your child learn to make healthy food choices away from home, too.

Mealtime Psychology

Helping your child become a healthy eater may take some mealtime psychology on your part. Keep these ideas in mind:

- Keep mealtimes calm and pleasant, with a chance for kids and adults to talk together. Mealtime stress can lead to emotional overeating or undereating for your child. Try to avoid fussing, nagging, arguing, or complaining at the table.
- Encourage healthy eating—without forcing or bribing your child.
- Reward your child with affection and attention—not food. Using food, including dessert, as a reward or a punishment promotes unhealthy attitudes about food and perhaps emotional overeating. Smiles, hugs, and compliments are better sweet treats.
- Respect food preferences. Give a young child freedom to choose and reject foods, just as older children and adults have. Encourage him or her to politely say "No, thank you." Making food choices is a competency children need to master.
- Stay positive! Avoid the notion of "forbidden" foods. That may cause your child to want them more. With discretion, almost any foods can be part of your child's healthy eating plan.
- Give yourself a break. No matter what your intent or how carefully you try, your child won't "eat right" every time.

Need more practical, easy ways to help kids eat healthy? Check here for "how-tos":

- Help your child with proper dental care; *see "A Closer Look . . . How to Keep Your Teeth and Gums Healthy," in chapter 25, page 737.*
- Help your child eat smart for sports; *see "Kids: Eating for Sports" in chapter 21, page 612.*
- Deal with food allergies or intolerances at home, at day care, in school, or in a restaurant; *see "A Closer Look . . . Helping Kids Deal with Food Allergies or Other Adverse Food Reactions," in chapter 23, page 658.*
- Find a credible nutrition expert experienced in issues for feeding kids if you need an answer; *see "How to . . . Find a Qualified Nutrition Expert" in chapter 26, page 761.*

FAMILY MEALTIME: A PRIORITY

The simple act of sharing a meal as a family nurtures family dynamics that can have important, long-lasting benefits. A shared meal means sitting together, facing each other, and interacting, not just eating the food. It's part of raising a healthy family.

Shared Meals Matter

Research on shared meals, while still sparse in this area, is growing. What's shown so far and what experts suggest is that frequent, regular family mealtimes can have several benefits:

- Kids and parents eat more healthfully. When kids eat with the family, they often consume more calcium, iron, and fiber; more of several vitamins; and less saturated and *trans* fats. They also eat more vegetables and/or fruits daily and may even learn to like a greater variety of foods.
- Eating together appears to promote kids' healthy weight, perhaps due to mindful eating and more-nourishing food choices. With scheduled mealtime, all—kids and adults—are more likely to eat the right amount for them. They come to the table hungry and stop when satisfied.
- Offering "talk time" for all, including toddlers, preschoolers, school-age children, and teens, enhances school performance and language development.
- Sharing meals appears to help prevent kids' behavioral problems and may reduce risky behaviors such as substance abuse and smoking. Perhaps this is because mealtime is a "touch point" in time between kids and parents, or because shared meals are one marker of healthy families.
- Mealtime provides a chance to teach social skills such as table manners and being polite and respectful. Kids learn by watching their parents, older siblings, and other caregivers.
- Eating together promotes family bonding and communication—a time to talk, to listen, to share stories and relate what's going on in order to help each other, and to create new family memories.

Family Mealtime Routine

In today's busy lives, it's not always easy to carve out time for a family meal every day. To encourage shared meals:

- Even if everyone can't be present all the time, eat as a family several times weekly and, if possible, daily. If it's breakfast, set the table the night before to save time and effort in the morning.
- If your family is always "on the go," especially when the teen years hit, designate family mealtimes together. Mark them on your calendars. Planning ahead makes it easier to fit family meals in.

✔ Your Healthy Eating Check-In

How Does Your Family Table Stack Up?

Family styles influence a child's eating and physical activity patterns and attitudes for life. What they eat and how much they move—and their attitudes toward both—have lifelong health implications. Take a moment to answer these questions and find out how well you're doing with your own family's eating and physical activity practices. As a parent, family member, or caregiver, do you:

	Never 1 point	Sometimes 2 points	Usually 3 points	Always 4 points
Share the family table together?				
1. Regularly eat your meals together as a family?	☐	☐	☐	☐
2. Serve meals and snacks on a regular schedule?	☐	☐	☐	☐
3. Make an effort to keep mealtimes pleasant?	☐	☐	☐	☐
4. Attempt to contain eating to the kitchen and dining room?	☐	☐	☐	☐
Share the family table together?				
5. Turn off the TV and limit cell phone use at the table during meals?	☐	☐	☐	☐
6. Involve your child in planning and preparing family food—and cleaning up?	☐	☐	☐	☐
Make healthy foods a priority?				
7. Offer a variety of nutrient-rich foods at meals and snacks?	☐	☐	☐	☐
8. Consider snacks an important part of the day's eating plan?	☐	☐	☐	☐
9. Expand food experiences by offering new foods and new food combinations?	☐	☐	☐	☐
10. Make breakfast an everyday habit?	☐	☐	☐	☐
11. Help your child learn to make healthy food choices at school and away from home?	☐	☐	☐	☐
Nurture positive eating behavior?				
12. Set a good example with your own food choices?	☐	☐	☐	☐
13. Give your child enough time to eat?	☐	☐	☐	☐
14. Avoid rewarding or punishing with food?	☐	☐	☐	☐
15. Avoid forcing a clean plate, and let your child stop eating when he or she feels full?	☐	☐	☐	☐
16. Give your child freedom to choose how much to eat from the foods offered?	☐	☐	☐	☐
Keep physically active?				
17. Encourage your child to play actively on most days?	☐	☐	☐	☐
18. Set a good example by being physically active yourself on most days?	☐	☐	☐	☐
19. Set limits on screen time (TV, computer, handheld devices)?	☐	☐	☐	☐
20. Enjoy physical activity regularly as a family (at least once or twice weekly)?	☐	☐	☐	☐
Subtotals	____	____	____	____

Add up your total points: ________

61 to 80 points: Excellent! You already nurture positive eating and physical activity patterns. Read on for more ideas.

41 to 60 points: Good. You're on the right track for feeding and exercising with your child. But you still have room to make positive changes in your family's lifestyle. Read on for more practical tips.

40 points or less: You've got lots of opportunity for healthier eating and activity patterns. Try to incorporate a few changes into your family's approach to food and physical activity. Read on for some steps to get you started.

"Do as I Do": Are You a Good Role Model?

Did you eat your vegetables today? Did you drink milk? Did you take a walk or do something physically active, not just sit by the TV or computer? Did you eat just a handful of chips or the whole bagful?

Whether you intend to or not, role modeling is probably the most powerful, effective way to help your child eat smart and move more. Children and teens learn their habits, attitudes, and beliefs about eating and physical activity by watching and interacting with you the parent, an older sibling, or another caregiver. By mimicking, they explore their world, try "grown-up" behavior, and hope to please you. Most young children want to do what others do!

So the next time you order a drink to go with a fast-food meal, eat when you're stressed or bored, or decide how you'll spend a leisurely afternoon, think about the messages you send. The best way to help your child eat healthier and be physically active is for you to do so, too!

- Remove distractions—TV and everyone's cell phones and other electronic devices—to make food and family the priority. This also helps to avoid mindless eating.
- Eat around a table, not side-by-side at the counter. It's better for conversation and eye contact.
- Keep family mealtime positive—and not rushed or unnecessarily prolonged. Use pleasant talk, and provide a chance for everyone (including your child) to share the day's events and to get attention.
- Set a good example by eating a variety of foods (including vegetables) yourself and showing your appreciation to those who prepared them.

See chapter 3, page 60, for more about meals and mealtime.

Learning about Food

For kids of any age, food offers a world of learning experiences. Because growing, buying, and preparing food are hands-on activities, everyday tasks that involve children and teens with food can encourage them to be food experimenters and healthy eaters. These tasks also help build family relationships and teach them so much more!

As you explore food together, teach two more *w*'s and another *h*: *what* the food is, *where* it comes from, and *how* it keeps them healthy.

Snacking for Good Nutrition

When it comes to healthy snacks, here's the key. Provide choices that are "visible," convenient, effortless, and tasty. Snacks can be thought of as mini-meals. For young children with small stomachs and for teens, whose nutrient and calorie demands are likely at an all-time high, planned snacks can fill in the nutrient gaps during the day. Time snacks so your child is hungry at mealtimes, and allow at least two hours between meals and snacks.

- Show your child or teen a variety of foods from each food group. Buy some to have on hand.
- "Walk" your child or teen through the kitchen so he or she knows where these foods are kept.
- Keep fresh fruit on the counter where your child or teen can see it.
- Wash, cut, and refrigerate fresh veggies so they're ready to eat. Keep yogurt dip on hand.
- Use see-through containers, clear plastic bags, or containers covered with plastic wrap so your child or teen can see what's inside.
- Put nutrient-rich foods where your child can reach them, perhaps on lower shelves in your refrigerator, pantry, or cabinet. Put "sometimes" foods such as cookies and chips away in cabinets where they're less convenient, especially for an impulse eater.
- Buy food in "single-serve" containers for grab-and-go eating—for example, baby carrots, fruit cups, juice, milk, pudding, and raisins. Or prepare "single-serve" portions yourself (with your child's help) to save money and packaging.

GROWING FOOD TOGETHER

Kids learn valuable lessons by planting, nurturing, and harvesting vegetables, fruits, and herbs, whether in a garden, in pots on a deck, or on a farm. Besides being fun, growing food is a lesson in science and environmental care, and provides a chance to be physically active and an opportunity for quality family time. Kids enjoy eating vegetables and fruits they grow themselves—even unusual types.

To grow garden vegetables, fruits, and herbs together:

- Encourage your child to help decide what to plant, perhaps by visiting a garden or reading a children's book about growing things. Try cherry tomatoes for eating with small hands, pumpkins for something big, purple carrots for something funny, or beets for something that grows underground. Or plant fruit trees or bushes in the spring.

- Grow vegetables and herbs from seeds or small starter plants in your backyard garden or plant pots. Perhaps start seeds in paper cups on your windowsill in early spring to transplant later.
- Talk about what plants need to grow: soil, water, and sunlight. Especially if your child is younger, talk about what he or she needs in order to grow, too.
- Plant herbs: basil, chives, mint, parsley, or rosemary. They're easy to grow, and kids often like to smell their aromas and pick the herbs to use in a salad, soup, or main dish for mealtime. *See "Herbs—and Spices, Too!" in chapter 8, page 266, for more about growing, storing, and using herbs.*
- Use gardening as a chance to teach environmental responsibility. Gather garden waste for composting. Use water wisely; don't waste water by overwatering.
- Before a meal, let your child or teen harvest and prepare his or her crops.

See "Grow a Family Garden!" on this page, for more tips.

SHOPPING FOR FOOD TOGETHER

When food shopping can be more than a quick in-and-out, make it an opportunity for food and nutrition education—and a chance to encourage healthy eating:

- As you walk through the produce section of your supermarket, farmers' market, or farm stand, encourage your child to name the vegetables and fruits. Talk about their colors, shapes, sizes, and texture. For fun, make it a scavenger hunt.
- Ask kids to help decide what foods to buy. Before shopping, you might show younger kids pictures of vegetables and fruits. Have them pick the ones they want to prepare for a family meal. Older kids and teens can help you plan the menu, make a shopping list, and fill the shopping cart.
- Challenge kids—even teens—to find one new food to try each time you shop together. Talk about it later as you prepare and taste it.
- As you shop, encourage kids to name the food group category of different foods they see in the store: vegetables, fruits, grain foods, dairy foods, and protein foods (meat, poultry, fish, beans, and nuts.)

At home, as you take vegetables out of grocery bags, talk about the part of the plant where each one grows: leaf (cabbage, greens, lettuce),

Grow a Family Garden!

Gardening offers family fun. In a garden, your whole family can be active or relaxed, and spend time together. Growing vegetables or herbs teaches kids that plants, like people, need tender-loving care to grow and stay healthy: soil (food), water, sunshine (smiles), and nurturing. Caring for plants helps develop responsibility. It also builds self-esteem when kids see what they can grow. A garden can teach your child about new foods. Kids are usually eager to taste what they grow.

Most kids are proud of what they grow. Even when gardening is messy, your child is learning. He or she can help with almost any gardening task. It's okay if the garden isn't planted perfectly.

Tip: Contact your county Cooperative Extension Service if you need guidance. *See "Resources You Can Use," page 765, to help locating it.*

WHAT YOU NEED:

- Containers for city gardens: milk and juice cartons, empty cans, rinsed empty bleach bottles, dishpans, plastic buckets, fish bowls, or bushel baskets
- Garden plot: a two-foot-square plot is big enough. (Preparing soil is hard for young children.)
- Child-size tools: watering can, hose, shovel, old spoon and fork, rake, digging stick, hoe, spade, and sticks to label plants
- Seeds or seedlings (young plants)
- Water for your hose or watering can
- Soil for container gardens
- Fertilizer: compost, manure, chemical types

If you live in a city, you can grow vegetables and herbs in a sunny place on the roof, fire escape, or balcony, or you could volunteer as a family to help plant and care for a community garden. You can also visit local farmers' markets.

EASY FOODS FOR KIDS TO GROW:

- In containers: carrots, chard, cherry tomatoes, cucumbers, herbs, lettuce, onions, peppers, spinach, tomatoes, zucchini
- In the ground: foods listed above, plus beets, collard greens, green beans, kale, okra, pumpkins
- In windowsill pots: herbs, seeds to germinate and replant as young plants in the garden

Source: Written by R. Duyff for *Nibbles for Health*, Food and Nutrition Service, USDA.

roots and tubers (beets, carrots, potatoes), stalk (asparagus, celery), flower (artichoke, broccoli, cauliflower), and seed (corn, green beans, peas).

Show your child or teen how to keep groceries clean and safe in your shopping cart. Give him or her responsibility for bringing clean, reusable shopping bags to be "green shoppers." *See "Food Safety and Quality: From Store to Home" and "Shopping Green: Opportunity, Responsibility" in chapter 6, pages 188 and 187.*

COOKING TOGETHER

Your kitchen is a learning laboratory. Just like learning to read and write, becoming self-sufficient and able to prepare nourishing and safe meals or snacks (and clean up, too) are essential life skills. Childhood and adolescence are times to learn.

For parents, teaching kitchen skills is often more than shared time together. In a busy family schedule, children and teens may need to take on some responsibilities for preparing healthy family meals. They may be expected to feed themselves sometimes. Learning good food-prep skills may also help kids prepare foods that promote a healthy weight.

Kids learn by watching adults and others in the kitchen. When children are ready, they can do simple tasks to help with family meals. Depending on a child's level of development, he or she can help with food preparation, serving, and cleanup.

Teaching Kids How to Cook

Working together in the kitchen offers many ways to nurture kids and to teach much more than healthy eating. Preparing food helps them learn, practice, and reinforce skills such as these:

- By reading a recipe together, your child learns new words and practices reading. He or she identifies foods and learns their qualities as ingredients are gathered.
- By preparing a recipe, your child practices measuring, counting, timing, sequencing, and following directions. These are all math and reading skills.
- By slicing, pouring, rolling dough, shaping meat patties, and doing other food preparation activities, your child develops small-muscle movement and eye-hand coordination.
- By watching dough rise, seeing eggs coagulate, or observing how sugar dissolves in water, your child experiences the practical side of science.
- By preparing food to eat themselves and to share with others, your child builds self-esteem and learns skills to become independent. This promotes social and emotional development. Most important, helping to prepare food promotes together time.
- By trying and exploring foods and eating utensils of other cultures as well as respecting the similarities and differences, your child gets a social studies lesson.

Cooking experiences. To help make cooking with your child successful, consider these tips:

- Choose foods and recipes that match your child's abilities. For a younger child, choose recipes with simple steps and few ingredients. Even preschoolers can tear apart lettuce leaves for a salad or break green beans into smaller pieces. As your child becomes more skilled and develops more fine motor skills, the recipes can become more complex. For foods that your child might prepare alone, make them together the first time. *See "'I Can Help': Kitchen Tasks for Kids of Every Age" in this chapter, page 498.*
- For a young, school-age cook, choose illustrated children's cookbooks that show the foods, measurements, and steps along the way. Go over the safety and sanitation tips often outlined at the front of a children's cookbook.

Microwave Oven Safety for Kids

Because burns are a common hazard related to microwave oven use, make sure kids know how to use a microwave oven safely.

- Make sure the microwave oven is on a sturdy stand—one that's low enough for kids. If it's too high to reach easily, your child may pull a hot dish down on him- or herself.
- Teach kids to read the controls on the microwave oven—the time, the power level, and the "start" and "stop" controls. If your child can't read them, he or she is too young to operate a microwave oven alone.
- Keep microwave-safe containers in one place—within your child's reach. Teach what is safe and what isn't.
- Always have your child use a child-size kitchen mitt to remove heated food from the microwave oven—whether the food is hot or not. In that way, it becomes a habit. Keep pot holders handy for kids.
- Teach your child to stir heated food before tasting to distribute the heat and avoid hot spots that can cause burns.
- Show your child how to open containers so that steam escapes away from his or her face. This includes packages of popped microwave popcorn.
- Until you're sure that your child has mastered the art of microwaving, provide supervision.

See "Microwaving Food Safely" in chapter 7, page 214, for more tips on using a microwave oven.

Click Here!
Links to Know . . .

These sites have easy recipes that children can prepare:

- Kids Eat Right, Academy of Nutrition and Dietetics
  www.eatright.org/resources/kids-eat-right-listing/?active=recipes
- ChopChop Magazine
  www.chopchopmag.org/recipes

- Ask your child to suggest foods he or she would like to make. Honor those choices when you can. Make cooking together a total experience that starts with shopping for ingredients together, too.
- Besides cooking together, have your child help you store food properly. Use this activity to show him or her how to handle food to keep it clean and safe from spoilage and foodborne illness.
- Pick a time to cook together when you're not rushed. Being relaxed and having fun is important.
- Relax! Food preparation can be messy, especially for young cooks; the end result doesn't need to be perfect. Patiently help your child learn with your guidance and encouragement, and with chances to try again if he or she makes mistakes.
- As you prepare food, talk about the directions, ingredients, measuring, how food changes form, and more. This is a teachable moment!
- Help your child become "green" in the kitchen and responsibly manage resources to limit wasted food and water. *See "The Waste-Less Kitchen" in chapter 8, page 243, to learn how.*
- Make cleanup an important part of cooking together, too.
- Sign up for a cooking class where kids and parents cook together. Volunteer to help with food activities in after-school programs. Suggest a summer cooking camp for your child. For a tween or teen, see if he or she can take a foods class at school.
- Watch cooking TV shows together, especially with your tween or teen. Besides good entertainment, some shows might inspire him or her—and you. After the show, prepare some of the dishes together for a family meal.

Alert! Kitchen Safety and Kids

With all that goes on in a kitchen, food preparation sends some "red flags" for kids' safety. Cooking is safe—if your child learns to be careful and if properly supervised. Even teens need kitchen safety reminders.

- Remind your child that the first step is always to wash hands with soap and water before and after handling food as shown here in "Hand-Washing Basics." Dry them well with a clean towel. Follow good cleanliness habits yourself. Review safety precautions.
- Supervise your child in the kitchen and point out what's not safe to touch, such as stovetops, hot pans, and turned-on mixers and blenders. *See "Safe from Kitchen Injuries" in chapter 7, page 196, and "Microwave Oven Safety for Kids" in this chapter, page 495, for kitchen safety rules.*
- Identify tasks for kids and tasks for grown-ups. Set limits on what your child can—and can't—do without proper supervision. For example, your child can't use the stove if a grown-up isn't home.
- Remind your child to be aware of his or her clothes and hair before using the stove. Large, loose-fitting garments and long hair can catch fire.
- Be a good kitchen role model. Your child will take kitchen-safety cues from you. Among the things to learn and practice: using clean utensils for different foods and using a food thermometer. *See chapter 7, page 191, for more guidance on food safety.*
- Practice what to do in case of fire. That includes "drop and roll" to smother the flames in case clothes catch fire. Keep a fire extinguisher (that's in working order) in view, and teach your child how to use it.
- Try to keep food and utensils your child will use within easy reach. Provide utensils that are safe for his or her skill level. Keep a sturdy stool handy for reaching higher places.

Hand-Washing Basics

Kids can't see them—but germs that can cause illness are everywhere. Because kids have less immunity than adults, proper hand washing and food safety are especially important.

Teach kids (and remind teens of) good hand-washing habits—always before and after handling food and eating, and after using the bathroom, touching a pet, combing hair, blowing their nose, or coughing or sneezing into their hands.

- Invest in a safe stool so, if needed, your child can reach the sink, the faucet, the soap, and a towel.
- Show your child how to wash his or her hands with soap and warm water, rubbing the palms together for twenty seconds. (It's good counting practice, too.) Singing "The Alphabet Song" while hand washing takes about twenty seconds. Show how to dry hands well with a clean towel, too.
- Practice with your child. Rub a little cinnamon and oil on your child's hands. Watch what happens with poor washing. Cinnamon that stays on hands represents germs.
- Be a good role model. Always wash and dry your hands properly, too.

- Remind your child not to climb on the counters or on a wobbling stool!
- Teach your child—even as a preschooler—to call 9-1-1 (or emergency numbers such as those for the fire department, poison control center, or police in your area). Post the phone numbers in your kitchen where your child can see them easily.
- Know first aid for choking. *See "Alert: What to Do If Someone's Choking" in chapter 7, page 196.*
- Keep a first-aid kit handy and stocked. Teach your child how to use it for a minor cooking injury. *See "Safe from Kitchen Injuries" in chapter 7, page 196, to know how the avoid kitchen injuries.*

EXPLORING MORE ABOUT FOOD

Opportunities to learn about food extend beyond the kitchen or grocery store:

- Read books about food, perhaps vegetables, with your child. Then taste those foods together. Ask a librarian, teacher, or head of the children's department in a bookstore for title suggestions. Find recipes for some foods in the stories that you can prepare together.
- Visit a farm, orchard, pick-your-own farm, or botanical garden to learn more about how food is grown or produced. Talk to farmers or gardeners, if you can. Ask how they handle compost and care for the environment.
- Use eating implements from different cultures, such as chopsticks and banana leaves, to make learning about food fun.

Kitchen Nutrition

Healthy, No-Cook Snacks for Kids

When kids have a case of the after-school munchies, offer snacks like these. They're easy and fun to make—and depending on your child's age, require little or no adult supervision to prepare.

	Grain	Vegetable	Fruit	Dairy	Protein Foods
Ants on a Log. Fill celery with peanut butter. Arrange raisins along the top.		●	●		●
Banana Pop. Peel a banana. Dip it in yogurt, then roll it in crushed breakfast cereal. Freeze until firm.	●		●	●	
Fruit Shake-ups. Put ½ cup low-fat fruit yogurt and ½ cup cold fruit juice in an unbreakable, covered container. Make sure the lid is tight. Shake it up and then pour into a cup.			●	●	
Fruit Slices and Peanut Butter. Spread peanut butter on apple or banana slices.			●		●
Fruits and Veggies with Dip. Offer strawberries and cutup fruits such as apples, bananas, and pears. Cut carrots, celery, cucumbers, or zucchini into sticks or coins. To eat, dip veggies into hummus or prepared salsa, or dip veggies and fruits into plain or flavored Greek yogurt.		●	●	●	
Ice Cream–wiches. Put a small scoop of ice cream or frozen yogurt between two oatmeal cookies or frozen whole-wheat waffles. Make a batch of these sandwiches and freeze until firm.	●			●	
Peanut Butter Balls. Mix peanut butter and bran or cornflakes in a bowl. Shape the mixture into balls with clean hands. Then roll them in crushed graham crackers.	●				●
Salsa Quesadilla. Fill a soft tortilla with low-fat cheese and salsa, then fold it over. Heat in a microwave oven until cheese is melted.	●	●		●	
Sandwich Cutouts. Using cookie cutters with fun shapes like dinosaurs, hearts, and stars, cut slices of low-fat cheese, lean meat, and whole-grain bread. Then put them together to make silly sandwiches. Eat the edges, too.	●			●	●

Feeding Concerns

No one ever said that helping kids become healthy and competent eaters was easy. Nearly every parent and caregiver faces feeding challenges and concerns, and nearly all parents want their child or teen to be adequately nourished, not over- or undernourished, in order to grow and develop normally.

VEGETABLES AND KIDS: COMMON CHALLENGE

What's a parent to do when vegetables are greeted with a chorus of "yuck"? For one reason or another, kids, including teens, often come up short on vegetables. Evidence indicates that eating enough vegetables and fruits is a marker of good nutrition.

The strong flavors of some vegetables make them more challenging for some kids' palates. With several unpressured tries, over time, even kids who are supertasters and find some flavors too strong, can learn to enjoy them. As a parent, you can turn "yuck" into "yes," starting with being a good role model yourself.

Trying new foods should be about discovery, not punishment. Remember that kids' food preferences change. Here are some tips to work vegetables into your child's meals and snacks:

- Introduce new vegetables without pressure. Let your child see them and talk about them at the store and at home. When he or she is ready, it's time to taste. It may take many attempts before tastings turn to liking new vegetables.
- Add veggies to foods your child already enjoys. Add shredded carrots, peas, or zucchini to burgers, chili, lasagna, macaroni and cheese, mashed potatoes, or spaghetti sauce. Or use them as pizza toppings.
- Offer raw finger-food veggies. Many kids prefer crisp, uncooked vegetables in mini sizes with herb-flavored yogurt dips.

"I Can Help": Kitchen Tasks for Kids of Every Age

Helping in the kitchen encourages kids to try new foods. They feel good about doing something "grown up." Give them small jobs to do. Praise their efforts. They are less likely to reject foods that they help to make. As children grow and develop more motor skills, they can help with different kitchen tasks. While these age-specific suggestions are typical, kids develop kitchen skills at different ages. You know your child best.

At 2 years:

Wipe tables.

Hand items to adult to put away (such as grocery shopping).

Place things in the trash.

Tear lettuce or greens.

Help "read" a cookbook by turning the pages.

Make "faces" out of pieces of vegetables and fruits.

Rinse vegetables or fruits.

Snap green beans.

At 3 years:

All that a 2-year-old can do, plus:

Add ingredients.

Talk about cooking.

Scoop or mash potatoes.

Squeeze citrus fruits.

Knead and shape dough.

Rinse produce in a large bowl filled with water.

Stir simple ingredients such as pancake batter.

Name and count foods.

Help assemble a pizza.

Use cookie cutters.

Use a pastry brush to oil meat, vegetables, and other food.

At 4 years:

All that a 3-year-old can do, plus:

Peel hard-cooked eggs and some fruits, such as bananas and oranges.

Set and help clear the table.

Crack eggs.

Help measure dry ingredients.

Help make sandwiches and tossed salads.

At 5 years:

All that a 4-year-old can do, plus:

Measure liquids.

Cut soft fruits and vegetables with a dull knife.

Use a whisk to beat eggs.

"I Can Help": Kitchen Tasks for Kids of Every Age *(continued)*

At 6 to 7 years:

All that a 5-year-old can do, plus:

Crack eggs into a bowl.

Use a vegetable peeler.

De-seed peppers and tomatoes.

Shuck and rinse corn.

Use blunt scissors to cut green onions and herbs.

Stir and prepare instant pudding.

Prepare lettuce for a salad.

At 8 to 9 years:

All that a 6- to 7-year-old can do, plus:

Rinse and clean vegetables.

Use a can opener.

Measure and mix dry ingredients.

Use a food thermometer.

Juice citrus fruits.

Pound chicken on a cutting board.

At 10 to 12 years:

All that a 8- to 9-year-old can do, plus:

Boil pasta and vegetables.

Simmer ingredients on the stove top.

Follow a simple step-by-step recipe.

Slice and chop vegetables.

Bake and microwave foods.

Adapted from Sources: Center for Nutrition and Public Policy, USDA, www.choosemyplate.gov/kitchen-helper-activities and Academy of Nutrition and Dietetics, www.eatright.org/resource/food/resources/eatright-infographics/kid-friendly-kitchen-tasks

Have you ever wondered?

. . . what to do if you think your child or teen has a food allergy? Talk to your child's doctor; don't make the diagnosis yourself. *See "Food Allergies: A Growing Concern" in chapter 23, page 654, to learn about food allergies and how to manage them.*

. . . what to do if you think your child or teen is lactose intolerant? You know that kids need the nutrients in dairy foods for growth and health. The good news: lactose intolerance, or difficulty digesting the sugar in milk, is often a matter of degree. And it's easy to manage—often by giving smaller, more frequent portions of milk. Also easier to digest are yogurt and cheese, which have milk's nutrients without much lactose. *See "Lactose Intolerance: A Matter of Degree" in chapter 23, page 666, for more tips.*

Lactose intolerance is more common than a milk allergy. If you suspect a lactose sensitivity, seek advice from your child's doctor, pediatric nurse, or a registered dietitian nutritionist. Don't simply give up milk! Your child or teen depends on you for calcium and other nutrients that milk provides for proper growth. Find alternative foods with comparable nutrition.

. . . if there's a link between nutrition and autism? There's no known cause for autism, but both genetics and environment are believed to play a role. Some speculate that a gluten-free, casein-free diet for those with autism may improve symptoms, but no evidence has proven this to be true. Self-prescribed, this approach can have unhealthy side effects. A small percentage of children with autism may benefit by eliminating artificial-color additives, according to some research. More research is needed to determine which foods or ingredients to avoid.

If you are the parent or caregiver of an autistic child, work with your health care team, including a registered dietitian nutritionist. Address eating behavior that is common in autistic children because it may lead to health concerns: limited food selection and strong food dislikes; not eating enough food; constipation due to limited food choices; and medical interactions with medications used to treat autism.

. . . if going gluten free is good for your child? If he or she is diagnosed with celiac disease or with non-celiac gluten sensitivity, the answer is "yes." Otherwise, gluten is harmless for children and teens. *See "Gluten Free: When It's a Must" in chapter 23, page 670, to understand the issues related to both these conditions and how to manage them.*

A gluten-free diet for kids without these health conditions can have unintended health consequences. Among them, your child may miss out on important nutrients such as iron and B vitamins from enriched and fortified foods such as breakfast cereal, pasta and bread, and fiber from whole-wheat products. If you think your child has symptoms of celiac disease or non-celiac gluten sensitivity, have him or her medically tested before starting a gluten-free diet.

- On the other hand, cook some vegetables to make them more appealing to your child. Steam, stir-fry, or microwave them in small amounts of water to keep their bright colors and crisp textures.
- "Fortify" ready-to-eat soups with extra vegetables or canned (rinsed and drained) beans.
- Start a "veggie club." Try to taste vegetables from A to Z, and check off letters of the alphabet as you go! When you shop, let your child pick a new vegetable as a family "adventure." Post a tasting chart on the refrigerator door to recognize family tasters.
- Nothing works? Offer more fruit, which also provides vitamins A and C, fiber, and phytonutrients.
- If your child doesn't like a new vegetable, say that it's okay and he or she can try it another time. Remind him or her that their taste preferences change, which is part of growing up.

See "Fruits and Vegetables: Fit More In!" in chapter 8, page 246, for more ideas for meals and snacks.

NUTRITION AND LEARNING

Well-nourished kids are ready to learn. They're more likely to have the energy, stamina, memory, mental clarity, and self-esteem to enhance their learning potential. In addition, school-age children and teens who are better nourished have fewer absences from school and often better classroom behavior, which creates a better learning environment for everyone.

Breakfast: Links to Learning

Does your child start the day with a nourishing breakfast? A morning meal is a key strategy for school success! It provides power to learn, helping kids do their personal best. Studies indicate that breakfast eaters tend to have higher school attendance and fewer hunger-induced stomachaches in the morning. And they may have better memory, better concentration, the ability to solve problems more easily, and better muscle coordination. Conversely, regular breakfast-skipping is linked to lower school achievement and performance.

Kids who eat breakfast may have a healthier body weight and are more likely to get enough of the nutrients they need for growth and

Quick School-Day Breakfasts

Breakfast—with a variety of nutrient-rich foods including protein foods—improves school performance, provides important nutrients, and puts kids on a path to a healthy weight. What's for breakfast? Even if kids are on their own in the morning, most can make these easy breakfasts. And they go down even "healthier" with juice or milk!	Grain	Vegetable	Fruit	Dairy	Protein Foods
Low-fat cheese slices served with—or melted on—whole-wheat toast; 100% fruit juice	●		●	●	
Iron-fortified cereal and low-fat or fat-free milk, topped with banana slices	●		●	●	
Peanut butter spread on toasted whole-grain bread or a waffle, or rolled inside a wheat tortilla; tangerine	●		●		●
Fruit—bananas, raisins, strawberries—on instant oatmeal made with milk	●		●	●	
Cold meat-and-veggie pizza	●	●		●	●
Leftover macaroni and cheese; banana or other fruit	●		●	●	
Apple and low-fat cheese slices between whole-wheat crackers or graham crackers	●		●	●	
Breakfast cereal topped with fresh fruit and yogurt	●		●	●	
Toasted frozen waffle, topped with low-fat yogurt and berries	●		●	●	

See "Why Breakfast?" in chapter 3, page 62, for more about the impact it has on your child's health.

health. The association between eating breakfast and body weight isn't fully understood, however. It may be that eating breakfast is something that people who are of normal weight do, and not that eating breakfast is the reason for normal weight.

Nutrients shortchanged when kids skip breakfast, such as calcium, iron, B vitamins, and vitamin D, typically aren't made up during the day. *See "Breakfast Matters" in chapter 3, page 60, and "Quick School-Day Breakfasts" in this chapter, page 500, for more about breakfast and solutions to breakfast-skipping or skimping.*

Undernutrition: Effects on Learning

Meal-skipping and poor food choices can lead to mild undernutrition for kids, even in economically stable families. Other kids may be poorly nourished because they don't have reliable access to enough affordable, nutritious food at all times of the year.

Although not easily recognized, mild undernutrition of some vitamins and minerals can inhibit mental abilities and concentration and affect learning. For example, even a mild iron deficiency can affect brain function. Severe nutrient deficiencies may be linked to improper or delayed growth, mental delays and disabilities, and very low energy levels, as well as hindering learning.

As a parent, caregiver, or community member, you have an important role in helping kids gain access to enough nourishing food. Supporting food programs in schools and communities is one way to do that. *See "Eating Right at School" in this chapter, page 505, and "Credible Support for Healthy Eating" in chapter 26, page 763.*

GROWTH AND WEIGHT

How do you know if the weight of your child or teen is healthy? Growth and weight can't be assessed by comparisons to other kids. They grow at different rates. Even at the same age, their heights and shapes differ widely.

Your Child's or Teen's Healthy Weight

Kids, especially school-age kids, like to measure their progress from year to year on a growth chart. You likely enjoy watching the progress, too. However, growth charts have an even more important role in monitoring a child's or teen's development.

Tracking Kids' Growth

Growth charts—using the body mass index (BMI) designed for children aged two to nineteen—track growth, and a child's or teen's weight in relation to height and gender. These charts, *shown in the appendix, page 777,* are used to assess whether a child may be underweight, overweight, obese, or at a healthy weight. Growth charts also assure parents and kids that there's a wide range of "normal." A muscular kid isn't necessarily fat, and a slim kid isn't necessarily underweight. They're simply different.

As kids mature, it's normal for their body fat to change, which is why adult BMI charts aren't meant for kids and the reason why it's important to track growth over time. Each child's growth clock, body size, muscularity, and shape is individual; girls differ from boys, too. Some kids plump up before puberty to prepare for their next rapid growth spurt. *Remember:* Your child will likely grow at the same way as one of his or her birth parents did at a similar age.

As a parent, you, along with your child's doctor, can use growth charts to help track your child's growth. Be aware that even the extremes—5th percentile or 95th percentile—don't necessarily mean your child is at an unhealthy weight. Kids can be fit at any size.

You may think your child or teen is really just "big boned," not overweight. If the BMI chart for children indicates that your child is overweight (when looking at weight in relation to height), take heed—even if your family is big. Your child's doctor should work with you to make the judgment.

At each pediatric visit, the doctor will screen your child or teen and determine whether his or her weight is within a healthy range, by assessing more than growth patterns. It's up to you as a parent to then follow up on any guidance to help your child reach or maintain the weight that's right for him or her.

Health care providers use several growth charts:

- The 2006 World Health Organization International growth charts often are used to assess the growth of infants and toddlers from birth to twenty-four months.
- The CDC Growth Charts are commonly used as an indicator to measure the size and growth patterns of children and teens in the United States. They show BMI-for-age weight status categories in percentiles, as *shown in the appendix, page 777.* You can also see these online sources of growth charts from the CDC and the US Department of Agriculture (USDA):
  - nccd.cdc.gov/dnpabmi/Calculator.aspx
  - www.choosemyplate.gov/preschoolers-growth-chart
  - www.cdc.gov/growthcharts/clinical_charts.htm

A growth chart, recorded at regular health exams, will track height and weight and show how your child or teen fits within a healthy range. The goal isn't a single, target weight but is instead a range that is considered normal for him or her.

What if you think your child or teen seems overweight or underweight? Be aware that some kids gain a little extra weight to support an upcoming growth spurt, and some may appear too slim as they shoot up in height. Your child's size may be normal. If you have concerns, discuss them with your child's doctor or a registered dietitian nutritionist who is trained to assess his or her weight. Never assess a child's or teen's body weight by adult standards. BMI charts for adults aren't meant for kids.

Overweight Children: Incidence, Reasons, and Risks

Overweight among children and teens is a significant public health issue—both short- and long-term. It has been described as the most common health problem among American youth today.

Although overweight children don't automatically become overweight or obese adults, there's reason for concern. Because eating and activity patterns for life often are established during childhood, the risk of being overweight as teens and adults is higher if they were overweight as children. Research also says those who are overweight as teens have a significantly greater chance of ongoing health concerns such as type 2 diabetes when they are adults.

The incidence. The CDC reports that being overweight has more than doubled among children and quadrupled in adolescents over the past thirty years. Although the rates seem to have stopped rising (and perhaps declined for the youngest children), more than one-third of children and adolescents were considered obese in 2012, according to government statistics. Nearly 18 percent of six- to eleven-year-olds and about 21 percent of youth aged twelve to nineteen years are considered obese, according to National Health and Nutrition Examination Survey (NHANES) data.

The reasons. The easy explanation is that overweight and obesity result from energy imbalance: a child or teen consumes more calories than his or her body uses. However, the underlying reasons—genetic, behavioral, and environmental—are complex and interrelated.

Do genetics factor in? Yes, as does family lifestyle. A child with one or two overweight parents has a higher risk. Certain genetic factors increase the chance of extra body weight. Although hormone imbalance is often blamed, it probably isn't the cause among children.

If a child has a genetic propensity for being overweight, family environment and interaction can make a difference. Kids often mimic the eating and lifestyle habits they see at home. Heavy snacking, irregular meals, and easy access to high-calorie foods are factors, as is a lot of sit-down time, such as TV and computer time. However, parents can control the home environment and hence the risk for being overweight.

Although rare, obesity is linked to some genetic and metabolic disorders such as Prader-Willi or Cushing's syndrome. Talk to your child's doctor if these are concerns.

Family lifestyles, genes, and health conditions aren't the only issues that factor into the epidemic of being overweight in childhood. Other issues may play a role:

- Many communities aren't designed for physical activity. Lacking sidewalks, bike paths, and parks, many kids don't have places for safe, active play.
- Physical education at school may be limited.
- Kids may spend much of their free time sitting: watching TV, playing electronic games, or engaging in social media. Screen time often fosters snacking; media ads may encourage less healthy food choices.
- Large portions (often as fast food), frequent snacking on high-calorie foods, and too many sugary beverages may be factors, too.

A child with a family history of overweight and obesity isn't destined to become an overweight teen or adult, although the chance goes up as the child gets older if he or she still carries excess weight. A physically active lifestyle and balanced, healthy eating are essentials to helping prevent a child from becoming overweight. Addressing weight problems early is important—and may trigger a commitment for others in the family to take steps to reach or keep their healthy weight, too!

The risks. Excess body weight during these early years can have physical and psychological consequences, both immediate and later in life.

- Even during youth, overweight children and teens are more likely to have risk factors related to heart disease (such as high blood pressure and high blood cholesterol levels). In a population sample of five- to seventeen-year-olds, 70 percent of the obese children had at least one risk factor for cardiovascular disease, while 39 percent of obese children had two or more risk factors.
- Overweight kids may have sleep apnea (short cessation of breathing while sleeping), problems with balance or ease of moving, and early puberty.
- With early puberty (more likely among overweight girls), girls have more estrogen over a lifetime, which may increase the risk for breast and ovarian cancer later on.
- There's also a link to asthma, especially if excess body fat is around the abdomen, and to bone and joint problems.
- When coupled with low calcium intake and weakened bones, overweight kids have more forearm fractures when they try to catch themselves during a fall.
- Overweight kids are more likely to develop prediabetes, when blood glucose levels indicate a high risk for diabetes. Type 2 diabetes, often seen in overweight adults, now is being seen in children and teens as well. Complications from diabetes are appearing sooner, too. *See "Children, Teens, and Diabetes" in chapter 24, page 712.*

- Overweight kids are at greater risk of being teased or bullied, feeling stigmatized, or isolating themselves from their peers, teachers, and family. This can result in a loss of self-esteem, a poor body image, or emotional stress. A bullied child may feel reluctant to go to school; absences can result in low grades and in further lowering of self-esteem and chances of success in life. *See "Bullying and Body Size" in this chapter, page 504.*
- Compared with their normal-weight peers, overweight kids are more likely to become obese adults who are more prone to health problems such as diabetes, heart disease, high blood pressure, stroke, osteoarthritis, gallbladder disease, and some forms of cancer.

Growing into a Healthy Weight

Healthy eating habits, combined with plenty of active play, can help most overweight kids grow into their healthy weight. These kids should be helped to limit their rate of weight gain, so their height catches up with their weight and so their BMI-for-age percentile won't increase over time.

For growing, developing bodies, weight loss generally isn't the best approach. A diet that's too restrictive, including too few calories, may not supply the food energy and nutrients your child needs and can trigger unhealthy binge eating if he or she feels too deprived.

Consult your child's doctor for a medical evaluation. Talk with your doctor, a registered dietitian nutritionist, or the school nurse for an appropriate way to manage weight. Weight-loss approaches for adults aren't meant for children or teens. *See "How to . . . Find a Qualified Nutrition Expert" in chapter 26, page 761.*

Promoting a Healthy Weight

Prevent overweight at an early age! Sometimes increased physical activity, rather than eating fewer calories, is enough to help a youngster maintain a healthy weight. But that depends on total calorie intake.

Families, schools, and communities can support healthy weight initiatives for all kids—weight issues or not. In addition to other guidance in this chapter, consider this advice, even if your child's weight seems healthy.

Remember that weight problems aren't just about food. Emotions, family problems, lifestyle, and self-image intertwine with eating behavior. As you address weight management, recognize the whole child—emotionally, socially, mentally, and physically. Lifestyle changes—often for the whole family—offer a good approach for helping an overweight child or teen manage his or her weight.

Establish a "healthy weight" mindset. These are ways you can help your youngster develop habits for a healthy weight:

- Be a role model. Involve the whole family in healthy eating so your overweight child or teen won't feel singled out.
- Give your child or teen more control. That may seem counterintuitive; however, when parents pressure or restrict food choices too much, kids don't learn self-regulation and may limit important nutrients. If they don't learn to read their hunger and fullness (satiety) cues, they may overeat. Restrictive eating also may lead to sneaking food, and then to guilt, self-condemnation, or overeating later.
- Observe and talk together about your child's feelings and subsequent behavior. Together, look for ways other than eating to address emotions. Even though eating may feel good for a while, food can't solve problems. Kids may say they're hungry when they're bored or want attention. Probe a little. Offer a snack, perhaps a cracker or an apple. If neither appeals, your child is probably bored, not hungry.
- Avoid undue attention to eating. For example, forget rewarding or punishing your child with food. In that way, you won't reinforce an emotional link to eating.
- Stay positive. Talk about being at a "healthy weight." The terms "overweight," "obese," and "underweight" are medical terms, not meant for talk with kids.

Control meal and snack nutrition. As a parent or caregiver, these are ways you can manage the eating environment:

- Tailor portion sizes that you serve to your child. Use smaller plates so less looks like more. Large portions encourage overeating. A still-hungry child can ask for more. Think about proportions, too, with plenty of vegetables and fruits offered in a meal.
- Establish snack times. Stock your kitchen with easy-to-reach, low-calorie snacks such as raw vegetables, fruits, low-fat or fat-free milk, or whole-grain wafers. Meals, rather than snacks, should provide most of your child's nutrients and calories.
- Be careful about bringing high-calorie foods and sugary drinks into the house. Hiding or forbidding access to certain foods and drinks makes them more attractive.
- Encourage plain water instead of sugary drinks for snacks. Some data supports that cutting back on sugary drinks is one way to consume fewer calories.
- Avoid labeling food as "good" or "bad." Instead, show how any food can fit, even an occasional cookie or a piece of candy. In fact, kids probably need a high-calorie snack from time to time for their energy needs. The whole eating plan is what counts.
- Eat as a family, when possible, away from the TV or computer screen. It's easy for kids to eat more when attention is shifted away from the meal and their fullness cues to a screen.

Encourage a healthy lifestyle. These are ways you can help kids be more physically active:

- Set limits on screen time. The AAP guidelines, released in 2016, identify screen time as time spent with digital media for entertainment, not for other uses such as online homework. Parents are urged to create a personalized Family Media Use Plan; see www.healthychildren.org/English/family-life/Media/. The AAP makes these recommendations:

- For infants aged eighteen months and younger, exposure to screen media is discouraged.
- For kids aged two to five, no more than one hour of screen time daily is advised.
- For kids, who are aged six and older, parents can determine screen time restrictions, and monitor the type of digital media (such as video games, mobile devices, computers, and TV) that their children use.
- Balance fun time with their appropriate use for homework and as learning tools. Screen time becomes an issue when it displaces physically active play and doing other active things.

- Encourage physical activities your child enjoys, but don't encourage excessive exercise. Besides burning calories, physical activity indirectly affects eating—for example, appetite control, stress release, and mental diversion from eating. Make physical activity a family affair. When parents are physically active, their kids are often active, too.

  Overweight children are often self-conscious in organized or competitive games. If your child or teen feels this way, encourage activities such as walking the dog or biking, where skill and an audience are less important.
- Encourage enough sleep. Besides being a health essential, adequate sleep may lower the risk for being overweight and obese, notes some research. *See "Sleep Tight, Sweet Dreams" on this page, for tips on healthy sleep habits.*

See "Weight: Right-Sized?" in this chapter, page 530, for more about body weight and image in the teen years.

Underweight: Fear of Gaining Weight

A desire to be overly thin, often prompted by media messages and by what parents say and do, is occurring in children as young as age three. Mostly girls, sometimes as young as age six, express concerns about their body image and weight gain. Inappropriate weight loss can interfere with growth—and may lead to eating disorders down the road.

Parents may play an even bigger role than media in shaping a child's or teen's body image. Even before adolescence:

- Strive for a positive eating relationship with your child or teen. Teach healthy eating habits.
- Focus on your child's or teen's inner qualities, not looks or weight. Avoid pressure to conform to any body size or shape.
- Refrain from negative comments about your own weight or anyone else's weight. Expressing thoughts about your own body image—your hips, your thighs, your abs—strongly influences how kids feel about theirs.
- Set a good example. Talk positively about how you manage your weight and feel about your body image. Skip the lure of fad dieting yourself.
- Encourage physical activity for building muscles and coordination. And work to develop your child's or teen's social skills, self-confidence, and self-esteem.

See "Eating Disorders: More Than a Nutrition Issue" in chapter 25, page 732, and "Pressure to Be Thin" in this chapter, page 531.

Bullying and Body Size

Overweight kids are more likely to be bullied, teased, and harassed. Underweight kids can be the brunt of bullying, too. Whether physical or verbal, this abuse can have a tremendous, even dangerous, effect on their self-esteem and well-being.

While bullying behavior often comes from peers, teasing and bullying can come from home, too. With concerns about childhood overweight, parents may nag, tease, or pressure kids, trying to inspire weight loss. That strategy usually backfires and may reinforce poor food habits. A sibling may tease or exclude an overweight sister or brother. Food may instead become an emotional tool to replace the comfort or support so needed from the family.

Sleep Tight, Sweet Dreams

Adequate sleep is essential to a healthy lifestyle for all ages. Kids are no exception. Adequate sleep is important for mental health (cognitive development) and reduces the chances of behavioral problems such as ADHD and mood swings that may impact an ability to learn in school, notes the National Sleep Foundation. Inadequate sleep may also be linked to pediatric overweight.

The AAP advises:

Age	Amount of Sleep
3 to 10 years old	12 hours daily
11 to 12 years old	About 10 hours daily
13 to 19 years old	About 9 hours daily

To encourage healthy sleep habits for your child:

- Teach him or her about healthy sleep habits. Be a good role model.
- Stick to a regular, consistent bedtime routine and sleep schedule.
- Keep the television, computer, cell phone, and other devices out of the bedroom.
- Make your child's bedroom conducive to sleep—dark, cool, and quiet.
- Avoid making caffeinated drinks available.

Rather than taking blame or feeling shame, kids with weight issues need empathy, open and supportive communication, inclusion, and encouragement for healthy food choices and physical activity.

- Encourage your child's school to support nutrition and physical education that promotes health at every body size—and to address the issue of bullying and body weight.
- Make the school counselor or administrator aware of any bullying behavior. Express your concerns.
- If your child is being bullied because of his or her size or weight, get professional help from a registered dietitian nutritionist or a specialist who addresses the connection between food, self-esteem, and body image.

On another note: Whether or not kids have a weight problem, it is important for them to be thoughtful and supportive classmates, friends, and siblings to those who are overweight or underweight. Remind your child that dealing with weight problems isn't easy and that all kids have the same basic needs and lots to offer, no matter what their body size. Teasing or bullying isn't caring, respectful, or fair and can lead to dangerous consequences.

EATING RIGHT AT SCHOOL

Breakfast, lunch, snacks: how do they fit into your kid's school day? From grade school through high school, students' meal and snack choices at school can positively affect their health, weight, and school success—academically and in extracurricular activities such as after-school sports. New regulations are making any food sold during the school day healthier.

School Breakfast and Lunch

Both public and nonprofit private schools provide affordable, convenient, and nutritious solutions for one, possibly two, meals daily for students: lunch and sometimes breakfast. Most school meals are regulated so they contribute positively to your child's overall nutrient and energy intake.

By law, meals served as part of the National School Food Service Program (NSFSP) of the USDA must be nourishing—and planned to promote kids' healthy weight. Menus must comply with national nutrition standards that reflect Dietary Reference Intakes (DRIs) and the 2015–2020 Dietary Guidelines for Americans. *See "Nutrients: How Much?" and "Eat Smart: Dietary Guidelines for Americans" in chapter 1, pages 6 and 8.* If schools meet these menu patterns, they can receive federal reimbursement for each meal served.

Today's school meals are getting healthier, as directed by the Healthy, Hunger-Free Kids Act of 2010. Under this law, many changes you may have made at home are happening gradually at school, too: more whole-grain foods, vegetables, and fruits every day; only milk that is low-fat or fat-free; right-sized portions to limit calories; and reduced saturated fats, *trans* fats, and sodium. Menu items must also provide nutrients identified as underconsumed. Local schools can determine how to follow the regulations: which foods to serve and how to prepare them.

Children who get school meals may have choices on the cafeteria line, perhaps for the types of vegetables or fruit, or type of milk including unflavored and flavored fat-free options. Choices help students build smart eating skills—and help ensure healthy meals.

Because most public and some private school meals have federal financial support, kids of all income levels have access to nutritious meals during school at a low cost. Some kids qualify for free or reduced-price meals.

In addition, schools must provide free drinking water during lunchtime; water can't be an alternative to milk. That's typically done with water fountains, cups, and water pitchers on lunch tables or free bottled water.

School breakfast. Your child deserves the chance to power up for school with a healthy breakfast. For kids who aren't hungry when they wake up in the morning, school breakfast, if available at your school, may offer the perfect solution to a hectic morning schedule.

As part of the NSFSP program, the meal pattern in the School Breakfast Program (SBP) must provide a variety of foods daily within a calorie range based on the student's grade in school. Menu standards give specific amounts of three required food components:

- 100% juice, vegetables, or fruit
- Low-fat (unflavored) or fat-free (flavored or unflavored) milk
- Grain foods, at least half of the grains must be whole grains

There are options for meat or a meal alternative. Less than 10 percent of calories can come from saturated fats. Sodium must be reduced gradually by school year 2022–23.

Some schools provide another breakfast option, called "Offer versus Serve." They can offer at least four food items. Students must choose at least three, one of which must be one-half cup of vegetables or fruits.

School lunch. Lunch is another opportunity for a nutritionally balanced meal during the school day. The National School Lunch Program (NSLP) also requires that menus meet nutrition standards with a variety of foods daily, within a calorie range based on the student's grade in school. Menu standards for lunch give specific amounts daily for five menu components:

- Vegetables—with a weekly requirement for variety (dark-green, red/orange; legumes; starchy and other vegetables)
- Fruits
- Meat or meat alternative
- Low-fat (unflavored) or fat-free (flavored or unflavored) milk
- Grain foods—at least half of the grains must be whole grains

As with breakfast, less than 10 percent of calories in school lunch menus can come from saturated fats, and sodium in lunch menus must be reduced gradually by school year 2022–23.

"Offer versus Serve" is required for school lunch at the senior-high level. All five menu components must be served. Students only need to take three in the required serving sizes, but for the same price as four or five; one selection must be at least one-half cup of either vegetables or fruit. This helps reduce food waste and lets students skip foods they don't plan to eat.

More improvements in today's school menus. With new menu regulations, many school menus are expanding the variety of nutrient-dense foods offered to students:

- Menus may include more fresh vegetables, fruits, salad bars or packaged salads, and different types of whole-grain foods, including whole-grain-rich pizza crusts, wraps, and rice bowls. Some grain products are a blend of whole grains and refined, enriched grains to make the color and texture more acceptable to kids.
- When offered, fries are oven-baked and may be sweet potato fries; chicken nuggets are baked, not fried; cheese may be low-fat or fat-free; foods are seasoned with more spices and herbs and less sodium. Look for more menu changes in the future.
- Schools are now encouraged to offer beans, tofu, and soy yogurt as meat alternatives for vegetarian students. They may offer beans on salad bars, black bean soup, hummus wraps, vegetarian chili, and vegetarian taco salads.
- Increasingly, schools engage in farm-to-school initiatives, with local foods appearing on school menus. Where possible, school gardens may provide some produce.
- Local chefs and farmers are bringing their culinary or agriculture know-how into the school to help kids learn more about food and promote healthy foods in school. Two programs—Chefs Move to Schools and Farm to School—are initiatives within USDA's Child Nutrition Programs.
- Cafeteria staff often offer tastings of new foods, sometimes as different vegetables are introduced.
- Many schools include parent and student input in planning school meal initiatives.

Snacks at school. With Smart Snacks in School standards, foods and drinks sold to your child during the school day must also meet nutrition standards: less than or equal to 200 calories with strict limits on sodium, fats (total, saturated, and *trans*), and total sugars. That includes foods sold in the à la carte line, the school store, and vending machines. For example, one ounce of peanuts or low-fat tortilla chips, a four-ounce fruit cup made with 100% juice, an eight-ounce granola bar (oats, fruit, nuts), and no-calorie flavored water must fit the standards.

Many school districts, counties, and states have additional policies about selling foods outside of school meals at schools and school events. Ask the administration about your Local School Wellness Policy.

Parent power. You can support healthy school foods in your community and influence the menus, vending machine choices, fundraiser options, and physical activity during and after school hours.

- Familiarize yourself with school menus. Find them on your school's website. Many school nutrition departments have a web page with menus, ingredients, nutritional facts, allergen information, and more. If not, ask for nutrition information about menus from the school's food-service director.
- Go over current menus with your child. Talk about choices on the cafeteria line; some menus have alternate choices, such as entree salads and sandwiches, in addition to the daily special. Talk about vegetable and fruit choices, too, and encourage your youngster to try new items. Practice picking from the menu as you talk together at home.
- If your child restricts food for any reason—perhaps a food allergy, religious or cultural reason, or preference to eat vegetarian—address options with a school administrator and school food-service staff. If they know ahead, most schools can match your child's unique needs. *See "Handle Food Allergies and Other Sensitivities" in chapter 23, page 653 for guidance.*
- Join or help to set up a school wellness committee. Get on the agenda of parents' association meetings at school, or start a parent group online. Most public schools and some private schools are part of the NSFSP. They must have School Wellness Policies set by each school or school district. Parents can be involved.
- Have lunch—or breakfast—with your child occasionally in the school cafeteria. Check with the principal or cafeteria manager first about visitor policies. See for yourself how school meals look and taste, how food is served, and what the cafeteria atmosphere is like. Ask questions about food preparation. You may be surprised to find out that many traditional favorites are now made with whole grains and with less fat and sodium.
- Get to know the school food-service staff. Volunteer to help with meal events, with tastings, or at regular meal hours. Help in a school garden. Express support. As you build relationships, share constructive suggestions.
- Support school nutrition education. Help your child practice at home what he or she learns at school. Find sound, often interactive, nutrition education for kids and families on websites, such as kids.usa.gov. *See "Unravel the Online Information 'Web'" in chapter 26, page 755.*
- Encourage school clubs and parent associations to serve healthier snacks and drinks at athletic and fundraising events and at school parties. Instead of sugary sodas and desserts, how about selling fresh fruit and flavored water? Or perhaps sponsor a carwash or walkathon where kids get exercise instead of selling food.
- Advocate for physical education (PE) as part of the school curriculum—to the school board, administration, and other parents. Recess before lunch encourages more physical activity, too. Encourage your grade-school child to play actively during recess. Recess is a wonderful and cost-effective way to get kids moving!

Balancing stringent academic standards with physical activity during the school day is challenging for schools. However, being physically active helps children stay healthy and ready to learn.

Brown-Bagging to School

If your child or teen prefers a bag lunch, make it nourishing, safe, and easy to carry. For younger kids, make it fun, too.

- What tote: brown bag, insulated bag, or lunch box? Ask what your child or teen prefers. For many, having the "right" tote is important. A lunch box is easier to clean; it may keep food cool longer. Wash it after every use. Always use a clean, new paper bag.
- For perishable foods, such as a meat sandwich, include a small, frozen cold pack. Remind your child or teen bring it home. An insulated bag, a frozen pouch, or a frozen juice box also helps keep food cool.
- Plan easy-to-eat foods. Good options include sandwiches, raw vegetable pieces (carrots, cherry tomatoes, cucumbers, red or green bell peppers), whole fruits, low-fat cheese slices or cubes, string cheese, crackers, individual containers of pudding, or an oatmeal cookie. If you pack an orange, score the rind so it's easy to peel—or tuck in a tangerine instead.

  It's okay to pack a brownie or a small bag of chips, but only as part of a healthy bag lunch. Kids may need the extra calories these foods supply.
- Expect your child to help plan and prepare his or her school lunch. At the store or farmers' market, ask him or her to choose foods to enjoy in a packed lunch for school. When involved, kids will probably eat every morsel—rather than trade those raw veggies for someone else's cookie.
- Teach your child how to pack his or her own lunch. Many kids can start helping to make their own lunch as young as first grade. Especially for tweens and teens, you don't need to do it! Just have nourishing brown-bag foods and packing supplies on hand and within easy reach. *Hint:* A lunch your child packs is more likely eaten and enjoyed.
- Remind your child or teen to store carried meals at school in a clean, safe place—away from sunlight and the heat vent in the classroom and not in a dirty gym bag.

> **?** Have you ever wondered?
>
> **. . . if a bag lunch would be a better option than a school lunch?** Not necessarily. In a study comparing lunches from home with a USDA-funded school lunch, the school meal provided significantly more dairy foods, vegetables, and fruits, contained less fat, and provided more food variety. If you decide to send a packed lunch, provide variety (lean protein foods, whole-grain bread, plenty of veggies and fruits, and milk money), and, if you pack them, include only a small portion of chips, cookies, or sweets.

- Add extra pleasure to a carried meal with an occasional surprise tucked inside—a riddle, a comic, or a note that says, "You're somebody special!" Knowing that someone cares is "nourishing" in its own way.

See "Packing Meals and Snacks Safely" in chapter 7, page 217, for food safety tips.

EATING OUT

Make restaurant meals a positive experience for the whole family. It's a chance for kids to learn how to behave when eating away from home—and how to make healthy food choices.

With Kids of Every Age

No matter what the age of your child—toddler to teen—these considerations help make a restaurant meal enjoyable for the whole family:

- Consider timing when you eat out. When meals are delayed, children can't compensate for hunger pangs as adults can, and you'll end up with a cranky meal companion! Perhaps offer a small snack ahead of time.
- Go early, before the rush. Call ahead for reservations to avoid waiting, and provide the full order the first time you're asked so the waiting time for food is shorter.
- Set parameters to help your child order, especially if you eat out often. Suggest healthy options, but let your child pick and even place the order if he or she wants to. (Avoid pressuring him or her.) This encourages independence and gives your child control. Limit sweets: one per meal, either a sweet dessert or a soda, not both. Talk about a price range, too, before ordering.
- Engage in pleasant table talk as you wait for your food—as for any family meal.
- In quick-service restaurants have your child or teen take responsibility for his or her own cleanup.
- Talk about uneaten food. If your child ordered more than can be eaten, discuss solutions for next time so food isn't wasted.

Especially with Young and School-Age Kids

These are a few more ways to make eating out a great family affair and a learning experience for kids who are school-age and younger:

- Choose a restaurant that caters to kids. A place that serves food quickly is best; waiting too long at the table is hard for a child. If you have a toddler or preschooler, request a high chair or booster seat. Save upscale table service for older kids.
- Set expectations before eating out and consequences for inappropriate restaurant behavior. Follow through, even if you need to leave the restaurant and opt for take-out. Reinforce positive behavior.

- When you're seated, childproof your table.
- Before ordering, ask about the preparation. If your child likes plain foods, ask for sauce or dressing on the side. Ask about substituting, perhaps carrot sticks in place of fries or milk instead of soda.
- Even though the kids' menu makes ordering easier, look beyond it for good alternatives. Instead of fried chicken nuggets and fries, which are popular on kids' menus, use this as a chance to expose your child to unfamiliar foods, perhaps the small portions from the appetizer menu. Good news: In many restaurants, more vegetables, fruits, and other healthy options are trending on kids' menus.
- If regular portions are too big, ask for appetizer portions. Or split an order between your child and another family member. Bring the leftovers home safely instead of expecting your child to "polish" the plate.
- Curb your child's appetite while you wait. Ask for a small portion of raw vegetables or bread—enough to take the edge off hunger, but not enough to interfere with a meal. Ask for drinks with the meal, not before, so your child doesn't fill up on liquids.
- Remain patient and positive. Mastering table and eating-out manners, including sitting still and being quiet, takes skill and practice—and your gentle guidance and role modeling.

If a Young Child Gets Fussy

Eating out isn't always easy for young, active toddlers or preschoolers. These tactics may help if your child gets fussy:

- Prepare. Bring along a stuffed animal to "share" the fun.
- Ask if the restaurant has a paper placemat to color or draw on. Bring your own crayons and paper or a travel game—just in case.
- Excuse yourselves from the table. Take a short walk.
- Talk in a calm, quiet, and positive way.
- Avoid forcing your child to eat. Instead, have the meal packed to take home.

See chapter 9, page 275, for more about restaurant ordering.

Toddlers and Preschoolers: Food and Active Play

Young children are like sponges, absorbing all the sights, sounds, and tastes around them. They are impressionable, as well as ready and eager to learn. That makes the toddler and preschool years a great time to nurture positive attitudes and skills as children learn to eat and enjoy a variety of foods. Establishing good eating habits and active lifestyles early starts lifelong patterns.

EARLY CHILDHOOD: GOOD NUTRITION FROM THE START

Every parent and caregiver knows that good nutrition from meals and snacks is essential for active, growing toddlers and preschoolers.

Toddlers and preschoolers grow at a slower rate than infants. Although normal growth differs from one child to another, between the ages of two and five, children, on average, grow two-and-a-half inches and gain four to five pounds each year.

Nutrient and Calorie Needs

Young children need the right amount of nutrients for energy, active play, learning, and the next stages of growth. Good nutrition and active play set them on the healthy path for reducing the chance of overweight and obesity, type 2 diabetes, heart disease, cancer, and other chronic diseases later in life.

Calories: How much? That depends on a child's age, growth rate, body size, and level of physical activity. Most moderately active to active children aged three to five need 1,200 to 1,600 calories a day. Two-year-olds typically need somewhat less, about 1,000 calories a day.

Carbohydrates: In the form of starches and mostly naturally occurring sugars, carbohydrates should provide about half of a child's daily calories. Fiber, another form of carbohydrate, is important, too. Like adults, many youngsters don't consume enough. For children aged one to three, the Institute of Medicine advises 19 grams of total fiber daily, and for children aged four to eight, 25 grams daily. Finding ways to help your child eat more whole grains, vegetables, fruits, and beans helps to provide enough fiber.

See "Carbs: Sugars, Starches, and Fiber" in chapter 11, page 345.

Protein: Children need enough high-quality protein for the growth of all body cells, including bones, and for the body substances (hormones and enzymes) that stimulate body processes. For children aged one to three, 5 to 20 percent of their total calories should come from protein, and for those aged four and older, 10 to 30 percent. *See "Protein: How Much? What Kind?" in chapter 12, page 377.*

Fat: A concentrated energy source, fat supports a young child's rapid growth, learning, and play. In fact, two fatty acids—linoleic and alpha-linolenic acid—are essential for growth and brain development. Food

- Nutrition.gov, National Agricultural Library, USDA
  www.nutrition.gov/life-stages/toddlers

Preschoolers: Food Behavior Markers

The preschool years are an important time for developing healthy habits for life. During this time, children grow and develop in ways that affect behavior in all areas, including eating. The timing of these milestones may vary with each child.

About two years

- Can use a spoon and drink from a cup
- Can be easily distracted while eating
- Experiences slower growth and a reduction in appetite
- Can be very messy with food
- May suddenly refuse certain foods

About three years

- Makes simple either/or food choices, such as a choice of apple or orange slices
- Pours liquid with some spills
- Is comfortable using a fork and spoon
- Can follow simple requests such as "Please use your napkin"
- Likes to imitate cooking
- May suddenly refuse certain foods

About four years

- Is influenced by TV, media, and peers
- May dislike many mixed dishes
- Rarely spills with a spoon or cup
- Knows what table manners are expected
- Can be easily sidetracked
- May suddenly refuse certain foods

About five years

- Has fewer demands
- Will usually accept the food that's available
- Eats with minor supervision

Source: USDA

must supply them because the body can't make them. Kids also need some fat from foods to help their bodies use vitamins A, D, E, and K and to make nourishing food appealing.

Restricting dietary fat isn't advised before the age of two, so for toddlers aged twelve to twenty-four months, whole milk, rather than low-fat, is advised. They need the essential fatty acids and food energy (calories) that whole milk provides. For ages two and older, low-fat (1 percent) or fat-free milk is advised.

Note: In 2008, the AAP advised that reduced-fat milk (2 percent) is appropriate for children aged twelve to twenty-four months—if overweight is a concern or if they have a family history of obesity, high cholesterol, or heart disease.

The Dietary Reference Intakes (DRIs) advise 30 to 40 percent of calories from fat for those aged one to three years. For those aged four to eighteen, fat intake should gradually match that of their parents. The advice is 25 to 35 percent of calories from fat, mostly unsaturated. *See "Fats: How Much? What Kind? How Much?" in chapter 13, page 394.*

Vitamins and minerals. All are essential. Several have been identified in the Dietary Guidelines for Americans as nutrients that are underconsumed for the general population, aged two and older: calcium, magnesium, and potassium, as well as vitamins A, C, D, and E, and choline. For young children, iron is often low, too.

The reason for the shortfall of these nutrients is unhealthy food patterns. To fit enough of those nutrients in, your child needs enough vegetables, fruits, and dairy foods. Eggs are a good source of choline and iron. Protein foods—lean meat, poultry, fish, and beans and peas—provide iron. Fruits with vitamin C, such as orange juice, enhance the absorption of iron from beans, eggs, grain products, and vegetables.

For young children, iron-deficiency anemia is a common nutrition problem. That's why children are screened for anemia in regular checkups. Children need enough iron to support growth, replace normal iron loss, and produce energy for learning, play, and normal cognitive development. A doctor may advise liquid iron supplements or chewable multivitamins for some children.

See "Vitamins and Minerals"in chapter 14, page 408.

Water. It's one of the most essential nutrients. Besides plain water, low-fat and fat-free milk and 100 percent juice are good sources; they also deliver other important nutrients. If you choose to offer 100 percent fruit juice, try to limit it to four to six ounces a day.

Have you ever wondered?

. . . about lead in the water supply and the health risks to children? Infants and children are at higher risk for lead poisoning than others. Among other problems, lead that builds up in the body over time can cause brain damage. Health experts advise that children get screened at ages one and two, perhaps more often if there's a risk. *See "Water: Concerns about Lead and Nitrates" in chapter 4, page 84, for more about screening and addressing lead in drinking water.*

Thirst signals if your child has not had enough water, but it's not a foolproof way to know. *See "Dietary Reference Intakes" in the appendix, page 780, for recommended amounts for young children. See "Water: A Fluid Asset" in chapter 15, page 443, for more about water.*

Healthy Meals and Snacks

A variety of foods with different textures, tastes, and colors—in adequate amounts (but not too much)—provides the nutrients and calories (energy) a child needs to thrive. So what makes up a healthy eating pattern for young children?

Their meals and snacks should have many of the same attributes as yours: a variety of nutrient-rich foods and beverages in the right amounts, child-size portions, limits on added sugars and solid fats (saturated and *trans* fats) and a day's food intake at the calorie level that's right for them. Whole grains, vegetables, fruits, low-fat dairy, and other protein-rich foods should supply most of a young child's calories. Access to foods with added sugars, such as sugary soda, fruit drinks, cookies, candy, and other foods with added sugars should be limited.

Most children do best with a routine—when meals and snacks are served at about the same time each day. Younger children may need to eat five to six times a day because their small stomachs don't hold much. For example, children aged two to five usually need to eat every two to three hours.

Even in these early years, children can learn to experience a wide variety of new foods. If your child resists, it's okay. Just relax; give him or her time to outgrow it. Still offer a variety of foods, and enjoy them yourself. *See "Tasting Something New" in this chapter, page 514, for tips on introducing them.*

Food guide. The USDA Eating Patterns are useful daily food guides for planning healthy meals and snacks for children aged two to five; *see "A Plan for Healthy Eating: From MyPlate to Your Plate" in chapter 2, page 25, and "Eating Patterns, 2015–2020 Guidelines for Americans" in the appendix, page 771,* to learn about food group amounts. Remember, it's not what your child eats at a single meal, or even in one day, that counts. Instead your child's overall eating plan for several days is important for now—and for lifelong health.

Toddlers need a variety of nutrient-dense foods too. A toddler-size portion is about one-quarter the size of a reasonable adult-size portion. As a rule-of- thumb for toddlers, some experts advise one tablespoon of each food you offer, for every year of your child's age. As calorie needs go up, preschoolers' portions need to be somewhat larger. Trust your child's appetite to know how much.

Finger foods. Toddlers, as well as preschoolers, like finger foods. By feeding themselves, they develop a sense of independence and learn when they are full. Self-feeding with fingers also helps toddlers explore so they can be familiar and comfortable with new foods.

Some healthy finger foods for these children include a baked potato cut into strips and dipped in low-fat dressing; grilled chicken cut into strips with honey-mustard sauce; a bagel topped with pizza sauce; graham crackers dipped in applesauce; and wedges of peeled apple, peach, or pear with a yogurt dip. (Dipping is easy for self-feeding.)

What about fries, chicken nuggets, and cheese? Restricting any food just makes it more desirable. An occasional child-size portion is fine if overall choices are low in solid fats and added sugars, and match a child's calorie needs.

See "For Starters: Meal and Snack Patterns for Preschoolers" in this chapter, page 513, for daily amounts that meet the nutrient and energy needs of most young children.

Snacks. Young children like to snack. With their small stomachs, eating just three meals a day may not meet their nutrition and calorie (energy) needs. Think of planned snacks as mini-meals that fill any gaps left by their regular meals.

If snacks conjure up images of high-calorie, low-nutrient foods—think again! Wise snack foods for young children come mostly from a variety of nutrient-rich foods. Low-fat or fat-free milk is a good snack drink; go easy on 100 percent fruit juice.

- Plan for two to three food-group snacks plus three meals a day.
- Let snacks supplement meals, not replace them.
- Plan ahead by keeping food-group snacks handy. An occasional piece of candy is okay, but avoid labeling it as a "special treat" to avoid undue emphasis. Just be matter-of-fact about it.
- Offer snacks two hours or more before meals so youngsters are hungry at mealtime. "Pacifier snacks" eaten while standing in line at the supermarket—or snacks just a half-hour before a meal—may interfere with your child's appetite and eating routine.
- Offer snacks when your child is hungry, not to calm tears or reward behavior. Otherwise, he or she will learn a pattern of emotional overeating. Maybe your child just needs attention, not food.
- Offer vegetables, fruits, or whole-grain foods at snack time if meals come up short on their nutrients.
- Offer small snack portions. Let your child ask for more if he or she is still hungry.
- Think "fun" at snack time: brightly colored vegetables and fruits; the aroma of freshly cut watermelon; the different textures of soft, creamy cheese with crisp, crunchy crackers.
- Encourage tooth brushing after snacks of any kind, not just after sweets. *See "A Closer Look . . . How to Keep Your Teeth and Gums Healthy" in chapter 25, page 737, for more about dental care.*

ENOUGH TO EAT, WITHOUT OVERFEEDING

You can lead a young child to the table, but you can't make him or her eat—nor should you! Let your child's appetite guide how much food is

Healthy Snacks for Kids Under Four

For kids under age four, avoid popcorn, nuts, seeds, and other hard, small, whole foods to prevent choking. Chop raw carrots and grapes and cooked hot dogs into small pieces.

Food Group	Food
Grains Go for whole-grain varieties whenever possible.	animal crackers bagel crackers English muffin graham crackers pita (pocket) bread pretzels rice cake toast tortilla unsweetened cereal (dry or with milk)
Vegetables	any raw vegetable (cut into strips or rounds) salsa vegetable soup
Fruits	any fresh fruit (sliced for finger food) applesauce canned or frozen fruits (in juice or water) dried fruits fruit juice* fruit leather
Dairy	cheese stick frozen yogurt pudding string cheese whole milk (12 to 24 months unless otherwise advised by your child's doctor) and low-fat or fat-free milk (after 24 months) yogurt
Protein Foods	bean soup hard-cooked egg hummus peanut butter tuna salad meat or poultry cubes

**See "Have you ever wondered . . . are fruit juices and fruit drinks are good choices for kids?" in this chapter, page 517, for advice about fruit juice.*

enough. If your toddler or preschooler is truly hungry and healthy, he or she will eat. After the first birthday, as growth slows, children's appetites often decrease.

How much is enough? Too much? Although no longer babies, young children aren't ready for adult-size portions. Adult servings can overwhelm small appetites and lead to overeating and too many calories. A pattern of overeating, starting in these early years, can lead to him or her to being overweight. Even among two- to five-year-olds, the percentage of overweight children is of significant concern, according to data from the CDC.

In contrast, underfeeding can cause feelings of deprivation and poor nutrition. Being too restrictive can even lead to weight gain if a child sneaks food to satisfy hunger. Trust your child's appetite, even if you need to decide what food to offer, when, and where. To become a competent eater, your healthy child needs to decide how much to eat of the foods you provide—and whether to eat them.

? Have you ever wondered?

. . . how to make sure food is safe for your young child? Infants and young children are at greater risk for foodborne illness than older children and adults; *chapter 7, page 191, offers plenty of advice to keep food safe.* Among the many lessons to teach your child are proper hand washing and skipping the urge to eat raw cookie dough!

Choking is another food safety issue. Avoid offering foods your child could choke on. Hard, smooth foods and round, firm foods, as well as chewing gum, can get lodged in a child's windpipe. Because children don't master chewing with a grinding motion until about age four years, choking is a significant danger until about age five. The AAP advises against whole peanuts until age seven or older. *See "Safety from Choking: Infants, Toddlers, and Preschoolers" in chapter 16, page 486, for more advice.*

. . . what to do if a child starts choking? Know what to do in advance! You might save a life.

For children aged one to four years, the AAP offers this advice: If your child has breathing difficulties but can still speak and has a strong cough, let the coughing itself dislodge the object. However, if he or she can't breathe or speak and has just a weak cough, have someone call 9-1-1 immediately. Then give quick inward and upward abdominal thrusts just above the navel and well below the bottom tip of the breastbone and rib cage until the object is coughed up.; *see "Alert: What to Do If Someone's Choking" in chapter 7, page 196.* If the child becomes unconscious, use the tongue-jaw lift to remove the object, and begin CPR; see the AAP's website www.healthychildren.org for instructions.

- Serve small helpings—smaller than yours. Let your child ask for more if he or she is still hungry.
- Respect your child's hunger and fullness cues. When he or she starts to play with food, becomes restless, or sends signals of "no more," remove the food.
- Space meals and snacks far enough apart so your child is hungry at each.
- Do away with the "clean plate" club. This practice may encourage overeating or a food aversion—habits that could set up your child for weight or eating problems later. If he or she always leaves food on the plate, serve less; you may be offering too much.

Day-to-day and meal-to-meal appetite fluctuations are normal; sometimes a child wants more and sometimes less. In fact, expect your child to pick at meals occasionally. Chances are that he or she will make up for it later. If your child is growing normally, seems healthy, and has energy to play, he or she probably is eating enough. Unsure? Talk to your child's doctor.

MEALTIME TACTICS FOR CHOOSY TODDLERS AND PRESCHOOLERS

Does your child refuse green foods? Does he or she suddenly react to an all-time favorite food with "I don't like this," or just "no"? Are you concerned because your youngster won't eat vegetables?

Bouts of independence are part of being a toddler or preschooler. "Choosy" eating may be your child's early attempts to make decisions and be assertive—a natural part of growing up. It may reflect a smaller appetite as his or her growth rate slows a bit. Or "no" may really mean "I want your attention."

Sometimes, at about age two, children start avoiding bitter-tasting vegetables. This may be nature's way of protecting them from poisonous plants, which typically are bitter, too. Young children also have more taste buds and may be more sensitive to flavors than you are.

Here are some tips to help you deal with a picky eater:

- Relax; be patient. Arm yourself with practical solutions to handle the "downs and ups" of child feeding. Your child won't starve if you consistently offer healthy choices with reasonable alternatives. Remember, there's a fine line between encouraging your child to eat well and pressuring him or her to eat.
- Rather than asking open-ended questions such as, "What do you want to eat?", offer two or three food choices. Deciding between or among them gives your child a feeling of control. It's also good practice for learning to make food decisions.
- Make food simple and recognizable. "Unmix" the food if that's an issue. Put aside some ingredients for mixed dishes before assembling the recipe, even a salad or sandwich. Then let your child put food together as he or she likes.
- Involve your child. Even young choosy eaters eat foods they help plan, buy, or make. Together, plan a meal around foods your child likes. When you shop, ask your child to pick a new food for the family to try. Ask for a kitchen helper; even small children can wash fresh fruit or put meat between bread slices for a sandwich. *See "'I Can Help': Kitchen Tasks for Kids of Every Age" in this chapter, page 498.*
- Encourage your child to practice serving him- or herself—for example, pouring milk from a small pitcher, spreading peanut butter on bread, or spooning food from a serving bowl to their plate. Even though spills are messy, that's part of becoming independent.
- Stock your kitchen with child-size dishes and utensils that your child can use with ease: cups easy to get his or her hands around; broad, straight, short-handled utensils; spoons with a wide mouth; forks with blunt tines; and plates with curved lips.
- If your child won't eat certain foods, perhaps spinach, don't worry. Just offer a food with similar nutrients, maybe broccoli. If sweet potatoes are rejected, carrots and cantaloupe are good sources of vitamin A. If plain milk is rejected, try low-fat fruit yogurt or low-fat cheese. Foods from the same food group supply similar nutrients.
- For your toddler or preschooler—school-age kids, too—make mealtime fun with a variety of colors and textures. Cut food into interesting shapes; arrange them attractively on the plate.
- Moisten dry foods such as meat if they're hard to chew. A little cheese sauce or vegetable or fruit juice might help. Serve drier foods alongside naturally moist foods such as mashed potatoes or cottage cheese. Or offer "dipping" sauces, such as yogurt dips, hummus, or salsa, with finger foods—kids love to dip!

Have you ever wondered?

. . . what to do you do when kids get "stuck" on a food? If your child keeps asking for the same food meal after meal, he or she is on a "food jag." Food jags are common in the toddler years and are more frustrating for you than harmful for your child. You're smart to stay low-key; the more you focus on this behavior, the longer it lasts.

Actually, it's okay to offer the food your child wants again and again and again! Just include other foods alongside to encourage variety. Most "monotonous diners" soon tire of eating the same food so often. If your child rejects whole categories of food—such as all vegetables or all dairy foods—for more than two weeks, talk to your child's doctor or a registered dietitian nutritionist to address any health issues—and perhaps get more advice.

For Starters: Meal and Snack Patterns for Preschoolers

A day's worth of meals and snacks for preschoolers can be planned in different ways to provide enough food from all five food groups, with many different menus. Here are menu suggestions for 1,000 calories a day, the amount estimated for preschoolers who are two years of age. They're based on the USDA's recommended daily amounts for each food group:

USDA Food Patterns Plan (1,000 Calories)	Total Amount for the Day
Grain Group	3 ounces
Vegetable Group	1 cup
Fruit Group	1 cup
Dairy* Group	2 cups
Protein Foods Group	2 ounces

Use USDA's MyPlate to plan a day's meals and snacks at a higher calorie level—1,200, 1,400, and 1,600 calories daily—for preschoolers aged three to five. *See "A Plan for Healthy Eating: From MyPlate to Your Plate," in chapter 2, page 25.*

Meals/Snacks	Sample Menus		
Breakfast	**Cereal and Banana, Milk**	**Toast, Fruit, and Yogurt**	**Applesauce-Topped Pancake, Milk**
1 ounce Grains ½ cup Fruit ½ cup Dairy*	1 cup crispy rice cereal ½ sliced banana ½ cup milk*	1 slice whole-wheat toast ⅓ cup plain yogurt* 4 sliced strawberries	1 small pancake ½ cup applesauce ½ cup milk*
Morning Snack	**Bread and Fruit**	**Cereal and Fruit**	**Graham Cracker and Fruit**
½ ounce Grains ½ cup Fruit	½ slice cinnamon bread ½ large orange	½ cup toasted oat cereal ½ cup diced pineapple	1 graham cracker (2 squares) ½ cup sliced banana
Lunch	**Chicken Sandwich and Salad**	**Soft Taco (meat or veggie)**	**Tuna Bagel Sandwich, Milk**
1 ounce Grains ¼ cup Vegetables ½ cup Dairy* 1 ounce Protein Foods	1 slice whole-wheat bread 1 ounce sliced chicken 1 slice American cheese* ¼ cup baby spinach (raw) 2 Tbsp. grated carrots	1 small tortilla 1 ounce cooked ground beef or ¼ cup refried beans ½ cup salad greens** 2 Tbsp. chopped tomatoes 2 Tbsp. shredded cheese*	1 mini whole-grain bagel 1 ounce canned tuna ¼ cup sliced cherry tomatoes ¼ cup diced celery ½ cup milk*
Afternoon Snack	**Veggie and Yogurt**	**Veggie and Milk**	**Veggie Juice and Cheese**
¼ cup Vegetables ½ cup Dairy*	¼ cup sugar snap peas ½ cup yogurt*	¼ cup carrot sticks ½ cup milk*	¼ cup tomato juice 1 string cheese*
Dinner	**Chicken and Potatoes with Peas, Milk**	**Spaghetti and Meatballs with Corn, Milk**	**Rice and Beans with Broccoli, Milk**
½ ounce Grains ½ cup Vegetables ½ cup Dairy* 1 ounce Protein Foods	1 ounce chicken breast ¼ cup mashed potato ¼ cup green peas ½ small whole-wheat roll ½ cup milk*	¼ cup cooked pasta 2 Tbsp. tomato sauce 1 meatball (1 ounce) ½ medium ear corn on the cob ½ cup milk*	¼ cup cooked brown rice ¼ cup black beans ¼ cup bell pepper ¼ cup broccoli ½ cup milk*

If a menu above has no beverage, water is a good drink option.
*Offer your child low-fat or fat-free milk, yogurt, and cheese.
** In the Vegetable Group, ½ cup fresh greens counts as ¼ cup vegetables.

Adapted from: Meal and Snack Pattern A. ChooseMyPlate.gov. Accessed December 1, 2016.

- Ensure that your child is seated—and seated high enough on the chair to easily see and reach the food. This makes trying new foods more pleasant. He or she may need a booster seat. Discourage eating while standing, walking, or lying down.
- Even in this fast-paced world, give your child enough time to eat. Remember: At this age kids are just learning to feed themselves. Time pressure puts stress on eating and takes the pleasure away.
- Trust your child's appetite. If your youngster seems to be picky, he or she may instead be full. Respecting hunger and fullness cues helps your child learn to eat the right amount.
- Most of all, relax. And be a good role model. Eat your veggies with a smile, not a frown. Drink your milk, too.
- Avoid conflict and criticism at mealtime; otherwise, your child may use food for "table control." Focus your attention on the positives in your child's eating behavior, not on your child's food. And unless you're prepared for a self-fulfilling prophecy, skip labeling your child as a "picky eater."

Remember: What your child eats over several days—not just one meal—is what really counts!

Tasting Something New

The tasting adventure continues throughout childhood—even into adulthood. More variety increases the chance for good nutrition and adds interest and fun to eating.

Helping children be willing food "tryers" is part of learning about food. At first, trying may mean touching, smelling, licking, and even spitting it out into a napkin. Here are some tips on how to encourage experimentation:

- Before offering the new food, talk about it: color, texture, size, shape, aroma, taste—sweet, bitter, salty, or tart. Don't dwell on whether your child likes it.
- Let your child help you prepare the food. He or she will be more willing to taste.
- Offer new foods at the start of meals. That's when kids are hungriest. Make the rest of the meal familiar with at least one food you know your child likes.
- Allow ample time for your child to eat and try new foods; however, excuse him or her after a reasonable time, say twenty to thirty minutes.
- Keep quiet about foods that you don't like. Your food dislikes may keep your child from trying new foods.
- Serve the same new food in different forms—for example, raw carrot sticks and cooked carrot coins.
- If your child doesn't like it? Just be matter-of-fact and perhaps say, "Maybe you'll like it next time," or "Maybe you'll like it when you get your grown-up tastes." Don't force a child to taste a food.
- Keep trying! Your child may need to taste a food at least eight to ten times before he or she learns to like it. Accept a fact of life: it's okay not to like every food.

FOOD AND PLAY IN CHILD CARE

Warm and caring staff, a safe environment, opportunities for development and self-expression—that's what most parents look for when choosing child care. Important, too, are the quality and safety of meals and snacks, the eating environment, and opportunities for active play.

Besides adequate nourishment, the eating skills and food attitudes learned and reinforced in child care can have a long-lasting impact on food behavior, health, and body weight. That's especially important for children who eat two or more meals and snacks in a child-care center.

Food safety is top priority! Child-care settings offer many opportunities for spreading illness: food service, diapering, toileting, and close contact with others. Cleanliness and safe food handling are "musts." Infants and young children with immature immune systems are more vulnerable to catching a cold, the flu, or another illness from others. Food safety extends to finding out how food allergies and other food-related issues are handled.

To help establish a lifelong habit of active living, children regularly involved in child care need a program with safe, fun, and developmentally appropriate ways to move more and sit less. Besides being healthy, active play teaches social skills and helps develop muscle and body skills.

The Child-Care Setting: Check It Out!

If you choose child care, look for high standards of cleanliness, nutrition, and active play. Here are some issues to look for:

Food preparation and storage areas:

- Neat and very clean
- Properly labeled and well-covered foods
- Adequate refrigeration and heating equipment
- Perishable foods stored in the refrigerator or freezer

Hand-washing area:

- Child-size sinks, or safe stepping stools for adult-size sinks
- Soap and paper towels

Mealtime and snack time:

- Meal and snack menus with a variety of nutrient-rich foods. Many child-care settings have specific menu guidelines for food types and amounts from each food group—grains, vegetables, fruits, dairy, and protein foods. They're matched to the nutrient and calorie needs of children. Ask to see the menus.
- Menus that reflect a family's religious and cultural practices. Some foods may need to be avoided, such as pork for many Jewish and Muslim children.

- Tables and chairs appropriately sized for children's comfort, or high chairs or booster seats
- Child-size utensils and cups to help young children master their feeding skills
- Adult supervision at mealtimes and snack times, as well as adequate staffing for feeding infants and children with special needs

Diaper-changing and toilet areas:

- Very clean
- Located away from food, and eating and play areas
- Closed containers for soiled diapers, tissues, and wipes
- Daily removal of soiled items

Other areas:

- Separate storage for each child's toothbrush, comb, and clothing
- Ample space between cots, nap rugs, or cribs

Parents as Child-Care Partners

For the many kids in child care, feeding is a shared responsibility. Together, parents and child-care providers offer foods that nourish kids. And together they help kids develop skills and a positive attitude about eating. Here's what you can do as a parent or parent figure:

- If your child has a feeding issue—perhaps a food allergy—make a plan with your child and the child-care staff.
- Ask for a meal and snack menu. Identify new foods.

Child Care: Questions to Ask

As you check out a child-care setting, you should be able to answer "yes" to all these food- and nutrition-related questions. For more guidance on choosing a child-care center, visit the AAP website www.HealthyChildren.org.

1. Do children, staff, and volunteers wash and dry their hands before and after eating and participating in food activities?
2. Do children wash and dry their hands after outdoor play, toileting, touching animals, sneezing, or wiping their nose?
3. Do child-care providers and parents wash their hands thoroughly after every diaper check and change?
4. Does each child have his or her own washcloth?
5. Are bottles and foods that are brought from home refrigerated and, if necessary, heated safely? (*Hint:* When you send food, always label it with your child's name. Transport perishable foods in an insulated sack with a cold pack.)
6. For infant care, is space provided for moms to breastfeed when they can be present?
7. Is food left over on a child's plate discarded properly?
8. Do children each have their own dish, cup, and utensils, rather than having to share?
9. Does an adult eat with the children, helping them learn table skills and serving as a good role model?
10. Can you volunteer or drop in from time to time including during meal and snack times?
11. Are menus posted online or on a bulletin board, or are they sent home with the children?
12. Are the foods appropriate for the ages of the children (e.g., no foods that may be choking hazards)?
13. Are plates, cups, and utensils washed and sanitized after each use?
14. Are the program's policies on meals, active play, and other issues consistent with yours?
15. Are toys that go into a child's mouth sanitized regularly?
16. Are food-related activities such as tasting parties, food preparation, growing foods from seed, field trips, and circle-time topics part of the child-care program?
17. Is safe, physically active indoor and outdoor play part of the daily routine? Is it well supervised? Does it match the abilities of the children? Do adults direct some activities?
18. Can you talk to the staff regularly and comfortably, especially about sensitive issues?

- Talk about and prepare unfamiliar foods at home before they're offered at school. After they're tried in child care, offer them again at home to reinforce the new food experience.
- Practice hand washing at home before your child starts child care. *See "Hand Washing Basics" in this chapter, page 496.*
- If schedules and policies allow, volunteer in a child-care setting to support the center's nutrition program. Offer to help with meal planning. Occasionally eat with children or help chaperone a food-related field trip. You might gather empty food packages and other kitchen supplies to use in play areas or for food activities. Early childhood educators appreciate help.

ACTIVE PLAY: TODDLERS AND PRESCHOOLERS

Run, jump, throw, kick! Active play helps your child develop and learn a variety of body skills, mental skills, and social skills, and it begins a habit of lifelong active living and a healthy weight.

Those skills develop with maturity when structured play develops physical (motor) skills and when kids have opportunities to move in their daily life. As a parent, it's up to you to encourage free and structured play that's physically active. Here are some ideas:

- Balance quiet play (such as reading together) with plenty of active play. Limit sitting time to thirty to sixty minutes at a stretch.
- Choose child care that makes safe, active play a priority.
- Set aside time each day to play together, perhaps tossing a ball, playing tag, or taking a family walk.
- Designate an inside and an outside area that's safe, where your child can freely jump, roll, and tumble.
- Pick toys that "move"—perhaps a ball or tricycle.
- Join a play group together.
- Limit screen time, *as noted in "Encourage a healthy lifestyle" on page 503 in this chapter.* Substitute human interaction and unstructured play for those under age two. For those ages two and older, encourage active "follow me" videos and computer games that encourage moving in their screen time.

School-Age Kids: Eat Smart, Move More

School-age youngsters—no longer preschoolers, not yet teens—are establishing habits that last a lifetime. For their good health and healthy weight, nutrition and physical activity should rank as high priorities.

During these years, children gain control of the world around them. They push for independence, associate more with their peers, and make more choices of their own. Because they're away from home more often, people other than family have a growing role in shaping their food decisions.

Parents, teachers, and schools provide much of kids' nutrition education. However, advertising in all kinds of media, including websites and social media—even phone apps—also influences kids' food decisions. A parent's challenge is to help their children access youth-focused websites, apps, and games that provide sound nutrition information.

KIDS: NUTRITION TO GROW ON

Kids aged six to twelve years old grow about two inches and gain about five pounds yearly. To look at it another way, they grow one to two feet and almost double their weight during these years.

Before you compare your child with another, remember that kids' body sizes, shapes, and growth patterns vary. Most grow in a pattern that's more like a birth parent than an unrelated friend. (Get out your family photo album for a visual memory.)

A school-age child's appetite gradually increases; most eat more just before a growth spurt. During childhood, growth is gradual, accelerating just prior to and during early adolescence. Generally, for girls this is from ages ten through fourteen, and for boys, from ages twelve through sixteen.

Kids don't need any special foods for their growth, energy, and health, just enough calories, or food energy (but not too much), and nutrients. They need the same nutrients as their parents do, only in different amounts. *See "A Closer Look . . . Tracking Kids' Growth" in this chapter, page 501.*

Calories. Energy (calorie) balance is key to fueling your child's growth and active life—and to maintaining your child's healthy weight.

Age, gender, and activity level determine your child's calorie needs. How do you know if your child is getting enough calories? By tracking his or her weight and height, your child's doctor will advise if he or she is consuming adequate calories for healthy growth or consuming too many or too few. If your child's growth pattern is normal, the food energy (calories) in his or her food choices is enough; *see "Estimated Calorie Needs per Day by Age, Gender, and Physical Activity Levels" in the appendix, page 770.* Calorie estimates help you plan, but your child's internal hunger cues are the best gauge.

Most calories should come from grain-based foods (at least half as whole grain), vegetables, fruits, low-fat or fat-free dairy foods, and other protein foods (lean meat, poultry, fish, eggs, beans and peas, and nuts). Limit foods high in either solid fats, added sugars, or both, such as cakes, candy, cookies, and sugary drinks.

- Nutrition.gov, National Agricultural Library, USDA
  www.nutrition.gov/life-stages/children
- Kids.gov, US government
  kids.usa.gov

Have you ever wondered?

. . . are fruit juices and fruit drinks good choices for kids? Actually, that takes a two-part answer.

- *Fruit juices:* You know that kids are urged to eat fruit every day; 100% fruit juice is one option, but be aware that too much juice can add up to a lot of calories, or crowd out other nourishing foods and beverages such as milk, and can spoil appetites. An excessive amount can also lead to diarrhea and intestinal discomfort. Sipping a lot of juice even promotes tooth decay. For children and teens, the AAP advises:

Age	Daily Juice Recommendations
1 to 6 years old	Limit to ½ to ¾ cup (4 to 6 ounces) of fruit juice daily. For children older than 6 months, fruit juice offers no nutritional benefits over whole fruits. Whole fruits also provide fiber and other nutrients.
7 to 18 years old	Limit to 1 to 1½ cups (8 to 12 ounces) of fruit juice daily

For food safety's sake, avoid unpasteurized juice.

- *Juice drinks:* They have some juice and perhaps added vitamin C or calcium, but offer fewer nutrients than 100% fruit juice or milk. Juice drinks also have added sugars. Juice drinks and fruit drinks cannot replace 100 percent fruit juice. Read the Nutrition Facts label and the ingredient list to compare. *See "Juice, Juice Drink, or Fruit Drink?" in chapter 4, page 88.*

. . . about iron poisoning—how does it happen? Iron poisoning from adult iron capsules or tablets—or from vitamin pills with iron—occurs when children accidentally swallow them. This can happen, too, if iron tablets meant for children aren't taken as directed, but instead at a higher dosage within a short period of time. If your doctor prescribes an iron supplement for your child, give it only as directed.

Iron poisoning can cause serious injury, even death. Call your doctor or a poison control center immediately if your child accidentally swallows an adult supplement with iron. Keep all pills in child-safe containers where your child can't reach them. *Note:* A healthy diet with iron-fortified foods won't cause iron poisoning! *See "Iron" in chapter 14, page 438, for more about iron and consuming excess amounts.*

. . what kind of snacks can help keep your child cavity free? *See "Oral Health: Your Healthy Smile" in chapter 25, page 735.*

Today's concerns about overweight youth recognize that many kids consume more calories than their bodies use—especially inactive kids. What foods often deliver excess calories? Perhaps too many energy-dense foods and drinks, over-sized portions, or poorly chosen snacks and drinks. On the flip side, kids also may need to burn more calories with more physical activity.

Macronutrients: carbohydrates, protein, and fats. Your child's main energy source is carbohydrates: 45 to 65 percent of total calories. Going low-carb isn't advised since kids need carbs to fuel growth, physical activity, brain power, and other body processes. The best carbohydrate foods deliver vitamins, minerals, and fiber, too. *See "Carbohydrates in Foods and Drinks" in chapter 11, page 358.*

Kids need high-quality protein for their growing bodies. This isn't an issue for kids who consume enough from the dairy group and protein foods group. Although not a main energy source, protein should provide 10 to 30 percent of a child's calories. The Recommended Dietary Allowance (RDA) is 19 grams daily for those aged four to eight years old, and 34 grams daily for those aged nine to thirteen. Advice: Make the most of these choices by choosing foods limited in added sugars and solid fats. *See chapter 12, page 373, to learn about protein.*

Regarding fat, another calorie source, the Institute of Medicine advises between 25 to 35 percent of calories from fat for kids aged four to eighteen. Most fats should come from foods such as fish, nuts, and vegetable oils that are higher in polyunsaturated and monounsaturated fatty acids. Like adults, kids need to limit solid fats in foods such as cakes and cookies. *See chapter 13, page 385, to learn more about dietary fat.*

Vitamins, minerals, and fiber. For school-age children, what nutrients may need special attention? The Dietary Guidelines for Americans identifies calcium, magnesium, potassium, vitamins A, C, D, and E, and choline as nutrients that may be low. Getting enough zinc, which is important for growth, and enough iron may be concerns for some children, as well. Fiber, a type of complex carbohydrate, often comes up short.

The reason for these shortfalls? For healthy kids, it's because they aren't consuming enough whole grains, vegetables, fruits, and dairy, which contain these nutrients. The solution? It's encouraging kids to eat daily meals and snacks that follow food-group guidelines; *see "A Plan for Healthy Eating: From MyPlate to Your Plate" in chapter 2, page 25.* Consuming two to three cups of low-fat or fat-free milk, or an equivalent, deliver calcium and vitamin D, as well as magnesium and potassium.

Eating more vegetables and whole fruits delivers vitamins A and C, as well as fiber; some are good sources of potassium. Whole-grain foods are good sources of many nutrients as well as fiber. Eggs deliver choline. And, lean meat, poultry, and fish are among the good sources of iron and zinc.

A comment about vitamin D: The RDA is 15 micrograms, or 600 IU (International Units), daily for children aged one to eighteen. Low-fat and fat-free milk are your child's best food source with 3 micrograms (120 IU) of vitamin D in an eight ounces of milk. Kids also get vitamin D benefits from outdoor time since the body makes vitamin D from sun exposure (except during winter months in northern latitudes). That's another reason to encourage playing outdoors, caring for a small garden, reading together outside, or taking messy activities such as painting outdoors—with sunscreen! With these strategies, a vitamin D supplement likely isn't needed.

See chapters 11 and 14, pages 345 and 408, to learn how vitamins, minerals, and fiber promote growth and health.

Water. For most school-age kids, getting enough water from beverages and foods isn't an issue. It's their beverage choices that need attention. Instead of sugary drinks, encourage plain water as a snack beverage and, with meals, low-fat or fat-free milk (flavored or unflavored), fortified soy beverages, and 100 percent fruit juice. *See chapter 4, page 81, for more about drink options and "Water: A Fluid Asset" in chapter 15, page 443, for more about water as a nutrient.*

See "Dietary Reference Intakes" in the appendix, page 780, for all nutrient recommendations for school-age kids.

HEALTHY MEALS AND SNACKS FOR SCHOOL-AGE KIDS

"Eat Right. Exercise. Have Fun": The USDA Food Patterns, *discussed in chapter 2, page 23,* are healthy eating guides for all family members, including kids. Among the goals: to help combat obesity, starting at a young age. Use these strategies to do so:

- Provide a variety of foods to your child each day from all five food groups—grain, vegetable, fruit, dairy, and protein foods—plus oils. Encourage many colorful vegetables, not just typical kid favorites (corn and potatoes); fruit as a sweet snack, and low-fat or fat-free milk to drink with meals, not sugary drinks such as soda.
- Plan meals and snacks for your child that match his or her food group needs. *See "Eating Patterns, 2015–2020 Dietary Guidelines for Americans" in the appendix, page 771, for amounts recommended for each food group.* And visit the website www.ChooseMyPlate.gov. Most children need more vegetables and fruits than they eat. *See "Vegetables and Kids: Common Challenge" in this chapter, page 498, for tips.* Most children need more whole-grain foods, too. Choose whole-grain crackers, breakfast cereals, and sandwich bread. And they need dairy group foods for bone-building calcium and vitamin D.
- Offer foods from each food group that are more nutrient dense—for example, whole-grain crackers instead of cookies; yogurt rather than ice cream; broiled chicken fingers, not fried chicken nuggets; raw veggies instead of chips; fruit in place of fruit pies.
- If your child doesn't like a certain food, offer options with similar nutrients. Instead of plain milk, offer low-fat flavored milk or a smoothie made with milk or yogurt. Instead of a sweet potato, offer carrots.
- Limit foods with added sugars, such as most cookies, candy, and juice drinks, as well as all sugar-sweetened drinks, including regular sodas. If kids fill up on these foods and drinks, they may miss out on the nutrient-rich foods they need; drinking a lot of sugary drinks increases the chance of unhealthy weight gain, too.

? Have you ever wondered?

. . . if your active child gets enough to drink? Children perspire with active play, even outside in cold weather when they're bundled up. Active children need eight or more cups of water during the day, as you do. It comes from all kinds of beverages, including milk and 100 percent juice. Just plain water is great for replenishing fluids; bring some along if you plan to be out for longer than an hour or on an extended car trip. Kids may drink more water if it's offered in appealing reusable "sports bottles."

See Chapter 21, "Fluids: Caution for kids" page 612, if your child is involved in sports.

Kids: Sweet Ideas with Less Added Sugars

- Shopping with kids? Choose the checkout line without the candy display.
- Snack beverage? Offer smoothies made with yogurt and fruit or 100 percent fruit juice, not fruit drinks or sodas.
- Dessert? Offer whole fruit or frozen 100 percent juice bars.
- Sweets? Provide only small portions, occasionally, in small plates or bowls.
- Kids don't eat a meal? Remind them that cookies, snack bars, chips, and candy are not meal replacements.

Foods to "Chews"

Chances are that some of your child's favorite foods may be high in food energy and low in nutrients. To get the most nutrition for the calories, encourage eating:

More often . . .	Less often . . .
Baked or grilled chicken fingers	Fried chicken strips and nuggets
Baked potato, baked sweet potato, colorful veggies	French fries, deep-fat-fried veggies
Graham crackers, animal crackers, fig bars	Chocolate-chip cookies, cupcakes
Low-fat or fat-free milk, 100 percent fruit juice	Soft drinks, fruit drinks, sports drinks
Nuts, dried fruits, plain popcorn, pretzels	Most potato chips, cheese puffs
Raw vegetable snacks (perhaps with hummus or salsa dip), fruit	Candy
Whole-grain bagels or English muffins, corn tortillas	Doughnuts, breakfast pastries
Yogurt, including Greek yogurt	Ice cream

Supplements for Kids?

Does your child eat a variety of foods? Do his or her meals and snacks have enough nutrient-rich foods from each food group? If so, your child probably doesn't need a nutrient supplement. Well-chosen meals and snacks likely supply enough vitamins and other nutrients for growth and health. In any event, food is the best nutrient source.

Before you give your child a supplement, talk to his or her doctor or a registered dietitian nutritionist! The AAP advises that healthy children who eat a well-balanced diet do not need vitamin supplements that exceed the RDAs for their age and gender.

If your child has a feeding problem that lasts for several weeks or if you're unsure about his or her nutrient intake, get expert advice. If your child is short on vitamin D, perhaps due to a milk allergy, a vitamin D supplement may be advised.

An appropriate supplement may be recommended if your child avoids an entire food group due to a food dislike, allergy, or intolerance, or if your child is a strict vegetarian. If your water supply isn't fluoridated, a fluoride supplement may be advised by your dentist.

Beware of claims for supplements targeted to help children get over colds, depression, or attention deficit disorder, among others. These claims aren't supported by sound science; such supplements may be harmful.

If your child's doctor recommends a nutrient supplement:

- Buy what's advised, perhaps a supplement made specifically for children. Check with the pharmacist if you need help. It should have no more than 100 percent of the Daily Values (DV). Unless stated otherwise, the % DVs stated on the Supplement Facts panel are meant for children aged four and older, as well as for adults. On supplements for younger children, look for the % DV for children under age four. *Beware:* An adult iron supplement can be dangerous for children! *See "Have you ever wondered . . . about iron poisoning—how does it happen" in this chapter, page 517.*
- Choose a supplement with a childproof cap. Store it out of your child's reach.
- Give a supplement only in the safe, advised dose.
- *Remember:* Supplements are just that—supplements—not an excuse to forgo smart eating.
- Remind children that supplements aren't candy, even if they come in fun names, colors, shapes, and packages.
- Remember that enriched and fortified foods may have the same added nutrients as the supplement. Read labels so your child doesn't get too much.

See chapter 10, page 315, to learn more about supplements.

Feeding Vegetarian Kids

Not surprisingly, vegetarian parents often raise vegetarian kids. Today, an awareness of and concern for animals also may prompt kids' interest in becoming vegetarians. Some teens opt for an eating style to be independent or to reflect their emerging beliefs.

Whatever the reason, a vegetarian eating pattern for growing, active school-age kids and teens can be healthy—if well planned and carefully followed. Even a vegan plan, with no animal-based foods, can supply enough nourishment, but the planning takes effort by everyone—kids, parents, and other caregivers.

The potential benefit is that vegetarian diets generally encourage nutrient-rich foods that many kids need more of: whole grains, vegetables, fruits, low-fat and fat-free dairy foods, and beans and peas. That can mean meals and snacks have more fiber and polyunsaturated fats, and less solid fats and fewer calories.

Vegetarian diets vary, and so do the nutrition concerns for vegetarian kids:

- *Lacto-ovo-vegetarian kids:* Eating dairy foods and eggs makes it easier to get enough nutrients. However, without meat, iron, zinc, and some other minerals may come up short, which may delay kids' normal growth and healthy weight gain. Milk, yogurt, cheese, and eggs each provide all the essential amino acids (proteins) for normal growth.
- *Vegan kids:* A vegan diet, if poorly planned, may not supply all the nutrients kids need to grow properly. Calcium, vitamin B_{12}, and vitamin D, as well as iron and zinc, need special attention. Although some vegetables provide calcium, it's generally not enough for bone growth. Without milk, kids also need another vitamin D source for bone growth, too, often advised in supplement form. Read the Nutrition Facts label to determine the calcium and vitamin D content of fortified soy beverages, a potential milk alternative. (*See "Nondairy Drinks: Soy, Almond, and More" in chapter 4, page 92.*) For vitamin B_{12}, many fortified breakfast cereals are options. To support growth, vegan kids need the right balance of essential amino acids from several sources, such as from beans and peas, soybeans, nuts, and seeds.

Ensuring that a vegetarian child or teen gets enough food energy, or calories, for proper growth and health is another concern. Because vegetarian meals can be low in fat and high in fiber ("bulky"), they may fill kids up without supplying enough calories.

To meet the nutrient and calorie demands of growth, offer your child or teen frequent meals and snacks. Provide some foods with more unsaturated fats such as avocadoes, nuts, nut butters, and seeds. Foods with some added sugars, such as oatmeal cookies and ice cream, may provide calories, but go easy on them. Nutrient-rich snacks provide calories, too: a peanut butter sandwich and milk; ready-to-eat breakfast cereal; raw vegetables with hummus or tofu dip; finger-food veggies; fruits; dried fruits; and nuts.

Your child's doctor may advise a nutrient supplement, especially if your child or teen is a vegan.

VEGETARIAN KIDS AND WEIGHT CONTROL

Is it okay for your teen to control weight with a vegetarian diet? Yes, if his or her food choices are varied and balanced as he or she maintains a healthy weight. However, vegetarian eating isn't always lower-calorie eating! The calorie content of food depends on your teen's overall food choices.

Be watchful: Make sure that vegetarian eating doesn't lead to or attempt to camouflage an eating disorder. If he or she loses too much weight or shows other signs of disordered eating, be concerned. Eating disorders can be harmful, even life-threatening. *See "Eating Disorders: More Than a Nutrition Issue" in chapter 25, page 732.*

SCHOOL MEALS FOR VEGETARIAN KIDS

If your school-age child or teen is a vegetarian, help him or her make smart choices from the array of foods that fit into vegetarian diets.

- Review school menus together and discuss what to order. If the school doesn't provide menus to parents, ask the school staff for help.
- Suggest the salad bar as a nutritious option—if it's available—and milk. A salad bar can be a good place to go for fresh vegetables and possibly for other nutrient-packed choices, including fruits, beans and peas, sunflower seeds, cheese, or hard-cooked eggs.
- When the school menu doesn't offer a vegetarian choice, a packed lunch is an option. A peanut butter sandwich is always popular (if your child or teen doesn't have a peanut allergy and if peanuts are permitted in school), as are egg salad sandwiches, cheese, and hummus with veggies.

ADVICE FOR FAMILY MEALS

If your child or teen decides to be a vegetarian, support the decision with food options that continue to promote growth, health, and a healthy weight. A vegetarian eating plan can supply enough of the nutrients and food energy needed—without overdoing on calories—if kids know how to make smart choices. Most of all, be supportive and learn how to make healthy vegetarian choices together. Here's how you might help:

- Together, make a shopping list of food-group foods that fit your child's or teen's vegetarian "style"—and keep those foods on hand: perhaps hummus, cheese, and crackers; raw veggies; fruit; milk; calcium-fortified soy beverage; yogurt; trail mix with nuts; and other quick, portable vegetarian snacks. Filling up on mostly cookies, chips, sugary drinks, ramen noodles, and fries may be vegetarian, but it's not healthy.
- Plan vegetarian dishes that your whole family can enjoy, such as bean tacos, chili with beans, or vegetarian pizza so you aren't a short-order cook preparing several different meals. *See "Meatless on the Menu" in chapter 3, page 73.*
- For some dishes, prepare them two ways with just a simple substitution: a veggie burger for your child or teen and beef burgers for the rest of the family. *See "Recipe Makeovers: Healthy Vegetarian" in chapter 8, page 237.*
- Prepare vegetarian foods that can be the main dish for your child or teen and a side dish for others—for example, pasta primavera or rice and beans. Offer low-fat or fat-free milk.
- Encourage your child or teen to plan and help prepare the menu to practice the basics of healthy vegetarian eating.
- Talk about eating-out options so your child or teen is prepared to make wise choices with peers.

See "The Healthy Vegetarian Way" in chapter 2, page 53, for guidance on vegetarian eating.

Eating Tactics for School-Age Kids

Kids' appetites and food preferences are changeable. Eating just small amounts or refusing certain foods may simply mean that your child is testing the flavors of food or exerting independence. To help your child eat well, be a role model for healthy eating, and take time for family meals. Here are some other ways to help:

- Stick to a regular meal schedule. That's how most school-age kids do best. When meals aren't regular or are missed, they may snack more throughout the day, so they're less hungry at mealtime. Breakfast skipping can affect learning and more; *see "Nutrition and Learning" in this chapter, page 500, and "Breakfast Matters" in chapter 3, page 60.*
- Serve snacks at least two hours before a meal. Since snacks can help supply the nutrients and food energy that growing, active kids need and that otherwise may be missing, make them nutrient rich. Two or three snacks per day are enough for most children. Kids who use more energy in active play, organized sports, or after-school activities need more calories—and perhaps more snacks—than kids who watch a lot of TV, play electronic games, spend time on a computer, or have a sedentary after-school routine.

  See "Snacking for Good Nutrition" in this chapter, page 493, and "Snacks Count!" in chapter 3, page 75.
- Support healthy eating at school; *see "Eating Right at School" in this chapter, page 505.* Encourage healthy snacks and physical activity choices with after-school programs or activities, too. Some programs and clubs offer "junior chef" or gardening activities.
- Reinforce and support what your child learns at school about healthy eating and physical activity, and why both matter. With your child, try this:
  - Using advice from www.ChooseMyPlate.gov and the food groups, plan a family meal or a day's snacks together. *See "A Plan for Healthy Eating: From MyPlate to Your Plate" in chapter 2, page 25.*
  - Count how many colorful vegetables your child eats each day.
  - Prepare foods (perhaps with vegetables or fruits) at home that your child learned about at school.
  - Track the type of physical activities and the time your child spends on them each day.
- Start with one new, good healthy-eating tactic at a time. Repeat and reinforce it. Once your child masters it, add another new one. If it's rejected, move on and try something else.
- Build trust with transparency. Avoid "tricking" a child by sneaking a veggie a child doesn't like into a food favorite.
- Make daily physical activity part of daily "family time." Help your child be physically active for sixty minutes of moderate activity on most days! *See "Get Up and Move!" in this chapter, page 522, for more about the health benefits and suggested activities.*

A Closer Look . . .

Should Kids' Cholesterol Levels Be Checked?

Until recently, cholesterol screening was only advised for kids considered at higher risk (family history) of heart disease. However, in 2011, the National Heart, Lung, and Blood Institute of the National Institutes of Health, with the endorsements of the AAP and the American Heart Association (AHA), provided new cholesterol-screening recommendations. They advise screening for every child between the ages of nine and eleven years old, and again between ages seventeen and twenty-one—even if they have no family history of cardiovascular disease.

In addition, the AAP recommends cholesterol testing for these groups of children, no later than ten years of age:

- Those whose parents or grandparents have had heart attacks or have been diagnosed with blocked arteries or disease affecting the blood vessels, such as stroke, before the age of fifty-five in men or sixty-five in women
- Those whose parents or grandparents have total blood cholesterol levels of 240 mg/dL or higher
- Those whose family health background is not known (such as many adopted children), or those who have characteristics associated with heart disease, such as high blood pressure, diabetes, smoking, or obesity

The reasons for these recommendations? While usually no symptoms are evident, high cholesterol levels early in life may play a role in developing atherosclerosis in adulthood, so identifying and lowering levels in youth may have benefits. The growing obesity epidemic among youth is another reason for the advice.

If your school-age child or teen has a higher than normal blood cholesterol level, don't panic. High cholesterol levels among children don't necessarily predict high levels in adulthood. When children come from high-risk families, it's prudent to check with a doctor and work with a registered dietitian nutritionist to bring the levels down. That's also good advice for the whole family!

For cardiovascular health, kids aged two through nineteen should maintain acceptable blood cholesterol levels, established by the National Cholesterol Education Program's Expert Panel on Blood Cholesterol in Children and Adolescents:

Levels	Total Cholesterol (mg/dL)	LDL Cholesterol (mg/dL)
High	200 or higher	130 or higher
Borderline	170 to 199	110 to 129
Acceptable	Less than 170	Less than 110

HDL levels should be greater than or equal to 35 mg/dL; triglycerides should be less than or equal to 150 mg/dL. Compelling evidence shows that fatty buildup in arteries begins in childhood and is more likely to occur with higher blood cholesterol levels. It slowly progresses into adulthood, often resulting in heart disease. For that reason, the AHA offers advice for children and teens to reduce cholesterol levels and fatty buildup in arteries:

- Cigarette smoking: discourage it.
- Regular aerobic exercise: encourage it.
- High blood pressure: identify and treat it.
- Overweight: avoid or reduce it.
- Diabetes: diagnose and treat it.
- Kids aged two and older should be encouraged to eat four to five cups of vegetables and fruits daily and eat a wide variety of foods that are low in saturated fats and *trans* fats.

See "Your Healthy Heart" in chapter 24, page 680, to learn about heart disease risks, prevention, and management.

For more about cardiovascular health for infants, children, and adolescents, visit the AHA website www.heart.org/ to learn more about heart health in kids. Consult a registered dietitian nutritionist or your doctor for a treatment approach that includes heart-healthy eating and physical activity if your child or teen is diagnosed with high blood cholesterol levels.

Many feeding strategies you used during the preschool years apply now, too. *See "Smart Tactics for Feeding Healthy Kids" and "Mealtime Tactics for Choosy Toddlers and Preschoolers" in this chapter, pages 490 and 512.*

GET UP AND MOVE!

Being physically active is part of a healthy start in life. When family, school, and community provide opportunities for active play and sports, kids are likely to participate.

Inactivity is linked to the dramatic rise of overweight among children, as well as teens. Consider some reasons why many kids are less physically active today than in times past:

- Today's kids too often play online games, text, participate in other digital media, or watch TV during their "prime time" for active play. Kids with too much screen time (for entertainment purposes) may not get enough physical exercise or time for creative activity and may miss out on human interaction.

- Many parents are concerned about safe outdoor play, especially if they work and aren't home to supervise. With less focus on physical education, kids have less chance at school for noncompetitive play.
- Kids often ride to school in a bus or car instead of walking or riding a bicycle.

Why Active Play for School-Age Kids?

Good physical health and a healthy body weight are just two reasons for active play, appropriate sports, and other physical activities for kids of every age. Free and structured play also does this:

- *Helps promote a child's physical development.* It builds muscular strength, including a strong heart muscle. Strong muscles promote good posture, which, in turn, affects a child's health and self-image. Weight-bearing activities such as running and skating help strengthen growing bones. Being active also helps build stamina, a quality that promotes learning and play. Once kids master basic physical skills, they can feel self-confident in their movements, which in turn can lead to enjoying physical activities more and being more active.
- *Promotes a healthy body weight.* Increased physical activity is one of the best ways for kids to keep their healthy weight.
- *Develops motor skills and coordination.* Playing catch develops eye-hand coordination. Hopscotch or jumping rope helps teach spatial relationships, while soccer helps develop manipulative skills.
- *Develops social skills.* As kids play actively with others, they share, cooperate, communicate, support each other, and act as a team.
- *Builds self-esteem.* Succeeding at any physical activity (not just team sports)—riding a bike, swimming a lap, or catching a ball—helps build self-confidence and a positive self image.
- *Keeps kids fit to protect themselves from injury and even danger.* When fit, they are more capable of running from danger and getting help in an emergency.
- *Comes with the joy of childhood!* Physical activity that's enjoyable is more likely to become a lifelong habit. An active child probably will be an active adult. A lifestyle that includes regular physical activity lowers the risk of many chronic diseases.

Activity for Kids: How Much? What Kind?

The CDC's Physical Activity Guidelines advise at least sixty minutes of moderate or vigorous physical activity every day for kids aged six to seventeen years. It doesn't have to be all at once. Activities that are vigorous (such as running), that build strength (such as climbing), and that build bones (such as jumping rope)—at least three times a week—are important.

Competitive sports aren't necessary and may not be right for some kids—especially if they create unnecessary pressure and take the fun out of being active.

Click Here!
Links to Know . . .

- Kidnetic (fun games to play inside or outside), International Food Information Council Foundation
  www.kidnetic.com
- BAM! Body and Mind (healthy eating and physical inactivity fun for kids and teens), Centers for Disease Control and Prevention
  www.cdc.gov/bam

Active play—biking, in-line skating, playing tag, swimming, or tossing a Frisbee, for example—can offer enough exercise for most kids. School recess is a great time for active play. Even household chores count: sweeping can be fun.

Next time your child says he or she doesn't know what to do, suggest something active. However, let your child take responsibility for what to do and for overcoming his or her own "boredom." *See "Ten Things for Kids to Do Instead of Screen Time" in this chapter, page 524.* *for ideas.*

Active Kids: Your Role as a Parent

To prevent your school-age child from joining the next generation of "couch potatoes," make physical activity a fun part of your family routine.

- Give your child enough free time for active play. Balance it with time for homework and activities such as reading, writing, and art.
- Join in when you can—perhaps hike together as a weekend outing, ride bikes after dinner, play a quick game of catch or hopscotch after work, clean up a local nature trail, try a rock-climbing gym, or take an active vacation. Walking together in the park or neighborhood provides more than exercise. It's a good time to talk and requires no equipment or planning, and it's free.
- Set limits on screen time, *as noted in "Encourage a healthy lifestyle" in this chapter, page 503.* Set a "media curfew" time. Keep the television, tablets, smart phones, video games, and charging stations out of your child's bedroom. Be consistent about your expectations.
- Offer a chance to try a group activity or a sport organized for kids. But trust your child's interest in the activity. If he or she is uninterested or feels embarrassed about not being good enough in a sport, help him or her find something else active to do. Instead of giving up right away, you can practice together at home to get better.
- Look for individual activities or sports if your youngster prefers that. Some kids are natural athletes and do well in group sports; others enjoy riding a bike or taking nature walks.

- Provide a safe place to play. Kids also need appropriate safety gear such as helmets, knee pads, or life jackets, as well as sunscreen (even in cold weather) and appropriate clothing.
- Until children are teens, avoid the urge to compete seriously against them in sports. Your child is likely no match for your adult strength and skill. Instead play together, and keep score if appropriate; just don't play to your full ability.
- Encourage "personal best" if your child participates in sports.
- Encourage after-school physical activities such as Scouting groups and those at outdoor centers, recreational and community centers, or your child's school. Consider after-school gymnastics, dance, karate, or swim classes.
- Encourage fun activities as the main event at kids' parties: perhaps swimming, bowling, or skating. Going to a party? Give gifts that encourage physical activity, such as sporting equipment, kites, balls, or physically active games.
- If your child has a physical disability, talk to his or her doctor about the appropriate amount and types of physical activities. Create chances for your child to try them.
- Be a role model! Make time for your own regular physical activity.

See "Kids: Eating for Sports" in chapter 21, page 612, for nutrition and fluid advice for youngsters involved in sports.

Ten Things for Kids to Do Instead of Screen Time

1. Encourage your child to jump rope. If he or she is older, try going "double Dutch" with two ropes. (A Hula-Hoop contest is fun, too.)
2. Take the dog for a brisk walk or play fetch. No dog? If your child is younger, have him or her take a teddy bear for a walk instead. Walking as a family is good talking time!
3. Give your child colored chalk to create a sidewalk mural or draw a hopscotch game—to play alone or together.
4. Don't let rainy days put a damper on fun! Dance or do jumping jacks or burpees inside.
5. Start a "hundred" walking club. Who's first in your family to walk a hundred times up and down the sidewalk or the stairs in your house?
6. Play tag or kickball in the playground, park, or backyard.
7. If there's snow, make a snowman or go sledding. Or take the family skating at an ice rink—even in July!
8. On warm days, go in-line skating or roller skating, ride bikes (remember the helmet and pads), or run through sprinkler "rain."
9. Hike together in a nearby park. Have your child find ten points of natural interest to enjoy as you hike.
10. Host a neighborhood bicycle or scooter wash outside—or a dog wash, instead.

Feeding the Teen Machine

Seeing teenagers make wise food choices is your reward for providing healthy food and teaching good nutrition in their younger years. By adolescence, many kids make most of their own food decisions. Other than filling the refrigerator and kitchen shelves with food and preparing family meals, parents have far less control over what their adolescent eats.

Teenagers themselves exert stronger influence over family eating than before, too, perhaps sharing the shopping, food preparation, and cleanup. Compared with their childhood years, they tend to consume more food and beverages away from home.

Chances are, teenagers know the basics of nutrition and healthy eating—learned at school and from parents. However, peer pressure, busy schedules, a sense of independence, sometimes unrealistic notions about body weight, weight expectations for sports, and an evolving self-image are among the barriers to healthy eating for many teens. Their food

Hey Teens, Did You Know?

- Unhealthy dieting can stop you from growing to your full height. Your body needs calories and other nutrients to grow and develop fully. Most teens shouldn't "diet."
- Your bones take in the most calcium during your teen years. The best sources are milk, yogurt, and low-fat cheese. Most teens need the equivalent of three to four cups of milk daily.
- If you don't eat breakfast, you may not have enough energy to concentrate in school or play a morning sport.
- Eating cookies, candy, or other sweet foods before an athletic event won't give you an energy boost.
- Girls lose iron during a menstrual period. If they don't eat iron-rich foods to replace this loss, they may feel weak and tired.
- Pizza and flatbread are healthier if you eat sensible amounts and know which toppings to choose such as veggies, fruits (such as pineapple), chicken, shrimp, and beans. *See "Pizza and Flatbread: Made to Order" in chapter 9, page 294, to learn how to build healthy ones.*
- Eating smart and moving more help you feel good, look good, and do your best.

choices may not reflect what teens really need. And to them, health issues of older age seem a long, long way off!

The same holds true for physical activity. Teens know why they should move more and be physically active, but that too, is fraught with barriers. In a nutshell, teens often don't connect their immediate food and physical activity patterns to their long- or short-term health. Many teens live in a wonderful world of invulnerability. Others follow misguided advice: supplements for muscle building, unsafe dieting for weight loss, and energy drinks for energy!

Many eating dilemmas that adults face are issues for teens. They too must pay attention to calorie-dense snacking, meal skipping, mindless eating, too-big portions, fad diets, eating too few vegetables and fruits, vegetarian eating, fast-food choices, and sports nutrition.

TEEN YEARS: FOOD, NUTRIENTS, AND GROWTH

Second only to infancy, adolescence is the fastest growth stage in life. Even when teens reach their adult height (for girls sooner than for boys), their bodies are still growing and developing.

Puberty marks the start of adolescent growth, the biggest growth spurt since infancy. When it starts and ends differs for each teen. For girls, puberty typically begins at about age twelve, about two years younger than for boys. During that time, the average youngster grows to be about 20 percent taller and about 50 percent heavier by his or her teen years. Body changes that happen as kids mature are stressful for some and may affect their self-image and perhaps the choices they make about eating and physical activity.

When and how your teen grows has more to do with genes than with food choices. However, smart eating does help determine if your teen grows to his or her full height potential—with strong bones, a fit body, and a healthy weight. As a parent, appreciate that your teen's normal growth pattern is normal, rather than make comparisons to a teenage friend.

What's good nutrition for teens? Calorie and nutrient needs increase to meet the growth and energy demands of adolescence. *See "Dietary Reference Intakes" in the appendix, page 780, to see how much.*

Calories: How Much?

Gender, body size, growth rate, and physical activity level determine how many calories teens need. The amount is somewhat more than when they were a bit younger—and, because of their growth spurt, more than at any other time in life.

Teenage boys on average need 1,800 to 2,600 calories a day when they're eleven to thirteen years old, and 2,200 to 3,200 calories a day when they're fourteen to eighteen. Boys who are who tall and big, and who do a lot of strenuous physical activity such as soccer, basketball, football, or other sports, may need 3,500 calories daily.

Teenage girls on average need 1,800 to 2,200 calories a day when they're eleven to thirteen, and 1,800 to 2,400 calories a day when fourteen to eighteen.

Let internal hunger cues, rather than charts and tables, be the guide to how much food your teen needs. As your teen's growth spurt slows down, so will his or her appetite. *See "Growth and Weight" in this chapter, page 501, for more about teens maintaining a healthy weight.*

Nutrients: Special Attention

All teens need enough calcium and vitamin D for bone growth and strength, protein for every body cell including muscles; carbohydrates and fats for energy; vitamins and minerals for the "sparks" that make all these body processes happen; and enough water.

Several nutrients may need attention because they often come up short in a teen's diet: calcium, iron, potassium, and vitamin D, as well as fiber; magnesium, vitamins A, C, and E, and choline may be underconsumed, as well.

Other nutrients—saturated fats, *trans* fats, added sugars, and sodium—may need attention for the opposite reason. As for adults, it's all too common for teens to consume too much of them due to poor food choices.

Calcium and vitamin D. "I'm sixteen, and I've stopped growing. So why do I need milk?" Milk and other dairy foods provide nutrients for bone growth and health, and more.

Teens are advised to consume enough foods rich in calcium and vitamin D so their bones become as strong as they can be. The RDA for calcium is 1,300 milligrams daily, and for vitamin D, it's 15 micrograms (600 IU) daily. An eight-ounce glass of milk has about 300 milligrams of calcium and 3 micrograms (120 IU) of vitamin D.

What foods are teens' best calcium sources? Milk (preferably low-fat or fat-free) as a beverage option with meals or as snacks, instead of sugary drinks, is a good option. Milk also contains other nutrients essential to healthy bones: vitamins A, D, and B_{12}, magnesium, potassium, and protein. Yogurt, cheese, and fortified soy beverages with meals or as snacks are calcium-rich, bone-building foods, too. Tofu (processed with calcium), as well as calcium-fortified juice and dark-green vegetables, also provide calcium.

See chapter 14, page 408, for more about calcium, vitamin D, and their sources.

For teens, especially girls, who choose diet soda over milk, often because they think milk will make them fat, help them understand: an eight-ounce glass of fat-free milk has just 80 calories. That's not much, especially when you also consider all the calcium and other nutrients it delivers—diet soda has none. Too often, soft drinks edge out milk and other calcium-rich beverages, resulting in a diet with much less calcium.

- Nutrition.gov, National Agricultural Library, USDA
  www.nutrition.gov/life-stages/adolescents

Bone Health: A Teen Issue

Bones keep on developing into the adult years. Even when teenagers reach their adult height, bones continue to strengthen as they become more dense. Almost half of an adult's bone mass forms during the teen years. The stronger bones become during adolescence, the lower the risk of osteoporosis later on.

Osteoporosis manifests itself in later years; however, it often begins in adolescence. Teenagers—children, too—who don't consume enough calcium put their bones at risk for the long term. They may start their adult years with a calcium deficit in their bones. With bone loss that comes as a natural part of aging, they have less to draw on, and their risk for osteoporosis, or brittle bone disease, increases.

In the United States, only 10 percent of girls and 42 percent of boys aged fourteen to eighteen consume the recommended amount of calcium daily. And many are short-changed on vitamin D. Getting enough of these bone-building nutrients, as well as getting enough protein, magnesium, and certain vitamins, is essential for bone health. Regular weight-bearing activities such as dancing, soccer, running, weight lifting, tennis, and volleyball are important because they trigger bone tissue to form.

Poor bone health can also result in stress fractures. These tiny cracks in the bone, usually from overuse, are among the most common sport injuries, especially for those who are involved in basketball, dance, gymnastics, tennis, and track and field. *See chapter 21, page 599, for more about sports nutrition.*

Smoking factors in to poor bone health, too. Both the nicotine and toxins in cigarettes can have a negative effect on forming maximum bone mass. Smoking triggers changes in cells and organs, as well as hormones that are needed to build bones. Nicotine and free radicals formed during smoking affect osteoblasts, or bone-building cells. Teens who smoke are smart to kick the habit for this and many other reasons!

See "A Closer Look . . . Calcium, Vitamin D, and Bone Health" in chapter 14, page 427, and "Osteoporosis and Bone Health" in chapter 25, page 738.

Iron. Does your teen seem chronically tired? Fatigue may come from too little sleep, an exhausting schedule, strenuous activity (a good kind of fatigue), or the emotional ups and downs of adolescence. Feeling tired also may be a symptom of low iron levels in the blood.

Iron is part of blood's hemoglobin, which carries oxygen to body cells. Once there, oxygen helps cells produce energy. When iron is in short supply, there's less oxygen available to produce energy—hence fatigue.

Iron needs go up dramatically in the teen years. For boys and girls aged nine to thirteen, the RDA is 8 milligrams daily. For adolescents, because more muscle mass and a greater blood supply demand more iron, the RDA for girls aged fourteen to eighteen jumps to 15 milligrams daily to replace iron losses from their menstrual flow. *See "The Menstrual Cycle: Nutrition Issues" in chapter 18, page 533.* For boys that same age, the RDA is 11 milligrams daily. Some experts advise more iron for teens who are heavily involved in sports.

For many teens—girls especially—paying attention to iron-rich foods is especially important. Two common reasons account for low intakes: poor food choices or restricting food in order to lose weight. Girls who don't eat protein foods regularly may not consume enough iron, either.

Iron comes from a variety of foods: meat, poultry, and fish. Beans and peas, enriched grain products, eggs, and some vegetables provide iron, too, although in a form that's less bioavailable, or useable by the body than iron from meat.

Vitamin C makes iron from eggs and plant sources more bioavailable, so teens who drink orange juice with their morning toast, cereal, or eggs get an iron boost. And those who skip the juice and just grab toast to eat at the bus stop don't get the full benefit of the iron in toast. *See "Iron" in chapter 14, page 438, for more about iron in a healthy diet.*

Other vitamins and minerals. A variety of nutrient-rich foods supplies enough of the vitamins and minerals teens need, including potassium and zinc. Vegetables, fruits, and milk are all great sources of potassium. Zinc, a nutrient important for growth and immunity, may be a concern for vegetarian teens who avoid lean meat, poultry, and fish, which are good sources of zinc; *see "Feeding Vegetarian Kids" in this chapter, page 520, and chapter 14, page 408, for more about these and other nutrients.*

Macronutrients: carbohydrates, fats, and protein. Most teens consume enough of all three naturally through healthy eating. The AMDRs for macronutrients for teens are as follows:

Carbohydrates	45 to 65 percent of total calories
Protein	10 to 30 percent of total calories The Recommended Dietary Allowance (RDA) level, a minimum recommended amount, is 46 grams daily for girls aged fourteen to eighteen and 52 grams daily for boys that age.
Dietary fat	25 to 35 percent of total calories

Teens are advised to limit solid fats (saturated and *trans* fats) and added sugars. *See chapters 11, page 345, 12, page 373, and 13, page 385, for more about carbohydrates, protein, and fats.* Most teens also need to consume significantly more fiber.

Water. For most teens, getting enough water isn't a problem. The issue is their choice of beverage. Instead of sugary and energy drinks, they're nutritionally better off choosing water, low-fat or fat-free milk (flavored or unflavored), fortified soy beverages, or 100 percent fruit juice. *See "Soda, Energy Drinks, and Enhanced Beverages" in chapter 4, page 100, for more about options and concerns about sugary and energy drinks; and "Water: A Fluid Asset" in chapter 15, page 443.*

See "Dietary Reference Intakes" in the appendix, page 780, for specific nutrient recommendations for teens.

HEALTHY EATING PLANS FOR TEENS

The advice about eating from the five food groups and oils, *described in chapter 2, page 21,* is meant for healthy people aged two and older—so that means teens, too! How much from each food group? That depends on how many calories teens need. The more active they are, the more calories they need—and the more they can eat.

Teens should choose enough and choose wisely from each food group. Here's top-line advice tailored for teens:

- *Grain group:* Make calories count. Carbs should provide the most food energy (calories). The best sources are grain foods with more fiber and less solid fats and added sugars. At least half of the choices should be from whole grains. Some ways to do this are to order pizza on whole-grain crust, make sandwiches on whole-wheat bread, and snack on plain popcorn or whole-wheat crackers.
- *Vegetable and fruit groups:* Eat more. Veggies and fruits deliver vitamins, minerals, fiber, and more, generally with fewer calories than other sources. Choose with variety in mind. Opt for those prepared or processed with less sodium and little or no added sugars. Go for color. Ease up on fries.
- *Dairy group:* Eat enough. Choose low-fat or fat-free dairy foods for calcium and vitamin D and their nutrient partners for a lifetime of healthy bones. If being a vegan or lactose intolerant are barriers, find other practical ways to get enough calcium and vitamin D. *See "A Closer Look . . . Feeding Vegetarian Kids" in this chapter, page 520, and "Lactose Intolerance: A Matter of Degree" in chapter 23, page 666, for advice.*
- *Protein foods group:* Eat enough. Lean meat and beans and peas supply the iron your body needs. These foods, along with poultry, fish, eggs, and nuts, provide protein, too. Go easy on fried chicken and fried fish.
- *Oils:* Choose an amount within your calorie budget. Choose vegetable oils, oily fish such as salmon, and foods such as avocadoes and nuts, instead of foods with more saturated and *trans* fats.

The amount advised from each food group depends on your teen's calorie needs. *See "Estimated Calorie Needs per Day by Age, Gender, and Physical Activity Level," and "Eating Patterns, 2015–2020 Dietary Guidelines for Americans" in the appendix, pages 770 and 771, to estimate calorie needs to find a food-group pattern that matches.*

See "Kids: Eating for Sports," chapter 21, page 612, for more nutrition guidance for teens involved in sports.

Make School Meals Count

Chosen well, lunch from the school cafeteria can provide at least one-third of the nutrients and calories that teens need in a day—and more if they eat school breakfast, too.

If your teen buys lunch at school, encourage him or her to choose the full variety of foods offered on the lunch menu—and to make school meals a chance to drink milk. *For more about school meals, see "Eating Right at School" in this chapter, page 505.* A variety of nutrient-rich foods equates to a healthy carried lunch or a la carte meal—not just pizza or a burger on most days.

Snacks: Filling the Gaps

With their high energy and nutrient needs, especially during their growth spurt, teens snack to refuel. Active, growing boys especially may need snacks to fill their bottomless pit. Snacks can also help to fill in nutrient gaps; if your teen doesn't drink milk for lunch, a snack of yogurt is great, and hummus and baby carrots is a way to fit veggies in.

Also important: snacking is part of hanging out when teens get together—even when they aren't really hungry! *Tip for teens:* It's okay to hang out without snacks. The real issue with teen snacking isn't whether they do or don't. Instead, it's about what and how much. These snack habits are among the nutrition concerns:

? Have you ever wondered?

. . . if you should be concerned when your teen skips meals? That depends. If meals are missed occasionally and replaced with healthy snacks, that's likely okay. It happens in busy teen lives.

However, if your teen skips meals regularly, the nutrients needed for growth, development, and health may come up short. Some teenage girls habitually skip breakfast or lunch to cut out calories, missing out on nutrient-rich foods. If later they satisfy their hunger with high-calorie, high-fat snack foods and sugary drinks, the net result is more calories and fewer nutrients than needed, and a potential for weight issues.

. . . how pregnancy affects a teenage girl's nutrition needs? During any pregnancy, the need for nutrients and calories goes up. For teens, the nutrient recommendations during pregnancy are higher than for adult women to support their own growth and development as well as the developing fetus. *See "Pregnancy During Adolescence" in chapter 18, page 548, for nutrition advice.*

Have you ever wondered?

. . . what foods may control teenage acne? Although all kinds of foods get blamed, teen acne is linked to hormonal changes, rarely to food choices. The best approach to healthy skin is for your teen to eat an overall varied and balanced diet, keep his or her skin clean, get enough rest—and wait. After the body matures, most acne clears up. If problems are severe or persist, talk to a dermatologist. Sometimes a skin application that contains a derivative of vitamin A is prescribed; simply taking a vitamin A tablet won't clear the skin.

Caution: If the doctor prescribes Accutane® (isotretinoin) to treat severe acne, avoid supplements containing vitamin A. Taken together, Accutane and vitamin A have toxic effects. Accutane can also raise cholesterol and blood lipid (fat) levels until the treatment stops. Because Accutane has many potential side effects, both psychological (depression, lack of concentration, irritability, and suicidal thoughts, among others) and physical (including unusual fatigue and appetite loss), make sure your teen follows dosage directions carefully, under close supervision of his or her doctor. Accutane can cause birth defects.

. . . if chocolate causes acne? No, chocolate doesn't cause acne or make acne worse. Hormones and hygiene, rather than any substance in chocolate, are the more likely culprits. A true food allergy to chocolate is rare. Instead, any reaction to a chocolate bar may come from other ingredients mixed in, such as nuts or milk.

. . . if kids who wear braces should avoid eating raw vegetables and fruits? No! It's true that hard, crunchy, or sticky foods can damage braces. But kids don't need to give up vegetables and fruits. Instead, they might choose softer types: perhaps a banana or ripe peach rather than a crisp apple; cucumber sticks rather than a whole, raw carrot; or sliced carrots or broccoli, softened in a microwave oven. Or they might cut these foods into bite-size pieces instead of eating them whole. Consult your teen's orthodontist for a list of foods that might damage braces.

- High-calorie snacks that replace nutrient-rich foods
- Mindless or emotional snacking that adds excess calories
- Large, even oversized, portions that add too many calories
- Overdoing on drinks and snacks that are high in solid fats, sodium, or added sugars, such as regular soft drinks, sweetened tea, candy, chips, cookies, and fruit pies

Here are some tips to help teens make healthy snack choices:

- Stock the kitchen with easy-to-grab nutrition. Ease is one reason why kids reach for chips or cookies, so make nutrient-rich snacks that take little or no effort available: for example, whole fruit (apples, bananas, grapes, tangerines), cut-up veggie sticks, hummus, string cheese, whole grain bagels or crackers, air-popped popcorn, low-fat plain and flavored milk, yogurt, and frozen yogurt.
- Fill your fridge with flavored milk, yogurt drinks, or fortified soy beverages so that sugary drinks and energy drinks won't compete. Look for low-fat and fat-free dairy options. If milk is cold, convenient, and "cool," your teen more likely will drink it.

See "Snacking for Good Nutrition" in this chapter, page 493, for more ideas.

Teens' Food Choices: Parenting Tactics

Bigger appetites, busy lifestyles, emotional swings, struggles for independence, peer pressure: they all challenge how and what teens eat. Still, you can influence your teen's eating habits—subtly:

- Despite teen lifestyles, make time for family meals. Schedule them around after-school activities and jobs. Put family meals on the calendar days in advance. Why? First, it's a good time to connect with your busy teen. (Save stressful conversations for another time.) What's more, research suggests that for teens, eating family meals is linked to consuming more vegetables, fruits, and milk, as well as fewer soft drinks and fried, high-fat, and sugar-laden foods. Some research also links family meals with better emotional health; fewer risk-taking behaviors, such as alcohol and drug abuse; and better school performance.

  See "Family Mealtime: A Priority" in this chapter, page 491, for more benefits and tips for shared meals.
- Come up with ways to help your teen fit breakfast in on school mornings. Teens, eager for a few more moments of sleep, are notorious breakfast skippers on school mornings. *See "Beating Breakfast Barriers" in chapter 3, page 64, for solutions.*
- Encourage your son or daughter to take a class at school in foods (cooking), nutrition and wellness, or consumer health to learn the practical basics of sound nutrition and healthy eating. These classes are also full of applied science, math, and social studies. *See "Learning about Food" in this chapter, page 493, for ways you and your teen can explore all things food together.*
- Help your teen build culinary skills. He or she can help you plan, shop for, and cook family meals. The kitchen is a place to practice what's learned in a foods class. (Some of today's TV cooking shows with teens might inspire them.) *Some tips in "Cooking Together" in this chapter, page 495, might help younger teens.*
- When you're eating out together, seek out healthier options in fast-food restaurants, vending machines, and convenience stores. Your teen may be unaware of all the choices available. Many fast-food restaurants, even some convenience stores, carry fresh fruit.

Look for wraps, trail mix, nuts, and flavored milk. Help teens tune into portion size, too. A small bag of chips can be as much fun to eat as a bigger bag, with far fewer calories! The same goes for soft drinks.

- In your talk time, tie smart eating and active living to what matters to your teen—growing normally; feeling good; looking good; and doing well in school, sports, or a personal interest (music, drama, art, whatever). Even if he or she seems to disregard your suggestions, your teen likely will "hear" your encouragement, concern, and example.
- Set a good example for wellness and lifestyle with regular physical activity, lower-fat eating, sensible portions, and not smoking. Kids notice when adults "walk the talk."
- Help your teen deal with peer pressure by coming up with ways to follow personal goals for smart eating, rather than going with the crowd. *See "Reaching SMART Goals, One Step at a Time!" in chapter 1, page 18.*
- Is your teen a vegetarian? *See "Feeding Vegetarian Kids" in this chapter, page 520, to be supportive.*

Alert: Teenage Drinking

"It's just beer; it's not like I'm using drugs!" That's common logic for some teens. But scientific evidence, the Dietary Guidelines for Americans, and the law are clear: Teens, do not drink!

What may start as social drinking with a seemingly "safe" sweet wine cooler or beer can turn high risk. Alcohol in wine coolers (wine plus carbonated fruit drink) and beer can quickly add up to dangerous levels of blood alcohol. Effects are faster and stronger for some than others; there's no way to predict how a teen will be affected. Add a high-caffeine energy drink, and it's more dangerous yet.

Besides being illegal, alcohol use by young people can have serious outcomes. For one, it can contribute to alcohol-related problems later on. Driving accidents, with potentially life-altering and fatal consequences, are among the obvious risks of drunkenness for anyone, not just for alcoholics.

As a parent, talk openly with your teen about the risks. Practice ways your teen can refuse alcoholic drinks and leave situations where alcohol is being consumed. Be mindful of alcohol use among your teen's peers and within the community so you can help him or her avoid it. Show by example your responsible use of alcoholic beverages, if you choose to drink them. *See "Alcoholic Beverages: In Moderation" in chapter 4, page 102, for more about drinking alcohol.*

MOVE IT: SPORTS AND MORE!

Does your teen move in high gear on a "24/7" schedule—from school to after-school activities and perhaps to a job, with homework, time with friends, and hours of texting or being online in between? Research shows that unless kids are involved in sports, their physical activity drops dramatically when they hit the teen years. Remember: A busy schedule may not be an active lifestyle!

Moving more promotes benefits that are dear to teenage hearts: looking good, being in shape, being strong, feeling energetic, being self-confident, doing well in school, and having a good outlook on life to become the adult they hope to be.

Being active also helps teens keep their healthy weight and helps reduce the risk for developing some chronic health problems later, including type 2 diabetes, heart disease, obesity, and osteoporosis. Reducing risk is especially true for teens who make active living a lifelong habit.

For teens, the Physical Activity Guidelines for Americans from the CDC advises sixty minutes or more of physical activity each day. Teens, take note:

- Divide the sixty minutes into smaller chunks of activity time spread throughout the day if you prefer.
- Do plenty of aerobic activity (moderate or vigorous).
- At least three days a week, fit in vigorous activity, muscle-strengthening activities, and bone-strengthening activities.
- Get a good balance of activities that stretch your muscles, strengthen your body, and give your heart a workout.

Has your teen walked, run, or biked 100 miles? How long did it take? Self-tracking physical activity, perhaps with an app or a step counter, helps your teen see his or her own progress, independent of organized sports. It's a great motivator for many!

See "A Closer Look . . . Ten Reasons to Get Up and Move!" in chapter 1, page 17, and "Get Up and Move" in this chapter, page 520, for more about guidelines and benefits of physical activity.

Teens on the Move: Overcoming Barriers

Why does it seem that more and more teenagers are less and less active? Perhaps it's the family pattern they "inherited," the world around them, or today's teen lifestyles. For every reason teens give to move less, check out the tactics for parents to try, and easy, often fun solutions for teens to move more.

REASON: Video games, social media, computers, and TV take precedence in free time. While the mental exercise of interactive computer and app games is great, teens'—and everyone's—eyes, brain, and body need a physically active break from sitting, too. In fact, brain synapses may work faster for those who take time for physical activity.

Tactics: Encourage your teen to balance social media and online and TV time with physically active time, either with friends and family or on his or her own. As a parent, set limits on screen time, *as noted in "Encourage* *a healthy lifestyle" in this chapter, page 503*. Have a "screen-free" zone in your home and a "landing place" for computers and digital devices that is within adult control—not in your teen's bedroom. (And a fridge doesn't belong in the bedroom, either.)

Teen Solutions:

- Do something active while watching TV: perhaps lift weights, do push-ups or sit-ups, or dance!
- Find active video games and websites that make your body move, not just sit. As an example, the BAM (Body and Mind) website from the CDC offers a chance for active gaming or moving while online: www.cdc.gov/bam/activity/index.html.
- Set limits on social media and TV time for yourself.

REASON: Teens say, "It's too far to walk there." So they ride in or drive cars nearly everywhere: to school, the mall, friends' homes, or work.

Tactic: Encourage independence and the physical activity benefits of getting to nearby places by foot or bike.

Teen Solutions:

- Get a foot scooter, in-line skates, or a bike. (Remember to get a helmet and perhaps knee pads for safety.)
- Walk or bike when possible rather than expecting someone to be your chauffeur.

REASON: Teens say they don't have time, especially if they work after school or if they're involved in after-school activities.

Tactic: Help your teen find ways to fit physical activity into the schedule and to balance homework with being physical active.

Teen Solutions:

- Read a book while pedaling a stationary bike. Study on a large balance ball while doing homework at a desk or table.
- Pick household chores that take more movement, such as washing the car, raking leaves, or sweeping sidewalks.
- If there's no time for a school sport or local sports league, see if a local gym has a teen membership. If so, sign up to go before or after school and on weekends.
- Make social time with friends an active time: walk, bike, or hike; dance; or play a pickup game of a favorite sport.

REASON: School doesn't require much PE.

Tactic: Make physical activity a lifestyle priority, not just a school requirement.

Teen Solutions:

- Sign up for PE at school whether required or not, and not just as a summer course. Ask a parent to support efforts to include physical education at school.
- Take a community class, perhaps in rock climbing, hip-hop dance, kickboxing, swimming, or martial arts.

REASON: Some teens feel self-conscious about sports, especially if they aren't athletic or they're overweight.

Tactic: Put the emphasis on fun, not performance.

Teen Solutions:

- Try individual physical activities, such as biking, walking, and in-line skating.
- Download music to listen to as you walk to keep up a quick pace.

REASON: Teens (especially girls) say, "I don't want to sweat or mess up my hair."

Tactic: Shift the mind-set. Even if your teen sweats, fitness is more important.

Teen Solutions:

- Do everyday activities such as walking to school or household tasks that don't work up a sweat.
- Come up with an active-day "look."
- Be active with friends so all have an active, "sweaty look." *See "Get Fit with a Friend" in this chapter, page 531.*

WEIGHT: RIGHT-SIZED?

Body image is a big issue for most teens, who are eager for acceptance, want to be attractive, and are self-conscious about body changes. Despite different body sizes, shapes, and growth stages, many do weigh within a healthy range.

At the same time, teenage overweight and obesity are national health concerns. Teenage eating disorders are all too common. And some teens use misguided approaches to achieve an unrealistic or unhealthy weight or body size.

As you help your teen grow and reach his or her healthy weight, remember: The "right weight" is a range, not a single number—and not the same weight as a friend's. The most important concern is health and a healthy weight for the individual teen, not simply appearance or the right weight for sports.

If Your Teen Is Overweight

Adult weight-loss diets aren't meant for teens—nor are quick-fix, fad diets. For many, growing into an appropriate weight is healthier than dieting—if the teen eats sensibly and gets enough physical activity. Dieting may deprive a growing teen of needed nutrients. *See "Weight Management: Strategies that Work!" in chapter 22, page 637.*

Unless a doctor advises it, the teen years aren't a time for a weight-loss diet. Teens who truly are overweight—or at risk for it—need a healthy, realistic, and safe way to manage weight. That includes both physical activity and smart eating, not "dieting."

Weight is a sensitive issue for everyone, especially teens. The best approach for parents to take with overweight teens is positive—no nagging, no forbidden foods, no criticism. A negative approach is a surefire route to defeat. Instead, understanding, love, and support go a long way in helping teens cope with and address weight issues.

The AAP advises parents to encourage healthy eating habits and to help provide teens with healthy meals and snacks and a regular exercise routine and to steer clear of encouraging dieting. You can offer your support in these ways:

- Help eliminate eating triggers, such as the sight of high-calorie snacks on the kitchen counter.
- Reassess your family's eating style. Make gradual improvements together. Gradual changes often become permanent ones.
- Do fun, physically active things together. You both benefit!
- Talk, listen, and offer support and alternatives for emotional issues that trigger eating.
- Gather resources your teen needs. Keep nutritious, lower-calorie foods, including vegetables and fruits, on hand. Prepare family meals that support your teen's strategies for managing weight.
- Make this book available for your teen to read. It's full of good-tasting ways to eat healthy at home, at school, or out with friends.
- Most of all, be accepting. Your love doesn't depend on your teen's weight loss. Unconditional acceptance goes a long way in promoting a positive self-image, which helps promote a healthy weight.

Pressure to Be Thin

To many teens, looks are almost everything! As their bodies develop and take on adult shapes, it's normal to focus on body image. Often, however, teens have unrealistic notions about their own weight and body size. Many girls, especially those aged nine to fifteen years old, view themselves as overweight when they really aren't. Although less common, many boys in this age group do, too.

Pressure to be thin is closely linked to the pressure to fit in and be accepted by peers. Thin people are viewed as successful, popular, and attractive. This message gets reinforced by media images and celebrities—and often by parents and friends. However, even the celebrities that teens try to emulate may not really have a "perfect look"; computers are often used to manipulate and retouch their photo images.

Teenage girls tend to diet, often poorly, as their main approach to having an attractive body, while boys often put more emphasis on exercise and body building. For girls, the pursuit of thinness often leads to fad dieting—usually ineffective, often dangerous. These diets are especially risky during adolescence, when teens' nutrient needs for growth and energy are high. Trying to lose weight fast to "look good" for a dance or a swim party is neither realistic nor healthy. *See "Popular Diets: Truths and Half Truths" in chapter 22, page 648, for more on fad diets.*

Get Fit with a Friend

Is your teenager looking for something to do? Suggest these active ways to get fit with a friend—and have fun!

- Do something active: play table tennis, go in-line skating, go hiking, or enjoy dancing. *Hint:* You don't need a partner for line dancing.
- Walk while talking on the phone with your friends.
- Sign up for a school or community sports team. You don't need to "play varsity" to get health benefits.
- Join the marching band if you play a musical instrument. Try out for cheerleading, majorettes, or the pom-pom squad.
- Volunteer as a stagehand for school plays. You'll get plenty of exercise doing stage chores.
- Do community service—perhaps at a community garden, home-building project, children's day camp, community cleanup, or animal center.
- Babysit. Play actively with children.
- Get a neighborhood job: mow lawns, shovel snow, wash cars, do yard work, walk a neighbor's dog.
- Enjoy interactive computer and video games that promote physical activity—instead of sitting and texting.

See "Quick Tips to Move More" in chapter 22, page 638, for more physical activity ideas that teens might do.

Teens who truly are overweight—or at risk for being overweight—need a realistic, safe, and healthy way to manage their weight. That includes both physical activity and a healthy eating plan, not "dieting."

Eating disorders. Sometimes a teen's pursuit of thinness leads to obsession, perhaps caused by a traumatic event or a life change. Although not overweight, and perhaps even underweight, some teens see themselves as fat. Sometimes a distorted body image begins as teens develop sexual characteristics.

A distorted body image may lead to an eating disorder. Teens, whose nutrient needs are high, instead may eat very little or may purge with self-induced vomiting or laxative abuse. This can result in extreme undernourishment and weight loss—even death. Because eating disorders are linked to psychological problems, attention from a mental health professional, as well as your child's doctor, is essential if there is an eating disorder.

Most victims of eating disorders—anorexia nervosa, bulimia, and binge eating—are teenage girls and young women. Although less common, teenage boys, in increasing numbers, have eating disorders, too. Binge eating is a common eating disorder of obese people. *See "Body Image and Eating Disorders: An Issue for Men, Too" in chapter 19, page 565 and "Eating Disorders: More than a Nutrition Issue" in chapter 25, page 732.*

Bodybuilding

Most teens want to build muscle (have great "abs") to look good and to perform well in sports. Many know the value of weight training. But for some, the size and shape of their muscles become obsessions that lead to seemingly constant weight lifting and workouts. They may also have the misguided notion that eating more protein builds muscle mass. Some opt for more meat portions, perhaps at the expense of whole-grain starchy foods; others take protein supplements and "bulk-up" drugs such as steroids. Muscle-building steroids are dangerous; *see "Ergogenic Aids: No Training Substitute" in chapter 21, page 619.*

Although protein needs go up during the teen years, an extra amount likely has no added bodybuilding benefits. Following food-group recommendations supplies the protein that most teens need—whether they're involved in weight training or not. Like extra carbohydrates or dietary fats, extra calories from protein are deposited in the body as fat, not muscle. *See Chapter 21, "Kids: Eating for Sports," page 612 for advice about the variety and amounts of food for teen athletes.*

A high-protein diet may contribute a higher percentage of calories from fat. That's especially true when teens opt for fewer foods high in carbohydrates, such as bread, cereal, pasta, and rice. The best advice for teenage bodybuilders? Follow the healthy eating guidelines in *chapter 2, page 21,* and be sensible with a weight-training program.

The key to building muscle is a good exercise program and enough nutrient-rich foods to fuel longer workouts. Through exercise, which creates a demand for more muscle, protein enters the muscles and makes them larger. *See "Muscle Myths" in chapter 21, page 608, to learn why just consuming extra protein doesn't build more muscle.*

"Making Weight"

Some teens are concerned with achieving a particular weight for wrestling or football. Others want to develop a lean, strong body for gymnastics, figure skating, or cheerleading.

Unhealthy weight management—either to gain or lose weight—can be dangerous for anyone, including young athletes. Cutting down on food and beverages, along with excessive exercising, overtraining, and sweating off water weight, can lead to dehydration, heat stress, and other health problems—and certainly does not enhance performance. Instead of gaining strength, muscles may get weaker and smaller, even for those who consume protein.

Without enough calories, the body burns some protein in muscles for energy. Crash dieting for sports and body image, along with a poor self-image, are factors that can lead to disordered eating and decreased performance.

See "Making Weight" in chapter 21, page 614, for more on food for sports and making weight.

? Have you ever wondered?

. . . if drinking milk will make your teen fat? Many teenage girls misguidedly link milk drinking to their fear of getting fat. Yet those who watch calories could consume fat-free dairy foods for fewer calories than drinking the same amount of a soft drink or juice. Eight ounces of fat-free milk has 85 calories and calcium and vitamin D, too. Eight ounces of regular soda has about 100 calories—but most soda is sold in twelve-ounce cans for about 150 calories or twenty-ounce bottles for about 250 calories!

. . . how to help your teen avoid the "freshman fifteen"? That number refers to the belief that many teens gain fifteen unwanted pounds during their first year at college. In fact, that amount may be overstated since some extra pounds probably result from adolescent development. Unwanted pounds may be the result of poor food habits prompted by academic pressure, the stress of being away from home, less physical activity, unlimited access to food on campus and nearby, and not having a parent around. As an antidote, encourage your teen to eat smart and take time for physical activity, perhaps as a study break. You might send your college student a "care package" with healthier and lower-calorie snack foods, too.

18

Manage Women's Unique Nutrition Concerns

In this chapter, find out about . . .

Food and PMS, fertility, and more uniquely female health issues

Healthy eating for pregnancy, breastfeeding, and post-delivery

Eating for midlife issues: menopause, bone health, and reducing health risks

Women: this chapter is meant especially for your unique nutrition needs. At one time, women's health needs were projected in studies done mostly with men. Except for a focus on reproductive health, women's particular health concerns were largely ignored. Today, medical research, health promotion, and healthcare address gender differences. And nutrition is center stage in many initiatives for women's health.

Women need the same nutrients that men do—perhaps more of some, depending on their age. Yet, they likely need fewer calories to deliver those nutrients. Unless men shift their physical activity level, the nutrition needs of healthy males don't change much over a lifetime. That's not true for women. Complexities of the reproductive system, the ups and downs of female hormones, and the physical demands of childbearing affect nutrition needs and healthcare. Menstruation, pregnancy, breastfeeding, and menopause all have nutrition implications.

Healthy eating fuels women's busy lifestyles and provides nourishment and energy for the unique issues of every age and stage in a woman's life. Regular physical activity makes a positive difference, too. Caring for yourself is part of caring for others. Whether you're fueling yourself for health and wellness in your twenties, forties, or sixties—or somewhere in between or beyond—follow the guidance on healthy eating *in chapter 2, page 21*.

The Childbearing Years

Healthy eating, active living, and hormones are intertwined in the complex issues of women's health. Whether or not you choose to have children, the choices you make now during your childbearing years affect the quality and length of your life for the long run. Many of those choices are uniquely female.

THE MENSTRUAL CYCLE: NUTRITION ISSUES

Some food and nutrition issues are linked to a woman's reproductive system and hormones—some food decisions you make can help you manage them.

Menstruation: Increased Iron Needs

In your childbearing years, you need more iron than men do to replace iron loss from menstrual flow. On average, women lose about ¼ cup of blood with each menstrual period. Those with heavy flows may lose more iron. For women who don't replace it, the lost iron—combined with low iron

Did You Know?

. . . you can practice healthy eating and living habits now to reduce the risk of unhealthy weight gain and type 2 diabetes later on?

. . . you can be slim and trim yet still have high blood cholesterol?

. . . even if you're fit and work out religiously and vigorously—yoga, running, biking—you can't effectively lower your risk for heart disease if you have poor eating habits, smoke, or have high blood cholesterol levels?

. . . most women (70 to 80 percent) who get breast cancer don't have a family history of this disease?

. . . breastfeeding in your childbearing years is protective against breast cancer later?

. . . having a family history of heart disease or breast cancer doesn't mean you'll get either one? Healthy eating, physically active living, and regular screenings protect you from both!

Girlfriends: A Support Network for Health

Whether you're twenty-five, fifty, or seventy-five years old, most women value the support and social interaction that comes from being with other women. Getting together doesn't need to involve food. If it does, make it an opportunity for a fitness and food adventure, with health as a priority.

- Set workout dates together, or walk the neighborhood as you talk. It's easier to stick to an exercise plan when you don't want to let someone else down.
- Share healthy recipes. You or your friends may have a great makeover recipe—with more vegetables and whole grains (and fewer calories)—that are already family tested!
- Snack on baby carrots, bell peppers, berries, or grapes when friend time is also food time. Quench your thirst with ice water flavored with a citrus slice or berries, instead of sugary drinks.
- Be each other's best cheerleader. Surround yourself with women who make positive food and lifestyle choices. Encourage one another to eat healthy and stay active.
- Start your own "gourmet club": couples or just girlfriends. Pick a theme; plan healthy menus to match—perhaps with a small indulgence.
- If you use social media, tweet, text, or e-mail a healthy meal idea or recipe, a great value at a farmers' market, or an active play-day idea for your kids, grandkids, nieces, or nephews.

intake, frequent dieting, and a low vitamin C intake—can contribute to an iron deficiency and even to anemia.

With anemia, body cells cannot produce enough energy, resulting in fatigue, a lack of concentration, weakness, irritability, and more symptoms. Consuming an inadequate amount of iron is one cause of anemia. *See "Anemia: 'Tired Blood'" in chapter 25, page 722, for other causes and treatment.*

For women aged nineteen to fifty, the Recommended Dietary Allowance (RDA) for iron is 18 milligrams daily. During pregnancy, it increases to 27 milligrams daily. To compare, adult men need 8 milligrams of iron daily. With menopause, a woman's need for iron drops to that of men.

To ensure that you meet your daily needs, eat enough iron-rich foods. There are two types of dietary iron: heme iron and nonheme iron. Heme iron comes from animal-based foods such as meat and poultry; nonheme iron comes from eggs and plant-based foods such as greens, soy, beans and peas, and nuts, as well as fortified and enriched grain products. Heme iron is better absorbed by the body, but foods with either heme or nonheme iron are good sources.

Consuming foods with nonheme iron along with vitamin C–rich foods allows your body to absorb iron better. You might eat citrus fruit or strawberries with iron-enriched cereal or a scrambled egg, or red bell pepper strips with whole-wheat pasta. *See "Iron" in chapter 14, page 438.*

Consult your doctor to determine if an iron supplement would be appropriate for you. *See "A Closer Look . . . Calcium and Iron Supplements" in chapter 10, page 320, to learn the best way to take it.*

PMS: Reducing Discomfort

Do you experience the discomfort of premenstrual syndrome (PMS)? Women describe as many as two hundred symptoms ranging from physical (such as abdominal pain; acne; backaches; bloating; headaches; swelling of the feet, hands, and ankles; tender breasts; weight gain) and food cravings to psychological (such as anxiety, irritability, and insomnia).

PMS—a condition, not a disease—starts as early as fourteen days before a woman's period and stops when menstrual flow starts. Shifts in hormone levels are the likely cause. Because body water fluctuates during the menstrual cycle, the body may retain fluids prior to the onset of a woman's period that disappear soon after it's over.

PMS gets attention in women's media, yet there's little consensus on its causes or treatment, and little conclusive research on links between nutrition and its symptoms. Despite claims, no evidence links PMS and nutritional deficiencies. Here's what's known—and unknown—about managing PMS with your food decisions.

- *Calcium* may help reduce fluid retention and regulate mood-related brain chemicals, but research isn't conclusive. Regardless, there's good reason to boost your calcium intake anyway. Calcium is essential for lifelong bone health; most women don't get

- American College of Obstetricians and Gynecologists
  www.acog.org/patients
- Academy of Nutrition and Dietetics
  www.eatright.org/resources/for-women
- Women's Health: MedlinePlus
  medlineplus/womenshealth.html
- Office on Women's Health, US Department of Health and Human Services
  www.womenshealth.gov
- National Agricultural Library, US Department of Agriculture
  www.nutrition.gov/life-stages/women

enough. Sources of calcium include dairy foods, tofu made with calcium sulfate, soymilk, dark-green leafy vegetables, edamame and other beans and peas, salmon with edible bones, and some fortified cereals and juices. *See "Calcium" in chapter 14, page 425, for more about calcium and its food sources.*

- *Phytoestrogens* are weak, naturally occurring plant estrogens that may help relieve some PMS symptoms. Science hasn't yet determined how much could be enough, or the interaction between phytoestrogens and other hormones. Still, foods with phytoestrogens such as tofu, tempeh, soy beverages, and many other soy foods are worth enjoying for their potential health benefits.
- *Salt.* If you retain a lot of water (five pounds or more) before your period, try cutting down on salt for a week to ten days before your period commences. *See "Sodium" in chapter 14, page 431, for ways you might do that.* Research suggests that higher progesterone levels before a period cause the body to excrete sodium naturally. Do not limit fluid because water will help flush out some of the excess sodium in your body.

  Should your water retention be more significant or should it cause extreme discomfort, consider consulting with your doctor about whether or not a diuretic would be appropriate.
- *Dietary supplements?* Despite anecdotal claims, no conclusive research indicates that vitamin B_6, vitamin E, or magnesium alleviate PMS symptoms—and furthermore, megadoses of vitamin B_6—can cause nerve damage. Except for any psychological effect, large doses of other vitamins, herbals, or botanicals such as evening primrose oil don't alleviate the symptoms, either, and they also may be harmful. *See chapter 10, page 315, to learn about the risks, benefits, and recommendations for dietary supplements.*

Mirror, Mirror: Body Image and Women

Positive or negative, body image—weight and appearance—preoccupies many women, especially those of a younger age. Today's culture in America is biased towards being physically attractive, rather than what's much more important: who a woman really is. Media, family, peers, and others typically reinforce the value of a female ideal for a body that's unattainable for most, even unhealthy for many who try.

In truth, women come in many sizes and shapes. Being healthy in the body you have and recognizing that a positive self-image and good self-esteem shouldn't depend on your physical attributes are keys to your well-being. Trying to reach unrealistic goals about body weight can result in poor food choices and, perhaps more seriously, to an eating disorder, which can be dangerous. *See "Eating Disorders: More Than a Nutrition Issue," in chapter 25, page 752.*

Having a healthy relationship with food, physical activity, and your body are what matters. They can lead to overall health and better body image.

See chapter 22, page 625, to learn effective and healthy ways to reach and maintain your personal best weight.

Until more is known, general guidelines for good health may help you cope with PMS if it's a problem. Live a physically active lifestyle. Relax, and learn how to alleviate stress and cope with mood swings. Get plenty of rest, and limit caffeine six to eight hours before sleeping. Eat an overall healthy diet.

The American College of Obstetricians and Gynecologists (ACOG) suggests simple dietary changes for relief as long as you keep calorie intake within your calorie needs. Eat foods rich in complex carbohydrates and calcium; eat less fat, salt, and added sugars; and avoid caffeine and alcohol. Learn smart strategies to overcome any food cravings, especially if they lead to excess calorie intake; *see chapter 3, page 80, for guidance on planning healthy meals and snacks.*

Physical activity may help. A good workout stimulates the release of brain endorphins, which can help relieve PMS moodiness related to low endorphin levels common just before your period. Moreover, if you tend to eat more before your period or experience food cravings, exercise can help you keep your intake under control and your weight stable. And sweating may help reduce bloating if you retain fluid.

Consult your doctor if PMS symptoms incapacitate you. Before you attribute ongoing symptoms to PMS, talk to your doctor. Diabetes, pelvic infections, depression, and other health problems may be misperceived as simply PMS.

? Have you ever wondered?

. . . if you need extra vitamins if you use oral contraceptives? No. An overall eating plan that's varied and balanced can supply enough nutrients if you're on the pill. However, taking an oral contraceptive over a period of time may exacerbate symptoms of a nutrient deficiency. Vitamin B_6 deficiency may trigger mood-related side effects related to oral contraceptives; vitamin B_6—found in, meat, poultry, and fish, as well as whole grain, beans and peas and some fortified breakfast cereals—helps the body produce serotonin, which helps regulate mood and pain.

. . . if drinking cranberry juice helps protect you from urinary tract infections? Many women suffer from urinary tract infections sometime in their lives. Although urine is normally bacteria free, bacteria can travel from the rectum, across the skin surface, and into the bladder and cause infection. It appears that substances in cranberries and blueberries (same berry family) may help prevent certain infection-causing bacteria from sticking to the urinary tract wall. Studies are investigating the role of drinking cranberry juice in reducing urinary tract bacteria.

If you feel the symptoms—frequent and urgent need to urinate, painful urination, cloudy or bloody urine, or lower back or abdominal pain—seek advice for proper treatment from your doctor. Drink water.

. . . if food choices can reduce symptoms of fibromyalgia? A syndrome more common in women in their twenties and thirties than in men, fibromyalgia results in chronic pain in fibrous tissues, muscles, tendons, and other connective tissues. It also may cause sleeplessness and may have links to depressions, although this is unclear.

For those suffering from fibromyalgia, studies haven't shown specific foods to eat or avoid. Some sufferers, however, report being sensitive to certain foods or ingredients; even that varies from person to person. Keeping a journal to specifically record the foods eaten and any resulting symptoms may offer clues to triggers, as would eliminating them for a short while. Consider consulting a registered dietitian nutritionist.

Although there's no known cure, a healthy weight helps keep pain in check by putting less pressure on the muscles and tissues around joints. Also important, continue to follow healthy eating advice, be physically active, get enough rest, and relieve stress. Avoiding caffeine six to eight hours before you sleep may also help; *see "Drink Smart—and Get Your Zzzzs!" in chapter 4, page 97, for tips.* Some herbal supplements are touted for relief, but research isn't conclusive; some may be harmful.

. . . why an eating disorder or missed periods can affect bone health? Estrogen levels may drop from over-exercising, from eating so little that a significant—unhealthy—amount of weight is lost, or from disorders of the ovaries or the pituitary gland, which directs hormone production by the ovaries. Low estrogen levels can result in missed periods and can lower the body's ability to form new bone in the ongoing process of bone turnover. That, in turn, promotes bone loss. *See "Eating Disorders: More Than a Nutrition Issue," in chapter 25, page 732.*

HEALTH CONCERNS: A FOOD OR NUTRITION LINK?

Food decisions may help manage some health issues that are unique to women. That includes vaginal yeast infections, fibrocystic breast disease, and polycystic ovary syndrome.

Vaginal Yeast Infections

Do food choices either promote or prevent vaginal yeast infections, or *Candida vulvovaginitis*? *Candida* is a fungus that commonly lives in the mouth, intestinal tract, vagina, and other moist, warm, and dark body areas.

For teenage girls and women, *Candida* may cause several symptoms: vaginal itching, redness, or pain; a thick, white, "cottage cheese-like" vaginal discharge; discomfort during urination; and perhaps white or yellow skin patches around the vaginal area. Recent use of antibiotics; uncontrolled diabetes; pregnancy; high-estrogen contraceptives; immunodeficiency; thyroid or endocrine disorders such as diabetes; overweight; and corticosteroid therapy are among the risk factors linked to yeast infections.

Does eating yogurt with live cultures prevent it? Friendly bacteria, such as *Lactobacillus acidophilus* in yogurt, has been proposed to help keep yeast cells under control. However, most research doesn't support this benefit. Regardless, that same six-ounce carton of yogurt does supply 225 to 335 milligrams of calcium—important for bone health. *See "Prebiotics and Probiotics: A Bioactive Duo" in chapter 15, page 453.*

To refute a common myth, no scientific evidence shows that eating sugary foods contributes to yeast infections. Neither do processed foods, fruit, or milk. Avoiding these foods or taking certain dietary supplements or antifungal drugs doesn't appear to prevent it.

The best way to properly diagnosis and determine appropriate treatment is with help from your doctor. If you're prone to yeast infections,

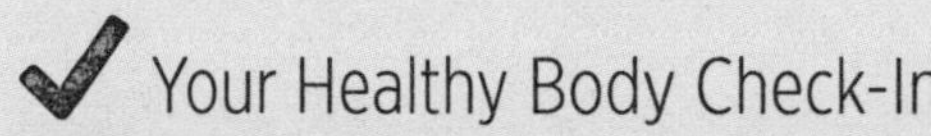

Your Healthy Body Check-In

Screening Tests for Women: Do You Keep Up?

Screening is key to promoting health and preventing disease. Many chronic health problems are linked to food choices or nutrition in one way or another, *as discussed throughout this book*. Use the chart below to find out which tests are appropriate for your age, then during your regular checkups, talk to your doctor about getting the ones you need. This chart is a general guideline; your doctor will personalize the timing of these tests for your needs. For the complete chart, which includes other important tests (including chlamydia, gonorrhea, HIV, and syphilis), visit www.womenshealth.gov/screening-tests-and-vaccines/screening-tests-for-women.

Take the opportunity at your regular checkups to ask about other health issues, too: overweight and obesity, alcohol use, and vaccines, such as for the flu, shingles, and pneumonia as you get older.

Screening Test	Ages 18–39	Ages 40–49	Ages 50–64	Ages 65 and Older
Blood pressure test	Get tested at least every 2 years if you have normal blood pressure (lower than 120/80).	Get tested at least every 2 years if you have normal blood pressure (lower than 120/80).	Get tested at least every 2 years if you have normal blood pressure (lower than 120/80).	Get tested at least every 2 years if you have normal blood pressure (lower than 120/80).
	Get tested once a year if you have blood pressure between 120/80 and 139/89.	Get tested once a year if you have blood pressure between 120/80 and 139/89.	Get tested once a year if you have blood pressure between 120/80 and 139/89.	Get tested once a year if you have blood pressure between 120/80 and 139/89.
	Discuss treatment with your doctor or nurse if you have blood pressure 140/90 or higher.	Discuss treatment with your doctor or nurse if you have blood pressure 140/90 or higher.	Discuss treatment with your doctor or nurse if you have blood pressure 140/90 or higher.	Discuss treatment with your doctor or nurse if you have blood pressure 140/90 or higher.
Bone mineral density test (osteoporosis screening)	N/A	N/A	Discuss with your doctor or nurse if you are at risk for osteoporosis.	Get this test at least once at age 65 or older. Talk to your doctor or nurse about repeat testing.
Breast cancer screening* (mammogram)	N/A	Discuss with your doctor or nurse.	Starting at age 50, get screened every 2 years.	Get screened every 2 years through age 74. Age 75 and older, ask your doctor or nurse if you need to be screened.
Cervical cancer screening (Pap test)	Get a Pap test every 3 years if you are 21 or older and have a cervix. If you are 30 or older, you can get a Pap test and HPV test together every 5 years.	Get a Pap test and HPV test together every 5 years if you have a cervix.	Get a Pap test and HPV test together every 5 years if you have a cervix.	Ask your doctor or nurse if you need to get a Pap test.

(continued)

Your Healthy Body Check-In *(continued)*

Screening Test	Ages 18–39	Ages 40–49	Ages 50–64	Ages 65 and Older
Cholesterol test	Starting at age 20, get a cholesterol test regularly if you are at increased risk for heart disease. Ask your doctor or nurse how often you need your cholesterol tested.	Get a cholesterol test regularly if you are at increased risk for heart disease. Ask your doctor or nurse how often you need your cholesterol tested.	Get a cholesterol test regularly if you are at increased risk for heart disease. Ask your doctor or nurse how often you need your cholesterol tested.	Get a cholesterol test regularly if you are at increased risk for heart disease. Ask your doctor or nurse how often you need your cholesterol tested.
Colorectal cancer screening† (using fecal occult blood testing, sigmoidoscopy, or colonoscopy)	N/A	N/A	Starting at age 50, get screened for colorectal cancer. Talk to your doctor or nurse about which screening test is best for you and how often you need it.	Get screened for colorectal cancer through age 75. Talk to your doctor or nurse about which screening test is best for you and how often you need it.
Diabetes screening	Get screened for diabetes if your blood pressure is higher than 135/80 or if you take medicine for high blood pressure.	Get screened for diabetes if your blood pressure is higher than 135/80 or if you take medicine for high blood pressure.	Get screened for diabetes if your blood pressure is higher than 135/80 or if you take medicine for high blood pressure.	Get screened for diabetes if your blood pressure is higher than 135/80 or if you take medicine for high blood pressure.

N/A is no advice.

*The American Cancer Society recommends the following for women at average risk of breast cancer. At age forty years, talk with your doctor about when to begin screening; you have the opportunity to start screening if you choose. At age forty-five years begin to have yearly mammograms. At age fifty-five years, transition to mammograms every other year or continue with annual mammography, depending on your preferences. Continue to have regular mammograms for as long as you're in good health. (2016).

†Guidelines from the American Cancer Society are more specific.

Source: Office on Women's Health, US Department of Health and Human Services, www.womenshealth.gov/. Accessed December 1, 2016.

lower your risk by maintaining good hygiene, avoiding vaginal sprays and douches since they may change the normal balance of healthy bacteria in the vagina, wearing cotton undergarments that don't hold in moisture and heat, and changing out of a wet bathing suit immediately after swimming.

Fibrocystic Breast Disease

Between 10 and 20 percent of women experience fibrocystic breast disease (FBD), characterized by benign (noncancerous), but often painful, breast lumps. Despite anecdotal claims, no carefully controlled research evidence links noncancerous breast lumps to caffeine intake. In fact, both the National Cancer Institute and the American Medical Association's (AMA's) Council on Scientific Affairs report that FBD isn't associated with caffeine intake. To clarify, the use of vitamin E as a treatment is controversial, although it's not harmful.

Because FBD is linked to hormone levels, it usually subsides with menopause—unless a woman receives hormone replacement therapy.

As a safety check for breast health, examine your breasts carefully each month. Women in their twenties and thirties should have a clinical breast exam as part of their regular health exam by doctor, preferably every three years. *Also see "Your Healthy Body Check-In: Screening Tests for Women: Do You Keep Up?" above.* And consult your doctor immediately about any breast lumps.

Polycystic Ovary Syndrome

Polycystic ovary syndrome (PCOS) is an often undiagnosed hormonal problem with a cluster of symptoms, which may include obesity, ovarian cysts, irregular menstrual cycles, acne, excess facial hair, infertility, and male pattern hair thinning. PCOS also increases other health risks: type 2 diabetes, heart disease, high blood pressure, and uterine and breast cancers.

Although the causes of PCOS aren't known, it's a lifelong problem that may run in families and begin in adolescence. Insulin resistance (which affects the way the body uses blood glucose), obesity, and having a high level of male hormones such as testosterone may explain some symptoms. PCOS isn't easy to diagnose; however, blood tests for hormone levels and ultrasound exams for ovarian cysts reveal clues.

Because of the short- and long-term health implications, talk to your doctor if you suspect PCOS. Some women with PCOS show no signs. Treatment may include weight loss, hormone therapy, and regular physical activity. Some women also need treatment for diabetes or high blood pressure.

An individualized eating plan with whole grains, vegetables, fruits, fish, and beans and peas, as well as dairy foods that are low fat or fat free, may help with weight management since they reduce total calorie intake. For an eating plan that's right for you, consult a registered dietitian nutritionist.

FERTILITY: GOOD HEALTH MATTERS

Healthy eating not only prepares your body for pregnancy, but also can affect fertility in ways that aren't yet clear. If you're trying to get pregnant:

- Aim for your healthy weight. Either extreme underweight or extreme overweight may affect your menstrual cycle and ovulation and so reduce fertility. How? The body produces estrogen in the ovaries and in fat cells. If very thin, the body won't produce as much estrogen in fat cells. With obesity, the body's fat cells produce too much. Either condition throws off the delicate hormonal balance that promotes fertility.
- Exercise caution with dietary supplements touted to enhance fertility. Not enough is known about the risks of extra vitamins, minerals, or herbals and how they might affect the unborn baby.
- Limit alcoholic beverages. Drinking excessively is linked to ovulation disorders.
- If you smoke, quit. Even secondhand smoke can affect your fertility and the outcome of pregnancy—and your secondhand smoke can also affect male fertility.
- Relax; manage stress.

Fertility is a couple's issue. One-third of infertility cases are related to the male partner. For men, overall healthy eating and lifestyle choices have a positive effect on fertility and sperm count. Among the advice for men to promote conception: follow healthy eating guidelines, maintain a healthy weight, stay physically active without over-exercising, avoid steroids or artificial testosterone, limit alcoholic beverages, and avoid smoking. *See "Fertility: A Man's Health Counts" in chapter 19, page 567, for more advice.* For fertility, both hopeful parents benefit from healthy eating and active living.

Get advice from your doctor if you have concerns about fertility. If you're having difficulty getting pregnant, explore the reasons and seek a sound approach to addressing infertility with your doctor. You'll also rule out any health problems that you or your spouse may have. *See "Polycystic Ovary Syndrome" in this chapter, page 538, for its effects on fertility.*

PRENATAL NUTRITION: PREPARING FOR PREGNANCY

Thinking about pregnancy? Be fit and ready! Inventory your health and nutrition habits now. Initiating good health and nutrition habits before pregnancy—or simply nudging healthy eating and active living back into your lifestyle—promotes your health and normal weight, as well as establishes the healthy environment your baby needs to develop normally during pregnancy. Your baby develops rapidly during the first weeks of pregnancy, perhaps before you even know you're expecting.

Preparing for pregnancy or not, advice for all healthy women is the same: Get enough of the forty or so nutrients essential for your good health—and your baby's health, too. That includes iron, which is essential for the brain growth of the fetus. *See chapter 2, page 21, as your "before, during, and after" pregnancy guide for healthy eating.*

Healthy Prepregnancy Weight

Reaching a healthy weight in a healthy way before conceiving is important—and not just for you! A healthy weight—before and during pregnancy and between pregnancies—reduces obstetric risks. It also increases your chances of a normal infant birth weight and lowers the risk of obesity for you and your offspring later in life.

Especially for overweight and obese women, preconception counseling on nutrition and physical activity is important, along with access to contraception, to allow time to reach a healthy weight before conceiving. *See "Healthy Weight Matters: Every Age and Stage of a Woman's Life" in this chapter, page 540, and chapter 22, page 625, which addresses reaching and maintaining a healthy weight.*

If you have had bariatric surgery, talk with your doctor and a registered dietitian nutritionist prior to pregnancy to ensure you get adequate nutrition to support your health and a healthy pregnancy.

If You Have Diabetes or Prediabetes

You can have a healthy baby if you have diabetes or prediabetes–just manage it properly. Work with your doctor to learn how to get your blood glucose level under control before you get pregnant and during pregnancy. You might need to adjust your medication for diabetes and delay pregnancy.

Uncontrolled diabetes, starting in the first few weeks of pregnancy, increases the chances of miscarriage, premature delivery, stillbirth, or having a baby with a serious birth defect. *See "Diabetes and Pregnancy" in this chapter, page 551.*

Folic Acid: Prevent Birth Defects

To prepare for pregnancy, all nutrients are essential. One merits special consideration: folate, or folic acid (a B vitamin). Folic acid is the form of folate in fortified foods and supplements. Not only is it essential to good health, your body needs folate to manufacture new cells and genetic

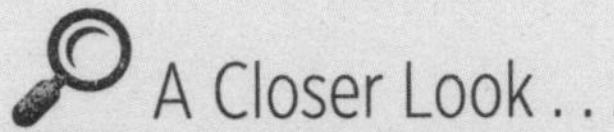

Healthy Weight Matters: Every Age and Stage of a Woman's Life

FOR SCHOOL-AGE GIRLS

A healthy weight during childhood offers protection for the long term: protects against adult obesity, overweight, and type 2 diabetes, and helps maintain healthy levels of blood cholesterol and triglycerides. During the growing-up years, a healthy weight boosts self-esteem, important for emotional, mental, and social development. Overweight increases the chance of early puberty. A healthy weight now helps ensure a healthy weight by the time young women become pregnant for the first time.

FOR TEENS AND YOUNG-ADULT WOMEN

As for school-age girls, a healthy weight during the teen and young adult years reduces the chances of adult obesity later and helps ensure a healthy pregnancy and nursing. Beyond that, maintaining a healthy weight promotes physical health in other ways. It lowers the risk for high blood cholesterol levels, type 2 diabetes, and high blood pressure, as well as arthritis in later life; and perhaps promotes easier breast cancer detection. On the flip side, a healthy weight—not underweight—helps teens and young women develop and maintain strong bones for peak bone mass. For emotional health, a healthy weight feels good and boosts self-esteem.

FOR WOMEN IN THEIR CHILDBEARING YEARS

The benefits of a healthy weight mirror those of the teen and young-adult years. In addition, a healthy weight promotes fertility and helps reduce the risk for gallbladder disease. For babies of women who are overweight, there's increased risk of congenital abnormalities and macrosomia (when the fetus grows very large), with possible birth injury.

FOR PREGNANT AND BREASTFEEDING WOMEN

Most important, healthy weight gain (not dieting) helps ensure a healthy pregnancy. It promotes normal fetal development and improves the chances of a healthy, full-term birth. When maternal weight is healthy, childbirth is easier and safer. Obesity increases the risk for high blood pressure, gestational diabetes, caesarean section, premature delivery, birth defects, and stillbirth. Maternal overweight and obesity may also affect a child's health in other ways, including increased risk of obesity during childhood and later in life. During breastfeeding, a healthy weight helps maintain the quality and volume of breast milk. For all these reasons, gradually returning to a healthy weight after delivery (postpartum) and between pregnancies is important.

FOR WOMEN AFTER MENOPAUSE

As earlier in life, a healthy weight protects against some health problems, including breast cancer, some other cancers, heart disease, and type 2 diabetes. That includes preventing risky abdominal weight gain as weight shifts after menopause.

FOR OLDER WOMEN

A healthy weight continues to protect against some cancers, heart disease, and type 2 diabetes. A healthy weight—not underweight—helps bones remain strong, cushions bones and organs from fracture and other injury (in case of a fall), and protects against wasting related to serious illness.

See chapter 22, page 625, to learn more about reaching and maintaining a healthy weight.

material. Soon after conception, folate helps develop the neural tube, which becomes your baby's spinal cord and brain.

Women who consume enough folate, particularly in the weeks prior to conception and during the first three months of pregnancy, may reduce the risk of neural tube defects, which occur when the neural tube does not close completely. As many as 75 percent of serious birth defects in the spine and neural tube (spina bifida) and brain (anencephaly) might be prevented if women consumed enough folic acid at this critical time.

The Recommended Dietary Allowance (RDA) for folate increases significantly with pregnancy. The RDA for nonpregnant women and teenage girls is 400 micrograms daily. During pregnancy it increases to 600 milligrams daily and while breastfeeding, 500 milligrams daily.

Since 1998, when it became law for many refined-grain products to be fortified with folic acid, the incidence of these types of birth defects has gone down significantly.

Folate from food. To consume enough:

- Eat a variety of foods with naturally occurring folate—for example, beans and peas, citrus fruits and juices, dark-green leafy vegetables, liver, and nuts.
- Read food labels to identify and choose foods fortified with folic acid—for example, most foods made with refined grains, such as breads, cornmeal, crackers, farina, flour, pasta, and rice. If folic acid is added to breakfast cereals, it's listed on the Nutrition Facts label.

For fortified foods, the package label may carry a health claim—that adequate folate intake may decrease the risk for neural tube defects.

- If you're limiting grain foods to cut calories or eat gluten free, eat other good sources of folate, such as folic acid–fortified foods.
- Know that whole-grain products, such as brown rice, may not be folic acid fortified. If most of your grains are whole grains, your choices may not provide much folate.

Folate from supplements. Even a varied, well-balanced eating plan may not supply enough folate to protect against birth defects. Nutrition experts advise that all nonpregnant women of childbearing age consume 400 micrograms of folic acid daily from fortified foods, vitamin supplements, or a combination, in addition to the folate naturally found in foods.

Consult your doctor or a registered dietitian nutritionist about appropriate levels of supplements with folic acid. Taking too much folate (more than 1,000 micrograms a day) can hide the symptoms of pernicious anemia, which can cause nerve damage. (Pernicious anemia may result from a vitamin B_{12} deficiency.) Taking large doses from vitamin pills, not food sources, is the usual reason why symptoms may go undetected.

Even if pregnant women do consume enough folate, obesity increases the chance of neural tube defects. *See "Folate (Folic Acid or Folacin)" in chapter 14, page 419.*

More Prepregnancy Advice

- Consume enough iron-rich foods. If you're iron deficient before pregnancy, it's harder to make it up during pregnancy. *See "Iron" in chapter 14, page 438.*
- Refrain from practices that may harm your developing baby: smoking, drinking alcoholic beverages, and inappropriate drug use. Important stages in your baby's development start right after conception. Before you know you're pregnant, potentially harmful substances may have effects.
- Discuss over-the-counter and prescription medications you take with your doctor. They may be harmful to your unborn baby.
- Stay physically active, or initiate moderate physical activity in your daily life. That will help prepare you to be "fit" and at your healthy weight for pregnancy.
- Handle food safely! During pregnancy, your immune system is weakened and your growing baby's immunity isn't well developed. Pregnant women are especially susceptible to three foodborne risks: listeriosis, methylmercury poisoning, and toxoplasmosis. *See "Food Safety Precautions" in this chapter, page 557, and "Bacteria: Hard Hitters" in chapter 7, page 220.*

You're Expecting!

Being a nurturing parent begins even before delivery. Although you can't change your age or genetic traits, there's plenty you can do during the nine months of pregnancy to ensure your well-being and that of your unborn baby: eat wisely, maintain a healthy pregnancy weight, stay physically active, and get plenty of rest.

More advice: See your doctor regularly, stop smoking (if that's a habit), and avoid alcoholic drinks and recreational drugs. The likely outcome is fewer complications during pregnancy, labor, and delivery, and a healthier baby—and perhaps another successful pregnancy in the future. Your food and lifestyle choices during pregnancy also influence your baby's long-term health and mental development.

PREGNANCY WEIGHT

"How much weight should I gain?" That's one of the top questions expectant mothers ask. In the last twenty-six weeks of pregnancy, your baby will grow fast, gaining about one ounce every day. Besides "baby weight," weight gain supports changes in your body and helps prepare you for breastfeeding. Appropriate weight gain helps ensure a healthy outcome.

If you don't gain enough, your chance for delivering a low-birth weight infant goes up. Babies who weigh less than five and a half pounds at birth are at greater risk for developmental difficulties and health problems.

Excess Weight Gain

Forget this myth: "The more weight I gain, the healthier and stronger my baby will be." Excessive weight gain during pregnancy can be risky and may trigger more discomfort such as backaches, hemorrhoids, and leg cramps. Both delivery and returning to a prepregnancy weight may be harder with too much weight gain.

As research reveals, health professionals share these concerns for the health of both mother and baby.

- For mom, gaining too much weight during pregnancy increases the risk of obesity later on because excess weight gained often isn't lost.
- Excess weight gain also can lead to back and joint problems, gestational diabetes, a complicated labor and delivery (including a baby being born too large, which can result in birth injury) or a cesarean section, and difficulty with breastfeeding.
- Overweight during pregnancy increases the chance of developing insulin resistance, high blood glucose, high blood pressure, and type 2 diabetes later in life. It also increases risks related to surgery and anesthesia. *See chapter 24, page 680, which addresses all these health concerns.*
- Babies born to overweight mothers tend to be heavier at and after birth and are at greater risk for overweight or obesity in childhood and for developing type 2 diabetes, high blood pressure, or heart disease later in life.

If you were dieting for weight loss before pregnancy, put that regimen aside for these nine months. Pregnancy is not a good time to skimp on calories, follow a weight-loss diet, or restrict weight gain. A doctor may advise modest weight loss during pregnancy

Pregnancy: How Much Weight Gain?

Talk to your doctor about the right weight gain for your pregnancy. Given for different pre-pregnancy BMI categories, these recommendations can help keep you from gaining too much weight and from adding to the burden of health problems that put you and your baby at risk.

You can also use this calculator along with your doctor's guidance: www.calculator.net/pregnancy-weight-gain-calculator.html. Or track your weight gain (and belly photos) with the free CineMama app from the March of Dimes.

BMI Before Pregnancy	Pregnant with One Baby		Pregnant with Twins
	Total Weight Gain (pounds)	**Weight Gain* per Week (pounds)** During 2nd and 3rd Trimester	**Total Weight Gain (pounds)**
Underweight (BMI <18.5)	28–40	1–1.3	(Insufficient data for guidelines)
Normal weight (BMI 18.5–24.9)	25–35	0.8–1	37–54
Overweight (BMI 25.0–29.9)	15–25	0.5–0.7	31–50
Obese (BMI ≥30.0)	11–20	0.4–0.6	25–42

*Calculations assume a 1.1 to 4.4 pound weight gain in the first trimester.

Adapted from source: Institute of Medicine, 2009.

Where Does Weight Gain Go?

Your baby may weigh about seven to eight pounds at birth—but you'll gain more than that. Why? Many parts of your body support pregnancy. Your blood volume expands by about 50 percent. Your breasts increase in size. Your body stores fat to sustain the baby's rapid growth and to provide energy for labor, delivery, and breastfeeding.

	Average Weight Gain
Baby	7½ pounds
Placenta	1½ pounds
Amniotic fluid (water around the baby)	2 pounds
Mother	
Breast growth	2 pounds
Uterus growth	2 pounds
Maternal stores (body's protein and fat)	7 pounds
Increased blood volume	4 pounds
Body fluids	4 pounds

Source: American College of Obstetricians and Gynecologists, 2010.

for a woman with a BMI of 40 or higher, but that should only happen under a doctor's care.

If you have had bariatric surgery, talk with your doctor and a registered dietitian nutritionist throughout your pregnancy to ensure you get adequate nutrition to support your health and a healthy pregnancy.

Weight Gain: What's Right for You

How much should you expect to gain during pregnancy? It's not necessarily the same as the weight gain advised for your mother or sister. Because every woman is unique, your doctor will advise a weight-gain range that's right for you. That depends on:

- *Your weight before pregnancy.* For a healthy pregnancy outcome, the Institute of Medicine provides general guidelines for weight gain based on prepregnancy BMI. For teens, adult BMIs should be used; the CDC growth charts in the *appendix, page 777,* may underestimate growth gain.

  See "Pregnancy: How Much Weight Gain?" in this chapter, page 542. Your doctor can help calculate your body mass index (BMI). *See "Body Mass Index" in chapter 22, page 627, for more about BMI and a link to an online BMI calculator.*

- *Your age.* Young, normal-weight teens (until age eighteen) may need to gain at the higher end of the weight-gain range. Teens are at greater risk for delivering low–birth weight babies. Pregnancy puts greater demands on their own growing, developing bodies.

- Academy of Nutrition and Dietetics
  www.eatright.org/resources/health/pregnancy
- Pregnancy Weight Gain Calculator
  www.choosemyplate.gov/pregnancy-weight-gain-calculator
- March of Dimes
  www.marchofdimes.org/pregnancy.aspx
- US Department of Health and Human Services
  www.womenshealth.gov/pregnancy

See "For Pregnancy during Adolescence" in this chapter, page 548, for more about their prenatal needs.

- *Expecting multiples? See "Pregnancy: How Much Weight Gain?" in this chapter, page 542, for recommendations for twins.*

Weight Gain: Slow and Steady

Your rate of weight gain during pregnancy is as important as the amount. Expect two to four pounds of weight gain during your first three months as an adult; for teens, expect four to six pounds. (More than that is likely body fat with no added benefit to mother or baby.) After your first trimester, you'll probably gain somewhat faster. From month to month, you may gain a little more or a little less.

If your doctor advises you to cut calories—without depriving yourself or your baby of nutrients—consider these tips:

- Substitute lower-fat or fat-free milk, yogurt, and cheese for whole-milk products. And choose lean meat, poultry, and fish.
- Broil, bake, grill, or stir-fry foods instead of frying them.
- Eat smaller portions. *See "Portions: Be Size Wise!" in chapter 3, page 78, for tips.*
- Cut down on foods that are high in fats, added sugars, and calories but are low in nutrients, such as candy, cake, pastries, and rich desserts. Eat more nutrient-rich foods such as vegetables and fruits instead.
- Increase your physical activity within your doctor's guidelines. *See "Pregnancy and Breastfeeding: Food and Sports" in chapter 21, page 613, if you're an athlete.*

See chapters 2 and 3, pages 21 and 60, for advice on healthy eating and "Weight Management: Strategies that Work" in chapter 22, page 637, for tips on managing calories.

NUTRIENTS AND CALORIES: FOR YOU AND BABY

During pregnancy, your need for most nutrients and calories goes up somewhat. Eating the right amounts from a variety of nutrient-dense foods is the best way to get what you need. An inadequate diet may impair your baby's development, and he or she may be underweight at birth.

For an eating plan that's right for your individual pregnancy, *see chapter 2, page 21, for more about healthy eating plans.* Unless you're overweight or obese, you probably need a food plan with 2,200 to 2,900 calories a day, depending on your level of physical activity.

Caution: If you've been pregnant recently or if you've breastfed within the past year, your body's nutritional reserves may be low. Problems during a previous pregnancy are another reason to make an effort to eat wisely for a healthy pregnancy. Always consult their doctor or a registered dietitian nutritionist to determine what's best for you during pregnancy.

See "Dietary Reference Intakes" in the appendix, page 780, for specific nutrient recommendations during pregnancy. If you're vegetarian, see "The Vegetarian Mom" in this chapter, page 546.

Fuel for Your Pregnancy

Did you know that, for a single birth, it takes about 75,000 calories for a healthy pregnancy (for the fetus and changes in the mother's body)? Your baby needs a constant supply of energy—every single minute for about 280 days! To do this, your body also needs an adequate energy supply. Otherwise, your body uses protein for energy instead of cell building.

How much? Eating for two (or more!) doesn't mean your calorie needs double. In fact, it's not that different from eating for one. After all, your growing baby needs far fewer calories for health than you do.

During the first trimester, energy (calorie) needs for most pregnant women are the same as before pregnancy. However, the Dietary Reference Intakes (DRIs) advise an additional 340 calories daily during the second trimester and 452 calories more during the third trimester for a pregnancy with a single fetus. Carrying more than one baby increases calorie needs.

How many calories for you? That's an individual matter that will depend on your prepregnancy BMI, rate of weight gain, age, physical activity level, and appetite. If you're overweight or obese prior to

Use this interactive tool to create a healthy eating plan to follow prior to and throughout your pregnancy.

- Center for Nutrition and Public Policy, USDA, Pregnancy and Breastfeeding: Health and Nutrition Information
  www.ChooseMyPlate.gov/moms-pregnancy-breastfeeding

pregnancy, you may be advised to consume somewhat fewer calories. If you're underweight before pregnancy, the advice may be to consume more calories. Consult with your doctor and a registered dietitian nutritionist for recommendations that are right for you.

What foods? Just a few more nutrient-rich food foods can supply the relatively small increase in calories needed for pregnancy. Nutrient-rich foods provide a healthy dose of nutrients, too. Beyond that, your food choices during pregnancy also may help to shape your baby's food preferences—even before he or she tastes solid food. The first taste may come from flavors that transfer through amniotic fluid.

A nutrient-rich snack, such as low-fat yogurt or fruit, during the day might be your best strategy for getting those extra calories or nutrients. If sugary sodas have been your snack drink, switch to low-fat or fat-free milk. How might 340 additional calories translate to "real food"—either as a snack or extra at meals? Here are three examples:

- One ounce of cold cereal, one banana, and one cup of fat-free milk
- One baked potato with skin, topped with one-half cup each of broccoli and cauliflower, and one ounce of low-fat cheese
- Three-quarters cup of cut-up fruit, one six-ounce low-fat yogurt, and one (three-and-a-half-inch) oatmeal cookie

See chapter 2, page 21, for more guidelines on healthy eating.

Carbs for Energy

Most of your calories, or food energy, should come from nutrient-dense carbohydrate foods. How much? The RDA is 175 grams of carbohydrates daily, which is the minimum glucose for both mother and baby. That's 700 calories a day. For overall nourishment during pregnancy, you need more; the Acceptable Macronutrient Distribution Range (AMDR) is 45 to 65 percent of total calories from carbohydrates. That's, on average, about 300 grams daily, or about 1,200 calories daily from carbs. Let carbohydrates come from nutrient-rich grain products (including whole grains), vegetables, fruits, and beans and peas. *See chapter 11, page 345, for more about carbohydrates.*

Baby-Building Protein

The structural components of body cells—your baby's and yours—are mostly protein. Changes in your own body, particularly the placenta, also require protein. An eating plan that follows advice for the USDA Food Patterns, *discussed in chapter 2, page 21*, provides enough protein for a healthy pregnancy.

Pregnancy requires somewhat more protein. The RDA is 71 grams of protein daily during pregnancy compared with 46 grams before pregnancy. To put the extra in perspective, a three-ounce meat patty has about 20 grams of protein, and eight ounces of milk have about 8 grams of protein. The RDA is really a minimum recommendation. The AMDR allows a higher percent of total calories from protein. Your doctor or a registered dietitian nutritionist can advise how much. *See chapter 12, page 373, for more about protein.*

? Have you ever wondered?

. . . if nonnutritive sweeteners are safe to consume during pregnancy? Current research shows no reason to avoid foods and beverages with nonnutritive sweeteners, such as acesulfame potassium, aspartame, neotame, saccharin, stevia, sucralose, or tagatose.

Exception: Women with the rare genetic disorder called phenylketonuria (PKU) should avoid foods sweetened with aspartame starting even before pregnancy. Women with PKU cannot break down phenylalanine, which is an amino acid in aspartame. When that happens, phenylalanine can reach high levels in the mother's blood and may affect the developing baby. Studies show that women with the PKU gene, but not the disease, metabolize aspartame well enough to protect their unborn baby from abnormal phenylalanine levels. If you have PKU or carry the gene, talk to your doctor.

Nonnutritive sweeteners in moderation can be useful to pregnant women with diabetes or to pregnant women who enjoy sweet flavors without adding calories. Instead of calorie-free soft drinks and candies, more nutritious foods and beverages may be better choices. Drink low-fat milk, juice, and water. *See "Nonnutritive Sweeteners: Flavor without Calories" in chapter 11, page 369, for more about low-calorie sweeteners and about aspartame and PKU.*

Dietary Fat—and Some Essentials

The advised percentage of calories from fat doesn't change during pregnancy. So follow the advice *in "Fats: The Right Amount for You" in chapter 13, page 394*. Still limit saturated fats and *trans* fats, and switch to sources of healthy oils.

For your baby's central nervous system, you need enough essential fatty acids. The Institute of Medicine advises an Adequate Intake (AI) of 13 grams of omega-6 fatty acids and 1.4 grams of omega-3s daily during pregnancy.

DHA and EPA (forms of omega-3s) are especially important for your baby's brain and eye development and function. That's why you're advised to consume two to three servings (at least eight and up to twelve ounces) of a variety of fish per week while you're pregnant, including oily fish that are high in omega-3s yet lower in methylmercury. Other nutrients in fish also offer a positive impact on health.

See "Foodborne Illness and Pregnancy" in this chapter, page 551, for types of fish to avoid for safety reasons. See "Fats: Not Created Equal" chapter 13, page 385, for more about these essential fatty acids.

Vital Vitamins

If carbohydrates are the fuel of human life, vitamins are sparks that make body processes happen. Although all vitamins are important during pregnancy, some need special attention, including those important for cell division and the formation of new life. Those vitamins that may need special attention are addressed here.

A varied and balanced approach to eating is the best way to get the vitamins you and your unborn baby need. Your doctor may prescribe a prenatal vitamin/mineral supplement, too. *See "Dietary Supplements: More Than Vitamin Pills" in chapter 10, page 316.*

Vitamin A. Vitamin A promotes the growth and health of cells and tissues throughout the body—yours and your baby's. Your everyday food choices can provide enough vitamin A for pregnancy.

Vitamin A supplements are not advised—retinyl acetate or retinyl palmitate (preformed vitamin A), beta-carotene (provitamin A), or a combination. Too much vitamin A from supplements—3,000 micrograms (2,800 micrograms for teens), or 10,000 IU (9,000 IU for teens) of preformed vitamin A daily—during pregnancy can increase the risk of birth defects.

Only with your doctor's advice should you take low levels of vitamin A in a supplement. Read the Supplement Facts on product labels, and choose one with no more than 100 percent of the Daily Value (DV) for vitamin A. Eating plenty of vegetables and fruits high in beta-carotene isn't a problem. Beta-carotene does not convert to vitamin A when blood levels of vitamin A are normal.

See "Vitamin A (and Provitamin A Carotenoids)" in chapter 14, page 410, for more about its role and sources.

Folate and other B vitamins. By consuming an extra 340 to 452 calories a day in your second and third trimester, you'll consume enough extra of most B vitamins (except for folate). During pregnancy, you need more thiamin, riboflavin, and niacin in order to use the extra energy from food. And you need more vitamin B_6 to help protein make new body cells, and somewhat more vitamin B_{12}, which helps nervous system development.

Folate takes special attention. Consuming enough during the first three months is especially critical for lowering a newborn's risk for defects of the neural tube, or brain and spinal cord. The RDA increases from 400 micrograms daily before pregnancy to 600 micrograms daily during pregnancy.

Get 400 micrograms daily of folate from fortified foods and/or supplements and the remaining 200 micrograms daily from foods with naturally occurring folate. For women who have had a child with a neural tube defect or who are taking certain drugs, a doctor may advise more. *See "Prenatal Nutrition: Preparing for Pregnancy" in this chapter, page 539, for more about folate needs prior to and during pregnancy.*

Caution: Pregnant women and teens who avoid products with wheat, perhaps to eat gluten free or low carb, or who eat only whole-wheat products may get shortchanged on folic acid. If you need to eat gluten free, talk to your doctor about a folic acid supplement and other food sources of folate, even before pregnancy.

Vitamin B_{12} is found naturally in foods of animal origin such as milk, cheese, eggs, meat, poultry, and fish. Pregnant women who consume little or no animal-based foods need a reliable source such as vitamin B_{12}–fortified cereal or a supplement. The Adequate Intake for vitamin B_{12} during pregnancy increases somewhat from 2.4 micrograms daily before pregnancy, to 2.6 micrograms per day.

Choline. The recommendation for choline, a vitamin-like substance that's often grouped with B vitamins, is needed for normal cell functioning. The need goes up during pregnancy and breastfeeding, yet many women don't consume enough. Although not fully understood, it appears that choline is important for an infant's development. It works with folic acid during pregnancy to develop the brain and nervous system. Egg yolks are an excellent source; milk, meat, poultry, and nuts provide it, too. *See "Choline" in chapter 14, page 422, to learn more about its roles and sources.* Infant formulas often contain choline.

Vitamin C. The need for vitamin C goes up a bit, but keep in mind that ¾ cup of 100 percent orange juice supplies enough for a day. Besides its other functions, vitamin C helps your body absorb iron from plant sources of food, which is important because your iron needs increase by about 50 percent during pregnancy. *See "Vitamin C (Ascorbic Acid)" in chapter 14, page 422.*

Vitamin D. Consuming enough vitamin D is important to help your body absorb the calcium needed for pregnancy. It's a nutrient that often comes up short in the diets of many women because they don't drink enough

Have you ever wondered?

. . . if you need a nutrient supplement during pregnancy? Check with your doctor or a registered dietitian nutritionist. A balanced diet with a variety of foods during pregnancy can provide healthy women with enough of most nutrients that are needed. A prenatal multivitamin/mineral supplement is often recommended to help ensure that you get enough iron, folic acid, and other nutrients.

A supplement is advised during pregnancy if you have iron-deficiency anemia, follow a poor-quality diet, or eat little or no foods from animal sources. When pregnant with multiples (such as twins), you may also need a multivitamin/mineral supplement. Talk to your doctor.

See "Nutrient Supplements" in chapter 10, page 316, for more information.

The Vegetarian Mom

Can a vegetarian eating plan promote a healthy pregnancy? What about breastfeeding? Yes, if you plan your food choices carefully.

A lacto-ovo-, lacto-, or strict (vegan) vegetarian eating plan can supply most of the nutrients and the food energy needed to support the increased needs of both mother and baby. Those more likely to come up short are iron, vitamins D and E, and choline. Adjusting for pregnancy and breastfeeding is easier if you've already mastered vegetarian eating skills. If, however, you decide to become a vegetarian during pregnancy, first consult a registered dietitian nutritionist.

For a vegetarian approach to eating during pregnancy or breastfeeding, follow the nutrition advice for all pregnant women and teens—*and for more about the nutrients noted below (their recommendations, roles, and sources), check elsewhere in this book*. Keep this additional advice in mind if you're a vegetarian mom:

- *Weight gain.* Keep tabs on your weight gain during pregnancy. Research shows that babies born to vegetarian moms are similar in birth weight to babies born to nonvegetarian moms—as long as the mother is well nourished during pregnancy.

  Caution: If a vegetarian eating plan doesn't provide enough calories during pregnancy, you may not gain enough weight to sustain normal fetal development, which may result in a low–birth weight baby. If your calorie intake is too low while nursing, your body may not produce enough breast milk.

- *Protein.* Get enough high-quality protein. Eggs and dairy foods can provide enough protein for lacto-ovo-vegetarians. With proper planning, vegans who consume plenty of grain products, beans and peas, nuts, and seeds can get enough high-quality protein, too, if they eat a variety of food, *as discussed in chapter 2, page 21.*

- *Omega-3s.* If you're a vegan or avoid fish, consume enough essential fatty acids from sources of alpha-linolenic acid (ALA), an essential omega-3 fatty acid that your body can convert to DHA and EPA, although somewhat inefficiently. And choose a vegetarian source of DHA, perhaps in fortified foods.

  Only small amounts of ALA—in foods such as canola oil, flaxseed, ground flaxseed, soy oils, and walnuts—convert to DHA. That's why your doctor may advise a supplement with DHA. During pregnancy and breastfeeding, consuming enough essential fatty acids is not only healthy for mom, but is important for your baby's brain and visual development.

- *Folate.* Get enough folate prior to and during pregnancy to avoid neural tube (spinal cord) defects in the fetus. A vegetarian diet may provide enough folate since many plant-based foods are good sources: dark-green leafy vegetables, beans and peas, some fruits, wheat germ, and grain products fortified with folic acid. Be aware that whole-grain foods may not be folic acid–fortified. As for women who aren't vegetarians, a folic acid supplement and/or folic acid–fortified foods is advised during and perhaps prior to pregnancy.

- *Vitamin B_{12}.* Consume foods that supply a reliable vitamin B_{12} source—perhaps fortified breakfast cereals—or a vitamin B_{12} supplement, especially if you're a vegan. Vitamin B_{12} is found naturally only in foods of animal origin.

  Pregnancy requires more vitamin B_{12} for your developing baby and your own increased blood supply. Without enough vitamin B_{12} during pregnancy and breastfeeding, and even before pregnancy, your baby is put at greater risk for anemia and nerve damage.

- *Vitamin D.* Consume enough vitamin D. Among other reasons, you need it to help absorb calcium. Milk fortified with vitamin D is great for lacto-ovo-vegetarians. Vegans likely need a vitamin D supplement, especially if exposure to sunlight is limited. Other sources: foods fortified with vitamin D such as cereals, juice, soy drinks, and other food products.

- *Calcium.* Consuming enough calcium is easier if you consume dairy products, and perhaps more challenging if you're a vegan. Either way, a calcium supplement may be advised; check with your doctor.

- *Iron.* As for nonvegetarians, take an iron supplement. Follow the recommended dosage. Too much iron can interfere with zinc absorption, putting your newborn at risk for a zinc deficiency. Not getting enough iron can affect fetal brain development.

- *Zinc.* Take a zinc supplement if your food choices come up short. The need for zinc increases by 50 percent during pregnancy. Vegetarian food sources of zinc include fortified cereals, wheat germ, milk, hard cheeses such as Parmesan and Asiago, beans and peas, nuts, and seeds.

Before you take any dietary supplement, talk to your doctor. *See chapter 10, page 315, for more about supplements.*

See chapter 12, page 373, for more about protein; chapter 13, page 385, for more about omega-3s; and chapter 14, page 408, for more about these and other vitamins and minerals

See "For Vegetarian Babies" in chapter 16, page 477, if you choose a vegetarian eating plan for your infant, too.

milk. The RDA is 15 micrograms (600 IU) cholecalciferol, daily. Vitamin D–fortified milk is a good source. Calcium-fortified foods with vitamin D such as juice, soy drinks, cereals, and other food products are options. *See "Vitamin D" in chapter 14, page 413.*

See "Vitamins: From A to K" in chapter 14, page 409, for more about these and other vitamins in a healthy eating plan.

Minerals: Giving Body Structure

Minerals are part of a baby's bones and teeth. Along with protein and vitamins, minerals help your body make blood cells and other body tissues, too. Minerals also take part in many body processes that support pregnancy. A few minerals require special attention during pregnancy: calcium, iron, and sometimes zinc.

Calcium. You need enough calcium now for two reasons: developing your baby's bones and preserving your own. Without enough calcium, your body will withdraw calcium from your bones to build your baby's bones. You can't afford the loss! Research suggests that you also may reduce the risks of developing toxemia and high blood pressure if you consume enough calcium.

The calcium recommendation doesn't change for pregnancy. The body absorbs calcium more efficiently during pregnancy. The RDA is 1,000 milligrams of calcium daily for pregnant adult women and 1,300 milligrams daily for teens. Yet before, during, and after pregnancy, many adults and teens don't get enough calcium to protect against osteoporosis later in life. *See "Osteoporosis and Bone Health" in chapter 25, page 738, for more about the risks and effects.*

The equivalent of three cups of milk from the dairy group supply nearly all the calcium adult women and teens need daily. An eight-ounce serving of milk or yogurt provides about 300 milligrams of calcium. *See "Calcium" in chapter 14, page 425.*

Calcium supplement. Your doctor may prescribe a supplement for you if you don't consume enough calcium-rich foods. But the advice is to consume calcium rich foods and calcium-fortified foods first, then take a calcium supplement for any shortfall. *See "Nutrient Supplements" in chapter 10, page 316, for more about calcium supplements. See "Lactose Intolerance: A Matter of Degree" in chapter 23, page 666, if dairy is an issue for you.*

Iodine. Some pregnant and breastfeeding women are marginally iodine deficient, perhaps because salt in processed foods isn't iodized. Iodine is important for brain development in the developing baby and for protecting against the effects of some environmental pollutants.

Before pregnancy, the RDA is 150 micrograms daily, and during pregnancy, it's 220 micrograms daily. Besides iodized salt, some sources are saltwater fish, especially cod but also shrimp and tuna, and reduced-fat milk. The American Thyroid Association advises taking a nutrient supplement with iodine and avoiding environmental pollutants, perhaps methylmercury from some fish, while pregnant and breastfeeding.

When you use salt—just enough to match your taste—use iodized salt. *See "Salty Terms" in chapter 6, page 186, to learn about different types of salt, and "Iodine" in chapter 14, page 437.*

Iron. Why do you need so much more iron during pregnancy—up from 18 to 27 milligrams daily for adult women and from 15 to 27 milligrams daily for teens? Iron is essential for making hemoglobin, a component of blood. During pregnancy your blood volume increases by about 50 percent. Hemoglobin carries oxygen throughout your body, including to the placenta for your unborn baby. Adequate iron is also essential for brain growth of the fetus, and later, for infants and children. Once these stages of development pass, the brain cannot catch up.

Even if you follow food guidance for pregnancy and breastfeeding, you may not get enough iron. To get enough, consume good iron sources every day: iron-fortified grain products; dark-green, leafy vegetables; lean meat, poultry, eggs, and beans and peas. Include good sources of vitamin C, such as broccoli, tomatoes, citrus fruits and juices, and kiwifruit in your eating plan, too. Vitamin C helps your body absorb iron from eggs and plant-based foods. *See "Iron," in chapter 14, page 438.*

Iron supplement. Besides an iron-rich diet, your doctor probably will prescribe a low-dose (30 milligrams per day) iron supplement or a prenatal vitamin supplement with iron. Why? Iron deficiency, the most common nutritional deficiency during pregnancy, increases the risk for low birth weight and possibly premature delivery or perinatal death; fatigue that may come with a deficiency may impair the interaction between mother and baby. (Perinatal is the period shortly before and after birth.)

Although widely available in food, iron isn't always well absorbed. Your best bet is to take the supplement on an empty stomach or with vitamin C–rich juice, but not with meals. Taking an iron supplement with coffee, tea, or other caffeine containing drinks may decrease its absorption. Calcium supplements also interfere with iron absorption and should be taken at a different time.

Iron itself can interfere with the absorption of some other minerals, such as zinc. An iron supplement with 15 milligrams of zinc and 2 milligrams of copper is recommended. Because many women start pregnancy with marginal iron stores, which increases the chance for anemia, your doctor may prescribe a higher dosage.

Iron supplements during pregnancy may cause side effects such as nausea, constipation, and appetite loss. If that happens, try taking the supplement with meals even though the iron may not be absorbed as well. Then make sure you eat more food sources of iron. A lower dosage might help, too; talk to your doctor. *See "Nutrient Supplements" in chapter 10, page 316.*

Zinc. The need for zinc, essential for cell growth and brain development, increases by 50 percent during pregnancy. The RDA is 11 milligrams daily for pregnant women and 12 milligrams daily for teens. Zinc comes in a variety of foods, but its best sources are meat, poultry, and fish. Eggs and some dairy foods supply zinc in smaller amounts. Beans and peas, nuts, and whole-grain products have zinc, too, but it's not absorbed as well. Most women and teens, except some vegetarian women, get enough zinc during pregnancy from their everyday food choices. Ask about a zinc supplement. *See "Zinc," in chapter 14, page 441.*

Sodium. Pregnant or not, choosing and preparing foods that contain little salt (and less sodium) and more potassium-rich foods such as vegetables and fruits is good advice. The sodium intake level doesn't change for pregnancy, so the AI remains 1.5 milligrams daily. You don't need to further restrict sodium during pregnancy—unless your doctor advises you to do so. If you limited your sodium intake before pregnancy, continue as your doctor recommends. *See "A Closer Look . . . Sodium and Potassium: A Salty Subject" in chapter 14, page 433.*

See "Minerals—Major and Trace" in chapter 14, page 425, for more about these and other minerals in a healthy eating plan.

Fiber

Hormone changes during pregnancy may cause digestive problems, such as constipation and hemorrhoids. Getting enough fiber—from whole-grain foods, vegetables, fruits, beans and peas, nuts, and seeds—may help lower the chance during pregnancy. The Adequate Intake (AI) is 28 grams daily—likely more than normally consumed. *See "Fiber and Health" in chapter 11, page 350.*

See "Dietary Reference Intakes" in the appendix, page 780, to find specific recommendations for other nutrients for healthy women during pregnancy.

FLUIDS MATTER

Remember: water is a nutrient. As part of your body's transportation system, it carries other nutrients to body cells and carries waste products away. That includes nourishment that passes through the placenta to your baby.

You need fluids—about twelve cups (about three liters) daily—for your own and your baby's increased blood volume. When you feel thirsty, drink more! *See "Water: A Fluid Asset" in chapter 15, page 443.*

Getting about ten cups of water from beverages daily is likely enough. Milk and 100 percent juice are better options than sugary drinks. High-moisture foods such as vegetables and fruits can supply the rest: about 20 to 25 percent of a pregnant woman's daily water intake.

Avoiding energy drinks during pregnancy is advised. Many contain ingredients such as ginseng that haven't been studied for safety during pregnancy. *See chapter 4, page 81, for more about drink options.*

PREGNANCY DURING ADOLESCENCE

Most teenagers don't plan to get pregnant. When it happens, it's high risk for both mother and baby. A teen is more likely to deliver a low–birth weight baby. Chances of anemia, premature delivery, and preeclampsia (or toxemia) are higher. Untreated, preeclampsia is potentially life-threatening to mother and baby.

? Have you ever wondered?

. . . if caffeinated drinks are okay during pregnancy? There's no conclusive evidence about the effects of caffeine on fetal development. If you're pregnant or breastfeeding, the ACOG advises limits: up to 200 milligrams of caffeine a day, which is the average amount of caffeine in twelve ounces of caffeinated coffee (depending on factors such as preparation method and roasting degree of coffee beans). Still, it's wise for pregnant women to monitor their caffeine consumption, listen to body cues, and talk to their doctor about consuming caffeine; individual sensitivities vary.

See "Caffeine and Health" in chapter 4, page 94.

Teen Pregnancy: Why High Risk?

Teens often don't get timely prenatal care. Their bodies are still growing, perhaps competing with the unborn baby for calories and nutrients. Their needs for calories, protein, and some vitamins and minerals are higher than for an adult pregnant woman. School, activities, social schedules, and emotional ups and downs often take good nutrition off a teen's "top ten" list.

Typical teen eating patterns—meal skipping and eating high-calorie/low-nutrient foods and drinks—don't prepare the teenage body for a healthy pregnancy or provide the ongoing supply of nutrients that a teen and her unborn baby need. Poor nourishment can set the stage for a problematic pregnancy experience and outcome, even in the first few weeks before a teen knows she's pregnant.

Another issue: figure-conscious teens may be reluctant to gain weight during pregnancy. However, they need to understand that pregnancy isn't the time to restrict calories or follow a weight-control diet. Pregnancy is just a temporary body change. The extra pounds gained during pregnancy are more than the fetus; weight gain is also for other parts of a mother's body that support pregnancy, delivery, and breastfeeding. *See "Where Does Weight Gain Go?" in this chapter, page 542.*

Advice for Pregnant Teens

Adequate health care is absolutely essential during a teenage pregnancy! Being a teen and being pregnant each have higher and unique nutritional needs. To meet both physical demands, guidance for proper nutrition and care from a doctor and a registered dietitian nutritionist is essential.

Until age eighteen, pregnant teens may need to gain more weight than adult women do. Most healthy, normal-weight young mothers gain twenty-five to thirty-five pounds by the end of their pregnancy. Gaining at the upper end of the suggested range helps the teen mother deliver a healthier, normal–birth weight baby.

A varied, balanced eating plan that the teen plans with her doctor or a registered dietitian nutritionist can provide enough calories (food energy) and nutrients during pregnancy. A multivitamin/mineral supplement may be prescribed by her doctor to supplement, not replace, meals or snacks. Regular physical activity, enough sleep, and prenatal care are essential to a healthy pregnancy.

See "Feeding the Teen Machine" in chapter 17, page 524, for more about nutrition during adolescence.

DISCOMFORTS OF PREGNANCY

With so many changes taking place in your body, occasional discomforts during pregnancy aren't surprising. They're especially common during the first trimester. A few changes in what—and how—you eat may relieve discomforts such as nausea, vomiting, constipation, heartburn, and swelling.

Nausea and Vomiting

Often referred to as "morning sickness," nausea or vomiting is experienced by many moms-to-be. Hormonal changes, particularly rising estrogen levels, are likely responsible. Somewhat of a misnomer, "morning sickness" may occur at any time—day or night—and usually goes away after the first three months of pregnancy.

Mild queasiness isn't harmful to you or your baby. These suggestions might keep nausea at bay:

- Avoid foods with strong flavors (perhaps spicy foods) or aromas if they trigger nausea. Pregnant women often have an exaggerated sense of smell, making a common aroma seem unappealing.
- Before getting out of bed, eat starchy foods such as crackers, plain toast, or dry cereal to help remove stomach acid. Get out of bed slowly.
- Enjoy small meals every two to three hours to prevent an empty stomach. Drink beverages between meals, and stay well hydrated. Take small sips for best tolerance of fluids.
- Eat easy-to-digest carbohydrate foods, such as crackers, plain pasta, rice, potatoes, other vegetables, and fruits, and low-fat protein foods such as lean meat, poultry, fish, and eggs. Limit fried and other high-fat foods if they cause discomfort.
- Savor every bite! Eat meals slowly. In fact, try to make your surroundings stress free. Turn on some gentle music, and open a window to let in fresh air.
- Before bedtime, eat a small snack such as peanut butter on crackers and milk, or cereal and milk.
- Experiment with beverages that may calm a queasy stomach: ginger ale, lemon or ginger tea, lemonade, or water flavored with lemon or ginger.

Pregnancy and Alcoholic Beverages Don't Mix!

Your blood passes through every organ in your body, through the placenta, and into the circulatory system of your unborn baby. Your baby will be exposed to any alcohol or drugs in your blood.

The Dietary Guidelines for Americans advises that women who are pregnant or who may be pregnant should not drink alcoholic beverages. Especially in the first few months of pregnancy, there may be negative behavioral or neurological consequences for the baby.

Drinking during pregnancy is linked to serious birth defects. Fetal alcohol syndrome (FAS) is associated with excessive drinking. Infants with FAS may be born with birth defects including retarded growth, mental impairment, or physical malformations. Drinking alcoholic beverages during pregnancy can lead to a wide range of lifelong physical, behavioral, and intellectual disabilities referred to as fetal alcohol spectrum disorders (FASDs). FAS is just one of these.

Even moderate levels (one drink a day) during pregnancy may lead to behavioral or developmental problems for your baby and may affect your child's future intelligence. The risks are greater for older moms and binge drinkers.

There is no known safe level for alcohol intake during pregnancy. Health experts don't know if babies differ in their sensitivity to alcohol. If you're trying to conceive or you're already pregnant, health experts advise you to avoid beer, wine, and other alcoholic beverages completely. As soon as you know you're pregnant, stop drinking! If you've had a glass of wine or two before you knew, you likely don't need to worry—still, stop.

As a reminder, alcoholic beverages carry a label warning about the dangers of drinking during pregnancy and its relation to birth defects.

> GOVERNMENT WARNING:
>
> (1) ACCORDING TO THE SURGEON GENERAL, WOMEN SHOULD NOT DRINK ALCOHOLIC BEVERAGES DURING PREGNANCY BECAUSE OF THE RISK OF BIRTH DEFECTS. (2) CONSUMPTION OF ALCOHOLIC BEVERAGES IMPAIRS YOUR ABILITY TO DRIVE A CAR OR OPERATE MACHINERY, AND MAY CAUSE HEALTH PROBLEMS.

- Choose foods that appeal to you and that "stay down." Even if your food choices aren't "nutritionally perfect," that's okay if queasiness doesn't last longer than a few days. If the problem persists, talk to your doctor or a registered dietitian nutritionist.
- Skip the urge to take a supplement to relieve nausea, unless advised by your doctor. There is only limited evidence to show that taking vitamin B_6 or ginger products offer relief for morning sickness without adverse effects to mom or baby. Some herbals may have harmful side effects.
- Get enough rest!

Some women experience hyperemesis, or persistent, severe nausea with spells of vomiting. This can leave pregnant women at risk for dehydration and weight loss. The cause is likely related to a rise in hormone levels. Consult your doctor, especially if severe nausea and vomiting continue after fourteen weeks, or if you have any of these problems: a small amount of dark-colored urine, inability to keep liquids down, dizziness when standing up, a racing or pounding heart, or bloody vomit.

Constipation

Since becoming pregnant, do you occasionally feel constipated? Many women do. Hormonal changes relax muscles to accommodate your expanding uterus, and that slows the action in your intestines. Taking an iron supplement can aggravate constipation, too. For some women, constipation, along with pressure from the baby, leads to hemorrhoids, which are large, swollen veins in the rectum.

To prevent or ease constipation and perhaps the discomfort of hemorrhoids, these tips may help:

- Consume more fluids. The guideline for pregnancy is about twelve cups of water daily, from beverages and some foods. Besides water, include milk, fruit juice, and perhaps broth in your fluid allowance. *See "Water: A Fluid Asset" in chapter 15, page 443.*
- Eat high-fiber foods: whole-grain foods, 100 percent bran cereals, vegetables, fruits, and beans and peas.
- Get the natural laxative effect of dried plums (prunes), prune juice, and figs.
- Be physically active every day if you can. Like swimming and prenatal exercise classes, walking is good exercise during pregnancy. Regular activity stimulates normal bowel function.
- Unless your doctor prescribes them, don't take laxatives. For hemorrhoids, ask your doctor to recommend a safe suppository or ointment.

Heartburn (Acid Reflux)

Especially during the last trimester, you may complain about heartburn, perhaps from hormonal changes that slow the movement of food through your digestive tract. To relieve your discomfort, these tips may help:

- Eat small meals frequently, every two to three hours.
- Avoid foods that may cause heartburn such as caffeinated and carbonated drinks, tomatoes, highly acidic citrus products, and greasy and highly seasoned food.
- Walk after you eat to help gastric, or stomach, juices go down, not up.
- Avoid lying down for three hours after eating.
- Sleep with your head elevated to avoid acid reflux.
- Ask your doctor about taking antacids. Calcium-based antacids may give fast relief and appear to pose low risk of adverse reactions. Some contain sodium bicarbonate (baking soda), which can interfere with nutrient absorption.

Swelling: Part of Pregnancy

Swelling is normal, especially in the last trimester. Water retained in your ankles, hands, and wrists is a reservoir for your expanded blood volume. It offsets the water lost during delivery, and it's used later for breast milk. Even with swelling, drink plenty of water. Unless your doctor advises otherwise, avoid diuretics that increase water loss through urination. There's no need to limit salt to prevent swelling.

To relieve the discomfort of moderate swelling, these tips may help:

- When you sit, put your feet up. Periodically, get up and stretch to improve your circulation.
- Try not to stand for long periods of time.
- Rest on your left side to aid circulation.
- Wear comfortable shoes, perhaps a larger size.
- Avoid tight clothes, tight stockings, tight-fitting rings, and anything else that restricts circulation.

Preeclampsia. Excessive swelling may signal preeclampsia, once referred to as toxemia. A complication of pregnancy, preeclampsia is indicated by high blood pressure and a high level of protein in the urine, which is a signal of organ damage, often the kidneys. Other signs of preeclampsia can include sudden weight gain, severe headaches, abdominal pain, changes in reflexes, excessive urine or no urine, excessive nausea and vomiting, and vision changes. It typically appears during the second half of pregnancy.

Advise your doctor right away if you develop these symptoms. The earlier it's caught, the easier it is to manage. Untreated, preeclampsia can be dangerous later in pregnancy, resulting in a premature birth and other serious complications for both you and baby. It even can be life-threatening for you both.

The causes of preeclampsia are not fully understood, but inadequate blood flow to the uterus, and genetics, as well as poor nutrition and high body fat (reflected in a high BMI), may be among the factors. Low calcium and low protein intake during pregnancy may factor in also. Cutting back on sodium won't prevent it, as once believed.

DIABETES AND PREGNANCY

Gestational diabetes—which may start around the middle of pregnancy and end after delivery—is a health problem for some pregnant women. To screen for gestational diabetes, the American Diabetes Association recommends that all women undergo an Oral Glucose Tolerance Test during their pregnancy.

Who's at risk? Women who have a family history of diabetes, those who are overweight or obese, those with previous gestational diabetes or who have delivered a baby who was large for his or her gestational age, and those with polycystic ovary syndrome are among those at risk. Most pregnant women are routinely tested for gestational diabetes at about twenty-four to twenty-eight weeks.

Whether it's preexisting or gestational, diabetes during pregnancy increases the risk for high blood pressure and preeclampsia, a dangerous condition, as discussed. Women with gestational diabetes often have big babies, who may be difficult to deliver, and these women may need a cesarean delivery. The risk for getting diabetes later in life is higher among women who develop gestational diabetes—and their babies may be more prone to overweight or obesity during childhood or adolescence, too.

If you have diabetes, you can deliver a healthy baby. Controlling existing diabetes before pregnancy is important. Your doctor should also monitor your pregnancy carefully and prescribe treatment, typically a combination of diet and physical activity. A registered dietitian nutritionist can help you develop an eating plan to control your blood glucose levels. *See "Diabetes: A Growing Concern" in chapter 24, page 698, to learn more about diabetes and how to effectively manage it.*

HIGH BLOOD PRESSURE AND PREGNANCY

Gestational hypertension, or high blood pressure—another health risk—happens in 12 to 22 percent of pregnancies in the United States. A significant number of these women develop preeclampsia, a serious health risk for mother and baby. Some risk factors for gestational hypertension are obesity, a multiples pregnancy, being African American or Hispanic, and being age thirty-five years or older.

Healthy eating and healthy weight can reduce the risk. Your doctor will monitor your blood pressure and treat hypertension if it develops. *See "Blood Pressure: Under Control?" in chapter 24, page 693, to learn about its risks and effects, and how to manage hypertension.*

FOODBORNE ILLNESS AND PREGNANCY

Handling food properly to avoid foodborne illness is always essential. For the safety of you and your baby, pregnancy is no exception.

Foodborne Illness Alert!

Some types of foodborne illness are of special concern during pregnancy:

- *Listeria monocytogenes*, a bacterium that causes listeriosis, may contaminate unpasteurized milk and foods made from it such as some soft cheeses, as well as raw and undercooked meat, poultry, and fish. Pregnant women are advised to avoid hot dogs, lunch meats, deli meats, and refrigerated smoked fish, unless properly reheated to steaming hot (or 165°F). These foods can cause miscarriage in the first trimester and serious illness, premature birth, or stillbirth later. Pregnant women are twenty times more susceptible than other healthy adults.
- *Toxoplasma gondii*, the parasite that causes toxoplasmosis, is linked to raw and undercooked meat and poultry, and to unwashed vegetables and fruits. It can pass from mother to unborn baby and cause severe symptoms including infant death or mental retardation. Because cat feces carry this parasite, avoid handling cat litter, always wash your hands well with soap and water after handling a cat, and keep your cat indoors.
- *Salmonella*, a bacterium that can contaminate raw or undercooked meat, poultry, fish, eggs, and unpasteurized milk cheese, and juice, poses as much risk during pregnancy as before becoming pregnant. Although rare in the United States, one

? Have you ever wondered?

. . . if herbal or other botanical supplements are safe during pregnancy and breastfeeding? There's not enough scientific evidence yet to recommend safe levels for herbal supplements for pregnant or nursing moms. Some are known to be harmful to a baby—for example, comfrey may cause liver damage, blue cohosh may cause heart defects, and pennyroyal may cause spontaneous abortions. Other herbs identified as potentially harmful include aloe, black cohosh, buckthorn, burdock, cascara, chamomile, coltsfoot, cornsilk, devil's claw root, Dong quai, ephedra, feverfew, gerrymander, ginseng, goldenseal, hawthorne, horseradish, licorice, lobelia, margosa oil, mate, mistletoe, rue, sassafras, skullcap, senna, St. John's wort, uva ursi, and yarrow. *See "Herbals and Other Botanicals" in chapter 10, page 320, for more about the safety and effectiveness of these supplements.*

. . . if herbal teas are okay to drink during pregnancy? Some, but not all, are considered safe if you enjoy no more than two to three cups a day. Blackberry, citrus peel, ginger, lemon balm, orange peel, and rosehip teas are among those considered safe if they've been processed according to government safety standards.

type—*Salmonella typhi*—may be passed to the developing baby and can cause a miscarriage, premature labor, or stillbirth.

- *E. coli 0157:H7*, a bacterium associated with raw and undercooked meat and unpasteurized milk or cider, is highly toxic. This bacteria can also come from water that is contaminated in private wells. This life-threatening strain, which can cause severe kidney, intestinal, and brain damage, can pass to your unborn baby.
- Lead exposure during pregnancy is linked to miscarriage and stillbirth, low–birth weight babies, and damage to a baby's nervous system. Over the long term lead poisoning can cause learning disabilities, organ damage, and even death. Among the sources of lead: water from lead pipes or pipes with lead solder, food served on ceramic plates with improperly applied lead glaze, and beverages kept and served in lead crystal decanters or glasses. *See "Water: Concerns about Lead and Nitrates" in chapter 4, page 84, and "Caution—Decorative Dishes" in chapter 7, page 216, for more about lead poisoning.*
- Methylmercury, a chemical pollutant found in high amounts in some fish, are especially harmful to unborn babies and young children, whose bodies are just developing. Mercury poisoning, for example, may damage the nervous system. No matter how you prepare or cook fish, you can't get rid of the methylmercury.

  That said, fish is a good source of protein, omega-3 fatty acids, and other essential nutrients with positive health benefits. The Food and Drug Administration and Environmental Protection Agency currently advises avoiding several types of fish (king mackerel, marlin, orange roughy, shark, swordfish, tilefish) from the Gulf of Mexico, and bigeye tuna because of their potential high levels of methylmercury and instead eat fish that are lower in mercury. These contaminants may be passed on to your baby if consumed during pregnancy or breastfeeding. *See "Have you ever wondered . . . if mercury in fish is risky?" in chapter 7, page 225.*

Food Safety Precautions

In addition to general food safety precautions, be sure to follow this advice during your pregnancy:

- Choose fish carefully. During pregnancy and breastfeeding, limit white (albacore) tuna to six ounces per week; it has more methylmercury than light canned tuna. Grouper, mahi mahi, monkfish, snapper, and tuna (yellowfin) are some other fish to limit to one serving (about four ounces cooked) a week. Follow advisories from local and state health department, state fishery agency, or Sea Grant office for a current safety status about fish from local streams, rivers, and lakes too; that includes fish you catch. If there is no advice, limit these options to only one serving a week (no other fish that week).

  Eat up to 12 ounces a week of fish that are lower in mercury, including some common options: canned light tuna, catfish, cod, pollock, salmon, shrimp, and tilapia.

  To learn about the 2017 advisory on eating fish during pregnancy, and see a complete list of fish that are "best choices" to eat two or three times a week and those that are "good choices" to eat in limited amounts, go to www.FDA.gov/fishadvice.
- Avoid raw or undercooked fish, especially during pregnancy and breastfeeding, to reduce the risks of viral and bacterial infections. That includes foods such as sashimi, sushi, or seviche, as well as partially cooked shellfish such as shrimp or crab.
- Avoid unpasteurized (raw) juice or milk or foods made from unpasteurized milk, such as some soft chesses (blue-veined cheeses, Brie, Camembert, feta, panela, queso blanco, and queso fresco). If you eat soft cheese, check the label to sure it's made from pasteurized milk. Pay special attention to juice, milk, and cheese sold from farmers' markets which may not carry labels.
- Avoid deli and luncheon meats (ham, turkey, beef), hot dogs, fermented or dry sausage, and refrigerated smoked fish (often labeled as kippered, jerky, lox, nova-style, or smoked) unless reheated to steaming hot (165°F) to kill *Listeria*, the bacteria that causes listeriosis. Canned smoked fish in a casserole or cooked dish is okay.
- Avoid premade meat and fish salads, such as chicken, ham, salmon, and tuna, from salad bars and delis, as well as unpasteurized and/or refrigerated pâtés or meat spreads. They too may carry *Listeria*.
- Avoid raw sprouts (alfalfa, clover, mung bean, and radish), which can carry harmful bacteria. To eat sprouts, cook them well first.

See chapter 7, page 191, for more food and water safety guidance.

Have you ever wondered?

. . . if drinking raw or unpasteurized milk and milk products during pregnancy, infancy, or childhood can protect against autism or allergies? No. Moreover, these dairy products may result in bacterial infections such as from *Campylobacter jejuni, E. coli 0157:H7, Listeria monocytogenes*, and *Salmonella*. Pregnant women, their unborn babies, and children are especially vulnerable; miscarriages can result. Neither the American Academy of Pediatrics (AAP) nor the FDA support consuming raw or unpasteurized milk or other dairy products during pregnancy and childhood. No scientifically valid evidence supports claims that pasteurized milk is linked to autism, allergic reactions, and asthma—or that drinking raw milk offers protection from these conditions.

Pass the Pickles: Cravings and Food Aversions

Whether it's pickles, chocolate, ice cream, or other foods, cravings as well as food aversions are common during pregnancy. Although the exact cause is unknown, taste perceptions may change along with hormonal changes.

Food aversions—often to coffee, tea, fried or fatty foods, spicy foods, meat, or eggs—are harmless unless the foods you regularly crave replace more nutritious ones. Instead, substitute nutritionally similar foods. For instance, if broccoli loses its appeal, substitute another vegetable that you enjoy and tolerate.

Caution: Cravings for nonfood substances, a condition called pica, can be dangerous. The cultural practice of craving ashes, burnt matches, chalk, clay, cornstarch, ice, laundry starch, or other odd substances comes from folklore that started hundreds of years ago. It was believed that eating a particular substance might decrease nausea, promote a healthy baby, or ease delivery. There's no evidence that this practice works—and it can be harmful to you and your baby. Some substances contain lead or other toxicants.

Craving ice may indicate an iron deficiency. Usually, once the iron-deficiency anemia is corrected, the craving for ice goes away. Consult with your doctor if you have cravings for or are consuming large quantities of ice so your iron levels can be checked.

A GLUTEN-FREE DIET AND PREGNANCY

Pregnant women with undiagnosed or untreated celiac disease have a greater risk for miscarriage, low-birth weight, stillbirth, and other pregnancy-related complications.

Whether you have celiac disease or not, a gluten-free diet can be low in several important nutrients—carbohydrates, niacin, folic acid, calcium, iron, phosphorus, and zinc—and low in fiber. If you must be gluten free, a registered dietitian nutritionist can help you create a nourishing food plan. Going gluten free by going "low carb" can set you up for inadequate nutrition. *See "Gluten Free: When It's a Must" in chapter 23, page 670, for guidance.*

PHYSICAL ACTIVITY AND PREGNANCY

Unless you have a medical reason that limits physical activity, mild to moderate physical activity benefits a pregnant mom—and won't affect an unborn child. If you're healthy, physical activity will not increase your chances of miscarriage, low-birth weight, or early delivery.

See "Pregnancy, Breastfeeding: Food and Sports" in chapter 21, page 613, if you're an athlete.

Being Active: The Benefits

Being active offers relief for some normal discomforts of pregnancy. Regular physical activity:

- Helps you look and feel good as your body changes
- May lower the risks for gestational diabetes and preeclampsia
- Promotes muscle tone, stamina, and strength
- Helps reduce leg and back pain, constipation, swelling, and bloating
- Promotes blood circulation, may help prevent varicose veins, and helps keep your lungs healthy
- Helps your posture and balance—important as your center of gravity shifts
- Helps you sleep better
- Prepares your body for labor and childbirth
- After delivery, helps your body get back in shape!

Your "Keep Moving" Plan

For healthy women during and after pregnancy, the Physical Activity Guidelines for Americans advises at least 150 minutes per week of moderate-intensity aerobic activity. You can spread it out over the week.

- Talk with your doctor about physical activity during pregnancy—including the type of sport or activities you plan to do. Doctors may advise against exercise for a high-risk pregnancy: high blood pressure induced by pregnancy, symptoms or a history of early contractions (preterm labor), vaginal bleeding, or early rupture of membranes. Other ongoing health conditions, such as heart or lung disease or high blood pressure, may limit physical activity.
- With your doctor, make an activity plan that keeps you fit, matches your health needs and lifestyle, and prepares you for delivery. With minor changes, you may be able to continue your regular physical activity routine.

  With moderate intensity, most pregnant women—even beginners—can do these activities: bike, low-impact and water aerobics, swim, and walk. Include strength-building and endurance activities; stretch before and afterward. The right intensity depends on your health and how active you were before pregnancy. (Later in pregnancy, recumbent or stationary biking might be best since you'll be more prone to falling.) Your clinic, health club, or hospital may offer an exercise program for pregnant women with exercises to help with labor.
- If you are just starting, build up slowly. Start with low-intensity activity as your doctor advises. Work up to a daily routine of about thirty minutes on most days. Now isn't the time to stop and start with bursts of heavy exercise. Remember to start with a five-to-ten-minute warmup of light activity and stretching, and end with

five to ten minutes of a slower activity and then stretch to cool down.

- If you were regularly and vigorously active prior to pregnancy, perhaps with strength training or running, you likely don't need to cut back—if you stay healthy. Talk to your doctor about how and when to modify your routine. For example, as your balance shifts, your risk of falling during some upright sports, such as racquet sports, may increase.
- Choose physical activities that are safe and comfortable. Avoid activities that increase your risk of falling or abdominal injury, such as horseback riding, downhill and water skiing, gymnastics, and contact sports such as soccer or basketball. Scuba diving is also risky; the water pressure can put your unborn baby at risk for decompression sickness.

Physical Activity: Cautions!

Physical activity is important—but exercise with care.

- Avoid jerky, bouncy movements—and don't overdo it. As your body shape changes and you gain weight, your center of gravity shifts. That puts more stress on your muscles and joints, particularly in your lower back and pelvis. Your balance changes, too. Some activities get harder to do, especially during the last three months. Injury is more likely as your hormones cause ligaments in your joints to stretch.
- Avoid overexercising. With the added weight of pregnancy, your body must work harder as you exercise. Overexertion isn't healthy for you or your unborn baby. If he or she becomes overheated at a critical time of development, the risk for birth defects goes up.
- After the first trimester, avoid exercises that require you to lie on your back. In that position, it may be harder for your blood to circulate, as well.
- Wear a supportive bra to protect your breasts.
- Drink plenty of water—before, during, and after physical activity—and wear appropriate clothing to avoid getting overheated and dehydrated. Avoid brisk exercise in hot, humid temperatures.
- Remember: pregnancy isn't the time to exercise in order to lose or keep from gaining weight!
- If you feel tired, stop before you feel exhausted. If you can talk as you move, your level of physical activity is right. Talk with your doctor about the right target heart rate for you. *See "Your Physical Activity: How Intense?" in chapter 21, page 600, to learn how to measure your heart rate.*
- If you experience any problems, stop your activity; consult your doctor right away. These are warning signs from the American College of Obstetricians and Gynecologists: chest pain, headaches, pain (in general or in your back or pubic area), calf pain or swelling, muscle weakness, dizziness or feeling faint, increased shortness of breath, vaginal bleeding or other fluid leaking from your vagina, uterine contractions, or decreased fetal movement.

NEW MOMS: AFTER DELIVERY

If you made some lifestyle changes for a healthy pregnancy, keep them up. Perhaps you stopped smoking, ate healthier foods, drank more milk, or exercised more routinely. Continue to take care of your body now that it's all yours again.

Shedding "Baby Weight"

Delivering your baby may be the fastest weight you ever lose! Between the baby and fluid loss, some moms lose up to ten pounds right after delivery, and another five pounds within the first month or so. For others, weight comes off gradually over a longer period. Most women continue to lose weight slowly and steadily for six to twelve months after delivery.

Even if you're planning another pregnancy, try to return to your prepregnancy weight. Having another baby before losing "baby weight" may cause problems during delivery. Moreover, accumulated weight gain from one pregnancy to the next isn't healthy—for your long-term health or a future pregnancy.

Returning to your prepregnancy weight is easier after a first pregnancy, harder after later pregnancies. It's also important for having the energy and health for parenting. How fast you shed "baby weight" depends on how physically active you are, what your calorie intake is, and, if you breastfeed, how long you do it. Losing "baby weight" may require a shift in your lifestyle, not just in your eating pattern. New demands of parenthood can make that challenging, but it's worth the effort!

See "Weight Management: Strategies That Can Work!" in chapter 22, page 637, for more guidance on healthy weight loss.

Postpartum Physical Activity Routine

When you recover from delivery and get your strength back, resume your prepregnancy activity routine—or start a new one. Besides the physical health benefits, physical activity can offer postpartum-mood benefits. Check with your doctor first, and then make physical activity a family affair.

Start with walking, then work up to more strenuous activity. Use a stroller or a front/back carrier so your baby can go on walks with you. Play actively together with your baby. Look for a postpartum exercise class in your community.

Gestational Diabetes

If you had gestational diabetes, get a blood glucose screening at six weeks after delivery and perhaps at your regular medical checkups later—even if the symptoms disappear. You're at higher risk for type 2 diabetes later in life.

Breastfeeding—Your Choice

The decision to breastfeed is personal. If you decide it's right for you and your baby, make good nutrition a priority. Your needs for calories and some nutrients are higher now than during pregnancy.

WHY BREASTFEED?

If you're able, breastfeeding is good for your baby—and for you. Besides the physical and emotional benefits to your baby, breastfeeding has benefits for new mothers:

- Nurtures a close emotional bond between you and your baby
- Reduces your risk of postpartum depression
- Helps reduce bleeding after delivery and helps you return to your prepregnancy shape faster than with formula-feeding. Breastfeeding releases the hormone oxytocin, which helps your uterus return to its normal size faster.
- May promote weight loss.
- May provide other health benefits to you later in life, although research evidence is inconclusive.

See "Nursing: Good for Mom" and "Human Milk: Good for Baby" in chapter 16, pages 461 and 460, for more about the benefits of breastfeeding.

For some women, it's better not to breastfeed. If you have HIV or active tuberculosis, breastfeeding could pass the infection to your baby. If you've had breast surgery, talk to your doctor about whether breastfeeding is an option for you.

CALORIES: HOW MUCH?

Your fuel supply for milk production comes from two sources: energy stored as body fat during pregnancy and extra energy (calories) from food choices. If you breastfeed exclusively, you need about 670 more calories a day, which come from body fat stores and from your food and drinks.

To produce breast milk, your body uses about 100 to 150 calories a day from the fat stored during pregnancy. That's why breastfeeding may help many new mothers lose pregnancy weight—in the short term.

To make up the difference, you need to consume more calories than your nonpregnancy recommendation: about 500 calories more daily for the first six months and an extra 400 calories daily for the second six months. Because women differ in their milk production, physical activity levels, and weight loss during breastfeeding, their energy needs may be somewhat different.

Small amounts of nutrient-rich foods can provide enough extra food energy (calories) and nutrients to support breastfeeding. *See "A Plan for Healthy Eating: From MyPlate to Your Plate" in chapter 2, page 25, for guidance.*

After you've established your breastfeeding routine, evaluate your calorie intake. Consider your physical activity level and your weight gain during pregnancy. Ask your lactation counselor or a registered dietitian nutritionist for guidance.

Breastfeeding and Weight Loss

Breastfeeding can help you return to your prepregnancy weight faster. However, the impact of nursing alone on weight loss is likely small and short term—and depends on how much and how long you breastfeed.

Losing two to four pounds a month probably won't affect your milk supply; gradual weight loss is healthier anyway. Losing more than four to five pounds a month after the first month isn't advised. Dipping below 1,800 calories daily may decrease your milk volume and compromise your nutritional status. Conversely, overweight and obesity may also decrease milk production.

To help you return to your prepregnancy weight and maintain a healthy weight, work out a plan with your doctor. Steer away from restrictive weight-loss regimens.

NUTRIENTS: JUST A LITTLE MORE

The need for most nutrients increases a bit while breastfeeding. A few need special attention, especially if you breastfeed longer than two or three months. *Also see "The Vegetarian Mom" in this chapter, page 546.*

Macronutrients

Your need for protein, essential fatty acids, and carbohydrates is higher if you breastfeed. Your everyday food choices can supply enough if chosen wisely and if you follow a healthy eating plan, *as discussed in chapter 2, page 21.*

Consuming at least eight and up to twelve ounces of a variety of fish weekly, including fish high in omega-3 fatty acids (in particular DHA) and low in methylmercury, may increase the DHA in breast milk and so promote your baby's brain and visual development. In fact, this is the reason DHA is now added to infant formula. Breast milk is best for baby. But scientific advances in formula research have brought formula closer to the composition of breast milk.

See "Foodborne Illness and Pregnancy" in this chapter, page 551, for guidance on safe fish intake during pregnancy and breastfeeding.

Vitamins and Minerals

Your need for a few vitamins and minerals are a bit higher than before your pregnancy to support breastfeeding. Everyday food choices, chosen wisely, in a healthy eating plan, can supply enough, *as discusssed* in *chapter 2, page 21.*

Folate. Especially if you're considering another pregnancy soon, consume the recommended 500 micrograms daily of folate—from fortified grain products and supplements as well as from vegetables and fruits—while breastfeeding. That recommendation is the same for women and teenage girls. *See "Folic Acid: Prevent Birth Defects" in this chapter, page 539.*

Vitamin B_6. The need for this B vitamin goes up, yet breastfeeding mothers often don't consume enough. The recommendation, given as an Adequate Intake level, for vitamin B_6 is 2 milligrams daily for women and teenage girls. Poultry, fish, and meat are the best sources, followed by whole grain products and beans and peas. Fortified cereals may be good sources, too.

Vitamin B_{12}. Consume enough to ensure an optimal amount of this vitamin in breast milk. The RDA is somewhat higher than before pregnancy, to 2.8 micrograms daily now. If you eat meat, poultry, fish, eggs, and dairy products, you're likely getting enough vitamin B_{12}. Some fortified foods may contain vitamin B_{12}.

Choline. The recommendation for choline, important for nervous system development, increases for women who breastfeed to 550 milligrams per day. Eggs are among the good sources. Breast milk supplies choline; infant formula is fortified with it.

Vitamin D. Breast milk doesn't have much vitamin D. If your meals and snacks are low in vitamin D or if you aren't exposed to sunlight, your breast milk may have less.

For you, milk is a good source because it's fortified with vitamin D. Some other good sources are calcium-fortified foods with vitamin D such as juice, soy drinks, cereals, and other food products. Sunlight helps your body produce it. Vitamin D recommendations are the same now as before your pregnancy.

See "Supplement Advice: For Breastfed Babies" in chapter 16, page 469, for advice about a vitamin D supplement for infants who are breastfed exclusively or along with formula-feeding.

Calcium. Your calcium needs don't change when you're breastfeeding. For teens the RDA remains at 1,300 milligrams daily; for adult women, 1,000 milligrams daily. Still, make sure you consume enough. If you come up short, your body may draw from calcium in your bones to keep the calcium content in breast milk adequate. Bone loss puts you at greater risk for osteoporosis later in life. Periodontal problems also may crop up after pregnancy and nursing, perhaps related to calcium drain.

Enjoy three cups of milk or its dairy food group equivalent (yogurt, cheese, calcium-fortified soymilk) daily. Calcium-fortified juice and cereals, tofu made with calcium sulfate, dark-green leafy vegetables, fish

? Have you ever wondered?

. . . if your food choices affect the flavor or color of breast milk? Yes, eating strongly flavored foods such as onions, garlic, broccoli, cabbage, cauliflower, or "hot" spicy food may give breast milk a noticeable flavor. These flavors make some babies fussy; other babies don't notice. In breast milk, babies also subtly experience the flavors of family foods, which may lead to their acceptance and enjoyment. If some foods seem to upset your baby, eat less of them, less often. What you eat may cause a harmless color change. Breast milk usually is white or bluish-white.

. . . if your body can produce enough milk to feed your baby? About 50 percent of mothers in the United State express that concern, yet only 5 percent aren't physically able to produce enough. Keep in mind that giving your baby a supplemental bottle—just in case—reduces your baby's suckling at the breast. This can reduce your milk production. Talk to your doctor to help you determine if your milk supply is sufficient. More frequent breastfeeding will help stimulate greater milk product to meet your baby's need.

. . . if you can drink caffeinated beverages while you're breastfeeding? Yes, enjoy your morning coffee or tea, or a soft drink for a snack, in moderation. The AAP notes that breast milk usually contains less than 1 percent of the caffeine a mom ingests. While caffeine does pass into breast milk and may affect baby's sleep or feeding, the caffeine in no more than three cups of coffee, consumed throughout the day, likely won't bother your baby. There is no evidence that caffeine decreases milk supply. *See "Caffeine and Health" in chapter 4, page 94, for more information.*

. . . if you can pass food allergens through breast milk to your baby? For starters, allergic reactions from allergies in human milk are extremely rare. No current convincing evidence shows that avoiding known food allergens during pregnancy or while breastfeeding prevents allergies—although limited research says avoiding certain foods while nursing may prevent eczema.

The AAP advises that pregnant and nursing women don't need to avoid eating peanuts and other potential allergens. If a baby has a natural parent or sibling with allergies, or if a baby already has a known allergy, then a doctor may advise a nursing mom to avoid certain food allergens.

If you suspect an allergy, never make the diagnosis yourself. Talk to your doctor. Then get help from a registered dietitian nutritionist to help you manage any allergy, and continue breastfeeding. *See "Food Allergies: A Growing Concern" in chapter 23, page 654.*

with edible bones are good calcium sources. *See "Osteoporosis and Bone Health" in chapter 25, page 738, to learn more about the importance of calcium in maintaining healthy bones.*

Zinc. Breastfeeding increases the need for zinc. The RDA for women is 12 milligrams daily and for teenage girls, 13 milligrams daily. Zinc's best sources are red meats, poultry, and fish. Eggs and some dairy foods supply zinc in smaller amounts. Beans and peas, nuts, and whole grain products contain zinc, but in a form that isn't absorbed in the body as well.

Multivitamin/Mineral Supplement

If you took a prenatal vitamin/mineral supplement during pregnancy, your doctor may recommend that you continue during breastfeeding. However, you probably can get enough nutrients from food—if you choose wisely. If your own food choices come up short on nutrients, in most cases your breast milk still will be sufficient to support your baby's growth and development—but at the expense of your own nutrient reserves! *See "Nutrient Supplements" in chapter 10, page 316, for guidance on meeting your needs.*

See chapter 14, page 408, for details about these and other nutrients including specific recommendations for healthy women during breastfeeding.

FLUIDS: DRINK ENOUGH

To ensure an adequate milk supply and to prevent dehydration, drink enough fluids to satisfy your thirst. That's the amount needed to keep your urine pale yellow or nearly colorless. During breastfeeding, you need about fifteen cups of water daily—more if you're thirsty. That includes water from beverages and food sources. If you're constipated or if your urine is concentrated (dark yellow), drink more.

Tip: Keep water, milk, or 100 percent juice handy to sip as you breastfeed. Milk and juice supply other nutrients you need in extra amounts while breastfeeding: calcium from milk and vitamin C from most fruit juices.

NONFOODS: EFFECTS ON BREAST MILK

While breastfeeding, take the same precautions you did during pregnancy: what you consume may be passed to your baby.

Alcoholic Beverages

Alcohol passes into breast milk. If you breastfeed, be especially cautious about habitually drinking alcoholic beverages. Contrary to popular belief, no scientific evidence suggests that an alcoholic drink promotes the "let-down" reflex. In fact, heavy drinking may inhibit that reflex. So steer away from beer, wine, or spirits for relaxation. Drinking alcoholic beverages also can decrease (not increase) milk production. *See "Breastfeeding Cautions" in chapter 16, page 466, to learn more about the effects of alcoholic beverages on breastfeeding and infant health.*

Smoking

Nicotine passes into breast milk. If you're a smoker and quit during pregnancy, breastfeeding isn't the time to start again. Nicotine can reduce your milk supply and increase your baby's chance for colic, a sinus infection, or fussiness. Too close to a nursing session, smoking may inhibit your "let-down" reflex. Smoking by anyone near your baby exposes him or her to the risks of secondhand smoke and possibly to getting burned. *See "Breastfeeding Cautions" in chapter 16, page 466.*

Medications

Talk to your doctor about any prescription and over-the-counter medications you're taking, even an aspirin and herbal supplements. Most pass into breast milk in concentrations that pose no harm to your infant, but there are some exceptions. Some may affect milk production and the let-down reflex. Take medications after nursing, not before—even if they're safe for babies. Recreational drugs—which pass into breast milk—are never considered safe for you or your baby. *See "Breastfeeding Cautions" in chapter 16, page 466.*

Food Safety Precautions

In addition to general food safety precautions, be sure to follow the same advice for breastfeeding as you did for pregnancy. That includes prevention of foodborne illness and exposure to contaminants such as methylmercury. *See "Food Safety Precautions" earlier in this chapter, page 552, for details.*

PHYSICAL ACTIVITY AND BREASTFEEDING

Being active likely won't affect the amount or composition of breast milk or your baby's growth. If you're highly active, your milk may have more lactic acid right after exercise, which may affect flavor but doesn't appear harmful to infants. *See "New Moms: After Delivery" earlier in this chapter, page 554, for more about physical activity, and see "Pregnancy, Breastfeeding: Food and Sports, chapter 21, page 613, if you're an athlete.*

Women: Midlife and Beyond

Turning forty or fifty? Experiencing weight gain for the first time? Concerned about bone health? Feeling a loss of muscle tone and stamina? Suffering the discomforts of menopause? Concerned about breast cancer or heart disease? Good health takes on new meaning—and staying healthy takes on renewed urgency—with the physical changes that come with midlife.

Launched in 1993, the Women's Health Initiative, a long-term national health study of the National Heart, Lung, and Blood Institute in the National Institutes of Health (NIH), has addressed many health issues of postmenopausal women related to how women age. With more than thirty years of research, much more is understood about strategies for preventing heart disease, breast and colorectal cancer, and osteoporotic fractures.

Being female and fit at forty, fifty, and beyond is all about being proactive. So relax. Accept the changes as normal and very individual. Eat smart and be physically active to keep your healthy weight, promote heart and bone health, and reduce your risks for heart disease, diabetes, and cancer.

What causes menopause? Hormones. With age, hormone levels slowly drop as ovaries produce less estrogen and progesterone, two of the main hormones involved in reproduction. As reproductive hormones diminish, every body cell—particularly in the cardiovascular, skeletal, and reproductive systems—is affected. This natural midlife passage in a woman's life cycle commonly occurs at about age fifty-one. The menopausal years are gradual, and the transition, called perimenopause, starts earlier.

Perimenopause typically starts in a woman's middle forties, but may start earlier or later, and lasts for four to six years as the ovaries gradually produce less estrogen and progesterone. One of the first signs of the "menopausal transition" is that periods may become irregular and be unusually heavy or light, perhaps with more time in between. Menopause is twelve months after the last period; postmenopause follows. Taking care of yourself makes this normal midlife transition easier. An active lifestyle also can reduce the discomforts of menopause.

- Menopause Map (a guide through the stages), The Endocrine Society
www.hormone.org/menopausemap

See chapter 20, page 517, for more about healthy aging; and chapters 24 and 25, pages 679 and 721, for many other health issues that affect women from midlife and beyond.

WEIGHT GAIN: A NEW CHALLENGE

At age forty or fifty, many women gain unwanted weight—perhaps for the first time in life. That likely doesn't feel good. It can be uncomfortable and cause low self-esteem. But that's not all. Weight gain is related to increased health risks including high cholesterol, high blood pressure,

? Have you ever wondered?

. . . if foods designed for women are worth it? "Feminine foods," or those nutritionally designed for women's needs, may offer health benefits—for example, soy beverage products, cereals fully fortified with folic acid, and juice with added calcium and vitamin D. Read food labels, then decide if you need what they provide. These foods often cost more. If you already consume enough nutrients from other foods, you may not need them.

. . . if feeling tired could signal a thyroid problem? Perhaps. Symptoms of hypothyroidism, or low thyroid function, include fatigue and mood swings. However, with mild hypothyroidism, you may feel fine. Cold intolerance; dry, brittle hair and skin; hoarseness; difficulty swallowing; forgetfulness; weight gain; and muscle stiffness are other symptoms, usually associated with more severe hypothyroidism. Those with hypothyroid disease are more likely to develop celiac disease, and vice versa.

The American Thyroid Association (ATA) estimates that 12 to 18 percent of the US population have hypothyroidism. Most are women and elderly people. Hashimoto's disease is a common cause of hypothyroidism, which occurs more often in women during middle age and leads to slower metabolism. A gluten-free diet for those with both celiac disease and hypothyroidism helps both conditions. It's not clear if a gluten-free diet can help with the routine treatment of those with just thyroid disease.

Wondering about eating broccoli, cauliflower, kale, and other cruciferous vegetables if you have hypothyroidism? They contain a natural substance called goitrogens that may affect production of the thyroid hormone; however, cooking inactivates them. If you eat a lot of these vegetables—in their raw form—consult your doctor, just in case. Soy products also may interfere with thyroid mediation.

Consult a registered dietitian nutritionist for a healthy eating plan, perhaps to manage your weight as well as other symptoms. Consider asking your doctor about a hormone supplement to manage a thyroid problem. Do not take an iodine supplement unless directed by your doctor. It is effective only when an iodine deficiency causes hypothyroidism.

and insulin resistance (a condition in which your body cannot use insulin correctly, which can lead to type 2 diabetes).

Gaining about one pound per year is common in the mid-life years. The reasons: partly lifestyle shifts and partly the lowering hormone levels associated with menopause, as well as the metabolic impact of natural physical aging. Metabolic rate, or the speed at which the body uses energy, also slows as hormone levels change: less female estrogen and then less progesterone with menopause. With less estrogen, the body metabolizes fat differently, with fat stored as subcutaneous, or under-the-skin, fat.

Why do many middle-aged women gain more belly fat and a thicker midsection that results in a "muffin top"? Hormone shifts—and perhaps more stress and less sleep—promote more visceral fat, which surrounds vital organs and accumulates under the abdominal wall. Abdominal, or visceral, body fat affects insulin sensitivity and glucose metabolism, and it appears to increase the risk for heart disease, higher cholesterol levels, high blood pressure, and insulin resistance as mentioned above—especially for many women who are overweight or obese. The greater the abdominal fat, the greater the waist size and the greater the health risks.

Another reality: By midlife, lifestyles often get more sedentary—perhaps if active work transitions to a sit-down job—demanding less food energy (calories). Caloric intake may not go down enough to compensate. With inactivity, muscle loss happens, too; less muscle means that fewer calories are needed to maintain weight. *Bottom line:* Inactivity and excess calories contribute to weight gain and to muscle mass being replaced by body fat.

While body changes are normal, you don't need to be resigned to excessive weight gain after forty. And there's no magic bullet to avoid weight gain. Plan for your body's natural metabolic slow down: make healthy food choices, avoid oversized portions to control calories, and stay physically active to build and maintain muscle, a firmer body composition, and energy balance. Consuming enough protein also helps preserve muscle mass as you age.

To maintain your healthy weight or to drop a few pounds if needed, adjust your food choices to reduce calories if pounds start to creep on. Follow healthy eating guidelines; *see chapter 2, page 21.* Move more—that includes strength training to maintain muscle and to keep your bones healthy. *See "What's a Healthy Weight?" in chapter 22, page 624.*

MUSCLE LOSS: A CHALLENGE

The body shape of women in their twenties often starts to shift in their thirties and forties. Hormonal and lifestyle changes factor in to the loss of lean muscle. If you're inactive, you can expect to lose about one percent of your lean muscle a year. But you have some control.

Regular physical activity—including activities that build strength, endurance, and flexibility—helps keep and build muscle mass, and limits muscle loss. *See "Move More! Physical Activity Guidelines" in chapter 1, page 15, and "Twenty Ways to Move More" in chapter 22, page 640.*

Nutritionally speaking, consuming enough protein can also help your body preserve muscle mass—and a healthy weight. Research indicates that consuming 25 to 30 grams of protein at each of three meals is optimal. So skip the notion of eating just toast and juice for breakfast, or a vegetable salad for lunch. Eating a meal with protein is a smarter way to help keep your youthful shape.

As an aside, protein may also help your body absorb calcium, which may improve bone health. *See chapter 12, page 373, for more about protein.*

NUTRIENT NEEDS: THE DOWNS AND UPS

Healthy eating—with plenty of vegetables, fruits, and whole grains, and enough low-fat or fat-free dairy foods and lean protein foods—continues to be strong advice for staying healthy during and after menopause. That includes consuming enough calcium, vitamin D, potassium, and fiber, which are linked to many health issues, yet many women under-consume them. And it means avoiding excessive amounts of saturated fats, added sugars, and sodium. *See chapters 11 through 15 for details about these and other nutrients, and "Dietary Reference Intakes" in the appendix, page 780, for recommended amounts for healthy women from midlife and beyond.*

Menopause: Iron and Folate Needs

With menopause, your iron need drops—the RDA decreases from 18 to 8 milligrams of iron daily. No longer having menstrual loss, the risk for iron deficiency decreases. Unless your doctor advises otherwise, stop taking iron supplements. Consuming too much iron, typically from a supplement, can be harmful—especially if you have a genetic disorder called hemochromatosis. With this condition, iron is absorbed more readily and can build up in body organs, causing irreparable damage.

Women in menopause don't need folate to protect against birth defects. However, the RDA remains at 400 micrograms daily, as for younger women who aren't pregnant. If you take supplements, talk to your doctor and likely shift to one with less folic acid. Emerging research suggests that too much folic acid from supplements and fortified foods may increase some health risks, perhaps for some cancers.

See "Iron" and "Folate (Folic Acid or Folacin)" in chapter 14, pages 438 and 419, for more about these nutrients, including more about hemochromatosis.

Bone Health: Calcium and Vitamin D Needs Go Up

Bone loss is part of aging. With a drop in estrogen levels during menopause, women lose bone faster, so calcium needs increase. In the first years after menopause, women lose at least 3 to 5 percent of bone mass per year and 1 percent per year after age sixty-five. Since ovaries produce most of the estrogen, that's also true for those who go through early menopause or have an early hysterectomy.

The smart advice: If you're not quite there, enter menopause with healthy bones and enough bone density to protect you from bone loss due to aging. That window, until a few years after menopause begins, is important.

Boosting your calcium and vitamin D intake and regular weight-bearing exercise helps slow bone loss and reduce risks for osteopenia/osteoporosis and fractures. Women are at greater risk for osteoporosis due to the rapid decline of estrogen that comes with menopause.

For women aged fifty-one and older, the RDA is 1,200 milligrams of calcium daily. For vitamin D the RDA is 15 micrograms (600 IU) daily for ages fifty-one to seventy years, and 20 micrograms (800 IU) over age seventy. As a reference, eight ounces of milk supply about 300 milligrams of calcium and 3 micrograms (120 IU) of vitamin D. Taking a calcium supplement with vitamin D is often advised; however, the benefits aren't clear for adults over age fifty.

For bone health, phytoestrogens haven't been shown to prevent osteopenia/osteoporosis, or lower fracture risk. While hormone therapy may help reduce bone loss, any benefit must be balanced against the increased risk of heart disease and breast cancer.

See "Osteoporosis and Bone Health" in chapter 25, page 738, for more about bone health; and "Vitamin D" and "Calcium" in chapter 14, pages 413 and 425.

Have you ever wondered?

. . . if hormone therapy may ease menopausal discomforts? Perhaps so for some women in early menopause, who are bothered by hot flashes, night sweats, interrupted sleep, and other discomforts. It may also help reduce the risk for osteoporosis. For some women, however, there's an increased risk for heart disease, stroke, and breast cancer with the use of hormone therapy medications that combine estrogen and progesterone.

According to the American Heart Association and the Office of Women's Health, hormone therapy is not advised for the prevention of heart disease, stroke, or other chronic conditions; for women with heart disease or who have had a heart attack or stroke; for women with a history of certain cancers such as breast and uterine; and for women with liver disease or a history of blood clots.

Since there has been a change of thinking on this issue in recent years, discuss with your doctor whether the benefits of hormone therapy outweigh your personal risks. If nutrition and lifestyle strategies aren't effective for relieving your menopausal discomforts, talk to your doctor to see if a low dose for as short a time as needed is appropriate for you. If you choose to use hormone therapy, see your doctor regularly. If you already use hormone therapy, reconsider your options. As an aside, research doesn't show that hormone therapy causes weight gain.

. . . why you may feel bloated with abdominal discomfort during menopause, as you did during your menstrual cycle? Again, fluctuations in hormones may be one reason. Beyond that, with age, your body may produce less lactase, creating some discomfort when consuming some dairy foods. *Follow the advice in "Lactose Intolerance: A Matter of Degree" in chapter 23, page 666, if dairy seems to be an issue.* Consume probiotics to keep your gut bacteria in balance; *see "Prebiotics and Probiotics: A Bioactive Duo" in chapter 15, page 453.* Talk to your doctor for advice and to rule out other health issues.

HOT FLASHES, INSOMNIA, AND OTHER MENOPAUSAL DISCOMFORTS

Menopausal symptoms vary with every woman. Many uncomfortable symptoms such as hot flashes, mood swings, night sweats, vaginal dryness, urinary problems, and sleeplessness persist during perimenopause and menopause. Nutrition and lifestyle strategies—rather than hormone therapy—may help. Talk to your doctor about the best approach for you. Nonhormonal medications may be prescribed.

Hot Flashes and Night Sweats

Hot flashes, or a short-term feeling of heat, perhaps accompanied by sweating (often at night) and a flushed face and neck, are common as hormone levels decline. They typically last about one year, or at least become less severe in time. For some women, they many continue longer, perhaps up to five years.

To manage the discomfort, avoid or control some common triggers, such as alcoholic drinks, caffeine, cigarette smoke, heat, spicy foods, stress, and tight clothing. Some lifestyle changes may help you cope, too. Sleep in a cool room, wear clothes that don't make you too warm, minimize stress, and stay physically active. Slow, deep breathing may also help.

Insomnia or Sleep Disturbances

Trouble sleeping affects about 61 percent of postmenopausal women, notes the National Sleep Foundation. But why? Shifts in hormone levels may account for some sleep disturbances, as a rapid rise in body temperature causes you to suddenly wake up. Emotional swings of midlife are among other contributors.

To encourage undisturbed sleep, try consuming milk or yogurt (low-fat or fat-free) at bedtime, most likely a "comfort food," and perhaps taking a relaxing shower. Enjoy your last caffeinated drink at least four to six hours before bedtime, and last alcoholic drink a few hours before, too. Follow a regular sleep routine. Keep physical activity, preferably early in the day, in your daily routine; done later, it may keep you awake at night. Go to bed when you're truly tired.

Have you ever wondered?

. . . if herbal and other botanical supplements are safe, effective treatments for menopausal symptoms or rebalancing hormones? Even though they're "natural," herbal and other botanical supplements may not be safe or effective. Evidence of their benefits is inconclusive.

- *Black cohosh* may act like estrogen. It may offer some relief from hot flashes, night sweets, or other menopausal symptoms, but evidence isn't conclusive. Side effects may include nausea, headache, or rash. For safety's sake, products with black cohosh may offer this label warning: "Discontinue use and consult a healthcare practitioner if you have a liver disorder or develop symptoms of liver trouble, such as abdominal pain, dark urine, or jaundice."
- *Flaxseed*, with its lignans, may offer some relief of mild symptoms (reducing hot flashes) for some women.
- *Red clover* has natural estrogens, but so far, research shows no significant menopause benefits. Long-term use could increase the risk of uterine cancer.
- *St. John's wort* may help relieve mild depression and mood swings tied to menopause, perhaps no more effective than a placebo.
- *Soy foods and their isoflavones* in amounts in food are safe and perhaps mildly helpful against hot flashes. Soy isoflavone supplements may reduce hot flashes in women after menopause although results are inconsistent; while safe for short periods, they may cause minor stomach and bowel problems.
- *Wild or Mexican yam* contains a substance promoted as an alternative to estrogen therapy. While it seems to have some estrogen-like effects, it is not converted to estrogen in the body.
- Other products without proof of effectiveness for relieving menopausal symptoms include *chasteberry, dong quai, evening primrose oil, ginseng, and valerian root*. Again, they're probably not worth the money. Ginseng may help improve sleep and boost mood.

Before you take herbal or other botanical supplements to reduce menopause symptoms, talk to your doctor or pharmacist. They may interfere with other medications you're taking. Some of these dietary supplements may affect hormone levels. They shouldn't be taken by women with a hormone-sensitive condition such as breast cancer or by younger women on birth control pills. Some may also cause allergic reactions.

See "Herbals and Other Botanicals" in chapter 10, page 320, for more about these and other dietary supplements. Also see Dietary Supplements Fact Sheets, ods.od.nih.gov/factsheets/list-all.

If you're concerned about weight gain, be aware that sleeplessness can affect your feelings of hunger, causing ghrelin, the hunger hormone, to increase and leptin, the satiety hormone, to decrease.

See "Have you ever wondered . . . why sleep is important to your health" in chapter 1, page 5, for more about the benefits.

Mood Swings

Many women experience mood swings such as irritability, anxiety, or depression, as well as memory or concentration problems, particularly during perimenopause. The causes aren't clear. Getting enough sleep, eating in a healthy way, and staying physically active helps, as does staying mentally active.

BREAST CANCER: REDUCING THE RISK

Breast cancer: it's a common fear for good reason. Breast cancer is the most common cancer among North American women, striking over 230,000 women annually. Followed by lung cancer, it's the second most common cause of cancer death for women.

Who's at Risk?

All women are vulnerable to breast cancer—and getting older is a key factor—although some have more risk than others. The CDC cites that risk comes from a combination of factors including:

- A family or personal history of breast cancer (although most women diagnosed with breast cancer don't have a family history of the disease)
- Early menstruation (before age twelve), due to longer exposure to hormones
- Late menopause (after age fifty-five), due to longer exposure to hormones
- Inherited gene mutations (most commonly BRCA1 and BRCA2); they are also at higher risk of ovarian cancer.
- Older-age pregnancy of first child (after age thirty) or no full-term pregnancy
- Radiation treatment to the chest or breasts before age thirty years

- Combination hormone therapy (estrogen plus progesterone) for more than five years
- Being physically inactive
- Being overweight or obese after menopause hormone therapy (estrogen plus progesterone) for more than five years
- Drinking alcoholic beverages, with a higher risk as intake goes up
- Having dense breasts with more connective than fatty tissue, which makes it harder to see tumors on a mammogram
- Simply getting older; most breast cancers are diagnosed after age fifty years.

After menopause, weight gain is linked with increased cancer risk, perhaps related to estrogens formed in the body's fat tissues. Are you a "pear" or an "apple"? The place where extra pounds of body fat settle on your body may make a difference. Early research suggests that women who carry excess body fat around the abdomen (apple shape) may have an increased breast cancer risk. After menopause, more excess weight accumulates there. This visceral fat, which accumulates around internal organs, increases the risk for insulin resistance and, in turn, type 2 diabetes. Visceral fat also increases risk for heart disease, some cancers, and perhaps dementia.

Some women choose to use alcoholic beverages in an attempt to induce sleep or decompress. However, excessive alcoholic beverage consumption may increase breast cancer risk. A daily limit of twelve ounces of beer, five ounces of wine, or one-and-a-half ounces of 80-proof distilled spirits is recommended. If you're at high risk for breast cancer, you may be better off enjoying nonalcoholic drinks instead. *See chapter 4, page 81, for beverage alternatives and more about drinking alcoholic beverages.*

Reducing Breast Cancer Risk

While you need to be "breast cancer aware," having risk factors doesn't make cancer inevitable. Although the causes of breast cancer aren't fully understood, healthy eating, with plenty of vegetables and fruits, maintaining a healthy weight throughout life, exercising regularly, and reducing alcoholic-beverage consumption may help protect you from breast lesions and cancer. Breastfeeding for at least several months in younger years is being studied for its possible role in reducing breast cancer risk. No data currently supports taking dietary supplements for breast cancer prevention.

The best protection is a well-balanced diet and regular physical activity, as well as a normal body weight. Make early detection a habit: monthly self-examination, regular mammograms, and routine breast examinations by your doctor. It's key to increased survival. *See "Your Healthy Body Check-In: Screening Tests for Women: Do You Keep Up?" in this chapter, page 537.*

The American Cancer Society's (ACS's) guidance for diet and cancer prevention relates to reducing the risk for breast cancer as well as other cancers, and to cardiovascular disease as well. *See "American Cancer Society Guidelines on Nutrition and Physical Activity" in chapter 24, page 715, for current recommendations. See "Cancer Connection" in chapter 24, page 713, for more about nutrition and cancer.*

? Have you ever wondered?

. . . if soy foods with their phytoestrogens (the isoflavone genistein) promote breast cancer? Enjoy tofu, tempeh, and edamame! The American Cancer Society notes that human research hasn't shown harm from eating soy foods—and that eating moderate amounts of soy food seems safe for both the general population and for cancer survivors; it may even help lower breast cancer risk. New research also suggests that phytoestrogens in soy are selective and don't have much effect on breast tissue. Dietary soy supplements aren't advised; more research is needed on their effects.

That said, still talk to your doctor before adding soy to your meals and snacks if you have breast cancer, if you're at high risk for breast cancer, or if you're taking tamoxifen, a hormone-blocking drug related to estrogen. Research is underway to explore flaxseed, which contains a type of phytoestrogen called lignan that may protect against hormone-sensitive cancers.

HEART DISEASE: A WOMAN'S ISSUE

For younger women, the incidence of cardiovascular disease is slightly lower than for men. Because estrogen production is highest during childbearing years, younger women usually have better protection from developing heart disease than in their older years.

While estrogen affects nearly every body tissue and organ system, its effects on cardiovascular health aren't fully understood. As estrogen levels drop with menopause, women no longer have the same protection from heart disease and high blood pressure that estrogen gives. HDL ("good") cholesterol levels drop; LDL ("bad") cholesterol levels rise. This is linked to the buildup of fat and cholesterol in the arteries that contributes to heart attack and stroke. That's true whether menopause is natural or surgical.

Studies show that from age fifty-five on, women's heart-disease risks parallel those of men—but seven to ten years later in her life! The death rate for women goes up, perhaps due to increased age or more risk factors. In fact, heart disease (not breast cancer) is the top killer and disabler of American women over age sixty-five. A woman is three times more likely to develop cardiovascular disease than breast cancer. About two-thirds of women who die of heart disease had no previous symptoms.

Ninety percent have one or more risk factors for developing heart disease, according to the American Heart Association (AHA).

Symptoms: Different for Women

The signs of heart disease for women often differ from those of men—and may go unrecognized or ignored. Women often have angina first, rather than a heart attack, and a lower HDL ("good") cholesterol level. When their HDL level drops, women are twice as likely to have a heart attack than men are. A woman's symptoms may be intermittent: unexplained heartburn, profound fatigue, nausea and vomiting, shortness of breath, and back or jaw pain.

Treadmill stress tests for diagnosis are less reliable for women than for men, too. Also less reliable is taking a low-dose aspirin for protection. If you haven't done so already, make heart-healthy choices. Start with small steps, then work your way up. This book is full of practical advice.

Reducing Heart Disease Risk

The AHA's Diet and Lifestyle Recommendations focus on nutrient-dense foods and healthy eating patterns instead of focusing on specific nutrients. They recognize that nutrients in food probably work together with synergistic interactions. *See "Your Healthy Heart" in chapter 24, page 679, for current AHA recommendations.*

The AHA reports that healthy choices have resulted in 330 fewer women dying from heart disease each day. This heart-health advice can make a difference to you. Here are some tips that may help:

- Don't smoke. Quit if you do.
- Control your blood glucose level. Manage diabetes if you have it. A healthy weight lowers your risk of type 2 diabetes. Diabetes increases heart disease risk, for women even more than for men. Aim for a normal blood glucose level. *See "Diabetes: A Growing Concern" in chapter 24, page 698, for guidance.*
- Know your risk factors. Know your heart health numbers. Know your family history.
- Get your blood pressure under control. Lower your blood pressure to optimal levels if you need to. *See "Blood Pressure: Under Control" in chapter 24, page 693, to learn more.*
- Lower your total blood cholesterol and LDL ("bad") cholesterol levels if you need to. *See "Heart Disease: The Blood Lipid Connection" in chapter 24, page 684, to learn about managing cholesterol.*
- Maintain a healthy weight. Trim down if you need to. *See "Weight Management Strategies that Work!" in chapter 22, page 637, for guidance.*
- Eat in a healthy way, *as discussed throughout this book.*
- Live actively. Take time to fit in physical activity. *See "Move More! Physical Activity Guidelines" in chapter 1, page 15, and "Twenty Ways to Move More" in chapter 22, page 640, for physical activity guidelines and ways to fit it in.*
- Control everyday stress, especially if it leads to overeating, smoking, or other risky behaviors.

Need more tips specific to women's health?

Check here for "how-tos":

- Help an adolescent girl address some nutrition issues that start during puberty; *see "Feeding the Teen Machine" in chapter 18, page 524.*
- Follow a safe, effective strategy for reaching and maintaining your healthy weight after pregnancy, menopause, or at any other time of life; *see chapter 22, page 624.*
- Address other issues related to aging; *see chapter 20, page 574.*
- Protect yourself from—or deal with—chronic health problems that afflict women: heart disease, diabetes, cancer (including breast cancer), osteoporosis, and anemia; *see chapters 24 and 25, pages 679 and 721.*
- Choose a supplement ("multi," calcium, iron) if you need it; *see "If You Take a Supplement . . ." in chapter 10, page 335.*
- Find a nutrition expert experienced in women's health issues; *see "How to . . . Find a Qualified Nutrition Expert" in chapter 26, page 759.*

19

Tackle Men's Nutrition Issues

In this chapter, find out about . . .

Healthy food for an active life

Food and fertility for men

The "andropause" and nutrition connection

Eating for a healthy waist, heart, and prostate

On your game? Do you care for your body as well as your car? Good health, strength, and energy matter for men at virtually any age. Among their priorities, most guys want to look good, perform at their best (work, sports, and/or other leisure activity), recover from injury, and avoid health problems along the way.

Making healthy eating and regular physical activity your priorities can help you stay on top of your game—with advice about both addressed throughout this book. Pair that with keeping in shape, getting enough good sleep, taming any work or life stress, drinking alcohol only in moderation (if at all), giving up or not starting tobacco (if you smoke or use chewing tobacco), and keeping a positive outlook on life.

Most advice for healthy eating that applies to adults works for both men and women. As a guy, the major difference is that your energy (calorie) and nutrient needs are a bit higher. The reason: most guys have more muscle and a larger body than most women have. That said, some nutrition and healthy eating advice needs a male perspective. With good health you can make the most of your life now and into the future. If you suspect a health issue at any point in life, take action early!

Guys: Your 20s, 30s—Any Age

Food does more than just power your muscles. How you look and feel and how much energy you have throughout your workday, for sports and then into your free or family time depends in large part on what you eat and drink. How often you make time for a workout or for sports—and how vigorous it is—matters for fitness, too. Together, they help set you up to remain strong, healthy, and in great shape for the long run.

BEYOND MEAT, POTATOES, AND BEER

Are you a meat-and-potatoes kind of guy? Is beer your "go-to" beverage? If so, now's a good time to expand your thinking and shift your options. Even if this isn't your style of eating, this chapter still applies to you!

Many men believe that more protein equals more muscle. That's not necessarily true, unless you do more strength-building activities, too. Another belief: red meat is more masculine than other protein foods, so many guys make steaks their center plate as often as they can. The fact is, other protein choices are good, too—and you don't need huge portions. *See "Muscle Myths" in chapter 21, page 608.*

Body Image and Eating Disorders: An Issue for Men, Too

For guys, the "perfect" athletic male body with muscle mass, leanness, and toned "abs" is the image that's projected in the media. The message is that this is the right body for competing well at work and sports and for romantic success.

These unrealistic media images can lead to misconceived notions about weight, physique, and muscularity—and perhaps masculinity—and can make some men self-conscious of what they deem as their physical flaws. For some, experiencing teasing or bullying in younger years exacerbates the issue. Concerns about body image and a desire for control can lead to eating disorders.

Those involved in sports with weight restrictions are at risk for eating disorders. Self-induced vomiting has become an acceptable, although unhealthy, practice in some circles, as is the use of anabolic steroids to build muscle, also related to body image.

That said, eating disorders are gender neutral. Binge eating disorder is more common among men, while anorexia and bulimia are more common among women.

Among the damaging effects of eating disorders among males are depression, social withdrawal, constipation, electrolyte problems, irregular heart rate, tooth enamel erosion, and low testosterone levels.

Males don't often acknowledge their eating disorder, a problem commonly overlooked by family and doctors, which results in eating disorders commonly under- or undiagnosed in males.

If you notice signs of binge eating or another eating disorder, seek help. Getting professional help is a sign of strength, not weakness.

See "Eating Disorders: More Than a Nutrition Issue" in chapter 25, page 732.

? Have you ever wondered?

. . . if you get enough protein—for your health and muscle strength? On average, most men do, according to the National Health and Nutrition Examination Survey (NHANES) data. In fact, most men exceed the Recommended Dietary Allowance (RDA), which is minimum advice for protein, at 56 grams of protein daily for men.

For more protein benefits, the Dietary Reference Intakes (DRIs) give advice as a range: 10 to 35 percent of your total calories from protein. If you're a moderately active guy aged twenty-six to forty-five years who needs about 2,600 calories daily, that's 65 to 227 grams of protein daily. If you follow food group advice, *discussed in chapter 2, page 21*, you're easily within that range. Choose lean protein foods and low-fat or fat-free dairy foods to limit saturated fats while getting plenty of protein. Ideally, it's best to spread out your protein intake between your meals and snacks.

See "RDAs for Protein: Figuring the Minimum" in chapter 12, page 379, to determine your daily protein target, and also see "Protein: Muscles and More" in chapter 21, page 607, for a list of the protein amounts in many foods.

So . . . when you think "nutrition," protein may come to mind first. Yet, food variety that includes enough of all nutrients and enough calories (but not to excess) is your real asset for strength, health, and more. This sums up the basics of healthy eating advice, *discussed in chapters 2, 3, and 4*:

- Enjoy red meat that's lean and in right-size portions. You don't need a half-pound burger or a twelve-ounce steak to get enough protein. A smaller portion, perhaps five to six ounces, is likely enough in a meal. Combine that with whole-grain or enriched-grain foods, vegetables, fruits, and low-fat or fat-free dairy foods to balance your plate with variety, more nutrients, and enough food energy (calories).

  Lean meat doesn't need to be a steak or burger, either. Any lean beef, pork, or other cut of meat provides similar amounts of protein, zinc, iron, and other nutrients. So do poultry and fish. Among its many roles, zinc from these foods helps your body make testosterone; *see "Zinc" in chapter 14, page 441.*

  Be aware: The American Cancer Society advises to limit processed meat (sausage, ham, jerky, bacon, and cold cuts) and red meat as part of a healthy diet with an emphasis on plant-based foods.
- Switch frequently from red meat to skinless poultry as well as fish. These lean protein foods are great sources of protein for muscle health and more. So are eggs and plant-based protein foods such as beans and peas, nuts, seeds, tempeh, and tofu.
- Make plant-based protein foods the center of your plate occasionally—perhaps with meat or poultry on the sidelines. Think of a pot of chili or bean enchiladas. Besides their protein, beans and peas are great fiber sources, which, down the line, can help keep your blood cholesterol at healthy levels and provide protection from some cancers.
- Like potatoes? Great! They're a good source of several vitamins, complex carbs, and, with their skins on, fiber, too. Switch to sweet potatoes sometimes. Their orange color is your clue to their benefits: they're rich in beta-carotene, which forms vitamin A.
- Go beyond potatoes with more vegetable variety. That will provide more nutrients and antioxidants, too. Get the benefits of flavonoids in leafy greens and deep-green, red, orange, and yellow

vegetables. Some flavonoids, a category of phytonutrients, raise levels of a hormone that triggers the body to make testosterone.

- Want something sweet? Rather than reach for cookies or donuts, grab a piece of fruit. Besides the naturally occurring sugars that provide energy, fruit delivers nutrients and fiber you need to keep fit.
- Switch to more whole-grain "carb" choices from the grain group: maybe a breakfast bowl of oatmeal, a hearty sandwich on whole-grain bread, and brown rice at dinner. They not only deliver complex carbs for energy, but their fiber is good for gastrointestinal health and more. Men typically don't consume enough fiber.
- Keep your body functioning well and your bones strong with enough low-fat or fat-free dairy foods. Ensuring bone health is important now and for the years ahead. (It's not just a women's issue.) Dairy foods are loaded with calcium, vitamin D, potassium, and protein—important for muscle, bones, and more. As an aside, vitamin D from milk, as well as oily fish such as salmon and mackerel, plays an important role in hormone production, including testosterone.

  Make low-fat or fat-free milk or fortified soy alternatives your drink of choice with meals and snacks. Yogurt's a great option, too.
- Keep the lid on fatty foods and foods with added sugars; their calories add up. On the positive side, avocados, canola and olive oils, oily fish (such as salmon), nuts, and seeds all have heart-healthy fats. (Although trendy, coconut oil is high in saturated fats and isn't heart healthy.) *See "Solid Fats and Oils: How Do They Compare?" in chapter 13, page 386, to learn more.*
- If you drink alcoholic beverages, enjoy a beer now and then, but skip drinking the whole six-pack during a game—or whatever takes up your spare time. Twelve ounces times six cans adds up to 900 calories! Same goes for adding on more calories with a third or fourth glass of wine or mixed drink at a party or business function. Set limits: no more than two drinks a day; *see "Alcoholic Beverages: In Moderation" in chapter 4, page 102.*

  A bit of trivia that raises a flag of concern: Data from early estimates in the National Health Interview Survey in 2014 showed that more than 31 percent of men aged eighteen years and older had consumed five or more drinks in one day at least once in the past year.
- Keep portions and snacking under control so you don't overdo on calories and put on extra fat tissue. If you're less athletic or physically active now than in younger years (if you're no longer involved in active sports), body fat can sneak up on you without your realizing it. You need to shift your eating and drinking habits. *See "Waist Management, Guys" in this chapter, page 569, to learn more.*

For more guidance on healthy eating and drinking, see chapter 2, page 21; chapter 3, page 60; and chapter 4, page 81. For specific nutrient recommendations for healthy men in their twenties, thirties, and beyond, see "Dietary Reference Intakes" in the appendix, page 782.

Supplements Targeted to Men

Mass gainers, testosterone boosters, creatine, pre-workout supplements—do you need them? While some may offer benefits, getting regular workouts, perhaps from your favorite sport, working out at the gym, jogging, or cycling, along with healthy eating and plenty of food variety, are healthier and more effective.

Side effects from some ergogenic, or muscle-building, supplements may have side effects that actually hinder performance. Some may be harmful, especially in the long run. Anabolic steroids can lower your testosterone level. Some evidence also suggests that the use of supplements with creatine or androstenedione may be linked to a higher risk of testicular cancer, especially among men who begin using them before age twenty-five, who use various types of supplements for muscle building, or who use them for a long time. It's unknown what ingredients might be responsible.

Research reports show mixed results on the effectiveness of testosterone supplements for improving sexual function, especially among men who are healthy.

Learn more about supplements here:

- Vitamin, mineral, herbal, and botanical supplements in *chapter 10, page 315.*
- Whey protein for muscle building in *"Have you ever wondered . . . what casein is? What whey protein is?" in chapter 12, page 382, and "Protein Sources: What Foods? When?" in chapter 21, page 609.*
- Muscle building: hormone supplements ("andro" and DHEA) and dietary supplements (amino acids, creatine) in *"Hormone Supplements for Sports: Uses and Concerns" in chapter 21, page 620.*

"Bro science" is often quackery, or misinformation, presented in a masculine way to capture your interest. Be wary of websites that offer information about nutrition and "super foods" or supplements—*and* sell products, perhaps as body builders or testosterone boosters. *See "Unravel the Online Information 'Web'" in chapter 26, page 754, for ways to judge the credibility of a website or app.*

If you are considering taking a supplement, talk to your doctor or a registered dietitian nutritionist about its potential benefits and risks before taking it.

PHYSICAL ACTIVITY: GO THE DISTANCE

Did you play sports as a teen? And did everyday living keep your body moving even when you weren't involved in sports?

Even if responsibilities of work, home life, and parenting shift your lifestyle, don't move exercise to the sidelines. Get and stay on track with physical activity. If you have a desk job, sinking into a chair by the TV or computer after work needs to be balanced with physically active time.

Being just a "weekend warrior" isn't the answer, either. For your good health, looks, strength, and energy, make a variety of physical activities a nearly daily habit:

- *Strength training and building.* Use free weights, push-ups, pull-ups, and crunches, and perhaps weight machines, to improve and keep up your strength, burn calories, build muscles, firm up, and, if you need to, trim off excess fat tissue and weight.
- *Aerobic activity.* Walk, jog, swim, bike, or spin for fitness, endurance, and mental well-being, as well as to burn calories. This helps maintain a healthy weight.
- *Flexibility and stretching.* Activities such as yoga, tai chi, and stretching before and after a workout reduce your risk for injury, improve your blood flow, and help you recover from muscle soreness.

Did You Know?

. . . the workout notion of "no pain, no gain" isn't necessary? More important, working out until your body hurts can cause injury. Regular and varied physical activity (moderate or more intense), not pain, is what matters. *See chapter 21, page 599, for more about physical activity level and sports.*

. . . guys may be more susceptible to overeating in social situations than women are? According to a Cornell University study, men tend to feel empowered to overeat around others. "Outeating" other guys, perhaps in competitive eating contests, as a way to showcase virility and strength to spectators may seem "cool" and exhilarating. For a healthier way to show the "macho" spirit, challenge friends a healthy arm wrestle.

. . . getting enough sleep (seven to nine hours per day) can reduce your risk of type 2 diabetes, heart disease, obesity, and depression? The quality and length of your sleep pattern can affect your metabolic rate, your immunity, your ability to deal with workday and life stresses, and even your hunger patterns. *See "Have you ever wondered . . . why sleep is important to your health?" in chapter 1, page 5.*

. . . although perhaps embarrassing, that passing gas or burping is normal and usually not a health concern? Your body makes gas when food is digested. Passing gas up to twenty times a day is normal. So are three or four burps after a meal, often caused by swallowing air. Pay attention to what may affect you; a few changes in what you eat and drink may help reduce the amount or discomfort of gas. *See "How to. . . Deal with Intestinal Gas" in chapter 11, page 354, for ways to reduce gas from eating beans and other high-fiber foods.*

Be aware that some health conditions such as lactose intolerance or a bowel obstruction can cause excessive gas. And sometimes people dismiss symptoms of a heart attack as "just gas." In either case, these require medical attention.

Click Here! Links to Know . . .

- Men's Health: MedlinePlus
  www.nlm.nih.gov/medlineplus/menshealth.html
- Men's Health Network
  www.menshealthnetwork.org
- Nutrition.gov, National Agricultural Library, USDA
  www.nutrition.gov/life-stages/men

- *Sports.* Whether it's pickup or organized, play volleyball, basketball, tennis, or some other active sport for your fitness, strength, and coordination, as well as to burn calories. Sports adds variety to your "game plan."
- *Everyday moves.* Your activity doesn't need to come only from sports. Mow the lawn, shovel snow, wash your car, and take the stairs to burn some calories and reduce your health risks throughout life.

See "Move More! Physical Activity Guidelines" in chapter 1, page 620, for more advice about daily physical activity and chapter 21, page 620, to learn about sports nutrition and peak physical performance. Data from early estimates in the National Health Interview Survey in 2014 show that only about half of men aged eighteen years and older met the 2008 federal physical-activity guidelines for aerobic activity through leisure-time aerobic activity.

FERTILITY: A MAN'S HEALTH COUNTS

Eager to be a dad? Pregnancy is about your fertility, not just that of your female partner. A man's food choices, lifestyle, and overall health are as important as a woman's for conceiving a healthy baby. In fact, about a third of infertility cases are linked to guys.

How so? Your food and lifestyle choices affect your reproductive health. Among the common causes of sperm-related infertility are low sperm count, slow-moving sperm, abnormally shaped and sized sperm, and insufficient semen to carry a sperm to the egg.

Even if your food and lifestyle decisions need improvement, a few months of better choices can get your reproductive health in better shape. The cycle of sperm production takes about three months. Positive changes in your food and lifestyle may improve fertility and sperm health in just a few months:

- Make healthy eating your priority. Good nutrition (balanced, varied, and adequate) can impact sperm production. Follow guidelines for healthy eating throughout this book.
- Maintain a healthy weight. Too much body fat tissue can disturb the balance of your sex hormones, which in turn affect fertility.

Being underweight can decrease sperm count or affect sperm function, too. In either case, working toward a healthier weight may positively affect your testosterone level.

As discussed earlier in this chapter, eat smart, and balance your calorie intake with physical activity. *See "Weight: What's Healthy?" in chapter 22, page 625, for more about body composition and a healthy weight.*

- Stay physically active. However, avoid excessive endurance exercise: too much or for too long. Overactivity may put your hormones out of balance, indirectly lowering your testosterone level and sperm count. Talk to your doctor about the type of sports you do; for example, strenuous, regular mountain biking is linked to a lower sperm count and scrotum abnormalities.
- Avoid anabolic steroids or artificial testosterone, used to increase muscle mass and improve athletic performance. These can cause testicular damage and lower your testosterone level. *See "Hormone Supplements for Sports" in chapter 21, page 620, to learn more.*
- If you drink alcoholic beverages, limit your intake. Excessive intake, which may throw off your body's hormonal balance, is linked to poor production of healthy sperm. Set limits: no more than two drinks a day; less may be best. Twelve ounces of beer, five ounces of wine, or one and a half ounces of distilled spirits, such as vodka, whiskey, or gin, count as one drink. *See "Alcoholic Beverages: In Moderation" in chapter 4, page 102, for more about drink equivalents and limiting your intake.*
- If you smoke, stop. Tobacco use in any form—including cigarettes, cigars, smokeless tobacco (chewing tobacco and snuff), pipes, hookahs (water pipes), and other tobacco products—is linked with a low sperm count and slow-moving sperm. Restricted blood flow, due to nicotine in the bloodstream, also can result in erectile dysfunction. Even your secondhand smoke can affect the fertility of a woman and the outcome of a pregnancy—and a woman's secondhand smoke can also affect male fertility.

  E-cigarettes, or "vaping"? The jury's out on health implications. While they may be less harmful than regular cigarettes, their secondhand smoke and long-term effects are yet unknown.

  As an aside: Infants and children exposed to secondhand smoke are sick more often than others. Evidence shows that kids with parents who smoke have more frequent and severe asthma attacks, respiratory infections, ear infections, and sudden infant death syndrome.
- Talk to your doctor about other factors that can affect your fertility and your sperm health, including medications, even over-the-counter medications. And avoid recreational drugs.

? Have you ever wondered?

. . . if eating soy foods will cause feminine characteristics (breasts) or impair fertility? No—so you don't need to worry about losing a male physique if foods with isoflavones (as weak phytoestrogens) such as edamame, soymilk, and tofu are a regular part of your meals. Clinical research doesn't show that soy foods lower the testosterone level or sperm concentration, or cause gynecomastia, or male breast tissue. Obesity (too much fat tissue), genetics, and some medications may play a role in male breast-tissue growth. On the flip side, some evidence indicates that soy foods may help protect against prostate cancer.

. . . if beer drinking really causes a beer belly? Yes, it can. Like too many calories from any source, a few extra beers—or other alcoholic drinks—can end up as unhealthy, unsightly belly fat. Those calories, added to the snacks that often go with drinking, can quickly add up to a "beer belly." Remember that a twelve-ounce beer has 150 calories, and many cans and bottles of beer hold more. Over time, especially when one beer leads to another, that adds up.

. . . if, like wine in moderation, drinking beer may have some health benefits? Maybe so—in moderation (no more than one to two beers, or twelve to twenty-four ounces, daily for adult men), but not as a six-pack! Starting to drink for health benefits isn't advised.

Like wine, beer contains polyphenols, which have antioxidant qualities that may help your heart. Beer is also a source of B vitamins. Other research suggests (but doesn't confirm) that it may reduce the risk of kidney stones as compared to drinking other alcoholic beverages. This may be due to its diuretic effect, its high water content, or the compounds in hops that may slow the release of calcium from bone, which may be linked to kidney stones.

. . . if BMI is a good tool for assessing your body weight? Body mass index (BMI) is one indicator, but it doesn't give the full story of muscle tissue and body composition, *as discussed in "Weight: What's Healthy?" in chapter 22, page 626.* For men with more muscle mass, their BMI may go above the "healthy range" on a BMI chart even though body fat isn't excessive. A BMI in the "overweight range" isn't a metabolic concern if the reason is more muscle. It is a concern if the reason is too much body fat. Talk to your doctor to accurately assess your body composition and BMI.

Dad's Role: Parenting Healthy Kids

From conception on, dads are as important to children and teens—and their overall health and well-being—as moms are. The food and lifestyle decisions you make as a father, or father figure, serve as good examples for your kids. And the health decisions you make for yourself affect their health and lives, too, directly and indirectly.

Parenting begins even before birth, starting out as a supportive, encouraging dad to a new mom during pregnancy and then to mom and baby during breastfeeding or bottle feeding; and from then on, it means also "being there" in the many ways a child or teen is nourished and nurtured for growth, development, and overall health. Healthy parents provide the guidance and setting for healthy kids. That's a slam dunk!

To help your kids grow strong and healthy:

- Take your turn with infant feeding. Do you feel clumsy, anxious, and uneasy with bottle feeding—or with helping test a first try with a spoon? Your confidence with infant feeding will come with practice and by assuming part of the responsibility. A benefit to dad and baby: building closer bonds with each other.
- What's your role in breastfeeding? Your support, encouragement, and confidence given to a new mother are often key to her success, especially if a mom's lack of sleep and hormonal changes make breastfeeding seem too challenging. And, you can be an advocate among other soon-to-be dads. *See "Help from Dad" in chapter 16, page 468, for ways you can help with infant feeding.*
- Whenever you can, share meals at the table (without the TV or cell phone) with your child or children—including your teenage kids. Family mealtime not only builds relationships, but evidence shows that children and teens who eat with their families have better nutrition, healthier weights, better learning success, and in their teen years, less substance abuse.
- Be your child's role model for healthy eating. Offer healthy foods and help him or her learn to make healthy food choices. That includes snacks and drinks. Kids watch and model what they see. So, if vegetables and fruits haven't caught your attention, now's the time to give them an important place on your plate. The same is true for low-fat or fat-free milk as your beverage of choice instead of sodas.
- Take your turn at food shopping and food prep with your kids. It's another way to help your kids learn to make healthy food choices and to spend time together. *See chapters 6, page 141, and 8, page 230, for a refresher on shopping and cooking for good health.*
- Encourage your child to enjoy active play for at least an hour a day. As he or she gets older, this might involve sports, both noncompetitive and competitive. The activity helps strengthen bones and muscles, build stamina, and develop motor skills. If you're active together, it builds your relationship—and it's fun! (An added benefit: it's a way to get your own daily exercise in, too.)

See chapter 17, page 489, to learn about good nutrition for kids, the family table, role modeling, active play, and more to help you as a parent or parent figure.

Men: Middle Years and Beyond

Whatever your age, keep your eye on the ball. Looking after your own health matters, and it's never too late to start.

Two sobering statistics: On average, men live about five to six years less than women. The death rate for most leading causes of death, including cancer, heart disease, diabetes, and suicide, is higher for men. Mental health can also be an issue, too, especially for older men.

Prevention matters for better health. Yet men typically schedule far fewer preventative medical visits than women do. See your doctor regularly, even when you're not sick. Discuss changes you notice in your physical or emotional health, and from any medications or supplements you take.

Know your family health history. Regular health screening and checkups, plus tracking your key health numbers and keeping them within a healthy range, reduces your risk for many chronic diseases such as heart disease, stroke, diabetes, and many types of cancer. Talk with your doctor about health issues common with aging such as heart disease, prostate and urinary problems, type 2 diabetes, depression, and Alzheimer's disease.

See "Your Healthy Body Check-In: Screening Tests for Men. Do You Keep Up?" in this chapter, page 572, and "Do You Know Your Numbers?" in chapter 24, page 681.

See chapter 20, page 574, for more about healthy aging and chapters 24, page 679, and 25, page 721, for more about several health concerns. For specific nutrient recommendations for healthy men in their middle years and beyond, see "Dietary Reference Intakes" in the appendix, page 782.

WAIST MANAGEMENT, GUYS

As for anyone, being overweight (from too much body fat) or obese may pose risks for men for a number of health concerns; *see "Obesity: The Risks" in chapter 22, page 630, for more about possible health risks.* So now's the time to get rid of any excess pounds of fat tissue you may have been carrying around for the past few years. An interesting statistic: the Centers for Disease Control and Prevention (CDC) indicates that

American men on average weigh about fifteen pounds more than they did two decades ago.

As men transition from the more muscular shape of youth toward the middle years, many gain weight in the midriff area. Men have more adipocytes, or fat-storing cells, around their abdomen, while women have more in their thighs, buttocks, and breasts. This is visceral fat, buried in the abdomen around internal organs such as the liver, pancreas, and intestines.

Visceral fat may play a role in developing insulin resistance, which boosts the risk for type 2 diabetes. In fact, it seems to have more potential health risks than the fat layer beneath the skin (subcutaneous fat) and fat in other parts of the body. Visceral fat may also increase the risk for heart disease, high blood pressure, and some cancers, and may be linked to dementia.

Get out the tape measure. If your waist measures forty inches around or more, it's time to shed some belly fat, slowly and healthfully. Dropping just 5 to 10 percent of your body weight may improve your overall health. To get your midsection under control, cut your portion sizes, engage in physical activity to balance the calories from food and drink with those you burn off, lower your stress level, cut back on alcoholic drinks, and try for seven to eight hours of sleep daily.

See "Weight Management: Strategies That Work" in chapter 22, page 637.

"ANDROPAUSE": AGING MALE SYNDROME

Testosterone, a hormone mainly secreted by the testicles, helps maintain sperm production, sex drive, bone density, facial and body hair, and muscle strength and mass. It also affects red blood cell production and fat distribution in the body.

As men get older, the body produces less testosterone than it did in the adolescent and early adult years. That's normal. Researchers indicate that natural decline may be about one percent a year after about age thirty to forty. With less testosterone, often called "low T," than earlier in life, men still remain fertile. However, as hormone levels go down—in differing amounts for different men—guys may notice some changes: weight gain, problems with sleeping, increased urination, less energy, emotional changes or depression, changes in sex drive, and bone, hair, and muscle loss.

The only way to identify "low T" is with a blood test. How might you minimize the hormonal shifts and changes that come with it? Healthy eating, regular physical activity, reducing stress, and adequate sleep may help. In fact, food and lifestyle strategies may be the most effective strategies for healthy life and sexual functions:

- Lose weight in a healthy way if you need to, or keep from gaining weight. Excessive abdominal fat tissue can lead to low testosterone levels. Excessive weight gain also can lead to other health issues; *see "Weight and Health" in chapter 22, page 628.*
- Strength train to help preserve muscle tissue and stimulate testosterone secretion. With physical activity, your brain signals a need for more testosterone. For raising testosterone levels, strength training has more benefits than cardio workouts, but overdoing can have the reverse effect.
- Find ways to control stress. Being overstressed, perhaps from working long hours, releases a steady amount of a hormone called cortisol, which affects the body's ability to create testosterone.
- Get enough good sleep. Lack of sleep affects many body chemicals and hormones and is linked to low testosterone levels in many men. If you have trouble sleeping, remember that sleep disorders are linked to weight gain. Seek ways to get a good night's rest (seven to eight hours per night). *See "Have you ever wondered . . . why sleep is important to your health?" in chapter 1, page 5.*

HEART DISEASE: A TOP HEALTH ISSUE FOR MEN

Just being a guy makes your risk for cardiovascular disease higher at an earlier age than for women. In fact, heart disease is the leading cause of death among men. Having excessive fat tissue, eating fatty foods, smoking cigarettes, and being inactive puts you at a greater risk. Rather than becoming a statistic, minimize the risk factors to live a longer and healthier active life.

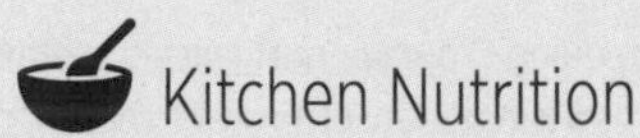

Man the Grill

Fair or not, an outdoor grill often gets appropriated to men. When grilling a great meal, try this:

- Mind the meat; go lean. Choose flank steak; sirloin; 95 percent lean ground beef; pork tenderloin; lean lamb; bison (buffalo); boneless, skinless chicken breast; or nearly any kind of fish. Use a grill basket for delicate fish. Try black bean burgers or grilled tofu as a meat-free option.
- Boost flavor without using marinades that are full of oil, sugar, or sodium. Instead, use dry herb rubs, salt-free spice blends, cayenne pepper, or hot sauce to kick up the flavor—or use a low-sodium prepared marinade with under 5 grams of sugar per serving.
- Go green—make room on the grill for vegetables, such as asparagus, broccoli, and green bell peppers, as well as corn, eggplant, summer squash, sweet potato, and zucchini. Brush on a little oil to keep them from sticking to the grill. Grilling brings out new flavors of vegetables you may not have experienced before.
- Go for sweet success. You can grill fruit too, as a side or for dessert. Try pineapple slices or halved peaches or plums; grill just until tender.

See "Grilling Food Safely," in chapter 7, page 215, for more about grilling.

The signs of a heart attack or stroke differ somewhat for men and women. For men, symptoms of a heart attack may be:

- Chest discomfort with a feeling of pressure, pain, or squeezing (the most common sign of a heart attack)
- Shortness of breath
- Sweating
- Feeling nauseated or lightheaded
- Discomfort in the abdomen, arms, back, jaw, or neck

Numbness or weakness in your face or limbs, often on one side of the body, are some signs of a stroke; confusion, imbalance, vision changes, and an intense headache are some others. *See "Warning Signs: Heart Attack, Stroke, and Cardiac Arrest" in chapter 24, page 692, for more information about symptoms that differ from symptoms among women. See "Symptoms: Different for Women" in chapter 18, page 563.*

This heart-health advice can keep you in the game:

- Know your personal risk factors: how your "health numbers" (blood glucose levels, blood pressure, body mass index, total and LDL cholesterol levels, and waist circumference) stack up and whether you have a family history of heart disease, stroke, or type 2 diabetes. Discuss this with your doctor—and manage what you need to. *See "Your Healthy Heart" and "Diabetes: A Growing Concern" in chapter 24, page 680, and page 698.*
- Know the early signs of a heart attack or stroke, *as just discussed.* Recovery for you or someone else depends on the speed of proper treatment—and a quick 9-1-1 call!
- Eat in a heart-healthy way. Choose lean meats and more plant-based foods such as whole-grain foods, vegetables, fruits, beans, and heart-healthy oils, as well as animal based foods such as low-fat and fat-free dairy foods, and lean protein foods (meat, skinless poultry, and fish). *Be aware:* eating excessive amounts of meat is linked to heart disease, as well as colon cancer. *Heart healthy eating is discussed throughout this book and in "Your Healthy Heart" and "Blood Pressure: Under Control?" in chapter 24, pages 680, and 693.*
- Manage your weight. Lose excess pounds if you need to through physical activity and reducing calories as part of healthy eating. Being overweight or obese, especially if you carry extra fat tissue in your abdomen, is linked to a higher risk for heart disease.
- Make physical activity a habit. Find an activity you enjoy, perhaps hitting the gym before work, playing tennis with a buddy, or walking your dog after dinner with your spouse or kids. Just thirty minutes a day, five days a week can reduce your risk significantly; being a "couch potato" ups the risk. Aerobic activity—walking, swimming, bicycling—is best for heart health. These activities make your heart beat faster, allowing more blood flow to your muscles and then to your lungs; make your capillaries widen, transferring more oxygen to your muscles; and make you breathe deeper and faster, putting more oxygen in your bloodstream. If you have a family history of heart disease or type 2 diabetes and are over age forty, talk to your doctor about strenuous activity.
- Don't use tobacco. The CDC estimates that smoking quadruples the risk of heart disease. Inhaling secondhand smoke puts you at risk, too.
- Control everyday stress, especially if it leads to overeating, smoking, alcohol abuse, or other risky behaviors.

See chapter 24, page 680, to learn more about preventing and managing heart disease, stroke, and hypertension.

Have you ever wondered?

. . . if men can get breast cancer? Although rare, it can happen. Among the risk factors: older age, alcoholism, obesity, chronic liver problems, a genetic condition linked to high estrogen levels, and having a family member—female or male—with breast cancer. Talk with your doctor if you think you may be at risk.

. . . if osteoporosis is also a man's health issue? Although less common than for women, older men can be at risk for osteoporosis. In fact, the National Osteoporosis Foundation (NOF) notes: Men older than age fifty are more likely to break a bone due to osteoporosis than they are to get prostate cancer. Surprised?

Men's larger bone structure gives protection, and they don't experience bone loss from the rapid hormone shifts of menopause. However, both physical and lifestyle factors can put them at higher risk: low intake of bone-building nutrients (including calcium and vitamin D), low level of testosterone, gastrointestinal disease, aging, lack of physical mobility, alcohol abuse, smoking, and anabolic steroid use.

The NOF also notes that low estrogen levels in men can also lead to bone loss, as well as having medical conditions such as chronic kidney, lung, or gastrointestinal disease; prostate cancer; and certain autoimmune disorders such as rheumatoid arthritis. For older men, the older the age, the greater the risk.

To keep your bones healthy, get enough calcium and vitamin D daily from food and perhaps supplements, too. Participate in regular weight-bearing and strength-training activities at least twice weekly. Avoid smoking. Limit alcoholic drinks to two a day. Talk to your doctor about your bone health. If appropriate, ask for a bone-density test and take prescribed medications. *See "Osteoporosis and Bone Health" in chapter 25, page 738.*

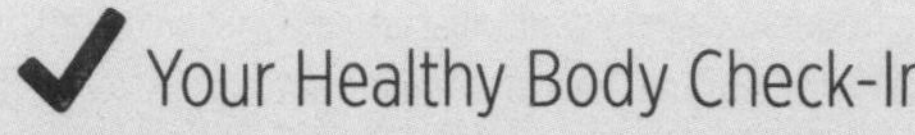

Your Healthy Body Check-In

Screening Tests for Men: Do You Keep Up?

Screening is key to promoting health and preventing disease. Many chronic health problems are linked to food choices or nutrition in one way or another, *as discussed throughout this book*. Use the chart below to find out which tests are appropriate for your age, then during your regular checkup, talk to your doctor about getting the ones you need. This chart is a general guideline; your doctor will personalize the timing of these tests for your needs. For the complete chart, which includes other important tests (abdominal aortic aneurysm screening, HIV test, and syphilis screening), visit www.womenshealth.gov/screening-tests-and-vaccines/screening-tests-for-men.

Take the opportunity at your regular checkups to ask about other health issues, too: overweight and obesity, alcohol use, and vaccines, such as for the flu, shingles, and pneumonia as you get older.

Screening Test	Ages 18–39	Ages 40–49	Ages 50–64	Ages 65 and Older
Blood pressure test	Get tested at least every 2 years if you have normal blood pressure (lower than 120/80).	Get tested at least every 2 years if you have normal blood pressure (lower than 120/80).	Get tested at least every 2 years if you have normal blood pressure (lower than 120/80).	Get tested at least every 2 years if you have normal blood pressure (lower than 120/80).
	Get tested once a year if you have blood pressure between 120/80 and 139/89.	Get tested once a year if you have blood pressure between 120/80 and 139/89.	Get tested once a year if you have blood pressure between 120/80 and 139/89.	Get tested once a year if you have blood pressure between 120/80 and 139/89.
	Discuss treatment with your doctor or nurse if you have blood pressure 140/90 or higher.	Discuss treatment with your doctor or nurse if you have blood pressure 140/90 or higher.	Discuss treatment with your doctor or nurse if you have blood pressure 140/90 or higher.	Discuss treatment with your doctor or nurse if you have blood pressure 140/90 or higher.
Cholesterol test	Starting at age 20 and continuing to age 35, get a cholesterol test if you are at increased risk for heart disease. Starting at age 35 and continuing to age 39, get a cholesterol test regularly. Ask your doctor or nurse how often you need your cholesterol tested.	Get a cholesterol test regularly. Ask your doctor or nurse how often you need your cholesterol tested.	Get a cholesterol test regularly. Ask your doctor or nurse how often you need your cholesterol tested.	Get a cholesterol test regularly. Ask your doctor or nurse how often you need your cholesterol tested.
Colorectal cancer screening (using fecal occult blood testing, sigmoidoscopy, or colonoscopy)	No screening needed.	No screening needed.	Starting at age 50, get screened for colorectal cancer. Ask your doctor or nurse which screening test is best for you and how often you need it.	Get screened for colorectal cancer through age 75. Ask your doctor or nurse which screening test is best for you and how often you need it.
Diabetes screening	Get screened for diabetes if your blood pressure is higher than 135/80 or if you take medicine for high blood pressure.	Get screened for diabetes if your blood pressure is higher than 135/80 or if you take medicine for high blood pressure.	Get screened for diabetes if your blood pressure is higher than 135/80 or if you take medicine for high blood pressure.	Get screened for diabetes if your blood pressure is higher than 135/80 or if you take medicine for high blood pressure.

Source: Office on Women's Health, US Department of Health and Human Services, www.womenshealth.gov/mens-health. Accessed December 1, 2016.

Have you ever wondered?

. . . if drinking green tea or pomegranate juice can reduce your risk for or treat prostate cancer? The jury's out on both counts. While some studies suggest that green tea, with its polyphenols (antioxidants) may protect against some types of cancer, including prostate cancer, clinical trials are only in their early stages. Evidence hasn't yet shown that green tea is an effective treatment.

Some research suggests that drinking pomegranate juice may help slow the rise in PSA or perhaps the growth of cancer cells, and so slow the progression of prostate cancer. The evidence is unclear. Before making pomegranate juice a daily habit, talk to your doctor; it may interact with some medications taken to control blood cholesterol levels or high blood pressure.

. . . if any supplements can protect against hair loss? For guys, nearly all hair loss comes from a genetic trait called male pattern baldness. There's no cure and no evidence that taking any dietary supplement makes a difference. As always, a healthy way of eating along with good hygiene and hair care can help you make the most of the hair you have.

PROSTATE HEALTH: REDUCING CANCER RISK

Aside from some types of skin cancer, prostate cancer is the most common cancer among men in the United States. Each year, more than 220,000 men are diagnosed with prostate cancer. Fortunately, it's highly treatable if caught early. *See "Cancer Connection" in chapter 24, page 713, to learn about the prevention of other cancers and about cancer treatment*

What's your risk? Being age sixty-five or older increases the chances, as does having a father, brother, or son with prostate cancer or being African American. Healthy eating, active living, and reducing stress to promote your overall health may help reduce your risk of developing prostate cancer, even as you get older or if you have a genetic risk.

- Eat for good health. Although not proven, making food choices for overall good health, with plenty of vegetables and fruits and limited dietary fat may lower your risk for prostate cancer. That same approach to eating also helps maintain a healthy weight, promotes heart health, and may be the best defense against nearly all types of cancer.

  Eating at least two and a half cups of vegetables and two cups of fruits per day appears protective. Deep-colored vegetables and fruits, such as red and orange bell peppers, spinach, tomatoes, and all kinds of berries have higher levels of many carotenoids, including lycopene, and other beneficial nutrients. Unfortunately, no single nutrient, vegetable or fruit, has been proven to reduce prostate cancer risk.

  Replacing solid fats (saturated and *trans* fats) and foods high in solid fats with healthy alternatives may be protective, too. Choose canola, olive, and other oils, and foods containing healthy oils, such as avocados, oily fish such as salmon, and nuts. These alternatives have been linked to a lower risk of prostate cancer, but the associations are yet unknown.
- Manage your weight. Lose excess pounds if you need to through physical activity and reducing calories as part of healthy eating. Being overweight or obese, especially if you carry extra fat tissue in your abdomen, is associated with a higher risk for prostate cancer.
- Be wary of dietary supplements with claims of preventing prostate cancer. In fact, some research suggests that high levels of some nutrients from supplements, including vitamin E and selenium, actually may increase the risk. Any nutrients that may be protective should come from food, not supplements.
- Stay physically active. Ramp up your daily activity, especially if your day (work and home) is mostly sedentary. Most evidence indicates that regular physical activity reduces the risk of prostate cancer. Beyond that, exercise promotes heart health, promotes a healthy weight, and reduces the risk for other cancers and health problems.
- Talk to your doctor about screening for prostate cancer—and the benefits and risks of screening for you. If advised, screening typically includes a Prostate Specific Antigen (PSA) blood test to measure a protein in blood produced by prostate cells. Note that an elevated PSA does not necessarily indicate cancer; it may mean an enlarged prostate or an infection.

Many men don't experience any symptoms of prostate cancer in the early stages. That said, it's important to find prostate cancer early when it's most treatable and hasn't spread elsewhere in the body.

20

Eat Healthy Beyond Midlife

In this chapter, find out about . . .

Eating right for healthy aging

Keeping the biomarkers of good health

Solutions for the food challenges of aging

Are you age sixty plus, or do you have an older relative or a friend? Are you in the "sandwich generation"—caught between caring for kids and older parents?

Adults whose ages span nearly half a century—from their sixties into their hundreds—can't be described singly or simply. Diversity describes every decade of the older years. In fact, today's sixty often is considered to be the new forty—with a different mind-set and a healthier body and lifestyle—than in past generations. Many people live full, active lives that differ little from life in their forties or fifties. Others are limited by health and lifestyle challenges. Of course, life and health change gradually as the years go by. That's part of life. Yet person by person, aging differs. If you're active and healthy, the latter part of this chapter may not apply to you; but especially if you are a caregiver, it may offer insights to help an older family member or friend, including one who may live alone.

Except for a few shifts in nutrient and calorie needs, overall health and attitude define aging more than calendar age does. That said, as an age group, older adults are at risk for developing chronic illnesses and related disabilities, including arthritis, congestive heart failure, dementia, and type 2 diabetes—because they're older.

So, with what you know now, if you were twenty, thirty, or forty again, would you make smarter food choices? Fit more physical activity into your life? Deal with stress better? Try to sleep more? You can't change the past—or stop the clock. Antiaging is impossible, but the choices made now, or at any age with many health conditions, can slow the changes and minimize the challenges that come with getting older, and may even extend your youth.

Being positive about aging as a natural process—rather than dwelling on negatives that come, too—can help you both physically and mentally. Whatever your age, start now to eat smarter and move more, and continue the many opportunities in your life's journey. From cover to cover, this book is all about the many strategies that promote healthy aging—yours and that of family and friends—throughout life. In this chapter, you'll find additional insights into the changes that occur during the sixty-plus years.

- If you're healthy and active, *check "Healthy Eating and Active Living Matter," page 575, for advice.*
- For advice on how lifestyle and physical changes that come with aging affect food-related decisions, *turn to "When Lifestyles Change," page 587.*

Healthy Eating and Active Living Matter

It's no secret: How you eat—and how active you are—have plenty to do with your biological age. Smart food choices and active living today not only keep your mind sharp, but may also help you feel younger; stay healthier, stronger, and more productive as well as self-sufficient; and enjoy a healthier, higher quality of life.

Looking positively at aging may even add a few more healthy years. You may also spend less money and time on health care. *See "How 'Old' Are You? Biomarkers of Age" in this chapter, page 576.*

FOOD FOR HEALTHY AGING

It's all about the food. Whatever your age, you need all the same nutrients that food provides—proteins, carbohydrates, fats, vitamins, minerals, and water—but perhaps in slightly different amounts, and the right amount of calories (food energy).

Calories: How Many?

As you get older, you likely use less energy (calories) than in your younger years. In fact, your calorie needs may go down by as much as 25 percent for two reasons:

- First, the obvious: if you're less physically active, your body burns fewer calories.
- Second, your basic body processes use energy at a slower rate as you age. With less lean body mass (in skeletal muscle, smooth muscle, and body organs), the body uses less energy to maintain itself. A slower metabolism doesn't equate to the need for less of most nutrients, however, just fewer calories. In fact, for some nutrients, they're a bit higher.

How many calories do you need if you're an older adult? Likely fewer now than in younger years—and that varies. Considering activity level, gender, health status, and age, as well as height and weight, many sedentary women aged sixty and older need just 1,600 calories daily, and 1,800 calories if they're moderately active. Many sedentary men of the same age need about 2,000 to 2,200 calories daily—with a little more if moderately active. Doesn't seem like many calories? *See "Calorie Basics" in chapter 1, page 7, for more about energy needs.*

For every age, consuming enough calories without overdoing it helps keep you at your healthy weight. The benefits of a healthy weight as you hit these older years? Better quality of life, ease of handling any disabilities if they arise, and less risk for many chronic health problems, such as type 2 diabetes and heart disease.

Chosen carefully, foods that deliver calories can—and should—also be nutrient rich. Know your calorie goal, and make your calories count, as discussed below. Balance calories in and out. Pay attention to your food and drink portions, perhaps having smaller portions.

Meals and Snacks: Make Calories Count!

Healthy eating should be about the foods you enjoy. The challenge for many healthy older adults, even those as young as sixty, is this: getting about the same amount of nutrients in meals and snacks as before, but probably with fewer calories. The smart-eating food guidelines *in chapter 2* still apply:

- Focus on food variety. Get the nutrients your body needs in the right amounts from a variety within each of the five food groups. Use one of the healthy eating patterns or the DASH diet for planning a day's worth of healthy meals and snacks. *See chapter 2, page 21, for a refresher on the food groups and eating patterns.* Pay special attention to getting enough of the nutrients *discussed in "Nutrients That Need Attention" in this chapter, page 577.*
- Choose mostly nutrient-packed foods that are lower in calories: whole-grain and enriched breads and cereals; dark-colored vegetables; fruits; low-fat and fat-free milk and milk products; lean meat, poultry, fish, eggs, and beans and peas.
- Eat your veggies and fruits (as you've likely reminded your kids, nieces and nephews, or grandkids). Colorful and nourishing, they're mostly nutrient rich and provide plenty of phytonutrients, or substances in vegetables, fruits, and other plant-based foods that offer health benefits. Along with their many health-promoting benefits, their fiber can help overcome constipation. Their potassium may help counter the effects of sodium on blood pressure, and their antioxidants may provide properties that may reduce disease risk.
- Make at least half your grains whole, to get their fiber benefits.

> **Did You Know . . . ?**
>
> Due to better health care, longer life expectancy, and the aging of the baby boom generation, the number of Americans aged sixty plus is on the rise—significantly! Statistically, people living to age sixty-five have an average life expectancy of nearly nineteen more years. And many of them have family members or friends whose ages stretch beyond these years.
>
> - By 2020, more than seventy-five million Americans are projected to be age sixty or older according to the US Administration on Aging.
> - By 2030, that number is projected to rise to about ninety-one million Americans.
> - Compare that to a decade or so ago in 2000 when about forty-six million were age sixty or older.
>
> The group expected to grow the fastest? Eighty-five years plus!

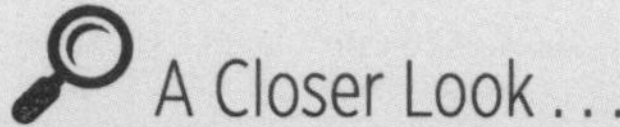

A Closer Look . . .

How "Old" Are You? Biomarkers of Age

Eager to slow the physical changes of aging? Want to feel healthy and energetic as you age? Rather than wait until you notice signs of aging, a fitness routine—healthy eating and regular physical activity—can help slow or reverse "biomarkers," or changes, that can come with getting older.

- *Your muscle mass and strength.* Stamina, ease of movement, ability to handle heavy objects, feeling energetic, and even physical appearance depend on muscle strength and flexibility. Yet, with age, muscle size and strength decrease naturally. After age thirty years or so, adults lose 3 to 8 percent of muscle mass per decade, notes the National Center for Biotechnology Information of the National Institutes of Health; muscle loss accelerates in the later years.

  This natural loss of lean muscle is called sarcopenia. Sarcopenia is the age-related, progressive loss of muscle, and, as a result, loss of strength and potentially mobility, physical function, independence, and more. Regular weight-bearing physical activity helps maintain muscle size, strength, and many other qualities of youth. *See "Protein: Pump It Up" in this chapter, page 578, and "Muscle, Sarcopenia, and Protein" in chapter 12, page 376, for more about sarcopenia.*
- *The rate at which your body uses energy.* Metabolic rate declines with age, about 2 to 3 percent for every decade. Loss of lean body tissue (muscle mass), along with hormone changes, is part of the reason. If you're physically active and keep your muscle mass, your body burns energy a little faster; muscle burns more energy than body fat.
- *Your percentage of body fat.* With age, body composition gradually shifts proportionally: more body fat, less muscle. Some extra body fat can be beneficial. However, besides losing that firm, muscular shape of youth, extra body fat increases your risk for high blood pressure, heart disease, stroke, some cancers, type 2 diabetes, arthritis, and breathing problems. "Midriff bulge" is a sure sign that you're probably not twenty-five anymore! The bottom line: Try to keep your body lean.
- *Your bone density.* Healthy bones let you enjoy physical activity as you age with less risk of fractures. Yet bone loss is a natural part of aging. If you keep your bones strong, you also may avoid fractures if you fall and are less likely to develop a "dowager's hump," which often appears with osteoporosis and compression fractures along the spine. This can affect your breathing and displace your organs. *See "Osteoporosis and Bone Health" in chapter 25, page 738, for ways to slow bone loss.*
- *Your serum cholesterol levels.* Age is one reason why total and LDL ("bad") cholesterol rise. As a heart-healthy strategy, maintaining a healthy weight, regular physical activity, and smart eating can help bring or keep down your total and LDL cholesterol levels, lower your triglyceride levels, and raise your HDL ("good") cholesterol levels. *See "Heart Disease: The Blood Lipid Connection" in chapter 24, page 684, for more about these lipids.*
- *Your blood glucose tolerance.* With age, blood glucose levels may rise for several reasons. In part, your body may not produce as much insulin. Physical activity, along with keeping a healthy weight, can help keep blood glucose levels within normal range and help you avoid type 2 diabetes.
- *Your body's "thermostat."* Fluids are your body's natural cooling system. As you get older, your sense of thirst may diminish, putting you at greater risk for dehydration if you don't drink enough. Still, your body needs at least nine to twelve-and-a-half cups of water daily from foods and beverages. Physical activity helps your body regulate its internal temperature.
- *Your aerobic capacity.* As you age, your body's ability to use the oxygen you breathe efficiently declines. With continued vigorous physical activity such as fast walking, your body pumps more oxygen to your muscles.

Why is all of this so important? It's preserving your physical function and independence, and helping to maintain the quality of your life. You'll also save on the costs of health care.

- Fit in lean protein foods and low-fat or fat-free dairy foods. You need their protein to maintain your muscle mass and other nutrients for your overall well-being. Dairy foods promote bone health and much more.
- Replace solid fats (saturated and *trans* fats) with healthy oils such as canola, corn, olive, and soybean, which are higher in poly- and monounsaturated fats. That may help to manage risk factors for heart disease and other chronic health problems. Omega-3s from fatty fish and some oils have unique health benefits.

  Remember: One gram of fat supplies more than twice the calories that a gram of either carbohydrate or protein does. Watching your total fat intake is a healthy way to ease up on calories.
- Limit added sugars—from sugar-sweetened drinks, sugary desserts, and more. Their calories add up; these foods are also nutrient

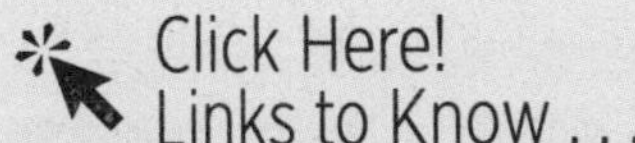

- Academy of Nutrition and Dietetics
  www.eatright.org/resources/for-seniors
- Aging in Motion (sarcopenia and age-related functional decline)
  aginginmotion.org
- NIH Senior Health, National Institutes of Health
  nihseniorhealth.gov/eatingwellasyougetolder
- What's on *Your* Plate? (smart food choices for healthy aging)
  www.nia.nih.gov/health/publication/whats-your-plate
- National Agricultural Library, USDA
  www.nutrition.gov/life-stages/seniors

poor. Want something sweet? Enjoy fruit instead; for more fiber, eat the edible skin.

Use the Nutrition Facts on food labels to check and compare calories and nutrients per serving. *See "Nutrition: Fact Check!" in chapter 6, page 144.*

Note: If you have diabetes, high blood pressure, or other health problems (or if you're at risk for them), your food and nutrient needs may differ from those outlined above. Medications, being older, and some health conditions may require adjustments in your food choices, too. Get advice from a registered dietitian nutritionist or your doctor. *See chapter 24, page 680, and chapter 25, page 722, to learn more about some common health issues.*

NUTRIENTS THAT NEED ATTENTION

As early as age fifty, a few nutrients may need special attention. Among the reasons? Physical changes that can accompany aging affect how your body digests food, absorbs its nutrients, and excretes wastes—and the ability and motivation to enjoy eating. If you take medication, it may interact with some nutrients.

Why Do You Age? Can You Slow Aging?

Those questions have kindled the search for the "fountain of youth" throughout history. Today's science is beginning to find answers.

Genetics has a lot to do with it, as do the food and lifestyle choices people make and the environment they live in. So does the reality of simply getting older. That said, aging is a progression, differing from person to person, with multiple causes, yet not well understood.

Oxidative stress, which damages DNA, body proteins, and lipids (fats), is a major factor. Damage comes from free radicals that form in the body, resulting from inflammation, infection, smoking, alcohol abuse, and more. *See "Vitamins as Antioxidants" in chapter 14, page 423, to learn about free radicals and antioxidants.*

The length of the body's telomeres offers more insights into aging, according to emerging research. Telomeres are the DNA on the caps at the ends of chromosomes in body cells. They protect genetic material and let your cells divide. Every time cells divide, they get a little shorter; that's normal. So whether a sign of aging or an effect, telomeres shorten with age. Some health conditions, such as inactivity, obesity, cancer, smoking, stress, and environmental pollutants are linked to shorter telomeres.

The rate of telomere shortening may predict the pace of aging. Perhaps, researchers say, those with longer telomeres might live longer, but that's unknown. Neither do we know how to retain their length or even lengthen them. It does appear that eating wisely with plenty of antioxidants from vegetables and fruits and omega-3s from fish, regular physical activity, and managing stress are linked to longer telomeres. Science is investigating other physiological and environmental factors that contribute to aging. Stay tuned.

Despite all we don't know about aging, we do know some ways to help slow the process. Longevity studies offer insights into factors that matter:

- An environment where physical activity is a natural part of daily living. There's no need for costly gyms or workout equipment.
- Social networks, including family and friend support, help shape healthy behavior—in other words, be with those who eat wisely, who don't drink heavily or smoke, and who live positively and with as little stress as possible.
- Having a positive purpose that's worth getting up for in the morning may possibly add several years to life expectancy.
- Smart eating and managing weight, *as discussed throughout this book,* helps prevent, delay, or manage health conditions associated with aging.
- Also important: participation in your own health care is key.

To quote the New England Centenarian Study, "The older you get, the healthier you've been."

So that you get enough of them, focus on these: calcium, vitamins D, E, and K, potassium, and fiber. Understandably, vitamin and mineral intake often declines as calorie intake declines, creating a health risk. You need enough protein, too. This all goes to explain why nutrient-dense foods are so important!

Sodium is typically overconsumed. Foods high in fats and added sugars are sometimes consumed at the expense of nutrient-dense foods from the five food groups.

See "Dietary Reference Intakes" in the appendix, page 782, for specific nutrient recommendations for healthy adults aged fifty-one through seventy and those seventy-one and older. Recommended amounts may differ for those with specific health problems. *See chapters 24, page 680, and 25, page 722, to learn more about some common health issues*—and talk with your doctor.

Protein: Pump It Up

If you follow advice from the protein foods group in one of the healthy eating patterns, *discussed in chapter 2, page 21*, you may be consuming enough. So what's the issue? Many aging adults don't meet the recommendations for protein.

- The Recommended Dietary Allowance (RDA) for those aged fifty-one years and older is 46 grams daily for women and 56 grams daily for men. That may not be enough. Emerging research suggests that healthy older adults may benefit from somewhat more protein than the RDA to help retain muscle and reduce the risk of sarcopenia. *See "Muscle, Sarcopenia, and Protein" in chapter 12, page 376.*
- The Acceptable Macronutrient Distribution Ranges (AMDR) recommended for protein is 10 to 35 percent of total calories. For a 2,000-calorie daily eating that's 50 to 175 grams of protein, or 200 to 700 calories from protein, per day. (Your calorie need may be more or less than that.)

Eating 25 to 30 grams of protein at each meal, from a high-quality protein food, helps retain muscle mass. Some experts advise more at this point in life: 40 grams of protein per meal. That could be 75 to 100 grams of protein daily, which fits within the Acceptable Macronutrient Distribution Ranges (AMDR), recommended for protein.

Consuming enough protein and getting enough regular strength-building exercise has benefits that you may overlook. As you age, enough protein plus enough physical activity helps to retain skeletal muscle and maintain your strength, and lowers your sarcopenia risk. Enough protein also may be linked to bone health; sarcopenia is linked to weak bones (osteoporosis), diabetes, and middle-age weight gain. Even if you're physically active and eat enough protein, you'll lose some skeletal muscle and strength with aging.

Why might protein intake come up short? If meat and poultry are hard to chew and swallow, they may be left on the plate. Those on fixed incomes with limited finances might avoid meat, poultry, or fish because they're often costly. Other people may have trouble digesting milk, another good protein source. To deal with these challenges:

- Combine lean meat, poultry, and fish—perhaps ground, chopped, or flaked—with less-expensive protein sources, such as eggs, beans and peas, and peanut butter.
- Include dairy products, an economical protein source: milk, cheese, and yogurt and foods made with these ingredients. If milk disagrees with you, try cheese, yogurt, or a soy-based alternative, *as discussed earlier in this chapter. See "Lactose Intolerance: A Matter of Degree" in chapter 23, page 666, if you're lactose sensitive.*
- Consult a registered dietitian nutritionist for other ways to ensure enough high-quality protein in your food choices. *See "Chewing Problems? Adjusting Texture" in this chapter, page 594, for protein foods that are easier to chew.*

See chapter 12, page 373, for more about protein, its benefits, the amounts in different foods, and how to fit enough into meals.

Calcium and Vitamin D: As Important as Ever

Since you aren't growing, why do calcium and vitamin D remain important? Bone health is a key reason. Loss of bone density is a natural part of aging, and since people live to be eighty plus, their bones need to survive longer, too. This means they need enough of these nutrients to ensure bone health. Together, calcium and vitamin D help protect you from fractures and bone loss (osteopenia, when bone density is lower than normal, and osteoporosis and osteomalacia, which is a more severe reduction in bone mass, due to depletion of calcium and bone protein).

The risk for osteoporosis goes up with age. By age seventy, between 30 and 40 percent of all women have had at least one fracture linked to osteoporosis. Even before that, many are diagnosed with osteopenia. The percentage continues to climb, even for men, who may develop bone disease later in life. *See "A Closer Look . . . Calcium, Vitamin D, and Bone Health" in chapter 14, page 427, and "Osteoporosis and Bone Health" in chapter 25, page 738, for more about these conditions.*

Age is only one reason why older adults have a higher risk for bone disease. Many don't consume enough calcium-rich foods, especially if dairy foods or calcium-fortified alternatives aren't a regular part of meals or snacks. With age, the body doesn't absorb calcium from food as well. In addition, many older adults don't get enough weight-bearing exercise, which helps to keep bones stronger. Vitamin D, which helps the body use calcium, may be limited in food choices, too, and it isn't absorbed as well as it once was.

Calcium and vitamin D aren't the only nutrients important for bone health. Others, including protein, vitamins A and K, and magnesium, as well as phytoestrogens, play a role—another reason why overall healthy eating is so important to reducing the risk of osteoporosis.

? Have you ever wondered?

. . . why milk doesn't seem to agree with you anymore? Some older adults have trouble digesting milk, even though they had no problem in younger years. The reason? With age, the small intestine may no longer produce as much lactase. Lactase, an enzyme, digests the natural sugar, called lactose, in milk and some milk products.

If you're feeling some discomfort with milk, you don't need to (and shouldn't) give up dairy foods. In fact, calcium is one nutrient needed in a greater amount after age fifty. To enjoy milk and reap its nutrient benefits, try this: Drink milk in small amounts; usually your body can handle a little at a time. Try buttermilk, yogurt, cheese, or lactose-reduced milk. Custard, pudding, and cream soup may be tolerated better. Calcium- and vitamin D–fortified soymilk, yogurt, and cheese can be alternatives. Try other foods that supply calcium, including some dark-green leafy vegetables and canned fish (salmon, sardines) with bones. *See "Lactose Intolerance: A Matter of Degree" in chapter 23, page 666, for more tips.*

. . . if you should avoid animal-based foods (meat, eggs, milk, cheese), which contain fat and cholesterol, to protect yourself from heart disease? There's no reason for "fat or cholesterol phobia." Thinking that you need to avoid meat, eggs, and dairy foods to protect against heart disease is unfounded—especially if that means missing out on these nutrient-rich foods. They supply other nutrients that often end up short in the eating patterns of older adults: calcium, iron, zinc, and vitamins B_6 and B_{12}. If you don't have heart disease, and if your blood cholesterol levels are within a healthy range, be sensible—and enjoy these foods in moderation.

Know, too, that saturated fats, found mostly in animal-based foods, and *trans* fats from partially hydrogenated fats in processed foods affect blood cholesterol levels more than dietary cholesterol does. So does physical inactivity, excessive body weight, heredity, aging, and gender. Current evidence shows that dietary cholesterol doesn't play a major role in blood cholesterol levels.

. . . if extra vitamin E will keep you young? We all dream of the fountain of youth. Many claims made for vitamin E are really distortions of research done with animals, not humans. Taking vitamin E supplements won't stop or reverse the aging process. And research doesn't show that older adults lower their chances of heart disease, cancer, or mental decline by taking vitamin E.

That said, research is exploring the potential benefits of taking extra amounts of vitamin E. As an antioxidant, it may play a protective role against some health problems including cataract formation. It's too soon to advise levels higher than the RDA of 15 milligrams of alpha-tocopherol (a form of vitamin E) a day.

Until more is known, choose foods that supply enough vitamin E such as nuts and wheat germ. Vegetable oils, such as cottonseed, safflower, or sunflower oil, also supply vitamin E; follow advice for oils, *discussed in chapter 2, page 21.* If you take a supplement, choose one with no more than 100 percent of the Daily Value (DV) for vitamin E. And talk to a registered dietitian nutritionist to help you sort through current research about vitamin E. *See "Vitamin E" in chapter 14, page 415, for more about this nutrient.*

. . . if dietary supplements can prevent macular degeneration? The first line of defense against age-related macular degeneration (AMD) for those who don't have it—or those who want to slow its progression—is simple, good health advice: regular physical activity, nourishing food including dark-green leafy vegetables and fish, and not smoking.

Research suggests that taking a certain combination of vitamins and minerals may help somewhat with intermediate or late AMD slow vision loss, but research regarding age-related macular degeneration is inconclusive. Talk to your eye-care professional or doctor to see if a supplement is right for you.

. . . why sleep is essential to healthy aging—and how to get a better night's sleep? As people get older, changes in sleep patterns are common. Some are normal. Other changes may be linked to medical conditions, medications, sleep disorders, stress, or poor sleep habits—and may need professional attention.

That said, a good night's sleep is essential to promote your immunity, repair the normal wear and tear on your body cells, and improve your memory formation and concentration. Among other health benefits, adequate rest also may help avoid increasing the risks of some chronic health conditions, *as noted in "Have you ever wondered . . . why sleep is important to your health?" in chapter 1, page 5.*

To get a better night's sleep, stay physically active during the day, but go easy within a few hours of bedtime. Exercise releases endorphins that boost mood and reduce everyday stress. Try eating a lighter meal in the evening and a bigger meal at lunchtime. Limit caffeine, alcoholic drinks, and nicotine, as all interfere with sleep. Alcoholic drinks suppress REM (rapid eye movement) sleep, which in turn, is linked to restless and light sleep and waking up at night. *Caution:* Don't combine sleeping pills and alcoholic drinks. Create a dark, quiet, and cool place to sleep, and be consistent with your sleep habits.

? Have you ever wondered?

. . . if taking a multivitamin/mineral supplement is recommended now? Consuming a wide variety of foods, in sufficient amounts, is the best approach to adequate nutrition no matter what your age if you're healthy. However, your doctor may suggest a multivitamin/mineral supplement meant for older adults, especially if you limit your food choices. For adults over age fifty, supplements with vitamin B_{12}, vitamin D, and perhaps calcium are often recommended. Talk to your doctor about any supplement, including an herbal supplement, before you take it.

There's good news if you're an older adult: Even if you haven't been consuming enough calcium and vitamin D all along, it's not too late to consume more now. You still can reduce your risk of bone fractures. At the same time, consume enough vitamin D, and do some weight-bearing exercise, such as walking. The stronger your bones are, the better equipped you'll be to handle aging. *See "Never Too Late to Move More" in this chapter, page 585, for more tips for physical activity.*

Calcium. Calcium benefits go well beyond bone health and reducing the risks of osteopenia and osteoporosis, or brittle-bone disease. That's true for both men and women. As you age, calcium also may promote cardiovascular health and help lower the risk for breast cancer.

After age fifty, calcium needs are higher. To help maintain bone mass, calcium recommendations increase by 20 percent. For women aged fifty-one and older, the RDA increases from 1,000 to 1,200 milligrams of calcium daily; for men, that increase happens after age seventy. That's almost as much as growing children and teens need daily.

Which foods supply calcium? Milk, yogurt, and cheese have the highest amount along with some calcium-fortified foods. *See "Calcium" in chapter 14, page 425, for more about this nutrient.*

Hint: Calcium in food is more bioavailable than from a supplement. But if you do take a calcium supplement, choose one with vitamin D, too. Check to see if the supplement should be taken with or between meals. *See "A Closer Look . . . Calcium and Iron Supplements," in chapter 10, page 320, for tips.*

Vitamin D. Healthy bones aren't vitamin D's only health benefit. Emerging research suggests that adequate vitamin D also promotes health and may reduce the risks for some cancers, diabetes, and autoimmune conditions, among other possible benefits. Of concern, the majority of adults over age fifty don't consume enough. Increasingly, a vitamin D supplement is recommended for older adults.

Vitamin D is unique. Known as the sunshine vitamin, your body makes it after sunlight or ultraviolet light hits your skin. With age, however, the body doesn't make vitamin D from sunlight as easily. By age seventy, the body makes 50 to 75 percent less vitamin D than for someone age twenty. The body doesn't convert vitamin D to its active form or absorb vitamin D from food as well as it once did, either. Adding to the risk, some older adults are housebound or covered up when they go outside, especially in northern climates, so sun exposure is limited. And if they don't drink milk or another beverage that is vitamin D–fortified, or don't eat oily fish (that provide vitamin D), they likely don't consume enough, either.

Like calcium, the need for vitamin D goes up after age seventy. In fact, the Adequate Intake level goes up from 15 micrograms (600 International Units, or IU), daily for ages fifty-one through seventy, to 20 micrograms (800 IU), daily after age seventy.

Choose foods that provide more vitamin D, such as dairy foods, soy beverages, juice, and cereals that are fortified with vitamin D. Even if you drink milk regularly and eat vitamin D–fortified cereal, you may need a vitamin D supplement. Consult your doctor or registered dietitian nutritionist and ask about the dosage. Taking high doses from a dietary supplement can be harmful. Taking too much vitamin D over time may lead to confusion, kidney stones or damage, and problems with heart rhythm. Signs of toxicity include nausea, vomiting, poor appetite, constipation, weakness, and weight loss. The Tolerable Upper Limit (UL) for vitamin D is 100 micrograms (4,000 IU), daily for adults of any age. Vitamin D toxicity almost always occurs from overuse of supplements and not from overexposure to sunlight.

See "Vitamin D" in chapter 14, page 413, for more about this nutrient, and its sources.

Vitamin C–Iron Connection

Food choices that come up short on iron, vitamin C, or both can increase the chance of anemia. Anemia can make you feel weak, tired, and irritable, or lose concentration. *See "Anemia: 'Tired Blood' " in chapter 25, page 722.*

Vitamin C. Although iron and vitamin C come from very different foods, they work together. Vitamin C helps your body absorb iron from eggs and plant sources of food. Vitamin C is especially important for this function if you rely heavily on beans, whole-grain foods, and iron-enriched cereals as iron sources.

Vitamin C functions in many ways in your body. Among them, as an antioxidant, vitamin C (found in citrus fruits, melons, berries, other fruits and some vegetables) also may help lower the risk for cataracts and some cancers. *See "Vitamin C (Ascorbic Acid)" and "Iron" in chapter 14, pages 422 and 438, for more about these nutrients.*

For adult men of any age, the RDA is 90 milligrams daily, and for women, it's 75 milligrams daily. As for any nutrient, try to get enough vitamin C from food first, not a supplement, since food provides a variety of nutrients. Many vitamin C–rich foods contain potassium as well as phytonutrients that promote health. Excessively high amounts of vitamin C from supplements can be harmful, especially if you have

Vegetarian Fare for Sixty-Plus Adults

As an older vegetarian, your overall nutrition needs and concerns are similar to those of others your age, and the nutrition issues are like those of any vegetarian. However, vitamin B_{12} and vitamin D need special attention.

With age, the body may not absorb vitamin B_{12} efficiently. Since vitamin B_{12} isn't found naturally in foods from plant sources, vegetarians, especially vegans, must rely on foods fortified with vitamin B_{12} or take a vitamin B_{12} supplement to prevent a deficiency.

If you don't consume dairy foods and don't get regular exposure to sunlight, you may be vitamin-D deficient. Choose juice, soymilk, cereal, and other vitamin D–fortified foods. You may need a vitamin D supplement, too.

Protein should not be a problem, except if you're on a very-low-calorie diet. For vegans, eating a variety of protein-rich plant-based foods daily, such as beans and peas, tofu, and soy beverages, likely can provide enough. Dairy foods and eggs—both good protein sources—fit in some vegetarian diets. Fiber, often higher in a vegetarian eating plan, may help older adults avoid constipation.

In later years, people are at greater risk for some health problems if they don't get the variety of nutrients they need, especially when recovering from illness. A healthy approach to vegetarian eating is essential—and a unique challenge for those vegetarians needing medical nutrition therapy. *See "The Healthy Vegetarian Way" in chapter 2, page 53, for guidance.*

hemochromatosis (*discussed in the next section*), recurring kidney stones or kidney disease.

Iron. Widely available in food, iron is an essential nutrient: heme iron from meat, poultry, and eggs and nonheme iron from eggs and iron-fortified cereals. Its role in carrying oxygen to every body cell for energy production, as well as boosting immunity and aiding memory and concentration, are among its many functions.

For adults aged fifty-one and older, the RDA is 8 milligrams daily. For women, that's less than half of what's needed before menopause. For adults over fifty, too much iron—taken in supplement form—is usually more of a concern than too little. A supplement with too much iron can be harmful for aging adults with a genetic illness called hemochromatosis. With this condition, iron is absorbed more readily and can build up in body organs, causing irreparable damage. Consult with your doctor before taking an iron supplement.

An iron deficiency can result from a low intake of iron and also from blood loss. Ulcers, hemorrhoids, or other health problems, and medications (perhaps too many aspirins) can cause blood loss. Reduced iron absorption may occur as the body secretes less digestive juices or when antacids interfere.

See "Iron" in chapter 14, page 438, for more about this nutrient and its sources, as well as hemochromatosis.

Vitamin A and Antioxidants

Antioxidants—in the form of some vitamins, minerals, and phytonutrients—appear to help protect against some signs of aging and health risks; *see "Vitamins as Antioxidants" in chapter 14, page 423.* According to some evidence, this may include some protection against cognitive decline and dementia in older adults—another reason to eat a variety of nutrient-dense foods, including vegetables, fruits, and whole-grain foods.

Carotenoids and vitamin A. Vitamin A helps your eyes adjust to darkness, which is important for your continued safety at any age. It comes from eggs, milk, fish oils, and liver, and from some carotenoids such as beta carotene (preformed vitamin A) that convert to vitamin A in foods such as carrots, broccoli, cantaloupe, and winter squash.

Other carotenoids, especially lutein and zeaxanthin, also may help reduce the risk of age-related macular degeneration and cataracts. Colorful vegetables and fruits such as kale, spinach, and citrus fruit are among the good food sources of these carotenoids.

For men aged fifty-one and older, the RDA is 900 micrograms Retinol Activity Equivalent (RAE) daily (equivalent to 3,000 IU), and for women, it's 700 micrograms RAE (equivalent to 2,333 IU) daily.

Should you take a supplement with vitamin A or beta carotene? Consult with a registered dietitian nutritionist or your doctor first. With age, the liver can't handle excess vitamin A as well. Too much from supplements can be especially harmful. *See "Vitamin A (and Provitamin A Carotenoids)" in chapter 14, page 410, for more about this nutrient.*

B Vitamins: 6, 12, and Folate

Vitamin B_6, or pyrodixine. This vitamin helps your body produce proteins, insulin, antibodies, hemoglobin, and other body substances and helps regulate metabolism, among other functions. Not getting enough vitamin B_6 also can lead to a type of anemia and other health conditions.

Vitamin B_6 may come up short for some adults over age fifty. The RDA for vitamin B_6 goes up slightly, from 1.3 milligrams daily for both

Brain Health: Can Nutrition Boost Your Memory?

For many, memory and the process of learning changes with aging. It's not uncommon to gradually have difficulty with multitasking, finding the right words and names, and keeping as attentive. It's a common frustration for those who constantly misplace eyeglasses, keys, or shoes. Can you slow these changes?

BRAIN FOOD

An eating pattern that nourishes a healthy heart is good for your brain and so your memory, too. Some evidence suggests that the foods in a Mediterranean-style eating plan encourage alertness, cognitive function, and memory. *See "The Mediterranean Route to Healthy Eating" in chapter 2, page 52.*

Possibly diet-related and certainly important to brain function is managing health conditions such as high blood pressure, high cholesterol levels, diabetes, and depression. Getting enough sleep may protect your memory, too. A healthy body makes for a healthy brain, ready to learn new things and create new memories.

SUPPLEMENTS FOR MEMORY?

Especially as people age, supplements and drugs marketed to enhance memory and cognitive function grab attention. Taking antioxidant supplements to treat memory loss hasn't been shown to be effective; some formulations can have side effects. Although limited memory-enhancement research is underway for herbals such as gingko biloba, no studies conclusively show that taking herbal supplements improves memory, thinking, or learning.

Recently, nootropics, or "smart pills," have emerged as a category of supplements and drugs meant to enhance cognitive function. They're often sold (and hyped) online without much regulation. Many of these so-called "natural enhancing supplements" are simply vitamins, herbals, and caffeine or another stimulant. Stimulants may promote alertness in the short run, but whether they offer other benefits to brain function is unclear.

The concept of nootropics is, however, of research interest. The idea is to find a way to adjust a metabolic or nutritional facet of brain function, perhaps one that involves memory or attention. With a mechanism that's so complex, high-quality research needs to be done to determine possible effectiveness and use.

BOTTOM LINE

Brain function depends on good blood flow to your brain. For brain health and optimizing cognitive function, there are factors in your control that are known to make a difference. These include eating regular meals with good nutrition, limiting alcohol, avoiding recreational drugs, doing regular physical activity, getting enough quality sleep, reducing stress, and keeping connections with others. And remember to keep your mind active with mentally stimulating activities.

men and women for those aged nineteen to fifty, to 1.7 milligrams daily for men and 1.5 milligrams daily for women for ages fifty-on and over. Among the good sources: fortified cereals, meat, poultry, fish, and pork, beans and peas, and some vegetables and fruits. *See "Vitamin B_6 (Pyridoxine)" in chapter 14, page 418.*

Vitamin B_{12}, or cobalamin. This vitamin works to keep nerve and blood cells healthy and to make DNA, which is the genetic material in cells. A low level of vitamin B_{12} is linked to memory loss. It also helps prevent a type of anemia that can cause weakness and fatigue. With coexisting conditions, other symptoms of vitamin B_{12} deficiency may go unrecognized.

Why might this happen? With aging, many older adults can't absorb naturally occurring vitamin B_{12} as well as they once did. Called atrophic gastritis, the stomach has less acidity, or has less hydrochloric acid (HCl) secretion, which impairs absorption of this vitamin. Lower HCl levels might also increase normal intestinal bacteria that use vitamin B_{12}. This reduces even further the amount of vitamin B_{12} available to the body.

For adults of any age, the RDA is 2.4 micrograms daily. Meat, poultry, fish, eggs, and dairy foods are all good sources. Those aged fifty-one and older are advised to consume foods fortified with vitamin B_{12}, such as fortified cereals or dietary supplements since their body may not be able to absorb naturally occurring vitamin B_{12}. The crystalline form of vitamin B_{12} in fortified foods and supplements is well absorbed by most people. *See "Vitamin B_{12} (Cobalamin)" in chapter 14, page 420, for more about this nutrient and its sources.*

Folate. Folate, a B vitamin, helps the body make DNA and other genetic material. It's needed to help cells divide, and works with vitamin B_{12} to make red blood cells. Not consuming enough over time may lead to anemia.

The RDA is 400 micrograms daily for adults of any age. Since refined flour and uncooked cereals are fortified with folic acid, a form of folate, you likely get enough. Many fruits, vegetables, and beans and peas are good sources of naturally occurring folate.

If you take a supplement with folic acid (folate), you may consume over the Tolerable Upper Intake Level (UL) of 1,000 micrograms daily, which is too much. Too much folate, most likely from a supplement, may mask a vitamin B_{12} deficiency as well as interfere with some medications. While folic acid supplements do lower blood homocysteine levels, they don't decrease the risk of heart disease as once thought.

Advice for those aged fifty-one and older: So you don't exceed the UL, choose a supplement that delivers no more than 400 micrograms of

Antiaging Miracles? Dream On

Marketers in magazines, on television, and online often prey on older adults with promises of easy cures or "antiaging" products. Many of the items they peddle are foods, substances from food, or supplements—with no substantial evidence for claims that these products help to treat arthritis, cancer, Alzheimer's disease, or other maladies, or promote longevity.

Many "miracle" products are costly. Money used to buy them is better spent on healthy, flavorful foods or proper medical care. Their harm may go further than the pocketbook. These remedies may mask symptoms, offer false hope, or worse yet, keep people from seeking reliable health care. These products also may interfere with the action of prescribed medications—or perhaps with the absorption of nutrients in food.

Always be cautious of promises that seem too good to be true. *See "Case against Health Fraud" in chapter 26, page 757, to learn how to judge these claims.* And always consult your doctor or a registered dietitian nutritionist before trying these products—or any alternative health care. *See chapter 10, page 315, for what's known and unknown about many supplements.*

folic acid (the form of folate in fortified foods and supplements) daily—if you're advised to take a folic acid supplement, talk to your doctor about a need for additional vitamin B_{12}. More research is needed to know of any benefits of folate supplementation for older adults.

Enriched-grain products (such as enriched white rice, pasta, and bread) are fortified with folic acid by law; that's not required for whole-grain products. If you eat mostly whole-grain foods such as whole-wheat bread, choose some that are folic acid–fortified. Check the Nutrition Facts label to find out. Dark-green leafy vegetables, some fruits, beans and peas, and liver are among the fruits and vegetables that are good sources of naturally occurring folate.

See "Folate (Folic Acid or Folacin)" in chapter 14, page 419, for more about this nutrient and its sources.

Other Vitamins

Two other nutrients may be of concern, as well: vitamin E and vitamin K. *See "Vitamin E" and "Vitamin K" in chapter 14, pages 415 and 416, for more about these nutrients.*

Sodium and Potassium

Sodium and potassium maintain fluid balance, so your body can do its most work. These minerals also help send messages from your brain to your muscles and regulate your blood pressure.

As people get older, the risk for prehypertension and hypertension, or high blood pressure, goes up. At the same time, blood pressure becomes more sodium (salt) sensitive. (Salt is sodium chloride.) Of concern, most adults consume much more sodium than they need. Yet, among many adults, as sodium intake goes down, so does blood pressure. High blood pressure contributes to heart disease, stroke, and kidney disease. On the other hand, potassium blunts sodium's effects on blood pressure for people of all ages, including older adults.

For those aged fifty-one through seventy, the AI for sodium decreases from 1,500 milligrams daily to 1,300 milligrams daily; for those over seventy, it decreases further to 1,200 milligrams daily. The recommendation for potassium stays the same: the AI is 4,700 milligrams daily.

To reduce the risk of high blood pressure, limit the sodium you take in, perhaps by following the DASH eating plan, *described in "DASH to Health" in chapter 2, page 21.* Most sodium comes from processed foods, so read Nutrition Facts labels to choose lower-sodium foods. And replace salt in your food preparation with herbs and spices, *See "Herbs—and Spices, Too!" in chapter 8, page 266.*

Consume more potassium-rich foods, too—fruits and many vegetables. Beans and peas, dairy foods, meat, poultry, fish, and nuts deliver potassium, too. Most Americans—including most older adults—don't consume enough potassium.

See "Sodium" and "Potassium" in chapter 14, pages 431 and 430, and "A Closer Look . . . Sodium and Potassium, A Salty Subject" in chaper 14, page 433, for more about these nutrients and their sources.

Zinc

Zinc is yet another essential nutrient. Among its functions it helps the body fight infections and repair body tissue. Among the areas of research, zinc might help slow the progression of age-related macular degeneration.

Yet absorption decreases with age. Even a marginal deficiency may affect the ability to taste, heal wounds, and provide immunity. And too much over time may lead to low copper levels, lower immunity, and low levels of HDL ("good") cholesterol.

For adult men of any age, the RDA for zinc is 11 milligrams daily; for women, it's 8 milligrams daily. Zinc comes from foods such as meat, poultry, and fish. Eggs and milk have smaller amounts. Beans and peas, nuts, and whole grains have zinc, too, in a form that's less bioavailable. *See "Zinc" in chapter 14, page 441, for more about this nutrient and its sources.*

Fiber

Fiber-rich foods aid digestion and help prevent the discomfort of constipation—nutrition concerns that arise with aging. Beyond that, fiber plays a role in heart health and reduced cholesterol levels, blood glucose control, weight management, lower colorectal cancer risk, and more. Many fiber-rich foods—whole grains, vegetables, fruits, beans and peas, and nuts—also deliver important vitamins, minerals, and antioxidants.

After age fifty, the AI for total fiber decreases: for men, from 38 grams daily to 30 grams daily, and for women, from 25 grams daily to 21 grams daily. Still, many older adults come up short on fiber, especially if they don't eat enough vegetables, fruits, and whole grains. *See chapter 11, page 345, for more about fiber and its sources.*

Water

The average healthy adult loses about 2½ quarts or more (about 10 or more cups) of water daily by urinating, perspiring, breathing, and eliminating other body wastes. To avoid dehydration, you need to replace these fluids. Thirst is your signal to drink more.

With age come changes that may affect your fluid intake. The sense of thirst often diminishes. At some point and for some older adults, thirst is no longer a primary reminder to drink. Kidneys may not conserve fluids as well as they once did, either, so the body holds on to less water. Those who have trouble getting around, perhaps due to arthritis, may deliberately limit fluid intake to avoid bathroom trips. Fear of incontinence also keeps some older people from drinking enough. Medication may contribute to dehydration, too.

Day to day, the amount of water you need varies, depending on your physical activity level, the weather, how much you perspire, and other factors. Consuming about 11 ½ to 15 ½ cups daily from drinking water, beverages, and food, depending on your gender, is a good guideline; *see "Water: A Fluid Asset" in chapter 15, page 443.*

Food typically provides about 20 percent of a person's fluid intake, leaving about nine to thirteen cups of fluids to come from what you drink. All beverages—100 percent juice, milk, tea, coffee, soft drinks—supply water. Low-fat and fat-free milk, 100 percent juice, and soup, offer other nutrients as well. *See chapter 4, to compare different beverages.*

If you can't recall how much water you drank at the end of the day, try this: Fill a jug (or two) or a jar with at least nine cups (seventy-two ounces) of water each morning. Place it in your refrigerator. Use that water for drinking and for making juice, lemonade, soup, tea, or coffee. When the water is gone, you've probably met your day's fluid goal. That said, remember that other fluids and food are water sources, too. Another option: Carry a clean, refillable water bottle with calibrated measurements with you.

Dehydration. This is a health concern for those who don't drink enough fluids, especially in hot weather. While fluids help keep kidneys healthy, dehydration can result in constipation and kidney problems. In older adults, dehydration may cause symptoms that seem like dementia, or impaired mental function, or might worsen existing dementia. In extreme cases, dehydration can lead to death. *See "Dehydration: Body Signals" in chapter 15, page 444, for additional effects.*

Other health issues. You need enough water to help rid your body of wastes. With less fluid, the chance of constipation increases.

Many older adults don't have as much saliva as they used to, which interferes with chewing and swallowing. Drinking water or other liquids with meals makes food easier to eat. Some medications need to be taken with water. Others, such as diuretics, cause the body to lose fluids. Understand how your medications may affect your hydration status.

If urinary incontinence is an issue, talk to your doctor about how to handle bladder control. *See "Have you ever wondered . . . if any dietary changes can help with bladder control?" in chapter 25, page 728, to learn more.*

See "Water: A Fluid Asset" in chapter 15, page 443, for more about water as a nutrient and the risks of dehydration.

Alcoholic Drinks: Be Cautious

Take a renewed look at your drinking habits as you age. Your body likely metabolizes alcohol more slowly as an older adult, lowering your tolerance. As a result, you may feel the effects of a single glass of wine, beer, or mixed drink more and faster now—even if your drinking habits don't change. That can increase your risk for falling or getting into an accident.

Taking medication, perhaps daily? Many medicines—both prescription and over-the-counter medications, as well as herbal remedies—can interact with alcohol, making them either less effective or more potent. Among them: aspirin, acetaminophen, cold and allergy medicine, cough syrup, sleeping pills, pain medication, and anxiety or depression medicine. The effects with a single drink may be sleepiness, dizziness, and lightheadedness and may impair your judgment, coordination, and skill. You may feel the effects even if you drink several hours after taking medication. Check with your doctor or pharmacist about interactions with any medications you take.

Heavy drinking is associated with increased risks for some health conditions, such as high blood pressure, liver problems, and several forms of cancer, and the chance of falling and injuries. Excessive drinking also increases diabetes risks and can lead to brain and heart damage, cirrhosis of the liver, and an inflamed pancreas.

The National Institute of Alcohol Abuse and Alcoholism advises healthy adults over age sixty-five who do not take medication to have no more than seven drinks a week, with no more than three in a single day. The Dietary Guidelines for Americans advises no more than one drink a day for women, and not more than two drinks a day for men. If you have a health problem such as liver disease, pancreatitis, or high triglyceride levels or take certain medications, you may need to drink less or not at all.

Don't consume alcoholic beverages if you take prescription or over-the-counter medications (including some herbal remedies) that can interact with alcohol, or if you have certain medical problems. Always ask your doctor about any interactions between medication you take and alcoholic drinks.

See "Alcoholic Beverages: In Moderation" in chapter 4, page 102, to learn more about the risks and advice about alcohol consumption.

NEVER TOO LATE TO MOVE MORE

No matter what your age—sixty, seventy, eighty, or perhaps even pushing ninety—it's never too late to get moving. Regardless of overall health, most people can participate in some form of enjoyable physical activity.

Physical Activity Matters

Regular physical activity just may be one of the most important health-promoting things you can do—even if you've been sedentary for awhile. It may prevent many health problems, including muscle loss, that seem to come with age, or at least slow their progression. Regular physical activity provides many benefits:

- Uses calories. By helping you balance energy out with energy in, active living helps you keep your healthy weight, especially when you control your energy, or calorie, intake, too. Beyond that, it helps speed up your metabolism, especially if you build up more muscle mass.
- Helps reduce your bone disease risk. Activities that cause your bones to bear weight, such as walking, help preserve bone density.
- Minimizes muscle loss, improves balance and agility, and keeps muscles strong. Strength helps reduce your risk of falling and helps you remain independent.
- May aid digestion and stimulate appetite—a benefit if food loses its appeal.
- Helps keep your heart and lungs healthier. Do some aerobic activity if you can; ask your doctor first.
- Helps keep your blood pressure, blood cholesterol, and blood glucose levels normal. That reduces risks related to health problems, such as high blood pressure, heart disease, diabetes, and metabolic syndrome.
- Helps relieve arthritis pain and aids joint function.
- Helps promote sleep. Changes in sleep patterns often come with getting older.
- Boosts your mental outlook and energy levels. Some studies even indicate that physical activity, including strength training, may promote better memory and mental abilities—even into the nineties! Being active can be an antidote for depression and perhaps "senior moments" of memory loss.

Physical Activity: How Much?

Any physical activity is better than none. Being inactive isn't healthy, no matter what your age or health condition. The more you move, the greater the benefits. If you're generally fit with no limiting health conditions, the Physical Activity Guidelines for Americans for older adults advises:

AGES FIFTY TO SIXTY-FOUR

For substantial health benefits, do one of the following: 150 minutes of moderate-intensity aerobic activity (such as brisk walking) every week; seventy-five minutes of vigorous-intensity aerobic activity (such as jogging or swimming) every week; or an equivalent mix of moderate- and vigorous-intensity aerobic activity. Bonus: If you do more, you get more health benefits. Plus, do muscle-strengthening activities on two or more days a week that work all major muscle groups (legs, hips, back, abdomen, chest, shoulders, and arms).

If 150 minutes seem like a lot, remember that you don't need to do them all at once. Break them up; spread them out during the day and week. As long as you're moderately or vigorously active for at least ten minutes at a time, you get the benefits. An activity that's of moderate intensity for one person may be vigorous for another. Talk to your doctor.

AGE SIXTY-FIVE AND OLDER

Follow the adult guidelines above, but if you can't meet those guidelines, be as physically active as your abilities and health allow. Just walking up stairs and lifting body weight strengthens your legs and hips. If you're at risk of falling, do exercises to maintain or improve your balance. Understand if and how any chronic health conditions affect your ability to do regular physical activity safely. *The bottom line:* The right physical-activity approach is all about you, how fit you are, what you feel comfortable doing, and your overall health.

For more about these guidelines and about activities defined as moderate and vigorous intensity, see "Move More! Physical Activity Guidelines" in chapter 1, page 15, and "The Physical Activity Guidelines for Americans" in the appendix, page 769.

Being Active: Overcoming Barriers

The key to fitting physical activity into your everyday routine is to make it fun and match it to your abilities. Even low-intensity activity can make a difference. Choose a variety of activities that improve endurance, strength, and flexibility.

- Walk—around the block or around the mall. Walk a dog, or invite a friend if you'd like companionship. If you don't have a sidewalk, a morning of mall walking is an option—especially in bad weather. Wear sturdy shoes.
- Do some gardening with manual, not electric, tools.
- Go swimming. Or try aqua exercises, such as stretching, water walking, or water aerobics—a good approach if you're not steady on your feet. These activities may help relieve some arthritis pain and aid joint function that accompanies arthritis.
- If you play golf, "go the course"—without the cart.
- Go dancing. Even a moderate two-step is good exercise—and a great way to be with other people.
- Take a class in Tai Chi, a series of slow, controlled movements, or try balance training that may include backward walking, sideways walking, heel walking, and toe walking.

Alert: Food Safety for Older Adults

Older adults are at greater risk for foodborne illness. Why? Their immune system can't always fight off bacteria and serious illness as easily as it did in the past. That's especially true for the frail elderly and those battling other health issues, such as an organ transplant or liver disease, or those dealing with some cancer treatments. With age, stomach acids, which help reduce intestinal bacteria, decrease, and weakened kidneys are less able to filter bacteria from the blood.

By age sixty-five, many adults have been diagnosed with one or more chronic conditions such as arthritis, cancer, cardiovascular disease, or diabetes, and may be taking at least one medication. These conditions may weaken the immune system, increasing the susceptibility to foodborne illness. Even mild foodborne illness can have a serious effect on health and, once contracted, can be hard to treat and may reoccur. Keep yourself and food preparation areas clean; wash your hands often.

Although the kitchen seems clean, poor eyesight or inadequate lighting may keep people from noticing food spills or visual signs of food spoilage. For those with less energy, proper cleaning may be hard to do.

TIPS FOR FOOD SAFETY

As an older adult, practice the four simple steps of clean, separate, cook, and chill, *discussed in chapter 7, page 191*. Follow this advice, too:

- If you need glasses, wear them when you handle food.
- Turn up the lights. Mature adults may have more trouble with glare from one light source, and so several might be more effective.
- Label perishable food with a date. Use a dark marker that's easy to read. Don't count on memory alone to know your own "use by" date.
- Don't rely on your sight, smell, or taste to determine if food is safe to eat, either. Contaminated food may not have an off flavor or off odor. With impaired vision, cross-contamination between salad vegetables and raw meat juices may not be obvious. Odors that signal spoilage may not be detected, either.
- Cook simply, to save your energy for cleanup. For example, buy prechopped, frozen vegetables instead of doing all the prep work yourself.
- Feeling short on energy? Set up a support system of family and friends to help with kitchen tasks when your energy is low.
- Refrigerate leftovers right away, and reheat them to the proper temperature before eating. *See "Reheating Leftovers Safely" in chapter 7, page 216.*
- Portions too big when you eat out? If you bring food home, but be sure to refrigerate it right away. Reheat it to steaming or boiling before you eat it.

See chapter 7, page 191, for more guidelines for keeping food safe as well as more about foodborne illnesses.

- To keep your arms strong, do strength exercises. Use canned foods from your kitchen shelves, bean bags, or one- to five-pound hand or ankle weights.
- Learn some chair exercises—good if you aren't steady on your feet or have degenerative joint disease. You can "sit and be fit" even if you're confined to a wheelchair or need a walker.
- Fit in some stretching activities that increase the range of motion in your ankles, knees, hips, shoulders, neck, and back—important for keeping your ability to do everyday tasks such as bending for a newspaper, reaching an upper shelf, or making a bed.
- Sign up for an exercise class or an individual fitness program especially designed for older adults. Check with your community center or area hospital for special classes. Some health insurance plans include free gym membership.
- Stop if you feel dizzy or short of breath or have pain.

See "Twenty Ways to Move More" in chapter 22, page 640, for more ideas.

Note: If you haven't been physically active or if you have a health condition such as heart disease, arthritis, or diabetes, or a physical disability, talk to your doctor before getting started. Together, plan activities and a sensible approach that's safe, effective, and right for you.

Even with health conditions like these, you can be physically active—and doing so can improve your quality of life, help manage your condition, and even reduce your risk of other health problems. Most important, start slowly, work toward your goal gradually, and

- Go4Life, National Institute on Aging, National Institutes of Health (ways to put physical activity into your life) go4life.nia.nih.gov

enjoy! *Tip:* No matter what activity you're involved in, drink plenty of water before, during, and afterward.

When Lifestyles Change

Lifestyle changes accompany each stage in life. Think about the independence that came with becoming an adult, the responsibility with parenthood, or the freedom of having kids finally "leave the nest." At some point, the adult years also bring new lifestyles and health conditions that impact what, where, when, and even with whom you eat. Retiring can change social interactions that impact food decisions, as do losing a spouse and moving away from a lifelong community.

EATING ALONE? MAKE MEALTIME ENJOYABLE

For many, eating provides a time to enjoy the company of others. That's especially true for those who've spent their time cooking for a family.

 Your Healthy Eating Check-In

Older Adults: Nutritionally Healthy?

If you're an older adult, use this checklist for insight into your nutritional health. If you care for an older adult, use it to be a better caregiver.

Read each statement. If it applies to you or someone you know, circle the number in the "yes" column. Then tally up the points to find out where you stand with your nutritional health.

	"Yes" Points
1. I have an illness or a condition that made me change the kind and/or amount of food I eat.	2
2. I eat fewer than two meals each day.	3
3. I eat few vegetables, fruits, or milk products.	2
4. I have three or more alcoholic drinks almost every day: beer, wine, or spirits.	2
5. I have tooth or mouth problems that make it hard for me to eat.	2
6. I don't always have enough money to buy the food I need.	4
7. I eat alone most of the time.	1
8. I take three or more different prescribed or over-the-counter drugs every day.	1
9. Without wanting to, I have lost or gained ten pounds in the past six months.	2
10. I am not always physically able to shop, cook, and/or feed myself.	2
Add up your total points:	____

If your score is . . .

0–2: *Good!* But check again in six months.

3–5: *You're at moderate nutritional risk.* Try to make some changes—suggested in this chapter—that improve your eating habits and lifestyle. Get advice from a registered dietitian nutritionist or another qualified nutrition professional, or from an office on aging, a senior citizens' center, a health department, or a senior nutrition program. And check again in three months.

6 or more: *You're at high nutritional risk.* The next time you see your doctor, registered dietitian nutritionist, or other qualified health or social service professional, bring this checklist. Talk about any problems, and ask for help to improve your nutritional health. He or she may use a more robust assessment, too. *Read on in this chapter for practical ways to follow their advice.*

Adapted with permission from: Nutrition Screening Initiative, a project of the American Academy of Family Physicians, the American Dietetic Association, and the National Council on Aging, Inc., and funded in part by a grant from Ross Products Division, Abbott Laboratories, Inc.

For another interactive assessment tool from Eat Right Ontario, visit www.nutritionscreen.ca/escreen/default.aspx.

For those who now live alone, pleasure and interest in preparing food, even eating, may diminish. Eating alone can feel boring or depressing—or feel like too much effort. Over time, social separation and isolation can have negative health and emotional consequences. Looking forward to a pleasant mealtime can boost your appetite and your morale. If you dine solo at home, consider these tips:

- Adjust your cooking style to small-scale food prep. Find recipes for one or two, perhaps online.
- Create a relaxed, attractive setting with soft music or flowers on the table. Set a place at the table, perhaps with a placemat, napkin, your best dishes, and a centerpiece. You'll feel more like you've had a meal—with more enjoyment—than just eating from the cooking pot.
- Eat in different places: the kitchen, patio or deck, dining room, or perhaps on a tray by the fireplace or a window for a change of pace. Take your meal to a park.
- Treat yourself to a meal out occasionally. Go for lunch and early-bird specials. Portions are usually smaller and prices lower. You might try restaurants with senior-citizen discounts. *See chapter 9, page 279, for tips on eating out, including dining alone.*

Kitchen Nutrition

Meal in Minutes

Prepare this nourishing meal with little effort and easy cleanup.

1. Place sliced carrots or other firm vegetables, such as cut-up butternut squash or sweet potato, and perhaps green beans or asparagus in a small baking dish lined with foil. Toss with 2 teaspoons of olive oil and crushed dry or chopped fresh herbs.
2. In the same baking dish, place one chicken breast or two smaller pieces of chicken. Sprinkle with lemon juice, olive oil, and herbs, or balsamic salad dressing before placing it in the oven.
3. Bake the vegetables and the chicken in the oven at 350°F for about 30 minutes. Check the internal temperature of the chicken with a food thermometer; the chicken is done when it reaches 170°F, about as long as it takes to roast the vegetables.
4. Set the table. Make a salad, if you'd like. Relax with a book or television program for about 20 minutes.
5. Fill a bowl with sliced, fresh fruit, berries, or canned peaches packed in juice, topped with Greek yogurt.
6. Heat a whole-wheat dinner roll. Use a little soft margarine or hummus as a spread.
7. Pour a tall glass of cold, low-fat milk.
8. Enjoy your dinner!

Setting the Table with Others

As a "single," you don't need to always dine alone.

- Set a standing date with a friend or relative (or a grandchild) for lunch or dinner at your home.
- Organize a dining club of friends who also want meal companionship so you have someone to cook for.
- Cut the effort. Get together with other older adults for weekly or monthly potluck suppers. Take turns as host.
- Eat out occasionally. Consider splitting an order with someone else, or take home half for another meal if restaurant portions seem too large.
- Take advantage of meals offered at senior and community centers. Many serve full midday meals on weekdays. Usually the price is right. In some communities, religious centers and schools serve meals for older adults.

  Added benefits: These meals offer a place to meet old friends and make new ones. You can enjoy a meal that takes more work to prepare than you may want to do for yourself. If you go to a community center, take advantage of an exercise class if they have one.

SHORT ON ENERGY? FAST, SIMPLE, AND HEALTHY MEALS

Some older adults say they have no time to cook. They're too busy living life to its fullest. For others, lack of inclination or energy, or perhaps less mobility, require quick and easy solutions to mealtime. And some get bored eating the same easy-to-fix foods over and over, so a variety of nutrient-rich foods from meal to meal is often lacking.

Whatever the reason, make food preparation and menus easy, varied, and healthy. Here are a few ideas as starters:

- For a quick breakfast, add milk to instant hot cereal and heat. It's almost as fast to prepare as ready-to-eat cereals.
- Prepare food ahead of time to eat in a day or two, or to freeze to eat later. For example, make lower-fat meatballs with lean, ground turkey or beef. Brown them, drain any grease, and then combine them with tomato sauce. Serve over pasta on one day, over brown rice the next, and freeze the rest for later. For a lower-sodium version, use salt-free tomato sauce, and flavor it with herbs.
- Freeze homemade soups, stews, lasagna, and other casserole dishes in single-serving containers. Thaw enough for one or two meals at a time. Label and date your packages to track what's in the freezer.

"DETERMINE" the Warning Signs of Poor Nutrition

If you're an older adult or if you care for someone older, be alert for these warning signs of poor nutrition. They spell the word "determine." Anyone with three or more of these risk factors should consult a doctor, a registered dietitian nutritionist, or other healthcare professional. These warning signs suggest risk but don't diagnose any health condition.

Disease

Eating poorly

Tooth loss or mouth pain

Economic hardship

Reduced social contact

Multiple medicines

Involuntary weight loss or gain

Needs assistance in self care

Elder years above age eighty

Reprinted with permission from: Nutrition Screening Initiative, a project of the American Academy of Family Physicians, the American Dietetic Association, and the National Council on Aging, Inc., and funded in part by a grant from Ross Products Division, Abbott Laboratories Inc.

- For easy-to-prepare salads, wash, tear, and dry salad greens. Store them in a plastic container for three to four days. Or purchase prewashed, precut salad greens in a bag. When you want a salad, just top the greens with sliced tomatoes, grated carrots, sliced deli meat, cheese, or canned kidney beans. Serve alongside low-fat or fat-free milk, whole-wheat bread, and canned fruit, packed in juice, not heavy syrup.
- Keep frozen prepared entrées on hand for quick cooking and easy cleanup, or buy single-serve prepared entrées at your supermarket. Check the sodium and calorie content before you buy. Team them with a salad, a whole-grain roll, a piece of fruit, and low-fat or fat-free milk for a hearty meal that takes little effort.
- Visit the supermarket salad bar for single servings of washed and chopped vegetables and fruits.

See chapter 3, page 60, for tips on planning easy-to-prepare, healthy meals and snacks.

FIXED INCOME? "MAXING" YOUR FOOD DOLLAR

Another adjustment may affect food decisions: learning to live and eat on a fixed income. If medical and prescription costs go up at the same time, you may not have as much money to spend on food. That said, healthy eating doesn't need to be costly. As a savvy shopper, you can buy plenty of nutrition for your food dollar. *See "Your Food Dollar: More Nutrition, Less Waste" in chapter 6, page 154.*

Concerned that fresh produce might take a bite out of your pocketbook? Buy seasonal vegetables and fruits when they typically cost less. Stock up on canned and frozen vegetables and fruits, as well as dried fruits, especially when they're on sale. Some canned fish such as tuna is easy to keep on hand, and it's healthy and low cost, as are canned, dried, or frozen beans and peas, which are good sources of protein.

Depending on income, some older adults qualify for SNAP (Supplemental Nutrition Assistance Program) food benefits (formerly the Food Stamp Program), handled by the US Department of Agriculture. Provided through an electronic benefits card, it works like cash at most grocery stores, giving access to healthy eating and nutrient-rich foods. If you're helping an older adult who's never used or qualified for SNAP, be sensitive; he or she may feel there's a social stigma with signing up or accepting SNAP benefits. Usually, SNAP benefits aren't for dining out, although for older adults, some restaurants are authorized to accept them in exchange for low-cost meals; ask before you order. Some older, low-income adults qualify for food assistance from farmers' markets.

Other government programs also provide food and nutrition assistance for older adults who qualify. *See "Credible Support for Healthy Eating" in chapter 26, page 761, for more information about these programs.* To find out if you—or someone you know—qualifies for SNAP or other food assistance, talk to a registered dietitian nutritionist, a social worker, or your local senior center. Or check the government pages in your phone book for your local SNAP office.

PHYSICAL LIMITS? HASSLE-FREE SHOPPING

As people get older, popping in and out of the car and the store may take more effort than you can easily handle. To shop with fewer hassles if you have physical limits, consider these tips:

- Start your shopping trip before you get to the store. Plan ahead. Make a grocery list so you won't need to retrace your steps through the store.
- Shop at quiet times, such as weekday mornings, when stores aren't crowded. Daytime shopping, when it's easier to see curbs and potholes, is safer, anyway, especially if you have trouble with night vision. If you must shop at night, pick a store with a well-lit parking lot, or ask someone to go with you.
- Feeling less stable? Use the shopping cart for balance—even to buy just a few items.
- If you're less mobile, shop in stores that provide battery-powered, sit-down grocery carts. It's a courtesy service that your supermarket may offer.
- If you have trouble reading food labels and unit price codes on shelves, take a magnifying glass.

- Keep a supply of nonperishable foods: canned foods (vegetables, fruits, juice, tuna, soup, stew, beans), cereal, dried fruit, nonfat dry milk or boxed (UHT shelf-stable) milk, and peanut butter; check for sodium and added sugars before buying. Then you won't need to shop when it's raining or snowing.
- Ask for help loading the groceries in your car. This also means extra security for you in the parking lot.
- If you qualify, get a sticker for your car that lets you park in handicapped spots.
- Don't drive or use public transportation? Check with your local area's Agency on Aging or Community Action Center for shopping assistance. Your community may offer shopping transportation for adults. Or if physical limitations keep you mostly homebound, hire a home health aide to shop and cook for you.
- Ask about special services from your supermarket: home delivery or phone orders. If you're computer savvy, you might do your food shopping online. *See "Shopping for Food Online" in chapter 6, page 158, for tips.*
- If you have ideas to make shopping more convenient for older shoppers, talk with the store manager. With the growing numbers of older customers, they'll likely listen.

AT-HOME AND RESIDENTIAL CARE: FOOD SERVICES

When food shopping, meal prep, and clean up for everyday meals is physically challenging or no longer pleasurable, you have choices. And you don't need to abandon your goal to eat healthy enjoyable meals.

Community Services

Can't easily cook anymore? That doesn't necessarily mean giving up living on your own. Many communities offer services for older adults to assure access to nutritious meals. In fact, the Older Americans Act, first funded more than fifty years ago, supports home and community services for adults aged sixty and older. These services are meant to reduce hunger and food insecurity; promote socialization, health, and well-being; and delay health problems. Look for these services in your community:

- Meals on Wheels brings food to housebound people. You can ask for vegetarian menus and menus for special dietary needs such as low sodium. If you get a home-delivered meal, remember: it's meant as the right nourishment for one meal, not two. Saving half for later can leave you shortchanged on nutrients. Trying to keep leftovers may pose a food safety risk.
- Home health aides help by shopping and preparing meals for older disabled people.
- Community centers offer hot meals. Some are part of adult day programs. Minivans may be available to take you to the center.
- Many churches, synagogues, mosques, and other faith-based and community organizations provide volunteers who help older adults with shopping and food preparation. For assistance, talk to a registered dietitian nutritionist or a social worker, or call your local Agency on Aging. *See "Credible Support for Healthy Eating" in chapter 26, page 761.*

Food Service in Adult Day Care and Healthcare Communities

Meals offer more than nourishment to daily life. That's especially true for many older adults, who look forward to meals as a time to be with others. Today's dining programs in adult day care and healthcare communities offer different types of food service: buffet-style dining, family-style dining, five (not just three) mealtimes, and "neighborhood" living with rooms clustered around an open kitchen and dining and living areas. *See "Adult Care: Questions to Ask" in this chapter, page 591, to help you explore care for older adults.*

Sandwiched In?

Are you among the many adults who fit in the "sandwich generation," with children or teens yet to raise and an elder parent to care for? If so, learn to cope without becoming overly stressed:

- Start by taking care of you: Eat smart, fit regular physical activity in, and try to stay rested. Overcome stress or handle pressures on time so they don't become barriers. You'll be more effective in all your family roles as parent, son or daughter, or perhaps spouse—and perhaps in the workforce or in your volunteer work.
- Plan openly with your family, including kids and an elder parent(s), so that goals, responsibilities, and expectations are clear. That includes activities that surround eating: shopping, food preparation, cleanup, eating schedules, and family meals.
- Share responsibilities as a family rather than attempt to do everything yourself. Try to avoid neglecting one family member to care for another.
- Put together a support network that may include adult day programs, home-delivered meals if you work all day, and other senior citizen services for your parent. Ask for help, and accept when it's offered.
- Accept the fact that you'll be tired and perhaps frustrated sometimes. Try to discard any feelings of guilt when you can't do all you want to do. Instead, get help so you can have a break, even if it's just for a few hours. Maybe it's a good time to do something physically active. If negative feelings trigger eating, find another emotional outlet.
- Respect the privacy, dignity, and independence of your elder parent(s).

✔ Adult Care: Questions to Ask

As you look for adult day care or a home life center (healthcare community) for yourself, or for a friend or family member, learn about the food service. You should be able to answer "yes" to all these food- and nutrition-related questions:

DINING AREA

1. Is the dining area clean, safe, comfortable, and attractive?
2. Are menus printed with lettering that's big enough for older people to read?
3. Is the dining area well lighted throughout, not just "mood" lighting or single lights that cause glare?
4. Does the dining area encourage socializing?
5. Can the resident decide where, when, and what he or she wants to eat—and with whom?
6. Is the dining table at a height appropriate for proper and comfortable seating?
7. Does the dining service have a high safety and sanitation record?

FOOD

8. Are people given freedom to make food choices and given a voice in meal planning and dining programs?
9. Are beverages and snacks available throughout the day?
10. Are the menus changed often so the menu cycle doesn't get monotonous?
11. Are fresh vegetables and fruits served often?
12. Do menus reflect the personal, cultural, and ethnic choices of the residents?
13. Do the menus show icons next to options that are lower in fat, added sugars, or sodium to help individuals make appropriate choices?
14. Is food served attractively and at the right temperature?
15. Are portion sizes acceptable? Are second helpings available if medically allowed?
16. Are religious and cultural food restrictions honored and respected? How about food preferences?
17. Are holidays and special events celebrated with special menus or appropriate foods?
18. Are special meals, such as low-sodium, diabetic, or soft-textured meals, provided to those who need them?
19. Are food and nutrition needs given individual attention? Are special utensils offered if needed?

STAFF

20. Is mealtime viewed as important to daily life?
21. Is a registered dietitian nutritionist on staff?
22. Are residents or guests encouraged to eat in a common dining room? Are they offered assistance to get there?
23. Do staff or volunteers help those needing assistance, perhaps cutting food or helping them eat?
24. Do staff or volunteers wear sanitary gloves when helping residents or guests eat so they don't spread infection?
25. Are residents or guests given enough time to eat, and not rushed?
26. For those who can't leave their rooms, is food brought on attractive trays and properly set for ease of in-room dining?
27. If residents or guests need assistance, is it given promptly so food doesn't get cold? Are trays removed promptly?
28. For a long-term care facility, does the staff track each person's weight and how much he or she eats and drinks?

Physical Changes: Challenges and Smart Strategies

What's changed? That depends. If you've inherited a great set of genes and taken care of yourself throughout life, you have a better chance of living a long, vital life. You may feel "fit as a fiddle" without many apparent physical signs of aging. Wrinkles and gray hairs hardly seem to count. In fact, they make you look wise and distinguished.

In the long run, some physical changes are inevitable. The reasons that the human body ages—and the rate of change—are still scientific speculation. But disease, environment, genetics, lifestyle, and nutrition are among the reasons. *See "Why Do You Age? Can You Slow Aging?" in this chapter, page 577.*

Both physical and lifestyle changes can affect food choices, nutrition, and levels of physical activity. Some changes can be debilitating. For example, older adults are at high risk for developing chronic illnesses and related disabilities, including arthritis, congestive heart failure, dementia, and type 2 diabetes. *See chapters 24, page 680, and 25, page 722, for more about these and other common health issues.*

Medications may have side effects related to food or nutrition. *See "Food and Medicine: Some Don't Mix" in chapter 25, page 743, to learn about interactions and tips for managing them.*

FLAVOR LOSS? AGING WITH "TASTE"

"That recipe just doesn't taste the way I remember!" You might hear that from an older adult. Maybe you've said it yourself. The truth is, the senses of smell, taste, and touch decline gradually, with loss of acuity starting at about age sixty. Some people notice the effects more than others.

Less "Sense-Able" with Age

You've probably given it little thought, but from the time of your earliest memories, smell and taste have affected the quality of your life, your overall health, and your personal safety. Think about simple pleasures: the variety of flavors in a holiday meal, the aromas of bread baking or turkey roasting in the oven, the sounds of popping popcorn, or the sizzle of food on the grill. Food's wonderful flavors encourage a healthy appetite and help stimulate digestion.

Flavor is really several perceptions: the senses of smell (olfaction) and taste (gustation), as well as touch (temperature and mouth feel). With aging, taste buds and olfactory nerves and receptors may not be as sensitive or as numerous. When flavors seem to change, people often mistakenly think they can't taste as well. However, the gradual loss of smell is often greater than the loss of taste. Taste is rather stable across the life span.

Age isn't the only reason why foods may seem to have a different flavor. Reducing the salt, added sugars, or fat in food choices for health benefits may alter familiar flavors. Differences in saliva (composition and amount) and problems with chewing and swallowing can affect flavor, too. Medications and health problems also may interfere. Some medicines leave a bitter flavor that affects saliva and, as a result, flavor. Some cause nausea, resulting in appetite loss, or dry mouth. Medicines may suppress taste and smell.

Health problems such as diabetes, high blood pressure, cancer, and liver disease, common among older people, may alter taste and smell. Loss of smell also can indicate other health problems such as Parkinson's and Alzheimer's diseases.

If nutrient-rich foods don't smell or taste appetizing, eating itself may become less pleasurable. Some older people may reach for the salt shaker or the sugar bowl, perhaps more often than before. Others may lose interest in eating. In each case, sensory changes, small appetites, and skipped meals can result in poor nutrition and the "anorexia" of aging. *See "Flavor and Health" in chapter 8, page 238.*

Senses: A First Alert

Your senses can't be taken for granted. They provide clues to the off flavor or appearance of deteriorating food, or perhaps to a kitchen fire or a gas leak in the kitchen stove. Sensory experiences that change due to age and health problems can pose potential health risks. That said, you often can overcome, or at least accommodate to, many sensory changes that gradually affect your food experiences and thus your personal health. For example:

- Have trouble reading food labels, recipes, an oven thermometer, or medication instructions? Get glasses for the first time, change your eyeglasses or contact lens prescription, or keep a magnifying glass handy. Large-print cookbooks are useful, too.
- Have trouble hearing a kitchen timer, food bubbling over on the stove, or a faucet you forgot to turn off? How about hearing the answers to your questions in a restaurant or supermarket? Find out from a doctor if you need a hearing aid.
- Experience a loss of smell and taste? When food "just doesn't taste as good as it used to," give it a flavor boost, *as discussed below.*

"Sage" Advice for a Flavor Boost

Compensating for a diminished sense of taste or smell is within your control. So, perhaps, is making special, restricted diets more appealing. You might intensify the flavor and aroma of food, vary the temperature and texture, or make food more visually appealing. And consider: Sensory loss may not be the issue; soft, colorless, and bland food and mushy vegetables don't appeal to most people. To add meal appeal, you might:

- Perk up flavors with more herbs and spices and some lemon juice—not with more salt or sugar. To compensate for age-related taste loss, you might need two to three times as much herb or spice and twice the flavor extract as you did in younger years. Despite a common myth, older adults can tolerate spicy foods. *Hint:* If any spices do cause stomach irritation, stick with herbs.

- Unless you're sensitive to it, use MSG, not salt. It has one-third of the sodium as the same amount of salt. One-half teaspoon can season a pound of meat or two to three cups of cooked vegetables.
- Add crunch. Texture adds to food's mouth feel and flavor. A variety of textures helps make up for a loss of taste and smell. Add whole-grain breads, whole-grain cereals, and cooked beans for more texture. What else is easy? Crushed crackers on soup, chopped nuts on vegetables or rice, and crushed cornflakes on pudding.
- Use strong-flavored ingredients: garlic, onions, sharp cheese, flavored vinegars and oils, concentrated fruit sauce, and jam.
- For less fat and fewer calories, impart flavor with herb rubs instead of gravy or sauces. Fat carries flavor, too. Use small amounts of flavorful oils such as olive and peanut oils for health benefits, too. A little dribble will do!
- Include foods of different temperatures in a single meal.
- Serve hot foods hot, not lukewarm, to enhance their flavor. Extreme hot or cold temperatures, however, tend to lessen flavors.
- Avoid overcooking. Steaming or microwaving vegetables for a shorter time retains more flavor and crunch.
- Serve colorful, attractive foods. Visual appeal is another way to make food more appetizing. A simple lemon or tomato slice on the plate adds appeal.
- Chew well to enjoy the foods' full flavors.
- If you smoke, stop. Smoking reduces your ability to perceive flavors (and leads to other health risks).
- Limit overexposing your taste buds to strong or bitter flavors, perhaps from unsweetened tea or coffee or bitter greens such as kale. While they have health benefits, they can temporarily affect sensitivity to other flavors.
- If you've lost interest in eating, talk to your doctor, and consult a registered dietitian nutritionist about other ways to make food more appealing. *Be aware:* Sensory loss may signal one or more serious health problems; tell your doctor.

See "Flavor on the Menu" in chapter 8, page 238, for ways to make food more flavorful and appealing.

Have you ever wondered?

. . . if taking mineral oil helps keep you regular as you get older? Taking mineral oil isn't recommended. It can promote the loss of fat-soluble vitamins (A, D, E, and K), which are essential to health.

CONSTIPATION? KEEPING REGULAR

Constipation is a persistent problem for many people as they get older. The reason? The digestive system may get a little sluggish. Not getting enough fluid or fiber and being inactive may compound the problem.

With constipation, stools get hard and can't be passed out of the body without straining. And the body's normal elimination schedule may change. Drinking enough fluids, eating enough fiber, and being physically active are ways to stay regular and avoid constipation—a healthier approach than using more laxatives. Here's how to prevent it:

- Drink enough water or other fluids. Fluids help your stools stay softer and bulkier, making them easier to eliminate.
- Fiber up. Fiber gives bulk to stools, enabling them to pass more easily through the colon. Further, it won't interfere with the digestion and absorption of nutrients, as laxatives might. *See "Fiber and Health" in chapter 11, page 350, for more about fiber, including fiber pills and powders.*
- Keep physically active and get enough rest. Both help keep your body regular.
- Listen to nature's call. The longer waste remains in your large intestine, the more difficult it is to eliminate. The body continues to draw out water, so stools get harder.

Avoid taking laxatives, as well as fiber pills and powders, unless your doctor recommends them. They may cause foods to pass through your intestinal tract faster than their vitamins and minerals can be absorbed. And some may cause your body to lose fluids and potassium. A cup of tea or warm water with lemon, taken first thing in the morning, can act as a gentle, natural laxative. If none of this works, ask a registered dietitian nutritionist or your doctor for more advice. *See "Digestive Health: GI Upsets and Conditions" in chapter 25, page 727, for more about dealing with constipation.*

NOT HUNGRY? DEALING WITH APPETITE LOSS

While many older adults say they just don't have an appetite, there's no single cause for that comment. As noted, sensory loss plays a role. Some have digestive problems that cause appetite loss. Body changes that come with age may cause someone to feel full sooner than at a younger age. And medication or health problems also may be a cause. For some, the problem is psychological: loneliness, depression, or anxiety, among others.

Regardless, people who don't eat adequately increase their chances for poor nutrition and its negative consequences. If you're not hungry, skipping meals actually may suppress your appetite—especially if you already have appetite loss. And skipping meals may cause your blood glucose level to drop too low and then surge too high later with a big meal. To perk up a tired appetite:

- Try to identify the problem with your doctor. If certain foods cause heartburn or gas, find alternatives. Talk to your doctor about your medication; if it's the cause, something else might be prescribed.

- Take advantage of the "up" times. When you feel well and your appetite is good, eat and enjoy!
- Learn to cope with appetite loss. Consuming enough calories may be easier if you eat by the clock rather than relying on hunger.
- Start the day with breakfast, when your appetite is likely at its best. Then try to eat something at every meal.
- Eat four to six smaller meals; keep portions small. You can take seconds if you're hungry for more. Plus, smaller meals may be easier to digest.
- Give yourself enough time to eat. Rushing through a meal can cause discomfort.
- To get your digestive juices flowing, serve foods hot. Heat brings out the aroma of food, usually making it more enticing.
- Fill the house with enticing food aromas such as freshly baked bread, cakes, or cookies.
- Make your overall meal look and taste more appealing. As mentioned earlier, food that's attractively arranged and served may help bring your appetite back. Giving foods a flavor boost may help, too. Colorful foods, different textures, and appetizing aromas make food more appealing.
- Drink a glass of beer or wine before a meal—if you drink, and only in moderation, *as defined in "Alcoholic Beverages: In Moderation," in chapter 4, page 102.* This often gives an appetite a jump start. But check with your doctor about any medication interactions or health conditions first.
- If possible, increase your physical activity. Doing so may promote a healthier appetite.
- If you're confined to bed, ask for help to keep your room pleasant. Remove bedpans and other unpleasant things. Enjoy a plant; turn on music!

CHEWING PROBLEMS? ADJUSTING TEXTURE

For many mature adults, poor appetite isn't much of a nutrition problem. Instead, tooth loss or mouth pain may be. An astounding number of adults lose all their teeth by age sixty-five. Many also have poorly fitting dentures that cause chewing problems and mouth sores.

What's at the root of oral health problems? Cavities may come to mind first. Yet gum, or periodontal, disease is the most common cause of tooth loss among older adults. As a result, many have missing, loose, or diseased teeth and sore, diseased gums. People with dentures may be able to eat all the foods they've always enjoyed if dentures fit right. If not, the resulting discomfort and mouth pain may keep them from eating a well-balanced diet. Osteoarthritis also can hinder chewing if it affects the lower jaw.

As discussed earlier, a dry mouth is another problem that may cause chewing and swallowing difficulties, especially if food is dry and hard to chew. As people get older, they may not have as much saliva flow to help soften food and wash it down. Medications, some health problems, and treatments such as chemotherapy also may decrease saliva flow or cause chewing and swallowing problems. *See "Cancer Treatment: Handling Food-Related Side Effects" in chapter 24, page 719.*

If you have chewing problems, make sure oral problems don't become a barrier to good nutrition:

- Have your teeth and gums (and perhaps dentures) checked. See your dentist, or go to a dentist who specializes in care for older adults. Many oral health problems can be treated. Have poorly fitted dentures adjusted.
- Choose softer foods that are easier to chew. Chop, grate, grind, puree, or cook hard vegetables or fruits to reduce your risk of choking. These nutrient-rich foods are softer and easier to eat:
    - *Grain group:* cooked cereal, cooked pasta, cooked rice, soft bread or rolls, softer crackers
    - *Vegetable group:* mashed or baked sweet and baking potatoes; salads with soft vegetables and chopped lettuce; steamed or microwaved cauliflower, peas, spinach, and squash; stewed tomatoes; vegetable juice
    - *Fruit group:* avocados, cooked or canned fruits, 100 percent fruit juice, ripe bananas, soft fruits such as sliced kiwi or peaches
    - *Dairy group:* low-fat and fat-free milk, cheese, ice cream, milk shakes, pudding, yogurt
    - *Protein foods group:* chopped lean meat, chopped chicken or turkey, canned fish, tender cooked fish, eggs, tofu, hummus, peanut butter
- Drink water or other fluids with meals and snacks to make swallowing easier.
- Consult a registered dietitian nutritionist. Together, you can plan meals with foods that you can eat comfortably without compromising your nutrient intake.

Tooth loss and chewing difficulty aren't inevitable parts of aging. Good oral care—starting now, whatever your age—can help you keep the teeth you were born with. *See "Oral Health: Your Healthy Smile" in chapter 25, page 735.*

Gum disease is highly preventable with proper brushing, daily flossing, and regular cleaning by a dentist or hygienist. If you can, have your teeth cleaned twice a year, and perhaps more often if you have gum disease. *See "A Closer Look . . . How to Keep Your Teeth and Gums Healthy" in chapter 25, page 737.*

WEIGHT LOSS—OR GAIN? MANAGING FOR HEALTH

Does clothing fit as it did before? Too loose? Have you lost weight as a result of a poor appetite or health problems? Or have extra pounds crept on? Maintaining or improving your weight may be a health step you need to take. Weigh yourself, or have someone weigh you, every so often to check for changes. Your doctor or a registered dietitian nutritionist can help you determine the weight that's healthy for you.

In later adult years, some evidence suggests that a high BMI is less predictive of mortality, or death, than it is among younger adults. In fact, being underweight with a BMI that's too low in later years appears to be a greater risk than having a high BMI. *See "Body Mass Index" in chapter 22, page 627, to figure your BMI.*

Weight Loss: A Concern

Weight loss may signal a health problem, especially if losing weight isn't your intention. If that happens, first and foremost, find out why.

Maybe you aren't consuming enough calories. Perhaps the reason is poor oral health or appetite loss. Or maybe immobility makes grocery shopping or food preparation difficult. Perhaps smaller meals and fewer snacks lower your food expense. Weight loss may signal an emotional problem, perhaps depression and/or bereavement, or social isolation. Unexpected weight loss also is a symptom for some serious health problems, including cancer.

Weight loss may be linked to physical weakness when muscle mass, not just body fat, is lost. Loss of physical strength and frailty increase the risk for falls and, as a result, bone fractures and other health problems that affect quality of life and health. Being significantly underweight for any reason may lead to serious malnutrition. It also may slow recovery from sickness or surgery. Severe weight loss may be life-threatening.

Whatever the reasons, talk to your doctor before you start trying to gain weight about an effective, safe approach that matches your health needs. Besides weight loss, talk about chewing or digestive problems, depression, and medications. Ask for screenings to detect nutrition-related problems.

To gain weight or avoid losing it:

- Eat enough. *See chapter 2, page 21, for your guide for consuming enough among and within the five food groups.*
- Eat five or six small meals a day if you fill up quickly at three bigger meals.
- Stick to a regular meal schedule so you don't forget to eat.
- Keep healthy, easy snack foods handy: cereal, cheese, crackers, fruits, hummus, milk, peanut butter, vegetables, whole-wheat bread, yogurt—even ice cream. Unsalted nuts and nut butters are nutrient dense and provide protein, too.
- Instead of coffee or tea, choose drinks that supply nutrients and calories such as hot cocoa, 100 percent juice, and milk. Or add milk to your coffee or tea for calories and milk's many nutrients.
- Fortify casseroles, soups, stews, and side dishes with more nourishing ingredients for more calories, too. For example: beans, dry milk, nuts, rice, pasta, shredded cheese, or wheat germ.
- Talk to a registered dietitian nutritionist or your doctor about ways to boost calories and nutrients in your meals and snacks.
- Ask about a protein bar, shake, or supplement to consume between meals, after dinner, or before mealtime. A protein bar or shake should not replace a meal.
- Find an appropriate way to stay physically active so you maintain your body's muscle mass—and your strength. Talk to your doctor and perhaps a physical therapist who works with older adults.

Be aware that some medications, including low-dose antidepressant drugs, may enhance appetite; others may interfere with appetite, digestion, or nutrient absorption.

See "What If You Need a Healthy Way to Gain Weight?" in chapter 22, page 651, for tips.

Weight Gain: An Issue, Too

As you get older, you need fewer calories to maintain your weight. It's not surprising, then, to gain a few pounds—especially if you're more sedentary and still eat as you always have. The concern is that being overweight or obese increases your risks for high blood pressure, heart disease, type 2 diabetes, and certain cancers.

If you have one of these problems already, or if you're carrying extra weight, dropping just a few pounds may lower your blood pressure, total blood cholesterol level, or blood glucose level. Extra body weight affects how easily you move and intensifies the discomfort of arthritis. It also can contribute to disabilities, which may lead to an earlier death.

As older adults lose muscle mass they typically gain body fat. Loss of strength increases the chance for becoming frail and of falling. Before you start trying to lose weight, talk to your doctor about an effective, safe approach that matches your health needs.

Note: Intentional weight loss among overweight and obese older adults often is advised and linked to lower risk of type 2 diabetes and to improved cardiovascular health.

To lose weight or avoid gaining it:

- Know your calorie target. Eat the recommended amount of nutrient-dense foods from the five food groups as well as healthy oils, based on your calorie target. That may mean smaller portions. *See chapter 2, page 21, for a healthy eating plan to match your calorie needs.*
- Eat regular meals. Meal skipping often leads to snacking and possibly overeating.
- Choose snacks carefully: breakfast cereal, vegetables, fruits, low-fat or fat-free milk, low fat yogurt, and frozen yogurt.
- Opt for foods with less fat and added sugars to cut calories. Choose lean meats and trim visible fat. *See chapter 8, page 230, for ways to trim calories from fat, and added sugars in food preparation.*
- If you drink alcoholic beverages, go easy. If you take medication or have some health conditions, you might need to avoid alcoholic drinks altogether. *See "Alcoholic Drinks: Be Cautious" in this chapter, page 584.*

- Keep busy so you don't eat from boredom or loneliness. And pay attention to your body's hunger and satiety (fullness) signals.
- Find safe, appropriate ways to move more and sit less. You'll get more health-promoting benefits than weight control alone.
- Beware of weight-loss plans with unrealistic promises. *See "Popular Diets: Truths and Half Truths" in chapter 22, page 648.*

See "Weight Management: Strategies That Work!" in chapter 22, page 637, for more about successful weight management.

LESS MOBILITY? TIPS FOR FOOD-PREP INDEPENDENCE

Some older adults move with the same grace, stamina, and dexterity of their earlier years. For others, health problems limit physical abilities. For example, arthritis, diabetes, osteoporosis, Parkinson's disease, respiratory diseases, and strokes can cause problems. Even healthy, mature adults who become gradually less active may have less strength and stamina for everyday tasks than when they were younger.

Rather than avoid certain categories of foods due to physical limitations, accept food preparation help if you need it. It's important to get nourishment from a variety of foods.

If you enjoy independent living, arrange your kitchen, equipment, and eating utensils for ease, accessibility, and safety.

Kitchen Arrangement

Make your kitchen space more workable, safe, and accessible:

- If you use a walker, scooter, or wheelchair, talk to a registered dietitian nutritionist or an occupational therapist about ways to change your kitchen for independent living. For example, you will need a clear space in the kitchen and eating area that's big enough to accommodate it.
- Ask about kitchens that meet universal design specifications, meaning they are accessible to anyone, including older adults with physical disabilities.
- Organize your kitchen for efficiency—everything within easy reach. Keep mixers, blenders, and other heavy, small appliances on the counter. Keep heavy pots and pans on lower shelves, too.
- Be careful of loose rugs by the sink or other places in your kitchen. They may feel good underfoot, but they're easy to trip over or slip on.
- If you're unsteady or need a cane, use a rolling tea cart to move food, dishes, and kitchen equipment from place to place.
- Have a counter that's the right height for you—with work surfaces that are three inches shorter than your elbow height, as specified by universal design.
- Counters at several levels are helpful if you need to sit to work sometimes.
- If you need one, choose a wheelchair or walker with a flat seat that can be used to move things, too. Check with a medical supply store.
- Plan to sit while you work. Use the kitchen table for food preparation, or get a stable chair or stool that's high enough for working at the counter or stove.

Kitchen Equipment

Make food prep and cooking equipment work better for you:

- Get a loud kitchen timer if you have trouble hearing. Especially if you're forgetful, using a timer when you cook can avoid burned food and kitchen fires.
- Cooking for just one? Use a microwave or toaster oven rather than the conventional oven.
- If you have vision problems, keep a magnifying glass handy, and have your eyes checked and fitted for glasses. That will make it easier to read expiration dates and small type on food labels.

Need more practical, easy ways to eat smart as the years go by?

Check here for "how-tos":

- Make a personal plan for healthy eating; *"Reaching SMART Goals: One Step at a Time!" in chapter 1, page 18, and chapter 2, page 21, for a healthy eating plan.*
- Find smart ways to lose, gain, or maintain your weight; *see chapter 22, page 625.*
- Make quick, simple meals if you don't have a lot of energy; *see chapter 3, page 60.*
- Get more for your food dollar on a fixed income; *see "Your Food Dollar: More Nutrition, Less Waste" in chapter 6, page 154.*
- Protect yourself from foodborne illness; *see chapter 7, page 191.*
- Prepare food to get more nutrition for fewer calories; *see chapter 8, page 230.*
- Perk up food's flavor with herbs and spices if it no longer tastes as good. Improve food's look, too; *see "Herbs—and Spices, Too!" in chapter 8, page 266.*
- Eat out, yet still match your health needs; *see chapter 9, page 275.*
- Eat to manage health problems; *see chapters 24, page 680, and 25, page 722.*
- Get easy, personalized tips from a nutrition expert; *see "Nutrition Advice to Trust" in chapter 26, page 758.*

- Use a cutting board with contrasting colors if you have trouble with vision. For example, it may be hard to safely cut an onion on a white plastic cutting board. Place a wet paper towel under the cutting board so it doesn't move around.
- Do you have trouble with manual tasks such as opening jars and cans, or perhaps cutting? Kitchen devices and utensils with large grips and other design features are sold to make food preparation easier for people with arthritis or other problems, and for those partly paralyzed by a stroke. Again, check with a medical supply store.
- If you use a wheelchair, buy an oven with front controls and a side-hinged door. Install it next to the sink or your work area, not across the kitchen. Put in low countertops and "pull-outs," such as cutting boards, in your kitchen. Talk to a physical therapist or registered dietitian nutritionist about other kitchen solutions.

Dishes and Eating Utensils

Set your table to make mealtime easier:

- Use an all-in-one fork and spoon if you have trouble with one hand. Check with a medical supply store or catalog to find one.
- Drink soup from a mug. It's easier than using a soup spoon—and there's one less utensil to wash.
- Get dishes with high rims and rubberized, nonslip backs. The rim helps you push food onto your spoon or fork.
- Shaky with a cup? Get a covered cup with a drinking spout or place for a straw.
- Set your table with plastic or nonslip placemats. They're easy to clean, and dishes won't slide on them as they might on the table surface.

Caregivers: Give a Helping Hand

For people who are sick, weak, or injured, good nutrition and someone to share a meal with are often the best medicine. Meals give a feeling of security, meaning, and structure to an older person's day and provide a sense of control over his or her surroundings. To make eating a pleasant experience, visit during mealtime, or invite (or bring) someone you care about to your home for a meal.

Regardless of age, those with difficulty feeding themselves may need a caring helping hand. If you offer help, make mealtime pleasant:

- Help with hand washing before and after eating. Use a wet, soapy washcloth, premoistened towels, or a hand sanitizer if the person can't get to the sink. Offer a towel for drying.
- Make sure that the food is the right consistency if chewing is difficult. Chop, grind, or puree the food as needed.
- Let the person decide what foods to eat first, next, and so on. Even when people can't feed themselves, most still want to feel in control.
- For dignity's sake, provide a napkin, a clothing protector, or an apron to help him or her keep clean.
- Offer some finger foods to eat independently. For example, try banana slices, orange sections, bread (cut into quarters), a soft roll, cheese sticks, or meat (sliced into strips).
- Offer a drink between bites to help with chewing and swallowing. Provide a straw and a cup that's not too big. You can always pour more.
- Consider how far the person can reach for a cup or dish. Arrange the place setting for easy reach.
- Offer small bites, and suggest a spoon rather than a fork. It's easier for holding food and less likely to jab his or her mouth.
- Sit together at the same level when you offer food.
- Share pleasant conversation in a normal tone, even if you need to do all the talking. To be sure you understand a response, repeat or rephrase it.
- Relax; be patient. Encourage self-expression of any kind. Meals should not feel rushed, especially if the person has trouble chewing or swallowing.
- If you can, eat your meal at the same time to continue the normalcy of social interaction at mealtime.
- Clean up spills right away. Keep a clean cloth handy.
- Most important, respect the person's needs and desires. Expect frustration, and handle it without a negative reaction. Counting on others for personal care can be emotionally difficult.
- Let the nurse or other caregivers know what and how much the person has eaten. In that way, other meals and snacks can be adjusted accordingly.

While healthy eating is very important, familiar routines and food choices may be difficult for those with Alzheimer's disease. For caring tips for someone with Alzheimer's disease, visit the website of the Alzheimer's Disease Education and Referral (ADEAR) Center, a service of the National Institute on Aging: www.nia.nih.gov/alzheimers/about-adear-center.

Safety Tips

Make your kitchen safer yet:

- Keep your cell phone handy and charged. You won't need to dash to the phone while you're cooking. It's a good safety measure, too, in case you fall and need to call for help.
- Give yourself time. Things may take a little longer to do as you get older. Rushing creates accidents.
- Does your floor seem slippery? Wear flat, rubber-soled shoes in the kitchen. And wipe up spills immediately so you don't slip.
- Have someone regularly check the smoke alarm in your kitchen to make sure it's working.
- Avoid using your oven as a room heater. If heating is a problem where you live, let someone know—a relative, landlord, building manager, or social worker, among others.

See "Safe from Kitchen Injuries" in chapter 7, page 196, for more tips.

With the growth of the aging population, new devices to help older people live independently and socially are being introduced. The US Department of Education's AbleData assistive technology website (abledata.com) provides information on products to help people live independent lives. This demographic shift also has spawned a field called gerontechnology, connecting technology to the health, housing, mobility, communication, leisure, and work of older adults to help them live in good health, comfort, and safety. An occupational therapist or a registered dietitian nutritionist with a specialty in gerontology might offer help, too.

SPECIAL DIET? TALK WITH YOUR DOCTOR

Almost 80 percent of older adults have one chronic health condition; more than half have two or more, according to the Centers for Disease Control and Prevention. Five of the eight common causes of death in those over age sixty-five have a nutrition connection.

Many health problems—physical and emotional—that arise with aging require major changes in what and how people eat. Discuss that with your doctor during your regular checkups—annually or more often as your doctor advises. Never self-diagnose an ongoing disease or prescribe your own special diet or dietary supplement to treat it. And be careful of so-called miracle cures.

For any health condition, there's no one recommended diet. Because needs differ so much, individualized nutrition advice is essential. Sometimes more than one health problem needs to be treated at the same time.

To manage your health condition, your food choices—medical nutrition therapy—may need as much of your attention as following directions for medications. If your doctor prescribes a special (therapeutic) diet for you, consult a registered dietitian nutritionist for guidance. Have your progress monitored, as advised. *See "Have you ever wondered . . . what medical nutrition therapy is?" in chapter 25, page 687.* For a referral to a registered dietitian nutritionist, ask your doctor. *See "Qualified Experts: Please Stand Up" in chapter 26, page 758, to learn more about finding and working with nutrition experts.*

21

Eat Smart for Sports

In this chapter, find out about . . .

Nutrient advice for athletes

High-performance diets

Reaching your competitive weight

Eating to compete: before, during, and after

Supplements and sports

On your mark . . . get set . . . go! Whether you train for competitive sports, or work out for your own good health or just for fun, what you eat and drink—and when—can be part of your formula for athletic success. Good nutrition can't replace training, effort, talent, and personal drive for peak performance. But what you eat and drink over time promotes your ability to do your personal best.

Whether competitive or recreational, physical activity puts extra demands on your body. You use more energy, lose more body fluids, and put extra stress on your muscles, joints, and bones. Fortunately, your well-chosen "training table" can help increase your endurance and help prevent dehydration and injury. Most important, healthy eating helps you feel good, stay fit, and have a positive "mental edge"!

For more about the benefits of regular physical activity and physical activity guidelines for the general public, see "Move More! Physical Activity Guidelines" in chapter 1, page 15.

Nutrients for Active Living

Good nutrition is fundamental to fitness. No matter what your level of physical activity, your nutrient needs are similar to others of your same age and gender. However, if you're highly active, you may need slightly more of some nutrients. That includes more water to replace fluid loss during high activity and more energy-supplying nutrients, especially carbohydrates.

Even then, nutrition goals and needs, especially for serious athletes, aren't static. Instead, they change during training and for competition and recovery. These targets must be personalized, taking into account the specific and unique needs of the event, performance goals, practical challenges, and food preferences.

For some athletes, advice for sports must go further. For example, for those managing a health condition such as diabetes, consulting their doctor or a registered dietitian nutritionist about the right food and beverage plan is essential for health and performance.

For serious or elite athletes who want to maximize their training and performance, consulting a registered dietitian nutritionist who specializes in sports nutrition can be a valuable asset. Much of that advice goes beyond the scope of this book.

Did You Know?

. . . heat stroke, associated with dehydration, ranks second among the reported causes of death among high school athletes?

. . . muscles are made of more than protein? Actually, 15 to 20 percent is protein; 70 to 75 percent is water; and 5 to 7 percent is fat, glycogen, and minerals.

. . . matching your carbohydrate intake to your activity level can boost your endurance?

THIRST FOR SUCCESS!

Do you drink plenty of water, but not to excess? Your optimal health and physical endurance, strength, and performance depend on it!

When physically active, even with recreational activity, you lose more fluids than usual, as sweat evaporates from your skin. Sweating is a good thing. It helps to dissipate body heat generated by muscle work, often intensified in hot weather. This helps keep your body temperature within a safe range.

As you breathe, often heavily, you exhale moisture. A 150-pound athlete can lose one-and-a-half quarts, or about three pounds, of fluid in just one hour. That equals six eight-ounce glasses of water. With heavy training, fluid loss can be higher. When you perspire heavily, you lose more than water. Sweat contains substantial, but variable, amounts of sodium—and smaller amounts of potassium, calcium, and magnesium.

Dehydration is the process of losing body fluids. Too much fluid loss, without replacing it, can lead to hypohydration, whereby the body's volume of fluid is inadequate for normal functioning. This can be life-threatening. ("Hypo-" means "under.")

Fluids for Peak Performance

What's the risk if you begin physical activity even slightly dehydrated or you lose too much fluid while you're active? Dehydration can affect strength, endurance, and aerobic capacity, as well as cardiovascular function and your body's temperature control—especially with severe fluid loss, or hypohydration.

Fluid losses, resulting in 2 percent or more of body weight, may hinder mental and physical performance, particularly during hot weather. That's about three pounds for a 150-pound person. Greater deficits have even more pronounced effects. *See "Fluids: How Much Is Enough" in chapter 15, page 377, to learn more about proper hydration.*

For energy production. Fluids are part of the energy-production cycle. As part of blood, water helps carry oxygen and glucose to muscle cells. There, oxygen and glucose help produce energy. Blood removes waste by-products as muscle cells generate energy and then passes them to urine. Fluid losses decrease blood volume; as a result, your heart must work harder to deliver enough oxygen to cells.

For cooling down. Exercising muscles generates ten to twenty times more heat than resting muscles, as a by-product of energy production. As you move, your overall temperature goes up, and you sweat. As sweat evaporates, your skin and the blood just under your skin cool you down. Cooler blood that flows throughout your body helps protect you from overheating. In higher humidity, perspiring is less effective in ridding the body of excess heat. If you don't replace lost fluids, your body's fluid balance is thrown off—becoming a bigger problem as working muscles continue to generate heat.

For transporting nutrients. Your bloodstream carries other nutrients for performance, including electrolytes, which help maintain body fluid balance.

Your Healthy Body Check-In

Your Physical Activity: How Intense?

Light, moderate, or intense? Estimate your activity level, and determine if your heart rate is within your target zone.

1. *Decide on your goal:*
   - *Moderate intensity:* Your target heart rate should be 50 to 70 percent of your maximum heart rate.
   - *Vigorous intensity:* Your target heart rate should be 70 to 85 percent of your maximum heart rate.
2. *Figure your maximum heart rate.* It's 220 minus your age. So, if you're 50 years old, your maximum heart rate is 170 beats per minute (bpm):

   220 – Your Age = Maximum Heart Rate

   220 – 50 = 170 bpm
3. *Determine your target zone.* Multiply your maximum heart rate by your workout intensity range. For example, for moderate activity, your target workout intensity is 50% to 70%:

   Maximum Heart Rate × Workout Intensity = Target Zone

   170 bpm × 50% to 70% = 85 to 119 bpm
4. *Take your heart rate.* Stop exercising. With your index and middle fingers, take your pulse at your neck, wrist, or chest. Count the beats for 60 seconds; the first beat is zero. (Or count for 30 seconds, then double it for bpm.)

The talk-sing test is a quick way to assess your workout intensity. *See "Have you ever wondered . . . if your own exercise level is of moderate intensity?" in chapter 1, page 17.*

Click Here!
Links to Know . . .

- Academy of Nutrition and Dietetics
  www.eatright.org/resources/fitness
- United States Olympic Committee
  www.teamusa.org/About-the-USOC/Athlete-Development/Sport-Performance/Nutrition

Various sports have their own organizations and websites. Some of the websites provide sound sports nutrition, written by qualified sports nutrition experts.

As a cushion. The fluid around your body's tissues and organs offers protection from all the jostles and jolts that go along with exercise.

For protection from dehydration and hypohydration. Fluid loss—beyond the early stages—increases your chances of heat injury, such as heat cramps, heat exhaustion, and heat stroke. Severe dehydration can be life-threatening. *See "Dehydration Alert!" in this chapter, page 602, and "Water: A Fluid Asset" in chapter 15, page 443.*

Fluids: Enough, Not Too Much

To adequately hydrate, make a personal fluid plan for your workout or competition to replace as much sweat loss as practical. Avoid drinking too much, as well.

PROPER HYDRATION

No matter what your sport—running, bicycling, swimming, tennis, even walking and golfing—or rigorous activity, drinking enough fluid is essential. Drink fluids before, during, and after exercise, especially in conditions when you sweat more. Getting enough isn't always easy, and fluid needs vary for active adults and competitive athletes.

- **Before you start, drink.** Avoid starting with a fluid deficit. That can happen for several reasons including recent, prolonged training in the heat, or competing in several events during the day. If you try to dehydrate as a way to "make weight" for a sport, you may not be able to get adequately hydrated before a workout or competition.

  Wear lightweight, loose-fitting clothing that wicks moisture, especially in warm weather. Fabrics that hold heat—such as tights, body suits, and heavy gear—as well as helmets and other protective gear, won't let sweat evaporate. That said, don't give up your gear; just be aware that they often hold in body heat.

- **During physical activity, drink.** Drink early and often—but not too much. Drink fluids every fifteen minutes during activity—even when you don't feel thirsty. Your thirst mechanism may not send thirst signals when you're exercising. Thirst signals dehydration; drink fluids before that happens. *Follow the schedule provided in "Physically Active: How Much Fluid?" in this chapter, page 603.*

Sweat rates differ among different people, different sports, climates (temperature and humidity), and elevations. Be especially careful if you exercise intensely in warm, humid weather. Consider how much hotter you feel on humid days. Sweat doesn't evaporate from your skin as quickly, so you don't get the cooling benefits. That's why on humid days it's easier to get hyperthermia, or overheated, as you exercise. Hyperthermia can lead to heat stroke, which can be fatal.

On the Road? Keep Moving!

Planes, trains, and automobiles get you where you're going. But to keep physically active when you travel—or perhaps keep up a training regimen—plan ahead.

- Pack comfortable workout clothes and footwear. Take a jump rope, running or walking shoes, or plastic dumbbells to fill with water. If music gets you "pumped," download music on your handheld device; bring your earbuds.
- Check the hotel television for a fitness channel, or find a YouTube workout to use when you travel.
- Bring your wearable activity tracker if you use one.
- Choose a hotel with exercise equipment, and then make time to use it. Before you make your reservation, ask about the facilities: an indoor or outdoor pool; tennis courts; bicycle rentals; and gym equipment such as a treadmill, step machine, or rowing machine.
- If you belong to a health club at home, check ahead for membership benefits elsewhere.
- At the airport, wait for your flight by walking the concourse. Skip people movers, or walk as they move you. On a long train or plane trip, walk up and down the aisle several times, if allowed. Ask for an aisle seat to avoid disturbing or climbing over fellow passengers. Do simple stretches to avoid stiffness.
- Set your alarm for an early wake-up so you can get a jump start on your day with a thirty-minute power walk or jog. Get a guidebook to map out your way—or ask at the hotel's front desk for a walking map.
- Skip the taxicab. If the distance is reasonable and it's safe, walk to business meetings, museums, shops, or restaurants in comfortable walking shoes.
- If you're driving, take regular breaks. You'll ride more comfortably after some physical activity.

Know the signs of dehydration and hypohydration. Some early signs are flushed skin, fatigue, increased body temperature, and faster breathing and pulse rate. Later signs are dizziness, weakness, and labored breathing with exercise. Replace fluids before symptoms get serious. *See "Dehydration: Body Signals!" in chapter 15, page 444.*

Carry a water bottle in a bottle belt or fluid pack, especially if you have no other available water source. Or find out where you can get fluids: a store (bring money), a water fountain, or a water bottle refilling station.

Stop to drink if you need fluids. You'll more than make up for any lost time with better performance. Drink, rather than suck ice or pour water over your head. Drinking is the only way to rehydrate and cool your body from the inside out.

- **After physical activity, drink.** Rehydrating after activity helps you recover faster, physically and mentally. Replace lost water weight. Weigh yourself before and after a workout. (Weigh yourself before a workout after urinating.) Don't wear the same clothing when you weigh yourself afterwards because it will be heavy with sweat, and weigh yourself before urinating.

  Replace each pound of weight lost during exercise with two-and-a-half to three cups of water, carbohydrate drink, or other fluids to bring your fluids back into balance. With too much of a fluid deficit, plan to drink more before and during your next work out. If you weigh more after exercise, you may have drank too much during activity; drink somewhat less while exercising next time.

Check the color of your urine. Dark-colored urine can be an indication of dehydration. Drink more fluids so your urine is pale and nearly colorless before exercising again. (*Note:* Some vitamin supplements also can cause dark-colored urine.)

See "Fluids: Caution for Kids" in this chapter, page 612, for more about adequate hydration for physically active children.

OVERHYDRATION

Be cautious about overdrinking, even water and sports drinks. Too much can lead to hyponatremia, or an abnormally low sodium level in the blood when too much water dilutes the sodium concentration in the blood. Kidneys can't remove excess body water before it moves into body cells, including brain cells. The extra pressure affects vital functions, with potentially fatal outcomes.

The cause of hyponatremia, sometimes called water intoxication, is overhydration. Anyone can be a victim. However, it's more common among recreational athletes who think they need to drink more but who actually have a lower work output and sweat rate than competitive athletes do. Also, women are at greater risk than men because they generally have a smaller body size. and therefore tend to have a lower sweat rate.

To avoid overhydrating:

- Make a hydration plan by measuring your hourly sweat rate. Weigh yourself before and after hour-long training sessions in different weather conditions. Add the amount of fluid weight lost to

? Have you ever wondered?

. . . if swimmers need to worry about dehydration? Like any athlete, swimmers perspire to keep from overheating. However, they may not notice their sweat—at least not while they're in the water. They, too, need to drink plenty of fluids before, during, and after rigorous swimming.

. . . if dehydration is a concern with cold-weather sports such as ice skating or skiing? Even in a cool or cold environment, you sweat. Attire for cold weather sports such as downhill skiing, snowmobiling, and ice hockey doesn't "breathe" or allow the body to cool down, either.

. . . if coconut water is as good as water or as a sports drink to replace fluids? For rehydration and recovery, according to promising researched evidence, coconut water appears to have the benefits of water and sports drinks to keep you hydrated—if you drink enough and if you like the taste. However, unsweetened coconut water is lower in carbohydrates (and calories) and sodium compared to most sports drinks, so it may not offer enough after a long workout. Coconut water is an excellent source of potassium, a nutrient that falls short in typical diets.

Coconut water comes from the inside of a young coconut. Coconut milk is different; it's produced from coconut "meat." *See "Nondairy Drinks: Soy, Almond, and More" in chapter 4, page 92, for more about coconut milk.*

Dehydration Alert

As you exercise, be alert for conditions that increase your fluid loss through sweat. With more perspiration, your body dehydrates faster.

- *Temperature.* The higher the temperature, the greater your sweat loss.
- *Intensity.* The harder you work out, the greater your sweat loss.
- *Body size.* The larger you are, the greater the sweat loss.
- *Duration.* The longer the workout, the greater your fluid loss.
- *Fitness.* Well-trained athletes sweat more, starting at a lower body temperature. With training, the body cools down more efficiently.

the amount of fluid consumed to get your total fluid loss, or sweat rate per hour. Once you know that, you know how much to drink to properly hydrate without overdoing. *Remember:* Balance your electrolytes, too, as they are lost in perspiration.

- Know the symptoms of early hyponatremia: for example, dizziness, confusion, or being bloated in the stomach, ankles and toes, and fingers and wrists. Other signs include nausea, vomiting, headache, delirium, seizures, respiratory distress, and loss of consciousness. This condition requires prompt medical attention because serious symptoms can lead to death if untreated.

Fluids for Sports: What's Best?

For workouts of less than thirty minutes of continuous activity and recreational walking, water, sports drinks, and juices all have a place.

Water. Water helps lower and normalize your body's core (internal) temperature when you're hot. Water moves quickly from your digestive tract to your tissues. At any time of year, cool water, preferred by many exercisers, may enhance performance.

Cold water is fine, too. Contrary to myth, drinking cold water during physical activity doesn't cause stomach cramps. For outside activity in cold weather, drink water that's warm or at room temperature to help protect you from hypothermia, or low body temperature.

Sports drinks. For many sports, plain water is as good a fluid replacement as a sports drink for those who do regular, daily physical activity.

That said, sports drinks basically water with sugar (glucose, sucrose, fructose) and electrolytes (sodium, potassium, chloride) can benefit athletes who exercise hard for more than sixty minutes. For them, sports drinks with 6 to 8 percent carbohydrate (14 to 19 grams of carbohydrate per eight ounces) may be better than water or diluted fruit juice for fluid replacement. More than 8 percent carbohydrate solution may decrease the rate of fluid absorption and take longer to leave the stomach.

If you're a long-distance runner or long-distance cyclist or are involved in other endurance events (longer than sixty minutes), sports drinks offer performance benefits. Research also shows a benefit for high-intensity activity (perhaps sprinting or playing hockey) lasting thirty minutes or more.

Glucose (simple form of carbohydrate) in sports drinks is a more immediate fuel, or energy, source for working muscles. It may help prevent muscle glycogen from depleting too fast and so help lengthen performance time. (Muscle glycogen is carbohydrate stored in muscle.) Glucose in sports drinks also helps fluid get out of the gut and into the bloodstream. Compared to juice or soft drinks, sports drinks are more diluted, so their fluid and glucose can be absorbed and used faster by the body.

Sports drinks supply electrolytes, which can replace the very small amounts of sodium and other electrolytes lost through perspiration. For most athletes, normal meals and snacks replace what's lost. The amount of sodium and other electrolytes in sport drinks is low compared to typical foods: 100 to 110 milligrams of sodium per eight ounces. During exercise that lasts longer than sixty minutes, or for exercise performed in high heat or humidity, drinks with electrolytes help to enhance fluid absorption. *See "Electrolytes: Sweat 'Em!" in this chapter, page 609.*

Sports drinks with extra vitamins? You don't lose vitamins when you sweat, so you don't need the extra. Eating more to boost your energy (calorie) intake provides any extra B vitamins you need for energy production. Do you need the caffeine, chromium, or amino acids that some supply? Food delivers sufficient amounts of both chromium and amino acids; extra caffeine may offer some benefits; *see "Have you ever wondered . . . if caffeine can boost your physical performance?" in this chapter, page 604.* Some of these sports drinks may cause gastrointestinal discomfort.

For endurance sports, experiment with sports drinks and other fluids during practices and low-key competition. If the flavor encourages you to drink more fluids—or if they give you a psychological boost—enjoy them, but don't overdo. Watching your weight? *Remember:* Sports drinks supply calories.

Fruit juice or soft drinks. Compared with sports drinks, sugars in fruit juices and soft drinks are more concentrated: 10 to 15 percent carbohydrate. They aren't recommended during exercise because of their high sugar content and, for soft drinks, their carbonation. Drinks with more sugar take longer to be absorbed, and they may cause cramps, diarrhea, or nausea. Carbonation can make you feel full and make your throat burn,

Physically Active: How Much Fluid?

Make a point of drinking fluids at all times during the day—not just after your workout or competition. How much fluid is enough? Here's a general schedule that can keep you from becoming dehydrated.

When to Drink	About How Much (*One medium mouthful of fluid = about 1 ounce; 1 cup – 8 ounces.*)
2 to 3 hours before activity	2 to 3 cups (and drink plenty with meals)
15 minutes before activity	1 to 1½ cups
Every 15 minutes during activity	½ to 1½ cups, enough to minimize body weight loss, without overdrinking
After activity	2 to 3 cups for each pound of body weight lost

Adapted from: Sports Nutrition: A Practice Manual for Professionals, 5th ed., Academy of Nutrition and Dietetics, 2012.

so you drink less fluid. You can also dilute fruit juice with water—if you like the flavor. Add a dash of salt, and you'll have a homemade sports drink.

Energy drinks. These typically contain more carbohydrates than commercial sport drinks. They're also usually higher in caffeine, and perhaps inositol and taurine (an amino acid). But energy drinks don't have unique energy-boosting power. Food is the best source of nutrients that supply energy.

The American Academy of Pediatrics (AAP) advises against energy drinks for children and teens, including those who are young athletes. AAP notes these reasons: (1) health risks posed by the stimulants in energy drinks for young people (children and teens) and (2) increased risk of overweight, obesity, and dental caries with routine intake of carbohydrate-containing sports drinks by children and teens. In addition, high school and college athletes should check the rules for consuming caffeinated energy drinks.

Most energy drinks aren't formulated for athletes' needs, yet their caffeine may enhance athletic performance by delaying the onset of fatigue. For adult athletes, they're generally okay if used in moderation and if the athlete has no underlying heart condition or high blood pressure. If you're an athlete, be aware of any caffeine sensitivity, and check with your doctor before consuming energy drinks.

See "Energy Drinks" in chapter 4, page 101.

Alcoholic drinks. They can impair, not enhance, your physical performance. Skip alcoholic drinks—at least until after you replenish the fluids lost in your workout—for these reasons:

- If you're looking for a carbohydrate source, look elsewhere. A twelve-ounce can of beer has less than a third of the carbs provided by a twelve-ounce serving of orange juice. Calories from alcohol don't fuel muscles. And they may lead to weight gain in the form of body fat.
- Alcohol works as a depressant, affecting your brain's ability to reason and make judgments.
- For endurance sports, there's another effect. When you drink a beer, wine, or a mixed drink, your liver works to detoxify and metabolize the alcohol. That can interfere with the liver's job of forming extra blood glucose for prolonged physical activity. Possible result? Early fatigue and slower recovery.
- Alcoholic drinks don't mix with sports. They can impair your motor skills: your reaction time and muscle reflexes, coordination, balance, stamina, speed, strength, visual perception, and more. The effects can last up to seventy-two hours. What's more, they can increase your risk of injury and swelling after injury.

After competition or a workout, follow the advice of your team's and sport's rules about alcohol use. It's wise to minimize or avoid alcoholic drinks post exercise when issues of recovery and injury repair are priorities.

See "Alcoholic Beverages: In Moderation" in chapter 4, page 102, for more about risks related to alcoholic drinks.

? Have you ever wondered?

. . . if caffeine can boost your physical performance? Maybe—and maybe not. People react to caffeine in different ways. Caffeine stimulates the central nervous system, increasing dopamine in the brain, which affects focus, vigilance, and perceived fatigue. Some evidence shows that caffeine, consumed before physical activity, may improve performance, reaction time, and endurance.

For caffeine-sensitive athletes, however, caffeine may exacerbate pre-event anxiety, disrupt sleep patterns, and cause gastrointestinal distress, among other symptoms. When consumed in high amounts, perhaps from energy or caffeine tablets, caffeine can impair motor skills.

If you choose to drink coffee, tea, soft drinks, or energy drinks with caffeine, or an energy gel or energy bites with caffeine, experiment during training, not competition. A single cup may help—or at least not hinder—your performance. But avoid caffeine overdose. More is not better!

The National Collegiate Athletic Association (NCAA) limits caffeine concentration to no more than 15 micrograms per milliliter of urine. You likely won't reach this level (equivalent to seventeen caffeinated, twelve-ounce sodas) from caffeine in food or drinks. But athletes who consume three 200-milligram caffeine tablets or some herbal sources of caffeine may exceed this limit. The challenge is that some products don't disclose the caffeine dose or may also contain other stimulants. Beginning in 2004, the International Olympic Committee no longer prohibits caffeine intake. Instead, it monitors caffeine content in urine.

If you want a caffeinated drink before a workout, choose wisely—within recommended amounts. A twelve-ounce low-fat latte, for example, can provide 10 grams of protein, naturally occurring sugars, and 75 milligrams of caffeine for 120 calories.

Also be aware that caffeine in moderation doesn't cause dehydration or electrolyte imbalance. *See "Caffeine and Health" in chapter 4, page 94.*

ENERGY TO BURN: FUELING YOUR WORKOUT

How much energy per day? That's an individual matter, too. A 200-pound body builder has very different needs from an 80-pound gymnast or a 130-pound jogger, walker, or cyclist. Physical training itself may use 500 to 3,000 or more calories daily—a huge range!

The harder, longer, and more often you work out, the more energy is required for muscle work. Any activity, such as cycling, power walking, or swimming is a bigger energy burner if done more vigorously.

Not surprisingly, some sports burn more energy than others. That's simply because they're more intense or their duration is longer. Both a golf game and downhill skiing may last several hours, but skiing uses more energy since it's more physically demanding for larger muscle groups. *See "Physical Activity: How Many Calories Will Your Body Burn" in chapter 1, page 8.* Body size (consider a male football player and a female gymnast) also makes a big difference. When two people ski together at the same intensity, the person weighing more likely burns more calories.

What are the risks of energy intake that's too low? Among the consequences for athletes are a loss of muscle mass; menstrual dysfunction; for adolescent girls and women a loss of or failure to gain bone density; and a higher chance for fatigue, injury, illness, and a longer recovery process.

See "How Many Calories? Figuring Your Energy Needs" in the appendix, page 771, to estimate your energy needs. Or have a registered dietitian nutritionist help you determine how much food energy you need for your physical activity.

? Have you ever wondered?

. . . how you can avoid "hitting the wall"? When endurance athletes run out of their source of glycogen, they're too tired to continue exerting themselves. To maintain your supply for as long as possible for endurance sports, follow a pre-exercise eating regimen that's high in carbohydrates. Have a sports drink if your workout lasts an hour or more. Eat a carbohydrate-rich snack right afterward when your body can store glycogen at a faster rate. Regular physical training also helps; your muscles adapt, gradually storing more glycogen for future intense workouts.

. . . if you should do your morning workout before breakfast? You'll turn in a better performance if you eat at least part of your breakfast before you exercise and the rest afterwards. Your body needs nourishment to replenish liver glycogen and steady your blood sugar level. Consuming 100 to 300 calories of an easily digested food can settle well and boost your energy. Not hungry for solid food? Then instead of solid food, enjoy a fruit smoothie or liquid meal replacement, along with a beverage.

. . . how to get enough carbs if you must eat gluten free? With so many grain foods on the market that are naturally gluten free or processed to be gluten free, supermarkets carry many options, just within the grain group. Beyond that, beans and peas and starchy vegetables are other great sources of carbs. *See "Gluten Free: When It's a Must" in chapter 23, page 670, for tips.*

CARBS: YOUR MAIN ENERGY SOURCE

For sports and everyday living, carbohydrates are your body's foremost energy source—and the main fuel for working muscles.

Carbs and the Athlete: How Much?

Most of your calories should come from carbohydrates. How much depends on the individual athlete's body composition, training schedule, and the sport. The daily guideline for carbohydrates to meet the needs for your muscles and central nervous system depends on the level and duration of your physical activity and your body weight.

To estimate how many grams you need daily as carbohydrates, first convert your body weight to kilograms (1 pound = 0.45 kilograms; 1 kilogram = 2.2 pounds). Then multiply that by the carbs needed per kilogram of your body weight for your activity level as shown in the chart below. For example, if you are involved in general training and weigh 120 pounds (55 kilograms), that's 275 to 385 grams of carbohydrate daily. If you weigh 175 pounds (80 kilograms), that's 400 to 560 grams of carbs daily.

Activity Level		**Carbohydrate Recommendation** (per kilogram of body weight)
Light	Recreational activity (low-intensity or skill-based activities with light training)	3 to 5 grams
Moderate	General training (moderate intensity, sixty minutes daily), for most athletes	5 to 7 grams
High	Endurance exercise (moderate to high intensity, one to three hours daily)	6 to 10 grams
Very high	Endurance exercise (moderate- to high-intensity exercise, four to five hours daily)	8 to 12 grams

Along with training, a high-carbohydrate eating plan promotes overall fitness and offers a competitive edge. With carbs (not fats or proteins) as the main fuel, you can maintain rigorous activity longer. Training helps your body use carbohydrates efficiently and store more as muscle glycogen, which is fuel ready to power your physical activity.

Carbs as Fuel

Carbohydrates supply fuel, or energy, for both your muscles and your central nervous system. For peak physical performance, it's important to match your carbohydrate intake and your body's carbohydrate stores with the physical demands of your sport.

To power working muscles, stored energy comes mostly from glycogen in muscles or the liver and from blood glucose. Glycogen is your body's storage form of carbohydrate. Depending on the intensity and duration of the exercise, fat and, for endurance athletes, some protein supplies energy, too. For activities that take high-intensity, short bursts of energy, both carbohydrates and fats supply energy for longer activity.

Blood glucose. Carbohydrates from food break down during digestion and convert to glucose. Some is used immediately for energy. The rest is either stored as glycogen in muscles and the liver, or it's converted to fat if you consume excess calories. The more muscle glycogen you can store, the more you have to power your muscles for physical activity.

Glycogen. Your body's glycogen stores are continually used and replenished. For more energy, your body fuels muscles with a mix of both carbohydrate (glycogen) and fat. The higher the immediate intensity of an activity, the more glycogen used; depleting muscle glycogen is linked to fatigue resulting in a decrease of stamina for intense, sustained exercise. Lower-intensity and longer-lasting activities use more stored body fat and less glycogen.

- For sports that require short, intense energy spurts (anaerobic activities), muscle glycogen is the main energy source used. These include tennis, volleyball, baseball, weight lifting, sprinting, and bowling.
- Sports requiring intensity and endurance use mostly muscle glycogen. Basketball and football are examples.
- For endurance activities (aerobic activities) such as long-distance running or cycling, your body uses glucose, glycogen, and fat for fuel; the proportion depends mainly on the activity's intensity and duration.

Going "low carb" for sports has unintended consequences. It not only affects your energy level, but possibly your thinking and concentration, too. This eating approach can cause muscle fatigue and breakdown, and an inability to perform at a higher physical intensity.

See chapter 11, page 345, for more about carbohydrates.

Carbs: Foods That Deliver More

Carbohydrates—starches and sugars—are an athlete's best energy source. Make carbohydrate-rich choices that are nutrient rich and deliver other nutrients, too. Consume enough every day to replenish your muscle and liver glycogen stores.

Starches come from breads, cereals, pasta, rice, and other grain foods; vegetables; and beans and peas. Foods with naturally occurring sugars (whole fruits, 100 percent fruit juice, and milk) are your best choices. Foods such as cakes, candy, cookies, and soft drinks provide added sugars; limit them. *See "Carbohydrates in Food: An Athlete's Rule of Thumb" in this chapter, page 607.*

Get creative by enjoying flavorful, nourishing mixed dishes that deliver carbs:

- *Made with breads, cereals, pasta, rice, and other grains:* couscous, pasta, polenta, or risotto dishes; sandwiches made with a bagel, bread, or pita bread; wraps made with soft tortillas; tabbouleh made with bulgur or other grains; or quinoa salad.
- *Made with vegetables or fruits:* baked potato stuffed with veggies and cheese; fresh fruit salad with chopped nuts; fruit smoothie with yogurt or kefir; pancakes topped with fruit; raw vegetables with yogurt dip.
- *Made with beans and peas:* bean enchiladas, beans and rice, chili with beans, hummus and pita; split pea soup with ham.

Reminder: In your normal training diet, most of your calories should come from carbohydrate foods.

Carbohydrate Loading

Your muscles and liver store glycogen—but only a limited amount—which must be replaced after each bout of exercise. Endurance athletes worry that they may "hit the wall," or feel extremely fatigued, before finishing. When this happens, they're out of glycogen.

Those involved in sports that last longer than ninety minutes, such as long-distance running or cycling, may benefit from higher glycogen stores. Carbohydrate loading (or glycogen loading) may help you "stockpile" two to three times more glycogen in your muscles for extended activity.

Carbohydrate loading won't make you run faster or pedal harder, but it may help you perform longer before getting tired. The more glycogen you store, the longer it lasts. To "load up" your muscles for endurance sports, combine training, rest, and eating extra carbohydrates.

- Starting about a week before the endurance event, taper off on training to rest your muscles so they can "re-stock" muscle glycogen. Completely rest the day before competing.
- Consume at least 10 to 12 grams of carbohydrate per kilogram of your body weight daily for about two days before your event. For example, if you weigh 175 pounds, that's 800 to 960 grams of carbohydrates daily. This may be about 70 percent of your day's calories. You will likely need to cut back on foods higher in fat to offset the calories from more carbohydrates. *See "Carbs and the Athlete: How Much?" in this chapter, page 605, for the formula to calculate the amount.*

What sports might you "carb load" for? If you're a trained athlete, try it for endurance events such as marathons and triathlons that last longer than ninety minutes, or for all-day events such as swim meets, a series of tennis matches, long-distance cycling, or soccer games. For shorter events, a normal, carbohydrate-rich eating plan supplies your muscles with enough glycogen—there's no need for carbohydrate loading.

Caution: If you have diabetes or high blood triglycerides, talk to your doctor and a registered dietitian nutritionist before trying this regimen.

Carbohydrates in Food: An Athlete's Rule of Thumb

Food	Carbohydrates
Breads and cereals: 1 slice bread *or* ½ cup rice or pasta *or* 1 ounce dry cereal	About 15 grams
Vegetables (not starchy): ½ cup cooked or raw	About 5 grams
Starchy vegetables: ½ cup	About 15 grams
Fruits: ½ cup *or* 1 small to medium whole fruit	10 to 15 grams
Milk: 1 cup	About 12 grams

See "Your Healthy Heart" and "Diabetes: A Growing Concern" in chapter 24, pages 680 and 698, for more about these health conditions.

FATS: WISELY CHOSEN

Fat also fuels working muscles. In fact, it's a more concentrated energy source than carbohydrates or protein. Fat performs other body functions, such as transporting fat-soluble vitamins and providing essential fatty acids.

Fat as Fuel

For energy, fat helps power activities of longer duration such as hiking or marathon running. Because fat doesn't convert to energy as fast as carbohydrates do, fat doesn't power quick energy spurts, such as the energy to return a tennis serve or run a 100-yard dash.

Unlike glycogen, fat needs oxygen for energy metabolism, which is why endurance sports, fueled in part by fat, are called aerobic activities. "Aerobic" means "with oxygen," and aerobic activities require a continuous intake of oxygen. The more you train, the more easily you breathe during longer activity; the oxygen you take in helps convert fat to energy.

No matter its source—carbohydrates, fats, or proteins—your body stores extra energy as body fat. Fat stores supply energy for aerobic activity. Even if you're lean, you likely have enough fat stores to fuel prolonged or endurance activity.

Fat and the Athlete: How Much?

Advice for athletes is the same as that for all healthy people. For good health, consume fat as one source of fuel, limit saturated fats to less than ten percent of total calories, try to avoid *trans* fats, and include sources of unsaturated fatty acids.

To get enough calories for sports, a day's eating plan with 20 to 35 percent of total calories from fat is a good guideline. Consuming an amount equal to or less than 20 percent of calories from fat doesn't benefit performance. And it may not provide enough calories or enough fat for the body's many functions. Extreme fat restriction may also limit the variety of foods and nutrients that promote overall heath and performance.

Besides a calorie shortfall, consuming too little fat, perhaps to keep weight and body fat down, has other health risks. Among them, young athletes on a very-low-fat diet may not consume enough essential fatty acids for normal growth and development. For female athletes (often dancers, gymnasts, and skaters) a low-calorie, low-fat diet may interfere with menstrual cycles, having lifelong health implications.

If your calorie needs are higher, your total fat intake may need to be higher, too. That's often true for football linemen and weight lifters, who may use 4,000 calories or more a day. Consume sources of healthy fats, such as nuts, olives, peanuts, and oils such as canola, olive, and peanut oils. Eating healthy fats shouldn't lead to heart disease. Still, fats shouldn't contribute more than 35 percent of total energy intake, as advised by the Dietary Reference Intakes, Acceptable Macronutrient Distribution Ranges.

With a high-fat diet, your carbohydrate or protein intake may come up short. Evidence doesn't support claims that a high-fat, low-carb eating plan benefits the physical performance of competitive athletes.

If you need to trim fat and boost carbohydrates for food energy, try simple strategies like these: eat a baked potato more often than fries, or replace a donut with a whole-grain bagel. Remember that fat isn't stored as muscle glycogen; carbs are.

See chapter 13, page 385, for more about dietary fat.

PROTEIN: MUSCLES AND MORE

Why is protein important to athletes? Does an athlete need more protein than a nonathlete? You know that your body uses protein for many purposes, *as discussed in chapter 12, page 373*. Athletes have reasons such as these:

- Protein is important for building muscles and for remodeling body proteins (resorption and formation) within bones, ligaments, and tendons.
- Protein is essential in many metabolic functions: for example, to make enzymes, hormones, and other body chemicals; to transport nutrients; to make muscles contract; to support immune functions; and to regulate body processes such as water balance.
- Without sufficient carbohydrates for high-energy demands, the body uses protein for energy instead. That's counterproductive to physical and athletic goals, however.

Protein and the Athlete: How Much?

Many athletes need somewhat more protein than sedentary people do—but optimal amounts are still unknown. Because athletes usually eat more, they tend to easily get what they need.

? Have you ever wondered?

. . . if eating a candy bar right before rigorous activity supercharges your body? For endurance activities of ninety minutes or longer, a sugary snack food, energy bar, or drink before exercise (or even during an event) may enhance your stamina. Bananas, fig bars, graham crackers, and raisins work, too. Drink water along with these snacks.

If you have a sugary snack or drink, keep it small: no more than 200 to 300 calories. Too much sugar may slow the time it takes water to leave your stomach; then your body won't replace fluids as quickly. A sports drink has some sugar to fuel your muscles—but not enough to impair rehydration.

. . . if energy bars, bites, or gels give you extra energy? Ingredients in these products are no remedy for fatigue and don't have special energy-boosting properties. Most have carbs or protein to sustain a short power surge; some contain caffeine. Those with fiber may have more staying power. They may be an option when snack choices are limited or if other solid foods in the middle of a workout create digestive discomfort, but not to replace a nourishing meal. They're also costly.

For overall fitness or strength building, extra protein—significantly beyond the amount recommended—hasn't been shown to offer added performance benefits. And, although protein supplies energy, extra amounts aren't the best fuel. If you've already consumed enough calories, additional calories from protein are stored as body fat, and not used for energy.

For anyone, protein should supply 10 to 35 percent of overall calorie intake. If you're trying to lose weight and limit calories, consuming 30 to 35 percent of calories from protein might help preserve lean muscle mass and help you lose body fat—if you're physically active, too, and stay within your calorie limit.

- *Most recreational exercisers:* 0.5 to 0.75 gram of protein per pound of body weight daily. For a 150-pound athlete, that's about 75 to 115 grams of protein each day, and just two to four ounces more of meat, chicken, or fish a day than recommended for nonathletes.
- *Endurance and strength training athletes:* 0.6 to 0.7 gram of protein per pound of body weight daily. Adults building muscle mass, including weight lifters and football players, may need 0.7 to 0.8 gram of protein daily per pound. Teen athletes need enough for growth and muscle building: 0.7 to 0.9 gram of protein per pound.

For reference, three ounces of lean beef supply about 20 to 25 grams of protein, eight ounces of milk supply 8 grams of protein, and one slice of bread has 2 grams of protein or more.

Caution about excess protein: Many people may consume a very-high-protein diet without harm. That said, extra protein is not stored in your body for future use as protein. Instead, it's either used as energy or stored as body fat. A high-protein diet also may be high in fat. And too much protein may displace carbohydrate foods, which are especially important for endurance sports and for weight training lasting sixty minutes or longer. Side effects may include metabolic imbalance, toxicity, nervous system disorders, and perhaps problems for those with existing kidney disease. Excess protein or amino acids can be harmful for those with unhealthy kidneys, such as those with diabetes or prediabetes.

When you consume excess protein, you need more water to excrete urea, a waste product formed when protein is broken down. So, excess protein increases the chances of dehydration as well as the need to urinate—an inconvenience during a workout. Excess protein could also increase calcium loss in urine, a concern for bone health.

Muscle Myths

You've likely heard the myth: Extra protein builds more muscle. In truth, only athletic training builds muscle strength and size. It's true that protein is important for athletes, but consuming more protein—from food or dietary supplements—won't make a difference. Consuming more than 2 grams of protein per kilogram of body weight hasn't been shown to offer muscle-building benefits when energy needs are adequate.

Can amino acid supplements build muscle? Despite claims, they won't increase muscle size or strength. Amino acids are building blocks of protein. Twenty different amino acids link to make proteins in food and in body tissue. To your body, amino acids in supplements are no different from those in food. From food, they "taste" better and likely cost much less.

Protein Foods: 20 Grams of High-Quality Protein

Food	Portion Size
Egg whites	6 large
Lean meat, poultry, or fish	3 ounces
Whole eggs	3 large
Tofu	1 cup
Cheese	3 ounces
Cottage cheese	1½ ounces
Low-fat milk	20 ounces
Low-fat Greek yogurt	8 ounces
Low-fat yogurt	13 ounces
Plain soymilk	23 ounces

Most athletes get enough protein—and enough amino acids—from food. Protein-rich foods supply other essential nutrients, too. Amino acid supplements supply just that—only amino acids. *The bottom line:* To build muscle, consume enough calories from carbs, follow advice to get protein from food, *as noted in this chapter*, and train regularly.

See "Ergogenic Aids: No Training Substitute" in this chapter, page 619, for more about dietary supplements for athletes.

Protein Sources: What Foods? When?

Foods—or a combination of foods—with high-quality protein (all essential amino acids) are the best choices for muscle synthesis and remodeling other body proteins. No evidence shows that protein supplements have advantages over food sources. In fact, protein foods deliver many other essential nutrients that protein supplements don't provide.

Optimal protein sources. Meat, poultry, fish, eggs, and dairy foods are excellent sources of high-quality protein. Beans and peas, tofu, nuts, seeds, and peanut butter also are great protein sources. Cereal, breads, and vegetables contain smaller amounts of lower-quality protein. If you're a vegetarian, choose a variety of protein-containing foods carefully to get all the essential amino acids. *See "Protein in Foods and Drinks" in chapter 12, page 378.*

What about whey, casein, and soy protein? Milk protein is a great protein source since it contains two proteins: whey (20 percent) and casein (80 percent). Whey is absorbed faster than casein, making it useful for recovery after a workout and somewhat more effective for muscle growth than casein alone or soy protein. Whey's branched-chain amino acids, including leucine, may trigger the body to make lean muscle when combined with resistance exercise. Soy protein is somewhat less effective than just whey.

The average American diet supplies more than enough protein. Just six to seven ounces total daily of lean meat, poultry, or fish—or the equivalent from eggs, beans and peas, nuts, or seeds—along with protein from dairy and grain foods, supply enough protein for most athletes. Athletes involved in endurance sports and weight lifters need somewhat more. Consider this: Instead of getting most protein in a meal from one source, enjoy a combination, with smaller portions of several protein foods.

A protein supplement? As an option if food sources of protein aren't convenient or available. Talk to a registered dietitian nutritionist to identify a quality protein supplement. Still, use it conservatively, mostly to optimize muscle recovery after a workout—and as part of your overall eating plan for sports.

Also note: Getting enough food energy (calories), especially from carbohydrates to match your energy needs, is important. That spares amino acids so they can be used to make body proteins.

Timing protein foods. The way you time and distribute your protein foods matters. And that can fluctuate based on many factors, including your training (frequency and intensity) and how fit you are:

- Instead of focusing on total protein for the whole day, as advised in the past, shift your mindset. Spread moderate amounts of high-quality protein foods throughout the day, including after strenuous training. That promotes muscle building; protein repair in bones, tendons, and ligaments; amino acid use in the body; and immunity. Consuming at least 20 to 25 grams of protein at each of your three daily meals plus your snacks, helps optimize muscle growth.
- A high-quality protein snack or meal (such as meat, poultry, fish, eggs, dairy foods, or soy) within two hours after exercise—either alone or with carbohydrate—helps stimulate muscle repair and growth. The protein might come from protein foods, a protein shake, or a protein bar.

See "Protein in Food: Complete and Incomplete" in chapter 12, page 375, for more about high-quality protein.

VITAMINS AND MINERALS: SENSE AND NONSENSE

Vitamins and minerals trigger body processes for physical performance. They don't supply energy, but some help produce energy from carbohydrates, fats, and proteins. Some help muscles relax and contract. Others are part of hemoglobin in blood that carries oxygen to cells to power aerobic activity. Still others keep your bones strong to physically support all the demands of sports. *See chapter 14, page 408, to learn more about vitamins and minerals.*

If you burn more energy, you need more of some vitamins and minerals. By eating enough from each of the five food groups, you likely consume enough vitamins and minerals. For those who might need slightly more, eating more food probably provides the extra. In fact, an athlete with a hearty appetite has a better chance of consuming enough vitamins and minerals than someone who's less active and eats less.

However, athletes who try to lose weight by consuming too few calories or by eliminating whole food groups are at greater risk for a number of vitamin and mineral shortcomings, frequently calcium, vitamin D, iron, and some antioxidant nutrients. For enough vitamins and minerals, eat recommended amounts of food group foods; *see chapter 2, page 21*. Taking a single vitamin or mineral supplement generally is not appropriate unless advised by a physician for medical reasons.

Electrolytes: Sweat 'Em!

Sweat is made of water along with electrolyte minerals, including sodium, chloride, and potassium. Among their functions, electrolytes help maintain your body's fluid balance—crucial for athletes. They help your muscles, including your heart muscle, contract and relax. And they help transmit nerve impulses.

As you perspire during a physical workout, your body loses small amounts of electrolytes, mostly sodium. Most athletes replace sodium and other electrolytes with foods they normally eat. Since you probably consume more than enough sodium to replace losses, there is no need for extra sodium.

If you're just moderately active, you likely don't need a drink for electrolyte replacement. Just stay hydrated. Endurance athletes, who sweat heavily for long periods, may need to replace sodium and other electrolytes, however. A sports drink with electrolytes, plus salty foods such as crackers and cheese, probably offer enough. Sodium from those sources helps speed rehydration. *See "Sports Drinks" in this chapter, page 603. See "Major Minerals: Electrolytes" in chapter 14, page 429.*

Iron and Athletes

Athletes, your muscle cells need iron to produce energy. Iron is part of hemoglobin, the component of red blood cells that carries oxygen to your body cells. Oxygen is used in energy metabolism, specifically for aerobic activities where fat converts to energy. An iron shortfall, even small, can affect physical performance.

Getting enough iron may be an issue—especially if you're female or if most of your iron comes from foods of plant origin such as beans and peas and grains. Women who engage in vigorous, prolonged activity may be at special risk for iron depletion, and vegetarian athletes may be, as well.

Even if you consume enough iron, you may be iron depleted if you're involved in endurance sports. Prolonged exercise such as marathon running and long-distance cycling promotes iron loss. With more exercise, you sweat more, losing some iron through perspiration. Endurance athletes may lose iron through urine, feces, and intestinal bleeding. If you're an endurance athlete, have your doctor check your iron status periodically. You may be advised to consume iron at a level higher than the Recommended Dietary Allowance.

Unless prescribed by your doctor, don't take an iron supplement. It is not an ergogenic aid for those who aren't iron depleted. Be aware that iron supplementation is harmful to those with a genetic disorder called hemochromatosis. It may also cause unwanted gastrointestinal issues.

See "Iron" in chapter 14, page 438, for more about recommended amounts and food sources; also see "Menstruation: Increased Iron Needs" in chapter 18, page 533.

Calcium, Vitamin D, and Weight-Bearing Exercise: Bone-Building Trio

Calcium, vitamin D, and weight-bearing exercise are a winning combination for building and maintaining the strong, healthy bones you need for sports. Maximize your calcium stores early in life to later minimize the loss that comes with age. Consuming enough calcium, at least 1,000 to 1,300 milligrams daily, depending on your age, and enough vitamin D offers protection against bone loss. For vitamin D, the RDA is 15 micrograms (600 IUs) daily for men and women aged 19 and older, and then 20 micrograms (800 IUs) daily over age 70.

Vitamin D also regulates the absorption of calcium and phosphorus, and emerging research suggests a role in the function of skeletal muscles. Outdoor athletes likely get enough vitamin D because their skin is exposed to sunlight; indoor athletes may not. Besides bone health, calcium is important to athletes because it helps regulate muscle contraction, nerve conduction, and with injuries, normal blood clotting.

Weight-bearing activity such as running, cross-country skiing, tennis, and soccer promotes the deposit of calcium into the matrix, or structure, of bones. While swimming and cycling offer many benefits of physical activity, they aren't weight-bearing, so they don't help to build bone.

See "Calcium" and "Vitamin D" in chapter 14, pages 425 and 413, for more about these nutrients.

Calcium and the female athlete triad. With inadequate food choices, many females, including teens, don't consume enough calcium and vitamin D for bone health. This concern is complicated by the female athlete triad, which is when three factors—low calorie intake, disrupted menstrual function, and bone health—come together.

Active women who repeatedly consume too few calories—perhaps due to disordered eating—to meet their training needs risk having their menstrual periods stop. This hinders the deposit of calcium into the bones of teens and young women at a time when bones should be developing at their maximum rate. Female athletes who've stopped menstruating are at special risk for developing stress fractures, decreased bone mineral density, and other bone problems. Sports that focus on leanness and aesthetics, such as cheerleading, diving, distance running, figure skating, and gymnastics, increase the risk.

? Have you ever wondered?

. . . if heavy training causes "sports anemia"? Perhaps, early in training. "Sports anemia" isn't really anemia. Because blood volume increases in the early weeks of endurance training, iron concentration in blood dilutes slightly as the body adapts to more physical activity. If you develop sports anemia, that's normal. It will disappear once your training program is off and running. With endurance training, your blood's capacity to carry oxygen and your athletic performance will improve. Taking iron supplements isn't helpful or advised.

Feeling tired may result from other aspects of training. If fatigue persists, or if you think you're at risk for other types of anemia, check with your doctor. *See "Anemia: 'Tired Blood'" in chapter 25, page 438.*

. . . if taking salt tablets prevents muscle cramps? Sodium loss is only one factor that contributes to muscle cramping during exercise. Muscle fatigue and dehydration also increase the chance of cramping. Athletes who sweat heavily and whose skin becomes encrusted with a salt residue can replace sodium with foods, such as soup, ham-cheese-mustard sandwiches, or pasta with tomato sauce, which are better options than salt tablets.

Women and teenage girls: Pay attention if your periods stop! Talk to your doctor. This is not a normal outcome of physical activity. Stress fractures from weakened bones can affect your physical performance. The long-range impact: increased osteoporosis risk. Besides changes in your training to normalize your menstrual cycle, your doctor may advise a higher calcium intake or a calcium supplement. *See "Osteoporosis and Bone Health" in chapter 25, page 738, for more about the risks.*

Vitamin Supplements: Not "Energy Charged"

Contrary to unscientific claims, there's likely no need for vitamin, mineral, or antioxidant supplements for sports if you're already well nourished. The "extra" won't offer an energy boost or added physical benefits—immediately or over the long run. Even if you're deficient in one or more nutrients, popping a supplement pill right before physical activity has no immediate effect.

Although B vitamins help your body use energy from food, no vitamin supplies energy. Since you likely eat more when you're physically active, you'll get the extra B vitamins you need from food—if your food choices are varied and nutrient rich.

If you take a supplement, choose a "multi" with no more than 100 percent of the Daily Values (DVs) for vitamins and minerals—unless your doctor prescribes more for special health reasons. *See "Dietary Supplements: More than Vitamin Pills" in chapter 10, page 316.*

A High-Performance Diet

Good nutrition, along with physical training, prepares you to achieve and maintain strength, flexibility, and endurance—key to putting in your best physical performance, whether you're a serious or recreational athlete.

What's the best training diet? One that's varied, moderate, and balanced, and that meets your energy (calorie) needs without overconsuming. Sound familiar? It's an eating plan that's high in carbohydrates, with enough proteins, vitamins, minerals, and water, and it limits the amount of saturated and *trans* fats, *as discussed earlier.* In addition to these basics, the right eating plan is customized for you, your training and competition (if you compete), and your sport.

FOOD GUIDES FOR ATHLETES

Except for calories, healthy eating advice for athletes and those with a rigorously active lifestyle doesn't differ much from advice for nonathletes. Both on- and off-season, the food patterns for athletes and nonathletes, *discussed in chapter 2, page 21,* offer healthy eating guidelines for different calorie needs. For some sports and athletes, calorie needs may exceed the levels in these food patterns, so food group amounts may need to be increased.

There's no single eating plan for sports, and instead you can customize. The difference is often due to calorie needs. For many athletes, energy needs are high—as many as 6,000 calories a day, for example, for some football players. To meet higher energy demands, choose more nutrient-rich, carbohydrate-rich foods, mostly from the grain, vegetable, and fruit food groups. A high-fat diet offers concentrated energy (from fat); saturated fats should be limited and *trans* fats avoided to reduce the risks for heart disease—even for highly active people.

The "Eating Patterns" *in the appendix, page 773,* can help you determine how much from each food group for your calorie needs. If your calorie needs are higher than provided in these patterns, a registered dietitian nutritionist can help revise the plan for your unique needs.

Whether it's a wristband, a watch, an earpiece, or biometric clothing, a wearable fitness tracker can be a useful tool in making a food plan and tracking your progress and the calories you burn. Many come with a mobile or web app and also track your food intake or scan bar codes to upload nutrition information.

An added reminder: Drinking enough fluids during training is also part of a high-performance diet. It's a good time to practice drinking "on schedule," not just for thirst. *See "Physically Active: How Much Fluid?" in this chapter, page 603.*

Different Sports, Different Eating Plans

No matter what your sport, the food patterns, *discussed in chapter 2, page 21,* provide a basic eating guide that can promote high performance. The most significant nutrition differences from sport to sport are how many calories and perhaps how much water is needed. The duration and intensity of the sport, as well as body size, make the difference. For example:

- A 200-pound football player uses more energy than a ninety-pound gymnast.
- A baseball player uses less energy than a soccer player, who's almost constantly in motion.
- An endurance cross-country skier or a long-distance runner likely uses more energy overall than a tennis player or golfer, who uses spurts of energy for a shorter time.

As discussed, every sport demands adequate fluids to replace perspiration and breathing losses. In sports with prolonged, intense activity, athletes may perspire more—especially during hot and humid weather.

Endurance sports. Cross-country and marathon running, cross-country skiing, distance cycling, field and ice hockey, long-distance swimming, and soccer: they all require more food energy for training and competition than non-endurance sports do. Because these sports last several hours, glycogen stores get depleted. The body needs other energy sources:

- Carbohydrate consumed during exercise helps endurance athletes maintain a fast pace.
- As exercise continues, fat is used more efficiently for fuel.
- Protein is a minor fuel source during endurance exercise. Endurance athletes don't need more protein than strength-training athletes; adult endurance athletes should aim for 0.6 to 0.7 gram of protein per pound of body weight.

? Have you ever wondered?

. . . how to eat after you're no longer in serious physical training? Many athletes never address that—but need to! Whether you're a college athlete who stops training or an elite athlete who retires, "retrain" for healthy eating. You'll likely need fewer calories, even though your nutrient needs remain about the same. If you don't cut back on your food and energy (calorie) intake, you'll likely gain weight. *See chapter 22, page 624, for guidance.*

An elite athlete in these sports may need 4,000 to 6,000 (or more) calories daily, depending on his or her body size, the duration of the activity, and overall effort. *Best sources:* a carbohydrate-rich diet with nutrient-dense and calorie-dense foods from all food groups.

Non-endurance sports. Baseball, bowling, golf, martial arts, softball, speed skating, sprint swimming, tennis, track and field, volleyball, and weight lifting: non-endurance sports are fueled by short bursts of energy, perhaps just for two or three minutes or even several seconds. While these sports take an intense, all-out effort, they don't use as much energy overall as endurance sports do. Still, non-endurance sports might be of high or moderate intensity. The overall energy demand depends not only on the duration but also on the intensity and the athlete's body size.

The overall nutrient needs of athletes involved in endurance and non-endurance sports are about the same. However, the energy (calorie) need differs with the intensity and duration of the sport. For that reason, the amount of macronutrients (carbohydrate, protein, and fat) will differ, but should still fit within their AMDR, or range of daily recommendations.

KIDS: EATING FOR SPORTS

Although much of this chapter may seem focused on older teens and adults, school-age and young adolescents also participate in competitive or noncompetitive sports, dance, or vigorous play. Their food and beverage choices power all they do: first and foremost for growth and development, and second for the added demands of physical activity.

Many situations, often unplanned, affect what kids eat and, as a result, their physical performance. That includes early lunch hours and after-school competition, practice that goes into family meal hours, sports fatigue that preempts homework and meals, lack of healthy food choices at home or away, and nervousness that causes food carried to eat before competition to go uneaten.

These challenges need smart, practical snack and meal solutions. Young, two-sport athletes, with little time to recover from one sport before competing in a different one, may have special meal and nutrition demands.

Nutrients for active kids. Except for calories and fluids, healthy eating guidelines and nutrient needs for young athletes and nonathletes are about the same. For serious young athletes who train intensely, a doctor or registered dietitian nutritionist can provide guidance. Getting enough iron, calcium, and vitamin D, for example, may be issues. Growing bones are more susceptible to sports injury from impact and excessive use. Remember that teen athletes need enough protein for growth and muscle building: 0.7 to 0.9 grams of protein per pound of body weight.

To fit healthy meals in between kids' sports schedules, help them do the following:

- Always start the day with a nourishing breakfast. Try to include a protein food. Whole-grain cereal with low-fat milk or yogurt along with sliced fruit or 100 percent juice is a quick option. *See "Breakfast Matters in chapter 3, page 60, and "Breakfast: Links to Learning" in chapter 17, page 500, for more about breakfast and kids.*
- Arm your kids with carried, healthy snacks to enjoy before and after sports practice and competition: cut-up raw vegetables, whole fruits, raisins or dried cranberries, whole-grain crackers and string cheese, pretzels, or trail mix. Include bottled water. *See "Healthy, No-Cook Snacks for Kids" and "Snacks: Filling the Gaps" in chapter 17, pages 497 and 527.*
- Make healthy meals and snacks a habit, even in the off-season, so it's an expectation during the sports season. Adjust your family's meal schedule if needed. Evidence shows that children and teens eat healthier when they regularly eat meals with their families. Talk with your child or teen athlete about ways to work meals into his or her practice or event schedule. *See "Eating Right at School" in chapter 17, page 505.*

Food energy for active kids. Does your highly active child consume enough calories? Here's a clue: Watch his or her performance. Kids who tire easily may not be eating enough. Another clue: Monitor your child's growth with your doctor. If your child is growing normally, his or her energy (calorie) intake is likely okay. If you're still unsure, ask your doctor to refer you to a registered dietitian nutritionist who can help you create a meal and snack plan to match your child's calorie needs and food preferences.

Energy needs depend on age, growth stage, body size, and the intensity, type, and length of the physical activity. *See "Estimated Calorie Needs Per Day by Age, Gender, and Physical Activity Level" in the appendix, page 772.* Some very active kids may need more calories than others to fuel activity.

Fluids: Caution for kids. Children are more likely than adults to get overheated from strenuous activity. As a result, they're at greater risk for the effects of dehydration caused by physical exertion. Even when they play actively in the backyard, kids need plenty of fluids before, during, and afterwards. The AAP advises against energy drinks for children and teens.

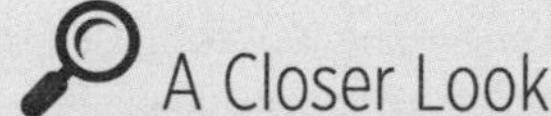

A Closer Look

Weight—for Young Athletes

For all children and teens, normal growth and development should be the top priority. In most cases, their weight should not be manipulated to meet goals required for sports.

Young athletes aren't the same as adult athletes. Because they're growing and because their growth spurts aren't always predictable, their body composition can't be judged in the same way. At certain times—for example, before puberty—a child's body naturally stores more body fat to prepare for the next growth spurt. Each child and teen matures at his or her own time and rate, due to differences in his or her genes. Each has different hormonal and metabolic responses to exercise, too. Let your child or teen grow to be the height and healthy weight that he or she is meant to be—even if smaller or larger body sizes are preferred for some sports.

An eating approach for sports can't change the genetic "body clock," either, and so speed up physical changes that enhance athletic performance. Supplements and ergogenic aids that are promoted to build muscle, prevent fat gain, or improve performance are never appropriate for children or teens and can be harmful. Neither is attempting to help teens gain weight to bulk up faster for a sport; that can increase body fat, not muscle. *See chapter 17, page 489, for more about healthy eating during childhood and adolescence.*

For young athletes—children and teens—weight goals should be healthy ones. A distorted body image that drives overexercising and undereating can lead to serious developmental and health problems. Making weight for wrestling is a common issue for teenage boys; *see "Making Weight" in chapter 17, page 532.* For teenage girls in many sports, it's the "female athlete triad": a syndrome of low calorie intake (often from disordered eating), low bone density, and amenorrhea (cessation of menstruation). *See "Calcium and the Female Athlete Triad," in this chapter, page 610.*

Being physically active is important for all kids of all ages, including those who are overweight or obese. Yet too much weight affects physical performance: balance, agility, endurance, chance of injury, among others.

Always talk to your doctor about the best weight for your child or teen. An inaccurate assessment may result in a weight goal that isn't healthy. Unhealthy weight-loss or weight-grain strategies for sports can be harmful to kids.

See "Growth and Weight" in chapter 17, page 501, and "Competition in a Weight Category?" in this chapter, page 616, for more about body weight.

Why is the risk for heat-related illness higher? Because children perspire less than teens and adults, their body's "air-conditioning" system is less effective. Kids generate more body heat with exercise, and their "thermostat" doesn't adjust as quickly in hot weather. Protective gear for many sports, such as hockey and football, hinders the ability to cool off, too.

Once they're thirsty, kids may be on the way to dehydration if not addressed right away. To protect them and ensure they are adequately hydrated:

- Encourage them to drink plenty of cool fluids before, during, and after physical activities. Water or 100 percent fruit juice diluted with water is refreshing; skip sodas, especially those with caffeine. For some sports, drinks with electrolytes are appropriate.
- Offer regular "time-outs" (every fifteen minutes) and ensure that fluids are readily available. Give them a water bottle for each practice and game.
- Weigh your child before and after exercise, and then replace fluids: three 8-ounce cups per pound of weight loss.
- Supervise them carefully, especially on hot and humid days, when fluid needs are even greater.
- Help them use time between events, perhaps in a tournament, to replace lost fluids.
- Teach them how to monitor their own need to rehydrate.

See chapter 17, page 489, for more about healthy eating advice for all kids, including those who are physically active.

PREGNANCY AND BREASTFEEDING: FOOD AND SPORTS

Pregnancy. Being physically active during pregnancy offers many benefits, among them a psychological lift, optimal weight gain, better aerobic fitness, and an easier labor and delivery. With a doctor's approval, active women may continue their sport. Less active women may start low-level activities gradually—again with their doctor's approval.

If you're pregnant, or planning to be, ask your doctor about precautions. Overheating your body from exercise, a sauna, or a steam room early in pregnancy can affect the development of your unborn baby. If you have anemia, hypertension, diabetes, or other health problems, rigorous activity during pregnancy may not be advised.

All the nutritional issues that relate to a healthy pregnancy apply to female athletes. Eat a varied and balanced diet—with enough calories to support your pregnancy, your own needs, and the demands of physical activity. If your calorie intake is too low, you may not gain enough weight, and your baby may not grow adequately.

Fluid replacement, always important, has even more health implications now. During pregnancy you need more fluids as your own and your baby's blood volume increase. If you don't drink enough, you're at greater risk for dehydration and overheating. *See "You're Expecting!" in chapter 18, page 541.*

Breastfeeding. With a doctor's guidance, most women can engage in sports or some other form of regular physical activity while they're breastfeeding. It's important to consider the calories needed for breastfeeding, as well as the calories for fueling a sport. With more physical activity, you need more calories; the actual amount depends on the duration and the intensity of your workout.

For athletes and nonathletes alike, the food patterns, *discussed in chapter 2, page 21*, offer guidance for planning a varied, balanced, and moderate eating plan during breastfeeding. Your fluid needs increase during breastfeeding, too. When you work out, drink more.

Most important: Take the guidance of your doctor as you make a food and hydration plan that matches the needs of pregnancy or breastfeeding, your own health, and the demands of your recreational or competitive sport. *See chapter 18, page 533, for more about healthy eating and physical activity during pregnancy and breastfeeding.*

See "Physical Activity and Pregnancy" and "Physical Activity and Breastfeeding" in chapter 18, pages 553 and 557, for more about the benefits and precautions.

THE VEGETARIAN ATHLETE

A vegetarian approach to eating, *as described in "The Healthy Vegetarian Way" in chapter 2, page 53*, is flexible enough to provide sufficient fuel and nutrition for sports. As with any high-performance diet, carbohydrate-rich foods should provide the most calories, or food energy—usually not an issue for vegetarians. However, consuming enough calories from an eating plan of bulky, plant-based foods may be challenging since the high fiber content may fill you up before eating enough calories. Eating six to eight meals or snacks of nutrient-dense foods a day is one practical solution. With good planning, special foods or supplements aren't generally needed.

Try to fit in high-quality protein foods at each meal. You can build muscle on a well-balanced vegetarian diet. The protein in eggs has a perfect balance of the nine essential amino acids; it's easily digestible, too. Other protein foods with easily digestible high-quality protein include low-fat dairy milk and yogurt, quinoa, and soy foods, such as edamame, soymilk, soy yogurt, and tofu. Fit in beans, nuts, and seeds, too.

Besides attention to getting enough food energy (calories) and enough high-quality protein, some vegetarian athletes may also be at risk of having low intakes of omega-3 fatty acids and key micronutrients such as riboflavin, vitamin B_{12}, calcium, iron, and zinc.

A registered dietitian nutritionist, who specializes in sports nutrition, can provide expert advice on helping you create a personalized vegetarian eating plan that meets your individual needs for your sport.

Making Weight

For some athletes, making weight to compete is an issue. That can be a challenge for those who weigh more during their off-season and who then need to drop a few pounds before training and competition. Others may need to "bulk up" to train and compete in contact sports.

Whatever your sport, for your peak performance, enter the competitive season at your best weight. Instead of trying to make weight quickly in order to train and compete, stay at your best weight year-round. Try to avoid weight cycling (losing and gaining, losing and gaining) during a competitive season.

BODY COMPOSITION: FIT, NOT FAT

For athletic performance (strength, speed, endurance), your body composition is more important than your weight—even if you compete in a weight category. (That's true for the strength, endurance, and overall fitness of nonathletes, too.) Body composition is the proportion of body muscle, fat, bone, and water.

There's no single and accepted body fat standard or range for athletes. The optimal percentage varies from athlete to athlete, sport to sport, and even for a specific position or event on a team. The right target range for body fat depends on the body type you were born with, your gender, and your sport, for example:

- *Different sports:* For a female tennis player, a body fat target might be 15 to 24 percent, and for a female soccer player, 13 to 18 percent of body mass.
- *Same sport, different position:* In American football, the target for a male lineman may be 15 to 19 percent body fat, and for a male back, 9 to 12 percent of body mass.
- *Different gender:* For a male gymnast, a body fat target of 5 to 12 percent of body mass may be advised; for a female gymnast, 10 to 16 percent.

Why is there a target range? For an individual athlete, body fat content varies over a sport's season and over his or her athletic career. Essential body fat for women likely varies for reasons of childbearing and hormonal differences.

How much is too low for health? In general, less than 5 percent body fat for men and less than 12 percent body fat for women is considered risky for health. The percentage of body fat that's risky for you individually may differ.

You can't measure your own body fat or composition accurately. Instead, seek a trained health expert who uses professional methods for measurement, such as skinfold measurements, air displacement, or bioelectrical impedance (done with a computer).

Caution: Intense training—without a dietary change—can lead to a condition called RED-s (relative energy deficiency in sport). It's more likely among young female athletes than male athletes. When energy (calorie) intake doesn't change to meet the needs of intense training, as well as growth and development, bone health, cardiovascular health, immune response, menstrual cycle for females, protein synthesis, and psychological health can be affected. This condition can lead to the "female athlete triad." *See "Calcium and the Female Athlete Triad," in this chapter, page 610.*

An exercise physiologist, a qualified trainer, or a registered dietitian nutritionist can help you determine the best target range for you. If you're a serious or perhaps an elite athlete, target goals for a healthy weight and for body fat composition are likely lower than that for most other active healthy people. *See "What's a Healthy Weight" in chapter 22, page 624, for more about body composition.*

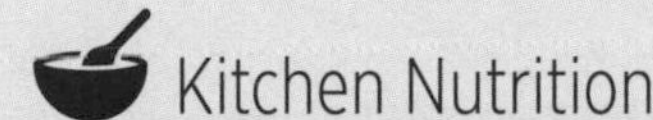

Kitchen Nutrition

Choices at the Training Table

For meals that are high in carbohydrates, provide a good protein source, and have limits on saturated fats, try these meal combos. The amounts of these nutrients depend on portion sizes.

- Chili made with kidney beans and lean ground beef, turkey, or chicken, or with soy crumbles or tempeh, served with whole-grain bread or rolls
- Stir-fry with vegetables and lean pork, chicken, shrimp, or tofu served over rice (prepared with healthy oil)
- Soft corn tortillas filled with vegetarian refried beans and topped with tomato sauce or salsa, and cheese
- Grilled fish kabobs (chunks of fresh fish alternating with cherry tomatoes, green bell peppers, and pineapple on a skewer) served over brown rice
- Lentils (alone or mixed with lean ground beef) in spaghetti sauce over whole-wheat pasta
- Green bell peppers stuffed with a lean ground turkey–brown rice mixture. Add a mixed green salad. Finish the meal with angel food cake topped with strawberries.
- Lean roast sirloin strips with a baked potato, steamed carrots, cauliflower, and whole-wheat rolls
- Chicken salad (with reduced-calorie mayonnaise, grated lemon peel, and tarragon) on whole-grain bread with tomato slices and sprouts. Serve with vegetable soup, whole-wheat crackers, and cantaloupe

WEIGHT LOSS: LOSING FAT, NOT MUSCLE

If you need to lose weight to make weight, to gain an advantage for competition, or to perform at your best, use an approach that allows you to lose fat, not muscle. The reason is that rapid weight loss with excessive calorie restriction may result in a loss of glycogen stores, in hypohydration, and in other outcomes that impair health and athletic performance. Instead, do this:

- Start your weight-loss strategies at the start of training season or well before competition so you don't compromise your athletic performance by trying to make weight.
- Set a weight goal that's realistic and healthy for you—one that considers your body composition and offers the best competitive edge for your sport.
- Increase your protein to preserve your muscle mass, while losing weight and body fat, as you take in somewhat fewer calories (energy). A higher-protein diet may help you increase your feeling of fullness more than a high-carb diet. Some evidence suggests that eating more protein is linked to eating fewer calories and to losing more body fat while keeping more muscle.
- Don't skimp on carbs, however. They're the fuel that working muscles need. Get most of your calories from starches (complex carbohydrates): grain products, including whole grains, vegetables, fruits, and beans and peas. Limit high-fat foods.
- As you cut back on calories, follow guidelines for the food patterns, *discussed in chapter 2, page 21*, to get enough vitamins and minerals from nutrient-rich food group foods, at a calorie level that's somewhat lower than what your body uses. *See "Food Guides for Athletes" in this chapter, page 611.*
- Make your weight loss gradual. Minimizing weight loss to less than one percent per week is better for athletic performance. With many quick weight-loss regimens, you may lose muscle along with body fat and deplete your stores of muscle glycogen, which may interfere with physical performance by shorting your energy supply. Quick weight loss may be partly water loss—a problem for athletes, who need to keep adequately hydrated.
- Even in off season, keep your training and physical activity level up. It does more than burn calories. Exercise boosts your metabolic rate, or the rate at which your body uses energy. Muscles use more energy than body fat does. In your off-season training, maintain your weight at the best weight for your sport.

See "Weight Management: Strategies That Work!" in chapter 22, page 637, for ways to lose weight in a healthy way.

Leanest: Not Always Better!

The notion that you can never be too thin or too lean may compromise physical performance. Athletes obsessed with a lean, thin body risk eating disorders and all the dangers (some life-threatening) that accompany severe weight loss. Among other concerns for athletes, a poorly fueled body that's too lean may not sweat and cool down properly, and so the possibility of dehydration goes up.

Remember that having some body fat has benefits. Fat cushions body organs, providing protection from injury. During endurance sports, both carbohydrate and fat provide energy for working muscles. If you're too lean, you may tire quickly. Restricting calorie intake too much to avoid body fat may result in a nutrient deficiency.

If you, someone you train with, or your child or teen show signs of an eating disorder, seek help. Share your concern with family, friends, or the coach, as well. *See "Eating Disorders: More Than a Nutrition Issue" in chapter 25, page 732.*

WEIGHT GAIN: GAINING MUSCLE, NOT FAT

Hockey and football are among the sports where extra body weight aids performance. Trying to "bulk up" too fast, however, may put on more fat than muscle—especially if you eat extra calories without enough exercise. If you're already in strenuous training, gaining weight may not be as easy as it sounds. You may use energy faster than you consume it.

To build muscle, engage in strength-building activity and consume enough calories. Contrary to myth, you don't need a lot of extra protein to help build muscle. *See "Muscle Myths" in this chapter, page 608.*

As with weight loss, the key to weight gain is "gradual and steady": about one-half to one pound a week. To get the extra energy to fuel exercise and build muscle:

- Increase portions of nutrient-rich foods at mealtime.
- Snack between meals, *as described in "Snacks Count!" in chapter 3, page 75.* Make your choices nutrient rich—and not high in added sugars or saturated fats.
- Drink extra low-fat chocolate milk, 100 percent juice, or fruit smoothies.
- Get most of your extra calories from nutrient-dense, high-carbohydrate foods—for example, granola or muesli topped with nuts or dried fruit. *See "What If You Need a Healthy Way to Gain Weight?" in chapter 22, page 732, for guidance.*

COMPETITION IN A WEIGHT CATEGORY

Body weight is critically important in sports such as body building, boxing, rowing, weight lifting, and wrestling, which have weight categories. Being the heaviest competitor in a lower weight class often is believed to provide a competitive edge. But hitting that target can be tricky. Even an extra pound or two may affect the weight class (category) you can compete in or your performance.

For good health, endurance, strength, and best performance, the better advice is to compete in a weight class that's realistic for your body composition and to maintain your optimal weight throughout the competitive season, rather than cycle to make weight in unhealthy ways for competition.

Water weight is not unnecessary body weight, so sweating off pounds in a sauna or rubber suit or with diuretics to make weight for wrestling—or any other sport—can potentially hinder performance. Because it may lead to hypohydration, losing as little as 2 to 3 percent of body weight from sweat (e.g., three to four pounds, or six to nine cups of fluid, for a 150-pound athlete) can lead to cramping and early fatigue, limit athletic performance, and may be dangerous to health.

Fasting, or drastically cutting back on food, to make weight in a short period of time, isn't healthy or performance enhancing either. It restricts carbohydrates and other nutrients needed for athletic performance. Feeling hungry is distracting. Never advised, fasting often causes fatigue, the potential for muscle loss, dehydration, and decreased performance. With fasting, the body won't store muscle glycogen as energy for training and competition. Overexercising to make weight depletes stored muscle glycogen that you need to compete in your sport.

A healthy eating plan—that starts well before weigh-in—is the smartest way to reach and stay in your weight class. Without ongoing, sensible weight management all season long, you might continue with the same weight dilemma and "weight cycle" for the next competition—and the next and the next!

The Game Plan

It's the day of the big event. You're excited and perhaps a bit anxious. You've trained hard. What should you eat to maximize your performance? Your game plan now—what you eat before, during, and after competition or a heavy workout—makes a difference.

For endurance events, think further ahead—before your pre-event meal. Several days beforehand, you might eat more carbohydrates and gradually rest your muscles. In that way, you'll store extra muscle glycogen and won't tire as quickly during the event. *See "Carbohydrate Loading" in this chapter, page 606.*

For any sport, think about what you eat well ahead for peak performance. Most energy for competition comes from foods eaten in the meals the day(s) before your pre-event meal. On competition day, carefully planned meals can't make up for a poor training diet. Read on for general advice.

BEFORE YOU COMPETE: PRE-EVENT FOOD AND DRINK

Choose a pre-event meal or snack—light, easy to digest, high carbohydrate—that matches your physical performance goals so you won't tire too soon. A light meal or snack helps prevent the distraction of hunger pangs and supplies energy for exercise that lasts an hour or more. Drink enough to fully hydrate before strenuous exercise.

The "right" pre-event meal or snack differs from athlete to athlete, event to event, and time of day. During training experiment with different foods, food combinations, amounts, and timing.

Timing. Finish eating one to four hours before your workout or competition. Make choices that contribute to your body's carb stores. This allows enough time for food to digest so you don't feel full or uncomfortable. Morning competition? Eat a hearty, high-carbohydrate dinner and bedtime snack the night before. In the morning, eat a light, high-carbohydrate meal or snack. Eating two hours before exercise helps replenish your liver glycogen and satisfy hunger.

Small meals. Choose a small meal or snack. The amount depends on what makes you feel comfortable.

High carbs. For faster digestion and absorption, enjoy a high-carb meal or snack that's moderate in protein and low in fat. (About 0.5 gram to 2 grams of carbohydrate per pound of body weight is about right.) Make pasta, rice, potatoes, or bread the "center" of your plate. A high-fat meal may cause indigestion or nausea with heavy exercise. *See "Athlete's Plate: Pre-Event, High-Carb Meals" in this chapter, page 618.*

Contrary to common belief, eating small amounts of fatty foods won't keep your body from storing muscle glycogen. In fact, a little fat adds flavor and helps you meet your overall energy needs.

A steak meal? The fats and proteins in steak take longer to digest than carbohydrates do. If steak gives you a "mental edge," enjoy a small portion along with carbohydrate-rich foods: perhaps a baked potato, pasta, or rice; carrots; a dinner roll; a fruit salad; and frozen yogurt for dessert. Allow several hours for the meal to digest before you compete.

No discomfort-causing foods. Skip foods that may cause intestinal discomfort during competition: gas-causing foods such as beans, cabbage, cauliflower, onions, and turnips; and bulky, high-fiber foods such as raw vegetables and fruits with seeds and tough skin; bran, nuts, and seeds.

Familiar and "feel-good" foods. Enjoy familiar foods and beverages. This isn't the time to try something new that may disagree with you. If a certain food or meal seems to enhance your performance, enjoy it—if you can fit it into your pre-event eating strategy.

Enough fluids. About two to three hours ahead, drink at least two cups of fluids. Then about fifteen minutes ahead, drink another one to one-and-a-half cups. Milk's okay. Stress and loss of body fluids—not milk—often slow saliva flow, causing "cotton mouth," or a dry mouth.

DURING COMPETITION: NOURISHED TO KEEP MOVING

Nourishment you choose now depends on your sport.

- *During most sports*, drinking plenty of fluids is the only real issue. Every fifteen or so minutes, drink enough to minimize loss of body weight without overdoing: one-half to one-and-a-half cups every fifteen minutes.
- *During endurance sports of sixty minutes or more*, a slightly sweetened carbohydrate drink (sports drink) or snack may help maintain your blood glucose levels, boost your stamina, and enhance your performance. Figure about 0.5 gram of carbohydrate per pound of your body weight per hour. Sports drinks are easy to digest, especially during intense activity. And they count as fluids. Their flavor may encourage their consumption, especially among children. Drink fluids every fifteen minutes or so! *See "Sports Drinks" in this chapter, page 603.*
- *During day-long events or regional tournaments*, snack on high-carbohydrate, low-fat foods. Between matches, sets, or other competitive events, bagels, crackers, rice cakes, apples, bananas, orange slices, and fruit bars are good choices. Bring snacks so you don't need to rely on a concession stand. Consuming fluids all day long remains important.

AFTER YOU COMPETE: NUTRITION FOR RECOVERY

Your cool-down exercise routine is as important as your warm-up. And what you eat and drink for recovery after a workout is as important as your pre-event eating routine. Start with a snack or meal within fifteen to sixty minutes after practice or competition. If you're a serious athlete, involved in strenuous exercise, a recovery plan, developed with a qualified trainer or registered dietitian nutritionist, specializing in sports nutrition,

Have you ever wondered?

. . . about competing on an empty stomach? You're better off eating. Food consumed within four hours of physical activity is fuel for working muscles. For morning events, eating is especially important for endurance. It replenishes liver glycogen and helps maintain your blood glucose level. Don't skip breakfast; if you don't have much of an appetite, at least eat something light!

. . . what to eat before competition if you feel too nervous to eat? Drinking a liquid meal supplement or a fruit smoothie might help. It provides nutrients and fluids needed for competition. And it might be more easily digested and absorbed than a full meal.

. . . if a "complete nutrition supplement," perhaps an energy bar or drink or a power gel, aids performance? Energy bars and drinks may be an energy source but typically don't supply the variety and amounts of other nutrients found in a meal. Power gels supply carbs, too, but usually few vitamins or minerals. A quick check of the Nutrition Facts reveals their calorie and nutrient contribution. Energy bars, drinks, or gels may be convenient during an endurance event; enjoy a carbohydrate-protein combination food afterward, such as low-fat chocolate milk or a fruit yogurt.

is essential. If you're a recreational, casual athlete, a regular plan of balanced eating is likely fine.

Make fluids your first priority. After competition or a heavy workout, replace your fluid loss. The amount depends on how much weight you lose through exercise. Simply weigh yourself before and afterward; the difference is your water weight. Replenish the loss: For every pound you lose, drink three cups of fluid. (That's more fluid than lost, but it gives you a safety net.) Continue to drink fluids throughout the day or several days until you return to your pre-exercise weight.

What fluids are best? Plain water and watery foods, such as soup, watermelon, and grapes, are good fluid recovery foods for short-term, low-intensity activity. For more intense activity, drink fluids with carbohydrates, such as juice or sports drinks. They replace fluids and electrolytes lost in sweat and help your body replenish muscle glycogen.

Beverages with protein help with muscle recovery for longer-duration activity. Flavored low-fat milk with a ratio of 4:1 carbohydrate-to-protein can be an alternative to commercial recovery beverages.

See chapter 4, page 81, for more about beverages and "Water: A Fluid Asset" in chapter 15, page 443.

Refuel your muscles with carbohydrates. Within the first several hours after competition or a heavy workout, eat a carbohydrate-rich meal or snack. For muscle recovery, the sooner, the better. For every pound of body weight, strive for about 0.5 gram of carbohydrates. For example, if you weigh 150 pounds, eat at least 75 grams of carbohydrates. That's easy to do with a high-carbohydrate snack or meal. For strenuous exercise that lasts ninety minutes or longer, consume that much carbohydrate within thirty minutes after exercise, and continue for four to six hours to optimize resynthesis of muscle glycogen. If you aren't hungry right after a training session, drink juice or a sports drink for fluids and carbs.

Because sports drinks are a diluted source of "carbs," double the amount of sports drink to get the same amount of carbohydrates—for example, thirty-two ounces of a sports drink and sixteen ounces of 100-percent juice each supply about 50 grams of carbohydrates. When your hunger returns, enjoy a high-carb meal or snack.

How about electrolytes? Through perspiration, you lose electrolytes such as sodium. Your meal—and perhaps a sports drink—after endurance sports will undoubtedly provide enough sodium and other electrolytes to replace your losses.

Protein for recovery. High-quality protein foods (20 to 25 grams) within two hours after exercise and eaten with carbohydrate foods—perhaps milk with cereal, chocolate milk, a shake, a protein bar, yogurt and berries,

Athlete's Plate: Pre-event, High-Carb Meals

There's no single menu prescribed for pre-event eating, but these three high-carbohydrate meals show what might be eaten by a 150- to 180-pound athlete one to two hours before an event.

Meal 1	Meal 2	Meal 3
1 cup cornflakes	2 cups beef noodle soup	2 six-inch pancakes with 2 tbsp. syrup
1 small banana	6 whole-wheat crackers	1 large scrambled egg
8 oz. fat-free milk	1 medium baked potato	½ cup sliced strawberries
1 three-inch bagel with 1 tbsp. peanut butter and 1 tbsp. jelly	8 oz. low-fat fruit yogurt	1 cup apple juice
¾ cup cranberry juice drink		
Calories 715	**Calories** 670	**Calories** 685
Carbohydrates 139 grams	**Carbohydrates** 115 grams	**Carbohydrates** 106 grams

? Have you ever wondered?

. . . where to get sports-specific nutrition advice—or to find out if your food choices help or hinder your training? Talk to a sports dietitian, a registered dietitian nutritionist with a specialty in sports nutrition, or other qualified expert for help in determining your energy needs, evaluating your eating plan, and strategizing ways to eat for peak performance. *Be aware:* "Personal trainer" isn't a regulated professional specialty. Some trainers are highly qualified exercise specialists; others aren't. To find a local sports dietitian, use the referral network from the Academy of Nutrition and Dietetics: www.SCANdpg.org.

. . . if drinking milk before a heavy workout causes stomach cramps? Contrary to myth, drinking milk before physical exertion doesn't cause stomach discomfort or digestive problems. If you have any discomfort after drinking milk, you may be sensitive to lactose, the naturally occurring sugar in milk. *See "Lactose Intolerance: A Matter of Degree" in chapter 23, page 666, to learn about lactose malabsorption and intolerance.* Besides its role in bone health, calcium in milk is needed for muscle contraction.

or a turkey sandwich—help to repair damaged muscle tissue and stimulate the development of new tissue. That's especially important if you're involved in high-intensity training that may damage muscle tissue (e.g., resistance training, interval sessions). With two protein sources—whey and casein—milk is a good recovery drink.

Ergogenic Aids: No Training Substitute

"Blast your body with energy!" "Guaranteed for muscle growth!" "For faster muscle recovery and longer endurance!" Chances are you've seen these and other supplement claims. "Ergogenic" means potential to increase work output. But, the fact is, only proper training and nutrition can do that.

Of course, you want to make the most of every workout and increase your competitive edge. But do you take supplements, hoping to enhance your physical performance, stamina, or recovery, without questioning their merits? Have you had a professional nutrition assessment to know if you need them?

It's easy to be lured by advertising claims that dietary and hormonal supplements improve strength, endurance, or recovery time, especially when anatomical graphics make the claims seem well researched. Yet valid and invalid advice often appear side-by-side in fitness magazines and online.

What about "proven results"? Perceived performance benefits of ergogenic aids often come from individual reports, from misunderstood physiology, or from product claims taken out of scientific context—even if labeled with an effective or safe dose. Some may have impurities or undeclared steroids. Benefits may be more psychological than physical. It's well documented that the side effects of taking many ergogenic aids may hinder performance and may cause harm, especially in the long run.

The NCAA advises school athletes to check with the athletics staff before using supplements; some are banned, and others may contain banned substances not listed on the supplement label. The NCAA also warns that dietary supplements are not well regulated and may cause a positive drug test, resulting in a loss of eligibility for the sport, and that supplements are taken at your own risk. The World Anti-Doping Agency also provides a list of prohibited substances.

Carrying a supplement claim such as "100 percent pure," "free of banned substances," or "pharmaceutical grade," or having a drug identification number does not guarantee that it's free of banned substances.

Snacks and Meals for Recovery

Snack Ideas

- Smoothie made with yogurt and frozen berries
- Sports drink (carbohydrate, electrolyte fluid) + sports bar (carbohydrate, protein)
- Graham crackers with peanut butter + low-fat chocolate milk + banana

Meal Ideas

- Whole-wheat pita sandwich or wrap with turkey and veggies + pretzels + low-fat milk
- Rice bowl with avocado, beans, cheese, and salsa + whole-grain tortilla chips or whole-wheat tortilla
- Stir-fry with lean steak, bell peppers, broccoli, and carrots + brown rice

DIETARY SUPPLEMENTS FOR SPORTS: USE AND CONCERNS

Some supplements can fill nutrient gaps in an athlete's diet or perhaps help improve the ability to train and recover after strenuous workouts. Yet the effectiveness and safety of many supplements, sold in supermarkets, fitness clubs, and online, are undetermined. And they're costly.

As you weigh the options, look for unbiased reviews, not only information from supplement makers about their products. Consider whether the cost is worth the benefit if you use them. And, for those that may deliver benefits, know that their value is greatest when added to a well-chosen eating plan.

Amino acids. Amino acid supplements such as arginine, branched-chain amino acids (BCAAs, or isoleucine, leucine, and valine), and ornithine are said to promote muscle growth, reduce muscle breakdown during exercise, and increase fat loss.

Most athletes consume more than enough amino acids from food, which makes these products unnecessary. What's more, they tend to be costly. That said, exercise itself spurs muscle growth, so taking these extra amino acids doesn't make a significant difference. BCAA can provide fuel for endurance activity but has not been shown to delay fatigue as a result. Growing research suggests it may play a role.

For healthy athletes, BCAAs are considered safe; those with kidney or liver disease may be at risk. *See "Muscle Myths" in this chapter, page 608.* *Note:* Supplements with isolated protein from whey, casein, soy, or egg may offer a boost when taken right after a workout.

Beet root juice. Early research suggests that the high amount of naturally occurring nitrates in beet root juice may improve blood flow, increase the efficiency of skeletal muscles, help you exercise longer (at least for non-elite athletes), and may help lower blood pressure. In the body, nitrates are changed into nitric acid, which aids blood flow and blood pressure. That may help lower oxygen demand in endurance athletes, but its effectiveness among elite athletes is unclear. Be aware that drinking beet root juice may give urine and stools a reddish appearance, which is normal. It also may cause gut discomfort. *Note:* Cooked beets don't provide as much nitrates as beet root juice does because the cooking process takes away some benefits.

Beta-alanine. This nonessential amino acid is produced naturally in the body. It helps produce a compound called carnosine that may help muscle endurance during short, high-intensity exercise such as sprinting or weight lifting before getting tired. However, the evidence for its effectiveness is insufficient.

Carnitine. Promoted for more energy, aerobic power, and body fat reduction, carnitine is composed of two essential amino acids, lysine and methionine. Carnitine is found in muscles and used for energy production; the human body produces adequate amounts. Foods of animal origin are good sources. Although safe in recommended doses, there's no need for extra. For improved athletic performance or to increase fat burning, it's ineffective when taken as a supplement.

Chromium picolinate. No scientific evidence shows that taking a chromium supplement improves physical performance, builds muscle, burns body fat, or prolongs youth. For that matter, the role of chromium in your overall health isn't well understood, although early research suggests benefits to some people with diabetes or glucose intolerance. It does play a role in using glucose. There is insufficient support for its use in weight loss and body composition changes, and it may cause oxidative damage. Chromium isn't recommended. There are safety concerns about doses over 200 micrograms or about forms with a high bioavailability.

Whole-grain foods, ready-to-eat cereals, apples, bananas, beef, beans and peas, and peanuts are some sources of chromium. Most people get enough from their normal diet. Supplements aren't advised; chromium supplements may interfere with the work of iron in the blood.

Creatine. As an ergogenic aid, it's promoted to increase muscle mass and strength, enhance energy, and delay fatigue especially for high-intensity workouts. In fact, creatine is a nitrogen-containing compound that's found naturally in meat and fish, is produced naturally in the human body, and is used for energy production. Research suggests that creatine supplements may promote muscle strength, help increase body weight, and aid recovery after strength training or short bouts of high-intensity activity, such as weightlifting. Creatine supplements aren't advised for teenage athletes, who need to learn what their bodies can do with hard training.

Medium-chain triglycerides (MCT): This type of fat is made up of medium-chain fatty acids, which are rapidly absorbed compared to other fats. Claims for these fatty acids are for increased endurance and fat burning in long-duration exercise. However, evidence doesn't support enhanced performance, and it may cause stomach upset when used as a supplement. Because it may increase blood lipid levels, MCT is not recommended.

Pyruvate: This is the end product of carbohydrate metabolism. Evidence doesn't support claims for its use in increasing endurance and decreasing body fat, or for promoting weight loss. Side effects may include adverse gastrointestinal effects, such as gas and nausea.

Spirulina. Spirulina, a blue-green algae, is marketed as a high-energy food. It's high in protein with small amounts of vitamin B_{12} but has no unique energy-producing qualities. Much of its vitamin B_{12} is inactive and cannot be absorbed by humans.

Note: Ephedra is now banned by the FDA for sale as a supplement, although the ruling has been challenged. Some over-the-counter medications may contain ephedrine.

See chapter 10, page 315, for more about dietary supplements. A registered dietitian nutritionist can help you sort through the pros and cons of supplements available to athletes. Unless your doctor prescribes them for medical reasons, taking vitamin or mineral supplements, in amounts beyond the Recommended Dietary Allowances, offers no added advantage for athletic performance. *See chapter 14, page 408, for daily recommendations.*

HORMONE SUPPLEMENTS FOR SPORTS: USES AND CONCERNS

Hormone supplements, or steroids, are another type of supplement that may increase muscle mass—but at a potential price to health. An ergogenic aid, they're powerful yet dangerous drugs!

Teens should never use steroids. Contrary to many a boy's wish, steroids won't bulk up muscles before puberty. Adolescents who use them may not grow to their normal height.

Androstenedione, or "andro," is an anabolic steroid that acts like testosterone, a male sex hormone. "Anabolic" refers to the metabolic processes of synthesizing body tissue. Steroids can help build bigger muscles, as well as increase strength, alter mood, and decrease body fat. However, they don't ensure better physical performance.

Of concern, their use can have dangerous and often permanent side effects. For example, in men, steroids may cause acne, testicular damage, enlarged breasts, and a lower sperm count. Used by women, steroids

These sports-supplement certification programs identify supplements that contain substances that are banned for sports:

- Banned Substances Control Group (BSCG) Certified Drug Free®
  www.bscg.org
- Informed-Choice
  www.informed-choice.org

Need more tips specific to eating for active living?

Check here for "how-tos":

- Manage weight sensibly; *see chapter 22, page 624.*
- Sort through claims for ergogenic dietary supplements; *see chapter 10, page 315.*
- Exercise safely during pregnancy and breastfeeding; *see "Physical Activity and Pregnancy" and "Physical Activity and Breastfeeding" in chapter 18, pages 553 and 557.*
- Spot the signs of eating disorders in athletes; *see "Eating Disorders: More than a Nutrition Issue" in chapter 25, page 732.*
- Seek advice from a sports dietitian, especially if you're an athlete who aspires to peak performance, an elite or professional athlete, or a physically active person with a health condition; *see "How to . . . find a qualified nutrition expert" in chapter 26, page 732.*

may cause masculine qualities: a lower voice, facial hair, smaller breasts, and loss of (or irregular) menstrual cycle.

Other potential risks: increased risk for injury, blood clots, and gastrointestinal problems, as well as liver damage, heart disease, and cancer. Steroid use is banned by the International Olympic Committee (IOC) and most other sports governing bodies and condemned by the American Academy of Pediatrics and the American College of Sports Medicine. In the Anabolic Steroid Control Act, androstenedione is a controlled substance, listed as a banned anabolic steroid and an illegal performance-enhancing drug.

Dehydroepiandrosterone (DHEA) is neither safe nor effective. It is sold as an alternative to anabolic steroids, is an androgenic steroid, and is banned by the IOC and the NCAA. "Androgenic" refers to the development of male characteristics. Evidence doesn't back up claims to increase energy, decrease body fat, counteract stress, and slow aging. In the short run, DHEA can have unpleasant side effects, including facial hair growth, acne, enlarged liver, rapid heartbeat, and testicular damage. With its potential effect on testosterone and estradiol (a female steroid produced in the ovaries) levels, its use may be risky for people with a family history of prostate or breast cancer. *See "Muscle Myths" in this chapter, page 608.*

PART V

Smart Eating: Preventing and Managing Health Issues

22

Reach and Maintain Your Healthy Weight

In this chapter, find out about . . .

Your healthy weight and calorie target

The risks of overweight and obesity

Strategies to maintain a healthy weight

Smart ways to lose or gain weight if needed

Fad diets and other weight-loss ploys

We often take it for granted, but good health is one of the most precious gifts of life. A healthy weight—maintained throughout life—helps you achieve good health in many ways: you look your best, feel your best, and reduce your risk for many serious and ongoing weight-related health problems.

The smart approach to your best weight is really no secret. A healthy lifestyle, with regular physical activity and a sensible eating pattern, make all the difference. An eating plan for your healthy weight should meet your nutrient needs and food preferences, within your calorie limits.

Calories matter: the calories consumed and the calories used for physical activity and metabolism. Managing them in and out may sound simple—and for some people, it is. Yet the dynamics of metabolism, along with the environment, culture, and social network you live in, and the everyday habits you have, may contribute to the challenges of achieving and maintaining a healthy weight.

From food shopping to food prep to eating out, this chapter—and others—provides practical and positive ways to help you reach and keep your healthy weight—and your healthy life.

What's a Healthy Weight?

The answer isn't as simple as stepping onto a bathroom scale and then comparing your weight to a chart. For the population overall, a healthy weight is often considered as a range, statistically related to a greater likelihood of good health.

PERSONALLY SPEAKING: YOUR HEALTHY WEIGHT

Your healthy weight is what's best for you—not necessarily the lowest weight you think you can be. It's one that "fits" your body, your overall good health, and your positive sense of self. Your best weight is also a weight you can maintain. It probably differs from the weight of others you know who are about the same height, gender, and age. Why a difference? Genes play a role because they determine your height, the size and shape of your body frame, and your general body composition.

Genetics isn't the only physiological reason for weight differences. Your metabolic rate, or the rate at which your body burns energy, factors in and is partly dependent on your genes, too, and your body composition. Muscle burns more calories than body fat does. Your overall health helps define where your weight fits within a healthy range, too.

Fit at Different Sizes

Healthy people come in many sizes and shapes: tall or short, stocky or lanky, smaller or bigger, muscular or not. These differences are unique to being human. There's no such thing as a "perfect body," or an ideal body weight, shape, or size, that everyone should strive for.

Whatever your body size and shape, you can be fit—and so live a full, productive life and reduce your risks for health problems. Make these your priorities:

- Be active—no matter what your body size—and eat for health. This duo helps offset any risks related to being overweight.
- Assess other health habits. Make choices with health in mind: get enough sleep, limit alcoholic drinks, and quit smoking. Each of these has an impact on both health and body weight.
- Get regular physical checkups.
- Monitor your "numbers" (blood cholesterol, triglycerides, blood pressure, fasting blood glucose levels). Keep them within a healthy range; *see chapter 24, page 679.*
- Make fitness and your personal healthy weight your goals, not some unattainable target. Even with a commitment to healthy eating and physical activity, losing weight, or maintaining a healthy weight, is harder for some.

WEIGHT: WHAT'S HEALTHY?

Your doctor or a registered dietitian nutritionist can help you determine a healthy weight range for you. Maybe the best goal is just weight maintenance, or maybe dropping or gaining a few pounds will reduce your health risks.

By itself, a bathroom scale isn't an adequate judge of body weight. A doctor or other healthcare professional will take several other things into account when assessing your weight: the location and amount of body fat; your mass index (BMI), or weight in relation to height; and as important, your overall health and risks for weight-related conditions such as diabetes, heart disease, and high blood pressure. With these assessments, you can set personal weight goals that you can achieve and maintain over time.

Body Shape and Composition

For a healthy weight, your body shape, waist size, and body composition are factors to consider.

Body shape. Stand in front of a full-length mirror, preferably nude. How do you look? Be your own judge. Are you shaped like an apple or a pear? For health, being an "apple" can be riskier than being a "pear." The place your body stores fat is one clue to your weight status.

Because it's metabolically active, abdominal or upper body fat (apple-like shape) especially increases some health risks for type 2 diabetes, high cholesterol levels, early heart disease, and high blood pressure, among other conditions. That can be true even when a BMI, *page 627,* falls within a healthy range. In contrast, excess weight carried on the hips, buttocks, and thighs (pear-like shape) doesn't appear to increase risks for health problems. There are some exceptions: varicose veins and orthopedic problems.

For the most part, being an "apple" or a "pear" is inherited. Where your body fat resides is influenced partly by your genes. However, after

Your Healthy Eating Check-In

Lose or Maintain?

Assessing weight and health risk involves three key measures:

1. Body mass index (BMI)
2. Waist circumference
3. Risk factors for diseases and conditions linked to obesity.* Along with being overweight or obese, the following conditions will put you at greater risk for heart disease and other conditions:

    High blood pressure

    High LDL ("bad") cholesterol

    Low HDL ("good") cholesterol

    High triglycerides

    High blood glucose

    Family history of premature heart disease

    Physical inactivity

    Cigarette smoking

People who are considered obese (BMI of 30 or higher)—or for those who are overweight (BMI of 25 to 29.9) and have two or more risk factors—are advised to lose weight.

People who are overweight but do not have a high waist measurement and who have fewer than two risk factors may need to prevent further weight gain rather than lose weight.

Talk to your doctor to see if you are at an increased risk and whether you should lose weight. Your doctor will evaluate your BMI, waist measurement, and other risk factors for heart disease. The good news is even a small weight loss (between 5 and 10 percent of your current weight) will help lower your risk of developing diseases associated with obesity.

**See chapter 24, page 679, for more about these diseases.*

Reference: National Heart, Lung, and Blood Institute, www.nhlbi.nih.gov/health/educational/lose_wt/risk.htm. Accessed November 15, 2016.

menopause, many women tend to add weight around the midriff. Smoking and drinking too many alcoholic beverages also seem to increase abdominal fat, and so increase the risk of weight-related health problems. Conversely, vigorous exercise can help to reduce body fat everywhere, including the abdomen, helping to decrease these health risks.

Waist size. Health risks go up as waist size increases, with more body fat around the middle. That's especially true when waist circumference measures more than thirty-five inches for a woman or more than forty inches for a man.

A simple tape measure is all you need for this assessment. Stand and measure your waist around your bare abdomen, just above your hipbone. (*Hint:* Relax, breathe out, and measure. Don't cinch in the tape measure or pull in your stomach.)

Body composition. Muscle weight or body fat? Body composition refers to the percentage of muscle, bone, fat, and water that makes up the body. Knowing your body composition helps assess fitness and weight, and may be measured in several ways:

- A health or fitness professional might use a skinfold caliper to measure the fat layer on several parts of your body, such as your arm, midriff, and thigh.
- Some health clubs offer body composition analysis with bioelectrical impedance, ultrasound, or air displacement plethysmography.
- Today's electronic scales and other digital devices also can provide an estimate of body fat percentages. Be aware that these body fat percentages are figured with an algorithm that isn't always accurate—one more reason for several assessment tools.

For most people, and unless you're a serious athlete, body composition analysis likely isn't needed. Your waist size, BMI, and health risks are better indicators of a healthy weight for you.

Note: Men generally have a lower percentage of body fat in relation to total weight than women do, but that in itself may not lower health risks.

Body Mass Index

Body mass index (BMI) doesn't measure body fat directly—and it isn't meant as the only factor to assess weight. Instead it's a measure of body weight in relation to height, considered a reasonably reliable indicator of total body fat. People with a higher percentage of body fat tend to have a higher BMI.

BMI indicates risk for weight-related diseases. The higher your BMI, the greater your risk for diseases such as heart disease, high blood pressure, type 2 diabetes, gallstones, breathing problems, and certain cancers. Having a very low BMI increases different health risks. Gaining or losing weight within the BMI ranges doesn't necessarily change your health risks, however.

BMI isn't a perfect indicator, however. It may overestimate body fat in athletes and others with a muscular build and may underestimate body fat in older persons and others who have lost muscle.

Age, gender, and ethnicity may affect BMI. For those under age sixty-five, health risks related to a higher BMI appear to be the same, regardless of age.

What is your BMI? Figuring BMI for adults of any age is the same. For your adult BMI (both men and women), *check "Does Your BMI Put You in the Risky Zone," below,* or use the online BMI calculator: www.nhlbi.nih.gov/health/educational/lose_wt/BMI/bmicalc.htm, where you'll also find information for a BMI calculator phone app.

- *BMI of 18.5 to 24.9.* This range is considered healthy for a given height. Take steps to keep it there, especially if your BMI starts to creep up. *Be aware:* Some people fit within the healthy range but still have excess body fat and little muscle.

  The BMI range allows for individual differences. Higher weights within this healthy range typically apply to people with more muscle and a large body frame. Why? Muscle and bone weigh more than fat.

  Even if your BMI falls into the "healthy" range, your risk of health problems is higher if you smoke cigarettes, don't participate in regular physical activity, and make poor food choices. Some people with a "healthy" BMI carry too much body fat, making them more prone to obesity-related health conditions, despite their BMI. *See "Your Healthy Eating Check-In: Lose or Maintain?" in this chapter, page 626, for risk factors.*

- *BMI of 25 to 29.9.* For most people, that's less healthy—unless the extra body weight comes from muscle and bone, not body fat. For adults, this range is considered overweight. If you fall within this

DOES YOUR BMI PUT YOU IN A RISKY ZONE?*

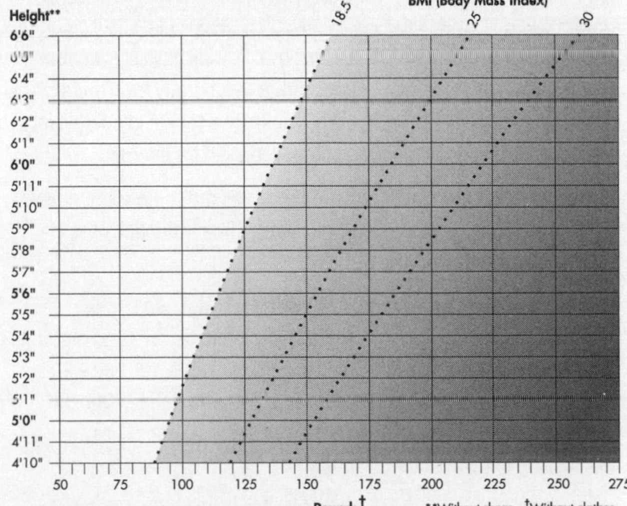

* BMI ranges shown above are for adults.

Directions: Find your weight on the bottom of the graph. Go straight up from that point until you come to the line that matches your height. Then look to find your weight group.

- BMI 18.5 to 24.9: not a risk factor for weight-related health problems
- BMI 25 to 29.9: some increased risk for weight-related health problems
- BMI 30 or higher: significant increased risk for weight-related health problems

range, try to be at the lower end, engage in regular physical activity, and keep your blood pressure, blood glucose, and cholesterol levels within normal limits

For some older people and for those with some chronic health issues, this somewhat higher BMI—with a little extra body fat—may be protective.

- *BMI of 30 and above.* For adults, this is considered obese. To put a BMI of 30 into context: that includes a woman who is 5 feet 4 inches tall and weighs 180 pounds or more and a man who is 5 feet 10 inches tall and weighs 209 pounds or more.

  The higher your BMI is above the healthy range, the greater your risk for weight-related problems. Shifting your BMI down even a bit can result in positive health changes, such as reduced blood pressure, cholesterol levels, blood glucose levels, and inflammation.

  Talk to your doctor about your whole picture of health and what your BMI means. You may be advised to take steps to reduce your weight and then maintain a healthier BMI.

- *BMI under 18.5.* This is below the healthy range. It may be okay for you, but it also may suggest a health problem.

  For women, a BMI under 18.5 may indicate increased risk for menstrual irregularity or infertility, and for men and women, risk for osteoporosis or weakened immunity. A low-normal or below-normal BMI also may be an early symptom of another health problem or an eating disorder. Check with your doctor if you lose weight suddenly or unexpectedly.

Use BMI only as a guideline. Age, gender, and ethnicity impact how it relates to body fat. Your BMI alone doesn't determine whether your weight is healthy. Remember that the location and amount of body fat you carry and your weight-related risk factors, including your family history of health problems, count, too.

Note: Adult BMI charts are not meant for children. Growth charts with BMIs for children and teens differ, taking their individual growth patterns and variations in body fat for their gender and age into account. *See "Growth and Weight" in chapter 17, page 501, for more about your child's or teen's healthy weight and "BMI: What Does It Mean?" in the appendix, page 777, for child and teen growth charts,* or visit www.cdc.gov/growthcharts.

Weight and Health

Your best weight feels good on you! Keeping a healthy weight gives you energy to enjoy life, achieve your life's goals, and feel good about yourself.

Have you ever wondered?

. . . why your body needs some body fat? Besides being a form of stored energy, body fat, or adipose tissue, is necessary to cushion and position your body organs, to protect your bones from injury, and to be a fat layer under your skin (subcutaneous fat) for insulation and helping you stay warm on a cold day. Soft fat pads on your buttocks and the palms of your hands protect your body from bumps, bangs, and jolts. While some body fat can be a source of energy, fat that's stored around your organs isn't accessed for energy.

Fat that circulates in the bloodstream carries fat-soluble vitamins (A, D, E, and K). Fat cells are also linked to the production of some hormones, such as estrogen.

. . . how overweight and obesity differ? As defined by the National Institutes of Health, overweight refers to an excess amount of body weight that may come from muscles, bone, fat, and water, while obesity refers to an excess amount of body fat. In 2013, the American Medical Association (AMA) recognized obesity as a disease needing medical attention.

. . . what it means to be "skinny fat"? It can be called "normal-weight obesity," or having a BMI within the healthy range yet having proportionally high body fat in relation to muscle mass. Being "skinny fat" can result in having the same health risks—type 2 diabetes, high blood pressure, and high cholesterol levels—as being considered obese.

Who is more likely to have normal-weight obesity? Svelte younger people who rarely exercise and eat poorly may look healthy on the outside but have metabolic risk factors. Older adults and others who have lost muscle mass due to inactivity or illness are also at risk. *Bottom line:* BMI is just one tool for assessing health risks. Knowing your whole health picture is essential!

. . . why clothes look different on a mannequin than on you? Most store mannequins don't represent average body shape or size of women or men in the United States. Mannequins for women are typically 5 feet 11 inches tall with a 34-inch bust, 24- to 25-inch waist, and 36-inch hips, say their manufacturers. And the body type you generally see in advertising or on a runway? Only about 5 percent of American females have that shape naturally. Most male mannequins have slimmed down in recent years, too, with some measuring in at 6 feet 1 inch tall, with a 38- to 40-inch chest and a 30- to 32-inch waist. The good news: in recent years some mannequins are being produced with more realistic body shapes.

Moreover, a healthy weight reduces your chances of developing many conditions that undermine your health and well-being.

Despite the many benefits of having a healthy weight, overweight and obesity have become epidemic in the United States among those of all ages—and in many other parts of the world, too. In the United States, the incidence has doubled over the past four decades, and among some demographics it has tripled.

UPS AND DOWNS: REASONS WHY

Overweight or underweight: it's easy to say someone eats too much or too little. If you struggle with your weight, you know it's far more complicated than that. Or you may blame weight gain on the natural shift in metabolism that comes with age.

The simple answer to weight gain is calorie imbalance, meaning more calories consumed than used. However, the underlying reasons are more complex and involve genetics, environment, unhealthy lifestyles, and social and psychological factors.

Sedentary Lifestyles

Today's lifestyles are often overscheduled, leaving little time for physical activity. Sound familiar? Your community may be designed for driving, not walking or bicycling. And what about the physical demands in your work environment?

Inactivity has become a way of life, making weight control an everyday challenge. The more you sit, the less energy you need, and the more likely you are to gain weight if your food intake stays the same. Weight gain results from fewer calories out, not just more in.

Technology adds to the mix of sedentary living. The amount of screen time—computers and tablets, smart phones, TV, and video games—is arguably linked to sedentary lifestyles and the rise in the number of people who are overweight.

Today, people also expend far fewer calories in daily tasks. Think of the impact of the computer and other digital devices over the past forty years. Before that, a typist on a manual typewriter burned fifteen more calories more per hour than someone doing the same work on a computer today. For four hours of work, that's sixty calories a day, or 300 calories over a work week. Add up the impact of escalators and moving sidewalks, cars and motorbikes, work-saving appliances, electric car-door openers, TV remote controls, and more!

Food Environment

The availability, quality, and quantity of food has shifted in recent years, too. Consider the temptation and marketing of convenient, very palatable, inexpensive, and calorie-dense foods nearly anywhere.

Compared to the 1970s, 600 more calories a day, on average, are available to eat. Bigger portions, served on bigger plates and in bigger cups, encourage many of these excess calories. *See "Portion Shift: How They've Changed" in chapter 3, page 79.*

Genetics and Family Influences

Genetics affect body weight too. Especially if conditions are right, genes may predispose someone to obesity. For example, people who inherit a "sluggish" metabolism are more likely to have a weight problem.

Family lifestyles, surroundings, and upbringing factor in as well, since family members typically share common eating and lifestyle habits. With one obese parent, the chances of being overweight are 40 percent; that doubles when both parents are obese. Some research suggests that overweight and obese mothers may be increasing an unborn baby's obesity risk. That said, you can manage your weight if others in your family have weight issues. But it may take some effort.

Hormones and Health Conditions

Several hormones appear to affect body weight. When out of balance, losing or maintaining weight is much harder. Among them:

- *Ghrelin,* the "hunger" hormone, secreted in your gut signals brain cells to stimulate your appetite. That also may drive emotional eating.
- *Leptin,* secreted by fat cells, signals satiety. Those who are overweight may be resistant to the satiety signal. Insulin resistance, a condition among many who are overweight or obese, can block the leptin signal. Insulin is a pancreatic hormone. Stimulated in part by weight loss and fitness, another hormone released from fat cells, called adiponectin, can partner with leptin to reverse insulin resistance.
- *Thyroxine,* the thyroid hormone, regulates your basal metabolic rate (BMR), or how fast your body burns calories. With hypothyroidism, the body lacks enough of this thyroid hormone, resulting in a slower metabolism, which in turn means your body requires fewer calories and you may gain weight.
- Hormones (cortisol produced in the adrenal glands) from prolonged or chronic stress may increase appetite and promote fat production and deposits, especially in the abdomen. Short-term stress, as a result, may increase your BMR; ongoing stress may slow it down to conserve energy. The role of chronic stress in weight is an area of research.

Other health factors, some genetically related, also are linked to weight gain, obesity, or problems with weight loss. These include certain health conditions, such as binge eating disorder, and Cushing's, polycystic ovary, and Prader-Willi syndromes. Some medications, such as anti-inflammatory steroid medications, may stimulate appetite, cause water retention, or affect your BMR. Check with your doctor.

Sleep Deprivation

Getting about seven-and-a-half or so hours of quality sleep daily is important. Sleep deprivation, according to current research, may lead to more body fat and may be a risk factor for obesity. Several reasons may factor in.

? Have you ever wondered?

. . . if my weight problem is really a thyroid problem? Often a thyroid problem is blamed for weight gain. But check with your doctor, who may order a test to find out and prescribe proper treatment. Hypothyroidism—when the thyroid gland doesn't produce enough of the hormone thyroxine—is the most common form of thyroid disease. One of the many symptoms is weight gain. Anyone can have an under active thyroid; among the risk factors: being a woman over age sixty, having an autoimmune disease, and having a family history of thyroid disease. Conversely, an overactive thyroid causes hyperthyroidism, perhaps resulting in weight loss despite increased appetite.

Good nutrition supports thyroid health. For example, iodine from iodized salt, seafood, and seaweed, and selenium from fish and organ meats help to make the thyroxine bioactive. *See "Have you ever wondered . . . if high blood cholesterol could be linked to a thyroid problem?" in chapter 24, page 683.*

. . . why it seemed easy to lose weight in your teens and twenties, and why it's so hard now? There could be several reasons—a less active lifestyle in adulthood, different eating habits, or physical changes in your body. Metabolism slows during each decade of your adult years.

Being sedentary is a contributing factor, too—if you lose muscle mass but gain body fat. The reason is that fat tissue requires fewer calories to maintain than muscle does. The remedy? Get moving again! Physical activity burns fat and can build muscle, making weight loss easier. Increased physical activity can boost the rate at which your body uses energy for your basic energy needs, too.

Sleeping less may result in eating more calories and snacking more for those who are awake longer. And if you're tired, you may not have the energy for physical activity. Sleep deprivation also affects hormones that regulate hunger and satiety. When you're tired, your body makes more ghrelin, the hormone that makes you feel hungry, and less leptin, a hormone that signals when you're full. When you feel hungry, it's easy to overeat. Being sleep deprived also may slow metabolism. That prompts a question: Because about one-quarter of women report sleep problems, could this be another link to midlife weight gain? Maybe.

Type 2 diabetes, cardiovascular disease, and lowered immunity, too, may be linked to not sleeping enough. Snooze enough, and stay tuned! *See "Have you ever wondered . . . why sleep is important to your health?" in chapter 1, page 5.*

Other Links to Weight Gain

Among other links to the obesity epidemic, mindless and emotional eating may result from uncontrolled anxiety and stress. Culture plays a role when higher-calorie foods are part of family and other social norms, and when food is frequently part of family traditions. Poverty—with possible links to poor and limited food choices—is associated with obesity, too, as is quitting smoking. *See "Have you ever wondered . . . why do people gain weight when they stop smoking?" in this chapter, page 644.*

Other reasons? Talk to your doctor if you're concerned about any unexplained weight gain. If you're treating a health condition with prescribed medication, don't stop; talk to your doctor to determine the cause and perhaps adjust medication. To refute a common misconception, birth control pills may cause some short-term water retention, but not weight gain.

OBESITY: THE RISKS

Spend an hour or so carrying around a five-pound bag of flour or a ten-pound bag of potatoes. Tiring? This will give you an idea of the extra burden on your body and heart when you carry excess pounds of body fat. The more you have, the greater that burden can be. Every body system—including the heart, the lungs, and the skeleton—has to work harder.

Obesity is defined as a chronic disease that needs medical attention. Many health problems, as well as premature death, are associated with obesity and perhaps overweight. That doesn't mean they're the cause, but the links are well recognized. *See chapters 24, page 679, and 25, page 721, for more about the links between excessive body weight and heart disease, type 2 diabetes, osteoarthritis, some cancers, and other health issues.*

Obesity can lead to a cycle of inactivity, which is in itself unhealthy. Often extra body weight makes physical activity more tiring—even for everyday activities such as walking upstairs or through a mall. Inactivity then can lead to more weight gain, more muscle loss, and many health risks.

The stigma of obesity can have emotional and social price tags, including poor self-esteem and social isolation. Although inequitable, prejudice, discriminatory practices, and assumptions of others, including employers and educators, can impact work and school opportunities, wages, relationships, and quality of life.

For America's youth, the epidemic of childhood overweight can affect their self-image and self-esteem, having an impact on almost every aspect of their lives, including school and friendships now—and well into adulthood. Often being less physically active, kids miss out on the benefits of regular exercise. Their chances of developing weight-related health problems—such as high blood cholesterol, high blood pressure, and type 2 diabetes—in childhood are higher. In the past, these conditions were primarily found among adults. *See "Growth and Weight" in chapter 17, page 501, for helping young people reach and maintain a healthy weight.*

See "A Closer Look . . . Healthy Weight Matters at Every Age and Stage of a Woman's Life" in chapter 18, page 540 and "Waist Management, Guys," in chapter 19, page 569, for the benefits of maintaining a healthy weight.

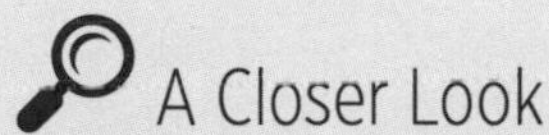

A Closer Look

Overweight and Obesity: Known Health Risks

Health Condition	How Is It Linked to Overweight and Obesity?	How Might Weight Loss Help if You're at Risk?
Type 2 diabetes *(see "Diabetes: A Growing Concern" in chapter 24, page 698)*	About 80 percent of people with type 2 diabetes are overweight or obese. Overweight may cause cells to become resistant to the hormone insulin. When someone is insulin resistant, blood glucose (sugar) cannot be taken up by body cells, resulting in high blood glucose. Cells that produce insulin must work extra hard to try to keep the blood glucose level normal. This may cause these cells to gradually fail.	If you are at risk, losing weight may help prevent or delay the onset of diabetes. If you have type 2 diabetes, losing weight and becoming more physically active can help you control your blood glucose levels and prevent or delay health problems. Losing weight and exercising more may also allow you to reduce the amount of diabetes medicine you take.
High blood pressure *(see "Blood Pressure: Under Control?" in chapter 24, page 693)*	Having a large body size may increase blood pressure because the heart needs to pump harder to supply blood to all body cells. Excess fat may also damage the kidneys, which help regulate blood pressure.	Weight loss that gets you close to the normal BMI range may greatly lower high blood pressure.
Heart disease *(see "Your Healthy Heart" in chapter 24, page 679)*	People who are overweight or obese may have increased heart disease risks: high blood pressure, high cholesterol, and high blood glucose. Excess weight also may cause changes to the heart that make it work harder to send blood to all body cells.	Losing 5 to 10 percent of your body weight may lower your chances of developing heart disease. Weight loss may improve blood pressure, cholesterol levels, and blood flow.
Stroke *(see "Your Healthy Heart" in chapter 24, page 679)*	Overweight and obesity increase blood pressure, the main cause of strokes. Excess weight also increases the chances of developing other problems linked to strokes, including high cholesterol, high blood glucose, and heart disease.	Losing weight may help you lower your blood pressure. It may also improve your cholesterol and blood glucose levels, which may then lower your risk for stroke.
Cancer—breast (after menopause), colon and rectum, endometrium (lining of the uterus), gallbladder, and kidney *(see "Cancer Connection" in chapter 24, page 713)*	Gaining weight as an adult increases the risk for several cancers, even if weight gain doesn't result in overweight or obesity. It isn't specifically known how being overweight increases cancer risk. Fat cells may release hormones that affect cell growth, leading to cancer. Eating or physical activity habits that may lead to overweight may also contribute to cancer risk.	Avoiding weight gain may prevent a rise in your cancer risk. Healthy eating and physical activity habits may lower your risk. Weight loss may also lower your risk, although studies have been inconclusive.
Sleep apnea	Obesity is the key risk factor for sleep apnea, or when breathing pauses one or more times during sleep. It has its own risks because it may cause daytime sleepiness, difficulty focusing, and even heart failure. An overweight person may have more fat stored around the neck. This may make the airway smaller. A smaller airway can make breathing difficult or loud (because of snoring), or breathing may stop altogether for short periods of time. Fat stored in the neck and throughout the body may produce substances that cause inflammation. Inflammation in the neck is a risk factor for sleep apnea.	Weight loss usually improves sleep apnea. Weight loss may help to decrease your neck size and lessen inflammation.

(continued)

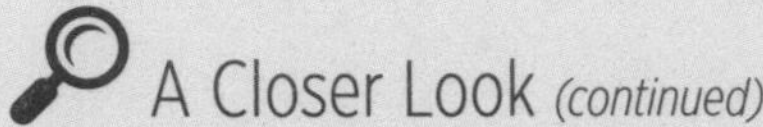

A Closer Look *(continued)*

Health Condition	How Is It Linked to Overweight and Obesity?	How Might Weight Loss Help if You're at Risk?
Osteoarthritis *(see "Arthritis: Getting Relief" in chapter 25, page 726)*	Being overweight is one of the risk factors for osteoarthritis, along with joint injury, older age, and genetic factors. Extra weight may place extra pressure on joints and cartilage (the hard but slippery tissue covering the ends of bones at a joint), causing them to wear away. People with more body fat may have higher blood levels of substances that cause inflammation. Inflamed joints may increase the risk for osteoarthritis.	Losing weight may help reduce the risk of developing osteoarthritis. Weight loss of at least 5 percent of your body weight may decrease stress on your knees, hips, and lower back and lessen inflammation in your body. If you have osteoarthritis, losing weight may help improve your symptoms. Exercise is one of the best treatments for osteoarthritis. Exercise can improve mood, decrease pain, and increase flexibility.
Fatty liver disease	The cause of fatty liver disease is still not known. The disease most often affects people who are middle-aged, overweight or obese, and/or diabetic. Fatty liver disease may also affect children.	With no specific treatment, those diagnosed with this disease are generally advised to lose weight, eat a healthy diet, increase physical activity, and avoid drinking alcoholic beverages. Lowering your body weight to a healthy range may improve your liver tests and reverse the disease somewhat.
Kidney disease	Obesity increases the risk of type 2 diabetes and high blood pressure, the most common causes of chronic kidney disease. Recent studies suggest that even in the absence of these risks, obesity itself may promote chronic kidney disease and quicken its progress.	In the early stages of chronic kidney disease, losing weight may slow the disease and keep your kidneys healthier longer. It's also important to choose foods with less salt (sodium), keep your blood pressure under control, and keep your blood glucose level in the target range.
Pregnancy problems—gestational diabetes, preeclampsia, needing a C-section (so taking longer to recover after giving birth) *(see "Diabetes and Pregnancy" and "Swelling: Part of Pregnancy" in chapter 18, pages 551 and 550)*	Pregnant women who are overweight are more likely to develop insulin resistance, high blood glucose, and high blood pressure. Being overweight also increases the risks associated with surgery and anesthesia, and severe obesity increases surgery time and blood loss. Gaining too much weight during pregnancy can have long-term effects for both mother and child. These effects include that the mother will be overweight or obese after the child is born. Another risk is that the baby may gain too much weight later as a child or as an adult. Babies of overweight or obese mothers are at an increased risk of being premature, being stillborn, or having neural tube defects.	If you are overweight or obese and would like to become pregnant, talk to your doctor about losing weight first. Reaching a normal weight before becoming pregnant may reduce your risks of weight-related problems. If you are pregnant and overweight or obese, talk to your doctor about limiting weight gain and being physically active during your pregnancy. Losing excess weight after delivery may help women reduce their health risks. For example, if a woman developed gestational diabetes, losing weight may lower the risk of diabetes later in life.

Adapted from source: National Institute of Diabetes and Digestive and Kidney Diseases/National Institutes of Health, www.niddk.nih.gov/health-information/health-topics/weight-control/health_risks_being_overweight/Pages/health-risks-being-overweight.aspx. Accessed December 1, 2016.

WEIGHT LOSS: IF ADVISED

Weight loss can reduce the risks of many health conditions for those considered obese or overweight. Whether you need to lose or maintain weight depends on your own risks for health problems, such as having heart disease or type 2 diabetes, and your age, gender, and ethnicity.

For those who would benefit from weight loss, the American College of Cardiology, American Heart Association, and The Obesity Society advise a sustained weight loss of 3 to 5 percent of body weight at a minimum to help improve the factors that increase the risk for some chronic diseases. Within six months, getting that up to 5 to 10 percent of weight loss is advised. For someone weighing 200 pounds, that's a loss of ten to twenty pounds. Slow and steady weight loss of up to two pounds per week is the safest way to lose weight.

If you are considered overweight or obese, that 5 to 10 percent of weight loss may improve your health and quality of life and may help you avoid or manage some health problems, such as high blood pressure, type 2 diabetes, high blood cholesterol, or arthritis.

Weight Cycling

Have you gained and lost the same ten, twenty, or even thirty pounds over and over again? Weight cycling is often an outcome of quick-fix diets, weight-loss gimmicks, and other risky strategies, and it may be a symptom of disordered eating, *described in "A Closer Look . . . Disordered Eating" in chapter 25, page 734.*

The cycle of repeatedly losing and regaining weight is common among many who go on weight-loss diets, not without possible consequences. It may lead to feelings of frustration, failure, and poor self-esteem. According to some studies, weight cycling may even increase the risk for ongoing health problems such as high blood pressure, high cholesterol levels, and gallbladder disease.

Most research indicates that weight cycling doesn't affect or lower your metabolic rate, according to the National Institutes of Health, Weight-Control Information Network. Most people return to their original weight if their activity level and calorie intake return to about the original levels, too. However, if someone is physically inactive, weight regain may result in a greater proportion of overall body fat.

If repeated "ups and downs" of dieting describe your weight, shift your approach to lifetime weight management, rather than short-term results. Make gradual and permanent changes in the way you eat, your physical activity level, and your lifestyle. It's the only way to be healthy—for life. *See "Reach SMART Goals One Step at a Time!" in chapter 1, page 18.*

Calories: A Matter of Balance

How do calories affect your weight? In principle, the answer may seem easy:

- *To maintain weight:* Balance the calories you consume from foods and beverages with calories expended.
- *For weight loss:* Consume fewer calories than you burn each day. To do that, cut back on calories in—and move more.
- *For weight gain:* Take in more calories than your body uses—and keep moving!

Calorie balance is about calories out (energy burned in physical activity) and calories in (energy consumed from foods and beverages). Your metabolic rate factors in, too.

CALORIES OUT: METABOLISM AND PHYSICAL ACTIVITY

Powering your body can be compared to fueling your car. Both need an energy source just to keep idling. When you move, your body (and your car) burns more fuel to go faster and farther. Like cars, some bodies are more fuel efficient than others, using less energy to do the same amount of work.

Metabolism: Energy for Body Basics

Energy for basal metabolism (basic needs) is the energy your body burns on "idle" to stay alive. In scientific terms, basal metabolic rate (BMR) is the energy level that keeps your involuntary processes going:

How Does Your Body Use Energy?

Your need for energy, or calories, never stops. Every minute of every day, your body needs a constant supply to stay alive and to function well.

If you're like most people, here's how your body uses the energy it "burns" each day:

Basic energy needs (basal metabolism)	60%
Physical activity (all movements)	30%
Digestion of food and absorption of nutrients	10%
Total energy use for the day	**100%**

Click Here!
Link to Know . . .

- Academy of Nutrition and Dietetics
www.eatright.org/resources/health/weight-loss
- Weight-control Information Network (WIN)
www.niddk.nih.gov/health-information/health-communication-programs/win

for example, pumping your heart, breathing, generating body heat, perspiring, transmitting brain messages, and producing thousands of body chemicals. For most people, basal metabolism represents about 60 percent of their energy needs.

Age, gender, genetics, and body composition and size, among other factors, affect the energy burn for these basic needs. The degree of "fuel efficiency" partly explains why one person can consume more calories day after day and never seem to gain a pound, while another of the same age, height, and activity level finds weight control a constant challenge.

Age. From infancy through adolescence, young people need more calories for their weight than adults do. That's not surprising since their bones, muscles, and other tissues are growing. During infancy, energy needs are higher per pound of body weight than at any other time in life. And watch a teenage boy eat; you know that his energy needs are high to fuel his growth spurt.

By adulthood, food energy (calorie) needs—and BMR—start to decline: about 2 to 3 percent for each decade. Body composition and hormones change with age. With less physical activity, muscle mass decreases; body fat may take its place. Because body fat burns less energy than muscle, fewer calories are needed to maintain body weight. This contributes to a slower metabolic rate, which can be counteracted partly with regular physical activity to help lessen muscle decline.

Genes. Genetic makeup and inherited body build account for some differences among people in their BMR—differences you can't change.

Body composition. A lean, muscular body has a higher metabolic rate than a softly rounded body with more fat tissue. Ounce for ounce, muscle burns more energy than body fat does. This means that at the same weight, people with lean, muscular bodies likely need more calories to function and maintain weight than people with a higher percentage of body fat. A softly rounded body type also has a greater tendency to store body fat than a lean, muscular body. *Tip:* Stay physically active to maintain your muscle mass—and give your BMR a slight boost.

Gender. The ratio of muscle to fat differs with gender, accounting for differences in BMRs, too. Up to age ten or so, energy needs for boys and girls are about the same, but puberty triggers change. As boys develop more muscle, they need more calories. Their added height and size demand more energy, too.

By adulthood, men usually have less body fat and 10 to 20 percent more muscle than women of the same age and weight. That's one reason why men's basic energy needs are higher. In contrast, women's bodies naturally keep body fat stores in reserve for pregnancy and breastfeeding, when a woman's energy needs go up.

Temperature. Outside temperature affects internal energy production. On chilly days, your BMR "burns" a little higher to keep you warm during prolonged exposure to cold. Shivering and moving to keep warm use energy, too. In hot temperatures, your body's air conditioning system burns a bit more energy, too—for example, as you perspire to cool down.

Diet factor. Very-low-calorie eating plans can make the body more energy efficient and slow your BMR. It's part of the body's survival mode, as it requires slightly fewer calories to perform the same processes.

Physical Activity: An Energy Burner

Movement of any kind—a blink of your eye, a wave of your hand, or a jog around the block—uses energy. In fact, about 30 percent of the energy your body uses powers all physical activity—not just what you do at the gym. At best, that estimate is imprecise because activity levels differ so much from person to person—and even by the same person from time to time.

Have you ever wondered?

. . . if chile peppers, or green tea or green coffee extracts can give your metabolism a boost? It's wishful thinking to hope that foods or drinks can speed up your metabolism or curb your appetite as claimed. Even if a food or drink could give a lift, it wouldn't be enough to offset the calories.

The Federal Trade Commission has dismissed fat-burning claims for green coffee extract as baseless and without scientific support. There's not enough evidence to rate the effect of green tea extract either.

. . . if knowing your BMR can help you lose weight? Not likely; it's not a weight-loss tool. (And to clarify: BMR isn't the same as BMI.) Eating enough nutrient-dense foods while limiting calories and modifying your lifestyle to burn more calories through physical activity are more important. Some people, perhaps athletes in training, may choose to monitor their BMR. If so, a health or fitness professional, especially a registered dietitian nutritionist, can help determine how.

Very active people need more calories, maybe 40 percent of their total energy intake, for physical activity.

The amount of energy to power physical activity actually depends on three things, often referred to as FIT: frequency (how often), intensity (how vigorous), and time (how long). Walking up stairs takes more calories than using an escalator. If you walk with a friend of the same age and body size, the one who pumps his or her arms and takes an extra lap around the block burns more energy for the same activity.

Digestion: An Energy Burner, Too

Eating itself actually burns calories, too. Digesting food and absorbing nutrients use about 10 percent of your day's energy expenditure—about 200 calories if you consume 2,000 calories daily. But don't count on these body processes as a miracle way to burn up all the energy in something you eat!

CALORIES IN: FOODS AND DRINKS

Many tools—food labels, calorie-counting books, apps, and websites—show that nearly all foods and drinks supply calories, some foods more than others. What accounts for the differences? Nutrient content—and portion size.

Carbohydrates, proteins, and fats (macronutrients), as well as alcohol, supply calories in foods and beverages. Gram for gram, fat and alcohol supply more than either carbohydrate or protein. Fats provide 9 calories per gram; alcohol, 7 calories per gram; and carbohydrates and proteins, each 4 calories per gram. Most foods provide a combination of macronutrients. Vitamins, minerals, and water don't provide calories. Neither does cholesterol.

A food's characteristics offer clues to its calorie density. Solid foods that are fibrous, watery, or watery-crisp, such as lettuce, celery, and watermelon, tend to have fewer calories and more volume than foods that are fatty or greasy-crisp, such as bacon and fried foods. For example, celery has more water and fiber and fewer calories than french fries do.

Calories: Myths or Truths

Myth: A rich, fudgy brownie before bedtime is more fattening than the same brownie eaten at lunchtime.

Truth: What you eat, not when, is the key issue. Weight gain from late-night snacking may come from eating out of habit, boredom, or stress—not hunger—and from eating more calories than you realize. To avoid late-night snacking, eat dinner a little later, skip TV snacks, save dessert for later, or go to bed earlier. That said, there's nothing wrong with a light, nourishing snack in the evening—if the calories fit into your calorie budget.

Another consideration: Limited research suggests that the body may store more calories as fat at night when cortisol levels tend to be somewhat higher; so far, the jury's still out. Cortisol is a body hormone, which may promote fat production and deposits. Also your BMR slows down a bit as you sleep at night.

Myth: Potatoes and bread are fattening.

Truth: By themselves, they're not high in calories—134 calories for a small potato and 70 calories for an average-size slice of bread. However, the calories in high-fat toppings or spreads can add up. Consider the calories in one tablespoon of sour cream (about 30 calories), butter or stick margarine (about 100 calories), and regular mayonnaise (about 100 calories).

Myth: Skip nuts for weight loss.

Truth: A small portion (an ounce or two) of nuts can take the edge off hunger. Enjoy them in small amounts for their healthy oils, protein, fiber, and magnesium. Be prudent: a half ounce (small handful) of mixed nuts has about 84 calories. If a bowl of nuts is within arm's reach, being prudent may not be easy!

Myth: Going vegetarian is a sure way to lose weight.

Truth: Not necessarily. Although a vegetarian eating plan is often lower in calories, cutting out meat, poultry, and dairy foods won't automatically mean fewer calories. Even vegetarians can overeat—with excessive portions and too many high-calorie foods. *See "The Healthy Vegetarian Way" in chapter 2, page 53, for guidelines.*

Myth: Carbs cause weight gain.

Truth: Excess calories from any source are the issue: carbohydrates, proteins, and fats. Limited research notes that carbohydrate-rich foods may promote weight gain in insulin-resistant people. For these individuals, it's speculated that the body reacts to sugars and starches by overproducing insulin—and so causes too much carbohydrate to be stored as fat. However, most people don't gain weight on a high-carbohydrate diet unless it provides excess calories. And most only lose on a low-carb diet because they restrict calories, too. *See "A Closer Look . . . Metabolic Syndrome" in chapter 24, page 686, for more about insulin resistance.*

Myth: Some foods—celery, lettuce, and watermelon—have negative calories.

Truth: It's enticing to think that some foods burn more calories to chew, digest, and absorb than they actually contain, but no valid studies support this claim. And these foods still have some calories. You can't hope that eating unlimited amounts will melt away pounds. That said, being low in calories and high in fiber, with water at more than ninety percent by weight, makes these good food choices on a weight loss diet.

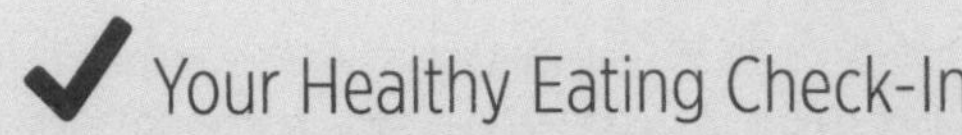

Your Healthy Eating Check-In

What About Weight Change?

Your attitude affects your ability to succeed at weight loss—and weight management. If you need to drop a few pounds, you'll be more successful if you're mentally ready before you begin.

Mark each statement as "yes" or "no" for you. Answer the way you really think—not how you'd like to think!

	Yes	No
1. I have thought a lot about my eating habits and physical activities. I know what I might change.	☐	☐
2. I know that I need to make permanent, not temporary, changes in how I eat and get exercise.	☐	☐
3. I will feel successful only if I lose a lot of weight.	☐	☐
4. I know that it's best if I lose weight slowly.	☐	☐
5. I'm thinking about losing weight now because I want to, not because someone else thinks I should.	☐	☐
6. I think losing weight would solve other problems in my life.	☐	☐
7. I am willing and able to increase my regular physical activity.	☐	☐
8. I can lose weight successfully if I have no slip-ups.	☐	☐
9. I am willing to commit time and effort each week to organize and plan my food and activity choices.	☐	☐
10. Once I lose a few pounds but reach a plateau (I can't seem to lose more), I usually lose the motivation to keep going.	☐	☐
11. I want to start a weight-loss program even though my life is unusually stressful right now.	☐	☐

SCORE YOURSELF

For items 1, 2, 4, 5, 7, and 9, score "1" point if you answered "yes" and "0" if you answered "no." For items 3, 6, 8, 10, and 11, score "0" for each "yes" answer and "1" point for each "no" answer. The higher your total score, the more likely you'll be successful at weight loss.

8 points or higher: You probably have good reasons to lose weight now. And you know some steps to success.

5 to 7 points: Reevaluate your reasons for losing weight and the strategies you'd follow.

4 points or less: Now may not be the right time to start. You may succeed initially, but you may not sustain the effort to reach or maintain your goal weight. Reconsider your reasons and approach.

INTERPRET YOUR ANSWERS

Your answers give clues to stumbling blocks to your weight management success. Any item you scored as "0" suggests a misconception about weight loss or a problem area for you. Look at each item more closely.

1. You can't change what you don't know. That includes eating and physical activity habits. Keep records for a week to pinpoint when, what, why, and how much you eat—and move. Track obstacles, too.
2. Your food and activity plans should be healthy ones that you can enjoy and sustain. Highly restrictive changes in eating habits or intense physical activity don't lead to permanent, healthy weight loss.
3. Many people fantasize about reaching a weight goal that's unrealistically low. Sound like you? Then rethink your meaning of success. A reasonable goal takes body type into consideration.

Your Healthy Eating Check-In *(continued)*

4. "Quick-fix" approaches often backfire when faced with the challenges of keeping weight off. The best and healthiest approach is slow—with small, achievable "mile markers" along the way, while learning ways to change habits for life.
5. A desire for and commitment to weight loss must come from within you. Long-term success comes by taking responsibility for weight goals and choosing your own approach.
6. While body image and self-esteem are strongly linked, thinking you can solve social problems by losing weight may set you up for disappointment. Being overweight is rarely the single cause.
7. Regular, moderate physical activity is key to successfully losing weight—and keeping it off. It doesn't need to be strenuous. Just enjoy it and do it regularly.
8. Perfection in following a weight-loss strategy isn't realistic. Instead of seeing lapses as catastrophes, view them as opportunities to learn what triggers your lapses and develop strategies to handle them.
9. Success requires planning, commitment, and time. Take time to assess your challenges, then develop an approach that's best for you.
10. A plateau is perfectly normal—don't give up too soon! Think about past efforts that failed, then identify strategies to help overcome hurdles.
11. Try to resolve other life stressors first if possible. And try to keep from eating for stress relief. Know that regular physical activity may help you manage stress.

Weight Management: Strategies That Work!

Trying to lose weight to fit into a bathing suit before vacation or to look good for your class reunion? Short-term motivation generally doesn't lead to long-term results.

The key to managing your weight is lifetime food and lifestyle changes, a positive attitude, knowledge of calories and food, and sensible strategies for calorie control. Internal motivators—health, increased energy, self-esteem, and feeling in control—increase your chances for lifelong success.

Whether for weight loss, gain, or maintenance, an effective plan requires healthy eating, regular physical activity, and being realistic about the weight you can achieve—in a healthy way, *as discussed throughout this book*. Keeping your healthy weight over time is better, even easier, than trying to lose weight after you gain.

If your weight is excessive, and especially if you have health problems, talk to your doctor before starting a weight-loss plan. Children, pregnant women, people with chronic diseases, and those over age sixty-five shouldn't attempt weight loss without advice from their doctor.

Weight-Loss Plan: Check It Out!

Ready to start a healthy and effective weight-control plan? Before you begin, ask yourself if the approach includes:

- A variety of foods from all the food groups and in the right amounts (enough, not too much)? (*See chapter 2, page 21, for guidance.*)
- Appealing foods you will enjoy eating for the rest of your life, not just a few weeks or months?
- Foods that are available where you usually shop?
- Flexibility with the chance to eat your favorite foods—in fact, any foods—in reasonable amounts?
- Eating strategies that fit your lifestyle and budget?
- Enough regular physical activity?

More "yes" answers indicate a weight-loss program you'll more likely stay with. Weight loss and maintenance can happen with healthy, permanent changes in your eating and physical activity habits.

1. CONSIDER YOUR CALORIE TARGET AND PERSONAL HEALTH

Eating for weight control and good health are one and the same: a varied and balanced food plan, partnered with regular physical activity, that follows a healthy food pattern at a calorie target that's right for you.

Personal health. Your personal health, family health history, and genetics should be factored in as you set a weight-loss and daily calorie target.

Calorie target. To set a calorie target for weight loss or maintenance:

- Start by estimating how many calories your body uses, on average, in a day. You'll figure this based on your age, gender, and level of physical activity. *See "How Many Calories? Figuring Your Energy Needs" in the appendix, page 771, to learn how.*

  Or use the Body Weight Planner from the National Institute of Health, an online tool to figure the calories and physical activity you need to reach your weight goal. It's meant for adults aged eighteen years or older, but not for women who are pregnant or breastfeeding. Visit www.niddk.nih.gov/health-information/health-topics/weight-control/body-weight-planner/pages/bwp.aspx/.
- To lose weight, consume less. Reducing calorie intake by 500 to 750 calories daily from your usually intake is recommended.

  Caution: Very-low-calorie diets with less than 800 calories daily are recommended only when deemed medically necessary and must be medically supervised.

For weight loss, there's no one dietary approach, as long as you hit your calorie target for weight loss and the amount of carbohydrate, protein, and fat in your overall food and drink choices fit within the recommended range (Acceptable Macronutrient Distribution Ranges), *noted in the appendix, page 780*. But don't short-change yourself on protein. The fewer calories you consume overall, the greater the percentage of calories that should come from protein. Along with weight-bearing physical activity, you need enough protein as you lose weight to retain your muscle mass.

Gone: The "3,500-Calorie Rule"

You probably heard this weight-loss advice in the past: "A pound of body fat adds up to 3,500 calories. So to lose one pound in seven days, eat 500 calories less a day (or burn 500 calories more a day). Keep it up every week for six months (about twenty-six weeks), and you'll lose twenty-six pounds." Problem is: It probably won't happen.

A weight-loss trajectory isn't that simple. While this rule-of-thumb may work for short-term weight loss and dropping just a few pounds, it's not effective advice over time. It may overestimate the rate and amount of weight loss that can be achieved. Today, experts recognize metabolic and genetic differences among people. Even your own metabolic rate may change over time as your body changes. That needs to be factored in.

Bottom line: Weight loss is generally slower than the old "3,500-calorie rule" suggests. The online Body Weight Planner, *referred to above*, can more accurately help you project long-term weight loss.

2. COMMIT TO ACTIVE LIVING

Move it to lose it! Physical activity is an important strategy for weight management. Although less efficient for weight loss, physical activity is important for maintaining muscle mass and promoting fat loss on a weight-loss regimen, and preventing weight gain once you reach your goal. Calories burned are as important as calories consumed. You don't need to be an exercise fanatic. However, you may need to modify your lifestyle to move more and sit less.

Daily Goal for Physical Activity

As advised by the National Institutes of Health, make physical activity a regular habit for a healthy weight:

- To manage body weight and prevent gradual weight gain, aim for at least 150 minutes (2 hours and 30 minutes) of moderate-intensity aerobic activity or 75 minutes (1 hour and 15 minutes) of vigorous-intensity aerobic activity each week. Or a combination of both.
- To lose weight, and keep it off you may need to boost your level of physical activity further. *See "Moderate Activity: What Is It?" in chapter 1, page 18.*

Quick Tips to Move More

Any moderate, consistent physical activity that you enjoy and stay with is a benefit. But fit in cardiovascular activities, strength-training, and core activities, too. You can boost your "calorie burn" with physical activity in three ways—longer, more frequent, and more intense:

- Do it all at once, or spread it out. For example, for moderate activity, ten minutes of brisk walking during your lunch hour, fifteen minutes of leisure bike riding after supper, and five minutes of sidewalk sweeping at home. That's already thirty minutes.
- Fit in muscle-building activities at least twice weekly: legs, hips, back, chest, stomach, shoulders, and arms. For kids, three times weekly for these activities is advised.
- If you haven't been physically active, then build up gradually. Even a little more physical activity—and a little less TV and computer time—can make a difference.
- Step it up. Get a pedometer to count your steps; work up to 10,000 steps a day. Find ways to be more active throughout the day: walk

Physical Activity: Matters

An active lifestyle is key to calorie balance. Study after study shows that those who keep physically active are more successful at managing their weight and keeping off extra pounds of body fat. Among the reasons why physical activity promotes a healthy weight:

- *Burns calories.* The longer, more frequently, and more vigorously you move, the more calories you burn. When you burn more than you consume, your body uses its energy stores, and you lose weight. Adding just thirty minutes of brisk walking to your day can make a difference!
- *Helps keep and build muscle, and lose body fat.* Without physical activity, you tend to lose lean body tissue when you eat fewer calories. Muscle burns more calories at rest.
- *Helps relieve stress and promote better sleep.* Stress may lead to the production of the hormone cortisol, noted earlier, which may promote fat production and deposits, and nibbling and consuming more calories than your body needs. *See "Sleep Deprivation" in this chapter, page 629, for links between sleep and body weight.*
- *Creates a "trimmer" mind-set.* As people get more physically active, they often opt for foods with fewer calories, less fat, and less added sugars, too.
- *Feels good.* A firm, lean body from physical activity feels stronger and trimmer, even at the same weight. Think of your body as a "package" of lean tissue and body fat; muscles take less space than body fat.

Weight control is just one reason to keep physically active. A physically active lifestyle offers many more rewards—from heart health to strong bones to stress relief and more. *See "Ten Reasons to Get Up and Move" in chapter 1, page 17.*

? Have you ever wondered?

. . . if you can lose weight in the problem places by spot exercising or reducing? Even though some weight-loss regimens make those promises, your body can't get rid of fat in just the problem spots. Abdominal crunches alone won't help you lose weight around your stomach—but it can help firm your muscles. As you exercise and burn more calories than you consume, your body draws energy from all its fat stores, including the problem spots.

while you talk on the phone, take an extra lap around the block when you walk the dog, and get up and move during TV commercials.

- Keep a log of your active minutes each week to stay accountable to yourself and hit your daily and weekly goals.

See "Physical Activity Guidelines for Americans" in the appendix, page 769, for more tips.

3. ADOPT AND STAY WITH A HEALTHY EATING PLAN

Single foods aren't "fattening." It's the calories in your total diet that matter. So what makes up a healthy eating plan for weight loss or weight maintenance? Can it provide the nutrients your body needs, within your calorie target? How can you stick with it?

First, make sure the plan is right and realistic for you by taking into account your overall health, family health history, genetics, food preferences, and more. It also needs to be sustainable in the long run—and not leave you feeling hungry, deprived, or food obsessed. *See "Reaching SMART Goals, One Step at a Time!" in chapter 1, page 18.*

Should it be low carb, low fat, or something else? Any approach with a calorie-intake deficit can result in weight loss. The important factor is this: It should deliver enough food variety with enough nutrient-dense foods and fewer calories than you eat now without compromising the nutrients needed for your overall good health. Remember that when you alter the amount of one macronutrient, you need to change others, too, to reach your calorie goal. Find what works for you.

Eating Plan for Healthy Weight

Follow advice from any one of the USDA Healthy Eating Patterns, as well as the DASH diet, at your target calorie level. *See chapter 2, page 21, for guidance, and the appendix, page 769, for recommended food group amounts for your calorie target.* Planning promotes success:

- Eat enough whole-grain foods, vegetables, and fruits. Being high in fiber and usually low in calories, they help you feel full faster. *Bonus:* These foods may take more time to chew, which may help you eat less.
- Fit lean protein foods, including lean meat, poultry, fish, eggs, and/or beans and peas, into each meal and perhaps snacks. Protein is satiating, so it may deter overeating. Along with physical activity, protein also helps preserve muscle as you cut back on calories. *See chapter 12, page 373, for more about protein.*
- Choose low-fat or fat-free dairy foods. Switching from whole to fat-free milk saves 80 calories per eight ounces, without changing the amounts of milk's other nutrients.
- Limit calories from solid fats (saturated and *trans* fats) and added sugars—small amounts, less often—since they contribute to your overall calorie intake. *See chapters 11, page 345, and 13, page 385, to learn about food sources for added sugars and fats.*

Twenty Ways to Move More

Fitting physical activity into your life may be easier than you think—even if you lead a busy life. These everyday activities count toward your day's total if they're done with moderate intensity. Most take only a little extra time. Fit activity in ten minutes at a time.

1. Start or end the day with a brisk walk. To keep yourself going, recruit your spouse, friend, or neighbor to join you. If you have an infant, use a baby carrier on your back as you walk. Or get a stroller you can gently push as you walk or run.
2. Make more of your commute. Walk or bike if you can. Or if you take mass transit, get off a stop ahead and walk the rest of the way. Walk or pedal a bike around your neighborhood, to visit a friend, or to do errands—if it's safe to do.
3. Use a standing desk. Or replace your desk chair with a stability ball. Neither may result in more calories burned, but both will strengthen muscles and perhaps improve your posture.
4. Ask others for walking meetings. Walk to talk personally with coworkers, rather than communicate by computer or cell phone.
5. Give yourself at least a five-minute activity break for every hour or two of computer time: walk to the water fountain or go up and down a few flights of stairs.
6. Walk around your building—outside or inside—during your lunch or work break. Join a work or mall walking club. It may boost your mood and help you relieve work stress, too. If the area isn't safe, do living room exercises.
7. Keep your sneakers and workout clothes in the car or at work. You'll be prepared when you have unexpected free time for a brisk walk or a quick workout.
8. Download a playlist of music to pump up your cardio workout. Or tune in to an online or YouTube workout.
9. Use the fitness club (if you've paid for it) or the one at your worksite if provided. Or use the athletic courts, pool, or walking trails in your local park. Your tax dollars paid for them, too.
10. Get a dog—walk and play. No dog? "Borrow" a neighbor's dog. Some dogs like to play with a Frisbee as much as kids do!
11. Take up gardening. (*Bonus:* Grow fresh vegetables and herbs if you can.) In the fall, rake leaves.
12. Play actively with your kids or grandkids. Shoot hoops. Play catch. Have fun.
13. Do household hobbies or projects as you watch television, such as refinishing furniture.
14. Catch up with household chores: wash the windows, reorganize a closet, sweep the floor or sidewalk, clean the garage or basement, or fix a fence. Forget the drive-through car wash. Wash the car yourself. *Bonus:* You'll save money, too.
15. Use exercise equipment you already own. Multitask: ride your exercise bike while you watch the morning news or read a book. Download a favorite TV show onto your notebook device to watch while you work out on the treadmill. Or work out as you listen to a podcast or audiobook.
16. If you're fit, push the lawn mower instead of using the power-assisted drive, and shovel snow by hand instead of relying on a snow blower.
17. Make homemade bread. Knead the dough by hand, not with a food processor or mixer.
18. Skip the movies. Go dancing instead!
19. Plan active family vacations or outings, perhaps canoeing, hiking, or snow skiing. Do active water sports at the beach or pool, rather than sunbathe.
20. Volunteer for a cause. Many local initiatives have built-in physical activity: community cleanup, scouting, coaching, and building homes (such as Habitat for Humanity).

- Limit sugary drinks and alcoholic beverages. Their calories can add up. Strong evidence shows that young people who consume more sugar-sweetened beverages also have higher body weights. That's also an issue for adults.

  Alcoholic drinks—wine, beer, spirits, and other alcoholic drinks—are top calorie contributors for many adults. Downing a six-pack of beer on a hot summer day can add up to 900 calories! Splitting a one-liter bottle of wine can supply 360 calories or more. Drinking alcoholic beverages also can stimulate your appetite (and lower your inhibitions), so you may eat more. *See "Alcoholic Beverages: In Moderation" in chapter 4, page 102.*

Eating Habits for Success

Everyday habits make a difference:

- Start your day with breakfast. Studies indicate that those who do have a lower BMI. However, evidence doesn't show that eating breakfast results in more weight loss. *See "Beating Breakfast Barriers" in chapter 3, page 64, for breakfast tips.*

- "Make over" higher-calorie foods that you eat often to cut calories and make them healthier. Take cooking classes, or hire a personal chef, to teach you if needed. *See "Culinary Know-How: Flavor Plus Health" in chapter 8, page 246, for kitchen nutrition help.*
- Remember that snacks count. Figure them into your healthy eating plan.
- Control your surroundings. Keep higher-calorie foods "out of sight, so out of mind."
- Skip the notion of "never." Instead, learn to occasionally fit small amounts of indulgent foods you like into your plan. Sticking to your weight-loss or maintenance plan is easier if you don't totally deprive yourself. Besides, no one food can make you fat. It's your total calorie intake over several days that counts.
- Keep your day's calorie target in mind as you choose foods and drinks. Nutrition Facts on food labels show the approximate calories in a label serving. *Remember:* A serving isn't necessarily the whole package. *See "Nutrition: Fact Check!" in chapter 6, page 148, to learn more about reading labels.*

  A calorie counter is a useful tool for finding or comparing foods. Two handy sources: a calorie counter app on a handheld device to scan barcodes, or an online tool to find nutrition information on thousands of foods: www.supertracker.usda.gov/foodapedia.aspx.
- Ask a registered dietitian nutritionist for more weight-loss help.

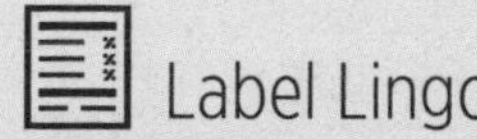

Label Lingo

Calories

Nutrition Facts on the food label list the calories in a single serving. In addition, "calorie lingo" on the package can alert you to lower-calorie food products as you search supermarket displays.

Label Term . . .	Means . . .
CALORIE-FREE	Contains fewer than 5 calories
LOW-CALORIE	Contains 40 calories or fewer
REDUCED OR FEWER CALORIES	Contains at least 25 percent fewer calories*
LIGHT OR LITE	Contains one-third fewer calories or 50 percent less fat*; if more than half the calories are from fat, fat content must be reduced by 50 percent or more
LOW-CALORIE MEALS	Contains 120 calories or fewer per 100 grams
LIGHT MEAL	"Low-fat"† or "low-calorie" meal

*As compared with a standard serving size of the regular food.

†A "low-fat meal" contains 3 grams or less fat per 100 grams and 30 percent or fewer calories from fat per serving.

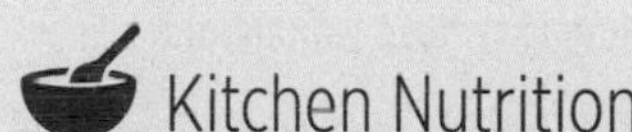

Kitchen Nutrition

Sweet Snacks, Fewer Calories

Next time you crave a sweet snack, make your calories count for more. Reach for fruit! Besides satisfying a taste for sweets, fruit is packed with nutrients and phytonutrients—and delivers fiber, too.

- *Frozen bananas.* Push a wooden stick into half of a peeled banana. Roll it in yogurt or give it a light coating of chocolate syrup, then roll it in crunchy cornflakes. Wrap and freeze.
- *Frozen chips.* Slice bananas into thin rounds. Spread them flat on a baking sheet. Cover and freeze. Serve frozen as a fun snack. (The same technique works for seedless grapes or berries.)
- *Fruit mix.* Mix a zipper-top bag of dried fruits of your choice: apple slices, apricots, blueberries, cherries, cranberries, pear slices, and raisins, among others.
- *Fruit pops.* For a nutritious fruit pop, pour pureed fruit (apricot, mango, papaya) or fruit juice into ice cube trays or paper cups. Place a craft stick in each "pop." Freeze.

Eat What You Crave

Restricting food choices too much may "feed" a so-called food craving—and set you up to overindulge!

A strong desire for certain foods may be physiological, psychological, or both. Perhaps it's linked to a physical need to resupply the body with nutrients it lacks. Or maybe it's psychological, reinforced by positive emotional and social links to certain foods.

What's the best way to handle a food craving? Studies suggest that avoiding certain foods altogether often makes them more irresistible. And giving in to an irresistible food may lead to overeating it. Then guilt creeps in. Trying to resist those foods once again may only lead to overindulging and feeling guilty again. A better approach? Eat a small, infrequent portion of a food you enjoy—even if it's higher in calories.

Even when you're trying to shed pounds, you can enjoy some high-calorie foods if your overall meals and snacks are healthy and you eat fewer calories than your body uses. Another option: try to satisfy your palate with a low-calorie version.

? Have you ever wondered?

. . . if drinking a glass of water before a meal can help you lose weight? Maybe. Although it's not a magic weight-loss beverage, it has no calories. Whether it affects satiety isn't clear since body mechanisms for hunger and thirst are separate. However, if you feel fuller after drinking water, you may take in fewer calories. That said, foods with a high water content such as vegetables, fruits, and soups may increase short-term satiety and so lead to consuming fewer calories. Give them a try!

. . . if the glycemic index is a useful tool for a weight-loss diet? The glycemic index (GI) measures how individual foods affect blood glucose levels. But it's not easily applied to the total diet or to weight loss. Choosing carbohydrate foods and drinks with a low GI isn't effective for weight loss, according to strong research evidence. Currently there is no standard definition for a low-glycemic index or low-glycemic load diet. *See "A Closer Look . . . Glycemic Index" in chapter 11, page 351.*

. . . if skipping a meal can jumpstart weight loss? Weight loss is all about creating an energy deficit—ingesting fewer calories than your body expends each day—but creating a calorie deficit that's too large can backfire. Because your body is programmed for survival, severely limiting calories can make your body think it's entering a famine and that it needs to do more with fewer calories. Your body adapts and uses fewer calories to perform the same tasks. *Bottom line:* meal skipping offers no real benefit.

. . . if low-fat and low-carb foods are low calorie, too? Neither one means "low calorie." Fat may be replaced with carbs, and vice versa. Either way, these foods may be similar in their calorie amounts to regular versions (or to each other), or have even more. Read the Nutrition Facts on the label to find out.

. . . if you should skip salad dressing to keep your salad "low cal"? While it may sound counterintuitive, the oil in your salad dressing is healthy—just "dress lightly." The fat-soluble vitamins (A, D, E, and K) in salad ingredients—carrots, kale, tomatoes, and more—only get absorbed if fat is present.

Need specific strategies to be more portion savvy?

Check here for "how-tos":

- Size up your servings; *see "Visual Guide to Portion Size" in chapter 2, page 24.*
- Be aware of portion size; *see "Portions: Be Size Wise!" in chapter 3, page 78.*
- Control restaurant portions; *see "Control Your Restaurant Portions" in chapter 9, page 279.*

4. GET PORTION SAVVY

Smaller portions mean fewer calories, so keep tabs on portion sizes to manage calories in. Even lower-calorie foods can add up to a hefty calorie count when portions get big. Portions that are just ten to twenty percent smaller than usual can add up to calorie savings!

How portion savvy are you? Without using a measuring cup, try pouring one cup of dry cereal—or scooping a half cup of ice cream—into a bowl. Now check the size with a measuring cup. Chances are, you've overestimated. Most people do. That's one reason why many people innocently overdo on calories. To ensure proper portions:

- Eat from plates, not packages. When you nibble chips or crackers from a package or snack on ice cream from the carton, you may not know how much you've eaten. It may be more—much more—than you think!
- Plate your food in the kitchen—no serving bowls at the table—to control the amounts.
- Get instant portion control with smaller bowls and dinner plates. Then smaller portions look like more.
- Replace large portions of higher-calorie foods, such as fries and sugary desserts, with lower-calorie foods, such as raw vegetables and fruits.
- Put leftovers away before eating to remove temptation.

The "Eating Patterns, *2015–2020 Dietary Guidelines for Americans*" *in the appendix, page 771*, provide food group guidelines in household measures. Use measuring cups and spoons, and perhaps a kitchen scale, to see how your helpings fit within the total food group recommendations for the day, or with serving sizes listed on the Nutrition Facts of food labels. *See "Portions: Be Size Wise!" in chapter 3, page 78.*

5. EAT MORE MINDFULLY

Examine your eating habits. Do you eat—perhaps often without thinking—to quickly get on with your day? Do you nibble unconsciously as you watch TV or work at your computer? If so, shift your food behavior to eat with the positive intention of discovering what and how to eat to feel well, not just to lose weight. You'll likely eat less—and enjoy your meals and snacks more if you do.

Mindful eating changes what you eat, and perhaps when and how. It may be more effective for calorie control than focusing simply on calories. To switch from mindless to mindful eating:

- Pause before reaching for food. Ask yourself: Am I hungry or thirsty? Is this food or drink worth the calories? Does it meet my physical needs—or emotions?

- Make eating your only event—do one thing at a time—and enjoy it. Eating when distracted by watching television, talking on the phone, or driving may lead to more food or drinks than you think. If you do eat as you watch TV, portion out just a small serving.
- Sit down to eat rather than nibble while you do other things or stand at the counter. Focus on your food so you know that you've eaten.
- Stop eating after you leave the table. Avoid the urge to nibble on leftovers as you clean up.
- Consciously choose foods that take more time to eat. For example, peeling and eating an orange takes longer than drinking a glass of orange juice.
- Other mindful strategies: Plan to prepare your own meals more often so that you're in control of the calories. When you eat out, consider the calories before ordering.

See "Eating: Mindless or Mindful?" in chapter 3, page 78, for more tips.

6. LISTEN TO YOUR BODY SIGNALS

Learn your body's signals for fullness and real hunger. This too is part of mindful eating:

- Eat when you're hungry; stop when you're satisfied, not full. For get the "clean-plate club." You don't need to "polish the plate" if you're already satisfied. Take less food from the start to avoid waste.
- Eat slowly. Savor the flavor of each bite. Put down your fork between bites. Swallow before refilling your fork. Eat with chopsticks if they slow you down. Take a sip of water between bites. Sip, rather than gulp, beverages. Remember, it takes about twenty minutes for your stomach to signal your brain that you're full—which curbs your urge for seconds.
- Plan nourishing meals and snacks ahead. Haphazard eating often becomes high-calorie eating. Being stuck in a food rut may not be mindful, either.
- When you get the urge to nibble (especially if you're not hungry), do something else.
- Try to be mindful about a regular eating schedule. (There's no hard-and-fast rule about eating three meals a day.) Missed meals may lead to impulsive snacking and overeating when you're hungry and may lower the rate at which your body burns energy.

7. OVERCOME EATING TRIGGERS

You have the best intentions. Then something triggers "food"—even though you're not hungry. Maybe it's the bell of the ice cream truck, the sight of cookies on the table, the aroma of popcorn at a movie theater, or simply plopping down in front of the TV, or feeling stressed.

Research indicates that habitually overeating in response to food cues, or being susceptible to them, is linked to weight gain. Whatever your triggers, be aware of the situations and emotions that lead to eating or drinking. And find mindful outcomes or alternatives:

- Keep a food log for a week or two to track what prompted a trigger or urge for a food or drink.
- Be aware of the influence of others. You don't need to eat the cake, muffins, or cookies in the break room just because your officemate brought them. Nor do you need to eat the dry snacks served at happy-hour meetings.
- Learn to differentiate between physical hunger and emotionally driven hunger, perhaps from boredom or stress. Instead of looking inside the fridge or diving into a bowl of snacks, divert your attention. Jog, call or text a friend, walk the dog, step out into your garden, or play with your kids.
- Accomplished something special? Reward yourself, but not with food. Treat yourself to a massage. Buy something new to wear or read. Or go to a play, concert, or sports event.
- Watch out for seasonal triggers: perhaps nibbling while watching fall and winter sports on television, "cooling off" in hot weather with a few beers or an extra-large soft drink, or eating a lot during the holidays.
- *Remember:* Out of sight, out of mind. If the sight of candy, chips, and other high-calorie foods lures you, store them in an inconvenient place such as on higher shelves or in the freezer. Store food in opaque containers to reduce temptation. Keep fresh fruit on the counter in a pretty container to encourage eating it.
- Shop on a full stomach to help avoid the temptation to buy extra goodies (including snacks at the checkout counter) or to nibble on free samples. Write your shopping list when you're not hungry.

Emotional Overeating: Take Control!

To relax, quell anger, or overcome depression or loneliness, mood-triggered eating may feel good—at first. But eating to cope with emotions can lead to more negative feelings (guilt, lack of personal control, and poor self-esteem) and perhaps to a cycle of mood-triggered eating and excessive calorie intake. Also important, using food to satisfy emotions may distract you from handling serious life issues.

On the plus side, learning to control mood-triggered eating promotes feelings of personal power and self-esteem. Learn to deal with emotions in a positive, appropriate way. Address the real problems. Resolve your moods with positive self-talk or a brief change of scenery. Compared with nibbling, physical activity—perhaps a brisk walk, bike ride, or tennis game—is a great stress buster!

? Have you ever wondered?

. . . why some people gain weight when they stop smoking? First, when smokers quit, they may feel hungry. Generally this lasts only for the first few weeks. Second, they may snack or consume more alcoholic drinks after they stop. Third, now as nonsmokers, they may burn slightly fewer calories during the day; smoking makes the body temporarily burn calories faster. For those who do gain weight, the average gain is about ten pounds.

Weight gain keeps some smokers from quitting. To limit weight gain, or better yet, help keep those ten pounds off, work with a registered dietitian nutritionist to work out a plan to reduce weight gain without undermining your plan to quit smoking. One quick tip: take a walk instead of lighting a cigarette.

Kitchen Nutrition

Celebration Meals Go Lean!

Celebration menus—or almost any meal—may be modified to lower the calories by trimming portions and cutting back on added sugars or high-fat sauces. Often differences go almost unnoticed. Compare this traditional menu with its lower-calorie version. *See "Culinary Know-How: Flavor Plus Health" and "Recipe Makeovers: Healthier, Easier" in chapter 8, pages 246 and 236, for ways to prepare healthy meals and snacks.*

Original Menu	Lower-Calorie Menu
3½ oz. roasted turkey with skin	3½ oz. skinless, roasted turkey
½ cup stuffing	½ cup wild rice pilaf
½ cup broccoli with 2 Tbsp. hollandaise sauce	½ cup broccoli topped with grated lemon peel
½ cup cranberry relish	¼ cup cranberry relish
1 medium crescent roll	1 whole-grain roll
1 slice pecan pie	1 slice pumpkin pie
Total calories: 1,140	**Total calories: 735**

8. HAVE A PARTY PLAN

Enjoying parties, holiday meals, and work events doesn't need to derail healthy food habits. And depriving yourself of special holiday or party foods, or feeling guilty when you do enjoy them, is neither a healthy strategy nor part of the spirit of getting together.

Beyond that, trying to lose weight during the holidays may be self-defeating. Instead, strive to maintain your weight. These tips may help you hold the line on high-calorie indulgences:

- Think ahead. Balance party eating with other meals. Eat small, lower-calorie meals during the day so you can enjoy celebration foods, too—while still being calorie aware.
- Take the edge off hunger beforehand. Eat a small, low-calorie snack such as fruit or whole-grain toast. Hunger can sabotage willpower!
- When you arrive, take your time greeting others first—conversation is calorie free! Settle into the festivities. Get a beverage, preferably with few calories. And avoid rushing to the food.
- Ask for sparkling water and a lime twist rather than wine, champagne, or a mixed drink. Sparkling water doesn't supply calories. Take control of calories in alcoholic drinks and other beverages; *see chapter 4, page 81.*
- Make just one trip to the party buffet. And be selective. Only choose foods you really want to eat; keep portions small. Often just a taste satisfies a craving or curiosity.
- Opt for lower-calorie party foods. Enjoy raw vegetables with a small dollop of dip, just enough to coat the end of the vegetable. Try boiled shrimp with cocktail sauce or lemon. Go easy on fried appetizers and cheese cubes.
- Move socializing away from the buffet to avoid nibbling unconsciously.
- Bringing a dish? Make it healthfully delicious—and low calorie so something with fewer calories is available. A platter of fresh fruit such as berries is usually a great bet.
- If you're the cook, perhaps for a family gathering, consider healthier, and perhaps lower-calorie, makeovers for traditional dishes.
- Enjoying a sit-down dinner party? Make your first helping small—especially if your host or hostess expects you to take seconds.

9. GATHER YOUR SUPPORT TEAM

Sticking to a plan for weight loss or weight control is often easier and more effective when others—friends, family, a health expert or a support group—give you support and cheer you on.

Friends and Family

Who influences your food decisions? Likely those you live, work, and socialize with. Their choices, actions, and judgments may affect yours, simply because you're together. Evidence indicates that the odds of being obese are much higher for those who have an obese friend or sibling—likely the reverse is true, too. Family and friends not only influence your food habits but also when and where you get exercise, and your body image. Having others support your weight goals encourages success:

- Take a family approach. Involve everyone in healthy eating and regular physical activity to manage weight or to lose it. That includes making healthier foods easily available at home, sharing family meals, doing active things together, giving social support and communicating sensitively with each other, and making health (not weight) the focus of talk time. *See "Family Meals Matter" in chapter 3, page 73, and "Family Mealtime: A Priority" in chapter 17, page 491 for ways to make shared meals a priority.*
- Get fit and stay fit with a friend or a family member. A partner increases the enjoyment factor of physical activity and healthy eating.
- Ask others to help keep you on track, if you're comfortable with that. Accountability is supportive.
- Watch for, and perhaps avoid, those who attempt to sabotage your efforts.

Qualified Health Professionals

If you have weight issues or questions about weight control, seek outside advice and help. But be wary. Not every weight-loss counselor is qualified.

Face-to-face weight-loss counseling can offer good support—with a qualified healthcare provider such as a registered dietitian nutritionist.

Judging Weight-Loss Programs

Millions of Americans participate in organized weight-loss programs each year. Today, the Internet also provides links to online weight-loss programs. Many of these programs are run by qualified medical and nutrition experts who can effectively help their clients lose weight and keep it off permanently. However, others make overblown claims and tout products that are ineffective and costly, and their staff may not have appropriate credentials.

As you look into different programs, consider what you've learned in this chapter and book, and use this list of questions to assess the quality of each one. Before you sign on the dotted line, make sure all these questions are answered to your satisfaction:

1. What is the approach? What rate of weight loss does the program aim for?
2. What are the health risks?
3. How will you assess my health status before recommending the program? (Many programs recommend a medical checkup before starting.)
4. Will the program include instruction, guidance, and skill building to help me learn to eat in a positive, healthy way for the long term? How?
5. Will the program include self-monitoring tools and techniques? What kind? Do I need a hand-held device, tablet, or computer?
6. Will you monitor my success with me at three- to six-month intervals and then help me modify my plan if needed? How?
7. Will the program include guidance on physical activity for a lifetime? How?
8. Does the program address challenges like eating at social gatherings or on the road?
9. What data shows that the program works? What has been written about the program's success besides individual testimonials?
10. Do customers keep off the weight after they leave the diet program? How much, on average, do they regain long term? (Ask for results over two to five years. The Federal Trade Commission requires weight-loss companies to back up their claims.)
11. What are the costs for membership, weekly fees, maintenance, and counseling? What's the payment schedule? Are any costs covered under health insurance? Do you give refunds if I drop out?
12. Am I required to buy specially formulated foods or supplements? What is the cost?
13. What is the maintenance and follow-up program? Is it part of the package, or does it cost extra?
14. What kind of professional support is provided? What are the credentials and experiences of these professionals? (Detailed information should be available on request.)
15. What are the program's requirements? Are there special menus or foods, counseling visits, or exercise plans? Can I make changes based on my food preferences or food allergies?

In addition to addressing weight advice and goals, a qualified healthcare professional will discuss other topics that have an impact on weight such as health problems, personal lifestyle, and food preferences, to devise a weight-loss plan specifically for you.

Logging on to an online or telehealth site may offer support for weight loss, too. Some people like the anonymity; others like personalized help with feedback at home. Some research suggests that well-designed, interactive programs, perhaps with smartphone texts or email messages and immediate access for support, are effective—at least in the short term. The challenge is finding a site that offers reliable guidance and privacy of personal data, rather than one that's mostly in business to sell products.

See "Nutrition Advice to Trust" in chapter 26, page 758, for tips on finding a qualified weight-loss expert.

Group Weight-Loss Programs

Should you join a support group or weight-loss program in your community or workplace? Perhaps, but that's up to you. Besides helping you craft personalized goals and strategies, group programs can offer psychological support. That may help you lose weight more effectively than trying on your own. Many group weight-loss programs, but not all, are coordinated by qualified nutrition experts.

The human resource department where you work may coordinate a wellness program, a fitness center onsite or offsite, or walking areas. Your workplace may offer a cafeteria menu with healthier food options, as well.

Recent research acknowledges that the most effective group programs provide group meetings, mobile applications, and online tools. The program may offer incentives. In the end, your own motivation is what matters. A program with self-monitoring, a maintenance plan that includes physical activity, and counseling that focuses on realistic behavioral changes is more effective for permanent success.

If you need help finding a weight-loss program, talk with a registered dietitian nutritionist, who is trained to help you figure out what kind of program will best fit your lifestyle. If you choose to join a group weight-loss program, attend regularly so you reap its full benefits. After you choose a weight-loss program, go prepared to talk with the program's healthcare professional about any health conditions you have. *See "Thirteen Tips to Make the Most of Nutrition Counseling" in chapter 26, page 760, for getting support from a qualified expert.*

Body Image: Dissatisfied, Distorted—or Not?

In a society that values thinness as the ideal, body weight and shape too often impact body image and inappropriately define self-worth—especially among teens and young women.

The so-called "ideal body" that is often portrayed in media reflects cultural values, not what's realistic for most or best for health. Some experts estimate that only 5 percent of American females naturally have the so-called "ideal shape" often portrayed in advertising and the fashion world. In addition, family and peer expectations and reactions from others influence a person's body image and, ultimately, self-worth.

When a poor body image leads to loss of self-esteem, many aspects of life suffer: the way people socialize, build relationships, participate in physical activities, and function psychologically at school and work and in daily life. Being dissatisfied with one's body image is both a symptom and a risk factor for distorted eating, and also for anorexia nervosa and bulimia nervosa, among other health risks. *See "Eating Disorders: More Than a Nutrition Issue" in chapter 25, page 732, for more about anorexia and bulimia.*

To help build a positive body image for yourself and others, reflect on your own ideas of body size and image. Recognize that healthy people come in many sizes and shapes. Skip comments that reinforce body size stereotypes, such as "I feel fat today." Talk about other personal qualities, and make them positive.

10. KEEP A POSITIVE MIND-SET

Those who succeed with weight loss and maintenance are more likely to engage positively in their "self-talk" and their overall mind-set about food—and they enjoy it, too. To engage your own positivity:

- Consider keeping a journal as a place for your own positive reinforcement. Be honest with yourself—but keep it judgment free.
- Be realistic with your self-talk. Skip absolutes—"always," "never," and "must"—in your tactics. "I'll never eat another french fry." "I must swim twenty laps every other day." Get rid of "shoulds," too. "I should get up early and walk."
- Cut yourself some slack. Nobody's perfect. Allow for occasional slipups in your eating strategies, without feeling guilty.
- Plan to indulge sensibly. You may be more successful in the long run. Occasional treats and splurges are okay.
- Give it time. For women, weight gain from water retention may be a normal part of a monthly menstrual cycle. Usually that passes in a few days.
- Expect success. Reaching life's goals is often self-fulfilling. Positive self-talk and an enthusiastic approach to weight management can set you up for success!
- Celebrate any success (but not by eating). If you carry around excess pounds, even small changes can make a difference in your health and reduce your disease risk.
- Enjoy how good your healthy weight feels. Reward yourself with a new garment, bouquet of flowers, or special outing, such as a sporting event or concert. Still, there's no greater motivation or reward than knowing you're in control, caring for yourself, and improving your health!

11. MONITOR YOUR PLAN, TRACK YOUR PROGRESS

It can make a difference! Those who keep a food and lifestyle log and track their weight, food choices, and physical activities are more likely to succeed at weight management than those who don't, studies show.

Self-monitoring makes you more accountable to yourself and helps you identify your problem spots. It may also help you think twice before indulging in a high-calorie snack when you're not hungry—or sitting out a workout. Tracking can be motivating, especially when you see success. *See "Digital Tracking: The Benefits" in chapter 26, page 763, for ways to use today's technology to track your progress.*

Food and Physical Activity Logs

Log on! Keep a record of what you eat and how active you are on a phone app, on an online website, or in a hand-written journal. Some online tracking tools are linked to databases with thousands of foods to help you keep track of calories and nutrients. You might look for an app with a calorie counter that scans barcodes on food packages.

The SuperTracker is one online example: www.supertracker.usda.gov/foodapedia.aspx. It lets you set nutrition and physical activity goals and track your food choices and physical activities, and then it tells how you stack up. Whatever system you use, you'll want to track what, when, why, where, and how you eat—for all your meals and snacks:

- *What foods and beverages and how much.* That includes sauces, condiments, spreads, dressings, and the snacks and snack drinks that are easily overlooked. A calorie counter on a handheld device might be useful.
- *Your mood and your hunger level.* These may help you identify eating triggers or food cues.
- *Time, place, with whom.* This information, too, may uncover eating triggers.

As you track your physical activity, record what you do and for how long. Log your perceived level of physical exertion, too. You might get a pedometer or other physical-activity tracking device to keep your records objective.

Regular Weighing

Weighing yourself—measuring your waist size, too—is also part of self-monitoring. Track your weight-loss progress—daily or weekly, whichever helps keep you on track. If daily weighing is confusing or discouraging, once a week is enough.

- Be aware that weight fluctuates from day to day due to fluid loss and retention. Always weigh yourself at the same time of day, on the same scale, nude or with the same amount of clothing.

? Have you ever wondered?

. . . if your stomach shrinks when you eat less? No, your body doesn't work that way. Although your stomach can expand to accommodate a large amount of food, it doesn't stretch out indefinitely. As your stomach contents pass into your intestines, it goes back to its normal size. When you cut back on calories, your stomach keeps its normal size, even if your appetite isn't as big.

. . . if every person's body has a unique set point, or a preset weight, that it tries to return to? That's a theory without conclusive evidence. Even if a set point exists, it's probably a range that can be set a little lower with more physical activity and food choices with fewer calories. For someone who's too thin, eating a few extra calories may help adjust the set point a bit higher.

. . . what to do when your weight seems to plateau? Be patient. Plateaus are normal with weight loss. Your body requires fewer calories to function as you lose weight. A metabolic shift can account, in part, for a plateau, which typically occurs on long-term weight-loss plans and during slower weight loss. If you hit a plateau, stick to your weight-loss plan. Adjust if you need to. Gradually adding more activity may help nudge you off the weight plateau. Reduce calories because your body may need fewer calories after weight loss.

Need more strategies for sensible, effective weight management?

Check here for "how-tos":

- Snack smart for fewer calories; *see "Snacks Count!" in chapter 3, page 75.*
- Get "calorie-wise" as you shop; *see "Nutrition: Fact Check!" in chapter 6, page 148.*
- Cut calories by trimming fats and added sugars during food prep; *see "Culinary Know-How: Flavor Plus Health" in chapter 8, page 246.*
- Eat out with calorie savvy; *see "Eating Out for Health and Pleasure" in chapter 9, page 276.*
- Help your child or teen keep a healthy weight; *see "Growth and Weight" in chapter 17, page 501.*
- Encourage your kids to move more and sit less; *see "Active Play: Toddlers and Preschoolers," "Get Up and Move!," and "Move It: Sports and More!" in chapter 17, pages 516, 522, and 529.*
- Stay physically active in your later years; *see "Never Too Late to Move More" in chapter 20, page 585.*
- Gain, maintain, or lose weight as an older adult; *see "Weight Loss—or Gain? Managing for Health" in chapter 20, page 594.*

- After you reach your goal, continue to weigh yourself regularly to help maintain your healthy weight.

Fitness Tracking

Although costly, today's technology offers wearable monitoring to clip onto your clothes or wear on your wrist. These sophisticated electronic devices can monitor the calories you expend 24/7. Some track your heart rate and blood pressure; some are linked to online health experts. Talk to your doctor if you think this is right for you. *See "How to . . . Use mHealth (Mobile)" in chapter 26, page 760.*

With weight management as part of your everyday lifestyle, healthy eating and physical activity become second nature.

Popular Diets: Truths and Half Truths

Every year Americans spend billions of dollars on the weight-loss industry—often for diet plans, diet books, services, and gimmicks that don't work! The lure of quick, easy weight loss is hard to resist, especially for those unwilling to make a commitment to lifelong behavioral changes.

Although these diets are typically ineffective in the long run, weight-loss hopefuls willingly give the next craze a chance. The result? Perhaps temporary success, but overall, wasted money, weight regained, a feeling of failure, and perhaps damage to health. *The bottom line:* If a diet or product sounds too good to be true, it probably is. And any diet that's taken to the extreme can add up to trouble.

The next dieting craze is often a past craze that's simply resurfaced with a new name, a new twist, yet still no sound science to back up the claims. Fad diets typically rely on nonscientific, unproven claims, personal stories, testimonials, or poorly controlled studies. Not surprisingly, many people feel confusion and diet fatigue as they sort through contradictory popular approaches to weight loss. Sound familiar? For those who try one fad diet after another, weight cycling becomes a common, frustrating problem.

PROMISES AND CAUTIONS: THE TRUTHS

Popular diets may not work—at least not in the long run—if they promote:

- **Rapid weight loss.** Quick weight loss is often muscle and water loss, too—not just body fat—typically regained quickly afterwards. Losing weight slowly and steadily is more likely to last than a rapid and dramatic weight change.
- **No need to exercise.** The best way to keep a healthy weight, lose body fat, and build muscle is to eat smart and move more. Regular physical activity is essential for good health and healthy weight management. Find physical activities that you enjoy, then aim for thirty to sixty minutes of activity on most days of the week to maintain weight—more for weight loss.

Have you ever wondered?

. . . if a high-protein/low-carb diet has any weight-loss advantage? If your total calorie intake is lower than your calorie expenditure, you'll lose weight, no matter where your calories come from. A high-protein diet won't lead to loss of body fat unless your overall calories are low enough. The best approach is a healthy eating pattern you can stick with—within the recommended ranges for energy nutrients (carbohydrate, protein, and fat).

- Low- to moderate-carbohydrate diets for weight loss may be advised for those with insulin resistance. Talk to your doctor.
- A moderate-carbohydrate diet with more protein may help some people lose body fat while maintaining muscle as they lose weight. For this diet, choose mostly lean protein foods (lean meat, skinless poultry, fish, and beans and peas).
- A high-protein diet may be risky for those with some chronic diseases, such as kidney disease. A high-protein diet is commonly defined as providing at least twenty percent of energy (calories) from protein. Talk to your doctor if this is an issue for you.

. . . if you can lose weight if you go gluten free? Gluten free is neither no-carb nor low-calorie. Instead, it's an eating plan for those with celiac disease or non-celiac gluten sensitivity, who can't tolerate gluten in foods made with wheat, barley, or rye; *see "Gluten-Free: When It's a Must" in chapter 23, page 670.* Other grain products replace these foods, but not their calories. In fact, gluten-free foods may have more calories than their regular counterparts if fats or sugars replace some gluten-containing ingredients.

For women who are or may become pregnant, there also are risks related to avoiding grain products such as bread that are fortified with folic acid, a nutrient that protects against birth defects.

If going gluten free helps some people trim down, they simply may be eating fewer calories because they're skipping pasta, pastries, and other baked goods—or they're making healthier food and lifestyle choices overall. Better than going gluten free, focus on choosing fiber-rich whole grains, without added sugars and solid fats—and just limiting the portions.

- **Rigid meal and snack plans.** Rigid plans can take a lot of effort and may not match your own food preferences or lifestyle. With any new diet, always ask yourself: "Can I eat this way for the rest of my life?" If the answer is "no," the plan is not for you.
- **Specific food combinations.** No scientific evidence suggests that combining certain foods or eating them in careful sequence, perhaps at specific times of day, aids weight loss. Eating the "wrong" combinations of food doesn't cause them to turn to body fat immediately or to produce toxins in your intestines, as some plans claim.
- **Unlimited amounts of some foods; severe restrictions of others.** Ditch diets that allow unlimited amounts of a single food (such as rice, grapefruit, or cabbage soup), that eliminate an entire food group (such as dairy foods), or that try to eliminate a nutrient (such as carbohydrates) or food substance (such as gluten). These diets have no unique ability to melt body fat and help you lose weight.

  Because they lack food variety, they likely won't provide all the nutrients needed for health, especially if some food categories are off-limits. This can have unintended health consequences, such as potential bone loss if, for instance, dairy is eliminated to save calories without replacing dairy's nutrients. Even by taking a multivitamin supplement, you'd miss some essential nutrients. And a diet plan that requires you to eat the same foods over and over is monotonous and hard to stick to.
- **Very-low-calorie diet, without medical supervision.** Without medical supervision, a diet plan that's very low in calories isn't advised. It won't provide adequate nutrition and may have unhealthy side effects. For people with some health problems, such as insulin-dependent diabetes or kidney disease, a very-low-calorie liquid diet can be harmful. Since people usually don't stay with them, there's usually no long-term weight loss.

  (*Note:* Very-low-calorie liquid formulas have been developed for short-term use—under a doctor's supervision. To help some obese people, they may aid short-term weight loss—if there's also a commitment to new habits for eating and active living. Used as a liquid diet without other foods, they provide only 400 to 800 calories a day.)

The bottom line: No super food or food combination can reverse weight gain resulting from physical inactivity and overeating. Eliminating a food or food category doesn't work, either. Also, because these diets don't teach new eating habits, people usually don't stick with them.
See the "Ten Red Flags of Junk Science" in chapter 26, page 758, for hints to misinformation.

FASTING, CLEANSING, AND DETOXING

As a tactic, does fasting jump-start weight loss? And do cleansing and detoxing making you healthier?

Fasting and starvation-type diets can peel off pounds. As with very-low-calorie diets, fasting deprives the body of energy and nutrients needed for normal functions. Most rapid weight loss is mostly water and muscle loss, which will come back as fast as it's lost. Fasting also may cause fatigue and dizziness, with less energy for physical activity. And it feeds the cycle of "yo-yo" dieting.

Other misconceptions: fasting or drinking only juice "cleans out" the system, removing toxic waste that accumulates from poor eating habits. If you're healthy, your body does that naturally as part of its metabolic processes, whether you fast, detox, cleanse, or not.

Note: Fasting is an important part of some religious observances, such as Ramadan for Muslims and some Hindu practices. Like other food patterns, both fasting and breaking the fast later in the day can be done in a healthy way. When breaking a fast, drink enough fluids to avoid dehydration, and choose nutrient-rich foods, perhaps with more protein and fiber, that help you feel full longer.

WEIGHT-LOSS SUPPLEMENTS

"Magic diet pill!" "Lose 30 pounds in 30 days—without diet or exercise." "Melt away fat." "Block the absorption of carbohydrates." "Speed your metabolism." Weight loss isn't easy. And promises from herbal remedies and other supplements can be tempting to try.

Despite the claims, no herbal remedies or other supplements can burn fat or shift your genetic code. Little scientific evidence indicates that weight-loss supplements really work. Besides being ineffective, some ingredients in supplements and herbal products can be dangerous—even deadly for some people. Some interfere with medications. And they can be costly, diverting money away from buying nutrient-rich foods.

Among those weight-loss supplements getting attention are bitter orange, chitosan, chromium picolinate, conjugated linoleic acid, ephedra, green coffee extract, green tea extract, guar gum, hoodia, and yohimbe. *See chapter 10, page 315, for more about the use and safety of these weight-loss and other supplements.* *Also visit this website: ods.od.nih.gov/factsheets/WeightLoss-Consumer.* If you are considering any of these weight-loss supplements, talk with your doctor before taking them—especially if you have a health condition such as diabetes, heart disease, or high blood pressure or if you take medication.

As with other supplements, the FDA does not test the effectiveness and safety of weight-loss supplements before they appear in the marketplace, and it advises that they may contain untested ingredients that have not been examined for safety or effectiveness. Makers of supplements are responsible for their safety and for the truthfulness of the claims. If testing has been done by the manufacturer, the number of people in the study is typically small and the study short term.

Possible product contamination is a safety concern for both children and adults. Some weight-loss supplements have been found to contain hidden medications or other compounds. The FDA may remove a product from the marketplace and, with the Federal Trade Commission, may take legal action against the manufacturer if a product is tainted with an undeclared drug or chemical ingredient.

Have you ever wondered?

. . . if over-the-counter diet pills help with weight loss? Over-the-counter diet pills, or appetite suppressants, work by curbing appetite, but usually just for a few weeks. Some have unpleasant side effects, and some can be addictive, with potential damage to the heart and the nervous system with long-term use. They may be prescribed to help a person start a lifelong program for weight management, but they're not a substitute for healthy eating habits over the long term. If you don't adjust your eating habits, you'll simply regain the weight you lost. They should only be used under a doctor's supervision.

. . . if obesity can be controlled with medication? For some people, medication may be prescribed—under a doctor's care—as part of an obesity treatment program. Medication may be prescribed if someone hasn't been able to lose weight while on a program to modify food and lifestyle behavior—and if he or she has a BMI of at least 30 for men or at least 27 for women, as well as a condition that may be related to being overweight such as high blood pressure or type 2 diabetes.

The FDA has approved several such medications for long-term use. Available over-the-counter or at a higher dose with a prescription, orlistat (Xenical®), approved for long-term use, reduces the absorption of dietary fat. However, its use may also reduce the absorption of fat-soluble vitamins (A, D, E, and K) temporarily, so a multivitamin supplement is often advised. The FDA warns that in rare cases orlistat can cause severe liver injury. This medication isn't effective for everyone and can have gastrointestinal side effects (cramps, gas, stool leakage, oily spotting) that may worsen when eating high-fat foods. With a lower-fat diet, these side effects may be lessened.

The FDA also has approved several appetite suppressants: phentermine for short-term use and some others (Belviq®, Contrave®, Qsymia®, and Saxenda®) for long-term use. Each has possible side effects (for some, serious and harmful) and should be taken under a doctor's supervision. Research continues on medications to manage obesity.

. . . if meal replacements are effective for weight loss? Research has shown that meal replacements (liquid drinks, meal bars, and portion-controlled meals) can be an effective weight-management aid for some. They can offer convenience, ease, and portion and calorie control, and perhaps reduce sensory stimulation from food itself. Like any food, they should be nutrient rich.

. . . if surgery and liposuction are options for weight loss? Not for most people. Bariatric surgery isn't an "easy way out." It should only be considered for those who have been unable to lose weight by modifying food choices and lifestyles—and only then if their BMI is 40 or more, or 35 or more if they have obesity-related health conditions or risks, such as type 2 diabetes, high blood pressure, sleep apnea, or high blood cholesterol. A doctor will also assess other factors, including health risks.

Gastric bypass, a type of bariatric surgery, done by bypassing part of the small intestine or by making a smaller stomach pouch, is used to help severely obese people lose weight. It reduces food intake and alters hormones in the gastrointestinal tract. Side effects and potential complications can have lifelong implications. Another approach, called adjustable gastric banding, can alter stomach capacity and emptying time. These surgeries either help restrict food intake or interrupt the way food is digested so that some calories and nutrients aren't absorbed. Healthy eating patterns and regular exercise, along with changes in lifestyles and eating behavior, are essential after surgery to sustain a healthy weight.

Liposuction, the surgical removal of fat tissue from various body areas, is often only a short-term solution. If eating and exercise habits remain the same, the weight is likely to be regained.

GIMMICKS AND OTHER "MIRACLES"

Promoters advertise even more "easy ways to weight loss"—weight-loss patches, electric muscle stimulators, starch and fat blockers, creams that melt fat away, and many others.

No products can magically melt fat while you watch TV, sleep, or sweat. While these products may claim to help you lose weight and get rid of cellulite, none has proven effective. Cellulite is simply normal body fat under the skin that looks lumpy when the fat layer gets thick, allowing connective tissue that holds fat in place to show. The lumpy look can lessen or disappear with normal weight loss.

You may have seen weight-loss "aids" that sweat off extra weight. Sweating in a sauna—or wearing a rubber belt or nylon clothes that make you perspire during exercise—may cause weight loss. However, the pounds that disappear are water loss, not body fat. When you drink or eat, the weight returns. Instead of helping to achieve a healthy weight goal, "sweating off" pounds may damage health through dehydration.

What if You Need a Healthy Way to Gain Weight?

There's plenty written about weight loss. But what if you're healthy—and you think you need to gain weight? Perhaps you lost weight after an illness. Or maybe you're an athlete wanting to bulk up with more muscle to perform better. Maybe you're thin. Or maybe you lost weight unintentionally for one reason or another.

If your BMI is low (under 18.5), that may be okay for you. Before trying to self-diagnose, check with your doctor to rule out any medical conditions that result in low weight or in sudden or unexpected weight loss.

RECOGNIZE THE REASONS FOR BEING UNDERWEIGHT

If you're healthy, the reasons for being underweight can be as complex as being overweight. Again, energy imbalance is the simple answer: fewer calories consumed than used, or not eating enough. Other reasons that may factor in, too:

- *Heredity.* Genetics plays a major role in physical build and musculature. If you are thin and healthy, that may be okay. Your natural shape may be like that of your birth parents and siblings. Some people inherit a speedy metabolism.
- *Growth spurt.* During adolescence, some teens may not seem able to eat enough to keep up with their growing body; maturity usually takes care of that.
- *Insufficient appetite signals.* Some people may not eat enough because they feel full even when they're not. The brain's appetite center may not signal hunger.
- *Emotions.* Feeling stressed or depressed can affect the brain's appetite control center.
- *Overexercising.* Other people may overexercise and not adequately compensate by eating enough food for calories burned.

Illness, pain, fatigue, medication, disease, or a combination can also affect the brain's appetite control center. Conditions such as Crohn's disease and irritable bowel disease, which affect the body's ability to absorb nutrients from food, and medications and medical treatments also may result in appetite loss or stomach discomfort.

If you lose weight suddenly and don't know why, talk to your doctor. This may be an early symptom of another health problem. Unintended weight loss may signal a health decline for older adults and those with health conditions such as cancer.

If you are underweight, the top priority is to determine why—under the care of your doctor. Address and properly manage any medical conditions first, if they exist.

EAT WISELY FOR WEIGHT GAIN

Gaining or regaining weight can be as challenging as losing weight. A mindful, healthy plan is as important for weight gain as for weight loss. And many of the same principles apply. The obvious approach for weight gain: consume more energy (calories) than your body burns.

The quality of your food choices should take precedence over the quantity of calories. The goal is to gain muscle or bone mass without gaining excess body fat.

Supplements promoted to bulk up muscles for weight may appeal to skinny teenage boys. However, they don't provide anything that food doesn't provide. *See "Bodybuilding" in chapter 17, page 532.*

To eat wisely for weight gain, follow this advice:

- Pay attention. "Hear" your body's hunger cues. Schedule meals or snacks if you sometimes get too busy to eat or simply forget.
- Eat more nutrient-rich foods. To make your calories count for good nutrition, follow one of the food patterns, *discussed in chapter 2, page 21.* Follow the pattern at a higher calorie level than you eat now. *See the "Eating Patterns, 2015–2020 Dietary Guidelines for Americans" in the appendix, page 771, for recommended food-group amounts at various calorie levels.*
- Eat frequent mini-meals if your appetite is small. Five or six small meals a day may be easier to handle than two or three large meals.
- Boost calories in nutrient-rich foods with other nourishing ingredients. Layer sandwiches with avocado slices, nut butter, or peanut butter. Garnish soups, salads, and cooked dishes with cheese, chopped nuts, dried cranberries, olives, or sesame or sunflower seeds. Fortify or top casseroles, meatloaf, soups, and chilis with dry milk powder and grated cheese.
- Even though higher-fat foods deliver more calories, be fat savvy. Keep your overall eating plan low in foods that are high in saturated fats. Replace solid fats with oils—and perhaps add a little canola, olive, or another healthy oil to your food prep, including salads. *See chapter 13, page 385, for more about dietary fat.*
- If they fill you up, limit beverages with meals so you have enough room for food. That said, still drink enough throughout the day. Milk, 100 percent juice, chai, or lattes provide nutrients plus some calories.
- Keep healthy snacks (energy bars, nuts, trail mix) on hand at work or home to eat when you're hungry. Something sweet? Fruit, dried fruit, or yogurt parfait.

(continued)

What if You Need a Healthy Way to Gain Weight? *(continued)*

- Drink more calories—if it's easier than chewing solid foods. Enjoy shakes and smoothies if you can't get enough calories from regular meals and snacks. Boost the calories and nutrition by adding avocado, cottage cheese, dry milk, dry oats, nut butter, protein powder, tofu, or yogurt. Or try a commercial liquid meal replacement; high in protein, too. Avoid filling up on diet sodas.
- Use the Nutrition Facts on food labels to choose nutrient-rich foods, which also supply somewhat more calories. Still limit added sugars as well as saturated and *trans* fats. *See "Nutrition: Fact Check!" in chapter 6, page 148, to learn more about label reading.*
- Stay away from unpleasant or unsettling topics of conversation at mealtimes if stress is an issue for you.
- If appetite loss is an ongoing problem for you, *see "Not Hungry? Dealing with Appetite Loss" in chapter 20, page 593, for strategies to stimulate a healthy appetite.*
- Get more guidance from a registered dietitian nutritionist to help you develop an eating plan to gain weight in a healthy and enjoyable way. *See "How to . . . Find a Qualified Nutrition Expert" in chapter 26, page 759.*

Note: Guidance here is not meant for those with eating disorders, whose weight problems are complex and often life-threatening, or for people with chronic disease.

MAKE PHYSICAL ACTIVITY A PRIORITY

To gain weight, there's no need to cut back on physical activity unless physical activity is excessive—or if your doctor advises a slower pace.

- Walk before meals if it helps stimulate your appetite.
- Stay physically active with strength-building and weight-bearing activity. It helps you build muscle, protect your bones, and feel energetic. *Tip:* Muscle weighs more than body fat.

UNDERWEIGHT: POTENTIAL RISKS

If the reason for being underweight is not eating enough, health risks may relate to undernutrition: not enough calories or enough food variety with adequate nutrients for energy and health, and for children, growth.

A low-normal or below-normal BMI may be an early symptom of another health problem. A doctor may advise weight gain, perhaps to replace lost weight and aid recovery after a prolonged illness or surgery, or to help withstand some medical treatments, perhaps cancer treatment. Stabilizing weight and even adding a few pounds may help improve longevity.

A below-normal BMI might also signal an eating disorder, which requires medical attention. *See "Eating Disorders: More Than a Nutrition Issue" in chapter 25, page 732, for risks of underweight related to these disorders.*

23

Cope with Food Allergies and Other Food Sensitivities

In this chapter, find out about . . .

Food allergies: managing the symptoms

Lactose intolerance: fitting dairy in

Celiac and non-celiac: eating gluten free

Other food sensitivities: managing them, too

A queasy stomach, itchy skin, or diarrhea—must be a reaction to something you ate, right? Maybe. But it may not be what you think. Before blaming food, take time to explore the cause.

Any food sensitivities that cause adverse reactions are health concerns. Some reactions cause discomfort. Others can seriously affect and disrupt the quality of life. And some reactions can be life-threatening. The causes are more numerous, and perhaps more complex, than you may think.

Food allergies. A food allergy rallies the body's disease-fighting (immune) system to action, creating unpleasant, sometimes serious, symptoms in response to a food component, usually a protein. Some severe reactions can be potentially fatal. The immune system starts to work even though the person isn't sick. That's why symptoms appear. If the immune system isn't the cause of a food reaction, it isn't an allergy.

Food intolerances. Different food intolerances have different causes. For various reasons, people may not be able to digest a component of certain foods, perhaps because a digestive enzyme such as lactase is deficient. Naturally occurring substances such as theobromine in coffee and tea or serotonin in bananas and tomatoes may cause reactions, but they aren't life-threatening. Since food intolerances may prompt some similar symptoms (nausea, diarrhea, abdominal cramps), they're often mislabeled as food allergies.

Other food sensitivities. Celiac disease is an example. As an autoimmune disorder, celiac disease is a gluten-related condition, whereby the intestinal villi, which absorb important nutrients, are damaged or destroyed. Oral allergy syndrome, not a true allergy, is another example.

In addition, infectious organisms such as bacteria, parasites, or viruses, which cause foodborne illness, or waterborne contaminants where fish is harvested, can cause adverse body reactions. *See "Foodborne Illness: More Common Than you Think" in chapter 7, page 218, to learn about those foodborne illnesses.*

Feelings of discomfort after eating also can be wrapped up with emotions. Even with no physiological reason, just thinking about, smelling, or tasting a certain food that someone associates with an unpleasant experience can make him or her feel sick. Simply misperceiving a food as harmful may trigger discomfort for some people, too!

So . . . how should you manage a food reaction? For some conditions, you must completely avoid certain foods to avoid harmful consequences; for others, a small amount may be tolerable.

Most important, if a certain food or type of food seems to bother you, skip the temptation to self-diagnose. Your doctor should diagnose your symptoms so you treat symptoms properly. This chapter can help familiarize you with possible causes, health risks, and ways to handle common adverse reactions to food.

Food Allergies: A Growing Concern

Have you ever heard parents say that their child is allergic to milk, then remark that he or she has no problems drinking chocolate milk? Or maybe you avoid a particular food yourself, believing you're allergic to it?

People often use the term "allergy" loosely to describe almost any physical reaction to food—even if it's psychological. Why? Because the symptoms of food allergies can mimic other adverse food reactions such as foodborne illness and food intolerances. The number of people who claim to have food allergies is likely far higher than the number who truly have them, notes the Centers for Disease Control and Prevention (CDC).

However, since reactions may be severe, even life-threatening, food allergies can't be taken lightly. Although the reasons are unclear, food allergies—and related severe reactions—appear to be on the rise. The true incidence is hard to determine.

FOOD ALLERGIES: WHO'S AT RISK?

Anyone, at any age and of all races and ethnicity, can develop a food allergy. But it's usually identified early in life. Young children are much more likely to have food allergies and often outgrow them. However, food allergies can occur in adulthood without a prior history of allergies. A family history of allergies (asthma, eczema, food allergies, or environmental allergies such as hay fever) increases the risk.

As many as 15 million Americans may have a food allergy reports Food Allergy Research and Education (FARE). And an estimated 4 percent (9 million) adults and 8 percent (6 million) children, more often young children, in the United States suffer from them. The CDC reports a 50 percent increase in food allergies among children since the late 1990s; research hasn't yet identified why.

ALLERGIES: AN IMMUNE RESPONSE

Certain foods may cause a physical reaction but don't cause someone to develop an allergic reaction. A true food allergy is an adverse physical response that happens when the body's disease-fighting (immune) system reacts to a component in food. That component is usually a protein, which is normally harmless. The body's immune system reacts even though the person isn't sick, sometimes called food hypersensitivity. The allergen sets off a chain of immune system reactions.

The most common allergic reaction involves immunoglobulin E (IgE) antibodies. An IgE-mediated reaction happens within an hour or so, as the body scrambles to protect itself by making antibodies that trigger the release of body chemicals, including histamine. In turn, these body chemicals cause uncomfortable symptoms associated with allergies, such as a runny nose, itchy skin, nausea, diarrhea, even a rapid heartbeat, or in severe cases, anaphylaxis.

A non-IgE reaction involves other components of the immune system—and *not* IgE antibodies. Unlike IgE-mediated reactions, non-IgE reactions are typically delayed—and can happen three to four hours or even longer after ingesting a problem food. These allergies aren't as well understood as IgE-mediated allergies. Common symptoms include eczema, abdominal discomfort, vomiting, and diarrhea and aren't life threatening. Sometimes they're mistaken for a foodborne illness.

Itching for a Cause?

An hour after eating peanut butter with crackers, your child has broken out with an itchy rash. Is your child allergic to peanuts, or perhaps wheat? Maybe, or maybe not. In any case, a call to the child's doctor is certainly in order. And how about adults? The onset of allergies can happen in adulthood, too.

More than 170 foods are known to cause allergic reactions in susceptible people. However, eight foods are more likely to set off a reaction than others. Milk, eggs, wheat, soy, fish (such as bass, cod, flounder, halibut, salmon, and tuna), crustacean shellfish (such as crab, crawfish, lobster, and shrimp), peanuts, and tree nuts (such as pecans or walnuts) are the most common foods containing allergens, and they cause about 90 percent of allergic reactions in the United States. Even trace amounts can cause a reaction.

FARE notes that sesame is also an allergen that affects hundreds of thousands of Americans, but it isn't currently listed as a common allergy for food-allergen labeling. It also advises that virtually any food may cause an allergic reaction for someone. Although rare, food allergies have been reported from corn, gelatin, meat and chicken, seeds (poppy, sesame, and sunflower being the most common), and spices (caraway, coriander, garlic, mustard, etc.); visit the website www.foodallergy.org/allergens/other-allergens to learn more about them.

By the age of ten—and often by age five—most kids outgrow milk, egg, soy, and wheat allergies. However, allergies to peanuts, tree nuts, fish, and crustacean shellfish are often lifelong. Only about 20 percent outgrow a peanut allergy, and only about 10 percent outgrow a tree nut

What Food Allergies Are Most Common?

- *Adults:* peanuts, tree nuts (such as almonds, Brazil nuts, cashews, hazelnuts, macadamias, pecans, pine nuts, pistachios, walnuts), fish (such as bass, cod, flounder, haddock, salmon, tuna), crustacean shellfish (such as crab, crawfish, lobster, shrimp)
- *Children:* peanuts, tree nuts, milk, eggs, wheat, soy

allergy. A board-certified allergist (certified by the American Academy of Allergy, Asthma, and Immunology) should determine whether a person has outgrown an allergy by giving a food-challenge test.

ALLERGIES: SIGNS, SYMPTOMS, AND DANGERS

Different people react to the same allergen in different ways. Even if a food contains a common allergen, you can't predict whether you might have an allergic reaction if you're allergy prone. Being allergic to more than one food is common.

For most food allergies, the first symptoms appear within the first few minutes to two hours after eating. Sometimes more symptoms, called biphasic reactions, start one to four hours after eating the food that triggers the reaction. In exceptionally sensitive people, just skin contact or inhaling the allergen (perhaps steam from cooking or flour dust) can provoke a reaction!

Symptoms? Something to Sneeze About

The most common symptoms include swelling, sneezing, and nausea. Most symptoms affect the skin, respiratory system, stomach, or intestines. A severe allergic reaction also may cause anaphylaxis, which can cause a drop in blood pressure, loss of consciousness, and even death.

SKIN REACTIONS:

- Hives
- Swelling of the lips, tongue, and face
- Itchy eyes
- Rash (eczema)

RESPIRATORY TRACT REACTIONS:

- Dry or raspy cough
- Runny nose
- Shortness of breath
- Swelling, itching, and/or tightness in the throat
- Wheezing (asthma)

DIGESTIVE TRACT REACTIONS:

- Abdominal cramps
- Diarrhea
- Nausea
- Vomiting

Keep in mind: other food- or nonfood-related conditions may cause these symptoms. To date, there's no known scientific link between food allergies and arthritis, behavioral problems, ear infections, migraine headaches, or urinary tract infections, although research is underway. Recent studies show a link between food allergies and severe asthma in children.

Food Allergies: The Dangerous Side

For most people with food allergies, reactions are more unsettling and unpleasant than life-threatening. In rare cases, an anaphylactic reaction can occur. When many different body systems react at the same time, the allergic response to food can be severe. Just a tiny bite of a food—and in rare instances, a touch or a whiff—can be harmful. With an anaphylactic reaction, symptoms often develop quickly—within seconds or minutes after eating—and progress quickly from mild to severe, even fatal. Symptoms may start with itching, tingling, or a metallic taste in the mouth, then progress to extreme itching, a swollen throat that makes breathing difficult, sweating, rapid or irregular heartbeat, low blood pressure, nausea, diarrhea, loss of consciousness, cardiac arrest, and shock. Without immediate medical attention, the affected person may die; minutes matter!

What foods may cause a severe reaction? Although rare, any food can cause anaphylactic reactions; most severe reactions are caused by proteins in peanuts, tree nuts, eggs, or crustacean shellfish. Those with asthma in addition to a food allergy, especially peanut and tree nut allergies, are at highest risk.

Reactions to a food allergen aren't predictable. Mild symptoms at first can get much more serious very fast. Someone with mild reactions in the past could have severe reactions when exposed another time. Severity depends on how allergic a person is and how much allergen is consumed.

Warning! If you—or a family member—experience true food allergies, plan ahead with your allergist how to handle accidental ingestion of the trigger allergen. The person should wear an identification bracelet

? Have you ever wondered?

. . . if foods with histamine can cause physical reactions? Yes, some people react, but a histamine intolerance isn't a true food allergy.

Histamine is a compound in nearly all body cells. It can be released in times of stress or as part of an allergic response. The symptoms can mimic those of a food allergy, such as itchy eyes, sneezing, wheezing, a headache, hives, or a rash, among others. To put this in familiar terms, you likely know about antihistamine medications, used to manage allergy symptoms.

Many foods contain histamine or cause the body to release histamine when consumed. Although not a complete list, some histamine-rich foods include aged cheese, beer and wine (especially red wine), fermented foods, mushrooms, processed meats, smoked fish, vinegar, and yogurt. Other foods have histamine in smaller amounts.

If you think you may have a histamine intolerance, talk with your doctor to check for and exclude conditions with "look-alike" symptoms. The only way to identify a histamine intolerance is through an elimination diet to see if your symptoms improve, then to slowly reintroduce foods to identify possible trigger foods. Consult with a registered dietitian nutritionist to identify food triggers while eating for your overall health.

or necklace to alert others and should carry epinephrine (a type of adrenalin) to inject quickly to counter the allergen and open the airway and blood vessels. A doctor will provide a prescription. Because the body's responses can be life-threatening, call 911 or an ambulance immediately if someone has severe allergic reactions.

DIAGNOSIS: TESTING FOR ALLERGIES

If you have symptoms, never try to self-diagnose. For an accurate diagnosis, you need a complete medical evaluation by a board-certified allergist. Someone with a food allergy should be under a doctor's care.

True food allergies can be measured and evaluated clinically—with no need for guessing. In that way, unrelated medical conditions are eliminated. Typically, the diagnosis includes a medical history, a physical exam, a food journal, an elimination diet, and laboratory tests. An initial screening is typically a skin test; an allergist then confirms a food allergy with more definitive tests.

Pass the Test?

Proven, standardized medical tests and ideally a blended food challenge help diagnose a food allergy but not its possible severity.

- *A skin-prick test (SPT)* measures the presence of IgE antibodies for a suspect food. These antibodies, released by the immune system, signal a reaction to an allergen. Small amounts of diluted food extracts are "pricked" into the skin. If the skin reacts with a mosquito-bite-like red bump (wheal) within about fifteen to thirty minutes, you may have a food allergy. Other tests are advised, too, since skin-prick testing has a high false-positive rate.
- *Blood tests* check for IgE antibodies to specific foods. An enzyme-linked immunosorbent assay (ELISA or EIA test) measures the amount of allergen-specific antibodies in the blood. (The radioallergosorbent, or RAST, test usually isn't used now.)
- In an *oral food-challenge test*, likely given in a doctor's office, the patient starts with a very small sample that's either the suspected food allergen or a placebo. The placebo won't produce an allergic reaction. The response is watched carefully. With no symptoms, the challenge gets repeated with higher doses. This test is the gold standard. It must be done under a doctor's supervision—never on your own.

Be aware: Negative results for allergy testing may not tell the whole story; the test won't detect allergies to foods not being tested, as well as those less-common food allergies that don't involve IgE antibodies.

Keeping track of physical reactions to a specific food one time after another may help you identify a possible food allergy or intolerance. Still, avoid self-diagnosis. The cause may be a more serious medical problem. Eliminating groups of foods from your eating pattern based only

? Have you ever wondered?

. . . if avoiding certain foods during pregnancy can prevent food allergies in the baby? There's no conclusive evidence that restricting foods during pregnancy makes a difference. In fact, it's not recommended. Babies born to mothers who have restricted their diets during pregnancy often have lower birth weights. Eating a known food allergen during pregnancy won't cause a food allergy in the infant, either. *See "Food Sensitivities and Your Baby" in chapter 16, page 479, for more guidance.*

. . . if breastfeeding can prevent food allergies in the baby? *As discussed in "Breastfeeding: Ideal for Babies" in chapter 16, page 460,* breastfeeding has many health benefits for babies. For those with a family history of allergies, there's no strong evidence that breastfed babies are less likely to have food allergies. That being said, breast milk is least likely to trigger an allergic reaction, and it strengthens a baby's immune system. Exclusive breastfeeding for the first four to six months may possibly reduce early eczema, wheezing, and cow's milk allergy.

. . . how you might reduce the chance that your child will develop a peanut allergy? New guidelines, released in early 2017 from the National Institute of Allergy and Infectious Disease (part of the National Institutes of Health), indicates that exposing infants to peanuts early, as young as four to six months of age, may prevent or reduce the chance of developing a peanut allergy later. The timing and way to introduce peanuts depends on an infant's risk, such as whether he or she already has eczema, an egg allergy, or both, and should be with a doctor's guidance. Peanuts should be in a form that won't cause choking, such as thinned peanut butter, perhaps mixed in apple sauce. In all cases, infants should start other solid foods before they are introduced to peanut-containing foods.

. . . if and when you should have your child tested for food allergies? Right away if you suspect signs of a food allergy. No age is too young.

. . . if it's okay to offer a small amount of the food if you think your child has outgrown the food allergy? No. Your allergist needs to test your child to be sure.

on a hunch may limit nutrients and other food substances needed for overall good health.

For the Record

Suspect a food allergy? During a medical exam you'll need to describe your symptoms and give some medical history. Prepare to answer such questions as:

- What are your symptoms?
- How long does it take for symptoms to appear after eating the food in question?
- How much of the food must you eat before you get a reaction?
- Do symptoms occur every time you eat the food?
- What else, such as physical activity or drinking alcoholic beverages, brings on symptoms?
- Does a family member have allergies? Food allergies?

You may need to keep a food journal, with all the foods, beverages (including alcoholic beverages), and medications you consume over a determined period. That includes brand names of commercially prepared foods. Also keep track of your physical reactions and how soon after eating they appear. By itself, a journal can't confirm a cause-and-effect relationship between a food and symptoms, but the information you record can suggest a connection to investigate.

An elimination diet also may help uncover a cause. Your doctor may instruct you to completely avoid the suspicious food for a while. If the symptoms go away, then reappear when you eat the food again, you may be allergic to it. If your symptoms aren't life-threatening, your doctor may recommend a re-challenge where the suspected allergen or allergens are reintroduced, one at a time.

Keeping a food journal or following an elimination diet may seem easy. However, detecting ingredients in prepared foods that cause allergic reactions may not be. A registered dietitian nutritionist has the expertise to help you. *See "How to . . . Find a Qualified Nutrition Expert" in chapter 26, page 759.* An electronic food journal can help you identify foods that trigger allergic reactions by tracking what you eat and drink and how you feel. *See "Digital Tracking: The Benefits" in chapter 26, page 761.*

Click Here!
Links to Know . . .

- Food Allergy Research and Education (FARE)
  www.foodallergy.org/allergens
- SafeFARE (food allergy–aware restaurants)
  www.safefare.org

MANAGING FOOD ALLERGIES

If you're diagnosed with a true food allergy, what's next? There's no cure—although new research for treatments is underway—and no pill to avoid a reaction. Instead, managing food allergies is life altering and requires constant attention, often by family and friends who support you, too.

If you have a food allergy, the only way to prevent an allergic reaction is to strictly avoid troublesome foods. Even tiny bites are risky. Prepare and choose meals and snacks with care!

- Seek professional help. Get a written plan for emergency care, including medication, from your doctor. Stay connected with your allergist and doctor and for regular annual follow ups.
- Often, a specific plan for your child or teen is needed to manage exposure to food allergens during school. *See "Helping Kids Deal with Food Allergies or Other Adverse Food Reactions" in this chapter, page 658.*
- Ask a registered dietitian nutritionist to help you identify safe foods, avoid unsafe foods, and still eat for good nutrition:
  - Check food labels for allergen labeling three times, for every item, every time—once at purchase, again when storing, and finally before preparing or eating the item. Foods can change at any time, due to ingredient substitutions and reformulations by the manufacturer. *See "Label Lingo: Words That Identify Food Allergens," in this chapter, page 660.*
  - Learn to make food substitutions when you prepare food at home and eat away from home, *as discussed in "Kitchen Nutrition: Handy Substitutions for Allergen-Free Cooking" in this chapter, page 665.*
  - Ask about a supplement in case you need to make up for any nutrients missed in an allergen-free diet. *See "Dietary Supplements: More than Vitamin Pills" in chapter 10, page 316, to learn about supplements.*
- Prepare for emergencies. Always carry injectable epinephrine (such as an EpiPen®, Auvi-Q™ or Adrenaclick®) at all times once a food allergy has been diagnosed—and make sure it hasn't expired or been damaged. Keep an antihistamine and a bronchodilator handy, in case you accidentally consume a food allergen and prepare to use it as directed. Get immediate medical help if needed. Wear an identification necklace or bracelet that identifies your allergy. *Be aware:* Antihistamine addresses symptoms but won't help with anaphylaxis.
- Tell others: family, coworkers, and friends. Let them know how they can help minimize your exposure to allergens—and what to do if you do have a reaction. Join a support group for help in managing emotional well-being, while managing food allergies.

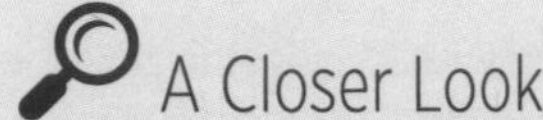

A Closer Look

Helping Kids Deal with Food Allergies or Other Adverse Food Reactions

Whether your child—or his or her pal—has a food allergy, parents and kids need to learn how to deal with it. The same basic advice holds for celiac disease or any other food sensitivity.

Contact your child's school:

- Find out how the school manages food allergies. Food allergies are considered a disability; a reasonable plan must be in place. Section 504 is a statute that requires the needs of students with disabilities must be met as adequately as those of non-disabled students. Visit the website www.kidswithfoodallergies.org for information on a Section 504 plan and how to set one up.
- Get a letter from your child's doctor stating your child's name, diagnosis, the effect of the allergy on him or her, the treatment (with suitable ingredient substitutions for meals and snacks), and what to do if he or she accidentally consumes the food allergen. Provide emergency contact information.
- Create a written plan. An allergic student should have an Emergency Anaphylaxis Plan in place with school personnel: the administration, nurse, food service staff, teachers, and perhaps coach and bus driver. Together, develop an approach for avoiding allergens without making your child feel "different" or isolated. Include food-related events in the plan: parties, birthday treats, in-class and after-school food activities, recess, field trips, and foods that children bring from home to share.
- With your doctor, other responsible adults, and your child, make a plan for epinephrine administration (for severe reactions) or antihistamine (for milder reactions) if needed for reactions caused by food allergies. Come up with a way your child can signal for help—fast!

Advise babysitters and other caregivers:

- Explain the allergy or other food sensitivity, foods to avoid, and safety precautions, including the dangers of cross contact. Make sure the caregiver knows the symptoms of a reaction and what to do if reactions occur; that may include giving epinephrine.
- Have safe foods ready for your child, so there's no need for food prep. If the caregiver is providing food, teach him or her to read food labels to identify and avoid problem foods.
- Provide contact information for someone to call in case of an emergency. For severe reactions, that may include 911; the caregiver should act first and then call you. Provide your cell phone number or another easy way to reach you.
- Plan your outings to avoid mealtime, if possible, perhaps in the evening after your child goes to bed.
- Keep all the instructions and information about your child's allergy or food sensitivity where the caregiver can easily access it.

Help your child cope:

- Make sure your child knows the signs or an allergic reaction, and how and when to tell an adult when he or she is having an allergy-related problem.
- Visit the cafeteria with your child before school starts so he or she can meet staff who can help. Choose a place to sit, perhaps an allergy-free table, to avoid cross contact with allergen-containing foods. Arrange for a responsible lunch buddy to help.
- Go over the menu with your child to identify safe and unsafe foods. Plan for food substitutes—with the food service staff—or for home-prepared food.
- Teach your child why and how to avoid "food swapping" and ignore pressure to try foods that are unfamiliar as a safety measure. Talk about strategies to avoid exposure to unsafe food. Role-play scenarios so your child will know how to react in these situations.
- Equip your child. When old enough to be responsible, children and teens who have severe reactions should carry an injectable form of epinephrine (and know how to use it), a personal emergency card (perhaps in a fun cardholder), a medical-alert necklace or bracelet, and a parent's phone number. Antihistamine may be enough for milder reactions.
- Be aware of bullying, a serious issue that allergic kids may face. *See "Bullying and Body Size" in chapter 17, page 504, for ways to handle bullying.*

Teach your child to be a caring friend to those who may or do have a food allergy:

- Take friends seriously if they say they have a food allergy or other food issue. Be thoughtful about friends' food choices at school, with foods you offer them at home, and with party foods.
- Don't swap or share food—even if you think it's okay.
- When you're nearby, avoid eating a food that's allergenic to a friend.
- Wash your hands after you eat so you don't transfer food to other things your friend may touch.
- Get immediate help if your friend gets sick.

Using Food Labels to Find Allergen-Free Foods

Food Allergen Labeling and Consumer Protection Act (FALCPA). Packaged foods regulated by the US Food and Drug Administration (FDA) must follow allergen labeling laws. The FDA regulates the labeling of all foods, except for poultry, most meats, certain egg products, and most alcoholic beverages.

- The top eight food allergens, or ingredients that contain the allergen, must be labeled in the common name of the allergen: milk, egg, fish, crustacean shellfish, tree nuts, wheat, peanuts, and soybeans. Sesame is not currently labeled.
- The specific types must be stated for tree nuts (e.g., cashews, walnut), fish (e.g., salmon, tuna), and shellfish (e.g., crab, shrimp).
- Major food allergens used in spices, flavorings, additives, and colorings must be listed, too.
- For food allergen labeling, the package will be labeled in one of two ways:
    - A "Contains" statement—for example, "Contains milk, egg, peanuts"—at the end of the ingredient list
    - The common name of the allergen from which the ingredient is derived—for example, "albumin (egg)"—listed in parentheses after the ingredient within the ingredient list

The FALCPA law doesn't apply to restaurant, deli, or bakery foods in a carry-out box or wrapper for an individual customer order. Alcoholic beverages such as beer may be labeled voluntarily. This law doesn't apply to fresh food items (such as fresh meat, fish, vegetables and fruits), and to certain meat, poultry, and/or egg products.

Some labels carry precautionary labeling such as "may contain," "processed in a facility that also processes," or "made on equipment with." This is voluntary, not currently regulated, and means "possible," so it's wise to avoid those foods. A food manufacturer, for example, may use the term if there is a chance, even small, that an allergen might be introduced through cross contact during production. The manufacturer can't use precautionary labeling as a substitute for good manufacturing practices, however; the statement must be truthful and not misleading.

How to Use Allergen Labeling. Here's how to use food labels to identify foods to avoid:

- Check for allergens in the ingredient list on food labels carefully every time you buy or use even familiar foods. If, for example, you're allergic to eggs, remember that eggs are common ingredients in mayonnaise, many salad dressings, and ice cream. No package label? Make a different choice. *See "Label Lingo: Words That Identify Food Allergens" in this chapter, page 660, for some ingredients to watch for.*
- Keep up-to-date on ingredients in food products. Periodically, food manufacturers change ingredients and production practices, perhaps using shared equipment. Also, the same food from different manufacturers likely has a different "recipe." Even if you're a long-time consumer of a certain food, check the label's ingredient list every time you buy it.
- If you have a milk or casein allergy, be cautious about kosher foods labeled as "pareve" or "parve." For religious purposes, these foods are milk free, or perhaps have only a very small amount of milk. Although appropriate for those with lactose intolerance, the food may not be milk free from a food-science perspective or for those with food allergies. If a "D" appears next to a kosher symbol, the product has an ingredient derived from milk or was produced in equipment shared with a dairy operation or processor. "F" printed near the kosher symbol indicates that it contains fish ingredients. *See "Kosher Symbols" in chapter 6, page 155, for examples of other symbols.*
- In doubt? Contact food manufacturers with your questions about allergens in their products. The company name, address, and perhaps a toll-free consumer information number or website are on the food label.
- Check labels on medications and on body care and oral care products. They also may contain food allergens such as milk, eggs, wheat, and tree nuts; allergen labeling required for foods regulated by the FDA doesn't apply to medications and body care and oral care products.
- Get help from the supermarket's registered dietitian nutritionist if this service is available.

Storing and Preparing Allergen-Free Food at Home

Store, prepare, and serve food to avoid cross contact so a food allergen from one food won't creep into an allergy-safe food. Even invisible traces on a utensil or from a splatter can cause a reaction! The same rule applies when you shop. For example, if you're concerned about a milk allergy, avoid deli-sliced meats since cheese and meat may be cut with the same slicer. Just cooking a food, or removing or scraping off the allergenic food (e.g., peanuts) won't make it safe for food allergy sufferers.

It may seem obvious to just leave the ingredient out of the recipe or off the plate, but a few other "how-tos" can help ensure a reaction-free meal or snack and avoid cross contact with a food allergen:

- Wash your hands with warm, soapy water before handling and serving allergen-free foods. Completely clean anything that came in contact with the allergen. Sanitizing gels or just water aren't enough to remove the allergen.
- Cook the allergen-free meal first. To avoid cross contact with other foods, cover it and set it aside until serving it.

continued on page 664

Label Lingo

Words That Identify Food Allergens

- All FDA-regulated manufactured food products that contain a "major food allergen" (milk, eggs, fish, peanuts, crustacean shellfish, tree nuts, peanuts, wheat, and soybeans) as an ingredient are required by US law to list that allergen on the product label in simple terms. For fish, crustacean shellfish, and tree nuts, the specific type of fish or nut must be listed.
- Read all product labels carefully before purchasing and consuming any item.
- Be aware of unexpected sources of allergens, such as the ingredients listed below.

Note: The lists that follow do not imply that the allergen is always present in these foods. It is intended to serve as a reminder to always read the label and ask questions about ingredients.

FOR A PEANUT-FREE DIET

Avoid foods that contain peanuts or any of these ingredients:

artificial nuts
beer nuts
cold-pressed, expeller-pressed, or extruded peanut oil
goobers
ground nuts
mixed nuts
monkey nuts
nut meat
nut pieces
peanut butter
peanut flour
peanut protein hydrolysate

Peanut is sometimes found in the following:

African, Asian (*especially Chinese, Indian, Indonesian, Thai, and Vietnamese*), and Mexican dishes
baked goods (*e.g., pastries, cookies*)
candy (*including chocolate candy*)
chili
egg rolls
enchilada sauce
marzipan
mole sauce
nougat

Keep the following in mind:

- Mandelonas are peanuts soaked in almond flavoring.
- The FDA exempts highly refined peanut oil from being labeled as an allergen. Studies show that most allergic individuals can safely eat peanut oil that has been highly refined (not cold-pressed, expeller-pressed, or extruded peanut oil). Follow your doctor's advice.
- A study showed that unlike other legumes, there is a strong possibility of cross-reaction between peanuts and lupine.
- Arachis oil is peanut oil.
- Many experts advise those allergic to peanuts to also avoid tree nuts.
- Sunflower seeds are often produced on equipment shared with peanuts.
- Some alternative nut butters, such as soy nut butter or sunflower seed butter, are produced on equipment shared with other tree nuts and, in some cases, peanuts. Contact the manufacturer before eating these products.

FOR AN EGG-FREE DIET

Avoid foods that contain eggs or any of these ingredients:

albumin (also spelled albumen)
egg (dried, powdered, solids, white, yolk)
eggnog
globulin
livetin
lysozyme
mayonnaise
meringue (meringue powder)
surimi
vitellin
words starting with "ovo" or "ova" (such as ovalbumin)

Egg is sometimes found in the following:

baked goods
breaded items
drink foam (*alcoholic, specialty coffee*)
egg substitutes
fried rice
ice cream
lecithin
marzipan
marshmallows
meatloaf or meatballs
nougat
pasta

Keep the following in mind:

- Individuals with egg allergy should also avoid eggs from duck, turkey, goose, quail, etc., as these are known to be cross-reactive with chicken egg.
- While the whites of an egg contain the allergenic protein, individuals with an egg allergy must avoid all eggs completely.

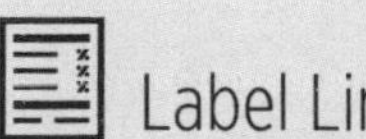

Label Lingo *(continued)*

FOR A TREE NUT–FREE DIET

Avoid foods that contain nuts or any of these ingredients:

almond
artificial nuts
beechnut
Brazil nut
butternut
cashew
chestnut
chinquapin nut
coconut*
filbert/hazelnut
gianduja (*a chocolate-nut mixture*)
ginkgo nut
hickory nut
litchi/lichee/lychee nut
macadamia nut
marzipan/almond paste
nangai nut
natural nut extract (*e.g., almond, walnut*)
nut butters (*e.g., cashew butter*)
nut meal/nut meat
nut milk
nut paste (*e.g., almond paste*)
nut pieces
pecan
pesto
pili nut
pine nut (*also referred to as Indian, pignoli, pigñolia, pignon, piñon, and pinyon nut*)
pistachio
praline
shea nut
walnut

Tree nuts are sometimes found in the following:

black walnut hull extract (*flavoring*)
natural nut extract
nut distillates/alcoholic extracts
nut oils (*e.g., walnut oil, almond oil*)
walnut hull extract (*flavoring*)

Keep the following in mind:

- Mortadella may contain pistachios.
- There is no evidence that coconut oil and shea nut oil/butter are allergenic.
- Many experts advise those allergic to tree nuts to also avoid peanuts.
- Talk to your doctor about other nuts not listed here.

*Coconut, the seed of a drupaceous fruit, has typically not been restricted in the diets of people with tree nut allergy. However, in October 2006, the FDA began identifying coconut as a tree nut. Medical literature documents a small number of allergic reactions to coconut; most occurred in people who were not allergic to other tree nuts. Ask your doctor if you need to avoid coconut.

FOR A MILK-FREE DIET

Avoid foods that contain milk or any of these ingredients:

butter, butter fat, butter oil, butter acid, butter ester(s)
buttermilk
casein
casein hydrolysate
caseinates (*in all forms*)
cheese
cottage cheese
cream
curds
custard
diacetyl
ghee
half-and-half
lactalbumin, lactalbumin phosphate
lactoferrin
lactose
lactulose
milk (*in all forms, including condensed, derivative, dry, evaporated, goat's milk and milk from other animals, low-fat, malted, milkfat, nonfat, powder, protein, skimmed, solids, whole*)
milk protein hydrolysate
pudding
Recaldent®
rennet casein
sour cream, sour cream solids
sour milk solids
tagatose
whey (*in all forms*)
whey protein hydrolysate
yogurt

Milk is sometimes found in the following:

artificial butter flavor
baked goods
caramel candies
chocolate
lactic acid starter culture and other bacterial cultures
luncheon meat, hot dogs, sausages
margarine
nisin
nondairy products
nougat

Keep the following in mind:

- Individuals who are allergic to cow's milk are often advised to also avoid milk from other domestic animals. For example, goat's milk protein is similar to cow's milk protein and may, therefore, cause a reaction in individuals who have a milk allergy.

Label Lingo *(continued)*

FOR A WHEAT-FREE DIET

Avoid foods that contain wheat or any of these ingredients:

bread crumbs
bulgur
cereal extract
club wheat
couscous
cracker meal
durum
einkorn
emmer
farina
hydrolyzed wheat protein
flour (*all purpose, bread, cake, durum, enriched, graham, high gluten, high protein, instant, pastry, self-rising, soft wheat, steel ground, stone ground, whole wheat*)
Kamut©
matzoh, matzoh meal (*also spelled as matzo, matzah, or matza*)
pasta
seitan
semolina
spelt
sprouted wheat
triticale
vital wheat gluten
wheat (*bran, durum, germ, gluten, grass, malt, sprouts, starch*)
wheat bran hydrolysate
wheat germ oil
wheat grass
wheat protein isolate
whole-wheat berries

Wheat is sometimes found in the following:

glucose syrup
oats
soy sauce
surimi
starch (*gelatinized starch, modified starch, modified food starch, vegetable starch*)

FOR A SOY-FREE DIET

Avoid foods that contain soy or any of these ingredients:

edamame
miso
natto
shoyu
soy (*soy albumin, soy cheese, soy fiber, soy flour, soy grits, soy ice cream, soymilk, soy nuts, soy sprouts, soy yogurt*)
soya
soybean (*curd, granules*)
soy protein (*concentrate, hydrolyzed, isolate*)
soy sauce
tamari
tempeh
textured vegetable protein (*TVP*)
tofu

Soy is sometimes found in the following:

Asian cuisine
vegetable broth
vegetable gum
vegetable starch

Keep the following in mind:

- The FDA exempts highly refined soybean oil from being labeled as an allergen. Studies show most allergic individuals can safely eat soy oil that has been highly refined (not cold-pressed, expeller-pressed, or extruded soybean oil).
- Most individuals allergic to soy can safely eat soy lecithin.
- Follow your doctor's advice regarding these ingredients.

FOR A FISH-FREE DIET

Fish is sometimes found in the following:

barbecue sauce
bouillabaisse
Caesar salad
caviar
deep-fried items
fish flavoring
fish flour
fish fumes
fish gelatin (*kosher gelatin, marine gelatin*)
fish meal
fish oil
fish sauce, imitation fish or shellfish, isinglass, lutefisk, maws (fish maw)
fish stock
nuoc mam (*Vietnamese fish sauce; be aware of other ethnic names*)
pizza (*anchovy topping*)
roe
salad dressing
seafood (fish) flavoring
shark cartilage
shark fin
surimi
sushi, sashimi
Worcestershire sauce

Keep the following in mind:

- If you have fish allergy, avoid seafood restaurants. Even if you order a nonfish item off the menu, cross contact of fish protein is possible.
- Asian cookery often uses fish sauce as a flavoring base. Exercise caution when eating this type of cuisine.
- Fish protein can become airborne in a steam released during cooking and may cause an allergic reaction. Stay away from cooking areas when fish is being prepared.

Label Lingo *(continued)*

FOR A SHELLFISH-FREE DIET

Avoid foods that contain shellfish or any of these ingredients:

barnacle
crab
crawfish (*crawdad, crayfish, ecrevisse*)
krill
lobster (*langouste, langoustine, Moreton bay bugs, scampi, tomalley*)
prawns
shrimp (*crevette, scampi*)

Your doctor may advise you to avoid mollusks or these ingredients:

abalone
clams (*cherrystone, geoduck, littleneck, pismo, quahog*)
cockle
cuttlefish
limpet (*lapas, opihi*)
mussels
octopus
oysters
periwinkle
scallops
sea cucumber
sea urchin
snails (*escargot*)
squid (*calamari*)
whelk (*turban shell*)

Shellfish are sometimes found in the following:

bouillabaisse
cuttlefish ink
fish stock
glucosamine
seafood flavoring (*e.g., crab or clam extract*)
surimi

Keep the following in mind:

- Any food served in a seafood (fish) restaurant may contain shellfish protein due to cross contact.
- For some individuals, a reaction may occur from inhaling cooking vapors or from handling fish or shellfish.
- Mollusks are not considered major allergens under food labeling laws and may not be fully disclosed on a product label.

FOR A SESAME-FREE DIET

Avoid foods that contain sesame or any of these ingredients:

benne, benne seed, benniseed
gingelly, gingelly oil
gomasio (*sesame salt*)
halvah
sesame flour
sesame oil
sesame paste
sesame salt
sesame seed
sesamol
sesamum indicum
sesemolina
sim sim
tahini, tahina, tehina
til

Sesame may sometimes be found in the following:

Asian cuisine (*sesame oil is commonly used in cooking*)
baked goods (*e.g., bagels, bread, breadsticks, hamburger buns, rolls*)
bread crumbs
cereals (*e.g., granola, muesli*)
chips (*e.g., bagel chips, pita chips, tortilla chips*)
crackers (*e.g., melba toast, sesame snap bars*)
dipping sauces (*e.g., baba ghanoush, hummus, tahini sauce*)
dressings, gravies, marinades, sauces
ethnic foods (*e.g., flavored rice, noodles, risotto, shish kebabs, stews, and stir fries*)
falafel
goma-dofu (*Japanese dessert*)
herbs, herbal drinks
margarine
pasteli (*Greek dessert*)
processed meats, sausages
protein and energy bars
snack foods (*e.g., candy, halvah, Japanese snack mix, pretzels, rice cakes*)
soups
sushi
tempeh
Turkish cake
vegetarian burgers

Keep the following in mind:

- Because sesame oil is not refined, it is recommended that it be avoided by individuals with sesame allergy.
- Sesame may be undeclared in ingredients such as flavors or spice blends. If you are unsure, call the manufacturer to ask about their ingredients and manufacturing practices. It is advised to specifically inquire if sesame is used as an ingredient, rather than simply asking what ingredients are used in a flavoring or spice blend.
- Sesame may also be found in nonfood items, including: cosmetics (including soaps and creams), medications, nutritional supplements, and pet foods. In nonfood items, the scientific name for sesame, *Sesamum indicum*, may appear on the label.

Source: Food Allergy Research and Education (FARE), www.foodallergy.org. Accessed December 1, 2016.

? Have you ever wondered?

. . . if a kiss can result in an allergic reaction? Yes, if it causes cross contact with a food allergen such as peanuts—especially if the allergen comes in contact with the eyes, mouth, or nose. If you have a food allergy, wait at least four hours before kissing someone who's eaten the problem food. (And if your hands come in contact with an allergen such as peanut butter, avoid rubbing your eyes.)

. . . if food allergy tests promoted in popular media are reliable? The National Institute of Allergy and Infectious Diseases (NIAID) cautions against unproven tests, such as hair analysis, pulse testing, muscle testing, IgG/IgG4 testing, and cytotoxicity. These tests can result in a false diagnosis and may not be validated by other labs. The risks? Useless avoidance of some foods or, more seriously, an allergic reaction, possibly severe, if a true food allergy isn't diagnosed. Talk to your allergist.

. . . if food allergies trigger asthma? Only in very rare cases. The usual triggers are allergens in dust, molds, pollen, and animals; pollutants in the air; respiratory infections; some medications; physical activity; and perhaps weather changes. If food appears to be a trigger, consult your doctor. Conversely, having asthma puts someone at greater risk for food allergies.

. . . if there's a cure for food allergies? At this time, no. Strictly avoiding foods with allergens is the only protective approach. The only medicine that stops anaphylaxis is injectable epinephrine.

continued from page 659

- Use different and clean (washed well in warm, soapy water) utensils (including knives and spatulas), containers, cutting boards, and serving utensils for foods prepared without the food allergen. For example:
  - *For a peanut allergy:* Just wiping off a knife used to spread peanut butter isn't enough. Use a clean, separate knife for other ingredients, perhaps jelly. The same holds true for another utensil, such as cleaning a blender after making an ice cream shake with peanut ingredients.
  - *For a wheat allergy:* Avoid intermixing bread makers and sifters that are used for wheat flours and for flours without wheat.
- Use different oils to cook allergenic and nonallergenic foods. Frying doesn't destroy allergens. For example:
  - *For a fish or crustacean shellfish allergy:* Use different cooking oil in a clean frying pan to deep-fry, and not what was used to fry shrimp and other fish or crustacean shellfish. Serve them on a separate plates with different utensils, too.
- Watch for allergenic ingredients. For example:
  - *For a tree nut allergy:* Ground-up nuts added to a muffin batter or a breading mix may go unnoticed. Even a bottle of barbecue sauce, pasta, or meat-free burgers may have nuts!
  - *For a fish allergy:* Bottled fish sauce in a stir-fry, Worcestershire sauce, or salad dressing could be an undetected problem. Anchovies flavor some Italian foods such as caponata.
  - *For an egg allergy:* Sometimes eggs are added to meatballs and fish croquettes so they hold their shape. They may be used in the foam for specialty coffee drinks, as an egg wash on pretzels, in some dry pasta, or in egg substitutes that contain egg whites.
  - *For a soy allergy:* Soy flours and soy protein are used in increasingly more baked goods and other prepared foods, and are often found in tuna.
  - *For a milk allergy:* Milk protein is in many brands of tuna. Currently, many foods labeled as "nondairy" have casein, a milk derivative. Meat may have casein as a binder.
  - *For a peanut allergy:* Peanuts are sometimes an unexpected substitute for tree nuts and may be found in some sauces, vegetarian foods, and other prepared foods.
- Experiment to find substitutions. Find a cookbook or online source of allergen-free recipes.

Eating Allergen Free Away from Home

If you struggle with a food allergy, eating away from home can be challenging. You're not in control of the ingredients or the food preparation. The good news: Some states have legislation meant to train those who work in restaurants to make food safer for those with allergies. When you eat out:

- Review the restaurant menu ahead when possible. Menus are often available online, or try to get a menu from the restaurant. Look for restaurants that advertise as allergy aware; call ahead. Perhaps avoid eating out at the busiest times of the week.
- Choose restaurants where you can special order. Many restaurants rely on premade foods, so an ingredient can't be removed; servers may not be aware of all the ingredients in some menu items, either. Chain restaurants usually give allergen information online.
- Make a chef card, *as shown in this chapter, page 666*, to explain your food allergy or sensitivity—and that your food must be cooked in a clean, safe area to avoid cross contact. Share it with your server and the chef when you order. If you travel to places English is not spoken or read, get a translation of the chef card as you prepare for your trip; check online sources for chef cards in different languages.

Handy Substitutions for Allergen-Free Cooking

Egg-free recipes—substitute for 1 egg*:

- 1 teaspoon baking powder + 1 tablespoon liquid + 1 tablespoon vinegar
- 1 teaspoon yeast dissolved in ¼ cup warm water
- 1½ tablespoons water + 1½ tablespoons oil + 1 teaspoon baking powder
- 1 packet plain unflavored gelatin + 2 tablespoons warm water (Don't mix until ready to use.)
- 2 tablespoons blended tofu
- 2 teaspoons ground flaxseed dissolved in 2 tablespoons warm water

Milk-free recipes—substitute for an equal amount of milk*:

- Fruit juice
- Nut, oat, potato, rice, soy, or hempseed beverages; and coconut milk
- Water

Wheat-free recipes—substitute for 1 cup wheat flour*:

- ¾ cup rice flour + ¼ cup cornstarch
- 1 cup fine cornmeal or corn flour
- ⅔ cup brown rice flour + ⅓ cup potato flour
- 1 cup soy flour + ¼ cup potato starch flour
- 1 cup of any of the following flours: amaranth, garbanzo/fava, quinoa, sorghum
- 1 tablespoon wheat flour equals:
  - 1½ teaspoons cornstarch, arrowroot, white rice flour, or potato starch
  - 2 teaspoons tapioca or uncooked rice
  - 1 tablespoon garbanzo or fava flour

*Experiment, because cooking or baking characteristics of the end result may differ with ingredient substitutions. Talk to a registered dietitian nutritionist about other substitutions.

- Explain your needs to your food server. Ask about the menu—ingredients and preparation—before ordering. The same dish prepared in different restaurants may not have the same ingredients. To play it safe, order plain foods such as grilled meats, steamed vegetables, and fresh fruits—but still ask questions!
- Ask for the chef or manager if your server seems unsure about the ingredients or preparation. It's okay to leave the restaurant or just enjoy the social time with your companions, but not eat, if your request isn't understood.
- Skip sauces, condiments, and fried foods—and other dishes if you're unsure of other ingredients. They may contain allergens.
- Let your fellow diner(s) know so they can support your choices and provide timely help if anaphylaxis occurs.
- Another option: bring allergen-safe food with you, just in case a restaurant can't accommodate your needs.

Risky Situations. If you have a food allergy, be cautious of these common situations:

- Buffet-style or family-style service—since the same serving utensils may be used for different dishes.
- Steak—since butter, which melts into meat, is often added to grilled meat for flavor, a possible issue exists if you have a milk allergy. Meat, poultry, or fish may also be dusted with flour. Actually, anything on a shared grill may be a problem.
- Fried foods—since the same oil may be used for different foods.
- Seafood (fish) restaurants if you have a fish allergy—since cooking utensils may come into contact with fish protein.
- Many African, Chinese, Indonesian, Malaysian, Mexican, Thai, and Vietnamese foods if you have a tree nut, peanut, or fish or crustacean shellfish allergy—peanuts, nuts, and fish sauce are common in some of these ethnic cuisines. Soy sauce contains wheat.
- Breaded foods if you have a wheat, milk, or egg allergy—since the problem protein may transfer if the same breading mix is used for different foods. Breaded foods may also have an egg wash.
- Scooped ice cream—since the scoopers for several flavors may be kept in the same tub of water.
- Desserts—since the server or chef may not know all the ingredients. Many restaurant desserts often come from specialty shops.
- Baked goods—since they're made with many common allergens, not just wheat, but soy flour, nuts, eggs, and milk. Today, more breads, pizza crusts, and other doughs are made with soy flour; wheat is often added to rye bread. Often sold unpackaged, baked goods are also at high risk for cross contact; tongs and other utensils are reused.

- For airline travel, advise of any peanut allergy when making the reservation and again at the departure gate. Consider an early morning flight when the plane is likely the cleanest. That said, airlines can't guarantee that the cabin will be free of peanut dust. Carry your own food on airlines. Ask for the peanut-free snack if you have a peanut allergy.
- If you're a guest in someone's home, offer to bring your own food or to help with food preparation.
- When you're the host, ask your guests about special food needs—in case they feel uncomfortable telling you. Adjust the menu or prepare some foods differently if needed to address their need, and be careful to avoid cross contact!

See chapter 9, page 275, for tips on eating smart away from home.

CHEF CARD: FOOD ALLERGY ALERT

I have severe food allergies.

In order for me to avoid a life-threatening reaction, I must avoid all foods that contain:

____

____

____

Please make sure that my food does not contain any of these ingredients and that any utensils and equipment used to prepare my meal, as well as the prep surfaces, are fully cleaned immediately before using. Thank you for your help.

Check here to download a chef card (in several languages):
FARE Chef Card: www.foodallergy.org/file/chef-card-template.pdf

Have you ever wondered?

. . . what the term "cross contact" means? It's when an allergen or gluten gets unintentionally introduced into a food product. That may happen during food processing or handling, or maybe with ineffective cleaning. Cross contact differs from cross-contamination, which generally refers to contact with unhealthy bacteria that can cause foodborne illness.

. . . if peanut, nut, or soy oils can cause an allergic response? Most peanut and soy oils are highly refined, making them free of the protein allergen. Research shows that people with peanut or soy allergies don't have reactions to these common oils; extremely sensitive people are still wise to be cautious. Cold-pressed peanut and tree nut oils are processed differently and may contain small amounts of protein allergens that can trigger a reaction.

. . . if you should avoid a food if the label says "Produced in a facility where products with peanuts are made"? Yes—if you need to avoid peanuts due to a peanut allergy. The product could have cross contact with the allergen in peanuts, even if there are no peanuts in the ingredient list.

. . . if foods modified by biotechnology contain allergens? It's possible. But no biotech foods to date contain protein from known allergenic foods. The FDA policy states that any protein taken from a food causing a known allergic reaction should be considered allergenic, too. It also must be listed on the label of a food produced by biotechnology. *See "Traditional and Modern Biotechnology" in chapter 5, page 124.*

. . . if a MMR (measles-mumps-rubella) vaccine or a flu shot is safe for someone with an egg allergy? Some vaccines contain a very small amount of egg protein since they're grown on egg embryos. If you have an egg allergy, talk to your doctor before getting a flu shot. The American Academy of Pediatrics acknowledges the safety of—and recommends—a single dose of MMR vaccine for children with egg allergies. Whether or not a flu shot is advised depends on the severity of the allergic reaction to eggs.

. . . if foods labeled as "nondairy" are okay for people with milk allergies? Carefully read the label to find out. For most people with a milk allergy, a key protein in milk called casein causes a reaction. Casein or caseinates are common additives.

. . . if soy is a good substitute for people with other allergies? Yes, if the person isn't allergic to soy, too. Calcium- and vitamin D–fortified soymilk can substitute for cow's milk—if you get enough of milk's other nutrients elsewhere. Soy nuts can substitute for peanuts or tree nuts.

. . . if eating local honey will help protect against seasonal allergic reactions? Sweet idea, but it's not a likely remedy because windborne pollens usually trigger seasonal allergies, not pollens spread by bees or other insects. Eating honey sourced from plants that don't cause allergy symptoms probably won't offer any benefit.

Have you ever wondered?

. . . what an exercise-induced food allergy is? It's a very infrequent reaction to eating a certain food before exercising. It's more common in teens and young adults. Allergic reactions may appear once exercising starts and the body temperature starts to rise. Anaphylaxis may even develop. Managing this allergy is easy: avoid eating the food that causes the reaction for a couple of hours before exercising. Evidence isn't clear whether this can happen only to those with a food allergy.

. . . if you should avoid coconut and water chestnuts if you have a tree nut allergy? Ask your doctor; a coconut is actually a fruit (a drupe), not a true nut. Any reaction is not from a nut allergy. Some people do react to coconut. Regarding water chestnuts, they're from a plant root, not a nut.

. . . if carrageenan is a problem if you're allergic to fish or crustacean shellfish? No; it's a seaweed extract, not a fish. An additive in many foods, it appears safe for people with allergies to fish and crustacean shellfish.

. . . why scallops and oysters don't need food allergen labeling? Like clams and mussels, they are molluscan shellfish (not crustacean shellfish) and aren't considered to be major food allergens.

. . . if there's such thing as a "hypoallergenic diet"? While popular media may offer this claim, no such diet exists. Why? Because bodies react differently. For reasons such as genetics, lifestyle, and health history, a diet that's "hypoallergenic" for one could cause a dangerous allergic response for another.

. . . if someone with an egg or milk allergy can eat baked foods with egg or milk? Research supports that the ingestion of cooked or baked egg or milk can be tolerated by some with these allergies; however, this may depend on the actual temperature achieved with cooking and the amount of protein in the product. The best advice: avoid unless your certified allergist advises otherwise. Most people with a food allergy need to totally eliminate the offending protein from their meals and snacks.

. . . if probiotics can prevent or treat a food allergy? To date, research has not shown that probiotics alone or probiotic supplements are effective in preventing or treating food allergies. A probiotic supplement may, however, reduce the risk for or speed recovery from atopic dermatitis, which is a risk factor for developing food allergies.

Lactose Intolerance: A Matter of Degree

Do you like milk but think that milk doesn't like you? Then you may be lactose intolerant—not allergic to milk or other dairy foods. The good news is that milk may be "friendlier" than you think!

WHAT IT IS—AND ISN'T

Lactose is a natural sugar in most dairy foods. During digestion, an intestinal enzyme called lactase breaks down lactose into smaller, more easily digested sugars—glucose and galactose. When it's not fully digested, lactose instead is fermented by "healthy" bacteria in the colon. This fermentation may produce uncomfortable symptoms—for example, abdominal gas or pain, bloating, cramping, diarrhea, and/or nausea.

Those with lactose intolerance (LI) have symptoms of gastrointestinal discomfort when they can't completely digest or absorb the amount of lactose they consume. Symptoms may begin from fifteen minutes to several hours after consuming foods or drinks containing lactose. The severity varies from person to person—based on how much lactose is consumed related to other foods.

Because lactase insufficiency, or deficiency, varies, most people with lactose intolerance can tolerate dairy products in varying amounts. Some may need to avoid lactose altogether. In varying degrees, after about ages two to five years, lactase activity may decline gradually and naturally. Although the body may not produce enough lactase to completely digest lactose, it may produce no (or just mild) symptoms.

To clarify a misconception, lactose intolerance differs from a milk allergy. Lactose intolerance results from an inability to adequately digest lactose, a milk sugar. Most people with lactose intolerance can consume dairy foods, *as discussed in "Managing Lactose Intolerance" in this chapter, page 668*. A milk allergy is an immune response to milk protein. It happens when the body's disease-fighting (immune) system reacts to a protein, such as casein, in milk. Those with a milk allergy usually must avoid all milk products unless they outgrow the allergy. A doctor's diagnosis, management, and treatment of a milk allergy is imperative. *See "Food Allergies: A Growing Concern" in this chapter, page 654.*

WHO'S AT RISK?

From birth, most infants produce the lactase enzyme, so lactose intolerance is rare in young children, at least until they're weaned. With age, however, the body gradually may produce less lactase. For those with a genetic tendency, lactose intolerance often starts in the late teens or early adulthood. If your child has ongoing gastrointestinal discomfort, talk to your child's doctor.

Not enough evidence exists to really know how many people have low levels of lactase, but lactose intolerance appears to be less common than once thought. Past estimates, which were higher, were based on studies of people consuming unrealistic amounts of lactose; today's estimates reflect real-life intake. On average, as few as 12 percent of the US population have this condition. Many people who think they're lactose intolerant really aren't; they may have some degree of lactose malabsorption instead, with few if any symptoms. Malabsorption is when substances such as lactose can't be fully absorbed into the bloodstream.

Certain ethnic and racial populations are more widely affected than others: African Americans, Asian Americans, Hispanics, and Native Americans. The condition is least common among persons of northern European descent, who tend to maintain adequate lactose levels throughout their lives; they descend from regions where dairy production began.

Lactose intolerance is sometimes linked to other health issues. It can be a side effect of chemotherapy or certain medical issues such as celiac disease, Crohn's disease, flu, gastric (stomach) surgery, or other intestinal diseases. And some medications may lower lactase production in the body. Depending on the cause, this type of lactose (dairy) intolerance may be remedied once the medical condition is treated.

Common Foods: How Much Lactose?

Those with lactose intolerance likely can handle the amount of lactose in about one cup of milk without any, or with just minor, symptoms.

LACTOSE IN COMMON DAIRY FOODS

Product	Portion	Grams
Milk: whole, 2%, 1%, fat-free	1 cup	12–13
Lactaid® milk (lactose-free)	1 cup	0
Buttermilk (cultured milk)	1 cup	12
Goat's milk	1 cup	9
Evaporated milk	1 cup	24
Nonfat dry milk	¼ cup	12
Cottage cheese: low-fat, 2%	4 oz.	2–3
Hard cheeses: e.g., Cheddar, Swiss, mozzarella	1 oz.	0.3–1
Processed cheese	1 oz.	2–3
Greek yogurt, plain	4–6 oz.	2–4
Yogurt, plain	1 cup	11–17
Sour cream	1 Tbsp.	<0.5
Ice cream	8 oz.	6–7
Whey, fluid	1 cup	13
Whey, dry	1 Tbsp.	2
Whey isolate powder	3 oz.	1

Sources: US Department of Agriculture, National Nutrient Database for Standard Reference, Release 28, 2016. N. S. Scrimshaw, et al., *American Journal of Clinical Nutrition* Supplement 48 (4), 1988; www.lactaid.com.

Lactose-free foods include:

- Broth-based soups
- Plain meat, fish, poultry
- Vegetables and fruits (plain)
- Tofu and tofu products
- Soy, rice, potato, nut, almond, oat, and hempseed beverages; coconut milk
- Bread, cereal, crackers, and desserts made without milk, dry milk, or whey

DIAGNOSIS: TESTING FOR LACTOSE INTOLERANCE

If you suspect a lactose intolerance, skip the urge to diagnose yourself. Instead, see your doctor for a medical diagnosis. Discomfort in your gut might be caused by another condition, such as irritable bowel syndrome or celiac disease, which can cause lactose intolerance and, in turn, other health risks.

Lactose intolerance is diagnosed by health professionals based on medical, family, and diet history, including a review of symptoms, a physical exam, and medical tests that measure the effect of lactose on the digestive system. Tests include the hydrogen breath test, or a stool acidity test for infants and young children.

MANAGING LACTOSE INTOLERANCE

Lactose intolerance (LI) is easy to manage. Most people with lower lactase levels can include some dairy and other lactose-containing foods in their meals and snacks. In fact, most can drink a cup of milk—or consume 12 grams of lactose—at a time with little or no discomfort.

Dairy Nutrition: For LI

Even if your doctor has diagnosed you with lactose intolerance, there's no reason to give up dairy foods—or to miss out on the nutrients they provide. Lactose intolerance isn't an "all or nothing" condition. Instead, it's a matter of degree. Whether you have lactose intolerance, or some lesser degree of malabsorption that comes with getting older, learn to manage the amount of lactose you consume. Know your tolerance level.

? Have you ever wondered?

. . . if goat's milk is a good substitute for cow's milk for someone with lactose intolerance or a milk allergy? Goat's milk has slightly less lactose: 9 grams of lactose per cup, compared with about 12 to 13 grams of lactose in one cup of cow's milk. For a milk allergy, the protein in goat's milk is similar to that of cow's milk; it's not a suitable alternative.

. . . if a nondairy creamer can replace milk for someone who's lactose intolerant? How about nonfat dry milk? No for both. Nondairy creamers may contain lactose. Check the ingredient list on the label. The nutrient content of creamer and milk differs; in a nondairy creamer, the protein quality and the amounts of calcium and vitamins A and D are lower than in milk. Regarding nonfat dry milk, remember that fat, not lactose, has been removed.

. . . if a/B milk offers unique health benefits? Milk with added a/B cultures (Acidophilus and Bifidobacteria cultures) is similar to the milk it's made from, so it is generally high in lactose. Although research isn't conclusive, these cultures may help improve lactose digestion, promote healthy bacteria in the GI tract, and lower blood pressure; however, a/B milk is not acceptable for a milk allergy.

Needlessly avoiding milk and other dairy foods—and perhaps trying to rely on a supplement for dairy's nutrients—may lead to nutrient shortfalls and, as a result, possible health risks. Remember that dairy foods deliver more than calcium. They're also important sources of protein, riboflavin, vitamins A and D, magnesium, phosphorus, potassium, and other nutrients essential for bone health and many other health functions.

Without milk and other dairy foods, meeting calcium and vitamin D recommendations can be challenging. Calcium and vitamin D are especially important for bone health. Adequate amounts help children and teens grow strong, healthy bones and help prevent the bone-thinning conditions called osteopenia and osteoporosis later in life. Since people are living longer, bones need to stay healthy for eighty years and more. *See "Osteoporosis and Bone Health" in chapter 25, page 738, for more about these conditions.* For children, adequate vitamin D helps prevent bone-softening rickets.

For children and teens with lactose intolerance, the American Academy of Pediatrics advises that dairy foods provide nutrients essential for growth. Lower-lactose dairy foods are options. The Special Supplemental Nutrition Program for Women, Infants, and Children (WIC) advises lactose-reduced and lactose-free dairy options first, before nondairy alternatives. Many heath organizations agree.

If you're lactose-intolerant, consult a registered dietitian nutritionist to help you plan meals and snacks adequate in calcium and vitamin D, while controlling lactose. In extreme cases or for children or pregnant women with lactose intolerance, a doctor or dietitian also may recommend a calcium supplement with vitamin D.

See "A Closer Look . . . Calcium, Vitamin D, and Bone Health" in chapter 14, page 427, for more about the potentially unintended consequences of avoiding dairy.

Lactose: Know Its Sources

Lactose usually comes from foods containing milk or milk solids. Prepared foods, even those labeled "nondairy," may contain lactose. If you're very lactose intolerant, check labels carefully.

- Check labels for ingredients that suggest lactose: milk, dry milk solids (including nonfat milk solids), buttermilk, sour or sweet cream, cheese, margarine, lactose, malted milk, whey, and whey protein concentrate.
- Be aware that baked and processed foods often contain small amounts of lactose: baking and pancake mixes, bread, candy and cookies, cold cuts and hot dogs, commercial sauces and gravies, cream soups, drink mixes, dry cereals, margarine, prepared foods (such as frozen pizza, lasagna, waffles), powdered meal-replacement supplements, salad dressings made with cheese or milk, and sugar substitutes.
- Know that some medications contain lactose. If you're lactose intolerant, consult your doctor or pharmacist about appropriate medications.

Tips for Dairy Tolerance

If you or someone in your family has one of these conditions, try these tips to comfortably enjoy lactose-containing foods:

- Consume smaller amounts at a time. For example, drink one-half- or three-quarter-cup servings of milk several times a day instead of drinking a one-cup serving one, two, or three times daily.
- Train your body to adapt. Start with small, more frequent portions of lactose-containing foods to help intestinal bacteria aid the digestion of lactose. Gradually increase the portion to your tolerance level. Research indicates that the amount of lactose that many people can tolerate can be changed in as few as two to three weeks.
- Enjoy lactose-containing foods as part of a meal or snack, not alone, along with solid foods, perhaps smoothies, soups, or breakfast cereal. That slows the release of lactose into the small intestine, making it easier to digest. Think of this as "diluting" the lactose.
- Choose dairy foods that are naturally lower in lactose, such as natural cheeses. When cheese is made, curds (or solids) separate from the whey (or watery liquid); most lactose is in the whey,

which is drained away. Natural cheeses such as Cheddar, Colby, Parmesan, and Swiss lose most of their lactose during processing and aging.

- Try buttermilk, kefir, and yogurt with active cultures. Their "friendly" bacteria help digest lactose. Not all cultured dairy foods contain live cultures. Look for the National Yogurt Association's seal "Live and Active Cultures" on the carton. Some kinds of yogurt, such as strained yogurt, have lower lactose levels, too.

  Kefir without active cultures and sweet acidophilus milk? *Be aware:* Most are no lower in lactose than other dairy foods; they're tolerated at least as well as milk.
- Opt for whole-milk dairy products. Their higher fat content may help to slow the rate of digestion, allowing a gradual release of lactose. In your overall food choices, choose other foods with less fat. Some research suggests that chocolate milk is tolerated better than unflavored milk, but if so, the reasons aren't clear.
- Enjoy a variety of nondairy calcium-rich foods daily: calcium- and vitamin-D fortified products such as bread, cereal, juice, soymilk, and tofu (prepared with calcium sulfate); chia seeds; some dark-green leafy vegetables; some legumes; teff; and canned sardines and salmon with bones. For canned fish, eat the bones to get the calcium. The amount of calcium from nondairy foods may be insufficient if these are your main calcium sources. For example, eating several cups of dark-green leafy vegetables each day to meet calcium needs may be unrealistic.
- Read food labels. Check the ingredient list for sources of lactose in processed and prepared foods, such as milk solids, cream, or whey; also see if the label says: "Contains milk." Casein, lactalbumin, lactate, and lactic acid come from milk but don't contain lactose. Check the label, too, for lactose-free and lactose-reduced products. *See "Lactose: Know Its Sources" in this chapter, page 669.*
- Ask a registered dietitian nutritionist or your doctor about taking calcium and vitamin D supplements to help fill in any gaps. *See "A Closer Look . . . Calcium and Iron Supplements" in chapter 10, page 320, for more about these supplements.*

If You Are Lactose Intolerant: More Ways to Fit Dairy In

Food products have been developed for people with lactose intolerance. Some are lactose reduced. Others contain lactase, the enzyme that digests milk sugar. If you're lactose intolerant and if the *"Tips for Dairy Tolerance" in this chapter, page 669*, aren't enough:

- Buy low-lactose or lactose-free milk and other dairy foods. Lactose-free milk is regular milk with little or no lactose. These products provide the same important nutrients.
- Add lactase enzyme, available in drops, to fluid milk before drinking it. You'll find instructions on the package. Your milk will taste slightly sweeter because added lactase does the work of digesting lactose for your body, breaking down the lactose in milk into simpler, sweeter sugars.
- Before eating lactose-rich foods, take lactase, often in capsule or tablet form. With a supplemental supply of lactase, you can eat limited amounts without discomfort. Read the timing and dosage instructions on the label.

Gluten Free: When It's a Must

If you are trying to avoid gluten, do you know what gluten is and its role in food? Do you have a true health need that's been medically diagnosed for avoiding it? Do you know that avoiding carbohydrate foods isn't the same as "gluten free"? Gluten is poorly understood by the general public.

Non-celiac gluten sensitivity and celiac disease are gluten-related disorders. While the body can't tolerate gluten, neither one is a food allergy or a true food intolerance.

Gluten is a general term for a group of proteins (prolamin *gliadin* and the glutelin *glutenin*) stored in certain grains (wheat, barley, rye), related grains (such as emmer, farro, kamut, and spelt), and foods made from them. (Oats are considered naturally gluten free, although they may contain gluten from cross contact, usually with gluten-containing ingredients.)

In today's discourse about gluten, gliadin has been misidentified in some media as a new protein, introduced into wheat in recent decades. It's not. It always has been part of wheat protein.

CELIAC VS. NON-CELIAC: WHAT'S THE DIFFERENCE?

Celiac disease is an autoimmune disorder, whereby the immune system attacks itself. As the body's natural defense system, the immune system normally protects the body from infection. However, with active celiac disease, gluten causes the immune system to react in a way that can cause intestinal inflammation and long-lasting damage. Celiac disease also is called celiac sprue, gluten-sensitive enteropathy, and nontropical sprue.

In unmanaged celiac disease, the immune system responds to gluten by damaging or destroying villi, the small, hairlike projections that line the small intestine. As a result, the intestine can't absorb nutrients properly into the bloodstream.

Without healthy villi, someone with celiac disease can become malnourished, even though he or she eats enough nourishing foods. Over time, and whether or not symptoms appear, damage from unmanaged

Hyperactivity: Any Food Link?

The notion of linking sugar, food additives, or gluten to hyperactive behavior or attention deficit hyperactivity disorder (ADHD) in children isn't supported by conclusive scientific evidence. Although the exact cause of ADHD isn't known, factors such as genetics and environmental influences have been suggested.

The Feingold diet, popularized in the past for its claimed ability to manage ADHD, has been touted for treating hyperactive children. It restricts foods containing salicylates, present in almonds; certain vegetables and fruits; artificial flavors and colors; and preservatives. However, its reported success was based on anecdotal data, not scientific research. Although many other studies have been conducted attempting to link foods with hyperactivity, a clear cause-and-effect link between food or cetain ingredients and hyperactivity hasn't been shown. Research is also investigating a potential link between ADHD, gluten, and celiac disease.

Until researchers learn more, the best management of ADHD includes behavioral modification and medication, if warranted by a doctor. If you choose to avoid food coloring or other additives, check the ingredient list on food labels.

See "Carbs and Health: Myths or Truths?" in chapter 11, page 349, for more about the misconceptions between sugar and behavior.

celiac disease increases many health risks, including anemia, arthritis, diabetes, gastrointestinal cancers, growth retardation in children, infertility, miscarriage and birth defects, delayed puberty, early osteoporosis, and thyroid conditions.

Non-celiac gluten sensitivity (NCGS) is clinically different. It's currently thought to be an innate immune-system response to gluten, not an auto-immune condition. Antibodies to gluten aren't formed. Experts note that new varieties of wheat, wheat hybrids, and the quality of grains that have been introduced in recent decades have been ruled out as causes.

Research on non-celiac gluten sensitivity is limited, but evolving. Among the issues being investigated: Could symptoms be caused by gluten or instead by other poorly digested carbohydrates, referred to collectively as FODMAPs (present in some gluten-containing grains and other foods)? Could consuming small amounts of gluten over time result in long-term health risks? *See "A Closer Look . . . FODMAPs" in chapter 25, page 730.*

WHO'S AT RISK?

Celiac disease is hereditary. If someone in your immediate family has celiac disease, your risk is much higher. But family history alone isn't always the best gauge.

Celiac disease is more common among people with European roots, but African, Asian including East Indian, Hispanic, and Middle Eastern populations are increasingly being diagnosed with celiac disease. The actual incidence of celiac disease in the United States is unknown since many cases aren't diagnosed. As many as one in 141 Americans has celiac disease, although most remain undiagnosed, notes the National Institute of Diabetes and Digestive and Kidney Diseases. However, the incidence is significantly higher for those with a genetic risk. Celiac disease can occur at any age. Symptoms may appear first during infancy after cereal is started. Most cases are diagnosed in adulthood, often four to five years after the first symptoms.

The longer celiac disease goes undiagnosed and untreated, the greater the chance of long-term health complications.

NCGS doesn't appear to be genetic, but does appear to be much more common than celiac disease. It can occur at any age as well as to those who have tolerated gluten before. An estimated 4 to 6 percent of Americans have this condition.

SYMPTOMS?

For people with celiac disease, up to 50 percent may have no gastrointestinal (GI) symptoms. For those who do, symptoms vary. Malabsorption may cause abdominal bloating, cramps, or gas; chronic constipation; diarrhea; and stomach pain—and perhaps appetite loss, fatigue, vomiting, and weight loss. Nerves and skin also can be involved. Some people experience a painful rash and perhaps eczema, joint pain, muscle cramps, and other symptoms. Malabsorption is when certain substances such as gluten can't be absorbed—or are poorly absorbed—into the bloodstream.

Temporary lactose malabsorption may accompany celiac disease, at least until the condition is under control and the small intestine heals. Healing may take months or years.

For children, chronic irritability could be a warning sign. For growth and development, a child's high energy and nutrient needs require adequate nourishment. Unmanaged celiac disease can affect a child's behavior and ability to grow and learn. Malabsorption of nutrients can lead to failure to thrive in infancy, delayed growth, short stature, delayed puberty, and dental enamel defects of permanent teeth.

Celiac disease is often misdiagnosed or significantly underdiagnosed. Why? Symptoms can imitate other health problems such as anemia, chronic fatigue syndrome, diverticulitis, inflammatory bowel disease, intestinal infections, and irritable bowel syndrome. Although many people with celiac disease have no symptoms, they still can develop complications over time. Often, celiac disease goes undetected until triggered by other body stresses: perhaps pregnancy, surgery, a viral infection, or severe emotional stress.

For people with NCGS, symptoms mimic celiac disease. Besides intestinal discomfort, they may include fatigue, headaches, a "foggy mind," and others. Intestinal symptoms are uncomfortable and often worsen over time, but this condition probably won't damage the intestine. A gluten-free diet relieves the symptoms.

Label Lingo

Words That Indicate Gluten

WHEAT, BARLEY, AND RYE: AVOID THEM!

Carefully read all food labels and ingredient lists to see if the food contains wheat, barley, or rye. Although many sources of these grains are obvious, others may not be. Use this information to help identify hidden sources of wheat, barley, and rye in ingredient lists.

OTHER TERMS FOR WHEAT

These words indicate the presence of wheat. No foods with any of these ingredients should be eaten:

- bromated flour
- durum flour
- enriched flour
- farina
- flour
- graham flour
- phosphated flour
- plain flour
- self-rising flour
- semolina
- white flour

Avoid oats unless labeled "gluten free" since production may result in cross contact with wheat—and only after consulting with your doctor or registered dietitian nutritionist.

These products also contain wheat gluten: bulgur, couscous, farro, Kamut®, matzoh meal/flour, spelt, and triticale.

If a food or an ingredient contains wheat or protein from wheat, "wheat" must be stated clearly on the food label. If another term for wheat is used in an ingredient list, "wheat" must appear on the food label in the ingredient list or in a "Contains" statement. For meat products, poultry products, and egg products, only the common or usual name of ingredients is required currently—and only on the ingredient list. *See "Food Labels: Decode the Package" in chapter 6, page 144, for more about reading ingredient lists.*

INGREDIENTS MADE FROM WHEAT

Some ingredients, including modified food starch, dextrin, and caramel color, may be derived from wheat. If a food has an ingredient (with protein from wheat) such as these, "wheat" must appear on the food label in the ingredient list or in a "Contains" statement. This applies to flavorings, colorings, and incidental additives as well. If a spice blend or seasoning mix contains wheat, it must be stated on the label.

FOODS AND INGREDIENTS MADE FROM BARLEY

Some foods and ingredients usually are made from barley (unless it is otherwise stated on the food label). Avoid foods with these ingredients:

- beer, ale, porter, stout, other fermented beverages (*Note:* Distilled alcoholic beverages, such as vodka and gin, are gluten free; gluten-free beers are available.)
- malt
- malt flavoring
- malt syrup or malt extract
- malt vinegar (*Note:* Other types of vinegar—such as cider, wine, and distilled—are gluten free.)
- malted beverages
- malted milk

PROCESSED FOODS THAT MAY CONTAIN WHEAT, BARLEY, OR RYE

These are some examples of processed foods that may contain wheat, barley, or rye. Check the ingredient list of all processed foods.

- brewer's yeast
- bouillon cubes
- brown rice syrup
- candy
- cold cuts, hot dogs, salami, and sausage
- communion wafers
- french fries
- gravy
- imitation fish
- matzo
- pasta
- rice mixes
- sauces
- seasoned tortilla chips and potato chips
- self-basting turkey
- seitan
- soups
- soy sauce
- vegetables in sauce

SUPPLEMENTS AND MEDICATIONS

Some medications—prescription and over-the-counter—and vitamin and mineral supplements may contain ingredients made from wheat or barley. Talk with your doctor and pharmacist about any medications you are taking. You also may want to contact the individual manufacturers and ask whether the supplement or medication contains any ingredients made from wheat or barley.

For dietary supplements, infant formulas, and medical foods that contain wheat or wheat protein, including flavoring, coloring, or incidental ingredients, "wheat" must be clearly stated on the label.

Adapted from *Nutrition Care Manual*, Academy of Nutrition and Dietetics. Accessed November 22, 2016.

DIAGNOSIS: TESTING FOR CELIAC DISEASE

If you think you have celiac disease or non-celiac gluten sensitivity, ask your doctor for a diagnosis *before* starting a gluten-free diet on your own. Eliminating gluten first can interfere with getting an accurate diagnosis. For an accurate test result, you need to be eating gluten at the time of testing to identify the biomarkers of celiac disease. There is no test for celiac disease for someone already on a gluten-free diet.

Why does it matter to know if the problem is celiac disease or NCGS, or something else? Self-diagnosis can lead to the wrong treatment, to harmful health consequences, or to an unnecessarily gluten-free diet. You wouldn't self-diagnose diabetes or heart disease; same goes for gluten-related disorders such as celiac disease or NCGS.

Celiac disease is diagnosed with blood tests, an intestinal biopsy, and other tests. During the testing, a form of lactose intolerance, may be detected. If celiac disease runs in your family, consider a genetic test even if you have no symptoms.

NCGS has no biomarkers. For that reason, no medical tests can confirm non-celiac gluten sensitivity. If you feel symptomatic, get tested first by a physician with expertise in celiac disease and food allergies. If these results are negative, then your doctor may advise a gluten-elimination diet, followed by a challenge with gluten. If symptoms improve when gluten is removed and reoccur when gluten is consumed again, you probably have a non-celiac gluten sensitivity.

NCGS is diagnosed by exclusion—and only if (1) celiac disease, a gluten or wheat allergy, and other related conditions have been ruled out, and (2) symptoms improve when gluten is removed but reoccur when gluten is reintroduced. *Be aware:* Saliva, blood, and stool tests are not validated or acceptable assessments for NCGS.

MANAGING GLUTEN-RELATED DISORDERS

For celiac disease, there is no cure or medical treatment. After a diagnosis, follow up with your doctor or a registered dietitian nutritionist is important. The only treatment is a strict gluten-free eating regimen for life. Once gluten is eliminated, the small intestine can start to heal. Nutrient absorption then improves, symptoms gradually disappear, damage can reverse, and associated health risks lessen.

Currently, the treatment for NCGS also is a gluten-free diet, but it's unclear whether this regimen needs to be lifelong. Those with either condition can live a long, healthy life—and enjoy nourishing, flavorful foods, too.

To eat gluten free to manage celiac disease or NCGS, follow this advice:

- Consult a registered dietitian nutritionist to learn how to eat gluten free, get all the nutrients you need from other sources, and enjoy eating. Ask about a supplement to fill in any nutrient gaps in a gluten-free diet. *Be aware:* Weight gain can be a side effect when someone with celiac disease starts a gluten-free diet. The reason is that the body is better able to absorb more nutrients and calories from food. *See "Nutrition Advice to Trust" in chapter 26, page 758, to find a qualified nutrition expert.*
- Find local and national support groups to share information and gluten-free recipes. Many support groups publish lists of acceptable food products by brand name, which can serve as a guide. A registered dietitian nutritionist can help you find a support group, a trustworthy blog, or online support.
- *If your child has celiac disease, see "A Closer Look . . . Helping Kids Deal with Food Allergies or Other Adverse Food Reactions" in this chapter, page 658, to ways to deal with celiac disease at school and elsewhere, and with friends.*

Note: Although not a treatment and not medically necessary, a gluten-free diet may offer some benefit to some people with other autoimmune disorders, such as multiple sclerosis, rheumatoid arthritis, or thyroid disease, or with autism. A doctor can determine if this may benefit someone with these conditions.

Gluten: Know Its Sources

Bagels, pasta, wheat tortillas, and whole-wheat bread are great sources of starches, other nutrients, and perhaps fiber. Those who react to gluten must get these nutrients from products that are gluten free.

Gluten free means no wheat, barley, rye, or their hybrids, no uncertified gluten-free oats, and no food or food component made from them. For those with celiac disease, even trace amounts of gluten can damage the small intestine. While gluten is mostly in food (including many processed foods), medicines and supplements may contain it, too.

Avoiding gluten from wheat can be challenging. That's because wheat is the main ingredient in many baked foods such as breads, breakfast cereals, breaded foods, crackers, pasta, and pretzels, among others.

Gluten-free labeling. "Gluten-free," "no gluten," "free of gluten," "without gluten." To make it easier to identify gluten-free products, the FDA released standards for voluntary labeling of "gluten-free" foods. The definition says that a product must contain less than 20 parts per million (ppm) of gluten, or contain no barley, rye, wheat, or other crossbred hybrids. It may be labeled "gluten-free" whether it is manufactured to be free of gluten or naturally gluten-free.

Testing by the manufacturer isn't required. The product may have a symbol to identify a food that meets these standards. *See "Gluten-Free Labeling" in chapter 6, page 152.* This FDA regulation doesn't apply to alcoholic beverages, prescription and over-the-counter drugs, pet foods, or cosmetics, which are regulated by a different agency—the Alcohol and Tobacco Tax and Trade Bureau (TTB). Nor does it cover products regulated by the US Department of Agriculture (USDA): meat, poultry, and certain egg products.

As an interim rule issued in 2014 by the TTB, alcoholic beverages made from ingredients that do *not* contain gluten may be labeled as "gluten-free." This includes wines fermented from fruit and spirits distilled from products other than grains with gluten. Alcoholic beverages made from gluten-containing grains may be labeled "Processed," "Treated," or "Crafted" to remove gluten. In that case, the claim must also show a qualifier, warning that the gluten content can't be determined and that the beverage may contain gluten.

Despite "gluten-free" claims, you still need to read further for ingredients listed on food labels. Unlike the eight common allergens, gluten doesn't need to appear on the ingredient list. And the word "gluten" won't appear in the Nutrition Facts. *See "Label Lingo: Words That Indicate Gluten" in this chapter, page 672.*

Shopping for Gluten-Free Foods—and More

If you—or someone you know—must eat gluten free, follow these shopping guidelines:

- Know that gluten free doesn't mean grain free. Choose among the many grain products and other starchy foods without gluten. Some of these grains may be unfamiliar, but they are used in gluten-free foods. Look for them on ingredient lists. *See "Gluten Free: Naturally!" in this chapter, page 674.*
- Ask your doctor or registered dietitian nutritionist about oats. In the past, people with celiac disease were advised to avoid oats. Evidence indicates that gluten-free oats in small amounts (½ cup dry oats or ¼ cup dry steel-cut oats)—not contaminated with wheat, barley, or rye during processing—are usually safe. If allowed, use only "gluten-free"–labeled oats. A small percentage of people with celiac disease can't tolerate gluten-free oats.
- Choose plain foods. All plain vegetables, fruits, meat, poultry, fish, eggs, milk, yogurt, cheese, nuts, seeds, and beans and peas are naturally gluten free. Remember that gluten-free labeling is voluntary so foods that are naturally gluten free may not be labeled "gluten-free."
- Look for products labeled as "gluten-free." Today, gluten-free bakery items, baking mixes, flour, pasta, pizza, snack foods, and soups are widely available in most grocery stores—often in a separate aisle in the store. You also can check specialty and health food stores, and online and mail order outlets.
- Look at the ingredient list and the "Contains" statement on a food label to identify gluten-containing ingredients. For example, flavored chips may be dusted with an ingredient made with wheat; malt flavoring, which is made from barley, is used in many dry cereals.

  If an ingredient such as modified food starch is made from wheat starch and contains wheat protein, allergen labeling on FDA-regulated food labels requires that "wheat" be declared. Malt would be on the ingredient list only; it's not included in allergen labeling. For USDA-regulated foods (egg, meat, and poultry

Gluten Free: Naturally!

Eating gluten free offers many nourishing, flavorful options. Besides vegetables, fruits, beans and peas, nuts, seeds, low-fat and fat-free dairy, fish, poultry, and meat,* try these grains, starches, and flours† that are gluten free:

Gluten-Free Grains

amaranth	quinoa
buckwheat	rice (brown, white)
corn (maize)	sorghum
Job's tears	teff
millet	wild rice
oats (labeled gluten free or pure/uncontaminated)	

Gluten-Free Starches

arrowroot	sago
cassava (manioc)	tapioca
corn	yucca
potato	

Gluten-Free Flours

flours from gluten-free grains	nut flours (e.g., almond, hazelnut, peanut)
legume and lentil flours (e.g., chickpea, fava, garfava)	soy flour

*Read food labels to make sure products don't contain ingredients with gluten. Be aware that many flours such as soy flours may have cross-contact with gluten-containing ingredients.

†Some grain products, such as millet and soy flours, are at higher risk for cross-contact with gluten. Some experts advise that all grain products eaten by those with celiac disease should be labeled "gluten free."

Adapted from: International Food Information Council Foundation.

? Have you ever wondered?

. . . if gluten-free products have less protein? That's an interesting question since gluten is a protein in some grains. The answer: It depends on what is used as a replacement. Use the Nutrition Facts on food labels to compare the amount of protein in gluten-free products to their traditional counterparts.

. . . if corn gluten is the same as gluten in wheat? No. In fact, this is a misnomer. The protein in corn is safe for those with celiac disease.

? Have you ever wondered?

. . . if a wheat allergy is the same as either celiac disease or NCGS? No; they're different conditions: different physiological responses, treated in somewhat different ways. With both a wheat allergy and celiac disease, wheat products and foods made with wheat products must be avoided. With celiac disease, barley and rye must be avoided, too. That's also the advice for NCGS.

Some with a wheat allergy may choose to go gluten free to be on the safe side. However, wheat substitutes, including barley and rye, are okay for a wheat allergy but not for celiac disease or NCGS. *See "Gluten Free: When It's a Must" in this chapter, page 670.*

Note: If wheat starch is specially processed to remove gluten, new FDA rules allow wheat starch in gluten-free foods.

. . . if modern wheat has more gluten than in the last century? There's no evidence that plant breeding over the past ninety or so years has increased the gluten content of wheat. And contrary to myth, world-wide, today's commercially available wheat—both modern and heirloom wheat—is derived from farmer selection and traditional breeding and is not genetically engineered. *See "A Closer Look . . . Understanding Biotechnology" in chapter 5, page 123, to learn about plant breeding.*

Some wheat varietals have more protein; others, less. The reason is their different uses. Pasta is made with wheat that has stronger gluten, while Asian noodles are made with wheat that has weaker gluten. Regardless, those with celiac disease and wheat allergy need to avoid them both.

. . . if glutinous rice has gluten? No. Its misleading name comes from its sticky, or glue-like, texture from the starch when it's cooked.

products), allergen labeling is voluntary, so the allergen "wheat" may not be shown. Only common or usual names, such as modified food starch or malt, are required.

- For gluten-free grain products made with refined grains, choose those that are enriched with B vitamins (thiamin, riboflavin, niacin) and iron, and fortified with folic acid. Be aware that fortification isn't required for gluten-free products that are whole grain.
- Check the label's ingredient list *every time* before consuming any product. Many commercially prepared foods—baked, canned, and frozen—have gluten-containing ingredients, but the ingredients may change. Contact the food manufacturer with ingredient questions. The company name, address, and perhaps a toll-free consumer information number or website are on the food label. *Remember:* "Wheat free" does not mean gluten free.
- Avoid bulk bins at grocery stores; ingredients can get into other bins. Gluten-free foods shelved under flour or loosely packaged bakery items can be a problem, too. Be aware that in a bakery, wheat flour can also stay in the air for several hours and expose surfaces, utensils, and gluten-free foods that aren't well packaged.
- Skip both alcoholic and nonalcoholic beer. Beer, including ale, lager, malt beverages, and stout, made from gluten-containing grains, is not distilled and so not gluten free. Avoid beer and other beverages identified as "gluten-removed" since it's not determined if they are safe for those with celiac disease.

  Instead, purchase beer made only with grains such as millet, rice, and sorghum. They are regulated by the FDA since they don't meet the TTB definition of beer. They may be labeled as "gluten-free." Unflavored distilled alcoholic beverages such as vodka and gin are gluten free. Those that are flavored may contain barley malt. Hard ciders and wine coolers also may contain added flavorings that have gluten.
- Ask your pharmacist if your medications contain wheat or gluten. Gluten may be an unexpected additive in some products. Read the ingredient list on labels for over-the-counter medications; ask the manufacturer. For prescriptions, ask your pharmacist. As a shortcut, visit the Gluten-Free Drugs website www.glutenfreedrugs.com, which lists many prescription and over-the-counter drugs. Regulations for gluten-free labeling for medications have been proposed, but not passed.

Storing and Preparing Gluten-Free Food at Home

Coping with celiac disease requires a strict food preparation and eating regimen. It's not just skipping the bun on the burger or scraping crusty breading off fried chicken. For those with celiac disease, even a trace of gluten such as a bread crumb can cause problems. Whether NCGS requires the same degree of strictness is unknown, but those with this disorder are advised to limit gluten until symptoms resolve.

While a gluten-free kitchen is challenging at first—especially in a shared kitchen—in time it becomes second nature. These tips can get you started:

- Store gluten-free ingredients separately from and above gluten-containing ingredients in your pantry or refrigerator.
- Purchase and use separate cutting boards, cooking equipment, and serving utensils for gluten-free foods, such as a second "gluten-free" toaster. Keep food preparation surfaces free of crumbs.
- Use good dishwashing and cleaning skills for all dishes, pots, pans, and utensils to remove any gluten ingredient.
- Substitute gluten-free flours for wheat flour in food prep. *See "Gluten Free: Naturally!" in this chapter, page 674.* Mix different flours. Because they give a different flavor and texture to baked goods,

using these flours takes practice and experimentation. (Gluten gives dough its elasticity, and bread, its structure.)

- *For baking and other food prep, also see the wheat-free substitutions in "Handy Substitutions for Allergen-Free Cooking" in this chapter, page 665.* Remember that wheat free is not gluten free.
- Avoid nonnutritive sweeteners if you have celiac disease because they affect friendly gut bacteria.
- Reduce the chance of cross-contact by having two sets of condiment jars for mayonnaise, mustard, or peanut butter to avoid cross-contact with utensils. Or get squeezable condiment containers.

Eating Gluten Free Away from Home

Eating away from home? You're in control of your own kitchen—not so when you eat out. The same grill may be used for eggs and pancakes; regular and gluten-free pasta may be cooked in the same pot of water; and the same fryer may be used for breaded and nonbreaded items.

When you eat out, follow this advice:

- Check ahead to find a restaurant with a gluten-free menu. Call, if possible, to discuss your needs. Be cautious about restaurants where language may be a communication challenge.
- Plan ahead. Dine early or late, when the restaurant has more time to handle your needs. Pack gluten-free bread to take with you if you want bread with your meal.
- Read restaurant menus carefully. Know that the FDA gluten-free labeling rule doesn't apply to restaurants, but the FDA suggests that they define gluten free in the same way.
- Ask questions as you order, not just about ingredients but how the food is prepared. Ask that food be prepared with separate and thoroughly cleaned equipment and surfaces.
- Create and present a chef card, *like the one in this chapter, page 666*, to explain your needs to the kitchen. Only those who prepare your food know what's in it.

Do You Have Celiac?

Use this online checklist from the National Foundation for Celiac Awareness to see if you should talk with your doctor:

- Celiac Disease Symptoms Checklist
  www.DoIHaveCeliac.org
- Celiac Disease Foundation
  celiac.org
- Celiac Support Association
  www.csaceliacs.org
- Gluten Intolerance Group
  www.gluten.org

Gluten: Clarifying Misconceptions

- Is a gluten-free diet effective for weight loss? That notion appears in popular media, but no evidence shows that simply going gluten-free results in weight loss. When people give up wheat, they're often skipping sweet desserts and snack foods that contain excess calories and perhaps eating more vegetables, fruits, and other nutrient-rich foods. They mistakenly attribute their weight loss with going gluten- or wheat-free. Ironically, some people gain weight when they go gluten-free!
- Does a gluten-free diet offer health benefits—even if you don't have celiac disease or non-celiac gluten sensitivity? Many people have given gluten-free eating a "health halo." Yet, scientific evidence shows health benefits *only* to those with diagnosed celiac disease, non-celiac gluten sensitivity, or another condition in which symptoms are improved without gluten in the diet.
- Are gluten-free foods healthier? "Gluten-free" doesn't signal better grain products, either. Some gluten-free packaged foods have more fat, added sugars, and calories than their regular counterparts.
- Will eliminating grain foods guarantee a gluten-free diet? No, gluten-containing ingredients are used in many processed foods, *as noted in "Words That Indicate Gluten" in this chapter, page 672*. Learn to be a label reader.

Risky situations. If you must eat gluten free, be cautious of these common situations:

- Buffet-style or family-style service—cross-contact with gluten-containing ingredients is likely, especially since the same serving utensils may be used for different dishes.
- Meats such as steak and prime rib—seasonings and au jus sauce may contain gluten. Imitation bacon bits and self-basting turkey need checking, too.
- Fried foods—the same oil may be used for different foods.
- Dairy foods—they may appear to be dairy, but nondairy foods (e.g., non-dairy creamer, whipped topping, "sour cream") may have gluten-containing ingredients. Ask, and read the ingredient list.
- Rice dishes, hash browns—prepackaged products may have gluten ingredients. Order plain steamed rice or rice cooked in water.
- Soups and sauces—soup bases, broth, bouillon, thickeners, and seasonings often have gluten-containing ingredients. It's safest to skip sauces, or ask if canned sauces or soups are used as ingredients.
- Salads—salad dressings may have unsafe ingredients. Ask for vinegar and oil, or a lemon wedge and oil on the side. Or bring your

own safe dressing from home. Skip the croutons and any imitation bacon bits.

- If you're a guest in someone's home, explain your special food needs ahead, preferably before the menu is planned. Offer to bring food to share. Ask if you can serve yourself first, before the chance of cross-contact with other foods may happen.

See chapter 9, page 275, for more restaurant tips.

Have you ever wondered?

. . . what wheat gluten is and how it's used in cooking? Wheat gluten, also known as seitan, is wheat protein. Sold in specialty stores, it has a chewy, meaty texture, making it a good, protein-rich ingredient in casseroles, soups, pasta sauces, and other recipes calling for chopped or ground meat or poultry. *Caution:* People with celiac disease, non-celiac gluten sensitivity, and wheat allergy should avoid wheat gluten.

. . . how to find gluten-free restaurant food? Today, more restaurants provide menu items that are gluten free and food-allergy friendly. Chefs, cooks, and servers are being trained to be food-allergy- and gluten-free-aware, and may provide gluten-free menus on request. Some restaurants participate in the Gluten-Free Food Service program of the Gluten Intolerance Group: www.gffoodservice.org/certified-directory/certified-food-services.

Some states are considering legislation for posting allergen signs in restaurants and for requiring servers to ask patrons if they have a known food allergy. The FDA says that restaurants making a gluten-free claim on their menus should keep their claims consistent with FDA's food labeling definition.

. . . if gluten-free communion wafers are available? Yes, both gluten-free (<20 ppm gluten) and low-gluten wafers that meet requirements of the Catholic Code of Canon Law are available. They may be used for communion with the permission of a priest or pastor. Even then, the possible risk of cross-contact by those handling regular communion wafers may be an issue. Communion with wine only may be another option. In most Protestant churches, a gluten-free option for bread is acceptable.

. . . if it's best to just avoid all grain foods when you need to eat gluten free? That isn't a smart option! Without enriched and fortified breads and cereals, you miss out on their B vitamins, including folate, and iron. By avoiding whole grains, you likely get shortchanged on fiber. Instead, check labels and choose gluten-free grain products that are fortified with folic acid and iron.

. . . how to stay gluten free if you're a vegetarian? The same advice applies, with some added advice: (1) find gluten-free protein sources; be aware that some protein foods enjoyed by vegetarians may contain gluten (barley-based miso, falafel, seitan, tempeh, veggie burgers); (2) find gluten-free grain alternatives for vegetarian dishes; and (3) choose gluten-free cereals that are with iron fortified.

. . . what to do if you love pasta? Check the gluten-free aisle of the store for options for pastas made with brown rice or quinoa. Look for other new sources, too, such as green banana pasta. Some alternatives have more calories and fat than traditional wheat pasta because fat is added for flavor appeal.

My Aching Head

Two to 20 percent of Americans suffer from migraines (severe head pain plus a range of other symptoms such as nausea, vomiting, or increased sensitivity to light, sound, and smells). Migraine headaches can affect anyone, but women are three times more likely than men to suffer; those with a family history of migraines are more susceptible. Migraines are most common between the ages of twelve and forty.

The causes of migraine headaches are complicated and not well understood. There's little agreement about the link between foods and headaches. And certain food components—natural or added—have been suspected, but not proven, to cause headaches in some people. For example, benzoic acid (a preservative), histamine (in red wine), nitrates (in processed meats), and tyrosine (in aged cheese, canned beans, and processed meats), are among the more common food-related triggers. Susceptible individuals may be affected by several factors, not just food.

If you experience chronic headaches, check with your doctor for a medical diagnosis. To determine which foods or drinks, if any, trigger migraine attacks, keep a journal, often for several weeks, of what you eat and drink, and how much.

If you're diagnosed with migraine headaches and feel you're susceptible to food triggers, a registered dietitian nutritionist can recommend substitutes for suspected triggers and ensure adequate nutrition. Some migraine sufferers may be advised to follow a diet with less tyramine. Tyramine is produced in foods when the amino acid tyrosine breaks down naturally; that happens in higher-protein foods with aging, fermentation, or longer storage.

Sensitive to Additives? Maybe, Maybe Not

Do you wonder what some ingredients on food labels do? Some improve the nutritional value. Some, such as spices and colors, enhance a food's flavor and appearance. Others prevent spoilage or give foods the consistency you expect. Without them, the food supply likely would be far more limited, less safe, and even less appealing. *See "Additives: Their Place on the Plate" in chapter 5, page 132.*

Consuming a food additive rarely causes adverse reactions. When it does, the response is commonly a sensitivity—not a true allergy. And the food itself, not the additive, is more often the cause. If you think you have a reaction to a certain additive, avoid it for a few days. Then get tested by your doctor. If the test is positive, learn how to avoid the additive and how to alert others if your reaction may be severe.

The FDA, which regulates food additives, considers food intolerances and allergies when approving their use. Preservatives, colors, and flavors are linked more commonly to food reactions than other additives. *See "Hyperactivity: Any Food Link?" in this chapter, page 671, for more about possible reactions to food additives.*

SULFITE SENSITIVITY: MILD TO SEVERE

Have you ever wondered why some dried apricots and dehydrated potatoes contain sulfites? Sulfites help prevent certain foods, such as vegetables, light-colored fruits, and dried fruits, from browning. In beer, wine, and other fermented foods, sulfites slow bacterial growth.

The term "sulfites" is a catchall, referring to several common food additives. Usually they have "sulf" in their names. Sulfites may be listed on food labels as sulfur dioxide, sodium sulfite, sodium or potassium bisulfite, sodium or potassium metabisulfite, sulfurous acid, and sodium dithionite.

For most people, sulfites in a varied diet pose no risk of side effects. However, the FDA estimates that one in a hundred people is sulfite sensitive. Asthmatics react more often to sulfites; the reaction may be severe. Among those without asthma, the incidence is considered rare.

For those who are sulfite sensitive, reactions may include diarrhea, hives, stomachache, swelling, or wheezing. Fortunately, side effects are mostly mild. However, reactions may become life-threatening for those who are very sensitive to sulfite. In rare cases, they may experience anaphylactic shock and require immediate medical care. *See "Symptoms? Something to Sneeze About" in this chapter, page 665, for more about anaphylaxis and other reactions.*

Consult your doctor for a medical evaluation if you think you're sulfite sensitive. Don't self-diagnose or self-impose dietary restrictions; that may lead to nutrient deficiencies. Because sulfites can trigger intense reactions in sulfite-sensitive asthmatics, the FDA prohibits using sulfites on vegetables (except potatoes) and fruits intended to be served or sold raw. In the past, sulfites sometimes were used to keep vegetables and fruits fresh longer on restaurant salad bars; that's no longer allowed.

Where Might You Find Sulfites?*

- Baked goods
- Beverages (vegetable and fruit juices, tea, beer, wine, and hard cider)
- Condiments and pickled cocktail onions
- Dried and sliced potatoes, sauerkraut, maraschino cherries, dried fruits, and fruit toppings
- Grape juice (white, pink, and red sparkling) and bottled lemon and lime juices
- Gravies, molasses, sauces, sauerkraut juice, and wine vinegar

*Check food labels for other sources. Some bulk foods may be sources as well.

Source: Nutrition Care Manual, Academy of Nutrition and Dietetics. Accessed November 22, 2016.

Managing a Sulfite Sensitivity

If you're among those who are sulfite sensitive, follow this advice:

- Check food labels to identify additives with sulfites, such as sulfur dioxide or sodium bisulfite. Be aware that they're used in varying amounts in many packaged foods, not just dehydrated potatoes, dried fruits, and fruit juices. By law, when sulfites are present in detectable amounts (10 ppm or more), the label must say so. *See "Where Might You Find Sulfites?" above.*
- Check alcoholic beverages. Labels on beer and wine must state "Contains Sulfites" if applicable above. De-alcoholized beer and wine still may contain sulfites.
- Ask about ingredients in restaurants before ordering. For example, ask if dried or canned foods, vegetables, or potato products contain—or were treated with—sulfites.
- Know that sulfites don't lose their effect with cooking.
- Make a plan with your doctor if you consume sulfites accidentally. Always carry a rescue inhaler!
- Be aware that some asthma and allergy medications contain sulfites. If you're sulfite sensitive, ask for another medication.
- Know that you can consume foods with *sulfates*. Sulfates such as calcium sulfate (an additive used to fortify foods with calcium) don't cause the same adverse reaction in sulfite-sensitive people.

COLOR ADDITIVES: RARE REACTIONS

Although the incidence is rare, a very small number—one or two of every ten thousand—of people are sensitive to a coloring added to food. FD&C Yellow No. 5, also called tartrazine, is a dye used to color foods, beverages, and medications. Research indicates that FD&C Yellow No. 5 may trigger hives, itching, and nasal congestion but not asthma attacks. This is the only food coloring known to cause such reactions.

When added to a food or a medication, FD&C Yellow No. 5 must be listed on the label or package insert. If you're sensitive to it, read labels carefully. Foods and beverages likely to contain tartrazine include candies; cheese dishes; flavor extracts; gelatins; ice cream; pudding, cake, and frosting mixes; salad dressings; seasoned salts; sherbets; and soft drinks.

ASPARTAME: PKU WARNING

Since their discovery, low-calorie or nonnutritive sweeteners—acesulfame K, aspartame, saccharin, sucralose, and tagatose—have been investigated thoroughly by regulatory agencies worldwide and by leading scientific organizations. Evidence indicates that their long-term intake is safe and not associated with adverse health effects. *See "Nonnutritive Sweeteners: Flavor without Calories" in chapter 11, page 369.*

With one exception, nonnutritive sweeteners don't cause symptoms of food sensitivity. People with the rare genetic disorder phenylketonuria (PKU) should avoid foods sweetened with aspartame. Aspartame is made from two amino acids (aspartic acid and phenylalanine) and methanol. The same amino acids are found naturally in meat, milk, vegetables, and fruits. Regardless of the source, people with PKU cannot metabolize phenylalanine properly, so they can consume only limited amounts of it. Unmanaged, PKU can cause tissue damage, and in infants, brain damage. As a precaution, all babies are screened for PKU at birth; that is when a diagnosis is made.

Need more strategies for handling food sensitivities?

Check here for "how-tos":

- Sharpen up on ingredient detection as you shop; *see chapter 6, page 150.*
- Ask the right menu questions when you eat out; *see chapter 9, page 278.*
- Monitor an infant's food-induced reactions; *see chapter 16, page 479.*
- Get more help from a registered dietitian nutritionist; *see chapter 26, page 758.*
- Find organizations that offer additional help; *see page 763.*

For those who suffer from this disorder, foods and beverages containing aspartame must carry a label warning stating "Phenylketonurics: Contains Phenylalanine." Aspartame, one of the most widely accepted food additives, is used in many products, including candy, carbonated and powdered soft drinks, frozen desserts, gelatin, hot beverage mixes, pudding, and yogurt. You'll find aspartame in the label's ingredient list. The PKU warning is a signal, too.

? Have you ever wondered?

. . . if you can be sensitive to MSG? Perhaps, but not likely. Some people describe varying symptoms, including body tingling, warmth, or headaches, after eating foods containing monosodium glutamate (MSG). The reported symptoms, usually mild, commonly last less than an hour. Collectively, the symptoms have been called "Chinese restaurant syndrome" because MSG was once common primarily in Chinese cuisine. Scientific evidence hasn't found a definitive link between MSG, Chinese food, and adverse side effects. MSG is not an allergen, according to the American College of Allergy, Asthma and Immunology, and it does not contain gluten.

MSG is just sodium and glutamate. If you want to moderate your MSG intake—or seem sensitive to it—ask to have your food prepared without added MSG in Asian restaurants. If the menu says "No MSG," it likely means no *added* MSG. MSG may be in other ingredients, such as soy sauce. Glutamate is naturally in most protein-containing foods. Check food labels. Glutamate-containing ingredients such as MSG, hydrolyzed protein, and autolyzed yeast extract appear on the ingredient list. MSG may be in a flavoring but may not be specifically identified, however. Glutamate that naturally occurs in food won't be listed. Consult a registered dietitian nutritionist for guidance. *See "MSG—Another Flavor Enhancer" in chapter 8, page 240.*

. . . why some people get a reaction from some fresh vegetables and fruits? Not a true food allergy, oral allergy syndrome (OAS) causes some people with pollen allergies and hay fever to react to certain raw vegetables and fruits such as celery, green bell peppers, tomatoes, apples, cherries, and kiwis, and to some nuts, seeds, and spices. Just touching them can cause a reaction. Mild symptoms (such as itchy or swelling mouth and lips, runny nose, watery eyes, sneezing, or rash) are like reactions to pollen. Rarely, symptoms may be more severe, and rarer still, life-threatening. This is usually a life-long condition. If you think you or a family member has OAS, talk to your doctor.

To help avoid and manage reactions, seek advice from a registered dietitian nutritionist, who may advise you to keep a food diary. You need to avoid only the foods that you react to. Handle foods you react to with kitchen gloves; remove any peels since they may cause a greater reaction; and cook the problem foods to break down the protein, or choose canned forms. For nuts, avoid both raw and cooked nuts since reactions to nuts may be more severe. An OAS reaction is not caused by pesticides, chemicals, or wax on fruit.

24

Manage Cardiovascular Disease, Diabetes, and Cancer

In this chapter, find out about . . .

Your key "numbers," or health markers

Your risks for heart disease, high blood pressure, diabetes, and cancer

Managing these health conditions with your food choices, if they arise

A healthy eating plan and lifestyle from the start are the best ways to stay healthy and prevent disease, or at least slow its course. That said, most health concerns don't start with a single event in life. Instead, they're a combination of factors. Some you can't control, such as your family history (genes), gender, or age; many you can. For any person, an early diagnosis and good medical care, along with consistent management, adequate nutrition, and positive attitude are the best medicine.

This chapter addresses several health issues—cardiovascular disease, high blood pressure, diabetes, and cancer—and their symptoms and management. Either directly or indirectly, these conditions eventually face most Americans.

This chapter may not apply to your unique or immediate health needs. And it's not meant for you to diagnose, manage, or treat these health conditions, or to answer all your questions. But it's good background for starters!

For health advice specific to you or to someone you care for, consult your doctor, a registered dietitian nutritionist, and other members of your healthcare team. For detailed information on the diet-related health conditions discussed in this chapter, visit the websites of the health organizations noted in this chapter and in *"Resources You Can Use" on page 762.*

Your Healthy Heart

You've likely heard the statistics. Heart disease is America's number one killer. Although its onset is slightly postponed for women, it's a disease that affects both genders. About 85.6 million people in the United States are living with some form of cardiovascular disease or the aftereffects of a stroke (2016 data, American Heart Association).

Truth is, many deaths from heart attacks or strokes are preventable. The American Heart Association's (AHA) goal is to improve the cardiovascular health of all Americans and to reduce deaths from cardiovascular disease and stroke significantly by the year 2020 with the *American Heart Association's "Life's Simple 7," shown in this chapter, page 684.*

WHAT IS HEART DISEASE? WHAT RISKS?

"Heart disease," or cardiovascular disease, describes several health problems that relate to the heart and blood vessels. Heart attacks and strokes may come to your mind first. However, high blood pressure, angina (chest pain), poor circulation, and abnormal heartbeats are among the other heart-related health concerns.

Damage control

Leading Causes of US Deaths

Of the ten leading causes of death in the United States, five are associated directly with diet, and five with excessive intake of alcoholic beverages. Paying attention to what you eat and drink can pay off with good health and longevity.

Rank and Cause	Risk Factors	
	Diet-Related	Alcohol-Related
1. Heart diseases	x	x
2. Cancers	x	x
3. Chronic lower respiratory diseases		
4. Accidents		x
5. Strokes	x	
6. Alzheimer's disease		
7. Diabetes	x	
8. Influenza and pneumonia		
9. Kidney diseases	x	x
10. Suicide		x

Source: National Vital Statistics Reports (reflecting 2014 data). Accessed November 30, 2016.

Click Here! Links to Know . . .

- Academy of Nutrition and Dietetics
  www.eatright.org
- American Heart Association
  www.heart.org
- American Diabetes Association
  www.diabetes.org
- American Cancer Society
  www.cancer.org
- Health Check Tools, National Institutes of Health
  medlineplus.gov/healthchecktools.html

HEART DISEASE: ARE YOU AT RISK?

High total and LDL ("bad") blood cholesterol levels mean greater risk for developing heart disease or having a heart attack. *See "Diagnosing Blood Lipid Levels" in this chapter, page 689.* High blood pressure is also a risk factor.

Knowing your risks for heart disease is the first step in creating a personal prevention plan; *see "Blood Pressure: Under Control?" in this chapter, page 693.* What increases your risk? Two factors aren't within your control: age and genetic tendency. Yet many other risk factors are.

Your Healthy Body Check-In

Do You Know Your Numbers?

Take care of you—and all those in your life! You can't control your age, gender, or family history, but there's plenty you can do to stay fit. For many health problems, the risk factors are the same, so the same smart living patterns may protect you from several chronic diseases.

How well are you protecting your health? If you can answer "yes" to the following questions and know your numbers, great! Fill in your own numbers in the blanks on the right. *Note:* Your numbers may vary from the recommended targets, depending on your individual age, gender, and certain health conditions.

YOUR BODY'S "MAINTENANCE" PROGRAM:	**Yes**	
1. Have you had a recent physical exam?	☐	
2. Do you know your numbers? Are they within a normal/optimal range:		
Body mass index (BMI) (recommended 18.5 to 24.9 for most people*)	☐	___ BMI
Waist circumference (recommended 35 inches or less for women, or 40 inches or less for men)	☐	___ inches

Continued on next page

✔ Your Healthy Body Check-In *(continued)*

Total blood cholesterol (recommended below 200 mg/dL†) ☐ ___ mg/dL

Blood pressure (recommended below 120/below 80 mm†) ☐ ___/___ mm Hg

Blood glucose (recommended A1C under 5.7%†) ☐ ___ %

Fasting blood glucose (normal is below 100 mg/dL†) ☐ ___ mg/dL

YOUR EATING HABITS:

3. Do you know about how many calories you need a day to maintain or lose weight? ☐

4. Do you eat portions appropriate for your weight and calorie need? ☐

5. Do you try to follow a healthy eating plan with these characteristics:

- Equivalent of about 6 ounces of breads, cereals, pasta, rice, and other grain products daily?‡ (One ounce is about 1 regular slice of bread, ½ cup of cooked rice or pasta, or 1 cup of ready-to-eat cereal.) ☐
- For grain products, at least half as whole grain?§ ☐
- At least 4½ cups or more of vegetables and fruits with a variety of colors and types daily?‡ ☐
- Enough calcium-rich dairy foods daily: 3 cups of low-fat or fat-free milk or an equivalent?‡ ☐
- Lean protein foods that add up to about 5½ ounces daily (e.g., lean meat, poultry, fish, eggs, beans and peas, and nuts)?‡ ☐
- Limited amounts of processed meats? ☐
- Beans and peas several times a week? ☐
- A variety of fish (about 8 ounces weekly) in place of some meat and poultry? ☐
- Limited amounts of saturated fats and little or no *trans* fatty acids most of the time? ☐
- Little or no salt added to foods and prepared food with little sodium? ☐
- Limited amounts of added sugars? ☐

YOUR LIFESTYLE HABITS:

6. Do you get at least 150 minutes a week of moderate, or at least 75 minutes of vigorous, physical activity a week, or a combination? ☐

Are some physical activities weight bearing (e.g., walking, dancing, tennis, basketball)? ☐

Are some physical activities muscle strengthening (e.g., push-ups, sit-ups, weight machines)? ☐

Are some physical activities aerobic (e.g., jogging, power walking, bicycling, swimming laps)? ☐

7. If you drink alcoholic beverages, do you do so in moderation (no more than one drink daily for women, or two for men)?** ☐

YOUR TOTAL POINTS: ___ × 4 = ___

Now count up all your "yes" answers, and give yourself 4 points for each one. What's your total score? How close does it come to 100? Of course, these eating and active-living strategies aren't the only ways to promote your good health. But the more often you said "yes," the better your chances are for a long, healthy life.

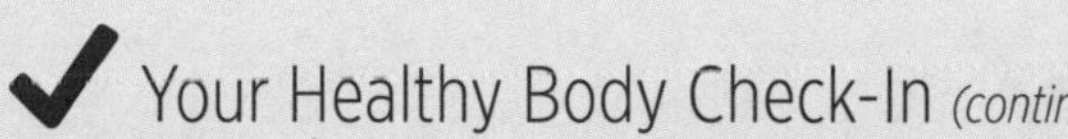

What does your score suggest? It only indicates how many different ways you already may be protecting yourself from health problems. And it suggests where you might improve.

Having a score of 50 compared with a perfect 100 doesn't mean you're twice as likely to develop heart disease, diabetes, cancer, or some other health problem. And this quick check-in is not meant for diagnosis, either. That's the role of your doctor in your regular physical checkups. However, your responses might point to risk factors that may contribute to health problems later. Read on to explore the role of nutrition and regular physical activity in common health conditions.

*See *"Body Mass Index" in chapter 22, page 627, to figure your BMI.*

†Some recommended levels may vary. Talk to your doctor about the right target for you based on your gender, health condition, and more.

‡For a 2,000-calorie daily diet. *See chapter 2 for more about a healthy eating plan and recommended amounts for you.*

§*See "Is It Really Whole Grain? Tricky to Know" in chapter 6, page 184.*

*** See chapter 4, page 102, for the definition of a standard drink.*

Have you ever wondered?

. . . if high blood cholesterol could be linked to a thyroid problem? Yes, it could. Hypothyroidism—when the thyroid gland doesn't produce enough of the hormone thyroxine—has many symptoms. Those with mild hypothyroidism may feel fine but be fatigued or have mood swings. Symptoms of more severe hypothyroidism can include a poor memory, dry skin and hair, cold intolerance, constipation, heavy menstrual flow, hoarseness or difficulty swallowing, muscle cramps or stiffness, and weight gain. Weight gain may lead to insulin resistance. Elevated LDL cholesterol may be another and serious side effect.

Treating hypothyroidism with medication—thyroid hormone—does more than treat a thyroid problem. It helps reduce high LDL cholesterol levels associated with this condition. Untreated, hypothyroidism can damage the cardiovascular system permanently.

As part of a routine physical exam, have your doctor check for thyroid problems. Hypothyroidism is much more common among women than among men. *See "Have you ever wondered . . . if feeling tired could signal a thyroid problem?" in chapter 18, page 558, for more about hypothyroidism.*

. . . if you need to worry about your cholesterol level if you're thin? Although people who are overweight or obese are at greater risk, any body type can have high cholesterol levels. And if you're among those who don't gain weight easily, you may be less aware of how much dietary fat, especially saturated and *trans* fats, you consume. Also consider other risk factors such as family history.

Risk Factors You Can't Control

Family history of heart disease. Having a family history of early heart disease (birth father or brother with heart attack or sudden death from it before age fifty-five; birth mother or sister, before age sixty-five) increases your risk.

African Americans, who are more likely to have high blood pressure, are at higher risk. So are Mexican Americans, Native Americans, Native Hawaiians, and some Asian Americans.

Age and gender. Getting older (men over age forty-five; women over age fifty five) increases your risk. Before menopause, women usually have lower cholesterol levels than men their age unless they have diabetes, after menopause, women's LDL cholesterol often rises. *See "Heart Disease: A Woman's Issue" in chapter 18, page 562, and "Heart Disease: A Top Health Issue for Men" in chapter 19, page 570.*

Risk Factors within Your Control

Current cigarette smoking. That includes cigarettes, e-cigarettes, cigars, pipe smoking, and smokeless tobacco, as well as exposure to secondhand smoke. For those who smoked in the past, risk for heart disease declines after quitting.

Physical inactivity, or a sedentary lifestyle. *See "Move More! Physical Activity Guidelines" in chapter 1, page 15, for guidelines for healthy people.*

Unhealthy eating pattern. Reducing calories from saturated and *trans* fats is strongly linked to lowering LDLs. So are emphasizing vegetables, fruits, and whole grains in your everyday food choices; choosing low-fat and fat-free dairy products, lean protein foods, and nontropical vegetable oils and nuts; and limiting sweets and sugary drinks. *Chapter 2,* *page 21, focuses on a healthy pattern of eating for the general healthy population. See "American Heart Association's Diet and Lifestyle Recommendations" in this chapter, page 688, for guidelines for healthy eating and lifestyles.*

Heavy drinking and too much stress. Too much alcohol intake can raise blood pressure, which can cause heart failure and lead to a stroke. And it can contribute to high triglycerides and irregular heartbeat. Stress can be a risk, too, as it often leads to overeating, smoking, and other factors that aren't heart healthy.

Contributing Health Conditions

Several health conditions can contribute to increased risk for heart disease:

Chronic inflammation. Food choices and lifestyle factors may contribute to an unhealthy form of inflammation, which in turn may play a role in heart disease. *See "A Closer Look . . . Inflammation, Health, and Food" in this chapter, page 699.*

Diabetes, even if under control. People with diabetes have a higher risk of dying from a heart attack. *See "Diabetes: A Growing Concern" in this chapter, page 698, to learn more about controlling diabetes.*

Overweight or obesity *(especially with excess abdominal fat).* The excess puts strain on the heart, raises blood pressure, raises total cholesterol and triglyceride levels, and lowers HDL cholesterol level. *See "Weight and Health" in chapter 22, page 628.*

High blood pressure. This condition causes the heart to work harder and so enlarge and weaken. Being treated for high blood pressure doesn't completely remove the risk. *See "Blood Pressure Levels: For Adults" in this chapter, page 696.*

American Heart Association's Life's Simple 7

The American Heart Association encourages everyone to take these seven steps for heart health.

1. Manage blood pressure.
2. Control cholesterol.
3. Reduce blood glucose (sugar).
4. Get active.
5. Eat better.
6. Lose weight.
7. Stop smoking.

To assess your heart health and get a heart-health plan, see the AHA website, mylifecheck.heart.org.

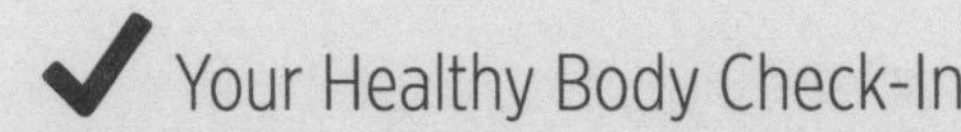

Your Healthy Body Check-In

Use this interactive calculator for your heart attack risk assessment:

- My Life Check, American Heart Association
  mylifecheck.heart.org/mobile/assessment.aspx

Heart Disease: Risk Outlook

Being at high risk doesn't mean you're sure to have a heart attack or stroke. That's good news! However, the more risk factors for heart disease you have—and the higher their level—the greater your statistical chances. For example, a total cholesterol level that's 300 mg/dL is riskier than one that's 250 mg/dL, although both are high risk (240 mg/dL and above). Changes in your food choices and lifestyle, and perhaps weight reduction and medication, can lower your risk score.

See "Heart Disease: A Woman's Issue" in chapter 18, page 562, and "Heart Disease: A Top Health Issue for Men" in chapter 19, page 570.

HEART DISEASE: THE BLOOD LIPID CONNECTION

High total and LDL cholesterol levels and high triglyceride levels are major risk factors for heart disease. Conversely, lowering these numbers and raising HDL cholesterol levels are better for heart health.

Serum (blood) cholesterol, a fatlike substance produced in the liver, is found in everyone's bloodstream. As part of every body cell, it's essential to human health and cell building. Since your body makes cholesterol, you don't need cholesterol from food.

What's the link, then, between blood cholesterol and heart disease? When total and LDL blood cholesterol levels are elevated or too high, deposits of cholesterol, called plaque, collect on arterial and other blood vessel walls. This condition is called atherosclerosis, or hardening of the arteries. As fatty plaques build up, arteries gradually become narrower and may slow or block the flow of oxygen-rich blood. Chest pain may result without enough oxygen to the heart. High HDL levels are protective. *See "A Closer Look . . . Blood Cholesterol: The 'Good' and 'Bad'" in this chapter, page 685.*

Plaque buildup happens silently, usually without symptoms. Warnings in the form of chest pains may not occur until vessels are about 75 percent blocked. Often a heart attack or a stroke strikes with no warning at all. A clot in a narrowed artery blocks blood flow to the heart, causing a heart attack.

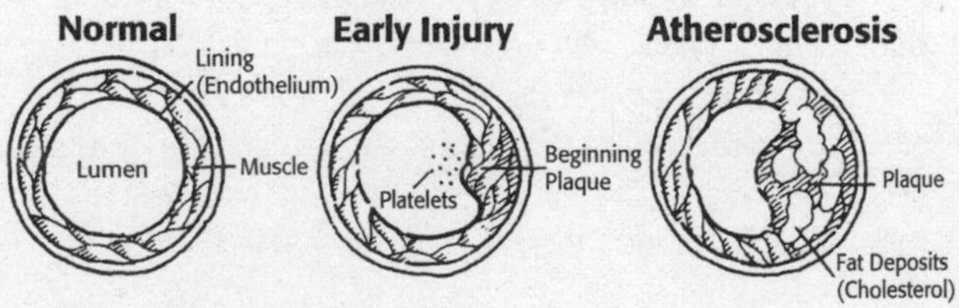

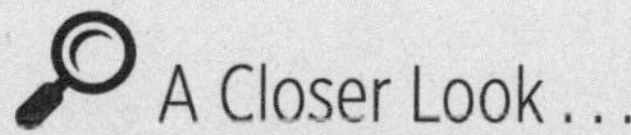

Blood Cholesterol: The "Good" and the "Bad"

Have you ever wondered what the terms "good" cholesterol and "bad" cholesterol really mean?

These terms don't refer to cholesterol in food. Instead, the nicknames "good" and "bad" blood cholesterol relate to risk factors for heart disease. High levels of HDL, or "good," cholesterol are linked to lower risk of heart disease; high levels of LDL, or "bad," cholesterol, to higher risk. Total blood cholesterol consists of both HDL and LDL cholesterol.

HDL AND LDL: TRANSPORT PACKAGES

Because cholesterol doesn't mix with water, it can't be carried along in your bloodstream. Instead, it's combined in "packages" with fats and proteins. These packages, called lipoproteins, carry cholesterol both to and from your body cells.

Two types of lipoproteins—HDLs and LDLs—transport "packages" of cholesterol through the bloodstream. Here's how:

- *High-density lipoproteins (HDLs)* act like waste-removal vehicles. They take cholesterol from the bloodstream and artery walls to the liver for removal from the body. A higher HDL level is desirable and will improve your total cholesterol level. According to the National Heart, Lung, and Blood Institute, an HDL level of 60 mg/dL or more is considered protective against heart disease. *Tip:* "H" stands for HDL and "healthy."

  People with a higher triglyceride level, *discussed in "Triglycerides: A Heart-Health Issue" in this chapter, page 686,* typically have lower HDLs. Several factors are linked to lower HDLs: genetic factors, type 2 diabetes, some medications (for example beta-blockers and anabolic steroids), being overweight, physical inactivity, and smoking.

- *Low-density lipoproteins (LDLs)* work like delivery vehicles. Produced naturally in the body, they keep blood cholesterol circulating in the bloodstream to all parts of the body, depositing plaque on artery walls along the way. With plaque buildup from too much LDL, heart disease risk goes up. To improve your total cholesterol level, keep LDLs down. *Tip:* "L" stands for LDLs and "less healthy."

HDL AND LDL: UPS AND DOWNS

Although HDL and LDL cholesterol aren't found in food, your food choices do influence your levels. So do your level of physical activity and your genes.

If you lower the saturated fats and *trans* fats in your diet, you'll likely bring down LDL blood cholesterol levels. And if you're physically active, you'll likely lower your LDL cholesterol and keep your HDL blood cholesterol higher. What you eat and your level of activity are just two of many factors that affect HDL, LDL, and total blood cholesterol levels, *as discussed in this chapter.*

- *To raise your HDL blood cholesterol:* Stay physically active and trim extra pounds of body fat if you're not at your healthy weight. Replacing some saturated fats with monounsaturated fats may raise HDL cholesterol. If you use tobacco products, quit.
- *To lower your LDL blood cholesterol:* Replace foods high in saturated fats and *trans* fats with those with more unsaturated fats. The 2015–2020 Dietary Guidelines for Americans advises less than 10% of calories from saturated fat, or no more than 22 grams of saturated fat for someone eating 2,000 calories a day. The advice for saturated fat from the American Heart Association is 5 to 6%. Keep *trans* fatty acids as low as possible. Soluble fiber and soy protein may help lower LDL cholesterol; *see chapters 11, page 345, and 12, page 373, for more about fiber and protein.* Keeping excess body weight off also may help.

LDL: NEW RESEARCH

The issue of LDL cholesterol may be more complicated than just being higher or lower, however. Emerging research suggests that the size and density of LDL particles may factor into cardiovascular risk. LDL particles that are large and buoyant may be linked to cardiovascular health, while those that are smaller and denser may be more prone to oxidation and so pose a greater risk. LDL particle size and density are influenced by genetics, diet, and body weight. Stay tuned!

With a stroke, blood can't flow to an area of the brain, depriving it of oxygen and blood glucose. The higher the blood cholesterol level, the greater the risk. When abnormally high total and LDL blood cholesterol levels go down, so does the risk for heart attack and stroke.

To limit the risk for atherosclerosis, aim to fit your blood cholesterol levels within a desirable range. Remember that high total blood cholesterol isn't the only risk factor for heart disease. Even a total cholesterol level of 200 or less won't automatically keep you safe. *Read on.*

See "Fats 101: A Dictionary of Terms" in chapter 13, page 387, to learn the meaning of fat-related terminology.

Blood Cholesterol Levels: Their Rise and Fall

There's no single reason for blood cholesterol levels being high or low. For some people, high or low blood cholesterol is an inherited tendency. In part, genetics affect how much cholesterol your body makes. However, families with heart disease share more than their genetic makeup. They

Metabolic Syndrome

Metabolic syndrome is a complex metabolic disorder defined as having several (three or more) risk factors at the same time: (1) a large waist circumference (more than 40 inches for men, more than 35 inches for women), (2) high blood pressure, (3) a high fasting blood glucose level, (4) a high triglyceride level, and/or (5) a low HDL ("good") cholesterol level. It's called "metabolic" because it involves body processes that keep the body functioning.

When multiple risk factors coexist, the risks for heart disease (heart attack and stroke) and diabetes, kidney disease, and some other conditions increase.

Several factors are among those that play a key role in developing metabolic syndrome: inactivity, overweight, obesity, and insulin resistance. Upper-body (abdominal) obesity adds to the problem. Genetics and older age also may play a role in causing metabolic syndrome. With the rise in obesity rates among adults, metabolic syndrome has become more common.

Insulin resistance happens when the body doesn't respond normally to the insulin it produces. Insulin, a hormone, helps move blood glucose into your body cells for energy production. If the body doesn't use insulin properly, the level of blood glucose starts to rise and can eventually lead to type 2 diabetes. Insulin resistance is closely tied to being overweight and obese.

To prevent or delay metabolic syndrome. Heart healthy lifestyle changes are the first line of prevention, delay, or treatment. It's important to first reduce the risk of coronary heart disease, and second to prevent the onset of type 2 diabetes. To do that, address all the risk factors at the same time; the recommendations for dealing with them are consistent. This includes increasing physical activity, achieving a healthy weight, and eating a healthy diet that's low in saturated fats (less than 10 percent of total calories). *See "The Mediterranean Route to Healthy Eating" in chapter 2, page 52,* as one food pattern to consider. Talk to your doctor.

Along with diet therapy and lifestyle changes, medications also may be prescribed to help control blood glucose, hypertension, and high blood lipids (cholesterol and triglycerides). Stop smoking if you smoke. *See "Diabetes: A Growing Concern" in this chapter, page 698.*

also grow up with similar lifestyle habits that may raise blood cholesterol levels—perhaps too much food with solid fats and excessive calories, physical inactivity, excessive alcohol intake, or smoking (or exposure to tobacco products). Age (being older) and gender are other factors, which you can't control.

Even if you inherited the genetic risk or if you're older, you can follow strategies, *discussed in "If You Need to Improve Your Lipid Levels . . ." in this chapter, page 689*, to reduce other risk factors and to bring your total and LDL cholesterol levels down. Know this:

- Compared to other dietary components, saturated fats and *trans* fats have the most significant LDL cholesterol–raising effect for most people. *As noted in "TFAs: The Ban" in chapter 13, page 404,* trans *fats are being phased out of the food supply.*
- Overweight and obesity not only raise total and LDL cholesterol, but also raise triglycerides and lower HDLs.
- Physical inactivity contributes to overweight and high blood pressure, but also can contribute to high total and LDL cholesterol levels and lower HDLs.

Triglycerides: A Heart-Health Issue

Whether they're saturated, polyunsaturated, or monounsaturated, triglycerides are the main form of fat in foods. Once consumed, they're processed by your liver. Excess calories from any source—carbohydrates, proteins, or fats—produce triglycerides for storage as body fat. Alcohol also can boost the liver's production of triglycerides.

Normal triglyceride levels vary by a person's age and gender. Your blood triglyceride level normally goes up after eating. The health risk comes from excess. Things that can increase your triglyceride levels to excess include being overweight, physical inactivity, cigarette smoking, excessive alcohol use, a very-high-carbohydrate diet, certain diseases and drugs, and genetic disorders. *Be aware:* Having high blood pressure multiplies the risk.

High blood triglycerides get much less attention than high cholesterol levels. Yet they, too, are significantly linked to heart disease, especially for those with other risk factors. A high triglyceride level, along with high LDL and low HDL levels, are linked to atherosclerosis, or the fatty buildup in artery walls that increases the risks for heart attack and stroke. As with high total and LDL cholesterol levels, high blood triglyceride levels don't mean you'll develop heart disease, but the chance goes up if you have other risk factors.

Because of the risk for heart disease, the National Heart, Lung, and Blood Institute recommends treating people with borderline-high and high triglyceride levels. If your blood triglyceride level consistently exceeds normal, then a healthier weight, regular physical activity, and perhaps medication may bring it down. (Normal is below 150mg/dL.) In fact, the advice for lowering total blood cholesterol levels also applies to reducing triglyceride levels. Of importance:

? Have you ever wondered?

. . . what medical nutrition therapy is? Often abbreviated as MNT, it's an essential part of comprehensive health care when you need it. For Medicare reimbursement, MNT is defined by the government as nutrition diagnoses, therapy, and counseling for the purpose of managing disease. Appropriate for many different health conditions and diseases, these services must be provided to you by a registered dietitian nutritionist or other nutrition professional. Referral usually comes from a doctor as part of your safe, effective, overall care. Medical nutrition therapy is always individualized, in-depth care that's provided over time, not in a single visit, to meet your very specific needs.

Most important, many people receiving care for health problems and illness can improve their health and well-being with medical nutrition therapy, and perhaps reduce their doctor visits, hospitalizations, and medication use.

. . . what nutrigenomics is and what it may mean for you? Nutrigenomics is the study of genes and their links to nutrition and health. It addresses how nutrients and other food components interact with a person's genetic makeup and how they may regulate particular genes to increase or decrease the risk for certain diseases. Nutrigenomics became possible with the decoding of the human genome, a feat completed only within this millennium.

As the study of nutrigenomics evolves, it can allow personalized nutrition as a way to approach health management and nutrition decisions. It offers a huge opportunity to customize advice for what someone eats for his or her own unique genetic makeup and nutritional needs. The goal: the potential to slow and even prevent all kinds of diseases—some directly nutrition related, such as heart disease, diabetes, cancer, celiac disease, and obesity, and others not, such as sickle cell disease, cystic fibrosis, and Alzheimer's disease—for those at risk.

Understanding functional foods and nutrigenomics goes hand in hand as science reveals unique ways in which foods' many substances work and interact within body cells. That said, a great deal of research is needed before gene-based nutrition advice becomes a reality. But the first steps are happening already. *See "A Closer Look . . . Functional Foods with Benefits Beyond the Basics" in chapter 5, page 134.*

- Maintain or improve your weight. Weight loss alone may significantly lower triglyceride levels.
- Reduce saturated fats and keep *trans* fats as low as possible in your meals and snacks. If you have high triglycerides, switching from more saturated fats as in butter and fatty meat to more unsaturated fats in foods such as canola oil, olive oil, or liquid margarine may improve those numbers. *See "The Mediterranean Route to Healthy Eating" in chapter 2, page 52,* as one food pattern to consider.

  Eating less fat and more carbohydrate may not be an effective strategy. In some people, this tactic may raise triglyceride levels and lower HDL cholesterol levels.
- *Be aware:* Low HDL ("good") cholesterol and/or high triglycerides can increase the risk for type 2 diabetes. If you have diabetes, your doctor may advise you to limit dietary cholesterol; *see "Cholesterol: If Advised to Cut Back" in chapter 13, page 406.*
- Eat vegetables, fruits, and low-fat or fat-free dairy products often.
- Eat oily fish, such as salmon and albacore tuna, since their omega-3 fatty acids may help lower triglycerides. *See "A Closer Look . . . Omega-3s and -6s" in chapter 13, page 392.*
- Get regular physical activity. *See "Move More! Physical Activity Guidelines" in chapter 1, page 15, for guidelines.*
- If you drink alcoholic beverages, consume less or skip them entirely. Even small amounts of alcoholic drinks can have a significant effect on blood triglyceride levels.

TESTING, TESTING: KNOW YOUR BLOOD CHOLESTEROL NUMBERS

Numbers don't tell the whole story of heart health, but they're good predictors. Know your total cholesterol number—whether or not you're at risk for heart disease and no matter what your adult age or gender. The total depends on your HDL, LDL, and triglyceride levels.

Lipoprotein profile. Blood lipid levels are measured from a blood sample. For a complete picture, you need a test for your fasting lipoprotein profile: total, HDL, and LDL cholesterol levels, as well as blood triglycerides and very low-density lipoproteins (VLDL). You need to fast for nine to twelve hours before the test, during which time you can't eat or drink anything but water.

Using your total and HDL cholesterol levels, your doctor may calculate your cholesterol ratio. This ratio is obtained by dividing your HDL cholesterol number into your total cholesterol number. For example, if your total cholesterol is 200 and your HDL is 50, then your ratio would be 4 to 1. The goal is to keep the ratio below 5 to 1; the optimum ratio is 3.5 to 1. The AHA provides this calculation: total blood (serum) cholesterol equates to HDL + LDL + 20 percent of your triglyceride level. A total cholesterol score of less than 180 mg/dL is considered optimal by the AHA, but your target may vary. *See "Diagnosing Blood Lipid Levels" in this chapter, page 689, for optimal levels.*

American Heart Association's Diet and Lifestyle Recommendations*

- Use up at least as many calories as you take in.
  - Start by knowing how many calories you should be eating and drinking to maintain your weight.
  - If you are trying not to gain weight, don't eat more calories than you know you can burn up every day.
  - Increase the amount and intensity of your physical activity to match the number of calories you take in.
  - Aim for at least 150 minutes of moderate physical activity or seventy-five minutes of vigorous physical activity—or an equal combination of both—each week. If you would benefit from lowering your blood pressure or cholesterol, the AHA recommends forty minutes of aerobic exercise of moderate to vigorous intensity three to four times a week
- Eat a variety of nutritious foods from all the food groups.
  - Eat an overall healthy dietary pattern that emphasizes a variety of whole grains, vegetables, fruits, low-fat dairy products, skinless poultry, fish, nuts, beans and peas, and nontropical vegetable oils.
  - Limit saturated fat, *trans* fat, sodium, red meat, sweets, and sugar-sweetened beverages. If you choose to eat red meat, compare labels, and select the leanest cuts available.
- Eat less of the nutrient-poor foods. Limit foods and beverages that are high in calories but low in nutrients. Also limit the amount of saturated fat, *trans* fat, and sodium you eat.
- As you make daily food choices, base your eating pattern on these recommendations:
  - Eat a variety of fresh, frozen, and canned vegetables and fruits without high-calorie sauces or added salt and sugars. Replace high-calorie foods with vegetables and fruits.
  - Choose fiber-rich whole grains for most grain servings.
  - Choose poultry and fish without skin, and prepare them in healthy ways without added saturated and *trans* fats. If you choose to eat meat, look for the leanest cuts available, and prepare them in healthy and delicious ways.
  - Eat a variety of fish at least twice a week, especially fish containing omega-3 fatty acids (for example, salmon, trout, and herring).
  - Select low-fat (1%) and fat-free (skim) dairy products.
  - Avoid foods containing partially hydrogenated vegetable oils to reduce *trans* fat in your diet.
  - Limit saturated and *trans* fats, and replace them with the better fats, monounsaturated and polyunsaturated. If you need to lower your blood cholesterol, reduce saturated fat to no more than 5 to 6 percent of total calories. For someone eating 2,000 calories a day, that's about 13 grams of saturated fat daily.
  - Cut back on beverages and foods with added sugars.
  - Choose foods with less sodium, and prepare foods with little or no salt. To lower blood pressure, aim to eat no more than 2,400 milligrams of sodium per day. Reducing daily intake to 1,500 milligrams is desirable because it can lower blood pressure even further. If you can't meet these goals right now, even reducing sodium intake by 1,000 milligrams per day can benefit blood pressure.
  - If you drink alcohol, drink in moderation. That means no more than one drink per day if you're a woman and no more than two drinks if you're a man.
  - Follow the AHA's recommendations when you eat out, and keep an eye on your portion sizes.
- Also, don't smoke tobacco—and avoid secondhand smoke.

*The AHA's advice—for the general population—is similar to the 2015–2020 Dietary Guidelines for Americans, from the US Department of Health and Human Services and the US Department of Agriculture (*see "Eat SMART: Dietary Guidelines for Americans" in chapter 1, page 8*).

Source: American Heart Association, www.heart.org. Accessed November 30, 2016.

Unless you're screened regularly, high lipid levels usually go unnoticed because high blood cholesterol has no symptoms. The AHA advises all adults aged 20 or older to have their cholesterol and other traditional risk factors checked every four to six years—and more often if you're considerably older or at risk for heart disease. If you have a birth father or brother with heart disease before age fifty-five, or a birth mother or sister before age sixty-five, health experts advise screening before age twenty. If your first results are high, your doctor may advise another test soon.

Before getting tested, follow the directions carefully from your doctor's office for accurate results. Let your doctor or a registered dietitian nutritionist interpret your test results—and guide you to achieve and maintain your cholesterol numbers at healthy levels. *See "Should Kids' Cholesterol Levels Be Checked?" in chapter 17, page 522.*

Other tests. Besides a standard lipoprotein panel to measure your risk for heart disease, your doctor might order other tests. For example:

Have you ever wondered?

. . . if cholesterol screenings at a mall or a health fair are a good idea? As an initial screening, these finger-stick tests may be good indicators, especially if your cholesterol levels are borderline high or high—or if you have other risk factors. Have them rechecked by your doctor. A finger-stick screening may be less accurate than a blood test done in your doctor's office or a health center. The most accurate and complete blood tests (standard lipoprotein panel) are done after fasting.

. . . about over-the-counter cholesterol tests? Done properly, they can be relatively accurate. However, home tests measure only total blood cholesterol levels, not HDLs, LDLs, or triglycerides. Like finger-stick tests, verify the results with your doctor—especially if your results are 200 mg/dL or more for total blood cholesterol and if you have other risk factors, such as a family history of heart disease. That said, you need blood tests from your doctor to track your blood lipid levels.

- *C-reactive protein* (CRP). This test assesses arteries for inflammation, which is a predictor of cardiovascular events. Inflammation is a protective immune reaction from an injury or infection. *See "A Closer Look . . . Inflammation, Health, and Food" in this chapter, page 699.*

  Many factors can cause CRP levels to rise and fluctuate, including high blood pressure, insulin resistance, high triglyceride levels, and tobacco and e-cigarette use. Regular physical activity, a healthy weight, and a heart-healthy diet with omega-3 fatty acids may help reduce inflammation. That said, the connection between high CRP levels and heart attack risk is not very well understood. Studies are being done to see if CRP testing can assess the risk for other health conditions, too, such as type 2 diabetes.
- *Metabolic syndrome marker.* This measures insulin sensitivity and blood glucose control. *See "A Closer Look . . . Metabolic Syndrome" in this chapter, page 686.*
- *Total LDL particle number.* This measures the total number of LDL particles. *See "LDLs: New Research" in "A Closer Look . . . Cholesterol: The 'Good' and the 'Bad'" in this chapter, page 685.*
- *Fibrinogen.* This measures clot formation within blood vessels, which signals atherosclerosis.
- *Lipoprotein-associated phospholipase A2.* (Lp-PLA2). This is a biomarker of vascular inflammation, which may predict cardiovascular events and a stroke.

Diagnosing Blood Lipid Levels

To lower your heart disease risk, strive to keep your blood lipid levels at desirable levels for life. If you don't know your blood cholesterol and triglyceride numbers, check soon. Then act on the results!

Level	Category
Total Cholesterol	
Less than 200 mg/dL	Desirable*
200–239 mg/dL	Borderline high
240 mg/dL and higher	High
LDL Cholesterol	
Less than 100 mg/dL	Optimal
100–129 mg/dL	Near optimal/above optimal
130–159 mg/dL	Borderline high
160–189 mg/dL	High
190 mg/dL and higher	Very High
HDL Cholesterol	
Less than 40 mg/dL	A major risk factor for heart disease
40–59 mg/dL	The higher, the better
60 mg/dL and higher	Considered protective against heart disease

Triglycerides also can raise your risk for heart disease. If your triglyceride level is borderline high (150–199 mg/dL) or high (200 mg/dL or higher), you may need treatment.

*The American Heart Association considers less than 180 mg/dL optimal.

Source: National Heart, Lung, and Blood Institute, National Institutes of Health, www.nhlbi.nih.gov/health/health-topics/topics/hbc/diagnosis. Accessed October 5, 2016.

IF YOU NEED TO IMPROVE YOUR LIPID LEVELS . . .

Bringing your cholesterol numbers down takes effort and commitment, changes in your eating and lifestyle, *as described here*, and perhaps the use of doctor-prescribed medication.

If you have diabetes and risk factors that affect LDLs, you may need more aggressive treatment to lower LDL and total cholesterol levels. Other heart-disease-related problems may require dietary changes not addressed below. Get advice from your doctor or a registered dietitian nutritionist.

Eat for Heart Health

With high or borderline high total or LDL cholesterol levels, shifting your food choices and lifestyle may bring your numbers to (or closer to) normal, and may even boost your HDLs. Even if these levels are normal or you take cholesterol-lowering medications (statins), the following guidelines make sense.

Follow the AHA's "Diet and Lifestyle Recommendations" *in this chapter, page 688*. In some cases, statin medication is also advised to prevent cardiovascular disease and stroke. Talk to your doctor. These are the basics behind eating for heart health:

- Limit saturated fats and keep *trans* fats as low as possible. Saturated and *trans* fats increase LDL blood cholesterol levels more than anything else you consume. The AHA recommends no more than 5 to 6 percent of calories from saturated fat; the 2015–2020 Dietary Guidelines for Americans advice is less than 10 percent. *See "Solid Fats: Eat Less and Switch" in chapter 13, page 399, to find out ways to limit saturated and* trans *fats.*
- Consume foods with enough dietary fiber. Viscous or gelatinous, soluble fibers gel or thicken in water and may enhance LDL cholesterol lowering. In the intestines, fiber binds to cholesterol-rich bile acids, passing them out of the body as waste rather than reabsorbing them. Fiber also may help improve the cholesterol ratio. *See "Fiber and Health" and "Fiber-Rich Foods" in chapter 11, page 362, for more about fiber, including viscous fiber, and its food sources.* No long-term studies show heart-healthy benefits from fiber supplements. They are not currently advised for reducing heart disease risk.
- Eat a variety of vegetables and fruits daily. Besides their fiber content, most are low in calories and fat. Emerging research also suggests potential benefits from their antioxidant nutrients and phytonutrients. *See "Fruits and Vegetables: Fit More In" in chapter 8, page 246.*
- Make some of your meals plant based. In other words, consider beans and peas and foods with soy protein as your key protein sources in these meals. *See "Meatless on the Menu" in chapter 3, page 73.*
- Eat only enough calories to reach and/or maintain your healthy weight. Ask your doctor or a registered dietitian nutritionist what a reasonable calorie level is for you. Drop a few pounds if you need to. *See "Weight and Health" in chapter 22, page 628, for more about the reasons for a healthy weight.*
- Your doctor may advise you to limit dietary cholesterol. Be prudent, as advised. The Dietary Guidelines for Americans notes that lower intakes of dietary cholesterol are linked to reduced risk of

? Have you ever wondered?

. . . if a food labeled "no cholesterol" is heart healthy? Not necessarily. It's higher amounts of saturated and *trans* fats from food that are the issue for most people, not the amount of cholesterol in food.

. . . if you can eat eggs as part of a heart-healthy diet? Unless your doctor advises against them, today's advice for most people is that there is no need to limit them. Eggs are a great protein source. Their cholesterol content doesn't appear to have much impact on blood cholesterol levels for most people. Evidence indicates that saturated and *trans* fats increase LDL cholesterol more than dietary cholesterol does.

If your doctor advises you to cut back on foods high in cholesterol, limit sources of solid fats (saturated fats and *trans* fats) and cholesterol, as recommended, too. To check the cholesterol and fat content in any packaged food, read the Nutrition Facts.

. . . if eating more olive oil may have a cholesterol-lowering effect? Likely so, but not if you end up eating a diet high in total fat and calories. You need to substitute foods that are higher in unsaturated fats for those higher in saturated fats—not simply add olive oil or other healthy oils to your food choices. Olive, canola, and safflower oils are among those high in unsaturated fats. *See "Solid Fats and Oils: How Do They Compare?" in chapter 13, page 386, to compare the types of fatty acids in solid fats and oils.*

. . . about the heart-health benefits and risks of other oils? Canola, safflower, and other vegetable oils are well known for the heart-healthy benefits of their unsaturated fat. But other plant-based oils—coconut oil, palm kernel oil, and palm oil are high in saturated fats.

When replacing foods high in saturated and *trans* fat, foods with both omega-3s and -6s (found in different proportions in plant-based oils) may reduce total and LDL cholesterol. Omega-6s also may improve insulin sensitivity. *See "A Closer Look . . . Omega-3s and -6s" in chapter 13, page 392, to learn more.*

. . . if fat replacers offer heart-healthy benefits? Perhaps—if you use them to replace full-fat foods and avoid consuming too many calories overall. In part, because these products are relatively new, no research shows long-term benefits. Until more is known, use them to give you flexibility with fat control. *See "Fat Replacers" in chapter 13, page 406.*

cardiovascular disease, but more research is needed for quantitative advice. *See "Cholesterol: Like Fat, Not Fat" in chapter 13, page 404, for more about dietary cholesterol.*

The Healthy Mediterranean-Style Eating Pattern and DASH diet, *described in chapter 2, page 21,* are both daily eating plans to follow for heart health. *For possible links between heart health and alcoholic drinks, see "A Closer Look . . . Wine: A Toast to Heart Health?" in this chapter, page 695.*

Maintain or Improve Your Weight

The more excess body fat you have, the greater your risk for heart disease. If you're overweight or obese, losing weight—even ten pounds—can help you lower LDL cholesterol. The 2013 guidelines from the American Heart Association and American College of Cardiology advises that for obese adults, a 3 to 5 percent weight loss can improve cholesterol levels and blood pressure. It also reduces risks for cardiovascular disease and diabetes. A 5 to 10 percent weight loss is better yet.

Weight loss is especially important if you have high triglycerides and/or low HDL cholesterol and carry excess abdominal fat. Those who carry a "spare tire" around their abdomen have a higher cardiac risk than those with extra padding around their hips and thighs.

See "Weight: What's Healthy" in chapter 22, page 626, for how to assess your body weight.

Keep Moving!

Regular, moderate activity is heart healthy in several ways. It helps normalize blood cholesterol and triglyceride levels, helping to boost HDLs and to lower LDLs and triglycerides. It also helps reduce blood pressure, helps your body control stress, helps reduce excess body weight as you burn energy, and helps improve insulin resistance for two to seventy-two hours. Aerobic activity that's more vigorous gives your heart muscle a good workout and ultimately helps your whole cardiovascular and respiratory systems stay fit. *See "Move More! Physical Activity Guidelines" in chapter 1, page 15, and "Commit to Active Living" in chapter 22, page 638, for more about physical activity and its benefits.*

Make Other Changes

Diet, weight management, and physical activity aren't the only ways to keep your heart healthy.

- If you have high blood pressure, get it under control. High blood pressure is a key risk factor for heart attack and stroke. *See "Blood Pressure: Under Control?" in this chapter, page 693.*
- If you use tobacco or e-cigarettes, give up the habit. It's a key factor in sudden death from cardiovascular disease. Smoking seems to raise blood pressure levels and heart rate. It may lower HDL cholesterol levels, too. And smoking may increase the tendency of blood to clot and so lead to a heart attack. For those who stop smoking, heart disease risk goes down over time, even for longtime smokers.
- If you have diabetes, keep your blood glucose level under control, *as discussed in "Diabetes: A Growing Concern" in this chapter, page 698.*

? Have you ever wondered?

. . . if garlic is good for your heart? Perhaps, but the research on the heart-health benefits of allium (a phytonutrient) in garlic and onions is preliminary. Best advice: Enjoy the flavor of garlic, but don't count on it for heart-healthy benefits. Follow medically sound advice to keep your blood cholesterol under control.

Although you can buy garlic pills and extracts, supplements may lack the phytonutrients that impart potential cholesterol-lowering benefits of garlic. Garlic supplements may cause stomach irritation and nausea.

. . . if fish-oil supplements can protect your heart? Fish-oil supplements are promoted for their omega-3 fatty acids and their potential for lowering the risk for blocked blood vessels and heart attacks. However, a proper dosage has not been determined; supplements can't cancel out the effects of a diet high in saturated and *trans* fats. Best guideline: Enjoy oily fish instead, and follow an overall moderate-fat eating plan.

High-quality, contaminant-free fish-oil supplements may be advised for people with high triglycerides who may benefit from consuming more omega-3s than their diet alone can provide. Some fish-oil supplements are high in vitamin A; check the Supplement Facts on the product label to avoid consuming toxic levels of vitamin A.

The AHA advises: Taking more than 3 grams of omega-3 fatty acids from a capsule should be done only under a doctor's care. *Be aware:* In some people, high intakes of omega-3s may impair blood clotting. Before taking fish-oil supplements, talk to your doctor.

. . . if folic acid and other B-vitamin supplements can help reduce heart disease risk? At one point, some scientists thought that folic acid supplements could reduce heart disease risk by lowering homocysteine levels. While they do lower homocysteine levels, they don't lower the risk for heart disease.

See "Dietary Supplements: More Than Vitamin Pills" in chapter 10, page 316, for more about these and other dietary supplements.

Consider Emerging Science

Other substances in food also may be cholesterol lowering. For some, research evidence is strong; for others, it's preliminary but promising.

Soy. Soybeans and soy products such as soy beverages, tofu, tempeh, and soyburgers (but not soybean oil) contain soy protein and several phytonutrients that may help promote heart health; isoflavones are the phytonutrients that get the most consumer attention. Although research can't confirm a direct benefit between soy intake and blood cholesterol levels, there may be an indirect benefit if soy replaces foods high in saturated fats. For adults, soy protein may have small effects on lowering total and LDL cholesterol levels; however, research findings are inconsistent.

See "A Closer Look . . . Soy: Protein and More" in chapter 12, page 383, for more about soy protein.

Plant stanols and sterols. Plant stanols and sterols, found naturally in vegetables, fruits, and plant oils, have an LDL cholesterol-lowering effect. They work by inhibiting the absorption of cholesterol (from foods and bile acids) in the intestine; instead, cholesterol passes out of the body through waste.

Some juices, soft gel capsules, spreads, and yogurts, are formulated to be high in plant stanols or sterols. These can be effective for lowering cholesterol for those with elevated LDLs. To be effective, you need to consume enough: 2 grams of plant stanols and sterols per day (or 1.6 to 3 grams daily if you have type 2 diabetes) with meals or other foods—as part of an eating plan that's low in saturated fat and cholesterol. *See "Functional Nutrition: Plant Stanols and Sterols" in chapter 13, page 405.*

Omega-3 fatty acids. Omega-3s from oily fish, such as salmon or tuna, may help reduce the risk of heart disease, although the data aren't conclusive. That's why the AHA recommends eating fish (preferably oily fish) at least twice a week, with each serving as 3½ ounces of cooked or ¾ cup of flaked fish. Omega-3 fatty acids from other sources—for example, canola, flaxseed, and soy oils; walnuts; and chia seeds—may have a similar effect.

See "A Closer Look . . . Omega-3s and -6s" in chapter 13, page 392.

Antioxidants. Nutrients and some phytonutrients that offer benefits may benefit your heart. For example, vitamin E may offer protection from blood clots and atherosclerosis, and vitamin C may help keep blood vessels flexible. However, the evidence is too limited to recommend vitamin supplements for heart health. Instead, enjoy a variety of nutrient-rich foods that supply antioxidant nutrients. Certain carotenoids, flavonoids, and lignans in plant-based foods may promote heart health. *See "Vitamins as Antioxidants" in chapter 14, page 423, to learn more about antioxidant benefits for heart health from certain nutrients and "Phytonutrients: Different from Nutrients" in chapter 15, page 448, to learn about phytonutrients.*

Warning Signs

Heart Attack, Stroke, and Cardiac Arrest

If you or someone you know experiences any of these warning signs, get medical help immediately—even if you're unsure. Pay attention to your body. A heart attack can start slowly with mild pain or discomfort. Minutes matter—call 911!

Heart Attack*

- Chest discomfort or pain: uncomfortable pressure, squeezing, fullness, or pain, usually in the center of the chest, that lasts more than a few minutes or that goes away and comes back
- Discomfort or pain in other areas of the upper body—for example, one or both arms, the back, neck, jaw, or stomach
- Shortness of breath—with or without chest discomfort
- Other signs: perhaps breaking out in a cold sweat, nausea, or light-headedness

Stroke

- Face drooping—sudden numbness or droopiness, especially on one side of the body. Ask if the person can smile.
- Arm weakness or numbness—can the person raise both arms? Does one arm drift downward?
- Speech difficulty, slurred speech, unable to speak, or hard to understand—can the person correctly repeat "the sky is blue"?

Cardiac Arrest

- Sudden loss of responsiveness; no response to tapping on shoulders
- No normal breathing: the person does not take a normal breath when you tilt the head up and check for at least five seconds.

*Warning signs for men and women may differ. Women will commonly feel chest pain and discomfort. But they're more likely than men to experience other symptoms, such as jaw ache, back pain, nausea, or vomiting. *See "Symptoms: Different for Women" in chapter 18, page 563.* Immediate care can safe a life. For a stroke, it may enable a full recovery.

Sources: American Heart Association; American Stroke Association, www.heart.org/HEARTORG/Conditions/911-Warnings-Signs-of-a-Heart-Attack_UCM_305346_SubHomePage.jsp#.

Cholesterol-Lowering Medication

Depending on your numbers, your risk factors, and if you have diabetes, your doctor may recommend cholesterol-lowering medication, along with heart-healthy eating and active living, which in turn may lessen the need for medication.

For those with certain cardiovascular risks, the AHA advised in 2013 that taking statins (rather than trying to hit a lower LDL target) should be the main treatment for preventing a heart attack or stroke. If you take these medications, ask about interactions with any foods, such as grapefruit and pomegranate: *see "Common Interactions Between Food and Some Medications" in chapter 25, page 744.*

For women, hormone therapy isn't an alternative for cholesterol-lowering medication. It is not recommended as a way to prevent heart disease or stroke or for those women with a history of heart disease, heart attack, or stroke. Talk to your doctor about specific prevention guidelines for heart disease for women and children.

Blood Pressure: Under Control?

Do you know your blood pressure (BP) reading? Normal blood pressure is considered less than 120 mm Hg systolic and less than 80 mm Hg diastolic. (Your BP target may differ, perhaps somewhat higher, if you have diabetes or other risk factors. Talk with your doctor about a target that's right for you.)

There's plenty you can do to control your blood pressure and keep it within a healthy range and so avoid high blood pressure, or hypertension. Start by knowing more about it.

WHAT IS HIGH BLOOD PRESSURE? WHAT RISKS?

You've heard the term "high blood pressure" many times. But do you know what it really is? And how it starts? For reasons that aren't yet clear, it happens when the body system that regulates blood flow malfunctions. Its medical name is hypertension.

Hypertension Defined

First, what it's not: Hypertension isn't emotional tension or stress, or being hyperactive, although stress may raise blood pressure temporarily. Even calm, relaxed people can have high blood pressure. For some, stress may be a factor, although the evidence of any link isn't clear-cut.

Blood pressure is the force of blood against artery walls. That pressure helps push blood through your arteries, blood vessels, and capillaries so oxygen can reach body cells. A blood pressure reading reflects two forces: systolic pressure, when the heart beats while pumping blood to your arteries, and diastolic pressure, when the heart rests between beats.

It's normal for blood pressure to rise and fall during the day. It's lower when you sleep and goes up when you're awake. It also goes up when you're excited, scared, or physically active. That's okay if it usually stays within a normal range and if it comes down to your normal baseline range when your activity stops.

High blood pressure, or hypertension, means consistently higher-than-normal pressure on blood vessel walls—in other words, too much force. It happens over time as blood gets pushed with more tension through arterioles, or small blood vessels, that become stretched, stiff, and constricted.

Hypertension-Related Health Risks

High blood pressure causes the heart to work harder to pump enough blood for the body's needs. The higher the pressure, the greater the work, the greater the risk of heart attack and stroke, and the greater the chance for permanent damage to the blood vessels of the heart, kidneys, eyes, and brain.

- Overstretched blood vessels are more prone to rupture. They can also tear, leaving scar tissue, which can trap plaque, cholesterol, and blood cells, narrowing the passage for blood. As plaque builds up in the arteries and blood flow is restricted, blood pressure goes higher.
- Narrowed arteries limit blood flow. Eventually, arteries or blood vessels may get blocked. Plaque might break off and block blood flow to the heart or brain, causing a heart attack or stroke, which can cause brain damage, heart failure, kidney failure, and paralysis.
- High blood pressure can cause aneurysms, or bulges in artery walls. They can occur anywhere, but commonly in the aorta (major artery from the heart), the spleen, the leg (behind the knee), the intestines, and in the brain (cerebral aneurysm). They can develop without symptoms, over many years.
- Other organs might get damaged, too, if they don't get enough oxygen. For example, pressure on blood vessels in the eye may damage the retina, impair vision, and even cause blindness.

High blood pressure often creeps up slowly and quietly. Until it's advanced, there usually are no symptoms. But undetected and uncontrolled, high blood pressure may cause damage to the brain, heart, and kidneys for years without someone knowing. Sometimes the first sign is a heart attack or stroke.

About one in three American adults has high blood pressure, yet many don't know they have it, according to CDC reports in 2016. Only about half of those with high blood pressure have it under control. About one in three American adults has prehypertension, or blood pressure numbers that are higher than normal but not yet in the high blood pressure range. Once high blood pressure develops, it usually lasts a lifetime.

HIGH BLOOD PRESSURE: ARE YOU AT RISK?

High blood pressure is a complex problem, and in most cases, its causes are still unknown. Yet health experts can identify people with increased risk. While more common after age thirty-five, high blood pressure can develop in children. Several factors contribute to your risk for high blood pressure.

Risk Factors You Can't Control

Family history of high blood pressure. There's a genetic tendency for high blood pressure. If your parents or close blood relatives have had high blood pressure, your chances are higher.

Certain racial or ethnic groups. African Americans have higher average blood pressure levels and tend to be more sodium sensitive than European Americans and tend to develop hypertension earlier. As a result, they're at greater risk for kidney disease as hypertension progresses and for death from heart disease and stroke. Some Asians also are at greater risk. The risks vary among different Hispanic American adults.

Age and gender. Blood pressure tends to go up with age, and blood vessels lose their flexibility. About 65 percent of those over age sixty have high blood pressure.

For men, it generally happens sooner, perhaps starting by ages forty-five to fifty, or even earlier. Women often are protected through menopause (unless they have diabetes). For most women, high blood

Lifestyle Changes to Treat High Blood Pressure

Lifestyle Change	Recommendation
Eat in a healthy way	Consume a diet that is heart healthy, limited in sodium and salt, and has more potassium. The DASH eating plan, *as discussed in "DASH to Health" in chapter 2, page 51,* is a good heart-healthy eating plan, even for those who don't have high blood pressure.
Be physically active	Engage in moderate—intensity aerobic exercise such as brisk walking or bicycling at least 2 hours and 30 minutes per week, or vigorous-intensity aerobic exercise for 1 hours and 15 minutes per week.
Maintain a healthy weight	If you are overweight or obese, try to lose weight. A loss of just 3 to 5 percent can lower your risk for health problems. Aim for a BMI below 25.
Limit alcohol intake	Limit consumption to no more than two drinks per day for men and no more than one drink per day for women and lightweight persons. (One drink is 12 ounces of beer, 5 ounces of wine, or 1½ ounces of 80-proof distilled spirits.)
Manage stress	Learn to manage stress, relax, and cope with problems to improve your emotional and physical health: for example, be physically active, listen to music, focus on something calm or peaceful, perform yoga or tai chi, or meditate.

If your doctor advises medications for blood pressure control, take them as directed and keep up your healthy lifestyle habits. For overall cardiovascular risk reduction, stop smoking and stop using other tobacco products.

Source: US Department of Health and Human Services, National Institutes of Health/National Heart, Lung, and Blood Institute, www.nhlbi.nih.gov/health/health-topics/topics/hbp/treatment, Accessed November 30, 2016.

pressure often starts about seven to ten years later than for men. Even if you don't have high blood pressure at age fifty-five, you have a 90 percent chance of developing it during your lifetime! Starting at about age sixty-five, the incidence is higher among women. That said, you can take steps to protect yourself from high blood pressure.

As an aside, blood pressure is often very low for newborns. By adolescence, normal blood pressure is similar to that of adults.

Medication: Sodium Alert for Hypertension

Are you on a sodium-modified eating plan? If so, talk to your doctor or pharmacist about any medications you take. Some contain sodium, including some antacids and alkalizers, headache remedies, laxatives, sedatives, and others.

If you take medication prescribed for high blood pressure, eating less sodium may let your medication work more effectively. If sodium reduction helps control your blood pressure, you may be able to reduce the dosage of antihypertensive medication.

Risk Factors Within Your Control

Sodium sensitivity. For many, an eating plan that's high in sodium may contribute to high blood pressure. There's no way to predict whose blood pressure may be sodium sensitive.

The Dietary Guidelines for Americans advises limiting daily sodium intake to less than 2,300 milligrams daily for children aged fourteen through eighteen and for adults. For those with prehypertension and hypertension, reducing sodium intake to 1,500 milligrams daily can result in even greater blood pressure reduction.

The AHA advises consuming no more than 2,400 milligrams of sodium daily to lower blood pressure—and reducing daily sodium intake to 1,500 is desirable because it can lower blood pressure even further. Even if you can't meet either of these guidelines, the AHA says reducing sodium intake by 1,000 milligrams daily can benefit blood pressure. To put that in context, most Americans, on average, consume more than 3,400 milligrams of sodium daily. For everyone, consuming more potassium-rich foods may help blunt sodium's effect on blood pressure.

See "A Closer Look . . . Sodium and Potassium, A Salty Subject" in chapter 14, page 433, for more about these nutrients.

Overweight or obesity. Extra body fat, especially around the waist and midriff, increases the risk for high blood pressure. Excessive weight puts more strain on the heart. Losing ten to twenty pounds can bring blood pressure down. *See "What's a Healthy Weight?" in chapter 22, page 625, for how to assess your body weight.*

Lifestyle. Inactivity can be a factor in overweight and obesity. Conversely, regular physical activity may help lower blood pressure since it's healthy for your circulatory system.

Long-lasting stress, smoking, and exposure to secondhand smoke, as well as sleep apnea, may contribute to high blood pressure, but scientific evidence doesn't prove them as causes. All are linked to other health risks, however. The AHA notes that while smoking isn't a proven cause of high blood pressure, each cigarette smoked increases blood pressure temporarily for many minutes after the cigarette is extinguished.

A Closer Look . . .

Wine: A Toast to Heart Health?

Does moderate drinking reduce the risk for heart disease? Maybe, although for heart-health benefits, people who don't drink aren't advised to start. And there's no conclusive answer to that question.

Research suggests that moderate drinking—red wine as well as white wine, beer, and distilled spirits—may offer heart-health benefits for some people, according to recent research. Possibly a small amount may help increase HDL ("good") blood cholesterol, and it may prevent some LDL ("bad") cholesterol from forming. However, factors other than ethanol (alcohol) also may play a role.

Phytonutrients such as resveratrol and tannins in wine may offer heart-health benefits. Resveratrol, a flavonoid in the skins and seeds of grapes, may function as an antioxidant, promoting heart health. It has estrogen-like qualities that may help increase HDLs or increase the oxidation, or breakdown, of LDLs. (Grape skins are needed to make red wine.)

Also speculated, resveratrol may help keep blood platelets from sticking together. It may boost the body's natural clot-dissolving enzyme; when blood platelets clot, they decrease blood flow, which can lead to a heart attack or stroke. Tannins also may inhibit platelet clotting. However, research hasn't shown if these phytonutrients are bioavailable.

There's a fine line between how much alcohol may be protective and how much instead may promote heart disease, high blood pressure, and strokes. Remember, alcohol also can raise triglyceride levels.

There's reason for caution. Scientists don't know enough to offer definitive advice on who may benefit. Even if a minor benefit exists, moderate drinking is only one factor related to heart health.

Other lifestyle factors may play a role—for example, wine drinkers may be more physically active, and they may drink wine with meals, which may affect blood lipid (fat) levels. Healthy eating, regular exercise, not smoking, and maintaining a healthy weight offer the most protection against heart disease!

It is known that excessive and binge drinking is risky. Besides potentially leading to high blood pressure, heart failure, and excess calories, too much drinking can lead to stroke, irregular heartbeat, and sudden cardiac death. For pregnant women, drinking is the leading known cause of birth defects; pregnant women are advised to avoid alcoholic beverages. Alcoholic beverages also supply extra calories, so if you're trying to control weight for heart health, control calories from alcoholic beverages, too.

If you don't drink, protecting your heart isn't a reason to start. If you do, one daily alcoholic drink may offer a benefit.

If you take aspirin regularly for heart health, your doctor may advise you to limit alcoholic beverages. *See "Alcoholic Beverages: In Moderation" in chapter 4, page 102, for more about alcoholic beverages in a healthy eating plan, with limits and a definition of moderate drinking.*

Too much drinking. Heavy and regular alcoholic drinking may increase the risk for high blood pressure and may lead to irregular heartbeat, stroke, and heart attack. *See "A Closer Look . . . Wine: A Toast to Heart Health," above.*

Contributing Health Conditions

Several health conditions can contribute to increased risk for hypertension:

Diabetes. Having type 2 diabetes or prediabetes increases the chance of developing high blood pressure if these conditions aren't managed carefully—another reason to control diabetes from its first diagnosis. *See "Diabetes: A Growing Concern" in this chapter, page 698.*

High blood lipids. If your blood lipids are high, they contribute to hypertension as well as to atherosclerosis. *See "Diagnosing Blood Lipid Levels" earlier in this chapter, page 689.*

? Have you ever wondered?

. . . what to do if you have prehypertension? Even high-normal blood pressure appears to increase cardiovascular risk significantly. If you fit into this category, you're smart to monitor your blood pressure regularly—and to make lifestyle and dietary changes, *described in this chapter,* now to bring your blood pressure levels down to a healthier level. That's equally important if you have high cholesterol levels, diabetes, or other cardiovascular risk factors, or if you're an older adult.

. . . how heart rate differs from blood pressure? Your heart rate is the number of heartbeats per minute. Your blood pressure is the amount of force exerted on your arteries when your heart beats.

Prehypertension. Even if your blood pressure is between 120/80 to 139/89 mm Hg, be cautious. With prehypertension, you'll likely develop high blood pressure later on. Take steps now to prevent it with healthy food and lifestyle choices.

TESTING, TESTING: KNOW YOUR BLOOD PRESSURE

A blood pressure measurement is two readings that look like a fraction. For example, an optimal reading is 120/80 mm Hg, expressed as "120 over 80" (mm Hg is millimeters of mercury). If it's somewhat less, that's okay.

- The higher number on top is systolic pressure. That's the pressure exerted when your heart (the ventricle) contracts, pumping blood out to your arteries.
- The bottom number, diastolic pressure, is the pressure exerted on your arteries between heartbeats, when your heart is at rest.

Whether you suspect high blood pressure or not, have your blood pressure checked regularly. If you're diagnosed with prehypertension, have it checked more often, and take steps to bring it down. Even children and teens should be checked as part of their regular physical exams, especially if they're overweight.

If your systolic, but not diastolic, pressure is high, you still have high blood pressure. The stage of hypertension you're in is the one with the highest number. With age, systolic blood pressure goes up; diastolic pressure does too until age fifty-five or so, then often it goes down. "Isolated systolic hypertension" is the most common type of high blood pressure for older Americans.

Blood pressure may fluctuate a bit during the day. Often the doctor's visit itself makes the number rise slightly. That's sometimes called "white-coat hypertension," which refers to elevated blood pressure perhaps due to the nervousness of seeing a doctor, who typically wears a white medical lab coat. To diagnose high blood pressure, you need two higher-than-normal readings taken one to several weeks apart.

If either your systolic or diastolic number, or both, are consistently at or above 140/90 mm Hg, there's cause for concern. The National Heart Lung, and Blood Institute advises that higher than 130/80 is considered high blood pressure for those with diabetes or kidney disease. Ranges for children differ. Usually high blood pressure is managed by a combination of medication, nutrition, and lifestyle changes.

Your local pharmacy may offer blood pressure readings as a free service. Or, buy an electronic blood pressure–measuring device to use at home. To check its accuracy, bring it to your next doctor's visit.

Blood Pressure Levels: For Adults*†

Category	Systolic†		Diastolic†
Normal	<120 mm Hg	and	<80 mm Hg
Prehypertension	120–139 mm Hg	or	80–89 mm Hg
High			
Stage 1	140–159 mm Hg	or	90–99 mm Hg
Stage 2	≥160 mm Hg	or	≥100 mm Hg

*These categories are for adults who have no short-term serious illnesses.

†Targets differ for those with diabetes and chronic kidney disease, who should keep their blood pressure below 130/80.

Source: US Department of Health and Human Services, National Institutes of Health/National Heart, Lung, and Blood Institute, www.nhlbi.nih.gov/health/health-topics/topics/hbp. Accessed November 30, 2016.

IF YOU'RE AT RISK OR ON MEDICATION . . .

Having a family history of high blood pressure doesn't necessarily mean you'll get it. And you can take preventive steps to reduce your risk, lower your blood pressure if needed, or make your blood pressure medication more effective.

Eat to Manage Blood Pressure

- Eat for heart health. Choose the right amounts of whole-grain and other high-fiber foods, vegetables, fruits, low-fat and fat-free dairy foods, lean meat, skinless poultry, fish (including oily fish with omega-3s), and beans and peas. Go low with solid fats (saturated and *trans* fats) and sodium, and limit added sugars. *See "DASH to Health" in chapter 2, page 51, for guidance on healthy eating patterns; see "DASH for Better Blood Pressure," in this chapter, page 697, for an introduction to the DASH eating plan.*
- Limit sodium. Keep it to less than 2,300 milligrams daily, as recommended in the Dietary Guidelines for Americans for those aged fourteen and older, and to 1,500 milligrams daily for further blood pressure reduction. And eat more potassium-rich foods because

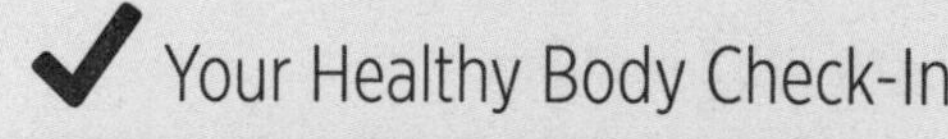

High Blood Pressure: Are You at Risk?

Use an interactive calculator to assess your high blood pressure risk:

- High Blood Pressure Health Risk Calculator, American Heart Association
  tools.bigbeelabs.com/aha/tools/hbp

DASH for Better Blood Pressure

The DASH (Dietary Approach to Stop Hypertension) Eating Plan, from the National Heart, Lung, and Blood Institute of the National Institutes of Health, emphasizes food rather than nutrients for lowering blood pressure. The DASH plan has been shown to lower blood pressure: down 2 to 8 mm Hg for systolic blood pressure. That's enough to lower hypertension risk significantly.

In research studies, the DASH plan worked fast—lowering blood pressure within two weeks. The benefits of the DASH plan were even better when combined with eating less sodium (down to 1,500 milligrams daily). Blood pressure dropped even more, especially for those with hypertension. Lower in fat, higher in potassium, and abundant in phytonutrients, the DASH plan also may help protect against some cancers, heart disease, and other health issues. *See "DASH to Health" in chapter 2, page 51, for more about this eating plan.*

they blunt the effects of sodium on blood pressure. Use the Nutrition Facts on food labels to make your food choices. *See "Major Minerals: Electrolytes" in chapter 14, page 429, for more about sodium, potassium, and salt substitutes.*

- Eat plenty of vegetables and fruits. The potassium and magnesium found in many vegetables and fruits may help control your blood pressure. *See "Potassium" and "Magnesium" in chapter 14, pages 430 and 428, for more about these nutrients and their food sources.*
- Put dairy and other calcium-rich foods on the menu. Three minerals—calcium, magnesium, and potassium—help regulate blood pressure. Calcium, and perhaps magnesium and potassium—all found in dairy foods—appear protective. No conclusive evidence shows that calcium and magnesium supplements offer extra benefits, however. *See "Calcium," "Magnesium," and "Potassium" in chapter 14, pages 425, 428, and 430, for more about these minerals.*
- Go easy on alcoholic beverages—if you drink. A limit of one drink per day for women and two for men appears safe. Alcoholic drinks may interfere with medication for hypertension. *See "Alcoholic Beverages: In Moderation" in chapter 4, page 102.*

Make Other Changes

- If you have a few pounds to shed, do it. Losing even ten pounds, through smart eating and physical activity, may bring your blood pressure down and reduce the strain on your heart—perhaps enough to avoid medication. As part of your weight loss plan, reducing solid fats and swapping in healthy oils lowers blood lipid levels, too—a benefit to heart health and diabetes management. *See "Weight Management: Strategies That Work" in chapter 22, page 637, to learn how to keep your healthy weight.*
- Fit in regular moderate to vigorous physical activity. Do at least thirty minutes a day, on most days. For example, moderate activity is walking two miles in thirty minutes. Sedentary living doesn't cause high blood pressure, but regular aerobic activity such as brisk walking, swimming, or biking may help bring it down. Moreover, physical activity can help you maintain a healthy weight. Talk to your doctor about a physical activity plan, including how to pace yourself and your level of exertion.
- Avoid tobacco smoke, including secondhand smoke. Although evidence doesn't show smoking to cause high blood pressure, tobacco smoke increases blood pressure for several minutes.
- Use hot tubs wisely if you have high blood pressure—and not if you're having a hypertensive crisis! Heat causes blood vessels to open, as does taking a brisk walk. If your doctor advises you to avoid moderate physical activity, skip the hot tub, too. Moving back and forth between cold water and a hot tub or sauna can raise blood pressure.
- Manage stress. It may lead to overeating, poor eating, smoking, or drinking alcoholic beverages, which all may increase your risk. Blood pressure may rise temporarily with the stress of a situation. The effects of chronic stress on blood pressure aren't known.

? Have you ever wondered?

. . . if caffeine causes high blood pressure? Since caffeine is a mild stimulant, you may think so. However, studies show that caffeine may result in only a very slight, temporary rise in blood pressure level. Ask your doctor if you should cut back on caffeine if your blood pressure is already high.

IF YOU HAVE HIGH BLOOD PRESSURE . . .

Relax. Although it's a lifelong condition, you can control high blood pressure and live a long, healthy life. The key is following your doctor's advice faithfully. Treatment likely will include a shift in your eating approach, weight loss (if you're overweight), more physical activity, tobacco cessation (if you use tobacco or e-cigarettes), and perhaps blood pressure medication.

- Make a plan of action with your doctor.
- If your doctor prescribes antihypertensive medication, take it as directed. If other tactics, like weight loss, lower your blood pressure level, taking medication may not be forever. Follow directions for medications carefully. Different blood pressure medications work in different ways. Some may interact with other medications—for example, for diabetes or kidney disease.
- If your doctor prescribes a sodium-modified diet, a registered dietitian nutritionist can help you plan, follow through, and monitor your sodium intake.

Diabetes: A Growing Concern

Diabetes is epidemic, affecting more than twenty-nine million Americans, as reported in 2016 by the CDC. Yet up to 25 percent of them—perhaps you or someone in your family—don't know they have it! If the current trends continue, one-third of American adults could have diabetes by 2050.

In 2016, the CDC also reported an estimated eighty-six million Americans have prediabetes, which sharply raises the risk for developing type 2 diabetes and increases the risk of heart disease and stroke.

Obesity and overweight are predictors of type 2 diabetes and insulin resistance. It's no surprise then that the worldwide rise in obesity parallels a rise in type 2 diabetes—which typically develops within a decade unless those who are obese make modest changes in their food choices and physical activity level and lose weight.

While an increasing number of people with type 2 diabetes and prediabetes goes undetected, knowledge about the condition, its causes, and its risks is one step toward its prevention.

WHAT IS DIABETES?

Diabetes is a physiological condition related to insulin, a hormone produced by the pancreas. People with diabetes either can't make insulin, can't make enough insulin, or can't use it. With an insufficient amount of insulin or an inability to use it properly, blood glucose (blood sugar) builds up in the bloodstream. That in turn affects energy metabolism, or the way the body converts sugar, starch, and other substances in foods to energy. Protein and fat metabolism are impacted, too.

Diabetes and Blood Glucose

For the record, eating affects everyone's blood glucose level—those with diabetes and those without. For someone without diabetes, blood glucose rises and falls within a normal range: a fasting level is under 100 mg/dL, and it is 140 mg/dL or less two hours after eating.

How does insulin work for healthy people? During digestion, glucose is released from carbohydrates in food and drinks and absorbed. It then circulates in the bloodstream as blood glucose to be used by body cells as an energy source. In those who don't have diabetes, insulin regulates blood glucose levels. It lets glucose pass from blood into body cells for energy production. Insulin helps blood glucose levels stay within a normal range so eating has little effect on blood glucose level.

For those with diabetes, however, their body can't control blood glucose levels normally. With type 1 diabetes, the pancreas doesn't make insulin or doesn't make enough to get glucose into the body's cells. Type 2 diabetes is insulin resistance, whereby the pancreas makes insulin (gradually not enough) but the body doesn't use it well. Either way, blood glucose levels rise higher than normal. This is called hyperglycemia.

Too little or no insulin, or the inability to use insulin properly, hinders the body's ability to use energy nutrients—carbohydrates, fats, and proteins. Instead of "feeding" cells, glucose accumulates in blood, causing blood glucose levels to rise. Since it can't be used for energy, blood glucose spills into urine, and some gets excreted. That makes extra work for the kidneys, causing frequent urination and excessive thirst.

When glucose can't be used adequately, it affects energy metabolism, or production. Over time, high blood glucose levels can lead to serious health conditions, *discussed in "Diabetes-Related Health Risks" later in this chapter, page 699.*

Categories of Diabetes

These are three main types of diabetes (type 1, type 2, and gestational), with prediabetes as a factor in developing type 2 diabetes. However, other health conditions may also result in diabetes.

What are the causes? Genetics play a role in both type 1 and type 2 diabetes; in either case, genes cannot be controlled. It's unclear what triggers the onset of type 1 diabetes. Lifestyle factors, which are in your control, may trigger type 2 diabetes; being overweight increases the risk. Other factors may play a role, for example, an older age for men and women, and for women, delivering a baby weighing more than nine pounds. To refute a myth, eating too much sugar or starches isn't the cause of diabetes.

Prediabetes. When a person's blood glucose level is higher than normal but not high enough for a diagnosis of type 2 diabetes, the diagnosis is prediabetes. Untreated, 15 to 30 percent of people diagnosed with prediabetes will develop type 2 diabetes within five years. In fact, most people who develop type 2 diabetes had prediabetes first. The heart and circulatory system can be damaged even in these early stages, so being tested is important.

To slow the progression to type 2 diabetes, blood glucose levels often may be controlled through food choices, weight control, and physical activity initially. Metformin therapy to prevent type 2 diabetes may be advised by a doctor, especially for those with a BMI greater than 35, those who are younger than sixty years, and those with prior gestational diabetes.

Type 1 diabetes. Type 1 diabetes, an autoimmune disease, accounts for 5 percent of diabetes cases. In this form of diabetes, the pancreas can't make insulin. Pancreatic beta cells that produce insulin have been destroyed, perhaps due to an inherited condition or to damage prompted by a virus. The causes aren't clear.

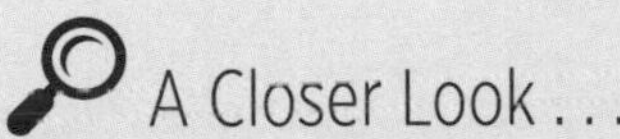

Inflammation, Health, and Food

On one hand, inflammation is a good thing. It's a natural and protective process that helps your body heal from injury, infection, or attack by a harmful substance. On the other hand, chronic, or ongoing, inflammation (pain, swelling, heat, and redness) of an affected organ or tissue happens when your immune system attacks healthy cells, leading to autoimmune diseases such as rheumatoid arthritis or Crohn's disease and contributing to heart disease, type 2 diabetes, cancer, obesity, Alzheimer's disease, and some allergic conditions.

Can the right food choices reduce ongoing inflammation? Maybe. Overall good nutrition, *as described in chapter 2, page 21,* enhances immunity and provides antioxidants that reduce the stress of inflammation. But specific foods? Some, such as oily fish (with their omega-3s and -6s), berries, some spices (such as cloves, ginger, and turmeric), and tart cherry juice, seem to suppress inflammation; how often or how much to consume is unknown. So far, the evidence is limited for these possible benefits, and there are no known anti-inflammatory miracles. Others, such as foods high in saturated and *trans* fats, may activate the inflammatory process.

While food choices are one factor linked to inflammation, there are others. For example, the quality and duration of sleep and other lifestyle factors can have a direct impact. *Bottom line:* Eat for good nutrition, maintain a healthy weight, get adequate sleep, and engage in regular physical activity.

Why is it an autoimmune disease? "Auto" refers to "self." The immune system, which normally protects the body from disease, instead attacks the beta cells that produce insulin.

People of any age can develop type 1 diabetes, but it often appears in youth. Its onset comes on suddenly. Daily insulin injections or an insulin pump, along with a careful eating and physical activity plan, are required to manage type 1 diabetes. Type 1 diabetes requires regular self-monitoring of blood glucose levels.

Type 2 diabetes. Type 2 diabetes, a metabolic disorder, accounts for 90 to 95 percent of diagnosed diabetes cases, with the incidence rising along with obesity rates, sedentary lifestyles, and an aging population, as well as better and early detection. The majority of those with type 2 diabetes are overweight.

With type 2 diabetes, the body doesn't respond to insulin normally (insulin resistance), even though the pancreas produces insulin. At first, the pancreas makes extra insulin to make up this inefficiency. However, over time, the pancreas cannot make enough insulin to normalize blood glucose levels. Type 2 diabetes often develops slowly with higher risk after age forty. Yet it's becoming more common among children and teens, as obesity has increased in these age groups.

In type 2 diabetes, blood glucose levels often may be controlled through food choices, weight control, and physical activity initially. However, because this condition is chronic and progressive, medication such as metformin therapy is typically needed when A1C rises. Adequate control is important from the start—and for life. The A1C test, *discussed in "Testing, Testing: Blood Glucose" in this chapter, page 701,* is a blood test used to diagnose type 1 and type 2 diabetes and to monitor how well someone manages it.

Taking glucose-lowering medicines may help the body produce more insulin or better use the insulin the body makes. Insulin given by injection or pump may be needed, too. Type 2 diabetes also requires regular self monitoring of blood glucose levels to gain feedback and drive individualized decisions. The course of care for type 2 diabetes is progressive over time.

Gestational diabetes. Gestational diabetes occurs in 2 to 10 percent of pregnancies, likely resulting from changes in hormone levels. Hormones from the placenta, needed for the baby's development, may block the action of the mother's insulin.

Screening for gestational diabetes is usually done at the first visit and then again twenty-four to twenty-eight weeks later. The risk is higher among obese and older women. About six to twelve weeks after a baby is born, the mother should be tested again, and if normal, every three years from then on or as recommended by her doctor.

Gestational diabetes needs careful control during pregnancy but usually disappears after delivery if blood glucose levels are within a target range. However, women with gestational diabetes are at increased risk for prediabetes and type 2 diabetes later in life. If planning for pregnancy, women with these conditions should prepare ahead and follow their doctor's advice for blood glucose levels. *See "Diabetes and Pregnancy" in chapter 18, page 551, for more information on gestational diabetes.*

Diabetes-Related Health Risks

If not managed properly, diabetes can have serious, even life-threatening, effects on health: eye problems (damage to blood vessels in the retina, cataracts, and glaucoma) and blindness; circulatory problems; nervous system disease (neuropathy); and diabetic kidney disease (nephropathy) and kidney failure; and serious, hard-to-treat infections which can lead to an amputation of toes, feet, or legs, among others. Diabetes also affects blood pressure and cholesterol levels, doubles the risk for heart attacks, and increases the risk of a stroke; two-thirds of those with diabetes die from these causes.

In fact, diabetes is the leading cause of blindness, leg and foot amputations, and kidney disease, and is the seventh-leading cause of death in the United States. To underscore the seriousness: More deaths result from diabetes each year than from breast cancer and AIDS combined.

Damage can add up. Even during prediabetes, some long-term damage, especially to the heart and circulatory system may occur. The best way to reduce the risks for these problems is to get diagnosed early and keep your blood glucose level near the normal range.

Good news: If you develop diabetes, you can live a long, healthy life. Learn how to manage it, and follow through. For those with prediabetes or type 2 diabetes, you may prevent or reduce its long-term consequences—with improvements in your overall food choices, your weight, and your physical activity.

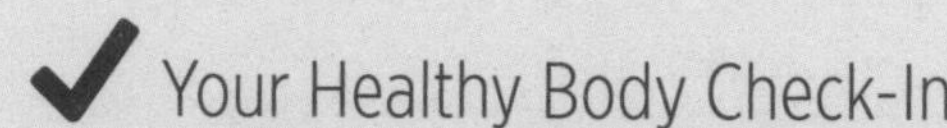

Diabetes: Are You at Risk?

Use these online interactive calculators to assess your diabetes health risk:

- Type 2 Diabetes Risk Test, American Diabetes Association www.diabetes.org/are-you-at-risk/diabetes-risk-test

Managing Prediabetes

Diagnosed with prediabetes? These strategies can help you manage it effectively and prevent or delay the onset of diabetes and its complications. In fact, a diabetes prevention program may reduce your risk of diabetes by nearly 60 percent.

- Reduce your body weight by 7 percent if you're overweight or obese. That's about fifteen pounds if you weigh 200 pounds. A 7 percent weight loss may not put you at your goal weight, but it is a step in the right direction toward managing your blood glucose levels and increasing your sensitivity to insulin. If you have trouble with weight loss, losing even ten to fifteen pounds can make a big difference. *See "Weight Management: Strategies That Work!" in chapter 22, page 637, for more about achieving and maintaining a healthy weight.*
- Get at least 150 minutes of exercise a week. A great way to get started is by walking. Aim for thirty minutes daily, such as brisk walking, five times a week. You might use an activity tracker or mobile activity tracking app for an objective measure to prompt and motivate you to move more. *"Digital Tracking: The Benefits" in chapter 26, page 761, for tips on tracking food and fitness information, "Move More! Physical Activity Guidelines" in chapter 1, page 15 and "Commit to Active Living" in chapter 22, page 638, offer more about physical activity and how to make it a regular habit.*
- Follow a healthy eating plan, *as described in chapter 2, page 21.* Eating meals at consistent times can help with weight loss and blood glucose control.

EARLY DETECTION: IMPORTANT!

The longer the body is exposed to high blood glucose levels, the greater the damage to the nervous and circulatory systems and to the blood vessels in the eyes, kidneys, heart, and feet.

Prediabetes and Diabetes: Symptoms (or Not)

According to the American Diabetes Association (ADA), many people don't know they have prediabetes or diabetes. Prediabetes has no clear symptoms. Some people with type 2 diabetes have no symptoms, and because some symptoms they have may seem harmless, diabetes goes undiagnosed. For those who do have symptoms:

- Common symptoms include extreme fatigue, frequent urination, unusual thirst, extreme hunger, unusual weight loss, and irritability.
- Those with type 2 diabetes also may experience frequent infections; cuts and bruises that heal slowly; blurred vision; numb or tingling hands or feet; or recurring skin, gum, or bladder infections.

How would you know if you have diabetes? A doctor's diagnosis, *with tests described later in "Testing, Testing: Blood Glucose" in this chapter, page 701,* and keeping tabs on your blood glucose level is the way to really know.

Type 2: Are You at Risk?

Knowing if you're at risk can help you take steps to prevent or manage diabetes as well as prediabetes. Some of these risk factors are within your control.

- Prediabetes, or an impaired glucose tolerance (IGT) and/or impaired fasting glucose (IFG)
- Age forty years or older. With age, the pancreas is less efficient at producing insulin. Starting at age forty-five, have your A1C checked, and then again every three years. Those with prediabetes need to be checked every one to two years.

- A close family member with diabetes. A genetic inherited tendency or shared circumstances increase risk. To refute a myth, diabetes isn't contagious.
- Certain racial or ethnic groups. Being of African American, Hispanic/Latino American, or Native American descent or being of Asian American, Hawaiian American, or other Pacific Islander descent increases diabetes risk and its complications.
- Being overweight or obese. With more body fat, body cells may become more insulin resistant. That said, many people who are overweight or obese do not develop diabetes, and those who do may be normal weight or slightly overweight. *See "What's a Healthy Weight?" in chapter 22, page 625, for how to assess your body weight.* Even if you're at risk for type 2 diabetes, with healthy eating, regular moderate exercise, and weight reduction, your odds drop, even if you're overweight.
- Sedentary lifestyle
- History of cardiovascular disease
- Low HDL cholesterol or high triglycerides levels, and high blood pressure
- Woman having had gestational diabetes or who delivered a baby weighing nine pounds or more
- Woman with polycystic ovary syndrome
- Other clinical conditions associated with insulin resistance

Chronic inflammation may play a role in diabetes. *See "A Closer Look . . . Inflammation, Health, and Food" in this chapter, page 699.*

TESTING, TESTING: BLOOD GLUCOSE

Testing blood glucose levels is done for two key reasons: for diagnosing prediabetes and, with a diagnosis of diabetes, for monitoring the "ups" and "downs" to manage and treat diabetes.

Diagnostic tests. Diabetes may be detected first by a urine test, given as a routine part of most physical exams. However, blood glucose readings are much more accurate and necessary for diagnosis. Starting at age forty-five, everyone should have a blood glucose test every three years, if healthy and at low risk. Those with prediabetes are advised to be tested annually.

For those at high risk, blood glucose checking should start sooner and be more frequent. Individuals of any age who are at higher risk include those who are overweight or obese, based on their BMI, or who have one or more additional type 2 diabetes risk factors, such as high blood pressure or previous gestational diabetes.

Testing should be done in a healthcare setting, such as a doctor's office. Be aware that screening checks, often done at community health events, aren't diagnostic, yet they can identify those at high risk who need further checking. The Glycated Hemoglobin (A1C) test, the Fasting Plasma Glucose (FPG) test, and the Oral Glucose Tolerance Test (OGTT) are used to diagnose diabetes:

- *A1C:* Measures your average blood glucose levels over two to three months and doesn't require overnight fasting. It assesses the percentage of hemoglobin that is glycated, or coated with sugar. Hemoglobin is a protein in red blood cells that carries oxygen. Diabetes is diagnosed by an A1C of greater than or equal to 6.5%; prediabetes is 5.7% to 6.4%.
- *FPG:* Measures your fasting blood glucose levels; usually done in the morning before breakfast after an eight-hour fast (no food or drink except water). Diabetes is diagnosed by a fasting blood glucose of greater than or equal to 126 mg/dL; prediabetes is 100 to 125 mg/dL.
- *OGTT:* Two-hour test that measures blood glucose levels before and two hours after a special sweet drink; tells how the body processes glucose. Diabetes is diagnosed by a two-hour blood glucose of greater than or equal to 200 mg/dL; prediabetes is 140 to 199 mg/dL.

For more information on diagnosing diabetes and learning about prediabetes, go to www.diabetes.org/diabetes-basics/diagnosis.

Self-monitoring. If you're diagnosed with diabetes, you need to self-monitor, or check your own blood glucose level. For example, your pre-meal goal may be 80–130 mg/dL and a post-meal goal (about 1 to 2 hours after beginning a meal) may be less than 180 mg/dL, according to the ADA's Standards of Medical Care in Diabetes—2017.

Target levels differ for young children, older adults, and those with gestational diabetes. Many factors determine the right blood glucose goals for someone with diabetes. While levels are recommended by the ADA, your healthcare team can provide guidance on when and how often to monitor realistic target blood glucose levels, individualized for you—for example, before meals, after meals, and at bedtime.

Also note: Those who aren't aware of their hypoglycemia lose their ability to feel blood glucose "lows."

Checking your blood glucose level is vital. Your doctor, registered dietitian nutritionist, or certified diabetes educator will show you how to check your blood glucose level:

- Once you get used to pricking your finger, forearm, or other alternate sites, it's easy: just a drop of blood on a test strip, read by a blood glucose meter.
- Record the results, the time, and the date. Or use a blood glucose meter that stores the readings for you.
- Log the information, perhaps with an online tool or diabetes mobile app. Share your log with your healthcare team to see if your diabetes care plan (eating, exercise, and medication), *as discussed in "If you Have Diabetes . . . " on page 702*, is working.

You might also use a Continuous Glucose Monitoring (CGM) system that provides real-time glucose readings, throughout the day and night, perhaps with an average as often as every five minutes. That enables you to see your glucose levels and track how fast they increase or decrease. You still need a blood glucose meter, but CGM provides more information to help you manage type 1 or type 2 diabetes.

Your registered dietitian nutritionist or certified diabetes educator can also help you understand what the numbers and patterns mean. He or she will guide you on changes to make, based on the results.

Once you become adept at self-monitoring, you can use your blood glucose reading to know if your diabetes treatment plan is on track or if you need to make adjustments. If your blood glucose level is too low (perhaps below 70 mg/dL) or too high (perhaps above 240 mg/dL), take action.

Monitoring tests: doctor visits. To control blood glucose levels and diabetes-related complications, ongoing monitoring means checking your "ABCs": A for hemoglobin A1C, B for blood pressure, and C for cholesterol (blood lipid) levels. Your goals will depend on your age, how long you've had diabetes, your health history, and other health conditions.

- *A:* Every three to six months, your doctor will run a glycated hemoglobin, or hemoglobin A1C, test. Like figuring a batting average for a baseball player, it measures your average blood glucose levels over the past two to three months, not just for a day. It indicates whether your blood glucose levels are under control over time, verifies your self-testing results, and shows how effective your health choices have been.

  See "Diagnosing Diabetes" in this chapter, page 701. Goals are individualized. An A1C goal may be as low as less than 6.5 or as high as 8 to 8.5. (The A1C target range for most pregnant women with diabetes is 6 to 6.5; talk to your doctor.)

  The estimated average glucose (eAG) is a newer way to report A1C, making it easier to see how well you are managing overall. It correlates with the units of measurement (mg/dL) on your blood glucose meter—so it would look familiar. Talk to your doctor to learn more about how these tests work.

- *B:* Since high blood pressure is common among those with prediabetes and diabetes, your doctor will check this, too, *as discussed in this chapter, page 701.*

- *C:* Abnormal blood cholesterol and triglyceride levels, *as discussed in this chapter, page 701,* often go hand-in-hand with diabetes.

If you have type 1 diabetes, your doctor also may advise a urine test for ketones, which are acids that may build up in urine to toxic levels. Without available insulin, body cells can't use glucose for energy, so your body turns to burning fat, not carbohydrates (glucose), for energy. And without glucose, body cells can't burn fat completely. Ketones form as a by-product of fat burning. When ketones build up, a condition called ketoacidosis can occur; left untreated, it can lead to a diabetic coma and even death.

Talk to your doctor about early symptoms of ketoacidosis, including excessive thirst, frequent urination, nausea, abdominal pain, weakness, fruity-scented breath, and confusion. Have an action plan to get immediate medical help if ketoacidosis develops.

Goals for Managing Diabetes

Whether you have been diagnosed with type 1, type 2, or gestational diabetes, your overall goals for managing the disease are the same.

- Keep blood glucose levels within the normal range or as close to normal as possible. This can prevent or reduce diabetes-related complications.
- Reduce your risk of heart disease and stroke, since people with diabetes are at risk for both. Keep blood pressure within normal levels and achieve healthy cholesterol levels.
- Adopt a healthy eating pattern and physically active lifestyle that are enjoyable and doable for you and can prevent, or at least slow, complications from diabetes.

IF YOU HAVE DIABETES . . .

Managing diabetes is complicated and sometimes even overwhelming. To simplify and help you manage it, team up with a registered dietitian nutritionist or certified diabetes educator. And control all the "ABCs"—your A1C level, blood pressure, and cholesterol and triglyceride levels.

Control your blood glucose levels so they stay as near to a target range as possible without frequent hypoglycemia; *see "Goals for Managing Diabetes" in this chapter, page 702.* Health problems occur when high blood glucose levels are sustained over time, not from an elevated blood glucose level after a single meal.

Like a teeter-totter, blood glucose levels go up and down. That's part of dealing with diabetes. Those swings can be dangerous when healthy eating, physical activity, and diabetes medication aren't balanced properly.

Blood glucose control: a balancing act. To keep blood glucose levels from going too high or too low, you need to balance the amount of carbohydrate you consume, the amount and types of insulin and/or diabetes medication you take, and the type and amount of physical activity you do:

- Too much food that contains carbohydrate or too little diabetes medication? Your blood glucose level can soar, affecting your health now and very seriously down the road.

Have you ever wondered?

. . . if going "low carb" would be a good approach for managing diabetes? Your goal should be to manage the carbohydrates in your food choices, not eliminate them. After all, you need the glucose (blood sugar) from carbohydrates as energy for your brain and other body cells. Remember: With diabetes, the issue is how insulin, which may be inadequate or not working properly, handles carbohydrates—not whether you need carbohydrates.

For weight maintenance, most women do well with 45 to 60 grams of carbohydrate per meal and most men do well with 60 to 75 grams of carbohydrate per meal. For weight loss, 30 to 45 grams of carbohydrate per meal may be a good target for women, and 45 to 60 grams of carbohydrate per meal, for men. Both men and women also may need a snack(s) with 15 grams of carbohydrates. Set your target with your doctor.

. . . if you need to give up fruit if you have diabetes? And what about avoiding white foods? For any of these foods, you just need to know how to "budget" them in your meals and snacks since all are carbohydrate foods. Get to know the portion size that contributes about 15 grams of carbohydrates, considered one choice if you use food lists as a tool for menu planning. Enjoy fruit in moderation since it delivers many nutrients you need for good health. Remember that the sweetness comes from fructose, a natural sugar, so go easy.

So-called white foods such as potatoes and bananas are sources of potassium. Enriched and fortified white bread, rice, and pasta are good sources of B vitamins (thiamin, riboflavin, niacin), iron, and folic acid. They, too, supply carbohydrates in the form of starch. Again, check the food lists for portions that contribute 15 grams of carbs.

. . . if taking a vitamin, mineral, or herbal supplement can help improve diabetes or have a glucose-lowering effect? Despite claims, no conclusive evidence shows that herbal products offer benefits for managing diabetes although some may have promise—and some may interact with diabetes medication. There may be safety concerns regarding the long-term use of antioxidant supplements such as vitamins C and E and carotenes.

Talk to your doctor first, if you choose to try them—and never use them in place of insulin or other prescribed medicine. *See chapter 10, page 705, for more about supplements.*

. . . if cinnamon can lower blood glucose levels? Some research has addressed this question as well as cinnamon's effect on blood pressure and blood cholesterol levels. However, evidence has been limited and conflicting. If you have diabetes, enjoy flavoring your food with cinnamon, but don't use it as a primary strategy for managing your blood glucose level.

- Too much exercise or too much insulin? Too little food or a delayed meal or snack time? Your blood glucose drops, and your body can't use blood glucose to produce enough energy.

To control "the ups and downs," carefully manage what you eat, how much, and when—no matter what type of diabetes you have. Eating raises your blood glucose level; physical activity and medication can lower it. For example, in the case of a low blood glucose level (<70 mg/dL), consume a small amount (15 grams) of a quick-acting carbohydrate, such as ½ cup juice or three to four glucose tablets. *See "Treating Low Blood Glucose" in this chapter, page 705, about the rule of 15.*

Diabetes management plan: an overview. For many people with type 2 diabetes, a management plan needs these three things: a healthy eating plan, regular physical activity, and strategies to prevent weight gain or achieve sensible weight loss if overweight. That may be enough to control a blood glucose level and to maintain good health. Others also need diabetes medication, prescribed by their doctor.

Different diabetes medications work in different ways: some lower blood glucose level; others help the body use insulin better. Medications may include pills and/or injections.

If you've just found out that you have diabetes, you may feel healthy. Even if it's hard to remember to stick with your eating and physical activity plan and—if prescribed by your doctor—a medication plan, the long-term benefits are well worth the effort!

Read on for general advice and six important strategies for managing diabetes and preventing its symptoms and complications. For individualized guidance, consult your doctor and a registered dietitian nutritionist. Some dietitians, pharmacists, and nurses are certified in one or both of these ways: Certified Diabetes Educator (CDE) or Board-Certified Advanced Diabetes Manager (BC-ADM).

1. Make a Daily Meal and Snack Plan

The game plan for smart eating with diabetes follows this general strategy: Eat about the same amount of food, in the right balance, at about the same time every day. To avoid weight gain, balance your day's food choices with regular physical activity. As you do so, enjoy the pleasure of food!

What is the "right balance"? It's *food variety* with a balance of different types of food; *portion savvy* to eat the right amount; and *control of energy-producing nutrients* (carbohydrates, fats, and proteins).

Diabetes: You're in Control!

If you have diabetes, these are seven areas you can focus on to manage your blood glucose levels. Ask for guidance from a certified diabetes educator or registered dietitian nutritionist.

1. *Healthy eating.* Having diabetes doesn't mean you have to give up your favorite foods or stop eating in restaurants. In fact, there is nothing you can't eat. But you need to know that the foods you eat affect your blood glucose.
2. *Being active.* Being active is not just about losing weight. It has many health benefits such as lowering cholesterol, improving blood pressure, lowering stress and anxiety, and improving your mood. If you have diabetes, physical activity can also help keep your blood glucose levels normal and help you keep your diabetes under control.
3. *Monitoring.* Checking your blood glucose levels regularly gives you vital information about your diabetes management. Monitoring helps you know when your blood glucose levels are on target, and it helps you make food and activity adjustments so that your body can perform at its best.
4. *Taking medication.* There are several types of medications often recommended for people with diabetes. Insulin, pills that lower your blood glucose, aspirin, blood pressure medication, cholesterol-lowering medication, or a number of others may work together to lower your blood glucose levels, reduce your risk of complications, and help you feel better.
5. *Problem solving.* Everyone encounters problems with their diabetes control. You can't plan for every situation you may face. However, there are some problem-solving skills that can help you prepare for the unexpected—and make a plan for dealing with similar problems in the future.
6. *Reducing risks.* Having diabetes puts you at a higher risk for developing other health problems. However, if you understand the risks, you can take steps now to lower your chance of diabetes-related complications.
7. *Healthy coping.* Diabetes can affect you physically and emotionally. It's natural to have mixed feelings about your diabetes management and to experience highs and lows. The important thing is to recognize these emotions as normal and then take steps to reduce the negative impact they can have on your self-care.

Source: AADE7 Self-Care Behaviors™, © 2010 American Association of Diabetes Educators.

You don't need special diabetic foods. Eating with diabetes follows principles of healthy eating for anybody aged two years and older: a variety of foods, including whole grains, vegetables, fruits, low-fat or fat-free dairy foods, healthy fats, and lean meats or meat alternatives. It's an approach that your whole family can follow, which makes meal management simpler and pleasurable. *See chapter 2, page 21, to learn about healthy eating plans.*

An eating plan: the big picture. There's no single eating plan for managing diabetes. In fact, the guidelines have built-in flexibility. Your doctor, along with a registered dietitian nutritionist and/or your certified diabetes educator, can help you plan what's right for you. Planning will address the following:

- *The amount and proportions of macronutrients: carbohydrates, fats, and proteins.* Your plan will depend on your food preferences, weight, blood cholesterol levels, and metabolic and medical goals. Besides controlling blood glucose levels, your plan also may help manage or improve your weight, blood pressure, and cholesterol levels. *See chapters 11, 12, and 13 to learn about macronutrients and their food sources.*

  As an adult, your carbohydrate target will likely be within a range of 45 to 65 percent of your calories, based on your metabolic goals. That range is the same as for the general population, set by the Dietary Reference Intakes. For a 2,000-calorie daily plan, that's 900 to 1,300 calories from total carbohydrates, or 225 to 325 grams of carbohydrate. (One carbohydrate gram supplies 4 calories.) Your personal carbohydrate target depends on your age, physical activity level, body size, and perhaps a weight-loss plan.

- *Portion sizes and amounts, and the kinds of food.* That's so you eat enough but not too much food or too much of one type of food. The ADA and Academy of Nutrition and Dietetics recommends 45 to 60 grams of carbohydrate per meal for women and 60 to 75 grams of carbs per meal for men. Specific food choices are up to you.

- *Overall timing.* You'll create a schedule to help you spread out your carbohydrates fairly evenly during the day. What if you skip a meal? With diabetes, you can't get away with skimping on lunch or breakfast to save up for an indulgent dinner. Instead, do trade-offs within a meal. With some diabetes medications, you may not be at risk for hypoglycemia if you occasionally skip a meal—still, it's not advised!

- *One or more meal and snack planning tools:* This may include healthy eating plans, food lists for diabetes, carbohydrate counting, and the plate method, *described below and in the next few pages.*

  For those with diabetes, there's no one ideal way to distribute calories among carbohydrates, fats, and proteins. An individual plan, while keeping total calories and metabolic goals in mind,

Treating Low Blood Glucose

How do you know if your blood glucose level is too low? Among the symptoms of hypoglycemia, or low blood glucose, are: Do you feel confused? Headachy or light-headed? Hungry? Irritable and anxious? Sweaty and shaky? Uncoordinated or confused? Weak or sleepy? Do you have a rapid heart rate? If so, these signs indicate that your blood glucose may be too low.

The way to know for sure is to check your blood glucose level with a meter. Many people, especially those with long-standing diabetes, have neuropathy, or a nervous system disease, which may make them unaware of having hypoglycemia. Others may think their blood glucose level is low when it's not. Low blood glucose generally is less than 70 mg/dL.

If it's under 70 mg/dL, use the "rule of 15" to treat it:

- Eat or drink something with 15 grams of carbohydrate so glucose can get into your blood. Each of these foods provide about 15 grams of carbohydrate: 3 or 4 glucose tablets; ½ cup (4 ounces) of fruit juice or regular soda (or ¾ cup [6 ounces] of ginger ale); 6 or 7 hard candies; or 1 tablespoon of sugar or honey.
- Rest for about fifteen minutes. Recheck your blood glucose level. If it's still low, eat or drink something with 15 grams of carbs again.
- Check to make sure your blood glucose level comes within a safe range. Then eat a small snack if your next meal or snack is more than an hour or two away.

Although this is an accepted treatment for hypoglycemia, the "rule of 15" should not replace the advice of your diabetes care team. Contact your doctor if low blood glucose continues.

Note: Protein should not be used to treat or prevent hypoglycemia.

Be prepared by keeping glucose tablets or a glucagon injection kit on hand for when you need it.

should be the goal. Instead, carbohydrate intake from whole grains, vegetables, fruits, dairy products, and beans and peas, with an emphasis on foods higher in fiber and lower in glycemic load, is advised.

Healthy eating plans for the day. Following a healthy eating plan for the day not only helps with blood glucose control, but also helps ensure good nutrition overall. Consult with your registered dietitian nutritionist or certified diabetes educator for the best plan for you:

- Eating patterns to use for daily menu planning for those with diabetes should be customized based on lifestyle and food preferences. This might include recommended food group choices for meals and snacks.
- The three USDA Healthy Eating Patterns, represented by MyPlate, are healthy eating guides for managing diabetes and for the whole family, as well. They're a good starting point for many, including those with prediabetes. Use them to manage carbohydrates and other energy nutrients (macronutrients) and to choose a variety of nutrient-rich foods. One of the USDA Healthy Eating Patterns is a vegetarian plan, *see chapter 2, page 53*. "The plate method," *described in this chapter, page 707*, is an easy way to apply this advice in a single meal.

Food lists for diabetes. Food lists are used as a way to estimate to plan meals for diabetes management. They're similar to food exchanges used in the past to estimate carbohydrate amounts. *See "Food Portions: How Many Carbs?"on the next page for examples of carbohydrate amounts in common foods.*

Food lists group foods together based on the similarity of their carbohydrate, fat, protein, and calorie content. Each food is given in a serving size within a list that has about the same carbohydrate, fat, protein, and calories as any of the other foods in the same list. You can trade one food on the list for any other on the same list and get about the same food value.

Using food lists works this way: Meals and snacks are planned with specific amounts from each list. The menu-planning goals are: (1) to get enough food variety and (2) to manage blood glucose levels by spreading out the carbohydrates, other energy-producing nutrients, and calories throughout the day. More comprehensive food lists also are published by the ADA and the Academy of Nutrition and Dietetics: "Choose Your Foods: Food Lists for Diabetes." If you want to use them, ask a registered dietitian nutritionist or certified diabetes educator to help you.

Carbohydrate counting. Carbohydrates (starches and sugars) affect blood glucose levels more than any other nutrient, which is why they need to be monitored and controlled.

Counting carbs is a useful meal and snack planning tool, allowing for more flexibility than other tools. It's simply adding up the total carbs—starches, naturally occurring sugars, and added sugars—in grams in your meals and snacks. Total carbs, not just sugars, matter since starches and sugars affect blood glucose levels in the same way.

To keep your blood glucose levels within the target range and prevent post-meal highs and lows, carbohydrate counting has an advantage. It lets you more precisely match rapid-acting medication (insulin) to the foods you eat. The more consistent your carbohydrate intake, the more stable your blood glucose level. Tight control is getting as close to a normal (nondiabetic) blood glucose level as safely possible.

With carb counting, you keep track of—and set limits on—the total carbohydrate grams you eat, trying to eat about the same number of carbohydrates, at the same time, each day. Alternatively, if you take mealtime insulin with an injection or pump, you may learn to adjust your insulin dose to cover the amount of carbohydrate you choose to eat.

Food Portions: How Many Carbs?

The following list provides the grams of carbohydrates, or "carb grams," in some common foods, in the portions noted.

Starches: 15 carb grams

Breads	
Bagel	¼ large (1 oz.)
Biscuit	1 (2½-inch diameter)
Bread, reduced calorie, light	2 slices (1½ oz.)
Bread, white or whole grain	1 slice (1 oz.)
Cornbread	1¾-inch cube (1½ oz.)
English muffin	½ muffin
Hamburger or hot dog bun	½ bun (¾ oz.)
Naan, chapati. or roti	1 oz.
Pancake	1 (4-inch diameter, ¼-inch thick)
Pita	½ (6-inch diameter)
Tortilla, corn or flour	1 small (6-inch diameter) or ⅓ large (10-inch diameter)
Waffle	1 (4-inch square)
Cereals and Grains (All grains and pasta measured as cooked)	
Barley, couscous, millet pasta, polenta, quinoa, or rice	⅓ cup
Bran cereal, shredded wheat (plain), or sugar-coated cereal	½ cup
Bulgur, kasha, tabbouleh, or wild rice	½ cup
Granola cereal	¼ cup
Hot cereal (oats, oatmeal, or grits)	½ cup
Unsweetened, ready-to-eat cereal	¾ cup
Starchy Vegetables (All measured as cooked)	
Cassava, dasheen, or plantain	⅓ cup
Corn, green peas, or parsnips	⅓ cup
Potato, with skin, baked	¼ large (3 oz.)
Potato, mashed with milk and fat	½ cup
Potatoes, french fries (oven baked)	1 cup (2 oz.)
Squash, winter	1 cup
Sweet potato or yam, plain	½ cup (3½ oz.)
Crackers and Snacks	
Crackers, animal	8 crackers
Crackers, graham	3 crackers (2 ½-inch squares)
Crackers, saltines or round butter type	6 crackers
Granola or snack bar	1 bar (¾ oz.)
Popcorn, popped	3 cups
Pretzels	¾ oz.
Rice cakes	2 cakes (4-inch diameter)
Snack chips, baked (pita, potato)	about 8 chips (¾ oz.)
Snack chips, regular (potato, tortilla)	about 13 chips (1 oz.)
Beans, Peas, and Lentils	
Baked beans, canned	⅓ cup
Beans, cooked or canned, drained and rinsed	½ cup

Fruits: 15 carb grams (weights listed include skin, core, and seeds)

Applesauce, unsweetened	½ cup
Banana	1 extra-small (about 4-inch long; 4 oz.)
Blueberries	¾ cup
Dried fruit	2 Tbsp.
Fruit, canned	½ cup
Fruit, whole (nectarine, orange, pear)	1 medium (6 oz.)
Fruit, whole (apple)	1 small (4 oz.)
Fruit juice, unsweetened	½ cup
Grapes	17 small (3 oz.)
Melon, diced	1 cup
Strawberries, whole	1¼ cup

Milk and Milk Alternates: 12 carb grams

Milk (fat-free, 1%, 2%, whole)	1 cup
Rice drink, plain, fat-free	1 cup
Yogurt (including Greek), plain or sweetened with artificial sweetener*	⅔ cup (6 oz.)

*Yogurts vary in carbohydrate content, so check the label.

Food Portions: How Many Carbs? *(continued)*

Nonstarchy Vegetables: 5 carb grams

Vegetable juice	½ cup
Vegetables, cooked	½ cup
Vegetables, raw	1 cup

Sweets and Desserts: 15 carb grams

Brownie, small, unfrosted	1 (1¼-inch square, ⅞-inch high; about 1 oz.)
Cake, unfrosted	1 piece (2-inch square; about 1 oz.)
Candy, hard	3 pieces
Ice cream, regular	½ cup
Pudding, sugar-free or sugar-and fat-free (made with fat-free milk)	½ cup
Sandwich cookie with crème filling	2 small (about ⅔ oz.)

Combination Foods: 15 carb grams

Soup (tomato, cream, broth types)	1 cup (8 oz.)
Stew (beef or other meats and vegetables)	1 cup (8 oz.)
Casserole-type entrees (tuna noodle, lasagna, spaghetti and meatballs, chili with beans, macaroni and cheese)	1 cup (8 oz.)
Pizza, thin crust	¼ (12-inch-diameter pizza) (5 oz.)
Potato or macaroni/pasta salad	½ cup

Combination Foods: 45 carb grams

Burrito (beef and bean)	1 (5 oz.)
Dinner-type healthy frozen meal (includes dessert and is usually less than 400 calories)	1 (about 9 to 12 oz.)

Source: Excerpted from Count Your Carbs: Getting Started. Academy of Nutrition and Dietetics/American Diabetes Association, 2014.

Carbohydrate counting isn't appropriate for everyone with diabetes. One reason: it takes effort, planning, and knowledge to track carbs. And underestimating (more common) or overestimating can significantly affect blood glucose levels.

With experience, however, many people can determine an accurate serving of carbohydrates just by eyeballing and know how certain foods will affect their blood glucose level. Many children with diabetes learn to count carbs, too, particularly for their favorite foods and with a bolus (dosage) wizard on their insulin pump.

So, how to do it: If counting carbs is your strategy, work with your healthcare team to set goals and make a plan that's right for you:

- Set your starting goal for weight maintenance at about 45 to 60 grams of carbohydrate per meal for women, or 60 to 75 grams per meal for men, and maybe 15 grams of carbohydrates for a snack.
- Match your food choices and portion sizes to your goal. Try to keep within 5 grams of your target. Remember, the more carbs consumed, the higher your blood glucose level may be. Take fat and protein into account when you consider total calories; they don't impact blood glucose.
- Know what counts as one serving of food with about 15 grams of carbohydrate; *see "For Carb Counters: Guesstimating Amounts in Foods" in this chapter, page 708*. Nutrition Facts labels, *discussed in chapter 6, page 144*, are a useful tool for counting carbs.
- Also remember: Carbohydrates can come from any food—not just bread, pasta, potatoes, and rice. Beans and peas, corn and other starchy vegetables, fruit and fruit juice, milk, and yogurt, as well as cake, candy, chips, cookies, and sodas have carbohydrates, too. Plain meat, poultry, and fish as well as oils don't. For meals and snacks, choose mostly nutrient-rich carbohydrate foods; they also supply vitamins, minerals, and phytonutrients.

Plate method. For a quick and easy tool to plan a meal, use the plate method (for when you don't require tight control for managing blood glucose). You don't need to do any counting, but you do need portion savvy. The goal: to eat sensible amounts, perhaps less overall, and to shift to bigger amounts of nonstarchy vegetables and smaller amounts of starchy foods and meats. This approach works not only for managing diabetes, but for managing your weight, too!

1. Draw an imaginary line through the middle of a nine-inch plate for lunch and dinner. Then divide one half in half again. You'll have three sections.

2. On half of the plate: Serve nonstarchy vegetables, such as bell peppers, bok choy, broccoli, carrots, cucumber, okra, spinach, salad greens, and tomatoes. That can provide 10 to 15 grams of carbohydrate.
3. On one-quarter of the plate: Serve starchy foods and grains, such as beans and peas, corn, grits, pasta, potatoes, rice, winter squash, whole-grain bread, low-fat crackers, and pretzels. This provides about 30 to 45 grams of carbohydrate.
4. On one-quarter of the plate: Serve lean meat, skinless chicken or turkey, fish, tofu or other plant-based protein, eggs, or low-fat cheese.
5. On the side: Serve 1 cup of low-fat or fat-free milk (for 12 carb grams) or 6 ounces of low-fat yogurt (about 12 carb grams). Or serve ½ cup of fruit or a small piece of fruit (about 15 carb grams). Or do both if your plan allows.
6. Fit in a small amount of healthy fats: *see "Oils: Go for Healthy Fats" in chapter 2, page 46, and "Healthy Oils: Replace Solid Fats," in chapter 13, page 395, for food preparation tips.*
7. Include a drink as a calorie-free beverage, such as water, unsweetened iced tea, or black, unsweetened coffee. Or use a nonnutritive sweetener.

If you have a combination food with starch and protein, such as a casserole or spaghetti with meat sauce, fill half your plate with the combination food. Fill the rest with nonstarchy vegetables.

With a slight variation, use the plate approach for breakfast, too. For a breakfast plate or bowl, fill half with starchy food, one-quarter with fruit, and one-quarter with meat or a meat substitute. Keep your portions small. Vegetables are eaten for breakfast in other countries; consider them for your breakfast, too.

2. Follow Your Eating Plan

Whatever plan, tool, or approach you use, know that sticking to it takes know-how, commitment, and consistency:

- Make the most of your carb choices. Remember that whole grains, vegetables, fruits, and low-fat and fat-free dairy foods are nutrient-rich; their carb content needs to be factored in. Just because they're nutritious doesn't mean you can eat as much of them as you want. *See "Carbohydrates in Foods and Drinks" in chapter 11, page 358.*
- Know how to fit sweetened foods, perhaps chocolate and sweet desserts, into your plan. You don't need to give them up, but instead eat a smaller portion; share with a friend; or save them for special occasions. Learn from your healthcare team how to prepare them differently, perhaps with a low-calorie sweetener.

  Remember that sugary foods are often low in nutrients yet high in calories and fat. Avoid sugar-sweetened drinks; that also helps reduce the risk for weight gain and higher cardiovascular risk.

For Carb Counters: Guesstimating Amounts in Foods

Knowing about how many carbohydrate grams a food has or estimating a carbohydrate serving takes practice and know-how—especially for mixed foods.

Use the Nutrition Facts on food labels: servings per package, serving size, and calories and nutrients per label serving. *See "Nutrition: Fact Check!" in chapter 6, page 148, to learn how to read Nutrition Facts labels.* Mobile apps, free online nutrient databases, and reference guides are other sources:

- Look at the grams of total carbohydrates per label serving. Divide the total grams of carbohydrate by 15 to determine the number of carbohydrate servings in one label serving. (One carbohydrate serving is the amount of food with 15 grams of carbohydrate.) Sugar isn't counted separately; it's part of total carbohydrates. Use food lists that can translate foods with 15 grams of carbohydrate into choices for your food plan. *See "Food Portions: How Many Carbs?" in this chapter, page 706.*
- If the food has significant fiber and sugar alcohols (which have less-digestible carbohydrates), you may wish to ask your registered dietitian nutritionist or certified diabetes educator to figure the carbohydrate impact.
- Ask about "free" foods and drinks, which have fewer than 20 calories and 5 grams or less of carbohydrates per serving. Some free foods contain sodium (salt); use them less often and in small amounts. Limit yourself to three servings or less of "free" foods and drinks a day, and spread them out. If you eat them all at once, the carbohydrate may raise your blood glucose level like one carbohydrate choice would.
- Use serving sizes on the Nutrition Facts label to help with your choices.
- As an aside, if you see label claims, such as "net carbs," "low carb," or "low-impact carbs," be wary. These claims aren't approved by the FDA. *See "Have you ever wondered . . . what 'net carbs,' 'low carb,' or 'net-impact carbs' mean—and don't mean?" in chapter 11, page 366, for more about carb-related claims.*

Unpackaged or restaurant foods? Find a book, website source, or app with carbohydrate facts to help you. By law, many restaurant chains provide nutrition information on their websites and at the restaurant. *See "Nutrition Labeling on the Menu: Your Right to Know" in chapter 9, page 285.*

Have you ever wondered?

. . . if people with diabetes should make food choices based on a food's glycemic index (GI)? GI as a tool may help "fine tune" blood glucose response when combined with carbohydrate counting for those whose blood glucose levels are already in control. However, it's not the first approach for managing food choices. In fact, research shows that the total amount of carbohydrate in a food predicts blood glucose response better than its GI does.

Whether or not there's a health benefit to selecting foods according to their glycemic index is controversial.

- On one hand, some research suggests that an overall eating plan with a lower glycemic response (glycemic load) may reduce insulin response and so help lower the chances of heart disease, diabetes, and obesity. Switching to lower-GI foods may help reduce after-meal blood glucose spikes.
- On the other hand, GI only has been established for single foods, and not for food combinations in meals and snacks or for meal size. And individual responses may differ.
- Having a low GI doesn't mean a food is high in nutrients. White bread has a higher GI that goes way down when spread with butter, high in saturated fats. Choosing foods based only on GI may keep you from eating some healthy, nutrient-rich foods, such as bananas and whole-wheat bread with other health benefits. Any food must be considered in a broader context of meals and snacks.

To date, there isn't enough evidence yet to show that using GI improves blood glucose levels. For now, stick to well-accepted approaches for diabetes management. If you want to use GI as an additional tool, get guidance from a registered dietitian nutritionist or certified diabetes educator.

In reality, you probably won't stop eating foods with a high GI. Instead, watch portions and count carbs so you know how to fit them in. *See "A Closer Look . . . Glycemic Index" in chapter 11, page 351.*

. . . if eating sugar or a carbohydrate-rich diet causes insulin resistance that results in weight gain? No, it's a common myth. Consuming carbohydrate-rich foods doesn't cause insulin resistance; excessive calories from any foods do. Those who are overweight and sedentary may have symptoms of insulin resistance, which are often diminished with moderate physical activity and weight loss.

. . . if drinking cow's milk during infancy causes type 1 diabetes? There's no scientific evidence that milk protein from cow's milk promotes type 1 diabetes in infants with an inherited tendency for diabetes. Regardless, the American Academy of Pediatrics (AAP) encourages breastfeeding for at least the first year of life for all babies, including those with a strong family history of type 1 diabetes. Some early research suggests that breastfeeding may reduce a mother's later risk for diabetes. For children aged one year or older with diabetes, the AAP recommends no restriction for cow's milk.

. . . if you can stop taking insulin if you take chromium supplements? No. Chromium supplements aren't an alternative to insulin. As a nutrient, chromium helps your body use blood glucose properly and helps break down proteins and fats. However, there isn't enough evidence on its safety or effectiveness to recommend routine chromium supplementation for blood glucose control. Its value for those with diabetes is inconclusive and controversial. Talk to your doctor before taking any supplements. Enjoy foods with chromium—eggs, cheese, meat, whole-grain products—to get what you need. *See "Other Supplements (Selected): Effectiveness, Cautions" in chapter 10, page 329, and "Chromium" in chapter 14, page 436, for more about this nutrient.*

Be aware: Fat-free foods such as cookies and candy may have more carbohydrates than their traditional counterparts.

- As a sweet option, consider foods with sugar alcohols, which have fewer calories or carbohydrate grams. Foods and drinks with low-calorie sweeteners (such as acesulfame potassium, aspartame, saccharin, and sucralose) may let you fit other foods in since they have little or no carbohydrates. Stevia or monk fruit extract may be options, too. *See "Nonnutritive Sweeteners: Flavor without Calories" in chapter 11, page 369, to learn about these sweeteners.*

  Warning: If you have the disorder phenylketonuria (PKU), avoid foods sweetened with aspartame. *See "Aspartame: PKU Warning" in chapter 23, page 679.*

  Reminder: "Sugar-free" doesn't mean "calorie free" or "carb free." *See "Sugar Alternatives" in chapter 11, page 368.* Sugar-free ice cream and candy may have as much carbohydrate as the regular options.

- Eat plenty of fiber-rich foods. Among the many health benefits, fiber helps you feel full after eating—an aid to weight control. How much? Figure about 14 grams of fiber for every 1,000 calories you consume. You may need more to get a metabolic effect; talk to your healthcare team for advice. *See "Fiber and Health" in chapter 11, page 350, for more about its benefits.*
- Choose mostly nutrient-rich lean, low-fat, and fat-free foods when you choose from the protein foods and dairy food groups. Instead

? Have you ever wondered?

. . . if you need to worry about a blood sugar spike after a meal if you have diabetes? A small rise in blood glucose is normal for those with diabetes and for those who don't have it. That said, every *high* blood glucose rise, or spike, has the potential to cause harm.

If you have diabetes, be aware of frequent post-meal blood glucose patterns, day after day, and try to keep your blood glucose level steady. Look for times when your blood glucose level typically runs high and when it's typically low. That indicates whether you need to change your medication, food choices, or physical activity. For women who are or trying to get pregnant, talk to your doctor.

The ADA advises a blood glucose level of less than 180 mg/dL for adults within one to two hours after eating; check with your doctor to find out the best goal for you. Even those who don't have diabetes may have a small rise before insulin arrives to "do its job"; for them, an after-meal blood glucose rise likely goes unnoticed.

. . . if diabetes will go away if you lose enough weight? Weight loss won't cure type 2 diabetes although it may allow you to use fewer medications and delay the progression of the disease. Remember: Other factors can also elevate blood glucose levels.

of foods high in saturated fats, choose those with healthy fats (oils) that are higher in unsaturated fats. They help keep your blood lipid levels within a healthy range.

A Mediterranean-style food pattern, which is high in monounsaturated fats, may improve glucose metabolism and lower cardiovascular disease risk. Also foods with omega-3 fatty acids such as oily fish, nuts, and seeds are advised for heart health. *See "The Mediterranean Route to Healthy Eating" in chapter 2, page 52.*

- Control salt/sodium in your food choices, too. Limit sodium to less than 2,300 milligrams per day, even less if you have high blood pressure. People with diabetes often have high blood pressure and a high risk for heart disease, or they acquire these conditions down the line. *See "Your Healthy Heart" and "Blood Pressure: Under Control?" in this chapter, pages 679 and 693. See chapter 13, page 385, and chapter 14, page 408, for ways to limit fat and sodium, respectively, in your food choices.*
- Be portion savvy. No matter what tool or approach you use—the USDA Food Patterns, food lists, carbohydrate counting, or the plate method—amounts are very important.

  Get out your measuring cups and spoons and the kitchen scale. Measure the volume of your coffee cups, mugs, glasses, bowls, and dishes. Measure out food and drink portions to get familiar with serving sizes that match your food plan and target amounts. For example, ⅓ cup of rice, or one carbohydrate exchange, provides 15 grams of carbohydrate.

  Learn to use your hand for quick estimates. Your fist equals about 1 cup; your palm is about ½ cup (3 to 5 ounces); and your thumb is about 1 tablespoon.
- Stick to your "clock." Keep to a regular meal and snack schedule—about the same amount of food at about the same time daily—to keep your blood glucose level steady. Skipping meals or following an irregular eating pattern may put your blood glucose level out of kilter. To compound the problem, meal skipping may lead to overeating later and to an eating pattern that won't match your plan for managing diabetes.

  Carry an emergency snack in case you must change your regular eating routine. A registered dietitian nutritionist can help you pick the best food choices for snacking.

  If you need insulin or other diabetes medication, take it on schedule, too. And don't stop taking it if your A1C drops to normal; if you do, it may go back up. Medication is meant to protect you for the long run.

3. Limit Alcoholic Drinks

Can you enjoy alcoholic drinks now and then? Discuss that question with your healthcare team before you drink alcoholic beverages. Some people with diabetes are wise not to drink at all.

What are some concerns and risks? The immediate concern is the risk of hypoglycemia soon after drinking and twelve hours or more afterward. The risk for hypoglycemia during sleep makes drinking hazardous for some. Be aware that others may confuse your symptoms of hypoglycemia, such as disorientation and dizziness, with drinking too much. You may not get the right help, which is another reason to wear a necklace or bracelet that identifies you as having diabetes.

Drinking can worsen some diabetes-related health problems such as high blood pressure, nerve damage from diabetes, and high triglyceride levels. Heavy drinking causes liver damage, which makes diabetes control harder. And alcoholic drinks contribute a significant amount of calories when you're trying to keep your weight under control.

You need to be cautious, too, if you take diabetes medications that work to lower blood glucose level. Combining these medications and alcohol may make your blood glucose level dangerously low!

If your blood glucose levels are under control and if your doctor indicates that alcoholic beverages in moderation are okay, a registered dietitian nutritionist or certified diabetes educator can help you work them into your meal plan. Keep these guidelines in mind:

- Check your blood glucose level before you decide if you should have a drink. If your blood glucose level is low or if you haven't eaten for a while, you shouldn't drink. If you do drink, check it again before bedtime; eat something with carbohydrate if your blood glucose level is low. Some people need to set an alarm to check during the night.
- As always, limit alcoholic drinks: no more than one drink a day for women, and two for men—the same limits as for people without

diabetes. A drink is defined as 12 ounces of beer, 5 ounces of wine, or 1½ ounces of 80-proof distilled spirits. Discuss your individual limits with your doctor and registered dietitian nutritionist. *See "Alcoholic Beverages: In Moderation" in chapter 4, page 102, for more about alcoholic drink equivalents.*

- *Always* eat when you have an alcoholic drink. Alcohol can lower blood glucose and cause hypoglycemia. When your liver is detoxifying alcohol, it doesn't produce as much glucose. Blood glucose that drops too low when drinking can be dangerous.
- As an alternative, choose low-alcohol beer, wine, or distilled spirits. They have fewer calories and less alcohol and carbohydrates than regular beer or sweet wine. Ask how they fit into your eating plan. While 5 ounces of red wine has less than 1 gram of carbohydrate, a 12-ounce beer has at least 15 grams of carbohydrate.
- Recognize that some wine coolers and mixed drinks (made with regular soda, juice, and regular mixers) contain sugars. Count them as part of your eating plan (as carbohydrate servings or carbohydrate grams). Mix drinks or spritzers with sugar-free mixers such as club soda, diet soft drinks, diet tonic, seltzer, or water.

See "Drink Responsibly!" in chapter 4, page 105, for more guidelines.

4. Get Moving

In several ways, active living is important for managing diabetes. For one, regular physical activity increases insulin sensitivity, helping glucose move out of blood more effectively. Second, being active can lower blood glucose as muscles use glucose for energy. Third, physical activity burns energy, making weight management easier; your body controls your blood glucose level better at a lower body weight. And fourth, regular physical activity helps reduce your risk for heart disease and high blood pressure, both linked to diabetes.

How much physical activity?

- Adults with diabetes are advised to engage in at least 150 minutes (2½ hours) weekly of moderate-intensity aerobic physical activity, spread over at least 3 days a week and no more than 2 consecutive days without exercise.
- If weight loss is your goal, aim to be physically active for at least 240 to 420 minutes (4 to 7 hours) per week.
- If able, people with type 2 diabetes are also advised to engage in strength training at least 2 days a week.
- Limiting sedentary time is important, too, as is breaking up extended time (90 minutes) sitting.

Be aware that for many with diabetes, intense exercise can actually raise blood glucose levels. The body draws glucose out of storage as part of a survival mechanism in case it's needed. That's another reason to talk with your registered dietitian nutritionist or certified diabetes educator about your physical activity plan.

Physical activity advice for those with diabetes:

- Before you start a physical activity plan, talk with your doctor, along with a registered dietitian nutritionist or certified diabetes educator. Balance exercise with eating to keep your blood glucose level within a target range. If you take insulin, planning for physical activity is trickier.
- Before you start an activity, check your blood glucose level. Depending on the number, you may need to take some action to manage your blood glucose level before you proceed:
    - 70 mg/dL or less: Treat hypoglycemia first, potentially with a snack having about 15 grams of fast-acting carbohydrate right away; wait about 15 minutes, then check again, *as noted in "Treating Low Blood Glucose" in this chapter, page 705*. The snack may depend on the duration and intensity of the activity and what you plan to eat at your next meal.
    - 70 to 100 mg/dL: For this blood glucose level, have a plan in place ahead of time with your healthcare team about your medication and overall glucose control to determine the best course of action for you and your sport.
    - 100 to 150 mg/dL: It's okay to start, but eat a light snack if you plan to be active for 30 minutes or more.
    - 240 mg/dL or more: Again, have a plan in place ahead of time with your healthcare team. It may be okay to engage in physical activity. Or you may be advised to wait, and get your blood glucose level down first. This advice is important if you're on glucose-lowering medication. (If your diabetes is managed by lifestyle changes, you don't have these same risks for hypoglycemia, or low blood glucose.)
- Take a carbohydrate-rich snack along when you're physically active—just in case you start feeling light-headed. If that happens, stop moving and eat it. Too much exercise and not enough food can lead to hypoglycemia.
- Get a buddy. Besides being more fun, it's safer. Let your partner know about your diabetes and what to do if you need help.
- Wear a tag, necklace, or bracelet with diabetes identification. And wear proper footwear to help ensure better circulation.
- Keep well hydrated. Water is a fine choice. Check with your doctor or a registered dietitian nutritionist about beverage choices if you need a fast-acting carbohydrate source; fruit juice, regular soda, or a sports drink may be advised then.

5. Control Your Weight

Whether you're overweight or not, manage your body weight as part of diabetes management. If you're overweight, losing 5 to 7 percent of your body weight may make blood glucose easier to control if you have type 2 diabetes. Why? A lower weight helps lower insulin resistance so that you may no longer need as much diabetes medication.

Children, Teens, and Diabetes

Type 1 diabetes is the most common form of diabetes among youth. With the rise in childhood overweight, more and more young people also are at risk for or diagnosed with type 2 diabetes, too. Dealing with diabetes during childhood and the teenage years adds to the challenges of growing up. Most kids don't want to be different.

The first guideline for addressing type 2 diabetes in youth is to try to prevent it. Before prediabetes or type 2 diabetes develops, help your child or teen maintain or grow into a healthy weight to reduce the chance. If he or she is overweight, ask your doctor about testing for diabetes at about age ten or at puberty if he or she has other risk factors for diabetes. *See "Growth and Weight" in chapter 17, page 501.*

If your child or teen is diagnosed with either type 1 or type 2 diabetes, accept and manage it together in a calm, careful, and positive way.

- Work closely with your child's or teen's healthcare team to manage diabetes and help him or her grow normally—physically, mentally, and emotionally.
- Gradually involve your child or teen in managing and taking responsibility for his or her diabetes. Encourage rather than nag, even when things aren't perfect. Help him or her learn when, how, and where to get help. Learning lifelong skills for diabetes management—and making them a habit—is part of growing up. Diabetes won't go away.
- Get advice from your healthcare team about special eating events such as birthday parties, sleepovers, field trips, and active play or sports.
- Be matter-of-fact, sensitive, and supportive as you help your child or teen learn about diabetes. A support group or diabetes camp for kids can help. Find a reliable website for kids about diabetes, or join a diabetes social media community with families and youth for support.
- Help teachers, babysitters, coaches, school food-service staff, the school nurse, and others who supervise your child or teen understand his or her diabetes and how they can support the diabetes healthcare plan. Meet with them and provide them with the instructions:
  - How to do blood glucose checks and give diabetes medication if needed
  - How to spot the symptoms of hypoglycemia and hyperglycemia and what to do if your child or teen has a reaction
  - Whether your child or teen has the ability and willingness to self-monitor and take medication
  - What the plans are for meals and appropriate snacking
  - Physical activity requirements
  - Phone numbers for you, your doctor, and other responsible adults
- Ensure that your child or teen has the time and privacy for diabetes care at school, in child care, and during after-school programs without discrimination.
- Help your child or teen feel comfortable about asking to leave class, recess or play, or school or community activities to monitor his or her blood glucose level and perhaps take insulin.
- Help your child or teen learn how to help others understand diabetes—and that it isn't contagious.
- Make diabetes management part of your parenting responsibility, but not the sole focus. Celebrate the joys of growing up and a healthy family life.

Be aware: The medical needs and fair treatment of children in all public and most private schools and day care centers are protected by law.

For more parenting tips, see chapter 17, page 489.

Other potential benefits of weight loss: lower blood lipid levels and lower blood pressure. Remember, with diabetes your risks for heart disease are higher.

Check with your healthcare team to see if weight loss is right for you. If so, consult a registered dietitian nutritionist about how much you need to lose, over what time frame, and how to eat for weight loss and diabetes management. Aiming for a weight loss of up to 2 pounds weekly is generally advised. *See chapter 22, page 624, for weight loss advice.*

6. Team Up for Health!

Seek advice from your healthcare team, whose specialties help you deal with the complexities of diabetes, such as your doctor, registered dietitian nutritionist, certified diabetes educator, and nurse, as well as an ophthalmologist, a podiatrist, and a pharmacist, among others. Follow through on your care plan.

You're the most important team member! For the team to work well, remember the advice discussed earlier:

- Set your target blood glucose levels with your doctor. Be realistic; you can't avoid some "ups and downs." Numbers that are mostly within a safe range reduce your risks for complications.
- Learn to check your own blood glucose level. Self-monitoring, perhaps several times daily, is wise with diabetes, especially if you're taking diabetes medication, if you're pregnant, or if your blood glucose levels are low or out of control.
- Log results to see how food, physical activity, and stress affect your blood glucose level. Share them with your healthcare team; ask about mobile health technologies for keeping track. *See "How to . . . Use mHealth (Mobile)" and "Digital Tracking: The Benefits" in chapter 26, pages 760 and 761.*

  You may choose to use a blood glucose monitor, which is a small, computerized machine that reads your blood glucose level. It's accurate if used correctly and if properly cleaned and maintained. An invasive blood glucose monitor, with a flexible catheter placed under the skin, provides continuous glucose monitoring. You may use it in conjunction with conventional blood glucose monitoring.
- Learn how to detect and safely treat an insulin reaction (hypoglycemia) and hyperglycemia—before you get into severe danger. "Hypo" means low, or too little, blood glucose; you need glucose. "Hyper" means high, or too much; you need insulin or exercise. Immediate, appropriate treatment, perhaps medical assistance, is essential! Wear a medical alert tag or carry a card to let others know what to do in case you pass out.
- Keep all appointments for checkups, counseling, and laboratory tests. If your blood glucose levels are under control, see your doctor two to four times a year; if not under control, go in more often. Can't make it? Change your appointment—don't skip it!
- Take diabetes medications as directed, even if you're sick. Tell your doctor or pharmacist about all other medicine and supplements (including herbal products) you take, both prescriptions and over-the-counter medications. Also tell your team about any side effects or problems you have with any medicine or supplement. Plan ahead; call for prescription refills well before you run out. If you take insulin, ask about an insulin pump, which gives a constant, small dose, or other newer devices.

  Caution: Diabetes medicines can't substitute for consistent healthy eating and physical activity for managing type 2 diabetes. Even for those with type 1 diabetes who must take insulin, a carefully planned diet and physical activity are important.
- Consult a registered dietitian nutritionist to create a healthy eating plan (perhaps with food lists, plate method, or carbohydrate counting) specific to you, including a plan for physical activity and managing weight. A dietitian also can offer specific advice on food shopping, label reading, eating out, and drinking alcoholic beverages.
- Get help with stress control or depression if needed. Under stress, it's harder to be diligent about diabetes care: staying active, eating smart, checking your blood glucose level, and perhaps controlling alcoholic beverages. Besides that, stress may raise your blood glucose level.
- Know that you don't need to struggle alone with diabetes. If your medications, eating plan, physical activity, or monitoring program cause problems or concerns, make an appointment to explore new strategies with your healthcare team. Managing diabetes can be complex—but your health now and later depends on it!

Cancer Connection

After heart disease, cancer is the second leading cause of illness and death in the United States, currently accounting for nearly one in four deaths. Men have nearly a one in two lifetime risk of developing cancer; for women, the risk is closer to one in three.

Lifestyle changes, along with early detection, can help prevent nearly half of the most common cancers, according to the American Institute for Cancer Research (AICR). Early detection, combined with new cancer treatments, have led to a dramatic improvement in five-year survival rates for all cancers.

Along with the roughly 1.7 million new cancer diagnoses in 2016, impressive improvements in cancer survival have led to an estimated 14.5 million Americans living with a history of cancer. Many of these survivors are considered to be living with cancer as a chronic disease, and at every stage of the disease. That includes before, during, and after treatment; during remission; during recurrence; and during palliative and hospice care. (Palliative means relieving pain or alleviating a problem without dealing with the underlying cause.) Good nutrition is critical for optimal outcomes and well-being.

WHAT IS CANCER?

The hallmark of cancer, which is an assortment of more than 100 diseases, is uncontrolled cellular growth with the ability of the original tumor to spread, or metastasize. That causes damage to other organs and other areas of the body.

Cancers are classified by the body tissues in which they start, such as the colon, breast, or skin. Recent, newer diagnostic tests and molecular methods allow cancers to be classified and treated based upon their genetic makeup, instead of tissue type.

Cancer starts with a single cell that divides abnormally. Because the DNA is damaged and the cell does not function as it should, it multiplies more rapidly than normal cells. The cancer cells use the body's resources, including nutrients, to continue to multiply.

Unlike normal cells that constantly are repaired or replaced, cancer cells grow out of control. With their damaged DNA, they invade other tissues. In the process, they disrupt and eventually destroy the normal function of the tissue or organ where they grow. These cancerous cells can metastasize, or spread through the bloodstream or the lymphatic system to other parts of the body, invading and destroying healthy body tissues and organs far from the original tumor.

There are many potential causes of cancer. For most cases, the exact cause isn't clear. A small number of cancers appear to be caused by inherited genes and to run in families. However, the majority of cancers result from environmental and lifestyle factors. In other words, cell DNA is damaged by the normal "wear and tear" of everyday life. In particular, it is damaged by exposure to cigarette smoke, alcohol intake beyond the recommended maximum of one drink per day for women and two drinks per day for men, excessive sun exposure, and a diet high in red and processed meats. Things that promote cancer, called carcinogens, also include viruses and chemicals.

Overweight and obesity are linked to cancers of the uterus and breast (among postmenopausal women), esophagus, kidney, colon, and other sites. It is not known exactly how obesity and excess body fat increase cancer risk. Body fat cells appear to produce hormones, such as insulin and estrogen, and other chemical messengers that may promote abnormal cell growth. Excess body fat appears to promote inflammation, which can cause cell damage.

REDUCE YOUR CANCER RISK

Since many cancer risk factors are out of your control, the best cancer prevention is to prevent the disease from developing in the first place. Based on the best scientific evidence, the ACS estimates that at least one-third of cancer deaths are due to overweight or obesity, physical inactivity, and poor nutrition—and could be prevented.

By focusing on the risk factors that are within your control, you can take a few small steps and potentially reduce your cancer risk significantly. If you smoke, stop. Limit your skin's exposure to sunlight. Stay physically active.

Eat for good health. Maintain your healthy weight and reduce your exposure to carcinogens, or cancer-causing agents. Even those people with an increased genetic risk for cancer may delay, or perhaps even prevent, its development with these strategies.

See "American Cancer Society's Guidelines on Nutrition and Physical Activity for Cancer Prevention" in this chapter, page 715; "Breast Cancer: Reducing the Risk" in chapter 18, page 561; and "Prostate Health: Reducing Cancer Risk" in chapter 19, page 575.

Eat Smart to Lower Cancer Risk

Nutrition guidelines for cancer prevention are similar to those for preventing other health problems, including heart disease, diabetes, and high blood pressure. Throughout this book, you'll find practical tips for healthy eating that also help to prevent cancer. Keep in mind that no single food or nutrient causes or prevents cancer.

- Maintain a healthy weight throughout your life. Balance your calorie intake by eating the right amounts of nutrient-rich foods and doing regular physical activity. If you are overweight or obese, aim to reach a healthy weight—and stay there for good. *See "Weight Management: Strategies That Work!" in chapter 22, page 21, for strategies for reaching and maintaining a healthy weight.*
- Focus on vegetables, fruits, beans and peas, and whole grains. These plant-based foods contain a complex mixture of vitamins, minerals, fiber, and phytonutrients, some of which appear to protect against some cancers—from the esophagus through the GI (gastrointestinal) tract to the rectum. These foods also may offer protection from bladder, endometrial (uterine), larynx, lung, and pancreatic cancers. *See chapter 2, page 21, for a healthy eating pattern to fit them in.*

  Many of these foods are high in fiber. That said, the links between fiber and cancer aren't clearly established. Although many high-fiber foods are low in fat, there's not much evidence to indicate that consuming more total fat increases cancer risk.
- Choose colorful vegetables and fruits for their potential antioxidant benefits and cell-protective benefits, which may help lower risks for some types of cancer. Vitamins and minerals (such as vitamins C and E and selenium) may help protect cells from damage caused by free radicals, *as discussed in "Vitamins as Antioxidants" in chapter 14, page 423*. So might their phytonutrients with antioxidant qualities and other health-promoting actions of the body; *see "Phytonutrients: Different from Nutrients" in chapter 15, page 448, for their sources and potential health benefits.*

  What about lycopene, the red-orange pigment in tomatoes, watermelon, and pink grapefruit? It may help reduce risk of some cancers. However, a cancer preventive link with any one specific food component is uncertain.

  Instead of a single phytonutrient, it appears that the combination of colorful phytonutrients in vegetables and fruits, from carotenoids (such as lycopene, lutein, and zeaxanthin) as well as flavonoids, offers the potential benefits. These countless food components work best together when coming from a varied diet with healthy plant-based foods, rather than from supplements.
- Fit in sources of calcium and vitamin D, such as fortified milk and yogurt. Emerging research suggests that higher calcium intake may be linked to lower risk of breast cancer; more vitamin D, to reduced risk of certain cancers; and both, perhaps to some cancers.

  A side note: In cultures where people eat a lot of salt-preserved foods (salt-cured and salt-pickled foods), the risk for stomach, nasopharyngeal, and throat cancers may be higher. No evidence suggests that the amounts of salt used in cooking or in flavoring foods affect cancer risk.
- Go easy on alcoholic beverages, if you drink them. Excessive drinking increases risks for esophagus, larynx, liver, mouth, and throat cancers—even more if you also smoke. As with other health problems, moderation is the key—no more than one drink daily for women, two for men. *See "Your Healthy Eating Check-In: Your Alcohol Calorie Calculator" in chapter 4, page 106, and "Alcoholic*

American Cancer Society's Guidelines on Nutrition and Physical Activity

FOR INDIVIDUAL CHOICES

Achieve and maintain a healthy weight throughout life.

- Be as lean as possible throughout life without being underweight.
- Avoid excess weight gain at all ages. For those who are overweight or obese, losing even a small amount of weight has health benefits and is a good place to start.
- Get regular physical activity and limit intake of high-calorie foods and drinks as keys to helping maintain a healthy weight.

Be physically active.

- *Adults:* Get at least 150 minutes of moderate-intensity or 75 minutes of vigorous-intensity activity each week (or a combination of these), preferably spread throughout the week.
- *Children and adolescents:* Get at least 1 hour of moderate- or vigorous-intensity activity each day with vigorous activity on at least 3 days each week.
- Limit sedentary behavior such as sitting, lying down, watching TV, and other forms of screen-based entertainment.
- Doing some physical activity beyond the usual activities, no matter what one's level of activity, can have many health benefits.

Eat a healthy diet, with an emphasis on plant-based foods.

- Choose foods and drinks in amounts that help you get to and maintain a healthy weight.
- Limit how much processed meat and red meat you eat.
- Eat at least 2½ cups of vegetables and fruits each day.
- Choose whole grains instead of refined-grain products.

If you drink alcohol, limit your intake.

- Drink no more than one drink per day for women or two per day for men.

FOR COMMUNITY ACTION

Public, private, and community organizations should work together at national, state, and local levels to apply policy and environmental changes that:

- Increase access to affordable, healthy foods in communities, places of work, and schools, and decrease access to and marketing of foods and drinks of low nutritional value, particularly to youth.
- Provide safe, enjoyable, and accessible environments for physical activity in schools and workplaces and for transportation and recreation in communities.

The American Institute for Cancer Research (AICR) also provides research-based cancer prevention recommendations related to nutrition, healthy weight, and physical activity. Visit the website www.aicr.org/reduce-your-cancer-risk/recommendations-for-cancer-prevention.

While specifically focused on cancer prevention, the American Cancer Society (ACS) and AICR recommendations parallel advice from the Dietary Guidelines for Americans (*see "Eat SMART: Dietary Guidelines for Americans" in chapter 1, page 8*).

Source: American Cancer Society, www.cancer.org. Accessed November 30, 2016.

Drink-Equivalents of Select Beverages" in the appendix, page 780, for alcoholic drink equivalents.

Some studies suggest that the risk of breast cancer may go up even with moderate drinking. Regular consumption of even a few drinks per week is linked to increased risk of breast cancer in women—especially for those who come up short on folate. Drinking also may increase the risk for colorectal and stomach cancers.

Live Smart to Lower Cancer Risk

- Be physically active. Besides helping you manage your weight, regular physical activity affects hormone levels and keeps your immune system working properly and so aids in protecting against cancer. Regular physical activity is linked to lower risk of breast (post-menopause), colon, endometrial (uterine), and prostate cancer. *See "Move More! Physical Activity Guidelines" in chapter 1, page 15, for more benefits of physical activity.*
- Make your life a "nonsmoking" zone. Smoking, chewing tobacco, and secondhand smoke are linked to more cancer deaths in the United States than any other cause. Although women fear breast cancer, more die annually of lung cancer linked to cigarette smoking. Smoking also lowers blood levels of some protective nutrients. In fact, smoking increases the chances of many other cancers, including bladder, cervical, esophageal, kidney, oral, pancreatic, stomach, and throat cancers, and some types of leukemia. By quitting, the risk gradually declines.

  For those who don't quit smoking, eat more vegetables and fruits. Many studies show that lung cancer risk goes down among

American Cancer Society's Warning Signs and Symptoms

In addition to cancer screening, be alert to these warning signs and symptoms of cancer.

General signs and symptoms

- Unexplained weight loss
- Fever
- Fatigue (doesn't get better with rest)
- Pain
- Skin changes: darker looking skin, yellowish skin, reddened skin, itching, excessive hair growth

Signs and symptoms of certain cancers

- Change in bowel or bladder habits
- Indigestion or trouble swallowing
- White patches inside the mouth or white spots on the tongue
- Nagging cough or hoarseness
- Recent change in a wart or mole, or any new skin change
- Sores that do not heal
- Thickening or lump in breast or elsewhere
- Unusual bleeding or discharge

See your doctor if you observe any of these signs or symptoms. And be aware that these symptoms can indicate other health issues.

Source: American Cancer Society, www.cancer.org. Accessed November 30, 2016.

smokers and nonsmokers when they consumed more vegetables and fruits.

No scientific evidence shows that supplements—beta-carotene, lycopene, vitamin E, for example—reduce cancer risk. In fact, high-dose beta-carotene supplements may increase lung cancer risk for some people (current and former smokers).

- Preventing skin cancer takes more than sunscreen. Limit your exposure to the sun, including especially midday sun. Limit the use of sunlamps and tanning booths to reduce your skin cancer risk. As part of your daily routine, wear protective clothing, UV-absorbing sunglasses (blocking 99 to 100 percent UV rays), wear a hat, and use sunblock to protect your skin.

Click Here! Links to Know . . .

- American Cancer Society, Cancer Screening by Age
  www.cancer.org/healthy/toolsandcalculators/reminders/screening-recommendations-by-age
- Centers for Disease Control and Prevention, Cancer Screening Tests
  www.cdc.gov/cancer/dcpc/prevention/screening.htm

A broad spectrum sunscreen with an SPF (sun protection factor) of at least 30 is advised by the American Academy of Dermatology and others. Many moisturizing creams come with built-in sunscreen. Try to avoid peak sun exposure: 10:00 A.M. to 4:00 P.M. (when your shadow is shorter than you are).

Unprotected skin produces vitamin D when exposed to sunlight of sufficient strength. Even so, many people fall short of getting enough vitamin D. To reduce cancer risks, limit sun exposure as a vitamin D source; it is best to get most of this nutrient from vitamin D–rich foods, such as oily fish and fortified dairy, and if needed, a vitamin D supplement.

TESTING, TESTING: CANCER SCREENING FOR EARLY DETECTION

Cancer develops gradually. The best cure: Stop cancer as soon as possible. That's why early detection is so important! On a monthly basis, perform self-exams: breast, testicular, skin. And make sure your regular physical checkups include routine cancer screening, as advised by your doctor. Cancer screening is done for early detection, to find cancer at an early stage before symptoms appear and when it's easier to treat or cure. For specifics on screening, check the American Cancer Society's website at www.cancer.org, and talk to your doctor.

IF YOU'RE DEALING WITH A CANCER DIAGNOSIS . . .

Food and nutrition advice differs for each type of cancer, its treatment, and your personal food preferences—also recognizing that dealing with cancer may change the way you eat when you don't feel well. Besides helping you feel stronger and better, good nutrition helps you handle the side effects of cancer treatment, reduce your chance of infection, and assist with your recovery from treatment or surgery.

The goals of eating advice? To help you maintain your weight, energy level, and strength. To do that, high-calorie foods and more protein are often advised. *See chapter 2, page 21, for tips on boosting calories with a healthy eating plan*. Some cancer treatments can cause weight gain. In that case, an eating pattern that helps to maintain a healthy weight is advised.

Safe food handling takes on even more importance since your body's immune response may not function as well. With a low white blood cell count (common with chemotherapy and radiation therapy), your body may not be able to fight infection or harmful foodborne bacteria effectively. *See chapter 7, page 191, for guidance on food safety.*

A registered dietitian nutritionist can help you make a plan for managing food choices if you're dealing with cancer. Ask your doctor for a referral.

Before Treatment or Surgery. . .

Prepare. Start with a positive mind-set. Eat for health. Being well nourished helps build your strength and energy reserves before surgery or treatment begins. Plan ahead by stocking your kitchen with foods you can eat while you're dealing with the possible side effects of treatment. Have nutrient-rich snacks on hand since you may not have the energy to prepare food or have an appetite after treatment. Let your support team know so you'll have help with food shopping and preparation, and companionship, if needed. Ask your doctor, nurse, social worker, or other healthcare professional about support groups.

During Chemotherapy or Radiation Therapy. . .

Cancer treatment often requires powerful medication or radiation therapy that not only kills cancer cells but may damage healthy body cells, possibly resulting in uncomfortable side effects. Careful food choices can help control some side effects that result from treatment.

Many side effects, such as lack of appetite and nausea, go away once treatment is over. Other side effects, such as lingering fatigue, may last longer. Changes in taste and smell due to radiation therapy to the head and neck regions also may last longer or, in some cases, may be permanent. Menopausal symptoms in women that are triggered by treatment tend to last beyond treatment as well, although relaxation techniques, such as mindfulness meditation, may help lessen symptom severity.

Working with a registered dietitian nutritionist to ensure you're eating a balanced diet, and getting tips for managing permanent taste and smell changes is very helpful. Acupuncture may help restore some salivary flow for some head and neck cancer survivors. If fatigue is very challenging, work with your doctor to rule out other contributors, such as thyroid dysfunction or other metabolic issues.

To deal with side effects of chemotherapy or radiation therapy that affect your ability to eat, try the strategies *described in "Cancer Treatment: Handling Food-Related Side Effects" in this chapter, page 719*. Frequent mini-meals, for example, might help. If you feel tired, ask your family or a friend for help with food shopping and meal preparation—or arrange for home-delivered meals. For more advice, especially if side effects persist, talk to a registered dietitian nutritionist.

Caution: Before you try them, ask your doctor about alternative or complementary therapies, such as herbal products, antioxidant vitamins, or minerals, that are promoted to relieve symptoms or improve the quality of your life. Although some are safe and harmless, others can interfere with the effects of radiation or chemotherapy or with your recovery from surgery. Some may have harmful side effects.

? Have you ever wondered?

. . . if cooking methods can increase cancer risk? First and foremost, adequate cooking is essential for cooking meat, poultry, and fish to safe temperatures to avoid foodborne illness.

High-heat methods such as charbroiling, grilling, broiling, and frying used to cook meat, poultry, and fish cause heterocyclic amines (HCAs) to form. Inconclusive research suggests that these substances may contribute to increased cancer risk for some people who eat large amounts of these foods; however, the possible risk is in the amount, and other substances in these foods may contribute, too. Braising, steaming, stewing, and microwaving meats produce fewer of these chemicals.

Charring creates other substances which are potential carcinogens. When fat from these foods drip onto fire, smoke and flames leave polycyclic aromatic hydrocarbons (PAHs).

The bottom line: There aren't enough HCAs and PAHs in properly cooked meat to make a difference. Sensible amounts of meat, poultry, and fish cooked with high heat, and occasional darkened or smoked meats are no cause for concern. *See "Grilling Food Safely" in chapter 7, page 215.*

. . . do processed meats increase colon cancer risk? First, a definition: processed meat, poultry, or fish has been cured, fermented, or smoked and has gone through other processes to enhance its color and/or flavor or to prevent bacterial growth.

The advice from the ACS is to limit processed meat, poultry, and fish. The reason is that some evidence has linked eating large amounts of them, perhaps in part due to the use of nitrites, to increased risk of colorectal and stomach cancers. An occasional hot dog, bacon strip, or ham sandwich is okay.

. . . if sugar feeds cancer cells? To refute a misperception, sugar doesn't increase cancer risk directly or speed the growth of cancer cells. Any indirect link to high sugar intake is inconclusive. A food pattern with a lot of sugary foods may, however, be short on the nutrient-rich vegetables, fruits, and whole grains that play unique roles in cancer prevention.

? Have you ever wondered?

. . . how to protect against breast cancer? Although there's no certain way to prevent it, you can reduce your risk and boost your odds of remission if you do get breast cancer.

Change risk factors that are within your control: Engage in regular physical activity, avoid or limit intake of alcoholic beverages, and stay at your healthy weight. The risk for many women from hormone therapy after menopause is small; however, not using hormone therapy may reduce your risk. Follow the ACS's guidelines (www.cancer.org/cancer/breastcancer) for finding breast cancer early.

If you are at higher risk for breast cancer, perhaps for genetic reasons, talk to your doctor. *See "Breast Cancer: Reducing the Risk" in chapter 18, page 561.* Although rare, men can develop breast cancer, too; older age, alcoholism, obesity, chronic liver problems, and a genetic condition linked to high estrogen levels are risk factors.

Chemotherapy. Chemotherapy uses oral or injected medications to stop or slow the progress of cancer cell growth. Among its common side effects are constipation or diarrhea, fatigue, mouth tenderness or sores, nausea and vomiting, and changes in the way food smells and tastes. To help you cope with the unpleasant effects of chemotherapy:

- Eat before your treatment. If it takes several hours, bring a light snack along unless a light snack is offered during your treatment.
- When your appetite is good between treatments, nourish yourself well. For many, breakfast is the best meal.
- Cut yourself some slack. Some people experience changes or loss of smell and taste from chemotherapy. Do your best when it's challenging to eat. Most oral and gastrointestinal (GI) side effects go away once treatment is over and your GI tract tissue has healed.

Radiation therapy. This form of therapy damages cancer cells with a series of daily treatments of radiation. Side effects depend on the area of the body being treated, the dosage, and the frequency of treatment. These can be a loss of appetite and taste, dry mouth, diarrhea, difficulty swallowing, nausea and vomiting, or a sore mouth or throat.

Many side effects contribute to eating problems, yet good nutrition is important during and after what may be several weeks of treatment.

To help you cope with the side effects of radiation:

- Eat before your treatment.
- If it takes time to get to a treatment center, bring along food to eat before and afterward. If you need to stay overnight, make plans ahead for convenient, easy, and nutritious meals and snacks.
- If you are receiving radiation therapy for head or neck cancer, your registered dietitian nutritionist may talk to you about the benefits of a feeding tube. This may sound unappealing and scary, but a feeding tube can be a lifesaver for those who cannot eat or swallow food during treatment.

  A feeding tube can allow the body to obtain the calories and nutrients needed for tolerating treatment, finishing treatment on time, and recovering. Feeding tubes may be recommended during treatment and for a few months after treatment to help you heal. It is then removed as you are able to begin eating more normally again.
- Give your body time to recover from any side effects. Often they don't appear right away but can last two to three weeks after treatments stop.

Other cancer treatment options may be recommended, such as biotherapy and antiangiogenic agents for some patients. They, too, have nutrition implications. Talk to your doctor or a registered dietitian nutritionist experienced with cancer treatment for an eating plan that's right for you.

Cancer Survival: After Treatment Ends. . .

While no special diet after cancer diagnosis and treatment is proven to prevent cancer recurrence, eating a well-balanced diet with plenty of plant-based foods, which also will help you maintain a healthy body weight, will go a long way toward keeping you healthy. This type of dietary pattern is associated with reduced risk of heart disease, diabetes, high blood pressure, stroke, dementia, and other chronic diseases. Everyone, those with and without a history of cancer, can benefit from it.

Cancer survivors are at greater risk for other cancers. And obesity is linked to breast cancer recurrence. However, healthy eating, appropriate weight, and a physically active lifestyle can make a difference for overall health, quality of life, and longevity—and help you gradually rebuild your strength.

Try to follow guidance from the Eating Patterns: 2015–2020 Dietary Guidelines for Americans; *see chapter 2, page 23, to learn more.* Drink alcoholic beverages in moderation, if at all. Prepare and store food safely. Consult with a registered dietitian nutritionist to manage any side effects that persist. *See "Resources You Can Use," page 763, for resources for cancer treatment and cancer survival.*

Cancer Treatment

Handling Food-Related Side Effects

Treatment and cancer itself often result in uncomfortable side effects that affect the desire and the ability to eat. If you experience these problems, first talk to your doctor to identify and address the causes. Follow food safety advice because you are more vulnerable to foodborne illness; *see "Foodborne Illness: More Common Than You Think" in chapter 7, page 218*. Here are some tips that might make eating easier and more appealing. Remember, good nutrition is part of your treatment and your feeling of well-being.

Note: For all of these conditions, ask for a referral to a registered dietitian nutritionist for help in their management.

If you have . . .	You can . . .
Changes in your senses of smell and taste	• Eat cooler foods rather than warm or hot foods. Hot foods may smell and taste stronger. As cold foods get warmer, a sweet taste may get more pronounced, which may or may not be desirable. • Cook foods with marinades and spices to mask strange tastes. • Use plastic utensils if metallic tastes are a problem. Avoid foods from a can or metal container. • Enhance the flavor of food with fat, acid, salt, and sweet. For example, put a pat of butter on hot cereal, add a few drops of lemon or lime juice to a smoothie, sprinkle sea salt on fresh melon cubes, or drizzle maple syrup on steamed carrots. • Maintain good oral hygiene by rinsing your mouth frequently with a bland rinse.* The National Cancer Institute advises rinsing the mouth three to four times daily, or as directed by a physician. • Place liquids with strong odors in a cup with a lid. Drink them through a straw. • Avoid mouthwashes or mouth rinses containing alcohol. • Talk to your doctor about taking a zinc supplement (50 milligrams) daily to improve your sense of taste. Limit its use to sixty days. • Talk to a registered dietitian nutritionist about ways to make food more appealing.
A poor appetite	• Eat small, more frequent meals and snacks. • Eat meals and snacks in a pleasant atmosphere. • Increase your intake of nutrient-rich foods. Eat high-calorie, high-protein foods. • Drink store-bought liquid food supplements or homemade drinks and smoothies. • Take advantage of times when you feel good, and eat then. • Try to be as physically active as you're able to stimulate your appetite. • Enlist help from others to help you buy and prepare food. • Talk to your doctor about an appetite stimulant.
Constipation	• Try to eat meals and snacks at the same times each day. • Increase your intake of high-fiber foods, such as whole-grain products; fresh or cooked vegetables and fruits, especially those with skins and seeds; dried fruits; beans and peas; and nuts. • Drink hot liquids to promote bowel movements. • Avoid gas-producing foods such as beans, broccoli, cabbage, and carbonated drinks. • Try to increase physical activity. • Eat probiotic-containing foods such as acidophilus milk, kefir, or pasteurized yogurt. • Talk to your doctor about the use of bulking agents, stool softeners, laxatives, or probiotic supplements.
Diarrhea	• Sip clear liquids (water, broth or bouillon, clear juices, gelatin, sports drinks, weak and tepid teas) throughout the day. • Eat small amounts of soft, bland foods. • Choose easy-to-digest protein foods such as chicken, turkey, fish, and eggs.

(continued)

Cancer Treatment *(continued)*

If you have . . .	**You can . . .**
Diarrhea	• Decrease intake of high-fiber foods such as whole-grain breads and cereals, raw vegetables and fruits, and nuts. • Avoid gas-causing foods that contain sugar alcohols (such as sorbitol, xylitol, mannitol) found in sugar-free candies, drinks, gums, and others. • Eat foods high in soluble fiber, such as applesauce, bananas, canned peaches, pasta, and white rice, which are easy to digest and can firm up the stool. • Eat foods at room temperature.
Mouth sores	• Maintain good oral hygiene by rinsing your mouth frequently with a bland rinse.* • Drink fluids throughout the day to keep your mouth moist. Use a straw to bypass mouth sores. • Eat foods at room temperature, cooled, or chilled. • Avoid dry, coarse, or rough-textured foods such as crackers, dry toast, granola, and raw vegetables and fruits. • Eat soft, moist foods with extra sauces, dressings, and gravies. • Avoid alcoholic and caffeinated drinks. • Avoid acidic foods such as citrus, pickled foods, tomatoes, and vinegar. • Avoid irritating ingredients such as hot peppers. • Talk to your doctor about medical foods or medications.
Throat irritation	• Eat soft, moist foods with extra sauces, dressings, and gravies. • Avoid dry, coarse, or rough-textured foods such as crackers, dry toast, granola, and raw vegetables and fruits. • Avoid alcoholic and caffeinated drinks. • Avoid acidic foods such as citrus, pickled foods, tomatoes, and vinegar. • Avoid irritating ingredients such as hot peppers. • Experiment with food temperatures (warm, cool, icy) to find the most soothing temperature(s).
Nausea or vomiting	• Eat small, more frequent meals and snacks. • Sip on cool or room-temperature clear liquids in small amounts. • Avoid high-fat, greasy, spicy, or overly sweet foods. • Place liquids with strong odors in a cup with a lid. Drink them through a straw. • Avoid foods with strong odors. • Try bland, easy-to-digest foods for days when you have a scheduled treatment. • Talk to your doctor about antinausea medication.
Thick saliva	• Maintain good oral hygiene by rinsing your mouth frequently with a bland rinse.* • Sip liquids throughout the day to keep your mouth moist. • Moisten room air with a cool-mist humidifier. Keep it clean to avoid the spread of bacteria. • Drink club soda, seltzer water, or papaya nectar. • Talk to your doctor about medication to manage thick secretions.
Dry mouth	• Eat soft, moist foods with extra sauces, dressings, and gravies. • Sip liquids throughout the day to keep your mouth moist. • Try sugar-free candy, gum, lozenges, or mints to stimulate saliva flow. Avoid chewing ice cubes, which can damage your teeth. • Try tart foods to stimulate saliva flow if open sores are not present. • Try mouth moisturizers or saliva substitutes to keep your mouth moist.

Cancer Treatment *(continued)*

If you . . .	You can . . .
Dry mouth	• Maintain good oral hygiene by rinsing your mouth frequently with a bland rinse.* • Talk to your doctor about medication to manage a dry mouth.
Unintended weight loss	• Eat small, more frequent, nutrient-dense meals and snacks; *see "Mini-Meals: Another Mealtime Approach" in chapter 3, page 75.* • Add protein and calories to favorite foods; *see "Breakfast: Six Ways to a Protein Boost" in chapter 3, page 63, and "Protein in Foods and Drinks" in chapter 12, page 378, for ideas.* • Try protein and energy supplements, such as whey or soy powder, in smoothies and other mixed foods. • Keep nutrient-dense foods on hand, and snack frequently. • Talk to your doctor about ways to stimulate your appetite and improve your food and drink intake.

*A solution of 4 cups water, ¾ teaspoon salt, and 1 teaspoon baking soda.

Adapted from: Grant, Barbara L. *Pocket Guide to the Nutrition Care Process and Cancer,* Chicago: Academy of Nutrition and Dietetics, 2015.

25

Manage Other Diet-Related Health Conditions

In this chapter, find out about . . .

Arthritis: relief, but no cure

Gut heath and GI conditions

Eating disorders and getting help

Oral health, cavities, and gum disease

Osteoporosis and bone health

And more!

Lifelong food and lifestyle decisions affect many health conditions—not just cardiovascular disease, cancer, and diabetes. From common concerns such as anemia, oral health, and osteoporosis . . . to health issues such as arthritis, gut health, and immunity that get more attention today . . . to eating disorders, this chapter provides an overview of their prevention, incidence, and management.

This chapter may not apply to your unique health conditions, nor is it meant to diagnose, manage, or treat them or to answer all your questions. For eating advice specific to you or to someone you care for, consult your doctor, a registered dietitian nutritionist, and other members of your personal healthcare team.

Anemia: "Tired Blood"

Have that "run-down" feeling? Perhaps you're overworked and under-rested. More sleep and relaxation may be what you need to get your energy back. Or perhaps fatigue is really a symptom of anemia. Actually, anemia isn't a disease, but instead a symptom of other health problems. And if you have anemia, you may—or may not—feel fatigued.

Hemoglobin, made with iron, is the protein in red blood cells that helps carry oxygen in the bloodstream to cells in organs and tissues throughout your body. It also helps transport carbon dioxide from your organs and tissues back to your lungs.

With anemia, the body either doesn't have enough red blood cells or red blood cells aren't big enough, to transport enough oxygen from the lungs to body cells. In turn, body cells can't produce enough energy since oxygen is in short supply. When that happens, symptoms such as fatigue, headache, an inflamed tongue, irritability, lack of concentration, pale skin, or weakness, may set in.

Often there's a nutrition connection to anemia. To produce enough healthy red blood cells, your body needs enough iron from your food choices, as well as enough folate and vitamin B_{12}.

ANEMIA: AN IRON DEFICIENCY?

Yes, one form of anemia—sometimes called "iron-poor blood"—can result from a food pattern that is too low in iron. In fact, an iron deficiency, with its effect on hemoglobin, is the most common form of anemia. It more likely affects adult women of child-bearing age, infants and children, and teenage girls. Without enough iron, the body can't make enough hemoglobin.

For this type of anemia, iron levels must be consistently low over time, which ultimately results in low levels of hemoglobin in the blood.

Click Here!
Links to Know . . .

- Academy of Nutrition and Dietetics
  www.eatright.org
- Health Check Tools, National Institute of Health
  medlineplus.gov/healthchecktools.html

Who's at Risk?

Infants and children. They need iron for their increasing blood volume and to grow and develop.

In the last trimester before birth, full-term babies have accumulated enough iron stores for the first four to six months of life. Premature and low–birth weight babies (weighing less than five-and-a-half pounds) don't have as much stored iron. Formula-fed infants are at risk if they take formula that's not iron fortified. Infants also are at risk for anemia if their mothers had a low iron status during pregnancy. At about six months of age, an infant's iron needs increase, which is when stored iron is used up. Breast milk and iron-fortified formula can provide iron in addition to that provided by solid foods.

Children are screened for iron deficiency anemia at regular checkups. Enough iron is important to support growth, replace normal iron loss, and produce energy for learning and play. The National Institutes of Health advises that children who have lead in their blood may be at risk for iron-deficiency anemia because lead can interfere with the body's ability to make hemoglobin.

Teens. For teens, restrictive or inconsistent eating, along with rapid growth, may put adolescents at risk. Being underweight increases the risk. The risk is higher, too, for teenage girls who have heavy periods.

Women. Before menopause, women need more iron than men do, so women are at higher risk. Why?

- Younger women need more iron due to monthly blood loss from menstruation. Women with heavy blood loss are at greater risk. Many may be unaware that their menses are unusually heavy.
- During pregnancy, women need 50 percent more iron than before: 27 milligrams a day, compared to 18 milligrams daily prior to pregnancy. The extra is needed for increased blood volume—at least three more pints of blood—which brings oxygen to the baby and for growing reproductive organs. Often a woman's stored iron gets used up to meet the demands of pregnancy.
- Women often don't consume enough iron-rich foods in their everyday food choices, perhaps because they restrict their food intake to control their weight or they may prefer mostly foods that are low in iron, such as many salads.
- Vegetarians, especially women, may be at risk with insufficient heme iron. Nonheme iron from plant sources and from eggs isn't absorbed as well as heme iron from meat, poultry, and fish. Pairing vitamin C–rich foods with foods containing nonheme iron helps absorption, *as discussed in "Iron" in chapter 14, page 438.*

Certain health conditions. Some health conditions such as diarrhea, intestinal disease, and gastric bypass surgery can cause inadequate iron absorption from food. So can some medications, including antacids and tetracycline. Before taking medication, talk with your doctor or pharmacist about interactions.

More nutrition connections. Iron absorption can be inhibited in varying degrees by substances in some foods. Some examples include tannins in tea and coffee (when consumed with a meal) and phytates in unrefined grains and soybeans. Large amounts of fiber may inhibit the absorption of nonheme iron. A food pattern that excludes iron-rich sources of food could be a reason, too.

For healthy children, teens, and adults, an iron-rich eating plan can prevent this most common type of anemia. For some, especially pregnant women, iron supplements might be recommended. Check with your doctor if you suspect anemia.

See "Iron" in chapter 14, page 438, to learn more about this nutrient; see chapters 16, page 408, and 18, page 533, to learn more about iron for infants and women.

? Have you ever wondered?

. . . why fair-skinned people often become pale with anemia? Hemoglobin gives blood its bright-red color. With less hemoglobin in circulation, skin is paler. For people with darker skin, the lining of the eye may become pale with anemia.

ANEMIA: MORE CAUSES

A lack of sufficient dietary iron isn't the only cause of anemia. Deficiencies in vitamin B_{12} or folate are other nutrition-related causes. Anemia is symptomatic of other health issues, too.

Anemia: Linked to Vitamin B_{12}

Anemia from a vitamin B_{12} deficiency doesn't have a single cause. It may result from poor food habits and a low intake of vitamin B_{12}. More often, it's pernicious anemia, caused by poor vitamin B_{12} absorption—perhaps due to a lack of intrinsic factor, or atrophic gastritis, or the surgical removal of part of the stomach or small intestine.

- What's intrinsic factor? It's a body chemical, produced in the stomach, that helps the body absorb vitamin B_{12} in the intestine. If gastric juices lack intrinsic factor, perhaps for genetic reasons,

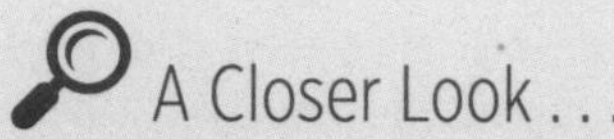

A Closer Look . . .

How to Build Your Immunity

A strong immune system doesn't guarantee that your body can fight off every cold, sniffle, flu bug, or infectious disease. But it is your best defense!

Immunity is the body's ability to use its highly complex, natural defense with highly specialized cells, organs, and a lymphatic system (a circulatory system separate from blood vessels). Even your first line of defense—your skin, hair, mucous membranes, tears, and saliva—helps protect your body from potentially harmful substances. Together they protect, defend, and clear your body from "attacks" by infectious bacteria, viruses, fungi, and parasites. A normal immune response ultimately offers protection from other health problems, too, including abnormal cell development, allergies, arthritis, and some cancers.

The immune response develops gradually from infancy on. Good nutrition, which includes handling food safely to avoid foodborne illness, is essential to keeping your immune system strong. A relatively mild deficiency of even one nutrient can make a difference in your body's ability to fight infection.

Among the nutrients well recognized for their many roles in building immunity and immune response are protein, vitamins A, C, and E, and zinc. Others, including vitamin B_6, folate, copper, iron, and selenium, as well as prebiotics and probiotics, also may influence immune response. Research is underway to investigate other nutrition-related issues that may play a role in immunity, including diabetes, hypoglycemia (low blood glucose), obesity, and overnutrition, and the role of lipids (fats).

To promote your own immunity, follow a healthy eating plan. A varied and balanced way of eating, *discussed in chapter 2,* can supply plenty of immune-boosting nutrients.

More immune-building advice: Get enough sleep. Schedule a flu shot if your doctor recommends it. Find ways to reduce stress. Move more. If you need a "nutrition safety net," take a multivitamin/mineral supplement, but be aware: High doses don't super immunize. Herbs? Use them with caution. Some (including echinacea and panax ginseng) may lower immunity. *See chapter 10, page 315, for more about using dietary supplements wisely.*

or if the secretion of stomach juices is impaired, vitamin B_{12} can't be absorbed properly.

- With age (typically over age sixty), atrophic gastritis, a condition that causes the acid content of stomach secretions decrease, can affect vitamin B_{12} absorption.
- Injury or surgical removal of part of the stomach also affects gastric juices and nutrient absorption.

Your doctor needs to diagnose these problems and offer advice. Because vitamin B_{12} comes only from animal sources of food (meat, poultry, fish, eggs, milk, and milk products), strict vegetarians, or vegans, can be at higher risk. They need a reliable source of vitamin B_{12}, perhaps a fortified breakfast cereal or a supplement, to protect against anemia.

See "Vitamin B_{12} (Cobalamin)" in chapter 14, page 420, for more about this nutrient.

Have you ever wondered?

. . . if you should heed the advice "Starve a cold and feed a fever"? Illness is no time to "starve" your body of nutrients. To fight infection, your body needs a supply of nutrients, from varied and balanced food choices, to build and maintain your natural defenses. Extra rest helps, too. With a fever, drink plenty of fluids: 100 percent juice, milk, soup, or water. If you don't have much appetite, eat bland, simple foods, perhaps more often.

How about vitamin C? It won't cure the common cold. No scientific evidence proves that a large dose, perhaps from a vitamin supplement, boosts immunity. However, more vitamin C may shorten the duration of a cold and decrease the severity of cold symptoms.

Zinc? *As noted in "Have you ever wondered . . . if zinc lozenges can help people with a cool feel better and recover faster?" in chapter 10, page 319,* the benefit from taking zinc supplements to prevent or shorten cold symptoms isn't clear. Research shows mixed results. Some research suggests that taking zinc lozenges or zinc syrup may slightly shorten the duration of a cold, especially if taken within a day of the first symptoms. No advice can be given for an effective dose. The best advice is to talk with your doctor before using a zinc supplement because large amounts can be toxic.

Anemia: Short on Folate

A deficiency of folate, essential for cell growth and development, can lead to anemia, too. Why? Without enough folate, red blood cells become enlarged and don't develop normally, so they can't carry oxygen to body cells as efficiently.

Whether or not you're at risk for anemia caused by folate deficiency, consume enough folate, especially if you're a woman planning to get pregnant—or if you already are pregnant. A folate deficiency may show up later in pregnancy when folate needs are high. Early in pregnancy, a shortage of folate may lead to birth defects of the spinal cord. *See "Folic Acid: Prevent Birth Defects" in chapter 18, page 539, for more about folate and pregnancy.*

Because most enriched-grain products are folic acid–fortified in the United States, most people consume enough to avoid anemia. Folate also comes from many vegetables (especially dark-green leafy vegetables, asparagus, and Brussels sprouts), some fruits (especially avocadoes and oranges), beans and peas, nuts, and peanuts. Some whole-grain foods and some gluten-free grain products are folic acid–fortified.

See "Folate (Folic Acid or Folacin) in chapter 14, page 419, for more about this nutrient.

Other Causes of Anemia

Anemia also may result from a large blood loss: hemorrhaging from an injury; bleeding hemorrhoids; internal bleeding from conditions such as a bleeding ulcer or colon cancer. Some medications, such as aspirin, also can cause internal bleeding. With few exceptions, if iron-deficiency anemia occurs in male adults, it likely results from blood loss.

Hereditary defects in blood cells (sickle-cell anemia), liver disease that affects body processes that use iron, and congestive heart failure are among other causes. Consult your doctor for a diagnosis and treatment. "Sports anemia," *discussed in "Have you ever wondered . . . if heavy training causes 'sports anemia' " in chapter 21, page 610,* isn't really anemia.

TESTING, TESTING: DO YOU HAVE ANEMIA?

Before you self-diagnose your fatigue as anemia and then pop an iron pill, consult your doctor about your symptoms. Ask for a blood test.

A hemoglobin test or a hematocrit test are simple, inexpensive blood tests to screen for the possibility of anemia; however, many conditions can affect the results. A hemoglobin test measures the amount of hemoglobin in your blood. The term "hematocrit" refers to the ratio of the volume of red blood cells to the total volume of blood. A hematocrit test tells if you have too few or too many red blood cells.

If the test results are positive, your doctor may conduct more specific tests, for example:

- For iron-deficiency anemia: serum ferritin or total iron-binding capacity (TIBC)
- For folate deficiency anemia: serum folate
- For vitamin B_{12} deficiency: serum vitamin B_{12} or a Schilling test

Proper diagnosis is essential for getting the right treatment since there are various types of anemia. The wrong treatment may have potentially harmful effects. For example, a folate supplement may "cure" blood-related symptoms of pernicious anemia but mask irreversible, potentially severe damage to the nervous system.

Treatment for sickle cell anemia—a genetic condition that's more common among those of African and Mediterranean descent—differs, too, from treatment for anemia that's diet related. This condition affects a child's growth patterns. Often a nutritionally adequate eating pattern with more protein and calories is prescribed, but both weight and growth for children must be monitored closely.

IF YOU'RE DIAGNOSED WITH ANEMIA . . .

If you or someone you care for is diagnosed with anemia, follow this advice:

- Consult your doctor or a registered dietitian nutritionist about appropriate treatment for the type of anemia you have. Follow prescribed treatment and professional advice, rather than simply take self-prescribed supplements. Keep any supplements and medication in a safe place where children can't reach them.

? Have you ever wondered?

. . . if treatments, such as herbal supplements, are safe and effective for many health conditions? Despite consumer attention to alternative treatments, little research backs up their safety or effectiveness. Although some have been used as traditional medicines for centuries, their success is shared mostly in individual reports, not scientific research. To gather sound research evidence to either support or dissuade their use, the National Center for Complementary and Integrative Health was established within the National Institutes of Health. Some treatments may offer promise in certain circumstances.

Until more is known, alternative approaches to healthcare shouldn't replace treatment that's known to be safe and effective. If you do choose to try alternative or complementary care, talk to your doctor first. Some alternative approaches may interfere with the effectiveness of your doctor's prescribed treatment. *See chapter 10, page 315, to learn the appropriate and safe use of dietary supplements.*

. . . if you can treat chronic fatigue with a special diet? Maybe. Studies are underway to determine the best treatment regimen for most sufferers. Of course, healthy eating, combined with adequate rest, regular physical activity, and stress management, can make a difference. So can better sleep habits and a schedule that times activities for when you have more energy. Skip unproven remedies, including dietary supplements that haven't shown effectiveness or safety. Talk with your doctor about other treatment approaches.

- Enjoy good food sources of all three nutrients: iron, vitamin B_{12}, and folate. Know that the body absorbs two to three times more iron from animal sources of food than from plant-based foods. Eating food with vitamin C, such as oranges, helps your body absorb iron from beans and peas and other plant-based sources.
- Follow up with your doctor, perhaps for appropriate blood tests to monitor your status.

Arthritis: Getting Relief

First be aware that there are different types of arthritis: (1) *rheumatoid arthritis (RA)*, an autoimmune disorder, causing chronic inflammation of joints and organs such as the lungs and eyes; (2) *osteoarthritis*, when cartilage in the joints starts to break down; and (3) *juvenile rheumatoid arthritis (JRA)*, among others.

Rheumatoid arthritis affects the lining of the wrist and small joints of the hands most often, including the knuckles and the middle joints of the fingers. The painful swelling that results can erode bones and deform joints. RA can start at any age, but most often after age forty and more likely among women.

If you suffer from RA, it likely has significant effects on your physical, emotional, and social functioning. Often those with RA are at increased risk for other health conditions, such as cardiovascular disease and osteoporosis.

The risks for osteoarthritis are higher for those who are overweight or obese, and for those who are older adults or who have had a joint injury. Excess body weight places more pressure on both joints and cartilage, and increases the chance for inflammation in the joints.

IF YOU'RE DIAGNOSED WITH ARTHRITIS . . .

To date, the best nutritional advice is: Follow a healthy and balanced eating plan, lower your risk for heart and bone diseases, and maintain a healthy weight, consistent with the Dietary Guidelines for Americans and advice from www.ChooseMyPlate.gov: nutrient dense, low in saturated and *trans* fats, and with a variety of foods, including vegetables and fruits, *as discussed in chapter 2, page 21*. Keeping a healthy weight is important so you don't put too much strain on arthritic joints and connective tissue.

To help protect bones, choose foods high in calcium. Choices include broccoli, dairy foods (such as low-fat or fat-free milk, cottage cheese, or yogurt), cooked greens (such as kale), orange juice with added calcium, soymilk, spinach, or tofu.

- Arthritis Foundation
  www.arthritis.org

? Have you ever wondered?

. . . if glucosamine or turmeric can relieve arthritis pain? Research suggests that, like aspirin and ibuprofen, glucosamine may help dull the pain of stiffening joints. Early findings indicate that it also may help slow the progression of osteoarthritis. However, not enough is known to confirm its safety or effectiveness. Research doesn't show that taking chondroitin sulfate and glucosamine—alone or in combination—reduces pain effectively for most people with osteoarthritis. If you have moderate to severe joint pain, talk to your doctor. Neither supplement is recommended by the Arthritis Foundation for treating arthritis. People with diabetes, shellfish allergies, and those taking blood-thinning medication or daily aspirin need to be especially cautious about taking glucosamine. Talk to your physician first before trying it.

Claims are made that turmeric, which contains curcumin, helps reduce inflammation and may help to control some pain from osteoarthritis, however, these claims aren't supported by strong research. Curcumin is being studied for this and other health issues; say tuned. Be aware that high doses or long-term use of turmeric may cause GI problems.

Be wary of lures for products, including vitamin supplements, copper bracelets, and magnets, that claim to help, or of taking too many aspirins to relieve pain. Over time, aspirin can irritate your stomach, causing bleeding that can lead to an iron deficiency. Talk to your doctor about a safe dosage.

. . . if lecithin can keep you healthy? Lecithin is a phospholipid, or a type of fat. Promoters make many claims for lecithin; for example, as a cure for or prevention of arthritis, gallstones, memory problems, nervous disorders, and skin problems, as well as for improved endurance. Others claim it dissolves cholesterol that's deposited in arteries. Because your body makes lecithin, taking it as a supplement doesn't appear to offer added benefits. Synthetic lecithin isn't well absorbed.

. . . if antioxidants can help protect your eyes from cataracts or macular degeneration? Maybe. Early research suggests that vitamins A and E, zinc, as well as lutein, zeaxanthin, and some fats may help prevent or slow (not restore) some eye changes that come with aging. Vitamin C may offer protection from cataracts. *See "Functional Nutrition: A Quick Look at Key Phytonutrients" in chapter 15, page 449, for lutein and zeaxanthin sources*. Talk to your eye-care professional about whether an antioxidant supplement is right for you.

For rheumatoid arthritis, medically accepted advice also may include moderate physical activity, prescribed medication, protection of joints, a multivitamin/mineral supplement with calcium and vitamin D, and hot and cold applications.

If you have other health conditions, make an eating and lifestyle plan with your doctor or a registered dietitian nutritionist. Managing weight and healthy eating are important to those with other types of arthritis, although they require a different treatment and management plan; talk to your doctor.

No specific nutrition therapy is advised just for people with osteoarthritis. Even small amounts of weight loss, perhaps five percent of body weight, for those with osteoarthritis may reduce joint inflammation and lessen the pain in the hips, knees, and lower back.

No conclusive research shows that any food or nutrient can effectively relieve the pain that comes with arthritis. Some foods and spices with anti-inflammatory effects may help some people and are being studied. *See "A Closer Look . . . Inflammation, Health, and Food" in chapter 24, page 669.*

Digestive Health: GI Upsets and Conditions

Constipation? Diarrhea? Heartburn? Stomachache? It's no surprise that discomfort and diseases of the gastrointestinal (GI) tract are linked to

A Closer Look . . .

How to Keep "Gut Healthy"

Your GI tract—from your stomach on—is amazingly important to your overall health. Somewhere between 500 to 1,000 different bacterial strains reside there—with potential roles that impact immunity, chronic disease risk, proper digestion, and perhaps nearly every disease that exists. Gut bacteria are also linked to brain function and perhaps to the ability to deal with stress.

So far, little is understood about the many roles of "friendly" gut bacteria. What is known, however, is that these gut bacteria help make some essential vitamins, help make body chemicals for brain function, and send signals to the immune system. Also known: short-chain fatty acids (SCFAs) produced in the gut by the action of bacteria and fermentable fiber help the body absorb calcium, iron, and magnesium. SCFAs also may reduce blood cholesterol and triglyceride levels and lower blood glucose response

Your body's unique microbiome* is established from your mother and ultimately is a result of your lifestyle and food choices. It's clear that the mix of gut bacteria of those with certain diseases differs from that of healthy people—and a diverse mix of gut bacteria is healthier.

ADVICE FOR GUT HEATH

Research on gut health is a hot topic these days. Even before research provides potential answers, you can help keep your gut healthy and your microbiome balanced in these ways:

- Consume a balanced diet. Choose a variety of foods from each food group, especially fiber-rich grains, vegetables, and fruits, as well as yogurt and other dairy foods with active cultures and fluids.
- Establish an eating routine. Eat regular meals to help promote consistent bowel movements.
- Eat small, more frequent meals. Aim for four to five small meals per day versus two to three large meals.
- Chew more. Digestion starts in the mouth. Chew thoroughly. Chewing can help with the needed breakdown of some nutrients.
- Remember a mealtime beverage. Fluids help move solids through the digestive system.
- Make half your plate veggies and fruits, and make at least half of your grains whole. Fiber-rich vegetables, fruits, and whole-grain foods can also provide prebiotics that support the growth of "good" bacteria in the digestive tract. Prebiotics are components of indigestible fibers that are food for probiotics.
- Eat yogurt, kefir, or other probiotics daily. Yogurts and kefir with live cultures contain probiotics that can help promote digestion. Probiotics are a group of live, active microorganisms (mostly bacteria, but other microbes such as yeast, too) that can deliver health benefits in the GI tract. Prebiotic and probiotic ingredients have a symbiotic relationship. Pairing them in recipes and meals allows them to work together for gut health. *See "Prebiotics and Probiotics: A Bioactive Duo" in chapter 15, page 453, to learn more.*
- Relax after eating. Give your body time to digest your meal before being active again.
- Avoid overeating. Excessive intake can burden the digestive system.
- Get moving. Focus on fitting physical activity into your day to help promote digestive health. Even slow activities like stretching and walking will promote good digestive health and release stress that may disrupt gut health.

See chapter 11, page 345, to learn about fiber, a gut-friendly component of many foods.

Adapted from International Food Information Council Foundation, 2011.

* The National Genome Research Institute (www.genome.gov) of the National Institutes of Health defines the humane microbiome as the collective genomes of the microbes (composed of bacteria, bacteriophage, fungi, protozoa and viruses) that live inside and on the human body. Humans have about ten times as many microbial cells as human cells.

Have you ever wondered?

. . . if antacids are okay for ongoing indigestion? Even though your body may produce less stomach acid with age, you may suffer from indigestion. Antacids, taken as directed, can help reduce or eliminate discomfort. However, excess amounts of antacids can deplete your body's phosphorus reserves, which may lead to softening of the bones, called osteomalacia. Taking antacids with calcium at mealtime may prevent your body from fully absorbing iron in food. Talk to your doctor about taking antacids. Symptoms that seem like indigestion could be something more serious.

. . . if milk or foods higher in fat can coat the stomach and protect it from stomach pain? No. Stomach secretions are produced even before food enters the stomach to prepare for digestion. Protein, found in milk, actually is one factor that stimulates more gastric (stomach) secretions. High-fat foods don't mix well within the stomach's water-soluble contents, so physically "coating" the stomach with fat isn't possible. High-fat foods do signal some hormones that slow the release of gastric acids and prepare for the intestinal phase of digestion. That doesn't physically protect the stomach.

. . . if any dietary changes can help with bladder control? Every situation and health condition, and every person, is different, but these tips might help. Ease up on caffeinated drinks since they work as diuretics, prompting an urge to urinate. Alcoholic drinks and acidic drinks such as juice can do that, too. Watch the amount of water you drink so you get enough to avoid dehydration, but don't overdo. If you're having problems with bladder control, check with your doctor.

. . . if cutting out certain carbs can ease IBS symptoms? Based on current research, the jury's still out on the effects of a low FODMAP diet, for managing irritable bowel syndrome (IBS). The idea is that the carbohydrates in certain foods aren't properly absorbed in the small intestine for those with IBS, causing their symptoms to get worse. For those who've been unsuccessful with other treatments, this may be an approach to try, supervised by a registered dietitian nutritionist who is experienced with the FODMAP diet, *as discussed in "A Closer Look . . . FODMAPs" in this chapter, page 730.*

nutrition. If you don't feel like eating, or if a health problem interferes with digestion or nutrient absorption, GI problems can affect your nutritional status.

For GI problems—those discussed here and others that aren't addressed in this book—always see a doctor for a diagnosis if problems persist, and seek guidance from your doctor and perhaps a registered dietitian nutritionist for eating advice.

HEARTBURN AND GASTRIC REFLUX DISEASE (GERD)

Heartburn. The discomfort of heartburn, or indigestion, occurs when digestive juices (hydrochloric acid) and food from the stomach back up into the esophagus. Your stomach lining is protected from acids that form during digestion, but your esophageal lining is sensitive to the burning sensation of stomach acids. That's what results in discomfort or pain.

Foods themselves don't cause heartburn, but some may aggravate the condition by stimulating stomach (gastric) acid production in some people. A problem with the esophageal sphincter may be involved, too.

Heartburn isn't dangerous, just uncomfortable. And it can be treated with antacids. If you regularly experience heartburn, consult your doctor about the best type for you; antacids can interfere with other medications. The danger can come if you ignore a heart attack, thinking it's simply heartburn. *See "Warning Signs: Heart Attack, Stroke, and Cardiac Arrest" in chapter 24, page 692.* If the pain continues or if it happens an hour or more after eating, call your doctor immediately!

GERD. Heartburn is a main symptom of gastroesophageal reflux disease (GERD); however, GERD is more serious and affects about 20 percent of Americans. With GERD, contents of the stomach flow backward into the esophagus. There are many physical and lifestyle factors that contribute to the malfunctioning of the ring of muscle that regulates the movement of food from the esophagus into the stomach.

The symptoms? Some people notice abdominal pain, bad breath, coughing, nausea, or vomiting. Besides heartburn and regurgitating stomach acid, symptoms include pain that feels like an ulcer, difficulty swallowing, or tooth erosion after awhile. If you have these ongoing symptoms, check with your doctor.

GERD is associated with several health conditions, such as abdominal pressure from obesity, a hiatal hernia, an increase of certain hormones (for example, gastrin, estrogen, and progesterone), as well as use of some medications and smoking.

An ongoing health problem, GERD needs attention. Inflammation of the esophagus is a risk factor for esophageal cancer and may lead to respiratory problems such as asthma, fluid in the lungs, chest congestion, wheezing, and pneumonia. A GERD diagnosis is based on symptoms, medical history, and testing such as an endoscopy.

If You Have Gastric Reflux Disease . . .

As part of your treatment, your doctor may recommend an eating plan that eliminates or reduces foods that irritate your esophagus or that cause reflux of stomach acids. Among the common foods and drinks to limit or avoid if they cause discomfort: alcoholic drinks, black pepper, caffeinated and decaffeinated coffee or tea, chocolate, mint, and any vegetable or fruit that causes symptoms. High-fat foods and large meals may cause problems, too.

Some people perceive that certain foods, such as spicy, tomato-based, or acidic foods (for example, oranges and other citrus), aggravate symptoms associated with GERD. However, these foods haven't been shown to abnormally increase stomach acid production. Whether to avoid them or not depends on an individual tolerance if you have GERD, try just small amounts, eaten with other foods. Since obesity increases the risk, your doctor may advise weight loss.

A registered dietitian nutritionist can provide guidelines for meals and snack planning. These eating-related tips also may help you manage GERD:

- Eat small, more frequent meals.
- Sit up while you eat, and sit or stand for forty-five to sixty minutes after you eat.
- Eat at least two to three hours before bedtime. Skip late-night meals or bedtime snacks.
- Wear loose-fitting clothes that don't put pressure on your abdomen.
- Start a weight-loss program if you are overweight.
- Sleep with your head slightly propped up.
- Quitting smoking if you smoke.

Your doctor also may suggest changes in your lifestyle and medication, and perhaps surgery.

DIVERTICULAR DISEASE

Diverticular disease is really two conditions. Diverticulosis is a condition in which pouches, called diverticula, develop in the weakened walls of the intestines, most often in the colon. Constipation makes the problem worse. These pouches can become inflamed and infected from bacteria in feces that get trapped there—a painful health problem called diverticulitis. Diverticulitis is generally considered a disease of the elderly, but as many as 20 percent of those who have it are under fifty years of age, and about a third of Americans develop it by age sixty.

The causes of diverticular disease aren't clear. However, it's likely linked to eating a low-fiber diet. Constipation and lack of exercise also may play a role. Inflammation may begin when bacteria or feces are caught in the diverticula.

Symptoms include abdominal pain, bloating, constipation, diarrhea, flatulence, nausea and vomiting, and a change in bowel habits. Getting a medical diagnosis is important.

If You Have Diverticular Disease . . .

- For diverticulosis, eat plenty of high-fiber foods to keep waste moving through the intestines to avoid constipation, and chew them well. A high-fiber diet is likely the only treatment you need. Studies don't support a link between inflammation of the diverticula and eating corn, nuts, popcorn, or seeds, according to the National Digestive Diseases Information Clearinghouse. Nuts and seeds are likely okay to eat.

  Since people with this condition differ in what and how much they can eat, decide what's best for you if you have diverticulosis. Keep a food journal to self-monitor and identify foods that may cause symptoms. *See "Fiber and Health" in chapter 11, page 350, for more about dietary fiber.*
- For diverticulitis, you need to clear up the infection and the inflammation. Treatment often includes antibiotics; perhaps a short-term liquid diet; bed rest; and, if the problem is severe, surgery.

IRRITABLE BOWEL SYNDROME (IBS)

Irritable bowel syndrome (IBS), an intestinal problem and not a disease, doesn't have a clear cause. However, abnormal contractions in the intestines, allergies, a genetic tendency, an infection, lactose intolerance, a low-fiber diet, lifestyle, or stress all may play a role. IBS also is known as colitis and spastic colon.

Studies estimate that 10 to 15 percent of adults have it, affecting twice as many women as men. Symptoms might be abdominal pain or cramps, as well as bloating, constipation, diarrhea, and gassiness, but symptoms aren't the same for everyone. If you have these symptoms, check with your doctor. They may be a sign of other serious diseases or disorders. Several tests are used to rule out other problems: complete blood count, stool examination, and sigmoidoscopy or colonoscopy.

Irritable bowel syndrome is different from inflammatory bowel disease (IBD)—including Crohn's disease and ulcerative colitis—which requires careful medical treatment. With IBD, a registered dietitian nutritionist helps a patient create an individualized approach to eating that not only helps manage GI symptoms, but also helps to prevent malnutrition and helps the GI tract to function normally.

If You Have Irritable Bowel Syndrome . . .

Stress or eating large meals or high-fat foods can trigger IBS. However, different people have different triggers. Food and eating habits are key to IBS management. Medication, probiotics, and stress management

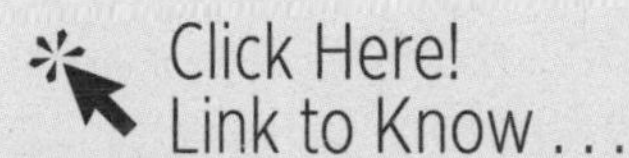

- Digestive Diseases, National Institute of Diabetes and Digestive and Kidney Diseases, US HHS
  www.niddk.nih.gov/health-information/digestive-diseases

may help, too. Many recommendations for managing IBS are good guidance for anyone. In addition to an overall healthful eating plan:

- Eat small, frequent meals. That helps ease the amount of food moving through the intestinal tract. Regular eating times help regulate bowels. Chew food well to aid digestion, and eat slowly to avoid swallowing a lot of air, which may cause gas.
- To prevent constipation, eat fiber-rich foods. Fiber helps move food through the intestines. Increase the amount slowly so your body can adjust, and so avoid feelings of abdominal gas, bloating, and cramping. *See "Fiber and Health" in chapter 11, page 350, for advice about dietary fiber.* Consult with your doctor or a registered dietitian nutritionist about the amount and type of fiber advised, as well as fiber sources that may aggravate IBS symptoms.
- If a food irritates or causes too much gas, keep track and avoid it. Beans and peas, broccoli, Brussels sprouts, cabbage, cucumber, cauliflower, corn, leeks, and onions are some foods that may cause gas.
- Limit any substance or food that makes symptoms worse: perhaps alcoholic drinks; caffeine; fruit canned in heavy syrup; high-fat foods; and sorbitol, a sugar alcohol. Sometimes fructose, the sugar in fruit and fruit drinks, isn't well tolerated. Talk to your doctor before avoiding types of food such as fruit if you suspect a problem. *Avoiding FODMAPs, described in "A Closer Look . . . FODMAPs" below, is sometimes a strategy for managing IBS.*
- Drink enough fluids to help prevent constipation. *See "Water: A Fluid Asset" in chapter 15, page 443, for advice about fluids.*
- Learn to manage stress. Anxiety may affect the speed at which food residues pass through the GI tract.
- If you have a food intolerance, learn to manage it, since IBS symptoms may worsen after drinking milk or eating dairy foods. *See "Lactose Intolerance: A Matter of Degree," in chapter 23, page 666.*
- Talk to your doctor about your medications. Some, such as antacids, may make symptoms worse. And some dietary supplements can have side effects that affect the GI tract—for example, aloe vera, black cohosh, garlic, ginkgo biloba, goldenseal, and saw palmetto, among others. *See "Herbals and Other Botanicals (Selected): Effectiveness, Cautions" in chapter 10, page 324, for more about these supplements.*

PEPTIC ULCERS

"Stress is giving me an ulcer!" In truth, it's not, although your body may secrete more stomach acid if you're under emotional strain.

Most ulcers in the esophagus, stomach, and small intestine are caused by bacteria called *Heliobactor pylori*. In addition, the use of some

FODMAPs

FODMAPs are getting attention these days. But what are they? And why the interest? It's all about "gut reactions."

This acronym—FODMAP—stands for Fermentable Oligosaccharides, Disaccharides, Monosaccharides, and Polyols. These are certain types of carbohydrates that may worsen the symptoms of some digestive disorders, such as irritable bowel syndrome (IBS) and inflammatory bowel disease (IBD). FODMAP carbohydrates may be poorly absorbed in the small intestine and fermented by gut bacteria, causing gas and distention. They are also highly osmotic, meaning that they pull water into the intestinal tract. These combined effects can lead to bloating, cramping, diarrhea, and increased gas—all symptoms of IBS.

Not all carbohydrates are considered FODMAPs. FODMAPs and their common food sources in the diet include:

- *Fructans*: garlic, inulin, onion, wheat, and others
- *Fructose*: fruit, high-fructose corn syrup, honey, and others
- *Galactans*: legumes, such as beans, lentils, and soybeans
- *Lactose*: dairy
- *Polyols*: stone fruits such as apricots, avocadoes, cherries, peaches, and plums; and sugar alcohols such as mannitol, sorbitol, and xylitol

A low-FODMAP diet may ease symptoms for those sensitive to these carbohydrates—but it is not a cure for IBS or IBD. It's a complex diet that is challenging to follow because FODMAP carbohydrates are found in so many different foods and ingredients.

Consult with a registered dietitian nutritionist if you want to try this approach—and when other conditions, such as celiac disease and non-celiac gluten sensitivity (NCGS), are ruled out. If used, health experts advise limiting sources of FODMAPs for six to eight weeks at first to determine whether this diet approach effectively reduces gastrointestinal symptoms. Regular follow-up with a dietitian is important to be sure you're meeting your nutritional needs on this limited diet, and to help you slowly reintroduce foods and determine if certain foods trigger your symptoms.

Many people with these conditions learn that they can tolerate smaller amounts of certain FODMAP-containing foods.

anti-inflammatory medications and having too much stomach acid, resulting from other health problems, are other causes. When the lining of the GI tract is impaired for any number of reasons, the cells underneath can't protect themselves from stomach acids. If the damage goes deep enough, the ulcer may bleed and cause pain. To refute another common myth, eating spicy foods doesn't cause ulcers either. In fact, no food choices cause or cure ulcers.

If You Have a Peptic Ulcer . . .

Antibiotics or antacids usually are prescribed to treat stomach ulcers: antibiotics to destroy the bacteria or antacids to suppress stomach acids. In addition, your doctor may recommend dietary treatment. To heal an ulcer, you don't need to eat bland foods, as once thought. Instead, this advice is generally given:

- Follow an overall, well-balanced eating plan.
- Limit foods and seasonings that stimulate the flow of gastric juices: black pepper, caffeinated drinks, chile powder, chocolate, cloves, and garlic. Decaffeinated coffee or tea may be a problem, too.
- Eat smaller, more frequent meals.
- Skip alcoholic beverages, aspirin, and smoking.
- Identify foods that directly irritate the gastric mucosa or are not individually tolerated. Unless a certain food causes repeated discomfort, enjoy any food you choose—as long as it fits within your healthy approach to eating.
- Avoid eating least two hours before bedtime.

SOME OTHER GI ISSUES

Some other GI issues may be less serious. However, they're still uncomfortable and unpleasant and may be symptoms of other serious health conditions.

Constipation and Hemorrhoids

Plenty of fiber-rich foods, plenty of fluids, and a physically active lifestyle help prevent constipation and hemorrhoids. It's also important to pay attention to your body's signals. Delaying a bowel movement can lead to constipation and hard, dry stools, which are difficult to pass. For travelers, a lack of access to safe water, sweat loss in a hot climate, or a dry airplane cabin may contribute to fluid loss that leads to constipation.

Hemorrhoids, which are swollen, inflamed veins in the anus and lower rectum, can be caused by straining during bowel movements. Pressure during pregnancy is among other causes.

To help prevent and treat constipation, eat a variety of fiber-rich foods, drink plenty of fluids, take regular bathroom breaks, and be physically active every day. Being active helps maintain muscle tone throughout your body, including your GI tract.

Constipation is a symptom of many other health-related conditions, too, including low fiber intake, physical inactivity, IBS, pregnancy, and obesity. It's also a symptom of some diseases including diabetes and thyroid disorders, as well as interactions with some medications and nutrient supplements. If constipation or hemorrhoids are chronic or painful problems, talk to your doctor. They might signal a more serious problem.

See "Digestive Health: Fiber Link" in chapter 11, page 352; "Constipation" (during pregnancy) in chapter 18, page 550; and "Cancer Treatment: Handling Food-Related Side Effects" in chapter 24, page 719.

Diarrhea and Vomiting

Both diarrhea and vomiting are symptoms of other health problems, some more serious than others. In either case, your body loses fluids that need replacing. These conditions can lead to dehydration and electrolyte imbalance. Diarrhea and vomiting can be especially dangerous for infants and older adults. If they persist, call your doctor immediately!

Diarrhea. What causes watery, loose stools, or diarrhea? Perhaps foodborne illness, contaminated water, infection, or medication. With diarrhea, waste passes through the intestines before fluids can be absorbed; body fluids may pass from the cells into the contents of the intestines. Among other possible causes: IBS and IBD.

For mild diarrhea, drink fluids, but avoid beverages with caffeine, added sugars, and sugar alcohols, as well as alcoholic beverages. It's also advisable to rest. Skip high-fiber and gas-producing foods, too, such as beans and peas, broccoli, cabbage, cauliflower, corn, and nuts, until diarrhea subsides. Prebiotic foods such as vegetables, fruits, and whole-grain foods, as well as probiotic foods such as cheese, kefir, and yogurt may help. Smaller, more frequent meals may be better tolerated. *See "Prebiotics and Probiotics: A Bioactive Duo" in chapter 15, page 453, to learn more about these foods.* For more severe or persistent diarrhea, see your doctor.

Vomiting. Vomiting may result from motion imbalance or be a normal reaction to an irritating substance, or it may be symptomatic of many different health problems. When you vomit, the normal rhythmic movements of digestion reverse their direction, expelling contents from your stomach, and perhaps intestines.

Usually the best "medicine" for vomiting is to drink fluids (in small, frequent amounts) and rest. Start with clear liquids, such as apple juice, broth, or gelatin. About eight hours after you stop vomiting, start to eat solid foods, one at a time in very small amounts. Foods that are odorless and low in fat and fiber are best for starters.

For persistent, projectile, or severe vomiting, check with your doctor immediately. You'll need proper rehydration, perhaps with electrolytes, and diagnosis and treatment of the underlying cause. *See "Cancer Treatment: Handling Food-Related Side Effects" in chapter 24, page 719, for more on dealing with diarrhea and vomiting.*

? Have you ever wondered?

. . . if what you eat or drink can lower the chance of urinary incontinence? Unintended loss of urine, a common issue for women after childbirth and perhaps for men with prostate treatment may be hard to avoid.

Keeping a healthy body weight may help, as those with excess body weight often have incontinence, too. It may be that some pelvic muscles are weakened by excess abdominal fat, but that's not yet known. Limiting foods or drinks that may be irritants, such as alcoholic and caffeinated drinks and citrus fruits, may help, but check with your doctor or a registered dietitian nutritionist. Being more physically active also may lower the chance of developing incontinence for middle-aged women, according to the Nurses' Health Study.

Eating Disorders: More Than a Nutrition Issue

At least thirty million Americans suffer from an eating disorder, according to the National Association of Anorexia Nervosa and Associated Disorders (ANAD). And those with eating disorders have the highest death rate of any mental illness. Yet despite the potential health risks, only 10 percent of those with eating disorders get treatment.

Eating disorders—anorexia nervosa, bulimia, and binge eating disorder—are actually distorted eating habits often related to emotional problems. All require qualified medical attention. Eating disorders differ from disordered eating, *discussed in "A Closer Look . . . Disordered Eating" in this chapter, page 734.*

- *Anorexia* typically results in low body weight. It is linked to menstrual irregularity, osteoporosis in women, and greater risk of early death in both women and men.
- *Bulimia* may or may not be linked to low body weight.
- *Binge eating disorder*, probably the most common, typically results in overweight and often in repeated weight gain and loss.

When does an eating disorder start? Generally it begins with an ordinary weight-loss diet, begun just before or after a major life change or trauma. There's no clear understanding of the exact causes, but they appear to be biologically and environmentally influenced. Someone with an eating disorder may look healthy but be quite ill.

Eating disorders are more than food problems. For its victims, their whole life—schoolwork or career, family life, overall health—gets wrapped up in eating issues.

ANOREXIA AND BULIMIA: WHAT ARE THEY?

Anorexia nervosa. It's sometimes called the "starvation sickness." Obsessed with food, thinness, and weight, people suffering from anorexia typically see themselves as overweight, deny their hunger, and refuse to eat—even after extreme weight loss.

Because they consume too few calories for their basic needs, their bodies slowly waste away. They may also lose weight with excessive exercise, self-induced vomiting, or misuse of laxatives, diuretics, or enemas.

By starving themselves, people with anorexia don't get the nutrients they need for normal bodily functions. The physical dangers include abdominal pain, constipation, dry skin, fine body hair, lack of menstrual periods, and low heart rate and blood pressure, as well as anemia, bone loss, changes in brain function, and kidney problems.

Bulimia nervosa. This condition is marked by binge eating and purging (self-induced vomiting). The person gorges, usually on high-calorie foods, and then intentionally vomits or uses laxatives or diuretics.

The consequences are serious: dehydration, internal bleeding from the stress of vomiting, organ damage, vitamin and mineral imbalance, and wearing down of tooth enamel from stomach acids in vomit. It also can result in long-lasting damage to the heart and digestive system. Unlike anorexia, people with bulimia may have a healthy weight for their age and height.

Many people with these eating disorders alternate between anorexia and bulimia. Among those affected: college-age women resort to bingeing, then purging to keep weight off.

Who's at Risk for Anorexia and Bulimia?

People of almost any age and either gender may develop an eating disorder, with incidence increasing among adults and even children as young as eight, nine, and ten years old. Who's at greater risk?

- *Females:* They're clearly more susceptible. About 90 to 95 percent of people with anorexia are women. It's estimated that as many as one in every 100 teenage girls in the United States will develop anorexia, according to ANAD.
- *Adolescents:* Anorexia is the third most common chronic illness among teens.

- National Association of Anorexia Nervosa and Associated Disorders
  www.anad.org

- *Athletes:* Dancers, gymnasts, wrestlers, and jockeys, who must control their weight, are susceptible.
- *Males:* Eating disorders are increasingly identified in males. An estimated 10 to 15 percent of those with anorexia or bulimia are male.

Anorexia and Bulimia: The Warning Signs

Eating disorders produce warning signs. If you or someone you know show any combination of these symptoms, be concerned!

People with anorexia may:

- Eat tiny portions, refuse to eat, deny hunger, diet continuously, and/or use diet pills.
- Be secretive, ritualistic, or preoccupied with food.
- Show abnormal weight loss—15 percent or more of body weight—or a large weight loss in a short time, and refuse to maintain a normal weight.
- Wear baggy clothes to hide their body shape.
- Act hyperactive, depressed, moody, or insecure; have low self-esteem and perhaps a perfectionist personality.
- Have an intense, persistent fear of being fat.
- See themselves as fat, wanting to lose more weight, even when they are very thin.
- Exercise excessively and compulsively.
- For females, have irregular or missing (at least three in a row) menstrual periods.
- Develop fine, downy hair on their arms and face because of inadequate protein intake.
- Experience hair loss, sunken eyes, and sensitivity to cold.
- Have constipation, stomach pain, low blood pressure and heart rate, and trouble sleeping.
- May binge eat, then purge, perhaps by vomiting.
- Abuse laxatives, diuretics, emetics, or diet pills to lose weight. Emetics such as syrup of ipecac induce vomiting.

In addition to the symptoms of anorexia, people with bulimia may:

- Binge eat, mainly in private, then purge or vomit.
- Disappear after eating—often to the bathroom, using running water to hide the sound of vomiting.
- Show great fluctuations in weight, and may be of normal weight or be overweight.
- Feel out of control when eating.
- Eat enormous meals but not gain weight.
- Feel ashamed and depressed after gorging.
- Develop dental problems caused by stomach acids from vomiting. Acids eat away at tooth enamel.
- Have swollen parotid glands. The parotid glands, near the ears, are one type of salivary glands.
- Have blood-shot eyes or bruised or callused knuckles.

BINGE EATING DISORDER (BED): MORE COMMON

First, what it's not: Binge eating disorder (BED) is different from occasionally overindulging or sometimes eating for comfort when feeling sad or upset. BED instead is the uncontrollable eating of large amounts of food in a short time—sometimes without even paying attention to how much.

Unlike bulimia, a person with BED usually doesn't purge, fast, abuse diuretics or laxatives, or overexercise. Both women and men have this disorder—many are obese or overweight. Issues are physical, psychological, and social:

- Foods eaten in large amounts by binge eaters are typically high in fats and added sugars, and may lack sufficient vitamins and minerals.
- Along with the likelihood of becoming overweight or obese from BED comes an increased risk for diabetes, gallbladder disease, heart disease, high blood pressure, and some cancers. The risk for arthritis, bone loss, and kidney disease is also higher.
- Binge eating often results in depression, embarrassment, and social isolation. Those with the disorder are often upset by both the related problems and their inability to control their eating.

Who's at Risk for Binge Eating Disorder?

Although the cause of BED isn't clear, it appears to be linked to depression and other negative emotions—not to being highly focused on food or being an overeater. Those at higher risk include people—more likely teens and young adults—with a family history of eating disorders, with low self esteem, or with a history since childhood of restrictive dieting. Among areas of research: the effect of brain chemicals and metabolism, and whether depression is a cause or result of BED.

Many people with BED are overweight or obese (often severely obese). Even normal-weight people have this disorder. More women than men deal with BED, but it's the most common eating disorder among men.

Binge Eating Disorder: The Warning Signs

Being overstuffed after an exceptional meal isn't necessarily a warning sign. Instead, people with binge eating disorder typically have several characteristics, as well as some noted for anorexia and bulimia:

- Feel out of control when eating.
- Eat unusually large amounts of food.
- Eat very fast.

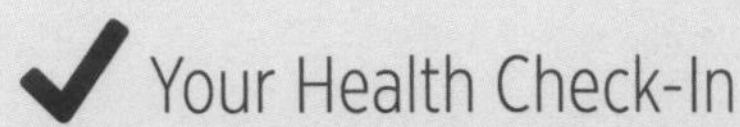

Your Health Check-In

Eating Disorder: Are You at Risk?

Use this interactive tool for a risk assessment:

- Online Eating Disorder Screening, National Eating Disorders Association www.nationaleatingdisorders.org/online-eating-disorder-screening

- Eat until they feel uncomfortable.
- Eat a lot, even when they aren't hungry.
- Feel embarrassed about the amount of food they eat and so eat alone.
- Feel disgusted, depressed, or guilty about overeating.
- Have high blood pressure, high cholesterol levels, or leg and joint pain.
- Have weight gain, diet chronically with or without weight loss.
- Have decreased physical activity.

The American Psychiatric Association identifies binging at least once per week for three months as a criterion.

GETTING HELP FOR EATING DISORDERS

If you suspect a friend or family member has anorexia, bulimia, or binge eating disorder, don't wait until a severe weight problem or a serious medical problem proves you are right. There's plenty you can do before that happens.

Act to get help. Speak to the person about your concern. Enlist assistance from family and friends. Talk to medical professionals, a social worker, or the school nurse or counselor, if the person is a student. Call your local mental health association. A registered dietitian nutritionist also can give an expert perspective on eating disorders. *See "Nutrition Advice to Trust" in chapter 26, page 758, to find a qualified expert in your area.*

A Closer Look . . .

Disordered Eating

Can someone have a problem with disordered eating without having an eating disorder? Yes. Although the terms sound similar, the conditions differ significantly.

Disordered eating describes a range of irregular eating habits that may or may not be diagnosed as a specific eating disorder. For example, compulsive or emotionally driven eating and chronic yo-yo dieting may not be diagnosed as eating disorders. Neither is night eating syndrome (not just eating at night) or orthorexia nervosa, a popular name for unhealthy obsessive, compulsive attitudes and behavior about eating only healthy or "pure" foods. Compulsive exercising is a related concern.

Signs and symptoms of disordered eating may include, but are not limited to:

- Chronic yo-yo dieting
- Frequent weight fluctuations
- Extremely rigid and unhealthy food and exercise regime
- Feelings of guilt and shame when unable to maintain food and exercise habits
- Preoccupation with food, body, and exercise that causes distress and has a negative impact on quality of life
- Compulsive or emotionally driven eating
- Use of compensatory measures, such as exercise, food restriction, fasting, and even purging or laxative use to "make up for" food consumed

Disordered eating can impact physical and mental health, increasing the risk for eating disorders, obesity, and other health conditions including bone loss and gastrointestinal disturbances, as well as significant stress, anxiety, depression, and social isolation. Yet its seriousness is often minimized or overlooked. Addressing it early on is important for long-term health.

Orthorexia is a different kind of issue. It often starts with intent to eat healthier: a good thing. But then when good intent moves on to extremes, entire food groups may get eliminated in a quest for a "perfect and clean" diet. Not only are important nutrients missed, but anxiety around food can result in losing a healthy relationship with food and sharing meals with others. Overcoming misunderstandings about food and nutrition is important, as is getting professional help.

A growing concern: There is the growing trend among some young women with diabetes to manipulate insulin as a way to lose weight.

A registered dietitian nutritionist is vital to the detection and treatment of disordered eating. *See "Nutrition Advice to Trust" in chapter 26, page 758, to find a qualified expert in your area.*

Three Things to Know about Eating Disorders

Experts aren't certain about the exact causes of eating disorders. But they do agree on these key points:

1. Food itself is not the primary problem. Instead, eating patterns are symptoms of serious psychological distress.
2. Early detection is crucial. The sooner the person gets help, the better the chance for permanent recovery.
3. Help is available. Team treatment, including medical and dental care, psychotherapy, nutrition education, and family counseling, provides the best results.

People with eating disorders may encourage these behaviors among others. Today, websites with private chat rooms and other social media spread and encourage these behaviors. If you're a parent, pay attention to whom your kids chat with online!

For people with BED, the condition needs to be treated first before addressing a weight-loss diet. Just losing weight isn't the answer. In fact, losing weight and keeping it off may be harder for those with BED (for physical and emotional reasons) than for people without an eating disorder. Normal-weight people with binge eating disorder shouldn't be on a weight-loss diet. Be aware that dietary supplements are sometimes misused by people with eating disorders to induce vomiting and control their weight.

The best treatment for eating disorders combines medical, nutrition, and psychological counseling. Participation in self-help groups for the patient, as well as group counseling for family members, are important parts of treatment.

Expect resistance. Someone with anorexia usually doesn't believe that he or she needs help or is in any danger. Someone with bulimia or BED may acknowledge the problem but refuse to seek help. The faster he or she gets help, the greater the chance for recovery.

Prepare for long-term treatment. Don't expect a teen to grow out of it. Recovery may take several months to several years. Symptoms and attitudes related to eating disorders rarely disappear quickly. Treatment includes helping people achieve an appropriate weight. Family support groups are particularly effective in helping relatives of those with eating disorders survive the long ordeal.

See "Your Child's Growth and Weight!" and "Pressure to Be Thin" in chapter 17, pages 501 and 531, for more guidance.

Oral Health: Your Healthy Smile

Imagine the wide smile that comes with those popular words from an old TV ad: "Look, Mom, no cavities!" Good oral hygiene and dental care, along with the widespread presence of fluoride toothpaste, fluoride rinses, sealants, and fluoridated water, have made smiles healthier than ever.

What else affects oral health? Heredity and the makeup and flow of saliva are part of it, as are nutritional status, use of medications, general health, and food choices as well as what and how often you eat.

And what makes dental health important for good nutrition and health? Chewing and swallowing are the first steps in digesting the nourishing foods you eat! Beyond that, compelling research evidence links flossing and overall gum health with reduced risk of heart disease. Good dental care is also strongly linked to many health conditions, such as diabetes.

TOOTH DECAY

What causes cavities, and how can you protect your teeth? Sugary foods may come to mind first, but sugars—both naturally occurring and added—aren't the only carbohydrates linked to cavity formation. Starches contribute to cavities (also called caries and dental decay), too.

A Plaque Attack!

Tooth decay starts when bacteria in your mouth mix with and feed off carbohydrates—both sugars and starches—to make acids. Bacteria are found in dental plaque, an invisible film that forms in your mouth and clings to the surfaces of your teeth and along your gum line.

Most bacteria that reside in your mouth don't cause decay. In fact, some are protective to teeth and gums. However, *Streptococcus mutans*, which may be familiar to you, is the main cause of tooth decay in humans.

Acids, produced by oral bacteria in plaque, can eat away tooth enamel, causing tooth decay and gum disease. Every time you eat sugars and starches, acids begin to bathe your teeth. Cavity-producing action continues for twenty minutes or more after you eat something starchy or sugary. You won't get cavities from just a few such occasions. However, over time this action can add up to promote cavity formation.

These two equations offer a quick summary of action that takes place in your mouth when bacteria in plaque mix with carbohydrates in food:

Plaque	+	Carbohydrates	=	Acid
Acid	+	Tooth Enamel	=	Potential Tooth Decay

A Sticky Issue

Hard candy offers no more threat to your teeth than pasta does. Surprised? Any food with carbohydrates—pasta, bread, rice, chips, fruit, even milk, as well as cake, cookies, and candy—can "feed" bacteria in plaque.

Likewise, table sugar, or sucrose, isn't the only sugar that affects oral health. Any sugar—whether it's added or naturally occurring—can promote cavities. Fructose in fruit and lactose in milk also cause bacteria to produce plaque acids. Cookies sweetened with juice have the same cavity-promoting potential as cookies made with table sugar.

Among young children, baby-bottle tooth decay happens when teeth or gums are exposed for extended periods of time to breast milk, formula, milk, fruit juice, or another sweet drink. When babies fall asleep sucking on a bottle or fall asleep frequently while breastfeeding, the chances go up. *See "Caring for Baby Teeth" in chapter 16, page 480, for more on baby-bottle tooth decay.*

Do some foods promote cavities more than others? No definitive list ranks the cavity-forming potential of foods. However, some factors make a difference.

Form of food. Solid or liquid, sticky or slow to dissolve—how long carbohydrate stays on tooth surfaces makes a difference. The faster food dissolves and leaves your mouth, the less chance it has to produce plaque acid.

Because some foods stick to your teeth, plaque acids continue their action long after you stop eating or drinking. The word "sticky" may conjure up thoughts of caramels. Yet caramels dissolve and leave your mouth faster than bread or chips that stick between your teeth or in the pits of your molars. It may take hours for their food particles to finally leave your mouth. Sticky dried fruit, granola bars, and raisins may stay on your teeth longer than a soft drink or hot fudge sundae.

Frequency. The more often sugary or starchy food contacts your teeth, the more chances plaque acid can attack tooth surfaces. For example, sucking hard candy or cough drops, nibbling chips, or slowly sipping a sugar-sweetened drink nourishes bacteria and bathes teeth with plaque acids for at least twenty minutes after each candy, nibble, or sip.

Snacking and a Healthy Smile

For everyone, especially children, smart snacking can lead to good oral health—and a healthy smile.

- Overcome the urge to snack frequently so acids from bacteria in plaque can't bathe your teeth as long.
- Choose snacks wisely for well-balanced eating. Eat raw vegetables, firm and crunchy fresh fruits, milk, plain yogurt, cheese, nuts, and popcorn.
- Even though sugars from hard candy, cough drops, and lollipops may leave your mouth faster than snacks that stick between your teeth, go easy on sugary snacks that dissolve slowly in your mouth. Sucking on foods prolongs the time that sugar bathes your teeth. Slowly sipping a sugar-sweetened beverage or soft drink has the same effect.
- Sip plain water (especially fluoridated water) or unsweetened coffee or tea—not juice, lemonade, soda, or sweetened tea or coffee. If you want a soda, make it the calorie-free type.
- Brush as soon as you can after snacking. This removes plaque and so stops the cavity-producing action of bacteria. Or at least rinse your mouth with water to get rid of food particles.

Will a box of raisins or bunch of grapes be more cavity promoting than a single raisin or single grape? Eaten at one time, portion size makes no difference. Any amount of carbohydrate gets the decay process going. It's the frequency of snacking that seems to have a bigger impact on cavity formation than snack size.

Other factors. The neutralizing effect on acids from other nutrients, *as noted below,* other foods eaten with carbohydrate foods, the order in which various foods are eaten, and acidic foods also can affect oral health.

Brushing after eating and flossing removes the decay duo of plaque and food particles. Swishing water around your mouth after meals and snacks may help rinse away food particles and sugars but won't remove plaque bacteria.

Cavities: Beyond Carbs

Carbohydrates aren't the only nutrition factor linked to dental health. Some medical conditions promote decay, as well.

Nutrients for dental health. For children, overall healthy eating promotes healthy teeth, making them stronger and more resistant to cavities. Several nutrients are especially important, including calcium, phosphorus, and vitamin D. These nutrients also build the jawbone, which helps keep teeth in place. For adults, calcium and vitamin D intake have little effect on keeping teeth healthy. But these same nutrients help keep the jawbone strong.

Fluoridation. Before fluoridation of water was common, tooth decay was much more prevalent. Now, adding fluoride to drinking water, toothpaste, and mouth rinses is one of the most effective ways to prevent cavities. Fluoride makes the structure of teeth stronger by helping to add minerals back to microscopic cavities on the surface of tooth enamel.

Bottled water generally isn't fluoridated. With more fluoride sources today, municipalities may adjust the fluoride level in their water supply to lower the chance of fluorosis, when teeth can become discolored or spotty from too much fluoride. *See "A Closer Look . . . Water: The Fluoride Connection" in chapter 4, page 83.*

Saliva flow. Saliva itself is beneficial. Your body produces up to one quart of saliva a day, especially if you drink enough fluids. That's good news because saliva helps protect your teeth from decay.

By washing away carbohydrates, leftover food particles, and acids from your mouth faster, saliva helps to reduce the time during which plaque acids can form. Minerals in saliva—calcium, fluoride, and phosphorus—may have a protective effect, too.

Food's potential to stimulate saliva flow also affects oral health. The high water content of firm, crunchy vegetables and fruits not only dilutes the effect of sugars, it stimulates saliva flow, neutralizing acid and washing away food particles. Crisp vegetables and fruits also can help clean plaque from teeth.

Some aged cheeses, such as sharp Cheddar, Monterey Jack, and Swiss, also may offer modest cavity protection. By increasing saliva flow, they lower acid levels. Both milk and cheese also contain nutrients, including calcium, phosphorus, and protein, that may help protect tooth enamel.

- American Dental Association/Mouth Healthy
  www.mouthhealthy.org

Medical conditions. Some medical conditions, such as GERD, which brings up stomach acid to the mouth, and eating disorders that cause vomiting, *both discussed earlier in this chapter, pages 728 and 732,* increase the risk of tooth-enamel erosion and cavities. So does dry mouth with less saliva flow.

GUM DISEASE

From an oral health standpoint, a cavity-free mouth doesn't get you home free! Gum, or periodontal, disease, which affects about three-quarters of American adults, is the main cause of tooth loss, which, in turn, can affect food choices and your nutrition status.

Some chronic health conditions have links to periodontal disease, including diabetes, heart disease, immune deficiency, and osteoporosis. Besides poor oral hygiene, tobacco use, hormonal changes for females, some medications, some chronic diseases such as AIDS and cancer, and a genetic tendency are risk factors.

When proper brushing and flossing don't remove plaque, it can harden into tartar, or hard deposits also called calculus. This hardened plaque attaches to tooth enamel and areas below the gum line.

As with tooth decay, bacteria in plaque and tartar are at the root of gum disease. In fact, these bacteria can thrive right along the gum line, causing inflammation and infection. You have inflammation if your gums get red and swollen and bleed when you brush or floss. This inflammation causes gingivitis, a mild type of gum disease. It can be reversed by proper dental hygiene and regular cleaning by a dentist or dental hygienist.

Untreated, gingivitis can progress to periodontitis, whereby gums pull away from teeth, leaving places for infections to thrive below the gum line. Besides inflammation, other symptoms may include bad breath that won't go away, loose or sensitive teeth, painful chewing, and teeth that look longer as gums recede. Constant infection causes the bone structure

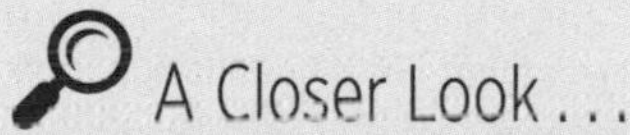

How to Keep Your Teeth and Gums Healthy

- Eat healthy! An adequate supply of nutrient-rich foods from all five food groups promotes healthy teeth and gums. Calcium, phosphorus, and vitamin A are important for tooth enamel, and vitamin C, for healthy gums. Vitamin D also plays a role in the density of the jawbone, where tooth sockets are. Good nutrition affects saliva, making your gums more resistant to infections caused by oral bacteria.
- Go easy on between-meal snacks. When you do snack, try to eat the snack at one time rather than over a longer period.
- Brush twice a day, in the morning and before bed; brush your tongue, too. Be aware that brushing too often may be abrasive to your tooth enamel. An antibacterial mouthwash can also be used to help keep oral bacteria at bay.
- Use a fluoride toothpaste with the American Dental Association (ADA) Seal of Acceptance. The optimal amount of fluoride from toothpaste comes from brushing twice a day, not any more often.
- Teach children over age two years to brush with just a pea-size amount of fluoride toothpaste and to spit out, not swallow, it. This reduces the chances of mottled teeth (dark spots) from too much fluoride. For kids under age two, talk to your doctor about fluoride toothpaste.
- Floss daily to help remove food particles and plaque between teeth where a toothbrush can't reach. Or use an interdental cleaner; ask your dentist if it's right for you. By removing plaque along the gum line, bacteria in plaque are less able to irritate your gums and cause inflammation.
- Use a fluoride mouth rinse with your dentist's advice; don't swallow it. A fluoride rinse for those under age six isn't advised.
- Have regular dental checkups, which include a thorough cleaning—commonly twice yearly. The dentist or dental hygienist will also check for other gum problems and oral cancer.
- Talk to your dentist about sealants, which protect against decay in the pits and fissures of your teeth (they're not just for kids).
- For infants, avoid the urge to pacify your baby with a bottle of juice, formula, or milk. If you choose to use a bottle as a pacifier, fill it with water only.
- For children, talk to your dentist, doctor, or pediatric nurse about what amount of fluoride your child should have. If you live in a community that doesn't have an optimal amount of fluoride in the water, supplements may be recommended.
- Don't smoke.

? Have you ever wondered?

. . . if presweetened cereals are more cavity promoting than unsweetened cereals? There's really no difference. Carbohydrates in both starches and sugars nourish bacteria that promote decay. The cavity factor depends on how long any cereal sticks between teeth or in the crevices in molars. Cavity-causing potential doesn't depend on the amount of starches or sugars. Although not a dental health issue, presweetened cereals are sources of added sugars, which most people need to reduce.

. . . if chewing gum will cause tooth decay? Actually, chewing sugarless gum may help keep your teeth healthy. The reasons: it helps stimulate saliva flow, which neutralizes mouth acids, and it helps dislodge food particles that stick to teeth. Look for sugarless chewing gum with the ADA Seal of Acceptance.

. . . what to do if your teeth feel sensitive when you sip hot coffee or eat ice cream? Check with your dentist. You may have a cavity, gum disease, or another dental health problem that causes the protective covering on tooth enamel to reach the nerves and cells in your tooth. Your doctor can suggest ways to treat sensitive teeth. Proper oral hygiene can prevent sensitive tooth pain.

. . . if you should brush your teeth before or after breakfast? After breakfast is best whenever possible. That reduces how long your teeth are exposed to fermentable carbohydrates. If you can't brush then, try to rinse your mouth out with water or chew sugarless gum.

. . . if switching from regular to diet soda eliminates the chance of cavities? Although there is no sugar in diet soda, it is acidic and may promote tooth erosion. If you cannot cut back, diet soda may be a better choice than regular sugared soda. However, a neutral beverage such as water would be the ideal choice to minimize the risk of caries from beverages.

of the jaw, the gums, and the connective tissue that support teeth to gradually deteriorate. Teeth may loosen and may need to be removed. Tooth loss, common among older adults, may be linked to periodontal disease.

Osteoporosis and Bone Health

Osteoporosis is often described as a disease of youth that manifests itself in the senior years. The signs usually don't show up until age sixty years or older. It's often called a silent disease because you can't feel your bones getting weaker. But you may notice that you're getting shorter or your upper spine is starting to curve forward.

WHAT IS OSTEOPOROSIS? WHAT RISKS?

Osteoporosis is a condition of gradually weakening, brittle bones. As bones lose calcium and other minerals, they become more fragile and porous. They may break under normal use or from just a minor fall, bump, or sudden strain—even a sneeze. Or a spontaneous break may cause a fall.

Because osteoporosis progresses slowly and silently, people often don't realize they have it until they fracture a bone. The spine, hip, and wrist are the most common fracture sites—but other bones can break, too.

Osteoporosis is common, affecting most Americans over age seventy, especially women. Men get it, too. In fact, if you add up all the cases of heart disease, stroke, and diabetes in a year, osteoporosis is more common. About fifty-four million Americans have osteoporosis and low bone mass, according to the National Osteoporosis Foundation; about one in two women and up to one in four men aged fifty and older will break a bone due to osteoporosis. Osteoporosis affects women and men of all races. More people have osteoporosis than report it, and many don't know they have it.

Many fractures, common among older adults, are linked to weakened bones, often overloaded by daily activities. Besides pain that may not go away, fractures cause changes in independence and may lead to isolation. A person may no longer be able to dress alone or walk across a room. Hip fractures also can be fatal. An average of 20 percent of people with hip fractures die from complications within a year after their fracture. Many survivors need long-term care.

Among older adults, a "dowager's hump" is an obvious sign of osteoporosis. Vertebrae in the spine collapse as a result of bone loss. Collapse of several vertebrae leads to a loss of height, back pain, and increasing disability.

Fractures have emotional consequences as well, such as depression. Besides a potential loss of self-esteem and body image, there's the worry of falling or future fractures.

OSTEOPOROSIS: WHO'S AT RISK?

Some risk factors for osteoporosis aren't within your control. Other risk factors can be.

Risk Factors You Can't Control

Gender. If you're female, you're about four times more likely than males to develop osteoporosis.

- On average, most women have thinner, smaller bones to start with than men—and women lose bone faster than men do as they get older.

- National Osteoporosis Foundation
  www.nof.org

How to Keep Your Bones Healthy

Keeping your bones healthy is a lifelong process of healthy eating and lifestyle habits. Ideally, your bone health strategies began during childhood and have continued throughout adulthood. But it's never too late to start.

Your bones are live tissue. Three key components keep them strong and flexible: collagen, a type of protein that gives flexibility; calcium-phosphate complexes that make bones hard and strong; and living bone cells that remove and replace sections of bone that get weak.

The denser your bones are before middle age, the better they can withstand bone loss that naturally happens with aging. Young women and teens have the best opportunity since their bones are still growing!

You can't control all factors that keep your skeleton healthy. But regardless of gender or body build—or your age now—you can slow the natural process of bone loss and so reduce your osteoporosis risk. The strategies: wise eating and lifestyle choices.

CLOSE THE CALCIUM AND VITAMIN D GAP

By now you're well aware of the link among calcium, vitamin D, and bone health. If your food choices come up short, it's time to close the nutrient gaps!

As an adult, you still need calcium; 1,000 milligrams daily is the Recommended Dietary Allowance (RDA) for men aged nineteen through seventy and women aged nineteen through fifty, and it's 1,200 milligrams daily for women aged fifty-one and older and for men aged seventy-one and older. Remember, an eight-ounce serving of milk, 6 ounces of yogurt, or one-and-a-half ounces of Cheddar cheese each supply about 300 milligrams of calcium. Teens need about 1,300 milligrams daily, although during this critical time of bone building, many switch from calcium-rich milk to other beverages and possibly start on a path toward osteoporosis later in life.

Vitamin D promotes calcium absorption. If you drink vitamin D–fortified milk, you may consume enough to protect against bone disease. If not, you need other food sources of vitamin D and perhaps a vitamin D supplement, particularly if you're over age seventy. *See "Vitamin D" and "Calcium" in chapter 14, pages 413 and 425, "Bone Health: Calcium and Vitamin D Needs Go Up" in chapter 18, page 559, (for women); and "Calcium and Vitamin D: As Important as Ever" in chapter 20, page 578.*

Consider other links to calcium. Caffeine can increase urinary loss of calcium, but moderate caffeine intake has little influence on bone health. One cup of regular coffee only prevents the absorption of the calcium found in one tablespoon of milk. If your caffeine intake is high, this effect can add up. To make up the difference, enjoy a latte (coffee with steamed milk) or tea with milk instead. Actually, sodium has a greater effect on calcium absorption than caffeine does; however, neither is significant if calcium intake is adequate.

Alcohol and smoking can block calcium absorption. Smoking can speed bone loss. For women, a lifelong habit of smoking a pack of cigarettes a day may lower bone density by menopause an extra 5 to 10 percent. If you smoke, consider the bone-healthy benefits of quitting. Excessive alcohol intake may inhibit some bone remodeling, increase calcium excretion, and increase the chance of falling. If you drink alcoholic beverages, drink only in moderation—for women, no more than one drink a day, and no more than two drinks daily for men. *See "Alcoholic Beverages: In Moderation" in chapter 4, page 102.*

For many women and men, supplements help ensure an adequate calcium and vitamin D intake and offer protection from osteoporosis. However, the main nourishment for healthy bones should come from food, not pills. If you take calcium and vitamin D pills, use them to supplement, not replace, nourishing foods. *See "Dietary Supplements: More Than Vitamin Pills" in chapter 10, page 316.*

To keep your bones healthy, help them become strong and dense when you're young. After that, help them stay strong by slowing the natural loss that comes with age. *See "A Closer Look . . . Calcium, Vitamin D, and Bone Health" in chapter 14, page 427.*

MOVE THOSE BONES!

Weight-bearing and resistance-training activities—at least three times weekly for adults—helps maintain bone density—if you consume enough calcium and vitamin D. If you're swimming, bicycling, or riding a stationary bike regularly, that's great. But these activities don't promote bone health because they aren't weight-bearing.

Instead, add activities such as these to your "activity repertoire": aerobic dancing, dancing, jogging, tennis, volleyball, walking, or weight lifting—even mowing the grass or shoveling snow. You don't need expensive equipment or a fitness club to lift weights. To build arm and shoulder strength, lift weight with things you have around your house, such as canned goods. *See "Calcium, Vitamin D, and Weight-Bearing Exercise: Bone-Building Trio" in chapter 21, page 610.*

- In young women, the hormone estrogen helps deposit calcium in bones. As estrogen levels drop with menopause, bones have less protection. For the first five to seven years after menopause, usually starting at age fifty, women lose bone faster. Estrogen deficiency from early menopause or from a hysterectomy also increases the risk.
- From the teen years on, women typically eat fewer calcium-rich foods than men do.
- If you're male, low hormone levels can put you at greater risk, too. Testosterone as well as estrogen protect men from bone loss. Drinking too many alcoholic beverages or eating too little can lower men's hormone levels. Check with your doctor.

Low body weight or small body frame. If you're underweight, you likely have less bone mass than someone with a healthy weight. Bone health is another benefit of keeping your weight within a healthy range throughout life.

Women with anorexia or bulimia and those who exercise very strenuously are at higher risk if estrogen levels decrease, causing menstrual periods to become irregular or stop. Women with eating disorders may not consume enough calcium- and vitamin D–rich foods, either. Men also can have eating disorders, which may put them at higher risk for bone loss and osteoporosis. *See "Eating Disorders: More Than a Nutrition Issue" in this chapter, page 732.*

Age. Bone is dynamic with an ongoing process of bone tissue replacement called remodeling. Older bone is replaced with new bone.

Until your early thirties, more bone tissue is remodeled than lost. Call it bones' preventive maintenance program. A few years later, that equation flips. During the first five to seven years after menopause, there is more rapid bone loss: 3 to 5 percent of bone loss per year. For both men and women, with advancing age, more bone is lost than remodeled—about 1 percent per year after age sixty-five. There are individual differences.

Certain racial and ethnic groups. Caucasians and Asians tend to be at higher risk than Latinos and African Americans, whose bones usually are stronger and more dense throughout their lives. Since anyone can develop osteoporosis, those in all race and ethnic groups are advised to consume the same amount of calcium.

That said, African Americans and Asian Americans are more likely to have lactose intolerance, which can make it harder to get enough calcium. In addition, African Americans more likely come up short on vitamin D intake and have a greater chance of getting some diseases that lead to osteoporosis, such as lupus.

Family history of osteoporosis. Osteoporosis runs in families. Not only do people inherit a genetic tendency toward bone fractures and osteoporosis, but families often live similar lifestyles and may follow similar eating patterns that increase risk.

Risk Factors Within Your Control

Lifestyle. Being inactive—perhaps with a desk job, sedentary leisure time, driving for long periods—weakens bones. However, regular weight-bearing activities such as walking, strength training, and dancing trigger

Have you ever wondered?

. . . if you can get kidney stones by drinking milk? That's a common myth. Instead, kidney stones (hard objects) form from substances—such as oxalate, uric acid, and calcium—in urine. When there is more waste than the fluid in urine can dilute, crystals begin to form. Research instead indicates that drinking milk may reduce the risk. A high-calcium diet may decrease the absorption of oxalate, a substance in some plant-based foods that can form calcium oxalate kidney stones. To lower your risk, drink plenty of fluids, eat plenty of vegetables and fruits, and get calcium and potassium from food, not supplements. Limit foods high in oxalates, such as almonds and spinach, if you've experienced a kidney stone already.

. . . if phytoestrogens in soybeans protect your bones? Maybe, since they act much like mild estrogens in the body. After menopause, as natural estrogen declines, phytoestrogens in soy products may help prevent some bone loss.

. . . if estrogen therapy can help prevent bone loss that comes with menopause? It may be advised for some women to control menopausal symptoms. However, for some women, this treatment can increase the risks for breast cancer, stroke, and heart attacks. Discuss this treatment—its risks and benefits for you—with your doctor. *See "Have you ever wondered . . . if hormone therapy may ease menopausal discomforts?" in chapter 20, page 560, for more about hormone therapy.*

. . . how osteoporosis, osteopenia, osteomalacia, and osteoarthritis differ? Because "osteo" refers to bone, their names suggest similarity. But they're different medical conditions. You know that osteoporosis refers to weakened bones; osteopenia is bone density lower than its peak and not yet diagnosed as osteoporosis. Osteomalacia is a softening of bones, often resulting from a vitamin D deficiency and a disorder in the body's bone-building process. Osteoarthritis is a chronic condition of the joints—"wear and tear"—when the cartilage between joints breaks down, causing pain, swelling, and stiffness.

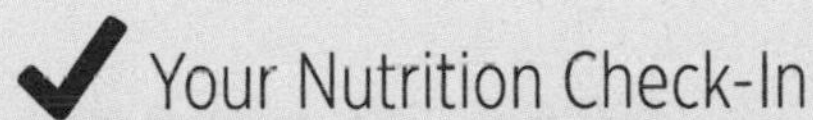

Osteoporosis: Are You at Risk?

While bone loss is a natural part of aging, osteoporosis and fractures don't need to be, according to the National Osteoporosis Foundation. As with any health problem, some women and men are at greater risk than others.

What's your risk? Check all those that apply to you. Then for the risk factors you can control, make a plan to change!

RISK FACTORS YOU *CAN'T* CONTROL. ARE YOU . . .

- Female? ☐
- Small-boned, with a slight body frame? ☐
- Caucasian or Asian? ☐
- Over age fifty-five? ☐
- From a family with a history of osteoporosis or hip fracture? ☐

RISK FACTORS YOU *CAN* CONTROL. ARE YOU . . .

- Physically inactive? ☐
- Consuming an overall eating plan that's low in calcium and vitamin D? ☐
- Maintaining a low body mass index (BMI)? ☐
- Taking high doses of thyroid medication, or high or prolonged doses of cortisone-like medication for arthritis, asthma, or other diseases? ☐
- A current smoker? ☐
- A heavy drinker of alcoholic beverages (three drinks or more per day)? ☐

Source: Adapted from National Osteoporosis Foundation

your body to deposit calcium in your bones, making or keeping them stronger and more dense.

Calcium and vitamin D intake. Throughout life, these nutrients are bone builders. If intake is consistently inadequate before ages thirty to thirty-five, bones may never be as dense as they could be; less bone gets built. After that, adults may lose bone faster if food choices don't supply enough.

Smoking. For men and women, smoking may lower calcium absorption and so promote bone loss. Among women, smoking lowers estrogen levels, which further contributes to bone loss. If you smoke, that's another good reason to quit.

Heavy drinking. Although the reasons aren't clear, heavy drinking is linked to weaker bones. Perhaps heavy drinkers don't consume enough food with calcium and vitamin D, or maybe it's a metabolic link.

Contributing Health Conditions

Some medications and medical problems. Taken in high doses or for a long time, ongoing use of steroids, thyroid medicine, and cortisone-like medications are among medications linked to increased osteoporosis risk. Steroid medications for conditions such as rheumatoid arthritis or asthma are especially risky.

Some health conditions such as chronic kidney, lung, and GI disease, prostate cancer, and some autoimmune disorders such as rheumatoid arthritis can lead to bone loss. Celiac disease and gastric bypass surgery can also contribute to osteoporosis. Talk to your doctor.

TESTING, TESTING: A BONE DENSITY SCAN

Bone density tests are the only way to diagnose osteoporosis before a bone breaks. These tests aren't invasive and take just five to ten minutes, scanning the spine, hip, and perhaps wrist. Exposure to radiation is minimal: less than 10 percent of the amount from flying roundtrip between the east and west coasts of the United States.

Results from a bone density scan are compared to standards of someone age-matched to you and someone younger at peak bone mass. The results may show bone health as normal or as a progression from osteopenia (low bone mass) to osteoporosis. This testing can be used to help determine if you need medication.

The National Osteoporosis Foundation (NOF) advises scans of the hip and spine. Bone density scanning may be covered by Medicare for many people. If you fit within one of the following groups, the NOF advises testing so that osteopenia or osteoporosis can be diagnosed while it can be treated effectively:

- Women and men who have had a fracture after age fifty
- All women aged sixty-five and older, and men aged seventy and older
- Women of menopause age with risk factors for osteoporosis, such as amenorrhea, early menopause, a fracture from a minor strain, low body weight, or a family history of osteoporosis

  Not at risk? Still, a bone density test at menopause offers a baseline for later, especially if you're contemplating estrogen or other drug therapy. Consult your doctor.
- Postmenopausal woman under age sixty-five with risk factors
- Men aged fifty through sixty-nine who have certain risk factors for osteoporosis

Your doctor may advise bone density testing if you have other health conditions or if you take high-risk medication, perhaps for arthritis. Testing isn't recommended for children, teens, healthy young men, or premenopausal women.

IF YOU HAVE OSTEOPOROSIS . . .

Prevent and treat osteoporosis with enough calcium and vitamin D, weight-bearing physical activity, and perhaps medication to help protect your bones from further deterioration. *See "A Closer Look . . . How to Keep Your Bones Healthy" in this chapter, page 739.*

- Protect yourself from slips and falls, which may easily fracture a bone, especially if you're over age sixty. Poor lighting, slippery floors and sidewalks, loose rugs, obstacles in walkways, and no assistive devices in bathrooms increase your risk of falling. Another precaution: check your vision.
- Consult with your doctor about new medications that may help prevent bone loss or treat osteopenia or osteoporosis. Equally important, talk to your doctor about other medications and supplements you take. Thyroid hormones, oral glucocortoids (steroids), and chemotherapy, among others, may promote bone loss.
- Enjoy plenty of calcium- and vitamin D–rich foods to slow or help prevent more bone loss. They provide more nourishment (magnesium, phosphorus, potassium, protein, and vitamin K) for bones—and overall health—than supplements do.
- If food and drinks can't provide enough calcium and vitamin D, you may be advised to take a calcium–vitamin D supplement and perhaps osteoporosis medication. Ask a registered dietitian nutritionist or your doctor about the right dosage and type, and if it should be taken with food to enhance absorption.

  Evidence indicates that taking a calcium–vitamin D supplement is effective for reducing fractures and falls (which can cause fractures) in older adults in institutionalized care. The benefits aren't clear for other adults over age fifty.

Other health conditions and problems are addressed in these chapters:

- Breast cancer: *see chapter 18, page 561*
- Cancer: *see chapters 18, page 561; 19, page 564; and 24, page 713*
- Cardiovascular disease: *see chapters 18, page 562; 19, page 570; and 24, page 680*
- Celiac disease: *see chapter 23, page 670*
- Choking (Heimlich maneuver): *see chapters 7, page 196, and 16, page 486 (infants under one year)*
- Constipation and hemorrhoids: *see chapters 11, page 350; 18, page 548; and 20, page 583*
- Dehydration: *see chapters 15, page 443, and 21, page 600*
- Dental cavities: *see chapter 16, page 469 (infants)*
- Diabetes: *see chapter 24, page 698*
- Eating disorders: *see chapters 17, page 504 (teens), and 19, page 565 (men)*
- Fibrocystic breast disease: *see chapter 18, page 538*
- Fibromyalgia: *see chapter 18, page 565*
- Food allergies: *see chapters 16 (infants) page 479; and 23, page 653*
- Foodborne illness: *see chapters 7, page 191; and 18, page 551*
- High blood pressure (hypertension): *see chapter 24, page 693*
- Lactose intolerance: *see chapter 23, page 666*
- Metabolic syndrome: *see chapter 24, page 686*
- Migraine headaches: *see chapter 23, page 677*
- Non-celiac gluten sensitivity: *see chapter 23, page 670*
- Overweight and obesity: *see chapters 17 (children and teens) page 502, and 22, page 626*
- Polycystic ovary syndrome: *see chapter 18, page 538*
- Prostate cancer: *see chapter 19, page 573*
- Reactive hypoglycemia: *see chapter 11, page 349*
- Sarcopenia: *see chapters 12, page 376, and 20, page 576*
- Vaginal yeast infections: *see chapter 18, page 536*

Doctor Prescribed: Diets and Medications

EATING PLAN TO MANAGE HEALTH ISSUES

Like medication, a doctor-prescribed eating plan—perhaps sodium-modified, high-fiber, gluten-free, or pureed—may be essential to managing a health condition. A special diet may be part of medical nutrition therapy. If your doctor prescribes a special diet:

- Get enough guidance to successfully comply. Ask for a referral to a registered dietitian nutritionist for help with planning and monitoring. The diet should match your physical needs, your food preferences, your lifestyle, and any cultural or religious needs. *Caution:* Let your doctor or registered dietitian nutritionist know about supplements or medications you take.
- Follow the nutrition plan faithfully. Record what you eat, your challenges, and your success with your doctor or a dietitian, especially if this is a long-term change in your eating regimen.
- Use Nutrition Facts and ingredient lists on food labels as information aids. Ask your dietitian for help use label facts effectively—and perhaps direct you to more reliable resources: websites, apps, digital monitoring devices, organizations, or support groups.
- Get family and friend support. Their encouragement and help with food shopping and preparation can make a special diet easier to follow—and may be healthy for others. For example, nearly everyone can benefit by eating more vegetables, fruits, and low-fat dairy foods and by cutting back on sodium on a DASH diet.

See "Thirteen Tips to Make the Most of Nutrition Counseling" in chapter 26, page 760.

FOOD AND MEDICINE: SOME DON'T MIX

Taking medications may not seem like a nutrition issue. Yet, when food and medicines are taken together, they may interact—for the good, or not.

Some medications alter appetite, taste, or smell, and may cause mouth sores or a dry mouth, making swallowing difficult. Others may induce nausea, irritate the GI tract, or make changes in metabolism.

The chemistry of the stomach and the intestines differs before and several hours after eating. Food, as well as substances released in your body during digestion, may either enhance or hinder the absorption, effectiveness, or excretion of some medications.

For the full benefits of both food and medications, even aspirin, take as directed.

- Some medications should be taken with meals. With food, they're less likely to irritate the stomach. Aspirin and ibuprofen are two examples.
- Some medications should be taken on an empty stomach, perhaps an hour before or three hours after eating. Food may slow their absorption and action. That's true of some antibiotics, for example.
- Some medications should be taken with plenty of water. That's true of most cholesterol-lowering medications.
- Some foods and medications shouldn't be consumed within several hours of each other. For example, fruit juice (including grapefruit juice) and other high-acid foods can destroy one type of penicillin. Calcium in dairy foods and in calcium supplements binds with tetracycline, so it passes through the body without being absorbed.
- Many medications shouldn't be taken with alcoholic beverages. Alcohol can block the effects of some medications, and amplify the effects of others to potentially harmful levels. Medication also can intensify the effects of alcohol in your body.

How do you know if you should take medicine with a meal or on an empty stomach? You can't know about the potential interactions between all medicines and food.

- Always read the directions and drug warnings printed on the container or on an accompanying information sheet with directions about when, how much per dose, how long to take the medication—and if it should be taken with food or not. It also may state what to do if you miss a dose. You can ask that directions be printed in large type.
- Ask your doctor, pharmacist, or a registered dietitian nutritionist about which foods or other drugs to avoid while taking the medication. *Note:* With the long-term use of some medications, your doctor also may prescribe a dietary supplement. *See chapter 10, page 315, for more about dietary supplements.*

MEDICATION: FOR SAFETY'S SAKE

If you take over-the-counter or prescription medications, or both, their safe, effective medical use is your responsibility.

- Keep medicines in their original containers with directions intact. Store them out of a child's reach.
- Always take medicine in a well-lighted place. Put on your glasses if you wear them! Otherwise you might take the wrong medication or the wrong amount.
- Only take medicines prescribed for you, even if your symptoms seem similar to someone else's.
- Talk to your doctor or pharmacist about all the medications you take, including over-the-counter medications and dietary supplements, such as herbal products, to avoid harmful interactions.
- Always take the medication as prescribed. If you don't take enough or stop too soon, the medication may not work. Taking too much, too often can be dangerous. Depending on the medication, excessive amounts also may keep your body from absorbing essential nutrients or deplete your supply.
- Talk to your pharmacist or check online for the best way to dispose of unused or expired medicines. Some can safely be flushed, but others should be disposed of differently.
- With each checkup, review your medication plan with your doctor to make sure it's still right for you.

Common Interactions between Food and Some Medications

MEDICINE CABINET **Prescription Drugs and Over-the-Counter Products**	**KITCHEN CABINET** **Common Food and Drug* Interactions** (For specific information about your medications, ask your doctor or pharmacist.)
Pain relievers • Aspirin (e.g., Anacin®, Bayer®) • Ibuprofen (e.g., Advil®, Motrin®, Nuprin®)	Take these with food to avoid irritating your stomach. Also limit other stomach irritants, such as alcohol and caffeine.
Antibiotics • Tetracycline (e.g., Achromycin®, Sumycin®) • Penicillin (e.g., Pen-Vee K®)	The calcium in dairy foods and in calcium and iron supplements can block the absorption of tetracycline-based products. Take these medications one hour or more before or after consuming dairy products or calcium supplements. When taken together, citrus fruits and fruit juices can destroy a type of penicillin.
Blood-thinning medication/ anticoagulants • Warfarin (e.g., Coumadin®, Dicoumerol®)	Eat in moderation a consistent (don't suddenly increase or decrease) amount of foods with vitamin K, such as dark-green leafy greens; kale; spinach; turnip greens; green tea; and some soy burgers. Too much vitamin K can decrease the ability of blood thinners to prevent clotting. Vitamin E supplements can increase the risk of bleeding. A natural ingredient in black licorice, called glycyrrhiza, can breakdown warfarin. This causes an increase in the body's clotting mechanism and can also make blood pressure medications less effective. Artificially flavored black licorice isn't a problem.
Cholesterol-lowering statins (most)	Furanocoumarins in grapefruit juice and perhaps pumelo and Seville oranges alter these medications, increasing their absorption. Grapefruit juice can also affect many other medications, including antihistamines, birth control drugs, blood pressure drugs, the cough suppressant dextromethorphan, stomach acid-blocking drugs, and thyroid replacement drugs. Other citrus juices do not contain furanocoumarins.
Antidepressants • MAO inhibitors (e.g., Marplan®, Parnate®)	When taken with foods high in tyramine (an amino acid found in protein foods), these medications may lead to increased blood pressure, fever, headache, vomiting, and possible death. Ask your doctor or a registered dietitian nutritionist for a list of foods to avoid, such as aged cheese, avocados, chocolate, cured meats, draft beer, fermented soy foods, red wine, sour cream, and yeast products. Drugs used to treat the symptoms of Parkinson's disease also interfere with the breakdown of tyramine.
Antacids containing • Aluminum (e.g., Amphojel®, Maalox®) • Calcium (e.g., Tums®) • Sodium (e.g., Alka-Seltzer®)	Wait two to three hours after taking an aluminum-containing antacid before you drink or eat citrus fruits. Citrus fruits can increase the amount of aluminum your body absorbs. Antacids with aluminum also can cause a loss of bone-building calcium. Some antacids can weaken the absorption of heart-regulating medications such as digoxin (e.g., Lanoxin). Some antacids can weaken the effect of anti-ulcer medication (e.g., Tagamet®) or drugs that treat high blood pressure (such as Inderal). Be sure to read all the alerts on the labels. If you have high blood pressure, read the label of antacids for the amount of sodium present.
Garlic pills	It is important for your blood to clot if you suffer a cut or undergo surgery. Substances in garlic appear to thin the blood. If you are already taking aspirin or other blood-thinning medications, taking garlic supplements may thin the blood too much.
Corticosteroids (Hydrocortisone®, Prednisone®, Solumedrol®)	Because these medications increase sodium and water retention, which may lead to edema, go easy on foods high in sodium, such as cheese, ham and other cured meats, pickled vegetables (pickled beets, olives, pickles, sauerkraut, others), processed foods, salty snacks, and salt added in cooking and at the table.
Medications for cancer treatment (Methotrexate®, Tamoxifen®)	Flavonoids in citrus fruits can help tamoxifen inhibit cancer cell growth. Methotrexate promotes folate deficiency; a folate supplement may be prescribed.

*Many supplements including herbal products may interact with medications, too. *See "Warning: Supplement-Drug Interactions!" in chapter 10, page 335.* The Vitamin and Mineral Fact Sheets from the Office of Dietary Supplements, National Institutes of Health, provide more details about nutrient-medication interactions for each nutrient; visit the website ods.od.nih.gov/factsheets/list-VitaminsMinerals.

Adapted from *To Your Health! Food & Activity Tips for Older Adults* (National Council on Aging, National Institute on Aging, President's Council on Physical Fitness and Sports, and Food Marketing Institute). Used with permission.

PART VI

Resources for Healthy Eating

26

Keep "Well" Informed

In this chapter, find out about . . .

Judging food and nutrition news and studies

Spotting truths and half-truths

Finding qualified nutrition advice and assistance

Do you rely on popular media—TV, magazines, or social and digital media such as blogs, mobile apps, podcasts, and Twitter—for food and nutrition advice and updates? Well-qualified food, nutrition, and health experts share trustworthy information through every kind of popular media, from print to digital—offering profound opportunities to help you make informed decisions that promote your health. Yet, these outlets and more also dispense nutrition hype, misleading headlines, and half-truths.

Can you easily find reliable information when you need it? Do you ever feel confused by conflicting information? For that matter, how do know you're getting the facts and current, sound advice?

The sheer volume of food and healthy-eating information can be overwhelming, often making it difficult to discern accurate, science-based information from misinformation. Today's social media provides new challenges: you're in charge of your own newsfeeds and can engage in them directly. Connecting with credible sources is essential!

Healthy Eating: Ten Reasons for Expert Advice

When do you need expert, science-based eating advice? Nearly every day! Sometimes you need a little more—if you:

1. Need to manage a health condition—perhaps a digestive issue, a food allergy, diabetes, cardiovascular problems, or high blood pressure—and if you're faced with the challenges of getting the right nutrition.
2. Want advice and support to help you lose or gain weight—or maintain a healthy weight for a lifetime—but don't want to give up all your favorite foods.
3. Want to improve your performance in sports—and need help setting healthy-eating goals to achieve results, whether you're running a marathon, skiing, or jogging with your dog.
4. Are pregnant—or you're trying to get pregnant—and want to make sure you're well nourished for a healthy pregnancy, delivery, and baby. (Fertility issues related to nutrition arise for men, too.)
5. Need guidance and confidence for breastfeeding—and want to make sure you get the right nutrition for you and your infant.
6. Are a parent or caregiver and want to make sure you're feeding your kids properly and helping them learn to be healthy eaters.

7. Care for an aging parent, other relative, or friend—and need help understanding his or her unique food and nutrition needs—such as food and drug interactions, a special diet, or changing ways that older adults experience food.
8. Are deciding if a dietary supplement is right for you and, if so, which one and how much.
9. Want simply to eat smarter and more mindfully—or perhaps want to learn how to make nourishing meals that taste good, choose healthy food when you shop, or navigate a menu wisely when you eat out.
10. Want to sort through the clutter of food and nutrition headlines and information in today's media or judge what you see in social media.

For these reasons and more, talk to a registered dietitian nutritionist or other qualified nutrition expert, *as discussed in this chapter, page 758*. Your health—and that of your family—depend on it!

Truth or Half-Truth: Read Between the Headlines

Every day, nutrition and health news makes headlines. "Boring" headlines or results may not make it to publication, but catchy titles and "surprising data" do because they grab interest. Striving to inform and capture attention, media often present information in a simple and absolute way. Despite threads of truth, media messages also may be laced with misinformation, opinions, or advice that don't apply to you. Sensational headlines, conflicts, and scares can be more compelling (and profitable) than substantiated science. Misinterpreted research results, inexperienced reporting, and marketing bias can propagate misinformation or simply present a limited perspective that may be out of context. And that news can be distorted or blown out of proportion each time it gets repeated.

Anyone, qualified or not, can dispense healthy eating and nutrition advice. Reliable information from qualified health professionals often appears alongside advice from uncredentialed "experts" and the general public.

If media is your "go-to" source for nutrition and health information, advice, and updates, there's good news. Many well-qualified food, nutrition, and health experts share science-based information through every kind of popular media, from traditional print and television to blogs, websites, twitter chat, and other forms of social media. It's your role to judge food and nutrition messages as you try to sort through the clutter.

BREAKING NEWS: JUDGING NUTRITION RESEARCH

In this age of instant communication, research often hits the media before nutrition experts can review and interpret the findings. Adding to the challenge, reporters assigned to medical stories usually need to report complex medical news quickly and often oversimplify the results. The potential outcomes? Misinterpretation, confusion, and increased perceptions of risks or hazards.

Scientists aren't out to mislead you. Responsible journalists aren't, either. Uncovering the mysteries of nutrition and the human body is complex. As new findings emerge, research may seem to contradict itself. Scientists may express opposing viewpoints on the same study or subject matter. Differences between two or more reports reflect how scientists continue to learn—sharing research and questioning each step along the way. Real science responds to new research evidence; scientific debate leads to more studies.

Advice may shift with new evidence, too. As an example, after careful review of current research, advice from the 2015–2020 Dietary Guidelines for Americans about cholesterol differs from the 2010 Dietary Guidelines. Experts acknowledged that the scientific evidence doesn't show a strong influence of dietary cholesterol on blood cholesterol and that most people don't overconsume cholesterol from their food choices.

Today's popular media allows you to listen to the scientific debate and early findings. Just keep in mind that it may take years of study before recommendations based on sound science (repeated, conclusive evidence) can be shared with the public. In fact, as science unravels more about the links among nutrition, health, and chronic disease, findings from today's reports may eventually be disproven and replaced by reports with new findings and recommendations. That's the scientific process!

Nutrition Research: Thirteen Ways to Judge the Findings

You can't dissect every research report. But you can use caution and common sense. Before you jump to conclusions and, as a result, change your food choices and lifestyle decisions, consider the following:

1. Go beyond the headlines. An attention-grabbing headline, a sound bite, or a tweet may leave a different impression than the full newspaper article, or news or research brief. Sometimes headlines don't match the story's facts. Read or listen to the whole story for the complete context. Often, helpful responses from other experts or "bottom-line" advice appears at the story's end.
2. Keep a healthy skepticism. Every study has strengths and weaknesses. Before you accept the conclusion, consider: Could there be a different explanation? Make nutrition and health decisions based on sound, consensus science. *See "Case against Health Fraud" in this chapter, page 755.*
3. Check the source. Credible research comes from credible institutions and scientists and is reported in credible, peer-reviewed scientific and professional journals. Before being published, research must meet well-established standards. If attributed simply to "they" or some elusive source, be wary of its results. Credible research also discloses conflicts of interest, which don't automatically discredit the research.
4. Recognize preliminary findings and unpublished data for what they are—preliminary. Read them with interest, but wait for

more evidence before making major changes in your food decisions.

5. Remember, once isn't enough! A single study, taken alone, seldom "proves" anything. And results from one study usually shouldn't be enough to change your food choices. Media typically doesn't show how this one study agrees or doesn't agree with previous studies, and replication studies may not make media headlines. Avoid the urge to view the latest study as the final word.

   One study is just one piece of a bigger scientific puzzle. Scientific studies gather evidence in a systematic way. True nutrition breakthroughs take years of study and support from repeated findings in many scientific studies. That's why health organizations, government agencies, and health experts may appear more conservative than headline news; their guidance reflects consistent, well-researched findings.

6. Know what the words mean. Credible nutrition reports are careful not to mislead you. Research results may "suggest," but that isn't the same as "prove." "Linked to," "contributes to," and "associated with" don't mean "cause." And "can" and "may" don't mean "will." Be aware that popular media mostly covers new research that shows association, rather than cause.

   The term "breakthrough" is so overworked that it's often meaningless. Real breakthroughs—for example, the discovery of penicillin or the polio vaccine—happen only infrequently.

   Many people think that "significant" means "major" or "important." However, a result is "statistically significant" only when the association between two factors is more than what might happen at random, as determined by a mathematical formula.

   What about "risky," "doubles the risk," or "triples the risk"? To be meaningful, you need to know what the risk was in the first place. If the risk was one in a million, and you double it, that's still only 1 in 500,000. If the risk was 1 in 100 and doubles, that's a much greater risk: 1 in 50.

   Watch out for absolutes, too. Responsible scientists don't claim "proof" or "cause" until repeated studies show conclusive findings.

7. Look for the human dimension. Animal studies may be among the first steps in researching a hypothesis. Even if the media implies it, the results may not apply to humans.

8. Read carefully before applying research conclusions to you—even if they are studies with human subjects. Ask yourself:

   - Are the people studied like me—perhaps in age, gender, health, ethnicity, geographic location, and lifestyle? For example, results of a study conducted among men may not apply to women and children.
   - Did the study include a large group of people? If a study sample is small, the results could be due to chance; when hundreds and thousands are in the study, the results are more convincing.
   - Was the study long range? Longer studies, with more people, are more likely to produce valid results.
   - Are other studies cited to support the evidence of a single study? And does it build on what scientists know already? Responsible scientists and careful journalists report research within the context of other studies and what's already known. One study rarely changes their nutrition advice.
   - Does the analysis of the results make sense? Are the conclusions supported by the data?
   - Does the study tell how the findings relate to overall food choices, lifestyle, and other research? A responsible report offers implications that fit the real world.

   Even with the answers to these questions, understanding research methods and findings can be challenging.

9. Keep your eyes out (and ears open) for follow-up reports. Breaking scientific news is often followed by review and advice from nutrition experts. For example, registered dietitian nutritionists often appear in media, helping to interpret news reports on food and nutrition issues.

   Even when research has been well conducted, scientists may view the results differently. It may take time for nutrition experts to study the research methods and findings. Don't always expect an immediate response from experts.

10. Check the disclosure statement for funding sources. Many research studies are funded, which helps to support the advancement of science, but funding can bias results if the research and its conclusions don't remain objective. Scientists are expected to uphold a commitment to objective methods and analysis, and avoid any form of bias that may influence the results.

11. Consider who is reporting the results. Legitimate scientific findings can get distorted once they leave the scientists' desks. Media

Have you ever wondered?

. . . how to access credible scientific journals? University, medical school, and large urban libraries have them. With Internet access, you can check online through the National Library of Medicine, a division of the US National Institutes of Health (www.nlm.nih.gov), to order full-text copies of articles from a medical library (local fees and delivery methods vary). Some journals are online with articles that may be available at no charge; others charge a small fee for individual articles.

Hierarchy of Scientific Evidence

Research studies aren't all created equal. The study design signals the strength of the results, or scientific evidence. The hierarchy ranges from the strongest evidence, based on meta-analyses, systematic reviews, and randomized controlled trials, to weaker evidence based on case reports.

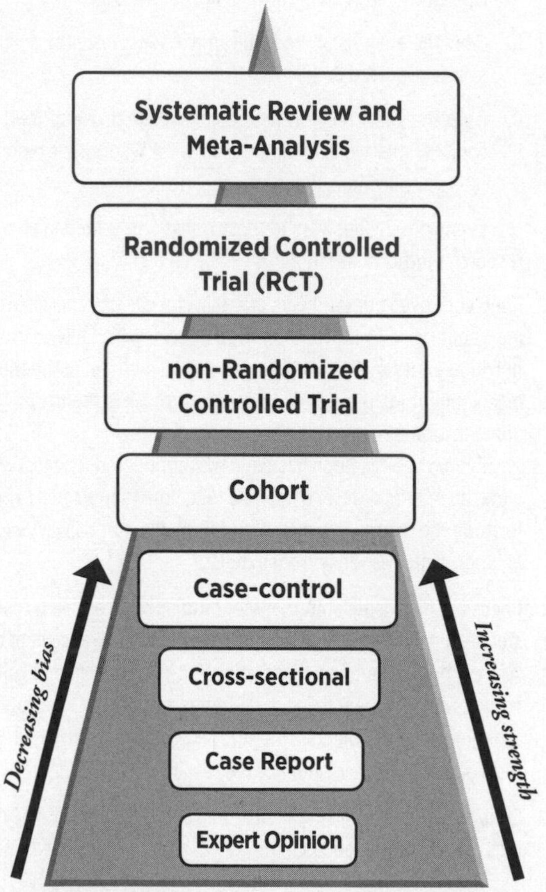

SYSTEMATIC REVIEW AND META-ANALYSIS A way to pool quantitative data from many studies to see what overall conclusions can be drawn, such as the pooling of more than twenty-five studies on soy protein to show their links to cholesterol lowering.

RANDOMIZED CONTROLLED TRIAL (RCT) Uses a random group of people who don't know (blind study) if they're in the experimental or placebo group until after the study is over. In a double-blind study, the researchers don't know, either.

NON-RANDOMIZED CONTROLLED TRIAL Uses different treatment groups that are assigned by the researchers or that participants choose. The participants and the researchers know what group they are in.

COHORT STUDY Follows a group of people with common characteristics and assesses whether or not exposure to a certain risk factor leads to a certain outcome.

CASE-CONTROL Follows specific groups of people (cases vs. controls for a certain outcome) who differ only by exposure to a risk factor.

CROSS-SECTIONAL STUDY Examines links at a single point in time to assess the prevalence of exposure to a risk factor or disease outcome.

CASE REPORT Looks at a single person or group with the goal of generalizing to others.

EXPERT OPINION Opinion isn't evidence. Instead, qualified experts can help interpret research findings for each level of this hierarchy, ask more questions, and put research in context.

Adapted with permission from the International Food Information Council Foundation, Washington, D.C. www.foodinsight.org

with health or medical reporters—trained to interpret research and complicated scientific information—are generally a better source.

12. Ask a qualified expert. Before you change your food choices, ask a registered dietitian nutritionist, another qualified nutrition expert, or your doctor to weigh in. Even promising research may not apply to you. For example, a report may suggest that red wine is heart healthy, but if you take an MAO inhibitor (an antidepressant), the combination may raise your blood pressure.

13. Put scientific reports into your own life's reality. For any advice, weigh the benefits and risks, as they apply to you, as an individual. Recognize that there's no such thing as "zero risk" for practically anything. And avoid cherry picking research findings to match what you hope or want to be true.

To explore the scientific evidence about a nutrition headline or topic, you can check an evidence-based library. Some are free; others require a subscription. *See "Resources You Can Use" in this book, page 763, to find an evidence-based library and other credible sources of nutrition information.*

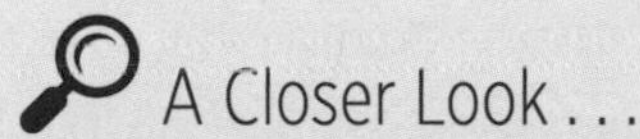

Scientific Studies: Research Terms Worth Understanding

ASSOCIATION, OR LINK	Relationship between two or more characteristics (also called variables or factors). If one variable changes, another may predictably change, too. An association doesn't necessarily mean that one variable causes the other.
BIAS	Any factor, recognized or not, that distorts the findings. In research studies, bias can influence the observations, results, and conclusions of the study and make them less accurate or believable.
CAUSATION	An association between two variables in which changing one causes the other to change. Causation does not mean that the variables are correlated; two variables can have a causal relationship and have little or no correlation.
CONFOUNDING VARIABLE	An unforeseen, and unaccounted for, variable (such as age, gender, smoking) that jeopardizes the reliability and validity of the study outcome.
CONTROL GROUP	The study group that doesn't receive the treatment. A control group is used to know if a treatment has an effect.
CORRELATION	An association between two research variables, such as eating lycopene and reduced risk for prostate cancer. A correlation does not mean that one variable causes the other; two variables can have a causal relationship and not be correlated.
EXPERIMENTAL GROUP	The study group that receives the treatment.
GENERALIZABILITY	Describes to what degree the research results apply to the general population of people who are like the studies' subjects.
INCIDENCE	The number of new cases of a disease or health condition reported as of a specific date for a defined population.
***IN VITRO* STUDY**	Laboratory study using cells or tissue samples, usually done before an *in vivo* study.
***IN VIVO* STUDY**	Study using living subjects, either animal or human.
MORBIDITY	Number of deaths in relation to a population.
MORTALITY	Number of people with an illness in relation to a population.
PLACEBO	A "fake" treatment, perhaps a sugar pill, which appears to be the same as the treatment under study. It's used to remove bias when study subjects don't know which treatment they have.
PLACEBO EFFECT	Positive results among subjects who think they're getting the real treatment.
PREVALENCE	The number of existing cases of a disease or health condition as of a specific date for a defined population.
RANDOM SAMPLE	A way to choose study subjects whereby everyone from a target population has an equal chance of being selected. In that way, the results can be generalized more easily to a larger group.
RELIABILITY	The extent to which a research measure, procedure, or instrument has been carefully controlled so the results are the same when the study is repeated.
RISK	The probability that something (perhaps a heart attack, stroke, cancer, diabetes, osteoporosis) will happen. "Risk" doesn't necessarily mean something will happen.
RISK FACTOR	A variable that's statistically linked to the incidence of disease, such as a high BMI as a risk factor for heart disease. Again, it doesn't necessarily mean cause and effect.
STATISTICAL SIGNIFICANCE	The probability that an observed effect in a study is occurring because of chance. It's typically shown as a probability value, or P-value ($p<0.05$). Simplistically speaking, the lower the P-value, the more statistically significant the result may be.
VALIDITY	The degree to which a study accurately reflects or assesses what it meant to study. A research method can be reliable, consistently measuring the same thing, but not be valid.
VARIABLE	A factor such as age, gender, or food choices in a study that differs among the people being studied. An independent variable is the one being studied; a dependent variable, perhaps lower blood glucose level or LDL cholesterol level, happens as a result of the treatment.

(continued)

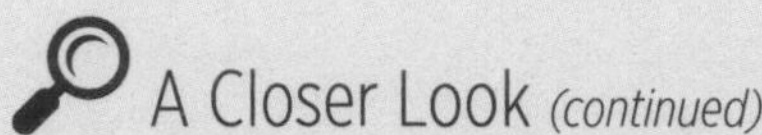

A Closer Look *(continued)*

MORE STUDY TERMS AND TYPES

In addition to the studies *defined in the "Hierarchy of Scientific Evidence," page 750*, you might see references to these types of studies:

EPIDEMIOLOGICAL OR ECOLOGICAL STUDY	A study that assesses the rate (incidence and prevalence) of a health condition among a specific group of people, such as neural tube defects among newborns.
EXPERIMENTAL STUDIES	*Clinical trials* use a particular type of person or group of people and follow a predefined intervention plan (or no intervention) so the effects can be evaluated. *Diagnostic trials* screen a particular type of person or group of people and follow a predefined intervention plan; screening is examining or testing a group of people to identify those who have an undiagnosed disease or to detect those who are at high risk. *Preventative trials* use healthy individuals to assess illness prevention via an intervention.
OBSERVATIONAL STUDY	A study that identifies a link between a health condition and behavior, such as overweight and TV watching, but doesn't prove cause and effect. All the variables aren't controlled; other factors may be responsible for the results. Although the study can't prove or disprove results, it can help develop the hypothesis. Cohort, case-control, cross-sectional, and ecological studies are all observational studies.
PROSPECTIVE STUDY	A study that poses the research questions, then follows groups of people, often for decades.
RETROSPECTIVE STUDY	A study that uses recorded data or recall of the past. Because the study relies on memory or some variables that can't be easily controlled, this type of research has limitations.

Adapted with permission from the International Food Information Council Foundation, Washington, D.C. www.foodinsight.org

FOOD AND NUTRITION "INFO": JUDGING THE MESSAGE

Coming from a best-selling book, a well-trafficked online site, or a highly visible medical talk show doesn't mean that the nutrition information and advice is sound, and it may not encourage informed decision-making. Give what you read and hear a reliability and validity check—no matter what the source, whether it's print, broadcast, or online media (even wikis).

To be a savvy consumer of healthy eating advice and information, find answers to these questions to help you make a judgment:

- Who wrote or said it? Check the author's or reviewer's qualifications. No matter what the media, credible information comes from qualified nutrition experts. A reputable nutrition author usually is educated in the field of nutrition, medicine, or a related specialty, with a degree or degrees from an accredited college or university. He or she usually is a credentialed member of a credible nutrition organization—for example, a registered dietitian nutritionist. *See "Qualified Experts: Please Stand Up" in this chapter, page 758.*
- Why was it published? Try to analyze what's being said or implied. If it's not clear, ask a qualified nutrition expert. For sound eating advice, find resources with a balanced nutrition message meant to inform, not advertise.
- Is the nutrition advice from credible sources? Check the cited sources. Reliable advice is backed up with credible sources such as:
    - Government entities. For example, the Health and Medicine Division (HMD) of the National Academies of Science, Engineering, and Medicine (NASEM); the US Department of Health and Human Services (DHHS); the US Department of Agriculture (USDA); and the Centers for Disease Control and Prevention (CDC) base their healthy eating and lifestyle guidelines on current evidence and consensus from scientific experts. Among guidance often cited and addressed throughout this book are Dietary Reference Intakes, 2015–2020 Dietary Guidelines for Americans, Physical Activity Guidelines for Americans, the DASH Eating Plan, and the CDC's body mass index (BMI).
    - Credible professional nutrition and health organizations. They base their advice on the most current, sound scientific evidence and government guidelines. If you want to know more, some, such as the Academy of Nutrition and Dietetics and the American Academy of Pediatrics, have position papers on their websites, which reflect scientific evidence on a variety of topics.
    - Peer-reviewed scientific journals. Research reported in peer-reviewed journals goes through the scrutiny of experts before it can be printed, so in medical news stories, look for

the journal citation. If you choose, you can read the original research. Among the many peer-reviewed journals: *New England Journal of Medicine, Lancet, Journal of the American Medical Association*, and *Journal of the Academy of Nutrition and Dietetics*.

Credible nutrition experts don't claim to have all the answers. If scientific evidence isn't conclusive or if the issues are controversial, they say so. At the same time, good science reporting shares the context of the findings and the limitations of the study and research design.

See "Resources You Can Use" page 763, for websites of government and health agencies, professional organizations, and food industry groups that provide credible, science-based information.

- Does it distinguish fact from opinion? Does it cite sources for the facts? Opinions and advice should be presented as such. Content from other websites or sources should be clearly credited and cited.
- What do qualified experts say about it? Look for their reviews. For a book, start inside or on the cover itself, where you may find a list of reviewers. Like those of the author, reviewers' credentials or affiliations help you judge their reliability.

  For an expert judgment, contact a registered dietitian nutritionist or other qualified expert connected with a local college, university, hospital, Cooperative Extension program, public health department, or who is in private practice.

Unravel the Online Information "Web"

Food and nutrition information—credible, or less so—proliferates in today's connected, online world. Online media instantaneously spreads food and nutrition news and advice, food prep tips, food safety recalls, and food product information—as well as food scares and "urban nutrition myths." All too often, headlines, fake news, and scares go viral, spreading faster than qualified experts can respond with a credible perspective.

Consider this. If you ask a question on a search engine, a countless number of possible answers may appear on your screen in a fraction of a second—with many of those answers appearing authoritative, yet being half-truths, biased, or advertising instead. And without a trustworthy link, even a tweet from a credible source that's 140 characters or less can't communicate much when it comes to scientific evidence, context, and fact.

Today's social and digital media allows anyone to become a publisher. How do you determine if a website, blog, online community, podcast, phone app, tweet, or other social media source provides trustworthy information? How do you know if credible sources are quoted just to "spin" a sense of legitimacy to unreliable sources? And how do you avoid falling victim to attention-grabbling "fake food news" that may appear online?

Two government agencies—the Federal Trade Commission (FTC) and the US Food and Drug Administration (FDA)—are responsible for helping to protect consumers from false or misleading health claims for products sold on the Internet. However, online content isn't overseen by any regulatory agency, nor is it checked for accuracy. Search engines don't rank or distinguish between accurate and inaccurate content, either. And search engines and search-engine optimization can make less credible sites more visible than trustworthy sites.

You need to use the same healthy skepticism with information from online media that you use to evaluate nutrition information from any source. That includes the growing amount of visual content that appears in online and digital media. In addition, judging online requires yet another layer of evaluation:

- Is the purpose clear? Is it designed to educate objectively, or to sell a product with a hidden guise of "sound" nutrition advice?

  Government and nonprofit sites don't have advertising. If it's promotional, the information is likely biased or reframed for marketing and sales. Look for a link to information about the site, often called "About Us" or "About This Site," to help you judge.

- Does it link to credible online sites? Reliable online health sites generally hyperlink only to sites that meet certain criteria, or their policy may not allow links. *Caution:* A disreputable site may hyperlink to a credible site—perhaps a government nutrition site—for a trustworthy perception.

  As you surf the Internet, keep track of your path. You may be unaware when you pass from a reliable to an unreliable source of information.

- Does the site have clickbait, or provocative content or a headline that attracts reader curiosity or attention, with click-throughs to another webpage? Clickbait often is paid for by advertisers.
- Who owns and operates the site? That's your clue to the site's perspective, its potential bias, and its intent. Remember that anyone can put up a website or blog. Look for contact information for the site.

  The three-letter suffix on a website address is your first clue. Those that end in .edu (educational institutions), .gov (government agencies), and perhaps .org (organizations, often nonprofit) tend to be the most credible. Those ending in .com are commercial (business) sites, and those ending in .net often denote networks, but can be used by individuals or organizations, including companies.

  Many .com sites have responsible consumer information. Many registered dietitian nutritionists who work as consultants or in private practice have websites, blogs, or other social media sites. You can verify their qualification (RDN or RD credential) by contacting the Commission on Dietetic Registration, the credentialing agency for the Academy of Nutrition and Dietetics. If they have a consultant or sponsor relationship to the content, that should be disclosed for transparency. *See "Resources You Can Use" page 763, for contact information.*

- What's the difference between "http" and "https" addresses? The https (with an "s") means that this is a secure version of http. The "s" stands for "secure"; the communication between your browser and the website is encrypted. Using an https link is important when you transmit sensitive information through the connection.
- Who wrote or created it? Is the credential identified? And what about disclosure? Much science-based information on blogs, websites, and social media, as well as other online content, is written by registered dietitian nutritionists. While the content from a qualified expert can be trusted, any sponsor or client relationship should be disclosed.

  In any type of media, including social media, disclosures of competing interests by the writer, site owner, or operator should be clear, prominent, and easily viewed. For example, disclosures in tweets may be identified as "#sponsored," "#ad," or "#client," and in blogs, "company x gave me this product to review."
- Is the information and advice current? Credible websites are updated frequently. Being current is crucial for health and nutrition information. The most recent date should be posted. *Caution:* Being current doesn't necessarily make it accurate.
- Does it explain how any personal information gathered from you online will—and will not—be used? Decide if you want to share what's requested. Read and understand the privacy policy; don't sign up if you don't fully understand its use. Your data may be used for unexpected marketing purposes. Remember that websites routinely track the path users take through their sites to determine what pages are being used.
- Is the information balanced, stating caveats and more than one perspective on an issue? Does it pass other credibility tests, *noted in this chapter?* Anyone can launch a site. Like any media report, being on the Internet doesn't ensure reliability.

Click Here! Websites and Blogs to Know . . .

- "Evaluating Internet Health Information," Medline Plus, US HHS, NIH
  medlineplus.gov/webeval/webeval.html
- *Food and Nutrition Magazine* app reviews
  www.foodandnutrition.org/Nutrition-Apps
- Healthfinder, US government gateway
  healthfinder.gov
- Nutrition Blog Network, blogs by registered dietitian nutritionists
  www.nutritionblognetwork.com
- Office of Disease Prevention and Health Promotion, US government gateway
  health.gov

- For discussion groups on food and nutrition, or online support or community groups for dieting or other nutrition-focused health issues, conditions, or diseases, does it have a registered dietitian nutritionist or other qualified nutrition expert as host? Be aware and look for the terms of using the service. Before you join in, follow the discussion and then decide if you'll participate. When you do join in, add to the conversation with thought, peer-to-peer support, and not "noise."
- Can you contact the online site's owners with problems, feedback, and questions?

A word about tweets and other online networks: Although they can offer a wealth of information, they, too, need to be assessed for accuracy of information—whether you just follow that social media handle or hashtag or also share what's posted. Determine if those you follow are credible sources. Pay attention to their network of followers and what they contribute to the conversation. Be aware that the more often content is shared and reinterpreted, the more likely it can be distorted. Take care to be factual and considerate if you make a comment or post information online or in a tweet.

How to . . . Find "Well"-Connected Links

Internet search engines can produce staggering amounts of results with no filtering or rating system. Credible sources and less reliable websites may appear side-by-side. To find health-related links with high standards, do this:

- Speed your search by using gateway sites that link to responsible organizations—for example, the US government's site (www.nutrition.gov). The US Department of Health and Human Services' Healthfinder (healthfinder.gov) provides hyperlinks to hundreds of responsible sites.
- Review more than one reliable website or blog on the same nutrition topic. When information is presented in short bites, one site usually isn't complete enough.
- Ask a nutrition expert, such as a registered dietitian nutritionist, who can identify nuances of online bias and inaccuracy. If you find news of interest on the Internet, perhaps about a phytonutrient link to health, or a dietary supplement, print the information with the name and address of the website or blog, and take it to your doctor or a nutrition expert for a qualified perspective.

  Some websites carry symbols for their credibility and ethics:

  - The HONcode shows adherence to the Health On the Net Foundation (HON) principles of providing health information to citizens that respects ethical standards (visit www.healthonnet.org for more information). This nonprofit, nongovernmental organization is accredited by the United Nations Economic and Social Council and dedicated to protecting citizens from misleading health information.

? Have you ever wondered?

. . . how to judge food scares and avoid nutrition scams that circulate through email? Being 100 percent sure about these food scares takes research. What appears unsolicited in your email or in social media is likely a hoax if (1) the email address that claims to be the e-mail sender doesn't to match, (2) you're asked to forward the email, (3) it claims not to be a hoax or an urban legend, (4) it appeals to your emotions, and/or (5) it doesn't cite a legitimate source or credible website.

If you're still not sure, you might check websites that debunk common food myths, scares, and scams, such as the American Council on Science and Health's www.acsh.org and the National Council against Health Fraud's www.quackwatch.org.

To minimize your chance of becoming a victim, read critically for obvious false claims, poor logic, and lack of common sense. Don't trust unsolicited email. Treat email attachments with caution, and skip the urge to click links in the email. Filter spam. Install antivirus software and a personal firewall; keep them updated.

- Another symbol identifies a URAC-accredited health website, which also offers a clue to its reliability. URAC sets high standards for helpful and timely health information (visit www.urac.org for more information).

Both symbols indicate voluntary compliance for standards of credible health and medical websites. However, many credible, ethical websites also provide reliable information even though they don't display a HONcode or URAC symbol. You always need to be a careful and savvy online consumer of health and nutrition information.

See "Resources You Can Use" page 763, to find reliable nutrition and health websites and blogs.

Case against Health Fraud

"Lose weight while you sleep." "No more arthritic pain." "Proven to enhance memory." "Scientific breakthrough," "secret ingredient," "ancient remedy," "proven science," and "miracle cure."

Americans spend billions of dollars annually on products and services that sound too good to be true. Some offer a money-back guarantee. Some are available from only one source, perhaps with payment required in advance. Some share testimonials with "amazing results" or use impressive-sounding medical terms, but offer no sound scientific

Your Healthy Eating Check-In

Can You Spot Truths, Half-Truths, and Non-Truths?

Sound too good to be true? To weigh the allure, arm yourself with these ten questions—even when you aren't suspicious!

Does the promotion of a nutrition product, regimen, service, treatment, or device . . .	**Yes**	**No**
1. Try to attract you with scare tactics, emotional appeals, or perhaps a "money-back guarantee"?	☐	☐
2. Promise to "revitalize," "detoxify," or "balance your body with nature"? Or claim to increase your stamina, stimulate your body's healing power, or boost your energy level?	☐	☐
3. Use personal anecdotes or testimonials as "proof" rather than use sound science?	☐	☐
4. Advise supplements as "insurance" for everyone? Recommend very large doses of nutrients? "Very large" is significantly more than 100 percent of the Daily Values. *See "% Daily Values: What are They Based On?" in the appendix, page 786,* to know the amount in metric measures for the Daily Value of specific nutrients.	☐	☐
5. Claim it can "treat," "cure," or "prevent" diverse health problems—from arthritis to cancer to sexual impotence?	☐	☐
6. Make unrealistic claims: "reverse the aging process," "cure disease," or "quick, easy approach"?	☐	☐
7. Blame the food supply as the source of health or behavior problems? Belittle government regulations? Or discredit the advice of recognized medical authorities?	☐	☐
8. Claim that its "natural" benefits surpass those of "synthetic" products?	☐	☐
9. Mention a "secret formula"? Fail to list ingredients on its label or state possible side effects?	☐	☐
10. Come from a "nutrition expert" without accepted credentials? Does he or she also sell the product?	☐	☐

continued on next page

Your Healthy Eating Check-In *(continued)*

Now score yourself: The more "yeses" you checked, the more questionable the promotion. But in this test, you might spot quackery with just one "yes" answer. Here's why:

1. Playing on emotion, misinformation, or even fear is common among nonscientific pseudo-experts. Emotional words used to promote a product can be an instant tip-off to quackery: "guaranteed," "breakthrough," and "miraculous." So are false claims that foods or additives are "deadly poisons."
2. Pseudo-medical jargon such as "detoxify" or "balance your body chemistry" suggests misinformation. These terms have no meaning in physiology. A supplement can't increase your strength, immunity, stamina, or energy level, either. *See "Ergogenic Aids: No Training Substitute" in chapter 21, page 619, for more about supplements promoted to athletes.*
3. Nutrition is a science, based on fact and not emotion or belief. Be skeptical of case histories and testimonials from satisfied users—if that's the only proof that a product works. Instead, look for science-based evidence from a reputable institution or a qualified health expert. Without scientific evidence, a reported "cure" actually may be a placebo effect. Its benefit may be psychological, not physical. The person may have been misdiagnosed in the first place. Even chronic ailments don't always have symptoms all the time.
4. Everyone does not need vitamin supplements, so ignore the hype! On the contrary, taking too much may be harmful. *See "Dietary Supplements: More Than Vitamin Pills" in chapter 10, page 316.* Most healthy people can get enough nutrients with a varied, balanced eating plan. Quacks rarely say who does not need a supplement. *See chapter 2, page 21, for more about healthy eating.*
5. No nutrition regimen, device, service, treatment, or product can treat so many different problems that ail you. And they can't cure many health conditions, including arthritis, cancer, and sexual impotence. Even when they're part of credible treatment or prevention strategies, nutrition factors are typically just one part of an overall healthcare plan.
6. Claims that sound too good to be true probably are. They say what people want to hear: simple cures and magic ways to change what's imperfect. There's no such thing as a quick fix or a magic bullet.
7. Misleading tactics often belittle the food supply, government regulation, and the established medical community. They may claim that the traditional health community is suppressing their work. Instead, they may call for "freedom of choice"—and describe unproven methods as alternatives to current, proven methods. By discrediting traditional approaches, quacks attempt to funnel healthcare dollars toward their own financial gain.
8. There's nothing magical about supplements promoted as "natural." Even substances found in nature can have natural toxins, with potent, drug-like effects.
9. By law, a medication must carry product information on its packaging. That includes the product's ingredients, use, dosage, warnings, and precautions, as well as what to do if adverse reactions occur. However, products or regimens sold through quackery may not report all this information.
10. Be wary when someone tries to assess your health status and then offers to sell you a remedy, such as a routine dietary supplement. Invalid tests may be hard to distinguish from legitimate clinical assessments. Those often used by quacks include hair analysis, iridology, and herbal crystallization analysis, among others. Computerized questionnaires can't gather enough information, either, to determine your need for a supplement. Get an opinion from a qualified health professional instead.

Quackery underlies many weight loss or gain regimens, too. *See "Popular Diets: Truths and Half-Truths" in chapter 22, page 648, for tips to judge their effectiveness and safety.*

evidence. Still others, likely scams, promise effective cures for a range of unrelated ailments. Their websites may not provide a company name, physical address, phone number, or other contact information.

"Health fraud" means promoting, for financial gain, a health remedy that doesn't work—or hasn't yet been proven to work or isn't supported by sound scientific evidence. The remedy may be a device, a treatment, a service, a plan, special foods, or other product. Rampant health fraud is often linked to the promise of nutrition benefits—perhaps to promote a dietary supplement, an herbal product, a weight-loss device, or a new diet program.

Those who promote fraudulent remedies are sometimes referred to as quacks. The term "quackery" comes from the term "quacksalver," referring to medieval peddlers of salves who sounded like quacking ducks when talking to promote their wares. Their motivation may be strictly financial gain, but often, quacks sincerely believe in the value of their product (perhaps a supplement), treatment, or service but lack both scientific understanding and expertise backed by accredited credentials.

FRAUD: LURE AND CONSEQUENCES

Health fraud and misleading tactics have grown dramatically, in part due to an unprecedented interest in and responsibility taken for one's own personal healthcare and staying healthy. That interest has created a huge demand for health-focused products and services: both legitimate and not.

The lure. A common reason for growing health fraud is hope for a quick or easy "health fix." Some people may count on fraudulent products to undo the results of an unhealthy lifestyle. It's not that simple—even if misleading tactics might lead you to believe otherwise.

Nutrition fraud thrives among people who are desperate for help, overconfident about possible risks, uninformed or already misinformed, or alienated from traditional healthcare. They're more easily manipulated, perhaps with ploys that seem reasonable: "We really care about you." "What have you got to lose?" "Science doesn't have all the answers." "We treat medicine's failures."

Looser government regulation of dietary supplements has contributed to their hype, as well. It allows claims for supplements to appear more credible than they really are. *See chapter 10, page 315, for more about the use and misuse of supplements.*

Potential consequences. Nutrition quackery exploits consumers, and it carries significant health and economic risks. Many claims are simply useless; others, potentially harmful:

- *False hopes.* Quacks may promise quick fixes and guaranteed results—but unsound nutrition advice, products, or services won't prevent or cure disease or replace unhealthy living. Easy remedies are hard to resist!
- *Substitute for reliable healthcare.* False hopes, created through quackery, may delay or replace qualified medical care or follow-up treatment. If you follow quackery, you may lose something you can't retrieve: time for effective treatment. Health scams are the most common type of fraud aimed at older adults and others with chronic or incurable diseases. The fanfare of health fraud and quackery is leaving people more vulnerable than ever.
- *Interference with sound eating and lifestyle habits.* This happens when misinformation replaces science-based guidance and medical care.
- *Unneeded expense.* In the best case, some of these products and services simply don't work—yet cause no harm. Why waste hard-earned money on devices, products, and services that have no effect?
- *Potentially harmful health risks.* Taking very large doses of some vitamins and minerals, in the form of dietary supplements, can have toxic side effects. For example, excessive amounts of vitamin A during pregnancy increase the chances of birth defects. Inappropriate supplement use can lead to harmful drug-nutrient interactions. For instance, taking vitamin K can be risky if you take blood-thinning drugs. *See chapter 14, page 408, for more about specific vitamins and minerals.*

  Over-the-counter herbal products, marketed as dietary supplements, are sources of potent drugs. Yet, unlike medications, herbal products aren't well regulated. *See "Herbals and Other Botanicals" in chapter 10, page 320.*

Registered dietitian nutritionists—with their qualifications given in *"Who is a Registered Dietitian Nutrionist?" in this chapter, page 759*—must follow the Academy of Nutrition and Dietetics' Code of Ethics guidelines if they sell nutrition supplements.

NUTRITION SCAMS: DON'T FALL VICTIM

No one has to be the victim of nutrition and health fraud. To protect yourself, be smart, be aware, be careful. Know how to identify it and where to report it:

- Retain a healthy skepticism. Take time to be well informed before you invest in a nutrition product, treatment, or service. It must stand up to the same scrutiny and rigor as any media story or scientific research study. Testimonials and anecdotes aren't enough.
- *Never* give personal information such as a Medicare ID number in exchange for a free offer!
- Seek advice from reliable sources. If you're suspicious about a statement, product, or service, contact a credible nutrition source—a registered dietitian nutritionist, your public health department, the medical or nutrition department of a nearby college or university, or your county Cooperative Extension Service.
- Report nutrition fraud. If you suspect that a statement, product, or service is fraudulent or false, inquire with the appropriate government agency, or file a nonemergency complaint. Your reports provide the information needed to launch investigations and stop fraudulent practices.
  - *To the FDA:* To make inquiries or file nonemergency problems and complaints about FDA-regulated products, including false claims for dietary supplements, contact

Ten Red Flags of Junk Science

A new health or nutrition report? Before you jump to conclusions, check it out. Any combination of these signs indicate exaggerated or false claims.

1. Recommendations that promise a quick fix
2. Dire warnings of danger from a single product
3. Claims that sound too good to be true
4. Simple conclusions drawn from a complex study
5. Recommendations based on a single study
6. Dramatic statements that are refuted by reputable scientific organizations
7. Lists of "good" and "bad" foods
8. Recommendations made to help sell a product or by the manufacturer itself
9. Recommendations based on studies without peer review
10. Recommendations from studies that ignore differences among individuals or groups

Source: Food and Nutrition Science Alliance (FANSA).

them at 1-888-463-6332 or via www.fda.gov/Safety/ReportaProblem. Contact the FDA also for concerns about inadequate package labels.

- *To the FTC:* For questions or concerns about false or misleading claims in advertising or websites, contact the FTC at 1-877-FTC-HELP (1-877-382-4357) or via www.ftc.gov/complaint. Visit the FTC website www.ftc.gov, which may list diet scams it has prosecuted.

Nutrition Advice to Trust

Want answers to your food and nutrition questions? Need personal nutrition counseling? Looking for food assistance for a friend or family member? Who should you trust? Locally and regionally, many well-qualified resources are ready to help—when you know how and where to find them.

QUALIFIED EXPERTS: PLEASE STAND UP

With all these notes of caution, just who is a qualified nutrition expert? Sometimes it's hard to tell.

Qualified nutrition experts, with specific academic and training credentials, know the science of nutrition. Some are food scientists, as well. Their degrees in human nutrition, dietetics, public health, or related fields (such as biochemistry, physiology, medicine, or a nutrition specialty in family and consumer sciences) come from well-respected, accredited colleges, universities, or medical schools. The title "dietitian" or "nutritionist" often describes what they do; a credential from an accredited institution is important!

An "accredited" institution generally is certified by an agency recognized by the US Department of Education. You can check the reference department of your local library for an institution's accreditation.

Letters after someone's name don't necessarily qualify that person to provide food and nutrition services. Even when that person holds other academic degrees, nutrition may not be his or her specialty. Probe further.

The initials RDN for "registered dietitian nutritionist" or NDTR for "nutrition and dietetic technician, registered" do mean the person has met specific educational requirements in nutrition and health. Be aware that some may choose to use RD (registered dietitian) or DTR (dietetic technician, registered) as their credentials.

Most states have licensing for qualified nutrition experts to help ensure credible nutrition guidance and quality healthcare in a clinical practice. The credential may be designated LDN (licensed dietitian nutritionist) or LD (licensed dietitian), although states differ. Qualifications for licensing typically reflect the same education and training required to become an RDN. Many qualified nutrition experts also have advanced degrees, such as MS, MEd, ScD, MD, or PhD.

Being qualified in nutrition, dietetics, or any health field doesn't end when a degree is conferred, but continues with lifelong education. A qualified healthcare provider should be able to address current nutrition research and guidance or help you find a reliable source of nutrition guidance.

What about job titles such "nutritionist" or "diet counselor" (without the RDN or NDTR credential)? In many states, these titles aren't licensed or regulated, and they may be used by those not adequately qualified to give accurate nutrition information or sound counseling advice. Some with unlicensed titles have just a little nutrition training or only mail-order diploma-mill credentials. The US Department of Education defines a "diploma mill" as an organization awarding degrees without requiring its students to meet the established educational standards followed by reputable accredited institutions. These titles may appear impressive—but don't be fooled.

What about health coaches, fitness trainers, and others who provide nutrition advice? To determine if you can trust these sources of nutrition information, find out the extent and source of their academic education and training in nutrition—and if they are credentialed, the requirements and by whom. Do they partner their consulting or coaching work with a qualified expert such as a registered dietitian nutritionist?

Unqualified practitioners can put their clients at risk for adverse health effects. Be cautious of those with supplements or training programs to sell.

Just as accredited licensure of physicians protects you from those unqualified to practice medicine, registration and licensure of nutrition professionals protects you from those unqualified to work as nutrition professionals. Qualified experts, from sources *noted on the next few pages*, can help you assess the credentials of various nutrition services.

How to . . . Find a Qualified Nutrition Expert

Some health problems can be managed partly or completely by diet and perhaps physical activity. If so, your doctor may advise you to seek advice from a registered dietitian nutritionist.

Health, education, and social service organizations in your community, as well as registered dietitian nutritionists in private practice, may provide nutrition counseling services. In many states, private health insurance and managed-care plans cover nutrition counseling (also known as medical nutrition therapy) for some health conditions, such as diabetes. Check these sources for a referral to a qualified expert in your area:

- Your doctor, health maintenance organization (HMO), or local hospital
- Your state or local Academies of Nutrition and Dietetics, public health department, Cooperative Extension Service, or the nutrition department of an area college or university

A Closer Look . . .

Who Is a Registered Dietitian Nutritionist?

A registered dietitian nutritionist (RDN) is a food and nutrition expert, who can translate the science of nutrition into practical solutions for healthy living. RDNs use their nutrition expertise to help individuals make unique, positive lifestyle changes. They are advocates for advancing the nutritional status of Americans and people around the world.

RDNs have earned the credential by meeting academic and professional requirements established by the Commission on Dietetic Registration (CDR), the credentialing agency for the Academy of Nutrition and Dietetics. This includes earning a minimum of a bachelor's degree from a regionally accredited college or university and completing an accredited, supervised practice program with preprofessional experience at a healthcare facility, community agency, or food-service corporation. RDNs must pass a rigorous national exam, administered by the Commission on Dietetic Registration, and must engage in ongoing education to maintain the credential.

Some RDNs hold additional certifications in specialized areas of practice such as pediatric, maternal, or sports nutrition; oncology, cardiovascular, or renal nutrition; weight counseling; or diabetes education. These are awarded through the CDR, and/or other medical and nutrition organizations. They are recognized within the profession but are not required. In addition to RDN credentialing, many states have regulatory laws for dietitians and nutrition practitioners.

Registered dietitian nutritionists work in a wide variety of employment settings throughout the community, including hospitals, schools, public health clinics, nursing homes, fitness centers, supermarkets, food management, food- and nutrition-related business and industry, government agencies, universities, research, and private practice.

Someone with this credential may also choose to identify as an RD, or registered dietitian.

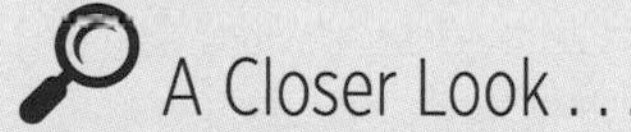

A Closer Look . . .

Who Is a Nutrition and Dietetic Technician, Registered?

The initials NDTR after someone's name stands for "nutrition and dietetic technician, registered." NDTRs are educated and trained at the technical level of nutrition and dietetics practice for the delivery of safe, culturally competent, quality food and nutrition services.

Nationally credentialed in food and nutrition, NDTRs are an integral part of health care and food-service management teams. They work under the supervision of a registered dietitian nutritionist when in direct patient/client nutrition care. They may work independently in providing general nutrition education to healthy populations.

NDTRs have earned at least a two-year degree from a regionally accredited college or university and have completed a dietetic technical program approved by the Academy of Nutrition and Dietetics' Accreditation Council for Education in Nutrition and Dietetics, including supervised practice experience in community programs, health care and food service. Alternatively, they can earn the credential by completing at least a bachelor's degree with successful completion of specified coursework and perhaps a supervised practice program.

Like RDNs, they must pass a national examination administered by the Commission on Dietetic Registration (CDR) and stay current with ongoing continuing education to maintain their NDTR credential.

Someone with this credential may also choose to identify as a DTR, or dietetic technician, registered.

Click Here!
Other Links to Know . . .

- Academy of Nutrition and Dietetics
  www.eatright.org
- Food and Nutrition Information Center
  www.nal.usda.gov/fnic
- International Food Information Council Foundation
  www.foodinsight.org
- QuackWatch
  www.quackwatch.com

- The Academy of Nutrition and Dietetics at www.eatright.org (click on "Find an Expert"). Or call 1-800-877-1600, ext. 5000.

Thirteen Tips to Make the Most of Nutrition Counseling

Whether you seek nutrition counseling on your own or as a follow-up from your doctor's referral, make the most of your office visit.

1. Have a medical checkup first. A qualified nutrition professional needs to know your health status before providing dietary guidance. Your doctor can share your blood pressure and information from blood tests, such as blood cholesterol, triglycerides, blood glucose, hemoglobin, and hematocrit levels, among others.
2. Share your goals. If you seek nutrition advice on your own, know what you want to accomplish. Do you want to lose weight? Have more stamina for sports? Improve your blood cholesterol levels? Live a healthier lifestyle?
3. Keep an ongoing personal health record—perhaps digitally—to share and aid decisions about your nutrition and health care. Some of this information may be kept in your electronic health record.
4. Be prepared to answer questions. Expect to talk about your eating habits, adverse reactions to foods, dietary supplements, weight history, food preferences, general medical history, family history of health problems, medications, special diets, any nutrition instruction you've had, and lifestyle habits. With those insights, a dietitian can customize food and nutrition advice for your lifestyle and health.
5. Ask for clarification. If you don't understand the terms used in the counseling session, ask. Terms such as "blood glucose level," "HDLs," "triglycerides," "anaphylactic reaction," and "*trans* fatty acids" are nutrition-related lingo. Know what they mean.
6. Be specific with your questions. You're the most important person on your healthcare team. You can only comply with dietary recommendations if you have a clear understanding of the advice offered.
7. Reveal all dietary supplements and medications you take, including herbal remedies and botanicals. Some supplements interact with medications (even over-the-counter types), rendering them ineffective or causing harmful side effects. *See "Common Interactions between Food and Some Medications: Talk to Your Doctor!" in chapter 25, page 744.* Dietary supplements taken in very large doses also may cause adverse health reactions; *see "Dietary Supplements: More than Vitamin Pills" in chapter 10, page 316, for more about the risks.*
8. For weight or sports nutrition counseling, expect to have your weight and body composition checked—usually height, weight, and a skinfold measurement in several spots on your body (or other techniques to measure body composition).
9. Be open to professional health advice. For example, if your doctor or others on your healthcare team talk about your weight or your child-feeding practices, it's for your benefit.
10. Keep careful eating records—if asked. Record everything you eat and drink, including snacks, perhaps for several days. Record amounts (in cups, ounces, tablespoons, or the like) and how foods were prepared, such as "fried" or "baked." If you suspect a food sensitivity, write reactions you think may be associated with the food or beverage. *See "Food and Physical Activity Logs" in chapter 22, page 647 for other tips to keep a food record.*
11. Involve your family. If you take a nutrition class or meet with a nutrition professional, bring a family member along. Support helps ensure success.
12. Forget miracles and magic bullets. A qualified nutrition professional will focus on changes in your lifestyle and food choices, not on quick results, miracle cures, or costly and unneeded dietary supplements.
13. Follow up, as advised, so your progress can be monitored and your questions answered. A positive change in body weight, blood pressure, blood cholesterol levels, and other physical conditions may take time. With your doctor or others on your healthcare team, plan for gradual results. Follow-up visits provide moral support, too!

How to . . . Use mHealth (Mobile)

Wearable fitness devices can monitor your personal biometrics. With a few clicks on your computer or handheld mobile device, you can calculate your BMI, assess your food choices, track your vital signs and self-health care, and even get your blood glucose level assessed. Technology can also tie in to online weight-control and fitness counseling. Before you use mobile health applications, referred to as mHealth apps, consider these guidelines:

- For a reliable diagnosis and prescribed eating plan, first work with qualified healthcare providers in person to review your medical history for reliable nutrition advice. Many registered dietitian nutritionists do online counseling. As with in-person counseling, check for credentials; state licensure laws typically apply to online counseling, too.

- Use quick, online nutrition assessments and counseling, as well as web-based self-monitoring, as support, but don't replace your healthcare provider. Use mHealth to complement your health care. *See "Digital Tracking: The Benefits," below, for ways to use today's technology.*

  For some interactive online tools, visit the USDA's www.nal.usda.gov/fnic/interactive-tools. Or visit MyPlate, www.ChooseMyPlate.gov. You'll also find a kids' section for food and nutrition games, video clips, and other interactive, fun activities.

- Even on trustworthy healthcare sites that do online nutrition assessments and counseling, there's a wrinkle: privacy. To protect the privacy of your records and avoid an onslaught of e-marketing, provide personal data only on encrypted, or secured, sites. If a "closed padlock" appears on the web page, the data you provide are encrypted and secure. And pay attention to "alarms" on the site that warn you when you're moving from secure to insecure parts of the website.

Digital Tracking: The Benefits

Today's technology offers many features that can make digital tracking of food and health information easy—and offers benefits that can help you reach your goals. Digital tracking is:

- *Fast.* Once you get the hang of the technology, using digital tracking is quicker than using pen and paper.
- *Easy.* Digital trackers do the math for you, adding up calories, nutrients, activity minutes, hours of sleep, and other information you decide to track.
- *Customized.* Most tracking apps use your personal information, such as your age, weight, level of activity, and other factors to help you determine your food and fitness goals.
- *Visual.* Digital trackers can turn the data you enter into graphs and charts to help you better understand the effects of your choices and the changes over time.
- *Fun.* Games, competitions, and rewards are built into many digital tracking tools, helping you stay motivated and, perhaps, connecting you to a community of like-minded supporters.
- *Shareable.* It's easy to share your tracking information with your doctor or registered dietitian nutritionist, so he or she can help modify the recommendations and help you reassess as you work toward your health goals.

Adapted with permission from: Moyer, Meagan F and Academy of Nutrition and Dietetics. *Bits & Bytes: A Guide to Digitally Tracking Your Food, Fitness, and Health.* Chicago, IL: Eatright Press, 2016.

CREDIBLE SUPPORT FOR HEALTHY EATING

Support for good nutrition and reliable information comes from many sources, in many places, for consumers of all ages. Know that many health professional organizations have adopted social media policies, governed by a code of ethics and content integrity.

Food and Nutrition Programs: Education, Government, and Not-for-Profit Sources

Many organizations, educational institutions, and government agencies are staffed with qualified nutrition experts. These are among programs that provide reliable food or nutrition information and services. Some also provide food assistance for those in need.

Cooperative Extension Service. Each US state and territory has a Cooperative Extension office that partners with the National Institute of Food and Agriculture, USDA, at its land-grant university and in a network of local or regional offices. Extension Service provides research-based consumer information on many food, nutrition, food safety, agriculture, and waste management topics. State land-grant universities employ qualified nutrition experts among their Extension Service staff.

Access your state's Extension Service's food and nutrition information online—or check websites for similar information from other states' extension offices.

Child nutrition programs. Schools, as well as many early childhood centers, after-school programs, and summer camps, provide nutritious breakfasts, lunches, milk, and often snacks for children and teens.

The USDA Food and Nutrition Service supports and strictly regulates many of these child nutrition programs, including nutrition education in schools. With strict nutrition guidelines, these programs include the National School Lunch Program, the School Breakfast Program, the Summer Food Service Program, the Fresh Fruit and Vegetable Program, and the Special Milk Program. Administered by state agencies, these programs help fight hunger and obesity by reimbursing organizations for providing healthy meals to children. Some students qualify for free and reduced-price meals available to those in need.

The USDA's Farm to School Program also supports these school foodservice programs. It helps to bring fresh vegetables and fruits to school cafeterias. And in some schools, it gives students hands-on ways to learn food and agriculture through farm visits and nutrition education.

See "Eating Right at School" in chapter 17, page 505, for ways you can learn more about the school nutrition programs in your local school.

Supplemental Nutrition Assistance Program (SNAP). Formerly called Food Stamps, SNAP provides food assistance to low-income families and individuals to buy food and nonalcoholic beverages. Qualified households receive an electronic benefits card that is used like cash in most grocery stores and many farmers' markets. SNAP at farmers' markets gives access to fresh vegetables and fruits.

To locate a nearby SNAP office, check your county public health department or the government pages of your phone book. SNAP is administered by state agencies and funded by the USDA. In a very few US states, the Restaurant Meals Program, a voluntary program, allows qualified elderly, disabled, and homeless SNAP recipients to buy food at authorized restaurants—if they don't have a place or the ability to store and cook food or have no access to a grocery store.

Women, Infants, and Children (WIC) Program. This federal government program offers food assistance, healthcare referrals, and nutrition education to low-income women who are pregnant; postpartum (shortly after delivery) women who are breastfeeding as well as non-breastfeeding; and to infants and children up to age five years who are at nutritional risk. It also has a Farmers' Market Nutrition Program.

To reach the WIC Program, check with your county or other local public health department.

Child and Adult Care Food Program (CACFP). This federally funded USDA program helps to provide nutritious meals and snacks daily to those in child- and adult-care institutions and family or group day-care homes. Nourishing food contributes to the wellness, healthy growth, and development of young children, and the health and wellness of older adults and chronically impaired disabled persons.

CACFP is administered at the state level. To reach this program, find a day-care home sponsor, or locate a facility that participates. Check here for your state CACFP agency: www.cacfp.org/resources/usda-stage-agencies.

More senior citizens' programs. In some communities, local not-for-profit agencies offer low-cost meals along with social contact for senior citizens. To find these services, check with a social worker, health department, faith-based group, or area Agency on Aging.

USDA's Senior Farmers' Market Nutrition Program (SFMNP) offers coupons to exchange for vegetables, fruits, honey, and fresh-cut herbs at participating farmers' markets, roadside stands, and community-supported agriculture programs. The SFMNP is administered at the state level, such as your State Department of Agriculture or Agency on Aging.

Home-delivered meals. People who can't leave their homes or who can't prepare food independently may seek services for home-delivered meals. For those who qualify, government or community agencies provide meals at low cost. If you or someone you know needs this help, check with a social worker, s faith-based group, or your state or area Agency on Aging.

Soup kitchens, food pantries, and more. For those who are homeless or have limited resources for food, not-for-profit and faith-based groups may provide food assistance at no cost. Check with social workers, social agencies, and religious groups for referrals.

As a local citizen, you might also volunteer to help with many of these efforts—or help initiate them. That includes volunteering in community gardens where fresh fruit and vegetables are grown for local residents.

Health (not-for-profit) organizations. The Academy of Nutrition and Dietetics, as well as many other health-focused organizations such as the American Heart Association, the American Diabetes Association, and FARE (Food Allergy Research and Education) provide the public and health professionals with a wealth of science-based food, nutrition, and health information. Check their websites and their local organizations. They may also provide you with a gateway to other credible food, nutrition, and health websites. *See "Resources You Can Use," page 763.*

For other government and not-for-profit food assistance programs, as well as food assistance for disaster relief, talk with your doctor, Cooperative Extension office, or local public health department for referrals.

FOOD AND NUTRITION INFORMATION: SUPERMARKETS, FOOD COMPANIES, AND MORE

Need or want to know more about a food or drink product than what's on a food label? Many food companies provide information about their products, including the nutrition and ingredient content, on their websites. That information may be especially important if you're managing a health issue such as a food allergy, celiac disease, or diabetes. Many brands also offer healthy eating and lifestyle information , food handling advice, food preparation ideas, and recipes. Their website or contact information is often printed on food packages.

As another information source, many food trade and commodity organizations provide general, nonbranded information. The scope of information is typically much broader. Their websites are generally funded by those who produce and perhaps process the food such as the farmers and ranchers, and not the branded companies. Many employ registered dietitian nutritionists to develop this information.

A number of supermarkets, other retail food stores, and farmers' markets, employ registered dietitian nutritionists or other food educators. Besides providing food and nutrition information on their websites and in their stores and e-magazines, these experts may be available in store to answer your questions, give store tours, assist with special diet needs, provide cooking classes, and much more.

Food industry resources need the same scrutiny as any source of food, nutrition, and health information. For example, is it written by a qualified expert, does it cite credible sources, and does it reflect sound science and the Dietary Guidelines for Americans? Review it carefully for balance and bias. Gather other balanced and reliable perspectives for controversial issues. Be aware of the differences between truly educational and promotional resources.

* * *

As stated at the start of this book . . . "Your life is filled with choices! Every day you make thousands of choices, many related to food. Some seem trivial. Others are important. A few may even set the course of your life. But as insignificant as a single choice may seem, when made over and over, it can have a major impact on your health—and your life!"

Choices based on sound science from trustworthy sources can lead you to better health, a longer life, and overall well-being.

Resources You Can Use

Looking for sound information and guidance about food, nutrition, and physical activity? Many reliable resources—professional associations, government agencies, health agencies, and credible nutrition newsletters—provide science-based food and nutrition information on websites, apps, blogs, forums, e-newsletters, RSS feeds, podcasts, videos, consumer hotlines, and print resources. They may also deliver programs and other initiatives you might find useful. Check your local hospital, public health, Cooperative Extension Service, and many food industry groups, as well.

Note: Check the general nutrition websites for information and guidance on topics of specific interest and concern, as well as sites focused on specific issues.

General Nutrition

Academy of Nutrition and Dietetics
120 South Riverside Plaza, Suite 2190
Chicago, IL 60606-6995
www.eatright.org

Find a Registered Dietitian Nutritionist
www.eatright.org/find-an-expert

Cooperative Extension Service
Contact your state's land-grant university.

Dietitians of Canada
www.dietitians.ca

International Food Information Council Foundation (IFIC)
www.foodinsight.org

Society for Nutrition Education and Behavior
www.sneb.org

Nutrition Research

Academy of Nutrition and Dietetics
www.andevidencelibrary.com
www.eal.org (subscription)

National Library of Medicine, National Institutes of Health (NIH)
www.nlm.nih.gov

Nutrition Evidence Library, US Department of Agriculture (USDA)
www.nel.gov

PubMed, National Center for Biotechnology Information, National Library of Medicine
www.ncbi.nlm.nih.gov/pubmed

Government Resources and Programs

Consumer

Dietary Guidelines for Americans
health.gov/dietaryguidelines/2015

Let's Move!
www.letsmove.gov

MyPlate
www.ChooseMyPlate.gov

Physical Activity Guidelines for Americans
www.health.gov/paguidelines

SuperTracker
www.supertracker.usda.gov
www.supertracker.usda.gov/foodapedia.aspx

Other

US Department of Agriculture (USDA)
www.nutrition.gov
www.usda.gov

Center for Nutrition Policy and Promotion (CNPP)
www.cnpp.usda.gov

Families, Food, and Fitness, Cooperative Extension System
articles.extension.org/families_food_fitness

Food and Nutrition Information Center (FNIC)
www.nal.usda.gov/fnic

Dietary Reference Intakes (DRI) Calculator
fnic.nal.usda.gov/fnic/interactiveDRI

Individual Dietary Assessment
fnic.nal.usda.gov/dietary-guidance/individual-dietary-assessment

Interactive Tools
fnic.nal.usda.gov/dietary-guidance/interactive-tools

Food and Nutrition Service (FNS)
www.fns.usda.gov

Child and Adult Care Food Program
www.fns.usda.gov/cacfp/child-and-adult-care food-program

Child Nutrition Programs
www.fns.usda.gov/school-meals/child-nutrition-programs

Supplemental Nutrition Assistance Program (SNAP)
www.fns.usda.gov/snap

Women, Infants, and Children's (WIC) Program
www.fns.usda.gov/wic

USDA Food Composition Databases
ndb.nal.usda.gov/ndb

US Department of Health and Human Services (HHS)
www.hhs.gov

Centers for Disease Control and Prevention (CDC)
www.cdc.gov

Food and Drug Administration (FDA)
www.fda.gov

Food and Nutrition: MedlinePlus, National Library of Medicine
medlineplus.gov/foodandnutrition.html

National Institutes of Health (NIH)
www.nih.gov

Office of Disease Prevention and Health Promotion (ODPHP)
www.health.gov
www.healthfinder.gov
www.healthypeople.gov

Surgeon General
www.surgeongeneral.gov

Agriculture and Food Production*

Agricultural Research Library, USDA
www.ars.usda.gov

Alliance to Feed the Future
www.alliancetofeedthefuture.org

American Community Gardening Association
communitygarden.org

Feeding America
healthyfoodbankhub.feedingamerica.org

Food and Agriculture Organization of the United Nations
www.fao.org/themes/en

Food and Drug Administration (FDA), HHS
www.fda.gov/Food/IngredientsPackagingLabeling/FoodAdditivesIngredients/ucm094211.htm

Food Waste Reduction Alliance, Grocery Manufacturers of America
www.foodwastealliance.org

Institute of Food Technologists
www.ift.org
www.ift.org/Knowledge-Center/Learn-About-Food-Science/Food-Facts.aspx

International Food Additives Council
foodingredientfacts.org

Know Your Farmer, Know Your Food, USDA
www.usda.gov/knowyourfarmer

National Agriculture in the Classroom
www.agclassroom.org

National Aquaculture Association
thenaa.net

National Institute of Food and Agriculture, USDA
nifa.usda.gov

Soil Science of America
www.soils.org

Sustainable Agriculture Research and Education, USDA
www.sare.org

US Farmers and Ranchers Alliance
www.fooddialogues.com

USDA Organic, USDA
www.usda.gov/organic

*See "Food and Beverage Industry Associations." Many links address farm-to-fork issues.

Dietary Supplements

Dietary Supplement Ingredient Database, USDA, ODS/NIH
dietarysupplementdatabase.usda.nih.gov

Drugs, Herbs and Supplements: MedlinePlus, National Library of Medicine
medlineplus.gov/druginformation.html

Food and Drug Administration (FDA), HHS
www.fda.gov/Food/DietarySupplements

National Agricultural Library, USDA
fnic.nal.usda.gov/dietary-supplements

National Center for Complementary and Integrative Health, NIH
nccih.nih.gov

Office of Dietary Supplements (ODS), NIH
www.ods.od.nih.gov

US Pharmacopeial Convention
www.usp.org/dietary-supplements

Eating Out/Traveling

Diet Facts
dietfacts.com

Healthy Dining Finder
www.healthydiningfinder.com

National Restaurant Association
www.restaurant.org

Traveler's Health, CDC
wwwnc.cdc.gov/travel/page/resources-for-travelers

Food Preparation and Menu Planning*

***Food & Nutrition Magazine*, Academy of Nutrition and Dietetics**
www.foodandnutrition.org

What's Cooking? USDA Mixing Bowl, FNS
www.whatscooking.fns.usda.gov

*See "Food and Beverage Industry Associations." Many links address food preparation.

Food Safety and Foodborne Illness

Academy of Nutrition and Dietetics, Home Food Safety
www.eatright.org/resources/homefoodsafety

American Association of Poison Control Centers
National hotline to local centers, 1-800-222-1222
www.aapcc.org

Centers for Disease Control and Prevention (CDC)
www.cdc.gov/foodsafety

Environmental Protection Agency (EPA)
www.epa.gov

Learn About Water
www.epa.gov/learn-issues/learn-about-water

National Lead Information Center
www.epa.gov/lead

Fight Bac, Partnership for Food Safety Education
www.fightbac.org

Food and Drug Administration (FDA)
(Or contact your regional FDA office.)
www.fda.gov/food

Food Safety, CDC
cdc.gov/foodsafety

Food Safety, HHS
www.foodsafety.gov

Meat and Poultry Hotline
1-888-MPHotline (1-888-674-6854)

Food Safety and Inspection Service (FSIS), USDA
www.fsis.usda.gov
www.fsis.usda.gov/wps/portal/informational/askkaren
www.befoodsafe.gov

NSF International
www.nsf.org

Water Quality Association
www.wqa.org

Food and Nutrition Misinformation

American Council on Science and Health
www.acsh.org

Federal Trade Commission (FTC)
(Or contact your regional FTC office.)
www.consumer.ftc.gov/topics/health-fitness

National Council against Health Fraud
www.ncahf.org
www.quackwatch.org

Food Shopping, Labeling, and Marketing

Farmers Market Coalition
farmersmarketcoalition.org

Food Labeling and Nutrition, FDA
www.fda.gov/Food/IngredientsPackagingLabeling/LabelingNutrition

Food Marketing Institute (FMI)
www.fmi.org

Food Value Analysis
www.foodvalueanalysis.org

Grocery Manufacturers of America (GMA)
www.gmaonline.org

National Farmers Market Directory, USDA
www.ams.usda.gov/local-food-directories/farmersmarkets

Life Cycle Nutrition

Infants, Children, and Adolescents

Academy of Nutrition and Dietetics, Kids Eat Right
www.eatright.org/kids

Action for Healthy Kids
www.actionforhealthykids.org

American Academy of Pediatrics (AAP)
www.healthychildren.org
www.aap.org

Bright Futures
www.brightfutures.org

Centers for Disease Control and Prevention (CDC)
www.cdc.gov/breastfeeding/resources/guide.htm

Children and Teenagers: MedlinePlus, National Library of Medicine, NIH
medlineplus.gov/childrenandteenagers.html

Food and Nutrition Service (FNS), USDA
www.fns.usda.gov/wic/breastfeeding-promotion-and-support-wic

Institute of Child Nutrition
www.nfsmi.org

La Leche League International
www.lalecheleague.org

March of Dimes
www.marchofdimes.com

National Agricultural Library, USDA
www.nutrition.gov/life-stages/infants
www.nutrition.gov/life-stages/toddlers
www.nutrition.gov/life-stages/children
www.nutrition.gov/life-stages/adolescents

National Healthy Mothers, Healthy Babies Coalition
www.hmhbpbc.org

Nemours
kidshealth.org

Office on Women's Health, HHS
www.womenshealth.gov/breastfeeding

School Nutrition Association
schoolnutrition.org

We Can! National Heart, Lung, and Blood Institute: NIH
www.nhlbi.nih.gov/health/educational/wecan

Older Adults

Aging in Motion
aginginmotion.org

Alliance for Aging Research
www.agingresearch.org

American Association of Retired Persons
www.aarp.org

Elder Care Locator, HHS
www.eldercare.gov/Eldercare.NET/Public/Index.aspx

Meals on Wheels America
www.mowaa.org

National Agricultural Library, USDA
www.nutrition.gov/life-stages/seniors

National Association of Area Agencies on Aging
www.n4a.org

National Association of Nutrition and Aging Services
www.nanasp.org

National Institute on Aging, NIH
www.nia.nih.gov
go4life.nia.nih.gov/get-started

NIH Senior Health, National Library of Medicine, NIH
nihseniorhealth.gov/eatingwellasyougetolder

Seniors' Health: MedlinePlus, National Library of Medicine, NIH
medlineplus.gov/seniorshealth.html

Men

Men's Health: MedlinePlus, National Library of Medicine, NIH
www.nlm.nih.gov/medlineplus/menshealth.html

Men's Health Network
www.menshealthnetwork.org

National Agricultural Library, USDA
www.nutrition.gov/life-stages/men

*Women**

American Congress of Obstetricians and Gynecologists
www.acog.org/patients

The Endocrine Society, Menopause Map
www.hormone.org/menopausemap

National Agricultural Library, USDA
www.nutrition.gov/life-stages/women

Office on Women's Health, HHS
www.womenshealth.gov

Women's Health: MedlinePlus, National Library of Medicine, NIH
medlineplus.gov/womenshealth.html

*See "Infants, Children, and Adolescents" for links on breastfeeding.

Health Conditions and Disease Prevention/Treatment

General

American Academy of Family Physicians
familydoctor.org
www.aafp.org

American Medical Association
www.ama-assn.org

American Public Health Association
www.apha.org

Centers for Disease Control and Prevention (CDC)
www.cdc.gov

MedlinePlus, National Library of Medicine
medlineplus.gov

The National Academies of Sciences, Engineering, and Medicine; Health and Medicine Division
www.nationalacademies.org/hmd

National Health Council
www.nationalhealthcouncil.org

National Health Information Center, ODPHP, HHS
health.gov/NHIC/

National Institutes of Health, HHS
www.nih.gov

National Wellness Institute, Inc.
www.nationalwellness.org

Office of Minority Health, HHS
www.minorityhealth.hhs.gov

US Department of Health and Human Services (HHS)
www.hhs.gov
www.healthfinder.gov

Alcohol Abuse and Alcoholism

National Council on Alcoholism and Drug Dependence, Inc.
www.ncadd.org

National Institute on Alcohol Abuse and Alcoholism, NIH
www.niaaa.nih.gov

Rethinking Drinking, HHS (alcoholic beverage calculators)
rethinkingdrinking.niaaa.nih.gov/ToolsResources/CalculatorsMain.asp

Arthritis

Arthritis Foundation
www.arthritis.org

Cancer

American Cancer Society
www.cancer.org

American Institute for Cancer Research
www.aicr.org

Cancers: MedlinePlus, National Library of Medicine, NIH
medlineplus.gov/cancers.html

National Cancer Institute, NIH
www.cancer.gov

Cardiovascular (Heart) Disease

American Heart Association
www.heart.org/HEARTORG

American Stroke Association
www.strokeassociation.org/STROKEORG

DASH Eating Plan, NIH
www.nhlbi.nih.gov/health/health-topics/topics/dash
www.dashdiet.org

Heart Diseases: MedlinePlus, National Library of Medicine, NIH
medlineplus.gov/heartdiseases.html

National Heart, Lung, and Blood Institute, NIH
www.nhlbi.nih.gov

Diabetes

American Diabetes Association
www.diabetes.org

Diabetes Mellitus: MedlinePlus, National Library of Medicine, NIH
medlineplus.gov/diabetesmellitus.html

Diabetes, National Institute of Diabetes and Digestive and Kidney Diseases, HHS
www.niddk.nih.gov/health-information/diabetes

JDRF
www.jdrf.org

Joslin Diabetes Center
www.joslin.org

Digestive Diseases

Beyond Celiac
www.beyondceliac.org

Celiac Disease Foundation
celiac.org

Celiac Support Association
www.csaceliacs.org

Digestive Disease National Coalition
www.ddnc.org

Digestive Diseases, National Institute of Diabetes and Digestive and Kidney Diseases, HHS
www.niddk.nih.gov/health-information/digestive-diseases

Gluten Free Watchdog
www.glutenfreewatchdog.org

Gluten Intolerance Group
www.gluten.org

Eating Disorders

National Association of Anorexia Nervosa and Associated Disorders
www.anad.org

National Eating Disorders Organization
www.nationaleatingdisorders.org

Overeaters Anonymous
www.oa.org

*Food Allergies and Sensitivities**

American Academy of Allergy, Asthma, and Immunology
www.aaaai.org

Food Allergy Research and Education (FARE)
www.foodallergy.org

Lactose Intolerance: MedlinePlus, National Library of Medicine, NIH
medlineplus.gov/lactoseintolerance.html

SafeFARE
www.safefare.org

*See "Digestive Diseases" for more links.

Obesity/Weight

The Center for Mindful Eating
thecenterformindfuleating.org

Obesity: MedlinePlus, National Library of Medicine, NIH
medlineplus.gov/obesity.html

Weight-control Information Network, National Institute of Diabetes and Digestive and Kidney Diseases, HHS
www.niddk.nih.gov/health-information/health-communication-programs/win

Oral Health

American Academy of Periodontology
www.perio.org/consumer/gum-disease.htm

American Dental Association, Mouth Healthy (consumer)
www.mouthhealthy.org/en

Osteoporosis and Bone Health

National Osteoporosis Foundation
www.nof.org

Osteoporosis: MedlinePlus, National Library of Medicine, NIH
www.nlm.nih.gov/medlineplus/osteoporosis.html

Physical Activity and Sports Nutrition*

American College of Sports Medicine
www.acsm.org

American Council on Exercise
www.acefitness.org

American Running Association
www.americanrunning.org

International Society of Sports Nutrition
www.sportsnutritionsociety.org

National Physical Activity Plan
www.physicalactivityplan.org

President's Council on Fitness, Sports & Nutrition, HHS
www.fitness.gov

Shape America: Society of Health and Physical Educators
www.shapeamerica.org

United States Olympic Committee
www.teamusa.org/About-the-USOC/Athlete-Development/Sport-Performance/Nutrition

Women's Sports Foundation
www.womenssportsfoundation.org

YMCA of the USA
www.ymca.net

*See "Dietary Supplements" for links on supplements and sports.

Vegetarian Eating

North American Vegetarian Society
www.navs-online.org

Vegetarian Resource Group
www.vrg.org

Food and Beverage Industry Associations

Alaska Seafood Marketing Institute
www.alaskaseafood.org

Almond Board of California
www.almonds.com

American Beverage Association
www.ameribev.org

American Egg Board
www.aeb.org

American Institute for Packaging and the Environment
www.ameripen.org

American Lamb Board
www.americanlamb.com

American Veal Association
www.americanveal.com

The Barley Council of Canada
gobarley.com

Beer Institute
www.beerinstitute.org

California Avocado Commission
www.californiaavocado.com

California Dried Plum Board
www.californiadriedplums.org

California Fig Advisory Board
californiafigs.com

California Olive Committee
calolive.org

California Olive Oil Council
www.cooc.com

California Raisin Marketing Board
www.calraisins.org

California Strawberry Commission
www.calstrawberry.com

California Walnuts
www.walnuts.org

Calorie Control Council
caloriecontrol.org

Can Manufacturers Institute
www.cancentral.com

Canned Food Alliance
www.mealtime.org

Canola Council of Canada
www.canolainfo.org

Cherry Marketing Institute
www.choosecherries.com

The Cranberry Institute
www.cranberryinstitute.org

Dairy Management, Inc.
www.dairy.org

Distilled Spirits Council of the United States
www.discus.org

Egg Nutrition Center
www.eggnutritioncenter.org

Flax Council of Canada
healthyflax.org

Frozen Food Foundation
www.frozenfoodfacts.org

Georgia Pecan Commission
georgiapecans.org

The Glutamate Association
www.msgfacts.com

GMO Answers
gmoanswers.com

Grain Foods Foundation
grainfoodsfoundation.org

Infant Nutrition Council of America
infantformula.org

The Institute for Scientific Information on Coffee and Health
coffeeandhealth.org

International Bottled Water Association
www.bottledwater.org

The International Tree Nut Council Research & Education Foundation
www.nuthealth.org

Juice Products Association
juiceproducts.org

McCormick Science Institute (herbs and spices)
www.mccormickscienceinstitute.com

Mushroom Council
www.mushroomcouncil.org

National Cattlemen's Beef Association
www.beefnutrition.org
www.beefitswhatsfordinner.com

National Chicken Council
www.eatchicken.com

National Coffee Association of USA
www.ncausa.org

National Dairy Council
www.nationaldairycouncil.org

National Fisheries Institute
www.aboutseafood.com

National Frozen and Refrigerated Foods Association
www.nfraweb.org

National Pasta Association
www.ilovepasta.org

National Peanut Board
nationalpeanutboard.org

National Pork Board
www.porkbeinspired.com

National Turkey Federation
www.eatturkey.com

National Watermelon Promotion Board
www.watermelon.org

North American Meat Institute
www.meatinstitute.org

North Carolina Sweet Potato Commission
www.ncsweetpotatoes.com

Oldways Whole Grains Council
wholegrainscouncil.org

Oregon Hazelnuts
oregonhazelnuts.org

Organic Trade Association
www.ota.com

The Peanut Institute
www.peanut-institute.org

Pistachio Health Institute
www.pistachiohealthinstitute.org

Potatoes USA
www.potatoesusa.com

Produce for Better Health Foundation
www.fruitsandveggiesmorematters.org
PBHFoundation.org

Produce Marketing Association
www.pma.com

Salt Institute
www.saltinstitute.org

SNAC International (formerly Snack Food Association)
snacintl.org

The Soyfoods Council
thesoyfoodscouncil.com

The Sugar Association
www.sugar.org

Tea Association of the U.S.A., Inc.
www.teausa.org

Tuna Council
www.aboutseafood.com/tuna-council-3

United Fresh Fruit & Vegetable Association
www.unitedfresh.org

United Soybean Board
www.soyconnection.com

US Dry Bean Council
www.usdrybeans.com

US Dry Pea & Lentil Council
www.usapulses.org

US Highbush Blueberry Council
www.blueberry.org

USA Pears
usapears.com

USA Rice Federation
www.usarice.com

Wheat Foods Council
www.wheatfoods.org

Newsletters, Websites, and Blogs

Academy of Nutrition and Dietetics, *Food & Nutrition Magazine*
www.foodandnutrition.org
www.foodandnutrition.org/Nutrition-Apps

Berkeley Wellness
www.berkeleywellness.com

Best Food Facts
www.bestfoodfacts.org

Environmental Nutrition
www.environmentalnutrition.com

Mayo Clinic Health Letter
healthletter.mayoclinic.com

Nutrition 411
www.nutrition411.com

Nutrition Blog Network: Powered by Dietitians (aggregate site)
nutritionblognetwork.com

Supermarket Savvy
www.supermarketsavvy.com

Tufts University Health and Nutrition Letter
www.nutritionletter.tufts.edu

WebMD
www.webmd.com

Women's Nutrition Connection
Weill Medical College of Cornell University
www.womensnutritionconnection.com

Appendix

Physical Activity Guidelines for Americans

In addition to following a healthy eating pattern, regular physical activity is one of the most important things Americans can do to improve their health. The Physical Activity Guidelines for Americans provides a comprehensive set of recommendations for the amounts and types of physical activity needed each day, as noted below. Just as individuals can achieve a healthy eating pattern in a variety of ways that meet their personal and cultural preferences, they can engage in regular physical activity in variety of ways throughout the day and by choosing activities they enjoy.

GUIDELINES FOR AGES 6 THROUGH 17

Children and adolescents should do 60 minutes (1 hour) or more of physical activity daily.

- Aerobic: Most of the 60 or more minutes a day should be either moderate[a]- or vigorous[b]-intensity aerobic physical activity and should include vigorous-intensity physical activity at least 3 days a week.
- Muscle-strengthening[c]: As part of their 60 or more minutes of daily physical activity, children and adolescents should include muscle-strengthening physical activity on at least 3 days of the week.
- Bone strengthening[d]: As part of their 60 or more minutes of daily physical activity, children and adolescents should include bone-strengthening physical activity on at least 3 days of the week.

It is important to encourage young people to participate in physical activities that are appropriate for their age, that are enjoyable, and that offer variety.

GUIDELINES FOR AGES 18 THROUGH 64

All adults should avoid inactivity. Some physical activity is better than none, and adults who participate in any amount of physical activity at all gain some health benefits.

- For substantial health benefits, adults should do at least 150 minutes (2 hours and 30 minutes) a week of moderate-intensity[a], or 75 minutes (1 hour and 15 minutes) a week of vigorous-intensity[b] aerobic physical activity, or an equivalent combination of moderate- and vigorous-intensity aerobic activity. Aerobic activity should be performed in episodes of at least 10 minutes, and preferably, it should be spread throughout the week.
- For additional and more extensive health benefits, adults should increase their aerobic physical activity to 300 minutes (5 hours) a week of moderate-intensity[a], or 150 minutes a week of vigorous-intensity[b] aerobic physical activity, or an equivalent combination of moderate- and vigorous-intensity activity. Additional health benefits are gained by engaging in physical activity beyond this amount.
- Adults should also include muscle-strengthening[c] activities that involve all major muscle groups on 2 or more days a week.

GUIDELINES FOR AGES 65 AND OLDER

Older adults should follow the adult guidelines. When older adults cannot meet the adult guidelines, they should be as physically active as their abilities and conditions allow.

- Older adults should do exercises that maintain or improve balance if they are at risk of falling.
- Older adults should determine their level of effort for physical activity relative to their level of fitness.
- Older adults with chronic conditions should understand whether and how their conditions affect their ability to do regular physical activity safely.

[a]Moderate-intensity physical activity: Aerobic activity that increases a person's heart rate and breathing to some extent. On a scale relative to a person's capacity, moderate-intensity activity is usually a 5 to 6 on a 1-to-10 scale. Brisk walking, dancing, swimming, and bicycling on a level terrain are examples.

[b]Vigorous-intensity physical activity: Aerobic activity that greatly increases a person's heart rate and breathing. On a scale relative to a person's capacity, vigorous-intensity activity is usually a 7 to 8 on a 1-to-10 scale. Jogging, singles tennis, swimming continuous laps, and bicycling uphill are examples.

[c]Muscle-strengthening activity: Physical activity, including exercise, that increases skeletal muscle strength, power, endurance, and mass. It includes strength training, resistance training, and muscular strength and endurance exercises.

[d]Bone-strengthening activity: Physical activity that produces an impact or tension force on bones, which promotes bone growth and strength. Running, jumping rope, and lifting weights are examples.

Adapted from US Department of Health and Human Services, *2008 Physical Activity Guidelines for Americans*, Washington DC: US Department of Health and Human Services, 2008. As published in the 2015–2020 Dietary Guidelines for Americans.

Estimated Calorie Needs per Day by Age, Gender, and Physical Activity Level

The total number of calories a person needs each day varies depending on a number of factors, including age, gender, height, and level of physical activity. In addition, a need to lose, maintain, or gain weight and other factors affect how many calories should be consumed. Estimated amounts of calories needed to maintain calorie balance for various gender and age groups at three different levels of physical activity are provided here. Due to reductions in basal metabolic rate (BMR) that occur with aging, calorie needs generally decrease for adults as they age.

These estimates are based on the Estimated Energy Requirements (EER)* equations, using the reference heights (average) and reference weights (healthy) for each age-gender group. For children and adolescents, reference height and weight vary. For adults, the reference man is five feet ten inches tall and weighs 154 pounds. The reference woman is five feet four inches tall and weighs 126 pounds.

These are only estimates, and approximations of individual calorie needs can be aided with online tools such as those available at www.supertracker.usda.gov.

Males				Females[d]			
Age	Sedentary[a]	Moderately Active[b]	Active[c]	Age	Sedentary[a]	Moderately Active[b]	Active[c]
2	1,000	1,000	1,000	2	1,000	1,000	1,000
3	1,200	1,400	1,400	3	1,000	1,200	1,400
4	1,200	1,400	1,600	4	1,200	1,400	1,400
5	1,200	1,400	1,600	5	1,200	1,400	1,600
6	1,400	1,600	1,800	6	1,200	1,400	1,600
7	1,400	1,600	1,800	7	1,200	1,600	1,800
8	1,400	1,600	2,000	8	1,400	1,600	1,800
9	1,600	1,800	2,000	9	1,400	1,600	1,800
10	1,600	1,800	2,200	10	1,400	1,800	2,000
11	1,800	2,000	2,200	11	1,600	1,800	2,000
12	1,800	2,200	2,400	12	1,600	2,000	2,200
13	2,000	2,200	2,600	13	1,600	2,000	2,200
14	2,000	2,400	2,800	14	1,800	2,000	2,400
15	2,200	2,600	3,000	15	1,800	2,000	2,400
16	2,400	2,800	3,200	16	1,800	2,000	2,400
17	2,400	2,800	3,200	17	1,800	2,000	2,400
18	2,400	2,800	3,200	18	1,800	2,000	2,400
19–20	2,600	2,800	3,000	19–20	2,000	2,200	2,400
21–25	2,400	2,800	3,000	21–25	2,000	2,200	2,400
26–30	2,400	2,600	3,000	26–30	1,800	2,000	2,400
31–35	2,400	2,600	3,000	31–35	1,800	2,000	2,200
36–40	2,400	2,600	2,800	36–40	1,800	2,000	2,200
41–45	2,200	2,600	2,800	41–45	1,800	2,000	2,200
46–50	2,200	2,400	2,800	46–50	1,800	2,000	2,200
51–55	2,200	2,400	2,800	51–55	1,600	1,800	2,200
56–60	2,200	2,400	2,600	56–60	1,600	1,800	2,200
61–65	2,000	2,400	2,600	61–65	1,600	1,800	2,000
66–70	2,000	2,200	2,600	66–70	1,600	1,800	2,000
71–75	2,000	2,200	2,600	71–75	1,600	1,800	2,000
76 and up	2,000	2,200	2,400	76 and up	1,600	1,800	2,000

*The EER is the average dietary energy intake that is predicted to maintain energy balance in healthy, normal weight individuals of a defined age, gender, weight, height, and level of physical activity consistent with good health.

[a] Sedentary means a lifestyle that includes only the physical activity of independent living.

[b] Moderately active means a lifestyle equivalent to walking about 1½ to 3 miles per day at 3 to 4 miles per hour, in addition to the activities of independent living.

[c] Active means a lifestyle that includes physical activity equivalent to walking more than 3 miles per day at 3 to 4 miles per hour, in addition to the activities of independent living.

[d] Estimates for females do not include women who are pregnant or breastfeeding.

Source: Institute of Medicine, *Dietary Reference Intakes for Energy, Carbohydrate, Fiber, Fat, Fatty Acids, Cholesterol, Protein, and Amino Acids*, Washington, DC: The National Academies Press, 2002. As published in the 2015–2020 Dietary Guidelines for Americans.

How Many Calories? Figuring Your Energy Needs

How much energy does your body need in a day? For a rough guesstimate, do the following "energy math."

1. *Figure your basic energy needs (BMR) by using the following formula.* If your Body Mass Index (BMI) indicates that you're overweight, use the average weight within the healthy-weight range for your height in *"Does Your BMI Put You in a Risky Zone?" in chapter 22, page 627.*

   Healthy Weight (in pounds) × (either 10 for women or 11 for men) = **Calories for Basic Energy Needs**

2. *Figure your energy needs for physical activity.* Check the activity level that matches your lifestyle for most days of the week:

   ___ Sedentary: mainly sitting, driving a car, lying down, sleeping, standing, reading, typing, or other low-intensity activities: 20%

   ___ Light Activity (for no more than two hours daily): light exercise such as light housework, grocery shopping, or walking leisurely: 30%

   ___ Moderate Activity: moderate exercise such as heavy housework, gardening, dancing, or brisk walking (and very little sitting): 40%

   ___ Very Active: active physical sports or a labor-intensive job such as construction work: 50%

   Multiply your basic energy needs from step 1 by the percentage that matches your activity level:

   Calories for Basic Needs × % Value (for physical activity level) = **Calories for Physical Activity**

3. *Figure your energy needs for digestion and absorbing nutrients by using the following formula.*

   (Calories for Basic Needs + Calories for Physical Activity) × 10% = **Calories for Digestion and Absorbing Nutrients**

4. Add up your total energy needs by adding the calories for each purpose.

   Calories for Basic Energy Needs + Calories for Physical Activity + Calories for Digestion and Absorbing Nutrients = **Calories for Total Energy Needs**

As an example, consider this 40-year-old female, who works at a desk and walks during her lunch hour. She weighs 125 pounds, which is healthy for her height.

Basic energy needs: 125 lbs × 10 = 1,250 calories

Energy for light physical activity: 1,250 calories × 0.30 = 375 calories

Energy for digestion and absorbing nutrients: (1,250 calories + 375 calories) × 0.10 = 162.5 calories

Total energy needs: 1,250 calories + 375 calories + 162.5 calories = **1,787.5 calories** (rounded to 1,800 calories daily)

See "Estimated Calorie Needs per Day by Age, Gender, and Physical Activity Level" earlier in this appendix, page 770, for total calorie estimates.

Eating Patterns, 2015–2020 Dietary Guidelines for Americans

Healthy eating patterns support a healthy body weight and can help prevent and reduce the risk of chronic disease throughout periods of growth, development, and aging as well as during pregnancy. The following principles apply to meeting the Key Recommendations of the 2015–2020 Dietary Guidelines for Americans, *as discussed in chapter 1:* 1) an eating pattern represents the totality of all foods and beverages consumed, 2) nutritional needs should be met primarily from foods, and 3) healthy eating patterns are adaptable.

The Dietary Guidelines for Americans provides three healthy eating patterns:

- Healthy US-Style Eating Pattern, page 772
- Healthy Mediterranean-Style Eating Pattern, page 774
- Healthy Vegetarian Eating Pattern, page 775

continued on next page

Healthy US-Style Eating Pattern*

Recommended Amounts of Food from Each Food Group at Twelve Calorie Levels

The Healthy US-Style Eating Pattern is based on the types and proportions of foods Americans typically consume, but in nutrient-dense forms and appropriate amounts. It is designed to meet nutrient needs while not exceeding calorie requirements and while staying within limits for overconsumed dietary components.

This pattern meets the RDA standards for almost all nutrients. For a few nutrients (vitamin D, vitamin E, choline, potassium), amounts in the pattern are marginal or below the RDA or AI standard for many or all age-sex groups. In most cases, an intake of these nutrients below the RDA or AI is not considered to be of public health concern.

To follow this pattern, identify the appropriate calorie level for you, choose a variety of foods from each group and subgroup over time in recommended amounts, and limit choices that are not in nutrient-dense forms so that the overall calorie limit is not exceeded.

For more information and tools to use this eating pattern, go to www.ChooseMyPlate.gov and health.gov/dietaryguidelines/2015/guidelines/appendix-3. *See "A Plan for Healthy Eating: From MyPlate to Your Plate" in chapter 2, page 25, for an explanation of the food groups and the recommendations for each.*

Calorie Level of Pattern[a]	**1,000**	**1,200**	**1,400**	**1,600**	**1,800**	**2,000**	**2,200**	**2,400**	**2,600**	**2,800**	**3,000**	**3,200**
Food Group[b]	**Daily Amount**[c] **of Food from Each Group** (vegetable and protein foods subgroup amounts are per week)											
Vegetables	**1 c-eq**	**1½ c-eq**	**1½ c-eq**	**2 c-eq**	**2½ c-eq**	**2½ c-eq**	**3 c-eq**	**3 c-eq**	**3½ c-eq**	**3½ c-eq**	**4 c-eq**	**4 c-eq**
Dark-green vegetables	½ c-eq/wk	1 c-eq/wk	1 c-eq/wk	1½ c-eq/wk	1½ c-eq/wk	1½ c-eq/wk	2 c-eq/wk	2 c-eq/wk	2½ c-eq/wk	2½ c-eq/wk	2½ c-eq/wk	2½ c-eq/wk
Red and orange vegetables	2½ c-eq/wk	3 c-eq/wk	3 c-eq/wk	4 c-eq/wk	5½ c-eq/wk	5½ c-eq/wk	6 c-eq/wk	6 c-eq/wk	7 c-eq/wk	7 c-eq/wk	7½ c-eq/wk	7½ c-eq/wk
Legumes (beans and peas)	½ c-eq/wk	½ c-eq/wk	½ c-eq/wk	1 c-eq/wk	1½ c-eq/wk	1½ c-eq/wk	2 c-eq/wk	2 c-eq/wk	2½ c-eq/wk	2½ c-eq/wk	3 c-eq/wk	3 c-eq/wk
Starchy vegetables	2 c-eq/wk	3½ c-eq/wk	3½ c-eq/wk	4 c-eq/wk	5 c-eq/wk	5 c-eq/wk	6 c-eq/wk	6 c-eq/wk	7 c-eq/wk	7 c-eq/wk	8 c-eq/wk	8 c-eq/wk
Other vegetables	1½ c-eq/wk	2½ c-eq/wk	2½ c-eq/wk	3½ c-eq/wk	4 c-eq/wk	4 c-eq/wk	5 c-eq/wk	5 c-eq/wk	5½ c-eq/wk	5½ c-eq/wk	7 c-eq/wk	7 c-eq/wk
Fruits	**1 c-eq**	**1 c-eq**	**1½ c-eq**	**1½ c-eq**	**1½ c-eq**	**2 c-eq**	**2 c-eq**	**2 c-eq**	**2 c-eq**	**2½ c-eq**	**2½ c-eq**	**2½ c-eq**
Grains	**3 oz-eq**	**4 oz-eq**	**5 oz-eq**	**5 oz-eq**	**6 oz-eq**	**6 oz-eq**	**7 oz-eq**	**8 oz-eq**	**9 oz-eq**	**10 oz-eq**	**10 oz-eq**	**10 oz-eq**
Whole grains[d]	1½ oz-eq	2 oz-eq	2½ oz-eq	3 oz-eq	3 oz-eq	3 oz-eq	3½ oz-eq	4 oz-eq	4½ oz-eq	5 oz-eq	5 oz-eq	5 oz-eq
Refined grains	1½ oz-eq	2 oz-eq	2½ oz-eq	2 oz-eq	3 oz-eq	3 oz-eq	3½ oz-eq	4 oz-eq	4½ oz-eq	5 oz-eq	5 oz eq	5 oz-eq
Dairy	**2 c-eq**	**2½ c-eq**	**2½ c-eq**	**3 c-eq**	**3 c-eq**	**3 c-eq**	**3 c-eq**	**3 c-eq**	**3 c-eq**	**3 c-eq**	**3 c-eq**	**3 c-eq**
Protein foods	**2 oz-eq**	**3 oz-eq**	**4 oz-eq**	**5 oz-eq**	**5 oz-eq**	**5½ oz-eq**	**6 oz-eq**	**6½ oz-eq**	**6½ oz-eq**	**7 oz-eq**	**7 oz-eq**	**7 oz-eq**
Meats, poultry, eggs	10 oz-eq/wk	14 oz-eq/wk	19 oz-eq/wk	23 oz-eq/wk	23 oz-eq/wk	26 oz-eq/wk	28 oz-eq/wk	31 oz-eq/wk	31 oz-eq/wk	33 oz-eq/wk	33 oz-eq/wk	33 oz-eq/wk
Seafood	3 oz-eq/wk	4 oz-eq/wk	6 oz-eq/wk	8 oz-eq/wk	8 oz-eq/wk	8 oz-eq/wk	9 oz-eq/wk	10 oz-eq/wk	10 oz-eq/wk	10 oz-eq/wk	10 oz-eq/wk	10 oz-eq/wk
Nuts, seeds, soy products	2 oz-eq/wk	2 oz-eq/wk	3 oz-eq/wk	4 oz-eq/wk	4 oz-eq/wk	5 oz-eq/wk	5 oz-eq/wk	5 oz-eq/wk	5 oz-eq/wk	6 oz-eq/wk	6 oz-eq/wk	6 oz-eq/wk
Oils	**15 g**	**17 g**	**17 g**	**22 g**	**24 g**	**27 g**	**29 g**	**31 g**	**34 g**	**36 g**	**44 g**	**51 g**
Limit on Calories for Other Uses												
Calories (% of calories)[e, f]	150 (15%)	100 (8%)	110 (8%)	130 (8%)	170 (9%)	270 (14%)	280 (13%)	350 (15%)	380 (15%)	400 (14%)	470 (16%)	610 (19%)

* One of three Eating Patterns in the 2015–2020 Dietary Guidelines for Americans, *as noted on page 771.*

[a] Food intake patterns at 1,000, 1,200, and 1,400 calories are designed to meet the nutritional needs of children 2 to 8 years old. Patterns from 1,600 to 3,200 calories are designed to meet the nutritional needs of children 9 years and older, and adults. If a child 4 to 8 years of age needs more calories and, therefore, is following a pattern at 1,600 calories or more, his/her recommended amount from the dairy group should be 2.5 cups per day. Children 9 years and older and adults should not use the 1,000-, 1,200-, or 1,400-calorie patterns.

Healthy US-Style Eating Pattern *(continued)*

[b] Foods in each group and subgroup are:

Vegetables

- *Dark-green vegetables:* All fresh, frozen, and canned dark-green leafy vegetables and broccoli, cooked or raw: for example, broccoli; kale; romaine; spinach; collard, mustard, and turnip greens.
- *Red and orange vegetables:* All fresh, frozen, and canned red and orange vegetables or juice, cooked or raw: for example, carrots, pumpkin, red peppers, sweet potatoes, tomatoes, tomato juice, and winter squash.
- *Legumes (beans and peas):* All cooked from dry or canned beans and peas: for example, black beans, chickpeas, edamame (green soybeans), kidney beans, lentils, pinto beans, split peas, and white beans. Does not include green beans or green peas.
- *Starchy vegetables:* All fresh, frozen, and canned starchy vegetables: for example, cassava, corn, green lima beans, green peas, plantains, and white potatoes.
- *Other vegetables:* All other fresh, frozen, and canned vegetables, cooked or raw: for example, cabbage, celery, cucumbers, green beans, green bell peppers, iceberg lettuce, mushrooms, onions, and zucchini.

Fruits

- All fresh, frozen, canned, and dried fruits and fruit juices: for example, apples and apple juice, bananas, berries, grapes, melons, oranges and orange juice, and raisins.

Grains

- *Whole grains:* All whole grain products and whole grains used as ingredients: for example, brown rice, oatmeal, popcorn, quinoa, whole-grain cereals and crackers, and whole-wheat bread.
- *Refined grains:* All refined-grain products and refined grains used as ingredients: for example, pasta, refined-grain cereals and crackers, white breads, and white rice. Refined-grain choices should be enriched.

Dairy

- All milk, including lactose-free and lactose-reduced products and fortified soy beverages (soymilk), cheeses, dairy desserts, frozen yogurt, and yogurt. Most choices should be low fat or fat-free. Cream, cream cheese, and sour cream are not included due to their low calcium content.

Protein Foods

- All seafood, meats, poultry, eggs, nuts, and seeds. Meats and poultry should be lean or low fat, and nuts should be unsalted. Legumes (beans and peas) can be considered part of this group as well as the vegetable group, but should be counted in one group only.

[c] Food group amounts are shown in cup-equivalents (c-eq) or ounce-equivalents (oz-eq). Oils are shown in grams (g). Quantity equivalents for each food are:

- *Vegetables and fruits, 1 cup equivalent is:* 1 cup raw or cooked vegetable or fruit, 1 cup vegetable or fruit juice, 2 cups leafy salad greens, ½ cup dried fruit or vegetable.
- *Grains, 1 ounce-equivalent is:* ½ cup cooked rice, pasta, or cereal; 1 ounce dry pasta or rice; 1 medium (1-ounce) slice bread; 1 ounce ready-to-eat cereal (about 1 cup flaked cereal).
- *Dairy, 1 cup-equivalent is:* 1 cup milk, yogurt, or fortified soymilk; 1½ ounces natural cheese such as Cheddar cheese; 2 ounces processed cheese.
- *Protein foods, 1 ounce-equivalent is:* 1 ounce lean meat, poultry, or seafood; 1 egg; ¼ cup cooked beans or tofu; 1 Tbsp. peanut butter; ½ ounce nuts or seeds.

[d] Amounts of whole grains in the patterns for children are less than the minimum of 3 oz-eq in all patterns recommended for adults.

[e] All foods are assumed to be in nutrient-dense forms, lean or low-fat, and prepared without added fats, sugars, refined starches, or salt. If all food choices to meet food group recommendations are in nutrient-dense forms, a small number of calories remain within the overall calorie limit of the pattern (i.e., limit on calories for other uses). The number of these calories depends on the overall calorie limit in the pattern and the amounts of food from each food group required to meet nutritional goals.

Nutritional goals are higher for the 1,200 to 1,600 calorie patterns than for the 1,000-calorie pattern, so the limit on calories for other uses is lower in the 1,200- to 1,600-calorie patterns. Calories up to the specified limit can be used for added sugars, added refined starches, solid fats, or alcohol, or to eat more than the recommended amount of food in a food group.

The overall eating pattern also should not exceed the limits of less than 10 percent of calories from added sugars and less than 10 percent of calories from saturated fats. At most calorie levels, amounts that can be accommodated are less than these limits.

For adults of legal drinking age who choose to drink alcohol, a limit of up to one drink per day for women and up to two drinks per day for men within limits on calories for other uses applies, and calories from protein, carbohydrate, and total fats should be within the Acceptable Macronutrient Distribution Ranges (AMDRs).

[f] Values are rounded.

Source: 2015–2020 Dietary Guidelines for Americans

Healthy Mediterranean-Style Eating Pattern*

Recommended Amounts of Food from Each Food Group at Twelve Calorie Levels

The Healthy Mediterranean-Style Eating Pattern is adapted from the Healthy US-Style Eating Pattern, modifying amounts recommended from some food groups to more closely reflect eating patterns that have been associated with positive health outcomes in studies of Mediterranean-style diets.

This pattern contains more fruits and seafood and less dairy than the Healthy US-Style Eating Pattern. It is similar to the Healthy US-Style Eating Pattern in nutrient content with the exception of calcium and vitamin D. Levels of calcium and vitamin D in this pattern are lower because less dairy is included for adults. See the table footnotes for amounts of dairy recommended for children and adolescents.

To follow this pattern, identify the appropriate calorie level, choose a variety of foods from each group and subgroup over time in recommended amounts, and limit choices that are not in nutrient-dense forms so that the overall calorie limit is not exceeded.

For more information and tools to use this eating pattern, go to www.ChooseMyPlate.gov and access the following table at health.gov/dietaryguidelines/2015/guidelines/appendix-4. *See "A Plan for Healthy Eating: From MyPlate to Your Plate" and "The Mediterranean Route to Healthy Eating" in chapter 2, pages 25 and 52, for an explanation of the food groups and the recommendations for each.*

Calorie Level of Pattern[a]	**1,000**	**1,200**	**1,400**	**1,600**	**1,800**	**2,000**	**2,200**	**2,400**	**2,600**	**2,800**	**3,000**	**3,200**
Food Group[b]	**Daily Amount**[c] **of Food from Each Group** (vegetable and protein foods subgroup amounts are per week)											
Vegetables	**1 c-eq**	**1½ c-eq**	**1½ c-eq**	**2 c-eq**	**2½ c-eq**	**2½ c-eq**	**3 c-eq**	**3 c-eq**	**3½ c-eq**	**3½ c-eq**	**4 c-eq**	**4 c-eq**
Dark-green vegetables	½ c-eq/wk	1 c-eq/wk	1 c-eq/wk	1½ c-eq/wk	1½ c-eq/wk	1½ c-eq/wk	2 c-eq/wk	2 c-eq/wk	2½ c-eq/wk	2½ c-eq/wk	2½ c-eq/wk	2½ c-eq/wk
Red and orange vegetables	2½ c-eq/wk	3 c-eq/wk	3 c-eq/wk	4 c-eq/wk	5½ c-eq/wk	5½ c-eq/wk	6 c-eq/wk	6 c-eq/wk	7 c-eq/wk	7 c-eq/wk	7½ c-eq/wk	7½ c-eq/wk
Legumes (beans and peas)	½ c-eq/wk	½ c-eq/wk	½ c-eq/wk	1 c-eq/wk	1½ c-eq/wk	1½ c-eq/wk	2 c-eq/wk	2 c-eq/wk	2½ c-eq/wk	2½ c-eq/wk	3 c-eq/wk	3 c-eq/wk
Starchy vegetables	2 c-eq/wk	3½ c-eq/wk	3½ c-eq/wk	4 c-eq/wk	5 c-eq/wk	5 c-eq/wk	6 c-eq/wk	6 c-eq/wk	7 c-eq/wk	7 c-eq/wk	8 c-eq/wk	8 c-eq/wk
Other vegetables	1½ c-eq/wk	2½ c-eq/wk	2½ c-eq/wk	3½ c-eq/wk	4 c-eq/wk	4 c-eq/wk	5 c-eq/wk	5 c-eq/wk	5½ c-eq/wk	5½ c-eq/wk	7 c-eq/wk	7 c-eq/wk
Fruits	**1 c-eq**	**1 c-eq**	**1½ c-eq**	**2 c-eq**	**2 c-eq**	**2½ c-eq**	**2½ c-eq**	**2½ c-eq**	**2 ½ c-eq**	**3 c-eq**	**3 c-eq**	**3c-eq**
Grains	**3 oz-eq**	**4 oz-eq**	**5 oz-eq**	**5 oz-eq**	**6 oz-eq**	**6 oz-eq**	**7 oz-eq**	**8 oz-eq**	**9 oz-eq**	**10 oz-eq**	**10 oz-eq**	**10 oz-eq**
Whole grains[d]	1½ oz-eq	2 oz-eq	2½ oz-eq	3 oz-eq	3 oz-eq	3 oz-eq	3½ oz-eq	4 oz-eq	4½ oz-eq	5 oz-eq	5 oz-eq	5 oz-eq
Refined grains	1½ oz-eq	2 oz-eq	2½ oz-eq	2 oz-eq	3 oz-eq	3 oz-eq	3½ oz-eq	4 oz-eq	4½ oz-eq	5 oz-eq	5 oz eq	5 oz-eq
Dairy[e]	**2 c-eq**	**2½ c-eq**	**2½ c-eq**	**2 c-eq**	**2 c-eq**	**2 c-eq**	**2 c-eq**	**2½ c-eq**	**2½ c-eq**	**2½ c-eq**	**2½ c-eq**	**2½ c-eq**
Protein foods	**2 oz-eq**	**3 oz-eq**	**4 oz-eq**	**5 ½ oz-eq**	**6 oz-eq**	**6½ oz-eq**	**7 oz-eq**	**7½ oz-eq**	**7½ oz-eq**	**8 oz-eq**	**8 oz-eq**	**8 oz-eq**
Meats, poultry, eggs	10 oz-eq/wk	14 oz-eq/wk	19 oz-eq/wk	23 oz-eq/wk	23 oz-eq/wk	26 oz-eq/wk	28 oz-eq/wk	31 oz-eq/wk	31 oz-eq/wk	33 oz-eq/wk	33 oz-eq/wk	33 oz-eq/wk
Seafood[f]	3 oz-eq/wk	4 oz-eq/wk	6 oz-eq/wk	11 oz-eq/wk	15 oz-eq/wk	15 oz-eq/wk	16 oz-eq/wk	16 oz-eq/wk	17 oz-eq/wk	17 oz-eq/wk	17 oz-eq/wk	17 oz-eq/wk
Nuts, seeds, soy products	2 oz-eq/wk	2 oz-eq/wk	3 oz-eq/wk	4 oz-eq/wk	4 oz-eq/wk	5 oz-eq/wk	5 oz-eq/wk	5 oz-eq/wk	5 oz-eq/wk	6 oz-eq/wk	6 oz-eq/wk	6 oz-eq/wk
Oils	**15 g**	**17 g**	**17 g**	**22 g**	**24 g**	**27 g**	**29 g**	**31 g**	**34 g**	**36 g**	**44 g**	**51 g**
Limit on Calories for Other Uses												
Calories (% of calories)[g, h]	150 (15%)	100 (8%)	110 (8%)	140 (9%)	160 (9%)	260 (13%)	270 (12%)	300 (13%)	330 (13%)	350 (13%)	430 (14%)	570 (18%)

* One of three Eating Patterns in the 2015–2020 Dietary Guidelines for Americans, *as noted on page 771.*

[a, b, c, d] *See footnotes for Healthy U.S.-Style Eating Pattern, page 772.*

[e] Amounts of dairy recommended for children and adolescents are as follows, regardless of the calorie level of the pattern: For 2-year-olds, 2 cup-eq per day; for 3- to 8-year-olds, 2½ cup-eq per day; for 9- to 18-year-olds, 3 cup-eq per day.

[f] The US Food and Drug Administration (FDA) and the US Environmental Protection Agency (EPA) provide joint guidance regarding seafood consumption for women who are pregnant or breastfeeding and for young children. For more information, see the FDA or EPA websites www.FDA.gov/fishadvice or www.EPA.gov/fishadvice, respectively.

[g, h] *See Healthy US-Style Eating Pattern, page 772, footnotes e though f.*

Source: 2015–2020 Dietary Guidelines for Americans

Healthy Vegetarian Eating Pattern*

Recommended Amounts of Food from Each Food Group at Twelve Calorie Levels

The Healthy Vegetarian Eating Pattern is adapted from the Healthy US-Style Eating Pattern. Amounts of soy products (particularly tofu and other processed soy products), legumes, nuts, seeds, and whole grains were increased, and meats, poultry, and seafood were eliminated. Dairy and eggs were included because they were consumed by the majority of these vegetarians.

This pattern can be vegan if all dairy choices are comprised of fortified soy beverages (soymilk) or other plant-based dairy substitutes.

The current Healthy Vegetarian Eating Pattern includes changes in food group composition and amounts, based on assessing the food choices of vegetarians. This pattern is similar in meeting nutrient standards to the Healthy US-Style Eating Pattern, but somewhat higher in calcium and fiber and lower in vitamin D due to differences in the foods included.

To follow this pattern, identify the appropriate calorie level, choose a variety of foods from each group and subgroup over time in recommended amounts, and limit choices that are not in nutrient-dense forms so that the overall calorie limit is not exceeded.

For more information and tools to use this eating pattern, go to www.ChooseMyPlate.gov and access the following table at health.gov/dietaryguidelines/2015/guidelines/appendix-5. *See "A Plan for Healthy Eating: From MyPlate to Your Plate" and "The Healthy Vegetarian Way" in chapter 2, pages 25 and 53, for an explanation of the food groups and the recommendations for each.*

Calorie Level of Pattern[a]	**1,000**	**1,200**	**1,400**	**1,600**	**1,800**	**2,000**	**2,200**	**2,400**	**2,600**	**2,800**	**3,000**	**3,200**
Food Group[b]	**Daily Amount**[c] **of Food from Each Group** (vegetable and protein foods subgroup amounts are per week)											
Vegetables	**1 c-eq**	**1½ c-eq**	**1½ c-eq**	**2 c-eq**	**2½ c-eq**	**2½ c-eq**	**3 c-eq**	**3 c-eq**	**3½ c-eq**	**3½ c-eq**	**4 c-eq**	**4 c-eq**
Dark-green vegetables	½ c-eq/wk	1 c-eq/wk	1 c-eq/wk	1½ c-eq/wk	1½ c-eq/wk	1½ c-eq/wk	2 c-eq/wk	2 c-eq/wk	2½ c-eq/wk	2½ c-eq/wk	2½ c-eq/wk	2½ c-eq/wk
Red and orange vegetables	2½ c-eq/wk	3 c-eq/wk	3 c-eq/wk	4 c-eq/wk	5½ c-eq/wk	5½ c-eq/wk	6 c-eq/wk	6 c-eq/wk	7 c-eq/wk	7 c-eq/wk	7½ c-eq/wk	7½ c-eq/wk
Legumes (beans and peas)[d]	½ c-eq/wk	½ c-eq/wk	½ c-eq/wk	1 c-eq/wk	1½ c-eq/wk	1½ c-eq/wk	2 c-eq/wk	2 c-eq/wk	2½ c-eq/wk	2½ c-eq/wk	3 c-eq/wk	3 c-eq/wk
Starchy vegetables	2 c-eq/wk	3½ c-eq/wk	3½ c-eq/wk	4 c-eq/wk	5 c-eq/wk	5 c-eq/wk	6 c-eq/wk	6 c-eq/wk	7 c-eq/wk	7 c-eq/wk	8 c-eq/wk	8 c-eq/wk
Other vegetables	1½ c-eq/wk	2½ c-eq/wk	2½ c-eq/wk	3½ c-eq/wk	4 c-eq/wk	4 c-eq/wk	5 c-eq/wk	5 c-eq/wk	5½ c-eq/wk	5½ c-eq/wk	7 c-eq/wk	7 c-eq/wk
Fruits	**1 c-eq**	**1 c-eq**	**1½ c-eq**	**1½ c-eq**	**1½ c-eq**	**2 c-eq**	**2 c-eq**	**2 c-eq**	**2 c-eq**	**2½ c-eq**	**2½ c-eq**	**2½ c-eq**
Grains	**3 oz-eq**	**4 oz-eq**	**5 oz-eq**	**5½ oz-eq**	**6½ oz-eq**	**6½ oz-eq**	**7½ oz-eq**	**8½ oz-eq**	**9½ oz-eq**	**10½ oz-eq**	**10½ oz-eq**	**10½ oz-eq**
Whole grains[e]	1½ oz-eq	2 oz-eq	2½ oz-eq	3 oz-eq	3½ oz-eq	3½ oz-eq	4 oz-eq	4½ oz-eq	5 oz-eq	5½ oz-eq	5½ oz-eq	5½ oz-eq
Refined grains	1½ oz-eq	2 oz-eq	2½ oz-eq	2½ oz-eq	3 oz-eq	3 oz-eq	3½ oz-eq	4 oz-eq	4½ oz-eq	5 oz-eq	5 oz-eq	5 oz-eq
Dairy	**2 c-eq**	**2½ c-eq**	**2½ c-eq**	**3 c-eq**	**3 c-eq**	**3 c-eq**	**3 c-eq**	**3 c-eq**	**3 c-eq**	**3 c-eq**	**3 c-eq**	**3 c-eq**
Protein foods	**1 oz-eq**	**1½ oz-eq**	**2 oz-eq**	**2½ oz-eq**	**3 oz-eq**	**3½ oz-eq**	**3½ oz-eq**	**4 oz-eq**	**4½ oz-eq**	**5 oz-eq**	**5½ oz-eq**	**6 oz-eq**
Eggs	2 oz/eq-wk	3 oz/eq-wk	3 oz/eq-wk	3 oz/eq-wk	3 oz/eq-wk	3 oz/eq-wk	3 oz/eq-wk	3 oz/eq-wk	3 oz/eq-wk	4 oz/eq-wk	4 oz/eq-wk	4 oz/eq-wk
Legumes (beans and peas)[d]	1 oz/eq-wk	2 oz/eq-wk	4 oz/eq-wk	4 oz/eq-wk	6 oz/eq-wk	6 oz/eq-wk	6 oz/eq-wk	8 oz/eq-wk	9 oz/eq-wk	10 oz/eq-wk	11 oz/eq-wk	12 oz/eq-wk
Soy products	2 oz/eq-wk	3 oz/eq-wk	4 oz/eq-wk	6 oz/eq-wk	6 oz/eq-wk	8 oz/eq- wk	8 oz/eq-wk	9 oz/eq-wk	10 oz/eq-wk	11 oz/eq-wk	12 oz/eq-wk	13 oz/eq-wk
Nuts, seeds, soy products	2 oz/eq-wk	2 oz/eq-wk	3 oz/eq-wk	5 oz/eq-wk	6 oz/eq-wk	7 oz/eq-wk	7 oz/eq-wk	8 oz/eq-wk	9 oz/eq-wk	10 oz/eq-wk	12 oz/eq-wk	13 oz/eq-wk
Oils	**15 g**	**17 g**	**17 g**	**22 g**	**24 g**	**27 g**	**29 g**	**31 g**	**34 g**	**36 g**	**44 g**	**51 g**
Limit on Calories for Other Uses												
Calories (% of calories)[f, g]	190 (19%)	170 (14%)	190 (14%)	180 (11%)	190 (11%)	290 (15%)	330 (15%)	390 (16%)	390 (15%)	400 (14%)	440 (15%)	550 (17%)

* One of three Eating Patterns in the 2015–2020 Dietary Guidelines for Americans, *as noted on page 771.*

[a, b, c] *See footnotes for Healthy US-Style Eating Pattern, page 772.*

[d] About half of total legumes are shown as vegetables, in cup-eq, and half as protein foods, in oz-eq. Total legumes in the patterns, in cup-eq, is the amount in the vegetable group plus the amount in the protein foods group (in oz-eq) divided by 4:

Calorie Level of Pattern[a]	1,000	1,200	1,400	1,600	1,800	2,000	2,200	2,400	2,600	2,800	3,000	3,200
Total Legumes (beans and peas) (c-eq/wk)	1	1	1½	2	3	3	3½	4	5	5	6	6

[e, f, g] *See Healthy US-Style Eating Pattern, page 772, footnotes d through f.*

Source: 2015–2020 Dietary Guidelines for Americans

DASH Eating Plan at Various Calorie Levels

The number of daily servings in a food group varies depending on calorie needs. Patterns from 1,600 to 3,100 calories meet the nutritional needs of adults. *See "DASH to Health" in chapter 2, page 51, for an explanation of this eating plan.*

	Number of Daily Servings by Calorie Level (unless the amount is noted per week)							
Food Group	**1,200 Calories**	**1,400 Calories**	**1,600 Calories**	**1,800 Calories**	**2,000 Calories**	**2,600 Calories**	**3,100 Calories**	**Serving Sizes**
Grains[a]	4 to 5	5 to 6	6	6	6 to 8	10 to 11	12 to 13	1 slice bread 1 oz. dry cereal[b] ½ cup cooked rice, pasta, or cereal[b]
Vegetables	3 to 4	3 to 4	3 to 4	4 to 5	4 to 5	5 to 6	6	1 cup raw leafy vegetable ½ cup cut-up raw or cooked vegetable ½ cup vegetable juice
Fruits	3 to 4	4	4	4 to 5	4 to 5	5 to 6	6	1 medium fresh fruit ¼ cup dried fruit ½ cup fresh, frozen, or canned fruit ½ cup fruit juice
Fat-free or low-fat milk and milk products[c]	2 to 3	2 to 3	2 to 3	2 to 3	2 to 3	3	3 to 4	1 cup milk or yogurt 1½ oz. cheese
Lean meats, poultry, and fish	3 or less	3 to 4 or less	3 to 4 or less	6 or less	6 or less	6 or less	6 to 9	1 oz. cooked meat, poultry, or fish 1 egg
Nuts, seeds, and legumes	3 per week	3 per week	3 to 4 per week	4 per week	4 to 5 per week	1	1	⅓ cup or 1½ oz. nuts 2 Tbsp. peanut butter 2 Tbsp. or ½ oz. seeds ½ cup cooked legumes (dried beans or peas)
Fats and oils[d]	1	1	2	2 to 3	2 to 3	3	4	1 tsp. soft margarine 1 tsp. vegetable oil 1 Tbsp. mayonnaise 1 Tbsp. salad dressing
Sweets and added sugars	3 or less per week	3 or less per week	3 or less per week	5 or less per week	5 or less per week	2 or less	2 or less	1 Tbsp. sugar 1 Tbsp. jelly or jam ½ cup sorbet or gelatin 1 cup lemonade
Maximum sodium limit[e]	2,300 mg/day	2,300 mg/day	2,300 mg/day	2,300 mg/day	2,300 mg/day	2,300 mg/day	2,300 mg/day	

[a] Whole grains are recommended for most grain servings as a good source of fiber and nutrients.

[b] Serving sizes vary between ½ cup and 1¼ cups, depending on cereal type. Check the Nutrition Facts label.

[c] For lactose intolerance, try either lactase enzyme pills with dairy products or lactose-free or lactose-reduced milk.

[d] Fat content changes the serving amount for fats and oils. For example, 1 Tbsp. regular salad dressing = one serving; 1 Tbsp. low-fat dressing = one-half serving; 1 Tbsp. fat-free dressing = zero servings.

[e] The DASH eating plan has a sodium limit of either 2,300 mg or 1,500 mg per day. *See "DASH to Health" in chapter 2, page 51, and "DASH for Better Blood Pressure" in chapter 24, page 697, to learn about the blood-pressure lowering benefits of lowered sodium levels.*

Source: www.nhlbi.nih.gov/health/health-topics/topics/dash/followdash. Accessed December 1, 2016.

BMI: What Does It Mean?

Body mass index (BMI) is a useful tool that can be used to estimate an individual's body weight status in relation to health risk. *See "Body Mass Index" in chapter 22, page 627, for a BMI chart and for an explanation and how to determine adult BMI.*

The terms "overweight" and "obese" describe weight ranges that are greater that what is considered healthy for a given height, while "underweight" describes a weight that is lower than what is considered healthy for a given height. These categories are a guide, and some people at a healthy weight also may have weight-responsive health conditions. Those with higher BMIs may have a higher composition of muscle, which accounts for added weight.

BMI charts for adults are not meant for children or teens. For that reason, growth charts, using BMIs and percentiles, were developed by the Centers for Disease Control and Prevention for girls and boys aged two through twenty to track their growth based on BMI.

BMI/growth charts are not meant to diagnose a child's or teen's weight status. BMI is, however, a reliable indicator of body fatness for most children and teens; it does not measure body fat. Because children and adolescents are growing, their BMI is plotted on growth charts for their gender and age. Their weight changes as they grow, even month by month. The percentile indicates the relative position of the child's BMI among children of the same gender and age. (A child and adolescent BMI calculator is available at nccd.cdc.gov/dnpabmi/calculator.aspx.) Healthcare professionals use these charts to track a child's or teen's growth over time. Your doctor should determine if your child has a weight problem and what action to take, if any, by considering many factors, not just BMI.

Weight Status	Children and Adolescents (BMI for Age Percentile Range)	Adults (BMI)
Underweight	Less than the 5th percentile	Less than 18.5
Healthy weight	5th percentile to less than the 85th percentile	18.5 to 24.9
Overweight	85th percentile to less than the 95th percentile	25.0 to 29.9
Obese	Equal to or greater than the 95th percentile	30.0 or greater

Source: Centers for Disease Control and Prevention

CDC Growth Charts

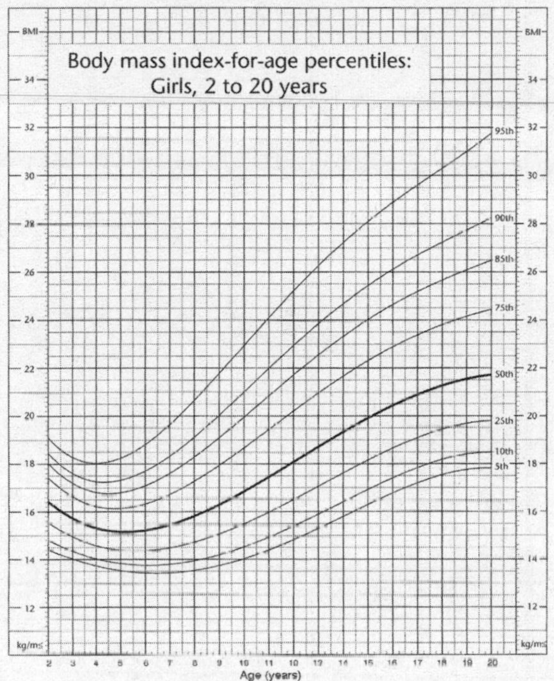

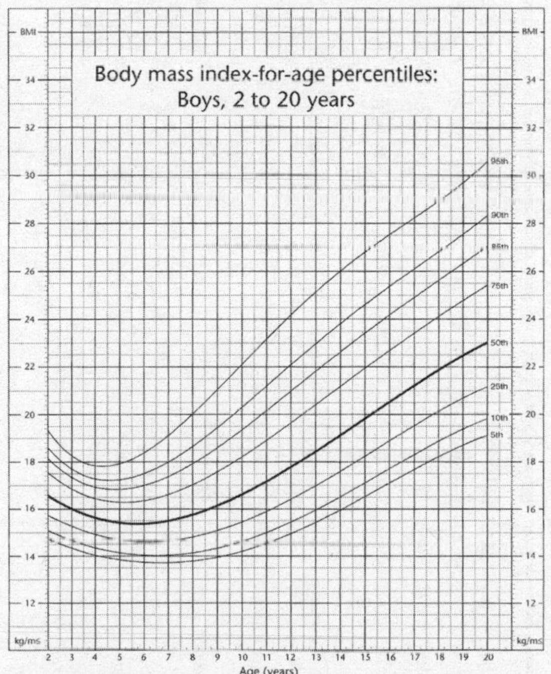

Source: Centers for Disease Control and Prevention, National Center for Health Statistics, CDC 2000 Growth Charts: United States. www.cdc.gov/growthcharts. Accessed November 30, 2016.

Sample Menus for a 2,000-Calorie Food Pattern

These seven-day menus are motivational tools to help put a healthy eating pattern into practice and to identify creative ideas for healthy meals. Averaged over a week, these menus provide the recommended amounts of key nutrients and foods from each food group. The menus feature many different foods to inspire ideas for adding variety to food choices. They are not intended to be followed day to day as a specific prescription for what to eat. Spices and herbs can be added for flavor. For sample two-week menus, go to:

choosemyplate-prod.asureedge.net/sites/default/files/budget/2WeekMenusAndFoodGroupContent.pdf

Day 1	Day 2	Day 3	Day 4	Day 5	Day 6	Day 7
Breakfast Creamy oatmeal (cooked in milk): *½ cup uncooked oatmeal* *1 cup fat-free milk* *2 Tbsp. raisins* *2 tsp. brown sugar* Beverage: 1 cup orange juice	**Breakfast** Breakfast burrito: *1 flour tortilla (8-in. diameter)* *1 scrambled egg* *⅓ cup black beans** *1 Tbsp. salsa* ½ large grapefruit Beverage: 1 cup water, coffee, or tea†	**Breakfast** Cold cereal: *1 cup ready-to-eat oat cereal* *1 medium banana* *½ cup fat-free milk* 1 slice whole-wheat toast *1 tsp. tub margarine* Beverage: 1 cup prune juice	**Breakfast** 1 whole-wheat English muffin *1 Tbsp. all-fruit preserves* 1 hard-cooked egg Beverage: 1 cup water, coffee, or tea†	**Breakfast** Cold cereal: *1 cup shredded wheat* *½ cup sliced banana* *½ cup fat-free milk* 1 slice whole-wheat toast *2 tsp. all-fruit preserves* Beverage: 1 cup fat-free chocolate milk	**Breakfast** French toast: *2 slices whole-wheat bread* *3 Tbsp. fat-free milk and ⅔ egg (in French toast)* *2 tsp. tub margarine* *1 Tbsp. pancake syrup* ½ large grapefruit Beverage: 1 cup fat-free milk	**Breakfast** Buckwheat pancakes with berries: *2 large (7 in.) pancakes* *1 Tbsp. pancake syrup* *¼ cup sliced strawberries* Beverage: 1 cup orange juice
Lunch Taco salad: *2 oz tortilla chips* *2 oz. cooked ground turkey* *2 tsp. corn/ canola oil (to cook turkey)* *¼ cup kidney beans** *½ oz. low-fat cheddar cheese* *½ cup chopped lettuce* *½ cup avocado* *1 tsp. lime juice (on avocado)* *2 Tbsp. salsa* Beverage: 1 cup water, coffee, or tea†	**Lunch** Roast beef sandwich: *1 small whole grain hoagie bun* *2 oz. lean roast beef* *1 slice part-skim mozzarella cheese* *2 slices tomato* *¼ cup mushrooms* *1 tsp. corn/canola oil (to cook mushrooms)* *1 tsp. mustard* Baked potato wedges: *1 cup potato wedges* *1 tsp. corn/canola oil (to cook potato)* *1 Tbsp. ketchup* Beverage: 1 cup fat-free milk	**Lunch** Tuna salad sandwich: *2 slices rye bread* *2 oz. tuna* *1 Tbsp. mayonnaise* *1 Tbsp. chopped celery* *½ cup shredded lettuce* 1 medium peach Beverage: 1 cup fat-free milk	**Lunch** White bean-vegetable soup: *1¼ cup chunky vegetable soup with pasta* *½ cup white beans** 6 saltine crackers* ½ cup celery sticks Beverage: 1 cup fat-free milk	**Lunch** Turkey sandwich: *1 whole-wheat pita bread (2 oz.)* *3 oz. roasted turkey, sliced* *2 slices tomato* *¼ cup shredded lettuce* *1 tsp. mustard* *1 Tbsp. mayonnaise* ¼ cup grapes Beverage: 1 cup tomato juice*	**Lunch** 3-bean vegetarian chili on baked potato: *¼ cup each cooked kidney beans,* navy beans,* and black beans** *½ cup tomato sauce** *¼ cup chopped onion* *2 Tbsp. chopped jalapeno peppers* *1 tsp. corn/canola oil (to cook onion and peppers)* *¼ cup cheese sauce* *1 large baked potato* ½ cup cantaloupe Beverage: 1 cup water, coffee, or tea†	**Lunch** New England clam chowder: *3 oz. canned clams* *½ small potato* *2 Tbsp. chopped onion* *2 Tbsp. chopped celery* *6 Tbsp. evaporated milk* *¼ cup fat-free milk* *1 slice bacon* *1 Tbsp. white flour* 10 whole-wheat crackers* 1 medium orange Beverage: 1 cup fat-free milk

Day 1	Day 2	Day 3	Day 4	Day 5	Day 6	Day 7
Dinner Spinach lasagna roll-ups: *1 cup lasagna noodles (2 oz. dry)* *½ cup cooked spinach* *½ cup ricotta cheese* *1 oz. part-skim mozzarella cheese* *½ cup tomato sauce** 1 oz. whole-wheat roll *1 tsp. tub margarine* Beverage: 1 cup fat-free milk	**Dinner** Baked salmon on beet greens: *4 oz. salmon fillet* *1 tsp. olive oil* *2 tsp. lemon juice* *⅓ cup cooked beet greens (sautéed in 2 tsp. corn/canola oil)* Quinoa with almonds: *½ cup quinoa* *½ oz. slivered almonds* Beverage: 1 cup fat-free milk	**Dinner** Roasted chicken: *3 oz. cooked chicken breast* 1 large sweet potato, roasted ½ cup succotash (limas and corn) *1 tsp. tub margarine* 1 oz. whole-wheat roll *1 tsp. tub margarine* Beverage: 1 cup water, coffee, or tea†	**Dinner** Rigatoni with meat sauce: *1 cup rigatoni pasta (2 oz. dry)* *2 oz. cooked ground beef (95% lean)* *2 tsp. corn/canola oil (to cook beef)* *½ cup tomato sauce** *3 Tbsp. grated parmesan cheese* Spinach salad: *1 cup raw spinach leaves* *½ cup tangerine sections* *½ oz. chopped walnuts* *2 tsp. oil and vinegar dressing* Beverage: 1 cup water, coffee, or tea†	**Dinner** Steak and potatoes: *4 oz. broiled beef steak* *⅔ cup mashed potatoes made with milk and 2 tsp. tub margarine* ½ cup cooked green beans *1 tsp. tub margarine* *1 tsp. honey* 1 oz. whole-wheat roll *1 tsp. tub margarine* Frozen yogurt and berries: *½ cup frozen yogurt (chocolate)* *¼ cup sliced strawberries* Beverage: 1 cup fat-free milk	**Dinner** Hawaiian pizza: *2 slices cheese pizza, thin crust* *1 oz. lean ham* *¼ cup pineapple* *¼ cup mushrooms* *1 tsp. safflower oil (to cook mushrooms)* Green salad: *1 cup mixed salad greens* *4 tsp. oil and vinegar dressing* Beverage: 1 cup fat-free milk	**Dinner** Tofu-vegetable stir-fry: *4 oz. firm tofu* *½ cup chopped Chinese cabbage* *¼ cup sliced bamboo shoots* *1 Tbsp. chopped sweet red peppers* *2 Tbsp. chopped green peppers* *1 Tbsp. corn/canola oil (to cook stir-fry)* *1 cup cooked brown rice (2 oz. raw)* Honeydew yogurt cup: *¾ cup honeydew melon* *½ cup plain fat-free yogurt* Beverage: 1 cup water, coffee, or tea†
Snacks 2 Tbsp. raisins 1 oz. unsalted almonds	**Snacks** 1 cup cantaloupe balls	**Snacks** ¼ cup dried apricots 1 cup flavored yogurt (chocolate)	**Snacks** 1 cup nonfat fruit yogurt	**Snacks** 1 cup frozen yogurt (chocolate) Beverage: 1 cup fat-free milk	**Snacks** 3 Tbsp. hummus 5 whole-wheat crackers*	**Snacks** 1 large banana spread with 2 Tbsp. peanut butter* 1 cup nonfat fruit yogurt

*Foods that are reduced sodium, low sodium, or no-salt added products. These foods can also be prepared from scratch with no added salt. All other foods are regular commercial products, which contain variable levels of sodium. The average sodium level of the seven-day menu assumes that no salt is added in cooking or at the table.

†Unless indicated, all beverages are unsweetened and without added cream or whitener.

Italicized foods are part of the dish or food that precedes it.

Source: www.ChooseMyPlate.gov

Alcoholic Drink-Equivalents of Select Beverages

The Dietary Guidelines for Americans defines a reference/standard drink[a] for regulatory purposes as a 12-ounce beer (5% alcohol), 5 ounces of wine (12% alcohol), or 1.5 ounces of 80-proof spirits. However, the alcohol content of packaged and mixed drinks varies, depending on the percentage of alcohol per volume of beer, wine, or spirits; the recipe if it's a mixed drink; and the size of the drink.

That's why a 12-ounce beer at 4.2 percent alcohol is less (0.8 drink) than one drink equivalent. A classic martini—made with 3 ounces of gin plus 0.5 ounce vermouth, both at 40 percent alcohol—add up to more than twice (2.3 drinks) that of a standard drink.

To consume alcoholic drinks in moderation, as advised by the Dietary Guidelines, you need to know the alcohol equivalent of whatever you drink. This chart shows how common alcoholic drinks compare to a standard drink (noted as 1 drink equivalent),[a] You can also do the calculation, as shown in the footnote below,[b] to figure how other alcoholic drinks compare to a standard drink.

Drink Description	Drink Equivalents[b]
Beer, beer coolers, and malt beverages	
12 fl. oz. at 4.2% alcohol (light beer)[c]	0.8
12 fl. oz. at 5% alcohol (reference/standard beverage)	1
16 fl. oz. at 5% alcohol	1.3
12 fl. oz. at 7% alcohol	1.4
12 fl. oz. at 9% alcohol	1.8
Wine	
5 fl. oz. at 12% alcohol (reference/standard beverage)	1
9 fl. oz. at 12% alcohol	1.8
5 fl. oz. at 15% alcohol	1.3
5 fl. oz. at 17% alcohol	1.4

Drink Description	Drink Equivalents[b]
Distilled spirits	
1.5 fl. oz. 80 proof distilled spirits (40% alcohol) (reference/standard beverage)	1
Mixed drink with more than 1.5 fl oz 80 proof distilled spirits (40% alcohol)	> 1[d]

[a] One alcoholic drink-equivalent is defined as containing 14 grams (0.6 fl. oz.) of pure alcohol. Drink-equivalents are not intended as a standard drink definition for regulatory purposes.

[b] To calculate drink equivalents, use the following formula. For example, a 16-fl.-oz. beer at 5% alcohol is 1.3 drink-equivalents. Here is how it is calculated:

(Volume of Beverage in Ounces	×	Alcohol Content in Percentage by Volume (ABV))	÷	0.6 Ounces of Alcohol per Drink-Equivalent	=	1 Drink-Equivalent
(16	×	0.05)	÷	0.6	=	1.3

[c] Light beer represents a substantial proportion of alcholic beverages consumed in the United States. Light beer is approximately 4.2% alcohol or 0.8 alcoholic drink-equivalents in 12 fluid ounces.

[d] Depending on factors, such as the type of spirits and the recipe, one mixed drink can contain a variable number of drink-equivalents.

Source: 2015–2020 Dietary Guidelines for Americans.

Dietary Reference Intakes

The Dietary Reference Intakes (DRIs) are nutrient reference values developed by the Institute of Medicine of The National Academies (now called The National Academies of Sciences, Engineering, and Medicine; Health and Medicine Division). They are intended to serve as a guide for good nutrition and provide the scientific basis for the development of eating guidelines in both the United States and Canada. These nutrient reference values are specified on the basis of age, gender and life stage, and cover more than 40 nutrient substances.

Pages 782 to 785 provide charts for the Recommended Dietary Allowances (RDAs) and Adequate Intakes (AIs) for water, macronutrients, vitamins, and elements (minerals), as well as Tolerable Upper Intake Levels (ULs) for vitamins and elements. The Acceptable Macronutrient Distribution Ranges (AMDRs) for Fat, Carbohydrate, and Protein are also provided. For other DRI charts, see www.nationalacademies.org/hmd/Activities/Nutrition/SummaryDRIs/DRI-Tables.aspx.

DRIs: Recommended Intakes for Individuals, Total Water and Macronutrients

Food and Nutrition Board, Institute of Medicine, National Academies

Life Stage Group	*Total* Water[a] (L/d)	Carbohydrate (g/d)	Total Fiber (g/d)	Fat (g/d)	Linoleic Acid (g/d)	α-Linolenic Acid (g/d)	Protein[b] (g/d)
Infants							
0 to 6 mo	0.7*	60*	ND	31*	4.4*	0.5*	9.1*
6 to 12 mo	0.8*	95*	ND	30*	4.6*	0.5*	**11.0**
Children							
1–3 y	1.3*	**130**	19*	ND[c]	7*	0.7*	**13**
4–8 y	1.7*	**130**	25*	ND	10*	0.9*	**19**
Males							
9–13 y	2.4*	**130**	31*	ND	12*	1.2*	**34**
14–18 y	3.3*	**130**	38*	ND	16*	1.6*	**52**
19–30 y	3.7*	**130**	38*	ND	17*	1.6*	**56**
31–50 y	3.7*	**130**	38*	ND	17*	1.6*	**56**
51–70 y	3.7*	**130**	30*	ND	14*	1.6*	**56**
> 70 y	3.7*	**130**	30*	ND	14*	1.6*	**56**
Females							
9–13 y	2.1*	**130**	26*	ND	10*	1.0*	**34**
14–18 y	2.3*	**130**	26*	ND	11*	1.1*	**46**
19–30 y	2.7*	**130**	25*	ND	12*	1.1*	**46**
31–50 y	2.7*	**130**	25*	ND	12*	1.1*	**46**
51–70 y	2.7*	**130**	21*	ND	11*	1.1*	**46**
> 70 y	2.7*	**130**	21*	ND	11*	1.1*	**46**
Pregnancy							
14–18 y	3.0*	**175**	28*	ND	13*	1.4*	**71**
19–30 y	3.0*	**175**	28*	ND	13*	1.4*	**71**
31–50 y	3.0*	**175**	28*	ND	13*	1.4*	**71**
Lactation							
14–18	3.8*	**210**	29*	ND	13*	1.3*	**71**
19–30 y	3.8*	**210**	29*	ND	13*	1.3*	**71**
31–50 y	3.8*	**210**	29*	ND	13*	1.3*	**71**

NOTE: This table (take from the DRI reports, see www.nap.edu) presents Recommended Dietary Allowances (RDA) in **bold type** and Adequate Intakes (AI) in ordinary type followed by an asterisk (*). An RDA is the average daily dietary intake level; sufficient to meet the nutrient requirements of nearly all (97-98 percent) healthy individuals in a group. It is calculated from an Estimated Average Requirement (EAR). If sufficient scientific evidence is not available to establish an EAR, and thus calculate an RDA, an AI is usually developed. For healthy breastfed infants, an AI is the mean intake. The AI for other life stage and gender groups is believed to cover the needs of all healthy individuals in the groups, but lack of data or uncertainty in the data prevent being able to specify with confidence the percentage of individuals covered by this intake.

[a] *Total* water includes all water contained in food, beverages, and drinking water.

[b] Based on g protein per kg of body weight for the reference body weight, e.g., for adults 0.8 g/kg body weight for the reference body weight.

[c] Not determined.

Dietary Reference Intakes (DRIs): Acceptable Macronutrient Distribution Ranges

Food and Nutrition Board, Institute of Medicine, National Academies

Macronutrient	Range (percent of energy) Children, 1–3 y	Children, 4–18 y	Adults
Fat	30–40	25–35	20–35
n-6 polyunsaturated fatty acids[a] (linoleic acid)	5–10	5–10	5–10
n-3 polyunsaturated fatty acids[a] (α-linolenic acid)	0.6–1.2	0.6–1.2	0.6–1.2
Carbohydrate	45–65	45–65	45–65
Protein	5–20	10–30	10–35

[a] Approximately 10% of the total can come from longer-chain *n*-3 or *n*-6 fatty acids.

Dietary Reference Intakes (DRIs): Recommended Dietary Allowances and Adequate Intakes, Vitamins

Food and Nutrition Board, Institute of Medicine, National Academies

Life Stage Group	Vitamin A (μg/d)[a]	Vitamin C (mg/d)	Vitamin D (μg/d)[b,c]	Vitamin E (mg/d)[d]	Vitamin K (μg/d)	Thiamin (mg/d)	Riboflavin (mg/d)	Niacin (mg/d)[e]	Vitamin B_6 (mg/d)	Folate (μg/d)[f]	Vitamin B_{12} (μg/d)	Pantothenic Acid (mg/d)	Biotin (μg/d)	Choline (mg/d)[g]
Infants														
0 to 6 mo	400*	40*	10	4*	2.0*	0.2*	0.3*	2*	0.1*	65*	0.4*	1.7*	5*	125*
6 to 12 mo	500*	50*	10	5*	2.5*	0.3*	0.4*	4*	0.3*	80*	0.5*	1.8*	6*	150*
Children														
1–3 y	300	15	15	6	30*	0.5	0.5	6	0.5	150	0.9	2*	8*	200*
4–8 y	400	25	15	7	55*	0.6	0.6	8	0.6	200	1.2	3*	12*	250*
Males														
9–13 y	600	45	15	11	60*	0.9	0.9	12	1.0	300	1.8	4*	20*	375*
14–18 y	900	75	15	15	75*	1.2	1.3	16	1.3	400	2.4	5*	25*	550*
19–30 y	900	90	15	15	120*	1.2	1.3	16	1.3	400	2.4	5*	30*	550*
31–50 y	900	90	15	15	120*	1.2	1.3	16	1.3	400	2.4	5*	30*	550*
51–70 y	900	90	15	15	120*	1.2	1.3	16	1.7	400	2.4[h]	5*	30*	550*
> 70 y	900	90	20	15	120*	1.2	1.3	16	1.7	400	2.4[h]	5*	30*	550*
Females														
9–13 y	600	45	15	11	60*	0.9	0.9	12	1.0	300	1.8	4*	20*	375*
14–18 y	700	65	15	15	75*	1.0	1.0	14	1.2	400[i]	2.4	5*	25*	400*
19–30 y	700	75	15	15	90*	1.1	1.1	14	1.3	400[i]	2.4	5*	30*	425*
31–50 y	700	75	15	15	90*	1.1	1.1	14	1.3	400[i]	2.4	5*	30*	425*
51–70 y	700	75	15	15	90*	1.1	1.1	14	1.5	400	2.4[h]	5*	30*	425*
> 70 y	700	75	20	15	90*	1.1	1.1	14	1.5	400	2.4[h]	5*	30*	425*
Pregnancy														
14–18 y	750	80	15	15	75*	1.4	1.4	18	1.9	600[j]	2.6	6*	30*	450*
19–30 y	770	85	15	15	90*	1.4	1.4	18	1.9	600[j]	2.6	6*	30*	450*
31–50 y	770	85	15	15	90*	1.4	1.4	18	1.9	600[j]	2.6	6*	30*	450*
Lactation														
14–18 y	1,200	115	15	19	75*	1.4	1.6	17	2.0	500	2.8	7*	35*	550*
19–30 y	1,300	120	15	19	90*	1.4	1.6	17	2.0	500	2.8	7*	35*	550*
31–50 y	1,300	120	15	19	90*	1.4	1.6	17	2.0	500	2.8	7*	35*	550*

NOTE: This table (taken from the DRI reports, see www.nap.edu) presents Recommended Dietary Allowances (RDAs) in **bold type** and Adequate Intakes (AIs) in ordinary type followed by an asterisk (*). An RDA is the average daily dietary intake level; sufficient to meet the nutrient requirements of nearly all (97-98 percent) healthy individuals in a group. It is calculated from an Estimated Average Requirement (EAR). If sufficient scientific evidence is not available to establish an EAR, and thus calculate an RDA, an AI is usually developed. For healthy breastfed infants, an AI is the mean intake. The AI for other life stage and gender groups is believed to cover the needs of all healthy individuals in the groups, but lack of data or uncertainty in the data prevent being able to specify with confidence the percentage of individuals covered by this intake.

[a] As retinol activity equivalents (RAEs). 1 RAE = 1 μg retinol, 12 μg β-carotene, 24 μg α-carotene, or 24 μg β-cryptoxanthin. The RAE for dietary provitamin A carotenoids is two-fold greater than retinol equivalents (RE), whereas the RAE for preformed vitamin A is the same as RE.

[b] As cholecalciferol. 1 μg cholecalciferol = 40 IU vitamin D.

[c] Under the assumption of minimal sunlight.

[d] As α-tocopherol. α-Tocopherol includes *RRR*-α-tocopherol, the only form of α-tocopherol that occurs naturally in foods, and the 2*R*-stereoisomeric forms of α-tocopherol (*RRR*-, *RSR*-, *RRS*-, and *RSS*-α-tocopherol) that occur in fortified foods and supplements. It does not include the 2*S*-stereoisomeric forms of α-tocopherol (*SRR*-, *SSR*-, *SRS*-, and *SSS*-α-tocopherol), also found in fortified foods and supplements.

[e] As niacin equivalents (NE). 1 mg of niacin = 60 mg of tryptophan; 0–6 months = preformed niacin (not NE).

[f] As dietary folate equivalents (DFE). 1 DFE = 1 μg food folate = 0.6 μg of folic acid from fortified food or as a supplement consumed with food = 0.5 μg of a supplement taken on an empty stomach.

[g] Although AIs have been set for choline, there are few data to assess whether a dietary supply of choline is needed at all stages of the life cycle, and it may be that the choline requirement can be met by endogenous synthesis at some of these stages.

[h] Because 10 to 30 percent of older people may malabsorb food-bound B_{12}, it is advisable for those older than 50 years to meet their RDA mainly by consuming foods fortified with B_{12} or a supplement containing B_{12}.

[i] In view of evidence linking folate intake with neural tube defects in the fetus, it is recommended that all women capable of becoming pregnant consume 400 μg from supplements or fortified foods in addition to intake of food folate from a varied diet.

[j] It is assumed that women will continue consuming 400 μg from supplements or fortified food until their pregnancy is confirmed and they enter prenatal care, which ordinarily occurs after the end of the periconceptional period—the critical time for formation of the neural tube.

SOURCES: *Dietary Reference Intakes for Calcium, Phosphorous, Magnesium, Vitamin D, and Fluoride* (1997); *Dietary Reference Intakes for Thiamin, Riboflavin, Niacin, Vitamin B_6, Folate, Vitamin B_{12}, Pantothenic Acid, Biotin, and Choline* (1998); *Dietary Reference Intakes for Vitamin C, Vitamin E, Selenium, and Carotenoids* (2000); *Dietary Reference Intakes for Vitamin A, Vitamin K, Arsenic, Boron, Chromium, Copper, Iodine, Iron, Manganese, Molybdenum, Nickel, Silicon, Vanadium, and Zinc* (2001); *Dietary Reference Intakes for Water, Potassium, Sodium, Chloride, and* Sulfate (2005); and *Dietary Reference Intakes for Calcium and Vitamin D* (2011).

Dietary Reference Intakes (DRIs): Recommended Dietary Allowances and Adequate Intakes, Elements

Food and Nutrition Board, Institute of Medicine, National Academies

Life Stage Group	Calcium (mg/d)	Chromium (μg/d)	Copper (μg/d)	Fluoride (mg/d)	Iodine (μg/d)	Iron (mg/d)	Magnesium (mg/d)	Manganese (mg/d)	Molybdenum (μg/d)	Phosphorus (mg/d)	Selenium (μg/d)	Zinc (mg/d)	Potassium (g/d)	Sodium (g/d)	Chloride (g/d)
Infants															
0 to 6 mo	200*	0.2*	200*	0.01*	110*	0.27*	30*	0.003*	2*	100*	15*	2*	0.4*	0.12*	0.18*
6 to 12 mo	260*	5.5*	220*	0.5*	130*	**11**	75*	0.6*	3*	275*	20*	**3**	0.7*	0.37*	0.57*
Children															
1–3 y	**700**	11*	**340**	0.7*	**90**	**7**	**80**	1.2*	**17**	**460**	**20**	**3**	3.0*	1.0*	1.5*
4–8 y	**1,000**	15*	**440**	1*	**90**	**10**	**130**	1.5*	**22**	**500**	**30**	**5**	3.8*	1.2*	1.9*
Males															
9–13 y	**1,300**	25*	**700**	2*	**120**	**8**	**240**	1.9*	**34**	**1,250**	**40**	**8**	4.5*	1.5*	2.3*
14–18 y	**1,300**	35*	**890**	3*	**150**	**11**	**410**	2.2*	**43**	**1,250**	**55**	**11**	4.7*	1.5*	2.3*
19–30 y	**1,000**	35*	**900**	4*	**150**	**8**	**400**	2.3*	**45**	**700**	**55**	**11**	4.7*	1.5*	2.3*
31–50 y	**1,000**	35*	**900**	4*	**150**	**8**	**420**	2.3*	**45**	**700**	**55**	**11**	4.7*	1.5*	2.3*
51–70 y	**1,000**	30*	**900**	4*	**150**	**8**	**420**	2.3*	**45**	**700**	**55**	**11**	4.7*	1.3*	2.0*
> 70 y	**1,200**	30*	**900**	4*	**150**	**8**	**420**	2.3*	**45**	**700**	**55**	**11**	4.7*	1.2*	1.8*
Females															
9–13 y	**1,300**	21*	**700**	2*	**120**	**8**	**240**	1.6*	**34**	**1,250**	**40**	**8**	4.5*	1.5*	2.3*
14–18 y	**1,300**	24*	**890**	3*	**150**	**15**	**360**	1.6*	**43**	**1,250**	**55**	**9**	4.7*	1.5*	2.3*
19–30 y	**1,000**	25*	**900**	3*	**150**	**18**	**310**	1.8*	**45**	**700**	**55**	**8**	4.7*	1.5*	2.3*
31–50 y	**1,000**	25*	**900**	3*	**150**	**18**	**320**	1.8*	**45**	**700**	**55**	**8**	4.7*	1.5*	2.3*
51–70 y	**1,200**	20*	**900**	3*	**150**	**8**	**320**	1.8*	**45**	**700**	**55**	**8**	4.7*	1.3*	2.0*
> 70 y	**1,200**	20*	**900**	3*	**150**	**8**	**320**	1.8*	**45**	**700**	**55**	**8**	4.7*	1.2*	1.8*
Pregnancy															
14–18 y	**1,300**	29*	**1,000**	3*	**220**	**27**	**400**	2.0*	**50**	**1,250**	**60**	**12**	4.7*	1.5*	2.3*
19–30 y	**1,000**	30*	**1,000**	3*	**220**	**27**	**350**	2.0*	**50**	**700**	**60**	**11**	4.7*	1.5*	2.3*
31–50 y	**1,000**	30*	**1,000**	3*	**220**	**27**	**360**	2.0*	**50**	**700**	**60**	**11**	4.7*	1.5*	2.3*
Lactation															
14–18 y	**1,300**	44*	**1,300**	3*	**290**	**10**	**360**	2.6*	**50**	**1,250**	**70**	**13**	5.1*	1.5*	2.3*
19–30 y	**1,000**	45*	**1,300**	3*	**290**	**9**	**310**	2.6*	**50**	**700**	**70**	**12**	5.1*	1.5*	2.3*
31–50 y	**1,000**	45*	**1,300**	3*	**290**	**9**	**320**	2.6*	**50**	**700**	**70**	**12**	5.1*	1.5*	2.3*

NOTE: This table (taken from the DRI reports, see www.nap.edu) presents Recommended Dietary Allowances (RDAs) in **bold type** and Adequate Intakes (AIs) in ordinary type followed by an asterisk (*). An RDA is the average daily dietary intake level; sufficient to meet the nutrient requirements of nearly all (97-98 percent) healthy individuals in a group. It is calculated from an Estimated Average Requirement (EAR). If sufficient scientific evidence is not available to establish an EAR, and thus calculate an RDA, an AI is usually developed. For healthy breastfed infants, an AI is the mean intake. The AI for other life stage and gender groups is believed to cover the needs of all healthy individuals in the groups, but lack of data or uncertainty in the data prevent being able to specify with confidence the percentage of individuals covered by this intake.

SOURCES: *Dietary Reference Intakes for Calcium, Phosphorous, Magnesium, Vitamin D, and Fluoride* (1997); *Dietary Reference Intakes for Thiamin, Riboflavin, Niacin, Vitamin B_6, Folate, Vitamin B_{12}, Pantothenic Acid, Biotin, and Choline* (1998); *Dietary Reference Intakes for Vitamin C, Vitamin E, Selenium, and Carotenoids* (2000); and *Dietary Reference Intakes for Vitamin A, Vitamin K, Arsenic, Boron, Chromium, Copper, Iodine, Iron, Manganese, Molybdenum, Nickel, Silicon, Vanadium, and Zinc* (2001); *Dietary Reference Intakes for Water, Potassium, Sodium, Chloride, and* Sulfate (2005); and *Dietary Reference Intakes for Calcium and Vitamin D* (2011). These reports may be accessed via www.nap.edu.

Dietary Reference Intakes (DRIs): Tolerable Upper Intake Levels, Vitamins

Food and Nutrition Board, Institute of Medicine, National Academies

Life Stage Group	Vitamin A (μg/d)[a]	Vitamin C (mg/d)	Vitamin D (μg/d)	Vitamin E (mg/d)[b,c]	Vitamin K	Thiamin	Riboflavin	Niacin (mg/d)[c]	Vitamin B_6 (mg/d)	Folate (μg/d)[c]	Vitamin B_{12}	Pantothenic Acid	Biotin	Choline (g/d)	Carotenoids[d]
Infants															
0 to 6 mo	600	ND[e]	25	ND	ND	ND	ND	ND	ND	ND	ND	ND	ND	ND	ND
6 to 12 mo	600	ND	38	ND	ND	ND	ND	ND	ND	ND	ND	ND	ND	ND	ND
Children															
1–3 y	600	400	63	200	ND	ND	ND	10	30	300	ND	ND	ND	1.0	ND
4–8 y	900	650	75	300	ND	ND	ND	15	40	400	ND	ND	ND	1.0	ND
Males															
9–13 y	1,700	1,200	100	600	ND	ND	ND	20	60	600	ND	ND	ND	2.0	ND
14–18 y	2,800	1,800	100	800	ND	ND	ND	30	80	800	ND	ND	ND	3.0	ND
19–30 y	3,000	2,000	100	1,000	ND	ND	ND	35	100	1,000	ND	ND	ND	3.5	ND
31–50 y	3,000	2,000	100	1,000	ND	ND	ND	35	100	1,000	ND	ND	ND	3.5	ND
51–70 y	3,000	2,000	100	1,000	ND	ND	ND	35	100	1,000	ND	ND	ND	3.5	ND
> 70 y	3,000	2,000	100	1,000	ND	ND	ND	35	100	1,000	ND	ND	ND	3.5	ND
Females															
9–13 y	1,700	1,200	100	600	ND	ND	ND	20	60	600	ND	ND	ND	2.0	ND
14–18 y	2,800	1,800	100	800	ND	ND	ND	30	80	800	ND	ND	ND	3.0	ND
19–30 y	3,000	2,000	100	1,000	ND	ND	ND	35	100	1,000	ND	ND	ND	3.5	ND
31–50 y	3,000	2,000	100	1,000	ND	ND	ND	35	100	1,000	ND	ND	ND	3.5	ND
51–70 y	3,000	2,000	100	1,000	ND	ND	ND	35	100	1,000	ND	ND	ND	3.5	ND
> 70 y	3,000	2,000	100	1,000	ND	ND	ND	35	100	1,000	ND	ND	ND	3.5	ND
Pregnancy															
14–18 y	2,800	1,800	100	800	ND	ND	ND	30	80	800	ND	ND	ND	3.0	ND
19–30 y	3,000	2,000	100	1,000	ND	ND	ND	35	100	1,000	ND	ND	ND	3.5	ND
31–50 y	3,000	2,000	100	1,000	ND	ND	ND	35	100	1,000	ND	ND	ND	3.5	ND
Lactation															
14–18 y	2,800	1,800	100	800	ND	ND	ND	30	80	800	ND	ND	ND	3.0	ND
19–30 y	3,000	2,000	100	1,000	ND	ND	ND	35	100	1,000	ND	ND	ND	3.5	ND
31–50 y	3,000	2,000	100	1,000	ND	ND	ND	35	100	1,000	ND	ND	ND	3.5	ND

NOTE: A Tolerable Upper Intake Level (UL) is the highest level of daily nutrient intake that is likely to pose no risk of adverse health effects to almost all individuals in the general population. Unless otherwise specified, the UL represents total intake from food, water, and supplements. Due to a lack of suitable data, ULs could not be established for vitamin K, thiamin, riboflavin, vitamin B_{12}, pantothenic acid, biotin, and carotenoids. In the absence of a UL, extra caution may be warranted in consuming levels above recommended intakes. Members of the general population should be advised not to routinely exceed the UL. The UL is not meant to apply to individuals who are treated with the nutrient under medical supervision or to individuals with predisposing conditions that modify their sensitivity to the nutrient.

[a] As preformed vitamin A only.

[b] As α-tocopherol; applies to any form of supplemental α-tocopherol.

[c] The ULs for vitamin E, niacin, and folate apply to synthetic forms obtained from supplements, fortified foods, or a combination of the two.

[d] β-Carotene supplements are advised only to serve as a provitamin A source for individuals at risk of vitamin A deficiency.

[e] ND = Not determinable due to lack of data of adverse effects in this age group and concern with regard to lack of ability to handle excess amounts. Source of intake should be from food only to prevent high levels of intake.

Sources: Dietary Reference Intakes for Calcium, Phosphorous, Magnesium, Vitamin D, and Fluoride (1997); *Dietary Reference Intakes for Thiamin, Riboflavin, Niacin, Vitamin B_6, Folate, Vitamin B_{12}, Pantothenic Acid, Biotin, and Choline* (1998); *Dietary Reference Intakes for Vitamin C, Vitamin E, Selenium, and Carotenoids* (2000); *Dietary Reference Intakes for Vitamin A, Vitamin K, Arsenic, Boron, Chromium, Copper, Iodine, Iron, Manganese, Molybdenum, Nickel, Silicon, Vanadium, and Zinc* (2001); and *Dietary Reference Intakes for Calcium and Vitamin D* (2011). These reports may be accessed via www.nap.edu.

Dietary Reference Intakes (DRIs): Tolerable Upper Intake Levels, Elements

Food and Nutrition Board, Institute of Medicine, National Academies

Life Stage Group	Arsenic[a]	Boron (mg/d)	Calcium (mg/d)	Chromium	Copper (μg/d)	Fluoride (mg/d)	Iodine (μg/d)	Iron (mg/d)	Magnesium (mg/d)[b]	Manganese (mg/d)	Molybdenum (μg/d)	Nickel (mg/d)	Phosphorus (g/d)	Selenium (μg/d)	Silicon[c]	Vanadium (mg/d)[d]	Zinc (mg/d)	Sodium (g/d)	Chloride (g/d)
Infants																			
0 to 6 mo	ND[e]	ND	1,000	ND	ND	0.7	ND	40	ND	ND	ND	ND	ND	45	ND	ND	4	ND	ND
6 to 12 mo	ND	ND	1,500	ND	ND	0.9	ND	40	ND	ND	ND	ND	ND	60	ND	ND	5	ND	ND
Children																			
1–3 y	ND	3	2,500	ND	1,000	1.3	200	40	65	2	300	0.2	3	90	ND	ND	7	1.5	2.3
4–8 y	ND	6	2,500	ND	3,000	2.2	300	40	110	3	600	0.3	3	150	ND	ND	12	1.9	2.9
Males																			
9–13 y	ND	11	3,000	ND	5,000	10	600	40	350	6	1,100	0.6	4	280	ND	ND	23	2.2	3.4
14–18 y	ND	17	3,000	ND	8,000	10	900	45	350	9	1,700	1.0	4	400	ND	ND	34	2.3	3.6
19–30 y	ND	20	2,500	ND	10,000	10	1,100	45	350	11	2,000	1.0	4	400	ND	1.8	40	2.3	3.6
31–50 y	ND	20	2,500	ND	10,000	10	1,100	45	350	11	2,000	1.0	4	400	ND	1.8	40	2.3	3.6
51–70 y	ND	20	2,000	ND	10,000	10	1,100	45	350	11	2,000	1.0	4	400	ND	1.8	40	2.3	3.6
> 70 y	ND	20	2,000	ND	10,000	10	1,100	45	350	11	2,000	1.0	3	400	ND	1.8	40	2.3	3.6
Females																			
9–13 y	ND	11	3,000	ND	5,000	10	600	40	350	6	1,100	0.6	4	280	ND	ND	23	2.2	3.4
14–18 y	ND	17	3,000	ND	8,000	10	900	45	350	9	1,700	1.0	4	400	ND	ND	34	2.3	3.6
19–30 y	ND	20	2,500	ND	10,000	10	1,100	45	350	11	2,000	1.0	4	400	ND	1.8	40	2.3	3.6
31–50 y	ND	20	2,500	ND	10,000	10	1,100	45	350	11	2,000	1.0	4	400	ND	1.8	40	2.3	3.6
51–70 y	ND	20	2,000	ND	10,000	10	1,100	45	350	11	2,000	1.0	4	400	ND	1.8	40	2.3	3.6
> 70 y	ND	20	2,000	ND	10,000	10	1,100	45	350	11	2,000	1.0	3	400	ND	1.8	40	2.3	3.6
Pregnancy																			
14–18 y	ND	17	3,000	ND	8,000	10	900	45	350	9	1,700	1.0	3.5	400	ND	ND	34	2.3	3.6
19–30 y	ND	20	2,500	ND	10,000	10	1,100	45	350	11	2,000	1.0	3.5	400	ND	ND	40	2.3	3.6
61–50 y	ND	20	2,500	ND	10,000	10	1,100	45	350	11	2,000	1.0	3.5	400	ND	ND	40	2.3	3.6
Lactation																			
14–18 y	ND	17	3,000	ND	8,000	10	900	45	350	9	1,700	1.0	4	400	ND	ND	34	2.3	3.6
19–30 y	ND	20	2,500	ND	10,000	10	1,100	45	350	11	2,000	1.0	4	400	ND	ND	40	2.3	3.6
31–50 y	ND	20	2,500	ND	10,000	10	1,100	45	350	11	2,000	1.0	4	400	ND	ND	40	2.3	3.6

NOTE: A Tolerable Upper Intake Level (UL) is the highest level of daily nutrient intake that is likely to pose no risk of adverse health effects to almost all individuals in the general population. Unless otherwise specified, the UL represents total intake from food, water, and supplements. Due to a lack of suitable data, ULs could not be established for vitamin K, thiamin, riboflavin, vitamin B_{12}, pantothenic acid, biotin, and carotenoids. In the absence of a UL, extra caution may be warranted in consuming levels above recommended intakes. Members of the general population should be advised not to routinely exceed the UL. The UL is not meant to apply to individuals who are treated with the nutrient under medical supervision or to individuals with predisposing conditions that modify their sensitivity to the nutrient.

[a]Although the UL was not determined for arsenic, there is no justification for adding arsenic to food or supplements.

[b]The ULs for magnesium represent intake from a pharmacological agent only and do not include intake from food and water.

[c]Although silicon has not been shown to cause adverse effects in humans, there is no justification for adding silicon to supplements.

[d]Although vanadium in food has not been shown to cause adverse effects in humans, there is no justification for adding vanadium to food and vanadium supplements should be used with caution. The UL is based on adverse effects in laboratory animals and this data could be used to set a UL for adults but not children and adolescents.

[e]ND = Not determinable due to lack of data of adverse effects in this age group and concern with regard to lack of ability to handle excess amounts. Source of intake should be from food only to prevent high levels of intake.

Sources: Dietary Reference Intakes for Calcium, Phosphorous, Magnesium, Vitamin D, and Fluoride (1997); *Dietary Reference Intakes for Thiamin, Riboflavin, Niacin, Vitamin B_6, Folate, Vitamin B_{12}, Pantothenic Acid, Biotin, and Choline* (1998); *Dietary Reference Intakes for Vitamin C, Vitamin E, Selenium, and Carotenoids* (2000); *Dietary Reference Intakes for Vitamin A, Vitamin K, Arsenic, Boron, Chromium, Copper, Iodine, Iron, Manganese, Molybdenum, Nickel, Silicon, Vanadium, and Zinc* (2001); *Dietary Reference Intakes for Water, Potassium, Sodium, Chloride, and Sulfate* (2005); and *Dietary Reference Intakes for Calcium and Vitamin D* (2011). These reports may be accessed via www.nap.edu.

% Daily Values: What Are They Based On?

Daily Values (DVs) for nutrients used on Nutrition Facts labels are used to calculate the % Daily Values you see on Nutrition Facts and Supplement Facts labels. Provided by the US Food and Drug Administration (FDA), these dietary references for nutrients are based on the RDAs or AIs. They're similar to the RDA or AI for those nutrients; however, you may need more or less.

The Nutrition Facts label shows %DVs. That helps you to see how much (what percentage) of various nutrients one serving of the food, drink, or supplement contributes to reaching the DVs, or your approximate nutrient needs.

For daily nutrient recommendations specific to your age and gender, *see the "Dietary Reference Intakes (DRIs)" earlier in this appendix, pages 782 to 785; DRIs are explained in "Nutrients: How Much?" in chapter 1, page 6.*

The following Daily Values are for adults and children aged four and older. Different DVs have also been set for foods marketed to infants through twelve months, children aged one through three years, and pregnant and lactating women.* For example, this means that food marketed to children aged one through three will show a %DVs specifically for this age group.

Listed here are the DVs, which add up to 100% DV, used for the original Nutrition Facts labeling as well as updated DVs used for the new Nutrition Facts labeling, *addressed in "A Closer Look . . . Nutrition Facts Update" in chapter 6, page 146*. The new values more closely align with the current RDAs for adults.

	100% DV Is Equal to This Amount	
Nutrient/Food Component	**Original†**	**New‡**
Total carbohydrate§	300 g	275 g
Dietary fiber§	25 g	28 g
Added sugars§	NA	50 g
Protein§	50 g	50 g
Total fat§	65 g	78 g
Saturated fat§	20 g	20 g
Cholesterol	300 mg	300 mg
Vitamin A	5,000 IU	900 mcg RAE
Vitamin D	400 IU (10 mcg)	20 mcg
Vitamin E	30 IU	15 mg
Vitamin K	80 mcg	120 mcg
Thiamin	1.5 mg	1.2 mg
Riboflavin	1.7 mg	1.3 mg
Niacin	20 mg	16 mg
Vitamin B_6	2 mg	1.7 mg
Folate	400 mcg	400 mcg
Vitamin B_{12}	6 mcg	2.4 mcg
Biotin	300 mcg	30 mcg

	100% DV Is Equal to This Amount	
Nutrient/Food Component	**Original†**	**New‡**
Pantothenic acid	10 mg	5 mg
Choline	NA	550 mg
Vitamin C	60 mg	90 mg
Calcium	1,000 mg	1,300 mg
Magnesium	400 mg	420 mg
Phosphorus	1,000 mg	1,250 mg
Chloride	3,400 mg	2,300 mg
Potassium	3,500 mg	4,700 mg
Sodium	2,400 mg	2,300 mg
Chromium	120 mcg	35 mcg
Copper	2 mg	0.9 mg
Iodine	150 mcg	150 mcg
Iron	18 mg	18 mg
Manganese	2 mg	2.3 mg
Molybdenum	75 mcg	45 mcg
Selenium	70 mcg	55 mcg
Zinc	15 mg	11 mg

* www.fda.gov/downloads/Food/GuidanceRegulation/GuidanceDocumentsRegulatoryInformation/LabelingNutrition/UCM513817.pdf

†These Daily Values are used for the original Nutrition Facts labels, authorized in 1990.

‡The Daily Values were revised in the final rule, "Food Labeling: Revision of the Nutrition and Supplement Facts Labels" (https://s3.amazonaws.com/public-inspection.federalregister.gov/2016-11867.pdf) for the new Nutrition Facts labels, with compliance by July 26, 2018.

§Based on the reference caloric intake of 2,000 calories for adult and children ages 4 year and older, and for pregnant women and lactating women.

Index

a/B milk, 671
açai, 39, 323, 324
Acceptable Macronutrient Distribution Ranges (AMDRs), 6
acesulfame potassium, 369
acid, and bacteria, 214
acid reflux (heartburn), 550, 728
acne, 528
acrylamide, 215
active living. *See* physical activity; sports
added sugars
  foods with, 364–65
  label lingo, 150, 367–68
  limiting, 48–50, 59, 290–91, 365–66
  recommended amounts, 12–13, 23, 356–57, 786
  vegetarian eating pattern, 59
addiction, 95, 350
additives, 119, 132–39, 678–79
Adequate Intakes (AIs), 6, 409
adipose tissue, 388
adolescents. *See* teenagers
adults. *See* men; women
adzuki (azuki) bean, 250
aerobic capacity, 576
African cuisine, 288
African horned melon, 39
age, as risk factor, 683, 693–94, 740
aging. *See* older adults
agriculture, 113–27, 163
aioli, 277
air travel, 309–10
AIs (Adequate Intakes), 6, 409
alcohol, cooking with, 266, 268
alcoholic drinks, 102–8
  air travel, 310
  for athletes, 604
  beer, 103, 105, 106, 107, 568
  and breastfeeding, 466, 557
  business travel, 311
  caffeinated, 101
  calories, 104, 106, 283, 301
  equivalents, 102–3, 780
  health benefits, 103–4, 568, 695
  health risks, 103, 104–5, 568, 695, 710–11, 741
  older adults, 584
  during pregnancy, 104, 549
  recommended amounts, 15, 23
  sobering effect of caffeine, 95
  teenage consumption, 529
  wine, 105, 106, 107, 695
alcoholism, 104, 108, 766
al dente, 277
alfredo sauce, 280
allergies. *See* food allergies; seasonal allergies
allulose, 370
almond milk, 92, 93, 381, 384, 480
almonds, 43, 281, 361, 381
aloe vera, 324
amaranth, 31, 253
AMDRs (Acceptable Macronutrient Distribution Ranges), 6
Amebiasis, 224
amino acids, 619
anabolic steroids. *See* steroids
ancient grains, 27
andropause (aging male syndrome), 570
androstenedione, 620–21
anemia, 722–26
anorexia nervosa, 732–33
antacids, 335, 728, 744
antiaging supplements, 323, 583
antibiotics, 121, 744
anticaking agents, 136
anticoagulants, 744
antidepressants, 744
antimicrobial soap, 196
antioxidants, 318, 335, 423–25, 581, 692, 726
antipasto, 297–98
anxiety, and caffeine, 95
appetite loss, 593–94, 651, 719
apples, 160, 360, 363, 402
appliances, 194, 233–34, 244–45
aquaculture, 119
arborio rice, 31
aristolochic acid, 322
aromatherapy, 393
arrabbiata sauce, 280
arthritis, 726–27, 766
arugula, 36
Asian pears, 39, 160
aspartame, 369–71, 679
asthma, 664
atemoya, 39
athletes. *See* sports
at risk populations. *See* health risks, people with
attention deficit disorder, 95
autism, 499, 552
azuki (adzuki) bean, 250

babies and baby foods, 459–88. *See also* breastfeeding
  almond, rice, coconut milk, 480
  anemia, 723
  avoid feeding from the jar, 485
  bottle-feeding, 471–76, 478
  breast- *vs.* formula-feeding, 460
  cereals, breads, and other grain foods, 478–79, 481
  choking prevention and safety, 486–88
  comforting, 478
  constipation, 482
  dad's role, 468, 569
  dental care, 480
  diabetes risk factors, 709
  feeding skills and readiness cues, 481, 483–84
  food allergies, 656
  food and nutrition programs, 762
  food safety, 488
  food sensitivities, 479
  food variety, 481–82
  fruit juices, 480
  healthy eating check-in, 461
  healthy growth, 478
  healthy weight, 471
  homemade baby food, 485–86
  honey, warning concerning, 480
  hunger cues, 464, 482
  infant formula, 471–76
  label lingo, 486
  lead poisoning, 482
  macronutrient needs, 781
  mealtime, 476
  mineral needs, 783, 785
  organic baby food, 482
  physical activity for, 475
  protein sources, 481–82
  solid foods, 476–88
  spoon feeding, 477–78
  teething, 478
  travel and day care, 485
  vegetables and fruits, 482
  vegetarian eating pattern, 477
  vitamin needs, 480, 782, 784
  warming baby's food, 482
  water needs, 463, 781
Bacillus cereus, 220, 227
bacon, 202, 254, 281, 282
bacteria
  and acid, 214
  basics, 220
  in cooked foods, 214
  foodborne illnesses, 219–21, 223
  and freezing foods, 205
  high-altitude cooking, 215
  and hot sauce, 214
  probiotic, 296
  in raw sprouts, 286
  in seafood, 214
  travelers' diarrhea, 313
bagels, 29, 79, 292, 402
baked goods, 185–86, 262–63, 266, 292, 396, 398. *See also specific products*
bakeware, 233
baking aisle, buying tips, 183–85
baking stone, 234
banh mi sandwich, 305
barbecue, 236, 293
barley, 31, 253, 360, 672
basal metabolic rate (BMR), 576, 633–34

basmati rice, 31, 32
basting, 233, 235
B-complex vitamins, 410, 417, 545, 691. *See also* vitamin B
beans and peas
- calorie counts, 281
- canned, 180, 265
- fitting more in, 251–52
- food preparation check-in, 247
- herbs and spices for, 272
- nutrients, 359, 397, 412, 706
- overview, 33
- preparation, 251–52
- recommended amounts, 34
- shopping for, 179–80
- types and uses, 250–51

béarnaise sauce, 280
béchamel sauce, 280
BED (binge eating disorder), 732, 733–34
beef
- cholesterol in, 406
- fat content, 396–97
- grain-finished and grass-finished, 121
- "grass-fed," 166
- ground, 201, 214, 381, 397, 406
- herbs and spices for, 272
- hormones used in production, 121
- lean cuts, 254, 256
- low-fat cooking methods, 256
- organic, 121
- protein content, 381
- stir-fry, 50
- storage of, 202
- tapeworm, 225
- temperature, cooked, 210, 213

beer, 103, 105, 106, 107, 568
beet greens, 36
beet root juice, 619–20
beriberi, 414
"best if used by" date, 153
beta-alanine, 620
beta-carotene, 424, 449
beurre blanc sauce, 280
beverages, 14, 81–108. *See also specific beverages*
- air travel, 310
- caffeine in, 98
- calories, limiting, 283, 291
- carbohydrates in, 358, 361–68
- fast-food, 296–97
- oxygen-enhanced, 88
- safety of, while traveling, 314
- shopping for, 180–81
- and sleep, 97
- sweeteners and calories, 182

BHA (butylated hydroxyanisole), 136
BHT (butylated hydroxytoluene), 136
binders, 137
binge eating disorder (BED), 732, 733–34
biological threats, 319
biotechnology, 123–27, 666
biotin, 319, 421, 782, 784, 786
bird flu, 221
bison, 46
bitter orange, 324
black beans, 71, 250
black cohosh, 324, 561
black currant oil, 331
black-eyed peas, 250, 381, 412
black rice, 31
bladder control, 728, 732
bleeding gums, 423
blenders, 233
blood (protein food), 258
blood (serum) cholesterol
- as age biomarker, 576
- and animal-based foods, 579
- basics, 404–5
- and cardiovascular disease, 684–87
- and chocolate, 391
- defined, 387
- and dietary fat, 390
- food-medication interactions, 744
- HDL ("good") cholesterol, 387, 685
- and high blood pressure, 695
- and hypothyroidism, 683
- improving lipid levels, 689–92
- LDL ("bad") cholesterol, 387, 576, 685
- testing, 687–89
- thin people, 683

blood glucose, 606, 698, 701–3, 705
blood glucose tolerance, 576
blood lipids. *See* blood (serum) cholesterol
blood orange, 39
blood pressure, 94, 537, 572, 695, 696. *See also* high blood pressure
blood-thinning medication, 744
blue-green algae, 332
BMI (body mass index), 568, 627–28, 777
BMR (basal metabolic rate), 576, 633–34
bodybuilding, 532
body composition, 576, 614–15, 627, 628, 634
body fat, need for, 628
body image, 535, 565, 646
body mass index (BMI), 568, 627–28, 777
body shape, 626–27
body weight. *See* weight
bok choy, 36, 161
bolognese sauce, 280
bone health
- and aging, 576
- and caffeine, 94
- calcium, vitamin D, and weight-bearing exercise, 427, 610, 739, 741
- and eating disorders, 536
- and menstruation, 536
- midlife and beyond, 559–60
- and osteoporosis, 738–42
- and protein, 376
- screening tests, 537, 741–42
- strategies for, 427
- of teenagers, 526

borage seed oil, 331
botanicals. *See* herbals and other botanicals
bottled water, 83, 85–87
bottle-feeding (babies), 471–76, 478
botulism, 220
bourguignonne sauce, 280
bovine spongiform encephalopathy (BSE), 223
bowl meals, 293
bowls (equipment), 233
BPA, safety of, 132
braces, dental, 528
brain (protein food), 258
brain health, 390, 391, 582
braising, 236, 260
Brazil nuts, 43
breadfruit, 36
breads
- for babies, 481–82
- calories, limiting, 283
- carbs and fiber in, 360
- dipping oils *vs.* butter, 282
- fat content, 396
- as fattening, 635
- herbs and spices for, 272
- portion size, 29
- potatoes as substitute for, 34
- sandwich choices, 294
- shopping for, 185–86

breakfast, 60–66
- baked goods, 292
- barriers, beating, 64, 66
- benefits of, 63
- calories, 63, 65
- cold foods, 292
- eggs, 291–92
- fast-food restaurants, 291–92
- and healthy body weight, 63
- hidden components, 66
- high-quality, 63–64
- hot entrées, 292
- and learning, 62–63, 500–501
- nutrients, 62
- protein foods, 63
- reasons for, 62–63
- on the road, 311–12
- sandwiches, 291–92
- school breakfasts, 505
- school-day, 500
- side dishes, 292
- two-minutes, 64
- vegetarian menu, 74

breakfast cereal
- for babies, 481–82
- fast-food meals, 292
- infant cereals, 478–79
- jazzed-up, 67
- nutrients, 360, 412, 414, 706
- overnight oatmeal, 67
- portion size, 29
- presweetened, 64, 738
- shopping for, 179

breast cancer, 537, 561–63, 571, 631, 718
breastfeeding, 555–57
- after breastfeeding, 464
- and alcoholic beverages, 104, 466, 557
- baby's healthy eating check-in, 461
- benefits, 460, 461–63, 555, 656
- and breast size, 462
- and caffeine, 556
- calories needed, 555
- cautions, 466
- color of breast milk, 556
- dad's role, 468, 569
- expressing (pumping) milk, 468–69
- and food allergies, 462, 556
- food and nutrition programs, 762
- food safety issues, 466, 557
- foreign travel, 313
- getting help, 466–67
- herbals and other botanicals, 551
- human milk bank, 469
- lactose sensitivity, 466
- latching on, 464
- macronutrient needs, 781
- maternal fluid intake, 557
- and medications, 466, 557
- mineral needs, 783, 785
- mother-baby bond, 461
- mother's health, 464–67
- nutrient requirements, 555–57
- and physical activity, 557, 614
- positions, 467
- premature babies, 462
- signs of success, 467–68
- and smoking, 466, 557
- storage and handling of breast milk, 470
- sufficient milk, 556
- supplemental bottles, 468
- supplements for babies, 469–70
- supplements for mother, 466
- techniques, 463–64, 465
- twins, 469
- vitamin needs, 782, 784
- water needs, 447, 781
- weaning, 470
- weight, mother's, 540, 555
- and working, 468–69

brining, and sodium content, 265
broad beans, 250
broccoli raab, 36
broiling, 236, 259
brown rice, 31, 253, 360
BSE (bovine spongiform encephalopathy), 223
Bt crops, 119
buckwheat, 31, 70, 253

buffalo meat, 46
buffets, 280–83, 286
bulgur, 29, 31, 253, 360, 381
bulimia, 732–33
bullying and body size, 504–5
burgers, 291, 293
burns, avoiding, 196
burping, 567
burritos, 50, 291
business trips, 311
butter, 238, 282, 393, 397, 400, 406
buttermilk, 93, 170
butylated hydroxyanisole (BHA), 136
butylated hydroxytoluene (BHT), 136
buying tips. *See* shopping

CACFP (Child and Adult Care Food Program), 762
cactus pads, 36
cactus pear, 40
Caesar salad dressing, 286, 298
caffeine
  in alcoholic drinks, 101
  for athletes, 604
  and blood pressure, 94, 697
  and health, 93–96
  in healthy eating plan, 16
  during pregnancy, 548
  sources, 98
  while breastfeeding, 556
calcium
  for athletes, 610–11
  and bone health, 427, 739, 741
  deficiencies, 426
  drug interactions, 335
  excess amounts, 426
  food sources, 56, 93, 170, 263–64, 303, 426, 428
  function, 425–26
  midlife and beyond, 559–60
  older adults, 578, 580
  during pregnancy, 547
  recommended amount, 426, 428, 783, 785, 786
  supplements, 320–21, 428
  for teenagers, 525
  while breastfeeding, 556–57
  for women, 610–11
calcium carbonate, 666
calcium propionate, 135
calories
  alcoholic drinks, 104, 106, 283, 301
  balance, 633–35
  basics, 7–8
  breakfast, 63, 311
  calorie-dense foods, 48
  children, 508, 516
  cooking method, 279
  cream, 172
  density, 635
  and energy needs, 771
  honey, 266
  label lingo, 641
  "low carb" foods, 366
  menu plans, 65
  myths and truths, 635
  need by age, gender, physical activity level, 770
  negative-calorie foods, 635
  number burned, by activity, 8, 18
  older adults, 575
  olive oils, 182
  in pregnancy, 543
  restaurants, 279, 283, 291
  salad ingredients, 280, 281
  sources, 7, 25
  sugar-free foods, 366
  sweetener type, 182, 346
  target, 7–8, 638
  teenagers, 525
  "3,500-calorie rule," 638
  and time of day, 635
  trade-offs, 48
  and weight maintenance, 633
Campylobacter jejuni, 220, 227
cancer
  chemotherapy, 717–18
  and cooking methods, 717
  defined, 713–14
  food-medication interactions, 744
  food-related side effects, 719–21
  management, 713–21
  overweight and obesity link, 631
  radiation therapy, 717–18
  risk reduction, 354, 377, 714–16, 717, 718
  screening tests, 537, 538, 572, 716
  survivors, 710
  treatment, 716–21
  warning signs and symptoms, 716
candy bars, 608
canned foods, 154, 175–77, 180, 197, 208–9
cannellini beans, 250, 298
cannelloni, 298
canning (food preservation), 130–31
cannoli, 298
canola oil, 398–99, 401
cape gooseberries, 39
carambola, 40
carbohydrate-based fat replacers, 407
carbohydrates, 345–72
  for athletes, 605–7, 618
  and body weight, 635, 648
  carbohydrate loading, 606
  for children, 508, 517
  counting, 705–8
  and diabetes, 703, 705–7
  digestion, 347
  fiber and health, 350, 352–55
  food sources, 358, 359–61, 361–68, 706–7
  as fuel, 347–48, 355–56, 605–6
  function, 6
  label lingo, 358, 366–68
  and mood, 353
  myths and truths, 349–50
  nutrient-rich, 361–62
  portion size, 706–7
  during pregnancy, 544
  quantity and type, 355–58
  recommended amounts, 355–56, 786
  simple and complex, 345–47
  sugar alternatives, 368–72
  for teenagers, 526
  terminology, 366
carbonara sauce, 280
carbon footprint, 114
cardiac arrest, warning signs, 692
cardiovascular disease
  and animal-based foods, 579
  and blood cholesterol, 684–92
  and caffeine, 95
  defined, 680
  and fats, 391
  management, 680–92
  in men, 570–71
  overweight and obesity link, 631
  and protein, 377
  risk factors, 681, 683–84
  in women, 562–63
cardiovascular health
  diet and lifestyle recommendations, 688, 690–91
  fats for, 390
  fiber for, 353
  nuts and seeds for, 400
  probiotics for, 454
  steps for, 684
  supplements for, 691
  wine for, 695
caregivers, 597
Caribbean cuisine, 70, 288, 307
carnitine, 329, 620
carotenoids, 424, 449, 450, 581
carpaccio, 286
carrageenan, 473, 667
casein, 382
cashews, 43
cassava, 36
casseroles, 50, 204, 210, 213, 237
cataracts, 726
CDC. *See* Centers for Disease Control and Prevention
celebration menus, 644
celeriac, 36, 161
celery, 161, 432
celiac disease, 278, 670–71, 673, 675, 676, 766. *See also* gluten-free foods
cell growth and repair, proteins for, 374
Centers for Disease Control and Prevention DC), 313, 314, 777
ceramics, caution concerning, 216
cereal. *See* breakfast cereal
cervical cancer, 537
chaparral, 322
chard, 36
chayote, 36
cheese
  calorie count, 281, 282
  equivalents, 264
  high risk foods and alternatives, 222
  limiting calories and saturated fats, 291
  mold on, 201
  nutrients, 381, 396, 400, 412
  pizza toppings, 295
  reducing food waste, 245
  sandwich choices, 294
  shopping for, 170–71
cheese dishes, vegetarian makeovers, 238
chemotherapy, 717–18
cherimoya, 39
chermoula sauce, 280
chewing gum, 738
chewing problems, 594
chia seeds, 43, 361, 383, 401
chicken. *See also* poultry
  brining, and sodium content, 265
  fast-food, 293
  fat content, 397
  free-range, 166
  herbs and spices for, 272
  lean choices, 293
  protein content, 381
  temperature, cooked, 210
  vitamin A in, 412
chickpeas, 250, 281
chicory, 36
chicory coffee, 96
Child and Adult Care Food Program (CACFP), 762
children, 489–532. *See also* babies; school-age children; teenagers; toddlers and preschoolers
  adult responsibilities, 489–90
  air travel, food for, 310
  alcohol risks, 104
  anemia, 723
  breakfast, 62–63, 64, 500
  bullying and body size, 504–5
  caffeine consumption, 96
  child nutrition programs, 761, 762
  children's responsibilities, 490
  chocolate milk for, 362
  choking prevention and safety, 486–88, 511
  cooking together, 495–97
  dad's role, 468, 569
  dehydration in, 612–13
  diabetes in, 712
  family meals, 73, 491–93
  fats, importance of, 390
  feeding concerns, 498–516
  fluid intake, 612–13
  food allergies, 499, 654, 656, 658
  food choices, 490–91
  food exploration, 497

children (*continued*)
  food safety, 490
  fruit juices and drinks, 517
  gardening, 493–94
  gluten free, 499
  growth and weight, 501–5, 777
  hand-washing basics, 496
  healthy eaters, raising, 489–93
  healthy eating check-in, 492
  home cooking, 230
  kitchen safety, 495, 496–97
  kitchen tasks for, 498–99
  label lingo, 486
  lactose intolerance, 499
  lead poisoning, 509
  learning about food, 493–97
  learning and nutrition, 500–501
  lifestyle, healthy, 503–4
  macronutrient needs, 781
  meals, healthy, 503, 510
  mealtime, 476, 491
  microwave oven safety, 495
  mineral needs, 783, 785
  nutrient and calorie needs, 508–10
  overweight, 502–3
  parents as role models, 493
  physical activity, 490, 569, 769
  physical activity, eating for, 612–13
  restaurant meals, 284, 290, 507–8
  school meals, 505–7
  sleep, 504
  snacks, healthy, 493, 497, 503, 510
  sugar, limiting, 518
  supplements, 337, 519
  underweight, 504
  and vegetables, 498, 500
  vegetarian eating pattern, 520–21
  vitamin needs, 782, 784
  water needs, 781
  weight, healthy, 501–2, 503, 613
chile peppers, 241, 634
chili, 204, 237
chimichurri sauce, 280
Chinese cuisine, 70, 71, 274, 288, 303–4
chips, 49
chitosan, 329
chloride, 429–30, 783, 785, 786
chlorine, in tap water, 85
chocolate, 98, 367, 391, 397, 402, 528
chocolate milk, 93, 98, 362
chocolate syrup, 98
choking, 196, 486–88, 511
cholesterol. *See also* blood (serum) cholesterol; dietary cholesterol
  basics, 404–7
  and calories, 406
  Daily Values (DVs), 786
  dictionary of terms, 387
  dietary *vs.* blood, 404–5
  and eggs, 255, 257, 292
  label lingo, 403
  screening tests, 522, 538, 572
cholesterol-free, defined, 403
choline, 422, 545, 556, 782, 784, 786
chondroitin, 331
chromium, 329, 436, 709, 783, 785, 786
chromium picolinate, 620
chronic fatigue, 725
chronic inflammation, 684
cider, 105
cilantro, 269
cinnamon, 325, 703
citric acid, 135
CLA (conjugated linoleic acid), 330
cleanliness. *See* food safety; kitchens
clean water, 87–88
"closed or coded" dates, 153
Clostridium botulinum, 220, 227
Clostridium perfringens, 220, 227
club soda, 88
cobalamin. *See* vitamin B_{12}
cocktails, 106
cocoa beverage, 98
cocoa butter, 391
coconut, 667
coconut milk, 92, 304, 400, 480
coconut oil, 391
coconut water, 94, 602
coenzyme Q10 (ubiquinone), 329
coffee, 79, 93–100, 296–97
coffee flour, 96
cognitive enhancers, 323
colander, 233
colloidal silver, 330
colon cancer, 717
color
  additives, 119, 137, 139, 678–79
  and flavor, 241
  of ground meats, 201, 214
  phytonutrient variety, 33, 452
colorectal cancer, 538, 572, 631
comfrey, 322
common cold, 319, 724
communion wafers, gluten-free, 677
Community Supported Agriculture (CSA), 163
complex carbohydrates, 345–47
condiments, 183, 291
conjugated linoleic acid (CLA), 330
constipation, 482, 550, 593, 719, 731
contaminated food, 199
continental breakfast, 311
convenience foods, 129, 132, 176–77
cooking, 230–74
  allergen-free foods, 659, 664
  with children, 495–97
  culinary basics, 231–33
  emergency supply checklist, 207
  flavor, 238–39, 241–43
  food safety, 209–16
  gluten-free food, 675–76
  healthy eating check-in, 247
  home cooking matters, 230–31
  meal kits, 276
  methods and cancer risk, 717
  methods and techniques, 236, 242–43, 259, 260, 717
  and mobility, 596–98
  with nonnutritive sweeteners, 267
  nutrient retention, 248
  recipes, 234–38
  skills to know, 232, 235
  tools, 233–34
  and vitamin content, 417
  waste-less kitchen, 243–44
cooking wine, 105
Cooperative Extension Service, 761
copper, 436, 783, 785, 786
corn, 34, 70, 161, 381
corn chips, 49
corned beef, 202
corn gluten, 674
cornmeal, 27
corn syrup, 182, 355
corn tortillas, 426
corticosteroids, 744
costs, food, 122, 129, 132, 155–59, 230
cottage cheese, 170, 281, 381, 396
coulis, 280
country of origin, on food labels, 153
coupons, 156
couscous, 27, 70, 272
cowpeas, 250, 381, 412
cow's milk. *See* milk
crabmeat, 168
crackers, 29, 181–82, 360, 706
cranberry juice, 536
cravings, 389, 553, 641
cream, 171–72, 235, 397
creamer, 671
creatine, 620
Crock-pot. *See* slow cooker
cross-breeding, 123–24
"cross contact," 666
cross-contamination, 195, 196
cruciferous vegetables, 34
cruise ships, 311
Cryptosporidium, 224, 227
CSA (Community Supported Agriculture), 163
Cuban cuisine, 307–8
cultured milks, 91–92
cupboards, food storage, 197–98
curing (food preservation), 131
curry spice blend, 274
cuts, avoiding, 196
cutting boards, 195, 196, 233
Cyclospora cayetanensis, 224, 227

daikon, 36, 161
Daily Values (DVs), 409, 786
dairy foods. *See also* lactose intolerance; *specific foods and beverages*
  calcium and vitamin D boost, 263–64
  calcium substitutes for, 428
  ethnic cuisine, 71, 299, 302, 305
  fast-food restaurants, 287
  fat content, 396
  food preparation check-in, 247
  freezing, 202, 204–5
  health benefits, 40–41
  healthy eating plan, 38, 40–42
  high risk foods and alternatives, 222
  key nutrients, 38, 40
  for lactose intolerant, 670
  meal planning, 71
  quick tips, 41–42, 58–59
  recommended amounts, 11, 23, 41
  reducing food waste, 245
  shopping for, 169–72
  spreads, 171
  storage of, 200, 202
  vegetarian eating pattern, 58–59, 238
  while traveling, 313
dal/dhal/dhall, 180
dark chocolate, 98
DASH (Dietary Approaches to Stop Hypertension), 51–52, 697, 776
dasheen, 36
dates (fruit), 39, 160, 360
day care, 485, 514–16
death, leading causes of, 681
deep-fried turkey, 257
degreasing pan juices, soups, and gravies, 261
dehydration, 444, 576, 584, 600, 601–2, 612–13
dehydroepiandrosterone (DHEA), 621
deli foods, 186, 203, 294
deli meats, 202, 204, 222
deli sandwiches. *See* sandwiches
demi-glace, 280
dental care. *See* oral health
depression, 323
desserts
  carbohydrates in, 707
  ethnic foods, 298, 300, 303–4
  fast-food, 296–97
  frozen, 174–75
  healthier options, 262–63, 283
  herbs and spices for, 273
  vegetarian recipe makeovers, 238
DHEA (dehydroepiandrosterone), 621
diabetes
  and alcoholic drinks, 710–11
  and blood glucose, 698, 701–3
  blood sugar spikes, post-meal, 710
  and carbohydrates, 349, 703, 705–7
  categories of, 698–99
  causes, 709
  children and teens, 712
  cinnamon for, 703
  diagnosis, 701
  doctor visits, 702
  early detection, 700–701
  and fiber, 352
  and fruits, 703
  gestational diabetes, 554, 632, 699
  and glycemic index (GI), 709

as heart disease risk factor, 684
and high blood pressure, 695
management, 698–713
meal and snack plan, 703–10
overweight and obesity link, 631
physical activity for, 711
and pregnancy, 539, 551
and protein, 376–77
related health risks, 699–700
risk factors, 700–701
screening tests, 538, 572
self-monitoring, 701–2
supplements for, 703, 709
symptoms, 700
type 1, 698–99, 709, 712
type 2, 699, 700–701, 712
weight control for, 710, 711–12
diarrhea, 220–21, 224–25, 313, 314, 447, 719–20, 731
Dietary Approaches to Stop Hypertension. *See* DASH
dietary cholesterol, 14, 387, 404–6, 579, 690
dietary fats. *See* fats
dietary fiber. *See* fiber
dietary guidelines, 8–15
Dietary Guidelines for Americans (2015–2020), 5, 8–16, 23, 355–57
Dietary Reference Intakes (DRIs), 5, 6–7, 409, 565, 780–85
dietary supplements. *See* supplements
diet soda, 102, 296, 375, 730
digestion, 347, 352–53, 635, 655, 727–31
digital trackers, 761
dim sum, 303
dinner, 65, 66, 73, 74
disaccharides, 346
disasters. *See* emergencies
dishcloths and towels, 192, 195
dishes, decorative, 216
dishwasher cooking, 214
disordered eating, 734
distilled spirits, 106
diuretic medications, 319
diverticular disease, 729
dragon fruit, 39
dressings. *See* salad dressing
dried beans. *See* beans
dried foods, buying tips, 175–76
drinks. *See* beverages
DRIs. *See* Dietary Reference Intakes
drive-in restaurants. *See* fast-food restaurants
driving and eating, 287
drugs. *See* medications
dry and shelf-stable foods, 198
dry heat, cooking methods, 259
drying (food preservation), 131
DVs. *See* Daily Values

EARs (Estimated Average Requirements), 6
East African cuisine, 288
eating disorders, 531–32, 536, 565, 732–35, 766
eating out. *See* restaurants
eating triggers, 643
echinacea, 325
E. coli, 220–21, 227, 552
eggs
allergens, 660, 664, 666, 667
blood spots on, 201
cage-free, 173
calorie count, 281
and cholesterol, 255, 257, 292, 406
cooking safely, 211–14
egg separator, 233
fast-food breakfasts, 291–92
fat content, 397
fertile, 173
food safety, 204
free-range, 173
freezing, 202, 204
in heart-healthy diet, 690
herbs and spices for, 272
high risk foods and alternatives, 222
lower-cholesterol, 173
modified-fat, 173
nutrients in, 173, 381, 412, 414, 428
organic, 173
in salad dressings, 286
shelf life, 202
shopping for, 172–73
storage of, 200, 202
substitutions, 665
temperature, cooked, 210, 213
vegetarian recipe makeovers, 237
einkorn, 31
electrolytes, 429–35, 609–10, 618. *See also* chloride; potassium; sodium
email scares and scams, 755
emergencies, 84, 205–8
emotional overeating, 643
emulsifiers, 130
endive, 36
endurance sports, 611–12
energy. *See also* calories; metabolic rate
body's use of, 633
from carbohydrates, 347–48, 355–56
conserving, 244
from fats, 389
proteins for, 375
energy bars, 608, 617
energy drinks, 98, 100–102, 604
enhanced beverages, 100–102
enriched, defined, 134, 419
Entamoeba histolytica, 224
environmental considerations
biotechnology, 125–26
energy conservation, 244–45
food waste, 243–44, 245
green shopping, 187–88
home kitchens, 243–46
organic foods, 123
resource conservation, 246
water safety and conservation, 87, 244
ephedrine, 322
equipment, kitchen, 233–34
escarole, 36
essential fatty acids, 54
essential oils, 393
Estimated Average Requirements (EARs), 6
estrogen therapy, 740
ethnic cuisine. *See also specific cuisines*
America's heritage, 116
flavor profiles, 239, 269
food guidelines, 24
meal planning, 70
restaurant meals, 297–309
sauces, 280
vegetarian dishes, 288–89
ethnicity, and health risk factors, 693, 740
ethylene gas, 119
evaporated cane juice, 347
evening primrose oil, 325, 331
exercise. *See* physical activity; sports
exercise-induced food allergy, 667
expert advice, 747–48, 758–61
extra lean, defined, 403
extras, in healthy eating plan, 48–51
eye health, 726

FALCPA (Food Allergen Labeling and Consumer Protection Act), 659
family
and bone health, 740
healthy eating check-in, 492
heart disease risk factors, 683
hypertension risk factors, 693
meals together, 73, 491–93
as support network, 644–45
and weight gain, 629
FAO (Food and Agriculture Organization), United Nations, 24
farmers' markets, 159
farming. *See* agriculture
farro, 31, 253
fast-food restaurants, 276, 287–97
fat, solid. *See* solid fat
fatback, 282
fat-based fat replacers, 407
fat-free, defined, 403
fatigue, chronic, 725
fats, 385–407. *See also* saturated fats
for athletes, 607
and body weight, 393–94
and cardiovascular disease, 391
children's needs, 508–9, 517
comparisons, 386
cravings for, 389
in cream, 172
deficiencies, 390
dictionary of terms, 387–88
fat replacers, 406–7, 690
and flavor, 246
in foods, 395–404
free-range chickens, 166
as fuel, 607
function, 6, 389–90
health concerns, 390–94
healthy eating check-in, 395
label lingo, 402–4
lean food choices, 261–62, 399–402
monounsaturated, 386, 388
"98% fat-free," 401
physiological effects, 390
polyunsaturated, 387, 388
as power source, 389
during pregnancy, 544
recommended amounts, 394–95
solid fats *vs.* oils, 386
substitutions, 262
for teenagers, 526
types of, 386
unsaturated, 385–87, 390, 396–97, 401
visible or not, 398–99
fat-separating pitcher, 233, 261
fat-soluble vitamins, 389–90, 409–17. *See also* vitamin A; vitamin D; vitamin E; vitamin K
fatty acids, 388
fatty liver disease, 632
fava beans, 250
FBD (fibrocystic breast disease), 538
FDA, supplement regulation, 328, 333
feet (hock), as protein food, 258
feijoa, 39
fennel, 36, 161
fenugreek, 325
fermentable oligosaccharides, disaccharides, monosaccharides, and polyols (FODMAPs), 353, 730
fermentation, 131, 353
fertility, 539, 567–68
fertilizers, 122
feta cheese, 281, 400
fevers, 724
fiber
in apples, 363
benefits, 350, 352–55
cancer protection, 354
children's needs, 517–18
as complex, 347
defined, 352
and digestive health, 352–53
food sources, 352, 359–64
and healthy weight, 350
for heart health, 353
label lingo, 367
older adults, 583
during pregnancy, 548
recommended amount, 357–58, 786
soluble and insoluble, 353
in soybeans and tofu, 173, 364
supplements, 357
and type 2 diabetes, 352

fiber (*continued*)
upper limit, 358
and whole grains, 358
fibrocystic breast disease (FBD), 538
fibromyalgia, 536
finger foods, 510
fingernails, as vitamin deficiency indicator, 319
first aid. *See* choking
fish. *See also* seafood
allergens, 662, 664
bacteria in, 214
as brain food, 391
calorie counts, 281
canned or pouched, 176
eating what you catch, 225
fast-food, 293
food safety, while traveling, 313–14
herbs and spices for, 272
high risk foods and alternatives, 222
lean choices, 257, 293
low-fat cooking methods, 254–55, 257
mercury in, 225
omega-3s and total fat in, 401
preparing safely, 209, 211, 247
raw, safety of, 286
serving size, 169
shopping for, 167–68, 176
storage of, 199–200, 202, 204
temperature, cooked, 210
vegetarian recipe makeovers, 237
fish-oil supplements, 330, 691
fitness. *See* physical activity; sports
"five-second rule," 196
flageolets, 250
flatbread, 294–95
flavonoids, 449, 451
flavor
additives for, 137–38
boosting, 592–93
and color, 241
cooking for, 230–74
culinary techniques, 242–43
defined, 238–39
enhancers, 240, 243
ethnic and regional foods, 239, 269
experience of, 239–40
fats, sugars, salt, 246
and food handling, 241
and food preparation, 241–43, 247
and food temperature, 241
garnishes, 243
and health, 238–41
MSG for, 240
and nutrition, 240–41
nuts, seeds, nut butters, 242
organic foods, 122
processed foods, 129
salt for, 434
and shape and size of foods, 241
and smell, 239
supertasters, 240
taste, 238–39
and texture, 241, 242
and touch, 239
variety for flavor appeal, 241
flavored vinegars, 271
flavor extracts, 269
flavor loss, in older adults, 592–93
flaxseed oil, 330
flaxseeds, 43, 254, 330, 361, 393, 401, 561
flour, 178, 183–85
flowers, edible, 238
fluoride
for breastfed babies, 469
deficiencies, 437
excess amounts, 437
function, 436
in infant formula, 472
recommended amount, 436–37, 783, 785
sources, 437
and tooth decay, 736
in water, 83
flu shots, 666
FODMAPs (fermentable oligo-saccharides, disaccharides, monosaccharides, and polyols), 353, 730
folate (folic acid / folacin)
deficiencies, 419–20, 725
drug interactions, 335
excess amounts, 420
food sources, 38, 420, 540–41
function, 419
and heart disease risk, 691
during menopause, 559
older adults, 582–83
during pregnancy, 545
preventing birth defects, 539–41
recommended amount, 419, 782, 784, 786
supplements, 541
while breastfeeding, 556
Food Allergen Labeling and Consumer Protection Act (FALCPA), 659
food allergies and allergens, 653–79. *See also specific allergens*
allergic reactions, 654–55
and asthma, 664
in babies, 656
and breastfeeding, 462, 556, 656
in children, 499, 656, 658
"cross contact," 666
cure for, 664
dangers, 655–56
defined, 653
diagnosis, 656–57, 664
exercise-induced, 667
"hypoallergenic diet," 667
immune response, 654–55
label lingo, 151–52, 659, 660–63
management, 657–59, 664–66
most common, 654
prevention, 552
and probiotics, 667
restaurant meals, 277, 278, 664–66, 667
at risk populations, 654
signs and symptoms, 655
substitutions, 665
and supplements, 336
Food and Agriculture Organization (FAO), United Nations, 24
Food-A-Pedia, 23
food bars, 280–83, 286
foodborne illness. *See* illness, foodborne
food deserts, 159
food insecurity, 114
food intolerances, 653, 655
food pantries, 762
food poisoning. *See* illness, foodborne
food preparation. *See* cooking
food processing, 127–40
additives, 132–39
continuum of choices, 129–30
defined, 127–28
fruits and vegetables, 127
making wise choices, 140
preserving food, 130–32
reasons for, 128–29
food processors, 233
food safety, 191–229. *See also* illness, foodborne
of additives, 136, 139
additives for, 135
for babies, 488
biotechnology, 125–26
and breastfeeding, 466, 470, 557
for children, 490, 511
common mistakes, 195
contaminated food, 199
cooking foods safely, 209–16
eggs with blood spots, 201
food bars, 286
ground beef, 201
kitchen cleanliness, 192–96
label lingo, 152
moldy cheese, 201
older adults, 586
organic foods, 122
during pregnancy, 552
principles, 16
processed foods, 128
raw-food diet, 208
restaurants, 285–86
road trips, 312
serving foods safely, 217
sprouts, 208
at the store, 188–89
storing foods safely, 197–208
transporting food safely, 190, 217–18
during travel, 310, 312–14
uncooked foods, preparation, 208–9
US food supply, 128
wild mushrooms, 201
food sensitivities, 136, 479, 653, 678–79, 766
food stamps. *See* SNAP
food storage
allergen-free foods, 659, 664
breast milk, 470
canned and jarred foods, 197
containers, 199, 234
cupboards and pantry, 197–98
dry and shelf-stable foods, 198
and flavor, 241
food safety, 197–208
freezer, 201–5
gluten-free food, 675–76
herbs and spices, 269–70
power outages, 205–8
refrigerator, 198–201
restaurant leftovers, 279
restaurant takeout foods, 286
supplements, 341
vacuum sealers, 199
what goes where, 197
food temperature, 210, 212, 241
food thermometers, 212, 213, 214, 233
food waste, 113, 153, 188, 243–46, 276, 286
foot-and-mouth disease, 223
forbidden rice. *See* black rice
foreign travel, food safety, 312–14
fortified, defined, 49, 134–35, 419
FOS (fructooligosaccharides), 348
foxglove, 335
fraudulent claims, 755–58
freekeh, 31
free radicals, 423
free-range chicken, 166
freeze-drying, 131
freezers/freezing/frozen foods, 131, 174–75, 199, 201–7
French cuisine, 288, 308
French toast, 292
fried foods, 291
friends, as support network, 531, 534, 644–45
frozen desserts, 238
frozen foods. *See* freezers/freezing/frozen foods
frozen yogurt, 41, 174, 296, 396, 402
fructooligosaccharides (FOS), 348
fruit drinks, 88–90, 173, 292, 517
fruit juices
for athletes, 603–4
for babies, 480
for children, 517
fast-food meals, 296
juicing, 90
label lingo, 88
nutrition, 89, 292, 414
shopping for, 90, 173
fruit pies, 50, 204, 397, 402
fruits
for babies, 482
calorie counts, 281

canned, jarred, dried, 175–76
carbohydrates in, 706
carbs and fiber in, 360
Chinese cuisine, 305
cooking and nutrition, 246
daily recommendations, 23
and diabetes, 703
Dietary Guidelines for Americans (2015–2020), 10
ethnic cuisine, 70
ethylene gas, 119
fast-food restaurants, 287
fat content, 396
fats in, 402
fitting more in, 246–51
food preparation check-in, 247
freshness of produce, judging, 160–62
frozen, 174
health benefits, 35
healthy eating plan, 35, 37–38, 39–40
heirloom, 163
herbs and spices for, 272
Italian cuisine, 299
judging freshness, 160–61
juicing, 90
key nutrients, 35
list of, 39–40
meal planning, 70
Mexican cuisine, 302
nutrient retention, 248
nutrients, sources of, 38
oral allergy syndrome (OAS), 679
preparing safely, 208
processed, 127
quick tips, 37–38, 57
recommended amounts, 35, 37
reducing food waste, 245
refrigerator storage of, 200
shopping for, 159–64, 174, 175–76
ugly, and nutrition, 163
vegetarian eating pattern, 57
wax coating, 128
fruit snacks, 176
fry pans, ribbed, 234
functional foods, 134–35, 453
functional qualities, additives for, 136–37
fusion cuisine, 239

game meat, 46
gamma-linolenic oil, 331
garam masala, 269
garbanzo beans, 250, 281
gardening, with children, 493–94
garlic, 325, 335, 691
garlic oils, 271
garlic pills, 744
garnishes, 243
gas, intestinal, 354, 567
gastric reflux disease (GERD), 728–29
gastrointestinal (GI) health, 453–55, 727–31
gelatin, 238
gender, as risk factor, 634, 683, 693–94
generally recognized as safe (GRAS) list, 139
genetic engineering, 154
genetics, and personal health, 629, 634, 651, 687, 740
GERD (gastric reflux disease), 728–29
German cuisine, 308
germander, 322
gestational diabetes, 554, 632, 699
ghee, 284, 400
GI (glycemic index), 351, 642, 709
Giardia lamblia, 224
GI health. *See* gastrointestinal health
ginger, 325
ginkgo biloba, 325–26, 335
ginseng, 326, 335
GL (glycemic load), 351
gleaning, 114
global cuisine. *See* ethnic cuisine; *specific cuisines*
gloves, plastic, 192
glucosamine, 331, 726
gluten-free foods. *See also* celiac disease; non-celiac gluten sensitivity
and carbohydrates, 605
for children, 499
communion wafers, 677
label lingo, 152, 672, 673–74
misconceptions, 676
natural choices, 674
as necessity, 670–77
during pregnancy, 553
restaurants, 676–77
shopping for, 674–75
storing and preparing, 675–76
for weight loss, 648
glutinous rice, 31, 675
glycemic index (GI), 351, 642, 709
glycemic load (GL), 351
glycogen, 606
goals, setting and reaching, 18–20
goat milk, 71, 92, 671
goji berry, 39
goldenseal, 326
gooseberries, 39
grading and inspection symbols, 154–55
graham flour, 27
grain-finished beef, 121
grains and grain products. *See also* whole grains
ancient grains, 27
for babies, 481–82
calories, limiting, 283
carbs and fiber in, 360, 706
cornmeal, 27
enriched and refined, 26
ethnic cuisine, 70, 299, 302, 305
fat content, 396
gluten-free, 677
health benefits, 28
healthy eating plan, 26–32
healthy recipe makeovers, 252–54
heirloom, 163
history, 130
key nutrients, 27–28
lean tips for, 261
list of, 31–32
meal planning, 70
nutrient retention, 248
portion size, 29
quick tips, 28, 30, 56–57
recommended amounts, 10–11, 23, 28
reducing food waste, 245
refrigerator storage of, 200
shopping for, 178–79
sprouted *vs.* unsprouted, 28
vegetarian eating pattern, 56–57
granadilla, 40
GRAS (generally recognized as safe) list, 139
grass-fed and grass-finished beef, 121, 166
graters, 233
gravies, degreasing, 261
great northern beans, 250
Greek cuisine, 274, 288, 300
Greek yogurt, 41, 71, 292, 381, 402
green beans, 250, 359
green coffee extracts, 326, 634
green haricot beans, 250
greens, 70, 161, 272, 281, 359
green shopping, 187–88
green tea, 99, 326, 573, 634
grilling, 215–16, 233, 236, 259, 570
grocery shopping. *See* shopping
ground meats
cholesterol in, 406
color of, 201, 214
fat content, 397
protein content, 381
storage of, 202
temperature, cooked, 210
thermometer placement, 213
growth, fats for, 390
guar gum, 331
guava (guayaba), 39
gum disease, 737
gut health. *See* gastrointestinal (GI) health

H1N1 (respiratory disease), 221
hair analysis, for vitamin or mineral deficiency, 416
hair loss, 573
Halal foods, 155
ham, 202, 210, 213, 254, 272, 281
hamburger. *See* ground meats
hamburgers, 291, 293
hand mixers, 233
hand sanitizer, 192
hand washing, 192, 195, 313, 496
hard cider, 105
hawthorn, 327
hazelnuts, 43
HDL ("good") blood cholesterol, 387, 686
health fraud, 755, 757–58
health risks, people with
age, as risk factor, 683, 693–94, 740
alcoholic beverages, 105
drinking water, 84
food allergies and allergens, 654
food alternatives, 222
gender, as risk factor, 634, 683, 693–94
race, as risk factor, 693, 740
supplement cautions, 337
health warnings, on food labels, 152
healthy, defined, 3–4
healthy eating
away from home, 275–314
basics, 22–25
choices and counterparts, 284
cooking for, 230–74
credible support for, 761–62
defined, and suggestions, 26
fueling fitness, 4
grains, 26–32
guidelines, 8–15, 771
home cooking, 230
plan, 25–51
readiness check-in, 4
recipe makeovers, 236–38
recommended amounts, 8–15, 23, 772–73, 774, 775
sample menus, 778–79
steps, 22
total diet focus, 9–10
tracking, 19
heart (protein food), 258
heart attack, 684, 692
heartburn (acid reflux), 550, 728
heart disease. *See* cardiovascular disease
heart health. *See* cardiovascular health
heart rate, 95, 695
Heimlich Maneuver, 196
heirloom vegetables, fruits, grains, 163
hemorrhoids, 731
hemp milk, 92–93
hemp seeds, 44, 401
hepatitis A, 224, 228
herbals and other botanicals, 320–28, 339–40, 551, 561, 725
herbal teas, 98–99, 551
herbed oils, 209, 271
herbed vinegars, 270
herbs
cooking with, 266, 270–74
defined, 267
ethnic flavor profiles, 269
growing, 267

herbs (*continued*)
history, 266
phytonutrients, 451
rub combos, 271
salt-free blends, 274
shopping for, 185
storage, 269–70
usage guide, 272–73
HFCS (high-fructose corn syrup), 182, 355
high-altitude cooking, 215
high blood pressure
and caffeine, 697
DASH (Dietary Approaches to Stop Hypertension), 51–52, 697, 776
defined, 693
food choices for, 696–97
health risks from, 693
as heart disease risk factor, 684
lifestyle changes for, 694
management, 693–98
medical plan for, 697–98
overweight and obesity link, 631
and pregnancy, 551
and protein, 377
risk factors, 693–95
and sodium, 433
testing for, 696
treatment, 694
high-fat foods, 57
high-fructose corn syrup (HFCS), 182, 355
high-oleic safflower and sunflower oils, 387
high-risk populations. *See* health risks, people with
histamines, 655
holiday menus, 644
Hollandaise sauce, 280, 286
home cooking. *See* cooking
home-delivered meals, 590, 762
hominy, 31, 253
honey, 266, 480, 666
hoodia, 327
hormones, 121, 560, 620–21, 629
hot-air popcorn popper, 233
hot dogs, 202, 222, 293, 397
hot flashes, 560
hot sauce, 214
humectants, 136
hunger signals, 464, 482, 643
hydration, 95, 447, 601–3
hydrogenation, 386, 387, 388
hydroponically grown foods, 119
hyperactivity, 95, 350
hypertension. *See* high blood pressure
"hypoallergenic diet," 667
hypoglycemia, 349
hyponatremia, 602
hypothyroidism, 683

IBS (irritable bowel syndrome), 728, 729–30
ice cream, 175, 396, 402, 412
illness, foodborne, 218–29
bacteria, 219–21, 223
mad cow disease, 223
molds, 226
older adults, 586
outbreaks, 219
parasites and viruses, 224–26
and pregnancy, 551–52
prevention, 219, 312–14
quick reference chart, 227–29
reporting, 224
restaurants, 285–86
symptoms, 223
tracking, 219
during travel, 312–14
treatment, 224, 226
when to call the doctor, 226
immersion blenders, 233
immune function, 454, 724
incontinence, 728, 732
Indian cuisine, 284, 288
indigestion, 728. *See also* digestion; gastrointestinal (GI) health
Indonesian cuisine, 288
indoor grills, 233
Indo-Pakistani cuisine, 308
infants. *See* babies and baby foods
inflammation, 684, 699
information, food and nutrition, 747–62
credible scientific journals, 749
email scares and scams, 755
expert advice, 747–48, 758–61
food and nutrition programs, 761–62
health fraud, 755, 757–58
judging the findings, 748–50
judging the message, 752–55
junk science, 758
nutrition advice to trust, 758–62
qualified experts, 758–61
read between the headlines, 748–55
scientific evidence hierarchy, 750
scientific studies, terms used in, 751–52
spotting truths, half-truths, and non-truths, 755–56
supermarkets, food companies, and more, 762
websites, 753–55, 760, 763–68
ingredient lists, on labels, 145, 150, 339, 340–41
injuries, kitchen, 196
insomnia, 560–61
inspection symbols, 154–55
instant-read thermometer. *See* food thermometers
insulin, 709
integrated pest management (IPM), 117–18
interesterified oil, 387
internal temperature. *See* food temperature
international cuisine. *See* ethnic cuisine
intestinal gas, 354, 567
intestines (protein food), 258
inulin, 348
iodine, 437, 547, 783, 785, 786
IPM (integrated pest management), 117–18
iron
for athletes, 610
for breastfed babies, 469
deficiencies, 438–39, 440, 722–23
excess amounts, 438–40
food pairings, 439
food sources, 440
function, 438
heme *vs.* nonheme, 439
in infant formula, 472
during menopause, 559
menstruating women, 533–34
older adults, 580–81
poisoning from, 517
during pregnancy, 547
recommended amount, 438, 783, 785, 786
supplements, 320–21
for teenagers, 526
in vegetarian eating pattern, 55
vitamin C connection, 580–81
irradiation (food preservation), 131–32, 221
irritable bowel syndrome (IBS), 728, 729–30
isoflavones, 332
isothiocyanates, 449
Italian cuisine, 71, 274, 289, 297–99

jams, 183
Japanese cuisine, 70, 71, 306–7
jarred foods, 175–76, 197, 208–9
jasmine rice, 31
Jerusalem artichoke, 36
jet lag, 310
jicama, 36, 70, 161
Job's tears, 31
JRA (juvenile rheumatoid arthritis), 726
juice. *See* fruit juices; vegetables
juice cleanse, 90
juice drinks. *See* fruit drinks
juicers, 233
junk science, 758
juvenile rheumatoid arthritis (JRA), 726

kale, 36, 161, 249
kamut, 31
kaniwa, 32
kasha, 31, 70, 253
kava, 322
kebobs, 237
kefir, 93
kelp, 36
ketchup, 199
kidney beans, 250, 251, 281, 359, 381
kidney disease, 632
kidney stones, 740
kids' menu (restaurants), 284, 290
kissing, 664
kitchens. *See also* cooking
arrangement for mobility, 596
cleanliness, 192–96, 285–86, 313, 496
equipment, 233–34, 596–97
reducing food waste, 243–46
safety, 196, 496–97
kitchen scale, 233
kitchen shears, 233
kiwano, 39
knives, 233, 235
kohlrabi, 36, 161
kombucha, 99, 456
Korean cuisine, 309
kosher foods, 155
kumquat, 39

labels, food
additives, 137
allergens, 145, 151–52, 659, 660–63
biotechnology, 126–27
calories, 641
carbohydrates, 358, 366–68
content claims, 146–48
country of origin, 153
decoding, 144–45, 155
dietary guidance statements, 151
fats, 401, 402–4
food safety and handling tips, 152
front-of-package, 148
genetic engineering, 154
gluten, 152, 672
grading and inspection symbols, 154–55
Halal foods, 155
health claims, 145, 150, 151
health warnings, 152
how to use, 151
for infants and young children, 486
ingredient lists, 145, 150
kosher foods, 155
manufacturer information, 153
marketing terms on, 154
meat labels, 165
"natural," meaning of, 154
net contents, 153
new labels, compared to old, 411
"98% fat-free," 401
nutrient content claims, 144, 146–48
Nutrition Facts, 144–49, 401, 403–4, 786
organic, 153–54
package dates, 153
probiotics, 455–56
protein, 380
restaurant menus, 283, 285
salt and sodium, 431, 435
seafood eco-labeling, 168
soy products, 384
structure/function claims, 145, 150–51

terms, meanings of, 155
type of food, 153
Universal Product Code (UPC), 155
unsaturated fats, 401
vitamins and minerals, 410
whole grains, 184
Zabiah Halal foods, 155
labels, supplements, 338–41
labneh (labna), 170
lactation. *See* breastfeeding
lactose-free milks, 92
lactose intolerance, 499, 666–70, 671
lactose sensitivity, 466
lamb
ethnic cuisine, 71
herbs and spices for, 272
lean cuts, 254, 255, 256
low-fat cooking methods, 256
storage of, 202
temperature, cooked, 210
thermometer placement, 213
lardo, 282
lardons, 282
lasagna, 50, 237
LDL ("bad") blood cholesterol, 387, 576, 685
lead exposure and poisoning, 84–85, 482, 509, 552
lean, defined, 403
lean meats, 254
learning, importance of nutrition to, 62–63, 500–501
leavening agents, 136–37
lecithin, 726
leeks, 36, 161
leftovers, safe use of, 200–201, 203, 204, 210, 216, 286
legumes. *See* beans and peas
lentils, 179–80, 250, 251–52, 359, 301, 700
less cholesterol, defined, 403
less fat, defined, 403
life expectancy, 575
light/lite, defined, 403, 641
lignan, 348
lignin, 348
lima beans, 250
lipid cholesterol. *See* blood (serum) cholesterol
lipids, 388, 390
lipoproteins, 388, 687–88
liposuction, 650
liquid smoke, 215
Listeria monocytogenes, 221, 228, 551
litchi. *See* lychee
liver (protein food), 258, 272, 397, 406, 412
livestock, organically raised, 122
local foods, 117, 276
longan, 39
longevity, 575
longevity rice, 31
loquat, 39
lotus root, 37
"low carb" foods, 366, 642
low cholesterol, defined, 403
low-fat foods, 57, 401, 403, 642
lunch
and afternoon sleepiness, 67
brown-bag, 217–18, 507
calorie levels, 65
hidden components, 66
school lunch, 505–6, 507
transporting safely, 217–18
two-minutes, 64
vegetarian menu, 74
luncheon meats. *See* deli meats
luo han guo, 371
lychee, 39, 70
lycopene, 449

macadamia nuts, 43, 391
macrobiotic diet, 57
macronutrients, 555, 781
macular degeneration, 579, 726
mad cow disease, 223
magnesium, 335, 428–29, 783, 785, 786
magnolia-stephania preparation, 322
major minerals, 425–35. *See also* calcium; electrolytes; magnesium; phosphorus
making weight, 532, 614–16
manganese, 440–41, 783, 785, 786
mangoes, 39, 70, 160, 412
mangosteen, 39
manioc, 36
manufacturer information, on labels, 153, 339
maple water, 90
margarine, 238, 397, 406
margaritas, 301
marinara, 280
matcha, 99
maturing and bleaching agents, 137
mayonnaise, 182–83, 217, 397
MCT (medium-chain triglycerides), 620
meal kits, 276
meal replacements, 650
meals, 60–80. *See also* breakfast; lunch; snacks
challenges and solutions, 71–73, 78–80
dinner, 65, 66, 73, 74
family meals, 73, 491–93
guidelines for mealtime, 69
meatless meals, 73–75
menu and calorie levels, 65
mindful eating, 78
mini-meals, 75
planning, 69–73
quick meals with foods on hand, 72
skipping meals for weight loss, 642
two-minutes, 64
measles-mumps-rubella (MMR) vaccine, 666
measuring cups and spoons, 233
meat. *See also specific meats*
for babies, 481–82
breakfast sides, 292
calories, 281, 283
canned or pouched, 176
color of ground beef, 201, 214
food preparation check-in, 247
herbs and spices for, 272
high risk foods and alternatives, 222
label lingo, 165
lean cuts, 120, 254, 256–57
low-fat cooking methods, 254–57
preparing safely, 209, 211
raw, safety of, 286
reducing food waste, 245
sandwich choices, 294
saturated fats, limiting, 254–55
servings per pound, 164
shopping for, 164–65, 176
storage of, 199–200, 202–3, 204
temperature, cooked, 210
terminology, 166
thermometer placement, 213
vegetarian recipe makeovers, 237
meatless diet. *See* vegetarian eating pattern
Meatless Monday campaign, 284
medical conditions, people with. *See* health risks, people with
medical nutrition therapy (MNT), 687
medications
and bone health, 741
and breastfeeding, 466, 557
cholesterol-lowering, 692
food interactions, 743, 744
for hypertension, 694
for obesity, 650
safety precautions, 743
supplements interactions, 323, 335
and vitamins, 411
Mediterranean-style eating pattern, 52–53, 774. *See also* Greek cuisine
medium-chain triglycerides (MCT), 620
melatonin, 310, 331
melons, 39, 160, 281, 360, 412
memory enhancers, 323, 582
men, health and nutrition, 564–73
andropause (aging male syndrome), 570
beyond meat, potatoes, and beer, 564–66
body image and eating disorders, 565
breast cancer in, 571
burping and passing gas, 567
as fathers, 468, 569
fertility, 567–68
grilling, 570
hair loss, 573
heart disease, 570–71
macronutrient needs, 781
middle years and beyond, 569–73
mineral needs, 783, 785
obesity, 569–70
osteoporosis, 571
overeating, 567
physical activity, 566–67
prostate health, 573
protein, 565
screening tests, 572
sleep, 567
soy foods, 568
supplements, 566, 573
vitamin needs, 782, 784
water needs, 781
menopause, 540, 558–61, 740
menstruation, 533–35, 536, 611
mental abilities, supplements for, 323
menus, healthy eating patterns, 778–79
menus, restaurants, 279
Italian cuisine, 297–98
kids' menus, 284, 290
labeling laws, 283, 285
menu language, 277
Mexican cuisine, 301
nutrition information, 282, 285
substitutions, 278
mercury, in fish, 225
metabolic rate, 576, 633–34
metabolic syndrome, 686
methylmercury, 552
Mexican cuisine, 70, 71, 274, 289, 301–3
Mexican yam, 561
mHealth, 760–61
microwaving
containers and wrappings, 214–15
equipment, 233
food safety, 214–15
how to, 260
safety for children, 495
and vitamins, 419
Middle Eastern cuisine, 71, 289, 309
midlife and beyond. *See also* older adults
andropause, 570
bone health, 559–60
heart disease, 570–71
menopause, 540, 558–61, 740
muscle loss, 559
nutrient needs, 559–60
obesity, 569–70
weight gain, 558–59
women, 557–63, 569–73
migraines, 677
milk, 90–92
a/B cultures, 671
allergens, 661, 664, 666, 667
aseptic packaging, 128
for athletes, 618
for babies, 472, 481–82
carbohydrates in, 706
chocolate milk, 362
cholesterol in, 406
cultured, 91–92
and diabetes, 709

milk (*continued*)
  fast-food meals, 292, 296
  fat content, 90–91, 396
  flavored, 91, 362
  freezing, 201
  goat's milk comparisons, 92
  healthy choices, 92, 93
  in infant formula, 472
  and kidney stones, 740
  lactose-free, 92
  nutrients, 91, 93, 248, 412, 414
  older adults, 579
  protein content, 381, 384
  raw *vs.* pasteurized, 201, 222
  shakes and smoothies, 297
  and sleep, 375
  soymilk comparisons, 92
  storage, 128, 201, 248
  substitutes, 665, 671
  and teenage weight gain, 532
milk chocolate, 98, 402
milk-fed veal, 166
milk thistle, 327
millet, 32, 253
mindfulness and mindless eating
  meals and snacks, 78
  restaurant meals, 276
  shopping, 156–58
  and weight management, 642–43
mineral oil, 593
minerals. *See* vitamins and minerals; *specific minerals*
mini food processor, 233
mini-meals, 64, 75
mixed foods
  carbohydrates in, 707
  casseroles, 50, 204, 210, 213, 237
  frozen, 174
  ingredient lists, 150
  lean tips for, 261
  shopping for, 174
  vegetarian recipe makeovers, 237
mixers, 233
MMR (measles-mumps-rubella) vaccine, 666
MNT (medical nutrition therapy), 687
mobility, and food preparation, 596–98
moist heat, cooking methods, 260
molasses, 346
mold, on cheese, 201
mold, and foodborne illness, 226
molybdenum, 441, 783, 785, 786
monosaccharides, 346
monosodium glutamate (MSG), 240, 303, 679
monounsaturated fatty acids (MUFAs), 386, 388
mood, 353, 561
morinda (noni), 331
Mornay sauce, 280
Moroccan cuisine, 70, 289
mouth feel, 239
movement. *See* physical activity; sports
MSG (monosodium glutamate), 240, 303, 679
MUFAs (monounsaturated fatty acids), 386, 388
muffins, 29, 79, 292, 360
mung beans, 250
muscles
  composition, 600
  cramps, 610
  loss with aging, 559, 576
  and protein, 376, 608–9
  and spinach, 440
mushrooms, 37, 70, 161, 201, 281, 414, 415
MyPlate (visual cue for healthy eating), 5, 15, 23, 25

nanotechnology, 138
Native American cuisine, 289
natto, 379, 381
natural additives, 136
"natural," meaning of, 154
natural sweeteners, 346
nausea and vomiting, 549–50, 720, 732
navy beans, 251, 359
NCGS. *See* non-celiac gluten sensitivity
NDTR (nutrition and dietetic technician, registered), 759
negative-calorie foods, 635
neotame, 371
"net carbs," 366
"net-impact carbs," 366
niacin, 418, 784, 786
night blindness, 414
night sweats, 560
nitrates, 84–85
non-celiac gluten sensitivity (NCGS), 670–71, 673, 675. *See also* gluten-free foods
nondairy foods
  beverages, 90, 92–93
  and milk allergies, 666, 671
  spreads, 171–72, 173–74
noni (morinda), 331
nonnutritive sweeteners, 267, 369–73, 544
nonstick pots and pans, 234
noodles, 293, 307. *See also* pasta
nopales, 36
"no refined sugar," 366
normal-weight obesity, 628
norovirus, 224–25, 228
"no sucrose," 366
"no sugar added," 150
nut butters, 180, 242, 359, 381, 397
nutrient-dense foods and beverages, 10, 49
nutrients, 343–456. *See also* carbohydrates; phytonutrients; probiotics; vitamins and minerals; water
  absorption, 454
  breakfast, 62
  Dietary Reference Intakes (DRIs), 6–7
  fat, 385–407
  label claims, 144, 146–48
  older adults, 577–85
  protein, 373–84
  recommendations, explanation of, 409
  retention, 248
  supplements, 316–20
  types and functions, 6
nutrigenomics, 687
nutrition. *See also specific foods and topics*
  additives for, 133–34
  cooked fruits and vegetables, 246
  counseling, 760
  and flavor, 240–41
  Food-A-Pedia, 23
  judging research findings, 748–50
  and learning, 62–63, 500–501
  organic foods, 122
  processed foods, 129
  scams, 757–58
  shopping savvy, 141–90
nutrition and dietetic technician, registered (NDTR), 759
Nutrition Facts
  content claims, 146–48
  Daily Values (DVs), 786
  for fact checking, 148–49
  fats, 403–4
  how to use them, 148–49
  reasons for using, 148
  unsaturated fats, 401
  updated labeling, 146–47
nuts
  calorie counts, 281
  carbs and fiber in, 361
  for flavor and texture, 242
  for heart health, 400
  list of, 43
  omega-3s and total fat in, 401
  shopping for, 180
  and weight loss, 635

OAS (oral allergy syndrome), 679
oatmeal, 29, 67, 292, 360, 396
oat milk, 93
obesity
  differed from overweight, 628
  health risks, 630–32, 684, 694
  medication for, 650
  in men, 569–70
  normal-weight, 628
offal. *See* variety meats
oils
  allergic response, 666
  vs. butter, 282
  defined, 388
  discolored, 215
  ethnic cuisines, 299, 302, 305
  fat content, 397
  food preparation check-in, 247
  healthy choices, 46–47, 395, 400, 402
  and heart health, 690
  herbed, 209
  high-oleic safflower and sunflower oils, 387
  hydrogenation, 386, 387, 388
  interesterified oil, 387
  key nutrients, 46
  lean tips for, 261–62
  liquid oil substitution for solid fat, 263
  olive oils, 182, 282, 393, 398, 690
  portion size, 47
  pump spray bottle, 234
  quick tips, 47, 59
  recommended amounts, 12, 23, 46–47
  refined and unrefined, 182
  shopping for, 182
  smelling bad, 215
  smoking when heated, 215
  vs. solid fats, 263, 386
  sources, 47
  vegetarian eating pattern, 59
older adults, 574–98
  adult day care, 590, 762
  aging as a progression, 577
  alcoholic beverages, 584
  antiaging miracles, 583
  appetite loss, 593–94
  at-home and residential care food services, 590–91
  biomarkers of age, 576
  brain health, 582
  calorie needs, 575
  caregivers, 597
  chewing problems, 594
  constipation, 593
  dishes and utensils, 597
  flavor loss, 592–93
  food and nutrition programs, 762
  foodborne illness, 586
  food dollar, maximizing, 589
  food for healthy aging, 575–77
  food safety, 586
  food shopping, 589–90
  healthy eating check-in, 587
  heart disease, 579
  kitchen arrangement, 596
  kitchen equipment, 596–97
  life expectancy, 575
  lifestyle changes, 587–91
  macular degeneration, 579
  meals and snacks, 575–76
  meals in minutes, 588–89
  memory, 582
  mobility and food preparation, 596–98
  nutrient needs, 577–85
  physical activity, 585–87, 769

physical challenges and strategies, 592–98
safety tips, 598
sandwich generation, 590
sleep, 579
slowing the aging process, 577
solo dining, 587–88
special diets, 598
supplements, 579, 580, 582
vegetarian eating pattern, 581
warning signs of poor nutrition, 589
weight gain, 594–96
weight loss, 594–95
oligosaccharides, 346
olive oils, 182, 282, 393, 398, 690
omega-3 fatty acids
advice, 393
and blood cholesterol, 692
in common foods (chart), 401
defined, 388
and health, 392
physiological effects, 390
recommended amounts, 394
supplements, 330, 392
omega-6 fatty acids, 388, 390, 392–93, 394
omega-7 fatty acids, 391
omega-9 MUFA, 390
omelets, 292
online grocery shopping, 158
ORAC (oxygen radical absorbance capacity), 424
oral allergy syndrome (OAS), 679
oral contraceptives, 536
oral health, 480, 735–38, 766
orange juice, 414
organic farming, 122–23
organic foods, 105, 121, 122, 123, 153–54, 482
organosulfur compounds, 451
osteoarthritis, 632, 726, 740
osteomalacia, 740
osteopenia, 740
osteoporosis, 571, 738–42, 766
ostrich, 46
oven-safe food thermometers, 213
overeating, 643
overhydration, 602
overweight
children, 502–3
differed from obesity, 628
health risks, 631–32, 684, 694
teenagers, 530–31
oxygen-enhanced drinks, 88
oxygen radical absorbance capacity (ORAC), 424
oysters, 210, 214, 225, 667

packaging
BPA in, 132
for freezing, 203–4
for microwaving, 214–15
pad Thai, 305
pain relievers, 744
pak choi. *See* bok choy
Paleo diet, 58
palm oil, 182
panbroiling, 236, 259
pancakes, 29, 292, 396
pancreas (protein food), 258
pan juices, degreasing, 261
pantothenic acid, 421, 422, 782, 784, 786
pantry
food storage, 197–98
quick meals with foods on hand, 72
staples, 234
papayas, 40, 70, 160
parasites, 205, 224–26
parsnips, 37, 161
partially hydrogenated oils (PHOs), 388
passion fruit, 40
pasta. *See also* noodles
carbs and fiber in, 360
gluten-free, 677
herbs and spices for, 272
Italian restaurants, 298
leftovers, food safety, 204
portion size, 29
sauces, 237, 280
shopping for, 177–78
volume, dried and cooked, 177
whole-wheat, 360
pâtés, 222
PCOS (polycystic ovary syndrome), 538–39
peanut allergies, 310, 656, 660, 664, 666
peanut butter, 180, 359, 381, 397
peanuts, 180, 359
pea protein, 382
peas. *See* beans and peas
pecans, 43, 381
pepino, 40
peptic ulcers, 730–31
pernicious anemia, 723–24
persimmon, 40
pest control, natural, 118
pesticides, 117, 118, 120, 122
pesto, 280, 298
pH control agents, 137
phenolic acids, 449
phenylalanine, 375
phenylketonuria (PKU), 679
PHOs (partially hydrogenated oils), 388
phosphorus, 429, 783, 785, 786
physical activity. *See also* sports
active living, 4–5
and blood cholesterol, 691
and bone health, 427, 739
and breastfeeding, 557
for busy lives, 640
calories burned, 8, 634–35
children, 475, 490, 516, 522–24, 569
choosing, 16–18
and diabetes, 711
fluid needs, 603
goals, 638
guidelines, 15–18, 769
habits for, 626
importance of, 639
infants, 475
intensity, measuring, 17
men, 566–67
monitoring, 647
older adults, 585–87
during pregnancy, 553–54
quick tips, 638–39
and salt needs, 432
teenagers, 529–30, 531
toddlers and preschoolers, 516
tracking, 648, 760–61
during travel, 311, 601
water needs, 447
weight management, 629, 638–39, 652
workday, 68
Physical Activity Guidelines for Americans, 5
phytoestrogens, 449–50, 562, 740
phytonutrients, 319, 448–53
phytosterols, 405
picnic foods, 217
pies, 50, 204, 263, 397, 402, 644
pigeon peas, 251, 429
pine nuts, 43
pinto beans, 251
pistachios, 43, 412
pizza, 50, 79, 204, 234, 237, 294–95
PKU (phenylketonuria), 679
plantains, 37, 70, 160
plant-based diets, defined, 52. *See also* vegetarian eating pattern
plant stanols and sterols, 405, 692
plastic gloves, 192
plumcot, 40
PMS (premenstrual syndrome), 534–35
poaching, 236, 260
pockets (sandwiches), 294
polycystic ovary syndrome (PCOS), 538–39
polyols (sugar alcohols), 368–69
polyunsaturated fatty acids (PUFAs), 387, 388
pomegranate, 40, 161
pomegranate juice, 573
pomelo, 40
popcorn, 29, 79, 233, 400
poppy seeds, 44
pork
brining and sodium content, 265
cholesterol in, 406
fatback, 282
fat content, 397
herbs and spices for, 272
lardo/lardons, 282
lean cuts, 254, 256
low-fat cooking methods, 256
protein content, 381
storage of, 202
tapeworm, 225
temperature, cooked, 210
thermometer placement, 213
portion size
and carbohydrates, 706–7
fast-food restaurants, 290
meals and snacks, 78–80
pizza, 295
plate method, 707–8
restaurant meals, 279
shift over time, 79
visual guide, 24
and weight management, 642
postpartum concerns, 554
potassium, 38, 319, 430, 433–34, 783, 786
potato chips, 49
potatoes, 34, 161, 204, 296, 359, 396, 635
pots and pans, 233, 234, 440
poultry
calorie counts, 281
canned or pouched, 176
healthy eating check-in, 247
herbs and spices for, 272
high risk foods and alternatives, 222
lean cuts, 254, 256–57
low-fat cooking methods, 254–57
organically raised, 122
preparing safely, 209, 211
reducing food waste, 245
saltwater solution, injected with, 265
servings per pound, 166
shopping for, 165–67, 176
storage of, 199–200, 202
temperature, cooked, 210
thermometer placement, 213
vegetarian recipe makeovers, 237
power outages, food storage safety, 205–8
prebiotics, 453–55, 456
precision farming, 117
prediabetes, 539, 698, 700
preeclampsia, 550–51, 632
pregnancy, 541–54
alcoholic beverages, 104, 549
caffeinated drinks, 548
carbohydrates, 544
constipation during, 550
cravings and food aversions, 553
diabetes, gestational, 551, 554, 632, 699
diabetes, preexisting, 551
dietary fat, 544
discomforts, 549–51
fiber, 548
and food allergies in baby, 656
food and nutrition programs, 762
food and sports, 613–14
and foodborne illness, 551–52
gluten-free diet, 553
heartburn (acid reflux), 550

pregnancy (*continued*)
herbals and other botanicals, 551
herbal teas, 551
and high blood pressure, 551
lead exposure, 552
macronutrient needs, 781
mineral needs, 547–48, 783, 785
nausea and vomiting, 549–50
nonnutritive sweeteners, safety of, 544
nutrients and calories, 539–41, 543–48, 781
nutrient supplements, 545
overweight and obesity risks, 632
physical activity, 553–54
postpartum concerns, 554
preeclampsia, 550–51
protein, 544
swelling, 550–51
teenagers, 527, 548–49
vegetarian eating pattern, 546
vitamin needs, 545, 547, 782, 784
water needs, 447, 781
weight, healthy, 540
weight gain, 541–43
prehypertension, 695, 696
premenstrual syndrome (PMS), 534–35
prenatal nutrition. *See* pregnancy
prepared foods, 186, 203
preparing foods. *See* cooking
preschoolers. *See* toddlers and preschoolers
preserving food, 128, 130–32, 133, 135
pressure cooker, 234
prickly pear, 40
primavera, defined, 277
prior-approved substances, 138–39
probiotics, 296, 323, 453–56, 473, 667
processed meats, 46, 717
processed poultry, 46
produce. *See* fruits; vegetables
productivity, workplace, 66–67
prostate health, 573
protein, 373–84
for athletes, 607–9, 618–19
for babies, 481–82
basics, 373–75
boosting, 382
breakfast, 63
building blocks, 373–74
for children, 508, 517
complete and incomplete, 375
ethnic cuisine, 71, 299, 302, 305
fast-food restaurants, 287
food sources, 378–84, 381
function, 6, 374
gluten-free foods, 674
health benefits, 44, 374–77
healthy eating plan, 42–46, 71, 380
key nutrients, 42, 44
label lingo, 380
for men, 565
muscle myths, 608–9
nutrients packaged with, 383
for older adults, 578
as percentage of body, 375
portion size, 45, 381
during pregnancy, 544
protein-based fat replacers, 407
quick tips, 45–46, 59
recommended amount, 11–12, 23, 44–45, 150, 377–78, 379, 786
satisfaction from, 377
shakes, 384
supplements, 382
for teenagers, 526
variety meats, 258
vegetarian eating pattern, 54, 59
and weight loss, 376, 648
provitamin A carotenoids, 410, 411, 412, 413
psyllium, 358
PUFAs (polyunsaturated fatty acids), 387, 388
pulses. *See* beans and peas
pumpkin seeds, 44, 381
pump spray bottles, 234
purple rice, 31
pyridoxine. *See* vitamin B_6
pyruvate, 620

quiche, 292
quinoa, 32, 253, 360, 381

RA (rheumatoid arthritis), 726–27
race, as risk factor, 693, 740
radiation therapy, 717–18
radicchio, 37
radishes, 36, 281
rambutan, 40
rapini, 36
raw foods, safety of, 208, 209, 286
raw milk, 201, 552
raw sugar, 347
RDAs (Recommended Dietary Allowances), 6, 409
RDN (registered dietitian nutritionist), 759
recalls of food, 221
recipes, 89, 91, 234–38, 268
Recommended Dietary Allowances (RDAs), 6, 409
red clover, 327, 561
red kidney beans, 251
red tide, 225, 314
reduced cholesterol, defined, 403
reduced fat, defined, 401, 403
reduction sauce, 280
refined sugar, 347
refreezing foods, 205
refrigerator
food storage safety, 198–201
packing food for, 198–99
power outages, food safety during, 206
shelf life of foods, chart of, 202–3
temperature, 198, 199, 234
regional cuisine, 24, 239. *See also* ethnic cuisine
registered dietitian nutritionist (RDN), 759
resistant starch, 348
restaurants, 275–314
added sugars, limiting, 290–91
annual sales, 275
bakery items, 292
balancing food choices, 277–78
bowl meals, 293
breakfast, 291–92
buffets, 280–83, 286
calories, 279, 283, 291
chicken, 293
with children, 284, 290, 507–8
cleanliness, 285–86
desserts, 296
dining alone, 285
drinks, 296–97
eating while driving, 287
ethnic cuisine, 288–89, 297–309
fast-food, 287–97
fish, 293
food allergens, 277, 278, 664–66, 667
food bars, 280–83, 286
food safety, 285–86
food waste, 276, 286
gluten-free meals, 676–77
healthy eating check-in, 290
leftover food, serving suggestions, 286
menu language, 277, 279, 297–98, 301
nutrition information, 282, 285
ordering your way, 278
pizza and flatbreads, 294–95
pleasures of, 276–77
portion size, 279, 290
salads, 280–83, 295–96
salt, limiting, 282, 290–91
sandwiches, 293, 294
saturated fats, limiting, 290–91
sauces, 280
side dishes, 296
social responsibility, 276
spa cuisine, 285
special needs, 277, 278
take-out foods, 186, 286
during travel, 309–14
trends, 276
vegetarian-style dining, 276, 283–84, 288–89
rheumatoid arthritis (RA), 726–27
rhubarb, 37
ribbed fry pan, 234
riboflavin. *See* vitamin B_2
rice
amount, dried *vs.* cooked, 178
cooking time, 253
glutinous, 31, 675
herbs and spices for, 272
leftovers, food safety, 204
nutrients, 360, 381, 396
portion size, 29
restaurant meals, 293, 298
shopping for, 178
types, 31, 32
rice cooker, 234
rice milk, 93, 384, 480
rickets, 414
road trips, 311–12
roasted turkey, 257
roasting, 234, 236, 249, 259
romesco (sauce), 280
rooibos tea (red bush tea), 99
rubs, 271
Russian cuisine, 309
rutabagas, 37, 161
rye, label lingo, 672
rye berries, 253

saccharin, 371
S-adenosyl methionine (SAM-e), 332
safety. *See* food safety; kitchens
salad dressing
calories, 281, 282, 283, 291, 642
fats, 291, 397, 399, 402
raw eggs in, 286
shopping for, 182–83
salads
calories, limiting, 283
fast-food, 295–96
fat, limiting, 257, 258, 260
herbs and spices for, 272
Italian restaurants, 298
leftovers, food safety, 204
salad bars, 280–83, 286
sodium, limiting, 283
salad spinner, 234
salmon, 119, 381, 397, 401, 406, 412, 414
Salmonella, 221, 228, 551–52
salsa, 34, 242, 402
salsify, 37
salt. *See also* sodium
in cooking water, 265
in cured meats, 254
and flavor, 246, 434
label lingo, 431
and muscle cramps, 610
preferences, 435
reducing, 264–65
in restaurant meals, 282
substitutes, 432
and thirst, 445
types, 186
uses, 434
salt pork, 254
SAM-e (S-adenosyl methionine), 332
sandwiches, 237, 291–92, 293, 294, 305
sandwich generation, 590
sanitation, emergency supply checklist, 207
sapodilla, 40

sarcopenia, 376, 576
sashimi, 286, 306
satiety, fats for, 390
saturated fats
  in foods (chart), 396–97
  label lingo, 403
  limiting, tips for, 50–51, 254–55, 290–91
  overview, 385–86
  physiological effects, 390
  recommended amount, 13–14, 23, 394, 398, 786
  substitutions, 262
  vegetarian eating pattern, 59
saturated fatty acids (SFAs), 388
sauces
  calories, limiting, 283
  Chinese cuisine, 303
  fats, reducing, 257–58
  fats in, 398
  herbs and spices for, 273
  list of, 280
  pizza, 294
  raw eggs in, 286
  shopping for, 183
sauerkraut, 293
sausage, 203
saw palmetto, 327
scale, kitchen, 233
school-age children, 516–24
  cholesterol levels, 522
  eating tactics, 521–22
  food allergies, 658
  healthy meals and snacks, 518–22
  healthy weight, 540
  nutrition and calorie needs, 516–18
  physical activity, 522–24
  vegetarian eating pattern, 520–21
  water needs, 518
school meals, 276, 505–7, 520, 527
science. *See* information
scombroid poisoning, 314
scurvy, 414
seafood. *See also* fish; shellfish
  bacteria in, 214
  eco-labeling, 168
  food safety, while traveling, 313–14
  raw seafood, safety of, 209, 286
  temperature, cooked, 210
seaphire, 37
seasickness, 311
seasonal allergies, 666
seasonings. *See* herbs; spices
seaweed, 37
seeds, 43–44, 180, 242, 281, 361, 400
selective breeding, 123–24
selenium, 441, 783, 785, 786
"sell by" or pull date, 153
seltzer, 88
senior citizens. *See* older adults
serum cholesterol. *See* blood cholesterol
sesame allergens, 663
sesame seeds, 44, 361
SFAs (saturated fatty acids), 388
shakes. *See* smoothies and shakes
shape and size of foods, 241
shark cartilage, 332
shears, kitchen, 233
shelf life, 128, 129, 197, 198
shellfish
  allergens, 663, 664, 667
  food safety, while traveling, 313, 314
  herbs and spices for, 272
  temperature, cooked, 210
Shigella, 221, 228
shipping food safely, 218
shopping, 141–90
  baking aisle, 183–85
  beans, peas, lentils, nuts, peanut and nut butters, 179–80
  beverages, 180–81
  breads and bakery products, 185–86
  canned, jarred, dried foods, 175–86
  cereals, 179
  with children, 494–95
  choices and decisions, 141–42
  condiments, sauces, jams, 183
  convenience foods, 176–77
  crackers and snack foods, 181–82
  dairy foods, 169–72
  deli, prepared, take-out foods, 186
  by department, 159
  dry seasonings, 185
  eggs, 172–73
  farmers' markets, 159
  fish, 167–69, 176
  food safety and quality, 188–90
  frozen foods, 174–75
  gluten-free foods, 674–75
  green shopping, 187–88
  hassle-free, 589–90
  healthy eating check-in, 144
  juice and juice drinks, 173
  label lingo, 144–55
  meat, 164–65, 176
  mindfully, 156–58
  oils and dressings, 182–83
  older adults, 589–90
  online, 158
  organic foods, 123
  pasta, rice, grains, 177–79
  perimeter of store, 159
  plan ahead, 156
  poultry, 165–67, 176
  produce, 159–64, 174, 175–76
  saving money, 155–58, 589
  shopping list for a healthy kitchen, 143
  small-household, 157
  soy, 175
  store excellence, 142
  supplements, 337–41
  timing your trip, 156
  tofu, tempeh, plant-based options, 173–74
shortening, 387
shrimp, 210, 281, 397, 406
side dishes, 204, 296
silicon, 785
simple carbohydrates, 345–47
sink cleanliness, 194
skin moisturizers, 416
skinny fat, 628
skyr yogurt, 170
sleep
  after lunch, 67
  apnea, 631
  and beverages, 97
  children, 504
  deprivation and weight gain, 629–30
  disturbances, postmenopausal, 560–61
  men, 567
  older adults, 579
  and physical health, 5
  and tryptophan, 375
sloppy joes, 237
slotted spoons, 234
slow cooker, 234
slow food, 78
smart eating. *See* healthy eating
SMART goals, 18–20
smell, and flavor, 239
smoking
  beta-carotene supplements, 424
  and bone health, 741
  and breastfeeding, 466, 557
  and fertility, 568
  heart disease risk factors, 683
  and weight gain, 644
smoothies and shakes, 292, 297, 384
snacks, 75–78
  benefits of smart snacking, 75–76
  calorie levels, 65
  carbohydrates in, 706
  for children, 493, 497, 510, 511, 518
  fats in, 402
  fruit snacks, 176
  mindful, 77–78
  myths, 76
  nutrient-rich options, 77
  oils in, 182
  and oral health, 736
  poor snacking, consequences of, 76–77
  at school, 506
  shopping for, 181–82
  sweet snacks, fewer calories, 641
  for teenagers, 527–28
  transporting safely, 217–18
  vegetarian menu, 74
SNAP (Supplemental Nutrition Assistance Program), 589, 761–62
soaps, antimicrobial, 196
social responsibility, of restaurants, 276
soda. *See* soft drinks
sodium. *See also* salt
  and blood pressure, 433, 694
  deficiencies, 432
  ethnic cuisine, 303, 305–7
  excess amounts, 432, 435
  food sources, 432, 435
  function, 431, 433–34
  ingredients with, 138
  label lingo, 431, 435
  older adults, 583
  during pregnancy, 548
  recommended amount, 14–15, 23, 431–32, 783, 785, 786
  reducing, 51, 279, 283, 290–91, 431, 434
  sensitivity, 432
  shopping tips, 177
  sources, 434–35
sodium nitrite, 135
soft drinks, 79, 98, 100–102, 296, 375, 738
solid fats, 263, 388, 394–95, 397, 398, 399–400
solo dining, 285, 587–88
sorghum, 32, 253
soup kitchens, 762
soups and stews
  defined, 236
  degreasing, 261
  fat, reducing, 257–58
  herbs and spices for, 273
  shopping for, 176–77
  storage of, 203, 204
  vegetarian recipe makeovers, 237
sour cream, 171, 397
sous vide, 132
South American cuisine, 289
soy
  allergens, 662, 664, 666
  and blood cholesterol, 691–92
  and breast cancer, 562
  label lingo, 384
  for men, 568
  for menopause symptoms, 561
  shopping for, 175
soybeans, 173, 251, 359, 364, 381, 740
soymilk, 92, 93, 381, 384, 414
soy protein, 332, 383, 384
spa cuisine, 285
Spanish cuisine, 289
special dietary needs, 277, 311, 598, 743. *See also specific health conditions*
spelt, 32, 253
spices, 185, 266–67, 269–74, 365, 451
spinach, 161, 281, 359, 412, 440
spirulina, 332, 620
sponges, kitchen, 194, 195
spoons, slotted, 234
sports, eating smart for, 599–621. *See also* physical activity
  after competition, 617–19
  breakfast, 605
  caffeine, 604
  candy bars, 608
  carbohydrates, 605–7, 618

sports (*continued*)
  children, 612–13
  during competition, 617
  electrolytes, 609–10, 618
  endurance sports, 611–12
  energy bars, 608, 617
  fats, 607
  fluid intake, 600–604, 618
  food guides, 611–12
  fueling your workout, 604–6
  game day, 616–19
  gluten free, 605
  healthy body check-in, 600
  high-performance diet, 611–14
  "hitting the wall," 605
  meal combos, 615
  milk, 618
  non-endurance sports, 612
  nutrients for, 599–611
  pre-event, 616–17, 618
  pregnancy and breastfeeding, 613–14
  protein, 607–9, 618–19
  supplements, 611, 619–21
  vegetarian athletes, 614
  vitamins and minerals, 609–11
"sports anemia," 610
sports drinks, 94, 603
spray bottles, 234
spreads
  dairy, 171
  fast-food breakfasts, 292
  lean tips for, 261, 291
  nondairy, 171–72, 173–74
  sandwich choices, 294
  trans fats, 401
  vegetarian recipe makeovers, 238
sprouts, 208, 222, 281, 286
squash, 37, 161, 359, 412
stabilizers, 137
Staphylococcus aureus (staph), 221, 228
staples, 234
starches, 346, 347–48, 362, 706. *See also* carbohydrates
starchy vegetables, 34
star fruit, 40
steak tartare, 286
steaming, 234, 236, 260
stearic acid, 388
steroids, 568, 620–21
stevia, 370
stewing, 260
stews. *See* soups and stews
sticky rice, 32
stir-fry, 50, 79, 236, 237, 259, 303
St. John's wort, 328, 335, 561
stomach lining (protein food), 258
stomach size, 647
strainers, 233
stroke, 631, 692
sucralose, 371–72
sugar. *See also* added sugars
  as addictive, 350
  alternatives, 368–72
  baking with, 266
  and cancer, 717
  and flavor, 246
  raw sugar, 347
  refined sugar, 347
  shopping for, 185
  sugar high, 350
  tips for reducing, 265–66
sugar alcohols (polyols), 368–69
sugar apple (sweetsop), 40
sugarcane, 347
sugar-free foods, 366
sugars (carbohydrates), 346, 347–48, 361–62, 367
sulfate, 430
sulfides/thiols, 450
sulfites, 136
sulfite sensitivity, 678
sunflower seeds, 44, 281, 381, 397
superfood, defined, 49
supermarkets. *See* shopping
supertasters, 240
supper. *See* dinner
Supplemental Nutrition Assistance Program (SNAP), 589, 761–62
supplements, 315–41
  adverse reactions, 336
  and allergies, 336
  antiaging, 323, 583
  antioxidants, 318, 425
  for athletes, 611, 619–21
  for babies, 469–70, 480
  benefits and risks, 321–22
  beta-carotene, 424
  and breastfeeding, 466, 469–70, 557
  calcium, 320–21, 428
  checklist, 338
  chelated minerals, 339
  for children, 337, 519
  claims, 340
  for diabetes, 703, 709
  dosage, 318–20
  drug interactions, 323, 335
  effectiveness, 324–35
  fats in, 339
  FDA regulated, 328, 333
  fiber, 357
  fish-oil, 330, 392, 691
  folate, 541
  hair loss, 573
  health warnings, 322–23
  in healthy diet, 49, 335–36
  herbals and other botanicals, 320–28, 339–40
  ingredients, 339, 340–41
  interactions, 320
  iron, 320–21
  label lingo, 319, 338–41, 672
  macular degeneration, 579
  medical advice concerning, 334, 336–37, 338
  for memory, 582
  for men, 566, 573
  myths and facts, 317
  nutrient supplements, 316–20
  for older adults, 579, 580
  omega-3 fatty acids, 330, 392, 691
  phytonutrients in, 319, 448
  during pregnancy, 545
  probiotics, 323, 456
  protein, 382
  quality standards, 328, 333
  risks, 318–20, 324–25
  science behind, 333–34
  shopping for, 337–41
  storage, 341
  usage guidelines, 335–41
  weight loss, 649–50
surgery, for weight loss, 650
surimi (imitation crabmeat), 168, 281
sushi, 286, 306
sustainable foods, 115, 129. *See also* food waste
sweet-and-sour sauce, 280
sweetbreads (protein food), 258
sweeteners, 138, 267, 346, 356. *See also* sugar; *specific sweeteners*
sweet rice, 32
sweetsop, 40
Swiss cuisine, 289
synbiotics, 453
syrup, storage safety, 199

Taenia saginata, 225
Taenia solium, 225
tagatose, 370
tail (protein food), 258
take-out foods, 186, 286
tamarillo, 40
tapeworm, 225
tap water. *See* water
taro, 37
taste experience, 238–39. *See also* flavor
tea, 93–100
teenagers, 524–32
  acne, 528
  alcohol risks, 104, 529
  anemia, 723
  bodybuilding, 532
  bone health, 526
  calories, 525
  diabetes in, 712
  eating disorders, 531–32
  fitness with a friend, 531
  food, nutrients, and growth, 525–27
  healthy eating plans, 527–29
  healthy food choices, 524
  nutrient needs, 525–27
  parenting tactics, 528–29
  physical activity, 529–30, 531
  pregnancy, 527, 548–49
  school meals, 527
  skipping meals, 527
  snacks, 527–28
  vegetarian eating pattern, 520–21
  weight, 501–2, 530–32, 540, 651
teething, 478
teff, 32
telomeres, 577
tempeh, 71, 173, 379, 381
temperature, food. *See* food temperature; food thermometers
testicles (protein food), 258
Texmati rice, 32
texture, and flavor, 241, 242
texturizers, 137
Thai cuisine, 304–6
thawing foods safely, 205
thermometers
  food, 212, 213, 214, 233
  refrigerator, 234
thiamin. *See* vitamin B_1
thickeners, 137
thirst, and salt, 445
thymus (protein food), 258
thyroid problems, 558, 630, 683
tocopherols. *See* vitamin E
toddlers and preschoolers, 508–16
  active living, 516
  amounts of food, 510–12
  in child-care setting, 514–16
  finger foods, 510
  food behavior markers, 509
  food guide, 510
  food jags, 512
  food safety, 511
  healthy meals and snacks, 510, 511
  meal and snack patterns, 513
  mealtime tactics, 512, 514
  new foods, 514
  nutrient and calorie needs, 508–10
tofu, 173, 281, 364, 381
Tolerable Upper Intake Levels (ULs), 6, 356, 409, 784, 785
tomatillos, 37, 70
tongue (protein food), 258
tooth care. *See* oral health
tortillas, 29, 426
total carbohydrates, 367
total fat, 396–97, 398, 401, 786
touch, and flavor, 239
Toxoplasma gondii, 225–26, 551
trace minerals, 425, 436–42. *See also* chromium; copper; fluoride; iodine; iron; manganese; molybdenum; selenium; zinc
trans fats
  ban on, 404
  defined, 387, 389
  label lingo, 150
  physiological effects, 390
  recommended amounts, 13–14, 394–95
  spreads, 401
  vegetarian eating pattern, 59
trans fatty acids (TFAs), 388

Transportation Security Administration (TSA), 310
transporting food safely, 190, 217–18, 286, 312
travel, 309–14
  airline food and drinks, 309–10
  baby foods, 485
  breakfast on the road, 311–12
  business travelers, 311
  cruise ships, 311
  diarrhea, 313, 314
  drinking water, 314
  driving and eating, 287
  food safety in faraway places, 312–14
  jet lag, 310
  physical activity during, 601
  precaution on your trip, 313–14
  pre-travel precaution, 313
  road trips, 312
  snacks, 77
tree nut allergies, 661, 664, 667
tree nuts, 43, 180
Trichinella spiralis, 226
trichinosis, 226
triglycerides, 388, 686–87
tripe, 258
triticale, 32, 253
tropical oils, 399
tryptophan, 375
TSA (Transportation Security Administration), 310
turkey, 166, 210, 257, 265, 272, 281
turmeric, 726
two-minute meals, 64
type 1 and 2 diabetes. *See* diabetes

ubiquinone (coenzyme Q10), 329
ugli fruit, 40
ulcers, 730–31
ULs. *See* Tolerable Upper Intake Levels
ultraviolet light, and vitamin D, 415
undernutrition, effects on learning, 501
underweight, 504, 651, 652, 740
United Nations Food and Agriculture Organization (FAO), 24
Universal Product Code (UPC), 155
unsaturated fats, 385–87, 390, 396–97, 401
unsweetened chocolate, caffeine in, 98
upper limits. *See* Tolerable Upper Intake Levels
urinary incontinence, 728, 732
urinary tract infections, 536
"use by" date, 153
utensils, cleanliness, 192, 195
UV light, and vitamin D, 415

vaccines, 666
vacuum sealers, 199
vaginal yeast infections, 536, 538
variety meats, 46, 203, 258
veal, 71, 166, 202, 210, 213, 256, 272
vegan eating pattern, 53–54, 379, 391, 520
vegetables. *See also specific vegetables*
  antioxidants, 425
  for babies, 482
  calories, 281, 283
  canned, jarred, dried, 175–76
  carbs and fiber in, 359, 706, 707
  for children, 498, 500
  by color, 33–34
  cooking and nutrition, 246
  cruciferous vegetables, 34
  ethnic cuisine, 70, 299, 302, 305
  ethylene gas, 119
  fast-food restaurants, 287, 296
  fat content, 260–61, 396
  fitting more in, 246–51
  food preparation check-in, 247
  freezing, 204
  freshness, determining, 161–62
  frozen, 174
  health benefits, 33
  healthy eating plan, 32–35, 36–37
  heirloom, 163
  herbs and spices for, 272, 273
  high risk foods and alternatives, 222
  juices, 89–90, 412, 619–20
  leftovers, food safety, 204
  list of, 36–37
  meal planning, 70
  nutrient retention, 246, 248
  nutrients, 32–33, 38
  oral allergy syndrome (OAS), 679
  preparing safely, 208
  processed, 127
  quick tips, 34–35, 57
  recommended amounts, 10, 23, 33–34
  reducing fat in, 260–61
  reducing food waste, 245
  roasting, 249
  sandwich choices, 294
  shopping for, 159–64, 174, 175–76
  starchy vegetables, 34
  storage of, 200
  ugly, and nutrition, 163
  vegetarian eating pattern, 57
  wax coating, 128
vegetarian eating pattern, 53–59
  for athletes, 614
  for babies, 477
  for children, 520–21
  dairy and dairy alternatives, 58–59
  definitions, 53–54
  ethnic cuisine, 288–89
  fat content of foods, 57
  fruit, 57
  glossary, 55
  gluten-free, 677
  grains, 56–57
  health benefits, 54
  how it works, 56–59
  meatless meals, 73–75
  nutrients to focus on, 54–56
  for older adults, 581
  omega-3s, 391
  during pregnancy, 546
  quick tips, 56–59
  recipe makeovers, 237–38
  recommended amounts, 74, 775
  restaurant meals, 276, 283–84
  sandwiches, 294
  stocking the kitchen, 187
  switching to, 57
  vegetables, 57
  for weight loss, 635
velouté, 280
vending machine snacks, 77
venison, 46
Vibrio, 221, 228
Vietnamese cuisine, 70, 304–6
vinaigrette, 280
vinegar, 182–83, 270, 271
viruses, and foodborne illnesses, 224–26
visual development, fats for, 390
vitamin A, 410–13
  deficiencies, 411, 414
  drug interactions, 335
  excess amounts, 411, 413
  food sources, 38, 412, 413
  function, 410
  older adults, 581
  during pregnancy, 545
  recommended amount, 410, 782, 784, 786
vitamin B. *See* B complex vitamins
vitamin B_1 (thiamin), 414, 417, 782, 784, 786
vitamin B_2 (riboflavin), 417–18, 782, 784, 786
vitamin B_6 (pyridoxine), 418–19, 556, 581–82, 784, 786
vitamin B_{12} (cobalamin), 420–21
  and anemia, 723–24
  deficiencies, 420
  excess amounts, 421
  food sources, 421
  function, 420
  older adults, 582
  recommended amount, 420, 782, 784, 786
  in vegetarian eating pattern, 56
  while breastfeeding, 556
vitamin C (ascorbic acid), 422–23
  as antioxidant, 424
  and common cold, 319
  deficiencies, 414, 422, 423
  excess amounts, 319, 422–23
  food sources, 38, 423
  function, 422
  iron connection, 580–81
  older adults, 580–81
  during pregnancy, 545
  recommended amount, 422, 782, 784, 786
  as water-soluble vitamin, 410
vitamin D, 413–15
  for athletes, 610–11
  and bone health, 427, 739, 741
  and breastfeeding, 469, 556
  for children, 469, 518
  deficiencies, 413–14
  excess amounts, 414
  as fat-soluble vitamin, 410
  food sources, 93, 263–64, 414–15
  function, 413
  in midlife and beyond, 559–60
  for older adults, 578, 580
  during pregnancy, 545, 547
  recommended amount, 413, 782, 784, 786
  for teenagers, 525
  in vegetarian eating pattern, 56
vitamin D_2, 319
vitamin D_3, 319
vitamin E, 410
  and aging, 579
  as antioxidant, 424–25
  Daily Values (DVs), 786
  deficiencies, 415
  Dietary Reference Intakes (DRIs), 782, 784
  drug interactions, 335
  excess amounts, 415
  food sources, 415–16
  function, 415
  as preservative, 136
  recommended amount, 415
  in skin moisturizers, 416
vitamin-enhanced beverages, 101–2
vitamin K, 416–17
  for breastfed babies, 469–70
  deficiencies, 416
  drug interactions, 335
  excess amounts, 416–17
  as fat-soluble vitamin, 410
  food sources, 416, 417
  function, 416
  recommended amount, 416, 782, 784, 786
vitamins and minerals, 408–42. *See also* supplements; *specific vitamins and minerals*
  as antioxidants, 423–25
  for athletes, 609–11
  for babies, 469–70, 480
  and breastfeeding, 469–70, 555, 557
  for children, 509, 517–18
  cooking's effect on, 417, 419
  deficiencies, 319, 414, 416
  drug interactions, 411
  fat-soluble vitamins, 389–90, 409–17
  food sources, 410
  function, 6, 408–9
  label lingo, 410
  major minerals, 425–35

vitamins and minerals (*continued*)
nasal sprays and patches, 319
during pregnancy, 545, 547–48
recommended amounts, 782, 783, 785
for teenagers, 525–26
trace minerals, 425, 436–42
water-soluble vitamins, 409, 410, 417–23
vomiting. *See* nausea and vomiting
vulnerable populations. *See* health risks, people with

waist size, 627
walnuts, 43, 361, 381, 401
waste. *See* environmental considerations; food waste
water
athletes' needs, 603
babies' needs, 463, 781
body's fluid balance, 447
bottled water, 85–87
children's needs, 509–10, 518, 781
chlorine in, 85
clean water, 87–88
conserving, 244
emergency supply, 84, 207
excess amounts, 445–46
filters, 88
flavored and nutrient-added, 86, 87, 102
fluoride in, 83
food sources, 444, 446
function, 6
glossary, 86
hard or soft, 84
healthy eating check-in, 445
healthy habits, 447–48
lead and nitrates in, 84–85
as nutrient, 443–48
older adults' needs, 584
recommended amount, 444–47, 781
regulations, 85–86
safety of, while traveling, 314
shopping for, 86–87
sodium in, 432
tap water, 81–85, 87, 314, 509
teenagers' needs, 526–27
testing, 85
treatment, 82
and weight loss, 642
water chestnuts, 667
water intoxication (hyponatremia), 602
water-soluble vitamins, 409, 410, 417–23. *See also* B-complex vitamins; vitamin C
wax coating on produce, 128
waxy rice, 32
weaning, 470
wearable fitness devices, 760–61
wehani rice, 32
weight, healthy
and blood cholesterol, 691
and BMI, 568, 627–28
body shape and composition, 626–27
body signals, 643
breakfast for, 63
and calories, 13, 633–35, 638
child's and teen's, 501–5, 613
determining, 625–28
and diabetes, 711–12
eating plan for, 639–41
eating triggers, 643
and fats, 393–94
fiber for, 350
healthy eating check-in, 636–37
mindful eating, 642–43
monitoring, 647–48
party plan, 644
and physical activity, 13, 638–39
portion savvy, 642
positive mind-set, 646
protein and, 376
as range, 647
reaching and maintaining, 625–52
support team, 644–46
waist size, 627
weight management strategies, 637–48
your personal healthy weight, 625–28
weight, making weight (athletes), 532, 614–16
weight-bearing exercise, 610
weight cycling, 633
weight gain
causes, 629–30
eating plan for, 651–52
midlife and beyond, 558–59
in older adults, 594–96
and smoking, 644
weight loss
and cancer treatment, 721
common questions, 642
and diabetes, 710
diet pills, 650
evaluating plans, 637, 645
fasting, cleansing, and detoxing, 649
gimmicks and "miracles," 650, 652
gluten free, 648
group programs, 646
health professionals, 645–46
high-protein/low-carb diet, 648
meal replacements, 650
in older adults, 594–95
plateaus, 647
popular diets, 648–50, 652
slow and steady approach, 633
spot reduction, 639
supplements, 323, 649–50
surgery and liposuction, 650
wellness, 3–5
wheat, 662, 664, 665, 672, 675
wheat berries, 32, 253
wheat bran, 178
wheat germ, 178
wheat gluten, 677
wheatgrass, 297
whey protein, 381, 382
white kidney beans, 250
white sapote, 40
whole grains
defined, 26, 27
fast-food restaurants, 287
and fiber, 358
food preparation check-in, 247
healthy recipe makeovers, 252–54
how to cook, 253
identifying, 184
nutrients, 27
portion size, 29
whole-wheat flour, 178
WIC (Women, Infants, and Children) Program, 762
wild mushrooms, 201
wild rice, 32, 253
wild yam, 561
willow bark, 322
wine, 105, 106, 107, 695
winter squash, 37, 359
woks, 234
wolfberry, 39
women, health and nutrition, 533–63. *See also* breastfeeding; pregnancy
alcoholic beverages, 104
anemia, 723
body image, 535
breast cancer, 561–63
childbearing years, 533–41
fertility, 539
foods designed for, 558
girlfriends as support network, 534
health concerns, 536–39
heart disease, 562–63
macronutrient needs, 781
menopause, 540, 558–61, 740
menstruation, 533–35, 536, 611
midlife and beyond, 557–63
mineral needs, 610–11, 783, 785
screening tests, 537–38
vitamin needs, 782, 784
water needs, 781
weight, healthy, 540
Women, Infants, and Children (WIC) Program, 762
workplace, healthy eating at, 66–68, 77
wormwood, 322
wraps (sandwiches), 294

yeast infections, 536, 538
yerba mate, 99
yogurt
fast-food meals, 292
frozen, 41, 174, 296, 396, 402
Greek yogurt, 41, 71, 292, 381, 402
nutrients in, 381, 396, 412, 414
portion size, 41
shopping for, 170, 174
skyr, 170
yohimbe, 322

Zabiah Halal foods, 155
zapote, 40
zinc, 441–42
and breastfeeding, 557
and common cold, 319
deficiencies, 442
excess amounts, 442
food sources, 442
function, 441–42
older adults, 583
during pregnancy, 547–48
recommended amount, 442, 783, 785, 786
in vegetarian eating pattern, 55–56
zoonutrients, 453

Chapter 16

Object-oriented Programming Foundations

This chapter will discuss object-oriented terms and definitions. As you prepare to enter the world of object-oriented programming, you should know that except for your current version of the Microsoft Visual C++ compiler, no special hardware is required.

When a program is written and compiled into an executable format, an .EXE file is created. Take a moment to think about just what that means. In file type terms, it means that a *.EXE is a *.EXE is a *.EXE. In other words, no matter if the source file was interpreted (as in the case of the BASIC language), compiled (as in assembly language, Pascal, FORTRAN, C, and C++), or compiled *and* interpreted (as in Java), once the translator generated the final executable form, they all ran on the same microprocessor!

This means that regardless of the source syntax, all of the program's instructions are translated down to machine language: adds, subtracts, compares, jumps, loops, and so on—native to the microprocessor. If you know assembly language, you already know just how close a language can be to the actual microprocessor's native tongue. As a language becomes more "high-level," you simply force the interpreter or compiler to do more work in getting your English-like statements translated to something the computer understands. And, in the case of all object-oriented languages, even more translation work is required.

However, the burden of work is on the translator. Since you do not buy a new computer to run object-oriented programs, object-oriented languages are inherently incapable of providing any additional microprocessor horsepower than, say, assembly language! Stop for a moment to ponder this last statement.

The real question to ask is "What is real different about object-oriented languages such as C++?" In a word—packaging! Consider this simple analogy. For the purpose of argument, imagine a program that declares and uses 100 integer variables. Messy, yes, but structurally possible. Now, imagine that you are in an intro computer course and your instructor begins teaching the topic of arrays. Ah, you say, what a logical and syntactical way to clean up this mess of 100 hundred separate, stand-alone integer variables! However, you also know that the rewritten array version did not give your program any more horsepower—it just streamlined logical and syntactical efficiency. In a similar sense, that is all that object-oriented programming does.

Object-oriented programming languages streamline and repackage concepts you, as a programmer, already know! What *are* new are those language constructs unique to C and C++, not found in other programming languages, that form the foundational building blocks to C++'s object-oriented capabilities. For example, C's keyword **static** is a non-object-oriented language feature. However, **static** can be used in object-oriented programs. If you are new to object-oriented design and syntax, your problem will not be learning how to repackage what you already know—such as how to write a function (called a member function or method in OOP terminology)—but rather how to incorporate C and C++'s new constructs in conjunction with the repackaging.

Here is one more fundamental concept you need to understand. You do not need to use object-oriented syntax to write a Windows 98 or NT application, and you can use object-oriented syntax to write DOS applications! Object-oriented syntax is a separate issue from what a program needs structurally to run under a multitasking operating system like Windows, or under the now fading command-line MS-DOS mode. Beginning OOPS and Windows programmers often view the two requirements as one entity.

More confusion is added to the mix by the product-specific recombinations of this packaging of "standard Windows syntax" used by companies. Using all of the objects available in the Visual C++ compiler package, for example, can be an overwhelming experience at first. To avoid this, Microsoft has preselected "standard" Windows objects and repackaged the already repackaged horsepower. Microsoft calls this double repackaging MFC (Microsoft Foundation Class) library.

With all of this information under your belt, sit back and relax. In this chapter you will see what you already know as a programmer become the underpinnings to object-oriented horsepower. They only thing standing in your way is terminology. Many of the procedural language fundamentals you already use have new names in an object-oriented world. For example, in this chapter you will learn how the C++ **class** type (an actual object-definition syntax/concept) is an outgrowth of the C **struct** type (a regular procedural language record-definition syntax/concept)!

There Is Nothing New Under the Sun

Advertisers know that a product will sell better if the word "new" appears somewhere on the product's label. If, however, the saying "There is nothing new under the sun" is applied to programming, the conclusion would have to be that object-oriented programming is not a new programming concept at all. Scott Guthery stated in 1989 that "object-oriented programming has been around since subroutines were invented in the 1940s" ("Are the Emperor's New Clothes Object Oriented?," *Dr. Dobb's Journal*, December 1989). The article continued by suggesting that objects, the foundation of object-oriented programming, have appeared in earlier languages, such as FORTRAN II.

Considering these statements, why are we only hearing about object-oriented programming in the closing decade of the 1900s? Why is it being touted as the newest programming technique of the century? It seems that the bottom line is packaging. OOP concepts may have been available in 1940, but we certainly didn't have them packaged in a usable container.

Early programmers, growing up with the BASIC language, often wrote large programs without the use of structured programming concepts. Pages and pages of programming code were tied together with one- or two-letter variables that had a global scope. The use of **goto** statements abounded. The code was a nightmare to read, understand, and debug. Adding new features to such a program was like unlocking Pandora's box. To say the least, the code was very difficult to maintain.

In the 1960s, structured programming concepts were introduced suggesting the use of meaningful variable names, global and local variable scope, and a procedure-oriented top-down programming approach. Applying these concepts made code easier to read, understand, and debug. Program maintenance was improved because the program could now be studied and altered one procedure at a time. Programming languages such as Ada, C, and Pascal encouraged a structured approach to programming problems.

Bjarne Stroustrup is considered the father of C++; he developed the language at Bell Labs in the early 1980s. He may well be the father of object-oriented programming as we know it in the C++ language. Jeff Duntemann stated that "Object-oriented programming is structured Structured Programming. It's the second derivative of software development, the Grand Unifying Theory of program structure" ("Dodging Steamships," *Dr. Dobb's Journal*, July 1989). Indeed, what you'll see as we go along is that object-oriented programming, using C++, builds upon foundations established earlier in the C language. Even though C++ is the foundational language for object-oriented programming, it is still possible to write unstructured code or procedure-oriented code. The choice is yours.

There might not be anything new under the sun if Scott Guthery's statements are taken to mean "programming concepts," but this chapter introduces you to the most elegant packaging method for a programming concept you have ever seen. At last we truly have the tools, with languages such as C++, to enter the golden age of object-oriented programming.

Traditional Structured Programming

The earlier chapters of this book were devoted to teaching traditional procedure-oriented structured programming techniques for solving C and C++ problems. These chapters introduced you to fundamental C and C++ syntax in a familiar programming environment. Procedure-oriented programming is common among all structured languages, including C, C++, Pascal, and PL/I. A procedure-oriented C or C++ program is structured in such a way that there is typically a main( ) function and possibly one or more functions (subroutines) that are called from the main( ) function. This is a top-down approach. The main( ) function is typically short, shifting the work to the remaining functions in the program. Program execution flows from the top of the main( ) function and terminates at the bottom of the same function.

In this approach, code and data are separate. Procedures define what is to happen to data, but the two never become one. You'll see that this changes in object-oriented programming. The procedural approach suffers from several disadvantages, chiefly program maintenance. When additions or deletions must be made to the program code, such as in a database program, the entire program must often be reworked to include the new routines. This approach takes enormous amounts of time in both development and debugging. A better approach toward program maintenance is needed.

Object-oriented Programming

Object-oriented programs (OOPs) function differently from the traditional procedural approach. They require a new programming strategy that is often difficult for traditional procedure-oriented programmers to grasp. In the next four chapters you will be introduced to the concepts that make up object-oriented programming in C++. If you have already written or examined program code for Windows 95, 98, or NT, you have had a taste of one of the concepts used in object-oriented programming—that a program consists of a group of objects that are often related. With C++, objects are formed by using the new class data type. A class provides a set of values (data) and the operations (methods or member functions) that act on those values. The resulting objects can be manipulated by using messages.

It is the message component of object-oriented languages that is also common to Windows and Presentation Manager programs. In object-oriented programming, objects hold not only the data (member data), but the methods (member functions) for working on that data. The two items have been combined into one working concept. Simply put, objects contain data and the methods for working on that data.

There are three distinct advantages offered to the programmer by object-oriented programming. The first is program maintenance. Programs are easier to read and understand, and object-oriented programming controls program complexity by allowing only the necessary details to be viewed by the programmer. The second advantage is program alteration (adding or deleting features). It is possible to make additions and deletions to programs, such as in a database program, by simply adding or deleting objects. New objects can inherit everything from a parent object, and they only need to add or delete items that differ. The third advantage is that you can use objects numerous times. Well-designed objects can be saved in a toolkit of useful routines that can easily be inserted into new code with few or no changes to that code.

In the earlier chapters of this book, you probably discovered that you could convert many C programs to C++, and vice versa, by making simple program alterations. For example, **printf** is switched to **cout** for I/O streams. This is an easy switch because the conversion is from a procedure programming structure to a procedural programming structure. However, object-oriented programming is exclusively in the C++ realm because C does not provide the vital link—the abstract data type class. It is therefore more difficult to convert a procedure-oriented program to object-oriented form. Programs have to be reworked, with traditional functions being replaced with objects. In some cases, it turns out to be easier to discard the old program and create an object-oriented program from the ground up. This can be considered a distinct disadvantage.

C++ and Object-oriented Programming

Object-oriented programming concepts cross language boundaries. Microsoft Pascal, for example, was one of the first languages to allow the use of objects. What does C++

have that makes it a suitable language for developing object-oriented programs? The answer is simply the class data type. It is C++'s **class** type, built upon C's **struct** type, that gives the language the ability to build objects. Also, C++ brings several additional features to object-oriented programming not included in other languages that simply make use of objects. C++'s advantages include strong typing, operator overloading, and less emphasis on the preprocessor. It is true that you can do object-oriented programming with other products and in other languages, but with C++, the benefits are outstanding. This is a language that was designed, not retrofitted, for object-oriented programming.

In the next section of this chapter, you will learn some object-oriented terminology. These terms and definitions will help you form a solid understanding of this programming technique. Be prepared; the new terminology will be your biggest hurdle as you enter the world of object-oriented programming.

Object-oriented Terminology

Much of the terminology of object-oriented programming is language independent—that is, it is not associated with a specific language such as Pascal or C++. Therefore, many of the following definitions apply to the various implementations of object-oriented languages. Chapter 17 discusses terms that are more C++ specific.

Object-oriented programming is a programming technique that allows you to view concepts as a variety of objects. By using objects, you can represent the tasks that are to be performed, their interaction, and any given conditions that must be observed. A data structure often forms the basis of an object; thus, in C or C++, the **struct** type can form an elementary object. Communicating with objects can be done through the use of messages, as mentioned earlier. Using messages is similar to calling a function in a procedure-oriented program. When an object receives a message, methods contained within the object respond. Methods, also called member functions, are similar to the functions of procedure-oriented programming. However, methods are part of an object.

The C++ class is an extension of the C and C++ **struct** type and forms the required abstract data type for object-oriented programming. The class can contain closely related items that share attributes. Stated more formally, an object is simply an instance of a class. In Figure 16-1, the **Lincoln automobile** class is illustrated.

Assume that the **Lincoln automobile** class is described in the program's code. This class might include a description of items that are common to all Lincolns and data concerning maintenance intervals. At run time, three additional objects of the **Lincoln** class can be created. They could include the **Lincoln Town Car**, the **Lincoln Mark**, and the **Lincoln Continental**. The additional objects might include details of features and data common to each individual model. For example, a **Mark VII** is an object that describes a particular type of Lincoln automobile. It is an instance of the **Lincoln** class.

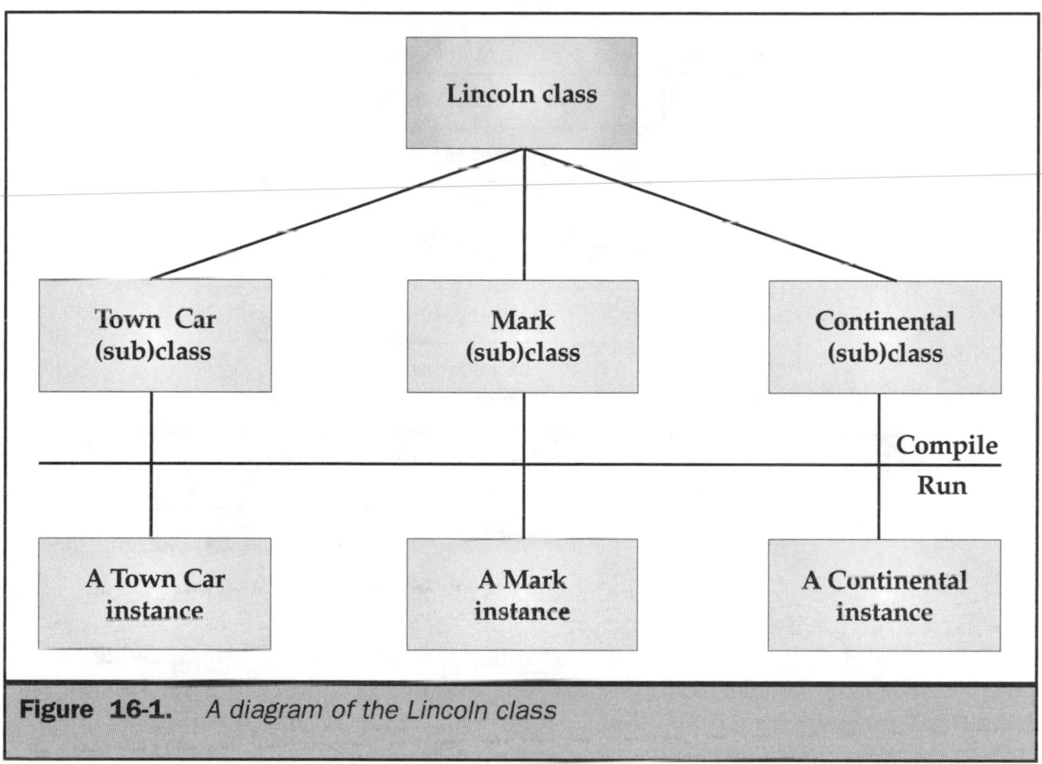

Figure 16-1. *A diagram of the Lincoln class*

If a message is sent to the instance of the **Lincoln** class (similar to a call to a function) with instructions to adjust the air suspension on all four wheels, that message could be utilized only by the **Mark** object of the class. Only the Lincoln Mark has four-wheel air suspension.

Ultimately, there should emerge class libraries containing many object types. Then, instances of those object types could be used to piece together program code. You will see interesting examples of this when Windows class libraries are described in Chapters 22 and 23.

Before you examine these terms in closer detail, it is a good idea to become familiar with several additional concepts that relate to C++ and object-oriented programming, as described in the next few sections.

Encapsulation

Encapsulation refers to the way each object combines its member data and member functions (methods) into a single structure. Figure 16-2 illustrates how you can combine data fields and methods to build an object.

Typically, an object's description is part of a C++ class and includes a description of the object's internal structure, how the object relates with other objects, and some form

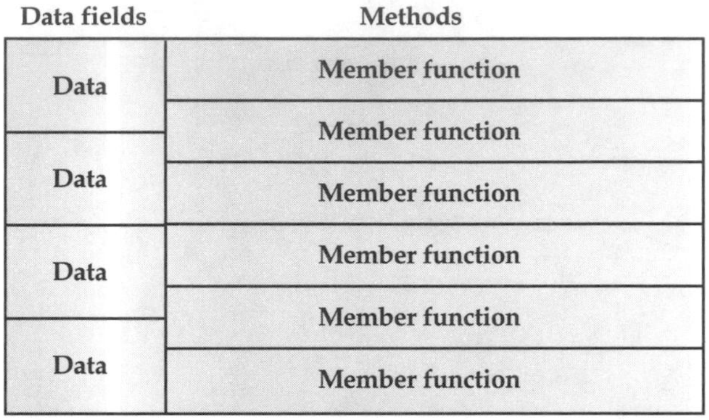

Data fields	Methods
Data	Member function
	Member function
Data	Member function
Data	Member function
	Member function
Data	Member function

Figure 16-2. *Data fields and methods combined to build an object*

of protection that isolates the functional details of the object from outside the class. The C++ class structure does all of this.

Functional details of the object are controlled in a C++ class by using private, public, and/or protected descriptors. In object-oriented programming, the public section is typically used for the interface information (methods) that makes the class reusable across applications. If data or methods are contained in the public section, they are available outside the class. The private section of a class limits the availability of data or methods to the class itself. A protected section containing data or methods is limited to the class and any derived subclasses.

Class Hierarchy

The C++ class actually serves as a template or pattern for creating objects. The objects formed from the class description are instances of the class. It is possible to develop a class hierarchy where there is a parent class and several child classes. In C++, the basis for doing this revolves around derived classes. Parent classes represent more generalized tasks, while derived child classes are given specific tasks to perform. For example, the **Lincoln** class discussed earlier might contain data and methods common to the entire Lincoln line, such as engines, instrumentation, batteries, braking ability, and handling. Child classes derived from the parent, such as **Town Car**, **Mark**, and **Continental**, could contain items specific to the class. For example, the Mark is the only car in the Lincoln line with four-wheel air suspension.

Inheritance

Inheritance, in object-oriented programming, allows a class to inherit properties from a class of objects. The parent class serves as a pattern for the derived class and can be altered in several ways. (In the next chapter you will learn that member functions can be overloaded, new member functions can be added, and member access privileges can be changed.) If an object inherits its attributes from a single parent, it is called single inheritance. If an object inherits its attributes from multiple parents, it is called multiple inheritance. Inheritance is an important concept since it allows reuse of a class definition without requiring major code changes. Inheritance encourages the reuse of code since child classes are extensions of parent classes.

Polymorphism

Another important object-oriented concept that relates to the class hierarchy is that common messages can be sent to the parent class objects and all derived subclass objects. In formal terms, this is called *polymorphism*.

Polymorphism allows each subclass object to respond to the message format in a manner appropriate to its definition. Imagine a class hierarchy for gathering data. The parent class might be responsible for gathering the name, social security number, occupation, and number of years of employment for an individual. You could then use child classes to decide what additional information would be added based on occupation. In one case, a supervisory position might include yearly salary, while in another case a sales position might include an hourly rate and commission information. Thus, the parent class gathers general information common to all child classes while the child classes gather additional information relating to specific job descriptions. Polymorphism allows a common data-gathering message to be sent to each class. Both the parent and child classes respond in an appropriate manner to the message. Polymorphism encourages extendability of existing code.

Virtual Functions

Polymorphism gives objects the ability to respond to messages from routines when the object's exact type is not known. In C++, this ability is a result of late binding. With late binding, the addresses are determined dynamically at run time rather than statically at compile time, as in traditional compiled languages. This **static** (fixed) method is often called early binding. Function names are replaced with memory addresses. Late binding accomplishes this by using virtual functions, which are defined in the parent class when subsequent derived classes will overload the function by redefining the function's implementation. When virtual functions are used, messages are passed as a pointer that points to the object instead of directly to the object.

Virtual functions utilize a table for address information. The table is initialized at run time by using a constructor. A constructor is invoked whenever an object of its class is created. The job of the constructor here is to link the virtual function with the table of address information. During the compile operation, the address of the virtual function is not known; rather, it is given the position in the table (determined at run time) of addresses that will contain the address for the function.

A First Look at the C++ Class

It has already been stated that the C++ class type is an extension of C's **struct** type. In this section, you learn how you can use the **struct** type in C++ to form a primitive class, complete with data and members. Next, you examine the formal syntax for defining a class and see several simple examples of its implementation. The section discusses the differences between a primitive **struct** class type and an actual C++ class and presents several simple examples to illustrate class concepts. (Chapter 17 is devoted to a detailed analysis of the C++ class as it applies to object-oriented programming.)

A Structure as a Primitive Class

Chapter 13 discussed structures for C and C++. In many respects, the structure in C++ is an elementary form of a class. You use the keyword **struct** to define a structure. Examine the following code:

```
//
//  sqroot.cpp
//  C++ program using the keyword "struct" to illustrate a
//  primitive form of class. Here several member functions
//  are defined within the structure.
//  Copyright (c) Chris H. Pappas and William H. Murray, 1998
//

#include <iostream.h>
#include <math.h>

struct math_operations {
  double data_value;

  void set_value(double ang) {data_value=ang;}
  double get_square(void) {double answer;
                           answer=data_value*data_value;
                           return (answer);}
  double get_square_root(void) {double answer;
                                answer=sqrt(data_value);
                                return (answer);}
} math;

main( )
{
  // set numeric value to 35.63
  math.set_value(35.63);
```

```
  cout << "The square of the number is: "
       << math.get_square( ) << endl;
  cout << "The square root of the number is: "
       << math.get_square_root( ) << endl;
  return (0);
}
```

The first thing to notice in this code is that the structure definition contains member data and functions. While you are used to seeing data declarations as part of a structure, this is probably the first time you have seen member functions defined within the structure definition. There was no mention of member functions in the discussion of the **struct** type in Chapter 13 because they are exclusive to C++. These member functions can act upon the data contained in the structure (or class) itself.

Recall that a class can contain member data and functions. By default, in a **struct** declaration in C++, member data and functions are public. (A public section is one in which the data and functions are available outside the structure.) Here is the output sent to the screen when the program is executed:

```
The square of the number is: 1269.5
The square root of the number is: 5.96909
```

In this example, the structure definition contains a single data value:

```
double data_value;
```

Next, three member functions are defined. Actually, the code for each function is contained within the structure:

```
void set_value(double ang) {data_value=ang;}
double get_square(void) {double answer;
                         answer=data_value*data_value;
                         return (answer);}
double get_square_root(void) {double answer;
                              answer=sqrt(data_value);
                              return (answer);}
```

The first member function is responsible for initializing the variable *data_value*. The remaining two member functions return the square and square root of *data_value*. Notice that the member functions are not passed a value; *data_value* is available to them as members of the structure. Both member functions return a **double**.

The program's main( ) function sets the value of *data_value* to 35.63 with a call to the member function, set_value( ):

```
math.set_value(35.63);
```

Notice that the name *math* has been associated with the structure *math_operations*.

The remaining two member functions return values to the **cout** stream:

```
cout << "The square of the number is: "
     << math.get_square( ) << endl;
cout << "The square root of the number is: "
     << math.get_square_root( ) << endl;
```

This example contains a structure with member data and functions. The functions are contained within the structure definition. You won't find an example simpler than this one.

In the next program, the **struct** keyword is still used to develop a primitive class, but this time the member functions are written outside the structure. This is the way you will most commonly see structures and classes defined.

This example contains a structure definition with one data member, *data_value*, and seven member functions. The member functions return information for various trigonometric values.

```
//
//  16TSTRUC.CPP
//  C++ program using the keyword "struct" to illustrate a
//  primitive form of class. This program uses a structure
//  to obtain trigonometric values for an angle.
//  Copyright (c) Chris H. Pappas and William H. Murray, 1998
//

#include <iostream.h>
#include <math.h>

const double DEG_TO_RAD=0.0174532925;

struct degree {
  double data_value;

  void set_value(double);
  double get_sine(void);
```

```
  double get_cosine(void);
  double get_tangent(void);
  double get_secant(void);
  double get_cosecant(void);
  double get_cotangent(void);
} deg;

void degree::set_value(double ang)
{
  data_value=ang;
}

double degree::get_sine(void)
{
  double answer;

  answer=sin(DEG_TO_RAD*data_value);
  return (answer);
}

double degree::get_cosine(void)
{
  double answer;

  answer=cos(DEG_TO_RAD*data_value);
  return (answer);
}

double degree::get_tangent(void)
{
  double answer;

  answer=tan(DEG_TO_RAD*data_value);
  return (answer);
}

double degree::get_secant(void)
{
  double answer;

  answer=1.0/sin(DEG_TO_RAD*data_value);
  return (answer);
```

```
}

double degree::get_cosecant(void)
{
  double answer;

  answer=1.0/cos(DEG_TO_RAD*data_value);
  return (answer);
}

double degree::get_cotangent(void)
{
  double answer;

  answer=1.0/tan(DEG_TO_RAD*data_value);
  return (answer);
}

main( )
{
  // set angle to 25.0 degrees
  deg.set_value(25.0);

  cout << "The sine of the angle is: "
       << deg.get_sine( ) << endl;
  cout << "The cosine of the angle is: "
       << deg.get_cosine( ) << endl;
  cout << "The tangent of the angle is: "
       << deg.get_tangent( ) << endl;
  cout << "The secant of the angle is: "
       << deg.get_secant( ) << endl;
  cout << "The cosecant of the angle is: "
       << deg.get_cosecant( ) << endl;
  cout << "The cotangent of the angle is: "
       << deg.get_cotangent( ) << endl;
  return (0);
}
```

Notice that the structure definition contains the prototypes for the member functions. The variable, *deg*, is associated with the degree structure type.

```
struct degree {
  double data_value;

  void set_value(double);
  double get_sine(void);
  double get_cosine(void);
  double get_tangent(void);
  double get_secant(void);
  double get_cosecant(void);
  double get_cotangent(void);
} deg;
```

Immediately after the structure is defined, the various member functions are developed and listed. The member functions are associated with the structure or class by means of the scope operator (::). Other than the use of the scope operator, the member functions take on the appearance of normal functions.

Examine the first part of the main( ) function:

```
// set angle to 25.0 degrees
deg.set_data(25.0);
```

Here, the value 25.0 is being passed as an argument to the set_value( ) function. Observe the syntax for this operation. The set_value( ) function itself is very simple:

```
void degree::set_value(double ang)
{
  data_value=ang;
}
```

The function accepts the argument and assigns the value to the class variable, *data_value*. This is one way of initializing class variables. From this point forward in the class, *data_value* is accessible by each of the six member functions. The job of the member functions is to calculate the sine, cosine, tangent, secant, cosecant, and cotangent of the given angle. The respective values are printed to the screen from the main( ) function with statements similar to the following:

```
cout << "The sine of the angle is: "
     << deg.get_sine( ) << endl;
```

Use the dot notation, commonly used for structures, to access the member functions. Pointer variables can also be assigned to a structure or class, in which case the arrow operator is used. You will see examples of this in Chapter 17.

The Syntax and Rules for C++ Classes

The definition of a C++ class begins with the **keyword** class. The class name (tag type) immediately follows the keyword. The framework of the class is very similar to the **struct** type definition you have already seen.

```
class type {
  type var1
  type var2
  type var3
      .
      .
      .
public:
  member function 1
  member function 2
  member function 3
  member function 4
      .
      .
      .
} name associated with class type;
```

Member variables immediately follow the class declaration. These variables are, by default, private to the class and can be accessed only by the member functions that follow. Member functions typically follow a public declaration. This allows access to the member functions from calling routines external to the class. All class member functions have access to public, private, and protected parts of a class.

The following is an example of a class that is used in the next programming example:

```
class degree {
  double data_value;

public:
  void set_value(double);
  double get_sine(void);
  double get_cosine(void);
  double get_tangent(void);
  double get_secant(void);
  double get_cosecant(void);
  double get_cotangent(void);
} deg;
```

This class has a type (tag name) **degree**. A private variable, *data_value*, will share **degree** values among the various member functions. Seven functions make up the function members of the class. They are set_value( ), get_sine( ), get_cosine( ), get_tangent( ), get_secant( ), get_cosecant( ), and get_cotangent( ). The name that is associated with this class type is *deg*. Unlike this example, the association of a variable name with the class name is most frequently made in the main( ) function.

Does this class definition look familiar? It is basically the structure definition from the previous example converted to a true class.

A Simple C++ Class

In a C++ class, the visibility of class members is, by default, private. That is, member variables are accessible only to member functions of the class. If the member functions are to have visibility beyond the class, you must explicitly specify that visibility.

The conversion of the last program's structure to a true C++ class is simple and straightforward. First, the **struct** keyword is replaced by the class keyword. Second, the member functions that are to have public visibility are separated from the private section of the class with the use of a public declaration. Examine the complete program:

```
//
//   tclass.cpp
//   C++ program illustrates a simple but true class and
//   introduces the concept of private and public.
//   This program uses a class to obtain the trigonometric
//   value for given angle.
//   Copyright (c) Chris H. Pappas and William H. Murray, 1998
//

#include <iostream.h>
#include <math.h>

const double DEG_TO_RAD=0.0174532925;

class degree {
  double data_value;

public:
  void set_value(double);
  double get_sine(void);
  double get_cosine(void);
  double get_tangent(void);
  double get_secant(void);
```

```
  double get_cosecant(void);
  double get_cotangent(void);
} deg;

void degree::set_value(double ang)
{
  data_value=ang;
}

double degree::get_sine(void)
{
  double answer;

  answer=sin(DEG_TO_RAD*data_value);
  return (answer);
}

double degree::get_cosine(void)
{
  double answer;

  answer=cos(DEG_TO_RAD*data_value);
  return (answer);
}

double degree::get_tangent(void)
{
  double answer;

  answer=tan(DEG_TO_RAD*data_value);
  return (answer);
}

double degree::get_secant(void)
{
  double answer;

  answer=1.0/sin(DEG_TO_RAD*data_value);
  return (answer);
}

double degree::get_cosecant(void)
```

```
{
  double answer;

  answer=1.0/cos(DEG_TO_RAD*data_value);
  return (answer);
}

double degree::get_cotangent(void)
{
  double answer;

  answer=1.0/tan(DEG_TO_RAD*data_value);
  return (answer);
}

main( )
{
  // set angle to 25.0 degrees
  deg.set_value(25.0);

  cout << "The sine of the angle is: "
       << deg.get_sine( ) << endl;
  cout << "The cosine of the angle is: "
       << deg.get_cosine( ) << endl;
  cout << "The tangent of the angle is: "
       << deg.get_tangent( ) << endl;
  cout << "The secant of the angle is: "
       << deg.get_secant( ) << endl;
  cout << "The cosecant of the angle is: "
       << deg.get_cosecant( ) << endl;
  cout << "The cotangent of the angle is: "
       << deg.get_cotangent( ) << endl;
  return (0);
}
```

In this example, the body of the program remains the same. The structure definition has been converted to a true, but elementary, class definition with private and public parts.

Note that the variable, *data_value*, is private to the class (by default) and as a result is accessible only by the member functions of the class. The member functions themselves have been declared public in visibility and are accessible from outside the class. Each class member, however, whether public or private, has access to all other class members, public or private.

Here is the output from the program:

```
The sine of the angle is: 0.422618
The cosine of the angle is: 0.906308
The tangent of the angle is: 0.466308
The secant of the angle is: 2.3662
The cosecant of the angle is: 1.10338
The cotangent of the angle is: 2.14451
```

Again, class member functions are usually defined immediately after the class has been defined and before the main( ) function of the program. Nonmember class functions are still defined after the function main( ) and are prototyped in the normal fashion. The next chapter examines the details of C++ classes more closely.

The Complete Reference

Chapter 17

Classes in C++

A primitive C++ class can be created by using the **struct** keyword, as you learned in the previous chapter. You also learned how to create several elementary C++ classes by using the **class** keyword. Both types of examples illustrated the simple fact that classes can contain member data and member functions (methods) that act on that data. In this chapter, you will learn more details about C++ classes—nesting of classes and structures, the use of constructors and destructors, overloading member functions, friend functions, operator overloading, derived classes, virtual functions, and other miscellaneous topics. These class structures create objects that form the foundation of object-oriented programs.

The programming flexibility offered to the C++ programmer is, to a large degree, a result of the various data types discussed in earlier chapters. The C++ class gives you another advantage: the benefits of a structure along with the ability to limit access to specific data to functions that are also members of the class. As a result, classes are one of the greatest contributions made by C++ to programming. The added features of the class over earlier structures include the ability to initialize and protect sensitive functions and data.

Consider, for example, the increase in programming power you have gained with each new data type. Vectors or one-dimensional arrays allow a group of like data types to be held together. Next, structures allow related items of different data types to be combined in a group. Finally, the C++ class concept takes you one step further with abstract data types. A class allows you to implement a member data type and associate member functions with the data. Using classes gives you the storage concept associated with a structure along with the member functions to operate on the member variables.

Features Specific to Classes

The syntax for correctly creating an elementary C++ class was illustrated in the previous chapter. However, classes have extended capabilities that go far beyond this simple syntax. This section is devoted to exploring these capabilities with an eye toward object-oriented programming. In the next chapter, class objects will be woven into more complicated object-oriented programs.

Working with a Simple Class

In this section, we'll present a short review of a simple class based on the definitions from Chapter 16. Remember that a class starts with the **keyword** class followed by a class name (tag). In the following example, the class tag name is **car**. If the class contains member variables, they are defined at the start of the class. Their declaration type is private, by default. This example defines three member variables: *mileage*, *tire_pressure*, and *speed*. Class member functions follow the member variable list. Typically, the member functions are declared public. A private declaration limits the member variables to member functions within the class. This is often referred to as data hiding. A public declaration makes the member functions available outside of the class:

```
class car {
  int   mileage;
  int   tire_pressure;
  float speed;

public:
  int maintenance(int);
  int wear_record(int);
  int air_resistance(float);
} mycar;
```

Notice that three member functions are prototyped within the class definition. They are maintenance( ), wear_record( ), and air_resistance( ). All three return an **int** type. Typically, however, the contents of the member functions are defined outside the class definition—usually, immediately after the class itself.

Let's continue the study of classes with a look at additional class features.

Nesting Classes

In Chapter 13, you learned that structures can be nested. This also turns out to be true for C++ classes. When using nested classes, you must take care not to make the resulting declaration more complicated than necessary. The following examples illustrate the nesting concept.

Nesting Structures Within a Class

The next listing is a simple example of how two structures can be nested within a class definition. Using nesting in this fashion is both common and practical. You can also use the **class** keyword in this manner.

```
//
//  wages.cpp
//  C++ program illustrates the use of nesting concepts
//  in classes. This program calculates the wages for
//  the named employee.
//  Copyright (c) Chris H. Pappas and William H. Murray, 1998
//

#include <iostream.h>

char newline;

class employee {
```

```
  struct emp_name {
    char firstname[20];
    char middlename[20];
    char lastname[20];
  } name;
  struct emp_hours {
    double hours;
    double base_sal;
    double overtime_sal;
  } hours;

public:
  void emp_input(void);
  void emp_output(void);
};

void employee::emp_input( )
{
  cout << "Enter first name of employee: ";
  cin >> name.firstname;
  cin.get(newline);    // flush carriage return
  cout << "Enter middle name of employee: ";
  cin >> name.middlename;
  cin.get(newline);
  cout << "Enter last name of employee:  ";
  cin >> name.lastname;
  cin.get(newline);

  cout << "Enter total hours worked:  ";
  cin >> hours.hours;
  cout << "Enter hourly wage (base rate):   ";
  cin >> hours.base_sal;
  cout << "Enter overtime wage (overtime rate): ";
  cin >> hours.overtime_sal;
  cout << "\n\n";
}

void employee::emp_output( )
{
  cout << name.firstname << " " << name.middlename
       << " " << name.lastname << endl;
  if (hours.hours <= 40)
```

```
    cout << "Base Pay:  $"
         << hours.hours * hours.base_sal << endl;
    else {
      cout << "Base Pay:  $"
           << 40 * hours.base_sal << endl;
      cout << "Overtime Pay: $"
           << (hours.hours-40) * hours.overtime_sal
           << endl;
      }
}

main( )
{
  employee acme_corp;     // associate acme_corp with class

  acme_corp.emp_input( );
  acme_corp.emp_output( );
  return (0);
}
```


In the next example, two classes are nested within the **employee** class definition. The use of nesting, as you can see, can be quite straightforward:

```
class employee {
  class emp_name {
    char firstname[20];
    char middlename[20];
    char lastname[20];
  } name;
  class emp_hours {
    double hours;
    double base_salary;
    double overtime_sal;
  } hours;

public:
  void emp_input(void);
  void emp_output(void);
};
```

The employee class includes two nested classes, **emp_name** and **emp_hours**. The nested classes, while part of the private section of the **employee** class, are actually available outside the class. In other words, the visibility of the nested classes is the same as if they were defined outside the **employee** class. The individual member variables, for this example, are accessed through the member functions (public, by default) emp_input( ) and emp_output( ).

The member functions, emp_input( ) and emp_output( ), are of type **void** and do not accept arguments. The emp_input( ) function prompts the user for employee data that will be passed to the nested structures (classes). The data collected includes the employee's full name, the total hours worked, the regular pay rate, and the overtime pay rate. Output is generated when the emp_output( ) function is called. The employee's name, base pay, and overtime pay will be printed to the screen:

```
Enter first name of employee: Peter
Enter middle name of employee: Harry
Enter last name of employee: Jones
Enter total hours worked: 52
Enter hourly wage (base rate): 7.50
Enter overtime wage (overtime rate): 10.00

Peter Harry Jones
Base Pay:  $300.00
Overtime Pay: $120.00
```

The main( ) function in this program is fairly short. This is because most of the work is being done by the member functions of the class:

```
employee acme_corp;    // associate acme_corp with class

acme_corp.emp_input( );
acme_corp.emp_output( );
```

The variable *acme_corp*, representing the Acme Computer Corporation, is associated with the **employee** class. To request a member function, the dot operator is used. Next, acme_corp.emp_input( ) is called to collect the employee information, and then acme_corp.emp_output( ) is used to calculate and print the payroll results.

An Alternate Nesting Form

There is an alternate way to perform nesting. The following form of nesting is also considered acceptable syntax:

```
class cars {
  int mileage;
```

```
public:
  void trip(int t);
  int speed(float s);
};

class contents {
  int count;
public:
  cars mileage;
  void rating(void);
{
```

Here, **cars** becomes nested within the **contents** class. Nested classes, whether inside or outside, have the same scope.

Working with Constructors and Destructors

A constructor is a class member function. Constructors are useful for initializing class variables or allocating memory storage. The constructor always has the same name as the class it is defined within. Constructors have additional versatility: they can accept arguments and be overloaded. A constructor is executed automatically when an object of the class type is created. Free store objects are objects created with the new operator and serve to allocate memory for the objects created. Constructors are generated by the Visual C++ compiler if they are not explicitly defined.

A destructor is a class member function typically used to return memory allocated from free store memory. The destructor, like the constructor, has the same name as the class it is defined in, preceded by the tilde character (~). Destructors are the complement to their constructor counterparts. A destructor is automatically called when the **delete** operator is applied to a class pointer or when a program passes beyond the scope of a class object. Destructors, unlike their constructor counterparts, cannot accept an argument and may not be overloaded. Destructors are also generated by the Visual C++ compiler if they are not explicitly defined.

A Simple Constructor and Destructor

The following listing represents the first example involving the use of constructors and destructors. Here a constructor and destructor are used to signal the start and end of a coin conversion example. This program illustrates that constructors and destructors are called automatically:

```
//
//  coins.cpp
```

```
//  C++ program illustrates the use of constructors and
//  destructors in a simple program.
//  This program converts cents into appropriate coins:
//  (quarters, dimes, nickels, and pennies).
//  Copyright (c) Chris H. Pappas and William H. Murray, 1998
//

#include <iostream.h>

const int QUARTER=25;
const int DIME=10;
const int NICKEL=5;

class coins {
  int number;

public:
  coins( ) {cout << "Begin Conversion!\n";}       // constructor
  ~coins( ) {cout << "\nFinished Conversion!";}  // destructor
  void get_cents(int);
  int quarter_conversion(void);
  int dime_conversion(int);
  int nickel_conversion(int);
};

void coins::get_cents(int cents)
{
  number=cents;
  cout << number << " cents, converts to:"
       << endl;
}

int coins::quarter_conversion( )
{
  cout << number/QUARTER << " quarter(s), ";
  return(number%QUARTER);
}

int coins::dime_conversion(int d)
{
  cout << d/DIME << " dime(s), ";
  return(d%DIME);
```

```
}

int coins::nickel_conversion(int n)
{
  cout << n/NICKEL << " nickel(s), and ";
  return(n%NICKEL);
}

main( )
{
  int c,d,n,p;

  cout << "Enter the cash, in cents, to convert: ";
  cin >> c;

  // associate cash_in_cents with coins class.
  coins cash_in_cents;

  cash_in_cents.get_cents(c);
  d=cash_in_cents.quarter_conversion( );
  n=cash_in_cents.dime_conversion(d);
  p=cash_in_cents.nickel_conversion(n);
  cout << p << " penny(ies).";
  return (0);
}
```


This program uses four member functions. The first function passes the number of pennies to the private class variable *number*. The remaining three functions convert cash, given in cents, to the equivalent cash in quarters, dimes, nickels, and pennies. Notice in particular the placement of the constructor and destructor in the class definition. The constructor and destructor function descriptions contain nothing more than a message that will be printed to the screen. Constructors are not specifically called by a program. Their appearance on the screen is your key that the constructor and destructor were automatically called when the object was created and destroyed.

```
class coins {
  int number;

public:
  coins( ) {cout << "Begin Conversion!\n";}       // constructor
  ~coins( ) {cout << "\nFinished Conversion!";}  // destructor
```

```
  void get_cents(int);
  int quarter_conversion(void);
  int dime_conversion(int);
  int nickel_conversion(int);
};
```

Here is an example of the output from this program:

```
Enter the cash, in cents, to convert: 159
Begin Conversion!
159 cents, converts to:
6 quarter(s), 0 dime(s), 1 nickel(s), and 4 penny(ies).
Finished Conversion!
```

In this example, the function definition is actually included within the constructor and destructor. When the function definition is included with member functions, it is said to be implicitly defined. Member functions can be defined in the typical manner or declared explicitly as inline functions.

Why not expand this example to include dollars and half-dollars!

Initializing Member Variables with Constructors

Another practical use for constructors is for initialization of private class variables. In the previous examples, class variables were set using separate member functions. In the next example, the original class of the previous program is modified slightly to eliminate the need for user input. In this case, the variable *number* will be initialized to 431 pennies:

```
class coins {
  int number;

public:
  coins( ) {number=431;}                          // constructor
  ~coins( ) {cout << "\nFinished Conversion!";}  // destructor
  int quarter_conversion(void);
  int dime_conversion(int);
  int nickel_conversion(int);
};
```

The route to class variables is always through class member functions. Remember that the constructor is considered a member function.

Creating and Deleting Free Store Memory

Perhaps the most significant reason for using a constructor is in utilizing free store memory. In the next example, a constructor is used to allocate memory for the **string1** pointer with the new operator. A destructor is also used to release the allocated memory back to the system when the object is destroyed. This is accomplished with the use of the **delete** operator.

```
class string_operation {
  char *string1;
  int  string_len;

public:
  string_operation(char *) {string1=new char[string_len];}
  ~string_operation( ) {delete string1;}
  void input_data(char *);
  void output_data(char *);
};
```

The memory allocated by new to the pointer **string1** can only be deallocated with a subsequent call to **delete**. For this reason, you will usually see memory allocated to pointers in constructors and deallocated in destructors. This also ensures that if the variable assigned to the class passes out of its scope, the allocated memory will be returned to the system. These operations make memory allocation dynamic and are most useful in programs that utilize linked lists.

The memory used by data types, such as **int** and **float**, is automatically restored to the system.

Overloading Class Member Functions

Class member functions can be overloaded just like ordinary C++ functions. Overloading functions means that more than one function can have the same function name in the current scope. It becomes the compiler's responsibility to select the correct function based upon the number and type of arguments used during the function call. The first example in this section illustrates the overloading of a class function named number( ). This overloaded function will return the absolute value of an **integer** or **double** with the use of the math functions abs( ), which accepts and returns **integer** values, and fabs( ), which accepts and returns **double** values. With an overloaded function, the argument types determine which member function will actually be used.

```
//
//  absol.cpp
//  C++ program illustrates member function overloading.
```

```
//  Program determines the absolute value of an integer
//  and a double.
//  Copyright (c) Chris H. Pappas and William H. Murray, 1998
//

#include <iostream.h>
#include <math.h>
#include <stdlib.h>

class absolute_value {
public:
  int number(int);
  double number(double);
};

int absolute_value::number(int test_data)
{
  int answer;

  answer=abs(test_data);
  return (answer);
}

double absolute_value::number(double test_data)
{
  double answer;

  answer=fabs(test_data);
  return (answer);
}

main( )
{
  absolute_value neg_number;

  cout << "The absolute value is "
       << neg_number.number(-583) << endl;
  cout << "The absolute value is "
       << neg_number.number(-583.1749) << endl;
  return (0);
}
```

Notice that the dot operator is used in conjunction with the member function name to pass a negative **integer** and negative **double** values. The program selects the proper member function based upon the type (**integer** or **double**) of argument passed along with the function name. The positive value returned by each function is printed to the screen:

```
the absolute value is 583
the absolute value is 583.1749
```

In another example, angle information is passed to member functions in one of two formats—a **double** or a **string**. With member function overloading, it is possible to process both types:

```
//
//  overld.cpp
//  C++ program illustrates overloading two class member
//  functions. The program allows an angle to be entered
//  in decimal or deg/min/sec format. One member function
//  accepts data as a double, the other as a string. The
//  program returns the sine, cosine, and tangent.
//  Copyright (c) Chris H. Pappas and William H. Murray, 1998
//

#include <iostream.h>
#include <math.h>
#include <string.h>

const double DEG_TO_RAD=0.0174532925;

class trigonometric {
  double angle;
  double answer_sine;
  double answer_cosine;
  double answer_tangent;

public:
  void trig_calc(double);
  void trig_calc(char *);
};

void trigonometric::trig_calc(double degrees)
{
```

```
  angle=degrees;
  answer_sine=sin(angle * DEG_TO_RAD);
  answer_cosine=cos(angle * DEG_TO_RAD);
  answer_tangent=tan(angle * DEG_TO_RAD);
  cout << "\nFor an angle of " << angle
       << " degrees." << endl;
  cout << "The sine is " << answer_sine << endl;
  cout << "The cosine is " << answer_cosine << endl;
  cout << "The tangent is " << answer_tangent << endl;
}

void trigonometric::trig_calc(char *dat)
{
  char *deg,*min,*sec;

  deg=strtok(dat,"d ");
  min=strtok(0,"m ");
  sec=strtok(0,"s");
  angle=atof(deg)+((atof(min))/60.0)+((atof(sec))/360.0);
  answer_sine=sin(angle * DEG_TO_RAD);
  answer_cosine=cos(angle * DEG_TO_RAD);
  answer_tangent=tan(angle * DEG_TO_RAD);
  cout << "\nFor an angle of " << angle
       << " degrees." << endl;
  cout << "The sine is " << answer_sine << endl;
  cout << "The cosine is " << answer_cosine << endl;
  cout << "The tangent is " << answer_tangent << endl;
}

main()
{
  trigonometric data;

  data.trig_calc(75.0);

  char str1[] = "35d 75m 20s";
  data.trig_calc(str1);

  data.trig_calc(145.72);

  char str2[] = "65d 45m 30s";
  data.trig_calc(str2);
```

```
  return (0);
}
```

This program makes use of a very powerful built-in function, strtok( ), prototyped in STRING.H. The syntax for using strtok( ) is straightforward:

```
char *strtok(string1,string2);  //locates token in string1
 char *string1;                 //string that has token(s)
 const char *string2;           //string with delimiter chars
```

The strtok( ) function will scan the first string, *string1*, looking for a series of character tokens. For this example, the tokens representing degrees, minutes, and seconds are used. The actual length of the tokens can vary. The second string, *string2*, contains a set of delimiters. Spaces, commas, or other special characters can be used for delimiters. The tokens in *string1* are separated by the delimiters in *string2*. Because of this, all of the tokens in *string1* can be retrieved with a series of calls to the strtok( ) function. strtok( ) alters *string1* by inserting a null character after each token is retrieved. The function returns a pointer to the first token the first time it is called. Subsequent calls return a pointer to the next token, and so on. When there are no more tokens in the string, a **null** pointer is returned.

This example permits angle readings formatted as decimal values or in degrees, minutes, and seconds of arc. For the latter case, strtok( ) uses the symbol (d) to find the first token. For minutes, a minute symbol (m) will pull out the token containing the number of minutes. Finally, the (s) symbol is used to retrieve seconds.

This program produces the following formatted output:

```
For an angle of 75 degrees.
The sine is 0.965926
The cosine is 0.258819
The tangent is 3.732051

For an angle of 36.305556 degrees.
The sine is 0.592091
The cosine is 0.805871
The tangent is 0.734722

For an angle of 145.72 degrees.
The sine is 0.563238
The cosine is -0.826295
The tangent is -0.681642
```

```
For an angle of 65.833333 degrees.
The sine is 0.912358
The cosine is 0.409392
The tangent is 2.228568
```

Class member function overloading gives programs and programmers flexibility when dealing with different data formats. If you are not into math or engineering programs, can you think of any applications that interest you where this feature might be helpful? Consider this possibility: if you are the cook in your household, you could develop an application that modifies recipes. You could write a program that would accept data as a decimal value or in mixed units. For example, the program might allow you to enter "1 pint 1.75 cups" or "1 pint 1 cup 2 tbsp".

Friend Functions

Classes have another important feature—the ability to hide data. Recall that member data is private by **default** in classes—that is, sharable only with member functions of the class. It is almost ironic, then, that there exists a category of functions specifically designed to override this feature. Functions of this type, called friend functions, allow the sharing of private class information with nonmember functions. Friend functions, not defined in the class itself, can share the same class resources as member functions.

Friend functions offer the advantage that they are external to the class definition, as shown here:

```
//
//  secs.cpp
//  C++ program illustrates the use of friend functions.
//  Program will collect a string of date and time
//  information from system. Time information will
//  be processed and converted into seconds.
//  Copyright (c) Chris H. Pappas and William H. Murray, 1998
//

#include <iostream.h>
#include <time.h>    // for tm & time_t structure
#include <string.h>  // for strtok function prototype
#include <stdlib.h>  // for atol function prototype

class time_class {
  long secs;
  friend char * present_time(time_class);  //friend
```

```
public:
  time_class(char *);
};

time_class::time_class(char *tm)
{
  char *hours,*minutes,*seconds;

  // data returned in the following string format:
  // (day month date hours:minutes:seconds year)
  // Thus, need to skip over three tokens, i.e.,
  // skip day, month and date
  hours=strtok(tm," ");
  hours=strtok(0," ");
  hours=strtok(0," ");

  // collect time information from string
  hours=strtok(0,":");
  minutes=strtok(0,":");
  seconds=strtok(0," ");

  // convert data to long type and accumulate seconds.
  secs=atol(hours)*3600;
  secs+=atol(minutes)*60;
  secs+=atol(seconds);
}

char * present_time(time_class);  // prototype

main( )
{
  // get the string of time & date information
  struct tm *ptr;
  time_t ltime;
  ltime=time(NULL);
  ptr=localtime(&ltime);

  time_class tz(asctime(ptr));

  cout << "The date/time string information: "
       << asctime(ptr) << endl;
  cout << "The time converted to seconds: "
```

```
        << present_time(tz) << endl;
  return (0);
}

char * present_time(time_class tz)
{
  char *ctbuf;
  ctbuf=new char[40];
  long int seconds_total;

  seconds_total=tz.secs;
  ltoa(seconds_total,ctbuf,10);
  return (ctbuf);
}
```

Notice in the class definition the use of the keyword **friend** along with the description of the present_time( ) function. When you examine the program listing, you will notice that this function, external to the class, appears after the main( ) function description. In other words, it is written as a traditional C++ function, external to member functions of the defined class.

This program has a number of additional interesting features. In the function main( ), the system's time is obtained with the use of *time_t* and its associated structure *tm*. In this program, *ltime* is the name of the variable associated with *time_t*. Local time is initialized and retrieved into the pointer, *ptr*, with the next two lines of code. By using *asctime(ptr)*, the pointer will point to an ASCII string of date and time information.

```
struct tm *ptr;
time_t ltime;
ltime=time(NULL);
ptr=localtime(&ltime);

time_class tz(asctime(ptr));
```

The date and time string is formatted in this manner:

```
day month date hours:minutes:seconds year \n \0
```

For example:

```
Mon Aug 10 13:12:21 1998
```

There is a more detailed discussion of built-in functions, including those prototyped in *TIME.H*, in Chapter 15.

The string information that is retrieved is sent to the class by associating *tz* with the class **time_class**:

```
time_class tz(asctime(ptr));
```

A constructor, **time_class**(char *), is used to define the code required to convert the string information into integer data. This is accomplished by using the strtok( ) function. The date/time information is returned in a rather strange format. To process this information, strtok( ) must use a space as the delimiter in order to skip over the day, month, and date information in the string. In this program, the variable *hours* initially serves as a junk collector for unwanted tokens. The next delimiter is a colon (:), which is used in collecting both hour and minute tokens from the string. Finally, the number of seconds can be retrieved by reading the string until another space is encountered. The string information is then converted to a **long** type and converted to the appropriate number of seconds. The variable *secs* is private to the class but accessible to the friend function.

The friend function takes the number of accumulated seconds, *tz.seconds*, and converts it back to a character string. The memory for storing the string is allocated with the new operator. This newly created string is a result of using the friend function.

The program prints two pieces of information:

```
The date/time string information: Mon Aug 10 09:31:14 1998

The time converted to seconds: 34274
```

First, **cout** sends the string produced by asctime( ) to the screen. This information is obtainable from time_t( ) and is available to the main( ) function. Second, the system time is printed by passing *present_time* to the **cout** stream.

While friend functions offer some interesting programming possibilities when programming with C++ classes, they should be used with caution.

The this Pointer

The keyword **this** is used to identify a self-referential pointer that is implicitly declared in C++, as follows:

```
class_name *this;   //class_name is class type.
```

The **this** pointer is used to point to the object for which the member function is invoked and is only accessible in member functions of the **class** (**struct** or **union**) type.

It can also be used to include a link on a doubly linked list or when writing constructors involving memory allocations, as you see in the following example:

```
class class_name {
  int x,y,z;
  char chr;

public:
  class_name(size) {this=new(size);}
  ~class_name(void);
};
```

Operator Overloading

You have learned that it is possible to overload member functions in a class. In this section, you will learn that it is also possible to overload C++ operators. In C++, new definitions can be applied to such familiar operators as **+**, **–**, *****, and **/** in a given class.

The concept of operator overloading is common in numerous programming languages, even if it is not specifically implemented. For example, all compiled languages make it possible to add two **integer**s, two **float**s, or two **double**s (or their equivalent types) with the **+** operator. This is the essence of operator overloading—using the same operator on different data types. In C++, it is possible to extend this simple concept even further. In most compiled languages, it is not possible, for example, to take a complex number, matrix, or character string and add them together with the **+** operator.

These operations are valid in all programming languages:

```
3 + 8
3.3 + 7.2
```

These operations are typically not valid operations:

```
(4 - j4) + (5 + j10)
(15d 20m 45s) + (53d 57m 40s)
"combine" + "strings"
```

If the last three operations were possible with the **+** operator, the workload of the programmer would be greatly reduced when designing new applications. The good news is that in C++, the **+** operator can be overloaded and the previous three operations can be made valid. Many additional operators can also be overloaded. Operator overloading is used extensively in C++. You will find examples throughout the various Microsoft C++ libraries.

Overloading Operators and Function Calls

In C++, the operators shown in Table 17-1 can be overloaded.

The main restrictions are that the syntax and precedence of the operator must remain unchanged from its originally defined meaning. Another important point is that operator overloading is valid only within the scope of the class in which overloading occurs.

Overloading Syntax

In order to overload an operator, the **operator** keyword is followed by the operator itself:

```
type operator opr(param list)
```

For example:

```
angle_value operator +(angle_argument);
```

Here, *angle_value* is the name of the class type, followed by the operator keyword, then the operator itself (+) and a parameter to be passed to the overloaded operator.

Within the scope of a properly defined class, several angles specified in degrees/minutes/seconds could be directly added together:

```
char str1[] = "37d 15m 56s";
 angle_value angle1(str1);

 char str2[] = "10d 44m 44s";
 angle_value angle2(str2);

 char str3[] = "75d 17m 59s";
 angle_value angle3(str3);

 char str4[] = "130d 32m 54s";
 angle_value angle4(str4);

 angle_value sum_of_angles;

 sum_of_angles=angle1+angle2+angle3+angle4;
```

In this example, the symbol for degrees is (d), for minutes (m), and for seconds (s).

<table>
<tr><td>+</td><td>–</td><td>*0</td><td>/</td><td>=</td><td><</td><td>></td><td>+=</td><td>–=</td></tr>
<tr><td>*0=</td><td>/=</td><td><<</td><td>>></td><td>>>=</td><td><<=</td><td>= =</td><td>!=</td><td><=</td></tr>
<tr><td>>=</td><td>++</td><td>--</td><td>%</td><td>&</td><td>^^</td><td>!</td><td>|</td><td>~</td></tr>
<tr><td>&=</td><td>^=</td><td>|=</td><td>&&</td><td>| |</td><td>%=</td><td>[]</td><td>( )</td><td>new</td></tr>
<tr><td>Delete</td><td></td><td></td><td></td><td></td><td></td><td></td><td></td><td></td></tr>
</table>

Table 17-1. *Operators that Can Be Overloaded in C++*

The carry information from seconds-to-minutes and from minutes-to-hours must be handled properly. A carry occurs in both cases when the total number of seconds or minutes exceeds 59. This doesn't have anything to do with operator overloading directly, but the program must take this fact into account if a correct total is to be produced, as shown here:

```
//
//  opover.cpp
//  C++ program illustrates operator overloading.
//  Program will overload the "+" operator so that
//  several angles, in the format degrees minutes seconds,
//  can be added directly.
//  Copyright (c) Chris H. Pappas and William H. Murray, 1998
//

#include <iostream.h>
#include <stdlib.h>
#include <string.h>

int totaldegrees, totalminutes, totalseconds;

class angle_value {
  int degrees, minutes, seconds;

  public:
  angle_value() {degrees=0,
                 minutes=0,
                 seconds=0;}  // constructor
  angle_value(char *);
```

```
    angle_value operator +(angle_value);
  };

angle_value::angle_value(char *angle_sum)
{
  degrees=atoi(strtok(angle_sum,"d"));
  minutes=atoi(strtok(0,"m"));
  seconds=atoi(strtok(0,"s"));
}

angle_value angle_value::operator+(angle_value angle_sum)
{
  angle_value ang;
  ang.seconds=(seconds+angle_sum.seconds)%60;
  ang.minutes=((seconds+angle_sum.seconds)/60+
              minutes+angle_sum.minutes)%60;
  ang.degrees=((seconds+angle_sum.seconds)/60+
              minutes+angle_sum.minutes)/60;
  ang.degrees+=degrees+angle_sum.degrees;
  totaldegrees=ang.degrees;
  totalminutes=ang.minutes;
  totalseconds=ang.seconds;
  return ang;
}

main()
{
  char str1[] = "37d 15m 56s";
  angle_value angle1(str1);

  char str2[] = "10d 44m 44s";
  angle_value angle2(str2);

  char str3[] = "75d 17m 59s";
  angle_value angle3(str3);

  char str4[] = "130d 32m 54s";
  angle_value angle4(str4);

  angle_value sum_of_angles;

  sum_of_angles=angle1+angle2+angle3+angle4;
```

```
  cout << "The sum of the angles is " << totaldegrees << "d "
       << totalminutes << "m " << totalseconds << "s"  << endl;

  return (0);
}
```

The following portion of code shows how the mixed units are added together. Here, the + operator is to be overloaded:

```
   .
   .
   .
  ang.seconds=(seconds+angle_sum.seconds)%60;
  ang.minutes=((seconds+angle_sum.seconds)/60+
              minutes+angle_sum.minutes)%60;
  ang.degrees=((seconds+angle_sum.seconds)/60+
              minutes+angle_sum.minutes)/60;
  ang.degrees+=degrees+angle_sum.degrees;
   .
   .
   .
```

The divide and modulus operations are performed on the sums to ensure correct carry information.

Further details of the program's operation are omitted since you have seen most of the functions and modules in earlier examples. However, it is important to remember that when you overload operators, proper operator syntax and precedence must be maintained.

The output from this program shows the sum of the four angles to be as follows:

```
The sum of the angles is 253d 51m 33s
```

Is this answer correct?

Derived Classes

A derived class can be considered an extension or inheritance of an existing class. The original class is known as a base or parent class and the derived class as a subclass or child class. As such, a derived class provides a simple means for expanding or customizing the capabilities of a parent class, without the need for re-creating the parent class itself. With a parent class in place, a common interface is possible to one or more of the derived classes.

Any C++ class can serve as a parent class, and any derived class will reflect its description. The derived class can add additional features to those of the parent class. For example, the derived class can modify access privileges, add new members, or overload existing ones. When a derived class overloads a function declared in the parent class, it is said to be a virtual member function. Throughout the remainder of this book, you will see that virtual member functions are very important to the concept of object-oriented programming.

Derived Class Syntax

You describe a derived class by using the following syntax:

```
class derived-class-type :(public/private/protected) . . .
        parent-class-type { . . . .};
```

For example, in creating a derived class, you might write

```
class retirement:public consumer { . . . .};
```

In this case, the derived class tag is **retirement**. The parent class has public visibility, and its tag is **consumer**.

A third visibility specifier is often used with derived classes—protected. A protected specifier is the same as a private specifier with the added feature that class member functions and friends of derived classes are given access to the class.

Using Derived Classes

The following example is used to illustrate the concept of a derived class. The parent class collects and reports information on a consumer's name, address, city, state, and ZIP code. Two similar child classes are derived. One derived child class maintains information on a consumer's accumulated airline mileage, while the second child class reports information on a consumer's accumulated rental car mileage. Both derived child classes inherit information from the parent class. Study the listing and see what you can discern about these derived classes.

```
//
//  dercls.cpp
//  C++ program illustrates derived classes.
//  The parent class contains name, street, city,
//  state, and zip information. Derived classes add
```

```
//  either airline or rental car mileage information
//  to parent class information.
//  Copyright (c) Chris H. Pappas and William H. Murray, 1998
//

#include <iostream.h>
#include <string.h>

char newline;

class consumer {
  char name[60],
       street[60],
       city[20],
       state[15],
       zip[10];
public:
  void data_output(void);
  void data_input(void);
};

void consumer::data_output( )
{
  cout << "Name: " << name << endl;
  cout << "Street: " << street << endl;
  cout << "City: " << city << endl;
  cout << "State: " << state << endl;
  cout << "Zip: " << zip << endl;
}

void consumer::data_input( )
{
  cout << "Enter The Consumer's Full Name: ";
  cin.get(name,59,'\n');
  cin.get(newline);       //flush carriage return
  cout << "Enter The Street Address: ";
  cin.get(street,59,'\n');
  cin.get(newline);
  cout << "Enter The City: ";
  cin.get(city,19,'\n');
  cin.get(newline);
  cout << "Enter The State: ";
```

```
  cin.get(state,14,'\n');
  cin.get(newline);
  cout << "Enter The Five Digit Zip Code: ";
  cin.get(zip,9,'\n');
  cin.get(newline);
}

class airline:public consumer {
  char airline_type[20];
  float acc_air_miles;
public:
  void airline_consumer( );
  void disp_air_mileage( );
};

void airline::airline_consumer( )
{
  data_input( );
  cout << "Enter Airline Type: ";
  cin.get(airline_type,19,'\n');
  cin.get(newline);
  cout << "Enter Accumulated Air Mileage: ";
  cin >> acc_air_miles;
  cin.get(newline);      //flush carriage return
}

void airline::disp_air_mileage( )
{
  data_output( );

  cout << "Airline Type: " << airline_type
       << endl;
  cout << "Accumulated Air Mileage: "
       << acc_air_miles << endl;
}

class rental_car:public consumer {
  char rental_car_type[20];
  float acc_road_miles;
public:
  void rental_car_consumer( );
  void disp_road_mileage( );
```

```
};

void rental_car::rental_car_consumer( )
{
  data_input( );
  cout << "Enter Rental_car Type: ";
  cin.get(rental_car_type,19,'\n');
  cin.get(newline);       //flush carriage return
  cout << "Enter Accumulated Road Mileage: ";
  cin >> acc_road_miles;
  cin.get(newline);
}

void rental_car::disp_road_mileage( )
{
  data_output( );

  cout << "Rental Car Type: "
       << rental_car_type << endl;
  cout << "Accumulated Mileage: "
       << acc_road_miles << endl;
}

main( )
{
  //associate variable names with classes
  airline jetaway;
  rental_car varooom;

  //get airline information
  cout << "\n--Airline Consumer--\n";
  jetaway.airline_consumer( );


  //get rental_car information
  cout << "\n--Rental Car Consumer--\n";
  varooom.rental_car_consumer( );

  //now display all consumer information
  cout << "\n--Airline Consumer--\n";
  jetaway.disp_air_mileage( );
  cout << "\n--Rental Car Consumer--\n";
```

```
  varooom.disp_road_mileage( );

  return (0);
}
```

In this example, the parent class is of type **consumer**. The private part of this class accepts consumer information for name, address, city, state, and zip code. The public part describes two functions, data_output( ) and data_input( ). You have seen functions similar to these used to gather class information in earlier programs. The first derived child class is **airline**.

```
class airline:public consumer {
  char airline_type[20];
  float acc_air_miles;
public:
  void airline_consumer(void);
  void disp_air_mileage(void);
};
```


This derived child class contains two functions, airline_consumer( ) and disp_air_mileage( ). The first function airline_consumer( ) uses the parent class to obtain name, address, city, state, and ZIP code, and attaches the airline type and accumulated mileage.

```
void airline::airline_consumer( )
{
  data_input( );
  cout << "Enter Airline Type: ";
  cin.get(airline_type,19,'\n');
  cin.get(newline);
  cout << "Enter Accumulated Air Mileage: ";
  cin >> acc_air_miles;
  cin.get(newline);       //flush carriage return
}
```

Do you understand how the derived class is being used? A call to the function data_input( ) is a call to a member function that is part of the parent class. The remainder of the derived class is involved with obtaining the additional airline type and accumulated mileage.

The information on accumulated air mileage can be displayed for a consumer in a similar manner. The parent class function data_output( ) prints the information gathered by the parent class (name, address, and so on) while disp_air_mileage( ) attaches the derived child class' information (airline type and mileage) to the output. The process is repeated for the rental car consumer.

Thus, one parent class serves as the data-gathering base for two derived child classes, each obtaining its own specific information.

The following is a sample output from the program:

```
--Airline Consumer--
Name: Peter J. Smith
Street: 401 West Summit Avenue
City: Middletown
State: Delaware
Zip: 19804
Airline Type: US AIR
Accumulated Air Mileage: 55321.0

--Rental Car Consumer--
Name: Harry Z. Beener
Street: 511 West Pacific Road
City: Longtown
State: New York
Zip: 25888
Rental Car Type: Audi
Accumulated Road Mileage: 33446.5
```

Experiment with this program by entering your own database of information. You might also consider adding additional member functions to the consumer class.

Now that you have learned about the class structure, you are ready for a complete look at I/O in C++ in the next chapter.

Chapter 18

Complete I/O in C++

Chapter 12 introduced the concept of the **iostream** objects, **cin**, and **cout**, along with the **put to** (insertion) operator, <<; and the **get from** (extraction) operator, >>. In this chapter, you will learn about the classes behind C++ I/O streams.

This chapter also introduces several additional topics relating to the development of C++ code, such as how to use C library functions in a C++ program.

Using enum Types in C++

User-defined enumerated types behave differently in C++ than their C counterparts. For example, C **enum** types are compatible with the type **int**. This means they can be cross-assigned with no complaints from the compiler. However, in C++ the two types are incompatible.

Another difference between C and C++ enumerated types involves the syntax shorthand when you define C++ *enum* variables. The following example program highlights the enumerated type differences between the two languages:

```
//
//  enum.cpp
//  C++ program demonstrates how to use enumerated types and
//  how C++ enumerated types differ from C enumerated types
//  Copyright (c) Chris H. Pappas and William H. Murray, 1998
//

#include <iostream.h>

typedef enum boolean { FALSE, TRUE };

void main(void)
{
// enum boolean bflag = 0; legal C, but illegal C++ statement
   boolean bcontinue, bflag = FALSE;

   bcontinue = (boolean)1;

   bflag = bcontinue;
}
```

This code starts by defining the enumerated type **boolean**, which is a standard type in several other high-level languages. Because of the ordering of the definition —FALSE, then TRUE—the compiler assigns a zero to FALSE and a 1 to TRUE. This is perfect for their logical use in a program.

The statement, commented out in the main( ) program, represents a legal C statement. Remember, when you define enumerated variables in C, such as *bflag*, you must use the **enum** keyword with the enumerated type's tag field—in this case, **boolean**. Since C **enum** types are compatible with **int** types, it is also legal to initialize a variable with an integer value. This statement would not get past the C++ compiler. The second statement in main( ) shows the legal C++ counterpart.

The final two statements in the program show how to use enumerated types. Notice that in C++, an explicit cast (**boolean**), is needed to convert the 1 to a **boolean**-compatible type.

User-defined types cannot be directly input from or output to a file, as you may recall. Either they must go through a conversion routine or you can custom overload the >> and << operators, as discussed in Chapter 12.

Reference Variables

The reference variable is a C++ feature that can really be appreciated because it simplifies the syntax and readability of the more confusing pointer notation. Remember that by using pointer parameters, a program could pass something to a function either call-by-reference or call-by-variable, which enabled the function to change the item passed. In contrast, call-by-value sends a copy of the variable's contents to the function. Any change to the variable in this case is a local change not reflected in the calling routine.

In the next example, the program passes an *stStudent* structure to a function using the three possible calling methods: call-by-value, call-by-reference with pointer notation, and call-by-reference using the simpler C++ reference type. If the program were sending the entire array to the subroutine, by default the array parameter would be passed call-by-reference. However, single structures within the array, by default are passed call-by-value.

```
//
//  refvar.cpp
//  C++ program demonstrating how the C++ reference type
//  eliminates the more confusing pointer notation.
//  The program also demonstrates how to pass a single
//  array element, call by value, variable, and reference.
//  Copyright (c) Chris H. Pappas and William H. Murray, 1998
//

#include <iostream.h>

struct stStudent {
```

```
  char   pszName[66],
         pszAddress[66],
         pszCity[26],
         pszState[3],
         pszPhone[13];
  int    icourses;
  float  GPA;
};

void vByValueCall     (stStudent   stAStudent);
void vByVariableCall  (stStudent *pstAStudent);
void vByReferenceCall (stStudent &rstAStudent);

void main(void)
{
  stStudent astLargeClass[100];

  astLargeClass[0].icourses = 10;

  vByValueCall     ( astLargeClass[0]);
  cout << astLargeClass[0].icourses << "\n"; // icourses still 10

  vByVariableCall  (&astLargeClass[0]);
  cout << astLargeClass[0].icourses << "\n"; // icourses = 20

  vByReferenceCall ( astLargeClass[0]);
  cout << astLargeClass[0].icourses << "\n"; // icourses = 30
}

void vByValueCall(stStudent  stAStudent)
{
  stAStudent.icourses += 10;    // normal structure syntax
}

void vByVariableCall(stStudent *pstAStudent)
{
  pstAStudent->icourses += 10;  // pointer syntax
}

void vByReferenceCall(stStudent &rstAStudent)
{
  rstAStudent.icourses += 10;   // simplified reference syntax
}
```

Notice that the following portion of code has spliced together each function's prototype, along with its matching invoking statement:

```
void vByValueCall      (stStudent  stAStudent);
     vByValueCall      ( astLargeClass[0]    );

void vByVariableCall   (stStudent *pstAStudent);
     vByVariableCall   (&astLargeClass[0]     );

void vByReferenceCall (stStudent &rstAStudent);
     vByReferenceCall ( astLargeClass[0]     );
```

One immediate advantage of this style is the simpler syntax needed to send a reference variable, *astLargeClass[0]* (the last statement), over the equivalent pointer syntax, *&astLargeClass[0]*. At this point, the difference may appear small. However, as your algorithms become more complicated, this simpler syntax can avoid unnecessary precedence-level conflicts with other operators such as the pointer **dereference** operator (*) and the period **member** operator (.), which qualifies structure fields.

The next three statements were pulled out of the program's respective functions to show the syntax for using the structure within each function:

```
stAStudent.icourses    += 10;  // normal structure syntax
pstAStudent->icourses += 10;  // pointer syntax
rstAStudent.icourses   += 10;  // simplified reference syntax
```

The last two statements make a permanent change to the passed *stStudent* structure because the structure was passed call-by-reference (variable). Notice that the last statement did not require the pointer operator.

The difference between the first and third statements is dramatic. Although they look identical, the first statement references only a copy of the *stStudent* structure. In this case, when *stAstudent.icourses* is incremented, it is done only to the function's local copy. Exiting the function returns the structure to bit oblivion, along with the incremented value. This explains why the program outputs 10, 20, 30, instead of 20, 30, 40.

Default Arguments

A function can be prototyped in C++ by using default arguments. This means that if the invoking statement omits certain fields, predefined default values will be supplied by the function. Default argument definitions cannot be spread throughout a function's prototype; they must be the last formal parameters defined. The following example program demonstrates how to define and use such a function:

```
//
//  defrag.cpp
//  C++ program demonstrates how to prototype functions
//  with default arguments. Default arguments must always
//  be the last formal parameters defined.
//  Copyright (c) Chris H. Pappas and William H. Murray, 1998
//

#include <iostream.h>

void fdefault_argument(char ccode='Q', int ivalue=0,
                       double fvalue=0);

void main(void)
{
  fdefault_argument('A',2,12.34);
  fdefault_argument( );

}

void fdefault_argument(char ccode, int ivalue, double fvalue)
{
  if(ccode == 'Q')
    cout << "\n\nUsing default values only.";
  cout << "\nivalue = " << ivalue;
  cout << "\nfvalue = " << fvalue;
}
```

Notice that in this program, all three formal parameter types have been given default values. The function fdefault( ) checks the *ccode* value to switch on or off an appropriate message. The output from the program is straightforward:

```
ivalue = 2
fvalue = 12.34

Using default values only.
ivalue = 0
fvalue = 0
```

Careful function prototyping, using default argument assignment, can be an important approach to avoiding unwanted side effects. This is one means of guaranteeing that dynamically allocated variables will not have garbage values if the user did not supply any. Another way to initialize dynamically allocated memory is with the function memset( ).

The memset( ) Function

The memset( ) function can be used to initialize a dynamically allocated byte, or bytes, to a specific character. The prototype for memset( ) looks like this:

```
void *memset(void *dest, int cchar, size_t count);
```

Once the memset( ) function is called, *dest* points to *count* bytes of memory initialized to the character *cchar*. The following example program demonstrates a dynamic structure declaration:

```
//
//  memset.cpp
//  C++ program demonstrating the function memset( ),
//  which can initialize dynamically allocated memory.
//  Copyright (c) Chris H. Pappas and William H. Murray, 1998
//

#include <iostream.h>
#include <memory.h>

struct keybits {
  unsigned char rshift, lshift,  ctrl,   alt,
                scroll, numlock, caplock, insert;
};

void main(void)
{
  keybits *pstkinitialized;

  pstkinitialized = new keybits;
  memset(pstkinitialized, 0, sizeof(keybits));
}
```

Because of the memset( ) function, the dynamically allocated structure pointed to by *pstkinitialized* contains all zeros. The call to the function memset( ) also used the sizeof( ) operator instead of hardwiring the statement to a "magic number." The use of sizeof( ) allows the algorithm to automatically adjust to the size of any object passed to it. Remember, too, that C++ does not require the **struct** keyword to precede a structure tag field (*keybits*) when defining structure variables, as is the case with *pstkinitialized*.

Formatting Output

The next example continues the development of C++ formatted output initially introduced in Chapter 12. The first program demonstrates how to print a table of factorials using **long doubles** with the **default** right justification:

```
//
//  fact1.cpp
//  A C++ program that prints a table of
//  factorials for the numbers from 1 to 25.
//  Program uses the long double type.
//  Formatting includes precision, width and fixed
//  with default of right justification when printing.
//  Copyright (c) Chris H. Pappas and William H. Murray, 1998
//

#include <iostream.h>
#include <iomanip.h>

main( )
{
  long double number,factorial;

  number=1.0;
  factorial=1.0;

  cout.precision(0);            // no decimal place
  cout.setf(ios::fixed);        // use fixed format

  for(int i=0;i<25;i++) {
    factorial*=number;
    number=number+1.0;
    cout.width(30);             // width of 30 characters
    cout << factorial << endl;
  }
```

```
  return (0);
}
```

The precision( ), width( ), and setf( ) class members functions were repeated in the loop. The output from the program takes on the following form:

```
                        1
                        2
                        6
                       24
                      120
                      720
                     5040
                    40320
                   362880
                  3628800
                 39916800
                479001600
               6227020800
              87178291200
            1307674368000
           20922789888000
          355687428096000
         6402373705728000
       121645100408832000
      2432902008176640000
     51090942171709440000
   1124000727777607680000
  25852016738884976640000
 620448401733239439360000
15511210043330985984000000
```

The next program/output pair demonstrates how to vary output column width and override the **default** right justification:

```
//
//  fact2.cpp
//  A C++ program that prints a table of
//  factorials for the numbers from 1 to 15.
//  Program uses the long double type.
//  Formatting includes precision, width, alignment,
```

```
//  and format of large numbers.
//  Copyright (c) Chris H. Pappas and William H. Murray, 1998
//

#include <iostream.h>
#include <iomanip.h>

main( )
{
  long double number,factorial;

  number=1.0;
  factorial=1.0;

  cout.precision(0);            // no decimal point
  cout.setf(ios::left);         // left justify numbers
  cout.setf(ios::fixed);        // use fixed format

  for(int i=0;i<25;i++) {
    factorial*=number;
    number=number+1.0;
    cout.width(30);             // width of 30 characters
    cout << factorial << endl;
  }

  return (0);
}
```

The left-justified output takes on the following form:

```
1
2
6
24
120
720
5040
40320
362880
3628800
39916800
479001600
6227020800
```

```
87178291200
1307674368000
20922789888000
355687428096000
6402373705728000
121645100408832000
2432902008176640000
51090942171709440000
1124000727777607680000
25852016738884976640000
620448401733239439360000
15511210043330985984000000
```

The next example prints out a table of numbers, their squares, and their square roots. The program demonstrates how easy it is to align columns, pad with blanks, fill spaces with zeros, and control numeric precision in C++.

```
//
//  sqrt.cpp
//  A C++ program that prints a table of
//  numbers, squares, and square roots for the
//  numbers from 1 to 15. Program uses the type
//  double. Formatting aligns columns, pads blank
//  spaces with '0' character, and controls
//  precision of answer.
//  Copyright (c) Chris H. Pappas and William H. Murray, 1998
//

#include <iostream.h>
#include <iomanip.h>
#include <math.h>

main( )
{
  double number,square,sqroot;

  cout << "num\t" << "square\t\t" << "square root\n";
  cout << "___________________________________________\n";

  number=1.0;
  cout.setf(ios::fixed);          // use fixed format

  for(int i=1;i<16;i++) {
```

```
    square=number*number;           // find square
    sqroot=sqrt(number);            // find square root

    cout.fill('0');                 // fill blanks with zeros
    cout.width(2);                  // column 2 characters wide
    cout.precision(0);              // no decimal place
    cout << number << "\t";

    cout.width(6);                  // column 6 characters wide
    cout.precision(1);              // print 1 decimal place
    cout << square << "\t\t";

    cout.width(8);                  // column 8 characters wide
    cout.precision(6);              // print 6 decimal places
    cout << sqroot << endl;

    number+=1.0;
  }
  return (0);
}
```

The formatted output takes on the following form:

```
num     square          square root
___________________________________
01      0001.0            1.000000
02      0004.0            1.414214
03      0009.0            1.732051
04      0016.0            2.000000
05      0025.0            2.236068
06      0036.0            2.449490
07      0049.0            2.645751
08      0064.0            2.828427
09      0081.0            3.000000
10      0100.0            3.162278
11      0121.0            3.316625
12      0144.0            3.464102
13      0169.0            3.605551
14      0196.0            3.741657
15      0225.0            3.872983
```

I/O Options

Chapter 16 introduced the concepts and syntax for object-oriented classes, constructors, destructors, member functions, and operators. This knowledge is required for a deeper understanding of C++ I/O.

C++, like C, does not have any built-in I/O routines. Instead, all C++ compilers come bundled with object-oriented **iostream** classes. These standard I/O class objects have a cross-compiler syntax consistency because they were developed by the authors of the C++ language. If you are trying to write a C++ application that is portable to other C++ compilers, you will want to use these **iostream** classes. The Visual C++ compiler provides the following five ways to perform C++ I/O:

- *ANSI C buffered I/O* C also supports buffered functions such as fread( ) and fwrite( ). These STDIO.H library functions perform their own buffering before calling the direct I/O base routines.
- *C console and port I/O* C provides additional I/O routines that have no C++ equivalent, such as _getch( ), _ungetch( ), and _kbhit( ). All non-Windows applications can use these functions, which give direct access to the hardware.
- *Microsoft Foundation Class library* The Microsoft CFile class found in the Foundation Class library provides C++, and especially Windows applications, with objects for disk I/O. Using this library of routines guarantees that your application will be portable and easy to maintain.
- *Microsoft iostream class library* The **iostream** class library provides C++ programs with object-oriented I/O. This I/O can be used in place of functions such as scanf( ), printf( ), fscanf( ), and fprintf( ). However, while these **iostream** classes are not required by C++ programs, many of the character-mode objects, such as **cin**, **cout**, **cerr**, and **clog**, are incompatible with the Windows graphical user interface.
- *Unbuffered C library I/O* The C compiler provides unbuffered I/O through functions such as _read( ) and _write( ). These functions are very popular with C programmers because of their efficiency and the ease with which they can be customized.

The iostream Class List

All of the I/O objects defined in the **iostream** class library share the same abstract stream base class, called **ios**, with the exception of the stream buffer classes. These derived classes fall into the four broad categories shown in Table 18-1.

Figure 18-1 illustrates the interrelationship between these **ios** stream classes.

Input Stream Classes	Description
Istream	Used for general-purpose input or as a parent class for other derived input classes
Ifstream	Used for file input
Istream_withassign	Used for cin input
Istrstream	Used for string input
Output Stream Classes	
Ostream	Used for general-purpose output or as a parent class for other derived output streams
Ofstream	Used for file output
Ofstream_withassign	Used for cout, cerr, and clog
ostrstream	Used for string output
Input/Output Stream Classes	
iostream	Used for general-purpose input and output, or as a parent class for other derived I/O streams
fstream	File I/O stream class
strstream	String I/O stream class
stdiostream	Standard I/O stream class
Stream Buffer Classes	
streambuf	Used as a parent class for derived object
filebuf	Disk file stream buffer class
strstreambuf	Stream buffer class for strings
stdiobuf	Stream buffer class for standard file I/O

Table 18-1. *The Four ios Class Categories*

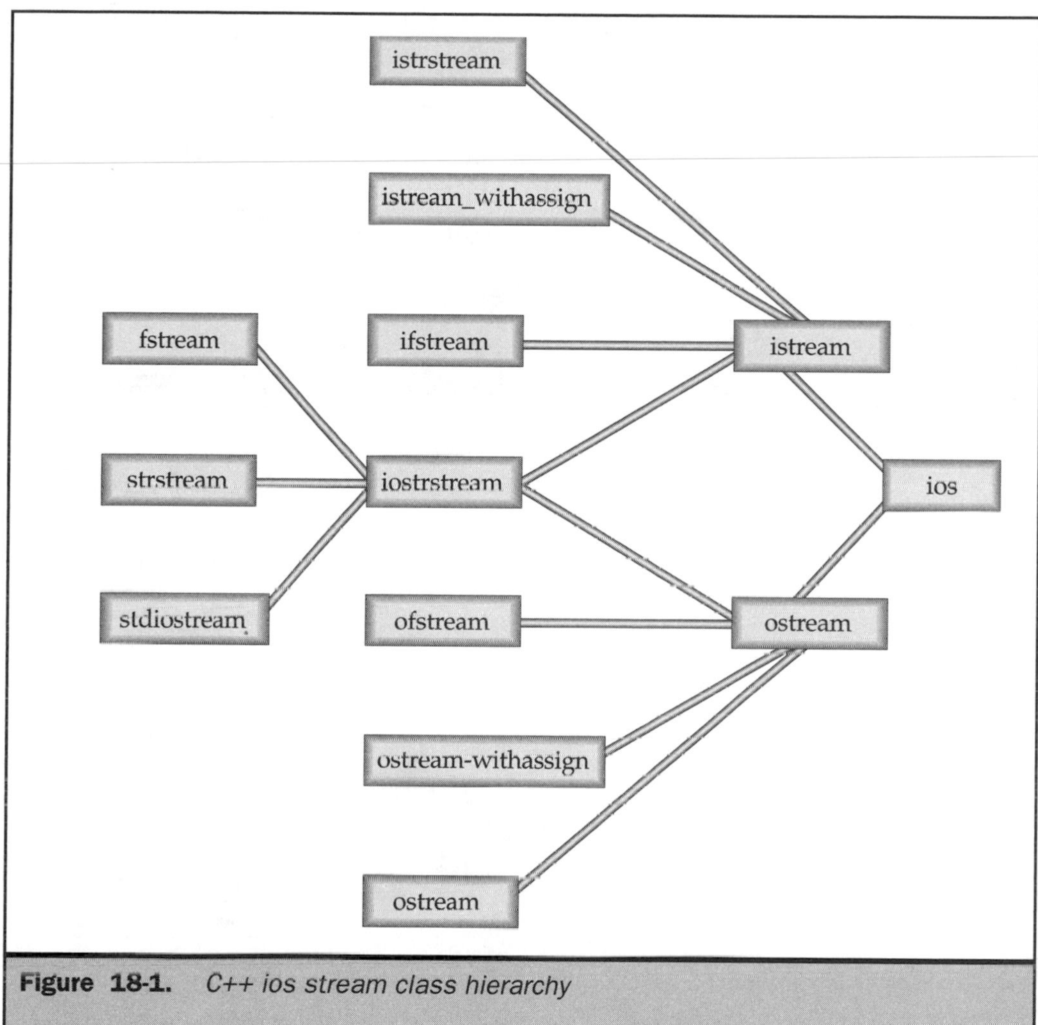

Figure 18-1. *C++ ios stream class hierarchy*

All **ios**-derived **iostream** classes use a **streambuf** class object for the actual I/O processing. The **iostream** class library uses the three derived buffer classes with streams as shown in Table 18-2.

Derived classes usually expand upon their inherited parent class definitions. This is why it is possible to use an operator or member function for a derived class that doesn't directly appear to be in the derived class' definition.

Often, because of this fact, it will be necessary to research back to the root or parent class definition. Since C++ derives so many of its classes from the **ios** class, a portion of **ios.h** follows. You will be able to use this as an easy reference for understanding any class derived from **ios**.

Buffered Class	Description
filebuf	Provides buffered disk file I/O
strstreambuf	Provides an in-memory array of bytes to hold the stream data
stdiobuf	Provides buffered disk I/O with all buffering done by the standard I/O system

Table 18-2. *Buffered Classes*

```
#ifndef EOF
#define EOF (-1)
#endif

class streambuf;
class ostream;

class ios {

public:
    enum io_state {  goodbit    = 0x00,
                     eofbit     = 0x01,
                     failbit    = 0x02,
                     badbit     = 0x04 };

    enum open_mode { in         = 0x01,
                     out        = 0x02,
                     ate        = 0x04,
                     app        = 0x08,
                     trunc      = 0x10,
                     nocreate   = 0x20,
                     noreplace  = 0x40,
                     binary     = 0x80 }; // not in latest spec.

    enum seek_dir { beg=0, cur=1, end=2 };

    enum {  skipws      = 0x0001,
            left        = 0x0002,
            right       = 0x0004,
```

```
        internal    = 0x0008,
        dec         = 0x0010,
        oct         = 0x0020,
        hex         = 0x0040,
        showbase    = 0x0080,
        showpoint   = 0x0100,
        uppercase   = 0x0200,
        showpos     = 0x0400,
        scientific  = 0x0800,
        fixed       = 0x1000,
        unitbuf     = 0x2000,
        stdio       = 0x4000
                            };

static const long basefield;   // dec | oct | hex
static const long adjustfield; // left | right | internal
static const long floatfield;  // scientific | fixed

ios(streambuf*);               // differs from ANSI
virtual ~ios( );

inline long flags( ) const;
inline long flags(long _l);

inline long setf(long _f,long _m);
inline long setf(long _l);
inline long unsetf(long _l);

inline int width( ) const;
inline int width(int _i);
inline ostream* tie(ostream* _os);
inline ostream* tie( ) const;

inline char fill( ) const;
inline char fill(char _c);

inline int precision(int _i);
inline int precision( ) const;

inline int rdstate( ) const;
inline void clear(int _i = 0);
```

```
//  NOTE: inline operator void*( ) const;
    operator void *( ) const { if(state&(badbit|failbit) ) \
                               return 0; return (void *)this; }
    inline int operator!( ) const;

    inline int  good( ) const;
    inline int  eof( ) const;
    inline int  fail( ) const;
    inline int  bad( ) const;
```

The programs in the following sections use a derived class based on some parent class. Some of the example program code uses derived class member functions, while other statements use inherited characteristics. These examples will help you understand the many advantages of derived classes and inherited characteristics. While these concepts may appear difficult or frustrating at first, you'll quickly appreciate how you can inherit functionality from a predefined class simply by defining a derived class based on the predefined one.

Input Stream Classes

The **ifstream** class used in the next example program is derived from **fstreambase** and **istream**. It provides input operations on a **filebuf**. The program concentrates on text stream input.

```
//
//  ifstrm.cpp
//  C++ program demonstrating how to use ifstream class,
//  derived from the istream class.
//  Copyright (c) Chris H. Pappas and William H. Murray, 1998
//
//  Valid member functions for ifstream include:
//        ifstream::open      ifstream::rdbuf
//
//  Valid member functions for istream include:
//        istream::gcount     istream::get
//        istream::getline    istream::ignore
//        istream::istream    istream::peek
//        istream::putback    istream::read
//        istream::seekg      istream::tellg

#include <fstream.h>
```

```
#define iCOLUMNS 80

void main(void)
{
  char cOneLine[iCOLUMNS];

  ifstream ifMyInputStream("IFSTRM.CPP",ios::in);
  while(ifMyInputStream) {
    ifMyInputStream.getline(cOneLine,iCOLUMNS);
    cout << '\n' << cOneLine;
  }
  ifMyInputStream.close( );
}
```

The **ifstream** constructor is used first to create an **ifstream** object and connect it to an open file descriptor, *ifMyInputStream*. The syntax uses the name of a file, including a path if necessary ("IFSTRM.CPP"), along with one or more open modes (for example, ios::in | ios::nocreate | ios::binary). The **default** is text input. The optional **ios::nocreate** parameter tests for the file's existence. The *ifMyInputStream* file descriptor's integer value can be used in logical tests such as **if** and **while** statements and the value is automatically set to zero on *EOF*.

The getline( ) member function inherited from the **iostream** class allows a program to read whole lines of text up to a terminating null character. Function getline( ) has three formal parameters: a **char** *, the number of characters to input—including the null character—and an optional delimiter (default = '\n').

cOneLine meets the first parameter requirement since **char** array names are technically pointers to characters. The number of characters to be input matches the array's definition, or *iCOLUMNS*. No optional delimiter was defined. However, if you knew your input lines were delimited by a special character—for example, '*'—you could have written the getline( ) statement like this:

```
ifMyInputStream.getline(cOneLine,iCOLUMNS,'*');
```

The example program continues by printing the string and then manually closes the file ifMyInputStream.close( ).

Output Stream Classes

All **ofstream** classes are derived from **fstreambase** and **ostream** and allow a program to perform formatted and unformatted output to a **streambuf**. The output from this program is used later in this chapter in the section entitled "Binary Files" to contrast text output with binary output.

The following example uses the **ofstream** constructor, which is very similar to its **ifstream** counterpart, described earlier. It expects the name of the output file, "MYOSTRM.OUT," and the open mode, **ios::out**.

```
//
// ostrm.cpp
// C++ program demonstrating how to use the ofstream class
// derived from the ostream class.
// Copyright (c) Chris H. Pappas and William H. Murray, 1998

// Valid ofstream member functions include:
//        ofstream::open     ofstream::rdbuf

// Valid ostream member functions include:
//        ostream::flush     ostream::ostream
//        ostream::put       ostream::seekp
//        ostream::tellp     ostream::write

#include <fstream.h>
#include <string.h>
#define iSTRING_MAX 40

void main(void)
{
  int i=0;
  long ltellp;
  char pszString[iSTRING_MAX] = "Sample test string\n";

  // file opened in the default text mode
  ofstream ofMyOutputStream("MYOSTRM.OUT",ios::out);

  // write string out character by character
  // notice that '\n' IS translated into 2 characters

  while(pszString[i] != '\0') {
    ofMyOutputStream.put(pszString[i]);
    ltellp = ofMyOutputStream.tellp( );
    cout << "\ntellp value: " << ltellp;
    i++;
  }
```

```
    // write entire string out with write member function

    ltellp = ofMyOutputStream.tellp( );
    cout << "\ntellp's value before writing 2nd string: "
         << ltellp;
    ofMyOutputStream.write(pszString,strlen(pszString));
    ltellp = ofMyOutputStream.tellp( );
    cout << "\ntellp's updated value: " << ltellp;

    ofMyOutputStream.close( );

  }
```

The initial **while** loop prints out the *pszString* character by character with the put( ) member function. After each character is output, the variable *ltellp* is assigned the current put( ) pointer's position as returned by the call to the tellp( ) member function. It is important that you stop at this point to take a look at the output generated by the program, shown at the end of this section.

The string variable *pszString* is initialized with 19 characters plus a '\0' null terminator, bringing the count to a total of 20. However, although the program output generates a *tellp* count of 1..20, the 20th character is not the '\0' null terminator. This is because in text mode, the *pszString*'s '\n' is translated into a 2-byte output, one for the carriage return (19th character) and the second for the linefeed (20th character). The null terminator is not output.

The last portion of the program calculates the output pointer's position before and after using the write( ) member function to print *pszString* as a whole string. Notice that the *tellp* values printed show that the function write( ) also translates the single null terminator into a two character output. If the character translation had not occurred, *tellp*'s last value would be 39 (assuming put( ) left the first count at 20, not 19). The abbreviated output from the program looks like this:

```
tellp value: 1
tellp value: 2
tellp value: 3
     .
     .
     .
```

```
tellp value: 17
tellp value: 18
tellp value: 20
tellp's value before writing 2nd string: 20
tellp's updated value: 40
```

Fortunately, **istream**-derived class member functions such as get( ) and read( ) automatically convert the 2-byte output back to a single '\n'. The program highlights the need for caution when dealing with file I/O. If the file created by this program was used later as an input file and opened in binary mode, a disaster would occur. Because binary files do not use such translation, the file positions and contents would be incorrect.

Buffered Stream Classes

The **streambuf** class is the foundation for C++ stream I/O. This general class defines all of the basic operations that can be performed with character-oriented buffers. The **streambuf** class is also used to derive file buffers (**filebuf** class) and the **istream** and **ostream** classes that contain pointers to **streambuf** objects.

Any derived classes based on the **ios** class inherit a pointer to a **streambuf**. The **filebuf** class, as seen in Figure 18-2, is derived from **streambuf** and specializes the parent class to handle files.

The following example begins by defining two **filebuf** handles, *fbMyInputBuf* and *fbMyOutputBuf*, using the open( ) member function to create each text file. Assuming there were no file-creation errors, each handle is then associated with an appropriate **istream** (input) and **ostream** (output) object. With both files opened, the **while** loop performs a simple echo print from the input stream is.get( ) to the output stream

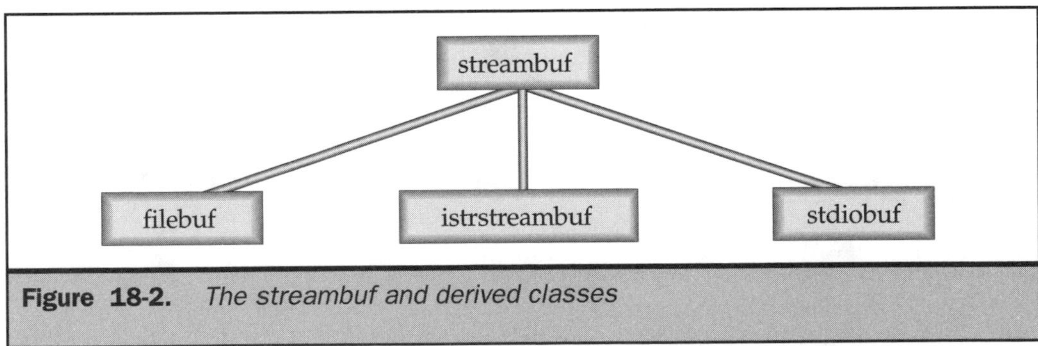

Figure 18-2. *The streambuf and derived classes*

os.put( ), counting the number of linefeeds, '\n'. The overloaded close( ) member function manually closes each file.

```
//
//  filbuf.cpp
//  C++ program demonstrating how to use filebuf class.
//  Copyright (c) Chris H. Pappas and William H. Murray, 1998
//
//  Valid member functions include:
//          filebuf::attach       filebuf::close
//          filebuf::fd           filebuf::~filebuf
//          filebuf::filebuf      filebuf::is_open
//          filebuf::open         filebuf::overflow
//          filebuf::seekoff      filebuf::setbuf
//          filebuf::sync         filebuf::underflow
//

#include <fstream.h>
#include <fcntl.h>
#include <process.h> // exit prototype

void main(void)
{
  char ch;
  int iLineCount=0;
  filebuf fbMyInputBuf, fbMyOutputBuf;

  fbMyInputBuf.open("c:\\FILBUF.CPP",_O_WRONLY | _O_TEXT);
  if(fbMyInputBuf.is_open( ) == 0) {
    cerr << "Can't open input file";
    exit (1);
  }

  istream is(&fbMyInputBuf);

  fbMyOutputBuf.open("c:\\output.dat",_O_WRONLY | _O_TEXT);
  if(fbMyOutputBuf.is_open( ) == 0) {
    cerr << "Can't open output file";
    exit (2);
  }
```

```
    ostream os(&fbMyOutputBuf);

    while(is) {
      is.get(ch);
      os.put(ch);
      iLineCount += (ch == '\n');
    }

    fbMyInputBuf.close( );
    fbMyOutputBuf.close( );

    cout << "You had " << iLineCount << " lines in your file";
}
```

String Stream Class

The **streambuf** class can be used to extend the capabilities of the **iostream** class. Figure 18-1, shown earlier, illustrated the relationship between the **ios** and derived classes. It is the **ios** class that provides the derived classes with the programming interface and formatting features. However, it is the **streambuf** public members and virtual functions that do all the work. All derived **ios** classes make calls to these routines.

All buffered **streambuf** objects manage a fixed memory buffer called a *reserve area.* This reserve area can be divided into a **get** area for input and a **put** area for output. If an application requires, the **get** and **put** areas may overlap. Your program can use protected member functions to access and manipulate the two separate **get** and **put** pointers for character I/O. Each application determines the behavior of the buffers and pointers based on the program's implementation of the derived class.

There are two constructors for **streambuf** objects. Their syntax looks like this:

```
streambuf::streambuf( );
streambuf::streambuf(char* pr, int nLength);
```

The first constructor is used indirectly by all **streambuf** derived classes. It sets all the internal pointers of the **streambuf** object to null. The second constructor creates a **streambuf** object that is attached to an existing character array. The following program demonstrates how to declare a string **strstreambuf** object derived from the **streambuf** base class. Once the *stbMyStreamBuf* object is created, the program outputs a single character using the sputc( ) member function and then reads the character back in with the sgetc( ) member function.

```
//
//  strbuf.cpp
//  C++ program demonstrating how to use the streambuf class.
//  Copyright (c) Chris H. Pappas and William H. Murray, 1998
//

#include <strstrea.h>
#define iMYBUFFSIZE 1024

 void main(void)
{
  char c;

  strstreambuf stbMyStreamBuf(iMYBUFFSIZE);
  stbMyStreamBuf.sputc('A');  // output single character to buffer
  c = stbMyStreamBuf.sgetc( );
  cout << c;
}
```

There are two separate pointers for **streambuf**-based objects, a *put to* and a *get from*. Each is manipulated independently of the other. The reason the sgetc( ) member function retrieves the 'A' is to return the contents of the buffer at the location to which the **get** pointer points. sputc( ) moves the **put** pointer but does not move the **get** pointer and does not return a character from the buffer.

Table 18-3 gives the names and explanations for all **streambuf** public members and highlights which functions manipulate the **put** and **get** pointers.

Public Member	Meaning
sgetc	Returns the character pointed to by the **get** pointer. However, **sgetc** does not move the pointer.
sgetn	Gets a series of characters from the **streambuf** buffer.
sputc	Puts a character in the **put** area and moves the **put** pointer.
sputn	Puts a sequence of characters into the **streambuf** buffer and then moves the **put** pointer.

Table 18-3. *Members of Streambuf*

snextc	Moves the **get** pointer and returns the next character.
sbumpc	Returns the current character and then moves the **get** pointer.
stossc	Advances the **get** pointer one position. However, **stossc** does not return a character.
sputbackc	Attempts to move the **get** pointer back one position. Character put back must match one from previous **get**.
out_waiting	Reports the number of characters in the **put** area.
in_avail	Reports the number of characters in the **get** area.
dbp	Outputs **streambuf** buffer statistics and pointer values.

Table 18-3. *Members of Streambuf* (continued)

Table 18-4 gives the names and explanations for all **streambuf** virtual functions.

Table 18-5 gives the names and explanations for all **streambuf** protected members.

The **streambuf** class comes equipped with almost every function a programmer could possibly need for manipulating a stream buffer. Since the **streambuf** class is used to derive file buffers (**filebuf** class) and **istream** and **ostream** classes, they all inherit **streambuf** characteristics.

Virtual Function	Meaning
seekoff	Seeks to the specified offset
seekpos	Seeks to the specified position
overflow	Clears out the **put** area
underflow	Fills the **get** area if necessary
pbackfail	Extends the sputbackc( ) function
setbuf	Tries to attach a reserve area to the **streambuf**
sync	Clears out the **put** and **get** areas

Table 18-4. *Virtual Functions of Streambuf*

Protected Member	Meaning
allocate	Allocates a buffer by calling **doalloc**
doallocate	Allocates a reserve area (virtual function)
base	Returns a pointer to the beginning of the reserve area
ebuf	Returns a pointer to the end of the reserve area
blen	Returns the size of the reserve area
pbase	Returns a pointer to the beginning of the **put** area
pptr	Returns the **put** pointer
gptr	Returns the **get** pointer
eback	Returns the lower bound of the **get** area
epptr	Returns a pointer to the end of the **put** area
cgptr	Returns a pointer to the end of the **get** area
setp	Sets all the **put** area pointers
setg	Sets all the **get** area pointers
pbump	Increments/decrements the **put** pointer
gbump	Increments/decrements the **get** pointer
setb	Sets up the reserve area
unbuffered	Sets or tests the **streambuf0** buffer state variable

Table 18-5. *Protected Members of streambuf*

Binary Files

Most of the example programs presented so far have used standard text files—or streams, as they are more appropriately called. This is not surprising since streams were originally designed for text, and text therefore is their default I/O mode.

Standard text files, or streams, contain a sequence of characters including carriage returns and linefeeds. In text mode, there is no requirement that individual characters remain unaltered as they are written to or read from a file. This can cause problems for certain types of applications. For example, the ASCII value for the newline character is a decimal 10. However, it could also be written as an 8-bit, hexadecimal 0A. In both C and C++ programs, it is considered to be the single character constant '\n'.

Under MS-DOS-compatible operations, the newline character is physically represented as a character pair—carriage return (decimal 13)/linefeed (decimal 10). Normally, this isn't a problem since the program automatically maps the two-character sequence into the single newline character on input, reversing the sequence on output. The problem is that a newline character occupies 1 byte, while the CR/LF pair occupies 2 bytes of storage.

Binary files, or streams, contain a sequence of bytes with a one-to-one correspondence to the sequence found in the external device (disk, tape, or terminal). In a binary file, no character translations will occur. For this reason, the number of bytes read or written will be the same as that found in the external device.

When an application is developed that needs to read an executable file, the file should be read as a binary file. Likewise, binary files should be used when reading or writing pure data files, like databases. Performing this action guarantees that no alteration of the data occurs except those changes performed explicitly by the application.

The following program is identical to OSTRM.CPP, described earlier in this chapter, except that the output file mode has been changed from text to **ios::binary**:

```
//
// binary.cpp
// This program is a modification of OSTRM.CPP and
// demonstrates binary file output.
// Copyright (c) Chris H. Pappas and William H. Murray, 1998
// Valid ofstream member functions include:
//        ofstream::open     ofstream::rdbuf
// Valid ostream member functions include:
//        ostream::flush     ostream::ostream
//        ostream::put       ostream::seekp
//        ostream::tellp     ostream::write

#include <fstream.h>
#include <string.h>
#define iSTRING_MAX 40

void main(void)
{
  int i=0;
  long ltellp;
  char pszString[iSTRING_MAX] = "Sample test string\n";
  // file opened in binary mode!
```

```
    ofstream ofMyOutputStream("MYOSTRM.OUT",ios::out | ios::binary);

    // write string out character by character
    // notice that '\n' is NOT translated into 2 characters!
    while(pszString[i] != '\0') {
      ofMyOutputStream.put(pszString[i]);
      ltellp = ofMyOutputStream.tellp( );
      cout << "\ntellp value: " << ltellp;
      i++;
    }

    // write entire string out with write member function
    ltellp = ofMyOutputStream.tellp( );
    cout << "\ntellp's value before writing 2nd string: " << ltellp;
    ofMyOutputStream.write(pszString,strlen(pszString));
    ltellp = ofMyOutputStream.tellp( );
    cout << "\ntellp's updated value: " << ltellp;

    ofMyOutputStream.close( );

}
```

The abbreviated output, seen in the following listing, illustrates the one-to-one relationship between a file and the data's internal representation:

```
tellp value: 1
tellp value: 2
tellp value: 3
     .
     .
     .
tellp value: 17
tellp value: 18
tellp value: 19
tellp's value before writing 2nd string: 19
tellp's updated value: 38
```

The string *pszString*, which has 19 characters plus a '\0' null string terminator, is output exactly as stored, without the appended '\0' null terminator. This explains why tellp( ) reports a multiple of 19 at the completion of each string's output.

Combining C and C++ Code

In earlier discussions (such as Chapter 6), you have seen how the **extern** keyword specifies that a variable or function has external linkage. This means that the variable or function referenced is defined in some other source file or later on in the same file.

In C and C++, the **extern** keyword can be used with a string. The string indicates that another language's linkage conventions are being used for the identifier(s) being defined. For C++ programs, the default string is "C++."

In C++, functions are overloaded by default. This causes the C++ compiler to assign a new name to each function. You can prevent the compiler from assigning a new name to each function by preceding the function definition with **extern** "C". This is necessary so that C functions and data can be accessed by C++ code. Naturally, this is only done for one of a set of functions with the same name. Without this override, the linker would find more than one global function with the same name. Currently, "C" is the only other language specifier supported by Visual C++. The syntax for using **extern** "C" takes this form:

```
extern "C" freturn_type fname(param_type(s) param(s))
```

The following listing demonstrates how **extern** "C" is used with a single-function prototype:

```
extern "C" int fprintf(FILE *stream, char *format, ...);
```

To modify a group of function prototypes, a set of braces, { }, is needed:

```
extern "C"
  {
      .
      .
      .
  }
```

The next code segment modifies the getc( ) and putc( ) function prototypes:

```
extern "C"
  {
     int getc(FILE *stream);
     int putc(int c, FILE *stream);
  }
```

The following example program demonstrates how to use **extern** "C":

```
//
//   clink.cpp
//   C++ program demonstrating how to link C++ code
//   to C library functions
//   Copyright (c) Chris H. Pappas and William H. Murray, 1998
//

#include <iostream.h>
#include <string.h>
#include <stdlib.h>

#define iMAX 9

extern "C" int imycompare(const void *pi1, const void *pi2);

void main(void)
{
  int iarray[iMAX] = { 1, 9, 2, 8, 3, 7, 4, 6, 5};

  for(int i = 0; i < iMAX; i++)
    cout << iarray[i] << " ";

  qsort(iarray,iMAX,sizeof(int),imycompare);

  for(i = 0; i < iMAX; i++)
    cout << iarray[i] << " ";
}

extern "C" int imycompare(const void *pi1, const void *pi2)
{
  return( *(int *)pi1 - *(int *)pi2);
}
```

All the Visual C++ include files use **extern** "C". This makes it possible for a C++ program to use the C run-time library functions. Rather than repeat **extern** "C" for every definition in these header files, the following conditional statement pair surrounds all C header file definitions:

```
// 3-statements found at the beginning of header file.
```

```
#ifdef __cplusplus
extern "C" {
#endif


// 3-statements found at the end of the header file.

#ifdef __cplusplus
}
#endif
```

When compiling a C++ program, the compiler automatically defines the __cplusplus name. This in turn makes the **extern** "C" { statement and the closing brace, }, visible only when needed.

Designing Unique Manipulators

The concept of stream manipulators was first introduced in Chapter 12. Manipulators are used with the insertion, <<, and extraction, >>, operators, exactly as if they represented data for output or variables to receive input. As the name implies, however, manipulators can carry out arbitrary operations on the input and output streams.

Several of the example programs used the built-in manipulators **dec**, **hex**, **oct**, **setw**, and **setprecision**. Now you will learn how to write your own custom manipulators. To gradually build your understanding of the syntax necessary to create your own manipulators, the example programs begin with the simplest type of manipulator, one with no parameters, and then move on to ones with parameters.

Manipulators Without Parameters

A custom manipulator can be created anytime to repeatedly insert the same character sequence into the output stream. For example, maybe your particular application needs to flag the user to an important piece of data. You may even want to beep the speaker to get the user's attention just in case he or she isn't looking directly at the monitor. Without custom manipulators, your output statements would look like this:

```
cout << '\a' << "\n\n\t\tImportant data: "
     << fcritical_mass << endl;
```

Every time you wanted to grab the user's attention, you would repeat the bell prompt, '\a', and the "...Important data: " string. An easier approach is to define a manipulator, called **beep**, that automatically substitutes the desired sequence. The **beep** manipulator also makes the statement easier to read:

```
cout << beep << fcritical_mass << endl;
```

The following program demonstrates how to define and use the beep( ) function:

```
//
//  beep.cpp
//  C++ program demonstrates how to create your own
//  non-parameterized manipulator
//  Copyright (c) Chris H. Pappas and William H. Murray, 1998
//

#include <iostream.h>

ostream& beep(ostream& os) {
  return os << '\a' << "\n\n\t\t\tImportant data: ";
}

void main(void)
{
 double fcritical_mass = 12459876.12;

 cout << beep << fcritical_mass;
}
```

The globally defined beep( ) function uses an **ostream&** formal parameter and returns the same **ostream&**. beep( ) works because it is automatically connected to the stream's **<<** operator. The stream's insertion operator, **<<**, is overloaded to accept this kind of function with the following inline function:

```
Inline ostream& ostream::operator<<(ostream& (*f)(ostream&)) {
  (*f)(*this);
  return *this;
}
```

The inline function associates the **<<** operator with the custom manipulator by accepting a pointer to a function passed an **ostream&** type and that returns the same. This is exactly how beep( ) is prototyped. Now when **<<** is used with beep( ), the compiler dereferences the overloaded operator, finding where function beep( ) sits, and then executes it. The overloaded operator returns a reference to the original **ostream**. Because of this, you can combine manipulators, strings, and other data with the << operators.

Manipulators with One Parameter

The **iostream** class library, prototyped in IOMANIP.H, defines a special set of macros for creating parameterized macros. The simplest parameterized macro you can write accepts either one **int** or **long** parameter.

The following application shows a prototype for such a manipulator, *fc*. The example program demonstrates the syntax necessary to create a single-parameter custom manipulator:

```
//
//  manip1.cpp
//  C++ program demonstrating how to create and use
//  one-parameter custom manipulators.
//  Copyright (c) Chris H. Pappas and William H. Murray, 1998
//

#include <iostream.h>
#include <iomanip.h>
#include <string.h>
#define iSCREEN_WIDTH 80


ostream& fc(ostream& os, int istring_width)
{
  os << '\n';
  for(int i=0; i < ((iSCREEN_WIDTH - istring_width)/2); i++)
    os << ' ';
  return(os);
}

OMANIP(int) center(int istring_width)
{
  return OMANIP(int) (fc, istring_width);
}

void main(void)
{
  char *psz = "This is auto-centered text!";
  cout << center(strlen(psz)) << psz;
}
```

The *center* custom-parameterized manipulator accepts a single value, *strlen(psz)*, representing the length of a string. IOMANIP.H defines a macro, OMANIP(int), and expands into the class **__OMANIP_int**. The definition for this class includes a constructor and an overloaded **ostream** insertion operator. When function center( ) is inserted into the stream, it calls the constructor that creates and returns an **__OMANIP_int** object. The object's constructor then calls the fc( ) function.

Manipulators with Multiple Parameters

The next example should be familiar. Actually, it is the same code (sqrt.cpp) seen earlier in the chapter to demonstrate how to format numeric output. However, the program has been rewritten using a two-parameter custom manipulator to format the data.

The first modification to the program involves a simple structure definition to hold the format manipulator's actual parameter values:

```
struct stwidth_precision {
  int iwidth;
  int iprecision;
};
```

When you create manipulators that take arguments other than **int** or **long**, you must use the **IOMANIPdeclare** macro. This macro declares the classes for your new data type. The definition for the *format* manipulator begins with the **OMANIP** macro:

```
OMANIP(stwidth_precision) format(int iwidth, int iprecision)
{
  stwidth_precision stWidth_Precision;
  stWidth_Precision.iwidth = iwidth;
  stWidth_Precision.iprecision = iprecision;
  return OMANIP (stwidth_precision)(ff, stWidth_Precision);
}
```

In this example, the custom manipulator is passed two integer arguments, *iwidth* and *iprecision*. The first value defines the number of spaces to be used by *format*, and the second value specifies the number of decimal places. Once *format* has initialized the stWidth_Precision structure, it calls the constructor, which creates and returns an **__OMANIP** object. The object's constructor then calls the ff( ) function, which sets the specified parameters:

```
static ostream& ff(ostream& os, stwidth_precision
                   stWidth_Precision)
{
```

```
  os.width(stWidth_Precision.iwidth);
  os.precision(stWidth_Precision.iprecision);
  os.setf(ios::fixed);
  return os;
}
```

The complete program follows. All of the code replaced by the call to *format* has been left in the listing for comparison. Notice how the *format* custom manipulator streamlines each output statement.

```
//
//  manip2.cpp
//  This C++ program is the same as sqrt.cpp, except
//  for the fact that it uses custom parameterized
//  manipulators to format the output.
//  A C++ program that prints a table of
//  numbers, squares, and square roots for the
//  numbers from 1 to 15. Program uses the type
//  double. Formatting aligns columns, pads blank
//  spaces with '0' character, and controls
//  precision of answer.
//  Copyright (c) Chris H. Pappas and William H. Murray, 1998
//

#include <iostream.h>
#include <iomanip.h>
#include <math.h>

struct stwidth_precision {
  int iwidth;
  int iprecision;
};

IOMANIPdeclare(stwidth_precision);

static ostream& ff(ostream& os, stwidth_precision
                   stWidth_Precision)
{
  os.width(stWidth_Precision.iwidth);
  os.precision(stWidth_Precision.iprecision);
  os.setf(ios::fixed);
  return os;
}
```

```
OMANIP(stwidth_precision) format(int iwidth, int iprecision)
{
  stwidth_precision stWidth_Precision;
  stWidth_Precision.iwidth = iwidth;
  stWidth_Precision.iprecision = iprecision;
  return OMANIP (stwidth_precision)(ff, stWidth_Precision);
}

main( )
{
  double number,square,sqroot;

  cout << "num\t" << "square\t\t" << "square root\n";
  cout << "___________________________________________\n";

  number=1.0;

//cout.setf(ios::fixed);          // use fixed format
  for(int i=1;i<16;i++) {
    square=number*number;         // find square
    sqroot=sqrt(number);          // find square root

    cout.fill('0');               // fill blanks with zeros
//  cout.width(2);                // column 2 characters wide
//  cout.precision(0);            // no decimal place
    cout << format(2,0) << number << "\t";

//  cout.width(6);                // column 6 characters wide
//  cout.precision(1);            // print 1 decimal place
    cout << format(6,1) << square << "\t\t";

//  cout.width(8);                // column 8 characters wide
//  cout.precision(6);            // print 6 decimal places
    cout << format(8,6) << sqroot << endl;

    number+=1.0;
  }
  return (0);
}
```

With the discussion of advanced C++ object-oriented I/O completed, you are ready to tackle object-oriented design philosophies. Chapter 19 explains how important good class design is to a successful object-oriented program solution.

Chapter 19

Working in an Object-oriented Environment

C++ appears to be the language of choice among object-oriented programmers; however, other languages are available. Every object-oriented language shares several common features. Bertrand Meyer, in his book *Object-Oriented Software Construction* (Prentice Hall, 1995), suggests that there are seven features standard to true object-oriented programs as a whole:

- Abstract data types
- Classes
- Inheritance
- Inheritance (multiple)
- Memory management (automatic)
- Object-based modularization
- Polymorphism

In Chapter 17 you learned that Visual C++ classes provide these features to the object-oriented programmer. You might also conclude that to do true object-oriented programming, you must work in a language, such as C++, that is itself object oriented. There are valid arguments against this notion, as you will see later in this book. For example, programs written for Microsoft's Windows contain many of the seven previously mentioned features, even though they can be written in C.

An Object-oriented Stack

Chapter 16 introduced many object-oriented concepts. For example, the C++ class was introduced as an abstract data type that provides the encapsulation of data structures and the operations on those structures (member functions). In this capacity, the C++ class serves as the mechanism for forming objects. The following simple example of object creation with a C++ class demonstrates the implementation of an object-oriented stack.

The traditional FILO (first in, last out) manner is used for the stack operations in this example. The stack class provides six member functions or methods: clear( ), top( ), empty( ), full( ), push( ), and pop( ). Examine the following listing and observe how these member functions are implemented:

```
//
//  stack.cpp
//  C++ program illustrates object-oriented programming
//  with a classical stack operation using a string of
//  characters.
//  Copyright (c) Chris H. Pappas and William H. Murray, 1998
```

```
//

#include <iostream.h>
#include <string.h>

#define maxlen 80

class stack {
  char str1[maxlen];
  int  first;

public:
  void clear(void);
  char top(void);
  int  empty(void);
  int  full(void);
  void push(char chr);
  char pop(void);
};

void stack::clear(void)
{
  first=0;
}

char stack::top(void)
{
  return (str1[first]);
}

int stack::empty(void)
{
  return (first==0);
}

int stack::full(void)
{
  return (first==maxlen-1);
}

void stack::push(char chr)
{
```

```
  str1[++first]=chr;
}

char stack::pop(void)
{
  return (str1[first--]);
}

main( )
{
  stack mystack;
  char str[11]="0123456789";

  // clear the stack
  mystack.clear( );

  // load the string, char-by-char, on the stack
  cout << "\nLoad character data on stack" << endl;
  for(int i=0; (int) i<strlen(str);i++) {
    if (!mystack.full( ))
      mystack.push(str[i]);
      cout << str[i] << endl;
  }

  // unload the stack, char-by-char
  cout << "\nUnload character data from stack" << endl;
  while (!mystack.empty( ))
    cout << mystack.pop( ) << endl;

  return (0);
}
```

In this application, characters from a string are pushed, one character at a time, onto the stack. Then the stack is unloaded one character at a time. Loading and unloading are done from the stack top, so the first character information loaded on the stack is pushed down most deeply in the stack.

Notice in the following listing that the character for the number zero was pushed onto the stack first. It should be no surprise that it is the last character popped off the stack.

```
Load character data on stack
0
1
2
3
4
5
6
7
8
9

Unload character data from stack
9
8
7
6
5
4
3
2
1
0
```

This example lacks many of the more advanced object-oriented concepts such as memory management, inheritance, and polymorphism. However, the example is a complete object-oriented program. The power of object-oriented thinking becomes more apparent as more and more of Meyer's seven points are actually implemented.

An Object-oriented Linked List in C++

A linked-list program was developed in Chapter 14 using a traditional procedural programming approach in C++. When using the procedure-oriented approach, you learned that the linked-list program is difficult to alter and maintain. In this chapter, a linked-list program using objects is developed that will allow you to create a list of employee information. It will also be possible to add and delete employees from the list. To limit the size of the linked-list program, no user interface will be used for gathering employee data. Data for the linked list has been *hardwired* in the main( ) function. Examples of how to make this program interactive and able to accept information from the keyboard have been shown in earlier chapters.

This program is slightly more involved than the application presented in Chapter 14. It includes, in addition to linked-list concepts, all seven of the object-oriented concepts listed earlier.

Creating a Parent Class

Several child classes derived from a common parent class are used in this example. The parent class for this linked-list example is named **NNR**. Here, the letters **NNR** represent the Nineveh National Research Company that develops computer-related books and software. The linked-list program is a database that will keep pertinent information and payroll data on company employees. The purpose of the parent class **NNR** is to gather information common to all subsequent derived child classes. For this example, that common information includes an employee's last name, first name, occupation title, social security number, and year hired at the company. The parent class **NNR** has three levels of isolation: public, protected, and private. The protected section of this class shows the structure for gathering data common to each derived child class. The public section (member functions) shows how that information will be intercepted from the function main( ).

```
// PARENT CLASS
class NNR {

friend class payroll_list;

protected:
  char lstname[20];
  char fstname[15];
  char job_title[30];
  char social_sec[12];
  double year_hired;
  NNR *pointer;
  NNR *next_link;

public:
  NNR(char *lname,char *fname,char *ss,
      char *job,double y_hired)
  {
    strcpy(lstname,lname);
    strcpy(fstname,fname);
    strcpy(social_sec,ss);
    strcpy(job_title,job);
    year_hired=y_hired;
    next_link=0;
  }
```

```
   .
   .
   .
   .
```

A **friend** class named **payroll_list** is used by the parent class and all derived child classes. When you study the full program listing in the section entitled "Examining the Complete Program" later in this chapter, notice that all derived child classes share this common variable, too. (Remember how the terms "private" and "public" relate to encapsulation concepts used by object-oriented programmers.)

A Derived Child Class

Four derived child classes are used in this program. Each of these is derived from the parent class **NNR** shown in the last section. This segment presents one child class, **salespersons**, which represents the points common to all four derived classes. A portion of this derived class is shown next. The derived child class satisfies the object-oriented concept of inheritance.

```
//SUB OR DERIVED CHILD CLASS
class salespersons:public NNR {

friend class payroll_list;

private:
  double disk_sales;
  double comm_rate;

public:
  salespersons(char *lname,char *fname,char *ss,
               char *job,double y_hired,
               double d_sales,double c_rate):
               NNR(lname,fname,ss,
               job,y_hired)
  {
    disk_sales=d_sales;
    comm_rate=c_rate;
  }
    .
    .
    .
    .
```

The **salespersons** child class gathers information and adds it to the information already gathered by the parent class. This in turn forms a data structure composed of last name, first name, social security number, year hired, the total sales, and the appropriate commission rate.

Here is the remainder of the child class description:

```
      .
      .
      .
      .

  void fill_sales(double d_sales)
  {
    disk_sales=d_sales;
  }

  void fill_comm_rate(double c_rate)
  {
    comm_rate=c_rate;
  }

  void add_info( )
  {
    pointer=this;
  }

  void send_info( )
  {
    NNR::send_info( );
    cout << "\n Sales (disks): " << disk_sales;
    cout << "\n Commission Rate: " << comm_rate;
  }

};
```

Instead of add_info( ) setting aside memory for each additional linked-list node by using the new free store operator, the program uses each object's **this** pointer. The *pointer* is being assigned the address of an **NNR** node.

Output information on a particular employee is constructed in a unique manner. In the case of the **salespersons** class, notice that send_info( ) makes a request to **NNR**'s send_info( ) function. **NNR**'s function prints the information common to each derived class; then the salespersons' send_info( ) function prints the information unique to the

the pointer until all employees have been printed. The next section of code shows how this is achieved:

```
        .
        .
        .
        .
void payroll_list::print_payroll_list( )
{
  NNR *present=location;

  while(present!=0) {
    present->send_info( );
    present=present->next_link;
  }
}
        .
        .
        .
```

The fact that the variable *pointer* contains the memory address of nodes inserted via add_info( ) was discussed earlier. This value is used by insert_employee( ) to form the link with the linked list. The insertion technique inserts data alphabetically by an employee's last name. Thus, the linked list is always ordered alphabetically by last name.

A correct insertion is made by the application by comparing the last name of a new employee with those already in the list. When a name (*node->lstname*) already in the list is found that is greater than the **current_node->lstname**, the first **while** loop ends. This is a standard linked-list insert procedure that leaves the pointer variable, **previous_node**, pointing to the node behind where the new node is to be inserted and leaves **current_node** pointing to the node that will follow the insertion point for the new node.

Once the insertion point is determined, the program creates a new link or node by calling node->add_info( ). The **current_node** is linked to the new node's **next_link**. The last decision that must be made is whether or not the new node is to be placed as the front node in the list or between existing nodes. The program establishes this by examining the contents of the pointer variable **previous_node**. If the pointer variable is zero, it cannot be pointing to a valid previous node, so *location* is updated to the address of the new node. If **previous_node** contains a nonzero value, it is assumed to be pointing to a valid previous node. In this case, **previous_node->next_link** is assigned the address of the new node's address, or **node->pointer**.

particular child class. For this example, this information includes the sales commission rate.

It would also have been possible to print the information about the sale completely from within the child class, but the method used allows another advantage of object-oriented programming to be illustrated, and that is the u *virtual* functions.

Using a Friend Class

The friend class, **payroll_list**, contains the means for printing the linked list and insertion and deletion of employees from the list. Here is a small portion of this

```
//FRIEND CLASS
class payroll_list {

private:
  NNR *location;

public:
  payroll_list( )
  {
    location=0;
  }

  void print_payroll_list( );

  void insert_employee(NNR *node);

  void remove_employee_id(char *social_sec);

};
      .
      .
      .
      .
```

Notice that messages that are sent to the member functions print_payroll_list( ), insert_employee( ), and remove_employee_id( ) form the functional part of the linked-list program.

Consider the function print_payroll_list( ), which begins by assigning the pointer to the list to the pointer variable **present**. While the pointer **present** is not zero, it will continue to point to employees in the linked list, direct them to **send_info**, and update

```
      .
      .
      .
      .
void payroll_list::insert_employee(NNR *node)
{
  NNR *current_node=location;
  NNR *previous_node=0;

  while (current_node != 0 &&
         strcmp(current_node->lstname,node->lstname) < 0) {
    previous_node=current_node;
    current_node=current_node->next_link;
  }
  node->add_info( );
  node->pointer->next_link=current_node;
  if (previous_node==0)
    location=node->pointer;
  else
    previous_node->next_link=node->pointer;
}
      .
      .
      .
      .
```


Items can be removed from the linked list only by knowing the employee's social security number. This technique adds a level of protection against accidentally deleting an employee.

As you examine remove_employee_id( ), shown in the next listing, note that the structure used for examining the nodes in the linked list is almost identical to that of insert_employee( ). However, the first **while** loop leaves the **current_node** pointing to the node to be deleted, not the node after the one to be deleted.

```
      .
      .
      .
      .
void payroll_list::remove_employee_id(char *social_sec)
{
  NNR *current_node=location;
  NNR *previous_node=0;
```

```
   while(current_node != 0 &&
         strcmp(current_node->social_sec,
         social_sec) != 0) {
     previous_node=current_node;
     current_node=current_node->next_link;
   }

   if(current_node != 0 && previous_node == 0) {
     location=current_node->next_link;
     delete current_node;
   }
   else if(current_node != 0 && previous_node != 0) {
     previous_node->next_link=current_node->next_link;
     delete current_node;
   }
 }
```

The first compound **if** statement takes care of deleting a node in the front of the list. The program accomplishes this by examining the contents of **previous_node** to see if it contains a zero. If it does, then the front of the list, *location*, needs to be updated to the node following the one to be deleted. This is achieved with the following line:

```
current_node->next_link
```

The second if statement takes care of deleting a node between two existing nodes. This requires the node behind to be assigned the address of the node after the one being deleted.

```
previous_node->next_link=current_node->next_link.
```

Now that the important pieces of the program have been examined, the next section puts them together to form a complete program.

Examining the Complete Program

The following listing is the complete operational object-oriented linked-list program. The only thing it lacks is an interactive user interface. When the program is executed, it will add nine employees, with their different job titles, to the linked list and then print the list. Next, the program will delete two employees from the list. This is accomplished by supplying their social security numbers. The altered list is then printed. The main( ) function contains information on which employees are added and deleted.

```
//
//  nnr.cpp
//  C++ program illustrates object-oriented programming
//  with a linked list. This program keeps track of
//  employee data at Nineveh National Research (NNR).
//  Copyright (c) Chris H. Pappas and William H. Murray, 1998
//

#include <iostream.h>
#include <string.h>

// PARENT CLASS
class NNR {

friend class payroll_list;

protected:
  char lstname[20];
  char fstname[15];
  char job_title[30];
  char social_sec[12];
  double year_hired;
  NNR *pointer;
  NNR *next_link;

public:
  NNR(char *lname,char *fname,char *ss,
      char *job,double y_hired)
  {
    strcpy(lstname,lname);
    strcpy(fstname,fname);
    strcpy(social_sec,ss);
    strcpy(job_title,job);
    year_hired=y_hired;
    next_link=0;
  }

  NNR( )
  {
    lstname[0]=NULL;
    fstname[0]=NULL;
    social_sec[0]=NULL;
    job_title[0]=NULL;
```

```
    year_hired=0;
    next_link=0;
  }

  void fill_lstname(char *l_name)
  {
    strcpy(lstname,l_name);
  }

  void fill_fstname(char *f_name)
  {
    strcpy(fstname,f_name);
  }

  void fill_social_sec(char *soc_sec)
  {
    strcpy(social_sec,soc_sec);
  }

  void fill_job_title(char *o_name)
  {
    strcpy(job_title,o_name);
  }

  void fill_year_hired(double y_hired)
  {
    year_hired=y_hired;
  }

  virtual void add_info( ) {
  }
  virtual void send_info( )
  {
    cout << "\n\n" << lstname << ", " << fstname
      << "\n Social Security: #" << social_sec;
    cout << "\n Job Title: " << job_title;
    cout << "\n Year Hired: " << year_hired;
  }

};

//SUB OR DERIVED CHILD CLASS
```

```
class administration:public NNR {

friend class payroll_list;

private:
  double yearly_salary;

public:
  administration(char *lname,char *fname,char *ss,
                char *job,double y_hired,
                double y_salary):
                NNR(lname,fname,ss,
                job,y_hired)
  {
    yearly_salary=y_salary;
  }

  administration( ):NNR( )
  {
    yearly_salary=0.0;
  }

  void fill_yearly_salary(double salary)
  {
    yearly_salary=salary;
  }

  void add_info( )
  {
    pointer=this;
  }

  void send_info( )
  {
    NNR::send_info( );
    cout << "\n Yearly Salary: $" << yearly_salary;
  }

};


//SUB OR DERIVED CHILD CLASS
```

```
class salespersons:public NNR {

friend class payroll_list;

private:
  double disk_sales;
  double comm_rate;

public:
  salespersons(char *lname,char *fname,char *ss,
               char *job,double y_hired,
               double d_sales,double c_rate):
               NNR(lname,fname,ss,
               job,y_hired)
  {
    disk_sales=d_sales;
    comm_rate=c_rate;
  }

  salespersons( ):NNR( )
  {
    disk_sales=0.0;
    comm_rate=0;
  }

  void fill_sales(double d_sales)
  {
    disk_sales=d_sales;
  }
  void fill_comm_rate(int c_rate)
  {
    comm_rate=c_rate;
  }

  void add_info( )
  {
    pointer=this;
  }

  void send_info( )
  {
    NNR::send_info( );
```

```
    cout << "\n Sales (disks): " << disk_sales;
    cout << "\n Commission Rate: " << comm_rate;
  }

};


//SUB OR DERIVED CHILD CLASS
class technicians:public NNR {

friend class payroll_list;

private:
  double hourly_salary;

public:
  technicians(char *lname,char *fname,char *ss,char *job,
              double y_hired,double h_salary):
              NNR(lname,fname,ss,job,y_hired)
  {
    hourly_salary=h_salary;
  }

  technicians( ):NNR( )
  {
    hourly_salary=0.0;
  }

  void fill_hourly_salary(double h_salary)
  {
    hourly_salary=h_salary;
  }

  void add_info( )
  {
    pointer=this;
  }

  void send_info( )
  {
    NNR::send_info( );
    cout << "\n Hourly Salary: $" << hourly_salary;
```

```
  }

};


//SUB OR DERIVED CHILD CLASS
class supplies:public NNR {

friend class payroll_list;

private:
  double hourly_salary;

public:
  supplies(char *lname,char *fname,char *ss,char *job,
           double y_hired,double h_salary):
           NNR(lname,fname,ss,
           job,y_hired)
  {
    hourly_salary=h_salary;
  }

  supplies( ):NNR( )
  {
    hourly_salary=0.0;
  }

  void fill_hourly_salary(double h_salary)
  {
    hourly_salary=h_salary;
  }

  void add_info( )
  {
    pointer=this;
  }

  void send_info( )
  {
    NNR::send_info( );
    cout << "\n Hourly Salary: $" << hourly_salary;
  }
```

```
};


//FRIEND CLASS
class payroll_list {

private:
  NNR *location;

public:
  payroll_list( )
  {
    location=0;
  }

  void print_payroll_list( );

  void insert_employee(NNR *node);

  void remove_employee_id(char *social_sec);

};

void payroll_list::print_payroll_list( )
{
  NNR *present=location;

  while(present!=0) {
    present->send_info( );
    present=present->next_link;
  }
}

void payroll_list::insert_employee(NNR *node)
{
  NNR *current_node=location;
  NNR *previous_node=0;
  while (current_node != 0 &&
         strcmp(current_node->lstname,node->lstname) < 0) {
    previous_node=current_node;
    current_node=current_node->next_link;
  }
```

```
  node->add_info( );
  node->pointer->next_link=current_node;
  if (previous_node==0)
    location=node->pointer;
  else
    previous_node->next_link=node->pointer;
}

void payroll_list::remove_employee_id(char *social_sec)
{
  NNR *current_node=location;
  NNR *previous_node=0;

  while(current_node != 0 &&
     strcmp(current_node->social_sec,social_sec) != 0) {
    previous_node=current_node;
    current_node=current_node->next_link;
  }

  if(current_node != 0 && previous_node == 0) {
    location=current_node->next_link;
    // delete current_node; needed if new( ) used in add_info( )
  }
  else if(current_node != 0 && previous_node != 0) {
    previous_node->next_link=current_node->next_link;
    // delete current_node; needed if new( ) used in add_info( )
  }
}

main( )
{
  payroll_list workers;

  // static data to add to linked list
  salespersons salesperson1("Harddrive","Harriet","313-56-7884",
                            "Salesperson",1985,6.5,7.5);
  salespersons salesperson2("Flex","Frank","663-65-2312",
                            "Salesperson",1985,3.0,3.2);
  salespersons salesperson3("Ripoff","Randle","512-34-7612",
                            "Salesperson",1987,9.6,6.8);
  technicians techperson1("Align","Alice","174-43-6781",
                            "Technician",1989,12.55);
```

```
    technicians techperson2("Tightscrew","Tom","682-67-5312",
                            "Technician",1992,10.34);
    administration vice_president1("Stuckup","Stewart",
                            "238-18-1119","Vice President",
                             1980,40000.00);
    administration vice_president2("Learnedmore","Lawrence",
                            "987-99-9653","Vice President",
                             1984,45000.00);
    supplies supplyperson1("Allpart","Albert","443-89-3772",
                            "Supplies",1983,8.55);
    supplies supplyperson2("Ordermore","Ozel","111-44-5399",
                            "Supplies",1988,7.58);

    // add the nine workers to the linked list
    workers.insert_employee(&techperson1);
    workers.insert_employee(&vice_president1);
    workers.insert_employee(&salesperson1);
    workers.insert_employee(&supplyperson1);
    workers.insert_employee(&supplyperson2);
    workers.insert_employee(&salesperson2);
    workers.insert_employee(&techperson2);
    workers.insert_employee(&vice_president2);
    workers.insert_employee(&salesperson3);

    // print the linked list
    workers.print_payroll_list( );

    // remove two workers from the linked list
    workers.remove_employee_id("238-18-1119");
    workers.remove_employee_id("512-34-7612");

    cout << "\n\n**********************************";

    // print the revised linked list
    workers.print_payroll_list( );

    return (0);
}
```

As you study the complete listing, see if you understand how employees are inserted and deleted from the list. If it is still a little confusing, go back and study each major section of code discussed in earlier sections.

Output from the Linked List

The linked-list program sends output to the monitor. The first section of the list contains the nine employee names that were used to create the original list. The last part of the list shows the list after two employees are deleted. Here is a sample output sent to the screen:

```
Align, Alice
 Social Security: #174-43-6781
 Job Title: Technician
 Year Hired: 1989
 Hourly Salary: $12.55

Allpart, Albert
 Social Security: #443-89-3772
 Job Title: Supplies
 Year Hired: 1983
 Hourly Salary: $8.55

Flex, Frank
 Social Security: #663-65-2312
 Job Title: Salesperson
 Year Hired: 1985
 Sales (disks): 3
 Commission Rate: 3.2

Harddrive, Harriet
 Social Security: #313-56-7884
 Job Title: Salesperson
 Year Hired: 1985
 Sales (disks): 6.5
 Commission Rate: 7.5

Learnedmore, Lawrence
 Social Security: #987-99-9653
 Job Title: Vice President
 Year Hired: 1984
 Yearly Salary: $45000

Ordermore, Ozel
 Social Security: #111-44-5399
 Job Title: Supplies
```

```
 Year Hired: 1988
 Hourly Salary: $7.58

Ripoff, Randle
 Social Security: #512-34-7612
 Job Title: Salesperson
 Year Hired: 1987
 Sales (disks): 9.6
 Commission Rate: 6.8

Stuckup, Stewart
 Social Security: #238-18-1119
 Job Title: Vice President
 Year Hired: 1980
 Yearly Salary: $40000

Tightscrew, Tom
 Social Security: #682-67-5312
 Job Title: Technician
 Year Hired: 1992
 Hourly Salary: $10.34

***********************************

Align, Alice
 Social Security: #174-43-6781
 Job Title: Technician
 Year Hired: 1989
 Hourly Salary: $12.55

Allpart, Albert
 Social Security: #443-89-3772
 Job Title: Supplies
 Year Hired: 1983
 Hourly Salary: $8.55

Flex, Frank
 Social Security: #663-65-2312
 Job Title: Salesperson
 Year Hired: 1985
 Sales (disks): 3
```

```
 Commission Rate: 3.2

Harddrive, Harriet
 Social Security: #313-56-7884
 Job Title: Salesperson
 Year Hired: 1985
 Sales (disks): 6.5
 Commission Rate: 7.5

Learnedmore, Lawrence
 Social Security: #987-99-9653
 Job Title: Vice President
 Year Hired: 1984
 Yearly Salary: $45000

Ordermore, Ozel
 Social Security: #111-44-5399
 Job Title: Supplies
 Year Hired: 1988
 Hourly Salary: $7.58

Tightscrew, Tom
 Social Security: #682-67-5312
 Job Title: Technician
 Year Hired: 1992
 Hourly Salary: $10.34
```

More OOPs

We're sure your interest in object-oriented has increased after working through this chapter. You will really be interested in the Windows applications developed in Chapters 22 through 26. These particular Windows applications make use of Microsoft's Foundation Class (MFC) library. This library contains the reusable classes that make programming under Windows 95, 98, and NT much easier. As you study these chapters, you will see the concepts you have mastered in this chapter applied to the Windows environment.

Part IV

Windows Programming Foundations

Chapter 20

Concepts and Tools for Windows Applications

Microsoft's main development language for 32-bit Windows applications is C or C++. In the past, assembly language has played a major role in speed-sensitive situations, but you will find that the majority of code for Windows itself is written in C or C++. Microsoft has provided all of the necessary tools with this version of the compiler for developing 32-bit Windows programs from within the language environment. This chapter will deal with the features that relate to a 32-bit procedure-oriented approach to Windows application development.

All of the Windows applications in this book are designed with the development tools provided with the Microsoft C++ compiler. When installing your Microsoft Visual C++ compiler, make sure that the setup program includes all of the available tools for Windows application development.

This chapter is divided into three major sections. The first section deals with the language, definitions, and terms used with Windows. This section also includes a discussion of the graphics-based environment. The second section is devoted to a discussion of those Windows items most frequently used by application developers. Here, Windows components such as borders, icons, bitmaps, and so on are examined. The third section includes a description of Windows resources and many of the Visual C++ tools provided for building them. Windows resources include icons, cursors, bitmaps, menus, hot keys, dialog boxes, and fonts.

Note *Throughout the remainder of this book the term Windows will refer to both the Windows 95, Windows 98, and Windows NT environments. If specific versions are important, then the terms "Windows 95," "Windows 98," or "Windows NT" will be used.*

Windows Fundamentals

Windows applications can be developed using a procedure-oriented approach in either C or C++. It is also possible to use an object-oriented approach when programming in C++. All approaches bring together point-and-shoot control, pop-up menus, and the ability to run applications written especially for the Windows environment. The purpose of this portion of the chapter is to introduce you to Windows concepts and vocabulary fundamentals. The graphics user interface is the interface of the future, and Windows gives you the ability to develop that code now!

The Windows Environment

Windows is a graphics-based multitasking operating system. Programs developed for this environment (those written specifically for Windows) all have a consistent look and command structure. To the user, this makes learning each successive Windows application easier.

To help in the development of Windows applications, Windows provides numerous built-in functions that allow for the easy implementation of pop-up menus, scroll bars, dialog boxes, icons, and many other features that represent a user-friendly interface. It is easy to take advantage of the extensive graphics programming language provided with Windows, and easily format and output text in a variety of fonts and pitches.

Windows permits the application's treatment of the video display, keyboard, mouse, printer, serial port, and system timers in a hardware-independent manner. Device or hardware independence allows the same application to run identically on a variety of computers with differing hardware configurations.

For those interested in the Java programming language, pay particular attention to this chapter. Many of the terms and concepts once relegated to C and C++ Windows development have found their way into many Java applications and applets.

Windows Advantages

There are numerous advantages for Windows users and programmers alike over the older DOS text-based environment. Windows provides several major programming capabilities that include a standardized graphics interface, a multitasking capability, an OOP approach in programming, memory control, hardware independence, and the use of dynamic link libraries (DLLs).

The Graphics User Interface (GUI)

The most noticeable Windows feature is the standardized graphics user interface, which is also the most important one for the user. All versions of Windows are based on the same standardized interface. The consistent interface uses pictures, or icons, to represent disk drives, files, subdirectories, and many of the operating system commands and actions. Figure 20-1 shows a typical Windows application.

Under Windows, program names appear in caption bars. Many of the basic file manipulation functions are accessed through the program's menus by pointing and clicking with the mouse. Most Windows programs provide both a keyboard and a mouse interface. Although you can access most Windows functions with just the keyboard, the mouse is the preferred tool of most users.

A similar look and feel is common to all Windows applications. Once a user learns how to manipulate common Windows commands, each new application becomes easier to master. For example, compare the Microsoft Excel screen shown in Figure 20-2 with the Microsoft Word screen shown in Figure 20-3.

These screens illustrate the similarity between applications, including common File and Edit options. Compare the options in both of these applications with the Paint application illustrated earlier in Figure 20-1.

The consistent user interface provides advantages for the programmer also. For example, it is possible to tap into built-in Windows functions for constructing menus and dialog boxes. All menus have the same style keyboard and mouse interface because Windows, rather than the programmer, handles its implementation.

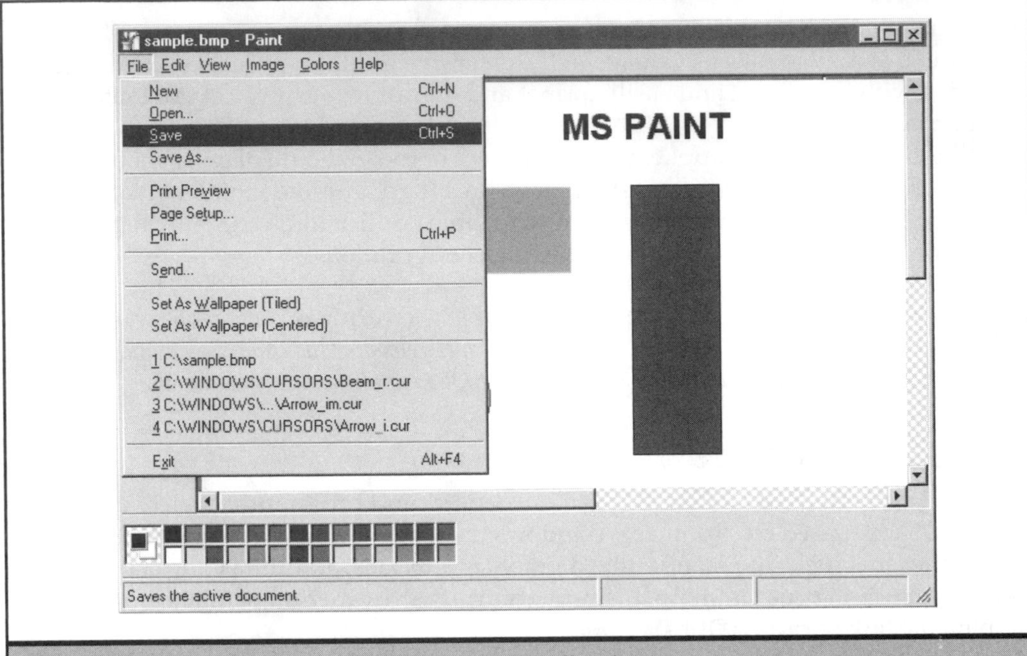

Figure 20-1. *Paint is a typical Windows application*

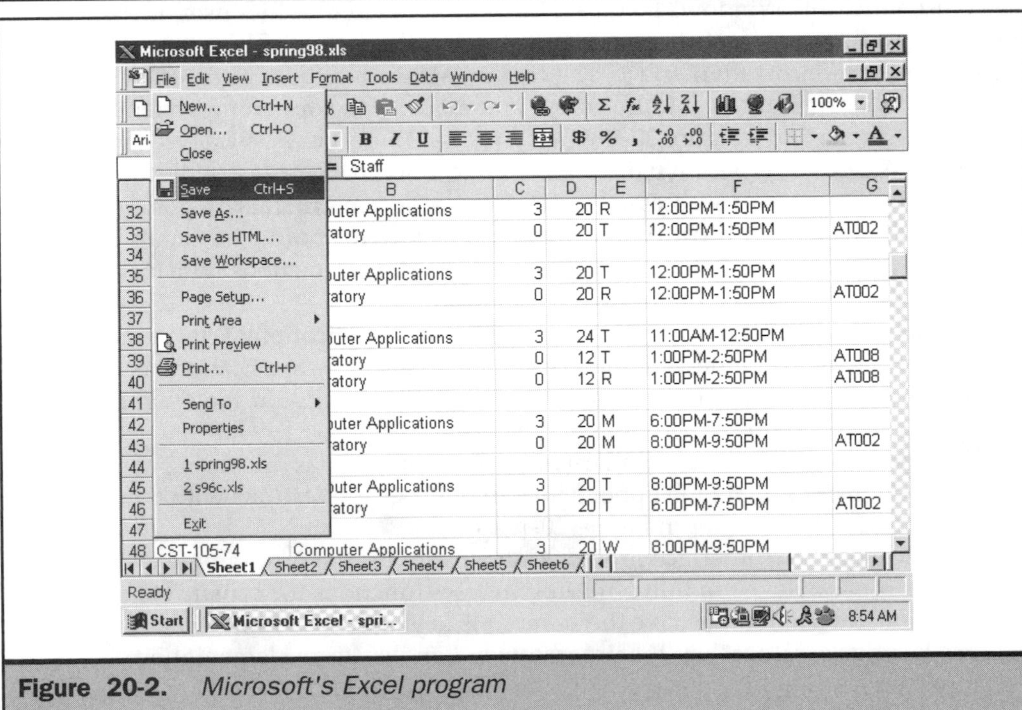

Figure 20-2. *Microsoft's Excel program*

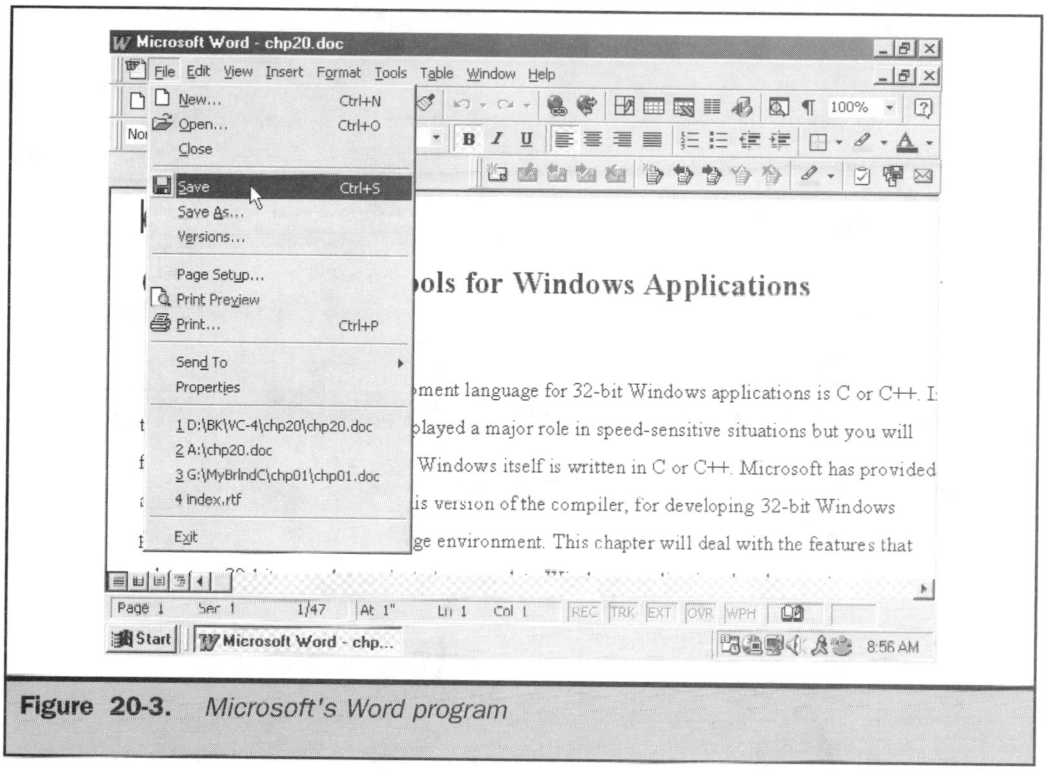

Figure 20-3. *Microsoft's Word program*

The Multitasking Environment

The Windows multitasking environment allows the user to have several applications, or several instances of the same application, running at the same time. The screen in Figure 20-4 shows two Windows applications running at the same time. Each application occupies a rectangular window on the screen. At any given time, the user can move the windows on the screen, switch between different applications, change the windows' sizes, and exchange information from window to window.

The example shown in Figure 20-4 is a group of two concurrently running processes—well, not really. In reality, only one application can be using the processor at any one time. The distinction between a task that is processing and one that is merely running is important. There is also a third state to consider. An application may be in the active state. An active application is one that is receiving the user's attention. Just as there can be only one application that is processing at any given instant, so too there can be only one active application at a time. However, there can be any number of concurrently running tasks. Partitioning of the microprocessor's processing time, called time slicing, is the responsibility of Windows. It is Windows that controls the

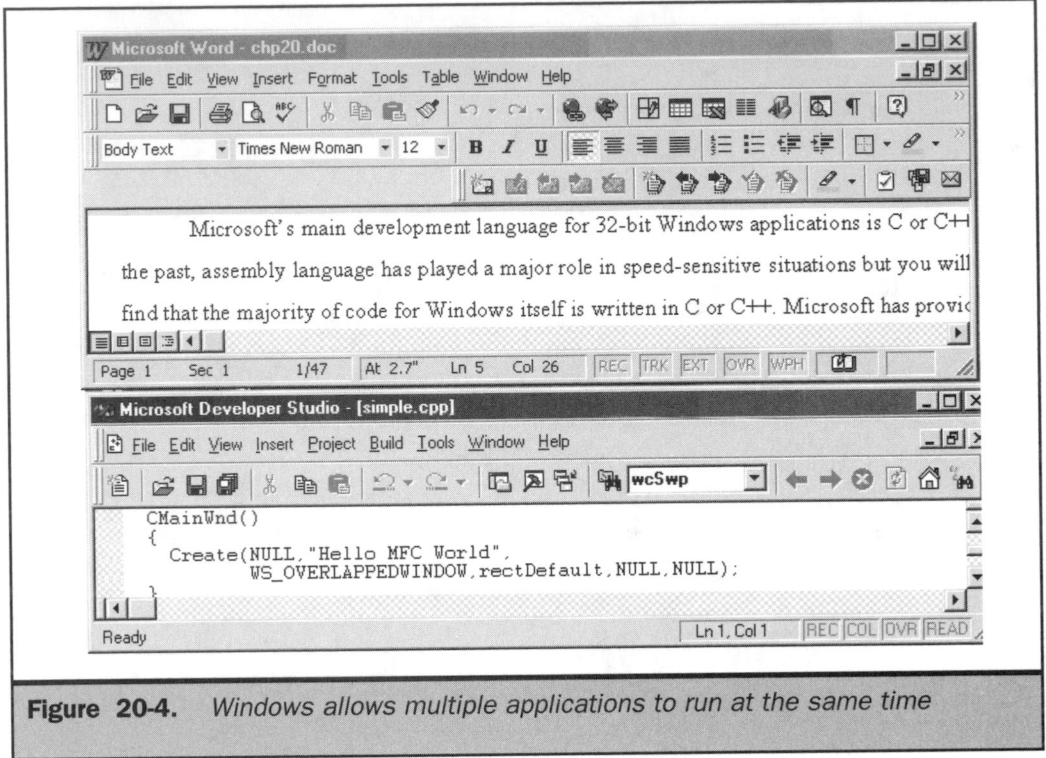

Figure 20-4. *Windows allows multiple applications to run at the same time*

sharing of the microprocessor by using a variety of techniques, including queued input or messages.

Before multitasking was achieved under Windows, applications assumed they had exclusive control of all the computer's resources, including the input and output devices, memory, the video display, and even the CPU itself. Under Windows, all of these resources must be shared. Thus, for example, memory management is controlled by Windows instead of by the application.

Advantages of Using a Queued Input

Memory, as you have learned, is a shared resource under Windows. However, so are most input devices such as the keyboard and mouse. Thus, when you develop a Windows program in C or C++, it is no longer possible to read directly from the keyboard with a getchar( ) function call or by using the C++ I/O stream. With Windows, an application does not make explicit calls to read from the keyboard or mouse. Rather, Windows receives all input from the keyboard, mouse, and timer in the system queue. It is the queue's responsibility to redirect the input to the appropriate program since more than one application can be running. This redirection is achieved by copying the message from the system queue into the application's queue. At this point, when the application is ready to process the input, it reads from its queue and dispatches a message to the correct window.

Input is accessed with the use of a uniform format called an *input message*. All input messages specify the system time, state of the keyboard, scan code of any depressed key, position of the mouse, and which mouse button has been pressed (if any), as well as information specifying which device generated the message.

Keyboard, mouse, and timer messages all have identical formats and are processed in a similar manner. Further, with each message, Windows provides a device-independent virtual keycode that identifies the key, regardless of which keyboard it is on, and the device-dependent scan code generated by the keyboard, as well as the status of other keys on the keyboard, including NUM LOCK, ALT, SHIFT, and CTRL.

The keyboard and mouse are a shared resource. One keyboard and one mouse must supply all the input information for each program running under Windows. Windows sends all keyboard input messages directly to the currently active window. Mouse messages, on the other hand, are handled differently. Mouse messages are sent to the window that is physically underneath the mouse cursor, the window with the *current focus*.

Another shared resource is timer messages. Timer messages are similar to keyboard and mouse messages. Windows allows a program to set a system timer so that one of its windows receives a message at periodic intervals. This timer message goes directly into the application's message queue. It is also possible for other messages to be passed into an application's message queue as a result of the program's calling certain Windows functions.

OOPs and Windows Messages

Object-oriented programming has recently become very popular, but Windows has always employed a pseudo-oops environment. The message system under Windows is the underlying structure used to disseminate information in the multitasking environment. From the application's perspective, a message is a notification that some event of interest has occurred that may or may not need a specific action. The user may initiate these events by clicking or moving the mouse, changing the size of a window, or making a menu selection. The events can also be initiated by the application itself. For example, a graphics-based spreadsheet could finish a recalculation that results in the need to update a graphics bar chart. In this situation, the application would send an "update window" message to itself.

Windows itself can also generate messages, as in the case of the "close session" message, in which Windows informs each application of the intent to shut down.

When considering the role of messages in Windows, use the following points. It is the message system that allows Windows to achieve its multitasking capabilities. The message system makes it possible for Windows to share the processor among different applications. Each time Windows sends a message to the application program, it also grants processor time to the application. In reality, the only way an application can get access to the microprocessor is when it receives a message. Second, messages enable an application to respond to events in the environment. These events can be generated by the application itself, by other concurrently running applications, by the user, or by Windows. Each time an event occurs, Windows makes a note and distributes an appropriate message to the interested applications.

Managing Memory

One of the most important shared resources under Windows is system memory. When more than one application is running at the same time, each application must cooperate to share memory in order not to exhaust the total resources of the system. Likewise, as new programs are started and old ones are terminated, memory can become fragmented. Windows is capable of consolidating free memory space by moving blocks of code and data in memory.

It is also possible to over-commit memory in Windows. For example, an application can contain more code than can actually fit into memory at one time. Windows can discard currently unused code from memory and later reload the code from the program's executable file.

Windows applications can share routines located in other executable files. The files that contain shareable routines are called dynamic link libraries (DLLs). Windows includes the mechanism to link the program with the DLL routines at run time. Windows itself is comprised of a large set of dynamic link libraries. To facilitate all of this, Windows programs use a new format of executable file, called the New Executable format. These files include the information Windows needs to manage the code and data segments and to perform the dynamic linking.

Independence from User Hardware

Windows also provides hardware or device independence. Windows frees the application developer from having to build programs that take into consideration every possible monitor, printer, and input device available for computers. For example, DOS applications had to be written to include drivers for every possible device the application would encounter. In order to make a DOS application capable of printing on any printer, the application designer had to furnish a different driver for every printer. This required many software companies to write essentially the same device driver over and over again—a LaserJet driver for Microsoft Word for DOS, one for Microsoft Works, and so on.

Under Windows, a device driver for each hardware device is written once. This device driver can be supplied by Microsoft, the application vendor, or the user. As you know, Microsoft includes a large variety of hardware drivers with Windows.

It is hardware independence that makes programming a snap for the application developer. The application interacts with Windows rather than with any specific device. It doesn't need to know what printer is hooked up. The application instructs Windows to draw a filled rectangle, for example, and Windows worries about how to accomplish it on the installed hardware. Likewise, each device driver works with every Windows application. Developers save time, and users do not have to worry about whether each new Windows application will support their hardware configuration.

Hardware independence is achieved by specifying the minimum capabilities the hardware must have. These capabilities are the minimum specifications required to ensure that the appropriate routines will function correctly. Every routine, regardless of its complexity, is capable of breaking itself down into the minimal set of operations required for a given device. This is a very impressive feature. For example, not every plotter is capable of drawing a circle by itself. As an application developer, however, you can still use the routines for drawing a circle, even if the plotter has no specific circle capabilities. Since every plotter connected to Windows must be capable of drawing a line, Windows is capable of breaking down the circle routine into a series of small lines.

Windows can specify a set of minimum capabilities to ensure that your application will receive only valid, predefined input. Windows has predefined the set of legal keystrokes allowed by applications. The valid keystrokes are very similar to those produced by the PC-compatible keyboard. Should a manufacturer produce a keyboard that contains additional keys that do not exist in the Windows list of acceptable keys, the manufacturer would also have to supply additional software that would translate these illegal keystrokes into Windows' legal keystrokes. This predefined Windows legal input covers all the input devices, including the mouse. Therefore, even if someone should develop a four-button mouse, you don't have to worry. The manufacturer would supply the software necessary to convert all mouse input to the Windows predefined possibilities of mouse-button clicks.

Dynamic Link Libraries (DLL)

Dynamic link libraries, or DLLs, provide much of Windows' functionality. They are used to enhance the base operating system by providing a powerful and flexible graphics user interface. Dynamic link libraries contain predefined functions that are linked with an application program when it is loaded (dynamically), instead of when the executable file is generated (statically). Dynamic link libraries use the .DLL file extension.

Storing frequently used routines in separate libraries was not an invention of the Windows product. For example, the C/C++ language depends heavily on libraries to implement standard functions for different systems. The linker makes copies of run-time library functions, such as getchar( ) and printf( ), and places them into a program's executable file. Libraries of functions save each programmer from having to re-create a new procedure for a common operation such as reading in a character or formatting output. Programmers can easily build their own libraries to include additional capabilities, such as changing a character font or justifying text. Making the function available as a general tool eliminates redundant design—a key feature in OOP.

Windows libraries are dynamically linked. In other words, the linker does not copy the library functions into the program's executable file. Instead, while the program is executing, it makes calls to the functions in the library. Naturally, this conserves memory. No matter how many applications are running, there is only one copy of the library in RAM at a given time, and this library can be shared.

When a call is made to a Windows function, the C++ compiler must generate machine code for a far intersegment call to the function located in a code segment in one of the Windows libraries. This presents a problem since until the program is actually running inside Windows, the address of the Windows function is unknown. Doesn't this sound suspiciously similar to the concept of late binding, discussed in the OOP section of this book? The solution to this problem in Windows is called *delayed binding* or *dynamic linking*. Starting with Windows 3.0 and Microsoft C 6.0, the linker allows a program to have calls to functions that cannot be fully resolved at link time. Only when the program is loaded into memory, to be run, are the **far** function calls resolved.

Special Windows import libraries are included with the C/C++ compiler; they are used to properly prepare a Windows program for dynamic linking. For example, the import library USER32.DLL is the import library that contains a record for each Windows function that your program can call. This record defines the Windows module that contains this function and, in many cases, an ordinal value that corresponds to the function in the module.

Windows applications typically make a call to the Windows PostMessage( ) function. When your application is linked at compile time, the linker finds the PostMessage( ) function listed in USER32.LIB. The linker obtains the ordinal number for the function and embeds this information in the application's executable file. When the application is run, Windows connects the call your application makes with the actual PostMessage( ) function.

The Executable Format for Windows

An executable file format was developed for Windows, and is called the *New Executable format*. This new format includes a new-style header capable of holding information about dynamic link library functions.

For example, DLL functions are included for the KERNEL, USER, and GDI modules. These libraries contain routines that help programs carry out various chores, such as sending and receiving messages. The library modules provide functions that can be called from the application program or from other library modules. To the module that contains the functions, the functions are known as *exports*. The New Executable format identifies these exported functions with a name and an ordinal number. Included in the New Executable format is an Entry Table section that indicates the address of each of these exported functions within the module.

From the perspective of the application program, the library functions that an application uses are known as *imports*. These imports use the various relocation tables and can identify the **far** calls that the application makes to an imported function. Almost all Windows programs contain at least one exported function. This window function is usually located in one of the library modules and is the one that receives window messages.

This new format also provides the additional information on each of the code and data segments in a program or library. Typically, code segments are flagged as moveable and discardable, while data segments are flagged as moveable. This allows Windows to move code and data segments in memory and even discard code segments if additional memory is needed. If Windows later decides it needs a discarded code segment, it can reload the code segment from the original executable file. Windows has another category called *load on call*. This defines a program or library code segment that will not be loaded into memory at all unless a function in the code segment is called from another code segment. Through this sophisticated memory-management scheme, Windows can simultaneously run several programs in a memory space that would normally be sufficient for only one program.

Originally, Windows depended on a module-definition file to specify the linker options just discussed. However, the linker provided with Visual C++ now provides equivalent command-line options for most module definition statements. Thus, a program now designed for Windows does not usually require a module definition file to access these capabilities.

Programming Concepts and Vocabulary for Windows

Windows programming is uniquely different for most programmers. The uniqueness occurs because Windows includes new programming concepts and its own special vocabulary. These new concepts and vocabulary can be broken down into two major categories: the features of Windows that are visible to the user, such as menus, dialog boxes, icons, and so on; and the invisible features such as messages, function access, and so on. There is a standard vocabulary associated with Windows programming development designed to give application developers the ability to communicate effectively with one another. Thus, all Windows features have been given a name and an associated usage. In this section, you will learn a variety of Windows terms that will give you the ability to confidently discuss and develop Windows applications.

What Is a Windows Window?

A Windows window appears to the user as a rectangular portion of the display device; its appearance is independent of the particular application at hand. To an application, however, the window is a rectangular area of the screen that is under the direct control of the application. The application has the ability to create and control everything about the main window, including its size and shape. When the user starts a program, a window is created. Each time the user clicks a window option, the application responds. Closing a window causes the application to terminate. Multiple windows convey to the user the multitasking capabilities of Windows. By partitioning the screen into different windows, the user can direct input to a specific application within the multitasking environment by using the keyboard or a mouse to select one of the concurrently running applications. Windows then intercepts the user's input and allocates any necessary resources (such as the microprocessor) as needed.

The Layout of a Window

Features such as borders, control boxes, About boxes, and so on, are common to all Windows applications. It is this common interface that gives Windows a comforting predictability from one application to another. Figure 20-5 illustrates the fundamental components of a typical Windows window.

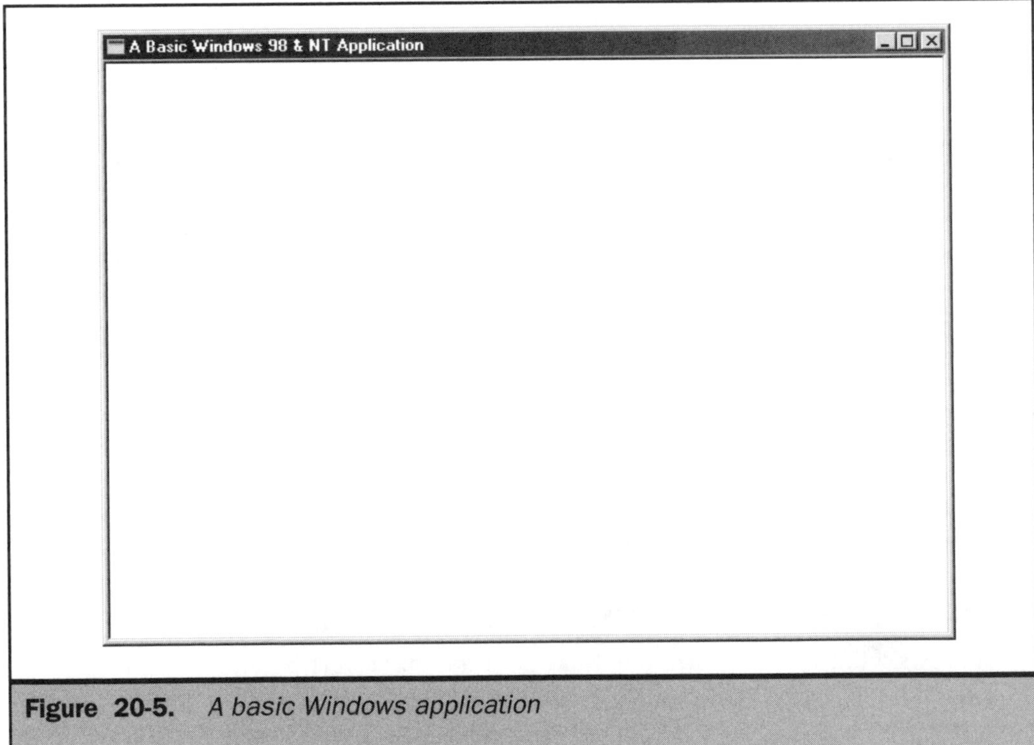

Figure 20-5. *A basic Windows application*

Border

A window has a border surrounding it. The border is made up of lines that frame the rectangular outline of the window. To the novice, the border may appear only to delineate one application's screen viewport from another. Upon closer examination of the border, however, a different conclusion will be drawn. For example, by positioning the mouse pointer over a border and holding down the left mouse button, the user can change the size of the active window.

Title Bar

The name of the application program is displayed at the top of the window in the title bar. Title bars are located at the top of each associated window. Title bars can be very useful in helping to remember which applications are currently running. By default, the active application uses a different color in the title bar area than a non-active application.

Control Icon

A control icon is used by each Windows application. The control icon is a small image in each window's upper-left corner. Clicking the mouse pointer on the control icon (referred to as clicking the control icon) causes Windows to display the system menu.

System Menu

The system menu is opened by clicking the mouse pointer on the control icon. The system menu provides standard application options such as Restore, Move, Size, Minimize, Maximize, and Close.

Minimize Icon

Each Windows application typically displays three iconic images in the upper-right corner of the window. The leftmost icon, a dash or underline symbol, allows the application to be minimized.

Maximize Icon

The maximize icon is in the middle of the three iconic images and appears as two very small windows. Use the maximize icon to make an application's window fill the entire screen. If this icon is selected, all other application windows will be covered.

Close Window Icon

The close window icon is on the right of the three iconic images and appears as an "X" symbol. Use the close window icon to quickly exit an application. When this icon is selected for an application, the application ends and other applications move to the foreground.

Vertical Scroll Bar

An application can show a vertical scroll bar, if desired. The vertical scroll bar is located against the right-hand edge of the application's window. The vertical scroll bar has opposite-pointing arrows at its extremes, a colored band, and a transparent window block. The transparent window block is used to visually represent the orientation between the currently displayed contents and the overall document (the colored band). Use the vertical scroll bar to select which of multiple pages of output are to be displayed. Clicking the mouse on either arrow typically shifts the display one line at a time. Clicking the mouse on the transparent window block, below the up arrow, and dragging it causes screen output to be quickly updated to any portion of the application's screen output. One of the best uses of the vertical scroll bar is for quickly moving through a multipage word processing document. Word processors such as Microsoft Word and WordPerfect take advantage of vertical scroll bars.

Horizontal Scroll Bar

It is also possible to display a horizontal scroll bar. The horizontal scroll bar is displayed at the bottom of each window. The horizontal scroll bar is similar in function to the vertical scroll bar. You use the horizontal scroll bar to select which of multiple columns of information you would like displayed. Clicking the mouse on either arrow causes the screen image to typically be shifted one column at a time. Clicking the mouse on the transparent window block, to the right of the left-pointing arrow, and dragging it causes the screen output to be quickly updated to any horizontally shifted portion of the application's screen output. One of the best uses for the horizontal scroll bar is for quickly moving through the multiple columns of a spreadsheet application, where the number of columns of information cannot fit into one screen width. Microsoft Excel makes good use of horizontal scroll bars.

Menu Bar

An optional menu bar can also be displayed just below the title bar in a window. Use the menu bar for making menu and submenu selections. Pointing and clicking the menu command or, alternately, using a hot-key combination makes menu selections. Hot-key combinations often use the ALT key in conjunction with the underlined letter in a command, such as the "F" is in the command File.

Client Area

The client area usually occupies the largest portion of each window. The client area is the primary output area for the application. Managing the client area is the responsibility of the application program. Additionally, only the application can output to the client area.

A Procedure-oriented Windows Class

The basic components of a window help define the standard appearance of an application. There are also occasions when an application will create two windows with a similar appearance and behavior. Windows Paint is one such example. The fashion in which Paint allows the user to clip or copy a portion of a graphics image is achieved by running two instances (or copies) of Paint. Information is then copied from one instance to the other. Each instance of Paint looks and behaves like its counterpart. This requires each instance to create its own window with an identical appearance and functionality.

Windows that are created in this manner look alike and behave in a similar fashion. These windows are said to be of the same **window** class. However, windows that you create can take on different characteristics. They may be different sizes, placed in different areas of the display, have different text in the caption bars, have different display colors, use different mouse cursors, and so on.

Every created window must be based on a **window** class. With applications developed in C using traditional function calls, several **window** classes are registered by the Windows application during its initialization phase. Your application may register additional classes of its own. In order to allow several windows to be created and based on the same **window** class, Windows specifies some of a window's characteristics as parameters to the CreateWindow( ) function, while others are specified in a **window** class structure. Also, when you register a **window** class, the class becomes available to all programs running under Windows. For object-oriented applications using Microsoft's Foundation Classes, much of this registration work is already done through the use of predefined objects. In Chapter 21 you will learn how to write 32-bit Windows applications in C/C++ using traditional function calls. Chapters 22 and 23 are designed to teach you how to write similar 32-bit object-oriented applications with the Microsoft Foundation Class (MFC) library.

Windows of similar appearance and behavior can be grouped together into classes, thereby reducing the amount of information that needs to be maintained. Since each **window** class has its own shareable **window** class structure, there is no needless replication of the **window** class' parameters. Also, two windows of the same class use the same function and any of its associated subroutines. This feature saves time and storage because there is no code duplication.

OOPs and Windows

Traditional C and C++ programs take on the characteristics of object-oriented programs under Windows. Recall that in object-oriented programming, an object is an abstract data type that consists of a data structure and various functions that act on the data structure. Likewise, objects receive messages that can cause them to function differently.

A Windows graphics object, for example, is a collection of data that can be manipulated as a whole entity and that is presented to the user as part of the visual interface. In particular, a graphics object implies both the data and the presentation of data. Menus, title bars, control boxes, and scroll bars are examples of graphics objects. The next sections describe several new graphics objects that affect the user's view of an application.

Icons

An icon is a small graphics object used to remind the user of a particular operation, idea, or product. For example, a spreadsheet application when minimized could display a very small histogram icon to remind the user that the application is running. Double-clicking the mouse on the histogram would then cause Windows to bring the application to active status. Icons can be very powerful tools. They are good for gaining the user's attention, as in the case of an error warning, and also when presenting choices to the user. Windows provides several stock icons, including a question mark, an exclamation point, an asterisk, an upturned palm icon, and so on. It is also possible to design your own device-independent color icons with the Microsoft C++ compiler's resource editor.

Cursors

Cursors are also Windows graphics symbols that are used to follow the movement of the pointing device. The graphics symbol is capable of changing shapes to indicate particular Windows actions. For example, the standard Windows arrow cursor changes to the small hourglass cursor to indicate a pause while a selected command is being executed. Windows provides several stock cursors: a diagonal arrow, a vertical arrow, an hourglass, a cross hair, an I-beam, and several others. You can also use the Microsoft C++ compiler's resource editor to create your own cursors.

Carets

Carets are symbols an application places in a window to show the user where input will be received. Carets are distinguished from other screen markers because they blink. Most of the time, mouse input is associated with a cursor and keyboard input with a caret. However, the mouse can move or change the input emphasis of a caret. To help clarify the difference between a cursor and a caret, Windows carets behave most similarly to the old DOS cursor. One of the carets provided for you automatically, when entering a dialog box, is the I-beam caret. Unlike in the cases of icons and cursors, an application must create its own carets using special functions. There are no stock carets.

Message Boxes

The message box is another common Windows graphics object. Message boxes are pop-up windows that contain a title, an icon, and a message. Figure 20-6 is the standard message box presented when terminating a Windows Notepad session:

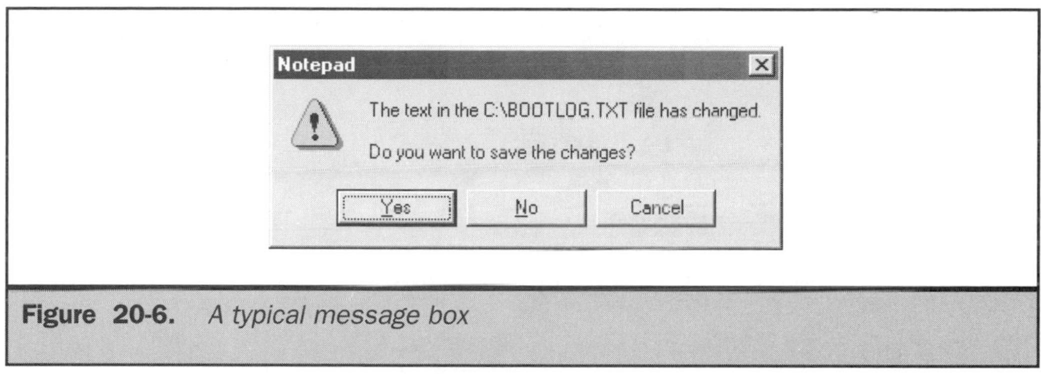

Figure 20-6. *A typical message box*

The application needs to supply the message title, the message itself, and instructions on which stock icon to use (if any), and indicate if a stock response is allowed (such as OK). Additional stock user responses include Yes/No, Yes/No/Cancel, OK/Cancel, and Retry/Cancel. Stock icons include IconHand, IconQuestion, IconExclamation, IconAsterisk, and so on.

Windows Dialog Boxes

A dialog box is similar to a message box in that it too is a pop-up window. Dialog boxes, however, are primarily used to receive input from the user rather than to just present output. A dialog box allows an application to receive information one field at a time or one box's worth of information at a time, rather than a character at a time. Figure 20-7 shows a typical Windows dialog box. Windows does the graphic design of a dialog box automatically for you. The layout of a dialog box is normally done with the compiler's resource editor.

Fonts

A font is a graphics object or resource that defines a complete set of characters from one typeface. These characters are all of a certain size and style that can be manipulated to give text a variety of appearances. A typeface is a basic character design, defined by certain serifs and stroke widths. For instance, your application can use any of the different fonts provided with Windows, including System, Courier, and Times Roman, or custom fonts that you define and include in the application program's executable file. By using built-in routines, Windows allows for the dynamic modification of a font, including boldface, italics, underline, and changing the size of the font. Windows provides all of the necessary functions for displaying text anywhere within the client area. Additionally, because of Windows device independence, an application's output will have a consistent appearance from one output device to the next. TrueType font technology, first introduced with Windows 3.1, provides improved fonts for the screen and printer under all current versions of Windows.

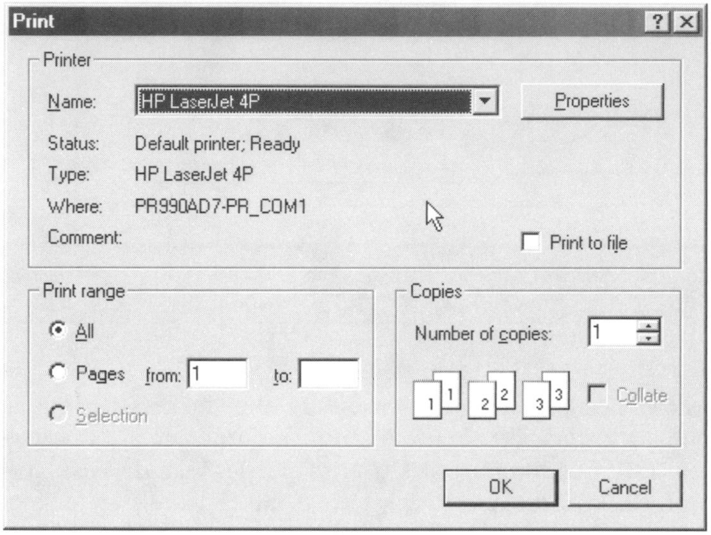

Figure 20-7. *A typical dialog box for Windows*

Bitmaps

Bitmaps serve as a photographic image of the display (in pixels) and are stored in memory. Bitmaps are used whenever an application must display a graphics image quickly. Since bitmapped images are transferred directly from memory, they can be displayed more quickly than by executing the code necessary to re-create the image. There are two basic uses for bitmaps. First, bitmaps are used to draw pictures on the display. For example, Windows uses many small bitmaps for drawing arrows in scroll bars; displaying the check marks when selecting pop-up menu options; and drawing the system menu box, the size box, and many others. Bitmaps are also used for creating brushes. Brushes allow you to paint and fill objects on the screen.

There are two disadvantages to using bitmaps. First, depending on their size, bitmaps can occupy an unpredictably large portion of memory. For each pixel that is displayed, there needs to be an equivalent representation in memory. Displaying the same bitmap on a color monitor versus a monochrome monitor would also require more memory. On a monochrome monitor, 1 bit can be used to define a pixel's being on or off. However, on a color monitor that can display 16 colors, each pixel would require 4 bits, or a nibble, to represent its characteristics. Also, as the resolution of the display device increases, so too does the memory requirement for the bitmap. Another disadvantage of bitmaps is that they contain only a static picture. For example, if an automobile is represented by a bitmap, there is no way to access the picture's various components, such as tires, hood, window, and so on. However, if the automobile had been constructed from a series of primitive drawing routines, an application would be able to change the data sent to these routines and modify individual items in the picture. For example, an application could modify the roofline and convert a sedan to a convertible. You can create or modify bitmaps with the compiler's resource editor.

Pens

Windows uses information on the current pen when it draws a shape on the screen. Pens are used to draw lines and outline shapes. Pens have three basic characteristics: line width, style (dotted, dashed, solid), and color. Windows always has a pen for drawing black lines and one for drawing white lines available to each application. It is also possible to create your own unique pens. For example, you might want to create a thick light-gray line to outline a portion of the screen or a dot-dash-dot line for spreadsheet data analysis.

Brushes

Windows uses brushes to paint colors and fill areas with predefined patterns. Brushes have a minimum size of 8 × 8 pixels and, like pens, have three basic characteristics: size, pattern, and color. With their 8 × 8-pixel minimum size, brushes are said to have a pattern, not a style as pens do. The pattern may be a solid color, hatched, diagonal, or any other user-definable combination.

Windows Messages

As you have learned, an application does not write directly to the screen under Windows. Neither does an application directly process hardware interrupts or output directly to the printer. Instead, an application uses the appropriate Windows functions or waits for an appropriate message to be delivered. Applications development under Windows must now incorporate the processing of the application and the user's view of the application through Windows.

The Windows message system is the underlying structure used to disseminate information in a multitasking environment. From the application's viewpoint, a message is seen as a notification that some event of interest has occurred that may or may not need a specific response. These events may have been initiated on the part of the user, such as clicking or moving the mouse, changing the size of a window, or making a menu selection. However, the signaled event could also have been generated by the application itself.

The overall effect of this process is that your application must now be totally oriented toward the processing of messages. It must be capable of awakening, determining the appropriate action based on the type of message received, taking that action to completion, and returning to sleep.

Windows applications are significantly different from their older DOS counterparts. Windows provides an application program with access to hundreds of function calls, directly or indirectly, through foundation classes. These function calls are handled by several main modules, including the KERNEL, GDI (graphics device interface), and USER modules. The KERNEL is responsible for memory management, loading and running an application, and scheduling. The GDI contains all of the routines to create and display graphics. The USER module takes care of all other application requirements.

The next section takes a closer look at the message system by examining the format and sources of messages and looking at several common message types and the ways in which both Windows and your application process messages.

The Windows Message Format

Messages are used to notify a program that an event of interest has occurred. Technically, a message is not just of interest to the application, but also to a specific window within that application. Therefore, every message is addressed to a window.

Actually, only one message system exists under Windows—the system message queue. However, each program currently running under Windows also has its own program message queue. The USER module must eventually transfer each message in the system message queue to a program's message queue. The program's message queue stores all messages for all windows in that program.

Four parameters are associated with all messages, regardless of their type: a window handle, a message type, and two additional 32-bit parameters. The first parameter specified in a window message is the handle of the window to which the message is addressed.

Note *These are the parameters for 32-bit Windows applications. The parameters used for earlier 16-bit Windows 3.x applications differed.*

Table 20-1 shows a list of data types frequently used with Win32 functions.

Handles are always used when writing procedure-oriented Windows applications. Remember that a handle is a unique number that identifies many different types of objects, such as windows, controls, menus, icons, pens and brushes, memory allocation, output devices, and even window instances. Under Windows, each loaded copy of a program is called an instance.

Because Windows allows you to run more than one copy of the same application at the same time, the operating system needs to keep track of each of these instances. It does this by attaching a unique instance handle to each running copy of the application.

The instance handle is usually used as an index into an internally maintained table. By referencing a table element rather than an actual memory address, Windows can dynamically rearrange all resources simply by inserting a new address into the resource's table position. For example, if Windows associates a particular application's

Data Type	Description
HANDLE	Defines a 32-bit **unsigned** integer that is used as a handle
HWND	Defines a 32-bit **unsigned** integer that is used as the handle to a window
HDC	Defines a handle to a device context
LONG	Specifies a 32-bit **signed** integer
LPSTR	Defines a 32-bit pointer
NULL	Specifies an integral zero value often used to trigger function **default** parameters or actions
UINT	Specifies a 32-bit **unsigned** integer
WCHAR	Specifies a 16-bit UNICODE character used to represent all of the symbols known for all of the world's written languages

Table 20-1. *Frequently Used Win32 Data Types*

resource with table lookup position 16, then no matter where Windows moves the resource in memory, table position 16 will contain the resource's current location.

Windows conserves memory resources because of the way multiple instances of the same application are handled. Several multitasking environments load each duplicate instance of an application just as if each was an entirely new application.

The instance of an application has a very important role. It is the instance of an application that defines all of the objects necessary for the functioning of the application. This can include controls, menus, dialog boxes, and much more, along with new **window** classes.

The second parameter in a message is the *message type*. This is one of the identifiers specified in several header files unique to Windows. These header files can be pointed to with the use of WINDOWS.H. With Windows, each message type begins with a two-character mnemonic, followed by the underscore character and, finally, a descriptor. The most frequently encountered type of message in traditional C and C++ Windows applications is the window message. Windows messages include WM_CREATE, WM_PAINT, WM_CLOSE, WM_COPY, WM_PASTE, etc. Other message types include control window messages (BM_), edit control messages (EM_), and list box messages (LB_). An application can also create and register its own message type. This permits the use of private message types.

The last two parameters provide additional information necessary to interpret the message. The contents of these last two parameters will therefore vary depending on the message type. Examples of the types of information that would be passed include which key was just struck, the position of the mouse, the position of the vertical or horizontal scroll bar elevators, and the selected pop-up menu item.

Generating Messages

It is the message-passing concept that allows Windows to be multitasking. Thus, Windows must process all messages. There are four basic sources for a message. An application can receive a message from the user, from Windows itself, from the application program itself, or from other applications.

User messages include keystroke information, mouse movements, point-and-click coordinates, any menu selections, the location of scroll bar elevators, and so on. The application program will devote a great deal of time to processing user messages. User-originated messages indicate that the person running the program wants to change the way the application is viewed.

A message is sent to an application whenever a state change is to take effect. An example of this would be when the user clicks an application's icon indicating that they want to make that application the active application. In this case, Windows tells the application that its main window is being opened, that its size and location are being modified, and so on. Depending on the current state of an application, Windows-originated messages can be processed or ignored.

In Chapter 21, you will learn how to write simple Windows applications in C and C++. When you do this, you will see that the program is broken down into specific procedures, with each procedure processing a particular message type for a particular window. One procedure, for example, will deal with resizing the application's window. It is quite possible that the application may want to resize itself. In other words, the source of the message is the application itself.

Currently, most applications written for Windows do not take full advantage of the fourth type of message source, intertask communication. However, this category will become increasingly important as more and more applications take advantage of this Windows integration capability. Microsoft's Dynamic Data Exchange protocol (DDE) was the first to take advantage of this feature.

Responding to Messages

Traditional C and C++ procedure-oriented Windows applications have a procedure for processing each type of message they may encounter. Different windows can respond differently to messages of the same type. For example, one application may have created two windows that respond to a mouse-button click in two different ways. The first window could respond to a mouse-button click by changing the background color, while the second window may respond to the mouse-button click by placing a crosshatch on a spreadsheet. It is because the same message can be interpreted differently by different windows that Windows addresses each message to a specific window within an application. Not only will the application have a different procedure to handle each message type, it will also need a procedure to handle each message type for each window. The window procedure groups together all the message-type procedures for an application.

The Message Loop

A basic component of all Windows applications is the message-processing loop. The location of the message loop in procedure-oriented applications is easy to identify. In object-oriented code, the message loop is processed in the CWinAPP foundation class.

Each C and C++ application performs the operation internally. These applications contain procedures to create and initialize windows, followed by the message-processing loop and, finally, some code required to close the application. The message loop is responsible for processing a message delivered by Windows to the main body of the program. Here, the program acknowledges the message and then requests Windows to send it to the appropriate window procedure for processing. When the message is received, the window procedure executes the desired action.

Two factors that can influence the sequence in which a message is processed are the message queue and the dispatching priority. Messages can be sent from one of two queues—either the system queue or the application's message queue. Messages, regardless of the source, are first placed in the system queue. When a given message reaches the front of the queue, it is sent to the appropriate application's message queue. This dual mode action allows Windows to keep track of all messages and permits each application to concern itself with only those messages that pertain to it.

Messages are placed in the queues as you would expect: FIFO (first in, first out) order. These are called synchronous messages. Most Windows applications use this type of dispatching method. However, there are occasions when Windows will push a message to the end of the queue, thereby preventing it from being dispatched. Messages of this type are called asynchronous messages. Care must be taken when sending an asynchronous message that overrides the application's normal sequence of processing.

Several types of asynchronous messages exist, including paint, timer, and quit messages. A timer message, for example, causes a certain action to take effect at a specified time, regardless of the messages to be processed at that moment. A timer message has priority, and will cause all other messages in the queue to be pushed farther from the queue front.

A few asynchronous messages can be sent to other applications. This is unique because the receiving application doesn't put the message into its queue. Rather, the received message directly calls the application's appropriate window procedure, where it is immediately executed.

How does Windows dispatch messages that are pending for several applications at the same time? Windows handles this problem in one of two ways. One method of message processing is called dispatching priority. Whenever Windows loads an application, it sets the application's priority to zero. Once the application is running, however, the application can change its priority. With everything else being equal, Windows will settle any message-dispatching contention by sending messages to the highest priority application.

One example of a high-priority program would be a data communications application. Tampering with an application's priority level is not recommended, and is very uncommon. Windows has another method for dispatching messages to concurrent applications of the same priority level. Whenever Windows sees that a particular application has a backlog of unprocessed messages, it hangs onto the new message while continuing to dispatch other new messages to the other applications.

Accessing Windows Functions

As you have learned, Windows provides the application developer with hundreds of functions. Examples of these functions include DispatchMessage( ), PostMessage( ), RegisterWindowMessage( ), and SetActiveWindow( ). For C++ programmers using the Microsoft Foundation Classes (MFC), many of these functions are dispatched automatically.

Calling Convention for Functions

Function declarations under 16-bit Windows 3.x included the **pascal** modifier, which was more efficient under DOS. Windows does not use this modifier for 32-bit applications. As you have learned, the parameters to all Windows functions are passed via the system stack. The parameters for the function are pushed from the rightmost parameter to the leftmost parameter, in a normal C and C++ fashion. Upon return from the function, the calling procedure must adjust the stack pointer to a value equal to the number of bytes originally pushed onto the stack.

The Windows Header File: WINDOWS.H

The WINDOWS.H header file provides a path to over a thousand constant declarations, **typedef** declarations, and hundreds of function prototypes. One of the main reasons a Windows application takes longer to compile than a non-Windows C or C++ program is the size of this and associated header files. The WINDOWS.H header file (and associated header files) is an integral part of all programs. Traditionally, WINDOWS.H is a required **include** file in all C and C++ Windows applications. When using the Microsoft Foundation Class library in C++, the WINDOWS.H header file is included via the AFXWIN.H header file.

Usually, the **#define** statements found in WINDOWS.H or its associated files map a numeric constant with a text identifier. For example:

```
#define WM_CREATE 0x0001
```

In this case, the Visual C++ compiler will use the hexadecimal constant 0x0001 as a replacement for WM_CREATE during preprocessing.

Other **#define** statements may appear a bit unusual. For example:

```
#define NEAR near
#define VOID void
```

In Visual C++, both **near** and **void** are reserved words. Your applications should use the uppercase NEAR and VOID for one very good reason: if you port your application to another compiler, it will be much easier to change the **#define** statements within the header file than to change all of the occurrences of a particular identifier in your application.

Components that Make Up a Windows Application

There are several important steps that are common in developing all Windows applications:

- Create the WinMain( ) and associated Windows functions in C or C++. You can also utilize foundation classes, such as CWinAPP, in C++.
- Create the menu, dialog box, and any additional resource descriptions and put them into a resource script file.
- (Optional) Use the appropriate resource editor in the Visual C++ compiler to create unique cursors, icons, and bitmaps.
- (Optional) Use the appropriate resource editor in the Visual C++ compiler to create dialog boxes.
- Compile and link all C/C++ language sources and resource files using a project file.

The actual creation of a Windows application requires the use of several new development tools. Before developing applications in C or C++, an understanding of these tools is needed. The next section briefly discusses the tools supplied with the Visual C++ compiler as they relate to creating a Windows application.

Visual C++ Windows Development Tools

The Visual C++ compiler contains several resource editors. The individual editors are available by selecting Insert | Resource from the compiler's main menu. These editors allow for the quick definition of icons, cursors, and bitmaps. They also provide a convenient method for creating your own unique fonts and make it easy to create dialog-box descriptions for data entry.

Resources have the capability of turning ordinary Windows applications into truly exciting graphical presentations. When you develop icons, cursors, menus, bitmaps, and more for your application, the graphical flare makes your programs presentation quality in appearance. Resource files also let you add user-interactive components to your program such as menus, keyboard accelerators, and dialog boxes.

Graphics objects such as icons, cursors, carets, message boxes, dialog boxes, fonts, bitmaps, pens, and brushes are all examples of resources. A resource represents data that is included in an application's executable file. Technically speaking, however, it does not reside in a program's normal data segment. When Windows loads a program into memory for execution, it usually leaves all of the resources on the disk. Consider, as an example, when the user first requests to see an application's About box. Before Windows can display the About box, it must first access the disk to copy this information from the program's executable file into memory.

The resource compiler, RC.EXE, is a compiler for Windows resources. Many times, a Windows application will use its own resources, such as dialog boxes, menus, and icons. Each one of these resources must be predefined in a file called a *resource file* or resource script file. These files are created with the resource editors previously mentioned. Resource script files can be compiled into resource files by the resource compiler. This information is then added to the application's final executable file. This method allows Windows to load and use the resources from the executable file.

The use of resources and additional compilers adds an extra layer of complexity to application development, but one that is easily incorporated with the project utility.

Project Files

Project files provide an efficient means of overseeing the compilation of resources and program code as well as keeping the executable version of an application up to date. They accomplish their incremental operation by keeping track of the dates and times of their source files.

Project files include information about the compile and link process for the particular program. Programmers often have the choice of changing libraries, hardware platforms, software platforms, etc. Project files are created within the integrated C and C++ editing environment. In many cases, the default project file setup can be used with just minor adjustments for program titles and a file list to include in the build operation.

Project files also support incremental compiles and links. For example, consider a Windows application that simulates the flight of an arrow. During the development process, you decide to create your own unique cursor instead of pointing with the standard arrow provided by Windows. You create a cursor that looks like an apple with an arrow through it. When the application is recompiled incrementally, the program only really needs to accommodate the changes in the cursor resource file, APPLE.CUR. The project utility will ensure that only the information about the new cursor is updated during recompilation, speeding up the overall operation.

Resources

Customizing a Windows application with your own icons, pointers, and bitmaps is easy when you use the resource editors provided with the C++ compiler. These editors give you a complete environment in which to develop graphical resources. The editors will also help you create menus and dialog boxes—the basic means of data entry in Windows. In this section, you learn how to use these editors to create icons, cursors, menus, and dialog boxes. The editors can also help you manipulate individual bitmaps, keyboard accelerators, and strings.

Resource Editors

Each editor is included within the Visual C++ environment and is an integral part of the compiler. As such, each editor is a completely integrated resource development environment designed to run under Windows. You can start each editor by first selecting the Insert | Resource menu options.

Icons, Cursors, and Bitmaps

This section describes the general operation of three editors. A specific editor is capable of producing icons, cursors, or bitmaps. Although each is a separate editor, they share many common features. As an example of the use of these image editors, a custom icon and cursor will be created for an application in the next chapter. Icons and cursors are really both small bitmaps. The resource editors for designing icons and cursors allow you to create device-independent bitmap images. The icons and cursors created with these editors are functionally device independent with respect to resolution.

This image-file format allows for the tailoring of a bitmap that has a consistent look on each particular display resolution. For example, one icon might consist of four definitions (called DIBs): one designed for monochrome displays, one for CGAs, one for EGAs, and one for VGAs. Whenever the application displays the icon, it simply refers to it by name; Windows then automatically selects the icon image best suited to the current display. Figure 20-8 shows the Editor window during the construction of a custom icon.

Initially, a color palette appears at the bottom of the editor for selecting the drawing color. Associated with this palette is a color box that shows the currently selected value. You can also create custom colors. A group of editing tools is also visible at the extreme right of the window.

A large editing area is provided for drawing the icons, cursors, or bitmaps. The area is initially divided into smaller cells with a 32 × 32 grid. The editor also provides a small View window to allow you to observe the graphics in true size.

Designing a Custom Icon and Cursor

Creating your first icon or cursor is simple. First, click on the compiler's Insert menu and select Resource. Now select the proper resource type (Bitmap, Icon, Cursor) from the resources listed. This action clears the editing area if any previous design is present, and gives you a clean canvas.

After selecting the icon or cursor resource, you will need to pick a drawing tool from the toolbox or use the default drawing pen.

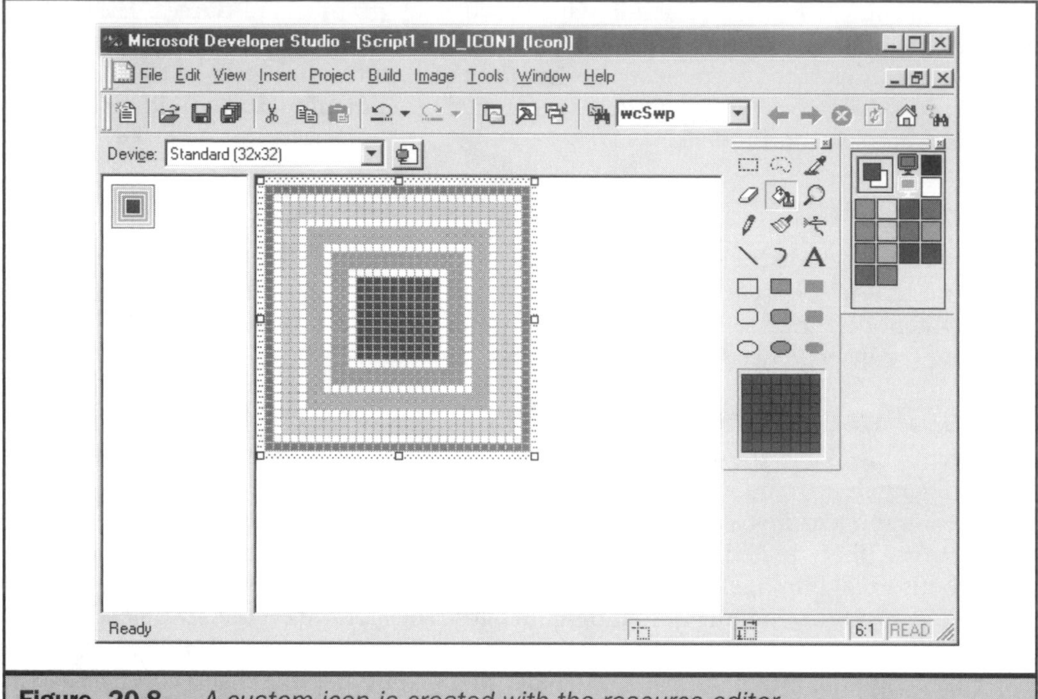

Figure 20-8. *A custom icon is created with the resource editor*

The editor can provide a broad spectrum of painting colors for icons and a selection of dithered colors for cursors. Click the color choice from the palette of colors shown. Now it is possible to draw the icon, cursor, or bitmap to your program's specification. You can also create custom colors. Be sure to save your final results by selecting the File menu and either the Save or Save As option.

Figure 20-9 shows the editor window with a completed cursor design. When looking at the completed icon or cursor designs, you will note that there are actually two renditions of the design. The larger one, within the editing area, allows you to easily visualize an image. The smaller version, to the left, represents the actual size of the design, as it will appear in the application's window.

It takes a great deal of patience and practice to create a meaningful icon, cursor, or bitmap. This process often requires several trial-and-error attempts. Whenever you come up with a design that looks good, stop and save a copy of it. It is too easy to get your design to a point where you really like it and make one additional change, only to ruin hours of work.

The first time you select the Save option from the File menu, the editor prompts you for a filename. If you are creating an icon, the file system will automatically

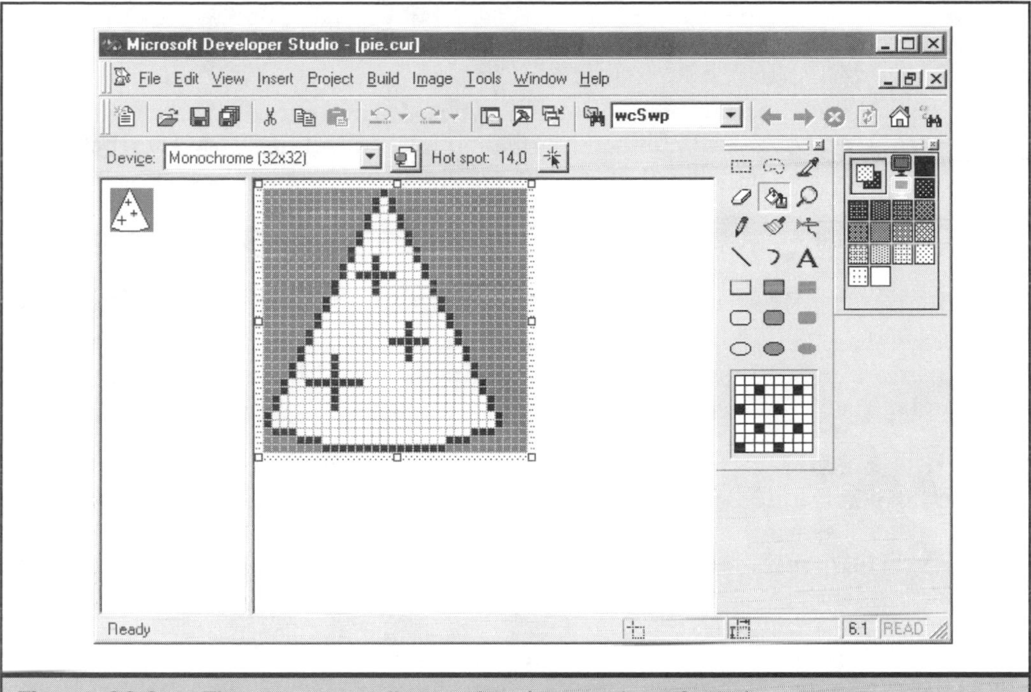

Figure 20-9. *The resource editor during the creation of a unique cursor*

append an .ICO file extension. The .CUR file extension is used for cursors. (Note that the file extension must be .ICO or .CUR, respectively.) If you are creating several possible designs, make certain you choose the Save As... option, not Save. Save overwrites your original file, but Save As... allows you to create multiple copies.

When you are creating cursors, you can select an optional hotspot. The Hotspot button is located just above the drawing palette. The cursor hotspot is a point that will be used to return the current screen coordinates during the application's use. The hotspot on the pie wedge cursor is located at the tip of the pie wedge.

Once you have selected the Hotspot button, a very small set of crosshairs appears in the drawing box. Simply place the crosshairs on the pixel you want to select as the hotspot and click the mouse. The coordinates of the selected hotspot will be added to the display box's list of statistics. Only one hotspot per cursor is allowed.

Designing Menus

Menus are one of Windows' most important tools for creating interactive programs. Menus form the gateway for easy, consistent interfacing across applications. In their simplest form, menus allow the user to point and click selections that have been predefined. These selections include screen color choices, sizing options, and file operations. More advanced menu options allow the user to select dialog boxes from the menu list.

Dialog boxes permit data entry from the keyboard. They allow the user to enter string, integer, and even real-number information for applications. However, before you can get to a dialog box, you typically must pass through a menu.

The menu created in this section is also used in the graphics application developed in the next chapter.

Menu Mechanics

The following sections describe what a menu is, what it looks like, how it is created, and the various menu options available to the programmer. Menus are very easy to create and implement in a program.

WHAT IS A MENU? A menu is a list of items or names that represent options that a user can take. In some cases, the list of items in a menu can even be bitmap images. The user can select an option by using the mouse, the keyboard, or a hot key. Windows, in turn, responds by sending a message to the application stating which command was selected.

CREATING A MENU The resource editor lets you select a menu resource. The menu will then be designed in the resource editor. An alternative technique is to use the compiler's text editor to specify a menu resource.

The resource editor is capable of creating or reading menu descriptions contained in resource script files (.RC) or compiled resource files (.RES). Resource script files are simply uncompiled text files. If a header file is available describing constants used in a menu's description, these can be added at the start of the menu's description. For example, the constant IDM_ABOUT might be identified with 40 in a header file.

Figure 20-10 shows a menu (PieMenu) being developed in the resource editor.

Different styles and attributes for application menus can be included in this file. These styles and attributes include checkmarks to indicate the status of an item or define styles for an item's text (normal or grayed) and separator lines to divide menus (menu bar breaks), align menu items in column format, and assign a help attribute to a menu item.

MENUS AND THE RESOURCE COMPILER By following a set of simple rules, Windows will draw and manage menus for you. In so doing, Windows will produce consistent menus from one application to another. The resource compiler will compile menu resource information. The compiled file, a file with a .RES file extension, will be combined with your application at link time. At this time, the compiler and linker will create the final executable file (.EXE).

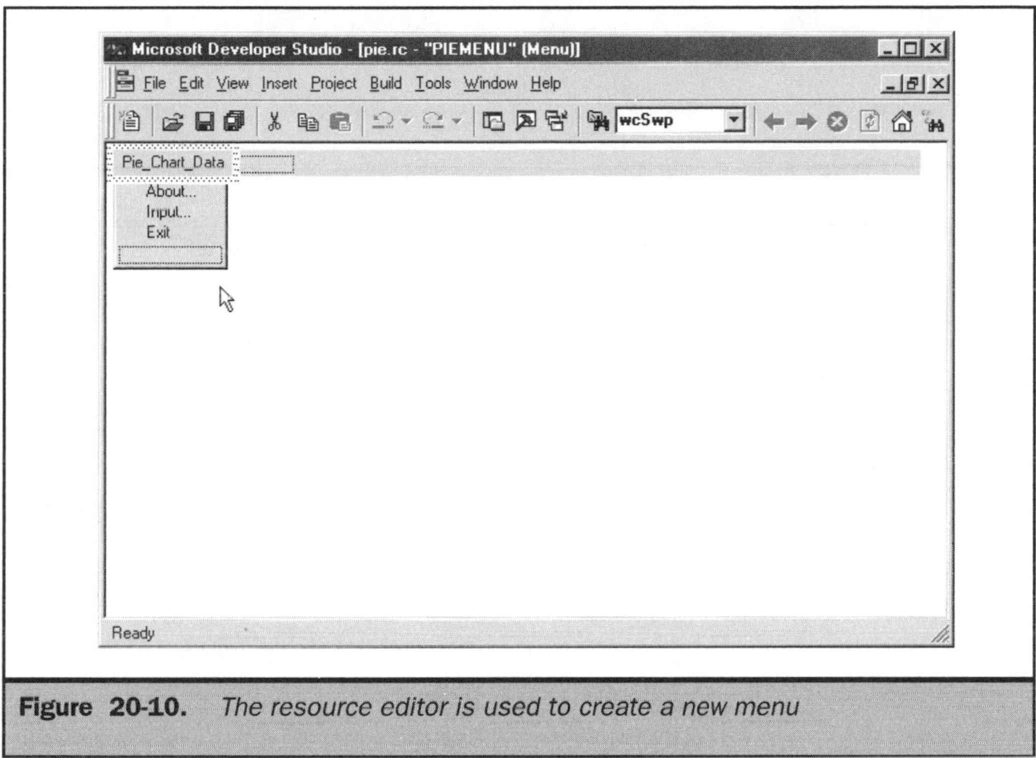

Figure 20-10. *The resource editor is used to create a new menu*

The structure of a simple menu is quite easy to understand. Here is a resource script file:

```
PIEMENU MENU DISCARDABLE
BEGIN
  POPUP "Pie_Chart_Data"
  BEGIN
    MENUITEM "About...", IDM_ABOUT
    MENUITEM "Input...", IDM_INPUT
    MENUITEM "Exit",     IDM_EXIT
  END
END
```


By studying this listing, you can identify a number of additional menu keywords such as MENU, POPUP, and MENUITEM. You can use brackets ({ }) instead of the keywords **begin** and **end**. It is also easy to identify the menu items that will appear in this menu: About Box..., Data Entry..., and Exit. The three dots following a menu selection indicate a dialog box to the user.

MENU KEYWORDS AND OPTIONS The name of this program's menu definition is PIEMENU. The menu definition name is followed by the keyword MENU. This particular example describes the pop-up menu Pie_Chart_Data, which will appear on the menu bar. Pop-up menus are arranged from left to right on the menu bar. If a large number of pop-up items are used, an additional bar is provided automatically. Only one pop-up menu can be displayed at a time.

You can use an ampersand to produce an underscore under the character that follows the ampersand in the selection list. The ampersand allows the menu item to be selected from the keyboard. The simple menu in the example does not take advantage of this feature, but if the "A" in the About Box... choice had been preceded with an ampersand, that selection could have been made with a key combination of ALT-A. With the example menu, the item can be selected by positioning the mouse pointer on the item and clicking the left button. When a pop-up menu is selected, Windows pops the menu to the screen immediately under the selected item on the menu bar. Each MENUITEM describes one menu item or name, for example, "Data Entry...."

Identification numbers or constants from a header file appear to the right of the menu items. If numbers are present, they can be replaced with values identified in header files—for example, IDM_ABOUT 40, IDM_INPUT 50, and IDM_EXIT 70. IDM stands for the identification number of a menu item. This form of ID has become very popular, but is not required. What is important, however, is that each menu item have a unique identification associated with it.

KEYBOARD ACCELERATORS Keyboard accelerators are most often used by menu designers as a sort of "fast-key" combination for selecting menu items. For example, a menu may have 12 color items for selecting a background color. The user can point and click the menu for each color in the normal fashion or, with a keyboard accelerator, simply hit a special key combination. If a keyboard accelerator is used, the function keys (F1 to F12), for example, could be used for color selection without the menu popping up at all.

Dialog Box Data Entry

You have already learned that menus are considered as a means of simple data entry. This section investigates a more significant means of data entry—the dialog box. While data can be entered directly into the application's client area, dialog boxes are the preferred entry form for maintaining consistency across Windows programs.

Dialog boxes allow the user to check items in a window list, set buttons for various choices, directly enter strings and integers from the keyboard, and indirectly enter real numbers (**floats**). A special form of control can also be used in a dialog box. Combo boxes allow a combination of a single-line edit field and list boxes. The dialog box is the programmer's key to serious data entry in Windows programs. The dialog box is also the programmer's secret for ease of programming since Windows handles all necessary program overhead.

Dialog boxes can be called when selected as a choice from a menu and appear as a pop-up window to the user. To distinguish a dialog box choice from ordinary selections in a menu, three dots (an ellipsis) follow the dialog option name. In the previous section, the About Box... and Data Entry... menu items referred to dialog box selections. Figure 20-11 shows a completed dialog box taken from an example that is developed in the next chapter.

Here is the resource script file for this dialog box:

```
PIEDLGBOX DIALOG DISCARDABLE  93, 37, 195, 159
STYLE DS_MODALFRAME|WS_POPUP|WS_VISIBLE|WS_CAPTION|WS_SYSMENU
CAPTION "Pie Chart Data"
FONT 8, "MS Sans Serif"
BEGIN
  GROUPBOX "Chart Title:",100,5,3,182,30,WS_TABSTOP
  GROUPBOX "Pie Wedge Sizes:",101,3,34,187,95,
           WS_TABSTOP
  LTEXT "Title: ",-1,10,21,30,8
  EDITTEXT DM_TITLE,40,18,140,12
  LTEXT "Wedge #1:  ",-1,10,50,40,8,NOT WS_GROUP
  LTEXT "Wedge #2:  ",-1,10,65,40,8,NOT WS_GROUP
  LTEXT "Wedge #3:  ",-1,10,80,40,8,NOT WS_GROUP
  LTEXT "Wedge #4:  ",-1,10,95,40,8,NOT WS_GROUP
  LTEXT "Wedge #5:  ",-1,10,110,40,8,NOT WS_GROUP
  LTEXT "Wedge #6:  ",-1,106,50,40,8,NOT WS_GROUP
  LTEXT "Wedge #7:  ",-1,106,65,40,8,NOT WS_GROUP
  LTEXT "Wedge #8:  ",-1,106,80,40,8,NOT WS_GROUP
  LTEXT "Wedge #9:  ",-1,106,95,40,8,NOT WS_GROUP
  LTEXT "Wedge #10:",-1,102,110,45,8,NOT WS_GROUP
  EDITTEXT DM_P1,55,45,30,12
  EDITTEXT DM_P2,55,60,30,12
  EDITTEXT DM_P3,55,75,30,12
  EDITTEXT DM_P4,55,90,30,12
  EDITTEXT DM_P5,55,105,30,12
  EDITTEXT DM_P6,150,44,30,12
  EDITTEXT DM_P7,150,61,30,12
  EDITTEXT DM_P8,150,76,30,12
  EDITTEXT DM_P9,149,91,30,12
  EDITTEXT DM_P10,149,106,30,12
  PUSHBUTTON "OK",IDOK,39,135,24,14
  PUSHBUTTON "Cancel",IDCANCEL,122,136,34,14
END
```

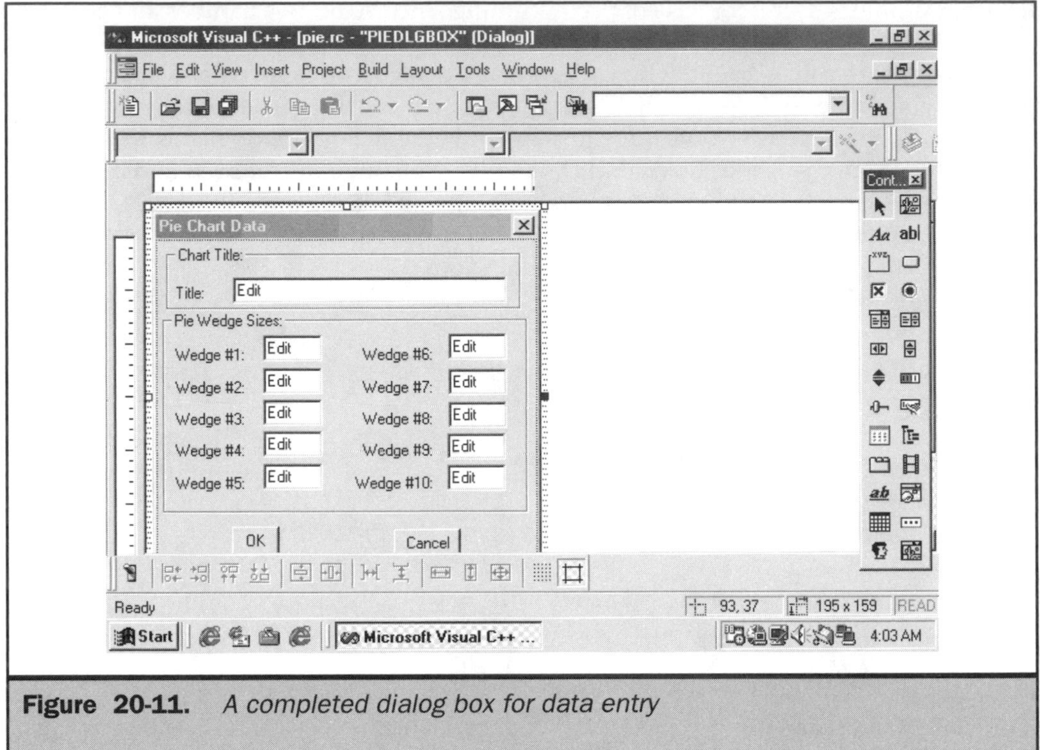

Figure 20-11. *A completed dialog box for data entry*

The specifications that make up a dialog box are typically produced with the resource editor. The resource editor is designed to read and save dialog resource files in the text (.RC) and compiled format (.RES). Text files make it easy to combine several menu and dialog box specifications in one file.

DIALOG BOX CONCEPTS Dialog boxes are actually "child" windows that pop up when selected from the user's menu. When various dialog box buttons, checkboxes, and so on are selected, Windows provides the means necessary for processing the message information.

Dialog boxes can be produced in two basic styles—modal and modeless. Modal dialog boxes are the most popular, and are used for the example developed in the next chapter. When a modal dialog box is created, no other options within the current program will be available until the user ends the dialog box by clicking an OK or Cancel button. The OK button will process any new information selected by the user, while the Cancel button will return the user to the original window without processing new information. Windows expects the ID values for these push buttons to be 1 and 2, respectively.

Modeless dialog boxes are more closely related to ordinary windows. A pop-up window can be created from a parent window, and the user can switch back and forth between the two. The same thing is permitted with a modeless dialog box. Modeless dialog boxes are preferred when a certain option must remain on the screen, such as a color select dialog box.

Dialog Box Design

There are two ways to enter the specifications for a dialog box. If you are entering information from a magazine or book listing, it will be easiest for you to use the compiler's text editor and simply copy the given menu and dialog box specifications into a resource script file, a file with an .RC file extension. When the resource script file is compiled, the resource compiler will create a file with an .RES file extension. If you are creating a new dialog box from scratch for your project, you should use the appropriate resource editor. The next few sections discuss the fundamentals of using the resource editor to create and modify a dialog box. Microsoft's online help utility will provide additional information for more advanced features and editing.

Reconsider the dialog box resource script file, shown earlier in this chapter, to convince yourself of the need for a resource editor for dialog boxes. The resource editor allows you to design the dialog box in a graphical environment.

Examine the dialog box resource script file shown earlier. Ask yourself the following questions. Where do all those terms come from? What do all those numbers mean? How could I figure all of this out without the resource editor? You would have to create, size, and place dialog boxes and their associated controls on the screen experimentally. The resource editor, on the other hand, will do all this for you automatically. Except for being able to make the claim that you created a dialog box without the resource editor at least once in your life, there is no reason for designing dialog boxes without the graphical environment of the editor.

Dialog Box Mechanics

If your dialog box information is entered in ASCII form from a book or magazine article, it must be compiled. This involves the use of the resource compiler. The resource compiler works in conjunction with the resource editor. On the other hand, if you are creating a new dialog box for a project from scratch, use the resource editor by selecting the Insert | Resource menu from the compiler's main menu bar. Then, select the Dialog Box option. A screen similar to the one in Figure 20-12 should appear.

The screen now contains the initial outline for the new dialog box. This initial dialog box can be moved about the screen and sized to fit your needs. The screen in Figure 20-13 shows the initial dialog box moved and sized with several controls in place.

PLACING TOOLBOX CONTROLS By far the most important aspect of using the resource editor when designing dialog boxes is an understanding of the various

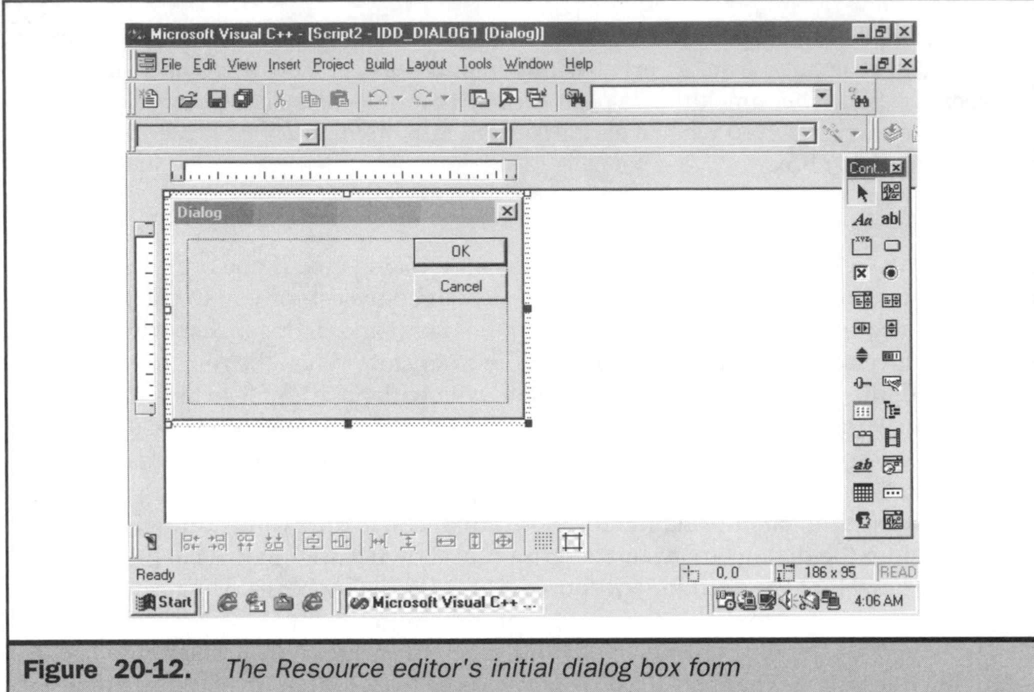

Figure 20-12. *The Resource editor's initial dialog box form*

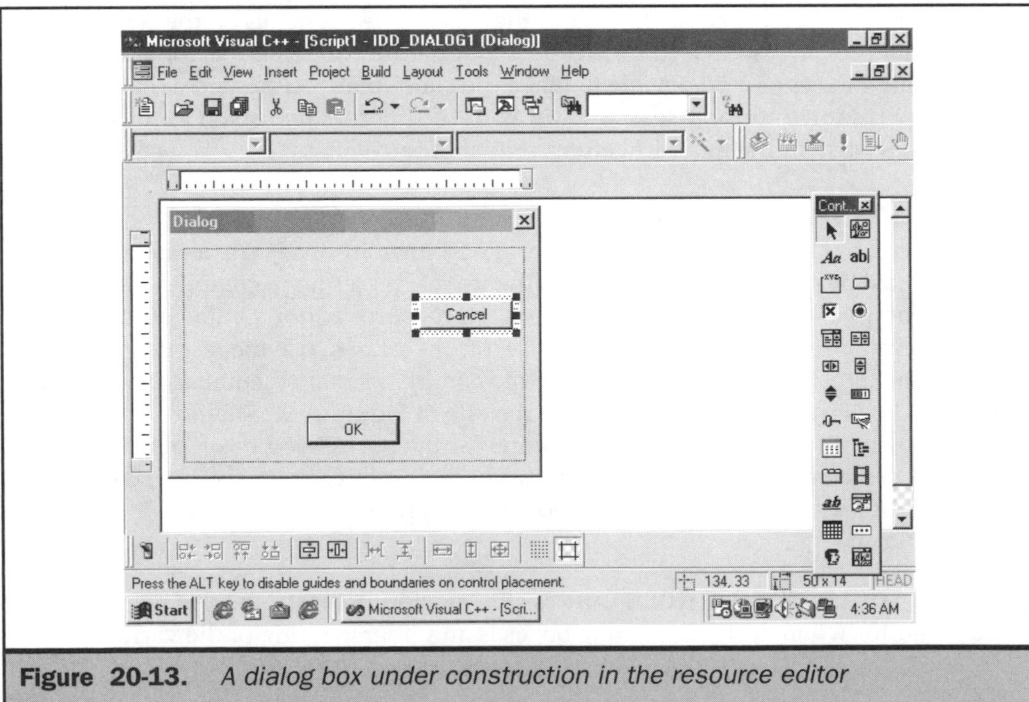

Figure 20-13. *A dialog box under construction in the resource editor*

controls that are provided for the user in the toolbox. Figure 20-14 shows the toolbox used by the resource editor when designing dialog boxes.

Here is a brief explanation of the toolbox controls.

- The *Static Text* control allows the insertion of labels and strings within the dialog box. These can be used, for example, to label an edit box. Select this control using the toolbox icon with the upper and lower case characters.
- The *Group Box* control creates a rectangular outline within a dialog box to enclose a group of controls that are to be used together. A group box contains a label on its upper-left edge. Select this control using the toolbox icon with the rectangular outline with text on the upper edge.
- The *Check Box* control creates a small square box, called a check box, with a label to its right. Check boxes are usually marked or checked by clicking with the mouse, but they can also be selected with the keyboard. Several check boxes usually appear together in a dialog box; they allow the user to check one or more features at the same time. Select this control using the toolbox icon with the "x" or check mark located in a small rectangular region.

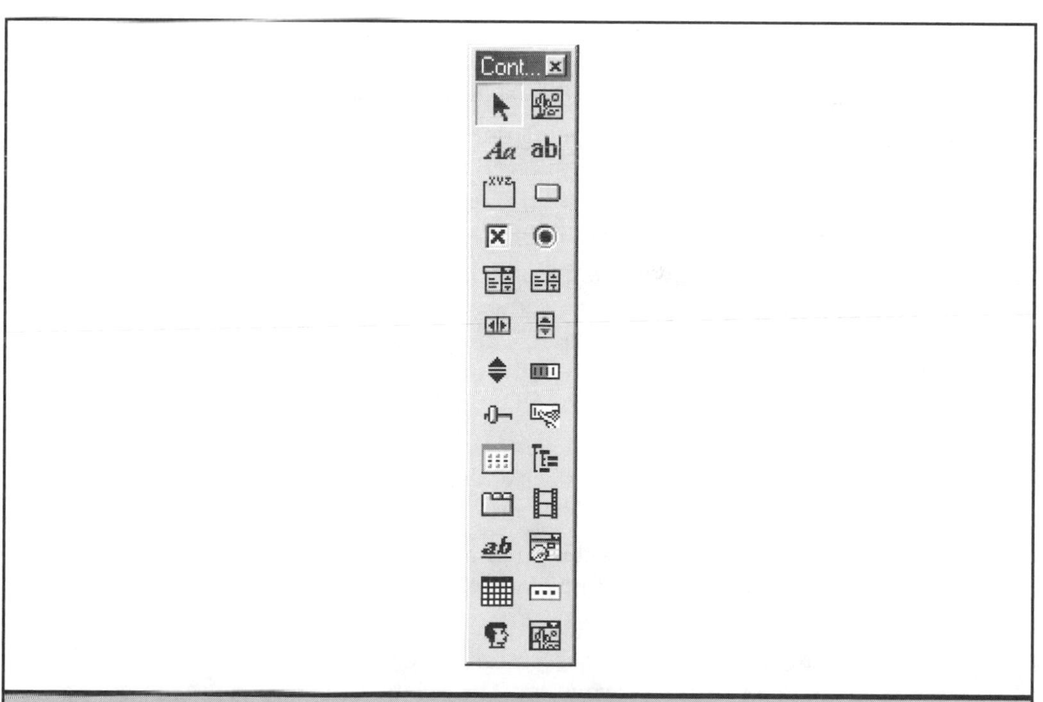

Figure 20-14. *The resource editor's toolbox for dialog boxes*

- The *Combo Box* control is made up of two elements. It is a combination of a single-line edit field (also called a Static Text control) and a List Box control. With a combo box, the user has the ability to enter something into the edit box or scroll through the list box looking for an appropriate selection. Windows provides several styles of combo boxes. Select this control using the toolbox icon with three rectangular areas. This control is located under the Check Box control.
- The *Horizontal Scroll Bar* controls allow horizontal scroll bars to be created for the dialog box. These are usually used in conjunction with another window or control that contains text or graphics information. Select this control using the toolbox icon with the left and right directional arrows.
- The *Spin* control creates two small rectangular areas, one on top of the other. The top area has an upward-pointing arrow and the bottom a downward-pointing arrow. This control functions like the thumb-wheel control on the new Microsoft mouse, allowing you to click selections up or down. Select this control using the toolbox icon with the two pyramid shapes (one upright and one upside down).
- The *Slider* control initially creates a horizontal slider button and track. The control can be changed to a vertical Slider control by changing the property of the control once it is placed in the dialog box. Slider controls are used frequently in place of scroll bars when simpler actions are required. Select this control using the toolbox icon with the Slider button and horizontal track.
- The *List* control contains a rectangular area for a list of items (these may be small iconic images) and a vertical scroll bar. This control is similar to the List Box control, but contains the vertical scroll bar. Select this control using the toolbox icon with the nine small images within the rectangular area.
- The *Tab* control is used when a dialog box is to contain a large amount of information. Instead of creating a complicated dialog box with one screen, the Tab control allows the user to flip to different pages within the dialog box. Each page then contains just a portion of the overall information. Select this control using the toolbox icon with the small tab folder.
- The *Rich Edit* control allows the user to enter and edit multiple lines of text. Formatting can be applied as well as embedded OLE objects. Select this control using the toolbox icon with underlined "ab" characters.
- The *Picture* control allows a rectangular area to be placed in the dialog box where a bitmapped image can be placed. Select this control using the toolbox icon with the small picture.
- The *Edit Box* control creates a small interactive rectangle on the screen in which the user can enter string information. The edit box can be sized to accept short or long strings. This string information can be processed directly as character or numeric integer data and indirectly as real-number data in the program. The

edit box is the most important control for data entry. Select this control using the toolbox icon with the lowercase "ab" characters.

- The *Button* control, is a small, slightly rounded, rectangular button that can be sized. The button contains a label within it. Buttons are used for making an immediate choice such as accepting or canceling the dialog box selections made. Select this control using the toolbox icon with rounded rectangular shape.
- The *Radio Button* control creates a small circle, called a radio button, with a label to its right. Radio buttons, like checkboxes, typically appear in groups. However, unlike checkboxes, only one radio button can be selected at a time in any particular group. Select this control using the toolbox icon with the small bull's-eye.
- The *List Box* control creates a rectangular outline with a vertical scroll bar. List boxes are useful when scrolling is needed to allow the user to select a file from a long directory listing. Select this control using the toolbox icon with the rectangular area and upward- and downward-facing arrows.
- The *Vertical Scroll Bar* control allows vertical scroll bars to be created for the dialog box. These are usually used in conjunction with another window or control that contains text or graphics information. Select this control using the toolbox icon with the upward- and downward-facing arrows.
- The *Progress* control produces a small bar that an application can use to indicate the progress of an operation. The progress bar is filled from left to right. Select this control using the toolbox icon with the small progress bar image.
- The *Hot Key* control enables the creation of a hot key. A hot key is a key or key combination that allows the quick selection of items such as menu selections and so on. Select this control using the toolbox icon with the button and finger combination.
- The *Tree* control displays a list of data in a tree structure. This control is helpful when you wish to convey to the user a hierarchical structure. Select this control using the toolbox icon with the small tree structure image
- The *Animate* control supports the displays of an AVI clip (audio video interleaved). The clip is created as a short series of bitmap frames. This is the technique used for making animated cursors. Select this control using the toolbox icon with the two file frames.
- The *Custom Control* control allows the use of existing custom or user controls. This technique has been replaced by the use of ActiveX controls and is included to be backward compliant. Developers should elect to use ActiveX controls. Select this control using the toolbox icon with the image of a person.

You can place controls in the current dialog box outline by selecting the appropriate control from the toolbox, positioning the mouse pointer in the dialog box, and clicking the mouse button. If the placement is not where you desired, you can use the mouse for repositioning. It is also possible to size the controls once they are placed.

Creating a Dialog Box

In this section, a simple About dialog box is created. About dialog boxes are used to identify the project and developers, give a copyright date, and so on. They usually contain only one push button—OK. They are the easiest dialog boxes to design. Figure 20-15 shows a sized and positioned dialog box outline awaiting the final placement of the Text and Button controls.

In this dialog box example, only two types of controls will be used—the Text and Button controls. You can use the mouse to place, size, and position the Text Box control in the dialog window. Clicking the mouse within the box after positioning it will allow editing of the actual text string. Figure 20-16 shows several controls where the text has been edited.

The string to be printed is entered in the Text window, where the word "Static" now appears. The ID value is automatically supplied. Now position the OK push button in the About box. To delete an existing control, such as "Cancel," click on the control and hit the DEL key. Clicking the mouse within the button allows you to enter the text for

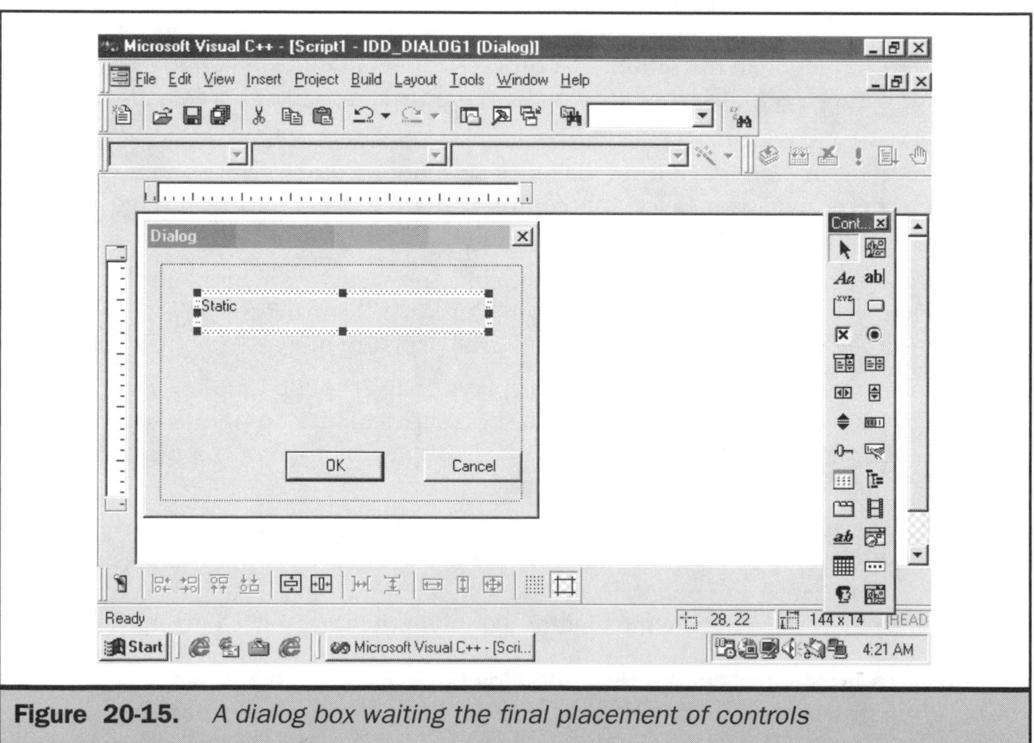

Figure 20-15. *A dialog box waiting the final placement of controls*

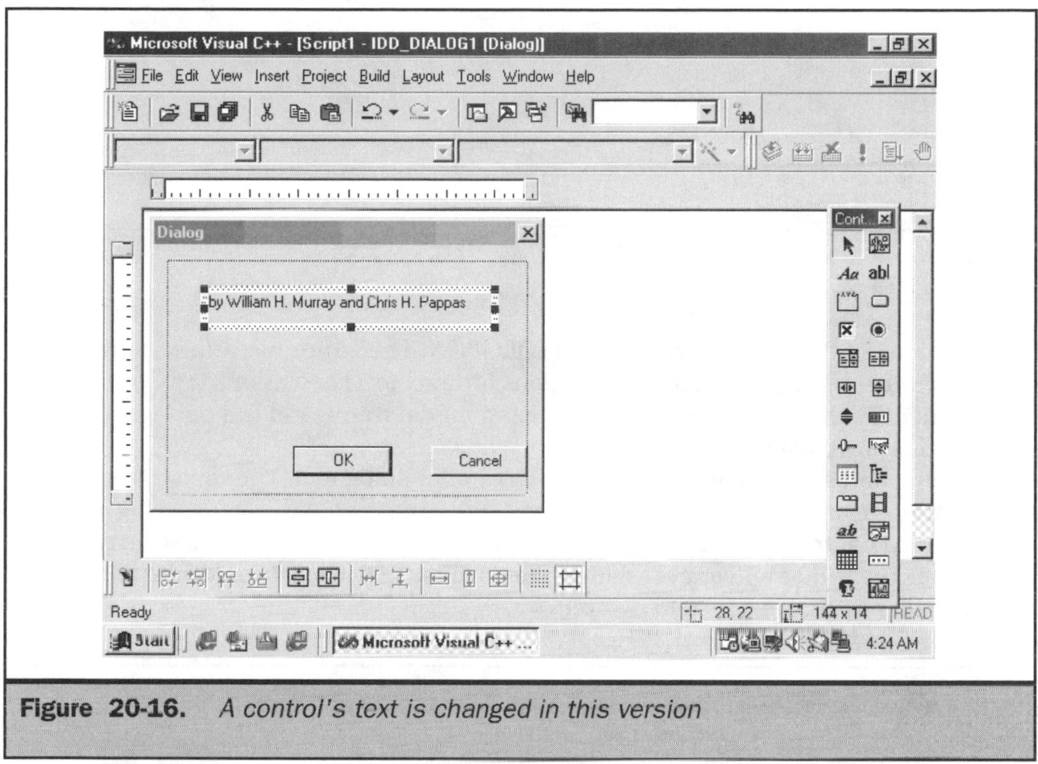

Figure 20-16. *A control's text is changed in this version*

the button. In this case, it will be "OK." Figure 20-17 shows the placement of the push button and the final dialog box.

You can then save the dialog box information by selecting the Save option from the File menu. Remember that the resource editor will save this file in the text (.RC) or compiled resource form (.RES). Using the resource editor to create dialog boxes is a skill learned with practice. Large dialog boxes, utilizing many controls, will initially take hours to design. Again, use the detailed information contained in the Help menu or your Microsoft user's manuals. Start with simple dialog boxes and work toward more complicated designs.

EXAMINING THE RESOURCE SCRIPT You can examine the script file information once the resource is saved as an .RC file. Use any ASCII text editor to see the About box description.

```
ABOUTDLGBOX DIALOG DISCARDABLE  50,300,180,84
STYLE DS_MODALFRAME|WS_POPUP|WS_VISIBLE|WS_CAPTION|WS_SYSMENU
```

```
CAPTION "About"
FONT 8, "MS Sans Serif"
BEGIN
  CTEXT "Microsoft C Pie Chart Program",-1,3,29,176,10
  CTEXT "by William H. Murray and Chris H. Pappas",-1,3,16,
         176,10
  PUSHBUTTON "OK",IDOK,74,51,32,14
END
```

The name of this dialog box is ABOUTDLGBOX. The editor has affixed various segment values along with size specifications for the box. The various style options further identify the dialog box as one that has a modal frame and is a pop-up type. Three controls are listed.

The first and second control specifications are for static text. The remaining specifications establish the text position and type.

The third control specifies an OK push button. The text within the first set of double quotes specifies what will appear within the push button. The labels for the ID values for the push button are a system default.

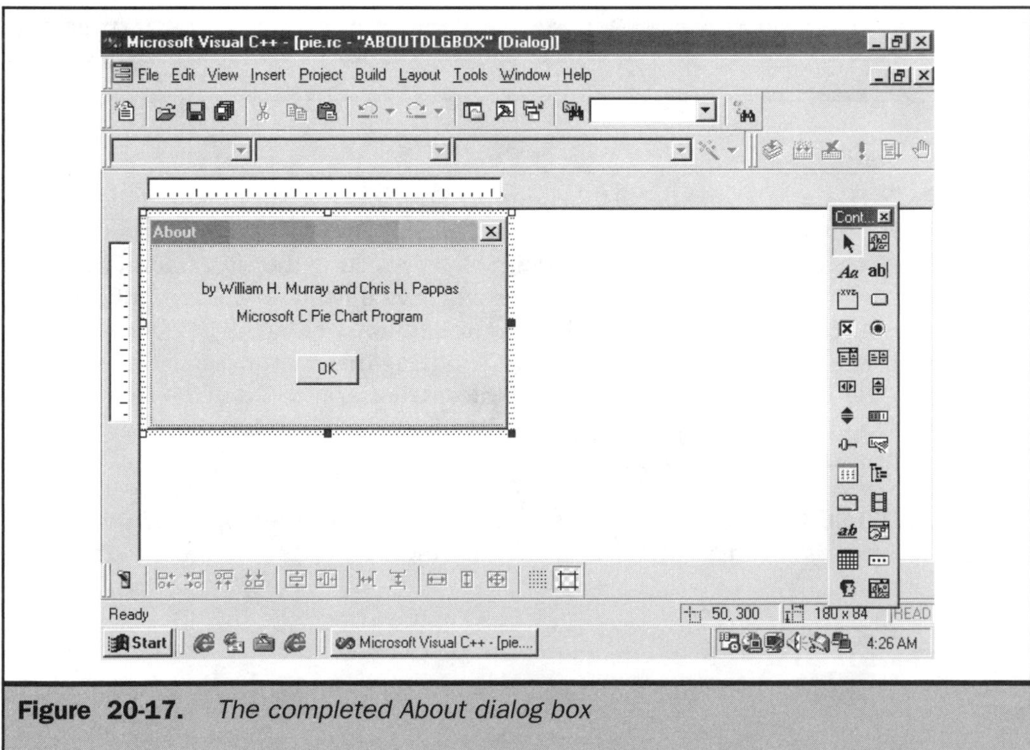

Figure 20-17. *The completed About dialog box*

Remember that it is not necessary to view this information at all. The resource editor will convert the graphics dialog box you see on the screen directly into a compiled resource file (.RES). The only time you will need this information is when you are entering dialog box specifications from a book or magazine.

The About dialog box we just created is used in the next chapter.

Resource Statements

You can also use resource script files for combining menu and dialog resources in one file.

Defining additional resources for an application is as simple as naming the resource ID followed by a resource compiler keyword and then the actual filename. Suppose you've created a resource script file called MYRES.RC:

```
myicon ICON myicon.ico
mycursor CURSOR mycursor.cur
mybitmap BITMAP mybitmap.bmp
```

Remember that MYRES.RC is a resource script or text file that defines three new resources. The names of the three resources are myicon, mycursor, and mybitmap. **Icon**, **cursor**, and **bitmap** are reserved keywords defining the type of the resource. These are followed by the actual filenames containing the resource information; for example: MYICON.ICO, MYCURSOR.CUR, and MYBITMAP.BMP.

There are five additional options that can be included with each single-line statement. These options follow the resource-type keyword and include **preload**, **loadoncall**, **fixed**, **moveable**, and **discardable**. The first two options define load options; the latter define memory options. For example:

```
resourceID resource-type [[load-option]] [[memory-option]]
          filename
```

The **preload** option automatically loads the resource whenever the application is run. **loadoncall** loads the resource only when it is called.

If a **fixed** memory option is selected, the resource remains at a fixed memory address. Selecting **moveable** allows Windows to move the resource to compact and conserve memory. The last choice, **discardable**, allows Windows to discard the resource if it is no longer needed. However, it can be reloaded should a call be made requesting the particular resource. For example, making mybitmap **loadoncall** and **discardable** is as simple as entering the following modified single-line statement into the resource script:

```
myicon ICON myicon.ico
mycursor CURSOR mycursor.cur
mybitmap BITMAP LOADONCALL DISCARDABLE mybitmap.bmp
```

Compiling Resources

Resource script files must be compiled into resource files. The resource compiler is responsible for this operation. The resource compiler can be run from the command line or, preferably, with the use of the project utility.

The command to run the resource compiler includes the name of the resource script file, the name of the executable file that will receive the compiler's binary format output, and any optional instructions.

The syntax for using the resource compiler from the command line is simple. From the command line, type

```
rc [[compiler options]] filename.rc [[executable filename]]
```

For example, invoking the resource compiler with the example resource script described earlier would look like one of the following three lines:

```
rc myres
rc myres.rc
rc -r myres.rc
```

The first two examples read the MYRES.RC resource script file, create the compiled resource file MYRES.RES, and copy the resources into the executable file MYRES.EXE. The third command performs the same actions, except that it does not put the resource into MYRES.EXE. If the third command were executed, the MYRES.RES binary file could be added to the MYRES.EXE file at a later date by using the following command structure:

```
rc myres.res
```

This causes the resource compiler to search for the compiled resource file (.RES) and place it into the executable file (.EXE) of the same filename.

Additional Resource Information

In addition to the information contained in this chapter, the Microsoft user's guides provide a wealth of information on each of these topics. While using the various resource editors, avail yourself of the extensive built-in help engine that is available. Details on the creation of actual Windows resources can be found in the books mentioned in this and earlier chapters, and in various magazine articles. Developing serious Windows code is a major undertaking, but don't forget to have fun while learning.

The next chapter will put these programming concepts into practice as you learn how to develop traditional 32-bit procedure-oriented Windows applications.

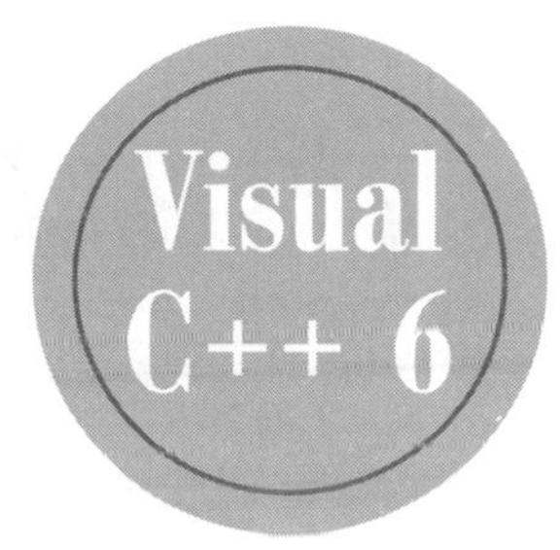

Chapter 21

Procedure-oriented Windows Applications

The previous chapter concentrated on Windows terms, definitions, and tools in order to prepare you for the procedure-oriented applications developed in this chapter. The most attractive features of Windows applications are the common visual interface, device independence, and concurrent execution. It is now time to put theory to practice and develop applications with these exciting features.

This chapter teaches you how to write Windows applications in C or C++. Chapters 22 and 23 introduce you to 32-bit object-oriented Windows applications. These applications incorporate the Microsoft's Foundation Class (MFC) library into your code. Even if you plan to do all of your development work in object-oriented C++, this is still an important chapter for you to study. By studying the applications developed in this chapter, you'll have a much better understanding of how the Microsoft Foundation Class library aids in C++ code development.

An Application Framework

This section describes the various components that make up a program called SWP.C (simple windows program). The SWP.C program incorporates all of the Windows components minimally necessary to create and display a window (a main window with a border, a title bar, a system menu, and maximize/minimize boxes), draw a diagonal line, print a text message, and allow you to gracefully exit the application. You'll also learn that the SWP.C program and its related files can serve as templates for future C or C++ Windows applications that you develop. Understanding code that is used over and over will save you time and help foster an understanding of how Windows applications are put together and why they work.

Table 21-1 summarizes frequently encountered data types that were discussed in Chapter 20.

There are a number of structures that are frequently encountered by Windows programmers. Table 21-2 will serve as a quick reference for these structures.

We're now ready to examine the components of a Windows application using these tools.

Windows Application Components

Windows applications contain two common and essential elements, the WinMain( ) function and a window function. The main body of your application is named WinMain( ). WinMain( ) serves as the entry point for the Windows application and acts in a way similar to the way that the main( ) function in standard C or C++ programs work.

The window function, not to be confused with WinMain( ), has a unique role. Recall that a Windows application never directly accesses any window functions. When a Windows application attempts to execute a standard window function, it makes a request to Windows to carry out the specified task. For this reason, all

Type	Description
CALLBACK	Replaces FAR PASCAL in application's call back routine.
HANDLE	A 32-bit unsigned integer that is used as a handle.
HDC	A handle to a device context.
HWND	A 32-bit unsigned integer that is used as the handle to a window.
LONG	A 32-bit signed integer
LPARAM	Type used for declaration of lParam.
LPCSTR	LPCSTR is the same as LPSTR, but is used for read-only string pointers.
LPSTR	A 32-bit pointer.
LPVOID	A generic pointer type. It is equivalent to (void *).
LRESULT	Used for the return value of a window procedure.
NULL	An integral zero value. It is frequently used to trigger default parameters or actions for a function.
UINT	An unsigned integer type. The host environment determines the size of UINT. For Windows 95 and NT, it is 32-bits.
WCHAR	A 16-bit UNICODE character. WCHAR is used to represent all of the symbols for all of the world's languages.
WINAPI	Replaces FAR PASCAL in API declarations.
WPARAM	Used for the declaration of wParam.

Table 21-1. *Frequently Encountered Win32 Types*

Structure	Description
MSG	Defines the fields of an input message
PAINTSTRUCT	Defines the paint structure used when drawing inside a window
RECT	Defines a rectangle
WNDCLASS	Defines a window class

Table 21-2. *Frequently Encountered Win32 Structures*

Windows applications must have a call back window function. The call back function is registered with Windows and is called back whenever Windows executes an operation on a window.

The WinMain( ) Function

A WinMain( ) function is required by all Windows applications. This is the point at which program execution begins and usually ends. The WinMain( ) function is responsible for the following:

- Creating and initiating the application's message processing loop (which accesses the program's message queue)
- Performing any required initializations
- Registering the application's **window** class type
- Terminating the program, usually upon receiving a WM_QUIT message

Four parameters are passed to the WinMain( ) function from Windows. The following code segment illustrates these required parameters as they are used in the SWP.C application:

```
int WINAPI WinMain(HINSTANCE hInst,HINSTANCE hPreInst,
                   LPSTR lpszCmdLine,int nCmdShow)
```

The first formal parameter to WinMain( ) is hInst, which contains the instance handle of the application. This number uniquely identifies the program when it is running under Windows.

The second formal parameter, hPreInst, will always contain a NULL indicating that there is no previous instance of this application.

Note *MS-DOS versions of Windows (Windows 3.3 and earlier) used hPreInst to indicate whether there were any previous copies of the program loaded. Under operating systems, such as Windows 95, 98, and NT, each application runs in its own separate address space. For this reason, under Windows 95, 98, and NT, hPreInst will never return a valid previous instance, just NULL.*

The third parameter, lpszCmdLine, is a long pointer to a null-terminated string that represents the application's command-line arguments. Normally, lpszCmdLine contains a NULL if the application was started using the Windows Run command.

The fourth and last formal parameter to WinMain( ) is nCmdShow. The **int** value stored in nCmdShow represents one of the many Windows predefined constants defining the possible ways a window can be displayed, such as SW_SHOWNORMAL, SW_SHOWMAXIMIZED, or SW_MINIMIZED.

WNDCLASS

The WinMain( ) function registers the application's main **window** class. Every **window** class is based on a combination of user-selected styles, fonts, caption bars, icons, size, placement, and so on. The **window** class serves as a template that defines these attributes.

Note *Under earlier versions of Windows running over DOS, registered* ***window*** *classes became available to all programs running under Windows. For this reason, the programmer had to use caution when naming and registering classes to make certain that those names used did not conflict with any other application* ***window*** *classes. Windows 95, 98, and NT require that every instance (each copy of an application) must register its own* ***window*** *class.*

Basically, the same standard C and C++ structure type is used for all Windows class definitions. The following example is taken directly from WINUSER.H, which is an **#include** file referenced in WINDOWS.H. The header file contains a **typedef** statement defining the structure type WNDCLASSW (a UNICODE-compatible definition), from which WNDCLASS is derived:

```
typedef struct tagWNDCLASSW {
    UINT         style;
    WNDPROC      lpfnWndProc;
    int          cbClsExtra;
    int          cbWndExtra;
    HANDLE       hInstance;
    HICON        hIcon;
    HCURSOR      hCursor;
    HBRUSH       hbrBackground;
    LPCWSTR      lpszMenuName;
    LPCWSTR      lpszClassName;
} WNDCLASSW, *PWNDCLASSW, NEAR *NPWNDCLASSW, FAR *LPWNDCLASSW;
```

Windows provides several predefined **window** classes, but most applications define their own. To define a **window** class, your application must define a structure variable of the following type:

```
WNDCLASS wcApp;
```

The wcApp structure is then filled with information about the **window** class. The following sections describe the various fields within the WNDCLASS structure. Some of the fields may be assigned a NULL, directing Windows to use predefined values, while others must be given specific values.

STYLE The style field names the **class** style. The styles can be combined with the bitwise OR operator. The style field is made up of a combination of the values shown in Table 21-3.

LPFNWNDPROC lpfnWndProc receives a pointer to the window function that will carry out all of the tasks for the window.

CBCLSEXTRA cbClsExtra gives the number of bytes that must be allocated after the **window** class structure. It can be set to NULL.

CBWNDEXTRA cbWndExtra gives the number of bytes that must be allocated after the window instance. It can be set to NULL.

Value	Meaning
CS_BYTEALIGNCLIENT	Aligns a client area on a byte boundary
CS_BYTEALIGNWINDOW	Aligns a window on the byte boundary
CS_CLASSDC	Provides the window class a display context
CS_DBLCLKS	Sends a double-click message to the window
CS_GLOBALCLASS	States that the window class is an application
Global class:	
CS_HREDRAW	Redraws the window when horizontal size changes
CS_NOCLOSE	Inhibits the close option from the system menu
CS_OWNDC	Each window receives an instance for its own
Display context (DC):	
CS_PARENTDC	Sends the parent window's display context (DC)
To the window class:	
CS_SAVEBITS	Saves that part of a screen that is covered by another window
CS_VREDRAW	Redraws the window when the vertical size changes

Table 21-3. *Frequently Used Windows Styles*

HINSTANCE hInstance defines the instance of the application registering the **window** class. This must be an instance handle and cannot be set to NULL.

HICON hIcon defines the icon to be used when the window is minimized. This can be set to NULL.

HCURSOR hCursor defines the cursor to be used with the application. This handle can be set to NULL. The cursor is valid only within the application's client area.

HBRBACKGROUND hbrBackground provides the identification for the background brush. This can be a handle to the physical brush or it can be a color value. Color values must be selected from one of the standard colors in the following list. A value of 1 must be added to the selected color.

COLOR_ACTIVEBORDER
COLOR_ACTIVECAPTION
COLOR_APPWORKSPACE
COLOR_BACKGROUND
COLOR_BTNFACE
COLOR_BTNSHADOW
COLOR_BTNTEXT
COLOR_CAPTIONTEXT
COLOR_GRAYTEXT
COLOR_HIGHLIGHT
COLOR_HIGHLIGHTTEXT
COLOR_INACTIVEBORDER
COLOR_INACTIVECAPTION
COLOR_MENU
COLOR_MENUTEXT
COLOR_SCROLLBAR
COLOR_WINDOW
COLOR_WINDOWFRAME
COLOR_WINDOWTEXT

If hbrBackground is set to NULL, the application paints its own background.

LPSZMENUNAME lpszMenuName is a pointer to a null-terminated character string. The string is the resource name of the menu. This item can be set to NULL.

LPSZCLASSNAME lpszClassName is a pointer to a null-terminated character string. The string is the name of the **window** class.

WNDCLASSEX

Windows offers an expanded definition for WNDCLASS named WNDCLASSEX that allows a small icon to be used for applications. Here is WNDCLASSEX structure:

```
typedef struct _WNDCLASSEX {
    UINT     style;
    WNDPROC  lpfnWndProc;
    int      cbClsExtra;
    int      cbWndExtra;
    HANDLE   hInstance;
    HICON    hIcon;
    HCURSOR  hCursor;
    HBRUSH   hbrBackground;
    LPCTSTR  lpszMenuName;
    LPCTSTR  lpszClassName;
    HICON    hIconSm;
} WNDCLASSEX;
```

You can see that these two structures are identical, except that WNDCLASSEX includes the hIconSm member, which is the handle of the small icon associated with a **window** class.

Predefined **window** classes are available, but most programmers define their own **window** class.

Defining a Window Class

An application can define its own **window** class by defining a structure of the appropriate type and then filling the structure's fields with the information about the **window** class.

The following listing is from the SWP.C application and demonstrates how the WNDCLASS structure has been defined and initialized.

```
char szProgName[]="ProgName";
               .
               .
               .
WNDCLASS wcApp;
               .
               .
               .
wcApp.lpszClassName=szProgName;
wcApp.hInstance    =hInst;
```

```
wcApp.lpfnWndProc   =WndProc;
wcApp.hCursor       =LoadCursor(NULL,IDC_ARROW);
wcApp.hIcon         =NULL;
wcApp.lpszMenuName  =szApplName;
wcApp.hbrBackground=GetStockObject(WHITE_BRUSH);
wcApp.style         =CS_HREDRAW|CS_VREDRAW;
wcApp.cbClsExtra    =0;
wcApp.cbWndExtra    =0;
if (!RegisterClass (&wcApp))
  return 0;
```

The SWP.C template application is assigned the generic name szProgName and is assigned to the window's wcApp.lpszClassName.

The second field in WNDCLASS, wcApp.hInstance, is assigned the value returned in hInst after WinMain( ) is invoked. This indicates the current instance of the application. lpfnWndProc is assigned the pointer address to the window function that will carry out all of the window's tasks. For the SWP.C application, the function is called WndProc( ).

Note *WndProc( ) is a user-defined function name—not a predefined function name. The function must be prototyped before the assignment statement.*

The wcApp.hCursor field is assigned a handle to the instance's cursor, which in this example is IDC_ARROW (representing the default tilted arrow cursor). This assignment is accomplished through a call to the LoadCursor( ) function. Since the SWP.C application has no default icon, wcApp.hIcon is assigned a value of NULL.

When wcApp.lpszMenuName is assigned a value of NULL, Windows understands that the class has no menu. If it did, the menu would have a name, which would appear within quotation marks. The GetStockObject( ) function returns a handle to a brush used to paint the background color of the client area of windows created from this class. For the SWP.C application, the function returns a handle to one of Windows predefined brushes; WHITE_BRUSH.

The wcApp.style **window** class style has been set to CS_HREDRAW or CS_VREDRAW. All **window** class styles have identifiers in WINUSER.H that begin with "CS_". Each identifier represents a bit value. The bitwise OR operation | is used to combine these bit flags. The two parameters used (CS_HREDRAW and CS_VREDRAW) instruct Windows to redraw the entire client area whenever the horizontal or vertical size of the window is changed.

The last two fields, wcApp.cbClsExtra and wcApp.cbWndExtra, are frequently assigned 0. These fields are used to optionally indicate the count of extra bytes that may have been reserved at the end of the **window** class structure and the window data structure used for each **window** class.

From previous discussions about instances, you may recall that under earlier 16-bit versions of Windows, an application had to register a **window** class if it was the first instance or copy loaded. Here is a portion of code that was used for that purpose:

```
if (!hPreInst)
{
        .
        .
        .
  if (!RegisterClass (&wcApp))
    return FALSE;
}
```

Windows checks the number of instances by examining the hPreInst parameter, which will always be NULL, and then registers the class.

There are two **if** statements in the code segment. The first **if** takes care of filling the WNDCLASS structure when this is the first instance. The second **if** statement registers the new **window** class. It does this by sending RegisterClass( ) a long pointer to the **window** class structure. If Windows cannot register the **window** class, which can happen if sufficient memory is not available, RegisterClass( ) will return a 0, terminating the program.

Creating a Window

All windows are patterned after some predefined and registered class type. Defining and then registering a **window** class has nothing to do with actually displaying a window in a Windows application.

A window is created with a call to the CreateWindow( ) function. This process is common for all versions of Windows. While the **window** class defines the general characteristics of a window, allowing the same **window** class to be used for many different windows, the parameters for CreateWindow( ) specify more detailed information about the window. If the function call is successful, CreateWindow( ) returns the handle of the newly created window. Otherwise, the function returns a NULL value.

The parameter information for the CreateWindow( ) function falls under the following categories: the class, title, style, screen position, window's parent handle, menu handle, instance handle, and 32 bits of additional information. For the SWP.C application, this function would take on the following appearance:

```
hWnd=CreateWindow(szProgName,"Simple Windows Program",
                  WS_OVERLAPPEDWINDOW,CW_USEDEFAULT,
                  CW_USEDEFAULT,CW_USEDEFAULT,
```

```
                    CW_USEDEFAULT,(HWND)NULL,(HMENU)NULL,
                    (HANDLE)hInst,(LPSTR)NULL);
```

The first field, szProgName (assigned earlier), defines the window's class, followed by the title to be used for the window's title bar (Simple Windows Program). The style of the window is the third parameter (WS_OVERLAPPEDWINDOW). This standard Windows style represents a normal overlapped window with a caption bar; a system menu icon; minimize, maximize and terminate icons; and a window frame.

The next six parameters (either CS_USEDEFAULT or NULL) represent the initial *x* and *y* positions and *x* and *y* sizes of the window, along with the parent window handle and window menu handle. Each of these fields has been assigned a **default** value. The hInst field contains the instance of the program, followed by no additional parameters (NULL).

Showing and Updating a Window

Under Windows, the ShowWindow( ) function is needed to actually display a window. The following portion of code, from the SWP.C application, demonstrates this:

```
ShowWindow(hWnd,nCmdShow);
```

The handle of the window created by the call to CreateWindow( ) is held in the hWnd parameter. The second parameter to ShowWindow( ), nCmdShow, determines how the window is initially displayed. This display mode is also referred to as the window's visibility state.

The nCmdShow parameter can specify that the window be displayed as a normal window (SW_SHOWNNORMAL) or in several other possible forms. For example, substituting nCmdShow with the WINUSER.H constant SW_SHOWMINNOACTIVE, as shown in the following line of code, causes the window to be drawn as an icon:

```
ShowWindow(hWnd,SW_SHOWMINNOACTIVE);
```

Other display possibilities include SW_SHOWMAXIMIZED, which causes the window to be active and fill the entire display, along with its counterpart, SW_SHOWMINIMIZED.

The final step in displaying a window requires a call to the Windows UpdateWindow( ) function:

```
UpdateWindow(hWnd);
```

A call to ShowWindow( ) with a SW_SHOWNORMAL parameter causes the function to erase the window's client area with the background brush specified in the window's class. It is the call to UpdateWindow( ) that generates the familiar WM_PAINT message, causing the client area to be painted.

The Message Loop

With everything in place, the application is ready to perform its main task: processing messages. Recall that Windows does not send input from the mouse or keyboard directly to an application. Windows places all input into the application's message queue. The message queue can contain messages generated by Windows or messages posted by other applications.

The application needs a message-processing loop once the call to WinMain( ) has created and displayed the window. The most common approach is to use a standard **while** loop:

```
while (GetMessage(&lpMsg,NULL,0,0))
{
  TranslateMessage(&lpMsg);
  DispatchMessage(&lpMmsg);
}
```

THE GETMESSAGE( ) FUNCTION The next message to be processed from the application's message queue can be obtained with a call to the Windows GetMessage( ) function. GetMessage( ) copies the message into the message structure pointed to by the **long** pointer, lpMsg, and sends the message structure to the main body of the program.

The NULL parameter instructs the function to retrieve any of the messages for any window that belongs to the application. The last two parameters, 0 and 0, tell GetMessage( ) not to apply any message filters. Message filters can restrict retrieved messages to specific categories such as keystrokes or mouse moves. These filters are referred to as wMsgFilterMin and wMsgFilterMax and specify the numeric filter extremes to apply.

Control can be returned to Windows at any time before the message loop is begun. For example, an application will normally make certain that all steps leading up to the message loop have executed properly. This can include making sure that each **window** class is registered and has been created. However, once the message loop has been entered, only one message can terminate the loop. Whenever the message to be processed is WM_QUIT, the value returned is FALSE. This causes the processing to proceed to the main loop's closing routine. The WM_QUIT message is the only way for an application to get out of the message loop.

THE TRANSLATEMESSAGE( ) FUNCTION Virtual-key messages can be converted into character messages with the TranslateMessage( ) function. The function call is required only by applications that need to process character input from the keyboard. This ability can be very useful because it allows the user to make menu selections without having to use the mouse.

The TranslateMessage( ) function creates an ASCII character message (WM_CHAR) from a WM_KEYDOWN and WM_KEYUP message. As long as this function is included in the message loop, the keyboard interface will also be in effect.

THE DISPATCHMESSAGE( ) FUNCTION Windows sends current messages to the correct window procedures with the DispatchMessage( ) function. This function makes it easy to add additional windows and dialog boxes to your application. DispatchMessage( ) automatically routes each message to the appropriate window procedure.

The Window Function

Recall that all applications must include a WinMain( ) function and a Windows call back function. Since a Windows application never directly accesses any Windows function, each application must make a request to Windows to carry out any specified operation.

A call back function is registered with Windows and is called back whenever Windows executes an operation on a window. The length of the actual code for the call back function will vary with each application. The window function itself may be very small, processing only one or two messages, or it may be large and complex.

The following code segment (minus application-specific statements) shows the call back window function WndProc( ) as it is used in the SWP.C application:

```
LRESULT CALLBACK WndProc(HWND hWnd,UINT messg,
                         WPARAM wParam,LPARAM lParam)
{
  HDC hdc;
  PAINTSTRUCT ps;

  switch (messg)
  {
    case WM_PAINT:
      hdc=BeginPaint(hWnd,&ps);
              .
              .
              .
      VailidateRect(hWnd,NULL);
      EndPaint(hWnd,&ps);
      break;
```

```
    case WM_DESTROY:
      PostQuitMessage(0);
      break;

    default:
      return(DefWindowProc(hWnd,messg,wParam,lParam));
  }
  return(0);
}
```

Windows expects the name referenced by the wcApp.lpfnWndProc field of the **window** class structure definition to match the name used for the call back function. WndProc( ) will be the name used for the call back function for all subsequent windows created from this **window** class.

The following code segment reviews the placement and assignment of the call back function's name within the **window** class structure:

```
    .
    .
    .
wcApp.lpszClassName=szProgName;
wcApp.hInstance    =hInst;
wcApp.lpfnWndProc  =WndProc;
    .
    .
    .
```

Windows has several hundred different Windows messages that it can send to the window function. These messages are labeled with identifiers that begin with "WM_". For example, WM_CREATE, WM_SIZE, and WM_PAINT are used quite frequently. These identifiers are also known as symbolic constants.

The first parameter to WndProc( ) is hWnd. hWnd contains the handle to the window to which Windows will send the message. Since it is possible for one window function to process messages for several windows created from the same **window** class, this handle is used by the window function to determine which window is receiving the message.

The second parameter to the function, messg, specifies the actual message being processed as defined in WINUSER.H. The last two parameters, wParam and lParam, specify any additional information needed to process each specific message. Frequently, the value returned to each of these parameters is NULL. This means that they can be ignored. At other times, the parameters contain a 2-byte value and a pointer, or two word values.

The WndProc( ) function continues by defining two variables: hdc specifies the display context handle, and ps specifies a PAINTSTRUCT structure needed to store client area information.

The call back function is used to examine the type of message it is about to process and then select the appropriate action to be taken. This selection process usually takes place within a standard C **switch** statement.

Processing WM_PAINT Messages

The first message that WndProc( ) will process in this template is WM_PAINT. This message calls the Windows function BeginPaint( ), which prepares the specified window for painting and fills a PAINTSTRUCT (&ps) with information about the area to be painted. The BeginPaint( ) function also returns a handle to the device context for the given window.

Because Windows is a multitasking operating system, it is possible for one application to display its window or dialog box over another application's client area. This creates a problem whenever the window or dialog box is closed: a hole appears on the screen where the dialog box was displayed. Windows handles this problem by sending the active application a WM_PAINT message. In this case, Windows requests that the active application update its client area.

Except for the first WM_PAINT message, which is sent by the call to UpdateWindow( ) in WinMain( ), additional WM_PAINT messages are sent under the following conditions:

- When forcing a WM_PAINT message with a call to the InvalidateRect( ) or InvalidateRgn( ) function
- When resizing a window
- When using the ScrollWindow( ) function
- Whenever a portion of a client area has been hidden by a menu or dialog box that has just been closed

Here is how the process works. Any portion of an application's client area that has been corrupted by the overlay of a dialog box, for example, has that area of the client area marked as invalid. Windows makes the redrawing of a client area efficient by keeping track of the diagonal coordinates of this invalid rectangle. It is the presence of an invalid rectangle that prompts Windows to send the WM_PAINT message.

If several portions of the client area are invalidated, Windows will adjust the invalid rectangle coordinates to encapsulate all invalid regions. In other words, Windows does not send a WM_PAINT message for each invalid rectangle.

The call to InvalidateRect( ) allows Windows to mark the client area as invalid, thereby forcing a WM_PAINT message. An application can obtain the coordinates of the invalid rectangle by calling the GetUpdateRect( ) function. A call to the ValidateRect( ) function validates any rectangular region in the client area and deletes any pending WM_PAINT messages.

The EndPaint( ) function is called when the WndProc( ) function ends its processing of the WM_PAINT messages. This function is called whenever the application is finished outputting information to the client area. It tells Windows that the application has finished processing all paint messages and that it is now OK to remove the display context.

Processing the WM_DESTROY Message

When the Close option is selected by the user from an application's system menu, Windows posts a WM_DESTROY message to the application's message queue. The application terminates after it retrieves this message.

The DefWindowProc( ) Function

The DefWindowProc( ) function call, in the default section of WndProc( )'s **switch** statement, is needed to empty the application's message queue of any unrecognized and/or unprocessed messages. This function ensures that all of the messages posted to the application are processed.

A Module Definition File

As you learned earlier, LINK provides a command-line equivalent to the module definition files once required by all Windows applications. A module definition file can be used to provide the linker with definitions and descriptive information so that it knows how to organize the application's executable file for Windows. This information becomes part of the header section of the New Executable file format.

Under Windows 95, 98, and NT, it is very unlikely that you will have to create a module definition file. This information is provided for completeness and backward compatibility.

A module definition file for the SWP.C application might take on the following appearance:

```
NAME        swp
DESCRIPTION 'Simple Windows Program'
EXETYPE     WINDOWS
CODE        PRELOAD MOVEABLE DISCARDABLE
DATA        PRELOAD MOVEABLE MULTIPLE
HEAPSIZE    4096
EXPORTS     WndProc       @1
```

The **name** statement defines SWP.C as a Windows program (not a dynamic link library) and gives the module a name. This name should be the same name as the program's executable (.EXE) file.

The **description** line copies the text into the executable file. Often this is used to embed added information such as a release date, version number, or copyright notice.

The **exetype** refers to the type of executable file to create.

Both the **code** and **data** segments have been marked as preloadable and moveable, allowing Windows to relocate them for any dynamic memory allocation requests. The **multiple** statement also instructs Windows to create unique data segments for each instance of the application. The use of **discardable** allows Windows to discard unused program code. This code can be automatically reloaded if necessary.

The **heapsize** statement specifies an amount of extra, expandable, local memory from within the application's data segment. The **stacksize** has been set to 9216. You can experiment with various sizes. Larger values may be necessary for applications with large non-static variables or those applications using recursion.

Finally, the **exports** statement identifies the application's dynamic link entry point and specifies the name of the procedure, in this case, WndProc.

Using a Make or Project Utility

There are two ways of putting your Windows applications together: from the command line or from within the integrated environment of the compiler. If you are building applications from the command line, you will need to write a make file. If you are building applications from within the integrated environment, you will need to use the project utility. We very strongly recommend the latter.

The nmake Utility

Microsoft provides a command-line program maintenance utility named NMAKE.EXE. The nmake utility is important when compiling command-line applications that use multiple source code or data segments. The use of the nmake utility requires the development of another text file, called the make file. Make files often do not have a file extension. Thus, for our first example, a command-line make file would be named SWP. The syntax for building an application from the command-line is as simple as typing the following:

```
nmake swp
```

The nmake utility is responsible for calling the Visual C++ compiler, linker, and resource compiler with the proper options. Make files also do partial builds of the application. For example, if the source code has changed but the resource code remains unchanged, the make file will just recompile the source code on subsequent operations.

A simple make file, such as one that could be used for the SWP.C application, will look something like this:

```
all : swp.exe

swp.obj: swp.c
  cl -c -AS -Gsw -Oas swp.c

swp.exe: swp.obj swp.def
  link /NOD swp,,,libw slibcew, swp.def
```

In a make file, the file named to the left of the colon is the file the nmake utility will update if any of the component files to the right of the colon have been updated. The action taken by the utility is restricted to the appropriate indented lines. Note that a command-line make file is a text file created in any text editor.

However, once again, we recommend the use of the project utility discussed in the next section as the preferred alternative to the command-line nmake utility.

PROJECT UTILITY

Seasoned users will choose to remain within the integrated environment of the Visual C++ compiler and compile and link their applications with the help of the Project utility. The Project utility will create an additional file on your disk with a .DSP file extension. So, in this example, the project file would be named SWP.DSP. Project files are not text files, so we can't show you the contents of the file, only tell you how to create one. If a project is built within a unique workspace, another file with a .DSW file extension will be created on your disk. The process of using a project file to manage your files is so simple that you will probably never choose to build applications from the command-line again!

To start a new project, use the compiler's File | New menu to open the New dialog box. Use the Projects folder and select a Win32 Application, as shown in Figure 21-1.

The project name for this example is TestApp, as you can see in Figure 21-1. Click the OK button to arrive at an initially blank screen.

To write code for the project, use the compiler's Project | Add To Project | New... menu selection, as shown in Figure 21-2.

When this selection is made, a New dialog box appears. Using the Text File option, as shown in Figure 21-3, enter the name of the file. In this example, it is TESTAPP.C.

It is also possible to select the C++ Source File as the file type; just be sure to name the file TESTAPP.C.

It is now possible to type your source code into this file, as shown in Figure 21-4.

When the source code is complete, use the File menu to save the project.

If your application requires other files, such as resource files and so on, they can be added to the project at this point. Use the Project | Add To Project | Files... menu selection, to specify the filename.

For all remaining applications in this book, we'll be developing our own project files and building our applications from within the integrated environment.

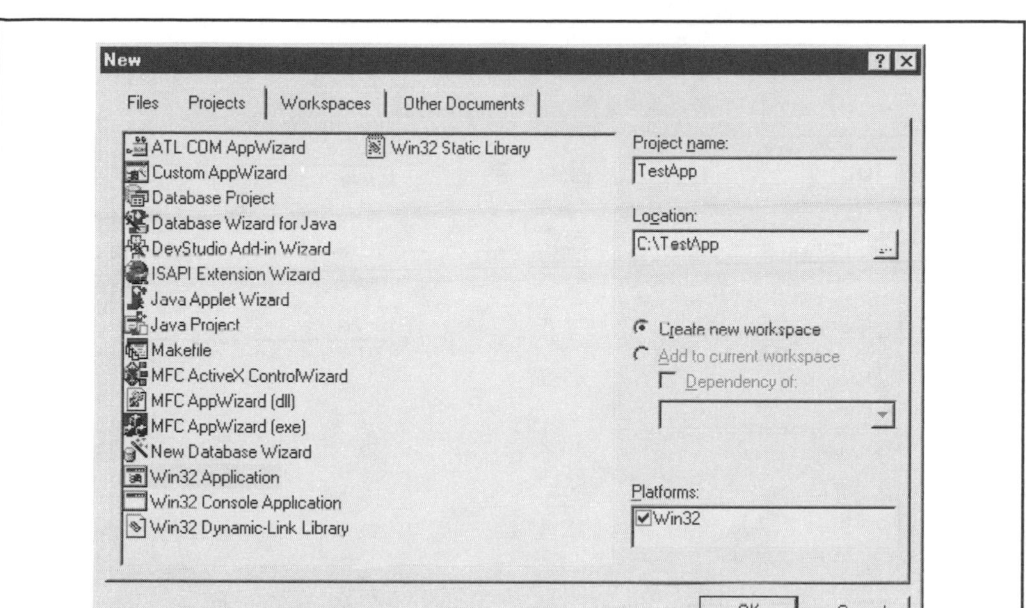

Figure 21-1. *A Win32 application is selected for the new TestApp project*

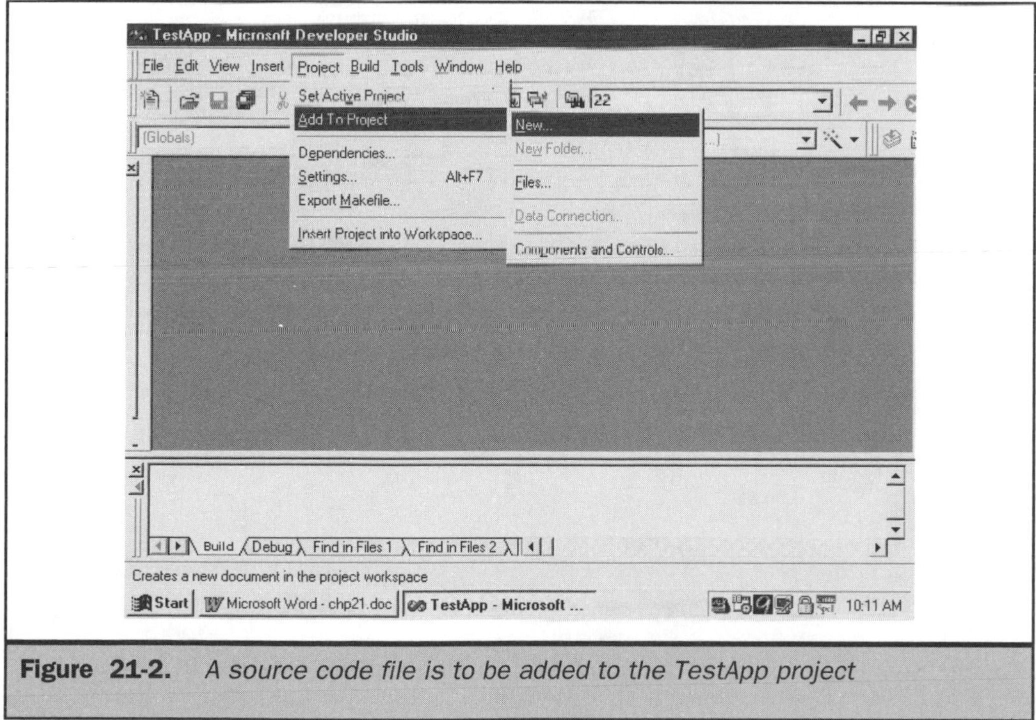

Figure 21-2. *A source code file is to be added to the TestApp project*

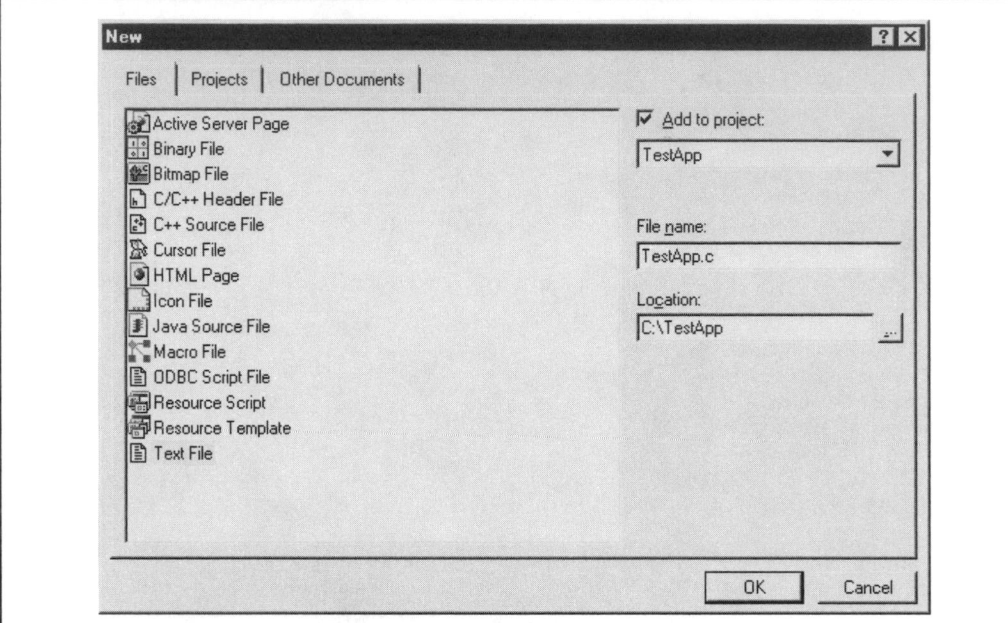

Figure 21-3. *A blank text file named TESTAPP.C will be the source code file for this example*

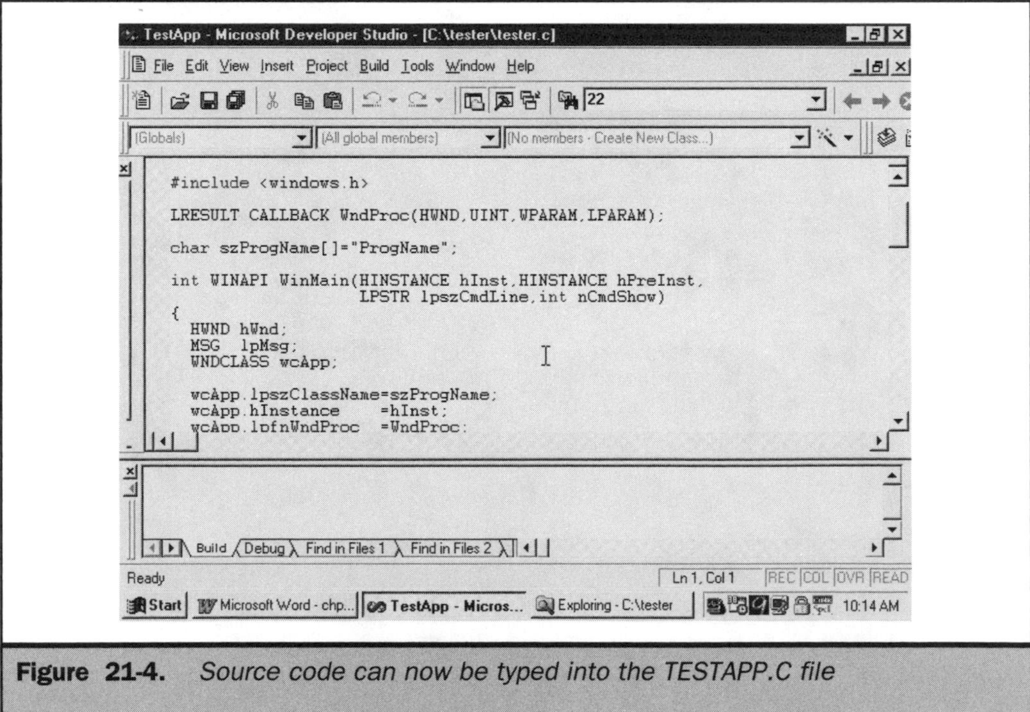

Figure 21-4. *Source code can now be typed into the TESTAPP.C file*

The next step in creating a new application is using the Project utility to build an executable file. Before building an application, it is important that all switches are set properly to build a Windows application. The command-line make utility, nmake, allows you to specify this in text form within the file, but the Project utility requires that these switches be set from within the integrated environment. These switches can be set from the Project | Settings... menu. When the Project Settings dialog box is visible, you will be provided with a number of folders. From the General folder, make sure the Microsoft Foundation Class Option is set to "Not Using MFC," as you can see in Figure 21-5.

Files are created and saved in a Debug subdirectory by default. When you have completed the project and are ready to generate a release candidate, change to the Release option.

Switch to the C/C++ folder. If you have not changed the defaults, your folder should appear similar to Figure 21-6.

The default options are satisfactory for almost all applications. As a check, make sure your project options match those shown in the Project Options list in Figure 21-6.

Switch to the Link folder. It should appear similar to Figure 21-7.

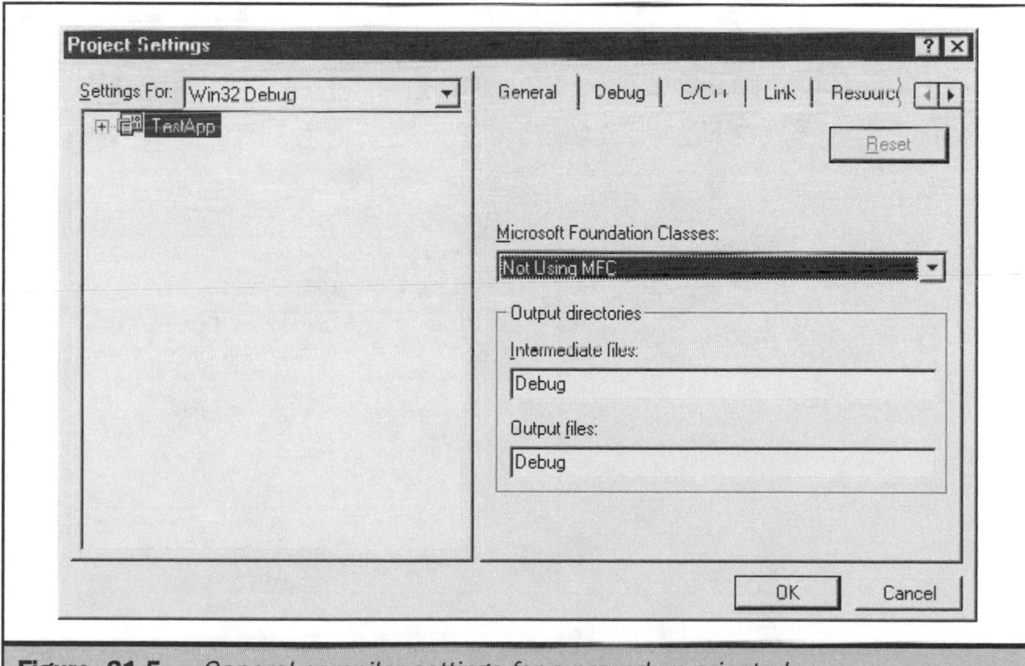

Figure 21-5. *General compiler settings for a procedure-oriented Windows application*

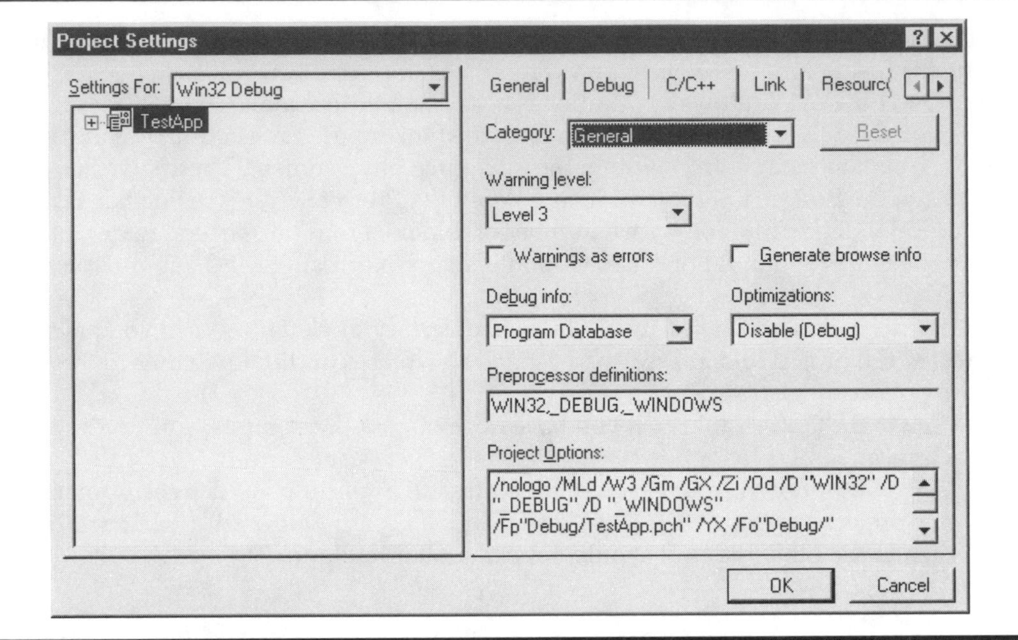

Figure 21-6. *C/C++ compiler settings for a Windows application*

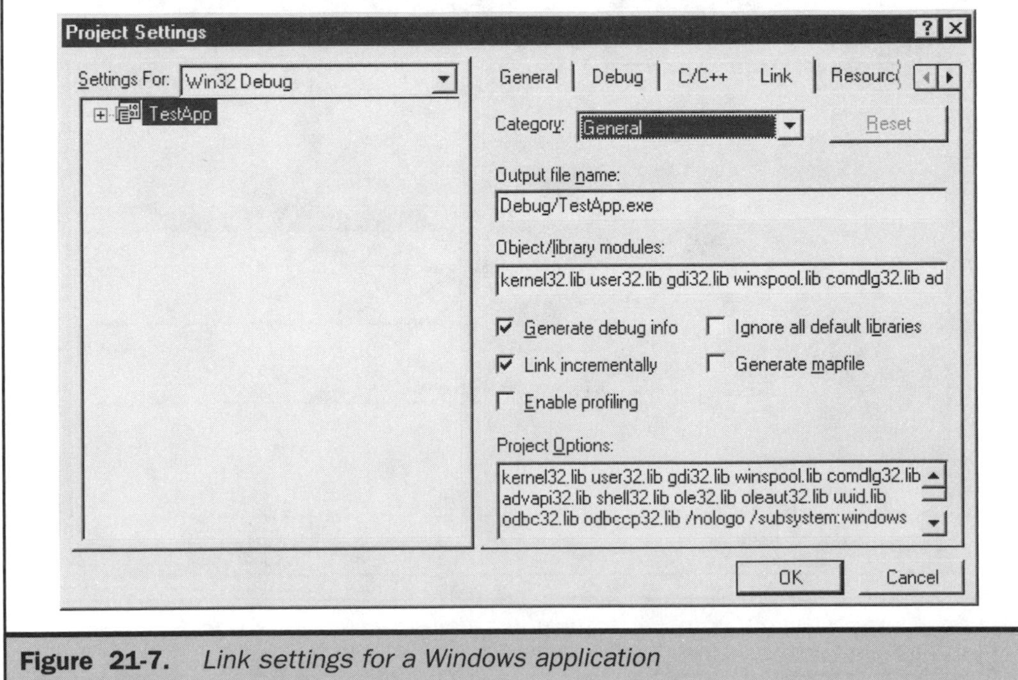

Figure 21-7. *Link settings for a Windows application*

Compare your project options with those shown in Figure 21-3. It is very important that the subsystem be set to /subsystem:windows and not to /subsystem:console. If it is not set in this manner, your application will compile but not link correctly.

A Complete Windows Program

We have been discussing portions of a complete program throughout the previous sections of this chapter. For your convenience, the following is a complete listing of all the code necessary to create the Simple Windows Program

The source code file, SWP.C, is straightforward. However, long listings warrant extra care when entering each line of code.

```
/*
*   swp.c
*   Simple Windows Program
*   Copyright (c) William H. Murray and Chris H. Pappas, 1998
*/

#include <windows.h>

LRESULT CALLBACK WndProc(HWND,UINT,WPARAM,LPARAM);

char szProgName[]="ProgName";

int WINAPI WinMain(HINSTANCE hInst,HINSTANCE hPreInst,
                   LPSTR lpszCmdLine,int nCmdShow)
{
  HWND hWnd;
  MSG  lpMsg;
  WNDCLASS wcApp;

  wcApp.lpszClassName=szProgName;
  wcApp.hInstance    =hInst;
  wcApp.lpfnWndProc  =WndProc;
  wcApp.hCursor      =LoadCursor(NULL,IDC_ARROW);
  wcApp.hIcon        =0;
  wcApp.lpszMenuName =0;
  wcApp.hbrBackground=GetStockObject(WHITE_BRUSH);
  wcApp.style        =CS_HREDRAW|CS_VREDRAW;
  wcApp.cbClsExtra   =0;
  wcApp.cbWndExtra   =0;
  if (!RegisterClass (&wcApp))
```

```
    return 0;

  hWnd=CreateWindow(szProgName,"Simple Windows Program",
                    WS_OVERLAPPEDWINDOW,CW_USEDEFAULT,
                    CW_USEDEFAULT,CW_USEDEFAULT,
                    CW_USEDEFAULT,(HWND)NULL,(HMENU)NULL,
                    (HANDLE)hInst,(LPSTR)NULL);
  ShowWindow(hWnd,nCmdShow);
  UpdateWindow(hWnd);
  while (GetMessage(&lpMsg,0,0,0)) {
    TranslateMessage(&lpMsg);
    DispatchMessage(&lpMsg);
  }
  return(lpMsg.wParam);
}

LRESULT CALLBACK WndProc(HWND hWnd,UINT messg,
                         WPARAM wParam,LPARAM lParam)
{
  HDC hdc;
  PAINTSTRUCT ps;

  switch (messg)
  {
    case WM_PAINT:
      hdc=BeginPaint(hWnd,&ps);

      MoveToEx(hdc,0,0,NULL);
      LineTo(hdc,639,429);
      MoveToEx(hdc,300,0,NULL);
      LineTo(hdc,50,300);

      TextOut(hdc,120,30,"<- a few lines ->",17);

      ValidateRect(hWnd,NULL);
      EndPaint(hWnd,&ps);
      break;
    case WM_DESTROY:
      PostQuitMessage(0);
      break;
    default:
```

```
        return(DefWindowProc(hWnd,messg,wParam,lParam));
        break;
    }
    return(0);
}
```

Recall, from earlier discussions, that the bulk of this code is required to define and register a window. The code that draws two lines and text in the client area is small in comparison.

```
MoveToEx(hdc,0,0,NULL);
LineTo(hdc,639,429);
MoveToEx(hdc,300,0,NULL);
LineTo(hdc,50,300);

TextOut(hdc,120,30,"<- a few lines ->",17);
```

It is at this location in the application's code that you can experiment with a wide variety of Windows GDI graphics drawing functions, which are called drawing primitives.

Compile and link your application by using the compiler's Build menu. You can choose the Build, Rebuild All, or Execute menu items. The Build menu item builds just the current file. The Rebuild All menu item rebuilds all project files (there is only one in this project). The Execute menu item attempts to run the application. When it finds no executable file, it will prompt you for permission to build and execute the application.

If everything goes okay during the build process, you'll end up with several additional files in your subdirectory. The executable file will be in the Debug subdirectory, specified as a project default.

Figure 21-8 shows the application's window. This application draws two diagonal lines on the screen and prints a short text message.

You can experiment with other GDI graphics primitives such as ellipses, chords, pie wedges, and rectangles. Let's see how these GDI primitives work.

Drawing an Ellipse

The Ellipse( ) function is used for drawing an ellipse or a circle. The center of the ellipse is also the center of an imaginary rectangle described by the points *x*1,*y*1 and *x*2,*y*2, as shown in Figure 21-9.

An ellipse is a closed figure. An ellipse is filled with the current brush. The handle for the device context is given by **hdc**. All other parameters are of type **int**. This function returns a type BOOL.

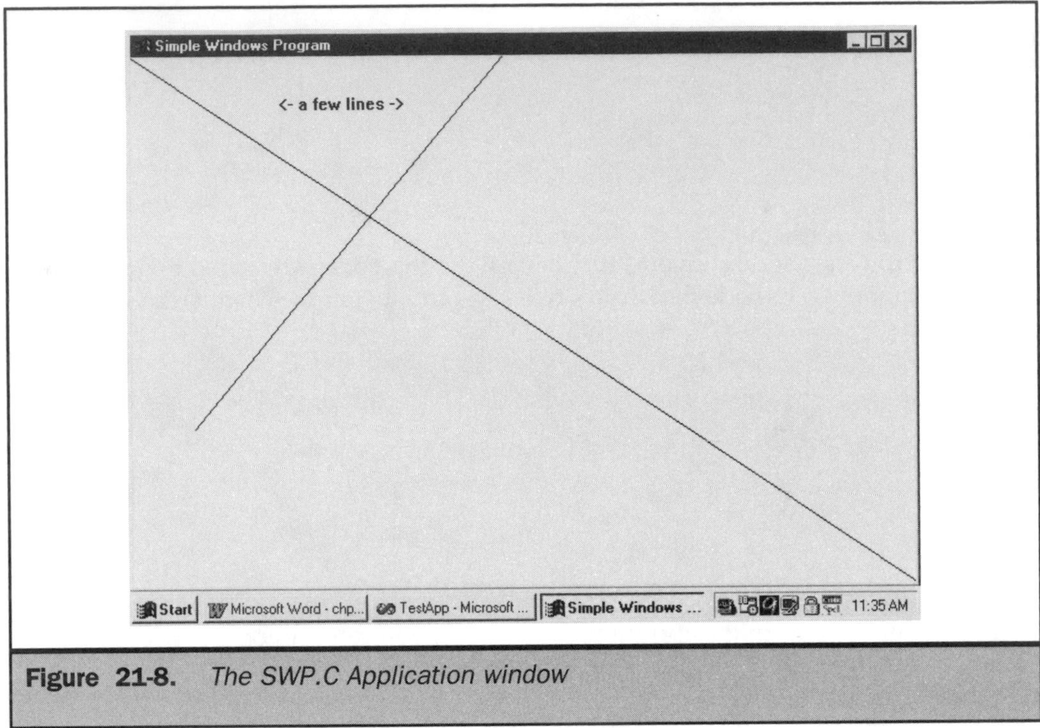

Figure 21-8. *The SWP.C Application window*

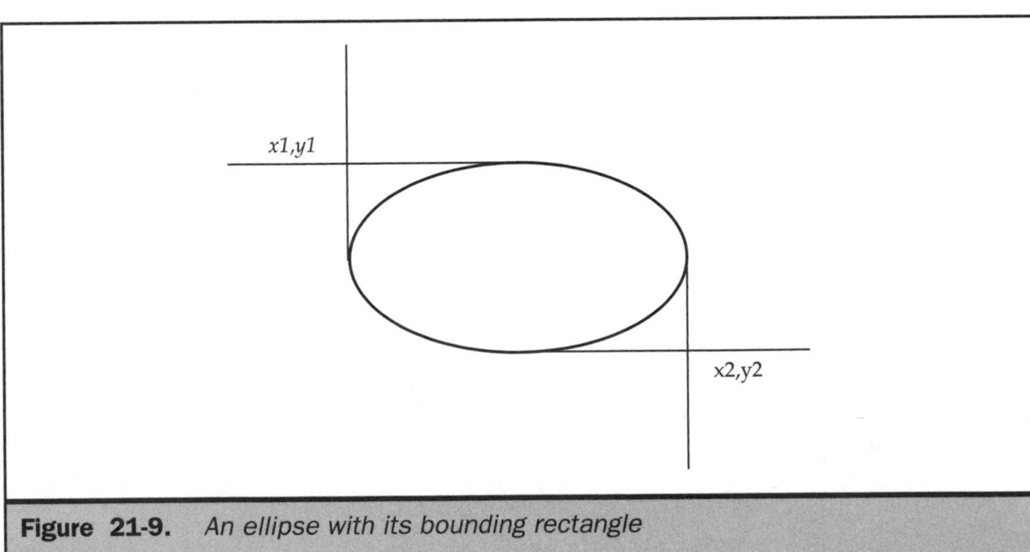

Figure 21-9. *An ellipse with its bounding rectangle*

The syntax for the command is

```
Ellipse(hdc,x1,y1,x2,y2)
```

For example, the following code draws a small ellipse in the user's window:

```
Ellipse(hdc,200,200,275,250);
TextOut(hdc,210,215,"<- an ellipse",13);
```

Figure 21-10 shows how the ellipse will appear on the screen.

Drawing a Chord

The Chord( ) function is a closed figure with a line between two arc points, *x3,y3* and *x4,y4*. Figure 21-11 shows these points. A chord is filled with the current brush.

The handle for the device context is given by **hdc**. All other parameters are of type **int**. This function returns a type BOOL.

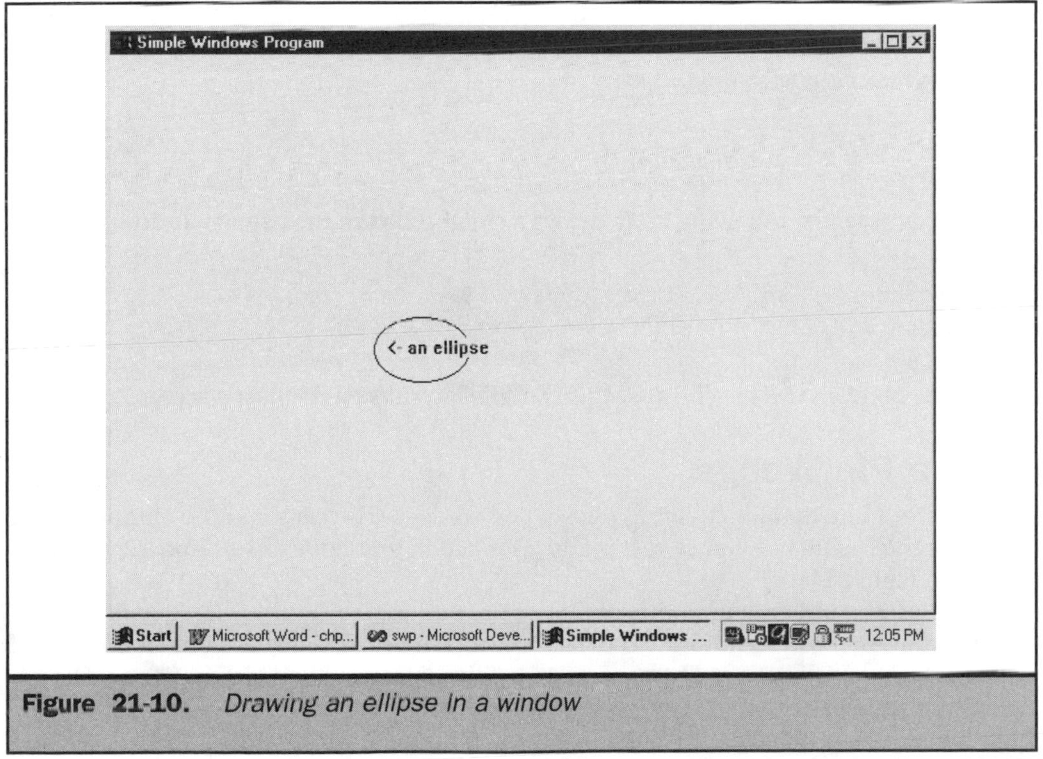

Figure 21-10. *Drawing an ellipse in a window*

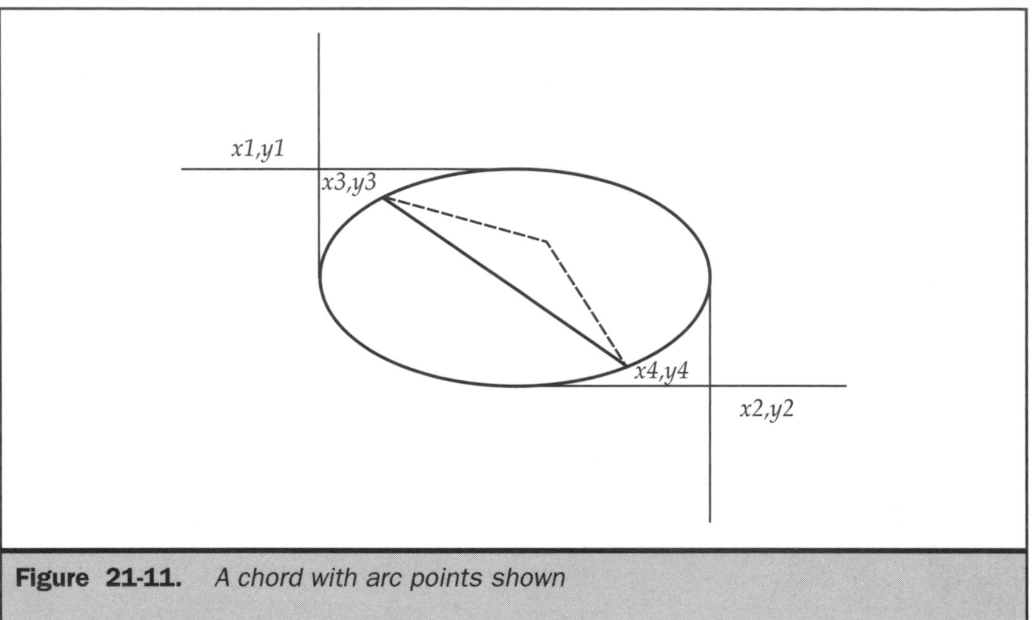

Figure 21-11. *A chord with arc points shown*

The syntax for the command is

```
Chord(hdc,x1,y1,x2,y2,x3,y3,x4,y4)
```

For example, the following code draws a small chord in the user's window:

```
Chord(hdc,550,20,630,80,555,25,625,70);
TextOut(hdc,470,30," A Chord ->",11);
```

Figure 21-12 shows the chord section and its location on the user's screen.

Drawing a Pie Wedge

Use the Pie( ) function for drawing pie-shaped wedges. The center of the elliptical arc is also the center of an imaginary rectangle described by the points *x1,y1* and *x2,y2*, as shown in Figure 21-13.

The starting and ending points of the arc are points *x3,y3* and *x4,y4*. Two lines are drawn from each endpoint to the center of the rectangle. Drawing is done in a counterclockwise direction. The pie wedge is filled because it is a closed figure. The handle for the device context is given by **hdc**. All other parameters are of type **int**. This function returns a type BOOL.

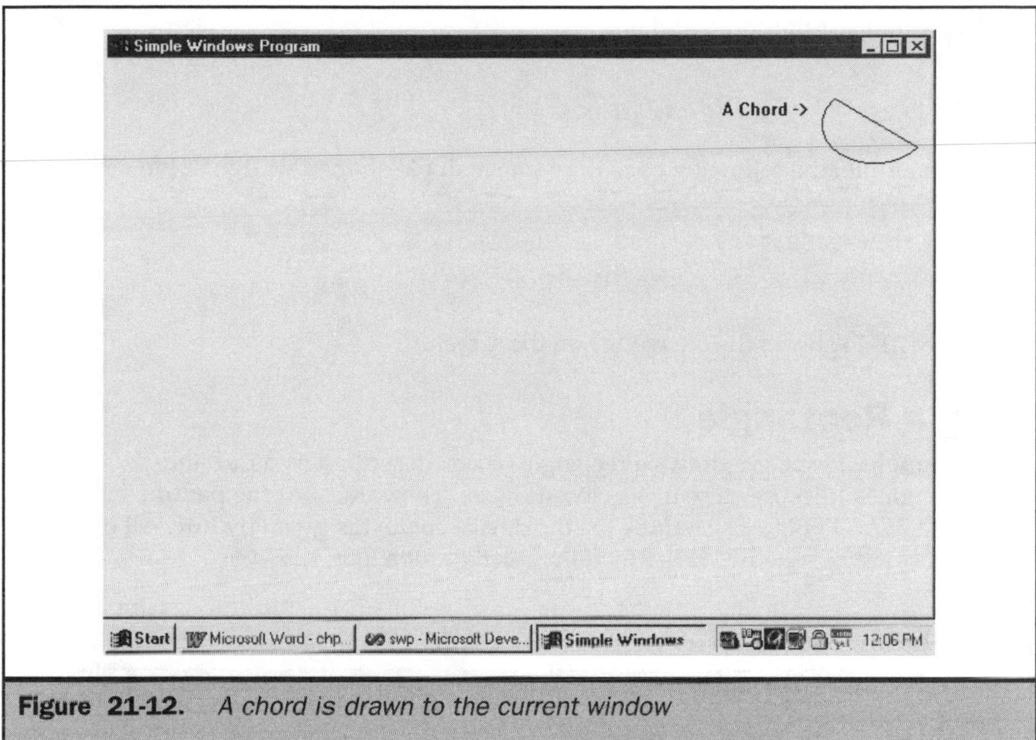

Figure 21-12. *A chord is drawn to the current window*

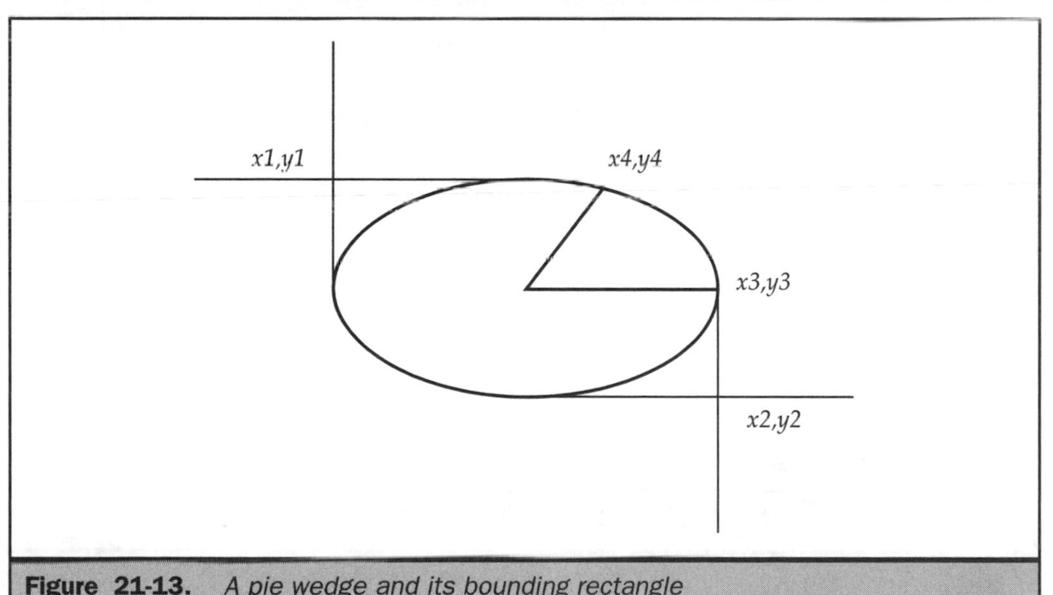

Figure 21-13. *A pie wedge and its bounding rectangle*

The syntax for the command is

```
Pie(hdc,x1,y1,x2,y2,x3,y3,x4,y4)
```

For example, the following code draws a small pie-shaped wedge in the window:

```
Pie(hdc,300,50,400,150,300,50,300,100);
TextOut(hdc,350,80,"<- A Pie Wedge",14);
```

Figure 21-14 shows the pie wedge on the screen.

Drawing a Rectangle

The Rectangle( ) function draws a rectangle or box described by *x1*,*y1* and *x2*,*y2*. Again, the rectangle is filled because it is a closed figure. The values for the parameters cannot exceed 32,767 (7FFFH). The handle for the device context is given by **hdc**. All other parameters are of type **int**. This function returns a type BOOL.

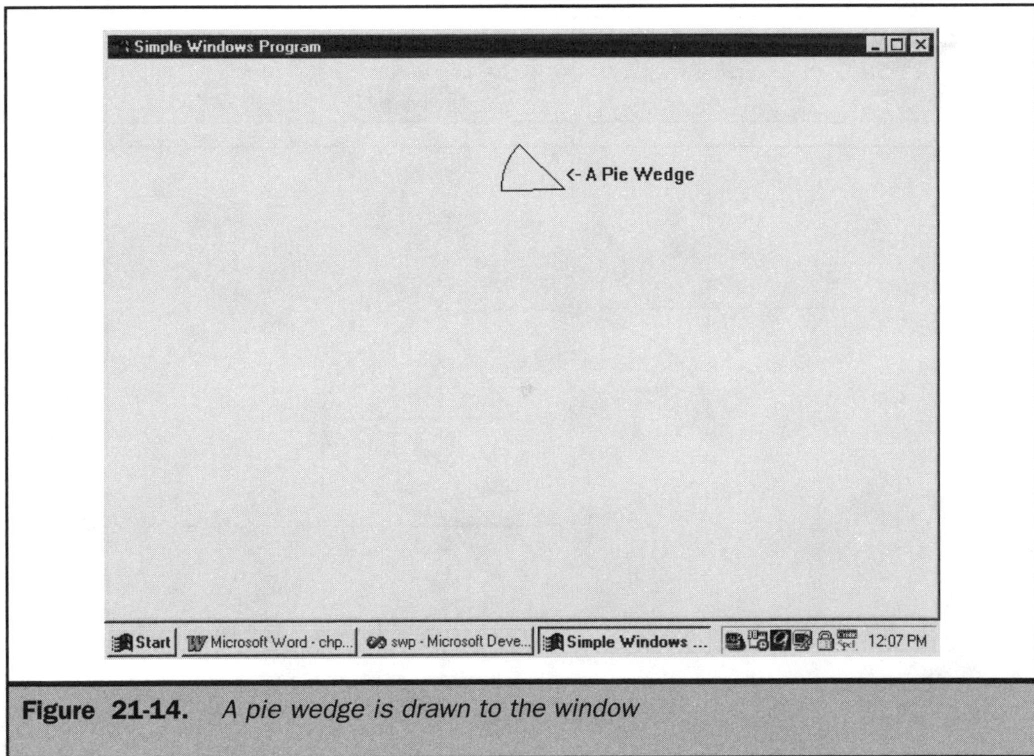

Figure 21-14. *A pie wedge is drawn to the window*

The syntax for the command is

```
Rectangle(hdc,x1,y1,x2,y2)
```

As an example, the following code draws a rectangular figure in the user's window:

```
Rectangle(hdc,50,300,150,400);
TextOut(hdc,160,350,"<- A Rectangle",14);
```

Figure 21-15 shows the rectangle produced on the screen.

Using SWP.C as a Template

The previous section described the development of a simple application. That application can now serve as a template that will allow you to experiment with additional Windows functions. This template serves as the basis of many simple

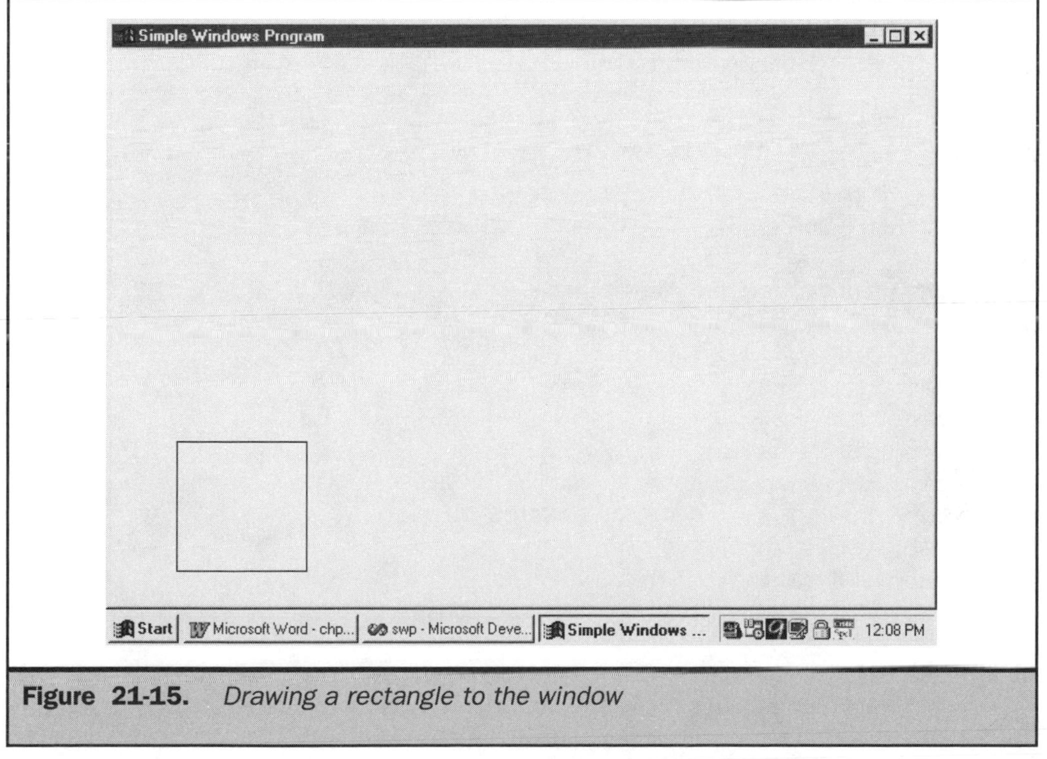

Figure 21-15. *Drawing a rectangle to the window*

applications requiring only minor changes in coding. The next example illustrates how you can use the template to design a simple application that will draw a sine wave in the client area of a window.

Here is the SWP.C code modified to become the SINE.C application.

```
/*
* Sine.c
* An application that draws a sine wave.
* Developed using swp.c as a template.
* Copyright (c) William H. Murray and Chris H. Pappas, 1998
*/

#include <windows.h>
#include <math.h>

#define pi 3.14159265359

LRESULT CALLBACK WndProc(HWND,UINT,WPARAM,LPARAM);

char szProgName[]="ProgName";

int WINAPI WinMain(HINSTANCE hInst,HINSTANCE hPreInst,
                   LPSTR lpszCmdLine,int nCmdShow)
{
  HWND hWnd;
  MSG  lpMsg;
  WNDCLASS wcApp;

  wcApp.lpszClassName=szProgName;
  wcApp.hInstance    =hInst;
  wcApp.lpfnWndProc  =WndProc;
  wcApp.hCursor      =LoadCursor(NULL,IDC_ARROW);
  wcApp.hIcon        =NULL;
  wcApp.lpszMenuName =NULL;
  wcApp.hbrBackground=GetStockObject(WHITE_BRUSH);
  wcApp.style        =CS_HREDRAW|CS_VREDRAW;
  wcApp.cbClsExtra   =0;
  wcApp.cbWndExtra   =0;
  if (!RegisterClass (&wcApp))
    return 0;

  hWnd=CreateWindow(szProgName,"A Sine Wave",
```

```
                    WS_OVERLAPPEDWINDOW,CW_USEDEFAULT,
                    CW_USEDEFAULT,CW_USEDEFAULT,
                    CW_USEDEFAULT,(HWND)NULL,(HMENU)NULL,
                    (HANDLE)hInst,(LPSTR)NULL);
  ShowWindow(hWnd,nCmdShow);
  UpdateWindow(hWnd);
  while (GetMessage(&lpMsg,0,0,0)) {
    TranslateMessage(&lpMsg);
    DispatchMessage(&lpMsg);
  }
  return(lpMsg.wParam);
}

LRESULT CALLBACK WndProc(HWND hWnd,UINT messg,
                         WPARAM wParam,LPARAM lParam)
{
  HDC hdc;
  PAINTSTRUCT ps;

double y;
int i;

  switch (messg)
  {
    case WM_PAINT:
      hdc=BeginPaint(hWnd,&ps);

/* draw the x & y coordinate axes */
MoveToEx(hdc,100,50,NULL);
LineTo(hdc,100,350);
MoveToEx(hdc,100,200,NULL);
LineTo(hdc,500,200);
MoveToEx(hdc,100,200,NULL);

/* draw the sine wave */
for (i=0;i<400;i++) {
  y=120.0*sin(pi*i*(360.0/400.0)/180.0);
  LineTo(hdc,i+100,(int) (200.0-y));
}

      ValidateRect(hWnd,NULL);
```

```
      EndPaint(hWnd,&ps);
      break;
    case WM_DESTROY:
      PostQuitMessage(0);
      break;
    default:
      return(DefWindowProc(hWnd,messg,wParam,lParam));
      break;
  }
  return(0);
}
```

In addition to the SINE.C file just shown, you will need a project file in order to compile and link the application within the integrated environment.

Examine the C source code and compare it with the previous SWP.C application. As you can see, this application makes only minor changes to the SWP.C template of the previous section.

Notice that new variables are declared in WndProc( ):

```
double y;
int i;
```

The actual sine wave plotting takes place under WM_PAINT. The coordinate axes are drawn with several calls to the MoveToEx( ) and LineTo( ) functions:

```
/* draw the x & y coordinate axes */
MoveToEx(hdc,100,50,NULL);
LineTo(hdc,100,350);
MoveToEx(hdc,100,200,NULL);
LineTo(hdc,500,200);
MoveToEx(hdc,100,200,NULL);
```

The sine wave is drawn and scaled in one operation. In this application, the waveform will extend 120 pixels above and below the horizontal axis. The sin( ) function from MATH.H is used to generate the sine values. The use of the constant **PI** is needed to convert angles from degrees to radians.

```
/* draw the sine wave */
for (i=0;i<400;i++) {
```

```
    y=120.0*sin(pi*i*(360.0/400.0)/180.0);
    LineTo(hdc,i+100,(int)(200.0-y));
}
```

Since this application was designed to work in the default drawing mode, the program draws directly in screen pixels. On a VGA monitor, the figure will fill the entire screen. Figure 21-16 shows the output of the program on a VGA screen. If a high-resolution monitor operating in 1024 × 768 graphics mode is used, the figure will be drawn in the upper-left corner of the monitor. Changes in figure size such as this are usually considered undesirable, and you'll see a technique for avoiding these variations in the PIE.C example that follows.

Creating a Pie Chart Application

A pie chart is a useful business application that also allows you to incorporate many of the resources studied in the last chapter into a presentation-quality program. This particular pie chart will use a menu, an About dialog box, and a data entry dialog box

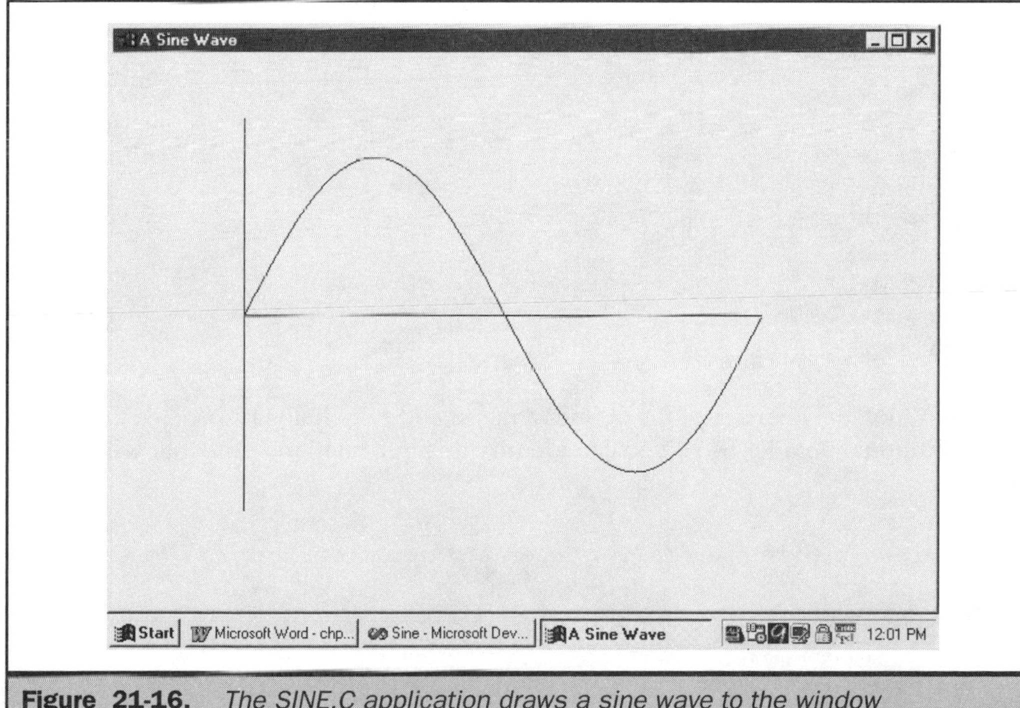

Figure 21-16. *The SINE.C application draws a sine wave to the window*

for user input. All three items, you might recall, were designed in the previous chapter. The data entry dialog box will prompt the user to enter up to ten numbers that define the size of each pie wedge. These integer numbers are then scaled in order to make each pie slice proportional in the 360-degree pie chart. Slices are colored in a sequential manner. The sequence is defined by the programmer and contained in the global array lColor[]. The program also allows the user to enter a title for the pie chart, which is centered below the pie figure. You may wish to continue the development of this example by adding a legend, label, or value for each pie slice.

Before compiling and linking, you will need to enter four separate files: PIE.H, PIE.RC, PIE.C, and PIE.CUR. The cursor was created with the resource editor, too.

Start this project by creating a new project file named PIE.DSP. If you are entering the code from the following listings, you will simply open several empty text files with the Project | Add | Files… menu selection, and name them appropriately.

Here is the PIE.H header file containing unique identification numbers for menu, dialog, and other resource items:

```
#define IDM_ABOUT     10
#define IDM_INPUT     20
#define IDM_EXIT      30

#define DM_TITLE     160
#define DM_P1        161
#define DM_P2        162
#define DM_P3        163
#define DM_P4        164
#define DM_P5        165
#define DM_P6        166
#define DM_P7        167
#define DM_P8        168
#define DM_P9        169
#define DM_P10       170
```

The PIE.RC resource script file defines a menu and two dialog boxes (See Chapter 20 for additional details). See if you can identify this information in the following listing:

```
//Microsoft Developer Studio generated resource script.
//
#include "resource.h"

#define APSTUDIO_READONLY_SYMBOLS
/////////////////////////////////////////////////////////////////
```

```
//
// Generated from the TEXTINCLUDE 2 resource.
//
#include "pie.h"
#define APSTUDIO_HIDDEN_SYMBOLS
#include "windows.h"
#undef APSTUDIO_HIDDEN_SYMBOLS

/////////////////////////////////////////////////////////////
#undef APSTUDIO_READONLY_SYMBOLS

/////////////////////////////////////////////////////////////
// English (U.S.) resources

#if !defined(AFX_RESOURCE_DLL) || defined(AFX_TARG_ENU)
#ifdef _WIN32
LANGUAGE LANG_ENGLISH, SUBLANG_ENGLISH_US
#pragma code_page(1252)
#endif //_WIN32

/////////////////////////////////////////////////////////////
//
// Cursor
//

PIECURSOR CURSOR DISCARDABLE "pie.cur"

/////////////////////////////////////////////////////////////
//
// Menu
//

PIEMENU MENU DISCARDABLE
BEGIN
  POPUP "Pie_Chart_Data"
  BEGIN
    MENUITEM "About...", IDM_ABOUT
    MENUITEM "Input...", IDM_INPUT
    MENUITEM "Exit",     IDM_EXIT
  END
END
```

WINDOWS PROGRAMMING FOUNDATIONS

```
/////////////////////////////////////////////////////////////////////////////
//
// Dialog
//

ABOUTDLGBOX DIALOG DISCARDABLE  50, 300, 180, 84
STYLE DS_MODALFRAME|WS_POPUP|WS_VISIBLE|WS_CAPTION|WS_SYSMENU
CAPTION "About"
FONT 8, "MS Sans Serif"
BEGIN
  CTEXT "Microsoft C Pie Chart Program",-1,3,29,176,10
  CTEXT "by William H. Murray and Chris H. Pappas",-1,3,16,
        176,10
  PUSHBUTTON "OK",IDOK,74,51,32,14
END

PIEDLGBOX DIALOG DISCARDABLE  93, 37, 195, 159
STYLE DS_MODALFRAME|WS_POPUP|WS_VISIBLE|WS_CAPTION|WS_SYSMENU
CAPTION "Pie Chart Data"
FONT 8, "MS Sans Serif"
BEGIN
  GROUPBOX "Chart Title:",100,5,3,182,30,WS_TABSTOP
  GROUPBOX "Pie Wedge Sizes:",101,3,34,187,95,WS_TABSTOP
  LTEXT "Title: ",-1,10,21,30,8
  EDITTEXT DM_TITLE,40,18,140,12
  LTEXT "Wedge #1: ",-1,10,50,40,8,NOT WS_GROUP
  LTEXT "Wedge #2: ",-1,10,65,40,8,NOT WS_GROUP
  LTEXT "Wedge #3: ",-1,10,80,40,8,NOT WS_GROUP
  LTEXT "Wedge #4: ",-1,10,95,40,8,NOT WS_GROUP
  LTEXT "Wedge #5: ",-1,10,110,40,8,NOT WS_GROUP
  LTEXT "Wedge #6: ",-1,106,50,40,8,NOT WS_GROUP
  LTEXT "Wedge #7: ",-1,106,65,40,8,NOT WS_GROUP
  LTEXT "Wedge #8: ",-1,106,80,40,8,NOT WS_GROUP
  LTEXT "Wedge #9: ",-1,106,95,40,8,NOT WS_GROUP
  LTEXT "Wedge #10:",-1,102,110,45,8,NOT WS_GROUP
  EDITTEXT DM_P1,55,45,30,12
  EDITTEXT DM_P2,55,60,30,12
  EDITTEXT DM_P3,55,75,30,12
  EDITTEXT DM_P4,55,90,30,12
  EDITTEXT DM_P5,55,105,30,12
  EDITTEXT DM_P6,150,44,30,12
```

```
  EDITTEXT DM_P7,150,61,30,12
  EDITTEXT DM_P8,150,76,30,12
  EDITTEXT DM_P9,149,91,30,12
  EDITTEXT DM_P10,149,106,30,12
  PUSHBUTTON "OK",IDOK,39,135,24,14
  PUSHBUTTON "Cancel",IDCANCEL,122,136,34,14
END

#ifdef APSTUDIO_INVOKED
//////////////////////////////////////////////////////////////
//
// TEXTINCLUDE
//

1 TEXTINCLUDE DISCARDABLE
BEGIN
  "resource.h\0"
END

2 TEXTINCLUDE DISCARDABLE
BEGIN
  "#include ""pie.h""\r\n"
  "#define APSTUDIO_HIDDEN_SYMBOLS\r\n"
  "#include ""windows.h""\r\n"
  "#undef APSTUDIO_HIDDEN_SYMBOLS\r\n"
  "\0"
END

3 TEXTINCLUDE DISCARDABLE
BEGIN
  "\r\n"
  "\0"
END

#endif    // APSTUDIO_INVOKED

#endif    // English (U.S.) resources
//////////////////////////////////////////////////////////////


#ifndef APSTUDIO_INVOKED
```

```
////////////////////////////////////////////////////////////
//
// Generated from the TEXTINCLUDE 3 resource.
//

////////////////////////////////////////////////////////////
#endif    // not APSTUDIO_INVOKED
```

Remember that the PIE.RC file is simply the text file equivalent to the menu and dialog boxes that were developed by the resource editors and discussed in the previous chapter.

The PIE.C source code is the last listing in this group of files. The length of this file has grown when compared to previous source code files because of the dialog box procedures. However, as you study the listing, you should still be able to locate elements of the SWP.C template.

```
/*
*   PIE.C
*   A Pie Chart Application with Resources
*   Copyright (c) William H. Murray and Chris H. Pappas, 1998
*/

#include <windows.h>
#include <string.h>
#include <math.h>
#include "pie.h"

#define radius      180
#define maxnumwedge 10
#define pi          3.14159265359

LRESULT CALLBACK WndProc(HWND,UINT,WPARAM,LPARAM);
BOOL CALLBACK AboutDlgProc(HWND,UINT,WPARAM,LPARAM);
BOOL CALLBACK PieDlgProc(HWND,UINT,WPARAM,LPARAM);

char szProgName[]="ProgName";
char szApplName[]="PieMenu";
char szCursorName[]="PieCursor";

char szTString[80]="(pie chart title area)";
```

```
unsigned int iWedgesize[maxnumwedge]={5,20,10,15};
long lColor[maxnumwedge]={0x0L,0xFFL,0xFF00L,0xFFFFL,0xFF0000L,
                          0xFF00FFL,0xFFFF00L,0xFFFFFFL,
                          0x8080L,0x808080L};

int WINAPI WinMain(HINSTANCE hInst,HINSTANCE hPreInst,
                   LPSTR lpszCmdLine,int nCmdShow)
{
  HWND hWnd;
  MSG  lpMsg;
  WNDCLASS wcApp;

  wcApp.lpszClassName=szProgName;
  wcApp.hInstance    =hInst;
  wcApp.lpfnWndProc  =WndProc;
  wcApp.hCursor      =LoadCursor(hInst,szCursorName);
  wcApp.hIcon        =LoadIcon(hInst,szProgName);
  wcApp.lpszMenuName =szApplName;
  wcApp.hbrBackground=GetStockObject(WHITE_BRUSH);
  wcApp.style        =CS_HREDRAW|CS_VREDRAW;
  wcApp.cbClsExtra   =0;
  wcApp.cbWndExtra   =0;
  if (!RegisterClass (&wcApp))
    return 0;

  hWnd=CreateWindow(szProgName,"Pie Chart Application",
                    WS_OVERLAPPEDWINDOW,CW_USEDEFAULT,
                    CW_USEDEFAULT,CW_USEDEFAULT,
                    CW_USEDEFAULT,(HWND)NULL,(HMENU)NULL,
                    (HANDLE)hInst,(LPSTR)NULL);
  ShowWindow(hWnd,nCmdShow);
  UpdateWindow(hWnd);
  while (GetMessage(&lpMsg,0,0,0))
  {
    TranslateMessage(&lpMsg);
    DispatchMessage(&lpMsg);
  }
  return(lpMsg.wParam);
}

BOOL CALLBACK AboutDlgProc(HWND hdlg,UINT messg,
```

```
                                    WPARAM wParam,LPARAM lParam)
{
  switch (messg)
  {
    case WM_INITDIALOG:
      break;
    case WM_COMMAND:
      switch (wParam)
      {
        case IDOK:
          EndDialog(hdlg,TRUE);
          break;
        default:
          return FALSE;
      }
      break;
    default:
      return FALSE;
  }
  return TRUE;
}

BOOL CALLBACK PieDlgProc(HWND hdlg,UINT messg,
                         WPARAM wParam,LPARAM lParam)
{
  switch (messg)
  {
    case WM_INITDIALOG:
      return FALSE;
    case WM_COMMAND:
      switch (wParam)
      {
        case IDOK:
          GetDlgItemText(hdlg,DM_TITLE,szTString,80);
          iWedgesize[0]=GetDlgItemInt(hdlg,DM_P1,NULL,0);
          iWedgesize[1]=GetDlgItemInt(hdlg,DM_P2,NULL,0);
          iWedgesize[2]=GetDlgItemInt(hdlg,DM_P3,NULL,0);
          iWedgesize[3]=GetDlgItemInt(hdlg,DM_P4,NULL,0);
          iWedgesize[4]=GetDlgItemInt(hdlg,DM_P5,NULL,0);
          iWedgesize[5]=GetDlgItemInt(hdlg,DM_P6,NULL,0);
          iWedgesize[6]=GetDlgItemInt(hdlg,DM_P7,NULL,0);
```

```
            iWedgesize[7]=GetDlgItemInt(hdlg,DM_P8,NULL,0);
            iWedgesize[8]=GetDlgItemInt(hdlg,DM_P9,NULL,0);
            iWedgesize[9]=GetDlgItemInt(hdlg,DM_P10,NULL,0);
            EndDialog(hdlg,TRUE);
            break;
          case IDCANCEL:
            EndDialog(hdlg,FALSE);
            break;
          default:
            return FALSE;
        }
        break;
      default:
        return FALSE;
    }
    return TRUE;
}

LRESULT CALLBACK WndProc(HWND hWnd,UINT messg,
                         WPARAM wParam,LPARAM lParam)
{
  HDC hdc;
  PAINTSTRUCT ps;
  HBRUSH hBrush;
  static FARPROC lpfnAboutDlgProc;
  static FARPROC lpfnPieDlgProc;
  static HWND hInst1,hInst2;
  static int xClientView,yClientView;

  unsigned int iTotalWedge[maxnumwedge+1];
  int i,iNWedges;

  iNWedges=0;
  for (i=0;i<maxnumwedge;i++) {
    if(iWedgesize[i]!=0) iNWedges++;
  }

  iTotalWedge[0]=0;

  for (i=0;i<iNWedges;i++)
    iTotalWedge[i+1]=iTotalWedge[i]+iWedgesize[i];
```

```
switch (messg)
{
  case WM_SIZE:
    xClientView=LOWORD(lParam);
    yClientView=HIWORD(lParam);
    break;
  case WM_CREATE:
    hInst1=((LPCREATESTRUCT) lParam)->hInstance;
    hInst2=((LPCREATESTRUCT) lParam)->hInstance;
    lpfnAboutDlgProc=MakeProcInstance(AboutDlgProc,
                                      hInst1);
    lpfnPieDlgProc=MakeProcInstance(PieDlgProc,hInst2);
    break;
  case WM_COMMAND:
    switch (wParam)
    {
      case IDM_ABOUT:
        DialogBox(hInst1,"AboutDlgBox",hWnd,
                  lpfnAboutDlgProc);
        break;
      case IDM_INPUT:
        DialogBox(hInst2,"PieDlgBox",
                  hWnd,lpfnPieDlgProc);
        InvalidateRect(hWnd,NULL,TRUE);
        UpdateWindow(hWnd);
        break;
      case IDM_EXIT:
        SendMessage(hWnd,WM_CLOSE,0,0L);
        break;
      default:
        break;
    }
    break;
  case WM_PAINT:
    hdc=BeginPaint(hWnd,&ps);

    SetMapMode(hdc,MM_ISOTROPIC);
    SetWindowExtEx(hdc,500,500,NULL);
    SetViewportExtEx(hdc,xClientView,-yClientView,NULL);
    SetViewportOrgEx(hdc,xClientView/2,yClientView/2,NULL);
```

```
        if (xClientView > 200)
          TextOut(hdc,strlen(szTString)*(-8/2),
                  240,szTString,strlen(szTString));

        for(i=0;i<iNWedges;i++) {
          hBrush=CreateSolidBrush(lColor[i]);
          SelectObject(hdc,hBrush);
          Pie(hdc,-200,200,200,-200,
             (int)(radius*cos(2*pi*iTotalWedge[i]/
                   iTotalWedge[iNWedges])),
             (int)(radius*sin(2*pi*iTotalWedge[i]/
                   iTotalWedge[iNWedges])),
             (int)(radius*cos(2*pi*iTotalWedge[i+1]/
                   iTotalWedge[iNWedges])),
             (int)(radius*sin(2*pi*iTotalWedge[i+1]/
                   iTotalWedge[iNWedges])));
        }


        ValidateRect(hWnd,NULL);
        EndPaint(hWnd,&ps);
        break;
      case WM_DESTROY:
        PostQuitMessage(0);
        break;
      default:
        return(DefWindowProc(hWnd,messg,wParam,lParam));
    }
    return(0);
}
```

In the next sections, we'll look at the important components that make up the complete pie project.

The Project File

Use the Project utility from within the integrated environment to build a project file for this application. Include the PIE.C and PIE.RC files in the project's file list.

The PIE.H Header File

The header file PIE.H contains identification information for various menu and dialog items. Additionally, note the ten unique identification numbers, which represent the ten values for wedge sizes. The user eventually enters these values.

The PIE.RC Resource File

The resource file PIE.RC contains information in script form for the pointer (PieCursor), menu (PieMenu), and two dialog boxes (AboutDlgBox and PieDlgBox). Figure 21-17 shows the About box and Figure 21-18 shows the data entry dialog box.

The design of both of these dialog boxes was discussed in the previous chapter. The resource editor created this composite resource script file as each resource was added to the project. When using the resource editor to add dialog boxes, you must have a fairly clear idea of how you want to represent various data fields and so on before starting the design. The control values are used to determine the position, size, and so on of dialog box items. The resource editor calculates these values. If you are entering

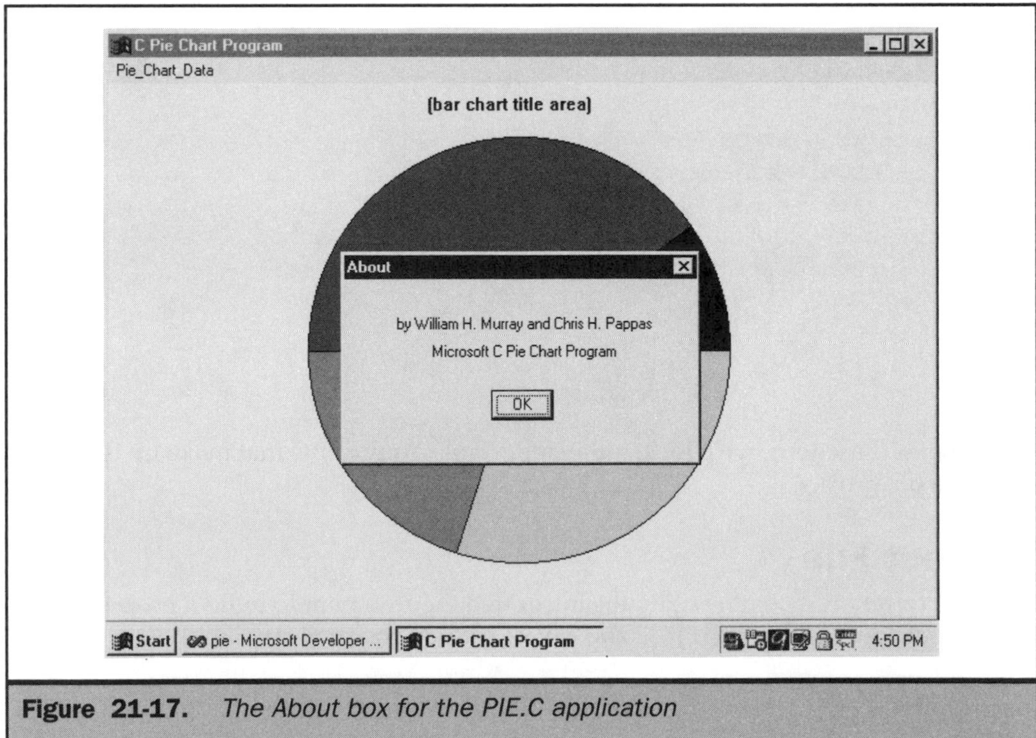

Figure 21-17. *The About box for the PIE.C application*

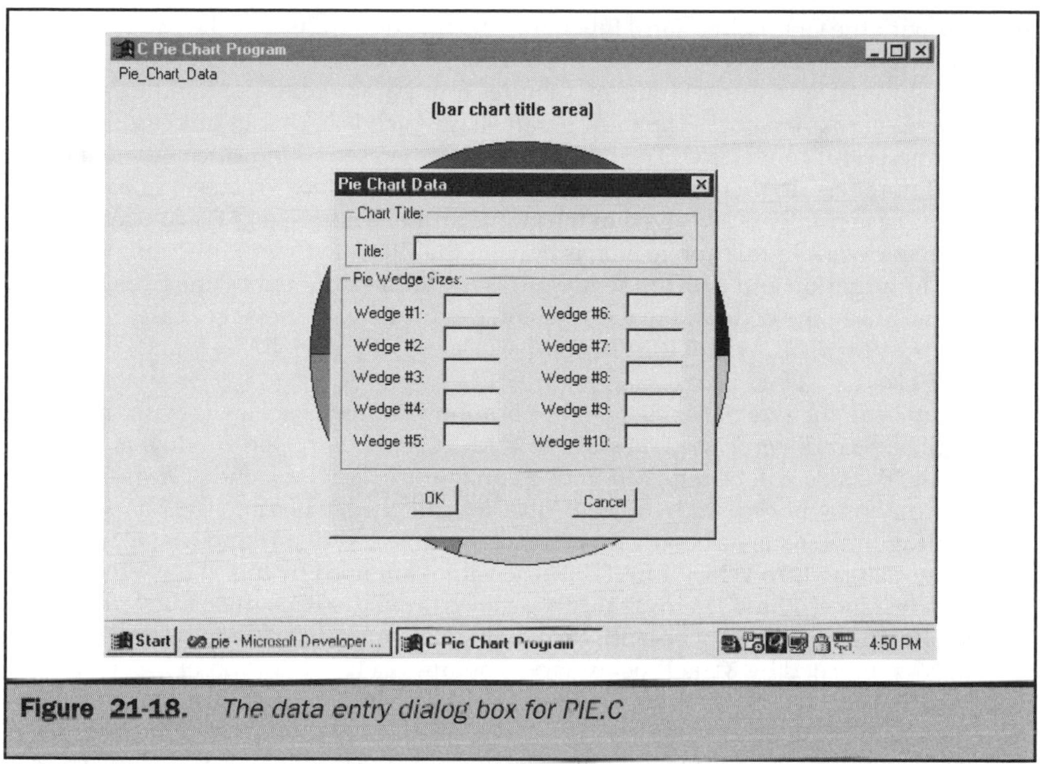

Figure 21-18. *The data entry dialog box for PIE.C*

this program, it will be easiest for you just to type this resource file as it appears in the listing.

The PIE.C Source Code

The C source code for PIE.C allows the user to develop a pie chart with as many as ten slices. An application will allow the user to input the data on pie-slice sizes directly to a dialog box. In addition to data on pie sizes, the user may enter the title of the pie chart. Don't let the size of this code listing scare you; much of the code you see is an extension of the SWP.C template code developed in the first example of this chapter. It would be a good idea to compare the SWP.C and PIE.C code at this time and discover the exact differences in the listings. This example concentrates on the new concepts for the application by extracting each important feature from the listing.

Dialog box information is processed with the **case** IDOK statement under the PieDlgProc. When the user selects the data entry item (a dialog box) from the program's menu, they will be allowed to enter a pie chart title and the data for up to ten pie slices. This data is accepted when the user selects the OK push button. The title is returned as a text string with the GetDlgItemText( ) function. Numeric information is returned with the GetDlgItemInt( ) function. This function translates the "numeric" string information entered by the user into an integer that can be a **signed** or **unsigned** number. The GetDlgItemInt( ) function requires four parameters. The handle and ID number are self-explanatory. The third parameter, which is NULL in this case, is used to flag a successful conversion. The fourth parameter is used to indicate **signed** and **unsigned** numbers. In this case, a zero states that the dialog box is returning **unsigned** numbers. These numbers are saved in the global array iWedgesize[ ] for future use.

The major work in this application is done in the WindowProc( ) function. Various pieces of information and data are sent as messages and examined by the five **case** statements. Study the code and make sure you can find these "message" **case** statements: WM_SIZE, WM_CREATE, WM_COMMAND, WM_PAINT, and WM_DESTROY.

Determining the size of the client or application window is achieved with the help of WM_SIZE. Windows sends a message to WM_SIZE any time the window is resized. In this case, the size will be returned in two variables, *xClientView* and *yClientView*. This information will be used by WM_PAINT to scale the pie chart to the window.

The program's instance handle is obtained and saved as hInst1 and hInst2 when processing messages to WM_CREATE. These values are used by the MakeProcInstance( ) function to create an instance thunk for each dialog box procedure or function. This is necessary because each dialog box procedure is a **far** procedure. The address returned by MakeProcInstance( ) points to a fixed portion of memory called the instance thunk. Two are required in this case because two dialog box procedures are being used.

Dialog boxes can be opened with messages sent to WM_COMMAND. Notice that WM_COMMAND contains three **case** statements. IDM_ABOUT is the ID for the About Box procedure, while IDM_INPUT is the ID for the data entry dialog box. IDM_EXIT allows a graceful exit from the application.

The routines for actually drawing the pie wedges are processed under WM_PAINT.

The mapping mode is changed to MM_ISOTROPIC from MM_TEXT. The **default** mapping mode is MM_TEXT. When in the MM_TEXT mapping mode, drawings are made in "pixel" coordinates with point 0,0 in the upper-left corner of the window. This is why the SINE.C example remained unchanged as the number of pixels changed in the client area.

```
SetMapMode(hdc,MM_ISOTROPIC);
SetWindowExtEx(hdc,500,500,NULL);
SetViewportExtEx(hdc,xClientView,-yClientView,NULL);
SetViewportOrgEx(hdc,xClientView/2,yClientView/2,NULL);
```

Table 21-4 shows additional mapping modes available under Windows.

MM_ISOTROPIC allows you to select the extent of both the x and y axes. The mapping mode is changed by calling the function SetMapMode( ). When the function SetWindowExt( ) is called with both parameters set to 500, the height and width of the

Value	Meaning
MM_ANISOTROPIC	Maps one logical unit to an arbitrary physical unit. The *x* and *y* axes are scaled.
MM_HIENGLISH	Maps one logical unit to 0.001 inch. Positive *y* is up.
MM_HIMETRIC	Maps one logical unit to 0.01 millimeter. Positive *y* is up.
MM_ISOTROPIC	Maps one logical unit to an arbitrary physical unit; *x* and *y* unit lengths are equal.
MM_LOENGLISH	Maps one logical unit to 0.01 inch. Positive *y* points up.
MM_LOMETRIC	Maps one logical unit to 0.1 millimeter. Positive *y* points up.
MM_TEXT	Maps one logical unit to one pixel. Positive *y* points down. This is the **default** mode.
MM_TWIPS	Maps one logical unit to 1/20 of a printer's point. Positive *y* points up.

Table 21-4. *Mapping Modes for Windows Applications*

client or application areas are equal. These are logical sizes that Windows adjusts (scales) to fit the physical display device. The display size values are used by the SetViewportExt( ) function. The negative sign for the *y* coordinate specifies increasing *y* values from the bottom of the screen. It should be no surprise that these are the values previously obtained under WM_SIZE.

For this example, the pie chart will be placed on a traditional *x,y* coordinate system, with the center of the chart at 0,0. The SetViewportOrgEx( ) function is used for this purpose.

The pie chart title is printed to the screen using the coordinates for the current mapping mode. The program centers the title on the screen by estimating the size of the character font and knowing the string length. For really small windows, the title is not printed.

```
if (xClientView > 200)
  TextOut(hdc,strlen(szTString)*(-8/2),
          240,szTString,strlen(szTString));
```

Before actually discussing how the pie wedges are plotted, let's return to the beginning of the WndProc procedure in order to gain an understanding of how the wedges are scaled to fit a complete circle. There are several pieces of code that are very important.

This code determines how many wedges the user has requested:

```
iNWedges=0;
for (i=0;i<maxnumwedge;i++) {
  if(iWedgesize[i]!=0) iNWedges++;
}
```

It is assumed that there is at least one wedge of some physical size, so the array *iWedgesize[ ]* can be scanned for the first zero value. For each nonzero value returned, *iNWedges* will be incremented. Thus, when leaving this routine, *iNWedges* will contain the total number of wedges for this plot.

A progressive total on wedge size values will be returned to the *iTotalWedge[ ]* array. These values will help determine where one pie slice ends and the next begins. For example, if the user entered 5, 10, 7, and 20 for wedge sizes, *iTotalWedge[ ]* would contain the values 0, 5, 15, 22, and 42. Study the following code to make sure you understand how these results are achieved:

```
iTotalWedge[0]=0;
for (i=0;i<iNWedges;i++)
  iTotalWedge[i+1]=iTotalWedge[i]+iWedgesize[i];
```

The values contained in *iTotalWedge[ ]* are needed in order to calculate the beginning and ending angles for each pie wedge. You might recall that the Pie( ) function accepts nine parameters. The first parameter is the handle, and the next four specify the coordinates of the bounding rectangle. In this case, for the mapping mode chosen, they are -200, 200, 200, and -200. The remaining four parameters are used to designate the starting *x,y* pair and the ending *x,y* pair for the pie arc. To calculate *x* values, the cosine function is used, and to calculate *y* values, the sine function is used. For example, the first *x* position is determined by multiplying the radius of the pie by the cosine of *2*pi*iTotalWedge[0]*. The *2*pi* value is needed in the conversion of degrees to radians. The *y* value is found with the sine function in an identical way. Those two values serve as the *x,y* starting coordinates for the first slice. The ending coordinates are found with the same equations, but using the next value in *iTotalWedge[ ]*. In order to scale each of these points to make all slices proportional and fit a 360-degree pie, each coordinate point is divided by the grand total of all individual slices. This total is the last number contained in *iTotalWedge[ ]*. Observe how this calculation is achieved in the next piece of code:

```
for(i=0;i<iNWedges;i++) {
```

```
    hBrush=CreateSolidBrush(lColor[i]);
    SelectObject(hdc,hBrush);
    Pie(hdc,-200,200,200,-200,
        (int)(radius*cos(2*pi*iTotalWedge[i]/
                iTotalWedge[iNWedges])),
        (int)(radius*sin(2*pi*iTotalWedge[i]/
                iTotalWedge[iNWedges])),
        (int)(radius*cos(2*pi*iTotalWedge[i+1]/
                iTotalWedge[iNWedges])),
        (int)(radius*sin(2*pi*iTotalWedge[i+1]/
                iTotalWedge[iNWedges])));
}
```

In order to draw and fill all slices, a loop is used. This loop will index through all *iNWedge* values.

Figure 21-19 shows the default pie chart plot, and Figure 20 shows a unique pie chart application.

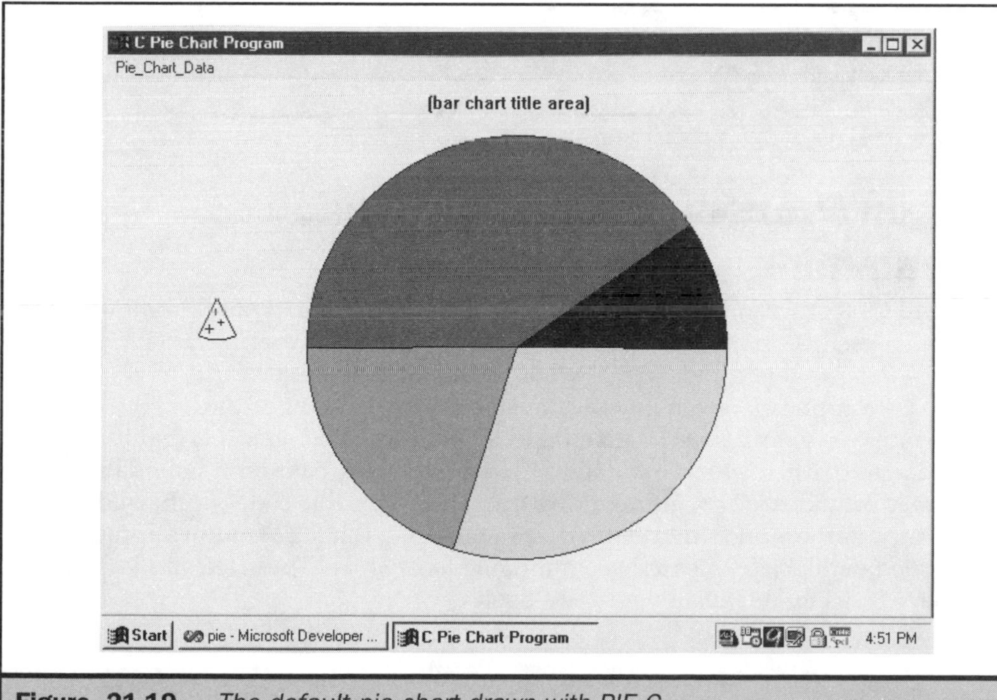

Figure 21-19. *The default pie chart drawn with PIE.C*

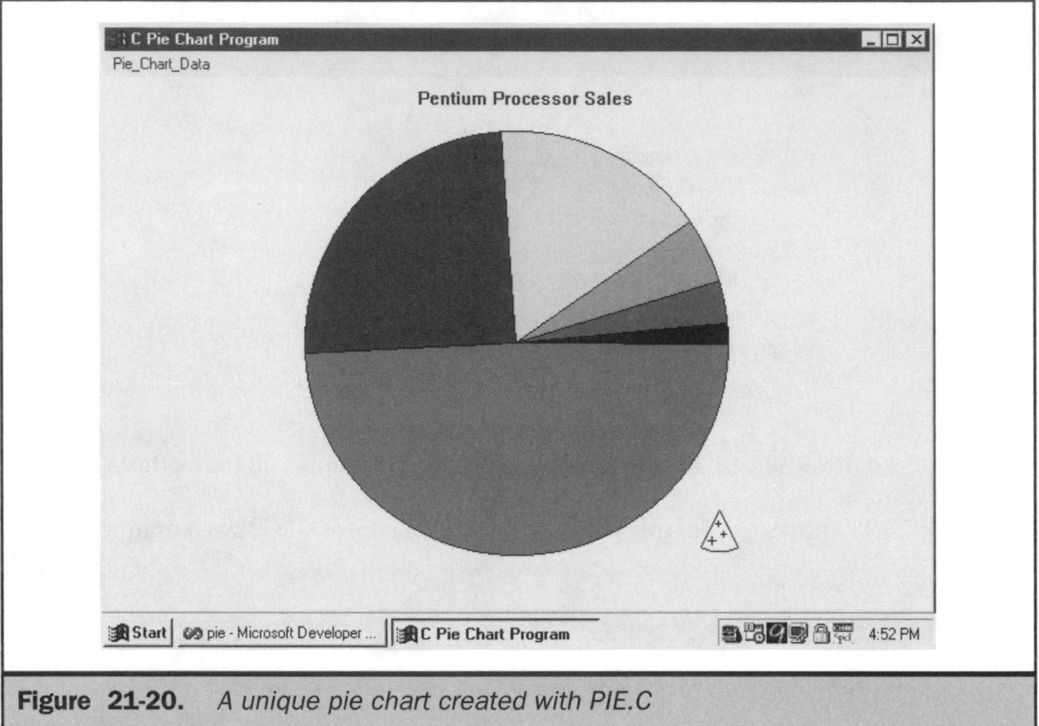

Figure 21-20. *A unique pie chart created with PIE.C*

More on Procedure-oriented Windows Programming

Most C and C++ programmers have used the procedure-oriented programming techniques presented in this chapter when developing Windows applications. You will find code similar to this C code in many books and magazine articles.

While C++ applications can have a similar structure and appearance to the C code in this chapter, they can also take advantage of object-oriented concepts and include the advantages of Microsoft's Foundation Class library. The Microsoft Foundation Class library provides the programmer with access to reusable code—a chief advantage of C++. Many authors and programmers are suggesting that all Windows applications be developed with object-oriented programming techniques. These techniques will be the primary focus in the remainder of this book.

Chapter 22

The Microsoft Foundation Class Library: Fundamentals

In the previous chapter you learned that even the simplest Windows applications, when created with the standard API function calls, are difficult and time consuming to develop. For example, the bare-bones SWP.C template developed in Chapter 21 contains over two pages of C code and Windows function calls. It is also obvious that much of that code can be used repeatedly from application to application. That base code is required just to establish a window on the screen. While Windows applications have been easy to use, procedure-oriented applications have certainly not been a joy to write or maintain.

Microsoft's Visual C++ compiler provides an up-to-date 32-bit Foundation Class library containing a new set of object-oriented programming tools for the exclusive development of 32-bit Windows applications. The Microsoft Foundation Class (MFC) library encapsulates all normal procedure-oriented Windows functions and provides support for control bars, property sheets, OLEO, ActiveX controls, and more. In addition, database support is provided for a wide range of database sources, including DAO and ODBC. You'll also find that the MFC supports the development of Internet applications in C++.

This chapter discusses the advantages of using the Microsoft Foundation Class library for Windows code development. The MFC library will make Windows application development easier. Also examined in this chapter are MFC terms, definitions, and techniques that are common across all MFC versions. The material you learn in this chapter can be applied to all of the MFC application code developed in the remaining chapters of this book. It is easy to determine the role of the MFC library when you realize that one chapter of this book was devoted to conventional procedure-oriented programming while all of the remaining chapters are devoted to object-oriented programming with the MFC!

We recommend that you take the time to review object-oriented terminology and programming techniques, discussed earlier in Chapters 15 through 18, before tackling the MFC terminology presented in this chapter.

The MFC is a powerful toolkit for the object-oriented programmer. Consider this analogy. If procedure-oriented Windows developers could be considered as having a hammer and crosscut saw in their toolkit, the object-oriented C++ Windows developer, using the MFC, is equipped with a pneumatic hammer and circular power saw.

The Need for a Foundation Class Library

The MFC library provides programmers with easy-to-use objects. Windows, from its very inception, has followed many principles of object-oriented programming design, within the framework of a non-object-oriented language like C. Many of these features were discussed in the previous two chapters. The marriage of C++ and Windows was a natural that can take full advantage of object-oriented features. The MFC development team designed a comprehensive implementation of the Windows Application Program

Interface (API). This C++ library encapsulates the most important data structures and API function calls within a group of reusable classes.

Class libraries such as the MFC offer many advantages over the traditional function libraries used by C programmers and discussed in the previous two chapters.

The following list includes many of the usual advantages of C++ classes:

- Elimination of function and variable name collisions
- Encapsulation of code and data within the class
- Inheritance
- Often, reduced code size resulting from well-designed class libraries
- Resulting classes appearing to be natural extensions of the language

With the use of the MFC library, the code required to establish a window has been reduced to approximately one-third the length of a conventional application. This allows you, the developer, to spend less time communicating with Windows and more time developing your application's code.

MFC Design Considerations

The Foundation Class library design team set rigorous design principles that had to be followed in the implementation of the MFC library. These principles and guidelines include the following:

- Allow the mixing of traditional function calls with the use of new class libraries.
- Balance power and efficiency in the design of class libraries.
- Make the transition from standard API function calls to the use of class libraries as simple as possible.
- Produce a class library that can migrate easily to evolving platforms, such as Windows 3.1 and 95 to Windows 98 and NT.
- Utilize the power of C++ without overwhelming the programmer.

The design team felt that good code design had to start with the MFC library itself. The C++ foundation classes are designed to be small in size and fast in execution time. Their simplicity makes them very easy to use, and their execution speed is close to the bulkier function libraries of C.

These classes were designed in a fashion that requires minimal relearning of function names for seasoned Windows programmers. Careful naming and designing of classes achieved this feature. As a matter of fact, Microsoft identifies this feature as the "single characteristic that sets the MFC apart from other class libraries…"

The MFC team also designed the Foundation Class library to allow a "mixed-mode" operation. That is, classes and traditional function calls can be intermixed in the same source code. Functions, such as SetCursor( ) and GetSystemMetrics( ) require direct calls, even when using the MFC.

Microsoft was also aware that class libraries should be usable. Some class libraries, provided earlier by other manufacturers, were designed with too high a level of abstraction. These "heavy classes," as Microsoft called them, tended to produce applications that were large in size and slow in execution. The MFC library provides a reasonable level of abstraction while keeping code sizes small.

The development team designed the original MFC library to be dynamic rather than static. The dynamic architecture has allowed the classes to be scaled to the growing Windows 95, 98, and NT environments we now have.

Key Features of the MFC Library

Class libraries for Windows are available from other compiler manufacturers, but Microsoft claims several real advantages for its MFC library, including the following:

- An extensive exception-handling design that makes application code less subject to failure. Support for "out of memory" and so on is provided.
- Better diagnostics support through the ability to send information about objects to a file. Also included is the ability to validate member variables.
- Complete support for all Windows functions, controls, messages, GDI (Graphics Device Interface) graphics primitives, menus, and dialog boxes.
- Determination of the type of a data object at run time. This allows for the dynamic manipulation of a field when classes are instantiated.
- Elimination of many **switch/case** statements that are a source of error. All messages are mapped to member functions within a class. This direct message-to-method mapping is available for all messages.
- Small code with a fast implementation. As mentioned earlier, the MFC library adds only a small amount of object code overhead and executes almost as quickly as conventional C Windows applications.
- Support for the Component Object Model (COM).
- Use of the same naming convention as the conventional Windows API. Thus, the action of a class is immediately recognized by its name.

The experienced Windows programmer will immediately appreciate two of these features: the familiar naming convention and the message-to-method mapping. If you reexamine the source code for the applications developed in Chapter 21, you will see extensive use of the error-prone **switch/case** statements. Also notice that these applications make extensive use of API function calls. Both groups of problems are eliminated or reduced when you use the MFC.

Professional developers will certainly appreciate Microsoft's dedication to better diagnostics and the small code overhead imposed by the MFC library. Now, programmers can take advantage of the MFC library without gaining a size penalty on their application's code.

The bottom line is that the MFC library is the only real ballgame in town! The MFC has become the de facto standard used by the majority of C++ compiler manufacturers.

It All Begins with CObject

Libraries such as the MFC library often start with a few parent classes. Additional classes are then derived from the parent classes. **CObject** is one parent class used extensively in developing Windows applications. The MFC library header files located in the MFC/INCLUDE subdirectory provide a wealth of information on defined classes.

Let's take a brief look at an edited version of **Cobject** that is defined in the AFX.H header file:

```
/////////////////////////////////////////////////////////////////
// class CObject is the root of all compliant objects

class CObject
{
public:

// Object model (types, destruction, allocation)
  virtual CRuntimeClass* GetRuntimeClass( ) const;
  virtual ~CObject( );  // virtual destructors are necessary

  // Diagnostic allocations
  void* PASCAL operator new(size_t nSize);
  void* PASCAL operator new(size_t, void* p);
  void PASCAL operator delete(void* p);

#if defined(_DEBUG) && !defined(_AFX_NO_DEBUG_CRT)
  // for file name/line number tracking using DEBUG_NEW
  void* PASCAL operator new(size_t nSize,
                            LPCSTR lpszFileName,
                            int nLine);
#endif
```

```
// Disable the copy constructor and assignment by default
// so you will get compiler errors instead of unexpected
// behavior if you pass objects by value or assign objects.

protected:
  CObject( );
private:
  CObject(const CObject& objectSrc);      //no implementation
  void operator=(const CObject& objectSrc);

// Attributes
public:
  BOOL IsSerializable( ) const;
  BOOL IsKindOf(const CRuntimeClass* pClass) const;

// Overridables
  virtual void Serialize(CArchive& ar);

  // Diagnostic Support
  virtual void AssertValid( ) const;
  virtual void Dump(CDumpContext& dc) const;

// Implementation
public:
  static const AFX_DATA CRuntimeClass classCObject;
#ifdef _AFXDLL
  static CRuntimeClass* PASCAL _GetBaseClass( );
#endif
};
```

This code has been edited slightly for clarity, but is essentially the same code that you will find in the header file.

Upon inspection of the **CObject** listing, notice the components that make up this class definition. First, **CObject** is divided into public, protected, and private parts. **CObject** also provides normal and dynamic type checking and serialization. Recall that dynamic type checking allows the type of object to be determined at run time. The state of the object can be saved to a storage medium, such as a disk, through a concept called persistence. Object persistence allows object member functions to also be persistent, permitting retrieval of object data.

Child classes are derived from parent classes. **CGdiObject** is an example of a class derived from **CObject**. Here is the **CGdiObject** definition as found in AFXWIN.H. Again, this listing has been edited for clarity.

```
////////////////////////////////////////////////////////////////
// CGdiObject abstract class for CDC SelectObject

class CGdiObject : public CObject
{
  DECLARE_DYNCREATE(CGdiObject)
public:

// Attributes
  HGDIOBJ m_hObject;  // must be first data member
  operator HGDIOBJ( ) const;
  HGDIOBJ GetSafeHandle( ) const;

  static CGdiObject* PASCAL FromHandle(HGDIOBJ hObject);
  static void PASCAL DeleteTempMap( );
  BOOL Attach(HGDIOBJ hObject);
  HGDIOBJ Detach( );

// Constructors
  CGdiObject( ); // must create a derived class object
  BOOL DeleteObject( );

// Operations
  int GetObject(int nCount, LPVOID lpObject) const;
  UINT GetObjectType( ) const;
  BOOL CreateStockObject(int nIndex);
  BOOL UnrealizeObject( );
  BOOL operator==(const CGdiObject& obj) const;
  BOOL operator!=(const CGdiObject& obj) const;

// Implementation
public:
  virtual ~CGdiObject( );
#ifdef _DEBUG
  virtual void Dump(CDumpContext& dc) const;
  virtual void AssertValid( ) const;
#endif
};
```


CGdiObject and its member functions (methods) allow drawing items such as stock and custom pens, brushes, and fonts to be created and used in a Windows application. Classes such as **CPen** are further derived from the **CGdiObject** class.

Microsoft has provided complete source code for the MFC library in order to allow the utmost in programming flexibility and customization. However, for the beginner, it is not even necessary to know how the various classes are defined in order to use them efficiently.

For example, in traditional procedure-oriented Windows applications, the DeleteObject( ) function is called with the following syntax:

```
DeleteObject(hBRUSH);  /*hBRUSH is the brush handle*/
```

In object-oriented applications, using the MFC library, the same results can be achieved by accessing the member function with the following syntax:

```
newbrush.DeleteObject( ); //newbrush is current brush
```

As you can see, switching between procedure-oriented Windows function calls and class library objects can be intuitive. Microsoft has used this approach in developing all Windows classes, making the transition from traditional function calls to MFC library objects very easy.

Key MFC Classes

The following is an abbreviated list of important 32-bit MFC classes derived from **Cobject**:

```
CObject
    CException
        CMemoryException
        CFileException
        CArchiveException
        CDaoException
        CNotSupportedException
        CUserException
        COleException
        COleDispatchException
        CDBException
        CResourceException
    CFile
        CStdioFile
        CMemFile
```

```
        COleStreamFile
        CSocketFile
    CDC
        CClientDC
        CWindowDC
        CPaintDC
        CMetaFileDC
    CGdiObject
        CPen
        CBrush
        CFont
        CBitmap
        CPalette
        CRgn
    CMenu
    CArray
    CByteArray
    CWordArray
    CDWordArray
    CPtrArray
    CObArray
    CStringArray
    CUIntArray
    CList
    CPtrList
    CObList
    CStringList
    CMap
    CMapWordToPtr
    CMapPtrToWord
    CMapPtrToPtr
    CMapWordToOb
    CMapStringToPtr
    CMapStringToOb
    CMapStringToString
    CDatabase
    CRecordSet
    CLongBinary
    CCmdTarget
        CWinThread
```

```
        CWinApp
            COleControlModule
    CDocTemplate
        CSingleDocTemplate
        CMultiDocTemplate
    COleObjectFactory
        COleTemplateServer
    COleDataSource
    COleDropSource
    COleDropTarget
    COleMessageFilter
    CConnectionPoint
CDocument
    COleDocument
        COleLinkingDoc
            COleServerDoc
                CRichEditDoc
CDocItem
    COleClientItem
        CRichEditCntrItem
    COleServerItem
CWnd
    CFrameWnd
        CMDIChildWnd
        CMDIFrameWnd
        CMiniFrameWnd
        COleIPFrameWnd
    CControlBar
        CToolBar
        CStatusBar
        CDialogBar
        COleResizeBar
    CSplitterWnd
    CPropertySheet
    CDialog
        CCommonDialog
            CColorDialog
            CFileDialog
            CFindReplaceDialog
            CFontDialog
            COleDialog
                COleInsertDialog
                COleChangeIconDialog
```

```
            COlePasteSpecialDialog
            COleConvertDialog
            COleBusyDialog
            COleLinksDialog
                COleUpdateDialog
            COleChangeSourceDialog
            COlePageSetupDialog
            CPrintDialog
    COlePropertyPage
    CPropertyPage
CView
    CCtrlView
        CEditView
        CListView
        CRichEditView
        CTreeView
CScrollView
    CFormView
        CDaoRecordView
        CRecordView
CAnimateCtrl
CButton
    CBitmapButton
CComboBox
CEdit
CHeaderCtrl
CHotKeyCtrl
CListBox
    CCheckListBox
    CDragListBox
CListCtrl
COleControl
CProgresCtrl
CRichEditCtrl
CScrollBar
CSliderCtrl
CSpinButtonCtrl
CStatic
CStatusBarCtrl
CTabCtrl
CToolbarCtrl
CToolTipCtrl
CTreeCtrl
```

From this list you can see and understand the general strategy in deriving one class or a group of classes from a parent class. The next list is an abbreviated list of the 32-bit runtime object model support provided by the MFC:

```
CArchive
CDumpContext
CRuntimeClass
CString
CTime
CTimeSpan
CRect
CPoint
CSize
CFileStatus
CCreateContext
CPrintInfo
CMemoryState
CCommandLineInfo
CDataExchange
CFieldExchange
CCmdUI
CDataFieldExchange
CWaitCursor
CFontHolder
CPictureHolder
COleCurrency
COleDateTime
COleDateTimeSpan
COleVariant
CMultiLock
CSingleLock
CPropExchange
COleDataObject
COleDispatchDriver
CRectTracker
CTypedPtrArray
CTypedPtrList
CTypedPtrMap
```

You'll want to put a bookmark at this spot. These two lists will help you as you continue to study the MFC library in the remaining chapters of this book.

A Simplified MFC Application

Before writing more complicated application code, let's see what is required to just establish a window on the screen. In the last chapter, you learned to do this in C with a program that spanned two pages in length. When you use the power of the MFC library, the initial program code can be reduced to one-third this size!

This section examines the simplest possible Windows application, SIMPLE.CPP. The simple application will establish a window on the screen and place a title in its title bar area.

Establishing a Window with SIMPLE.CPP

In order to compile this MFC application, you need to enter the source code that follows. The source code file, while initially strange in appearance, is certainly shorter than its procedure-oriented counterparts.

```
//
//  simple.cpp
//  The code needed to establish a window with
//  the Microsoft Foundation Class library
//  Copyright © William H. Murray and Chris H. Pappas, 1998
//

#include <afxwin.h>

class CTheApp : public CWinApp
{
public:
  virtual BOOL InitInstance( );
};

class CMainWnd : public CFrameWnd
{
public:
  CMainWnd( )
  {
    Create(NULL,"Hello MFC World",
           WS_OVERLAPPEDWINDOW,rectDefault,NULL,NULL);
  }
};

BOOL CTheApp::InitInstance( )
{
```

```
    m_pMainWnd=new CMainWnd( );
    m_pMainWnd->ShowWindow(m_nCmdShow);
    m_pMainWnd->UpdateWindow( );

    return TRUE;
}

CTheApp TheApp;
```

Once this C++ file is entered, you can compile this application from the integrated environment by creating a project file that includes the use of the MFC library.

Note *Make sure you set the option in the Project menu to include the static MFC library.*

The following sections examine how each piece of code works in establishing the window on the screen.

Using the AFXWIN.H Header File

The AFXWIN.H header file is the gateway to Windows programming with the MFC library. This header file calls all subsequent header files, including WINDOWS.H, as they are needed. Using one header file also aids in creating precompiled header files. Precompiled header files save time when repeated compilation is being done during application development.

It might be a good idea to print a copy of AFXWIN.H for your reference as you develop your own applications using the MFC library. However, be warned, this header file has grown and approaches 100 pages in the current version because of support for OLE features and so on.

Deriving a Class from CWinApp

This application starts by deriving a class, **CTheApp**, from the MFC parent class, **CWinApp**. The programmer defines this new object.

```
class CTheApp : public CWinApp
{
public:
  virtual BOOL InitInstance( );
};
```

The class **CTheApp** overrides the member function InitInstance( ) of **CWinApp**. You will find that overriding member functions occurs frequently. By overriding InitInstance( ), you can customize the initialization and execution of the application. In

CWinApp, it is also possible to override InitApplication( ), ExitInstance( ), and OnIdle( ), but for most applications, this will not be necessary.

Here is an edited portion of the **CWinApp** class description as found in the AFXWIN.H header file:

```
//////////////////////////////////////////////////////////////////
// CWinApp - the root of all Windows applications

class CWinApp : public CWinThread
{
  DECLARE_DYNAMIC(CWinApp)
public:

// Constructor
  CWinApp(LPCTSTR lpszAppName = NULL);  //app defaults
                                        //to EXE name

// Attributes
  // Startup args (do not change)
  HINSTANCE m_hInstance;
  HINSTANCE m_hPrevInstance;
  LPTSTR m_lpCmdLine;
  int m_nCmdShow;

  // Running args (can be changed in InitInstance)
  LPCTSTR m_pszAppName;
  LPCTSTR m_pszRegistryKey;   // used for registry entries
  CDocManager* m_pDocManager;

public:  // set in constructor to override default
  LPCTSTR m_pszExeName;       // executable name (no spaces)
  LPCTSTR m_pszHelpFilePath;  // default based on module path
  LPCTSTR m_pszProfileName;   // default based on app name

// Initialization Operations - should be done in InitInstance
protected:
  void LoadStdProfileSettings(UINT nMaxMRU = _AFX_MRU_COUNT);
  void EnableShellOpen( );

  void SetDialogBkColor(COLORREF clrCtlBk = RGB(192,192,192),
        COLORREF clrCtlText = RGB(0, 0, 0));
    // set dialog box and message box background color
```

WINDOWS PROGRAMMING FOUNDATIONS

```
  void SetRegistryKey(LPCTSTR lpszRegistryKey);
  void SetRegistryKey(UINT nIDRegistryKey);
    // enables app settings in registry instead of INI files
    //  (registry key is usually a "company name")

#ifdef _MAC
  friend void CFrameWnd::OnSysColorChange( );
  friend void CDialog::OnSysColorChange( );
#endif

  BOOL Enable3dControls( ); //use CTL3D32.DLL for 3D controls
#ifndef _AFXDLL
  BOOL Enable3dControlsStatic( );  //link CTL3D.LIB instead
#endif

  void RegisterShellFileTypes(BOOL bCompat=FALSE);
    // call after all doc templates are registered
  void RegisterShellFileTypesCompat( );
    // for backwards compatibility
  void UnregisterShellFileTypes( );

// Helper Operations - usually done in InitInstance
public:
  // Cursors
  HCURSOR LoadCursor(LPCTSTR lpszResourceName) const;
  HCURSOR LoadCursor(UINT nIDResource) const;
  HCURSOR LoadStandardCursor(LPCTSTR lpszCursorName) const;
  HCURSOR LoadOEMCursor(UINT nIDCursor) const;

  // Icons
  HICON LoadIcon(LPCTSTR lpszResourceName) const;
  HICON LoadIcon(UINT nIDResource) const;
  HICON LoadStandardIcon(LPCTSTR lpszIconName) const;
  HICON LoadOEMIcon(UINT nIDIcon) const;
     .
     .
     .
  // overrides for implementation
  virtual BOOL InitInstance( );
  virtual int ExitInstance( ); // return app exit code
  virtual int Run( );
```

```
    virtual BOOL OnIdle(LONG lCount);
    virtual LRESULT ProcessWndProcException(CException* e,
                                            const MSG* pMsg);

public:
    virtual ~CWinApp( );
        .
        .
        .
protected:
    //{{AFX_MSG(CWinApp)
    afx_msg void OnAppExit( );
    afx_msg void OnUpdateRecentFileMenu(CCmdUI* pCmdUI);
    afx_msg BOOL OnOpenRecentFile(UINT nID);
    //}}AFX_MSG
    DECLARE_MESSAGE_MAP( )
};
```

The **CWinApp** class is responsible for establishing and implementing the Windows message loop. The Windows message loop was discussed in Chapter 21. This action alone eliminates many lines of repetitive code.

CFrameWnd

The application's window, established by the **CMainWnd** class, is defined from the base class, **CFrameWnd,** as shown in the following segment of code:

```
class CMainWnd : public CFrameWnd
{
public:
  CMainWnd( )
  {
    Create(NULL,"Hello MFC World",
           WS_OVERLAPPEDWINDOW,rectDefault,NULL,NULL);
  }
};
```

The constructor for the class, CMainWnd( ), calls the Create( ) member function to establish initial window parameters. In this application, the window's style and caption are provided as parameters. You'll see in Chapter 23 that it is also possible to specify a menu name and an accelerator table when this member function is used.

Here is an edited portion of **CFrameWnd,** also found in the AFXWIN.H header file:

```
/////////////////////////////////////////////////////////////////
// CFrameWnd - base class for SDI and other frame windows

class CFrameWnd : public CWnd
{
  DECLARE_DYNCREATE(CFrameWnd)

// Constructors
public:
  static AFX_DATA const CRect rectDefault;
  CFrameWnd( );

  BOOL LoadAccelTable(LPCTSTR lpszResourceName);
  BOOL Create(LPCTSTR lpszClassName,
        LPCTSTR lpszWindowName,
        DWORD dwStyle = WS_OVERLAPPEDWINDOW,
        const RECT& rect = rectDefault,
        CWnd* pParentWnd = NULL,        // != NULL for popups
        LPCTSTR lpszMenuName = NULL,
        DWORD dwExStyle = 0,
        CCreateContext* pContext = NULL);

  // dynamic creation - load frame and associated resources
  virtual BOOL LoadFrame(UINT nIDResource,
        DWORD dwDefaultStyle = WS_OVERLAPPEDWINDOW |
                               FWS_ADDTOTITLE,
        CWnd* pParentWnd = NULL,
        CCreateContext* pContext = NULL);

  // special helper for view creation
  CWnd* CreateView(CCreateContext* pContext,
                 UINT nID = AFX_IDW_PANE_FIRST);
   .
   .
   .
  // control bar docking
  void EnableDocking(DWORD dwDockStyle);
  void DockControlBar(CControlBar* pBar, UINT nDockBarID = 0,
    LPCRECT lpRect = NULL);
  void FloatControlBar(CControlBar* pBar, CPoint point,
```

```
    DWORD dwStyle = CBRS_ALIGN_TOP);
  CControlBar* GetControlBar(UINT nID);
   .
   .
   .
// Implementation
public:
  virtual ~CFrameWnd( );
  int m_nWindow;
  HMENU m_hMenuDefault;        // default menu resource
  HACCEL m_hAccelTable;        // accelerator table
  DWORD m_dwPromptContext;     // current help prompt
  BOOL m_bHelpMode;            // if TRUE, help mode is active
  CFrameWnd* m_pNextFrameWnd; // CFrameWnd in app global list
  CRect m_rectBorder;          // OLE border space negotiation
  COleFrameHook* m_pNotifyHook;

  CPtrList m_listControlBars; // array of control bars that
                               // have this window as dock site
  int m_nShowDelay;            // SW_ command for delay show/hide

     .
     .
     .
  // Windows messages
  afx_msg int OnCreate(LPCREATESTRUCT lpCreateStruct);
  afx_msg void OnDestroy( );
  afx_msg void OnClose( );
  afx_msg void OnInitMenuPopup(CMenu*, UINT, BOOL);
  afx_msg void OnMenuSelect(UINT nItemID, UINT nFlags,
                            HMENU hSysMenu);
  afx_msg LRESULT OnPopMessageString(WPARAM wParam,
                                     LPARAM lParam);
  afx_msg LRESULT OnSetMessageString(WPARAM wParam,
                                     LPARAM lParam);
   .
   .
   .
protected:
#ifndef _MAC
  afx_msg LRESULT OnDDEInitiate(WPARAM wParam,
                                LPARAM lParam);
```

```
  afx_msg LRESULT OnDDEExecute(WPARAM wParam,
                               LPARAM lParam);
  afx_msg LRESULT OnDDETerminate(WPARAM wParam,
                                 LPARAM lParam);
  afx_msg LRESULT OnRegisteredMouseWheel(WPARAM wParam,
                                         LPARAM lParam);
#endif
#ifdef _MAC
  afx_msg void OnActivateApp(BOOL bActive, HTASK hTask);
  afx_msg void OnPaint( );
#endif
  DECLARE_MESSAGE_MAP( )

  friend class CWinApp;
};
```

The first parameter in the Create( ) member function allows a class name to be specified in compliance with the traditional Windows API RegisterClass( ) function. Normally, this will be set to NULL in the applications you develop (a parent window) and a class name will not be required.

Implementing the InitInstance( ) Member Function

Recall that the derived **CTheApp** class object overrode the InitInstance( ) member function. Here is how this application implements InitInstance( ):

```
BOOL CTheApp::InitInstance( )
{
  m_pMainWnd=new CMainWnd( );
  m_pMainWnd->ShowWindow(m_nCmdShow);
  m_pMainWnd->UpdateWindow( );

  return TRUE;
}
```

The new operator invokes the constructor CMainWnd( ), discussed in the previous section. The *m_pMainWnd* member variable (*m_* indicates a member variable) holds the location for the application's main window. The ShowWindow( ) member function is required to display the window on the screen. The parameter, *m_nCmdShow,* is initialized by the application's constructor. UpdateWindow( ) displays and paints the window being sent to the screen.

The Constructor

The last piece of code invokes the application's constructor at startup:

```
CTheApp TheApp;
```

The application code for this example is very simple and straightforward. The application merely establishes a window; it does not permit you to draw anything in the window.

In the next chapter, you will create a more generalized template, as you did in Chapter 21. This template will allow you to use basically the same MFC code from one application to another. In addition, this template code will allow you to draw in the client area of the window.

Running the SIMPLE.CPP Application

Figure 22-1 shows a window similar to the one that will appear on your screen. While the application didn't draw anything in the client area of the window, it did give the application a new title!

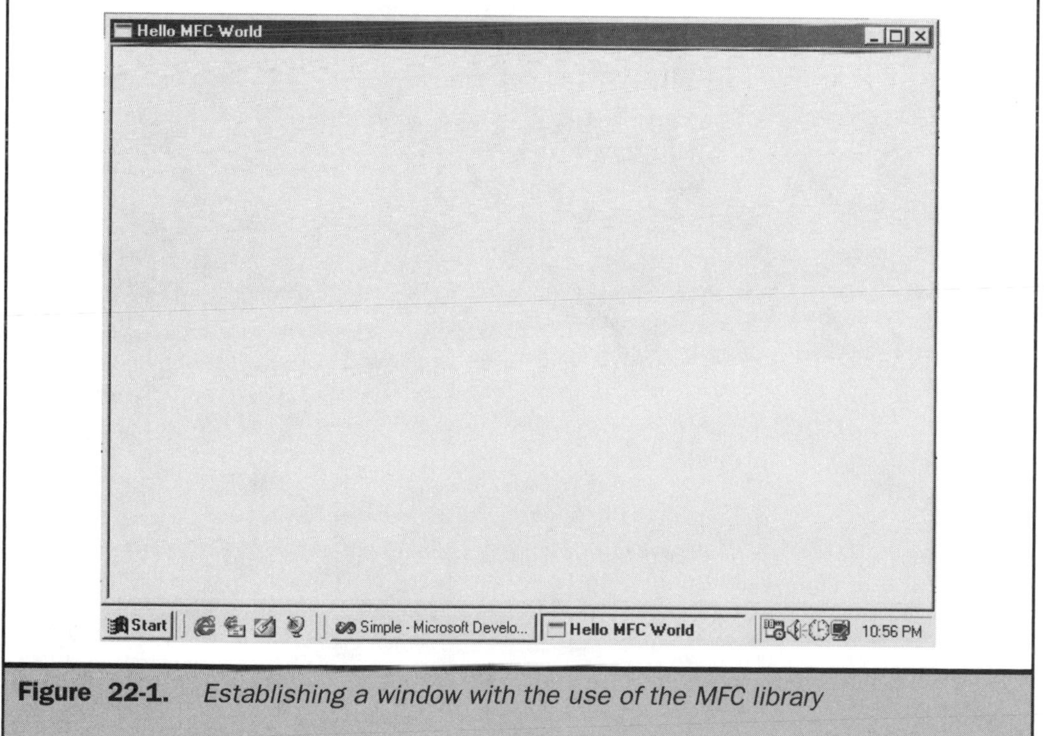

Figure 22-1. *Establishing a window with the use of the MFC library*

This code forms the foundation for all Windows MFC library applications developed in this book. You might want to review the important details one more time before going on to the applications created in Chapter 23.

Application Maintenance Is Easy with the MFC

Reusable classes are one of the main drawing cards in C++ for simplified design and application maintenance. The MFC library for Windows allows C++ to be extended in a natural way, making these classes appear to be part of the language itself. In the next chapter you'll explore many additional features of the MFC library as you develop applications that range from a simple program template to a robust charting program using menus and dialog boxes.

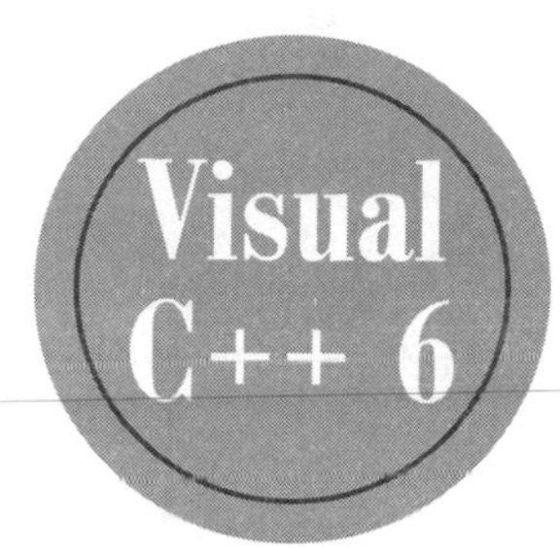

Chapter 23

Windows Applications Using the MFC

Chapters 20 and 21 contained information on various Windows building blocks such as menus, dialog boxes, keyboard accelerators, and so on. In Chapter 22, you learned the theory and specifications of the Microsoft Foundation Class (MFC) library. This chapter combines all of previously discussed Windows building blocks and builds applications using 32-bit object-oriented MFC tools.

In this chapter, you will find four complete MFC library Windows applications that will help you understand the MFC library even better. The examples in this chapter are graded—that is, each example builds upon the knowledge you gain from the previous example. It is imperative, therefore, that you study each of the applications in the order in which they appear. By the time you get to the fourth application, you will be working with a complex Windows application that uses several Windows resources, depends heavily on the MFC library, and produces a useful commercial-grade application.

The program listings for each application are quite long. If you are entering them from the keyboard, do so carefully. Remember, as you type that these listings are still far shorter than their procedure-oriented counterparts from Chapter 21.

A Simple Application and Template

In Chapter 22, techniques for establishing a window on the screen with the MFC library were introduced. That example serves as a gateway to all such Windows applications that utilize the client area for printing and drawing.

The first application in this chapter, named MFCSWP, simply prints a message in the window's client area. The name of this program is derived from the acronym for "MFC simple windows program."

Before beginning the discussion of the important aspects of the application, let's examine a complete program listing. The listing that follows includes a header file and a C++ source code file. The information in the header file was essentially contained in the source code file in the previous chapter. The header file provides information on how our application's classes are derived from the MFC library. This is a style of coding that is promoted by Microsoft. Here is the MFCSWP.H header file listing:

```
class CMainWnd : public CFrameWnd
{
public:
  CMainWnd( );
  afx_msg void OnPaint( );
  DECLARE_MESSAGE_MAP( );
};

class CmfcswpApp : public CWinApp
{
```

```
public:
  BOOL InitInstance( );
};
```

The C++ source code file is straightforward. As you examine the following MFCSWP.CPP file, pay particular attention to the overall length of the listing:

```
//
//  mfcswp.cpp
//  A Simple Windows Program using the MFC.
//  This code can serve as a template for the development
//  of other MFC applications.
//  Copyright (c) William H. Murray and Chris H. Pappas, 1998
//

#include <afxwin.h>
#include "mfcswp.h"

CmfcswpApp theApp;

CMainWnd::CMainWnd( )
{
  Create(NULL,"A MFC Windows Application",
         WS_OVERLAPPEDWINDOW,rectDefault,NULL,NULL);
}

void CMainWnd::OnPaint( )
{
  CPaintDC dc(this);
  dc.TextOut(200,200,"Using the MFC Library",21);
}

BEGIN_MESSAGE_MAP(CMainWnd,CFrameWnd)
  ON_WM_PAINT( )
END_MESSAGE_MAP( )

BOOL CmfcswpApp::InitInstance( )
{
  m_pMainWnd=new CMainWnd( );
  m_pMainWnd->ShowWindow(m_nCmdShow);
  m_pMainWnd->UpdateWindow( );
```

```
    return TRUE;
}
```

This composite listing gives you a chance to examine all of the code necessary to produce a working application. The next sections examine those details that are unique to this example.

The MFCSWP.H Header File

As you examine the applications in this chapter, you will find two types of header files. The first type, shown in this section, is used to indicate class definitions that are unique to the application. As a matter of style, the filename and the .H extension—for example, MFCSWP.H—will always identify this type of header file. The second style of header file is the type used earlier in Chapter 21. This style header file can contain menu and dialog box resource identification values. When this second style of header file is used, it is identified with an additional "R" (standing for "resource") at the end of the filename. For example, if the application in this section had used a resource ID header file, it would have been named MFCSWPR.H. You'll see this second style of header file used in the final two examples in this chapter.

The definitions for two classes are contained here: **CMainWnd** is derived from **CWinApp**, and **CmfcswpApp** is derived from **CFrameWnd**.

```
class CMainWnd : public CFrameWnd
{
public:
  CMainWnd( );
  afx_msg void OnPaint( );
  DECLARE_MESSAGE_MAP( );
};

class CmfcswpApp : public CWinApp
{
public:
  BOOL InitInstance( );
};
```

Recall that these classes were part of the body of the SIMPLE.CPP application and were explained in Chapter 21. Putting them in a separate header file is just a matter of style—one encouraged by Microsoft.

Notice, in particular, that **CMainWnd** contains a member function declaration, OnPaint( ), and the addition of a message map. For member functions such as OnPaint( ), the **afx_msg** keyword is used instead of virtual. The OnPaint( ) member function belongs to the **CWnd** class that the **CMainWnd** class overrides. This allows the client area of the window to be altered. The OnPaint( ) function is automatically called when a WM_PAINT message is sent to a **CMainWnd** object.

DECLARE_MESSAGE_MAP is used in virtually all MFC Windows applications. This line states that the class overrides the handling of certain messages. (See the body of the application.) Microsoft uses message maps instead of virtual functions because it is more space efficient.

The MFCSWP.CPP Source Code File

The majority of this application's code is the same as the SIMPLE.CPP example from Chapter 21. However, notice the addition of the OnPaint( ) message handler function.

Examine the portion of code shown here:

```
void CMainWnd::OnPaint( )
{
  CPaintDC dc(this);

  dc.TextOut(200,200,"Using the MFC Library",21);
}
```

A device context is created for handling the WM_PAINT message. Now, any Windows GDI functions that are encapsulated in the device context can be used in this member function. This code is similar in concept to the procedure-oriented template created in Chapter 21. When the OnPaint( ) function has finished, the destructor for **CPaintDC** is called automatically.

This application uses a fairly short message map, as the following code indicates:

```
BEGIN_MESSAGE_MAP(CMainWnd,CFrameWnd)
  ON_WM_PAINT( )
END_MESSAGE_MAP( )
```

Two classes are specified by BEGIN_MESSAGE_MAP: **CMainWnd** and **CFrameWnd**. **CMainWnd** is the target class, and **CFrameWnd** is a class derived from **CWnd**. The ON_WM_PAINT( ) function handles all WM_PAINT messages and directs them to the OnPaint( ) member function just discussed. In upcoming applications, you'll see many additional functions added to the message map.

The biggest advantage of using a message map is the elimination of many error-prone **switch/case** statements that are so typical of procedure-oriented Windows applications.

Running the MFCSWP Application

When you create your project file for your Visual C++ compiler, make sure that you mark this application as an MFC application. Otherwise, you will get a series of strange errors when compiling and linking. Once you have entered the application code and received an error-free compilation, run the program. The screen should be similar to the one shown in Figure 23-1.

If you want to experiment with other GDI primitives, just remove the TextOut( ) function call and insert the function of your choice into the template code. You can choose from such functions as: Rectangle( ), Ellipse( ), LineTo( ), and so on. The next example will illustrate the use of several graphics functions that will draw a line, a chord, an arc, and more.

Drawing in the Client Area

The second application in this chapter is named GDI. The GDI application will draw several graphics shapes in the window's client area. These are the same GDI drawing primitives discussed (and used separately) in Chapter 21.

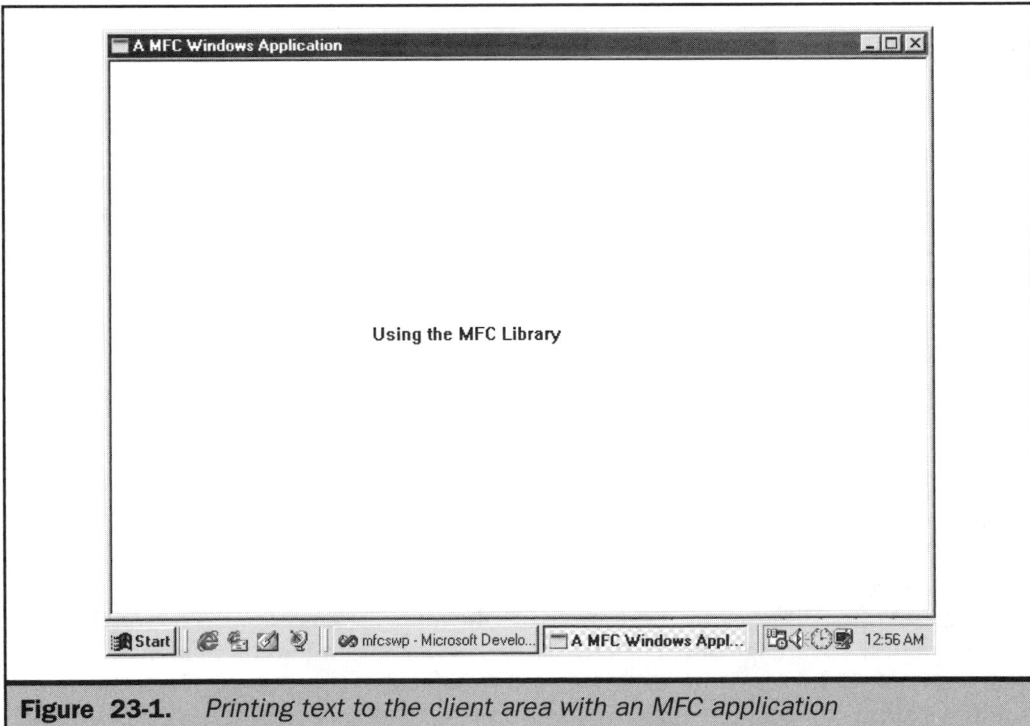

Figure 23-1. *Printing text to the client area with an MFC application*

This application also requires two files: the header file, GDI.H, and the source code file, GDI.CPP.

Enter each of the files carefully. When both files have been entered, the application can be compiled. Remember to state that this is an MFC application when building your application with the Project utility. The GDI.H header file, which follows, is similar in structure to the previous example:

```
class CMainWnd : public CFrameWnd
{
public:
  CMainWnd( );
  afx_msg void OnPaint( );
  DECLARE_MESSAGE_MAP( );
};

class CgdiAApp : public CWinApp
{
public:
  BOOL InitInstance( );
};
```

The source code file for the GDI.CPP application follows:

```
//
//  gdi.cpp
//  An extension of the mfcswp.cpp application
//  that allows experimentation with graphics
//  drawing primitives.
//  Copyright (c) William H. Murray and Chris H. Pappas, 1998
//

#include <afxwin.h>
#include "gdi.h"

CgdiAApp theApp;

CMainWnd::CMainWnd( )
{
  Create(NULL,"Experimenting With GDI Primitives",
         WS_OVERLAPPEDWINDOW,rectDefault,NULL,NULL);
}
```

```
void CMainWnd::OnPaint( )
{
  static DWORD dwColor[9]={RGB(0,0,0),          //black
                           RGB(255,0,0),        //red
                           RGB(0,255,0),        //green
                           RGB(0,0,255),        //blue
                           RGB(255,255,0),      //yellow
                           RGB(255,0,255),      //magenta
                           RGB(0,255,255),      //cyan
                           RGB(127,127,127),    //gray
                           RGB(255,255,255)};   //white
  short xcoord;
  POINT polylpts[4],polygpts[5];

  CBrush newbrush;
  CBrush* oldbrush;
  CPen  newpen;
  CPen* oldpen;

  CPaintDC dc(this);
  // draws a wide black diagonal line
  newpen.CreatePen(PS_SOLID,6,dwColor[0]);
  oldpen=dc.SelectObject(&newpen);
  dc.MoveTo(0,0);
  dc.LineTo(640,430);
  dc.TextOut(70,20,"<-diagonal line",15);
  // delete pen objects
  dc.SelectObject(oldpen);
  newpen.DeleteObject( );

  // draws a blue arc
  newpen.CreatePen(PS_DASH,1,dwColor[3]);
  oldpen=dc.SelectObject(&newpen);
  dc.Arc(100,100,200,200,150,175,175,150);
  dc.TextOut(80,180,"small arc->",11);
  // delete pen objects
  dc.SelectObject(oldpen);
  newpen.DeleteObject( );

  // draws a wide green chord
  newpen.CreatePen(PS_SOLID,8,dwColor[2]);
  oldpen=dc.SelectObject(&newpen);
```

```
dc.Chord(550,20,630,80,555,25,625,70);
dc.TextOut(485,30,"chord->",7);
// delete pen objects
dc.SelectObject(oldpen);
newpen.DeleteObject( );

// draws and fills a red ellipse
newpen.CreatePen(PS_SOLID,1,dwColor[1]);
oldpen=dc.SelectObject(&newpen);
newbrush.CreateSolidBrush(dwColor[1]);
oldbrush=dc.SelectObject(&newbrush);
dc.Ellipse(180,180,285,260);
dc.TextOut(210,215,"ellipse",7);
// delete brush objects
dc.SelectObject(oldbrush);
newbrush.DeleteObject( );
// delete pen objects
dc.SelectObject(oldpen);
newpen.DeleteObject( );

// draws and fills a blue circle with ellipse function
newpen.CreatePen(PS_SOLID,1,dwColor[3]);
oldpen=dc.SelectObject(&newpen);
newbrush.CreateSolidBrush(dwColor[3]);
oldbrush=dc.SelectObject(&newbrush);
dc.Ellipse(380,180,570,370);
dc.TextOut(450,265,"circle",6);
// delete brush objects
dc.SelectObject(oldbrush);
newbrush.DeleteObject( );
// delete pen objects
dc.SelectObject(oldpen);
newpen.DeleteObject( );

// draws a black pie wedge and fills with green
newpen.CreatePen(PS_SOLID,1,dwColor[0]);
oldpen=dc.SelectObject(&newpen);
newbrush.CreateSolidBrush(dwColor[2]);
oldbrush=dc.SelectObject(&newbrush);
dc.Pie(300,50,400,150,300,50,300,100);
dc.TextOut(350,80,"<-pie wedge",11);
```

```
// delete brush objects
dc.SelectObject(oldbrush);
newbrush.DeleteObject( );
// delete pen objects
dc.SelectObject(oldpen);
newpen.DeleteObject( );

// draws a black rectangle and fills with gray
newbrush.CreateSolidBrush(dwColor[7]);
oldbrush=dc.SelectObject(&newbrush);
dc.Rectangle(50,300,150,400);
dc.TextOut(160,350,"<-rectangle",11);
// delete brush objects
dc.SelectObject(oldbrush);
newbrush.DeleteObject( );

// draws a black rounded rectangle and fills with blue
newbrush.CreateHatchBrush(HS_CROSS,dwColor[3]);
oldbrush=dc.SelectObject(&newbrush);
dc.RoundRect(60,310,110,350,20,20);
dc.TextOut (120,310,"<------rounded rectangle",24);
// delete brush objects
dc.SelectObject(oldbrush);
newbrush.DeleteObject( );

// draws several green pixels
for(xcoord=400;xcoord<450;xcoord+=3)
  dc.SetPixel(xcoord,150,0L);
dc.TextOut(455,145,"<-pixels",8);

// draws several wide magenta lines with polyline
newpen.CreatePen(PS_SOLID,3,dwColor[5]);
oldpen=dc.SelectObject(&newpen);
polylpts[0].x=10;
polylpts[0].y=30;
polylpts[1].x=10;
polylpts[1].y=100;
polylpts[2].x=50;
polylpts[2].y=100;
polylpts[3].x=10;
polylpts[3].y=30;
```

```
    dc.Polyline(polylpts,4);
    dc.TextOut(10,110,"polyline",8);
    // delete pen objects
    dc.SelectObject(oldpen);
    newpen.DeleteObject( );

    // draws a wide cyan polygon and
    // fills with diagonal yellow
    newpen.CreatePen(PS_SOLID,4,dwColor[6]);
    oldpen=dc.SelectObject(&newpen);
    newbrush.CreateHatchBrush(HS_FDIAGONAL,dwColor[4]);
    oldbrush=dc.SelectObject(&newbrush);
    polygpts[0].x=40;
    polygpts[0].y=200;
    polygpts[1].x=100;
    polygpts[1].y=270;
    polygpts[2].x=80;
    polygpts[2].y=290;
    polygpts[3].x=20;
    polygpts[3].y=220;
    polygpts[4].x=40;
    polygpts[4].y=200;
    dc.Polygon(polygpts,5);
    dc.TextOut(70,210,"<-polygon",9);
    // delete brush objects
    dc.SelectObject(oldbrush);
    newbrush.DeleteObject( );
    // delete pen objects
    dc.SelectObject(oldpen);
    newpen.DeleteObject( );
}

BEGIN_MESSAGE_MAP(CMainWnd,CFrameWnd)
  ON_WM_PAINT( )
END_MESSAGE_MAP( )

BOOL CgdiAApp::InitInstance( )
{
  m_pMainWnd=new CMainWnd( );
  m_pMainWnd->ShowWindow(m_nCmdShow);
  m_pMainWnd->UpdateWindow( );
```

```
    return TRUE;
}
```

This example uses a variety of pens and brushes, in addition to investigating various GDI graphics primitives. Let's look at the code in more detail.

The GDI.H Header File

Examine the GDI.H header file. Did you notice that only the name of the application has changed from the previous example? Basically, this feat is possible because of the simplicity of the example—no menus, dialog boxes, or other external resources.

The GDI.CPP Source Code File

Here is a portion of code the source code listing contained in the OnPaint( ) message handler function. An array is created to hold the RGB values for nine unique brush and pen colors. You'll see shortly how colors are picked from this array:

```
static DWORD dwColor[9]={RGB(0,0,0),          //black
                         RGB(255,0,0),        //red
                         RGB(0,255,0),        //green
                         RGB(0,0,255),        //blue
                         RGB(255,255,0),      //yellow
                         RGB(255,0,255),      //magenta
                         RGB(0,255,255),      //cyan
                         RGB(127,127,127),    //gray
                         RGB(255,255,255)};   //white
```

The **CBrush** and **CPen** classes permit brush or pen objects to be passed to any CDC (base class for display context) member function. Brushes can be solid, hatched, or patterned, and pens can draw solid, dashed, or dotted lines. Here is the syntax that is required to create a new brush and pen object for this example:

```
CBrush newbrush;
CBrush* oldbrush;
CPen  newpen;
CPen* oldpen;
```

Since each GDI primitive's code is somewhat similar to the others in the group, we will only examine two typical sections. The first piece of code is used to draw a wide black diagonal line in the window:

```
// draws a wide black diagonal line
newpen.CreatePen(PS_SOLID,6,dwColor[0]);
oldpen=dc.SelectObject(&newpen);
dc.MoveTo(0,0);
dc.LineTo(640,430);
dc.TextOut(70,20,"<-diagonal line",15);
// delete pen objects
dc.SelectObject(oldpen);
newpen.DeleteObject( );
```

The pen object is initialized by the CreatePen( ) function to draw black solid lines, six logical units wide. Once the pen is initialized, the SelectObject( ) member function is overloaded for the **pen object** class and attaches the pen object to the device context. The previously attached object is returned. The MoveTo( ) and LineTo( ) functions set the range for the diagonal line that is drawn by the selected pen. Finally, a label is attached to the figure with the use of the TextOut( ) function.

Brushes can be handled in a similar way. In the following code, the brush is initialized to be a hatch-brush filled with blue crosses (HS_CROSS). The brush object is selected in the same way the pen object was selected.

```
// draws a black rounded rectangle and fills with blue
newbrush.CreateHatchBrush(HS_CROSS,dwColor[3]);
oldbrush=dc.SelectObject(&newbrush);
dc.RoundRect(60,310,110,350,20,20);
dc.TextOut (120,310,"<------rounded rectangle",24);
// delete brush objects
dc.SelectObject(oldbrush);
newbrush.DeleteObject( );
```

The RoundRect( ) function draws a rounded rectangle in black at the given screen coordinates. A label is also printed for this figure.

The remaining shapes are drawn to the screen using a similar technique.

Running the GDI Application

Build the application by creating a project file specifically requesting the inclusion of the MFC library. Run the application and note the results that appear on your screen.

This application has a minor drawback, as you may have observed! All coordinate points for the GDI functions are set to pixel values valid for VGA monitors. What happens if you are using a super VGA display, for example? If you are using a higher-resolution display, such as a super VGA, the image will fill in only the upper-left part of your screen.

To eliminate this problem, your application can determine your display's characteristics and adjust accordingly. This determination adds an extra layer of complexity to the application code, which has been kept as simple as possible to this point. However, the final two examples in this chapter will teach you how to scale your figures to fit the current display type. All of this can be done automatically if your program is properly written.

When you run this application, your screen should look something like that shown in Figure 23-2 if you are using a VGA monitor. The various GDI objects are displayed in very vivid colors.

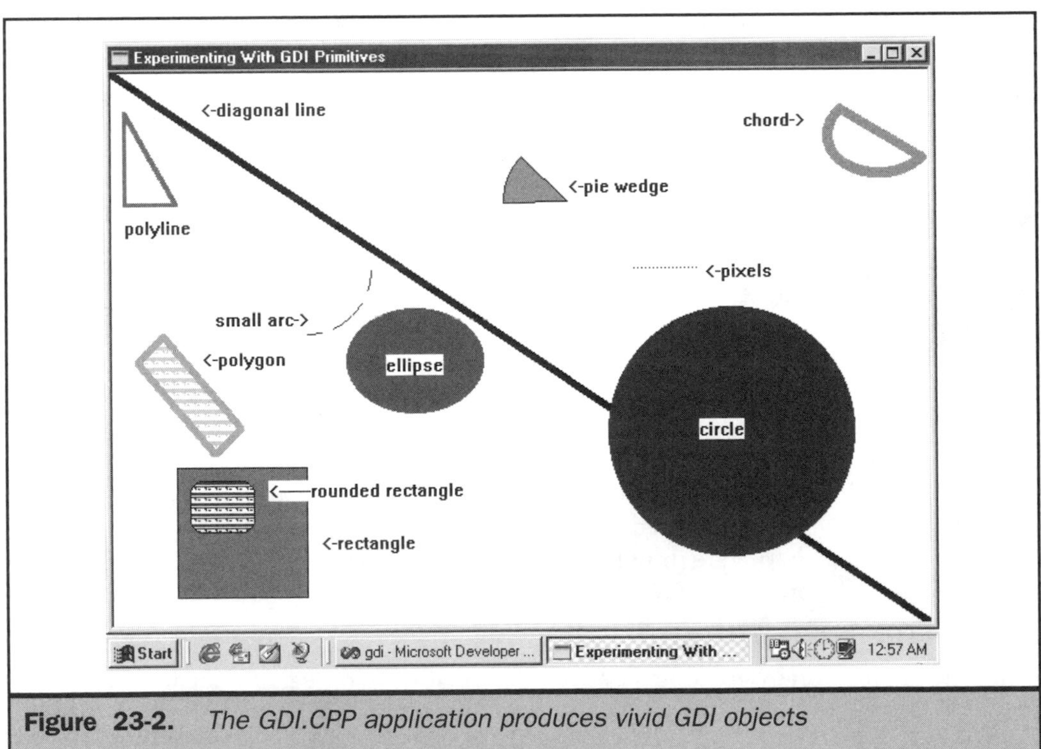

Figure 23-2. *The GDI.CPP application produces vivid GDI objects*

A Fourier Series Application with Resources

The next application in this chapter, FOURIER.CPP, will draw a Fourier series waveform in the window's client area. This application uses two Windows resources: a menu and a dialog box. You may want to refer to Chapter 21 for details on the techniques for creating each of these resources.

As the complexity of each application grows, so does the list of files required for compiling and linking. This application requires a header file named FOURIER.H, a resource header file named FOURIERR.H (note the addition of the extra "R"), a resource script file named FOURIER.RC, and the source code file named FOURIER.CPP.

Enter each file carefully. When all the files have been entered, the application can be compiled and linked. Also, remember to include FOURIER.RC, and FOURIER.CPP in your project file's list of files needed for the build process.

One header file is used for class information, as you can see in the FOURIER.H file that follows:

```
class CMainWnd : public CFrameWnd
{
public:
  CMainWnd( );
  afx_msg void OnPaint( );
  afx_msg void OnSize(UINT,int,int);
  afx_msg int  OnCreate(LPCREATESTRUCT cs);
  afx_msg void OnAbout( );
  afx_msg void OnFourierData( );
  afx_msg void OnExit( );
  DECLARE_MESSAGE_MAP( )
};

class CTheApp : public CWinApp
{
public:
  virtual BOOL InitInstance( );
};

class CFourierDataDialog : public CDialog
{
public:
  CFourierDataDialog(CWnd* pParentWnd=NULL)
                      : CDialog("FourierData",pParentWnd)
                      {  }
```

WINDOWS PROGRAMMING FOUNDATIONS

```
  virtual void OnOK( );
};
```

Another header file contains the traditional ID values needed by menus and dialog boxes. This file is named FOURIERR.H.

```
#define IDM_FOUR   100
#define IDM_ABOUT  110
#define IDM_EXIT   120
#define IDD_TERMS  200
#define IDD_TITLE  201
```

The resource script file, FOURIER.RC, for this example includes a description for a menu and two dialog box descriptions. The dialog box descriptions are for a simple About box and a data entry dialog box.

```
//Microsoft Developer Studio generated resource script.
//
#include "fourierr.h"

#define APSTUDIO_READONLY_SYMBOLS
/////////////////////////////////////////////////////////////////
//
// Generated from the TEXTINCLUDE 2 resource.
//
#define APSTUDIO_HIDDEN_SYMBOLS
#include "windows.h"
#undef APSTUDIO_HIDDEN_SYMBOLS
#include "afxres.h"

/////////////////////////////////////////////////////////////////
#undef APSTUDIO_READONLY_SYMBOLS

/////////////////////////////////////////////////////////////////
// English (U.S.) resources

#if !defined(AFX_RESOURCE_DLL) || defined(AFX_TARG_ENU)
#ifdef _WIN32
LANGUAGE LANG_ENGLISH, SUBLANG_ENGLISH_US
#pragma code_page(1252)
```

```
#endif //_WIN32

/////////////////////////////////////////////////////////////////////////////
//
// Menu
//

FOURIERMENU MENU DISCARDABLE
BEGIN
  POPUP "Fourier Data"
  BEGIN
    MENUITEM "Fourier Data...", IDM_FOUR
    MENUITEM "Fourier About...", IDM_ABOUT
    MENUITEM "Exit", IDM_EXIT
  END
END

/////////////////////////////////////////////////////////////////////////////
//
// Dialog
//

ABOUTBOX DIALOG DISCARDABLE  14, 22, 200, 75
STYLE WS_POPUP | WS_CAPTION
CAPTION "About Box"
BEGIN
  CTEXT "A Fourier Series Waveform",-1,30,5,144,8
  CTEXT "A MFC Application",-1,30,17,144,8
  CTEXT "By William H. Murray and Chris H. Pappas",
        -1,28,28,144,8
  CTEXT "(c) Copyright 1998",201,68,38,83,8
  DEFPUSHBUTTON   "OK",IDOK,84,55,32,14,WS_GROUP
END

FOURIERDATA DIALOG DISCARDABLE  74, 21, 142, 70
STYLE WS_POPUP | WS_CAPTION
CAPTION "Fourier Data"
BEGIN
  LTEXT "Title: ",-1,6,5,28,8,NOT WS_GROUP
  EDITTEXT IDD_TITLE,33,1,106,12
  LTEXT "Number of terms: ",-1,6,23,70,8,NOT WS_GROUP
  EDITTEXT IDD_TERMS,76,18,32,12
```

```
  PUSHBUTTON "OK",IDOK,25,52,24,14
  PUSHBUTTON "Cancel",IDCANCEL,89,53,28,14
END

#ifdef APSTUDIO_INVOKED
/////////////////////////////////////////////////////////////
//
// TEXTINCLUDE
//

1 TEXTINCLUDE DISCARDABLE
BEGIN
  "resource.h\0"
END

2 TEXTINCLUDE DISCARDABLE
BEGIN
  "#define APSTUDIO_HIDDEN_SYMBOLS\r\n"
  "#include ""windows.h""\r\n"
  "#undef APSTUDIO_HIDDEN_SYMBOLS\r\n"
  "#include ""afxres.h""\r\n"
  "\0"
END

3 TEXTINCLUDE DISCARDABLE
BEGIN
  "\r\n"
  "\0"
END

#endif    // APSTUDIO_INVOKED

#endif    // English (U.S.) resources
/////////////////////////////////////////////////////////////

#ifndef APSTUDIO_INVOKED
/////////////////////////////////////////////////////////////
//
// Generated from the TEXTINCLUDE 3 resource.
//

/////////////////////////////////////////////////////////////
#endif    // not APSTUDIO_INVOKED
```

The source code file, FOURIER.CPP, is slightly more complicated than the previous example because it must handle a menu and two dialog box resources. See if you can find this additional code as you examine the following listing:

```
//
//  fourier.cpp
//  Drawing A Fourier Series with the use of
//  the MFC library.
//  Copyright (c) William H. Murray and Chris H. Pappas, 1998
//

#include <afxwin.h>
#include <string.h>
#include <math.h>
#include "fourierR.h"    // resource IDs
#include "fourier.h"

int m_cxClient,m_cyClient;
char mytitle[80]="Title";
int nterms=1;

CTheApp theApp;

CMainWnd::CMainWnd( )
{
  Create((AfxRegisterWndClass(CS_HREDRAW|CS_VREDRAW,
         LoadCursor(NULL,IDC_CROSS),
         (HBRUSH) (GetStockObject(WHITE_BRUSH)),NULL)),
         "Fourier Series Application with the MFC",
         WS_OVERLAPPEDWINDOW,rectDefault,NULL,"FourierMenu");
}

void CMainWnd::OnSize(UINT,int x,int y)
{
  m_cxClient=x;
  m_cyClient=y;
}

void CMainWnd::OnPaint( )
{
  CPaintDC dc(this);
  static DWORD dwColor[9]={RGB(0,0,0),          //black
                           RGB(245,0,0),        //red
```

```
                                RGB(0,245,0),      //green
                                RGB(0,0,245),      //blue
                                RGB(245,245,0),    //yellow
                                RGB(245,0,245),    //magenta
                                RGB(0,245,245),    //cyan
                                RGB(127,127,127),  //gray
                                RGB(245,245,245)}; //white

int i,j,ltitle,ang;
double y,yp;
CBrush newbrush;
CBrush* oldbrush;
CPen newpen;
CPen* oldpen;

// create a custom drawing surface
dc.SetMapMode(MM_ISOTROPIC);
dc.SetWindowExt(500,500);
dc.SetViewportExt(m_cxClient,-m_cyClient);
dc.SetViewportOrg(m_cxClient/20,m_cyClient/2);

ang=0;
yp=0.0;

newpen.CreatePen(BS_SOLID,2,RGB(0,0,0));
oldpen=dc.SelectObject(&newpen);

// draw x & y coordinate axes
dc.MoveTo(0,240);
dc.LineTo(0,-240);
dc.MoveTo(0,0);
dc.LineTo(400,0);
dc.MoveTo(0,0);
// draw actual Fourier waveform
for (i=0; i<=400; i++) {
  for (j=1; j<=nterms; j++) {
    y=(150.0/((2.0*j)-1.0))*sin(((j*2.0)-1.0)*0.015708*ang);
    yp=yp+y;
  }
  dc.LineTo(i,(int) yp);
  yp-=yp;
```

```
    ang++;
  }

  // prepare to fill interior of waveform newbrush.
  newbrush.CreateSolidBrush(dwColor[7]);
  oldbrush=dc.SelectObject(&newbrush);
  dc.ExtFloodFill(150,10,dwColor[0],FLOODFILLBORDER);
  dc.ExtFloodFill(300,-10,dwColor[0],FLOODFILLBORDER);

  // print waveform title
  ltitle=strlen(mytitle);
  dc.TextOut(200-(ltitle*8/2),185,mytitle,ltitle);

  // delete brush objects
  dc.SelectObject(oldbrush);
  newbrush.DeleteObject( );
}

int CMainWnd::OnCreate(LPCREATESTRUCT)
{
  UpdateWindow( );
  return (0);
}

void CMainWnd::OnAbout( )
{
  CDialog about("AboutBox",this);
  about.DoModal( );
}

void CFourierDataDialog::OnOK( )
{
  GetDlgItemText(IDD_TITLE,mytitle,80);
  nterms=GetDlgItemInt(IDD_TERMS,NULL,0);
  CDialog::OnOK( );
}

void CMainWnd::OnFourierData( )
{
  CFourierDataDialog dlgFourierData(this);
  if (dlgFourierData.DoModal( )==IDOK) {
```

```
      InvalidateRect(NULL,TRUE);
      UpdateWindow( );
    }
  };

  void CMainWnd::OnExit( )
  {
    DestroyWindow( );
  }

  BEGIN_MESSAGE_MAP(CMainWnd,CFrameWnd)
    ON_WM_PAINT( )
    ON_WM_SIZE( )
    ON_WM_CREATE( )
    ON_COMMAND(IDM_ABOUT,OnAbout)
    ON_COMMAND(IDM_FOUR,OnFourierData)
    ON_COMMAND(IDM_EXIT,OnExit)
  END_MESSAGE_MAP( )

  BOOL CTheApp::InitInstance( )
  {
    m_pMainWnd=new CMainWnd( );
    m_pMainWnd->ShowWindow(m_nCmdShow);
    m_pMainWnd->UpdateWindow( );
    return TRUE;
  }
```

The FOURIER.H Header File

As the code segment below shows, **CMainWnd** now contains several function declarations and a message map. The member functions include OnPaint( ), OnSize( ), OnCreate( ), OnAbout( ), OnFourierData( ), and OnExit( ). The **afx_msg** keyword is used instead of **virtual**. The OnPaint( ) member function is found in the **CWnd** class. The **CWnd** class is overridden by the **CMainWnd** class. This allows the client area of the window to be altered.

```
afx_msg void OnPaint( );
afx_msg void OnSize(UINT,int,int);
afx_msg int  OnCreate(LPCREATESTRUCT cs);
afx_msg void OnAbout( );
afx_msg void OnFourierData( );
afx_msg void OnExit( );
```

The OnPaint( ) function is automatically called when a WM_PAINT message is sent to a **CMainWnd** object by Windows or the application. The OnSize( ) function is called whenever a WM_SIZE message is generated by a change in the size of the window. This information will be useful for scaling graphics to the window size. The OnCreate( ) function points to a structure that contains information about the window being created. This structure contains information on the size, style, and other aspects of the window. The functions OnAbout( ), OnFourierData( ), and OnExit( ) are user-defined functions that respond to WM_COMMAND messages. WM_COMMAND messages are generated when the user selects an option from a menu or dialog box.

DECLARE_MESSAGE_MAP is used again to state that the class overrides the handling of certain messages. (See the body of the application.) Recall that this technique is more space efficient than the use of **virtual** functions.

The MFC library supports regular and modal dialog boxes with the **CDialog** class. For very simple dialog boxes such as About boxes, the MFC can be used directly. For data entry dialog boxes, however, the class will have to be derived. The dialog box for this example will permit the user to enter an optional graph title and an integer for the number of harmonics to be drawn in the window. The **CFourierDataDialog** class is derived from the **CDialog** foundation class. Modal dialog boxes must be dismissed before other actions can be taken in an application, as shown in the following portion of code:

```
class CFourierDataDialog : public CDialog
{
public:
  CFourierDataDialog(CWnd* pParentWnd=NULL)
                    : CDialog("FourierData",pParentWnd)
                    { }
  virtual void OnOK( );
};
```

In a derived modal dialog class, member variables and functions can be added to specify the behavior of the dialog box. Member variables can also be used to save data entered by the user or to save data for display. Classes derived from **CDialog** require their own message maps, with the exception of the OnInitDialog( ), OnOK( ), and OnCancel( ) functions.

In this simple example, the CfourierDataDialog( ) constructor supplies the name of the dialog box, "FourierData," and the name of the dialog box's owner. The parent window is the owner for this modal dialog box.

The dialog box will actually return data to the application when the user clicks on the OK dialog box button. If either the OK or the Cancel button is clicked, the dialog box closes and is removed from the screen. When the dialog box closes, the member functions access their member variables to retrieve information entered by the user. Dialog boxes requiring initialization can override the OnInitDialog( ) member function for this purpose.

The Resource Files

The FOURIERR.H resource header file and the FOURIER.RC resource script file are used by the resource compiler to produce a single compiled Windows resource.

The FOURIERR.H resource header file contains five identification values. IDM_FOUR, IDM_ABOUT, and IDM_EXIT are used for menu selection choices, while IDD_TERMS and IDD_TITLE are for the data entry dialog box.

The resource script file also contains a description of the application's menu and dialog boxes. The menu is shown in Figure 23-3. Compare the menu title and features to the text used to create the menu in the resource file.

This application also uses two dialog boxes. Figure 23-4 shows the About dialog box for this application.

Figure 23-5 shows the data entry dialog box for this application.

Take a minute to compare the text file for each dialog box with the actual screen figures. Remember that the dialog box resources used the resource editor to construct both dialog boxes.

The FOURIER.CPP Source Code File

The complexity of the application file for this example has increased greatly because of the inclusion of menus and dialog boxes. Other features, which you might want to include in your own programs, have also been added. In the following sections, you'll see how to:

- Determine the size of the current window
- Draw and fill an object in the window
- Select a new cursor
- Set a new viewport and origin for drawing

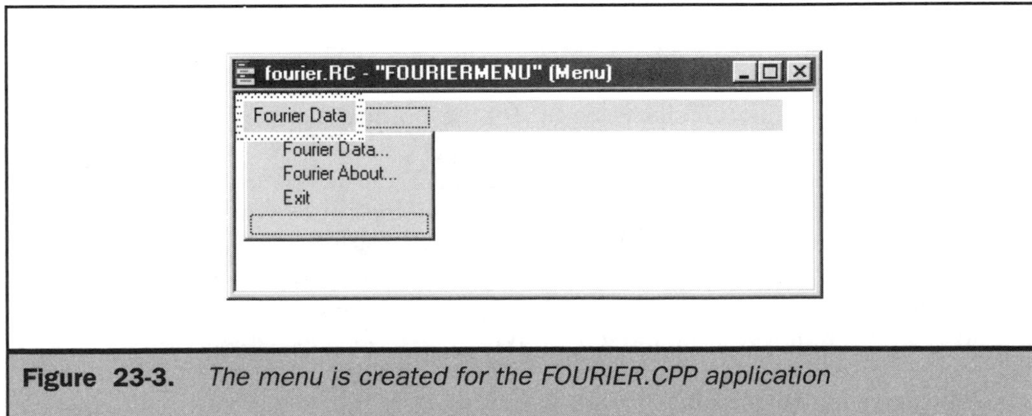

Figure 23-3. *The menu is created for the FOURIER.CPP application*

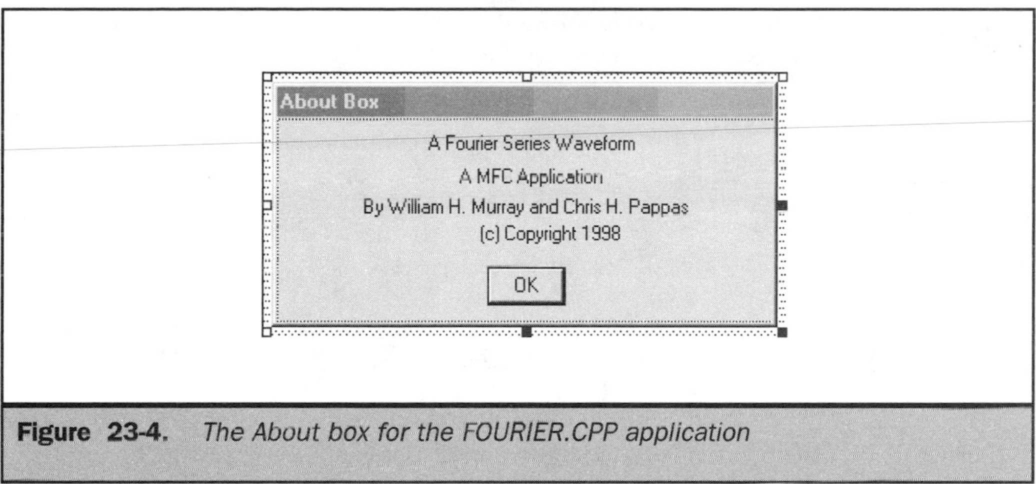

Figure 23-4. *The About box for the FOURIER.CPP application*

- Set the background color

Let's examine these features as they appear in the program.

Creating a Custom CMainWnd Class

Using **AfxRegisterWndClass** to create a **registration** class can customize the **CMainWnd** class. A **registration** class has many fields, but four are easily altered: style, cursor, background, and the Minimize icon.

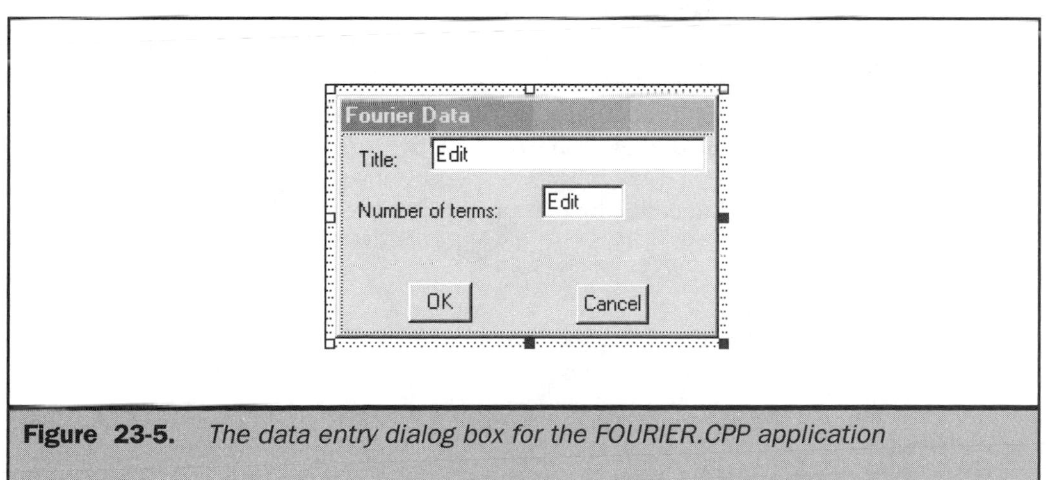

Figure 23-5. *The data entry dialog box for the FOURIER.CPP application*

The following small piece of code shows the syntax for changing the cursor to a stock cross shape (IDC_CROSS) and setting the brush that paints the background to a WHITE_BRUSH:

```
CMainWnd::CMainWnd( )
{
  Create((AfxRegisterWndClass(CS_HREDRAW|CS_VREDRAW,
        LoadCursor(NULL,IDC_CROSS),
        (HBRUSH) GetStockObject(WHITE_BRUSH),NULL)),
        " Fourier Series Application with the MFC",
        WS_OVERLAPPEDWINDOW,rectDefault,NULL,"FourierMenu");
}
```

Also note that the menu name is identified in the Create( ) member function.

Determining the Window's Current Size

The OnSize( ) member function returns the size of the current client window. A WM_SIZE message is generated whenever the window is resized. As shown here, the current window size is saved in two variables, *m_cxClient* and *m_cyClient*:

```
void CMainWnd::OnSize(UINT,int x,int y)
{
  m_cxClient=x;
  m_cyClient=y;
}
```

These values will be used to scale the graphics the application draws to fit the current window's dimensions.

Drawing the Fourier Waveform

In order to prevent the scaling problems described in the previous example, a scalable drawing surface is created. You may wish to review the purpose of these functions in Chapter 21.

As shown in the following code, the mapping mode is changed to MM_ISOTROPIC with the SetMapMode( ) function. The MM_ISOTROPIC mapping mode uses arbitrary drawing units.

```
dc.SetMapMode(MM_ISOTROPIC);
```

The next line of code shows the window's extent set to 500 units in both the *x* and *y* directions:

```
dc.SetWindowExt(500,500);
```

This simply means that the *x* and *y* axes will always have 500 units, regardless of the size of the window. The viewport extent is set to the currently reported window size, as shown here:

```
dc.SetViewportExt(m_cxClient,-m_cyClient);
```

In this case, you will see all 500 units in the window.

Note *Using a negative value when specifying the y viewport extent forces y to increase in the upward direction.*

As the following code shows, the viewport origin is set midway on the *y* axis a short distance (a fifth of the length) from the left edge of the *x* axis:

```
dc.SetViewportOrg(m_cxClient/20,m_cyClient/2);
```

Next, *x* and *y* coordinate axes are drawn in the window. Compare the values shown here to the axes shown in screen shots later in this section:

```
// draw x & y coordinate axes
dc.MoveTo(0,240);
dc.LineTo(0,-240);
dc.MoveTo(0,0);
dc.LineTo(400,0);
dc.MoveTo(0,0);
```

The technique for drawing the Fourier wave, shown below, uses two **for** loops. The *i* variable controls the angle used by the sine function, and the *j* variable holds the value for the current Fourier harmonic. Each point plotted on the screen is a summation of all the Fourier harmonics for a given angle. Thus, if you request that the application draw 1,000 harmonics, approximately 400,000 separate calculations will be made.

```
// draw actual Fourier waveform
for (i=0; i<=400; i++)
{
  for (j=1; j<=nterms; j++)
  {
    y=(150.0/((2.0*j)-1.0))*sin(((j*2.0)-1.0)*0.015708*ang);
```

```
      yp=yp+y;
    }
    dc.LineTo(i,(int) yp);
    yp-=yp;
    ang++;
  }
```

The LineTo( ) function is used to connect each calculated point, forming a waveform drawn with a solid line. This waveform will have its interior region filled with a gray color by the ExtFloodFill( ) function. The ExtFloodFill( ) function requires the coordinates of a point within the fill region and the bounding color that the figure was drawn with. The FLOODFILLBORDER parameter fills to the boundary color. You can determine these values from the following code:

```
// prepare to fill interior of waveform newbrush.
  newbrush.CreateSolidBrush(dwColor[7]);
  oldbrush=dc.SelectObject(&newbrush);
  dc.ExtFloodFill(150,10,dwColor[0],FLOODFILLBORDER);
  dc.ExtFloodFill(300,-10,dwColor[0],FLOODFILLBORDER);
```

Before the figure is completed, a title is printed in the window and the brush object is deleted, as shown here:

```
// print waveform title
ltitle=strlen(mytitle);
dc.TextOut(200-(ltitle*8/2),185,mytitle,ltitle);

// delete brush objects
dc.SelectObject(oldbrush);
newbrush.DeleteObject( );
```

Remember that all objects drawn within the client area will be scaled to the viewport. This program eliminates the sizing problem of earlier examples and requires only a little additional coding.

The About Dialog Box

About boxes are very easy to create and implement. About boxes are used to communicate information about the program, the program's designers, the copyright date, and so on.

A modal dialog box is created when the user selects the Fourier About... option from the application's menu. The OnAbout( ) command handler requires only a few lines of code:

```
void CMainWnd::OnAbout( )
{
  CDialog about("AboutBox",this);
  about.DoModal( );
}
```

The constructor for **CDialog** uses the current window as the parent window for the object. The **this** pointer is typically used here and refers to the currently used object. The DoModal( ) member function is responsible for drawing the About box in the client area. When the OK button in the About box is clicked, the box is removed and the client area is repainted.

The Data Entry Dialog Box

Dialog boxes that allow user input require a bit more programming than simple About boxes do. A data input dialog box can be selected from the application's menu by selecting Fourier Data....

An illustration of this dialog box was shown earlier. The user is permitted to enter a chart title and an integer representing the number of Fourier harmonics to draw. If the user clicks on the OK button, the data entry dialog box is removed from the window and the client area is updated, as shown in the following portion of code:

```
void CMainWnd::OnFourierData( )
{
  CFourierDataDialog dlgFourierData(this);
  if (dlgFourierData.DoModal( )==IDOK)
  {
    InvalidateRect(NULL,TRUE);
    UpdateWindow( );
  }
};
```


CFourierDataDialog was derived from **CDialog** in the header file, FOURIER.H, as discussed earlier. Notice, however, that it is at this point in the application that data is retrieved. The user entered this data in the dialog box. Here is a portion of code that returns this information when the dialog box's OK push button is clicked:

```
void CFourierDataDialog::OnOK( )
{
  GetDlgItemText(IDD_TITLE,mytitle,80);
  nterms=GetDlgItemInt(IDD_TERMS,NULL,0);
  CDialog::OnOK( );
}
```

The GetDlgItemText( ) function returns chart title information to mytitle in the form of a string. The dialog box location for this information is identified by IDD_TITLE. Integer information can be processed in a similar manner with the GetDlgItemInt( ) function. Its dialog box identification value is IDD_TERMS, and the integer retrieved by the function is returned to the variable *nterms*. The second parameter is used to report translation errors, but is not used in this application. If the third parameter is nonzero, a check will be made for a signed number. In this application, only positive numbers are possible.

Responding to OnExit( )

The final application menu option is Exit. Exit will destroy the client window by calling the DestroyWindow( ) function:

```
void CMainWnd::OnExit( )
{
  DestroyWindow( );
}
```

This application menu option gives the user a method of exiting the application without using the system menu.

The Message Map

Two classes are specified in BEGIN_MESSAGE_MAP: **CMainWnd** and **CFrameWnd**. **CMainWnd** is the target class, and **CFrameWnd** is a class based on **CWnd**. The ON_WM_PAINT( ) function handles all WM_PAINT messages and directs them to the OnPaint( ) member function. ON_WM_SIZE( ) handles WM_SIZE messages and directs them to the OnSize( ) member function. The ON_WM_CREATE( ) function handles WM_CREATE messages and directs them to the OnCreate( ) member function. There is an ON_COMMAND( ) function for each application menu item. Message information on menu items is processed and then returned to the appropriate member function. Here is the message map for this example:

```
BEGIN_MESSAGE_MAP(CMainWnd,CFrameWnd)
  ON_WM_PAINT( )
  ON_WM_SIZE( )
```

```
    ON_WM_CREATE( )
    ON_COMMAND(IDM_ABOUT,OnAbout)
    ON_COMMAND(IDM_FOUR,OnFourierData)
    ON_COMMAND(IDM_EXIT,OnExit)
END_MESSAGE_MAP( )
```

As mentioned in an earlier example, the use of message maps has eliminated the need for error-prone **switch/case** statements.

Running FOURIER

Compile the application with the Project utility. When the FOURIER application is executed, a default waveform is drawn in the client area. A default value of one harmonic produces a sine wave, as shown in Figure 23-6. Figure 23-7 shows ten harmonics, and Figure 23-8 shows 50 harmonics.

As the number of harmonics increases, the figure drawn in the client area will approach a perfect square wave. You can experiment with various values and note how the drawing time increases for very large numbers of harmonics.

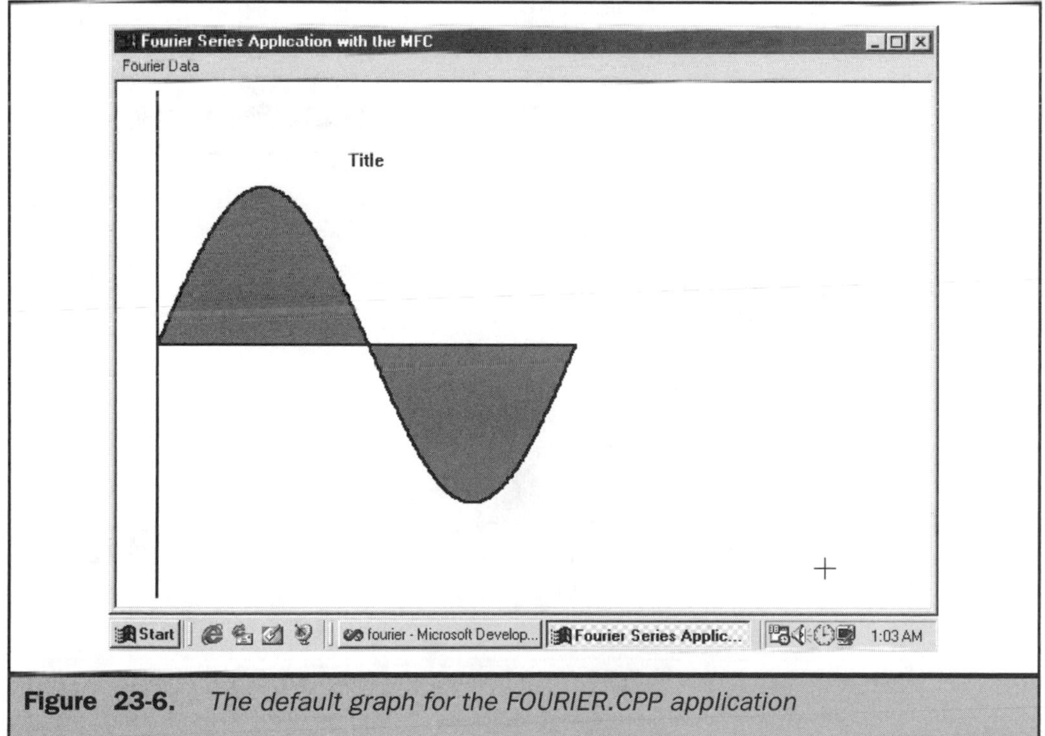

Figure 23-6. *The default graph for the FOURIER.CPP application*

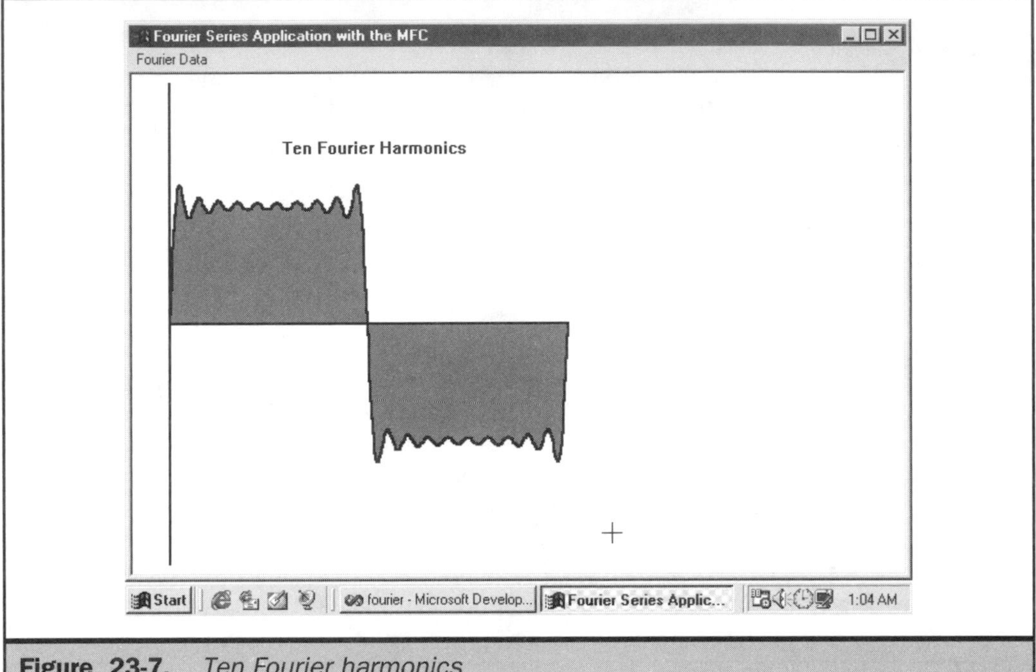

Figure 23-7. *Ten Fourier harmonics*

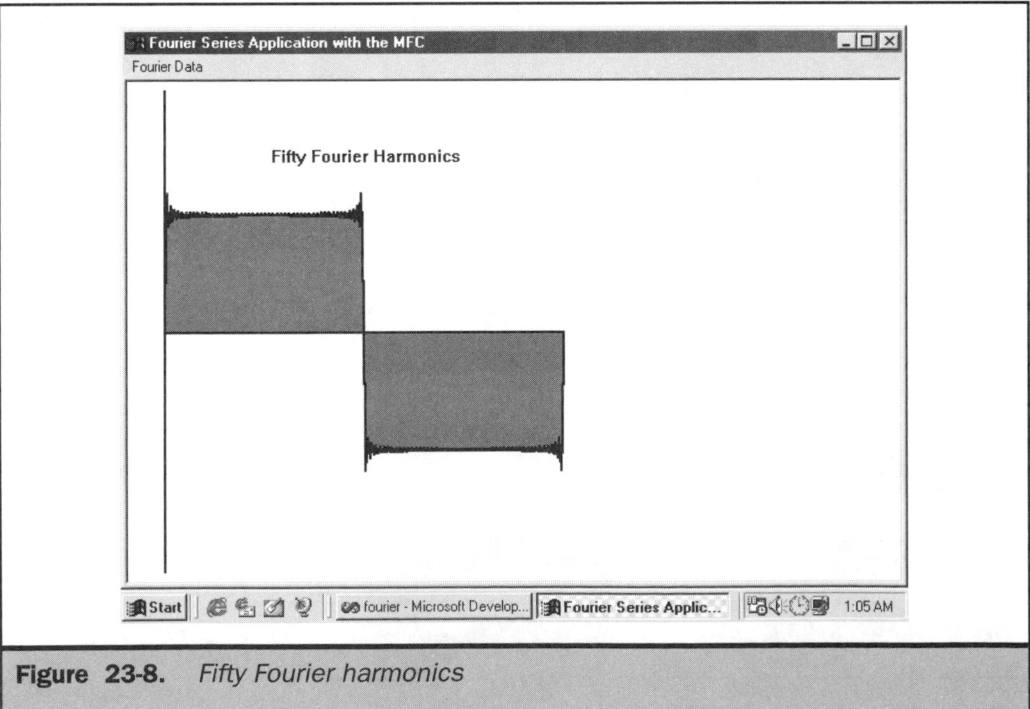

Figure 23-8. *Fifty Fourier harmonics*

A Bar Chart with Resources

The final application in this chapter, BARCHART.CPP, will draw a presentation-quality bar chart in the window's client area. This application also makes use of several Windows resources, including a menu, an About dialog box, and a data entry dialog box.

The complete application is compiled and linked with four separate files. These files include the header file, BARCHART.H, the resource header file, BARCHARTR.H, the resource script file, BARCHART.RC and the source code file, BARCHART.CPP.

Enter each file carefully. You will also need to create a project file. Remember to mark this as a MFC application. The BARCHART.RC and BARCHART.CPP must be named in the project file's list of files to include for the build. When all files have been entered, the application can be compiled and linked.

The BARCHART.H header file gives our class descriptions for **CMainWnd**, **CTheApp**, and **CBarDataDialog**. These classes are children of MFC library classes.

```
class CMainWnd : public CFrameWnd
{
public:
  CMainWnd( );
  afx_msg void OnPaint( );
  afx_msg void OnSize(UINT,int,int);
  afx_msg int  OnCreate(LPCREATESTRUCT cs);
  afx_msg void OnAbout( );
  afx_msg void OnBarData( );
  afx_msg void OnExit( );
  DECLARE_MESSAGE_MAP( )
};

class CTheApp : public CWinApp
{
public:
  virtual BOOL InitInstance( );
};

class CBarDataDialog : public CDialog
{
public:
  CBarDataDialog(CWnd* pParentWnd=NULL)
                : CDialog("BarDlgBox",pParentWnd)
                {  }
  virtual void OnOK( );
};
```

The BARCHARTR.H resource header file contains the ID values that will be used for the menu and two dialog boxes:

```
#define IDM_ABOUT     10
#define IDM_INPUT     20
#define IDM_EXIT      30
#define DM_TITLE     300
#define DM_XLABEL    301
#define DM_YLABEL    302
#define DM_P1        303
#define DM_P2        304
#define DM_P3        305
#define DM_P4        306
#define DM_P5        307
#define DM_P6        308
#define DM_P7        309
#define DM_P8        310
#define DM_P9        311
#define DM_P10       312
```

The BARCHART.RC resource script file defines the application's menu and dialog boxes:

```
//Microsoft Developer Studio generated resource script.
//
#include "resource.h"
#include "barchartr.h"

#define APSTUDIO_READONLY_SYMBOLS
/////////////////////////////////////////////////////////////////////////////
//
// Generated from the TEXTINCLUDE 2 resource.
//
#define APSTUDIO_HIDDEN_SYMBOLS
#include "windows.h"
#undef APSTUDIO_HIDDEN_SYMBOLS
#include "afxres.h"

/////////////////////////////////////////////////////////////////////////////
#undef APSTUDIO_READONLY_SYMBOLS

/////////////////////////////////////////////////////////////////////////////
```

```
// English (U.S.) resources

#if !defined(AFX_RESOURCE_DLL) || defined(AFX_TARG_ENU)
#ifdef _WIN32
LANGUAGE LANG_ENGLISH, SUBLANG_ENGLISH_US
#pragma code_page(1252)
#endif //_WIN32

/////////////////////////////////////////////////////////////
//
// Menu
//

BARMENU MENU DISCARDABLE
BEGIN
  POPUP "Bar_Chart"
  BEGIN
    MENUITEM "About Box...", IDM_ABOUT
    MENUITEM "Bar Values...", IDM_INPUT
    MENUITEM "Exit", IDM_EXIT
  END
END

/////////////////////////////////////////////////////////////
//
// Dialog
//

ABOUTDLGBOX DIALOG DISCARDABLE  14, 22, 200, 75
STYLE WS_POPUP | WS_CAPTION
CAPTION "About Box"
BEGIN
  CTEXT "A Bar Chart Application",-1,30,5,144,8
  CTEXT "A Simple MFC Windows Application",-1,30,17,144,8
  CTEXT "By William H. Murray and Chris H. Pappas",
         -1,28,28,144,8
  CTEXT "(c) Copyright 1998",-1,68,38,83,8
  DEFPUSHBUTTON   "OK",IDOK,84,55,32,14,WS_GROUP
END

BARDLGBOX DIALOG DISCARDABLE  42, 65526, 223, 209
```

```
STYLE WS_POPUP | WS_CAPTION
CAPTION "Bar Chart Data"
BEGIN
  GROUPBOX "Bar Chart Title:",100,5,11,212,89,WS_TABSTOP
  GROUPBOX "Bar Chart Heights",101,5,105,212,90,WS_TABSTOP
  LTEXT "Title: ",-1,43,35,28,8,NOT WS_GROUP
  EDITTEXT DM_TITLE,75,30,137,12
  LTEXT "x-axis label:",-1,15,55,55,8,NOT WS_GROUP
  EDITTEXT DM_XLABEL,75,50,135,12
  LTEXT "y-axis label:",-1,15,75,60,8,NOT WS_GROUP
  EDITTEXT DM_YLABEL,75,70,135,12
  LTEXT "Bar #1: ",-1,45,125,40,8,NOT WS_GROUP
  LTEXT "Bar #2: ",-1,45,140,40,8,NOT WS_GROUP
  LTEXT "Bar #3: ",-1,45,155,40,8,NOT WS_GROUP
  LTEXT "Bar #4: ",-1,45,170,40,8,NOT WS_GROUP
  LTEXT "Bar #5: ",-1,45,185,40,8,NOT WS_GROUP
  LTEXT "Bar #6: ",-1,130,125,40,8,NOT WS_GROUP
  LTEXT "Bar #7: ",-1,130,140,40,8,NOT WS_GROUP
  LTEXT "Bar #8: ",-1,130,155,40,8,NOT WS_GROUP
  LTEXT "Bar #9: ",-1,130,170,40,8,NOT WS_GROUP
  LTEXT "Bar #10:",-1,130,185,45,8,NOT WS_GROUP
  EDITTEXT DM_P1,90,120,30,12
  EDITTEXT DM_P2,90,135,30,12
  EDITTEXT DM_P3,90,150,30,12
  EDITTEXT DM_P4,90,165,30,12
  EDITTEXT DM_P5,90,180,30,12
  EDITTEXT DM_P6,180,120,30,12
  EDITTEXT DM_P7,180,135,30,12
  EDITTEXT DM_P8,180,150,30,12
  EDITTEXT DM_P9,180,165,30,12
  EDITTEXT DM_P10,180,180,30,12
  PUSHBUTTON "OK",IDOK,54,195,24,14
  PUSHBUTTON "Cancel",IDCANCEL,124,195,34,14
END

#ifdef APSTUDIO_INVOKED
/////////////////////////////////////////////////////////////////////////////
//
// TEXTINCLUDE
//
```

```
1 TEXTINCLUDE DISCARDABLE
BEGIN
  "resource.h\0"
END

2 TEXTINCLUDE DISCARDABLE
BEGIN
  "#define APSTUDIO_HIDDEN_SYMBOLS\r\n"
  "#include ""windows.h""\r\n"
  "#undef APSTUDIO_HIDDEN_SYMBOLS\r\n"
  "#include ""afxres.h""\r\n"
  "\0"
END

3 TEXTINCLUDE DISCARDABLE
BEGIN
  "\r\n"
  "\0"
END

#endif    // APSTUDIO_INVOKED

#endif    // English (U.S.) resources
/////////////////////////////////////////////////////////////

#ifndef APSTUDIO_INVOKED
/////////////////////////////////////////////////////////////
//
// Generated from the TEXTINCLUDE 3 resource.
//

/////////////////////////////////////////////////////////////
#endif    // not APSTUDIO_INVOKED
```


It took a while to get here, but we're now ready to look at the source code for the BARCHART.CPP application. Examine this code and note the inclusion of various resources such as menus, dialog boxes, etc.

```
//
//  barchart.cpp
//  A Presentation Quality Bar Chart Application
```

```
//  using the MFC Library.
//  Copyright (c) William H. Murray and Chris H. Pappas, 1998
//

#include <afxwin.h>
#include <string.h>
#include <math.h>
#include <stdlib.h>
#include "barchartr.h"   // resource IDs
#include "barchart.h"

#define maxnumbar 10
char szTString[80]="(bar chart title area)";
char szXString[80]="x-axis label";
char szYString[80]="y-axis label";
int iBarSize[maxnumbar]={20,10,40,50};
int m_cxClient,m_cyClient;

CTheApp theApp;

CMainWnd::CMainWnd( )
{
  Create((AfxRegisterWndClass(CS_HREDRAW|CS_VREDRAW,
        LoadCursor(NULL,IDC_CROSS),
        (HBRUSH) GetStockObject(WHITE_BRUSH),NULL)),
        "Bar Chart Application with the MFC",
        WS_OVERLAPPEDWINDOW,rectDefault,NULL,"BarMenu");
}

void CMainWnd::OnSize(UINT,int x,int y)
{
  m_cxClient=x;
  m_cyClient=y;
}

void CMainWnd::OnPaint( )
{
  CPaintDC dc(this);
  static DWORD dwColor[10]={RGB(0,0,0),         //black
                            RGB(245,0,0),       //red
                            RGB(0,245,0),       //green
                            RGB(0,0,245),       //blue
```

```
                                    RGB(245,245,0),     //yellow
                                    RGB(245,0,245),     //magenta
                                    RGB(0,245,245),     //cyan
                                    RGB(0,80,80),       //blend 1
                                    RGB(80,80,80),      //blend 2
                                    RGB(245,245,245)}; //white

    CFont newfont;
    CFont* oldfont;
    CBrush newbrush;
    CBrush* oldbrush;
    int i,iNBars,iBarWidth,iBarMax;
    int ilenMaxLabel;
    int x1,x2,y1,y2;
    int iBarSizeScaled[maxnumbar];
    char sbuffer[10],*strptr;

    iNBars=0;
    for (i=0;i<maxnumbar;i++) {
      if(iBarSize[i]!=0) iNBars++;
    }

    iBarWidth=400/iNBars;

    // Find bar with maximum height and scale
    iBarMax=iBarSize[0];
    for(i=0;i<iNBars;i++)
      if (iBarMax<iBarSize[i]) iBarMax=iBarSize[i];

    // Convert maximum y value to a string
    strptr=_itoa(iBarMax,sbuffer,10);
    ilenMaxLabel=strlen(sbuffer);

    // Scale bars in array.  Highest bar = 270
    for (i=0;i<iNBars;i++)
      iBarSizeScaled[i]=iBarSize[i]*(270/iBarMax);

    // Create custom viewport and map mode
    dc.SetMapMode(MM_ISOTROPIC);
    dc.SetWindowExt(640,400);
    dc.SetViewportExt(m_cxClient,m_cyClient);
```

```
dc.SetViewportOrg(0,0);

// Draw text to window if large enough
if (m_cxClient > 200) {
newfont.CreateFont(12,12,0,0,FW_BOLD,
                   FALSE,FALSE,FALSE,OEM_CHARSET,
                   OUT_DEFAULT_PRECIS,
                   CLIP_DEFAULT_PRECIS,
                   DEFAULT_QUALITY,
                   VARIABLE_PITCH|FF_ROMAN,
                   "Roman");
oldfont=dc.SelectObject(&newfont);
dc.TextOut((300-(strlen(szTString)*10/2)),
            15,szTString,strlen(szTString));
dc.TextOut((300-(strlen(szXString)*10/2)),
            365,szXString,strlen(szXString));
dc.TextOut((90-ilenMaxLabel*12),70,strptr,ilenMaxLabel);
// delete font objects
dc.SelectObject(oldfont);
newfont.DeleteObject( );

newfont.CreateFont(12,12,900,900,FW_BOLD,
                   FALSE,FALSE,FALSE,
                   OEM_CHARSET,OUT_DEFAULT_PRECIS,
                   CLIP_DEFAULT_PRECIS,
                   DEFAULT_QUALITY,
                   VARIABLE_PITCH|FF_ROMAN,
                   "Roman");
oldfont=dc.SelectObject(&newfont);
dc.TextOut(50,200+(strlen(szXString)*10/2),
           szYString,strlen(szYString));
// delete font objects
dc.SelectObject(oldfont);
newfont.DeleteObject( );
}

// Draw coordinate axis
dc.MoveTo(99,49);
dc.LineTo(99,350);
dc.LineTo(500,350);
dc.MoveTo(99,350);
```

```
  // Initial values
  x1=100;
  y1=350;
  x2=x1+iBarWidth;

  // Draw Each Bar
  for(i=0;i<iNBars;i++) {
    newbrush.CreateSolidBrush(dwColor[i]);
    oldbrush=dc.SelectObject(&newbrush);
    y2=350-iBarSizeScaled[i];
    dc.Rectangle(x1,y1,x2,y2);
    x1=x2;
    x2+=iBarWidth;
    // delete brush objects
    dc.SelectObject(oldbrush);
    newbrush.DeleteObject( );
  }
}

int CMainWnd::OnCreate(LPCREATESTRUCT)
{
  UpdateWindow( );
  return (0);
}

void CMainWnd::OnAbout( )
{
  CDialog about("AboutDlgBox",this);
  about.DoModal( );
}

void CBarDataDialog::OnOK( )
{
  GetDlgItemText(DM_TITLE,szTString,80);
  GetDlgItemText(DM_XLABEL,szXString,80);
  GetDlgItemText(DM_YLABEL,szYString,80);
  iBarSize[0]=GetDlgItemInt(DM_P1,NULL,0);
  iBarSize[1]=GetDlgItemInt(DM_P2,NULL,0);
  iBarSize[2]=GetDlgItemInt(DM_P3,NULL,0);
  iBarSize[3]=GetDlgItemInt(DM_P4,NULL,0);
  iBarSize[4]=GetDlgItemInt(DM_P5,NULL,0);
```

```
  iBarSize[5]=GetDlgItemInt(DM_P6,NULL,0);
  iBarSize[6]=GetDlgItemInt(DM_P7,NULL,0);
  iBarSize[7]=GetDlgItemInt(DM_P8,NULL,0);
  iBarSize[8]=GetDlgItemInt(DM_P9,NULL,0);
  iBarSize[9]=GetDlgItemInt(DM_P10,NULL,0);
  CDialog::OnOK( );
}

void CMainWnd::OnBarData( )
{
  CBarDataDialog dlgBarData(this);
  if (dlgBarData.DoModal( )==IDOK) {
    InvalidateRect(NULL,TRUE);
    UpdateWindow( );
  }
};

void CMainWnd::OnExit( )
{
  DestroyWindow( );
}

BEGIN_MESSAGE_MAP(CMainWnd,CFrameWnd)
  ON_WM_PAINT( )
  ON_WM_SIZE( )
  ON_WM_CREATE( )
  ON_COMMAND(IDM_ABOUT,OnAbout)
  ON_COMMAND(IDM_INPUT,OnBarData)
  ON_COMMAND(IDM_EXIT,OnExit)
END_MESSAGE_MAP( )

BOOL CTheApp::InitInstance( )
{
  m_pMainWnd=new CMainWnd( );
  m_pMainWnd->ShowWindow(m_nCmdShow);
  m_pMainWnd->UpdateWindow( );
  return TRUE;
}
```

When all of these files are entered, build the application with the Visual C++ Project utility.

The BARCHART.H Header File

This application will use many of the features of the previous application. For example, note the similar function declarations in **CMainWnd** and the message map:

```
afx_msg void On Paint( );
afx_msg void OnSize(UINT,int,int);
afx_msg int  OnCreate(LPCREATESTRUCT cs);
afx_msg void OnAbout( );
afx_msg void OnBarData( );
afx_msg void OnExit( );
```

The creation of the About and data entry dialog boxes parallels the last example. In this application, however, the data entry dialog box will process more user input than in the previous example. You may want to review the information dealing with dialog boxes in the previous example at this time.

The Resource Files

The BARCHARTR.H and BARCHART.RC files are combined by the Microsoft Resource Compiler into a single compiled Windows resource, BARCHART.RES.

The BARCHARTR.H resource header file contains three menu identification values: IDM_ABOUT, IDM_INPUT, and IDM_EXIT.

Thirteen identification values are also included for use by the modal dialog box. Three are for the title and labels: DM_TITLE, DM_XLABEL, and DM_YLABEL. The remaining ten values, DM_P1 to DM_P10, are for retrieving the height of the individual bars. They will be represented with integer values.

The resource script file, BARCHART.RC, contains a description of the application's menu and dialog boxes. The menu is shown in Figure 23-9. Compare the menu title and features to the text used to create the menu in the resource file.

The application contains two dialog boxes. The About box is almost identical to that used in the previous application. The data entry dialog box is a bit more complex, and is shown in Figure 23-10.

The resource editor was used to construct both the About dialog box and the data entry dialog box.

The BARCHART.CPP Source Code File

This section concentrates on those features of the bar chart application that were not addressed in the applications developed earlier in this chapter. The BARCHART.CPP application will allow the user to draw a presentation-quality bar chart in the client area of a window. With the use of a modal dialog box, the user can specify a chart title, axis labels, and the heights of up to ten bars. The chart will then be correctly scaled to the window, with each bar's color selected from an array of predefined values.

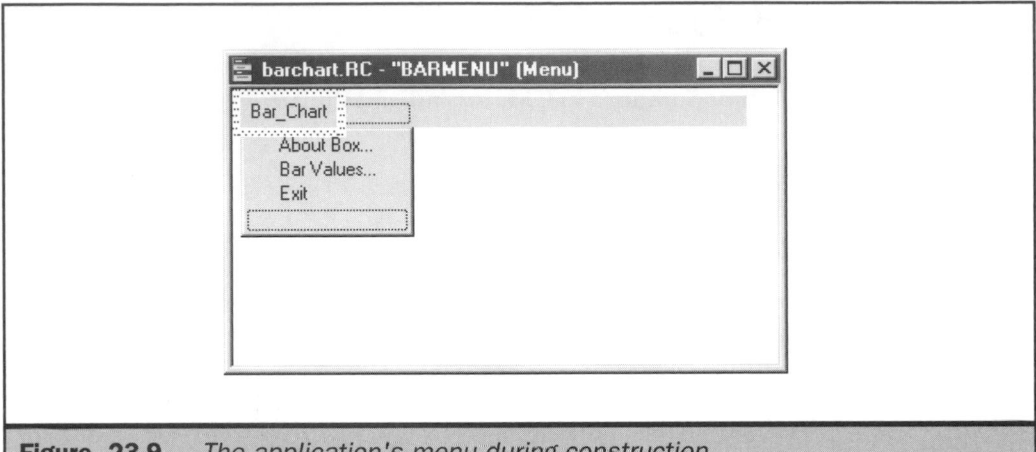

Figure 23-9. *The application's menu during construction*

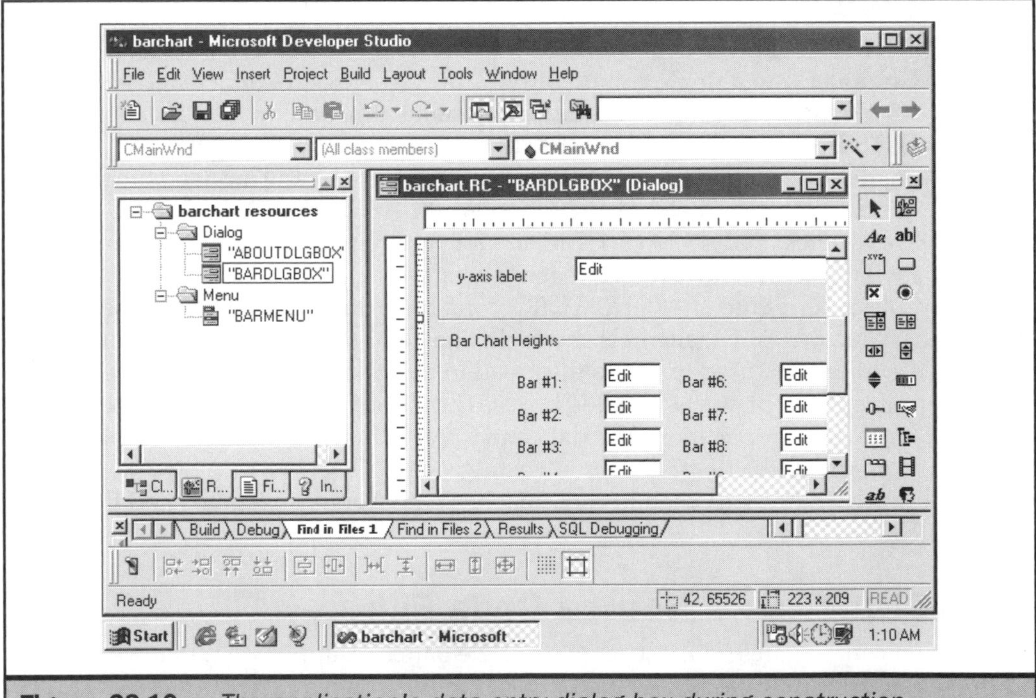

Figure 23-10. *The application's data entry dialog box during construction*

The maximum number of bars, *maxnumbar*, is set to ten at the start of the application:

```
#define maxnumbar 10
```

This value can be changed slightly, but remember that a good bar chart doesn't crowd too many bars onto a single chart.

As you can see in the following code, global data types hold initial bar chart values for titles, axis labels, and bar heights:

```
char szTString[80]="(bar chart title area)";
char szXString[80]="x-axis label";
char szYString[80]="y-axis label";
int iBarSize[maxnumbar]={20,10,40,50};
```

The size of the client area will also be saved as a global value. These are the same variable names used in the previous example:

```
int m_cxClient,m_cyClient;
```

Because the application keeps track of the client area size, this bar chart can be scaled to fit the current window size.

Bar colors are selected from the *dwColor* array in a sequential manner. If the bar chart has three bars, they will be black, red, and green. Colors can be exchanged if you so desire.

The **CFont** and **CBrush** classes permit a font or brush object to be passed to any CDC (base class for display context) member function. New fonts will be needed to draw the chart title and axis labels. Brushes were discussed earlier in this chapter. Here is the syntax used to create a new font and brush object:

```
CFont newfont;
CFont* oldfont;
CBrush newbrush;
CBrush* oldbrush;
```


Manipulating Bar Data

Before plotting a bar chart, it is first necessary to determine how many bar values are being held in the global array *iBarSize*. This can be determined by counting values until the first zero value is encountered:

```
iNBars=0;
for (i=0;i<maxnumbar;i++)
{
  if(iBarSize[i]!=0) iNBars++;
}
```

Data values are returned to this array whenever the data entry dialog box is closed. The width of each bar drawn in the chart is dependent upon the total number of bars. The chart will always be drawn to the same width. Individual bar width is determined with this calculation:

```
iBarWidth=400/iNBars;
```

The height of each bar is determined relative to the largest bar value entered by the user. The largest bar value is always drawn to the same chart height. The size of the largest bar value is easy to determine:

```
// Find bar with maximum height and scale
iBarMax=iBarSize[0];
for(i=0;i<iNBars;i++)
  if (iBarMax<iBarSize[i]) iBarMax=iBarSize[i];
```

This chart will also print the height of the largest bar value next to the vertical axis. The _itoa( ) function is used to convert this value to a string:

```
// Convert maximum y value to a string
strptr=_itoa(iBarMax,sbuffer,10);
ilenMaxLabel=strlen(sbuffer);
```

The remaining bars in the array are then scaled to the largest bar's value:

```
// Scale bars in array. Highest bar = 270
for (i=0;i<iNBars;i++)
  iBarSizeScaled[i]=iBarSize[i]*(270/iBarMax);
```

Preparing the Window

Before the application begins drawing in the window's client area, the mapping mode, window extent, viewport extent, and origin are set with the following portion of code:

```
// Create custom viewport and map mode
dc.SetMapMode(MM_ISOTROPIC);
dc.SetWindowExt(640,400);
dc.SetViewportExt(m_cxClient,m_cyClient);
dc.SetViewportOrg(0,0);
```

This same action was taken in the previous example to ensure that when the window changes size, the chart will remain proportional to the window size. See the previous application for additional details on these function calls.

Drawing Text to the Window

The previous application drew text to the screen using the Windows default font. When several fonts or orientations are required, various font functions must be used. This application requires several font sizes and orientations. Let's look at how these can be created. There are actually two ways to create and manipulate fonts in Windows: CreateFont( ) and CreateFontIndirect( ). This example uses the CreateFont( ) function.

WHAT IS A FONT? A font can be defined as a complete set of characters of the same typeface and size. Fonts include letters, punctuation marks, and additional symbols. The size of a font is measured in points. For example, 12-point Arial, 12-point Times New Roman, 14-point Times New Roman, and 12-point Lucida Bright are all different fonts. A point is the smallest unit of measure used in typography. There are 12 points in a pica and 72 points (6 picas) in an inch.

A typeface is a basic character design that is defined by a stroke width and a serif (a smaller line used to finish off a main stroke of a letter, as you can see at the top and bottom of the uppercase letter "M"). As mentioned above, a font represents a complete set of characters from one specific typeface, all with a certain size and style, such as italics or bold. Usually, the system owns all of the font resources and shares them with application programs. Fonts are not usually compiled into the final executable version of a program.

Applications such as BARCHART.CPP treat fonts like other drawing objects. Windows supplies several fonts: System, Terminal, Courier, Helvetica, Modern, Roman, Script, and Times Roman, as well as several TrueType fonts. These are called GDI_supplied fonts.

THE CREATEFONT( ) FUNCTION SYNTAX The CreateFont( ) function is defined in the WINDOWS.H header file. This function selects a logical font from the GDI's pool of physical fonts that most closely matches the characteristics specified by the developer in the function call. Once created, this logical font can be selected by any device. The syntax for the CreateFont( ) function is

```
CreateFont(Height,Width,Escapement,Orientation,Weight,
Italic,Underline,StrikeOut,CharSet,
OutputPrecision,ClipPrecision,Quality,
PitchAndFamily,Facename)
```

Using CreateFont( ), with its 14 parameters, requires quite a bit of skill. Table 23-1 gives a brief description of the CreateFont( ) parameters.

The first time the CreateFont( ) function is called by the application, the parameters are set to the following values:

Height = 12
Width = 12
Escapement = 0
Orientation = 0
Weight = FW_BOLD
Italic = FALSE
Underline = FALSE
StrikeOut = FALSE
CharSet = OEM_CHARSET
OutputPrecision = OUT_DEFAULT_PRECIS
ClipPrecision = CLIP_DEFAULT_PRECIS
Quality = DEFAULT_QUALITY
PitchAndFamily = VARIABLE_PITCH | FF_ROMAN
Facename = "Roman"

An attempt will then be made by Windows to find a font to match the preceding specifications. This font will be used to print a horizontal string of text in the window. The next time CreateFont( ) is called, the parameters are set to the following values:

Height = 12
Width = 12
Escapement = 900
Orientation = 900
Weight = FW_BOLD
Italic = FALSE
Underline = FALSE
StrikeOut = FALSE
CharSet = OEM_CHARSET
OutputPrecision = OUT_DEFAULT_PRECIS
ClipPrecision = CLIP_DEFAULT_PRECIS
Quality = DEFAULT_QUALITY
PitchAndFamily = VARIABLE_PITCH | FF_ROMAN
Facename = "Roman"

CreateFont( ) Parameters	Description
(LONG) Height	Desired font height in logical units
(LONG) Width	Average font width in logical units
(LONG) Escapement	Angle (in tenths of a degree) for each line written in the font
(LONG) Orientation	Angle (in tenths of a degree) for each character's baseline
(LONG) Weight	Weight of font (from 0 to 1,000); 400 is normal, 700 is bold
(BYTE) Italic	Italic font
(BYTE) Underline	Underline font
(BYTE) StrikeOut	Struck out fonts (redline)
(BYTE) CharSet	Character set (ANSI-CHARSET, OEM-CHARSET)
(BYTE) OutputPrecision	How closely output must match the requested specifications (OUT-CHARACTER PRECIS, OUT-DEFAULT-PRECIS, OUT-STRING-PRECIS, OUT-STROKE-PRECIS)
(BYTE) ClipPrecision	How to clip characters outside of clipping range (CLIP-CHARACTER PRECIS, CLIP-DEFAULT-PRECIS, CLIP-STROKE-PRECIS)
(BYTE) Quality	How carefully the logical attributes are mapped to the physical font (DEFAULT-QUALITY, DRAFT-QUALITY, PROOF-QUALITY)
(BYTE) PitchAndFamily	Pitch and family of font (DEFAULT-PITCH, FIXED-PITCH, PROOF-QUALITY, FF-ROMAN, FF-SCRIPT, FF-DECORATIVE, FF-DONTCARE, FF-MODERN, FF-SWISS)
(CHAR) Facename	A string pointing to the typeface name of the desired font

Table 23-1. *CreateFont( ) Parameters*

Again, an attempt will be made by Windows to find a match to the preceding specifications. Examine the listing and notice that only Escapement and Orientation were changed. Both of these parameters use angle values specified in tenths of a degree. Thus, 900 represents an angle of 90.0 degrees. The Escapement parameter rotates the line of text from horizontal to vertical. Orientation rotates each character, in this application, by 90.0 degrees. This font will be used to print a vertical axis label in the application.

Here is how the vertical axis label was printed in this application:

```
newfont.CreateFont(12,12,900,900,FW_BOLD,
                   FALSE,FALSE,FALSE,
                   OEM_CHARSET,
                   OUT_DEFAULT_PRECIS,
                   CLIP_DEFAULT_PRECIS,
                   DEFAULT_QUALITY,
                   VARIABLE_PITCH|FF_ROMAN,
                   "Roman");
oldfont=dc.SelectObject(&newfont);
dc.TextOut(50,200+(strlen(szXString)*10/2),
          szYString,strlen(szYString));
```

When you develop your own applications, be sure to examine the online documentation on the CreateFont( ) function and the additional typefaces that may be available for your use.

Drawing the Axes and Bars

Simple *x* and *y* coordinate axes are drawn with the use of the MoveTo( ) and LineTo( ) functions:

```
// Draw coordinate axis
dc.MoveTo(99,49);
dc.LineTo(99,350);
dc.LineTo(500,350);
dc.MoveTo(99,350);
```

The program then prepares for drawing each bar. As the following code shows, the first bar always starts at position 100,350 on the chart, as defined by $x1$ and $y1$. The width of the first bar and all subsequent bars is calculated from the last drawing position and the width of each bar. The second *x* value is defined by $x2$.

```
// Initial values
x1=100;
y1=350;
x2=x1+iBarWidth;
```

Bars are drawn (by the program) by retrieving the scaled bar height value from *iBarSizeScaled*. This scaled value, saved in *y2*, is used in the Rectangle( ) function. Since the Rectangle( ) function draws a closed figure, the figure will be filled with the current brush color. The color value selected from the array is incremented during each pass through the loop. Here is a portion of code to show how this is achieved:

```
// Draw Each Bar
for(i=0;i<iNBars;i++)
{
  newbrush.CreateSolidBrush(dwColor[i]);
  oldbrush=dc.SelectObject(&newbrush);
  y2=350-iBarSizeScaled[i];
  dc.Rectangle(x1,y1,x2,y2);
  x1=x2;
  x2+=iBarWidth;
}
```

After each bar is drawn, the values in *x1* and *x2* are updated to point to the next bar's position. This process is repeated in the **for** loop until all the bars are drawn.

Running BARCHART

Compile the BARCHART application within the Project utility. When you execute the application, a default bar chart similar to the one in Figure 23-11 will be drawn in the window. You can create a custom bar chart, as shown in Figure 23-12, by entering a chart title, axis labels, and unique bar values.

You can continue the development of this application by adding axis tick marks, a legend, and so on. Customization is limited only by your imagination.

What's Next?

The examples in this chapter were built upon an MFC application (MFCSWP.CPP) that served as a template. This template was static in the sense that nothing in the template changed unless you changed the code yourself. In the next chapter, you will learn how to use various wizards that work in conjunction with the MFC library to produce dynamic templates. As you build applications using wizards, code will automatically be generated to your specifications!

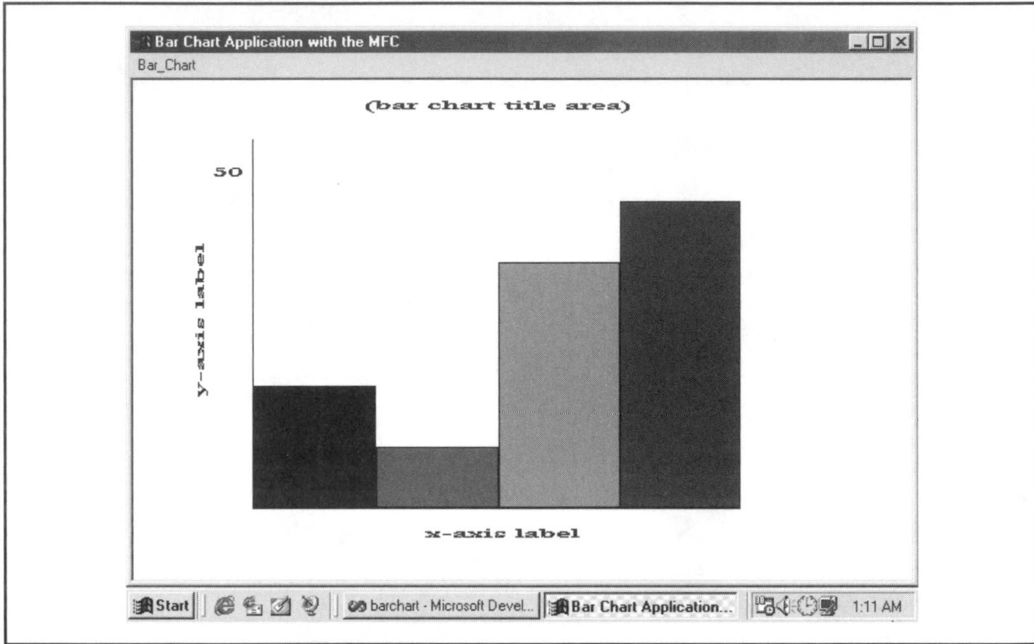

Figure 23-11. *The default chart for the BARCHART application*

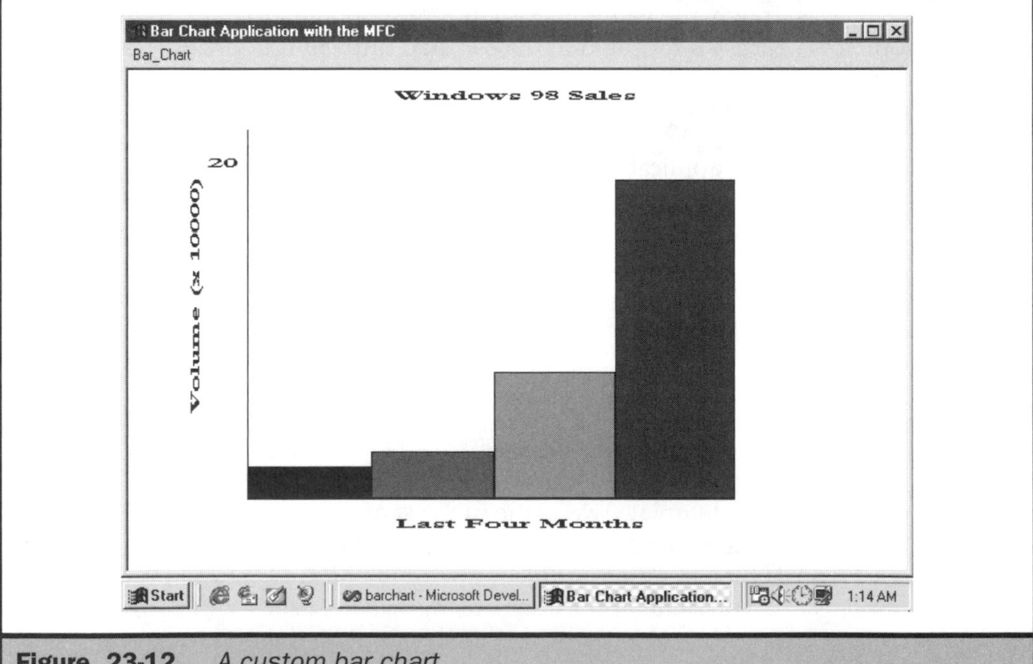

Figure 23-12. *A custom bar chart*

Part V

Wizards

Chapter 24

Application and Class Wizards

In the previous four chapters, you learned how to develop 32-bit Windows 95, 98, and NT applications with a procedure-oriented and object-oriented approach using Microsoft Foundation Class libraries. These chapters relied heavily on the use of templates for code development. Templates allow programmers to use redundant code over and over again, freeing them to concentrate on the new features of a particular application. We view these as static templates that you merely reuse from one application to another.

Sometimes, however, static templates are not enough. Imagine an application where you want to incorporate file I/O capabilities, such as creating a new file, opening an existing file, saving a file, and so forth. Perhaps you'll also want to include editing capabilities, such as cutting, copying, pasting, and so on. Features such as these use a familiar menu style already incorporated in our static templates. Now extend your thinking a little farther and imagine creating applications with a multiple document interface (MDI) and object linking and embedding (OLE) features. No single static template will allow us to pick and choose from this extended list of programming features.

Microsoft's solution was to create a dynamic template generator called the AppWizard. The AppWizard depends heavily on the Microsoft Foundation Class library and generates object-oriented code. To select the AppWizard, when starting a new project, select the File menu in the Visual C++ compiler. Then choose New and select the MFC AppWizard from the list of options. The AppWizard generates a code template that will allow you to select only those features you need for your application. However, as was the case with the static templates in this book, it is still up to you to write the remainder of the code for your unique application.

A close relative of the AppWizard is the ClassWizard. The ClassWizard allows you to add classes or customize existing classes. The ClassWizard can be used after the template code is created by the AppWizard. The ClassWizard is selected using the View menu and selecting the ClassWizard menu item.

This chapter will explore the use of these two wizards and help you understand how they can be put to work for you. Two applications will be developed as examples. The first will use the bare minimum AppWizard code to create an application with a client area that contains simple graphics. The second will use several wizard features. This application will be a simple text editor that can work with multiple documents (MDI), display a toolbar at the top of the application, and incorporate file I/O and editing capabilities.

Be warned, however, that there is a learning curve that you must overcome before you will become comfortable using these new tools. We strongly recommend that you review Chapters 22 and 23 before proceeding. These chapters deal with the MFC library. Wizards only generate object-oriented code; they rely on the MFC library for their power.

The Graph Application

In this section, you will learn all of the steps necessary to create a basic application using the AppWizard and ClassWizard tools. This is a mechanical process, requiring that certain steps be completed in a specific order. The steps discussed here will take you through the development of code that will be used to create the first program, named Graph.

If your compiler is up and running, follow the steps along with us as we create this application.

The AppWizard

From the Microsoft Visual C++ menu bar, select the File menu and then the New item from the menu list. As shown in Figure 24-1, a dialog box will appear that will allow you to start a new project by selecting the MFC AppWizard (exe) option.

Name the new project Graph, as shown in Figure 24-1. After you have named the project, you can start developing it using the AppWizard. Notice the project location shown in Figure 24-1. Now, simply click on OK to start the AppWizard.

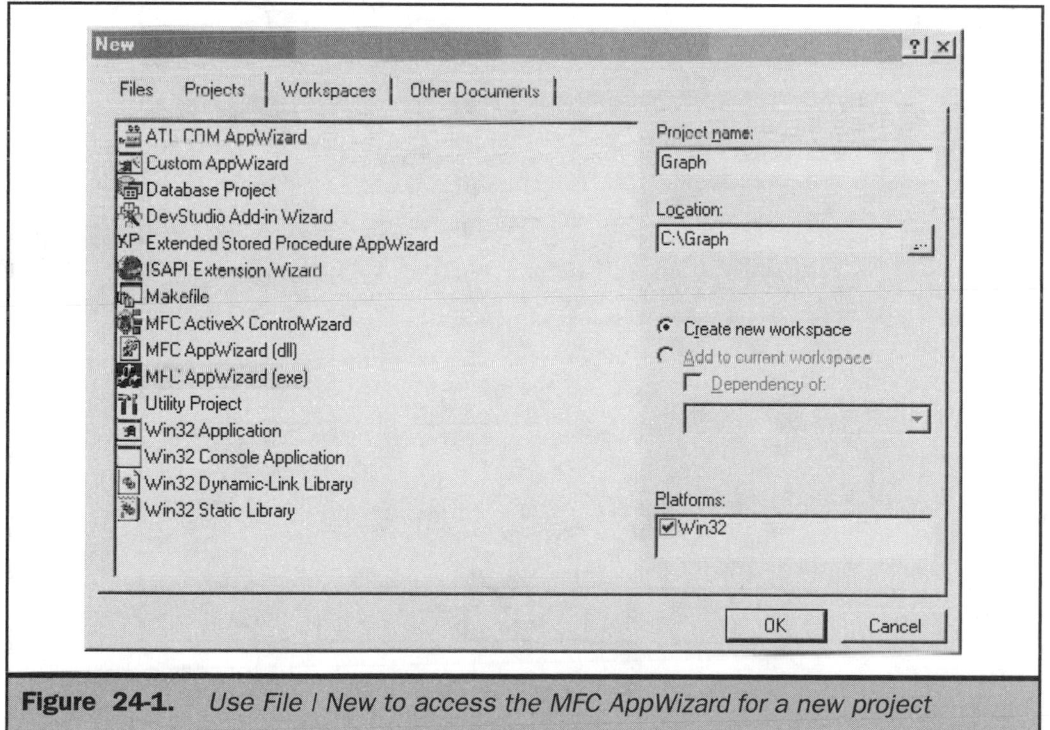

Figure 24-1. *Use File / New to access the MFC AppWizard for a new project*

The first step in generating a project with the AppWizard involves making a decision about whether the project will handle single, multiple, or dialog-based documents, as shown in Figure 24-2.

Single-document interfaces are the simplest, since multiple-document communications will not be required for this example. Make sure the Document/View architecture support option is checked. Accept the default for the resource language option. Click on the Next button to start Step 2, shown in Figure 24-3.

Step 2 is used only when you want to include database support. For this example, None is selected. Click on the Next button to start Step 3, shown in Figure 24-4.

Step 3 allows you to specify the type of OLE support: containers or servers. For this example, None is selected. You'll learn more about this option in Chapter 25. Click on the Next button to start Step 4, shown in Figure 24-5.

Step 4 gives you the opportunity to add special features to the project. For example, a toolbar or status bar could be added at this point. In our first example, however, no special features are needed. Click on the Next button to start Step 5, shown in Figure 24-6.

Select the options shown in Figure 24-6 for Step 5. Now, click the Next button to start Step 6 as Figure 24-7.

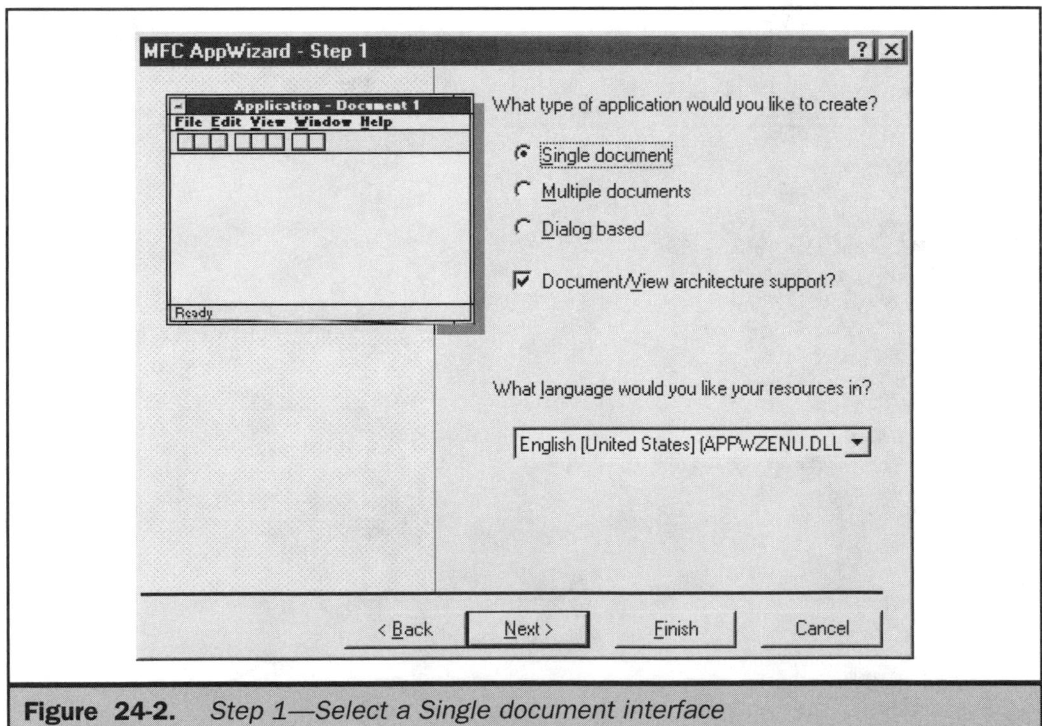

Figure 24-2. *Step 1—Select a Single document interface*

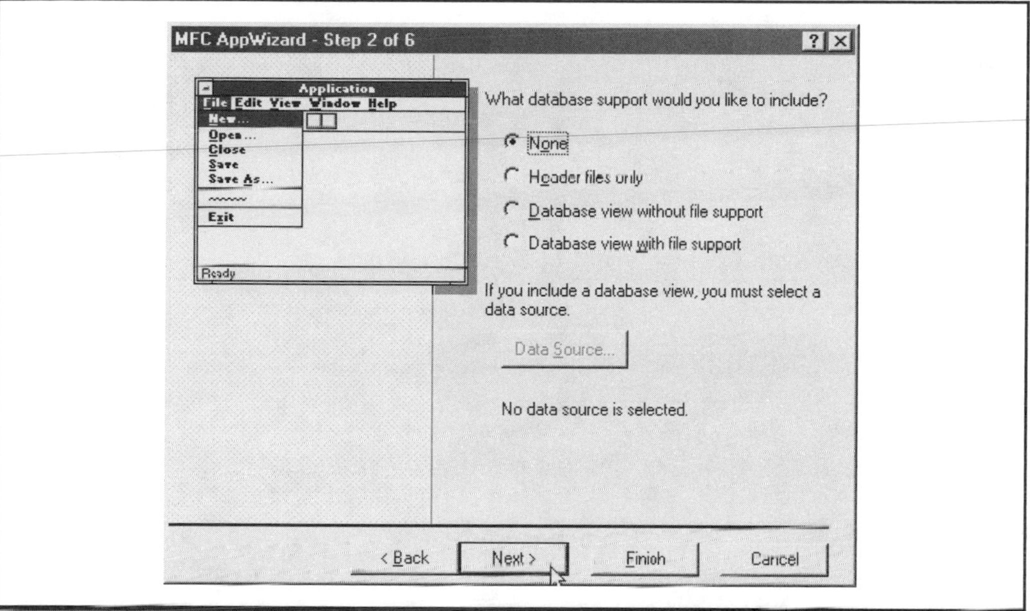

Figure 24-3. *Step 2—Select None since no database support is needed*

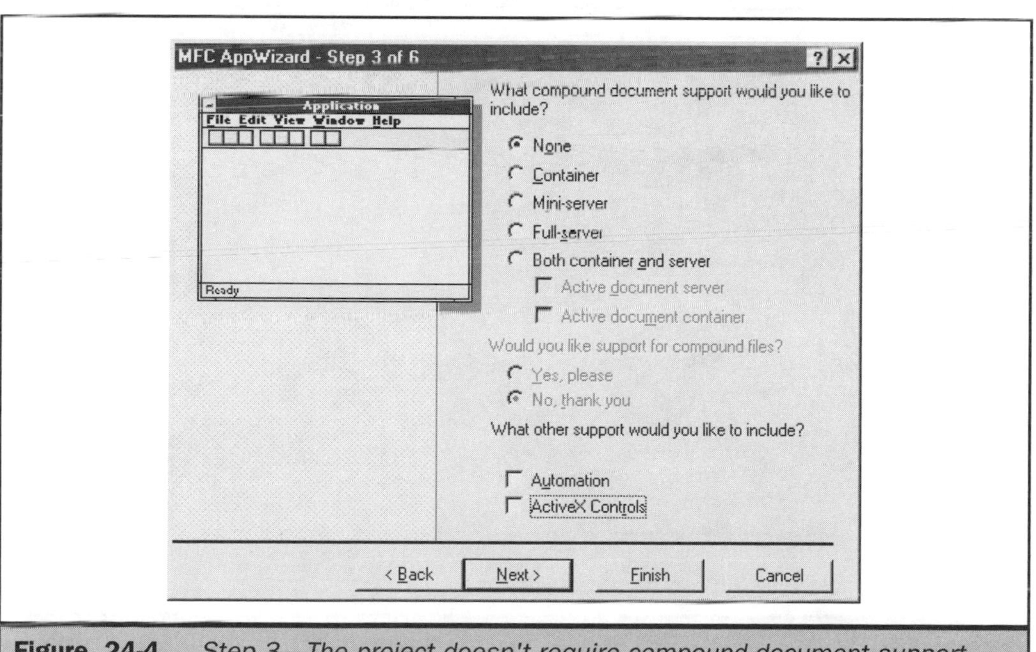

Figure 24-4. *Step 3—The project doesn't require compound document support*

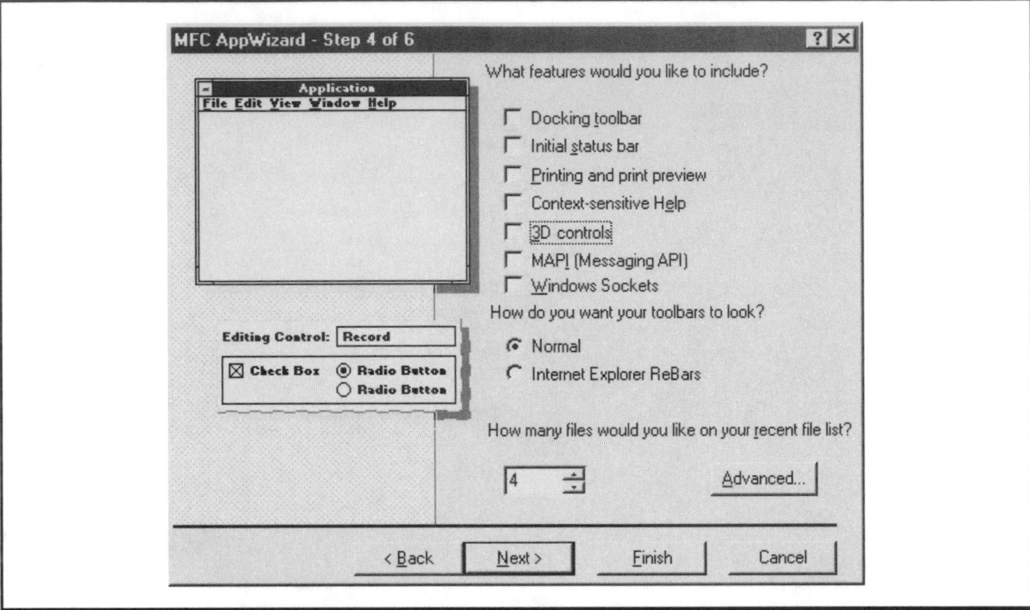

Figure 24-5. *Step 4—Allows special application features to be added*

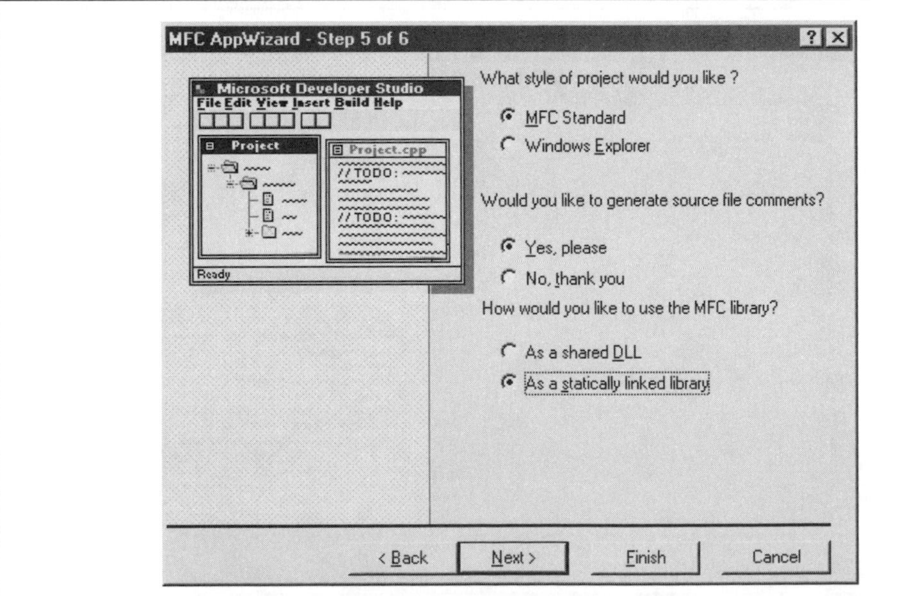

Figure 24-6. *Step 5—Allows the MFC project type, inclusion of source comments, and the identification of the MFC library*

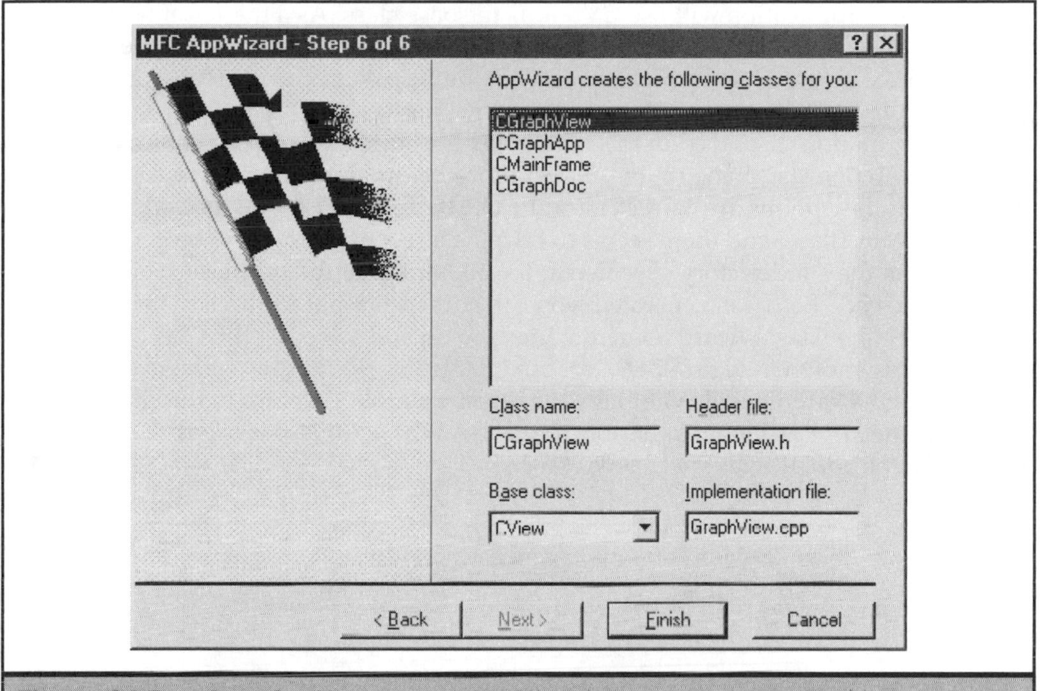

Figure 24-7. *Step 6—Allows a review of the classes to be generated by the AppWizard*

Step 6 is the final step used to specify project features. Here, you will see a listing of the new classes that the AppWizard will automatically generate. The four classes that will be created for this application are **CGraphApp**, **CMainFrame**, **CGraphDoc**, and **CGraphView**.

If you select **CGraphView** in the list box, shown in Figure 24-7, the Base class list box will expand so that you can specify whether you want the **CGraphView** class to be derived from the **CEditView**, **CFormView**, **CScrollView**, or **CView** base class.

The **CView** class, derived from the **CWnd** class, is used to create the base for user-defined view classes. A view serves as a buffer between the document and the user, and is actually a child of a frame window. It produces an image of the document on the screen or on the printer and uses input from the keyboard or the mouse as an operation on the document.

Two of the classes mentioned above, **CFormView** and **CEditView**, are derived from the **CView** base class. **CFormView** describes a scrollable view that is based on a dialog template resource and includes dialog box controls. **CEditView** describes a text editor. **CEditView** is used in the second application developed in this chapter.

The Graph application will use **CView** as the base class. As a matter of fact, all of the default classes shown in the Base class list box are acceptable. Click on the Finish button and see a description summary of what the AppWizard will create for this project. Figure 24-8 shows the information for this project.

The information displayed in this dialog box is a summary of your choices, and this box offers you one last chance to make alterations before the template code is generated. If the options are correct, click the OK button to generate the code.

The various files—and there seems to be quite a few of them—will be generated and stored in the subdirectory specified at the beginning of the project.

After the code has been generated, you can add additional features to the project code by selecting ClassWizard using the View menu and selecting the ClassWizard… menu item, as shown in Figure 24-9.

Our Graph example will eventually draw some simple graphics to the client area. Therefore, the application must be able to process WM_PAINT messages. The message handler can be added with the ClassWizard.

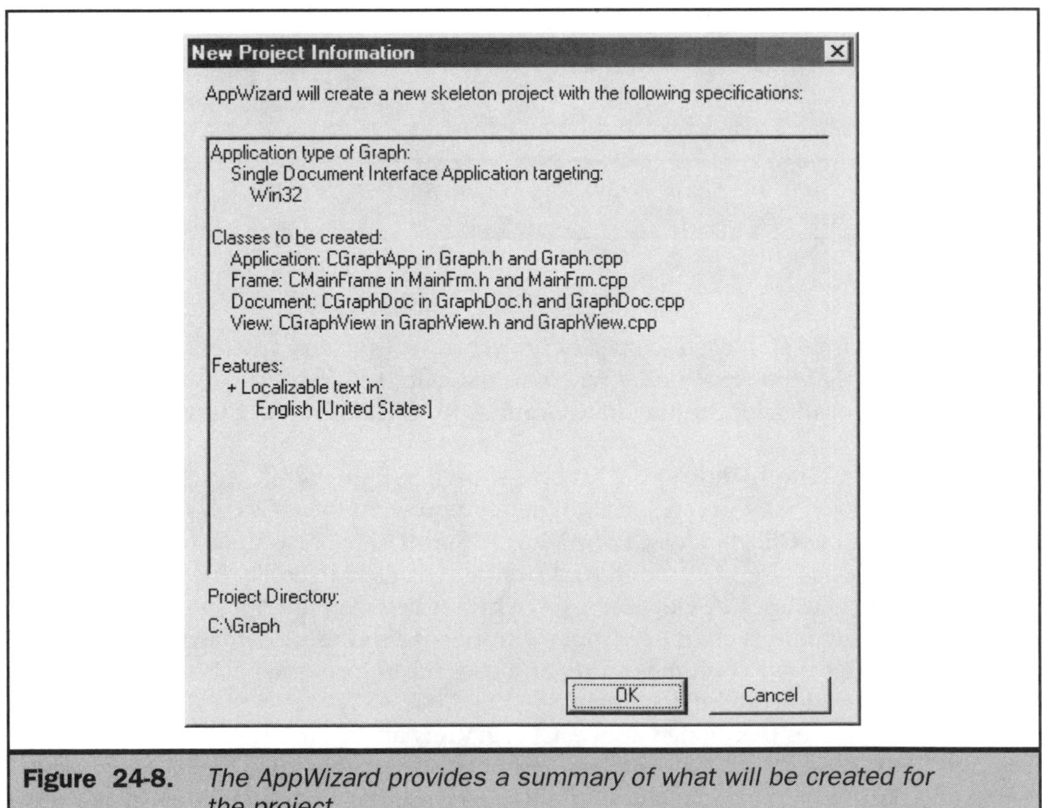

Figure 24-8. *The AppWizard provides a summary of what will be created for the project*

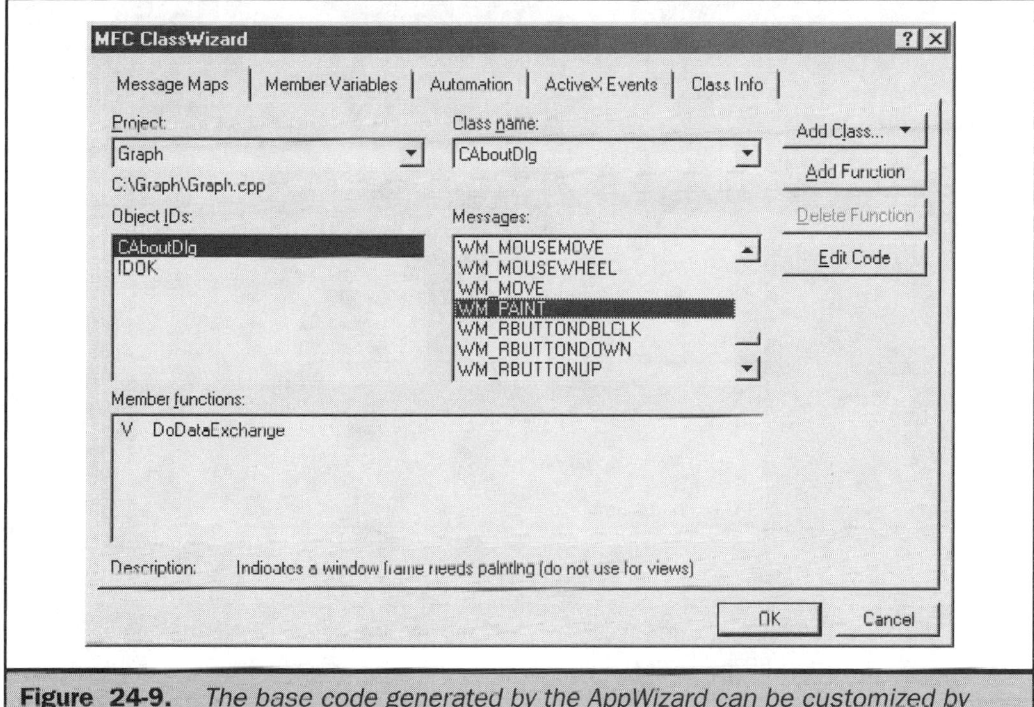

Figure 24-9. *The base code generated by the AppWizard can be customized by using the ClassWizard*

The ClassWizard

The ClassWizard generates additional code for the application. This code can be used to support the processing of messages such as WM_PAINT, WM_MOUSEMOVE, and so forth. The ClassWizard, as mentioned in the previous section, is started from the View menu by selecting the ClassWizard menu item. Figure 24-10 shows the initial ClassWizard dialog box.

In this application, an OnPaint( ) member function will be added to our program code to process WM_PAINT messages. To add this support code, select **CGraphView** in the Class name text entry box. From the Object IDs list box, choose **CGraphView**, as shown in Figure 24-10.

When **CGraphView** is selected, a list of messages will be shown in the Messages list box. When the WM_PAINT message is selected from the Messages list box, the OnPaint( ) member function will be shown in the Member functions list.

The GRAPHVIEW.CPP file will now contain this inserted code, as shown in Figure 24-11.

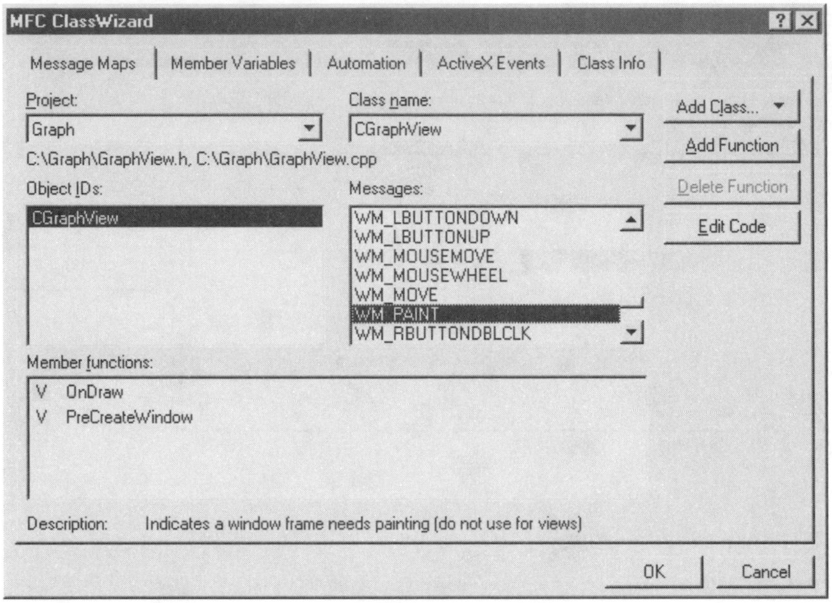

Figure 24-10. *The initial ClassWizard dialog box with the WM_Paint message handler added to the project*

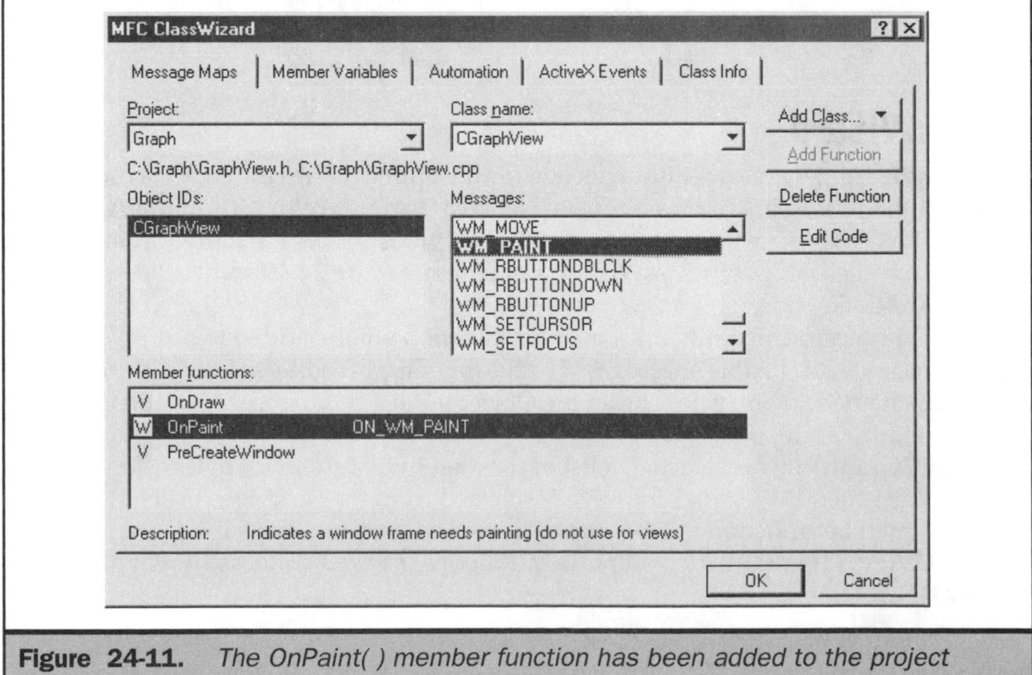

Figure 24-11. *The OnPaint( ) member function has been added to the project*

At this point, various graphics functions can be added to this member function to make this application unique. You'll see how this is done before we conclude this example.

The next step is to compile and test the basic application.

Building the Application

When all of the message handlers have been added to the program's code with the ClassWizard, the application can be compiled and linked. Select the Rebuild All menu item from the compiler's Build menu, as shown in Figure 24-12.

During the build operation, details of the operation are displayed to the screen. Figure 24-13 shows the steps performed in the compile and link process for this application.

Notice in particular that four source code files—GRAPH.CPP, MAINFRM.CPP, GRAPHDOC.CPP, and GRAPHVIEW.CPP—will be compiled and then linked. In terms of sheer numbers, these four files are just the tip of the iceberg. When compilation is complete, examine the subdirectory in which these files are stored; you'll see more than 30 files stored there. Automation has its price!

An executable file is also present in the appropriate subdirectory. Execute the program. Your screen should look something like Figure 24-14.

The initial screen is empty because no graphics functions have been added at this point. Worse, none of the menu items work, with the exception of the About box from the Help menu. This is because the code for processing these messages must

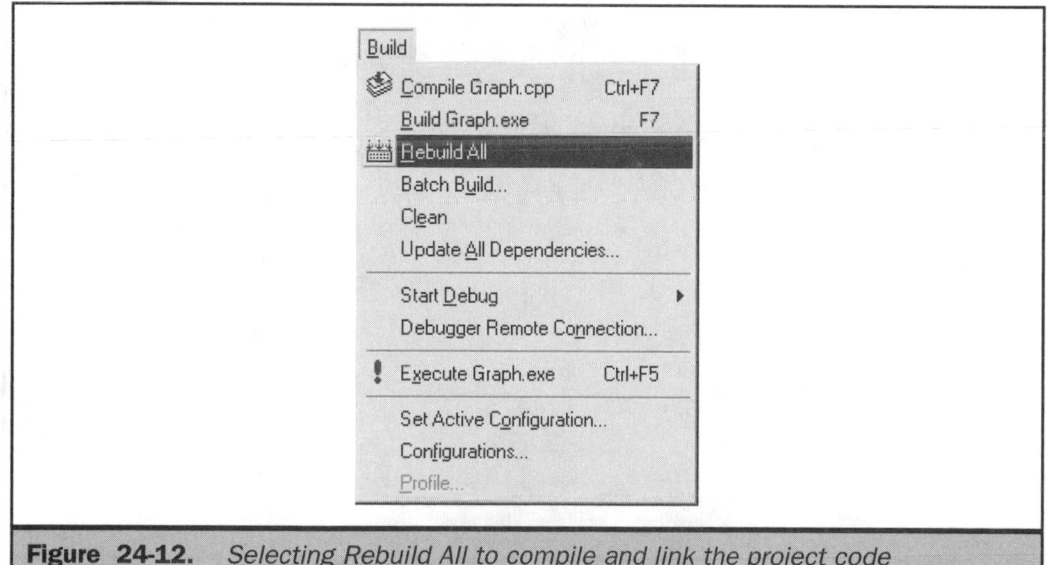

Figure 24-12. *Selecting Rebuild All to compile and link the project code*

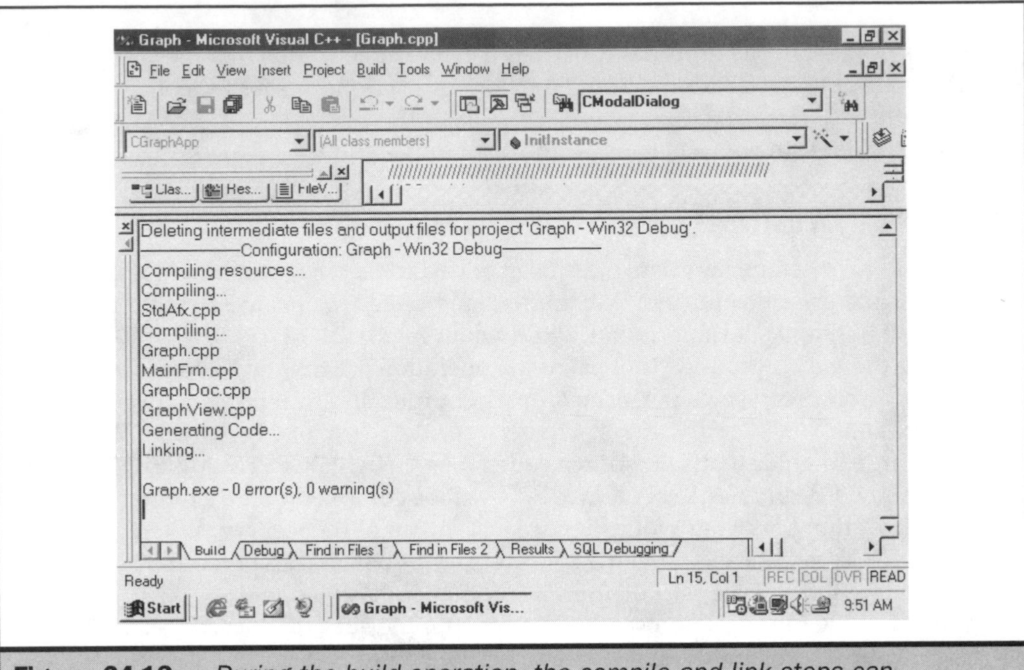

Figure 24-13. *During the build operation, the compile and link steps can be viewed*

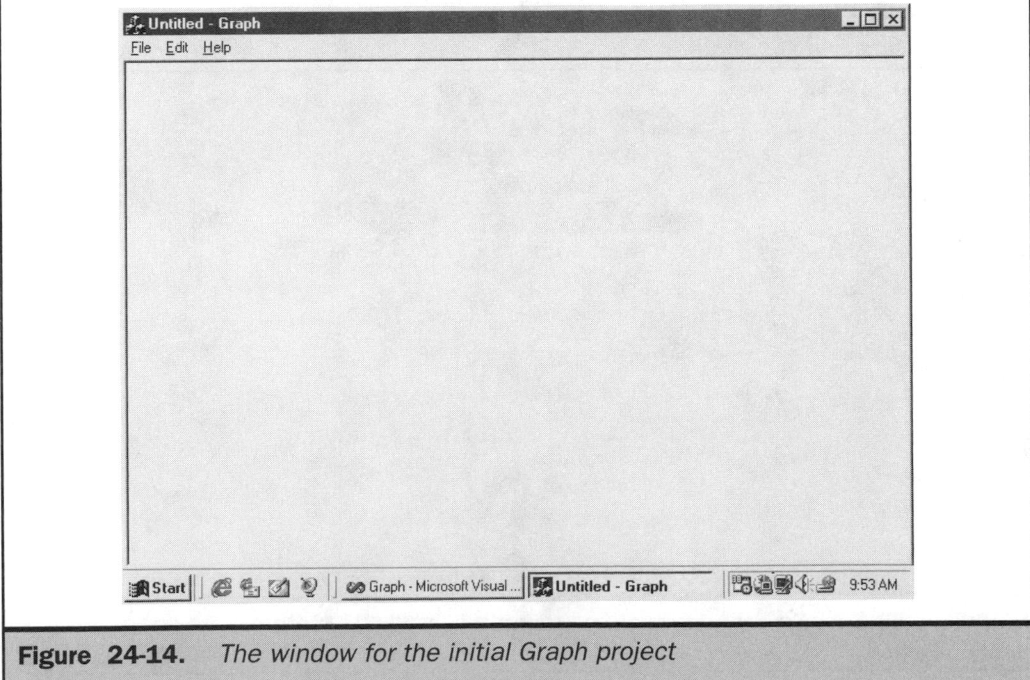

Figure 24-14. *The window for the initial Graph project*

be added by you—it is not automatically generated. However, if you have gained a good understanding of the MFC library from previous chapters, developing this code will not be too difficult. The final example in this chapter will make use of all of these features.

Examining AppWizard Code

The AppWizard, with a little help from the ClassWizard, generated four important C++ files for the initial Graph application. These files were named GRAPH.CPP, MAINFRM.CPP, GRAPHDOC.CPP, and GRAPHVIEW.CPP. Each of these C++ files has an associated header file: GRAPH.H, MAINFRM.H, GRAPHDOC.H, and GRAPHVIEW.H. The header files contain the declarations of the specific classes in each C++ file. The purpose of each C++ file will be examined in the following sections.

THE GRAPH.CPP FILE The GRAPH.CPP file, shown here, serves as the main file for the application. It contains the **CGraphApp** class.

```
// Graph.cpp : Defines class behaviors for the application.
//

#include "stdafx.h"
#include "Graph.h"

#include "MainFrm.h"
#include "GraphDoc.h"
#include "GraphView.h"

#ifdef _DEBUG
#define new DEBUG_NEW
#undef THIS_FILE
static char THIS_FILE[] = __FILE__;
#endif

/////////////////////////////////////////////////////////////////////////////
// CGraphApp

BEGIN_MESSAGE_MAP(CGraphApp, CWinApp)
  //{{AFX_MSG_MAP(CGraphApp)
  ON_COMMAND(ID_APP_ABOUT, OnAppAbout)
    // NOTE - the ClassWizard will add and remove mapping
    // macros here.
    //    DO NOT EDIT what you see in these blocks of
    // generated code!
```

WIZARDS

```
  //}}AFX_MSG_MAP
  // Standard file based document commands
  ON_COMMAND(ID_FILE_NEW, CWinApp::OnFileNew)
  ON_COMMAND(ID_FILE_OPEN, CWinApp::OnFileOpen)
END_MESSAGE_MAP()

/////////////////////////////////////////////////////////////////
// CGraphApp construction

CGraphApp::CGraphApp()
{
  // TODO: add construction code here,
  // Place all significant initialization in InitInstance
}

/////////////////////////////////////////////////////////////////
// The one and only CGraphApp object

CGraphApp theApp;

/////////////////////////////////////////////////////////////////
// CGraphApp initialization

BOOL CGraphApp::InitInstance()
{
  // Standard initialization
  // If you are not using these features and wish to reduce
  // the size of your final executable, you should remove
  // from the following the specific initialization routines
  // you do not need.

  // Change the registry key under which our settings are
  // stored.  You should modify this string to be something
  // appropriate  such as the name of your company or
  // organization.
  SetRegistryKey(_T("Local AppWizard-Generated Applications"));

  LoadStdProfileSettings();  // Load INI file options
                             // (including MRU)
```

```
  // Register the application's document templates.  Document
  // templates  serve as the connection between documents,
  // frame windows and views.

  CSingleDocTemplate* pDocTemplate;
  pDocTemplate = new CSingleDocTemplate(
    IDR_MAINFRAME,
    RUNTIME_CLASS(CGraphDoc),
    RUNTIME_CLASS(CMainFrame),        // main SDI frame window
    RUNTIME_CLASS(CGraphView));
  AddDocTemplate(pDocTemplate);

  // Parse command line for shell commands, DDE, file open
  CCommandLineInfo cmdInfo;
  ParseCommandLine(cmdInfo);

  // Dispatch commands specified on the command line
  if (!ProcessShellCommand(cmdInfo))
    return FALSE;

  // The one and only window is initialized - show and update.
  m_pMainWnd->ShowWindow(SW_SHOW);
  m_pMainWnd->UpdateWindow();

  return TRUE;
}


/////////////////////////////////////////////////////////////////////////////
// CAboutDlg dialog used for App About

class CAboutDlg : public CDialog
{
public:
  CAboutDlg();

// Dialog Data
  //{{AFX_DATA(CAboutDlg)
  enum { IDD = IDD_ABOUTBOX };
  //}}AFX_DATA
```

```
  // ClassWizard generated virtual function overrides
  //{{AFX_VIRTUAL(CAboutDlg)
  protected:
  virtual void DoDataExchange(CDataExchange* pDX);
  //}}AFX_VIRTUAL

// Implementation
protected:
  //{{AFX_MSG(CAboutDlg)
  // No message handlers
  //}}AFX_MSG
  DECLARE_MESSAGE_MAP()
};

CAboutDlg::CAboutDlg() : CDialog(CAboutDlg::IDD)
{
  //{{AFX_DATA_INIT(CAboutDlg)
  //}}AFX_DATA_INIT
}

void CAboutDlg::DoDataExchange(CDataExchange* pDX)
{
  CDialog::DoDataExchange(pDX);
  //{{AFX_DATA_MAP(CAboutDlg)
  //}}AFX_DATA_MAP
}

BEGIN_MESSAGE_MAP(CAboutDlg, CDialog)
  //{{AFX_MSG_MAP(CAboutDlg)
  //}}AFX_MSG_MAP
END_MESSAGE_MAP()

// App command to run the dialog
void CGraphApp::OnAppAbout()
{
  CAboutDlg aboutDlg;
  aboutDlg.DoModal();
}
```

```
//////////////////////////////////////////////////////////////
// CGraphApp commands
```

The message map, near the top of the listing, belongs to the **CGraphApp** class. This message map specifically links the ID_APP_ABOUT, ID_FILE_NEW, and ID_FILE_OPEN messages with their member functions: OnAppAbout( ), CWinApp::OnFileNew( ), and CWinApp::OnFileOpen( ). Also notice in the listing that a constructor, an initial instance InitInstance( ), and a member function OnAppAbout( ) are implemented.

The About dialog box is derived from the **CDialog** class. If you examine the lower portion of the code you will notice a message map, a constructor, and a member function CDialog::DoDataExchange( ) for this derived dialog class.

There are no initial **CGraphApp** commands, as you can see from the end of `the listing.

THE MAINFRM.CPP FILE The MAINFRM.CPP file, shown below, contains the frame class **CMainFrame**. This class is derived from **CFrameWnd** and is used to control all single-document-interface (SDI) frame features.

```
// MainFrm.cpp : implementation of the CMainFrame class
//

#include "stdafx.h"
#include "Graph.h"

#include "MainFrm.h"

#ifdef _DEBUG
#define new DEBUG_NEW
#undef THIS_FILE
static char THIS_FILE[] = __FILE__;
#endif

//////////////////////////////////////////////////////////////
// CMainFrame

IMPLEMENT_DYNCREATE(CMainFrame, CFrameWnd)

BEGIN_MESSAGE_MAP(CMainFrame, CFrameWnd)
  //{{AFX_MSG_MAP(CMainFrame)
```

```
    // NOTE - the ClassWizard will add and remove mapping
    // macros here.
    //    DO NOT EDIT what you see in these blocks of
    // generated code !
  //}}AFX_MSG_MAP
END_MESSAGE_MAP()

/////////////////////////////////////////////////////////////
// CMainFrame construction/destruction

CMainFrame::CMainFrame()
{
  // TODO: add member initialization code here

}

CMainFrame::~CMainFrame()
{
}

BOOL CMainFrame::PreCreateWindow(CREATESTRUCT& cs)
{
  if( !CFrameWnd::PreCreateWindow(cs) )
    return FALSE;
  // TODO: Modify the Window class or styles here by modifying
  //  the CREATESTRUCT cs

  return TRUE;
}

/////////////////////////////////////////////////////////////
// CMainFrame diagnostics

#ifdef _DEBUG
void CMainFrame::AssertValid() const
{
  CFrameWnd::AssertValid();
}

void CMainFrame::Dump(CDumpContext& dc) const
{
```

```
    CFrameWnd::Dump(dc);
}

#endif //_DEBUG

/////////////////////////////////////////////////////////////////////////////
// CMainFrame message handlers
```

When you examine this listing, you'll notice that the message map, constructor, and destructor initially contain no code. The member functions AssertValid( ) and Dump( ) use definitions contained in the parent class. Also note that **CMainFrame** initially contains no message handlers.

THE GRAPHDOC.CPP FILE The GRAPHDOC.CPP file, shown here, contains the **CGraphDoc** class, which is unique to your application. This file is used to hold document data and to load and save files.

```
// GraphDoc.cpp : implementation of the CGraphDoc class
//

#include "stdafx.h"
#include "Graph.h"

#include "GraphDoc.h"

#ifdef _DEBUG
#define new DEBUG_NEW
#undef THIS_FILE
static char THIS_FILE[] = __FILE__;
#endif

/////////////////////////////////////////////////////////////////////////////
//////////
// CGraphDoc

IMPLEMENT_DYNCREATE(CGraphDoc, CDocument)

BEGIN_MESSAGE_MAP(CGraphDoc, CDocument)
  //{{AFX_MSG_MAP(CGraphDoc)
    // NOTE - the ClassWizard will add and remove mapping macros here.
```

```
    //    DO NOT EDIT what you see in these blocks of generated
          code!
  //}}AFX_MSG_MAP
END_MESSAGE_MAP()

//////////////////////////////////////////////////////////////////////
//////////
// CGraphDoc construction/destruction

CGraphDoc::CGraphDoc()
{
  // TODO: add one-time construction code here

}

CGraphDoc::~CGraphDoc()
{
}

BOOL CGraphDoc::OnNewDocument()
{
  if (!CDocument::OnNewDocument())
    return FALSE;

  // TODO: add reinitialization code here
  // (SDI documents will reuse this document)

  return TRUE;
}



//////////////////////////////////////////////////////////////////////
//////////
// CGraphDoc serialization

void CGraphDoc::Serialize(CArchive& ar)
{
  if (ar.IsStoring())
  {
    // TODO: add storing code here
  }
```

```
  else
  {
    // TODO: add loading code here
  }
}

////////////////////////////////////////////////////////////////////
//////////
// CGraphDoc diagnostics

#ifdef _DEBUG
void CGraphDoc::AssertValid() const
{
  CDocument::AssertValid();
}

void CGraphDoc::Dump(CDumpContext& dc) const
{
  CDocument::Dump(dc);
}
#endif //_DEBUG

////////////////////////////////////////////////////////////////////
//////////
// CGraphDoc commands
```

Examine this listing and you will again notice that the message map, constructor, and destructor contain no code. Four member functions can be used to provide vital document support. OnNewDocument( ) uses the definition provided by the parent class. Serialize( ) supports persistent objects. Our second programming example will use this member function to help with file I/O. The member functions AssertValid( ) and Dump( ) use definitions contained in the parent class. There are no initial **CGraphDoc** commands.

THE GRAPHVIEW.CPP FILE The GRAPHVIEW.CPP file, shown here, provides the view of the document. In this implementation, **CGraphView** is derived from the **CView** class. **CGraphView** objects are used to view **CGraphDoc** objects.

```
// GraphView.cpp : implementation of the CGraphView class
//
```

```
#include "stdafx.h"
#include "Graph.h"

#include "GraphDoc.h"
#include "GraphView.h"

#ifdef _DEBUG
#define new DEBUG_NEW
#undef THIS_FILE
static char THIS_FILE[] = __FILE__;
#endif


//////////////////////////////////////////////////////////////
// CGraphView

IMPLEMENT_DYNCREATE(CGraphView, CView)

BEGIN_MESSAGE_MAP(CGraphView, CView)
  //{{AFX_MSG_MAP(CGraphView)
  ON_WM_PAINT()
  //}}AFX_MSG_MAP
END_MESSAGE_MAP()

//////////////////////////////////////////////////////////////
// CGraphView construction/destruction

CGraphView::CGraphView()
{
  // TODO: add construction code here

}

CGraphView::~CGraphView()
{
}

BOOL CGraphView::PreCreateWindow(CREATESTRUCT& cs)
{
  // TODO: Modify the Window class / styles here by modifying
```

```
  //  the CREATESTRUCT cs

  return CView::PreCreateWindow(cs);
}

/////////////////////////////////////////////////////////////////////////////
// CGraphView drawing

void CGraphView::OnDraw(CDC* pDC)
{
  CGraphDoc* pDoc = GetDocument();
  ASSERT_VALID(pDoc);

  // TODO: add draw code for native data here
}

/////////////////////////////////////////////////////////////////////////////
// CGraphView diagnostics

#ifdef _DEBUG
void CGraphView::AssertValid() const
{
  CView::AssertValid();
}

void CGraphView::Dump(CDumpContext& dc) const
{
  CView::Dump(dc);
}

CGraphDoc* CGraphView::GetDocument() // non-debug version
{
  ASSERT(m_pDocument->IsKindOf(RUNTIME_CLASS(CGraphDoc)));
  return (CGraphDoc*)m_pDocument;
}
#endif //_DEBUG

/////////////////////////////////////////////////////////////////////////////
// CGraphView message handlers

void CGraphView::OnPaint()
```

```
{
  CPaintDC dc(this); // device context for painting

  // TODO: Add your message handler code here

  // Do not call CView::OnPaint() for painting messages
}
```

Normally, the message map would be empty, but remember that we used the ClassWizard to add ON_WM_PAINT message-handling abilities. The constructor and destructor are empty.

The OnDraw( ) member function uses the pointer **pDoc** to point to the document. The member functions AssertValid( ) and Dump( ) use definitions contained in the parent class.

The message handler, OnPaint( ), is described at the end of this listing. Simple graphics commands, such as those shown in earlier chapters, can be inserted here.

Drawing in the Client Area

In the initial design phase of the Graph application, a single-document interface (SDI) application was created using the AppWizard and the ClassWizard. The view class was derived from the parent class, **CView**. Recall that the ClassWizard allowed us to add the WM_PAINT message handler to this code.

This is the perfect platform from which to draw simple graphics to the client area with very little additional work. To see how easy this can be, add the following code to the OnPaint( ) message handler shown in the previous listing:

```
// CGraphView message handlers

void CGraphView::OnPaint( )
{
  static DWORD dwColor[9]={RGB(0,0,0),          //black
                           RGB(255,0,0),        //red
                           RGB(0,255,0),        //green
                           RGB(0,0,255),        //blue
                           RGB(255,255,0),      //yellow
                           RGB(255,0,255),      //magenta
                           RGB(0,255,255),      //cyan
                           RGB(127,127,127),    //gray
                           RGB(255,255,255)};   //white
```

```
POINT polylpts[4],polygpts[5];
int xcoord;

CBrush newbrush;
CBrush* oldbrush;
CPen newpen;
CPen* oldpen;

CPaintDC dc(this); // device context for painting

// draws and fills a red ellipse
newpen.CreatePen(PS_SOLID,1,dwColor[1]);
oldpen=dc.SelectObject(&newpen);
newbrush.CreateSolidBrush(dwColor[1]);
oldbrush=dc.SelectObject(&newbrush);
dc.Ellipse(275,300,200,250);
dc.TextOut(220,265,"ellipse",7);
dc.SelectObject(oldbrush);
newbrush.DeleteObject( );
dc.SelectObject(oldpen);
newpen.DeleteObject( );

// draws and fills a blue circle with ellipse function
newpen.CreatePen(PS_SOLID,1,dwColor[3]);
oldpen=dc.SelectObject(&newpen);
newbrush.CreateSolidBrush(dwColor[3]);
oldbrush=dc.SelectObject(&newbrush);
dc.Ellipse(375,75,525,225);
dc.TextOut(435,190,"circle",6);
dc.SelectObject(oldbrush);
newbrush.DeleteObject( );
dc.SelectObject(oldpen);
newpen.DeleteObject( );

// draws several green pixels
for(xcoord=400;xcoord<450;xcoord+=5)
  dc.SetPixel(xcoord,350,0L);
dc.TextOut(460,345,"<- pixels",9);

// draws a wide black diagonal line
```

```
newpen.CreatePen(PS_SOLID,6,dwColor[0]);
oldpen=dc.SelectObject(&newpen);
dc.MoveTo(20,20);
dc.LineTo(100,100);
dc.TextOut(60,20,"<- diagonal line",16);
dc.SelectObject(oldpen);
newpen.DeleteObject( );

// draws a blue arc
newpen.CreatePen(PS_DASH,1,dwColor[3]);
oldpen=dc.SelectObject(&newpen);
dc.Arc(25,125,175,225,175,225,100,125);
dc.TextOut(50,150,"small arc ->",12);
dc.SelectObject(oldpen);
newpen.DeleteObject( );

// draws a wide green chord
newpen.CreatePen(PS_SOLID,8,dwColor[2]);
oldpen=dc.SelectObject(&newpen);
dc.Chord(125,125,275,225,275,225,200,125);
dc.TextOut(280,150,"<- chord",8);
dc.SelectObject(oldpen);
newpen.DeleteObject( );

// draws a black pie slice and fills with green
newpen.CreatePen(PS_SOLID,1,dwColor[0]);
oldpen=dc.SelectObject(&newpen);
newbrush.CreateSolidBrush(dwColor[2]);
oldbrush=dc.SelectObject(&newbrush);
dc.Pie(200,0,300,100,200,50,250,100);
dc.TextOut(260,80,"<- pie wedge",12);
dc.SelectObject(oldbrush);
newbrush.DeleteObject( );
dc.SelectObject(oldpen);
newpen.DeleteObject( );

// draws a black rectangle and fills with gray
newbrush.CreateSolidBrush(dwColor[7]);
oldbrush=dc.SelectObject(&newbrush);
dc.Rectangle(25,300,150,375);
dc.TextOut(50,325,"rectangle",9);
```

```
 dc.SelectObject(oldbrush);
 newbrush.DeleteObject( );

 // draws a black rounded rectangle and fills with blue
 newbrush.CreateHatchBrush(HS_CROSS,dwColor[3]);
 oldbrush=dc.SelectObject(&newbrush);
 dc.RoundRect(350,250,400,290,20,20);
 dc.TextOut(410,270,"
rectangle",20);
 dc.SelectObject(oldbrush);
 newbrush.DeleteObject( );

 // draws several wide magenta lines with polyline
 newpen.CreatePen(PS_SOLID,3,dwColor[5]);
 oldpen=dc.SelectObject(&newpen);
 polylpts[0].x=10;
 polylpts[0].y=30;
 polylpts[1].x=10;
 polylpts[1].y=100;
 polylpts[2].x=50;
 polylpts[2].y=100;
 polylpts[3].x=10;
 polylpts[3].y=30;
 dc.Polyline(polylpts,4);
 dc.TextOut(10,110,"polyline",8);
 dc.SelectObject(oldpen);
 newpen.DeleteObject( );

 // draws a wide cyan polygon and
 // fills with diagonal yellow
 newpen.CreatePen(PS_SOLID,4,dwColor[6]);
 oldpen=dc.SelectObject(&newpen);
 newbrush.CreateHatchBrush(HS_FDIAGONAL,dwColor[4]);
 oldbrush=dc.SelectObject(&newbrush);
 polygpts[0].x=40;
 polygpts[0].y=200;
 polygpts[1].x=100;
 polygpts[1].y=270;
 polygpts[2].x=80;
 polygpts[2].y=290;
 polygpts[3].x=20;
```

```
    polygpts[3].y=220;
    polygpts[4].x=40;
    polygpts[4].y=200;
    dc.Polygon(polygpts,5);
    dc.TextOut(80,230,"<- polygon",10);
    dc.SelectObject(oldbrush);
    newbrush.DeleteObject( );
    dc.SelectObject(oldpen);
    newpen.DeleteObject( );

  // Do not call CView::OnPaint( ) for painting messages
}
```

This should be familiar code since it employs simple GDI graphics functions. Compile and execute the revised version of this application. Your screen should be similar to the one shown in Figure 24-15.

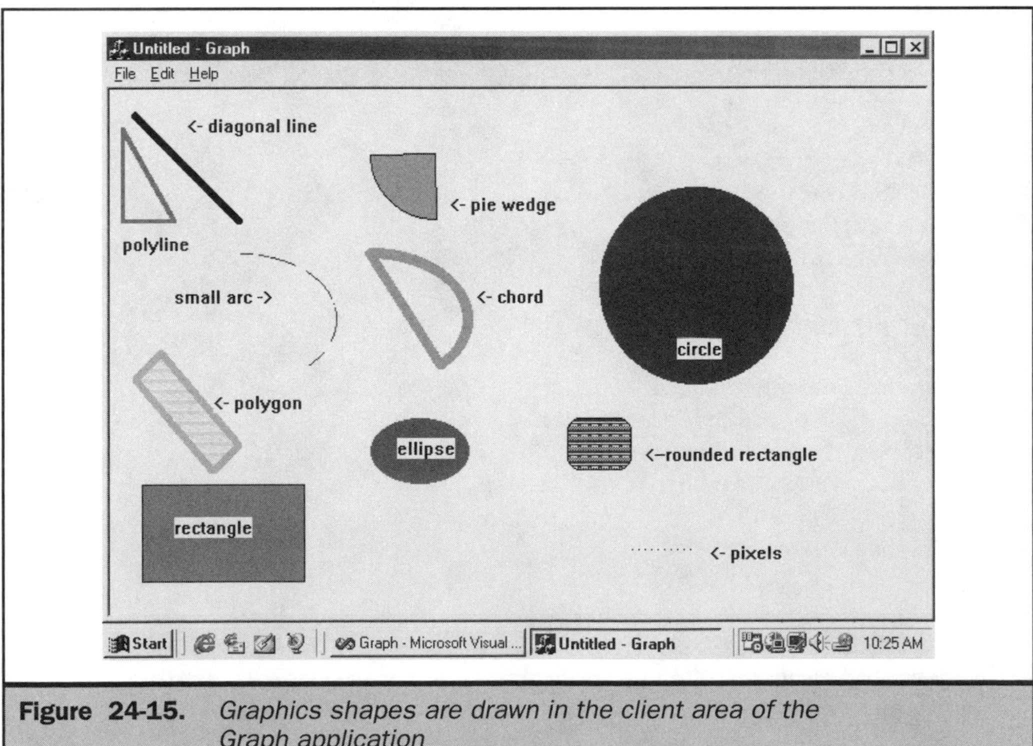

Figure 24-15. *Graphics shapes are drawn in the client area of the Graph application*

The AppWizard generated a template with a menu bar containing the File, Edit, and Help menus, along with the various graphics shapes. The default About box is viewed from the Help menu, as shown in Figure 24-16.

Remember that the other menus and menu items are not functional. Why? Because no additional code was added to the template to handle those responses.

If you diligently went through the AppWizard's template and removed code not used by this application, you would arrive at a static template very similar to the one we created and used in Chapter 23.

The next example will use an entirely new AppWizard template to generate a simple text editor. Enhancements will be made to the template code to add additional functionality to the application.

The Word Processor Application

Here is an application that will allow you to do simple text editing. From the Microsoft Visual C++ main menu bar, select the File menu and then the New menu item. The list box in the New dialog box will allow you to select the MFC AppWizard (exe) option to

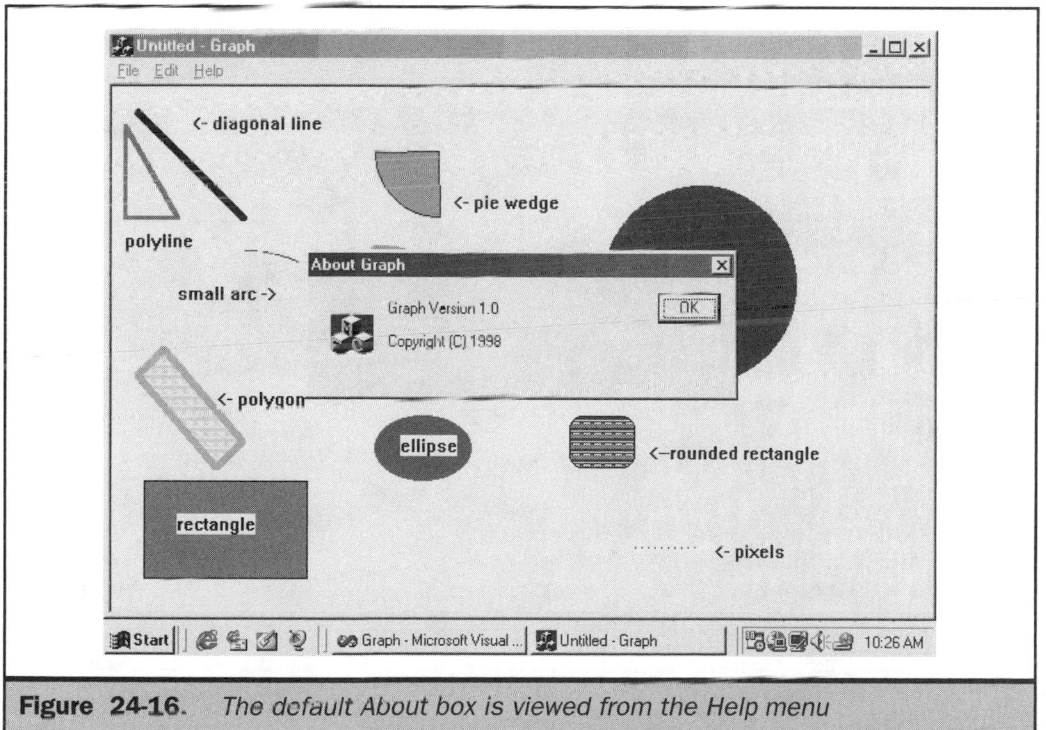

Figure 24-16. *The default About box is viewed from the Help menu*

generate a new project. Remember to enter the name of the project, as shown in Figure 24-17.

The AppWizard will simultaneously create a new subdirectory by the same name beneath the currently selected directory and path. Now you can begin the six-step process that the AppWizard uses to build new applications. In Step 1, shown in Figure 24-18, you can see that this application will permit the user to work with multiple documents.

Figures 24-19 and 24-20 show that no database or compound document support will be included with this project.

In Step 4, shown in Figure 24-21, select options that allow this application to include a toolbar, a status bar, 3-D controls, and the ability to print the documents.

In Step 5, shown in Figure 24-22, no source code comments were requested and this project's library option was set to a statically linked library.

Step 6 shows the five classes that will be created for this application: **CEditorApp**, **CMainFrame**, **CChildFrame**, **CEditorDoc**, and **CEditorView**. This final dialog box can be seen in Figure 24-23.

When **CEditorView** is selected in the list box, the Base class list box will expand so that you can specify whether you want the **CEditorView** class to be derived from the **CEditView**, **CFormView**, **CListView**, **CRichEditView**, **CScrollView**, **CTreeView**, or **CView** base class.

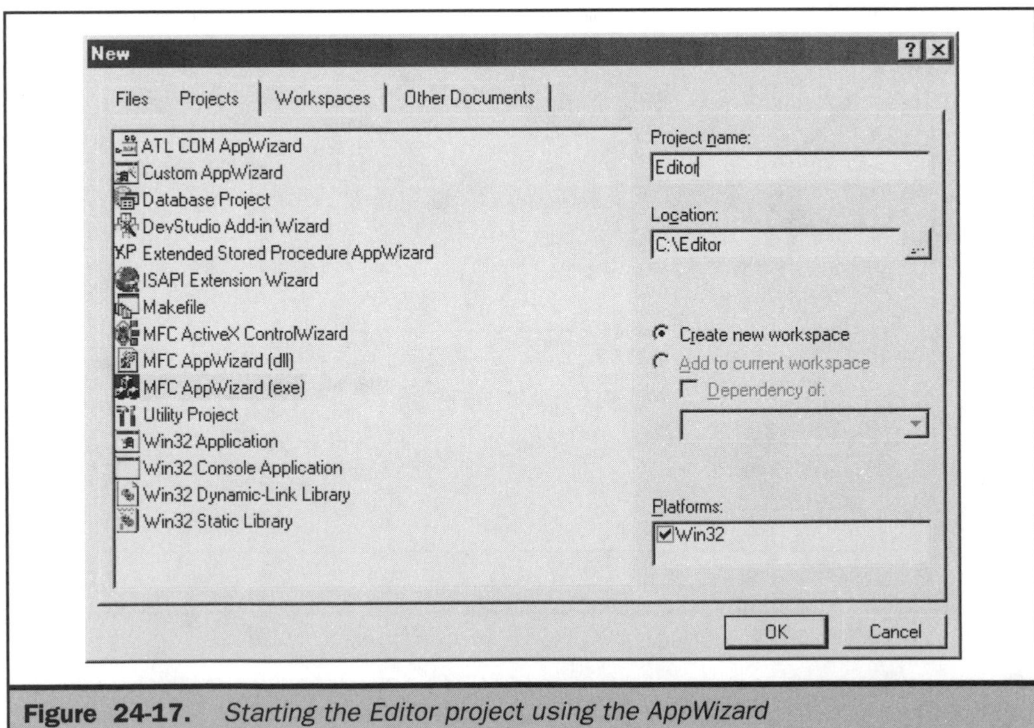

Figure 24-17. *Starting the Editor project using the AppWizard*

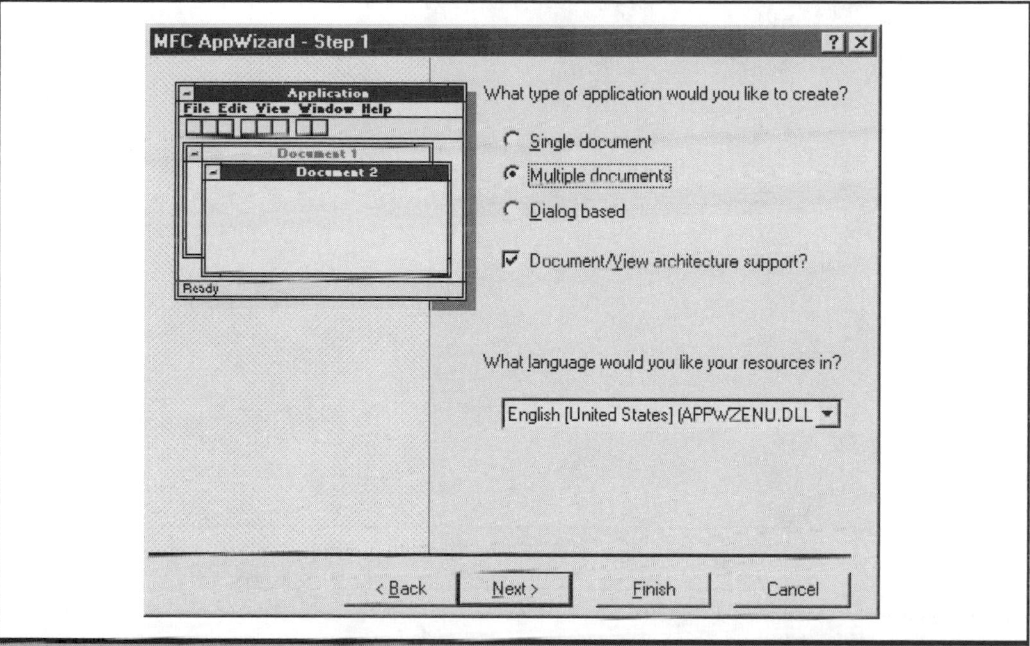

Figure 24-18. *Step 1—Use the Multiple document interface for this project*

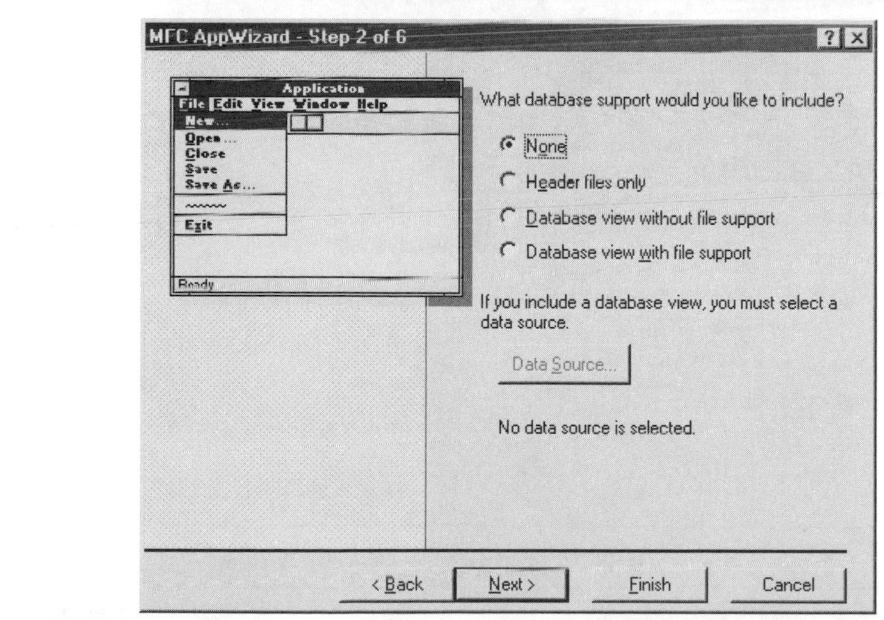

Figure 24-19. *Step 2—Checking None indicates that no database support is needed for this project*

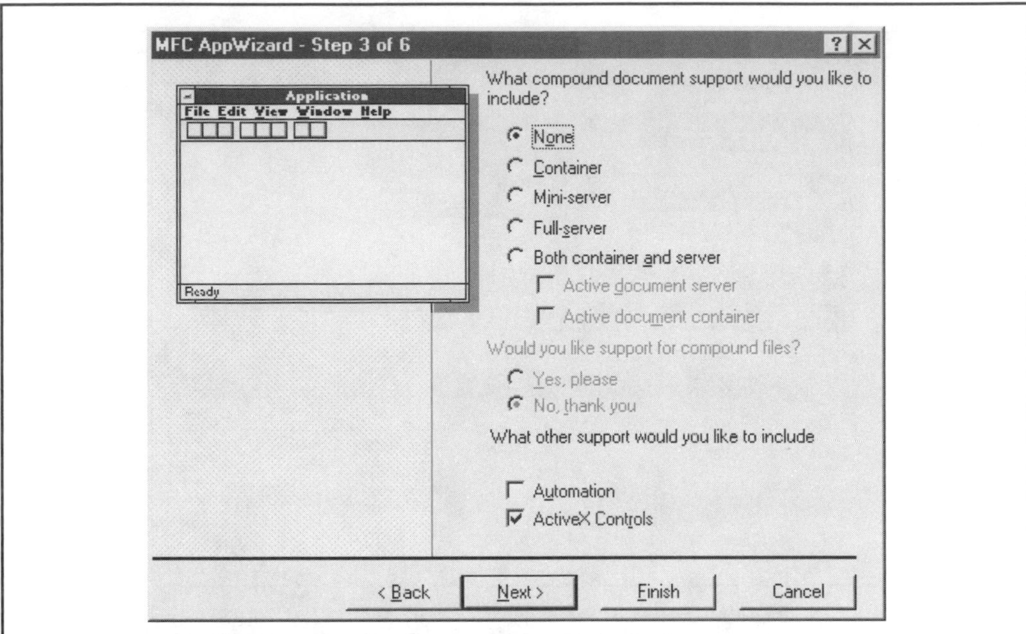

Figure 24-20. *Step 3—This project does not support compound documents but will use ActiveX controls*

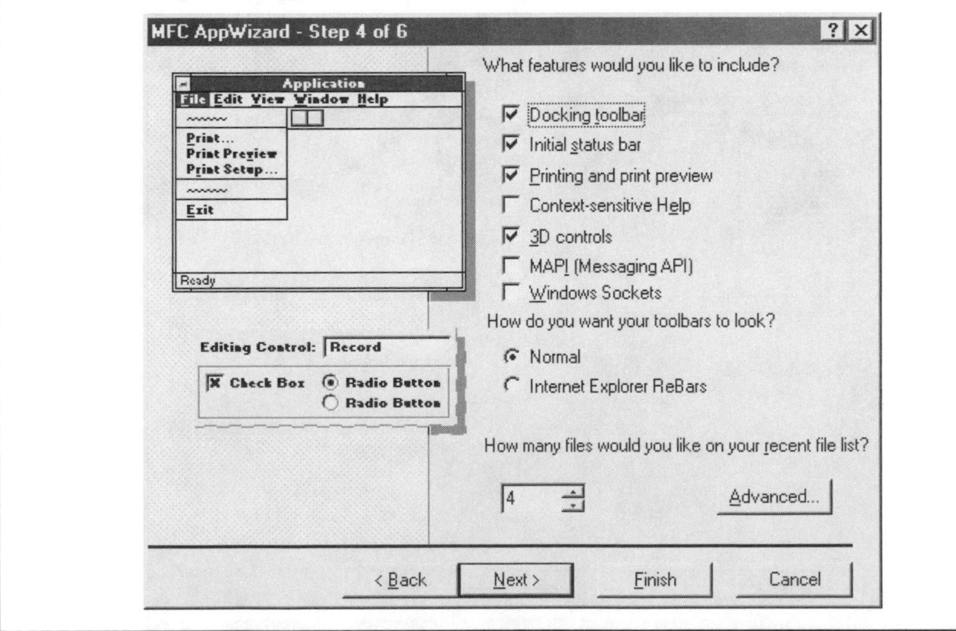

Figure 24-21. *Step 4—This project uses a toolbar, status bar, and 3-D controls. Documents can also be printed*

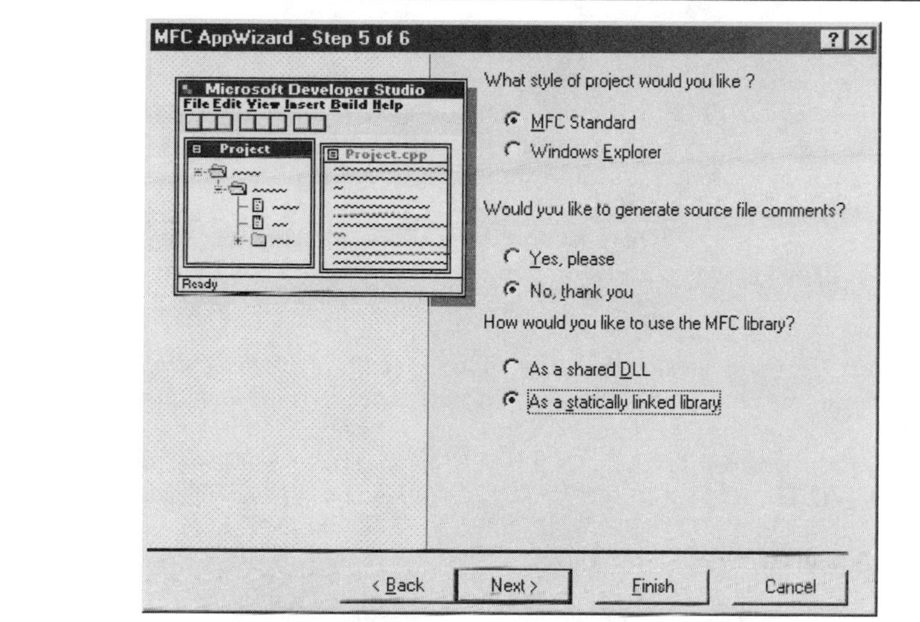

Figure 24-22. *Step 5—No comments are requested in the source code. A statically linked library is requested*

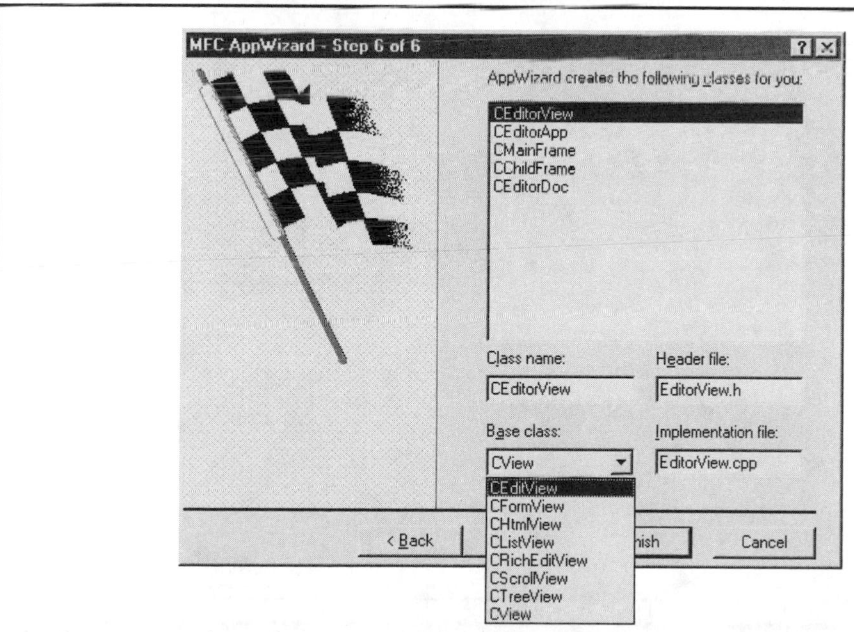

Figure 24-23. *Step 6—Five unique classes will be generated to support the Editor application*

In this example the **CEditorView** class, derived from the **CEditView** class, is used to create the base for this application's user-defined view classes. **CEditView** describes a class that can be used to develop a simple text editor. After selecting the class, select the Finish button. A summary of the AppWizard's development process is then shown. Figure 24-24 shows the summary for this example application.

Select the OK button in this dialog box to start the code-generation process. Figure 24-25 shows the project file list when the AppWizard's build process is complete.

These files will be generated and stored in the subdirectory specified at the start of the project.

Note *The* ***CEditView*** *class supplies the necessary functionality of an edit control. Now your template can print, find and replace, cut, copy, paste, clear, and undo. Since the* ***CEditView*** *class is derived from the* ***CView*** *class, its objects can be used with documents and document templates. As a default, this class handles ID_FILE_PRINT, ID_EDIT_CUT, ID_EDIT_COPY, ID_EDIT_PASTE, ID_EDIT_CLEAR, ID_EDIT_UNDO, ID_EDIT_SELECT_ALL, ID_EDIT_FIND, ID_EDIT_REPLACE, and ID_EDIT_REPEAT.*

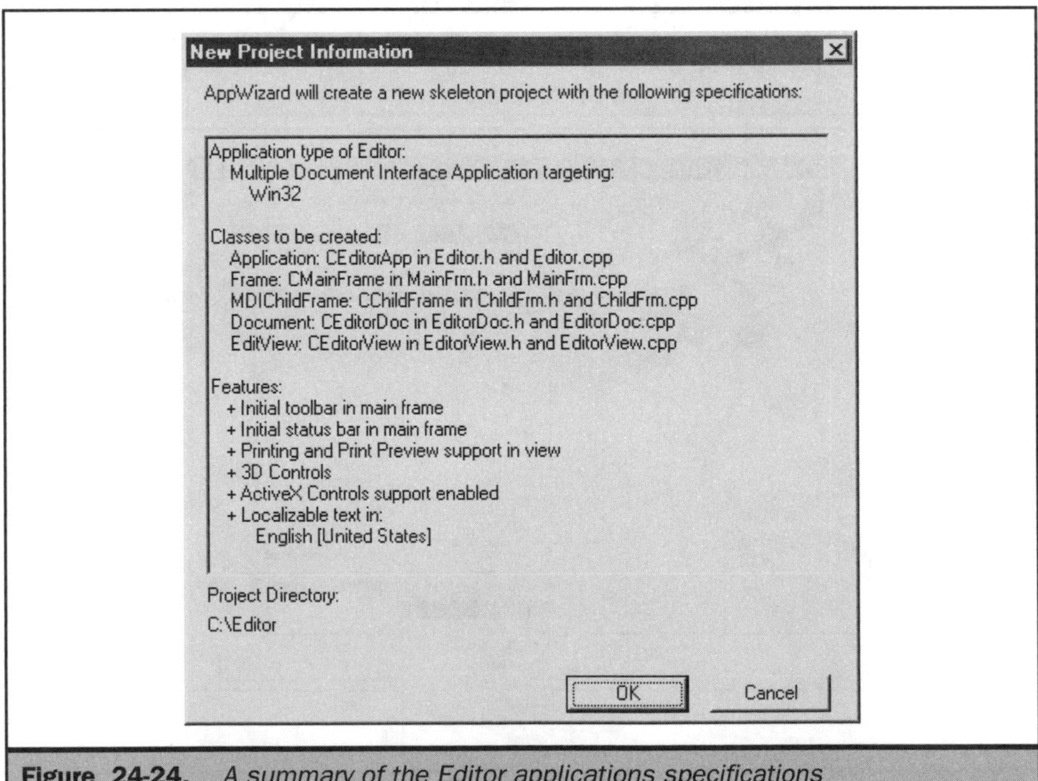

Figure 24-24. *A summary of the Editor applications specifications*

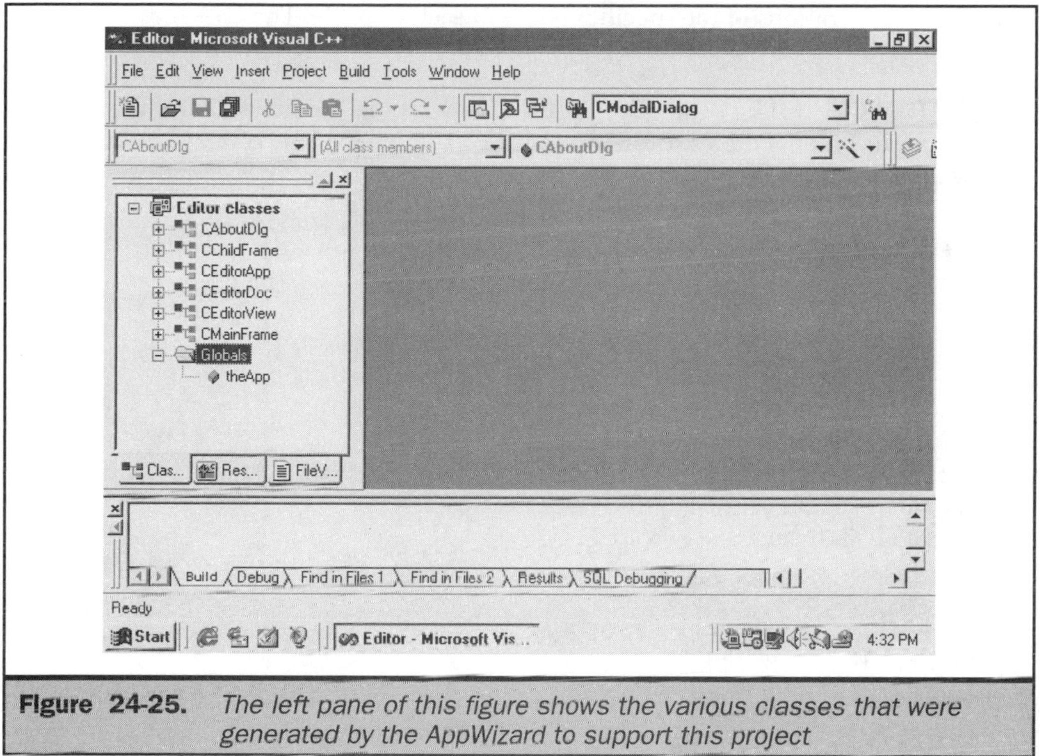

Figure 24-25. *The left pane of this figure shows the various classes that were generated by the AppWizard to support this project*

The Editor application currently being built will eventually use one message handler, but we're saving the details on that message handler for later!

Building the Application

This application can now be compiled and linked in the normal manner. When the compile and link process has been completed, an executable file will be present in the appropriate subdirectory. Run the application from the Build menu. You should be able to open existing text files or create new files.

Let's examine the code produced by the AppWizard and discuss several additions we've added to the project.

Examining AppWizard Code

The AppWizard generates five C++ files for the initial Editor application. These files are named EDITOR.CPP, MAINFRM.CPP, EDITORDOC.CPP, CHILDFRM.CPP, and EDITORVIEW.CPP. Each of these C++ files has an associated header file: EDITOR.H, MAINFRM.H, EDITORDOC.H, CHILDFRM.H, and EDITORVIEW.H. The header files contain the declarations of the specific classes in each C++ file. The C++ files will be examined in the following sections.

THE EDITOR.CPP FILE The EDITOR.CPP file serves as the main file for the application. It contains the **CEditorApp** class. You'll note that the code we've added to this file appears in a bolded font.

```
// Editor.cpp : Defines the class behaviors for application.
//

#include "stdafx.h"
#include "Editor.h"

#include "MainFrm.h"
#include "ChildFrm.h"
#include "EditorDoc.h"
#include "EditorView.h"

#ifdef _DEBUG
#define new DEBUG_NEW
#undef THIS_FILE
static char THIS_FILE[] = __FILE__;
#endif

/////////////////////////////////////////////////////////////
// CEditorApp

BEGIN_MESSAGE_MAP(CEditorApp, CWinApp)
  //{{AFX_MSG_MAP(CEditorApp)
  ON_COMMAND(ID_APP_ABOUT, OnAppAbout)
  //}}AFX_MSG_MAP
  // Standard file based document commands
  ON_COMMAND(ID_FILE_NEW, CWinApp::OnFileNew)
  ON_COMMAND(ID_FILE_OPEN, CWinApp::OnFileOpen)
  // Standard print setup command
  ON_COMMAND(ID_FILE_PRINT_SETUP, CWinApp::OnFilePrintSetup)
END_MESSAGE_MAP()

/////////////////////////////////////////////////////////////
// CEditorApp construction

CEditorApp::CEditorApp()
```

```
{
}

/////////////////////////////////////////////////////////////////
// The one and only CEditorApp object

CEditorApp theApp;

/////////////////////////////////////////////////////////////////
// CEditorApp initialization

BOOL CEditorApp::InitInstance()
{
COLORREF clrCtlBk, clrCtlText;

  // Set dialog background color to blue, text to white
  SetDialogBkColor(clrCtlBk=RGB(0,0,255),
                   clrCtlText=RGB(255,255,255));

  AfxEnableControlContainer();

  // Standard initialization

#ifdef _AFXDLL
  Enable3dControls();       // Call when using as shared DLL
#else
  Enable3dControlsStatic();  // Call when statically linking
#endif

  // Change the registry key under which settings are stored.
  SetRegistryKey(_T("Local AppWizard-Generated Applications"));

  LoadStdProfileSettings();  // Load standard INI file options

  // Register document templates

  CMultiDocTemplate* pDocTemplate;
  pDocTemplate = new CMultiDocTemplate(
    IDR_EDITORTYPE,
    RUNTIME_CLASS(CEditorDoc),
    RUNTIME_CLASS(CChildFrame), // custom MDI child frame
```

```
    RUNTIME_CLASS(CEditorView));
  AddDocTemplate(pDocTemplate);

  // create main MDI Frame window
  CMainFrame* pMainFrame = new CMainFrame;
  if (!pMainFrame->LoadFrame(IDR_MAINFRAME))
    return FALSE;
  m_pMainWnd = pMainFrame;

  // Parse command line for standard shell commands, etc.
  CCommandLineInfo cmdInfo;
  ParseCommandLine(cmdInfo);

  // Dispatch commands specified on the command line
  if (!ProcessShellCommand(cmdInfo))
    return FALSE;
  pMainFrame->ShowWindow(m_nCmdShow);
  pMainFrame->UpdateWindow();

  return TRUE;
}


/////////////////////////////////////////////////////////////////
// CAboutDlg dialog used for App About

class CAboutDlg : public CDialog
{
public:
  CAboutDlg();

// Dialog Data
  //{{AFX_DATA(CAboutDlg)
  enum { IDD = IDD_ABOUTBOX };
  //}}AFX_DATA

  // ClassWizard generated virtual function overrides
  //{{AFX_VIRTUAL(CAboutDlg)
  protected:
  virtual void DoDataExchange(CDataExchange* pDX);
  //}}AFX_VIRTUAL
```

```
// Implementation
protected:
  //{{AFX_MSG(CAboutDlg)
    // No message handlers
  //}}AFX_MSG
  DECLARE_MESSAGE_MAP()
};

CAboutDlg::CAboutDlg() : CDialog(CAboutDlg::IDD)
{
  //{{AFX_DATA_INIT(CAboutDlg)
  //}}AFX_DATA_INIT
}

void CAboutDlg::DoDataExchange(CDataExchange* pDX)
{
  CDialog::DoDataExchange(pDX);
  //{{AFX_DATA_MAP(CAboutDlg)
  //}}AFX_DATA_MAP
}

BEGIN_MESSAGE_MAP(CAboutDlg, CDialog)
  //{{AFX_MSG_MAP(CAboutDlg)
    // No message handlers
  //}}AFX_MSG_MAP
END_MESSAGE_MAP()

// App command to run the dialog
void CEditorApp::OnAppAbout()
{
  CAboutDlg aboutDlg;
  aboutDlg.DoModal();
}


/////////////////////////////////////////////////////////////////////////////
// CEditorApp commands
```

The message map, near the top of the listing, belongs to the **CEditorApp** class. This message map specifically links the ID_APP_ABOUT, ID_FILE_NEW, ID_FILE_OPEN, and ID_FILE_PRINT_SETUP messages with their member functions OnAppAbout( ), CWinApp::OnFileNew( ), CWinApp::OnFileOpen( ), and CWinAppOnFilePrintSetup( ). Also notice in the listing that a constructor, an initial instance InitInstance( ), and a member function OnAppAbout( ) are implemented.

One change that has been made to the AppWizard's code is a change in the background and foreground colors for all dialog boxes used by this application. The portion of code required for this change is shown in bold in the previous listing.

Also, as the following code shows, this application will use a multiple-document interface instead of the single-document interface used in the previous example:

```
// Register document templates
CMultiDocTemplate* pDocTemplate;
pDocTemplate = new CMultiDocTemplate(
  IDR_EDITORTYPE,
  RUNTIME_CLASS(CEditorDoc),
  RUNTIME_CLASS(CChildFrame), // custom MDI child frame
  RUNTIME_CLASS(CEditorView));
AddDocTemplate(pDocTemplate);
```

The About dialog box is derived from the **CDialog** class just as in the previous example. There are no initial **CEditorApp** commands, as you can see from the end of the listing.

THE MAINFRM.CPP FILE The MainFrm.cpp file, shown here, contains the frame class **CMainFrame**. This class is derived from **CFrameWnd** and is used to control all multiple-document-interface (MDI) frame features. Pay particular attention to the portion of the listing set in a bold font.

```
// MainFrm.cpp : implementation of the CMainFrame class
//

#include "stdafx.h"
#include "Editor.h"

#include "MainFrm.h"

#ifdef _DEBUG
#define new DEBUG_NEW
#undef THIS_FILE
static char THIS_FILE[] = __FILE__;
#endif
```

```
////////////////////////////////////////////////////////////////////
//////////
// CMainFrame

IMPLEMENT_DYNAMIC(CMainFrame, CMDIFrameWnd)

BEGIN_MESSAGE_MAP(CMainFrame, CMDIFrameWnd)
  //{{AFX_MSG_MAP(CMainFrame)
  ON_WM_CREATE()
  //}}AFX_MSG_MAP
END_MESSAGE_MAP()

static UINT indicators[] =
{
  ID_SEPARATOR,           // status line indicator
  ID_INDICATOR_CAPS,
  ID_INDICATOR_NUM,
  ID_INDICATOR_SCRL,
};

////////////////////////////////////////////////////////////////////
//////////
// CMainFrame construction/destruction

CMainFrame::CMainFrame()
{
}

CMainFrame::~CMainFrame()
{
}

int CMainFrame::OnCreate(LPCREATESTRUCT lpCreateStruct)
{
  if (CMDIFrameWnd::OnCreate(lpCreateStruct) == -1)
    return -1;

  if (!m_wndToolBar.CreateEx(this, TBSTYLE_FLAT, WS_CHILD |
                            WS_VISIBLE | CBRS_TOP |
                            CBRS_GRIPPER | CBRS_TOOLTIPS |
                            CBRS_FLYBY | CBRS_SIZE_DYNAMIC) ||
```

```
  !m_wndToolBar.LoadToolBar(IDR_MAINFRAME))
{
  TRACE0("Failed to create toolbar\n");
  return -1;      // fail to create
}

if (!m_wndStatusBar.Create(this) ||
  !m_wndStatusBar.SetIndicators(indicators,
    sizeof(indicators)/sizeof(UINT)))
{
  TRACE0("Failed to create status bar\n");
  return -1;      // fail to create
}

  m_wndToolBar.EnableDocking(CBRS_ALIGN_ANY);
  EnableDocking(CBRS_ALIGN_ANY);
  DockControlBar(&m_wndToolBar);

  return 0;
}

BOOL CMainFrame::PreCreateWindow(CREATESTRUCT& cs)
{
  if( !CMDIFrameWnd::PreCreateWindow(cs) )
    return FALSE;
  return TRUE;
}

//////////////////////////////////////////////////////////////////////
//////////
// CMainFrame diagnostics

#ifdef _DEBUG
void CMainFrame::AssertValid() const
{
  CMDIFrameWnd::AssertValid();
}

void CMainFrame::Dump(CDumpContext& dc) const
{
  CMDIFrameWnd::Dump(dc);
```

```
}

#endif //_DEBUG

/////////////////////////////////////////////////////////////////////
//////////
// CMainFrame message handlers
```

When you examine this listing, you will notice that the message map does handle ON_WM_CREATE messages. The constructor and destructor, however, still contain no code.

However, notice the inclusion of this small portion of code:

```
static UINT indicators[] =
{
  ID_SEPARATOR,           // status line indicator
  ID_INDICATOR_CAPS,
  ID_INDICATOR_NUM,
  ID_INDICATOR_SCRL,
};
```

Recall that the AppWizard was asked to generate a template with an initial toolbar and status bar. This group of custom controls will require ID values for the various status line indicators.

The inclusion of the toolbar and status bar is handled by the second portion of bolded code, shown in the MAINFRM.CPP listing.

The member functions AssertValid( ) and Dump( ) use definitions contained in the parent class. **CMainFrame** initially contains no message handlers.

THE EDITORDOC.CPP FILE The EDITORDOC.CPP file, shown here, contains the **CEditorDoc** class, which is unique to this application. This file is used to hold document data and to load and save files.

```
// EditorDoc.cpp : implementation of the CEditorDoc class
//

#include "stdafx.h"
#include "Editor.h"

#include "EditorDoc.h"
```

```
#ifdef _DEBUG
#define new DEBUG_NEW
#undef THIS_FILE
static char THIS_FILE[] = __FILE__;
#endif

/////////////////////////////////////////////////////////////////////
// CEditorDoc

IMPLEMENT_DYNCREATE(CEditorDoc, CDocument)

BEGIN_MESSAGE_MAP(CEditorDoc, CDocument)
  //{{AFX_MSG_MAP(CEditorDoc)
  //}}AFX_MSG_MAP
END_MESSAGE_MAP()

/////////////////////////////////////////////////////////////////////
// CEditorDoc construction/destruction

CEditorDoc::CEditorDoc()
{
}

CEditorDoc::~CEditorDoc()
{
}

BOOL CEditorDoc::OnNewDocument()
{
  if (!CDocument::OnNewDocument())
    return FALSE;

  return TRUE;
}



/////////////////////////////////////////////////////////////////////
// CEditorDoc serialization

void CEditorDoc::Serialize(CArchive& ar)
```

```
{
    ((CEditView*)m_viewList.GetHead())->SerializeRaw(ar);
}

/////////////////////////////////////////////////////////////////
// CEditorDoc diagnostics

#ifdef _DEBUG
void CEditorDoc::AssertValid() const
{
  CDocument::AssertValid();
}

void CEditorDoc::Dump(CDumpContext& dc) const
{
  CDocument::Dump(dc);
}
#endif //_DEBUG

/////////////////////////////////////////////////////////////////
// CEditorDoc commands
```

When you examine this listing, you will again notice that the message map, constructor, and destructor contain no code. Several member functions can be used to provide vital document support. OnNewDocument( ) uses the definition provided by the parent class. Serialize( ) supports persistent objects. This line of code, set in bold type in the previous listing, provides the functionality to the file I/O menu commands, allowing text files to be created, opened, and saved.

The member functions AssertValid( ) and Dump( ) use definitions contained in the parent class. There are no initial **CEditorDoc** commands.

THE EDITORVIEW.CPP FILE The EDITORVIEW.CPP, shown next, provides the view of the document. In this implementation, **CEditorView** is derived from the **CEditView** class.

```
// EditorView.cpp : implementation of the CEditorView class
//

#include "stdafx.h"
#include "Editor.h"
```

```
#include "EditorDoc.h"
#include "EditorView.h"

#ifdef _DEBUG
#define new DEBUG_NEW
#undef THIS_FILE
static char THIS_FILE[] = __FILE__;
#endif


/////////////////////////////////////////////////////////////////////////////
// CEditorView

IMPLEMENT_DYNCREATE(CEditorView, CEditView)

BEGIN_MESSAGE_MAP(CEditorView, CEditView)
  //{{AFX_MSG_MAP(CEditorView)
  ON_WM_RBUTTONDOWN()
  //}}AFX_MSG_MAP
  // Standard printing commands
  ON_COMMAND(ID_FILE_PRINT, CEditView::OnFilePrint)
  ON_COMMAND(ID_FILE_PRINT_DIRECT, CEditView::OnFilePrint)
  ON_COMMAND(ID_FILE_PRINT_PREVIEW, CEditView::OnFilePrintPreview)
END_MESSAGE_MAP()

/////////////////////////////////////////////////////////////////////////////
// CEditorView construction/destruction

CEditorView::CEditorView()
{
}

CEditorView::~CEditorView()
{
}

BOOL CEditorView::PreCreateWindow(CREATESTRUCT& cs)
{
```

```
  BOOL bPreCreated = CEditView::PreCreateWindow(cs);
  cs.style &= ~(ES_AUTOHSCROLL|WS_HSCROLL);  // Enable
word-wrapping

  return bPreCreated;
}

/////////////////////////////////////////////////////////////////////
// CEditorView drawing

void CEditorView::OnDraw(CDC* pDC)
{
  CEditorDoc* pDoc = GetDocument();
  ASSERT_VALID(pDoc);
}

/////////////////////////////////////////////////////////////////////
// CEditorView printing

BOOL CEditorView::OnPreparePrinting(CPrintInfo* pInfo)
{
  // default CEditView preparation
  return CEditView::OnPreparePrinting(pInfo);
}

void CEditorView::OnBeginPrinting(CDC* pDC, CPrintInfo* pInfo)
{
  CEditView::OnBeginPrinting(pDC, pInfo);
}

void CEditorView::OnEndPrinting(CDC* pDC, CPrintInfo* pInfo)
{
  CEditView::OnEndPrinting(pDC, pInfo);
}

/////////////////////////////////////////////////////////////////////
// CEditorView diagnostics

#ifdef _DEBUG
void CEditorView::AssertValid() const
{
```

```
  CEditView::AssertValid();
}

void CEditorView::Dump(CDumpContext& dc) const
{
  CEditView::Dump(dc);
}

CEditorDoc* CEditorView::GetDocument() // non-debug version is
inline
{
  ASSERT(m_pDocument->IsKindOf(RUNTIME_CLASS(CEditorDoc)));
  return (CEditorDoc*)m_pDocument;
}
#endif //_DEBUG

///////////////////////////////////////////////////////////////////////
//////////
// CEditorView message handlers

void CEditorView::OnRButtonDown(UINT nFlags, CPoint point)
{
  char szTimeStr[20];
  CTime tm=CTime::GetCurrentTime( );

  sprintf(szTimeStr, "It's now  %02d:%02d:%02d",
          tm.GetHour( ),tm.GetMinute( ),
          tm.GetSecond( ));

  MessageBox(szTimeStr, "Is it time to quit yet?",
             MB_OK);


  CEditView::OnRButtonDown(nFlags, point);
}
```

When you examine the message map, you will see that it contains ON_WM_RBUTTONDOWN, which was added by the ClassWizard, and ID_FILE_PRINT and ID_FILE_PREVIEW, which are provided when the **CEditorView** class is used. The constructor and destructor are empty.

The OnDraw( ) member function uses the pointer *pDoc* to point to the document. **CEditorView** handles document printing with OnPreparePrinting( ), OnBeginPrinting( ), and OnEndPrinting( ). The member functions AssertValid( ) and Dump( ) use definitions contained in the parent class.

The message handler code for OnRButtonDown( ) is an easy enhancement to the application. Use the ClassWiz ard, shown in Figure 24-26, to add WM_RBUTTONDOWN message capabilities and the **OnRButtonDown** class.

Double-click the mouse on the **OnRButtonDown** member function, shown in Figure 24-26, to move directly to the **CEditorView** message handler section of EDITORVIEW.CPP. Figure 24-27 shows the point where the code was inserted.

Now, if the user clicks the right mouse button while using the text editor, a small dialog box will pop up on the screen and display the current time.

Figure 24-28 shows the application running with two text files opened for inspection.

Want to know what time it is while you are working? Maybe it's time to quit? Depress the right mouse button while over a document to pop up a message box with the current time. Figure 24-29 shows an example of this message box.

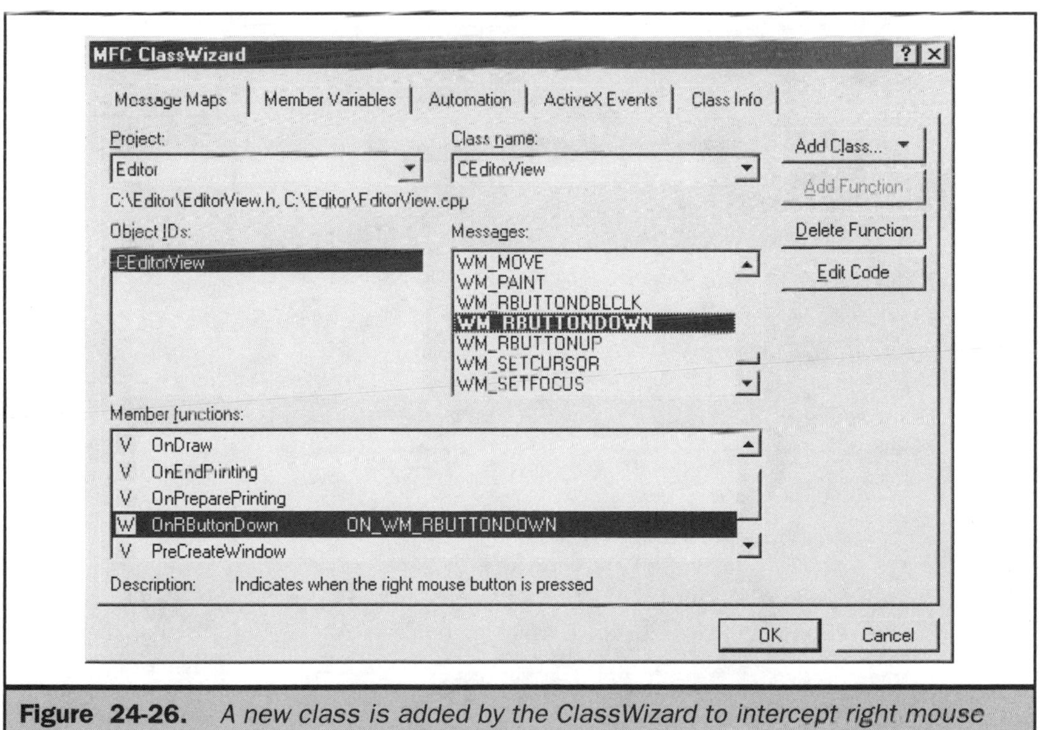

Figure 24-26. *A new class is added by the ClassWizard to intercept right mouse button down messages*

WIZARDS

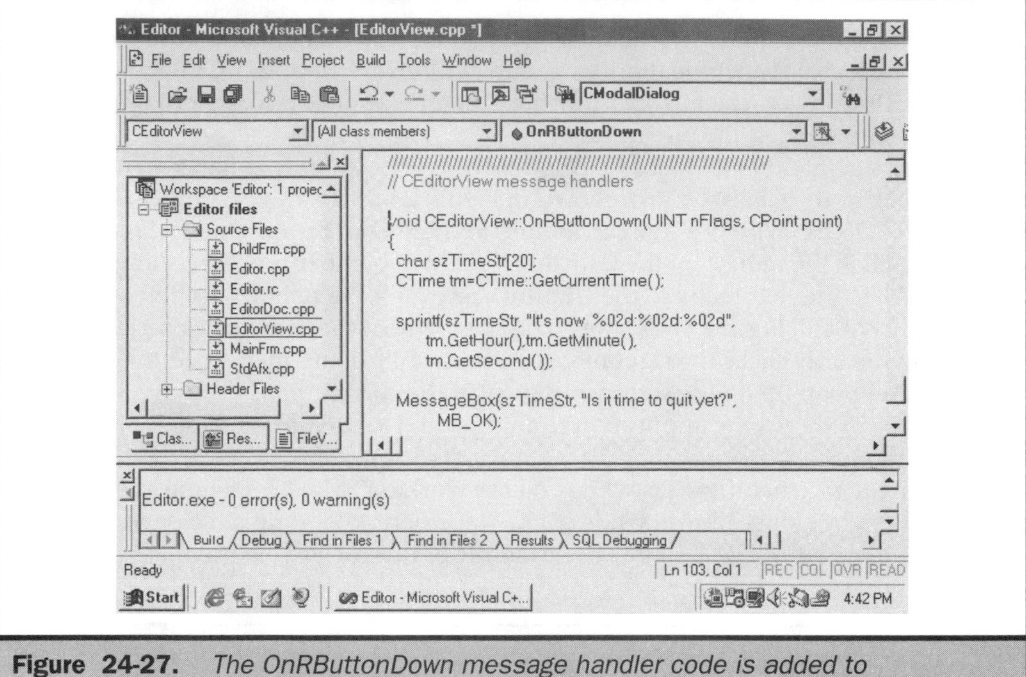

Figure 24-27. *The OnRButtonDown message handler code is added to the application*

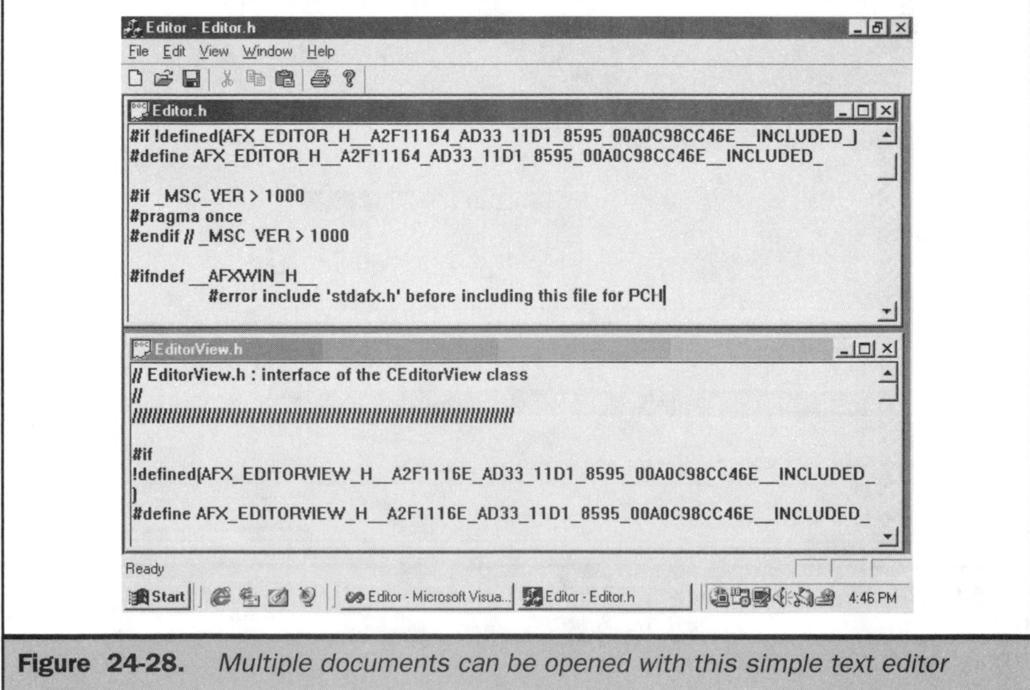

Figure 24-28. *Multiple documents can be opened with this simple text editor*

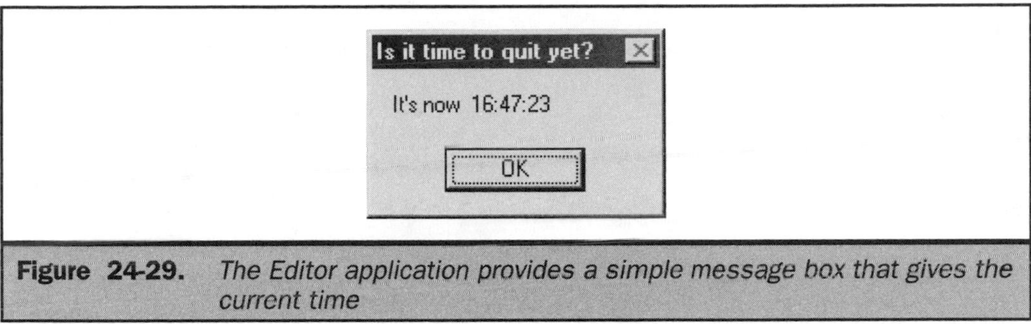

Figure 24-29. *The Editor application provides a simple message box that gives the current time*

What's Coming?

The next chapter uses the knowledge you have gained in this chapter about the AppWizard and the ClassWizard to develop applications that deal with compound document support.

Chapter 25

Getting Started with OLE

The concepts and definitions used with the tools in Microsoft OLE are introduced in this chapter. OLE, at its inception, simply stood for Object Linking and Embedding. However, as Microsoft expanded its power and features, its abilities exceeded this definition. Microsoft no longer refers to this product as anything but OLE. By definition, OLE is an object-based technology for sharing information and services across process and machine boundaries.

OLE tools allow programmers to develop interconnected applications—*compound documents*—which are dynamically linked together. These compound documents include linked or embedded objects in addition to data.

Developing OLE-compliant containers and servers without the use of Microsoft's wizards and the MFC is foolish, because you'd have to write literally thousands of lines of code, much of it redundant from application to application.

This chapter shows you how to build OLE-compliant applications with the AppWizard. This powerful tool, first discussed in Chapter 24, is great for developing applications with OLE features. The program developer can transcend the mundane tasks of repetitive programming code by using the AppWizard's dynamic templates. The AppWizard also allows you, the programmer, to introduce features into your applications without having to worry about the details of the implementation. With the AppWizard, implementing OLE in an application has become very, very simple!

A container application is developed in this chapter with the use of the AppWizard. The information you learn from this application can be applied to a server application that you can develop on your own.

OLE Features and Specifications

OLE offers additional features that are not directly related to compound documents. These features specify methods for handling drag-and-drop, data transfer, file management, and so on. This section contains an overview of these concepts.

Objects

Procedure-oriented Windows programming makes extensive use of API function calls. Sometimes it is difficult to see the implementation language (C or C++) because these applications seem to contain nothing but function calls!

In Chapters 22 and 23 you observed a movement away from a procedure-oriented programming approach and toward an object-oriented approach. The MFC library provides the tools for this transition. With OLE, additional tools for object-oriented programming have become available.

The object-oriented *component object model* is a binary specification or standard that allows two unrelated applications to communicate with each other. The communication takes place through interfaces implemented on the object. When an object conforms to this standard, it is called a *Component Object Model* or *COM object*.

A component object can be instantiated through a component object library—which contains functions that support this instantiation. A *component object* is a Windows object with a unique class ID. The object's functions, contained in the library and referred to as an *interface*, can be called via a returned pointer. This process allows the creation of objects that are not dependent upon the programming language. The library also *marshals* how function calls and function parameters are handled between processes.

Files

OLE allows the use of stream and storage objects—*compound files*—that streamline file manipulation. The stream object most closely resembles a single file, and the storage object resembles a file directory. This structured storage concept shields you from the actual location of data on a disk.

Microsoft's long-range plans include the development of a common file structure so that all files can be easily browsed.

Data

Uniform data transfers are made through a *data object*. OLE uses pointers to a data object. This helps connect the data source to the data receiver. The data object, in turn, handles how data is actually exchanged. Thus, to the programmer, data transfers that use the Clipboard will be handled in the same manner as those that use drag-and-drop.

Embedding

Compound documents can hold information from a variety of unrelated sources. For example, a Microsoft Word document can contain an Excel chart and a Paint bitmap.

Before OLE, items such as charts and bitmaps could be copied to other documents via the Clipboard. Once the objects were "pasted" into the receiving document, they retained no knowledge of their former life. They were static, dead images. If changes eventually had to be made to these objects, the user had to return to the application that originally generated the object, make the changes on the original, and go through the cut-and-paste transfer process once again.

In this case, the Word document would be called the *container*, and Excel and Paint would be called the servers. A container holds an object or objects created by other applications, whereas a server is the source of an object or objects used by other applications.

An Embedded Object

As an example, this section will teach you how to embed a Paint object into a Microsoft Word document. Word will be the container, and Paint will be the server.

Open Microsoft Word. Figure 25-1 shows a typical Word screen with a small amount of text written in the window.

From the Microsoft Word Insert menu, select the Object... menu item, as shown in Figure 25-2.

Once the menu item is selected, the Object dialog box will appear, as shown in Figure 25-3.

From the Object dialog box, choose Paintbrush Picture as the object to embed. Paint will be opened automatically, as shown in Figure 25-4, and the drawing surface will float over the top of the Word document. You will now be in the Page Layout view mode of Word.

The next step is to use Paint to draw the object that you wish to embed in the Word document. In this example, a little text and several simple graphics shapes were drawn in the Paint drawing area, as shown in Figure 25-5.

When you are done creating the object, select the Save menu item in Paint's File menu.

Now click on the Word document to return to Microsoft Word and close the Paint application. Figure 25-7 shows the Word document containing the embedded object while in the Page Layout mode.

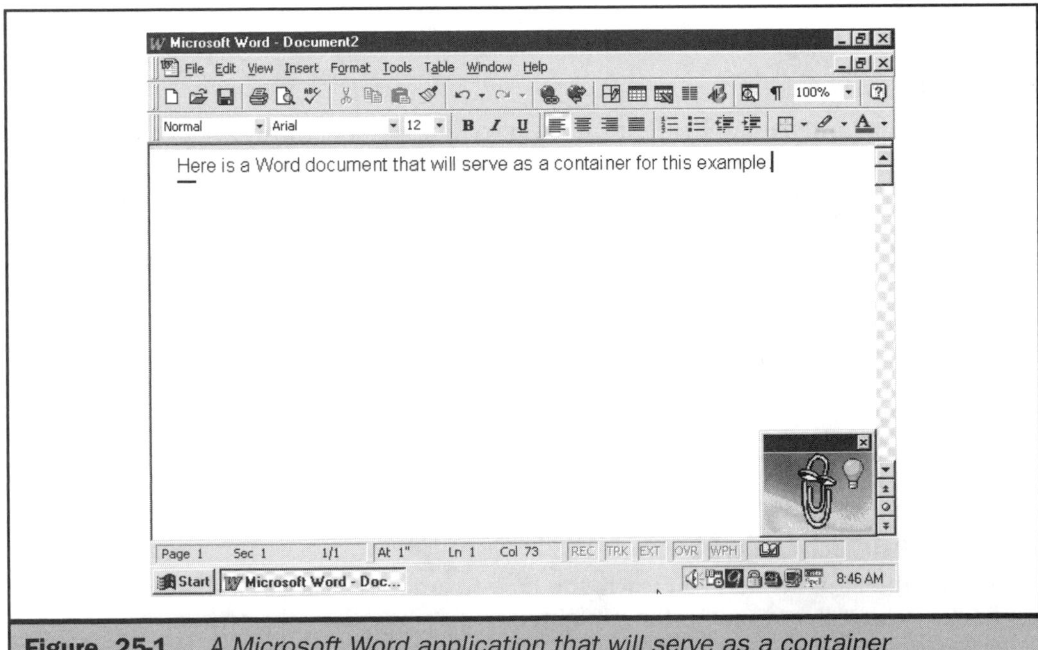

Figure 25-1. *A Microsoft Word application that will serve as a container*

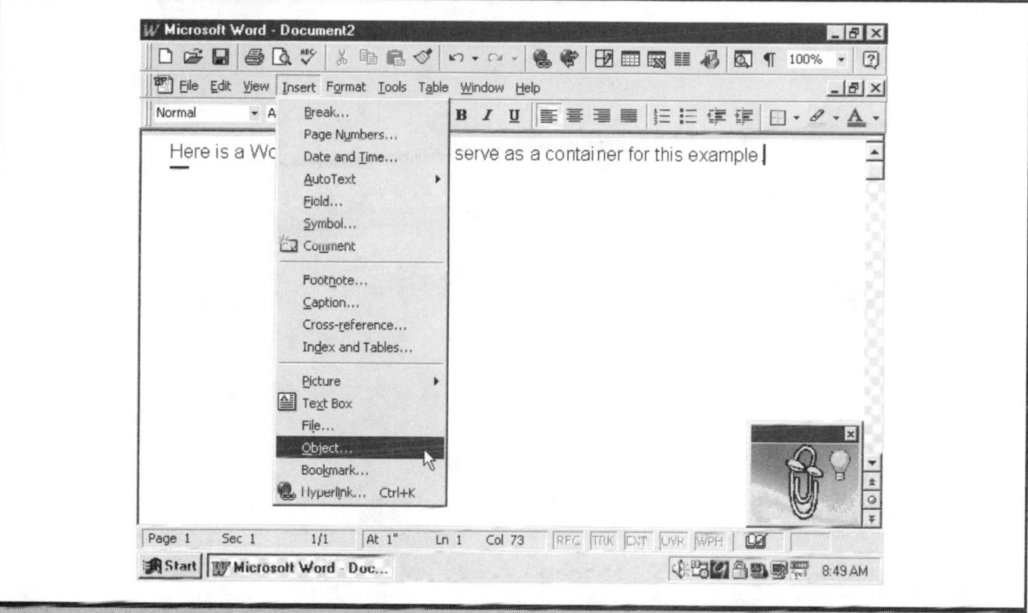

Figure 25-2. *Use the Insert menu to select the Object... menu item*

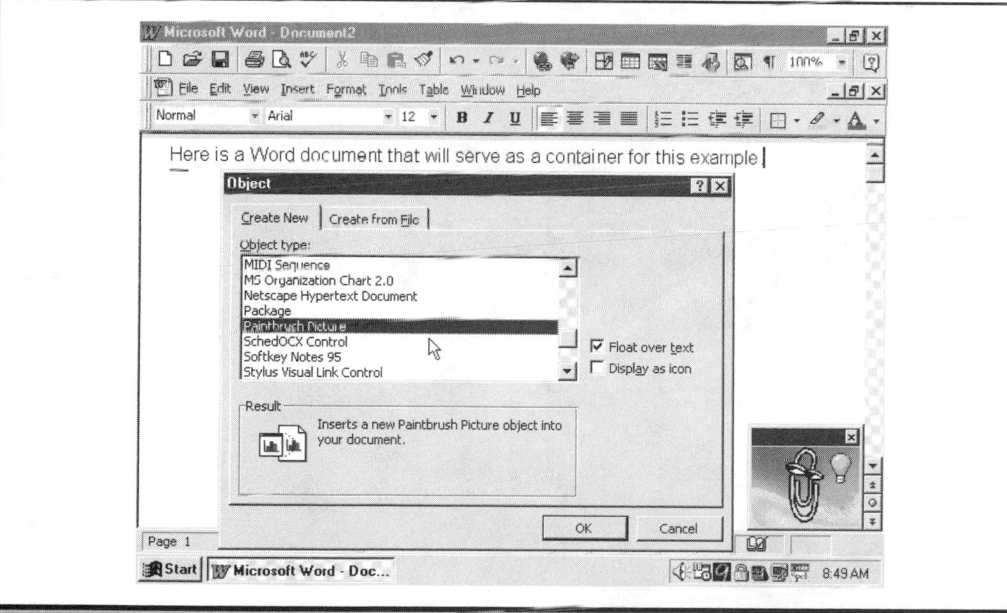

Figure 25-3. *The Object dialog box allows the type of object to be identified*

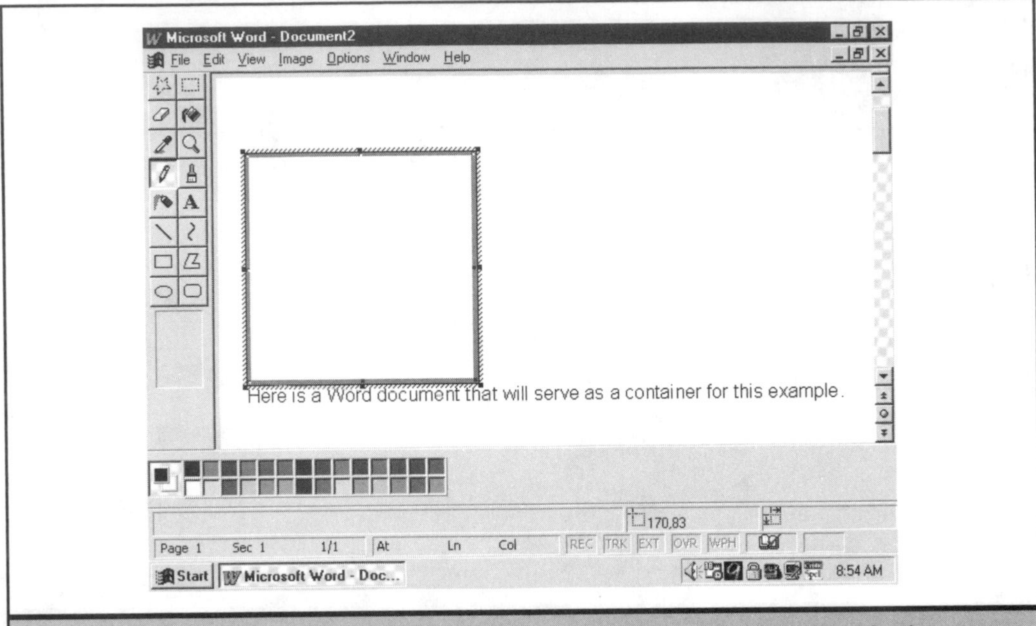

Figure 25-4. *Paint has been identified as the object to be embedded in the Word document*

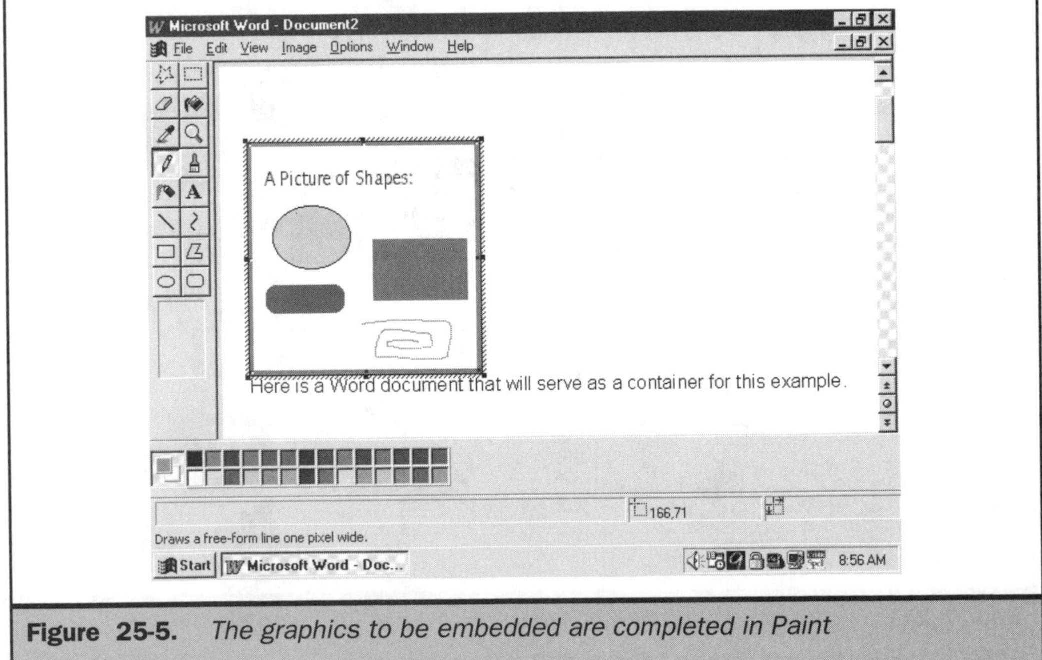

Figure 25-5. *The graphics to be embedded are completed in Paint*

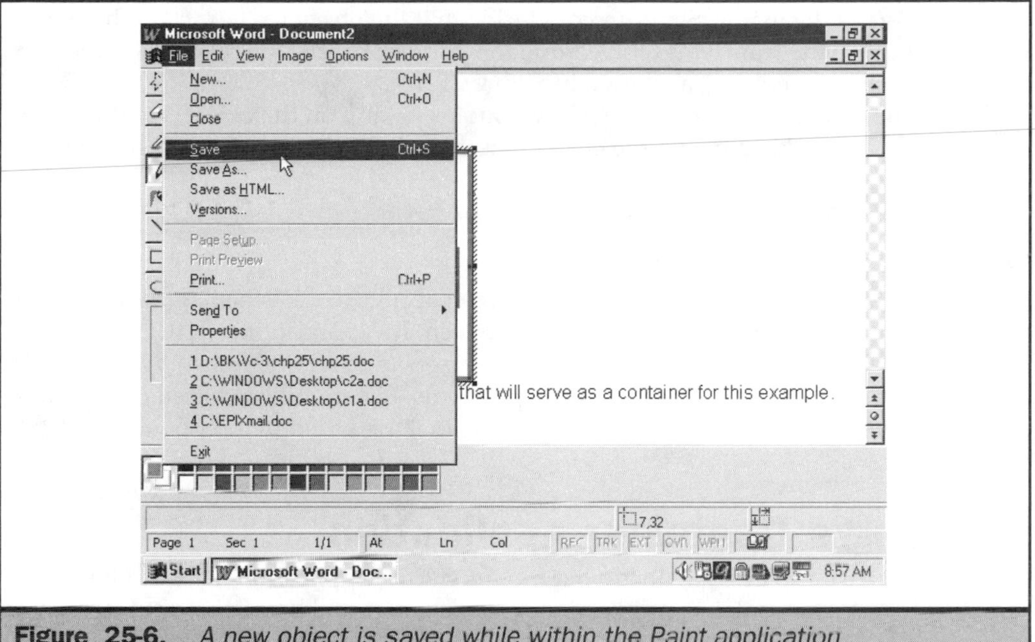

Figure 25-6. *A new object is saved while within the Paint application*

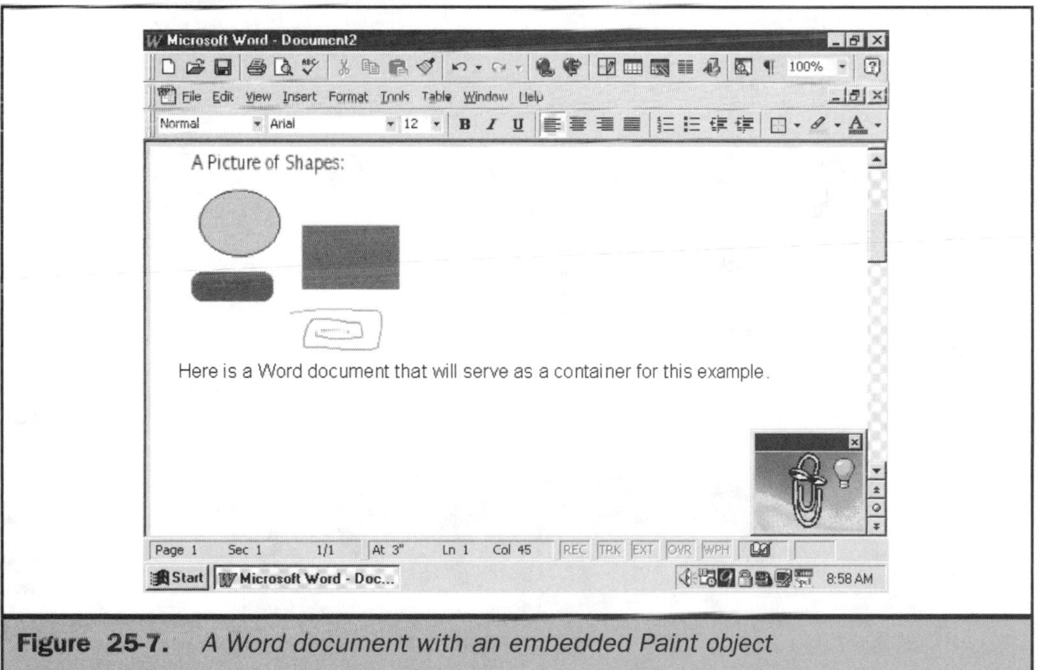

Figure 25-7. *A Word document with an embedded Paint object*

Now, here is the magic. Suppose you decide that the object isn't exactly what you wanted. Because the transfer is OLE compliant, you can simply single-click on the object to block it for editing, as shown in Figure 25-8.

When the object is selected in Word by double-clicking on the object, Paint is immediately opened again with the currently selected object ready for editing. Figure 25-9 shows this process.

Linking

OLE supports a dynamic linking process between applications. When applications are linked, data can be shared instantaneously between the applications. In the past, linking was difficult because it was too easy for users to break the links. With OLE, *file monikers* prevent most of the link breakage problems. File monikers, based on a path in the file system, are used to identify COM objects that are saved in their own files.

Creating a Container Application

In Chapter 24, a simple single-document interface (SDI) application named "Graph" was developed. The container application in this chapter will be patterned closely after that example. We'll call this application "Cnt."

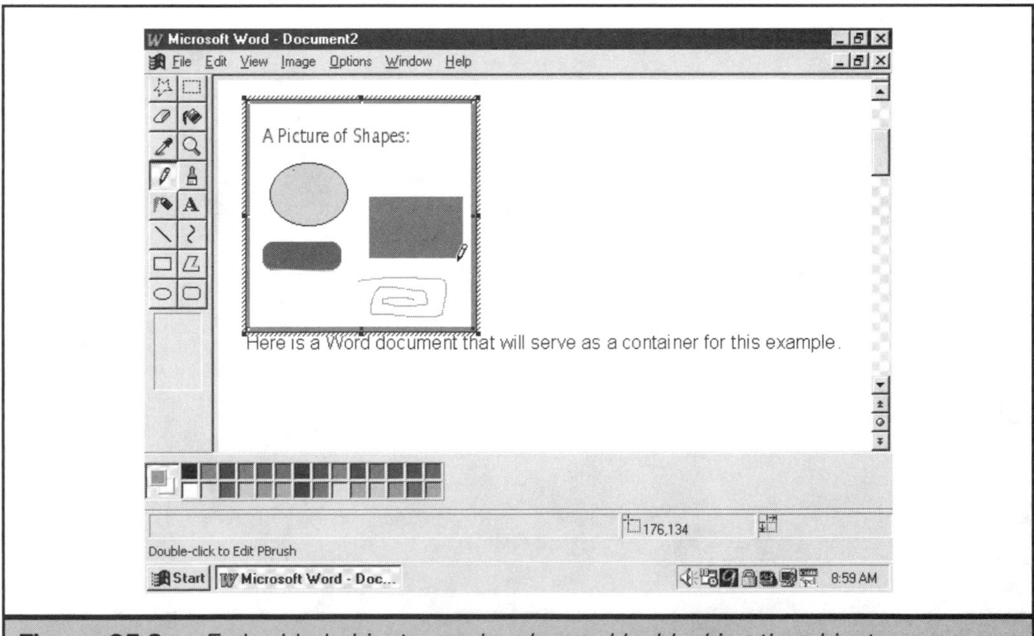

Figure 25-8. *Embedded objects can be changed by blocking the object*

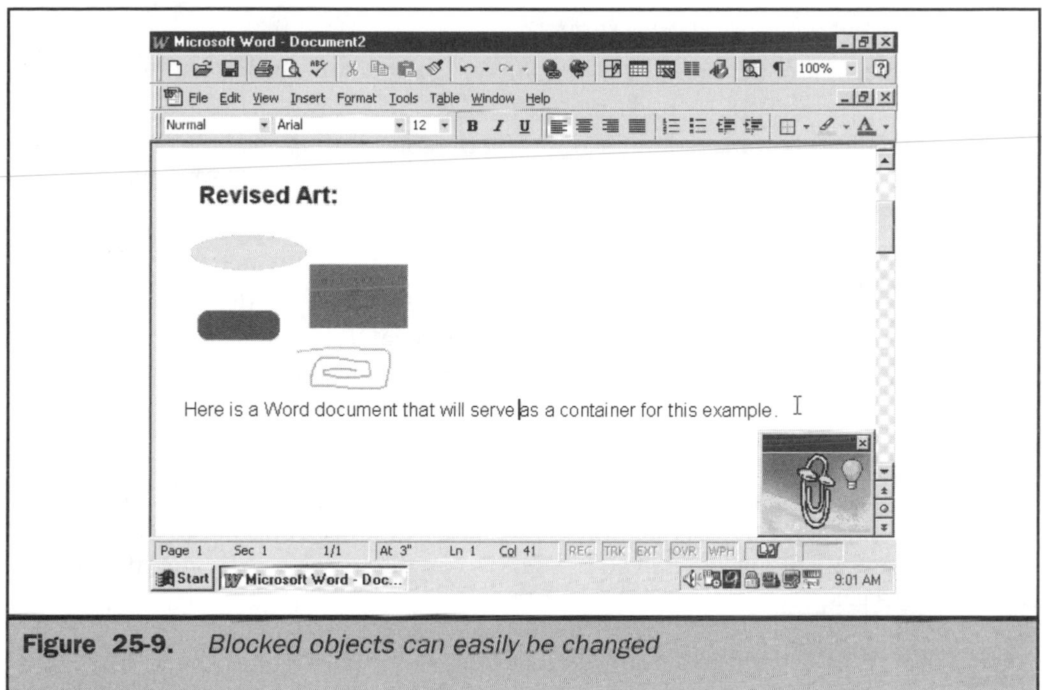

Figure 25-9. *Blocked objects can easily be changed*

This application uses two important OLE classes, **COleClientItem** and **COleDocument**. **COleDocument** manages a list of **COleClientItem** items. **COleClientItem** itself manages the embedded or linked objects and the required communications.

The important thing to remember as you view the container code in the next sections is that the code is completely generated by the AppWizard. This container template code can be enhanced with your specific application features to turn it into a full-blown product. In this chapter, however, no additional features were added to the basic template.

Working with the AppWizard

The AppWizard is used here in the same way it was used in Chapter 24. You might want to review that chapter for a more detailed explanation of each step in the creation process. This section will examine the most important steps, in an abbreviated form, for building the container application, Cnt:

- Use the Microsoft Visual C++ File menu to start a new project.
- Select the MFC AppWizard (.EXE) to start the six-step process:

  1. Create a single-document interface.

2. Do not include database support.
3. Select a Container as the OLE compound document. Include support for ActiveX controls.
4. Include all of the default features for the container application.
5. Select a MFC Standard project, source code comments, and then pick a statically linked library.
6. Examine the list of classes to be generated, making any necessary changes. Click on the Finish button to complete the specification process.

- The AppWizard will generate a summary screen. If this information is correct, click on the OK button to generate the project's code.
- The panel, to the left of your display, should now show the various classes and files created for the project.

Finally, build the executable file by selecting the Rebuild All option from the compiler's Build menu. When the process is complete, the appropriate subdirectory will contain an executable file named CNT.EXE. We will test this container in another section of this chapter.

AppWizard Files

The files generated by the AppWizard produce a fully operable container application named Cnt. When the files have been generated by the AppWizard, your subdirectory will contain the following unique C++ files: CNT.CPP, MAINFRM.CPP, CNTDOC.CPP, CNTVIEW.CPP, and CNTRITEM.CPP. Also in this subdirectory will be a host of supporting header files, resource files, and so on.

The Container File: CNT.CPP

The code used in the container CNT.CPP file is almost identical to that used in the Graph example in Chapter 24. Compare the two files and notice the similarities. You might also want to return to Chapter 24 if you need more details on the message map and the classes used in this file.

The file is listed here, so the application's code for this chapter will be complete:

```
// Cnt.cpp : Defines the class behaviors for the application.
//

#include "stdafx.h"
#include "Cnt.h"

#include "MainFrm.h"
#include "CntDoc.h"
```

```
#include "CntView.h"

#ifdef _DEBUG
#define new DEBUG_NEW
#undef THIS_FILE
static char THIS_FILE[] = __FILE__;
#endif

/////////////////////////////////////////////////////////////////
// CCntApp

BEGIN_MESSAGE_MAP(CCntApp, CWinApp)
  //{{AFX_MSG_MAP(CCntApp)
  ON_COMMAND(ID_APP_ABOUT, OnAppAbout)
    // NOTE - the ClassWizard will add\remove mapping macros.
    //    DO NOT EDIT these blocks of generated code!
  //}}AFX_MSG_MAP
  // Standard file based document commands
  ON_COMMAND(ID_FILE_NEW, CWinApp::OnFileNew)
  ON_COMMAND(ID_FILE_OPEN, CWinApp::OnFileOpen)
  // Standard print setup command
  ON_COMMAND(ID_FILE_PRINT_SETUP, CWinApp::OnFilePrintSetup)
END_MESSAGE_MAP()

/////////////////////////////////////////////////////////////////
// CCntApp construction

CCntApp::CCntApp()
{
  // TODO: add construction code here,
  // Place all significant initialization in InitInstance
}

/////////////////////////////////////////////////////////////////
// The one and only CCntApp object

CCntApp theApp;

/////////////////////////////////////////////////////////////////
// CCntApp initialization

BOOL CCntApp::InitInstance()
```

```
{
  // Initialize OLE libraries
  if (!AfxOleInit())
  {
    AfxMessageBox(IDP_OLE_INIT_FAILED);
    return FALSE;
  }

  AfxEnableControlContainer();

  // Standard initialization
  // If not using these features you can reduce the size
  //  of the final executable; remove from the following
  //  the specific initialization routines you do not need.

#ifdef _AFXDLL
  Enable3dControls();       //Call when using MFC in shared DLL
#else
  Enable3dControlsStatic(); //Call when linking statically
#endif

  // Change the registry key under which settings are stored.
  // Modify this string to be something appropriate
  // such as the name of your company or organization.
  SetRegistryKey(_T("Local AppWizard-Generated Applications"));

  LoadStdProfileSettings();  //Load standard options

  // Register the application's document templates.
  //  Document templates serve as the connection between
  // documents, frame windows and views.

  CSingleDocTemplate* pDocTemplate;
  pDocTemplate = new CSingleDocTemplate(
    IDR_MAINFRAME,
    RUNTIME_CLASS(CCntDoc),
    RUNTIME_CLASS(CMainFrame),       // main SDI frame window
    RUNTIME_CLASS(CCntView));
  pDocTemplate->SetContainerInfo(IDR_CNTR_INPLACE);
  AddDocTemplate(pDocTemplate);
```

```
  // Parse command line for standard shell commands
  CCommandLineInfo cmdInfo;
  ParseCommandLine(cmdInfo);

  // Dispatch commands specified on the command line
  if (!ProcessShellCommand(cmdInfo))
    return FALSE;

  // The window has been initialized, show and update.
  m_pMainWnd->ShowWindow(SW_SHOW);
  m_pMainWnd->UpdateWindow();

  return TRUE;
}


/////////////////////////////////////////////////////////////////////////////
// CAboutDlg dialog used for App About

class CAboutDlg : public CDialog
{
public:
  CAboutDlg();

// Dialog Data
  //{{AFX_DATA(CAboutDlg)
  enum { IDD = IDD_ABOUTBOX };
  //}}AFX_DATA

  // ClassWizard generated virtual function overrides
  //{{AFX_VIRTUAL(CAboutDlg)
  protected:
  virtual void DoDataExchange(CDataExchange* pDX);
  //}}AFX_VIRTUAL

// Implementation
protected:
  //{{AFX_MSG(CAboutDlg)
    // No message handlers
  //}}AFX_MSG
  DECLARE_MESSAGE_MAP()
```

```
};

CAboutDlg::CAboutDlg() : CDialog(CAboutDlg::IDD)
{
  //{{AFX_DATA_INIT(CAboutDlg)
  //}}AFX_DATA_INIT
}

void CAboutDlg::DoDataExchange(CDataExchange* pDX)
{
  CDialog::DoDataExchange(pDX);
  //{{AFX_DATA_MAP(CAboutDlg)
  //}}AFX_DATA_MAP
}

BEGIN_MESSAGE_MAP(CAboutDlg, CDialog)
  //{{AFX_MSG_MAP(CAboutDlg)
    // No message handlers
  //}}AFX_MSG_MAP
END_MESSAGE_MAP()

// App command to run the dialog
void CCntApp::OnAppAbout()
{
  CAboutDlg aboutDlg;
  aboutDlg.DoModal();
}


/////////////////////////////////////////////////////////////////
// CCntApp commands
```

There is an interesting section of code in this file that deserves a mention. Under OLE, in-place editing is supported. *In-place editing* means that when an object is embedded in a container, such as our Cnt application, its menu replaces the container's menu. For example, if an Excel spreadsheet object is embedded in Cnt, Cnt's menu will change to that of Excel's!

This menu change is handled by MFC, via OLE, almost automatically. MFC makes this possible by having three menu sources available: IDR_MAINFRAME, IDR_DOCTYPE, and IDR_CNTR_INPLACE (the name of the last IDR is specific to your application). When no object is embedded in the container application,

IDR_MAINFRAME is used. When a document is opened, IDR_DOCTYPE is used. Finally, when an object has been embedded in the container, IDR_CNTR_INPLACE is used.

The Container File: MAINFRM.CPP

The code used in the container MAINFRM.CPP file is the same as that used in the Graph example in Chapter 24. Again, return to Chapter 24 if you need more details on the message map and classes used in this file.

For completeness, the file is listed here:

```
// MainFrm.cpp : implementation of the CMainFrame class
//

#include "stdafx.h"
#include "Cnt.h"

#include "MainFrm.h"

#ifdef _DEBUG
#define new DEBUG_NEW
#undef THIS_FILE
static char THIS_FILE[] = __FILE__;
#endif

/////////////////////////////////////////////////////////////////////////////
// CMainFrame

IMPLEMENT_DYNCREATE(CMainFrame, CFrameWnd)

BEGIN_MESSAGE_MAP(CMainFrame, CFrameWnd)
  //{{AFX_MSG_MAP(CMainFrame)
    // ClassWizard will add and remove mapping macros here.
    //    DO NOT EDIT these blocks of generated code !
  ON_WM_CREATE()
  //}}AFX_MSG_MAP
END_MESSAGE_MAP()

static UINT indicators[] =
{
  ID_SEPARATOR,           // status line indicator
  ID_INDICATOR_CAPS,
  ID_INDICATOR_NUM,
```

```
  ID_INDICATOR_SCRL,
};

/////////////////////////////////////////////////////////////////////////////
// CMainFrame construction/destruction

CMainFrame::CMainFrame()
{
  // TODO: add member initialization code here

}

CMainFrame::~CMainFrame()
{
}

int CMainFrame::OnCreate(LPCREATESTRUCT lpCreateStruct)
{
  if (CFrameWnd::OnCreate(lpCreateStruct) == -1)
    return -1;

  if (!m_wndToolBar.CreateEx(this, TBSTYLE_FLAT, WS_CHILD |
    WS_VISIBLE | CBRS_TOP | CBRS_GRIPPER | CBRS_TOOLTIPS |
    CBRS_FLYBY | CBRS_SIZE_DYNAMIC) ||
    !m_wndToolBar.LoadToolBar(IDR_MAINFRAME))
  {
    TRACE0("Failed to create toolbar\n");
    return -1;      // fail to create
  }

  if (!m_wndStatusBar.Create(this) ||
    !m_wndStatusBar.SetIndicators(indicators,
      sizeof(indicators)/sizeof(UINT)))
  {
    TRACE0("Failed to create status bar\n");
    return -1;      // fail to create
  }

  // TODO: Delete these lines to if toolbar is not to
  //  be dockable
  m_wndToolBar.EnableDocking(CBRS_ALIGN_ANY);
```

```
  EnableDocking(CBRS_ALIGN_ANY);
  DockControlBar(&m_wndToolBar);

  return 0;
}

BOOL CMainFrame::PreCreateWindow(CREATESTRUCT& cs)
{
  if( !CFrameWnd::PreCreateWindow(cs) )
    return FALSE;
  // TODO: Modify the Window class or styles here by modifying
  //  the CREATESTRUCT cs

  return TRUE;
}

/////////////////////////////////////////////////////////////////
// CMainFrame diagnostics

#ifdef _DEBUG
void CMainFrame::AssertValid() const
{
  CFrameWnd::AssertValid();
}

void CMainFrame::Dump(CDumpContext& dc) const
{
  CFrameWnd::Dump(dc);
}

#endif //_DEBUG

/////////////////////////////////////////////////////////////////
// CMainFrame message handlers
```

The Container File: CNTDOC.CPP

The code used in the container CNTDOC.CPP file, shown here, contains some additional code that does not appear in the Graph application in Chapter 24. Compare the two files and notice the differences.

```
// CntDoc.cpp : implementation of the CCntDoc class
//

#include "stdafx.h"
#include "Cnt.h"

#include "CntDoc.h"
#include "CntrItem.h"

#ifdef _DEBUG
#define new DEBUG_NEW
#undef THIS_FILE
static char THIS_FILE[] = __FILE__;
#endif

/////////////////////////////////////////////////////////////////
// CCntDoc

IMPLEMENT_DYNCREATE(CCntDoc, COleDocument)

BEGIN_MESSAGE_MAP(CCntDoc, COleDocument)
  //{{AFX_MSG_MAP(CCntDoc)
    // NOTE - the ClassWizard will add and remove macros here.
    //    DO NOT EDIT these blocks of generated code!
  //}}AFX_MSG_MAP
// Enable default OLE container implementation
ON_UPDATE_COMMAND_UI(ID_EDIT_PASTE,
                     COleDocument::OnUpdatePasteMenu)
ON_UPDATE_COMMAND_UI(ID_EDIT_PASTE_LINK,
                     COleDocument::OnUpdatePasteLinkMenu)
ON_UPDATE_COMMAND_UI(ID_OLE_EDIT_CONVERT,
                     COleDocument::OnUpdateObjectVerbMenu)
ON_COMMAND(ID_OLE_EDIT_CONVERT,
           COleDocument::OnEditConvert)
ON_UPDATE_COMMAND_UI(ID_OLE_EDIT_LINKS,
                     COleDocument::OnUpdateEditLinksMenu)
ON_COMMAND(ID_OLE_EDIT_LINKS,
           COleDocument::OnEditLinks)
ON_UPDATE_COMMAND_UI_RANGE(ID_OLE_VERB_FIRST,
                       ID_OLE_VERB_LAST,
                       COleDocument::OnUpdateObjectVerbMenu)
END_MESSAGE_MAP()
```

```
/////////////////////////////////////////////////////////////////
// CCntDoc construction/destruction

CCntDoc::CCntDoc()
{
// Use OLE compound files
EnableCompoundFile();

  // TODO: add one-time construction code here

}

CCntDoc::~CCntDoc()
{
}

BOOL CCntDoc::OnNewDocument()
{
  if (!COleDocument::OnNewDocument())
    return FALSE;

  // TODO: add reinitialization code here
  // (SDI documents will reuse this document)

  return TRUE;
}



/////////////////////////////////////////////////////////////////
// CCntDoc serialization

void CCntDoc::Serialize(CArchive& ar)
{
  if (ar.IsStoring())
  {
    // TODO: add storing code here
  }
  else
  {
    // TODO: add loading code here
```

```
    }

    // Calling the base class COleDocument enables serialization
    //  of the container document's COleClientItem objects.
    COleDocument::Serialize(ar);
}

/////////////////////////////////////////////////////////////////
// CCntDoc diagnostics

#ifdef _DEBUG
void CCntDoc::AssertValid() const
{
    COleDocument::AssertValid();
}

void CCntDoc::Dump(CDumpContext& dc) const
{
    COleDocument::Dump(dc);
}
#endif //_DEBUG

/////////////////////////////////////////////////////////////////
// CCntDoc commands
```

The most significant change in this file comes with the expansion of the message map, as shown in bold type.

The message map will now allow the implementation of the default OLE container. You can also see that the constructor calls the EnableCompoundFile( ) function. This is required for a container application.

The Container File: CNTVIEW.CPP

The container CNTVIEW.CPP file also has some major changes in comparison to the Graph application in Chapter 24. Examine the following file and note the additions to the message map.

```
// CntView.cpp : implementation of the CCntView class
//

#include "stdafx.h"
#include "Cnt.h"
```

```
#include "CntDoc.h"
#include "CntrItem.h"
#include "CntView.h"

#ifdef _DEBUG
#define new DEBUG_NEW
#undef THIS_FILE
static char THIS_FILE[] = __FILE__;
#endif


/////////////////////////////////////////////////////////////////
// CCntView

IMPLEMENT_DYNCREATE(CCntView, CView)

BEGIN_MESSAGE_MAP(CCntView, CView)
  //{{AFX_MSG_MAP(CCntView)
    // NOTE - the ClassWizard will add and remove macros.
    //    DO NOT EDIT these blocks of generated code!
  ON_WM_DESTROY()
  ON_WM_SETFOCUS()
  ON_WM_SIZE()
  ON_COMMAND(ID_OLE_INSERT_NEW, OnInsertObject)
  ON_COMMAND(ID_CANCEL_EDIT_CNTR, OnCancelEditCntr)
  //}}AFX_MSG_MAP
  // Standard printing commands
  ON_COMMAND(ID_FILE_PRINT, CView::OnFilePrint)
  ON_COMMAND(ID_FILE_PRINT_DIRECT, CView::OnFilePrint)
  ON_COMMAND(ID_FILE_PRINT_PREVIEW, CView::OnFilePrintPreview)
END_MESSAGE_MAP()

/////////////////////////////////////////////////////////////////
// CCntView construction/destruction

CCntView::CCntView()
{
  m_pSelection = NULL;
  // TODO: add construction code here

}
```

```
CCntView::~CCntView()
{
}

BOOL CCntView::PreCreateWindow(CREATESTRUCT& cs)
{
  // TODO: Modify the Window class or styles here by modifying
  //  the CREATESTRUCT cs

  return CView::PreCreateWindow(cs);
}

///////////////////////////////////////////////////////////////
// CCntView drawing

void CCntView::OnDraw(CDC* pDC)
{
  CCntDoc* pDoc = GetDocument();
  ASSERT_VALID(pDoc);

  // TODO: add draw code for native data here
  // TODO: also draw all OLE items in the document

  // Draw the selection at an arbitrary position.
  //  This code should be removed once your real drawing
  //  code is implemented.  This position corresponds exactly
  //  to the rectangle returned by CCntCntrItem,
  //  to give the effect of in-place editing.

  // TODO: remove this code when final draw code is complete.

  if (m_pSelection == NULL)
{
    POSITION pos = pDoc->GetStartPosition();
    m_pSelection = (CCntCntrItem*)pDoc->GetNextClientItem(pos);
}
if (m_pSelection != NULL)
  m_pSelection->Draw(pDC, CRect(10, 10, 210, 210));
}

void CCntView::OnInitialUpdate()
```

```
{
  CView::OnInitialUpdate();


  // TODO: remove this code when final code is written
  m_pSelection = NULL;    // initialize selection

}

//////////////////////////////////////////////////////////////
// CCntView printing

BOOL CCntView::OnPreparePrinting(CPrintInfo* pInfo)
{
  // default preparation
  return DoPreparePrinting(pInfo);
}

void CCntView::OnBeginPrinting(CDC* /*pDC*/,
                               CPrintInfo* /*pInfo*/)
{
  // TODO: add extra initialization before printing
}

void CCntView::OnEndPrinting(CDC* /*pDC*/,
                             CPrintInfo* /*pInfo*/)
{
  // TODO: add cleanup after printing
}

void CCntView::OnDestroy()
{
  // Deactivate the item on destruction; this is important
  // when a splitter view is being used.
   CView::OnDestroy();
   COleClientItem* pActiveItem = GetDocument()->
                               GetInPlaceActiveItem(this);
   if (pActiveItem != NULL && pActiveItem->
                            GetActiveView() == this)
   {
```

```
      pActiveItem->Deactivate();
      ASSERT(GetDocument()->
             GetInPlaceActiveItem(this) == NULL);
   }
}


/////////////////////////////////////////////////////////////////
// OLE Client support and commands

BOOL CCntView::IsSelected(const CObject* pDocItem) const
{
  // The implementation below is adequate if your selection
  //  consists of only CCntCntrItem objects.  To handle
  //  different selection mechanisms, the implementation
  //  here should be replaced.

  // TODO: implement this function that tests for a selected
  // OLE client item

  return pDocItem == m_pSelection;
}

void CCntView::OnInsertObject()
{
  // Invoke standard Insert Object dialog box for information
  //  for new CCntCntrItem object.
  COleInsertDialog dlg;
  if (dlg.DoModal(COleInsertDialog::DocObjectsOnly) != IDOK)
    return;

  BeginWaitCursor();

  CCntCntrItem* pItem = NULL;
  TRY
  {
    // Create new item connected to this document.
    CCntDoc* pDoc = GetDocument();
    ASSERT_VALID(pDoc);
    pItem = new CCntCntrItem(pDoc);
    ASSERT_VALID(pItem);
```

```
    // Initialize the item from the dialog data.
    if (!dlg.CreateItem(pItem))
      AfxThrowMemoryException();  // any exception will do
    ASSERT_VALID(pItem);

    // If item created from class list, not from file, launch
    //  the server to edit the item.
    if (dlg.GetSelectionType() ==
            COleInsertDialog::createNewItem)
      pItem->DoVerb(OLEIVERB_SHOW, this);

    ASSERT_VALID(pItem);

    // As an arbitrary interface, this sets the selection
    //  to the last item inserted.

    // TODO: reimplement selection as for your application

    m_pSelection = pItem;   // set to last inserted item
    pDoc->UpdateAllViews(NULL);
  }
  CATCH(CException, e)
  {
    if (pItem != NULL)
    {
      ASSERT_VALID(pItem);
      pItem->Delete();
    }
    AfxMessageBox(IDP_FAILED_TO_CREATE);
  }
  END_CATCH

  EndWaitCursor();
}

// The following command handler provides standard keyboard
//  user interface to cancel an in-place editing session.
//  The container (not the server) causes the deactivation.
void CCntView::OnCancelEditCntr()
{
```

```
  // Close any in-place active item on this view.
  COleClientItem* pActiveItem = GetDocument()->
                              GetInPlaceActiveItem(this);
  if (pActiveItem != NULL)
  {
    pActiveItem->Close();
  }
  ASSERT(GetDocument()->GetInPlaceActiveItem(this) == NULL);
}

// Special handling of OnSetFocus and OnSize is required for
//  a container when an object is being edited in-place.
void CCntView::OnSetFocus(CWnd* pOldWnd)
{
  COleClientItem* pActiveItem = GetDocument()->
                              GetInPlaceActiveItem(this);
  if (pActiveItem != NULL &&
    pActiveItem->GetItemState() ==
                COleClientItem::activeUIState)
  {
    // need to set focus to this item if in the same view
    CWnd* pWnd = pActiveItem->GetInPlaceWindow();
    if (pWnd != NULL)
    {
      pWnd->SetFocus();   // don't call the base class
      return;
    }
  }

  CView::OnSetFocus(pOldWnd);
}

void CCntView::OnSize(UINT nType, int cx, int cy)
{
  CView::OnSize(nType, cx, cy);
  COleClientItem* pActiveItem = GetDocument()->
                              GetInPlaceActiveItem(this);
  if (pActiveItem != NULL)
    pActiveItem->SetItemRects();
}
```

```
////////////////////////////////////////////////////////////////
// CCntView diagnostics

#ifdef _DEBUG
void CCntView::AssertValid() const
{
  CView::AssertValid();
}

void CCntView::Dump(CDumpContext& dc) const
{
  CView::Dump(dc);
}

CCntDoc* CCntView::GetDocument() // non-debug version
{
  ASSERT(m_pDocument->IsKindOf(RUNTIME_CLASS(CCntDoc)));
  return (CCntDoc*)m_pDocument;
}
#endif //_DEBUG

////////////////////////////////////////////////////////////////
// CCntView message handlers
```

So that it can handle drawing (i.e., inserted objects) for CCntView container, the OnDraw( ) member function has to be altered by the AppWizard. This portion of code was shown in bold type in the file. Here is just a small portion of that code:

```
if (m_pSelection != NULL)
    m_pSelection->Draw(pDC, CRect(10, 10, 210, 210));
}
```

This code, by default, places the object at a prearranged location designated by CRect( ) at 10,10 and 210,210. These values can be changed manually or automatically.

Other additions include OnInitialUpdate( ), IsSelected( ), OnInsertObject( ), OnCancelEdit( ), OnSetFocus( ), and OnSize( ). These signal when an OLE object is selected or otherwise being manipulated. OnInsertObject( ) runs **COleInsertDialog**. Any additional code for these functions must be supplied by you, the programmer.

The Container File: CNTRITEM.CPP

The container CNTRITEM.CPP file, shown here, is responsible for the implementation of the **CCntCntrItem** class

```
// CntrItem.cpp : implementation of the CCntCntrItem class
//

#include "stdafx.h"
#include "Cnt.h"

#include "CntDoc.h"
#include "CntView.h"
#include "CntrItem.h"

#ifdef _DEBUG
#define new DEBUG_NEW
#undef THIS_FILE
static char THIS_FILE[] = __FILE__;
#endif

/////////////////////////////////////////////////////////////////////////////
// CCntCntrItem implementation

IMPLEMENT_SERIAL(CCntCntrItem, COleClientItem, 0)

CCntCntrItem::CCntCntrItem(CCntDoc* pContainer)
  : COleClientItem(pContainer)
{
  // TODO: add one-time construction code here

}

CCntCntrItem::~CCntCntrItem()
{
  // TODO: add cleanup code here

}

void CCntCntrItem::OnChange(OLE_NOTIFICATION nCode,
                            DWORD dwParam)
{
  ASSERT_VALID(this);
```

```
  COleClientItem::OnChange(nCode, dwParam);

  // When an item is being edited (in-place or fully open)
  //  it sends OnChange notifications for changes in the state
  //  of the item or visual appearance of its content.

  // TODO: invalidate the item by calling UpdateAllViews
  //  (with hints appropriate to your application)

  GetDocument()->UpdateAllViews(NULL);
    // for now just update ALL views/no hints
}

BOOL CCntCntrItem::OnChangeItemPosition(const CRect& rectPos)
{
  ASSERT_VALID(this);

  // In-place activation CCntCntrItem::OnChangeItemPosition
  //  is called to change the position of the in-place
  //  window. This is a result of the data in the server
  //  document changing when the extent has changed or as a
  //  result of in-place resizing.
  //
  // The default is to call the base class, which will call
  //  COleClientItem::SetItemRects to move the item
  //  to the new position.

  if (!COleClientItem::OnChangeItemPosition(rectPos))
    return FALSE;

  // TODO: update any cache of the item's rectangle/extent

  return TRUE;
}

void CCntCntrItem::OnGetItemPosition(CRect& rPosition)
{
  ASSERT_VALID(this);

  // In-place activation, CCntCntrItem::OnGetItemPosition
  //  will determine the location of this item.  The default
```

```
  //  implementation simply returns a hard-coded
  //  rectangle. This rectangle would reflect the current
  //  position of the item relative to the view used
  // for activation.
  // Obtain the view by calling CCntCntrItem::GetActiveView.

  // TODO: return correct rectangle (in pixels) in rPosition

  rPosition.SetRect(10, 10, 210, 210);
}

void CCntCntrItem::OnActivate()
{
    // Allow only one inplace activate item per frame
    CCntView* pView = GetActiveView();
    ASSERT_VALID(pView);
    COleClientItem* pItem = GetDocument()->
                            GetInPlaceActiveItem(pView);
    if (pItem != NULL && pItem != this)
        pItem->Close();

    COleClientItem::OnActivate();
}

void CCntCntrItem::OnDeactivateUI(BOOL bUndoable)
{
  COleClientItem::OnDeactivateUI(bUndoable);

    // Hide the object if it is not an outside-in object
    DWORD dwMisc = 0;
    m_lpObject->GetMiscStatus(GetDrawAspect(), &dwMisc);
    if (dwMisc & OLEMISC_INSIDEOUT)
        DoVerb(OLEIVERB_HIDE, NULL);
}

void CCntCntrItem::Serialize(CArchive& ar)
{
  ASSERT_VALID(this);
```

```
  // Call base class to read in COleClientItem data.
  // This sets up the m_pDocument pointer returned from
  //  CCntCntrItem::GetDocument, it is a good idea to call
  //  the base class Serialize first.
  COleClientItem::Serialize(ar);

  // now store/retrieve data specific to CCntCntrItem
  if (ar.IsStoring())
  {
    // TODO: add storing code here
  }
  else
  {
    // TODO: add loading code here
  }
}

/////////////////////////////////////////////////////////////////
// CCntCntrItem diagnostics

#ifdef _DEBUG
void CCntCntrItem::AssertValid() const
{
  COleClientItem::AssertValid();
}

void CCntCntrItem::Dump(CDumpContext& dc) const
{
  COleClientItem::Dump(dc);
}
#endif

/////////////////////////////////////////////////////////////////
```

The main purpose of this file is to help monitor the position and size of the item in the drawing. Examine the portion of code set in bold type. Have you seen these coordinates before?

In the next section, you'll see how to use the container application to accept an object from a server.

Testing the Container Application

The container application can now be tested. Remember that the container application was produced as a template, without additional functionality added. However, what you will see in the next few pages is a very complete and functioning application.

The container application can be started by typing **Cnt** at the command line or run directly from the integrated environment of the Visual C++ compiler. Figure 25-10 shows the initial container window.

This container can use objects from any server. For this example we'll insert an Excel spreadsheet into the container. To select Excel as the server, open the container's Edit menu and use the Insert New Object… menu option. This will open the Insert Object dialog box, as shown in Figure 25-11.

From the Insert Object dialog box, choose Microsoft Excel Worksheet as the object to embed in the container.

Figure 25-12 shows the initial insertion of the object into the container document with data entered in various cells.

Don't forget, you gained all of this functionality without writing one line of code. The AppWizard has made it very easy to develop OLE container and server applications. As a little project, why not create your own server application.

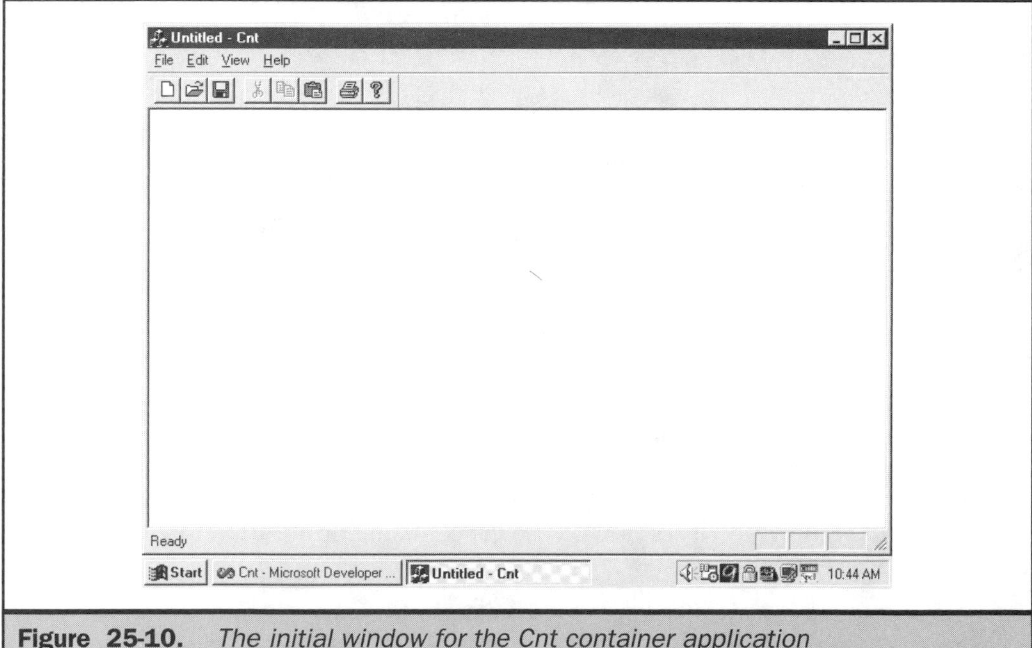

Figure 25-10. *The initial window for the Cnt container application*

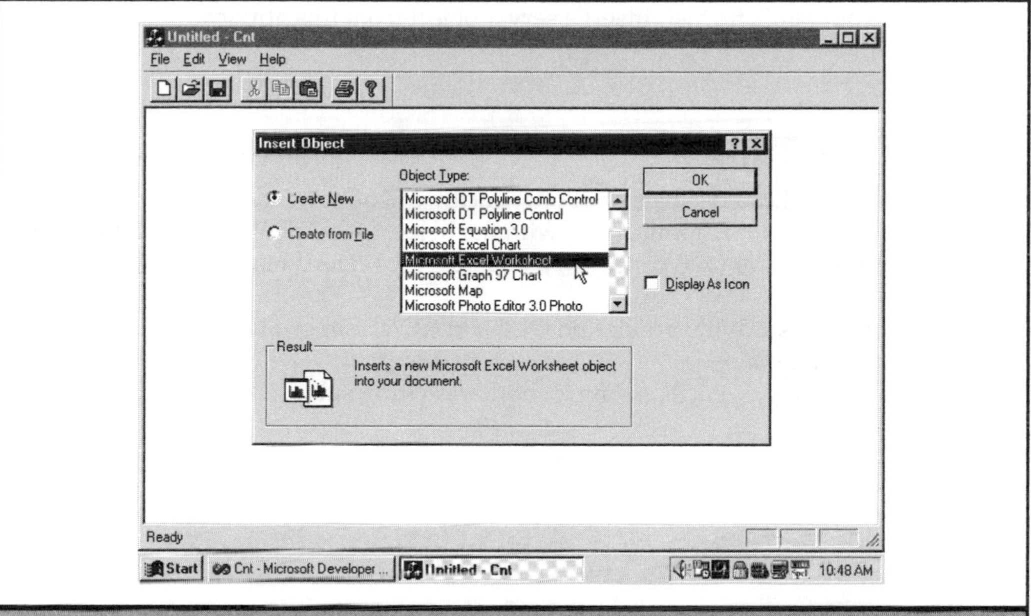

Figure 25-11. *The Insert Object dialog box allows the selection of an Excel worksheet*

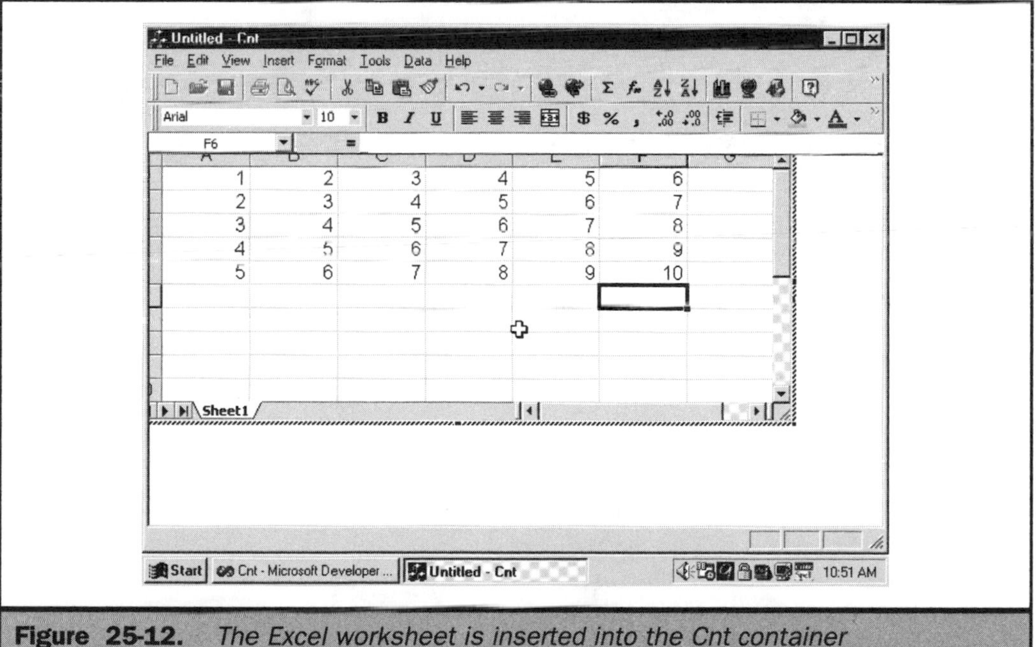

Figure 25-12. *The Excel worksheet is inserted into the Cnt container*

Then, to test your skills further, insert a server object from this application into the Cnt container.

What's Coming?

OLE is truly a complicated subject, but one worthy of your attention. The smart money is on building OLE applications with the help of the AppWizard and the MFC library. Once you master OLE concepts, using the AppWizard makes actual project creation a snap.

We recommend studying articles on OLE and COM that can be found in the *Microsoft Systems Journal*.

In the next chapter, we will examine another exciting subject: ActiveX controls.

The Complete Reference

Chapter 26

Getting Started with ActiveX Controls

You are already familiar with a wide variety of Windows controls such as radio buttons, checkboxes, list boxes, and so on. Many developers also design their own controls. This special group of controls is known as ActiveX or custom controls. As Windows evolved from 3.*x* to Windows 95, 98, and NT, so have custom controls. Custom controls really had their beginning with Microsoft's Visual Basic programming language. Visual Basic made it easy to implement new controls that were not part of the standard group of Windows controls. These custom controls, originally known as VBXs (after their original file extension .VBX), were specialty items. They were actually small dynamic link libraries (DLL) with .VBX file extensions. Custom controls have now evolved into 32-bit controls with new abilities. These new controls use an .OCX file extension. A good example of a custom control is a custom slide bar that might be used to control the volume in a CD-ROM player application.

There is a commercial market for well designed custom controls. However, custom controls developed commercially can also be much more complicated. Some include complete spreadsheet, image, and database capabilities within the control!

Many programmers have developed custom controls using Visual Basic and then incorporated them into their C/C++ applications. Obviously, the C/C++ language has needed its own mechanism for creating custom controls. At the same time Microsoft was developing a solution, they began the migration from 16-bit Windows 3.1 to 32-bit Windows 95 and NT. As it turns out, the hardware-specific 16-bit VBX controls will not serve the new 32-bit multiple platform environments as well as programmers desired. Thus, Microsoft decided that rather than expand the VBX specifications, it would redesign the custom control architecture to include the 32-bit platforms; thus, the new control specifications with .OCX file extensions. Under Windows 95, 98, and Windows NT, OCX controls are the natural replacement for the older VBX custom controls of Visual Basic. These new custom controls will also serve container applications such as Microsoft Access, Excel, Word, PowerPoint, and so on. The term "custom control" has largely been replaced with "ActiveX control."

The good news concerning controls for the C++ developer is that ActiveX controls have a built-in Microsoft C++ wizard that helps build the control. This wizard is officially called the *MFC ActiveX ControlWizard*. The wizard builds the ActiveX control using object-oriented C++ code and takes full advantage of the MFC.

During development, your controls can be tested with the ActiveX Test Container tool. Once the ActiveX control is complete, it can be incorporated into any application that supports OLE objects. Microsoft Word, Excel, and Access are typical applications that support ActiveX controls.

Note *There is another aspect to Windows controls—controls that involve the COM object-model. This group of controls allows control usage independent of the container and thus is ideal for languages such as Visual Basic, Visual C++, and even dynamic HTML.*

ActiveX Controls

ActiveX controls can be placed alongside standard controls such as radio buttons, push buttons, checkboxes, and so on. Therefore, you might find a dialog box containing a few radio buttons, checkboxes, and an ActiveX control. ActiveX controls, however, are inherently more difficult to implement.

Unless a commercial vendor has supplied an ActiveX control, you, the programmer, will be responsible for the design and complete implementation of the control and its properties. The problem is now twofold. First, during the design phase you must create, write, and compile the code that draws the control and implements all of the control's, methods, and so on. This code eventually becomes a tiny dynamic link library (see Appendix C for more information on DLLs) with an .OCX file extension. Second, the application that is to use the ActiveX control must now interface with the control's methods, data, and so on. You also must properly design this interface.

A properly designed ActiveX control must be independent from the application in which it is used. In other words, it must be completely reentrant. Remember that an ActiveX control is really a separate dynamic link library that is not linked to any particular application. A separate instance for data for each use of the control is required for reentrance in a DLL. The only communications allowed between an application and an ActiveX control are via messages. Hence, an ActiveX control must be defined in a dynamic link library.

Control Design Criteria

When entering the design phase for an ActiveX control, several decisions must be made to create an ActiveX control as appealing and functional as possible.

First, you must decide how the ActiveX control will be drawn and displayed. Here, some talent will be required to produce ActiveX controls that are both functional and attractive.

Next, the ActiveX control should be designed to take advantage of changes in control properties resulting from the automation interface of the control. Note that for ActiveX controls, so designed, property pages will allow the user to change properties at run time. Arguments should be assigned ActiveX controls in order to control events, set their names, and determine when they should be fired. A control's methods should be defined in terms of arguments and return types.

Finally, the persistence of a control's various property states must be determined and implemented.

The COleControl *Class*

ActiveX controls are derived from MFC's COleControl class. Examine the code in the next listing. This listing contains an edited portion of the AFXCTL.H header file. If you are interested in examining the full header file, you should be able to locate it in the MFC's INCLUDE subdirectory. Be warned, however, that this file is approximately 30 pages in length.

```
// This is part of the MFC C++ library.
// Copyright (C) 1992-1998 Microsoft Corporation
// All rights reserved.
//
// This source code is only intended as a supplement to the
// Microsoft Foundation Classes Reference and related
// electronic documentation provided with the library.
// See these sources for detailed information regarding the
// Microsoft Foundation Classes product.

/////////////////////////////////////////////////////////////////////////////
// AFXCTL.H - MFC OLE Control support
   .
   .
   .
/////////////////////////////////////////////////////////////////////////////
// Stock events

#define EVENT_STOCK_CLICK() \
  {afxEventStock,DISPID_CLICK,_T("Click"),VTS_NONE},

#define EVENT_STOCK_DBLCLICK() \
  {afxEventStock,DISPID_DBLCLICK,_T("DblClick"),VTS_NONE},

#define EVENT_STOCK_KEYDOWN() \
  {afxEventStock,DISPID_KEYDOWN,_T("KeyDown"),VTS_PI2 VTS_I2},

#define EVENT_STOCK_KEYPRESS() \
  {afxEventStock,DISPID_KEYPRESS,_T("KeyPress"),VTS_PI2},

#define EVENT_STOCK_KEYUP() \
  {afxEventStock,DISPID_KEYUP,_T("KeyUp"),VTS_PI2 VTS_I2},

#define EVENT_STOCK_MOUSEDOWN() \
  {afxEventStock,DISPID_MOUSEDOWN,_T("MouseDown"),\
    VTS_I2 VTS_I2 VTS_XPOS_PIXELS VTS_YPOS_PIXELS},

#define EVENT_STOCK_MOUSEMOVE() \
```

```
  {afxEventStock,DISPID_MOUSEMOVE,_T("MouseMove"),\
    VTS_I2 VTS_I2 VTS_XPOS_PIXELS VTS_YPOS_PIXELS},

#define EVENT_STOCK_MOUSEUP() \
  {afxEventStock,DISPID_MOUSEUP,_T("MouseUp"),\
    VTS_I2 VTS_I2 VTS_XPOS_PIXELS VTS_YPOS_PIXELS},

#define EVENT_STOCK_ERROREVENT() \
  {afxEventStock,DISPID_ERROREVENT,_T("Error"),\
VTS_I2 VTS_PBSTR VTS_SCODE VTS_BSTR VTS_BSTR VTS_I4 VTS_PBOOL},

#define EVENT_STOCK_READYSTATECHANGE() \
{afxEventStock,DISPID_READYSTATECHANGE,_T("ReadyStateChange"),\
    VTS_I4},
    .
    .
    .
/////////////////////////////////////////////////////////////////
// Stock properties

#define DISP_PROPERTY_STOCK(theClass,szExternalName,dispid,
                              pfnGet,pfnSet,vtPropType) \
  {_T(szExternalName),dispid,NULL,vtPropType,\
    (AFX_PMSG)(void (theClass::*)(void))&pfnGet,\
    (AFX_PMSG)(void (theClass::*)(void))&pfnSet,
    0,afxDispStock},\

#define DISP_STOCKPROP_APPEARANCE() \
  DISP_PROPERTY_STOCK(COleControl,"Appearance",
  DISPID_APPEARANCE,\
    COleControl::GetAppearance,COleControl::SetAppearance,
    VT_I2)

#define DISP_STOCKPROP_BACKCOLOR() \
  DISP_PROPERTY_STOCK(COleControl,"BackColor",
  DISPID_BACKCOLOR,\
    COleControl::GetBackColor,COleControl::SetBackColor,
    VT_COLOR)

#define DISP_STOCKPROP_BORDERSTYLE() \
  DISP_PROPERTY_STOCK(COleControl,"BorderStyle",
  DISPID_BORDERSTYLE,\
```

```
    COleControl::GetBorderStyle,COleControl::SetBorderStyle,
    VT_I2)

#define DISP_STOCKPROP_CAPTION() \
  DISP_PROPERTY_STOCK(COleControl,"Caption",DISPID_CAPTION,\
    COleControl::GetText,COleControl::SetText,VT_BSTR)

#define DISP_STOCKPROP_ENABLED() \
  DISP_PROPERTY_STOCK(COleControl,"Enabled",DISPID_ENABLED,\
    COleControl::GetEnabled,COleControl::SetEnabled,VT_BOOL)

#define DISP_STOCKPROP_FONT() \
  DISP_PROPERTY_STOCK(COleControl,"Font",DISPID_FONT,\
    COleControl::GetFont,COleControl::SetFont,VT_FONT)
    .
    .
    .
/////////////////////////////////////////////////////////////////
// Stock methods

#define DISP_FUNCTION_STOCK(theClass,szExternalName,dispid,
                          pfnMember,vtRetVal,vtsParams) \
  {_T(szExternalName),dispid,vtsParams,vtRetVal,\
    (AFX_PMSG)(void (theClass::*)(void))&pfnMember,
    (AFX_PMSG)0,0,\
    afxDispStock},\

#define DISP_STOCKFUNC_REFRESH() \
  DISP_FUNCTION_STOCK(COleControl,"Refresh",DISPID_REFRESH,\
      COleControl::Refresh,VT_EMPTY,VTS_NONE)

#define DISP_STOCKFUNC_DOCLICK() \
  DISP_FUNCTION_STOCK(COleControl,"DoClick",DISPID_DOCLICK,\
      COleControl::DoClick,VT_EMPTY,VTS_NONE)
    .
    .
    .
  // Firing events
  void AFX_CDECL FireEvent(DISPID dispid,BYTE* pbParams,...);

// Firing functions for stock events
  void FireKeyDown(USHORT* pnChar,short nShiftState);
```

```
    void FireKeyUp(USHORT* pnChar,short nShiftState);
    void FireKeyPress(USHORT* pnChar);
    void FireMouseDown(short nButton,short nShiftState,
      OLE_XPOS_PIXELS x,OLE_YPOS_PIXELS y);
    void FireMouseUp(short nButton,short nShiftState,
      OLE_XPOS_PIXELS x,OLE_YPOS_PIXELS y);
    void FireMouseMove(short nButton,short nShiftState,
      OLE_XPOS_PIXELS x,OLE_YPOS_PIXELS y);
    void FireClick();
    void FireDblClick();
    void FireError(SCODE scode,LPCTSTR lpszDescription,
                   UINT nHelpID = 0);
    void FireReadyStateChange();
     .
     .
     .
// Type library
    BOOL GetDispatchIID(IID* pIID);

    // Connection point container
    virtual LPCONNECTIONPOINT GetConnectionHook(REFIID iid);
    virtual BOOL GetExtraConnectionPoints(CPtrArray* pConnPoints);

    // Events
    static const AFX_DATA AFX_EVENTMAP_ENTRY _eventEntries[];
    virtual const AFX_EVENTMAP* GetEventMap() const;
    static const AFX_DATA AFX_EVENTMAP eventMap;
    const AFX_EVENTMAP_ENTRY* GetEventMapEntry(LPCTSTR pszName,
      DISPID* pDispid) const;
    void FireEventV(DISPID dispid,BYTE* pbParams,
                    va_list argList);

    // Stock events
    void KeyDown(USHORT* pnChar);
    void KeyUp(USHORT* pnChar);
    void ButtonDown(USHORT iButton,UINT nFlags,CPoint point);
    void ButtonUp(USHORT iButton,UINT nFlags,CPoint point);
    void ButtonDblClk(USHORT iButton,UINT nFlags,CPoint point);
     .
     .
     .
// Stock properties
```

```
  OLE_COLOR m_clrBackColor;       // BackColor
  OLE_COLOR m_clrForeColor;       // ForeColor
  CString m_strText;              // Text/Caption
  CFontHolder m_font;             // Font
  HFONT m_hFontPrev;              // Prev select font object
  short m_sAppearance;            // Appearance
  short m_sBorderStyle;           // BorderStyle
  BOOL m_bEnabled;                // Enabled
  long m_lReadyState;             // ReadyState
   .
   .
   .
// Message Maps
protected:
  //{{AFX_MSG(COleControl)
  afx_msg void OnKeyDown(UINT nChar,UINT nRepCnt,UINT nFlags);
  afx_msg void OnKeyUp(UINT nChar,UINT nRepCnt,UINT nFlags);
  afx_msg void OnChar(UINT nChar,UINT nRepCnt,UINT nFlags);
  afx_msg void OnMouseMove(UINT nFlags,CPoint point);
  afx_msg void OnLButtonDown(UINT nFlags,CPoint point);
  afx_msg void OnLButtonUp(UINT nFlags,CPoint point);
  afx_msg void OnLButtonDblClk(UINT nFlags,CPoint point);
  afx_msg void OnMButtonDown(UINT nFlags,CPoint point);
  afx_msg void OnMButtonUp(UINT nFlags,CPoint point);
  afx_msg void OnMButtonDblClk(UINT nFlags,CPoint point);
  afx_msg void OnRButtonDown(UINT nFlags,CPoint point);
  afx_msg void OnRButtonUp(UINT nFlags,CPoint point);
  afx_msg void OnRButtonDblClk(UINT nFlags,CPoint point);
  afx_msg void OnInitMenuPopup(CMenu*,UINT,BOOL);
  afx_msg void OnMenuSelect(UINT nItemID,UINT nFlags,
                            HMENU hSysMenu);
  afx_msg LRESULT OnSetMessageString(WPARAM wParam,
                                     LPARAM lParam);
  afx_msg void OnEnterIdle(UINT nWhy,CWnd* pWho);
  afx_msg void OnCancelMode();
  afx_msg void OnPaint(CDC* pDC);
  afx_msg BOOL OnEraseBkgnd(CDC* pDC);
  afx_msg void OnSysKeyDown(UINT nChar,UINT nRepCnt,
                            UINT nFlags);
  afx_msg void OnSysKeyUp(UINT nChar,UINT nRepCnt,
                          UINT nFlags);
  afx_msg int  OnMouseActivate(CWnd *pDesktopWnd,
```

```
                                UINT nHitTest,UINT message);
    afx_msg LRESULT OnSetText(WPARAM wParam,LPARAM lParam);
    afx_msg BOOL OnNcCreate(LPCREATESTRUCT lpCreateStruct);
    afx_msg void OnDestroy();
    afx_msg  void OnKillFocus(CWnd* pNewWnd);
    afx_msg void OnSetFocus(CWnd* pOldWnd);
    afx_msg void OnNcPaint();
    afx_msg void OnNcCalcSize(BOOL bCalcValidRects,
                              NCCALCSIZE_PARAMS* lpncsp);
    afx_msg UINT OnNcHitTest(CPoint point);
    afx_msg void OnNcLButtonDown(UINT nHitTest,CPoint point);
    afx_msg BOOL OnSetCursor(CWnd* pWnd,UINT nHitTest,
                             UINT message);
    afx_msg UINT OnGetDlgCode();
    afx_msg int OnCreate(LPCREATESTRUCT lpCreateStruct);
    afx_msg void OnSize(UINT nType,int cx,int cy);
    afx_msg void OnMove(int x,int y);
    afx_msg void OnShowWindow(BOOL bShow,UINT nStatus);
    //}}AFX_MSG

    afx_msg LRESULT OnOcmCtlColorBtn(WPARAM wParam,
                                     LPARAM lParam);
    afx_msg LRESULT OnOcmCtlColorDlg(WPARAM wParam,
                                     LPARAM lParam);
    afx_msg LRESULT OnOcmCtlColorEdit(WPARAM wParam,
                                      LPARAM lParam);
    afx_msg LRESULT OnOcmCtlColorListBox(WPARAM wParam,
                                         LPARAM lParam);
    afx_msg LRESULT OnOcmCtlColorMsgBox(WPARAM wParam,
                                        LPARAM lParam);
    afx_msg LRESULT OnOcmCtlColorScrollBar(WPARAM wParam,
                                           LPARAM lParam);
    afx_msg LRESULT OnOcmCtlColorStatic(WPARAM wParam,
                                        LPARAM lParam);

    DECLARE_MESSAGE_MAP()

    // button handler helpers
    void OnButtonUp(USHORT nButton,UINT nFlags,CPoint point);
    void OnButtonDown(USHORT nButton,UINT nFlags,CPoint point);
    void OnButtonDblClk(USHORT nButton,UINT nFlags,
                        CPoint point);
```

```
// Interface Maps
public:
  // IPersistStorage
BEGIN_INTERFACE_PART(PersistStorage,IPersistStorage)
    INIT_INTERFACE_PART(COleControl,PersistStorage)
    STDMETHOD(GetClassID)(LPCLSID);
    STDMETHOD(IsDirty)();
    STDMETHOD(InitNew)(LPSTORAGE);
    STDMETHOD(Load)(LPSTORAGE);
    STDMETHOD(Save)(LPSTORAGE,BOOL);
    STDMETHOD(SaveCompleted)(LPSTORAGE);
    STDMETHOD(HandsOffStorage)();
  END_INTERFACE_PART_STATIC(PersistStorage)
   .
   .
   .
  // IOleInPlaceObject
  BEGIN_INTERFACE_PART(OleInPlaceObject,
                       IOleInPlaceObjectWindowless)
    INIT_INTERFACE_PART(COleControl,OleInPlaceObject)
    STDMETHOD(GetWindow)(HWND*);
    STDMETHOD(ContextSensitiveHelp)(BOOL);
    STDMETHOD(InPlaceDeactivate)();
    STDMETHOD(UIDeactivate)();
    STDMETHOD(SetObjectRects)(LPCRECT,LPCRECT);
    STDMETHOD(ReactivateAndUndo)();
    STDMETHOD(OnWindowMessage)(UINT msg,WPARAM wParam,
                               LPARAM lparam,
      LRESULT* plResult);
    STDMETHOD(GetDropTarget)(IDropTarget **ppDropTarget);
  END_INTERFACE_PART(OleInPlaceObject)

  // IOleInPlaceActiveObject
  BEGIN_INTERFACE_PART(OleInPlaceActiveObject,
                       IOleInPlaceActiveObject)
    INIT_INTERFACE_PART(COleControl,OleInPlaceActiveObject)
    STDMETHOD(GetWindow)(HWND*);
    STDMETHOD(ContextSensitiveHelp)(BOOL);
    STDMETHOD(TranslateAccelerator)(LPMSG);
```

```
    STDMETHOD(OnFrameWindowActivate)(BOOL);
    STDMETHOD(OnDocWindowActivate)(BOOL);
    STDMETHOD(ResizeBorder)(LPCRECT,LPOLEINPLACEUIWINDOW,
                            BOOL);
    STDMETHOD(EnableModeless)(BOOL);
END_INTERFACE_PART(OleInPlaceActiveObject)
  .
  .
  .
```

Our intention in showing this partial listing was not to explain each section of the listing in detail, but to provide you with a reference as we introduce some new terms used with ActiveX controls. You'll find several of the captions for those sections set in a bold font.

Events

Events are actions or responses that are triggered by the control's reaction to an action on the control—for example, a keypress or mouse button click. KeyUp and KeyDown are examples of stock events.

Since your class will be derived from Microsoft's **COleControl** class, it will be able to use a new map that enables messages. These messages or events are sent to the application using the control. This application is called the *control container*. The application or container will receive information about an event when something happens to the control. This event could be as simple as clicking the mouse within the control. Using event parameters can provide additional information. Examine the message map area of the previous listing.

A control communicates with its application (container) by firing events. ActiveX provides stock and custom events to be used by your control. See the sections marked stock events in the previous listing. Stock events are handled by the **COleControl** as a default. Custom events might be used to signal the application (container) when a control event occurs, such as receiving a message.

Methods and Properties

The control must expose a set of methods (functions) and properties (interface) to the application using the control in order to make an ActiveX control interactive. Methods are control functions that permit external code to alter characteristics of the control. Typical characteristics include appearance, properties, or behavior. Control properties, on the other hand, include the color, text, font, and other elements used in the control. Methods and properties form the basic mechanism whereby the application (container) communicates with the control. This communication allows the appearance and values of the control to be changed. The developer, while using Microsoft's ClassWizard, defines methods and properties. Find the section defining stock methods in the previous listing. Stock methods are implemented automatically by the **COleControl** class. The programmer can add custom methods if additional custom features are needed by the control.

A primary interface to the control allows early bound access to the control's methods and properties. Here, object methods are exposed as methods, and properties as get/set method pairs. **IDispatch** is used for late bound access. The application using the control (container) decides which type of binding is provided the user. **IProvideClassInfo** returns a **CoClass TypeInfo**, which describes the control.

ActiveX controls also provide extended properties, methods, and events. Usually this is control-specific information needed only by the application (container).

Persistence

Controls support persistence to streams through **IPersistStream** and persistence to storage through **IPersistStorage**. Both implementations can be found in the interface maps section of the previous listing. **IPersistStorage** is necessary for continued support of compound document applications (containers). **IPersistStream** allows embedded controls to be saved to streams, where feasible.

Persistence permits the ActiveX control to read or write property values to and from a file or stream. An application (container) can use persistence to store property values for the control. These values can then be retrieved if a new instance of the control is created.

An example, not shown in the previous listing, is the parameter PX_Blob that is used to exchange a control property that stores Binary Large Object (BLOB) data. In a similar manner, PX_Bool is used to exchanges a control property of type BOOL.

Containers that Can House ActiveX Controls

The standard compound document interface required for an in-place embedding container has the attributes necessary for a control container. In addition to the container attributes inherent in this type of container, the container must also provide two additional items: events and ambient properties.

An ActiveX control actually serves as a converter when dealing with events. As such, a control must convert events from the user into events that are meaningful to the container. For each event so converted, the container must supply an entry point in order to respond to the event.

Ambient properties refers to container properties that typically apply to all controls in the container. These include default colors and fonts.

Creating a Simple ActiveX Control with the MFC

In this section, you will learn the step-by-step approach to creating a simple ActiveX control template. Then we will modify the template to create a unique control for our use.

Remember that all of Microsoft's wizards generate MFC library code. If you need to review object-oriented coding techniques using the MFC, study the material in Chapters 22 through 25.

From this point on, the MFC ActiveX ControlWizard will be referred to simply as the ControlWizard.

Creating a Basic ActiveX Control

From the Microsoft Visual C++ menu bar, select the File | New menu item. From the New dialog box, select the MFC ActiveX ControlWizard, as shown in Figure 26-1. Name this project TDCtrl.

Step 1, in the two-step process, allows you to select a variety of options including the number of controls, source code comments, and so on. Accept the default settings, as shown in Figure 26-2.

Step 2 allows additional design features to be added to the control. Again, accept the default settings as shown in Figure 26-3.

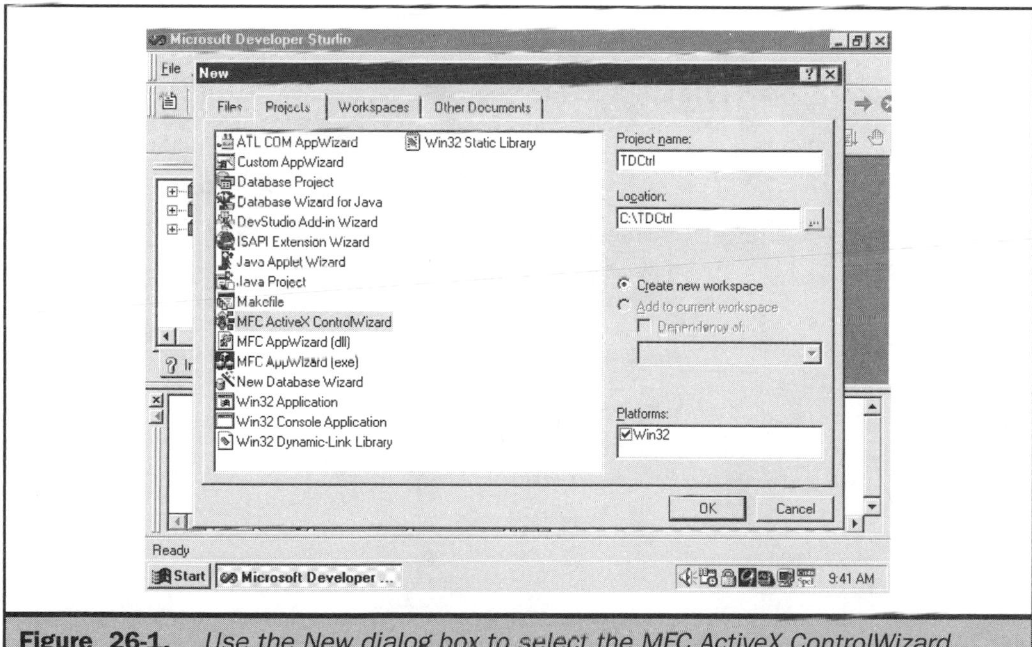

Figure 26-1. *Use the New dialog box to select the MFC ActiveX ControlWizard*

WIZARDS

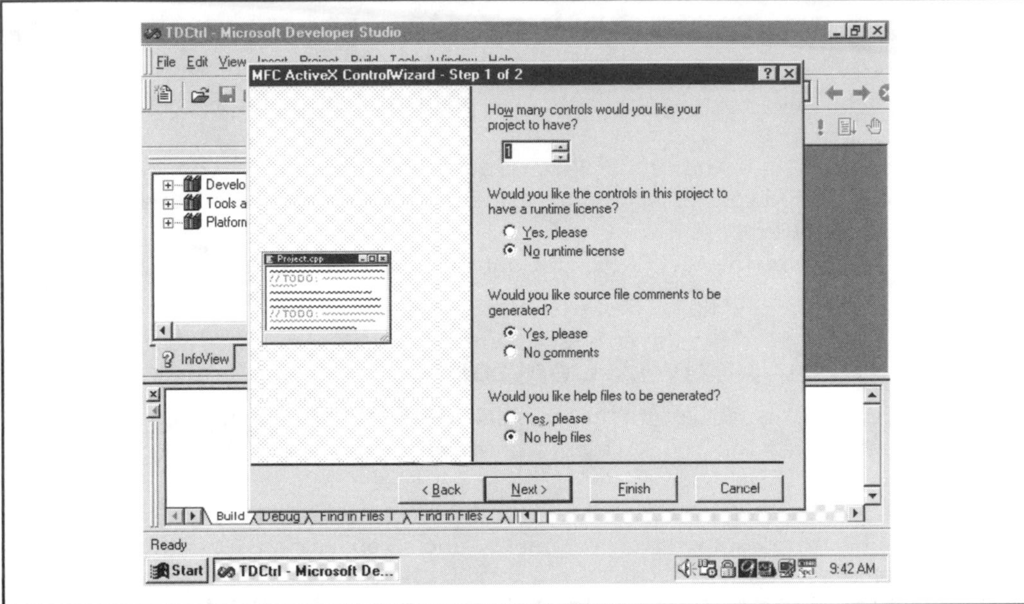

Figure 26-2. *Step 1—Accept the ActiveX control design defaults for this initial control*

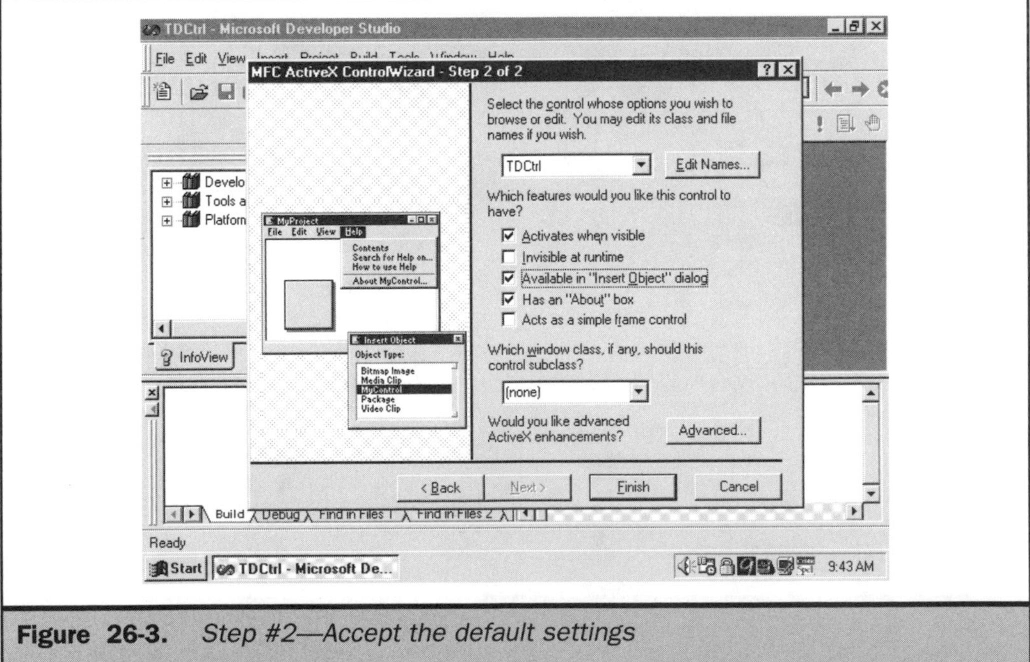

Figure 26-3. *Step #2—Accept the default settings*

Figure 26-4 shows a summary of the new control's specifications just prior to generating the code.

When the OK button is clicked in the New Project Information dialog box, the ControlWizard will generate the files necessary to create the basic control. Figure 26-5 shows a list of classes and global values for this control.

The TDCtrl control can now be built using the Build | Build or Build | Rebuild All menu selection. When this operation is complete, a new control with the filename TDCTRL.OCX will be located in the appropriate subdirectory.

ActiveX controls are small DLL files that can be tested in the appropriate container. Until the control is complete, it is best to use a test container to examine your control's operation. Microsoft provides the ActiveX Control Test Container. This container is accessed from the Tools menu, as shown in Figure 26-6.

When you start the test container, you will have to select the TDCtrl control from the test container's Edit | Insert New Control menu. When this selection is made, the Insert Control dialog box will display a list of registered controls. Scroll down the list till you find the TDCtrl control, as shown in Figure 26-7.

The registered control list will vary as you increase and decrease registered controls on your system. You should be able to find the TDCtrl, however.

When you click the mouse on the OK button in the Insert Control dialog box, the control will be brought into the test container, as you can see in Figure 26-8.

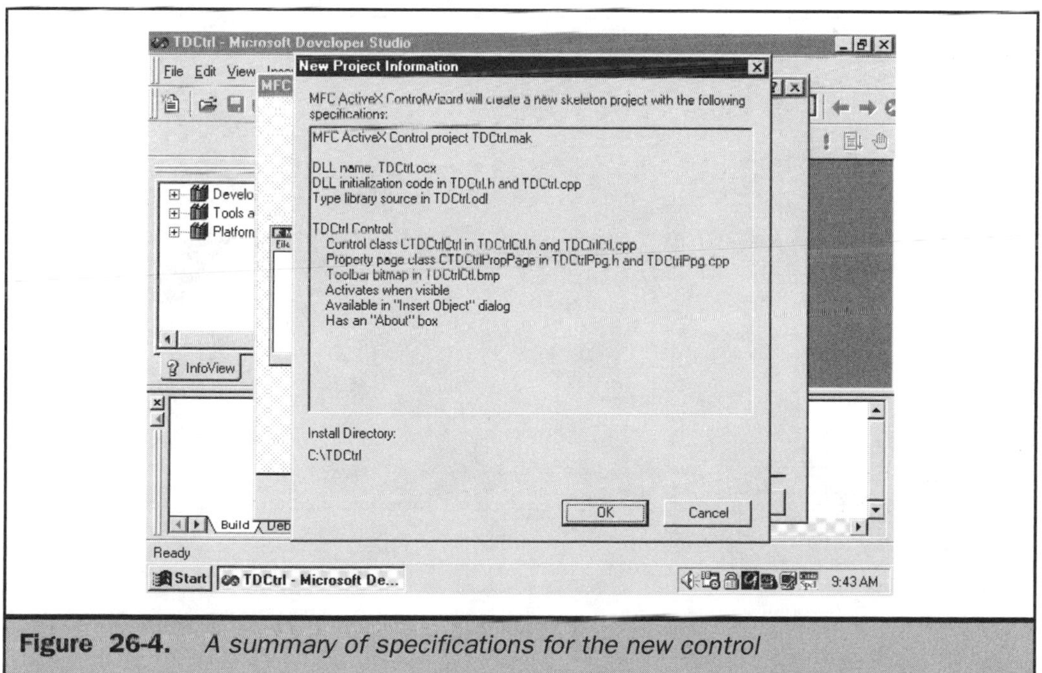

Figure 26-4. *A summary of specifications for the new control*

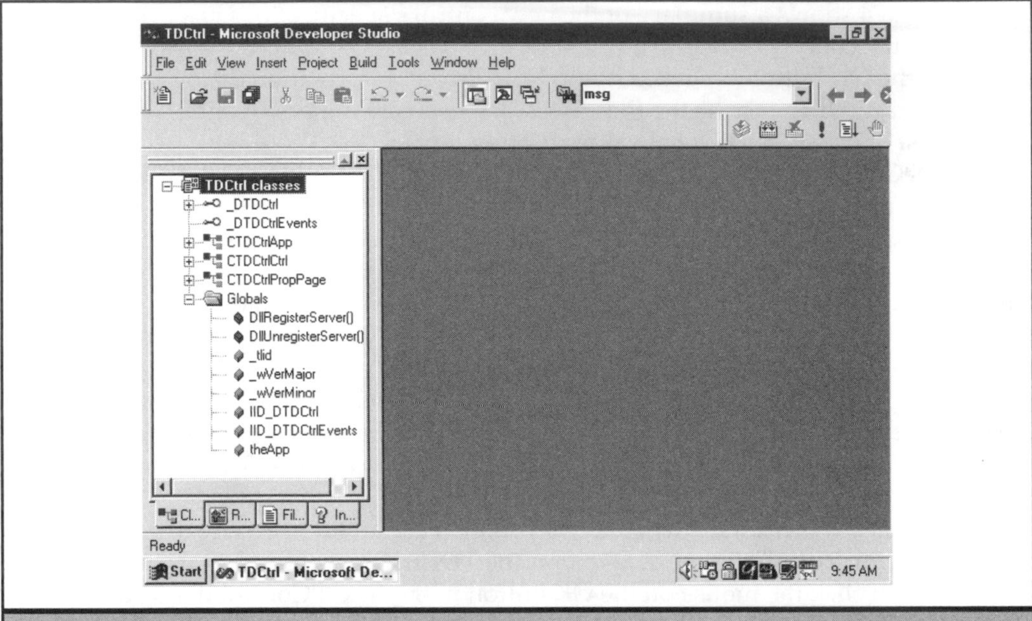

Figure 26-5. *A list of classes and globals for the TDCtrl ActiveX control*

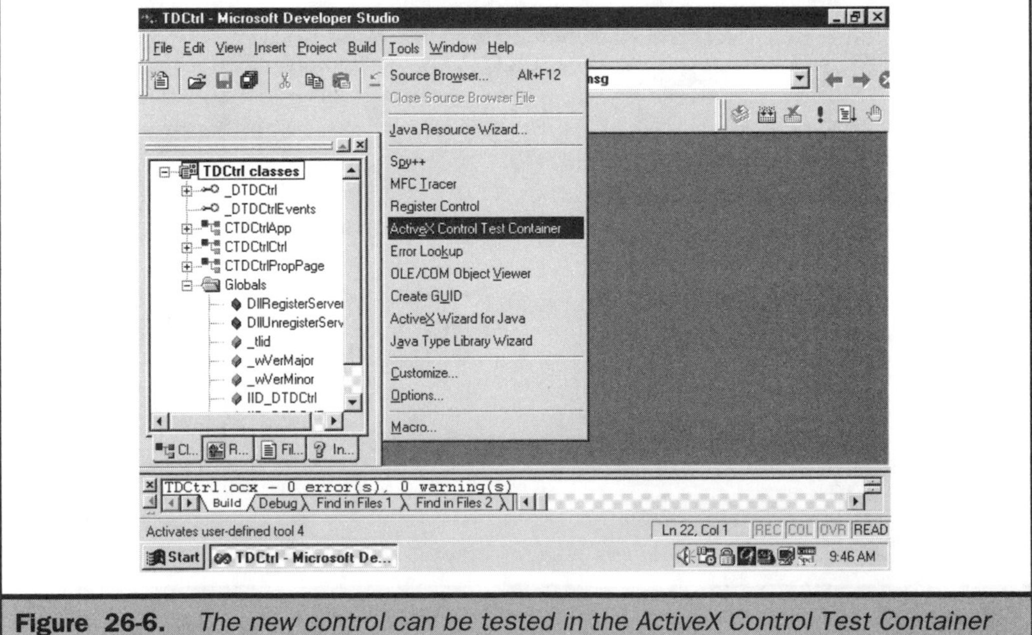

Figure 26-6. *The new control can be tested in the ActiveX Control Test Container*

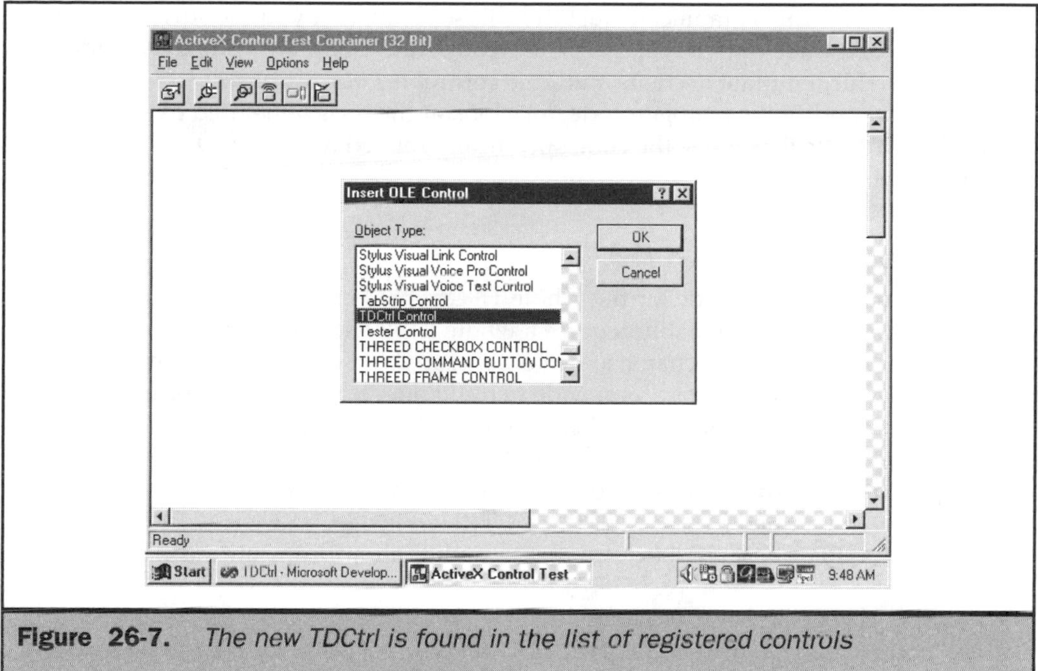

Figure 26-7. *The new TDCtrl is found in the list of registered controls*

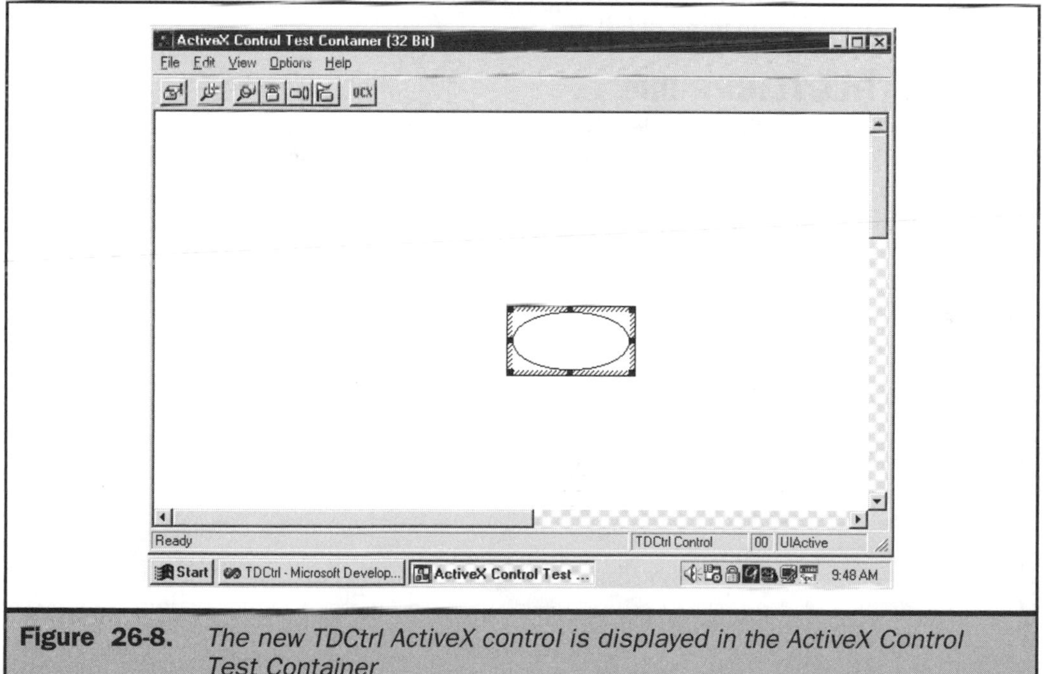

Figure 26-8. *The new TDCtrl ActiveX control is displayed in the ActiveX Control Test Container*

The actual control is graphically just the ellipse shape that you see surrounded by a design frame. At this point the control is not really functional. We will have to add some code to this template to create a unique control for our purposes.

Before we modify the template code, let's look at the code generated by the ControlWizard. We'll examine the code specifically related to the changes we're about to make to the template.

A Look at Important Code

A detailed analysis of the code for the whole TDCtrl project is beyond the scope of this book. Actually, it would probably require a whole book itself. However, you don't have to be an automobile mechanic to drive a car, and you certainly don't have to understand every nuance of program code to build effective ActiveX controls. You have learned the basics of how the MFC combines object-oriented objects into complete applications.

The ControlWizard generates four C++ files for most ActiveX controls. In this example they are named STDAFX.CPP, TDCTRL.CPP, TDCTRLCTL.CPP, and TDCTRLPPG.CPP. These files are supported with their appropriate support header files.

The STDAFX.CPP file is used to include all the standard header files that your ActiveX control will need. The TDCTRL.CPP file is responsible for the implementation of the **CTDCtrlApp** class and the registration of the subsequent DLL file.

In the following sections we examine the role of the TDCTRLCTL.CPP and TDCTRLPPG.CPP files in more detail.

The TDCTRLCTL.CPP File

The TDCTRLCTL.CPP file provides the actual implementation of the ActiveX control's OLE class. In this example, that class is **CTDCtrlCtrl**. This is the file you will most likely spend most of your time editing. In this file, you will be able to create unique implementations of your ActiveX control from the default ActiveX control created by the ControlWizard.

Let's examine the specific code allotted to the default ActiveX control. Study the following listing:

```
// TDCtrlCtl.cpp : the CTDCtrlCtrl ActiveX Control class.

#include "stdafx.h"
#include "TDCtrl.h"
#include "TDCtrlCtl.h"
#include "TDCtrlPpg.h"
```

```
#ifdef _DEBUG
#define new DEBUG_NEW
#undef THIS_FILE
static char THIS_FILE[] = __FILE__;
#endif


IMPLEMENT_DYNCREATE(CTDCtrlCtrl, COleControl)


/////////////////////////////////////////////////////////////////////////////
// Message map

BEGIN_MESSAGE_MAP(CTDCtrlCtrl, COleControl)
  //{{AFX_MSG_MAP(CTDCtrlCtrl)
  // NOTE - ClassWizard will add/remove message map entries
  //    DO NOT EDIT these blocks of generated code !
  //}}AFX_MSG_MAP
  ON_OLEVERB(AFX_IDS_VERB_PROPERTIES, OnProperties)
END_MESSAGE_MAP()


/////////////////////////////////////////////////////////////////////////////
// Dispatch map

BEGIN_DISPATCH_MAP(CTDCtrlCtrl, COleControl)
  //{{AFX_DISPATCH_MAP(CTDCtrlCtrl)
  // NOTE - ClassWizard will add/remove dispatch map entries
  //    DO NOT EDIT these blocks of generated code !
  //}}AFX_DISPATCH_MAP
  DISP_FUNCTION_ID(CTDCtrlCtrl, "AboutBox", DISPID_ABOUTBOX,
                   AboutBox, VT_EMPTY, VTS_NONE)
END_DISPATCH_MAP()


/////////////////////////////////////////////////////////////////////////////
// Event map

BEGIN_EVENT_MAP(CTDCtrlCtrl, COleControl)
  //{{AFX_EVENT_MAP(CTDCtrlCtrl)
  // NOTE - ClassWizard will add/remove event map entries
  //    DO NOT EDIT these blocks of generated code !
```

```
  //}}AFX_EVENT_MAP
END_EVENT_MAP()


/////////////////////////////////////////////////////////////////////////////
// Property pages

// TODO: Add more property pages as needed.
// Also increase the count!
BEGIN_PROPPAGEIDS(CTDCtrlCtrl, 1)
  PROPPAGEID(CTDCtrlPropPage::guid)
END_PROPPAGEIDS(CTDCtrlCtrl)


/////////////////////////////////////////////////////////////////////////////
// Initialize class factory and guid

IMPLEMENT_OLECREATE_EX(CTDCtrlCtrl, "TDCTRL.TDCtrlCtrl.1",
                       0xc0377506, 0xb276, 0x11d1, 0xba, 0xe9,
                       0, 0xa0, 0xc9, 0x8c, 0xc4, 0x6e)


/////////////////////////////////////////////////////////////////////////////
// Type library ID and version

IMPLEMENT_OLETYPELIB(CTDCtrlCtrl,_tlid,_wVerMajor,_wVerMinor)


/////////////////////////////////////////////////////////////////////////////
// Interface IDs

const IID BASED_CODE IID_DTDCtrl =
    { 0xc0377504, 0xb276, 0x11d1, { 0xba, 0xe9, 0, 0xa0, 0xc9,
                                   0x8c, 0xc4, 0x6e } };
const IID BASED_CODE IID_DTDCtrlEvents =
    { 0xc0377505, 0xb276, 0x11d1, { 0xba, 0xe9, 0, 0xa0, 0xc9,
                                   0x8c, 0xc4, 0x6e } };


/////////////////////////////////////////////////////////////////////////////
// Control type information
```

```
static const DWORD BASED_CODE _dwTDCtrlOleMisc =
  OLEMISC_ACTIVATEWHENVISIBLE |
  OLEMISC_SETCLIENTSITEFIRST |
  OLEMISC_INSIDEOUT |
  OLEMISC_CANTLINKINSIDE |
  OLEMISC_RECOMPOSEONRESIZE;

IMPLEMENT_OLECTLTYPE(CTDCtrlCtrl,IDS_TDCTRL,_dwTDCtrlOleMisc)


///////////////////////////////////////////////////////////////
// CTDCtrlCtrl::CTDCtrlCtrlFactory::UpdateRegistry -
// Adds or removes system registry entries for CTDCtrlCtrl

BOOL CTDCtrlCtrl::CTDCtrlCtrlFactory::UpdateRegistry \
     (BOOL bRegister)
{
  // TODO: Verify control follows apartment-model threading
  // rules.
  // Refer to MFC TechNote 64 for more information.
  // If your control does not conform to the apartment-model
  // rules, then modify the code below, changing the 6th
  // parameter from afxRegApartmentThreading to 0.

  if (bRegister)
    return AfxOleRegisterControlClass(
      AfxGetInstanceHandle(),
      m_clsid,
      m_lpszProgID,
      IDS_TDCTRL,
      IDB_TDCTRL,
      afxRegApartmentThreading,
      _dwTDCtrlOleMisc,
      _tlid,
      _wVerMajor,
      _wVerMinor);
  else
    return AfxOleUnregisterClass(m_clsid, m_lpszProgID);
}


///////////////////////////////////////////////////////////////
```

```
// CTDCtrlCtrl::CTDCtrlCtrl - Constructor

CTDCtrlCtrl::CTDCtrlCtrl()
{
  InitializeIIDs(&IID_DTDCtrl, &IID_DTDCtrlEvents);

  // TODO: Initialize your control's instance data here.
}


/////////////////////////////////////////////////////////////////////////////
// CTDCtrlCtrl::~CTDCtrlCtrl - Destructor

CTDCtrlCtrl::~CTDCtrlCtrl()
{
  // TODO: Cleanup your control's instance data here.
}


/////////////////////////////////////////////////////////////////////////////
// CTDCtrlCtrl::OnDraw - Drawing function

void CTDCtrlCtrl::OnDraw(
      CDC* pdc, const CRect& rcBounds, const CRect& rcInvalid)
{
  // TODO: Replace following code with your own drawing code.
  pdc->FillRect(rcBounds,
  CBrush::FromHandle((HBRUSH)GetStockObject(WHITE_BRUSH)));
  pdc->Ellipse(rcBounds);
}


/////////////////////////////////////////////////////////////////////////////
// CTDCtrlCtrl::DoPropExchange - Persistence support

void CTDCtrlCtrl::DoPropExchange(CPropExchange* pPX)
{
  ExchangeVersion(pPX, MAKELONG(_wVerMinor, _wVerMajor));
  COleControl::DoPropExchange(pPX);

  // TODO: Call PX_ functions for persistent custom property.
```

```
}


//////////////////////////////////////////////////////////////////////
// CTDCtrlCtrl::OnResetState - Reset control to default state

void CTDCtrlCtrl::OnResetState()
{
  COleControl::OnResetState();

  // TODO: Reset any other control state here.
}


//////////////////////////////////////////////////////////////////////
// CTDCtrlCtrl::AboutBox - Display an "About" box to the user

void CTDCtrlCtrl::AboutBox()
{
  CDialog dlgAbout(IDD_ABOUTBOX_TDCTRL);
  dlgAbout.DoModal();
}


//////////////////////////////////////////////////////////////////////
// CTDCtrlCtrl message handlers
```

The message map, dispatch map, and event map are automatically created and edited by the Microsoft wizards. Under most circumstances, you will not edit these maps directly.

Recall that message maps are important because they provide an alternative to the **switch** statement used in procedure-oriented programs to handle messages. Automation includes techniques to call methods and access properties across several applications. These requests are dispatched via the dispatch map. The event map helps process ActiveX control events.

Examine the listing and notice the section of code used to implement the type library. In general, ActiveX controls need to exchange information concerning various properties and methods. The best way to provide this information is through a type library.

As you continue reading down the listing, you will see code for updating the system registry as well as constructor code for initializing instances of the control.

The OnDraw( ) member function is going to be of immediate interest to us, because it is this section of code that draws the graphics for the control. In the default control provided by the ControlWizard, the default shape is an Ellipse( ).

```
/////////////////////////////////////////////////////////////////////////////
// CTDCtrlCtrl::OnDraw - Drawing function

void CTDCtrlCtrl::OnDraw(
      CDC* pdc, const CRect& rcBounds, const CRect& rcInvalid)
{
  // TODO: Replace following code with your own drawing code.
  pdc->FillRect(rcBounds,
CBrush::FromHandle((HBRUSH)GetStockObject(WHITE_BRUSH)));
  pdc->Ellipse(rcBounds);
}
```

The ControlWizard also designed a default About box for this project. The contents of this simple dialog box can be edited to suit your project's needs or used as is. You'll find the resource information in the TDCTRL.RC resource file. The About dialog box is brought to the screen with the following portion of code:

```
/////////////////////////////////////////////////////////////////////////////
// CTDCtrlCtrl::AboutBox - Display an "About" box to the user

void CTDCtrlCtrl::AboutBox()
{
  CDialog dlgAbout(IDD_ABOUTBOX_TDCTRL);
  dlgAbout.DoModal();
}
```

Notice that the default About box is a standard modal dialog box of the type we have been using since Chapter 22.

The TDCTRLPPG.CPP File

This file derives the **CTDCtrlPropPage** class from Microsoft's **COlePropertyPage** class. Examine the following listing:

```
// TDCtrlPpg.cpp : the CTDCtrlPropPage property page class.

#include "stdafx.h"
#include "TDCtrl.h"
```

```
#include "TDCtrlPpg.h"

#ifdef _DEBUG
#define new DEBUG_NEW
#undef THIS_FILE
static char THIS_FILE[] = __FILE__;
#endif


IMPLEMENT_DYNCREATE(CTDCtrlPropPage, COlePropertyPage)


/////////////////////////////////////////////////////////////////
// Message map

BEGIN_MESSAGE_MAP(CTDCtrlPropPage, COlePropertyPage)
  //{{AFX_MSG_MAP(CTDCtrlPropPage)
  // NOTE - ClassWizard will add/remove message map entries
  //    DO NOT EDIT these blocks of generated code !
  //}}AFX_MSG_MAP
END_MESSAGE_MAP()


/////////////////////////////////////////////////////////////////
// Initialize class factory and guid

IMPLEMENT_OLECREATE_EX(CTDCtrlPropPage,
                       "TDCTRL.TDCtrlPropPage.1",
                       0xc0377507, 0xb276, 0x11d1, 0xba, 0xc9,
                       0, 0xa0, 0xc9, 0x8c, 0xc4, 0x6e)


/////////////////////////////////////////////////////////////////
// CTDCtrlPropPage::CTDCtrlPropPageFactory::UpdateRegistry -
// Adds or removes system registry entries for CTDCtrlPropPage

BOOL CTDCtrlPropPage::CTDCtrlPropPageFactory::UpdateRegistry \
     (BOOL bRegister)
{
  if (bRegister)
    return AfxOleRegisterPropertyPageClass \
          (AfxGetInstanceHandle(),
```

```
            m_clsid, IDS_TDCTRL_PPG);
    else
      return AfxOleUnregisterClass(m_clsid, NULL);
}


/////////////////////////////////////////////////////////////////////////////
// CTDCtrlPropPage::CTDCtrlPropPage - Constructor

CTDCtrlPropPage::CTDCtrlPropPage() :
  COlePropertyPage(IDD, IDS_TDCTRL_PPG_CAPTION)
{
  //{{AFX_DATA_INIT(CTDCtrlPropPage)
  // NOTE: ClassWizard will add member initialization here
  //    DO NOT EDIT these blocks of generated code !
  //}}AFX_DATA_INIT
}


/////////////////////////////////////////////////////////////////////////////
// CTDCtrlPropPage::DoDataExchange - Moves data between
// page and properties

void CTDCtrlPropPage::DoDataExchange(CDataExchange* pDX)
{
  //{{AFX_DATA_MAP(CTDCtrlPropPage)
  // NOTE: ClassWizard will add DDP, DDX, and DDV calls here
  //    DO NOT EDIT these blocks of generated code !
  //}}AFX_DATA_MAP
  DDP_PostProcessing(pDX);
}


/////////////////////////////////////////////////////////////////////////////
// CTDCtrlPropPage message handlers
```

The AfxOleRegisterPropertyPageClass( ) function is used to register the property page class with the registration database. This permits the property page to be used by other containers that are made aware of ActiveX controls. The registry, with the property page name and its location on the system, will be updated after this function is called.

Notice in this file that COlePropertyPage, from which our **CTDCtrlPropPage** class is derived, can use the constructor to identify the dialog-template resource on which the property page is based and also the string resource containing the caption.

The DoDataExchange( ) function is generally used by the framework to exchange and validate dialog data. Here, the specific job is to move data between the page and properties of the control.

Customizing the Initial Control

The ClassWizard can be used to modify the default custom control produced by the ControlWizard. To modify the default custom control described in the previous section, the following features will be added to the project:

- The TDCtrl control will always draw a rectangle instead of the default ellipse.
- The TDCtrl surface will be a unique color.
- The TDCtrl control will respond to a mouse event within the control and print the current system time and date within the control.

All of these new features can be added to the control by just working with the TDCtrlCtl.cpp and TDCtrlCtl.h files. In the next section, we'll add several of the new features.

Changing the Shape, Size, and Colors of the TDCtrl

From within the Visual C++ compiler, use the View menu to select the ClassWizard menu item. The following modifications allow the shape and color properties of the control to be modified:

1. Select the Automation tab from within the ClassWizard dialog box.
2. Select CTDCtrlCtrl from the Class name list box.
3. Use the Add Property button to display the Add Property dialog box. See Figure 26-9.
4. Enter the name **TDShape** as the External name.
5. Select Member variable as the Implementation.
6. Choose BOOL from the drop-down Type list box. Notice that the Notification function edit control contains OnTDShapeChanged. The member variable is *m_tDShape*.

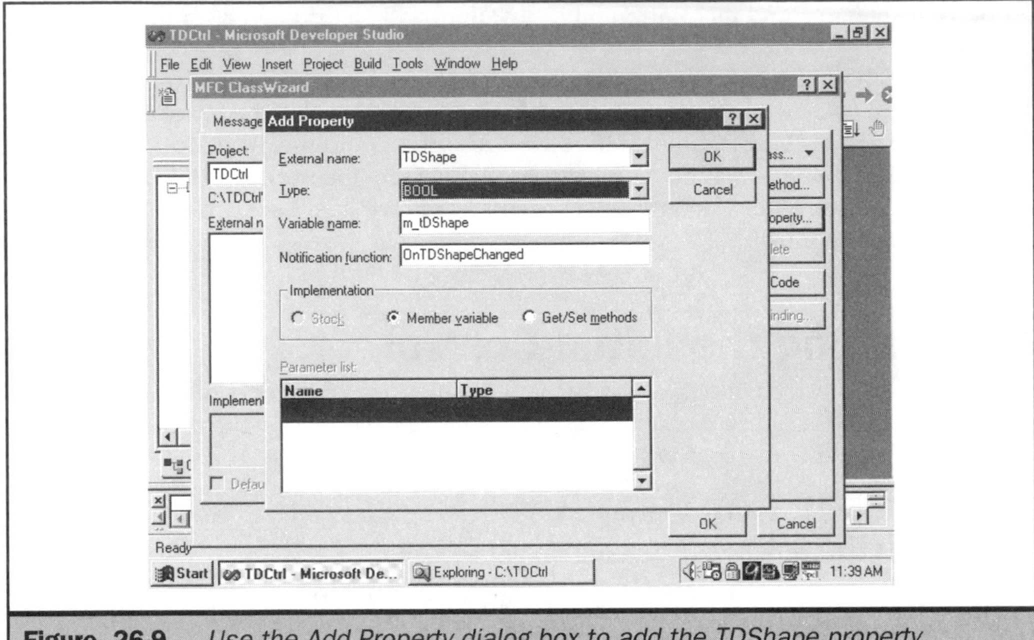

Figure 26-9. *Use the Add Property dialog box to add the TDShape property*

7. Accept these values with the OK button, and return to the OLE Automation tab.
8. Select the Add Property button again, and display the Add Property dialog box.
9. In the edit control of the External name combo box, select BackColor from the drop-down list of available items.
10. For an Implementation, select Stock.
11. Accept these values with the OK button, and return to the Automation tab. The MFC ClassWizard dialog box should be similar to Figure 26-10.
12. Use the OK push button to accept the choices and close the ClassWizard.

The ClassWizard will create the code to add the TDShape and BackColor properties to the **CTDCtrlCtrl** class. The **CTDCtrlCtrl** class's dispatch map will be altered to accommodate the TDShape property. A declaration for the OnTDShapeChanged( ) function is added to the TDCTRLCTL.H header file.

The previous changes are added automatically by the ClassWizard. Now it becomes our job to write the code that reacts to these changes.

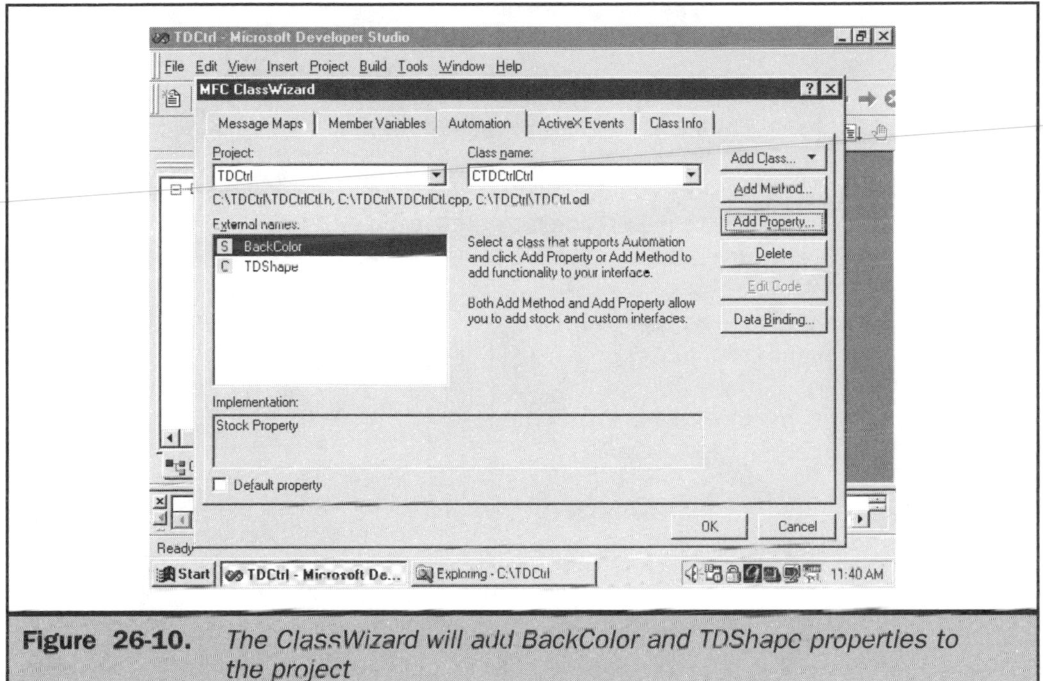

Figure 26-10. *The ClassWizard will add BackColor and TDShape properties to the project*

Return to the TDCTRLCTL.CPP File

The following listing shows the code we've modified in the TDCTRLCTL.CPP file. This file is identical to the default file returned by the ControlWizard, except for the lines of code set in a bold font. Make these changes to your file, too:

```
/////////////////////////////////////////////////////////////////////////////
// CTDCtrlCtrl::OnDraw - Drawing function

void CTDCtrlCtrl::OnDraw(CDC* pdc, const CRect& rcBounds,
                         const CRect& rcInvalid)
{
  CBrush* pOldBrush;
  CBrush NewBrush;
  CPen* pOldPen;
  CPen NewPen;

  pdc->FillRect(rcBounds,CBrush::FromHandle((HBRUSH) \
```

WIZARDS

```
    GetStockObject(WHITE_BRUSH)));

    NewPen.CreatePen(PS_SOLID,3,RGB(0,0,0));
    pOldPen=(CPen*)pdc->SelectObject(&NewPen);

    // Create a yellow brush
    NewBrush.CreateSolidBrush(RGB(255,255,0));
    pOldBrush=(CBrush*)pdc->SelectObject(&NewBrush);

    // Draw and fill the rectangle
    pdc->Rectangle(rcBounds);

    pdc->SelectObject(pOldPen);
    pdc->SelectObject(pOldBrush);
}
```

The modified control is drawn with the Rectangle( ) function and filled with a yellow brush.

Responding to Mouse Events

In this section, you'll learn how to make the TDCtrl control respond to a mouse event. If the cursor is on the TDCtrl control when the left mouse button is depressed, the TDCtrl will change to a light gray color and report the system date and time to the control. The color change, date, and time information are indicators that a control "hit" has occurred.

Here is a list of steps needed to implement the "hit" features:

1. Select the Automation tab from the MFC ClassWizard dialog box.
2. Select **CTDCtrlCtrl** from the Class name list box.
3. Select the Add Property button and display the Add Property dialog box.
4. In the edit control of the External names combo box, type **HitTDCtrl**.
5. For an Implementation, check to make sure Member Variable is selected.
6. Select OLE_COLOR from the Type list box, and clear the Notification function edit control.
7. Close the Add Property dialog box by selecting the OK button, and return to the Automation tab. Your screen should look similar to Figure 26-11.
8. Select the Message Maps tab.

9. Select **CTDCtrlCtrl** from the Class name list box.
10. From the Object IDs list box, select **CTDCtrlCtrl** and then view a list of messages in the Messages list box.
11. Select WM_LBUTTONDOWN from the Messages list box.
12. Choose the Add Function button.
13. Repeat this process by selecting WM_LBUTTONUP. Your screen should look similar to Figure 26-12.
14. Select the OK push button to accept the choices and close the ClassWizard.

The ClassWizard will automatically create the code to add the HitTDCtrl property and the outlines for the above function implementations for the **CTDCtrlCtrl** class.

These changes are added by the ClassWizard, but we must now write the code that reacts to these events.

The TDCTRLCTL.H Header File

An additional insertion must be made in the header file to accommodate a new function. The function is used to change the control's color when a hit occurs. Insert the

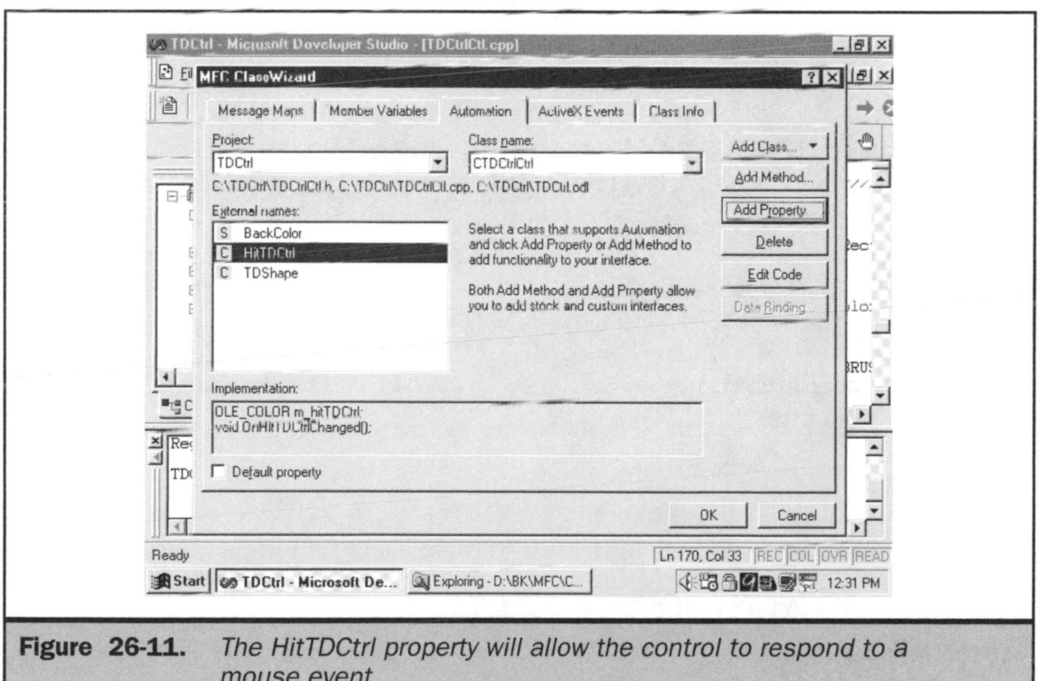

Figure 26-11. *The HitTDCtrl property will allow the control to respond to a mouse event*

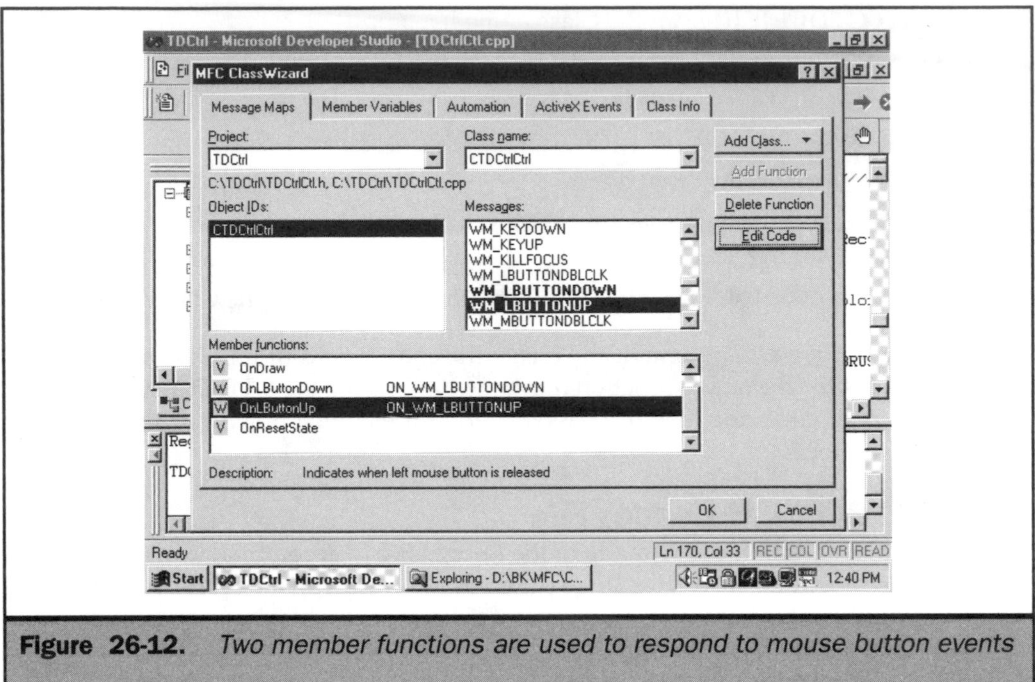

Figure 26-12. *Two member functions are used to respond to mouse button events*

function prototype HitTDCtrl( ), just under the destructor shown in the following partial listing of the TDCTRLCTL.H header file:

```
// Implementation
protected:
  ~CTDCtrlCtrl( );

void HitTDCtrl(CDC* pdc);              // Blink the color
.
      .
      .
```

The code will now be added for detecting mouse clicks within the control.

Return to the TDCTRLCTL.CPP File

The control's face will change color when the user clicks the left mouse button within the rectangular area. The event notification, in part, is handled by the DoPropExchange( ) function. Here is the DoPropExchange( ) function and modification showing the new line in a bold font:

```
//////////////////////////////////////////////////////////////
// CTDCtrlCtrl::DoPropExchange - Persistence support

void CTDCtrlCtrl::DoPropExchange(CPropExchange* pPX)
{
  ExchangeVersion(pPX, MAKELONG(_wVerMinor, _wVerMajor));
  COleControl::DoPropExchange(pPX);

  // TODO: Call PX_ functions for persistent custom property.

// Use a light-gray color to show a hit
PX_Long(pPX,_T("HitTDCtrl"), (long &)m_hitTDCtrl,
        RGB(200, 200, 200));
}
```

This function is responsible for initializing the *m_hitTDCtrl* member variable to a light gray color. The variable *m_hitTDCtrl* must be cast to a **long** since it is an **unsigned long** value.

The ClassWizard added the OnLButtonDown( ) and OnLButtonUp( ) function outlines. The following listing shows the modifications we made to each function in a bold font.

This code checks to make sure the left mouse button was clicked within the face of the clock. If it was, the HitTDCtrl( ) function will be called to change the color of the clock face from yellow to light gray.

When the left mouse button is released, the OnLButtonUp( ) function merely invalidates the control, forcing a repaint in the face to yellow.

The InFace( ) function is used to determine if the left mouse button was depressed within the clock face. All of the following code must be added to the end of the CLOCKCTL.CPP listing:

```
void CTDCtrlCtrl::OnLButtonDown(UINT nFlags, CPoint point)
{
  // TODO: Add message handler code here and/or call default

CDC* pdc;

  //Blink a color change for control
pdc = GetDC( );
HitTDCtrl(pdc);
ReleaseDC(pdc);

  COleControl::OnLButtonDown(nFlags, point);
}
```

```
void CTDCtrlCtrl::OnLButtonUp(UINT nFlags, CPoint point)
{
  // TODO: Add message handler code here and/or call default

InvalidateControl( );

  COleControl::OnLButtonUp(nFlags, point);
}
```

This function first locates the center of the TDCtrl control and then determines if the hit occurred within the rectangle.

If the point falls within the rectangle, the HitTDCtrl( ) function is called. All of the code in the following function must be added to the end of the TDCTRLCTL.CPP listing:

```
void CTDCtrlCtrl::HitTDCtrl(CDC* pdc)
{

  CBrush* pOldBrush;
  CBrush hitBrush(TranslateColor(m_hitTDCtrl));
  CRect rc;
  TEXTMETRIC tm;
  struct tm *date_time;
  time_t timer;

  // Background mode to transparent
  pdc->SetBkMode(TRANSPARENT);

  GetClientRect(rc);

  pOldBrush=pdc->SelectObject(&hitBrush);

  // Draw and fill the rectangle
  pdc->Rectangle(rc);

  // Get time and date
  time(&timer);
  date_time=localtime(&timer);
  const CString& strtime = asctime(date_time);

  // Get Font information then print
  pdc->GetTextMetrics(&tm);
```

```
    pdc->SetTextAlign(TA_CENTER | TA_TOP);
    pdc->ExtTextOut((rc.left + rc.right) / 2,
                    (rc.top + rc.bottom - tm.tmHeight) /2,
                    ETO_CLIPPED, rc, strtime,
                    strtime.GetLength( ) - 1, NULL);
    pdc->SelectObject(pOldBrush);
}
```

The code in this function selects the light gray brush, defined earlier, and repaints the entire TDCtrl control area. The time and date information is accessed with normal C functions.

Testing the TDCtrl ActiveX Control

The Test Container can be used, once again, to test the final version of the TDCtrl control.

For this example, open the test container while in Visual C++ and insert the control by selecting it from the list of registered controls. When the control is inserted it can be resized as shown in Figure 26-13.

Now position the cursor over the control and click the left mouse button to see the current time and date information on a light gray background, as shown in Figure 26-14.

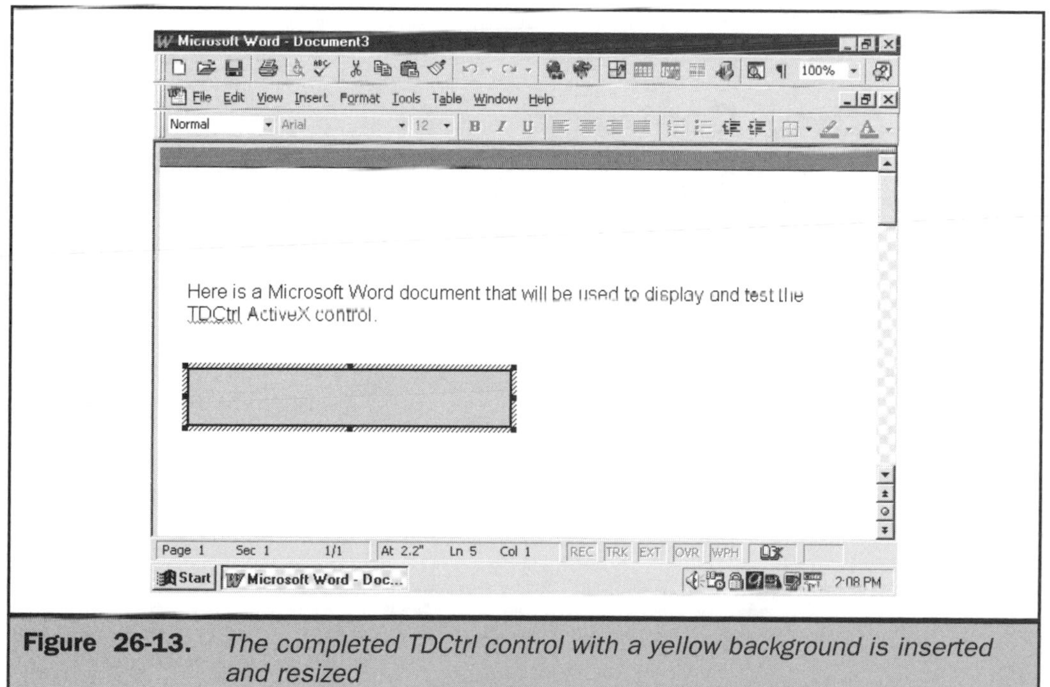

Figure 26-13. *The completed TDCtrl control with a yellow background is inserted and resized*

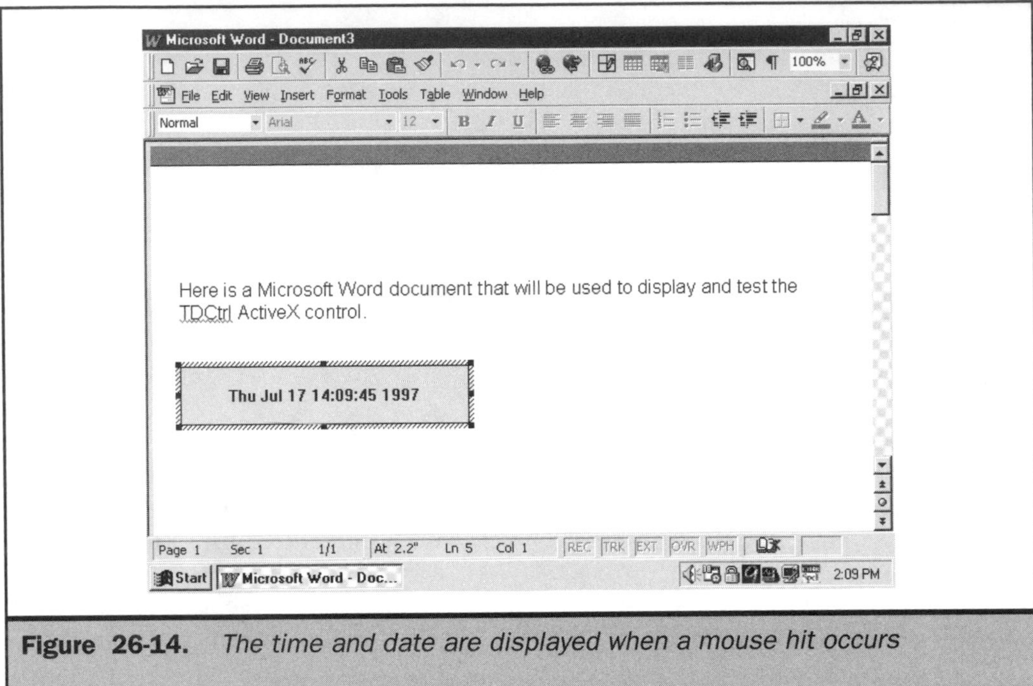

Figure 26-14. *The time and date are displayed when a mouse hit occurs*

More ActiveX Controls?

If the topic of ActiveX controls is of real interest to you, you'll want to read additional sources of information. The *Microsoft Systems Journal* contains a wealth of material on ActiveX controls.

ActiveX controls can also be designed in Microsoft's Visual Basic. Some programmers prefer the use of Visual Basic when designing ActiveX controls because of its drag-and-drop design capabilities.

The Complete Reference

Chapter 27

COM and DHTML

In Chapters 25 and 26 you learned that OLE and ActiveX are built on the COM "object model." The COM object model defines how an object exposes itself and how the exposure works across processes. This chapter will introduce you to another powerful component of the COM family—the ATL. ATL stands for the Active Template Library. The ATL can easily be used to create COM objects, ActiveX controls, and more. The ATL also provides built-in support for many basic COM interfaces.

The ATL provides classes that fit into the following categories:

- Class Factories
- Class information
- COM modules
- Connection points
- Controls: general support
- Data transfer
- Data types
- Dual interfaces
- Error information
- Interface Pointers
- IUnknown implementation
- Object safety
- Persistence
- Properties and Property Pages
- Registry support
- Running objects
- Site information
- Tear-Off interfaces
- Thread Pooling
- Threading models and Critical Sections
- UI support
- Windows support

You might note that many of these classes were supported and used in Chapters 25 and 26.

In the following sections, we'll develop a simple ATL application that blends the Microsoft Polygon ATL tutorial application with the functionality of the ActiveX control developed in Chapter 26. However, this ATL application will go a step further.

The COM object will be used in a DHTML document that can be viewed in Microsoft's Internet Explorer!

Creating the ATL Polygon Project

ATL projects are created by using the ATL COM AppWizard. Use the following steps to create the basic ATL Polygon project:

1. From within Visual C++, select the File | New menu item, then choose the Projects tab.
2. Choose the ATL COM AppWizard.
3. Name the project **Polygon**, as shown in Figure 27-1.

When you select OK, the ATL COM AppWizard dialog box will open, as shown in Figure 27-2.

Select the Dynamic Link Library (DLL) option, then select Finish to complete the process. The New Project Information dialog box, as shown in Figure 27-3, will open and display the information for the ATL project.

Select OK to generate the basic files for the ATL Polygon project.

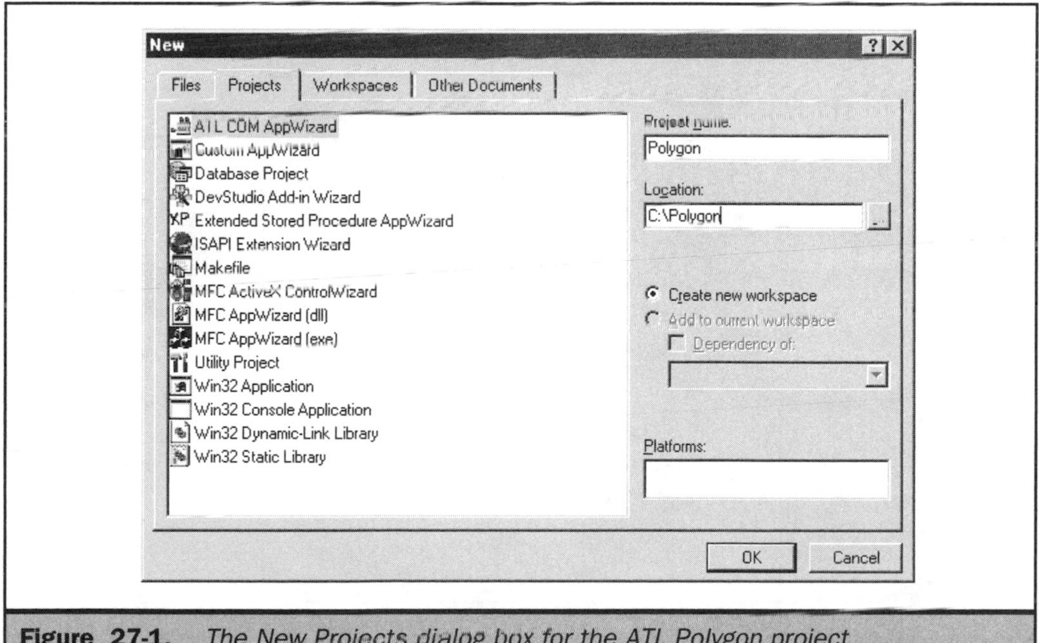

Figure 27-1. *The New Projects dialog box for the ATL Polygon project*

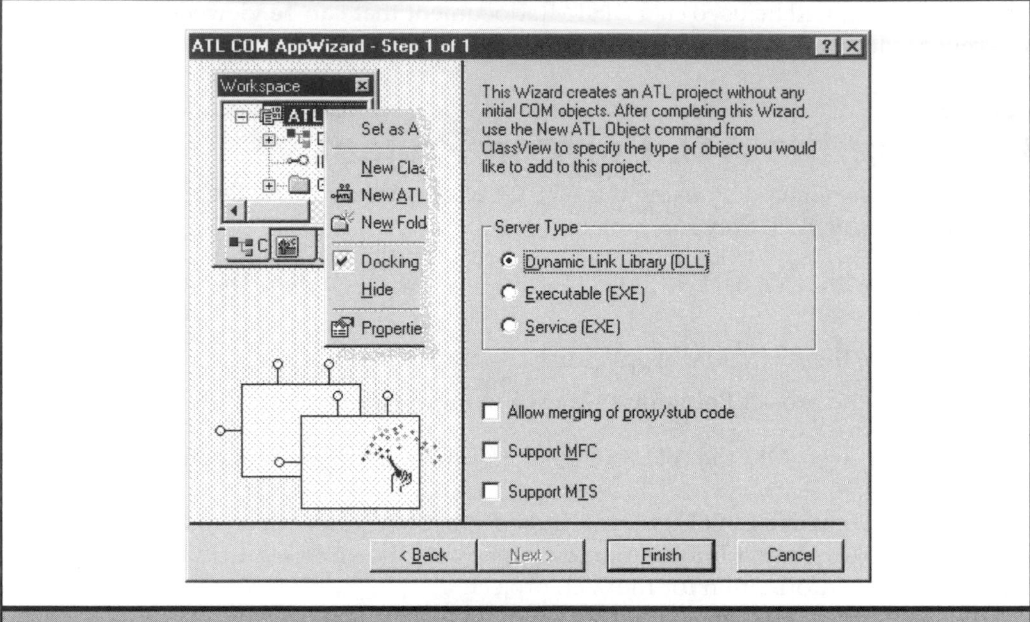

Figure 27-2. *The ATL COM AppWizard dialog box*

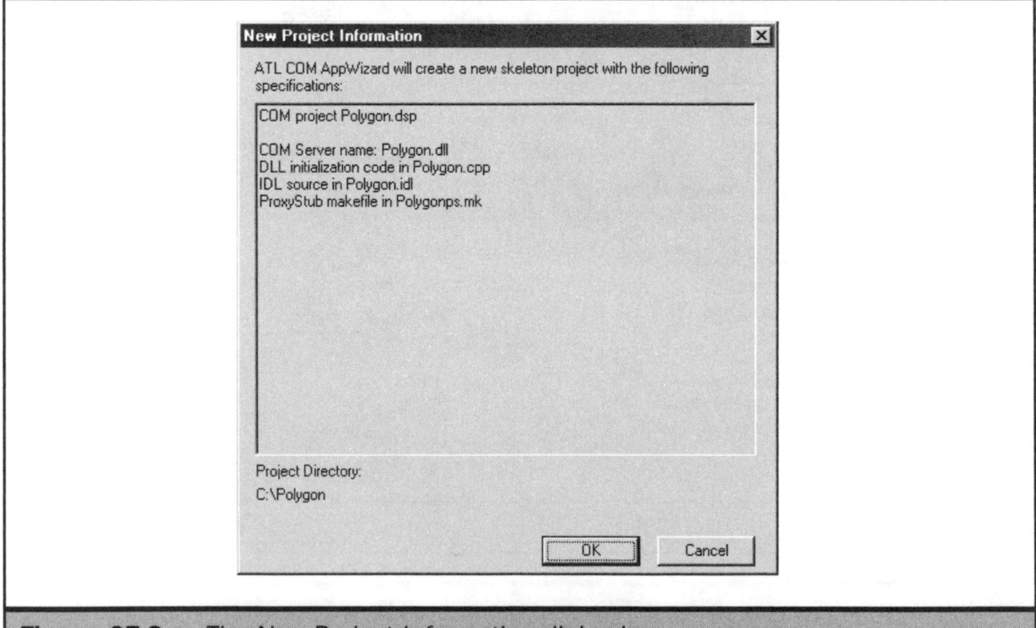

Figure 27-3. *The New Project Information dialog box*

In order to make this project functional, a control will be added to the basic code. Use the Insert | New ATL Object... menu item to open the ATL Object Wizard dialog box, as shown in Figure 27-4.

Select the Full Control option and select the Next button. You will now be allowed to set various configurations for the control using the property pages of the ATL Object Wizard Properties dialog box, as shown in Figure 27-5.

Using the Names tab in this dialog box, enter the name **PolyCtl** in the Short Name edit box. All other entries will be completed automatically. See Figure 27-5 once again.

Next select the Attributes tab and check both support checkboxes as shown in Figure 27-6.

Now, select the Stock Properties tab and enable support for Fill Color as shown in Figure 27-7.

Select OK and return to the developer's screen. If you now open the FileView window, as shown in Figure 27-8, you will see the list of files generated for this project.

There now exists enough information to build the ATL project. From the menu, select the Build | Rebuild All option and compile and link the project. To test the initial control, select the Tools | ActiveX Control Test Container menu item.

Use the Test Container's Edit | Insert New Control menu item to open the Insert Control dialog box. Scroll down the list of available controls until you locate the **PolyCtl** Class control. Select this control and it will be placed in the editor, as shown in Figure 27-9.

This control will not really be functional until we add various properties, events, and property pages to the control.

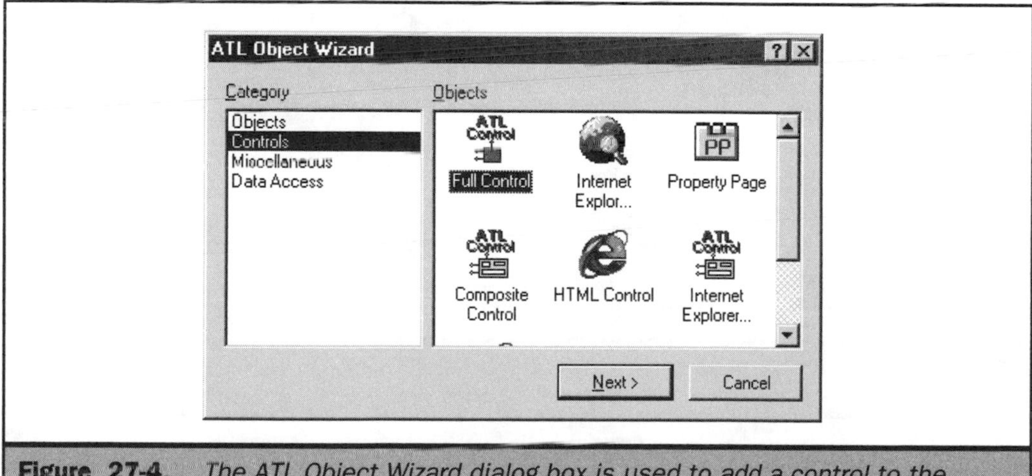

Figure 27-4. *The ATL Object Wizard dialog box is used to add a control to the project*

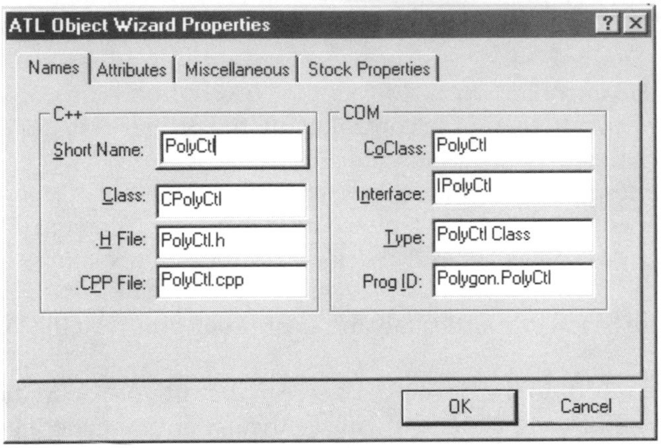

Figure 27-5. *The ATL Object Wizard Properties dialog box will permit various control configurations to be set*

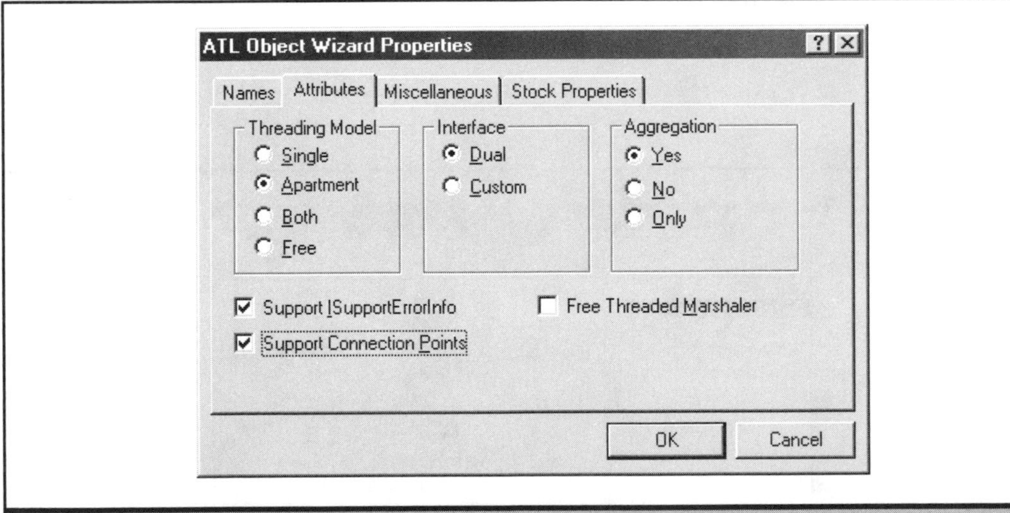

Figure 27-6. *The Attributes tab is used to select ISupportErrorInfo and Connection Points*

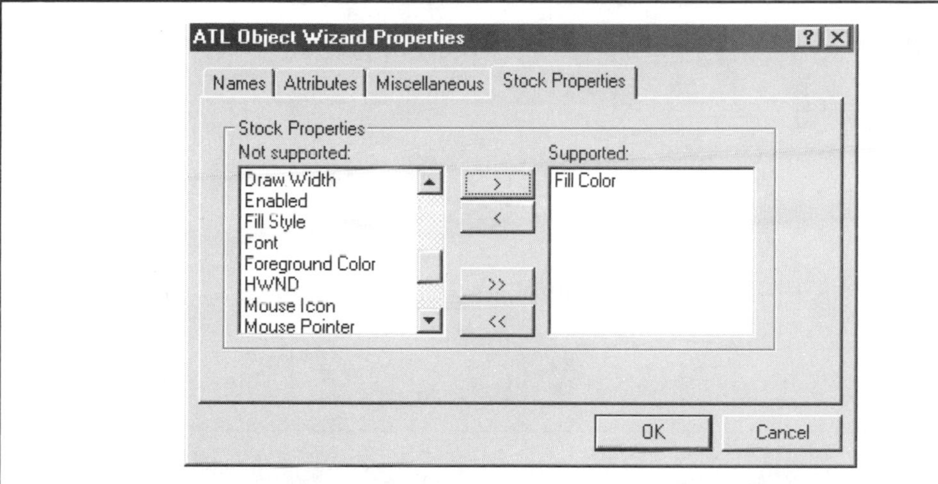

Figure 27-7. *The Stock Properties tab allows specific stock properties to be supported by the project*

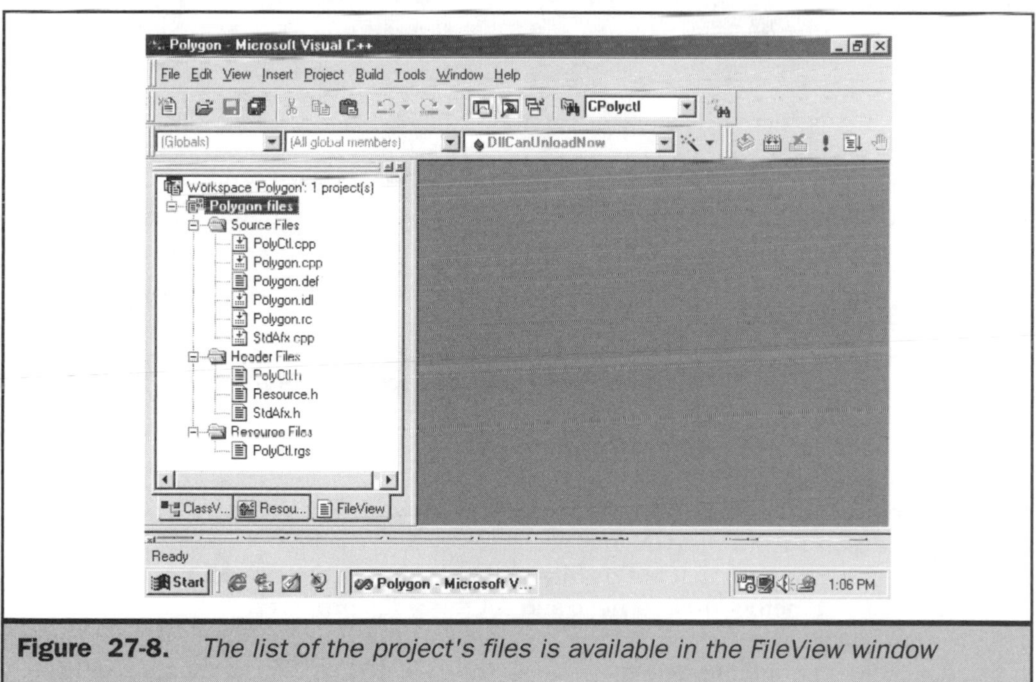

Figure 27-8. *The list of the project's files is available in the FileView window*

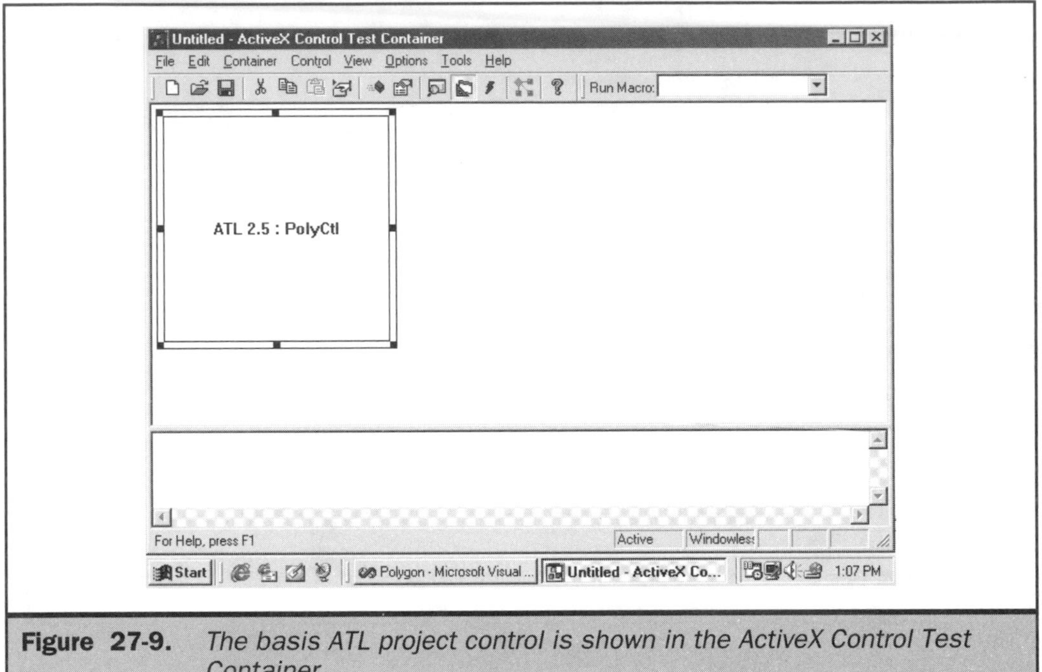

Figure 27-9. *The basis ATL project control is shown in the ActiveX Control Test Container*

Adding and Modifying the Project's Code

In this section, we'll make several modifications to various files in the ATL Polygon project that will make it functional.

Adding a Property

IPolyCtl is used to contain custom methods and properties for the project. To add a new property, use the Visual C++ ClassView to select the **IPolyCtl** class, then right-click the mouse to open a menu box. From the menu box, choose the Add Property… item. This selection will open the Add Property to Interface dialog box, as shown in Figure 27-10.

Select the property type, short, from the drop-down list of property types. Then use the name **Sides** as the Property Name. Select OK to add the new property.

The MIDL (a program that builds files with .idl file extensions) defines a **get** method and a **put** method that retrieve and set the Sides property.

In addition, **get** and **put** function prototypes are added to the POLYCTL.H header file and a skeleton implementation of each to the POLYCTL.CPP file. You'll see this implementation when we view the completed file in the next section.

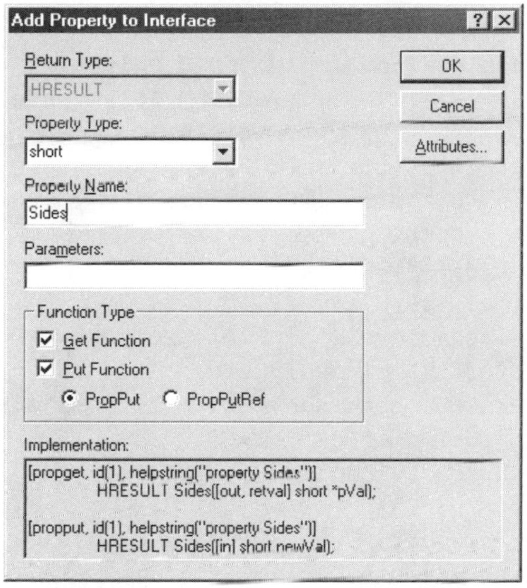

Figure 27-10. *The Add Property to Interface dialog box allows the "Sides" property to be added to the control*

Drawing a Better Control

In this section, we'll examine all of the changes that we have made to the basic ATL program code to make it more functional. Most of these changes have been made to the POLYCTL.H and POLYCTL.CPP files.

This is the code for the header file, POLYCTL.H. Additions and changes to the basic code are shown in a bold font.

```
// PolyCtl.h : Declaration of the CPolyCtl

#include <math.h>
#include "resource.h"       // main symbols
#include "CPPolygon.h"

/////////////////////////////////////////////////////////////////
// CPolyCtl
class CPolyCtl :
  public CComObjectRoot,
  public CComCoClass<CPolyCtl, &CLSID_PolyCtl>,
  public CComControl<CPolyCtl>,
  public CStockPropImpl<CPolyCtl, IPolyCtl,
```

```
                          &IID_IPolyCtl,
                          &LIBID_POLYGONLib>,
  public IProvideClassInfo2Impl<&CLSID_PolyCtl,
                                &DIID__PolyEvents,
                                &LIBID_POLYGONLib>,
  public IPersistStreamInitImpl<CPolyCtl>,
  public IPersistStorageImpl<CPolyCtl>,
  public IQuickActivateImpl<CPolyCtl>,
  public IOleControlImpl<CPolyCtl>,
  public IOleObjectImpl<CPolyCtl>,
  public IOleInPlaceActiveObjectImpl<CPolyCtl>,
  public IViewObjectExImpl<CPolyCtl>,
  public IOleInPlaceObjectWindowlessImpl<CPolyCtl>,
  public IDataObjectImpl<CPolyCtl>,
  public IPersistPropertyBagImpl<CPolyCtl>,
  public ISupportErrorInfo,
  public ISpecifyPropertyPagesImpl<CPolyCtl>,
  public CProxy_PolyEvents<CPolyCtl>,
  public IConnectionPointContainerImpl<CPolyCtl>,
  public IPropertyNotifySinkCP<CPolyCtl>,
  public IObjectSafetyImpl<CPolyCtl>
{
public:
  CPolyCtl()
  {
    m_nSides = 6;                        // initial hexagon
    m_clrFillColor = RGB(0xFF, 0xFF, 0); // use yellow fill
  }

DECLARE_REGISTRY_RESOURCEID(IDR_PolyCtl)

BEGIN_COM_MAP(CPolyCtl)
  COM_INTERFACE_ENTRY(IPolyCtl)
  COM_INTERFACE_ENTRY(IDispatch)
  COM_INTERFACE_ENTRY_IMPL(IViewObjectEx)
  COM_INTERFACE_ENTRY_IMPL_IID(IID_IViewObject2,
                               IViewObjectEx)
  COM_INTERFACE_ENTRY_IMPL_IID(IID_IViewObject,
                               IViewObjectEx)
  COM_INTERFACE_ENTRY_IMPL(IOleInPlaceObjectWindowless)
  COM_INTERFACE_ENTRY_IMPL_IID(IID_IOleInPlaceObject,
                               IOleInPlaceObjectWindowless)
```

```
    COM_INTERFACE_ENTRY_IMPL_IID(IID_IOleWindow,
                                IOleInPlaceObjectWindowless)
    COM_INTERFACE_ENTRY_IMPL(IOleInPlaceActiveObject)
    COM_INTERFACE_ENTRY_IMPL(IOleControl)
    COM_INTERFACE_ENTRY_IMPL(IOleObject)
    COM_INTERFACE_ENTRY_IMPL(IQuickActivate)
    COM_INTERFACE_ENTRY_IMPL(IPersistStorage)
    COM_INTERFACE_ENTRY_IMPL(IPersistStreamInit)
    COM_INTERFACE_ENTRY_IMPL(IPersistPropertyBag)
    COM_INTERFACE_ENTRY_IMPL(ISpecifyPropertyPages)
    COM_INTERFACE_ENTRY_IMPL(IDataObject)
    COM_INTERFACE_ENTRY(IProvideClassInfo)
    COM_INTERFACE_ENTRY(IProvideClassInfo2)
    COM_INTERFACE_ENTRY(ISupportErrorInfo)
    COM_INTERFACE_ENTRY_IMPL(IConnectionPointContainer)
    COM_INTERFACE_ENTRY(IObjectSafety)
END_COM_MAP()

BEGIN_CONNECTION_POINT_MAP(CPolyCtl)
    CONNECTION_POINT_ENTRY(DIID__PolyEvents)
    CONNECTION_POINT_ENTRY(IID_IPropertyNotifySink)
END_CONNECTION_POINT_MAP()

BEGIN_PROPERTY_MAP(CPolyCtl)
    PROP_ENTRY("Sides", 1, CLSID_PolyProp)
    PROP_PAGE(CLSID_CColorPropPage)
END_PROPERTY_MAP()

BEGIN_MSG_MAP(CPolyCtl)
    MESSAGE_HANDLER(WM_PAINT, OnPaint)
    MESSAGE_HANDLER(WM_GETDLGCODE, OnGetDlgCode)
    MESSAGE_HANDLER(WM_SETFOCUS, OnSetFocus)
    MESSAGE_HANDLER(WM_KILLFOCUS, OnKillFocus)
    MESSAGE_HANDLER(WM_LBUTTONDOWN, OnLButtonDown)
END_MSG_MAP()

// ISupportsErrorInfo
    STDMETHOD(InterfaceSupportsErrorInfo)(REFIID riid);

// IViewObjectEx
    STDMETHOD(GetViewStatus)(DWORD* pdwStatus)
    {
```

```
      ATLTRACE(_T("IViewObjectExImpl::GetViewStatus\n"));
      *pdwStatus = VIEWSTATUS_OPAQUE;
      return S_OK;
    }

// IPolyCtl
public:
    STDMETHOD(get_Sides)(/*[out, retval]*/ short *newVal);
    STDMETHOD(put_Sides)(/*[in]*/ short newVal);

    HRESULT OnDraw(ATL_DRAWINFO& di);
    LRESULT OnLButtonDown(UINT uMsg, WPARAM wParam,
                          LPARAM lParam, BOOL& bHandled);

    short m_nSides;
    OLE_COLOR m_clrFillColor;
    POINT m_arrPoint[10];
};
```

As you examine the listing, notice the **get** and **put** function prototypes mentioned earlier. Also, notice in the constructor that the initial number of sides for the polygon is set to six and the initial fill color to yellow. This project will allow polygons with 3 to 10 sides to be drawn.

Note *Microsoft's Polygon project set the limit to 100.*

A connection point interface and a connection point container interface are also needed for this project. A COM object can have multiple connection points, so the COM object also implements a connection point container interface. The IConnectionPoint interface implements the connection point. The IConnectionPointContainer interface is used to implement a connection point container.

An ATL proxy generator is used to create the IConnectionPoint interface by reading the type library and creating a function for each event that can be fired. A type library must be generated before using the proxy generator. To build a type library, right-click on the POLYGON.IDL file while in FileView and generate the POLYGON.TLB file by selecting Compile POLYGON.IDL. This file is the type library.

Now, right-click on CpolyCtl and select the Implement Connect Point menu item. The CPPOLYGON.H file has a class called **CProxy_PolyEvents** that is derived from IConnectionPointImpl and two methods, **Fire_ClickIn** and **Fire_ClickOut**. These methods are used to fire control events.

IConnectionPointContainer is exposed through the QueryInterface( ) function when it is added to the COM map in POLYCTL.H.

The IConnectionPointContainer is notified of available points by using a connection point map. Here is a small portion of the POLYCTL.H file:

```
BEGIN_CONNECTION_POINT_MAP(CPolyCtl)
  CONNECTION_POINT_ENTRY(DIID__PolyEvents)
  CONNECTION_POINT_ENTRY(IID_IPropertyNotifySink)
END_CONNECTION_POINT_MAP()
```

A WM_LBUTTONDOWN event handler is added to detect when a user clicks the left mouse button. The prototype is included in this file and the implementation in the POLYCTL.CPP file.

The following listing shows the POLYCTL.CPP file containing all of the additions for the project. The code additions are shown in a bold font.

```
// PolyCtl.cpp : Implementation of CPolyCtl
#include "stdafx.h"
#include "Polygon.h"
#include "PolyCtl.h"
#include <time.h>
#include <string.h>


////////////////////////////////////////////////////////////////
// CPolyCtl

STDMETHODIMP CPolyCtl::InterfaceSupportsErrorInfo(REFIID riid)
{
  static const IID* arr[] =
  {
    &IID_IPolyCtl,
  };
  for (int i=0;i<sizeof(arr)/sizeof(arr[0]);i++)
  {
    if (InlineIsEqualGUID(*arr[i],riid))
      return S_OK;
  }
  return S_FALSE;
}

HRESULT CPolyCtl::OnDraw(ATL_DRAWINFO& di)
```

```
{
struct tm *date_time;
time_t timer;
static TEXTMETRIC tm;

RECT& rc = *(RECT*)di.prcBounds;
HDC hdc = di.hdcDraw;

COLORREF colFore;
HBRUSH hOldBrush, hBrush;
HPEN hOldPen, hPen;

// Translate m_colFore into a COLORREF type
OleTranslateColor(m_clrFillColor, NULL, &colFore);

// Create and select the colors to draw the circle
hPen = (HPEN)GetStockObject(BLACK_PEN);
hOldPen = (HPEN)SelectObject(hdc, hPen);
hBrush = (HBRUSH)GetStockObject(WHITE_BRUSH);
hOldBrush = (HBRUSH)SelectObject(hdc, hBrush);

const double pi = 3.14159265358979;
POINT  ptCenter;
double  dblRadiusx = (rc.right - rc.left) / 2;
double  dblRadiusy = (rc.bottom - rc.top) / 2;
double  dblAngle = 3 * pi / 2;
double  dblDiff  = 2 * pi / m_nSides;
ptCenter.x = (rc.left + rc.right) / 2;
ptCenter.y = (rc.top + rc.bottom) / 2;

// Calculate the points for each side
for (int i = 0; i < m_nSides; i++)
{
m_arrPoint[i].x = (long) \
                  (dblRadiusx*cos(dblAngle)+ptCenter.x+0.5);
m_arrPoint[i].y = (long) \
                  (dblRadiusy*sin(dblAngle)+ptCenter.y+0.5);
dblAngle += dblDiff;
}
Ellipse(hdc, rc.left, rc.top, rc.right, rc.bottom);

// Create/select brush used to fill the polygon
```

```
hBrush = CreateSolidBrush(colFore);
SelectObject(hdc, hBrush);
Polygon(hdc, &m_arrPoint[0], m_nSides);


// Print date and time
time(&timer);
date_time=localtime(&timer);

const char* strtime;

strtime  = asctime(date_time);

SetBkMode(hdc,TRANSPARENT);

SetTextAlign(hdc, TA_CENTER | TA_TOP);
ExtTextOut(hdc, (rc.left + rc.right)/2,
          (rc.top + rc.bottom - tm.tmHeight)/2,
          ETO_CLIPPED, &rc, strtime,
          strlen(strtime)-1, NULL);

// Select old pen and brush and delete created brush
SelectObject(hdc, hOldPen);
SelectObject(hdc, hOldBrush);
DeleteObject(hBrush);

return S_OK;
}

LRESULT CPolyCtl::OnLButtonDown(UINT uMsg, WPARAM wParam,
                                LPARAM lParam, BOOL& bHandled)
{
HRGN hRgn;
WORD xPos = LOWORD(lParam);  // horiz. position of cursor
WORD yPos = HIWORD(lParam);  // vertical position of cursor

// Create a region from our list of points
hRgn = CreatePolygonRgn(&m_arrPoint[0], m_nSides, WINDING);

// If the clicked point is in polygon, fire the ClickIn
//  event otherwise we fire the ClickOut event
if (PtInRegion(hRgn, xPos, yPos))
```

```
    Fire_ClickIn(xPos, yPos);
  else
    Fire_ClickOut(xPos, yPos);

  // Delete the region that we created
  DeleteObject(hRgn);
  return 0;
}

STDMETHODIMP CPolyCtl::get_Sides(short *pVal)
{
  *pVal = m_nSides;
  return S_OK;
}

STDMETHODIMP CPolyCtl::put_Sides(short newVal)
{
  if (newVal > 2 && newVal < 11)
  {
    m_nSides = newVal;
    FireViewChange();
    return S_OK;
  }
  else
    return Error(_T("Must have between 3 and 10 sides"));
}
```

When Microsoft developed the polygon project, they used the sin( ) and cos( ) functions from MATH.H to calculate the polygon points. See if you can find that portion of code in the previous listing. Our project modifies the original polygon project by limiting the number of sides to 10 instead of 100 and includes the code necessary to print the local date and time within the control. As a matter of fact, the date and time will be updated each time a "hit" occurs within the polygon shape. We used code similar to this in the ActiveX control developed in Chapter 26.

The **put_Sides** method (near the end of the listing) is changed in order to force a call via the FireViewChange( ) function, which in turn calls the InvalidateRect( ) function, forcing a repainting of the control. If this isn't done, the figure will not update when "hits" occur.

In order to fire events, a small portion of code must be added to the POLYGON.IDL file. The additions to this file are shown in a bold font.

```
#include <olectl.h>
// Polygon.idl : IDL source for Polygon.dll
//

// This file will be processed by the MIDL tool to
// make the type library (Polygon.tlb) and marshalling code.
import "oaidl.idl";
import "ocidl.idl";

  [
    object,
    uuid(4CBBC675-507F-11D0-B98B-000000000000),
    dual,
    helpstring("IPolyCtl Interface"),
    pointer_default(unique)
  ]
  interface IPolyCtl : IDispatch
  {
    [propput, id(DISPID_FILLCOLOR)]
    HRESULT FillColor([in]OLE_COLOR clr);
    [propget, id(DISPID_FILLCOLOR)]
    HRESULT FillColor([out, retval]OLE_COLOR* pclr);
    [propget, id(1), helpstring("property Sides")] \
    HRESULT Sides([out, retval] short *newVal);
    [propput, id(1), helpstring("property Sides")] \
    HRESULT Sides([in] short newVal);
  };
[
  uuid(4CBBC673-507F-11D0-B98B-000000000000),
  version(1.0),
  helpstring("Polygon 1.0 Type Library")
]
library POLYGONLib
{
  importlib("stdole32.tlb");

[
    uuid(4CBBC677-507F-11D0-B98B-000000000000),
    helpstring("Event interface for PolyCtl")
  ]
  dispinterface _PolyEvents
  {
    properties:
```

WIZARDS

```
    methods:
    [id(1)] void ClickIn([in]long x, [in] long y);
    [id(2)] void ClickOut([in]long x, [in] long y);
  };

  [
    uuid(4CBBC676-507F-11D0-B98B-000000000000),
    helpstring("PolyCtl Class")
  ]
  coclass PolyCtl
  {
    [default] interface IPolyCtl;
    [default, source] dispinterface _PolyEvents;
  };


  [
    uuid(A3121F30-516B-11D0-B98C-000000000000),
    helpstring("PolyProp Class")
  ]
  coclass PolyProp
  {
    interface IUnknown;
  };
};
```

The ClickIn( ) and ClickOut( ) methods use the x and y coordinates of the clicked point as parameters.

A property page can be added to the control with the use of the ATL Object Wizard. Use the Insert | New ATL Object… menu item to open the ATL Object Wizard dialog box, as shown in Figure 27-11.

Select the Property Page option and select the Next button. You will now be allowed to set various configurations for the control using the property pages of the ATL Object Wizard Properties dialog box, as shown in Figure 27-12.

Using the Names tab in this dialog box, enter the name **PolyProp** in the Short Name edit box. All other entries will be completed automatically. See Figure 27-12 once again.

Next, select the Strings tab and enter the Title and Doc String as shown in Figure 27-13.

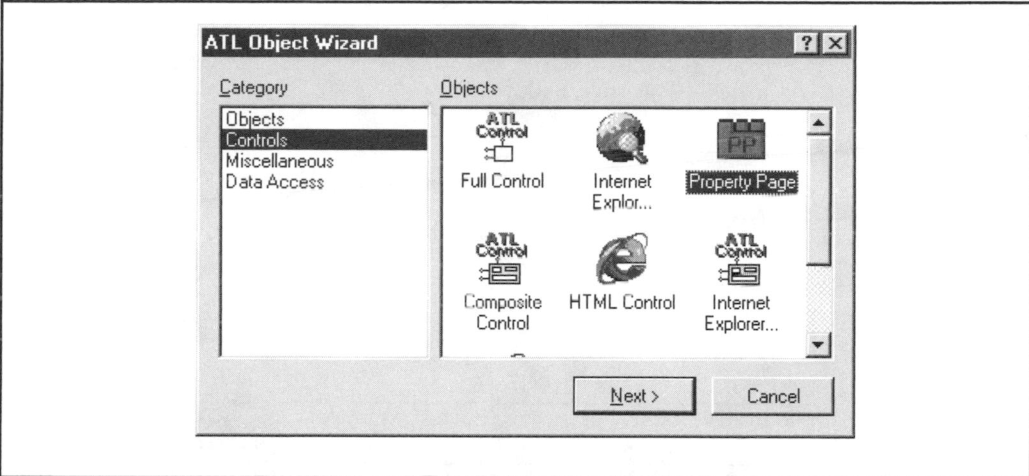

Figure 27-11. *The ATL Object Wizard dialog box is used to add a property page control to the project*

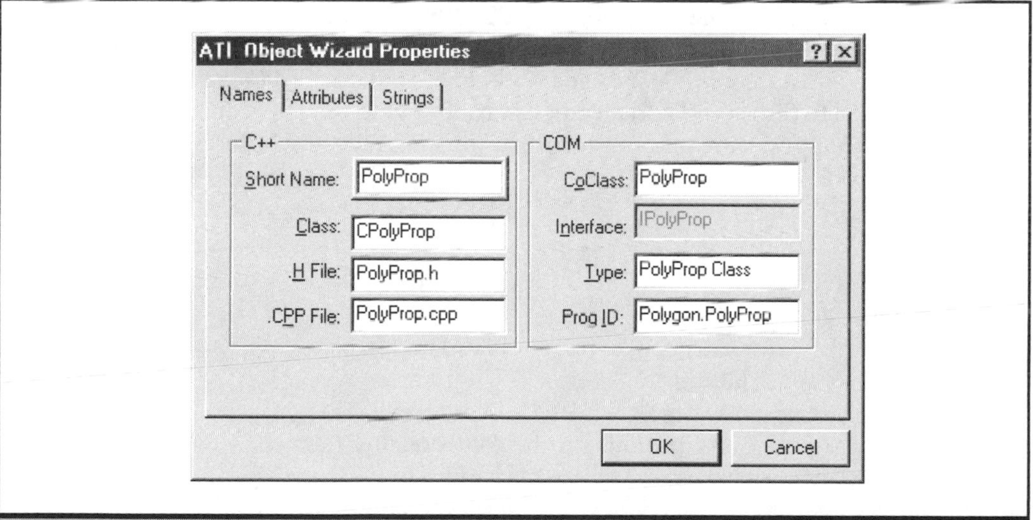

Figure 27-12. *The ATL Object Wizard Properties dialog box will permit various control configurations to be set*

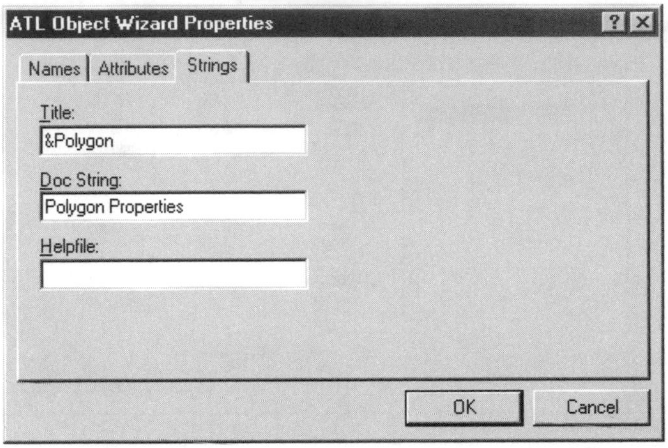

Figure 27-13. *The Strings tab is used to set the Title and Doc String for the property page*

When you select OK the POLYPROP.H, POLYPROP.CPP and POLYPROP.RGS files will be generated. In addition, a new property page is added to the object entry map.

Use the ResourceView, while in Visual C++, to open the IDD_POLYPROP dialog box. Change the label to **Sides:** and add an edit box control with the IDC_SIDES ID value.

Make the changes, shown here in bold, to the POLYPROP.H file

```
// PolyProp.h : Declaration of the CPolyProp

#include "resource.h"       // main symbols
#include "Polygon.h"

EXTERN_C const CLSID CLSID_PolyProp;

/////////////////////////////////////////////////////////////////
// CPolyProp
class CPolyProp :
  public CComObjectRoot,
  public CComCoClass<CPolyProp, &CLSID_PolyProp>,
  public IPropertyPageImpl<CPolyProp>,
  public CDialogImpl<CPolyProp>
{
public:
```

```
  CPolyProp()
  {
    m_dwTitleID = IDS_TITLEPolyProp;
    m_dwHelpFileID = IDS_HELPFILEPolyProp;
    m_dwDocStringID = IDS_DOCSTRINGPolyProp;
  }

  enum {IDD = IDD_PolyProp};

DECLARE_REGISTRY_RESOURCEID(IDR_PolyProp)

BEGIN_COM_MAP(CPolyProp)
  COM_INTERFACE_ENTRY_IMPL(IPropertyPage)
END_COM_MAP()

BEGIN_MSG_MAP(CPolyProp)
  COMMAND_HANDLER(IDC_SIDES, EN_CHANGE, OnSidesChange)
  CHAIN_MSG_MAP(IPropertyPageImpl<CPolyProp>)
END_MSG_MAP()

  STDMETHOD(Apply)(void)
  {
    USES_CONVERSION;
    ATLTRACE(_T("CPolyProp::Apply\n"));
    for (UINT i = 0; i < m_nObjects; i++)
    {
      CComQIPtr<IPolyCtl, &IID_IPolyCtl> pPoly(m_ppUnk[i]);
      short nSides = (short)GetDlgItemInt(IDC_SIDES);
      if FAILED(pPoly->put_Sides(nSides))
      {
        CComPtr<IErrorInfo> pError;
        CComBSTR      strError;
        GetErrorInfo(0, &pError);
        pError->GetDescription(&strError);
        MessageBox(OLE2T(strError), _T("Error"), MB_ICONEXCLAMATION);
        return E_FAIL;
      }
    }
    m_bDirty = FALSE;
    return S_OK;
  }
```

```
    LRESULT OnSidesChange(WORD wNotify, WORD wID, HWND hWnd, BOOL&
            bHandled)
    {
      SetDirty(TRUE);
      return 0;
    }
  };
```

A property page could have more than one client attached to it at a time, so the Apply( ) function is used to loop around and call put_Sides on each client with the value obtained from the edit box.

The property page is now added to the control by adding the following line to the POLYCTL.H header file:

```
PROP_ENTRY("Sides", 1, CLSID_PolyProp)
```

Now, we're ready to test the control on an actual Web page.

Testing the ATL Control on a Web Page

The ATL Object Wizard creates the initial control along with an HTML file that contains the control. This file is named PolyCtl.htm and can be opened in Microsoft's Internet Explorer. Here, you will be able to view and test the ATL control on an actual Web page.

Add the following changes, shown in a bold font, to the POLYCTL.HTM while in the Visual C++ environment:

```
<HTML>
<HEAD>
<TITLE>ATL 2.0 test page for object PolyCtl</TITLE>
</HEAD>
<BODY>
<OBJECT ID="PolyCtl" <
 CLASSID="CLSID:4CBBC676-507F-11D0-B98B-000000000000">
>
</OBJECT>
<SCRIPT LANGUAGE="VBScript">
<!--
Sub PolyCtl_ClickIn(x, y)
PolyCtl.Sides = PolyCtl.Sides + 1
End Sub
```

```
Sub PolyCtl_ClickOut(x, y)
PolyCtl.Sides = PolyCtl.Sides - 1
End Sub
-->
</SCRIPT>
</BODY>
</HTML>
```

Now, start the Microsoft Internet Explorer and open the POLYCTL.HTM file. Your screen should initially appear like Figure 27-14.

Continue to test the control by clicking the left mouse button within and without the control's figure. Figure 27-15 shows the control after two additional clicks (hits) within the control.

Notice that the number of sides to the polygon increased.

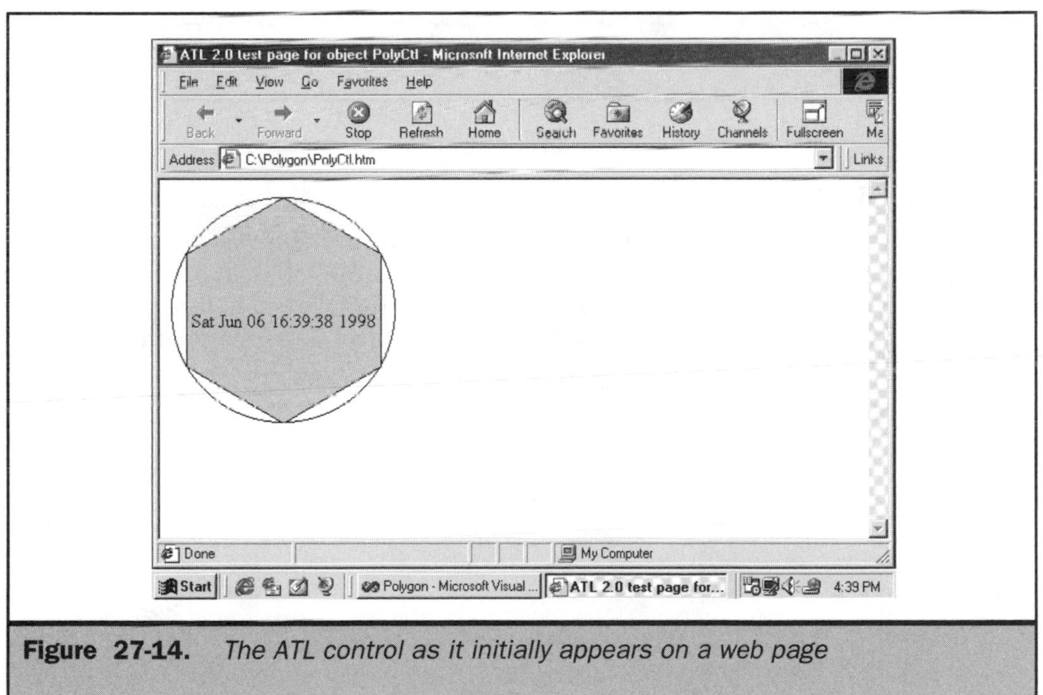

Figure 27-14. *The ATL control as it initially appears on a web page*

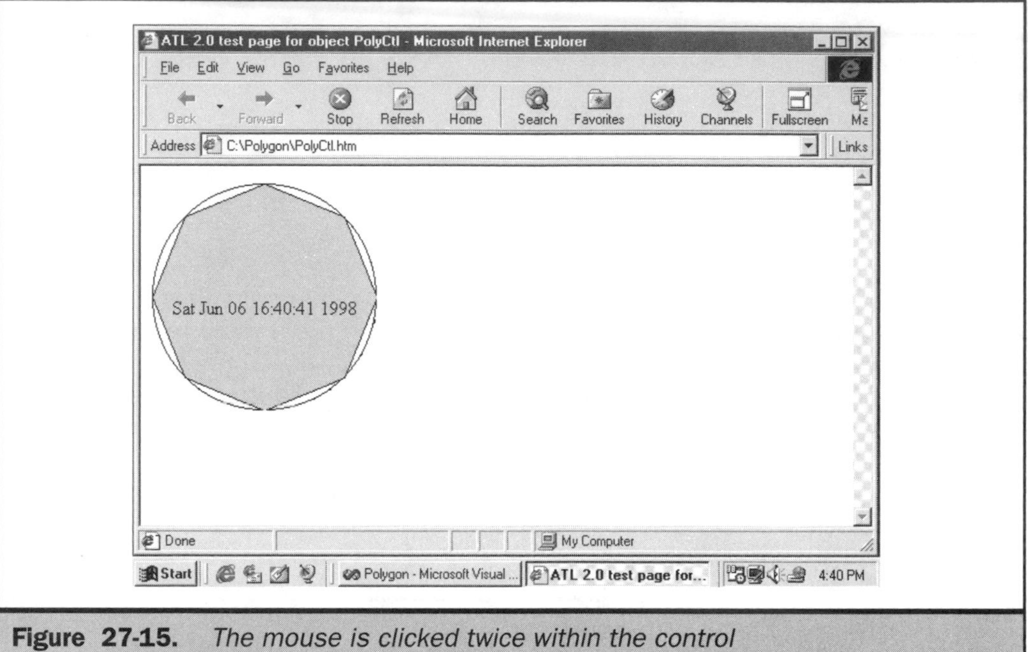

Figure 27-15. *The mouse is clicked twice within the control*

ATL vs. ActiveX

Microsoft claims that the use of ATL is easier than the use of the MFC for many applications. Did you find the development of the ATL control in this chapter simpler than the development of the ActiveX control in Chapter 26? We think they are about the same. ATL is certainly a reasonable alternative to control development in the MFC.

Appendix A

Extended ASCII Table

Decimal	Hexadecimal	Symbol	Decimal	Hexadecimal	Symbol
0	0	(blank)	32	20	(blank)
1	1	☺	33	21	!
2	2	☻	34	22	"
3	3	♥	35	23	#
4	4	♦	36	24	$
5	5	♣	37	25	%
6	6	♠	38	26	&
7	7	✚	39	27	'
8	8	◘	40	28	(
9	9	○	41	29	)
10	A	◙	42	2A	*
11	B	♂	43	2B	+
12	C	♀	44	2C	,
13	D	♪	45	2D	-
14	E	♫	46	2E	.
15	F	☼	47	2F	/
16	10	►	48	30	0
17	11	◄	49	31	1
18	12	↕	50	32	2
19	13	‼	51	33	3
20	14	¶	52	34	4
21	15	§	53	35	5
22	16	▬	54	36	6
23	17	↨	55	37	7
24	18	↑	56	38	8
25	19	↓	57	39	9
26	1A	→	58	3A	:
27	1B	←	59	3B	;
28	1C	∟	60	3C	<
29	1D	↔	61	3D	=
30	1E	▲	62	3E	>
31	1F	▼	63	3F	?

Decimal	Hexadecimal	Symbol	Decimal	Hexadecimal	Symbol
64	40	@	96	60	`
65	41	A	97	61	a
66	42	B	98	62	b
67	43	C	99	63	c
68	44	D	100	64	d
69	45	E	101	65	e
70	46	F	102	66	f
71	47	G	103	67	g
72	48	H	104	68	h
73	49	I	105	69	i
74	4A	J	106	6A	j
75	4B	K	107	6B	k
76	4C	L	108	6C	l
77	4D	M	109	6D	m
78	4E	N	110	6E	n
79	4F	O	111	6F	o
80	50	P	112	70	p
81	51	Q	113	71	q
82	52	R	114	72	r
83	53	S	115	73	s
84	54	T	116	74	t
85	55	U	117	75	u
86	56	V	118	76	v
87	57	W	119	77	w
88	58	X	120	78	x
89	59	Y	121	79	y
90	5A	Z	122	7A	z
91	5B	[	123	7B	{
92	5C	\	124	7C	|
93	5D	]	125	7D	}
94	5E	^	126	7E	~
95	5F	_	127	7F	⌂

Decimal	Hexadecimal	Symbol	Decimal	Hexadecimal	Symbol
128	80	Ç	160	A0	á
129	81	ü	161	A1	í
130	82	é	162	A2	ó
131	83	â	163	A3	ú
132	84	ä	164	A4	ñ
133	85	à	165	A5	Ñ
134	86	å	166	A6	ª
135	87	ç	167	A7	º
136	88	ê	168	A8	¿
137	89	ë	169	A9	⌐
138	8A	è	170	AA	¬
139	8B	ï	171	AB	½
140	8C	î	172	AC	¼
141	8D	ì	173	AD	¡
142	8E	Ä	174	AE	«
143	8F	Å	175	AF	»
144	90	É	176	B0	░
145	91	æ	177	B1	▒
146	92	Æ	178	B2	▓
147	93	ô	179	B3	│
148	94	ö	180	B4	┤
149	95	ò	181	B5	╡
150	96	û	182	B6	╢
151	97	ù	183	B7	╖
152	98	ÿ	184	B8	╕
153	99	Ö	185	B9	╣
154	9A	Ü	186	BA	║
155	9B	¢	187	BB	╗
156	9C	£	188	BC	╝
157	9D	¥	189	BD	╜
158	9E	Pt	190	BE	╛
159	9F	ƒ	191	BF	┐

Decimal	Hexadecimal	Symbol	Decimal	Hexadecimal	Symbol
192	C0	└	224	E0	α
193	C1	┴	225	E1	β
194	C2	┬	226	E2	Γ
195	C3	├	227	E3	π
196	C4	─	228	E4	Σ
197	C5	┼	229	E5	σ
198	C6	╞	230	E6	µ
199	C7	╟	231	E7	τ
200	C8	╚	232	E8	φ
201	C9	╔	233	E9	θ
202	CA	╩	234	EA	Ω
203	CB	╦	235	EB	δ
204	CC	╠	236	EC	∞
205	CD	═	237	ED	∅
206	CE	╬	238	EE	∈
207	CF	╧	239	EF	∩
208	D0	╨	240	F0	≡
209	D1	╤	241	F1	±
210	D2	╥	242	F2	≥
211	D3	╙	243	F3	≤
212	D4	╘	244	F4	⌠
213	D5	╒	245	F5	⌡
214	D6	╓	246	F6	÷
215	D7	╫	247	F7	≈
216	D8	╪	248	F8	°
217	D9	┘	249	F9	•
218	DA	┌	250	FA	•
219	DB	█	251	FB	√
220	DC	▄	252	FC	n
221	DD	▌	253	FD	2
222	DE	▐	254	FE	■
223	DF	▀	255	FF	(blank)

Appendix B

DOS 10H, 21H, and 33H Interrupt Parameters

This appendix contains the most popular DOS, BIOS, and Mouse interrupts and parameters.

Screen Control with BIOS-Type 10H Interrupts

Syntax: INT 10H (when the following parameters are set to the required values).

Interface Control of the CRT

AH Value	Function	Input	Output
AH = 0	Set the mode of display	AL = 0	40×25 color text
		AL = 1	40×25 color text
		AL = 2	80×25 color text
		AL = 3	40×25 color text
		AL = 4	320×200 4-color graphics
		AL = 5	320×420 4-color graphics
		AL = 6	640×200 2-color graphics
		AL = 7	80×25 monochrome text
		AL = 13	320×200 16-color graphics
		AL = 14	640×200 16-color graphics
		AL = 15	640×350 monochrome graphics
		AL = 16	640×350 16-color graphics
		AL = 17	640×480 2-color graphics
		AL = 18	640×480 16-color graphics
		AL = 19	320×200 256-color graphics
AH = 1	Set cursor type	CH =	Bits 4–0 start of line for cursor
		CL =	Bits 4–0 end of line for cursor
AH = 2	Set cursor position	DH =	Row
		DL =	Column
		BH =	Page number of display (0 for graphics)
AH = 3	Read cursor position		DH = row
			DL = column

AH Value	Function	Input	Output
			CH = cursor mode
			CL = cursor mode
			BH = page number of display
AH = 4	Get light pen position		AH = 0, switch not down/triggered
			AH = 1, valid answers as follows:
			DH = row
			DL = column
			CH = graph line (0 to 99)
			BX = graph column (0 to 319/639)
AH = 5	Set active display page	AL =	New page value
			(0 to 7) modes 0 and 1
			(0 to 3) modes 2 and 3
AH = 6	Scroll active page up	AL =	Number of lines, 0 for entire screen
		CH =	Row, upper-left corner
		CL =	Column upper-left corner
		DH =	Row, lower-right corner
		DL =	Column, lower-right corner
		BH =	Attribute to be used
AH = 7	Scroll active page down	AL =	Number of lines, 0 for entire screen
		CH =	Row, upper-left corner
		CL =	Column, upper-left corner
		DH =	Row, lower-right corner
		DL =	Column, lower-right corner
		BH =	Attribute to be used

Handling Characters

AH Value	Function	Input	Output
AH = 8	Read attribute/ character at cursor position	BH =	Display page
		AL =	Character read
		AH =	Attribute of character
AH = 9	Write attribute/ character at cursor position	BH =	Display page
		CX =	Count of characters to write
		AL =	Character to write
		BL =	Attribute of character
AH = 10	Write character at cursor position	BH =	Display page
		CX =	Count of characters to write
		AL =	Character to write

Graphics Interface

AH Value	Function	Input	Output
AH = 11	Select color palette	BH =	Palette ID (0 to 127)
		BL =	Color for above ID
			0—background (0 to 15)
			1—palette
			0—green(1), red(2), yellow(3)
			1—cyan(1), magenta(2), white(3)
AH = 12	Draw dot on screen	DX =	Row (0 to 199)
		CX =	Column (0 to 319/639)
		AL =	Color of dot
AH = 13	Read dot information	DX =	Row (0 to 199)
		CX =	Column (0 to 319/639)
		AL =	Value of dot

ASCII Teletype Output

AH Value	Function	Input	Output
AH = 14	Write to active page	AL =	Character to write
		BL =	Foreground color
AH = 15	Get video state	AL =	Current mode
		AH =	Number of screen columns
		BH =	Current display page
AH = 16	(Reserved)		
AH = 17	(Reserved)		
AH = 18	(Reserved)		
AH = 19	Write string	ES:BP =	Point to string
		CX =	Length of string
		DX =	Cursor position for start
		BH =	Page number
		AL = 0	BL = attribute (char, char, char,...char) cursor not moved
		AL = 1	BL = attribute (char, char, char,...char) cursor is moved
		AL = 2	(char, attr, char, attr...) cursor not moved
		AL = 3	(char, attr, char, attr...) cursor is moved
AH = 1A	R/W display combination code		
AH = 1B	Return functionality state information		
AH = 1C	Save/restore video state		

Specifications and Requirements for the DOS 21H Interrupt

Syntax: INT 21H (when the following parameters are set to the required values).

AH Value	Function	Input	Output
AH = 0	End of program		(similar to INT 20H)
AH = 1	Wait and display keyboard character with CTRL-BREAK check		AL = character entered
AH = 2	Display character with CTRL-BREAK check	DL =	Character to display
AH = 3	Asynchronous character input		AL = character entered
AH = 4	Asynchronous character output	DL =	Character to send
AH = 5	Character to write	DL =	Character to write
AH = 6	Input keyboard character	DL =	0FFH if character entered, 0 if none
AH = 7	Wait for keyboard character (no display)		AL = character entered
AH = 8	Wait for keyboard character (no display—CTRL-BREAK check)		AL = character entered
AH = 9	String displayed	DS:DX	Address of string; must end with $ sentinel
AH = A	Keyboard string to buffer	DS:DX =	Address of buffer. First byte = size, second = number of characters read
AH = B	Input keyboard status		AL–no character = 0FFH character = 0
AH = C	Clear keyboard buffer and call function	AL =	1,6,7,8,0,A (function #)
AH = D	Reset default disk drive	None	None

AH Value	Function	Input	Output
AH = E	Select default disk drive		Al = number of drives DL–0 = A drive 1 = B drive, etc.
AH = F	Open file with unopened FCB	DS:DX =	Location AL = 0FFH if not found AL = 0H if found
AH = 10	Close file with FCB	DS:DX =	Location (same as AH = OFH)
AH = 11	Search directory for match of unopened FCB	 DS:DX =	AL = 0FFH if not found 00000AL = 0H if found Location DTA contains directory entry
AH = 12	Search (after AH = 11) for other files that match wildcard specifications		(Same as AH = 11H)
AH = 13	Delete file named by FCB	DS:DX =	Location (same as AH = 11H)
AH = 14	Sequential read of open file. Number of bytes in FCB (record size)	DS:DX =	Location AL = 0 transfer OK AL = 1 end of file AL = 2 overrun DTA segment AL = 3 EOF/partial read
AH = 15	Sequential write of open file. Transfer from DTA to file, with FCB update of current record	DS:DX =	Location AL = 0 transfer OK AL = 1 disk full/ROF AL = 2 overrrun DTA segment
AH = 16	Create file (length set to zero)	DS:DX =	Location (same as AH = 11H)
AH = 17	Rename file	DS:DX	Location AL = 0 rename OK AL = 0FFH no match found
AH = 18	(DOS internal use)		
AH = 19	Drive code (default)		AL–0 = A drive 1 = B drive, etc.
AH = 1A	Set Data Transfer Add	DS:DX =	Points to location

AH Value	Function	Input	Output
AH = 1B	File Allocation Table	DS:DX =	Address of FAT DX = number of units AL = record/alloc. unit CX = sector size (same as AH = 1B)
AH = 1C	Disk drive FAT information	DL =	Drive number: 0 = default, 1 = A, 2 = B
AH = 1D	(DOS internal use)		
AH = 1E	(DOS internal use)		
AH = 1F	(DOS internal use)		
AH = 20	(DOS internal use)		
AH = 21	Random read file	DS:DX =	Location of FCB (same as AH = 14H)
AH = 22	Random write file	DS:DX =	(same as AH = 21H)
AH = 23	Set file size	DS:DX =	Location of FCB AL = 0 if set AL = 0FFH if not set
AH = 24	Random record size	DS:DX =	Location of FCB
AH = 25	Set interrupt vector (change address)	DS:DX = AL =	Address of vector table Interrupt number
AH = 26	Create program segment	DX =	Segment number
AH = 27	Random block read	DS:DX =	Address of FCB AL–0 read OK 1 EOF 2 wrap around 3 partial record
AH = 28	Random block write	DS:DX =	Address of FCB AL–0 write OK 1 lack of space
AH = 29	Parse file name	DS:SI = DS:DI =	Point to command line Memory location for FCB AL = bits to set options

AH Value	Function	Input	Output
AH = 2A	Read date		CX = year (80 to 99) DH = month (1 to 12) DL = day (1 to 31)
AH = 2B	Set date		CX and DX (same as previous) AL–0 if valid 0FF if not valid
AH = 2C	Read time		CH = hours (0 to 23) CL = minutes (0 to 59)
AH = 2D	Set time		CX and DX (same as previous) AL–0 if valid 0FF if not valid
AH = 2E	Set verify state	DL = AL =	0 0 = verify off 1 = verify on
AH = 2F	Get DTA	ES:BX =	Get DTA into ES
AH = 30	Get DOS version		AL = version number AH = sub number
AH = 31	Terminate and remain resident		AL = exit code DX = memory size in paragraphs
AH = 32	(DOS internal use)		
AH = 33	CTRL-BREAK check	AL = AL =	0 = request state 1 = set the state DL = 0 for off DL = 1 for on
AH = 34	(DOS internal use)		
AH = 35	Read interrupt address	AL =	Interrupt number ES:BX point to vector address
AH = 36	Disk space available	DL =	Drive (0 = default, 1 = A, 2 = B, etc.) AX = sectors/cluster (FFFF if invalid) BX = number of free clusters CX = bytes per sector DX = total number of clusters

AH Value	Function	Input	Output
AH = 37	(DOS internal use)		
AH = 38	Country-dependent information (32-byte block)	DS:DX =	Location of memory Date/time Currency symbol Thousands separator Decimal separator
AH = 39	Make directory	DS:DX =	Address of string for directory
AH = 3A	Remove directory	DS:DX =	Address of string for directory
AH = 3B	Change directory	DS:DX =	Address of string for new directory
AH = 3C	Create a file	DS:DX = CX =	Address of string for file AX = file handle File attribute
AH = 3D	Open a file	DS:DX = AL =	Address of string for file 0 = open for reading 1 = open for writing 2 = open for both AX returns file handle
AH = 3E	Close a file handle	BX =	File handle
AH =3F	Read a file or device	BX = CX = DS:DX =	File handle Number of bytes to read Address of buffer AX = number of bytes read
AH = 40	Write a file or device	BX = CX = DS:DX =	File handle Number of bytes to read Address of buffer AX = number of bytes written
AH = 41	Delete a file	DS:DX =	Address of file string
AH = 42	Move file pointer	BX = AL = CX:DX DX:AX	File handle Pointer's starting location Number of bytes Current file pointer
AH = 43	Set file attribute	AL = 1 CX = DS:DX =	 Attribute Address of file string
AH = 45	Duplicate file handle	BX	File handle AX = returned file handle

Output

File handle
CX = second file handle

Drive number (0 = default,
1 = A drive, 2 = B drive)
Buffer address
DS:SI returns address of string

Number of paragraphs
AX = allocated blocks

Segment of returned block

Segment block
New block size

Location of ASCIIZ string
(drive/path/filename)
AL–0 = load and execute
3 = load/no execute

Binary return code (all files
closed)

AX returns exit code of another
program

Location of ASCIIZ string
(drive/path/filename)
CX = search attribute
DTA completed

(AH = 4EH called first)

AL–0 if verify off
1 if verify on

Address of string for old
information
Address of string for new
information

AH Value	Function	Input	Output
AH = 57	Get/set file date/time	AL	00 (return) 01 (set)
		BX	File handle
		DX and CX	Date and tin
AH = 59	Extended error code	BX =	DOS versior AX = error c BH = class o BL = suggest CH = where
AH = 5A	Create temporary file		CX = file attr CF = Set on e AX = error co
		DS:DX =	Points to strin
AH = 5B	Create a new file		(same as prev

For DOS versions above 2.0, use AH = 36H for file management.

Mouse Control Functions Accessed Through Interrupt 33H

Syntax: INT 33H (when the following parameters are set to the requir

AH Value	Function	Input	Output
AX = 0	Install flag and reset	BX = CX = DX =	If AX = 0 and B Mouse support AX = –1, then B supported mous
AX = 1	Show pointer	BX =	Does nothing if otherwise
		CX =	increments the p flag by 1
		DX =	Shows pointer in pointer-draw fla

AH Value	Function	Input	Output
AX = 2	Hide pointer	BX =	Does nothing if already hidden, otherwise
		CX =	decrements the pointer-draw flag
		DX =	Value of –1 hides image
AX = 3	Get position and button status	BX = CX = DX =	For 2- or 3-button mice, BX returns which button pressed: 0 = leftmost, 1 = rightmost, 2 = center button. Button 3 to 15 reserved. CX = x coordinate; DX = y coordinate of pointer in pixels
AX = 4	Set pointer position	CX =	New horizontal position in pixels
		DX =	New vertical position in pixels For values that exceed screen boundaries, screen maximum and minimum are used
AX = 5	Get button press information	BX =	Button status requested, where 0 = leftmost, 1 = rightmost, 2 = center button. AX–bit 0 (leftmost) = 0 or 1 bit 1 (rightmost) = 0 or 1 bit 2 (center) = 0 or 1 If 0 button up, and if 1 button down. BX = number of times button pressed since last call CX = horizontal coordinate of mouse DX = vertical coordinate of mouse
AX = 6	Get button release information	BX =	Button status requested, same format as for AX = 5 previosly described. AX, BX, CX, and DX as previously described. If 0, button up; 1 if button down

AH Value	Function	Input	Output
AX = 7	Set minimum and maximum horizontal position	CX =	Minimum virtual-screen horizontal coordinate in pixels
		DX =	Maximum virtual-screen horizontal coordinate in pixels
AX = 8	Set minimum and maximum vertical position	DX =	Maximum virtual-screen vertical coordinate in pixels
AX = 9	Set graphics pointer block	BX=	Pointer hot-spot horizontal coordinate in pixels
		CX =	Pointer hot-spot vertical coordinate in pixels
		DX =	Address of screen/pointer masks
		ES =	Segment of screen/pointer masks
AX = 10	Set text pointer	BX =	Pointer select value
		CX =	Screen mask value/hardware cursor start scan line
		DX =	Pointer mask value/ hardware cursor stop scan line BX = 0 select software text pointer BX = 1 select hardware cursor CX and DX bit map to: 0 to 7 character 8 to 10 foreground color 11 intensity 12 to 14 background color 15 blinking
AX = 11	Read mouse motion counters	BX =	CX = horizontal count
		CX =	DX = vertical count
		DX =	Range –32,768 to +32, 768 read in mickeys

AH Value	Function	Input	Output
AX = 12	Set user-defined subroutine	CX = DX = ES =	Call mask Offset of subroutine Segment of subroutine CX word bit map: 0 pointer position changed 1 leftmost button pressed 2 leftmost button released 3 rightmost button pressed 4 rightmost button released 5 center button pressed 6 center button released 7 to 15 reserved = 0 Following values loaded when subroutine is called: AX = condition of mask BX = button status CX = pointer horizontal coordinate DX = pointer vertical coordinate SI = last vertical mickey count read DI = last horizontal mickey count read
AX = 13	Light pen emulation on	BX = CX = DX =	Instructs mouse driver to emulate a light pen Vertical mickey/pixel ratio Ratios specify number of mickeys per 8 pixels
AX = 14	Light pen emulation off	BX = CX = DX =	Disables mouse driver light pen emulation (Same as AX = 13)
AX = 15	Set mickey/pixel ratio	CX = DX =	Horizontal mickey/pixel ratio (Same as AX = 13)

AH Value	Function	Input	Output
AX = 16	Conditional off	CX = DX = SI = DI =	Left column coordinate in pixels Upper row coordinate in pixels Right column coordinate in pixels Lower row coordinate in pixels Defines an area of the screen for updating
AX = 19	Set double speed threshold	BX = DX =	Doubles pointer motion Threshold speed in mickeys/second
AX = 20	Swap user-defined subroutine	CX = DX = ES =	Call mask Offset subroutine Segment of subroutine Sets hardware interrupts for call mask and subroutine address, returns previous values CX word call mask: 0 pointer position changed 1 leftmost button pressed 2 leftmost button released 3 rightmost button pressed 4 rightmost button released 5 center button pressed 6 center button released 7 to 12 reserved = 0 Following values loaded when subroutine is called: AX = condition of mask BX = button status CX = pointer horizontal coordinate DX = pointer vertical coordinate SI = last vertical mickey count read DI = last horizontal mickey count read

AH Value	Function	Input	Output
AX = 21	Get mouse state storage requirements	BX = CX = DX =	Gets size of buffer in bytes needed to store state of the mouse driver BX = size of buffer in bytes
AX = 22	Save mouse driver state	BX = CX = DX = ES =	Saves the mouse driver state Offset of buffer Segment of buffer
AX = 23	Restore mouse driver state	BX = CX = DX = ES =	Restores the mouse driver state from a user buffer Offset of buffer Segment of buffer

Appendix C

Dynamic Link Libraries

Dynamic link libraries (DLLs) are in many ways similar to other Visual C++ libraries in that they give the programmer an easy way to distribute new functions and other resources. DLLs differ from other Visual C++ libraries in that they are linked to the application at run time rather than during the compile/link cycle. This process is described as dynamic linking rather than static linking. Static linking occurs when linking C++ run-time libraries to an application at compile/link time. DLLs also offer the advantage in multitasking environments of sharing both functions and resources.

DLLs can be divided into two distinct categories: conventional API-based DLLs written in C or C++ (without objects), and MFC object-based DLLs. API DLLs have the advantage of being portable from one compiler to another. DLLs based on the MFC are, of course, restricted to compilers using a licensed version of the MFC.

Since our focus in this book has been on the MFC, we'll demonstrate the development of a simple DLL with the use of the MFC library.

An MFC-based Dynamic Link Library

An MFC-based DLL can be created and compiled in a manner similar to the MFC Windows applications of Chapters 24 through 26 in this book, but with some subtle changes. To build the example FRAMER.DLL dynamic link library, use the AppWizard to create all necessary header, resource, and source code files. Follow these steps to complete the Framer project.

1. Use the Visual C++ File | New menu option to bring up the New dialog box, as shown in Figure C-1.
2. Name the new MFC AppWizard (DLL) project *Framer*.
3. Click OK to start the MFC AppWizard (DLL).
4. For step 1 of the DLL AppWizard, make sure the Regular DLL using shared MFC DLL option is selected, as shown in Figure C-2.
5. For remaining steps, use the defaults suggested by the AppWizard.
6. Click Finish, review the options as shown in Figure C-3, then generate the base code for the project by selecting OK.

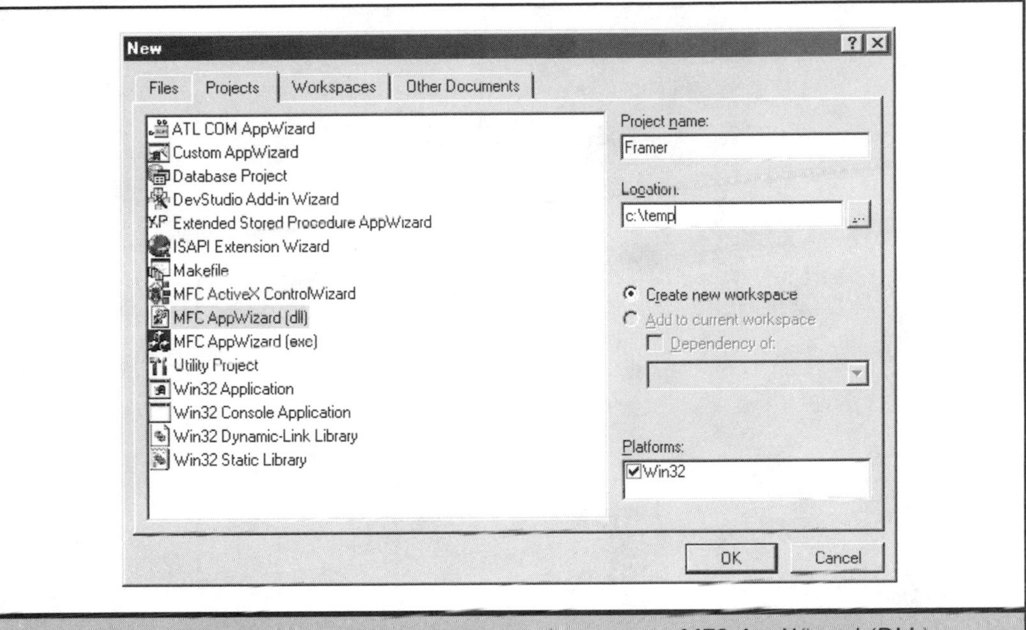

Figure C-1. *The New dialog box allows you to create a MFC AppWizard (DLL) project*

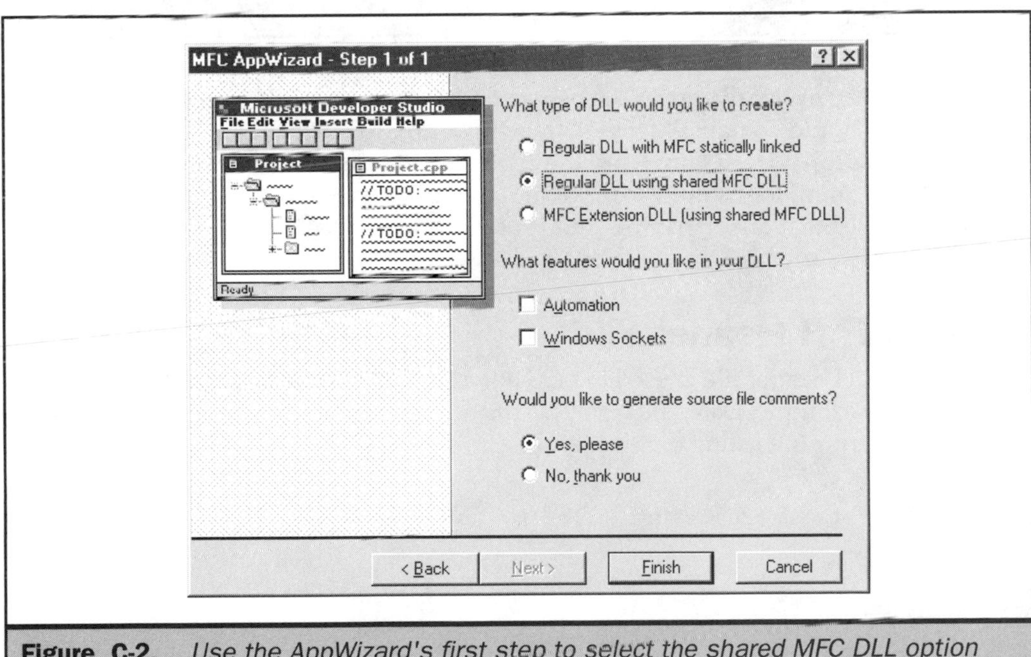

Figure C-2. *Use the AppWizard's first step to select the shared MFC DLL option*

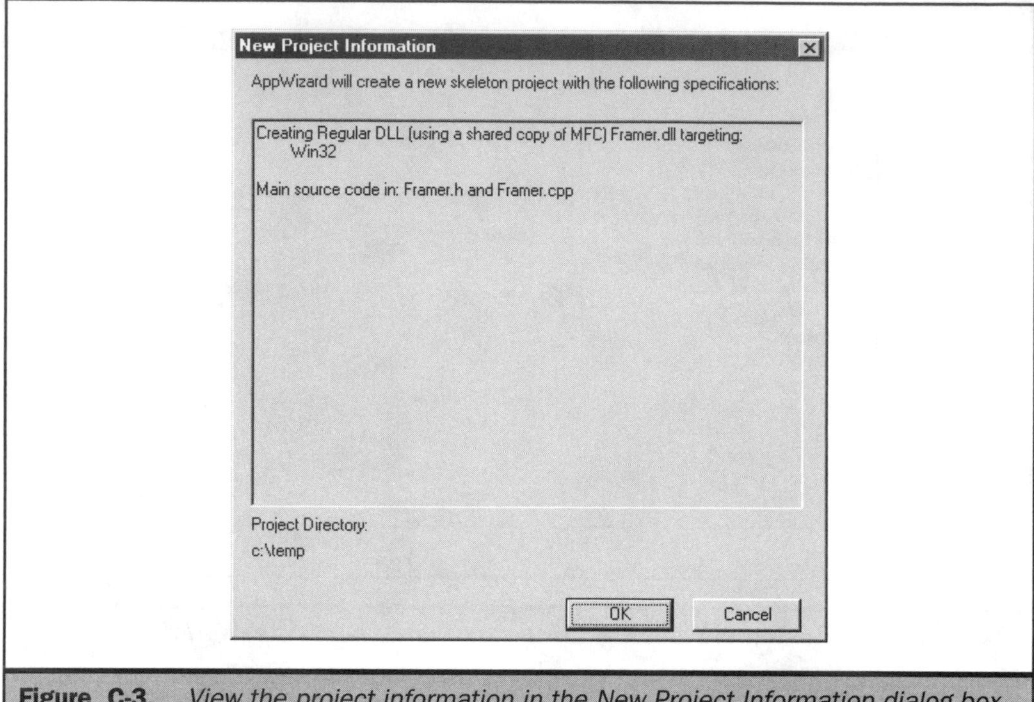

Figure C-3. *View the project information in the New Project Information dialog box*

When the AppWizard creates the base code for the Framer project, your subdirectory should contain the files shown in Figure C-4.

Like other AppWizard templates, the code that was generated is functional—it just doesn't do anything for us until we add our own unique code.

The two files that are of greatest interest to us are the FRAMER.H and FRAMER.CPP files.

The FRAMER.H Header File

The FRAMER.H header file is used to hold any function prototypes that we wish to export. In this example, DateAndTime( ) is the only function we've included in this code. Here is a partial listing of this file.

```
// Framer.h : main header file for the FRAMER DLL
//

    .
    .
    .
```

```
#ifndef __AFXWIN_H__
  #error include 'stdafx.h' before including this file for PCH
#endif

#include "resource.h"                    // main symbols


__declspec( dllexport ) void WINAPI DateAndTime();

//////////////////////////////////////////////////////////////////
// CFramerApp
// See Framer.cpp for the implementation of this class
//

class CFramerApp : public CWinApp
    .
    .
    .
```

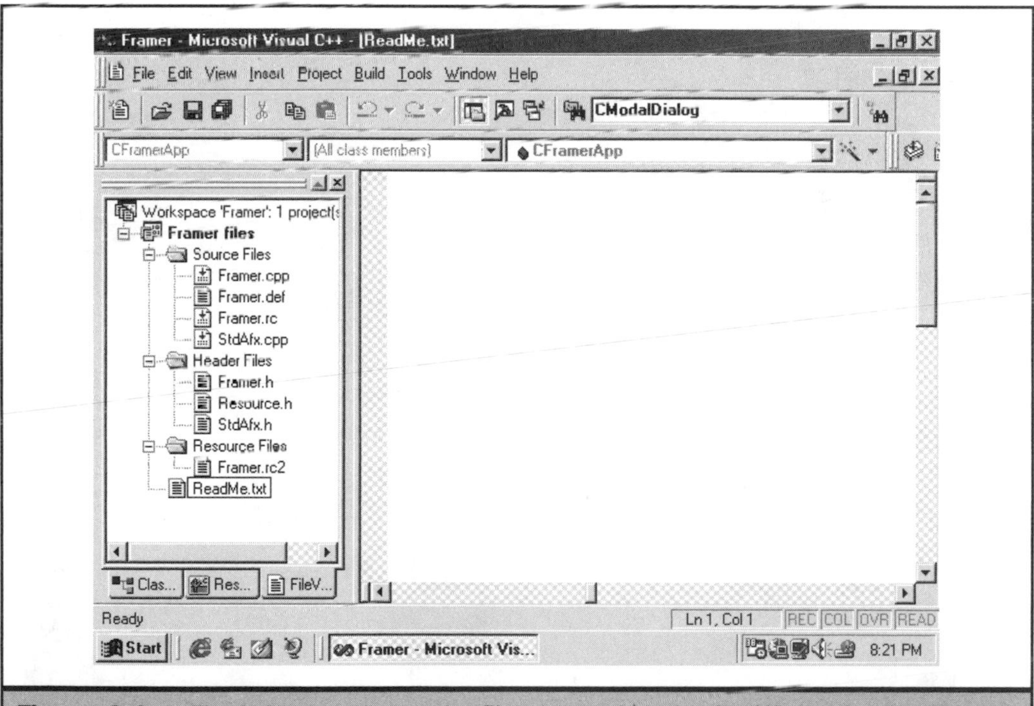

Figure C-4. *The left pane shows the files created by the AppWizard for the Framer DLL project*

Microsoft uses the extended attribute syntax—for example, __declspec—for simplifying and standardizing Microsoft-specific extensions to the C++ language. Here, the **__declspec** keyword indicates that an instance of the type will be stored with a Microsoft-specific storage-class attribute.

The explicit use of the **dllexport** keyword has eliminated the need for EXPORT statements in the module definition file (FRAMER.DEF). Developers of C-based DLLs are familiar with the practice of identifying all exported functions in the module definition file. That practice is now outdated.

The FRAMER.CPP Source Code File

The specific DLL code is added to the FRAMER.CPP file. In the following complete listing, that code is shown in a bold font:

```
// Framer.cpp : The initialization routines for the DLL.
//

#include "stdafx.h"
#include "Framer.h"

#ifdef _DEBUG
#define new DEBUG_NEW
#undef THIS_FILE
static char THIS_FILE[] = __FILE__;
#endif

//
//  Note!
//
//    If this DLL is dynamically linked against the MFC
//    DLLs, any functions exported from this DLL which
//    call into MFC must have the AFX_MANAGE_STATE macro
//    added at the very beginning of the function.
//
//    For example:
//
//    extern "C" BOOL PASCAL EXPORT ExportedFunction()
//    {
//      AFX_MANAGE_STATE(AfxGetStaticModuleState());
//      // normal function body here
```

```
//    }
//
//    It is very important that this macro appear in each
//    function, prior to any calls into MFC.  This means that
//    it must appear as the first statement within the
//    function, even before any object variable declarations
//    as their constructors may generate calls into the MFC
//    DLL.
//
//    Please see MFC Technical Notes 33 and 58 for additional
//    details.
//

/////////////////////////////////////////////////////////////////////////////
// CFramerApp

BEGIN_MESSAGE_MAP(CFramerApp, CWinApp)
  //{{AFX_MSG_MAP(CFramerApp)
    // NOTE - the ClassWizard will add and remove mapping
    // macros here.
    //    DO NOT EDIT what you see in these blocks of
    // generated code!
  //}}AFX_MSG_MAP
END_MESSAGE_MAP()

/////////////////////////////////////////////////////////////////////////////
// CFramerApp construction

CFramerApp::CFramerApp()
{
  // TODO: add construction code here,
  // Place all significant initialization in InitInstance
}

/////////////////////////////////////////////////////////////////////////////
// The one and only CFramerApp object

CFramerApp theApp;

__declspec( dllexport ) void WINAPI DateAndTime()
```

```
{
AFX_MANAGE_STATE(AfxGetStaticModuleState());

  // get current date and time information
struct tm *date_time;
time_t timer;

  time(&timer);
date_time=localtime(&timer);

const CString& strtime = asctime(date_time);

  // Draw a message box to the window
AfxMessageBox(strtime, MB_OK, 0);
}
```

As you learned while examining this listing, if this DLL is dynamically linked against the MFC DLLs, certain considerations must be made. Specifically, all exported functions that call into the MFC must have the **AFX_MANAGE_STATE** macro added at the start of the function.

The next six lines of code are used to retrieve the date and time information from the system. This information is then placed in a string, *strtime*.

When a call is made to this DLL, the DLL will in turn draw a message box to the window. The message box reports the date and time that the DLL was called. The message box can be canceled by clicking on the OK button.

Building the FRAMER.DLL

Build the DLL by selecting the appropriate build option from the compiler's Build menu. When the build cycle is complete, the DEBUG subdirectory will contain several important files.

The FRAMER.DLL is the dynamic link library, and FRAMER.LIB is the associated library. Both files must be placed in specific locations:

- Copy FRAMER.DLL to your Windows subdirectory containing system DLLs. This is usually C:\WINDOWS\SYSTEM.
- Copy FRAMER.LIB to the DEBUG subdirectory of the application that will use the DLL. The subdirectory for this example will be named C:\DLLDEMO\DEBUG.

In order to test the DLL, we will have to build a standard MFC application and call the DLL.

An Application that Calls a DLL

In this section, you will build an application designed to take advantage of the FRAMER.DLL dynamic link library. This application, named DLLDemo, will make a single call to the DateAndTime( ) function in the DLL created in the previous section.

Use the following steps to create the DLLDemo base code with the AppWizard:

1. Use the Visual C++ File | New menu option to bring up the New dialog box, as shown in Figure C-5.
2. Name the project DLLDemo. Click OK to start the MFC AppWizard.
3. Follow the normal project creation steps and create an application with a single-document interface using the Document/View architecture support as shown in Figure C-6.
4. Use wizard defaults for all other steps and build as a shared DLL.
5. Review and accept the classes as shown in the review list. Click the Finish button to generate the project files.

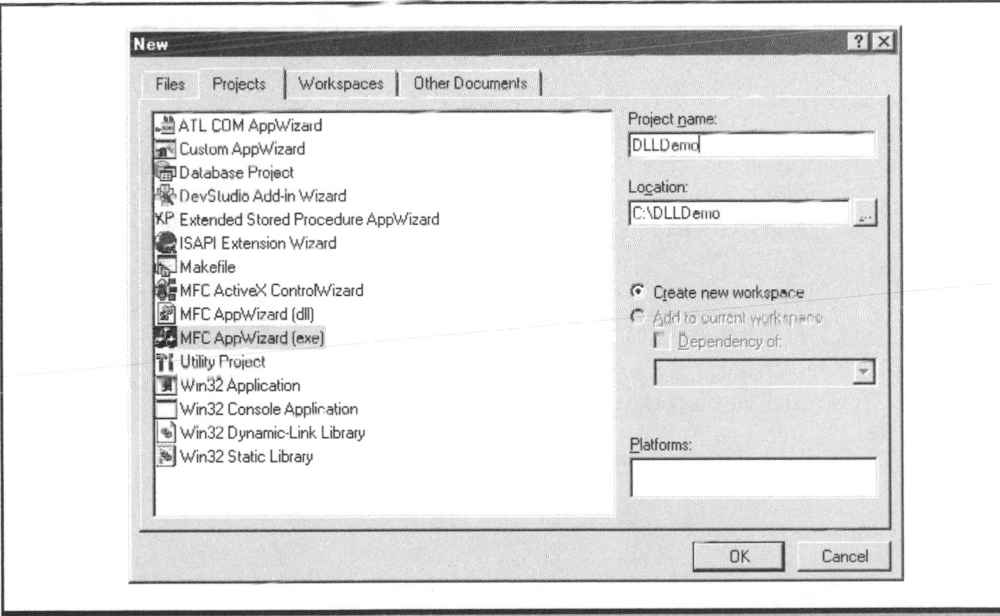

Figure C-5. *Use the New dialog box to create a new MFC AppWizard application named DLLDemo*

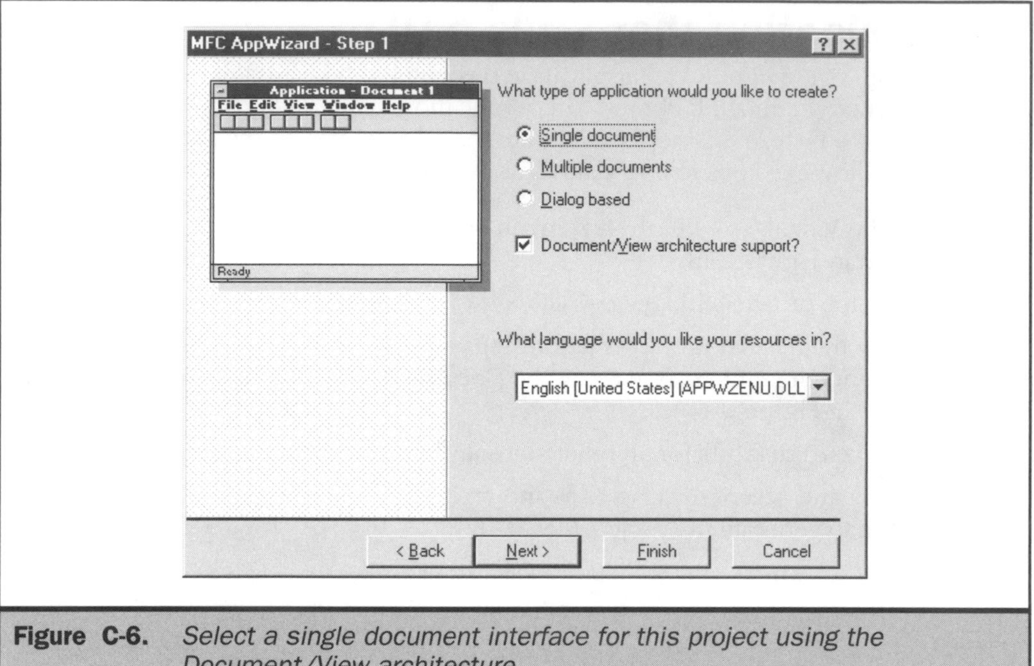

Figure C-6. *Select a single document interface for this project using the Document/View architecture*

It is now up to us to add the application-specific code to the above base code. As you will recall from Chapters 24 through 26, the AppWizard generated numerous files to support each application. In this case, there will be five source code files and their associated header files.

There are two files that are of interest to us. The first is DLLDEMOVIEW.H and the second is DLLDEMOVIEW.CPP.

The DLLDEMOVIEW.H Header File

The DLLDEMOVIEW.H header file is used to hold any function prototypes that we wish to import. In this example, DateAndTime( ) is the only function we wish to use. Here is a partial listing of this file.

```
// DLLDemoView.h : interface of the CDLLDemoView class
//
/////////////////////////////////////////////////////////////////////
    .
    .
    .
```

```
extern void WINAPI DateAndTime( );

class CDLLDemoView : public CView
{
    .
    .
    .
```

The **extern** keyword alerts the compiler that this function is external to the body of the current program. During the build process, the linker will look for this function. If the linker cannot find DateAndTime( ) in an appropriate library, you will receive a short but sweet error message.

The DLLDEMOVIEW.CPP Source Code File

In order to handle WM_PAINT messages, you'll want to add the OnPaint( ) member function and associated message handlers. To do this, follow these steps:

1. Use the View | ClassWizard... menu selection to open the MFC ClassWizard dialog box.
2. Select WM_PAINT from the Messages list box and add the OnPaint( ) member function.
3. Double-click the mouse on the OnPaint( ) member function to add and edit the member-specific code.

The following is a partial listing of the DLLDEMOVIEW.CPP source code file. The code specific to the OnPaint( ) member function is the only portion of code that is altered from the original listing. The file contains a single line of code in a bold font. This is the location where the DateAndTime( ) DLL function is called.

```
// DLLDemoView.cpp : implementation of CDLLDemoView
//

    .
    .
    .

/////////////////////////////////////////////////////////////////////
// CDLLDemoView message handlers

void CDLLDemoView::OnPaint( )
{
```

```
    CPaintDC dc(this); // device context for painting

    dc.TextOut(280,100,"Send a little text to the Window",32);

    // Call the DLL
  DateAndTime( );

    // Do not call CView::OnPaint( ) for painting messages
  }
```

Before building this project, there is one more critical step that must be taken. The DLL FRAME.LIB must be identified so the linker can resolve the external functions. This is done using the compiler's Project | Settings… menu selection to open the Project Settings dialog box. Figure C-7 shows this dialog box and the Link tab selected.

You can now build the application by making the appropriate build selection from the compiler's Build menu.

Run the program from within the IDE. You should see a screen similar to Figure C-8.

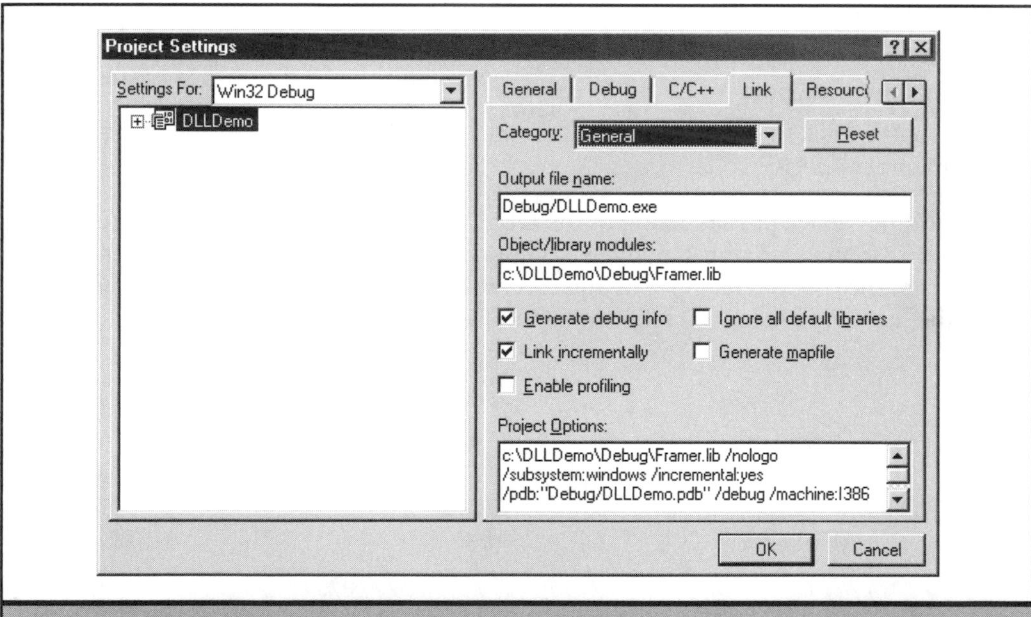

Figure C-7. *Use the Link tab to identify the FRAME.LIB in the linker's object/library module*

The DLLDemo application will draw the message box on the screen anytime a WM_MOUSE message is received. This action allowed us to keep the application as simple as possible and yet it demonstrates all of the steps necessary in incorporating a DLL.

More DLLs?

DLLs are considered an advanced programming topic by most developers. We included this appendix because of our discussion of ActiveX controls, which are really small DLLs.

If you are interested in expanding your knowledge of DLLs, we can only recommend one book. It is Steve Holzner's *Advanced Visual C++ Programming* (by M&T Books, 1996). Steve devotes a whole chapter to this advanced but important topic.

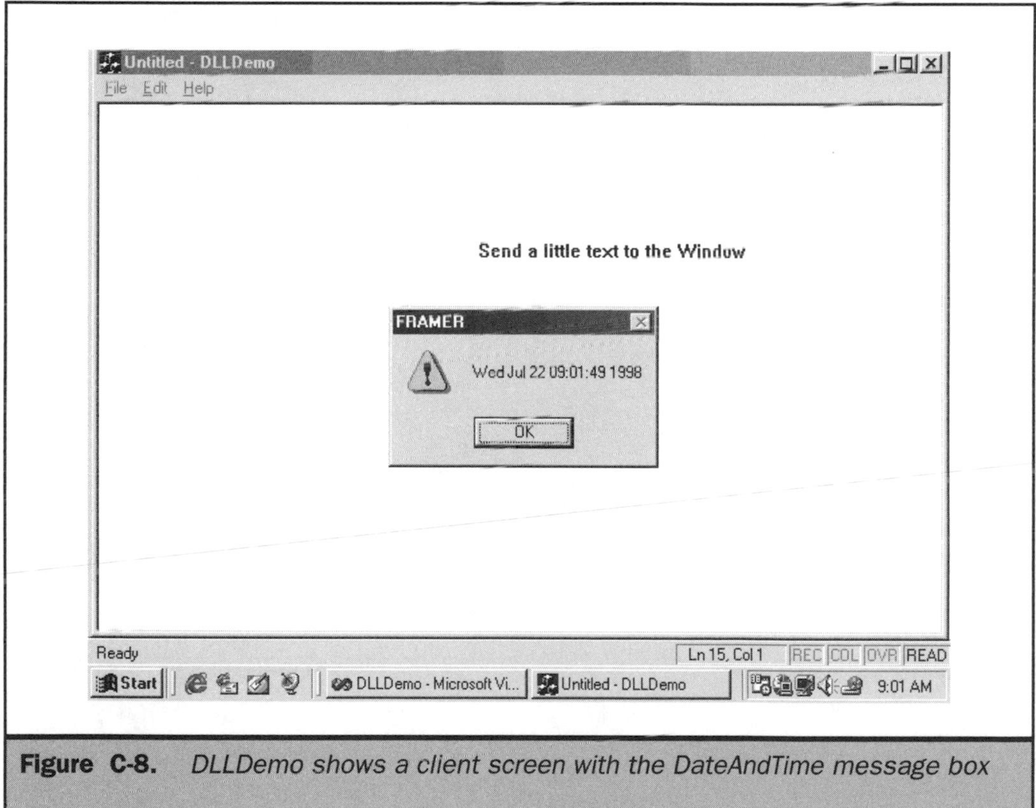

Figure C-8. *DLLDemo shows a client screen with the DateAndTime message box*

Index

! (NOT), 164-165
!= (non-equality), 162-166, 627 628
!0 (non-zero), 165
(concatenation operator), 464-465
#, 322, 371, 464
#@ (charizing operator), 465-466
#define statements, 658-659
#define, 144-145, 190, 451-457, 467
#elif, 460-461
#else, 460
#endif, 458
#error, 461
#if, 459
#ifdef, 458, 460
#ifndef, 459-460, 467
#include, 115, 130, 467
#line, 461
#pragma, 462
#undef, 459
% (modulus operator), 548-549, 369
    C output formatting control, 368-376
& (address operator), 117, 154, 269, 381, 425
    bitwise AND, 156-158
    creating C++ reference type, 349
&& (logical AND), 164-165, 168
:: (scope resolution operator), 222
*,
    const void, 325-326
    pointer operator, 155, 299-351
** (pointer to pointer), 338-344
*=, 580
: (derived classes), 564-570, 625-626
:: (scope operator), 533, 537-539, 542-543
?: (conditional operator), 166-168, 185-187, 240, 294-295, 336
[] (array subscript), 263-264

with array of pointers, 336-338
\ (line continuation symbol), 194, 456
\?, 121
\\, 121, 365
\', 121
\", 121
\0 (null terminator), 590-591
\0 (null-string terminator), 266, 274, 334, 364
with string pointers, 336-338
^ (XOR), 157-158
^Z (EOF), 182, 210
{ } (compound block), 178-196
| (bitwise OR), 157-158
| | (logical OR), 164-165, 168
~ (NOT), 158
~ (tilde character), 547
' ' (format prefix), 371
+ (addition), 160, 336-338
++ (increment), 159-160, 314, 336-338
+=, 557, 563, 574, 582
< (less than), 162-166
< (redirection), 356
<< (put to/insertion – C++), 123, 386-395
<= (less than or equal), 162-166
= (assignment operator), 160-161
== (equality), 162-166
==, 627-628
-> (arrow operator), 425-435, 474-476
> (greater than), 162-166
->, 575
->, 627-628
>= (greater than or equal), 162-166
>> (get from/extraction – C++), 123, 386-395
16-bit C/C++ environment, 148, 314
32-bit C/C++ environment, 148, 321-322

A

abort( ), 481-491
About Visual C++, 52
abs( ),186-187, 481-491, 508-511
abstract data type, 525, 610
access modifiers, 143-146
accessing,
array elements, 267-269
identifiers (internal vs. external), 255-260
out-of-scope identifiers, 254-260
structure members, 417-418
acos( ), 508-511
acosl( ), 508-511
Active Template Library (ATL), 930-952
ActiveX Controls, 894-928
COleControl class, 895-903
containers, 904
control design criteria, 895
customizing simple ActiveX control, 919-927
events, 903
methods, 903-904
mouse events, 922-927
persistence, 904
properties, 903-904
shape, size, and colors, 919-922
Wizard, 894
Ada, 99
AddDocTemplate( ), 821
adding files to project, 61-62
addition (+), 160
AFX.H, 735
AFX_DATA_INIT, 845
AFX_DATA_MAP, 845
AFX_MSG, 756, 774
AFX_MSG_MAP, 819
AFX_VIRTUAL, 822
AFX_VIRTUAL, 844
AfxEnableControlContainer( ), 870
AfxGetInstanceHandle( ), 913
AfxMessageBox( ), 883
AfxOleRegisterControlClass( ), 913
AfxOleRegisterPropertyPageClass( ), 918
AfxOleUnregisterClass( ), 913
AfxRegisterWndClass, 771, 777
AfxThrowMemoryException( ), 883

AFXWIN.H, 736, 743-744, 755
Algol 60, 98-99
allocate( ), 597
allocation (memory dynamic), 472-478
altering stream buffer in C, 357-358
ambient properties (ActiveX), 904
AND,
&, 156-158
logical - &&, 164-165, 168
animate control, 673
anonymous unions, 110
ANSI (American National Standards Institute), 99, 105-107, 216-217, 448
ANSI_CHARSET, 801
APL, 101, 733
Application and Class Wizards, 808-857
AppWizard, 809-814, 836-841
ClassWizard, 814-817
Editor application, 836-857
Graph application, 817-835
Arc( ), 760, 831-834
argc, 245-249, 335-338
argument,
array type, 279-289
command line, 244-249
function types, 224-236
list (varying length), 252-254
passing, 219-221
type (reference), 111
varying-length, 111
argv[], 245-249, 335-338
arithmetic operators, 160
pointer, 313-318
array, 234-236, 261-295
and pointer arithmetic, 316-318
of string pointers, 344-348
pointers, 308-309, 335-338
structures (passing), 428-431
structures, 422-425
types, 449-450
ASCII table, 954-957
asctime( ), 511-518, 557-559, 926, 943
asin( ), 508-511
asinl( ), 508-511
assembly language (interface), 102
ASSERT( ), 829
ASSERT_VALID( ), 829
AssertValid( ), 824, 848, 851
assigning pointer address (illegal type), 301
assignment operator (=), 160-162
atan( ), 508-511
atan2( ), 508-511
atan2l( ), 508-511
atanl( ), 508-511
atexit( ), 214-216, 481-491
atof( ), 249, 481-491, 554
atoi( ), 247-248, 336, 338, 481-491, 563
atol( ), 481-491, 557-559
auto, 151-156

B

B (Basic language), 98-99
bad( ), 410
base conversion, 237-238
base( ), 597
basefield, 396, 405
BCPL (Basic Combined Programming Language), 98-99, 101
BEGIN, 715, 769
BEGIN_MESSAGE_MAP( ), 755, 757, 763, 774
BeginPaint( ), 691, 702, 711
BeginWaitCursor( ), 882
Binary Large Object (BLOB), 904
binary, 237-238, 381, 409
bit-fields, 436-437
bitmap (creating), 82-86
BITMAP, 677
bitwise operators, 156-158
BLACK_PEN, 942
blen( ), 597
block ({}), 178-196
scope, 109
books online, 86-87

BOOL, 703-709
boolean, 572-573
Breakpoints, 76-79
brushes, 653
BS_SOLID, 772
bsearch( ), 481-491
buffer (altering stream in C), 357-358
Build menu, 42-45
button control, 673

C

C, 98-101, 121
 console and port I/O, 583
 formatting input, 381-383
 output formatting, 368-376
 vs. C++, 109-114, 249-254, 417, 443
 vs. older high-level languages, 100-101
C/C++, 132-143, 168-176
C/C++ libraries, 480-518
C++, 108-114
 character output, 404-405
 data type (new bool), 142-143
 file I/O, 407-411
 for loop, 197-198
 I/O introduction, 385-411
 numeric formatting, 406
 object-oriented programming, 105-107
 reference type, 348-351
 string formatting, 405
 structures, 417
CAboutDlg, 822
calculating array dimensions, 269-272
call back function, 682
CALLBACK, 681
calloc( ), 481-491
CAnimateCtrl, 741
CAPTION, 716, 769
capturing extended keys, 363
CArchive, 742
CArchiveException, 738
CArray, 739
carriage return, 590-591
cast (cast type), 444, 454
 char, 398
 enum type, 444
 explicit, 151
 int, 398, 404
 pointer type, 328
 pointers, 331-333
CATCH, 883
CBitmap, 739
CBitmapButton, 741
CBRS_ALIGN_ANY, 848, 874-875
CBRS_FLYBY, 847
CBRS_GRIPPER, 847
CBRS_SIZE_DYNAMIC, 847
CBRS_TOOLTIPS, 847
CBRS_TOP, 847
CBrush, 739, 760, 797
CButton, 741
CByteArray, 739
CCheckListBox, 741
CClientDC, 739
CCmdTarget, 739
CCmdUI, 742
CColeLinksDialog, 741
CComboBox, 741
CCommandLineInfo, 742, 821
CCommonDialog, 740
CConnectionPoint, 740
CControlBar, 740
CCreateContext, 742
CCtrlView, 741
CDaoException, 738
CDaoRecordView, 741
CDatabase, 739
CDataExchange, 742
CDateFieldExchange, 742
CDBException, 738
CDC, 739, 797
cdecl, 146, 148
CDialog, 740, 821
CDialogBar, 740

CDocItem, 740
CDocTemplate, 740
CDocument, 740, 825-827
CDragListBox, 741
CDumpContext, 742
CDWordArray, 739
CEdit, 741
CEditView, 741, 813, 836
ceil( ), 508-511
ceill( ), 508-511
cerr, 386, 395, 407
CException, 738
CFieldExchange, 742
CFile, 738
CFileDialog, 740
CFileException, 738
CFileStatus, 742
CFindReplaceDialog, 740
CFont, 739, 797
CFontDialog, 740
CFontHolder, 742
CFormView, 741, 813, 836
CFrameWnd, 740, 743, 747-750, 754, 823-824
CGA, 82
CGdiObject, 736-739
char, 134-136, 226-227, 238-239
    cast, 398
    output in C++, 404-405
character functions (CTYPE.H), 491-497
character(s) in string, 500-501, 504-505
character,
    arrays, 289-295
    I/O, 361-363
    output in C++, 404-405
characters, 134-136
charizing operator (#@), 465-466
CHeaderCtrl, 741
check box control, 671
checking,
    compiler of pointer type, 301
    types (limited), 102, 104
child,
    class, 528, 614
    window, 668
Chord( ), 706, 761, 831-834
CHotKeyCtrl, 741
cin, 386-395, 418, 434
CIN.FLAGS( ), 139
CIN.GET( ), 332, 394-395, 434
CIN.GETLINE( ), 206
class, 525-527, 542
    factories, 930
    libraries, 733
    style, 684
classes (C++), 109, 542-570, 610
    constructors and destructors, 547-551
    delete operator, 547, 551
    derived classes (:), 113, 564-570
    free store memory, 551
    friend functions, 556-559
    inheritance, 564
    initializing member variables, 550
    member functions/methods (::), 542-543
    nesting, 543-547
    null pointer, 555
    operator overloading, 560-564
    overloading member functions, 551-556
    parent, 565
    private, 542, 565
    protected, 565
    public, 542, 565
    simple, 542-543
    this pointer, 559-560
    tilde character(~), 547
    virtual member function, 565
clear( ), 410
clear/load buffer, 502
client area, 648
CLIP_CHARACTER_PRECIS, 801
CLIP_DEFAULT_PRECIS, 792, 801

CLIP_STROKE_PRECIS, 801
CList, 739
CListBox, 741
CListCtrl, 741
CListView, 741, 836
clog, 395
CLongBinary, 739
close( ), 127, 360, 407-408
closing streams, 359-360
CMainWnd, 744, 747, 750, 755
CMap, 739
CMapPtrToPtr, 739
CMapPtrToWord, 739
CMapStringToPtr, 739
CMapStringToString, 739
CMapStrToOb, 739
CMapWordToOb, 739
CMapWordToPtr, 739
CMDIChildWnd, 740
CMDIFrameWnd, 740
CMemFile, 738
CMemoryException, 738
CMemoryState, 742
CMenu, 739
CMetaFileDC, 739
CMiniFrameWnd, 740
CMultiLock, 742
CMultipleDocTemplate, 740
CNotSupportedException, 738
CObArray, 739
CObject (contents), 738-740
CObList, 739
code,
    editing, 58
    size (optimal), 101
CODE, 694-695
COleBusyDialog, 741
COleChangeIconDialog, 740
COleChangeSourceDialog, 741
COleClientItem, 740, 867
COleControl, 741
COleControlModule, 740
COleConvertDialog, 741
COleCurrency, 742
COleDataObject, 742
COleDataSource, 740
COleDateTime, 742
COleDateTimeSpan, 742
COleDialog, 740
COleDispatchDirver, 742
COleDispatchException, 738
COleDocument, 740, 867
COleDropSource, 740
COleDropTarget, 740
COleException, 738
COleInsertDialog( ), 882-883
COleInsertDialog, 740, 882
COleIPFrameWnd, 740
COleLinkingDoc, 740
COleMessageFilter, 740
COleObjectFactory, 740
COlePageSetupDialog, 741
COlePasteSpecialDialog, 741
COlePropertyPage, 741, 916, 919
COleResizeBar, 740
COleServerDoc, 740
COleServerItem, 740
COleStreamFile, 739
COleTemplateServer, 740
COleUpdateDialog, 741
COleVariant, 742
color palette, 661
COLORREF, 843, 942
COM(component object model), 860, 894
    interface, 861
    modules, 930
COM and DHTML, 930-952
combo box control, 672
comma operator (,), 168
command line arguments, 106, 244-249
comment,
    block, 115-117
    syntax, 109
compatibility of types, 448-451
compiling resources, 678
compiling simple programs, 53-80

compound,
assignment, 161-162
block ({}), 178-196
files (COM), 861
concatenation operator (##), 464-465
conditional, 462-464
controls, 178-196
debugging, 462-463
CONIO.H, 480-481
connection points, 930
constructors and destructors, 112, 529
container (OLE), 861
context-sensitive help, 24-25
continuing lines (\), 194
control,
characters (output), 120
container, 903
icon, 647
key capture, 363
program statements, 177-216
Z (^Z), 182
conversions,
base, 237-238
data type, 149-151
hierarchy of, 149-151
cos( ), 508-511, 533, 538, 554, 723
cosh( ), 508-511
coshl( ), 508-511
cosl( ), 508-511
cout, 386-411, 418, 434
fill( ), 400, 406
flags( ), 140
precision( ), 402, 406
put( ), 393
setf( ), 140
unsetf( ), 398, 405-406
width( ), 192, 400, 406
write( ), 399, 402, 405
CPaintDC, 739, 755, 757, 760
CPalette, 739
CPen, 737, 739, 760, 764, 772
CPictureHolder, 742
CPL (Combined Programming Language), 98-99
CPoint, 742
CPrintDialog, 741
CPrintInfo, 742
CProgressCtrl, 741
CPropertySheet, 740
CPropExchange, 742
CPtrArray, 739
CPtrList, 739
CR / LF, 598
Create( ), 743, 747, 755
CreateEx( ), 847, 874
CreateFont( ), 792, 802
CreateHatchBrush( ), 762-763, 831-834
CreateItem( ), 883
CreatePen( ), 760-761, 765, 831-834, 922
CreatePolygonRgn( ), 943
CreateSolidBrush( ), 723, 761-763, 831-834, 922
CREATESTRUCT, 824
CreateWindow( ), 688-689, 702, 710-711, 719
CRecordSet, 739
CRecordView, 741
CRect, 742
CRectTracker, 742
CResourceException, 738
CRgn, 739
CRichEditCntrItem, 740
CRichEditCtrl, 741
CRichEditDoc, 740
CRichEditView, 741, 836
cross-platform portability, 103
CRuntimeClass, 742
CS_BYTEALIGNCLIENT, 684
CS_BYTEALIGNWINDOW, 684
CS_CLASSDC, 684
CS_DBLCLKS, 684
CS_GLOBALCLASS, 684
CS_HREDRAW, 684, 687, 701, 771
CS_NOCLOSE, 684
CS_OWNDC, 684

CS_PARENTDC, 684
CS_SAVEBITS, 684
CS_VREDRAW, 684, 687, 701, 771
CScrollBar, 741
CScrollView, 741, 813, 836
CSingleDocTemplate, 740, 821
CSingleLock, 742
CSize, 742
CSliderCtrl, 741
CSocketFile, 739
CSpinButtonCtrl, 741
CSplitterWnd, 740
CStatic, 741
CStatusBar, 740
CStatusBarCtrl, 741
CStdioFile, 738
CString, 742
CStringArray, 739
CStringList, 739
CTabCtrl, 741
CTDCtrlPropPage, 916, 919
CTEXT, 716, 769
ctime( ), 511-518
CTime, 742
CTimeSpan, 742
CTollBar, 740
CToolbarCtrl, 741
CToolTipCtrl, 741
CTreeCtrl, 741
CTreeView, 741, 836
CTRL key capture, 363
CTYPE.H, 135, 209-211, 480-481, 491-497
CTypedPtrArray, 742
CTypedPtrList, 742
CTypedPtrMap, 742
CUIntArray, 739
cur, 409-410
CURSOR, 677
cursor hotspot, 85-86
CUserException, 738
customizable toolbars and menus, 14
customization (compiler option), 20
CView, 741, 813, 828, 836
CW_USEDEFAULT, 688-689, 702
CWaitCursor, 742
CWinApp, 740, 743-745, 754, 819
CWindowDC, 739
CWinThread, 739
CWnd (contents), 740-741
CWnd, 740, 813
CWordArray, 739

D

DAO, 732
data conversions,
    float to string, 483-484
    string to long integer, 484-485
data,
    encapsulation, 112
    types, 133-143, 149-151, 196
DATA, 694-695
data object (OLE), 861
DataObject viewer, 11-12
dbp( ), 596
dc( ), 755, 757, 771, 790, 831
DDE, 656
Deactivate( ), 882
debugging,
    conditional statements, 462-463
    programs, 53-80
dec, 247-86, 398
declarations (external-variable), 152-154
DECLARE_MESSAGE_MAP( ), 754, 756
declaring,
    arrays, 263-264
    functions (external level), 156
    loop control in C++, 197-198
    pointers, 299-301
    variables, 117
DEFAULT_PITCH, 801
DEFAULT_QUALITY, 792, 801
DEFPUSHBUTTON, 769
DefWindowProc( ), 692, 694, 703, 712
delayed binding, 644
Delete( ), 883

DeleteObject( ), 738, 760-763, 765, 831-834
delimiter, 555, 559
derived classes, 113, 614, 615-617
DestroyWindow( ), 774, 782
destructors (and constructors), 112
Developer Studio, 54-55
DIALOG, 716, 769
dialog box, 85, 637, 651, 666-677
DialogBox( ), 722
DIBs, 82
difftime( ), 511-518
dimensions (calculating array), 269-272
discardable, 644, 677
DISCARDABLE, 769
dispatching priority, 657-658
DispatchMessage( ), 691, 702, 711
div( ), 481-491
division (/), 160
DLL (Dynamic Link Libraries), 643-644, 978-989
doallocate( ), 597
DockControlBar( ), 848, 875
docking toolbar, 26-27
Document / View architecture, 810
DoDataExchange( ), 822, 844
DoModal( ), 773, 781, 793-794, 822, 882
DoPreparePrinting( ), 881
DoPropExchange( ), 924-925
DOS interrupt parameters, 960-962
DoVerb( ), 883, 888
do-while, 205-206
DRAFT_QUALITY, 801
Draw( ), 880, 885
DS_MODALFRAME, 716
dual interfaces, 930
Dump( ), 829, 848
DWORD, 771
dynamic,
    linking, 642
    memory allocation, 327-330, 472-478

E

early bound access, 904
eback( ), 597
ebuf( ), 597
edit box control, 672-673
EDITTEXT, 716, 769, 788
EGA, 82
egptr( ), 597
element, 262
Ellipse( ), 705, 761, 831, 914
else, 545
embedded controls, 904
Enable3dControls( ), 843
Enable3dControlsStatic( ), 843
EnableCompoundFile( ), 877
EnableDocking( ), 848, 874
encapsulation, 610, 733
END, 363, 715, 769
END_CATCH, 883
END_MESSAGE_MAP( ), 755, 757, 763
EndDialog( ), 720-721
endl, 392-393, 544-545, 548
EndPaint( ), 691, 694, 702, 712
EndWaitCursor( ), 883
enum, 141-142, 442-33, 821
enumerated types, 109, 140-142, 196, 449-450, 466
enumeration set, 140-142
eof (look-ahead), 366, 410
EOF, 161, 355, 362, 368, 589
epptr( ), 597
errno, 470
error,
    handling, 470-471
    messages, 64-55:13
Error Lookup, 46-47
ES_AUTOHSCROLL, 853
escape sequences, 120
ETO_CLIPPED, 927
exception-handling, 734
executable format, 644-645
EXETYPE, 694-695

exit( ), 142, 204, 211-214, 335-336, 481-491, 593
EXIT_FAILURE, 214
EXIT_SUCCESS, 214
exp( ), 508-511
expansion (macros), 453-455
expl( ), 508-511
EXPORTS, 694-695
extended key capture, 363
extern, 151-156, 222, 458, 466, 600
ExtFloodFill( ), 773, 779
extraction, 123
  operator (>>), 386-395
ExtTextOut( ), 927, 943

F

fabs( ), 508-511, 552
fabsl( ), 508-511
factorials (table of), 578-581
fail( ), 410
false, 142-143
far, 146, 148-149, 321-322
fast, 102
fclose( ), 126, 359-360
fcloseall( ), 359:360
FCNTL.H, 593
fdopen( ), 355
feof( ), 366, 368
FF_DECORATIVE, 801
FF_DONTCARE, 801
FF_MODERN, 801
FF_ROMAN, 792, 801
FF_SCRIPT, 801
FF_SWISS, 801
fflush( ), 358
fgetc( ), 204, 361-362, 377-381
fgetchar( ), 362-363
fgets( ), 289-291, 363-365
File menu, 27-30
  Close, 28
  Exit, 30
  New, 27-28
  Open, 28
  Page Setup, 29
  Print, 29-30
  Recent file list, 30
  Recent workspace list, 30
  Save, 28
  Save All, 29
  Save As, 29
file,
  comparisons (with WinDiff), 93
  handle, 355
  I/O in C++, 407-411
  mode (binary), 381
  modes, 125
  monikers (OLE), 866
  pointer, 376-381
  position marker, 376-381
FILE, 124
files,
  adding to project, 61-62
  proper use of header, 466
  saving, 58-59
fill( ), 400, 406, 582, 607
FillRect( ), 914, 921
FILO, 610
find and replace, 65-67
find string within a string, 506-507
Fire_ClickIn( ), 944
Fire_ClickOut( ), 944
FireViewChange( ), 944
firing,
  events, 903
  functions (ActiveX), 898-899
FIXED_PITCH, 801
flags( ), 139, 140
float, 117, 150, 228-233, 242-243
FLOAT.H, 469, 471-472
floatfield, 396
floating toolbar, 26-27
floating-point, 134, 137-140
FLOODFILLBORDER, 773, 780
floor( ), 508-511

floorl( ), 508-511
flush carriage return, 566-568
flushall( ), 423
fmod( ), 508-511
fmodl( ), 508-511
FONT, 716
fonts, 651, 799-803
fopen( ), 124, 347, 355-356, 359
for, 196-202, 772, 779
formal argument list, 224-236
format control symbols, 121-122
format( ), 607
formatting,
    IDE File Print, 30
    input in C, 381-383
    numeric in C++, 406
    output in C, 368-376
    strings in C++, 405
FORTRAN, 100, 147
foundations (C/C++ programming), 84
fprintf( ), 124, 371-376
fputc( ), 204, 361-362
fputchar( ), 362-363
fputs( ), 204, 289-291, 358, 363-365
fread( ), 379-381
free store memory, 328
free( ), 327-330, 339, 344, 481-491
freopen( ), 355
frexp( ), 508-511
frexpl( ), 508-511
friend class, 615, 617-621
friends, 113
fscanf( ), 124, 359, 381-383
fseek( ), 376-381, 396
fstream, 409
FSTREAM.H, 407, 590-591, 593
ftell( ), 376-381
function,
    arguments, 224-236
    inlining, 19
    key capture, 363
    overloading, 111, 250-252
    pointers to, 323-327
    prototypes, 466, 658
    prototyping, 216-219
    return types, 236-244
    types, 450
functions, 215-260
    C vs. C++, 249-254
    declaring external level, 156
    returning addresses, 350-351
    stream, 355-360
    virtual, 113-114
fundamental components of C/C++ program, 114-128
FW_BOLD, 792
fwrite( ), 379-381

G

gbump( ), 597
GDI, 644, 654, 703
generating messages, 656
get from operator (>>), 123, 386-395
get( ), 331, 333, 407, 391, 394-395, 434, 477, 544, 566-569
GetActiveView( ), 881
getc( ), 226, 361-362, 382
getcar( ), 161, 168
getch( ), 226-227, 382
getchar( ), 210-211, 226, 362-363, 382
getche( ), 226
GetClientRect( ), 926
GetCurrentTime( ), 854
GetDlgItemInt( ), 720-721, 773, 782, 793-794
GetDlgItemText( ), 720, 773, 782, 793
GetDocument( ), 829, 853, 880-882
GetDrawAspect( ), 888
getenv( ), 481-491
GetHour( ), 854
GetInPlaceActiveItem( ), 881
GetItemState( ), 884
getline( ), 206
GetMessage( ), 690, 702, 711
GetMinute( ), 854

GetMiscStatus( ), 888
GetNextClientItem( ), 880
gets( ), 289-291, 363-365, 417-419
GetSecond( ), 854
GetSelectionType( ), 883
GetStartPosition( ), 880
GetStockObject( ), 687, 701, 771, 922, 942
GetTextMetrics( ), 926
GetUpdateRect( ), 693
getw( ), 365-368
global data, 327
gmtime( ), 511-518
good( ), 410-411
gptr( ), 597
GROUPBOX, 716
group box control, 671
GUI (graphical user interface), 637-639

H

HANDLE, 655, 681
HBRBACKGROUND, 685
HBRUSH, 683, 771, 942
HCURSOR, 683, 685
HDC, 655, 681
header files, 130, 168-176, 480-481
heap, 327
HEAPSIZE, 694-695
heavy classes, 734
help,
    context-sensitive, 24-25
    topics (printing), 89-90
Help menu, 50-52
Help Workshop, 12
hex, 247-248, 398, 404-405
hexadecimal character constants, 106
HICON, 683, 685
hierarchy of conversions, 149-151
high-level languages (older vs. C), 100-101
HINSTANCE, 682, 685
HOME, 363
homogenous data type, 262
horizontal scroll bar control, 672
horizontal scroll bar, 648
hot key control, 673
Hotspot
    button, 663
    editor, 85-86
HPEN, 942
HS_CROSS, 762, 765, 833
HS_FDIAGONAL, 763, 833
huge, 146, 148-149, 321-322
Hungarian notation, 131
HWND, 655, 681
hypot( ), 229, 508-511

I/O (C++), 572-607
    binary files, 597-599
    buffered stream (streambuf), 592-594
    combining C and C++ code, 600-602
    default arguments, 575-577
    enum types, 572-573
    formatting output, 578-583
    I/O options, 583
    ifstream, 588-589
    input stream (ifstream), 588-589
    iostream class list (ios), 583-586
    manipulators (multiple parameters), 605-607
    manipulators (one parameter), 604-605
    manipulators (zero parameters), 602-604
    memset( ) function, 577-578
    ofstream, 589-592
    output stream (ofstream), 589-592
    reference variables, 573-575
    streambuf, 592-594
    string stream (strstreambuf), 594-597
    strstreambuf, 594-597

icons, 82-86, 637, 650
ICON, 677
ID_CANCEL_EDIT_CNTR, 879
ID_EDIT_CLEAR, 840
ID_EDIT_COPY, 840
ID_EDIT_CUT, 840
ID_EDIT_FIND, 840
ID_EDIT_PASTE, 840, 876
ID_EDIT_PASTE_LINK, 876
ID_EDIT_REPEAT, 840
ID_EDIT_REPLACE, 840
ID_EDIT_SELECT_ALL, 840
ID_EDIT_UNDO, 840
ID_FILE_NEW, 842, 846, 869
ID_FILE_OPEN, 842, 845, 869
ID_FILE_PRINT, 840, 852, 879
ID_FILE_PRINT_DIRECT, 852, 879
ID_FILE_PRINT_PREVIEW, 852, 879
ID_FILE_PRINT_SETUP, 842, 845, 869
ID_INDICATOR_CAPS, 847, 849, 873
ID_INDICATOR_NUM, 847, 849, 873
ID_INDICATOR_SCRL, 847, 849
ID_OLE_EDIT_CONVERT, 876
ID_OLE_EDIT_LINKS, 876
ID_OLE_INSERT_NEW, 879
ID_OLE_VERB_FIRST, 876
ID_OLE_VERB_LAST, 876
ID_SEPARATOR, 847, 849, 873
IDC_ARROW, 701
IDC_CROSS, 771, 778
IDE (Integrated Development Environment), 23-52
    understanding menus, 25-26
    print options, 30
identical type, 448-449
identifier scope, 155, 222
identifiers,
    out-of-scope, 254-260
    variable names, 130-132
IDP_FAILED_TO_CREATE, 883
IDP_OLE_INIT_FAILED, 870
IDR_CNTR_INPLACE, 870, 872
IDR_DOCTYPE, 872
IDR_EDITORTYPE, 846
IDR_MAINFRAME, 848, 870
if, 178-196, 620, 688
    -else, 180-196
    -else-if, 184-185
ifstream, 396, 407-408, 410
illegal,
    identifiers, 130-132
    pointer assignment (type), 301
IMPLEMENT_DYNACREATE, 823-824
IMPLEMENT_OLECREATE_EX( ), 912, 917
IMPLEMENT_OLECTLTYPE( ), 913
IMPLEMENT_OLETYPELIB( ), 912
imports, 644
IN_AVAIL( ), 596
include,
    files, 658
    subdirectory, 8
index, 262
    out of bounds, 272-273
inherit, 525
inheritance, 610, 733
initial value, 140
initializing
    arrays, 264-267
    pointers, 306-307
InitInstance( ), 743-744, 755-756, 763
inline functions, 111, 249-250
input,
    formatting in C, 381-383
    redirection, 356-357
input message, 641
Insert menu, 39-40
insertion operator (<<), 123, 386-395
instantiated classes, 734
int, 136, 150, 227-228, 240-241
    cast, 398, 404
integer,
    I/O, 365-368
    values, 134
integrated debugger (using), 72-80

interface,
  assembly language, 102
  COM, 861
  maps, 904
  pointers, 930
introduction to I/O in C++, 385-411
InvalidateControl( ), 926
InvalidateRect( ), 693, 722, 774, 781
InvalidateRgn( ), 693
IO.H, 480-481
IOMANIP.H, 139, 578-582, 604
ios stream class hierarchy, 585
ios::, 396-410
ios::binary, 599
ios::fixed, 578, 580-582
ios::left, 580
ios::out, 590-591, 599
iostream, 395, 480-481, 572-607
IOSTREAM.H, 116-117, 386, 395-411
IS_INDICATOR_SCRL, 873
isalnum( ), 491-497
isalpha( ), 491-497
isascii( ), 209-211, 491-497
iscntrl( ), 491-497
isdigit( ), 491-497
isgraph( ), 491-497
IsKindOf( ), 854, 885
islower( ), 491-497
isprint( ), 210-211, 491-497
ispunct( ), 210-211, 491-497
isspace( ), 210-211, 491-497
IsStoring( ), 826, 877
istream, 395
isupper( ), 491-497
isxdigit( ), 491-497

K

KERNEL, 644, 654
keyboard,
  accelerators, 666
  message, 641
keywords, 132-133

L

labs( ), 481-491, 508-511
langauges, 100-102
ldexp( ), 508-511
ldexpl( ), 508-511
ldiv( ), 481-491
leading underscore, 130
left, 400, 406
left shift (<<), 158-159
legal identifiers, 130-132
length of string, 506
level,
  declaring functions external, 156
  external, 152-154
  internal, 154-155
  operator precedence, 167-168
libraries (C/C++), 168-176, 480-518
  CONIO.H, 480-481
  CTYPE.H, 480-481, 491-497
  IO.H, 480-481
  IOSTREAM.H, 480-481, 573-607, 621
  MATH.H, 480-481, 508-511, 552, 581-582
  STDIO.H, 480-481
  STDLIB.H, 480-491, 552, 556
  stream, 114
  STRING.H, 480-481, 498-508, 556, 621
  TIME.H, 480-481, 511-518
library,
  modules, 644
  routines, 103
limited type checking, 102, 104
LIMITS.H, 469-470
line continuation symbol (\), 194, 456
linefeed, 590-591
LineTo( ), 702-703, 760, 831-834
linked list, 471-478
  oops, 613-632
linker, 643
list box control, 673
list control, 672

literal string, 119
load on call, 644, 677
LoadCursor( ), 701, 710, 771, 778, 790
LoadStdProfileSettings( ), 820, 843
LoadToolBar( ), 848
localtime( ), 511-518, 557-559, 926, 943
log( ), 508-511
log10( ), 508-511
log10l( ), 508-511
logical operators, 162-166
logl( ), 508-511
long double, 508
LONG, 655, 681
look-ahead eof, 366
lowercase/uppercase conversions, 496-497, 507-508
low-level I/O, 360
LPARAM, 681
LPCREATESTRUCT, 722
LPCSTR, 681
LPSTR, 655, 681
LPVOID, 681
LRESULT, 681
lseek( ), 360
LTEXT, 716, 769
ltoa( ), 558-559
lvalue, 144

M

m_cxClient, 771-772, 778
m_cyClient, 771-772, 778
m_nCmdShow, 750, 755
m_pDocument, 829
m_pMainWnd, 750, 755, 821
m_pSelection, 879-881
m_wndToolBar, 875
machine-oriented languages, 101
macro, 249-250
  using stringsize operator (#), 322-323
macros, 451-457
main( ), 115-116, 216
MakeProcInstance( ), 722
malloc( ), 327-330, 339, 344, 420, 481-491
mapping modes, 727
marshals (COM), 861
mask, 203
math functions (MATH.H), 508-511
maximize icon, 647
MDG, 681
member,
  access privilege, 529
  accessing, 417-418
  data, 525, 532
  function, 525, 532, 535-537, 539, 610
  operator (.), 575
  variable, 535, 536-537
  variable validation, 734
  structure accessing, 417-418
memccpy( ), 498-508
memchr( ), 498-508
memcmp( ), 498-508
memcpy( ), 498-508
memicmp( ), 498-508
memmove( ), 498-508
memory (system), 642
memory,
  allocation (dynamic), 472-478
  dynamic, 327-330
  efficient, 103
  management, 610, 642
MEMORY.H, 577
memset( ), 498-508
menu bar, 648
MENU, 715, 769
MENUITEM, 715, 769
menus, 25-26, 664-666
message, 525
  boxes, 650-651
  format, 654-656
  loop, 657-658
  map, 782-783
  map (ActiveX), 900-903
  queue, 657
  type, 655

MessageBox( ), 854
messages, 112, 641-642, 653-658
viewing with Spy++, 91-92
warning and error, 64-65
method, 525, 532, 535-537, 539
Microsoft Foundation Class (MFC)
Fundamentals, 732-752
design considerations, 733-734
key classes, 738-742
key features, 734-735
Microsoft Foundation Class (MFC)
Windows Applications, 754-804
bar chart application, 785-804
current window size, 778
drawing a Fourier waveform, 778-779
drawing in the client area, 758-766
fonts, 799-802
Fourier series application, 767-784
GDI.CPP source code file, 764-765
GDI.H header file, 764
MFCSWP.CPP source code file, 757
MFCSWP.H header file, 756-757
running the GDI application, 765-766
running the simple application, 758
simple application and template, 754-758
minimize icon, 647
mixed-mode operations, 149-151, 734
MM_ANISOTROPIC, 727
MM_HIENGLISH, 727
MM_HIMETRIC, 727
MM_ISOTROPIC, 722, 726-727, 772
MM_LOENGLISH, 727
MM_LOMETRIC, 727
MM_TEXT, 726-727
MM_TWIPS, 727
modal (dialog box), 668, 775
mode (binary), 381
modeless (dialog box), 668-669
modes file, 125
modf( ), 508-511
modfl( ), 508-511
modifiable lvalue, 144
modifiers (access), 143-146
modular structure, 102
monikers (OLE file), 866
mouse message, 641
MoveTo( ), 760, 765, 831-834
MoveToEx( ), 702-703, 711
moving file pointer, 376-381
multidimensional arrays, 276-289
multiplication (*), 160
multitasking environment, 639-640

N

naming variables (identifiers), 130-132
near, 146, 148-149, 321-322
nested if-else, 183-196
nesting structures, 435-436
New Executable Format, 642, 644-645
NMAKE.EXE, 695-696
nocreate, 409
noreplace, 408-409
NULL, 355, 366, 474, 655, 681-682
pointer comparison, 320
with pointers, 329
null-string terminator, 266, 274, 334, 364
numeric formatting in C++, 406

O

object-based modularization, 610
Object-oriented programming, 105-107, 525, 522-540, 610-632
C++ and oops, 525-526
class hierarchy, 528-529
class syntax and rules, 536-537
encapsulation, 527-528
inheritance, 528-529
object-oriented linked list, 613-632
object-oriented stack, 610-613
polymorphism, 529
simple class, 537-540

structure as a class, 530-535
terminology, 526-527
traditional structured programming, 524
virtual functions, 529
oct, 247-248, 398
OCX, 894
ODBC, 732
OEM_CHARSET, 792, 801
offset, 321-322
ofstream, 396, 407-408
OLE,
AppWizard, 867-890
data, 861
embedded object, 861-866
embedding, 861
examining and modifying code, 873-890
features and specifications, 860-866
files, 861
linking, 866
objects, 860-861
OLE container application, 866-892
subdirectory, 8
testing OLE container application, 890-892
OLE_NOTIFICATION, 886
OLEIVERB_HIDE, 888
OLEMISC_INSIDEOUT, 888
OleTranslateColor( ), 942
ON_COMMAND( ), 774, 782, 794, 819-820, 869, 876
ON_UPDATE_COMMAND_UI( ), 876
ON_UPDATE_COMMAND_UI_RANGE( ), 876
ON_WM_CREATE( ), 774, 782, 794
ON_WM_DESTROY( ), 879
ON_WM_PAINT( ), 755, 757, 763, 774, 782, 794
ON_WM_RBUTTONDOWN, 854
ON_WM_SETFOCUS( ), 879
ON_WM_SIZE( ), 774, 782, 794, 879
OnAbout( ), 767, 773-775,785, 793, 795
OnActivate( ), 888
OnBeginPrinting( ), 853, 881
OnCreate( ), 767, 774-775, 785, 795
OnDeactivateUI, 888
OnDestroy( ), 881
OnDraw( ), 829, 853, 880, 914, 916, 921, 940-941
OnEndPrinting( ), 853, 881
OnExit( ), 767, 774-775, 782, 785, 795
OnFileNew( ), 846
OnFileOpen( ), 846
OnFilePrintSetup( ), 846
OnLButtonDown( ), 925, 940
OnLButtonUp( ), 925
OnNewDocument( ), 826, 877
OnPaint( ), 754-757, 829
OnPreparePrinting( ), 853
OnSize( ), 767, 771, 884
open file modes, 125
open( ), 360, 408
opening streams, 355-356
operations (mixed-mode), 149-151
operators, 156-167
overloading, 562
optimal code size, 101
optimizations (compiler option), 20
optional tag field, 442
OR (|), 157-158
ostream, 395, 408
ostrstream, 398, 405
out, 408
OUT_CHARACTERPRECIS, 801
OUT_DEFAULT_PRECIS, 792, 801
OUT_STRING_PRECIS, 801
OUT_STROKE_PRECIS, 801
out_waiting( ), 596
out-of-scope identifiers, 254-260
output,
characters in C++, 404-405
control characters, 120
control symbols, 121
formatting in C, 368-376
redirection, 356-357
overflow( ), 596
overloading,
functions, 111, 250-252
operators, 113, 388, 560

P

paint message, 657
PAINTSTRUCT, 681, 693
parameter,
  default values, 111
  list (varying length), 252-254
  type (reference), 111
parameters,
  array type, 279-289
  command line, 244-249
  function types, 224-236
  passing, 219-221
parent class, 525, 528, 614
ParseCommandLine( ), 821
Pascal, 146-147
passed by value, 219-220
passing,
  arguments, 219-221
  array of structures, 420-422, 428-431
  arrays, 279-289
  pointers to array, 428-431
pbackfail( ), 596
pbase( ), 597
pbump( ), 597
p-code, 15-16
pDocTemplate, 821
pens, 653
perror( ), 470-471
persistence, 930
PGDN, 363
PGUP, 363
picture control, 672
Pie( ), 708, 723, 729, 761, 831-834
piping, 357
POINT, 760, 831
pointer, 134
  arithmetic (with arrays), 316-318
  data type, 103
  file moving, 376-381
  portability, 321
  types, 451, 106, 112, 330-333
pointers, 297-351
  16-bit, 321-322
  32-bit, 321-322
  arrays of string, 344-348
  casting, 331-333
  comparing, 320-321
  returned from functions, 350-351
  type checking, 301
  void, 330-333
polygon project (ATL), 930-952
Polygon( ), 763, 831-834
Polyline( ), 763, 831-834
polymorphism, 113-114, 610
pop-up menu, 636
POPUP, 715, 769
postfix, 143, 160
PostQuitMessage( ), 692, 702, 712
pow( ), 234, 279, 508-511
pow10( ), 508-511
pow10l( ), 508-511
powl( ), 508-511
pptr( ), 597
precedence level,
  operator, 167-168
  table, 163-164
precision( ), 402, 406, 578, 580, 582
precompiled header files, 468-469
PreCreateWindow( ), 824, 828, 848, 853, 875, 880
predefined macros, 457
prefix, 143, 160
preload, 677
preprocessor,
  operators, 464-466
  statement, 115
  statements (advanced), 457-466
  formatting codes, 30
print help topics, 89-90
printf( ), 117-118, 371-376, 386-387, 419
private, 528, 614
problem-oriented languages, 101
problems with macros, 453-455

Procedure-oriented Windows
  applications, 680-730
    application framework, 680-699:16
    chord, 705-706
    components, 680-682
    creating a window, 688-689
    DefWindowProc( ) function, 694
    DispatchMessage( ), 691
    ellipse, 703-705
    GetMessage( ) function, 690
    message loop, 690-691
    module definition file, 694-695
    nmake utility, 695-696
    pie, 706-708
    pie chart application, 713-730
    PIE.C source code file, 725-730
    PIE.H header file, 724
    PIE.RC resource script file, 724-725
    project file, 723-724
    project utility, 696-701
    rectangle, 708-709
    showing and updating a window, 689-690
    simple procedure-oriented application, 701-709
    sine wave application, 709-712
    TranslateMessage( ), 690-691
    Window class, 686-688
    Window function, 691-693
    WM_DESTROY messages, 694
    WM_PAINT messages, 693-694
    WNDCLASS, 683-685
    WNDCLASSEX, 686-690
PROCESS.H, 211-213, 246-249, 593
Processes Viewer, 91-93
program,
    control 177-216
    creating first, 55-57
    fundamental components, 114-128
programs (simple),
    compiling, 53-80
    debugging, 53-80
    writing, 53-80
progress control, 673
project files, 660
Project menu, 40-42
    Add to Project, 41
    Dependencies, 42
    Export Makefile, 42
    Insert Project into Workspace, 42
    Set Active Project, 41
    Settings, 42
    Source Control, 41
projects (subdirectory), 8
PROOF_QUALITY, 801
properties, 930
    array, 262-263
property pages, 930
protected, 528, 536, 614, 621
prototypes, 466, 540
    overloading, 250-252
prototyping functions, 106, 216-219
PS_DASH, 760, 832
PS_SOLID, 760-763, 831
public, 528, 531, 614, 621
PUSHBUTTON, 716, 770
put to operator (<<), 123, 386-395
put( ), 393, 407
putc( ), 361-362
putchar( ), 210-211, 362-363, 377-381
puts( ), 289-292, 363-365
putw( ), 365-368

Q

qsort( ), 323-327, 481-491
queued input, 640-641
QuickWatch, 79-80
quit message, 657

R

radio button control, 673
radix, 368
rand( ), 481-491

random number generator, 489-490
.RC file, 675-676
rdstate( ), 410
read( ), 360
realloc( ), 481-491
rebuild all, 63
RECT, 681
Rectangle( ), 708-709, 831-834
rectDefault, 743, 755
recursion, 222-223
redirection, 356-357
reentrant, 895
reference,
  argument type, 111
  type (C++), 220-221, 348-351
RegisterClass( ), 688, 701, 710
registration class, 777
registry support, 930
relational operators, 162-166
replace (and find), 65-67
.RES file, 678
Resource,
  compiler, 660
  editors, 661-678
  script file, 660, 675-677
  statements, 677
resources, 660-661
return type (function), 216-219, 236-244
return( ), 116
returning addresses from functions, 350-351
rewind( ), 376-381
RGB( ), 760, 764, 771-772, 790-791
rich edit control, 672
right shift (>>), 158-159
Ritchie, Dennis, 98-99
ROT viewer, 13
rotating bits, 490-491
RoundRect( ), 762, 765, 831-834
runtime object model support (list), 742
RUNTIME_CLASS, 471, 843-844, 870

S

saving files, 58-59
sbumpc( ), 596
scanf( ), 117-118, 381-383, 386-387, 419
scope, 155, 222, 255-260
  block, 109
  pointer data type, 328
  rules, 155
screen output, 119-120
scroll bar, 637
ScrollWindow( ), 693
searches and sorts, 485-488
SEEK_CUR, 376-381
SEEK_END, 376-381
SEEK_SET, 376-381
seekg( ), 410
seekoff( ), 596
seekp( ), 409
seekpos( ), 596
SelectObject( ), 723, 760-763, 765, 831-834
SendMessage( ), 722
sequential underscores, 130
Serialize( ), 826, 850-851, 877-878
setb( ), 597
SetBkMode( ), 926, 943
setbuf( ), 357-358, 596
SetContainerInfo( ), 870
SetDialogBkColor( ), 843
setf( ), 140, 396, 406, 578
SetFocus( ), 884
setg( ), 597
SetIndicators( ), 848
SetItemRects( ), 884
SetMapMode( ), 722, 726-727, 772, 778
setp( ), 597
SetPixel( ), 762, 831-834
SetRect( ), 888
SetRegistryKey( ), 820, 843
SetTextAlign( ), 927, 943
setting breakpoints, 76-79
setvbuf( ), 357-359

SetViewportExt( ), 772, 779
SetViewportExtEx( ), 726-727
SetViewportOrg( ), 772
SetViewportOrgEx( ), 726-727
SetWindowExt( ), 772, 779
SetWindowExtEx( ), 726-727
sgetc( ), 595
sgetn( ), 595
showpos, 400, 406
ShowWindow( ), 689, 744, 755, 821
signed, 137, 139, 449
simple programs, 53-80
sizeof( ), 106, 269-272, 324
    with 16-bit pointers, 321-322
    with pointer data type, 315
sin( ), 508-511, 533, 554, 711, 772
sinh( ), 508-511
sinhl( ), 508-511
sinl( ), 508-511
sizeof( ), 577
slider control, 672
snextc( ), 596
sorting integers, 486-487
source code (editing), 58
spin control, 672
spring( ), 289-291
sprintf( ), 854
sputbackc( ), 596
sputc( ), 595
sputn( ), 595
Spy++, 91
sqrt( ), 508-511, 582
square roots (table of), 581-582, 606-607
srand( ), 481-491
sscanf( ), 381-383
stack, 327
standard,
    C/C++ libraries, 168-176
    data types, 133-143
    library functions (STDLIB.H), 481-491
static text control, 671
statically loaded, 643
status bar, 810
STDARG.H, 252-254
stdaux, 355-359
STDDEF.H, 315
stderr, 355-359
stdin, 355-359
STDIO.H, 358-360, 480-481
STDLIB.H, 213-215, 480-481
stdout, 355-359
storage classes, 151-156, 221-222
stossc( ), 596
strcat( ), 291-295, 498-508
strchr( ), 498-508
strcmp( ), 498-508
strcmpi( ), 498-508
strcoll( ), 498-508
strcpy( ), 291-295, 498-508
strcspn( ), 498-508
strdup( ), 498-508
stream,
    altering buffer in C, 357-358
    functions, 355-360
    libraries, 114
STREAM.H, 395-411
streampos, 409
streams (closing), 359-360
strerror( ), 498-508
strftime( ), 511-518
stricmp( ), 498-508
string,
    array pointers of, 344-348
    formatting in C++, 405
    functions (character array), 289-295, 498-508
    I/O, 273-276, 363-365
    literal, 119
    pointers, 311-313
stringize operator (#), 322-323, 464
strlen( ), 291-295, 334, 498-508, 773, 779, 798
strlwr( ), 498-508
strncat( ), 498-508
strncmp( ), 291-295, 498-508

strncpy( ), 498-508
strnicmp( ), 498-508
strnset( ), 498-508
strong typing, 526
Stroustrup, Bjarne, 108
strpbrk( ), 498-508
strrchr( ), 498-508
strrev( ), 498-508
strset( ), 498-508
strspn( ), 498-508
strstr( ), 498-508
STRSTREA.H, 396, 404
strtod( ), 481-491
strtok( ), 498-508, 554-555, 557-559, 563
strtol( ), 481-491
strtoul( ), 481-491
struct, 449, 473, 526, 542, 578
structures,
    and bit-fields, 436-437
    and pointers, 425-435
    and union types, 450-451
    array of, 422-425
    definitions, 466
    differences between
        C and C++, 417
    member accessing, 417-418
    nesting, 435-436
    passing pointers to array, 428-431
strupr( ), 498-508
struture differences between
  C and C++, 417
strxfrm( ), 498-508
STYLE, 716, 769
subscript, 262
subtracting pointers, 320
subtraction (-), 160
SVGA, 82
SW_MINIMIZED, 682
SW_SHOW, 871
SW_SHOWMAXIMIZED, 682, 689
SW_SHOWMINIMIZED, 689
SW_SHOWMNNOACTIVE, 689
SW_SHOWNORMAL, 682, 689-690
switch / case, 187-196, 734
switching views, 67-68
sync( ), 596
syntax,
    function prototyping, 216-219
    identifiers, 130-132
system,
    memory, 642
    menu, 647
    queue, 657
system( ), 481-491

T

TA_CENTER, 927, 943
TA_TOP, 927, 943
tab control, 672
tabs (\t), 194-195
tag,
    field, 415, 417, 442
    name, 537
tan( ), 508-511, 533, 538, 554
tanh( ), 508-511
tanhl( ), 508-511
tanl( ), 508-511
TBSTYLE_FLAT, 847
tear-off interfaces, 930
tellp( ), 409
test container, 907
TEXTMETRIC, 942
TextOut( ), 702, 755, 757, 760-763, 765,
  773, 792, 831-834
this pointer, 616, 623-626
Thompson, Ken, 98-99
thread pooling, 930
threading models, 930
time and date structures, 512
time delay routine, 517-518
time( ), 511-518, 557-559, 926, 943
TIME.H, 480-481, 511-518
timer message, 641, 657
title bar, 647
tm, 512, 557-559, 854

toascii( ), 491-497
tokens, 555, 559
tolower( ), 135-136, 491-497
toolbar, 26-27, 810
toolbox controls, 669-674
Tools menu, 45-48
  ActiveX Control Test Container, 47
  Close Source Browser File, 46
  Customize, 48
  Error Lookup, 46-47
  Macro, 48
  MFC Tracer, 47
  OLE/COM Object Viewer, 47
  Options, 48
  Play, 48
  Record, 48
  Register Control, 48
  Source Browser, 46
  Spy++, 47
  Visual Component Manager, 47
topic search (beginning), 88-89
toupper( ), 135-136, 491-497
TranslateMessage( ), 690-691, 702, 711
translating, 130
TRANSPARENT, 926, 943
tree control, 673
trigonometric calculations, 508-511
trigraphs, 107
TRUE (!0), 165
TrueType font, 651
trunc, 409
type,
  C++ reference, 348-351
  checking (limited), 102, 104
  checking (pointers), 301
  compatibility, 448-451
typedef, 327, 379-380, 440-442
types,
  array, 449-450
  array argument, 279-280
  enumerated, 449-450
  function return, 236-244
  pointer, 451
  structure and union, 450-451
tzset( ), 511-518

U

UI support, 930
UINT, 655, 681
unbuffered C library, 583
unbuffered( ), 597
underflow( ), 596
underscore (_), 130-132
understanding menus (IDE), 25-26
UNICODE, 683
union, 437-440, 450-451
UNIX, 98
unlink( ), 360
unsetf( ), 398, 405-406
unsigned, 136-137, 139, 203, 449
unsized (array initialization), 266-267
UpdateAllViews( ), 883
UpdateWindow( ), 689-690, 744, 773-774
uppercase / lowercase conversions, 405, 496-497, 507-508
USER, 644, 654
USER32.LIB, 644, 654

V

ValidateRect( ), 691, 693, 702, 711
variable,
  declarations, 152-155
  naming conventions, 130-132
  scope, 155, 222
VARIABLE_PITCH, 792
variables,
  declaring, 117
  out-of-scope, 254-260
  pointer, 298-299
variant record, 437

varying length argument lists, 111, 252-254
VBScript macros, 48
VBX, 894
vertical scroll bar, 648
vertical scroll bar control, 673
VGA, 82
View menu, 36-39
viewing messages (Spy++), 91-92
virtual functions, 113-114
Visual Basic, 894
Visual C++ advanced features, 81-94
vitrual keycode, 641
void *, 321, 327-328, 331-333
    const, 325-326

W

warning messages, 64-65
WCHAR, 655, 681
while, 202-205, 590-594, 619
white space, 381
WHITE_BRUSH, 687, 701, 771, 778, 942
width( ), 192, 368, 400, 582, 607
Win32 Console Application, 55
WINAPI, 681
WinDiff, 93
WINDING, 943
window class, 649, 683, 686-688, 692
window layout, 646-648
Window menu, 48-50
Windows Concepts and Tools, 636-678
    advantages, 637-644
    animate control, 673
    bitmaps, 652-653
    border, 647
    brushes, 653
    button control, 673
    carets, 650
    check box control, 671
    client area, 648
    close window icon, 647
    combo box control, 672
    compiling resources, 678
    components, 659
    concepts and vocabulary, 645-659
    control icon, 647
    cursors, 650
    custom control, 673
    development tools, 659-678
    dialog boxes, 651, 666-677
    DLL (dynamic link libraries), 643-644
    edit box control, 672-673
    environment, 634-637
    executable format, 644-645
    fonts, 651
    generating messages, 656
    group box control, 671
    GUI (graphical user interface), 637-639
    hardware independence, 642-643
    horizontal scroll bar control, 672
    horizontal scroll bar, 648
    hot key control, 673
    icons, 650
    keyboard accelerators, 666
    list box control, 673
    list control, 672
    maximize icon, 647
    memory management, 642
    menu bar, 648
    menus, 663-666
    message boxes, 650-651
    message format, 654-656
    message loop, 657-658
    messages, 641-642, 653-658
    minimize icon, 647
    multitasking environment, 639-640
    oops and Windows, 649-650
    pens, 653
    picture control, 672

progress control, 673
project files, 660
queued input, 640-641
radio button control, 673
resource editors, 661-678
resource script file, 675-677
resource statements, 677
resources, 660-661
responding to messages, 656-657
rich edit control, 672
slider control, 672
spin control, 672
static text control, 671
system menu, 647
tab control, 672
title bar, 647
toolbox controls, 669-674
tree control, 673
vertical scroll bar, 648
vertical scroll bar control, 673
window class (procedure-oriented), 649
window layout, 646-648
Windows functions, 658
Windows window, 645-646
WINDOWS.H, 658-659
Windows functions, 679-804
Windows hardware independence, 642-643
WinMain(( ), 680-682, 687, 701, 710, 719
WINUSER.H, 692
wizards, 15
WM_CHAR, 691
WM_CLOSE, 655
WM_COMMAND, 720, 726, 775
WM_COPY, 655
WM_CREATE, 655, 692, 726, 782
WM_DESTROY, 692, 694, 726
WM_INITDIALOG, 720
WM_KEYDOWN, 691
WM_KEYUP, 691
WM_LBUTONDOWN, 923
WM_LBUTTONUP, 923
WM_PAINT, 655, 690, 691, 693, 726, 775, 782
WM_PASTE, 655
WM_QUIT, 682, 690
WM_SIZE, 692, 726, 727, 782
WNDCLASS, 681
WPARAM, 681
write( ), 360, 399, 402, 405
WS_CAPTION, 716, 769
WS_CHILD, 847
WS_GROUP, 769
WS_HSCROLL, 853
WS_OVERLAPPEDWINDOW, 688-689, 702, 743, 755
WS_POPUP, 716, 769
WS_SYSMENU, 716
WS_VISIBLE, 716, 847

XOR (^), 157-158

Z

zero, 142-143
with pointer comparison, 320